Ex. Lib. (Reprint- #9900) Used - $30.00

SOUTHERN COLORADO STATE COLLEGE LIBRARY

DISCARDED BY
USC LIBRARY

D1773174

SOLD

A CONCORDANCE

TO

THE POETICAL WORKS

OF

WILLIAM COWPER

BY

JOHN NEVE

"Nulla dies sine linea."
TULLY.

GREENWOOD PRESS, PUBLISHERS
NEW YORK

Originally published in 1887
by Sampson Low, Marston, Searle & Rivington

First Greenwood Reprinting, 1969

Library of Congress Catalogue Card Number 68-57632

SBN 8371-1073-4

PRINTED IN UNITED STATES OF AMERICA

DEDICATED

TO MY DAUGHTERS.

PREFACE.

This Concordance is compiled from the Poetical Works of William Cowper in the Aldine Edition of the British Poets. It does not include translations, except the more important ones from Vincent Bourne, and only a few of the Minor Poems, including "To Mary" and "The Castaway."

EXPLANATION OF ABBREVIATIONS.

A.C.	Report of an Adjudged Case.	M.D.	The Morning Dream.
A.S.	Alexander Selkirk.	M.F.	Mutual Forbearance.
A.T.	Anti-Thelypthora.	Miss —	Lines to Miss —
A.T. ii	On Martin Madan's Answer to same.	M.P.	On receipt of My Mother's Picture.
A.T. iii	Impromptu on same.	Mor.	The Moralizer corrected.
A.T. iv	On a review of same.	Mrs. M.	On Mrs. Montagu's Feather Hangings.
B.	Boadicea.	N.	To the Rev. Mr. Newton.
B.B.	Biographia Britannica.	N.A.	The Needless Alarm.
Beau	On a spaniel—called Beau.	N.C.	The Negro's Complaint.
B.R.	Beau's reply.	N.G.	The Nightingale and Glowworm.
C.	Catharina.	N.Y.G.	The Poet's New Year's Gift.
Cast.	The Castaway.	O. i	Ode to Apollo.
Ch.	Charity.	O. ii	,, to Peace.
Comp. i	A Comparison.	P.	The Poet, the Oyster, and Sensitive Plant.
Comp. ii	Comparison addressed to a Young Lady.		
Con.	Conversation.	P.A.	Pity for Poor Africans.
C.G.	The Cock Fighter's Garland.	Pat.	The Modern Patriot.
Dr.	Dr. Darwin—Lines to.	P.B.	The Pine Apple and the Bee.
D.W.	The Dog and the Water Lily.	P.E.	Progress of Error.
E. i	Epistle to Lady Austen.	P.F.	The Poplar Field.
E. ii	,, to a Protestant Lady.	P.T.	Pairing Time Anticipated.
E. iii	,, to Joseph Hill.	Q.V.	On the Queen's Visit to London.
E. iv	,, to Robert Lloyd.	R.	Retirement.
Ep. i	Epitaph on Hamilton.	R.C.	The Retired Cat.
Ep. ii	,, on a Hare.	R.G.	On the Loss of the *Royal George*.
Ep. iii	,, on Dr. Johnson.	R.H.	Reflection on Horace, Book ii., Ode x.
Ex.	Expostulation.	S.	The Shrubbery.
F.	Friendship.	S. i	Sonnet to Henry Cowper.
F.A.	The Four Ages.	S. ii	,, a Young Lady.
F.B.	The Faithful Bird.	St. i	Stanzas for 1787.
F.M.	The Flatting Mill.	St. ii	,, ,, 1788.
G.	On a Goldfinch starved to death in his cage.	St. iii	,, ,, 1789.
Gr.	Gratitude.	St. iv	,, ,, 1790.
H.	Hope.	St. v	,, ,, 1792.
Her.	Heroism.	St. vi	,, ,, 1793.
H.F.	Human Frailty.	T.	Truth.
J.G.	John Gilpin.	T. i	Task, Book i. The Sofa.
J.P.	Judgment of the Poets.	T. ii	,, ,, ii. The Time-piece.
J.T.	In Memory of John Thornton.	T. iii	,, ,, iii. The Garden.
L.R.	The Lily and the Rose.	T. iv	,, ,, iv. The Winter Evening.
L.W.	Love of the World reproved.	T. v	,, ,, v. The Winter Morning Walk.
M.	To Mary.	T. vi	,, ,, vi. The Winter Walk at Noon.
M. i	On the burning of Lord Mansfield's Library.	T.B.	On the death of Mrs. Throgmorton's Bullfinch.
M. ii	On the same.		
M.B.	On a Mischievous Bull.	Th.	On Promotion of Lord Thurlow.

EXPLANATION OF ABBREVIATIONS.

Tir.	Tirocinium; or, Review of Schools.	*U.*	To the Rev. W. C. Unwin.
Trans. i	The Glowworm.	*V.*	The Valediction.
Trans. ii	The Jackdaw.	*W.N.*	The Winter Nosegay.
Trans. iii	The Cricket.	*Y.D*	The Yearly Distress.
Trans. iv	The Parrot.	*Y.O.*	Yardley Oak.
Trans. H.	Horace, Book ii., Ode x.	1789.	Annus Memorabilis 1789.
T.T.	Table Talk.		

CONCORDANCE.

ABANDON.
And forced to *a.* what she bravely sought *T.* v 368
ABANDONED.
Cruel, *a.*, glorying in her shame! *T.* iii 68
A. as unworthy of our love *T.* iii 731
A. and, which still I more regret *T.* iv 692
ABANDONING.
Lost by *a.* her own relief *R.* 758
ABASED.
I shrink *a.*, and yet aspire to thee *R.* 94
ABATE.
Still there is room for pity to *a. Ch.* 198
In part *a.*, that happiness were small *Na.* 112
But difficulties soon *a. Tran.* iv 40
In human bosoms, quench it, or *a. T.* iv 747
ABATED.
That fire *a.* which impels rash youth *Con.* 641
ABBÉ.
Ere long some bowing, smirking, smart *a. P.E.* 385
ABBEY.
Where mouldering *a.* walls o'erhang the glade *H.* 351
ABDICATE.
But Christ as soon would *a.* his own *T.* 77
ABDICATED.
And hoped to seize his *a.* helm *Ex.* 577
ABDOMINOUS.
Gorgonius sits, *a.* and wan *P.E.* 217
ABEL.
Since *A.* worshipped, or the world began *H.* 644
ABHOR.
Through fear, not love; and Heaven *a.* the fee *Ch.* 46
A. constraint, and dares not feign a zeal *Con.* 713
Hast thou (a sacrilege his soul *a.*) *Ex.* 346
His soul *a.* a mercenary thought *H.* 332
And him as deeply who *a.* it not *H.* 333
A. the craft he boasted of before *H.* 522
You would *a.* to do me wrong *N.G.* 17
A. each other. Mountains interposed *T.* ii 17
And all that I *a.* thou freckled fair *T.* iii 839
And he *a.* the jest by which he shines *T.* v 617
The lie that flatters I *a.* the most *T.T.* 88
ABHORRED.
Perish, hopeless and *a. B.* 15
A. the sacrifice, and cursed the priest *P.E.* 340
Perish the virtue, as it ought, *a. T.* 503
Few transient years, won from the abyss *a. T.* i 286
The most remote from his *a.* resort *T.* vi 398

ABHORRENCE.
And spits *a.* in the Christian's face *H.* 662
Heaven turns from with *a.* and disdain *T.* 72
Her own *a.*, and as much your scorn *T.* 510
With just *a.* of so mean a part *Tir.* 455
ABIDE.
No Friendship will *a.* the test *F.* 37
Thee we reject, unable to *a. T.* v 879
Nor heed what guests there enter and *a. Tir.* 888
ABILITY.
And wiser men's *a.*, pretence *Con.* 628
They had indeed *a.* to smooth *T.* v 692
ABJECT.
At thought of her forlorn and *a.* state *T.* i 659
It is the *a.* property of most *T.* v 246
ABJURE.
Shall I *a.* thee not to court thy shame? *Ex.* 655
ABLE.
'Tis clear that they were always *a. P.T.* 3
With gazing, when they see an *a.* man *T.* v 256
ABLER.
Should turn to writers of an *a.* sort *R.* 716
Is Christ the *a.* teacher, or the schools? *T.* ii 534
Of *a.* votaries to cleanse the stain *T.T.* 635
ABLUTION.
A Jordan for the *a.* of our woes *Con.* 566
ABODE.
Has made the new-born creature her *a. Con.* 754
And marks the bounds of our *a. E.* i 38
No traveller ever reached that blest *a. E.* ii 11
To fill with fragrance his *a.* above *H.* 122
The world, no longer thy *a.*, not thee *J.T.* 10
Following, that led me to my own *a. Na.* 128
Within her master's snug *a. R.C.* 34
Where, in his own oracular *a. T.* 389
My visit still, but never mine *a. T.* i 251
And clammy, of his dark *a.* have bred *T.* i 439
Down falls the venerable pile, the *a. T.* iii 767
And harmless pleasures in the thronged *a. T.* iv 782
Ye horrid towers, the *a.* of broken hearts *T.* v 384
Precipitate the loathed *a.* of man *T.* vi 376
Who, when she formed, designed theem an *a. T.* vi 580
Wheresoe'er be thine *a. Tran.* iii 3
ABOUND.
Nor even shrubs *a. A Tale* 2
Where covert guile and artifice *a. Ch.* 285
Streams never flow in vain; where streams *a. Comp.* i 9
Happy the nation where such men *a. Ex.* 653
Earn if you want; if you *a.*, impart *P.E.* 253
Poisoning the waters where their swarms *a. P.E.* 481

The path to bliss *a*. with many a snare *T.* 301
That life holds out to all, should most *a*. *T.* i 752
Therefore in towns and cities they *a*. *Tir*. 519
Are such men rare? perhaps they would *a*. *Tir*. 700
Where most nectareous sweets *a*. 1789, 20

ABOUNDED.
The dead in whom that good *a*. most *J. T.* 4

ABOUNDING.
Than she supplies from her *a*. store *Ch*. 102

ABRAHAM.
For whom God heard his *A*. plead in vain *T*. iii 848

ABRIDGE.
A. him of his just and native rights *T*. v 436
Tyranny sends the chain that must *a*. *T.T.* 474

ABROAD.
He walked *a*., o'ertaken in the rain *Con*. 277
Lest he should trespass, begged to go *a*. *E*. iii 23
To sound his horn, and publish it *a*. *H*. 311
Now let the bright reverse be known *a*. *H*. 710
The trumpet sounds, your legions swarm *a*. *Her*. 53
And when he next doth ride *a*. *J. G*. 251
And fanged with brass the demons are *a*. *Na*. 182
Obsequious when *a*., though proud at home *R*. 440
That field of promise, how it flings *a*. *T*. 453
We have no slaves at home :—then why *a*. *T*. ii 37
Pours she not all her choicest fruits *a*. *T*. ii 85
Pure, from so foul a pool, to shine *a*. *T*. ii 798
Dressed to his taste, inviting him *a*. *T*. iii 358
And drenched conservatory breathes *a*. *T*. iii 498
Each opening blossom, freely breathes *a*. *T*. iii 622
A., and desolating public life *T*. iii 683
Raging *a*., and the rough wind, endear *T*. iv 309
Now goes the nightly thief prowling *a*. *T*. iv 432
And drop the night-bolt!—ruffians are *a*. *T*. iv 568
The great proficiency he made *a*. *T*. iv 654
When man was multiplied and spread *a*. *T*. v 221
He looks *a*. into the varied field *T*. v 738
That calls the unwonted villager *a*. *T*. vi 300
And Æthiopia spreads *a*. the hand *T*. vi 812
Snuffs up the wind and flings himself *a*. *T.T.* 669
Though *a*. they are frozen and dead *W.N.* 8

ABROGATE.
And *a*., as roundly as she may *T*. i 742

ABRUPT.
A. and horrid as the tempest roars *R*. 533

ABSENCE.
A. of occupation is not rest *R*. 623
That such short *a*. may endear it more *T*. i 517
Against unkindness, *a*., and neglect *T*. vi 627
Of love by *a*. chilled into respect *Tir*. 576

ABSENT.
Shall mourn her *a*. lord, for he is gone *A.T.* 104
An *a*. friend's fidelity and love *Con*. 308
Tender idolater of *a*. charms *R*. 220
Or charged with amorous sighs of *a*. swain *T*. iv 20
Graced with the name of a long *a*. friend *V*. 40

ABSOLUTE.
Sits *a*. on his unshaken throne *H*. 474
Should be a despot *a*., and boast *T*. v 311
Vast was his empire, *a*. his power *T*. vi 357
The hallowed bench from *a*. contempt *Tir*. 431
From total night, and *a*. disgrace *T.T.* 665

ABSOLUTION.
His worthless *a*. all the prize *Ex*. 525

ABSORBED.
A. in that immensity I see *R*. 93
Were tasked to his full strength, *a*. and lost *T*. iv 301

ABSORBS.
And dark oblivion soon *a*. them all *B.R.* 8
Whate'er this world produces, it *a*. *Ch*. 564
And vanity *a*. at length *E*. i 81

ABSTAIN.
Good Mussulman, *a*. from pork *L.W.* 2
Cry in his startled ear, "*a*. from sin!" *P.E.* 38
He that *a*. and he alone, does right *P.E.* 585

ABSTINENCE.
Hollow-eyed *a*., and lean Despair *H*. 58
The precept that enjoins him *a*. *P.E.* 236
His works, his *a*., his zeal allowed *T*. 91
Than *a*., and beggary, and lice *T*. 124

ABSURD.
Quite as *a*., though not so light, as he *Con*. 296
And half the night? fanatic and *a*. *Con*. 578
As once *a*. in all discerning eyes *Con*. 806
Of all that was *a*., profane, impure *Con*. 888
Their learning legendary, false, *a*. *Ex*. 127
When some hypothesis *a*. and vain *P.E.* 444
Less impious than *a*., and owing more *T*. vi 656

ABSURDEST.
'Tis grave Philosophy's *a*. dream *H*. 65

ABSURDITY.
By sparks *a*. strikes out of Pride *Con*. 148

ABSURDLY.
A., not his office, but himself *T*. ii 548

ABUNDANCE.
Begets its likeness. Rank *a*. breeds *T*. i 686
Laughs with *a*.; and the land, once lean *T*. vi 766

ABUNDANT.
That good diffused may more *a*. grow *Con*. 443
The *a*. harvest, recompense divine *H*. 770
After long drought, when rains *a*. fall *N.A.* 59
It thrives in misery, and *a*. grows *T*. 125
Traps to catch youth are most *a*. too *Tir*. 522

ABUSE.
Ranks its *a*. among the foulest deeds *Ch*. 209
To teach good manners, and to curb *a*. *Con*. 164
They dare not wait the riotous *a*. *Con*. 261
The fruitful parent of *a*. and wrong *Con*. 461
That thankless waste and wild *a*. destroy *Ex*. 679
Time wasted, violated laws, *a*. *F.A.* 14
Man may improve the crisis, or *a*. *P.E.* 26
There stand, and justify the foul *a*. *P.E.* 144
Still hurtful in the *a*., or by the excess *P.E.* 228
But if to wrong the judgment and *a*. *P.E.* 304
If clemency revolted by *a*. *P.E.* 596
With what superior skill we can *a*. *T*. i 637
Will reckon with us roundly for the *a*. *T*. vi 606
Where fashion shall not sanctify *a*. *T*. vi 852
Would deem it no *a*., or waste of pains *Tir*. 627
The *a*. of her sacred charge, the press *T.T.* 633
If Acrimony, Slander, and *A*. *T.T.* 762

ABUSED.
The insidious witch that had his wits *a*. *A.T.* 176
But Grace *a*. brings forth the foulest deeds *Ex*. 212
And life *a*., and not to be suborned *H*. 224
By all whom sentiment has not *a*. *Tir*. 538
See wealth *a*., and dignities misplaced *Tir*. 815

ABUSERS.
And profligate *a*. of a world *T*. iii 696

ABYSS.
Deep in the *a.* of Silver-end *E.* i 42
On steady wing sails through the immense *a. H.* 163
Fast anchored in the deep *a.* of space *R.* 84
Few transient years, won from the *a.* abhorred *T.* i 286
Of elevation down into the *a. T.* ii 93
That seems half quenched in the immense *a. T.* iii 216
Profounder, in the fathomless *a. T.* v 594
That show like beacons in the blue *a. T.* v 839

ACADEMIC.
With *a.* dignity devout *H.* 106
Or *a.* tutors, teaching youths *N.A.* 79
Of *a.* fame (howe'er deserved) *T.* iii 15

ACADEMIES.
And small *a.* win all the praise? *Tir.* 504

ACADEMUS.
Of *A.* is this false or true? *T.* ii 533

ACCENT.
Hear the sweet *a.* of his tuneful voice *R.* 771
And colleges, untaught; sells *a.*, tone *T.* ii 359

ACCEPT.
A. the tribute of a stranger's pen *Ch.* 291
A. it only, and the boon is yours *H.* 327
Forgive their evil, and *a.* their good *T.* 582
Adore him? Will he hear, *a.* and bless? *T.* ii 515

ACCEPTANCE.
No works shall find *a.*, in that day *Ch.* 557

ACCESS.
Its destined goal of difficult *a. T.* vi 277

ACCESSIBLE.
A., and prayer prevail, she will *T.T.* 407

ACCOMMODATE.
To furnish and *a.* a world *Ch.* 124
Than when employed to *a.* the fair *T.* i 73

ACCOMPANIED.
Stillness, *a.* with sounds so soft *T.* vi 83

ACCOMPLISHED.
And when *a.* in her wayward school *Con.* 465
In chains of error our *a.* minds *H.* 484
With all the charms of an *a.* taste *R.* 510
And luxury the *a.* sofa lost *T.* i 88
A more *a.* world's chief glory now *T.* i 724
He sighs, departs, and leaves the *a.* plan *T.* iii 785
And tongue *a.* in the fulsome cant *T.* vi 289
Scenes of *a.* bliss! which who can see *T.* vi 760
Thus, half *a.* ere he yet began *Tir.* 234

ACCOMPLISHING.
The sun *a.* his early march *N.A.* 29

ACCOMPLISHMENTS.
Though all *a.*, all knowledge meet *Ch.* 601
A. have taken virtue's place *P.E.* 417
Say, what *a.* at school acquired *Tir.* 577

ACCORD.
The wrangler, rather than *a.* with you *Con.* 111
Thus harmony and family *a. T.* vi 379

ACCOSTED.
And thus *a.* him *J. G.* 164

ACCOUNT.
A. them implements of mischief still *Ch.* 556
But all shall give *a.* of every wrong *Con.* 25
Are all upon your own *a. P.* 48
You think him humble—God *a.* him proud *T.* 92
She half an angel in her own *a. T.* 149
The good he scorned, all carried to *a. T.* 546
Dissolve in pity, and *a.* the learn'd *T.* iii 183
That, while it gives us worth in God's *a. T.* iii 283
When He shall call his debtors to *a. T.* iii 365
O happy! and, in my *a.*, denied *T.* iv 357
Then most deserving in their own *a. T.* v 261
A. it music; that it summons some *T.* v 409
Thee I *a.* still happy, and the chief *T.* v 460
And just in his *a.*, why bird and beast *T.* vi 389
A. him an encumbrance on the state *T.* vi 958
A. him no just mark for idle wit *Tir.* 726
The world *a.* an honourable man *Tir.* 738
That we *a.* most durable below! *Y.O.* 71

ACCOUNTABLE.
A., and God, some future day *T.* vi 605

ACCOUTRED.
One was *a.* when the cry began *A.T.* 135

ACCRUE.
Know, your arrears with every hour *a. Con.* 491

ACCURSED.
This does Profusion, and the *a.* cause *T.* ii 697

ACCUSE.
'Tis senseless arrogance to *a. F.* 52

ACCUSTOMED.
Ears long *a.* to the pleasing lute *Ex.* 68
And held *a.* conference with my heart *F.A.* 9
The man to solitude *a.* long *N.A.* 55
None, *a.* to the sound *St.* iv 7
From his *a.* perch. Hard-faring race! *T.* i 564
He from the stack carves out the *a.* load *T.* v 33

ACHE.
My heart of thoughts that made it *a. Ep.* ii 35
His head and his heart are both likely to *a. F.M.* 15
Shall make your scribbling fingers *a. J.P.* 39
With present ills his heart must *a. N.* 11 [*Tir.* 801
Whose hearts will *a.*, once told what ills may reach
'Tis not, as heads that never *a.* suppose *R.* 323

ACHIEVE.
Yet time at length (what will not time *a.*?) *Her.* 29
Has business; feels himself engaged to *a. T.* iii 377
Trivial, and worthy of disdain, *a. T.* v 699

ACHIEVED.
This process *a.*, it is doomed to sustain *F.M.* 9
A. a labour which had, far and wide *Y.O.* 108

ACHIEVEMENT.
The *a.* of Art may amuse *C.* 37
Beyond the *a.* of successful flight *T.* i 692
Of old *a.*, and despair of new *T.* ii 254
Or what *a.* of immortal fame *T.* vi 923
In little bosoms such *a.* strike *Tir.* 232.

ACHING.
With *a.* heart, and discontented looks *R.* 471
And many an *a.* wish, your beamy fires *T.* v 838
His crimes and follies with an *a.* eye *Tir.* 62

ACKNOWLEDGE.
Till none but beasts *a.* him a man *Con.* 426
The grand effect; *a.* with joy *T.* iii. 227
Unless thy conscious heart *a.* none *Tir.* 580

ACKNOWLEDGED.
From worn-out follies, now *a.* such *F.A.* 3
Must stand *a.*, while the world shall stand *T.* ii 334

A., others may admire it too *T.* iii 704
To earth's *a.* Sovereign, finds at once *T.* v 803

ACQUAINT.
A. thyself with God, if thou wouldst taste *T.* v 779

ACQUAINTANCE.
The new *a.* soon became a guest *Con.* 531

ACQUAINTED.
A. with the woes that fear or shame *Con.* 495
Too well *a.* with their smiles, slides off *T.* i 511

ACQUIESCED.
I heard and *a.*; then to and fro *F.A.* 18

ACQUIESCENCE.
He seeks, and *a.* of his soul *T.* v 597

ACQUIRE.
There form connections, but *a.* no friend *T.* ii 634
They may *a.* that confident address *Tir.* 349
Heroic song from thy free touch *a. T.T.* 292

ACQUIRED.
Add to such erudition, thus *a. T.* ii 765
With wholesome learning, yet *a.* with ease *Tir.* 118
Pretend to all that parts have e'er *a. V.* 15
Say, what accomplishments, at school *a. Tir.* 577

ACQUISITION.
An *a.* rather rare *F.* 31

ACQUITTED.
Here see, *a.* of all vain pretence *Ch.* 412

ACRES.
Those naked *a.* to a sheltering grove *T.* iii 773
His hungry *a.* stinks, and is no use *T.* iv. 503

ACRID.
Their *a.* temper turns, as soon as stirred *Ch.* 503
With *a.* salts, his very heart athirst *T.* i 448

ACRIMONY.
If *A.*, Slander, and Abuse *T.T.* 762

ACT.
Could *a.* extortion, and the worst of crimes *Ex.* 148
A. but an honest and a faithful part *Ex.* 556
Some *a.* upon this prudent plan *F.* 181   [*A.T.* 53
And promised they should *a.* the wild-goose part
A. without aim   nk little, and feel less *H.* 8
And though in *a.* unwearied, secret still *J.T.* 37
But reveries (for human minds will *a.*) *R.* 637
Must move and *a.* for him alone *R.C.* 114
One *a.*, that from a thankful heart proceeds *T.* 223
Put so much of his heart into his *a. T.* ii 249
Then *a.* in Nature's office, brings to pass *T.* iii 542
The stress of a continual *a.*, the pain *T.* vi 208
To give such *a.* and utterance as they may *T.* vi 339
Vicious in *a.*, in temper savage—fierce *T.* vi 487
A necessary *a.* incurs no blame *T.* vi 573
And righteous limitation of its *a. T.* vi 596
To show the world how Garrick did not *a. T.* vi 677
A. with a force, and kindles with a zeal *T.T.* 482
Some *a.* by the delicate mind *The Rose* 14
Unpurified by an authentic *a. Y.O.* 12

ACTION.
Brings every thought, word, *a.* to the test *P.E.* 34
And grace his *a.* ere the curtain fall *R.* 34
By ceaseless *a.* all that is subsists *T.* i 367
Of *a.* and reaction. He has found *T.* ii 193
Whose *a.* say that they respect themselves *T.* ii 377
His every nerve in *a.* and at stretch *T.* iii 90

His every *a.*, and imbrutes the man *T.* iv 461
His speech, his form, his *a.* full of grace *T.T.* 346

ACTIVE.
The rest, alert and *a.*, as became *A.T.* 133
We feel thy force still *a.* at this hour *Ch.* 272
'Tis always *a.* on the side of Truth *Con.* 602
Sordid as *a.*, ignorant as loud *R.* 22
Post away swiftly to more *a.* scenes *R.* 273
His *a.* years with indolent repose *R.* 618
Not such the alert and *a.*   Measure life *T.* i 396
Let *a.* Laws apply the needful curb *T.T.* 314

ACTIVITY.
Supplies with warm *a.* and force *T.T.* 220

ACTOR.
Outscolds the ranting *a.* on the stage *T.* iv 45
The self-complacent *a.*, when he views *T.* iv 200
Though the chief *a.* died upon the stage *T.T.* 341
Next, busy *a.* on a meaner stage *V.* 27

ACUTE.
Our sensibilities are so *a. Con.* 351
Save that his scent is less *a.* than theirs *P.E.* 85
Some, more *a.*, and more industrious still *T.* iii 155

ADAGIO.
The *a.* and andante it demands *T.* ii 361

ADAM.
Slept in *A.* ? and in those from him *F.A.* 24
Is that *A.*'s offspring may be saved *T.* 183
Of thickest shades like *A.* after taste *Y.O.* 15

ADAMANTINE.
Turns to the stroke his *a.* scales *T.* ii 324

ADD.
And graced with all Philosophy can *a. Ch.* 342
Can Nature *a.* a charm, or Art confer *Ex.* 5 [*H.* 430
And *a.* Right Reverend to Smug's honoured name
A. nothing now to the degraded dead *H.* 269
A. joy to duty, makes me glad to pay *M.P.* 70
And *a.* a smile to what was sweet before *R.* 10
Or bind them faster on, and *a.* still more ? *T.* 186
A. to such erudition, thus acquired *T.* ii 765 [*T.* 344
Prayer would *a.* faith, and faith would fix them there
And *a.* two-thirds of the remaining half *T.* iii 131
I shall not *a.* myself to such a chase *T.* iv. 786
And *a.* his rapture to the general praise *T.* v 890
A. tenfold bitterness to death by pangs *T.* vi 395
Works magic wonders, *a.* a brighter hue *Tir.* 23
A., as he can, his tributary mite *T.T.* 112   [585
A. too, that, thus estranged, thou canst obtain *Tir.*
And if he *a.*, a blessing shared by few *V.* 89

ADDED.
The comfort of a few poor, *a.* days *H.* 729
The baby seems to smile with *a.* charms *P.E.* 519
Compensating his loss with *a.* hours *T.* iv. 134
Come then, and, *a.* to thy many crowns *T.* vi 902 ;
                                          [*T.* vi 855
ADDICTED.
Was much *a.* to inquire *R.C.* 3

ADDISON.
In front of these came *A.*   In him *T.T.* 642

ADDLED.
Themselves were chilled, their eggs were *a. P.T.* 55

ADDRESS.
Hearing a lawyer, grave in his *a. Con.* 69
When called to *a.* myself to you *E.* i 28
That I presume to *a.* the Muse *E.* iv 12
For men of their appearance and *a. P.E.* 388

How shall I speak thee, or thy power a. *P.E.* 460
Refines his speech and fashions his a. *R.* 240
Genteel in figure, easy in a. *T.* 203
With such a. from themes of sad import *T.* ii 300
And tender in a., as well becomes *T.* ii 406
Pathetic exhortation; and to a. *T.* ii 469
A. himself who will to the pursuit *T.* iv 784
From nature's bounty—that humane a. *T.* v 469
To manage with a., to seize with power *T.T.* 358
And the tear that is wiped with a little a. *Rose* 19
They may acquire that confident a. *Tir.* 349
He had not made his own with more a. *Tir.* 582
And his a., if not quite French in ease, *Tir.* 670

ADDRESSED.
Nor he alone a. the wayward fair *A.T.* 34
With verse a. to me? *B.R.* 28
The lady thus a. her spouse. *M.F.* 1
A ram, the ewes and wethers, sad, a. *N.A.* 82
But, "Thus far and no farther," when a. *P.E.* 600
The turtle thus a. her mate *The Doves* 7
Ye knew at least, by constant proofs a. *Tir.* 273
Your smooth eulogium, to our crown a. *T.T.* 91

ADEPT.
And beaus, a. in everything profound *H.* 347
Made just the a. that you designed your son *Tir.* 237

ADEQUATE.
Is more than a. to all I seek *Tir.* 386

ADHERING.
By congregated loads a. close *T.* iv. 344

ADIEU.
Entreated "Help!" or cried—"A." *Cast.* 42
"A., dear Sir! lest you should lose it now" *Con.* 282
"A.," Vinosa cries, ere yet he sips *H.* 357
"A. to all morality, if Grace *H.* 359
A long, long sigh, and wept a last a.! *M.P.* 31
A. and farewells are a sound unknown *M.P.* 33
Earth, seas, and sun a.! *St.* iii 10
I bid you both a long and last a. *V.* 5

ADJOINING.
A. close to Kilwick's echoing wood *N.A.* 3

ADJURATIONS.
With a. every word impress *Con.* 70

ADJUST.
And periwig nicely a. *Gr.* 24
To a. the fragrant charge of a short tube *T.* v 55

ADJUSTED.
Ice upon ice, the well a. parts *T.* v 146

ADMINISTER.
To a., to guard, to adorn the state *T.* v 342

ADMINISTERED.
"Whate'er is best a. is best" *Tir.* 508

ADMIRABLY.
With hesitation a. slow *Con.* 123

ADMIRAL.
When a., extolled for standing still *T.T.* 192
Of some flagged a.; and tortuous arms *Y.O.* 96

ADMIRATION.
While A., feeding at the eye *T.* i 157
And be our a. and our praise" *T.* v 259

ADMIRE.
Such often, like the tube they so a. *Con.* 249
He soon replied,—"I do a." *J.G.* 17

"Did you a. my lamp," quoth he *N.G.* 15
A. his learning, and almost adore *P.E.* 507
A. the work, but slips the lesson by *R.* 214
But Nature's works far lovelier. I a. *T.* i 421
None more a., the painter's magic skill *T.* i 422
Dote not too much, nor spoil what ye a. *T.* ii 498
What we a. we praise, and when we praise *T.* iii 702
Acknowledged, others may a. it too *T.* iii 704
Much that I love, and more that I a. *T.* iii 838
Man views it and a., but rests content *T.* v 791
How would the world a.! but speaks it less *T.* vi 128
The deeds that men a. as half divine *T.T.* 3
A wish to copy what he must a. *Tir.* 649

ADMIRED.
Needs only to be seen to be a. *Ex.* 493
For its beauty a. and its use *Gr.* 26
Your Hope shall stand unblamed, perhaps a. *H.* 616
See the sage hermit, by mankind a. *T.* 87
If more a. than she *L.R.* 2 [*T.* ii 434
Though learned with labour, and though much a.
Less worthy of applause, though more a. *T.* v 127
Priests have invented, and the world a. *Tir.* 185
Be great, be feared, be envied, be a. *V.* 16

ADMIRER.
With smiles alluring her a., man *H.* 40
A., and be destined to divide *T.* iii 726

ADMIRING.
Then each might show, to his a. friends *Con.* 199
With fierce and envious yet a. eyes *Ex.* 204
Have risen at length on your a. eyes *H.* 492
A., terrified, the novel strain *N.A.* 49
Her slighted works to your a. view *R.* 543
Engaged my wonder, and a. still *T.* iv 715
And still a., with regret supposed *T.* iv 716

ADMIT.
A. it true, the consequence is clear *Con.* 165
The Southern sash a. too strong a light *Con.* 331
And all the world a. them *F.* 162
This only spares no lust, a. no plea *H.* 645
The grave a. no cure for guilt or sin *St.* ii 30
A. me to a share; the guiltless eye *T.* i 333
May claim this merit still—that she a. *T.* iii 102
Dire disappointment that a. no cure *T.* iii 557
The heart's insanity a. no cure *T.* vi 523
Its squeezed contents, and more than it a. *T.* vi 671
And the world cheerfully a. the claim *T.T.* 715

ADMITTED.
Pleasure a. in undue degree *P.E.* 269
A. freely, may afford their aid *T.* iii 425
His works. A. once to his embrace *T.* v 780
And, if a. at thy board he sit *Tir.* 725

ADMONISH.
Alike a. not to roam *S.* 22
Must prompt him, and a. how to catch *T.* iii 507

ADMONISHED.
A., scorn the caution and the friend *E.* ii 17
But thus a., we can walk erect *T.* ii 593

ADMONITION.
A thousand awful a. scorned *St.* ii 27
Which a. can alone disperse *Tir.* 600

ADO.
I marry without more a. *P.T.* 36

ADOLESCENCE.
Of a., or a firmer age *Con.* 46

ADOLESCENT.
Detain their a. charge too long *Tir.* 219

ADOPT.
Once more I would a. the graver style Ch. 489
A. his own, 'tis equally in vain Con. 109
To a. the chymist's golden dream F. 143
With all that bigotry a., inspired T. 88 [785
Too proud to a. the thoughts of one unknown Tir.
Because that world a. it. If it bear T. vi 982

ADOPTED.
Friends, not a. with a schoolboy's haste R. 725

ADOPTING.
A. their mistake, profoundly thinks T. v 270

ADORATION.
In language soft as A. breathes! T. ii 495

ADORE.
"This triple realm a. thee; thou art come" Ch. 270
Admire his learning, and almost a. P.E. 507
A. a creature, and devout in vain R. 227
A. him? Will he hear, accept, and bless? T. ii 515
With truth from heaven, created thing a. Y.O. 7

ADORED.
Thy parliaments a., on bended knees Ex. 538
Ye devotees to your a. employ P.E. 75
A. and praised in all that thou hast wrought R. 92
Deserves to be beloved, but not a. R. 272
Thou art not known where Pleasure is a. T. iii 51
A. through fear, strong only to destroy T. v 445

ADORING.
Thy name a., and then preach thee man! T. vi 887

ADORN.
All consecrated to adorn the fair A.T. 16
When scarlet fruits the russet hedge a. A.T. 72
And unless you a. it, a nausea follows F.M. 24
One Georgian star a. the skies Q.V. 75
A. his intellects as well as shelves T. 423
To a. the sofa with eulogium due T. iii 12
To administer, to guard, to a. the state T. v 342
Not so. The virtue still a. our age T.T. 340
A. the polished periods as they fall T.T. 766
A., though differing in its kind U. 15

ADORNED.
Two nymphs a. with every grace D.W. 7
With helmet heads, and dragon-scales a. R. 69
Not sumptuously a., nor needing aid T. iv 251
Her head, a. with lappets pinned aloft T. iv 540
And prop the pile they but a. before T. v 116
'Tis not the wreath that once a. thy brow T.T. 370

ADORNING.
"A. May, that peevish maid" J.P. 35

ADRIFT.
If self-exalting claims be turned a. H. 530
Turn him a. upon a rolling sea Tir. 868

ADULT.
So language in the mouths of the a. Con. 15

ADULTERY.
A., neighing at his neighbour's door Ex. 39

ADULTRESS.
Than to release the a. from her bond T. iii 63
The a.! what a theme for angry verse! T. iii 64

ADUST.
A. with stripes told out for every crime T. 83

ADVANCE.
'Tis hard if all is false that I a. Con. 95
Proud to a. it all they can Mrs. M. 14
Exert their influence, and a. their cause P.E. 463
Where it a. far into the deep T. i 619
A. it into notice, that its worth T. iii 703
That may a., but cannot hinder, thine T. vi 955
And, felt alike by each, a. both Tir. 485

ADVANCED.
On all the wings of chivalry a. A.T. 149
That flight in circles urged a. them nought N.A. 52
Will stand a. a step above the rest R. 722
His predecessor's coat a. to wear T. 145
The globe and its concerns, I seem a. T. iv 95

ADVANCEMENT.
Forbids the a. of the soul he binds R. 236
And, as thou wouldst the a. of thine heir Tir. 708

ADVANCING.
A. Fashion to the post of Truth T. i 744
In Honour's field a. his firm foot T.T. 16

ADVANTAGE.
Placed with a. at his listening ear A.T. 181
Honesty shines with great a. there H. 402
No mean a. from a kindred cause T. i 387
It may enjoy the a. of the worth T. iii 771
Receives a. from his noiseless hours T. vi 944

ADVENT.
The dawn of thy last a., long desired T. vi 866

ADVENTURES.
With all the a. of his early life Tir. 325

ADVENTUROUS.
And after poising her a. wings R. 671
Escaped with pain from that a. flight T. i 4
The expedience of a less a. course Tir. 804

ADVERSE.
Let nothing a., nothing unforeseen Ch. 131
Is a. Providence, when pondered well Ex. 310
Providence a. in events like these? Ex. 313
Just then, by a. fate impressed T.B. 43
Of a. fortune's power Trans. H. 3

ADVERTISE.
To a. in verse a public pest T. iv 501
An art contrived to a. a joke T.T. 539
And though I would not a. them yet Tir. 915

ADVERTISED.
Then a., and auctioneered away T. iii 756

ADVICE.
Though sage a. of friends the most sincere R. 249
Could give a., could censure or commend R. 291

ADVISE.
But whom do I a.? the fashion-led Tir. 779

ADVISER.
Than to neglect a good a. P.T. 61

ADVOCATE.
Well spoken, a. of sin and shame Con. 587

ÆSOP.
Æ., and Phædrus, and the rest? Why not Tir. 546

ÆTHEREAL.
Æ. journeys, submarine exploits T. iv 85

ÆTHIOPIA.
And Æ. spreads abroad the hand T. vi 812

ÆTNA'S.
There was a time when Æ.'s silent fire Her. 1
Behold in Æ.'s emblematic fires Her. 45
But Æ. of the suffering world ye sway? Her. 78

AFFABLE.
A., humble, diffident, and mild *P.E.* 537
Gentle, and a., and full of grace *T.* vi 500

AFFAIRS.
Who makes no bustle with his soul's a. *Con.* 580
With proof, that we, and our a. *E.* i 57
By which Heaven rules the mixed a. of man *H.* 16
Assembled on a. of love *P.T.* 14
An aspect stern on man's a. *P.T.* 48
But ask the noble drudge in state a. *R.* 407
The smooth and equal course of his a. *T.* ii 173

AFFECT.
If neither horse nor groom a. the squire *Con.* 419
Nor can he much a. the neighbouring peer *R.* 441
Though many boast thy favours, and a. *T.* iii 294
Or nymphs responsive, equally a. *T.* iv 21

AFFECTATION.
Of idle mirth and a. coy *S.* ii 10
All a. 'Tis my perfect scorn *T.* ii 417

AFFECTION.
That guides and governs our a. *E.* i 35
Enfeeble his a. *F.* 156
Skins may differ, but a. *N.C.* 15.
A. lights a brighter flame *U.* 27
Farewell, false hearts! whose best a. fail *V.* 1
Proof of an old a. still alive *V.* 24

AFFECTIONATE.
A., a mother lost so long *M.P.* 14
May feel it too; a. in look *T.* ii 405
Patient, a., of high command *Tir.* 602

AFFECTS.
A. indeed a most humane concern *Ch.* 495
Done to the nobler part a. it long *Tir.* 491

AFFIRMANCE.
They swear it, till a. breeds a doubt *Con.* 66

AFFLICTION.
Gives even a. a grace *A.S.* 55
What their a. was, and begged a share *Con.* 524
That scorns a. mercifully meant *R.* 760
To bid *A.'s* eye no longer stream *S.* ii 12
Galled by a.'s heavy chain *St.* v 11

AFFLUENT.
And dint of genius, to an a. lot *T.T.* 677

AFFORD.
A. them place of rest? *A Tale* 26
Or all that this earth can a. *A.S.* 28
Some succour yet they could a. *Cast.* 25
A. a plea allowable, or just *Con.* 47
And with it every joy it can a. *H.* 679
Or spendthrift's prodigal excess a. *J.T.* 16
For the sweets your cane a. *N.C.* 24
The richest earthly boon his hands a. *R.* 271
That could a. retirement, or could not? *R.* 488
Can British Paradise no scenes a. *P.E.* 257
Dearly obtains the refuge it a. *T.* i 238   [*P.F.* 10
Where the hazels a. him a screen from the heat
By its true worth, the comforts it a. *T.* i 397
May feed excesses she can ill a. *T.* ii 650
With pleasure more than even their fruits a. *T.* iii 410
Admitted freely, may a. their aid *T.* iii 425
Friendly to vital motion, may a. *T.* iii 509
A. the smaller minstrels no supply *T.* v 84
And they that can a. the expense of more *Tir.* 694

AFFORDING.
Thus war a. field for the display *T.* v 238

AFFRIGHT.
One falls—the rest, wide scattered with a. *St.* ii 23

AFFRONT.
Will not a. me, and no other can *Con.* 194
Yet please not, but a. you to your face *Con.* 228
That air of insolence a. your God *Con.* 487
That, while it courts, a. and does you wrong *R.* 550
Retorts the a. against the Crown of Pride *T.* 502
To quell the faction that a. the throne *T.T.* 67
Courage, ungraced by these, a. the skies *T.T.* 378

AFFRONTED.
Not more a. by avowed neglect *T.* 73

AFLOAT.
I dreamed that on ocean a. *M.D.* 5
Sweet moralist! a. on life's rough sea *R.H.* 3

AFRAID.
Were not a. to plough the brine *A Tale* 71
So man, the moth, is not a., it seems *T.* vi 211

AFRICA.
For *A.'s* once loved, benighted shore *Ch.* 241
From *A.'s* sorrowful shore *M.D.* 32
A.'s coast I left forlorn *N.C.* 2
A.'s sons should undergo *N.C.* 37
By our blood in *A.* wasted *N.C.* 41
In *A.'s* torrid clime, or India's fiercest heat *T.T.* 297

AFTER-GAMES.
To him that wears it. What can a. *T.* ii 762

AFTER-THRIFT.
Sad waste! for which no a. atones *St.* ii 29

AGE.
Might learn from the wisdom of a. *A.S.* 23
They court the notice of a future a. *B.B.* 4
That tells his name, his worth, his a. *Cast.* 51
Nor a. nor infancy could find thee there *Ch.* 48
Of adolescence, or a firmer a. *Con.* 46   [*Ch.* 171
The beasts are chartered—neither a. nor force
But when the breath of a. commits the fault *Con.* 49
Credulous infancy, or a. as weak *Con.* 225
Well—what are a., and the lapse of time *Con.* 547
Vigorous in a. as in the flush of youth *Con.* 601
Could fetch from records of an earlier a. *Con.* 615
Yet a., by long experience well informed *Con.* 639
No—shame upon a self-disgracing a. *Con.* 735
The praise of names for a. obsolete *Con.* 828
And call up evidence from every a. *Ex.* 162   [647
The fruits of a., less fair, are yet more sound *Con.*
But a., in spite of weakness and of pain *Ex.* 251
For a. safe beneath his sheltering hand *Ex.* 563
Their names, alas! in vain reproach an a. *Ex.* 660
By repetition palled, by a. obtuse *H.* 22
Would a. in thee resign his wintry reign *H.* 33
That only future a. can restore *Her.* 40
As youth or a. persuades, and neither true *H.* 70
But down to latest a., from earliest youth *H.* 232
And bore the pelting scorn of half an a. *H.* 557
The scoff of withered a. and beardless youth *H.* 743
Two nymphs, both nearly of an a. *J.P.* 1   [i 132
Some youthful grace that a. would gladly keep *T.*
But a. yet to come shall mourn *M.* i 11
Proof against sickness and old a. *M.F.* 50
And still to be so to my latest a. *M.P.* 69
Could I believe, that winds for a. pent *N.A.* 85
From thoughtless youth to ruminating a. *P.E.* 24
Lay his old a. upon the lap of ease *R.* 12
And at the root of a. *St.* i 24   [*T.* iv 124
Than those of a., thy forehead wrapped in clouds
To a. in a world of pain *St.* v 9
To a., where he goes *St.* v 10
Conscious of a., she recollects her youth *T.* 153
He, praised perhaps for a. yet to come *T.* 333

Those barbarous *a*. past, succeeded next *T.* i 16
Even *a*. itself seems privileged in them *T.* i 403
For second childhood; and devote old *a*. *T.* ii 637
In wintry *a*. to feel no chill *M.* 42 [*T.* ii 728
Was quenched in rheums of *a*., his voice unstrung
In Christian charity (good-natured *a*.!) *T.* iii 95
To Moses, was mistaken in its *a*. *T.* iii 154
Impaired by *a*., his unrelenting hand *T.* iii 416
That toiling *a*. have but just matured *T.* iii 450
Are wedded thus, like beauty to old *a*. *T.* iii 660
Improvement too, the idol of the *a*. *T.* iii 764
And lilies for the brows of faded *a*. *T.* iv 80
To *a*., if he might *St.* v 8 [226
E'en misses, at whose *a*. their mothers wore *T.* iv
Grant it :—I still must envy them an *a*. *T.* iv 529
I marvelled much that at so ripe an *a*. *T.* iv 713
That monarchs have supplied, from *a*. to *a*. *T.* v 386
But the *a*. of virtuous politics is past *T.* v 493
A distant *a*. asks where the fabric stood *T.* v 535
A. of hopeless misery. Future death *T.* v. 607
That reared us. At a thoughtless *a*., allured *T.* vi 38
A. after *a*., than to arrest his course? *T.* vi 131
Slow circling *a*. are as transient days *T.* vi 227
That *a*. or injury has hollowed deep *T.* vi 311 [790
Holds its due course, nor fears the frosts of *a*. *T.* vi
Exclaimed, "that me, the lullabies of *a*." *T.* vi 506
Or can, the more than Homer of his *a*.? *T.* vi 647
More golden than that *a*. of fabled gold *T.* vi 996
While Alfred's name the father of his *a*. *T.T.* 105
Not so. The virtue still adorns our *a*. *T.T.* 340
A. elapsed ere Homer's lamp appeared *T.T.* 556
And *a*. ere the Mantuan Swan was heard *T.T.* 557
To give a Milton birth, asked *a*. more *T.T.* 559
Was lumber in an *a*. so void of taste *T.T.* 619
Of rank obscenity, debauched their *a*. *T.T.* 631
With all the skill of *a*. *Th.* 8 [730
Which heaven has heard for *a*., have an end *T.* vi
Shall cheer our latest *a*. *The Doves* 12 [*Tir.* 14
With truths poured down from every distant *a*.
A book (to please us at a tender *a*. *Tir.* 121
Their childhood pleased them at a riper *a*. *Tir.* 148
And such an *a*. as ours balks no expense *Tir.* 257
We feel it e'en in *a*., and at our latest day *Tir.* 317
As, hid from *a*. past, God now displays *Tir.* 638
Health's last farewell, a staff to thine old *a*. *Tir.* 878
That would reclaim a vicious *a*. *U.* 6
Amusement-monger of a trifling *a*. *V.* 28
Relics of *a*.! Could a mind, imbued *Y.O.* 6
When tempests could not. At thy firmest *a*. *Y.O.* 93
But since, although well qualified by *a*. *Y.O.* 137

AGED.

"Princess!" if our *a*. eyes *B.* 9
He, still more *a*., feels the shocks *Ep.* ii 41
Muse, hang this harp upon yon *a*. beech *Ex.* 718
One comfort yet shall cheer thine *a*. heart *Tir.* 897
Lives not, *a*. though he be *Tran.* iii 31

AGENCY.

An *a*. divine, to make him know *T.* vi 130

AGENTS.

A. of his will to use? *N.C.* 32

AGGLOMERATED.

The *a*. pile, his frame may front *T.* iii 472

AGGRIEVED.

From your *a*. Bow-wow *B.R.* 24

AGHAST.

E'en Leeuwenhoek himself would stand *a*. *P.E.* 485

AGILE.

And lightly, shaking it with *a*. hand *T.* iii 478

AGITATE.

Began to *a*. the matter *P.T.* 16

Winds from all quarters *a*. the air *T.* i 373
The wisest heads might *a*. in vain *Tir.* 130
The force that *a*. not unimpaired *Y.O.* 83

AGITATION.

Delight in *a*., yet sustain *Y.O.* 82

AGOG.

Six precious souls, and all *a*. *J.G.* 39

AGONIES.

Whom now despairing *a*. destroy *H.* 172
A fever's *a*., and fed on drugs *T.* i 446
And *a*. of human and of brute *T.* ii 105
With eloquence that *a*. inspire *T.* iii 330

AGONIZED.

Bled, groaned, and *a*., and died in vain *P.E.* 624

AGREE.

Not oft so well *a*.) *Dr.* 2
First, for a thought—since all *a*. *E.* iv 35
Each man of common sense *a*.) *E.* iv 68
Your faith and mine substantially *a*. *H.* 398
And all, impatient of dry land, *a*. *R.* 523
And heart that cannot rest *a*.! *S.* 4
Give saintship, then all Europe must *a*. *T.* 111

AGREED.

Where parties are *a*., retired the scene *A.T.* 89
A. But would you sell or slay your horse *T.T.* 304

AGRIPPA.

As bold as, in *A*.'s presence, Paul *Ex.* 445

AGUISH.

And *a*. east, till time shall have tranformed *T.* iii 772

AID.

When, snatched from all effectual *a*. *Cast.* 63
This genial intercourse, and mutual *a*. *Ch.* 93
Let supposition lend her *a*. once more *Ch.* 383
And He that gives conception *a*. the birth *Con.* 434
A beam that *a*., but never grieves the sight *Con.* 600
In *a*. of our defective sight *E.* i 62
To listen is to lend him *a*. *F.* 101
And in her eye, and by her *a*. *Mrs. M.* 49
In *a*. of her design *Q.V.* 34
Emblems of health and heavenly *a*. *Q.V.* 47
And hold the world indebted to your *a*. *R.* 665
Yet never ask his *a*.! *St.* vi 20 [*T.* ii 368
That grave and learned clerks should need such *a*.
His prayer preferred to saints that cannot *a*. *T.* 85
Benevolence, and peace, and mutual *a*. *T.* ii 48
Its bergamot, or *a*. the indebted eye *T.* ii 452
Admitted freely, may afford their *a*. *T.* iii 425
Must lend its *a*. to illustrate all their charms *T.* iii 591
Uninjured, but expect the upholding *a*. *T.* iii 658
Not sumptuously adorned, nor needing *a*. *T.* iv 251
Of distribution; liberal of their *a*. *T.* iv 413
Need no such *a*. as Superstition lends *T.* vi 510
In *a*. of our defects. In some are found *T.* vi 611
Kind Providence attends with gracious *a*. *T.T.* 249

AIDED.

For *a*. both by ear and scent *T.B.* 49

AIDING.

A. a dubious and deficient sight *Ch.* 329
And she the works of Phœbus *a*. *Mrs. M.* 55
In *a*. helpless indigence, in works *T.* vi 964
Where, stillness *a*. study, and his mind *Tir.* 773

AILING.

Touch but his nature in its *a*. part *Tir.* 161

AILS. [272
What *a*. thee, restless as the waves that roar *Ex.*

AIM.

(Charity chosen as my theme and *a.*) *Ch.* 295
Pure in her *a.*, and in her temper mild *Ch.* 422
Such as our motive is our *a.* must be *Ch.* 567
The mark at which my juster *a.* I take *Con.* 105
Transformed to blessings, miss their cruel *a. E.* ii 38
Candid and just, with no false *a.* in view *Ex.* 648
Act without *a.*, think little, and feel less *H.* 8
His happiness, her dear, her only *a. H.* 64
So void of all utility or *a. H.* 88
The inquirer's *a.*, that remedy, is Hope *H.* 114
His *a.* was mischief, and his zeal pretence *H.* 564
Glory your *a.*, but justice your pretence *Her.* 44
When, exercise and air my only *a. N.A.* 31
Who studiously make peace their *a. N.G.* 36
Whose hand is feeble, or his *a.* untrue *P.E.* 571
Calls him away from selfish ends and *a. R.* 19
Or shoot the careless with a surer *a. R.* 218
Her smile his *a.*, all higher *a.* farewell! *R.* 246
Sick of a thousand disappointed *a.*) *R.* 366
Your useful labours, and important *a. R.* 664
Me poetry (or rather notes that *a.*) *R.* 801
And the foe's unerring *a. St.* iv 12
Pants for it, *a.* at it, enters it, and dies *T.* 6
Are his sole *a.*, and all his glory now *T.* iv 658
And figure of the man, his secret *a. T.* vi 618
And *a.* them at the shield of truth again *T.* vi 875
They take perhaps a well directed *a. T.T.* 206
Prompt his endeavour, and engage his *a. T.T.* 747
At first he *a.* at what he hears *Tran.* iv 19

AIMED.

But yet successful, being *a.* at him *Con.* 540 [591
Which, *a.* at him, have pierced the offended skies *H.*

AIMING.

For ever *a.* at the world's esteem *Con.* 367

AIR.

Soft *a.* and gentle heavings of the wave *Ch.* 127
Snuffs up the morning *a.*, forgets the rein *Ch.* 175
As ever dressed a bank, or scented summer *a. Ch.* 259
He hides behind a magisterial *a. Ch.* 493
Bowed at the close with all his graceful *a. Con.* 73
That *a.* of insolence affronts your God *Con.* 487
And asked them, with a kind, engaging *a. Con.* 523
Divest the rougher sex of female *a. Con.* 843
The noon was shady, and soft *a. D.W.* 1
That cleaves the yielding *a.* unheard *E.* i 88
O balmy gales of soul-reviving *a. E.* ii 27
Yet He was gentle as soft summer *a. Ex.* 133
Enjoyed the open *a. F.B.* 3
Time was when I was free as *a. G.* 1
The screaming nations, hovering in mid *a. H.* 353
Soft *a.* and genial moisture feed and cheer *H.* 489
To storm the citadels they build in *a. H.* 626
Long as I draw ethereal *a. Miss* — 67
The sober cordial of sweet *a. Mor.* 10   [iv 772
To range the fields and treat their lungs with *a. T.*
When, exercise and *a.* my only aim *N.A.* 31
Upborne into the viewless *a. O.* i 13   [iii 539
From flower to flower, and even the breathing *a. T.*
Hark! how it floats upon the dewy *a.*! *P.E.* 63
A simpering countenance, and a trifling *a. P.E.* 206
Or whether clearer skies and softer *a. P.E.* 409
Up-spouted by a whale in *a. Q.V.* 19   [*T.* i 589
And breathing wholesome *a.*, and wandering much
Once prone on earth, now buoyant upon *a. R.* 66
Frowning in storms, or breathing gentle *a. R.* 194
The suitor's *a.* indeed he soon improves *R.* 237
Soft *a.*, nocturnal vigils, and day dreams *R.* 260
And sends the patient into purer *a. R.* 282
Breathes clouds of dust, and calls it country *a. R.* 486

The breathings of the lightest *a.* that blows *R.* 530
Where neither cold might come, nor *a. R.C.* 31
Would give a barbarous *a.* to British song *T.* 102
And sails with lappet head and mincing *a. T.* 139
Fearless of humid *a.* and gathering rains *T.* 212
And so two citizens who take the *a. T.* i 79
Respiring freely the fresh *a.*, that makes *T.* i 138
Winds from all quarters agitate the *a. T.* i 373
The *a.* salubrious of her lofty hills *T.* i 428
In catching smoke and feeding upon *a. R.* 38
Receive our *a.*, that moment they are free *T.* ii 41
And mortal nuisance into all the *a. T.* ii 98
Then, with an *a.* most gracefully performed *T.* ii 447
As move derision, or by foppish *a. T.* ii 562
And sheltered sofa, while the nitrous *a. T.* iii 32
I cannot analyze the *a.*, nor catch *T.* iii 214   [443
As the sun peeps, and vernal *a.* breathe mild *T.* iii
At measured distances, that *a.* and sun *T.* iii 424
If fanned by balmy and nutritious *a. T.* iii 524
The maid who views with pensive *a. P.B.* 23   [732
But are not wholesome *a.*, though unperfumed *T.* iii
Sermons, and city feasts, and favourite *a. T.* iv 84
Of the infirm, is wholesome *a.* to thee *T.* iv 365
He steps right onward, martial in his *a. T.* iv 640
Prove it. A breath of unadulterate *a. T.* iv 750
While *a.* impregnated with incense play *M.P.* 94
Streams far behind him, scenting all the *a. T.* v 57
With melting *a.*, or martial, brisk, or grave *T.* vi 3
And guiltless of offence, they range the *a. T.* vi 575
If all we find possessing earth, sea, *a. Tir.* 91 [687
The mulberry-tree was hymn'd with dulcet *a. T.* vi
But how? resides such virtue in that *a. Tir.* 373
The pedagogue, with self-complacent *a. Tir.* 527
And not at last evaporate in *a. Tir.* 772   [294
Place me where winter breathes his keenest *a. T.T.*
Must find a colder soil and bleaker *a. Tir.* 851
Perhaps some bonny Caledonian *a. T.T.* 534
With artless *a.* and concerts of her own *T.T.* 697
In praise harmonious the first *a.* he drew *Y.O.* 155
And strangers to the *a.* of courts 1789, 62

AIRY.

Who long had marked her *a.* lodge *A Fable* 25
A. del Castro was as bold a knight *A.T.* 1
They sport like wanton doves in *a.* rings *A.T.* 32
Proves after all a wind-gun's *a.* charge *Con.* 274
As erst with *a.* self-conceit *R.C.* 100
They bound, and *a.*, o'er the sunny glade *St.* ii 22
How *a.* and how light the graceful arch *T.* i 341
From reveries so *a.*, from the toil *T.* iii 188
Thither he wings his *a.* flight *Tran.* ii 14   [iv 525
Vain wish! those days were never; *a.* dreams *T.*

AKIN.

A. to rapture, when the bauble finds *T.* vi 276
Formed as if *a.* to thee *Tran.* iii 18

ALACRITY.

We never feel the *a.* and joy *T.T.* 242.

À-LA-MORT.

What makes some sick, and others *à. Con.* 292

ALARM.

Better dwell in the midst of *a. A.S.* 7
I may *a.* thee, but I fear the shame *Ch.* 294
That, while they please, possess us with *a. Ch.* 546
And sucked a breast that panted with *a. Ex.* 473
The Maker fills the nations with *a. Ex.* 585
They felt the rude *a. M.* 26   [185
Great crimes *a.* the conscience, but it sleeps *T.* iii
Might well *a.* the most unguarded mind *P.E.* 58
The lover too shuns business and *a. R.* 219
Contingence might *a.* him, and disturb *T.* ii 172

Grieves, but *a.* me not. I mourn the pride *T.* iv 102
Of sounding an *a.* assaults these doors *T.* iv 146
With all the prettiness of feign'd *a. T.* vi 319

ALBION.
No braver chief could *A.* boast *Cast.* 7
Nor ever ship left *A.'s* coast *Cast.* 9
Thou, as a gallant bark from *A.'s* coast *M.P.* 88
In *A.'s* happy isle. The lumber stood *T.* i 58
The sons of *A.*; fearing each to lose *T.* iii 599
O Queen of *A.*, queen of isles! 1789, 56 [v 517
And hewed them link from link. Then *A.'s* sons *T.*

ALCOVE.
This china that decks the *a. Gr.* 33
Look where he comes; in this embowered *a. R.* 283
The summit gained, behold the proud *a. T.* i 278
Sacred to neatness and repose, the *a. T.* vi 571

ALDERMAN.
An *A.* of Cripplegate contrived *T.* i 61

ALDERS.
Those *a.* quivering to the breeze *S.* 6

ALERT.
The rest, *a.* and active, as became *A.T.* 133
Not such the *a.* and active. Measure life *T.* i 396
Grow on the gamester's elbows, and the *a. T.* iii 761
Let magistrates *a.* perform their parts *T.T.* 311

ALEXIS.
Thyrsis, *A.*, or whatever name *R.* 247

ALFRED.
On such a stool immortal *A.* sat *T.* i 22
While *A.'s* name, the father of his age *T.T.* 105

ALGEBRA.
The scales are false, or *a.* a lie *Con.* 22

ALIENATED.
Thou well deservest an *a.* son *Tir.* 579

ALIGHT.
The clumsy swains *a. Y.D.* 22

ALIGHTING.
My Lord, *a.* at his usual place *R.* 585
A. in far distant fields, finds out *T.* ii 109
A., turns the key in her own door *T.* ii 653
Softly *a.* upon all below *T.* iv 328

ALIVE.
To make a blaze—that's roasting him *a. Con.* 334
Far more *a.* than other men *E.* i 10
Of critics now *a.* or long since dead *H.* 426
To strip them off, 'tis being flayed *a. P.E.* 583
Men that if now *a.*, would sit content *T.* ii 541
Man praises man. The rabble, all *a. T.* vi 694
And keeps *a.* his fierce but noble fires *T.T.* 223
Proof of an old affection still *a. V.* 24
Finds thee not less *a.* to her sweet force *Y.O.* 133

ALLAYED.
No voice divine the storm *a. Cast.* 61

ALL-BESTOWING.
Had not his Maker's *a.* hand *Con.* 429

ALL-CONQUERING.
Then the proud eagles of *a.* Rome *Ex.* 209

ALL-CREATING.
Why did *a.* Nature? *N.C.* 17
Of *a.* energy and might *T.* v 554

ALL-DEVOURING.
In *a.* flame *M.* 22

ALLEGIANCE.
Had they maintained *a.* firm and sure *Ex.* 207

ALLEY.
This moss-grown *a.* musing, slow *S.* 18
Or tinkle in 'Change *A.*, to amuse *T.T.* 186

ALLIANCE.
Of close *a.* to the Eternal Mind *J.T.* 44

ALLIED.
Might feel themselves *a.* to all the race *Ch.* 22

ALLOT.
Hour after hour delightfully *a. R.* 373

ALLOTMENT.
It is the *a.* of the skies *E.* i 33

ALLOTTED.
Nature, employed in her *a.* place *H.* 145

ALLOW.
And, such as storms *a. Cast.* 26
All men of common sense *a. E.* iv 69

ALLOWABLE.
Affords a plea *a.*, or just *Con.* 47

ALLOWANCE.
Where vice has such *a.*, that her shifts *T.* iii 106

ALLOWED.
Though common sense, *a.* a casting voice *Con.* 663
I could be well content, *a.* the use *F.A.* 1
But yet was not *a. J.G.* 34
His works, his abstinence, his zeal *a. T.* 91

ALLOWS.
She yet *a.* herself that boy behind *T.* 142
A. short time for play, and none for sloth *Tir.* 484

ALL-PURIFYING.
Cleansed in thine own *a.* blood *T.* 581

ALL-QUICKENING.
The soul, whose sight *a.* grace renews *Ch.* 395

ALL-SEEING.
And hide past folly from *a.* eyes? *Ex.* 405
The scrutiny of those *a.* eyes *T.* 271
Proofs of the wisdom of the *a.* mind *Tir.* 94

ALLURE.
Or one whom blood *a. Beau.* 14
Who labour hard to *a.* and draw *E.* i 23

ALLURED.
A. by my report: but sure no less *T.* iii 699
That reared us. At a thoughtless age, *a. T.* vi 38

ALLUREMENTS.
Hourly *a.* on his passions press *P.E.* 61

ALLURING.
With smiles *a.* her admirer, man *H.* 40

ALLY.
Her natural *a. Miss —* 90

ALMIGHTY.
Ought at the view of an *A.* power *Con.* 658
So rich an interest in *A.* love? *Ex.* 166
Themselves secured beneath the *A.* wing *Ex.* 189
Insensible of truth's *a.* charms *H.* 655
" Die then, if power *A.* save you not *P.E.* 589
And though the *A.* Maker has throughout *T.* iv 73
That form, the labour of *A.* skill *Tir.* 7
'Tis power *a.* bids him shine *Tran.* i 23

ALMS.

To lull the painful malady with *a*. *Ch*. 448
No charity but *a*. aught values she *Ch*. 459
My prayers and *a*., imperfect and defiled *T*. 577
They live, and live without extorted *a*. *T*. iv 403

ALOFT.

Within that cavity *a*. *A Tale* 37
Pleased she beheld *a*. portrayed *Q.V*. 45
Her head, adorned with lappets pinned *a*. *T*. iv 540
Repays their labour more; and perched *a*. *T*. v 91
As if an eagle flew *a*., and then *T.T*. 552

ALONE.

'Tis Providence *a*. secures *A Fable* 30
I must finish my journey *a*. *A.S*. 10
Nor he *a*. addressed the wayward fair *A.T*. 34
If John marries Mary, and Mary *a*. *A.T*. iii 1
'Tis Nature *a*. that we love *C*. 36
Catharina *a*. can rejoice *C*. 42
A. could rescue them *Cast*. 34
We perished, each *a*. *Cast*. 64 [208
He from whose hands *a*. all power proceeds *Ch*.
But Charity not feigned intends *a*. *Ch*. 449
The founder of that name *a*. inspires *Ch*. 600
"Sir!" I believe it on that ground *a*. *Con*. 233
Save from the subjects of that work *a*. *Con*. 740
That great defect would cost him, not *a*. *Con*. 763
The path of sorrow, and that path *a*. *E*. ii 9
By letting poetry *a*. *E*. iv 10
The scenes to which not youth *a*. resorts *Ex*. 24
Or, waking at the call of lust *a*. *Ex*. 101
'Twas theirs *a*. to dive into the plan *Ex*. 235
The busy trifler dreams himself *a*. *Ex*. 322
And while he ruled thee by the sword *a*. *Ex*. 490
Held by the tenure of his will *a*. *Ex*. 673
And truth *a*., where'er my life be cast *Ex*. 732
An architect requires *a*. *F*. 164
You must not live *a*. *F.B*. 27
But still the imputed tints are those *a*. *H*. 73
Seems, as it is, the fountain whence *a*. *H*. 708
Not kindred minds *a*. are called to employ *H*. 738
That Hope which can *a*. exclude despair *H*. 751
But ours *a*. can ne'er prevail *H.F*. 21
The loss was his *a*. *M*. i 10
I will obey, not willingly *a*. *M.P*. 15
The Heaven that thou *a*. canst make? *O*. ii 14
If the matter depended *a*. upon me *P.A*. 37
Nor these *a*., whose pleasures less refined *P.E*. 57
'Tis not *a*. the grape's enticing juice *P.E*. 271
And toil to polish its rough coat *a*. *P.E*. 420
He that abstains, and he *a*. does right *P.E*. 585
Choose not *a*. a proper mate *P.T*. 64
By right of worth, not blood *a*. *Q.V*. 3
Save love of George *a*. *Q.V*. 64
And calls a creature formed for God *a*. *R*. 17
Nor these *a*. profer a life recluse *R*. 169
Such as its symptoms can *a*. express *R*. 288
A sacred art! to which *a*. life owes *R*. 749
'Tis love like his that can *a*. defeat *R*. 781
Must move and act for him *a*. *R.C*. 114
Thou art not voice *a*., but hast beside *S*. i 9
These *a*., so often heard *St*. iv 30
He lives who lives to God, *a*., *St*. vi 1
And worships Chance *a*.! *St*. vi 28 [201
The livelong night: nor these *a*., whose notes *T*.
Such lunacy is ignorance *a*. *T*. 450
Brings not *a*. the more conspicuous part *T*. 561
And well-tried virtues, could *a*. inspire *T*. i 148
Nor rural sights *a*., but rural sounds *T*. i 181
Nor does the chisel occupy *a*. *T*. i 705
That can *a*. make sweet the bitter draught *T*. i 751
Of his own works, his dreadful part *a*. *T*. ii 82
Knots of worthy solution, which *a*. *T*. ii 520
or taste *a*., and well-contrived display *T*. iii 603
My charmer is not mine *a*.; my sweets *T*. iii 719
Blown in its native bed; 'tis there *a*. *T*. iv 660
'Tis Liberty *a*. that gives the flower *T*. v 446
Is work for him that made him. He *a*. *T*. v 697
The death he had deserved, and died *a*. *T*. vi 556
Thou who *a*. art worthy! It was thine *T*. vi 857
When flowers *a*. I knew would little please *T*. vi 1010
Though want of due restraint *a*. have bred *Tir*. 533
Unenvied there, he may sustain *a*. *Tir*. 535
Which admonition can *a*. disperse *Tir*. 600
Wise for himself and his few friends *a*. *Tir*. 675
He deems it hard to vegetate *a*. *Tir*. 724
His head *a*. remained to tell *T.B*. 65
I fear lest thee *a*. they seize *The Doves* 23
By silent magnanimity *a*. *T.T*. 68
Though discontent *a*. can find out where *T.T*. 197
Subserviency his praise, and that *a*. *T.T*. 361
One man *a*., the father of us all *Y.O*. 144
By sufferers like herself *a*. 1789, 49

ALOOF.

God stood not, though he seemed to stand *a*. *Ch*. 59
Bid nations leagued against thee stand *a*. *Ex*. 565
Fancy may stand *a*. from the design *H*. 672

ALOUD.

And snorts *a*. to cast the mist aside *A.T*. 164
He reads wise lectures, and describes *a*. *Ch*. 389
Some whispered softly, and some twanged *a*. *Ch*. 518
And many a tomb, like Hamilton's *a*. *Ep*. i 9
Cry *a*., thou that sittest in the dust *Ex*. 267
Publishing to all *a*. *St*. iv 14 [318
And perks his ears, and stamps, and cries *a*. *T*. vi
They cry *a*. in every careless ear *T.T*. 434
And calls *a*. for sack *Tran*. iv 15
But soon articulates *a*. *Tran*. iv 22

ALPHABETS.

As *a*. in ivory employ *Con*. 11

ALPINE.

Some *a*. mountain, wrapped in snow *Miss* — 33

ALPS.

The cloud-surmounting *a*., the fruitful vales *R*. 79

ALTAR.

Thine *a*., sacred Liberty, should stand *Ch*. 256
To build our *a*., confident and bold *Con*. 849
And serves the *a*., in my soul I loathe *T*. ii 416
On Fortune's velvet *a*. offering up *T*. ii 657
Shall have its *a*.; and the world shall go *T*. vi 668

ALTER.

Much less could he *a*. her mind *Gr*. 48
To check, or *a*. from its course *Miss* — 59

ALTERED.

His *a*. gait and stateliness retrenched *T*. v 76
Your *a*. heart—and so, my Lord, farewell! *V*. 26

ALTERNATE.

And then *a*., with a sickly hope *T*. v 428
Calm and *a*. storm, moisture and drought *Y.O*. 77

ALTERNATELY.

A. the nations learn and teach *Ch*. 120
Beating *a*., in measured time, *T.T*. 528

ALTERNATIVE.

(Awful *a*.! believed, beloved *Ex*. 688

ALTHÆA.

A. with the purple eye; the broom *T*. vi 170

ALTITUDES.
Leaves saints to enjoy those *a.* they teach *Con.* 585

AMAIN.
John coming back *a. J.G.* 222

AMARANTHINE.
And laid her soft in *a.* flowers *A.T.* 8
Plucks *a.* joys from bowers of bliss *H.* 164
The only *a.* flower on earth *T.* iii 268

AMASSES.
For her, *a.* an unbounded store *Tir.* 15

AMAZE.
His road, deriding much the blank *a. T.* vi 536

AMAZED.
A. that shadows should obscure the sight *H.* 534
The calender, *a.* to see *J.G.* 161
Tremble and be *a.* at thine escape *T.* ii 159

AMBASSADOR.
As God's *a.*, the grand concerns *T.* ii 464

AMBIGUITIES.
His *a.* his total sum *Con.* 143

AMBIGUOUS.
Inquisitive, the less *a.* past *Y.O.* 44

AMBITION.
Speaks a divine *a.*, and a zeal *Ch.* 307
Of all *a.* man may entertain *Con.* 221
From mean self-interest and *a.* clear *Ex.* 439
From avarice and *a.* free *O.* ii 8
Here various motives his *a.* raise *P.E.* 53
A., avarice, and the lust of fame *P.E.* 273
Of pride, *a.*, or impure desires *R.* 110
'Twas his *a.* to be seen of men *T.* 53
To fill the *a.* of a private man *T.* ii 236
The *a.* of one meaner far, whose powers *T.* iii 458
A., Avarice, Penury incurred *T.* iii 811
That tempts *A.* On the summit see *T.* iv 58
Tend downward; his *a.* is to sink *T.* v 592
A. in a boy supplied *Th.* 7
The wretch, to naught but his *a.* true *T.T.* 30
By low *a.* and the thirst of praise *T.T.* 591

AMBITIOUS.
A., not to shine or to excel *Con.* 623
A. of brushing the sky *Gr.* 4
The mischiefs your *a.* pride inspires! *Her.* 46
A. of a shelter there *Mrs. M—* 44
That courts display before *a.* eyes *R.* 178
And yet *a.* not to sing in vain *T.* ii 312
A. of preferment for its gold *T.* ii 387
And vain enough to be *a.* still *T.* v 338

AMBLING.
To cross his *a.* pony day by day *R.* 467
A. and prattling scandal as he goes *T.* ii 382

AMBROSIAL.
A. gardens, in which Art supplies *Ex.* 11

AMEN.
And answer all—"*A.!*" *St.* i 36
Hail, Sternhold then, and Hopkins hail! *A.T.T.* 760

AMENABLE.
Say to what bar *a.* were man? *P.E.* 28

AMENDS.
In honourable bumps his rich *a. Con.* 200
Not unemployed, and finding rich *a. T.* iv 729

AMISS.
In characters uncouth, and spelt *a. T.* i 283
May exercise *a.* his proper powers *T.* v 339
The few that pray at all pray oft *a. T.* vi 54
And yet his judgment was not framed *a. T.T.* 390
Of argument, employed too oft *a. Y.O.* 31

AMITY.
On terms of *a.* complete *F.* 116
To live on terms of *a.* with vice *T.* v 658

AMNESTY.
Of *a.*, the meed of blood divine *Y.O.* 13

AMOMUM.
The *a.* there with intermingling flowers *T.* iii 576

AMOROUS.
He called her Posy, with an *a.* art *A.T.* 21
To watch yon *a.* couple in their play *T.* 136
Or charged with *a.* sighs of absent swains *T.* iv 20

AMOUNT.
Shall find them rated at their full *a. T.* 545
Your feelings in their full *a. P.* 47
Which *a.* to possession time out of mind *A.C.* 12

AMPLE.
Loose fly his forelock and his *a.* mane *Ch.* 176
Thy soul as *a.* as thy bounds are small *Ex.* 696
To whom an atom is an *a.* field *R.* 62
Deception innocent—give *a.* space *T.* i 353
To all the nations. *A.* was the boon *T.* v 199
And folly in as *a.* measure meet *T.* v 309
Its *a.* area 'gan explore *T.B.* 38
For her, the Memory fills her *a.* page *Tir.* 13
That grazed it stood beneath that *a.* cope *Y.O.* 54

AMPLER.
Provides the faculties an *a.* range *Ch.* 334
And transplantation in an *a.* space *T.* iii 533
Resplendent less, but of an *a.* round *T.* iv 258
And more aspiring, and with *a.* spread *T.* vi 145

AMUSE.
The achievements of Art may *a. C.* 37
A trifle if it move but to *a. P.E.* 303
Servile employ; but such as may *a. T.* iii 406
While fields of pleasantry *a.* us there *T.* iv 76
Or tinkle in 'Change Alley, to *a. T.T.* 186

AMUSED.
While thoughtful man is plausibly *a. T.* iii 186
The wish to shine, the thirst to be *a. T.* iii 829
Nor less *a.*, have I quiescent watched *T.* iv 291
Some have *a.* the dull, sad years of life *T.* v 180
A. spectators of this bustling stage *T.* v 878

AMUSEMENT.
Business or vain *a.*, care or mirth *R.* 647
A. and true knowledge hand in hand *R.* 702
Their least *a.* where he found the most *T.* ii 310
But is *a.* all? Studious of song *T.* ii 311
Made vocal for the *a.* of the rest *T.* iv 159
To such *a.* as ingenious woe *T.* v 416
Much to the *a.* of the crowd *Tran.* iv 23

AMUSEMENT-MONGER.
A. of a trifling age *V.* 28

ANACREON.
A., Horace, played in Greece and Rome *T.T.* 608

ANALYSE.
I cannot *a.* the air, nor catch *T.* iii 214

ANARCHY.
Spread *a.* and terror all around? *T.T.* 303

ANCESTRY.
Long lines of a., renowned of old *Tir.* 817
Our a., a gallant Christian race *T.T.* 372

ANCHOR.
Has dropped her a., and her canvas furled *Ch.* 443
Hope, as an a. firm and sure, holds fast *H.* 167

ANCHORED.
Of life, long since has a. by thy side *M.P.* 99
Fast a. in the deep abyss of space *R.* 84

ANCHORITE.
"Past all dispute, yon a.," say you *T.* 106

ANCIENT.
"The blood of a. worthies in his veins" *A.T.* 116
Oh! could their a. Incas rise again *Ch.* 65
While Conscience, happier than in a. years *Ch.* 274
Where stands that monument of a. power *Ch.* 549
The heathen lawgivers of a. days *Con.* 35 [167
Where dwell they now? Where dwelt in a. day *Ex.*
('Twas therefore much the same in a. days) *E.* iii 7
Mere shadows now, their a. pomp forgot *Ex.* 262
Babbler of a. fables, leaves a doubt *Ex.* 503
A hollow scooped, I judge, in a. time *N.A.* 17
Nor a., will be so, preserved with care *P.E.* 400
So, a. poets say, serene *Q.V.* 69
And cultivate a taste for a. song *R.* 375
The estate his sires had owned in a. years *R.* 579
Yon a. prude, whose withered features show *T.* 131
And such in a. halls and mansions drear *T.* i 24
Of a. growth, make music not unlike *T.* i 185
Invites us. Monument of a. taste *T.* i 253
Their a. barriers, deluging the dry? *T.* ii 56
A prince with half his people! *A.* towers *T.* ii 121
In colleges and halls, in a. days *T.* ii 699
So once were ranged the sons of a. Rome *T.* iii 596
To reverence what is a., and can plead *T.* v 300
An a., not a legendary tale *T.* vi 479
By a. covenant ere Nature's birth *T.* vi 858
Renowned in a. song; not vexed with care *T.* vi 997
Caught from the deeds of a. fame *Tir.* 645
Feats of renown, though wrought in a. days *T.T.* 22
Now, from the dust of a. days, bring forth *T.T.* 376
Nineveh, Babylon, and a. Rome *T.T.* 432
Embowelled now, and of thy a. self *Y.O.* 110
Much a. chronicle, and long 1789, 2

ANDANTE.
The adagio and a. it demands *T.* ii 361

ANGEL.
'Tis e'en as if an a. shook his wings *Ch.* 438
Where 'tis an a.'s happiness to stray) *Con.* 472
Like a. in the service of their Lord *Ex.* 674
Mysteries are food for a.; they digest *F.A.* 55
Nor all an a.'s eloquence explain *H.* 126
So may your guiding a. give *Miss —* 95
She, half an a. in her own account *T.* 149
As a. use, the Gospel whispers peace *T.* ii 342
And a. choirs attended. Wondering stood *T.* vi 352
A devil's purpose with an a.'s face *T.T.* 130
Let me, the charge of some good a., find *V.* 77

ANGEL-HEADS.
Like a. in stone with pigeon wings! *Con.* 576

ANGELIC.
The dews condensed into a. food *Ex.* 182
"True," answered an a. guide *Mor.* 39
A. gratulations rend the skies *T.* 587
Milton, whose genius had a. wings *T.* iii 255

ANGER.
His a. who can waste thee with a word *Ex.* 341
And a. insignificantly fierce *T.* vi 320
Is that which a. hourly for surprise *Con.* 223

ANGRY.
Frowns in the storm with a. brow *A Fable* 38
And if perhaps made a., soon appeased *Ch.* 429
The a. Muse thus sings thee forth *M.B.* 23
But a., coarse, and harsh expression *M.F.* 59
Or bury me in ocean's a. tide! *T.* 270   [212
And perilous lightnings from the a. clouds *T.* iii
A. and sad, and his last crust consumed *T.* i 246
The adultress! what a theme for a. verse! *T.* iii 64
So soon succeeding such an a. night *T.* vi 259
Or growl'd defiance in such a. sort *T.* vi 377

ANGUISH.
Dimness and a., all thy beams obscured *Ex.* 393
With eyes of a., execrate their lot *T.* ii 665

ANIMAL.
Not a. alone, but shrubs and trees *N.A.* 57
The fiercest a. with magic charms) *R.* 254
With sight of a. enjoying life *T.* vi 325
Each a., of every name, conceived *T.* vi 373
The flesh of a. in fee, and claim *T.* vi 452
The blameless a., without rebuke *T.* vi 469
May stand between an a. and woe *T.* vi 727
In all that live, plant, a., and man *Y.O.* 79

ANIMATE.
Nor a. the soul to Christian deeds *H.* 300
His soul exults, Hope a. his lays *R.* 777
Becomes the soul that a. them all *T.* v 275
That were a theme might a. the dead *T.T.* 202

ANIMATED.
Discourse may want an a.—No *Con.* 101
But a. Nature sweeter still *T.* 198
So I with a. hopes behold *T.* v 837

ANIMATING.
Her a. smile withdrawn *S.* 15

ANKLE-DEEP.
Hence, a. in moss and flowery thyme *T.* i 270

ANNA.
Dear *A.*—between friend and friend *E.* i 1
Say, *A.*, had you never known *E.* i 67
Which Mary to *A.* conveyed *The Rose* 2

ANNALS.
What nation will you find, whose a. prove *Ex.* 165

ANNEX'D.
Have each their record, with a curse a. *T.* vi 441

ANNIHILATE.
We persecute, a. the tribes *T.* iii 309

ANNOUNCE.
A. to the world his own and theirs *T.* ii 357
The simple clerk, but loyal, did a. *T.* vi 661

ANNOY.
Pernicious weed. Whose scent the fair a. *Con.* 251
The flinty soil indeed their feet a. *E.* ii 31
So numerous are the follies that a. *Tir.* 597

ANNOYANCE.
No rough a. rankling in his mind *R.* 428

ANNUAL.
And by Philomel's a. note *C.* 47
No longer prey upon our a. rents *Ch.* 616
This a. tribute Death requires *St.* i 11
By public exigence, till a. food *T.* v 458

ANNUL.
Of holy writ, she has presumed to *a*. *T*. i 741

ANSON.
Is wet with *A*.'s tear *Cast*. 52

ANSWER.
Prose *a*. every common end *E*. i 2
In *a*. to the fiat of his word *Ex*. 154   [536
Shall *a*.—" Hope, sweet Hope, has set me free " *H*.
His only *a*. was a blameless life *H*. 577
Makes *a*. quite beside the mark *M.F*. 10
Ah, that maternal smile! it *a*.—" Yes " *M.P*. 27
Hark! he *a*.—Wild tornadoes *N.C*. 33
Where his whirlwinds *a*.—" No " *N.C*. 40
On purpose to *a*. you, out of my mint *P.A*. 19
Their *a*. to the call is—" Not at home " *P.E*. 168
Wins in return an *a*. of disdain *R*. 228
Vast as it is, it *a*., as it flows *R*. 529
And *a*. all—" Amen! " *St*. i 36
Devised by self to *a*. selfish ends *T*. 110
That question has its *a*.—What is man? *T*. 382
A Deity could solve. Their *a*., vague *T*. ii 521
He purposes, and he shall *a*.—" None " *T*. vi 934
Bid fair enough to *a*. in the proof *Tir*. 564
Deserves an *a*. similar, or none *Tir*. 904

ANSWERED.
" True," *a*. an angelic guide *Mor*. 39
Him *a*. then his loving mate and true *N.A*. 105
The happiness of *a*. prayers 1789, 64   [*P.A*. 23
He was shocked, sir, like you, and *a*.—" Oh no! "

ANTARCTIC.
Towards the *A*.   Even the favoured isles *T*. i 620

ANTHEMS
Re-echoing pious *a*.! while beneath *T*. i 343

ANTICIPATE.
Toils to *a*. in vain *E*. i 66
A. a day it never sees *Ep*. i 8
Watches your eye, *a*. command *T*. 214
Would oft *a*. his glad return *T*. i 543
A. perforce some dire event *T*. v 524
To soar, and to *a*. the skies *T*. v 723

ANTICIPATED.
He snuffs far off the *a*. joy *P.E*. 219
A. rents, and bills unpaid *R*. 559

ANTIPATHIES.
A. are none. No foe to man *T*. vi 777

ANTIQUARIAN.
Craze *a*. brains with endless doubt *P.E*. 394

ANTIQUATED.
Are such an *a*. scene *M.F*. 7

ANTIQUITY.
Him blind *a*. profaned, not served *T*. vi 231

ANVIL.
Of lust, and on the *a*. of despair *T*. v 665

ANXIETY.
Where, all his long *a*. forgot *R*. 7
He feels the *a*. of life, denied *T*. ii 302
Careless of all the *a*. he feels *T.T*. 145

ANXIOUS.
To every pang that racks an *a*. mind *Ex*. 571
With *a*. meaning, Heavenward turn his eye! *St*. ii 8
Then *a*. to be longer spared *St*. v 25   [140
From *a*. thoughts how wealth may be increased *R*.

A. in vain to find the distant floor *T*. i 48
And *a*. mainly that the flock he feeds *T*. ii 404
If *a*. only that their boys may learn *Tir*. 513
Nor ceased till, ever *a*. to redress *T.T*. 632

APACE.
So Self starts nothing but what tends *a*. *Ch*. 565

APE.
And would degrade her votary to an *a*. *Con*. 460
God's work may serve an *a*. upon a stage *Con*. 736
Profusion *a*. the noble part *F*. 4   [854
With lean performance *a*. the work of Love *T*. vi
Their whole attention, and *a*. all his tricks *Tir*. 225

APOCALYPSE.
See Mercy's grand *a*. displayed! *H*. 448

APOLLO.
A., hast thou stolen away *O*. i 11

APOLOGISTS.
Of all that grave *a*. may write *Ex*. 383

APOSTATE.
But transformation of *a* man *T*. v 695
The young *a*. sickens at the view *Tir*. 167

APOSTLE.
Such was the portrait an *a*. drew *Ch*. 432
From such *a*., O ye mitred heads *T*. ii 392

APOSTOLIC.
His *a*. charity the same *H*. 583
If *a*. gravity be free *P.E*. 146

APPAREL.
Conspicuous, and in bright *a*. clad *T*. v 25

APPARELLED.
A. in exactest sort *R.C*. 19

APPARENT.
Blown on the summit of the *a*. fruit *T*. iii 536

APPEAL.
To Justice she may make her bold *a*. *T*. 498

APPEALED.
A. to many a poet's page *L.R*. 11

APPEAR.
" In behalf of the Nose, it will quickly *a*. *A.C*. 9
'Tis called a satire, and the world *a*. *Ch*. 515
As frequent as the want of it *a*. *Ch*. 605   [*A.C*. 21
" On the whole it *a*., and my argument shows "
And savage in its principle *a*. *Con*. 171
Where 'tis a shame to be ashamed to *a*. *Con*. 376
The pillar of the eternal plan *a*. *Con*. 558
And Virtue with peculiar charms *a*. *Con*. 637
A brighter scene beyond that vale *a*. *Con*. 882
No shepherds' tents within thy view *a*. *E*. ii 54
Why weeps the Muse for England? What *a*. *Ex*. 1
Then wherefore weep for England? What *a*. *Ex*. 30
Say Wrath is coming, and the storm *a*. *Ex*. 270
Those rights that millions envy thee *a*. *Ex*. 681
That man, when smoothest he *a*. *F*. 23
May I myself at last *a*. *F*. 214
Thus tortured and squeezed, at last it *a*. *F.M*. 5
This cap, that so stately *a*. *Gr*. 1
The sun, obedient, at her call *a*. *H*. 43
The rose or lily *a*. blue or green *H*. 72
The monarch most that seldom will *a*. *H*. 502
Could those few pleasant days again *a*. *M.P*. 80
Of happier times *a*. *N*. 22
I could be much composed, nor should *a*. *N.A*. 89
Sounds are but sounds, and till the cause *a*. *N.A*. 119

Grey dawn *a*. ; the sportsman and his train *P.E.* 82
'Tis granted, and no plainer truth *a. P.E.* 353
Eternity's unknown expanse *a. R.* 149
That so much death *a*. ? *St.* i 8
Though not a grace *a*. on strictest search *T.* 151
Channel her cheeks, a Niobe *a. T.* 174
Fair fields *a*. below, such as he left *T.* i 452
For such unmeasurable woe *a. T.* i 459
That softly swelled and gaily dressed *a. T.* iii 629
The omnipotent magician, Brown, *a. T.* iii 766
The rest *a*. a wilderness of strange *T.* iv 78
Noiseless, *a*. a moving hill of snow *T.* iv 346
A. a spot upon a vestal's robe *T.* iv 554
But here and there an ugly smutch *a. T.* iv 608
The glory of thy work, which yet *a. T.* v 866
That scarce a leaf *a*. ; mezereon too *T.* vi 167
Fulfil the purpose, and *a*. design'd *Tir.* 93
Each dreams that each is just what he *a. Tir.* 448
He speaks, and they *a*. ; to him they owe *T.T.* 356
The promise of delicious fruit *a. V.* 52
And long before the day *a. G.D.* 11 [650
Such knowledge, gained betimes, and which *a. Tir.*

APPEARANCE.
Till thy *a*. chased the gloom, forlorn *J.T.* 21
For men of their *a*. and address *P.E.* 388
The dark *a*. will not last *Trans. H.* 26

APPEARED.
Or smiled when a Sabbath *a. A.S.* 32
Sent to do more than he *a*. to have done *Con.* 518
A. two lovely foes *L.R.* 6
Wherever his glory *a. M.D.* 20
Though not a hound from whom it burst *a. N.A.* 46
Nor ever frowned, or sad *a. St.* iii 23
Ages elapsed ere Homer's lamp *a. T.T.* 556

APPEAREST.
Ah, treat them kindly ! rude as thou *a. T.* iv 370

APPEARING.
She smiles, *a*., as in truth she is *T.* iii 49

APPEASED.
And if perhaps made angry, soon *a. Ch.* 429

APPETITE.
May rove at will, where *a*. shall lead *A.T.* 60
Occasion prompt, and *a*. so keen *A.T.* 90
What health and sober *a*. demand *H.* 158
If *A*., or what divines call lust *H.* 385
To take the bend his *a*. ordain *H.* 603
Like thine, her *a*. is keen *P.B.* 27
What then !—are *a*. and lusts laid down *P.E.* 102
Receives from her both *a*. and treat *P.E.* 210
First *A*. enlists him Truth's sworn foe *P.E.* 542
That *a*. can ask, or wealth provide *R.* 744
Sighs if perhaps your *a*. should fail *T.* 215
Guiltless of pampered *a*. obscene *T.* i 104
Hard fare ! but such as boyish *a. T.* i 123
To bind the roving *a*., and lead *T.* ii 525
Though *A*. raise outcries at the cost ? *T.* ii 621
Of critic *a*., no sordid fare *T.* iii 461
By traitor *A*., and armed with darts *T.* iii 685
Takes part with *A*., and pleads the cause *T.* v 630
" Hath God indeed given *a*. to man " *T.* v 635
As must create an *a*. for prayer ? *Tir.* 374

APPLAUSE.
Its sordid nourishment from man's *a. Con.* 672
And gave misplaced *a. J.P.* 20
I should deserve to forfeit all *a*.) *P.E.* 511
Or plead its silence as its best *a. R.* 414
Speaks with reserve, and listens with *a. R.* 448
O Popular *A*. ! what heart of man *T.* ii 481

And thus gives Virtue indirect *a. T.* iii 104
Less worthy of *a*., though more admired *T.* v 127
When most extravagant in his *a. T.* v 262
Deserves at least *a*. for her attempt *T.* v 369
Such mischiefs after it, with much *a. Tir.* 494
But that they catch at popular *a. T.T.* 144
Levied a tax of wonder and *a. T.T.* 650

APPLE.
But *a*. we want, and *a*. we'll have *P.A.* 30
If not, you shall have neither *a*. nor pear " *P.A.* 32
Opposite in the *a*. tree *P.T.* 31   [*P.A.* 38
His *a*. might hang till they dropped from the tree
An *a*. tree, or lofty pear *R.C.* 12

APPLICATION.
On *a*. to its noblest end *J.T.* 28
Who pant with *a*. misapplied *T.* vi 273

APPLIED.
He spoke indignant, and his spurs *a. A.T.* 191
A bold remark, but which, if well *a. Ch.* 535
May furnish illustration, well *a. Con.* 206
You laugh—'tis well—the tale *a. L.W.* 23
Like Isaac, with a mind *a. Mor.* 11
Whose fires to sacred Truth *a. Mrs. M—* 32
To every pane his trunk *a. P.B.* 8
In praise *a*., to the same part—his head *P.E.* 533
To hourly use *a. St.* iii 20
By medicine well *a*., but without grace *T.* vi 522
With all thy faculties elsewhere *a. Tir.* 659
And never meant the rule should be *a. T.T.* 11
My busy search, I next *a*. 1789, 12

APPLY.
The warder at the door his key *a. H.* 720
Turn eastward now, and fancy shall *a. T.* 97
And catechise it well ; *a*. thy glass *T.* iii 203
Let active Laws *a*. the needful curb *T.T.* 314

APPOINTED.
While they passed through to their *a*. land *Ex.* 186
But guests that sought it in the *a*. one *H.* 307
Stars countless, each in his *a*. place *R.* 83
Wafts the rich prize to its *a*. use *T.* iii 540
A. sage preceptor to the Will *Tir.* 32
In him thy well *a*. proxy see *Tir.* 676

APPREHENSION.
Nor in her own fond *a. R.C.* 101

APPREHENSIVE.
Such teachable and *a*. parts *T.* vi 612

APPRISED.
There, undisturbed by Folly. and *a. T.* iii 34
(*A*. that he is such) a careless boy *Tir.* 906

APPROACH.
My quick *a*., and soon he dropped *D.W.* 35
Starts at her first *a*., and sounds To arms ! *H.* 656
Ere long *a*. life's evening shades *Mor.* 35
A step if fair, and if a shower *a. R.* 491
With the *a*. of Death *St.* v 28
She quakes at his *a*.   Her hollow womb *T.* ii 88
None but his steel *a*. them. What is weak *T.* iii 414
Take step for step ; and, as I near *a. T.* v 18
Is made familiar, watches his *a. T.* v 423   [iv 295
Though still deceived, some stranger's near *a. T.*
His long love-ditty for my near *a. T.* vi 309
" Where is the promise of your Lord's *a*. ? " *T.* vi 871

APPROACHING.
Each some *a*. good divines *A Tale* 63
But most before *a*. showers *Ep.* ii 27

On good that seems *a. F.* 81
She now presaged *a.* doom *R.C.* 74

APPROBATION.
And warbling out his *a. N.G.* 24
Attested, glad, his *a. P.T.* 40
Whose *a.*—prosper even mine *T.* vi 1024

APPROPRIATES.
A. nature as his Father's work *T.* v 761

APPROVE.
Man to maintain, and such as God *a. Con.* 538
I grant it dangerous, and *a.* your fear *Con.* 653
And free from bias, must *a.* the choice *Con.* 664
And you, fond maid, *a. Miss —* 94
Warns him or prompts, *a.* him or restrains *P.E.* 35
Not that I mean to *a.*, or would enforce *R.* 117
For once I can *a.* the patriot's voice *R.* 387
Thus Heaven *a.*, as honest and sincere *T.* 225
Were he on earth, would hear, *a.*, and own *T.* ii 396
With such a zeal to be what they *a. T.* ii 791
And what they will not taste must yet *a. T.* iii 701
Condemns, *a.*, and with a faithful voice *Tir.* 33

APPROVED.
Which hue she most *a.*, she chose them all *T.* vi 161
Or stained with guilt, beneficent, *a. T.* vi 998
That are of chief and most *a.* report *Tir.* 459
A. their method in all other things *T.T.* 95

APPROVING.
The polish'd counter, and *a.* none *T.* vi 281
The man *a.* what had charm'd the boy *Tir.* 149

APRIL.
'Twas *A.*, as the bumpkins say *A Fable* 8
On rippling waters in an *A.* day *A.T.* 24
Himself as bountiful as *A.* rains *H.* 304
Then *A.* with her sister May *N.* 17

APRON.
The livelong night. A tattered *a.* hides *T.* i 549

APT.
A. emblem of a virtuous maid *Comp.* ii 2
Poets, are sometimes *a.* to maul the thing *Con.* 290
This simile were *a.* enough *E.* iv 47
Humility is gentle, *a.* to learn *Ex.* 454
Attend;—an *a.* similitude shall show *T.* 236 [661
Thus Fancy paints thee, and though *a.* to err *T.* i
Or vicious, and not therefore *a.* to teach *T.* ii 550
Wit, undistinguishing, is *a.* to strike *T.T.* 101
Too *a.* to play the wanton with her powers *T.T.* 301

AQUILINE.
Terribly arched and *a.* his nose *T.* iii 192

ARBITER.
The *a.* of this terraqueous swamp *T.* v 281
Quick-sighted *a.* of good and ill *Tir.* 31

ARBITRARY.
Such hard and *a.* measure here *E.* iii 55
Thy monarchs *a.*, fierce, unjust *Ex.* 528
Dare step across his *a.* views *H.* 193
A Briton's scorn of *a.* chains? *T.T.* 201

ARBITRATES.
Who waits to dress us, *a.* their date *T.* ii 600

ARBITRATION.
And *a.* wise of the Supreme *T.* ii 165

ARBITRESS.
Fell Discord, *a.* of such debate *T.* iv 482

ARBOUR.
An *a.* near at hand of thickest yew *A.T.* 81

ARBUTHNOT.
Her serious mirth, to *A.* and Swift *T.T.* 657

ARCADIAN.
And nowhere, but in feigned *A.* scenes *H.* 9
And those *A.* scenes that Maro sings *T.* iv 515
'Tis a bower of *A.* sweets *W.N.* 9

ARCH.
For the close-woven *a.* of limes *C.* 29 [*N.A.* 30
His lamp now planted on Heaven's topmost *a.*
Hers is the spacious *a.*, the shapely spire *Ch.* 105
"Can this be true?"—an *a.* observer cries *Con.* 231
As if, like *a.* built with skilful hand *Ex.* 286
It stands, like the cerulean *a.* we see *T.* 26
You have two servants—Tom, an *a.* sly rogue *T.* 201
How airy and how light the graceful *a. T.* i 341
Our *a.* of empire, steadfast but for you *T.* i 773

ARCHBISHOP.
Let Comus rise *A.* of the land *P.E.* 184

ARCHED.
The cock his *a.* tail's azure show *Mrs. M—* 7
Her eye-brows *a.*, her eyes both gone astray *T.* 135
Terribly *a.* and aquiline his nose *T.* iii 192

ARCHER.
Shot by an *a.* strong *I.G.* 154
Been hurt by the *a.* In his side He bore *T.* iii 113

ARCHITECT.
Built by that *A.* who built the skies *Con.* 560
An *a.* requires alone *F.* 164

ARCTIC.
Hard task indeed o'er *a.* seas to roam! *H.* 548

ARDENT.
More *a.* as the disk emerges more *T.* v 4
To press with energy your *a.* thought *V.* 10

ARDENTLY.
What *a.* I wished, I long believed *M.P.* 38

ARDOUR.
Of that which called his *a.* forth *Mor.* 44
Catching its *a.* as I mused along *R.* 376
And *a.* in the Christian race *St.* vi 23
The country, with what *a.* he contrives *T.* iv 778

ARDUOUS.
But in his *a.* enterprise to close *R.* 617
And not soon spent, though in an *a.* task *T.* i 401
Aware of nothing *a.* in a task *T.* ii 307
That not to attempt it, *a.* as he deems *T.* vi 757
The labour, were a task more *a.* still *T.* vi 758

AREA.
Its ample *a.* 'gan explore *T.B.* 38

ARGUE.
Could *a.* once, could jest, or join the song *R.* 290
And could discriminate and *a.* well *T.* v 289

ARGUED.
So Tongue was the lawyer, and *a.* the cause *A.C.* 5

ARGUMENT.
"On the whole it appears, and my *a.* shows *A.C.* 21
But what were his *a.* few people know *A.C.* 27
The tender *a.* of kindred blood *Ch.* 32
What will not *a.* sometimes suppose?) *Ch.* 380

ARGUMENT—ARRIVE

The clash of *a.* and jar of words *Con.* 85
Your thread of *a.* is snapped again *Con.* 110
An *a.* of cogence, we may say *Con.* 293
(I hate long *a.* verbosely spun) *E.* iii 44
Needs no expense of *a. F.* 140
From stuccoed walls smart *a.* rebound *H.* 346
With senseless noise, his *a.* the sword *H.* 660
Your scruples and *a.* bring to my mind *P.A.* 17
Shall prove (what *a.* could never yet) *T.* 431
The method clear, and *a.* exact ? *T.* iii 279
"We find sound *a.*, we read the heart" *T.* v 654
Will need no stress of *a.* to enforce *Tir.* 803
Of *a.*, employed too oft amiss *Y.O.* 31

ARISE.

"Will none *a.*, no knight who still retains *A.T.* 115
Other Romans shall *a. B.* 21
And Faith, the root whence only can *a. Ex.* 111
When God *a.*, with an awful frown *Ex.* 249
A Man *a.*, a man whom God has taught *H.* 623
And from their prison-house below *a. N.A.* 87
Ere another such grove shall *a.* in its stead *P.F.* 16
When piping winds shall soon *a. T.B.* 17
Or bids the rocks in ruder pomp *a. Tir.* 28

ARISTÆUS.

In such a palace *A.* found *T.* v 135

ARK.

To Gaul, to Greece, and into Noah's *a. R.* 694
Presume to lay their hand upon the *a. T.* ii 231

ARM.

Called for his *a.*, and for his princely steed *A.T.* 124
Sounds not *a.* shall win the prize *B.* 23
Walks *a.* in *a.* with Nature all his way *Ch.* 314
Spreads wide her *a.* of universal love *Ch.* 596
For thou wast born amid the din of *a. Ex.* 472
To waste thy life in *a.*, or lay it down *Ex.* 536
'Tis thus, extending his tempestuous *a. Ex.* 584
A world is up in *a.*, and thou, a spot *Ex.* 694
Were all collected in thy single *a. Ex.* 704
Though, clasped and cradled in his nurse's *a. H.* 179
If *a.* engage him, he devotes to sport *H.* 207
Starts at her first approach, and sounds to *a.* ! *H.* 656
His eyes are sunk, *a.* folded, head reclined *H.* 689
There Beauty woos him with expanded *a. P.E.* 55
Go, fool ; and *a.* in *a.* with Clodio, plead *P.E.* 197
Committed once into the public *a. P.E.* 518
The recompense that arts or *a.* can yield *R.* 101
A. hanging idly down, hands clasped below *R.* 286
Carries her Bible tucked beneath his *a. T.* 147
The self-restoring *a.* of human power *T.* 402
I never trusted in an *a.* but thine *T.* 575 [164
And holds them dangling at *a.*'s length in scorn *T.*
Whose *a.* this twentieth winter I perceive *T.* i 145
And ash far-stretching his umbrageous *a. T.* i 311
Frowning as if in his unconscious *a. T.* i 381
Each in his field of glory ; one in *a. T.* ii 241
Of heavenly temper, furnishes with *a. T.* ii 346
Fall back into our seat, extend an *a. T.* ii 448
A palsy struck his *a.*, his sparkling eye *T.* ii 727
So when the Jewish leader stretched his *a. T.* ii 825
Thou art the nurse of Virtue. In thine *a. T.* iii 48
And wandering eyes, still leaning on the *a. T.* iii 53
(But that the basket dangling on her *a. T.* iv 547
The rich, and they that have an *a.* to check *T.* iv 587
Perhaps timidity restrains his *a. T.* iv 599 [567
See that your polished *a.* be primed with care *T.* iv
A., through the vanity and brainless rage *T.* iv 619
Is Liberty : a flight into his *a. T.* v 577
Not seldom, his avenging *a.*, to smite *T.* vi 464
Man praises man. Desert in arts or *a. T.* vi 632
Courage in *a.*, and ever prompt to show *T.T.* 276

Nature in *a.*, her elements at strife *T.T.* 448 [125
Thine *a.* have left thee ! Winds have rent them off *Y.O.*
Of some flagged admiral ; and tortuous *a. Y.O.* 96
Of chiefs whose single *a.* could boast 1789, 5

ARMED.

A. at all points, with terror in his brow *A.T.* 140
Truth *a.* it with a point so keen, so just *A.T.* 145
A. with thunder, clad with wings *B.* 27
Their leader *a.* with meekness, zeal, and love *Ex.* 187
Gone thither *a.* and hungry, returned full *Ex.* 368
But Winter, *a.* with terrors here unknown *H.* 473
Like Pallas springing *a.* from Jove *Mrs. M—* 26
And *a.* himself in panoply complete *T.* ii 345
With such artillery *a.* Vice parries wide *T.* ii 810
By traitor Appetite, and *a.* with darts *T.* iii 685
A. for a work too difficult for thee *Tir.* 677 [497
And *a.* with strength surpassing human powers *T.T.*

ARMOUR.

What though in scaly *a.* dressed *Miss* — 41

ARMOURY.

The *a.* of Winter ; where his troops *T.* v 139

ARMY.

"Come ten, come twenty, should an *a.* call *A.T.* 185
Proud of thy fleets and *a.*, stolen the gem *Ex.* 348
Shall raise no feuds for *a.* to suppress *T.T.* 317
They trust in *a.*, and their courage dies *T.T.* 468
Church, *a.*, physic, law *Tran.* ii 27

AROMATIC.

Her sweetest flowers, her *a.* gums *T.* ii 86

AROSE.

Between Nose and Eyes a strange contest *a. A.C.* 1
Much controversy straight *a. L.W.* 15

ARRAIGNED.

Of the robed pedagogue ! Else let the *a. T.* ii 823

ARRAIGNS.

A. him, charges him with every wrong *T.* 262

ARRANGEMENT.

Yet just *a.*, rarely brought to pass *T.* iii 588

ARRANT. [301

(Oh cast them from thee !) are weeds, *a.* weeds *H.*

ARRAY.

To gaze at Nature in her green *a. T.* i 449
Misdeems it, dazzled by its bright *a. T.* iv 685
The lilac, various in *a.*, now white *T.* vi 157

ARRAYED.

But above all, in her own light *a. H.* 447
With eager step, and carelessly *a. R.* 187
Fit for the power in which he stands *a. Tir.* 98

ARREAR.

Know, your *a.* with every hour accrue *Con.* 491
Oh think, if chargeable with deep *a. Ex.* 608
Is not the pardon of thy long *a. F.A.* 13
He has incurred a long *a. St.* v 31

ARREST.

To *a.* the fleeting images that fill *T.* ii 290
Can but *a.* the light and smoky mist *T.* v 105
Age after age, than to *a.* his course ? *T.* vi 131

ARRIVE.

That thought is joy, *a.* what may to me *M.P.* 107
"When my last hour *a.*" *St.* iii 34
To the far distant goal, *a.* and dies *T.* vi 430

ARRIVED.
A., a night like noon she sees *Q.V.* 41
Is but a transient guest, newly *a*. *T.* iii 750
A., he feels an unexpected change *Tir.* 567

ARRIVING.
At length a ship *a*. brought *A Tale* 23

ARROGANCE.
'Tis senseless *a*. to accuse *F.* 52
In vain : the slave of *a*. and pride *P.E.* 548

ARROGANT.
'Tis narrow, selfish, *a*. and draws *Con.* 671
Lewd, avaricious, *a*., unjust *Ex.* 56
The pride of *a*. distinctions fall *R.* 659
The plea of works, as *a*. and vain *T.* 71

ARROW.
And the swift-winged *a*. of Light *A.S.* 44
So like an *a*. swift he flew *J.G.* 153
None sends his *a*. to the mark in view *P.E.* 570
And the barbed *a*. of a frowning God *R.* 304
In which are kept our *a*. Rusting there *T.* ii 804
Long since : with many an *a*. deep infixed *T.* iii 109
And lays his *a*. by *Tran. H.* 30

ARROWY.
The gloomy clouds, find weapons, *a*. sleet *T.* v 140
The lambent homage of his *a*. tongue *T.* vi 782

ART.
He called her Posy, with an amorous *a*. *A.T.* 21
She tutored some in Dædalus's *a*. *A.T.* 52
" O cursed Hypothesis ! your hellish *a*." *A.T.* 113
The achievements of *a*. may amuse *C.* 37 [*Con.* 811
A. once esteemed may be with shame dismissed
Tricked out of all his royalty by *a*. *Ch.* 53
Ingenious *a*., with her expressive face *Ch.* 97
These are the gifts of *A*. ; and *A*. thrives most *Ch.*113
And slaying man would cease to be an *a*. *Ch.* 619
May be esteemed a gift, and not an *a*. *Con.* 4
Whose deeds had left, in spite of hostile *a*. *Con.* 513
Grace him again with long forgotten *a*. *Con.* 839
May prove, though much beside the rules of *a*.*Con.*869
Can Nature add a charm, or *A*. confer *Ex.* 5
Ambrosial gardens, in which *A*. supplies *Ex.* 11
To modest cheeks, and borrowed one from *A. Ex.* 48
The pharisee the dupe of his own *a*. *Ex.* 93
In other climes perhaps creative *A. Ex.* 229
From fading good derives, with chemic *a*. *H.* 159
Where busy *a*. are never at a stand *H.* 440 [*H.* 497
What were they ? What some fools are made by *a*.
But speaks with plainness *a*. could never mend *H.*451
Hence all that is in man, pride, passion, *a*., *H.* 653
Whose lines uniting by an honest *a*. *H.* 756
Which *a*. can only darken and disguise *H.* 769
Increasing commerce and reviving *a*. *Her.* 73
Through all his *a*. we view *H.F.* 14
And all thy threads with magic *a*. *M.* 18
The *A*. come smiling in the close *Miss* — 81
(Blest be the *a*. that can immortalize *M.P.* 8
The *a*. that baffles Time's tyrannic claim *M.P.* 9
By what unseen and unsuspected *a*. *P.E.* 3
And of all *a*. sagacious dupes invent *P.E.* 435
And seemed by some Magician's *a*. *Q.V.* 59
The recompense that *a*. or arms can yield *R.* 101
Parks in which *A*. preceptress Nature weds *R.* 335
But versed in *a*. that while they seem to stay *R.* 383
Wild without *a*., or artfully subdued *R.* 416
O sacred *a*. ! to which alone life owes *R.* 749
These, these are *a*. pursued without a crime *R.* 799
And while I teach an *a*. too little known *R.* 807
The Christian has an *a*. unknown to thee *R.H.* 4

To steer with nicest *a*. betwixt the extreme *S.* ii 9
Nice-fingered *A*. must emulate in vain *T.* 202
By culinary *a*., unsavoury deems *T.* i 125
Lovely indeed the mimic works of *A*. *T.* i 420
His nature, and though capable of *a*. *T.* i 576
The manners and the *a*. of civil life *T.* i 596
From all that Science traces, *A*. invents *T.* i 627
I do confess them nurseries of the *a*. *T.* i 693
Each province of her *a*. her equal care *T.* i 707
But such as *A*. contrives, possess ye still *T.* i 757
Then to dispose his copies with such *a*. *T.* ii 294
Of gallery critics by a thousand *a*. *T.* ii 365
In *a*. like yours. I cannot call the swift *T.* iii 211
That may disgrace his *a*., or disappoint *T.* iii 422
Food for the vulgar merely—is an *a*. *T.* iii 449
Not so when winter scowls. Assistant *A*. *T.*iii 541
Oh innocent, compared with *a*. like these *T.* iii 801
No powdered pert proficient in the *a*. *T.* iv 145
Once simple, are initiated in *a*. *T.* iv 493
And touches of his hand, with so much *a*. *T.* iv 736
With forms so various, that no powers of *a*. *T.* v 108
Thus Nature works as if to mock at *A*. *T.* v 122
His *a*. survived the waters ; and ere long *T.* v 220
And thou hast need of discipline and *a*. *T.* v 467
By which the magic *a*. of shrewder wits *T.* vi 99
Uninjured, with inimitable *a*. *T.* vi 195
Man praises man. Desert in *a*. or arms *T.* vi 632
Exhausted all materials of the *a*. *T.* vi 717
By no kind *a*. his confidence again *Tir.* 586
Low in the world, because he scorns its *a*. *Tir.* 672
See volunteers in all the vilest *a*. *Tir.* 835
Sustained with so much grace and *a*. *Tran.* iv 35
To nurse with tender care the thriving *A*. *T.T.* 69
Those *a*. be theirs that hate his gentle reign *T.T.* 89
His galleries with the works of *a*. well graced *T.T.*162
When ministers and ministerial *a*. *T.T.* 190
Guards well what *A*. and Industry have won *T.T.* 280
Let Discipline employ her wholesome *a*. *T.T.* 310
Quite unindebted to the tricks of *a*. *T.T.* 525
An *a*. contrived to advertise a joke *T.T.* 539
Had faded, poetry was not an *a*. *T.T.* 585
And *a*. revived beneath a softer day *T.T.* 621
Made poetry a mere mechanic *a*. *T.T.* 654
Too proud for *a*., and trusting in mere force *T.T.* 683
Than ever blazed by *a*. *U.* 28
A. has in a measure supplied *W.N.* 3
Transports not chargeable with *a*. 1789, 60

ARTFUL.
To study Culture, and with *a*. toil *R.* 785
'Tis not in *a*. measures, in the chime *T.* vi 1020

ARTFULLY.
Wild without art, or *a*. subdued *R.* 416

ARTHRITIC.
From pangs *a*. that infest the toe *T.* i 105

ARTICLE.
Or in one *a*. of vice reclaimed *Tir.* 241

ARTICULATE.
I think, *a*., I laugh and weep *T.* iii 198
Heard to *a*. like other men *Tir.* 667
But soon *a*. aloud *Tran.* iv 22

ARTICULATION.
Have all *a*. in his ears *N.A.* 68
Nor owed *a*. to his ear *Y.O.* 148

ARTIFICE.
Where covert guile and *a*. abound *Ch.* 285
Rhetoric is *a*., the work of man *Ex.* 136
And lest the fulsome *a*. should fail *P.E.* 291
Where eloquence and *a*. shall fail *R.* 658

ARTIFICER.

Respectful of the smutched *a. T.* ii 491
The first *a.* of death; the shrewd *T.* v 213
Might well suppose the *a.* divine *T.* v 561
The great *a.* of all that moves *T.* vi 207
To which the unwashed *a.* repairs *T.T.* 152

ARTIFICIAL.

And vex their flesh with *a.* sores *T.* i 582

ARTILLERY.

And deems her sharp *a.* mere straw *H.* 597
With such *a.* armed. Vice parries wide *T.* ii 810

ARTIST.

Find the sweet lyre on which an *a.* plays *Con.* 900
A., attend! Your brushes and your paint *T.* 171
Peace to the *a.* whose ingenious thought *T.* 210
The inferior wonders of an *a.'s* hand *T.* i 419

ARTLESS.

Suspicion lurks not in her *a.* breast *Ch.* 426
He shine with all a cherub's *a.* charms *H.* 180
This *a.* vow may Heaven receive *Miss —* 93
Who bidst me honour with an *a.* song *M.P.* 13
Thy genuine charms, and guide an *a.* hand *R.* 204
Heaven's easy, *a.*, unencumbered plan! *T.* 22
To *a.* ingenuity and skill *T.* iv 797
Her *a.* manners, and her neat attire *T.* iv 536
The stamp of *a.* piety impress'd *Tir.* 153
And, *a.* as thou art, whom thou wilt choose *Tir.* 856
Wild *a.* airs and concerts of her own *T.T.* 697

ASCEND.

Compasses earth, dives into it, *a. Ch.* 315
Knows he his origin? can he *a. F.A.* 22 [*T.* vi 317
A. the neighbouring beech; there whisks his brush
But as a scale, by which the soul *a. R.* 111
In spiral rings *a.* the trunk, and lays *R.* 231
Close at his heels, a demagogue *a. T.* iv 61
A. his top mast, through his peering eyes *T.* iv 115
Have raised you high as talents can *a. V.* 13

ASCENDED.

Heard shouts that *a.* the sky *M.D.* 39

ASCENDING.

Sometimes *a.*, debonair *R.C.* 11
The *a.* damps; then leisurely impose *T.* iii 477
A., fires the horizon; while the clouds *T.* v 2

ASCENT.

Is this the rugged path, the steep *a. P.E.* 71
Swift pace or steep *a.* no toil to me *T.* i 139

ASCERTAIN.

Its value, what no thought can *a. H.* 125

ASCRIBE.

And some *a.* the invention to a priest *T.* i 62
Views him in all; *a.* to the grand cause *T.* iii 226

ASCRIBED.

Jotham *a.* to his assembled trees *T.* v 322

ASH.

"Beauty for *a.*" is a gift indeed *Ch.* 230 [*R.* 230
Rough elm, or smooth grained *a.*, or glossy beech
Of *a.*, or lime, or beech, distinctly shine *T.* i 303
And *a.* far-stretching his umbrageous arm *T.* i 311
His *a.*, where, and in what weal or woe? *T.* ii 519
Houses in *a.*, and the fall of stocks *T.* iv 16; [v 726
And chased them up to Heaven. Their *a.* flew *T.*
Thy scattered hair with sleet like *a.* filled *T.* iv 121
The next mere dust and *a.* in the grave *Tir.* 60

ASHAMED.

"The guiltiest still are ever least *a. A.T.* 188.
By softer methods, must be made *a. Ch.* 498
Where 'tis a shame to be *a.* to appear *Con.* 376
And chaste themselves, are not *a.* to own *T.* iii 74
The modest speaker is *a.* and grieved *T.* iv 66
With decent duty, not *a.* to pray *Tir.* 176 [293
Return *a.*, without the wreaths they sought *Ex.*

ASHORE.

No! Soon as from *a.* he saw *A Tale* 49 [145
Shall roll themselves *a.*, and reach him there *T.* ii

ASIATIC.

With *A.* vices stored thy mind *Ex.* 372

ASININE.

'Tis the most *a.* employ on earth *Con.* 209

ASK.

She strikes out all that Luxury can *a. Ch.* 103
To find the medicine *a.* some share of wit *Con.* 879
A. now of History's authentic page *Ex.* 161
A. what is human life—the sage replies *H.* 1
And *a.*, and fancy they find, blessings there *H.* 243
What are England's rights, I *a. N.C.* 10
A. him, if your knotted scourges *N.C.* 29 [525
Kneels and *a.* Heaven to bless the dear deceit *P.E.*
Man's coltish disposition *a.* the thong *P.E.* 360
To tell them more than they have wit to *a. P.E.* 390
I shall not *a.* Jean Jacques Rousseau *P.T.* 1
A. wealth of Heaven, and gain a real prize *R.* 162
A. not the boy, who when the breeze of morn *R.* 395
But *a.* the noble drudge in state affairs *R.* 407
That appetite can *a.*, or wealth provide *R.* 744
Yet never *a.* his aid! *St.* vi 20 [crazed! *T.* i 556
Though pinched with cold, *a.* never—Kate is
Go, dress thine eyes with eyesalve; *a.* of him *T.*ii 203
Or *a.* of whomsoever he has taught *T.* ii 204
Now make our own. Posterity will *a. T.* ii 577
Though at their own destruction. She *a. T.* ii 642
To them that *a.* it?—Freely.—'Tis his joy *T.* iii 273
That *a.* robust, tough sinews, bred to toil *T.* iii 405
A. egress; which obtained, the overcharged *T.*iii 497
To no mean hand, and *a.* the touch of taste *T.* iii 632
These *a.* with painful shyness, and, refused *T.* iii 418
Ye all can swallow, and she *a.* no more *T.* iv 512
A distant age *a.* where the fabric stood *T.* v 535
And such well pleased to find it, *a.* no more *T.* v 795
Nor *a.* his leave to slumber or to play *T.* vi 405
By budding ills, that *a.* a prudent hand *T.* vi 591
A. him, indeed, what trophies he has raised *T.* vi 932
Then *a.* not, whether limited or large? *Tir.* 511
The encroaching nuisance *a.* a faithful hand *Tir.* 601
Oracular, I would not curious *a. Y.O.* 42 [120
And *a.*, with busy scorn, "Was this the man?" *T.T.*

ASKANCE.

Provokes me to a smile. With eye *a. T.* v 14

ASKED.

And *a.* them, with a kind, engaging air *Con.* 523
Whate'er was *a.*, too timid to resist *Ex.* 540 [ii 512
And spring-time of the world; *a.*, whence is man? *T.*
A. of the waves that broke upon his coast *Ex.* 572
And *a.* him to go and assist in the job *P.A.* 24
Were soon conjoined; nor other cement *a. T.* v 147
Of its own taunting question, *a.* so long *T.* vi 870
A., when in Hell, to see the royal jail *T.T.* 94
To give a Milton birth, *a.* ages more *T.T.* 559

ASKING.

And *a.* of the surge that bathes thy foot *T.* i 655
Would urge a wiser suit than *a.* more *T.* vi 56

ASLANT.
Blown all *a.*, a driving, dashing rain *T.* 239
Then downward and then upward, then *a. T.* v 427

ASLEEP.
A. at the dawn of the day *M.D.* 2
As natural as when *a.* to dream *R.* 636

ASP.
Of temper as envenomed as an *a. T* 159
Of *a.* their venom, overpowering strength *T.* v 702
A brood of *a.*, or quicksands in his way *Tir.* 870

ASPASIO.
So spake *A.*, firm possessed *St.* iii 13
Such lived *A.*; and at last *St.* iii 29

ASPECT.
An *a.* stern on man's affairs *P.T.* 48

ASPERITY.
And with *a.* replied *P.* 20

ASPERSION.
A. is the babbler's trade *F.* 100

ASPIRE.
To joys forbidden man *a. P.B.* 15
I shrink abased, and yet *a.* to Thee *R.* 94

ASPIRING.
A. to the rank of Queen *L.R.* 7
Plant behind plant *a.*, in the van *T.* iii 593
Some, more *a.*, catch the neighbour shrub *T.* iii 665
And more *a.*, and with ampler spread *T.* vi 145

ASS.
O weariness beyond what *a.* feel *H.* 99
Stubborn and sturdy, a wild *a.*'s colt *H.* 182
For while he spake, a braying *a. J.G.* 203
The *a.*; for he, we know, has lately strayed *N.A.* 96
An *a.*'s burden, and, when laden most *T.* iv 441

ASSAILANT.
"Oh, shame to knighthood!" his *a.* cried *A.T.* 179

ASSAILED.
A. by scandal and the tongue of strife *H.* 576
Whom Truth and Soberness *a.* in vain *T.* ii 480
That promised once more firmness, so *a. T.* v 526

ASSAILS.
Whoe'er *a.* thee, thy success is sure *Ev.* 701

ASSASSINED.
A. by a thief! *T.B.* 6

ASSASSINS.
The wild *a.* start into the street *Ch.* 507

ASSAULTS.
From all *a.* of evil, proving still *T.* iii 680
Of sounding an alarm *a.* these doors *T.* iv 146
From the cruel *a.* of the clime *W.N.* 12

ASSEMBLE.
Chased, never to *a.* more 1789, 41

ASSEMBLED.
A. on affairs of love *P.T.* 14
Jotham ascribed to his *a.* trees *T.* v 322

ASSEMBLING.
Of Tityrus, *a.*, as he sang *T.* iv 707

ASSEMBLY.
The moles and bats in full *a.* find *Ev.* 630
O Sin! an *a.* such as earth *T.* vi 816

ASSENT.
Her utmost reach, historical *a. Con.* 777
Virtue engages his *a. H.F.* 11
To cheat themselves and gain the world's *a. P.E.* 436
They gain at last his unreserved *a. T.* v 663

ASSERT.
"To *a.* the charter of the chaste and fair *A.T.* 117
A. the nose upon his face his own *Con.* 122
Which god *a.* his own *St.* vi 26
A. the rights of his offended Lord *T.* 263
A. the skies, and vindicate her due *T.* 490
A. precedence, and bespeaks control *Tir.* 9
A. the native evil of his heart *Tir.* 162
Thus graced, the man *a.* a poet's name *T.T.* 714

ASSERTION.
And were I called to prove the *a.* true *E.* iii 12

ASSEVERATION.
A. blustering in your face *Con.* 59

ASSIDUOUS.
A. sips at every flower 1789, 18

ASSIGNED.
And bind the task *a.* thee to thine heart *Ex.* 651
When, earth's *a.* duration at an end *R.* 653
God drave asunder, and *a.* their lot *T.* v 198

ASSIMILATES.
A. all objects. Earth receives *T.* iv 329

ASSIST.
But finds that though his tubes *a.* the sight *Ch.* 387
To *a.* his foe's down-fallen beast to rise *T.* vi 444

ASSISTANCE.
Calls for the kind *a.* of a tune *R.* 712
And needing none *a.* of the storm *T.* ii 144
Her cause demands the *a.* of your throats *T.* iv 511

ASSISTANT.
Not so when winter scowls. *A.* Art *T.* iii 541

ASSOCIATE.
To *a.* all the branches of mankind *Ch.* 84
Henceforth *a.* in one common herd *Con.* 76
The friend of Truth, the *a.* of sound sense *R.* 696
Good health, and, its *a.* in the most *T.* i 399
Since then, with few *a.*, in remote *T.* iii 117
With few *a.*, and not wishing more *T.* iii 120
That form, indeed, the *a.* of a mind *Tir.* 5

ASSOCIATED.
But man *a.* and leagued with man *T.* iv 663

ASSUAGE.
My sorrows I then might *a. A.S.* 21
To *a.* the throbbings of the festered part *R.* 321
Its foul inhabitant. But to *a. T.* iii 501
And thou wilt need some comfort to *a. Tir.* 877

ASSUME.
The snowy robe her wintry state *a. R.* 195
The backstring and the bib, *a.* the dress *T.* iv 227
What character, what turn thou wilt *a. Tir.* 853
Touched with a coal from Heaven, *a.* the lyre *T.T.* 735

ASSUMED.
Than that heroic strut *a.* before *Con.* 490
Habits are soon *a.*, but when we strive *P.E.* 582
But when the Second Charles *a.* the sway *T.T.* 620

ASSUMING.
Nature *a.* a more lovely face *R.* 357.
A. thus a rank unknown before *T.* ii 370
Pale, wan, and livid, but *a.* soon *T.* iii 523

ASSURANCE.
And confident *a.* of the rest *T.* v 576
" That give *a.* of their own success *T.* v 843

ASSURE.
But I can *a.* you I saw it in print *P.A.* 20

ASSURED.
The peasant's hopes, and not in vain *a. Her.* 9
Speaks him a criminal, *a. St.* vi 35
The soul reposing on *a.* relief *T.* 455

ASSYRIA.
Long time *A.* bound them in her chain *Ex.* 73

ASTONISH.
To *a.* and to grieve his gazing friends *T.* iv 655
The *a.* vulgar trembled, while He tore *Ex.* 139
The storm of music shakes the *a.* crowd *T.T.* 491

ASTRIDE.
Briskly, *a.* upon the parlour broom *Tir.* 367

ASTRONOMIC.
With more than *a.* eyes *Q.V.* 73

ASTRONOMY.
In which, or *a.* lies *Gr.* 15

ASTRUT.
Inflated and *a.* with self-conceit *T.* v 268

ATE.
Daniel *a.* pulse by choice—example rare *P.E.* 215

ATHANASIAN.
By *A.* nonsense, or Nicene) *H.* 394

ATHEIST.
They were by nature, *a.*, head and heart *H.* 498
What *a.* call him, a designing knave *P.E.* 108
And *a.*, if Earth hear so base a slave) *P.E.* 615
That live an *a.* life ; involves the Heaven *T.* ii 180
Of God and goodness, *a.* in ostent *T.* vi 486
To combat *a.* with in modern days *Tir.* 639

ATHENIAN.
Liberty taught him her *A.* strain *T.T.* 343

ATHENS.
To *A.* or to Rome, for wisdom short *T.* ii 536

ATHIRST.
With acrid salts, his very heart *a. T.* i 448

ATHLETIC.
Make him *a.* as in days of old *Con.* 841
If one, his equal in *a.* frame *H.* 191
Of manners rough, and coarse *a.* cast *P.E.* 187
When health demands it, of *a.* sort *Tir.* 653

ATHWART.
Strikes the rough thread of error right *a. Ex.* 330

ATLANTIC.
The *A.* billows roared *Cast.* 2
On the other side the *A. Pat*[t] 6
Snore to the murmurs of the *A.* wave ? *T.* iv 27

ATLAS.
The disencumbered *A.* of the state *R.* 394

ATOM.
Discordant *a.* meet, ferment, and fight *Ex.* 297
To whom an *a.* is an ample field *R.* 62
Of *a.*, sparkling in the noonday beam *T.* i 361

Measures an *a.*, and now girds a world ? *T.* i 718
Noiseless, an *a.*, and an *a.* more *Y.O.* 106

ATONES.
Sad waste ! for which no after-thrift *a. St.* ii 29
A slight gratuity *a.* for all *T.* 288
On principle, where foppery *a. T.* iv 689

ATONEMENT.
The *a.* a Redeemer's love has wrought *T.* 505

ATONING.
And mad, the symbols of *a.* grace *Ex.* 378

ATROCIOUS.
To judge the lands, to purge *a.* crimes *A.T.* 141
Have justly doomed, for some *a.* cause *H.* 713

ATTACHED.
Else more *a.* to pleasures found at home *R.* 518

ATTACHES.
By various ties *a.* man to man *Ch.* 16

ATTACHMENT.
For sea-born Venus her *a.* shows *Con.* 265
And, proud to make his firm *a.* known *T.* 219
Where love is mere *a.* to the throne *T.* v 361
A. never to be weaned or changed *T.* vi 625
This fond *a.* to the well-known place *Tir.* 314
Complain not if *a.* lewd and base *Tir.* 889

ATTACK.
"But guard thee well, expect no feigned *a. A.T.* 189

ATTAIN.
And if, ere he *a.* his end *Mor.* 53
But me, scarce hoping to *a.* that rest *M.P.* 100
A. not to the dignity of thought *R.* 640
To *a.* perfection in this nether world *T.* i 85
Diffused, *a.* the surface ; when, behold ! *T.* iii 493
The mind *a.*, beneath her happy reign *T.T.* 262
The growth that Nature meant she should *a. T.T.* 263

ATTAINABLE.
Truths useful and *a.* with ease *F.A.* 32

ATTAINED.
Pride has *a.* its most luxuriant growth *T.* 115

ATTAINING.
We sought without *a. F.* 36

ATTAINMENTS.
That man's *a.* in his own concerns *T.* vi. 613

ATTEMPT.
Oh fond *a.* to give a deathless lot *B.B.* 1
And wins mankind, as his *a.* prevail *Ch.* 335
His odoriferous *a.* to please *Con.* 287
Poets *a.* the noblest task they can *J.T.* 1
Urged his *a.* on every side *P.B.* 7
A. no task it cannot well fulfil *R.* 280
Presuming an *a.* not less sublime *T.* iii 459
But censure profits little : vain the *a. T.* iv. 500
Thwart his *a.*, or envy his success *T.* iv. 787
Deserves at least applause for her *a T.* v 369
So oft, and wearied in the vain *a. T.* v 628
And that to bind him is a vain *a. T.* v 777
So cheaply the renown of that *a. T.* vi 534
That not to *a.* it, arduous as he deems *T.* vi. 757
Desperate *a.*, till trees shall speak again ! *Y.O.* 49

ATTEND.
On all the vestiges of truth *a. Con.* 219
May such success *a.* the pious plan *Con.* 837
That no success *a.* on spears and swords *Ex.* 352

And if success his steps *a. F.* 82
A. to finish what the sword begun *Her.* 60
And ecstasy *a.* the tear *Miss* — 55
Death, and the pains of Hell *a.* him there *P.E.* 547
True Wisdom will *a.* his feeble call *R.* 33
Man shall be summoned and the dead *a.* ? *R.* 654
Artist, *a.*! your brushes and your paint *T.* 171
No Fear *a.* to quench his glowing fires *T.* 189
A.;—an apt similitude shall show *T.* 236
Some trivial slips their daily walk *a. T.* 286
He that *a.* to his interior self *T.* iii 373
All well repaid, demand him, he *a. T.* iii 398
A. him; drives his cattle to a march *T.* iv 647
His dog *a.* him, close behind his heel *T.* v 47
"*A.* to their own music? Have they faith *T.* v 647
Kind Providence *a.* with gracious aid *T.T.* 249
And every Muse *a.* her in her way *T.T.* 619
A. superior worth *Th.* 16
No Muses in these lines *a. U.* 29
If they who on thy state *a.* 1789, 66

ATTENDANT.
A train, *a.* on their queen *Miss* — 71
A. at the senior's side *Mor.* 40
To yon fair Sun and his *a.* Earth? *Tir.* 36
If the *a.*, and if such as these *T.T.* 164

ATTENDED.
For Reynard, close *a.* at his heels *N.A.* 124
"Was ever cat *a.* thus? *R.C.* 54
And angel choirs *a.*, wondering stood *T.* vi 352

ATTENDING.
Ungenial blasts *a.* curl the streams *T.T.* 213

ATTENTION.
The *a.* Pleasure has so much engrossed *Ch.* 631
They fix *a.*, heedless of your pain *Con.* 63
The repetition makes *a.* lame *Con.* 214
At least, we moderns, our *a.* less *Con.* 791
Mutual *a.* is implied *F.* 49
First fixes our *a. F.* 177
With nice *a.* in a righteous scale *H.* 367
Ensured him mute *a.* and regard *H.* 687
Becomes not weary of *a. M.F.* 52
Solicits kind *a.* to his dream *P.E.* 523
Habits of close *a.*, thinking heads *R.* 705
A theme for all the world's *a. R.C.* 102
Pleasure's call *a.* wins *St.* iv. 25
Inquisitive *a.*, while I read *T.* iv. 52
Would waste *a.* at the checker'd board *T.* vi 265
Their whole *a.*, and ape all his tricks *Tir.* 225
Where all the *a.* of the faithful host *Tir.* 769
Should claim my fixed *a.* more than you *T.T.* 181
If human woes her soft *a.* claim *T.T.* 484

ATTENTIVE.
(*A.* when thou readest) of England's peers *S.* i 3
Wisdom in minds *a.* to their own *T.* vi 91
So bountiful, in whose *a.* ear *T.* vi 460
They see the *a.* crowds his talents draw *Tir.* 362
Its various parts to his *a.* note *Tir.* 642

ATTEST.
Conspiring, may *a.* his bright design *T.* iii 654

ATTESTED.
A., glad, his approbation *P.T.* 40

ATTIC.
Of *A.* phrase and senatorial tune *S.* i 11
Sublimity and *A.* taste combined *T.T.* 644

ATTIRE.
The bride, while yet her bride's *a.* is on *A.T.* 103
The sycamore, capricious in *a. T.* i 318
And quaint in its deportment and *a. T.* ii 461

Her artless manners, and her neat *a. T.* iv 536
For cleanly riddance than for fair *a. T.* vi 994

ATTIRED.
Religion, if in heavenly truths *a. Ex.* 492
Though leafless, well *a.*, and thick beset *T.* vi 168

ATTITUDE.
Therefore, avaunt all *a.*, and stare *T.* ii 430

ATTRACT.
A. us, and neglected Nature pines *T.* iii 730

ATTRACTED.
Touched with the magnet, had *a.* his *Con.* 272

ATTRACTIVE.
Nor less *a.* is the woodland scene *T.* i 300
And most *a.*, is the fair result *T.* iii 639

ATTRIBUTES.
God and His *a.* (a field of day *Con.* 471
His gracious *a.*, and proves the share *H.* 139
Reflect his *a.* who placed them there *Tir.* 92

AUBURN.
Thy silver locks, once *a.* bright *M.* 25
A tooth or *a.* lock, and by degress *T.* i 133
The *a.* nut that held thee, swallowing down *Y.O.* 20

AUCTION.
Frequents the crowded *a.*; station'd there *T.* vi 286
Or turn them into shops and *a.* rooms *Tir.* 902

AUCTIONEERED.
Then advertised, and *a.* away *T.* iii 756

AUDACIOUS.
The *a.* convict whom he dares not bind *T.* iv 602

AUDIT.
Corruption! Whoso seeks an *a.* here *T.* iv 610

AUDITORS.
Are fittest *a.* for such to seek *Con.* 226

AUGMENT.
Nor feels their happiness *a.* his own *T.* vi 326

AUGUR.
Of whom I needs must *a.* better things *T.* ii. 582

AUGUST.
His creature thwart not his *a.* design *H.* 142
And show the *a.* tribunal of the skies *R.* 656
The theme though humble, yet *a.* and proud *T.* i 6
Sofa, and couch, and high built throne *a. T.* v 164
And are *a.*, but this transcends them all *T.* v 552

AURORA.
With which *A.* decks the skies *T.B.* 16

AUSONIA.
With all her vines; nor for *A.*'s groves *T.* ii 214
Live there, and prosper. Those *A.* claims *T.* iii 582

AUSPICIOUS.
Or pass unheeded this *a.* morn *S.* ii 4
The *a.* moment, when the tempered heat *T.* iii 508

AUSTERE.
Fruits of a blighted size, *a.* and crude *T.* 494
The bramble, black as jet, or sloes *a. T.* i 122
Milder, among a people less *a. T.* v 488
Religion, harsh, intolerant, *a. T.T.* 612

AUTHENTIC.
As Time improves the grape's *a.* juice *Con.* 643
Ask now of History's *a.* page *Ex.* 161
The unequivocal, *a.* deed *T.* v 653
Unpurified by an *a.* act *Y.O.* 12

AUTHOR.

She speaks of Him, her *a.*, guardian, friend *Ch.* 399
Just as the sapience of an *a.'s* brain *Ch.* 519
Their *a.'s* frailty, and return to dust *Con.* 554
Hence *a.* of illustrious name *F.* 85
Himself sole *a.* of his own disgraces *H.* 317
Praising the *a.* of all good in man *J.T.* 2
"Oh! if my Sovereign *A.* please *Miss* — 25
None but an *a.* knows an *a.'s* cares *P.E.* 516
Till *a.* hear at length one general cry *R.* 707
As the necessities their *a.* feel *T.* ii 672
Of Nature, overlooks her *a.* more *T.* iii 237
You the regardless *a.* of its woes *T.* v 350
But not its *A.* Unconcerned who formed *T.* v 793
The *A.* of her beauties, who, retired *T.* v 893
If, *a.* of no mischief and some good *T.* vi 953
Had not its *a.* dignified the plan *Tir.* 51
He too might make his *a.'s* wisdom clear *Tir.* 100
That *a.* are most useful pawned or sold *Tir.* 211

AUTHORITY.

Blasphemed the *a.* from which it sprung *Ex.* 156
Divine *a.* within his breast *P.E.* 33
Implies *a.* that never can *P.E.* 602
And centering all *a.* in modes *T.* i 745
A. herself not seldom sleeps *T.* iv 593
A father, whose *a.*, in show *T.* vi 30
But if *a.* grow wanton, woe *T.T.* 226
When he usurped *a.* just place *T.T.* 320
She clothed him with *a.* and awe *T.T.* 344

AUTUMN.

Nor *A.* yet had brushed from every spray *N.A.* 21
Now green, now tawny, and ere *A.* yet *T.* i 319
Hence Summer has her riches, *A.* hence *T.* iii 427
Till *A.'s* fiercer heats and plenteous dews *Tir.* 47

AUTUMNAL.

'Twas on the noon of an *a.* day *A.T.* 70
And like the stores *a.* suns mature *Con.* 649
A. rains had made it chill *Mor.* 13
Unwelcome vapours quench *a.* beams *T.T.* 212
But Fate thy growth decreed; *a.* rains *Y.O.* 23

AVAIL.

Where no prevarication shall *a. R.* 657

AVARICE.

Low in the pits thine *a.* has made *Ch.* 72
And, *A.* being judge, with ease succeeds *Ch.* 195
Extravagance and *A.* shall subscribe *Ch.* 467
A. in thee was the desire of wealth *J.T.* 25
From *a.* and Ambition free *O.* ii 8
A. shows, and virtue is the price *P.E.* 52
Will *A.* and Concupiscence give place *P.E.* 104
Ambition, *a.*, and the lust of fame *P.E.* 273
The lure of *a.*, or the pompous prize *R.* 177
Ambition, *A.*, Penury incurred *T.* iii 811
And *a.* that make man a wolf to men *T.* iv 103
When *A.* starves, and never hides his face *T.T.* 422

AVARICIOUS.

Lewd, *a.*, arrogant, unjust *Ex.* 56
Fierce, *a.*, proud, there must be war *T.T.* 10

AVAUNT.

Therefore, *a.* all attitude, and stare *T.* ii 430

AVENGE.

To *a.* than to prevent the breach of law *T.* i 731

AVENGED.

Which God *a.* on Pharaoh—the Bastille *T.* v 383

AVENGING.

Remember, Heaven has an *a.* rod *Ch.* 216
He heard the wheels of an *a.* God *Ex.* 57
Not seldom, his *a.* arm, to smite *T.* vi 464

AVENUES.

Ye fallen *a.*! once more I mourn *T.* i 338

AVERSE.

Some minds by Nature are *a.* to noise *R.* 175

AVERTED.

But, with *a.* eyes, the omniscient Judge *T.* 227

AVERTS.

In vain he closes or *a.* his eyes *T.* 470

AVON.

Of *A.* famed in song. Ah pleasant proof *T.* vi 682

AVOWED.

Not more affronted by *a.* neglect *T.* 73

AWAIT.

If toil *a.* me, or if dangers new *T.* iii 20

AWAITED.

No sofa then *a.* my return *T.* i. 126

AWAKE.

A. at Duty's call *D.W.* 42
But man, all-feeling and *a. N.* 9
And, like an infant, troublesome *a. T.* 427
A. sometimes the Muses too *Tran. H.* 29
Ye reasoners broad *a.*, whose busy search *Y.O.* 30

AWAKENED.

A. by the shock (cried Puss) *R.C.* 53

AWAKENS.

And Death *a.* from that dream too late *T.T.* 126

AWAKING.

Who brought the lamp that with *a.* beams *Ex.* 500

AWARD.

Heaven *a.* the vengeance due *B.* 42
"The strife now stands upon a fair *a. Con.* 851

AWARE.

A. that flight, in such a sea *Cast.* 33
A. of wintry storms *M.B.* 6
The worm, *a.* of his intent *N.G.* 13
But few that court Retirement are *a. R.* 609
A. of nothing arduous in a task *T.* ii 307
Not waste it, and *a.* that human life *T.* iii 363
Not soon deceived; *a.* that what is base *T.* vi 989
A. then how much danger intervenes *Tir.* 883

AWE.

Whose beauty impressed me with *a. M.D.* 11 [156
Regards with scorn, though once received with *a. Tir.*
A monarch clothed with majesty and *a. T.* 405
That rule, pursued with reverence and with *a. T.* 536
Truth, Hope, and Charity, and touched with *a. T.* i 2
With solemn *a.*, that bids me well beware *T.* ii 327
Shook the delinquent with such fits of *a. T.* ii 722
To touch the sword with conscientious *a. T.T.* 77
She clothed him with authority and *a. T.T.* 344

AWE-STRUCK.

A., before thy presence bend 1789, 67

AWFUL.

Of his sweet but *a.* lyre *B.* 36
Before his presence, at whose *a.* throne *Con.* 659
When God arises, with an *a.* frown *Ex.* 249

And in whose *a*. sight all nations seem *Ex.* 344
(*A*. alternative ! believed, beloved *Ex.* 688
But Conscience, in some *a*., silent hour *H.* 215
Those *a*. syllables, Hell, Death, and Sin *H.* 690
And stands a witness at Truth's *a*. bar *Her.* 81
Bound on a voyage of *a*. length *H.F.* 17
The depth, how *a*.! falling there, we burst *N.A.* 110
Read, ye that run, the *a*. truth *St.* i 21
A thousand *a*. admonitions scorned *St.* ii 27
The dying, trembling at the *a*. close *T.* 436
Yet *a*. as the consecrated roof *T.* i 342
Of her magnificent and *a*. cause? *T.* ii 232
Himself, as conscious of his *a*. charge *T.* ii 403
Start at his *a*. name, or deem his praise *T.* iv 180
By the unimpeachable and *a*. oath *T.* v 549
And utter now and then an *a*. voice *T.* vi 34
To occupy a sacred, *a*. post *Tir.* 414

AWKWARD.
Such drunken reelings, have an *a*. look *Con.* 862
With rash and *a*. force the chords he shakes *Con.* 901
But gently to rebuke his *a*. fear *H.* 61
With *a*. gait, stretched neck, and silly stare *P.E.* 380

They sidle to the goal with *a*. pace *P.E.* 562
No longer blushing for her *a*. load *T.* iv 551
His *a*. gait, his introverted toes *T.* iv 633

AWOKE.
A. and found it true *T.B.* 48.

AXE.
The *a*. will smite at God's command *St.* i 15
The cheerful haunts of man ; to wield the *a. T.* v. 42
But the *a*. spared thee. In those thriftier days *Y.O.* 100

AXLE.
As *a*. sometimes kindle as they go *P.E.* 407
Spin round upon her *a*., ere the warmth *T.* iii 491

AZORES.
Levantine regions these, the *A*. send *T.* iii 583

AZURE.
The cock his arched tail's *a*. show *Mrs. M.* 7
His radiant glories, *a*., green, and gold *T.* 61
His *a*. eyes, is tinctured black and red *T.* iv. 216
To stroke his *a*. neck, or to receive *T.* vi 781

B.

BAAL.
Then B. is the God, and worship him" *Con.* 854
A priesthood such as *B.'s* was of old *T.* ii 678

BABBLER.
B. of ancient fables, leaves a doubt *Ex.* 503
Aspersion is the *b.'s* trade *F.* 100
That *b*., called philosophers, devise *Tir.* 158

BABE.
Delighted with her *b*., the enchantress smiled *A.T.* 9
With doubtful credit, told to frighten *b. T.* iv 564
B. in the cause of freedom, and should fear *T.* v 291
The father, who designs his *b*. a priest *Tir.* 364
Which *b*. might play with; and the thievish jay *Y.O.* 18

BABEL.
Of the great *B*., and not feel the crowd *T.* iv 90
When B. was confounded, and the great *T.* v 193

BABOONS.
B. are free from, upon human race? *Ex.* 417

BABY.
The *b*. seems to smile with added charms *P.E.* 519
Of heroes, whose infirm and *b*. minds *T.* v 190
And binds a wreath about their *b*. brows *T.T.* 124

BABY-FEATURED.
Both *b*., and of infant size *P.E.* 201

BABYLON.
Saw *B*. set wide her two-leaved brass *Ex.* 59
But made long since, like B. of old *T.* 391
Increasing London? *B*. of old *T.* i 722
By him of *B*., life stands a stump *T.* v 401
Nineveh, *B*., and ancient Rome *T.T.* 432

BABYLONIAN.
The *B*. tyrant with a nod *P.E.* 130

BACCHANAL.
Then Genius danced a *B*.; he crowned *T.T.* 602

BACCHANALIAN.
Even *B*. madness has its charms *P.E.* 56

That bind the sinner's *B*. brow *T.* 462
So when, by *B*. torn *T.B.* 62
There waiter Dick, with *B*. lays *Tir.* 214

BACK.
" And guard behind the sorceress at thy *b*.!" *A.T* 190
And set up his *b*., and clawed like a cat *A.T.* ii 5
And conscious of an unincumbered *b. Ch.* 174
Call legions up from Hell to *b*. the deed *Con.* 691
And proves by thumps upon your *b. F.* 170
What thing upon his *b*. had got *J.G.* 95
The bottles twain behind his *b. J.G.* 123 [*P.E.* 115
Cries—" Well done, Saint!" and claps him on the *b*.
These choose the *b*., the belly those *L.W.* 16
Think how many *b*. have smarted *N.C.* 23
But restless was the chair; the *b*. erect *T.* i 44
We wear it at our *b*. There, closely braced *T.* ii 586
News from all nations lumbering at his *b. T.* iv 7
His murderer on his *b*., and, push'd all day *T.* vi 428
But though the felon on his *b*. could dare *T.* vi 516
But bends his sturdy *b*. to any toy *Tir.* 549
Leave kingly *b*. to cope with kingly cares *T.T.* 174

BACKED.
Below the exigence, or be not *b. T.* ii 557
Long *b*., long-tailed, with whiskered snout *T.B.* 35
The force of discipline when *b*. by love *Tir.* 681
B. with a modest sheet of humble prose *V.* 20

BACKSTRING.
The *b*. and the bib, assume the dress *T.* iv 227

BACKWARD.
Yet, *b*. as they are, and long have been *Tir.* 919

BACON.
All her reflected features. *B*. there *T.* i 702

BAD.
Till perjuries are common as *b*. pence *Ex.* 387 [*Con.* 323
They thought they must have died, they were so *b*.
Resistless in so *b*. a cause, but lame *T.* iv 439 [683
B. men, profaning Friendship's hallowed name *Con.*
What none but *b*. men wish exploded, must *T.* v 613

BADE.
B. rise in haste a dark and drizzling fog *A.T.* 94
Unless the power that *b.* him stand, restore *Ch.* 348
Given him a soul, and *b.* him understand *Con.* 430
"No doubt, my dear, I *b.* him come *M.F.* 11 [116
He drew them forth, and healed, and *b.* me live *T.* iii
And equal; and he *b.* them dwell in peace *T.* v 201

BADGER-COLOURED.
And *b.* hide *T.B.* 36

BAFFLED.
And at his feet the *b.* billows die *T.* i 525
B. his rider, saved against his will *T.* vi 520

BAFFLES.
The art that *b.* Time's tyrannic claim *M.P.* 9

BAG.
And music of the bladder and the *b. T.* i 585
And having dropped the expected *b.*, pass on *T.* iv 11
To his voracious *b.*, struggling in vain *T.* iv 450
Each lugging out his *b. Y.D.* 52

BAGOT.
We sometimes see a Lowth or *B.* there *Tir.* 435

BAITS.
And *b.* its hook with prodigies and lies *Con.* 224
Alas! expect it not. We found no *b. T.* i. 672

BAITED.
Nor *b.* hook deceive the fish's eye *T.* iii 313

BAKER'S
Dependent on the *b's.* punctual call *T.* i 244

BAKING.
For *b.* earth, or burning rock to lime *N.A.* 18

BALAAM.
He hates the hardness of a *B's.* heart *T.* vi 467

BALANCE.
While Chief Baron Ear sat to *b.* the laws *A.C.* 7
And having struck the *b.*, now proceed *Con.* 798
The partial *b.* and deceitful weight *Ex.* 41
That *b.* the wings of every hour *Ex.* 321
To make his *b.* true *J.G.* 72
Upon the ticklish *b.* of suspense *T.* iii 550
In *b.* on his conduct of a pin? *T.* vi 271
The *b.* in the highest place *Th.* 11

BALCONY.
From the *b.* spied *J.G.* 142

BALD.
Praise from the rivelled lips of toothless, *b. T.* ii 488
Teeth for the toothless, ringlets for the *b. T.* iv 81
With rueful faces and *b.* pates *Y.D.* 23

BALKS. [*R.* 421
Green *b.* and furrowed lands, the stream that spreads
O sweet retirement! who would *b.* the thought *R.* 487
Can always *b.* the tomb *St.* i 28
And such an age as ours *b.* no expense *Tir.* 257

BALL.
Was smooth and even as an ivory *b. A.T.* 47
Know then, that Heavenly Wisdom on this *b. Ex.* 314
Fandango, *b*, and rent! *F.B.* 33
Blame, cynic, if you can, quadrille or *b. P.E.* 175
Crape and cocked pistol, and the whistling *b.T.* iii 802
To theatre, or jocund feast, or *b. T.* v 410
To trivial toys, and, pushing ivory *b. T.* vi 274

To pitch the *b.* into the grounded hat *Tir.* 308
The moons of Jove, and Saturn's belted *b. Tir.* 634
Thou wast a bauble once, a cup and a *b. Y.O.* 17

BALLOTED.
Is *b.* and trembles at the news *T.* iv 627

BALM.
By way of *b.* for healing *F.* 96
With lenient *b.* may Oberon hence *Miss* — 21
The *b.* of care, Elysium of the mind *P.E.* 180

BALMY.
And shed the *b.* blessings on the lips *Con.* 442
O *b.* gales of soul-reviving air! *E.* ii 27
From Flora's *b.* store *M.* 2, 10
If fanned by *b.* and nutritious air *T.* iii 524
Their *b.* odours, and imparts their hues *T.* vi 243

BANANAS.
Thy cocoas, and *b*, palms and yams *T.* i 640

BAND.
Again—the *b.* of commerce was designed *Ch.* 83
The soul can mix with the celestial *b. Con.* 717
Have burst the *b.*, and cast the yoke away *Ex.* 465
The jocund Loves in Hymen's *b. Miss* — 73
Of union, and converts the sacred *b. T.* ii 686
The tasselled cap and the spruce *b.* a jest *T.* ii 749
Himself enslaved by terror of the *b. T.* iv 601
Great cause occurs to save him from a *b. Tir.* 696
To see a *b.* called patriot, for no cause *T.T.* 143

BANDITTI.
But to divert a fierce *b. E.* iv 13
The fierce *b.* which I mean *E.* iv 19

BANE.
Nor his who for the *b.* of thousands born *R.* 687

BANEFUL.
The comet's *b.* influence is a dream *P.E.* 100

BANISH.
To *b.* hesitation, and proclaim *H.* 63
These Flora *b.*, and gives the fair *T.* i 460
And bids the world take heart and *b.* fear *T.* ii 195

BANISHING.
Thy worst effect is *b.* for hours *Con.* 253

BANK.
On southern *b.* the ruminating sheep *A.T.* 78
On the *b.* of our river, I know *C.* 30 [*P.F.* 6
Of my favourite field, and the *b.* where they grew
Disdains the *B.* and throws the golden sands *Ch.* 248
As ever dressed a *b.*, or scented summer air *Ch.* 259
A cottage on the *b.* of Ouse *E.* i 48 [sounds *H.* 45
B. clothed with flowers, groves filled with sprightly
A western *b.'s* still sunny side *Mor.* 18 [185
Streams swelled above the *b.*, enjoined to stand *Ex.*
A narrow brook, by rushy *b.* concealed *N.A.* 9
Unfolds his flock, then under *b.* or bush *R.* 397
Fast by the *b.* of the slow-winding Ouse *R.* 804
Washed by the sea, or on the gravelly *b. T.* i 13
To enjoy a ramble on the *b.* of Thames *T.* i 115
Delighted. There, fast rooted in their *b. T.* i 166
Deep in the loamy *b.* Uptorn by strength *T.* iv 438
And see where it has hung the embroidered *b.T.* v107
And called the world to worship in the *b. T.* vi 681
Thus as the bee, from *b.* to bower 1789, 17

BANKRUPT.
"Battered and *b.* fortunes mended here" *T.* iii 824
He gives, what *b.* Nature never can *V.* 95

BANNERS.
And all the *b.* been unfurled *Q.V.* 23

BANQUET.
The *b.* of thy smiles ? *O.* ii 12

BANQUETING.
Sits *b.*, and God provides the feast *P.E.* 166

BAPTIZED.
B. her fleet Invincible in vain *Ex.* 569
Then all is plain. Philosophy *b. T.* iii 243

BAR. [337
None *b.* Him out from his most secret thought *Ex.*
Or send another shivering to the *b. Con.* 187
Learned at the *b.*, in the palæstra bold *Con.* 842
To flourish and parade with at the *b. Ex.* 665
When a *b.* of pure silver or ingot of gold *F.M.* 1
Begin their march to meet thee at the *b. H.* 226
And stands a witness at Truth's awful *b. Her.* 81
Say to what *b.* amenable were man ? *P.E.* 28
And *b.* the door the moment they intrude *P.E.* 160
Your cause before a *b.* you little dread *P.E.* 198
The *b.*, the senate, or the tented field *R.* 102 [745
Of headstrong youth were broken; *b.* and bolts *T.* ii
The folded gates would *b.* my progress now *T.* i 330
The sooty films that play upon the *b. T.* iv 292

BARB. [*A.T.* 193
The *b.* sprang forward, and his lord, whose force

BARBARITY.
(As if *b.* were high desert) *T.* vi 435

BARBAROUS.
And at the bottom *b.* still and rude *Con.* 167
Would give a *b.* air to British song *T.* 102
Those *b.* ages past, succeeded next *T.* i 16
And *b.* climes, where violence prevails *T.* i 604
In *b.* prostitution of your son *Tir.* 405
Oh, *b.*! wouldst thou with a Gothic hand *Tir.* 899

BARBED.
And the *b.* arrows of a frowning God *R.* 304

BARD.
Such the *B.'s* prophetic words *B.* 33 [iv 704
No *b.* could please me but whose lyre was tuned *T.*
And tears by *b.* or heroes shed *Cast.* 53
And deem the *B.*, whoe'er he be *D.* 21
Happy the *b.* (if that fair name belong *H.* 754
Thy unbound spirit into *b.* again *M.P.* 87
All, all alike, transport the glowing *b. R.* 197
Mute as e'er gazed on orator or *b. S.* i 8
O happy peasant! O unhappy *b.*! *T.* 331
Their eulogy; those sang the Mantuan *b. T.* iii 453
The Sabine *b.* O evenings, I reply *T.* iv 190
No *b.* embalms and sanctifies his song *T.* v 728
No *b.*, howe'er majestic, old or new *T.T.* 180
And every hallowed Druid was a *b. T.T.* 503
In less illustrious *b.* his beauty shone *T.T.* 574
'Twere new indeed to see a *b.* all fire *T.T.* 734
Already by some happier *b.* 1789, 10

BARE. [*Ch.* 54
That stripped him *b.*, and broke his honest heart
In Scotland's realm, forlorn and *b. A Tale* 9
His own offences, and strips others *b. Ch.* 494
Usurps God's office, lays his bosom *b. Con.* 745
But half a coat, and show his bosom *b. E.* iii 51
B. trees and shrubs but ill, you know *P.T.* 52
The Bramin kindles on his own *b.* head *T.* 99
Presented *b.* against the storm, plods on *T.* iv 353
Of those that *b.* them, in whatever cause *T.* iv 620

BAREHEADED.
Say why *b.* you are come *J.G.* 167
Who, with *b.* and obsequious bows *T.* iii 819

BARGAIN.
What, but a sordid *b.* for the skies *T.* 76
A senseless *b.* When I see such games *T.* iii 176
Swears 'tis a *b.*, rails at his hard fate *T.* vi 293

BARGE-LADEN.
The Nen's *b.* wave *St.* i 2

BARK.
Impede the *b.* that ploughs the deep serene *Ch.* 132
The sapless wood, divested of the *b. Con.* 53
The dogs did *b.*, the children screamed *J.G.* 109
Thou, as a gallant *b.* from Albion's coast *M.P.* 88
Crossing in your *b.* the main *N.C.* 44
Or ploughed perhaps by British *b.* again *T.* i 631
Then shakes his powdered coat, and *b.* for joy *T.* v 51

BARON.
While Chief *B.* Ear sat to balance the laws *A.C.* 7

BARONET.
By some lewd earl, or rakehell *b. P.E.* 314

BARRELS.
Like *b.* with their bellies full *Y.D.* 47

BARREN.
So *b.* sands imbibe the shower *F.* 184 [419
But *b.*, at the expense of neighbouring twigs *T.* iii
He rears unchanged his *b.* head *Miss* — 39
Near *b.* rocks, in palaces, or cells *R.* 540
That meet (no *b.* interval between) *T.* iii 409
B. as lances, among which the wind *T.* vi 142

BARRENNESS.
To *b.*, and solitude, and tears *T.* v 441
Of *b.* is past. The fruitful field *T.* vi 765

BARRIERS.
Their ancient *b.*, deluging the dry ? *T.* ii 56
A faithful *b.*, not o'erleaped with ease *T.* iii 681
Sheer o'er the craggy *b.*, and immersed *T.* vi 554
How weak the *b.* of mere Nature proves *Tir.* 169

BASE.
Its head as guarded as its *b.* is sure *Con.* 556
Or, in his words who damned the *b.* desire *Ex.* 422
From crimes as *b.* as any charged on me ? *Ex.* 711
But men unqualified and *b. F.* 2
Complain not if attachments lewd and base *Tir.* 889
Unworthy, *b.* and insincere *F.* 215
They were, what *b.* credulity believes *H.* 507
Begetting and conceiving all that's *b. P.E.* 569
And Atheist, if Earth bear so *b.* a slave) *P.E.* 615
He pressed him much to quit his *b.* employ *R.* 594
Scorns the *b.* hireling, and the slavish drudge *T.* 228
And deem his *b.* stupidity no crime *T.* 542
With *b.* materials, sat on well-tanned hides *T.* i 51
Profusion unrestrained, with all that's *b. T.* ii 675
Society, and that saps and worms the *b. T.* ii 816
So coveted, else *b.* and disesteemed *T.* iii 448
Sheltering the *b.* with its projected eaves *T.* iii 483
For ever dribbling out their *b.* contents *T.* iv 506
Or his *b.* gluttony, are causes good *T.* vi 388
O'er the green summit of the rocks, whose *b. T.* vi 496
Not soon deceived; aware that what is *b. T.* vi 989
To such *b.* hopes, in many a sordid soul *Tir.* 460
Is *b.* in kind, and born to be a slave *T.T.* 28
Wanting its proper *b.* to stand upon *T.T.* 54
If monarchy consist in such *b.* things *T.T.* 139
While no *b.* fear impedes her in her course *T. T.* 267

BASELY.
Paid with the blood that he had *b.* spared *T.* iii 91

BASENESS.
To lure me to the b. of a lie *T.T.* 86

BASER.
In b. souls unnumbered evils meet *Ch.* 37

BASEST.
Worse than a poniard in the b. hand *P.E.* 305
Is profanation of the b. kind *T.T.* 758

BASHFUL.
I pity b. men, who feel the pain *Con.* 347
The squire, once b., is shamefaced no more *P.E.* 403
As b., yet impatient to be seen *T.* i 325
The meek and b. boy will soon be taught *Tir.* 338

BASHFULNESS.
Sweet b.! it claims at least this praise *T.* iv 70

BASIS.
And must be made the b. *F.* 57

BASK.
In hope to b. a little yet *Mor.* 21
To frisk awhile, and b. in the warm sun *T.* vi 314
Graze with the fearless flocks; all b. at noon *T.* vi 774

BASKET.
Now b. up the family of plagues *T.* ii 667
(But that the b. dangling on her arm *T.* iv 547
The swains their b. make *T.B.* 30

BASKING.
Were b. hot, and all in blow *P.B.* 2

BASTED.
As they had b. been *J.G.* 128

BASTILLE.
Which God avenged on Pharaoh—the B. *T.* v 383

BASTIONS.
As b. set point blank against God's will *Con.* 688

BATH.   [516
Content with Bristol, B., and Tunbridge Wells *R.*

BATHES.
And asking of the surge that b. thy foot *T.* i 655
And b. their eyes with nectar, and includes *T.* vi 244

BATS.
The moles and b. in full assembly find *Ex.* 630
As useless to the moles and to the b. *T.* vi 880

BATTERED.   [834
"His country's weather-bleached and b. rocks *T.* v
"B. and bankrupt fortunes mended here" *T.* iii 824

BATTLE.
Rushed to b., fought and died *B.* 39
But shipwreck, earthquake, b., fire, and flood *Ch.* 232
"Speed us away to b. and to fame!" *Ex.* 289
Unblest, and that the b. is the Lord's? *Ex.* 353
Pants to be told of b. won or lost *R.* 476
It was not in the b. *R.G.* 17

BAUBLE.
The ring a b., and the priest a knave *A.T.* 66
To make the sun a b. without use *H.* 81
Delighted with my b. coach, and wrapped *M.P.* 50
Akin to rapture, when the b. finds *T.* vi 276
I give the b. but the second place *Tir.* 388
Thou wast a b. once, a cup and ball *Y.O.* 17

BAULK.   [135
Yet, though he tease and b. your listening ear *Con.*

BAWL.
As loud as he could b. *J.G.* 112
"Yes, truly—one must scream and b. *M.F.* 27

BAYS.
Lolls at his ease behind four handsome b. *R.* 392
Green as the b. tree, ever green *St.* i 17   [*T.* 365
They swarm around thee, and thou stand'st at b. *T.*
In village or in town, the b. of curs *T.* i 230
Shall royal institutions miss the b. *Tir.* 503
Where Nichol swung the birch and twined the b. *V.* 36

BEACH.
Methinks I see thee straying on the b. *T.* i 654
That pressed the b., and hasty to depart *T.* ii 118
Their offspring, left upon so wild a b. *Tir.* 802

BEACONS.
Have kindled b. in the skies, and the old *T.* ii 59
"That show like b. in the blue abyss *T.* v 839

BEADS.
Book, b., and maple dish, his meagre stock *T.* 80
Like a swarth Indian with his belt of b. *T.* iv 749

BEAGLE.
True b. as the staunchest hound he keeps *P.E.* 87

BEAK.
Entreated, opening wide his b. *P.T.* 19
And parrots with twin cherries in their b. *T.* i 38
He left poor Bully's b. *T.B.* 54
That b. whence issued many a lay *T.B.* 56
Or kites with cruel b. *The Doves* 34

BEAKER.
He lives, and o'er his brimming b. boasts *T.* vi 434

BEAM.
But she, inconstant as the b. that play *A.T.* 23
"By Dian's b.," Sir Marmadan exclaimed *A.T.* 187
Blessed the glad b. of that propitious day *A.T.* 205
Too scanty for the exertion of his b. *Ch.* 590
A b. that aids, but never grieves the sight *Con.* 600
Of Revelation's ineffectual b. *Con.* 830   [611
The b. of heavenly truth have swelled the debt! *Ex.*
That b. delight? a heart untaught to sigh *Ep.* i 6
Dimness and anguish, all thy b. obscured *Ex.* 393
Who brought the lamp that with awaking b. *Ex.* 500
Save for the fruits his heavenly b. produce *H.* 82
In b. of inextinguishable light *H.* 134   [*H.* 503
And though his b., that quicken where they shine
Suppose the b. should dip on the wrong side *H.* 374
But brighter b. than his who fires the skies *H.* 491
His noonday b. were never half so bright *H.* 737
Than golden b. of orient light *M.* 27
Pay tribute to thy glorious b. *O.* i 7
Hatched by the b. of truth, denies him rest *P.E.* 241
In counterpoise, flies up and kicks the b. *T.* 356
Some b. of rectitude she yet displays *T.* 485
While he that scorns the noonday b., perverse *T.* 523
Of atoms, sparkling in the noonday b. *T.* i 361
Beneath the rosy cloud, while yet the b. *T.* i 495
In which they flourish most; where, in the b. *T.* i 694
The fence withdrawn, he gives them every b. *T.* iii 444
The eclipse that intercepts truth's heavenly b. *T.* v 683
That shows by night a lucid b. *Tran.* i 3
Watch every b. Philosophy imparts *T.T.* 78
Unwelcome vapours quench autumnal b. *T.T.* 212
If brighter b. than all he threw not forth *T.T.* 680
Transmitting cloudless, and the solar b. *Y.O.* 75

BEAMING.
And all his country b. in his face *T.T.* 347

BEAMY.
"And many an aching wish, your b. fires T. v 838

BEANS. [23
But corn was housed, and b. were in the stack N.A.

BEAR.
To improve the fortitude that b. the load Ch. 160
Tried, as it should be, by the fruit it b. Con. 172
Because a b. is rude and surly? No—Con. 192
And b. the marks upon a blushing face Con. 349
While Honour, Virtue, Piety, b. sway Ex. 326
And are indeed a bog that b. F. 124
To pardon or to b. it F. 174
That cannot b. the blaze of Scripture light H. 298
To b. it, suffered shame where'er he went H. 587
In which I b. my trusty sword J.G. 63
No virtuous wish can b. a date Mor. 57
The choicest flowers she b. Pat. 14
Or Fancy's fondness for the child she b. P.E. 517
And Atheist, if Earth b. so base a slave) P.E. 615
And Destiny, that sometimes b. P.T. 47
B. proof of an intelligence divine R. 208
A mind unnerved, or indisposed to b. R. 677
And b. the brand of blasphemy burnt in T. 348
And strained to the last screw that he can b. T. 385
We b. our shades about us; self-deprived T. i 259
May b. us smoothly to the Gallic shore T. ii 262
We may with patience b. our moderate ills T. iv 339
Upon their jutting chests. He, formed to b. T. iv 350
The plump convivial parson often b. T. iv 595
A noble cause, which none who b. a spark T. iv 614
To b. his burdens, drawing in his gears T. v 273
But is it fit, or can it b. the shock T. v 305
All b. the royal stamp that speaks them his T. v 551
While sloth seduces more, too weak to b. T. vi 107
The Lion, and the libbard, and the b. T. vi 773
Custom and prejudice shall b. no sway T. vi 838
Because that world adopts it. If it b. T. vi 982
And b. the palm away" Th. 12 [329
And fierce Licentiousness should b. the blame T.T.
B. witness, long ere his dismission come Tir. 561
He b. it with meek manliness of soul T.T. 225

BEARDS.
Long b., long noses, and pale faces M.F. 6 [iv 123
Fringed with a b. made white with other snows T.
Then, with his silver b. and magic wand P.E. 183
The veteran shows, and gracing a grey b. T. i 406
And shamed as we have been, to the very b. T. ii 271

BEARDED.
The youth now b., and yet pert and raw, Tir. 155
And having known thee b. and full-grown V. 37

BEARDLESS.
The scoff of withered age and b. youth H. 743

BEARER.
A pedler's pack, that bows the b. down T. i 465
Till the stout b. lift the corpse again T. i 481

BEARING.
Well, I protest 'tis past all b.!" M.F. 25

BEAST.
The b. that roam over the plain A.S. 13
The b. is laid down in his lair A.S. 50
The b. are chartered—neither age nor force Ch. 171
The noble b. judge otherwise, his groom Con. 414
Till none but b. acknowledge him a man Con. 426
The snorting b. began to trot J.G. 83
Birds of all feather, b. of every name N.A. 65
Envy the b., then, on whom Heaven bestows P.E. 267
Drives to their dens the obedient b. of prey R. 766
Weeps when she sees inflicted on a b. T. ii 25
On bird and b., the other charged for man T. iv 249
Thy waggon is thy wife, and the poor b. T. iv 367
And just in his account, why bird and b. T. vi 389
To assist his foe's down-fallen b. to rise T. vi 444
That oft the b. has seem'd to judge the man T. vi 478
A longer date to the far nobler b. T. vi 529
A b. forth sallied on the scout T.B. 34

BEAT. [vi 497
B. back the roaring surge, scarce heard so high T.
Let Dares b. Entellus black and blue Con. 198
After all he must b. it as thin and as fine F.M. 21
"Where tempests never b. nor billows roar" M.P. 97
B. in the breast of man, that even a few T. i 285
B. high within them at a mother's wrongs T. v 519
Playing, at b. of drum, their martial pranks T.T. 136

BEATEN.
Confine the million in the b. track T.T. 667

BEATING.
B. alternately, in measured time T.T. 528

BEAU.
A spaniel, B., that fares like you Beau 1
The sight's enough—no need to smell a b. Con. 285
B. marked my unsuccessful pains D.W. 21
B. trotting far before D.W. 30
And b., adepts in every thing profound H. 347
A praying, synagogue-frequenting b. T 57
Her crimson honours; and the spangled b. T. iii 578

BEAUTEOUS.
Her b. form reflected clear below M.P. 93
Now sanguine, and her b. head now set T. vi 158

BEAUTIFUL.
A b. and perfect whole E. i 64
Scenes must be b. which, daily viewed T. i 177
Or what he views of b. or grand T. vi 249
And weighed down its b. head The Rose 4
On the b. bosom of May W.N. 16

BEAUTIFY.
Might b. and cheer the night" N.G. 22

BEAUTY.
That all the various b. we survey A.T. 48
"Starts at the call of b. in distress A.T. 120
"B. for ashes" is a gift indeed Ch. 230
But are we so to wit and b. blind Con. 257
Their b. I intent surveyed D.W. 15
The b. of a rose full blown E. i 68
And praised the wrath that laid her b. waste Ex. 427
The graces and the b. F. 45
For its b. admired and its use Gr. 26
Wine has no taste, and b. has no charms H. 705
Whose b. impressed me with awe M.P. 11
Whilst b. decks the plain Miss — 40
There B. woos him with expanded arms P.E. 55
Where unassisted sight no b. sees R. 56.
Borrowing a b. from the works of grace R. 358
B. he lately slighted as he passed R. 425
He views it not, or sees no b. there R. 470
Graced with such wisdom, how would b. shine R. 557
Sighs o'er the b. of the charming scene R. 566
Has lost its b. and its powers S. 16
His Maker has no b. in his sight T. 414
Of hedge-row b. numberless, square tower T. i 173
Her b., her fertility. She dreads T. i 370
And mar the face of B., when no cause T. i 458
Till half their b. fade; the weary sight T. i 510
Gives more than female b. to a stone T. i 703
That so much b. would do well to purge T. i 726

Where *b.* oft and lettered worth consume *T.* ii 123
Displaying his own *b.*, starves his flock *T.* ii 429
Poured forth by *B.* splendid and polite *T.* ii 494
That gives society its *b.*, strength *T.* ii 681
And charmed with rural *b.*, to repose *T.* iii 28
Some traces of her youthful *b.* left) *T.* iii 299
There blooms exotic *b.*, warm and snug *T.* iii 568
And covetous of Shakespeare's *b.*, seen *T.* iii 601
And by contrasted *b.* shining more) *T.* iii 635
Are wedded thus, like *b.* to old age *T.* iii 660
As twice seven years, his *b.* had then first *T.* iv 714
That all discern a *b.* in his works *T.* iv 739
Smit with the *b.* of so fair a scene *T.* v 560
So clothed with *b.*, for rebellious man? *T.* v 754
The Author of her *b.*, who, retired *T.* v 893
The *b.* of the wilderness are his *T.* vi 186   [764
And clothe all climes with *b.*; the reproach *T.* vi
To see thy *b.*, and to share thy joy *T.* vi 815
Strength joined with *b.*, dignity with grace *Tir.* 2
The prize of *b.* in a woman's eyes *Tir.* 472
That like some cottage *b.*, strikes the heart *T.T.* 524
In less illustrious bards his *b.* shone *T.T.* 574
And as the sun in rising *b.* dressed *T.T.* 706
See, Mary, what *b.* I bring *W.N.* 5

BECAME.
The rest, alert and active, as *b. A.T.* 133
The new acquaintance soon *b.* a guest *Con.* 531
They felt what it *b.* them much to feel *Con.* 543
The debt, which justly *b.* due *E.* iv 23
That trot *b.* a gallop soon *J.G.* 87
The new machine, and it *b.* a Chair *T.* i 43
'Gan murmur, as *b.* the softer sex *T.* i 71
And Virtue fled. The schools *b.* a scene *T.* ii 735
B. stone blind; precedence went in truck *T.* ii 741
Were burnished into heroes, and *b. T.* v 280

BECAMEST.
Fostering propitious, thou *b.* a twig *Y.O.* 39

BECKONS.
B. the legions of his storms away *H.* 477

BECKONING.
Where *b.* Pleasure leads them wildly stray *Ex.* 464

BECOME.
B. at length so splendid in our own *Con.* 370
Now, in a posture that *b.* you more *Con.* 489
Who waits for heaven ere he *b.* divine *Con.* 584
B. a mockery and a standing jest *Ex.* 110
The rich poor, the poor *b.* purse-proud *H.* 18
B. not weary of attention *M.F.* 52
'Tis now *b.* a history little known *M.P.* 52
Ere yet the pleasing toil *b.* a pain *P.E.* 70
B. more rare as dissipation spreads *R.* 706
There touched by Reynolds, a dull blank *b. T.* i 700
And tender in address, as well *b. T.* ii 406
We are *b.* so candid and so fair *T.* iii 93
He speaks. The lake in front *b.* a lawn *T.* iii 774
B. a dice-box, and a billiard mace *T.* iv 221
Less dainty than *b.* his grave outside *T.* iv 605
That instant he *b.* the serjeant's care *T.* iv 631
He stands erect; his slouch *b.* a walk *T.* iv 639
B. a loathsome body, only fit *T.* iv 674
B. the soul that animates them all *T.* v 275
Thou couldst *b.* unkind at last *The Doves* 31
B. their pattern, upon whom they fix *Tir.* 224
Thy popularity, and art *b. Y.O.* 57

BECOMING.
But unattired in that *b.* vest *T.T.* 722

BED.
Relate how many weeks they kept their *b. Con.* 315

And who is hanged, and who is brought to *b. Con.* 396
Would give relief of *b.* and board to none *H.* 306
Nor gardens interspersed with flowery *b. R.* 336
He left his *b.*, he trod the floor *R.C.* 91
Then stepped the poet into *b. R.C.* 107
Come hither, ye that press your *b.* of down *T.* i 362
Whose headaches nail them to a noonday *b. T.* i 500
Finds a cold *b.* her only comfort left *T.* ii 655 [827
Spawned in the muddy *b.* of Nile, came forth *T.* ii
The *b.* the trusted treasure of their seeds *T.* iii 650
Saves the small inventory, *b.*, and stool *T.* iv 401
Blown in its native *b.*; 'tis there alone *T.* iv 660
Where, on his *b.* of wool and matted leaves *T.* vi 312

BEDEW.
And the first thankful tears *b.* his cheeks *H.* 727

BEDIGHT.
With russet specks *b. A Tale* 42

BEDLAM.
See *B.'s* closeted and handcuffed charge *Tir.* 819
This *B.* part; and others nearer home *T.T.* 609

BEDSIDE.
Dagger in hand, steals to your *b. Ch.* 187

BEE.
Perhaps might prosper with a swarm of *b. Con.* 288
Their memory, like the *b.* that fed *M.* 29
And *b.* in hives as idly wait *N.* 3
A *b.* of most discerning taste *P.B.* 3
The silly unsuccessful *b. P.B.* 22.
As all by instinct, like the *b. Q.V.* 43
The *b.* transports the fertilizing meal *T.* iii 538
He travels and expatiates, as the *b. T.* iv 107
Of his lost *b.* to her maternal ear *T.* v 137
Thus as the *b.*, from bank to bower 1789, 17

BEECH.   [*T.* vi 317
Ascends the neighbouring *b.*; there whisks his brush
Muse, hang this harp upon yon aged *b. Ex.* 718
Of ash, or lime, or *b.*, distinctly shine *T.* i 303
The maple, and the *b.* of oily nuts *T.* i 315   [230
Rough elm, or smooth-grained ash, or glossy *b. R.*
For ere the *b.* and elm have cast their leaf *T.* iii 466
The rustic throng beneath his favourite *b. T.* iv 708

BEER.
But knew no medium between guzzling *b. R.* 601

BEFALL.
To tell us what is to *b. A Fable* 22
His sole opinion, whatsoe'er *b. Con.* 133   [10
True. Changes will *b.*, and friends may part *E.* iii
Or (which is likelier to *b.*) *P.T.* 34

BEFELL.   [*P.E.* 464
By thee worse plagues than Pharaoh's land befell

BEFIT.
But what old Chaucer's merry page *b. A.T.* 84
That constancy *b.* them *F.* 159
That royal residence might well *b. T.* v 157

BEFRIEND.   [421
Shall much *b.* you. Time shall give increase *T.* iv
B. thee, of all other friends bereft *Tir.* 881

BEG.
B. you for once to take his part *St.* 135
He *b.* their flattery with his latest breath *T.* 315
She *b.* an idle pin of all she meets *T.* i 553   [573
Loud when they *b.*, dumb only when they steal *T.* i
Can dig, *b.*, rot, and perish, well content *T.* iii 805
B. a warm office, doomed to a cold jail *T.* iii 820
To engross a moment's notice; and yet *b. T.* iv 67

B. a propitious ear for his poor thoughts *T.* iv 68
And *b.* for exile, or the pangs of death? *T.* v 434
And looks as if he came to *b. G.D.* 31 [iv 405
To soothe their honest pride, that scorns to beg *T.*

BEGAN.
One was accounted when the cry *b. A.T.* 135
Home to the goal where it *b.* the race *Ch.* 566
Which this day's incident *b.? E.* i 84
See Nature gay as when she first *b. H.* 39
As useless as the moment it *b. H.* 96
Since Abel worshipped, or the world *b. H.* 644
The snorting beast *b.* to trot *J.G.* 83
B. to feel, as well he might *N.G.* 5
B. to agitate the matter *P.T.* 16
Her climbing she *b.* to find *R.C.* 25
Thus war *b.* on earth; these fought for spoil *T.* v 228
Was registered in Heaven ere time *b. T.* v 530
And learn with wonder how this world *b. Tir.* 127
Time was he closed as he *b.* the day *Tir.* 175

BEGAT.
The tasted sweets of property *b. T.* v 224
B. a tranquil confidence in all *T.* vi 366

BEGET.
Which idleness and weariness *b. R.* 762
B. its likeness. Rank abundance breeds *T.* i 686
Increase of power *b.* increase of wealth *T.* iv 580
The eyesight of Discovery; and *b. T.* v 452
Remorse *b.* reform. His master-lust *T.* v 618
B. no thunder-clouds to trouble life *V.* 76

BEGETTING.
B. and conceiving all that's base *P.E.* 569

BEGGARS.
B. Invention, and makes Fancy lame *R.* 710 [ii 656
Wives *b.* husbands, husbands starve their wives *T.*

BEGGARED.
Though lean and *b.*, every twentieth pace *T.* iv 468

BEGGARLY.
And force the *b.* last doit, by means *T.* v 316

BEGGARY.
Than abstinence, and *b.*, and lice *T.* 124

BEGGED.
And *b.* an interest in his frequent prayers *Con.* 74
What their affliction was, and *b.* a share *Con.* 524
Lest he should trepass, *b.* to go abroad *E.* iii 23
Ye are bid, *b.*, besought to entertain *P.E.* 264

BEGGING.
Of fluttering, loitering, cringing, *b.*, loose *T.* iii 832

BEGINS.
'Tis in the church the leprosy *b. Ex.* 96
B. their march to meet thee at the bar *H.* 226
And where his danger and God's wrath *b. H.* 609
That folly ends where genuine Hope *b. H.* 637
His journey to *b. J.G.* 50
B. a long look out for distant land *R.* 433
Lashed into foaming waves, *b.* to roar *T.* 260
Exposed to his cold breath, the task *b. T.* iii 469
Just when our drawing-rooms *b.* to blaze *T.* iv 267
My pleasures too *b.* But me, perhaps *T.* v 272
In all directions, he *b.* again—*T.* v 431
Thus, half accomplished ere ye yet *b. Tir.* 234
Of classic food *b.* to be his care *Tir.* 319
That here *b.* with most that long complaint *Tir.* 587
Who, just when industry *b.* to snore *Tir.* 745
Look up—your brains begin to swim *Tran.* ii 10
When children first *b.* to spell *Tran.* iv 37
Ere yet his race *b.*, its glorious close *T.T.* 708

Or ere the wheels of verse *b.* to roll *T.T.* 711
At length the busy time *b. Y.D.* 49

BEGINNING.
Whose Love knew no *b.*, knows no end *Ch.* 400
Runs round; still ending, and *b.* still *T.* iii 627

BEGIRT.
The villas with which London stands *b. T.* iv 748

BEGONE.
B.! the whip and bell in that hard hand *Ch.* 212

BEGOT.
Of self-congratulating Pride, *b. T.* v 622

BEGOTTEN.
Their zeal *b.*, as their works rehearse *Ch.* 505

BEGUILE.
For he would oft *b. Ep.* ii. 34
Which labour of his frown *b. Mrs. M.* 29
No meretricious graces to *b. T.* 23
B. their woes, and make the woods resound *T.* i 586
B. the night, and set a keener edge *T.* iv 164
For, after all, if merely to *b. T.T.* 740

BEGUILED.
So fares it with the multitudes *b. H.* 278
By expectation every day *b. M.P.* 40
Fretful unless diverted and *b. R.* 108.

BEGUN.
Produced a friendship, then *b. E.* i 101
Attend to finish what the sword *b. Her.* 60
Wretch even then, life's journey just *b.? M.P.* 24
His morning course, the enchantment was *b. P.E.* 68
In tribes and clans, and had *b.* to call *T.* v 222
Egregious purpose! worthily *b. Tir.* 404

BEHALF.
" In *b.* of the Nose, it will quickly appear *A.C.* 9
He pleaded again in *b.* of the eyes *A.C.* 26
Much more in *b.* of your wish might be said *P.A.* 14
On God's *b.*, lays waste his fairest works *T.* ii 136

BEHELD.
Nor him *b.*, nor her again *Cast.* 12
B. with joy the lovely scene defaced *Ex.* 426
Pleased she *b.* aloft portrayed *Q.V.* 45
B. their progress with the deepest dread *T.T.* 325

BEHEST.
'Twas Nature, Sir, whose strong *b. B.R.* 7

BEHOLD.
B. a Christian!—and without the fires *Ch.* 599
Whoever boasts that name—*b.* a cheat! *Ch.* 603
While eager Hodge *b.* the prize *E.* iv 43
And hope, in due time, to *b. Gr.* 31
B. in Ætna's emblematic fires *Her.* 45
And now in the grass *b.* they are laid *P.F.* 7
B. in these what leisure hours demand *R.* 701
The summit gained, *b.* the proud Alcove *T.* i 278
B. the picture!—Is it like?—Like whom? *G.* ii 408
Diffused, attain the surface; when, *b.*! *T.* iii 493
With all its generations; I *b. T.* iv 99
B. the schools in which plebeian minds *T.* iv 492
In other heavens than these that we *b. T.* v 571
" So I with animated hopes *b. T.* v 837
All we *b.* is miracle; but, seen *T.* vi 132
B. the measure of the promise filled *T.* vi 798
B. your bishop! well he plays his part *Tir.* 420
B. that figure, neat, though plainly clad *Tir.* 664

BEHOVES.
Now theirs was converse such as it *b. Con.* 537

BEING.
Gives Charity her *b.* and her birth *Ch.* 378
A *b.* of less equity than man *H.* 384
Have a *b.* less durable even than he *P.F.* 20
Mounts from inferior *b.* up to God *R.* 114
His *b.* end where death dissolves the bond *Tir.* 67

BELIE.
B. their name, and offer nothing new *R.* 714

BELIED.
Unless *b.* by common fame *F.* 86

BELIEF.
Each man's *b.* is right in his own eyes *H.* 283
Is tremontane, and stumbles all *b. T.* iv 533
" And gesture, they propound to our *b.? T.* v 649
'Tis your *b.* the world was made for man *T.T.* 47

BELIEVE.
For seamen much *b.* in signs *A Tale* 61
The worst suggested, she *b.* the best *Ch.* 427
' Sir! I *b.* it on that ground alone *Con.* 233
Will they *b.*, though credulous enough *Con.* 721
That while she dotes, and dreams that she *b. Con.* 775
His unsuspecting sheep *b.* it pure *Ex.* 103
'Tis to *b.* what men inspired of old *Ex.* 646
But prove as ready to *b. F.* 17
" I never will *b.*," the colonel cries *H.* 381
They were, what base credulity *b. H.* 507
That few *b.* the wonders thou hast wrought *H.* 667
Could I *b.*, that winds for ages pent *N.E.* 85
Stand the soul-quickening words—*B.* and Live *T.* 31
The book shall teach you; read, *b.*, and live! *T.* 274
B., rush forward, and possess the prize *T.* 374

BELIEVED.
A close designer not to be *b. Con.* 477
A truth still sacred, and *b.* of old *Ex.* 351
(Awful alternative! *b.*, beloved *Ex.* 688
What ardently I wished, I long *b. M.P.* 38
Till others have the soothing tale *b. P.E.* 493
This once *b.*, 'twere logic misapplied *Tir.* 103

BELIEVER.
Ploughs up the roots of a *b.'s* care *T.* 460
All joy to the *b.*! He can speak—*T.* 571
Nor judge by statute a *b.'s* hope *T.T.* 72

BELINDA.
B., maids are soon preferred *Tran.* iv 7
B. and her bird! 'tis rare *Tran.* iv 31

BELL.
But the sound of the church-going *b. A.S.* 29
Begone! the whip and *b.* in that hard hand *Ch.* 212
Unto the *B.* at Edmonton *J.G.* 11
That drove them to the *B. J.G.* 218
I heard the *b.* tolled on thy burial day *M.P.* 28
No more move us than the *b. St.* iv 31
Duly as clink of *b.* to morning prayers *T.* 140
Seems what it is, a cap and *b.* for fools *T.* 368
Tall spire, from which the sound of cheerful *b. T.* i 174
Sportive and jingling her poetic *b. T.* iv 702
How soft the music of those village *b. T.* vi 6
True to the jingling of our leader's *b. Tir.* 254

BELLES.
Your prudent grandmammas, ye modern *b. R.* 515

BELLY.
These choose the back, the *b.* those *L.W.* 16
Like barrels with their *b.* full *Y.D.* 47

BELLOW.
If Winter *b.* from the north *Trans. H.* 22

BELL-ROPE.
Girt with a *b.* that the Pope has blessed *T.* 82

BELONG.
To which the said spectacles ought to *b. A.C.* 4
If sentence of eternal pain *b. H.* 389
Say man's a worm, and power *b.* to God *H.* 711
Happy the bard (if that fair name *b. H.* 754
All these *b.* to virtue, and all prove *b. P.E.* 247
That prize *b.* to none but the sincere *P.E.* 578
That it *b.* to freemen, would disgust *T.* v 482
Such reasonings (if that name must needs *b. T.* v 655
But no prophetic fires to me *b. T.T.* 504

BELOVED.
Reduced to practice, his *b.* rule *Con.* 139
(Awful alternative! believed, *b. Ex.* 688
And all the love of the *b.* John *H.* 625
Deserves to be *b.*, but not adored *R.* 272
From pleasures left, but never more *b. R.* 564
I would not be a king to be *b. T.* v 359
That country, if at all, must be *b. ? T.* v 508
Who is *b.* where never seen 1789, 71

BELSHAZZAR.
Which shook *B.* at his wine *Q.V.* 51

BELT.
My leathern *b.* likewise *J.G.* 62
Through which the *b.* he drew *J.G.* 70
Like a swarth Indian with his *b.* of beads *T.* iv 749

BELTED.
With *b.* waist and pointers at their heels *T.* ii 753
The moons of Jove, and Saturn's *b.* ball *Tir.* 134

BEMAZED.
With intellects *b.* in endless doubt *T.* v 848

BENCH.
Your only one, till sides and *b.* fail *T.* ii 475
From tippling *b.*, cellars, stalls, and styes *T.* vi 695
The *b.* on which we sat while deep employed *Tir.* 302
The hallowed *b.* from absolute contempt *Tir.* 431

BENDS.
And *b.* the tough materials to his will *Ch.* 464
Though twice a Cæsar could not *b.* thee now *Ex.* 477
Could *b.* one knee, engage one votary there *H.* 506
To take the *b.* his appetites ordain *H.* 603
And when I *b.*, retire, and shrink *P.* 35 [557
B. the straight rule to their own crooked will *P.E.*
Hebrew or Syriac, shall be forced to *b. P.E.* 499
But *b.* his sturdy back to any toy *Tir.* 549
And *b.* her polished neck beneath his hand *T.T.* 411
Awe-struck, before thy presence *b.* 1789, 67

BENDED.
Thy parliaments adored, on *b.* knees *Ex.* 538

BENDING.
B. as he swept the chords *B.* 35
The shivering urchin, *b.* as he goes *T.* 143

BENEFACTOR.
Serving a *b.*, I am free *Ch.* 242

BENEFACTRESS.
His *b.* blushes at the deed *P.E.* 212

BENEFICENT.
Of God, *b.* in all His ways *R.* 556
Or stained with guilt, *b.*, approved *T.* vi 998

BENEFITS.
Receiving *b.* and rendering none *T.* vi 959

BENEVOLENCE.
B., and peace, and mutual aid *T.* ii 49

BENEVOLENT.
Come, prompt me with *b.* desires *Ch.* 11
Is sober, meek, *b.*, and prays *H.* 520
Been less, or less *b.* than strong *T.* v 852
Impart to the *b.*, who wish *T.* vi 344

BENEVOLUS.
Thanks to *B.*—he spares me yet *T.* i 262

BENIFICENCE.
And whose *b.* no charge exhausts *T.* vi 230

BENIGHTED.
For Africa's once loved, *b.* shore *Ch.* 241

BENIGNITY.
B., friendship, and truth *Gr.* 44

BENT.
Full many a champion *b.* on daring deed *A.T.* 123
B., wool, and feathers mixed *A Tale* 40
For tell some men that pleasure, all their *b. Con.* 875
B. all on pleasure, heedless of its end *E.* ii 18
The bow well *b.*, and smart the spring *H.F.* 5
That, though on pleasure she was *b. J.G.* 31
B. knees, round shoulders, and dejected looks *T.* iv 634
Beneath the dazzling deluge; and the *b. T.* v 22

BEREFT.
Of friends, of hope, of all *b. Cast.* 5
See Judah's promised king, *b.* of all *R.* 767
Befriend thee, of all other friends *b. Tir.* 881

BERGAMOT.
Its *b.*, or aids the indebted eye *T.* ii 452

BERRIES.
Not yet the hawthorn bore her *b.* red *N.A.* 19
Or blushing crabs, or *b.* that emboss *T.* i 121

BERRY-BEARING.
Lie covered close; and *b.* thorns *T.* v 82

BESET.
Peeps at the vale below; so thick *b. T.* i 225
Not rude and surly, and *b.* with thorns *T.* i 601
Though leafless, well attired, and thick *b. T.* vi 168
B. with every ill but that of fear *T.T.* 363

BESOTTED.
Step forth to notice; and, *b.* thus *T.* v 257

BESOUGHT.
Ye are bid, begged, *b.* to entertain *P.E.* 264

BESPEAKS.
And every drop *b.* a Saviour thine *E.* ii 48
" B. at least a stubborn soil *E.* iv 82
For 'tis a union that *b. F.* 47
That sound *b.* Salvation on her way *H.* 455
To Him whose works *b.* his nature, Love *J.T.* 46
May rival these; these all *b.* a power *T.* i 431
That's noble, and *b.* a nation proud *T.* ii 43
Still they are frowning signals, and *b. T.* ii 68
Prepare for happiness; *b.* him one *T.* vi 912
Asserts precedence, and *b.* control *Tir.* 9
B. a land, once Christian, fallen, and lost *T.T.* 428

BESPOKE.
B. at least a man that knew mankind *E.* iii 41
The Lily's height *b.* command *L.R.* 13
B. him past the bounds of freakish youth *T.* ii 704

BEST.
That every tribe, though placed as he sees *b. Ch.* 19

On man, a mourner in his *b.* estate *Ch.* 156
At my *b.* home, if not exiled from thee " *Ch.* 243
The worst suggested, she believes the *b. Ch.* 427
From motives such as his, though not the *b. Ch.* 481
B. for the public, and my wisest part *Con.* 870
They *b.* can judge a poet's worth *Dr.* 5
That moving signal summoning when *b. Ex.* 179
Thus fell the *b.* instructed in her day *Ex.* 225
As ever Roman had in Rome's *b.* days *Ex.* 591
To read the news, or fiddle, as seems *b. H.* 76
Till the *b.* tongue, or heaviest hand, prevails *H.* 196
Whose temper was the *b. J.P.* 4   [568
The world's *b.* comfort was, his doom was passed *H.*
His powers of *b.* exertion there *Mor.* 32
Those Christians *b.* deserve the name *N.G.* 35
Might prove a mischief, or at *b.* a toy *P.E.* 302
And having done, we think the *b.* we can *P.E.* 367
Or plead its silence as its *b.* applause *R.* 414
Seems at the *b.* but dreaming life away *R.* 468
Is thine;—*b.* gift, the unfailing source of joy *S.* ii 12
His *b.* concerns aright *St.* v 6
Recoil from weary life's *b.* hour *St.* v 19   [505
The scholar's pitch (the scholar *b.* knows why *P.E.*
His love as *b.* we may *St.* vi 6   [709
Should *b.* secure them, and promote them most *T.* iii
Or ford the rivulets, are *b.* at home *T.* 217
The worst of men, and curses of the *b. T.* 434
Or vermin, or at *b.* of cock purloined *T.* i 563
The wisest and the *b.* feel urgent need *T.* ii 483
There they are happiest who dissemble *b. T.* ii 639
Oh friendly to the *b.* pursuits of man *T.* iii 290
For plunder; much solicitous how *b. T.* iv 433
Of little worth, an idler in the *b. T.* vi 952
So the *b.* courser on the plain *Th.* 17   [29
Some friend is gone, perhaps his son's *b.* friend *T.* vi
Are *b.* disposed of where with most success *Tir.* 848
Church ladders are not always mounted *b. Tir.* 381
In which the *b.* and worthiest tremble most *Tir.* 415
A piece of mere church furniture at *b. Tir.* 425
Boys are, at *b.*, but pretty buds unblown *Tir.* 446
" Whate'er is *b.* administered is *b.*" *Tir.* 508 [717
And all the instructions of thy son's *b.* friend *Tir.*
And thou at *b.*, and in thy soberest mood *Tir.* 753
Every dish, and spoil the *b. Tran.* iii 14
Free to prove all things, and hold fast the *b. T.T.* 273
Satire has long since done his *b.*, and curst *T.T.* 728
And the winter of sorrow *b.* shows *W.N.* 23
The future, *b.* unknown, but at thy mouth *Y.O.* 43
Of their *b.* tone their dissolution owe *Y.O.* 85

BESTIAL.
B., a meagre intellect, unfit *T.* v 454

BESTOW.
Delayed not to *b. Cast.* 28
To quit the bliss thy rural scenes *b. Ch.* 299
Not less effectual than what love *b. Ch.* 483
And shines as if impatient to *b. Ch.* 591
The largess He *b.*, prescribes the terms *H.* 325
To take with gratitude what heaven *b. H.* 430
Nor spurn away a gift a God *b. H.* 547
Envy the beast, then, on whom Heaven *b. P.E.* 267
Woman indeed, a gift he would *b. R.* 269
His portion in the good that Heaven *b. T.T.* 20
With joy beyond what victory *b. T.T.* 80

BESTOWED.
Divinely *b.* upon man *A.S.* 18
Empire is on us *b. B.* 43
Grief is itself a medicine, and *b. Ch.* 159
With all that man e'er wished, or Heaven *b.? Ex.* 196
B. on man, like all that we partake *H.* 117
The fragrant waters on my cheeks *b. M.P.* 62
And he that deems his leisure well *b. R.* 505

BESTOWED—BID

To taste a joy like that he has *b. R.* 632
Fair recompense of labour well *b. T.* iii 430
The praise *b.* was just and wise *Th.* 13
By such a lamp *b. Tran.* i 14

BESTRIDES.
B. the wintry flood, in which the moon *T.* iv 3

BETIDE.
At what such a dream should *b.? M.D.* 42

BETIMES.
B. into the mould of heavenly truth *Tir.* 106
Shall blush *b.,* and there his glory rise *Tir.* 396

BETRAY.
Too oft *b.* the votaries of his fires *A.T.* 30
Who yet *b.* his secret by his works *Con.* 80
With naught in charge, he could *b.* no trust *P.E.* 29
B. the secret of their silent course *T.* 196
That speech *b.* at once a bigot's tongue *T.* 519
Flash desperation, and *b.* their pangs *T.* i 502
But if, with all his genius, he *b. Tir.* 529
B. thee, while professing to defend *T.T.* 333

BETRAYED.
Perhaps his confidence just then *b. E.* iii 36
Where the *b.,* forsaken, and oppressed *T.* 437
The slippery seat *b.* the sliding part *T.* i 46

BETTER.
B. dwell in the midst of alarms *A.S.* 7
"And *b.* spear I smite you where you stand" *A.T.* 170
But N. liked it never the *b.* for that *A.T.* ii 6
Some *b.* things are found *A Tale* 4
And Conversation, in its *b.* part *Con.* 3
Or if, deserving of a *b.* doom *Con.* 413
Or such as might be *b.* shown *E.* iv 9
And cannot see, though few see *b. E.* iv 33
God's *b.* gift they scoff at, and refuse *Ex.* 459
Prove it;—if *b.,* I submit and bow *Ex.* 633
To form the *b.* prayer *Miss —* 20
'Twere *b.* to be born a stone *P.* 11
And e'en the child who knows no *b. P.T.* 5
Their noxious growth, starve every *b.* seed *R.* 44
And ignorance of *b.* things makes man *R.* 503
Far more intelligent, and *b.* taught *R.* 673
The *b.* part of man unblessed *St.* vi 31
Ingenious Fancy, never *b.* pleased *T.* i 72
Now scorned, but worthy of a *b.* fate *T.* i 254
There often wanders one, whom *b.* days *T.* i 534
Saw *b.* clad, in cloak of satin trimmed *T.* i 535
The *b.* hand, more busy, gives the nose *T.* ii 451
Of whom I needs must argue *b.* things *T.* ii 582
Should speak to purpose, or with *b.* hope *T.* iii 25
To all the virtues of those *b.* days *T.* iii 745
To *b.* deeds, he bundles up the spoil *T.* iv 440
Nor does the boarded hovel *b.* guard *T.* iv 443
And *b.* never learned, or left behind *Tir.* 584
Find him a *b.* in a distant spot *Tir.* 759 [*T.T.* 42
And Death's own scythe would *b.* speak his power
Not *b.* much than spectacles a brute *Tir.* 782
No—guard him *b.* Is he not thine own *Tir.* 873
Slaves fight for what were *b.* cast away *T.T.* 282

BETTY.
When B. screaming came down stairs *J.G.* 59

BEVERAGE.
And, heavy laden, brings his *b.* home *T.* i 242
He drinks his simple *b.* with a gust *T.T.* 240

BEWAIL.
Bewildered once, must he *b.* his loss *P.E.* 612
And if I must *b.* the blessing lost *T.* v 485
would at least *b.* it under skies *T.* v 487

BEWARE.
B. no negligence of yours *F.* 154
B. of desperate steps. The darkest day *N.A.* 132
B. of too sublime a sense *R.C.* 109
Truth will intrude—she bids him yet *b. T.* 471
With solemn awe, that bids me well *b. T.* ii 327
Of judgment and of mercy, should *b. T.* ii 465

BEWILDERED.
B. once, must he bewail his loss *P.E.* 612

BEWRAY.
Which filthily *b.* and sore disgrace *Tir.* 593

BIAS.
And free from *b.,* must approve the choice *Con.* 664
Free from the wayward *b.* bigots feel *P.E.* 454
The *b.* of the purpose. How much more *T.* ii 493
He gives the local *b.* all its sway *Tir.* 334

BIASED.
As Interest *b.* knaves, or Fashion fools *Ex.* 38
Or seeking with a *b.* mind *F.* 209

BIB.
One that still needs his leading-string and *b. P.E.* 531
The backstring and the *b.,* assume the dress *T.* iv 227

BIBLE.
That dropped upon his *B.* was sincere *H.* 575
Carries her *B.* tucked beneath her arm *T.* 147
Just knows, and knows no more, her *B.* true *T.* 327
The *B.* only stands neglected there *T.* 425
The *B.* an imposture and a cheat? *T.* 432

BIBLE-OATH.
A *b.* to be whate'er they please *T.* iv 629

BICKERINGS.
In causeless feuds and *b.* of their own *Ex.* 537
But oh! the strife! the *b.,* and debate *H.* 342
This civil *b.* and debate *L.R.* 17

BID.
An earthquake may be *b.* to spare *A Fable* 34
B. suffer it awhile, and kiss the rod *Ch.* 166
Else I would say, and as I spake *b.* fly *Ch.* 268
'Tis heavy, bulky, and *b.* fair to prove *Con.* 307
And Jupiter *b.* fair to rule again *Con.* 822
And *b.* a dawning sky display *E.* i 77 [*Con.* 444
And speech may praise the power that *b.* it flow
Had *b.* defiance to the warring world *Ex.* 212
B. rottenness invade, and bring to dust *Ex.* 332
That He *b.* thousands fly when none pursue *Ex.* 360
B. nations leagued against thee stand aloof *Ex.* 565
Who *b.* him shine, or if he shine or not *H.* 84
And *b.* the mountains he has built stand fast *H.* 476
Clothes it with earth, and *b.* the produce live *Her.* 30
And *b.* us fear the same *M.* ii 4
'Tis Nature *b.,* and whilst the laws *Miss —* 49
When virtue *b.* it flow *Miss —* 56
B. me and Mary mourn *N.* 14
Has He *b.* you buy and sell us *N.C.* 27
But know, the law that *b.* the drunkard die *P.E.* 199
Ye are *b.,* begged, besought to entertain *P.E.* 264
Hence the same word, that *b.* our lusts obey *P.E.* 496
To *b.* the pleadings of Self-love be still *R.* 129
And *b.* her mountains and her hills rejoice *R.* 362
B. these in elegance of form excel *R.* 793 [2
Than *b.* me shun the deep, and dread the shore *R.H.*
Where Duty *b.* he confidently steers *R.H.* 6
To *b.* Affliction's eye no longer stream *S.* ii 12
Go, *b.* the winter cease to chill the year *T.* 399
Truth will intrude—she *b.* him yet beware *T.* 471
He *b.* him glow with unremitting love *T.* 557

When Custom *b.*, but no refreshment find *T.* i 390
And gives them all their fury; *b.* a plague *T.* ii 182
And *b.* the world take heart and banish fear *T.* ii 195
With solemn awe, that *b.* me well beware *T.* ii 327
That *b.* defiance to the united powers *T.* ii 769
Impervious to the wind. First he *b.* spread *T.* iii 475
And undebauched. But we have *b.* farewell *T.* iii 744
Even as he *b.*! The enraptured owner smiles *T.* iii 780
That he has let it pass—But never *b. T.* vi 294
Or *b.* the rocks in ruder pomp arise *Tir.* 28
B. fair enough to answer in the proof *Tir.* 564
To *b.* the traveller, as he went *Tran.* i 15
'Tis power almighty *b.* him shine *Tran.* i 23
Nor *b.* him shine in vain *Tran.* i 24   [213
And *b.* them hide themselves in earth beneath *T.* iii
The glass that *b.* man mark the fleeting hour *T.T.* 41
Nor draw it, but when Duty *b.* him draw *T.T.* 78
B. equity throughout his works prevail *T.T.* 250
I *b.* you both a long and last adieu *V.* 5   [509
Drink and be mad then; 'tis your country *b.*! *T.* iv

BIDDING.
The post that at his *b.* speeds away *Ex.* 355
And waste it at the *b.* of his hand *T.T.* 451

BIDST.
Who *b.* me honour with an artless song *M.P.* 13

BIER.
As if they met around a father's *b. Con.* 874
And e'en the star, that glitters on the *b. H.* 270

BIG.
Or scare the nation with its *b.* contents *Ch.* 617
A despot *b.* with power obtained by wealth *Ex.* 370
"My head is twice as *b.* as yours *J.G.* 187
For why?—they were too *b. J.G.* 212   [498
Have proved them truths too *b.* to be expressed *Con.*
Burly and *b.*, and studious of his ease *T.* i 63
To ecstasy too *b.* to be suppress'd *T.* vi 340
Is kept to strut, look *b.*, and talk away *T.T.* 233

BIGOT.
So he called him a *b.*, a wrangler, a monk *A.T.* ii 3
Then Ceremony leads her *b.* forth *Ex.* 115
No blinder *b.*, I maintain it still *H.* 594
Free from the wayward bias *b.* feel *P.E.* 454
That speech betrays at once a *b.*'s tongue *T.* 519

BIGOTRY.
Who though devout, yet *b.* had none *Con.* 68
Themselves the slaves of *b.* or lust *Ex.* 529
While *B.*, with well dissembled fears *H.* 657
With all that *b.* adopts, inspired *T.* 88

BILK.
He cannot drink five bottles, *b.* the score *P.E.* 193

BILKING.
In *b.* tavern bills, and spouting plays *Tir.* 327

BILLIARDS.
Returns at noon to *b.*, or to books *R.* 472
Becomes a dice-box, and a *b.* mace *T.* iv 221

BILLOW.
The *b.* and the blast defied *A Tale* 55
The Atlantic *b.* roared *Cast.* 2
Whom the winds waft where'er the *b.* roll *Ex.* 19
"Where tempests never beat nor *b.* roar *M.P.* 97
O'er the raging *b.* borne *N.C.* 4
And at his feet the baffled *b.* die *T.* i 525
Tormented into *b.*, heaves and swells *T.* ii 101
By many a *b.* tossed *Tran.* iv 3

BILLOWY.
And fearless of the *b.* scene *Q.V.* 71

BILLS.
Anticipated rents, and *b.* unpaid *R.* 559
In bilking tavern *b.*, and spouting plays *Tir.* 327

BIND.
"The marriage bond has lost its power to *b. A.T.* 101
To *b.* the lawless, and to punish guilt *Ch.* 281
The ties of Nature do but feebly *b. Ch.* 371
And *b.* the task assigned thee to thine heart *Ex.* 651
The pride of lettered ignorance that *b. H.* 483
The keenest frost that *b.* the stream *N.* 5
No. But his own engagement *b.* him fast *P.E.* 106
Delusions strong as Hell shall *b.* him fast *P.E.* 609
Forbids the advancement of the soul he *b. R.* 236
Or *b.* them faster on, and add still more? *T.* 186
That *b.* the sinner's Bacchanalian brow *T.* 462
B. man, the lord of all. Himself derives *T.* i 386
B. all his faculties, forbids all growth *T.* i 613
Reclaims the wanderer, *b.* the broken heart *T.* ii 314
To *b.* the roving appetite, and lead *T.* ii 525
And *b.* the shoulders flat. We prove its use *T.* ii 589
What longest *b.* the closest, forms secure *T.* iii 480
The audacious convict, whom he dares not *b. T.* iv 602
No frost can *b.* it there; its utmost force *T.* v 104
Oppression, prisons, have no power to *b. T.* v 543
And that to *b.* him is a vain attempt *T.* v 777
And *b.* a wreath about their baby brows *T.T.* 124
The chain that *b.* them, and a tyrant's sway *T.T.* 283

BIRCH.   [36
Where Nichol swung the *b.* and twined the bays *V.*

BIRD.
(For ravens, though, as *b.* of omen *A Fable* 20
The homeless *b.* a nest? *A Tale* 28
Not even *b.* can hide *A Tale* 66
But you have killed a tiny *b. Beau* 5
Sir, when I flew to seize the *b. B.R.* 1
If killing *b.* be such a crime *B.R.* 25
A captive *b.* into the boundless sky *Ch.* 269
To learn the twittering of a meaner *b.? Con.* 448
It passed unnoticed, as the *b. E.* i 87
Blush when I tell you how a *b. F.B.* 34
No groves have ye; nor cheerful sound of *b. H.* 169
The *b.* put off their every hue *Mrs. M—* 1
B. of all feather, beasts of every name *N.A.* 65
If *b.* confabulate or no *P.T.* 2
The *b.*, conceiving a design *P.T.* 11
A last year's *b.*, who ne'er had tried *P.T.* 28
But though the *b.* were thus in haste *P.T.* 45
The fall of waters, and the song of *b. R.* 183
Sweet *b.* in concert with harmonious streams *R.* 259
The self-applauding *b.*, the peacock see *T.* 58
B. warbling all the music. We can spare *T.* i 764
On *b.* and beast, the other charged for man *T.* iv 249
He gives the princely *b.*, with all his wives *T.* iv 449
Of other tenants than melodious *b. T.* iv 574
He sees me, and at once, swift as a *b. T.* vi 316
And just in his account, why *b.* and beast *T.* vi 389
The young to let the parent *b.* go free *T.* vi 446
He cannot skim the ground like summer *b. T.* vi 921
Oft water fairest meadows, and the *b. T.* vi 930
Dire foe alike of *b.* and mouse *T.B.* 20
Thus sang the sweet sequestered *b. The Doves* 37
There is a *b.* who, by his coat *Tran.* ii 1
Thrice happy *b.*! I too have seen *Tran.* ii 31
Sweet Poll! the mimic *b.* replies *Tran.* iv 14
Belinda and her *b.*! 'tis rare *Tran.* iv 31
When *b.* are to be taught to prate *Tran.* iv 41
To weaving nets for *b.* fruit *T.* iv 263

BIRKS.
All *b.* and braes, though he was never there *T.T.* 535

BIRTH.

The gems of India, Nature's rarest *b*. *Ch.* 134
Gives Charity her being and her *b*. *Ch.* 378
As He ordains things sordid in their *b*. *Ch.* 561
To hear them tell of parentage and *b*. *Con.* 210
When wine has given indecent language *b*. *Con.* 263
And He that gives conception aids the *b*. *Con.* 434
Partakers of a new ethereal *b*. *Con.* 724 [343
Regret would rouse them, and give *b*. to prayer *T.*
The pangs of a poetic *b*. *Dr.* 7 [*b. R.* 35
Souls that have long since despised their heavenly
Perhaps 'twas mere good humour gave it *b*. *E.* iii 38
And theirs, by *b*., the Saviour of us all *Ex.* 202
Creates, gives *b*. to, guides, consummates all *Ex.* 315
The cradle that received thee at thy *b. Ex.* 469
Pants for the place of her ethereal *b. H.* 162
Of one, whose *b*. was in a land of light *H.* 535
She teemed and heaved with an infernal *b. Her.* 13
My boast is not that I deduce my *b. M.P.* 108
Would mock the majesty of man's high *b. R.* 71
Shall seem to start into a second *b. R.* 356
To *b*. or wit, nor gives nor takes offence *R.* 450
In vain they pushed inquiry to the *b. T.* ii 511
Hangs over mortal eyes, blind from the *b. T.* iii 234
B., deaths, and marriages, epistles wet *T.* iv 17
He is indeed a freeman. Free by *b. T.* v 763
"And systems of whose *b*. no tidings yet *T.* v 827
When all creation started into *b. T.* vi 199
By ancient covenant ere Nature's *b. T.* vi 858
Why did the fiat of a God give *b. Tir.* 35
The great indeed, by titles, riches, *b., Tir.* 346
To give a Milton *b*. asked ages more *T.T.* 559
That once lived here thy brethren! At my *b. Y.O.* 2
So much thy juniors, who, their *b*. received *Y.O.* 135

BIRTHDAY.

The *b*. of Invention; weak at first *T.* i 17

BIRTH-PLACE.

His *b*. and his dam? The country mourns *T.* ii 814

BIRTHRIGHT.

His *b*. shaken, and no longer clear *Con.* 765
Thee of thy *b*., gentle Bob *E.* iv 2
Where I am free by *b*., not at all *T.* v 479

BISCUIT.

The *b*., or confectionary plum *M.P.* 61

BISHOP.

Supposed the man a *b*., or at least *Con.* 71
And though a *B*. toil to cleanse the stain *Ex.* 384
Go, cast your orders at your *B*.'s feet *P.E.* 120
Not all the plenty of a *B*.'s board *T.* 121
They knew not, what some *b*. may not know *T.* 451
Behold your *b*.! well he plays his part *Tir.* 420

BISHOP-LIKE.

Where, *b*., he finds a perch *Tran.* ii 5

BIT.

Thus *b*. by *b*. the world is swallowed *L.W.* 34
Always at speed, and never drawing *b. T.T.* 685

BITCH-FOX.

Where oft the *b*. hides her hapless brood *N.A.* 4

BITE.

And, when he could, would *b. Ep.* ii 12 [iii 581
The winter's frown, if screened from his shrewd *b. T.*
The creature is so sure to kick and *b. P.E.* 540
Grow frantic with her pangs, and *b*. the ground *T.*444

BITTER.

Yet *b*. felt it still to die *Cast.* 35
Else he was seldom *b*. or morose *E.* iii 35
Wept till all Israel heard his *b*. cry *Ex.* 63
That can alone make sweet the *b*. draught *T.* i 751
Unmixed with drops of *b*., which neglect *T.* iii 46
And she that sweetens all my *b*. too *T.* iii 720

BITTERNESS.

Adds tenfold *b*. to death by pangs *T.* vi 395

BLACK.

Let Dares beat Entellus *b*. and blue *Con.* 198
That, with a *b*. infernal train *E.* iv 15
Fleecy locks and *b*. complexion *N.C.* 13
Dwells in white and *b*. the same *N.C.* 16
Though *b*. and foul before *O.* i 20
But while they get riches by purchasing *b. P.A.* 15
The poisonous, *b*., insinuating worm *P.E.* 7
As yet *b*. breeches were not, satin smooth *T.* i 10
Lapdog and lambkin with *b*., staring eyes *T.* i 37
The bramble, *b*. as jet, or sloes austere *T.* i 122
His azure eyes, is tinctured *b*. and red *T.* iv 216
Serves but to show how *b*. is all beside *Tir.* 844
His *b*. interpreter the charge disdained *T.T.* 99

BLACKBIRD.

The *b*. has fled to another retreat *P.F.* 9
The warblings of the *b*., clear and strong *R.* 569

BLACKEN.

Give it a charge to *b*. and traduce *T.T.* 763

BLACK-SCEPTRED.

To the *b*. rulers of slaves *M.D.* 47

BLADDER.

And music of the *b*. and the bag *T.* i 585

BLADE.

Or *b*. that might redeem it from despair *Her.* 28
And tender *b*., that feared the chilling blast *T.* iv 331
From every herb and every spiry *b. T.* v 9
Such were not they of old, whose tempered *b.T.*v 515
To the green *b*. that twinkles in the sun *T.* vi 251

BLAME.

(A fault philosophers might *b. A Fable* 5
To scourge him, weariness his only *b. Ch.* 215
Satire is, more than those he brands; to *b. Ch.* 492
Not that all freedom of dissent I *b. Con.* 97
And he that *b*. what they have blindly chose *H.* 284
B., cynic, if you can, quadrille or ball *P.E.* 175
B. his own indolence, observes, though late *R.* 477
Poor Jack—no matter who—for when I *b. R.* 575
Now *b*. we most the nurslings or the nurse? *T.* ii 771
Perfect and unimpeachable of *b. T.* v 867
A necessary act incurs no *b. T.* vi 573
What none could reverence all might justly *b. Tir.* 87
I *b*. not those who, with what care they can *Tir.* 261
Or, if I *b*., 'tis only that they dare *Tir.* 263
The great and small deserve one common *b. Tir.* 515
And fierce Licentiousness should bear the *b. T.T.* 329

BLAMED.

He *b*. and protested, but joined in the plan *P.A.* 43

BLAMELESS.

Though *b*., had incurred perpetual strife *Con.* 512
His only answer was a *b*. life *H.* 577
('Tis *b*., be it what it may) *N.Y.G.* 19
The *b*. animal, without rebuke *T.* vi 469

BLAME-WORTHY.

Thee therefore still, *b*. as thou art *T.* v 456

BLANK.

As bastions set point *b*. against God's will *Con.* 688
Not yet so *b*., or fashionably blind *H.* 92
Of *b*. oblivion, seem a glorious prize *T.* i 287
There touched by Reynolds, a dull *b*. becomes *T.* i 700
The streams are lost amid the splendid *b. T.* v 96

BLANK—BLESSING

His road, deriding much the b. amaze T. vi 536
The tomb take all, and all be b. beyond Tir. 68
If not a scene of pleasure, a mere b. Tir. 752

BLASPHEME.
The Truth she loves a sightless world b. Ch. 416
B. his creed, as founded on a plan Tir. 159

BLASPHEMED.
B. the authority from which it sprung Ex. 156

BLASPHEMY.
Impudent b.! So Folly pleads Ch. 194
That Scripture lies, and b. is sense P.E. 595
Was b. his sin? Or did he stray T. 48
And bears the brand of b. burnt in T. 348
The mouth with b., the heart with woe T. i 505

BLAST.
Lest the rude b. should snap the bough A Fable 14
The billows and the b. defied A Tale 55
But so the furious b. prevailed Cast. 21
Had heard his voice in every b. Cast. 45
That since the flowers of Eden felt the b. Con. 751
Chill b. of trouble nip their springing joys E. ii 32
Was rocked by many a rough Norwegian b. Ex. 470
And while, at intervals, a cold b. snip Ex. 720
The Christian vessel, and defies the b. H. 168
Thus braves the whirling b. Miss — 34   [vi 60
And where the woods fence off the northern b. T.
Me howling b. drive devious, tempest-tossed M.P. 102
Nor b. that shake the dripping bower Mrs. M— 16
Come fiend, come fury, giant, monster, b. N.A. 121
Sent us a wind to parch us at a b.? P.E. 256
Slips to his hammock, and forgets the b. R. 436
The rising waves obey the increasing b. R. 532
Unnumbered branches waving in the b. T. i 188
The impression of the b. with proud disdain T. i 380
And desolates a nation at a b. T. ii 188   [iii 441
The plenteous bloom, that no rough b. may sweep T.
And potent to resist the freezing b. T. iii 465
At evening, till at length the freezing b. T. iv 303
And tender blade, that feared the chilling b. T. iv 331
Or shed impervious to the b. Resigned T. v 72
Of wintry b.; the loftiest tower Trans. H. 14
Who for the sake of filling with one b. T.T. 31
Ungenial b. attending curl the streams T.T. 213

BLASTED.
And what his storms have b. and defaced T. vi 745

BLAZE.
How dark the veil that intercepts the b. Ch. 57
To make a b.—that's roasting him alive Con. 334
The b. of a meridian day E. i 78
That cannot bear the b. of Scripture light H. 298
This earth shall b., and a new world succeed H. 749
To thee the dayspring, and the b. of noon R. 347
Tight boxes neatly sashed, and in a b. R. 483
And spreads his hopes before the b. of day T. iii 445
Just when our drawing-rooms begin to b. T. iv 267
Resemble most some city in a b. T. v 5
Occasion needs but fan them, and they b. T. v 207
As set the midnight riot in a b. Tir. 287

BLAZED.
Than ever b. by art U. 28

BLAZING.
Refreshing change! where now the b. sun? T. i 335
Her scanty stock of brushwood, b. clear T. iv 381
And b. London seemed a second Troy T.T. 323

BLAZON.
Retires to b. his own worthless name R. 217

BLEACHED.
A splintered stump b. to a snowy white Y.O. 128

BLEAK.
But where, however b. the view A Tale 3

BLEAKER.
Must find a colder soil and b. air Tir. 851

BLEAR.   [168
Should ever tease the lungs and b. the sight T. iii

BLEATING.
Known by thy b., Ignorance thy name Con. 588
Nor herds have ye to boast, nor b. flocks H. 466
And sheep-walks populous with b. lambs T. vi 111

BLED.
And while the victim slowly b. to death Ex. 498
B., groaned, and agonized, and died in vain P.E. 624
For which our Hampdens and our Sidneys b. T. v 486
B. nobly, and their deeds, as they deserve T. v 705

BLEED.
B. gold for ministers to sport away T. iv 508

BLEEDING.
B. from the Roman rods B. 2
Lay b. under that soft hand of thine P.E. 338
And staunch the b. of a broken heart R. 322
Not knowing thee, we reap with b. hands R. 753
With stripes, that Mercy, with b. brows T. vi 239
Who wore the platted thorns with a b. heart T. ii 24
With b. sides and flanks that heave for life T. vi 429

BLEMISH.
That none are free from b. since the fall Ch. 204
Some b. in due time made known F. 146
A b., or a sense impaired M.F. 43
Who reckon every touch a b. P. 56

BLEND.
To him that b. no fable with his song H. 755
To b. good sense and elegance and ease S. ii 11

BLESS.
Your golden moments b. Miss — 102   [vi 699
To gaze in his eyes and b. him. Maidens wave T.
Kneels and asks Heaven to b. the dear deceit P.E. 525
Adore him? Will he hear, accept, and b.? T. ii 515

BLESSED.
B. the glad beams of that propitious day A.T. 205
B. with all wealth can give thee, to resign Ch. 297
Blessing and b. where'er she goes Comp. i 8   [438
Should range where Providence has b. the soil Con.
He b. the bread, but vanished at the word Con. 533
O b. within the enclosure of your rocks H. 465
Yet b. the guardian care that kept M. ii 7
O b. proficiency! surpassing all R. 99   [P.E. 316
Heaven b. the youth, and made him fresh and fair
B., rather cursed, with hearts that never feel R. 307
Girt with a bell-rope that the Pope has b. T. 82
O b. effect of penury and want T. 361
Or only with a whistle b. T.B. 10

BLESSING.
For the chief b. of my fairest days Ch. 265
B. and blessed where'er she goes Comp. i 8
And shed the balmy b. on the lips Con. 442
Friendship a b. cheap or small E. i 92
Transformed to b., miss their cruel aim E. ii 38
The b. of the most indebted land Ex. 164
He brought thy land a b. when he came Ex. 484
Given thee his b. on the clearest proof Ex. 564
That b. truly sacred, and when given Ex. 684
A b. to my country and mankind Ex. 727
And bliss not seen by b. understood H. 148

All witnesses of *b.* foully scorned *H.* 223
And ask, and fancy they find, *b.* there *H.* 243
Deem life a *b.* with its numerous woes *H.* 546
By gales of *b.* driven *St.* iii 32
Shall find the *b.* unimproved, a curse *T.* 521
And jealous of the *b.*   Spread it then *T.* ii 44
From whom are all our *b.*, business finds *T.* iii 366
And if I must bewail the *b.* lost *T.* v 485
But had a *b.* in its darkest frown *T.* vi 35
Those *b.*'s of our early youth *The Doves* 11
Unworthy of the *b.* of the brave *T.T.* 27
A *b.*, freedom is the pledge of all *T.T.* 257
And if he add, a *b.* shared by few *V.* 89

BLEST.
Oh! never seen but in thy *b.* effects *Ch.* 7
But souls that carry on a *b.* exchange *Con.* 693
That there are *b.* inhabitants of earth *Con.* 723
And *b.* reforms that I have never heard *Con.* 804
No traveller ever reached that *b.* abode *E.* ii 11
A people, planted, watered, *b.* as they? *Ex.* 168
Except a few with Eli's spirit *b. Ex.* 448   [377
The Saviour's feast, his own *b.* bread and wine *Ex.*
(*B.* be the art that can immortalize *M.P.* 8
In wedded love already *b. N.Y.G.* 11   [592
B. he, though undistinguished from the crowd *T.* i
Love makes the music of the *b.* above *P.E.* 77
What says the prophet? Let that day be *b. P.E.* 157
Once the *b.* residence of truth divine *T.* 387
Oh *b.* seclusion from a jarring world *T.* iii 675
Thus *b.*, I draw a picture of that bliss *T.* iii 694
B. with an infant's ignorance of all *T.* iv 624
In that *b.* moment, Nature throwing wide *T.* v 891
Try now the merits of this *b.* exchange *Tir.* 173
A father *b.* with an ingenious son *Tir.* 543
Perhaps a father, *b.* with any brains *Tir.* 626
Churchmen, in whose esteem their *b.* employ *Tir.* 823
B. country, where these kingly glories shine! *T.T.* 81
B. England, if this happiness be thine! *T.T.* 82

BLEW.
The ruffling wind, scarce conscious that it *b. T.* i 156

BLIGHT.
The garden fears no *b.*, and needs no fence *T.* vi 771

BLIGHTED.
Fruits of a *b.* size, austere and crude *T.* 494

BLIGHTING.
Infectious as impure, your *b.* power *Con.* 41

BLIND.
B. was he born, and his misguided eyes *Ch.* 357
Grown dim in trifler studies, *b.* he dies *Ch.* 358
Endued with reason, yet by nature *b. Ch.* 382
She sees a world stark *b.* to what employs *Ch.* 404
He might as well be *b.*, and deaf, and dumb *Con.* 144
But are we so to wit and beauty *b. Con.* 257   [375
But counterfeit is *b.*, and skulks through fear *Con.*
Spurious, and only current with the *b. E.* ii 8
B. to the working of that secret Power *Ex.* 320
On special search, the keen-eyed eagle *b. Ex.* 631
And whether being crazed or *b. F.* 208
Not yet so blank, or fashionably *b. H.* 92
And teach the world, if not perversely *b. H.* 138
The gross idolatry *b.* heathens teach *H.* 499
The lawless herd, with fury *b. M.* ii 13
To faults compassionate or *b. M.F.* 56
Within no bounds—the *b.* that lead the *b. P.E.* 477
Not *b.* by choice, but destined not to see *T.* 530
B. nature to a God not yet revealed *T.* ii 526
Prepares it for its ruin, hardens, *b. T.* ii 690
Became stone *b.*; precedence went in truck *T.* ii 741

Hangs over mortal eyes, *b.* from the birth *T.* iii 234
And snow, that often *b.* the traveller's course *T.* v 142
Yours, a *b.* instinct, crouches to the rod *T.* v 355
Their progress in the road of science; *b. T.* v 451
Thou shalt perceive that thou wast *b.* before *T.* v 781
We give to Chance, *b.* Chance, ourselves as *b. T.* v 865
Him *b.* antiquity profaned, not served *T.* vi 231
B., and in love with darkness! yet e'en these *T.* vi 885
"Ah, *b.* to bright futurity, untaught *Tir.* 379
Look round you on a world perversely *b. Tir.* 813
Merely to gratify so *b.* a guide? *Tir.* 864   [iv 223
Thus decked, he charms a world whom Fashion *b. T.*

BLINDED.
The spells and charms that *b.* you before *P.E.* 619

BLINDER.
No *b.* bigot, I maintain it still *H.* 594

BLINDLY.
And he that blames what they have *b.* chose *H.* 284

BLISS.
To quit the *b.* thy rural scenes bestow *Ch.* 299
True *b.*, if man may reach it, is composed *Con.* 679
Invite thee, woo thee, to the *b.* they share *Ex.* 627
A scene of fancied *b.* and heart-felt care *H.* 5
And *b.* not seen by blessings understood *H.* 148
That *b.*, revealed in Scripture, with a glow *H.* 149
Plucks amaranthine joys from bowers of *b. H.* 164
That man will freely take an unbought *b. H.* 335
O *b.* precarious, and unsafe retreats! *Her.* 33
That there is *b.* prepared in yonder sky *J.T.* 13
At once both *b.* and woe! *Miss* — 8
Perhaps a tear, if souls can weep in *b. M.P.* 26
Full *b.* is *b.* divine *N.Y.G.* 14
Lead to the *b.* she promises the wise *P.E.* 73
To stand a way-mark in the road to *b.? P.E.* 117
His only *b.* is sorrow for her sake *R.* 244
All *b.* beside a shadow or a sound *R.* 354
Yet how fallacious is all earthly *b. R.* 457
Deceitful views of future *b.*, farewell! *T.* 9
The path to *b.* abounds with many a snare *T.* 301
That endless *b.* (how strange soe'er it seem) *T.* 355
Was *b.* reserved for happier days;—so slow *T.* i 83
Domestic Happiness, thou only *b. T.* iii 41
But foolish man foregoes his proper *b. T.* iii 296
Thus blest, I draw a picture of that *b. T.* iii 694
That flattered me with hopes of earthly *b. T.* iv 696
These, and a thousand images of *b. T.* vi 341
Scenes of accomplish'd *b.*! which who can see *T.* vi 760
Therefore in contemplation is his *b. T.* vi 924

BLITHE.
And Bonner, *b.* as shepherd at a wake *Ex.* 614
They sang as *b.* as finches sing *F.B.* 7
The priest he merry is and *b. Y.D.* 5

BLOATED.
As *b.* spiders draw the flimsy line *P.E.* 495
Into his overgorged and *b.* purse *T.* i 737
Strange that such folly as lifts *b.* man *T.* v 283
And *b.* spider, till the pampered pest *T.* v 422

BLOCKHEAD.
If I mistake not—*B.*! with a fork! *H.* 362

BLOOD.
"The *b.* of ancient worthies in his veins *A.T.* 116
In the *b.* that she has spilt *B.* 14
Or one whom *b.* allures *Beau* 14
The tender argument of kindred *b. Ch.* 32
Trade in the *b.* of innocence, and plead *Ch.* 182
By an oath dipped in sacramental *b.? Ex.* 381
And when he laid them on the scent of *b. Ex.* 520
Received the seal of martyrdom in *b. Ex.* 617
Who write in *b.* the merits of your cause *Her.* 42

BLOOD—BLUSH

No crested warrior dips his plume in *b. Her.* 86
With *b.* of his subjects imbrued *M.D.* 36
By our *b.* in Afric wasted *N.C.* 41
By right of worth, not *b.* alone *Q.V.* **3**
My penitential stripes, my streaming *b. T.* 95
Cleansed in thine own all-purifying *b. T.* 581
Nor yet the mariner, his *b.* inflamed *T.* i 447
A plague into his *b.*; and cannot use *T.* ii 140
Paid with the *b.* that he had basely spared *T.* iii 91
Search it, and prove now if it be not *b. T.* iii 204
To fill with riot, and defile with *b. T.* iii 307
Who starves his own; who persecutes the *b. T.* iv 463
Build factories with *b.*, conducting trade *T.* iv 681
Cain had already shed a brother's *b. T.* v 208
Bought with His *b.* who gave it to mankind *T.* v 546
Have fallen in her defence. A Patriot's *b. T.* v 714
And win it with more pain. Their *b.* is shed *T.* v 719
With *b.* of their inhabitants impaled *T.* vi 391
And the *b.* thrills and curdles at the thought *T.* vi 514
With sounding whip, and rowels dyed in *b. T.* vi 527
Is not; the pure and uncontaminate *b. T.* vi 789
And overpaid its value with thy *b. T.* vi 860
Of amnesty, the meed of *b.* divine *Y.O.* 13

BLOOD-BOUGHT.
Cheap though *b.*, and thrown away when sold *T.T.* 331

BLOOD-EXTORTING.
Matches, *b.* screws *N.C.* 30

BLOODY.
And eats into his *b.* sword like rust *T.T.* 8

BLOOM.
To exhibit, in full *b.* disclosed *F.* 44   [iii 441
The plenteous *b.*, that no rough blast may sweep *T.*
Sweet smiles, and *b.* less transient than her own *T.* i 461
On all that *b.* below, or shines above *H.* 136
Deserted of its *b.*, the flaccid, shrunk *T.* i 392
And dangerous to the touch, has yet its *b. T.* i 528
There *b.* exotic beauty, warm and snug *T.* iii 568
His faculties, expanded in full *b. T.* iv 661
Hypericum all *b.*, so thick a swarm *T.* vi 165

BLOOMED.
Might have *b.* with its owner a while *The Rose* 18

BLOOMEST.
Deem not, sweet rose, that *b.* midst many a thorn *S.* ii 1

BLOOMING.
Crowned with the garland of life's *b.* years *Con.* 638
The *b.* groves that girdled her around *Her.* 6
Nor gales that catch the scent of *b.* groves *R.* 337
And putrify the breath of *b.* Health *T.* ii 184
Designs the *b.* wonders of the next *T.* vi 197
The mulberry-tree was hung with *b.* wreaths *T.* vi 685
Her sunshine and her rain, her *b.* spring *T.* vi 946

BLOSSOM.
Each opening *b.*, freely breathes abroad *T.* iii 622
Her *b.*: and luxuriant above all *T.* vi 172
Spring hangs her infant *b.* on the trees *Tir.* 43
Thy *b.* deck our unsuspecting years *V.* 51

BLOSSOM-BRUISING.
Skin-piercing volley, *b.* hail *T.* v 141

BLOT.
A *b.* that will be still a *b.*, in spite *Ex* 382
The very butt of Slander, and the *b. H.* 558
And say, "*B.* out my sin, confessed, deplored *H.* 592
While through the Stygian veil that *b.* the day *Her.* 17
As human nature's broadest, foulest *b. T.* ii 22
No shades of superstition *b.* the day *T.T.* 270

BLOW.
But in the sunshine strikes the *b. A Fable* 39
And, Phineas-like, transfixed them at a *b. A.T.* 196
Deprived of her and freedom at a *b. Ch.* 149
May *b.* up self-conceit, and nourish pride *Ch.* 376
While you, my friend, whateverwind should *b. E.* iii 60
Unless a zeal for virtue guide the *b. Ex.* 437 [43
Who strike the *b.*, then plead your own defence *Her.*
The wind did *b.*, the cloak did fly *J.G.* 101
Were shattered at a *b. J.G.* 124
But screened from every storm that *b. Mrs. M—* 18
The wildest wind that *b. N.* 6
By all the winds that *b. O.* i 16
Were basking hot, and all in *b. P.B.* 2
The breathings of the lightest air that *b. R.* 530
Nor those in which the stage gives vice a *b. R.* 685
The spark of life. The sportive wind *b.* wide *T.* i 567
B. mildew from between his shrivelled lips *T.* ii 186
Too weak for those decisive *b.* that once *T.* ii 273
A wreath, that cannot fade, of flowers that *b. T.* iv 156
From what point *b.* the weather *Tran.* ii 9
Skill to direct, and strength to strike the *b. T.T.* 357
If Mercy then put by the threatening *b. T.T.* 404
As the fairest and sweetest that *b. W.N.* 15

BLOWING.
But just at eve the *b.* weather *A Fable* 16

BLOWN.
His lilies newly *b. D.W.* 14
The beauties of a rose full *b. E.* i 68
The flower of Israel's infamy full *b. Ex.* 222
B. all aslant, a driving, dashing rain *T.* 239
B. on the summit of the apparent fruit *T.* iii 536
B. in its native bed; 'tis there alone *T.* iv 660

BLUE.
Let Dares beat Entellus black and *b. Con.* 198
From the *b.* rim, where skies and mountains meet *H.* 94
The rose or lily appears *b.* or green *H.* 72
And just when evening turns the *b.* vault grey *H.* 79
"And pinch your noses *b.*" *J.P.* 40.
Induced a splendid cover, green and *b. T.* i 32
And such expense as pinches parents *b. T.* ii 756
Feeds a *b.* flame, and makes a cheerful hearth *T.* iii 33
"That show like beacons in the *b.* abyss *T.* v 839
And has the warmth of May. The vault is *b. T.* vi 62

BLUNDERER.
Your *b.* is as sturdy as a rock *P.E.* 539

BLUNDERS.
And when I hope his *b.* are all out *Con.* 117

BLUNT.
With every herb that *b.* the sense *Miss —* 23
And forced the *b.* and yet unbloodied steel *T.* v 215
And *b.* his pointed fury; in its case *T.* vi 193

BLUNTED.
He gleans the *b.* shafts that have recoiled *T.* vi 874

BLUSH.
And only *b.* in the proper place *Con.* 374
Forgot the *b.* that virgin fears impart *Ex* 47
B., if thou canst; not petrified, thou must *Ex.* 555
B. when I tell you how a bird *F.B.* 34
B., Calumny! and write upon his tomb *H.* 588
His benefactress *b.* at the deed *P.E.* 212 [415
But oft-times deaf to suppliants who would *b. T.* iv
And having human feelings, does not *b. T.* ii 27
Shall *b.* betimes, and there his glory rise *Tir.* 396
He will not *b.*, that has a father's heart *Tir.* 547
He *b.*, hangs his head, is shy and strange *Tir.* 568

BLUSHED.
That *b.* at its own praise; and press the youth *T.* ii [712
B. on the pannels. Mirror needed none *T.* v 160
Liberty *b.*, and hung her drooping head *T.T.* 324
B. that effects like these she should produce *T.T.* 326

BLUSHING.
And bear the marks upon a *b.* face *Con.* 349
Unveiled her *b.* cheek, looked on and smiled *Ex.* 425
And *b.* at the tameness of the rest *Ex.* 543
Or *b.* crabs, or berries that emboss *T.* i 121
With *b.* fruits, and plenty not his own *T.* iii 429
No longer *b.* for her awkward load *T.* iv 551
With *b.* wreaths, investing every spray *T.* vi 169

BLUSTERING.
Asseveration *b.* in your face *Con.* 59

BOARD.
Washed headlong from on *b. Cast.* 4
Would give relief of bed and *b.* to none *H.* 306
Sir Smug," he cries (for lowest at the *b. H.* 413
Lolling at your jovial *b. N.C.* 22
Sits long and late at the carousing *b. T.* 50
Not all the plenty of a bishop's *b. T.* 121
Since pulpits fail, and sounding *b.* reflect *T,* iii 21
Placed at some vacant corner of the *b, T.* iv 230
Would waste attention at the checker'd *b. T.* vi 265
And, if admitted at thy *b.* he sit *Tir.* 725
And thankful at my frugal *b.* 1789, 35

BOARDED.
Nor does the *b.* hovel better guard *T.* iv 443

BOAST.
For husband there and wife may *b. A Tale* 5
No braver chief could Albion *b. Cast.* 7
Whoever *b.* that name—behold a cheat! *Ch.* 603
Youth has a sprightliness and fire to *b. Con.* 635
Or seem to *b.* a fire he does not feel *Con.* 714
She *b.* a confidence she does not hold *Con.* 768
And thou hadst neither fleet nor flag to *b. Ex.* 553
Will boast it their possession *F.* 3 [*T.* vi 146
Shall *b.* new charms, and more than they have lost
Since fickle creatures *b.* a soul *F.* 109
That *b.* the treasure, all at his command *H.* 176
Without good works, whatever some may *b. H.* 363
Nor herds have ye to *b.*, nor bleating flocks *H.* 466
Ah! luckless speech, and bootless *b. J.G.* 201
My *b.* is not that I deduce my birth *M.P.* 108
Whate'er they *b.* of rich and gay *Mrs. M—* 12
It *b.* a splendour ever new *Mrs. M—* 19
At length a bullfinch, who could *b. P.T.* 17 [186
The world can *b.*, and her chief favourites share *R.*
What once I valued and could *b.*, a friend *R.* 378
And highest in renown, can justly *b. R.* 676 [404
From grudging hands; but other *b.* have none *T.* iv
We *b.* some rich ones whom the Gospel sways *T.* 377
Then *b.* (but wait for that unhoped-for hour) *T.* 401
The *b.* of mere pretenders to the name *T.* i 492
Can *b.* but little virtue; and inert *T.* i 623 [282
Laugh ye, who *b.* your more mercurial powers *T.* iv
Time was when it was praise and *b.* enough *T.* ii 233
Some small pre-eminence; we justly *b. T.* ii 275
Such powers I *b.* not—neither can I rest *T.* iii 217
Though many *b.* thy favours, and affect *T.* iii 294
Shines there, and flourishes. The golden *b. T.* iii 571
And cherries hangs her twigs. Geranium *b. T.* iii 577
Was but to *b.* his own peculiar good *T.* iii 717
Should be a despot absolute, and *b. T.* v 311 [346
Mark now the difference, ye that *b.* your love *T.* v
And stately tone of moralists, who *b. T.* v 690
He lives, and o'er his brimming beaker *b.' T.* vi 434
But he may *b.*, what few that win it can *T.* vi 974
Much zeal in virtue's cause all teachers *b. Tir.* 517

And *b.* its splendour too *Tran.* i. 28
And, of all lies (be that one poet's *b.*), *T.T.* 87
All that should be the *b.* of British song *T.T.* 369
Of chiefs whose single arm could *b.* 1789, 5

BOASTED.
The solemn trifler, with his *b.* skill *Ch.* 355 [79
The sword shall light upon thy boasted powers *Ch.*
Abhors the craft he *b.* of before *H.* 522
Tarnish all your *b.* powers *N.C.* 54
New-fangled sentiment, the *b.* grace *Tir.* 539

BOASTING.
What! silent? Is your *b.* heard no more *T.* 567

BOAT.
While the billows high-lifted the *b. M.D.* 7

BOAZ.
The Jachin and the *B.* of them all *Tir.* 500

BOB.
Thee of thy birthright, gentle *B. E.* iv 2

BOBBINS.
Pillow and *b.* all her little store *T.* 318

BODILY.
They left these *b.* concerns at large *A.T.* 130

BODING.
The jay, the pie, and even the *b.* owl *T.* 205

BODY.
He feels his *b's* bondage in his mind *Ch.* 152
Tell not as new what every *b.* knows *Con.* 237
But how a *b.* so fantastic, trim *T.* ii 460
Becomes a loathsome *b.*, only fit *T.* iv 674
Stripes, and a dungeon; and his *b.* serves *T.* v 582
His *b.* bound, but knows not what a range *T.* v 775

BŒOTIAN.
Like a gross fog *B.*, rising fast *T.* iii 495

BOG.
From many a streaming lake and reeking *b. A.T.* 93
Of Tiber's marshes and the papal *b. Ex.* 511
(As Irish *b.* are always green) *F.* 122
And are indeed a *b.* that bears *F.* 124

BOIL.
Kindle a fiery *b.* upon the skin *T.* ii 183

BOLD.
Airy del Castro was as *b.* a knight *A.T.* 1
So may the wolf, whom famine has made *b. Ch.* 184
A *b.* remark, but which, if well applied *Ch.* 535
Learned at the bar, in the palæstra *b. Con.* 842
To build our altar, confident and *b. Con.* 849
As *b.* as, in Agrippa's presence, Paul *Ex.* 445
And wilt thou join to this *b.* enterprise *Ex.* 698
His *b.* intrusion on their dark retreat *H.* 356
Where *b.* inquiry, diving out of sight *H.* 443
I am a linendraper *b. J.G.* 21
Pushing her *b.* inquiry to the date *R.* 669
To Justice she may make her *b.* appeal *T.* 498
Than all invective is his *b.* harangue *T.* ii 354
Or harmless flocks is hazardous and *b. T.* iv 575
To be as *b.* and forward as he ought *Tir.* 339
When infamous Venality grown *b. T.T.* 416
Surly and slovenly, and *b.* and coarse *T.T.* 682
To the four-quartered winds robust and *b. Y.O.* 98

BOLDER.
A *b.* still, a contest with the skies *Ex.* 699

BOLDEST.
The *b.* patriot might be proud to feel *Ch.* 308

BOLDLY.
No knave but *b.* will pretend *F.* 13
Of popular disgust, yet *b.* still *T.* iii 706

BOLDNESS.
Stood trembling at the *b.* of thy power *Ex.* 597

BOLE.
Thou hadst within thy *b.* solid content *Y.O.* 94

BOLT.
Shoots back the *b.*, and all his courage dies *H.* 721
The infidel has shot his *b.* away *T.* vi 872 [ii 745
Of headstrong youth were broken; bars and *b. T.*
The *b.* that spare the mountains side *Trans. H.* 16

BOLTED.
That sweeps the *b.* shutter, summons home *T.* iv 304

BON-MOTS.
B. to gall the Christian and the Jew *T.* 308

BOND.
" The marriage *b.* has lost its power to bind *A.T.* 101
All *b.* of nature, in that moment end *Ch.* 142
It does not feel for man. The natural *b. T.* ii 9
And wear the *b.*, than fasten them on him *T.* ii 36
A dissolution of all *b.* ensued *T.* ii 743
Than to release the adultress from her *b. T.* iii 63
By regal warrant, or self-joined by *b. T.* iv 664
Gives *b.* in stone and ever-during brass *T.* v 710
" Our mutual *b.* of faith and truth *The Doves* 9
His being end where death dissolves the *b. Tir.* 67
The practice was a *b.* upon his heart *Tir.* 177
To keep the matrimonial *b.* unstained *T.T.* 74

BONDAGE.
He feels his body's *b.* in his mind *Ch.* 152
But we, in mutual *b.* knit *Dr.* 17
You chains and *b.* for a tyrant's sake *T.* v 352
Her house of *b.*, worse than that of old *T.* v 382

BONDMAN.
I was a *b.* on my native plain *Ch.* 236

BONE. [184
Shortlived themselves to immortalize their *b. T.* v
Which stuck in M.'s stomach as cross as a *b. A.T.* ii 8
And buy the muscles and the *b.* of man? *Ch.* 140
Thy *b.* not fashioned, and thy joints not knit *Ex.* 475
They left their *b.* beneath unfriendly skies *Ex.* 524
Dewdrops may deck the turf that hides the *b. St.* ii 31
From gaiety that fills the *b.* with pain *T.* i 504
The prominent and most unsightly *b. T.* ii 588
B. of my *b.*, and kindred souls to mine *T.* iii 220
Thyself in miniature, thy flesh, thy *b.*? *Tir.* 874
On future broken *b.* and bruises *Tran.* ii 20 [364
That breathes the spleen, and searches every *b. T.* iv
Proportioned well, half muscle and half *b. T.T.* 219

BONNER.
And *B.*, blithe as shepherd at a wake *Ex.* 614

BONNY.
Perhaps some *b.* Caledonian air *T.T.* 534

BONY.
With *b.* and unkerchiefed neck defies *T.* 137
Then grace the *b.* phantom in their stead *T.T.* 43

BOOBIES.
Then let the *b.* stay at home *Y.D.* 65

BOOK.
Small need of Prayer *B.*, or of priest, I ween *A.T.* 88
M. quarrels with N. because M. wrote a *b. A.T.* ii 1
With her *b.*, and her voice, and her lyre *C.* 49
Though such continual zigzags in a *b. Con.* 861
What walks we take, what *b.* we choose *E.* i 6
Kiss the *b.*'s outside, who ne'er look within? *Ex.* 389
The sacred *B.*, its value understood *Ex.* 616
The *b.* of all the world that charmed me most *H.* 427
The Sacred *B.* no longer suffers wrong *H.* 449
Stoppled his cruise, replaced his *b. Mor.* 7
Well tutored learning, from his *b. Mrs. M—* 37
A critic on the sacred *b.* should be *P.E.* 452
Returns at noon to billiards, or to *b. R.* 472 [274
The *b.* shall teach you; read, believe, and live!" *T.*
B., therefore, not the scandal of the shelves *R.* 683
B., beads, and maple dish, his meagre stock *T.* 80
The Scripture was his jest *b.*, whence he drew *T.* 307
His *b.* well trimmed, and in the gayest style *T.* 421
But rare at home, and never at his *b. T.* ii 383
What's that which brings contempt upon a *b. T.* iii 277
Friends, *b.*, a garden, and perhaps his pen *T.* iii 355
Which neatly she prepares; then to his *b. T.* iii 392
To *b.*, to music, or the poet's toil *T.* iv 262
And learning wiser grow without his *b. T.* vi 87
B. are not seldom talismans and spells *T.* vi 98
He notes it in his *b.*, then raps his box *T.* vi 292
That His most holy *b.*, from whom it came *T.* vi 650
Better than all the *b.* he found *T.B.* 41 [114
What friends we sort with, or what *b.* we read *Tir.*
A *b.* (to please us at a tender age *Tir.* 121 [147
'Twere well with most if *b.* that could engage *Tir.*
'Tis called a *b.*, though but a single page) *Tir.* 122
Deeper in none than in their surgeon's *b. Tir.* 289
Not to be found by poring on a *b. Tir.* 384

BOON.
What uses of his *b.* the giver would *Con.* 436
Accept it only, and the *b.* is yours *H.* 327
The richest earthly *b.* his hands afford *R.* 271
Would he improve the *b. St.* v 4
To all the nations. Ample was the *b. T.* v 199
And with the *b.* gives talents for its use *T.* v 860
But if he grant a friend, that *b.* possessed *V.* 91

BOOR.
Of Indian fume, and guzzling deep, the *b. T.* iv 473

BOORISH.
The *b.* driver leaning o'er his team *T.* i 298

BOOT.
Oh spare them, ye knights of the *b. Gr.* 19 [*T.* iv 6
With spatter'd *b.*, strapp'd waist, and frozen locks
In ponderous *b.* beside his reeking team *T.* iv 342

BOOTED.
Spendthrifts, and *b.* sportsmen, oftener seen *T.* ii 752

BOOTLESS.
Ah! luckless speech, and *b.* boast *J.G.* 201
'Twere wild profusion all, and *b.* waste *Tir.* 49

BORDERING.
A rich deposit, on the *b.* lands *Ch.* 249

BORDERS.
That overhangs the *b.* of thy Tomb *H.* 38

BORE.
And *b.* the worthless prize away *A Fable* 29 [491
Thy Druids struck the well-strung harps they *b. Ex.*
And *b.* the pelting scorn of half an age *H.* 557
A scourge hung with lashes he *b. M.D.* 30 [277
Finds, by degrees, the truths that once *b.* sway *P.E.*
I saw the hearse that *b.* thee slow away *M.P.* 29
Not yet the hawthorn *b.* her berries red *N.A.* 19
B. on his branch, luxuriant then and rude *T.* 493
Been hurt by the archers. In his side He *b. T.* iii 113

Cyrene, when he *b.* the plaintive tale *T.* v 136 [150
Or having, kept concealed. Some drill and *b. T.* iii

BORED. [iv 44
And *b.* with elbow points through both his sides *T.*

BORN.
In fairy land was *b.* the matchless dame *A.T.* 5
To names ignoble *b.* to be forgot! *B.B.* 2
Blind was he *b.*, and his misguided eyes *Ch.* 357
For thou art *b.* sole heir, and single *E.* iv 3
For thou wast *b.* amid the din of arms *Ex.* 472
At length his destined moment to be *b.? F.A.* 26
Of sensual evil, and thus Hope is *b. H.* 152
B. capable indeed of heavenly truth *H.* 231
'Twere better to be *b.* a stone *P.* 11 [iv 265
When they command whom man was *b.* to please *T.*
To serve the Sovereign we were *b* to obey *R.* 50
Nor his who, for the bane of thousands *b. R.* 687
Well *b.*, well disciplined, who placed apart *R.* 727
In happier days to brighter prospects *b.! S.* ii 5
That we were *b.* her children. Praise enough *T.* ii 235
Much. I was *b.* of woman, and drew milk *T.* iii 196
'Tis *b.* with all, the love of Nature's works *T.* iv 731
Thenceforth they are his cattle: drudges *b. T.* v 272
Remember Handel? Who, that was not *b. T.* vi 645
Proclaim him *b.* to sway *Th.* 10
Few boys are *b.* with talents that excel *Tir.* 509
B. in a climate softer far than ours *T.T.* 234
Who, *b.* a gentleman, hast stooped too low *V.* 33
B. from above and made divinely wise *V.* 94

BORNE.
B. far away on elevated wings *A.T.* 31
Was briskly *b.* along *A Tale* 54
Now *b.* upon the wings of Truth sublime *Ex.* 466
May press the eye too closely to be *b. H.* 551
If chance, on heavy pinions slowly *b. H.* 716
O'er the raging billows *b. N.C.* 4
For evils daily felt and hardly *b. R.* 752
And ready to be *b.* to court *R.C.* 20
Has slackened to a pause, and we have *b. T.* i 155
Possess ye, therefore, ye who, *b.* about *T.* i 754
Learning has *b.* such fruit in other days *T.* iii 248
Oh thou, whom, *b.* on fancy's eager wing *Tir.* 131
But if a deed not tamely to be *b. T.T.* 488

BOROUGHS.
Hence chartered *b.* are such public plagues *T.* iv 671

BORROWS.
From her the canvass *b.* light and shade *Ch.* 107
But cannot play them, *b.* a friend's hand *T.* i 473
But *b.* all its grandeur from the soul *Tir.* 10 [669
The strength they *b.* with the grace they lend *T.* iii

BORROWED.
To modest cheeks, and *b.* one from Art *Ex.* 48
On *b.* wheels away she flies *Q.V.* 37

BORROWING.
B. a beauty from the works of grace *R.* 358
And, at the watchman's lantern *b.* light *T.* ii 654

BOSOM.
Felt them in her *b.* glow *B.* 38
And brings, at his return, a *b.* charged *Ch.* 321
Two *b.* friends, each pensively inclined *Con.* 507
Usurps God's office, lays his *b.* bare *Con.* 745
But half a coat, and show his *b.* bare *E.* iii 51
Should spring within thy *b.*, drive it thence *Ex.* 709
The glowing *b.* swell *Miss* — 16
Our self-approving *b.* draws *Miss* — 51 [*N.A.* 37
Sheep grazed the field; some with soft *b.* pressed
" Still may my melting *b.* cleave *Miss* — 85
Speckle the *b.* of the distant plain *P.E.* 83
In every *b.* where her nest is made *P.E.* 240

Nor Ouse on his *b.* their image receives *P.F.* 4
Her peaceful *b.* laves *Q.V.* 72
The *b.* of his God *St.* iii 16
A *b.* heaved with never ceasing sighs *T.* i 552
Within its reeking *b.*, threatening death *T.* iii 503
Unfolds its *b.*; buds, and leaves, and sprigs *T.* iv 153
In human *b.*, quench it or abate *T.* iv 747
Even in the stifling *b.* of the town *T.* iv 753
As in the *b.* of the slaves he rules *T.* v 310
His *b.* of the hue *T.B.* 15
His counsellor and *b.* friend shall prove *Tir.* 216
In little *b.* such achievements strike *Tir.* 232
Writes on his *b.*, "To be let or sold" *T.T.* 417
On the beautiful *b.* of May *W.N.* 16

BOTANIST.
Say, *b.*, within whose province fall *H.* 286
" When, cry the *b.*, and stare *P.* 21

BOTTLE.
And—pardon me, the *b.* stands with you " *H.* 380
Had two stone *b.* found *J.G.* 66
Each *b.* had a curling ear *J.G.* 69
And hung a *b.* on each side *J.G.* 71
The *b.* he had slung *J.G.* 106
A *b.* swinging at each side *J.G.* 107
The *b.* twain behind his back *J.G.* 123
For all might see the *b.* necks *J.G.* 131
He cannot drink five *b.*, bilk the score *P.E.* 193

BOTTLED.
Like *b.* wasps upon a southern wall *R.* 494

BOTTOM.
And at the *b.* barbarous still and rude *Con.* 167
Runs in a *b.*, and divides the field *N.A.* 10
A drawer, it chanced, at *b.* lined *R.C.* 35

BOTTOMLESS.
The *b.* demands of contest waged *Y.O.* 102

BOUGH.
Lest the rude blast should snap the *b. A Fable* 14
Hung not far off upon a myrtle *b. A.T.* 174
Here and there one upon the topmost *b. T.* 380
Of thorny *b.*: have loved the rural walk *T.* i 112
Their pendant *b.*, stooping as if to drink *T.* i 269
Seems sunk, and shortened to its topmost *b. T.* i 306
Shot through the *b.*, it dances as they dance *T.* i 346
His garlands from the *b.* Again, as oft *T.* iii 442
The *b.* in which are bred the unseemly race *Tir.* 594
The nightingale may claim the topmost *b. T.T.* 576
Thy yet close-folded latitude of *b. Y.O.* 21 [403
Still lives, though all its pleasant *b.* are gone *T.* v
For owls to roost in. Once thy spreading *b. Y.O.* 52

BOUGHT.
Whose bounty *b.* me but to give me light *Ch.* 235
Love is not pedler's trumpery, *b.* and sold *H.* 330
Men from England *b.* and sold me *N.C.* 5
That sinews *b.* and sold have ever earned *T.* ii 32
B. with His blood who gave it to mankind *T.* v 546

BOUND.
Held within modest *b.*, the tide of speech *Con.* 889
And marks the *b.* of our abode *E.* i 38
And to domestic *b.* confined *Ep.* ii 7
Whereon he loved to *b. Ep.* ii 22
Long time Assyria *b.* them in her chain *Ex.* 73
Then thou art *b.* to serve him, and to prove *Ex.* 560
Thy soul as ample as thy *b.* are small *Ex.* 696
My gravelly *b.*, from self to human kind *F.A.* 20
B. in the fetters of an unknown tongue *H.* 450
Fast by the stream that *b.* your just domain *Her.* 47
B. on a voyage of awful length *H.F.* 17

Within no *b.*—the blind that lead the blind *P.E.* 477
They *b.*, and airy, o'er the sunny glade *St.* ii 22
E'er since, a truant boy, I passed my *b. T.* i 114
To narrow *b.* The Grove receives us next *T.* i 354
The law by which all creatures else are *b. T.* i 385
B. homeward, and in hope already there *T.* i 522
With lace, and hat with splendid riband *b. T.* i 536
Bespoke him past the *b.* of freakish youth *T.* ii 704
Than in the *b.* of duty? What was learned *T.* ii 754
One common Maker *b.* me to the kind? *T.* iii 209
Like flowers selected from the rest and *b. T.* iv 667
Fast *b.* in chains of silence, which the fair *T.* iv 53
And they that never pass their brick-wall *b. T.* iv 771
The king who loves the law, respects his *b. T.* v 332
Was sure to intoxicate the brows it *b. T.* v 245
No narrow *b.*; her cause engages him *T.* v 395
His body *b.*, but knows not what a range *T.* v 775
He marks the *b.* which Winter may not pass *T.* vi 192
Not so when, held within their proper *b. T.* vi 574
That we are *b.* to cast the minds of youth *Tir.* 105
As *b.* in duty, would confirm the choice *Tir.* 419
To more than he is hired or *b.* to teach *Tir.* 732
But never peep beyond the thorny *b. T.T.* 582
The brimming goblet, seized the Thyrsus *b. T.T.* 603

BOUNDARY.
Virtue and vice had *b.* in old time *T.* iii 75
One step beyond the *b.* of the laws *T.T.* 228

BOUNDED.
Or *b.* only by a law, whose force *T.* vi 358

BOUNDING.
Consult Life's silent clock, thy *b.* vein *E.* i 3
The chariots *b.* in her wheel-worn streets *Ex.* 21
The *b.* fawn, that darts across the glade *T.* vi 327
For *b.* and curvetting in his course *T.T.* 305

BOUNDLESS.
Hills, valleys, rivers, and the *b.* sea *A.T.* 49
And if a *b.* plenty be the robe *Ch.* 85
A captive bird into the *b.* sky *Ch.* 269
To uphold the *b.* scenes of his command *Ch.* 582
Far from the flock, and in a *b.* waste *E.* ii 42
To distribution *b.* of thy own *J.T.* 32
In *b.* oceans, never to be passed *T.* i 629
Some *b.* contiguity of shade *T.* ii 2
And *b.* as it is, a crowded coop *T.* iii 834
Now quenching in a *b.* sea of clouds *Y.O.* 76

BOUNTEOUS.
By *b.* heaven designed *Miss* — 2
But, O Thou *b.* giver of all good! *T.* v 903

BOUNTIFUL.
Himself as *b.* as April rains *H.* 304
So *b.*, in whose attentive ear *T.* vi 460

BOUNTY.
Whose *b.* bought me but to give me light *Ch.* 235
Royally, freely, for his *b.* sake *H.* 118
Thy *b.* all were Christian, and I make *J.T.* 47
Thy morning *b.* ere I left my home *M.P.* 60
Thy power divine, and *b.* beyond thought *R.* 91
And share the joys your *b.* may create *R.* 790
The wretch who slights the *b.* of the skies *T.* 543
From Nature's *b.*—that humane address *T.* v 469
" The use of his own *b.*?—making first *T.* v 639
'Tis grace, 'tis *b.*, and it calls for praise *V.* 87

BOURN.
And where the land slopes to its watery *b. N.A.* 13

BOUT. [*Tir.* 245
Where neither **strumpet's charms**, nor drinking *b.*

BOW.
Struck thrice the point upon his saddle *b. A.T.* 166
I interrupt him with a sudden *b. Con.* 281
Horatio's servant once, with *b.* and cringe *E.* iii 20
They learn to *b.*, to kneel, to sit, to stand *Ex.* 120
The Roman taught thy stubborn knee to *b. Ex.* 476
Prove it;—if better, I submit and *b. Ex.* 633
Wreathed into an elegant *b. Gr.* 7
Bright as the covenant-ensuring *b. H.* 150
The *b.* well bent, and smart the spring *H.F.* 5
To place it in thy *b. O.* i 26 [left *Y.O.* 127
With *b.* and shaft have burnt them. Some have
Of drunkards, or the music-drawing *b. St.* ii 12
A pedler's pack, that *b.* the bearer down *T.* i 465
And craving Poverty, and in the *b. T.* ii 490
And *b.* obsequious, hide their hate of her *T.* ii 646
Who, with bare-headed and obsequious *b. T.* iii 819
In pilgrimage to *b.* before his shrine *T.* vi 669
The God that strings the silver *b. Tran. H.* 28
Before whose infant eyes the flatterer *b. TT.* 123
Then like a *b.* long forced into a curve *T.T.* 622
Fancy that from the *b.* that spans the sky *T.T.* 702
Starts from its office like a broken *b. V.* 70

BOWED. [*R.* 599
Jack *b.* and was obliged—confessed 'twas strange
B. at the close with all his graceful airs *Con.* 73

BOWELS.
Would creep into the *b.* of the hills *T.* vi 867

BOWER.
There Fancy nursed her in ideal *b. A.T.* 7
Plucks amaranthine joys from *b.* of bliss *H.* 164
Of all that deck the lanes, the fields, the *b. H.* 288
Nor blasts that shake the dripping *b. Mrs. M*— 16
Shall chase him from the *b. N.* 18
'Tis Harmony from you sequestered *b. P.E.* 65
'Tis a *b.* of Arcadian sweets *W.N.* 9 [iv 728
Though stretched at ease in Chertsey's silent *b. T.*
While Peace possessed these silent *b. S.* 14
And long protracted *b.*, enjoyed at noon *T.* i 257
Forth from thy native *b.*, to show thee here *T.* i 636
Of golden fruitage, and her myrtle *b. T.* ii 215
Thus as the bee, from bank to *b.* 1789, 17

BOWING.
And now, as he went *b.* down *J.G.* 121
Ere long some *b.*, smirking, smart Abbé *P.E.* 385

BOWL.
The carriage *b.* along and all are pleased *P.E.* 438
He dips his *b.* into the weedy ditch *T.* i 241

BOW-WOW.
From your aggrieved *B. B. R.* 24

BOX.
And partner once of Tiny's *b. E.P.* ii 43
Tight *b.* neatly sashed, and in a blaze *R.* 483
Nor his who quits the *b.* at midnight hour *T.* i 98
Suspend their crazy *b.*, planted thick *T.* iv 774
He notes it in his book, then raps his *b. T.* vi 292
That they must soon learn Latin, and to *b. Tir.* 323

BOXEN.
With many a *b.* bush, close-clipped between *A.T.* 82

BOY.
Hour after hour, the yet unlettered *b. Con.* 12
B. care but little whom they trust *F.* 20
Yon roaring *b.*, who rave and fight *Pat.* 5
Ask not the *b.*, who when the breeze of morn *R.* 395
She yet allows herself that *b.* behind *T.* 142
E'er since, a truant *b.*, I passed my bounds *T.* i 114

BOY—BRAVED

The sturdy swain diminished to a *b*.! *T*. i 162
And vicious pleasures; buys the *b*. a name *T*. ii 759
The *b*.'s neglected sire! a mother too *T*. vi 43
And when the bush-exploring *b*., that seized *T*. vi 445
" Ambition in a *b*. supplied *Th*. 7   [*Tir*. 654
Would make him—what some lovely *b*. have been
Train him in public with a mob of *b*. *Tir*. 206
Ye nurseries of our *b*., we owe to you *Tir*. 248
B. as ye were, the gravity of men *Tir*. 272
The meek and bashful *b*. will soon be taught *Tir*. 338
B. are, at best, but pretty buds unblown *Tir*. 446
B., once on fire with that contentious zeal *Tir*. 470
The mind and heart of every sprightly *b*. *Tir*. 598
Few *b*. are born with talents that excel *Tir*. 509
If anxious only that their *b*. may learn *Tir*. 513
That youth takes pleasure in, to please his *b*. *Tir*. 550
Alas, poor *b*.!—the natural effect *Tir*. 575
The man approving what had charm'd the *b*. *Tir*. 149
Safe under such a wing, his *b*. shall show *Tir*. 684
And say, my *b*., the unwelcome hour is come *Tir*. 849
(Apprised that he is such) a careless *b*. *Tir*. 906
The little *b*. and all? *Y.D*. 34   [840
That though school-bred the *b*. be virtuous still *Tir*.

BOYISH.
Whose friendship from his *b*. years he chose *Con*. 424
When *b*. innocence was all my praise!) *R*. 372
Hard fare! but such as *b*. appetite *T*. i 123
The struggling efforts of my *b*. tongue *T*. iv 711
A *b*. friendship may so soon decline *Tir*. 453

BOYLE.
Such was Sir Isaac, and such *B*. and Locke *P.E*. 538

BRACE.
The citizen, and *b*. his languid frame! *T*. iv 752

BRACED.
With leathern girdle *b*. *J.G*. 130   [*T*. i 350
And now, with nerves new *b*. and spirits cheered
Of texture firm a lattice-work, that *b*. *T*. i 42
We wear it at our backs. There, closely *b*. *T*. ii 586

BRACELETS.
Sees watches, *b*., rings, and lockets *P.B*. 25

BRAES.
All birks and *b*., though he was never there *T.T*. 535

BRAIN.
The wildest project of her teeming *b*. *A.T*. 57
Just as the sapience of an author's *b*. *Ch*. 519
With oaths like rivets forced into the *b*. *Con*. 64
Useless in him alike both *b*. and speech *Con*. 141
The worst that can invade a sickly *b*. *Con*. 222
A shallow *b*. behind a serious mask *Con*. 297
Your elevated voice goes through the *b*. *Con*. 328
And puzzling set his puppy *b*. *D.W*. 23
Which busy man's inventive *b*. *E*. i 65
Make cruel inroads in my *b*. *E*. iv 16
What web too weak to catch a modern *b*.? *Ex*. 629
O querulous and weak!—whose useless *b*. *H*. 29
Patron of all those luckless *b*. *O*. i 1
Craze antiquarian *b*. with endless doubt *P.E*. 394
Has filled with all its fumes a critic's *b*. *P.E*. 445
Faults in the life breed errors in the *b*. *P.E*. 564
Nor yet the swarms that occupy the *b*. *R*. 644
These are the sober, in whose cooler *b*. *T*. 38
To fill the void of an unfurnished *b*. *T*. iv 209
So loose to private duty, that no *b*. *T*. v 512
The frenzy of the *b*. may be redressed *T*. vi 521
If shrewd, and of a well constructed *b*. *Tir*. 523
Perhaps a father, blest with any *b*. *Tir*. 626
Look up—your *b*. begin to swim *Tran*. ii 10

With much sufficiency in royal *b*. *T.T*. 52   [*V*. 9
Your *b*. well furnished, and your tongue well taught
Feels himself spent, and fumbles for his *b*. *T.T*. 537

BRAINLESS.
Arms, through the vanity and *b*. rage *T*. iv 619

BRAKE.
Ten thousand rove the *b*. and thorns among *H*. 280
That he may follow them through *b*. and brier *N.A*. 6
As one who long in thickets and in *b*. *T*. iii 1

BRANCH.
To associate all the *b*. of mankind *Ch*. 84
Bore on his *b*., luxuriant then and rude *T*. 493
Unnumbered *b*. waving in the blast *T*. i 188
On all her *b*. Piety has found *T*. iii 249
The *b*., sturdy to his utmost wish *T*. iii 530
Must smooth be shorn away; the sapless *b*. *T*. iii 613
With clasping tendrils, and invest his *b*. *T*. iii 666
A leafless *b*. thy sceptre, and thy throne *T*. iv 125
That trickle down the *b*., fast congealed *T*. v 114
In fancied peace beneath his dangerous *b*. *T*. v 325
Whose outspread *b*. overarch the glade *T*. vi 72

BRANCHING.
Environed with a ring of *b*. elms *T*. i 223

BRAMBLE.
And horrid *b*. intertwine below *N.A*. 16
Or should the *b*., interposed, our fall *N.A*. 111
The *b*., black as jet, or sloes austere *T*. i 122
In the shadow of a *b*., and reclined *T*. v 324

BRAMIN.
The *B*. kindles on his own bare head *T*. 99
I say the *B*. has the fairer claim *T*. 108
Where hermits and where *B*. meet with theirs *T*. 168

BRAND.
Satire is, more than those he *b*., to blame *Ch*. 492
Or, if it does not, *b*. him to the last *P.E*. 107
And bears the *b*. of blasphemy burnt in *T*. 348
And verse of mine shall never *b*. the wretch *T*. iii 72

BRANDISHES.
He *b*. his pliant length of whip *T*. iv 355

BRASS.
That *b*. and steel should make so fine a show *Ch*. 554
No; marble and recording *b*. decay *Con*. 551
Saw Babylon set wide, her two-leaved *b*. *Ex*. 59
And fanged with *b*. the demons are abroad *N.A*. 102
And filleted about with hoops of *b*. *T*. v 402
Ah, tinkling cymbal and high-sounding *b*. *T*. v 681
Gives bond in stone and ever-during *b*. *T*. v 710
Not rough with wire of steel or *b*. *T.B*. 26

BRAT.
Then cast them, closely bundled, every *b*. *T*. ii 673

BRAVE.
Built a *b*. world, which cannot yet subsist *Ch*. 192
And veil your daring crest that *b*. the skies *Con*. 486
A soldier may be anything, if *b*. *H*. 209
Thus *b*. the whirling blast *Miss* — 34
Toll for the *b*.! *R.G*. 1
The *b*. that are no more! *R.G*. 2
Eight hundred of the *b*. *R.G*. 5
Toll for the *b*.! *R.G*. 13
B. Kempenfelt is gone *R.G*. 14
A *b*. man knows no malice, but at once *T*. ii 268
They *b*. the season, and yet find at eve *T*. iv 378
Mark now the proof I give thee, that the *b*. *T*. vi 509
Unworthy of the blessings of the *b*. *T.T*. 27

BRAVED.
B. and defied, and in our own sea proved *T*. ii 272

BRAVELY.
Who *b.* breaks the most *Pat.* 12
And forced to abandon what she *b.* sought *T.* v 368

BRAVER.
No *b.* chief could Albion boast *Cast* 7

BRAWL.
Or flushed with fierce dispute, a senseless *b. T.* v 472

BRAY.
Or heard we that tremendous *b.* alone *N.A.* 93
Meantime, noise kills not. Be it Dapple's *b. N.A.* 115

BRAYING.
For while he spake, a *b.* ass *J.G.* 203

BRAZEN.
She ploughs a *b.* field, and clothes a soil *T.* i 709
Hear the faint echo of those *b.* throats *T.* iv 104

BRAZEN-CLAWED.
Demons produce them doubtless, *b. N.A.* 101

BREACH. [281
The *b.*, though small at first, soon opening wide *P.E.*
To avenge than to prevent the *b.* of law *T.* i 731
Lost favour back again, and closed the *b. T.* ii 724

BREAD.
He blessed the *b.*, but vanished at the word *Con.* 533
His diet was of wheaten *b. Ep.* ii 13   [iii 342
Yes—thou may'st eat thy *b.*, and lick the hand *T.*
The Saviour's feast, his own blest *b.* and wine *Ex.* 377
The life of multitudes, a nation's *b.* ! *Her.* 56
Besides the man's poor, his orchard's his *b. P.A.* 27
Earth gives too little, giving only *b. T.* 365
And sleep not: see him sweating o'er his *b. T.* i 363
When I am hungry for the *b.* of life ? *T.* ii 426
Fish up his dirty and dependent *b. T.* iii 808
At his own wonder, wondering for his *b. T.* iv 87

BREADTH.
By just degrees an overhanging *b. T.* iii 482

BREAK.
And he that splits his cranium, *b.* at most *A.T.* 44
I ventured once to *b. B.R.* 10
He *b.* the cord that held him at the rack *Ch.* 173
Thy worn-out heart will *b.* at last *M.* 51
Ne'er roughened by those cataracts and *b. M.P* 66
Who bravely *b.* the most *Pat.* 12
One *b.* the glass, and cuts his fingers *P.B.* 34
Girt with a chain he cannot wish to *b. R.* 243
Those flimsy webs that *b.* as soon as wrought *R.* 639
To *b.* a jest, when pity would inspire *T.* ii 468
Shall *b.* into its preconceived display *T.* iii 652
Though eloquent themselves, yet fear to *b. T.* iv 54
To *b.* some maiden's heart and his mother's heart *T.* iv 656
B. on the soul, and by a flash from Heaven *T.* v 884
This widowed heart would *b.*" *The Doves* 36
He *b.* away, and seek the distant plain ? *T.T.* 307

BREAKING.
If *b.* windows be the sport *Pat.* 10
Regardless of wringing and *b.* a heart *The Rose* 15

BREAST.
A raven, while with glossy *b. A Fable* 1
The Spring drew near, each felt a *b. A Tale* 13
You cried,—"Forbear!"—but in my *b. B.R.* 5
Suspicion lurks not in her artless *b. Ch.* 426
Each heart would quit its prison in the *b. Ch.* 610
Give it the *b.*, or stop its mouth with pap ! *Con.* 480
And spread the sacred treasures of the *b. Con.* 573
And every moment's calm, that soothes the *b. E.* ii 39
Hast thou, though suckled at fair freedom's *b. Ex.* 364
Against an innocent unconscious *b. Ex.* 431
And sucked a *b.* that panted with alarms *Ex.* 473
Will thrust a dagger at your *b. F.* 94

Religion ruling in the *b. F.* 203
But nature works in every *b. F.B.* 13
There dwells a consciousness in every *b. H.* 636
Dwells there a wish in such a *b. Miss* — 5
The shafts of woe—in such a *b. Miss* — 43
Divine authority within his *b. P.E.* 33
And proves a raging scorpion in his *b. P.E.* 241
Felt each a mortal stab in her own *b. P.E.* 339
To the wild wave, or wilder human *b. P.E.* 601
With a turf on my *b.*, and a stone at my head *P.F.* 15
Thus Conscience pleads her cause within the *b. R.* 15
To measure all that passes in the *b. R.* 133
The love of change that lives in every *b. R.* 171
His undissembling virtue to my *b. R.* 380
Though one, I grant it, in the generous *b. R.* 721
These and a thousand plagues that haunt the *b. R.* 763
Beats in the *b.* of man, that even a few *T.* i 285
Displeasure in his *b.* who smites the earth *T.* ii 69
As sweet as charity from human *b. T.* iii 197
Tempered in hell, invades the throbbing *b. T.* iii 686
The seeds of murder in the *b.* of man *T.* v 210
By kind tuition on his yielding *b. Tir.* 154
May never more be stamped upon his *b. Tir.* 763
Oh friendship ! cordial of the human *b.* ! *V.* 49
Our Queen's long-agitated *b.* 1789, 47

BREATH.
And each endures, while yet he draws his *b. Ch.* 143
But when the *b.* of age commits the fault *Con.* 49
Divert the champions prodigal of *b. Con.* 89
Upon the rolling chords rung out his dying *b. Ex.* 499
In dying sighs my little *b. G.* 11
That poor Jonquil, with almost every *b. H.* 89
The *b.* of Heaven must swell the sail *H.F.* 23
Away went Gilpin, out of *b. J.G.* 157
Man mourns his fleeting *b. St.* v 26
Till man resigns his *b. St.* vi 34
He begs their flattery with his latest *b. T.* 315
Conspire against him. With his *b.* he draws *T.* ii 139
And putrify the *b.* of blooming Health *T.* ii 184
And suffocates the *b.* at every turn *T.* ii 819
Exposed to his cold *b.*, the task begins *T.* iii 469
And his head thumps to feed upon the *b. T.* iv 47
Thy *b.* congealed upon thy lips, thy cheeks *T.* iv 122
The pent-up *b.* of an unsavoury throng *T.* iv 196
While every *b.*, by respiration strong *T.* iv 348
Prove it. A *b.* of unadulterate air *T.* iv 750
Thus idly do we waste the *b.* of praise *T.* vi 711
The *b.* of Heaven has chased it. In the heart *T.* vi 786
Their *b.* a sample of last night's regale *Tir.* 834
To float a bubble on the *b.* of Fame *T.T.* 746
One *b.* of Heaven, that cried—" Restore !" 1789, 40

BREATHE.
Which *b.* the low desire *Miss* — 10
The marble *b.*, the canvass glows *Miss* — 83
Where spices *b.* and brighter seasons smile *M.P.* 91
B. clouds of dust, and calls it country air *R.* 486
Slaves cannot *b.* in England ; if their lungs *T.* ii 40
And, charged with putrid verdure, *b.* a gross *T.* ii 97
The nose of nice nobility. *B.* soft *T.* ii 259
In language soft as Adoration *b.* ! *T.* ii 495   [iii 738
Whose Stygian throats *b.* darkness all day long *T.*
As the sun peeps, and vernal airs *b.* mild *T.* iii 443
And drenched conservatory *b.* abroad *T.* iii 498
Each opening blossom, freely *b.* abroad *T.* iii 622
That *b.* the spleen, and searches every bone *T.* iv 364
And man would *b.* but for his Maker's shame *Tir.* 88
And will it *b.* into him all the zeal *Tir.* 375
Place me where Winter *b.* his keenest air *T.T.* 294

BREATHED.
Those *b.* from lips of everlasting love *E.* ii 30
They *b.* in faith their well-directed prayers *Ex.* 239

The wind, of late *b.* gently forth *P.T.* 50
Then *b.* his soul into his rest *St.* iii 15
Complacency has *b.* a gentle gale *T.* 419

BREATHING.
Frowning in storms, or *b.* gentle airs *R.* 194
The *b.* of the lightest air that blows *R.* 530
And *b.* wholesome air, and wandering much *T.* i 589
From flower to flower, and even the *b.* air *T.* iii 539

BRED. [*Tir.* 838
All these, and more like these, were *b.* at schools
A moral, sensible, and well *b.* man *Con.* 193
Peers are not always generous as well *b. R.* 597
And clammy, of his dark abode have *b. T.* i 439
The thirst than slaked it, and not seldom *b. T.* ii 509
And *b.*, within the memory of no few *T.* ii 677
That ask robust, tough sinews, *b.* to toil *T.* iii 405
Though want of due restraint alone have *b. Tir.* 533
The boughs in which are *b.* the unseemly race *Tir.* 594

BREECHES.
As yet black *b.* were not, satin smooth *T.* i 10

BREED.
They swear it, till affirmance *b.* a doubt *Con.* 66
'Tis such a light as putrefaction *b. Con.* 675
Of man's superior *b. D.W* 40
The want of both denotes a meaner *b. H.* 292
Faults in the life *b.* errors in the brain *P.E.* 564
Nor such as useless conversation *b. R.* 643
The slavish dread of solitude, that *b. T.* i 488
Begets its likeness. Rank abundance *b. T.* i 686
Profusion *b.* them; and the cause itself *T.* ii 820
To check the procreation of a *b. Tir* 603

BREEDING.
Good *b.* and good sense gave all a grace *H.* 683
Whose wit is rudeness, whose good *b.* tires *R.* 438
Swept with a woman's neatness, *b.* else *T.* iii 616

BREEDING-PLACE.
Long-time a *b.* they sought *A Tale* 21

BREEZE.
Ask not the boy, who when the *b.* of morn *R.* 395
And the fresh-blowing *b.* never failed *M.D.* 8
Those alders quivering to the *b. S.* 6
And riots in the sweets of every *b. T.* i 444
Upon the wanton *b.* Strew the deck *T.* ii 256
Rock'd in the cradle of the western *b. Tir.* 44
By slender threads, and swinging in the *b. Tir.* 592

BRENTFORD.
So sit two kings of *B.* on one throne *T.* i 78

BRETHREN.
His free-born *b.* of the southern pole *Ch.* 34
And *b.* in calamity should love *T.* ii 74
Clothe the twin *b.* in each other's dress *T.T.* 45
That once lived here thy *b.*! At my birth *Y.O.* 2

BRIBE.
While Fame and Self-complacence are the *b. Ch.* 468
No wealth can *b.*, no prayers persuade to slay *Comp.* i 4
No *b.* the heart can win *Miss —* 58
"Worlds should not *b.* me back to tread *St.* iii 5
Foh! 'twas a *b.* that left it; he has touched *T.* iv 609
Fidelity that neither *b.* nor threat *T.* vi 628
Will sneer, and charge you with a *b. T.T.* 84

BRIBED.
And judgment drunk, and *b.* to lose his war *P.E.* 450
And must be *b.* to compass earth again *T.* i 675

BRICKBATS.
To find it stuffed with *b.*, earth, and stones *Con.* 310

BRICKS.
B. line the sides, but shivered long ago *N.A.* 15

BRICK-WALL.
And they that never pass their *b.* bounds *T.* iv 771

BRIDE.
"Now is the time to make the maid a *b.*!" *A.T.* 69
The *b.*, while yet her *b.*'s attire is on *A.T.* 103

BRIDGE.
As wide as the *b.* of the Nose is; in short *A.C.* 15
A sudden steep upon a Rustic *B. T.* i 267
Hark! 'tis the twanging horn o'er yonder *b. T.* iv 1

BRIDGET'S.
Scrawled upon glass Miss *B.*'s lovely name *T.* 156

BRIDGEWATER.
Not Brindley nor *B.* would essay *T.T.* 182

BRIDLE.
Whose *b.*, while he cropped the grass below *A.T.* 173
The flirted fan, the *b.*, and the toss *H.* 344

BRIDLING.
Dick heard, and tweedling, ogling, *b. P.T.* 38

BRIEF. [*Ex.* 512
Then priests with bulls, and *b.*, and shaven crowns
The *b.* proclaimed, it visits every pew *Ch.* 469

BRIEFLY.
Delivered *b.* thus his mind *P.T.* 22

BRIER.
That he may follow them through brake and *b. Na.* 6
Who found not thorns and *b.* in his road *E.* ii 12
Picked from the thorns and *b.* of reproof *T.* vi 1013

BRIGHT.
The *b.* original was one he knew *Ch.* 433
Can hopes of Heaven, *b.* prospects of an hour *Con.* 591
Had wit as *b.* as ready to produce *Con.* 614
Thou hast as *b.* an interest in her rays *Ex.* 590
By their's whose *b.* example, unimpeached *Ex.* 656
How *b.* soe'er the prospect seems *F.* 73
B. as the covenant-ensuring bow *H.* 150
Yes, but an object *b.* as orient morn *H.* 550
Now let the *b.* reverse be known abroad *H.* 710
His noonday beams were never half so *b. H.* 737
Which is both *b.* and clear" *J.G.* 28
Thy silver locks, once auburn *b. M.* 25
With torches ever *b. Miss —* 74
Of some tall temple playing *b. Mrs. M—* 36
With yon *b.* regent of the day *Mrs. M—* 52
But warm, and *b.*, and calm as May *P.T.* 10
B. shone the roofs, the domes, the spires *Q.V.* 13
His *b.* perfections at whose word they rose *R.* 200
Now came the cane from India, smooth and *b. T.* i 39
Have changed the woods, in scarlet honours *b. T* i 320
B. as his own, and trains by every rule *T.* ii 347
Ficoides, glitters *b.* the winter long *T.* iii 579
Conspiring, may attest his *b.* design *T.* iii 654
Sees her unwrinkled face reflected *b. T.* iv 4
Misdeems it, dazzled by its *b.* array *T.* iv 685
Conspicuous, and in *b.* apparel clad *T.* v 25
To a keen edge and made it *b.* for war *T.* v 216
Yellow and *b.*, as bullion unalloy'd *T.* vi 17 1
The *b.* profusion of her scatter'd stars *T.* vi 176
He sets the *b.* procession on its way *T.* vi 190
B. as the sun the sacred city shines *T.* vi 800
A glory, *b.* as that of all the signs *Tir.* 282
And destines their *b.* genius to be shown *Tir.* 336
Ah, blind to *b.* futurity, untaught *Tir.* 379
In that *b.* quarter his propitious skies *Tir.* 395
O *b.* occasions of dispensing good *T.T.* 63
I read of *b.* embattled fields 1789, 3

BRIGHTEN.

Whose wit can b. up a wintry day *Con.* 581
Reclaim his taste, and b. up his parts *Con.* 840

BRIGHTER.

Wait for the dawning of a b. day *Ch.* 167
Than those a b. season pours around *Con.* 648
A b. scene beyond that vale appears *Con.* 882
To darker climes, or climes of b. day *Ex.* 18
But b. beams than his who fires the skies *H.* 491
A b. prize than that he meant *Mor.* 55
Where spices breathe and b. seasons smile *M.P.* 91
And pant for b. days *N.* 12
Views constellations b. than her own *P.E.* 178
New life ordained and b. scenes to share *R.* 65
In happier days, to b. prospects born ! *S.* ii 5
But let not him that shares a b. day *T.* 539
Shone b. still, once called to public view *T.* v 521
But Martyrs struggle for a b. prize *T.* v 718
" And to possess a b. Heaven than yours ? " *T.* v 831
Works magic wonders, adds a b. hue *Tir.* 23
Not b. than in theirs the scholar's prize *Tir.* 473
Expect a b. sky *Trans. H.* 27
Were b. than the sleekest mole *T.B.* 14
If b. beams than all he threw not forth *T.T.* 680
Affection lights a b. flame *U.* 27

BRIGHTEST.

And make it b. at its latest date *Con.* 604
The b. wonders of an endless day *H.* 753
Howe'er performed, it was their b. part *T.* 579
The b. truths that man has ever seen *T.* ii 555

BRIGHTLY.

Which fate shall b. gild *N.Y.G.* 18

BRIGHTNESS.

Conspicuous as the b. of a star *T.* 29

BRIGHT-STUDDED.

B. to dazzle the eyes *Gr.* 13

BRILLIANT.

A truth the b. Frenchman never knew *T.* 328
And play his b. parts before my eyes *T.* ii 425
Peace to them all ! those b. times are fled *Tir.* 284

BRIMMING.

He lives, and o'er his b. beaker boasts *T.* vi 434
The b. goblet, seized the Thyrsus, bound *T.T.* 603

BRINDLEY.

Not B. nor Bridgewater would essay *T.T.* 182

BRINE.

Were not afraid to plough the b. *A Tale* 71
Not long beneath the whelming b. *Cast.* 13

BRING.

Or was the merchant charged to b. *A Tale* 27
To traverse seas, range kingdoms, and b. home *Ch.* 301
And b., at his return, a bosom charged *Ch.* 321
'Tis wrong to b. into a mixed resort *Con.* 291
And b. the trifler under rigorous sway *Con.* 596
To b. the passions under sober sway *Con.* 831
B. forth that unexpected hour *E.* i 30
Good each, we know not what to-morrow b. *E.* iii 8
But Grace abused b. forth the foulest deeds *Ex.* 213
Bids rottenness invade, and b. to dust *Ex.* 332
Reclaim the wandering thousands, and b. home *Ex.* 720
Sometime occasion b. to light *F.* 148
B. many a precious pearl of truth to light *H.* 444
B. to the distant ear a sullen sound *Her.* 36
" Good lack ! " quoth he, " yet b. it me *J.G.* 61
" This shall be yours, when you b. back *J.G.* 219
So did he fly—which b. me to *J.G.* 155 [*M.P.* 81
Might one wish b. them, would I wish them here ?
Your scruples and arguments b. to my mind *P.A.* 17
B. every thought, word, action, to the test *P.E.* 34
And Pleasure b. as surely in her train *P.E.* 43
Like a slain deer, the tumbrel b. him home *P.E.* 94
B. not alone the more conspicuous part *T.* 561
And, heavy laden, b. his beverage home *T.* i 242
That b. the planets home into the eye *T.* iii 230
What's that which b. contempt upon a book *T.* iii 277
Or dives not for it, or b. up instead *T.* iii 384
She b. her infants forth with many smiles *T.* iii 437
Then acts in Nature's office, b. to pass *T.* iii 542
Yet careless what he b., his one concern *T.* iv 9
To-morrow b. a change, a total change ! *T.* iv 322
B. its own evil with it, makes it less *T.* v 770
B. into doubt the wisdom of the skies *Tir.* 72
A public school shall b. to pass with ease *Tir.* 372
B. he, to sweeten fruits so undesired *Tir.* 578
Saved from his home, where every day b. forth *Tir.* 757
B. down the warrior's trophy to the dust *T.T.* 7
Now, from the dust of ancient days b. forth *T.T.* 376
B. colours dipped in Heaven, that never die *T.T.* 703
Whate'er we write, we b. forth nothing new *T.T.* 733
See, Mary, what beauties I b. *W.N.* 5

BRINGING.

Are b. into vogue their heathen train *Con.* 821
Ye once were justly famed for b. forth *Tir.* 279
Thus b. home to him the most remote *Tir.* 643

BRINK.

Carelessly nods and sleeps upon the b. *Ex.* 99
They gathered close around the old pit's b. *Na.* 53
Then doubtless many a trifler, on the b. *St.* ii 13
O'er hills, through valleys, and by river's b. *T.* i 113

BRISK.

He cherups b. his ear-erecting steed *T.* iii 9
With melting airs, or martial, b., or grave *T.* vi 3
The Frenchman, easy, debonair, and b. *T.T.* 236

BRISKER.

Its b. and its graver strains fall short *R.* 294
May run in cities, with a b. force *R.* 454

BRISKLY.

Was b. borne along *A Tale* 54
B., astride upon the parlour broom *Tir.* 367
More b. moved by his severer toil *T.* iv 389

BRISTOL.

Content with B., Bath, and Tunbridge Wells *R.* 516

BRITAIN.

Steered B.'s oak into a world unknown *Ch.* 25
Oh, happy B. ! we have not to fear *E.* iii 54
In B.'s isle, beneath a George's reign ! *Her.* 90
Of all your empire ; that where B.'s power *T.* ii 46
As dwell at large in B.'s chartered land *T.T.* 259

BRITISH.

" For B. nymphs, whose lords were lately true *A.T.* 109
When the B. warrior queen *B.* 1
But raise the shrillest cry in B. ears *Ex.* 271
The fairest B. fair *L.R.* 26
Then farewell B. freedom *Pat.* 24
Can B. Paradise no scenes afford *P.E.* 257
With limbs of B. oak, and nerves of wire *R.* 311
Would give a barbarous air to B. song *T.* 102
Or ploughed perhaps by B. bark again *T.* i 631
Our B. Themis gloried with just cause *T.* iii 257
Of B. natures, wanting its excuse *T.* v 481
Poll gains at length the B. shore *Tran.* iv 4
And fill with discontent a B. isle *T.T.* 253

All that should be the boast of *B.* song *T.T.* 369
Hence, *B.* poets too the priesthood shared *T.T.* 502

BRITON.
A *B.* knows, or if he knows it not *Ch.* 200
It seems as if we *B.* were ordained *Con.* 363
A *B.'s* scorn of arbitrary chains? *T.T.* 201

BRITTLE.
Her *b.* toys, restores me to myself *T.* iv 307
So stood the *b.* prodigy; though smooth *T.* v 154
Whose noblest coin is light and *b.* man *V.* 96

BROAD.
Ocean exhibits, fathomless and *b. R.* 525
Exposes, and holds up to *b.* disgrace *T.* ii 553
His *b.* keen knife into the solid mass *T.* v 35
In nature, from the *b.* majestic oak *T.* vi 250
Ye reasoners *b.* awake, whose busy search *Y.O.* 30

BROADEST.
As human nature's *b.*, foulest blot *T.* ii 22

BROAD-CLOTH.
B. without, and a warm heart within *E.* iii 63

BROILING.
B. beneath a July sun *E.* iv 50

BROILS.
Successive loads succeeding *b.* impose *Ex.* 308
Such civil *b.* are my delight *Pat.* 17

BROKE.
That stripped him bare, and *b.* his honest heart *Ch.* 54
Dispelled thy gloom, and *b.* away thy dreams *Ex.* 501
Asked of the waves that *b.* upon his coast *Ex.* 572
And every post, and where the chaise *b.* down *P.E.* 374
Worse than the deeds of galley-slaves *b.* loose *T.T.* 327

BROKEN.
Informed, He gathered up the *b.* thread *Con.* 525
"A threefold cord is not soon *b. E.* i 106
Fell *b.* and defaced at their own door, *Ex.* 506
She sung of the slave's *b.* chain *M.D.* 19
Only by a *b.* heart *N.C.* 48
And staunch the bleedings of a *b.* heart *R.* 322
Reclaims the wanderer, binds the *b.* heart *T.* ii 344
Of headstrong youth were *b.*; bars and bolts *T.* ii 745
See then the quiver *b.* and decayed *T.* ii 803
The dangers we have 'scaped, the *b.* snare *T.* iv 185
Ye horrid towers, the abode of *b.* hearts *T.* v 384
That the wind severs from the *b.* wave *T.* vi 156
On future *b.* bones and bruises *Tran.* ii 20
Starts from its office like a *b.* bow *V.* 70

BROOD.
"'Tis over, and the *b.* is safe" *A Fable* 19
A lawless *b.*, and curse thee to thy face *Ex.* 283
Where oft the bitch-fox hides her hapless *b. Na.* 4
And slumbering oscitancy mars the *b.*? *T.* ii 774
A *b.* of asps, or quicksands in his way *Tir.* 870

BROOK.
And N. did not like it, which M. could not *b. A.T.* ii 2
A narrow *b.*, by rushy banks concealed *Na.* 9
Nor noise was heard but of the hasty *b. Na.* 39
Can least *b.* management, however mild *R.* 252
And like a Summer *b.* are past away *R.* 296
To draw the incautious minnow from the *b. R.* 402
A cheap but wholesome salad from the *b. T.* vi 304
Like shallow *b.* which summer suns exhale! *V.* 2

BROOKED.
Trouble is grudgingly and hardly *b. Ch.* 218

BROOM.
Althæa with the purple eye; the *b. T.* vi 170
Briskly, astride upon the parlour *b. Tir.* 367

BROTHELLERS.
For gamesters, jockeys, *b.* impure *T.* ii 751

BROTHER.
Hate their own likeness in a *b.'s* face *Con.* 158
Had each a *b.'s* interest in his heart *H.* 579
That *b.* should not war with *b. N.G.* 29
That thought that meditates a *b.'s* wrong *T.* 560
Thus man devotes his *b.*, and destroys *T.* ii 20
All are not such. I had a *b.* once— *T.* ii 780
Cain had already shed a *b.'s* blood *T.* v 208

BROTHERHOOD.
The priestly *b.*, devout, sincere *Ex.* 438
Of *b.* is severed as the flax *T.* ii 10
To cut the link of *b.*, by which *T.* iii 208

BROUGHT.
At length a ship arriving *b. A Tale* 23
Collect at evening what the day *b.* forth *Con.* 19
And who is hanged, and who is *b.* to bed *Con.* 396
Ere yet they *b.* their journey to an end *Con.* 521
As if not Love, but Wrath, had *b.* Him down *Ex.* 132
And having trucked thy soul, *b.* home the fee *Ex.* 374
B. fire from Heaven, the sex-abusing crime *Ex.* 415
He *b.* thy land a blessing when he came *Ex.* 484
Who *b.* the lamp that with awaking beams *Ex.* 500
The morning came, the chaise was *b. J.G.* 33
'Twas my distress that *b.* thee low *M.* 7
By our sufferings since ye *b.* us *N.C.* 45
Chafed him, and *b.* dull nature to a glow *P.E.* 408
"Since the dear hour that *b.* me to thy foot *T.* 573
With summer fruits *b.* forth by wintry suns *T.* iii 552
Yet just arrangement, rarely *b.* to pass *T.* iii 588
Then he, of all that Nature has *b.* forth *Tir.* 69
The powers that Sin has *b.* to a decline *T.T.* 383
So when remote futurity is *b. T.T.* 492
Polite, yet virtuous, who has *b.* away *V.* 79

BROW.
Frowns in the storm with angry *b. A Fable* 38
Wreaths for her *b.*, and girdles for her waist *A.T.* 14
Armed at all points, with terror on his *b. A.T.* 140
And there resume an unembarrassed *b. Con.* 401
Taxed till the *b.* of Labour sweats in vain *Ex.* 305
When Sin has shed dishonour on thy *b. Ex.* 394
That bind the sinner's Bacchanalian *b. T.* 462
Had shed immortal glories on your *b. T.* 569
And overbuilt with most impending *b. T.* iii 193
And lilies for the *b.* of faded age *T.* iv 80
A star or two, just twinkling on thy *b. T.* iv 253
Was sure to intoxicate the *b.* it bound *T.* v 245
It yields them, or recumbent on its *b. T.* v 787
Who wore the platted thorns with bleeding *b. T.* vi 239
And binds a wreath about their baby *b. T.T.* 124
'Tis not the wreath that once adorned thy *b. T.T.* 370
His *b.* with ivy, rushed into the field *T.T.* 604
Sat fast on George's *b.* again 1789, 45

BROWN.
The omnipotent magician, *B.*, appears! *T.* iii 766
The golden harvest, of a mellow *b. T.* iv 314
Just when the day declined, and the *b.* loaf *T.* iv 393
That mingles all my *b.* with sober gray *Tir.* 144
The inestimable Estimate of *B. T.T.* 384

BRUISED.
He *b.* beneath his feet the infernal powers *Ch.* 584
And *b.* the side, and, elevated high *T.* i 66

BRUISES.
On future broken bones and *b. Tran.* ii 20

BRUNT.
Worse than the mortal *b.* of rival swords *Con.* 86

Endurest the *b.*, and darest defy them all *Ex.* 697
The pelting *b.* of the tempestuous night *T.* iv 351

BRUSH. [*b. T.* vi 317
Ascends the neighbouring beech; there whisks his
To *b.* the surface, and to make it flow *Con.* 102
Artist, attend! your *b.* and your paint *T.* 171
So I, with *b.* in hand and pallet spread *T.* iv 239
And half on foot, they *b.* the fleecy flood *T.* v 63

BRUSHED.
His long red cloak, well *b.* and neat *J.G.* 75
Nor Autumn yet had *b.* from every spray *N.A.* 21
B. by the wind. So sportive is the light *T.* i 345

BRUSHING.
Ambitious of *b.* the sky *Gr.* 4

BRUSHWOOD.
Her scanty stock of *b.*, blazing clear *T.* iv 381

BRUTAL.
And joining the freethinker's *b.* roar *P.E.* 593
With *b.* lust as ever Circe made *T.T.* 629

BRUTALIZE.
In human mould, should *b.* by choice *T.* i 575

BRUTE.
I am lord of the fowl and the *b. A.S.* 4
His manners with his fate puts on the *b. Ch.* 154
Seem our nation *b.* no longer *N.C.* 49
Made nothing but a *b.*, the slave of sense *P.E.* 214
B. capable would tell you 'tis a lie *P.E.* 261
He proves less happy than his favoured *b. R.* 633
And agonies of human and of *b. T.* ii 105 [vi 614
Matched with the expertness of the *b.* in theirs *T.*
Should some contagion, kind to the poor *b. T.* iii 208
The wonder; humanizing what is *b. T.* v 700
B. graze the mountain-top, with faces prone *T.* v 785
Of the poor *b.*, seems wisely to suppose *T.* v 437
Feed on the slain, but spare the living *b.! T.* vi 458
That claims forbearance even for a *b. T.* vi 466
And taught a *b.* the way to safe revenge *T.* vi 559
If not the virtuous, yet the worth of *b. T.* vi 724
Not better much than spectacles a *b. Tir.* 782

BUBBLES.
Eternity for *b.* proves at last *T.* iii 175
To float a *b.* on the breath of Fame *T.T.* 746

BUBBLING.
Thou ever *b.* spring of endless lies *P.E.* 467
And while the *b.* and loud hissing urn *T.* iv 38

BUCKETS.
Of dropping *b.* into empty wells *T.* iii 189

BUCKLED.
B. his helm, and to his steed repaired *A.T.* 172

BUCKRAM.
To *b.* out the memory of a man *T.* vi 652

BUD.
Ye worms that eat into the *b.* of youth! *Con.* 40
By looking on the *b.*, descry *E.* i 70
A worm is in the *b.* of youth *St.* i 23
And ventilate and warm the swelling *b. T.* iii 426
To some shrewd sharper, ere it *b.* again *T.* iii 754
Unfolds its bosom; *b.*, and leaves, and sprigs *T.* iv 153
To weep for the *b.* it had left with regret *The Rose* 7
Boys are, at best, but pretty *b.* unblown *Tir.* 446
When Discipline helps opening *b.* of sense *T.T.* 508
The *b.* inserted in the rind *U.* 13
The *b.* of peach or rose *U.* 14

BUDDING.
By *b.* ills, that ask a prudent hand *T.* vi 591

BUDGE.
The solemn fop, significant and *b. Con.* 299

BUDGET.
His *B.*, often filled, yet always poor *Ch.* 614
But O the important *b.!* ushered in *T.* iv 23

BUFFET.
Which here people call a *b. Gr.* 34

BUFFETED.
But tossed and *b.* about *P.* 9

BUFFOON.
The dear-bought placeman, and the cheap *b. Con.* 30
Our Sabbaths closed with mummery and *b. P.E.* 153

BUILD.
But found not where to *b. A Tale* 16
Thy *b.* each other up with dreadful skill *Con.* 687
To *b.* our altar, confident and bold *Con.* 849
B. by whatever plan caprice decrees *H.* 614
To storm the citadels they *b.* in air *H.* 626 [v 132
When thou wouldst *b.*; no quarry sent its stores *T.*
That *b.* its glory on its Maker's praise *R.* 210
He seeks a favoured spot; that where he *b. T.* iii 471
B. factories with blood, conducting trade *T.* iv 681
B. him a pedestal, and say, "Stand there *T.* v 258
We *b.* with what we deem eternal rock *T.* v 534
The mere materials with which wisdom *b. T.* vi 93

BUILDING.
Or *b.* hospitals on English ground? *Ch.* 44
To finish a fine *b. F.* 165
At *b.* human wonders mountain high *T.* v 179
Nor write on each—This *b.* to be let *Tir.* 916

BUILT.
They paired, and would have *b.* a nest *A Tale* 15
B. a brave world, which cannot yet subsist *Ch.* 192
B. by no mercenary vulgar hand *Ch.* 257
Prisons expect the wicked, and were *b. Ch.* 280
B. by that architect who *b.* the skies *Con.* 560
As if, like arches *b.* with skilful hand *Ex.* 286
And bids the mountains he has *b.*, stand fast *H.* 476
Discover huge cathedrals *b.* with stone *P.E.* 381
All paired, and each pair *b.* a nest *P.T.* 44 [688
B. God a church, and laughed his word to scorn *R.*
His well *b.* systems, philosophic dreams *T.* 8
That having wielded th' elements, and *b. T.* iii 170
Sofa, and couch, and high *b.* throne august *T.* v 164
Were *b.*, the fountains opened, or the sea *T.* v 765
But runs the road of wisdom. Thou hast *b. T.* v 849
See Salem *b.*, the labour of a God! *T.* vi 799
Large *b.* and latticed well *T.B.* 24 [v 753
That planned, and *b.*, and still upholds a world *T.*
You told me, I remember, glory *b. T.T.* 1

BULK.
Goliath, might have seen his giant *b. T.* iv 270
Slow after century, a giant *b. Y.O.* 63 [*R* 67
Whose shape would make them, had they *b.* and size

BULKY.
'Tis heavy, *b.*, and bids fair to prove *Con.* 307

BULL. [61
Free as the lordly *b.* that ranges o'er the mead *A.T*
A story of a cock and *b. P.T.* 7 [*Ex.* 512
Then priests with *b.*, and briefs, and shaven crowns

BULLFINCH.
At length a *B.*, who could boast *P.T.* 17

BULLION.
Yellow and bright, as *b*. unalloyed *T*. vi 171

BULLY.
And *B*.'s cage supported stood *T.B.* 22
For *B*.'s plumage sake *T.B.* 27
A dream disturbed poor *B*.'s rest *T.B.* 44
He left poor *B*.'s beak *T.B.* 54

BULWARKS.
Despise his *b*., and unpeople earth *R*. 72

BUMPER.
The purple *b*. trembling at his lips *H*. 358
And drank the little *b*. every day *T*. 158

BUMPKIN.
'Twas April as the *b*. say *A Fable* 8
Each *b*. of the clan *Y.D.* 26

BUMPS.
In honourable *b*. his rich amends *Con*. 200

BUNCH.   [674
Shall stuff his shoulders with King Richard's *b. T*. vi

BUNDLE.
It can't be a match —'tis a *b*. of matches *A.T.* iii 4
Of the plague spread by *b*. left behind *P.E.* 352
To better deeds, he *b*. up the spoil *T*. iv 440

BUNDLED.
Then cast them, closely *b*., every brat *T*. ii 673
And *b*. close to fill some crowded vase *T*. iv 668

BUOYANT.
Once prone on earth, now *b*. upon air *R*. 66
And spirits *b*. with excess of glee *T*. vi 329

BURDEN.
War lays a *b*. on the reeling state *Ex*. 306
An ass's *b*., and, when laden most *T*. iv 441
To bear his *b*., drawing in his gears *T*. v 273
Earth groans beneath the *b*. of a war *T*. vi 392
The *b*. of my song *Y.D.* 4

BURGHERS.
And *b*., men immaculate perhaps *T*. iv 672

BURIAL.
I heard the bell tolled on thy *b*. day *M.P.* 28

BURIED.
The verdure of the plain lies *b*. deep *T*. v 21

BURLY.
B. and big, and studious of his ease *T*. i 63

BURN.
Might *b*. his useless Machiavel, and sleep *Ch*. 613
Our wasted oil unprofitably *b. Con*. 357
Did they not *b*. within us by the way?" *Con*. 536
Till the last fire *b*. all between the poles *Con*. 756
The puny tyrant *b*. to subjugate *H*. 189
Can trace the torrent as it *b*. along? *Her*. 20
Kindled in Heaven, that it *b*. down to earth *T*. ii 134
He *b*. with most intense and flagrant zeal *T*. iii 794
I *b*. to set the imprisoned wranglers free *T*. iv 34
With every lust with which frail Nature *b. Tir*. 66
A kindred spark: they *b*. to do the like *Tir*. 233
The spirit of that competition *b. Tir*. 474
What *b*. at home, or threatens from afar *T.T.* 447

BURNED.
But she has *b*. her mask, not needed here *T*. iii 105
And if, soon after having *b*., by turns *Tir*. 65

BURNING.
Every *b*. word he spoke *B*. 7

B. and scorched into perpetual dearth *Ex*. 421
And grinds his crown beneath her *b*. wheels *H*. 652
The *b*. of his own *M*. i 12
For baking earth, or *b*. rock to lime *N.A.* 18
With which she gazes at yon *b*. disk *T*. i 713
Yet feel the *b*. instinct: over-head *T*. iv 773

BURNISHED.
Were *b*. into heroes, and became *T*. v 280

BURNT.
Has *b*. to tinder a stale last year's news *B.B.* 10
Have *b*. to dust a nobler pile *M*. i 3   [*Y.O.* 127
With bow and shaft have *b*. them. Some have left
There pages mangled, *b*., and torn *M*. i 9
And bears the brand of blasphemy *b*. in *T*. 348

BURST.
Their wisdom *b*. into this sage reply *Con*. 877
Have *b*. the bands, and cast the yoke away *Ex*. 465
Though not a hound from whom it *b*. appeared *N.A.* 46
The depth, how awful! falling there, we *b. N.A.* 110
Weep tears of joy, and *b*. into a song *T*. 458
When Tumult lately *b*. his prison door *T.T.* 318
Didst *b*. thine egg, as theirs the fabled twins *Y.O.* 35

BURSTING.
(Unfelt the fury of those *b*. mines) *Her*. 8
Of patriots, *b*. with heroic rage *T*. iv 48

BURY.
Or *b*. me in ocean's angry tide! *T*. 270
B. herself in solitude profound *T*. 443

BUSH.
With many a boxen *b*., close-clipped between *A.T.* 82
Unfolds his flock, then under bank or *b. R*. 397
On the flourishing *b*. where it grew *The Rose* 8

BUSH-EXPLORING.
And when the *b*. boy, that seized *T*. vi 445

BUSIED.
Sought their own village, *b*. as they went *Con*. 509
Where Policy is *b*., all night long *Ex*. 300

BUSIEST.
And may be feared amid the *b*. scenes *R*. 121
As theirs who bustle in the *b*. scene *R*. 734

BUSINESS.
As mendicants, whose *b*. is to roam *Con*. 859
(For 'tis my *b*. to reply) *T*. iv 80
If *B*., constant as the wheels of time *Ex*. 604
B. is labour, and man's weakness such *H*. 19
Pastime and *b*. both, it should exclude *P.E.* 159
Hackneyed in *b*., wearied at that oar *R*. 1
Or scorned where *b*. never intervenes *R*. 122
The Lover too shuns *b*. and alarms *R*. 219
That whirl away from *b*. and debate *R*. 393
The man of *b*. and his friends compressed *R*. 495
Shakes hands with *b*., and retires indeed *R*. 514
A *b*. with an income at its heels *R*. 615
B. or vain amusement, care or mirth *R*. 647
From whom are all our blessings, *b*. finds *T*. iii 366
Has *b*.; feels himself engaged to achieve *T*. iii 377
Where nothing feeds it. Neither *b*. crowds *T*. iv 744
Its customs and its *b. Tran*. ii 28
Votaries of *b*. and of pleasure prove *V*. 71

BUSKIN.
To live by *b*., sock, and raree-show *V*. 34

BUSTLE.
We *b*. up with unsuccessful speed *Con*. 215

Who makes no b. with his soul's affairs *Con.* 580
As theirs who b. in the busiest scene *R.* 734
The b. and the raree-show *Tran.* ii 16
And all the crowds that b. life away *V.* 74

BUSTLER.
Forgive him then, thou b. in concerns *T.* vi 951

BUSTLING.
Placed for his trial on this b. stage *P.E.* 23
Amused spectators of this b. stage *T.* v 878

BUSY.
Where commerce has enriched the b. coast *Ch.* 114
Far from the world's gay b. throng *Comp.* ii 4
The Mind despatched upon her b. toil *Con.* 437
Which b. man's inventive brain *E.* i 65
Her peaceful shores, where b. commerce waits *Ex.* 13
Display with b. and laborious hand *Ex.* 163
The b. trifler dreams himself alone *Ex.* 322
The b. heralds hang the sable scene *H.* 264
Where b. arts are never at a stand *H.* 440
Though b., trifling; empty though refined *P.E.* 426
The b. race examine and explore *R.* 151
Lips b., and eyes fixed, foot falling slow *R.* 285
Nor view of waters turning b. mills *R.* 334
But when his lord would quit the b. road *R.* 631
The rest too b., or too gay, to wait *T.* 40
His wrath is b., and his frown is felt *T.* ii 94
The better hand, more b., gives the nose *T.* ii 451
He picks clean teeth, and, b. as he seems *T.* ii 627
Esteems that b. world an idler too! *T.* iii 354
What is it but a map of b. life *T.* iv 55

But here the needle plies its b. task *T.* iv 150
The world o'erlooks him in her b. search *T.* vi 915
Too b. to intend a meaner care *Tir.* 660
And some perhaps, who, b. as they are *Tir.* 799
And ask, with b. scorn, "Was this the man?" *T.T.* 120
Next, b. actor on a meaner stage *V.* 27
At length the b. time begins *Y.D.* 49
Ye reasoners broad awake, whose b. search *Y.O.* 30
My b. search, I next applied 1789, 12

BUTLER.
Though B.'s wit, Pope's numbers, Prior's ease *T.T.* 764

BUTT.
The very b. of slander, and the blot *H.* 558

BUTTER.
Of savoury cheese, or b. costlier still *T.* iv 395

BUTTERFLY.
The gilded b. pursues *E.* iv 51

BUTTON.
Till, loop and b. failing both *J.G.* 103

BUY.
And b. the muscles and the bones of man? *Ch.* 140
B. what is woman-born, and feel no shame? *Ch.* 181
Has He bid you b. and sell us *N.C.* 27 [*P.A.* 2
And fear those who b. them and sell them, are knaves
If we do not b. the poor creatures, they will *P.A.* 11
And vicious pleasures; b. the boy a name *T.* ii 759
What pearl is it that rich men cannot b. *T.* iii 285

C.

CABIN.
And I to my c. repair *A.S.* 52
And sends thee to thy c., well prepared *T.* i 670

CABINET.
By diving into c. intrigue *T.T.* 154

CADENCE.
In c. sweet, now dying all away *T.* vi 8

CÆRULEAN.
Hangs out her lamp in yon c. height *A.T.* 138

CÆSAR.
Regions C. never knew *B.* 29
Though twice a C. could not bend thee now *Ex.* 477
Till C.'s image is effaced at last *P.E.* 280
Some headless hero, or some C. shows *P.E.* 395
The laurels that a C. reaps are weeds *T.* vi 939

CAFFRARIA.
C.; foreigners from many lands *T.* iii 585

CAGE.
Might smooth her feathers, and enjoy her c. *Ch.* 306
So settling on his c., by play *F.B.* 25
Ye dungeons and ye c. of despair *T.* v 385
Her favourite, even in his c. *T.B.* 4
And Bully's c. supported stood *T.B.* 22
A rat fast clinging to the c. *T.B.* 46
His teeth were strong, the c. was wood *T.B.* 53
And in his c., like parrot fine and gay *T.T.* 232

CAGED.
For caught and c., and starved to death *G.* 10

CAIN.
C. had already shed a brother's blood *T.* v 208

CALAMITOUS.
Of that c. mischief has been found *T.* ii 821

CALAMITY.
Thy fastings, when c. at last *Ex.* 400
And brethren in c. should love *T.* ii 74

CALCULATE.
Employed to c. the enormous sum *P.E.* 486
With which she c., computes, and scans *T.* i 716

CALEDONIA.
C.'s traffic and pride! *Gr.* 18

CALEDONIAN.
Perhaps some bonny C. air *T.T.* 534

CALENDER.
And my good friend the c. *J.G.* 23
Till, at his friend the c.'s *J.G.* 159
The c., amazed to see *J.G.* 161
And thus unto the c. *J.G.* 171
The c., right glad to find *J.G.* 177

CALL.
" Starts at the c. of beauty in distress *A.T.* 120
" Come ten, come twenty, should an army c. *A.T.* 185
The tree they c. a mast *A Tale* 34

No land but listens to the common c. Ch. 91
C. Nature from her ivy-mantled den Ch. 95
These have an ear for his paternal c. Ch. 250
Though Wisdom hail them, heedless of her c. Ch. 406
To c. the few that trust in him his friends Ch. 588
But fear to c. a more important cause Con. 397
C. gentleman whom she has made a fool Con. 466
That fools, as you have done, shall c. a dream Con. 504
C. legions up from Hell to back the deed Con. 691
Awake at Duty's c. D.W. 42
Not that I dream, or mean to c. E. i 91
Or, waking at the c. of lust alone Ex. 101
And c. up evidence from every age Ex. 162
There were the prophets, theirs the priestly c Ex. 201
With none on earth that thou canst c. thine own Ex. 266
Which here people c. a buffet Gr. 34
But what the gods c. it above Gr. 35
The sun, obedient, at her c. appears H. 43
If appetite, or what divines c. lust H. 385
With prudence always ready at our c. H. 431
Their great inspirer c. J.P. 30
But no—what here we c. our life is such M.P. 84
The c. of early Spring N. 4
Which rural gentlemen c. sport divine N.A. 8
These c. him loudly to pursuit of more P.E. 50
What atheists c. him, a designing knave P.E. 108
Hear him again. He c. it a delight P.E. 163
Their answer to the c. is—" Not at home " P.E. 168
That pleasures, therefore, or what such we c. P.E. 225
And c. her charms to public notice forth P.E. 296
If a wish wander that way, c. it home P.E. 586
And c. a creature formed for God alone R. 17
C. him away from selfish ends and aims R. 19
True Wisdom will attend his feeble c. R. 33
I may resemble Thee, and c. Thee mine " R. 98
That men erroneously their glory c. R. 100
C. thee to cope with enemies, and first R. 267
Can c. up life into his faded eye R. 339
Breathes clouds of dust, and c. it country air R. 486
C. for the kind assistance of a tune R. 712
Flowers by that name promiscuously we c. R. 723
" Shall c. to supper, when, no doubt R.C. 63
Faces a thousand dangers at her c. R.H. 7
Pleasure's c. attention wins St. iv 25
To c. up Plenty from the teeming earth T. 181
Not so; the silver trumpets' heavenly c. T. 349
Grant her indebted to what zealots c. T. 483
Dependant on the baker's punctual c. T. i 244
He c. for Famine, and the meagre fiend T. ii 185
Of heroes little known, and c. the rant T. iii 140
That He will judge the earth, and c. the fool T. iii 178
In arts like yours. I cannot c. the swift T. iii 211
C. idle, and who justly, in return T. iii 353 [iii 399
The welcome c., conscious how much the hand T.
When He shall c. his debtors to account T. iii 365
That c. the past to our exact review T. iv 184
C. comedy, to prompt him with a smile? T. iv 199
Gloriously drunk, obey the important c.! T. iv 510
In tribes and clans, and had begun to c. T. v 222
Which have their exigencies too, and c. T. v 240
All that the contest c. for; spirit, strength T. v 376
Comes at his c., and serves him for a friend T. v 424
Who c. for things that are not, and they come T. v 687
C. the delightful scenery all his own T. v 741
Or promising with smiles to c. again T. vi 282
That c. the unwonted villager abroad T. vi 300
Man scarce had risen, obedient to his c. T. vi 348
It may succeed; and, if his sins should c. Tir. 410
And c. aloud for sack Tran. iv 15 [v 61
Come trooping at the housewife's well-known c. T.
Religion, virtue, truth, whate'er we c. T.T. 286
Can c. her smiling down, and fix her here T.T. 413
'Tis grace, 'tis bounty, and it c. for praise V. 87

CALLED.
The legislature c. it May A Fable 9
He c. her Posy, with an amorous art A.T. 21
C. for his arms, and for his princely steed A.T. 124
So he c. him a bigot, a wrangler, a monk A.T. ii 3
'Tis c. a satire, and the world appears Ch. 515
Those seeds of science c. his A.B.C. Con. 14
His evidence, if he were c. by law Con. 125 [278
C. on a friend, drank tea, stepped home again Con.
When c. to address myself to you E. i 28
C. for a cloud to darken all their years E. ii 25
And were I c. to prove the assertion true E. iii 12
C. thee away from peaceable employ Ex. 534
Leaped out of nothing, c. by the Most High Ex. 639
Sighs for his exit, vulgarly c. death H. 90 [6
Thus, while gray evening lulled the wind and c. F.A.
Not kindred minds alone are c. to employ H. 738
They gentle c., and kind and soft J.P. 21
Of that which c. his ardour forth Mor. 44
That once we c. the pastoral house our own M.P.53
Did plants c. sensitive grow there?" P. 22
C. to these crystal streams, do ye turn off P.E. 265
C. to the temple of impure delight P.E. 584
Darkness, O queen! ne'er c. before Q.V. 35
Who comes when c., and at a word withdraws R.447
C. up from earth to heaven St. iii 30
If cushion might be c., what harder seemed T. i 55
I c. the low-roofed lodge the Peasant's nest T. i 227
Illusive of philosophy, so c. T. ii 505 [vi 1006
It shall not grieve me, then, that once, when c. T.
There dwelt a sage c. Discipline. His head T. ii 702
So I, designing other themes, and c. T. iii 11
Not as the prince in Shushan, when he c. T. iii 714
Shone brighter still, once c. to public view T. v 521
And c. the world to worship on the banks T. vi 681
'Tis c. a book, though but a single page) Tir. 122
That babblers, c. philosophers, devise Tir. 158
To see a band, c. patriot, for no cause T.T. 143
To hear it c. extravagance and waste T.T. 163
He may be c. to give up health and gain V. 63

CALLING.
A huge throat c. to the clouds for drink Y.O. 112

CALLOUS.
Obduracy takes place; c. and tough T.T. 458

CALM.
And make a c. of human life F. 134 [ii 39
And every moment's c., that soothes the breast E.
A c. succeeds—but Plenty, with her train Her. 63
But thou canst taste no c. delight M.B. 17
Their ruffled plumage c. refit Mrs. M— 46
The flock grew c. again, and I, the road N.A. 127
But warm, and bright, and c. as May P.T. 10
Conveyed her c. along Q.V. 68. [259
Come then, and thou shalt find thy votary c. T. iv
And c. descend to yours St. v 36 [391
Sweet converse, sipping c. the fragrant lymph T. iii
And finding in the c. of truth-tried love T. iii 56
How c. is my recess, and how the frost T. iv 308
But 'twas a transient c. A storm was near T. vi 544
Before a c., that rocks itself to rest T. vi 739 [77
C. and alternate storm, moisture and drought Y.O.

CALUMNY.
Blush, C.! and write upon his tomb H. 588

CALVES.
Cured of the golden c., their fathers' sin Ex. 215

CAM.
From school to C. or Isis, and thence home P.E. 369

CAMBRIAN.
But more discreet than he a C. ewe N.A. 106

CAME.

The morning c., when neighbour Hodge *A Fable* 24
She c.—she is gone—we have met *C.* 1
C., not expected in that humble guise *Ex.* 87
He brought thy land a blessing when he c. *Ex.* 484
The morning c., the chaise was brought *J.G.* 33
But soon c. down again *J.G.* 48
So down he c. ; for loss of time *J.G.* 53
When Betty screaming c. downstairs *J.G.* 59
Until he c. unto the Wash *J.G.* 135
I c. because your horse would come *J.G.* 173
Whence straight he c. with hat and wig *J.G.* 181
'Twas for your pleasure you c. here *J.G.* 199
To a slave-cultured island we c. *M.D.* 26
Thus many a sad to-morrow c. and went *M.P.* 42
And heedless whither, to that field I c. *N.A.* 32
On eager wing the spoiler c. *P.B.* 5
The leaves c. on not quite so fast *P.T.* 46
Yet glad she c. that night to prove *Q.V.* 29
When in c., housewifely inclined *R.C.* 49
Then c. the maid, and it was closed *R.C.* 58
The evening c., the sun descended *R.C.* 65
And puss c. into mind no more *R.C.* 71
Nor plague nor famine c. *St.* i 10   [*T.* 155
Who spanned her waist, and who where'er he c.
Ere yet it c., the traveller urged his steed *T.* 244
Celestial, though they knew not whence it c. *T.* 532
Marshalling all his terrors as he c. *T.* 547   [39
Now c. the cane from India, smooth and bright *T.* i
Spawned in the muddy beds of Nile, c. forth *T.* ii 827
That His most holy book, from whom it c. *T.* vi 650
In front of these c. Addison.   In him *T.T.* 642
And looks as if he c. to beg *Y.D.* 31

CAMPAIGN.
O'erhung the c. ; and the numerous flock *Y.O.* 53

CANAAN'S.
Let Egypt's plagues, and C.'s woes proclaim *Ex.* 169

CANCEL.
Lost innocence, or c. follies past *T.* iii 678

CANDID.
Clean, c., and witty—Thelypthora dies *A.T.* iv 2
C. and just, with no false aim in view *Ex.* 648
C., and generous, and just *F.* 19
C. and learned, dispassionate and free *P.E.* 453
We are become so c. and so fair *T.* iii 93

CANDIDATES.
That c. for such a prize should feel *Tir.* 376

CANDIDLY.
Or c. confess yourself a dunce *T.T.* 571

CANDLE.
And useless as a c. in a skull *Con.* 780

CANDLELIGHT.
By daylight or c.—eyes should be shut *A.C.* 32

CANDOUR.
Their thirst of knowledge, and their c. too! *T.* ii 544

CANE.
Has God then given its sweetness to the c. *Ch.* 190
With c. extended far, I sought *D.W.* 17
Dangling his c. about, and taking snuff *H.* 27
Supple and flexible as Indian c. *H.* 602
For the sweets your c. affords *N.C.* 24   [39
Now came the c. from India, smooth and bright *T.* i

CANKERED.
The c. spoil corrodes the pining state *Ch.* 63
But being c. now, and half worn out *P.E.* 393

CANT. [289
And tongue accomplished in the fulsome c. *T.* vi

CANTING.
C. and whining out all day the word *Con.* 577
Sometimes a c. hypocrite is found *T.* 233

CANVASS.
From her the c. borrows light and shade *Ch.* 107
Heaven speed the c., gallantly unfurled *Ch.* 123
Has dropped her anchor, and her c. furled *Ch.* 443
A trick upon the c., pointed flame *Con.* 782
The marble breathes, the c. glows *Miss* — 83
To teach the c. innocent deceit *R.* 797
Spreads all his c., every sinew plies *T.* 5.
In shirt of hair, and weeds of c. dressed *T.* 81
With all his c. set, and inexpert *T.* ii 486
Take half thy c. in *Tran H.* 36

CAP.
To take his honour's orders, c. in hand *Con.* 416
This c., that so stately appears *Gr.* 1
This c. to my cousin I owe *Gr.* 5
Seems what it is, a c. and bell for fools *T.* 368
His c. well-lined with logic not his own *T.* ii 737
The tasselled c. and the spruce band a jest *T.* ii 749

CAPABLE.
Born c. indeed of heavenly truth *H.* 231
Brutes c. would tell you 'tis a lie *P.E.* 261
His nature, and though c. of arts *T.* i 576
Cultured and c. of sober thought *T.* iii 324
All that are c. of pleasure pleased *T.* vi 345
But all are c. of living well *Tir.* 510

CAPACIOUS.
But overcharges her c. hand *Ch.* 100
The treasured sweets of the c. plan *Ch.* 323
Than a c. reservoir of means *T.* ii 201

CAPACITY.
By our c. of grace divine *T.* vi 602

CAPER.
Than c. in the morris-dance of verse *T.T.* 519

CAPITAL.
The fairest c. of all the world *T.* i 698
On pleasure, haunt the c., and thus *T.* iv 590

CAPPED.
In scarlet mantle warm, and velvet c. *M.P.* 51

CAPRICE.
Wherever chance, c., or fancy guide *Con.* 794
Build by whatever plan, c. decrees *H.* 614
Or aught He does, is governed by c. *T.* 346
And by c. as multiplied as his *T.* ii 597
And sweating in his service; his c. *T.* v 274

CAPRICIOUS.
C. Taste itself can crave no more *Ch.* 101
The sycamore, c. in attire *T.* i. 318
C., in which fancy seeks in vain *T.* v 120

CAPTAIN.
Their God their c., lawgiver, and king *Ex.* 190
A trainband c. eke was he *J.G.* 3
The stout tall c., whose superior size *Tir.* 222
Part of the c. precious store *Tran.* iv 5

CAPTIOUS.
And c. cavil and complaint subside *H.* 144
A c. question, sir (and yours is one) *Tir.* 903

CAPTIVATE.
To c. the tempting prey *E.* iv 54
And while they c., inform the mind *H.* 759

CAPTIVATING.
When *c*. lusts have lost their power *H.* 216

CAPTIVE.
A *c*. bird into the boundless sky *Ch.* 269
Captivity led *c*., rose to claim *Ch.* 585
Her princes *c*., and her treasures spoiled *Ex.* 62

CAPTIVITY.
C. led captive, rose to claim *Ch.* 585

CAR.
Sounds forth the signal, as she mounts the *c. H.* 647
A sliding *c*., indebted to no wheels *T.* iv 126 [vi 740
For He, whose *c*. the winds are, and the clouds *T.*
Some shout him, and some hang upon his *c. T.* vi 698

CARAVANS.
In coaches, chaises, *c*., and hoys *R.* 521

CARCASS.
That owns a *c*., and not quake for fear? *N.A.* 100
Like an unburied *c*. tricked with flowers *T.* vi 992

CARD.
The gamester may have cast his *c*. away *Con.* 813
A snug and friendly game at *c. L.W.* 28
As inoffensive, what offence in *c*.? *P.E.* 149
C. with what rapture, and the polished die *P.E.* 171
The paralytic, who can hold her *c. T.* i 472   [207
C. were superfluous here, with all the tricks *T.* iv
Or with his pen, save when he scrawls a *c. T.* ii 384
Of *c*. devoted Time, and night by night *T.* iv 229
Paint *c*. and dolls, and every idle thing *T.* iv 241

CARD-PLAYING.
Or hadst thou a polite, *c*. wife *Tir.* 743

CARE.
His time, his talents, and his ceaseless *c. A.T.* 15
The fears and hopes of a commercial *c. Ch.* 279
Wherever found (and all men need thy *c*.) *Ch.* 47
And make colloquial happiness your *c. Con.* 82
The path of narrative with *c*. pursue *Con.* 217
When, 'scaped from literary *c. D.W.* 3
Are part of a Jehovah's *c. E.* i 58
Who, nursed with tender *c. Ep.* ii 6
From which no *c*. can save *Ep.* ii 42
If God Himself be not beneath her *c. Ex.* 603
Boys *c*. but little whom they trust *F.* 20
Your unparticipated *c. F.* 125
A scene of fancied bliss and heartfelt *c. H.* 5
Not that his hours devoted all to *c. H.* 57
His offspring hold in his paternal *c. H.* 140
Their mind a wilderness through want of *c. H.* 233
The common *c*. that waits on all beside *H.* 539
Hard task! for one who lately knew no *c. H.* 696
Without a soil to invite the tiller's *c. Her.* 27
Yet bless the guardian *c*. that kept *M.* 27
I *c*. not whether east or north *M.B.* 21
Extend no *c*. beyond themselves *Miss* — 63
Nor ancient, will be so, preserved with *c. P.E.* 400
Quavering and semiquavering *c*. away *P.E.* 127
The balm of *c*., Elysium of the mind *P.E.* 180
Mortals whose pleasures are their only *c. P.E.* 289
None but an author knows an author's *c. P.E.* 516
For threescore years employed with ceaseless *c. R.* 37
Thine, and upheld by thy paternal *c. R.* 89
With *c*. collect what in their eyes excels *R.* 153
Gives Melancholy up to Nature's *c. R.* 281
As ever recompensed the peasant's *c. R.* 332
Escaped from office and its constant *c. R.* 408
Business or vain amusement, *c*. or mirth *R.* 647
To learned *c*. or philosophic toil *R.* 662
The weight of subjects worthiest of her *c. R.* 678
She left the *c*. of life behind *R.C.* 47
And, doubtful what, with prudent *c. R.C.* 85
But fixed, unalterable *c. S.* 9   [iii 83
And taught the unblemished to preserve with *c. T.*
Ploughs up the roots of a believer's *c. T.* 460
Each province of her heart her equal *c. T.* i 707
Were precious, and inculcated with *c. T.* ii 701
Or if the garden with its many *c. T.* iii 397
Her want of *c*., screening and keeping warm *T.*iii 440
And which no *c*. can obviate. It were long *T.* iii 558
Unsung, and many *c*. are yet behind *T.* iii 606
Not less dispersed by daylight and its *c. T.* iv 138
Thy days roll on exempt from household *c. T.* iv 366
Thine helpless charge, dependent on thy *c. T.* iv 369
With all the thrift they thrive not all the *c. T.* iv 399
That instant he becomes the serjeant's *c. T.* iv 631
He severs it away; no needless *c. T.* v 38
Clean riddance quickly made, one only *c. T.* v 70
Are yet his *c*., and have an interest all *T.* vi 448
Renowned in ancient song; not vexed with *c. T.*vi 997
Though that of all most worthy of his *c. T.* 426
And lay it at its ease with gentle *c. T.* ii 449   [773
Through want of *c*.; or her whose winking eye *T.* ii
And slight the hovel as beneath her *c. T.* ii 459
Beneath his *c*., a thriving vigorous plant *T.* ii 714
The worth of what she mimics with such *c. T.* iii 103
Fearless, and wrapt away from all his *c. T.* iii 311
Whom ten long years' experience of my *c. T.*iii 338
Grudge not the cost. Ye little know the *c. T.* iii 547
And more laborious; *c*. on which depends *T.* iii 607
And constant occupation without *c. T.* iii 693
With sweet oblivion of the *c*. of day *T.* iv 250
Her train and her umbrella all her *c. T.* iv 552
So manifold in *c*., whose every day *T.* v 769   [567
See that your polished arms be primed with *c. T.*iv
Of unremitted vigilance and *c. T.* vi 209   [*T.* v 202
Peace was awhile their *c*.; they ploughed and sowed
Still sacred, and preserves with pious *c. T.* vi 690
A mother's lecture and a nurse's *c. Tir.* 196
Of classic food begins to be his *c. Tir.* 319   [193
Whose only *c*., might truth presume to speak *Tir.*
What dream they of, that, with so little *c. Tir.* 358
May raise such fruits as shall reward his *c. Tir.* 771
Yet make their progeny their dearest *c. Tir.* 800
And trust for safety to a stranger's *c. Tir.* 852
That then, in recompense of all thy *c. Tir.* 879
Our parents yet exert a prudent *c. Tir.* 115   [261
I blame not those who, with what *c*. they can *Tir.*
While colts and puppies cost us so much *c*.? *Tir.* 295
Though there, in spite of all that *c*. can do *Tir.* 521
Dismiss their *c*. when they dismiss their flock *Tir.* 624
Too busy to intend a meaner *c. Tir.* 660
In all good faculties beneath his *c. Tir.* 709
Whom *c*. and cool deliberation suit *Tir.* 781
To nurse with tender *c*. the thriving Arts *T.T.* 69
Leave kingly backs to cope with kingly *c. T.T.* 174
His fostering power, and tutelary *c. T.T.* 257
Ye patriots, guard it with a miser's *c. T.T.* 335
Her sovereign's tutelary *c.* 1789, 39

CAREER.
Makes Justice still the guide of his *c. Ex.* 715
View him at Paris in his last *c. T.* 311
Fruitful and young as in their first *c.*? *Tir.* 42
" Stop, while ye may; suspend your mad *c. T.T.* 435
Short his *c*., indeed, but ably run *T.T.* 671

CAREFUL.
Now mistress Gilpin (*c*. soul!) *J.G.* 65
Be *c*. where he trod *Tran.* i 16

CAREFULLY.
Divine Communion, *c*. enjoyed *R.* 747

CARELESS.
Is rather c. of her sister's fame *Ch.* 454
While thousands, c. of the damning sin *Ex.* 388
Take, if ye can, ye c. and supine *P.E.* 9
Yet c. what he brings, his one concern *T.* iv 9
The roving eye misleads the c. heart *R.* 126
Or shoot the c. with a surer aim *R.* 218
Preserve the church! and lay not c. hands *T.* ii 393
C. of their Creator. And that low *T.* v 587
Too c. often, as our years proceed *Tir.* 113
(Apprised that he is such) a c. boy *Tir.* 906
C. of all the anxiety he feels *T.T.* 145
Or if, when ridden with a c. rein *T.T.* 306
They cry aloud in every c. ear *T.T.* 434
He struck the lyre in such a c. mood *T.T.* 686
Cold in his cause, and c. of his woes *V.* 4

CARELESSLY.
C. nods and sleeps upon the brink *Ex.* 99
With eager step, and c. arrayed *R.* 187

CARGOES.
For merchants rich in c. of despair *Ch.* 138

CARING.
Not knowing, and too oft not c., why *Tir.* 7 4

CARNIVOROUS.
Thanks for thy food. C., through sin *T.* vi 457

CAROLS.
With which he shouts and c., "Vive le Roy!" *T.T.* 243

CAROUSING.
Sit long and late at the c. board? *T.* 50

CARP.
Nor c. at every flaw you may discern *Con.* 92

CARPET.
A Turkey c. was his lawn *Ep.* ii 21
These c., so soft to the foot *Gr.* 17

CARRIAGE.
The c. bowls along and all are pleased *P.E.* 438
To sleep within the c. more secure *T.* i 92
To slumber in the c. more secure *T.* i 99
If the gilt c., and the pampered steed *T.T.* 133

CARRIED.
The good he scorned, all c. to account" *T.* 546

CARRIES.
"He c. weight!" "He rides a race!" *J.G.* 115
C. her Bible tucked beneath his arm *T.* 147

CORROSION.
By ceaseless sharp c. *F.* 63

CARROT.
Sliced c. pleased him well *Ep.* ii 2

CARRY.
And c., in contusions of his skull *Con.* 201
But souls that c. on a blest exchange *Con.* 693
But still he seemed to c. weight *J.G.* 129
This lesson seems to c. *P.T.* 63
To c. me, to fan me while I sleep *T.* ii 30
They have their weight to c., subjects theirs *T.T.* 175
To c. nature lengths unknown before *T.T.* 558

CARVE.
Weigh sunbeams, c. a fly, or spit a flea *Ch.* 354
To c. his rustic name upon a tree *R.* 400
He from the stack c. out the accustomed load *T.* v 33
Should c. himself a wife in gingerbread *T.T.* 555

CARVED.
Skillet, and old c. chest, from public sale *T.* iv 402
The very name we c. subsisting still *Tir.* 301

CARVERS.
By rural c., who with knives deface *T.* i 281

CARVING.
The c. and the gilding *F.* 168

CASCADES.
For clumps, and lawns, and temples and c. *H.* 247
Now murmuring soft, now roaring in c. *T.* iii 779

CASE.
('Tis a c. that has happened, and may do again) *A.C.* 18
Its semblance in another's c. *Cast.* 60
Makes contradiction such a hopeless c. *Con.* 60
And though self-idolized in every c. *Con.* 157
I give him over as a desperate c. *Con.* 406
'Tis time, however, if the c. stands thus *Con.* 847
To comprehend the c. *D.W.* 24
Or how do justice in this c.? *E.* 72
In England's c. to move the Muse to tears? *Ex.* 2
In England's c. to move the Muse to tears? *Ex.* 31
Are observations on the c. *F.* 160
Could he with reason murmur at his c. *H.* 316
Make works a vain ingredient in the c. *H.* 360
Contrived to suit frail nature's crazy c. *H.* 604
Be in a hungry c." *J.G.* 192
Respecting in each other's c. *N.G.* 33 [246
Now drenched throughout, and hopeless of his c *T.*
Are all enchantments in a c. like thine *R.* 261
And blunts his pointed fury; in its c. *T.* vi 193
Free man and slave then, if the c. be such *T.T.* 254

CASED.
That he was c. in such enchanted steel *A.T.* 183

CASEMENTS.
What are the c. lined with creeping herbs *T.* iv 762

CASH.
To tease for c., and quarrel with all day *P.E.* 372

CASHIERED.
By selfish views, thus censured and c. *Tir.* 496

CASK.
The c., the coop, the floated cord *Cast.* 27
An oracle within an empty c. *Con.* 298
Of all this riot and ten thousand c. *T.* iv 505

CASKETS.
Kept snug in c. of close-hammered steel *R.* 308

CASSIOPËIA.
Fair C. sat *Gr.* 16

CASSOCKED.
A c. huntsman, and a fiddling priest! *P.E.* 111

CAST.
On every mind some mighty spell she c. *A.T.* 37
And snorts aloud to c. the mist aside *A.T.* 164
The gamester may have c. his cards away *Con.* 813
Ah! be not sad, although thy lot be c. *E.* ii 41
" And thus o'er all a lustre c. *E.* iv 77
Have burst the bands, and c. the yoke away *Ex.* 465
And truth alone, where'er my life be c. *Ex.* 732
Who first misuse, then c. their toys away *H.* 128
Is a pearl c., completely c., away *H.* 259 [301
(Oh c. them from thee!) are weeds, arrant weeds *H.*
The other was of gentler c. *J.P.* 13
And should my future lot be c. *M.* 49
An oyster c. upon the shore *P.* 1
Go, c. your orders at your Bishop's feet *P.E.* 120

Of manners rough, and coarse athletic c. *P.E.* 187
Luxury gives the mind a childish c. *R.* 703
Nature perhaps herself had c. her *R.C.* 8
And mercy c. away *St.* vi 40
And c. his filthy raiment at them all *T.* 235
I c. them at thy feet—my only plea *T.* 583
Strange! that a creature rational, and c. *T.* i 574
Then c. them, closely bundled, every brat *T.* ii 673
His patrimonial timber c. its leaf *T.* iii 752
For ere the beech and elm have c. their leaf *T.* iii 466
Shakes her encumbered lap, and c. them out *T.* iv 499
Can wind around him, but he c. it off *T.* v 736
Insulted and traduced, are c. aside *T.* vi 879
That we are bound to c. the minds of youth *Tir.* 105
New situations give a different c. *Tir.* 440
Thence the prevailing manners take their c. *Tir.* 913
And move the lips of poets c. in lead *T.T.* 203
Slaves fight for what were better c. away *T.T.* 282
God's curse can c. away ten thousand sail! *T.T.* 467
Verse in the finest mould of fancy c. *T.T.* 618
And, like his Lordship, c. thy friend away *V.* 48

CASTALIAN.
Has flowed from lips wet with *C.* dews *T.* iii 251

CASTING.
Though common sense, allowed a c. voice *Con.* 663

CASTLE.
And seeing the old c. of the state *T.* v 525

CASTRO.
Airy del *C.* was as bold a knight *A.T.* 1

CAT.
And set up his back, and clawed like a c. *A.T.* ii 5
A poet's c., sedate and grave *R.C.* 1
C. also feel, as well as we *R.C.* 23
"Was ever c. attended thus? *R.C.* 54
Forth skipped the c., but now replete *R.C.* 99
No c. had leave to dwell *T.B.* 21

CATALOGUE.
With glass at eye, and c. in hand *T.* vi 288

CATARACTS.
Ne'er roughened by those c. and breaks *M.P.* 66
C. of declamation thunder here *T.* iv 73

CATARRH. [392
And coughs, and rheums, and phthisic, and c. *Con.*

CATCH.
Could c. the sound no more *Cast.* 46
He c. all improvements in his flight *Ch.* 115
Yes—you may c. him tripping, if you can *Con.* 120
To c. the triflers of the time *E.* i 20
C. from each other a contagious spot *Ex.* 105
What web too weak to c. a modern brain? *Ex.* 629
And c. in its progress a sensible glow *F.M.* 20
To c. the wandering notice of mankind *H.* 137
How glad they c. the largess of the skies *N.A.* 62
At such a sight to c. the poet's flame *R.* 85
From all he sees he c. new delight *R.* 189
That I may c. a fire but rarely known *R.* 205
Nor gales that c. the scent of blooming groves *R.* 337
All c. the frenzy, downward from her Grace *T.* ii 647
I cannot analyse the air, nor c. *T.* iii 214
Must prompt him, and admonish how to c. *T.* iii 507
Some, more aspiring, c. the neighbour shrub *T.* iii 665
Where, diligent to c. the first faint gleam *T.* v 59
From distant mountains c. the flying joy *T.* vi 795
Traps to c. youth are most abundant too *Tir.* 522
Just c. at the sound *Tran.* iv 21

To c. renown by ruining mankind *T.T.* 60
But that they c. at popular applause *T.T.* 144
An eye like his to c. the distant goal *T.T.* 710

CATCHING.
That fire is c. if you draw too near *Con.* 654
Would run most dreadful risk of c. cold *E.* iii 59
By c. at his rein *J.G.* 224
In c. smoke and feeding upon air *R.* 38
C. its ardour as I mused along *R.* 376

CATCHPOLE-CLAWS.
And gibbeted, as fast as c. *T.* ii 684

CATERER.
Grand c. and dry nurse of the church! *T.* ii 371

CATECHISE.
And c. it well; apply thy glass *T.* iii 203

CATERPILLARS.
Like c., dangling under trees *Tir.* 591

CATGUT.
With wire and c. he concludes the day *P.E.* 126

CATHARINA.
C. has fled like a dream *C.* 5
C., Maria, and I *C.* 10
C., did nothing impede *C.* 27
C. alone can rejoice *C.* 42

CATHARTIC.
How an emetic or c. sped *Con.* 316

CATHEDRALS.
Discover huge c. built with stone *P.E.* 381

CATTLE.
Of spacious meads with c. sprinkled o'er *T.* i 164
Attends him; drives his c. to a march *T.* iv 647
The c. mourn in corners, where the fence *T.* v 27
Thenceforth they are his c.: drudges born *T.* v 272
And his own c. must suffice him soon *T.* vi 710

CAUGHT.
Worms may be c. by either head or tail *Ch.* 528
But still the prize, though nearly c. *D.W.* 19
For c. and caged, and starved to death *G.* 10
But soon my ear c. the glad news *M.D.* 43 [134
A courteous knighthood, c. the generous flame *A.T.*
C. in a delicate, soft, silken net *P.E.* 312
But if you pass the threshold you are c. *P.E.* 588
I know not where she c. the trick *R.C.* 7
Ocean has c. the frenzy, and upwrought *T.* ii 111
His horse, as he had c. his master's mood *T.* vi 549
C. from the deeds of men of ancient fame *Tir.* 645
Hast c. the cold distemper of the day *V.* 47

CAUSE.
So Tongue was the lawyer, and argued the c. *A.C.* 5
It has always been reckoned a just c. of strife *A.T.* ii 9
Man to the centre of the common c. *Ch.* 328
The c. of Virtue could not be his view *Ch.* 542
Who prostitute it in the c. of vice *Con.* 27
The c. is plain, and not to be denied *Con.* 159
And hazard life for any or no c. *Con.* 184
The c. perhaps inquiry may descry *Con.* 363
But fear to call a more important c. *Con.* 397
Of virtue, and religion's glorious c. *Con.* 686
And constituted guardians of his c. *Ex.* 200
He pours contempt on them, and on their c. *Ex.* 329
In such a c. they could not dare to fear *Ex.* 621
If lawyer, loud whatever c. he plead *H.* 201
This only can; for this plain c. expressed *H.* 340
If thus the important c. is to be tried *H.* 373

CAUSE—CEASING

Have justly doomed, for some atrocious *c*. *H*. 713
Who write in blood the merits of your *c*. *Her*. 42
The nymphs referred the *c*. *J.P.* 18
Must *c*. him shame or discontent *Mor*. 46
For such a *c*., to feel the slightest fear *N.A.* 90
Sounds are but sounds, and till the *c*. appear *N.A.* 119
Such *c*. of terror in an empty sound *N.A.* 130
Your *c*. before a bar you little dread *P.E.* 198
Strange the recital! from whatever *c*. *P.E.* 401
Exert their influence, and advance their *c*. *P.E.* 463
Ye ladies! (for indifferent in your *c*. *P.E.* 510
Be flowery, and he see no *c*. of fear *P.E.* 546
Thus Conscience pleads her *c*. within the breast *R*. 15
For such a *c*. the Poet seeks the shade *R*. 188
Shall own itself a stammerer in that *c*. *R*. 413
C. to provide for a great future day *R*. 652
The sprightly morn her *c*. renewed *R.C.* 69
The *c*. is Conscience;—Conscience oft *St*. v 21
Who judged the Pharisee? What odious *c*. *T*. 44
Ye have much *c*. for envy—but not all *T*. 376
No mean advantage from a kindred *c*. *T*. i 387
And mar the face of Beauty, when no *c*. *T*. i 458
But far beyond the rest, and with most *c*. *T*. i 632
To enforce the wrong, for such a worthy *c*. *T*. ii 14
And principles; of *c*., how they work *T*. ii 191
Thou fool! Will thy discovery of the *c*. *T*. ii 196
And learn, though late, the genuine *c*. of all *T*. ii 205
Of her magnificent and awful *c*.? *T*. ii 232
Support, and ornament of Virtue's *c*. *T*. ii 336
That he is honest in the sacred *c*. *T*. ii 375
No: he was serious in a serious *c*. *T*. ii 476
This does Profusion, and the accursed *c*. *T*. ii 697
Of such deep mischief has itself a *c*. *T*. ii 698
Profusion breeds them; and the *c*. itself *T*. ii 820
Views him in all; ascribes to the grand *c*. *T*. iii 226
From instrumental *c*. proud to draw *T*. iii 238
Our British Themis gloried with just *c*. *T*. iii 257
By *c*. not to be divulged in vain *T*. iii 371
The *c*. of piety, and sacred truth *T*. iii 707
Her interests, or that gives her sacred *c*. *T*. iii 792
Resistless in so bad a *c*., but lame *T*. iv 439 [511
Her *c*. demands the assistance of your throats *T*. iv
Lamented change! to which full many a *c*. *T*. iv 576
A noble *c*., which none who bears a spark *T*. iv 614
Of those that bare them in whatever *c*. *T*. iv 620
Babes in the *c*. of freedom, and should fear *T*. v 291
To serve him nobly in the common *c*. *T*. v 344
And pity for her loss. But that's a *c*. *T*. v 370
No narrow bounds; her *c*. engages him *T*. v 395
Wherever pleaded! 'Tis the *c*. of man *T*. v 396
And lack of knowledge, and with *c*. enough *T*. v 501
Can he be strenuous in his country's *c*. *T*. v 506
Takes part with Appetite, and pleads the *c*. *T*. v 630
Spare not in such a *c*. Spend all the powers *T*. v 676
Patriots have toiled, and in their country's *c*. *T*. v 704
Made such by thee, we love thee for that *c*. *T*. v 881
Is *c*. of half the poverty we feel *T*. vi 52
Familiar with the effect we slight the *c*. *T*. vi 121
And under pressure of some conscious *c*.? *T*. vi 220
Whose *c*. is God. He feeds the secret fire *T*. vi 224
And fear as yet was not, nor *c*. for fear *T*. vi 367
Or his base gluttony, are *c*. good *T*. vi 388
Does law, so jealous in the *c*. of man *T*. vi 432
To interfere though in so just a *c*. *T*. vi 473
What *c*. move us, knowing as we must *Tir*. 292
And you are staunch indeed in learning's *c*. *Tir*. 492
Much zeal in virtue's *c*. all teachers boast *Tir*. 517
Great *c*. occurs to save him from a band *Tir*. 696
From education, as the leading *c*. *Tir*. 911
And will prevail or perish in her *c*. *T.T.* 18 [204
The *c*., though worth the search, may yet elude *T.T.*
To see a band, called patriot, for no *c*. *T.T.* 143
Fires him at once in Freedom's glorious *c*. *T.T.* 229
The noblest *c*. mankind can have at stake *T.T.* 285
Sing where you please, in such a *c*. I grant *T.T.* 298
Her sacred *c*., but trembled when he rose *T.T.* 351
When profanation of the sacred *c*. *T.T.* 426
Unchangeably connected with its *c*.) *T.T.* 443
Cold in his *c*., and careless of his woes *V*. 4
But worn by frequent impulse, to the *c*. *Y.O.* 84

CAUSELESS.

In *c*. feuds and bickerings of their own *Ex*. 537
C., and daubed with undiscerning praise *T*. v 360

CAUTION.

Admonished, scorn the *c*. and the friend *E*. ii 17
A decent *c*. and reserve at least *H*. 404
With *c*. and good heed *J.G.* 80
Counsel and *c*. from a voice like mine *P.E.* 10
With *c*. taste the sweet Circean cup *P.E.* 580
And while experience *c*. us in vain *R*. 755
Of all their *c*. in thy gentlest gales *T*. ii 484
Prayer to the winds, and *c*. to the waves *Tir*. 183
Except of *c*. and of common sense *Tir*. 258

CAUTIOUS.

Till I, with slow and *c*. hand *F.B.* 29
My friends! be *c*. how ye treat *P.T.* 23
Descending now (but *c*., lest too fast) *T*. i 266
C. he pinches from the second stalk *T*. iii 527

CAVES.

That shoot into your darkest *c*. the day *H*. 493
To distant *c*. the lonely wanderer flies *R*. 769
The wilderness is theirs with all its *c*.'s *T*. vi 401
And Time hath made thee what thou art—a *c*. *Y.O.* 51

CAVERN.

Each creek and *c*. of the dangerous shore *R*. 152
And fiery *c*., roars beneath his feet *T*. ii 90

CAVIL.

And captious *c*. and complaint subside *H*. 144
And *c*. at with ease, but none refute *T*. 360

CAVITY.

Within that *c*. aloft *A Tale* 37

CAW.

And says—what says he?—*C. Tran*. ii 30

CAWING.

But *c*. rooks, and kites that swim sublime *T*. 203

CEASE.

But still a soul thus touched can never *c*. *Ch*. 420
Must *c*. for ever when the poor shall *c*. *Ch*. 452
Relenting forms would lose their power or *c*. *Ch*. 608
And slaying man would *c*. to be an art *Ch*. 619
The guide to pleasures which can never *c*. *S*. ii 14
Go, bid the winter *c*. to chill the year *T*. 399
And comforts *c*. Dress drains our cellar dry *T*. ii 614

CEASED.

Nor *c*. till, ever anxious to redress *T.T.* 632

CEASELESS.

His time, his talents, and his *c*. care *A.T.* 15
By *c*. sharp corrosion *F*. 63
For threescore years employed with *c*. care *R*. 37
To *c*. service by a *c*. force *T*. vi 219
By *c*. action all that is subsists *T*. i 367
The hills and valleys with their *c*. songs *T*. v 78

CEASING.

A bosom heaved with never *c*. sighs *T*. i 552
Descending, and with never *c*. lapse *T*. iv 327

CEDARS.
For *c.* famed, fair Lebanon supplied *A.T.* 143
The *c.* and the hyssop on the wall *H.* 287

CEILING.
And gild our chamber *c.* as they pass *T.* ii 649
The shadow to the *c.*, there by fits *T.* iv 275

CELEBRATE.
The man we *c.* must find a tomb *T.* iii 264
That poets *c.*; those golden times *T.* iv 514
Rejoice in him, and *c.* his sway *T.* v 326

CELESTIAL.
Pregnant with *c.* fire *B.* 34
The soul can mix with the *c.* bands *Con.* 717
And lend *c.* fire *Miss* — 82
C., though they knew not whence it came *T.* 532
Misled by custom, strain *c.* themes *T.* ii 438

CELL.
Wast thou in monkish *c.* and nunneries found *Ch.* 43
Near barren rocks, in palaces, or *c. R.* 540
With easy force it opens all the *c. T.* vi 11

CELLAR. [614
And comforts cease. Dress drains our *c.* dry *T.* ii
From tippling benches, *c.*, stalls, and styes *T.* vi 695

CEMENT.
Were soon conjoined; nor other *c.* asked *T.* v 147

CEMENTED.
That has *c.* us in one *E.* i 102

CENSOR.
Through reverence of the *c.* of thy son *Tir.* 734
The weekly *c.* of a laughing town *V.* 38

CENSORIOUS.
C., and her every word a wasp *T.* 160

CENSURE.
And all her *c.* of the work of grace *Con.* 784 [182
Lest fops should *c.* us, and fools should sneer *Con.*
But public *c.* speaks a public foe *Ex.* 436
By useless *c.*, whom we cannot mend *H.* 273
These move the *c.* and illiberal grin *H.* 744
His *c.* reached them as he dealt it *P.* 65
Could give advice, could *c.*, or commend *R.* 291
Religion does not *c.* or exclude *R.* 783
But truce with *c.* Roving as I rove *T.* iv 232
But *c.* profits little: vain the attempt *T.* iv 500
Seems to imply a *c.* on the rest *T.T.* 92
Thus free from *c.*, overawed by fear *T.T.* 115
And *c.* oft as useless. Stillest streams *T.* vi 929

CENSURED.
By selfish views, thus *c.* and cashiered *Tir.* 496
But to be rudely *c.* when they fail *T.T.* 158

CENTERING.
C. at last in having none at all *Con.* 134
There *c.* in a focus round and neat *Con.* 239
And *c.* all authority in modes *T.* i 745

CENTRE.
From the *c.* all round to the sea *A.S.* 3
Man to the *c.* of the common cause *Ch.* 328
From the same *c.* of enlightening grace *Ch.* 364
Another's good;—theirs *c.* in their own *Ch.* 450
The *c.* of a glowing heart *E.* i 14
Pierced to the very *c.* of the realm *Ex.* 576
What treasures *c.*, what delights, in thee *H.* 174
To exchange the *c.* of a thousand trades *H.* 246
Ethelred's house, the *c.* of six ways *H.* 302

The *c.* of delights he may not taste? *P.E.* 230
Discordant motives in one *c.* meet *R.* 173
Resistless from the *c.* he should seek *T.* v 590
Thou art the source and *c.* of all minds *T.* v 896
The mulberry-tree stood *c.* of the dance *T.* vi 686
Subsist and *c.* in one point—a friend *Tir.* 390

CENTURY.
Somebody proved it, *c.* ago *P.E.* 501
Then twig; then sapling; and, as *c.* rolled *Y.O.* 62
Slow after *c.*, a giant bulk *Y.O.* 63

CEREMONY.
Made half their maids, sans *c.* wives *A.T.* 128
Then *C.* leads her bigots forth *Ex.* 115

CEREMONIAL.
And solemn *c.* of the day *T.* vi 680

CERTAIN.
C. invisibles as shrewd as he *Con.* 738
That *c.* feasts are instituted now *Con.* 823

CERULEAN.
It stands, like the *c.* arch we see *T.* 26

CHAFED.
C. him, and brought dull nature to a glow *P.E.* 408

CHAFF. [Ex. 303
That yields them *c.* and dust, and nothing more
Its patient drudges with dry *c.* and weeds *R.* 48
Full on the destined ear. Wide flies the *c. T.* i 359

CHAFFINCH.
A *c.* and his mate *A Tale* 12

CHAIN.
And snap the *c.* the moment when you may *Ch.* 168
Would heal his heart, and melt his *c* away *Ch.* 229
Sin forged, and Ignorance made fast, the *c.* 237
C. up the wolves and tigers of mankind *Ch.* 287
Long time Assyria bound them in her *c. Ex.* 73
That ever dragged a *c.*, or tugged an oar *Ex.* 527
In *c.* of error our accomplished minds *H.* 484
She sung of the slave's broken *c. M.D.* 19
Ere our necks received the *c. N.C.* 42
Girt with a *c.* he cannot wish to break *R.* 243
Not to be led in *c.*, but to subdue *R.* 266
Galled by affliction's heavy *c. St.* v 11
The freeborn Christian has no *c.* to prove *T.* 187
Or, if a *c.*, the golden one of love *T.* 188
C. him, and tasks him, and exacts his sweat *T.* ii 23
So many maniacs dancing in their *c. T.* ii 663
Fast bound in *c.* of silence, which the fair *T.* iv 53
You *c.* and bondage for a tyrant's sake *T.* v 352
In forging *c.* for us, themselves were free *T.* v 392
C. nowhere patiently, and *c.* at home *T.* v. 478
C. are the portion of revolted man *T.* v 581
And all are slaves beside. There's not a *c. T.* v 734
His spirit takes, unconscious of a *c. T.* v 776
A Britain's scorn of arbitrary *c.? T.T.* 201 [283
The *c.* that binds them, and a tyrant's sway *T.T.*
Tyranny sends the *c.* that must abridge *T.T.* 474

CHAINED.
Which thousands once fast *c.* to quit no more *R.* 2
C. to the routs that she frequents for life *Tir.* 744

CHAIR.
I twirl my thumbs, fall back into my *c. Con.* 115
This wheel-footed studying *c. Gr.* 9.
Produce them—take a *c.*—now draw a saint *T.* 172
And shakes the sceptic in the scorner's *c. T.* 472

CHAIR—CHAPEL

The new machine, and it became a *C. T.* i 43
But restless was the *C.*; the back erect *T.* i 44
Convenience next suggested Elbow *C. T.* i 87

CHAISE.
All in a *c.* and pair *J.G.* 12
Will fill the *c.*; so you must ride *J.G.* 15
The morning came, the *c.* was brought *J.G.* 33
So three doors off the *c.* was stayed *J.G.* 37 [374
And every post, and where the *c.* broke down *P.E.*
'Tis done—he steps into the welcome *c. R.* 391
In coaches, *c.*, caravans, and hoys *R.* 521
Close packed and smiling, in a *c.* and one *T.* i 80
His skill in coachmanship, or driving *c. Tir.* 326

CHALKY.
And fling their foam against thy *c.* shore *Ex.* 273
The *c.* ring, and knuckle down at taw *Tir.* 307

CHALLENGER.
The impious *c.* of power divine *T.* vi 546

CHALLENGING.
C. human scrutiny, and proved *T.* v. 868

CHAMBER.
As private as the *c.* where they slept *Ex.* 144
Far other paintings grace the *c.* now *H.* 262
Thy nightly visits to my *c.* made *M.P.* 58
And gild our *c.* ceilings as they pass *T.* ii 649
Nor palaces, nor even *c.*, 'scaped *T.* ii 831
Through all the heart's dark *c.*, and reveal *T.* iii 241
The *c.* or refectory, may die *T.* vi. 572
But, if thou guard its sacred *c.* sure *Tir.* 891

CHAMBERMAID.
The *c.*, and shut it fast *R.C.* 50

CHAMPION.
Full many a *c.*, bent on daring deed *A.T.* 123
Divert the *c.* prodigal of breath *Con.* 89
Or serves the *c.* in forensic war *Ex.* 664
And sickly, while her *c.* wear their hearts *T.* v 511

CHANCE.
And from a *c.* so new *A Tale* 62
A fool must now and then be right by *c. Con.* 96
Wherever *c.*, caprice, or fancy guide *Con.* 794
If Envy *c.* to creep in *F.* 75
But friends that *c.* to differ *F.* 135
If *c.*, on heavy pinions slowly borne *H.* 716
A hermit (or if '*c.* you hold *Mor.* 1
For with a race like theirs no *c.* I see *N.A.* 113
That night, by *c.*, the poet watching *R.C.* 77
And worship *c.* alone! *St.* vi 28 [29
Where *c.* may throw me, beneath elm or vine *T.* iii
For property stripped off by cruel *c. T.* i 503
The greatest oft originate) could *c. T.* ii 168
If e'er it chanced, as sometimes *c.* it must *T.* ii 717
If *c.* at length he find a greensward smooth *T.* iii 7
What *c.* that I, to fame so little known *T.* iii 23
The hope of better things, the *c.* to win *T.* iii 828
We give to *C.*, blind *C.*, ourselves as blind *T.* v 865
But *C.* is not; or is not where Thou reignest *T.* v 870
He journeyed ; and his *c.* was as he went *T.* vi 488
And if it *c.*, as sometimes *c.* it will *Tir.* 839
If he should *c.* to fall *Tran.* ii 21

CHANCED.
This history *c.* of late *A Tale* 10
That zeal, not vanity, has *c.* to make *Ch.* 635
A warm dispute once *c.* to wage *J.P.* 3
The goddess *c.* to hear *L.R.* 18
It *c.* then on a winter's day *P.T.* 9
This observation, as it *c.*, not made *R.* 463

A drawer, it *c.* at bottom lined *R.C.* 35
If e'er it *c.*, as sometimes chance it must *T.* ii 717

CHANCE-MEDLEY.
Is all *c.*, and unknown to me *Tir.* 858

CHANGE.
In every *c.*, both mine and yours *A Fable* 31 [845
The *c.* shall please, nor shall it matter aught *Con.*
He reads the skies, and, watching every *c. Ch.* 333
Who shifts and *c.* all things but his shape *Con.* 459
Great *c.* and new manners have occurred *Con.* 803
True, *c.* will befall, and friends may part *E.* iii 10
But distance only cannot *c.* the heart *E.* iii 11
And feels no *c.*, unshaken and serene *Ex.* 587
By such a *c.*, thy darkness is made light *Er.* 640
The love of *c.* that lives in every breast *R.* 171
That so retired he should not wish a *c. R.* 600
Whatever hopes a *c.* of scene inspires *R.* 679
Must *c.* her nature, or in vain retires *R.* 680
But love of *c.*, it seems, has place *R.C.* 21
Refreshing *c.*! where now the blazing sun? *T.* i 335
Of desultory man, studious of *c. T.* i 507
Can *c.* their whine into a mirthful note *T.* i 583
A new possessor, and survives the *c. T.* ii 110
But *c.* with every moon. The sycophant *T.* ii 599
Through every *c.* that Fancy, at the loom *T.* ii 608
For thou art meek and constant, hating *c. T.* iii 55
To-morrow brings a *c.*, a total *c.*! *T.* iv 322
And loudly wondering at the sudden *c. T.* iv 451
Lamented *c.*! to which full many a cause *T.* iv 576
Grows conscious of a *c.*, and likes it well *T.* iv 638
'Twere well if his exterior *c.* were all *T.* iv 649
But not to warp or *c.* it. We are his *T.* v 343
To count the hour-bell, and expect no *c. T.* v 404
By dint of *c.* to give his tasteless task *T.* v 429
Grace makes the slave a freeman. 'Tis a *c. T.* v 688
Garden of God, how terrible the *c. T.* vi 371
By any *c.* of fortune; proof alike *T.* vi 626.
Arrived, he feels an unexpected *c. Tir.* 567
Or tinkle in *C.* Alley, to amuse *T.T.* 186
C. is the diet on which all subsist *Y.O.* 72
Created changeable, and *c.* at last *Y.O.* 73

CHANGED.
As she had *c.* her kind *A Tale* 46
From things terrestrial, and divinely *c. Con.* 723
Alas, how *c.*! expressive of his mind *H.* 688
And though she *c.* her mood so oft *J.P.* 23 [i 320
Have *c.* the woods, in scarlet honours bright *T.*
Where penury is felt the thought is *c. T.* iv 397
Attachment never to be weaned or *c. T.* vi 625
Since all thy tears were *c.* to smiles 1789, 57

CHANGEABLE.
Created *c.*, and change at last *Y.O.* 73

CHANGEFUL.
And no condition of this *c.* life *T.* v 768

CHANGING.
And finds a *c.* clime a happy source *Con.* 387

CHANNEL.
C. her cheeks, a Niobe appears *T.* 174

CHANTICLEER.
Where *c.* amidst his harem sleeps *T.* iv 447

CHAOS.
C. of contrarieties at war *Ex.* 295
Thy *c.* order, and thy weakness might *Ex.* 641

CHAPEL.
So in the *c.* of old Ely House *T.* vi 658

CHAPLAIN.
Just made fifth *c.* of his patron lord *H.* 414

CHAPLET.
And fragrant *c.*, recompensing well *T.* iii 668

CHAPTERS.
And deans, no doubt, and *c.*, with one voice *Tir.* 418

CHARACTER.
But if she touch a *c.*, it dies *Ch.* 456
Christ and his *c.* their only scope *Con.* 541
That form the *c.* he seeks *F.* 46
In *c.* uncouth, and spelt amiss *T.* i 283
In *c.* has littered all the land *T.* ii 676
Whom matrons now, of *c.* unsmirched *T.* iii 73
And paint his person, *c.* and views *T.* iii 143
Is seen no more. The *c.* is lost! *T.* iv 539
Whose *c.*, yet undebauched, retains *Tir.* 809
What *c.*, what turn thou wilt assume *Tir.* 853
The public *c.* its colours draws *Tir.* 912
Each *c.* in every part *Tran.* iv 34
Skilled in the *c.* that form mankind *T.T.* 705.

CHARACTERED.
Were *c.* on every statesman's door *T.* iii 823

CHARGE.
But not the mitred few, the soul their *c. A.T.* 129
Proves after all a wind-gun's airy *c. Con.* 274
Or, if excused that *c.*, at least deceived *Con.* 478
Retort the *c.*, and let the world be told *Con.* 767
And first, let no man *c.* me, that I mean *Con.* 871
To thrust the *c.* of deeds that I detest *Ex.* 430
How freely will they meet and *c.*! *F.* 137
If priest, supinely droning o'er his *c. H.* 198
(Yet *c.* not heavenly skill with having planned *H.* 542
And while his tongue the *c.* denies *H.F.* 15
Such Mahomet's mysterious *c. L.W.* 7
With naught in *c.*, he could betray no trust *P.E.* 29
With which I *c.* my page *St.* i 22
C. not, with light sufficient and left free *T.* 19
At such a season, and with such a *c. T.* 219
Arraigns him, *c.* him with every wrong *T.* 262
The poor are near at hand, the *c.* is small *T.* 287
C. not a God with such outrageous wrong" *T.* 520
The loaded wain, while lightened of its *c. T.* i 296
Upridged so high, and sent on such a *c. T.* ii 116
Himself, as conscious of his awful *c. T.* ii 403
That he had ta'en in *c.* He would not stoop *T.* ii 478
Sticks close, a Mentor worthy of his *c. T.* ii 595
The nurse, no doubt. Regardless of her *c. T.* ii 775
Stand up unconscious, and refute the *c. T.* ii 824
That ran through all his purposes, and *c. T.* iii 148
These therefore are his own peculiar *c. T.* iii 412
True to his *c.*, the close packed load behind *T.* iv 8
Thine helpless *c.*, dependent on thy care *T.* iv 369
To adjust the fragrant *c.* of a short tube *T.* v 55
Receive proud recompense. We give in *c. T.* v 706
But how should matter occupy a *c. T.* vi 216
And whose beneficence no *c.* exhausts *T.* vi 230
Summer in haste the thriving *c.* receives *Tir.* 45
His pride resents the *c.*, although the proof *Tir.* 163
Detain their adolescent *c.* too long *Tir.* 219 [512
But, watch they strictly, or neglect their *c.? Tir.*
See Bedlam's closeted and handcuffed *c. Tir.* 819
If thou desert thy *c.*, and throw it wide *Tir.* 887
But 'tis her own important *c. Tran.* iv 10
Will sneer, and *c.* you with a bribe *T.T.* 84
His black interpreter the *c.* disdained *T.T.* 99
The abuses of her sacred *c.*, the press *T.T.* 633
Give it a *c.* to blacken and traduce *T.T.* 763
Let me, the *c.* of some good angel, find *V.* 77

CHARGEABLE.
Oh think, if *c.* with deep arrears *Ex.* 608
C. only with a human shape *H.* 514
Stand *c.* with guilt, and to the shafts *T.* ii 155
Transports not *c.* with art 1789, 60

CHARGED.
Or was the merchant *c.* to bring *A Tale* 27
C. with a freight transcending in its worth *Ch.* 133
And brings, at his return, a bosom *c. Ch.* 321
And *c.* Hostility and Hate to roar *Ex.* 566
From crimes as base as any *c.* on me? *Ex.* 711
And *c.* with octavos and twelves *Gr.* 27
C. with the folly of his life's mad scene *P.E.* 88
One, and one only, *C.* with deep regret *P.E.* 349
Full *c.* with England's thunder *R.G.* 31 [*T* iii 6
Of close-rammed stones has *c.* the encumbered soil
(Such were the sins with which he *c.* his Lord) *T.* 51
And, *c.* with putrid verdure, breathe a gross *T.* ii 97
My panting side was *c.*, when I withdrew *T.* iii 110
Or *c.* with amorous sighs of absent swains *T.* iv 20
On bird and beast, the other *c.* for man *T.* iv 249
But God will never. When he *c.* the Jew *T.* vi 443
And *c.* perhaps with venom, that intrudes *T.* vi 569
The rottenness which Time is *c.* to inflict *Y.O.* 67
Minority. No tutor *c.* his hand *Y.O.* 157

CHARIOT.
The *c.* bounding in her wheel-worn streets, *Ex.* 21
The nymph between two *c.* glasses *P.B.* 20
In *c.* and sedans, know no fatigue *T.* i 755
Of order from the *c.* to the plough *T.* iv 586
Propitious in his *c.* paved with love *T.* vi 744
With half the *c.* and sedans in town *Tir.* 748

CHARIOTEER.
Long ere the *c.* of day had run *P.E.* 67

CHARIOTED.
No:—let her pass, and *c.* along *T.* iii 69

CHARITY.
Whether we name thee *C.* or Love *Ch.* 3 [41
Where wast thou then, sweet *C.?* Where then *Ch.*
The o'erflowing well of *C.* springs here" *Ch.* 366
Gives *C.* her being and her birth *Ch.* 378
The reign of genuine *C.* commence *Ch.* 413
But *C.* not feigned intends alone *Ch.* 449
No *C.* but alms aught values she *Ch.* 459
To Peace and *C.*, is mere pretence *Ch.* 534
True *C.*, a plant divinely nursed *Ch.* 573
(*C.* chosen as my theme and aim) *Ch.* 295
Did *C.* prevail, the press would prove *Ch.* 623
Let *C.* forgive me a mistake *Ch.* 634
C. may relax the miser's fist *Con.* 812
Judging, in *c.* no doubt, the town *H.* 250
His apostolic *c.* the same *H.* 583
Such was thy *c.*; no sudden start *J.T.* 41
Truth, Hope, and *C.*, and touched with awe *T.* i 2
And there, unless when *C.* forbids *T.* i 548
In Christian *c.* (good-natured age!) *T.* iii 95
As sweet as *c.* from human breasts *T.* iii 197
Against the *c.* of domestic life *T.* iv 677
Who slights the *c.* for whose dear sake *T.* v 507
The *c.* that warmed his heart was moved *T.* vi 498

CHARLES. [vi 659
When wandering *C.*, who meant to be the third *T.*
The dinner served, *C.* takes his usual stand *T.* 213
"*C.*, without doubt," say you—and so he ought *T.* 222
They dream of little *C.* or William graced *Tir.* 360
But when the second *C.* assumed the sway *T.T.* 620

CHARM.
O Solitude! where are the *c. A.S.* 5

No spell or *c.* was proof against the thrust *A.T.* 146
But shine with cruel and tremendous *c. Ch.* 545
And Virtue with peculiar *c.* appears *Con.* 637
Can Nature add a *c.*, or Art confer *Ex.* 5 [551
That clips thy shores, had no such *c.* for thee *Ex.*
To *c.* to sleep the threatening of the skies *Ex.* 404
By every *c.* that smiles upon her face *Ex.* 668
Ten thousand *c.*, that only fools despise *H.* 51
He shine with all a cherub's artless *c. H.* 180
Insensible of Truth's almighty *c. H.* 655
Wine has no taste, and beauty has no *c. H.* 705
And all the *c.* of a Sicilian year *Her.* 24 [iv 223
Thus decked, he *c.* a world whom Fashion blinds *T.*
Of numerous *c.* possessed *J.P.* 2 [146
Shall boast new *c.*, and more than they have lost *T.* vi
In short, the *c.* her sister had *J.P.* 27 [245
Where neither strumpet's *c.*, nor drinking bout *Tir.*
Yet me they *c.*, whate'er the theme *M.* 23
Give life her every *c. Miss —* 80 [*T.T.* 696
And *c.* the woodland scenes, and wilds unknown
Fancy shall weave a *c.* for my relief *M.P.* 18
Even Bacchanalian madness has its *c. P.E.* 56
And call her *c.* to public notice forth *P.E.* 296
The baby seems to smile with added *c. P.E.* 519
The spells and *c.* that blinded you before *P.E.* 619
Amid the *c.* of a sequestered spot *R.* 8
Thy genuine *c.*, and guide an artless hand *R.* 204
Tender idolater of absent *c. R.* 220
The fiercest animals with magic *c.*) *R.* 254
Or *c.* the sorrows of a drooping friend *R.* 292
What *c.* he sees in Freedom's smile expressed *R.* 409
That does not *c.* the more for being new *R.* 462
With all the *c.* of an accomplished taste *R.* 510
To dance on earth, and *c.* all human eyes *R.* 796
Can e'er forget the *c.* he left behind *S.* ii 3
And still has power to *c. St.* v 16 [32
Too many shocked at what should *c.* them most *T.*
Not so the pheasant on his *c.* presumes *T.* 66
That hails the rising moon, have *c.* for me *T.* 206
Still soothing, and of power to *c.* me still *T.* i 143
No tree in all the grove but has its *c. T.* i 307
Not senseless of its *c.*, what still we love *T.* i 516
Their former *c.* ? And having seen our state *T.* i 642
So sterile with what *c.* soe'er she will *T.* i 710
Is proof against thy sweet seducing *c. ? T.* ii 482
C. he may have, but he has frailties too *T.* ii 497
The *c.* of virtue in their just esteem *T.* ii 796
Must lend its aid to illustrate all their *c. T.* iii 591
Vainglorious of her *c.*, his Vashti forth *T.* iii 715
From clamour, and whose very silence *c. T.* iii 735
These are the *c.* that sully and eclipse *T.* iii 825
The *c.* of Nature. 'Tis the cruel gripe *T.* iii 826
Then Milton had indeed a poet's *c. T.* iv 709
A garden in which nothing thrives, has *c. T.* iv 754
C. the deaf serpent wisely. Make him hear *T.* v 671
Smitten in vain ! Such music cannot *c. T.* v 682
C. more than silence. Meditation here *T.* vi 84
To *c.* his ear, whose eye is on the heart *T.* vi 1022
No. Freedom has a thousand *c.* to show *T.T.* 260
That *c.* down fear they frolic it along *T.T.* 463
Without a creamy smoothness has no *c. T.T.* 513
Where the flowers have the *c.* of the spring *W.N.* 7
The *c.* of the late-blowing rose *W.N.* 21

CHARMED. [Grace ?"*P.E.*105

C. by the sounds, "your Reverence," or "your
And much was she *c.* with a tone *C.* 14 [*T.* vi 704
Why ? what has *c.* them ? Hath he saved the state ?
The world is *c.*, and Scrib escapes the law *Ch.* 526
C. with the sight, "The world," I cried *D.W.* 37
The book of all the world that *c.* me most *H.* 427
Has *c.* me much (not e'en Occiduus more) *P.E.* 139
And the scene where his melody *c.* me before *P.F.* 11

So sings he, *c.* with his own mind and form *T.* 411
Or *c.* me young, no longer young, I find *T.* i 142
And *c.* with rural beauty, to repose *T.* iii 28
The man approving what had *c.* the boy *Tir.* 149
Rose like a paper-kite and *c.* the town *T.T.* 385

CHARMER.

My *c.* is not mine alone ; my sweets *T.* iii 719

CHARMING.

Its odour perished, and its *c.* hue *Con.* 43
Must constitute the *c.* whole *F.* 59
O *c.* Paradise of short-lived sweets ! *Her.* 34
Sighs o'er the beauties of the *c.* scene *R.* 566
And in the *c.* strife triumphant still *T.* iv 163

CHARTER.

" To assert the *c.* of the chaste and fair *A.T.* 117
And in that *c.* reads, with sparkling eyes *T.* 329
By *c.*, and that *c.* sanctioned sure *T.* v 548
The *c.* was conferred, by which we hold *T.* vi 451

CHARTERED.

The beasts are *c.*—neither age nor force *Ch.* 171
Hence *c.* boroughs are such public plagues *T.* iv 671
As dwell at large in Britain's *c.* land *T.T.* 259

CHASE.

Tho reeking, roaring hero of the *c. Con.* 405
And *c.* the splenetic dull hours away *Con.* 582
By joys possessed, and joys still held in *c. Ex.* 669
And others shooting and the *c. L.W.* 32
That first engaged him in the *c.*" *Mor.* 38
To urge the fruitless *c.* be lost *Mor.* 42
" Grieve not, my child, *c.* all thy fears away ! *M.P.* 6
Shall *c.* him from the bowers *N.* 18
For persevering *c.*, and headlong leaps *P.E.* 86
Lived in his saddle, loved the *c.*, the course *R.* 577
Nor those of learned philologists who *c. R.* 691
Divine Communion *c.*, as the day *R.* 765
War and the *c.* engross the savage whole *T.* i 608
The *c.* for sustenance, precarious trust ! *T.* i 611
To which the mind resorts, in *c.* of terms *T.* ii 288
In *c.* of fancied happiness, still wooed *T* iii 126
I shall not add myself to such a *c. T.* iv 786
In feast or in the *c.*, in song or dance *T.* v 758
Liberty *c.* all that gloom away *T.T.* 271

CHASED.

Three sparks ensued that *c.* it all away *A.T.* 167
For him, though *c.* with furious heat *Beau* 11
Till thy appearance *c.* the gloom, forlorn *J.T.* 21
Fled, *c.* by her melody clear *M.D.* 22
And *c.* them up to Heaven. Their ashes flew *T.* v 726
The breath of heaven has *c.* it. In the heart *T.* vi 786
C., never to assemble more 1789, 41

CHASING.

C. the darkness and the damps *Q.V.* 7

CHASM.

That theme exhausted, a wide *c.* ensues *Con.* 393
The yawning *c.* of indolence supply ! *P.E.* 172

CHASTE.

To assert the charter of the *c.* and fair *A.T.* 117
Silent and *c.* she steals along *Comp.* ii 3
And he grown *c.* that was the slave of lust *Con.* 810
And plain in manner; decent, solemn, *c. T.* ii 401
And *c.* themselves, are not ashamed to own *T.* iii 74
And *c.*, though unconfined, whom I extol *T.* iii 713
O for a world in principle as *c. T.* vi 836
Not very sober though, nor very *c. Tir.* 750
Extravagant or sober, loose or *c. Tir.* 914
Is so refined, and delicate, and *c. T.T.* 511

CHASTENING.
A Father's frown, and kiss his *c.* hand *R.* 346

CHASTER.
The *c.* Muse of modern days omits *A.T.* 85

CHASTISE.
It may correct a foible, may *c. T.* ii 316

CHATHAM'S.
And *C.'s* eloquence to marble lips *T.* i 704 [367
Once *C.* saved thee, but who saves thee next? *T.T.*
That *C.'s* language was his mother tongue *T* ii 237
And *C.*, heart-sick of his country's shame *T.* ii 244
They made us many soldiers. *C.* still *T.* ii 245
And the last left the scene when *C.* died *T.T.* 339

CHATTELS.
And *c.* of leisure and ease *Gr.* 50

CHATTER.
And with much twitter, and much *c. P.T.* 15

CHATTERING.
As idle as the *c.* of a daw *A.T.* 63
Let fashion, leader of a *c.* train *Con.* 457

CHAUCER.
But what old *C.'s* merry page befits *A.T.* 84

CHEAP. [*T.T.* 331
C. though blood-bought, and thrown away when sold
The dear-bought placeman, and the *c.* buffoon *Con.* 30
Friendship a blessing *c.* or small! *E.* i 92
But above all reflect, how *c.* soe'er *Ex.* 680
A *c.* but wholesome salad from the brook *T.* vi 304

CHEAPER.
And play the fool, but at a *c.* rate *R.* 562

CHEAPLY.
So *c.* the renown of that attempt *T.* vi 534

CHEAPSIDE.
As if *C.* were mad *J.G.* 44
Should purl amidst the traffic of *C. T.T.* 185

CHEAT.
Whoever boasts that name—behold a *c.*! *Ch.* 603
And always friendly, we were wont to *c. E.* iii 4
Scripture employed to sanctify the *c. Ex.* 92
To *c.* themselves and gain the world's assent *P.E.* 436
And daily more enamoured of the *c. P.E.* 524
The Bible an imposture and a *c.*? *T.* 432
To zigzag manuscript, and *c.* the eyes *T.* ii 364
Can *c.*, or move a moment's fear in me? *T.* vi 508
Will *c.* him if he can *Y.D.* 28

CHEATED.
And he that will be *c.* to the last *P.E.* 607

CHECK.
To *c.* the vessel's course *Cast.* 20
To *c.*, or alter from its course *Miss* — 59
Till He that rides the whirlwind *c.* the rein *R.* 535
C. vegetation in the torpid plant *T.* iii 468
The rich, and they that have an arm to *c. T.* iv 587
Not so where, scornful of a *c.*, it leaps *T.* v 101
That scruple *c.* him. Riot is not loud *T.* v 614
Defies the *c.* of winter, haunts of deer *T.* vi 110
To *c.* them. But, alas! none sooner shoots *T.* vi 592
To *c.* the procreation of a breed *Tir.* 603

CHECKED.
O'erheard and *c.* this idle talk *P.* 40
And never *c.* by what impedes the wise *T.* 373

CHECKER'D.
Would waste attention at the *c.* board *T* vi 265

CHECKING.
Nor freezing sky nor sultry, *c.* me *T.* vi 297

CHEEK.
She saw, and turned her rosy *c.* away *A.T.* 87
To modest *c.*, and borrowed one from art *Ex.* 48
At which I oft shave *c.* and chin *Gr.* 23 [425
Unveiled her blushing *c.*, looked on and smiled *Ex.*
And the first thankful tears bedew his *c. H.* 727
The seat of empire is her *c. L.R.* 27
The fragrant waters on my *c.* bestowed *M.P.* 62
But when the huntsman with distended *c. N.A.* 43
Channel her *c.*, a Niobe appears *T.* 174 [iv 352
With half-shut eyes and puckered *c.* and teeth *T.*
For none they need: the languid eye, the *c. T.* i 391
His *c.* recovers soon its healthful hue *T.* i 441
Two empirics he stands, and with swoln *c. T.* ii 352
With tears, that trickled down the writer's *c. T.* iv 18
But gay confusion; roses for the *c. T.* iv 79
Thy breath congealed upon thy lips, thy *c. T.* iv 122
And stroke his polished *c.* of purest red *Tir.* 847
And wet his *c.* with sorrows not his own *V.* 66

CHEEK-DISTENDING.
The *c.* oath, not to be praised *T.* iv 488

CHEER.
C. what were else a universal shade *Ch.* 94
That *c.* the silent journey of the night *Ch.* 320
To *c.* the rude forefathers of mankind *Con.* 454
By night a fire, to *c.* the gloomy way *Ex.* 178
Nor *c.* the spirit, nor refresh the sight *H.* 299
Soft airs and genial moisture feed and *c. H.* 489
And *c.* the drooping flowers, unheard, unseen *J.T.* 40
The love that *c.* life's latest stage *M.F.* 49
Might beautify and *c.* the night" *N.G.* 22
Ten thousand warblers *c.* the day, and one *T.* 200
Greets with three *c.* exulting. At his waist *T.* i 523
C. all their seasons with a grateful smile *T.* i 622
That *c.* but not inebriate, wait on each *T.* iv 40
The glimpse of a green pasture, how they *c. T.* iv 751
How find the myriads that in summer *c. T.* v 77
Shall *c.* our latest age *The Doves* 12
One comfort yet shall *c.* thine aged heart *Tir.* 897

CHEERED.
And be *c.* by the sallies of youth *A.S.* 24
And *c.* her with a song *A Tale* 56
C. as they go by many a sprightly strain *E.* ii 14
That cordial thought her spirit *c. Q.V.* 65 [350
And now, with nerves new braced and spirits *c. T.* i

CHEERFUL.
No groves have ye, nor *c.* sound of bird *H.* 469
Both sad and in a *c.* mood *N.Y.G.* 3
True Piety is *c.* as the day *T.* 176
Content though mean, and *c.* if not gay *T.* 319
Tall spire, from which the sound of *c.* bells *T.* i 174
Of *c.* days, and nights without a groan *T.* i 366
Feeds a blue flame, and makes a *c.* hearth *T.* iii 33
Cold and yet *c.*: messenger of grief *T.* iv 13
The *c.* haunts of man; to wield the axe *T.* v 42

CHEERFULLY.
Like him, crossed *c.* tempestuous seas *H.* 584
Would *c.* these limbs resign *Tran.* ii 34
And the world *c.* admits the claim *T.T.* 715

CHEERING.
The *c.* fragrance of her dewy vales *T.* i 429

CHEESE.
Of savoury *c.*, or butter costlier still *T.* iv 395

CHEMIC.
From fading good derives, with *c.* art *H* 159.

CHEQUER.
In all the good and ill that *c.* life! *T.* ii 162

CHEQUERED.
The *c.* earth seems restless as a flood *T.* i 344
C. with all complexions of mankind *T.* iii 836

CHERISH.
To *c.* virtue in an humble state *R.* 789

CHERISHED.
An era *c.* long by me 1789, 33

CHERRIES.
And parrots with twin *c* in their beak *T.* i 38 [577
And *c.* hangs her twigs. Geranium boasts *T.* iii

CHERRY-STONES.
Sits linking *c.*, or platting rush *R.* 398

CHERTSEY. [iv 728
Though stretched at ease in *C.*'s silent bowers *T.*

CHERUB.
He shine with all a *c.*'s artless charms *H.* 180
Would hiss the *c.* Mercy from the stage *T.* 478

CHERUP.
But with a *c.* clear and strong *D.W.* 25
He *c.* brisk his ear-erecting steed *T.* iii 9

CHEST.
Half open in the topmost *c. R.C.* 40
Something imprisoned in the *c. R.C.* 84
Anything rather than a *c. R.C.* 106 [402
Skillet, and old carved *c.*, from public sale *T.* iv
Deals him out money from the public *c. T.* iii 796
Upon their jutting *c.* He, formed to bear *T.* iv 350

CHESTNUTS.
These *c.* ranged in corresponding lines *T.* i 263

CHICKEN.
Her *c.* prematurely counted *A Fable* 4
Faint as a *c.*'s note that has the pip *Con.* 356

CHID.
From labour; and the lover, who has *c. T.* v 412
He *c.* the tardiness of every post *R.* 475

CHIEF.
While *C.* Baron Ear sat to balance the laws *A.C.* 7
Sat the Druid, hoary *c. B.* 6
No braver *c.* could Albion boast *Cast.* 7
C. grace below, and all in all above *Ch.* 4
For the *c.* blessings of my fairest days *Ch.* 265
Unfriendly to society's *c.* joys *Con.* 252
And his *c.* glory, was the gospel theme *Con.* 620
Presumes itself *c.* favourite of the skies *Con.* 674
But *c.*, myself I will enjoin *D.W.* 41
But the *C.* Shepherd even there is near *E.* ii 44
Of the *c.* strength and glory of the frame *Ex.* 335
Thy *c.*, the lords of many a petty fee *Ex.* 532 [186
The world can boast, and her *c.* favourites share *R.*
His flock the *c.* concern he ever knew *R.* 404 [239
Of virtue, made one *c.*, whom times of peace *T.* v
The hardy *c.*, upon the rugged rock *T.* i 12 [38
C. monster that has plagued the nations yet! *T.T.*
A more accomplished world's *c.* glory now *T.* i 724
But elegance, *c.* grace the garden shows *T.* iii 638
We the *c.* patron of the common wealth *T.* v 349
Thee I account still happy, and the *c. T.* v 460
Whose *c.* distinction is their spotless name *Tir.* 355
That are of *c.* and most approved report *Tir.* 459
Though the *c.* actor died upon the stage *T.T.* 341
These were the *c.*; each interval of night *T.T.* 572
Which formed the *c.* display *Q.V.* 10
Of *c.* whose single arm could boast 1789, 5

CHIEFLY.
And *c.* when religion leads the way *Con.* 704
Food *c.* for the mind *T.B.* 42
Lurks the contagion *c.* to be feared *Tir.* 689
Where vile example (yours I *c.* mean *Tir.* 761

CHIEN SAVANT.
"Friend Robert, thus like *c. E.* iv 87

CHILD.
So when a *c.*, as playful children use *B.B.* 9 [10
And graced with all her gifts the favourite *c. A.T.*
Her wisdom seems the weakness of a *c. Ch.* 423
And was his plaything often when a *c. E.* iii 33
My sister, and my sister's *c. J.G.* 13 [*M.P.* 6
"Grieve not, my *c.*, chase all thy fears away!"
"*C.*! I am rather hard of hearing" *M.F.* 26
Dupe of to-morrow even from a *c. M.P.* 41
And without discipline the favourite *c. P.E.* 361
Or Fancy's fondness for the *c.* she bears *P.E.* 517
Patient of contradiction as a *c. P.E.* 536
And e'en the *c.* who knows no better *P.T.* 5
Not as the plaything of a froward *c. R.* 107 [iii 432
Makes needful still; whose Spring is but the *c. T.*
Were but the feeble efforts of a *c. T.* 578 [623
The clown, the *c.* of nature, without guile *T.* iv
But spurious and short-lived; the puny *c. T.* v 621
Soon see your wish fulfilled in either *c. Tir.* 344
To double all thy pleasure in thy *c. Tir.* 682 [880
Thy *c.* shall show respect to thy gray hairs *Tir.*

CHILDHOOD.
From infancy through *c.*'s giddy maze *H.* 187
The same that oft in *c.* solaced me *M.P.* 4
I seem to have lived my *c.* o'er again *M.P.* 115
For second *c.*; and devote old age *T.* ii 637
To sports which only *c.* could excuse *T.* ii 638
If aught was learned in *c.*, is forgot *T.* ii 755
Their *c.* pleased them at a riper age *Tir.* 148

CHILDISH.
'Tis *c.* dotage, a delirious dream! *Ch.* 417
Luxury gives the mind a *c.* cast *R.* 703
A *c.* waste of philosophic pains *Tir.* 76
C. in mischief only and in noise *Tir.* 207
To take in *c.* plays a *c.* part *Tir.* 548

CHILDLIKE.
Such was thy wisdom, Newton, *c.* sage! *T.* iii 252

CHILDREN.
So when a child, as playful. *c.* use *B.B.* 9
Peasants and *c.* all around us *E.* i 40
The very *c.* watch for thy disgrace *Ex.* 282
Men deal with life as *c.* with their play *H.* 127
Myself, and *c.* three *J.G.* 14
The dogs did bark, the *c.* screamed *J.G.* 109
C. not thine have trod my nursery floor *M.P.* 47
Then think of his *c.*, for they must be fed *P.A.* 28
Where *c.* would with ease discern the way *P.E.* 434
That we were born her *c.* Praise enough *T.* ii 235
He gave them in his *c.* veins, and hates *T.* iv 464
When *c.* first begin to spell *Tran.* iv 37 [124
Which *c.* use, and parsons—when they preach *Tir.*
In tales, in trifles, and in *c.*'s play *T.T.* 731 [772
The *c.*, crooked, and twisted, and deformed *T.* ii

CHILL.
C. blasts of trouble nip their springing joys *E.* ii 32
In wintry age to feel no *c. M.* 42
Autumnal rains had made it *c. Mor.* 13
With her *c.* hand, the mellow leaves away *N.A.* 22
Go, bid the winter cease to *c.* the year *T.* 399
And *c.* and darkness a wide-wandering soul *T.* v 684

CHILLED.
C. more his else delightful way *Mor.* 16
Themselves were c., their eggs were addled *P.T.* 55
Of love by absence c. into respect *Tir.* 576

CHILLING.
And tender blade, that feared the c. blast *T.* iv 331
By drunken howlings; and the c. tale *T.* iv 562
A c. flood on summer's drooping flowers *T.T.* 211

CHIME.
Musical as the c. of tinkling rills *P.E.* 14
Streams tinkle sweetly in poetic c. *R.* 568
'Tis not in artful measures, in the c. *T.* vi 1020

CHIMING
Through the cleft rock, and, c. as they fall *T.* 193

CHIN.
An honest man, close-buttoned to the c. *E.* iii 62
At which I oft shave cheek and c. *Gr.* 23
C. fallen, and not an eye-ball to be seen *P.E.* 137
To show the peeping down upon his c. *Tir.* 235
The money chinks, down drop their c. *Y.D.* 51

CHINA.
No matter where, in C. or Japan *E.* iii 47
This c. that decks the alcove *Gr.* 33

CHINESE.
Like a fat squab upon a C. fan *P.E.* 218

CHINK.
And where, secure as mouse in c. *R.C.* 5 [*T.* v 86
Thins all their numerous flocks. In c. and holes
The money c., down drop their chins *Y.D.* 51

CHIRP.
And c., and kiss, he seemed to say *F.B.* 26
While the poor grasshopper must c. below *T.T.* 577

CHIRPING.
C. on my kitchen hearth *Tran.* iii 2

CHISEL.
Nor does the c. occupy alone *T.* i 705

CHIT. [318
Hark! how the sire of c., whose future share *Tir.*
While yet thou wast a grovelling puling c. *Ex.* 474

CHIVALRY.
On all the wings of c. advanced *A.T.* 149

CHLOE.
And C. from her garland picks the weed *H.* 293

CHOICE.
The scene of her sensible c.! *C.* 44
Or make the parrot's mimicry his c.! *Con.* 449.
And free from bias, must approve the c. *Con.* 664
That cried "Repent"—and gloried in thy c.? *Ex.* 399
Dared to suppose the subject had a c. *Ex.* 544
Nice in its c., and of a tempered heat *J.T.* 36
Must be supplied with objects of his c. *P.E.* 46
Daniel ate pulse by c.—example rare! *P.E.* 215
And make the course he recommends my c. *R.* 388
Not blind by c., but destined not to see *T.* 530
Each to his c.; soon whiten all the land *T.* i 294
Recoils from its own c.—at the full feast *T.* i 467
In human mould, should brutalize by c. *T.* i 575
Subordinate, and diligence was c. *T.* ii 716 [ii 793
Than they themselves by c., for wisdom's sake *T.*
And left them to an undirected c. *T.* ii 802
Had I the c. of sublunary good *T.* iii 689
My fancy, ere yet liberty of c. *T.* iv 698 [vi 107
And swallowing, therefore, without pause or c. *T.*

The victim of his own tremendous c. *T.* vi 558
Guides the decision of a doubtful c. *Tir.* 34 [857
Though much depends on what thy c. shall be *Tir.*
Ah, happy designation, prudent c. *Tir.* 342 [vi 910
Would make his fate his c.; whom peace, the fruit *T.*
As bound in duty, would confirm the c. *Tir.* 419
May here and there prevent erroneous c. *Tir.* 798

CHOICEST.
The c. raptures to impart *Miss* — 3
The c. flowers she bears *Pat.* 14
Pours she not all her c. fruits abroad *T.* ii 85

CHOIRS.
And angel c. attended, wondering stood *T.* vi 352

CHOKE.
Inveterate habits c. the unfruitful heart *R.* 41

CHOKED.
Are a stream c., or trickling to no end *Tir.* 718

CHOOSE.
Serve him with venison, and he c. fish *Con.* 335
But conversation, c. what theme we may *Con.* 703
What walks we take, what books we c. *E.* i 6
Are come from distant Loire to c. *E.* i 47
Denied that earthly opulence they c. *Ex.* 458
These c. the back, the belly those *L.W.* 16
To make them grow just where she c. *P.* 24
Free in his will to c. or to refuse *P.E.* 25
C. not alone a proper mate *P.T.* 64
He c. company, but not the squire's *R.* 437
Grace leads the right way; if you c. the wrong *T.* 17
Of wrath obnoxious, God may c. his mark *T.* ii 156
Drink, when we c. it, at the fountain head *T.* ii 502
To understand and c. thee for their own *T.* iii 295
Or covet more than freemen c. to grant *T.* v 340
Is pleased with it, and, were he free to c. *T.* vi 909
And, artless as thou art, whom thou wilt c. *Tir.* 856
He c. it the rather *Tran.* ii 12

CHOOSING.
For ye are worthy; c. rather far *T.* iv 403

CHORD.
Bending as he swept the c. *B.* 35 [901
With rash and awkward force the c. he shakes *Con.*
Strike on the deep-toned c. the sum of all *P.E.* 605
Man is a harp whose c. elude the sight *R.* 325 [499
Upon the rolling c. rung out his dying breath *Ex.*
An instrument whose c., upon the stretch *T.* 384
The solemn c., and with a trembling hand *T.* i 3
The voice of singing and the sprightly c. *T.* ii 78
Some c. in unison with what we hear *T.* vi 4 [161
The touch from many a trembling c. shakes out *T.* iv

CHORISTER.
With many a c. the woods among *A.T.* 77

CHORUS.
(Her rosy c.) fly *Miss* — 72

CHOSE.
Whose friendship from his boyish years he c. *Con.* 424
The tender theme on which they c. to dwell *Con.* 528
And he that blames what they have blindly c. *H.* 284
'Tis plain the creature, whom he c. to invest *Tir.* 95
Ennobling every reason that he c. *T.T.* 562
Forgetful of the man whom once ye c. *V.* 3 [161
Which hue she most approved, she c. them all *T.* vi

CHOSEN.
(Charity c. as my theme and aim) *Ch.* 295
And having c. evil, scorned the voice *Ex.* 398
Shall be my c. theme, my glory to the last *Ex.* 734
Nor would he quit that c. stand *F.B.* 28

His object c., wealth or fame *Mor.* 27
But c. with a nice discerning taste *R.* 726
Was c. leader; him they served in war *T.* v 233
His phrase well c., clear, and full of force *Tir.* 669

CHRIST.

C. and his character their only scope *Con.* 541
That love of C. in all its quickening power *Con.* 562
Paul's love of C., and steadiness unbribed *H.* 580
To prove that without C. all gain is loss *H.* 631
Pay!—follow C., and all is paid *St.* v 33
But C. as soon would abdicate his own *T.* 77
Is C. the abler teacher, or the schools? *T.* ii 534
If C., then why resort at every turn *T.* ii 535

CHRISTIAN.

And C. marrying may convert the Turks *A.T* 160
Canst thou, and honoured with a C. name *Ch.* 180
Behold a C.!—and without the fires *Ch.* 599
Names almost worthy of a C.'s praise *Con.* 36
A C.'s wit is inoffensive light *Con.* 599
A veteran warrior in the C. field *Con.* 607
The C., in whose soul, though now distressed *Con.* 707
Peruses closely the true C.'s face *Con.* 743
That in her heart the C. she reveres *Con.* 787
To learn in God's own school the C. part *Ex.* 650
The C. vessel, and defies the blast *H.* 168
Nor animate the soul to C. deeds *H.* 300
The C. Hope is—Waiter, draw the cork—*H.* 360
True C. are, dissemblers, drunkards, thieves *H.* 508
Throughout mankind, the C. kind at least *H.* 635
And spits abhorrence in the C.'s face *H.* 662
Thy bounties all were C., and I make *J.T.* 47
Those C. best deserve the name *N.G.* 35
The C. has an art unknown to thee *R.H.* 4
And ardour in the C. race *St.* vi 23
The free-born C. has no chains to prove *T.* 187
Bon-mots to gall the C. and the Jew *T.* 308
Its odour o'er the C.'s thorny road! *T.* 454
"Is virtue then, unless of C. growth *T.* 515
That guides the C. in his swifter race *T.* 534
In C. charity, (good-natured age!) *T.* iii 95
C. in name, and infidel in heart *Tir.* 421
Our ancestry, a gallant C. race *T.T.* 372
Bespeaks a land, once C., fallen and lost *T.T.* 428
Drew a rough copy of the C. face *T.T.* 614

CHRISTIANLIKE.

He, C., retreats with modest mien *T.* 68

CHRONICLE.

Much ancient c., and long 1789, 2

CHURCH.

The c. warmed, they would no longer hold *Ch.* 606
'Tis in the c. the leprosy begins *Ex.* 96
Such, when the Teacher of his c. was there *Ex.* 123
Built God a c., and laughed his word to scorn *R.* 688
But that she fasts, and item goes to c. *T.* 152
Grand caterer and dry nurse of the c.! *T.* ii 371
Preserve the c.! and lay not careless hands *T.* ii 393
By monitors that mother c. supplies *T.* ii 576
Well may the c. wage unsuccessful war *T.* ii 809
Trees, c., and strange visages, expressed *T.* iv 288
So fares thy c. But how thy c. may fare *T.* vi 838
C. ladders are not always mounted best *Tir* 381
A piece of mere c. furniture at best *Tir.* 425
A great frequenter of the c. *Tran.* ii 4
C., army, physic, law *Tran.* ii 27

CHURCH-BRED.

"Fallible man," the c. youth replies *H.* 421

CHURCH-GOING.

But the sound of the c. bell *A.S.* 29

CHURCHILL.

C., himself unconscious of his powers *T.T.* 672

CHURCH-JUGGLER.

A mere c., hypocrite, and slave *P.E.* 109

CHURCHMAN.

Than in a c. slovenly neglect *T.* ii 456
C., in whose esteem their blest employ *Tir.* 823

CHURCH-QUACKS.

C., with passions under no command *P.E.* 474

CHURL.

Heedless of all his pranks, the sturdy c. *T.* v 52
Let reverend c. his ignorance rebuke *Tir.* 401

CHURLISH.

Yet half mankind maintain a c. strife *H.* 322
Of c. Winter, in her froward moods *T.* iii 433

CHYMIST.

To adopt the c.'s golden dream *F.* 143

CINDERS.

Rake well the c., sweep the floor *E.* iv 41
In the red c., while with poring eye *T.* iv 289

CIPHER.

And silent c., while her proxy plays *T.* i 477
Deems him a c. in the works of God *T.* vi 943

CIRCASSIANS.

"Ye fair C.! all your lutes employ *A.T.* 107

CIRCE.

With brutal lust as ever C. made *T.T.* 629

CIRCEAN.

With caution taste the sweet C. cup *P.E.* 580

CIRCLE.

The c. formed, we sit in silent state *Con.* 379
That flight in c. urged advanced them naught *N.A.* 52
In still repeating c., screaming loud *T.* 204
The Rout is Folly's c., which she draws *T.* ii 629
The silent c. fan themselves, and quake *T.* iv 149
Shall fill the c. of those eyes *The Doves* 15
Retired from all the c. of the gay *V.* 73

CIRCLING.

That shook the c. seas and solid earth *Her.* 14
C. around and limiting his years *R.* 150
Slow c. ages are as transient days *T.* vi 227
Yon c. worlds, their distance, and their size *Tir.* 633

CIRCUIT.

Immortal fragrance fills the c. wide *Ch.* 439
That tread the c. of the cistern wheel! *H.* 100
Runs the great c., and is still at home *T.* iv 119

CIRCULATE.

And let it c. through every vein *T.* ii 45

CIRCUMSCRIBE.

That no restraints can c. them more *T.* ii 792

CIRCUMSPECTLY.

As c. as you can *F.* 152

CIRCUMVENTION.

Sly c., unrelenting hate *T.* i 615

CISTERN.

That tread the circuit of the c. wheel! *H.* 100

CITADELS.

To storm the c. they build in air *H.* 623

CITIZEN.
John Gilpin was a c. *J.G.* 1
Delight the c., who gasping there *R.* 485
And so two c. who take the air *T.* i 79
To which the insipid c. resorts *T.* iii 642
The c., and brace his languid frame! *T.* iv 752

CITY.
Than aught that the c. can show *C.* 32
Had found one c. not to be o'ercome *Ex.* 210
The night his c. fell *Q.V.* 52
From c. humming with a restless crowd *R.* 21
May run in c. with a brisker force *R.* 454
Yet not in c. oft; in proud, and gay *T.* i 681
And gain-devoted c. Thither flow *T.* i 682
In c. foul example on most minds *T.* i 685
In gross and pampered c., sloth, and lust *T.* i 687
In c., vice is hidden with most ease *T.* i 689
And show this queen of c., that so fair *T.* i 727
Have rambled wide. In country, c., seat *T.* iii 14
She loses all her influence. *C.* then *T.* iii 729
Ten righteous would have saved a c. once *T.* iii 843
Sermons, and c. feasts, and favourite airs *T.* iv 84
That men immured in c., still retains *T.* iv 766
Resemble most some c. in a blaze *T.* v 5   [iv 466
Pass where we may, through c. or through town *T.*
Of no mean c., planned or ere the hills *T.* v 764
Bright as a sun the sacred c. shines *T.* vi 800
Therefore in towns and c. they abound *Tir.* 519
What follows next, let c. of great name *T.T.* 430
Here c. won, and fleets dispersed 1789, 13

CITY-LIFE.
Nor habits of luxurious c. *T.* iv 745

CIVET.
I cannot talk with c. in the room *Con.* 283

CIVETED.
C. fellows, smelt ere they are seen *Tir.* 830

CIVIL.
Thy senate is a scene of c. jar *Ex.* 294
This c. bickering and debate *L.R.* 17
Such c. broils are my delight *Pat.* 17
That c. war embitters all his life *T.* 468
The manners and the arts of c. life *T.* i 596

CIVILIZES.
The sex whose presence c. ours *Con.* 254

CLAD.
Armed with thunder, c. with wings *B.* 27
That man, in Nature's richest mantle c. *Ch.* 341
Of peace or ease to creatures c. as we *N.A.* 114
With reverend tutor, c. in habit lay *P.E.* 371
Saw better c., in cloak of satin trimmed *T.* i 535
Conspicuous, and in bright apparel c. *T.* v 25
Then each, in its peculiar honours c. *T.* vi 147
Behold that figure, neat, though plainly c. *Tir.* 664

CLAIM.
Not Mexico could purchase kings a c. *Ch.* 214
The foe of virtue has no c. to thee *Ch.* 288
Captivity led captive, rose to c. *Ch.* 585
No!—there I grant the privilege I c. *Con.* 98
And c. a reverence in its shortening day *Con.* 645
And all her love of God a groundless c. *Con.* 781
And c. a right to scamper and run wide *Con.* 793
And c. for ever, as his royal right *Ex.* 362
Peace (if insensibility may c.) *H.* 235
May c. some right to be esteemed divine *H.* 504
If self-exalting c. be turned adrift *H.* 530
The art that baffles Time's tyrannic c. *M.P.* 9
Cannot forfeit Nature's c. *N.C.* 14
'Tis God's just c., prerogative divine *R.* 278
C. most compassion, and receives the least *R.* 302
And never waves his c. *St.* i 12
I say the Brahmin has the fairer c. *T.* 108
The vellum of the pedigree they c. *T.* i 569
At least superior jockeyship, and c. *T.* ii 276
May c. this merit still—that she admits *T.* iii 102
Live there, and prosper. Those Ausonia c. *T.* iii 582
Sweet bashfulness! it c. at least this praise *T.* iv 70
Such c. compassion in a night like this *T.* iv 375
The sword and falchion their inventor c. *T.* v 218
In confirmation of the noblest c. *T.* v 720
Our c. to feed upon immortal truth *T.* v 721
The flesh of animals in fee, and c. *T.* vi 452
That c. forbearance even for a brute *T.* vi 466
Or safety interfere, his rights and c. *T.* vi 582
C. more than half the praise as his due share *Tir.* 528
For since (so fashion dictates) all, who c. *Tir.* 690
Should c. my fixed attention more than you *T.T.* 181
And Freedom c. him for her firstborn son *T.T.* 281
If human woes her soft attention c. *T.T.* 484
The nightingale may c. the topmost bough *T.T.* 576
And c. the palm for purity of song *T.T.* 636
And the world cheerfully admits the c. *T.T.* 715
Urged loud a c. to be rehearsed 1789, 14

CLAIMED.
C. all the glory of thy prosperous wars? *Ex.* 347

CLAIMING.
Involves the combatants; each c. Truth *T.* iii 162

CLAMMY.
And c., of his dark abode have bred *T.* i 439

CLAMOUR.
Oh that the voice of c. and debate *Ch.* 309
Such is the c. of rooks, daws, and kites *H.* 349
Might be supposed to c. for a guide *N.A.* 98
Safe from the c. of perverse dispute *R.* 145
And c. of the field? Detested sport *T.* iii 326
From c., and whose very silence charms *T.* iii 735

CLAMOROUS.
The law grown c., though silent long *T.* 261
And infants c. whether pleased or pained *T.* i 232
To c. importunity in rags *T.* iv 414
The inglorious feat, and c. in praise *T.* vi 436

CLAN.
For interest sake or swarming into c. *T.* iv 665
In tribes and c., and had begun to call *T.* v 222
O'erwatch the numerous and unruly c. *Tir.* 262
Each bumpkin of the c. *Y.D.* 26

CLANG.
Or with the high-raised horn's melodious c. *N.A.* 35

CLAP.
He c. his lens, if haply they may see *Ch.* 385
C. spectacles on her sagacious nose *Con.* 742
And c. the gate behind thee *M.B.* 24   [*P.E.* 115
Cries—"Well done, Saint!" and c. him on the back
Pleased Fancy c. her pinions at the sight *R.* 190

CLARIONETS.
Ye c., and softer still, ye lutes *T.* ii 260

CLASH.
The c. of arguments and jar of words *Con.* 85
Hence all that interferes and dares to c. *P.E.* 427

CLASP.
Which, crooked into a thousand whimsies, c. *Y.O.* 118

CLASPED.
Though, c. and cradled in his nurse's arms H. 179
Arms hanging idly down, hands c. below R. 286

CLASPING.
With c. tendrils, and invest his branch T. iii 666

CLASS.
The heart of merit in the meaner c. T. iv 618

CLASSIC.
The gift of nature, or the c. store Con. 896
Whose wit well managed, and whose c. style R. 717
Of c. food begins to be his care Tir. 319

CLASSICAL.
Weigh, for a moment, c. desert Tir. 488

CLATTER.
From the c. of street-pacing steeds C. 46

CLAWS. [A.T. iii 3
Should John wed a score, oh the c. and the scratches!

CLAWED.
And set up his back, and c. like a cat A.T. ii 5

CLAY.
Too weak to struggle with tenacious c. T. 216
May be indifferent to her house of c. T. ii 458

CLEAN.
C., candid, and witty—Thelypthora dies A.T. iv 2
And keep the polish of the manners c. R. 733
To conjure c. away the gold they touch T. i 571
He picks c. teeth, and, busy as he seems T. ii 627
His milkwhite hand; the palm is hardly c. T. iv 607
C. riddance quickly made, one only care T. v 70
To cultivate and keep the morals c. Tir. 920

CLEANLIER.
But now with pleasant pace a c. road T. iii 17

CLEANLY.
For c. riddance than for fair attire T. vi 994

CLEANSE.
And though a Bishop toil to c. the stain Ex. 384
Of abler votaries to c. the stain T.T. 635

CLEANSED. [206
The spot he loathed so much for ever c. away A.T.
C. in thine own all-purifying blood T. 581
All feel the freshening impulse, and are c. T. i 376

CLEAR.
Decisive and c., without one if or but A.C. 30
Here stay thy foot, how copious and how c. Ch. 365
They always are decisive, c. and strong Con. 150
Admit it true, the consequence is c. Con. 165
A tale should be judicious, c., succinct Con. 235
His birthright shaken, and no longer c. Con. 765
But with a cherup c. and strong D.W. 25
And tell them truths divine and c. E. i 21
Will make the dark enigma c. E. i 54
To watch the fountain, and preserve it c. Ex. 98
And graced with c. credentials from above Ex. 188
Too just to wink, or speak the guilty c. Ex. 256
With sums Peruvian mines could never c. Ex. 285
From mean self-interest and ambition c. Ex. 439
And Dick, although his way was c. F.B. 22
Which is both bright and c." J.G. 28
Did sing most loud and c. J.G. 204
From all such frenzy c. J.P. 14
Fled, chased by her melody c. M.D. 22
Her beauteous form reflected c. below M.P. 93
The c. harangue, and cold as it is c. P.E. 19
And with a c. and shining lamp supplied P.E. 558
Tis c. that they were always able P.T. 3
Or half so c., as in the rural scene R. 456
The warblings of the blackbird, c. and strong R. 569
And prejudice have left a passage c.) T. 114 [T. v 151
Gleamed through the c. transparency, that seemed
With c. exemption from its own defects T. i 404
The sport of every wave? No: none are c. T. ii 153
His office sacred, his credentials c. T. ii 339
The method c., and argument exact? T. iii 279
Sought in still water, and beneath c. skies T. iii 382
And overlaid with c. translucent glass T. iii 485
By roses, and c. suns though scarcely felt T. iii 733
And the c. voice, symphonious, yet distinct T. iv 162
With lights, by c. reflection multiplied T. iv 268
Her scanty stock of brushwood, blazing c. T. iv 381
A c. escape from tyrannizing lust T. v 579 [vi 260
And these dissolving snows, and this c. stream T.
C. and sonorous, as the gale comes on! T. vi 10
The morning sharp and c. But now at noon T. vi 58
In modern eyes), shall make the doctrine c. T. vi 482
And unambitious course, reflecting c. T. vi 723
The stamp and c. impression of good sense T. vi 983
He too might make his author's wisdom c. Tir. 100
His phrase well chosen, c., and full of force Tir. 669
Unimpaired, and shrill, and c. Tran. iii 23

CLEARED.
Had poured the day, and c. the Roman skies Ex. 228

CLEARER.
Sheds every hour a c. light E. i 61
Or, whether c. skies and softer air P.E. 409

CLEAREST.
Given thee his blessing on the c. proof Ex. 564
Its c. tone, the rapture it inspires T.T. 293

CLEARLY.
Thy words, more c. than thy works, display R. 96
So that the jest is c. to be seen T.T. 540

CLEAVE.
Like theirs that c. the flood or graze the field Con. 423
That c. the yielding air unheard E. i 88
" Still may my melting bosom c. Miss — 85
So Sophistry c. close to and protects P.E. 287
And c. through life inseparably close T. ii 761

CLEFT.
Through the c. rock, and, chiming as they fall T. 193
That hides the seamew in his hollow c. T. i 519

CLEMENCY.
If c. revolted by abuse P.E. 596
For long forbearing C. to wait T.T. 401

CLERGY.
Ye c., while your orbit is your place P.E. 96
He hails the c., and defying shame T. ii 356
Or c. made so fine? Y.D. 62

CLERK.
And there scarce less illustrious goes the c. B.B. 14
And while the c. just puzzles out the psalm Ch. 473
For many a grave and learned c. P. 31
So prays your C. with all his heart St. i 33
So your Verse-man I, and C. St. iv 9 [ii 368
That grave and learned c. should need such aid T.
And sweet the c. below. But neither sleep T. i 96
Nor yet the dozings of the c., are sweet T. i 101
The simple c., but loyal, did announce T. vi 661
By learned c., and Latinists professed Tir. 382
A scrivener's c., or footman out of place Tir. 407

CLICKING.
Grows drowsy as the c. of a clock H. 104

CLIENTS.
The poor thy *c.*, and Heaven's smile thy fee! *Ch.* 312

CLIFF. [552
Rushed to the *c.*, and having reached it, stood *T.* vi

CLIMATE.
Each *c.* needs what other climes produce *Ch.* 89
And knit the unsocial *c.* into one *Ch.* 126
Who seek it in his *c.* and his frame *T.T.* 207
Born in a *c.* softer far than ours *T.T.* 234

CLIMBED.
C., like a squirrel to his dray *A Fable* 28

CLIMBEST.
Thou *c.* the mountain top, with eager eye *T.* i 664

CLIMBING.
Her *c.*, she began to find *R.C.* 25

CLIMBS.
He *c.*, he pants, he grasps them! at his heels *T.* iv 60

CLIME.
Each climate needs what other *c.* produce *Ch.* 89
And finds a changing *c.* a happy source *Con.* 387
To darker *c.*, or *c.* of brighter day *Ex.* 18
In other *c.* perhaps creative Art *Ex.* 229
With which from *c.* to *c.* he sped his course *P.E.* 406
And stepped at once into a cooler *c. T.* i 337
And barbarous *c.*, where violence prevails *T.* i 604
In every *c.*, and travel where we might *T.* ii 234
And wise precaution, which a *c.* so rude *T.* iii 431
Unconscious of a less propitious *c. T.* iii 567
He sucks intelligence in every *c. T.* iv 111 [ii 209
Shall be constrained to love thee. Though thy *c. T.*
My native nook of earth! Thy *c.* is rude *T.* v 462
Feel all the rigour of thy fickle *c. T.* v 484
And clothe all *c.* with beauty; the reproach *T.* vi 764
Into all lands. From every *c.* they come *T.* vi 814
In Afric's torrid *c.*, or India's fiercest heat *T.T.* 297
And shot a dayspring into distant *c. T.T.* 561
From the cruel assaults of the *c. W.N.* 12

CLING.
As creeping ivy *c.* to wood or stone *P.E.* 285
So Love, that *c.* around the noblest minds *R.* 235
Themselves love life, and *c.* to it, as he *T.* i 483

CLINGING.
A rat fast *c.* to the cage *T.B.* 46

CLINK.
Duly as *c.* of bell to morning prayers *T.* 140

CLINKING.
Incessant, *c.* hammers, grinding wheels *T.* i 231

CLIP. [551
Except that office *c.* it as it goes *Ch.* 484
That *c.* thy shores, had no such charms for thee *Ex.*

CLOAK. [30
"And fetch my *c.*; for, though the night be raw *E.* iii
His long red *c.*, well brushed and neat *J.G.* 75
The wind did blow, the *c.* did fly *J.G.* 101
Saw better clad, in *c.* of satin trimmed *T.* i 535
Worn as a *c.*, and hardly hides, a gown *T.* i 550
Or wrap himself in Hamlet's inky *c. T.* vi 675

CLOCK.
Consult Life's silent *c.*, thy bounding vein *Ep.* i 3
Grows drowsy as the clicking of a *c. H.* 104
He hears the notice of the *c.*, perplexed *H.* 700
Precisely when the *c.* strikes four" *M.F.* 14
While fancy, like the finger of a *c. T.* iv 118

Machines themselves, and governed by a *c. Tir.* 625
The *c.* of history, facts and events *Y.O.* 46

CLOCKWORK.
The *c.* tintinnabulum of rhyme *T.T.* 529

CLOD. [637
May turn the *c.*, and wheel the compost home *T.* iii
Beneath the frozen *c.*; all seeds of herbs *T.* v 81
To a vile *c.*, so draws him, with such force *T.* v 589
Thou fellest mature; and, in the loamy *c. Y.O.* 33

CLODIO.
The rank debauch suits *C.*'s filthy taste *P.E.* 188
Wonders at *C.*'s follies, in a tone *P.E.* 191
Go, fool; and arm-in-arm with *C.*, plead *P.E.* 197

CLOG.
Thus Conscience freed from every *c. L.W.* 21
No clustering ornaments to *c.* the pile *T.* 24

CLOGGED.
To the *c.* wheels; and in its sluggish pace *T.* iv 345

CLOISTER.
Thy friend, though to a *c.*'s shade consigned *S.* ii 2

CLOSE.
Designed to sit *c.* to it just like a saddle *A.C.* 16
Dagger in hand, steals *c.* to your bedside *Ch.* 187
C. to the part where vision ought to be *Ch.* 386
Pinched *c.* between his finger and his thumb *Ch.* 477
Forcibly drawn from many a *c.* recess *Ch.* 529
Includes creation in her *c.* embrace *Ch.* 598
Bowed at the *c.* with all his graceful airs *Con.* 73
Perhaps at last *c.* scrutiny may show *Con.* 177
And new or old, still hasten to a *c. Con.* 238
As if in *c.* committee on the sky *Con.* 385
A *c.* designer not to be believed *Con.* 477
Enjoy the stillness of some *c.* retreat *Con.* 570
And finds Hypocrisy *c.* lurking there *Con.* 746
To *c.* in sable every social scene *Con.* 872
To steer it *c.* to land *D.W.* 18
But somewhat at that moment pinched him *c. E.* iii 34
And sighing millions prophesy the *c. Ex.* 309
And Hell's *c.* mischief naked in his sight *Ex.* 339
And thanks for this effectual *c. G.* 14
Through mere necessity to *c.* his eyes *H.* 85
Life without hope can *c.* but in despair *H.* 274
Were copied *c.* in him, and well transcribed *H.* 581
The shameful *c.* of all his misspent years *H.* 715
Of *c.* alliance to the Eternal Mind *J.T.* 44
The Arts come smiling in the *c. Miss —* 81
Shades slanting at the *c.* of day *Mor.* 15
Adjoining *c.* to Kilwick's echoing wood *N.A.* 3
They gathered *c.* around the old pit's brink *N.A.* 53
For Reynard, *c.* attended at his heels *N.A.* 124
Oh what a dying, dying *c.* was there! *P.E.* 64
The snug, *c.* party, or the splendid hall *P.E.* 176
Your pleasures with no curses in the *c. P.E.* 268
So sophistry cleaves *c.* to and protects *P.E.* 287
Where works of man are clustered *c.* around *R.* 25
Stand *c.* concealed, and see a statue move *R.* 284
But in his arduous enterprise to *c. R.* 617
Habits of *c.* attention, thinking heads *R.* 705
Its happiest seasons, and a peaceful *c. R.* 750
To *c.* life wisely, may not waste my own *R.* 868
To the *c.* copse, or far sequestered green *T.* 69
Her elbows pinioned *c.* upon her hips *T.* 133
'Tis perched upon the green hill top, but *c. T.* 222
The dying, trembling at the awful *c. T.* 436
In vain he *c.* or averts his eyes *T.* 470
And woven *c.*, or needlework sublime *T.* i 34
C. packed and smiling, in a chaise and one *T.* i 80
Of grassy swarth, *c.* cropped by nibbling sheep *T.* i 110

To wait the *c.* of all ? But grant her end *T.* ii 65
And with a well-bred whisper *c.* the scene ! *T.* ii 413
And having spoken wisely, at the *c. T.* ii 442
Sticks *c.*, a Mentor worthy of his charge *T.* ii 595
And cleaves through life inseparably *c. T.* ii 761
Enjoy *c.* shelter, wall, or reeds, or hedge *T.* iii 474
He shuts it *c.*, and the first labour ends *T.* iii 489
C. interwoven, where they meet the vase *T.* iii 612
True to his charge, the *c.* packed load behind *T.* iv 8
Now stir the fire, and *c.* the shutters fast *T.* iv 36
C. at his heels, a demagogue ascends *T.* iv 61
I saw the woods and fields at *c.* of day *T.* iv. 311
By congregated loads adhering *c. T.* iv 344 [ii 713
C. to his side that pleased him.   Learning grew *T.*
And bundled *c.* to fill some crowded vase *T.* iv 668
His dog attends him. *C.* behind his heel *T.* v 47
Lie covered *c.* ; and berry-bearing thorns *T.* v 82
And listening *c.* with both his ears *Tran.* iv 20
With *c.* fidelity and love unfeigned *T.T.* 73
To sheath it, in the peace-restoring *c. T.T.* 79
Ere yet his race begins, its glorious *c. T.T.* 709
Down to the *c.* of life's fast fading scene *V.* 85

CLOSE-BUTTONED.

An honest man, *c.* to the chin *E.* iii 62

CLOSE-CLIPPED.

With many a boxen bush, *c.* between *A.T.* 82

CLOSED.

His hours of study *c.* at last *Mor.* 5
Our sabbaths, *c.* with mummery and buffoon *P.E.* 153
Then came the maid and it was *c. R.C.* 58
Lost favour back again, and *c.* the breach *T.* ii 724
The volume *c.*, the customary rites *T.* iv 167
Time was he *c.* as he began the day *Tir.* 175

CLOSE-FOLDED.

Thy yet *c.* latitude of boughs *Y.O.* 21

CLOSE-HAMMERED.

Kept snug in caskets of *c.* steel *R.* 308

CLOSELY.

Peruses *c.* the true Christian's face *Con.* 743
May press the eye too *c.* to be borne *H.* 551
We wear it at our backs. There, *c.* braced *T.* ii 586
Then cast them, *c.* bundled, every brat *T.* ii 673

CLOSE-PENT.

Sad witnesses how *c.* man regrets *T.* iv 777

CLOSE-RAMMED.   [646
Of *c.* stones has charged the encumbered soil *T.* iii

CLOSEST.

Of friendship's *c.* tie *Dr.* 18
The *c.* knot that may be tied *F.* 62
What longest binds the *c.*, forms secure *T.* iii 480

CLOSETS.

Nor *c.* up his thoughts, whate'er he thinks *H.* 410
Yet this dull room, and that dark *c. M.F.* 4
Steal to the *c.* of young innocence *P.E.* 316

CLOSETED.

See Bedlam's *c.* and handcuffed charge *Tir.* 819

CLOSE-WOVEN.

For the *c.* arches of limes *C.* 29

CLOSING.

C. at last in darkness and despair *H.* 6

CLOTH.

Nor frown, unless he vanish with the *c. Tir.* 730
Holds up the *c.* before *Y.D.* 44

CLOTHE.   [*T.* vi 113
Peeps through the moss that *c.* the hawthorn root
The power to *c.* that reason with his word *Con.* 432
Taught thee to *c.* thy pinked and painted hide *Ex.* 486
C. it with earth, and bids the produce live *Her.* 30
Humility may *c.* an English Dean ? *T.* 118   [i 555
Though pressed with hunger oft, or comelier *c. T.*
She ploughs a brazen field, and *c.* a soil *T.* i 709
Some *c.* the soil that feeds them, far diffused *T.* iii 662
And *c.* all climes with beauty ; the reproach *T.* vi 764
C. the twin brethren in each other's dress *T.T.* 45

CLOTHED.   [sounds *H.* 45
Banks *c.* with flowers, groves filled with sprightly
Is she not *c.* with a perpetual smile ? *Ex.* 4 [*Ex.* 390
Hast thou, when Heaven has *c.* thee with disgrace
A monarch *c.* with majesty and awe *T.* 405
So *c.* with beauty, for rebellious man ? *T.* v 754
She *c.* him with authority and awe *T.T.* 344

CLOTHING.

Time was, when *c.*, sumptuous or for use *T.* i 8
Of flowers, like flies *c.* her slender rods *T.* vi 166

CLOUD.

Called for a *c.* to darken all their years *E.* ii 25
A *c.*, to measure out their march by day *Ex.* 177
Soon raised a *c.* that darkened every land *Ex.* 509
Them without light, and thee without a *c. Ex.* 717
The *c.* that flit, or slowly float away *R.* 192
Seen through the medium of a *c.* like thine *R.* 352
Breathes *c.* of dust, and calls it country air *R.* 486
The sloping land recedes into the *c. T.* i 171
Beneath the rosy *c.*, while yet the beams *T.* i 495
And perilous lightnings from the angry *c. T.* iii 212
And drunk no moisture from the dripping *c. T.* iii 515
Than those of age, thy forehead wrapped in *c. T.* iv 124
There sit, involved and lost in curling *c. T.* iv 472
Ascending, fires the horizon; while the *c. T.* v 2
That fumes beneath his nose : the trailing *c. T.* v 56
The gloomy *c.*, find weapons, arrowy sleet *T.* v 140
" Beneath a vault unsullied with a *c. T.* v 824
Without a *c.*, and white without a speck *T.* vi 63 [33
Whose favour, like the *c.* of spring, might lower *T.* vi
For He, whose car the winds are, and the *c. T.* ii 740
'Tis in the *c.*—that pleases him *Tran.* vi 11
And marks whatever *c.* may interpose *T.* 707
Now quenching in a boundless sea of *c. Y.O.* 76
A huge throat calling to the *c.* for drink *Y.O.* 112
For then the *c.* of eighty-eight, 1789, 36

CLOUD-CAPPED.

She towered a *c.* pyramid of snow *Her.* 4
His *c.* eminence divide *Trans. H.* 17

CLOUDLESS.

Transmitting *c.*, and the solar beam *Y.O.* 75

CLOUD-SURMOUNTING.

The *c.* Alps, the fruitful vales *R.* 79

CLOWN.

And even to a *c.*—Now roves the eye *T.* i 288
The *c.*, the child of nature, without guile *T.* iv 623
Without the *c.* that pay *Y.D.* 68

CLOY.

And if the feast of freedom *c.* thee not *Ex.* 671

CLOYING.

With never *c.* odours, early and late *T.* vi 164

CLUB.

Oh ! to the *c.*, the scene of savage joys *Con.* 421
Ensanguined hearts, *c.* typical of strife *T.* iv 218

To be the Table Talk of *c.* up stairs *T.T.* 151
When Labour and when Dullness *c.* in hand *T.T.* 526

CLUE.
Still making probability your *c. Con.* 218   [357
And through life's labyrinth holds fast the *c. P.E.*

CLUMPS.
For *c.*, and lawns, and temples, and cascades *H.* 247

CLUMSY.
Their sovereign nostrum is a *c.* joke *R.* 313
Dull in design, and *c.* to perform *T.* i 18
But with his *c.* port the wretch has lost *T.* iv 650
Resumes her powers, and spurns the *c.* fraud *Tir.* 188
The *c.* swains alight *Y.D.* 22

CLUSTERED.
These most resembling *c.* stars *Q.V.* 11
Where works of man are *c.* close around *R.* 25
Like homely-featured Night, of *c.* gems *T.* iv 252

CLUSTERING.
No *c.* ornaments to clog the pile *T.* 24

CLUTCH.
That his own humour dictates, from the *c. T.* v 317

COACH.
Delighted with my bauble *c.*, and wrapped *M.P.* 50
In *c.*, chaises, caravans, and hoys *R.* 521
In *c.* with purple lined, and mitres on its side *Tir.* 369

COACHBOX.
Who quits the *c.* at the midnight hour *T.* i 91

COACH-CROWDED.
Flies, winged with joy, to some *c.* door *Tir.* 746

COACHMANSHIP.
His skill in *c.*, or driving chaise *Tir.* 326

COAL.   [*T.T.* 735
Touched with a *c.* from Heaven, assume the lyre

COALESCENCE.
A friendly *c. F.* 132

COARSE.
The school of *c.* good fellowship and noise *Con.* 422
But angry, *c.*, and harsh expression *M.F.* 59
I scorn your *c.* insinuation *P.* 27
Of manners rough, and *c.* athletic cast *P.E.* 187
To wear a tattered garb however *c. T.* iv 416 [831
Else *c.* and rude in manners, and their tongue *Tir.*
Surly and slovenly, and bold and *c. T.T.* 682
Oh! why are farmers made so *c. Y.D.* 61

COARSENESS.
Themselves will hide its *c.* with a veil *P.E.* 292
And rustic *c.* would. A heavenly mind *T.* ii 457

COARSER.
And *c.* grass, upspearing o'er the rest *T.* v 23

COARSEST.
Fine passing thought, e'en in her *c.* works *Y.O* 81

COAST.
Proved kinder to them than the *c. A Tale* 31
Nor ever ship left Albion's *c. Cast.* 9
Where commerce has enriched the busy *c. Ch.* 114
When other nations flew from *c.* to *c. Ex.* 552
Asked of the waves that broke upon his *c. Ex.* 572
To reach the distant *c. H.F.* 22
Thou, as a gallant bark from Albion's *c. M.P.* 88
Afric's *c.* I left forlorn *N.C.* 2
Fly to the *c.* for daily, nightly joys *R.* 522
Vengeance at last pours down upon their *c. T.T.* 472

COAT.
But half a *c.*, and show his bosom bare *E.* iii 51
Yet nothing feel in that rough *c. P.* 51
And toil to polish its rough *c.* alone *P.E.* 420
His predecessor's *c.* advanced to wear *T.* 145 [51
Then shakes his powdered *c.*, and barks for joy *T.* v
There is a bird, who by his *c. Tran.* ii 7

COBBLER.
Smith, *c.*, joiner, he that plies the shears *T.* iv 476

COBHAM.
And *C.'s* groves, and Windsor's green retreats *R.* 571

COBWEBS.
Entangled in the *c.* of the schools *T.* iv 726

COCK.
The *c.* his arched tail's azure show *Mrs. M*— 7
A story of a *c.* and bull *P.T.* 7
Or vermin, or at best of *c.* purloined *T.* i 563
And the first larum of the *c.'s* shrill throat *T.* iv 569
To sad necessity, the *c.* foregoes *T.* v 73

COCKADE.
With the king's shoulder-knot and gay *c. T.T.* 44

COCKED.
Crape and *c.* pistol, and the whistling ball *T.* iii 802

COCOAS.
Thy *c.* and bananas, palms and yams *T.* i 640

COEVAL.
And oaks *c.* spread a mournful shade *H.* 352
His own *c.* took but little note *T.* iii 142

COFFEE.
What, give up our desserts, our *c.*, and tea! *P.A.* 8

COGENCE.
An argument of *c.*, we may say *Con.* 293

COGENT.   [411
The tongue whose strains were *c.* as commands *R.*

COIN.
A *c.* by Craft for Folly's use designed *E.* ii 7
If paid in any other *c. E.* iv 26
So *c.* grows smooth, in traffic current passed *P.E.* 279
Whose noblest *c.* is light and brittle man *V.* 96

COINCIDENT.
C., exhibit lucid proof *T.* ii 374

COINED.
A story so pat, you may think it is *c. P.A.* 18

COLD.
So, when the *c.* damp shades of night prevail *Ch.* 527
Such frozen figures, stiff as they are *c. Ch.* 607
Reports it hot or *c.*, or wet or dry *Con.* 386 [333
He shakes with *c.*—you stir the fire and strive *Con.*
Such men are not forgot as soon as *c. Con.* 630
A *c.* misgiving, and a killing dread *Con.* 770
Would run most dreadful risk of catching *c. E.* iii 59
Or where does *c.* Reflection less intrude? *Ex.* 8
With *c.* disgust, or philosophic pride *Ex.* 691
And while, at intervals, a *c.* blast sing *Ex.* 720
The clear harangue, and *c.* as it is clear *P.E.* 19
With some *c.* moral think to quench the fire *P.E.* 320
By *c.* submersion, razor, rope, or lead *R.* 584
Was *c.* and comfortless within *R.C.* 28
Where neither *c.* might come, nor air *R.C.* 31
Of loathsome diet, penury, and *c. T.* i 591 [*T.* i 556
Though pinched with *c.*, asks never.—Kate is crazed!
Finds a *c.* bed her only comfort left *T.* ii 655

Exposed to his *c*. breath, the task begins *T*. iii 469
C. as its theme, and like its theme the fruit *T*. iii 564
Begs a warm office, doomed to a *c*. jail *T*. iii 820
C. and yet cheerful: messenger of grief *T*. iv 13
The piercing *c*., but feels it unimpaired *T*. iv 361
Dangled along at the *c*. finger's end *T*. iv 392 [176
Treacherous and false; it smiled and it was *c*. *T*. v
In converse, either starved by *c*. reserve *T*. v 471
And we are deep in that of *c*. pretence *T*. v 494
Is *c*. on this. She execrates indeed *T*. v 730 [iii 554
The process. Heat and *c*., and wind and steam *T*.
A *c*. stagnation on the intestine tide *T*. vi 139
Their noble qualities all quenched and *c*. *Tir*. 818
C. in his cause, and careless of his woes *V*. 4
C. in my turn, and unconcerned like you *V*. 6
Hast caught the *c*. distemper of the day *V*. 47

COLDER.
Must find a *c*. soil and bleaker air *Tir*. 851

COLLAR.
Slips the slave's *c*. on, and snaps the lock *T.T.* 477

COLLECT.
C. at evening what the day brought forth *Con*. 19
With care *c*. what in their eyes excels *R*. 153
C. the scattered truths that Study gleans *R*. 274

COLLECTED.
Were all *c*. in thy single arm *Ex*. 704
With all a July sun's *c*. rays *R*. 484

COLLEGE.
And *c*., untaught; sells accent, tone *T*. ii 359
In *c*. and halls, in ancient days *T*. ii 699
So *c*. and halls neglected much *T*. ii 731
He graced a *c*., in which order yet *T*. ii 785
Send him to *c*. If he there be tamed *Tir*. 240
Survey our schools and *c*., and see *Tir*. 909

COLLISION.
Secure from *c*. and dust *Gr*. 22

COLLOQUIAL.
And make *c*. happiness your care *Con*. 82
And sweet *c*. pleasures are but few! *T*. iv 398

COLONEL.
I never will believe," the *c*. cries *H*. 381

COLONNADE.
And the whispering sound of the cool *c*. *P.F.* 2
Not distant far, a length of *c*. *T*. i 253

COLOUR.
Poetry may, but *c*. cannot paint *Con*. 384
Than the *c*. of our kind *N.C.* 52
In *c*. these, and those delight the smell *R*. 794
Their length and *c*. from the locks they spare *T*. i 134
With *c*. mixed for a far different use *T*. iv 240
The public character its *c*. draws *Tir*. 912
Brings *c*. dipped in Heaven, that never die *T.T.* 703

COLOURED.
So Flora's wreath through *c*. crystal seen *H*. 71
Not *c*. like his own, and having power *T*. ii 13

COLT.
Stubborn and sturdy, a wild ass's *c*. *H*. 182
While *c*. and puppies cost us so much care *Tir*. 295

COLTISH.
Man's *c*. disposition asks the thong *P.E.* 360

COLUMN.
I see a *c*. of slow-rising smoke *T*. i 557

Lie scattered where the shapely *c*. stood *T*. ii 76
Throws up a steamy *c*., and the cups *T*. iv 39

COMBAT.
A Trojan *c*. would be something new *Con*. 197
To *c*. may be glorious, and success *T*. iii 687
To *c*. atheists with in modern days *Tir*. 639

COMBATANT.
And teach the *c*. a woman's part? *Ex*. 359
No *c*. are stiffer *F*. 138
Involves the *c*.; each claiming Truth *T*. iii 162

COMBATING.
Suffered by virtue *c*. below? *J.T.* 18.

COMBINE.
Though various foes against the Truth *c*. *T*. 473
In thee some virtuous qualities *c*. *V*. 31

COMBINED.
Sweet scent, or lovely form, or both *c*. *H*. 290
"Since thus ye have *c*.," he said *J.P.* 33
The soft relations, which, *c*. *Miss* — 79
Their periwigs of wool and fears *c*. *N.A.* 75
C. with millions more *O*. i 18
And earthly sounds, though sweet and well *c*. *P.E.* 79
His master's interest and his own *c*. *T*. 193
What happy skill and industry *c*. *T*. 430
In all their private functions, once *c*. *T*. iv 673
Sublimity and Attic taste *c*. *T.T.* 644

COMBINING.
It is *c*. fire with smoke *F*. 119

COMBUSTION.
Who, kindling a *c*. of desire *P.E.* 319

COME.
"*C*. ten, *c*. twenty,—should an army call *A.T.* 185
C., prompt me with benevolent desires *Ch*. 11
We *c*. with joy from our eternal rest *Ch*. 73
"This triple realm adores thee;—thou art *c*. *Ch*. 270
Oh *c*. not ye near innocence and truth *Con*. 39
His wit invites you by his looks to *c*. *Con*. 303
The visit paid, with ecstasy we *c*. *Con*. 399
Of dangers past, and wonders yet to *c*. *Con*. 572
That *c*. to waft us out of sorrow's power *Con*. 592
He feels a gentle tingling *c*. *E*. i 11
Are *c*. from distant Loire to choose *E*. i 47
Whence *c*. it then, that in the wane of life *E*. iii 14
Till gentler Puss shall see *c*. *Ep*. ii 40
Who seeks a friend should *c*. disposed *F*. 43
Till half the world *c*. rattling at his door *H*. 77
Nor hope have they, nor fear of aught to *c*. *H*. 254
C., prophet, drink, and tell us what think you" *H*. 418
Than he who must have pleasure, *c*. what will *H*. 595
Three customers *c*. in *J.G.* 52
Say why bareheaded you are *c*. *J.G.* 167
Or why you *c*. at all?" *J.G.* 168
"I came because your horse would *c*. *J.G.* 173
But ages yet to *c*. shall mourn *M*. i 11
"No doubt, my dear, I bade him *c*. *M.F.* 11
C., then fair maid (in nature wise) *Miss* — 13
The Arts *c*. smiling in the close *Miss* — 81
And suns to *c*., as round they wheel *Miss* — 101
C. fiend, *c*. fury, giant, monster, blast *N.A.* 121
C., peace of mind, delightful guest! *O*. ii 1
I only wish 'twould *c*. *Pat*. 2
But triflers are engaged and cannot *c*. *P.E.* 167
Had known their sovereign *c*. *Q.V.* 44
Look where he *c*.; in this embowered alcove *R*. 283
The wreck of what I was, fatigued I *c*. *R*. 386
Nor yet the parson's who would gladly *c*. *R*. 439
Who *c*. when called, and at a word withdraws *R*. 447
Where neither cold might *c*., nor air *R.C.* 31

COME—COMMENCE

"Susan will *c*. and let me out" *R.C.* 64
We seek it, ere it *c*. to light *R.C.* 97
And those of sorrows yet to *c*. *S*. 24
For yet an hour to *c*. *St.* i 26
Duly at my time I *c*. *St.* iv 13
Spirit of instruction! *c*. *St.* iv 35
Oh for a shelter from the wrath to *c*.! *T*. 268
C., then—a still, small whisper in your ear *T*. 297
He, praised perhaps for ages yet to *c*. *T*. 333
But *c*. at last the dull and dusky eve *T*. i 669
Nor is it well, nor can it *c*. to good *T*. i 739
Fall prone; the pale inhabitants *c*. forth *T*. ii 125
Forth *c*. the pocket mirror.—First we stroke *T*. ii 445
Than once, and others of a life to *c*. *T*. iii 123
Is fed with many a victim. Lo! he *c*. *T*. iii 765
And now perhaps the glorious hour is *c*. *T*. iii 790
He *c*., the herald of a noisy world *T*. iv 5
That it foretells us, always *c*. to pass *T*. iv 72
C., Evening, once again, season of peace *T*. iv 243
C. then, and thou shalt find thy votary calm *T*. iv 259
C. trooping at the housewife's well known call *T*. v 61
C. at his call, and serves him for a friend *T*. v 424
Who calls for things that are not, and they *c*. *T*. v 687
Clear and sonorous, as the gale *c*. on! *T*. vi 10
Again the harmony *c*. o'er the vale *T*. vi 65
An unsuspected storm. His hour was *c*. *T*. vi 545
A pompous and slow-moving pageant *c*. *T*. vi 697
The time of rest, the promised Sabbath, *c*. *T*. vi 733
Into all lands. From every clime they *c*. *T*. vi 814
C. then, and, added to thy many crowns *T*. vi 855
Shows somewhat of that happier life to *c*. *T*. vi 907
Suffer his justice in a world to *c*. *Tir*. 102
And, as maturity of years *c*. on *Tir*. 236
Your son *c*. forth a prodigy of skill *Tir*. 525
Bears witness, long ere his dismission *c*. *Tir*. 561
Find it expedient, *c*. what mischief may *Tir*. 692
Disease or *c*. not, or finds easy cure *Tir*. 766
Of pleasures past, or follies yet to *c*. *Tir*. 776
And say, My boy, the unwelcome hour is *c*. *Tir*. 849
C. heaviest to the ground *Trans. H.* 15
Soon the sweet Spring *c*. dancing forth *Trans. H.* 23
Here, Sally, Susan, *c*., *c*. quick *Tran.* iv 29
He thought the dying hour already *c*. *T.T.* 392
Is punished, and down *c*. the thunderbolt *T.T.* 403
Speak to the present times and times to *c*. *T.T.* 433
C., ponder well, for 'tis no jest *Y.D.* 1
For then the farmers *c*. jog, jog *Y.D.* 13
So in they *c*.—each makes his leg *Y.D.* 29
The dinner *c*., and down they sit *Y.D.* 37
" *C*., neighbours, we must wag " *Y.D.* 50

COMEDY.
Call *c*., to prompt him with a smile? *T*. iv 199

COMELIER.
Though pressed with hunger oft, or *c*. clothes *T*. i 555

COMELINESS.
The praise of wisdom, *c*., and worth *P.E.* 295

COMELY.
Each *c*. in its kind *J.G.* 184

COMET.
The *c.'s* baneful influence is a dream *P.E.* 100
Replace the wandering *c*. in his sphere *T*. 400

COMFORT.
The world's best *c*. was his doom was passed *H*. 568
The *c*. of a few poor, added days *H*. 729
But happier far, who *c*. those that wait *H*. 762
The *c*. of the wedded state *M.F.* 46
Thus grief itself has *c*. dear *Miss* — 53
No pleasure! Are domestic *c*. dead? *P.E.* 243
Where should they find (those *c*. at an end *T*. 439
By its true worth, the *c*. it affords *T*. i 397 [538
Grace, knowledge, *c*.—an unfathomed store? *T*. ii
And *c*. cease. Dress drains our cellar dry *T*. ii 614
Finds a cold bed her only *c*. left *T*. ii 655
And all the *c*. that the lowly roof *T*. iv 141
Nor *c*. else, but in their mutual love *T*. iv 406
The *c*. of a reasonable joy *T*. vi 347
Some taste of *c*. in a world of woe *T*. vi 966
Would die at last in *c*., peace, and joy *Tir*. 150
And thou wilt need some *c*. to assuage *Tir*. 877
One *c*. yet shall cheer thine aged heart *Tir*. 897
And may as rich in *c*. prove *U*. 11

COMFORTLESS.
Was cold and *c*. within *R.C.* 28
Oh *c*. existence! hemmed around *T*. v 432
But ere he gain the *c*. repose *T*. v 596

COMING.
Say Wrath is *c*., and the storm appears *Ex*. 270
John *c*. back amain *J.G.* 222 [ii 614
And hates their *c*. They (what can they less?) *T*.
Which seen delights him not; then *c*. home *T*. iv 236

COMMAND.
Shall a wider world *c*. *B*. 28
In spite of your *c*. *B.R.* 2
That flies, like Gabriel on his Lord's *c*. *Ch*. 135
Are hateful ensigns of usurped *c*. *Ch*. 213
To uphold the boundless scenes of his *c*. *Ch*. 582
Once take the shell beneath his just *c*. *Con*. 904
As soldiers watch the signal of *c*. *Ex*. 119
As fortune, vice, or folly may *c*. *H*. 12
That boasts the treasure, all at his *c*. *H*. 176
Oh! see me sworn to serve thee, and *c*. *H*. 669
The Lily's height bespoke *c*. *L.R.* 13
Oh that a verse had power, and could *c*. *P.E.* 323
The youth, obedient to his sire's *c*. *P.E.* 377
Church-quacks, with passions under no *c*. *P.E.* 474
Ten thousand rivers poured at his *c*. *R*. 75
The tongue whose strains were cogent as *c*. *R*. 411
Influence, and power, were all at his *c*. *R*. 596
The axe will smite at God's *c*. *St.* i 15
If scorn of God's *c*., impressed *St.* vi 29
Sees, far as human optics may *c*. *T*. 3
Watches your eye, anticipates *c*. *T*. 214
And Justice, guardian of the dread *c*. *T*. 277
The occasion—for the Fair *c*. the song *T.* i 7
Exults in its *c*. The sheepfold here *T.* i 290
Though wondrous, He *c*. us, in his word *T*. iii 223
When they *c*. whom man was born to please *T*. iv 265
Such men are raised to station and *c*. *T.T.* 354
To stoop to Tyranny's usurped *c*. *T.T.* 440
When He *c*. in whom they place no trust *T.T.* 471
The Muse imparts, and can *c*. the lyre *T.T.* 481
An ell or two of prospect we *c*. *T.T.* 581
The laurel seemed to wait on his *c*. *T.T.* 688
At her *c*. winds rise and waters roar *Tir*. 25
A task as much within your own *c*. *Tir*. 552
Patient, affectionate, of high *c*. *Tir*. 602
His heart, now passive, yields to thy *c*. *Tir*. 885

COMMANDER.
See great *c*. making war a trade *Tir*. 821

COMMEMORATING.
And, next, *c*. worthies lost *J.T.* 3

COMMEMORATION.
C. mad; content to hear *T*. vi 635

COMMENCE.
The reign of genuine charity *c*. *Ch*. 413
Of the last meal *c*. A Roman meal *T*. iv 168

COMMEND.
Could give advice, could censure, or *c. R.* 291

COMMENDATION.
And, more than all, with *c.* due *Tir.* 646

COMMENDED.
Much to be pitied or *c. P.* 44

COMMENDING.
That were not; and *c.* as they would *T.* vi 236

COMMENT.
Hence *c.* after *c.*, spun as fine *P.E.* 494

COMMERCE.
Again—the band of *c.* was designed *Ch.* 83
Where *c.* has enriched the busy coast *Ch.* 114
And *C.* partially reclaims mankind *Ch.* 372
Her peaceful shores, where busy *C.* waits *Ev.* 13
Increasing *c.* and reviving art *Her.* 73
In London. Where has *c.* such a mart *T.* i 719
Of riper joys, and *c.* with the world *T.* ii 763
And to the stir of *C.*, driving slow *T.* iii 739
There, in his *c.* with the liveried herd *Tir.* 688

COMMERCIAL.
The fears and hopes of a *c.* caro *Ch.* 279
Thee, therefore, of *c.* fame, but more *J.T.* 5
Of innocent *c.* Justice red *T.* iv 683

COMMISSION.
When sent with God's *c.* to the heart *T.* ii 471

COMMIT.
But when the breath of age *c.* the fault *Con.* 49
C. no wrong, nor wastes what it enjoys *T.* i 334
And glossy, he *c.* to pots of size *T.* iii 512
And conscious of the outrage he *c. T.* vi 599
C. her eggs, incautious, to the dust *Tir.* 791

COMMITTEE.
As if in close *c.* on the sky *Con.* 385

COMMITTED.
The secret just *c. F.* 69
C. once into the public arms *P.E.* 518
Though *c.* every day *St.* iv 28

COMMODIOUS.
We have at least *c.* standing here *N.A.* 120
Convivial table and *c.* seat *T.* v 162
(What seemed at least *c.* seat) were there *T.* v 163

COMMON.
One man the *c.* father of the kind *Ch.* 18
No land but listens to the *c.* call *Ch.* 91
Man to the centre of the *c.* cause *Ch.* 328
Henceforth associate in one *c.* herd *Con.* 76
Religion, Virtue, Reason, *C.* Sense *Con.* 77
Rove where you please, 'tis *c.* all around *Con.* 100
Though *c.* sense, allowed a casting voice *Con.* 663
Prose answers every *c.* end *E.* i 2
Each man of *c.* sense agrees *E.* iv 68
All men of *c.* sense allow *E.* iv 69
Till perjuries are *c.* as bad pence *Ex.* 387
Unless belied by *c.* fame *F.* 86
The *c.* care that waits on all beside *H.* 539
His speech rebellion against *c.* sense *H.* 565
In *c.* to the lot of all *M.F.* 42
Faith, want of *c.* sense *St.* vi 22
The *c.*, overgrown with fern, and rough *T.* i 526
As to a *c.* and most noisome sewer *T.* i 683
And stand exposed by *c.* peccancy *T.* ii 72
"Defend me therefore, *C.* Sense," say *T.* iii 187
One *c.* Maker bound me to the kind? *T.* iii 209
For mercy and the *c.* rights of man *T.* iv 680

That being parcel of the *c.* mass *T.* v 247
To serve him nobly in the *c.* cause *T.* v 344
Of the same grove, and drink one *c.* stream *T.* vi 776
And, *c.* sense diffusing real day *Tir.* 189
Except of caution and of *c.* sense *Tir.* 258
For more than *c.* punishment, it shall *Tir.* 411
The great and small deserve one *c.* blame *Tir.* 515
With savoury truth and wholesome *c.* sense *Tir.* 629

COMMONPLACE
That savour much of *c. F.* 161

COMMONWEALTH.
From pools and ditches of the *c. T.* iii 809
We the chief patron of the *c. T.* v 349

COMMUNICATE.
Pants to *c.* her noble fires *Ch.* 403
Feeds sparingly, *c.* his store *H.* 521
'Tis generous to *c.* your skill *T.* ii 282
C., with joy, the good she finds *T.T.* 275

COMMUNICATIVE.
C. of the good he owns *T.* i 332

COMMUNION.
When one that holds *c.* with the skies *Ch.* 435
And flow in free *c.* with the rest *Ch.* 611
When souls drawn upwards in *c.* sweet *Con.* 569
From such *c.* in their pleasant course *Con.* 698
Divine *C.*, carefully enjoyed *R.* 747
Divine *C.* chases as the day *R.* 765

COMPACT.
So polished and *c.* from head to heel *A.T.* 184
Nor more harmonious or *c. Mrs. M—* 40
The uplifted frame, *c.* at every joint *T.* iii 484
In verse well disciplined, complete *c. T.T.* 647

COMPANION.
Whose only fit *c.* is his horse *Con.* 412
Keep still the dear *c.* at their side? *Con.* 734
Should deem it by our old *c.* made *N.A.* 95
And witness, dear *c.* of my walks *T.* i 144
That drag the dull *c.* to and fro *T.* iv 368
The rude *c.* smiled, as if transformed *T.* vi 543

COMPANY.
In *c.* with man *A Tale* 72
And give good *c.* a face severe *Con.* 873
He chooses *c.* but not the squire's *R.* 437

COMPARE.
C. what then thou wast, with what thou art *Ex.* 557
So, fire with water to *c. Q.V.* 17
To spread the page of Scripture, and *c. R.* 131
Reverenced no less. Who could with him *c.? T.* v 235

COMPARED.
C. with the speed of its flight *A.S.* 42
C. with this sublimest life below *R.* 103
All evils then seem light, *c. St.* v 27
C. with the repose the Sofa yields *T.* i 102
Oh innocent, *c.* with arts like these *T.* iii 801
Of Nature, and though poor perhaps *c. T.* v 739
Worthy, *c.* with sycophants, who kneel *T.* vi 886
And never withering wreaths, *c.* with which *T.* vi 938
Half a span, *c.* with thee *Tran.* iii 32

COMPARING.
Though cannot spend itself, *c.* still *Y.O.* 86

COMPARISON.
Lost nothing by *c.* with ours? *T.* i 648

COMPASS.
C. earth, dives into it, ascends *Ch.* 315

And give the strain the c. it demands Con. 718 [103
Sails ripped, seams opening wide, and c. lost M.P.
His ship half foundered, and his c. lost T. 2
And must be bribed to c. earth again T. i 676
To c. that good end, forecast the means Tir. 884

COMPASSED.
Thus c. about with the goods Gr. 49

COMPASSION.
With much c. undertakes the task P.E. 389
Claims most c., and receives the least R. 302
In kind c. of his failing strength R. 626
Such claim c. in a night like this T. iv 375
Man may dismiss c. from his heart T. vi 442

COMPASSIONATE.
Learns to c. the sick she sees Ch. 411.
To faults c. or blind M.F. 56

COMPATRIOT.
And Wolfe's great name c. with his own T. ii 238

COMPENSATE.
He may c. for a day of sloth T. iv 434

COMPENSATING.
C. his loss with added hours T. iv 134
Of rural scenes, c. his loss T. iv 768
But well c. her sickly looks T. vi 163

COMPETENCE.
The road that leads from c. and peace T. iv 496

COMPETENT.
And he was c. whose purse was so T. ii 742

COMPETITION.
Few c. but engender spite Con. 161
The spirit of that c. burns Tir. 474
To scenes where c., envy, strife V. 75

COMPLACENCE.
With looks of some c. he resumed T. vi 535

COMPLACENCY.
He views it with c. supreme P.E. 522
C. has breathed a gentle gale T. 419

COMPLAIN.
To prove an evil of which all c. E. iii 43
Thy racked inhabitants repine, c. Ex. 304
How sweet soe'er the verse c. Miss — 11
C. of being thus exposed P. 50
C. not if attachments lewd and base Tir. 889

COMPLAINED.
Few Frenchmen of this evil have c. Con. 359
In gentle sounds it seems as it c. Con. 905
The wrong was his who wrongfully c. H. 321
C., though incommodiously pent in T. i 69

COMPLAINING.
Nor is it wise c. F. 33
C. in a speech well worded P. 3

COMPLAINT.
And captious cavil and c. subside H. 144
Their long c. is self-inflicted woe T. iv 430
That here begins with most that long c. Tir. 587
And 'tis the sad c., and almost true T.T. 732

COMPLETE.
To make the shining prodigy c. Ch. 602
Though various yet c. Dr. 10
On terms of amity c. F. 116

The palace were but half c. F. 166
The worth of each had been c. J.P. 5
With all her crew c.! R.G. 12
And armed himself in panoply c. T. ii 345
Of their c. effect. Much yet remains T. iii 605
And a c. recovery struck him dumb T.T. 393
In verse well disciplined, c., compact T.T. 647

COMPLETELY.
Is a pearl cast, c. cast away H. 259
But makes him, if at all, c. free H. 646
Not yet by time c. silvered o'er T. ii 703

COMPLEX.
Oh how unlike the c. works of man T. 21

COMPLEXION.
Fleecy locks and black c. N.C. 13
Hence the c. of his future days T. 280
Chequered with all c. of mankind T. iii 836

COMPLIANCE.
C. with his will your lot ensures H. 326.

COMPLIED.
C. with, and were graciously dismissed Ex. 541

COMPLIMENT.
But first the squire's, a c. but due Ch. 470
And many a c. politely penned T.T. 721

COMPLY.
Which men c. with e'en because they must H. 386
Some to c. with humour, and a mind R. 605
But to c. with feelings, and to give V. 23

COMPOSE.
C. their useless wing N. 2
An eyebrow, next c. a straggling lock T. ii 446
C. the passions, and exalt the mind T. iii 305
Serve to c. a spirit well inclined T. v 657

COMPOSED.
True bliss, if man may reach it, is c. Con. 679
I could be much c., nor should appear N.A. 89
" For soon as I was well c. R.C. 57

COMPOST.
May turn the clod, and wheel the c. home T. iii 637

COMPOSURE.
Nor less c. waits upon the room T. 190
How perfect the c. of his soul! T. 481
Or make me so. C. is thy gift T. iv 260

COMPOUND.
No papist more desirous to c. T. 291
Is an ingredient in the c., man T. iv 732
Or rather a gross c., justly tried Tir. 466

COMPOUNDED.
C. and made up like other men T. v 307

COMPREHEND.
To c. the case D.W. 24
What simplest minds can soonest c. H. 452
Are qualities that seem to c. P.E. 423

COMPREHENSION.
In which all c. wanders lost T. iv 75

COMPREHENSIVE.
A c. faculty that grasps T. v 251
Such c. views the spirit takes T. vi 15

COMPRESS.
C. the sum into its solid worth Con. 20
And neatly fitted, it c. hard T. ii 587

COMPRESSED—CONDENSED

COMPRESSED.
The man of business and his friends c. R. 495

COMPRESSION.
Fades rapidly, and by c. marred T. iv 669

COMPRISED.
Of giddy joys c. St. vi 10

COMPROMISE.
Then c. had place, and scrutiny T. ii 740

COMPUNCTIONS.
Of laughter his c. are sincere T. v. 616

COMPUTE.
Whether he measure earth, c. the sea Ch. 353
And "Hence," he said, "my mind c. Mor. 25
With which she calculates, c., and scans T. i 716

COMRADES.
His c. who before Cast. 44
And went with his c. the apples to seize P.A. 42
And sighs for the smart c. he has left T. iv 648

COMUS.
Let C. rise archbishop of the land P.E. 184

CONCEAL.
Are insincere, meant only to c. Con. 785
Successfully c. her loathsome form P.E. 8
More tattered still; and both but ill c. T. i 551
And show the name ye might c. at home T. ii 279
C. the mood lethargic with a mask T. iv 299

CONCEALED.
C. within an unsuspected part Con. 365
He found, c. beneath a fair outside Ex. 89
Where'er they flow, now seen, and now c. H. 48
With nothing here that wants to be c. H. 406
A narrow brook, by rushy banks c. N.A. 9
Stand close c., and see a statue move R. 284
My partners in retreat. Disgust c. T. iii 38
Or having, kept c. Some drill and bore T. iii 150

CONCEALING.
Sin's rotten trunk c. its defects P.E. 288

CONCEALMENT.
And waits, in snug c. laid Ep. ii 39

CONCEIT. [618
The strange c., vain projects, and wild dreams H.
A silly fond c. of his fair form T. ii 420

CONCEIVE.
He first c., then perfects his design Ex. 318
The impatient fervour which it first c. T. iii 502
However trivial all that he c. T. iv 69 [374
But slaves that once c. the glowing thought T. v

CONCEIVED.
This fits not nicely, that is ill c. T. ii 603
Each animal, of every name, c. T. vi 373

CONCEIVING.
Begetting and c. all that's base P.E. 569
The birds c. a design P.T. 11
C. thunders, through a thousand deeps T. ii 89

CONCEPTION.
And He that gives c. aids the birth Con. 434
For their c., which they cannot move T. v 254

CONCERN.
They left these bodily c. at large A.T. 130
Right reverend sirs! was no c. of theirs A.T. 132
Affects indeed a most humane c. Ch. 495
The system of a world's c. E. i 74
Her grave c., her kind suspicions, there H. 516
Thy maidens grieved themselves at my c. M.P. 36
His flock the chief c. he ever knew R. 404
His best c. aright St. v 6
The least of our c. (since from the least T. ii 167
As God's ambassador, the grand c. T. ii 464
Yet careless what he brings, his one c. T. iv 9
Its fluctuations, and its vast c. ? T. iv 56
The globe and its c., I seem advanced T. iv 95
In lucrative c. Examine well T. iv 606
The incumbrance of his own c., and spare T. vi 206
That man's attainments in his own c. T. vi 613
Forgive him, then, thou bustler in c. T. vi 951
But truths on which depends our main c. Tir. 77
While morals languish, a despised c. Tir. 514
Is no c. at all of his Tran. ii 29

CONCERNED.
An ordinance it c. them much to know H. 313
For Providence, that seems c. to exempt Tir. 430

CONCERT.
Some love a c. or a race L.W. 31
Sweet birds in c. with harmonious streams R. 259
With artless airs and c. of her own T.T. 697

CONCERTO.
The full c. swells upon your ear P.E. 128

CONCISE.
And finished his c. repast Mor. 6

CONCLUDE.
C. his unfeigned love of him, a feint Con. 748
We should unwarily c. F. 28
With wire and catgut he c. the day P.E. 126

CONCLUSION.
And gains remote c. at a jump Con. 154
C. retrograde, and mad mistake T. iii 239
And in c. mar them. Nature's threads Y.O. 80

CONCOCTED.
And meliorate the well c. juice T. 496

CONCUPISCENCE.
Will Avarice and C. give place P.E. 104

CONCUSSION.
Thrives by the rude c. of the storm T. i 378

CONDEMN.
With a reasoning the court will never c. A.C. 22
Their haste himself c. Cast. 32
She makes excuses where she might c. Ch. 424
Seen in another they at once c. Con. 156
C. the prattler, for his idle pains R. 547
C. the injurious deed, the slanderous tongue T. 559
And making prize of all that he c. T. ii 604
C., approves, and with a faithful voice Tir. 33
Which, though in plain plebeians we c. Tir. 352
The rest will slight thy counsel, or c. Tir. 805
C. the unfatherly, the imprudent part Tir. 866
Maintaining yours, you cannot theirs c. T.T. 49

CONDEMNED.
"Ah, hapless wretch! c. to dwell P. 5
Like fabled Tantalus, c. to hear P.E. 231
Immured though unaccused, c. untried T. v 393
Perversely, which of late she so c. T. v 631

CONDENSED.
The dews c. into angelic food Ex. 182
And fast c. upon the dewy sash T. iii 496

CONDESCEND.
That throned above all height he c. *Ch.* 587
The just Creator c. to write *H.* 133

CONDESCENDING.
A man whom marks of c. grace *R.* 445
More nourish pride, that c. vice *T.* 123
While c. Majesty looks on *T.T.* 138

CONDITION.
His hard c. with severe constraint *T.* i 612
And no c. of this changeful life *T.* v 768

CONDUCT.
Than while his c. proves his heart sincere *Con.* 766
They could have held the c. they pursue *H.* 256
The mind and c. mutually imprint *P.E.* 566
Our c. with the laws engraven there *R.* 132
And Conscience and our C. judge us all? *R.* 660
Of all his c. this the genuine sense *T.* 94
Whence springs the c. that offends you so *T.* 237
His c., to the test, but tries his heart *T.* 562
C. the eye along his sinuous course *T.* i 165
Is to c. it to the destined inn *T.* iv 10   [v 650
"Nay—c. hath the loudest tongue. The voice *T.*
C. the unguarded nose to such a whiff *T.* iv 469
In balance on his c. of a pin? *T.* vi 271
By their own c. they must stand or fall *T.T.* 108

CONDUCTED.
C. on a manageable scale *Tir.* 703

CONDUCTING.
Build factories with blood, c. trade *T.* iv 681

CONDUIT.
"As freely as a c. spout! *E.* iv 86

CONE.
Such reasoning falls like an inverted c. *T.T.* 53

CONFABULATE.
If birds c. or no *P.T.* 2

CONFECTIONARY.
The biscuit, or c. plum *M.P.* 61

CONFEDERACY.
A dark c. against the laws *Con.* 685
C. of projectors wild and vain *T.* v 194

CONFEDERATE.
Of Earth and Hell c. take away *T.* v 541
That hellish foes, c. for his harm *T.* v 735

CONFER.
Can Nature add a charm, or Art c. *Ex.* 5

CONFERENCE.
And held accustomed c. with my heart *F.A.* 9
Sweet C.; inquires what strains were they *T.* v 818

CONFERRED.
The charter was c., by which we hold *T.* vi 451

CONFESS.
A distant virtue we can all c. *H.* 552
I do c. them nurseries of the arts *T.* i 693
True, I am no proficient, I c. *T.* iii 210
Nor need one; I am conscious and c. *T.* iv 284
To see their sovereign, and c. his sway *T.* vi 356
Then let the supercilious great c. *T.* vi 967
(Forgive the crime) I wish them, I c. *Tir.* 921
Or candidly c. yourself a dunce *T.T.* 571

CONFESSED.
C. the wonder, and with daring tongue *Ex.* 155
And God's disposing providence c. *Ex.* 558

And say ;—"Blot out my sin, c., deplored *H.* 592
Are hurtful is a truth c. by all *P.E.* 226
Jack bowed and was obliged;—c.'twas strange *R.*599
Can a Truth, by all c. *St.* iv 21
That grace was Cowper's—his, c. by all *T.* 119
A power, c. so lately on his knees *Tir.* 180
C. a God; they kneeled before they fought *T.T.* 374

CONFIDENCE.
"Honour, esteem and c. forgot *A.T.* 111
He mounts at once—such c. infused *A.T.* 175
And, with a fearless c., make known *Con.* 695
She boasts a c. she does not hold *Con.* 768
Perhaps his c. just then betrayed *E.* iii 36
Shall win my c. again *F.* 190
Fresh c. the speculatist takes *P.E.* 490
For I have gained thy c., have pledged *T.* iii 346
But who, with filial c. inspired *T.* v 745
Begat a tranquil c. in all *T.* vi 366
By no kind arts his c. again *Tir.* 586

CONFIDENT.
To build our altar, c. and bold *Con.* 849
Trembling yet happy, c. yet meek *T.* 572
And c. assurance of the rest *T.* v 576
They may acquire that c. address *Tir.* 349
Most c., when palpably most wrong *T.T.* 143

CONFIDENTLY.
By some 'tis c. said *L.W.* 17
Where Duty bids he c. steers *R.H.* 6

CONFINE.
To muse in silence, or at least c. *T.* iii 36
For he who values Liberty c. *T.* v 393
Nor penury, can cripple or c. *T.* v 772
Within the c. of their wild domain *T.* vi 407   [96
"But where, good sir, do you c. your kings"? *T.T*
C. the million in the beaten track *T.T.* 667

CONFINED.
The swell of pity, not to be c. *Ch.* 246
Or only what in cottages c. *Ex.* 29
And to domestic bounds c. *E.P.* ii 7
But Tom was still c. *F.B.* 21
Than that to which he keeps c. *Mrs. M—* 41
Discoverers of they know not what, c. *P.E.* 476
However humble and c. the sphere *T.T.* 166

CONFIRM.
Because the deed, by which his love c. *H.* 324
Then obstinate self-will c. him so *P.E.* 543
They may c. his habits, rivet fast *T.* ii 767
As bound in duty, would c. the choice *Tir.* 419

CONFIRMATION.
In c. of the noblest claim *T.* v 720

CONFIRMED.
C. by long experience of thy worth *T.* i 147
Takes deeper root, c. by what they see *T.* ii 568

CONFLAGRATION.
A c., or a wintry flood *Ch.* 465
The thought of c. *F.* 108
A c. labouring in her womb *Her.* 12

CONFLICT.
Points out a c. with thyself, the worst *R.* 268
With c. of contending hopes and fears *T.* i 668

CONFOUND.
Our softer satellite. Your songs c. *T.* i 766
(If power she be that works but to c.) *T.* v 872

CONFOUNDED.
When Babel was c., and the great *T.* v 193

CONFUSION.
But gay c.; roses for the cheeks *T.* iv 79

CONFUTATION.
Formed for the c. of the fool *T.* v 567

CONGEALED.
Thy breath c. upon thy lips, thy cheeks *T.* iv 122
That trickle down the branches, fast c. *T.* v 114

CONGENIAL.
C. with thine own; and if it be *T.* iii 205

CONGRATULATE.
Is to c., not to praise *E.* ii 2

CONGREGATED.
By c. loads adhering close *T.* iv 344

CONJECTURE.
C. gripes the victims in his paw *Ch.* 525
C. and remark, however shrewd *T.T.* 205

CONJECTURED.
C., sniffing round and round *T.B.* 40

CONJOINED.
Were soon c.; nor other cement asked *T.* v 147

CONJUGATED.
But c. verbs and nouns declined? *Tir.* 619

CONJUGATION.
Of an immediate c. *P.T.* 41

CONJURE.
To c. clean away the gold they touch *T.* i 571

CONJURED.
And that my raptures are not c. up *T.* i 151

CONJURERS.
They teach both c. and old women *A. Fable* 21

CONNECTED.
For vicious ends c. *F.* 42
In early years c., time unbinds *Tir.* 439
Unchangeably c. with its cause) *T.T.* 443

CONNECTING.
He too has a c. power, and draws *Ch.* 327

CONNEXION.
And plans and orders our c. *E.* i 36
There form c., but acquire no friend *T.* ii 634
Have oft-times no c., knowledge dwells *T.* vi 89
C. formed for interest, and endeared *Tir.* 495

CONNIVE.
But ye c. at what ye cannot cure *Tir.* 275

CONQUER.
Sure not to c., and sure not to yield *Ch.* 621
To c. those by jocular exploits *T.* ii 479
Generals, who will not c. when they may *T.T.* 194

CONQUERED.
When Obstinacy once has c. Grace *Ex.* 152
Lords of the c. soil, there rooted fast *Ex.* 192
Exported slavery to the c. East? *Ex.* 365

CONQUERING.
Like a proud swan, c. the stream by force *T.T.* 523

CONQUEROR.
And at this hour the c. feels the proof *Ch.* 60
How much the country to the c. owes *Ex.* 481
Renew the quarrel on the c.'s part *Her.* 74

CONQUEST.
And, cursed with c., finally succeed *Con.* 692
Proclaims the soil a c. he has won *H.* 479
Thy word fulfilled, the c. of a world! *T.* vi 905
Secure of c. where the prize *Th.* 15

CONSCIENCE.
While C., happier than in ancient years *Ch.* 274
Some seek, when queasy c. has its qualms *Ch.* 447
Hast thou, with heart perverse and c. seared *Ex.* 396
But C., in some awful, silent hour *H.* 215
That c. there performs her proper part *H.* 692
His c. owns it true *H.F.* 16
Heaven from above, and C. from within *P.E.* 37
Thus c. freed from every clog *L.W.* 21 [*P.E.* 246
Good sense, good health, good c. and good fame?
Thus C. pleads her cause within the breast *R.* 15
Is there, as Reason, C., Scripture say *R.* 651
And C. and our Conduct judge us all? *R.* 660
The cause is c.; —c. oft *St.* v 21
His c., like a glassy lake before *T.* 259
Their judge was C., and her rule their law *T.* 535
Soon follows, and the curb of c. snapped *T.* ii 571
And warps the c. of public men *T.* ii 691
Great crimes alarm the c., but it sleeps *T.* iii 185
And self-reproaching c.? He foresees *T.* v 600
He slights the strokes of c. Nothing moves *T.* v 666
With c. and with thee. Lust in their hearts *T.* vi 895
He by the test of c., and a heart *T.* vi 988
In early days the c. has in most *Tir.* 109
Though c. will have twinges now and then *T.T.* 425
Imagined sanctity. The c., yet *Y.O.* 11

CONSCIENTIOUS.
To touch the sword with c. awe *T.T.* 77

CONSCIOUS.
Shrieked at the sight, and, c., fled the place *A.T.* 200
And c. of an unincumbered back *Ch.* 174
That, c. of her crimes, she feels instead *Con.* 769
Hope! let the wretch, once c. of the joy *H.* 171
When, c. of no danger from below *Her.* 3
Say, wast thou c. of the tears I shed? *M.P.* 22
C. of weakness in its noblest powers *R.* 124
C. of jeopardy incurred *R.C.* 76
C. of age, she recollects her youth *T.* 153
Then, c. of her meritorious zeal *T.* 497
The ruffling wind, scarce c. that it blew *T.* i 156
Himself, as c. of his awful charge *T.* ii 403
The welcome call, c. how much the hand *T.* iii 399
Nor need one; I am c. and confess *T.* iv 284
What, c. of your virtues, we can spare *T.* iv 425
Grows c. of a change, and likes it well *T.* iv 638
C. and fearful of too deep a plunge *T. v.* 64
C. of impotence they soon grow drunk *T.* v 255
Is weakness when opposed; c. of wrong *T.* v 372
And under pressure of some c. cause? *T.* vi 220
And, c. of some danger, either fled *T.* vi 375
And c. of the outrage he commits *T.* vi 599
Yes—ye are c.; and on all the shelves *Tir.* 269
Unless thy c. heart acknowledge—none *Tir.* 580
Nor say, go thither, c. that there lay *Tir.* 869

CONSCIOUSNESS.
There dwells a c. in every breast *H.* 636

CONSECRATE.
To c. our few remaining groves *Con.* 826

CONSECRATED.
All c. to adorn the fair *A.T.* 16
Thy Levites, once a c. host *Ex.* 263
With holiness and c. rest *P.E.* 158
Thus studied, used and c thus *R.* 105
Yet awful as the c. roof *T.* i 342

CONSECRATION.
'Tis *c.* of his heart, soul, time *R.* 223

CONSENT.
But sing and shine by sweet *c. N.G.* 31
When health required it, would *c.* to roam *R.* 517
With one *c.* to rush into the sea *R.* 524
And I *c.* you take it for your text *T.* ii 474
Their efforts, yet resolved with one *c. T.* vi 338
Nor would the Nine *c.* the sacred tide *T.T.* 184

CONSEQUENCE.
Admit it true, the *c.* is clear *Con.* 165
Of your own worth and *c. R.C.* 110
To prove a *c.* by none denied *Tir.* 104
Shall give him *c.*, heal all defects *Tir.* 392

CONSERVATORS.
Like *c.* of the public health *Con.* 390

CONSERVATORY.
And drenched *c.* breathes abroad *T.* iii 498

CONSIDER.
C. all injustice with a frown *Ch.* 210

CONSIDERATE.
With fixed *c.* face *D.W.* 22

CONSIDERED.
I passed, and next *c.*—what is man ? *F.A.* 21
With well *c.* steps, seems to resent *T.* v 75

CONSIGNED.
Thy friend, though to a cloister's shade *c. S.* ii 2

CONSIST.
Safety *c.* not in escape *A Fable* 32
If monarchy *c.* in such base things *T.T.* 139

CONSISTENT.
A pledge he gave for a *c.* part *Tir.* 178

CONSOLE.
Our groves were planted to *c.* at noon *T.* i 760

CONSOLED.
C. him and dispelled his fears *R.C.* 90
That soothe the rich possessor; much *c. T.* iv 755

CONSOLIDATED.
Forced downward, is *c.* soon *T.* iv 349

CONSORT.
Then, perching at his *c.'s* side *A Tale* 53
And thy loved *c.* on the dangerous tide *M.P.* 93

CONSPICUOUS.
C. as the brightness of a star *T.* 29
Brings not alone the more *c.* part *T.* 561
C. many a league, the mariner *T.* i 521
By more than one, themselves *c.* there *T.* ii 787
C., and in bright apparel clad *T.* v 25
Makes more *c.*, and illumines more *T.* vi 175

CONSPIRE.
C. to honour thee *Dr.* 4
C. against thy peace with one design *R.* 262
C. against him. With his breath, he draws *T.* ii 139
Inveterate, hopeless of a cure, *c. T.* iv 577

CONSPIRING.
C., may attest his bright design *T.* iii 654

CONSTABLE.
Then kill a *c.*, and drink five more *P.E.* 194

CONSTANCY.
That *c.* befits them *F.* 159

Or nothing much, his *c.* in ill *T.* v 667
And in the *c.* of nature's course *T.* vi 123
And *c.* sincere *The Doves* 14
With packhorse *c.* we keep the road *Tir.* 252
We hug the hopes of *c.* and truth *V.* 53

CONSTANT.
" Vain our delusive hope of *c.* knights *A.T.* 100
The *c.* creaking of a country sign *Con.* 10
Through *c.* dread of giving Truth offence *Con.* 129
Yet still, o'erclouded with a *c.* frown *Con.* 339
If Business, *c.* as the wheels of time *Ex.* 604
But ah ! by *c.* heed I know *M.* 45
Thy *c.* flow of love, that knew no fall *M.P.* 65
In *c.* exhalations *O.* i 8
Escaped from office and its *c.* cares *R.* 408
Thump after thump resounds the *c.* flail *T.* i 357
C. rotation of the unwearied wheel *T.* i 368
It is the *c.* revolution, stale *T.* i 462
So lately found, although the *c.* sun *T.* i 621
C. at routs, familiar with a round *T.* ii 385
For thou art meek and *c.*, hating change *T.* iii 55
And *c.* occupation without care *T.* iii 693
Who, *c.* only in rejecting thee *T.* vi 882
Ye knew at least, by *c.* proofs addressed *Tir.* 273
From *c.* converse with I know not whom *Tir.* 854

CONSTANTLY.
And *c.* supported *F.* 51

CONSTELLATION.
Or rather *c. F.* 12
Views *C.* brighter than her own *P.E.* 178
That *c.* set, the world in vain *T.T.* 660

CONSTITUTE.
Must *c.* the charming whole *F.* 59

CONSTITUTED.
And *c.* guardians of his cause *Ex.* 200

CONSTITUTIONAL.
Patient of *c.* control *T.T.* 224

CONSTITUTIONALLY.
Who *c.* pulls *Pat.* 15

CONSTRAIN.
That I should ill requite thee, to *c. M.P.* 86

CONSTRAINED.
Shall be *c.* to love thee. Though thy clime *T.* ii 200
Or by necessity *c.*, they live *T.* vi 413
The mind, released from too *c.* a nerve *T.T.* 622

CONSTRAINING.
Free too, and under no *c.* force *Tir.* 861

CONSTRAINT.
Each individual, suffering a *c. Con.* 383
Abhors *c.*, and dares not feign a zeal *Con.* 713
And, serving God herself through mere *c. Con.* 717
His hard condition with severe *c. T.* i 612
And we are weeds without it. All *c. T.* v 418

CONSTRUCTED.
If shrewd, and of a well *c.* brain *Tir.* 523

CONSTRUCTION.
So liberal in *c.*, and so rich *T.* iii 94

CONSULT.
Yet to *c.* a little seemed no crime *Con.* 865
C. life's silent clock, thy bounding vein *Ep.* i 3
C. all day your interest and your ease *T.* 217

CONSULTED.
C. and obeyed, to guide his steps *T.* v 674

CONSULTING.
C. England's happiness at home *T.* ii 246

CONSUME.
C. his soul with vain desires *P.B.* 16
Where beauty oft and lettered worth *c. T.* ii 123

CONSUMED.
How oft, my slice of pocket store *c. T.* i 118
Angry and sad, and his last crust *c. T.* i 246
In penury *c.* his idle hours *T.T.* 673

CONSUMMATE.
Would only prove him a *c.* fool *Con.* 140
Creates, gives birth to, guides, *c.* all *Ex.* 315

CONSUMMATION.
There was the *c.* and the crown *Ex.* 221

CONTACT.
In *c.* inconvenient, nose to nose *Con.* 270

CONTAGION.
To me their peace by kind *c.* spread *N.A.* 42
If such escape *c.*, and emerge *T.* ii 797
Should some *c.*, kind to the poor brutes *T.* iii 308
C., and disseminating death *T.* iii 617
Lurks the *c.* chiefly to be feared *Tir.* 689

CONTAGIOUS.
And dreaded more than a *c.* touch *Con.* 652
Catch from each other a *c.* spot *Ex.* 105
To the next rank *c.*, and in time *T.* iv 584

CONTAINS.
To guess and spell what it *c. E.* i 52

CONTAMINATING.
Should fly the world's *c.* touch *Ex.* 446

CONTEMNS.
Her dear five hundred friends, *c.* them all *T.* ii 643

CONTEMPLATE.
For can we find it less? *C.* first *N.A.* 109

CONTEMPLATING.
C. with small delight 1789, 24

CONTEMPLATION.
By *C.'s* help, not sought in vain *M.P.* 114
In *c.* of a turnpike-road *R.* 506
Scenes formed for *c.*, and to nurse *T.* iii 301
And *c.*, heart-consoling joys *T.* iv 781
To *c.*, and within his reach *T.* vi 263
Therefore in *c.* is his bliss *T.* vi 924

CONTEMPLATIVE.
See where he sits, *c.* and fixed *T.* 415
The mind *c.*, with some new theme *T.* iv 280
Thus men, whose thoughts *c.* have dwelt *T.T.* 168

CONTEMPORARIES.
C. all surpassed, see one *T.T.* 670

CONTEMPT.
He pours *c.* on them, and on their cause *Ex.* 329
That, through profane and infidel *c. T.* i 740
What's that which brings *c.* upon a book *T.* iij 277
The hallowed bench from absolute *c. Tir.* 431
See what *c.* is fallen on humankind *Tir.* 814

CONTEMPTIBLE.
Proof not *c.* of what she can *Y.O.* 131

CONTEND.
Live to no sober purpose, and *c. H.* 129

CONTENDING.
With conflict of *c.* hopes and fears *T.* i 663

CONTENT.
Or scare the nation with its big *c. Ch.* 617
C. on earth in earthly things to shine *Con.* 583
I could be well *c.*, allowed the use *F.A.* 1
Like him he laboured, and like him *c. H.* 586
Not for my own *c.* or ease *P.* 8
C. with Bristol, Bath, and Tunbridge Wells *R.* 516
C. if thus sequestered I may raise *R.* 805
Like thee, *c.* in every state may find *S.* ii 7
Than he contrives to suffer well *c. T.* 104
C. though mean, and cheerful if not gay *T.* 319
In modest mediocrity, *c. T.* i 50
Or make his house his grave: nor so *c. T.* ii 147
Men that if now alive, would sit *c. T.* ii 541
Can dig, beg, rot, and perish, well *c. T.* iii 805
Retires, *c.* to quake, so they be warmed *T.* iv 386
For ever dribbling out their base *c. T.* iv 506
To me an unambitious mind, *c. T.* iv 798
And reigns *c.* within them: him we serve *T.* v 333
Of that one feature can be well *c. T.* v 474
Man views it and admires, but rests *c. T.* v 791
The redbreast warbles still, but is *c. T.* vi 77
Commemoration mad; *c.* to hear *T.* vi 635
Its squeezed *c.*, and more than it admits *T.* vi 671
C. indeed to sojourn while he must *T.* vi 913
And is he well *c.* his son should find *Tir.* 617
To exchange *c.* for trouble, ease for pain *V.* 64
C. of heart, more praises still are due *V.* 90
Thou hadst within thy bole solid *c. Y.O.* 94

CONTENTED.
And I, *c.* with an humble theme *T.* vi 719
That slaves, howe'er *c.*, never know *T.T.* 261

CONTENTEDLY.
And lives *c.* between *Trans. H.* 8

CONTENTION.
The trumpet of *c. F.* 99
But where will fierce *c.* end *L.R.* 3

CONTENTIOUS.
Boys, once on fire with that *c.* zeal *Tir.* 470

CONTEST.
Between Nose and Eyes a strange *c.* arose *A.C.* 1
A bolder still, a *c.* with the skies? *Ex.* 699
He dies disputing, and the *c.* ends *P.E.* 553
Great *c.* follows, and much learned dust *T.* iii 161
All that the *c.* calls for; spirit, strength *T.* v 376
The bottomless demands of *c.* waged *Y.O.* 102

CONTIGUITY.
Some boundless *c.* of shade *T.* ii 2

CONTINGENCE.
C. might alarm him, and disturb *T.* ii 172

CONTINUAL.
Though such *c.* zigzags in a book *Con.* 861
His will and judgment at *c.* strife *T.* 467
His thorns with streamers of *c.* praise? *T.* v 330
The stress of a *c.* act, the pain *T.* vi 208

CONTINUE.
Resolved it should *c.* there *R.C.* 86
Return, sweet Evening, and *c.* long! *T.* iv 244

CONTINUING.
I grant that men *c.* what they are *T.T.* 9

CONTORTIONS.
By shrugs and strange *c.* of his face *P.E.* 414

CONTRABAND.
Who fill the world with doctrines *c. P.E.* 475

CONTRACT.
Till sympathy *c.* a kindred pain *R.* 299
C. defilement not to be endured *T.* iv 670

CONTRACTED.
No spots *c.* among grooms below *Tir.* 685

CONTRADICTION.
Makes *c.* such a hopeless case *Con.* 60
Is *c.* for its own dear sake *Con.* 106
Patient of *c.* as a child *P.E.* 536

CONTRARIETIES.
Chaos of *c.* at war *Ex.* 295

CONTRASTED.
And by *c.* beauty shining more) *T.* iii 635

CONTRIBUTE.
C. to the gorgeous plan *Mrs. M—* 13
C. most perhaps to enhance their fame *Tir.* 468

CONTRIBUTION.
Pay *c.* to the store he gleans *T.* iv 110

CONTRIVANCE.
C. intricate expressed with ease *R.* 55

CONTRIVE.
Than he *c.* to suffer well content *T.* 104
But such as Art *c.*, possess ye still *T.* i 757
As nations ignorant of God *c. T.* ii 574
C. creation; travel nature up *T.* iii 156
The country, with what ardour he *c. T.* iv 778
C., hard shifting, and without her tools *T.* v 417
Thus dream they, and *c.* to save a God *T.* vi 205
Could you *c.* the payment, and rehearse *T.T.* 178

CONTRIVED.
C. both for toil and repose *Gr.* 10
C. to suit frail nature's crazy case *H.* 604
An Alderman of Cripplegate *c. T.* i 61
That idleness has ever yet *c. T.* iv 208
An art *c.* to advertise a joke *T.T.* 539

CONTRIVER.
C. who first sweated at the forge *T.* v 214

CONTRIVING.
No cutting and *c. F.* 141
Lives by *c.* delicates for you) *T.* iii 546

CONTROL.
Nor would endure that any should *c. Ch.* 33
Round other systems under her *c. Ch.* 318
A Finch, whose tongue knew no *c. P.T.* 26
His passions tamed, and all at his *c. T.* 417
The limits of *c.*, his gentle eye *T.* ii 719
Or who so worthy to *c.* themselves *T.* v 236
Dispersed the shackles of usurped *c. T.* v 516
The oppression of a tyrannous *c. T.* vi 455
Asserts precedence, and bespeaks *c. Tir.* 9
A ubiquarian presence and *c. Tir.* 266
Watch his emotions, and *c.* their tide *Tir.* 610
Patient of constitutional *c. T.T.* 224
No. His high mettle, under good *c. T.T.* 303

CONTROLLED.
As if one master-spring *c.* them all *T.* iv 203
Unbidden, and not now to be *c. T.* vi 551
Of that *c.* ordinance they move *T.* vi 202

CONTROVERSIAL.
Of *c.* rage emits *F.* 104
They, strangers to the *c.* field *T.* 371

CONTROVERSY.
Much *c.* straight arose *L.W.* 15

CONTUSIONS.
And carry, in *c.* of his skull *Con.* 201.
C. hazarding of neck or spine *N.A.* 7

CONVENED.
The sovereignty they were *c.* to please *Ex.* 539
C. for purposes of empire less *T.* iii 62
They form one social shade, as if *c. T.* iii 586

CONVENIENCE.
Lodged with *c.* in the fork *R.C.* 13
C. next suggested Elbow Chairs *T.* i 87
C., and security, and use *T.* ii 682
The sum is this. If man's *c.*, health *T.* vi 581

CONVENIENT.
He found it *c.* to be poor *Ch.* 189
Oaths used as playthings or *c.* tools *Ex.* 37
Uplifted hands, that, at *c.* times *Ex.* 147
And thence with all *c.* speed to Rome *P.E.* 370
But wisely seeks a more *c.* friend *R.* 443

CONVENTICLE.
Heard at *c.*, where worthy men *T.* ii 437

CONVENTION.
In politic *c.*) put your trust *T.* v 323

CONVERSANT.
C. only with the ways of men *R.* 39
Nor *c.* with men or manners much *T.* iii 24
Much *c.* with Heaven, she often holds *T.* v 815

CONVERSATION.
And *C.*, in its better part *Con.* 3
And echo *c.* dull and dry *Con.* 211
But *C.*, choose what theme we may *Con.* 703
While *c.*, an exhausted stock *H.* 103
I wave just now, for *c.'s* sake" *H.* 436
Nor such as useless *c.* breeds *R.* 643
In *c.* frivolous, in dress *T.* ii 379

CONVERSE.
But talking is not always to *c. Con.* 8
Now theirs was *c.* such as it behoves *Con.* 537
Sweet *c.*, sipping calm the fragrant lymph *T.* iii 391
With social *c.* and instructive ease *T.* iv 135
In *c.*, either starved by cold reserve *T.* v 471
That *c.* which we now in vain regret *T.* vi 40
From constant *c.* with I know not whom *Tir.* 854

CONVERSED.
Since she and I *c.* together last *Con.* 800

CONVERT.
And Christians marrying may *c.* the Turks *A.T.* 160
Of union, and *c.* the sacred band *T.* ii 686

CONVEY.
C. to this desolate shore *A.S.* 34
C. a distant country into mine *T.* i 424

CONVEYANCE.
And mode of its *c.*, by such tricks *T.* ii 561
The neat *c.* hiding all the offence *T.* vi 980

CONVEYED.
From them to thee, *c.* along the tide *Ex.* 624
All seemed so peaceful, that from them *c. N.A.* 41
C. her calm along *Q.V.* 68
Which Mary to Anna *c. The Rose* 2

CONVEYING.
C. worthless dross into its place *T.* i 572

CONVICTS.
C. a man fanatic in the extreme *Con.* 665
The audacious *c.*, whom he dares not bind *T.* iv 602

CONVICTED.
C. once, should ever after wear *E.* iii 50

CONVICTION.
Flings at your head *c.* in the lump *Con.* 153

CONVINCED.
C. at last, upon a nearer view *R.* 591
Note their extravagance, and be *c. T.* ii 573

CONVIVIAL.
The plump *c.* parson often bears *T.* iv 595
C. table and commodious seat *T.* v 162

CONYERS.
"Because ye will not," *C.* would reply *T.* 358

COOING.
Sits *c.* in the pine-tree, nor suspends *T.* vi 308

COOK.
When *C.*—lamented, and with tears as just *Ch.* 23
While *C.* is loved for savage lives he saved *Ch.* 39

COOL.
Or *c.*, as the season demands *Gr.* 38.   [*T.* vi 533
His rage grew *c.*; and pleased perhaps to have earned
To enjoy *c.* nature in a country seat *H.* 245
And the whispering sound of the *c.* colonnade *P.F.* 2
Ill-clad and fed but sparely, time to *c. T.* iv 379
Whom care and *c.* deliberation suit *Tir.* 781

COOLER.
These are the sober, in whose *c.* brains *T.* 38
And stepped at once into a *c.* clime *T.* i 337

COOLING.
Its *c.* vapour o'er the dewy meads *R.* 422

COOLNESS.
The gloom and *c.* of declining day *T.* i 258

COOP.
The cask, the *c.*, the floated cord *Cast.* 27
And boundless as it is, a crowded *c. T.* iii 834

COPE.
Calls thee to *c.* with enemies, and first *R.* 267
Leave kingly backs to *c.* with kingly cares *T.T.* 174
That grazed it stood beneath that ample *c. Y.O.* 54

COPIED.
Were *c.* close in him, and well transcribed *H.* 581

COPIOUS.
Here stay thy foot; how *c.*, and how clear *Ch.* 365
There he was *c.* as old Greece or Rome *Con.* 621
C. of flowers the woodbine, pale and wan *T.* vi 162

COPIOUSLY.
When *c.* supplied, then most enlarged *Tir.* 19

COPSE.
In many an orchard, *c.*, and grove *P.T.* 13
To the close *c.*, or far sequestered green *T.* 69

COPY.
And teach the softer not to *c.* theirs *Con.* 844
Imbibes and *c.* what she hears and sees *P.E.* 356
If languages and *c.* all cry "No!" *P.E.* 500
Then to dispose his *c.* with such art *T.* ii 294
A wish to *c.* what he must admire *Tir.* 649
Drew a rough *c.* of the Christian face *T.T.* 614

CORD.
The cask, the coop, the floated *c. Cast.* 27
He breaks the *c.* that held him at the rack *Ch.* 173
"A threefold *c.* is not soon broken" *E.* i 106

CORDIAL.
Some *c.* endearing report *A.S.* 35
The sober *c.* of sweet air *Mor.* 10
That *c.* thought her spirit cheered *Q.V.* 65
And give thy life its only *c.* left? *Tir.* 882
Oh friendship! *c.* of the human breast! *V.* 49

CORDIALLY.
Were witnesses how *c.* I pressed *R.* 379

CORK.
The Christian Hope is—Waiter, draw the *c. H.* 361

CORN.
Her fields, a rich expanse of wavy *c. Ex.* 9
But *c.* was housed, and beans were in the stack *N.A.* 23

CORNER.
The vainest *c.* of our own vain heart *Con.* 366
Placed at some vacant *c.* of the board *T.* iv 230
The cattle mourn in *c.*, where the fence *T.* v 27
But seeks the *c.* of some distant seat *Tir.* 571
Fops at all *c.*, lady-like in mien *Tir.* 829

CORNUBIAN.
And in the gulfs of her *C.* mines *H.* 458

CORONER.
The jury meet, the *c.* is short *T.* 447

CORONET.
The *c.*, placed idly at their head *H.* 268
And one who wears a *c.* and prays *T.* 378

CORPOREAL.
Can lift herself above *c.* things *T.* 487

CORPSE.
Till the stout bearers lift the *c.* again *T.* i 481

CORRECT.
It may *c.* a foible, may chastise *T.* ii 316
By thee I might *c.*, erroneous oft *Y.O.* 45

CORRECTED.
An error soon *c. F.* 21

CORRECTION.
She needs herself *c.*; needs to learn *T.* ii 776

CORRESPONDING.
Whose *c.* misses fill the ream *P.E.* 311
These chestnuts ranged in *c.* lines *T.* i 233
A *c.* tone in jovial souls *T.* iii 333

CORRODES.
The cankered spoil *c.* the pining state *Ch.* 63

CORROSIVE.
A pestilent and most *c.* steam *T.* iii 494

CORRUPT.
Stark naught because *c.* in their design *T.T.* 4

CORRUPTED.
That salt preserves thee; more *c.* else *T.* iii 845

CORRUPTER.
Greybeard *c.* of our listening youth *P.E.* 312

CORRUPTING.
Nor guiltless of *c.* other men *R.* 382

CORRUPTION.
Of honour, perjury, *c.*, frauds *T.* ii 669
C.! Whoso seeks an audit here *T.* iv 610

CORTEZ.
See *C.* odious for a world enslaved! *Ch.* 40

COST.

That great defect would c. him, not alone Con. 763
Their freedom purchased for them, at the c. Ev. 171
But whether all the time it c. Mor. 41.
Strange world, that c. it so much smart St. v 15
As Nature at her own peculiar c. T. 397
Than by the labour and the skill it c. T. ii 297
Though Appetite raise outcries at the c.? T. ii 621
Grudge not the c. Ye little know the cares T. iii 547
A mine to satisfy the enormous c. T. iii 783
While colts and puppies c. us so much care? Tir. 295
At folly's c., themselves unmoved the while T.T. 659
'Twould c. him, I dare say Y.D. 66

COSTLIER.

Our habits, c. than Lucullus wore T. ii 596
Of goddesses yet known, and c. far T. ii 659
Of savoury cheese, or butter c. still T. iv 395

COSTLY.

Of cucumber, while c. yet and scarce T. iii 462
And be not c. more than of true worth T. vi 984

COT.

Within some pious pastor's humble c. Tir. 760

COTTAGE.

A c. on the banks of Ouse E. i 48
Or only what in c. confined Ev. 29
A c., whither oft we since repair T. i 221
The c., walk along the plastered wall T. v 19
That like some c. beauty, strikes the heart T.T. 524

COTTAGER.

Let c., and unenlightened swains H. 240
Yon c., who weaves at her own door T. 317

COTTON.

No C., whose humanity sheds rays H. 205

COUCH.

To thy straw c., and slumber unalarmed T. iii 345
Sofa, and c., and high built throne august T. v 164

COUCHED.

He c. it firm upon his puissant thigh A.T. 147
Which, c. in prose, they will not hear E. i 22

COUGH. [148

C. their own knell, while, heedless of the sound T. iv
And c., and rheums, and phthisic, and catarrh Con.392

COUNCIL.

And one in c. Wolfe, upon the lap T. ii 242

COUNSEL.

C. of her country's gods B. 4
Disdained thy c., only in distress Ev. 530
C. and caution from a voice like mine! P.E. 10
For ghostly c., if it either fall T. ii 556
The rest will slight thy c., or condemn Tir. 805

COUNSELLOR.

His c. and bosom friend shall prove Tir. 216

COUNT.

Undazzled, and detects and c. his spots? T. i 714
To c. the hour-bell, and expect no change T. v 404

COUNTED.

Her chickens prematurely c. A Fable 4.

COUNTENANCE.

That the visage or c. had not a Nose A.C. 19
Stamped on each c. such marks of mind N.A. 76

A simpering c., and a trifling air P.E. 20
His c., his purse, his heart, his hand R. 595
Sees not a c. there that speaks of joy T. iv 205
Was but the graver c. of love T. vi 32

COUNTER.

The polished c., and approving none T. vi 281

COUNTERFEIT.

But c. is blind, and skulks through fear Con. 375
Shall c. the motions of the flood T. ii 148

COUNTERMARCHING.

Marching and c., with an eye T. vi 267

COUNTERPART.

And he that seemed our c. at first Tir. 442

COUNTERPOISE.

In c., flies up and kicks the beam T. 356

COUNTLESS.

Stars c., each in his appointed place R. 83
In grains as c. as the seaside sands T. vi 245
Whom ocean feels through all his c. waves Tir. 39

COUNTRY.

For whose lean c. much disdain A Tale 73
Counsel of her c.'s gods B. 4
And in his c.'s glory sought his own Ch. 26
Spreads foreign wonders in his c.'s sight Ch. 116
The constant creaking of a c. sign Con. 10
That all Olympus through the c. roves Con. 825
Their title to a c. not their own Ev. 173
And thou thyself o'er every c. sown Ev. 265
C. indebted to thy power, that shine Ev. 280
How much the c. to the conqueror owes Ev. 481
A blessing to my c. and mankind Ev. 727
Escaped from a cross c. ride! Gr. 20
To enjoy cool nature, in a c. seat H. 245
Forsaking c., kindred, friends, and ease H. 585
As when a fellow, whom his c.'s laws H. 712
Into the c. far away J.G. 215
Breathes clouds of dust, and calls it c. air R. 486
He likes the c., but in truth must own R. 573
Conveys a distant c. into mine T. i 424 [T. iii 757
The c. starves, and they that feed the o'ercharged
A patriot's for his c.; thou art sad T. i 658
To tempt us in thy c. Doing good T. i 673
God made the c., and man made the town T. i 749
It plagues your c. Folly such as yours T. i 770
They touch our c., and their shackles fall T. ii 42
My c.! and while yet a nook is left T. ii 207
And Chatham, heart-sick of his c.'s shame T. ii 244
His birth-place and his dam? The c. mourns T. ii 814
Have rambled wide. In c., city, seat T. iii 14
His c., or was slack when she required T. iii 89
They love the c., and none else, who seek T. iii 320
To serve his c. Ministerial grace T. iii 795
Unpeople all our c. of such herds T. iii 831
Discover c., with a kindred heart T. iv 116
Drink and be mad then; 'tis your c. bids! T. iv 509
The town has tinged the c.; and the stain T. iv 553
It knew not once, the c. wins me still T. iv 694
The c., with what ardour he contrives T. iv 778
Can he be strenuous in his c.'s cause T. v 506
That c., if at all, must be beloved? T. v. 508 [834
"His c.'s weather-bleached and battered rocks T. v
Patriots have toiled, and in their c.'s cause T. v 704
He serves his c., recompenses well T. vi 968
That, if his c. stand not by his skill T. vi 975
Where Duty placed them, at their c.'s side T.T. 24
Blest c., where these kingly glories shine! T.T. 81
E'en when he labours for his c.'s good T.T. 142
The c.'s need have scantily supplied T.T. 338

And all his c. beaming in his face T.T. 347
But when a c. (one that I could name) T.T. 414

COUPLE.

To watch yon amorous c. in their play T. 136

COURAGE.

Or c. die away Cast. 16
And fear, not c., is its proper source Con. 180
That C. is his creature; and Dismay Ex. 354
A soldier's best is c. in the field H. 405
Shoots back the bolt, and all his c. dies H. 721
Whose c. well was tried R.G. 6
Rouse all your c. at your utmost need T. 565
But be ye of good c. Time itself T. iv 420
To feel, and c. to redress her wrongs T. iv 795
For stratagem, or c., or for all T. v 232
Gives c. to their foes, who, could they see T. vi 865
With them is c.; his effrontery wit Tir. 227
Because forsooth thy c. has been tried Tir. 739
But c., man! methought the muse replied Tir. 787
Who with a c. of unshaken root T.T. 15
C. in arms, and ever prompt to show T.T. 276
C., ungraced by these, affronts the skies T.T. 378
They trust in armies, and their c. dies T.T. 468

COURAGEOUS.

C., and refreshed for future toil T. iii 19

COURSE.

To check the vessel's c. Cast. 20
Intent upon her destined c. Comp. ii 6
Winding a secret or an open c. Ch. 369 [431
The reasoning power vouchsafed of c. inferred Con.
Their nimble nonsense takes a shorter c. Con. 152
Some farrier should prescribe his proper c. Con. 411
From such communion in their pleasant c. Con. 698
Pursues it c. that truth and nature teach Con. 890
Are altogether gone a devious c. Ex. 463
Impelled thee more to that heroic c. J.T. 34
To check, or alter from its c. Miss — 59 [126
Through mere good fortune, took a different c. N.A.
Sets me more distant from a prosperous c. M.P. 105
His wonted c., yet what I wished is done M.P. 113
All is irregular, and out of c. P.E. 449 [406
With which from clime to clime he sped his c. P.E.
His morning c., the enchantment was begun P.E. 68
Those winding modestly a silent c. R. 78
A superstitious and monastic c. R. 118
And make the c. he recommends my choice R. 388
The tide of life, swift always in its c. R. 453
Lived in his saddle, loved the chase, the c. R. 577
Sad period to a pleasant c. ! St. vi 37
Obedient to the customs of the c. T. 14
Betrays the secret of their silent c. T. 196
Man's obligations infinite, of c. T. 197
Conducts the eye along his sinuous c. T. i 165
The smooth and equal c. of his affairs T. ii 173
His devious c. uncertain, seeking home T. iii 3
Maternal nature had reversed its c. T. iii 436
Meanders lubricate the c. they take T. iv 65
The c. of human things from good to ill T. iv 578
And snow, that often blinds the traveller's c. T. v 142
A c. of long observance for its use T. v 301
(As in a map the voyager his c.) T. vi 17
But trees, and rivulets whose rapid c. T. vi 109
And in the constancy of nature's c. T. vi 122
Age after age, than to arrest his c. ? T. vi 131
Prescribed their c., to regulate it now T. vi 204
(As is the c. of rash and fiery men) T. vi 542
And unambitious c., reflecting clear T. vi 723
Fulfill'd their tardy and disastrous c. T. vi 735
Holds its due c., nor fears the frosts of age T. vi 790
To ensure the perseverence of his c. Tir. 238

It pricks the genius forward in its c. Tir. 483
The expedience of a less adventurous c. Tir. 804
Unless the sway of custom warp thy c. Tir. 862
To turn the c. of Helicon that way T.T. 183 [461
But nothing scares them, from the c. they love T.T.
While no base fear impedes her in her c. T.T. 267
Give me the line that ploughs its stately c. T.T. 522
For bounding and curvetting in his c. T.T. 305 [160
Leaned on her elbow, watching Time, whose c. Y.O.

COURSED. [50

Then c. the field around, and c. it round again N.A.

COURSER.

So the best c. on the plain Th. 17
Perhaps some c. who disdains the road T.T. 668

COURT. [28

For the c. did not think they were equally wise A.C.
Then holding the spectacles up to the c.—A.C. 13
With a reasoning the c. will never condemn A.C. 22
They c. the notice of a future age B.B. 4
Sweet harmonist of Flora's c. ! Dr. 3
With tortured innocence in Mary's c. Ex. 613
Shall I abjure thee not to c. thy shame ? Ex. 655
All the grim honours of his ghastly c. H. 261
Secure of favour at her c. Mrs. M— 22
When lawless mobs insult the C. Pat. 9
Ye kings and rulers, what have c. to show ? R. 104
That c. display before ambitious eyes R. 178
That, while it c., affronts and does you wrong R. 550
But few that c. Retirement are aware R. 609
And ready to be borne to c. R.C. 20
And lunacy the verdict of the c. T. 448 [519
From c. dismissed, found shelter in the groves T. iv
To c. a grin, when you should woo a soul T. ii 467
On human grandeur and the c. of kings T. v 172
And in her streets, and in her spacious c. T. vi 809
A slave at c., elsewhere a lady's man Tir. 423 [855
Who there will c. thy friendship with what views Tir.
His c., the dissolute and hateful school T.T. 626
And strangers to the air of c. 1789, 62

COURTED.

Like a coy maiden, Ease, when c. most T. i 409

COURTEOUS.

A c. knighthood, caught the generous flame A.T. 134
A stranger joined them, c. as a friend Con. 522

COURTIER.

C. and Patriot cannot mix F. 127

COURTLY.

I still revere thee, c. though retired T. iv 727
True. While they live, the c. laureate pays T.T. 109

COUSIN.

This cap to my c. I owe Gr. 5

COVENANT.

Form, in its stead, a c. of shame Con. 684
By ancient c. ere Nature's birth T. vi 858

COVENANTED.

Upon the lap of c. rest Con. 574

COVENANT-ENSURING.

Bright as the c. bow H. 150

COVER.

To c. a pill for a delicate palate F.M. 12
C. us from every eye St. iv 34
Induced a splendid c., green and blue T. i 32

COVERED.

And c. with a fine-spun, specious veil P.E. 328

COVERED—CREATION

Lie *c.* close; and berry-bearing thorns *T.* v 82 [829
Were *c.* with the pest; the streets were filled *T.* ii
Start up sagacious, *c.* with the dust *T.T.* 170

COVERING.
C. his shame from his offended sight *T.* v 634

COVERT.
Where *c.* guile and artifice abound *Ch.* 285
Oft have I wished the peaceful *c.* mine *T.* i 233

COVET.
And *c.* longer woe? *St.* v 20
Made others *c.* what they saw so fair *T.* v 227
Or *c.* more than freemen choose to grant *T.* v 340
For there is none to *c.*, all are full *T.* vi 772

COVETED.
So *c.*, else base and diseesteemed *T.* iii 448
More to be prized and *c.* than yours *T.* iv 191

COVETOUS.
Too *c.* of drink *O.* i 10
And *c.* of Shakespeare's beauty, seen *T.* iii 601
C. only of a virtuous praise *T.T.* 95

COWERING.
And crowded knees, sit *c.* o'er the sparks *T.* iv 385

COWLEY.
Ingenious *C.*! and though now reclaimed *T.* iv 723

COWPER.
C., whose silver voice, tasked sometimes hard *S.* i 1
That grace was *C.'s*—his, confessed by all *T.* 119

COXCOMB.
A graver *c.* we may sometimes see *Con.* 295
With some unmeaning *c.* at your side *R.* 546
Like regimented *c.* rank and file *T.* 422
And pedantry that *c.* learn with ease *T.* vi 290

COY.
Of idle mirth and affectation *c. S.* ii 10
Like a *c.* maiden, Ease, when courted most *T.* i 409
Though apt, yet *c.*, and difficult to win *T.* ii 289

CRABS.
Or blushing *c.*, or berries that emboss *T.* i 121

CRAB-COMPUTING.
And own his *c.* powers o'ercome *P.E.* 487

CRACK.
C. the satiric thong? 'Twere wiser far *T.* iii 26

CRADLE.
The *c.* that received thee at thy birth *Ex.* 469
Rock'd in the *c.* of the western breeze *Tir* 44
Obsequious, from the *c.* to the throne *T.T.* 122
Designed thy *c.*; and a skipping deer *Y.O.* 25

CRADLED.
Though, clasped and *c.* in his nurse's arms *H.* 179
Even in the *c.* weakness of the world! *T.* v. 286

CRAFT.
A coin by *c.* for Folly's use designed *E.* ii 7
Abhors the *c.* he boasted of before *H.* 522

CRAFTSMAN.
The lackey, and the groom: the *c.* there *T.* iv 474

CRAGGY.
Here runs the mountainous and *c.* ridge *T.* iv 57
Sheer o'er the *c.* barrier, and immersed *T.* vi 554

CRAMP.
Crippling his pleasures with the *c.* of fear! *T.* 466

CRANIUM.
And he that splits his *c.*, breaks at most *A.T.* 44

CRANNIES.
And searched for *c.* in the frame *P.B.* 6
In every *c.* but the right *R.C.* 98

CRAPE.
C. and cocked pistol, and the whistling ball *T.* iii 802

CRASH.
And from within the wood that *c.* was heard *N.A.* 45

CRAVE.
Capricious Taste itself can *c.* no more *Ch.* 101

CRAVING.
And suck, and leave a *c.* maggot there! *P.E.* 326
And *c.* Poverty, and in the bow *T.* ii 490
Fails for the *c.* hunger of the state *T.* v. 459

CRAWLS.
That *c.* at evening in the public path *T.* vi 565

CRAZE.
C. antiquarian brains with endless doubt *P.E.* 394

CRAZED.
And whether being *c.* or blind *F.* 208   [*T.* i 556
Though pinched with cold, asks never.—Kate is *c.*!

CRAZY.
Contrived to suit frail nature's *c.* case *H.* 604
And *c.* earth has had her shaking fits *T.* ii 60
Suspend their *c.* boxes, planted thick *T.* iv 774

CREAKING.
The constant *c.* of a country sign *Con.* 10
To hear his *c.* panniers at the door *T.* i 245

CREAM.
The fruit of all her labour is whipped *c. T.T.* 551

CREAMY.
Without a *c.* smoothness has no charms *T.T.* 513

CREATE.
Starved by that indolence their mines *c. Ch.* 64
C., gives birth to, guides, consummates all *Ex.* 313
Most unavoidably *c. F.* 107
The tidings of unpurchased Heaven *c. H.* 343
Then farewell all that must *c. M.F.* 45
And share the joys your bounty may *c. R.* 790
As must *c.* an appetite for prayer? *Tir.* 374

CREATED.
C. and sustained *Q.V.* 60
Seem all *c.* since he travelled last *R.* 426
Joint-stools were then *c.*; on three legs *T.* i 19
As if *c.* only like the fly *T* iii 134
C. fair so much in vain for them *T.* iii 697
And streams, as if *c.* for his use *T.* iii 776
In silly dotage on *c.* things *T.* v 586
With truth from heaven, *c.* thing adore *Y.O.* 7
C. changeable, and change at last *Y.O.* 73

CREATING.
I gazed, myself *c.* what I saw *T.* iv 290

CREATION.
Includes *c.* in her close embrace *Ch.* 598
To drown it? What is his *c.* less *T.* ii 200
Contrive *c.*; travel nature up *T.* iii 156
Infused at the *c.* of the kind *T.* iv 733
Behind his own *c.*, works unseen *T.* v. 894
When all *c.* started into birth *T.* vi 199

CREATIVE.
n other climes perhaps *c*. Art *Ex*. 229

CREATOR.
Starts not aside from her *C*.'s plan *Con*. 452
To give the creature the *C*.'s due *E*. ii 3
That their *C*. had no serious end *H*. 130
The just *C*. condescends to write *H*. 133
Who make the good *C*. on their plan *H*. 383
Careless of their *C*. And that low *T*. v 587

CREATURE.
An isle possessed by *c*. of our kind *Ch*. 381
To tremble (as a *c*. of an hour *Con*. 657
Has made the new-born *c*. her abode *Con*. 754
To give the *c*. the Creator's due *E*. ii 3
That Courage is his *c*.; and Dismay *Ex*. 354
Some fickle *c*. boast a soul *F*. 109
His *c*. thwart not his august design *H*. 142
Field, fruit, and flower, and every *c*. here *H*. 490
C. of gentler race *M.B*. 4
Of peace or ease to *c*. clad as we *N.A*. 114
If we do not buy the poor *c*. they will *P.A*. 11
The *c*. is so sure to kick and bite *P.E*. 540
And calls a *c*. formed for God alone *R*. 17
Adores a *c*., and devout in vain *R*. 227
And lovers, of all *c*., tame or wild *R*. 251
The law by which all *c*. else are bound *T*. i 385
Strange! that a *c*. rational, and cast *T*. i 574
Played by the *c*. of a Power who swears *T*. iii 177
Of thought, the *c*. of a polished mind *T*. iii 640
Strange that so fair a *c*., should yet want *T*. iii 725
The *c*., summoned from their various haunts *T*. vi 355
We think them tedious *c*. *Tran*. iv 39
In vain thy *c*. testify of thee *T*. v. 856
From *c*. that exist but for our sake *T*. vi 603
All *c*. worship man, and all mankind *T*. vi 783
The *c*. is that God pronounces good *T*. vi 828
Stands self-impeached the *c*. of least worth *Tir*. 70
'Tis plain the *c*., whom he chose to invest *Tir*. 95
All *c*., with precision understood *Y.O*. 151

CREDENCE.
To win due *c*. to what follows next *N.A*. 72

CREDENTIALS.
And graced with clear *c*. from above *Ex*. 188
His office sacred, his *c*. clear *T*. ii 339

CREDIBLY.
How *c*., 'tis hard for me to state) *Con*. 816

CREDIT.
Thy rulers load thy *c*., year by year *Ex*. 284
Of *c*. and renown *J.G*. 2
With doubtful *c*., told to frighten babes *T*. iv 564
Soon lose their *c*., and are all effaced *Tir*. 200

CREDULITY.
They were, what base *C*. believes *H*. 507
That would have shocked *C*. herself *T*. ii 694
Deep in his soft *c*. the stamp *T*. v 497

CREDULOUS.
C. infancy, or age as weak *Con*. 225
Will they believe, though *c*. enough *Con*. 721

CREED.
My *c*. (whatever some creed-makers mean *H*. 393
My *c*. is, he is safe that does his best *H*. 395
My *c*. persuades me, well employed, may save *T*. 522
Blasphemes his *c*., as founded on a plan *Tir*. 159

CREED-MAKERS.
My creed (whatever some *c*. mean *H*. 393

CREEKS.
The wriggling fry soon fill the *c*. around *P.E*. 480
Each *c*. and cavern of the dangerous shore *R*. 152

CREEP.
And I had rather *c*. to what is true *Con*. 863 [145
Where men of judgment *c*., and feel their way *Con*.
If Envy chance to *c*. in *F*. 75
Of him that *c*. and him that flies *N.G*. 38
There from the sunburnt hayfield homeward *c. T*. i 295
Now *c*. he slow; and now, with many a frisk *T*. v 48
The vale of Nature, where it *c*. and winds *T*. vi 721
Would *c*. into the bowels of the hills *T*. vi 867
Nor always timorously *c*. *Trans*. *H*. 5

CREEPING.
As *c*. ivy clings to wood or stone *P.E*. 285
And lowly *c*., modest and yet fair *T*. iii 663
What are the casements lined with *c*. herbs *T*. iv 762
The *c*. vermin, loathsome to the sight *T*. vi 568
That *c*. pestilence is driven away *T*. vi 785

CRESCENT.
The *c*. moon, the diadem of night *R*. 82

CREST.
And veil your daring *c*. that braves the skies *Con*. 486
Which seems by the *c*. that it rears *Gr*. 3
But now wear *c*. of oven-wood instead *N.A*. 12
The subtlest serpent with the loftiest *c*. *T*. 476 [271
Whole without stooping, towering *c*. and all *T*. iv

CRESTED.
No *c*. warrior dips his plume in blood *Her*. 86
Stretch'd forth to dally with the *c*. worm *T*. vi 780

CREVICE.
That finds out every *c*. of the head *T*. vi 707

CREW.
With all her *c*. complete! *R.G*. 12

CREWEL.
Or scarlet *c*., in the cushion fixed *T*. i 54

CRIB.
These at his *c*., and some beneath his roof *T*. vi 415

CRIED. [179
"Oh, shame to Knighthood!" his assailant *c*. *A.T*.
"Fair fall the deed!" the Knight exulting *c*.*A.T*.68
In vain," they *c*., "are hymeneal rites *A.T*. 99 [169
To horse!" he *c*., " or by this good right hand *A.T*
You *c*.,—" Forbear "—but in my breast *B.R*. 5
A mightier *c*.—" Proceed "—*B.R*. 6
Entreated "Help!" or *c*.—" Adieu!" *Cast*. 42
Charmed with the sight, "The world," I *c.D.W*.37
" A friend!" Horatio *c*., and seemed to start *E*. iii 28
So, " Fair and softly," John he *c*. *J.G*. 85 [399
That *c*. " Repent!"—and gloried in thy choice? *Ex*.
But John he *c*. in vain *J.G*. 86
And every soul *c*. out, "Well done!" *J.G*. 111
And smiling divinely, she *c*.—*M.D*. 15
You are so deaf," the lady *c*. *M.F*. 15
See! with united wonder, *c*. *Th*. 5
Awakened by the shock (*c*. Puss) *R.C*. 53 [40
One breath of Heaven, that *c*.—" Restore!" 1789,

CRIME.
To judge the lands, to purge atrocious *c*. *A.T*. 141
If killing birds be such a *c*. *B.R*. 25
And when unstained with any grosser *c*. *Con*. 634
That, conscious of her *c*., she feels instead *Con*. 769
Yet to consult a little seemed no *c*. *Con*. 865
Could act extortion and the worst of *c*. *Ex*. 148
Brought fire from Heaven the sex-abusing *c*. *Ex*. 415

From c. as base as any charged on me? *Ex.* 711
His c. were such as Sodom never knew *H.* 562 [366
That Heaven will weigh man's virtues and his c. *H.*
Their only c., vicinity to you! *Her.* 52
Are c. so little to be spared *M.F.* 44
Slain at the foot of pleasure be no c. *P.E.* 182
And every thought that wanders is a c. *R.* 224
These, these are arts pursued without a c. *R.* 799
Adust with stripes told out for every c. *T.* 83
In faithful memory she records the c. *T.* 161
Past indiscretion is a venial c. *T.* 491
And deem his base stupidity no c. *T.* 542
The frequency of c. has washed them white *T.* iii 71
Great c. alarm the conscience, but it sleeps *T.* iii 185
And spotted with all c.; in whom I see *T.* iii 837
But many a c. deem'd innocent on earth *T.* vi 439
And suffer for its c.; would learn how fair *T.* vi 827
His c. and follies with an aching eye *Tir.* 62
(Forgive the c.) I wish them, I confess *Tir.* 921
Judged every effort of the Muse a c. *T.T.* 617
Then leave their c. for History to scan *T.T.* 119

CRIMINAL.
'Tis c. to leave a sinking state *R.* 478
Speaks him a c., assured *St.* vi 35

CRIMSON.
With here and there a tuft of c. yarn *T.* i 53
Take of the c. stream meandering there *T.* iii 202
Her c. honours; and the spangled beau *T.* iii 578

CRINGE.
Horatio's servant once, with bow and c. *E.* iii 20
Make just reprisals, and with c. and shrug. *T.* ii 645

CRINGING.
Of fluttering, loitering, c., begging, loose *T.* iii 832

CRIPPLE.
Nor penury, can c. or confine *T.* v 772

CRIPPLEGATE.
An alderman of C. contrived *T.* i 61

CRIPPLING.
C. his pleasures with the cramp of fear! *T.* 466

CRISIS.
Man may improve the c., or abuse *P.E.* 26
The c. of a dark decisive hour *T.T.* 359

CRITERION.
(Try the c., 'tis a faithful guide) *P.E.* 514

CRITIC.
Of c. now alive or long since dead *H.* 426
Has filled with all its fumes a c.'s brain *P.E.* 445
A c. on the sacred book should be *P.E.* 452
Like trout pursued, the c. in despair *P.E.* 502
Of gallery c. by a thousand arts *T.* ii 365
Of c. appetite, no sordid fare *T.* iii 461
Which not e'en c. criticise; that holds *T.* iv 51

CRITICISE.
Which not e'en critics c.; that holds *T.* iv 51

CRITIC-PROOF.
But I have another c.! *T.* iv 48

CROAKED. [282
Storks among frogs, that have but c. and died *T.* v

CROAKING.
The c. nuisance lurked in every nook *T.* ii 830

CROMWELL. [*T.T.* 610
When C. fought for power, and while he reigned

CRONY.
And you might grumble, c. mine *E.* iv 25

CROOKED.
Bend the straight rule to their own c. will *P.E.* 557
The children, c., and twisted, and deformed *T.* ii 772
C. or straight, through quags or thorny dells *Tir.* 253
Which, c. into a thousand whimsies, clasp *Y.O.* 118

CROP.
He thought to put him in his c. *N.G.* 12
The glad espousals, and ensures the c. *T.* iii 54

CROPPED.
Whose bridle, while he c. the grass below *A.T.* 173
I saw him, with that lily c. *D.W.* 33
Of grassy swarth, close c. by nibbling sheep *T.* i 110
And tail c. short, half lurcher and half cur *T.* v 46

CROSS.
Which stuck in M.'s stomach as c. as a bone *A.T.* ii 8
Escaped from a c. country ride! *Gr.* 20
All hope despair, that stands not on his c. *H.* 632
For ever and for ever? No—the C.! *P.E.* 613
The C. once seen is death to every vice *P.E.* 622
To c. his ambling pony day by day *R.* 467
Point to the cure, describe a Saviour's c. *Tir.* 165

CROSSED.
Like him, c. cheerfully tempestuous seas *H.* 584
(The storms all weathered and the ocean c.) *M.P.* 89

CROSSING.
C. in your barks the main *N.C.* 44

CROUCHES.
Yours, a blind instinct, c. to the rod *T.* v 355
Whose trade it is to smile, to c. to please *T.T.* 128

CROW.
Might be supposed a c. *Tran.* ii 3

CROWD.
A thousand names are tossed into the c. *Ch.* 517
A sense they know not, to the wondering c. *Ch.* 390
And will not punish, in one mingled c. *Ex.* 716
Vicissitude wheels round the motley c. *H.* 17
Proclaim their titles to the c. around *H.* 266
From cities humming with a restless c. *R.* 21
Blest he, though undistinguished from the c. *T.* i 592
And c. the roads, impatient for the town! *T.* iii 319
Of the great Babel, and not feel the c. *T.* iv 90
Where nothing feeds it. Neither business, c. *T.* iv 744
That c. away before the driving wind *T.* v 3
They see the attentive c. his talents draw *Tir.* 362
Much to the amusement of the c. *Tran.* iv. 23
The storm of music shakes the astonished c. *T.T.* 491
And all the c. that bustle life away *V.* 74

CROWDED.
Like c. forest-trees we stand, *St.* i 13
Others are dragged into the c. room *T.* i 478
In all our c. streets; and senates seem *T.* iii 61
The c. roots demand enlargement now *T.* iii 532
And boundless as it is, a c. coop *T.* iii 834
Sweats in the c. theatre, and squeezed *T.* iv 43
And c. knees, sit cowering o'er the sparks *T.* iv 385
And bundled close to fill some c. vase *T.* iv. 668
Frequents the c. auction: station'd there *T.* vi 286
C. with the garland of life's blooming years *Con.* 638

CROWN.
There was the consummation and the c. *Ex.* 221 [512
Then priests with bulls, and briefs, and shaven c. *Ex.*
And c. the soul, while yet a mourner here *H.* 165
And grinds his c. beneath her burning wheels! *H.* 652

Once more the spiry myrtle c. the glade *Her.* 31
To c. the smiling hours *N.* 20
The *C.*, took notice of an ostler's face *R.* 586
Retorts the affront against the c. of Pride *T.* 502
That c. it! yet not all its pride secures *T.* i 279
That picked the jewel out of England's c. *T.* ii 265
Where once your noble fathers won a c. ! *T.* iii 281
Perhaps may c. us, but to fly is safe *T.* iii 688
I c. the king of intimate delights *T.* iv 139
With modesty and meekness, and the c. *T.* v 243
Thou art of all thy gifts thyself the c. *T.* v 904
Come then, and, added to thy many c. *T.* vi 855
Receive yet one, the c. of all the earth *T.* vi 856
Come then, and, added to thy many c. *T.* vi 902
If you can c. a discipline, that draws *Tir.* 493
Your smooth eulogium, to one c. addressed *T.T.* 91
Indeed is treasure, and c. all the rest *V.* 92
And far the richest c. on earth 1789, 42

CROWNED. [10

How laughs the land with various plenty c. ! *Comp.* i
C. with a thousand victories, and at last *Ex.* 191
Humility is c., and Faith receives the prize *T.* 589
When he was c. as never king was since *T.* vi 350
And c. it with the majesty of man *Tir.* 52
Then Genius danced a Bacchanal; he c. *T.T.* 602

CRUDE.

Fruits of a blighted size, austere and c. *T.* 494

CRUEL.

Nor, c. as it seemed, could he *Cast.* 31
But shine with c. and tremendous charms *Ch.* 545
Transformed to blessings, miss their c. aim *E.* ii 38
Make c. inroads in my brain *E.* iv 16
Cry to the proud, the c., and unjust *Ex.* 268
Have done him c. wrong *M.* 214
But ah, the c. glass between !" *P.B.* 28
For property stripped off by c. chance *T.* i 503
C., abandoned, glorying in her shame ! *T.* iii 68
And in his hands and feet, the c. scars *T.* iii 114
Of c. man, exulting in her woes *T.* iii 336
The charms of Nature ! 'Tis the c. gripe *T.* iii 826
C. is all he does. 'Tis quenchless thirst *T.* iv 459
Where c. man defeats not her design *T.* vi 343
No c. purpose lurk'd within his heart *T.* vi 362
(What will not hunger's c. rage ?) *T.B.* 5
The c. death he died *T.B.* 66
Or kites with c. beak *The Loves* 34
From the c. assaults of the clime *W.N.* 12

CRUELLY.

C. spared, and hopeless of escape! *T.* v 399

CRUELTY.

More c. could none express *G.* 16
The seeds of c., that since have swell'd *T.* vi 381
Than c., most devilish of them all *T.* vi 594

CRUISE.

Stopped his c., replaced his book *Mor.* 7

CRUMBLING.

Or e'er his hoof had pressed the c. verge *T.* vi 519

CRUSH.

Had sought to c. them, guarded as they were *Ex.* 205
C. me, ye rocks; ye falling mountains, hide *T.* 269
An inadvertent step may c. the snail *T.* vi 564
Forgetful that the foot may c. the trust *Tir.* 792
Nor c. a worm, whose useful light *Tran.* i 17

CRUSHED.

Felt himself c. at the first word he spoke *T.T.* 353

CRUST.

Angry and sad, and his last c. consumed *T.* i 246

A dry but independent c., hard earned *T.* iv 409
And, feasting on an onion and a c. *T.T.* 241

CRUTCHES.

Halting on c. of unequal size *P.E.* 560

CRY.

One was accoutred when the c. began *A.T.* 135 [216
And in the saddest part c.—" Droll indeed ! " *Con.*
Can this be true ? " an arch observer c. *Con.* 231
Then mirth is sin, and we should always c. *Con.* 878
Wept till all Israel heard his bitter c. *Ex.* 63
C. aloud, thou that sittest in the dust *Ex.* 267
C. to the proud, the cruel, and unjust *Ex.* 268
But raise the shrillest c. in British ears *Ex.* 271
The c. in all thy ships is still the same *Ex.* 288
Lothario c., " What philosophic stuff! *H.* 28
C. to her universal realm, " Rejoice ! " *H.* 54
" No need," he c., " of gravity, stuffed out *H.* 105
" Renounce the world," the preacher c. *L.W.* 25
" Adieu,"; Vinosa c., ere yet he sips *H.* 357
I never will believe," the colonel c. *H.* 381
Sir Smug," he c. (for lowest at the board *H.* 413
And c., " Perhaps eternity strikes next ! " *H.* 701
They all at once did c. *J.G.* 146
They raised the hue and c. *J.G.* 236
" When, c. the botanists, and stare *P.* 21 [*P.E.* 115
C.—" Well done, Saint!" and claps him on the back
C. in his startled ear, " Abstain from sin ! " *P.E* 38
If languages and copies all c., " No ! " *P.E.* 500
Till authors hear at length one general c. *R.* 707
" His joys be mine," each Reader c. *St.* iii 33
Wakes the sooner for his c. *St.* iv 8 [*T.* 34
Heaven on such terms ! " they c. with proud disdain
" And is the soul indeed so lost," she c. *T.* 479 [229
Where dwell these matchless saints? " old Curio c. *T.*
C.—hem ! and reading what they never wrote *T.* ii 411
And perks his ears, and stamps, and c. aloud *T.* vi 318
One song employs all nations ; and all c. *T.* vi 791
Sweet Poll ! his doting mistress c. *Tran.* iv 13
They c. aloud in every careless ear *T.T.* 434

CRYING.

In being touched, and c.—" Don't ! " *P.* 38

CRYSTAL.

So Flora's wreath through coloured c. seen *H.* 71
Called to these c. streams, do ye turn off *P.E.* 265
To drink sweet waters of the c. well *T.* i 240
In vain to filter off a c. draught *T.* ii 507
Or Temper sheds into thy c. cup *T.* iii 47
And shrubs of fairy land. The c. drops *T.* v 113

CUCUMBER.

Of c., while costly yet and scarce *T.* iii 462

CUE.

He from Italian songsters takes his c. *P.E.* 112

CULINARY.

By c. arts, unsavoury deems *T.* i 125

CULLS.

But oh ! for him my Fancy c. *Pat.* 13

CULPRIT.

C. his liberty regains *E.* iv 59

CULTIVATE.

And c. a taste for ancient song *R.* 375
He c. These serve him with a hint *T.* iv 758
To improve and c. their just demesne *T.* v 226
To c. and keep the morals clean *Tir.* 920

CULTIVATED.

Distinguish every c. kind *H.* 291
And genial soil of c. life *T.* i 679
And Nature in her c. trim *T.* iii 357

CULTIVATED—CURTAIN

An upright heart, and c. mind *Tir.* 722
If he indulge a c. taste *T.T.* 161

CULTIVATION.
That c. glories in, are his *T.* vi 189

CULTURE.
On c., and the sowing of the soil *Con.* 6
To study c., and with artful toil *R.* 785
By c. tamed, by liberty refreshed *T.* i 606

CULTURED.
C. and capable of sober thought *T.* iii 324

CUMBROUS.
And through the c. throng *Q.V.* 66

CUNNING.
With all the c. of an envious shrew *T.* ii 266
Nor C. justify the proud man's wrong *T.* vi 844

CUP.
He wipes and scours the silver c. in vain *Ex.* 385
But if the rogue be gone a c. too far *P.E.* 440
With caution taste the sweet Circean c. *P.E.* 580
And mingle with our c. *R.G.* 27
Throws up a steamy column, and the c. *T.* iv 39
Or Temper sheds into thy crystal c. *T.* iii 47 [*Rose* 5
The c. was all filled, and the leaves were all wet *The*
One drop of Heaven's sweet mercy in his c. *T.* iii 804
Thou wast a bauble once, a c. and ball *Y.O.* 17

CUR.
In village or in town, the bay of c. *T.* i 230
And tail cropped short, half lurcher and half c. *T.* v 46

CURATE.
Sweet sleep enjoys the c. in his desk *T.* i 94
Nor sleep enjoyed by c. in his desk *T.* i 100

CURB.
To teach good manners, and to c. abuse *Con.* 164
By way of wholesome c. upon our pride *Con.* 361
Religion c. indeed its wanton play *Con.* 595
In spite of c. and rein *J.G.* 88 [571
Soon follows, and the c. of conscience snapped *T.* ii
The c. invented for the mulish mouth *T.* ii 744
Let active Laws apply the needful c. *T.T.* 314

CURD.
The milk of their good purpose all to c. *Ch.* 504

CURDLES.
And the blood thrills and c. at the thought *T.* vi 514

CURE.
And find submission more than half a c. *Ch.* 158
Springs from the mischief it intends to c. *Con.* 170
Physicians write in hopes to work a c. *Con.* 407 [887
Thus touched, the tongue receives a sacred c. *Con.*
And, tainted by the very means of c. *Ex.* 104
And c. of every ill! *G.* 15
Those evils it would gladly c. *M.F.* 58
And that a rope must c. them *Pat.* 20
Prevent the danger, or prescribe the c. *P.E.* 18
One sad epistle thence, may c. mankind *P.E.* 351
No c. for such, till God who makes them heals *R.* 342
No medicine, though it oft can c. *St.* i 27
The grave admits no c. for guilt or sin *St.* ii 30
That Scripture is the only c. of woe *T.* 452
Is obstinate, and c. beyond our reach *T.* iii 40
Dire disappointment that admits no c. *T.* iii 557
Inveterate, hopeless of a c., conspires *T.* iv 577
The heart's insanity admits no c. *T.* vi 523
Point to the c., describe a Saviour's cross *Tir.* 165
But ye connive at what ye cannot c. *Tir.* 275
Disease or comes not, or finds easy c. *Tir.* 766
Which now and then sweet Poetry may c. *T.T.* 743

CURED.
C. of the golden calves, their fathers' sin *Ex.* 215
But modest, sober, c. of all *R.C.* 103

CURIO. [*T.* 229
Where dwell these matchless saints?" old C. cries

CURIOSITY.
Or thine, but c., perhaps *T.* i 634

CURIOUS.
A great retailer of the c. ware *Con.* 229
With c. touch examines me *P.* 33
And gratify no c. eyes *Q.V.* 39
By c. eyes and judgments ill informed *T.* ii 435
And the mouse with c. snout *Tran.* iii 12
Oracular, I would not c. ask *Y.O.* 42

CURL.
Ungenial blasts attending c. the streams *T.T.* 213

CURLED.
C., scented, furbelowed, and flounced around *Ex.* 51

CURLING.
Each bottle had a c. ear *J.G.* 69
C. and whitening over all the waste *R.* 531
And c. tendrils gracefully disposed *T.* iv 154
There sit, involved and lost in c. clouds *T.* iv 472

CURRENT.
Vice passing c. by the stamp of law *A.T.* 156
With God's deep stamp upon its c. worth *Con.* 710
Spurious, and only c. with the blind *E.* ii 8
And day by day some c.'s thwarting force *M.P.* 104
So coin grows smooth, in traffic c. passed *P.E.* 279
But nowhere with a c. so serene *R.* 455
To winter, and the c. in his veins *T.* iv 388
And unperceived the c. steals away *T.* v 100
Till settling on the c. year 1789, 27

CURRIED.
C. his nag and looked another way *R.* 590

CURSE.
The wreath he won drew down an instant c. *Ch.* 61
Forgot to c., and only kneel to pray *Con.* 814
They drew a c. from an intended good *Ex.* 129
A lawless brood, and c. thee to thy face *Ex.* 283
Successful there, he wins a c. *Mor.* 48
Your pleasures with no c. in the close *P.E.* 268
Or c. the desert with a tenfold dearth? *T.* 182
Shall find the blessing unimproved a c. *T.* 524
The worst of men, and c. of the best *T.* 434
Before he eats it.—'Tis the primal c. *T.* i 364
Nothing is proof against the general c. *T.* iii 265
Dire is the frequent c., and its twin sound *T.* iv 487
Procure him many a c. By slow degrees *T.* iv 635
Have each their record, with a c. annex'd *T.* vi 441
Exults to see its thistly c. repealed *T.* vi 768
And not with c. on his heart, who stole *Tir.* 151
On fire with c., and with nonsense hung *Tir.* 832
God's c. can cast away ten thousand sail! *T.T.* 467

CURSED.
"O c. Hypothesis! your hellish arts *A.T.* 113
And, c. with conquest, finally succeed *Con.* 692
Abhorred the sacrifice, and c. the priest *P.E.* 340
Blessed, rather c., with hearts that never feel *R.* 307

CURST.
Lip-deep in what he longs for, and yet c. *P.E.* 233
Satire has long since done his best, and c. *T.T.* 728

CURTAIN.
Drew the grey c. of the fading west *Ch.* 263

You rise and drop the c.—now 'tis night *Con.* 332
These c., that keep the room warm *Gr.* 37
The c. drawn by Prejudice and Pride *H.* 571
And grace his action ere the c. fall *R.* 34
The trumpet—will it sound? the c. rise? *R.* 655
He drew the c. at his side *R.C.* 81
Let fall the c., wheel the sofa round *T.* iv 37
In letting fall the c. of repose *T.* iv 248

CURTAINED.
That c. round the scene where they reposed *A.T.* 95

CURVATURE.
With c. of slow and easy sweep *T.* i 352

CURVE.
Then like a bow long forced into a c. *T.T.* 622

CURVETTING.
For bounding and c. in his course *T.T.* 305

CUSHION.
May now and then their velvet c. take *H.* 248
Or scarlet crewel, in the c. fixed *T.* i 54
If c. might be called, what harder seemed *T.* i 55
On the same c. of habitual sloth *T.* iv 598

CUSTOM.
The fear of tyrant c., and the fear *Con.* 181
Women, whom c. has forbid to fly *P.E.* 504
We can escape from *C.*'s idiot sway *R.* 49
Obedient to the c. of the Course *T.* 14
When *C.* bids, but no refreshment find *T.* i 390
And c. of her own, till Sabbath rites *T.* i 746
Misled by c., strain celestial themes *T.* ii 438
By vicious *C.*, raging uncontrolled *T.* iii 682
The manners, c., policy of all *T.* iv 109
Such dupes are men to c., and so prone *T.* v 299
C. and prejudice shall bear no sway *T.* vi 838
The slaves of c. and established mode *Tir.* 251

Unless the sway of c. warp thy course *Tir.* 862
Its c. and its businesses *Tran.* ii 28

CUSTOMARY.
Within its c. nook *Mor.* 8
The volume closed, the c. rites *T.* iv 167

CUSTOMER.
Three c. come in *J.G.* 52
Twas long before the c. *J.G.* 57

CUT.
We have our similes c. short *E.* iv 65
One breaks the glass, and c. his fingers *P.B.* 34
And c. up all my follies by the root *T.* 574
To c. the link of brotherhood, by which *T.* iii 208
And truth c. short to make a period round *T.T.* 517
But oh! it c. him like a scythe *Y.D.* 7

CUTTING.
No c. and contriving *F.* 141

CYLINDERS.
It is passed between c. often, and rolled *F.M.* 3

CYMBAL.
Ah, tinkling c. and high-sounding brass *T.* v. 681

CYNIC.
Blame, c., if you can, quadrille or ball *P.E.* 175

CYNTHIO.
While *C.* ogles, as she passes *P.B.* 19

CYPRESS.
Of neighbouring c., or more sable yew *T.* vi 154

CYRENE.
C., when he bore the plaintive tale *T.* v 136

CYRUS.
And *C.*, with relenting pity moved *Ex.* 75

D.

DÆDALUS.
She tutored some in *D.*'s art *A.T.* 52

DAGGER. [there? *A.T.* 118
"Find out her treacherous heart, and plant a d.
D. in hand, steals close to your bedside *Ch.* 187
Will thrust a d. at your breast *F.* 94

DAGON.
As *D.* in Philistia long before *Ex.* 507

DAILY.
In d. musings and in nightly dreams *A.T.* 12
Murmuring and weary of our d. toil *Ch.* 221
D. derive increasing light and force *Con.* 697
And d. threaten to drive thence *E.* iv 17
I see thee d. weaker grow *M.* 6
And d. more enamoured of the cheat *P.E.* 524
Fly to the coast for d., nightly joys *R.* 522
Earth's millions d. fed, a world employed *R.* 553
For evils d. felt, and hardly borne *R.* 752
Some trivial slips their d. walk attend *T.* 286
Scenes must be beautiful which, d. viewed *T.* i 177
Please d., and whose novelty survives *T.* i 178
His d. fare as delicate. Alas! *T.* ii 626

DAINTY.
His d., and the World's more numerous half *T.* iii 545
Less d. than becomes his grave outside *T.* iv 605

DAIRY.
Too proud for d. work, or sale of eggs *T.* iv 549

DAISIES.
And prink their hair with d., or to pick *T.* vi 303

DALE. [*N.A.* 34
Told hill and d. that Reynard's track was found
That draw the sportsman over hill and d. *T.* iii 310

DALLY. [780
Stretch'd forth to d. with the crested worm *T.* vi
To d. much with subjects mean and low *T.T.* 544

DAM. [ii 814
His birth-place and his d.? The country mourns *T.*
Each sire and d., of an infernal race *P.E.* 568

DAME.
In fairy land was born the matchless d. *A.T.* 5
D. Gurton thus, and Hodge her son *E.* iv 39

DAMN.
And save or d. as these or those prevail H. 368
A hopeless task, and d. them if they fail H. 392
" And doth he reprobate and will he d. T. v 638

DAMNABLE.
Be d., then damned without excuse P.E. 597

DAMNED.
Or, in his words who d. the base desire Ex. 422
Die when he might, he must be d. at last H. 569
Be damnable, then d. without excuse P.E. 597

DAMNING.
While thousands careless, of the d. sin Ex. 388

DAMP.
So, when the cold d. shades of night prevail Ch. 527
They put on a d. night cap, and relapse Con. 322
Chasing the darkness and the d. Q.V. 7
The ascending d.; then leisurely impose T. iii 477

DANCE.
" Seraglios sing, and harems d. for joy! A.T. 108
The world may d. along the flowery plain E. ii 13
As in a d. the pair that take the lead H. 13
Laymen have leave to d., if parsons play P.E. 151
Then to the d., and make the sober moon P.E. 173
Footing it in the d. that Fancy leads P.E. 308
To d. on earth, and charm all human eyes R. 796
Shot through the boughs, it d. as they d. T. i 346
When safe occasion offers; and with d. T. i 584
Are silent. Revelry, and d., and show T. ii 79
Then shake them in despair, and d. again T. ii 666
Could pageantry and d., and feast and song T. iii 314
In feast or in the chase, in song or d. T. v 758
That leads the d. a summons to be gay T. vi 336
The mulberry tree stood centre of the d. T. vi 686

DANCED. [395
Who d. with whom, and who are like to wed Con.
Enjoyed the show and d. about the stake Ex. 615
To speak its excellence; I d. for joy T. iv 712 [517
The wretch, who once sang wildly, d. and laughed H.
Then Genius d. a Bacchanal; he crowned T.T. 602

DANCING.
She guides the finger o'er the d. keys Ch. 109
Not of the moral, but the d. school P.E. 190
D. uncouthly to the quivering flame T. iv 276
Soon the sweet Spring comes d. forth Trans. H. 23
So many maniacs d. in their chains T. ii 663
The d. Naiads through the dewy meads T.T. 693

DANES.
Besides, if we do, the French, Dutch, and D. P.A. 9

DANGER.
From d. of a frightful shape A Fable 33
The d. they discern not, they deny Ch. 418
Of d. past, and wonders yet to come Con. 572
But here again a d. lies F. 25
And where his d. and God's wrath begin H. 609
When, conscious of no d. from below Her. 3
And d. little known H.F. 18
Prevent the d., or prescribe the cure P.E. 18
The joy, the d. and the toil o'erpays P.E. 90
'Tis valued for the d.'s sake the more P.E. 521
Faces a thousand d. at her call R.H. 7
While d. passed is turned to present joy T. 256
His d. or escapes, and haply find T. ii 309
If toil await me, or if d. new T. iii 20
How great the d. of disturbing her T. iii 35
Ten thousand d. lie in wait to thwart T. iii 553
The d. we have 'scaped, the broken snare T. iv 185
Even daylight has its d.; and the walk T. iv 572

The scorn of d., and united hearts T. v 377
And, conscious of some d., either fled T. vi 375
Aware then how much d. intervenes Tir. 883

DANGEROUS.
Suggests it safe, or d., to be plain Ch. 520
I grant it d., and approve your fear Con. 653
In vain opinion's waste and d. wild H. 279
May prove a d. foe indeed F. 77
And thy loved consort on the d. tide M.P. 98
Safe in themselves, but d. in the excess P.E. 62
Each creek and cavern of the d. shore R. 152
And d. to the touch, has yet its bloom T. i 528
That it is d. sporting with the world T. ii 777
In fancied peace beneath his d. branch T. v 325

DANGLED.
D. along at the cold finger's end T. iv 392

DANGLING.
D. his cane about, and taking snuff H. 27
Still d. at his waist J.G. 132
That pressed it, and the feet hung d. down T. i 47
And holds them d. at arm's length in scorn T. 164
(But that the basket d. on her arm T. iv 547
Like caterpillars, d. under trees Tir. 591

DANIEL.
D. ate pulse by choice—example rare! P.E. 215

DANISH.
And D. howlings scared thee as they passed Ex. 471

DANK.
To sallow sickness, which the vapours, d. T. i 438
In volumes wheeling slow, the vapour d. T. iii 499

DAPPLE.
Meantime, noise kills not. Be it D.'s bray N.A. 115

DAPPLED.
Observe the d. foresters, how light St. ii 21
Looks to the westward from the d. east T.T. 706

DARE.
Who d. dishonour, or defile, the tongue Con. 26
Let D. beat Entellus black and blue Con. 198
They d. not wait the riotous abuse Con. 261
We d. not risk them into public view Con. 371
That he who d., when she forbids, be grave Con. 475
Abhors constraint, and d. not feign a zeal Con. 713
The man that d. traduce, because he can Ex. 432
O slave! with powers thou didst not d. exert Ex. 546
In such a cause they could not d. to fear Ex. 621
Alas for the poet! who d. undertake F.M. 13
D. step across his arbitrary views H. 193
Hence all that interferes and d. to clash P.E. 427
I d. not—" And you need not," God replies T. 272
Woe to the tyrant, if he d. intrude T. vi 406 [602
The audacious convict, whom he d. not bind T. iv
But though the felon on his back could d. T. vi 516
Nor could he d. presumptuously displease Tir. 179
Or, if I blame, 'tis only that they d. Tir. 263
'Twould cost him, I d. say Y.D. 66

DARED. [Con. 501
Touched by that power that you have d. to mock
Thou that hast wasted earth, and d. despise Ch. 69
D. to suppose the subject had a choice Ex. 544 [639
(For was it less, what heathen would have d. T. vi
And d. to look his master in the face T.T. 321
No sycophant or slave, that d. oppose T.T. 350

DAREST.
Endurest the brunt, and d. defy them all Ex. 697

DARING.
Full many a champion bent on d. deed A.T. 123

And veil your *d.* crest that braves the *Con.* 486.
Confessed the wonder, and with *d.* tongue *Ex.* 155
Forbid in vain to push his *d.* way *Ex.* 17 [230
His hairbreadth 'scapes, and all his *d.* schemes *Tir.*

DARK.

Bade rise in haste a *d.* and drizzling fog *A.T.* 94
And *d.* oblivion soon absorbs them all *B.B.* 8 [612
The statesman, skilled in projects *d.* and deep *Ch.*
How *d.* the veil that intercepts the blaze *Ch.* 57
Shines in the *d.*, but ushered into day *Con.* 677
A *d.* confederacy against the laws *Con.* 685
Will make the *d.* enigma clear *E.* i 54
The sense was *d.*; 'twas therefore fit *E.* iv 61
Not to be pierced in play, or in the *d. Ex.* 435
But thine, as *d.* as witcheries of the night *Ex.* 494
His bold intrusion on their *d.* retreat *H.* 356
A *d.* importance saddens every day *H.* 699
D. and voluminous the vapours rise *Her.* 15
Yet this dull room, and that *d.* closet *M.F.* 4
Sir Humphrey, shooting in the *d. M.F.* 9
In earth's *d.* womb have found at last a vent *N.A.* 86
A something shining in the *d. N.G.* 9
Sing, Muse (if such a theme, so *d.* so long *P.E.* 1
Start it at home, and hunt in the *d. R.* 693
With foliage of such *d.* redundant growth *T.* i 226
Disfigures Earth, and, plotting in the *d. T.* i 275
And clammy, of his *d.* abode have bred *T.* i 439
And all at random, fabulous and *d. T.* ii 522 [523
Left them as *d.* themselves. Their rules of life *T.* ii
And *d.* in things divine. Full often too *T.* iii 235
Deciduous, when now November *d, T.* iii 467 [241
Through all the heart's *d.* chambers, and reveal *T.* iii
A flowery island, from the *d.* green lawn *T.* iii 630
And made so sparkling what was *d.* before *T.* v 558
The deep *d.* green of whose unvarnish'd leaf *T.* vi 174
Such rare exceptions, shining in the *d. Tir.* 841
The *d.* appearance will not last *Trans. H.* 26
The crisis of a *d.* decisive hour *T.T.* 359
To throw his *d.* displeasure o'er the scene *T.T.* 445
The *d.* and sullen humour of the time *T.T.* 616
Are we then left—Not wholly in the *d. T.T.* 662

DARKEN.

Called for a cloud to *d.* all their years *E.* ii 25
Which art can only *d.* and disguise *H.* 769
Philosophers, who *d.* and put out *P.E.* 472
And chills and *d.* a wide-wandering soul *T.* v 684

DARKENED.

Soon raised a cloud that *d.* every land *Ex.* 509

DARKENING.

And *d.* and enlightening, as the leaves *T.* i 348

DARKER.

To *d.* climes, or climes of brighter day *Ex.* 18
Prefer the twilight of a *d.* time *T.* 541

DARKEST.

That shoot into your *d.* caves the day *H.* 493
Beware of desperate steps. The *d.* day *N.A.* 132
Vanish at once into the *d.* shade *St.* ii 24
But had a blessing in its *d.* frown *T.* vi 35
And throwing up into the *d.* gloom *T.* vi 153

DARKNESS.

They cannot give it, or make *d.* light *Ch.* 388
D. itself before his eye is light *Ex.* 338
So then;—as *d.* overspread the deep *Ex.* 636
By such a change, thy *d.* is made light *Ex.* 640
Error and *d.* occupy their place *Ex.* 693
Closing at last in *d.* and despair *H.* 6
Spent half the *d.*, and snored out the rest *H.* 510
Expects in *d.* and heart chilling fears *H.* 714

Winks hard, and talks of *d.* at noonday *P.E.* 451
Chasing the *d.* and the damps *Q.V.* 7
D. the skies had mantled o'er *Q.V.* 33
D., O Queen! ne'er called before *Q.V.* 35 [738
Whose Stygian throats breathe *d.* all day long *T.* iii
By works of *d.* and nocturnal wrong *T.* iv 435
Blind, and in love with *d.*! yet e'en these *T.* vi 885
And, tedious years of Gothic *d.* passed *T.T.* 564

DARLING.

Howe'er ingenious on his *d.* theme *Con.* 137
The text that sorts not with his *d.* whim *P.E.* 446
The Frenchman's *d.*? Are they not all proofs *T.* iv 765
The shipwright's *d.* treasure, didst present *Y.O.* 97

DART.

For every *d.* that malice ever shot *H.* 559
And he that forged, and he that threw the *d. H.* 578
D. to the mud, and finds his safety there *P.E.* 502
Swift beyond thought the lightnings *d.* away *T.* 243
With gentle force soliciting the *d. T.* iii 115
By traitor Appetite, and armed with *d. T.* iii 685
"From the green wave emerging, *d.* an eye *T.* v 835
The bounding fawn that *d.* across the glade *T.* vi 327
And *d.* his soul into the dawning plan *T.T.* 499

DARTED.

Grew stern, and *d.* a severe rebuke *T.* ii 720

DARTING.

And *d.* through his elm an eagle's eye *A.T.* 148

DARWIN.

Can gaze on even *D.'s* wit *Dr.* 19

DASH.

Strange! how the frequent interjected *d. Ch.* 521
To *d.* through thick and thin *J.G.* 40
The *d.* of Ocean on his winding shore *T.* i 186
The milldam, *d.* on the restless wheel *T.* v 102
To *d.* the pen through all that you proscribe *T.T.* 760

DASHED.

From the *d.* pane the deluge as it falls *T.* iii 488

DASHING.

The raving storm and *d.* wave defies *Con.* 559
This plumage, neither *d.* shower *Mrs. M—* 15
Blown all aslant, a driving, *d.* rain *T.* 239

DASTARDLY.

The practice *d.*, and mean, and low *Con.* 178

DATE.

A more enduring *d. Cast.* 58
And make it brightest at its latest *d. Con.* 604 [224
Their woes, not yet repealed, thence *d.* them all *Ex.*
Thence *d.* their sad declension, and their fall *Ex.* 223
To trace thee to the *d.* when yon fair sea *Ex.* 550
By reminiscence to his earliest *d.*? *F.A.* 23
And of a transient *d. G.* 9
His *d.* of life, so likely to be short *H.* 208
No virtuous wish can bear a *d. Mor.* 57
But short the *d.* of all we gather here *R.* 460
Pushing her bold inquiry to the *d. R.* 669
Who waits to dress us, arbitrates their *d. T.* ii 600
That He who made it, and revealed its *d. T.* iii 153
Old or of later *d.*, by sea or land *T.* v 381
All has its *d.* below; the fatal hour *T.* v 529
Hence *d.* the persecution and the pain *T.* vi 384
A longer *d.* to the far nobler beast *T.* vi 529
Far beyond the *d.* of man *Tran.* iii 28
There is a time, and justice marks the *d. T.T.* 400
Half a millenium since the *d.* of thine *Y.O.* 136

DAUB.

The difference of a Guido from a *d. T.* vi 285

DAUBED.
Causeless, and d. with undiscerning praise T. v 360
DAUGHTER.
Sends Nature forth, the d. of the skies R. 795
DAW.
As idle as the chattering of a d. A.T. 63
Such is the clamour of rooks, d., and kites H. 349
The very rooks and d. forsake the fields T. v 89
DAWN.
Grey d. appears; the sportsman and his train P.E. 82
The d. of thy last advent; long desired T. vi 866
There d. the splendour of his future years Tir. 394
Neither night nor d. of day Tran. iii 25
DAWNING.
Wait for the d. of a brighter day Ch. 167
The peep of morning shed a d. light Ch. 261
And bid a d. sky display E. i 77
And darts his soul into the d. plan T.T. 499
DAY.
Enjoyed at ease the genial d. A Fable 7
On rippling waters in an April d. A.T. 24
'Twas on the noon of an autumnal d. A.T. 70
The chaster Muse of modern d. omits A.T. 85
And set the unseemly pair in open d. A.T. 168
Blessed the glad beams of that propitious d. A.T. 205
And when your linnet on a d. B.R. 13
My numbers that d. she had sung C. 17
In number the d. of the year C. 26
Wait for the dawning of a brighter d. Ch. 167
Inform his mind; one flash of heavenly d. Ch. 228
For the chief blessings of my fairest d. Ch. 265
No works shall find acceptance in that d. Ch. 557
Collect at evening what the d. brought forth Con. 19
The heathen lawgivers of ancient d. Con. 35
A tasteless journal of the d. before Con. 276
God and his attributes (a field of d. Con. 471
O d. of heaven, and nights of equal praise! Con. 567
Serene and peaceful as those heavenly d. Con. 568
Canting and whining out all d. the word Con. 577
Whose wit can brighten up a wintry d. Con. 581
A dozen would-bes of the modern d. Con. 612
And claims a reverence in its shortening d. Con.645
Shines in the dark, but ushered into d. Con. 677
Make him athletic as in d. of old Con. 841
To express the occurrence of the d. E. i 4
But d. by d., and year by year E. i 53
The blaze of a meridian d. E. i 78
Which this d.'s incident began? E. i 84
('Twas therefore much the same in ancient d.E. iii 7
Some few that I have known in d. of old E. iii 58
Anticipates a d. it never sees Ep. i 8 [Ex. 16
Where dwelt they now? Where dwelt in ancient d.
To darker climes, or climes of brighter d. Ex. 18
A cloud to measure out their march by d. Ex. 177
Thus fell the best instructed in her d. Ex. 225 [228
Had poured the d., and cleared the Roman skies Ex.
Where shall a teacher look, in d. like these Ex. 450
Thou wast the veriest slave, in d. of yore Ex. 526
As ever Roman had in Rome's best d. Ex. 591
Heroes and worthies of d. past, thy sires? Ex. 658
To spend two hours in dressing for the d. H. 80
And if perchance, on some dull drizzling d. H. 371
A hand as liberal as the light of d. H. 408
The trumpet of a life-restoring d. H. 456
The sweet vicissitudes of d. and night H. 488
That shoot into your darkest caves the d. H. 493
And finds the modish manners of the d. H. 612
A dark importance saddens every d. H. 699
The comfort of a few poor, added d. H. 729
Their hours, their d., in listening to his joy H. 739

The brightest wonders of an endless d. H. 753
When on a d., like that of the last doom Her. 11 [17
While through the Stygian veil that blots the d. Her.
To-morrow is our wedding d. J.G. 9
Said John,—" It is my wedding d. J.G. 193
Was heard, one genial summer's d. J.P. 31
Asleep at the dawn of the d. M.D. 2
And something every d. they live M.F. 39
Shades slanting at the close of d. Mor. 15
I heard the bell tolled on thy burial d. M.P. 28
By expectation every d. beguiled M.P. 40
And where the gardener Robin, d. by d. M.P. 48
Could those few pleasant d. again appear M.P. 80
And d. by d. some current's thwarting force M.P.104
Where rises and where sets the d. Mrs. M— 11
With yon bright regent of the d. Mrs. M— 52
And pant for brighter d. N. 12
And weave fresh garlands every d. N. 19
Beware of desperate steps. The darkest d. N.A. 132
A nightingale, that all d. long N.G. 1
That wish on some fair future d. N.Y.G. 17
Why, stooping from the noon of d. O. i 9
Rebellion is my theme all d. Pat. 1
Thus having wasted half the d. P.B. 11
Long ere the charioteer of d. had run P.E. 67
'Tis exercise, and health, and length of d. P.E. 91
With wire and catgut he concludes the d. P.E. 126
A d. of luxury, observed aright P.E. 164 [157
What says the prophet? Let that d. be blest P.E.
To tease for cash, and quarrel with all d. P.E. 372
It chanced then on a winter's d. P.T. 9
'Tis well if, looked for at so late a d. R. 31
Happy, if full of d.—but happier far R. 45
Instruct me, guide me to that heavenly d. R. 95
From scenes of sorrow into glorious d. R. 168
The rising or the setting orb of d. R. 191
Soft airs, nocturnal vigils, and d. dreams R. 260
Ye saw me once (ah, those regretted d. R. 371
To cross his ambling pony d. by d. R. 467
Exempt from future service all his d. R. 628
Cause to provide for a great future d. R. 652
Can save us always from a tedious d. R. 745
Divine Communion chases as the d. R. 765
(With her indeed 'twas never d.) R.C. 68
Than if entombed the d. before R.C. 72
In happier d., to brighter prospects born! S. ii 5
To see again my d. o'erspread St. iii 7
He who sits from d. to d. St. iv 1
Though committed every d. St. iv 28
Who trample order; and the d. St. vi 25
Sport for a d., and perish in a night T. 42
From the strict duties of the sacred d.? T. 49
And drank the little bumper every d. T. 158
True Piety is cheerful as the d. T. 176
Ten thousand warblers cheer the d., and one T. 200
Consults all d. your interest and your ease T. 217
Hence the complexion of his future d. T. 280
Shuffling her threads about the livelong d. T. 320
But let not him that shares a brighter d. T. 539
Was bliss reserved for happier d.;—so slow T. i 83
The gloom and coolness of declining d. T. i 258
Of cheerful d., and nights without a groan T. i 366
'Tis free to all—'tis every d. renewed T. i 434 [547
The dreary waste; there spends the livelong d. T. i
There often wanders one, whom better d. T. i 534
To dream all night of what the d. denied T. i 671
My soul is sick, with every d.'s report T. ii 6
The terrors of the d. that sets them free T. ii 128
He grinds divinity of other d. T. ii 362 [T. iii 738
Whose Stygian throats breathe darkness all d. long
What was a Monitor in George's d.? T. ii 580
In colleges and halls, in ancient d. T.ii 699
Men too were nice in honour in those d. T. iii 85

Learning has borne such fruit in other *d. T.* iii 248
And spreads his hopes before the blaze of *d. T.* iii 445
That *d.* and night are exercised, and hang *T.* iii 549
To all the virtues of those better *d. T.* iii 745 [iii 786
That he has touched, retouched, many a long *d. T.*
Than Sodom in her *d.* had power to be *T.* iii 847
With sweet oblivion of the cares of *d. T.* iv 250
I saw the woods and fields at close of *d. T.* iv 311
Thy *d.* roll on exempt from household care *T.* iv 366
Warmed, while it lasts, by labour all *d.* long *T.* iv 377
He may compensate for a *d.* of sloth *T.* iv 434 [393
Just when the *d.* declined, and the brown loaf *T.* iv
Would I had fallen upon those happier *d. T.* iv 513
That favoured such a dream, in *d.* like these *T.* iv 530
Of smiling *d.*, they gossip'd side by side *T.* v 60
So manifold in cares, whose every *d. T.* v 769 [525
Vain wish! those *d.* were never; airy dreams *T.* iv
Then we are free. Then Liberty like *d. T.* v 883
Slow circling ages are as transient *d. T.* vi 227 [177
These have been, and these shall be in their *d. T.* vi
His murderer on his back, and, push'd all *d. T.* vi 428
Accountable, and God, some future *d. T.* vi 605
And give the *d.* to a musician's praise *T.* vi 644
And solemn ceremonial of the *d. T.* vi 680 [vi 696
Swarm in the streets. The statesman of the *d. T.*
And in his sportive *d. Th.* 2 [*Tir.* 757
Saved from his home, where every *d.* brings forth
Down to the sunset of their latest *d. Tir.* 82
In early *d.* the conscience has in most *Tir.* 109
Yet e'en in transitory life's late *d. Tir.* 143
Time was he closed as he began the *d. Tir.* 175
And, common sense diffusing real *d. Tir.* 189
We love the play place of our early *d. Tir.* 297
We feel it e'en in age, and at our latest *d. Tir.* 317
And labours to surpass him *d.* and night *Tir.* 480
The indented stick, that loses *d.* by *d. Tir.* 559
To combat Atheists with in modern *d. Tir.* 639
Not occupied in *d.* dreams, as at home *Tir.* 775
Which disappears by *d. Tran.* i 4
Neither night nor dawn of *d. Tran.* iii 25 [22
Feats of renown, though wrought in ancient *d. T.T.*
No shades of superstition blot the *d. T.T.* 270 [376
Now, from the dust of ancient *d.*, bring forth *T.T.*
Not prompted, as in our degenerate *d. T.T.* 590
And arts revived beneath a softer *d. T.T.* 621
Hast caught the cold distemper of the *d. V.* 47
The manners, not the morals, of the *d. V.* 80
If God give health, that sunshine of our *d.*! *V.* 88
And long before the *d.* appears *Y.D.* 11
In sooth the sorrow of such *d. Y.D.* 17 [100
But the axe spared thee. In these thriftier *d. Y.O.*

DAYLIGHT.

By *d.* or candlelight—Eyes should be shut *A.C.* 32
Not less dispersed by *d.* and its cares *T.* iv 138
Even *d.* has its dangers; and the walk *T.* iv 572

DAYSPRING.

To thee the *d.*, and the blaze of noon *R.* 347
Of *d.* overshoot his humble nest *T.* i 496
And shot a *d.* into distant climes *T.T.* 561

DAZZLE.

Bright-studded to *d.* the eyes *Gr.* 13
Or will he seek to *d.* me with tropes *T.* ii 423

DAZZLED.

Misdeems it, *d.* by its bright array *T.* iv 685

DAZZLING.

In *d.* streaks the vivid lightnings play *Her.* 18
Beneath the *d.* deluge, and the bents *T.* v 22
So *d.* in their eyes who set it on *T.* v 244
The *d.* splendour of the scene below *T.* vi 64

DEAD.

Alike immortalize the *d. Cast.* 54
Who live in pleasure, *d.* e'en while they live *H.* 230
Adds nothing now to the degraded *d. H.* 269
Of critics now alive or long since *d. H.* 426
Reveal (the man is *d.*) to wondering eyes *H.* 572
The *d.* in whom that good abounded most *J.T.* 4
My Mother! when I learned that thou wast *d. M.P* 21
No pleasure! Are domestic comforts *d.? P.E.* 243
At length when all had long supposed him *d. R.* 583
Man shall be summoned and the *d.* attend? *R.* 654
And all are *d.* beside *St.* vi 2
Are such a *d.*, preponderating weight *T.* 354
That man is *d.* in sin, and life a gift *T.* 514
Of lazy nurse who snores the sick man *d. T.* i 97
For interest sake, the living to the *d. T.* iii 661
Of sympathy, and therefore *d.* alike *T.* vi 323
Deaf as the *d.* to harmony, forgets *T.* vi 646
The incorrigibly wrong, the deaf, the *d.*! *Tir.* 780
That were a theme might animate the *d. T.T.* 202
Though abroad they are frozen and *d. W.N.* 8

DEAF.

He might as well be blind, and *d.*, and dumb *Con.* 144
Pleasure is *d.* when told of future pain *Ex.* 66
"You are so *d.*," the lady cried *M.F.* 15
"You are so sadly *d.*, my dear *M.F.* 17
And *d.* to all the impertinence of tongue *R.* 549 [415
But oft-times *d.* to suppliants who would blush *T.* iv
Charm the *d.* serpent wisely. Make him hear *T.* v 671
D. as the dead to harmony, forgets *T.* vi 646 [867
Thou wouldst not, *d.* to Nature's tenderest plea *Tir.*
The incorrigibly wrong, the *d.*, the dead! *Tir.* 780

DEAL. [*A.C.* 6

With a great *d.* of skill, and a wig full of learning
But such a tree! 'twas shaven *d. A Tale* 33
Sorting and puzzling with a *d.* of glee *Con.* 13
Who *d.* with Scripture, its importance felt *Con.* 729
Men *d.* with life as children with their play *H.* 127
To *d.* and shuffle, to divide and sort *T.* i 474
D. him out money from the public chest *T.* iii 796
Or doing nothing with a *d.* of skill *T.T.* 193
With stern severity. *d.* out the year *T.T.* 209

DEALINGS.

A lawyer's *d.* should be just and fair *H.* 401
Slaves of gold, whose sordid *d. N.C.* 53

DEALT.

As Tully with philosophy once *d. Con.* 730
For Israel *d.* in robbery and wrong *Ex.* 35
His censure reached them as he *d.* it *P.* 65
The painted tablets, *d.* and *d.* again! *P.E.* 170

DEAN.

But (I might instance in St. Patrick's *d.*) *Ch.* 499
Humility may clothe an English *D. T.* 118 [418
And *d.*, no doubt, and chapters, with one voice *Tir.*

DEAR.

"My *d.* deliverer out of hopeless night *Ch.* 234
"Adieu, *d.* Sir! lest you should lose it now" *Con.* 282
Is contradiction for its own *d.* sake *Con.* 106 [708
Lives the *d.* thought of joys he once possessed *Con.*
Keep still the *d.* companion at their side? *Con.* 734
D. Anna—between friend and friend *E.* i 1
Not dreaming of so *d.* a friend *E.* i 41
D. Joseph—five and twenty years ago— *E.* iii 3
One story more, *d.* Hill, and I have done *E.* iii 45
Of *d.* Mat Prior's easy jingle *E.* iv 4
If *d.* society be worth a thought *Ex.* 670
Thy *d.* delights while here below *F.* 212
His happiness, her *d.*, her only aim *H.* 64
Gethsemane! in thy *d.*, hallowed ground *H.* 297

DEAR—DEBONAIR

John Gilpin's spouse said to her d. *J.G.* 5
And you are she, my dearest d. *J.G.* 19
And for that wine is d. *J.G.* 26
For which he paid full d. *J.G.* 202
" No doubt, my d., I bade him come *M.F.* 11
" You are so sadly deaf, my d. *M.F.* 17
Thus grief itself has comforts d. *Miss —* 53
The meek intelligence of those d. eyes *M.P.* 7
Faithful remembrancer of one so d. *M.P.* 11
I would not trust my heart—the d. delight *M.P.* 82
Our d. delights are often such *P.B.* 29
O the d. pleasures of the velvet plain *P.E.* 169
My d. Dick Redcap, what say you? *P.T.* 37 [573
" Since the d. hour that brought me to thy foot *T.*
Their own d. virtue their unshaken trust *T.* 281
And witness, d. companion of my walks *T.* i 144
As d. to thee as once? And have thy joys *T.* i 647
No : d. as freedom is, and in my heart's *T.* ii 33 [643
Her d. five hundred friends, contemns them all *T.* ii
Who slights the charities for whose d. sake *T.* v 507
They prove too often at how d. a rate *T.* vi 416
A man deemed worthy of so d. a trust *Tir.* 711
Receive, d. friend, the truths I teach *Trans. H.* 1
Reward his memory, d. to every muse *T.T.* 14
And I will sing, at Liberty's d. feet *T.T.* 296
And thinking I might purchase it too d. *T.T.* 515
You sell it plaguy d. *Y.D.* 60
For that d. sorrow's sake forego 1789, 52

DEAR-BOUGHT.

The d. placeman, and the cheap buffoon *Con.* 30
Are not important always as d. *Tir.* 74

DEAREST.

And you are she, my d. dear *J.G.* 19
The occupation d. to his heart *T.* ii 709
The nurture of her youth, her d. pledge *T.* ii 779
Yet make their progeny their d. care *Tir.* 800 [359
They risk their hopes, their d. treasure, there? *Tir.*

DEARLY.

The wreath He won so d. in our name *Ch.* 586
The emphatic speaker d. loves to oppose *Con.* 269
D. obtains the refuge it affords *T.* i 238

DEARTH.

Burning and scorched into perpetual d. *Ex.* 421
Or curse the desert with a tenfold d. *T.* 182
The d. of information and good sense *T.* iv 71
From d. to plenty, and from death to life *T.* vi 181

DEATH.

But waged with D. a lasting strife *Cast.* 17
A stroke as fatal as the scythe of D. *Ch.* 144
And put the peaceably-disposed to d. *Con.* 90
Never, if honest ones, when d. is sure *Con.* 408
And while the victim slowly bled to d. *Ex.* 498
For caught and caged, and starved to d. *G.* 10
Sighs for his exit, vulgarly called d. *H.* 90 [*H.* 260
They die.—D. lends them, pleased and as in sport
And d.'s a doom sufficient for the rest " *H.* 396
Denouncing d. upon the sins of man *H.* 512 [627
And smite the untempered wall 'tis d. to spare *H.*
Those awful syllables, Hell, D., and Sin *H.* 690
D. and the pains of Hell attend him there *P.E.* 547
The Cross once seen is d. to every vice *P.E.* 622
Till d. exterminate us all *P.T.* 35
That so much d. appears? *St.* i 8
This annual tribute D. requires *St.* i 11
That, soon or late, d. also is your lot *St.* ii 35
The gulf of d. triumphant passed *St.* iii 31
D. at hand—yourselves his mark—*St.* iv 11
D. and Judgment, Heaven, and Hell *St.* iv 29
Why deem we d. a foe? *St.* v 18

And dread of D. ensues *St.* v 24
With the approach of D. *St.* v 28
His d. your peace ensures *St.* v 34
But rather d. disguised *St.* vi 12
Of everlasting d. *St.* vi 36
And d. or restitution is the word *T.* 264
And smothered in't at last is praised to d. *T.* 316
Life for obedience, d. for every flaw *T.* 550
She heard the doleful tidings of his d. *T.* i 455
That she is rigid in denouncing d. *T.* i 732
Life in the unproductive shades of d. *T.* ii 124
To seek a tranquil d. in distant shades *T.* iii 111
Within its reeking bosom, threatening d. *T.* iii 503
Contagion, and disseminating d. *T.* iii 617
Births, d., and marriages, epistles wet *T.* iv 17
The first artificer of d. ; the shrewd *T.* v 213
True to the d., but not to be his slaves *T.* v 345
And beg for exile, or the pangs of d. ? *T.* v 434
O'er all we feed on power of life and d. *T.* vi 453
Of folly, plunging in pursuit of d. *T.* v 595
Ages of hopeless misery. Future d. *T.* v 607
And d. still future. Not a hasty stroke *T.* v 608
But unrepealable enduring d. *T.* v 610
'Tis desperate, and he sleeps the sleep of d. *T.* v 669
Yet deemed oracular, lure down to d. *T.* v 863
Might he demand them at the gates of d. *T.* vi 45
From dearth to plenty, and from d. to life *T.* vi 181
Adds tenfold bitterness to d. by pangs *T.* vi 395
To steel their hearts against the dread of d." *T.* vi 511
Declined the d., and wheeling swiftly round *T.* vi 518
The d. he had deserved, and died alone *T.* vi 556
The cruel d. he died *T.B.* 66
D. never shall divide *The Doves* 28   [*T.T.* 42
And D. own scythe, would better speak his power
His being end where d. dissolves the bond *Tir.* 67
And D. awakens from that dream too late *T.T.* 126
Even where D. predominates. The spring *Y.O.* 132

DEATH-BELL.

To toll the d. of its own decease *T.* ii 51

DEATHLESS.

Oh fond attempt to give a d. lot *B.B.* 1
Thy d. wreaths, and triumphs all thine own *H.* 664

DEBARRED.

From the whole hog to be d. *L.W.* 12

DEBASED.

And that a nation shamefully d. *T.T.* 396
D. to servile purposes of Pride *T.T.* 748

DEBATE.

Oh that the voice of clamour and d. *Ch.* 309
A duel in the form of a d. *Con.* 84
But oh ! the strife, the bickering, and d. *H.* 312
Or if in masculine d. he shared *H.* 686
This civil bickering and d. *L.R.* 17
That whirl away from business and d. *R.* 393
Or do we grind her still ? The grand d. *T.* iv 30
Fell Discord, arbitress of such d. *T.* iv 482

DEBAUCH.

The rank d. suits Clodio's filthy taste *P.E.* 188
Of stale d., forth issuing from the styes *T.* iv 470
And tattered in the service of d. *T.* v 633

DEBAUCHED.

Of rank obscenity, d. their age *T.T.* 631

DEBILITATES.

From what d. and what inflames *R.* 20

DEBONAIR.

Sometimes ascending, d. *R.C.* 11
The Frenchman, easy, d., and brisk *T.T.* 236

DEBT.
I owed a trifle, and have paid the *d. Con.* 796
The *d.*, which justly became due *E.* iv 23 [*Ex.* 611
The beams of heavenly truth have swelled the *d.*!
Their measure filled, they too shall pay the *d. Ex.*712
Increasing taxes and the nation's *d. T.T.* 177

DEBTORS.
When He shall call his *d.* to account *T.* iii 365

DECAY.
No; marble and recording brass *d. Con.* 551
They flourish, and as these decline, *d. Ex.* 327
Shall live exempt from weakness and *d. H.* 752
Which first inspired the flame, *d. M.F.* 54
A falling empire, hasten its *d. R.* 384
Sprightly, and old almost without *d. T.* i 408
With most success when all besides *d. T.* iv 157
Neglected talents rust into *d. T.T.* 546
Slow, into such magnificent *d. Y.O.* 90

DECAYED.
See then the quiver broken and *d. T.* ii 803
D. by time, or withered by a frost *V.* 58

DECEASE.
That now and then a hero must *d. Con.* 175
To toll the death-bell of its own *d. T.* ii 51

DECEIT.
All but their own experience as *d.*! *Con.* 720
Their piety a system of *d. Ex.* 91
Kneels and asks Heaven to bless the dear *d. P.E.* 525
To teach the canvass innocent *d. R.* 797
Where rumour of oppression and *d. T.* ii 3

DECEITFUL.
The partial balance and *d.* weight *Ex.* 41
D. views of future bliss, farewell! *T.* 9

DECEIVE.
She mocks her Maker, and herself *d. Con.* 776
Nor any fool he would *d. F.* 16
Or may my friend *d.* me! *F.* 216
Nor baited hook *d.* the fish's eye *T.* iii 313
Not slothful; happy to *d.* the time *T.* iii 362
D. no student. Wisdom there and truth *T.* vi 114

DECEIVED.
With many a freakish trick *d.* his pains *A.T.* 25
Both sides *d.*, if rightly understood *Ch.* 622
But if, unhappily *d.*, I dream *Ch.* 632
Will judge himself *d.*, and prove it too *Con.* 112
Or, if excused that charge, at least *d. Con.* 478
And disappointed still, was still *d. M.P.* 39
And therefore prints, himself but half *d. P.E.* 492
If this be learning, most of all *d. T.* iii 184 [295
Though still *d.*, some stranger's near approach *T.* iv
Not soon *d.*; aware that what is base *T.* vi 989

DECENT.
Suffice it then in *d.* terms to say *A.T.* 86
And let them guide you to a *d.* end *Con.* 220
So manners *d.* and polite *F.* 178
A *d.* caution and reserve at least *H.* 404
And plain in manner; *d.*, solemn, chaste *T.* ii 401
Some, *d.* in demeanour while they preach *T.* ii 440
With *d.* duty, not ashamed to pray *Tir.* 176
Then *d.* Pleasantry and sterling Sense *T.T.* 638

DECENTLY.
My share of duties *d.* fulfilled *T.* vi 1001

DECEPTION.
No mockery meets you, no *d.* there *P.E.* 618
D. innocent—give ample space *T.* i 353

DECIDE.
D. no question with their tedious length *Con.* 87
A worthless form, than to *d.* aright *T.* vi 851

DECIDED.
Must be *d.* by the worth *Mor.* 43
In settled habit and *d.* taste *Tir.* 778

DECIDUOUS.
D., when now November dark *T.* iii 467
D., or its own unbalanced weight *T.* v 40

DECISION.
The event and sure *d.* of the fight? *Ex.* 363
Guides the *d.* of a doubtful choice *Tir.* 34

DECISIVE.
D. and clear, without one if or but *A.C.* 30
They always are *d.*, clear and strong *Con.* 150
Too weak for those *d.* blows that once *T.* ii 273
The crisis of a dark *d.* hour *T.T.* 359

DECK.
Oft pacing, as the mariner his *d. F.A.* 19
This china that *d.* the alcove *Gr.* 33
Of all that *d.* the lanes, the fields, the bowers *H.* 288
That *d.*, with all the splendour of the true *H.* 485
Whilst beauty *d.* the plain *Miss* — 40 [ii 31
Dewdrops may *d.* the turf that hides the bones *St.*
And *d.* itself with ornaments of gold *T.* i 529
Upon the wanton breezes. Strew the *d. T.* ii 256
Nor are these all. To *d.* the shapely knoll *T.* iii 628
He travels, and I too. I tread his *d. T.* iv 114
With which Aurora *d.* the skies *T.B.* 16 [*d. Y.O.* 95
That might have ribbed the sides and planked the
Thy blossoms *d.* our unsuspecting years *V.* 51

DECKED.
Presents it *d.* with every hue *Mor.* 30 [iv 223
Thus *d.*, he charms a world whom Fashion blinds *T.*
And winter is *d.* with a smile *W.N.* 4

DECLAIMERS.
Designed by loud *d.* on the part *T.* v 498

DECLAMATION.
Cataracts of *d.* thunder here *T.* iv 73

DECLARE.
And differing judgments serve but to *d. H.* 423

DECLARED.
For Time, the destroyer *d. Gr.* 45

DECLENSION.
Thence date their sad *d.*, and their fall *Ex.* 223
Must save it from *d. F.* 180
Preserved by virtue from *d. M.F.* 51
Of modest grandeur, and *d.* thence *Y.O.* 89

DECLINE.
Nor soon he felt his strength *d. Cast.* 15
That in the valley of *d.* are lost *Con.* 636
They flourish; and as these *d.*, decay *Ex.* 327
Partakers of thy sad *d. M.* 33
As life *d.*, speed rapidly away *T.* i 130
A boyish friendship may so soon *d. Tir.* 453
The powers that Sin has brought to a *d. T.T.* 383

DECLINED.
D. at length into the vale of years *T.* ii 726
Just when the day *d.*, and the brown loaf *T.* iv 393
D. the death, and wheeling swiftly round *T.* vi 518
But conjugated verbs and nouns *d. Tir.* 619

DECLINING.
"Till Sol, *d.* in the west *R.C.* 62
The gloom and coolness of *d.* day *T.* i 258

DECLIVITY.
Nor soft d. with tufted hills R. 333
Hence the d. is sharp and short T. i 326
Whose sharp d. shoots off secure T. iii 487

DECORUM.
So 'twas a hallow'd time; d. reign'd T. vi 691
He puts it on, and, for d. sake T. vi 985

DECOYED.
That none, d. into that fatal ring T. ii 631

DECREE.
'Tis an unalterable fixed d. Con. 467
The purport of his deep d. E. i 60
E'en as his will and his d. ordain Ex. 325
No! the d. was just and without flaw H. 318
Build by whatever plan caprice d. H. 614
And fixed by Heaven's d. Miss — 46
Your wilful suicide on God's d. T. 20

DECREED.
So his lordship d., with a grave solemn tone A.C. 29
D. that whosoever should offend E. iii 48
Theirs be the laurel-wreath d. E. iv 83
And when, as Justice has long since d. H. 748
But Fate thy growth d.; autumnal rains Y.O. 23

DECREPID.
Tradition, now d. and worn out Ex. 502

DECREPITUDE.
D., and in the looks of lean T. ii 489

DEDICATE.
And d. a tribute, in its use T. vi 712

DEDUCE.
My boast is not that I d. my birth M.P. 108

DEED.
" Fair fall the d.!" the knight exulting cried A.T. 68
Full many a champion bent on daring d. A.T. 123
Impelled me to the d. B.R. 8
Expedience as a warrant for the d.? Ch. 183
Ranks its abuse among the foulest d. Ch. 209
A stream of liberal and heroic d. Ch. 245
Should be the guerdon of a noble d. Ch. 293 [461
How many d. with which the world has rung Ch.
On Reason's verdict is a madman's d. Con. 190
Whose d. had left, in spite of hostile arts Con. 513
Call legions up from Hell to back the d. Con. 691
She did me wrong, I recompensed the d. Con. 797
Shall hear of this thy d. D.W. 38 [213
But Grace abused brings forth the foulest d. Ex.
To thrust the charge of d. that I detest Ex. 430
Nor animate the soul to Christian d. H. 300
Because the d., by which his love confirms H. 324
By d. in which the world must never mix P.E. 162
His benefactress blushes at the d. P.E. 212
To veil a d. of thine! Q.V. 36
On word and d., imply St. vi 30
Thought, word, and d., his liberty evince T. 195
Excels ten thousand mercenary d. T. 224 [T. 559
Condemns the injurious d., the slanderous tongue
To better d., he bundles up the spoil T. iv 440
And him in peace, for sake of warlike d. T. v 234
" The unequivocal, authentic d. T. v 653 [652
" May play what tune he pleases. In the d. T. v
Bled nobly, and their d., as they deserve T. v 705
And measure of the offence, rebukes a d. T. vi 655
That palliates d. of folly and of shame) Tir. 333
Caught from the d. of men of ancient fame Tir. 645
The d. that men admire as half divine T.T. 3
That takes not fire at their heroic d. T.T. 26 [327
Worse than the d. of galley-slaves broke loose T.T.
But if a d. not tamely to be borne T.T. 488
D. of unperishing renown 1789, 15

DEEM. [Ch. 589
That in the heaven of heavens, that space He d.
She d. all safe, for she has paid the price Ch. 458
And having felt the pangs you d. a jest Con. 497
As, having it, he d. the world's disdain Con. 762
And d. the bard, whoe'er he be Dr. 21
Not that I d., or mean to call E. i 91
To d. the wit a friend displays F. 88
Quite to forget, or d. it worth no thought H. 83
And d. her sharp artillery mere straw H. 597
D. life a blessing with its numerous woes H. 546
Should d. it by our old companion made N.A. 95
D. our nation brutes no longer N.C. 49
And minds that d. derided pain a treat R. 310
Does all, and d. too little, all he can R. 320
And he that d. his leisure well bestowed R. 505
Why d. we death a foe? St. v. 18 [thorn S. ii 1
D. not, sweet rose, that bloomest midst many a
Who d. his house a useless place St. vi 21
And d. his base stupidity no crime T. 542
By culinary arts, unsavoury d. T. i 125
Who d. religion frenzy, and the God T. iv 178
Start at his awful name, or d. his praise T. iv 180
We build with what we d. eternal rock T. v 534
He d. a thousand or ten thousand lives T. v 276
Nor d. he wiser him, who gives his noon T. vi 278
Of what he d. no mean or trivial trust T. vi 607
And I am recompensed, and d. the toils T. vi 725
That not to attempt it, arduous as he d. T. vi 757
Pursuing gilded flies; and such he d.T. vi 922
D. him a cipher in the works of God T. vi 943
He d. it hard to vegetate alone Tir. 724
D. his reward too great if he prevail Tir. 479
Would d. it no abuse, or waste of pains Tir. 627
D. it of no great moment whose, or where Tir. 784
(For what kings d. a toil, as well they may T.T. 155

DEEMED.
The Point of Honour has been d. of use Con. 163
Can ne'er be d. worth half so much E. iv 29
That men have d. substantial since the fall H. 154
Let each be d. a queen" L.R. 24
Has she no spark that may be d. her own? T. 482
Emerging, must be d. a labour due T. iii 631 [iv 546
Ill propped upon French heels; she might be d. T.
Yet d. oracular, lure down to death T. v 863 [881
They now are d. the faithful, and are praised T. vi
But many a crime d. innocent on earth T. vi 439
What all had d. his own Th. 20
A man d. worthy of so dear a trust Tir. 711

DEEP.
D. in ruin as in guilt B. 16
D. in the abyss of Silver-End E. i 42
The purport of his d. decrees E. i 60
Impede the bark that ploughs the d. serene Ch. 132
Yes, to d. sadness sullenly resigned Ch. 151 [612
The statesman, skilled in projects dark and d. Ch.
A d. memorial graven on their hearts Con. 514 [741
The World grown old her d. discernment shows Con.
Whose wisdom, drawn from the d. well of life Con. 564
With God's d. stamp upon its current worth Con. 710
Oh think, if chargeable with d. arrears Ex. 608
So then :—as darkness overspread the d. Ex. 636
That remedy, not hid in d. profound H. 111 [F.A.28
D. mysteries both! which schoolmen must have toiled
To search forbidden d., where mystery lies F.A. 33
Beneath the smiling surface of the d. H. 184
Thy d. repentance of thy thousand lies H. 590
Hates with a d. sincerity the true H. 642
No thunders shook with d. intestine sound Her. 5

And all their d. impressions, wear away P.E. 278
Fast anchored in the d. abyss of space R. 84
One, and one only, charged with d. regret P.E. 349
To dive into the secret d. within R. 135
Pursue their sport, and follow to the d. R. 160
To them the d. recess of dusky groves R. 181
He swathes about the swelling of the d. R. 527
Some swayed by fashion, some by d. disgust R. 607
Where it advances far into the d. T. i 619 [R.H. 2
Than bid me shun the d., and dread the shore?
Conceiving thunders, through a thousand d. T. ii 89
Gone with the refluent wave into the d. T. ii 120
Rise not, the waters of the d. shall rise T. ii 143
Of such d. mischief has itself a cause T. ii 698 [109
Long since: with many an arrow d. infixed T. iii
Immortal Hale! for d. discernment praised T. iii 258
The rage of fermentation, plunges d. T. iii 519
And spreads the honey of his d. research T. iv 112
Of d. deliberation, as the man T. iv 300 [438
D. in the loamy bank. Uptorn by strength T. iv
Of Indian fume, and guzzling d. the boor T. iv 473
The verdure of the plain lies buried d. T. v 21
D. plunging, and again d. plunging oft T. v 34
Conscious and fearful of too d. a plunge T. v 64
And we are d. in that of cold pretence T. v. 494
Die too: the d. foundations that we lay T. v. 532
D. in his soft credulity the stamp T. v 497 [174
The d. dark green of whose unvarnished leaf T. vi
In wisdom, and with philosophic d. T. v 297 [302
The bench on which we sat while d. employed Tir.
That age or injury has hollowed d. T. vi 311 [555
D. in the flood, found, when he sought it not T. vi
Not always tempt the distant d. Trans. H. 4 [628
Swarmed with a scribbling herd, as d. inlaid T.T.

DEEPER.
And whelmed in d. gulfs than he Cast. 66
Of d. green the elm; and d. still T. i 312
Takes d. root, confirmed by what they see T. ii 568
D. in none than in their surgeon's books Tir. 289

DEEPEST.
Beheld their progress with the d. dread T.T. 325

DEEPLY.
D. resolved to shut a Saviour out Con. 690
With fingers d. dyed in human gore Ex. 497
And him as d. who abhors it not H. 333
Ill fated race! how d. must they rue Her. 51
A thousand other themes less d. traced M.P. 57

DEEP-TONED.
Strike on the d. chord the sum of all P.E. 605

DEER. [94
Like a slain d., the tumbrel brings him home P.E.
Or forest where the d. securely roves R. 182
I was a stricken d. that left the herd T. iii 108
Defies the check of winter, haunts of d. T. vi 110
Poor England! thou are a devoted d. T.T. 362
Designed thy cradle; and a skipping d. Y.O. 25

DEFACE.
By rural carvers, who with knives d. T. i 281

DEFACED.
Beheld with joy the lovely scene d. Ex. 426
And what his storms have blasted and d. T. vi 745

DEFAULT.
The price of his d. But now—yes, now T. iii 92

DEFEAT.
To thwart its influence, and its end d. Ch. 38
'Tis love like his that can alone d. R. 781
To France than all her losses and d. T. v 380
Where cruel man d. not her design T. vi 343

DEFECT.
Their own d., invisible to them Con. 155
That great d. would cost him, not alone Con. 763
Our friend's d. long hid from sight F. 149
Sin's rotten trunk concealing its d. P.E. 288
With clear exemption from its own d. T. i 404
In aid of our d. In some are found T. vi 611
Shall give him consequence, heal all d. Tir. 392

DEFECTION.
That after man's d. laid all waste Con. 752

DEFECTIVE.
In aid of our d. sight E. i 62
D. only in his Roman nose P.E. 396
D. and unsanctioned, proved too weak T. ii 524

DEFENCE.
Say not (and if the thought of such d. Ex. 708 [43
Who strike the blow, then plead your own d. Her.
Have fallen in her d. A Patriot's blood T. v 714

DEFENCELESS.
His victims, robbed of their d. all T. iv 458
Waged with d. innocence, while he T. vi 393

DEFEND.
'Tis hard, indeed, if nothing will d. Con. 173
Till sinking in the quicksand he d. P.E. 552
"D. me therefore, Common Sense," say I T. iii 187
Betray thee, while professing to d. T.T. 333

DEFIANCE.
Had bid d. to the warring world Ex. 212
That bids d. to the united powers T. ii 769
And in d. of her rival powers T. v 123
Or growled d. in such angry sort T. vi 377

DEFICIENT.
Aiding a dubious and d. sight Ch. 329

DEFIED.
The billows and the blast d. A Tale 55
Each tender tie of life d. Miss — 29
Hear then how Mercy, slighted and d. T. 501
Braved and d., and in our own sea proved T. ii 272
Is never with impunity d. T. vi 548

DEFILE.
Who dare dishonour, or d., the tongue Con. 26
To fill with riot, and d. with blood T. iii 307

DEFILED.
Then Nature, injured, scandalized, d. Ex. 424
My prayers and alms, imperfect and d. T. 577
To them it flowed much mingled and d. T. ii 503
Is soon dishonoured and d. in most T. vi 590
The puppy pack that had d. the scene T.T. 641

DEFILEMENT.
Contracts d. not to be endured T. iv 670

DEFINED.
But that disease, when soberly d. Con. 667
Or something not to be d. F. 176

DEFORM.
No flaw d., no difficulty thwarts T. vi 229
As now, and with excoriate forks d. Y.O. 5

DEFORMED.
With prickly gorse, that, shapeless and d. T. i 527
Be fickle, and thy year, most part, d. T. ii 210
The children, crooked, and twisted, and d. T. ii. 772

DEFRAY.
With our expenditure d. his own T. ii 605

DEFY.
The raving storm and dashing wave d. Con. 559

DEFY—DELIGHT

Endurest the brunt, and darest d. them all Ex. 697
The Christian vessel, and d. the blast H. 168
Fired with a zeal peculiar, they d. H. 461
With bony and unkerchiefed neck d. T. 137
Here grotto within grotto safe d. T. v 117
D. the check of winter, haunts of deer T. vi 110
The worth of his three kingdoms I d. T.T. 85.

DEFYING.
He hails the clergy, and d. shame T. ii 356

DEGENERATE.
The features of the last d. times T. vi 900
Not prompted, as in our d. days T.T. 590

DEGRADE.
And would d. her votary to an ape Con. 460
Disturb good order, and d. true worth T. iii 674

DEGRADED.
Adds nothing now to the d. dead H. 269

DEGRADING.
O most d. of all ills that wait Ch. 155

DEGREE.
Though feeble in d., in kind the same Ch. 594
For God unfolds by slow d. E. i 59
Yet man, laborious man, by slow d. Her. 67
Finds, by d., the truths that once bore sway P.E. 277
Pleasure admitted in undue d. P.E. 269
There hardening by d., till double steeled P.E. 590
He sighs,—for after all, by slow d. R. 465
A tooth or auburn lock, and by d. T. i 133
The middle field; but scattered by d. T. i 293
But just d., an overhanging breadth T. iii 482
The licence of the lowest in d. T. iv 588
Procure him many a curse. By slow d. T. iv 635
He yet by slow d. puts off himself T. iv 637
Thus by d. self-cheated of their sound T. v 264
And wisely store the nursery by d. Tir. 117
May be as fervent in d. U. 9
On all around him; learned not by d. Y.O. 147

DEIFIED.
D. useless wood or senseless stone Ex. 238

DEIGN.
Scarce d. to notice him, or, if she see T. vi 942

DEIGNED.   [T.T. 718
The flowers would spring where'er she d. to stray
No pastime but with her he d. to take A.T. 17
Did not our hearts feel all He d. to say Con. 535
To Truth itself, that d. him no reply T. iii 271
Presents the prayer the Saviour d. to teach Tir. 123

DEIST.
There, and there only (though the d. rave P.E. 614
Where d., always foiled, yet scorn to yield T. 372

DEITY.
A D. could solve. Their answers, vague T. ii 521

DEJECTED.
Bent knees, round shoulders, and d. looks T. iv 634

DELAY.
Nor stops, till, overleaping all d. Ch. 178
It suffers interruption and d. P.E. 442
Vociferous, and impatient of d. T. i 299
To his young hopes, requires discreet d. T. iii 504
And patient of the slow-paced swain's d. T. v 32
Its long d., feels every welcome stroke T. v 413
Thy saints proclaim thee king; and thy d. T. vi 864

DELAYED.
Our progress was often d. C. 11
D. not to bestow Cast. 28

DELEGATE.
Legates and d., with powers from hell Ex. 514
Whom once, as d. of God on earth T. vi 399
Seem with one voice to d. to you? Tir. 554

DELIBERATION.
With slow d. he unties Ch. 471
Of deep d., as the man T. iv 300
Whom care and cool d. suit Tir. 781

DELICACY.
To virtue, d., truth, or sense P.E. 513

DELICATE.
With feet too d. to touch the ground Ex. 52
To cover a pill for a d. palate F.M. 12
'Tis gentle, d., and kind M.F. 55
Caught in a d., soft, silken net P.E. 313
Sounds harshly in so d. an ear R. 250
" Oh what a d. retreat! R.C. 60
More d. his timorous mate retires T. 214
You think, perhaps, so d. his dress T. ii 625
His daily fare as d. Alas! T. ii 626
Lives by contriving d. for you) T. iii 546
Some act by the d. mind The Rose 14
Is so refined, and d. and chaste T.T. 511
So nice his ear, so d. his touch) T.T. 653
To the d. growth of our isle W.N. 2

DELICIOUS.
D., when her patriots of high note T. iv 170
The promise of d. fruit appears V. 52

DELIGHT.
The seaman, with sincere d. A Tale 57
A lasting, a sacred d. C. 40
But misery still d. to trace Cast. 59
And injured, makes forgiveness her d. Ch. 431
On all the wings of holiday d.) Ch. 548
What neither yields us profit nor d. Con. 241
That fills the listening lover with d. Con. 446
And, farewell else all hope of pure d. Con. 681
To mar d. superior to its own E. ii 34
That beams d. ? a heart untaught to sigh ? Ep. i 6
In hopes of permanent d. F. 68
Thy dear d. while here below F. 212
But that d. they never knew F.B. 11
If he wish to instruct, he must learn to d. F.M. 17
She holds a Paradise of rich d. H. 60
What treasures centre, what d., in thee H. 174
Nature indeed vouchsafes for our d. H. 487
Of fools that hate thee and d. in sin H. 745
Seek to d., that they may mend mankind H. 758
To illumine with d. the saddest scenes J.T. 20
But thou canst taste no calm d. M.B. 17
That all the true d. of man Miss — 47
I would not trust my heart—the dear d. M.P. 82
Me from my d. to sever N.C. 11
Such civil broils are my d. Pat. 17
Our dear d. are often such P.B. 29
Where'er he turns, enjoyment and d. P.E. 47
Hear him again. He calls it a d. P.E. 163
D. us, by engaging our respect P.E. 208
The centre of d. he may not taste? P.E. 230
D. like these, ye sensual and profane P.E. 263
Called to the temple of impure d. P.E. 584
From all he sees he catches new d. R. 189
Shall fill thee with d. unfelt before R. 360
Nature in every form inspires d. R. 417
D. the citizen, who gasping there R. 485
Yet neither these d., nor aught beside R. 743
In colour these, and those d. the smell R. 794
Puss with d. beyond expression R.C. 43

98　　　　　　　　　DELIGHT—DEMOSTHENES

To make his precepts our *d. St.* vi 7
Himself so much the source of his *d. T.* 413
D. us, happy to renounce awhile *T.* i 515
Thy simple fare, and all thy plain *d. T.* i 646
Of gratulation and *d.*, her King ? *T.* ii 84
Scenes such as these, 'tis his supreme *d. T.* iii 306
D. which who would leave, that has a heart *T.* iii 22
I crown thee king of intimate *d. T.* iv 139
Which seen *d.* him not; then coming home *T.* iv 236
Is still the livery she *d.* to wear *T.* iv 760
Freely and with *d.*, who leaves us free *T.* v 334
Upon his heart-strings, trembling with *d. T.* v 414
Whom God *d.* in, and in whom He dwells *T.* v 778
Made pure, shall relish with divine *d. T.* v 783 [:28
When none pursues, through mere *d.* of heart *T.* vi
Such recollection of our own *d. Tir.* 311
That scorn of all *d.* but those of sense *Tir.* 351
To lead his son, for prospects of *d. Tir.* 630
From vicious inmates and *d.* impure *Tir.* 892
But still, while Virtue kindled his *d. T.T.* 598
And, dizzy with *d.*, profaned the sacred wires *T.T.* 607
To polish, furnish, and *d.* the mind *T.T.* 645
Mankind to share in the divine *d. T.T.* 753
D. in agitation, yet sustain *Y.O.* 82
Contemplating with small *d.* 1789, 24

DELIGHTED
D. with her babe, the enchantress smiled *A.T.* 9
D. with my bauble coach, and wrapped *M.P.* 50
D. There, fast rooted in their bank *T.* i 166
And smiles *d.* wth the eternal poise *T.* iv 486

DELIGHTFUL
From side to side of her *d.* isle *Ex.* 3
And this *d.* earth, and that fair sky *Ex.* 638
Chilled more his else *d.* way *Mor.* 16
Come, peace of mind, *d.* guest! *O.* ii 1
" O most *d.* hour by man *St.* iii 1
D. industry enjoyed at home *T.* iii 356
Calls the *d.* scenery all his own *T.* v 741

DELIGHTFULLY
Hour after hour *d.* allot *R.* 373

DELINQUENT
Shook the *d.* with such fits of awe *T.* ii 722
Denounce no doom on the *d.?* None *T.* vi 433

DELIRIOUS
'Tis childish dotage, a *d.* dream! *Ch.* 417

DELIRIUM
Intoxication and *d.* wild *T.* ii 510
Imposed a gay *d.* for a truth *T.* iv 528

DELIVERS
Legends prolix *d.* in the ears *S.* i 2

DELIVERANCE
The fast that wins *d.*, and suspends *Ex.* 406
Shall he, for such *d.* freely wrought *T.* 191
The disappointed foe, *d.* found *T.* iv 186

DELIVERED
Is note for note *d.* in our ears *Con.* 455
D. briefly thus his mind *P.T.* 22
But, once *d.*, kills them with a frown *T.* iii 438
Because *d.* down from sire to son *T.* v 303

DELIVERER
" My dear *d.* out of hopeless night *Ch.* 234
Viewed a *d.* with disdain and hate *Ex.* 217
To the *d.* of an injured land *T.* iv 793

DELLS.　　　　　　　　　　　　　　[253
Crooked or straight, through quags or thorny *d. Tir.*

DELUGE
To let the military *d.* pass *Ex.* 60
These like a *d.* with impetuous force *R.* 77
From the dashed pane the *d.* as it falls *T.* iii 488
Beneath the dazzling *d.*; and the bents *T.* v 22
The *d.* washed it out; but left unquenched *T.* v 209

DELUGING
Their ancient barriers, *d.* the dry ? *T.* ii 56
Profusion, *d.* a state with lusts *T.* ii 688

.DELUSION
Mere folly and *d.*—Sir, your toast *H.* 364
D. strong as Hell shall bind him fast *P.E.* 609
Each in his own *d.*; they are lost *T.* iii 125

DELUSIVE
" Vain our *d.* hope of constant knights *A.T.* 100
There no *d.* hope invites despair *P.E.* 617
D. most where warmest wishes are *T.* i 542

DEMAGOGUE
Close at his heels, a *d.* ascends *T.* iv 61

DEMAND
Not only fills Necessity's *d. Ch.* 99
And give the strain the compass it *d. Con.* 718
He knows that God *d.* his heart entire *Con.* 759
And gives him all his just *d.* require *Con.* 760
D. one moment of thy fleeting time *Ep.* i 2
Or cool, as the season *d. Gr.* 38
What health and sober appetite *d. H.* 158
Go now, and with important tone *d. H.* 528
The keen *d.* of appetite *N.G.* 6
Behold in these what leisure hours *d. R.* 701
The loud *d.*, from year to year the same *R.* 709
The grain, or herb, or plant that each *d. R.* 788
High in *d.*, though lowly in pretence *T.* 93
A soul redeemed *d.* a life of praise *T.* 279
More distant, and that prophecy *d. T.* ii 66
The adagio and andante it *d. T.* ii 361
Can lodge a heavenly mind—*d.* a doubt *T.* ii 462
All well repaid, *d.* him, he attends *T.* iii 398
The crowded roots *d.* enlargement now *T.* iii 582
Her cause *d.* the assistance of your throats *T.* iv 511
Might he *d.* them at the gates of death *T.* vi 45
So vast in its *d.*, unless impell'd *T.* vi 218
The exalted prize *d.* an upward look *Tir.* 383
When health *d.* it, of athletic sort *Tir.* 653
The bottomless *d.* of contest waged *Y.O.* 102

DEMANDING
Not tire, *d.* rather skill than force *T.* iii 407

DEMEANOUR
Hence a *d.* holy and unspecked *T.* 281
Some, decent in *d.* while they preach *T.* ii 440

DEMESNE
But that the lord of this enclosed *d. T.* i 331
To improve and cultivate their just *d. T.* v 223

DEMI-DEIFY
They *d.* and fume him so *T.* v 266

DEMIGOD
Surrounding throngs the *d.* revere *T.* 312

DEMON
Where a *D.*, her enemy, stood— *M.D.* 27
D. produced them doubtless, brazen-clawed *N.A.* 101
And fanged with brass the *d.* are abroad *N.A.* 102
Of *d.* uttered, from whatever lungs *N.A.* 118

DEMOSTHENES
In him, *D.* was heard again *T.T.* 342

DEMURE.
Observe each face, how sober and d.! *P.E.* 135

DEN.
Calls Nature from her ivy-mantled d. *Ch.* 95
And shut up every satyr in his d. *Con.* 38
Drives to their d. the obedient beasts of prey *R.* 766
A d. of mischiefs never to be told *T.* 392

DENIED.
She feels that frailty she d. so long *Ch.* 409
The cause is plain, and not to be d. *Con.* 159
D. that earthly opulence they choose *Ex.* 458
These, amidst scenes as waste as if d. *H.* 538
To dream all night of what the day d. *T.* i 671
He feels the anxieties of life, d. *T.* ii 302
O happy! and, in my account, d. *T.* iv 357
By the impure, and hears his power d. *T.* v 895
D. the endearments of thine eye *The Doves,* 35
To prove a consequence by none d. *Tir.* 104
What Nature, alas! has d. *W.N.* 1

DENOMINATES.
D. an itch for writing *E.* i 18

DENOTES.
The want of both d. a meaner breed *H.* 292

DENOUNCE.
D. no doom on the delinquent? None *T.* vi 433

DENOUNCING.
D. death upon the sins of man *H.* 512
That she is rigid in d. death *T.* i 732

DENSE.
Impelled through regions d. and rare *O.* i 15

DENY.
The danger they discern not, they d. *Ch.* 418
And while his tongue the charge d. *H.F.* 15
Hatched by the beams of truth, d. him rest *P.E.* 240
To seek that peace a tyrant's frown d. *R.* 770
Shall fall on her, when Heaven d. it thee *T.* 512
D. the power that wields it. God proclaims *T.* ii 178
Need help, d. them nothing but his name. *T.* iv 428
D. thy Godhead with a martyr's zeal. *T.* vi 883

DEPART.
Disbanded legions freely might d. *Ch.* 618 [785
He sighs, d., and leaves the accomplished plan *T.* iii
Our more harmonious notes: the thrush d. *T.* i 767
That pressed the beach, and hasty to d. *T.* ii 118

DEPARTED.
And Heaven is all d. as a scroll *H.* 747

DEPARTING.
From the d., they are lost, and rove *T.* v 893

DEPARTURE.
Are but d. from the first design *A.T.* 50

DEPEND.
Yet much d., as in the tiller's toil *Con.* 5
While truths on which eternal things d. *Ex.* 117
And if the genuine worth of gold d. *J.T.* 27
And more laborious; cares on which d. *T.* iii 607
Superior as we are, they yet d. *T.* vi 608
But truths on which d. our main concern *Tir.* 77
D. not much upon your golden dream *Tir.* 429[857
Though much d. on what thy choice shall be *Tir.*
Thus happiness d., as Nature shows *T.T.* 246

DEPENDANT.
D. on the baker's punctual call *T.* i 244

DEPENDED.
If the matter d. alone upon me *P.A.* 37

DEPENDENCE.
Is what it was, d. upon Thee *T.* 584

DEPENDENT.
Fish up his dirty and d. bread *T.* iii 803
Thine helpless charge, d. on thy care *T.* iv 369
D. upon man; those in his fields *T.* vi 414

DEPENDING.
His legs d. at the open door *T.* i 93
With handkerchief in hand d. low *T.* ii 450
Thus all success d. on an ear *T.T.* 514

DEPICTED.
The pattern grows, the well d. flower *T.* iv 151

DEPLORE.
Youth lost in dissipation, we d. *H.* 23
Ten thousand swains the wasted scene d. *Her.* 39
D. the wasted regions of her globe *Her.* 80
Thee to d., were grief misspent indeed *J.T.* 11

DEPLORED.
And say;—"Blot out my sin, confessed, d. *H.* 592
But though I less d. thee ne'er forgot *M.P.* 45
And worse than all, and most to be d. *T.* ii 21
Works the d. and mischievous effect *T.* iv 616

DEPORTMENT.
Manly d., gallant, easy, gay *H.* 407
A just d., manners graced with ease *P.E.* 421
And quaint in its d. and attire *T.* ii 461

DEPOSIT.
A rich d., on the bordering lands *Ch.* 249
D. in those shallows all their spawn *P.E.* 479

DEPRAVED.
Against a heart d. and temper hurt *Tir.* 489

DEPRECIATES.
D. and undoes us in our own? *T.* iii 284

DEPRIVED.
D. of her and freedom at a blow *Ch.* 149

DEPTH.
As men of d. in erudition use *Ch.* 392
The d., how awful! falling there, we burst *N.A.* 110
Of d. enough, and none to spare *R.C.* 41
To reach a d. profounder still, and still *T.* v 593

DERIDED.
(Though Vice d. with a just design *Ch.* 487
And minds that deem d. pain a treat *R.* 310

DERIDING.
His road, d. much the blank amaze *T.* vi 536

DERISION.
As move d., or by foppish airs *T.* ii 562
Grew tremulous, and moved d. more *T.* ii 729
Incurs d. for his easy faith *T.* v 500

DERIVE.
Daily d. increasing light and force *Con.* 697
From fading good d., with chemic art *H.* 159
Binds man, the lord of all. Himself d. *T.* i 386
D. from Heaven, pure as the fountain is *T.* vi 833
From which at least a grateful few d. *T.* vi 965
That man, the master of this globe d. *Tir.* 3

DERIVED.
D. from nature's noblest part *E.* i 13
With light d. from thee, would smother thine *Ex.* 281

DERIVED—DESIGNED

D. from the same source of light and grace *T.* 533
'Tis Liberty of Heart, *d.* from Heaven *T.* v 545

DESCANTS.
With merry *d.* on a nation's woes *T.* iv 77

DESCANTING.
D. on his fate *Cast.* 56

DESCEND.
His sun precipitate *d. Mor.* 54
And calm *d.* to yours *St.* v 36
With youthful smiles, *d.* towards the grave *T.* i 407
While the winds whistle, and the snows *d. T.* iii 509
That seizes first the opulent, *d. T.* iv 583
Shall visit earth in mercy; shall *d. T.* vi 743

DESCENDED.
The evening came, the sun *d. R.C.* 65

DESCENDING.
'Tis Heaven, all Heaven *d.* on the wings *H.* 732
Seem drops *d.* in a shower of light *R.* 350
Then swift *d.* with a seaman's haste *R.* 435
D. now (but cautious, lest too fast) *T.* i 266
D., and with never-ceasing lapse *T.* iv 327
Of his *d.* progeny was found *T.* v 212
And when *d.* he resigns the skies *Tir.* 37

DESCRIBE.
He reads wise lectures, and *d.* aloud *Ch.* 389
Hophni and Phineas may *d.* the rest *Ex.* 449
When Pope *d.* them, have a thousand sweets *R.* 572
Praise justly due to those that I *d. T.* i 180
Would I *d.* a preacher, such as Paul *T.* ii 395
A history : *d.* the man, of whom *T.* iii 141
Should seek the guiltless joys that I *d. T.* iii 698
D. and prints it, that the world may know *T.* iv 237
Point to the cure, *d.* a Saviour's cross *Tir.* 165

DESCRIED.
As here and there a twinkling star *d. Tir.* 843

DESCRY.
The cause perhaps inquiry may *d. Con.* 363
By looking on the bud, *d. E.* i 70
Impatient to *d.* the flags of France *Ex.* 291
Endued with reason only to *d. Tir.* 61

DESERT.
Hail, honoured land! a *d.* where *A Tale* 65
Where seas or *d.* part them from the rest *Ch.* 20
Verse cannot stoop so low as thy *d. Ex.* 547
Well spake the prophet,—"Let the *d.* sing *H.* 524
The foes of man, or make a *d.* sweet *R.* 782
Or curse the *d.* with a tenfold dearth? *T.* 182
D. their office; and themselves intent *T.* iv 589
(As if barbarity were high *d.*) *T.* vi 435
Man praises man. *D.* in arts or arms *T.* vi 632
Must shine by true *d.*, or not at all *Tir.* 357
Weigh, for a moment, classical *d. Tir.* 488
If thou *d.* thy charge, and throw it wide *Tir.* 887
Stands in the *d.* shivering and forlorn *T.T.* 724

DESERTED.
D. and his friends so nigh *Cast.* 36
D. of its bloom, the flaccid, shrunk *T.* i 392

DESERVE.
Those Christians best *d.* the name *N.G.* 35
D. not, if so soon offended *P.* 43
I should *d.* to forfeit all applause) *P.E.* 511
D. to be beloved, but not adored *R.* 272
Can life in them *d.* the name *St.* vi 13
What shall the man *d.* of human kind *T.* 429
And 'tis but seemly, that where all *d. T.* ii 71
Exposed to manacles, *d.* them well *T.* v 366
D. at least applause for her attempt *T.* v 369

Bled nobly, and their deeds, as they *d. T.* v 705
His steeds, usurp a place they well *d. T.* vi 703
Be it a weakness, it *d.* some praise *Tir.* 296
Should move a sneer at thy *d.* fame *Tir.* 142
The great and small *d.* one common blame *Tir.* 515
D. an answer similar, or none *Tir.* 904
Whose worth *d.* as warm a lay *U.* 3

DESERVED.
And having well *d.*, expects the worst *T.* 266
Of academic fame (howe'er *d.*) *T.* iii 15
The death he had *d.*, and died alone *T.* vi 556

DESERVEDLY.
Who scorns it, starves *d.* at home *T.* i 435

DESERVEST.
Thou well *d.* an alienated son *Tir.* 579

DESERVING.
Or if, *d.* of a better doom *Con.* 413
Because *d.*, silently retire *T.* iv 419
Then most *d.* in their own account *T.* v 261
D. honour, but for wisdom more *T.* vi 491

DESIGN.
Are but departures from the first *d. A.T.* 50
(Though Vice derided with a just *d. Ch.* 487
And one in heart, in interest, and *d. Con.* 701
As smiths or joiners perfect a *d. Con.* 790
Is made subservient to the grand *d. Con.* 897
Tis not that I *d.* to rob *E.* iv 1
Stiff in the letter, lax in the *d. Ex.* 125
He first conceives, then perfects his *d. Ex.* 318
Hast thou, by statute, shoved from its *d. Ex.* 376
And farther still the formed and fixed *d. Ex.* 429
His creature thwart not his august *d. H.* 142
By this, with nice precision of *d. H.* 606
Fancy may stand aloof from the *d. H.* 672
Phœbus, if such be thy *d. O* i 25
It falls at last, far wide of his *d. P.E.* 575
The birds conceiving a *d. P.T.* 11
In aid of her *d. Q.V.* 34
To trace in Nature's most minute *d. R.* 53
Manly *d.*, and learning's grave pursuits *R.* 242
Conspire against thy peace with one *d. R.* 262
And such as, in the zeal of good *d. R.* 697
Pride above all opposes her *d. T.* 474
Dull in *d.*, and clumsy to perform *T.* i 18
His master-strokes, and draw from his *d. T.* ii 398
The threads of politic and shrewd *d. T.* iii 147
Conspiring, may attest his bright *d. T.* iii 654
To grace the full pavilion. His *d. T.* iii 716
D. the blooming wonders of the next *T.* vi 197
Whose work is without labour; whose *d. T.* vi 223
Where cruel man defeats not her *d. T.* vi 343
Much less might serve, when all that we *d. T.* vi 642
To want of judgment than to wrong *d. T.* vi 657
The father, who *d.* his babe a priest *Tir.* 364
If, therefore, e'en when honest in *d. Tir.* 452
Stark naught, because corrupt in their *d. T.T.* 4
Distorted from its use and just *d. T.T.* 754

DESIGNATION.
Ah, happy *d.*, prudent choice *Tir.* 342
With *d.* of the finger's end *Tir.* 641

DESIGNED.
D. to sit close to it just like a saddle *A.C.* 13
Again—the band of commerce was *d. Ch.* 83
Let just Restraint, for public peace *d. Ch.* 286
The melody that was at first *d. Con.* 453
And touch the subject I *d.* at first *Con.* 868
A coin by Craft for Folly's use *d. E.* ii 7
In pity to the souls his Grace *d. E.* ii 23

But if a sweeter voice, and one *d. Ex.* 726
D., in honour of his endless love *H.* 121
She seemed *d.* for Flora's hand *L.R.* 15
By bounteous heaven *d. Miss* — 2
And sense of having well *d. Mor.* 52
That heralds ere *d. Q.V.* 24
When he *d.* a Paradise below *R.* 270
Master of all the enjoyments he *d. R.* 427
As they *d.* to mock me, at my side *T.* v 17
D. by loud declaimers on the part *T.* v 498
Of such a gulf as he *d.* his grave *T.* vi 515
Who, when she form'd, *d.* them an abode *T.* vi 580
And all the plan their destiny *d. Tir.* 86
Fulfil the purpose, and appear *d. Tir.* 93
Made just the adept you *d.* your son *Tir.* 237
Nor taint his speech with meannesses *d. Tir.* 686
D. by Nature wise, but self-made fools *Tir.* 837
Thus with a rigour, for his good *d. T.T.* 216
D. thy cradle; and a skipping deer *Y.O.* 25

DESIGNER.
But though we praise the exact *d.*'s skill *Ch.* 555
A close *d.* not to be believed *Con.* 477

DESIGNING.
What Atheists call him, a *d.* knave *P.E.* 103
So I, *d.* other themes, and called *T.* iii. 11
And still *d.* a more glorious far *T.* v 564

DESIRABLE.
Not e'en the sun, *d.* as rare *H.* 503
On so *d.* an end *Mor.* 34

DESIRE.
Come, prompt me with benevolent *d. Ch.* 11
And, in the glow of her intense *d. Ch.* 402
Found him as prompt, as their *d.* was true *Con.* 545
Their hopes, *d.*, and purposes estranged *Con.* 725
And while it shows the land the soul *d. Con.* 885
Or, in his words who damned the base *d. Ex.* 422
Which make that Heaven, if thou *d.* it thine *Ex.* 687
They drop through mere *d.* to prate *F.* 71
And Dick felt some *d. F.B.* 15
Renewed *d.* would grace with other speech *H.* 35
Man feels the spur of passions and *d. H.* 55
Avarice in thee was the *d.* of wealth *J.T.* 25
Which breathes the low *d. Miss* — 10
To thy whole heart's *d.? N.Y.G.* 12
Consumes his soul with vain *d. P.B.* 16
The world around solicits his *d. P.E.* 39
Who, kindling a combustion of *d. P.E.* 319
Of pride, ambition, or impure *d. R.* 110
Genius, and temper, and *d* of rest *R.* 172
We meet at last in one sincere *d. R.* 389
Give e'en a dunce the employment he *d. R.* 613
With visions prompted by intense *d. T.* i 451
Yet thousands still *d.* to journey on *T.* i 470
Of more; and industry in some *T.* v 225
"Love kindles as I gaze. I feel *d. T.* v 842
With what intense *d.* he wants his home *Tir.* 562
Who, wise yourselves, *d.* your sons should learn *Tir.*
Thou hast all thine heart's *d. Tran.* iii 16   [811

DESIRED.
The good so long *d. A Tale* 24
As hermit could have well *d. Mor.* 4
Seems so to be *d.*, perhaps I might *M.P.* 83
From objects too much dreaded or *d. R.* 144
The dawn of thy last advent, long *d. T.* vi 866

DESIRING.
And shines without *d.* to be seen *T.* 70

DESIROUS.
No Papist more *d.* to compound *T.* 291
D. to return, and not received *T.* iii 81.

DESK.
"Ye groves" (the statesman at his *d.* exclaims *R.* 365
Sweet sleep enjoys the curate in his *d. T.* i 94
Nor sleep enjoyed by curate in his *d. T.* i 100

DESOLATE.
Convey to this *d.* shore *A.S.* 34
And *d.* a nation at a blast *T.* ii 188
And regions long since *d.*, proclaim *T.T.* 431

DESOLATED.
Rolled over all our *d.* land *Ch.* 76

DESOLATING.
Abroad, and *d.* public life *T.* iii 683

DESPAIR.
Soon hurries me back to *d. A.S.* 48
Supported by *d.* of life *Cast.* 18
For merchants rich in cargoes of *d. Ch.* 138
By lean *d.* upon an empty purse *Ch.* 506
Is yet no subject of *d. F.* 32
Closing at last in darkness and *d. H.* 6
Hollow-eyed Abstinence, and lean *D. H.* 58
Life without hope can close but in *d. H.* 274
All hope *d.*, that stands not on his cross *H.* 632
And harder still as learnt beneath *d. H.* 697
That Hope which can alone exclude *d. H.* 751
Or blade that might redeem it from *d. Her.* 23
Like trout pursued, the critic in *d. P.E.* 502
There no delusive hope invites *d. P.E.* 617
And weeps a sad libation in *d. R.* 226
The prospect, such as might enchant *d. R.* 439
And must *d.* to pay *St.* v 32
Of old achievements, and *d.* of new *T.* ii 254
Then shake them in *d.*, and dance again *T.* ii 666
Ye dungeons and ye cages of *d. T.* v 385
"So strict, that less than perfect must *d.? T.* v 641
Of lust, and on the anvil of *d. T.* v 665
We could not teach, and must *d.* to learn *T.* vi 620
Promise a work of which they must *d. Tir.* 234
When Freedom, wounded almost to *d. T.T.* 196

DESPAIRING.
Whom now *d.* agonies destroy *H.* 172
As midnight, and *d.* of a morn *J.T.* 22
Plunging, and half *d.* of escape *T.* iii 6

DESPATCHED.
The mind *d.* upon her busy toil *Con.* 437

DESPERATE.
I give him over as a *d.* case *Con.* 406
Beware of *d.* steps. The darkest day *N.A.* 132
'Tis *d.*, and he sleeps the sleep of death *T.* v 669
As if their duty were a *d.* task *T.T.* 313
D. attempt, till trees shall speak again! *Y.O.* 49

DESPERATION.
Flash *d.*, and betray their pangs *T.* i 502

DESPISE.
Thou that hast wasted earth, and dared *d. Ch.* 69
As to *d.* the glory of our kind *Con.* 258
Ten thousand charms, that only fools *d. H.* 51
What they themselves, without remorse, *d. H.* 253
D. his bulwarks, and unpeople earth *R.* 72
D. the plain direction, and are lost *T.* 33
The favoured few—the enthusiasts you *d. T.* 231

DESPISED.
Patron of else the most *d.* of men *Ch.* 290

Pleasure o'ervalued, and his grace d. *Ex.* 252
And tells of laws d., at least not kept *H.* 220
Thy means so feeble, and d. so much *H.* 666
Souls that have long d. their heavenly birth *R.* 35
Shall be d. and overlooked no more *R.* 359
But which the poor, and the d. of all *T.* iii 287
Insipid else, and sure to be d. *T.* vi 1016
I name thee not, lest so d. a name *Tir.* 141
While morals languish, a d. concern *Tir.* 514
D. by thee, what more can he expect *Tir.* 712
See womanhood d., and manhood shamed *Tir.* 827
Will be d. and trampled on at last *T.T.* 397
O long d., but now victorious host *T.T.* 473

DESPISING.
D. all rebuke, still persevered *Ex.* 397

DESPOND.
And I can weep, can hope, and can d. *T.* iii 841

DESPONDENCE.
D., self-deserted in her grief *R.* 757
Nor is it yet d. and dismay *T.T.* 410

DESPOT.
A d. big with power obtained by wealth *Ex.* 370
Should be a d. absolute, and boast *T.* v 311

DESPOTISM.
As well be yoked by D.'s hand *T.T.* 258

DESSERTS.
What, give up our d., our coffee, and tea! *P.A.* 8

DESTINED.
And d. all the treasure there *A Fable* 26
Not d. to my tooth *B.R.* 18
When such a d. wretch as I *Cast.* 3
Intent upon her d. course *Comp.* ii 6
At length his d. moment to be born? *F.A.* 26
Through the ripe harvest lies their d. road *Her.* 54
Not blind by choice, but d. not to see *T.* 530
Full on the d. ear. Wide flies the chaff *T.* i 359
Heaven-born, and d. to the skies again *T.* iii 50
Admirers, and be d. to divide *T.* iii 726
Is to conduct it to the d. inn *T.* iv 10
Its d. goal of difficult access *T.* vi 277
Its d. office, yet with gentle stroke *T.* vi 1003

DESTINES.
And d. their bright genius to be shown *Tir.* 336

DESTINY.
His d. repelled *Cast.* 40
For which, alas! my d. severe *N.A.* 27
And D., that sometimes bears *P.T.* 47
And all the plan their d. design'd *Tir.* 86

DESTITUTE.
No, wrangler,—d. of shame and sense *P.E.* 235
For their support, so d. But they *T.* iv 455
And d. of means to raise themselves *T.* v 248

DESTROY.
That thankless waste and wild abuse d. *Ex.* 679
Whom now despairing agonies d. *H.* 172
Whose fruit, though fair, tempts only to d. *P.E.* 238
Thus man devotes his brother and d. *T.* ii 20
Let slip with such a warrant to d. *T.* ii 54
Adored through fear, strong only to d. *T.* v 445 [322
When the rude rabble's watchword was—"D.!" *T.T.*
D. them—skies uncertain, now the heat *Y.O.* 74

DESTROYED.
For them, the states to which they went d. *Ex.* 176
Destruction, with a zeal to be d. *T.* vi 526 [303
Though mangled, hacked, and hewed, not yet d. *Tir.*

DESTROYER.
For Time, the d. declared *Gr.* 45
To prove you their d., as ye are *Her.* 82

DESTRUCTION.
Though at their own d. She that asks *T.* ii 642
D., with a zeal to be destroyed *T.* vi 523

DESTRUCTIVE.
Well does the work of his d. scythe *T.* iv 222

DESULTORY.
Of d. man, studious of change *T.* i 507

DETACH. [74
D. the soul from earth, and speed her to the skies *P.E.*

DETACHED.
Must be d., and where it strews the floor *T.* iii 615

DETAIN.
D. their adolescent charge too long *Tir.* 219

DETAINED.
Struggling, d. in many a petty nook *N.A.* 40
" As one who long d. on foreign shores *T.* v 832

DETECT.
Undazzled, and d. and counts his spots? *T.* i 714
But soon, alas! d. the rash mistake *V.* 55

DETECTED.
What shifts he used, d. in a scrape *Tir.* 328

DETERMINED.
D., and possessing it at last *T.* iv 720

DETEST.
For scorning what they taught him to d. *Ch.* 56
To thrust the charge of deeds that I d. *Ex.* 430
Hypocrisy, d. her as we may *T.* iii 100

DETESTED.
And clamours of the field? D. sport *T.* iii 326

DETHRONED.
And seems d. and vanquished. Peace ensues *T.* v 620

DEVASTATION.
Havoc and d. in the van *Her.* 21

DEVIATIONS.
The needle's d. too *F.* 113

DEVICES.
With shallow shifts and old d., worn *T.* v 632

DEVIL.
A mere disguise, in which a d. lurks *Con.* 79
A d.'s purpose with an angel's face *T.T.* 136

DEVILISH.
Than cruelty, most d. of them all *T.* vi 594

DEVIOUS.
Are altogether gone a d. course *Ex.* 463
Me howling blasts drive d., tempest-tossed *M.P.* 102
Or lead him d. from the path of truth *P.E.* 60
His d. course uncertain, seeking home *T.* iii 3
Or drive it d. with a dexterous pat *Tir.* 309

DEVISE.
That earth has seen, or fancy can d. *Ch.* 255
And tricks and turns that fancy may d. *Ex.* 137
" The sanguinary schemes that some d. *H.* 382
And place, instead of quirks themselves d. *H.* 629
More hideous foes than fancy can d. *R.* 68
What is all righteousness that men d. *T.* 75

D., while he guards his tender trust *T.* iii 561
That babblers, called philosophers, *d. Tir.* 158

DEVISED.

D. by self to answer selfish ends *T.* 110
D. the Weatherhouse, that useful toy ! *T.* 211
Heard the sweet moan with pity, and *d. T.* i 74

DEVOTE.

If arms engage him, he *d.* to sport *H.* 207
That he *d.* not with a zeal like theirs *R.* 222
Dooms and *d.* him as his lawful prey *T.* ii 15
Thus man *d.* his brother, and destroys *T.* ii 20
For second childhood; and *d.* old age *T.* ii 637
And whether I *d.* thy gentle hours *T.* iv 261

DEVOTED.

Not that his hours *d.* all to care *H.* 57
Of card *d.* Time, and night by night *T.* iv 229
Poor England! thou art a *d.* deer *T.T.* 362

DEVOTEES.

Ye *d.* to your adored employ *P.E.* 75

DEVOTION.

Supplied such relics as *d.* holds *T.* vi 689

DEVOUR.

Of nations, sworn to spoil thee and *d. Ex.* 703
And worry and *d.* each other *N.G.* 30
Needless, and first torments ere he *d. T.* vi 396

DEVOURING.

Thunder, and earthquake, and *d.* flame *T.* 548

DEVOUT.

Who though *d.*, yet bigotry had none *Con.* 68
The priestly brotherhood, *d.*, sincere *Ex.* 438
With academic dignity *d. H.* 106
Adores a creature, and *d.* in vain *R.* 227
Skilful alike to seem *d.* and just *R.* 689

DEW.

Thy lips have shed instruction as the *d. Ch.* 238
So once in Gideon's fleece the *d.* were found *E.* ii 49
Whose foot ne'er tainted morning *d. Ep.* ii 3
The *d.* condensed into angelic food *Ex.* 182
My drink the morning *d. G.* 3
Why falls the Gospel like a gracious *d.? T.* 180
That dries his feathers, saturate with *d. T.* i 494
Has flowed from lips wet with Castalian *d. T.* iii 251
Nectareous essences, Olympian *d. T.* iv 83
To sweep away the *d. T.B.* 18
Till Autumn's fiercer heats and plenteous *d. Tir.* 47
Let laurels drenched in pure Parnassian *d. T.T.* 13

DEWDROP.

D. may deck the turf that hides the bones *St.* ii 31
With slipshod heels, and *d.* at his nose *T.* 144

DEWY.

That murmurs through the *d.* mead *O.* ii 16
Hark! how it floats upon the *d.* air! *P.E.* 63
Its cooling vapour o'er the *d.* meads *R.* 422
Prolific, and the lime at *d.* eve *T.* i 316
The cheering fragrance of her *d.* vales *T.* i 429
And fast condensed upon the *d.* sash *T.* iii 496
The dancing Naiads through the *d.* meads *T.T.* 693

DEXTEROUS.

And with a *d.* jerk soon twists him down *T.* iv 62
Or drive it devious with a *d.* pat *Tir.* 309

DIADEM.

Thy *d.* displaced, thy sceptre gone *Ex.* 258

The crescent moon, the *d.* of night *R.* 82
God set the *d.* upon his head *T.* vi 351
The *d.*, with mighty projects lined *T.T.* 59

DIAL.

Like figures drawn upon a *d.* plate *Con.* 380

DIALOGUE.

And snappish *d.*, that flippant wits *T.* iv 198

DIAMOND.

As *d.*, stripped of their opaque disguise *Ch.* 397
As with the *d.* on his lily hand *T.* ii 424
With spots quadrangular of *d.* form *T.* iv 217

DIAN.

"By *D.'s* beams," Sir Marmadan exclaimed *A.T.* 187

DIANAS. [517

Nymphs were *D.* then, and swains had hearts *T.* iv

DIARY.

An extract of his *d.*,—no more *Con.* 275

DIBBLING.

With pointed hoof *d.* the glebe prepared *Y.O.* 26

DICE. [171

Cards with what rapture, and the polished *d. P.E.*
Owes all its weight, like loaded *d.* to lead *Con.* 302

DICEBOX.

Becomes a *d.*, and a billiard mace *T.* iv 221

DICK.

And *D.* felt some desires *F.B.* 15
And *D.*, although his way was clear *F.B.* 22
My dear *D.* Redcap, what say you? *P.T.* 37
D. heard, and tweedling, ogling, bridling *P.T.* 38
There waiter *D.*, with bacchanalian lays *Tir.* 214

DICTATE.

How slow to learn the *d.* of his love *E.* ii 20
Of all that Wisdom *d.* this the drift *T.* 513 [413
Is Nature's *d.* Strange! there should be found *T.* i
That his own humour *d.*, from the clutch *T.* v 317
For since (so fashion *d.*) all, who claim *Tir.* 690

DIE.

Clean, candid, and witty—Thelypthora *d. A.T.* iv 2
Or courage *d.* away *Cast.* 16
Yet bitter felt it still to *d. Cast.* 35
Grown dim in trifling studies, blind he *d. Ch.* 358
Laugh at their only remedy, and *d. Ch.* 419
But if she touch a character, it *d. Ch.* 456
But being tied, it *d.* upon the lip *Con.* 355
Above all else, and wondered He should *d. Con.* 520
The stench remains, the lustre *d.* away *Con.* 678
That sick, she trembles, knowing she must *d. Con.* 773
His manna from the ground, or starve and *d. F.A.* 38
D. of disdain, or whistle off the sound *H.* 348 [*H.* 260
They *d.*—Death lends them, pleased, and as in sport
D. when he might, he must be damned at last *H.* 569
Shoots back the bolt, and all his courage *d. H.* 721
And glory for the virtuous when they *d. J.T.* 14
I saw him both sicken and *d. M.D.* 37
Leaps every fence but one, there falls and *d. P.E.* 93
But know, the law that bids the drunkard *d. P.E.* 199
He *d.* disputing, and the contest ends *P.E.* 553
D. then, if power Almighty save you not *P.E.* 589
And having lived a trifler, *d.* a man *R.* 14
Tickle and entertain us, or we *d. R.* 708
Where all good qualities grow sick and *d. R.* 738

D self-accused of life run all to waste? *St.* ii 28 [ii 6
On which the press might stamp him next to d. *St.*
Though 'tis his privilege to d. *St.* v 3
With life that cannot d. *St.* vi 32
Make us learn that we must d. *St.* vi 36
Pants for it, aims at it, enters it, and d. *T.* 6
Far distant, such as he would d. to find *T.* i 453
They love it, and yet loathe it; fear to d. *T.* i 435
And at his feet the baffled billows d. *T.* i 525
The rivers d. into offensive pools *T.* ii 96
Life's necessary means, but he must d. *T.* ii 141
Or heedless folly, by which thousands d. *T.* iii 219
It is a flame that d. not even there *T.* iv 743
As instinct prompts; self-buried ere they d. *T.* v 88
A splendid opportunity to d.? *T.* v 320
D. too : the deep foundations that we lay *T.* v 532
And, ere one flowery season fades and d. *T.* vi 196
To the far distant goal, arrives and d. *T.* vi 430
The chamber, or refectory, may d. *T.* vi 572
And useless while he lives, and when he d. *Tir.* 71
Would d. at last in comfort, peace, and joy *Tir.* 150
The meteor of the gospel d. away *Tir.* 190
Poor Poll is like to d.! *Tran.* iv 30   [703
Brings colours dipped in Heaven that never d. *T.T.*
They trust in armies, and their courage d. *T.T.* 468
As one at point to d. *Y.D.* 10

DIED.

Rushed to battle, fought, and d. *B:* 39   [*Con.* 323
They thought they must have d., they were so bad
D. by the sentence of a shaven priest *Ch.* 55
Soon after He that was our surety d. *Con.* 506 [625
Their streaming hearts poured freely when they d. *Ex.*
Had Paul of Tarsus lived and d. a Jew *H.* 257
Bled, groaned, and agonized and d. in vain *P.E.* 624
Lived long, wrote much, laughed heartily and d.*T.* 307
With one who left her, went to sea, and d. *T.* i 533
O'erlooked and unemployed, fell sick, and d. *T.* ii 733
Saved him, or the unrelenting seer had d. *T.* vi 471
The death he had deserved, and d. alone *T.* vi 556
The cruel death he d. *T.B.* 66   [*T.* v 282
Storks among frogs, that have but croaked and d
Tells of a few stout hearts that fought and d. *T.T.* 23
And the last left the scene when Chatham d. *T.T.* 339
Though the chief actor d. upon the stage *T.T.* 341
That he who d. below, and reigns above *T.T.* 738

DIET.

His d. was of wheaten bread *Ep.* ii 13
In lighter d. at a later hour *Ex.* 403
Of loathsome d., penury, and cold *T.* i 591
He gulps the windy d.; and ere long *T.* v 269
To improve this d., at no great expense *Tir.* 623
Prevented much by d. neat and plain *Tir.* 767
Change is the d. on which all subsist *Y.O.* 72

DIFFER.

But friends that chance to d. *F.* 135
Skins may d., but affection *N.C.* 15
Your sentence and mine d. What's a name? *T.* 107

DIFFERENCE.

A d. strikes at length the musing heart *Comp.* i 8
But here alas! the fatal d. lies *H.* 282
The d., though essential, fails to strike *P.E.* 204
Mark now the d., ye that boast your love *T.* v 346
The d. of a Guido from a daub *T.* vi 285

DIFFERENT.

Seem to reflection of a d. race *Ex.* 619
Thus things terrestial wear a d. hue *H.* 69
Through mere good fortune, took a d. course *N.A.* 123
With colours mixed for a far d. use *T.* iv 240
To join a traveller, of far d. note *T.* vi 489

New situations give a d. cast *Tir.* 440
D. in size, but in effect the same *Tir.* 516

DIFFERING.

D. in language, manners, or in face, *Ch.* 21
And d. judgments serve but to declare *H.* 423
Adorns, though d. in its kind *U.* 15

DIFFICULT.

So dimly writ, or d. to spell *Ex.* 311
So d. to spell *Q.V.* 50
A life of ease a d. pursuit *R.* 634
Though apt, yet coy, and d. to win *T.* ii 230
Its destined goal of d. access *T.* vi 277
Is d., their punishment obscene *Tir.* 221
Armed for a work too d. for thee *Tir.* 677

DIFFICULTY.

Gives d. all the grace of ease *Ch.* 110
No flaw deforms, no d. thwarts *T.* vi 229
But d. soon abate *Tran.* iv. 40

DIFFIDENT.

Affable, humble, d., and mild *P.E.* 537

DIFFUSE.

But groves, hills, and valleys d. *C.* 39
Thy fame d., praised not for utterance meet *S.* i 13

DIFFUSED.

That good d. may more abundant grow *Con.* 443
'Tis more—'tis God d. through every part *H.* 734
D., make Earth the vestibule of Hell *P.E.* 465
D., attain the surface; when, behold! *T.* iii 493
Some clothe the soil that feeds them, far d. *T.* iii 662
The Lord of all, himself through all d. *T.* vi 221

DIFFUSING.

D. odours; nor unnoted pass *T.* i 317
And, common sense d. real day *Tir.* 189

DIG.

If I survive thee, I will d. thy grave *T.* iii 349
Can d., beg, rot, and perish, well content *T.* iii 805

DIGEST.

Mysteries are food for angels; they d. *F.A.* 35
Or turn to nourishment, d. well *T.* iii 396
But wholesome, well d.; grateful some *T.* vi 1014

DIGNIFIED.

On man's most d. and happiest state *Ch.* 2
Now tell me, d. and sapient sir *T.* ii 531
So d., that she was hardly less *T.* iv 537
Had not its author d. the plan *Tir.* 51

DIGNITY.

Named with emphatic d., "The Tower" *Ch.* 550
In form a man, in d. a God *Ex.* 86
With academic d. devout *H.* 106
With all Elijah's d. of tone *H.* 624
Attain not to the d. of thought *R.* 640
"I am all splendour, d., and grace!" *T.* 65
By wealth or d., who dwells secure *T.* i 593
Paternal sweetness, d., and love *T.* ii 708
Of honour, d., and fair renown! *T.* iii 59
But d.'s, resentful of the wrong *T.* iii 79
To monarchs d.; to judges sense *V.* iv 796
Fortune and d.; the loss of all *T.* v 602
Strength joined with beauty, d. with grace *Tir.* 2
See wealth abused, and d. misplaced *Tir.* 815
Lifted at length by d. of thought *T.T.* 676
Your senatorial d. of face *V.* 11

DIGRESS.

Beyond the example of our sires d. *Con.* 792

DIGRESSION.
D. is so much in modern use *Con.* 855

DILATED.
His whispered theme, d. and at large *Con.* 273

DILATES.
And what d. the powers must needs refine *Ch.* 332

DILIGENCE.
Subordinate, and d. was choice *T.* ii 716

DILIGENT.
Where, d. to catch the first faint gleam *T.* v 59

DIM.
And Hymen, trimming his d. torch anew *A.T.* 201
Grown d. in trifler studies, blind he dies *Ch.* 358
Their views, indeed, were indistinct and d. *Con.* 539
Review thy d. original and prime *Ex.* 467 [265
With mournful scutcheons, and d. lamps between *H.*
Soon watery grew her eyes and d. *Q.V.* 53
And sees, by no fallacious light or d. *R.* 115
Seen in the d. horizon, turns thee pale *T.* i 667
And Nature with a d. and sickly eye *T.* ii 64
Man made for kings! those optics are but d. *T.T.* 55

DIMENSIONS.
Within the small d. of a point *R.* 58

DIMINISHED.
The sturdy swain d. to a boy! *T.* i 162

DIMINUTIVE.
D., well filled with well-prepared *T.* iii 513

DIMLY.
So d. writ, or difficult to spell *Ex.* 311
How d. seen, how faintly understood! *R.* 88

DIMNESS.
D. and anguish, all thy beams obscured *Ex.* 393

DIM-SIGHTED.
For our d. observation *E.* i 86

DIN.
For thou wast born amid the d. of arms *Ex.* 472
For all the savage d. of the swift pack *T.* iii 325

DINE.
If wife should d. at Edmonton *J.G.* 195
And I should d. at Ware" *J.G.* 196
"I am in haste to d. *J.G.* 198
A man o' the town d. late, but soon enough *T.* ii 622

DINGLEDERRY.
All Kilwick and all D. rang *N.A.* 36

DINNER.
"The d. waits, and we are tired" *J.G.* 147
The d. served, Charles takes his usual stand *T.* 213
The d. comes, and down they sit *Y.D.* 37

DINT.
By d. of change to give his tasteless task *T.* v 429
And d. of genius, to an affluent lot *T.T.* 677

DIP.
Suppose the beam should d. on the wrong side *H.* 374
No crested warrior d. his plume in blood *Her.* 86
He d. his bowl into the weedy ditch *T.* i 241
We pass a gulf in which the willows d. *T.* i 268

DIPPED.
And e'en the d. and sprinkled live in peace *Ch.* 609
By an oath d. in sacramental blood? *Ex.* 38

D. in the fountain of eternal love *T.* vi 863
Brings colours d. in Heaven, that never die *T.T.* 703

DIRE.
The d. effect of mercy without price *H.* 496
D. disappointment that admits no cure *T.* iii 557
D. is the frequent curse, and its twin sound *T.* iv 487
Anticipate perforce some d. event *T.* v 524
D. foe alike of bird and mouse *T.B.* 20
(A d. effect, by one of Nature's laws *T.T.* 442

DIRECT.
D. us in our distant road *E.* i 37
D. thee to that eminence they reached *Ex.* 657
Paul should himself d. me. I would trace *T.* ii 397
So did not Paul. D. me to a quip *T.* ii 472
Nor does he govern only, or d. *T.* iii 403
Skill to d., and strength to strike the blow *T.T.* 357

DIRECTED.
They breathed in faith their well d. prayers *Ex.* 239
Yet, by his ear d., guessed *R.C.* 83
They take perhaps a well d. aim *T.T.* 206

DIRECTING.
Pursue the track of his d. wand *T.* iii 777

DIRECTION.
Despise the plain d., and are lost *T.* 33
In all d., he begins again—*T.* v 431
And just d. sacred, to a thing *T.* vi 713

DIRECTLY.
D. to the First and Only Fair *T.* v 675

DIREST.
And gives his d. foe a friend's embrace *T.* ii 270

DIRT.
"But let me scrape the d. away *J.G.* 189

DIRTY.
Fish up his d. and dependent bread *T.* iii 808

DISABUSED.
At once the dreaming mind is d. *Tir.* 90

DISAGREE.
On Scripture ground are sure to d. *H.* 599
If flowers can d.? *L.R.* 4

DISAPPEAR.
Vines, olives, herbage, forests d. *Her.* 23
As duly as the swallows d. *T.* iii 814
Which d. by day *Tran.* i 4

DISAPPOINT.
That may disgrace his art, or d. *T.* iii 422
And d. the roots; the slender roots *T.* iii 611
Whose frown can d. the proudest strain *T.* vi 1023

DISAPPOINTED.
And d. still, was still deceived *M.P.* 39
Sick of a thousand d. aims) *R.* 366
And still are d. Rings the world *T.* iii 129
The d. foe, deliverance found *T.* iv 186

DISAPPOINTMENT.
But when unpacked your d. groans *Con.* 309
With d. lowering in his eyes *H.* 2
Man's d. must of course ensue *H.* 132
Dire d. that admits no cure *T.* iii 557
And d. all the fruit *P.B.* 18
A d. waits him even there *Tir.* 566
Hook d. on the public wheels *T.T.* 146

DISARMS.
His grief the world of all her power d. *H.* 704
Yet let a poet (Poetry d. *R.* 253

DISASTROUS.
Fulfilled their tardy and *d.* course *T.* vi 735

DISBANDED.
D. legions freely might depart *Ch.* 618

DISCARD.
And studious of mutation still, *d. T.* ii 610

DISCARDED.
And gods and goddesses *d.* long *Con.* 819

DISCERN.
The danger they *d.* not, they deny *Ch.* 418
Nor carp at every flaw you may *d. Con.* 92
D. a rival in a friend *F.* 83
Then might all people well *d. J.G.* 105
D. the fraud beneath the specious lure *P.E.* 17
Where children would with ease *d.* the way *P.E.* 434
But if the wanderer his mistake *d. P.E.* 610
Their real interest to *d. N.G.* 28
If, ere we yet *d.* life's evening star *R.* 46
We may *d.* the thresher at his task *T.* i 356
That all *d.* a beatuy in his works *T.* iv 739
D. in all things what, with stupid gaze *T.* v 808
And soothed into a dream that he *d. T.* vi 284

DISCERNED.
The floating wreath again *d. D.W.* 31
Have not, it seems, *d.* it *F.* 210
Thence with what pleasure have we just *d. T.* i 159

DISCERNING.
So famed for his talent in nicely *d. A.C.* 8
True Modesty is a *d.* grace *Con.* 373
As once absurd in all *d.* eyes *Con.* 806
A Bee of most *d.* taste *P.B.* 3
But chosen with a nice *d.* taste *R.* 726
Such rhapsodies our shrewd *d.* youth *Tir.* 191

DISCERNMENT.
The World grown old her deep *d.* shows *Con.* 741
Grant me *d.*, and I grant it you *P.E.* 535
Immortal Hale! for deep *d.* praised *T.* iii 258
And read with such *d.*, in the port *T.* vi 617
D., Eloquence, and Grace *Th.* 9

DISCHARGE.
Is to *d.* the duties of his sphere *H.* 400
D. but these kind offices, (and who *T.* iii 618

DISCHARGED.
What wonder, if *d.* into the world *T.* ii 806

DISCIPLINE.
And without *d.* the favourite child *P.E.* 361
That she is slack in *d.*; more prompt *T.* i 730
That fear no *d.* of human hands *T.* ii 325
Of holy *d.*, to glorious war *T.* ii 348
There dwelt a sage called *D.* His head *T.* ii 702
But *D.*, a faithful servant long *T.* ii 725
Their good old friend, and *D.* at length *T.* ii 732
And thou hast need of *d.* and art *T.* v 467
No meaner hand may *d.* the shoots *T.* iii 413
Schools, unless *d.* were doubly strong *Tir.* 218
If you can crown a *d.*, that draws *Tir.* 493
The force of *d.* when backed by love *Tir.* 681
Let *D.* employ her wholesome arts *T.T.* 310
Where *D.* helps opening buds of sense *T.T.* 508

DISCIPLINED.
Well born, well *d.*, who, placed apart *R.* 727
In verse well *d.*, complete, compact *T.T.* 647

DISCLAIM.
Woe to the man whose wit *d.* its use *R.* 211
For what poor toys they can *d. St.* vi 15
Else his own glorious rights He would *d. T.* 555

DISCLAIMING.
And Truth *d.* both; and thus they spend *T.* iii 163
Their nature; and, *d.* all regard *T.* iv 679

DISCLOSE.
O Nature! whose Elysian scenes *d. R.* 199
That trust them, and in the end *d.* a face *T.* ii 693
Her veil opaque, *d.* with a smile *T.* v 892.

DISCLOSED.
Of hearts in union mutually *d. Con.* 680.
To exhibit, in full bloom *d. F.* 44

DISCLOSING.
D. Paradise where'er He treads? *T.* ii 87

DISCOMFITED.
And sore *d.*, from slough to slough *T.* iii 5

DISCOMPOSE.
Shall drench again or *d. Mrs. M—* 17

DISCONCERT.
To *d.* what Policy has planned *Ex.* 299

DISCONTENT.
Serves merely as a soil for *d. H.* 97
Must cause him shame or *d. Mor.* 46
Murmuring and ungrateful *D.—R.* 759
In repining *d. Tran.* iii 30
Though *D.* alone can find out where *T.T.* 197
And fill with *d.* a British isle *T.T.* 253

DISCONTENTED.
With aching heart, and *d.* looks *R.* 471

DISCORD.
Yield only *d.* in his Maker's ear *T.* 386
Fell *D.*, arbitress of such debate *T.* iv 482

DISCORDANT.
D. atoms meet, ferment, and fight *Ex.* 297
D. motives in one centre meet *R.* 173
Of homogeneal and *d.* springs *T.* ii 190
No passion touches a *d.* string *T.* vi 787

DISCOURSE.
Whatever subject occupy *d. Con.* 57
D. may want an animated—No *Con.* 101
Of wise reflection and well timed *d. Con.* 388
D., as if released and safe at home *Con.* 571
To hold *d.*, at least in fable *P.T.* 4
D. ensues, not trivial, yet not dull *T.* iv 174
(As often as libidinous *d. T.* v 660
So on they fared. *D.* on other themes *T.* vi 539
No jester, and yet lively in *d. Tir.* 668
Foul with excess, and with *d.* obscene *Tir.* 736.
Myself the oracle, and will *d. Y.O.* 142

DISCOVER.
D. huge cathedrals built with stone *P.E.* 381
That fools *d.* it, and stray no more *T.* ii 530
Of Observation, and *d.*, else *T.* iii 231
D. him that rules them; such a veil *T.* iii 233
D. countries, with a kindred heart *T.* iv 116

DISCOVERER.
D. of they know not what, confined *P.E.* 476

DISCOVERING.
D. much the temper of her sire *T.* iii 434

DISCOVERY.
Enriched with the *d.* ye have made *R.* 666
The task of new *d.* falls on me *T.* 218

Thou fool! Will thy d. of the cause T. ii 196
And pregnant with d. new and rare T. iii 138
The eyesight of D.; and begets T. v 452
Then spread the rich d., and invite T.T. 752

DISCREDITS.
The noblest function, and d. much T. ii 554

DISCREET.
And she may now be as d. and wise Con. 805
Yet was thy liberality d. J.T. 35
But more d. than he a Cambrian ewe N.A. 106
To his young hopes, requires d. delay T. iii 504

DISCREETLY.
Reply d.—" To be sure—no doubt!" Con. 118
D. limited to two at most Tir. 770

DISCRETION.
And Dullness of D.—F. 6

DISCRIMINATE.
And could d. and argue well T. v 289

DISCRIMINATED.
D. each from each, by strokes T. iv 735

DISCRIMINATING.
That souls have no d. hue Ch. 202

DISCUSS.
And without this, whatever he d. Ch. 351

DISCUSSION.
Of rational d., that a man T. v 306

DISDAIN.
For whose lean country much d. A Tale 73
D. the Bank, and throws the golden sands Ch. 248
Of fancied scorn and undeserved d. Con. 348
As, having it, he deems the world's d. Con. 762
Viewed a deliverer with d. and hate Ex. 217
It shakes the sides of splenetic D. Ex. 548
Die of d., or whistle off the sound H. 318
And swelling with d. L.R. 10
Wins in return an answer of d. R. 228   [34
"Heaven on such terms!" they cry with proud d. T.
Heaven turns from with abhorrence and d. T. 72
D. not, nor the palate, undepraved T. i 124
The impression of the blast with proud d. T. i 380
Thy follies too; and with just d. T. ii 222
That feels for injured love! but I d. T. iii 66
Trivial and worthy of d., achieves T. v 699
From repartee, with jokes that he d. Tir. 728
That wants no driving and d. the lead T.T. 134
Perhaps some courser who d. the road T.T. 668

DISDAINED.
By mummeries He that dwelt in it d. Ex. 146
D. thy counsels, only in distress Ex. 530
His black interpreter the charge d. T.T. 99
And so d. the rules he understood T.T. 687

DISDAINFUL.
Though but a dream) art grown d. too V. 44

DISEASE.
And, from a knowledge of her own d. Ch. 410
And give us, in recitals of d. Con. 313
But that d., when soberly defined Con. 667
Punctually paid for lengthening out d. H. 204
The source of the d. that Nature feels T. ii 194
Vain tampering has but fostered his d. T. v 668
But all is harmony and love. D.—T. vi 788
May some d., not tardy to perform T. vi 1002
D. or comes not, or finds easy cure Tir. 766

DISEASED.
Who much d., yet nothing feel St. vi 17

DISENCUMBERED.
The d. Atlas of the state R. 394

DISENGAGE.
No time shall d. The Doves 10

DISENGAGED.
Long held, and scarcely d. at last T. iii 16

DISENTANGLE.
They d. from the puzzled skein T. iii 145

DISESTEEMED.
So glorious now, though once so d. Ch. 580
So coveted, else base and d. T. iii 448

DISFIGURES.
D. Earth, and, plotting in the dark T. i 275

DISGRACE.
So withered stumps d. the sylvan scene Con. 51
Who to please others will themselves d. Con. 227
Of needless shame, and self-imposed d. Con. 350
There sits and prompts him with his own d. Con. 463
The very children watch for thy d. Ex. 282
And do his errand of d. and shame Ex. 334   [390
Hast thou, when Heaven has clothed thee with d. Ex.
Whose horrid perpetration stamps d. Ex. 416
And that, judicially withdrawn, d. Ex. 692
Himself sole author of his own d. ? H. 317
Exposes, and holds up to broad d. T. ii 553
That may d. his art, or disappoint T. iii 422
Or fertile only in its own d. T. vi 767
High-minded, foaming out their own d. T. vi 898
Pressed on his part by means that would d. Tir. 406
Such vicious habits as d. his name Tir. 531
Which filthily bewray and sore d. Tir. 593
From total night and absolute d. T.T. 665

DISGRACED.
And, though d. and slighted, to redeem Ch. 13
D. as thou hast been, poor as thou art T. v 475
Our early notices of truth, d. Tir. 199
Great titles, offices, and trusts d. Tir. 816
Those ensigns of dominion, how d.! T.T. 40

DISGRACEFUL.
Vainly industrious, a d. prize T. iii 385.

DISGRACEFULLY.
D. on every trifler's tongue Ex. 663

DISGUISE.
When all d. shall be rent away Ch. 558
As diamonds, stripped of their opaque d. Ch. 397
A mere d., in which a devil lurks Con. 79
Will speak without d., and must impart Con. 711
Which art can only darken and d. H. 769
Jack knew his friend, but hoped in that d. R. 587
For monstrous novelty and strange d. T. ii 612
While innocence without d. The Doves 13

DISGUISED.
Howe'er d. the inflammatory tale P.E. 327
But rather death d. St. vi 12

DISGUST.
With cold d., or philosophic pride Ex. 691
Some swayed by fashion, some by deep d. R. 607
Object of my implacable d. T. ii 418
My partners in retreat. D. concealed T. iii 38
Of popular d., yet boldly still T. iii 706
That it belongs to freemen, would d. T. v 482

DISGUSTED.
Was hurt, d., mortified P. 19

DISH.
"Yon shapeless nothing in a *d. P.* 25
Book, beads, and maple *d.*, his meagre stock *T.* 80
Every *d.*, and spoil the best *Tran.* iii 14

DISHEARTENING.
Whose prospect shows thee a *d.* waste *H.* 32
Mov'd many a sigh at its *d.* length *T.* vi 22

DISHEVELLED.
Like the fair flower *d.* in the wind *T.* iii 262

DISHONOUR.
Who dare *d.*, or defile, the tongue *Con.* 26
When sin has shed *d.* on thy brow *Ex.* 394
D. with unhallowed play *St.* vi 27
Reflect *d.* on the land I love *T.* ii 224
Its own *d.* by a worse relapse *T.* v 626
"*D.* God, and makes a slave of man *T.* v 643
D., and be wronged with redress *T.* vi 822

DISHONOURED.
Send your *d.* gown to Monmouth Street *P.E.* 121
Or be *d.*, in the exterior form *T.* ii 560
Is soon *d.* and defiled in most *T.* vi 590
In his *d.* works himself endure *T.* vi 821

DISINCLINED.
To social scenes by nature *d. R.* 606

DISINGENUOUS.
Than Vice's mean and *d.* race *P.E.* 297

DISINTERESTED.
D. good, is not our trade *T.* i 674
The most *d.* and virtuous minds *Tir.* 438

DISJOINING.
D. from the rest, has unobserved *Y.O.* 107

DISK.
With which she gazes at yon burning *d. T.* i 713
The sun's meridian *d.*, and at the back *T.* iii 473
More ardent as the *d.* emerges more *T.* v 4

DISMANTLED.
Shall be *d.* of its fleecy load *T.* vi 179

DISMAY.
The positive pronounce without *d. Con.* 146
That Courage is his creature; and *D. Ex.* 354
Nor is it yet despondence and *d. T.T.* 410

DISMAYED.
Sir Airy, not a whit *d.* or scared *A.T.* 171

DISMISS.
"*D.* poor Harry!" he replies *M.F.* 19
Man may *d.* compassion from his heart *T* vi 442
D. me weary to a safe retreat *T.* vi 1004
D. their cares when they *d.* their flock *Tir.* 624

DISMISSED.
Unless his right to rule it be *d.? Ch.* 193
Arts once esteemed may be with shame *d. Con.* 811
Complied with, and were graciously *d. Ex.* 541
The man that mentioned him, at once *d. H.* 560
D. with grave, not haughty looks *Mrs. M—* 38
He teaches those to read, whom schools *d. T.* ii 358
From courts *d.*, found shelter in the groves *T.* iv 519

DISMISSING.
With whom, *d.* forms, he may unbend *R.* 414
Nor even then, *d.* as performed *T.* iii 655

DISMISSION.
Bears witness, long ere his *d.* come *Tir.* 561

DISOBEDIENCE.
My *d.* now *B.R.* 22

DISOBEY.
Would *d*, though sure to be shut out *H.* 315

DISORDER.
In wild *d.*, and unfit for use *T.* ii 805

DISOWN.
That Scripture, Justice, and Good Sense *d. Ex.* 503

DISPASSIONATE.
Candid and learned, *d.* and free *P.E.* 453

DISPATCH.
With reasonable forecast and *d. T* ii 623
Of pleasure and variety, *d. T.* iii 813

DISPELLED.
D. thy gloom, and broke away thy dreams *Ex.* 501
Consoled him and *d.* his fears *R.C.* 90

DISPENSE.
Though Nature weigh our talents, and *d. Con.* 1
For Nature, nice, as liberal to *d. P.E.* 213
Swallow the two grand nostrums they *d. P.E.* 594
"The teacher's office, and *d.* at large *T.* v 645

DISPENSED.
That only shadows are *d.* below *H.* 67

DISPENSERS.
Ye sage *d.* of poetic fame *T.* iii 457

DISPENSING.
O bright occasions of *d.* good *T.T.* 63

DISPERSE.
When the sun's shafts *d.* the gloom of night *Ex.* 479
May suddenly your joys *d. F.* 65
Which admonition can alone *d. Tir.* 600

DISPERSED.
But now, to gather up what seems *d. Con.* 867
Their glory faded, and their race *d. Ex.* 241
The family *d.*, and fixing thought *T.* iv 137
Not less *d.* by daylight and its cares *T.* iv 138
D. the shackles of usurped control *T.* v. 516
Here cities won, and fleets *d.* 1789, 13

DISPERSING.
D. all his dream *D.W.* 26

DISPLACE.
Retrench a sword blade, or *d.* a patch *T.* ii 318

DISPLACED.
Thy diadem *d.* thy sceptre gone *Ex.* 258
My shrubs *d.* from that retreat *F.B.* 2

DISPLAY.
And bid a dawning sky *d. E.* i 77
D. with busy and laborious hand *Ex.* 163
To deem the wit a friend *d. F.* 88
Like quicksilver, the rhetoric they *d. P.E.* 21
Which formed the chief *d. Q.V.* 10
Thy words, more clearly than thy works, *d. R.* 93
That courts *d.* before ambitious eyes *R.* 178
Some beams of rectitude she yet *d. T.* 485
Nor taste alone and well-contrived *d. T.* iii 603
Shall break into its preconceived *d. T.* iii 652
Thus war affording field for the *d. T.* v 238
His other works, the visible *d. T.* v 553
As, hid from ages past, God now *d. Tir.* 628
Thy magnanimity *d. Tran. H.* 32
And when recording History *d. T.T.* 21

DISPLAYED.
It was the time when Ouse d. *D.W.* 13
See mercy's grand apocalypse d.! *H.* 448
Then sweet to muse upon his skill d. *R.* 51
Just in the scene where he d. his own *Tir.* 337
So I, from theme to theme d. 1789, 21

DISPLAYING.
D., on its varied side, the grace *T.* i 172
D. his own beauty, starves his flock! *T.* ii 429

DISPLEASE.
Nor could he dare presumptuously d. *Tir.* 179

DISPLEASED.
His only pleasure is to be d. *Con.* 346

DISPLEASURE.
D. in his breast who smites the earth *T.* ii 69
His hot d. against foolish men *T.* ii 179
To throw his dark d. o'er the scene *T.T.* 445

DISPOSE.
Find place in his dominion, or d. *T.* ii 169
Then to d. his copies with such art *T.* ii 294
Large expectation, he d. neat *T.* iii 423
Replete with vapours, and d. much *T.* v 463
Not only Vice d. and prepares *T.T.* 438

DISPOSED.
In starry forms d. upon the wall *Ch.* 552
Who seeks a friend should come d. *F.* 43
Each yielding harmony, d. aright *R.* 326
He, therefore, who would see his flowers d. *T.* iii 648
And curling tendrils, gracefully d. *T.* iv 154
Lamps gracefully d., and of all hues *T.* v. 149
Are best d. of where with most success *Tir.* 318

DISPOSING.
And God's d. providence confessed *Ex.* 558
But by a master's hand, d. well *T.* iii 589

DISPOSITION.
Man's coltish d. asks the thong *P.E.* 360
When d., like a sail unfurled *Tir.* 450

DISPROVE.
So fancy dreams. D. it, if ye can *Y.O.* 29

DISPUTABLE.
A d. point is no man's ground *Con.* 99

DISPUTANTS.
No learned d. would take the field *Ch.* 620

DISPUTATION.
The sparks of d. *F.* 105

DISPUTE.
The point in d. was, as all the world knows *A.C.* 3
My right there is none to d. *A.S.* 2
She rather waives than will d. her right *Ch* 420
A warm d. once chanced to wage *J.P.* 3
D., though short, are far too long *P.* 45
Safe from the clamours of perverse d. *R.* 145
" Past all d., yon anchorite, say you *T.* 106
And he says much that many may d. *T.* 359
Fierce the d. whate'er the theme; while she *T.* iv 481
Or flushed with fierce d., a senseless brawl *T.* v 472
Whose lying heart d. against a God *T.* v 568
D. have been, and still prevail *Tran.* i 5

DISPUTING.
He dies d., and the contest ends *P.E.* 553

DISREGARD.
Thou wast not heard with drowsy d. *S.* i 5

Or d., or more presumptuous still *T.* ii 177
Or d. our follies, or that set *T.* v 877
I d. as much as once I loved *V.* 8

DISREGARDED.
Drops from the lips a d. thing *T.* ii 565

DISSECTION.
Under d. of the knotted scourge *T.* vi 419

DISSEMBLE.
There they are happiest who d. best *T.* ii 630

DISSEMBLED.
While Bigotry, with well d. fears *H.* 657

DISSEMBLERS.
But, grave d.! could not understand *Ex.* 159
True Christians are, d., drunkards, thieves *H.* 503
Than by the mere d.'s feigned respect *T.* 74

DISSEMINATING.
Contagion, and d. death *T.* iii 617

DISSENSION.
And rush into d. *F.* 102

DISSENT.
Not that all freedom of d. I blame *Con.* 97

DISSIMILAR.
To give d. yet fruitful lands *R.* 787

DISSIMULATION.
If smooth D., skilled to grace *T.T.* 129

DISSIPATE.
Prowess to d. a host 1789, 6

DISSIPATED
A social, not a d. life *T.* iii 376
Hopeless indeed that d. minds *T.* iii 695

DISSIPATION.
Youth lost in d., we deplore *H.* 23
Become more rare as d. spreads *R.* 706
Of fashion d., taverns, stews *T.* ii 770

DISSOLUTE.
His court, the d. and hateful school *T.T.* 626

DISSOLUTION.
A d. of all bonds ensued *T.* ii 743
For d., hurtful to the main *T.* iv 675
Of their best tone their d. owe *Y.O.* 85

DISSOLVE.
That makes seas stable, and d. the rock *Con.* 502
D. in pity, and account the learn'd *T.* iii 183
His being end where death d. the bond *Tir.* 67

DISSOLVED.
For them, the rocks d. into a flood *Ex.* 181

DISSOLVING.
And these d. snows, and this clear stream *T.* vi 230

DISTANCE.
But d. only cannot change the heart *E.* iii 11
Viewed from a d., and with heedless eyes *P.E.* 202
All d., motion, magnitude, and now *T.* i 717
At measured d., that air and sun *T.* iii 424
At a safe d., where the dying sound *T.* iv 92
Yon circling worlds, their d., and their size *Tir.* 633

DISTANCED.
Was quickly d., matched against a peer's *R.* 580

DISTANT.
" To d. wilds in quest of other game *A.T.* 106

Responsive to the *d.* neigh he neighs *Ch.* 177
Directs us in our *d.* road *E.* i 37
Are come from *d.* Loire to choose *E.* i 47
Groan heavily along the *d.* road *Ex.* 58
Thy language at this *d.* moment shows *Ex.* 480
Of *d.* wisdom shoots across his way *H.* 94
And scorns to share it with the *d.* sun *H.* 480
A *d.* virtue we can all confess *H.* 552
Brings to the *d.* ear a sullen sound *Her.* 36
A land that *d.* tyrants hate in vain *Her.* 89
To reach the *d.* coast *H.F.* 22
D. a little mile he spied *Mor.* 17
Sets me more *d.* from a prosperous course *M.P.*105
Speckle the bosom of the *d.* plain *P.E.* 83
And hills that echo to the *d.* herds *R.* 184
That melt and fade into the *d.* sky *R.* 424
Begins a long look out for *d.* land *R.* 433
To *d.* caves the lonely wanderer flies *R.* 769
And plough the *d.* main *R.G.* 32
Of *d.* floods, or on the softer voice *T.* 191
Anxious in vain to find the *d.* floor *T.* i 48
The *d.* plough slow-moving, and beside *T.* i 160
Not *d.* far, a length of Colonnade *T.* i 252
Within the twilight of their *d.* shades *T.* i 304
Conveys a *d.* country into mine *T.* i 424
Far *d.*, such as he would die to find *T.* i 453
To *d.* shores, and she would sit and weep *T.* i 510
If ever it has washed our *d.* shore *T.* i 656
More *d.*, and that prophecy demands *T.* ii 66
Alighting in far *d.* fields, finds out *T.* ii 109
To seek a tranquil death in *d.* shades *T.* iii 111
To *d.* worlds, and trifling in their own *T.* iii 166
But in a *d.* spot, where, more exposed *T.* iii 770
I mean the man who, when the *d.* poor *T.* iv 427
A *d.* age asks where the fabric stood *T.* v 535
From inland regions to the *d.* main *T.* v 790
Shall publish, even to the *d.* eye *T.* vi 148
To the far *d.* goal, arrives and dies *T.* vi 430
Though but in *d.* prospect, and not feel *T.* vi 761
From *d.* mountains catch the flying joy *T.* vi 795
With truths poured down from every *d.* age *Tir.* 14
But seeks the corner of some *d.* seat *Tir.* 571
Find him a better in a *d.* spot *Tir.* 759
Not always tempt the *d.* deep *Trans. H.* 4
He break away, and seek the *d.* plain? *T.T.* 307
In all her gates, and shakes her *d.* shores *T.T.* 453
The poet's heart; he looks to *d.* storms *T.T.* 495
And shot a dayspring into *d.* climes *T.T.* 561
An eye like his to catch the *d.* goal *T.T.* 710

DISTEMPER.

Now the *d.*, spite of draught or pill *Con.* 319
They saw *d.* healed, and life restored *Ex.* 153
Has caught the cold *d.* of the day *V.* 47

DISTEMPERED.

D., or has lost prolific powers *T.* iii 415

DISTENDED.

But when the huntsman with *d.* cheek *N.A.* 43

DISTICH.

To set a *d.* upon six and five *T.T.* 507

DISTILS.

Earth glitters with the drops the night *d. H.* 42

DISTINCT.

Not more *d.* from harmony divine *Con.* 9
Which seldom a *d.* report pervades *Con.* 802
Voice only fails, else how *d.* they say *M.P.* 5
And the clear voice, symphonious, yet *d. T.* iv 162

DISTINCTION.

The pride of arrogant *d.* fall *R.* 650

O'erwhelming all *d.* On the flood *T.* v 97
Whose chief *d.* is their spotless name *Tir.* 355.

DISTINCTLY.

Of ash, or lime, or beech, *d.* shine *T.* i 303
" *D.* scenes invisible to man *T.* v 823

DISTINGUISH.

D. every cultivated kind *H.* 291

DISTINGUISHED.

Nobly *d.* above all the six *P.E.* 161
With less *d.* than ourselves; that thus *T.* iv 338
D. much by reason, and still more *T.* vi 601

DISTORT.

And sullen sadness, that o'ershade, *d. T.* i 457

DISTORTED.

It views the truth with a *d.* eye *Con.* 639
Our own as much *d. F.* 54
D. from its use and just design *T.T.* 751
On thy *d.* root, with hearers none *Y.O.* 140

DISTORTION.

From rickets and *d.*, else our lot *T.* ii 592

DISTRACTING.

To fly for refuge from *d.* thought *T.* v 415

DISTRESS.

" Starts at the call of beauty in *d. A.T.* 120
Alas! his efforts double his *d. Con.* 343
Disdained thy counsels, only in *d. Ex.* 530
The poor, inured to drudgery and *d. H.* 7
'Twas my *d.* that brought thee low *M.* 7
Interpret to the marking eye *d. R.* 287
Yet he too finds his own *d.* in theirs *T.* iv 390

DISTRESSED.

Springs in due time supply for the *d. Ch.* 482
The Christian, in whose soul, though now *d. Con.* 707
So Jealousy looks forth *d. F.* 80
Always from port withheld, always *d. M.P.* 101
A mind quite vacant is a mind *d. R.* 624
D. the weary loins that felt no ease *T.* i 45
Are both alike *d. Y.D.* 20

DISTRESSFUL.

Fix on the wainscoat a *d.* stare *Con.* 116

DISTRIBUTION.

To *d.* boundless of thy own *J.T.* 32
Of *d.*; liberal of their aid *T.* iv 413
He gave them, in its *d.* fair *T.* v 200

DISTRUST.

And no *d.* of his intent in theirs *T.* vi 363

DISTURB.

That pleads for peace till it *d.* the state *Ch.* 310
And with a quiet, which no fumes *d. Con.* 267
When snoring she *d.* As sweetly he *T.* i 90
Contingence might alarm him, and *d. T.* ii 172
Is oft too welcome, and may much *d. T.* ii 492
D. good order, and degrade true worth *T.* iii 674
D. the economy of Nature's realm *T.* vi 579
To guard the Peace that Riot would *d. T.T.* 315

DISTURBANCE.

And sin without *d.* Often urged *T.* v. 659
Wrought this *d.* But the wane is near *T.* vi 709

DISTURBED.

More fixed below, the more *d.* above *T.* i 384
A dream *d.* poor Bully's rest *T.B.* 44

DISTURBING—DIVINELY

DISTURBING.
How great the danger of *d.* her *T.* iii 35

DISUSE.
Grew rusty by *d.*; and massy gates *T.* ii 746

DISUSED.
Now rust *d.*, and shine no more *M.* 11

DITCH.
O'er hedge and *d.*, through gaps and mews *E.* iv 52
He dips his bowl into the weedy *d. T.* i 241
From pools and *d.* of the commonwealth *T.* iii 809

DITTY.
Resounds with his sweet-flowing *d.* no more *P.F.* 12

DIVE.
Compasses earth, *d.* into it, ascends *Ch.* 315
'Twas theirs alone to *d.* into the plan *Ex.* 235
To *d.* into the secret deeps within *R.* 135
Or *d.* not for it, or brings up instead *T.* iii 384
Thus lovely halcyons *d.* into the main *T.T.* 566

DIVERGING.
D. each from each, like equal rays *H.* 303

DIVERSIFIED.
D. with trees of every growth *T.* i 301
D., that two were never found *T.* iv 737

DIVERSIFY.
Ingenious to *d.* dull life *R.* 520

DIVERSION.
Some seek *d.* in the tented field *T.* v 185

DIVERSITY.
The gay *d.* of leaf and flower *T.* iii 590
Was split into *d.* of tongues *T.* v 195

DIVERT.
D. the champions prodigal of breath *Con.* 80
But to *d.* a fierce banditti *E.* iv 13

DIVERTED.
Fretful unless *d.* and beguiled *R.* 108

DIVEST.
D. the rougher sex of female airs *Con.* 843

DIVESTED.
The sapless wood, *d.* of the bark *Con.* 53

DIVIDE.
Whom nothing could *d. A Tale* 68
A fretful temper will *d. F.* 61
No fertilizing streams your fields *d. H.* 467
Runs in a bottom, and *d.* the field *N.A.* 10
D. the frail inhabitants of earth *R.* 648
To deal and shuffle, to *d.* and sort *T.* i 474
Admirers, and be destined to *d. T.* iii 723
Two Gods *d.* them all. Pleasure and Gain *T.* vi 892
Death never shall *d. The Doves* 28
His cloud-capped eminence *d. Trans. H.* 17

DIVIDED.
She thus maintains *d.* sway *Mrs. M* — 51
United yet *d.*, twain at once *T.* i 77

DIVIDING.
The Ouse, *d.* the well-watered land *T.* i 323

DIVINE.
Effects of punishment and wrath *d. A.T.* 51
Each some approaching good *d. A Tale* 63
And gave them a grace so *d. C.* 18

No voice *d.* the storm allayed *Cast.* 61
And Love *D.* has paid one price for all *Ch.* 205
Speaks a *d.* ambition, and a zeal *Ch.* 307
All truth is precious, if not all *d. Ch.* 331
'Tis truth *d.*, exhibited on earth *Ch.* 377
Implies no trespass against Love *D.*) *Ch.* 488
And prove too weak for so *d.* a theme *Ch.* 633
Not more distinct from harmony *d. Con.* 9
But Truth *d.* for ever stands secure *Con.* 555
Who waits for heaven ere he becomes *d. Con.* 534
Gird up each other to the race *d. Con.* 702
For which Heaven formed the faculty *d. Con.* 893
And tell them truths *d.* and clear *E.* i 21
Thy tears all issue from a source *d. E.* ii 47
By power *d.*, and skill that could not err *Ex.* 206
As a mere instrument in hands *d. Ex.* 319
The word of prophecy, those truths *d. Ex.* 686
But know, that Wrath *D.*, when most severe *Ex.* 714
And import, of their oracles *d. Ex.* 126
For truth is unwelcome, however *d. F.M.* 23
If, led from earthly things to things *d. H.* 141
If appetite, or what *d.* call lust *H.* 385
May claim some right to be esteemed *d. H.* 504
That while I trembling trace a work *d. H.* 671
The abundant harvest, recompense *d. H.* 770
Which rural gentlemen call sport *d. N.A.* 8
For 'twas the self-same Power *D.—N.G.* 19
Full bliss is bliss *d. N.Y.G.* 14
And prove their owner half *d.*" *P.* 64
D. authority within his breast *P.E.* 33
The signature and stamp of power *d. R.* 54
Thy power *d.*, and bounty beyond thought *R.* 91
Bears proof of an intelligence *d. R.* 208
'Tis God's just claim, prerogative *d. R.* 278
Ye want but that to seem indeed *d. R.* 558
D. Communion, carefully enjoyed *R.* 747
D. Communion chases the day *R.* 765
No soil like poverty for growth *d. T.* 363
Once the blest residence of truth *d. T.* 387
Nor hoped, but in thy righteousness *d. T.* 576
The legate of the skies!—His theme *d. T.* ii 338
I seek *d.* simplicity in him *T.* ii 432
Who handles things *d.*; and all beside *T.* ii 433
Of Light *D.* But Egypt, Greece, and Rome *T.* ii 500
And waved his rod *d.*, a race obscene *T.* ii 826
And dark in things *d.* Full often too *T.* iii 235
And lineaments *d.* I trace a hand *T.* iii 722
Might well suppose the artificer *d. T.* v 561
From fool to wise, from earthly to *d. T.* v 696
Made pure, shall relish with *d.* delight *T.* v 783
Till then unfelt, what hands *d.* have wrought *T.* v 784
What prodigies can power *d.* perform *T.* vi 118
An agency *d.*, to make him know *T.* vi 129
The impious challenger of power *d. T.* vi 546
By our capacity of grace *d. T.* vi 602
A talent so *d.*, remember too *T.* vi 649
If he regard not, though *d.* the theme *T.* vi 1019
Of poets raised by you, and statesmen, and *d. Tir.* 233
Whate'er she meant, this truth *d. Tran.* i 21
The deeds that men admire as half *d. T.T.* 3
Than Virtue quickens, with a warmth *d. T.T.* 382
She pours a sensibility *d. T.T.* 486
Mankind to share in the *d.* delight *T.T.* 753
May kill a sound *d. Y.D.* 64
Of amnesty, the need of blood *d. Y.O.* 13
A theme for poetry *d.* 1789, 29

DIVINELY.
D. bestowed upon man *A.S.* 18
But Reason still, unless *d.* taught *Ch.* 337
True Charity, a plant *d.* nursed *Ch.* 573
From things terrestrial, and *d.* changed *Con.* 726
To walk with God, to be *d.* free *T.* v 722

On some fair theme; some theme d. fair T. vi 754
Born from above and made d. wise V. 94
DIVING.
Where bold Inquiry, d. out of sight H. 413
By d. into cabinet intrigue T.T. 154
DIVINITY.
He grinds d. of other days T. ii 362
That hides d. from mortal eyes T. vi 877
DIVORCE.
This riving stroke, this ultimate d. H. 640
DIVORCED.
And knees and hassocks are well nigh d. T. i 748
DIVULGED.
By causes not to be d. in vain T. iii 371
DIZZY. [607
And d. with delight, profaned the sacred wires T.T.
And sucked in d. madness with his draught H. 513
DOCTOR. [ii 351
But hark—the D.'s voice!—fast wedged between T.
A d.'s trouble, but without the fees Con. 314
Victorious seemed, and now the d.'s skill Con. 320
Are there who purchase of the D.'s ware? T. ii 366
DOCTRINE.
The d. warped to what they never meant Con. 778
While others at that d. rail L.W. 19
Who fill the world with d. contraband P.E. 475
In d. uncorrupt; in language plain T. ii 400 [373
Whose hands are pure, whose d. and whose life T. ii
In modern eyes), shall make the d. clear T. vi 482
Strange d. this! that without scruple tears T.T. 5
DODONA.
As in D. once thy kindred trees Y.O. 41
DOFFS.
Sheepish he d. his hat, and mumbling swears T. iv 628
DOG.
My d.! what remedy remains Beau 17
My d. shall mortify the pride D.W. 39
The d. did bark, the children screamed J.G. 109 [125
By panting d., tired man, and spattered horse N.A.
Unmissed but by his d. and by his groom P.E. 95
Receives the morsel—flesh obscene of d. T. i 562
His d. attends him. Close behind his heel T. v 47
DOGGISH.
And ease a d. pain Beau 10
DOG'S-EARED.
Who starve upon a d. Pentateuch Tir. 402
DOIT.
And force the beggarly last d., by means T. v 316
DOLE. [v 94
Pick up their nauseous d., though sweet to them T.
"Their weekly d. of edifying strains T. v 646
DOLEFUL.
With d. rumour and sad presage hung Ex. 357
She heard the d. tidings of his death T. i 545
DOLLS.
Paint cards and d., and every idle thing T. iv 211
DOLT.
Or such another d. as you P. 30
DOMAIN.
Fast by the stream that bounds your just d. Her. 47
Within the confines of their wild d. T. vi 407

DOMES.
Bright shone the roofs, the d., the spires Q.V. 13
DOMESTIC.
And to d. bounds confined Ep. ii 7
D. happiness and rural joy Ex. 535
Alas! and is d. strife M.F. 31
No pleasure! Are d. comforts dead? P.E. 213
D. Happiness, thou only bliss T. iii 41
D. life in rural leisure passed! T. iii 292
And under an old oak's d. shade T. iv 172
Against the charities of d. life T. iv 677
The feathered tribes d. Half on wing T. v 62
Upon the endearments of d. life T. v 438
And shining each in his d. sphere T. v 520
None that, in thy d. snug recess Tir. 581
Exchanged for the secure d. scheme Tir. 705
DOMINEERING.
Free from the d. power of Lust P.E. 458
DOMINION.
Holds a usurped d. o'er his tongue Con. 462
Strength in his heart, d. in his nod T. 409
Find place in his d., or dispose T. ii 169
With kingship and d. o'er the rest Tir. 96
Those ensigns of d., how disgraced! T.T. 40
DON. [98
"Indeed," replied the D., "there are but few" T.T.
DONOR.
With him, the D. of eternal life H. 323
DOOM.
Or if, deserving of a better d., Con. 413 [560
The world's best comfort was, his d. was passed H.
And death's a d. sufficient for the rest" H. 396
When on a day, like that of the last d. Her. 11
When wit and genius meet their d. M. ii 1
She now presaged approaching d. R.C. 74
D. and devotes him as his lawful prey T. ii 15 [53
To preach the general d. When were the winds T. ii
D. to the knife; nor does he spare the soft T. iii 417
And d. him for perhaps a heedless word T. v 440
Denounce no d. on the delinquent? None T. vi 433
D. him not then to solitary meals Tir. 719
And if He d. that people with a frown T.T. 456
DOOMED.
This process achieved, it is d. to sustain F.M. 9
Have justly d., for some atrocious cause H. 713
Eternal winter d. to know Miss — 35
Which future pages yet are d. to share T. 146
Begs a warm office, d. to a cold jail T. iii 820
D. it, as insufficient for his praise T. v 565
The tyranny that d. them to the fire T. v 731
"And hasting to a grave, yet d. to rise T. v 830
D. to the dust, or lodged already there T. vi 714
Who, d. to an obscure but tranquil state T. vi 903
D. to a no less ignominious fate Tir. 498
DOOMSDAY.
And writes a D. sentence on his heart H. 693
DOOR.
Passing his prison d. B.R. 14
Not he, but his emergence, forced the d. Ch. 183
Might swing at ease behind his study d. Ch. 615
Swinging the parlour d. upon its hinge E. iii 21
And sift the dust behind the d. E. iv 42
Adultery neighing at his neighbour's d. Ex. 39
Fell broken and defaced at their own d. Ex. 503
Till half the world comes rattling at his d. H. 77
And they might enter at his open d. H. 308

The warder at the *d.* his key applies *H.* 720
That wealth within is ruin at the *d. Her.* 76
To drive up to the *d.* lest all *J.G.* 35
So three *d.* off the chaise was stayed *J.G.* 37
And shall expect him at the *d. M.F.* 13
And bar the *d.* the moment they intrude *P.E.* 160
Stand starved at your inhospitable *d. P.E.* 250
Ducks paddle in the pond, before the *d. R.* 499
Yon cottager, who weaves at her own *d. T.* 317
His legs depending at the open *d. T.* i 93
To hear his creaking panniers at the *d. T.* i 245
Alighting, turns the key in her own *d. T.* ii 653
At the right *d.* Profusion is the sire *T.* ii 674
To pass us readily through every *d. T.* iii 99   [559
The unguarded *d.* was safe; men did not watch *T.* iv
Were charactered on every statesman's *d. T.* iii 823
Perhaps by moonlight at their humble *d. T.* iv 171
Of sounding an alarm assaults these *d. T.* iv 146
Unwrenched the *d.*, however well secured *T.* iv 446
The studs that thick emboss his iron *d. T.* v 426
He, entering at the study *d. T.B.* 17   [746
Flies, winged with joy, to some coach-crowded *d. Tir.*
And eyes the *d.*, and watches a retreat *Tir.* 572
Nor plagues that haunt the rich man's *d. Trans. H.* 11
When Tumult lately burst his prison *d. T.T.* 318

DORMITORY.
And *d.* too *Tran.* ii 6

DOSE.
In which I both scribble and *d. Gr.* 12

DOTAGE.
'Tis childish *d.*, a delirious dream! *Ch.* 417
What *d.* will not Vanity maintain? *Ex.* 628
In silly *d.* on created things *T.* v 586

DOTARDS.
And fantasies of *d.*, such as thou *T.* vi 507

DOTE.   [775
That while she *d.*, and dreams that she believes *Con.*
D. not too much, nor spoil what ye admire *T.* ii 498
Yet thus we *d.*, refusing while we can *T.* v 874

DOTING.
Were Love, in these the world's last *d.* years *Ch.* 604
Sweet Poll! his *d.* mistress cries *Tran.* iv 13

DOUBLE.
Alas! his efforts *d.* his distress *Con.* 343
With the *d.* employment of mallet and mill *F.M.* 16
There hardening by degrees, till *d.* steeled *P.E.* 590
And shock me. I should then with *d.* pain *T.* v 483
So God wrought *d.* justice; made the fool *T.* vi 557
To *d.* all thy pleasure in thy child *Tir.* 682
Keep Vice restrained behind a *d.* guard *T.T.* 66
With *d.*, toil, and shiver at their work *T.T.* 215

DOUBLED.
Witness a joy that thou hast *d.* long *T.* i 149

DOUBLY.
And slaves, by truth enlarged, are *d.* freed *Ch.* 231
Joys *d.* sweet to feelings quick as thine *Ch.* 298
Sweet always *d.* sweet *Q.V.* 28
Schools, unless discipline were *d.* strong *Tir.* 218

DOUBT.
They swear it, till affirmance breeds a *d. Con.* 66
Reply discreetly—"To be sure—no *d.*!" *Con.* 118
The punishment importing this, no *d. E.* iii 52
Babbler of ancient fables, leaves a *d. Ex.* 503
And if some Spartan soul a *d.* expressed *Ex.* 542
Judging, in charity no *d.*, the town *H.* 250

Then theirs, no *d.*, as well as mine, is sure *H.* 388
No *d.*, my dear, I bade him come *M.F.* 11
That sage they seemed, as lawyers o'er a *d. N.A.* 77
Will heartily thank us, no *d.*, for our pains *P.A.* 10
Craze antiquarian brains with endless *d. P.E.* 394
Eternal truth by everlasting *d. P.E.* 473
Shall call to supper, when, no *d. R.C.* 63   [222
" Charles without *d.*," say you—and so he ought *T.*
D. not hereafter with the saints to mount *T.* 150
And heaven, no *d.*, shall be their home at last *T.* 296
Can lodge a heavenly mind—demands a *d. T.* ii 462
'Tis Revelation satisfies all *d. T.* ii 527
The nurse, no *d.* Regardless of her charge *T.* ii 775
Are grand, no *d.*, and worthy of the Word *T.* v. 555
With intellects bemazed in endless *d. T.* v 848
Is register'd in heaven; and these no *d. T.* vi 440
Brings into *d.* the wisdom of the skies *Tir.* 72 [418
And deans, no *d.*, and chapters, with one voice *Tir.*
Some sneaking virtue lurks in him, no *d. Tir.* 244
You think, no *d.*, he sits and muses *Tran.* ii 19
To *d.* the love his favourites may pretend *T.T.* 159
And should, no *d.*, if they were all forgot *T.T.* 771

DOUBTED.
And he that never *d.* of his state *T.* 299

DOUBTFUL.
Her gloomy monarch, *d.*, and resigned *Ex.* 570
And, *d.* what, with prudent care *R.C.* 85
With *d.* credit, told to frighten babes *T.* iv 564
Guides the decision of a *d.* choice *Tir.* 34

DOUBTLESS.
Is *d.* left behind *A Tale* 48
D. it is. To which, of my own store *H.* 433
Demons produce them *d.*, brazen-clawed *N.A.* 101
And *d.* she in thine *N.Y.G.* 16
He *d.* is in sport, and does but droll *T.* ii 369

DOUGH.
And he that kneads the *d.*; all loud alike *T.* iv 477

DOVE.
Oh! had I the wings of a *d. A.S.* 19
They sport like wanton *d.* in airy rings *A.T.* 32
Time, as he passes us, has a *d.'s* wing *T.* iv 211
And soothed the listening *d. The Doves* 8

DOWN.
Starts from the *d.* on which she lately slept *H.* 219
D. that almost escape the inquiring eye *R.* 423
Come hither, ye that press your beds of *d. T.* i 362
To show the peeping *d.* upon his chin *Tir.* 235

DOWN-FALLEN.
To assist his foe's *d.* beast to rise *T.* vi 444

DOWNRIGHT.
Through *d.* inability to rise *T.* i 480

DOWN-STOOPING.
Where Night *d.* from her ebon throne *P.E.* 177

DOWNY.
The thistle's *d.* seed my fare *G.* 2
His mantling neck with *d.* gold *Mrs. M—* 6
Return and make thy *d.* nest *O.* ii 2
Fast falls a fleecy shower; the *d.* flakes *T.* iv 326

DOZEN.
A *d.* would-bes of the modern day *Con.* 612
Some half a *d.*, and some half a score *Tir.* 695

DOZING.
The *d.* sages drop the drowsy strain *Con.* 247
D. out all his idle noons *Ep.* ii 31
Nor yet the *d.* of the clerk, are sweet *T.* i 101

DRAG.
They swathe the forehead, d. the limping limb T. i 581
That d. the dull companion to and fro T. iv 368

DRAGGED.
That ever d. a chain, or tugged an oar Ex. 527
Others are d. into the crowded room T. i 478
Till Persecution d. them into fame T. v 725

DRAGON-SCALES.
With helmet heads, and d. adorned R. 69

DRAINED.
So rich, so thronged, so d., and so supplied T. i 720
D. to the last poor item of his wealth T. iii 784

DRAINING.
And d. its nutritious powers to feed R. 43

DRAINS.
And comforts cease. Dress d. our cellar dry T. ii 614

DRAMA.
What means the d. by the world sustained? R. 646

DRANK.
For then, by toil subdued, he d. Cast. 47
Called on a friend, d. tea, stepped home again Con. 278
And d. the little bumper every day T. 158

DRAUGHT.
Now the distemper, spite of d. or pill Con. 319
And sucked in dizzy madness with his d. H. 518
In vain to filter off a crystal d. T. ii 507

DRAVE.
God d. asunder, and assigned their lot T. v 198

DRAW.
And each endures, while yet he d. his breath Ch. 143
He too has a connecting power, and d. Ch. 327
That fire is catching if you d. too near Con. 654
'Tis narrow, selfish, arrogant, and d. Con. 671
Who labour hard to allure and d. E. i 23
Is to renounce hypocrisy; to d. Ex. 408
The Christian Hope is—Waiter, d. the cork H. 361
He laughs, whatever weapon Truth may d. H. 596
He d. upon life's map a zig-zag line H. 607
Ye monarchs, whom the lure of honour d. Her. 41
Our self-approving bosom d. Miss — 51
"Long as I d. ethereal air Miss — 67
Is almost enough to d. pity from stones P.A. 4
But he can d. a pattern, make a tart P.E. 195
His great improvement and new lights he d. P.E. 402
As bloated spiders d. the flimsy line P.E. 495
To d. the incautious minnow from the brook R. 402
Produce them—now d. a chair—now d. a saint T. i 172
The love of Nature, and the scenes she d. T. i 412
Or else vain-glory, prompted us to d. T. i 635
Conspire against him. With his breath, he d. T. ii 139
His master-strokes, and d. from his design T. ii 398
The Rout is Folly's circle, which she d. T. ii 629
From instrumental causes proud to d. T. iii 238
That d. the sportsman over hill and dale T. iii 310
Thus blest, I d. a picture of that bliss T. iii 694
To a vile clod, so d. him, with such force T. v 589
D. gross impurity, and likes it well T. vi 979
As happy as we once to kneel and d. Tir. 306
They see the attentive crowds his talents d. Tir. 362
If you can crown a discipline, that d. Tir. 493
The public character its colours d. Tir. 912
Plants it upon the line that justice d. T.T. 17
Nor d. it, but when Duty bids him d. T.T. 78
When tithing time d. near Y.D. 8

DRAWER.
A d., it chanced, at bottom lined R.C. 35
A d. impending o'er the rest R.C. 39
"The open d. was left, I see R.C. 55
He 'gan in haste the d. explore R.C. 92

DRAWING.
Exhibits elevations, d., plans P.E. 397
In d. pictures of forbidden joys R. 216
And growing old in d. nothing up!" T. iii 190
Just when our d. rooms begin to blaze T. iv 267
To bear his burdens, d. in his gears T. v 273
Always at speed, and never d. bit T.T. 685

DRAWL.
Their fleece his pillow, and his weekly d. H. 199

DRAWLING.
The tedious rector d. o'er his head T. i 95

DRAWN.
Forcibly d. from many a close recess Ch. 529
Like figures d. upon a dial plate Con. 380
Whose wisdom, d. from the deep well of life Con. 564
When souls d. upwards in communion sweet Con. 569
The curtain d. by Prejudice and Pride H. 571
To streams of popular opinion d. P.E. 478
D. from his refuge in some lonely elm T. vi 310
In measure, as by force of instinct d. T. vi 412

DRAY.
Climbed like a squirrel to his d. A Fable 28

DREAD.
Found oftenest in what least we d. A Fable 37
But slavery!—Virtue d. it as her grave Ch. 163
Preserve me from the thing I d. and hate Con. 83
Through constant d. of giving Truth offence Con. 129
Enlarge and fortify the d. redoubt Con. 689
A cold misgiving, and a killing d. Con. 770
A d. she would not, yet is forced to feel Con. 786
Pulled down the tyrants India served with d. Ex. 366
Your cause before a bar you little d. P.E. 198
Like Eden's d. probationary tree P.E. 468 [482
That d. the encroachment of our growing streets R.
Than bid me shun the deep, and d. the shore? R.H. 2
And d. of Death ensues St. v 24
Much menaced, nothing d. St. vi 18
A growing d. of vengeance at his heels T. 258
And Justice, guardian of the d. command T. 277
Her beauty, her fertility. She d. T. i 370   [i 487
Then wherefore not renounce them? No—the d. T.
The slavish d. of solitude, that breeds T. i 488
The joy of many, and the d. of more T. iii 281
Much of her vigilant instinctive d. T. iii 340
To steel their hearts against the d. of death" T. vi 511
Fixed motionless, and petrified with d. T. vi 538
A world that does not d. and hate his laws T. vi 826
The symptoms that you see with so much d. Tir. 534
Beheld their progress with the deepest d. T.T. 325

DREADED.
And d. more than a contagious touch? Con. 652
A tempest usher in the d. morn H. 717
From objects too much d. or desired R. 144
Once d. by our foes R.G. 26
And d. as thou art! Thou hold'st the sun T. iv 129

DREADFUL.
They build each other up with d. skill Con. 687
Would run most d. risk of catching cold E. iii 59
But ah! those d. yells what soul can hear N.A. 99
Of his own works, his d. part alone T. ii 82
As d. as the Manichean God T. v 444
The d. leap, more rational his steed T. vi 517
And while the d. risk foreseen forbids Tir. 860

DREADING.

D. a negative, and overawed *E.* iii 22

DREAM.

The land of *d.*, Hypothesis her name *A.T.* 6
In daily musings and in nightly *d. A.T.* 12
That forms material whatsoe'er we *d. A.T.* 40
Far other *d.* his feverish mind employed *A.T.* 153
Catharina is fled like a *d. C.* 5
I therefore purpose not, or *d. Cast.* 55
Philosophy, that does not *d.* or stray *Ch.* 313
'Tis childish dotage, a delirious *d.* ! *Ch.* 417
But if, unhappily deceived, I *d. Ch.* 632
A *d.* to any except those that *d. Con.* 482
That fools, as you have done, shall call a *d. Con.* 504
That while she dotes, and *d.* that she believes *Con.* 775
Dispersing all his *d. D.W.* 26
Still haunts, in hope to *d.* of youth again *Ex.* 26
Pronounced him frantic, and his fears a *d. Ex.* 70
Pronounced by greybeards a pernicious *d. Ex.* 114
With all the embroidery of poetic *d. Ex.* 234
The busy trifler *d.* himself alone *Ex.* 322 [*Ex.* 402
What mean they ? Can't thou *d.* there is a power
As grasshoppers, as dust, a drop, a *d.* ? *Ex.* 345
Dispelled thy gloom, and broke away thy *d. Ex.* 501
And did they *d.*, and art thou wiser now ? *Ex.* 632
And *d.* that he had found one *F.* 18
All thoughts of friendship are but *d. F.* 74
To adopt the chymist's golden *d. F.* 143
The poets will swear that I *d. Gr.* 55
'Tis grave Philosophy's absurdest *d. H.* 65
And, howsoever shadowy, no *d. H.* 124
Perhaps when sickness, or some fearful *d. H.* 217
Revere the laws they *d.* that Heaven ordains *H.* 241
The strange conceits, vain projects, and wild *d.H.* 618
Like language uttered in a *d. M.* 22
At what such a *d.* should betide ? *M.D.* 42
A momentary *d.*, that thou art she *M.P.* 20
The comet's baneful influence is a *d. P.E.* 100
With sentimental frippery and *d. P.E.* 312
Solicits kind attention to his *d. P.E.* 523 [598
Some *d.* that they can silence, when they will *P.E.*
Though his life be a *d.*, his enjoyments, I see *P.F.* 19
Thus laden, *d.* that they are rich and great *R.* 155
Soft airs, nocturnal vigils, and day *d. R.* 260
Forgery of fancy, and a *d.* of woes *R.* 324
As n. ural as when asleep to *d. R.* 636
Where *d.* of dress, intrigue, and pleasure reign *R.* 642
The man who *d.* himself so great *R.C.* 111
His well-built systems, philosophic *d. T.* 8
The *d.* of fancy, tranquil and secure *T.* i 236
And *d.* of transports she was not to know *T.* i 544
The *d.* is past; and thou hast found again *T.* i 639
To *d.* all night of what the day denied *T.* i 671
With hurtful error, prejudice, and *d. T.* ii 504
To tell its slumbers, and to paint its *d. T.* iii 13
And never won. *D.* after *d.* ensues *T.* iii 127
And still they *d.* that they shall still succeed *T.* iii 128
D., empty *d.* The million flit as gay *T.* iii 133 [317
Who *d.* they have a taste for fields and groves *T.* iii
Riches have wings, and grandeur is a *d. T.* iii 263
Laboured, and many a night pursued in *d. T.* iii 787
Soothed with a waking *d.* of houses, towers *T.* iv 287
Vain wish! those days were never; airy *d. T.* iv 525
That favoured such a *d.*, in days like these *T.* iv 530
My very *d.* were rural: rural too *T.* iv 700
Silently as a *d.* the fabric rose *T.* v 144 [492
And tremble at vain *d.* ? Heaven grant I may! *T.* v
Can *d.* them trusty to the general weal *T.* v 514
Thus *d.* they, and contrive to save a God *T.* vi 205
And soothed into a *d.* that he discerns *T.* vi 284
' And dost thou *d.*,'' the impenetrable man *T.* vi 505
Of which she little *d.* Perhaps she owes *T.* vi 945

A *d.* disturbed poor Bully's rest *T.B.* '44
Replete with *d.*, unworthy of a man *Tir.* 160
What *d.* they of, that, with so little care *Tir.* 358
They *d.* of little Charles or William graced *Tir.* 360
D. him episcopally such at least *Tir.* 365
Depend not much upon your golden *d. Tir.* 429
Each *d.* that each is just what he appears *Tir.* 448
Not occupied in day *d.*, as at home *Tir.* 775
And Death awakens from that *d.* too late *T.T.* 126
O Liberty! the prisoner's pleasing *d. T.T.* 175
Though but a *d.*!) art grown disdainful too *V.* 44
So Fancy *d.* Disprove it, if ye can *Y.O.* 29
Through tomes of fable and of *d.* 1789, 7

DREAMED.

He *d.* not of a foe, or if his fear *A.T.* 151
Foretold one, *d.* not of a foe so near *A.T.* 152
I *d.* what I cannot but sing *M.D.* 3
I *d.* that, on ocean afloat *M.D.* 5

DREAMER.

The rest are sober *d.*, grave and wise *T.* iii 137
Ingenious *d.*, in whose well-told tale *Tir.* 135

DREAMING.

" What, always *d.* over heavenly things *Con.* 575
Not *d.* of so dear a friend *E.* i 41
Seems at the best but *d.* life away *R.* 468
At once the *d.* mind is disabused *Tir.* 90
Of *d.* study and pedantic rust *T.T.* 171
Such is the folly of our *d.* youth *V.* 54

DREAMT.

He little *d.*, when he set out *J.G.* 99

DREAR.

And such in ancient halls and mansions *d. T.* i 24
And drive the wedge in yonder forest *d. T.* v 43

DREARY.

Neglected, leaves a *d.* waste behind *Comp.* i 12
Again life's *d.* waste *St.* iii 6
The *d.* waste; there spends the livelong day *T.* i 457
And prospect oft so *d.* and forlorn *T.* vi 21
Is *d.*, so with him all seasons please *T.* vi 255

DREGS.

The *d.* and feculence of every land *T.* i 684

DRENCH.

Shall *d.* again or discompose *Mrs. M—* 17

DRENCHED.

Now *d.* throughout, and hopeless of his case *T.* 246
And *d.* conservatory breathes abroad *T.* iii 498
Let laurels *d.* in pure Parnassian dews *T.T.* 13

DRESS.

Earth seems a garden in its loveliest *d. Her.* 57
To *d.* a room for Montagu *Mrs. M—* 2
Sweat of ours must *d.* the soil *N.C.* 20 [642
Where dreams of *d.*, intrigue, and pleasure reign *R.*
Her form with *d.* and lotion they repair *P.E.* 299
Go, *d.* thine eyes with eyesalve; ask of him *T.* ii 203
The freaks of fashion, regulate the *d. T.* ii 317
In conversation frivolous, in *d. T.* ii 379
Who waits to *d.* us, arbitrates their date *T.* ii 600
We sacrifice to *d.*, till household joys *T.* ii 613 [614
And comforts cease. *D.* drains our cellar dry *T.* ii
You think, perhaps, so delicate his *d. T.* ii 625
When gay Goodnature *d.* her in smiles *T.* ii 784
And *d.* the regular yet various scene *T.* iii 592
The backstring and the bib, assume the *d. T.* iv 227
To *d.* a sofa with the flowers of verse *T.* vi 1007
Clothe the twin brethren in each other's *d. T.T.* 45

DRESSED.

As ever *d.* a bank, or scented summer air *Ch.* 259

By Vanity's unwearied finger *d. Ex.* 46
What though in scaly armour *d. Miss* — 41
He knows indeed that whether *d.* or rude *R.* 415
In shirt of hair, and weeds of canvass *d. T.* 81
Some mansion, neat and elegantly *d. T.* 250
D. to his taste, inviting him abroad *T.* iii 358
That softly swelled and gaily *d.* appears *T.* iii 629
Though well perfumed and elegantly *d. T.* vi 991
So take my judgment in his language *d. Tir.* 507
In painted plumes superbly *d. Tran.* iv 1
And as the sun in rising beauty *d. T.T.* 706

DRESSING.
To spend two hours in *d.* for the day *H.* 80
Pant for the praise of *d.* to the taste *T.* iii 460

DREW.
The spring *d.* near, each felt a breast *A Tale* 13
The wreath he won *d.* down an instant curse *Ch.* 61
D. the grey curtain of the fading west *Ch.* 263
Such was the portrait an apostle *d. Ch.* 432
Or when a storm *d.* near *Ep.* ii 28
They *d.* a curse from an intended good *Ex.* 129
Through which the belt he *d. J.G.* 70
And still, as fast as he *d.* near *J.G.* 117
And, turning from my nursery window, *d. M.P.* 30
D. me to school along the public way *M.P.* 49
George ever *d.* from her *Q.V.* 56
He *d.* the curtain at his side *R.C.* 81 [iii 116
He *d.* them forth, and healed, and bade me live *T.*
And all his strength from Scripture *d. St.* iii 19
The Scripture was his jest book, whence he *d. T.* 307
D. from the stream below. More favoured, we *T.* ii 501
Much. I was born of woman, and *d.* milk *T.* iii 196
He *d.* the liturgy, and framed the rights *T.* vi 679
D. a rough copy of the Christian face *T.T.* 614
D. not his life from woman; never gazed *Y.O.* 145
In praise harmonious the first air he *d. Y.O.* 155

DRIBBLING.
The *d.* stream ne'er puts it out again *P.E.* 322
For ever *d.* out their base contents *T.* iv 506

DRIED.
With which when neatly peeled and *d. T.B.* 29

DRIFT.
Of all that Wisdom dictates the *d. T.* 513
Force not my *d.* beyond its just intent *Tir.* 505

DRIFTED.
Wide scampering, snatches up the *d.* snow *T.* v 49

DRILL. [150
Or having, kept concealed. Some *d.* and bore *T.* iii

DRILLED.
And *d.* in holes, the solid oak is found *T.* i 26

DRINK.
Fast as the thirsting ear can *d.* the sound *Ch.* 112
D. wisdom at the milky stream of light *Ch.* 319
While others poison what the flock must *d. Ex.* 100
My *d.* the morning dew *G.* 3 [418
Come, prophet, *d.*, and tell us what think you" *H.*
Must go to heaven—and I must *d.* his health *H.* 412
Too covetous of *d. O.* i 10
He cannot *d.* five bottles, bilk the score *P.E.* 193
Then kill a constable, and *d.* five more *P.E.* 194
Thou fountain at which *d.* the good and wise *P.E.* 466
He that sips often, at last *d.* it up *P.E.* 581
The sun, a world whence other worlds *d.* light *R.* 81
To *d.* sweet waters of the crystal well *T.* i 240
Their pendant boughs, stooping as if to *d. T.* i 269
D., when we choose it, at the fountain head *T.* ii 502

D. and be mad then; 'tis your country bids! *T.* iv 509
To swear, to game, to *d.*; to show at home *T.* iv 652
He *d.* his simple beverage with a gust *T.T.* 240[776
Of the same grove, and *d.* one common stream *T.* vi
A huge throat calling to the clouds for *d. Y.O.* 112

DRINKING.
Where neither strumpet's charms, nor *d.* bout *Tir.* 245

DRIPPING.
Nor blasts that shake the *d.* bower *Mrs. M—* 16
With *d.* rains, or withered by a frost *T.* ii 211
And drunk no moisture from the *d.* clouds *T.* iii 515
For a nosegay, so *d.* and drowned *The Rose* 10

DRIVE.
Who *d.* a loathsome traffic, gauge and span *Ch.* 139
Would *d.* them forth from the resort of men *Con.* 37
And daily threaten to *d.* them *E.* iv 17
Should spring within thy bosom, *d.* it thence) *Ex.* 709
D. through the realms of Sin, where Riot reels *H.* 651
To *d.* up to the door, lest all *J.G.* 35 [102
Me howling blasts *d.* devious, tempest-tossed *M.P.*
D. to their dens the obedient beasts of prey *R.* 766
Attends him; *d.* his cattle to a march *T.* iv 647
And *d.* the wedge in yonder forest drear *T.* v 43
Or *d.* it devious with a dextrous pat *Tir.* 309

DRIVEL.
Should ever *d.* out of human lips *T.* v 285

DRIVELING.
Sniveling and *d.* folly without end *P.E.* 310

DRIVELLER.
If some mere *d.* suck the sugared fib *P.E.* 530

DRIVEN.
Wherever *d.* by wind or tide *P.* 53
D. out an exile from the face of Saul *R.* 768
By gales of blessing *d. St.* iii 32
Plashed neatly, and secured with *d.* stakes *T.* iv 437
Were *d.* from Paradise: and in that hour *T.* vi 380
D. to the slaughter, goaded, as he runs *T.* vi 421
That creeping pestilence is *d.* away *T.* vi 785
To fairy land be *d. Miss* — 22

DRIVER.
The boorish *d.* leaning o'er his team *T.* i 298

DRIVING.
Blown all aslant, a *d.*, dashing rain *T.* 239
The mind He gave me; *d.* it, though slack *T.* iii 369
And to the stir of Commerce, *d.* slow *T.* iii 739
That crowd away before the *d.* wind *T.* v 3
His skill in coachmanship, or *d.* chaise *Tir.* 326
That wants no *d.* and disdains the lead *T.T.* 134

DRIZZLING.
Bade rise in haste a dark and *d.* fog *A.T.* 94
And if perchance, on some dull, *d.* day *H.* 371

DROLL.
And in the saddest part cry—" *D.* indeed!" *Con.* 216
He doubtless is in sport, and does but *d. T.* ii 369
With *d.* sobriety they raised a smile *T.T.* 658

DRONE-PIPE.
That's worse—the *d.* of an humblebee *Con.* 330

DRONING.
If priest, supinely *d.* o'er his charge *H.* 198

DROOP.
Should *d.* and wither where they grow *P.* 59

DROOPING.
And drought on all the *d.* herbs around *E.* ii 50

And cheers the d. flowers, unheard, unseen *J.T.* 40
Or charm the sorrows of a d. friend *R.* 292
A chilling flood on summer's d. flowers *T.T.* 211
Liberty blushed, and hung her d. head *T.T.* 324

DROP.

D. one by one from Fame's neglecting hand *B.B.* 6
He half exhibits, and then d. the sum *Ch.* 478
The dozing sages d. the drowsy strain *Con.* 247
You rise and d. the curtain—now 'tis night *Con.* 332
And every d. bespeaks a Saviour thine *E.* ii 48
As grasshoppers, as dust, a d., a dream? *Ex.* 345
They d. through mere desire to prate *F.* 71
Earth glitters with the d. the night distils *H.* 42
That Pity had engendered, d. one here *H.* 677
He d. at once his fetters and his fear *H.* 725
A poet's d. of ink? *O.* i 12
Illustrious d.! and happy then *O.* i 21   [396
First shakes the glittering d. from every thorn *R.*
Seem d. descending in a shower of light *R.* 350
He d. the rein, and leaves him to his pace *T.* 247
D. the red vengeance from his willing hand *T.* 278
Like kindred d. been mingled into one *T.* ii 19
D. from the lips a disregarded thing *T.* ii 565
Unmixed with d. of bitter, which Neglect *T.* iii 46
One d. of Heaven's sweet mercy in his cup *T.* iii 804
And d. the night-bolt;—ruffians are abroad *T.* iv 568
And shrubs of fairy land. The crystal d. *T.* v 113
From many a twig the pendant d. of ice *T.* vi 83
Here every d. of honey hides a sting *T.* vi 830
Must d. indeed the hope of public praise *T.* vi 973
The money chinks, down d. their chins *Y.D.* 51

DROPPED.

Has d. her anchor, and her canvass furled *Ch.* 443
My quick approach, and soon he d. *D.W.* 35
That d. upon his Bible was sincere *H.* 575   [38
His apples might hang till they d. from the tree *P.A.*
And, having d. the expected bag, pass on *T.* iv. 11

DROPPING.

Of d. buckets into empty wells *T.* iii 189

DROSS.

And made all pleasures else mere d. to me" *H.* 537
Left sensuality and d. behind *T.* 526
Conveying worthless d. into its place *T.* i 572

DROUGHT.   [iii 555

Moisture and d., mice, worms, and swarming flies *T.*
And d. on all the drooping herbs around *E.* ii 50
After long d., when rains abundant fall *N.A.* 59
That can alone make sweet the bitter d. *T.* i 751
Calm and alternate storm, moisture and d. *Y.O.* 77

DROVE.

That d. them to the Bell *J.G.* 218

DROWN.

And d. him in her dry and dusty gulfs *T.* ii 149
To d. it? What is his creation less *T.* ii 200
Nor drunk enough to d. it. In the midst *T.* v 615

DROWNED.

Others, that earth, ere Sin had d. it all *A.T.* 46
For a nosegay, so dripping and d. *The Rose* 10

DROWSY.

The dozing sages drop the d. strain *Con.* 247
Grows d. as the clicking of a clock *H.* 104
Thou was not heard with d. disregard *S.* 115

DRUDGE.

Its patient d. with dry chaff and weeds *R.* 48
But ask the noble d. in state affairs *R.* 407
Scorns the base hireling, and the slavish d. *T.* 228
Thenceforth they are his cattle : d. born *T.* v 272
And teach one tyrant pity for his d. *T.* vi 728

DRUDGERY.

The poor, inured to d. and distress *H.* 7

DRUG.

Thou art indeed the d. a gardener wants *Con.* 255
A fever's agonies, and fed on d. *T.* i 446

DRUGGED.

Or do they still, as if with opium d. *T.* iv 26

DRUID.

Sat the D., hoary chief *B.* 6   [496
Thy D. struck the well strung harps they bore *Ex.*
And every hallowed D. was a bard *T.T.* 503
When our forefathers D. in their oaks *Y.O.* 10

DRUM.

He hates the field, in which no fife or d. *T.* iv 646
Playing at beat of d., their martial pranks *T.T.* 136

DRUNK.   [ii 808

Their points obtuse, and feathers d. with wine! *T.*
Enthusiasts d. with an unreal joy *P.E.* 76
And judgment d., and bribed to lose his way *P.E.* 450
And d. no moisture from the dripping clouds *T.* iii 515
All learned, and all d. ! the fiddle screams *T.* iv 478
Gloriously d., obey the important call! *T.* iv 510
Conscious of impotence they soon grow d. *T.* v 255
Nor d. enough to drown it. In the midst *T.* v 615

DRUNKARDS.

True Christians are, dissemblers, d., thieves *H.* 508
But know, the law that bids the d. die *P.E.* 199
Of d., or the music-drawing bow *St.* ii 12

DRUNKEN.

Such d. reelings, have an awkward look *Con.* 862
By d. howlings; and the chilling tale *T.* iv 562
Shall win his heart, and have his d. praise *Tir.* 215

DRUNKENNESS.   [833

Now flushed with d., now with whoredom pale *Tir.*

DRY.

And echo conversations dull and d. *Con.* 211
Reports it hot or cold, or wet or d. *Con.* 386   [721
Through the d. leaves, and pants upon the string *Ex.*
Shall shine and d. the tear *N.* 24
Its patient drudges with d. chaff and weeds *R.* 48
And all, impatient of d. land, agree *R.* 523   [614
And comforts cease. Dress drains our cellar d. *T.* ii
A sleeping fog, and fancies it d. land *T.* 4 [*T.* i 566
Which, kindled with d. leaves, just saves unquenched
That d. his feathers, saturate with dew *T.* i 494
Their ancient barriers, deluging the d. ? *T.* ii 56
And drown him in her d. and dusty gulfs *T.* ii 149
Grand caterer and d. nurse of the church *T.* ii 371
D. fern or littered hay, that may imbibe *T.* iii 476
A d. but independent crust, hard earned *T.* iv 409

DRYADS.

Nereids or D., as the fashion leads *R.* 537

DUB.

Praise his proficiency, and d. him man *P.E.* 368

DUBIOUS.

Aiding a d. and deficient sight *Ch.* 329
Man on the d. waves of error tossed *T.* 1

DUBIUS.

D. is such a scrupulous good man *Con.* 119

DUCKS.

D. paddle in the pond, before the door *R.* 499

DUCTILE.

Smooth, d., and even his fancy must flow *F.M.* 18

DUE.

Heaven awards the vengeance d. B. 42
But first the squire's, a compliment but d. Ch. 470
Springs in d. time supply for the distressed Ch. 482
They fill their measure, and receive their d. Con. 34
And in d. time feeds heartily on both Con. 338 [750
(And in d. time the world shall know it too) Con.
Lest they miscarry of what seems their d. Con. 372
For mercy shown, while wrath is justly d. Con. 492
To give the creature the Creator's d. E. ii 3
The debt, which justly became d. E. iv 23
If Vice received her retribution d. Ex. 247
Some blemish in d. time made known F. 146
And hope, in d. time, to behold Gr. 31
While Passion turns aside from its d. scope H. 113
To win d. credence to what follows next N.A. 72
To give to Virtue what is Virtue's d. P.E. 294
Assert the skies, and vindicate her d. T. 490
Praise justly d. to those that I describe T. i 180
To adorn the Sofa with eulogium d. T. iii 12
Emerging, must be deemed a labour d. T. iii 631
And surfeited lewd town with her fair d. T. iii 758
D. sustenance, or where subsist they now? T. v 79
Where all was vitreous, but in order d. T. v 161
That in d. season he forgets it too T. v. 267 [790
Holds its d. course, nor fears the frosts of age T. vi
But fairer wreaths are d., though never paid T. v 712
D. to thy last, and most effectual work T. vi 904
Claims more than half the praise as his d. share Tir. 528
Though want of d. restraint alone have bred Tir. 533
And, more than all, with commendation d. Tir. 646
Content of heart, more praises still are d. V. 90

DUEL.

A d. in the form of a debate Con. 84

DUKE.

The parson knows enough who knows a d. Tir. 403
But, having found him, be thou d. or earl Tir. 706

DULCET.

The mulberry tree was hymn'd with d. airs T. vi 687

DULCIMER.

Psaltery and sackbut, d. and flute P.E. 133

DULL.

And echo conversations d. and dry Con. 211
And chase the splenetic d. hours away Con. 582
That truth itself is in her head as d. Con. 779
And the d. service of the lip were there Ex. 44
To fill the d. vacuity till four H. 78
A d. rotation, never at a stay H. 101
And if, perchance, on some d., drizzling day H. 371
Yet this d. room, and that dark closet M.F. 4 [408
Chafed him, and brought d. nature to a glow P.E.
Ingenious to diversify d. life R. 520 [355
Then Heaven, eclipsed so long, and this d. earth R.
Envy, ye great, the d. unlettered small T. 375
Torpid and d. beneath a frozen zone T. 481
D. in design, and clumsy to perform T. i 18 [700
There touched by Reynolds, a d. blank becomes T. i
I cannot think thee yet so d. of heart T. i 651
But comes at last the d. and dusky eve T. i 669
Discourse ensues, not trivial, yet not d. T. iv 174
That drag the d. companion to and fro T. iv 368
Some have amused the d. sad years of life T. v 180
To him whose moments all have one d. pace T. v 407
D. as it is, and satisfy a law T. vi 217 [380
The knowledge of the World, and d. of thought Tir.
The punch goes round, and they are d. Y.D. 45
He was excused the penalties of d. Y.O. 156

DULNESS.

Grave without d., learned without pride Con. 609
And D. of Discretion F. 6
Or shine the d. of still life away R. 746
To palliate d., and give time a shove T. iv 210
When Labour and when D., club in hand T.T. 526

DUMB. [Con. 32

Wrath stays him, or else God would strike them d.
He might as well be blind, and deaf, and d. Con. 144
As well for them had prophecy been d. H. 255 [573
Loud when they beg, d. only when they steal T. i
Of harmless Nature, d., but yet endued T. iii 329
And makes the task his own. Inspiring d. T. vi 474
Praise him on earth, or obstinately d. Tir. 101
D. as a senator, and as a priest Tir. 424
And a complete recovery struck him d. T.T. 393

DUNCE.

How much a d. that has been sent to roam P.E. 415
Excels a d. that has been kept at home P.E. 416
Give e'en a d. the employment he desires R. 613
Proceeding soon a graduated d. T. ii 739
And many a d., whose fingers itch to write T.T. 111
Or candidly confess yourself a d. T.T. 571
Would you your son should be a sot or d. Tir. 201

DUNGEON.

But knowledge such as only d. teach Ch. 303
Upon his d. walls the lightning play H. 718
What a mere d. is this house! M.F. 2
In some unwholesome d., and a prey T. i 437
Ye d. and ye cages of despair T. v 386
Stripes, and a d.; and his body serves T. v 582

DUPE.

And made her d. see all things with her eyes) A.T. 39
The pharisee the d. of his own art Ex. 93
D. of to-morrow even from a child M.P. 41
And of all hearts sagacious d. invent P.E. 435
He that hates truth shall be the d. of lies P.E. 607
The d. of pleasure, or the slaves of gain R. 24
Such d. are men to custom, and so prone T. v 299

DURABLE.

Have a being less d. even than he P.F. 20
Twas d.; as worthless as it seemed T. v 174
That we account most d. below Y.O. 71

DURATION.

When, earth's assigned d. at an end R. 653

DURHAM'S.

Though placed in golden D.'s second stall T. 120

DUSK.

Scarce noticed in the kindred d. of eve T. iv 321

DUSKY.

And wood and lawn in d. folds enclosed A.T. 96
To them the deep recess of d. groves R. 181
But comes at last the dull and d. eve T. i 669

DUST.

As ever mingled with heroic d. Ch. 24
Their author's frailty, and return to d. Con. 554
And sift the d. behind the door E. iv 42
Cry aloud, thou that sittest in the d. Ex. 267 [303
That yields them chaff and d., and nothing more Ex.
Bids rottenness invade, and bring to d. Ex. 332
As grasshoppers, as d., a drop, a dream? Ex. 345
Kneel now, and lay thy forehead in the d. Ex. 554
Secure from collision and d. Gr. 22
Have burnt to d. a nobler pile M. i 3
Breathes clouds of d., and calls it country air R. 486
Her palaces are d. In all her streets T. ii 77 [161
Great contest follows, and much learned d. T. iii
Minute as d. and numberless, oft work T. iii 556

DUST—EAGLE

And fairly laid the zodiac in the *d. T.* iii 647
They roll themselves before him in the *d. T.* v 260
And licks the foot that treads it in the *d. T.* v 356
We turn to *d.*, and all our mightiest works *T.* v 531
And in the *d.*, sifted and searched in vain *T.* v 536
Who form'd him from the *d.*, his future grave *T.* vi 349
Doomed to the *d.*, or lodged already there *T.* i 714
The *d.* that waits upon his sultry march *T.* vi 741
The next mere *d.* and ashes in the grave *Tir.* 60
Commits her eggs, incautious, to the *d. Tir.* 791
Brings down the warrior's trophy to the *d. T.T.* 7
Start up sagacious, covered with the *d. T.T.* 170
Now, from the *d.* of ancient days, bring forth *T.T.* 376

DUSTY.
And drown him in her dry and *d.* gulfs *T.* ii 149
Like that which sends him to the *d.* grave *T.* v 609

DUTCH.
Besides, if we do, the French, *D.*, and Danes *P.A.* 9

DUTY.
And laws and *d.* are neglected things *A.T.* 33
Awake at *D.*'s call *D.W.* 42
Against the well-known *d.* of a friend *E.* iii 49
Reciprocated *d. F.* 48
Is to discharge the *d.* of his sphere *H.* 400
Adds joy to *d.*, makes me glad to pay *M.P.* 70
Are the means that *d.* urges *N.C.* 31
Peace, both the *d.* and the prize *N.G.* 37
Is *d.* a mere sport, or an employ? *R.* 649
Where *D.* bids he confidently steers *R.H.* 6
From the strict *d.* of the sacred day? *T.* 49
Expert in all the *d.* of his place *T.* 206
Than in the bounds of *d.*? What was learned *T.* ii 754
So loose to private *d.*, that no brain *T.* v 512
My share of *d.* decently fulfilled *T.* vi 1001
With decent *d.*, not ashamed to pray *Tir.* 176
As bound in *d.*, would confirm the choice *Tir.* 419
Serene, and to his *d.* much inclined *Tir.* 774
Where *D.* placed them, at their country's side *T.T.* 24
Nor draw it, but when *D.* bids him draw *T.T.* 78
As if their *d.* were a desperate task *T.T.* 313

DWARFISH.
The *d.*, in the rear retired, but still *T.* iii 594

DWELL.
Better *d.* in the midst of alarms *A.S.* 7 [*Ex.* 167
Where *d.* they now? Where dwelt in ancient day
The tender theme on which they chose to *d. Con.* 528
While yet he *d.* below, must stoop to glean *F.A.* 37
Of those that walk at evening where ye *d. H.* 472
There *d.* a consciousness in every breast *H.* 636
A nation *d.*, not envious of your throne *Her.* 49
And *d.* there in a female heart *Miss* — 1
D. there a wish in such a breast *Miss* — 5
No joy can ever *d. Miss* — 44

D. in white and black the same *N.C.* 16
There *d.* some wish in every heart *N.Y.G.* 15
Where wilt thou *d.*, if not with me *O.* ii 7
"Ah, hapless wretch! condemned to *d. P.* 5
Votaries of Pleasure, where'er she *d. R.* 539 [*T.* 229
"Where *d.* these matchless saints?" old Curio cries
By wealth or dignity, who *d.* secure *T.* i 593
Whom God delights in, and in whom He *d. T.* v 778
And equal; and he bade them *d.* in peace *T.* v 201
There *d.* the most forlorn of human kind *T.* v 397
Have ofttimes no connexion. Knowledge *d. T.* vi 89
No cat had leave to *d. T.B.* 21
As *d.* at large in Britain's chartered land *T.T.* 259
To teach, no Spirit *d.* in thee, nor voice *Y.O.* 138

DWELLER.
Vain thought! the *d.* in that still retreat *T.* i 237
The *d.* in the vales and on the rocks *T.* vi 793

DWELLING.
His *d.* a recess in some rude rock *T.* 79

DWELT. [167
Where dwell they now? Where *d.* in ancient day *Ex.*
By mummeries He that *d.* in it disdained *Ex.* 146
Where once we *d.* our name is heard no more *M.P.* 46
And still unsated, *d.* upon the scene *T.* i 158
There *d.* a sage called Discipline. His head *T.* ii 702
D. young Misagathus; a scorner he *T.* vi 485
D. visibly the light-creating God *T.* 390 [*T.T.* 168
Thus men, whose thoughts contemplative have *d.*

DWINDLED.
Have *d.* into unrespected forms *T.* i 747

DYE.
The peacock sends his heavenly *d. Mrs. M*— 3
D. them at last in all their glowing hues *Tir.* 48

DYED.
With fingers deeply *d.* in human gore *Ex.* 497
Should suffer torture, and the streams be *d. T.* vi 390
With sounding whip, and rowels *d.* in blood *T.* vi 527

DYING.
D., hurled them at the foe *B.* 40 [499
Upon the rolling chords rung out his *d.* breath *Ex.*
In *d.* sighs my little breath *G.* 11
Oh what a *d.*, *d.* close was there! *P.E.* 64
The *d.*, trembling at the awful close *T.* 436
That feeds upon the sobs and *d.* shrieks *T.* iii 328
At a safe distance, where the *d.* sound *T.* iv 92
But *d.* soon, like all terrestrial joys *T.* iv 382
At the sword's point, and *d.* the white robe *T.* iv 682
In cadence sweet, now *d.* all away *T.* vi 8
The spaniel *d.* for some venial fault *T.* vi 418
And glistening even in the *d.* eye *T.* vi 631
He thought the *d.* hour already come *T.T.* 392

E.

EAGER.
Her *e.* thought, and feeds her flowing joys *Ch.* 405
Escaped my *e.* hand *D.W.* 20
While *e.* Hodge beholds the prize *E.* iv 43
On *e.* wing the spoiler came *P.B.* 5
Thou climbest the mountain top, with *e.* eye *T.* i 664
Oh thou, whom, borne on fancy's *e.* wing *Tir.* 131
With *e.* step, and carelessly arrayed *R.* 187 [73
Truths that the learned pursue with *e.* thought *Tir.*

EAGERLY.
When, looking *e.* around *N.G.* 7

EAGLE.
And darting through his helm an *e.*'s eye *A.T.* 148

Where his *e.* never flew *B.* 31
Then the proud *e.* of all-conquering Rome *Ex.* 209
On special search, the keen-eyed *e.* blind *Ex.* 631
Where finds Philosophy her *e.* eye *T.* i 712
As if an *e.* flew aloft, and then *T.T.* 552

EAGLE-EYED.
This truth, Philosophy, though *e. T.* ii 174

EAGLE-PINIONED.
But the Muse *e.*, has in view *P.E.* 331

EAR.
While Chief Baron *E.* sat to balance the laws *A.C.* 7
Shook the young leaves about her *e. A Fable* 12
Placed with advantage at his listening *e. A.T.* 181
Fast as the thirsting *e.* can drink the sound *Ch.* 112
These have an *e.* for his paternal call *Ch.* 250
Gathering around it, with erected *e. Ch.* 516 [135
Yet, though he tease and balk your listening *e. Con.*
Nose, *e.*, and eyes seem present on the spot *Con.* 318
Is note for note deliver'd in our *e. Con.* 455
Be never named in *e.* esteemed polite *Con.* 474
His rich materials, and regale your *e. Con.* 617
Nor *e.* heard huntsman's halloo *Ep.* ii 4 [451
For *e.* and hearts that he can hope to please? *Ex.*
E. long accustomed to the pleasing lute *Ex.* 68
But raise the shrillest cry in British *e. Ex.* 271
Whoever keeps an open *e. F.* 97
Like music it tinkles and rings in your *e. F.M.* 7
His eyes shut fast, his fingers in his *e. H.* 658
And laughter sounds like madness in his *e. H.* 703
The sound of pardon pierce his startled *e. H.* 724
Brings to the distant *e.* a sullen sound *Her.* 36
Each bottle had a curling *e. J.G.* 69
But soon my *e.* caught the glad news *M.D.* 43
The sweetest that *e.* ever heard *M.D.* 18 [*N.A.* 25
With tails high mounted, *e.* hung low, and throats
Though *e.'s* she gave me two, gave me no *e. N.A.* 28
Have all articulation in his *e. N.A.* 68
Falls soporific on the listless *e. P.E.* 20
Cry in his startled *e.*, "Abstain from sin!" *P.E.* 38
The full concerto swells upon your *e. P.E.* 128
The precious stream still purling in his *e. P.E.* 232
Sounds harshly in so delicate an *e. R.* 250
Yet by his *e.* directed, guessed *R.C.* 83
Saluting his poetic *e. R.C.* 89
Legends prolix delivers in the *e. S.* i 2
Oft repeated in your *e. St.* iv 18
His measured step were governed by his *e. T.* 63
The truth is (if the truth may suit your *e. T.* 113
To soothe and satisfy the human *e. T.* 199
Come, then—a still, small whisper in your *e. T.* 297
Yield only discord in his maker's *e. T.* 386
How does it grate upon his thankless *e. T.* 465
Taught the raised shoulders to invade the *e. T.* i 67
Just undulates upon the listening *e. T.* i 175 [187
And taints the golden *e.* He springs his mines *T.* ii
From such unpleasing sounds as haunt the *e. T.* i 229
Full on the destined *e.* Wide flies the chaff *T.* i 359
Might never reach me more! My *e.* is pained *T.* ii 5
Swarms in all quarters; meets the eye, the *e. T.* ii 818
Begs a propitious *e.* for his poor thoughts *T.* iv 68
Fall a soft murmur, on the uninjured *e. T.* iv 93
May prove a trumpet, summoning your *e. T.* iv 570
Ere yet her *e.* was mistress of their powers *T.* iv 703
Shaggy, and lean, and shrewd, with pointed *e. T.* v 45
Of his lost bees to her maternal *e. T.* v 137
With music such as suits their sovereign *e. T.* v 387
And goodness infinite, but speak in *e. T.* v 854
A voice is heard that mortal *e.* hear not *T.* v 886
Your house about your *e. Pat.* 16
And, as the mind is pitch'd, the *e.* is pleased *T.* vi 2
Falling at intervals upon the *e. T.* vi 7

So bountiful, in whose attentive *e. T.* vi 460 [502
Much to persuade, he plied his *e.* with truths *T.* vi
Is but to gratify an itching *e. T.* vi 643 [318
And perks his *e.'s*, and stamps, and cries aloud *T.* vi
To charm his *e.*, whose eye is on the heart *T.* vi 1022
The leathern *e.* of stockjobbers and Jews *T.T.* 187
They cry aloud in every careless *e. T.T.* 434
Thus all success depending on an *e. T.T.* 514
So nice his *e.*, so delicate his touch) *T.T.* 653
For aided both by *e.* and scent *T.B.* 49
To *e.* and eyes, the vices of the rest *Tir.* 274
A parent pours into regardless *e. Tir.* 590
And listening close with both his *e. Tran.* iv 20
In my own *e.* such matter as I may *Y.O.* 143
Nor owed articulation to his *e. Y.O.* 148

EAR-ERECTING.
He cherups brisk his *e.* steed *T.* iii 9

EARL.
Guy *E.* of Warwick and fair Eleanore *Con.* 243
By some lewd *e.*, or rakehell baronet *P.E.* 314
But, having found him, be thou duke or *e. Tir.* 706

EARLIER.
Could fetch from records of an *e.* age *Con.* 615

EARLIEST.
By reminiscence to his *e.* date? *F.A.* 23
To one, from our *e.* youth *Gr.* 42
But down to latest age, from *e.* youth *H.* 232
Our most important are our *e.* years *P.E.* 354

EARLY.
And to say truth, though in its *e.* prime *Con.* 633
Exclaims "Prepare thee for an *e.* shroud" *Ep.* i 10
Either too *e.* or too late *Mor.* 58
The call of *e.* Spring *N.* 4
The sun accomplishing his *e.* march *N.A.* 29
What *e.* philosophic hours he keeps *R.* 429
Round Thurlow's head in *e.* youth *Th.* 1
Those blessings of our *e.* youth *The Doves* 11
There we grow *e.* grey, but never wise *T.* ii 633
But there I laid the scene. There *e.* strayed *T.* iv 697
In the low vale of life, that *e.* felt *T.* iv 799
With never cloying odours, *e.* and late *T.* vi 164
In *e.* days the conscience has in most *Tir.* 109
Our *e.* notices of truth, disgraced *Tir.* 199
We love the play-place of our *e.* days *Tir.* 297
With all the adventures of his *e.* life *Tir.* 325
In *e.* years connected, time unbinds *Tir.* 439
Hurt too perhaps for life; for *e.* wrong *Tir.* 490
Where *e.* rest makes *e.* rising sure *Tir.* 765

EARN.
And echoing praises, such as fiends might *e. Her.* 61
E. if you want; if you abound, impart *P.E.* 253
Just *e.* a scanty pittance, and at night *T.* 321
Toils much to *e.* a monumental pile *T.* i 276
Well spent in such a strife, may *e.* indeed *T.* v 715

EARNED.
As ever *e.* a lady's love in fight *A.T.* 2
And *e.* too late, it wants the grace *Mor.* 37 [*T.* vi 533
His rage grew cool; and pleased perhaps to have *e.*
That sinews bought and sold have ever *e. T.* ii 32
Well-managed shall have *e.* its worthy price *T.* iii 800
A dry but independent crust, hard *e. T.* iv 409
So Gideon *e.* a victory not his own *T.T.* 360

EARNEST.
Is given in *e.* of eternal rest *E.* ii 40

EARNESTLY.
And, occupied as *e.* as she *T.* vi 917

EARTH—EASE
121

EARTH.

Or all that this e. can afford *A.S.* 28
Others, that e., ere Sin had drowned it all *A.T.* 46
Thou that hast wasted e., and dared despise *Ch.* 69
That e. has seen, or fancy can devise *Ch.* 254
Compasses e., dives into it, ascends *Ch.* 315
Whether he measure e., compute the sea *Ch.* 353
'Tis truth divine, exhibited on e. *Ch.* 377
To be resolved into their parent e. *Ch.* 562
Its fruit on e., its growth above the skies *Ch.* 578
'Tis the most asinine employ on e. *Con.* 209 [310
To find it stuffed with brickbats, e., and stones *Con.*
For all is perfect that God works on e. *Con.* 433
The time is short, and there are souls on e. *Con.* 493
Content on e. in earthly things to shine *Con.* 583
That there are blest inhabitants of e. *Con.* 723[266
With none on e. that thou canst call thine own *Ex.*
Where Paradise seemed still vouchsafed on e. *Ex.*420
This island, spot of unreclaimed rude e. *Ex.* 468
Thy thunders travel over e. and seas *Ex.* 582
They could not purchase e. with such a prize *Ex.* 622
And this delightful e., and that fair sky *Ex.* 638
E. glitters with the drops the night distils *H.* 42
And e. has no reality but woe" *H.* 68
Hope with uplifted foot, set free from e. *H.* 161
Peace be to those (such peace as E. can give) *H.* 229
This e. shall blaze, and a new world succeed *H.* 749
That shook the circling seas and solid e. *Her.* 14
Clothes it with e., and bids the produce live *Her.* 30
E. seems a garden in its loveliest dress *Her.* 57
From loins enthroned, and rulers of the e. *M.P.*109
For baking e., or burning rock to lime *N.A.* 18
In e. dark womb have found at last a vent *N.A.* 86
From e. or hell, we can but plunge at last *N.A.* 122
Diffused, make E. the vestibule of Hell *P.E.* 465
And atheist, if E. bear so base a slave) *P.E.* 615
Till yonder heaven and e. shall mingle *P.T.* 33
Their wishes all impregnated with e. *R.* 36 [*P.E.*74
Detach the soul from e., and speed her to the skies ?
Once prone on e., now buoyant upon air *R.* 66
Despise his bulwarks, and unpeople e. *R.* 72
E. made for man, and man himself for him *R.* 116
On e. what is, seems formed indeed for us *R.* 106
Then Heaven, eclipsed so long, and this dull e. *R.* 355
E.'s millions daily fed, a world employed *R.* 553
Divide the frail inhabitants of e. *R.* 648
When, e.'s assigned duration at an end *R.* 653
To dance on e., and charm all human eyes *R.* 796
E., seas, and sun, adieu ! *St.* iii 10
Called up from E. to Heaven *St.* iii 30
To call up Plenty from the teeming *E.*—*T.* 181
No slaves on e. more welcome were than they *T.* 352
E. gives too little, giving only bread *T.* 365
Supreme on e., and worthy of the skies *T.* 408
To all on E., and to Himself above *T.* 558
Disfigures E., and, plotting in the dark *T.* i 275
Tho chequered e. seems restless as a flood *T.* i 344
The E. was made so various, that the mind *T.* i 506
And fungus fruits of e., regales the sense *T.* i 532
And must be bribed to compass e. again *T.* i 676
Not more the glory of the e. than she *T.* i 723
Of wrong and outrage with which e. is filled *T.* ii 7
And crazy e. has had her shaking fits *T.* ii 60
Displeasure in his breast who smites the e. *T.* ii 69
How does the e. receive him? with what signs *T.* ii 83
Grows fluid ; and the fixed and rooted e. *T.* ii 1
Kindled in Heaven, that it burns down to e. *T.* ii 134
The e. shall shake him out of all his holds *T.* ii 146
Were he on e., would hear, approve, and own *T.* ii 396
The solid e., and from the strata there *T.* iii 151
That He will judge the e., and call the fool *T.* iii 178
And bid them hide themselves in e. beneath *T.* iii 213
The only amaranthine flower on e. *T.* iii 268
Though placed in Paradise (for e. has still *T.* iii 298
Thrice must the voluble and restless e. *T.* iii 490
These on the warm and genial e. that hides *T.* iii 516
Oh thou resort and mart of all the e. *T.* iii 835 [645
Has made a Heaven on e.; with suns and moons *T.* iii
Assimilates all objects. E. receives *T.* iv 329 [iv 82
Heaven, e., and ocean, plundered of their sweets *T.*
From Heaven to E., of lambent flame serene *T.* v 153
Thus war began on e. ; these fought for spoil *T.* v 228
Thy native nook of e. ! Thy clime is rude *T.* v 462
Of E. and Hell confederate take away *T.* v 541[803
To e.'s acknowledged Sovereign, finds at once *T. v.*
"And stored the e. so plenteously with means *T.* v 636
Praise that from e. resulting, as it ought *T.* v 802
To gratulate the new-created e. *T.* v 820 [*T.* v 80
E. yields them nought : the imprisoned worm is safe
And Flora, and Vertumnus, peopling e. *T.* vi 234
The forms with which he sprinkles all the e. *T.* vi 246
And e. be punish'd for its tenants' sake *T.* vi 257
E. groans beneath the burden of a war *T.* vi 392
Whom once, as delegate of God on e. *T.* vi 399
But many a crime deem'd innocent on e. *T.* vi 439
Shall visit e. in mercy ; shall descend *T.* vi 743
Rivers of gladness water all the e. *T.* vi 763
E. rolls the rapturous hosanna round *T.* vi 797
All kingdoms and all princes of the e. *T.* vi 801
O Sion ! an assembly such as e. *T.* vi 816 [vi 925
Whose power is such, that whom she lifts from e. *T.*
Receive yet one, the crown of all the e. *T.* vi 856
And mischief in their hands, they roam the e. *T.* vi 896
To yon fair Sun and his attendant E. ? *Tir.* 36
If all we find possessing e., sea, air *Tir.* 91
Praise him on e., or obstinately dumb *Tir.* 101
The wretch shall rise, and be the thing on e. *Tir.* 412
To spread the e. before him, and commend *Tir.* 640
The impoverished e. ; an overbearing race *T.* iii 672
That theme on e. exhausted, though above *T.T.* 594
A soul exalted above E., a mind *T.T.* 704 [460
E. shakes beneath them, and Heaven roars above *T.T.*
To fame as lasting as the e. pretend *V.* 17
While E. wears a mantle of snow *W.N.* 13
And far the richest crown on e. 1789, 42
The good on e. they valued most 1789, 51

EARTHLY.

Content on earth in e. things to shine *Con.* 583
Denied that e. opulence they choose *Ex.* 458
If, led from e. things to things divine *H.* 141
He now perceives where e. pleasure ends *H.* 695 [78
And e. sounds, though sweet and well combined *P.E.*
The richest e. boon his hands afford *R.* 271
Yet how fallacious is all e. bliss *R.* 457
Fond of the phantom of an e. rest *R.* 764
That flattered me with hopes of e. bliss *T.* iv 696
From fool to wise, from e. to divine *T.* v 696
Ghostly in office, e. in his plan *Tir.* 422

EARTH-RUST.

Where neither grub, nor root, nor e. now *T.* v 90

EARTHQUAKE.

An e. may be bid to spare *A Fable* 34
But shipwreck, e., battle, fire, and flood *Ch.* 282
Thunder and e., and devouring flames *T.* 548

EASE.

Enjoyed at e. the genial day *A Fable* 7
Well fed, and at his e. *Beau* 2
And e. a doggish pain *Beau* 10
Gives difficulty all the grace of e. *Ch.* 110
And, Avarice being judge, with e. succeeds *Ch.* 195
Might swing at e. behind his study door *Ch.* 615
To press your point with modesty and e. *Con.* 104
A life of e. would make them harder still *E.* ii 22

That Matthew's numbers run with *e. E.* iv 67
Yet fear, youth ofttimes healthful and at *e. Ep.* i 7
Thou canst not read, with readiness and *e. Ex.* 312
And all at home is pleasure, wealth, and *e. Ex.* 583
Truths useful and attainable with *e. F.A.* 32
With *e.*, and find them nutriment; but man *F.A.* 36
And chattels of leisure and *e. Gr.* 50
Forsaking country, kindred, friends, and *e. H.* 585
(Such is his thirst of opulence and *e.) Her.* 68
To live, unblessed, in torpid *e. Miss* — 27
Have speech for him, and understood with *e. N.A.* 58
Of peace or *e.* to creatures clad as we *N.A.* 114
Not for my own content or *e. P.* 8   [41
His scruples thus silenced, Tom felt more at *e. P.A.*
Where children would with *e.* discern the way *P.E.* 434
With the same *e.* that man puts on his gown ? *P.E.* 103
The mind, impressible and soft, with *e. P.E.* 355
A just deportment, manners graced with *e. P.E.* 421
Lay his old age upon the lap of *E.—R.* 12
Contrivance intricate expressed with *e. R.* 55
God in a moment executes with *e. R.* 328
Lolls at his *e.* behind four handsome bays *R.* 392
A life of *e.* a difficult pursuit *R.* 634
Sometimes her *e.* and solace sought *R.C.* 15
Recumbent at her *e.* ere long *R.C.* 45
To blend good sense and elegance and *e. S.* ii 11
Consults all day your interest and your *e. T.* 217
Think with what pleasure, safe and at his *e. T.* 253
And cavil at with *e.*, but none refute *T.* 360
Distressed the weary loins that felt no *e. T.* i 45
Burly and big, and studious of his *e. T.* i 63
And ill at *e.* behind. The ladies first *T.* i 70 [136
That mounts the stile with *e.*, or leaps the fence *T.* i
From strenuous toil his hours of sweetest *e. T.* i 388
Like a coy maiden, *E.*, when courted most *T.* i 409
In manners—victims of luxurious *e. T.* i 625
In cities, vice is hidden with most *e. T.* i 689
And lay it at its *e.* with gentle care *T.* ii 449
And winds his way with pleasure and with *e. T.* iii 10
Me, therefore, studious of laborious *e. T.* iii 361
A faithful barrier, not o'erleaped with *e. T.* iii 681
Thus sitting, and surveying thus at *e. T.* iv 94 [iv 728
Though stretched at *e.* in Chertsey's silent bowers *T.*
With social converse and instructive *e. T.* iv 135
Thus oft reclined at *e.*, I lose an hour *T.* iv 302
Hail, therefore, patroness of health and *e. T.* iv 780
A wish for *e.* and leisure, and ere long *T.* iv 800
Found here that leisure and that *e.* I wished *T.* iv 801
Great purposes with *e.*, that turns and wields *T.* v 252
With as much *e.* as Samson his green withes *T* v 737
With *e.*, and is at large. The oppressor holds *T* v 774
And pedantry that coxcombs learn with *e. T* vi 290
Engage no notice, and enjoy much *e. T* vi 957 [118
With wholesome learning, yet acquired with *e. Tir.*
The rude will scuffle through with *e.* enough *Tir.* 340
A public school shall bring to pass with *e. Tir.* 372
No longer takes, as once, with fearless *e. Tir.* 569
And his address, if not quite French in *e. Tir.* 670
Secure and at his *e. Tran.* ii 18
Must follow royalty, then welcome *e. T.T.* 165 [764
Though Butler's wit, Pope's numbers, Prior's *e. T.T.*
To exchange content trouble, *e.* for pain *V.* 64
Fulfilled with *e.* had you been so inclined *V.* 22 [19
Seeking her food, with *e.* might have purloined *Y.O.*

EASED.
Who, if from labour *e. Miss* — 62

EASIER.
With both our eyes, is *e.* than to think *Tir.* 256
Were occupation *e.* to be found *Tir.* 701

EASIEST.
For there the game they seek is *e.* found *Tir.* 520

EASILY.
Traced *e.* to its true source above *J.T.* 45

EAST.
From *E.* to West, no sorrow can be found *Ex.* 28
Exported slavery to the conquered *E.* ? *Ex.* 365
I care not whether *e.* or north *M.B.* 21
Now shifted *e.*, and *e.* by north *P.T.* 51   [772
And aguish *e.*, till time shall have transformed *T.* iii
A prisoner in the yet undawning *e. T.* iv 130
Thy vigorous pulse, and the unhealthful *E.—T.* iv 363
A native of the gorgeous *e. Tran.* iv 2
Looks to the westward from the dappled *e. T.T.* 706

EASTERN.
Of *e.* groves, and oceans floored with ice *Ex.* 16
'Tis heard where England's *E.* glory shines *H.* 457
She spreads the morning over *e.* hills *H.* 41
No pleasure ! Has some sickly *e.* waste *P.E.* 255
Is heard salvation. *E.* Java there *T.* vi 810

EASTWARD.
Some *e.*, and some westward, and all wrong *H.* 281
Turn *e.* now, and Fancy shall apply *T.* 97

EASY.
Of dear Mat Prior's *e.* jingle *E.* iv 4
That Robert's lines are *e.* too *E.* iv 70
Manly deportment, gallant, *e.*, gay *H.* 407
But 'tis not *e.* with a mind like ours *R.* 123
'Tis such an *e.* walk, so smooth and straight *R.* 489
'Tis *e.* to resign a toilsome place *R.* 621
Heaven's *e.*, artless, unencumbered plan ! *T.* 22
Rebel, because 'tis *e.* to obey *T.* 36
Genteel in figure, *e.* in address *T.* 203
O'er all his thoughts, and swelled his *e.* sail *T.* 420
But rude at first, and not with *e.* slope *T.* i 64
With curvature of slow and *e.* sweep *T.* i 352
Is obvious, placed within the *e.* reach *T.* i 598
An *e.* reckoning, and they think the same *T.* v 278
Incurs derision for his *e.* faith *T.* v 500
With *e.* force it opens all the cells *T.* vi 11
And levying thus, and with an *e.* sway *Tir.* 611
Disease or comes not, or finds *e.* cure *Tir.* 766
The Frenchman, *e.*, debonair, and brisk *T.T.* 236
And took, too often, there his *e.* nap *T.T.* 679

EAT.
Nor did you kill that you might *e. Beau* 9
Ye worms that *e.* into the bud of youth ! *Con.* 40
And stop and *e.*, for well you may *J.G.* 191
They might with safety *e.* the rest *L.W.* 10
Mahometans *e.* up the hog *L.W.* 22
With mouths made only to grin wide and *e. R.* 309
Before he *e.* it.—'Tis the primal curse *T.* i 364
A vagabond and useless tribe there *e. T.* i 559
It is a hungry vice ;—it *e.* up all *T.* ii 680 [iii 342
Yes—thou may'st *e.* thy bread, and lick the hand *T.*
And *e.* into his bloody sword like rust *T.T.* 8

EATEN.
Till quite from tail to snout 'tis *e. L.W.* 38
And *e.* with a sigh, than to endure *T.* iv. 410

EATING.
By worms voracious *e.* through and through *T.* i 27

EAVES.
Sheltering the base with its projected *e. T.* iii 483
The sparrows peep, and quit the sheltering *e. T.* v 65

EBB.
But which, when life at *e.* runs weak and low *R.* 3
Health suffers, and the spirits *e.* ; the heart *T.* i 466

EBON. [177
Where Night, down-stooping from her *e*. throne *P.E.*
The honours of his *e*. poll *T.B.* 13

EBRIETY.
Of ruinous *e*. that prompts *T.* iv 460

ECCENTRIC.
But if *e*. ye forsake your sphere *P.E.* 98
Of modest truth for wit's *e*. range *Tir.* 174

ECHO.
And *e*. conversations dull and dry *Con.* 211
And *E*. learns politely to repeat *Con.* 827
And hills that *e*. to the distant herds *R.* 184
Hear the faint *e*. of those brazen throats *T.* iv 104
Just *e*. thine, whose features are thine own *Tir.* 846
To *e*. sigh for sigh, and groan for groan *V.* 65

ECHOING. [180
"Oh, shame!" ten thousand *e*. nymphs replied *A.T.*
And *e*. praises, such as fiends might earn *Her.* 61
Adjoining close to Kilwick's *e*. wood *N.A.* 3

ECLIPSE.
(For thou hast known *e*., and endured *Ex.* 392
The splendour of your lamps, they but *e*. *T.* i 765
To be preferred to smoke, to the *e*. *T.* iii 736
These are the charms that sully and *e*. *T.* iii 825
The *e*. that intercepts truth's heavenly beam *T.* v 683

ECLIPSED.
Then Heaven, *e*. so long, and this dull earth *R.* 355

ECLIPSING.
That, quite *e*. Pleasure's painted face *T.T.* 649

ECONOMY.
Disturbs the *e*. of Nature's realm *T.* vi 579

ECSTACY.
The visit paid, with *e*. we come *Con.* 399
And *e*. attends the tear *Miss* — 55
E. sets her stamp on every mien *P.E.* 136
To *e*. too big to be suppress'd *T.* vi 340
As *e*., unmanacled by form *T.T.* 589

ECSTATIC.
Ring with *e*. sounds unheard before *R.* 780.

EDEN.
That since the flowers of *E*. felt the blast *Con.* 751
Like *E.*'s dread probationary tree *P.E.* 468
Traces of *E*. are still seen below *R.* 28
And thou enjoy an *E*. ere it fails *R.* 364
So *E*. was a scene of harmless sport *T.* vi 364
In *E*., ere yet innocence of heart *T.T.* 584

EDGE.
What *e*. of subtlety canst thou suppose *T.* iii 206
Beguile the night, and set a keener *e*. *T.* iv 164
To a keen *e*. and made it bright for war *T.* v 216
With his sly scythe, whose ever-nibbling *e*. *Y.O.* 105

EDGED.
Streams *e*. with osiers, fattening every field *H.* 47

EDIFICE.
Of the *e*. that policy has raised *T.* ii 817

EDIFIED.
Whoe'er was *e*., themselves were not! *T.* ii 444
Doubtless, much *e*., and all refreshed *T.* vi 693

EDIFYING.
Their weekly dole of *e*. strains *T.* v 646

EDMONTON.
Unto the Bell at *E*.—*J.G.* 11

Of *E*. so gay *J.G.* 136
At *E*., his loving wife *J.G.* 141
If wife should dine at *E*.—*J.G.* 195

EDUCATION.
That *E*. gives her, false or true *P.E.* 358
Say, muse (for *e*. made the song *Tir.* 290
Were *e*., else so sure to fail *Tir.* 702
From *e*., as the leading cause *Tir.* 911
Whom *E*. stiffens into state *T.T.* 125

EDUCE.
From mere minutiæ can *e*. *E.* i 75
Yet has the wondrous virtue to *e*. *H.* 155

EDWARD.
And the sixth *E*., grace the historic page *T.T.* 106

EFFACED.
Still outlives many a storm that has *e*. *M.P.* 56
Till Cæsar's image is *e*. at last *P.E.* 280
Then were not all *e*.; then speech profane *T.* iv 522
Soon lose their credit, and are all *e*. *Tir.* 200

EFFECT.
E. of punishment and wrath divine *A.T.* 51
Oh! never seen but in thy blest *e*. *Ch.* 7
Thy worst *e*. is banishing for hours *Con.* 253
(Hardly the *e*. of inclination *E.* i 99
With less excuse, and, haply, worse *e*.?" *F.A.* 17
The dire *e*. of mercy without price! *H.* 496
And the world's hatred, as its sure *e*. *T.* 282
O blessed *e*. of penury and want *T.* 361
Need other physic none to heal the *e*. *T.* i 590
Resolving all events, with their *e*. *T.* ii 163
By necessary laws their sure *e*. *T.* ii 192
Suspend the *e*., or heal it? Has not God *T.* ii 197
Of grossest nature and of worst *e*. *T.* ii 689
The grand *e*.; acknowledges with joy *T.* iii 227
Of their complete *e*. Much yet remains *T.* iii 605
The *e*. of laziness or sottish waste *T.* iv 431
Works the deplored and mischievous *e*. *T.* iv 616
Whose word leaps forth at once to its *e*. *T.* v 686
Familiar with th' *e*. we slight the cause *T.* vi 121
Nature is but a name for an *e*. *T.* vi 223
(O wonderful *e*. of music's power!) *T.* vi 636
Different in size, but in *e*. the same *Tir.* 516
Alas, poor boy!—the natural *e*. *Tir.* 575
Blushed that *e*. like these she should produce *T.T.* 326
A dire *e*., by one of Nature's laws *T.T.* 442
'Tis but the natural *e*. 1789, 68

EFFECTUAL.
When, snatched from all *e*. aid *Cast.* 63
Not less *e*. than what Love bestows *Ch.* 483
And thanks for this *e*. close *G.* 14
The most important and *e*. guard *T.* ii 335
Sovereign, and most *e*., to secure *T.* ii 590
Due to thy last and most *e*. work *T.* vi 904

EFFEMINACY.
But that *e*., folly, lust *T.T.* 394

EFFEMINATES.
Frown at *e*., whose very looks *T.* ii 223

EFFERVESCENCE.
Without an *e*. *F.* 129

EFFORT.
Alas! his *e*. double his distress *Con.* 343
That, after many a. vain *F.B.* 16
Were but the feeble *e*. of a child *T.* 578
The firstborn *e*. of my youthful muse *T.* iv 701
The struggling *e*. of my boyish tongue *T.* iv 711
Almost without an *e*., plans too vast *T.* v 253

Their *e.*, yet resolved with one consent *T.* vi 338
And every *e.* ends in push-pin play *T.T.* 547
Judged every *e.* of the Muse a crime *T.T.* 617

EFFRONTERY.
With them is courage; his *e.* wit *Tir.* 227

EGG.
Her new-laid *e.* she fondly pressed *A Fable* 2
Four ivory *e.* soon pave its floor *A Tale* 41
Remorse the fatal *e.* by Pleasure laid *P.E.* 239
Themselves were chilled, their *e.* were addled *P.T.* 55
The *e.* was laid from which he sprung *T.B.* 8
Should never game-fowl hatch her *e.* again *T.* iii 312
Enjoyed, spare feast! a radish and an *e.*! *T.* iv 173
Too proud for dairy work, or sale of *e. T.* iv 549
Commits her *e.*, incautious to the dust *Tir.* 791
Didst burst thine *e.*, as theirs the fabled twins *Y.O.* 35

EGLANTINE.
Nor grateful *e.* regales the smell *H.* 471

EGREGIOUS.
E. purpose! worthily begun *Tir.* 404

EGRESS.
Asks *e.*; which obtained, the overcharged *T.* iii 497

EGYPT.
Let *E.* plagues, and Canaan's woes proclaim *Ex.* 168
Of Light Divine. But *E.*, Greece, and Rome *T.* ii 500
Polluting *E.*: gardens, fields, and plains *T.* ii 828

EIGHT.
E. years and five round-rolling moons *Ep.* ii 29
E. hundred of the brave *R.G.* 5
And He and his *E.* Hundred *R.G.* 35

EIGHTEEN.
The management of tyros of *e. Tir.* 220

EIGHTY-EIGHT.
For then the clouds of *e.* 1789, 36

EIGHTY-NINE.
In memorable *e.* 1789, 31
The spring of *e.* shall be 1789, 32

EKE.
A trainband captain *e.* was he *J.G.* 3
And *e.* with all his might *J.G.* 92
And *e.* did rear right merrily, two staves *T.* vi 662

ELAPSED.
Twelve years have *e.* since I last took a view *P.F.* 5
Long time *e.* or e'er our rugged sires *T.* i 68
That hour *e.*, the incurable revolt *T.T.* 402
Ages *e.* ere Homer's lamp appeared *T.T.* 556

ELASTIC.
Or when it first forsakes the *e.* string *P.E.* 573
The *e.* spring of an unwearied foot *T.* i 135
His form robust and of *e.* tone *T.T.* 218

ELBOW.
All *e.* shake. Look in, and you would swear *P.E.* 129
Her *e.* pinioned close upon her hips *T.* 133
But *e.* still were wanting; these, some say *T.* i 60
The soft Settee; one *e.* at each end *T.* i 75
And in the midst an *e.* it received *T.* i 76
Convenience next suggested *e.* chairs *T.* i 87
Till prostitution *e.* us aside *T.* iii 60
Grow on the gamester's *e.*, and the alert *T.* iii 761
And bored with *e.* points through both his sides *T.* iv 44
Her *e.* ruffled, and her tottering form *T.* iv 545 [160
Leaned on her *e.*, watching Time, whose course *Y.O.*

ELEANORE.
Guy Earl of Warwick and fair *E. Con.* 243

ELECT.
The sacramental host of God's *e. T.* ii 349

ELECTION.
And having made *e. F.* 153

ELECTIVE.
Man, thus endued with an *e.* voice *P.E.* 45

ELEGANCE.
A sense of *e.* we rarely find *R.* 501
Bids these in *e.* of form excel *R.* 793
To blend good sense and *e.* and ease *S.* ii 11
A real *e.*, a little used *T.* ii 611
But *e.*, chief grace the garden shows *T.* iii 638

ELEGANT.
Wreathed into an *e.* bow *Gr.* 7
E. phrase, and figure formed to please *P.E.* 422
This *e.* rose, had I shaken it less *The Rose* 17
The jasmine, throwing wide her *e.* sweets *T.* vi 173
E. as simplicity, and warm *T.T.* 588

ELEGANTLY.
Some mansion, neat and *e.* dressed *T.* 250
Though well perfumed and *e.* dressed *T.* vi 991

ELEMENT.
Still to that *e.* from which she rose *Con.* 266
And fit the limpid *e.* for use *T.* i 374
Your *e.*; there only ye can shine *T.* i 758
And by the voice of all its *e. T.* ii 52
The very *e.*, though each be meant *T.* ii 137
That having wielded th' *e.*, and built *T.* iii 170
Of *e.* tumultuous, in whom lust *T.* v. 308
The infant *e.* received a law *T.* vi 200
Nature in arms, her *e.* at strife *T.T.* 448
And, all the *e.* thy puny growth *Y.O.* 38

ELEVATED.
Borne far away on *e.* wings *A.T.* 31
Your *e.* voice goes through the brain *Con.* 328
And bruised the side, and, *e.* high *T.* i 66
Its *e.* site forbids the wretch *T.* i 239

ELEVATION.
Exhibits *e.*, drawings, plans *P.E.* 397
Of *e.* down into the abyss *T.* ii 93
"If from your *e.*, whence ye view *T.* v. 825

ELI.
Except a few with *E.*'s spirit blest *Ex.* 448

ELIGIBLE.
I sought an *e.* theme 1789, 8

ELIJAH.
And say, as stern *E.* said of old *Con.* 850
With all *E.*'s dignity of tone *H.* 624

ELISHA.
E.'s eye, that, when Gehazi strayed *Tir.* 267

ELL.
An *e.* or two of prospect we command *T.T.* 581

ELM. [230
Rough *e.*, or smooth-grained ash, or glossy beech *R.*
Stand, never overlooked, our favourite *e. T.* i 167
Environed with a ring of branching *e. T.* i 223
Of deeper green the *e.*; and deeper still *T.* i 312

Between the upright shafts of whose tall *e. T.* i 355
For ere the beech and *e.* have cast their leaf *T.* iii 466
The walk, still verdant, under oaks and *e. T.* vi 70 [29
Where chance may throw me, beneath *e.* or vine *T.* iii
Drawn from his refuge in some lonely *e. T.* vi 310

ELOPE. [876
That, since thy strength must with thy years *e. Tir.*

ELOQUENCE.
His happy *e.* seemed there at home *Con.* 622
Nor all an angels's *e.* explain *H.* 126
Not all whose *e.* the fancy fills *P.E.* 13
Where *e.* and artifice shall fail *R.* 658
With spirit, genius, *e.*, supplied *T.* 305
And Chatham's *e.* to marble lips *T.* i 704
Of patriot *e.* to flash down fire *T.* ii 217
With *e.* that agonies inspire *T.* iii 330
Here rills of oily *e.* in soft *T.* iv 64
"Discernment, *E.* and Grace *Th.* 9

ELOQUENT.
As honest and more *e.* than mine *J.T.* 8
Harangued him thus, right *e. N.G.* 14
Though *e.* themselves, yet fear to break *T.* iv 54

ELUDE.
Where nought *e.* the persevering quest *H.* 445
Man is a harp whose chords *e.* the sight *R.* 325 [204
The cause, though worth the search, may yet *e. T.T.*

ELVES.
Peace to the phlegm of sullen *e. Miss* — 61

ELY.
So in the chapel of old *E.* House *T.* vi 658

ELYSIAN.
Shall steep me in *E.* reverie *M.P.* 19
O Nature! whose *E.* scenes disclose *R.* 199

ELYSIUM.
The balm of care, *E.* of the mind *P.E.* 180

EMANCIPATE.
That parts us, are *e.* and loosed *T.* ii 39
Familiar, serve to *e.* the rest! *T.* v 298

EMANCIPATED.
The soul, *e.*, unoppressed *T.T.* 272

EMBALMS.
No bard *e.* and sanctifies his song *T.* v 728

EMBALMED.
E. for ever in its own perfume *Con.* 632

EMBATTLED.
And roofs *e.* high, the gloomy scenes *T.* ii 122
And through the trees I view the *e.* tower *T.* vi 66
I read of bright *e.* fields 1789, 3

EMBELLISH.
May Mercury once more *e.* man *Con.* 833
Such lofty strains *e.* what you teach *T.T.* 478

EMBELLISHED.
Then, whether *e.* or rude *C.* 35
E. with—"He said," and "So said I" *Con.* 212

EMBELLISHING.
E. the scene around *P.* 58

EMBELLISHMENT.
Rich in *e.* as strong *Dr.* 11

EMBERS.
The few small *e.* left she nurses well *T.* iv 383

EMBITTERING.
E. all his state *Trans. H.* 12

EMBITTERS.
That civil war *e.* all his life *T.* 468

EMBLEM.
Apt *e.* of a virtuous maid *Comp.* ii 2
E. of health and heavenly aid *Q.V.* 47
Forth steps the man *e.* of myself *T.* i 213
And spades, the *e.* of untimely graves *T.* iv 219
There, like the visionary *e.* seen *T.* v 400

EMBLEMATIC.
Behold in Ætna's *e.* fires *Her.* 45

EMBODIED.
"Ordained to guide the *e.* spirit home *T.* v. 840

EMBOSS.
Or blushing crabs, or berries that *e. T.* i 121
The studs that thick *e.* his iron door *T.* v 426

EMBOSSED.
The sunbeam; there, *e.* and fretted wild *T.* v 118
Upheaved above the soil, and sides *e. Y.O.* 65

EMBOWELLED.
E. now, and of thy ancient self *Y.O.* 110

EMBOWERED.
Look where he comes; in this *e.* alcove *R.* 283

EMBRACE.
Includes creation in her close *e. Ch.* 598
Straitening its growth by such a strict *e. R.* 234
And gives his direst foe a friend's *e. T.* ii 270
His works. Admitted once to his *e. T.* v 780
Unless the world were all prepared to *e. Tir.* 917

EMBRACED.
But still, whoever wooed her, or *e. A.T.* 36

EMBROIDERED.
Sweet Nature, stripped of her *e.* robe *Her.* 79
And see where it has hung the *e.* banks *T.* v 107

EMBROIDERY.
With all the *e.* of poetic dreams *Ex.* 234

EMBRYO.
And all thine *e.* vastness, at a gulp *Y.O.* 22

EMERGE.
If such escape contagion, and *e. T.* ii 797
More ardent as the disk *e.* more *T.* v 4

EMERGED.
E. all splendour in our isle at last *T.T.* 565

EMERGENCE.
Not he, but his *e.*, forced the door *Ch.* 188

EMERGING.
E., must be deemed a labour due *T.* iii 631
"From the green wave *e.*, darts an eye *T.* v 835

EMETIC.
How an *e.* or cathartic sped *Con.* 316
O nauseous!—an *e.* for a whet! *P.E.* 222

EMINENCE.
Directs thee to that *e.* they reached *Ex.* 657
How oft upon yon *e.* our pace *T.* i 154
To *e.* fit only for a God *T.* v. 284
His cloud-capped *e.* divide *Trans. H.* 17

EMINENT.
One *e.* above the rest for strength *T.* v. 231

EMITS.
Of controversial rage *e. F.* 104

EMOLLIENTS.
And such *e.* as his friends could spare *R.* 305

EMOLUMENT.
Of honours, or *e.*, or fame *T.* iv 785
Her honours, her *e.*, her joys *T.* vi 923

EMOTION.
Watch his *e.*, and control their tide *Tir.* 610

EMPEROR.
Once on a time an *E.*, a wise man *E.* iii 46

EMPHASIS.
The *e.* in score, and gives to prayer *T.* ii 360
And by an *e.* of interest his *T.* v 749

EMPHATIC.
Named with *e.* dignity, "The Tower" *Ch.* 550
The *e.* speaker dearly loves to oppose *Con.* 269

EMPIRE.
Rome, for *e.* far renowned *B.* 17
E. is on us bestowed *B.* 43
The seat of *e.* is her cheeks *L.R.* 27
Its *e.* is not hers, not is it thine *R.* 277
A falling *e.*, hasten its decay *R.* 384
Our arch of *e.*, steadfast but for you *T.* i 773
True, we have lost an *e.*—let it pass *T.* ii 263
Of all your *e.*; that where Britain's power *T.* ii 46
Convened for purposes of *e.* less *T.* iii 62
With all thy loss of *e.*, and though squeezed *T.* v 457
Vast was his *e.*, absolute his power *T.* vi 357
His right of *e.* over all that lives *Tir.* 4

EMPIRICS.
Two *e.* he stands, and with swoln cheeks *T.* ii 352

EMPLOY.
"Ye fair Circassians! all your lutes *e. A.T.* 107
God's gift with pleasure in his praise *e. Ch.* 252
She sees a world stark blind to what *e. Ch.* 404
If Self *e.* us, whatsoe'er is wrought *Ch.* 569
As alphabets in ivory *e. Con.* 11
'Tis the most asinine *e.* on earth *Con.* 209
Some men *e.* their health, an ugly trick *Con.* 311
E. our present thoughts and pains *E.* i 51
Called thee away from peaceable *e. Ex.* 534
Not kindred minds alone are called to *e. H.* 738
Ye devotees to your adored *e. P.E.* 75
Turtle and venison all his thoughts *e. P.E.* 220
The sacred implement I now *e. P.E.* 301
His hours of leisure and recess *e. R.* 215
A secret thirst of his renounced *e. R.* 474
He pressed him much to quit his base *e. R.* 594
Is duty a mere sport, or an *e.? R.* 649
Is occupied as well, *e.* his hours *R.* 507
E., shut out from more important views *R.* 803
Nature inanimate *e.* sweet sounds *T.* 197
What glowing thanks his lips and heart *e. T.* 255
And did He not of old *e.* his means *T.* ii 199
Servile *e.*; but such as may amuse *T.* iii 406
All healthful, are the *e.* of rural life *T.* iii 625
Like those which modern senators *e. T.* iv 490
New faculties, or learns at least to *e. T.* v 806
One song *e.* all nations; and all cry *T.* vi 791
Churchmen, in whose esteem their blest *e. Tir.* 823
Wouldst thou, possessor of a flock, *e. Tir.* 905
E. his philosophic pate *Tran.* ii 23
His humorous talent next *e. Tran.* iv 26
When themes like these *e.* the poet's tongue *T.T.* 198
Let Discipline *e.* her wholesome arts *T.T.* 310
If Flattery, Folly, Lust, *e.* the pen *T.T.* 761

EMPLOYED.
Far other dreams his feverish mind *e. A.T.* 153
Scripture *e.* to sanctify the cheat *Ex.* 92
Nature, *e.* in her allotted place *H.* 145
E. to calculate the enormous sum *P.E.* 486
For threescore years *e.* with ceaseless care *R.* 37
Earth's millions daily fed, a world *e. R.* 553
A mind *e.* on so sublime a theme *R.* 668
My creed persuades me well *e.*, may save *T.* 522
Than when *e.* to accommodate the fair *T.* i 73
Happy the man who sees a God *e. T.* ii 161
Treads on thy sweeping train; one hand *e. T.* iv 247
That even our enemies, so oft *e. T.* v 391
With means that were not till by thee *e. T.* v 850
Witty, and well *e.*, and, like thy Lord *Tir.* 139
The bench on which we sat while deep *e. Tir.* 302
Of argument, *e.* too oft amiss *Y.O.* 31

EMPLOYMENT.
With the double *e.* of mallet and mill *F.M.* 16
So well that thought the *e.* seems to suit *P.E.* 132
Give e'en a dunce the *e.* he desires *R.* 613
How various his *e.* whom the world *T.* iii 352

EMPOWERED.
Were I *e.* to regulate the lists *Con.* 195

EMPTINESS.
From *e.* itself a real use *H.* 156

EMPTY.
By lean despair upon an *e.* purse *Ch.* 506
An oracle within an *e.* cask *Con.* 298
Lavish of life, to win an *e.* tomb *Ex.* 522
Such cause of terror in an *e.* sound *N.A.* 130
But sighs at thought of *e.* pockets *P.B.* 26
Though busy, trifling; *e.* though refined *P.E.* 426
In an old *e.* watering pot *R.C.* 16
Or all that we have left, is *e.* talk *T.* ii 253
Strutting and vapouring in an *e.* school *T.* ii 330
Most part an *e.* ineffectual sound *T.* iii 22
Dreams *e.* dreams. The million flit as gay *T.* iii 133
Of dropping buckets into *e.* wells *T.* iii 189
Imparting substance to an *e.* shade *T.* iv 527
A trifler vain, and *e.* of all good *Tir.* 754

EMULATE.
Nice-fingered Art must *e.* in vain *T.* 202

EMULATION.
Whose toe of *e.* treads too near *R.* 442
Then study languished, *E.* slept *T.* ii 734
And *e.* is its specious name *Tir.* 469
And *e.*, as engendering hate *Tir.* 497

EMULOUS.
E. always of the nearest place *H.* 238

ENACTING.
So frail a kind, and then *e.* laws *T.* v 640

ENAMOURED.
And daily more *e.* of the cheat *P.E.* 524
E. of its harm! *St.* v 14
For me, *e.* of sequestered scenes *T.* iii 27
Thee too *e.* of the life I loved *T.* iv 718

ENCHANT.
Whate'er *e.* them, are no snares to them *R.* 180
The prospect such as might *e.* despair *R.* 469

ENCHANTED.
That he was cased in such *e.* steel *A.T.* 183
Perhaps, *e.* with the love of fame *Ch.* 539
My poems *e.* I view *Gr.* 30

ENCHANTING.
Nature, *e*. Nature, in whose form *T*. iii 721
E. music and immortal wreaths *T*. iv 687
E. novelty, that moon at full *T*. vi 706

ENCHANTMENT.
His morning course, the *e*. was begun *P.E.* 68
Are all *e*. in a case like thine *R*. 261

ENCHANTRESS.
Delighted with her babe, the *e*. smiled *A.T.* 9

ENCLOSED.
But man, within a wider pale *e*. *A.T.* 59
And wood and lawn in dusky folds *e*. *A.T.* 96
You, in your grotto-work *e*. *P*. 49
But that the lord of this *e*. demesne *T*. i 331
Or Inspiration teaches; and *e*. *T*. i 628

ENCLOSURE.
O blessed within the *e*. of your rocks *H*. 465
Then snug *e*. in the sheltered vale *T*. i 513

ENCOMIUM.
E. in old time was poet's work *T*. vi 715

ENCOMPASSING.
E. his throne a few short years *T.T.* 132

ENCOUNTER.
They should *e*. with well loaded fists *Con*. 196
Of half the toils they must *e*. there *R*. 610

ENCOURAGE.
Was to *e*. goodness. He would stroke *T*. ii 710
He can *e*. slavery to a smile *T.T* 252
Or better managed, or *e*. less *Tir*. 922

ENCOURAGEMENT.
Here see the *e*. Grace gives to vice *H*. 495
Of warm *e*., and in the eye *T*. i 695

ENCOURAGING.
And Mercy, *e*. thought! *A.S.* 54

ENCROACH.
That man should thus *e*. on fellow man *T*. v. 435

ENCROACHING.
And hates him for *e*. *F*. 84.
The *e*. nuisance asks a faithful hand *Tir*. 601

ENCROACHMENT.
That dread the *e*. of our growing streets *R*. 482

ENCUMBERED. [646
Of close-rammed stones has charged the *e*. soil *T*. iii
Shakes her *e*. lap, and casts them out *T*. iv 499
The plentiful moisture *e*. the flower *The Rose* 3
Though laden, not *o*. with her spoil *Tir*. 17

ENCUMBRANCE.
Account him an *e*. on the state *T*. vi 958

END. [*A.T.* 127
Lest Rome should *e*. with her first founders' lives
To thwart its influence, and its *e*. defeat *Ch*. 38
Wise to promote whatever *e*. he means *Ch*. 87
All bonds of nature, in that moment *e*. *Ch*. 142
Whose Love knew no beginning, knows no *e*. *Ch*. 400
Perhaps—whatever *e*. he might pursue *Ch*. 541
His wise forbearance has their *e*. in view *Con*. 33
Mankind from quarrels, but their fatal *e*. *Con*. 174
And let them guide you to a decent *e*. *Con*. 220
Ere yet they brought their journey to an *e*. *Con*. 521
Rose answers every common *e*. *E*. i 2
Bent all on pleasure, heedless of its *e*. *E*. ii 18

"'Tis but a step, sir, just at the street's *e*." *E*. iii 26
For vicious *e*. connected *F*. 42
That their Creator had no serious *e*. *H*. 130
That folly *e*. where genuine Hope begins *H*. 637
He now perceives where earthly pleasure *e*. *H*. 695
On application to its noblest *e*. *J.T.* 28
But where will fierce contention *e*. *L.R.* 4
On so desirable an *e*. *Mor*. 34
And if, ere he attain his *e*. *Mor*. 53
Can trace her mazy windings to their *e*. *P.E.* 16
Sniveling and driveling folly without *e*. *P.E.* 310
He dies disputing, and the contest *e*. *P.E.* 553
Calls him away from selfish *e*. and aims *R*. 19 [645
Whence, and what are we? to what *e*. ordained ? *R*.
From mighty means to more important *e*. *R*. 112
When, earth's assigned duration at an *e*. *R*. 653
Or stabbed a man to serve some private *e*.? *T*. 47
Devised by self to answer selfish *e*. *T*. 110 [439
Where should they find (those comforts at an *e*.) *T*.
With designation of the finger's *e*. *Tir*. 641
The soft Settee; one elbow at each *e*. *T*. i 75
To wait the close of all? But grant her *e*. *T*. ii 65
That trust them, and in the *e*. disclose a face *T*. ii 693
He shuts it close, and the first labour *e*. *T*. iii 489
And Katerfelto, with his hair on *e*. *T*. iv 86
When shall I find an *e*., or how proceed? *T*. iv 233
Dangled along at the cold finger's *e*. *T*. iv 392
Ten thousand seek an unmolested *e*. *T*. v 87
Which heaven has heard for ages, have an *e*. *T*. vi 730
Of God and man, and peaceful in its *e*. *T*. vi 999
His being *e*. where death dissolves the bond *Tir*. 67
And ending, if at last its *e*. be gained *Tir*. 408 [487
The *e*., though plausible, not worth the means *Tir*.
And his *e*. sure, without one glimpse of hope *Tir*. 427
Are a stream choked, or trickling to no *e*. *Tir*. 718
To compass that good *e*., forecast the means *Tir*. 884
And every effort *e*. in push-pin play *T.T.* 547

ENDEAR.
That such short absence may *e*. it more *T*. i 517
When having no stake left, no pledge to *e*. *T*. iii 791
Raging abroad, and the rough wind, *e*. *T*. iv 309

ENDEARED.
Of hours that sorrow since has much *e*. *T*. i 117
Connexion formed for interest, and *e*. *Tir*. 495

ENDEARMENTS.
Upon the *e*. of domestic life *T*. v 438
Denied the *e*. of thine eye *The Doves* 35

ENDEARING.
Some cordial *e*. report *A.S.* 35
All this, and more *e*. still than all *M.P.* 64

ENDEAVOUR.
E. laudable engage *Mor*. 50
His high *e*., and his glad success *T*. v 901
Prompt his *e*., and engage his aim *T.T.* 747

ENDED.
My ramble *e*., I returned *D.W.* 29
Nor yet when eventide was *e*. *N.G.* 4

ENDING.
Runs round; still *e*., and beginning still *T*. iii 627
"From toilsome life to never *e*. rest *T*. v 841
And *e*., if at last its end be gained *Tir*. 408

ENDLESS.
And gains new vigour at her *e*. task *Ch*. 104
Fixed in the rolling flood of *e*. years *Con*. 557
A harbinger of *e*. good *E*. i 90
" Matthew" says Fame " with *e*. pains *E*. iv 73
Designed, in honour of his *e*. love *H*. 121

The brightest wonders of an *e.* day *H.* 753
Craze antiquarian brains with *e.* doubt *P.E.* 394
Thou ever bubbling spring of *e.* lies *P.E.* 467
An *e.* life above? *St.* vi 16
That *e.* bliss (how strange soe'er it seem) *T.* 355
Ten thousand sages lost in *e.* woe *T.* 517
By *e.* riot, Vanity, the Lust *T.* iii 812
With intellects bemazed in *e.* doubt *T.* v 848
And *e.* her increase. Thy rams are there *T.* vi 804

ENDOWED.
Where will you find a race like theirs *e. Ex.* 195
The soldier thus *e.*, who never shrinks *H.* 409
Men well *e.*, of honourable parts *Tir.* 836

ENDUED.
Fancy *e.* her in her natal hour) *A.T.* 92
So it is, when the mind is *e. C.* 33
E. with reason, yet by nature blind *Ch.* 382
Man, thus *e.* with an elective voice *P.E.* 45
Of harmless Nature, dumb, but yet *e. T.* iii 329
Refinement is *e.*, thrice happy thou! *T.* iv 359
E. with reason only to descry *Tir.* 61

ENDURE.
Nor would *e.* that any should control *Ch.* 33
And each *e.*, while yet he draws his breath *Ch.* 143
All other sorrows virtue may *e. Ch.* 157
Through wintry rigours unimpaired *e. Con.* 650
Such as a friend but ill *e. F.* 155
And will, with sympathy *e. M.F.* 57
Whatever evil it *e. P.* 42
Though some folks can't *e.* them *Pat.* 18
He just *e.*, and, with a sickly spleen *R.* 565
All plants of every leaf, that can *e. T.* iii 580
Few self-supported flowers *e.* the wind *T.* iii 657
And eaten with a sigh, than to *e. T.* iv 410
But once enslaved, farewell! I could *e. T.* v 477
In heaven-renouncing exile, he *e. T.* v 598
The playful humour; he could now *e. T.* vi 47
In his dishonor'd works himself *e. T.* vi 821
And evils not to be endured *e. Tir.* 276
Thine *e.* the winter long *Tran.* iii 22
That neither gave nor would *e.* offence *T.T.* 639
The tædium that the lazy rich *e. T.T.* 742

ENDURED.
(For thou hast known eclipses, and *e. Ex.* 392
He does not scorn it, who has long *e T.* i 445
Contracts defilement not to be *e. T.* iv 670
And evils not to be *e.* endure *Tir.* 276

ENDUREST.
E. the brunt, and darest defy them all *Ex.* 697

ENDURING.
A more *e.* date *Cast.* 58
But unrepealable *e.* death *T.* v 610

ENEMY.
Calls thee to cope with *e.*, and first *R.* 267
Has made, what *e.* could ne'er have done *T.* i 772
Make *e.* of nations who had else *T.* ii 18
Of flowers, that feared no *e.* but warmth *T.* v 159
That even our *e.*, so oft employed *T.* v 391

ENERGETIC.
Expressive, *e.*, and refined *Ex.* 482

ENERGY.
Or sought with *e.*, must fill the void *R.* 748
By native power and *e.* her own *T.* 396
Of all-creating *e.* and might *T.* v 554
Where now the vital *e.* that mov'd *T.* vi 134
To press with *e.* your ardent thought *V.* 10

ENERVATE.
E. and enfeeble, and needs must *T.T.* 395

ENFEEBLE.
E. his affection *F.* 156
Enervate and *e.*, and needs must *T.T.* 395

ENFOLDS.
As the leaf that *e.* what an invalid swallows *F.M.* 22

ENFORCE.
Not that I mean to approve, or would *e. R.* 117
To *e.* the wrong, for such a worthy cause *T.* ii 14
Will need no stress of argument to *e. Tir.* 803

ENFORCED.
On pangs *e.* with God's severest stroke *R.* 314

ENGAGE.
That men *e.* in it impelled by force *Con.* 179
Whom all the vanities they scorned *e. Ex.* 661
If arms *e.* him, he devotes to sport *H.* 207
Could bend one knee, *e.* one votary there *H.* 506
Virtue *e.* his assent *H.F.* 11
Endeavours laudable *e. Mor.* 50
'Tis a sight to *e.* me, if anything can *P.F.* 17
No narrow bounds; her cause *e.* him *T.* v 395
E. no notice, and enjoy much ease *T.* vi 957
'Twere well with most if books that could *e. Tir.* 147
At stated hours, his freakish thoughts *e. Tir.* 606
The fleeting forms of majesty *e. T.T.* 117
Will win her visits or *e.* her stay *T.T.* 411
Prompt his endeavour, and *e.* his aim *T.T.* 747

ENGAGED.
E. myself to be at home *M.F.* 12
That first *e.* him in the chase" *Mor.* 38
But triflers are *e.* and cannot come *P.E.* 167
Has business; feels himself *e.* to achieve *T.* iii 377
E. my wonder, and admiring still *T.* iv 715

ENGAGEMENT.
No. But his own *e.* binds him fast *P.E.* 106
From all his wearisome *e.* freed *R.* 513

ENGAGING.
And asked them, with a kind, *e.* air *Con.* 523
Delights us, by *e.* our respect *P.E.* 208

ENGENDER.
Few competitions but *e.* spite *Con.* 161
Or lust *e.*, and indulgence feeds *R.* 644

ENGENDERED.
That Pity had *e.*, drop one here *H.* 677

ENGENDERING.
And emulation, as *e.* hate *Tir.* 497

ENGINE.
In an *e.* of utmost mechanical strength *F.M* 4

ENGINEERING.
Though all your *e.* proves in vain *P.E.* 321

ENGLAND.
Might traverse *E.* safely to and fro *E.* iii 61
Why weeps the Muse for *E.* ? What appears *Ex.* 1
In *E.'s* case to move the Muse to tears? *Ex.* 2
Then wherefore weep for *E.*? What appears *Ex.* 30
In *E.'s* case to move the Muse to tears? *Ex.* 31
'Tis heard where *E.'s* Eastern glory shines *H.* 457
Men from *E.* bought and sold me *N.C.* 5
What are *E.'s* rights, I ask *N.C.* 10
For no such sight had *E.'s* Queen *Q.V.* 25
The tears that *E.* owes. *R.G.* 28
Full charged with *E.'s* thunder *R.G.* 31

ENGLAND—ENLISTED

(Attentive when thou readest) of *E.'s* peers *S.* i 3
For sight of ship from *E.* Every speck *T.* i 666
Slaves cannot breath in *E.*; if their lungs *T.* ii 40
Far guiltier *E.*! lest he spare not thee *T.* ii 160
E., with all thy faults, I love thee still *T.* ii 206 [226
Should *E.* prosper, when such things, as smooth *T.* ii
Consulting *E.'s* happiness at home *T.* ii 246
That picked the jewel out of *E.'s* crown *T.* ii 265
And folly in the heart; were *E.* now *T.* iii 742
What *E.* was, plain, hospitable, kind *T.* iii 743
And king in *E.* too, he may be weak *T.* v 337
For *E.'s* glory, seeing it wax pale *T.* v 510
Where *E.*, stretch'd towards the setting sun *T.* vi 483
Blest *E.*, if this happiness be thine! *T.T.* 82
Poor *E.*! thou art a devoted deer *T.T.* 362
That threatened *E.'s* trembling state 1789, 37

ENGLISH.

We *E.* often stood *A Tale* 74
Or building hospitals on *E.* ground? *Ch.* 44
As if 'twere treason against *E.* laws *Con.* 398
The virtues of old Rome for *E.* use *Con.* 836
Humility may clothe an *E.* Dean *T.* 118
Than some grave sinners upon *E.* ground *T.* 292
And throws Italian light on *E.* walls *T.* i 425
Where *E.* minds and manners may be found *T.* ii 208
There's not an *E.* heart that would not leap *T.* v 389
Not *E.* stiff, but frank, and formed to please *Tir.* 671
An *E.* poet's privilege to rant *T.T.* 299
Where most they flourish, upon *E.* ground *T.T.* 337

ENGRAVEN.

Were trusted with his own *e.* laws *Ex.* 199
Our conduct with the laws *e.* there *R.* 132
To read, *e.* on the mouldy walls *T.* v 418
Thy title is *e.* with a pen *T.* vi 862

ENGROSS.

War and the chase *e.* the savage whole *T.* i 608
To *e.* a moment's notice; and yet begs *T.* iv 67

ENGROSSED.

The attention Pleasure has so much *e Ch* 631

ENGULPHS.

London *e.* them all! The shark is there *T.* iii 816

ENHANCE.

Secure the favour, and *e.* the joy *Ex.* 678
Contributes most perhaps to *e.* their fame *Tir.* 468

ENHANCED.

Pure from the lees, which often more *e. T.* ii 508

ENHANCING.

Of vice in others but *e.* more *T.* ii 795

ENIGMA.

Will make the dark *e.* clear *E.* i 54

ENIGMATIC.

Unlike the *e.* line *Q.V.* 49

ENJOIN.

While Providence *e.* to every soul *Ch.* 121
But chief, myself I will *e. D.W.* 41
Then heaven *e,* the fallible and frail *H.* 391
The precept that *e.* him abstinence *P.E.* 236

ENJOINED.

Streams swelled above the bank, *e.* to stand *Ex.* 185
And, silence publicly *e. P.T.* 21

ENJOY.

Forget to *e.* the palm-tree's offered shade *Ch.* 222
E. immunity from priestly power *Ch.* 273
Might smooth her feathers, and *e.* her cage *Ch.* 306

E. the stillness of some close retreat *Con.* 570 [585
Leaves saints to *e.* those altitudes they teach *Con.*
To *e.* cool nature in a country seat *H.* 245
And ruminating flocks *e.* the shade *Her.* 32
And hate the tumult half the world *e. R.* 176
And thou *e.* an Eden ere it fails *R.* 364
Sweet sleep *e.* the curate in his desk *T.* i 94
To *e.* a ramble on the banks of Thames *T.* i 115
Commits no wrong, nor wastes what it *e. T.* i 334
Such health and gaiety of heart *e. T.* i 587
From all the rigours of restraint, *e. T.* ii 127
Or tasting long *e.* thee; too infirm *T.* iii 44
Will he be idle who has much to *e.? T.* iii 360
His warm but simple home, where he *e. T.* iii 389
E. close shelter, wall, or reeds, or hedge *T.* iii 474
Which he, thus occupied, *e.*! Retreat *T.* iii 676
It may *e.* the advantage of the north *T.* iii 771
He wanted, for a wealthier to *e.! T.* iii 789
That I, and mine, and those we love, *e. T.* iv 193
And the resplendent rivers. His to *e. T.* v 743
As free to live, and to *e.* that life *T.* vi 585
Engage no notice, and *e.* much ease *T.* vi 957
Let me *e.*, in some unthought-of spot *V.* 83

ENJOYED.

E. at ease the genial day *A Fable* 7
Of rights restored, variety *e. A.T.* 154
E. the show, and danced about the stake *Ex.* 615
E. the open air *F.B.* 3
In gathering plenty yet to be *e. R.* 554
Divine Communion, carefully *e. R.* 747
Nor sleep *e.* by curate in his desk *T.* i 100
And long protracted bowers, *e.* at noon *T.* i 257
Delightful industry *e.* at home *T.* iii 356
Forsaken, or through folly not *e. T.* iii 711
E., spare feast! a radish and an egg! *T.* iv 173
The silence and the warmth *e.* within *T.* iv 310

ENJOYING.

Might we view her *e.* it here *C.* 56
With sight of animals *e.* life *T.* vi 325

ENJOYMENT.

Where'er he turns, *e.* and delight *P.E.* 47
Are sweet Philosophy's *e.* run *P.E.* 259
Though his life be a dream, his *e.*, I see *P.F.* 19
Master of all the *e.* he designed *R.* 427
These tell me of *e.* past *S.* 23
Fireside *e.*, homeborn happiness *T.* iv 140

ENLARGE.

E. and fortify the dread redoubt *Con.* 689
He gives a tongue to *e.* upon, a heart *T.* iv 794

ENLARGED.

With rich instruction, and a soul *e. Ch.* 322
And slaves, by truth *e.*, are doubly freed *Ch.* 231
And still *e.* as she receives the grace *Ch.* 596
As London, opulent, *e.*, and still *T.* i 721
When copiously supplied, then most *e. Tir.* 19

ENLARGEMENT.

The crowded roots demand *e.* now *T.* iii 532

ENLIGHTENED.

Or from philosophy's *e.* page *Con.* 616
Than ye, when happiest, and *e.* most *R.* 675
The mind indeed, *e.* from above *T.* iii 225

ENLIGHTENING.

From the same centre of *e.* grace *Ch.* 364
And darkening and *e.*, as the leaves *T.* i 348

ENLISTED.

A graver fact, *e.* on your side *Con.* 205

ENLISTS.
First Appetite e. him Truth's sworn foe *P.E.* 542

ENLIVEN.
Storms but e. its unfading green *Ch.* 576

ENNOBLE.
That can e. man, and make frail life *T.* v 603
A theme to e. even mine 1789, 30

ENNOBLING.
And these the Grecian in e. strains *T.* iii 454
Lost without thee the e. powers of verse *T.T.* 291
E. every region that he chose *T.T.* 562

ENORMITY.
To swear to some e. he saw *Con.* 126

ENORMOUS.
Employed to calculate the e. sum *P.E.* 486
To an e. and o'erbearing height *T.* ii 112
A mine to satisfy the e. cost *T.* iii 783
To such gigantic and e. growth *T.* vi 382
Of girth e., with moss-cushioned root *Y.O.* 64

EN PASSANT.
"Lets fall a poem e. *E.* iv 88

ENRAGED.
E. the more by what might have reformed *T.* vi 524

ENRAPTURED.
Even as he bids! The e. owner smiles *T.* iii 780

ENRICH.
But time that should e. the nobler mind *Comp.* i 11
Sprightly and fresh, e. every theme *Con.* 894
To e. thy walls: but thou didst hew the floods *T.* v 133
Does but encumber whom it seems to e. *T.* vi 95
Why do the seasons still e. the year *Tir.* 41
Than how to e. thyself, and next, thine heir *Tir.* 661

ENRICHED.
Where commerce has e. the busy coast *Ch.* 114
The farther traced, e. them still the more *Con.* 516
May feel a heart e. by what it pays *R.* 209
E. with the discoveries ye have made *R.* 666

ENROLLED.
But though slave they have e. me *N.C.* 7

ENSANGUINED.
E. hearts, clubs typical of strife *T.* iv 218

ENSIGN.
Are hateful e. of usurped command *Ch.* 213
"Right," says an e., "and for aught I see *H.* 397
Those e. of dominion, how disgraced! *T.T.* 40

ENSLAVED.
See Cortez odious for a world e.! *Ch.* 40
From servile fear, or be the more e.? *T.* 184
Himself e. by terror of the band *T.* iv 601
But once e., farewell! I could endure *T.* v 477
Which whoso tastes can be e. no more *T.* v 544

ENSLAVES.
E. the will, nor leaves the judgment free *P.E.* 270

ENSNARING.
They stood the test of her e. smile *Ex.* 78

ENSUE.
That theme exhausted, a wide chasm e. *Con.* 393
Man's disappointment must of course e. *H.* 132
An Iliad, only not in verse, e. *H.* 194
And dread of death e. *St.* v 24
And never won. Dream after dream e. *T.* iii 127

Discourse e., not trivial, yet not dull *T.* iv 174 [620
And seems dethroned and vanquished. Peace e. *T.* v

ENSUED.
Three sparks e. that chased it all away *A.T.* 167
The evening gray again e. *R.C.* 70
A dissolution of all bonds e. *T.* ii 743
Minute the horrors that e. *T.B.* 52

ENSUING.
E. seemed to obliterate the past *T.* vi 540

ENSURE.
Compliance with his will your lot e. *H.* 326
His death your peace e. *St.* v 34
The glad espousals, and e. the crop *T.* iii 543
And for a time e., to his loved land *T.* v 716
To e. the perseverance of his course *Tir.* 238
Of grandeur that e. respect 1789, 69

ENSURED.
Their usefulness e. by zeal and love *Ex.* 443
E. him mute attention and regard *H.* 687
E. us mastery there, we yet retain *T.* ii 274

ENTANGLED.
Full many a knight had been e. there *A.T.* 35
E., winds now this way and now that *T.* iii 2
E. in the cobwebs of the schools *T.* iv 726

ENTELLUS.
Let Dares beat E. black and blue *Con.* 198

ENTER.
And they might e. at his open door *H.* 308
Pants for it, aims at it, e. it, and dies *T.* 6
'Tis open, and ye cannot e.—why? *T.* 357
I would not e. on my list of friends *T.* vi 560
Or, if it e., soon starved out again *Tir.* 768
Nor heed what guests there e. and abide *Tir.* 888

ENTERING.
The plough of wisdom never e. there *H.* 234
He, e. at the study door *T.B.* 37

ENTERPRISE.
And wilt thou join to this bold e. *Ex.* 698
But in his arduous e. to close *R.* 617

ENTERTAIN.
Is often useful, always e. *Con.* 204
Of all ambitions man may e. *Con.* 221
You speak with life, in hopes to e. *Con.* 327
I will by no means e. *F.* 191
Ye are bid, begged, besought to e. *P.E.* 264
Tickle and e. us, or we die *R.* 708
To e. a thief or two in pay *Tir.* 693

ENTERTAINMENT.
Their wonted e., all retire *T.* ii 303

ENTHRALL'D.
Holds an unthinking multitude e. *T.* vi 100

ENTHRONED.
From loins e., and rulers of the earth *M.P.* 109
'Twas the last trumpet—see the Judge e.! *T.* 564

ENTHUSIAST.
E. drunk with an unreal joy *P.E.* 76
No wild e. ever yet could rest *P.E.* 470
The favoured few—the e. you despise *T.* 231

ENTICE.
That, so refined, it might the more e. *P.E.* 344

ENTICED.
E. him from his oaths of knighthood far *A.T.* 27

ENTICING.
'Tis not alone the grape's *e.* juice *P.E.* 271

ENTITLED.
E. here to reign *Q.V.* 4

ENTIRE.
He knows that God demands his heart *e. Con.* 759
Slept unperceived, the mountain yet *e. Her.* 2

ENTOMBED.
Than if *e.* the day before *R.C.* 72

ENTRANCED.
To where the fond Sir Airy lay *e. A.T.* 150
Of error leads them, by a tune *e. T.* vi 104

ENTREATED.
E. "Help!" or cried—"Adieu!" *Cast.* 42
E., opening wide his beak *P.T.* 19

ENVELOPE.
And floating films *e.* every thorn *A.T.* 73

ENVENOMED.
Of temper as *e.* as an asp *T.* 159

ENVIED.
The *e.* tenants of some happier spot *T.* i 610
Be great, be feared, be *e.*, be admired *V.* 16

ENVIES.
Nor *e.* he aught more their idle sport *T.* vi 272

ENVIOUS.
An *e.* world will interpose its frown *E.* ii 33
With fierce and *e.* yet admiring eyes *Ex.* 204
An *e.* man, if you succeed *F.* 76
A nation dwells, not *e.* of your throne *Her.* 49
With all the cunning of an *e.* shrew *T.* ii 266
The minor heroes view with *e.* eyes *Tir.* 223

ENVIRONED.
E. with a ring of branching elms *T.* i 223

ENVY.
His glittering purse, that *e.* of all eyes *Ch.* 472
No *e.* mingles with our praise *Dr.* 13
Those rights that millions *e.* thee appear *Ex.* 681
If *e.* chance to creep in *F.* 75
As *E.* pines at good possessed *F.* 79
It hurts our pride, and moves our *e.* less *H.* 553
I *e.* that unfeeling shrub *P.* 15
E. the beast, then, on whom Heaven bestows *P.E.* 267
E., ye great, the dull unlettered small *T.* 375
Ye have much cause for *e.*—but not all *T.* 376
So farewell *e.* of the Peasant's Nest! *T.* i 247
Which all might view with *e.*, none partake *T.* iii 718
Grant it :—I still must *e.* them an age *T.* iv 529
Thwart his attempt, or *e.* his success *T.* iv 787
Of *e.*, hatred, jealousy, and pride *Tir.* 467
To scenes where competition, *e.*, strife *V.* 75

EPIC.
Is genius only found in *e.* lays? *T.T.* 568

EPICTETUS.
Has *E.*, Plato, Tully, preached! *T.* ii 540

EPIDEMIC.
Of *e.* throats, if such there are *Con.* 391

EPISCOPALLY.
Dreams him *e.* such at least *Tir.* 365

EPISTLE.
One sad *e.* thence, may cure mankind *P.E.* 351
Births, deaths, and marriages, *e.* wet *T.* iv 17

EQUAL.
Was *e.* to the swiftness of his horse *A.T.* 194
Are taught by rays that fly with *e.* pace *Ch.* 363
O days of heaven, and nights of *e.* praise! *Con.* 567
And *e.* truth on either side *F.* 50
If one, his *e.* in athletic frame *H.* 191
Diverging each from each, like *e.* rays *H.* 303
Was one, whom justice, on an *e.* plan *H.* 511
With *e.* grace below *O.* i 28
Each province of her art her *e.* care *T.* i 707
The smooth and *e.* course of his affairs *T.* ii 173
And *e.* ; and he bade them dwell in peace *T.* v 201
The sweets of Liberty and *e.* laws *T.* v. 717
A rhetoric *e.* to those parts of speech ? *Tir.* 398

EQUALLY.
Adopt his own, 'tis *e.* in vain *Con.* 109
A soul serene, and *e.* retired *R.* 143
Or nymphs responsive, *e.* affect *T.* iv 21

EQUIPAGE.
Of *e.*, our gardens, and our sports *T.* i 644
The gilded *e.*, and turning loose *T.* vi 702

EQUIPPED.
E. from top to toe *J.G.* 74

EQUITY.
A being of less *e.* than man *H.* 384
Where Peace, and *E.*, and Freedom smile *Her.* 84
He sees that human *e.* is slack *T.* vi 472
And *E.* ; not jealous more to guard *T.* vi 850
Bids *e.* throughout his works prevail *T.T.* 250

ERA.
An *e.* cherished long by me 1789, 33

ERADICATE.
E. him, tear him from his hold *T.* v 437

ERASED.
To impress a value, not to be *e. Tir.* 613

ERECT.
But Innocence, sedate, serene, *e. P.E.* 207
Her head *e.*, her fan upon her lips *T.* 134
But restless was the chair ; the back *e. T.* i 44
But thus admonished, we can walk *e. T.* ii 593
He stands *e.* ; his slouch becomes a walk *T.* iv 639
The stubborn soil, and hold thee still *e Y.O.* 119

ERECTED.
Gathering around it, with *e.* ears *Ch.* 516
Or mean self-love *e. F.* 39

ERR.
By power divine, and skill that could not *e. Ex.* 201
Than opportunity vouchsafed to *e. F.A.* 16
Or so resolved to *e. J.P.* 26
Whoever *e.*, the priest can ne'er be wrong *P.E.* 508
It *e.* but little from the intended line *P.E.* 574
Thus Fancy paints thee, and though apt to *e. T.* i 661
Perhaps *e.* little when she paints thee thus *T.* i 662
That *e.* not, and find raptures still renewed *T.* iii 723

ERRED.
Its error, if it *e.*, was merely this *T.T.* 391

ERRAND.
Impel the fleet whose *e.* is to save *Ch.* 128
And do his *e.* of disgrace and shame *Ex.* 334
Wild fowl or venison, and his *e.* speeds *T.* iv 612

ERRONEOUS.
By modern lights from an *e.* taste *T.* iv 724
May here and there prevent *e.* choice *Tir.* 798
By thee I might correct, *e.* oft *Y.O.* 45

ERRONEOUSLY.
That men *e.* their glory call *R.* 100

ERROR.
Infuses lies and *e.* of his own *Ex.* 102
Strikes the rough thread of *e.* right athwart *Ex.* 330
E., and darkness occupy their place *Ex.* 693
An *e.* soon corrected *F.* 21
Of fewer *e.*, on a second proof! *F.A.* 5
In chains of *e.* our accomplished minds *H.* 484
The serpent *E.* twines round human hearts *P.E.* 34
Then welcome *e.*, of whatever size *P.E.* 283
Tell him he wanders, that his *e.* leads *P.E.* 544
Faults in the life breed *e.* in the brain *P.E.* 564
Man on the dubious waves of *e.* tossed *T.* 1
He, lost in *e.* his vain heart prefers *T.* 335
With hurtful *e.*, prejudice, and dreams *T.* ii 504
Of *e.* leads them, by a tune entranced, *T.* vi 104
One Lord, one Father. *E.* has no place *T.* vi 784
And quit their office for their *e.*'s sake *T.* vi 884
But learns his *e.* in maturer years *Tir.* 449
A monarch's *e.* are forbidden game *T.T.* 114
Its *e.*, if it erred, was merely this *T.T.* 391

ERST.
As *e.* with airy self-conceit *R.C.* 100

ERUDITE.
"'Twere well," says one sage, *e.*, profound *T.* iii 191

ERUDITION.
As men of depth in *e.* use *Ch.* 392
Add to such *e.*, thus acquired *T.* ii 765
Let *e.* grace him, or not grace *Tir.* 387

ESCAPE.
Safety consists not in *e. A Fable* 32
The world is charmed, and Scrib *e.* the law *Ch.* 526
Alas, how time *e.*!—'tis even so *E.* iii 2
"To *e.* him at the idlest time *E.* iv 76
Might also have indulged with an *e. H.* 513
We can *e.* from custom's idiot sway *R.* 49
Downs that almost *e.* the inquiring eye *R.* 423
He might *e.* the most observing eyes *R.* 588
E. at last to liberty and light *T.* i 440
The wealth of Indian provinces, *e. T.* i 738
Tremble and be amazed at thine *e. T.* ii 159
His dangers or *e.*, and haply find *T.* ii 309
If such *e.* contagion, and emerge *T.* ii 797
Plunging, and half despairing of *e. T.* iii 6
Suffer his woes, and share in his *e. T.* iv 117
Unless by Heaven's peculiar grace, *e. T.* ii 632
E. unhurt beneath so warm a veil *T.* iv 332
To *e.* the impending famine, often scared *T.* v 68
Cruelly spared, and hopeless of *e.*! *T.* v 399
A clear *e.* from tyrannizing lust *T.* v 579
How he was flogged, or had the luck to *e. Tir.* 329

ESCAPED.
E. my eager hand *D.W.* 20
If we *e.* not, if Heaven spared not us *Ex.* 245
E. from a cross country ride! *Gr.* 20
E. from office and its constant cares *R.* 408
E. with pain from that adventurous flight *T.* i 4
One who has known, and has *e.* mankind *V.* 78

ESPECIALLY.
E. sugar, so needful we see? *P.A.* 7

ESPOUSALS.
The glad *e.*, and ensures the crop *T.* iii 543

ESSAY.
And, after many a vain *e. E.* iv 53
And fights again; but finds his best *e. T.* v 624
Not Brindley nor Bridgewater would *e. T.T.* 182
And place it in his first *e. U.* 21

ESSENCED.
And tender as a girl, all *e.* o'er *T.* ii 227

ESSENCES.
Nectareous *e.*, Olympian dews *T.* iv 83

ESSENTIAL.
I superadd a few *e.* more *H.* 434
The difference, though *e.*, fails to strike *P.E.* 204

ESTABLISHED.
The slaves of custom and *e.* mode *Tir.* 251

ESTATE.
On man, a mourner in his best *e.*! *Ch.* 156
Not to redeem his time, but his *e. R.* 561
The *e.* his sires had owned in ancient years *R.* 579
E. are landscapes, gazed upon awhile *T.* iii 755
(Made by a monarch) on her own *e. T.* v 171

ESTEEM.
"Honour, *e.* and confidence forgot *A.T.* 111
But has left a regret and *e. C.* 7
For ever aiming at the world's *e. Con.* 367
And wild as madness in the world's *e. Con.* 666
The sorrows sympathy *e.* us own *Con.* 696
Loses at once all value and *e. Ex.* 113
How he *e.* your merit *F.* 171
E. them, sow them, rear them, and protect *H.* 295
Yet let me stand excused, if I *e. R.* 667
But what is man in his own proud *e.*? *T.* 403
The charms of virtue in their just *e. T.* ii 796
E. that busy world an idler too! *T.* iii 354
Where he, that fills an office, shall *e. T.* vi 816
And schools, that have outlived all just *e. Tir.* 704
Churchmen, in whose *e.* their blest employ *Tir.* 823

ESTEEMED.
The longer I heard, I *e. C.* 21
May be *e.* a gift, and not an art *Con.* 4
Be never named in ears *e.* polite *Con.* 474
Arts once *e.* may be with shame dismissed *Con.* 811
May claim some right to be *e.* divine *H.* 504

ESTIMATE.
His well-poised *e.* of right and wrong *H.* 611
The inestimable *E.* of Brown *T.T.* 384

ESTIMATION.
Just *e.* prized above all price *T.* ii 34

ESTRANGE.
"Seduce our husbands, and *e.* their hearts *A.T.* 114

ESTRANGED.
Their hopes, desires, and purposes *e. Con.* 725
To live *e.* from God his total scope *Tir.* 426
Add too, that, thus *e.*, thou canst obtain *Tir.* 585

ETERNAL.
We come with joy from our *e.* rest *Ch.* 73
And all supplied from an *e.* source *Ch.* 370
To rush into a fixed *e.* state *Con.* 185
The pillar of the *e.* plan appears *Con.* 558
Is given in earnest of *e.* rest *E.* ii 40
While truths on which *e.* things depend *Ex.* 117
Received the transcript of the *E.* Mind *Ex.* 198
"Suffering the vengeance of *e.* fire" *Ex.* 423
Ere Nature rose from her *e.* sleep *Ex.* 637
With him the Donor of *e.* life *H.* 323
If sentence of *e.* pain belong *H.* 389

On icy plains, and in *e.* snows *H.* 464
Of an *e.*, universal war *H.* 648
These are thy glorious works, *e.* Truth *H.* 742
Of close alliance to the E. Mind *J.T.* 44
E. winter doomed to know *Miss* — 35
E. truth by everlasting doubt *P.E.* 473
Settling at last upon *e.* things *R.* 672
Worthy to live, and of *e.* use *R.* 700
In the pure fountain of *e.* love *T.* iii 244
Fruits of omnipotent *e.* love *T.* iv 188
And smiles delighted with the *e.* poise *T.* iv 486
We build with what we deem *e.* rock *T.* v 534
Meant it *e.*, had he not himself *T.* v 562
Their only point of rest, E. Word ! *T.* v 897
And that one season an *e.* spring *T.* vi 770
Dipped in the fountain of *e.* love *T.* vi 863
But let *e.* Infamy pursue *T.T.* 29

ETERNITY.

And cries, "Perhaps *e.* strikes next!" *H.* 701
E.'s unknown expanse appears *R.* 149
E. for bubbles proves at last *T.* iii 175
Trembling, as if *e.* were hung *T.* vi 270

ETHELRED.

E.'s house, the centre of six ways *H.* 302

ETHEREAL.

Partakers of a new *e.* birth *Con.* 724
Pants for the place of her *e.* birth *H.* 162
"Long as I draw *e.* air *Miss* — 67
Vast in its powers, *e.* in its kind *Tir.* 6

ETIQUETTE.

And has the Ladies' E. by heart *P.E.* 196

EULOGIUM.

To adorn the Sofa with *e.* due *T.* iii 12
Your smooth *e.*, to one crown addressed *T.T.* 91

EULOGY.

If honest *e.* can spare thee room *H.* 589
Their *e.*; those sang the Mantuan bard *T.* iii 453
Messiah's *e.* for Handel's sake *T.* vi 637

EUROPE.

Give saintship, then all E. must agree *T.* 111
The post-horns of all *E.*, lays her waste *T.T.* 32

EVANDER.

Of good *E.*, still where he was left *T.* vi 537
E., famed for piety, for years *T.* vi 490

EVANESCENT.

Of *e.* glory, once a stream *T.* v 167

EVANGELICAL.

Oh fie ! 'Tis *e.* and pure *P.E.* 133

EVAPORATE.

And not at last *e.* in air *Tir.* 772

EVE.

But just at *e.* the blowing weather *A Fable* 16
And here I wander *e.* and morn *M.B.* 11
Nor yet at *e.* his note suspended *N.G.* 3
Prolific, and the lime at dewy *e. T.* i 316
But comes at last the dull and dusky *e. T.* i 669
The pensive wanderer in their shades. At *e. T.* i 761
Scarce noticed in the kindred dusk of *e. T.* iv 321
They brave the season, and yet find at *e. T.* iv 378
From morn to *e.* his solitary task *T.* v 44
One silent *e.* I wandered late *The Doves* 5

EVEN.

Was smooth and *e.* as an ivory ball *A.T.* 47
Smooth, ductile, and *e.* his fancy must flow *F.M.* 18
Perched on the sign-post, holds with *e.* hand *T.* iv 483

EVENING.

Again, when *e.* in her sober vest *Ch.* 262
Collect at *e.* what the day brought forth *Con.* 19
His frisking was at *e.* hours *Ep.* ii 25
Thus, while gray *e.* lulled the wind and called *F.A.* 6
And just when *e.* turns the blue vault gray *H.* 79
Of those that walk at *e.* where ye dwell *H.* 472
Ere long approach life's *e.* shades *Mor.* 35
A poet, in his *e.* walk *P.* 39
For Sabbath *e.*, and perhaps as sweet *P.E.* 141
If, ere we yet discern life's *e.* star *R.* 46
The purple *e.* and resplendent moon *R.* 348
Nor quits till *e.* watch his giddy stand *R.* 434
The *e.* came, the sun descended *R.C.* 65
The *e.* gray again ensued *R.C.* 70
At *e.*, and at night retire secure *T.* iii 344
So let us welcome peaceful *e.* in *T.* iv 41
Not such his *e.*, who with shining face *T.* iv 42
Of long uninterrupted *e.* know *T.* iv 143
O *e.* worthy of the gods ! exclaimed *T.* iv 189
The Sabine bard. O *e.* I reply *T.* iv 190
Come, E., once again, season of peace *T.* iv 243
Return, sweet *E.*, and continue long ! *T.* iv 244
At *e.*, till at length the freezing blast *T.* iv 303
That crawls at *e.* in the public path *T.* vi 565

EVENING-RAMBLE.

The last *e.* we made *C.* 9

EVENING-TIDE.

To serious thought at E. *Mor.* 12

EVENT.

In musings worthy of the great *e. Con.* 510
E. of most important use E. i 76
Providence adverse in *e.* like these ? *Ex.* 313
The *e.*, and sure decision of the fight ? *Ex.* 363
Trifles pursued, whate'er the *e. Mor* 45
Resolving all *e.*, with their effects *T.* ii 163
Do I forbode impossible *e. T.* v 491
Anticipate perforce some dire *e. T.* v 524
The *e.* is sure; expect it, and rejoice ! *Tir.* 343
E. improbable and strange as these *Tir.* 370
Seizes *e.* as yet unknown to man *T.T.* 498
The clock of history, facts and *e. Y.O.* 46

EVENTFUL.

E., should supply her with a theme *Y.O.* 161

EVENTIDE.

It happened on a solemn *e. Con.* 505
Walks forth to meditate at *e. T.* vi 949

EVER-DURING.

Gives bond in stone and *e.* brass *T.* v 710

EVERLASTING.

Those breathed from lips of *e.* love *E.* ii 30
Eternal truth by *e.* doubt, *P.E.* 473
Of *e.* death *St.* vi 36
On the sad theme, their *e.* state *T.* 41
'Tis found as *e.* as his love *T.T.* 595

EVER-NIBBLING.

With his sly scythe, whose *e.* edge *Y.O.* 105

EVIDENCE.

His *e.*, if he were called by law *Con.* 125
And call up *e.* from every age *Ex.* 162
An *e.* and reprehension both *Tir.* 656

EVIL.

In baser souls unnumbered *e.* meet *Ch.* 37
Few Frenchmen of this *e.* have complained *Con.* 359
To prove an *e.* of which all complain *E.* iii 43
And having chosen *e.*, scorned the voice *Ex.* 398

Of *e.* yet unmentioned *F.* 195
It is an *e.* incident to man *F.A.* 30
Of sensual *e.*, and thus Hope is born *H.* 152
Can see his love, though secret *e.* lurks *H.* 544
Can see no *e.* in a play *L.W.* 30
Those *e.* it would gladly cure *M.F.* 58
Whatever *e.* it endures *P.* 42
Knowledge of good and *e.* is from thee *P.E.* 469
For *e.* daily felt and hardly borne *R.* 752
And *e.* felt within *St.* iii 26
All *e.* then seem light, compared *St.* v 27
Forgive their *e.*, and accept their good *T.* 582
Such *e.* Sin hath wrought, and such a flame *T.* ii 133
From all assaults of *e.*, proving still *T.* iii 680
Except what wisdom lays on *e.* men *T.* v 449
Is *e.*; hurts the faculties, impedes *T.* v 450
Brings its own *e.* with it, makes it less *T.* v 770
Yet, feeling present *e.*, while the past *T.* vi 23
That source of *e.* not exhausted yet *T.* vi 369
Assert the native *e.* of his heart *Tir.* 162
And *e.* not to be endured endure *Tir.* 276
But judge, where so much *e.* intervenes *Tir.* 486

EVINCE.
Thought, word, and deed, his liberty *e. T.* 195

EVINCED.
Incurable obduracy *e. T.* vi 532

EVINCING.
In heavenly truth; *e.*, as she makes *T.* vi 183

EWE.
A ram, the *e.* and wethers, sad, addressed *N.A.* 82
But more discreet than he, a Cambrian *e. N.A.* 106

EXACT.
But though we praise the *e.* designer's skill *Ch.* 555
Can length of years on God himself *e. Con.* 549
E. yet not precise, though meek, keen-eyed *Con.* 610
Their order on his shelves *e. Mrs. M*— 39
No—the man's morals were *e.*; what then ? *T.* 52
In London. Where her implements *e. T.* i 715
Chains him, and tasks him, and *e.* his sweat *T.* ii 23
The method clear, and argument *e.* ? *T.* iii 279
That calls the past to our *e.* review *T.* iv 184
And tutored with a relish more *e. T.* iv 741
E. and regular the sounds will be *T.T.* 530
Then Pope, as harmony itself *e. T.T.* 646
Now stars, two lobes, protruding, paired *e. Y.O.* 36

EXACTEST.
Apparelled in *e.* sort *R.C.* 19

EXALT.
To *e.* a people, and to place them high *Con.* 519
To gaze at his own splendour, and to *e. T.* ii 547
Compose the passions, and *e.* the mind *T.* iii 305

EXALTED.
And yet *e.* above God's own word *Ex.* 128
E. on his pedestal of pride *T.* 313
Let heathen worthies, whose *e.* mind *T.* 525
Whose heart with praise, and whose *e.* mind *T.* v 751
The *e.* prize demands an upward look *Tir.* 383
A soul *e.* above Earth, a mind *T.T.* 704

EXALTING.
As if *e.* him they raised themselves *T.* v 263

EXAMINE.
With curious touch *e.* me *P.* 33
The busy race *e.* and explore *R.* 151
In lucrative concerns. *E.* well *T.* iv 606

EXAMPLE.
Beyond the *e.* of our sires digress *Con.* 792
By theirs whose bright *e.*, unimpeach'd *Ex.* 656
And seem to pray, for good *e.* sake *H.* 249
Resort to this *e.* as a rock *P.E.* 143
Daniel ate pulse by choice—*e.* rare! *P.E.* 215
In cities foul *e.* on most minds *T.* i 685
That his *e.* had a magnet's force *T.* ii 250
And loose *e.*, whom he should instruct *T.* ii 552
Nor can *e.* hurt them: what they see *T.* ii 794
Of sad experience, nor *e.* set *T.* v 294
Shine with his fair *e.*, and though small *T.* vi 961
Whose fair *e.* may at once inspire *Tir.* 648
Where vile *e.* (yours I chiefly mean *Tir.* 761
O learn, from our *e.* and our fate *T.T.* 436

EXCEED.
Though the pleasures of London *e. C.* 25
But, if he play the glutton and *e. P.E.* 211
He finds the labours of that state *e. R.* 619

EXCEEDING.
He makes one useful point *e.* clear *Con.* 136
Then, with a voice *e.* low *M.F.* 29

EXCEL.
And stirs his own to match them, or *e. Ch.* 118
Ambitious, not to shine or to *e. Con.* 623
E. a dunce that has been kept at home *P.E.* 416
With care collect what in their eyes *e. R.* 153
Who will may pant for glory and *e. R.* 245
Her works must needs *e.* who fashioned you *R.* 544
Bids these in elegance of form *e. R.* 793
E. ten thousand mercenary deeds *T.* 224
Few boys are born with talents that *e. Tir.* 509

EXCELLENCE.
To speak its *e.*; I danced for joy *T.* iv 712

EXCELLENT.
The growth of what is *e.*, so hard *T.* i 84
Of what is *e.* in man, they thirst *T.* ii 790

EXCELLING.
Are luxuries *e.* all the glare *R.* 185

EXCEPTED.
And, thunderbolts *e.*, quite a God! *T.* 410

EXCEPTIONS.
Such rare *e.*, shining in the dark *Tir.* 841

EXCESS.
Their prayers made public, their *e.* kept *Ex.* 143
Or spendthrifts prodigal *e.* afford *J.T.* 16
Safe in themselves, but dangerous in the *e. P.E.* 62
Still hurtful in the abuse, or by the *e. P.E.* 228
Of libertine *e.* The Sofa suits *T.* i 106
And wantonness, and gluttonous *e. T.* i 688
May feed *e.* she can ill afford *T.* ii 651
Wealth luxury, and luxury *e. T.* iv 581
E., the scrofulous and itchy plague *T.* iv 582
And spirits buoyant with *e.* of glee *T.* vi 329
And Liberty, preserved from wild *e. T.T.* 316
Foul with *e.*, and with discourse obscene *Tir.* 736

EXCHANGE.
But souls that carry on a blest *e. Con.* 693
To *e.* the centre of a thousand trades *H.* 246
I would not yet *e.* thy sullen skies *T.* ii 212
Try now the merits of this blest *e. Tir.* 173
To *e.* content for trouble, ease for pain *V.* 64

EXCHANGED.
E. for the secure domestic scheme *Tir.* 705

EXCISE.
The *e.* is fattened with the rich result *T.* iv 504

EXCITE.
May even our wonder *e. C.* 38
The explosion of the levelled tube *e. H.* 350
The pleasing spectacle at once *e. Tir.* 310

EXCITING.
E. oft our gratitude and love *T.* iv 182

EXCLAIM.
E. " Prepare thee for an early shroud " *Ep.* i 10
" Spoke like an oracle," they all *e. H.* 437
And with a rapture like his own *e. R.* 86
" Ye groves," (the statesman at his desk *e. R.* 365
Sarcastic, would *e.*, and judge the song *T.* iii 563

EXCLAIMED.
" By Dian's beams," Sir Marmadan *e. A.T.* 187
O evenings worthy of the gods! *e. T.* iv 189
E., " that me; the lullabies of age *T.* vi 506
" And such," I *e.*, " is the pitiless part *The Rose* 13

EXCLAIMING.
And left them both *e.*, " 'Twas the Lord! *Con.* 534

EXCLUDE.
That Hope which can alone *e.* despair *H.* 751
Pastime and business both, it should *e. P.E.* 159
Religion does not censure or *e. R.* 783

EXCLUSION.
Shall sigh at their *e.*, and return *T.* vi 672

EXCLUSIVE.
Is sparkling wit the world's *e.* right *Con.* 589
While learning, once the man's *e.* pride *P.E.* 429

EXCLUSIVELY.
Peculiar, and *e.* her own *T.* i 432

EXCOMMUNICATION.
On pain of *e.*" *L.W.* 6

EXCORIATE.
As now, and with *e.* forks deform *Y.O.* 5

EXCURSIONS.
His wild *e.*, window-breaking feats *Tir.* 228

EXCURSIVE.
That Fancy finds in her *e.* flights *T.* iv 242

EXCUSE.
Let my obedience then *e. B.R.* 21
She makes *e.* where she might condemn *Ch.* 424
With less *e.*, and, haply, worse effect?" *F.A.* 17
But these, *e.* the liberty I take *H.* 435
Of sabbath hours with plausible *e.? P.E.* 145
Be damnable, then damned without *e. P.E.* 597
To sports which only childhood could *e. T.* ii 638
Unmasked, vouchsafing this their sole *e. T.* ii 695
Nor this to feed his own! 'Twere some *e. T.* iv 452
Of British natures, wanting its *e. T.* v 481
To *e.* in which reason has no part *T.* v 656
It seems idolatry with some *e. Y.O.* 9

EXCUSED.
Or, if *e.* that charge, at least deceived *Con.* 478
The veteran steed *e.* his task at length *R.* 625
Yet let me stand *e.*, if I esteem *R.* 667
E. the incumbrance of more solid worth *Tir.* 347
He was *e.* the penalties of dull *Y.O.* 156

EXECRATE.
With eyes of anguish, *e.* their lot *T.* ii 665
Is cold on this. She *e.* indeed *T.* v 730

EXECUTE.
And Vengeance *e.* what Justice wills *Ch.* 82
God in a moment *e.* with ease) *R.* 328

EXECUTED.
But measures planned and *e.* well *T.T.* 386

EXEMPLIFIED.
Its use and power *e.* in thee *J. T.* 50
Rarely *e.* among ourselves *T.* vi 624

EXEMPT.
Shall live *e.* from weakness and decay *H.* 752
E. from every ill beside *P.* 54
E. from future service all his days *R.* 628
That liberates and *e.* me from them all *T.* iv 97
Thy days roll on *e.* from household care *T.* iv 366
For Providence, that seems concerned to *e. Tir.* 430

EXEMPTED.
If quite *e.* from the same) *A Fable* 6
Oh! may I live *e.* (while I live *T.* i 103

EXEMPTION.
With clear *e.* from its own defects *T.* i 404

EXERCISE.
When I do *e.*" *J.G.* 64
When, *e.* and air my only aim *N.A.* 31
'Tis *e.*, and health, and length of days *P.E.* 91
And *e.* all functions of a man *T.* iii 199
May *e.* amiss his proper powers *T.* v 339

EXERCISED.
That day and night are *e.*, and hang *T.* iii 549

EXERT.
O slave! with powers thou didst not dare *e. Ex.* 546
E. their influence, and advance their cause *P.E.* 463
Our parents yet *e.* a prudent care *Tir.* 115

EXERTED.
Had been *e.* none *Q.V.* 62
Lest Power *e.*, but without success *Tir.* 277

EXERTING.
Nature *e.* an unwearied power *T.T.* 690

EXERTION.
Too scanty for the *e.* of his beams *Ch.* 590
His powers of best *e.* there *Mor.* 32

EXHALATIONS.
In constant *e. O.* i 8
Like fleeting *e.*, found no more *Tir.* 84

EXHALE.
Like shallow brooks which summer suns *e.! V.* 2

EXHAUST.
Noisome, and ever greedy to *e. T.* iii 671
And whose beneficence no charge *e. T.* vi 230
Sure to *e.* the plant on which they feed *Tir.* 604

EXHAUSTED.
That theme *e.*, a wide chasm ensues *Con.* 393
While conversation, an *e.* stock *H.* 103
E., has had genius to supply *T.* ii 609
E., he resorts to solemn themes *T.* v 661
That source of evils not *e.* yet *T.* vi 369
Till, his *e.* quiver yielding none *T.* vi 873
E. all materials of the art *T.* vi 717
That theme on earth *e.*, though above *T.T.* 594

EXHIBIT.
He half e., and then drops the sum *Ch.* 478
To e., in full bloom disclosed *F.* 44
E. elevations, drawings, plans *P.E.* 397
Ocean e., fathomless and broad *R.* 525
Coincident, e. lucid proof *T.* ii 374
Would fail to e. at the public shows *T.* ii 619
E. every lineament of these *T.* vi 901
Thence to e. to his wondering eyes *Tir.* 632

EXHIBITED.
'Tis truth divine, e. on earth *Ch.* 377

EXHIBITIONS.
What e. various hath the world *Y.O.* 69

EXHILARATE.
E. the spirit, and restore *T.* i 182

EXHORTATION.
Pathetic e.; and to address *T.* ii 469

EXIGENCE.
Below the e., or be not backed *T.* ii 557
Which have their e. too, and call *T.* v 240
By public e., till annual food *T.* v 458

EXILE.
Driven out an e. from the face of Saul *R.* 768
And seeking e. from the sight of men *T.* 442
And beg for e., or the pangs of death? *T.* v 434
In heaven-renouncing e., he endures *T.* v 598

EXILED.
At my best home, if not e. from thee" *Ch.* 243
Ah! I could pity thee e. *M.B.* 13

EXIST.
From creatures that e. but for our sake *T.* vi 603

EXISTED.
Fair as it is, e. ere it was *T.* v 799

EXISTENCE.
Oh comfortless e.! hemmed around *T.* v 432

EXIT.
Sighs for his e., vulgarly called death *H.* 90

EXOTIC.
Is hope e.? Grows it not at home? *H.* 549
There blooms e. beauty, warm and snug *T.* iii 568

EXPAND.
His high-bred steed e. his nostrils wide *A.T.* 163
Still as I touch the lyre, do thou e. *R.* 203
The toiling steeds e. the nostril wide *T.* iv 347

EXPANDED.
There Beauty woos him with e. arms *P.E.* 55
His faculties, e. in full bloom *T.* iv 661
Beneath the shade of her e. leaves *Tir.* 46

EXPANSE.
Her fields, a rich e. of wavy corn *Ex.* 9
Thy mariners explore the wild e. *Ex.* 290
Eternity's unknown e. appears *R.* 149

EXPATIATES.
He travels and e., as the bee *T.* iv 107

EXPECT.
"But guard thee well, e. no feigned attack *A.T.* 189
Prisons e. the wicked, and were built *Ch.* 280
E. in darkness and heart-chilling fears *H.* 714
And shall e. him at the door *M.F.* 13
And having well deserved, e. the worst *T.* 266
Alas! e. it not. We found no bait *T.* i 672
Uninjured, but e. the upholding aid *T.* iii 658
E. her soon with footboy at her heels *T.* iv 550
To count the hour-bell, and e. no change *T.* v 404
The event is sure; e. it, and rejoice! *Tir.* 343
With so much reason all e. from them *Tir.* 353
Despised by thee, what more can he e. *Tir.* 712
E. a brighter sky *Trans. H.* 27

EXPECTANT.
Stand motionless e. of its fall *T.* v 528

EXPECTATION.
Much less of pleasing e.) *E.* i 100
Or e. of the next, give leave *Ex.* 607
By e. every day beguiled *M.P.* 40
The folly of his e. *R.C.* 116
Large e., he disposes neat *T.* iii 423

EXPECTED.
Came, not e. in that humble guise *Ex.* 87
And, having dropped the e. bag, pass on *T.* iv 11
And view with tears the e. harvest lost *V.* 57
May be e. from thee, seated here *Y.O.* 139

EXPECTING.
A gift to his e. fair *A Fable* 27

EXPEDIENCE.
E. as a warrant for the deed? *Ch.* 183
The e. of a less adventurous course *Tir.* 804

EXPEDIENT.
Suggests the e. of a yearly fast *Ex.* 401
To be at least e. *F.* 201
The e. and inventions multiform *T.* ii 287
Too long, to tell the e. and the shifts *T.* iii 559
As God's e. to retrieve his loss *Tir.* 166
Find it e., come what mischief may *Tir.* 692

EXPELS.
Or soon e. him if it is *M.F.* 62

EXPEND.
But youth, health, vigour to e. *Mor.* 33

EXPENDING.
E. late on all that length of plea *S.* i 6

EXPENDITURE.
With our e. defrays his own *T.* ii 603

EXPENSE.
Needs no e. of argument *F.* 140
A laugh at his e., is slender praise *R.* 318
The unpitied victim of ill judged e. *R.* 512
And such e. as pinches parents blue *T.* ii 756
But barren, at the e. of neighbouring twigs *T.* iii 419
For loose e. and fashionable waste *Tir.* 204
And such an age as ours balks no e. *Tir.* 257
Those habits of profuse and lewd e. *Tir.* 350
To improve this diet, at no great e. *Tir.* 628
And they that can afford the e. of more *Tir.* 694
But seldom (as if fearful of e.) *T.T.* 698

EXPERIENCE.
Yet Age, by long e. well informed *Con.* 639
All but their own e. as deceit! *Con.* 720
Of passed e., and the wisdom gleaned *F.A.* 2
Now by the voice of his e. true *H.* 707
And while E. cautions us in vain *R.* 755
Confirmed by long e. of thy worth *T.* i 147
Whom ten long years' e. of my care *T.* iii 338
E., slow preceptress, teaching oft *T.* iii 505
Of sad e., nor examples set *T.* v 294

EXPERIENCED.
And many a pang *e.* still within *E.* ii 35
E. here below *St.* iii 2
The *e.* and the sage *Th.* 6

EXPERT.
E. to swim, he lay *Cast.* 14
E. in all the duties of his place *T.* 206
Learn from *e.* inquirers after truth *Tir.* 192

EXPERTNESS.
Matched with the *e.* of the brutes in theirs *T.* vi 614

EXPIRED.
And the moment the monster *e. M.D.* 38
And his three years of heroship *e. T.* iv 644

EXPLAIN.
Nor all an angel's eloquence *e. H.* 126
E. all mysteries, except her own *T.* ii 528

EXPLAINED.
E., illustrated, and searched so well *Con.* 527

EXPLODED.
What none but bad men wish *e.*, must *T.* v 613

EXPLOITS.
To conquer those by jocular *e. T.* ii 479
Æthereal journeys, submarine *e. T.* iv 85

EXPLORE.
Thy mariners *e.* the wild expanse *Ex.* 290
And woodpeckers *e.* the sides *M.B.* 7
The busy race examine and *e. R.* 151.
He 'gan in haste the drawers *e. R.C.* 92
Its ample area 'gan *e. J.B.* 38
The learned finger never need *e. T.* iv 362

EXPLORING.
E. far and wide the watery waste *T.* i 665

EXPLOSION.
At one immense *e. F.* 66
The *e.* of the levelled tube excites *H.* 350

EXPORTED.
E. slavery to the conquered East? *Ex.* 365

EXPOSED.
Complain of being thus *e. P.* 50
E. to view, but not to touch *P.B.* 30
E. her too much to the wind *R.C.* 26
E. him to the vengeance of the laws? *T.* 45
And stand *e.* by common peccancy *T.* ii 72
E. their inexperience to the snare *T.* ii 801
E. to his cold breath, the task begins *T.* iii 469
But in a distant spot, where, more *e. T.* iii 770
E. than others, with less scruple made *T.* iv 457
E. to manacles, deserves them well *T.* v 366

EXPOSES.
E., and holds up to broad disgrace *T.* ii 553

EXPOSTULATE.
Prompt to persuade, *e.*, and warn *Ex.* 441

EXPOUND.
I could *e.* the melancholy tone *N.A.* 94

EXPRESS.
To *e.* the occurrence of the day *E.* i 4
More cruelty could none *e. G.* 16
To *e.* unwieldy joy *Q.V.* 20
Such as its symptoms can alone *e. R.* 288
Moves without noise, and swift as an *e. T.* 204
When the great Sovereign would his will *e. T.* 551
I would *e.* him simple, grave, sincere *T.* ii 399

EXPRESSED.
Have proved them truths too big to be *e. Con.* 498
And if some Spartan soul a doubt *e. Ex.* 542
This only can; for this plain cause *e. H.* 340
(Had he the sinful part *e. L.W.* 9
Their sentiments so well *e. P.T.* 42
Contrivance intricate *e.* with ease *R.* 55
What charms he sees in Freedom's smile *e. R.* 409
Grow, by being oft *e. St.* iv 23
Well taught, he all the sounds *e. T.B.* 11
Trees, churches, and strange visages *e. T.* iv 288
Thus thy praise shall be *e. Tran.* iii 9
Is not to be *e. Y.D.* 18

EXPRESSION.
E. and the privilege of thought *Con.* 404
Thy indistinct *e.* seem *M.* 21
But angry, coarse, and harsh *e. M.F.* 59
Pass with delight beyond *e. R.C.* 43

EXPRESSIVE.
Ingenious Art, with her *e.* face *Ch.* 97
E., energetic, and refined *Ex.* 482
Alas, how changed! *E.* of his mind *H.* 688
And seem, if judged by their *e.* looks *Tir.* 288

EXPUNGE.
Propitious Spirit! yet *e.* a wrong *Ch.* 276

EXQUISITELY.
Rufillus, *e.* formed by rule *P.E.* 189
Harmony, strength, words *e.* sought *T.T.* 701

EXTEND.
E. no care beyond themselves *Miss* — 63
E. a larger sphere *Miss* — 100
Fall back into our seat, *e.* an arm *T.* ii 448
Sing, then—and *e.* thy span *Tran.* iii 27

EXTENDED.
With cane *e.* far, I sought *D.W.* 17

EXTENDING.
'Tis thus, *e.* his tempestuous arm *Ex.* 584

EXTENSIVE.
Opening the map of God's *e.* plan *R.* 147

EXTERIOR.
But lives when that *e.* grace *M.F.* 53
And Wisdom falls before *e.* grace *P.E.* 418
Or be dishonoured, in the *e.* form *T.* ii 560
'Twere well if his *e.* change were all *T.* iv 619
Less on *e.* things than most suppose *T.T.* 247

EXTERMINATE.
Till death *e.* us all *P.T.* 35

EXTERMINATED.
Peeled, scattered, and *e.* thus *Ex.* 246

EXTINCT.
The flame *e.*, he views the roving fire *B.B.* 11
Some place, a spark or two not yet *e. T.* vi 684

EXTINGUISH.
Religion should *e.* strife *F.* 133
Are paramount, and must *e.* theirs *T.* vi 583

EXTINGUISHED.
His eye relumines its *e.* fires *T.* i 442
The taper soon *e.*, which I saw *T.* iv 391

EXTOL.
We therefore pleased *e.* thy song *Dr.* 9
And chaste, though unconfined, whom I *e. T.* iii 713

EXTOLLED.
When admirals, e. for standing still T.T. 192

EXTORT.
To e. their truncheons from the puny hands T. v 189

EXTORTED.
They live, and live without e. alms T. iv 403

EXTORTION.
Could act e. and the worst of crimes Ex. 148

EXTRACT.
An e. of his diary,—no more Con. 275
E. a register, by which we learn T. iii 152

EXTRACTING.
In the lost kind, e. from the lips T. v 701

EXTRAVAGANCE.
E. and Avarice shall subscribe Ch. 467
Note their e., and be convinced T. ii 573
To hear it called e. and waste T.T. 163

EXTRAVAGANT.
When most e. in his applause T. v 262
E. or sober, loose or chaste Tir. 914

EXTREME.
Convicts a man fanatic in the e. Con. 665
Yours real, and pernicious in the e. P.E. 101
To steer with nicest art betwixt the e. S. ii 9
E., at once rapacious and profuse T. ii 380

EXTREMEST.
For he has touched them. From the e. point T. ii 92

EXUBERANT.
E. is the shadow it supplies Ch. 577
Though sickly samples of the e. whole T. iv 761

EXULTING.
"Fair fall the deed!" the knight e. cried A.T. 68
Scarce less e. in the sight A Tale 59
Greets with three cheers e. At his waist T. i 523
Of cruel man, e. in her woes T. iii 336

EXULT.
His soul e., Hope animates his lays R. 777
E. in its command. The sheepfold here T. i 290
E. to see its thistly curse repealed T. vi 768
E. in his miscarriage if he fail Tir. 478

EYE.
Between Nose and E. a strange contest arose A.C. 1
He pleaded again in behalf of the E.—A.C. 26 [32
By daylight or candlelight—E. should be shut A.C.
And made her dupes see all things with her e.) A.T. 39
And darting through his helm an eagle's e. A.T. 148
His feathered shipmates e. A Tale 58
Princess! if our aged e. B. 9
Blind was he born, and his misguided e. Ch. 357
(Two themes to Nature's e. for ever sealed) Ch. 362
His glittering purse, that envy of all e. Ch. 472
At every stroke wit flashes in our e. Ch. 543 [Con.232
"Yes" (rather moved) "I saw it with these e.!"
Nose, ears, and e. seemed present on the spot Con.318
Self-searching with an introverted e. Con. 364
In other e. our talents rarely shown Con. 369
Know then, and modestly let fall your e. Con. 485
It views the truth with a distorted e. Con. 669
As once absurd in all discerning e. Con. 806
With an unjaundiced e. Dr. 20
Could you, though luminous your e. E. i 69
In old grimalkin's glaring e. E. iv 44
Hast thou the vigour of thy youth? An e. Ep. i 5
The prophet wept for Israel; wished his e. Ex. 33 [53
They stretched the neck, and rolled the wanton e.Ex.
To sift and search them with unerring e. Ex. 88
With fierce and envious yet admiring e. Ex. 204
Philosophy indeed on Grecian e. Ex. 227
Darkness itself before his e. is light Ex. 338
And hide past folly from all-seeing e.? Ex. 405
Lest, having misapplied our e. F. 26
Bright-studded to dazzle the e. Gr. 13
With disappointment lowering in his e. H. 2
Whose e. reverted weeps o'er all the past H. 31
Or pride can look at with indifferent e. H. 52
Through mere necessity to close his e. H. 85
Each man's belief is right in his own e. H. 283
Where science points her telescopic e. H. 441
Have risen at length on your admiring e. H. 492
The poor reclaimed inhabitant, his e. H. 532
May press the e. too closely to be borne H. 551
Reveal (the man is dead) to wondering e. H. 572
(Though other follies strike the public e. H. 620
Lama Sabacthani before their e. H. 630
His e. shut fast, his fingers in his ears H. 658
His e. are sunk, arms folded, head reclined H. 689
With lustre-beaming e. Miss — 70
The meek intelligence of those dear e. M.P. 7
His rainbows and his starry e. Mrs. M— 4
And in her e., and by her aid Mrs. M— 43 [202
Viewed from a distance, and with heedless e. P.E.
Must watch his purpose with a steadfast e. P.E. 577
And gratify no curious e. Q.V. 39
Soon watery grew her e. and dim Q.V. 53
With more than astronomic e. Q.V. 73
The roving e. misleads the careless heart R. 126
With care collect what in their e. excels R. 153
A few forsake the throng; with lifted e. R. 161
That courts display before ambitious e. R. 178
Who studies Nature with a wanton e. R. 213
Teaches his e. a language, and no less R. 239
Lips busy, and e. fixed, foot falling slow R. 285
Interpret to the marking e. distress R. 287
Can call up life into his faded e. R. 339
She shines but little in his heedless e. R. 405
Downs that almost escape the inquiring e. R. 423
He might escape the most observing e. R. 588
To dance on earth, and charm all human e. R. 796
To bid affection's e. no longer stream S. ii 12 [ii 8
With anxious meaning, Heavenward turn his e.! S.
All Heaven unfolded to my e. St. iii 11
Cover us from every e. St. iv 34
Watches your e., anticipates command T. 214
To your weak sight her telescopic e. T. 98
Her eyebrows arched, her e. both gone astray T. 135
And tells, not always with an e. to truth T. 154
But, with averted e., the omniscient Judge T. 227
Even at your side, Sir, and before your e. T. 230
The scrutiny of those all-seeing e. T. 271
And in that charter reads, with sparkling e. T. 329
Grace in his mien, and glory in his e. T. 407
In vain he closes or averts his e. T. 470
Lap-dog and lambkin with black, staring e. T. i 37
For none they need: the languid e., the cheek T. i 391
While Admiration, feeding at the e. T. i 157
Conducts the e. along his sinuous course T. i 165
And even to a clown.—Now roves the e. T. i 288
Admits me to a share: the guiltless e. T. i 333
A sparkling e. beneath a wrinkled front T. i 405
Than please the e.—sweet Nature every sense T. i427
His e. relumines its extinguished fires T. i 442
The lowering e., the petulance, the frown T. i 456
And save me too from theirs whose haggard e. T.i501
Where frequent hedges intercept the e. T. i 514

EYE—FACE

Thou climbst the mountain top, with eager *e. T.* i 664
Of warm encouragement, and in the *e. T.* i 695
Where finds Philosophy her eagle *e. T.* i 712
And Nature with a dim and sickly *e. T.* ii 64
Seems, in their *e.*, a mercy, for thy sake *T.* ii 132
Did not his *e.* rule all things, and intend *T.* ii 166
Go, dress thine *e.* with eye-salve; ask of him *T.* ii 203
In foreign *e.!*—be grooms, and win the plate *T.* ii 280
To zig-zag manuscript, and cheats the *e. T.* ii 364
And play his brilliant parts before my *e. T.* ii 425
By curious *e.* and judgments ill informed *T.* ii 435
Grow wanton, and give proof to every *e. T.* ii 443
Its bergamot, or aids the indebted *e. T.* ii 452
Surveys his fair reversion with keen *e. T.* ii 601
With *e.* of anguish, execrate their lot *T.* ii 665
His *e.* was meek and gentle, and a smile *T.* ii 706
The limits of control, his gentle *e. T.* ii 719
A palsy struck his arm, his sparkling *e. T.* ii 727 [773
Through want of care; or her whose winking *e. T.* ii
Swarms in all quarters; meets the *e.*, the ear *T.* ii 818
And wandering *e.*, still leaning on the arm *T.* iii 53
That brings the planets home into the *e. T.* iii 230
Hangs over mortal *e.*, blind from the birth *T.* iii 234
Has *e.* indeed; and viewing all she sees *T.* iii 245
Nor baited hook deceive the fish's *e. T.* iii 313 [135
That spreads his motley wings in the *e.* of noon *T.* iii
Of lubbard Labour needs his watchful *e. T.* iii 400
In every flash of his far-beaming *e. T.* iii 602
The seals of office glitter in his *e. T.* iv 59 [iv 352
With half-shut *e.*, and puckered cheeks and teeth *T.*
Ascends his topmast, through his peering *e. T.* iv 115
His azure *e.*, is tinctured black and red *T.* iv 216
In the red cinders, while with poring *e. T.* iv 289
Provokes me to a smile. With *e.* askance *T.* v 14
To seize the fair occasion; well they *e. T.* v 66
So dazzling in their *e.* who set it on *T.* v 244
And He by means in philosophic *e. T.* v 698
Can lift to Heaven an unpresumptuous *e. T.* v 746
Whose *e.* they fill with tears of holy joy *T.* v 750
Thine *e.* shall be instructed, and thine heart *T.* v 782
And *e.* intent upon the scanty herb *T.* v 786
"From the green wave emerging, darts an *e. T.* v 835
Shall publish, even to the distant *e. T.* vi 148
Althæa with the purple *e.*; the broom *T.* vi 170
Where no *e.* sees them. And the fairer forms *T.* vi 188
And bathes their *e.* with nectar, and includes *T.* vi 244
Marching and countermarching, with an *e. T.* vi 267
With glass at *e.*, and catalogue in hand *T.* vi 288
In modern *e.*), shall make the doctrine clear *T.* vi 482
And glistening even in the dying *e. T.* vi 631 [vi 699
To gaze in his *e.*, and bless him. Maidens wave *T.*
(A sight to which our *e.* are strangers yet) *T.* vi 825
She judges of refinement by the *e. T.* vi 987
That hides divinity from mortal *e. T.* vi 877
To charm his ear, whose *e.* is on the heart *T.* vi 1022
Ye nymphs! if e'er your *e.* were red *T.B.* 1
Shall fill the circles of those *e. The Doves* 15
Denied the endearments of thine *e. The Doves* 35
His crimes and follies with an aching *e. Tir.* 62
The minor heroes view with envious *e. Tir.* 223
With both our *e.*, is easier than to think *Tir.* 256
Elisha's *e.*, that, when Gehazi strayed *Tir.* 267
To ears and *e.*, the vices of the rest *Tir.* 274
Which only a parental *e.* foresees *Tir.* 371
The prize of beauty in a woman's *e. Tir.* 472
And *e.* the door, and watches a retreat *Tir.* 572
And seems it nothing in a father's *e. Tir.* 615
Thence to exhibit to his wondering *e. Tir.* 632
Beneath thy roof, beneath thine *e.* to prove *Tir.* 680
Before whose infant *e.* the flatterer bows *T.T.* 123
Stand most revealed before the freeman's *e. T.T.* 269
An *e.* like his to catch the distant goal *T.T.* 710
The *e.*, that never saw thee, shine 1789, 58

EYEBALL.
Chins fallen, and not an *e.* to be seen *P.E.* 137

EYEBROW.
Her *e.* arched, her eyes both gone astray *T.* 135
An *e.*, next compose a straggling lock *T.* ii 446

EYELID.
If ever on thy *e.* stood the tear *H.* 676

EYESALVE.
Go, dress thine eyes with *e.*; ask of him *T.* ii 203

EYESIGHT.
The *e.* of Discovery; and begets *T.* v 452

F.

FABLE.
That *f.* old, that seemed for ever mute *Con.* 817
Might shine in *f.*, and grace idle themes *Ex.* 233
Babbler of ancient *f.*, leaves a doubt *Ex.* 503
To him that blends no *f.* with his song *H.* 755
To hold discourse, at least in *f. P.T.* 4
Like those in *f.* feigned *Q.V.* 58
Possess the heart, and *f.* false as hell *T.* v 862
O scenes surpassing *f.*, and yet true *T.* vi 759
Through times of *f.* and of dream 1789, 7

FABLED.
Like her the *f.* Phœbus wooed in vain *Ex.* 599
Like *f.* Tantalus, condemned to hear *P.E.* 231
More golden than that age of *f.* gold *T.* vi 996
Didst burst thine egg, as theirs the *f.* twins *Y.O.* 35

FABRIC.
Silently as a dream the *f.* rose *T.* v 144
A distant age asks where the *f.* stood *T.* v 535

FABULOUS.
And all at random, *f.* and dark *T.* ii 522
As if, like him of *f.* renown *T.* v 691

FACE.
That sages have seen in thy *f.? A.S.* 6
Differing in language, manners, or in *f. Ch.* 21
Ingenious Art, with her expressive *f. Ch.* 97
The smile of opulence in sorrow's *f. Ch.* 130
And Heaven reflected in her *f. Comp.* ii 10
Asseveration blustering in your *f. Con.* 59
Assert the nose upon his *f.* his own *Con.* 122
Hate their own likeness in a brother's *f. Con.* 158
Yet please not, but affront you to your *f. Con.* 228
And bear the marks upon a blushing *f. Con.* 349
Peruses closely the true Christian's *f. Con.* 743
Tell her again, the sneer upon her *f. Con.* 783
And give good company a *f.* severe *Con.* 873
With fixed considerate *f. D.W.* 22
The mask from *f.* never seen before *Ex.* 140

A lawless brood, and curse thee to thy *f.* *Ex.* 283
And long provoked, repaid thee to thy *f.* *Ex.* 391
Are proud and set their *f.* as a rock *Ex.* 457
By every charm that smiles upon her *f.* *Ex.* 668
If even her *f.* he has spared *Gr.* 47
Yesterday's *f.*, twin image of to-day *H.* 102
And spits abhorrence in the Christian's *f.* *H.* 662
That hangs upon your *f.* *J.G.* 190
Long beards, long noses, and pale *f.* *M.F.* 6
And while that *f.* renews my filial grief *M.P.* 17
Awhile they mused ; surveying every *f.* *N.A.* 73
Observe each *f.*, how sober and demure ! *P.E.* 134
To hide the shocking features of her *f.* *P.E.* 298
By shrugs and strange contortions of his *f.* *P.E.* 414
Nature assuming a more lovely *f.* *R.* 357
The Crown, took notice of an ostler's *f.* *R.* 586
Driven out an exile from the *f.* of Saul *R.* 768
F. a thousand dangers at her call *R.H.* 7
And mar the *f.* of Beauty, when no cause *T.* i 458
And pretty *f.*, in presence of his God ? *T.* ii 422
That trust them, and in the end disclose a *f.* *T.* ii 693
Sees her unwrinkled *f.* reflected bright *T.* iv 4
Not such his evening, who with shining *f.* *T.* iv 42
The slope of *f.*, from the floor to the roof *T.* iv 202
And sleeps and is refreshed. Meanwhile the *f.* *T.* iv 298
And slowly, and by most unfelt, the *f.* *T.* iv 324
Brutes graze the mountain-top, with *f.* prone *T.* v 785
Whose *f.* too was familiar to his view *T.* vi 494
A devil's purpose with an angel's *f.* *T.T.* 130
And dared to look his master in the *f.* *T.T.* 321
And all his country beaming in his *f.* *T.T.* 347
When Avarice starves, and never hides his *f.* *T.T.* 422
Drew a rough copy of the Christian *f.* *T.T.* 614
That, quite eclipsing Pleasure's painted *f.* *T.T.* 649
Your senatorial dignity of *f.* *v.* 11
With rueful *f.* and bald pates *Y.D.* 23

FACETIOUS.
The skittish fancy with *f.* tales *T.* ii 470

FACT.
A graver *f.*, enlisted on your side *Con.* 205
Or make that fiction which was once a *f.* *Con.* 550
Specious in show, impossible in *f.* *R.* 638
Else sure notorious *f.*, and proof so plain *Tir.* 259
The clock of history, *f.* and events *Y.O.* 46
Timing more punctual unrecorded *f.* *Y.O.* 47

FACTION.
In setting right what *F.* has set wrong *Ex.* 301
To quell the *f.* that affronts the throne *T.T.* 67

FACTION-MAD.
That, like the multitude made *f.* *T.* iii 673

FACTIOUS.
Healthful and undisturbed by *f.* fumes *T.* v 513

FACTORIES.
Build *f.* with blood, conducting trade *T.* iv 681

FACULTY.
Provides the *f.* an ampler range *Ch.* 334
The *f.* that seemed reduced to naught *Con.* 403
Obscure or quench a *f.* that finds *Con.* 593
For which Heaven formed the *f.* divine *Con.* 898
Far as the *f.* can stretch away *R.* 74
His utmost *f.*, severe indeed *R.* 620
Binds all his *f.*, forbids all growth *T.* i 613
His *f.*, expanded in full bloom *T.* iv 661
A comprehensive *f.* that grasps *T.* v 251
Is evil ; hurts the *f.*, impedes *T.* v 450
New *f.*, or learns at least to employ *T.* v 806
Fires all the *f.* with glorious joy *T.* v 885
With all thy *f.* elsewhere applied *Tir.* 659
In all good *f.* beneath his care *Tir.* 709

FADE.
And verse, more lasting, hues that never *f.* *Ch.* 108
Whose glory, with a light that never *f.* *Con.* 883
The glow that Fancy gave it *f.* *Mor.* 36
Shine safe without a fear to *f.* *Mrs. M—* 50
That melt and *f.* into the distant sky *R.* 424
Man thinks he *f.* too soon *St.* v 2
Till half their beauties *f.* ; the weary sight *T.* i 510
All flesh is grass, and all its glory *f.* *T.* iii 261 [156
A wreath that cannot *f.*, of flowers that blow *T.* iv
F. rapidly, and by compression marred *T.* iv 669
And *f.* not. There is Paradise that fears *T.* v 572
And, ere one flowery season *f.* and dies *T.* vi 196

FADED.
Their glory *f.*, and their race dispersed *Ex.* 241
Refreshes, where it winds, the *f.* green *J.T.* 39
Can call up life into his *f.* eye *R.* 339
But feels while grasping at his *f.* joys *R.* 473
And lilies for the brows of *f.* age *T.* iv 80 [313
Though *f.* ; and the lands were lately waved *T.* iv
And renovation of a *f.* world *T.* vi 124
Had *f.*, poetry was not an art *T.T.* 585

FADING.
Drew the grey curtain of the *f.* west *Ch.* 263
From *f.* good derives, with chemic art *H.* 159
Both Poet saves and Plume from *f.* *Mrs. M—* 55
Down to the close of life's fast *f.* scene *V.* 85

FAIL.
Give me the fidgets, and my patience *f.* *Con.* 208 [706
That strength would *f.*, opposed against the push *Ex.*
A hopeless task, and damns them if they *f.* *H.* 392
Voice only *f.*, else how distinct they say *M.P.* 5
The difference, though essential *f.* to strike *P.E.* 204
And lest the fulsome artifice should *f.* *P.E.* 291
From urns that never *f.*, through every land *R.* 76
Both *f.* beneath a fever's secret sway *R.* 295
And thou enjoy an Eden ere it *f.* *R.* 364
Where eloquence and artifice shall *f.* *R.* 658
Sighs if perhaps your appetite should *f.* *T.* 215
That never fail'd, nor shall it *f.* me now " *T.* 586
And pillars of our planet seem to *f.* *T.* ii 63
And under such preceptors, who can *f.* ? *T.* ii 284
Your only one, till sides and benches *f.* *T.* ii 475
Would *f.* to exhibit at the public shows *T.* ii 619
Since pulpits *f.*, and sounding boards reflect *T.* iii 21
From ill to worse, is fatal, never *f.* *T.* iv 579
F. for the craving hunger of the state *T.* v 459
That these ménageries *f.* their trust *Tir.* 293
Exults in his miscarriage if he *f.* *Tir.* 478
Were education, else so sure to *f.* *Tir.* 702
But to be rudely censured when they *f.* *T.T.* 158
They trust in navies, and their navies *f.* *T.T.* 466
Farewell, false hearts! whose best affections *f.* *V.* 1
When most relied on is most sure to *f.* *V.* 68
F. not, in virtue and in wisdom laid *Y.O.* 121

FAILED.
He shouted ; nor his friends had *f.* *Cast.* 19
And when his juicy salads *f.* *Ep.* ii 19
And the fresh-blowing breeze never *f.* *M.D.* 8
That never *f.*, nor shall it fail me now " *T.* 586

FAILING.
Of never *f.* love *A Tale* 52
Till, loop and button *f.* both *J.G.* 103
That *f.* left untold *J.P.* 24
'Tis wild good nature's never *f.* lot *R.* 582
In kind compassion of his *f.* strength *R.* 626

FAINT.
F. as a chicken's note that has the pip *Con.* 356
Led them, however faltering, *f.* and slow *T.* 537

Hear the *f.* echo of those brazen throats *T.* iv 104
With *f.* illumination, that uplifts *T.* iv 274
Where, diligent to catch the first *f.* gleam *T.* v 59
Of filial frankness lost, and love grown *f. Tir.* 588

FAINTER.
Thy spirits have a *f.* flow *M.* 5
While thus she spake, I *f.* heard the peals *N.A.* 123

FAINTLY.
How dimly seen, how *f.* understood! *R.* 88
Till she resemble *f.* what she views *R.* 298
F. impress the mind, or not at all *T.* vi 24

FAIR.
A gift to his expecting *f. A Fable* 27
All consecrated to adorn the *f. A.T.* 16
Nor he alone addressed the wayward *f. A.T.* 34 [68
F. fall the deed!" the knight exulting cried *A.T.*
October bright, but mild and *f.* as May *A.T.* 71
Ye *f.* Circassians! all your lutes employ *A.T.* 107 [110
Nymphs quite as *f.*, and happier once than you *A.T.*
"To assert the charter of the chaste and *f. A.T.* 117
A knight—(can he that serves the *f.* do less) *A.T.* 119
For cedars famed, *f.* Lebanon supplied *A.T.* 143
With fragrant turf, and flowers as wild and *f. Ch.* 258
Though *f.* without, and luminous within *Ch.* 343
Guy Earl of Warwick and *f.* Eleanore *Con.* 243 [251
Pernicious weed! whose scent the *f.* annoys *Con.*
'Tis heavy, bulky, and bids *f.* to prove *Con.* 307 [647
The fruits of age, less *f.*, are yet more sound *Con.*
And Jupiter bids *f.* to rule again *Con.* 822
"The strife now stands upon a *f.* award *Con.* 851
He found, concealed beneath a *f.* outside *Ex.* 89 [364
Hast thou, though suckled at *f.* Freedom's breast *Ex.*
To trace thee to the date when yon *f.* sea *Ex.* 550
And this delightful earth, and that *f.* sky *Ex.* 638
F. Cassiopeïa sat *Gr.* 16
Of all the ways that seem to promise *f. H.* 338
A lawyer's dealings should be just and *f. H.* 401
And whether at the toilet of the *f. H.* 684
Happy the bard, (if that *f.* name belong *H.* 754
So, "*F.* and softly," John he cried *J.G.* 85
A *f.* imperial flower *L.R.* 14
The fairest British *f. L.R.* 26
Come, then *f.* maid (in nature wise) *Miss* — 13
Shortlived possession! but the record *f. M.P.* 54
That wish on some *f.* future day *N.Y.G.* 17 [*P.E.* 216
Heaven blessed the youth, and made him fresh and *f.*
Whose fruit, though *f.*, tempts only to destroy *P.E.* 238
Then kiss their idol, and pronounce her *f. P.E.* 300
Ye pimps, who, under Virtue's *f.* pretence *P.E.* 315
Who fasten without mercy on the *f. P.E.* 325
That make Italian flowers so sweet and *f. P.E.* 410
This universal frame, thus wondrous *f. R.* 90
In sighs he worships his supremely *f. R.* 225
Then neither heathy wilds, nor scenes as *f. R.* 331
To the *f.* haven of my native home *R.* 385
How *f.* is Freedom?—he was always free *R.* 399
A step if *f.*, and if a shower approach *R.* 491
The occasion—for *F.* commands the song *T.* i 7
Than when employed to accommodate the *f. T.* i 73
My relish of *f.* prospect; scenes that soothed *T.* i 141
F. fields appear below, such as he left *T.* i 452
These Flora banishes, and gives the *f. T.* i 460
And show this queen of cities, that so *f. T.* i 727
A silly fond conceit of his *f.* form *T.* ii 420
And recognise the slow retiring *f. T.* ii 454
Surveys his *f.* reversion with keen eye *T.* ii 601
Of honour, dignity, and *f.* renown! *T.* iii 59
We are become so candid and so *f. T.* iii 93
Like the *f.* flower dishevelled in the wind *T.* iii 262
F. recompense of labour well bestowed *T.* iii 430
And most attractive, is the *f.* result *T.* iii 639

And lowly creeping, modest and yet *f. T.* iii 663
Created *f.* so much in vain for them *T.* iii 697 [725
Strange that so *f.* a creature should yet want *T.* iii
And surfeited lewd town with her *f.* dues *T.* iii 758
And all that I abhor; thou freckled *f. T.* iii 839
Fast bound in chains of Silence, which the *f. T.* iv 53
Follow the nimble finger of the *f. T.* iv 155
Than the *f.* shepherdess of old romance *T.* iv 538
A wrestling match, a footrace, or a *f. T.* iv 624
To seize the *f.* occasion; well they eye *T.* v 66
He gave them, in its distribution *f. T.* v 200
Made others covet what they saw so *f. T.* v 227
Smit with the beauty of so *f.* a scene *T.* v 560
Directly to the First and Only *F.*—*T.* v 675
F. as it is, existed ere it was *T.* v 799
With those *f.* ministers of light to man *T.* v 816
His presence, who made all so *f.*, perceived *T.* vi 253
On some *f.* theme, some theme divinely *f. T.* vi 754
And suffer for its crime; would learn how *f. T.* vi 827
Shine with his *f.* example, and though small *T.* vi 961
For cleanly riddance than for *f.* attire *T.* vi 994
I played awhile, obedient to the *f. T.* vi 1008
F. science poured the light of truth *Th.* 3
To yon *f.* Sun and his attendant Earth *Tir.* 36
But, *f.* although and feasible it seem *Tir.* 428
Though *f.* in promise, permanent and sound *Tir.* 437
Bid *f.* enough to answer in the proof *Tir.* 564
Whose *f.* example may at once inspire *Tir.* 648
To purchase at the fool-frequented *f. T.T.* 756
With flower as sweet, or fruit as *f. U.* 17
No firmer friendships than the *f.* have shown *V.* 82

FAIRER.
The *f.* scenes of sweet Saucerre *E.* i 46
To wish thee *f.* is no need *N.Y.G.* 5
I say the Bramin has the *f.* claim *T.* 108
But *f.* wreaths are due, though never paid *T.* v 712
Where no eye sees them. And the *f.* forms *T.* vi 188
Makes all still *f.*, as with him no scene *T.* vi 254

FAIREST.
F. and foremost of the train that wait *Ch.* 1
For the chief blessings of my *f.* days *Ch.* 265
And show the softest minds and *f.* forms *Con.* 259
The *f.* British fair *L.R.* 26
The *f.* capital of all the world *T.* i 698
On God's behalf, lays waste his *f.* works *T.* ii 133
Oft water *f.* meadows, and the bird *T.* vi 930
As the *f.* and sweetest that blow *W.N.* 15

FAIRLY.
Which is, that I may *f.* quit *E.* iv 22
I *f.* find myself pitchkettled *E.* iv 32
Faithfully, *f.*, by that sacred test *R.* 134
And *f.* laid the zodiac in the dust *T.* iii 647

FAIRY.
In *f.* land was born the matchless dame *A.T.* 5
To *f.* land be driven *Miss* — 22
And shrubs of *f.* land. The crystal drops *T.* v 113

FAITH.
That man by *F.* and Truth is made a slave *A.T.* 66
Her hope presumption, and her *f.* a lie *Con.* 774
If he be silent, *f.* is all a whim *Con.* 853
And *F.*, the root whence only can arise *Ex.* 111
And kept the *f.* immaculate and pure *Ex.* 208 [239
They breathed in *f.* their well directed prayers *Ex.*
Why having kept good *f.*, and often shown *Ex.* 276
Your *f.* and mine substantially agree *H.* 398
Of *f.*'s supporting rod *St.* iii 14
F., want of common sense *St.* vi 22 [344
Prayer would add *f.*, and *f.* would fix them there *T.*
Humility is crowned, and *F.* receives the prize *T.* 589
Incurs derision for his easy *f. T.* v 500

"Attend to their own music? Have they *f. T.* v 647
And all the mysteries to *f.* proposed *T.* vi 878
Of virtue, and whom virtue, fruit of *f. T.* vi 911
" Our mutual bond of *f.* and truth *The Doves* 9

FAITHFUL.

Act but an honest and a *f.* part *Ex.* 556
F., and faithfully informed, unfold *Ex.* 647
Will trust him for a *f.* generous part *H.* 336
The *f.* monitor's and poet's part *H.* 757
F. remembrancer of one so dear *M.P.* 11
(Try the criterion, 'tis a *f.* guide) *P.E.* 514
Virtuous and *f.* Heberden, whose skill *R.* 279
In *f.* memory she records the crimes *T.* 160
A *f.* likeness of the forms he views *T.* ii 293
But Discipline, a *f.* servant long *T.* ii 725
And *f.* to the foot, his spirits rise *T.* iii 8
A *f.* barrier, not o'erleaped with ease *T.* iii 681 [881
They now are deemed the *f.*, and are praised *T.* vi
Condemns, approves, and with a *f.* voice *Tir.* 33
The encroaching nuisance asks a *f.* hand *Tir.* 601
Where all the attention of his *f.* host *Tir.* 769
And *f.* in its sort *U.* 10

FAITHFULLY.

Faithful, and *f.* informed, unfold *Ex.* 647
F., fairly, by that sacred test *R.* 134

FAITHLESS.

F. alike in friendship and in love *V.* 72

FALCHION.

The sword and *f.* their inventor claim *T.* v 218

FALL.

On waxen pinions soar without a *f. A.T.* 54 [68
" Fair *f.* the deed!" the knight exulting cried *A.T.*
Lethæan gulfs receive them as they *f. B.B.* 7
That none are free from blemish since the *f. Ch.* 204
Thus taught, down *f.* the plumage of his pride *Ch.* 345
I twirl my thumbs, *f.* back into my chair *Con.* 115
You *f.* at once into a lower key *Con.* 329
Know then, and modestly let *f.* your eyes *Con.* 485
Lets *f.* a poem *en passant E.* iv 88 [223
Thence date their sad declension, and their *f. Ex.*
That men have deemed substantial since the *f. H.* 154
Say, botanist, within whose province *f. H.* 286
But if infirmities that *f. M.F.* 41
Thy constant flow of love, that knew no *f. M.P.* 65
After long drought, when rains abundant *f. N.A.* 59
Or should the brambles, interposed, our *f. N.A.* 111
F. soporific on the listless ear *P.E.* 20
And if he fell, would *f.* because he must *P.E.* 30
Leaps every fence but one, there *f.* and dies *P.E.* 93
And Wisdom *f.* before exterior grace *P.E.* 418
It *f.* at last, far wide of his design *P.E.* 575 [604
But, Muse, forbear; long flights forbade a *f. P.E.*
And grace his action ere the curtain *f. R.* 34
Ourselves, and our recovery from our *f. R.* 138
The *f.* of waters, and the song of birds *R.* 183
Its brisker and its graver strains *f.* short *R.* 294
The pride of arrogant distinctions *f. R.* 659
And some are marked to *f. St.* i 14
Who next is fated, and who next to *f. St.* ii 18 [23
One *f.*—the rest, wide-scattered with affright *St.* ii
Why *f.* the Gospel like a gracious dew? *T.* 180
Through the cleft rock, and, chiming as they *f. T.* 193
The task of new discoveries *f.* on me *T.* 218
Reproach a people with his single *f. T.* 234
Shall *f.* on her, when Heaven denies it thee *T.* 512
Pride *f.* unpitied, never more to rise *T.* 588
That seems to swing uncertain, and yet *f. T.* i 358
A mutilated structure, soon to *f. T.* i 774
That *f.* asunder at the touch of fire *T.* ii 11

They touch our country, and their shackles *f. T.* ii 42
The rocks *f.* headlong, and the valleys rise *T.* ii 95
F. prone; the pale inhabitants come forth *T.* ii 125
F. back into our seat, extend an arm *T.* ii 448
For ghostly counsel, if it either *f. T.* ii 556
Of Paradise that has survived the *f.! T.* iii 42
From the dashed pane the deluge as it *f. T.* iii 488
Down *f.* the venerable pile, the abode *T.* iii 767
Houses in ashes, and the *f.* of stocks *T.* iv 16
Let *f.* the curtains, wheel the sofa round *T.* iv 37
F. a soft murmur on the uninjured ear *T.* iv 93
In letting *f.* the curtain of repose *T.* iv 248
Fast *f.* a fleecy shower: the downy flakes *T.* iv 326
That lifts him into life, and lets him *f. T.* iv 791
That in its *f.* the liquid sheet throws wide *T.* v 106
Stand motionless expectants of its *f. T.* v 528
F. first before his resolute rebuke *T.* v 619
On fancied Innocence. Again he *f. T.* v 623
And, intercepting in their silent *f. T.* vi 74
Oft as the price-deciding hammer *f. T.* vi 291 [1011
Let *f.* the unfinished wreath, and roved for fruit *T.* vi
The task now *f.* into the public hand *T.* vi 718
At least his follies have not wrought her *f. T.* vi 976
The props of such proud seminaries *f. Tir.* 499
And save him from a *f. Tran.* i 20
If he should chance to *f. Tran.* ii 21
Such reasoning *f.* like an inverted cone *T.T.* 53
By their own conduct they must stand or *f. T.T.* 108
Adorn the polished periods as they *f. T.T.* 766

FALLACIOUS.

And sees, by no *f.* light or dim *R.* 115
Yet how *f.* is all earthly bliss *R.* 457

FALLACY.

Mere *f.*, or foolishness, or both? *T.* 516

FALLEN.

" Art thou too *f.*, Iberia? Do we see *Ch.* 67
Thy temple, once thy glory, *f.* and raised *Ex.* 259
Chins *f.*, and not an eyeball to be seen *P.E.* 137
F. from her glory, and too weak to rise *T.* 480
Ye *f.* avenues! once more I mourn *T.* i 338
The hope of such hereafter! They have *f. T.* ii 240
Would I had *f.* upon those happier days *T.* iv 513
Another moon new risen, or meteor *f. T.* v 152
To hear that ye were *f.* at last; to know *T.* v 390
Have *f.* in her defence. A Patriot's blood *T.* v 714
See what contempt is *f.* on humankind *Tir.* 814
Bespeaks a land, once Christian, *f.* and lost *T.T.* 428

FALLIBLE.

Then heaven enjoins the *f.* and frail *H.* 391
" *F.* man," the church-bred youth replies *H.* 421
" Is still found *f.*, however wise *H.* 422

FALLING.

And knows that *f.* he shall rise no more *Ch.* 347
The depth, how awful! *f.* there, we burst *N.A.* 110
Lips busy, and eyes fixed, foot *f.* slow *R.* 285
A *f.* empire, hasten its decay *R.* 384
Crush me, ye rocks; ye *f.* mountains, hide *T.* 269
F. at intervals upon the ear *T.* vi 7
And flee for safety to the *f.* rocks *T.* vi 868

FAL LOWS.

I saw far off the weedy *f.* smile *T.* iv 316

FALSE.

And *f.* ones are as rare almost *A Tale* 7
The scales are *f.*, or algebra a lie *Con.* 22
In every tale they tell, or *f.* or true *Con.* 61
Pronounce your human form a *f.* pretence *Con.* 78
'Tis hard if all is *f.* that I advance *Con.* 95
Is the *f.* fire of an o'erheated mind *Con.* 668

Their learning legendary, *f.*, absurd *Ex.* 127
Candid and just, with no *f.* aim in view *Ex.* 648
Friendship a *f.* ideal good *F.* 29
A vain pursuit of fugitive, *f.* good *H.* 4
"Your office is to winnow *f.* from true *H.* 417
A *f.* religion, is unknown to you *H.* 486
That Education gives her, *f.* or true *P.E.* 358
But such as Learning without *f.* pretence *R.* 695
Of Academies, is this *f.* or true? *T.* ii 533
So hollow and so *f.*—I feel my heart *T.* iii 182
Treacherous and *f.*; it smiled and it was cold *T.* v 176
Possess the heart, and fables *f.* as hell *T.* v 862
May no foes ravish thee, and no *f.* friend *T.T.* 332
Farewell, *f.* hearts! whose best affections fail *V.* 1

FALSEHOOD.
"*F.*! which whoso but suspects of truth *T.* v 642

FALSELY.
Is *f.* named, and no such thing *St.* vi 11
But *f.* Sages after sages strove *T.* ii 506

FALTERING.
Led them, however *f.*, faint, and slow *T.* 537

FAME.
Harmony the path to *f.* *B.* 24
Drop one by one from *F.'s* neglecting hand *B.B.* 6
Is rather careless of her sister's *f.* *Ch.* 454
While *F.* and self-complacence are the bribe *Ch.* 468
Perhaps, enchanted with the love of *f.* *Ch.* 539
"Matthew," says *F.*, "with endless pains *E.* iv 73
Speed us away to battle and to *f.*! *Ex.* 289
Unless belied by common *f.* *F.* 86
His *f.* soon spread around *J.G.* 114
Thee, therefore, of commercial *f.*, but more *J.T.* 5
His object chosen, wealth or *f. Mor.* 27 [*f.? P.E.* 246
Good sense, good health, good conscience, and good
  Ambition, avarice, and the lust of *f.* *P.E.* 273
Feebly and vainly, at poetic *f.* *R.* 802
Thy *f.* diffuse, praised not for utterance meet *S.* i 13
The Frenchman first in literary *f.* *T.* 303
Of academic *f.* (howe'er deserved) *T.* iii 15
What chance that I, to *f.* so little known *T.* iii 23
Ye sage dispensers of poetic *f.* *T.* iii 457   [491
Whose oath is rhetoric, and who swear for *f.* *T.* iv
Of honours, or emolument, or *f.* *T.* iv 785
With schemes of monumental *f.*; and sought *T.* v 182
The fatal issue to his health, *f.*, peace *T.* v 601
Till Persecution dragged them into *f.* *T.* v 725
F. had not left the venerable man *T.* vi 492
Or what achievements of immortal *f.* *T.* vi 933
Should move a sneer at thy deserved *f.* *Tir.* 142
And in the firmament of *f.* still shines *Tir.* 281
But families of less illustrious *f.* *Tir.* 354
His wealth, *f.*, honours, all that I intend *Tir.* 389
Contributes most perhaps to enhance their *f.* *Tir.* 468
Threaten his health, his fortune, and his *f.* *Tir.* 532
Caught from the deeds of ancient *f.* *Tir.* 645
A higher than a mere plebeian *f.* *Tir.* 691
To float a bubble on the breath of *F.*—*T.T.* 746
The poet's lyre, to fix his *f.* *U.* 25
To *f.* as lasting as the earth pretend *V.* 17

FAMED.
So *f.* for his talent in nicely discerning *A.C.* 8
For cedars *f.*, fair Lebanon supplied *A.T.* 143
F. for thy probity from shore to shore *J.T.* 6
And sound integrity, not more than *f.* *T.* iii 259
Evander, *f.* for piety, for years *T.* vi 490
Of Avon, *f.* in song. Ah pleasant proof *T.* vi 682
Ye once were justly *f.* for bringing forth *Tir.* 279

FAMILIAR.
And Thornton is *f.* with the joy *Ch.* 253

F. with the wonders of the sky *H.* 442
With such fine words *f.* to his tongue *P.E.* 509
To studies then *f.*, since forgot *R.* 374
And wilds *f.* with a lion's roar *R.* 779
Fastidious, seeking less *f.* scenes *T.* i 512
Constant at routs, *f.* with a round *T.* ii 385
Has made at last *f.*; she has lost *T.* iii 339
F., serve to emancipate the rest! *T.* v 298
Is made *f.*, watches his approach *T.* v 423
F. with the effect we slight the cause *T.* vi 121
Grown so *f.* with her frequent guest *T.* vi 306
Whose face too was *f.* to his view *T.* vi 494
She makes *f.* with a Heaven unseen *T.* vi 926
And, least *f.* where he should be most *Tir.* 573

FAMILY.
Now baskets up the *f.* of plagues *T.* ii 667
Not visible, his *f.* of worlds *T.* iii 232
The *f.* dispersed, and fixing thought *T.* iv 137
Its *f.* and tribe. Laburnum rich *T.* vi 149
Thus harmony and *f.* accord *T.* vi 379
But *f.* of less illustrious fame *Tir.* 354

FAMINE.
So may the wolf, whom *f.* has made bold *Ch.* 184
F., and Pestilence, her first-born son *Her.* 59
Did *F.* or did Plague prevail *St.* i 7
Nor Plague nor *F.* came *St.* i 10
He calls for *F.*, and the meagre fiend *T.* ii 185
Whom *f.* cannot reconcile to filth *T.* iv 417
To escape the impending *f.*, often scared *T.* v 68

FAMISHED.
Food for the *f.* rovers of the flood *Ch.* 532
Is *f.*—finds no music in the song *T.* i 468

FAMOUS.
Of *f.* London town *J.G.* 4

FAN.
The flirted *f.*, the bridle, and the toss *H.* 344
Sighs must *f.* it, tears must water *N.C.* 19
Like a fat squab upon a Chinese *f.* *P.E.* 218
Much less to feed and *f.* the fatal fires *R.* 109
There, wanting nothing save a *f.* *R.C.* 17
Her head erect, her *f.* upon her lips *T.* 134
Graced with a sword, and worthier of a *f.* *T.* i 771
To carry me, to *f.* me while I sleep *T.* ii. 30
That never tire, soon *f.* them all away *T.* iii 763
The silent circle *f.* themselves, and quake *T.* iv 149
Occasion needs but *f.* them, and they blaze *T.* v 207

FANATIC.
And half the night? *f.* and absurd! *Con.* 578
What is *f.* frenzy, scorned so much *Con.* 651
Convicts a man *f.* in the extreme *Con.* 665

FANCIED.
A *f.* head against a *f.* post *A.T.* 45
Of *f.* scorn and undeserved disdain *Con.* 348
We find the friends we *f.* we had won *E.* iii 16
A scene of *f.* bliss and heart-felt care *H.* 5
In chase of *f.* happiness, still wooed *T.* iii 126
In *f.* peace beneath his dangerous branch *T.* v 325
On *f.* Innocence. Again he falls *T.* v 623

FANCIFUL.
And it seemed to a *f.* view *The Rose* 6

FANCY.
There *F.* nursed her in ideal bowers *A.T.* 7
F. endued her in her natal hour) *A.T.* 92
The work of my *F.* the more *C.* 22
That earth has seen, or *f.* can devise *Ch.* 254
Suppose (when thought is warm, and *f.* flows *Ch.* 379

FANCY—FASCINATION

Wherever chance, caprice, or *f.* guide *Con.* 794
Thought is so rare, and *f.* so profuse *Con.* 856
And tricks and turns, that *F.* may devise *Ew.* 137
Smooth, ductile, and even his *f.* must flow *F.M.* 18
In many such *f.* as these *Gr.* 52
And *f.* I fear they will seem *Gr.* 53
And ask, and *f.* they find, blessings there *H.* 243
F. may stand aloof from the design *H.* 672
Or lively *f.* guess *Miss —* 104
The glow that *F.* gave it fades *Mor.* 36
F. shall weave a charm for my relief *M.P.* 18
And while the wings of *f.* still are free *M.P.* 118
There Genius, Learning, *F.*, Wit *Mrs. M—* 45
But oh! for him my *F.* culls *Pat.* 13
Not all whose eloquence the *f.* fills *P.E.* 13
Footing it in the dance that *F.* leads *P.E.* 308
From *F.*'s influence, and intemperate Zeal *P.E.* 455
Or *F.*'s fondness for the child she bears *P.E.* 517
More hideous foes than *f.* can devise *R.* 68
Then with a glance of *F.*, to survey *R.* 73
Wherever freakish *f.* points the way *R.* 128
Pleased *F.* claps her pinions at the sight *R.* 190
Forgery of *f.*, and a dream of woes *R.* 324
Beggar's Invention, and makes *F.* lame *R.* 710
A sleeping fog, and *f.* it dry land *T.* 4
Turn eastward now, and *F.* shall apply *T.* 97
Ingenious *F.*, never better pleased *T.* i 72
The dreams of *f.*, tranquil and secure *T.* i 236
The powers of *f.* and strong thought are theirs *T.* i 402
Her *F.* followed him through foaming waves *T.* i 539
At what a sailor suffers; *F.* too *T.* i 541
Thus *F.* paints thee, and though apt to err *T.* i 661
The skittish *f.* with facetious tales *T.* ii 470
Through every change that *F.*, at the loom *T.* ii 608
While *f.*, like the finger of a clock *T.* iv 118
Of *f.*, or proscribes the sound of mirth *T.* iv 176
That *F.* finds in her excursive flights *T.* iv 242
Me oft has *F.*, ludicrous and wild *T.* iv 286
The glassy threads with which the *F.* weaves *T.* iv 306
My *f.*, ere yet liberty of choice *T.* iv. 698
Capricious, in which *f.* seeks in vain *T.* v 120
Pushed with a madman's fury. *F.* shrinks *T.* vi 513
For her the *F.*, roving unconfined *Tir.* 21
Oh thou, whom, borne on *f.*'s eager wing *Tir.* 131
In *f.* sees him more superbly ride *Tir.* 368
Genius is thine, and thou art *F.*'s nurse; *T.T.* 290
That verse, whatever fire the *f.* warms *T.T.* 512
Verse in the finest mould of *f.* cast *T.T.* 618
F. that from the bow that spans the sky *T.T.* 702
F. has sported all her powers away *T.T.* 730
With all that *F.* can invent to please *T.T.* 765
So *F.* dreams. Disprove it, if ye can *Y.O.* 29

FANDANGO.
F., ball, and rout! *F.B.* 33

FANGED.
And *f.* with brass the demons are abroad *N.A.* 102

FANGS.
A quarry of stout spurs and knotted *f. Y.O.* 117

FANNED.
If *f.* by balmy and nutritious air *T.* iii 524

FANNING.
Around her, *f.* light her streamers gay *M.P.* 95

FANTASIES.
And *f.* of dotards, such as show *T.* vi 507

FANTASTIC.
But how a body so *f.*, trim *T.* ii 460
(*F.* misarrangement)! on the roof *T.* v 111

FAR-BEAMING.
In every flash of his *f.* eye *T.* iii 602

FARCE.
Till *f.* itself, most mournfully jejune *R.* 711
Of solemn *f.*, where Ignorance in stilts *T.* ii 736

FARE.
A Spaniel, Beau, that *f.* like you *Beau* 1
The thistle's downy seed my *f. G.* 2
So *f.* it with the multitudes beguiled *H.* 278
So *f.* it with the sinner, when he feels *T.* 257
Hard *f.*! but such as boyish appetite *T.* i 123
Thus *f.* the shivering natives of the north *T.* i 617
Thy simple *f.*, and all thy plain delights *T.* i 646
His daily *f.* as delicate. Alas! *T.* ii 626
So *f.* we in this prison-house, the world *T.* ii 661
Of critic appetite, no sordid *f. T.* iii 461
Ill *f.* the traveller now, and he that stalks *T.* iv 341
So *f.* thy church. But how thy church may *f. T.* vi 888
To feed our infant minds with proper *f. Tir.* 116

FARED.
So on they *f.* Discourse on other themes *T.* vi 539

FAREWELL. [79
Lay snug and warm;—'twas summer's *f.* peep! *A.T.*
F., my former joys! I sigh no more *Ch.* 240
And, *f.* else all hope of pure delight *Con.* 681
The freeman to a *f.* flight *F.B.* 20
Then *f.* all that must create *M.F.* 45
Adieus and *f.* are a sound unknown *M.P.* 33
And now, *F.*—Time unrevoked has run *M.P.* 112
F.! we meet no more? *O.* ii 24
Then *f.* British freedom *Pat.* 24
The poplars are felled;—*f.* to the shade *P.F.* 1
But *f.* promises of happier fruits *R.* 241
Her smile his aim, all higher aims *f.*! *R.* 246
Then *f.* all self-satisfying schemes *T.* 7
Deceitful views of future bliss, *f.*! *T.* 9
So *f.* envy of the Peasant's Nest! *T.* i 247
F. those honours, and *f.* with them *T.* ii. 239
And undebauched. But we have bid *f. T.* iii 744
But *f.* now to unsuspicious nights *T.* iv 565
But once enslaved, *f.*! I could endure *T.* v 477
But now *f.* all legendary tales *Tir.* 181
Health's last *f.*, a staff to thine old age *Tir.* 878
If this be kingly, then *f.* for me *T.T.* 149
F., false hearts! whose best affections fail *V.* 1
Your altered heart—and so, my Lord, *f.*! *V.* 26
First, *f.* Niger! whom now duly proved *V.* 7
Terentius, once my friend, *f.* to thee! *V.* 30

FARMER.
Woe to the gardener's pale, the *f.*'s hedge *T.* iv 436
For then the *f.* come jog, jog *Y.D.* 13
Oh! why are *f.* made so coarse *Y.D.* 61

FARRIER.
Their mildest physic is a *f.*'s purge *Ch.* 502
Some *f.* should prescribe his proper course *Con.* 411

FAR-SOUGHT.
I found the *f.* treasure near 1789, 28

FAR-SPREADING.
That sweep the skirt of some *f.* wood *T.* i 184

FAR-STRETCHING.
And ash *f.* his umbrageous arm *T.* i 311

FASCINATE.
All vanish there, and *f.* no more *P.E.* 620

FASCINATION.
Some to the *f.* of a name *T.* vi 101

FASHION.

Steps forth to *f*. and refine the race *Ch.* 98
Yet *F*., leader of a chattering train *Con.* 457
By *F*. taught, forbade them once to name *Con.* 496
As Interest bias'd knaves, or *F.* fools *Ex.* 38
That *F.*, Taste, or Luxury suggest *H.* 446
Has time worn out, or *f.* put to shame *P.E.* 245
Refines his speech and *f.* his address *R.* 240
Nereids or Dryads, as the *f.* leads *R.* 537
Some swayed by *f.*, some by deep disgust *R.* 607
A massy slab, in *f.* square or round *T.* i 21
Advancing *F.* to the post of Truth *T.* i 744
The freaks of *f.*, regulate the dress *T.* ii 317
Of *f.*, dissipation, taverns, stews *T.* ii 770   [223
Thus decked, he charms a world whom *F.* blinds *T.* iv
The worse for what it soils. The *f.* runs *T.* iv 555
Where *F.* shall not sanctify abuse *T.* vi 852
For since (so *f.* dictates) all, who claim *Tir.* 690

FASHIONABLE.
And just proportion, *f.* mien *T.* ii 421
For loose expense and *f.* waste *Tir.* 204

FASHIONABLY.
Not yet so blank, or *f.* blind *H.* 92

FASHIONED.
Thy bones not *f.*, and thy joints not knit *Ex.* 475
Or was he not, till *f.* in the womb? *F.A.* 27
To snare the mole, or with ill *f.* hook *R.* 401
Her works must needs excel who *f.* you *R.* 544
Much more who *f.* it, he gives it praise *T.* v 801

FASHIONING.
"And *f.* my softened heart *Miss* — 91

FASHION-LED.
But whom do I advise? the *f. Tir.* 779

FAST.
Seized *f.* the saddle and sprang up behind *A.T.* 178
F. as the thirsting ear can drink the sound *Ch.* 112
Sin forged, and Ignorance made *f.*, the chain *Ch.* 237
Lords of the conquered soil, there rooted *f. Ex.* 192
Seized *f.* his hand, held out to set them free *Ex.* 219
Suggests the expedient of a yearly *f. Ex.* 401
The *f.* that wins deliverance, and suspends *Ex.* 406
Hope, as an anchor firm and sure holds *f. H.* 167
And bids the mountains he has built stand *f. H.* 476
His eyes shut *f.*, his fingers in his ears *H.* 658
F. by the stream that bounds your just domain *Her.* 47
Seized *f.* the flowing mane *J.G.* 46
And still, as *f.* as he drew near *J.G.* 117
F. rooted against every rub " *P.* 16
No. But his own engagement binds him *f. P.E.* 106
Seems verging *f.* towards the female side *P.E.* 430
And through life's labyrinth holds *f.* the clue *P.E.* 357
The propagated myriads spread so *f. P.E.* 484
Delusions strong as Hell shall bind him *f. P.E.* 609
The leaves came on not quite so *f. P.T.* 46
Which thousands once *f* chained to quit no more *R.* 2
F. anchored in the deep abyss of space *R.* 84
F. by the banks of the slow-winding Ouse *R.* 804
The chambermaid, and shut it *f. R.C.* 50
F. by their native shore! *R.G.* 4
But that she *f.*, and, item, goes to church *T.* 152
And all their leaves *f.* fluttering, all at once *T.* 189
F. locked in mine, with pleasure such as Love *T.* i 146
Delighted. There, *f.* rooted in their bank *T.* i 166
Descending now (but cautious, lest too *f.*) *T.* i 266
Who then that has thee, would not hold thee *f. T.* ii 129
The mirror of the mind, and hold them *f. T.* ii 291
They gaze upon the links that hold them *f. T.* ii 664
And gibbeted, as *f.* as catchpole-claws *T.* ii 684
They may confirm his habits, rivet *f. T.* ii 767

Like a gross fog Bœotian, rising *f. T.* iii 495 [ii 351
But hark—the Doctor's voice!—*f.* wedged between *T.*
And *f.* condensed upon the dewy sash *T.* iii 496
F. as the periods from his fluent quill *T.* iv 19
Now stir the fire, and close the shutters *f. T.* iv 36
F. bound in chains of Silence, which the fair *T.* iv 53
By flocks, *f.* feeding and selecting each *T.* iv 318
F. falls a fleecy shower, the downy flakes *T.* iv 326
And heaviest, light of foot steals *f.* away *T.* iv 442
That trickle down the branches, *f.* congealed *T.* v 114
Recovering *f.* its liquid music, prove *T.* vi 261
A rat *f.* clinging to the cage *T.B.* 46
F. stuck within his own *T.B.* 60
Holds *f.* her office here, can ne'er forget *Tir.* 134
Either his gratitude shall hold him *f. Tir.* 893
He that holds *f.* the golden mean *Trans. H.* 7
Free to prove all things, and hold *f.* the best *T.T.* 273
Sat *f.* on George's brows again 1789, 45
Down to the close of life's *f.* fading scene *V.* 85

FAST-ANCHORED.
And we the righteous, whose *f.* isle *T.* ii 151

FASTEN.
Who *f.* without mercy on the fair *P.E.* 325
And wear the bonds, than *f.* them on him *T.* ii 36

FASTER.
And made him *f.* run *J.G.* 228
Or bind them *f.* on, and add still more? *T.* 186
Shakes it again, and *f.*, to the ground *T.* 241
But *f.* far, and more than all the rest *T.* iv 613

FASTIDIOUS.
F., seeking less familiar scenes *T.* i 512
F., or else listless, or perhaps *T.* ii 306

FASTING.
Thy *f.*, when calamity at last *Ex.* 400
All *f.* else, whate'er be the pretence *Ex.* 412
F. and prayer sit well upon a priest *H.* 403

FAT.
Like a *f.* squab upon a Chinese fan *P.E.* 218

FATAL.
A stroke as *f.* as the scythe of Death *Ch.* 144
Mankind from quarrels, but their *f.* end *Con.* 174
But here, alas! the *f.* difference lies *H.* 282
And pleasure's *f.* wiles? *O.* ii 9
Remorse, the *f.* egg by Pleasure laid *P.E.* 239
To *f.* ills; that though the path he treads *P.E.* 545
The least obliquity is *f.* here *P.E.* 599
Much less to feed and fan the *f.* fires *R.* 109
She sprang no *f.* leak *R.G.* 19
That none, decoyed into that *f.* ring *T.* ii 631
From ill to worse, is *f.*, never fails *T.* iv 579
All has its date below; the *f.* hour *T.* v 529
The *f.* issue to his health, fame, peace *T.* v 601
A flat and *f.* negative obtains *Tir.* 714
Some mischief *f.* to his future worth *Tir.* 758

FATALIST.
Else, on the *f.* unrighteous plan *P.E.* 27

FATE.
F. steals along with silent tread *A Fable* 36
But *F.* reserved Sir Airy to maintain *A.T.* 56
Descanting on his *f. Cast.* 56
His manners with his *f.*, puts on the brute *Ch.* 154
F. having placed all truth above his reach *Con.* 142
They tell us of the *f.* of Rome *M.* ii 3
Far be it from my *f. Miss* — 26
Which *f.* shall brightly gild *N.Y.G.* 18   [49
These for the rich: the rest, whom *F.* had placed *T.* i

Now scorned, but worthy of a better *f. T.* i 254
Your *f.* unmerited, once more rejoice *T.* i 339
Swears 'tis a bargain, rails at his hard *f. T.* vi 293
Just then, by adverse *f.* impressed *T.B.* 43 [*T.* vi 910
Would make his *f.* his choice ; whom peace, the fruit
Doomed to a no less ignominious *f. Tir.* 498
O learn, from our example and our *f. T.T.* 436
But *F.* thy growth decreed ; autumnal rains *Y.O.* 23

FATED.
Ill *f.* race ! how deeply must they rue *Her.* 51
Who next is *f.*, and who next to fall *St.* ii 18

FATHER.
One man the common *f.* of the kind *Ch.* 18
The tender ties of *f.*, husband, friend *Ch.* 141
As if they met around a *f.'s* bier *Con.* 874
Cured of the golden calves, their *F.'s* sin *Ex.* 215
And while she takes, as at a *f.'s* hand *H.* 157
A *F.'s* frown, and kiss his chastening hand *R.* 346
Our *f.* knew the value of a screen *T.* i 255
Where once your noble *f.* won a crown ! *T.* ii 281
That sits a stigma on his *f.'s* house *T.* ii 760
Who had survived the *f.*, served the son *T.* iii 748
And smiling say—My *F.* made them all !" *T.* v 747
Appropriates nature as his *F.'s* work *T.* v 761
A *f.*, whose authority, in show *T.* vi 30
All, in the universal *F.'s* love ? *T.* vi 449
One Lord, one *F.* Error has no place *T.* vi 784
Indulges all a *f.'s* heartfelt glee *Tir.* 321
The *f.*, who designs his babe a priest *Tir.* 364
A *f.* blest with an ingenuous son *Tir.* 543
F., and friend, and tutor, all in one *Tir.* 544
He will not blush, that has a *f.'s* heart *Tir.* 547
His favourite stand between his *f.'s* knees *Tir.* 570
And seems it nothing in a *f.'s* eye *Tir.* 615
Perhaps a *f.*, blest with any brains *Tir.* 626
And hopest thou not ('tis every *f.'s* hope) *Tir.* 875
While Alfred's name, the *f.* of his age *T.T.* 105
One man alone, the *f.* of us all *Y.O.* 144
Our *f.'s* triumphs and our own 1789, 16

FATHER-BIRD.
Soon every *f.* and mother *P.T.* 56

FATHOMLESS.
Ocean exhibits, *f.* and broad *R.* 525
Profounder, in the *f.* abyss *T.* v 594

FATHOMS.
But, if you please, some *f.* lower down *T.* 170

FATIGUE.
Incurring short *f.*: and though our years *T.* i 129
In chariots and sedans, know no *f. T.* i 755
The insupportable *f.* of thought *T.* vi 106
To indulge his genius, after long *f. T.T.* 153

FATIGUED.
The wreck of what I was, *f.* I come *R.* 386
F. me, never weary of the pipe *T.* iv 706

FATTENED.
The excise if *f.* with the rich result *T.* iv 504

FATTENING.
Streams edged with osiers, *f.* every field *H.* 47

FAULT.
(A *f.* philosophers might blame *A Fable* 5
But when the breath of age commits the *f. Con.* 49
Sometimes the *f.* is all our own *F.* 145
F. in the life breed errors in the brain *P.E.* 564
To *f.* compassionate or blind *M.F.* 56
Mark well the finished plan without a *f. R.* 551
England, with all thy *f.*, I love thee still *T.* ii 206

Is oft-times proof of wisdom, when the *f. T.* iii 39
The spaniel dying for some venial *f. T.* vi 418
Or looked for now, the *f.* must be his own *Tir.* 243
The whole reproach, the *f.* was all his own *Tir.* 536
A subject's *f.*, a subject may proclaim *T.T.* 113

FAUNS
The *F.* and Satyrs, a lascivious race *A.T.* 199

FAVOUR.
Were hushed in *f.* of thy generous plea *Ch.* 311
The *f.* poured upon the Jewish name *Ex.* 170
Secure the *f.*, and enhance the joy *Ex.* 678
Secure of *f.* at her court *Mrs. M—* 22
What *f.* then not yet possessed *N.Y.G.* 9
Yet seek him, in his *f.* life is found *R.* 353
Thankless for *f.* from on high *St.* v 1
Lost *f.* back again, and closed the breach *T.* ii 724
Though many boast thy *f.*. and affect *T.* iii 294 [33
Whose *f.*, like the clouds of spring, might lower *T.* vi
And trivial *f.*, lasting as the life *T.* vi 630
Religion, richest *f.* of the skies *T.T.* 268

FAVOURABLE.
Man's *f.* judgment, but his own *Con.* 764

FAVOURED.
And the most *f.* land, look where we may *Ex.* 226
Has he not hid thee, and thy *f.* land *Ex.* 562
And right toward the *f.* place *Mor.* 19
He proves, less happy than his *f.* brute *R.* 633
The *f.* few—the enthusiast you despise *T.* 231
And sinks, while *f.* with the means to rise *T.* 544
Who oftenest sacrifice are *f.* least *T.* i 411
Towards the Antarctic. Even the *f.* isles *T.* i 620
Drew from the stream below. More *f.*, we *T.* ii 501
He seeks a *f.* spot ; that where he builds *T.* iii 471
That *f.* such a dream, in days like these *T.* iv 530
With transports such as *f.* lovers feel *T.* iv 721
" *F.* as ours, transgressors from the womb *T.* v 829

FAVOURITE.
And graced with all her gifts the *f.* child *A.T.* 10
Presumes itself chief *f.* of the skies *Con.* 674
" My *f.* Nymph to slight *J.P.* 34
'Twas but a mile ; your *f.* horse *M.F.* 23
And without discipline the *f.* child *P.E.* 361
Of my *f.* field, and the bank where they grew *P.F.* 6
To spare no passion, and no *f.* sin *R.* 136
The world can boast, and her chief *f.* share *R.* 186
Stand, never overlooked, our *f.* elms *T.* i 167
Sermons, and city feasts, and *f.* airs *T.* iv 84
His *f.* herb ; while all the leafless groves *T.* iv 319
The rustic throng beneath his *f.* beech *T.* iv 708
A scene so friendly to his *f.* task *T.* vi. 264
With tears o'er hapless *f.* shed *T.B.* 2
Her *f.*, even in his cage *T.B.* 4   [231
Transport them, and are made their *f.* themes *Tir.*
His *f.* stand between his father's knees *Tir.* 570
To doubt the love his *f.* may pretend *T.T.* 159
She rears her *f.* man of all mankind *T.T.* 217

FAWN.
To skip and gambol like a *f. Ep.* ii 23   [327
The bounding *f.*, that darts across the glade *T.* vi

FEAR.
And filled her with a thousand *f. A Fable* 13
And all her *f.'s* were hushed together *A Fable* 17
F. seized the trembling sex ; in every grove *A,T.* 97
He dreamed not of a foe, or if his *f. A.T.* 151
Of virtue too well fenced to *f.* a flaw *A.T.* 155 [182
She whispered still that he had naught to *f. A.T.*
With little to hope or to *f. C.* 54   [*Ch.* 46
Through *f.*, not love ; and Heaven abhors the fee

FEAR—FEAT

The occasion of transmuting *f*. to love ? *Ch.* 225
Owns no superior but the God she *f. Ch.* 275
The *f*. and hopes of a commercial care *Ch.* 279
I may alarm thee, but I *f*. the shame *Ch.* 294
And *f*., not courage, is its proper source *Con.* 180
The *f*. of tyrant custom, and the *f. Con.* 181
The *f*. of being silent makes us mute *Con.* 352
To *f*. each other, fearing none beside *Con.* 362 [375
But counterfeit is blind, and skulks through *f. Con.*
But *f*. to call a more important cause *Con.* 397 [495
Acquainted with the woes that *f*. or shame *Con.*
I grant it dangerous, and approve your *f. Con.* 653
And while she seems to scorn him, only *f. Con.* 788
Oh, happy Britain! we have not to *f. E.* iii 54 [i 7
Yet *f*. Youth ofttimes healthful and at ease *Ep.*
For then he lost his *f. Ep.* ii 26
Forgot the blush that virgin *f*. impart *Ex.* 47
Pronounced him frantic, and his *f*. a dream *Ex.* 70
Knock at the gates of nations, rouse their *f. Ex.* 269
In such a cause they could not dare to *f. Ex.* 621
And thou couldst laugh away the *f*. of harm *Ex.* 705
And fancies I *f*. they will seem *Gr.* 53
But gently to rebuke his awkward *f. H.* 61
Nor hope have they, nor *f*. of aught to come *H.* 254
And silence every *f*. with, God is just *H.* 370
While Bigotry, with well dissembled *f. H.* 657
Expects in darkness and heart-chilling *f. H.* 714
He drops at once his fetters and his *f. H.* 725
And bid us *f*. the same *M.* ii 4   [6
"Grieve not, my child, chase all thy *f*. away!" *M.P.*
Shine safe without a *f*. to fade *Mrs. M—* 50   [67
The looks and gestures of their griefs and *f. N.A.*
Their periwigs of wool and *f*. combined *N.A.* 75
For such a cause, to feel the slightest *f. N.A.* 90
That owns a carcass and not quake for *f*.? *N.A.* 100
Prodigies ominous, and viewed with *f.P.E.* 99 [*P.A.* 2
And *f*. those who buy them and sell them, are knaves
Be flowery, and he see no cause of *f. P.E.* 546
I *f*. we shall have winter yet" *P.T.* 25
The love of virtue, and the *f*. of God *R.* 730
Consoled him and dispelled his *f. R.C.* 90
He holds no parley with unmanly *f. R.H.* 5
Wins no notice, wakes no *f. St.* iv 20
'Tis Judgment shakes him; there's the *f. St.* v 29
Their sin is plain, but what have we to *f. T.* 129
From servile *f*., or be the more enslaved? *T.* 184
No *F*. attends to quench his glowing fires *T.* 189
What *f*. he feels his gratitude inspires *T.* 190
The work of generous love and filial *f. T.* 226
The last impossible, he *f*. the first *T.* 265
He has no hope who never had a *f. T.* 298
Crippling his pleasures with the cramp of *f*.! *T.* 466
As Vengeance can inflict, or sinners *f. T.* 554
They love it, and yet loathe it; *f*. to die *T.* i 485
Reflection and remorse, the *f*. of shame *T.* i 489
With conflict of contending hopes and *f. T.* i 668
And bids the world take heart and banish *f. T.* ii 195
That *f*. no discipline of human hands *T.* ii 325
And find the total of their hopes and *f. T.* iii 132
And seem to smile at what they need not *f. T.* iii 575
Though eloquent themselves, yet *f*. to break *T.* iv 54
Then sleep was undisturbed by *F*., unscared *T.* iv 561
Babes in the cause of freedom, and should *f. T.* v 291
Adored through *f*., strong only to destroy *T.* v 445
And fade not. There is Paradise that *f. T.* v 572
Scripture is still a trumpet to his *f. T.* v 611
And *f*. as yet was not, nor cause for *f. T.* vi 367
A jealousy and an instructive *f. T.* vi 374
Can cheat, or move a moment's *f*. in me? *T.* vi 508
The garden *f*. no blight, and needs no fence *T.* vi 771
Holds its due course, nor *f*. the frosts of age *T.* vi 790
I *f*. lest thee alone they seize *The Doves* 23
And know no other *f. The Doves* 24

Preserved from guilt by salutary *f. Tir.* 111
Rejoices with a wholesome *f. Trans. H.* 20
Thus free from censure overawed by *f. T.T.* 115
Happy the state that has not these to *f. T.T.* 167
While no base *f*. impedes her in her course *T.T.* 267
Beset with every ill but that of *f. T.T.* 363
That charm down *f*., they frolic it along *T.T.* 463
And some wits flag through *f*. of losing it *T.T.* 521
He then is full of fright and *f. Y.D.* 9

FEARED.   [575

Then too much *f*., and now too much forgot *Ex.*
And may be *f*. amid the busiest scenes *R.* 121
A plague so little to be *f. M.F.* 33
Are neither felt nor *f*. by them *N.* 7
Sounds such as these, so worthy to be *f. N.A.* 84
Not else unworthy to be *f. Q.V* 67
That rule he prized, by that he *f. St.* iii 21
No want of timber then was felt or *f. T.* i 57
And tender blade, that *f*. the chilling blast *T.* iv 331
Of flowers, that *f*. no enemy but warmth *T.* v 159
They *f*., and as his perfect image love *T.* vi 400
Lurks the contagion chiefly to be *f. Tir.* 689
Be great, be *f*., be envied, be admired *V.* 16

FEARFUL.

Perhaps when sickness, or some *f*. dream *H.* 217
And 'tis a *f*. spectacle to see *T.* ii 662
Conscious and *f*. of too deep a plunge *T.* v 64
As *f*. of offending whom he wished *T.* vi 501
But seldom (as if *f*. of expense) *T.T.* 698

FEARING.

To fear each other, *f*. none beside *Con.* 362
The sons of Albion; *f*. each to lose *T.* iii 599

FEARLESS.

And, with a *f*. confidence, make known *Con.* 695
And *f*. of the billowy scene *Q.V.* 71
F. of humid air and gathering rains *T.* 212
F. of wrong, reposed his weary strength *T.* i 15
And stands an impudent and *f*. mark *T.* ii 812
F., and rapt away from all his cares *T.* iii 311
F., a soul that does not always think *T.* iv 285
Graze with the *f*. flocks; all bask at noon *T.* vi 774
No longer takes, as once, with *f*. ease *Tir.* 569

FEASIBLE.

But, fair although and *f*. it seem *Tir.* 428

FEAST.

And made so welcome at their simple *f. Con.* 532
That certain *f*. are instituted now *Con.* 823
The Savour's *f*., his own blest bread and wine *Ex.* 377
And if the *f*. of freedom cloy thee not *Ex.* 671
The full-gorged savage, at his nauseous *f. H.* 509
Sits banqueting, and God provides the *f. P.E.* 166
Let him your rubric and your *f*. prescribe *P.E.* 185
Beneath the open sky she spreads the *f. T.* i 433
Recoils from its own choice—at the full *f. T.* i 467
Could pageantry and dance, and *f*. and song *T.* iii 314
Sermons, and city *f*., and favourite airs *T.* iv. 84
Enjoyed, spare *f*.! a radish and an egg! *T.* iv 173
To theatre, or jocund *f*., or ball *T.* v 410
In *f*. or in the chase, in song or dance *T.* v 758

FEASTING.

And, *f*. on an onion and a crust *T.T.* 241

FEAT.

The *f*. of Vestris, or the naval force *Con.* 58
Some write a narrative of wars and *f. T.* iii 139
To Nature's praises. Heroes and their *f. T.* iv 705
Performing such inimitable *f. T.* v 125
The inglorious *f*., and. clamorous in praise *T.* vi 436

FEAT—FEEL

His wild excursions, window-breaking *f. Tir.* 228
F. of renown, though wrought in ancient days *T.T.* 22
The *f.* of heroes and the wrath of kings *T.T.* 597
For *f.* of sanguinary hue 1789, 25

FEATHER.
Bents, Wool, and *f.* mixed *A Tale* 40
And licked his *f.* smooth *B.R.* 20
Might smooth her *f.*, and enjoy her cage *Ch.* 306
Birds of all *f.*, beasts of every name *N.A.* 65
That dries his *f.*, saturate with dew *T.* i 494
Their points obtuse, and *f.* drunk with wine! *T.* ii 808
And fledged with icy *f.*, nod superb *T.* v 26
A soldier's *f.*, or a lady's glove *T.T.* 549

FEATHERED.
His *f.* shipmates' eyes *A Tale* 58
The *f.* tribes domestic. Half on wing *T.* v 62
The ostrich, silliest of the *f.* kind *Tir.* 789

FEATURE.
Ghastly in *f.*, and his stammering tongue *Ex.* 356
To hide the shocking *f.* of her face *P.E.* 298
Yon ancient prude, whose withered *f.* show *T.* 131
Pleasure and wonder in his *f.* mixed *T.* 416
All her reflected *f.* Bacon there *T.* i 702
Of that one *f.* can be well content *T.* v 474
The *f.* of the last degenerate times *T.* vi 900
Just echoes thine, whose *f.* are thine own *Tir* 846
That gild thy *f.*, show in theirs 1789, 65

FECULANCE.
The dregs and *f.* of every land *T.* i 684

FED.
Well *f.*, and at his ease *Beau* 2
F. by the Love from which it rose at first *Ch.* 574
Were fountains *f.* with infinite supplies *Ex.* 34
F. from the richest veins of the Mogul *Ex.* 369
That *f.* the flocks and herds of wealthy Lot *Ex.* 419
There Memory, like the bee that's *f. M.* ii 9   [28
Then think of his children, for they must be *f.*" *P.A.*
With which the fieldfare, wintry guest, is *f. N.A.* 20
Earth's millions daily *f.*, a world employed *R.* 553
Of malice *f.* while flesh is mortified *T.* 166
I *f.* on scarlet hips and stony haws *T.* i 120
A fever's agonies, and *f.* on drugs *T.* i 446
And *f.* on manna. And such thine, in whom *T.* iii 256
Is *f.* while a victim. Lo! he comes *T.* iii 765
Ill-clad and *f.* but sparely, time to cool *T.* iv 379
Still to be *f.*, and not to be surcharged *Tir.* 20

FEE.   [*Ch.* 46
Through fear, not love; and Heaven abhors the *f.*
The poor thy clients, and Heaven's smile thy *f.*! *Ch.* 312
A doctor's trouble, but without the *f. Con.* 314|374
And having trucked thy soul, brought home the *f. Ex.*
Thy chiefs, the lords of many a petty *f. Ex.* 532
Perhaps a grave physician, gathering *f. H.* 203
The flesh of animals in *f.*, and claim *T.* vi 452

FEEBLE.
Though *f.* in degree, in kind the same *Ch.* 594
And *f.* onset of a pigmy rush *Ex.* 707
But now and then perhaps a *f.* ray *H.* 93
To frown and roar, and shake his *f.* form *H.* 186
Thy means so *f.*, and despised so much *H.* 666
Whose hand is *f.*, or his aim untrue *P.E.* 571
True Wisdom will attend his *f.* call *R.* 33
Were but the *f.* efforts of a child *T.* 578

FEEBLENESS.
Such *f.* of limbs thou provest *M.* 37

FEEBLY.
The ties of Nature do but *f.* bind *Ch.* 371.
F. and vainly, at poetic fame) *R.* 802

FEED.
Her eager thought, and *f.* her flowing joys *Ch.* 405
And in due time *f.* heartily on both *Con.* 338
In fly-blown flesh, whereon the maggot *f. Con.* 676
Soft airs and genial moisture *f.* and cheer *H.* 489
F. sparingly, communicates his store *H.* 521
And hides the ruin that it *f.* upon *P.E.* 286
And draining its nutritious powers to *f. R.* 43
Sick of the service of a world that *f. R.* 47
Much less to *f.* and fan the fatal fires *R.* 109
And *f.* the fire that wastes thy powers away *R.* 264
Or lust engenders, and indulgence *f. R.* 644
And anxious mainly that the flock he *f. T.* ii 404
May *f.* excesses she can ill afford *T.* ii 651 [*T.* iii 757
The country starves, and they that *f.* the o'ercharged
F. a blue flame, and makes a cheerful hearth *T.* iii 33
That *f.* upon the sobs and dying shrieks *T.* iii 328
That *f* thee; thou may'st frolic on the floor *T.* iii 343
And succulent, that *f.* its giant growth *T.* iii 418
Some clothe the soil that *f.* them, far diffused *T.* iii 662
And his head thumps, to *f.* upon the breath *T.* iv 47
Nor this to *f.* his own! 'Twere some excuse *T.* iv 452
That like the filth with which the peasant *f. T.* iv 502
Where nothing *f.* it. Neither business crowds *T.* iv 744
That *f* the thrush (whatever some suppose) *T.* v 83
Our claim to *f.* upon immortal truth *T.* v 721
Whose cause is God. He *f.* the secret fire *T.* vi 224
O'er all we *f.* on power of life and death *T.* vi 453
Can find no warrant there. *F.* then, and yield *T.* vi 456
F. on the slain, but spare the living brute! *T.* vi 458
To *f.* our infant minds with proper fare *Tir.* 116
For public schools 'tis public folly *f. Tir.* 250
Sure to exhaust the plant on which they *f. Tir.* 604
No nourishment to *f.* his growing mind *Tir.* 618
Who *f.* a pupil's intellect with store *Tir.* 622   [907
And *f.* him well, and give him handsome pay *Tir.*
The stream that *f.* the wellspring of the heart *T.T.* 380

FEEDING.
In catching smoke and *f.* upon air *R.* 38
While Admiration *f.* at the eye *T.* i 157
By flocks, fast *f.* and selecting each *T.* iv 318

FEEL.
"*F.* all the meanness of your slavish lot *A.T.* 112
Would *f.* herself happier here *C.* 28
Might *f.* themselves allied to all the race *Ch.* 22
And at this hour the conqueror *f.* the proof *Ch.* 60
He *f.* his body's bondage in his mind *Ch.* 152
Buy what is woman-born, and *f.* no shame! *Ch.* 181
We *f.* thy force still active, at this hour *Ch.* 272
The boldest patriot might be proud to *f. Ch.* 308
He *f.* his need of an unerring guide *Ch.* 346
Flies to save some, and *f.* a pang for all *Ch.* 407
She *f.* that frailty she denied so long *Ch.* 409 [145
Where men of judgment creep, and *f.* their way *Con.*
I pity bashful men, who *f.* the pain *Con.* 347
Did not our hearts *f.* all He deigned to say *Con.* 535
They felt what it became them much to *f. Con.* 543
F. less the journey's roughness and its length *Con.* 699
Or seem to boast a fire he does not *f. Con.* 714
That, conscious of her crimes, she *f.* instead *Con.* 769
A dread she would not, yet is forced to *f. Con.* 786
He *f.* a gentle tingling come *E.* i 11
Should *f.* that itching and that tingling *E.* i 25
He, still more aged, *f.* the shocks *Ep.* ii 41
And *f.* no change, unshaken and serene *Ex.* 587
Act without aim, think little, and *f.* less *H.* 8
Man *f.* the spur of passions and desires *H.* 55
O weariness beyond what asses *f. H.* 99
Again the mountain *f.* the imprisoned foe *Her.* 37
In wintry age to *f.* no chill *M.* 42
To *f.* the most refined *Miss* — 4

With all a tender heart can *f.* *Miss* — 103
For such a cause, to *f.* the slightest fear *N.A.* 90
Began to *f.*, as well he might *N.G.* 5
If I can *f.* as well as he *P.* 34
Yet nothing *f.* in that rough coat *P.* 51
You would not *f.* at all—not you *P.* 60
Free from the wayward bias bigots *f. P.E.* 454
May *f.* a heart enriched by what it pays *R.* 209 [307
Blessed, rather cursed, with hearts that never *f. R.*
No wounds like those a wounded spirit *f. R.* 341
But *f.* while grasping at his faded joys *R.* 473
There *f.* a pleasure perfect in its kind *R.* 629
Cats also *f.*, as well as we *R.C.* 23
Forgoes not what she *f.* within *S.* 10
Forced to a pause, would *f.* it good to think *St.* ii 15
Who much diseased, yet nothing *f. St.* vi 17
What fear he *f.* his gratitude inspires *T.* 190
So fares it with the sinner, when he *f. T.* 257
F. herself happy amidst all her grief *T.* 456
Though on a Sofa, may I never *f. T.* i 108
We mount again, and *f.* at every step *T.* i 271 [376
All *f.* the freshening impulse, and are cleansed *T.* i
He seems indeed indignant, and to *f. T.* i 379
It does not *f.* for man. The natural bond *T.* ii 9
Is felt, mankind may *f.* her mercy too *T.* ii 47
The source of the disease that Nature *f. T.* ii 194
But I can *f.* thy fortunes, and partake *T.* ii 219
As any thunderer there. And I can *f. T.* ii 221
He *f.* the anxieties of life, denied *T.* ii 302
May *f.* it too; affectionate in look *T.* ii 405
The wisest and the best *f.* urgent need *T.* ii 483
As the necessities their authors *f. T.* ii 672
I mean to tread. I *f.* myself at large *T.* iii 18 [iii 411
Which, save himself who trains them, none can *f. T.*
That *f.* for injured love! but I disdain *T.* iii 66
So hollow and so false—I *f.* my heart *T.* iii 182
Has business; *f.* himself engaged to achieve *T.* iii 377
F. wrath and pity, when I think on thee! *T.* iii 842
Of the great Babel, and not *f.* the crowd *T.* iv 90
Thy frame, robust and hardy, *f.* indeed *T.* iv 360
The piercing cold, but *f.* it unimpaired *T.* iv 361
The man *f.* least, as more inured than she *T.* iv 387
With transports such as favoured lovers *f. T.* iv 721
Yet *f.* the burning instinct: over-head *T.* iv 773
To *f.*, and courage to redress her wrongs *T.* iv 795
They know not what it is to *f.* within *T.* v 250
Its long delay, *f.* every welcome stroke *T.* v 413
F. all the rigour of thy fickle clime *T.* v 484
With a propriety that none can *f. T.* v 744
" Love kindles as I gaze. I *f.* desires *T.* v 842
And *f.* a parent's presence no restraint *T.* vi 49
Is cause of half the poverty we *f T.* vi 52
Across a velvet level, *f.* a joy *T.* vi 275
Nor *f.* their happiness augment his own *T.* vi 326
'Twas his sublimest privilege to *f. T.* vi 359
Such is the impulse and the spur he *f. T.* vi 755
Though but in distant prospect, and not *f. T.* vi 761
" 'Tis then I *f.* myself a wife *The Doves* 25
Whom Ocean *f.* through all his countless waves *Tir.* 39
That *f.* not at that sight, and *f.* at none *Tir.* 299
We *f.*, it e'en in age, and at our latest day *Tir.* 317
That candidates for such a prize should *f. Tir.* 376
F. all the rage that female rivals *f. Tir.* 471
Of those who never *f.* in the right place *Tir.* 540
Arrived, he *f.* an unexpected change *Tir.* 567
F. all his happiest privileges lost *Tir.* 574
But recollect that he has sense, and *f. Tir.* 720
F. not the wants that pinch the poor *Trans. H.* 10
The tallest pines *f.* most the power *Trans. H.* 13
With all the savage thirst a tiger *f. T.T.* 36
Careless of all the anxiety he *f. T.T.* 145
We never *f.* the alacrity and joy *T.T.* 242
I know the mind that *f.* indeed the fire *T.T.* 480
Whate'er the theme, that others never *f. T.T.* 483
F. himself spent, and fumbles for his brains *T.T.* 537

FEELING.

Joys doubly sweet to *f.* quick as thine *Ch.* 298
With Friendship's finest *f. F.* 93
Fires all his *f.* with a noble scorn *H.* 151
How much his *f.* suffered, sat Sir Smug) *H.* 416
Powers of the mind, and *f.* of the heart *H.* 654
But man, all *f.* and awake *N.* 9
Prove that you have human *f. N.C.* 55
Of ruder shape, and *f.* none *P.* 12
Your *f.* in their full amount *P.* 47
These, these are *f.* truly fine *P.* 63
These both are pleasures to the *f.* heart *P.E.* 254
And having human *f.*, does not blush *T.* ii 27
To thaw him into *f.*; or the smart *T.* iv 197
And have a friend in every *f.* heart *T.* iv 376
Yet, *f.* present evils, while the past *T.* vi 23 [583
Though some, perhaps, that shock thy *f.* mind *Tir.*
Much less transfix his *f.* with an oath *Tir.* 729
But they have human *f.*—turn to them *Tir.* 806
Along the nerve of every *f.* line *T.T.* 487
But to comply with *f.*, and to give *V.* 23
Not hard by nature, in a *f.* part *V.* 42

FEE-SIMPLE.

The fixed *f.* of the vain and light? *Con.* 590

FEET.

Then would he say submissive at thy *f. Ch.* 232
He bruised beneath his *f.* the infernal powers *Ch.* 584
The treasure at my *f. D.W.* 36
With unshod *f.* they yet securely tread *E.* ii 16
The flinty soil indeed their *f.* annoys *E.* ii 31
With *f.* too delicate to touch the ground *Ex.* 52
Down to the very turf beneath thy *f. H.* 50
At every step beneath their *f.* they tread *Her.* 55
Beneath his well shod *f. J.G.* 82
Go, cast your orders at your Bishop's *f. P.E.* 120
When Winter soaks the fields, and female *f. T.* 215
I cast them at thy *f.*—my only plea *T.* 583 [47
That pressed it, and the *f.* hung dangling down *T.* i
And at his *f.* the baffled billows die *T.* i 525
And in his hands and *f.*, the cruel scars *T.* iii 114
Nor his, who patient stands till his *f.* throb *T.* iv 46
To horrid sounds of hostile *f.* within *T.* iv 571
And I will sing, at Liberty's dear *f. T.T.* 296

FEIGN.

Abhors constraint, and dares not *f.* a zeal *Con.* 713
But he that loves him has no need to *f. T.T.* 90

FEIGNED.

" But guard thee well, expect no *f.* attack *A.T.* 189
But Charity not *f.* intends alone *Ch.* 449
And nowhere, but in *f.* Arcadian scenes *H.* 9
Like those in fable *f. Q.V.* 58
Than by the mere dissemblers' *f.* respect *T.* 74
With all the prettiness of *f.* alarm *T.* vi 319

FEIGNING.

Yet even these, though, *f.* sickness oft *T.* i 580

FEINT.

Concludes his unfeigned love of him, a *f. Con.* 748

FELL. [72

Till the foe found them, and down *f.* the towers *Ex.*
Thus *f.* the best instructed in her day *Ex.* 225
F. broken and defaced at their own door *Ex.* 506
And if he *f.*, would fall because he must *P.E.* 30
The night his city *f. Q.V.* 52
A serving-maid was she, and *f.* in love *T.* i 537 [733
O'erlooked and unemployed, *f.* sick, and died *T.* ii

F. Discord, arbitress of such debate *T.* iv 482
The wonder of the North. No forest *f. T.* v 131
The tree-enchanter Orpheus *f. T. B.* 64
I snapped it, it *f.* to the ground *The Rose* 12
Shifted the wind that raised it, and it *f. T.T.* 387
Oaks *f.* not, hewn by thousands, to supply *Y.O.* 101

FELLED.
The poplars are *f.*—farewell to the shade *P.F.* 1

FELLER.
The *f.'s* toil which thou couldst ill requite *Y.O.* 115

FELLEST.
Thou *f.* mature; and, in the loamy clod *Y.O.* 33

FELLOW.
He finds the pasture where his *f.* graze *Ch.* 179
But marks the man that treads his *f.* down *Ch.* 211
Prefers his *f.* grooms, with much good sense *Con.* 417
"Go, *f.*!—whither?"—turning short about *E.* iii 24
He finds his *f.* guilty of a skin *T.* ii 12
That man should thus encroach on *f.* man *T.* v 435
Resents his *f.'s,* wishes it were less *Tir.* 477
Coveted *f.,* smelt ere they are seen *Tir.* 830
"Few, *f.*!—there are all that ever reigned *T.T.* 100
And, summoned to partake its *f.'s* woe *V.* 69

FELLOWSHIP.
The school of coarse good *f.* and noise *Con.* 422
For human *f.,* as being void *T.* vi 322

FELON.
As when a *f.,* whom his country's laws *H.* 712
Flies to the tempting pool, or *f.* knife *T.* 446 [813
Have we not tracked the *f.* home, and found *T.* ii
But though the *f.* on his back could dare *T.* vi 516

FELT.
The spring drew near, each *f.* a breast *A Tale* 13
F. them in her bosom glow *B.* 38
Nor soon he *f.* his strength decline *Cast.* 15
Yet bitter *f.* it still to die *Cast.* 35
Nor *f.* but in the soul that Heaven selects *Ch.* 8
And having *f.* the pangs you deem a jest *Con.* 497
They *f.* what it became them much to feel *Con.* 543
Who deal with Scripture, its importance *f. Con.* 729
That since the flowers of Eden *f.* the blast *Con.* 751
And Dick *f.* some desires *F.B.* 15
If ever thou hast *f.* another's pain *H.* 674
They *f.* the rude alarm *M.* ii 6
Are neither *f.* nor feared by them *N.* 7
And *f.* the sneer with scorn enough *P.* 18
And each by shrinking showed he *f.* it *P.* 66 [41
His scruples thus silenced, Tom *f.* more at ease *P.A.*
F. each a mortal stab in her own breast *P.E.* 339
But teems with powers he never *f.* before *P.E.* 404
Job *f.* it, when he groaned beneath the rod *R.* 303
But with a soul that ever *f.* the sting *R.* 315
Revered at home, and *f.* in foreign lands *R.* 412
No happiness is *f.,* except the true *R.* 461
For evils daily *f.* and hardly borne *R.* 752
And evil *f.* within *St.* iii 26
But when he *f.* it, heaved a sigh *St.* iii 27
Distressed the weary loins that *f.* no ease *T.* i 45
No want of timber then was *f.* or feared *T.* i 57
The spleen is seldom *f.* where Flora reigns *T.* i 455
Is *f.,* mankind may feel her mercy too *T.* ii 47 [73
To what no few have *f.,* there should be peace *T.* ii
His wrath is busy, no man his frown is *f. T.* ii 94 [733
By roses, and clear suns though scarcely *f. T.* iii
That never *f.* a stupor, know no pause *T.* iv 283
Where penury is *f.* the thought is changed *T.* iv 397
That *f.* their virtues; Innocence, it seems *T.* iv 518
In the low vale of life, that early *f. T.* iv 799
Would not reproach me with the loss I *f. T.* v 490

Were sons indeed; they *f.* a filial heart *T.* v 518 [972
The man, whose virtues are more *f.* than seen *T.* vi
Shall ne'er be *f.* by me *The Doves* 18
Or gently *f.,* and only so *The Doves* 19
And, *f.* alike by each, advances both *Tir.* 485
On situations that they never *f. T.T.* 169 [231
Is seldom *f.,* though sometimes seen and heard *T.T.*
F. himself crushed at the first word he spoke *T.T.* 353
So little *f.,* so fervently professed! *V.* 50

FEMALE.
Divest the rougher sex of *f.* airs *Con.* 843
The nymph must lose her *f.* friend *L.R.* 1
And dwells there in a *f.* heart *Miss* — 1
Seems verging fast towards the *f.* side *P.E.* 430
When Winter soaks the fields, and *f.* feet *T.* 215
Gives more than *f.* beauty to a stone *T.* i 703
On *f.* industry, the threaded steel *T.* iv 165
F. and male, Pomona, Pales, Pan *T.* vi 233
Feel all the rage that *f.* rivals feel *Tir.* 471

FENCE.
Leaps every *f.* but one, there falls and dies *P.E.* 93
Teach him to *f.* and figure twice a week *P.E.* 366
That mounts the stile with ease, or leaps the *f. T.* i 136
The *f.* withdrawn, he gives them every beam *T.* iii 444
The cattle mourn in corners, where the *f. T.* v 27
And where the woods *f.* off the northern blast *T.* vi 60
The garden fears no blight, and needs no *f. T.* vi 771
Or oaken *f.* that hems the paddock round *T.T.* 583

FENCED.
Of virtue too well *f.* to fear a flaw *A.T.* 155

FERMENT.
Discordant atoms meet, *f.* and fight *Ex.* 297

FERMENTATION.
The rage of *f.,* plunges deep *T.* iii 519

FERMENTING.
Impregnated with quick *f.* salts *T.* iii 464

FERN.
The common overgrown with *f.,* and rough *T.* i 526
Dry *f.* or littered hay, that may imbibe *T.* iii 476

FERRIED.
And they themselves once *f.* o'er the wave *T.* ii 38

FERTILE.
Or *f.* only in its own disgrace *T.* vi 767

FERTILITY.
Her beauty, her *f.* She dreads *T.* i 370

FERTILIZING.
No *f.* streams your fields divide *H.* 467
The bee transports the *f.* meal *T.* iii 538

FERVENCY.
F., freedom, fluency of thought *T.T.* 700

FERVENT.
His *f.* spirit labours. There he fights *T.* vi 936
May be as *f.* in degree *U.* 9

FERVENTLY.
So little felt, so *f.* professed! *V.* 50

FERVOUR.
The *f.* and the force of Indian skies *Ex.* 12
The impatient *f.* which it first conceives *T.* iii 502

FESTERED.
To assuage the throbbings of the *f.* part *R.* 321

FESTOON.
Else unadorned, with many a gay *f. T.* iii 667

FETCH.
Could *f.* from records of an earlier age *Con.* 615 [30
"And *f.* my cloak; for, though the night be raw *E.* iii

FETCHED.
Far *f.* and little worth; nor seldom waits *T.* i 243

FETTERS.
Bound in the *f.* of an unknown tongue *H.* 450
He drops at once his *f.* and his fear *H.* 725

FEUDS.
In causeless *f.* and bickerings of their own *Ex.* 527
Shall raise no *f.* for armies to suppress *T.T.* 317

FEVER.
Both fail beneath a *f.'s* secret sway *R.* 295
A *f.'s* agonies, and fed on drugs *T.* i 446

FEVERISH.
Far other dreams his *f.* mind employed *A.T.* 153

FIAT.
In answer to the *f.* of his word *Ex.* 154
Why did the *f.* of a God give birth *Tir.* 35

FIB.
If some mere driveller suck the sugared *f. P.E.* 530

FIBRES.
Their *f.* penetrate its tenderest part *R.* 42

FICKLE.
Some *f.* creatures boast a soul *F.* 109
In sorting flowers to suit a *f.* taste *H.* 767
Be *f.*, and thy year, most part, deformed *T.* ii 210
Of Novelty, her *f.*, frail support *T.* iii 54
Feel all the rigour of thy *f.* clime *T.* v 484
Thy Providence forbids that *f.* power *T.* v 871
"But oh! if, *f.* and unchaste *The Doves* 29

FICOIDES.
F., glitters bright the winter long *T.* iii 579

FICTION.
Or make that *f.* which was once a fact? *Con.* 555
For the unscented *f.* of the loom *T.* i 416
Sweet *f.* and sweet truth alike prevail *Tir.* 136

FICTITIOUS.
Or real, or *f.*, of the times *T.* 162

FIDDLE.
To read the news, or *f.*, as seems best *H.* 76
Strike the *f.*, let us all be gay! *P.E.* 150
All learned, and all drunk! the *f.* screams *T.* iv 478
Give him his lass, his *f.*, and his frisk *T.T.* 237

FIDDLING.
A cassocked huntsman, and a *f.* priest *P.E.* 111

FIDELITY.
An absent friend's *f.* and love *Con.* 308
By long *f.* and live *E.* i 104
F. that neither bribe nor threat *T.* vi 628
With close *f.* and love unfeigned *T.T.* 73

FIDGETS.
Give me the *f.*, and my patience fails *Con.* 208

FIE.
Thus life is spent (oh *f.* upon 't!) *P.* 37
Oh *f.*! 'Tis evangelical and pure *P.E.* 133

FIELD. [*A.T.* 186
"Thee to the *f.*, thou shouldst withstand them all"
No learned disputants would take the *f. Ch.* 620

God and his attributes (a *f.* of day *Con.* 471 [428
Like theirs that cleave the flood or graze the *f. Con.*
A veteran warrior in the Christian *f. Con.* 607
Her *f.*, a rich expanse of wavy corn *Ex.* 9
Streams edged with osiers, fattening every *f. H.* 47
Of all that deck the lanes, the *f.*, the bowers *H.* 288
A soldier's best is courage in the *f. H.* 405
No fertilizing streams your *f.* divide *H.* 467
F., fruit, and flower, and every creature here *H.* 490
There is a *f.*, through which I often pass *N.A.* 1
Runs in a bottom, and divides the *f. N.A.* 10 [*N.A.* 50
Then coursed the *f.* around, and coursed it round again
And heedless whither, to that *f.* I came *N.A.* 32 [37
Sheep grazed the *f.*; some with soft bosom pressed *N.A.*
Again, impetuous to the *f.* he flies *P.E.* 92
He takes the *f.*, the master of the pack *P.E.* 114 [6
Of my favourite *f.*, and the bank where they grew *P.F.*
Where mountain, river, forest, *f.* and grove *R.* 29
To whom an atom is an ample *f. R.* 62
The bar, the senate, or the tented *f. R.* 102
From every window, and the *f.* are green *R.* 498
When Winter soaks the *f.*, and female feet *T.* 215
They, strangers to the controversial *f. T.* 371
That *f.* of promise, how it flings abroad *T.* 453
The middle *f.*; but scattered by degrees *T.* i 293
Renounce the odours of the open *f. T.* i 415
Fair *f.* appear below, such as he left *T.* i 452
She ploughs a brazen *f.*, and clothes a soil *T.* i 709
And least be threatened in the *f.* and groves *T.* i 753
Alighting in far distant *f.*, finds out *T.* ii 109 [213
And *f.* without a flower, for warmer France *T.* ii
Each in his *f.* of glory; one in arms *T.* ii 241 [317
Who dream they have a taste for *f.* and groves *T.* iii
Polluting Egypt: gardens, *f.*, and plains *T.* ii 828
And clamours of the *f.*? Detested sport *T.* iii 326
While *f.* of pleasantry amuse us there *T.* iv 76
I saw the woods and *f.* at close of day *T.* iv 311
He hates the *f.*, in which no fife or drum *T.* iv 646
Hence to the *f.* of glory, as the world *T.* iv 684 [772
To range the *f.* and treat their lungs with air *T.* iv
Stretches a length of shadow e'er the *f. T.* v 10
The very rooks and daws forsake the *f. T.* v 89
Some seek diversion in the tented *f. T.* v 185
Thus war affording *f.* for the display *T.* v 238
He looks abroad into the varied *f. T.* v 738 [237
To each some province, garden, *f.* or grove *T.* vi
Dependent upon man; those in his *f. T.* vi 414
Or take their pastime in the spacious *f. T.* vi 576
Of barrenness is past. The fruitful *f. T.* vi 765
In Honour's *f.* advancing his firm foot *T.T.* 16
The varied *f.* of science, ever new *T.T.* 264
His brows with ivy, rushed into the *f. T.T.* 604 [692
Spreads the fresh verdure of the *f.*, and leads *T.T.*
I read of bright embattled *f.* 1789, 3

FIELDFARE.
With which the *f.*, wintry guest, is fed *N.A.* 20

FIEND.
And echoing praises, such as *f.* might earn *Her.* 61
Come *f.*, come fury, giant, monster, blast *N.A.* 121
He calls for Famine, and the meagre *f. T.* ii 185

FIERCE.
But to divert a *f.* banditti *E.* iv 13
The *f.* banditti which I mean *E.* iv 19
With *f.* and envious yet admiring eyes *Ex.* 204
Thy monarchs arbitrary, *f.*, unjust *Ex.* 528
A temper passionate and *f. F.* 64
But where will *f.* contention end *L.R.* 3
Where man, by nature *f.*, has laid aside *T.* i 594
Where *f.* Temptation, seconded within *T.* iii 684
Or flushed with *f.* dispute, a senseless brawl *T.* v 472

F. the dispute whate'er the theme; while she T. iv 481
And anger insignificantly f. T. vi 320
To prey upon each other; stubborn, f. T. vi 897
F., avaricious, proud, there must be war T.T. 10
And keeps alive his f. but noble fires T.T. 223 [329
And f. Licentiousness should bear the blame T.T.

FIERCENESS.
His f., having learnt, though slow to learn T. i 595

FIERCER.
Till Autumn's f. heats and plenteous dews Tir. 47

FIERCEST.
The f. animals with magic charms) R. 254
His manly forehead to the f. foe T.T. 277
In Afric's torrid clime, or India's f. heat T.T. 297

FIERY.
Whom f. suns, that scorch the russet spice Ex. 15
Where no volcano pours his f. flood Her. 85
And f. caverns, roars beneath his foot T. ii 90
Kindle a f. boil upon the skin T. ii 183
Are sown the sparks that kindle f. war T. v 206
(As is the course of rash and f. men) T. vi 542

FIFE.
He hates the field, in which no f. or drum T. iv 646

FIFTEEN.
To scribble as you scribbled at f. P.E. 318
Just f. minutes, huddle up their work T. ii 412

FIFTH.
Just made f. chaplain of his patron lord H. 414

FIFTY.
Some f. or a hundred lustrums hence T. ii 579

FIGHT.
As ever earned a lady's love in f. A.T. 2
Prepared to f. for shadows of no worth Ex. 116
But, though they f. as thine have ever fought Ex. 292
Discordant atoms meet, ferment and f. Ex. 297
The event and sure decision of the f. ? Ex. 363
Thy magnanimity in f. M.B. 19
Yon roaring boys, who rave and f. Pat. 5 [T. ii 230
And love when they should f.; when such as these
Which he that f. a season so severe T. iii 560
And f. again, but finds his best essay T. v 624
His fervent spirit labours. There he f. T. vi 936
To him that f. with Justice on his side T.T. 12
Slaves f. for what were better cast away T.T. 282
But they that f. for freedom, undertake T.T. 284
Siege after siege, f. after f. 1789, 23

FIGURE.
Such frozen f., stiff as they are cold Ch. 607
Like f. drawn upon a dial plate Con. 380
And grace thy f. with a soldier's pride Ex. 487
Teach him to fence and f. twice a week P.E. 366
Elegant phrase, and f. formed to please P.E. 422
Genteel in f., easy in address T. 203
And f. of the man, his secret aim T. vi 618
Behold that f., neat, though plainly clad Tir. 664
Like the two f. at St. Dunstan's stand T.T. 527
A wintry f. like a withered thorn T.T. 725

FILE.
Like regimented coxcombs rank and f. T. 422

FILIAL.
And while that face renews my f. grief M.P. 17
The work of generous love and f. fear T. 226

Were sons indeed; they felt a f. heart T. v 518
But who, with f. confidence inspired T. v 745
Of f. frankness lost, and love grown faint Tir. 588
And keep him warm and f. to the last Tir. 894

FILL.
Not only f. Necessity's demand Ch. 99
Immortal fragrance f. the circuit wide Ch. 439
They f. their measure, and receive their due Con. 34
That f. the listening lover with delight Con. 446
Happy to f. Religion's vacant place Ex. 121
Might give more life to marble, or might f. Ex. 231
The Maker f. the nations with alarm Ex. 585
To f. the dull vacuity till four H. 78
To f. with fragrance his abode above H. 122
Will f. the chaise; so you must ride J.G. 15
Not all whose eloquence the fancy f. P.E. 13
Whose corresponding misses f. the ream P.E. 311
Who f. the world with doctrines contraband P.E. 475
The wriggling fry soon f. the creeks around P.E. 480
And f. the world of traffic and the shades R. 120
Shall f. thee with delights unfelt before R. 360
Or sought with energy, must f. the void R. 748
And lull the spirit while they f. the mind T. i 187
All summer long, which winter f. again T. i 329
From gaiety that f. the bones with pain T. i 504
To f. the ambition of a private man T. ii 236
To arrest the fleeting images that f. T. ii 290
To f. with riot, and defile with blood T. iii 307 [428
And hence even Winter f. his withered hand T. iii
To f. the void of an unfurnished brain T. iv 209
And bundled close to f. some crowded vase T. iv 668
Just in the niche he was ordained to f. T. iv 792
Not to the man who f. it as he ought T. v 362
Whose eye they f. with tears of holy joy T. v 750
Yes—ye may f. your garners, ye that reap T. v 755
That f. the skies nightly with silent pomp T. v. 817
Where he, that f. an office, shall esteem T. vi 846
Shall f. the circles of those eyes The Doves 15
For her, the memory f. her ample page Tir. 13
But oh! if Fortune f. thy sail Trans. H. 34
And f. with discontent a British isle T.T. 253
She f. profuse ten thousand little throats T.T. 694

FILLED.
And f. her with a thousand fears A Fable 13
With genial instinct f. A Tale 14 [sounds H. 45
Banks clothed with flowers, groves f. with sprightly
Has f. his urn where these pure waters rise Ch. 436
His Budget, often f., yet always poor Ch. 614
F. up at last with interesting news Con. 394
With such a jest as f. with hellish glee Con. 737
Their measure f., they too shall pay the debt Ex. 712
With a whole gamut f. of heavenly notes N.A. 26
Has f. with all its fumes a critic's brain P.E. 445
Who stole her slipper, f. it with Tokay T. 157
Of wrong and outrage with which earth is f. T. ii 7
The pulpit, therefore, (and I name it f. T. ii 326 [829
Were covered with the pest; the streets were f. T. ii
Diminutive, well f. with well-prepared T. iii 513
Thy scattered hair with sleet like ashes f. T. iv 121
Unoccupied, has f. the void so well T. v 557
Behold the measure of the promise f. T. vi 798 [Rose 5
The cup was all f., and the leaves were all wet The
F. with as much true merriment and glee T.T. 244
To each his name significant, and, f. Y.O. 153

FILLETED.
And f. about with hoops of brass T. v 402

FILLING.
Who for the sake of f. with one blast T.T. 31

FILMS.

And floating *f*. envelope every thorn *A.T.* 73
The sooty *f*. that play upon the bars *T.* iv 292

FILTER.

In vain to *f*. off a crystal draught *T.* ii 507

FILTH.

The *f*. of rottenness and worm of pride *Ex.* 90
To purge and skim away the *f*. of vice *P.E.* 343
Whom famine cannot reconcile to *f. T.* iv 417 [502
That like the *f*. with which the peasant feeds *T.* iv

FILTHILY.

Which *f*. bewray and sore disgrace *Tir.* 593

FILTHY.

The rank debauch suits Clodio's *f*. taste *P.E.* 188
And cast his *f*. raiment at them all *T.* 235

FINALLY.

And, cursed with conquest, *f*. succeed *Con.* 692

FINCH.

They sang as blithe as *f*. sing *F.B.* 7
A *F*., whose tongue knew no control *P.T.* 26

FIND,   [there? *A.T.* 118

"*F*. out her treacherous heart, and plant a dagger
Nor age nor infancy could *f*. thee there *Ch.* 48 [*A.C.* 10
And your lordship," he said, "will undoubtedly *f*.
And *f*. submission more than half a cure *Ch.* 158
He *f*. the pasture where his fellows graze *Ch.* 179
But *f*. that though his tubes assist the sight *Ch.* 387
No works shall *f*. acceptance in that day *Ch.* 557 [310
To *f*. it stuffed with brickbats, earth, and stones *Con.*
And *f*. a changing clime a happy source *Con.* 387
Obscure or quench a faculty that *f. Con.* 593
But veneration or respect *f*. none *Con.* 739
And *f*. it a mere mask of sly grimace *Con.* 744
And *f*. Hypocrisy close lurking there *Con.* 746
To *f*. the medium asks some share of wit *Con.* 879
F. the sweet lyre on which an artist plays *Con.* 900
And all the floating thoughts we *f. E.* i 7
We *f*. the friends we fancied we had won *E.* iii 16
I fairly *f*. myself pitchkettled *E.* iv 32
And gammer *f*. it on her knees *E.* iv 45
He *f*. his long, last home *Ep.* ii 38
F. not, or hardly *f*., a single friend *Ex.* 118
What nation will you *f*.. whose annals prove *Ex.* 165
Where will you *f*. a race like theirs endowed *Ex.* 195
The moles and bats in full assembly *f. Ex.* 630
If every polished gem we *f. F.* 7
Shall *f*. me as reserved as he *F.* 188
Pursue the search, and you will *f. F.* 199
With ease, and *f*. them nutriment; but man *F.A.* 36
There *f*. a judge inexorably just *H.* 227
And ask, and fancy they *f*., blessings there *H.* 243
And *f*. the modish manners of the day *H.* 612
And he that *f*. his Heaven must lose his sins *H.* 638
F. out his weaker part *H.F.* 10
O'erjoyed was he to *f. J.G.* 30
The calendar, right glad to *f. J.G.* 177
And set their wit at work to *f. L.W.* 13
The flowers are gone—but still we *f. M.* ii 15
So I no more may *f*. thee *M.B.* 22
Will *f*. occasion to forbear *M.F.* 38
For can we *f*. it less ? Contemplate first *N.A.* 109
Till some reason ye shall *f. N.C.* 50
"Methinks," I said, "in thee I *f. P.B.* 13
May *f*. a Muse to grace it with a song) *P.E.* 2 [277
F., by degrees, the truth that once bore sway *P.E.*
Your sober thoughts will hardly *f*. it one *P.E.* 489
Darts to the mud, and *f*. his safety there *P.E.* 503
We *f*. a little isle, this life of man *R.* 148

You *f*. safe shelter in the next stage-coach *R.* 492
Forget their labours, and yet *f*. no rest *R.* 496
A sense of elegance we rarely *f. R.* 501
And he soon *f*. the talents it requires *R.* 614
He *f*. the labours of that state exceed *R.* 619
Grasps seeming Happiness, and *f*. it Pain *R.* 756
Her climbing she began to *f. R.C.* 25
Like thee, content in every state may *f. S.* ii 7
The Scripture yields) or hope to *f*. a friend ? *T.* 440
Where should they *f*. (those comforts at an end *T.* 439
Shall *f*. the blessing unimproved, a curse *T.* 524
Shall *f*. them rated at their full amount *T.* 545
Anxious in vain to *f*. the distant floor *T.* i 48
Or charmed me young, no longer young, I *f. T.* i 142
When custom bids, but no refreshment *f. T.* i 390
Far distant, such as he would die to *f. T.* i 453
Is famished—*f*. no music in the song *T.* i 468
Where *f*. Philosophy her eagle eye *T.* i 712
He *f*. his fellow guilty of a skin *T.* ii 12
Alighting in far distant fields, *f*. out *T.* ii 109
F. place in his dominion, or dispose *T.* ii 169
That each may *f*. its most propitious light *T.* ii 295
His dangers or escapes, and haply *f. T.* ii 309 [514
Where must he *f*. his Maker ?   With what rites *T.* ii
F. one ill made, another obsolete *T.* ii. 602
F. a cold bed her only comfort left *T.* ii 655   [iii 7
If chance at length he *f*. a greensward smooth *T.*
And *f*. the total of their hopes and fears *T.* iii 132
The man we celebrate must *f*. a tomb *T.* iii 264
Seek and obtain, and often *f*. unsought? *T.* iii 288
Would *f*. them hideous nurseries of the spleen *T.* iii 318
Vain tears, alas ! and sighs that never *f. T.* iii 332 [366
From whom are all our blessings, business *f. T.* iii
The morning *f*. the self-sequestered man *T.* iii 386.
That errs not, and *f*. raptures still renewed *T.* iii 723
With meaner objects even the few she *f*.! *T.* iii 727
Where shall I *f*. an end, or how proceed ? *T.* iv 233
F. happiness unblighted ; or, if found *T.* iv 334 [803
Sent through the traveller's temples ! He that *f. T.* iii
Come then, and thou shalt *f*. thy votary calm *T.* iv 259
That Fancy *f*. in her excursive flights *T.* iv 242
Yet he too *f*. his own distress in theirs *T.* iv 390
They brave the season, and yet *f*. at eve *T.* iv 378
But helpless, in few years shall *f*. their hands *T.* iv 423
How *f*. the myriads, that in summer cheer *T.* v 77
The gloomy clouds, *f*. weapons, arrowy sleet *T.* v 140
Where *f*. ye passive fortitude? Whence springs *T.* v 327
The wearied hireling *f*. it a release *T.* v 411
Opprobrious residence, he *f*. them all *T.* v 584
And fights again; but *f*. his best essay *T.* v 624
"We *f*. sound argument, we read the heart" *T.* v 654
In senseless riot ; but ye will not *f. T.* v 757
The Paradise he sees, but *f*. it such *T.* v 794
And such well pleased to *f*. it, asks no more *T.* v 795
To earth's acknowledged Sovereign, *f*. at once *T.* v 803
Happy who walks with him! Whom what he *f T.* vi 247
Akin to rapture, when the bauble *f. T.* vi 276 [vi 456
Can *f*. no warrant there. Feed then, and yield *T.*
Shall seek it, and not *f*. it, in his turn *T.* vi 600
That *f*. out every crevice of the head *T.* vi 707
F. in a sober moment time to pause *Tir.* 56
If all we *f*. possessing earth, sea and air *Tir.* 91
Is not to *f*. what they profess to seek *Tir.* 194
Nor gambling practices can *f*. it out *Tir.* 246
And is he well content his son should *f. Tir.* 617
F. it expedient, come what mischief may *Tir.* 692
F. him a better in a distant spot *Tir.* 759
Disease or comes not, or *f*. easy cure *Tir.* 766
Must *f*. a colder soil and bleaker air *Tir.* 851
Where, bishoplike, he *f*. a perch *Tran.* ii 5
And in reality to *f*. no friend *T.T.* 160
Though Discontent alone can *f*. out where *T.T.* 197
Communicates with joy, the good she *f. T.T.* 275

Let me, the charge of some good angel *f. V.* 77
F. thee not less alive to her sweet force *Y.O.* 133

FINDEST.
Friendship and truth to others, *f.* thou none ? *Ex.* 277

FINDING.
Till *f.*, what he might have found before *Ch.* 475
But *f.* soon a smoother road *J.G.* 81
And *f.* in the calm of truth—tried love *T.* iii 56
Not unemployed, and *f.* rich amends *T.* iv 729
That *f.* an interminable space *T.* v 556

FINE.
That brass and steel should make so *f.* a show *Ch.* 554
A *f.* puss-gentleman that's all perfume *Con.* 284
To finish a *f.* building *F.* 165
After all he must beat it as thin and as *f. F.M.* 21
Poet's goods are not often so *f. Gr.* 54
And sensibilities so *f.* ! *P.* 14
"And your *f.* sense," he said, "and yours *P.* 41
These, these are feelings truly *f. P.* 63
Hence comment after comment, spun as *f. P.E.* 494
With such *f.* words familiar to his tongue *P.E.* 509
He wore them as *f.* trappings for a show *T.* 56 [vi 561
(Though graced with polished manners and *f.* sense *T.*
Ere yet mortality's *f.* threads give way *T.* v 578
And in his cage, like parrot *f.* and gay *T.T.* 232
Or clergy made so *f.* ? *Y.D.* 62 [81
F. passing thought, e'en in her coarsest works *Y.O.*

FINE-SPUN.
And covered with a *f.*, specious veil *P.E.* 328

FINESSE.
But he (his musical *f.* was such) *T.T.* 652

FINEST.
With Friendship's *f.* feeling *F.* 93
Verse in the *f.* mould of fancy cast *T.T.* 618

FINGER.
She guides the *f.* o'er the dancing keys *Ch.* 109
Pinched close between his *f.* and his thumb *Ch.* 477
Down to his *f.* and his thumb *E.* i 12
By Vanity's unwearied *f.* dressed *Ex.* 46
With *f.* deeply dyed in human gore *Ex.* 497
Shows with a pointing *f.*, but no noise *H.* 221
His eyes shut fast, his *f.* in his ears *H.* 658
Shall make your scribbling *f.* ache *J.P.* 39
One breaks the glass, and cuts his *f. P.B.* 34
His *f.* held the pen *R.G.* 22
And hides his hands to keep his *f.* warm *T.* 148
While fancy, like the *f.* of a clock *T.* iv 118
Follow the nimble *f.* of the fair *T.* iv 155
The learned *f.* never need explore *T.* iv 362
Dangled along at the cold *f.'s* end *T.* iv 392
Touched by the Midas *f.* of the state *T.* iv 507
With designation of the *f.'s* end *Tir.* 641
And many a dunce, whose *f.* itch to write *T.T.* 111

FINISH.
I must *f.* my journey alone *A.S.* 10
To *f.* a fine building *F.* 165
Attend to *f.* what the sword begun *Her.* 60

FINISHED.
And *f.* his concise repast *Mor.* 6
Mark well the *f.* plan without a fault *R.* 551
That in good time the stripling's *f.* taste *Tir.* 203
'Tis *f.*, and yet, *f.* as it seems *T.* iii 781

FIR.
[H. 525
Where sprang the thorn, the spiry *f.* shall spring

FIRE.
Too oft betrays the votaries of his *f. A.T.* 30
Pregnant with celestial *f. B.* 34
The flame extinct he views the roving *f. B.B.* 11
Teach me to kindle at thy gentle *f. Ch.* 12 [282
But shipwreck, earthquake, battle, *f.*, and flood *Ch.*
Pants to communicate her noble *f. Ch.* 403
Behold a Christian !—and without the *f. Ch.* 599
Grows fungous, and takes *f.* at every spark *Con.* 54
Important trifles ! have more smoke than *f. Con.* 250
He shakes with cold—you stir the *f.* and strive *Con.* 333
That man should love his Maker, and that *f. Con.* 483
Youth has a sprightliness and *f.* to boast *Con.* 635
That *f.* abated which impels rash youth *Con.* 641
That *f.* is catching if you draw too near *Con.* 654
Is the false *f.* of an o'erheated mind *Con.* 668
Or seem to boast a *f.* he does not feel *Con.* 714
Till the last *f.* burn all between the poles *Con.* 756
By night a *f.*, to cheer the gloomy way *Ex.* 178 [415
Brought *f.* from Heaven, the sex-abusing crime *Ex.*
Suffering the vengeance of eternal *f. Ex.* 423 [*Ex.* 659
Or his, who touched their hearts with hallowed *f.* ?
Would hunt a Saracen through *f.* and flood *Ex.* 521
It is combining *f.* with smoke *F.* 119
F. all his feelings with a noble scorn *H.* 151
But brighter beams than his who *f.* the skies *H.* 491
There was a time when Ætna's silent *f. Her.* 1
Behold in Ætna's emblematic *f. Her.* 45
And lend celestial *f. Miss* — 82
Whose *f.* to sacred Truth applied *Mrs. M*— 32
And kindles in his soul a treacherous *f. P.E.* 40
With some cold moral think to quench the *f. P.E.* 320
To hang their momentary *f. Q.V.* 15
So, *f.* with water to compare *Q.V.* 17
Much less to feed and fan the fatal *f. R.* 109
That I may catch a *f.* but rarely known *R.* 205
And feed the *f.* that wastes thy powers away *R.* 264
The sacred *f.*, self-torturing his trade *T.* 100
No Fear attends to quench his glowing *f. T.* 189
His eye relumines its extinguished *f. T.* i 442
That falls asunder at the touch of *f. T.* ii 11
F. from beneath, and meteors from above *T.* ii 57
Of patriot eloquence to flash down *f. T.* ii 217
And keeps our larder lean ; puts out our *f. T.* ii 615
Now stir the *f.*, and close the shutters fast *T.* iv 36
Ascending, *f.* the horizon ; while the clouds *T.* v 2
The tyranny that doomed them to the *f. T.* v 731
"And many an aching wish, your beamy *f. T.* v 838
F. all the faculties with glorious joy *T.* v 885
Whose cause is God. He feeds the secret *f. T.* vi 224
Whose *f.* was kindled at the prophet's lamp *T.* vi 732
Boys, once on *f.* with that contentious zeal *Tir.* 470
On *f.* with curses, and with nonsense hung *Tir.* 832
Frisking thus before the *f. Trans.* iii 15
That takes not *f.* at their heroic deeds *T.T.* 26
And keeps alive his fierce but noble *f. T.T.* 223 [229
F. him at once in Freedom's glorious cause *T.T.*
Is but the *f.* without the sacrifice *T.T.* 379
I know the mind that feels indeed the *f. T.T.* 480
F. indignation and a sense of scorn *T.T.* 489
But no prophetic *f.* to me belong *T.T.* 504
That verse, whatever *f.* the fancy warms *T.T.* 512
The victim of his own lascivious *f. T.T.* 606
'Twere new indeed to see a bard all *f. T.T.* 734

FIRED.
F. with a zeal peculiar, they defy *H.* 461

FIRESIDE.
F. enjoyments, homeborn happiness *T.* iv 140

FIRM.
He couched it *f.* upon his puissant thigh *A.T.* 147
Had they maintained allegiance *f.* and sure *Ex.* 207

FIRM—FIVE

Hope, as an anchor *f*. and sure, holds fast *H*. 167
My *f*. persuasion is, at least sometimes *H*. 365
So spake Aspasio, *f*. possessed *St*. iii 13
Of texture *f*. a lattice-work that braced *T*. 42
And, proud to make his *f*. attachment known *T*. 219
Upborne they stood. Three legs upholding *f*. *T*. i 20
Than the *f*. oak of which the frame was formed *T*. i 56
And skirted thick with intertexture *f*. *T*. i 111
His *f*. stability to what he scorns *T*. i 383
F. as a rock. Nor wanted aught within *T*. v 156
In Honour's field advancing his *f*. foot *T.F*. 16 [195
F. friends to peace, to pleasure, and good pay *T.T*.

FIRMAMENT.
And in the *f*. of fame still shines *Tir*. 281

FIRMER.
Of adolescence, or a *f*. age *Con*. 46   [287
The more 'twere pressed the *f*. it would stand *Ex*.
No *f*. friendships than the fair have shown) *V*. 82

FIRMEST.
When tempests could not. At thy *f*. age *Y.O*. 93

FIRMNESS.
Had reached the sinewy *f*. of their youth *T*. v 288
That promised once more *f*., so assailed *T*. v 526

FIRST.
Are but departures from the *f*. design *A.T*. 50 [127
Lest Rome should end with her *f*. founders' lives *A.T*.
But *f*. the squire's, a compliment but due *Ch*. 470
Humility the parent of the *f*. *Con*. 377
And *f*., let no man charge me, that I mean *Con*. 871
" I'll see him too—the *f*. I ever saw " *E*. iii 31
F., for a thought—since all agree *E*. iv 35
The last of nations now, though once the *f*. *Ex*. 242
He *f*. conceives, then perfects his design *Ex*. 318
F. fixes our attention *F*. 177
The same we practised at *f*. sight *F*. 179
See Nature gay as when she *f*. began *H*. 39
Who *f*. misuse, then cast their toys away *H*. 128
Starts at her *f*. approach, and sounds to arms! *H*. 656
And the *f*. thankful tears bedew his cheeks *H*. 727
For he got *f*. to town *J.G*. 246
Since *f*. our sky was overcast *M*. 2
Which *f*. inspired the flame, decays *M.F*. 54
That *f*. engaged him in the chase " *Mor*. 38
For can we find it less? Contemplate *f*. *N.A*. 109
F. wish to be imposed on, and then are *P.E* 290
F. Appetite enlists him Truth's sworn foe *P.E*. 542
F. put it out, then take it for a guide *P.E*. 559
Or when it *f*. forsakes the elastic string *P.E*. 573
Calls thee to cope with enemies, and *f*. *R*. 267 [396
F. shakes the glittering drops from every thorn *R*.
The lowest *f*., and without stop *R. C*. 93
The last impossible, ho fears the *f*. *T*. 265
The Frenchman *f*. in literary fame *T*. 303
And ill as ease behind. The ladies *f*. *T*. i 70
Thus *f*. Necessity invented Stools *T*. i 86 [*T*. ii 198
Still wrought by means since *f*. He made the world?
Forth comes the pocket mirror.—*F*. we stroke *T*.ii 445
And planetary some; what gave them *f*. *T*. iii 159
Even as his *f*. progenitor, and quits *T*. iii 297 [475
Impervious to the wind. *F*. he bids spread *T*. iii
He shuts it close, and the *f*. labour ends *T*. iii 489
The impatient fervour which it *f*. conceives *T*.iii 502
And the *f*. larum of the cock's shrill throat *T*. iv 569
That seizes *f*. the opulent, descends *T*. iv 583 [714
As twice seven years, his beauties had then *f*. *T*. iv
Where, diligent to catch the *f*. faint gleam *T*. v 59
The *f*. artificer of death; the shrewd *T*. v 213
Contriver who *f*. sweated at the forge *T*. v 214
And the *f*. smith was the *f*. murderer's son *T*. v 219

Thus kings were *f*. invented, and thus kings *T*. v 279
Of these the *f*. in order, and the pledge *T*. v 575
Falls *f*. before his resolute rebuke *T*. v 619
" The use of his own bounty ?—making *f*. *T*. v 639
Directly to the *F*. and Only Fair *T*. v 675
And need not his immediate hand, who *f*. *T*. vi 203
The total herd receiving *f*. from one *T*. vi 335
Needless, and *f*. torments ere he devours *T*. vi 396
Fruitful and young as in their *f*. career ? *Tir*. 42
That *f*., or last, hereafter, if not here *Tir*. 99
And some street-pacing harlot his *f*. love *Tir*. 217
When *f*. we started into life's long race *Tir*. 315
When children *f*. begin to spell *Tran*. iv 37   [353
Felt himself crushed at the *f*. word he spoke *T.T*.
Flew to its *f*. position, with a spring *T.T*. 623
And place it in this *f*. essay *U*. 21
F., farewell Niger ! whom now duly proved *V*. 7
Of treeship—*f*. a seedling hid in grass *Y.O*. 61
In praise harmonious the *f*. air he drew *Y.O*. 155

FIRSTBORN
Famine, and Pestilence, her *f*. son *Her*. 59
The *f*. efforts of my youthful muse *T*. iv 701
And Freedom claims him for her *f*. son *T.T*. 281

FISH.
Serve him with venison, and he chooses *f*. *Con*. 335
You that are but almost a *f*. *P*. 26
Nor baited hook deceive the *f*'s eye *T*. iii 313
F. up his dirty and dependent bread *T*. iii 808
Propitious, pays his tribute, game or *f*. *T*. iv 611

FISTS.
They should encounter with well loaded *f*. *Con*. 196
Charity may relax the miser's *f*. *Con*. 812
And griping *f*., and unrelenting frowns *Ex*. 513

FIT.
Perhaps the man was in a sportive *f*. *Ch*. 537
Whose only *f*. companion is his horse *Con*. 412 [644
Mellows and makes the speech more *f*. for use *Con*.
The sense was dark; 'twas therefore *f*. *E*. iv 61
A Friendship that in frequent *f*. *F*. 103
Than this his Maker has seen *f*. to give *H*. 601
They therefore needs must *f*. *J.G*. 188
I hold it therefore wisest and most *f*. *N.A*, 103
She, for her humble sphere by nature *f*. *T*. 323
And *f*. the limpid element for use *T*. i 374
And crazy earth has had her shaking *f*. *T*. ii 60
This *f*. not nicely, that is ill conceived *T*. ii 603
Waste youth in occupations only *f*. *T*. ii 636
Shook the delinquent with such *f*. of awe *T*. ii 722
Of womanhood, *f*. pupils in the school *T*. iv 228
The shadow to the ceiling, there by *f*. *T*. iv 275
Becomes a loathsome body, only *f*. *T*. iv 674
To eminence *f*. only for a God *T*. v 284
But is it *f*., or can it bear the shock *T*. v 305
F. for the power in which he stands array'd *Tir*. 98
To *f*. thee for a nobler post than thine *V*. 32

FITNESS.
Of rectitude and *f*., moral truth *T*. v 672

FITTED.
And neatly *f*., it compresses hard *T*. ii 587
Till smooth'd and squar'd and *f*. to its place *T*. vi 94

FITTER.
Is but a garnished nuisance *f*. far *T*. vi 993

FITTEST.
Are *f*. auditors for such to seek *Con*. 226

FIVE.
Every *f*. minutes how the minutes go *Con*. 382
Dear Joseph—*f*. and twenty years ago *E*. iii 1

FIVE—FLAW

Eight years and *f.* round-rolling moons *Ep.* ii 29
He cannot drink *f.* bottles, bilk the score *P.E.* 193
Then kill a constable, and drink *f.* more *P.E.* 194
Her dear *f.* hundred friends, contemns them all *T.*ii 643
Else of a mannish growth, and *f.* in ten *Tir.* 208
To set a distich upon six and *f. T.T.* 507

FIX.

They *f.* attention, heedless of your pain *Con.* 63
F. on the wainscoat a distressful stare *Con.* 116
First *f.* our attention *F.* 177   [*T.* 344
Prayer would add faith, and faith would *f.* them there
The roving thought and *f.* it on themselves *T.* vi 119
Becomes their pattern, upon whom they *f. Tir.* 224
Can call her smiling down, and *f.* her here *T.T.* 413
The poet's lyre, to *f.* his fame *U.* 25

FIXED.

Their roofless home they *f. A Tale* 38
To rush into a *f.* eternal state *Con.* 185
'Tis an unalterable *f.* decree *Con.* 467
F. in the rolling flood of endless years *Con.* 557
The *f.* fee-simple of the vain and light ? *Con.* 590
With *f.* considerate face *D.W.* 22
And farther still the formed and *f.* design *Ex.* 429
And *f.* by Heaven's decree *Miss* — 46
F. their tyrants' habitations *N.C.* 38
Lips busy, and eyes *f.*, foot falling slow *R.* 285
But *f.*, unalterable care *S.* 9
See where he sits, contemplative and *f. T.* 415
Or scarlet crewel, in the cushion *f. T.* i 54
Ponderous, and *f.* by its own massy weight *T.* i 59
More *f.* below, the more disturbed above *T.* i 384
Grows fluid ; and the *f.* and rooted earth *T.* ii 100
And tell us whence the stars; why some are *f. T.* iii 158
Indurated and *f.*, the snowy weight *T.* v 98
As *f.* as marble, with a forehead ridged *T.* vi 268
F. motionless, and petrified with dread *T.* vi 538
Should claim my *f.* attention more than you *T.T.* 181

FIXING.

The family dispersed, and *f.* thought *T.* iv 137

FLACCID.

Deserted of its bloom, the *f.*, shrunk *T.* i 392

FLAG.

Now wantoned lost in *f.* and reeds *D.W.* 9
Impatient to descry the *f.* of France *Ex.* 291
And thou hadst neither fleet nor *f.* to boast *Ex.* 553
And some wits *f.* through fear of losing it *T.T.* 521

FLAGEOLET.

Of *f.* or flute *T.B.* 12

FLAGGED.

Of some *f.* admiral; and tortuous arms *Y.O.* 96

FLAGRANT.

He burns with most intense and *f.* zeal *T.* iii 794

FLAILS.

Where *f.* of oratory thresh the floor *Ex.* 302
Thump after thump resounds the constant *f. T.* i 357

FLAKES.

Fast falls a fleecy shower : the downy *f. T.* iv 326
The frequent *f.*, has kept a path for me *T.* vi 75

FLAMBEAUX.

Whose *f.* flash against the morning skies *T.* ii 648

FLAME: [134

A courteous Knighthood, caught the generous *f. A.T.*
The *f.* extinct, he views the roving fire *B.B.* 11
Unless a love of virtue light the *f. Ch.* 491
That sight imparts a never-dying *f. Ch.* 593
Out of the very *f.* of rage and hate *Con.* 186
But sage observers oft mistake the *f. Con.* 655
A trick upon the canvass, pointed *f. Con.* 782
That jewel of the purest *f. F.* 11
He followed Paul, his zeal a kindred *f. H.* 582
In all-devouring *f. M.* ii 2
Which first inspired the *f.*, decays *M.F.* 54
That glossy shine, or vivid *f. Mrs. M*— 10
At such a sight to catch the poet's *f. R.* 85
May least offend against so pure a *f. R.* 248
He reads his sentence at the *f.* of Hell *T.* 10
Thunder, and earthquake, and devouring *f. T.* 548
Their fortitude and wisdom were a *f. T.* 531
Such evil Sin hath wrought, and such a *f. T.* ii 133
Feeds a blue *f.*, and makes a cheerful hearth *T.* iii 33
Dancing uncouthly to the quivering *f. T.* iv 276
It is a *f.* that dies not even there *T.* iv 743
From Heaven to Earth, of lambent *f.* serene *T.* v 153
To teach his heart to glow with generous *f. Tir.* 644
Affection lights a brighter *f. U.* 27

FLAMING.

Where, *f.* in scarlet and gold *Gr.* 29

FLANKS.

Which made his horse's *f.* to smoke *J.G.* 127
With bleeding sides and *f.* that heave for life *T.* vi 429

FLASH.

Inform his mind ; one *f.* of heavenly day *Ch.* 228
At every stroke wit *f.* in our eyes *Ch.* 543
Thunder and *f.* upon the steadfast shores *R.* 534
F. desperation, and betray their pangs *T.* i 502
Of patriot eloquence to *f.* down fire *T.* ii 217   [648
Whose flambeaux *f.* against the morning skies *T.* ii
In every *f.* of his far-beaming eye *T.* iii 602
Breaks on the soul, and by a *f.* from Heaven *T.* v 884
" When lightnings *f.* among the trees *The Doves* 21
And *f.* thanksgivings to the skies ! 1789, 55

FLASHING.

Wit *f.* on Religion's side *Mrs. M*— 31
Now *f.* wide, now glancing as in play *T.* 242

FLAT.

And binds the shoulders *f.* We prove its use *T.* ii 589
A *f.* and fatal negative obtains *Tir.* 714

FLATTED.

Is sent to be *f.* or wrought into length *F.M.* 2

FLATTER.

Teach, while they *f.* him, his proper place *R.* 446
The lie that *f.* I abhor the most *T.T.* 88

FLATTERED.

That *f.* me with hopes of earthly bliss *T.* iv 696

FLATTERER.

Before whose infant eyes the *f.* bows *T.T.* 123

FLATTERY.

He begs their *f.* with his latest breath *T.* 315
By nature, or by *f.* made so, taught *T.* ii 546
If *F.*, Folly, Lust, employ the pen *T.T.* 761.

FLAVIA.

F., most tender of her good name *Ch.* 453

FLAVOUR.

That gives it all its *f.* We have run *T.* ii 607
Of *f.* or of scent in fruit or flower *T.* vi 248

FLAW.

Of virtue too well fenced to fear a *f. A.T.* 155
Nor carp at every *f.* you may discern *Con.* 92
No ! the decree was just and without *f. H.* 318

FLAW—FLIPPANT

From temper f. unsightly N.Y.G. 8
Life for obedience, death for every f. T. 550
No f. deforms, no difficulty thwarts T. vi 229
Union of hearts without a f. between V. 86

FLAX.
Of brotherhood is severed as the f. T. ii 10

FLAXEN.
And lay thine hand upon his f. head Tir. 848

FLAYED.
To strip them off, 'tis being f. alive P.E. 583

FLEA.
Weigh sunbeams, carve a fly, or spit a f. Ch. 354

FLED. [A.T. 200
Shrieked at the sight, and, conscious, f. the place
Catharina is f. like a dream C. 5
And mercy, f. to as the last resort H. 378
F., chased by her melody clear M.D. 22
Are all the nameless sweets of friendship f.? P.E. 244
The blackbird has f. to another retreat P.F. 9
And Virtue f. The schools became a scene T. ii 735
And, conscious of some danger, either f. T. vi 375
Had f. from William, and the news was fresh T. vi 660
Peace to them all! those brilliant times are f. Tir. 284
Of fruit proscribed, as to a refuge, f. Y.O. 16

FLEDGED. [214
Theirs, should I paint him, has his pinions f. T. iv
And f. with icy feathers, nod superb T. v 26

FLEE.
And f. for safety to the falling rocks T. vi 868

FLEECE.
So once in Gideon's f. the dews were found E. ii 49
Their f. his pillow, and his weekly drawl H. 199
With frictions of her f. M.B. 10

FLEECED.
Though heavenly in pretension, f. thee well Ex. 515

FLEECY.
F. locks and black complexion N.C. 13
Pours out its f. tenants o'er the glebe T. i 291
Fast falls a f. shower : the downy flakes T. iv 326
And half on foot, they brush the f. flood T. v 63
Shall be dismantled of its f. load T. vi 179

FLEET.
How f. is a glance of the mind A,S. 41
Impel the f. whose errand is to save Ch. 128
Proud of thy f. and armies, stolen the gem Ex. 348
And thou hadst neither f. nor flag to boast Ex. 553
Baptized her f. Invincible in vain Ex. 569
The horse as wanton, and almost as f. T. vi 330
Here cities won, and f. dispersed 1789, 13

FLEETING.
Demands one moment of thy f. time Ep. i 2
With self-indulgence winged the f. hours Ex. 71
Transient indeed as is the f. hour H. 119
Man mourns his f. breath St. v 26
To arrest the f. images that fill T. ii 290
That I myself am but a f. shade T. v 13
Of f. life its lustre and perfume T. v. 447
Like f. exhalations, found no more Tir. 84
The glass that bids man mark the f. hour T.T. 41
The f. forms of majesty engage T.T. 117

FLESH.
In fly-blown f., whereon the maggot feeds Con. 676
Pride may be pampered while the f. grows lean T. 117
Of malice fed while f. is mortified T. 166

Receives the morsel—f. obscene of dog T. i 562
And vex their f. with artificial sores T. i 582
There is no f. in man's obdurate heart T. ii 8
All f. is grass, and all its glory fades T. iii 261
The f. of animals in fee, and claim T. vi 452
Thyself in miniature, thy f., thy bone Tir 874

FLESH-FLIES.
Far, far away, these f. of the land P.E. 324

FLEW.
He f. to reach it, by a law A Tale 51
Where his eagles never f. B. 31
Which f. not till to-day Beau 6
Sir, when I f. to seize the bird B.R. 1
And ever as the minutes f. Cast. 41
And Time forbid to touch them as he f. Ex. 184
When other nations f. from coast to coast Ex. 552
At last it f. away J.G. 104
Up f. the windows all J.G. 110
So like an arrow swift he f. J.G. 153
Laid down his pipe, f. to the gate J.G. 163
F. open in short space J.G. 242
And f. to save, ere yet too late L.R. 19
And rockets f., self-driven Q.V. 14 [v 726
And chased them up to Heaven. Their ashes f. T.
At once the shock unseated him : he f. T. vi 553
As if an eagle f. aloft, and then T.T. 552
F. to its first position, with a spring T.T. 623

FLEXIBLE.
Supple and f. as Indian cane H. 602

FLIGHT.
Compared with the speed of its f. A.S. 42
Aware that f., in such a sea Cast. 33
He catches all improvements in his f. Ch. 115
With scarce a slower f. D.W. 12
No f. above the pitch of prose E. i 16
The freeman to a farewell f. F.B. 20 [74
Could Time, his f. reversed, restore the hours M.P.
Around their f. who highest soar Mrs. M—48 [52
That f. in circles urged advanced them nought N.A.
He trimmed his f. another way P.B. 12
But, muse, forbear; long f. forbode a fall P.E. 604
Escaped with pain from that adventurous f. T. i 4
Beyond the achievement of successful f. T. i 692
They shame their shooters with a random f. T. ii 807
That Fancy finds in her excursive f. T. iv 242
'Tis pusillanimous and prone to f. T. v 373
Is Liberty : a f. into his arms T. v 577
That wait on man, the f. performing horse T. vi 426
Thither he wings his airy f. Trans. ii 14

FLIMSY.
As bloated spiders draw the f. line P.E. 495
Those f. webs that break as soon as wrought R. 639
Hackneyed and worn to the last f. thread T.T. 727

FLING.
F. at your head conviction in the lump Con. 153.
And f. their foam against thy chalky shore? Ex. 273
To f. his glories o'er the robe she wears H. 44
That field of promise, how it f. abroad T. 453
Snuffs up the wind and f. himself abroad T.T. 669
And f. his head before Y.D. 30

FLINTY.
The f. soil indeed their feet annoys E. ii 31

FLIPPANT.
The f. and the scold J.P. 22
And snappish dialogue, that f. wits T. iv 198
The squirrel, f., pert, and full of play T. vi 315
With all their f. fluency of tongue T.T. 147

FLIRTED.
The *f.* fan, the bridle, and the toss *H.* 344

FLIT.
F. out of sight, and mocks his pains *E.* iv 60
The clouds that *f.*, or slowly float away *R.* 192 [133
Dreams empty dreams. The million *f.* as gay *T.* iii

FLITTING.
Pleased with his solitude, and *f.* light *T.* vi 79

FLOAT.
It *f.* a vapour now *O.* i 14
Hark! how it *f.* upon the dewy air! *P.E.* 63
The clouds that flit, or slowly *f.* away *R.* 192
And she may *f.* again *R.G.* 30
Now hoist the sail, and let the streamers *f. T.* ii 255
To *f.* a bubble on the breath of Fame *T.T.* 746

FLOATED.
The cask, the coop, the *f.* cord *Cast.* 27

FLOATING.
And *f.* films envelope every thorn *A.T.* 73
His *f.* home for ever left *Cast.* 6
The *f.* wreath again discerned *D.W.* 31
And all the *f.* thoughts we find *E.* i 7

FLOCK.
Far from the *f.*, and in a boundless waste *E.* ii 42
While others poison what the *f.* must drink *Ex.* 100
That fed the *f.* and herds of wealthy Lot *Ex.* 419
Alas, not so! the poorest of the *f. Ex.* 456
A *f.* so scattered, and so wont to roam *Ex.* 729
Nor herds have ye to boast, nor bleating *f. H.* 466
And ruminating *f.* enjoy the shade *Her.* 32
The *f.* grew calm again, and I, the road *N.A.* 127
Will not the sickliest sheep of every *f. P.E.* 142
Unfolds his *f.*, then under bank or bush *R.* 397
His *f.* the chief concern he ever knew *R.* 404
And anxious mainly that the *f.* he feeds *T.* ii 404
Displaying his own beauty, starves his *f.*! *T.* ii 429
By *f.*, fast feeding and selecting each *T.* iv 318
Or harmless *f.*, is hazardous and bold *T.* iv 575 [v 86
Thins all their numerous *f.* In chinks and holes *T.*
Then, as a shepherd separates his *f. T.* v 196
Graze with the fearless *f.*; all bask at noon *T.* vi 774
F. to that light; the glory of all lands *T.* vi 802
Nabaioth, and the *f.* of Kedar there *T.* vi 805 [624
Dismiss their cares when they dismiss their *f. Tir.*
Wouldst thou, possessor of a *f.*, employ *Tir.* 905
To see a people scattered like a *f. T.T.* 34
O'erhung the campaign; and the numerous *f. Y.O.* 53
No *f.* frequents thee now. Thou hast outlived *Y.O.* 56

FLOGGED.
How he was *f.*, or had the luck to escape *Tir.* 329

FLOOD.
But shipwreck, earthquake, battle, fire, and *f. Ch.* 282
A conflagration, or a wintry *f. Ch.* 465
Food for the famished rovers of the *f. Ch.* 532 [428
Like theirs that cleave the *f.* or graze the field *Con.*
Fixed in the rolling *f.* of endless years *Con.* 557
For them, the rocks dissolved into a *f. Ex.* 181
Would hunt a Saracen through fire and *f. Ex.* 521
Pours out a *f.* of splendour upon thine *Ex.* 589
A painful passage o'er a restless *f. H.* 3
Has wept a silent *f.*, reversed his ways *H.* 519
Where no volcano pours his fiery *f. Her.* 85
Thus swiftly dividing the *f. M.D.* 25
There sits quiescent on the *f.* that show *M.P.* 92
Scorned by the nobler tenants of the *f. P.E.* 482
Now in the *f.*, now panting in the meads *R.* 538
Of distant *f.*, or in the softer voice *T.* 191

The chequered earth seems restless as a *f. T.* i 344
Resistless. Never such a sudden *f. T.* ii 115
Shall counterfeit the motions of the *f. T.* ii 148
Bestrides the wintry *f.*, in which the moon *T.* iv 3
And half on foot, they brush the fleecy *f. T.* v 63
O'erwhelming all distinction. On the *f. T.* v 97 [133
To enrich thy walls; but thou didst hew the *f. T.* v
Deep in the *f.* found, when he sought it not *T.* vi 555
A chilling *f.* on summer's drooping flowers *T.T.* 211

FLOODGATES.
And forced the *f.* of licentious mirth *Con.* 264

FLOOR.
Four ivory eggs soon pave its *f. A Tale* 41
And panting pressed the *f. B.R.* 16
Rake well the cinders, sweep the *f. E.* iv 41
Where flails of oratory thresh the *f. Ex.* 302
Children not thine have trod my nursery *f. M.P.* 47
He left his bed, he trod the *f. R.C.* 91
Anxious in vain to find the distant *f. T.* i 48 [343
That feeds thee; thou may'st frolic on the *f. T.* iii
Must be detached, and where it strews the *f. T.* iii 615
The slope of faces, from the *f.* to the roof *T.* iv 202
One spits upon the *f. Y.D.* 42

FLOORED.
Of eastern groves, and oceans *f.* with ice *Ex.* 16

FLORA.
Sweet harmonist of *F.'s* court! *Dr.* 3
So *F.'s* wreath through coloured crystal seen *H.* 71
She seemed designed for *F.'s* hand *L.R.* 15
From *F.'s* balmy store *M.* ii 10
The spleen is seldom felt where *F.* reigns *T.* i 455
These *F.* banishes, and gives the fair *T.* i 460
And *F.*, and Vertumnus; peopling earth *T.* vi 234
Where *F.* is still in her prime *W.N.* 10

FLOUNCED.
Curled, scented, furbelowed, and *f.* around *Ex.* 51

FLOURISH.
They *f.*; and, as these decline, decay *Ex.* 327
To *f.* and parade with at the bar *Ex.* 665
In which they *f.* most; where, in the beams *T.* i 694
Shines there, and *f.* The golden boast *T.* iii 571
Where most they *f.*, upon English ground *T.T.* 337

FLOURISHING.
On the *f.* bush where it grew *The Rose* 8

FLOW.
Suppose (when thought is warm, and fancy *f. Ch.* 379
And *f.* in free communion with the rest *Ch.* 611 [19
Streams never *f.* in vain; where streams abound *Comp.*
To brush the surface, and to make it *f. Con.* 102 [444
And speech may praise the power that bids it *f. Con.*
Tastes of its healthful origin, and *f. Con.* 565
Should *f.* like waters after summer showers *Con.* 705
F. in a foreign land, but not in vain *E.* ii 46
Smooth, ductile, and even his fancy must *f. F.M.* 18
Where'er they *f.*, now seen and now concealed *H.* 48
Thy spirits have a fainter *f. M.* 5
When virtue bids it *f. Miss* — 56
Thy constant *f.* of love, that knew no fall *M.P.* 65
Vast as it is, it answers, as it *f. R.* 529
But tears of godly grief ne'er *f.* within *St.* ii 32
And gain-devoted cities. Thither *f. T.* i 682
F. into her; unbounded is her joy *T.* vi 803

FLOWED.
A wig that *f.* behind *J.G.* 182
To them it *f.* much mingled and defiled *T.* ii 503
Rotation; from what fountain *f.* their light *T.* iii 160
Has *f.* from lips wet with Castalian dews *T.* iii 251

FLOWER.

And laid her soft in amaranthine *f*. *A.T.* 8
With all the *f*. he found, he wove in haste *A.T.* 13
And only missed the *f*. that graced their side *A.T.* 75
With fragrant turf, and *f*. as wild and fair *Ch.* 258
Taints in its rudiments the promised *f*. *Con.* 42
Visiting every *f*. with labour meet *Con.* 439
That since the *f*. of Eden felt the blast *Con.* 751
The future splendour of the *f*.? *E.* i 72
Like some of Nature's sweetest *f*. *E.* i 94
The *f*. of Israel's infamy full blown *Ex.* 222
But render neither fruit nor *f*. *F.* 185 [sounds *H.* 45
Banks clothed with *f*., groves filled with sprightly
And yet the seed of an immortal *f*. *H.* 120   [289
What parts the kindred tribes of weeds and *f*. ? *H.*
Field, fruit, and *f*., and every creature here *H.* 490
In sorting *f*. to suit a fickle taste *H.* 767
And cheers the drooping *f*., unheard, unseen *J.T.* 40
If *f*. can disagree ? *L.R.* 4
The *f*. are gone—but still we find *M.* ii 15
He hears the herbs and *f*. rejoicing all *N.A.* 60
A fair imperial *f*. *L.R.* 14
When, playing with thy vesture's tissued *f*. *M.P.* 75
The choicest *f*. she bears *Pat.* 14
That make Italian *f*. so sweet and fair *P.E.* 410
F. by that name promiscuously we call *R.* 723
F. of rank odour upon thorny lands *R.* 754
That shuts within its seed the future *f*. *R.* 792
Her sweetest *f*., her aromatic gums *T.* ii 86
And fields without a *f*., for warmer France *T.* ii 213
Like the fair *f*. dishevelled in the wind *T.* iii 262
The only amaranthine *f*. on earth *T.* iii 268
Large foliage, overshadowing golden *f*. *T.* iii 535
From *f*. to *f*., and even the breathing air *T.* iii 539
The amomum there with intermingling *f*. *T.* iii 576
The gay diversities of leaf and *f*. *T.* iii 590
He, therefore, who would see his *f*. disposed *T.* iii 648
Few self-supported *f*. endure the wind *T.* iii 657 [728
Stripped of her ornaments, her leaves, and *f*. ! *T.* iii
From *f*. to *f*., so he from land to land *T.* iv 108
The pattern grows, the well depicted *f*. *T.* iv 151
A wreath, that cannot fade, of *f*. that blow *T.* iv 156
Man in society is like a *f*. *T.* iv 659
Like *f*. selected from the rest, and bound *T.* iv 667
Of *f*., that feared no enemy but warmth *T.* v 159
'Tis Liberty alone that gives the *f*. *T.* v 446   [137
Of leaf and *f*. ? It sleeps ; and the icy touch *T.* vi
Copious of *f*. the woodbine, pale and wan *T.* vi 162
Of *f*., like flies clothing her slender rods *T.* vi 166
Rules universal nature. Not a *f*. *T.* vi 240
Of flavour or of scent in fruit or *f*. *T.* vi 248
Happy to rove among poetic *f* *T.* vi 752
Worms wind themselves into our sweetest *f*. *T.* vi 831
Like an unburied carcass tricked with *f*. *T.* vi 992
To dress a Sofa with the *f*. of verse *T.* vi 1007
Whom *f*. alone I knew would little please *T.* vi 1010
The plentiful moisture encumbered the *f*. *The Rose* 3
With *f*. and fruit the wilderness supplies *Tir* 27
To show him in an insect or a *f*. *Tir.* 636 [*T.T.* 718
The *f*. would spring where'er she deigned to stray
A chilling flood on summer's drooping *f*. *T.T.* 211
Forms, colours, and gives scent to every *f*. *T.T.* 691
With *f*. as sweet, or fruit as fair *U.* 17
Where the *f*. have the charms of the spring *W.N.* 7
Assiduous sips at every *f*. 1789, 18

FLOWERY.

With many a wild, indeed, but *f*. spray *Ch.* 629
The world may dance along the *f*. plain *E.* ii 13
Tell where she lurks, beneath what *f*. shades *P.E.* 54
Be *f*., and he see no cause of fear *P.E.* 546
The fruits that hang on pleasure's *f*. stem *R.* 179
Nor gardens interspersed with *f*. beds *R.* 336

Kills too the *f*. weeds, where'er they grow *T.* 461
Hence, ankle-deep in moss and *f*. thyme *T.* i 270
A *f*. island, from the dark green lawn *T.* iii 630
And, ere one *f*. season fades and dies *T.* vi 196
By flowing numbers and a *f*. style *T.T.* 741

FLOWING.

Her eager thought, and feeds her *f*. joys *Ch* 405
These *f*. from the fount of grace above *E.* ii 29
Seized fast the *f*. mane *J.G.* 46
With wig prolix, down *f*. to his waist *Tir.* 361
Was natural as in the *f*. stream *T.T.* 592.
By *f*. numbers and a flowery style *T.T.* 741

FLUCTUATION.

Strange *f*. of all human things ! *E.* iii 9
Its *f*., and its vast concerns ? *T.* iv 56

FLUENT.

Fast as the periods from his *f*. quill *T.* iv 19

FLUENCY.

With all their flippant *f*. of tongue *T.T.* 147
Fervency, freedom, *f*. of thought *T.T.* 700

FLUID.

Grows *f*. ; and the fixed and rooted earth *T.* ii 100

FLUSH.

Vigorous in age as in the *f*. of youth *Con.* 601
And *f*. into variety again *T.* vi 180

FLUSHED.   [*Tir.* 833

Now *f*. with drunkenness, now with whoredom pale
Or *f*. with fierce dispute, a senseless brawl *T.* v 472

FLUTE.

Psaltery and sackbut, dulcimer and *f*. *P.E.* 133
Ye clarionets, and softer still, ye *f*. *T.* ii 260
Of flageolet or *f*. *T.B.* 12

FLUTTER.

" And *f*. loose, the sport of every wind *A.T.* 102
That *f*. loose on golden wing *F.B.* 8
That *f*. least is longest on the wing *T.* vi 931

FLUTTERED.

Had *f*. all his strength away *B.R.* 15
And sighed for every fool that *f*. by *Ex.* 54

FLUTTERING.

And all their leaves fast *f*., all at once *T.* i 189
Their *f*. rags, and shows a tawny skin *T.* i 568
Of *f*., loitering, cringeing, begging, loose *T.* iii 832

FLY.

That *f*., like Gabriel on his Lord's commands *Ch.* 135
Loose *f*. his forelock and his ample mane *Ch.* 176
Else I would say, and as I spake, bid *f*. *Ch.* 268
Weigh sunbeams, carve a *f*., or spit a flea *Ch.* 354
Are taught by rays, that *f*. with equal pace *Ch.* 363
F. to save some, and feels a pang for all *Ch.* 407
And if it weigh the importance of a *f*. *Con.* 21
That He bids thousands *f*. when none pursue *Ex.* 360
Should *f*. the World's contaminating touch *Ex.* 446
The wind did blow, the cloak did *f*. *J.G.* 101
So did he *f*.—which brings me to *J.G.* 155
Thus seeing Gilpin *f*. *J.G.* 234
(Her rosy chorus) *f*. *Miss* — 72
Of him that creeps and him that *f*. *N.G.* 38
Ordained perhaps, ere summer *f*. *O.* i 17
Again, impetuous to the field he *f*. *P.E.* 92
Women, whom custom has forbid to *f*. *P.E.* 504
On borrowed wheels away she *f*. *Q.V.* 37
F. to the levee, and, received with grace *R.* 479
F. to the coast for daily, nightly joys *R.* 522
To distant caves the lonely wanderer *f*. *R.* 769

Else, though unequalled to the goal he *f. T.* 15
In counterpoise, *f.* up and kicks the beam *T.* 356
F. to the tempting pool, or felon knife *T.* 446
Full on the destined ear. Wide *f.* the chaff *T.* i 359
As if created only like the *f. T.* iii 134 [*T.* iii 555
Moisture and drought, mice, worms, and swarming *f.*
Must *f.* before the knife ; the withered leaf *T.* iii 614
Perhaps may crown us, but to *f.* is safe *T.* iii 688
F. swiftly, and unfelt the task proceeds *T.* iv 166
To *f.* for refuge from distracting thought *T.* v 415
Of flowers, like *f.* clothing her slender rods *T.* vi 166
Pursuing gilded *f.* ; and such he deems *T.* vi 922
The shadows *f.*, philosophy prevails *Tir.* 1&2 [746
F., winged with joy, to some coach-crowded door *Tir.*
that unimproved those many moments *f. Tir.* 616
Spread little wings, and rather skip than *f. T.T.* 579
Time was when, settling on thy leaf, a *f. Y.O.* 91

FLY-BLOWN.

In *f.* flesh, whereon the maggot feeds *Con.* 676

FLYING.

From distant mountains catch the *f.* joy *T.* vi 795

FOAM.

And fling their *f.* against thy chalky shore ? *Ex.* 273
The *f.* upon the waters not so light *T.* 43

FOAMING.

Lashed into *f.* waves, begins to roar *T.* 260
Her Fancy followed him through *f.* waves *T.* i 539
High-minded, *f.* out their own disgrace *T.* vi 898

FOAMY.

Her silver globes, light as the *f.* surf *T.* vi 155

FOCUS.

There centring in a *f.* round and neat *Con.* 239

FODDER.

Their wonted *f.* ; not like hungering man *T.* v 30

FOE.

He dreamed not of a *f.*, or if his fear *A.T.* 151
Foretold one, dreamed not of a *f.* so near *A.T.* 152
Rushed with a whirlwind's fury on the *f. A.T.* 195
Dying, hurled them at the *f. B.* 40
The *f.* of virtue has no claim to thee *Ch.* 288
Snares in his path, and *f.* that lurk within *Con.* 470
Till the *f.* found them, and down fell the towers *Ex.* 72
But public censure speaks a public *f. Ex.* 436
Thy *f.* implacable, thy land at rest *Ex.* 581
What nation amongst all my *f.* is free *Ex.* 710
(Sworn *f.* to every thing that's witty!) *E.* iv 14
May prove a dangerous *f.* indeed *F.* 77
And *f.* of our perishing kind *Gr.* 46
Again the mountain feels the imprisoned *f. Her.* 37
Some *f.* to his upright intent *H.F.* 9
Appeared two lovely *f. L.R.* 6
Sworn *f.* to sense and law *M.* i 2
Thou polished and high-finished *f.* to truth *P.E.* 341
First Appetite enlists him Truth's sworn *f. P.E.* 542
More hideous *f.* than fancy can devise *R.* 68
The *f.* of man, or make a desert sweet *R.* 782
Once dreaded by our *f. R.G.* 26
And the *f.'s* unerring aim *St.* iv 12
Why deem we death a *f.? St.* v 18
Though various *f.* against the Truth combine *T.* 473
Upon thy *f.*, was never meant my task *T.* ii 218
And gives his direst *f.* a friend's embrace *T.* ii 270
The disappointed *f.*, deliverance found *T.* iv 186
As he whose prowess had subdued their *f.? T.* v 237
That hellish *f.*, confederate for his harm *T.* v 735
To assist his *f.'s* down-fallen beast to rise *T.* vi 444
Antipathies are none.   No *f.* to man *T.* vi 777

Gives courage to their *f.*, who, could they see *T.* vi 865
Dire *f.* alike of bird and mouse *T.B.* 26
His manly forehead to the fiercest *f. T.T.* 277
May no *f.* ravish thee, and no false friend *T.T.* 332
She has one *f.*, and that one *f.* the world *T.T.* 455

FOG.

Bade rise in haste a dark and drizzling *f. A.T.* 94
And thine was smothered in the stench and *f. Ex.* 510
A sleeping *f.*, and fancies it dry land *T.* 4.
Like a gross *f.* Bœotian, rising fast *T.* iii 495

FOH.   [609

F.! 'twas a bribe that left it : he has touched *T.* iv

FOIBLE.

It may correct a *f.*, may chastise *T.* ii 316

FOILED.

A man that would have *f.* at their own play *Con.* 611
Where deists, always *f.*, yet scorn to yield *T.* 372
Or having long in miry ways been *f. T.* iii 4
The State that strives for liberty, though *f. T.* v 367
Till Nature, unavailing Nature, *f. T.* v 627

FOLD.

And wood and lawn in dusky *f.* enclosed *A.T.* 96
To quit the forest and invade the *f. Ch.* 185
All night, we resting quiet in the *f. N.A.* 92
Russet and rude, *f.* up the tender germ *T.* vi 194

FOLDED,

His eyes are sunk, arms *f.*, head reclined *H.* 689
The *f.* gates would bar my progress now *T.* i 330

FOLIAGE.

With its new *f.* on *St.* i 18
With *f.* of such dark redundant growth *T.* i 226
Large *f.*, overshadowing golden flowers *T.* iii 535
Peep through their polished *f.* at the storm *T.* iii 574
Shall put their graceful *f.* on again *T.* vi 144
Forgotten as the *f.* of thy youth *Y.O.* 59

FOLIO.

This *f.* of four pages, happy work ! *T.* iv 50

FOLK.

For us plain *f.*, and all who side with us *Con.* 848
And yield so much to noble *f. F.* 118
Were never *f.* so glad *J.G.* 42
Though some *f.* can't endure them *Pat.* 18
Were e'er such hungry *f.*! *Y.D.* 38

FOLLOW.

And though the fox he *f.* may be tamed *Con.* 409
Nor swifter greyhound *f. Ep.* ii 2
And unless you adorn it, a nausea *f. F.M.* 24
That shows how far 'tis safe to *f.* sin *H.* 608
That he may *f.* them through brake and brier *N.A.* 6
To win due credence to what *f.* next *N.A.* 72
Peace *f.* Virtue as its sure reward *P.E.* 42
Pursue their sport, and *f.* to the deep *R.* 160
Pay !—*f.* Christ, and all is paid *St.* v 33
And all were swift to *f.* whom all loved *T.* ii 251
Soon *f.*, and the curb of conscience snapped *T.* ii 571
Great contest *f.*, and much learn'd dust *T.* iii 161
F. the nimble finger of the fair *T.* iv 155
To wandering sheep, resolved to *f.* none *T.* vi 891
To *f.* foolish precedents, and wink *Tir.* 255
Must *f.* royalty, then welcome ease *T.T.* 165
What *f.* next, let cities of great name *T.T.* 430

FOLLOWED.

I thence withdrew, and *f.* long *D.W.* 27
Showed that they *f.* all they seemed to shun *Ex.* 142

He *f.* Paul, his zeal a kindred flame *H.* 582
Reviled and loved, renounced and *f. L.W.* 33
Her Fancy *f.* him through foaming waves *T.* i 539
War *f.* for revenge, or to supplant *T.* i 609
May be *f.* perhaps by a smile " *The Rose* 20

FOLLOWER.
No friend or *f.* of mine *L.W.* 4

FOLLOWING.
F., that led me to my own abode *N.A.* 128
And thou a wretch, whom, *f.* her old plan *Tir.* 737

FOLLY.
Impudent blasphemy! So *F.* pleads *Ch.* 194
But God o'errules all human *f.* still *Ch.* 463
That mulish *f.*, not to be reclaimed *Ch.* 497
O *f.* worthy of the nurse's lap *Con.* 479
And lips unstained by *f.* or by strife *Con.* 563
It moves me more perhaps than *F.* ought *Con.* 625
A coin by Craft for *F.*'s use designed *E.* ii 7
And hide past *f.* from all-seeing eyes? *Ex.* 405
From worn-out *f.*, now acknowledged such *F.A.* 3
As fortune, vice, or *f.* may command *H.* 12
For he, with all his *f.*, has a mind *H.* 91
Mere *f.* and delusion—Sir, you toast *H.* 364
(Though other *f.* strike the public eye *H.* 620
That *f.* ends where genuine Hope begins *H.* 637
And *F.* pays, resound at your return *Her.* 62
'Tis here the *f.* of the wise *H.F.* 13
" The minx shall for your *f.*'s sake *J.P.* 37
F. the spring of his pursuit *P.B.* 17
Leave Vice and *F.* unsubdued behind *P.E.* 81
Charged with the *f.* of his life's mad scene *P.E.* 88
Wonders at Clodio's *f.*, in a tone *P.E.* 191
F. and Innocence are so alike *P.E.* 203
Yet *F.* ever has a vacant stare *P.E.* 205
In rushes *F.* with a full moon tide *P.E.* 282
Sniveling and driveling *f.* without end *P.E.* 310
The *f.* of his expectation *R.C.* 116
And look on *F.*'s pageantry with scorn *S.* ii 8
His *f.*, and his woe! *St.* iii 4
And cut up all my *f.* by the root *T.* 574
It plagues your country. *F.* such as yours *T.* i 770
Thy *f.* too: and with a just disdain *T.* ii 222
To those that need it. *F.* is soon learned *T.* ii 283
The Rout is *F.*'s circle, which she draws *T.* ii 629
His *f.*, but to spoil him is a task *T.* ii 768
There, undisturbed by *F.*, and apprised *T.* iii 34
Or heedless *f.*, by which thousands die *T.* iii 219
Lost innocence, or cancel *f.* past *T.* iii 678
Forsaken, or through *f.* not enjoyed *T.* iii 711
And *f.* in the heart; were England now *T.* iii 742
For *f.*, gallantry for every vice *T.* iv 690
Strange that such *f.* as lifts bloated man *T.* v 283
And *f.* in as ample measure meet *T.* v 309
Of *f.*, plunging in pursuit of death *T.* v. 595
Or disregard our *f.*, or that sit *T.* v 877
By ev'ry gilded *f.*, we renounced *T.* vi 39
At least his *f.* have not wrought her fall *T.* vi 976
His crimes and *f.* with an aching eye *Tir.* 62
For public schools 'tis public *f.* feeds *Tir.* 250
That palliates deeds of *f.* and of shame) *Tir.* 333
So numerous are the *f.* that annoy *Tir.* 597
From youthful *f.* than the same neglect *Tir.* 713
Of pleasures past, or *f.* yet to come *Tir.* 776
But that effeminacy, *f.*, lust *T.T.* 394
At *f.*'s cost, themselves unmoved the while *T.T.* 659
If Flattery, *F.*, Lust, employ the pen *T.T.* 761
Such is the *f.* of our dreaming youth *V.* 54

FOMENTATION.
Soft *f.*, and invite the seed *T.* iii 510

FOND.
Propitious to his *f.* intent there grew *A.T.* 80
To where the *f.* Sir Airy lay entranced *A.T.* 150
Oh *f.* attempt to give a deathless lot *B.B.* 1
And you, *f.* maid, approve *Miss* — 94
(A poet *f.* of Nature and your friend) *R.* 542
F. of the phantom of an earthly rest *R.* 764
Nor in her own *f.* apprehension *R.C.* 101
A silly *f.* conceit of his fair form *T.* ii 420
This *f.* attachment to the well known place *Tir.* 314
F. of the speculative height *Trans.* ii 13

FONDLED.
What pleasure can the miser's *f.* hoard *J.T.* 15

FONDLY.
Her new-laid eggs she *f.* pressed *A Fable* 2
Then thus the god whom *f.* they *J.P.* 29

FONDNESS.
Strange *f.* of the human heart *St.* v 13
Or Fancy's *f.* for the child she bears *P.E.* 517

FOOD.
Has left some hundreds without home or *f. Ch.* 466
F. for the famished rovers of the flood *Ch.* 532
The dews condensed into angelic *f. Ex.* 182
Mysteries are *f.* for angels; they digest *F.A.* 35
Restless as his who toils and sweats for *f. J.T.* 24
And hoards them in her sleeve; but needful *f. T.* i 554
F. for the vulgar merely—is an art *T.* iii 449
By public exigence, till annual *f. T.* v 458 [*P.F.* 483
Minnows and gudgeons gorge the unwholesome *f.*
Thanks for thy *f.* Carnivorous, through sin *T.* vi 457
F. chiefly for the mind *T.B.* 42
Of classic *f.* begins to be his care *Tir.* 319
For such is all the mental *f.* purveyed *Tir.* 620
Seeking her *f.*, with ease might have purloined *Y.O.* 19

FOOL.
A *f.* must now and then be right by chance *Con.* 96
Would only prove him a consummate *f. Con.* 140 [182
Lest fops should censure us, and *f.* should sneer *Con.*
Calls gentleman whom she has made a *f. Con.* 466
That *f.*, as you have done, shall call a dream *Con.* 504
And therefore 'tis a mark *f.* never hit *Con.* 880
As Interest biased knaves, or Fashion *f. Ex.* 38
And sighed for every *f.* that fluttered by *Ex.* 54
Nor any *f.* he would deceive *F.* 16
Ten thousand charms, that only *f.* despise *H.* 51
What were they? What some *f.* are made by art *H.* 497
And when by that of reason, a mere *f. H.* 567
Of *f.* that hate thee and delight in sin *H.* 745
To play the *f.* on Sundays, why not we? *P.E.* 147
Go, *f.*; and, arm in arm with Clodio, plead *P.E.* 197
And play the *f.*, but at a cheaper rate *R.* 562
In misery *f.* upon themselves impose *T.* 126
Seems what it is, a cap and bells for *f. T.* 368
And the *f.* with it, who insults his Lord *T.* 504.
Thou *f.*! Will thy discovery of the cause *T.* ii 196
That *f.* discover it, and stray no more *T.* ii 530
Till they can laugh at virtue, mock the *f. T.* ii 692
That He will judge the earth and call the *f. T.* iii 178
Formed for the confutation of the *f. T.* v 567
From *f.* to wise, from earthly to divine *T.* v 696
So God wrought double justice; made the *f. T.* vi 557
Designed by Nature wise, but self-made *f. Tir.* 837
E'en on the *f.* that trampled on their laws *T.T.* 651

FOOLISH.
The sight our *f.* heart inflames *P.B.* 31.
His hot displeasure against *f.* men *T.* ii 179
But *f.* man foregoes his proper bliss *T.* iii 296
To follow *f.* precedents, and wink *Tir.* 255

FOOLISHNESS.
Mere fallacy, or *f.*, or both ? *T.* 516.

FOOT.
And woman trembling at the *f.* of man *A.T.* 158
Here stay thy *f.* ; how copious, and how clear *Ch.* 365
Whose *f.* ne'er tainted morning dew *Ep.* ii 3
Stamped with his *f.*, and smote upon his thigh *Ex.* 64
These carpets, so soft to the *f. Gr.* 17
Hope with uplifted *f.*, set free from earth *H.* 161
I plant my *f.* upon this ground of trust *H.* 369
Slain at the *f.* of Pleasure be no crime *P.E.* 182
Lips busy, and eyes fixed, *f.* falling slow *R.* 285
" Since the dear hour that brought me to thy *f. T.* 573
The elastic spring of an unwearied *f. T.* i 135
Our *f.* half sunk in hillocks green and soft *T.* i 272
And asking of the surge that bathes thy *f. T.* i 655
And fiery caverns, roars beneath his *f. T.* ii 90
And faithful to the *f.*, his spirits rise *T.* iii 8
And heaviest, light of *f.* steals fast away *T.* iv 442
And half on *f.*, they brush the fleecy flood *T.* v 63
Intrinsically precious ; to the *f. T.* v 175
And licks the *f.* that treads it in the dust *T.* v 356
To rend a victim trembling at his *f. T.* vi 411
He sells protection. Witness at his *f. T.* vi 417
Who needlessly sets *f.* upon a worm *T.* vi 563
Forgetful that the *f.* may crush the trust *Tir.* 792
In Honour's field advancing his firm *f. T.T.* 16

FOOT-BOY.
Expect her soon with *f.* at her heels *T.* iv 550

FOOT-FREQUENTED.
To purchase, at the *f.* fair *T.T.* 756

FOOTING.
F. it in the dance that Fancy leads *P.E.* 308

FOOTMAN.
A scrivener's clerk, or *f.* out of place *Tir.* 407
By *f.* Tom for witty and refined *Tir.* 687

FOOT-RACE.
A wrestling match, a *f.*, or a fair *T.* iv 626

FOOTSTEPS.
The *f.* of Simplicity, impressed *T.* iv 520
The unambiguous *f.* of the God *T.* v 812

FOP. [182
Lest *f.* should censure us, and fools should sneer *Con.*
The solemn *f.*, significant and budge *Con.* 299
F. at all corners, lady-like in mien *Tir.* 829

FOPPERY.
On principle, where *f.* atones *T.* iv 689

FOPPISH.
As move derision, or by *f.* airs *T.* ii 562

FORBADE.
By Fashion taught, *f.* them once to name *Con.* 496

FORBEAR.
You cried—" *F.* ! "—but in my breast *B.R.* 5
Will find occasion to *f. M.F.* 38
But, muse, *f.* ; long flights forebode a fall *P.E.* 604
Oh, Muse ! *f.* to speak *T.B.* 51

FORBEARANCE.
His wise *f.* has their end in view *Con.* 33
That claims *f.* even for a brute *T.* vi 466

FORBEARING.
For long *f.* clemency to wait *T.T.* 401

FORBID.
That he who dares, when she *f.*, be grave *Con.* 475
F. in vain to push his daring way *Ex.* 17
And Time *f.* to touch them as he flew *Ex.* 184
He meant not to *f.* the head *L.W.* 18
F. him none but the licentious joy *P.E.* 237
Women, whom custom has *f.* to fly *P.E.* 504
F. the advancement of the soul he binds *R.* 236
The thousands whom the world *f.* to rest *T.* 438
Its elevated site *f.* the wretch *T.* i 239
And their inveterate habits, all *f. T.* i 490
And there, unless when Charity *f. T.* i 548
Binds ll his faculties, *f.* all growth *T.* i 613
Nor such as with a frown *f.* the play *T.* iv 175
F. their interference, looking on *T.* v 523
Thy Providence *f.* that fickle power *T.* v 871
And while the dreadful risk foreseen *f. Tir.* 860

FORBIDDEN.
If either on *f.* ground *F.* 34
To search *f.* deeps, where mystery lies *F.A.* 33
Nor hold *f.* joys in view *O.* ii 5
To joys *f.* man aspires *P.B.* 15
In drawing pictures of *f.* joys *R.* 216
A monarch's errors are *f.* game *T.T.* 114

FORBIDDEST.
Thou temptest none, but rather much *f. Y.O.* 114

FORBIDDING.
F. you the prey *Beau* 8
Sweet in itself, and not *f.* sport *Tir.* 652

FORBORNE.
Which God, though long *f.*, will not forget *Ex.* 713

FORCE. [193
The barb sprang forward, and his lord, whose *f. A.T.*
The beasts are chartered—neither age nor *f. Ch.* 171
We feel thy *f.* still active, at this hour *Ch.* 272
With gentle yet prevailing *f. Comp.* ii 5
The feats of Vestris, or the naval *f. Con.* 58
Where others toil with philosophic *f. Con.* 151
That men engage in it, impelled by *f. Con.* 179
Daily derive increasing light and *f. Con.* 697 [901
With rash and awkward *f.* the chords he shakes *Con.*
And *f.* me to a smile *Ep.* ii 36
The fervour and the *f.* of Indian skies *Ex.* 12
With *f.* not easily suppressed *F.B.* 14
Nature opposes with her utmost *f. H.* 639
And still by motives of religious *f. J.T.* 33
Thy hands their little *f.* resign *M.* 34
And day by day some current's thwarting *f. M.P.* 104
Whether increased momentum, and the *f. P.E.* 405
The Will made subject to a lawless *f. P.E.* 448
These like a deluge with impetuous *f. R.* 77
May run in cities, with a brisker *f. R.* 454
F. many a shining youth into the shade *R.* 560
That passion's *f.*, and so did she *R.C.* 24
His life should prove that he perceives their *f. T.* 198
That his example had a magnet's *f. T.* ii 250
And *f.* them sit, till he has pencilled off *T.* ii 292
Spent all his *f.*, and made no proselyte *T.* ii 331
With gentle *f.* soliciting the darts *T.* iii 115
Not tire, demanding rather skill than *f. T.* iii 407
From his pernicious *f.* Nor will he leave *T.* iv 445
With such undeviating and even *f. T.* v 37
No frost can bind it there ; its utmost *f. T.* v 104
And *f.* the beggarly last doit, by means *T.* v 316
To a vile clod, so draws him, with such *f. T.* v 589
With easy *f.* it opens all the cells *T.* vi 11 [vi 201
From which they swerve not since. That under *f. T.*
When most severe, and mustering all its *f. T.* vi 31
To ceaseless service by a ceaseless *f. T.* vi 219
Or bounded only by a lair, whose *f. T.* vi 358

In measure, as by *f.* of instinct drawn *T.* vi 412
The *f.* he spends against their fury vain *Tir.* 64
And give your monstrous project all its *f. Tir.* 239
The spur is powerful, and I grant its *f. Tir.* 482
F. not my drift beyond its just intent *Tir.* 505
His phrase well chosen, clear, and full of *f. Tir.* 669
The *f.* of discipline when backed by love *Tir.* 681
Free too, and under no constraining *f. Tir.* 861
Supplies with warm activity and *f. T.T.* 220
She ventures onward with a prosperous *f. T.T.* 266
Acts with a *f.*, and kindles with a zeal *T.T.* 482 [523
Like a proud swan, conquering the stream by *f. T.T.*
Too proud for art, and trusting in mere *f. T.T.* 683
A thousand ways the *f.* of genuine love *V.* 62
Swelling with vegetative *f.* instinct *Y.O.* 34
The *f.* that agitates not unimpaired *Y.O.* 83
Finds thee not less alive to her sweet *f. Y.O.* 133

FORCED.

Not he, but his emergence, *f.* the door *Ch.* 188
With oaths like rivets *f.* into the brain *Con.* 64
And *f.* the floodgates of licentious mirth *Con.* 264
A dread she would not, yet is *f.* to feel *Con.* 786
F. from home and all its pleasures *N.C.* 1
Hebrew or Syriac, shall be *f.* to bend *P.E.* 499
F. to a pause, would feel it good to think *St.* ii 15
F. downward, is cosolidated soon *T.* iv 349
And *f.* the blunt and yet unblooded steel *T.* v 215
And *f.* to abandon what she bravely sought *T.* v 368
Then like a bow long *f.* into a curve *T.T.* 622

FORCEFUL.

Upturned so lately by the *f.* share *T.* iv 315

FORCIBLY.

F. drawn from many a close recess *Ch.* 529

FORCING.

The meek and modest Truth, and *f.* her *T.* vi 840

FORD.

Or *f.* the rivulets, are best at home *T.* 217

FOREBODE.

And, if I well *f. J.G.* 174
But, muse, forbear; long flights *f.* a fall *P.E.* 604
Do I *f.* impossible events *T.* v 491
Infect his happiest moments, he *f. T.* v 606

FOREBODING.

Pendulous, and *f.*, in the view *T.* iv 293

FORECAST.

With reasonable *f.* and dispatch *T.* ii 623
F. the future whole; that when the scene *T.* iii 651
To compass that good end, *f.* the means *Tir.* 884

FOREFATHER.

To cheer the rude *f.* of mankind *Con.* 454
Like thy renowned *f.*, far and wide *S.* i 12
Of our *f.*—a grave, whiskered race *T.* iii 768
When our *f.* Druids in their oaks *Y.O.* 10

FOREGO.

What has he left that he can yet *f.? Ch.* 150
O Friendship! if my soul *f. F.* 211
The very sense of it *f.* its use *H.* 21
Its nature to *f. Miss* — 6.
All wish, or seem to wish, they could *f. R.* 4
F. not what she feels within *S.* 10
But foolish man *f.* his proper bliss *T.* iii 296
To sad necessity, the cock *f. T.* v 73
For that dear sorrow's sake *f.* 1789, 52

FOREGOING.

Than in *f.* years? *St.* i 6

FOREGONE.

More frequent, and *f.* her usual rest *T.* ii 61

FOREHEAD.

Kneel now, and lay thy *f.* in the dust *Ex.* 554
They swathe the *f.*, drag the limping limb *T.* i 581
Than those of age, thy *f.* wrapped in clouds *T.* iv 124
As fix'd as marble, with a *f.* ridged *T.* vi 268
Rise in his *f.*, and seem rank enough *Tir.* 164
His manly *f.* to the fiercest foe *T.T.* 277

FOREIGN.

Spreads *f.* wonders in his country's sight *Ch.* 116
Flow in a *f.* land, but not in vain *E.* ii 46
Sets off a wanderer into *f.* lands *P.E.* 378
Revered at home, and felt in *f.* lands *R.* 412
In *f.* eyes!—be grooms, and win the plate *T.* ii 280
" As one who long detained on *f.* shores *T.* v 832

FOREIGNER.

If *f.* likewise would give up the trade *P.A.* 13
Caffraria; *f.* from many lands *T.* iii 585

FORELOCK.

Loose fly his *f.* and his ample mane *Ch.* 176

FOREMOST.

Fairest and *f.* of the train that wait *Ch.* 1
To take the lead and be the *f.* still *Tir.* 377

FORENSIC.

Or serves the champion in *f.* war *Ex.* 664

FORERUNNER.

The foul *f.* of a general rot *Ex.* 106

FORESEEING.

He, *f.* what vexations *N.C.* 37

FORESEEN.

And while the dreadful risk *f.* forbids *Tir.* 860

FORESEES.

And self-reproaching conscience? He *f. T.* v 600
Which only a parental eye *f. Tir.* 371

FOREST.

From the *f.* of our land *B.* 26
To quit the *f.* and invade the fold *Ch.* 185
As when two pilgrims in a *f.* stray *H.* 276
Vines, olives, herbage, *f.* disappear *Her.* 23
Where mountain, river, *f.*, field, and grove *R.* 29
Or *f.* where the deer securely roves *R.* 182
Then *f.*, or the savage rock, may please *T.* i 518
There *f.* of no meaning spread the page *T.* iv 74
And drive the wedge in yonder *f.* drear *T.* v 43
The wonder of the North. No *f.* fell *T.* v 131
By men performed, made all the *f.* ring *Y.O.* 109
Long since, and rovers of the *f.* wild *Y.O.* 126

FORESTALL.

To *f.* sweet St. Valentine *P.T.* 12

FORESTER.

Like a neglected *f.*, runs wild *P.E.* 362
Observe the dappled *f.*, how light *St.* ii 21

FOREST-TREES.

Like crowded *f.* we stand *St.* i 13

FORETASTE.

His soul refreshed with *f.* of the joy? *T.* vi 762

FORETELLS.

That it *f.* us, always comes to pass *T.* iv 72

FORETOLD.
F. one, dreamed not of a foe so near *A.T.* 152
F. by prophets, and by poets sung *T.* vi 731

FOREWARN'D.
But he that has humanity, *f. T.* vi 566

FOREWENT.
His sheltering side, and wilfully *f. T.* vi 40

FORFEIT.
Cannot *f.* Nature's claim *N.C.* 14
I should deserve to *f.* all applause) *P.E.* 511
To which he *f.* even the rest he loves *T.* i 395
Gives him his praise, and *f.* not her own *T.* iii 247
Prove this, and *f.* all pretence to praise *T.T.* 569

FORFEITURE.
No *f.*, and of its fruits he sends *T.* v 573

FORGE.
Strong Genius, from whose *f.* of thought *Mrs. M—* 23
Contriver who first sweated at the *f. T.* v 214
Till hardened his heart's temper in the *f. T.* v 664

FORGED.
Sin *f.*, and Ignorance made fast, the chain *Ch.* 237
And he that *F*, and he that threw the dart *H.* 578

FORGERY.
F. of fancy, and a dream of woes *R.* 324
By *f.*, by subterfuge of law *T.* ii 670
What none can prove a *f.*, may be true *T.* v 612

FORGET.
Of her he loves, and never can *f. Ch.* 146
Snuffs up the morning air, *f.* the rein *Ch.* 175
F. to enjoy the palm-tree's offered shade *Ch.* 222
F. his harmony, with rapture heard *Con.* 447
Is madly to *f.* that life is short *Con.* 772
Which God, though long forborne, will not *f. Ex.* 713
If he could possibly *f. F.* 167
Quite to *f.*, or deem it worth no thought *H.* 83
Slips to his hammock, and *f.* the blast *R.* 436
F. their labours, and yet find no rest *R.* 496
Can e'er *f.* the charms he left behind *S.* ii 3
No;—the voluptuaries, who ne'er *f. T.* 341
F. her labour as she toils along *T.* 457
And having found his instrument, *f. T.* ii 176
F. in peace the injuries of war *T.* ii 269
That in due season he *f.* it too *T.* v 267
That he at last *f.* it. All his hopes *T.* v 591
Deaf as the dead to harmony, *f. T.* vi 646
Holds fast her office here, can ne'er *f. Tir.* 134

FORGETFUL.
F. of the glorious toils of war *A.T.* 28
F. that the foot may crush the trust *Tir.* 792
F. of the man whom once ye chose *V.* 3

FORGETTING.
I must incur, *f.* Howard's name *Ch.* 296
F. its important weight *F.* 70

FORGING.
In *f.* chains for us, themselves were free *T.* v 392

FORGIVE.
Let Charity *f.* me a mistake *Ch.* 634
To pity and perhaps *f. M.F.* 40
F. their evil, and accept their good *T.* 582
F. him then, thou bustler in concerns *T.* vi 951
(F. a transient thought) *The Doves* 30
(F. the crime) I wish them, I confess *Tir.* 921

FORGIVEN.
All former friends *f.*, and forgot *V.* 84

FORGIVENESS.
And injured, makes *f.* her delight *Ch.* 431·
F., and the privilege of hope *H.* 214

FORGOT.
"Honour, esteem and confidence *f. A.T.* 111
To names ignoble born to be *f.* ! *B.B.* 2
What he remembers seems to have *f. Con.* 132
Nothing is slightly touched, much less *f. Con.* 317
Such men are not *f.* as soon as cold *Con.* 630
F. to curse, and only kneel to pray *Con.* 814
F. the blush that virgin fears impart *Ex.* 47
Mere shadows now, their ancient pomp *f. Ex.* 262
Then too much feared, and now too much *f. Ex.* 575
But though I less deplored thee ne'er *f. M.P.* 45
So soon to be *f. O.* i 24
Left out his linchpin, or *f.* his tar *P.E.* 441
Where all his long anxieties *f. R.* 7
To studies then familiar, since *f. R.* 374
Jack vanished, was regretted and *f. R.* 581
These truths, though known, too much *f. St.* i 31
F. their office, opening with a touch *T.* ii 747
If aught was learned in childhood, is *f. T.* ii 755
They should go out in fume, and be *f.* ? *T.* iii 172
How! turn again to tales long since *f. Tir.* 545
And should, no doubt, if they were all *f. T.T.* 771
All former friends forgiven, and *f. V.* 84

FORGOTTEN.
Grace him again with long *f.* arts *Con.* 839
Who fret their hour and are *f.* things *V.* 46
F. as the foliage of thy youth *Y.O.* 59

FORK.
If I mistake not—Blockhead! with a *f.* ! *H.* 362
Lodged with convenience in the *f. R.C.* 13
From the full *f.*, the saturated straw *T.* iii 479
The peasants urge their harvest, ply the *f. T.T.* 214
As now, and with excoriate *f.* deform *Y.O.* 5

FORLORN.
In Scotland's realm, *f.* and bare *A Tale* 9
Till thy appearance chased the gloom, *f. J.T.* 21
Afric's coast I left *f. N.C.* 2
At thought of her *f.* and abject state *T.* i 659
There dwell the most *f.* of human kind *T.* v 397
And prospect oft so dreary and *f. T.* vi 21
Stands in the desert shivering and *f. T.T.* 724

FORM.
My *f.* with indifference see *A.S.* 14
That *f.* material, whatsoe'er we dream *A.T.* 40
That *f.* and rites are tricks of human law *A.T.* 62
F. or no *f.*, pluralities or pairs *A.T.* 131
In starry *f.* disposed upon the wall *Ch.* 552
To recollect that in a *f.* like ours *Ch.* 583
Relenting *f.* would lose their power, or cease *Ch.* 608
Pronounce your human *f.* a false pretence *Con.* 78
A duel in the *f.* of a debate *Con.* 84
And show the softest minds and fairest *f. Con.* 259
F., in its stead, a covenant of shame *Con.* 684
In *f.* a man, in dignity a God *Ex.* 86
With hollow *f.*, and gesture, and grimace *Ex.* 122
The requisites that *f.* a friend *F.* 14
That *f.* the character he seeks *F.* 46
My *f.* genteel, my plumage gay *G.* 5
And *f.* genteel were all in vain *G.* 8
These stoves that for pattern and *f. Gr.* 39
To frown and roar, and shake his feeble *f. H.* 186
Sweet scent, or lovely *f.*, or both combined *H.* 29
By this he *f.*, as pleased he sports along *H.* 610
Such at least was the *f.* that she wore *M.D.* 10
To *f.* the better prayer *Miss —* 20
Her beauteous *f.* reflected clear below *M.P.* 93

F. rise, to quick perfection wrought *Mrs. M*— 24
To *f.* an Iris in the skies *O.* i 19
Successfully conceals her loathsome *f. P.E.* 8
Her *f.* with dress and lotion they repair *P.E.* 299
To wonder at a thousand insect *f. R.* 63
And *f.* it to the taste of her he loves *R.* 238
Nature in every *f.* inspires delight *R.* 417
With whom, dismissing *f.*, he may unbend *R.* 444
Bids these in elegance of *f.* excel *R.* 793
So sings he, charmed with his own mind and *f. T.* 411
Gave them a twisted *f.* vermicular *T.* i 30
The richest scenery and the loveliest *f. T.* i 711
Have dwindled into unrespected *f. T.* i 747
A faithful likeness of the *f.* he views *T.* ii 293
A silly fond conceit of his fair *f. T.* ii 420
Or be dishonoured in the exterior *f. T.* ii 560
A *f.* not now gymnastic as of yore *T.* ii 591
A *f.* as splendid as the proudest there *T.* ii 620
There *f.* connexions, but acquire no friend *T.* ii 634
What longest binds the closest, *f.* secure *T.* iii 480
They *f.* one social shade, as if convened *T.* iii 586
Nature, enchanting Nature, in whose *f. T.* iii 721
With spots quadrangular of diamond *f. T.* iv 217
Her elbows ruffled, and her tottering *f. T.* iv 545
His *f.*, and movement; is as smart above *T.* iv 641
With *f.* so various, that no powers of art *T.* v 108
To be the tenant of man's noble *f. T.* v 455
A ray of heavenly light gilding all *f. T.* v 810
Where no eye sees them. And the fairer *f. T.* vi 188
The *f.* with which he sprinkles all the earth *T.* vi 246
As God was free to *f.* them at the first *T.* vi 586
A worthless *f.*, than to decide aright *T.* vi 851
It is not from his *f.*, in which we trace *Tir.* 1
That *f.*, indeed, the associate of a mind *Tir.* 5
That *f.*, the labour of Almighty skill *Tir.* 7
To *f.* thy son, to strike his genius forth *Tir.* 679
The fleeting *f.* of majesty engage *T.T.* 117
His *f.* robust and of elastic tone *T.T.* 218
His speech, his *f.*, his action full of grace *T.T.* 346
All are his instruments; each *f.* of war *T.T.* 446
As ecstasy, unmanacled by *f. T.T.* 589
F., opens, and gives scent to every flower *T.T.* 691
Skilled in the characters that *f.* mankind *T.T.* 705

FORMALITY.
Hypocrisy, *f.* in prayer *Ex.* 43

FORMED.
And farther still the *f.* and fixed design *Ex.* 429
Was *f.* to harden hearts and shock the sight *Ex.* 495
Who found thee nothing, *f.* thee for his praise *Ex.* 643
Elegant phrase, and figure *f.* to please *P.E.* 422
And calls a creature *f.* for God alone *R.* 17
Than the firm oak of which the frame was *f. T.* i 56
F. for his use, and ready at his will? *T.* ii 202
Seems *f.* for contemplation, and to nurse *T.* iii 301
Upon their jutting chests. He, *f.* to bear *T.* iv 350
Who, when she *f.*, designed them an abode *T.* vi 580
Resolved a union *f.* for life *The Doves* 27
Not English stiff, but frank, and *f.* to please *Tir.* 671
If guards, mechanically *f.* in ranks *T.T.* 135
Not *f.* like us, with such Herculean powers *T.T.* 235
F. with materials neat and soft *A Tale* 39
To look at him who *f.* us and redeemed *Ch.* 579
The circle *f.*, we sit in silent state *Con.* 379
For which Heaven *f.* the faculty divine *Con.* 898
Rufillus, exquisitely *f.* by rule *P.E.* 189
Which *f.* the chief display *Q.V.* 10
On earth what is, seems *f.* indeed for us *R.* 106
Next to that power who *f.* thee and sustains *R.* 201
Up!—God has *f.* thee with a wiser view *R.* 265
Why *f.* at all? And wherefore as he is? *T.* ii 513
Unapt to learn, and *f.* of stubborn stuff *T.* iv 636
I never framed a wish or *f.* a plan *T.* iv 695 [740
And all can taste them; minds that have been *f. T.* iv
F. for the confutation of the fool *T.* v 567
But not its Author. Unconcerned who *f. T.* v 793
Who *f.* him from the dust, his future grave *T.* vi 349
Thus *f.*, thus placed, intelligent, and taught *Tir.* 53
" Why *f.* at all, and wherefore as thou art?" *Tir.* 58
Connexion *f.* for interest, and endeared *Tir.* 495
As, wheresoever taught, so *f.*, he will *Tir.* 526
And *f.* of God without a parent's mind *Tir.* 790
F. as if akin to thee *Trans.* iii 18
A union *f.* as mine with thee *U.* 7

FORMER.
Farewell, my *f.* joys! I sigh no more *Ch.* 240
Not that the *F.* of us all, in this *T.* 345
Their *f.* charms? And having seen our state *T.* i 642
My *f.* partners of my peopled scene *T.* iii 119

FORNICATION.
How simple wedlock *f.* works *A.T.* 159

FORSAKE.
The vessel weighs, *f.* the shore *A Tale* 43
But if eccentric ye *f.* your sphere *P.E.* 98
Or when it first *f.* the elastic string *P.E.* 573
A few *f.* the throng; with lifted eyes *R.* 161
The very rooks and daws *f.* the fields *T:*v 89

FORSAKEN.
Forsaking, and *f.* of all friends *H.* 694
F. her retreat *Q.V.* 26
Where the betrayed, *f.*, and oppressed *T.* 437
F., or through folly not enjoyed *T.* iii 711

FORSAKING.
F. country, kindred, friends, and ease *H.* 585
F., and forsaken of all friends *H.* 694
F. thee, what shipwreck have we made *T.* iii 58

FORTIFY.
Enlarge and *f.* the dread redoubt *Con.* 689

FORTITUDE.
To improve the *f.* that bears the load *Ch.* 160
Their *f.* and wisdom were a flame *T.* 531
Where find ye passive *f.*? Whence springs *T.* v 327

FORTRESS.
A *f.* to which she retreats *W.N.* 11

FORTUITOUS.
By these *f.* and random strokes *T.* v 124

FORTUITOUSLY.
The world and I *f.* met *Con.* 795

FORTUNE.
Be it your *f.*, year by year *A Tale* 77
As *f.*, vice, or folly may command *H.* 12
Through mere good *f.*, took a different course *N.A.* 126
But I can feel thy *f.*, and partake *T.* ii 219
On *F.*'s velvet altar offering up *T.* ii 657
Their last poor pittance—*F.*, most severe *T.* ii 658
" Battered and bankrupt *f.* mended here" *T.* iii 824
F., and dignity; the loss of all *T.* v 602
By any change of *f.*; proof alike *T.* vi 626
Threaten his health, his *f.*, and his fame *Tir.* 532
Of adverse *f.*'s power *Trans. H.* 3
But oh! if *F.* fill thy sail *Trans. H.* 34
In wisdom, health, in *f.*, and in lies *T.T.* 469

FORTY.
She might be young some *f.* years ago *T.* 132

FORWARD.
To be as bold and *f.* as he ought *Tir.* 339

FOSTERED—FOUNDED

FOSTERED.
Vain tampering has but *f.* his disease *T.* v 668

FOSTERING.
His *f.* power, and tutelary care *T.T.* 257
F. propitious, thou becamest a twig *Y.O.* 39

FOUGHT.
Rushed to battle, *f.*, and died *B.* 39
But, though they fight as thine have ever *f. Ex.* 292
His last sea-fight is *f. R.G.* 15   [*T.T.* 610
When Cromwell *f.* for power, and while he. reigned
If any wronged her. Wolfe, where'er he *f. T.* ii 248
Thus war began on earth ; these *f.* for spoil *T.* v 228
Tells of a few stout hearts that *f.* and died *T.T.* 23
Confessed a God; they kneeled before they *f. T.T.* 374

FOUL.
The *f.* forerunner of a general rot *Ex.* 106
Though black and *f.* before *O.* i 20
There stand, and justify the *f.* abuse *P.E.* 144
In cities *f.* example on most minds *T.* i 685
May yet be *f.*; so witty, yet not wise *T.* i 728
Pure, from so *f.* a pool, to shine abroad *T.* ii 798
Its *f.* inhabitant. But to assuage *T.* iii 501
The way to glory by miscarriage *f. T.* iii 506
The triple purpose. In that sickly, *f. T.* v 583
F. with excess, and with discourse obscene *Tir.* 736

FOULEST.
Ranks its abuse among the *f.* deeds *Ch.* 209
But Grace abused brings forth the *f.* deeds *Ex.* 213
As human nature's broadest, *f.* blot *T.* ii 22

FOULLY.
All witnesses of blessings *f.* scorned *H.* 223

FOUND.
F. oftenest in what least we dread *A Fable* 37
With all the flowers he *f.*, he wove in haste *A.T.* 13
Some better things are *f. A Tale* 4
But *f.* not where to build *A Tale* 16
Wherever he *f.* man to nature true *Ch.* 27
The simple native of the new *f.* isle *Ch.* 30
Wast thou in monkish cells and nunneries *f. Ch.* 43
Wherever *f.* (and all men need thy care) *Ch.* 47
He *f.* it inconvenient to be poor *Ch.* 189
Till finding, what he might have *f.* before *Ch.* 475
Sure to succeed, the remedy they *f. Con.* 500
F. him as prompt, as their desire was true *Con.* 545
Hearts may be *f.* that harbour at this hour *Con.* 561
Nor shall be *f.* in unregenerate souls *Con.* 755
Sobriety perhaps may now be *f. Con.* 807
That Spaniel *f.* for me) *D.W.* 8
Thus we were settled when you *f.* us *E.* i 39
Who *f.* not thorns and briars in his road *E.* ii 12
So once in Gideon's fleece the dews were *f. E.* ii 49
That all was naught within, and all *f.* out *E.* iii 53
But ah! 'tis lost as soon as *f. E.* iv 58
From East to West, no sorrow can be *f. Ex.* 28
Till the foe *f.* them, and down fell the towers *Ex.* 72
He *f.*, concealed beneath a fair outside *Ex.* 891
Had *f.* one city not to be o'ercome *Ex.* 210
He will be *f.* impartially severe *Ex.* 255
He *f.* thee savage, and he left thee tame *Ex.* 485
F. thee a goodly sponge for Power to press *Ex.* 531
He *f.* the laurel only—happier you *Ex.* 600   [643
Who *f.* thee nothing, formed thee for his praise *Ex.*
Happy the man there seeking and there *f. Ex.* 652
Not quickly *f.*, if negligently sought *Ex.* 695
And dream that he had *f.* one *F.* 18
Or where it was not to be *f. F.* 35
Through numerous generations till he *f. F.A.* 25
Yet seldom sought where only to be *f. H.* 112 [275
'Twas there we *f.* them, and must leave them there *H.*
If wild in nature, and not duly *f. H.* 296

" Is still *f.* fallible, however wise *H.* 422
Had two stone bottles *f.*. *J.G.* 66
Told hill and dale that Reynard's track was *f. N.A.* 34
In earth's dark womb have *f.* at last a vent *N.A.* 86
Much wondered whither the silly sheep had *f. N.A.* 129
And *f.* a supper somewhere else *N.G.* 26
If all the plants that can be *f. P.* 57
She myriads *f.* below *Q.V.* 76
And works of God are hardly to be *f. R.* 26
Yet seek him, in his favour life is *f. R.* 353
Else more attached to pleasures *f.* at home *R.* 518
Some seeking happiness not *f.* below *R.* 604
Have *f.* their home, the grave *St.* i 4
Once went I forth, and *f.*, till then unknown *T.* 220
Sometimes a canting hypocrite is *f. T.* 233
Now scattered wide, and nowhere to be *f. T.* 394
And drilled in holes, the solid oak is *f. T.* i 26 [413
Is Nature's dictate. Strange! there should be *f. T.* i
So lately *f.*, although the constant sun *T.* i 621
The dream is past; and thou hast *f.* again *T.* i 639
Alas! expect it not. We *f.* no bait *T.* i 672 [*T.* i 641
And homestall thatched with leaves. But hast thou *f.*
And having *f.* his instrument, forgets *T.* ii 176
Of action and reaction. He has *f. T.* ii 193
Where English minds and manners may be *f. T.* ii 208
Their least amusement where he *f.* the most *T.* ii 310
But where are its sublimer trophies *f.? T.* ii 319
Till gowns at length are *f.* mere masquerade *T.* ii 748
Have we not tracked the felon home, and *f. T.* ii 813
Of that calamitous mischief has been *f. T.* ii 821
F. too where most offensive, in the skirts *T.* ii 822
There was I *f.* by one who had himself *T.* iii 112
On all her branches. Piety has *f. T.* iii 249
Such as the mistress of the world once *f. T.* iv 169
The disappointed foe, deliverance *f. T.* iv 186
Finds happiness unblighted; or if *f. T.* iv 334 [519
From courts dismissed, *f.* shelter in the groves *T.* iv
And manners profligate, were rarely *f. T.* iv 523
Had *f.* me, or the hope of being free *T.* iv 699
The joy half lost, because not sooner *f. T.* iv 717
Diversified, that two were never *f. T.* iv 737
F. here that leisure and that ease I wished *T.* iv 801
In such a palace Aristæus *f. T.* v 135
The same lubricity was *f.* in all *T.* v 165
Of his descending progeny was *f. T.* v 212
Some relish, till the sum, exactly *f. T.* v 430
For when was public virtue to be *f. T.* v 502
We miss'd that happiness we might have *f.! T.* vi 28
Deep in the flood *f.*, when he sought it not *T.* vi 555
In aid of our defects. In some are *f. T.* vi 611
Better than all the books he *f. T.B.* 41
Awoke and *f.* it true *T.B.* 48
Like fleeting exhalations, *f.* no more *Tir.* 84
Not to be *f.* by poring on a book *Tir.* 384
Besides, school-friendships are not always *f. Tir.* 436
For there the game they seek is easiest *f. Tir.* 520
Were occupation easier to be *f. Tir.* 701
But, having *f.* him, be thou duke or earl *Tir.* 706
Patriots, alas! the few that have been *f. T.T.* 336
Is genius only *f.* in epic lays? *T.T.* 568
'Tis *f.* as everlasting as his love *T.T.* 595
Pity Religion has so seldom *f. T.T.* 716
On other mighty ones, *f.* also thee *Y.O.* 68
But none I *f.*, or *f.* them shared 1789, 7
But rests on none till that be *f.* 1789, 19
I *f.* the far-sought treasure near 1789, 28

FOUNDATION.
On what *f.* virtue is to stand *H.* 529
Die too: the deep *f.* that we lay *T.* v 532
So stands a kingdom, whose *f.* yet *Y.O.* 120

FOUNDED.
Blasphemes his creed, as *f.* on a plan *Tir.* 159

FOUNDER. [127
Lest Rome should end with her first *f.s'* lives *A.T.*
The *f.* of that name alone inspires *Ch.* 600

FOUNDERED.
His ship half *f.*, and his compass lost *T.* 2

FOUNT.
These flowing from the *f.* of grace above *E.* ii 29

FOUNTAIN.
Or taste the *f.* in the neighbouring glade *Ch.* 223
Some men make gain a *f.*, whence proceeds *Ch.* 244
Where *f.* fed with infinite supplies *Ex.* 34
To watch the *f.*, and preserve it clear *Ex.* 98
Seems, as it is, the *f.* whence alone *H.* 708
Thou *f.* at which drink the good and wise *P.E.* 466
Of neighbouring *f.*, or of rills that slip *T.* 192
Drink, when we choose it, at the *f.* head *T.* ii 502
Rotation; from what *f.* flowed their light *T.* iii 161
In the pure *f.* of eternal love *T.* iii 244
Were built, the *f.* opened, or the sea *T.* v 765
Derives from Heaven, pure as the *f.* is *T.* vi 833
Dipped in the *f.* of eternal love *T* vi. 863

FOUR.
F. ivory eggs soon pave its floor *A Tale* 41
To fill the dull vacuity till *f. H.* 78
Precisely when the clock strikes *f.*" *M.F.* 14
Lolls at his ease behind *f.* handsome bays *R.* 392
With twice *f.* hundred men *R.G.* 24
Improved the simple plan, made three legs *f. T.* i 29
This folio of *f.* pages, happy work! *T.* iv 50

FOUR-QUARTERED.
To the *f.* winds, robust and bold *Y.O.* 98

FOWL.
I am lord of the *f.* and the brute *A.S.* 4
And seems to say—" Ye meaner *f.*, give place *T.* 64

FOX.
And though the *f.* he follows may be tamed *Con.* 409

FOX-FOLLOWER.
A mere *f.* never is reclaimed *Con.* 410

FRAGMENT.
Alas for Sicily! rude *f.* now *T.* ii 75
A *f.*, and the spoutless teapot there *T.* iv 776

FRAGRANCE.
Immortal *f.* fills the circuit wide *Ch.* 439
The selfsame gale that wafts the *f.* round *Her* 35
To fill with *f.* his abode above *H.* 122
Perceived the *f.* as he passed *P.B.* 4
The cheering *f.* of her dewy vales *T.* i 429

FRAGRANT.
With *f.* turf, and flowers as wild and fair *Ch.* 258
Their *f.* memory will outlast their tomb *Con.* 631
The *f.* grove, the inestimable mine *H.* 177
The *f.* waters on my cheeks bestowed *M.P.* 62
Sweet converse, sipping calm the *f.* lymph *T.* iii 391
And *f.* chaplet, recompensing well *T.* iii 668
Of orange, myrtle, or the *f.* weed *T.* iv 764
To adjust the *f.* charge of a short tube *T.* v 55

FRAIL.
But man is *f.*, and can but ill sustain *Ex.* 81
Then heaven enjoins the fallible and *f. H.* 391
Contrived to suit *f.* nature's crazy case *H.* 604
Perhaps a *f.* memorial, but sincere *M.P.* 72
Divide the *f.* inhabitants of earth *R.* 648
Was man (*f.* always) made more *f. St.* i 5
For he was *f.* as thou or I *St.* iii 25

Of Novelty, her fickle, *f.* support *T.* iii 54
That can ennoble man, and make *f.* life *T.* v 603
"So *f.* a kind, and then enacting laws *T.* v 640
With every lust with which *f.* Nature burns *Tir.* 66
But, being man, and therefore *f.*, he may ?) *Tir.* 896
The heart of man for such a task too *f. V.* 67

FRAILTY.
She feels that *f.* she denied so long *Ch.* 409
Their author's *f.*, and return to dust *Con.* 554
Charms he may have, but he has *f.* too *T.* ii 497

FRAME.
That none could *f.* or ratify but she *Con.* 468
F. many a purpose, and God works His own *Ex.* 323
Of the chief strength and glory of the *f. Ex.* 335
And youth invigorate that *f.* again *H.* 34
If one, his equal in athletic *f. H.* 191
And searched for crannies in the *f. P.B.* 6
But still in vain, the *f.* was tight *P.B.* 9
We long for pineapples in *f. P.B.* 32
This universal *f.*, thus wondrous fair *R.* 90
Than the firm oak of which the *f.* was formed *T.* i 56
But relaxation of the languid *f. T.* i 81
The agglomerated pile, his *f.* may front *T.* iii 472
The uplifted *f.*, compact at every joint *T.* iii 484
Thy *f.*, robust and hardy, feels indeed *T.* iv 360
The citizen, and brace his languid *f.! T.* iv 752
Who seek it in his climate and his *f. T.T.* 207
A tender sympathy pervades the *f. T.T.* 485

FRAMED.
I never *f.* a wish, or formed a plan *T.* iv 695
He drew the liturgy, and *f.* the rights *T.* vi 679
F. for the service of a free-born will *Tir.* 8
And yet his judgment was not *f.* amiss *T.T.* 390

FRANCE.
Impatient to descry the flags of *F.—Ex.* 291
And fields without a flower, for warmer *F.—T.* ii 213
True, we may thank the perfidy of *F.—T.* ii 264
To *F.* than all her losses and defeats *T.* v 380
To give thee what politer *F.* receives *T.* v 468

FRANK.
Not English stiff, but *f.*, and formed to please *Tir.* 671

FRANKINCENSE.
And fumed with *f.* on every side *T.* 314

FRANKNESS.
Of filial *f.* lost, and love grown faint *Tir.* 588

FRANTIC.
The sable warrior, *f.* with regret *Ch.* 145
Pronounced him *f.*, and his fears a dream *Ex.* 70
Played only gambols in a *f.* mood *H.* 541
But most so when most *f. Pat.* 8
Grow *f.* with her pangs, and bite the ground *T.* 444
But *f.* who thus spend it all for smoke? *T.* iii 174
Laughs at the *f.* sufferer's fury, spent *T.* vi 423

FRATERNAL.
As that of true *f.* love *U.* 12

FRAUD.
Discern the *f.* beneath the specious lure *P.E.* 17
Of honour, perjury, corruption, *f. T.* ii 669
And pocketed a prize by *f.* obtained *T.* iii 87
A Liberty which persecution, *f. T.* v 542 [188
Resumes her powers, and spurns the clumsy *f. Tir.*

FRAUGHT.
The show-glass *f.* with glittering ware *P.B.* 24

FREAK.

The *f.* of fashion, regulate the dress *T.* ii 317
Thy most magnificent and mighty *f. T.* v 130

FREAKISH.

With many a *f.* trick deceived his pains *A.T.* 25
The *f.* humour of the present time *Con.* 866
Wherever *f.* Fancy points the way *R.* 128
Bespoke him past the bounds of *f.* youth *T.* ii 704
At stated hours, his *f.* thoughts engage *Tir.* 606
Grow *f.*, and o'erleaping every mound *T.T.* 302

FRECKLE.

But shows some touch, in *f.*, streak, or stain *T.* vi 241

FRECKLED.

And all that I abhor; thou *f.* fair *T.* iii 839

FREE.

F. as the lordly bull that ranges o'er the mead *A.T.* 61
He made at first, though *f.* and unconfined *Ch.* 17
That has a heart and life in it, " Be *f.* !" *Ch.* 170
That none are *f.* from blemish since the fall *Ch.* 204
Serving a benefactor, I am *f. Ch.* 242
But let insolvent innocence go *f.*" *Ch.* 289
If this be servile, that can ne'er be *f. Ch.* 568
And flow in *f.* communion with the rest *Ch.* 611
And *f.* from bias, must approve the choice *Con.* 664
And *f.* from every taint but that of vice *Ex.* 150
Seized fast his hand, held out to set them *f. Ex.* 219
Thou that hast set the persecuted *f. Ex* 278
Baboons are *f.* from, upon human race? *Ex.* 417
And all from shore to shore is *f.* beside *Ex.* 595
Charge not, with light sufficient and left *f. T.* 19
Will seldom scruple to make *f. F.* 92
Time was when I was *f.* as air *G.* 1
Hope with uplifted foot, set *f.* from earth *H.* 161
The *f.* republic of the whip-gig state *H.* 190 [536
Shall answer—" Hope, sweet Hope, has set me *f. H.*
But makes him, if at all, completely *f. H.* 646
And while the wings of fancy still are *f. M.P.* 118
Still in thought as *f.* as ever *N.C.* 9
From Avarice and Ambition *f. O.* ii 8
If apostolic gravity be *f. P.E.* 146
Enslaves the will, nor leaves the judgment *f. P.E.*
Candid and learned, dispassionate and *f. P.E.* 453
F. from the domineering power of Lust *P.E.* 458
How fair is Freedom? he was always *f. R.* 399
From ostentation, as from weakness, *f. T.* 25
The gracious showers, unlimited and *f. T.* 511
'Tis *f.* to all—'tis every day renewed *T.* i 434
Receive our air, that moment they are *f. T.* ii 41
The terrors of the day that sets them *f. T.* ii 128
Is *f.* to all men—universal prize *T.* iii 724
Is India *f.*? and does she wear her plumed *T.* iv 28
I burn to set the imprisoned *f. T.* iv 34 [iv. 600
When he should strike, he trembles, and sets *f. T.*
Had found me, or the hope of being *f. T.* iv 699
Freely and with delight, who leaves us *f. T.* v 334
In reason, is judicious, manly, *f. T.* v 354
Of a superior, he is never *f. T.* v 364
In forging chains for us, themselves were *f. T.* v 392
Among the nations, seeing thou art *f. T.* v 461
Yet being *f.*, I love thee: for the sake *T* v 473
Where I am *f.* by birthright, not at all *T.* v 479
In scenes which, having never known me *f. T.* v 489
Haste now, philosopher, and set him *f. T.* v 670
To walk with God, to be divinely *f. T.* v 722
He is the freeman whom the Truth makes *f. T.* v. 733
He is indeed a freeman. *F.* by birth *T.* v 763
Then we are *f.* Then Liberty like day *T.* v 883
Unvisited by man. There they are *f. T.* vi 403
The young to let the parent bird go *f. T.* vi 446
Is pleased with it, and, were he *f.* to choose *T.* vi 909

Religion makes the *f.* by nature slaves *Tir.* 184
F. too, and under no constraining force *Tir.* 861
All kingship, and may I be poor and *f.*! *T.T.* 150
As if he heard his king say, " Slave be *f.*!" *T.T.* 245
Heroic song from thy *f.* touch acquires *T.T.* 292

FREEBORN.

His *f.* brethren of the southern pole *Ch.* 34
The *f.* Christian has no chains to prove *T.* 187
Framed for the service of a *f.* will *Tir.* 8
To him that treads upon his *f.* toe *T.T.* 227

FREED.

And slaves, by truth enlarged, are doubly *f. Ch.* 231
Thus Conscience *f.* from every clog *L.W.* 21
Or more ingenious, or more *f. N.Y.G.* 7
From all his wearisome engagements *f. R.* 513

FREEDOM.

Deprived of her and *f.* at a blow *Ch.* 149
Can quell the love of *f.* in a horse *Ch.* 172
Not that all *f.* of dissent I blame *Con.* 97
Their *f.* purchased for them, at the cost *Ex.* 171
Hast thou, though suckled at fair *f.*'s breast *Ex.* 364
F., in other lands scarce known to shine *Ex.* 588
True *f.* is where no restraint is known *Ex.* 592
Such *f.* is—and Windsor's hoary towers *Ex.* 596
And if the feast of *f.* clog thee not *Ex.* 671
Loudly resent the stranger's *f.* there *H.* 354
Where Peace, and Equity, and *F.* smile *Her.* 84
Then farewell British *f. Pat.* 24
How fair is *F.*? He was always free *R.* 399
What charms he sees in *F.*'s smile expressed *R.* 409
In *F.* lost so long, now repossessed *R.* 410
His *f.* is the *f.* of a prince *T.* 196
No; dear as *f.* is, and in my heart's *T.* ii 33
F.: whom they that lose thee so regret *T.* ii 130
Babes in the cause of *f.*, and should fear *T.* v 291
Whose *f.* is by sufferance, and at will *T.* v 363
Of *f.*, in that hope itself possess *T.* v 375
His *f.* is the same in every state *T.* v 767
When *F.*, wounded almost to despair *T.T.* 196
Fires him at once in *F.*'s glorious cause *T.T.* 229
But is not *F.*, at least, is not ours *T.T.* 300
No. *F.* has a thousand charms to show *T.T.* 260
And *F.* claims him for her first-born son *T.T.* 281
But they that fight for *f.*, undertake *T.T.* 284
A blessing, *f.* is the pledge of all *T.T.* 287
Fervency, *f.*, fluency of thought *T.T.* 700

FREELY.

Disbanded legions *f.* might depart *Ch.* 618
" As *f.* as a conduit spout! *E.* iv 86 [625
Their streaming hearts poured *f.* when they died *Ex.*
How *f.* will they meet and charge! *F.* 137
Royalty, *f.*, for his bounty's sake *H.* 118
He will give *f.*, or he will withhold *H.* 331
That man will *f.* take an unbought bliss *H.* 335
Shall he, for such deliverance *f.* wrought *T.* 191
The remedy you want I *f.* give *T.* 273
Respiring *f.* the fresh air, that makes *T.* i 137
To them that ask it?—*F.*—'Tis his joy *T.* iii 273
Admitted *f.*, may afford their aid *T.* iii 425
Each opening blossom, *f.* breathes abroad *T.* iii 622
F. and with delight, who leaves us free *T.* v 334

FREEMAN.

The *f.* to a farewell flight *F.B.* 20
" I go to make *F.* of slaves " *M.D.* 16
Himself the only *f.* of his land? *T.* v 312
Or covet more than *f.* choose to grant *T.* v 340
That it belongs to *f.*, would disgust *T.* v 482
Grace makes the slave a *f.* 'Tis a change *T.* v 688
He is the *f.* whom the Truth makes free *T.* v 733
He is indeed a *f.* Free by birth *T.* v 763

FREEMAN—FRIEND 169

. and slave then, if the case be such *T.T.* 254
tands most revealed before the *f.* eyes *T.T.* 269

FREETHINKER.
nd joining the *f.*'s brutal roar *P.E.* 593

FREEZING.
nd potent to resist the *f.* blast *T.* iii 465
t evening, till length the *f.* blast *T.* iv 303
or *f.* sky nor sultry, checking me *T.* vi 297

FREIGHT.
harged with a *f.* transcending in its worth *Ch.* 133

FREIGHTED.
o when a ship, well *f.* with the stores *Ch.* 441

FRENCH.
Besides, if we do, the *F.*, Dutch and Danes *P.A.* 9
His stock, a few *F.* phrases got by heart *P.E.* 375
An Indian mystic, or a *F.* recluse *T.* 128 [546
ll propped upon *F.* heels, she might be deemed *T.* iv
And his address, if not quite *F.* in ease *Tir.* 670

FRENCHMAN.
Few *F.* of this evil have complained *Con.* 359
praise the *F.*, his remark was shrewd *R.* 739
The *F.* first in literary fame *T.* 303
A truth the brilliant *F.* never knew *T.* 328
The *F.*'s darling? Are they not all proofs *T.* iv 765
The *F.*, easy, debonair, and brisk *T.T.* 236

FRENZY.
What is fanatic *f.*, scorned so much *Con.* 651
A tenfold *f.* seizes all the rest *H.* 634
From all such *f.* clear *J.P.* 14
Ocean has caught the *f.*, and upwrought *T.* ii 111
All catch the *f.*, downward from her Grace *T.* ii 647
Who deem religion *f.*, and the God *T.* iv 178
To gratify the *f.* of his wrath *T.* vi 387
The *f.* of the brain may be redressed *T.* vi 521
Surpassed in *f.* by the mad at large *Tir.* 820

FREQUENCY.
The *f.* of crimes has washed them white *T.* iii 71

FREQUENT.
Strange! how the *f.* interjected dash *Ch.* 521
As *f.* as the want of it appears *Ch.* 605
And begged an interest in his *f.* prayers *Con.* 74
With *f.* intercourse, and always sweet *E.* iii 3
A Friendship that in *f.* fits *F.* 103
The rustling straw sends up a *f.* mist *T.* i 360
Where *f.* hedges intercept the eye *T.* i 514
By *f.* lapse, can hope no triumph here *T.* i 691
Dire is the *f.* curse, and its twin sound *T.* iv. 487
The *f.* flakes has kept a path for me *T.* vi 75
T. the crowded auction; station'd there *T.* vi 286
Grown so familiar with her *f.* guest *T.* vi 306
Chained to the routs that she *f.* for life *Tir.* 744
No flock *f.* thee now. Thou hast outlived *Y.O.* 56
But worn by *f.* impulse, to the cause *Y.O.* 84

FREQUENTER.
A great *f.* of the Church *Trans.* ii 4

FRESH.
Or taxed invention for a *f.* supply *Ch.* 514
Revived, are hastening into *f.* repute *Con.* 818
Sprightly and *f.*, enriches every theme *Con.* 894
And to this hour, to keep it *f.* in mind *Ex.* 516
F. odours from the shrubbery at my side *F.A.* 7
By thy own hand, till *f.* they shone and glowed *M.P.* 63
And weave *f.* garlands every day *N.* 19 [*P.E.* 316
Heaven blessed the youth, and made him *f.* and fair
F. confidence the speculatist takes *P.E.* 490

Respiring freely the *f.* air, that makes *T.* i 138
Smells *f.*, and, rich in odoriferous herbs *T.* i 531
F. for his task, intend what task he may *T.* iii 387
Had fled from William, and the news was *f. T.* vi 660
And there obtains *f.* triumphs o'er himself *T.* vi 937
Spreads the *f.* verdure of the field, and leads *T.T.* 692
These pinks are as *f.*, and as gay *W.N.* 14

FRESH-BLOWING.
And the *f.* breeze never failed *M.D.* 8

FRESHENING.
F. his lazy spirits as he ran *P.E.* 411
All feel the *f.* impulse, and are cleansed *T.* i 376

FRESHNESS.
Knows what the *f.* of their hue implies *N.A.* 61

FRET.
Those humours, tart as wines upon the *f. R.* 761
Who *f.* their hour and are forgotten things *V.* 46

FRETFUL.
Some *f.* tempers wince at every touch *Con.* 325
A *f.* temper will divide *F.* 61
Froward at school, and *f.* in his plays *H.* 188
To gratify a *f.* passion *M.F.* 35
F. unless diverted and beguiled *R.* 108
F. if unsupplied; but silent, meek *T.* v 31

FRETTED.
The sunbeam; there, embossed and *f.* wild *T.* v 118

FRETTING.
The *f.* plague is in the public purse *Ch.* 62

FRICTIONS.
With *f.* of her fleece *M.B.* 10

FRIEND.
My *f.*, do they now and then send *A.S.* 37
Oh! tell me I yet have a *f. A.S.* 39
Though a *f.* I am never to see *A.S.* 40
Of *f.*, of hope, of all bereft *Cast.* 5
He shouted; nor his *f.* had failed *Cast.* 19
Deserted and his *f.* so nigh *Cast.* 36
Thou tutelary *f.* of helpless men? *Ch.* 42
The tender ties of father, husband, *f. Ch.* 141
She speaks of Him, her author, guardian, *f. Ch.* 399
But lest I seem to sin against a *f. Ch.* 485
To call the few that trust in him his *f. Ch.* 588
Then each might show, to his admiring *f. Con.* 199
Called on a *f.*, drank tea, stepped home again *Con.* 278
An absent *f.*'s fidelity and love *Con.* 308
Two bosom *f.*, each pensively inclined *Con.* 507
A stranger joined them, courteous as a *f. Con.* 522
Mine be the *f.* less frequent in his prayers *Con.* 579
Dear Anna—between *f.* and *f. E.* i 1
Not dreaming of so dear a *f. E.* i 41
Admonished, scorn the caution and the *f. E.* ii.17
True. Changes will befall, and *f.* may part *E.* iii 10
We find the *f.* we fancied we had won *E.* iii 10 [iii 27
"For what?"—"An please you, sir, to see a *f.*" *E.*
"A *f.*!" Horatio cried, and seemed to start *E.* iii 28
Against the well-known duties of a *f. E.* iii 49 [60
While you, my *f.*, whatever wind should blow *E.* iii
"F. Robert, thus like *chien savant E.* iv 87
Find not, or hardly find, a single *f. Ex.* 118
The requisites that form a *f. F.* 14
Who seeks a *f.* should come disposed *F.* 43
But not a *f.* worth keeping *F.* 78
Discerns a rival in a *f. F.* 83
To deem the wit a *f.* displays *F.* 88
But *f.* that chance to differ *F.* 135
Seeking a real *f.*, we seem *F.* 142
Our *f.*'s defect long hid from sight *F.* 149

Such as a *f.* but ill endures *F.* 155
That *f.* should be sincere and just *F.* 158
Is such a *f.* that one had need *F.* 172
Be very much his *f.* indeed *F.* 173
Or may my *f.* deceive me! *F.* 216
To leave his *f.* behind *F.B.* 24
A prison with a *f.* preferred *F.B.* 35
Forsaking country, kindred, *f.*, and ease *H.* 585
Forsaking, and forsaken of all *f. H.* 694
And my good *f.* the calender *J.G.* 23
Till, at his *f.* the calender's *J.G.* 159
His *f.* in merry pin *J.G.* 178
The nymph must lose her female *f. L.R.* 1
No *f.* or follower of mine *L.W.* 4
Like her a *f.* to peace *M.B.* 12
" *F.!* we have lived too long. I never heard *N.A.* 83
If stubborn Greek refuse to be his *f. P.E.* 498
" My *f.!* be cautious how ye treat *P.T.* 23
Though sage advice of *f.* the most sincere *R.* 249
Or charm the sorrows of a drooping *f. R.* 292
And such emollients as his *f.* could spare *R.* 305
F. such as his for modern Jobs prepare *R.* 306
What once I valued and could boast, a *f. R.* 378
But wisely seeks a more convenient *f. R.* 443
The man of business and his *f.* compressed *R.* 495
(A poet fond of Nature and your *f.*) *R.* 542
Jack knew his *f.*, but hoped in that disguise *R.* 587
The *f.* of Truth, the associate of sound Sense *R.* 696
F. (for I cannot stint as some have done *R.* 719
F., not adopted with a schoolboy's haste *R.* 725
Such *f.* prevent what else would soon succeed *R.* 731
But grant me still a *f.* in my retreat *R.* 741
Thy *f.*, though to a cloister's shade consigned *S.* ii 2
Had he seduced a virgin, wronged a *f. T.* 46
The Scripture yields) or hope to find a *f.? T.* 440
But cannot play them, borrows a *f.'s* hand *T.* i 473
And heard our music; are thy simple *f. T.* i 645
And gives his direst foe a *f.'s* embrace *T.* ii 270
One proof at least of manhood! while the *f. T.* ii 594
There form connections, but acquire no *f. T.* ii 634
Her dear five hundred *f.*, contemns them all *T.* ii 643
Their good old *f.*, and Discipline at length *T.* ii 732
F. in the *f.* of science, and true prayer *T.* iii 250
I knew at least one hare that had a *f. T.* iii 351
F., books, a garden, and perhaps his pen *T.* iii 355
And have a *f.* in every feeling heart *T.* iv 376
To astonish and to grieve his gazing *f. T.* iv 655
We too are *f.* to loyalty. We love *T.* v. 331
Comes at his call, and serves him for a *f. T.* v 424
Who loves no part? He be a nation's *f. T.* v 504
Who is, in truth, the *f.* of no man there? *T.* v 505
Some *f.* is gone, perhaps his son's best *f.! T.* vi 29
That softer *f.*, perhaps more gladly still *T.* vi 44
I would not enter on my list of *f. T.* vi 560
What *f.* we sort with, or what books we read *Tir.* 114
His counsellor and bosom *f.* shall prove *Tir.* 216
Subsist and centre in one point—a *f. Tir.* 390
A *f.*, whate'er he studies or neglects *Tir.* 391
Father, and *f.*, and tutor, all in one *Tir.* 544
E'en in his pastimes he requires a *f. Tir.* 607
Wise for himself and his few *f.* alone *Tir.* 675
And all the instructions of thy son's best *f. Tir.* 717
Befriend thee, of all other *f.* bereft *Tir.* 881
Receive, dear *f.*, the truths I teach *Trans. H.* 1
And in reality to find no *f. T.T.* 160
Firm *f.* to peace, to pleasure, and good pay *T.T.* 195
May no foes ravish thee, and no false *f. T.T.* 332
Virtue indeed meets many a rhyming *f. T.T.* 620
The kindness of a *f. U.* 2
I sink the poet in the *f. U.* 30
Made you a Peer, but spoiled you for a *f.! V.* 14
But not hereafter to the name of *f.! V.* 18
Terentius, once my *f.*, farewell to thee! *V.* 30

Graced with the name of a long-absent *f. V.* 40
And, like his Lordship, cast thy *f.* away *V.* 48
Whoever undertakes a *f.'s* great part *V.* 59
All former *f.* forgiven, and forgot *V.* 84
But if he grant a *f.*, that boon possessed *V.* 91
The truth of a *f.* such as you *W.N.* 24

FRIENDLY.

And always *f.*, we were wont to cheat *E.* iii 4
A *f.* coalescence *F.* 132
A snug and *f.* game at cards *L.W.* 28
At least are *f.* to the great pursuit *R.* 146
F. to peace, but not to me *S.* 2
Oh *f.* to the best pursuits of man *T.* iii 290
F. to thought, to virtue, and to peace *T.* iii 291
F. to vital motion, may afford *T.* iii 509
Strained through the *f.* mats, a vivid green *T.* iii 525
A scene so *f.* to his favourite task *T.* vi 264

FRIENDSHIP.

Society, *F.*, and Love *A.S.* 17
Whose *f.* from his boyish years he chose *Con.* 424
Bad men, profaning *f.'s* hallowed name *Con.* 683
Of *f.'s* closest tie *Dr.* 18
F. a blessing cheap or small *E.* i 92
Produced a *f.*, then begun *E.* i 101
F. and truth to others, findest thou none? *Ex.* 277
No wonder *F.* does the same *F.* 10
F. a false ideal good *F.* 29
No *F.* will abide the test *F.* 37
All thoughts of *f.* are but dreams *F.* 74
With *F.'s* finest feeling *F.* 93
A *F.* that in frequent fits *F.* 103
The noblest *F.* ever shown *F.* 205
O *F.!* if my soul forego *F.* 211
Of *F.*, satisfied with noise *F.B.* 32
Benignity, *f.*, and truth *Gr.* 44
F. and Love seemed tenderly at strife *H.* 680
And generous *F.* hand in hand *Miss* — 75
Are all the nameless sweets of *f.* fled? *P.E.* 244 [691
Health, leisure, means to improve it, *f.*, peace *T.* iii
A boyish *f.* may so soon decline *Tir.* 453
Who there will court thy *f.*, with what views *Tir.* 855
To love and *f.* both, that is not pleased *T.* vi 324
As ever *F.* penned *U.* 4
Oh *f.!* cordial of the human breast! *V.* 49
Faithless alike in *f.* and in love *V.* 72
No firmer *f.* than the fair have shown *V* 82

FRIGHTS.

I soon recover from these needless *f. H.* 375
He then is full of *f.* and fears *Y.D.* 9

FRIGHTED.

The *f.* steed he *f.* more *J.G.* 227

FRIGHTEN.

With doubtful credit, told to *f.* babes *T.* iv 564

FRIGHTFUL.

From dangers of a *f.* shape *A Fable* 33

FRINGED.

And from the trees that *f.* his hill *Mor.* 14 [123
F. with a beard made white with other snows *T.* iv

FRIPPERY.

With sentimental *f.*, and dream *P.E.* 312

FRISK. [48

Now creeps he slow; and now, with many a *f. T.* v
To *f.* awhile, and bask in the warm sun *T.* vi 314
Give him his lass, his fiddle, and his *f. T.T.* 237

FRISKING.

His *f.* was at evening hours *Ep.* ii 25
F. thus before the fire *Trans.* iii 15

FRITH.
Lands intersected by a narrow *f. T.* ii 16
FRIVOLOUS.
In conversation *f.*, in dress *T.* ii 379
FROG. [452
Yet gnats have had, and *f.* and mice, long since *T.* iii
Storks among *f.*, that have but croak'd and died *T.* v 282
FROLIC.
And *f.* where they list *F.B.* 9
That feeds thee; thou may'st *f.* on the floor *T.* iii 343
Retracing thus his *f.* ('tis a name *Tir.* 332
That charm down fear, they *f.* it along *T.T.* 463
FRONT.
The second milestone *f.* the garden gate *R.* 490
A sparkling eye beneath a wrinkled *f. T.* i 405
The agglomerated pile, his frame may *f. T.* iii 472
He speaks. The lake in *f.* becomes a lawn *T.* iii 774
FRONTED.
The prouder sashes *f.* with a range *T.* iv 763
FROST.
The keenest *f.* that binds the stream *N.* 5
With dripping rains, or withered by a *f. T.* ii 211
And introduces hunger, *f.*, and woe *T.* ii 616
How calm is my recess, and how the *f. T.* iv 308
No *f.* can bind it there; its utmost force *T.* v 104
Holds its due course, nor fears the *f.* of age *T.* vi 790
Decayed by time, or withered by a *f. V.* 58
One talks of mildew and of *f. Y.D.* 53
FROST-BOUND.
And slippery the materials, yet *f. T.* v 155
FROWARD.
F. at school, and fretful in his plays *H.* 188
Not as the plaything of a *f.* child *R.* 107
Of churlish Winter, in her *f.* moods *T.* iii 433
FROWN.
F. in the storm with angry brow *A Fable* 38
And made the mountains tremble at his *f.? Ch.* 78
Considers all injustice with a *f. Ch.* 210
Yet still, o'erclouded with a constant *f. Con.* 339
An envious world will interpose its *f. E.* ii 33
He judged them with as terrible a *f. Ex.* 131
When God arises with an awful *f. Ex.* 249
And griping fists, and unrelenting *f. Ex.* 513
'Twas but to prove how quickly, with a *f. Ex.* 578
The tide of pleasure, heedless of his *f. Ex.* 683
To *f.* and roar, and shake his feeble form *H.* 186
As with a *f.* to say, " Do this, and live *H.* 329 [650
Scorns with the same indifference *f.* and smiles *H.*
Her *f.* were seldom known to last *J.P.* 15
Which labour of his *f.* beguile *Mrs. M—* 29
A Father's *f.*, and kiss his chastening hand *R.* 346
To seek that peace a tyrant's *f.* denies *R.* 770
Your portion is with them; nay never *f. T.* 169
And if he but suspects a *f.*, turns pale *T.* 216
The lowering eye, the petulance, the *f. T.* i 456
His wrath is busy, and his *f.* is felt *T.* ii 94
F. at effeminates, whose very looks *T.* ii 223
Secured it by an unforgiving *f. T.* ii 247
His *f.* was full of terror, and his voice *T.* ii 721
But, once delivered, kills them with a *f. T.* iii 438
And groat per diem, if his patron *f. T.* iii 821 [581
The winter's *f.*, if screened from his shrewd bite *T.* iii
Nor such as with a *f.* forbids the play *T.* iv 175
The rugged *f.* and insolent rebuffs *T.* iv 411
But had a blessing in its darkest *f. T.* vi 35
Whose *f.* can disappoint the proudest strain *T.* vi 1023

Nor *f.*, unless he vanish with the cloth *Tir.* 730
And if He doom that people with a *f. T.T.* 456
The *f.* of a sky so severe *W.N.* 18
FROWNED.
F. oftener than she smiled *J.P.* 8
And in her humour, when she *f. J.P.* 9
(And raised her voice, and *f.* beside) *M.F.* 16
Nor ever *f.*, or sad appeared *St.* iii 23
FROWNING.
F. in storms, or breathing gentle airs *R.* 194
And the barbed arrows of a *f.* God *R.* 304
F. as if in his unconscious arm *T.* i 381
Still they are *f.* signals, and bespeak *T.* ii 68
FROZEN.
Such *f.* figures, stiff as they are cold *Ch.* 607
From the world's girdle to the *f.* pole *Ex.* 20
Piles up his stores amidst the *f.* waste *H.* 475
Torpid and dull beneath a *f.* zone *T.* 481 [6
With spatter'd boots, strapp'd waist and *f.* locks *T.* iv
Beneath the *f.* clod; all seeds of herbs *T.* v 81
Though abroad they are *f.* and dead *W.N.* 8
FRUGAL.
She had a *f.* mind *J.G.* 32
To her who, *f.* only that her thrift *T.* ii 650
The *f.* housewife trembles when she lights *T.* iv 380
And thankful at my *f.* board 1789, 35
FRUIT.
When scarlet *f.* the russet hedge adorn *A.T.* 72
Its *f.* on earth, its growth above the skies *Ch.* 578
Tried, as it should be, by the *f.* it bears *Con.* 172
F. of his love and wonders of his might *Con.* 473 [586
And plucks the *f.* placed more within his reach " *Con.*
The *f.* of age, less fair, are yet more sound *Con.* 647
But render neither *f.* nor flower *F.* 185
Save for the *f.* his heavenly beams produce *H.* 82
Field, *f.* and flower, and every creature here *H.* 490
And *f.* reward his honourable toil *H.* 761
Poor man! I would save him his *f.* if I could *P.H.* 35
And disappointment all the *f. P.B.* 18 [238
Whose *f.*, though fair, tempts only to destroy *P.E.*
The *f.* that hang on pleasure's flowery stem *R.* 179
Her summer heats, her *f.*, and her perfumes *R.* 196
But farewell promises of happier *f. R.* 241
Such are the *f.* of sanctimonious pride *T.* 165
F. of a blighted size, austere and crude *T.* 494
And fungous *f.* of earth, regales the sense *T.* i 532
And all her *f.* by radiant truth matured *T.* i 607
By other hopes and richer *f.* than yours *T.* i 677
Pours she not all her choicest *f.* abroad *T.* ii 85
Learning has borne such *f.* in other days *T.* iii 248
With pleasure more than even their *f.* afford *T.* iii 410
With blushing *f.*, and plenty not his own *T.* iii 429
Blown on the summit of the apparent *f. T.* iii 536
Cold as its theme, and like its theme the *f. T.* iii 564 [552
With summer *f.*, brought forth by wintry suns *T.* iii
F. of omnipotent eternal love *T.* iv 188 [*T.* vi 910
Would make his fate his choice; when peace, the *f.*
To weaving nets for bird-alluring *f. T.* iv 263
No forfeiture, and of its *f.* he sends *T.* v 573
Of flavour or of scent in *f.* or flower *T.* vi 248 [1011
Let fall the unfinished wreath, and roved for *f. T.* vi
Of virtue, and whom virtue, *f.* of faith *T.* vi 911
With flower and *f.* the wilderness supplies *Tir.* 27
Brings he, to sweeten *f.* so undesired *Tir.* 578
May raise such *f.* as shall reward his care *Tir.* 771
The *f.* of all her labour is whipped cream *T.T.* 551
With flower as sweet, or *f.* as fair *U.* 17
The promise of delicious *f.* appears *V.* 52
Of *f.* proscribed, as to a refuge, fled *Y.O.* 16

FRUITAGE.
Of golden *f.*, and her myrtle bowers *T.* ii 215

FRUITFUL.
God opens *f.* Nature's various scenes *Ch.* 88
No longer *f.*, and no longer green *Con.* 52
The *f.* parent of abuse and wrong *Con.* 461
Think on the *f.* and well watered spot *Ex.* 418
The cloud-surmounting Alps, the *f.* vales *R.* 79
To give dissimilar yet *f.* lands *R.* 787
Me *f.* scenes and prospects waste *S.* 21
And *f.* soil, that has been treasured long *T.* iii 514
Were sown in human nature's *f.* soil *T.* vi 383
Of barrenness is past. The *f.* field *T.* vi 765
F. and young as in their first career? *Tir.* 42

FRUITFULNESS.
And social, nip his *f.* and use *T.* v 439

FRUITLESS.
To urge the *f.* chase be lost *Mor.* 42
Our years, a *f.* race without a prize *H.* 25
Revolving seasons, *f.* as they pass *Her.* 25

FRY.
The wriggling *f.* soon fill the creeks around *P.E.* 480
And the land stank—so numerous was the *f.* *T* ii 832

FUEL.
They pick their *f.* out of every hedge *T.* i 565

FUGITIVE.
A vain pursuit of *f.*, false good *H.* 4
My *f.*, years are all hasting away *P.F.* 13
Multitudes, *f.* on every side *T.* ii 106
And *f.* in vain. The sylvan scene *T.* ii 107

FULFIL.
'Tis thus Omnipotence his law *f.* *Ch.* 81
To praise him, is to serve him, and *f.* *Ex.* 644
For though thou gladly wouldst *f.* *M.* 13
Attempts no task it cannot well *f.* *R.* 280
F. the purpose, and appear design'd *Tir.* 93

FULFILLED.
I wish it all *f.* *N.Y.G.* 20
F. their tardy and disastrous course *T.* vi 735
Thy word *f.*, the conquest of a world! *T.* vi 905
My share of duties decently *f.* *T.* vi 1001
Soon see your wish *f.* in either child *Tir.* 344
F. with ease had you been so inclined *V.* 22

FULL. [*A.C.* 6
With a great deal of skill, and a wig *f.* of learning
F. of rage and *f.* of grief *B.* 8
A satisfactory receipt in *f.* *Con.* 202
The beauties of a rose *f.* blown *E.* i 68
"Who both write well, and write *f.* speed! *E.* iv 84
The flower of Israel's infamy *f.* blown) *Ex.* 222
Gone thither armed and hungry, returned *f.* *Ex.* 368
Those holy men, so *f.* of truth and grace *Ex.* 618
The moles and bats in *f.* assembly find *Ex.* 630
To exhibit, in *f.* bloom disclosed *F.* 44
F. slowly pacing o'er the stones *J.G.* 79
His reeking head *f.* low *J.G.* 122
F. ten miles off, at Ware *J.G.* 152
For which he paid *f.* dear *J.G.* 202
F. bliss is bliss divine *N.Y.G.* 14
Your feelings in their *f.* amount *P.* 47
The *f.* concerto swells upon your ear *P.E.* 128
In rushes Folly with a *f.* moon tide *P.E.* 282
Happy if *f.* of days—but happier far *R.* 45
F. charged with England's thunder *R.G.* 31
Shall find them rated at their *f.* amount *T.* 545
F. on the destined ear. Wide flies the chaff *T.* i 359
Recoils from its own choice—at the *f.* feast *T.* i 467
Just please us while the passion is at *f.* *T.* ii 598
His frown was *f.* of terror, and His voice *T.* ii 721
And dark in things divine. *F.* often too *T.* iii 235
From the *f.* fork, the saturated straw *T.* iii 479
To grace the *f.* pavilion. His design *T.* iii 716
Stealing a sidelong glance at a *f.* house *T.* iv 201
Lamented change! to which *f.* many a cause *T.* iv 576
His faculties, expanded in *f.* bloom *T.* iv 661
And *f.* immunity from penal woe *T.* v 580 [*T.* iv 301
Were tasked to his *f.* strength, absorbed and lost
The squirrel, flippant, pert, and *f.* of play *T.* vi 315
That skims the spacious meadow at *f.* speed *T.* vi 331
Gentle, and affable, and *f.* of grace *T.* vi 500
Enchanting novelty, that moon at *f.* *T.* vi 706
For there is none to covet, all are *f.* *T.* vi 772
His phrase well chosen, clear, and *f.* of force *Tir.* 669
Little inmate, *f.* of mirth *Tran.* iii 1   [*T.T.* 97
"There," said his guide, "the group is *f.* in view"
His speech, his form, his action *f.* of grace *T.T.* 346
The shelves are *f.*, all other themes are sped *T.T.* 726
And having known thee bearded and *f.* grown *V.* 37
He then is *f.* of fright and fears *Y.D.* 9
Live barrels with their bellies *f.* *Y.D.* 47

FULL-BLOWN.
The *f.* rose, the shepherd and his lass *T.* i 36

FULL-GORGED.
The *f.* savage, at his nauseous feast *H.* 509

FULSOME.
And lest the *f.* artifice should fail *P.E.* 291
Now this is *f.*; and offends me more *T.* ii 455
And tongue accomplish'd in the *f.* cant *T.* vi 289

FUMBLE.
Feels himself spent, and *f.* for his brains *T.T.* 537

FUME.
And with a quiet, which no *f.* disturb *Con.* 267
Has filled with all its *f.* a critic's brain *P.E.* 445
They should go out in *f.*, and be forgot? *T.* iii 172
Of Indian *f.*, and guzzling deep, the boor *T.* iv 473
That *f.* beneath his nose: the trailing cloud *T.* v 56
They demi-deify and *f.* him so *T.* v 266
Healthful and undisturbed by factious *f.* *T.* v 513

FUMED.
And *f.* with frankincense on every side *T.* 314

FUNCTION.
The sacred *f.*, in your hands is made *P.E.* 122
Sad sacrilege! no *f.*, but a trade! *P.E.* 123
The noblest *f.*, and discredits much *T.* ii 554
And exercise all *f.* of a man *T.* iii 199
In all their private *f.*, once combined *T.* iv 673

FUNGOUS.
Grows *f.*, and takes fire at every spark *Con.* 54
And *f.* fruits of earth, regales the sense *T.* i 532

FUR.
Needs he the tragic *f.*, the smoke of lamps *T.* iv 195

FURBELOWED.
Curled, scented, *f.*, and flounced around *Ex.* 51

FUR-CLAD.
Imperial mistress of the *f.* Russ! *T.* v 129

FURIOUS.
For him, though chased with *f.* heat *Beau* 11
But so the *f.* blast prevailed *Cast.* 21
And in the *f.* inquest that it makes *T.* ii 135

FURLED—GALL

FURLED.
Has dropp'd her anchor, and her canvass *f. Ch.* 443

FURNISH.
To *f.* and accommodate a world *Ch.* 124
May *f.* illustration, well applied *Con.* 206
And *f.* us, perhaps at last *E.* i 55
F. always oil for its own wheels *R.* 616
Of heavenly temper, *f.* with arms *T.* ii 346
To polish, *f.*, and delight the mind *T.T.* 645

FURNISHED.
We will be *f.* with our own *J.G.* 27
Your brain well *f.*, and your tongue well taught *V.* 9

FURNISHING.
Who, far enough from *f.* their shelves *Tir.* 825

FURNITURE.
A piece of mere church *f.* at best *Tir.* 425

FURROWED.
Wild roses over *f.* ground *Mrs. M—* 28   [421
Green balks and *f.* lands, the stream that spreads *R.*
And *f.* into storms, and with a hand *T.* vi. 269

FURY.
Rushed with a whirlwind's *f.* on the foe *A.T.* 195
(Unfelt the *f.* of those bursting mines) *Her.* 8
And shake with *f.* to the ground *J.P.* 11
The lawless herd, with *f.* blind *M.* ii 13
Come fiend, come *f.*, giant, monster, blast *N.A.* 121
The force he spends against their *f.* vain *Tir.* 64
And gives them all their *f.*; bids a plague *T.* ii 182
And blunts his pointed *f.*; in its case *T.* vi 193
Laughs at the frantic sufferer's *f.*, spent *T.* vi 423
Pushed with a madman's *f.* Fancy shrinks *T.* vi 513
And tamer far for so much *f.* shown *T.* vi 541

FUTURE.
They court the notice of a *f.* age *B.B.* 4
Though *f.* pain may serve for present mirth *Con.* 494
The *f.* splendour of the flower ? *E.* i 72
Pleasure is deaf when told of *f.* pain *Ex.* 66
The *f.* tone and temper of the sky *Ex.* 158
That only *f.* ages can restore *Her.* 40
And should my *f.* lot be cast *M.* 49
That wish on some fair *f.* day *N.Y.G.* 17
And learned in *f.* to be wiser *P.T.* 60
Heaven grant us no such *f.* sight *Q.V.* 79
Exempt from *f.* service all his days *R.* 628
Cause to provide for a great *f.* day *R.* 652
That shuts within its seed the *f.* flower *R.* 792
Deceitful views of *f.* bliss, farewell ! *T.* 9
Which *f.* pages yet are doomed to share *T.* 146
Hence the complexion of his *f.* days *T.* 280
The *f.* shall obliterate the past *T.* 295
Courageous, and refreshed for *f.* toil *T.* iii 19
A pimple that portends a *f.* sprout *T.* iii 528
Forecasts the *f.* whole; that when the scene *T.* iii 651
Ages of hopeless misery. *F.* death *T.* v 607
And death still *f.* Not a hasty stroke *T.* v 608
Who form'd him from the dust, his *f.* grave *T.* vi 349
Accountable, and God, some *f.* day *T.* vi 605
Hark ! how the sire of chits, whose *f.* share *Tir.* 318
There dawns the splendour of his *f.* years *Tir.* 394
That instant upon all his *f.* pains *Tir.* 715
Some mischief fatal to his *f.* worth *Tir.* 758
On *f.* broken bones and bruises *Trans.* ii 20
The *f.*, best unknown, but, at thy mouth *Y.O.* 43

FUTURITY.
Then perish on *f.'s* wide shore *Tir.* 83
Ah, blind to bright *f.*, untaught *Tir.* 379
So, when remote *f.* is brought *T.T.* 492

G.

GABRIEL.
That flies, like *G.* on his Lord's commands *Ch.* 135

GAIETY.
But save me from the *g.* of those *T.* i 499
From *g.* that fills the bones with pain *T.* i 504
Such health and *g.* of heart enjoy *T.* i 587

GAILY.
That softly swelled and *g.* dressed appears *T.* iii 629

GAIN.
Yet from a richer nothing *g.* *A Tale* 75
And *g.* new vigour at her endless task *Ch.* 104 [244
Some men make *g.* a fountain, whence proceeds *Ch.*
But all he *g.* for his harangue is—" Well ! *Ch.* 393
In hopes to *g.*, what else I must have lost *Ch.* 630
And *g.* remote conclusions at a jump *Con.* 154
Instructed him at length to *g. F.B.* 17
To prove that without Christ all *g.* is loss *H.* 631
To cheat themselves and *g.* the world's assent *P.E.* 436
The dupes of pleasure, or the slaves of *g. R.* 24
Ask wealth of Heaven, and *g.* a real prize *R.* 162
A meaner than himself shall *g.* the prize *T.* 16
The poor should *g.* it, and the rich should not ? *T.* 340
Through plenty, lose in morals what they *g. T.* i 624
But ere he *g.* the comfortless repose *T.* v 596
They *g.* at last his unreserved assent *T.* v 663 [892
Two gods divide them all—Pleasure and *G.—T.* vi

Poll *g.* at length the British Shore *Trans.* iv 4
He may be called to give up health and *g. V.* 63

GAIN-DEVOTED.
And *g.* cities. Thither flow *T.* i 682

GAINED.
The summit *g.*, behold the proud Alcove *T.* i 278
For I have *g.* thy confidence, have pledged *T.* iii 346
And ending, if at last its end be *g. Tir.* 408 [650
Such knowledge, *g.* betimes, and which appears *Tir.*
The proud Protector of the power he *g. T.T.* 611

GAIT.   [380
With awkward *g.*, stretched neck, and silly stare *P.E.*
His awkward *g.*, his introverted toes *T.* iv 633
His altered *g.* and stateliness retrenched *T.* v. 76

GALE.
The *g.* informs us, laden with the scent *Ch.* 446
O balmy *g.* of soul-reviving air ! *E.* ii 27   [35
The selfsame *g.* that wafts the fragrance round *Her.*
Nor *g.* that catch the scent of blooming groves *R.* 337
By *g.* of blessing driven *St.* iii 32
Complacency has breathed a gentle *g. T.* 419
Of all their caution in thy gentlest *g. T.* ii 484
Clear and sonorous, as the *g.* comes on ! *T.* vi 10
With more than a propitious *g. Trans. H.* 35

GALL.
Bon mots to *g.* the Christian and the Jew *T.* 308

GALL—GATE

Remarks that *g.* so many, to the few *T.* iii 37

GALLANT.
Manly deportment, *g.*, easy, gay *H.* 407
Thou, as a *g.* bark from Albion's coast *M.P.* 88
New trimmed, a *g.* show! *Q.V.* 6
Our ancestry, a *g.* Christian race *T.T.* 372

GALLANTLY.
Heaven speed the canvass, *g.* unfurled *Ch.* 123

GALLANTRY.
For folly, *g.* for every vice *T.* iv 690

GALLED.
Which *g.* him in his seat *J.G.* 84
G. by affliction's heavy chain *St.* v 11
To loose the links that *g.* mankind before *T.* 185

GALLERY.
Of *g.* critics by a thousand arts *T.* ii 365
His *g.* with the works of art well graced *T.T.* 162

GALLEY-SLAVES.
Worse than the deeds of *g.* broke loose *T.T.* 327

GALLIC.
May bear us smoothly to the *G.* shore *T.* ii 262

GALLOP.
That trot became a *g.* soon *J.G.* 87

GALLOPED
And *g.* off with all his might *J.G.* 207

GAMBLING.
Nor *g.* practices can find it out *Tir.* 246

GAMBOL.
Played only *g.* in a frantic mood *H.* 541
These *g.* he did play *J.G.* 134
To skip and *g.* like a fawn *Ep.* ii 23
The very kine that *g.* at high noon *T.* vi 334
Together, or all *g.* in the shade *T.* vi 775

GAME.
"To distant wilds in quest of other *g. A.T.* 106
A snug and friendly *g.* at cards *L.W.* 28
Or other sublunary *g. Mor.* 28
A senseless bargain. When I see such *g. T.* iii 176
Learn every trick, and soon play all the *g. T.* iv 231
Propitious, pays his tribute, *g.* or fish *T.* iv 611
To swear, to *g.*, to drink; to show at home *T.* iv 652
But war's a *g.* which, were their subjects wise *T.* v 187
A monarch's errors are forbidden *g. T.T.* 114
Went with him, and saw all the *g.* he played ? *Tir.* 268
Playing our *g.*, and on the very spot *Tir.* 305
For there the *g.* they seek is easiest found *Tir.* 520

GAME-FOWL.
Should never *g.* hatch her eggs again *T.* iii 312

GAMESTER.
The *g.* may have cast his cards away *Con.* 813
For *g.*, jockeys, brothellers impure *T.* ii 751
Grow on the *g.'s* elbows, and the alert *T.* iii 761

GAMMER.
And *g.* finds it on her knees *E.* iv 45

GAMUT.
With a whole *g.* fill'd of heavenly notes *N.A.* 26

'GAN.
'*G.* make his instrument of music speak *N.A.* 44
He '*g.* in haste the drawers explore *R.C.* 92
'*G.* murmur, as became the softer sex *T.* i 71
Its ample area '*g.* explore *T.B.* 38

GANDER.
Swift as the proudest *g.* of them all *A.T.* 55

GAP.
O'er hedge and ditch, through *g.* and mews *E.* iv 52
Not in the words—but in the *g.* between *T.T.* 541

GARB.
Is Winter hideous in a *g.* like this ? *T.* iv 194
To wear a tattered *g.*, however coarse *T.* iv 416

GARDEN.
Ambrosial *g.*, in which Art supplies *Ex.* 11
Earth seems a *g.* in its loveliest dress *Her.* 57
Within the *g.'s* peaceful scene *L.R.* 5
Nor *g.* interspersed with flowery beds *R.* 336
The second milestone fronts the *g.* gate *R.* 490
Of equipage, our *g.*, and our sports *T.* i 644
Polluting Egypt: *g.*, fields, and plains *T.* ii 828
Friends, books, a *g.*, and perhaps his pen *T.* iii 355
Or if the *g.* with its many cares *T.* iii 397
Who loves a *g.*, loves a greenhouse too *T.* iii 566
But elegance, chief grace the *g.* shows *T.* iii 638
A *g.* in which nothing thrives has charms *T.* iv 754
To each some province, *g.*, field or grove *T.* vi 237
G. of God, how terrible the change *T.* vi 371
The *g.* fears no blight, and needs no fence *T.* vi 771
Robbery of *g.*, quarrels in the streets *Tir.* 229

GARDENER.
Thou art indeed the drug a *g.* wants *Con.* 255
And where the *g.* Robin, day by day *M.P.* 48
She watched the *g.* at his work *R.C.* 14
Woe to the *g.'s* pale, the farmer's hedge *T.* iv 436

GARLAND.
Crowned with the *g.* of life's blooming years *Con.* 638
And Chloe from her *g.* picks the weed *H.* 293
The *g.* that she wore *J.P.* 12
And weave fresh *g.* every day *N.* 19
His *g.* from the boughs. Again, as oft *T.* iii 442

GARMENT.
Their very *g.* sacred, old yet new *Ex.* 183

GARNER.
Yes—ye may fill your *g.*, ye that reap *T.* v 755

GARNISH.
That ye may *g.* your profuse regales *T.* iii 551

GARNISHED.
Is but a *g.* nuisance, fitter far *T.* vi 993

GARRICK.
And so, while *G.*, as renowned as he *T.* iii 598
Man praises man; and *G.'s* memory next *T.* vi 664
To show the world how *G.* did not act *T.* vi 677
For *G.* was a worshipper himself *T.* vi 678

GARRISON.
My little *g.* of sense *E.* iv 18

GASP.
At his last *g.*; but could not for a world *T.* iii 807

GASPING.
Delight the citizen, who *g.* there *R.* 485

GATE.
Hark! the Gaul is at her *g.'s*! *B.* 20
To pour his golden tide through all her *g. Ex.* 14
Knock at the *g.* of nations, rouse their fears *Ex.* 269
To hear plain truth at Judah's hallowed *g. H.* 763
Their *g.* wide open threw *J.G.* 120
Laid down his pipe, flew to the *g. J.G.* 163
And claps the *g.* behind thee *M.B.* 24
The second milestone fronts the garden *g. R.* 490
The folded *g.* would bar my progress now *T.* i 330
Grew rusty by disuse ; and massy *g. T.* ii 746
To hear the roar she sends through all her *g. T.* iv 91
No rattling wheels stop short before these *g. T.* iv 144

Might he demand them at the *g.* of death *T.* vi 45
In all her *g.*, and shakes her distant shores *T.T.* 453
Praise is in all her *g.*; upon her walls *T.* vi 808
Now, all unwelcome at his *g. Y.D.* 21

GATH.
Oh name it not in *G.*! it cannot be *T.* ii 367
From many a mirror, in which he of *G.*—*T.* iv 269

GATHER.
But now, to *g.* up what seems dispersed *Con.* 867
Can *g.* honey from a weed *P.B.* 36
But short the date of all we *g.* here *R.* 460
That learning is too proud to *g.* up *T.* iii 286
To *g.* kingcups in the yellow mead *T.* vi 302

GATHERED. [1012
Roved far, and *g.* much: some harsh, 'tis true *T.* vi
Informed, He *g.* up the broken thread *Con.* 525
They *g.* close around the old pit's brink *N.A.* 53

GATHERING.
G. around it, with erected ears *Ch.* 516
And *g.* all her treasures, sweet by sweet *Con.* 440
Perhaps a grave physician, *g.* fees *H.* 203
In *g.* plenty yet to be enjoyed *R.* 554
Fearless of humid air and *g.* rains *T.* 212 [492
Slow *g.* in the midst, through the square mass *T.* iii
And *g.*, at short notice, in one group *T.* iv 136

GAUDY.
But *g.* plumage, sprightly strain *G.* 7

GAUGE.
Who drive a loathsome traffic, *g.* and span *Ch.* 139

GAUL.
Hark! the *G.* is at her gates! *B.* 20
To *G.*, to Greece, and into Noah's ark *R.* 694

GAVE.
And *g.* them a grace so divine *C.* 18
Whate'er they *g.*, should visit more *Cast.* 30
But his who *g.* thee, and preserves thee mine *Ch.* 267
Perhaps 'twas mere good humour *g.* it birth *E.* iii 38
She *g.* it, and *g.* me beside *Gr.* 6
Good breeding and good sense *g.* all a grace *H.* 683
And *g.* misplaced applause *J.P.* 20 [19
That privilege was thine: Heaven *g.* thee means *J.T.*
The glow that Fancy *g.* it fades *Mor.* 36
Oft *g.* me promise of thy quick return *M.P.* 37
Though ears she *g.* me two, *g.* me no ear *N.A.* 28
No tempest *g.* the shock *R.G.* 18
From Sinai's top Jehovah *g.* the law *T.* 549
G. them a twisted form vermicular *T.* i 30
And planetary some; what *g.* them first *T* iii 159
The mind He *g.* me; driving it, though slack *T.* iii 369
He *g.* them in his children's veins, and hates *T.* iv 464
He *g.* them, in its distribution fair *T.* v 200
Bought with His blood who *g.* it to mankind *T.* v 546
A pledge he *g.* for a consistent part *Tir.* 178
Spoke from his lips, and in his looks *g.* law *T.T.* 245
That neither *g.* nor would endure offence *T.T.* 639
G. Virtue and Morality a grace *T.T.* 648

GAVEST.
Perhaps thou *g.* me, though unfelt, a kiss *M.P.* 25

GAY.
Far from the world's *g.* busy throng *Comp.* ii 4
My form genteel, my plumage *g. G.* 5
See Nature *g.* as when she first began *H.* 39
Manly deportment, gallant, easy, *g. H.* 407
Like streamer long and *g. J.G.* 102
Of Edmonton so *g. J.G.* 136
Around her, fanning light her streamers *g. M.P.* 95
Whate'er they boast of rich and *g. Mrs. M—* 12
The great, the *g.*, shall they partake *O.* ii 13
And many a *g.* unlettered spark *P.* 32

Strike the fiddles, let us all be *g.*! *P.E.* 150
But now alike, *g.* widow, virgin, wife *R.* 519
And whistling, as if unconcerned and *g. R.* 589
The *g.*, the thoughtless, have I seen *St.* i 19
The rest too busy, or too *g.*, to wait *T.* 40
Content though mean, and cheerful if not *g. T.* 319
Whom we call *g.*? That honour has been long *T.* i 491
The innocent are *g.*—the lark is *g. T.* i 493
Himself a songster, is as *g.* as he *T.* i 498
Yet not in cities oft: in proud, and *g. T.* i 681
Yet what can satire, whether grave or *g.*? *T.* ii 315
When *g.* Goodnature dresses her in smiles *T.* ii 784
Dreams empty dreams. The million flit as *g. T.* iii 133
The *g.* diversities of leaf and flower *T.* iii 590
Else unadorned, with many a *g.* festoon *T.* iii 667
But *g.* confusion; roses for the cheeks *T.* iv 79
Imposed a *g.* delirium for a truth *T.* iv 528
And ribands streaming *g.*, superbly raised *T.* iv 541
That makes so *g.* the solitary place *T.* vi 187
That leads the dance a summons to be *g. T.* vi 336
Not more intelligent, than loose and *g. Tir.* 530
And much too *g.* to have any of their own *Tir.* 786
With the king's shoulder-knot and *g.* cockade *T.T.* 44
And in his cage, like parrot fine and *g. T.T.* 232
Retired from all the circles of the *g. V.* 73
These pinks are as fresh, and as *g. W.N.* 14

GAYEST.
The *g.* I had to produce *Gr.* 28
His books well trimmed, and in the *g.* style *T.* 421
May teach the *g.*, make the gravest smile *Tir.* 138

GAZE.
Can *g.* on even Darwin's wit *Dr.* 19
To *g.* at Nature in her green array *T.* i 449
With which she *g.* at yon burning disk *T.* i 713
To *g.* at his own splendour, and to exalt *T.* ii 547
They *g.* upon the links that hold them fast *T.* ii 664
Discerns in all things what, with stupid *g. T.* v 808
"Love kindles as I *g.* I feel desires *T.* v 842 [699
To *g.* in his eyes, and bless him. Maidens wave *T.* vi

GAZED.
All huddling into phalanx, stood and *g. N.A.* 48
Mute as e'er *g.* on orator or bard *S.* i 8
Estates are landscapes, *g.* upon awhile *T.* iii 755
I *g.*, myself creating what I saw *T.* iv 290
Drew not his life from woman; never *g. Y.O.* 145

GAZETTE.
Then view him, self-proclaimed in a *g. T.T.* 37

GAZING.
We wonder, as we *g.* stand below *Ch.* 553
To astonish and to grieve his *g.* friends *T.* iv 655
With *g.*, when they see an able man *T.* v 256

GEARS.
To bear his burdens, drawing in his *g. T* v 273

GEHAZI.
Elisha's eye, that, when *G.* strayed *Tir.* 267

GEM. [22
And graved it on a *g.* and wore it next his heart *A.T.*
The *g.* of India, Nature's rarest birth *Ch.* 134
Proud of thy fleets and armies, stolen the *g. Ex.* 348
It sparkles with the *g.* he left behind *Ex.* 483
If every polished *g.* we find *F.* 7
Had he the *g.*, the spices, and the land *H.* 175
The *g.*, though luminous before *Mrs. M—* 33
With hopeful *g.* The rest, no portion left *T.* iii 421
Like homely-featured night, of clustering *g. T.* iv 252
The *g.* of truth from his unguarded soul *Tir.* 152
Since such a reptile has its *g. Trans.* i 27
Incomparable *g.*! thy worth untold *T.T.* 330

GENERAL.

And offers something to the g. use Ch. 90
A prouder station on the g. scale Ch. 336
The foul forerunner of a g. rot Ex. 106
He was a traitor by the g. voice Ex. 545
Gleans up the refuse of the g. spoil Her. 70
Till authors hear at length one g. cry R. 707
To preach the g. doom. When were the winds T. ii 53
Nothing is proof against the g. curse T. iii 266
Can dream them trusty to the g. weal T. v 514
And adds his rapture to the g. praise T. v 890
G., who will not conquer when they may T.T. 194

GENERATION.

Through numerous g. till he found F.A. 25
At length a g. more refined T. i 28
With all its g.; I behold T. iv 99

GENEROUS.

A courteous knighthood, caught the g. flame A.T. 134
And reddening with a just and g. pride A.T. 204
Puts off his g. nature, and, to suit Ch. 153
Were hushed in favour of thy g. plea Ch. 311
Candid, and g., and just F. 19
Was much too g. and sincere F.B. 23
Will trust him for a faithful g. part H. 336
From g. sympathy what joys Miss — 15
And g. Friendship hand in hand Miss — 75
Peers are not always g. as well bred R. 597
Though one, I grant it, in the g. breast R. 721
Thy g. powers, but silence honoured thee S. i 7
The work of g. love and filial fear R. 226
'Tis g. to communicate your skill T. ii 282
Of royal mercy, and through g. scorn T. vi 410
To teach his heart to glow with g. flame Tir. 644

GENIAL.

Enjoyed at ease the g. day A Fable 7
With g. instinct filled A Tale 14
This g. intercourse, and mutual aid Ch. 93
Soft airs and g. moisture feed and cheer H. 489
Was heard, one g. summer's day J. P. 31
No g. spring to taste Miss — 36
And g. soil of cultivated life T. i 679
These on the warm and g. earth that hides T. iii 516
The regular return of g. months T. vi 125
When thou, transplanted from thy g. home Tir. 850

GENIALLY.

Unfolded g. and spread the man P.E. 412

GENIUS.

To show my g. or my wit E. iv 7
When wit and g. meet their doom M. ii 1
Strong G., from whose forge of thought Mrs. M— 23
There G., Learning, Fancy, Wit Mrs. M— 45
And praise his g., he is soon repaid P.E. 532
G., and temper, and desire of rest R. 172
With spirit, g., eloquence, supplied T. 305
Exhausted, has had g. to supply T. ii 609
Milton, whose g. had angelic wings T. iii 255
And G. shed his rays Th. 4
And destines their bright g. to be shown Tir. 336
It pricks the g. forward in its course Tir. 483
But if, with all his g., he betray Tir. 529
To form thy son, to strike his g. forth Tir 679
To indulge his g., after long fatigue T.T. 153
G. is thine, and thou art Fancy's nurse T.T. 290
The substitute for g., sense, and wit T.T. 543
Thus g. rose and set at ordered times T.T. 560
Is g. only found in Epic lays? T.T. 568
Then G. danced a Bacchanal; he crowned T.T. 602
And dint of g., to an affluent lot T.T. 677
How are the powers of g misapplied! T.T. 749

GENTEEL.

My form g., my plumage gay G. 5

And form g. were all in vain G. 8
G. in figure, easy in address T. 203

GENTLE.

Teach me to kindle at thy g. fires Ch. 12
Soft airs and g. heavings of the wave Ch. 127
With g. yet prevailing force Comp. ii 5
In g. sounds it seems as it complained Con. 905
He feels a g. tingling come E. i 11
Thee of thy birthright, g. Bob E. iv 2
Yet He was g. as soft summer airs Ex. 133
Humility is g., apt to learn Ex. 454
Thanks, g. swain, for all my woes G. 13
Politely learned, and of a g. race H. 682
They g. called, and kind and soft J.P. 21
'Tis g., delicate, and kind M.F. 55
Frowning in storms, or breathing g. airs R. 194
Complacency has breathed a g. gale T. 419
And strength is lord of all; but g., kind T. i 605
Thee, g. savage! whom no love of thee T. i 633
And lay it at its ease with g. care T. ii 449
My very g. reader yet unborn T. ii 581
His eye was meek and g., and a smile T. ii 706
The limits of control, his g. eye T. ii 719
With g. force soliciting the darts T. iii 115
And whether I devote thy g. hours T. iv 261
We lov'd, but not enough, the g. hand T. vi 37
G., and affable, and full of grace T. vi 500
Its destined office, yet with g. stroke T. vi 1003
Those arts be theirs that hate his g. reign T.T. 89

GENTLEMAN.

Calls g. whom she has made a fool Con. 466
As some grave g. in Terence says E. iii 6
Six g. upon the road J.G. 233
Which rural g. call sport divine N.A. 8
So sweet to huntsman, g., and hound N.A. 131
"Methinks the g.," quoth she P.T. 30
Who, born a g., has stooped too low V. 33

GENTLER.

Till g. Puss shall come Ep. ii 40
The other was of g. cast J.P 13
Creatures of g. race M.B. 4
The g. Virtues too are joined Miss — 77
Why takes the g. Moon her turn to rise Tir. 38

GENTLEST.

Of all their caution in thy g. gales T. ii 484

GENTLY.

When g., as in June, the rivers glide A.T. 74
That men, if g. tutored, will not learn Ch. 496
Then lifts it g. from the ground E. iv 57
But g. to rebuke his awkward fear H. 61
Yet g. pressed, press g. mine M. 35
The wind, of late breathed g. forth P.T. 50
Or g. felt, and only so The Doves 19
O'er all his pleasures g. to preside Tir. 609

GENUINE.

The reign of g. Charity commence Ch. 413
" Nor needs his g. ore refine! E. iv 89
Man is the g. offspring of revolt H. 181
And Peace the g. offspring of her smile H. 482
That folly ends where g. hope begins H. 637
And if the g. worth of gold depend J.T. 27
That not a glimpse of g. light pervades P.E. 6
Thy g. charms, and guide an artless hand R. 204
Of all his conduct this the g. sense T. 94
But g., and art partner of them all T. i 153
And learn, though late, the g. cause of all T. ii 205
Undoubted scholarship and g. worth Tir. 280
A thousand ways the force of g. love V. 62

GEORGE.

In Britain's isle, beneath a G.'s reign Her. 90

G. took his seat again *Q.V.* 2
Where *G.*, recovered, made a scene *Q.V.* 27
G. ever drew from her *Q.V.* 56
And *G.* the theme of all *Q.V.* 48
Save love of *G.* alone *Q.V.* 64
Down went the Royal *G.*—*R.G.* 11
What was a Monitor in *G.*'s days? *T.* ii 580
Sung to the praise and glory of King *G.*! *T.* vi 663
Sat fast on *G.*'s brows again 1789, 45

GEORGIAN.
One *G.* star adorns the skies *Q.V.* 75

GERANIUM.
And cherries hangs her twigs. *G.* boasts *T.* iii 577

GERMS.
Then rise the tender *g.*, upstarting quick *T.* iii 521
Russet and rude, folds up the tender *g.* *T.* vi 194

GERMANY.
And still it spreads. See *G.* send forth *H.* 459

GESTURE.
With hollow form, and *g.*, and grimace *Ex.* 122
The looks and *g.* of their griefs and fears *N.A.* 67
And natural in *g.*; much impressed *T.* ii 402
" And *g.*, they propound to our belief? *T.* v 649

GET.
Where they did all *g.* in *J.G.* 38
He did again *g.* down *J.G.* 248
He will lose none by me, though I *g.* a few " *P.A.* 40
Reduce his wages, or *g.* rid of her *T.* 211

GETA.
From top to toe the *G.* now in vogue *T.* 202

GETHSEMANE!
G.! in thy dear, hallowed ground *H.* 297

GEWGAWS.
Made all his virtues *g.* of no price *T.* 55

GHASTLY.
G. in feature, and his stammering tongue *Ex.* 356
All the grim honours of his *g.* court *H.* 261

GHOST. [723
When Hope, long lingering, at last yields the *g.* *H.*

GHOSTLY.
So may the ruffian, who with *g.* glide *Ch.* 186
For *g.* counsel, if it either fall *T.* ii 556
Perhaps, though by profession *g.* pure *T.* iv 603
G. in office, earthly in his plan *Tir.* 422

GIANT.
Come fiend, come fury, *g.*, monster, last *N.A.* 121
And succulent, that feeds its *g.* growth *T.* iii 418
Goliath, might have seen his *g.* bulk *T.* iv. 270
Slow after century, a *g.* bulk *Y.O.* 63.

GIANT-KILLING.
Or *g.* Jack, would please me more *Con.* 244

GIBBETED.
And *g.*; as fast as catchpole-claws *T.* ii 684

GIBEON.
As once in *G.*, interrupt the race *T.* vi 126

GIDDY.
From infancy through childhood's *g.* maze *H.* 187
Nor quits till evening watch his *g.* stand *R.* 434
Of *g.* joys comprised *St.* vi 10   [*Tir.* 444
Young heads are *g.*, and young hearts are warm

GIDEON.
So once in *G.*'s fleece the dews were found *E.* ii 49
So *G.* earned a victory not his own *T.T.* 360

GIFT.
A *g.* to his expecting fair *A Fable* 27   [10
And graced with all her *g.* the favourite child *A.T.*
He soothed with *g.*, and greeted with a smile *Ch.* 29
"Beauty for ashes" is a *g.* indeed *Ch.* 230 [*Ch.* 113
These are the the *g.* of Art, and Art thrives most
God's *g.* with pleasure in his praise employ *Ch.* 252
May be esteemed a *g.*, and not an art *Con.* 4
The *g.* of nature, or the classic store *Con.* 896
Puffed up with *g.* they never understood *Ex.* 130
When *g.* perverted, or not duly prized *Ex.* 251'
God's better *g.* they scoff at, and refuse *Ex.* 459
Life is his *g.*, from whom whate'er life needs *H.* 115
With every good and perfect *g.*, proceeds *H.* 116
And grace be grace indeed, and life a *g.* *H.* 531
Nor spurn away a *g.* a God bestows *H.* 547
The well judged purchase, and the *g.* *M.* i. 7
The *g.* of Nature and of Grace *N.G.* 34
Woman indeed, a *g.* he would bestow *R.* 239
Is thine;—best *g.*, the unfailing source of joy *S.* ii 13
That man is dead in sin, and life a *g.*" *T.* 514
The *g.* of Providence, and squander life *T.* i. 638
What wonder then that health and virtue, *g. T.* i. 750
Or make me so. Composure is thy *g.* *T.* iv 260
And promise of a God. His other *g.* *T.* v 550
Thou art of all thy *g.* thyself the crown *T.* v. 904
Nature imparting her satiric *g.* *T.T.* 656
The *g.* whose office is the Giver's praise *T.T.* 750 [41
Might prove a welcome *g.*, and touch thine heart *V.*

GIGANTIC.
To such *g.* and enormous growth *T.* vi 382

GILD.
And the sun *g.* the shining spires again *Her.* 72
Which fate shall brightly *g.* *N.Y.G.* 18
And he shall *g.* yon mountain's height again *P.E.* 69
Or recollected only to *g.* o'er *R.* 9
And *g.* our chamber ceilings as they pass *T.* ii 649
That *g.* thy features, show in theirs 1789, 65

GILDED.
The *g.* butterfly pursues *E.* iv 51
By ev'ry *g.* folly, we renounced *T.* vi 39
The *g.* equipage, and turning loose *T.* vi 702
Pursuing *g.* flies; and such he deems *T.* vi 922

GILDING.
For such indulgence *g.* all thy years *Ex.* 609
The carving and the *g.* *F.* 168
A ray of heavenly light *g.* all forms *T.* v 810

GILPIN.
John *G.* was a citizen *J.G.* i
John *G.*'s spouse said to her dear *J.G.* 5
Quoth Mrs. *G.*,—" That's well said *J.G.* 25
John *G.* kissed his loving wife *J.G.* 29
John *G.* at his horse's side *J.G.* 45
Now mistress *G.* (careful you!) *J.G.* 65
Away went *G.*, neck or naught *J.G.* 97
Away went *G.*—who but he? *J.G.* 113
Said *G.*—" So am I!" *J.G.* 148
"Stop, stop, John *G.*!—Here's the house!" *J.G.* 145
Away went *G.*, out of breath *J.G.* 157
Now *G.*, had a pleasant wit *J.G.* 169
Away went *G.*, and away *J.G.* 209
Went *G.*'s hat and wig *J.G.* 210
Now Mistress *G.*, when she saw *J.G.* 213
Away went *G.*, and away *J.G.* 229
Thus seeing *G.* fly *J.G.* 234

That G. rode a race *J.G.* 214
And G., long live he *J.G.* 250

GILT.
If the g. carriage, and the pampered steed *T.T.* 133

GINGERBREAD.
Should carve himself a wife in g. *T.T.* 555

GIRD.
G. up each other to the race divine *Con.* 702
Measures an atom, and now g. a world? *T.* i 718

GIRDLE.
Wreaths for her brow, and g. for her waist *A.T.* 14
Trade is the golden g. of the globe *Ch.* 86
From the world's g. to the frozen pole *Ex.* 20
With leathern g. braced *J.G.* 130
A g. of half-withered shrubs he shows *T.* i 524

GIRDLED.
The blooming groves that g. her around *Her.* 6

GIRL.
And tender as a g., all essenced o'er *T.* ii 227

GIRT.
G. with a chain he cannot wish to break *R.* 243
G. with a bell-rope that the pope has blessed *T.* 82

GIRTH.
Of g. enormous, with moss-cushioned root *Y.O.* 64

GIVE.
G. even Affliction a grace *A.S.* 55
Oh fond attempt to g. a deathless lot *B.B.* 1
To g. the melancholy theme *Cast.* 57
G. difficulty all the grace of ease *Ch.* 110
To g. the pole the produce of the sun *Ch.* 125
Whose bounty bought me, but to g. me light *Ch.* 235
Blessed with all wealth can g. thee, to resign *Ch.* 297
G. Charity her being and her birth *Ch.* 378
They cannot g. it, or make darkness light *Ch.* 388
How the good squire g. never less than gold *Ch.* 480
All zeal for a Reform that g. offence *Ch.* 533
But all shall g. account of every wrong *Con.* 25
(For opposition g. opinion strength) *Con.* 88
G. me the fidgets, and my patience fails *Con.* 208
And g. us, in recitals of disease *Con.* 313
I g. him over as a desperate case *Con.* 406
And He that g. conception aids the birth *Con.* 434
G. it the breast, or stop its mouth with pap! *Con.* 480
But g. it usefulness unknown before *Con.* 597
And g. true piety that odious name *Con.* 656
And g. the strain the compass it demands *Con.* 718
And g. him all his just demands require *Con.* 760
And g. the moral springs their proper play *Con.* 832
And g. good company a face severe *Con.* 873
To Him who g. me all " *D.W.* 44
To g. the creature the Creator's due *E.* ii 3
G. him at length the lucky pat *E.* iv 55
Might g. more life to marble, or might fill *Ex.* 231
Creates, g. birth to, guides, consummates all *Ex.* 315
Or expectation of the next, g. leave *Ex.* 607
Of what He g., unsparing and profuse *Ex.* 677
And she g. largely more than he requires *H.* 56
To prove that what she g. she g. sincere *H.* 62
Peace be to those (such peace as Earth can g.) *H.* 229
Would g. relief of bed and board to none *H.* 306
And sure it is as kind to smile and g. *H.* 328
He will g. freely, or he will withhold *H.* 331
God g. the word, the preachers throng around *H.* 453
Here see the encouragement Grace g. to vice *H.* 495
Than this his Maker has seen fit to g. *H.* 601
G. life her every charm *Miss* — 80
So may your guiding angel g. *Miss* — 95

G. wit, that what is left may shine *O.* i 27
What, g. up our desserts, our coffee, and tea! *P.A.* 8
If foreigners likewise would g. up the trade *P.A.* 13
Will Avarice, and Concupiscence g. place *P.E.* 104
So g. to Virtue what is Virtue's due *P.E.* 294
That Education g. her, false or true *P.E.* 358
We g. some Latin, and a smatch of Greek *P.E.* 365
Whatever shocks, or g. the least offence *P.E.* 512
G. useful light though I should miss renown *R.* 206
No longer g. an image all thine heart *R.* 276
G. Melancholy up to Nature's care *R.* 281
Could g. advice, could censure, or commend *R.* 291
To birth or wit; nor g. nor takes offence *R.* 450
G. e'en a dunce the employment he desires *R.* 613
Pardon me, ye that g. the midnight oil *R.* 661
Nor those in which the stage g. vice a blow *R.* 685
Luxury g. the mind a childish cast *R.* 703
G. Truth a lustre, and make Wisdom smile *R.* 718
To g. dissimilar yet fruitful lands *R.* 787
Legible only by the light they g. *T.* 30
And seems to say—" Ye meaner fowl, g. place *T.* 64
Would g. a barbarous air to British song *T.* 102
He g. a perfect rule—what can He less? *T.* 552
That g. society its beauty, strength *T.* ii 681
G. saintship, then all Europe must agree *T.* 111
" The remedy you want I freely g. *T.* 273
Regret would rouse them, and g. birth to prayer *T.* 343
Earth g. too little, giving only bread *T.* 365
Deception innocent—g. ample space *T.* i 353
These Flora banishes, and g. the fair *T.* i 460
G. more than female beauty to a stone *T.* i 703
And g. them all their fury; bids a plague *T.* ii 182
And g. his direst foe a friend's embrace *T.* ii 270
The emphasis in score, and g. to prayer *T.* ii 360
Grow wanton, and g. proof to every eye *T.* ii 443
The better hand, more busy, g. the nose *T.* ii 451
That g. it all its flavour. We have run *T.* ii 607 [799
And g. the world their talents and themselves *T.* ii
And thus g. Virtue indirect applause *T.* iii 104
G. him his praise, and forfeits not her own *T.* iii 247
That, while it g. us worth in God's account *T.* iii 233
The fence withdrawn, he g. them every beam *T.* iii 444
Suffice to g. the marshalled ranks the grace *T.* iii 604
Sightly, and in just order, ere he g. *T.* iii 649
Her interests, or that g. her sacred cause *T.* iii 792
To palliate dullness and g. time a shove *T.* iv 210
And g. them voice and utterance once again *T.* iv 35
He g. the princely bird, with all his wives *T.* iv 449
Great talents; and God g. to every man *T.* iv 789
He g. a tongue to enlarge upon, a heart *T.* iv 794
By dint of change to g. his tasteless task *T.* v. 429
'Tis Liberty alone that g. the flower *T.* v 446 [iv 421
Shall much befriend you. Time shall g. increase *T.*
To g. thee what politer France receives *T.* v 468
Ere yet mortality's fine threads g. way *T.* v 578
Receive proud recompense. We g. in charge *T.* v 706
G. bond in stone and ever-during brass *T.* v 710
But g. the glorious sufferers little praise *T.* v 732
Much more who fashioned it, he g. it praise *T.* v 801
Who g. its lustre to an insect's wing *T.* v 813
" That g. assurance of their own success *T.* v 843
And with the boon g. talents for its use *T.* v 860 [865
We g. to Chance, blind Chance, ourselves as blind *T.* v
G. what Thou canst, without thee we are poor *T.* v 905
May g. an useful lesson to the head *T.* vi 86
Nor deems he wiser him, who g. his noon *T.* vi 278
To g. such act and utterance as they may *T.* vi 339
Mark now the proof I g. thee, that the brave *T.* vi 509
And g. the day to a musician's praise *T.* vi 644
To g. it praise proportioned to its worth *T.* vi 756
G. courage to their foes, who, could they see *T.* vi 865
Why did the fiat of a god g. birth *Tir.* 35
And g. your monstrous project all its force *Tir.* 239

GIVE—GLEANING

He *g.* the local bias all its sway *Tir.* 334
I *g.* the bauble but the second place *Tir.* 388
Shall *g.* him consequence, heal all defects *Tir.* 392
New situations *g.* a different cast *Tir.* 440
And *g.* thy life its only cordial left *Tir.* 882
And feed him well, and *g.* him handsome pay *Tir.* 907
G. him a modicum of light *Tran.* i 11
Some *g.* that honour to his tail *Tran.* i 7
Such a strain as I can *g. Tran.* iii 8
He scolds, and *g.* the lie *Tran.* iv 27
To *g.* Religion her unbridled scope *T.T.* 71 [*T.T.* 309
G. him Olympic speed, and shoots him to the goal
G. him his lass, his fiddle, and his frisk *T.T.* 237
He *g.* the word, and Mutiny soon roars *T.T.* 452
G. Liberty the last, the mortal shock *T.T.* 476 [522
G. me the line that ploughs its stately course *T.T.*
To *g.* a Milton birth, asked ages more *T.T.* 559
Forms, opens, and *g.* scent to every flower *T.T.* 691
G. it a charge to blacken and traduce *T.T.* 763
But to comply with feelings, and to *g. V.* 23
He may be called to *g.* up health and gain *V.* 63
If God *g.* health, that sunshine of our days! *V.* 88
He *g.*, what bankrupt nature never can *V.* 95
Yet not to *g.* offence or grieve *Y.D.* 43
Which it would *g.* in rivulets to thy root *Y.O.* 113

GIVEN.

Has God then *g.* its sweetness to the cane *Ch.* 190
When wine has *g.* indecent language birth *Con.* 263
G. him a soul, and bade him understand *Con.* 430
Is *g.* in earnest of eternal rest *E.* ii 40
Their wisdom pure, and *g.* them from above *Ex.* 442
G. thee his blessing on the clearest proof *Ex.* 564
That blessings truly sacred, and when *g. Ex.* 684
And yet our lot is *g.* us in a land *H.* 439
Surpassing all that mine or mint had *g. J.T.* 30
Nor rested till the Gods had *g.* it life *P.E.* 529
Of provocation *g.* or wrong sustained *T.* v 315
"Hath God indeed *g.* appetites to man *T.* v 635 [610
Their strength, or speed, or vigilance, were *g. T.* vi

GIVER.

What uses of his boon the *g.* would *Con.* 436
With some sincerity, on the *g.*'s part *T.* ii 559
But, O Thou bounteous *g.* of all good! *T.* v 903
The gift whose office is the *G.*'s praise *T.T.* 750

GIVING.

Through constant dread of *g.* Truth offence *Con.* 129
Earth gives too little, *g.* only bread *T.* 365
In playing tricks with Nature, *g.* laws *T.* iii 165
And sorted hues (each *g.* each relief *T.* iii 634
And *g.* one, whose heart is in the skies *V.* 93

GLAD.

Blessed the *g.* beams of that propitious day *A.T.* 205
Of the *g.* legions of the King of Kings *H.* 733
Were never folk so *g. J.G.* 42
The calender, right *g.* to find *J.G.* 177
The postboy's horse right *g.* to miss *J.G.* 231
'Twas in the *g.* season of spring *M.D.* 1
Adds joy to duty, makes me *g.* to pay *M.P.* 70
How *g.* they catch the largess of the skies *N.A.* 62
Attested, *g.*, his approbation *P.T.* 40   [*P.E.* 165
When the *g.* soul is made Heaven's welcome guest
Would oft anticipate his *g.* return *T.* i 543
The *g.* espousals, and ensures the crop *T.* iii 543
His high endeavour, and his *g.* success *T.* v 901
Yet *g.* she came that night to prove *Q.V.* 29

GLADE.

Or taste the fountain in the neighbouring *g. Ch.* 223
Sweet stream that winds through yonder *g. Comp.* ii 1
Where mouldering abbey walls o'erhang the *g. H.* 351
Once more the spiry myrtle crowns the *g. Her.* 31

They bound, and airy, o'er the sunny *g. St.* ii 22
Whose outspread branches overarch the *g. T.* vi 71
The bounding fawn that darts across the *g. T.* vi 327

GLADLY.

Some youthful grace that age would *g.* keep *T.* i 132
G. the thickening mantle; and the green *T.* iv 330
And *g.* would have done *J.G.* 226
For though thou *g.* wouldst fulfil *M.* 13
Those evils it would *g.* cure *M.F.* 58
But *g.*, as the precept were her own *M.P.* 16
Nor yet the parson's, who would *g.* come *R.* 439
Would *g.* stretch life's little span *St.* v 7

GLADNESS.

Suffering with *g.* for a Saviour's sake *R.* 776
Rivers of *g.* water all the earth *T.* vi 763

GLANCE.

How fleet is a *g.* of the mind *A.S.* 41
Then with a *g.* of Fancy to survey *R.* 73
Stealing a sidelong *g.* at a full house *T.* iv 201

GLANCED.

Of undesigned severity, that *g. T.* v 170

GLANCING.

Now flashing wide, now *g.* as in play *T.* 242

GLARE.

Are luxuries excelling all the *g. R.* 185
By short transition we have lost his *g.* i 336

GLARING.

In old grimalkin's *g.* eyes *E.* iv 44

GLASS.

Pure-bosomed as that watery *g. Comp. T.* ii 9
Sighing and smiling as he takes his *g. H.* 419
The nymph between two chariot *g. P.B.* 20
But ah, the cruel *g.* between! *P.B.* 28
One breaks the *g.*, and cuts his fingers *P.B.* 34
Scrawled upon *g.* Miss Bridget's lovely name *T.* 156
That, as with molten *g.*, inlays the vale *T.* i 170
And start theatric, practised at the *g. T.* ii 431
With opera *g.* to watch the moving scene *T.* ii 453
And catechise it well; apply thy *g. T.* iii 203
And overlaid with clear translucent *g. T.* iii 485
With *g.* at eye, and catalogue in hand *T.* vi 288
Unquestioned, though the jewel be but *g. Tir.* 463
The *g.* that bids man mark the fleeting hour *T.T.* 41

GLASSY.

This *g.* stream, that spreading pine *S.* 5
His conscience, like a *g.* lake before *T.* 259
Obdurate and unyielding, *g.* smooth *T.* i 52   [306
The *g.* threads with which the Fancy weaves *T.* iv
And make thy marble of the *g.* wave *T.* v 134

GLEAM.

Where, diligent to catch the first faint *g, T.* v 59

GLEAN.

While yet he dwells below, must stoop to *g. F.A.* 37
G. up the refuse of the general spoil *Her.* 70
Collect the scattered truths that Study *g. R.* 274
Pay contribution to the store he *g. T.* iv 110
He *g.* the blunted shafts that have recoiled *T.* vi 874

GLEANED.   [v 151

G. through the clear transparency, that seemed *T.*
Of passed experience, and the wisdom *g. F.A.* 2

GLEANING.

Repays their work—the *g.* only mine *H.* 771
Like *g.* of an olive tree they show *T.* 379

GLEBE—GLORY

GLEBE.
Pours out its fleecy tenants o'er the *g. T.* i 291
With pointed hoof dibbling the *g.* prepared *Y.O.* 26

GLEE.
Sorting and puzzling with a deal of *g. Con.* 13
With such a jest as filled with hellish *g. Con.* 737
And spirits buoyant with excess of *g. T.* vi 329
Indulges all a father's heartfelt *g. Tir.* 321
Filled with as much true merriment and *g. T.T.* 244

GLENS.
Its hollow *g.*, its thickets, and its plains *T.* vi 402

GLIDE.
When gently, as in June, the rivers *g. A.T.* 74
So may the ruffian, who with ghostly *g. Ch.* 186
I *g.* and steal along with heaven in view *H.* 379
So life *g.* smoothly and by stealth away *T.* vi 995
So *g.* my life away! and so at last *T.* vi 1000

GLIMPSE.
A *g.* of joy, that we have met *N.* 23
That not a *g.* of genuine light pervades *P.E.* 6
The *g.* of a green pasture how they cheer *T.* iv 751
And his end sure, without one *g.* of hope *Tir.* 427

GLISTENING.
G. at once with pity and surprise *H.* 533
And *g.* even in the dying eye *T.* vi 631

GLITTER.
Must tinkle and *g.* like gold to the sight *F.M.* 19
Earth *g.* with the drops the night distils *H.* 42
And e'en the star, that *g.* on the bier *H.* 270
Now *g.* in the sun and now retires *T.* i 324
Ficoides, *g.* bright the winter long *T.* iii 579
The seals of office *g.* in his eyes *T.* iv 59
With those whose mansions *g.* in his sight *T.* v 740
Not always *g.* in my view) 1789, 26

GLITTERING.
His *g.* purse, that envy of all eyes *Ch.* 472
Like a loose heap of ribbon, a *g.* show *F.M.* 6
The show-glass fraught with *g.* ware *P.B.* 24
G. in vain, or only to seduce *R.* 212
First shakes the *g.* drops from every thorn *R.* 396
Here *g.* turrets rise, upbearing high *T.* v 110
Is worth, with all its gold and *g.* store *T.T.* 61

GLOBE.
Trade is the golden girdle of the *g. Ch.* 86
Deplores the wasted regions of her *g. Her.* 80
The *g.* and its concerns, I seem advanced *T.* iv 95
Her silver *g.*, light as the foamy surf *T.* vi 155
That man, the master of this *g.* derives *Tir.* 3
The *g.* and sceptre in such hands misplaced *T.T.* 39

GLOBOSE.
The seas *g.* and huge, the o'erarching vault *R.* 552
With prominent wens *g.*; till at the last *Y.O.* 66

GLOOM. [479
When the Sun's shafts disperse the *g.* of night *Ex.*
Dispelled thy *g.*, and broke away thy dreams *Ex.* 501
"For lift thy palsied head, shake off the *g. H.* 37
Till thy appearance chased the *g.*, forlorn *J.T.* 21
The *g.* and coolness of declining day *T.* i 258
So spent in parlour twilight, such a *g. T.* iv 278
And throwing up into the darkest *g. T.* vi 153
Liberty chases all that *g.* away *T.T.* 271
Loved not the light, but, gloomy, into *g. Y.O.* 14

GLOOMY.
Are *g.* thoughts led on by Spleen *E.* iv 20
By night a fire, to cheer the *g.* way *Ex.* 178

Her *g.* monarch, doubtful, and resigned *Ex.* 570
The *g.* scene surveys *N.* 10
With all the *g.* past *St.* iii 8
And roofs embattled high, the *g.* scenes *T.* ii 122
The *g.* clouds, find weapons, arrowy sleet *T.* v 140
Loved not the light, but, *g.*, into gloom *Y.O.* 14

GLORIED.
That cried "Repent"—and *g.* in thy choice? *Ex.* 399
Our British Themis *g.* with just cause *T.* iii 257

GLORIFY.
We *g.* that Self, not him we ought *Ch.* 570

GLORIOUS.
Forgetful of the *g.* toils of war *A.T.* 28
So *g.* now, though once so disesteemed *Ch.* 580
Of virtue, and religion's *g.* cause *Con.* 686
Live from his lips, and spread the *g.* sound *H.* 454
Not e'en the *g.* sun, though men revere *H.* 501
These are thy *g.* works, eternal Truth *H.* 742
Then these thy *g.* works, and they who share *H.* 750
Pay tribute to thy *g.* beams *O.* i 7
"These are thy *g.* works, thou Source of good *R.* 87
From scenes of sorrow into *g.* day *R.* 168
G. as Solyma's interior shrine *T.* 388
Else his own *g.* rights He would disclaim *T.* 555
Of blank oblivion, seem a *g.* prize *T.* i 287
Of holy discipline, to *g.* war *T.* ii 348
To combat may be *g.*, and success *T.* iii 687
And now perhaps the *g.* hour is come *T.* iii 790
Pronounced it transient, *g.* as it is *T.* v 563
And still designing a more *g.* far *T.* v 564
But gives the *g.* sufferers little praise *T.* v 732
Fires all the faculties with *g.* joy *T.* v 885
Fires him at once in Freedom's *g.* cause *T.T.* 229
G. in war, but for the sake of peace *T.T.* 278
Ere yet his race begins, its *g.* close *T.T.* 708

GLORIOUSLY.
G. drunk, obey the important call! *T.* iv 510

GLORY.
And in his country's *g.* sought his own *Ch.* 26
Thy pomp is in the grave, thy *g.* laid *Ch.* 71
Reflect the noonday *g.* of the skies *Ch.* 398
Or sell their *g.* at a market price *Con.* 28
As to despise the *g.* of our kind *Con.* 258
To spread the newborn *g.* in their view *Con.* 546
And his chief *g.*, was the gospel theme *Con.* 620
Whose *g.*, with a light that never fades *Con.* 883
Jerusalem a prey, her *g.* soiled *Ex.* 61
Their *g.* faded, and their race dispersed *Ex.* 241
Thy temple, once thy *g.*, fallen and raised *Ex.* 259
Of the chief strength and *g.* of the frame *Ex.* 335
Claimed all the *g.* of thy prosperous wars? *Ex.* 347
Thy *g.*, and thy shame if unimproved) *Ex.* 689
Shall be my chosen theme, my *g.* to the last *Ex.* 734
To fling his *g.*, o'er the robe she wears *H.* 44
'Tis heard where England's Eastern *g.* shines *H.* 457
G. your aim, but Justice your pretence *Her.* 44
And *g.* for the virtuous when they die *J.T.* 14
Wherever her *g.* appeared *M.D.* 20
Yet let the *g.* of a night *Q.V.* 77
That men erroneously their *g.* call *R.* 100
Successive rhyme his *g.* and reward *R.* 198
That builds its *g.* on its Maker's praise *R.* 210
Who will may pant for *g.* and excel *R.* 245
His work of *g.* done *R.G.* 16
His radiant *g.*, azure, green, and gold *T.* 61
Though he too has a *g.* in his plumes *T.* 67
Restore to man the *g.* he has lost *T.* 398
Grace in his mien, and *g.* in his eyes *T.* 407
Fallen from her *g.*, and too weak to rise *T.* 480
Had shed immortal *g.* on your brow *T.* 569

Not more the g. of the earth than she T. i 723
A more accomplished world's chief g. now T. i 724
Each in his field of g.; one in arms T. ii 241
All flesh is grass, and all its g. fades T. iii 261
His g., and his nature to impart T. iii 274
The way to g. by miscarriage foul T. iii 506
Are his sole aim, and all his g. now T. iv 658
Hence too the field of g., as the world T. iv 684
Of evanescent g., once a stream T. v 167
For England's g., seeing it wax pale T. v 510
But these are not his g. Man, 'tis true T. v 559
The g. of thy work, which yet appears T. v 866
That cultivation g. in, are his T. vi 189
Sung to the praise and g. of King George! T. vi 663
Flock to that light; the g. of all lands T. vi 802
And shows him g. yet to be revealed T. vi 927
You told me, I remember, g., built T.T. 1
Blest country, where these Kingly g.'s shine! T.T. 81
A g., bright as that of all the signs Tir. 282
Shall blush betimes, and there his g. rise Tir. 396

GLORYING.
Cruel, abandoned, g. in her shame! T. iii 68

GLOSSARY.
And needs no g. to set him right N.A. 70

GLOSSY.
A raven, while with g. breast A Fable 1
That g. shine, or vivid flame Mrs. M— 10
Rough elm, or smooth-grained ash, or g. beech R. 230
And g., he commits to pots of size T. iii 512

GLOSSY-LEAVED.
Some g., and shining in the sun T. i 314

GLOVE.
As if the world and they were hand and g. T.T. 173
A soldier's feather, or a lady's g. T.T. 549

GLOW.
Felt them in her bosom g. B. 38
And, in the g. of her intense desires Ch. 402
And, warmed by the pressure, is all in a g. F.M. 8
And catch in its progress a sensible g. F.M. 20
That bliss, revealed in scripture, with a g. H. 149
Where late we saw the mimic landscape g. H. 263
A transport g. in all he looks and speaks H. 726
The marble breathes, the canvas g. Miss — 83
The g. that Fancy gave it fades Mor. 36
Chafed him, and brought dull nature to a g. P.E. 408
Set London in a g. Q.V. 8
He bids him g. with unremitting love T. 557
To teach his heart to g. with generous flame Tir. 644

GLOWED.
By thy own hand, till fresh they shone and g. M.P. 63

GLOWING.
When all his g. language issued forth Con. 709
The centre of a g. heart E. i 14
The g. tablets with a juster skill Ex. 232
The g. bosom swell Miss — 16
The little ones, unbuttoned, g. hot Tir. 304
Dye them at last in all their g. hues Tir. 48
All, all alike, transport the g. bard R. 197
No Fear attends to quench his g. fires T. 189
What g. thanks his lips and heart employ T. 255
The g. hearth may satisfy awhile T. iv 273
But slaves that once conceive the g. thought T. v 374
Only by gratitude and g. thought T.T. 587

GLOW-WORM.
And knew the g. by his spark N.G. 10

GLUED.
Was g. to the sword-hilt with Indian gore Ch. 50

GLUTTON.
But, if he play the g. and exceed P.E. 211

GLUTTONOUS.
And wantonness, and g. excess T. i 688

GLUTTONY.
Or his base g., are causes good T. vi 388

GNATS. [452
Yet g. have had, and frogs and mice, long since T. iii

GNOMON.
As if the g. on his neighbour's phiz Con. 271

GO.
But g. the male? Far wiser, he A Tale 47
There g. my lady, and there g. the squire B.B. 12
There g. the parson—O illustrious spark! B.B. 13
And there scarce less illustrious, g. the clerk B.B. 14
But let insolvent innocence g. free" Ch. 289
Except that office clips it as it g. Ch. 484
Blessing and blessed where'er she g. Comp. i 8
G., quit the rank to which ye stood preferred Con. 75
Your elevated voice g. through the brain Con. 328
Every five minutes how the minutes g. Con. 382
G. seek on Revelation's hallowed ground Con. 499
Ere life g. down, to see such sights again) Con. 606
Cheered as they g. by many a sprightly strain E. ii 14
And said, " G. spend them in the vale of tears" E. ii 26
"G., fellow!—whither?—turning short about E. iii24
Must g. to heaven—and I must drink his health H. 412
G. now, and with important tone demand H. 528
Will lend his horse to g." J.G. 24
G.! thou art all unfit to share M.B. 1
Thy prowess—therefore, g.! M.B. 20 [P.A. 26
What! rob our good neighbour! I pray you don't g.:
"I g. to make Freemen of Slaves" M.D. 16 [P.A.33
They spoke, and Tom pondered—"I see they will g.
And asked him to g. and assist in the job P.A. 24
If you will g. with us, you shall have a share P.A. 31
But since they will take them, I think I'll g. too P.A.39
G., cast your orders at your Bishop's feet P.E. 120
G., fool; and arm in arm with Clodio plead P.E. 197
As axles sometimes kindle as they g. P.E. 407
Thus men g. wrong with an ingenious skill P.E. 556
Ten thousand thousand strings at once g. loose R. 329
As useless if it g. as when it stands R. 682
To ages, where he g. St. v 10
The shivering urchin, bending as he g. T. 143
But that she fasts, and, item, g. to church T. 152
G., bid the winter cease to chill the year T. 399
And not a year but pilfers as he g. T. 131 [203
G. dress thine eyes with eyesalve; ask of him T. ii
Ambling and prattling scandal as he g. T. ii 382
He whistles as he g., light-hearted wretch T. iv 12
The wain g. heavily, impeded sore T. iv 343
Now g. the nightly thief prowling abroad T. iv 432
Forth g. the woodman, leaving unconcerned T. v 41
Makes wintry music, sighing as it g. T.vi 143 [vi 140
But let the months g. round, a few short months T.
And is not ere to-morrow's sun g. down T. vi 215
The young to let the parent bird g. free T. vi 446
Shall have its altar; and the world shall g. T. vi 668
Nor say, g. thither, conscious that there lay Tir. 869
The punch g. round, and they are dull Y.D. 45

GOADED.
Driven to the slaughter, g., as he runs T. vi 421

GOAL.

Home to the g. where it began the race Ch. 566
They sidle to the g. with awkward pace P.E. 562
Else. though unequalled to the g. he flies T. 15
Its destined g. of difficult access T. vi 277
To the far distant g., arrives and dies T. vi 430
And does but at the g. obtain Th. 19 [T.T. 309
Gives him Olympic speed and shoots him to the g.
An eye like his to catch the distant g. T.T. 710

GOBLET.

The brimming g.,seized the Thyrsus,bound T.T. 603

GOD

Counsel of her country's g.'s B. 4
G., working ever on a social plan Ch. 15 [59
G. stood not, though he seemed to stand, aloof Ch.
Art thou the G., the thunder of whose hand Ch. 75
G. opens fruitful Nature's various scenes Ch. 88
A herald of G.'s love to pagan lands Ch. 136
Or if the will and sovereignty of G.—Ch. 165
Has G. then given its sweetness to the cane Ch. 190
To smite the poor is treason against G.—Ch. 217
G.'s gift with pleasure in his praise employ Ch. 252
Owns no superior but the G. she fears Ch. 275
For self to self, and G. to man revealed Ch. 361
But G. o'errules all human follies still Ch. 463
Nor spring from love to G., or love to man Ch. 560
To see a G. stretch forth his human hand Ch. 581
G.'s name so much upon his lips, a priest Con. 72
For all is perfect that G. works on earth Con. 433
G. and his attributes (a field of day Con. 471 [Con. 32
Wrath stays him, or else G. would strike them dumb
That air of insolence affronts your G.—Con. 487
Man to maintain, and such as G. approves Con. 538
Can length of years on G. himself exact Con. 549
As bastions set point blank against G.'s will Con. 688
With G.'s deep stamp upon its current worth Con. 710
G.'s work may serve an ape upon a stage Con. 736
Usurps G.'s office, lays his bosom bare Con. 745 [747
And, serving G. herself through mere restraint Con.
Sincerity towards the heart-searching G.—Con. 753
He knows that G. demands his heart entire Con. 759
And all her love of G. a groundless claim Con. 781
And g. and goddesses discarded long Con. 819 [749
And yet, G. knows, look human nature through Con.
By stout substantial g. of wood and stone Con. 834
If Israel's Lord be G., then serve the Lord Con. 852
Then Baal is the G., and worship him" Con. 854
For G. unfolds by slow degrees E. 159
When G. and you know I have neither E. iv 8
Since twenty sheets of lead, G. knows E. iv 27
He heard the wheels of an avenging G. Ex. 57
In form a man, in dignity a G.—Ex. 86
Then G. own image on the soul impressed Ex. 109
And yet exalted above G.'s own word Ex. 128
Their G. their captain, lawgiver, and king Ex. 190
And the true G. the G. of truth was theirs Ex. 240
When G. arises with an awful frown Ex. 249 [323
Frames many a purpose, and G. works his own Ex.
The stroke that a vindictive G. intends Ex. 407
G.'s better gift they scoff at, and refuse Ex. 459
And G.'s disposing providence confessed Ex. 558
If G. himself be not beneath her care Ex. 603 [Ex. 504
But still light reached thee; and those G. of thine:
To learn in G.'s own school the Christian part Ex.650
Which G.,though long forborne,will not forget Ex.713
On points which G. has left at large F. 136
But what the g. call it above Gr. 35
And the barbed arrows of a frowning G.—R. 304
When G. and man stand opposite in view H. 131
And silence every fear with—G. is just H. 370
And—G. is merciful—Sets all to rights H. 376

Nor spurn away a gift a G. bestows H. 547 [453
G. gives the word, the preachers throng around H.
Scripture indeed is plain, but G. and he H. 598
And where his danger and G.'s wrath begin H. 609
A man arise, a man whom G. has taught H. 623
Except the few his G. may have impressed H. 633
Mighty to parry and push by G.'s word H. 659
G.'s holy word, once trivial in his view H. 706
Say man's a worm, and power belongs to G.—H. 711
'Tis more—'tis G. diffused through every part H. 734
'Tis G. himself triumphant in his heart H. 735
What scourges are the g.'s that rule below Her. 66
And, though G. made thee of a nature prone J.T. 31
Then thus the g. whom fondly they J.P. 29 [131
Had summoned them to serve his golden g. P.E.
G.'s worship and the mountebank between P.E. 156
Sits banqueting, and G. provides the feast P.E. 166
Thou g. of our idolatry, the Press? P.E. 461
Nor rested till the g. had given it life P.E. 529
Take leave of nature's G., and G. revealed P.E. 591
And calls a creature formed for G. alone R. 17
And works of G. are hardly to be found R. 26
Mounts from inferior beings up to G.—R. 114
Truth is not local, G. alike pervades R. 119
Opening the map of G.'s extensive plan R. 147
Up!—G. has formed thee with a wiser view R. 265
'Tis G.'s just claim, prerogative divine R. 278
On pangs enforced with G.'s severest stroke R. 314
G. in a moment executes with ease) R. 328 [342
No cure for such, till G. who makes them heals R.
Much of the power and majesty of G.—R. 526
Of G., beneficent in all His ways R. 556 [R. 688
Built G. a church, and laughed his word to scorn
The love of virtue, and the fear of G.—R. 730
And trusting in his G., surmounts them all R.H. 8
The axe will smite at G.'s command St. i 15
The bosom of his G.—St. iii 16
He lives who lives to G., alone St. vi 1
For other source than G. is none St. vi 3
To live to G. is to requite St. vi 5
Have wounds which only G. can heal St. vi 19
Which G. asserts his own St. vi 26
If scorn of G. commands, impressed St. vi 29
Yet so will G. repay St. vi 38
Your wilful suicide on G.'s decree T. 20 [92
You think him humble--G. accounts him proud T.
I dare not—" And you need not," G. replies T. 272
Dwelt visibly the light-creating G.—T. 390
And thunderbolts excepted quite a G.!—T. 410
Charge not a G. with such outrageous wrong T. 520
Prefer to the performance of a G.—T. i 418
The total ordinance and will of G.—T. i 743 [749
G. made the country, and man made the town T. i
While G. performs, upon the trembling stage T. ii 8
On G.'s behalf, lays waste his fairest works T. ii 136
Of wrath obnoxious, G. may choose His mark T. ii156
Happy the man who sees a G. employed T. ii 161
Then G. might be surprised, and unforeseen T. ii 171
Denies the power that wields it. G. proclaims T. ii 178
Suspend the effect, or heal it? Has not G.—T. ii 197
The sacramental host of G.'s elect T. ii 349
To make G.'s work a sinecure; a slave T. ii 390
And pretty face in presence of his G.?—T. ii 422
He that negotiates between G. and man T. ii 463
As G.'s ambassador, the grand concerns T. ii 464
When sent with G.'s commission to the heart T. ii 471
Blind nature to a G. not yet revealed T. ii 526
As nations ignorant of G. contrive T. ii 574 [T. iii 221
G. never meant that man should scale the heavens
As meant to indicate a G. to man T. iii 246 [iii 708
And virtue, and those scenes which G. ordained T.
Sagacious reader of the works of G.—T. iii 253 [272
And wherefore? Will not G. impart his light T. iii

That, while it gives us worth in *G.'s* account *T.* iii 283
For whom *G.* heard his Abraham plead in vain *T.* iii 848
Who deem religion frenzy, and the *G.*—*T.* iv 178
O evenings worthy of the *g.*! exclaimed *T.* iv 189
Great talents : and *G.* gives to every man *T.* iv 789
G. drave asunder, and assigned their lot *T.* v 198
To eminence fit only for a *G.*—*T.* v 284   [292
And quake before the *g.* themselves had made *T.* v
Which *G.* avenged on Pharaoh—the Bastille *T.* v 383
As dreadful as the Manichean *g.* *T.* v 444
And promise of a *G.* His other gifts *T.* v 550
Whose lying heart disputes against a *G.*—*T.* v 568
" Hath *G.* indeed given appetites to man *T.* v 635
" Dishonours *G.*, and makes a slave of man *T.* v 643
To walk with *G.*, to be divinely free *T.* v 722 [779
Acquaint thyself with *G.*, if thou wouldst taste *T.* v
Whom *G.* delights in, and in whom He dwells *T.* v 778
The unambiguous footsteps of the *G.*—*T.* v 812
Sent forth a voice, and all the sons of *G.*—*T.* v 821
G. such as gilt makes welcome ; *g.* that sleep *T.* v 876
See nought to wonder at. Should *G.* again *T.* vi 125
A soul in all things, and that soul is *G.*—*T.* vi 185
Thus dream they, and contrive to save a *G.*—*T.* vi 205
Whose cause is *G.* He feeds the secret fire *T.* vi 224
With tutelary goddesses and *g.* *T.* vi 235   [252
Prompts with remembrance of a present *G.*—*T.* vi
G. set the diadem upon his head *T.* vi 351
Garden of *G.*, how terrible the change *T.* vi 371
Whom once, as delegate of *G.* on earth *T.* vi 399
But *G.* will never. When he charged the Jew *T.* vi 443
Of *G.* and goodness, atheist in ostent *T.* vi 486 [557
So *G.* wrought double justice ; made the fool *T.* vi
As *G.* was free to form them at the first *T.* vi 586
Accountable, and *G.*, some future day *T.* vi 605
The *g.* of our idolatry once more *T.* vi 667
See Salem built, the labour of a *G.*! *T.* vi 799 [820
So *G.* has greatly purposed ; who would else *T.* vi
The creature is that *G.* pronounces good *T.* vi 828
Two *g.* divide them all—Pleasure and Gain *T.* vi 892
Deems him a cipher in the works of *G.*—*T.* vi 943
Of *G.* and man, and peaceful in its end *T.* vi 999
Why did the fiat of a *g.* give birth *Tir.* 35 [*Tir.* 54
Look where he will, the wonders *G.* has wrought
That taught of *G.* they may indeed be wise *Tir.* 107
And guides the Progress of a soul to *G.*—*Tir.* 146
As *G.'s* expedient to retrieve his loss *Tir.* 166
In sacrilege, in *G.'s* own house profaned *Tir.* 409
To live estranged from *G.* his total scope *Tir.* 426
That *G.* and nature, and your interest too *Tir.* 553
As, hid from ages past, *G.* now displays *Tir.* 638
And formed of *G.* without a parent's mind *Tir.* 790
The *G.* that strings the silver bow *Trans. H.* 28 [374
Confessed a *G.* ; they kneeled before they fought *T.T.*
Stamps *G.'s* own name upon a lie just made *T.T.* 420
G.'s curse can cast away ten thousand sail ! *T.T.* 467
And yet magnificent—a *G.* the theme ! *T.T.* 593
If *G.* give health, that sunshine of our days ! *V.* 87

GODDESS.
And gods and *g.* discarded long *Con.* 819
The *g.* chanced to hear *L.R.* 18
Of *g.* yet known, and costlier far *T.* ii 659
That reeling *g.* with the zoneless waist *T.* iii 52
With tutelary *g.* and gods *T.* vi 235

GODDESS-LIKE.
That *g.* woman he viewed *M.D.* 34

GODHEAD.
Deny thy *G.* with a martyr's zeal *T.* vi 883

GODLIKE.
Oh ! 'tis a *g.* privilege to save *Ch.* 226

GODLINESS.
Pretends a zeal for *g.* and grace *H.* 661

GODLY.
But tears of *g.* grief ne'er flow within *St.* ii 32

GOING.   [25
"Nay—stay at home—you're always *g.* out " *E.* iii
What ! hang a man for *g.* mad ! *Pat.* 23

GOLD.
More precious than silver and *g.* *A.S.* 27   [479
G., to be sure !—Throughout the town 'tis told *Ch.*
How the good squire gives never less than *g.* *Ch.* 480
As one of *g.*, and yours was such *E.* iv 30   [iii 18
Can *g.* grow worthless that has stood the touch ? *E.*
No ; *g.* they seemed, but they were never such *E.* iii 19
When a bar of pure silver or ingot of *g.* *F.M.* 1
Must tinkle and glitter like *g.* to the sight *F.M.* 19
Where, flaming in scarlet and *g.* *Gr.* 29
And if the genuine worth of *g.* depend *J.T.* 27
His mantling neck with downy *g.* *Mrs. M*— 6
Paid my price in paltry *g.* *N.C.* 6
Slaves of *g.*, whose sordid dealings *N.C.* 53
His radiant glories, azure, green, and *g.* *T.* 61
And decks itself with ornaments of *g.* *T.* i 529
To conjure clean away the *g.* they touch *T.* i 571
To peculators of the public *g.* *T.* i 735
Ambitious of preferment for its *g.* *T.* ii 387
Bleed *g.* for ministers to sport away *T.* iv 508
In streaming *g.* ; Syringa, ivory pure *T.* vi 150
More golden than that age of fabled *g.* *T.* vi 996
Is worth, with all its *g.* and glittering store *T.T.* 61
G., purer far than Ophir ever knew *V.* 97

GOLD-BEATER.
The thump after thump of a *g.* mallet *F.M.* 10

GOLDEN.
And spread her *g.* hopes below *A Fable* 15
And phillyrea of a *g.* green *A.T.* 83
Trade is the *g.* girdle of the globe *Ch.* 86
Disdains the Bank, and throws the *g.* sands *Ch.* 248
To pour his *g.* tide through all her gates *Ex.* 14
Cured of the *g.* calves, their fathers' sin *Ex.* 215
To adopt the chymist's *g.* dream *F.* 143
That flutter loose on *g.* wing *F.B.* 8
Than *g.* beams of orient light *M.* 27
Your *g.* moments bless *Miss* — 102
Like sunbeams on the *g.* height *Mrs. M*— 35
Had summoned them to serve his *g.* god *P.E.* 131
With *g.* wing and satin poll *P.T.* 27
Her *g.* tassels on the leafy sprays *R.* 232
Though placed in *g.* Durham's second stall *T.* 120
Or, if a chain, the *g.* one of love *T.* 188
And taints the *g.* ear. He springs his mines *T.* ii 187
Of *g.* fruitage, and her myrtle bowers *T.* ii 215
Large foliage, overshadowing *g.* flowers *T.* iii 535
Shines there, and flourishes. The *g.* boast *T.* iii 571
The Levee swarms, as if in *g.* pomp *T.* iii 822
The *g.* harvest, of a mellow brown *T.* iv 314
That poets ; celebrate those *g.* times *T.* iv 514
Her *g.* tube, through which a sensual world *T.* vi 978
More *g.* than that age of fabled gold *T.* vi 996
Depend not much upon your *g.* dream *Tir.* 429
He that holds fast the *g.* mean *Trans. H.* 7

GOLDFINCHES.
Two *g.*, whose sprightly song *F.B.* 4

GOLIATH.
G., might have seen his giant bulk *T.* iv 270

GONE.
But the sea-fowl is *g.* to her nest *A.S.* 49
" Shall mourn her absent lord, for he is *g.* *A.T.* 104
The mother-bird is *g.* to sea *A Tale* 45

She came—she is *g*.—we have met *C.* 1
'Tis *g.* again—plague on't! I thought *E.* iv 37
That useful thing, her needle *g. E.* iv 40
Thy diadem displaced, thy sceptre *g. Ex.* 258
G. thither armed and hungry, returned full *Ex.* 368
Are altogether *g.* a devious course *Ex.* 463
The flowers are *g.*—but still we find *M.* 215
But was it such?—it was.—Where thou art *g. M.P.* 32
But if the rogue be *g.* a cup too far *P.E.* 440
Brave Kempenfelt is *g. R.G.* 14
But Kempenfelt is *g. R.G.* 33
I passed—and they were *g. St.* i 20
Her eyebrows arched, her eyes both *g.* astray *T.* 135
Looked to the sea for safety? They are *g. T.* ii 119
G. with the refluent wave into the deep *T.* ii 120
I see that all are wanderers, *g.* astray *T.* iii 124 [403
Still lives, though all its pleasant boughs are *g. T.* v
Some friend is *g.*, perhaps his son's best friend! *T.*vi29

GOOD. [*A.T.* ii 4
With as many hard names as would line a *g.* trunk
"To horse!" he cried, "or by this *g.* right hand *A.T.*169
Though little need, to his *g.* palfrey's side *A.T.* 192
'Tis a very *g.* match between Mary and John *A.T.* iii 2
The *g.* so long desired *A Tale* 24
Each some approaching *g.* divines *A Tale* 63
Takes the resemblance of the *g.* she views *Ch.* 396
Another's *g.*; theirs centres in their own *Ch.* 450
Flavia, most tender of her own *g.* name *Ch.* 453
How the *g.* squire gives never less than gold *Ch.* 480
The milk of their *g.* purpose all to curd *Ch.* 504
Pelting each other for the public *g. Ch.* 622
Dubius is such a scrupulous *g.* man *Con.* 119
To teach *g.* manners, and to curb abuse *Con.* 164
Prefers his fellow grooms, with much *g.* sense *Con.* 417
The school of coarse *g.* fellowship and noise *Con.* 422
That *g.* diffused may more abundant grow *Con.* 443
The soul's sure interest in the *g.* she seeks *Con.* 728
And give *g.* company a face severe *Con.* 873
A harbinger of endless *g. E.* i 90
G. lack, we know not what to-morrow brings *E.* iii 8
Perhaps 'twas mere *g.* humour gave it birth *E.* iii 38
They drew a curse from an intended *g. Ex.* 129
Why, having kept *g.* faith, and often shown *Ex.* 276
That infidels may prove their title *g. Ex.* 380
That Scripture, Justice, and *G.* Sense disown *Ex.* 593
Friendship a false ideal *g. G.* 29
As Envy pines at *g.* possessed *G.* 79
On *g.* that seems approaching *G.* 81
G. sense and knowledge of mankind *G.* 200
Thus compassed about with the *g. Gr.* 49
Poets' *g.* are not often so fine *Gr.* 54
A vain pursuit of fugitive, false *g. H.* 4
With every *g.* and perfect gift, proceeds *H.* 116
By *g.* vouchsafed makes known superior *g. H.* 147
From fading *g.* derives, with chemic art *H.* 159
And seem to pray, for *g.* example sake *H.* 249
Without *g.* works, whatever some may boast *H.* 363
Who make the *g.* Creator on their plan *H.* 383
Wild as if Nature there, void of all *g. H.* 540
This man was happy—had the World's *g.* word *H.*678
G. breeding and *g.* sense gave all a grace *H.* 683
And my *g.* friend the calender *J.G.* 23
"*G.* lack!" quoth he, yet bring it me *J.G.* 61
With caution and *g.* heed *J.G.* 80
Praising the Author of all *g.* in man *J.T.* 2
The dead in whom that *g.* abounded most *J.T.* 4
Thou hadst an industry in doing *g. J.T.* 23
"*G.* Mussulman, abstain from pork *L.W.* 2 [126
Through mere *g.* fortune, took a different course *N.A.*
Maria! I have every *g. N.Y.G.* 1
But staying behind will do him no *g. P.A.* 36
Will Providence o'erlook the wasted *g.? P.E.* 223
G. sense, *g.* health, *g.* conscience, and *g.* fame? *P.E.* 246

But we, as if *g.* qualities would grow *P.E.* 363
Thou fountain at which drink the *g.* and wise *P.E.* 466
Knowledge of *g.* and evil is from thee *P.E.* 469
By his *g.* will would keep us single *P.T.* 32
Than to neglect a *g.* adviser *P.T.* 61
"These are thy glorious works, thou Source of *g.R.*87
And woo and win thee to thy proper *g. R.* 256
The *g.* we never miss we rarely prize *R.* 406
Whose wit is rudeness, whose *g.* breeding tires *R.* 438
'Tis wild *g.* nature's never failing lot *R.* 582
And such as, in the zeal of *g.* design *R.* 697
Where all *g.* qualities grow sick and die *R.* 738
To blend *g.* sense and elegance and ease *S.* ii 11
Forced to a pause, would feel it *g.* to think *St.* ii 15
Have purchased Heaven, and prove my title *g. T.* 96
Possess herself of all that's *g.* or true *T.* 489
The *g.* he scorned, all carried to account" *T.* 546
Forgive their evil, and accept their *g. T.* 582
Communicative of the *g.* he owns *T.* i 332
G. health, and, its associate in the most *T.* i 399
G. temper; spirits prompt to undertake *T.* i 400
To tempt us in thy country. Doing *g. T.* i 673
Disinterested *g.*, is not our trade *T.* i 674
It is not seemly, nor of *g.* report *T.* i 729
Nor is it well, nor can it come to *g. T.* i 739
In all the *g.* and ill that chequer life! *T.* ii 162
Their *g.* old friend, and Discipline at length *T.* ii 732
With such ingredients of *g.* sense and taste *T.* ii 789
Well-equipaged, is ticket *g.* enough *T.* iii 98
Disturb *g.* order, and degrade true worth *T.* iii 674
Had I the choice of sublunary *g. T.* iii 689
Was but to boast his own peculiar *g. T.* iii 717
The dearth of information and *g.* sense *T.* iv 71
But be ye of *g.* courage. Time itself *T.* iv 420
The course of human things from *g.* to ill *T.* iv 578
Seem most at variance with all moral *g. T.* iv 621
Your self-denying zeal, that holds it *g. T.* v 328
The surest presage of the *g.* they seek *T.* v 378
'Tis therefore sober and *g.* men are sad *T.* v 509
Be most sublimely *g.*, verbosely grand *T.* v 678
The loaded soil, and ye may waste much *g. T.* v 756
But, O Thou bounteous giver of all *g.! T.* v 903
Till time has stolen away the slightest *g. T.* vi 51
Or his base gluttony, are causes *g. T.* vi 388
Of *g.* Evander, still where he was left *T.* vi 537
To quadruped instructors, many a *g. T.* vi 622
The creature is that God pronounces *g. T.* vi 828
The occasion it presents of doing *g. T.* vi 847
If, author of no mischief and some *g. T.* vi 953
The stamp and clear impression of *g.* sense *T.* vi 983
Quick-sighted arbiter of *g.* and ill *Tir.* 31
That in *g.* time the stripling's finished taste *Tir.* 203
In all *g.* faculties beneath his care *Tir.* 709
A trifler vain, and empty of all *g. Tir.* 754
To compass that *g.* end, forecast the means *Tir.* 884
His portion in the *g.* that Heaven bestows *T.T.* 20
O bright occasions of dispensing *g. T.T.* 63 [96
"But where, *g.* sir, do you confine your kings?" *T.T.*
E'en when he labours for his country's *g. T.T.* 191
Patriots, who love *g.* places at their hearts *T.T.* 191
Firm friends to peace, to pleasure, and *g.* pay *T.T.* 195
Thus with a rigour, for his *g.* designed *T.T.* 216
Communicates with joy the *g.* she finds *T.T.* 275
No. His high mettle, under *g.* control *T.T.* 308
Always harbinger of *g. Trans.* iii 4
That holds in view the *g.* of man *U.* 24
Let me, the charge of some *g.* angel, find *V.* 77
To make their payments *g. Y.D.* 16
G. Mr. What-d'ye-call? *Y.D.* 36
The *g.* on earth they valued most 1789, 51

GOOD-BREEDING.
Nor smooth *G.* (supplemental grace) *T.* vi 853

GOODLY.
Found thee a *g.* sponge for Power to press *Ex.* 531

GOOD-NATURE.
When gay *G.* dresses her in smiles *T.* ii 784

GOOD-NATURED.
In Christian charity, (*g.* age !) *T.* iii 95

GOODNESS.
Wisdom and *G.* are twin-born, one heart *Ex.* 634
His names of wisdom, *g.*, power, and love *H.* 135
It were to weep that *g.* has its meed *J.T.* 12
Was to encourage *g.* He would stroke *T.* ii 710
And *g.* infinite, but speak in ears *T.* v 854
Of God and *g.*, atheist in ostent *T.* vi 486

GOOSE.
And promised they should act the wild *g.* part *A.T.* 53
Or a wild *g.* at play *J.G.* 140

GORE.
Was glued to the sword-hilt with Indian *g. Ch.* 50
With fingers deeply dyed in human *g. Ex.* 497

GORGE. [483
Minnows and gudgeons *g.* the unwholesome food *P.E.*

GORGEOUS.
Contribute to the *g.* plan *Mrs. M—* 13
A native of the *g.* East *Trans.* iv 2

GORGONIUS.
G. sits, abdominous and wan *P.E.* 217

GORSE.
With prickly *g.*, that shapeless and deformed *T.* i 527

GOSLING.
Surprised at all they meet, the *g.* pair *P.E.* 379

GOSPEL.
And his chief glory, was the *g.* theme *Con.* 620
This record of thee for the *G.*'s sake *J.T.* 48
Why falls the *G.* like a gracious dew ? *T.* 180
We boast some rich ones whom the *G.* sways *T.* 377
How readily, upon the *G.* plan *T.* 381
As angels use, the *G.* whispers peace *T.* ii 342
The meteor of the *G.* dies away *Tir.* 190
With *g.* lore, turn infidels themselves *Tir.* 826

GOSSIP'D.
Of smiling day, they *g.* side by side *T.* v 60

GOT.
And up he *g.*, in haste to ride *J.G.* 47
What thing upon his back had *g. J.G.* 95
Nor stopped till where he had *g.* up *J.G.* 247
His stock, a few French phrases *g.* by heart *P.E.* 375

GOTHIC.
Without it, all is *g.* as the scene *T.* iii 641
Oh, barbarous ! wouldst thou with a *G.* hand *Tir.* 899
And, tedious years of *G.* darkness passed *T.T.* 564

GOURD.
To raise the prickly and green-coated *g. T.* iii 446

GOUTY.
The *g.* limb, 'tis true ; but *g.* limb *T.* i 107

GOVERN.
That guides and *g.* our affections *E.* i 35
Nor does he *g.* only, or direct *T.* iii 403
That *g.* all things here, shouldering aside *T.* vi 839

GOVERNED.
His measured step were *g.* by his ear *T.* 63
Or aught He does, is *g.* by caprice *T.* 346

Machines themselves, and *g.* by a clock *Tir.* 625
Then, only *g.* by the selfsame rule *Tir.* 871

GOVERNMENT.
For skill in *g.*, at length made king *T.* v 241
I praise a school as Pope a *g. Tir.* 506

GOVERNOR.
The *G.* of all, himself to all *T.* vi 459

GOWN.
With the same ease that man puts on his *g. ? P.E.* 103
Send your dishonoured *g.* to Monmouth Street *P.E.* 121
Worn as a cloak, and hardly hides, a *g. T.* i 550
Till *g.* at length are found mere masquerade *T.* ii 748

GRACE.
Gives even Affliction a *g. A.S.* 55
And gave them a *g.* so divine *C.* 18
Chief *g.* below, and all in all above *Ch.* 4
Gives difficulty all the *g.* of ease *Ch.* 110
From the same centre of enlightening *g. Ch.* 364 [395
The soul, whose sight all-quickening *g.* renews *Ch.*
And would the *g.* I mean to recommend *Ch.* 486
And still enlarged as she receives the *g. Ch.* 597
Thus have I sought to *g.* a serious lay *Ch.* 628
True Modesty is a discerning *g. Con.* 373
Weak and imperfect in all *g.* beside *Con.* 758
And all her censures of the work of *g. Con.* 784
G. him again with long forgotten arts *Con.* 839
(Two nymphs adorned with every *g. D.W.* 7
In pity to the souls his *G.* designed *E.* i 23
These flowing from the fount of *g.* above *E.* ii 29
And had the *g.* in scenes of peace to show *Ex.* 79
The *g.* of a life that wins the skies *Ex.* 112
Had *g.* for other's sins, but none for theirs *Ex.* 134
When Obstinacy once has conquered *G.—Ex.* 152
But *G.* abused brings forth the foulest deeds *Ex.* 213
Might shine in fable, and *g.* idle themes *Ex.* 233
Pleasure o'ervalued, and his *g.* despised *Ex.* 252
And made the symbols of atoning *g. Ex.* 378
And *g.* thy figure with a soldier's pride *Ex.* 487
Peculiar is the *g.* by thee possessed *Ex.* 580
Those holy men, so full of truth and *g. Ex.* 618
What virtue, or what mental *g. F.* 1
The *g.* and the beauties *F.* 45
Renewed desire would *g.* with other speech *H.* 35
Is handmaid to the purposes of *g. H.* 146
To any throne, except the throne of *g. H.* 239
Far other paintings *g.* the chamber now *H.* 262
" Adieu to all morality, if *G.—H.* 359
Here see the encouragement *G.* gives to vice *H.* 495
And *g.* be *g.* indeed, and life a gift *H.* 531
And reconcile his lusts with saving *g. H.* 605
Pretends a zeal for godliness and *g. H.* 661
Good breeding and good sense gave all a *g. H.* 683
Those hangings with their worn-out *g. M.F.* 5
But lives when that exterior *g. M.F.* 53
And earned too late, it wants the *g. Mor.* 37
The gifts of Nature and of *G.—N.G.* 34
With equal *g.* below *O.* i. 28
May find a Muse to *g.* it with a song) *P.E.* 2 [*P.E.* 105
Charm'd by the sounds—Your Reverence, or your *G.*
The *G.* too, while Virtue at their shrine *P.E.* 337
Returning, he proclaims by many a *g. P.E.* 413
And Wisdom falls before exterior *g. P.E.* 418
And *g.* his action ere the curtain fall *R.* 34
Truth, wisdom, *g.*, and peace, like that above *R.* 163
But does a mischief while she lends a *g. R.* 233
Borrowing a beauty from the works of *g. R.* 358
A man whom marks of condescending *g. R.* 445
Flies to the levee, and, received with *g. R.* 479
But not to manage leisure with a *g. R.* 622
G. leads the right way ; if you choose the wrong *T.* 17

No meretricious g. to beguile T. 23
I am all splendour, dignity, and g.! T. 65
That g. was Cowper's—his, confessed by all T. 119
Though not a g. appears on strictest search T. 151
Reports a message with a pleasing g. T. 205
G. in his mien, and glory in his eyes T. 407
G. undeserved, yet surely not for all T. 484
Derived from the same source of light and g. T. 533
Some youthful g. that age would gladly keep T. i. 132
Displaying, on its varied side, the g. T. i 172
A messenger of g. to guilty men T. ii 407   [538
G., knowledge, comfort—an unfathomed store? T. ii
Unless by Heaven's peculiar g., escape T. ii 632
All catch the frenzy, downward from her G. T. ii 647
Suffice to give the marshalled ranks the g. T. iii 604
But elegance, chief g. the garden shows T. iii 638
The strength they borrow with the g. they lend T.iii669
To g. the full pavilion. His design T. iii 716
Hill wants a g., the loveliest it could show T. iii 782
To serve his country. Ministerial g. T. iii 795
Which some may practise with politer g. T. iv 494
Whom once her virgin modesty and g. T. iv 535
His hat, or his plumed helmet, with a g. T. iv 643
Of nightshade, or valerian, g. the well T. iv 757
And with poetic trappings g. thy prose T. v 679
G. makes the slave a freeman. 'Tis a change T. v 688
And seeking g. to improve the prize they hold T. vi 55
With which kind nature g. every scene T. vi 342
Gentle, and affable, and full of g. T. vi 500
By medicine well applied, but without g. T. vi 522
By our capacity of g. divine T. vi 602   [853
Nor smooth Good-breeding (supplemental g.) T. vi
"Discernment, Eloquence and G. Th. 9
Strength joined with beauty, dignity with g. Tir. 2
That g. and Nature have to wage through life Tir. 30
Let erudition g. him, or not g. Tir 387   [Tir. 397
Your Lordship, and your G.! what school can teach
Still keeps a seat or two for worth and g. Tir. 433
New-fangled sentiment, the boasted g. Tir. 539
Though thou hadst never g. enough to prove Tir. 741
Sustain'd with so much g. and art Trans. iv 35
Then g. the bony phantom in their stead T.T. 43
And the sixth Edward's, g. the historic page T.T. 106
If smooth Dissimulation, skilled to g. T.T. 129
His speech, his form, his action full of g. T.T. 346
Patterns of every virtue, every g. T.T. 373
Without the smile, the sweetness or the g. T.T. 615
Gave Virtue and Morality a g. T.T. 648   [745
Stamped on the well-bound quarto g. the shelf T.T.
Sound sense, intrepid spirit, manly g. V. 12
'Tis g., 'tis bounty, and it calls for praise V. 87

GRACED.

And g. with all her gifts the favourite child A.T. 10
And only missed the flowers that g. their side A.T. 75
Love g. the theme, and harmony the song A.T. 198
And g. with all Philosophy can add Ch. 342
And g. with clear credentials from above Ex. 188
That g. his lettered store M. i. 8
A just deportment, manners g. with ease P.E. 421
As he that slumbers in pavilions g. R. 509   [557
G. with such wisdom, how would beauty shine! R.
G. with a sword, and worthier of a fan T. i 771
G. caterer and dry nurse of the church! T. ii 371
He g. a college, in which order yet T. ii 785 [vi 561
(Though g. with polished manners and fine sense T.
Scenes rarely g. with rural manners now T. iv 557
They dream of little Charles or William g. Tir. 360
His galleries with the works of art well g. T.T. 162
Was g. with many an undulating light T.T. 573
Thus g., the man asserts a poet's name T.T. 714
G. with the name of a long absent friend V. 40
Seem g. with a livelier hue W.N. 22

GRACEFUL.

G. and useful all she does Comp. ii 7
Bowed at the close with all his g. airs Con. 73
How airy and how light the g. arch T. i 341
Shall put their g. foliage on again T. vi 144
Hence, in a Roman mouth, the g. named T.T. 500

GRACEFULLY.

Then, with an air most g. performed T. ii 447
And curling tendrils, g. disposed T. iv 154
Lamps g. disposed, and of all hues T. v 149
Can wear it e'en as g. as she T. vi 986

GRACING.

And, Truth and Wisdom g. all he said Con. 526
The veteran shows, and g. a grey beard T. i 406

GRACIOUS.

His g. attributes, and prove the share H. 139
And scorn, for its own sake, the g. way T. 37
Why falls the Gospel like a g. dew? T. 180
The g. shower, unlimited and free T. 511
But like his purpose, g., kind, and sweet T. vi 504
Kind Providence attends with g. aid T.T. 249

GRACIOUSLY.

Complied with, and were g. dismissed Ex. 541

GRADUATED.

Proceeding soon a g. dunce T. ii 739
Taints downward all the g. scale T. iv 585

GRAIN.

The g., or herb, or plant. that each demands R. 788
The scattered g., and thievishly resolved T. v 67
Of voided pulse or half-digested g. T. v 95
Then what were left of roughness in the g. T. v 480
In g. as countless as the sea-side sands T. vi 245

GRAINED.

Rough elm, or smooth g. ash, or glossy beech R. 230

GRANBY.

But G. was, meant truly what he said R. 598

GRAND.

Is made subservient to the g. design Con. 897
See Mercy's g. apocalypse displayed! H. 448
G. Metropolitan of all the tribe P.E. 186
Swallow the two g. nostrums they dispense P.E. 594
No g. inquisitor could worse invent T. 103
The g. retreat from injuries impressed T. i 280
As God's ambassador, the g. concerns T. ii 464
Views him in all; ascribes to the g. cause T. iii 226
The g. effect; acknowledges with joy T. iii 227
Or do we grind her still? The g. debate T. iv 30
Are g., no doubt, and worthy of the Word T. v 555
Be most sublimely good, verbosely g. T. v 678
More g. than it produces year by year T. vi 120
The g. transition, that there lives and works T. vi 184
Or what he views of beautiful or g. T. vi 249

GRANDEUR.

Riches have wings, and g. is a dream T. iii 263
With modest g. in thy purple zone T. iv 257
For g. or for use. Long wavy wreaths T. v 158
On human g. and the courts of kings T. v 172
But borrows all its g. from the soul Tir. 10
But thou, it seems (what cannot g. do V. 43
Of modest g. and declension, thence Y.O. 89
Of g. that ensures respect 1789, 69

GRANDMAMMAS.

Your prudent g., ye modern belles R. 515

GRANT.

But g. the plea, and let it stand for just Ch. 196

No!—there I g. the privilege I claim *Con* 98
I g. it dangerous, and approve your fear *Con.* 653
" Oh ! g., kind Heaven to me *Miss* — 66
G. me discernment, and I g. it you *P.E.* 535
Heaven g. us no such future sight *Q.V.* 79
Oh ! g. a poet leave to recommend *R.* 541
Though one, I g. it, in the generous breast *R.* 721
But g. me still a friend in my retreat *R.* 741
G. her indebted to what zealots call *T.* 483
To wait the close of all ? But g. her end *T.* ii 65
G. it :—I still must envy them an age *T.* iv 529
Or covet more than freemen choose to g. *T.* v 340
And tremble at vain dreams? Heaven g. I may! *T.* v 492
Which monarchs cannot g., nor all the powers *T.* v 540
The spur is powerful, and I g. its force *Tir.* 482
I g. that men continuing what they are *T.T.* 9
I g. the sarcasm is too severe *T.T.* 103
Sing where you please; in such a cause I g. *T.T.* 298
But if he g. a friend, that boon possessed *V.* 91

GRANTED.
'Tis g., and no plainer truth appears *P.E.* 353

GRAPE.
As Time improves the g.'s authentic juice *Con.* 643
'Tis not alone the g.'s enticing juice *P.E.* 271

GRASP.
Now stoops upon it, and now g. the prey *P.E.* 334
G. seeming Happiness, and find it Pain *R.* 756
In tempests; quits his g. upon the winds *T.* ii 181
He climbs, he pants, he g. them ! At his heels *T.* iv 60
A comprehensive faculty that g. *T.* v 251

GRASPED.   [125
So swarmed the Sabine youth, and g. the shield *A.T.*
He g. the mane with both his hands *J.G.* 91
Shines as it runs, but g. at, slips away *P.E.* 22

GRASPING.
But feels while g. at his faded joys *R.* 473

GRASS.
Whose bridle, while he cropped the g. below *A.T.* 173
Thick overspread with moss and silky g. *N.A.* 2
And now in the g. behold they are laid *P.F.* 7
In matted g., that with a livelier green *T.* 195
All flesh is g., and all its glory fades *T.* iii 261
And coarser g., upspearing o'er the rest *T.* v 23
Of treeship—first a seedling hid in g. *Y.O.* 61

GRASSHOPPERS.
As g., as dust, a drop, a dream ? *Ex.* 345
Happiest g. that are *Trans.* iii 20
While the poor g. must chirp below *T.T.* 577

GRASSY.
Of g. swarth, close cropped by nibbling sheep *T.* i 110

GRATE.
Soon passed the wiry g. *G.* 12
How does it g. upon his thankless ear *T.* 465
Well latticed—but the g. alas ! *T.B.* 25

GRATEFUL.
Nor g. eglantine regales the smell *H.* 471
That they proceeded from a g. heart *T.* 580
Cheer all their seasons with a g. smile *T.* i 622
So g. to the palate, and when rare *T.* iii 447
Here also g. mixture of well matched *T.* iii 633
From which at least a g. few derive *T.* vi 965
But wholesome, well digested; g. some *T.* vi 1014

GRATIFIED.
Are g. with mischief, and who spoil *T.* v 191

GRATIFY.
Too often rails to g. his spleen *Ch.* 500
To g. a fretful passion *M.F.* 35
And g. no curious eyes *Q.V.* 39
" To g. the hunger of his wish *T.* v 637
To g. the frenzy of his wrath *T.* vi 387
Is but to g. an itching ear *T.* vi 643
Merely to g. so blind a guide ? *Tir.* 864

GRATITUDE.
While G. and Love made service sweet *Ch.* 233
Hour after hour, thy g. and love *Ex.* 561
That g. and temperance in our use *Ex.* 676
To take with g. what heaven bestows *H.* 430
Till G. grew vocal in the praise *R.* 555
What fear he feels his g. inspires *T.* 190
Has he a world of g. and love ? *T.* 208
Thine unsuspecting g. and love *T.* iii 348
Its g., and thanks him with its sweets *T.* iii 623
Exciting oft our g. and love *T.* iv 182
Can move or warp ; and g. for small *T.* vi 629
Either his g. shall hold him fast *Tir.* 893
Only by g. and glowing thought *T.T.* 587

GRATUITY.
A slight g. atones for all *T.* 288

GRATULATE.
To g. the new-created earth *T.* v 820

GRATULATIONS.
Angelic g. rend the skies *T.* 587
Of g. and delight, her King ? *T.* ii 84

GRAVE.   [29
So his lordship decreed, with a g. solemn tone *A.C.*
Thy pomp is in the g., thy glory laid *Ch.* 71
But slavery !—Virtue dreads it as her g. *Ch.* 163
And land some g. optician on the shore *Ch.* 384
Hearing a lawyer, g. in his address *Con.* 69
That he who dares, when she forbids, be g. *Con.* 475
G. without dulness, learned without pride *Con.* 609
As some g. gentleman in Terence says *E.* iii 6
For matters of more g. import *E.* iv 66
Must soon partake his g. *Ep.* ii 44
But, g. dissemblers! could not understand *Ex.* 159
Of all that g. apologists may write *Ex.* 383
'Tis g. Philosophy's absurdest dream *H.* 65
Perhaps a g. physician, gathering fees *H.* 203
Her g. concern, her kind suspicions, there *H.* 516
Dismissed with g., not haughty looks *Mrs. M* — 38
To save our life leap all into the g.! *N.A.* 108
For many a g. and learned clerk *P.* 31
You speak very fine, and you look very g. *P.A.* 29
Manly designs, and learning's g. pursuits *R.* 242
Seeming a sanctuary, proves a g. *R.* 736
A poet's cat, sedate and g. *R.C.* 1
Have found their home, the g. *St.* i 4
The g. admits no cure for guilt or sin *St.* ii 30
And the next opening g. may yawn for you *St.* ii 36
Soon the g. must be your home *St.* iv 15
Think on the g. where He was laid *St.* v 35
Than some g. sinners upon English ground *T.* 292
With youthful smiles, descends towards the g. *T.* i 407
Or make his house his g.: nor so contend *T.* ii 147
Yet what can satire, whether g. or gay ? *T.* ii 315
I would express him simple, g., sincere *T.* ii 399 [368
That g. and learned clerks should need such aid *T.* ii
The rest are sober dreamers, g. and wise *T.* iii 137
And we that worship him, ignoble g. *T.* iii 265
If I survive thee, I will dig thy g. *T.* iii 349
Of our forefathers—a g., whiskered race *T.* iii 768
And spades, the emblem of untimely g. *T.* iv 219
Less dainty than becomes his g. outside *T.* iv 605
Like that which sends him to the dusty g. *T.* v 609

Of theological and *g*. import) *T*. v 662
" And hasting to a *g*., yet doomed to rise *T*. v 830
With melting airs, or martial, brisk or *g*. *T*. vi 3
Who form'd him from the dust, his future *g*. *T*. vi 349
Of such a gulf as he designed his *g*. *T*. vi 515
The next mere dust and ashes in the *g*. *Tir*. 60

GRAVED

And *g*. it on a gem and wore it next his heart *A.T.* 22

GRAVELLY.

My *g*. bounds, from self to human kind *F.A.* 20
Washed by the sea, or on the *g*. bank *T.* i 13

GRAVEN.

A deep memorial *g*. on their hearts *Con.* 514

GRAVER.

Once more I would adopt the *g*. style *Ch*. 489
A *g*. fact, enlisted on your side *Con.* 205
A *g*. coxcomb we may sometimes see *Con*. 295
And, like the *g*.'s memory, pass away *Con.* 552
Its brisker and its *g*. strains fall short *R*. 294
A jarring note. Themes of a *g*. tone *T.* iv 181
Was but the *g*. countenance of love *T*. vi 32

GRAVEST.

May teach the gayest, make the *g*. smile *Tir*. 138

GRAVING.

The wall on which we tried our *g*. skill *Tir*. 300

GRAVITATION.

And sordid *g*. of his powers *T*. v 588

GRAVITY.

"No need," he cries, " of *g*., stuffed out *H*. 105
If apostolic *g*. be free *P.E*. 146
In spite of *g*. and sage remark *T*. v 12
And with a *g*. beyond the size *T*. vi 654
Boys as ye were, the *g*. of men *Tir*. 272

GRAZE.

He finds the pasture where his fellows *g*. *Ch*. 179
Like theirs that cleave the flood or *g*. the field *Con.* 428
And turned into the park or mead to *g*. *R*. 627 [785
Brutes *g*. the mountain-top, with faces prone *T.* v
G. with the fearless flocks ; all bask at noon *T*. vi 774

GRAZED. [*N.A.* 37

Sheep *g*. the field ; some with soft bosom pressed
The sheep recumbent, and the sheep that *g*. *N.A.* 47
With verdure not unprofitable, *g*. *T*. iv 317
That *g*. it stood beneath that ample cope *Y.O.* 54

GREASED.

If Tom be sober, and the wheels well *g*. *P.E*. 439

GREAT. [*A.C*. 6

With a *g*. deal of skill, and a wig full of learning
Guns, halberts, swords and pistols, *g*. and small *Ch*.551
A *g*. retailer of this curious ware *Con*. 229
In musings worthy of the *g*. event *Con*. 510
That *g*. defect would cost him, not alone *Con.* 763
G. changes and new manners have occurred *Con.* 803
As needs they must, from *g*. to small ! *E*. i. 80
The *g*. and small but rarely meet *F*. 115
Honesty shines with *g*. advantage there *H*. 402
Their *g*. inspirer call *J.P*. 30
The happiest of the *g*. *M.B*. 16
'Tis woven in the world's *g*. plan *Miss* — 45
The *g*., the gay, shall they partake *O*. ii 13
His *g*. improvement and new lights he draws *P.E*.402
At least are friendly to the *g*. pursuit *R*. 146
Thus laden, dream that they are rich and *g*. *R*.155
Be thou the *g*. inspirer of my strains *R*. 202
Cause to provide for a *g*. future day *R*. 652
All such as manly and *g*. souls produce *R*. 699
The man who dreams himself so *g*. *R.C*. 111
Envy, ye *g*., the dull unlettered small *T*. 375

When the *g*. Sovereign would his will express *T*. 551
He, not unlike the *g*. ones of mankind *T*. i 274
G. skill have they in palmistry, and more *T*. i 570
And Wolfe's *g*. name compatriot with his own *T*. ii 238
How *g*. the danger of disturbing her *T*. iii 35
G. contest follows, and much learned dust *T*. iii 161
Of oracles like these ? *G*. pity too *T*. iii 169 [185
G. crimes alarm the Conscience, but it sleeps *T*. iii
Of the *g*. Babel, and not feel the crowd *T*. iv 90
Runs the *g*. circuit, and is still at home *T*. iv 119
Yet show that thou hast mercy, which the *g. T.* iv 371
The *g*. proficiency he made abroad *T*. iv 654
But slighted as it is, and by the *g*. *T*. iv 691
Some must be *g*. *G*. offices will have *T*. iv 788
G. talents : and God gives to every man *T*. iv 789
When Babel was confounded, and the *g*. *T*. v 193
G. purposes with ease, that turns and wields *T*. v 252
The *g*. artificer of all that moves *T*. vi 207 [*T*. v 177
G. princes have *g*. playthings. Some have played
Then let the supercilious *g*. confess *T*. vi 967
The wisdom of *g*. nations, now no more *Tir*. 16 [341
G. schools suit best the sturdy and the rough *Tir*.
The *g*. indeed, by titles, riches, birth *Tir*. 346
Deems his reward too *g*. if he prevail *Tir*. 479
G. schools rejected then, as those that swell *Tir*. 501
The *g*. and small deserve one common blame *Tir*. 515
To improve this diet, at no *g*. expense *Tir*. 628
G. cause occurs to save him from a band *Tir*. 696
Deem it of no *g*. moment whose or where *Tir*. 784
Securely placed between the small and *g*. *Tir*. 808
G. titles, offices, and trusts disgraced *Tir*. 816
See *g*. commanders making war a trade *Tir*. 821
G. lawyers, lawyers without study made *Tir*. 822
A *g*. frequenter of the church *Tran*. ii 3
He sees that this *g*. roundabout *Tran*. ii 25
The little and the *g*. *Trans*. *H*. 9
What follows next, let cities of *g*. name *T.T*. 430
Or, having whelped a prologue with *g*. pains *T.T*.536
Be *g*., be feared, be envied, be admired *V*. 16
Whoever undertakes a friend's *g*. part *V*. 59
The *g*. and little of thy lot, thy growth *Y.O*. 87

GREATER.

And raised thyself, a *g*., in their stead ? *Ex*. 367

GREATEST.

The *g*. oft originate) could Chance *T*. ii 168

GREATLY.

I pity them *g*., but I must be mum *P.A*. 5
So God has *g*. purposed; who would else *T*. vi 820

GRECIAN.

Philosophy indeed on *G*. eyes *Ex*. 227
And these the *G*., in ennobling strains *T*. iii 454

GREECE.

Not the proud monuments of *G*. or Rome *Ch*. 302
There he was copious as old *G*. or Rome *Con*. 621
To Gaul, to *G*., and into Noah's ark *R*. 694
Of Light Divine. But Egypt, *G*., and Rome *T*. ii 500
He sunk in *G*., in Italy he rose *T.T*. 563
Anacreon, Horace, played in *G*. and Rome *T.T*.608

GREEDY.

Noisome, and ever *g*. to exhaust *T*. iii 671

GREEK.

The little *G*. look trembling at the scales *H*. 195
Leuconomus (beneath well sounding *G*.—*H*. 554
We give some Latin, and a smatch of *G*.—*P.E*. 365
If stubborn *G*. refuse to be his friend *P.E*. 498
Small skill in Latin, and still less in *G*.— *Tir*. 385
'Tis not enough that *G*. or Roman page *Tir*. 605

GREEN.

And phillyrea of a golden *g*. *A.T*. 83

Storms but enliven its unfading g. *Ch.* 576
No longer fruitful, and no longer g. *Con.* 52 [626
When some g. heads, as void of wit as thought *Con.*
(As Irish bogs are always g.) *F.* 122 [46
The yellow tilth, g. meads, rocks, rising grounds *H.*
The rose or lily appears blue or g. *H.* 72
Refreshes, where it winds, the faded g. *J.T.* 39
And teach her, unexperienced yet and g. *P.E.* 317
From every window, and the fields are g. *R.* 498 [571
And Cobham's groves, and Windsor's g. retreats *R.*
G. as the bay tree, ever g. *St.* i 17 [*R.* 421
G. balks and furrowed lands, the stream that spreads
His radiant glories, azure, g., and gold *T.* 61
To the close copse, or far sequestered g. *T.* 69
In matted grass, that with a livelier g. *T.* 195
Induced a splendid cover, g. and blue *T.* i 32
'Tis perched upon the g. hill top, but close *T.* i 222
Our foot half sunk in hillocks g. and soft *T.* i 272
Of deeper g. the elm; and deeper still *T.* i 312
Now g., now tawny, and ere autumn yet *T.* i 319
To gaze at Nature in her g. array *T.* i 449 [525
Strained through the friendly mats a vivid g. *T.* iii
A flowery island, from the dark g. lawn *T.* iii 630
A variegated show; the meadows g. *T.* iv 312
Gladly the thickening mantle; and the g. *T.* iv 330
The glimpse of a g. pasture, how they cheer *T.* iv 751
That Nature lives; that sight-refreshing g. *T.* iv 759
With as much ease as Samson his g. withes *T.* v 737
" From the g. wave emerging, darts an eye *T.* v 835
The deep dark g. of whose unvarnish'd leaf *T.* vi 174
To the g. blade that twinkles in the sun *T.* vi 251
O'er the g. summit of the rocks, whose base *T.* vi 496

GREEN-COATED.

To raise the prickly and g. gourd *T.* iii 446

GREENHOUSE.

The g. is my summer seat *F.B.* 1
Who loves a garden, loves a g. too *T.* iii 566

GREENSWARD.

If chance at length he find a g. smooth *T.* iii 7

GREETED.

He soothed with gifts, and g. with a smile *Ch.* 29

GREETS.

G. with three cheers exulting. At his waist *T.* i 523

GREW.

Propitious to his fond intent there g. *A.T.* 80
Till both g. vexed and tired *A Tale* 22
And where unsightly and rank thistles g. *H.* 526
The flock g. calm again, and I, the road *N.A.* 127
The plant he meant g. not far off *P.* 17 [*P.F.* 6
Of my favourite field, and the bank where they g.
G. quarrelsome, and pecked each other *P.T.* 57
Soon watery g. her eyes and dim *Q.V.* 53
Till Gratitude g. vocal in the praise *R.* 555 [ii 713
Close to his side that pleased him. Learning g. *T.*
G. stern, and darted a severe rebuke *T.* ii 720
G. tremulous, and moved derision more *T.* ii 729
G. rusty by disuse; and massy gates *T.* ii 746 [vi 533
His rage g. cool; and pleased perhaps to have earned *T.*
On the flourishing bush where it g. *The Rose* 8 [129
And some memorial none where once they g. *Y.O.*

GREY.

Drew the g. curtain of the fading west *Ch.* 263 [6
Thus, while g. evening lulled the wind and called *F.A.*
And just when evening turns the blue vault g. *H.* 79
G. dawn appears; the sportsman and his train *P.E.* 82
Beneath your shades your g. possessor hide *R.* 368
The evening g. again ensued *R.C.* 70 [302
Alike yet various. Here the g. smooth trunks *T.* i
And of a wannish g.; the willow such *T.* i 309
The veteran shows, and gracing a g. beard *T.* i 406
There we grow early g. but never wise *T.* ii 633
That mingles all my brown with sober g. *Tir.* 144
Thy child shall show respect to thy g. hairs *Tir.* 880

GREYBEARD.

Pronounced by g. a pernicious dream *Ex.* 114
G. corrupter of our listening youth *P.E.* 342

GREYHOUND.

Nor swifter g. follow *Ep.* ii 2

GRIEF.

Full of rage and full of g. *B.* 8
G. is itself a medicine, and bestowed *Ch.* 159
Has one that notices his silent g. *Ch.* 207
That g., sequestered from the public stage *Ch.* 305
A long immunity from g. and pain *Ex.* 82 [iii 37
His g. might prompt him with the speech he made *E.*
His g. the world of all her power disarms *H.* 704
Thee to deplore were g. misspent indeed *J.T.* 11
Thus g. itself has comforts dear *Miss* — 53
And while that face renews my filial g. *M.P.* 17
The looks and gestures of their g. and fears *N.A.* 67
O'erwhelmed at once with wonder, g., and joy *R.* 593
Despondence, self-deserted in her g. *R.* 757
No womanish or wailing g. has part *R.* 773
But tears of godly g. ne'er flow within *St.* ii 32
Feels herself happy amidst all her g. *T.* 456
Cold and yet cheerful: messenger of g. *T.* iv 13
To him indifferent whether g. or joy *T.* iv 15
Oh! share Maria's g. *T.B.* 3

GRIEVANCE.

To stroke the prickly g., and to hang *T.* v 329

GRIEVE.

A beam that aids, but never g. the sight *Con.* 600
To mortify and g. me *F.* 213
" G. not, my child, chase all thy fears away!" *M.P.* 6
G., but alarms me not. I mourn the pride *T.* iv 102
To astonish and to g. his gazing friends *T.* iv 655
Yet not to give offence or g. *Y.D.* 43 [1006
It shall not g. me, then, that once, when called *T.* vi

GRIEVED.

Although it g. him sore *J.G.* 54
Thy maidens g. themselves at my concern *M.P.* 36
The modest speaker is ashamed and g. *T.* iv 66

GRIM.

All the g. honours of his ghastly court *H.* 261

GRIMACE.

Prescribes the theme, the tone, and the g. *Con.* 464
And finds it a mere mask of sly g. *Con.* 744
With hollow form, and gesture, and g. *Ex.* 122

GRIMALKIN.

In old g.'s glaring eyes *E.* iv 44

GRIN.

And g. with wonder at the jar he makes *Con.* 902
These move the censure and illiberal g. *H.* 744
But show peculiar light, by many a g. *P.E.* 383
With mouths made only to g. wide and eat *R.* 309
To court a g., when you should woo a soul *T.* ii 467
Relaxed into a universal g. *T.* iv 204

GRIND.

Oppression, labouring hard to g. the poor *Ex.* 40
And g. his crown beneath her burning wheels! *H.* 652
He g. divinity of other days *T.* ii 362
Or do we g. her still? The grand debate *T.* iv 30

GRINDING.

Incessant, clinking hammers, g. wheels *T.* i 231

GRIPE.

Conjecture g. the victims in his paw *Ch.* 525

The charms of Nature! 'Tis the cruel *g. T.* iii 826
GRIPING.
And *g.* fists, and unrelenting frowns *Ex.* 513
GRIST.
The total *g.* unsifted, husks and all *T.* vi 108
GROAN.
But when unpacked your disappointment *g. Con.* 309
G. heavily along the distant road *Ex.* 58
"Where'er is heard a *g. Miss* — 88   [*g. P.A.* 3
What I hear of their hardships, their tortures, their
And tortures and *g.* will be multiplied still *P.A.* 12
And happiest he that *g.* beneath his weight *R.* 156
Will weep indeed, and heave a pitying *g. T.* 177
Of cheerful days, and nights without a *g. T.* i 366
The sighs and *g.* of miserable men! *T.* v 388
Earth *g.* beneath the burden of a war *T.* vi 392
The *g.* of Nature in this nether world *T.* vi 729
To echo sigh for sigh, and *g.* for *g. V.* 65
GROANED.
Bled, *g.*, and agonized, and died in vain *P.E.* 624
Job felt it, when he *g.* beneath the rod *R.* 303
Hark! universal Nature shook and *g. T.* 563
GROAT.
And *g.* per diem, if his patron frown *T.* iii 821
GROOM.
The noble beast judge otherwise, his *g. Con.* 414
Prefers his fellow *g.*, with much good sense *Con.* 417
If neither horse nor *g.* affect the squire *Con.* 419
Unmissed but by his dogs and by his *g. P.E.* 95
In foreign eyes!—be *g.*, and win the plate *T.* ii 280
The lackey, and the *g.*: the craftsman there *T.* iv 474
No spots contracted among *g.* below *Tir.* 685
Or throw them up to livery-nags and *g. Tir.* 901
GROSS.
The *g.* idolatry blind heathens teach *H.* 499
In *g.* and pampered cities, sloth, and lust *T.* i 687
And, charged with putrid verdure, breathe a *g. T.* ii 97
Like a *g.* fog Bœotian, rising fast *T.* iii 495
As this is *g.* and selfish! over which *T.* vi 837
Draws *g.* impurity, and likes it well *T.* vi 979
Or rather a *g.* compound, justly tried *Tir.* 466
GROSSER.
And when unstained with any *g.* crime *Con.* 634
That, while thy truths my *g.* thoughts refine *R.* 97
GROSSEST.
Of *g.* nature and of worst effects *T.* ii 689
GROTTO.
Here *g.* within *g.* safe defies *T.* v 117
GROTTO-WORK.
"You, in your *g.* enclosed *P.* 49
GROUND.
Soon her pride shall kiss the *g. B.* 19
Or building hospitals on English *g.*? *Ch.* 44
And honest Merit stands on slippery *g. Ch.* 284
A disputable point is no man's *g. Con.* 99
Sir! I believe it on that *g.* alone *Con.* 233
Go seek on Revelation s hallowed *g. Con.* 499
That, while in health, the *g.* of her support *Con.* 771
Where once intoxication pressed the *g. Con.* 808
Then lifts it gently from the *g. E.* iv 57
With feet too delicate to touch the *g. Ex.* 52
If either on forbidden *g. F.* 34
His manna from the *g.*, or starve and die *F.A.* 38
The yellow tilth, green meads, rocks, rising *g. H.* 46
Gethsemane! in thy dear, hallowed *g. H.* 297
I plant my foot upon this *g.* of trust *H.* 369

On Scripture *g.* are sure to disagree *H.* 599
With what materials, on what *g.*, you please *H.* 615
And shake with fury to the *g. J.P.* 11
Wild roses over furrowed *g. Mrs. M.* — 28
He spied far off, upon the *g. N.G.* 8
And pleased at heart, because on holy *g. T.* 232
Shakes it again, and faster, to the *g. T.* 241
Than some grave sinners upon English *g. T.* 292
In science, win one inch of heavenly *g. T.* 338
Grow frantic with her pangs, and bite the *g. T.* 444
There, lost behind a rising *g.*, the wood *T.* i 305
I would not have a slave to till my *g. T.* ii 29
That we might try the *g.* again, where once *T.* vi 26
He cannot skim the *g.* like summer birds *T.* vi 921
I snapped it, it fell to the *g. The Rose* 12
Comes heaviest to the *g. Trans. H.* 15
Where most they flourish upon English *g. T.T.* 337
He trod the very selfsame *g.* you tread *T.T.* 388
A skilful guide into poetic *g.*! *T.T.* 717
GROUNDED.
To pitch the ball into the *g.* hat *Tir.* 308
GROUNDLESS.
And all her love of God a *g.* claim *Con.* 781
GROUP.   [97
"There," said his guide, "the *g.* is full in view" *T.T.*
And gathering, at short notice, in one *g. T.* iv 136
GROVE.   [sounds *H.* 45
Banks clothed with flowers, *g.* filled with sprightly
Fear seized the trembling sex; in every *g. A.T.* 97
But *g.*, hills, and valleys diffuse *C.* 39   [368
Some through the *g.*, some down the sloping hills *Ch.*
To consecrate our few remaining *g. Con.* 826
Of eastern *g.*, and oceans floored with ice *Ex.* 16
The fragrant *g.*, the inestimable mine *H.* 177 [*H.* 741
Rocks, *g.*, and streams, must join him in his praise
No *g.* have ye; nor cheerful sound of bird *H.* 469
The blooming *g.* that girdled her around *Her.* 6
The *g.*, and the sequestered shed *O.* ii 17
Ere another such *g.* shall arise in its stead *P.F.* 16
In many an orchard, copse, and *g. P.T.* 13
Where mountain, river, forest, field, and *g. R.* 29
To them the deep recess of dusky *g. R.* 181
Nor gales that catch the scent of blooming *g. R.* 337
"Ye *g.*," (the statesman at his desk exclaims *R.* 365
And Cobham's *g.*, and Windsor's green retreats *R.* 571
G., heaths, and smoking villages, remote *T.* i 176
No tree in all the *g.* but has its charms *T.* i 307
To narrow bounds. The *G.* receives us next *T.* i 354
And least be threatened in the fields and *g.*? *T.* i 753
Our *g.* were planted to console at noon *T.* i 760
With all her vines; nor for Ausonia's *g. T.* ii 214
Who dream they have a taste for fields and *g. T.* iii 317
And *g.*, if unharmonious yet secure *T.* iii 734
Those naked acres to a sheltering *g. T.* iii 773
His favourite herb; while all the leafless *g. T.* iv 319
From courts dismiss'd, found shelter in the *g. T.* iv 519
To each some province, garden, field, or *g. T.* vi 237
Thy *g.* and lawns then witness'd! Every heart *T.* vi 372
Of the same *g.*, and drink one common stream *T.* vi 776
And Saba's spicy *g.*, pay tribute there *T.* vi 807
GROVELLING.
While yet thou wast a *g.*, puling chit *Ex.* 474
GROW.
G. fungous, and takes fire at every spark *Con.* 54
That good diffused may more abundant *g. Con.* 443
Though Time will wear us, and we must *g.* old *Con.* 629
The rich *g.* poor, the poor become purse-proud *H.* 18
G. drowsy as the clicking of a clock *H.* 104   [18
Can gold *g.* worthless that has stood the touch? *E.* iii

Shall g. the myrtle, and luxuriant yew" H. 527
Is Hope exotic? G. it not at home? H. 549
I see thee daily weaker g. M. 6
Did plants called sensitive g. there?" P. 22
To make them g. just where she chooses P. 24
Should droop and wither where they g. P. 59
So coin g. smooth, in traffic current passed P.E. 279
But we, as if good qualities would g. P.E. 363
Where all good qualities g. sick and die R. 738
G., by being oft expressed St. iv 23
Pride may be pampered while the flesh g. lean T. 117
It thrives in misery, and abundant g. T. 125 [414
G. frantic with her pangs, and bite the ground T.
Kills too the flowery weeds where'er they g. T. 461
G. fluid; and the fixed and rooted earth T. ii 100
G. wanton, and give proof to every eye T. ii 443
Since Heaven would g. weary of a world T. ii 583
There we g. early grey, but never wise T. ii 633
G. on the gamester's elbows, and the alert T. iii 761
The pattern g., the well depicted flower T. iv 151
G. conscious of a change, and likes it well T. iv 638
Conscious of impotence they soon g. drunk T. v 255
And Learning wiser g. without his books T. vi 87
But if Authority g. wanton, woe T.T. 226
G. freakish, and o'erleaping every mound T.T. 302
The reprobated race g. judgment-proof T.T. 459
The stock whereon it g. U. 16

GROWING.
That dread the encroachment of our g. streets R. 482
A g. dread of vengeance at his heels T. 258
And g. old in drawing nothing up!" T. iii 190
The g. seeds of wisdom; that suggest T. iii 302
The g. wonder takes a thousand shapes T. v 119
No nourishment to feed his g. mind Tir. 618

GROWL'D.
Or g. defiance in such angry sort T. vi 377

GROWN.
G. dim in trifling studies, blind he dies Ch. 358 [741
The world g. old, her deep discernment shows Con.
And he g. chaste that was the slave of lust Con. 810
The law g. clamorous, though silent long T. 261
Thus often Unbelief, g. sick of life T. 445
Society, g. weary of the load T. iv 498
Can even now when they are g. mature T. v 296
Patriots are g. too shrewd to be sincere T. v 495
(Himself g. sober in the vale of tears) T. vi 48
G. so familiar with her frequent guest T. vi 306
Of filial frankness lost, and love g. faint Tir. 588
When infamous Venality g. bold T.T. 416
And having known thee bearded and full g. V. 37
Though but a dream) art g. disdainful too V. 44

GROWTH.
Its fruit on earth, its g. above the skies Ch. 578
Their noxious g., starve every better seed R. 44
Straitening its g. by such a strict embrace R. 234
Pride has attained its most luxuriant g. T. 115
No soil like poverty for g. divine T. 363
Pride, of a g. superior to the rest T. 475
" Is virtue then, unless of Christian g. T. 515
The g. of what is excellent, so hard T. i 84
Of ancient g., make music not unlike T. i 185
With foliage of such dark redundant g. T. i 226
Diversified with trees of every g. T. i 301
Binds all his faculties, forbids all g. T. i 613
And succulent, that feeds its giant g. T. iii 418 [529
And interdicts its g. Thence straight succeed T. iii
Large g. of what may seem the sparkling trees T. v 112
And of an humbler g., the other tall T. vi 152
To such gigantic and enormous g. T. vi 382
If unrestrained, into luxuriant g. T. vi 593

Else of a mannish g., and five in ten Tir. 208
Of the mere schoolboy's lean and tardy g. Tir. 657
The g. that Nature meant she should attain T.T. 233
To the delicate g. of our isle W.N. 2
But Fate thy g. decreed; autumnal rains Y.O. 23
And, all the elements thy puny g. Y.O. 38
The great and little of thy lot, thy g. Y.O. 87

GRUB.
As little mercy as the g. and worms? Con. 230 [90
Where neither g., nor root, nor earth-nut now T. v

GRUDGE.
G. not, ye rich, (since Luxury must have T. iii 544
G. not the cost. Ye little know the cares T. iii 547
And reaped their plenty without g. or strife T. v 203

GRUDGING.
From g. hands; but other boast have none T. iv 404

GRUDGINGLY.
Trouble is g. and hardly brooked Ch. 218

GRUMBLE.
And you might g., crony mine E. iv 25

GUARD.
" But g. thee well, expect no feigned attack A.T. 189
"And g. behind the sorceress at thy back!" A.T. 190
Remember, if He g. thee and secure Ex. 700
While all his purposes and steps to g. P.E. 41
And g. it with a sanction as severe T. 553
The most important and effectual g. T. ii 335
Devises, while he g. his tender trust T. iii 561
Nor does the boarded hovel better g. T. iv 443
To invade another's rights, or g. their own T. iv 560
To administer, to g., to adorn the state T. v 342
To g. them, and to immortalize her trust T. v 711
And Equity: not jealous more to g. T. vi 850
Keep Vice restrained behind a double g. T.T. 66
G. what you say; the patriotic tribe T.T. 83
If g., mechanically formed in ranks T.T. 135
G. well what Arts and Industry have won T.T. 230
To g. the Peace that Riot would disturb T.T. 315
Ye patriots, g. it with a miser's care T.T. 335
No—g. him better. Is he not thine own Tir. 873
But, if thou g. its sacred chambers sure Tir. 891

GUARDED.
Its head as g. as its base is sure Con. 556
Had sought to crush them, g. as they were Ex. 205
Is kept and g. as a sacred thing T. v 304

GUARDIAN.
She speaks of Him, her author, g., friend Ch. 399
And constituted g. of his cause Ex. 200
Yet blessed the g. care that kept M. ii 7
Whatever parents, g., schools, intend P.E. 424
And Justice, g. of the dread command T. 277

GUDGEONS. [183
Minnows and g. gorge the unwholesome food P.E.

GUERDON.
Should be the g. of a noble deed Ch. 293

GUESS.
To g. and spell what it contains E. i 52
Or g., with a prophetic power E. i 71
Or lively fancy g. Miss — 104

GUESSED.
Yet, by his ear directed, g. R.C. 83 [447
Whose scent and hues are rather g. than known Tir.

GUEST.
The new acquaintance soon became a g. Con. 531
But g. that sought it in the appointed One H. 307

O welcome g., though unexpected here! M.P. 12
With which the fieldfare, wintry g., is fed N.A. 20
Come, peace of mind, delightful g.! O. ii 1
To be a g. with them? O. ii 18 [P.E.165
When the glad soul is made Heaven's welcome g.
Man, Nature's g. by invitation sweet P.E. 209
Is but a transient g., newly arrived T. iii 750
Grown so familiar with her frequent g. T. vi 306
Nor heed what g. there enter and abide Tir. 888
Inoffensive, welcome g.! Trans. iii 10

GUIDE.

She g. the finger o'er the dancing keys Ch. 109
He feels his need of an unerring g. Ch. 346
Philosophy, without his heavenly g. Ch. 375
And let them g. you to a decent end Con. 220
Wherever chance, caprice, or fancy g. Con. 794
That g. and governs our affections E. i 35
Creates, gives birth to, g., consummates all Ex. 315
Unless a zeal for virtue g. the blow Ex. 437
Makes Justice still the g. of his career Ex. 715
To g. our use of it, is all in all H. 432
Which served my weak thought for a g. M.D. 44
" True," answered an angelic g. Mor. 39
Might be supposed to clamour for a g. N.A. 98
(Try the criterion, 'tis a faithful g.) P.E. 514
First put it out, then take it for a g. P.E. 559
Instruct me, g. me to that heavenly day R. 95
Thy genuine charms, and g. an artless hand R. 204
The g. to pleasures which can never cease S. ii 14
He that would win the race, must g. his horse T. 13
That g. the Christian in his swifter race T. 534
Consulted and obeyed, to g. his steps T. v 674
" Ordained to g. the embodied spirit home T. v 840
A skilful g. into poetic ground! T.T. 717 [97
" There," said his g., " the group is full in view" T.T.
G. the decision of a doubtful choice Tir. 34
And g. the progress of the soul to God Tir. 146
Merely to gratify so blind a g.? Tir. 864
To modern times, with Truth to g. 1789, 11

GUIDED.

With nice incision of her g. steel T. i 708

GUIDING.

So may your g. angel give Miss — 95

GUIDO.

The difference of a G. from a daub T. vi 285

GUILE.

Where covert g. and artifice abound Ch. 285
The clown, the child of nature, without g. T. iv 623

GUILT.

Deep in ruin as in g. B. 16
To bind the lawless, and to punish g. Ch. 281
With all the g. of such unnatural war Con. 188
The grave admits no cure for g. or sin St. ii 30
Her tale of g. renews St. v 22 [876
Gods such as g. makes welcome; gods that sleep T. v
Stand chargeable with g., and to the shafts T. ii 155
Or stained with g., beneficent, approved T. vi 998
Preserved from g. by salutary fears Tir. 111
On selfish principles, is shame and g. T.T. 2

GUILTIER.

Far g. England! lest he spare not thee T. ii 160

GUILTIEST.

" The g. still are ever least ashamed A.T. 188

GUILTLESS.

Nor g. of corrupting other men R. 382
G. of pampered appetite obscene) T. i 104
Admits me to a share: the g. eye T. i 333
Should seek the g. joys that I describe T. iii 698
Upon the g. passenger o'erthrown T. vi 424
And g. of offence, they range the air T. vi 575

GUILTY.

Too just to wink, or speak the g. clear" Ex. 256
He finds his fellow g. of a skin T. ii 12
A messenger of grace to g. men T. ii 407
And none than we more g. But where all T. ii 154
In g. splendour, shake the public ways T. iii 70
Cannot indeed to g. man restore T. iii 677
Or harms them there is g. of a wrong T. vi 578 [597
By which Heaven moves in pardoning g. man T. vi
Or g. soon relenting into tears Tir. 112
The g. and not g., both alike T.T. 102
Are but his rods to scourge a g. land T.T. 450

GUINEA.

Slides g. behind g. in his palm Ch. 474

GUISE.

Came, not expected in that humble g. Ex. 87
This more than monster in his proper g. H. 573
In merry g. he spoke J.G. 172

GULF.

Lethæan g. receive them as they fall B.B. 7
And whelmed in deeper g. than he Cast. 66
And in the g. of her Cornubian mines H. 458
Wide yawns a g. beside a ragged thorn N.A. 14
The g. of death triumphant passed St. iii 31
We pass a g. in which the willows dip T. i 268
And drown him in her dry and dusty g. T. ii 149
And wantons in the pebbly g. below T. v 103
Of such a g. as he designed his grave T. vi 515
Down to the g. from which is no return T.T. 465

GULP.

He does not swallow, but he g. it down Con. 340
And all thine embryo vastness, at a g. Y.O. 22

GULPHS.

He g. the windy diet, and ere long T. v 269

GUMS.

Her sweetest flowers, her aromatic g. T. ii 86

GUNS. [551

G., halberts, swords and pistols, great and small Ch.

GURTON.

Dame G. thus, and Hodge her son E. iv 39

GUST.

Such writers and such readers owe the g. P.E. 329
But swelled into a g.—who then, alas! T. ii 485
He drinks his simple beverage with a g. T.T. 240

GUY.

G. Earl of Warwick and fair Eleanore Con. 243

GUZZLING.

But knew no medium between g. beer R. 601
Of Indian fume, and g. deep, the boor T. iv 473

GYMNASTIC.

A form, not now g. as of yore T. ii 591

H.

HABIT.
With reverend tutor, clad in *h*. lay *P.E.* 371
H. are soon assumed, but when we strive *P.E.* 582
Inveterate *h*. choke the unfruitful heart *R.* 41
H. of close attention, thinking heads *R.* 705
And their inveterate *h*., all forbid *T.* i 490
Our *h*., costlier than Lucullus wore *T.* ii 596
They may confirm his *h*., rivet fast *T.* ii 767
Nor *h*. of luxurious city-life *T.* iv 745
Those *h*. of profuse and lewd expense *Tir.* 350
Of *h*., inclination, temper, taste *Tir.* 441
Such vicious *h*. as disgrace his name *Tir.* 531
In settled *h*. and decided taste *Tir.* 778

HABITATIONS.
Fixed their tyrants' *h*. *N.C.* 39

HABITUAL.
On the same cushion of *h*. sloth *T.* iv 598

HACKED. [*Tir.* 303
Though mangled, *h*., and hewed, not yet destroyed

HACKNEYS.
By public *h*. in the schooling trade *Tir.* 621

HACKNEYED.
H. in business, wearied at that oar *R.* 1
Is *h*. house unlackeyed; who, in haste *T.* ii 652
H; and worn to the last flimsy thread *T.T.* 727

HAGGARD.
And save me too from theirs whose *h*. eyes *T.* i 501

HAIL.
H., honoured land! a desert where *A Tale* 65
Though Wisdom *h*. them, heedless of her call *Ch.* 406
The man that *h*. you Tom or Jack *F.* 169
That *h*. the rising moon, have charms for me *T.* 206
He *h*. the clergy, and, defying shame *T.* ii 356
H., therefore, patroness of health and ease *T.* iv 780
Of multitudes unknown: *H*., rural life! *T.* iv 783
Skin-piercing volley, blossom-bruising *h*. *T.* v 141
H., Sternhold then; and, Hopkins, *h*.! Amen *T.T.* 760
And one of storms of *h*. *Y.D.* 54

HAIR.
The man that's strangled by a *h*. *A Fable* 35
Wide-elbowed, and wadded with *h*. *Gr.* 11
Will never look one *h*. the worse *M.F.* 24
Too rudely wanton with her *h*. *R.C.* 32
In shirt of *h*., and weeds of canvass dressed *T.* 81
And Katerfelto, with his *h*. on end *T.* iv 86
Thy scattered *h*. with sleet like ashes filled *T.* iv 121
And prink their *h*. with daisies, or to pick *T.* vi 303
Thy child shall show respect to thy gray *h*. *Tir.* 880

HAIR-BRAINED.
From every *h*. proselyte he makes *P.E.* 491

HAIR-BREADTH.
His *h*. 'scapes, and all his daring schemes *Tir.* 230

HALBERTS.
Guns, *h*., swords and pistols, great and small *Ch.* 551

HALCYONS.
Thus lovely *h*. dive into the main *T.T.* 566

HALE. [258
Immortal *H*.! for deep discernment praised *T.* iii

HALF.
Made *h*. their maids, sans ceremony, wives *A.T.* 128
And find submission more than *h*. a cure *Ch.* 158
He *h*. exhibits, and then drops the sum *Ch.* 478
Makes *h*. a sentence at a time enough *Con.* 246
And *h*. the night? fanatic and absurd! *Con.* 578
But *h*. a coat, and show his bosom bare *E.* iii 51
Can ne'er be deemed worth *h*. so much *E.* iv 29
The palace were but *h*. complete *F.* 166
All these are not *h*. that I owe *Gr.* 41
Till *h*. the world comes rattling at his door *H.* 77
To thrive in, an incumbrance ere *h*. spent *H.* 98
Yet *h*. mankind maintain a churlish strife *H.* 322
Spent *h*. the darkness, and snored out the rest *H.* 510
And bore the pelting scorn of *h*. an age *H.* 557
His noonday beams were never *h*. so bright *H.* 737
Time has but *h*. succeeded in his theft *M.P.* 120
And prove their owner *h*. divine" *P.* 64
Thus having wasted *h*. the day *P.B.* 11
But being cankered now, and *h*. worn out *P.E.* 393
Till *h*. mankind were like himself possessed *P.E.* 471
And therefore prints, himself but *h*. deceived *P.E.* 492
And hate the tumult *h*. the world enjoys *R.* 176
Or *h*. so clear, as in the rural scene *R.* 456
Of *h*. the toils they must encounter there *R.* 610
H. open in the topmost chest *R.C.* 40
His ship *h*. foundered, and his compass lost *T.* 2
She, *h*. an angel in her own account *T.* 149
She, never heard of *h*. a mile from home *T.* 334
Our foot *h*. sunk in hillocks green and soft *T.* i 272
Till *h*. their beauties fade; the weary sight *T.* i 510
A prince with *h*. his people! Ancient towers *T.* ii 121
To insure a side-box station at *h*. price *T.* ii 624
Plunging, and *h*. despairing of escape *T.* iii 6
With the vain stir. I sum up *h*. mankind *T.* iii 130
And add two-thirds of the remaining *h*. *T.* iii 131
That seems *h*. quenched in the immense abyss *T.* iii 216
H. so refined or so sincere as ours *T.* iv 206 [545
His dainties, and the World's more numerous *h*. *T.* iii
For more than *h*. the tresses it sustains *T.* iv 544
The joy *h*. lost, because not sooner found *T.* iv 717
Screens them, and seem *h*. petrified to sleep *T.* v 28
And tail cropped short, *h*. lurcher and *h*. cur *T.* v 46
The feathered tribes domestic. *H*. on wing *T.* v 62
And *h*. on foot, they brush the fleecy flood *T.* v 63
Is cause of *h*. the poverty we feel *T.* vi 52 [vi 78
With slender notes, and more than *h*. suppressed *T.*
Thus, *h*. accomplished ere he yet begin *Tir.* 234
Claims more than *h*. the praise as his due share *Tir.* 528
Some *h*. a dozen, and some *h*. a score *Tir.* 695
With *h*. the chariots and sedans in town *Tir.* 748
H. a span, compared with thee *Trans.* iii 32
The deeds that men admire as *h*. divine *T.T.* 3
Proportioned well, *h*. muscle and *h*. bone *T.T.* 219
Religion weaves for her, and *h*. undressed *T.T.* 723
Take *h*. thy canvass in *Trans. H.* 36
Sifts *h*. the pleasures of short life away *Y.O.* 32
H. a millennium since the date of thine *Y.O.* 136

HALF-A-CROWN.
She pulled out *h*. *J.G.* 216

HALF-DIGESTED.
Of voided pulse or *h*. grain *T.* v 95

HALF-EATEN.
Lodged on the shelf, *h*. without sauce *T.* iv 394

HALF-SHUT. [352
With *h*. eyes, and puckered cheeks, and teeth *T.* iv

HALF-WITHERED.
A girdle of *h.* shrubs he shows *T.* i 524

HALL.
Even till his spacious *h.* would hold no more *H.* 309
The snug, close party, or the splendid *h. P.E.* 176
And such in ancient *h.* and mansions drear *T.* i 24
In colleges and *h.*, in ancient days *T.* ii 699
So colleges and *h.* neglected much *T.* ii 731

HALLOO.
Nor ear heard huntsman's *h. Ep.* ii 4

HALLOWED.
Go seek on Revelation's *h.* ground *Con.* 499
Bad men, profaning friendship's *h.* name *Con.* 683
Or his, who touched their hearts with *h.* fires ? *Ex.* 659
Gethsemane ! in thy dear, *h.* ground *H.* 297
To hear plain truth at Judah's *h.* gate *H.* 763
So 'twas a *h.* time : decorum reign'd *T.* vi 691
And every *h.* Druid was a bard *T.T.* 503
The *h.* bench from absolute contempt *Tir.* 431

HALT.
Though *h.*, and weary of the path they tread *T.* i 471

HALTING.
Old Winter, *h.* o'er the mead *N.* 13
H. on crutches of unequal size *P.E.* 560

HAMILTON.
And many a tomb, like *H.'s* aloud *Ep.* i 9

HAMLET.
Village, or *h.*, of this merry land *T.* iv 467
Or wrap himself in *H.'s* inky cloak *T.* vi 675

HAMMER.
How I shall *h.* out a letter *E.* iv 34
Incessant, clinking *h.*, grinding wheels *T.* i 231
No sound of *h.* or of saw was there *T.* v 145
Oft as the price-deciding *h.* falls *T.* vi 291

HAMMOCK.
Slips to his *h.*, and forgets the blast *R.* 436

HAMPDENS.
For which our *H.* and our Sidneys bled *T.* v 486

HAND.
An arbour near at *h.* of thickest yew *A.T.* 81
The trumpet now spoke Marmadan at *h. A.T.* 161
"To horse!" he cried," or by this good right *h. A.T.* 169
Drop one by one from Fame's neglecting *h. B.B.* 6
The *h.* that slew till it could slay no more *Ch.* 49
Art thou the God, the thunder of whose *h. Ch.* 75
But overcharges her capacious *h. Ch.* 100
Dagger in *h.*, steals close to your bedside *Ch.* 187
He from whose *h.* alone all power proceeds *Ch.* 208
Begone ! the whip and bell in that hard *h. Ch.* 212
Built by no mercenary vulgar *h. Ch.* 237
Heaven held his *h.*, the likeness must be true *Ch.* 434
To see a God stretch forth his human *h. Ch.* 581
To take his honour's orders, cap in *h. Con.* 416
Had not his *h.*, the mellow Maker's all-bestowing *h. Con.* 429
But let the wise and well instructed *h. Con.* 903
Escaped my eager *h. D.W.* 20
The *h.* of the Supremely Wise *E.* i 34
Though duly from my *h.* he took *Ep.* ii 9
Uplifted *h.*, that, at convenient times *Ex.* 147
That Sin let loose speaks Punishment at *h. Ex.* 160
Display with busy and laborious *h. Ex.* 163
Seized fast his *h.*, held out to set them free *Ex.* 219
Provoke the vengeance of his righteous *h. Ex.* 253
As if, like arches built with skilful *h. Ex.* 286
As a mere instrument in *h.* divine *Ex.* 319

Weighing them in the hollow of his *h. Ex.* 343
For ages safe beneath his sheltering *h. Ex.* 563
Till I, with slow and cautious *h. F.B.* 29
Seem the work of Mulciber's *h. Gr.* 40
Riches are passed away from *h.* to *h. H.* 11
And while she takes, as at a father's *h. H.* 157
Till the best tongue, or heaviest *h.*, prevails *H.* 196
A *h.* as liberal as the light of day *H.* 408
A plaything world, unworthy of his *h. H.* 543
A painter's skill into a poet's *h. H.* 670
He grasped the mane with both his *h. J.G.* 91
She seemed designed for Flora's *h. L.R.* 15
Thy *h.* their little force resign *M.* 34
In his *h.*, as the sign of his sway *M.D.* 29
The scourge he let fall from his *h. M.D.* 35
And generous Friendship *h.* in *h. Miss* — 75
And, staff in *h.*, set forth to share *Mor.* 9 [63
By thy own *h.*, till fresh they shone and glowed *M.P.*
With her chill *h.*, the mellow leaves away *N.A.* 22
The sacred function, in your *h.* is made *P.E.* 122
Worse than a poniard in the basest *h. P.E.* 305
Lay bleeding under that scft *h.* of thine *P.E.* 338
Whose *h.* is feeble, or his aim untrue *P.E.* 571
Thy genuine charms, and guide an artless *h. R.* 204
The richest earthly boon his *h.* afford *R.* 271
Arms hanging idly down, *h.* clasped below *R.* 286
A Father's frown, and kiss his chastening *h. R.* 346
Kneels, kisses *h.*, and shines again in place *R.* 480
Shakes *h.* with business, and retires indeed *R.* 514
His countenance, his purse, his heart, his *h. R.* 595
An idler is a watch that wants both *h. R.* 681
Amusement and true knowledge *h.* in *h. R.* 702
Not knowing thee, we reap with bleeding *h. R.* 753
Death at *h.*—yourselves his mark *St.* ii 11
And hides his *h.* to keep his fingers warm *T.* 148
Drops the red vengeance from his willing *h. T.* 278
The poor are near at *h.*, the charge is small *T.* 287
The solemn chords, and with a trembling *h. T.* i 3
The inferior wonders of an artist's *h. T.* i 419
But cannot play them, borrows a friend's *h. T.* i 473
Of temperate wishes and industrious *h. T.* i 599
Presume to lay their *h.* upon the ark *T.* i 231
That fear no discipline of human *h. T.* ii 325 [ii 373
Whose *h.* are pure, whose doctrine and whose life *T.*
Preserve the church ! and lay not careless *h. T.* ii 393
As with the diamond on his lily *h. T.* ii 424
With handkerchief in *h.* depending low *T.* ii 450
The better *h.*, more busy, gives the nose *T.* ii 451
And mortifies the liberal *h.* of love *T.* ii 757
And in his *h.* and feet, the cruel scars *T.* iii 114 [342
Yes—thou may'st eat thy bread, and lick the *h. T.* iii
The welcome call, conscious how much the *h. T.* iii 399
Impaired by age, his unrelenting *h. T.* iii 416
No meaner *h.* may discipline the shoots *T.* iii 413
And hence even Winter fills his withered *h. T.* iii 428
And lightly, shaking it with agile *h. T.* iii 478
But by a master's *h.*, disposing well *T.* iii 589
To no mean *h.*, and asks the touch of taste *T.* iii 632
And lineaments divine I trace a *h. T.* iii 722 [247
Treads on thy sweeping train; one *h.* employed *T.* iv
So I, with brush in *h.* and pallet spread *T.* iv 239
Sat for the picture ; and the poet's *h. T.* iv 256
One *h.* secures his hat, save when with both *T.* iv 354
And while her infant race with outspread *h. T.* iv 384
From grudging *h.*; but other'boast have none *T.* iv 404
But helpless, in few years shall find their *h. T.* iv 423
Perched on the sign-post, holds with even *h. T.* iv 483
Indebted to some smart wig-weaver's *h. T.* iv 543
To all the violence of lawless *h. T.* iv 591
His milk-white *h.* ; the palm is hardly clean *T.* iv 607
And touches of his *h.*, with so much art *T.* iv 736
To extort their truncheons from the puny *h. T.* v 189
Till then unfelt, what *h.* divine have wrought *T.* v 784

We lov'd, but not enough, the gentle *h. T.* vi 37
And need not his immediate *h.,* who first *T.* vi 203
And furrow'd into storms, and with a *h. T.* vi 269
With glass at eye, and catalogue in *h. T.* vi 288
He spoke, and to the precipice at *h. T.* vi 512
By budding ills, that ask a prudent *h. T.* vi 591
The task now falls into the public *h. T.* vi 718
And smiles to see, her infant's playful *h. T.* vi 779
And Æthiopia spreads abroad the *h. T.* vi 812
The veil is rent, rent too by priestly *h. T.* vi 876
And mischief in their *h.,*they roam the earth *T.* vi 896
But all is in His *h.,* whose praise I seek *T.* vi 1017
Then why resign into a stranger's *h. Tir.* 551
The encroaching nuisance asks a faithful *h. Tir.* 601
So sure to spoil him, and so near at *h. Tir.* 697
And lay thine *h.* upon his flaxen head *Tir.* 848
Secure it thine, its key is in thine *h. Tir.* 886
Oh, barbarous! wouldst thou with a Gothic *h.Tir.*899
But this is sure—The *h.* of might *Trans.* i 9
The globe and sceptre in such *h.* misplaced *T.T.* 39
As if the world and they were *h.* and glove *T.T.* 173
As well be yoked by Despotism's *h. T.T.* 258
He stood as some inimitable *h. T.T.* 348
And bend her polished neck beneath his *h. T.T.* 441
And waste it at the bidding of his *h. T.T.* 451
When Labour and when Dullness club in *h. T.T.* 526
He snatched it rudely from the Muse's *h. T.T.* 689
Minority. No tutor charged his *h. Y.O.* 157

HANDCUFFED.

See Bedlam's closeted and *h.* charge *Tir.* 819

HANDEL.

Messiah's eulogy for *H.'s* sake *T.* vi 637
Remember *H.?* Who, that was not born *T.* vi 645

HAND-IN-HAND.

Like *H.* insurance plates *F.* 106

HANDKERCHIEF.

With *h.* in hand depending low *T.* ii 450

HANDLED.

Had *h.* been before *J.G.* 94

HANDLES.

Who *h.* things divine; and all beside *T.* ii 433

HANDMAID.

Is *h.* to the purposes of grace *H.* 146

HANDSOME.

Some *h.* present, as your hopes presage *Con.* 306
Lolls at his ease behind four *h.* bays *R.* 392
And feed him well, and give him *h.* pay *Tir.* 907

HANG.

H. out her lamp in yon cærulean height *A.T.* 138
Though syllogisms *h.* not on my tongue *Con.* 93
Would *h.* an honest man, and save a thief *Con.* 128
Muse, *h.* this harp upon yon aged beech *Ex.* 718
The busy heralds *h.* the sable scene *H.* 264
And *h.* their horrors in the neighbouring skies *Her.*16
That *h.* upon your face *J.G.* 190   [*P.A.* 38
His apples might *h.* till they dropped from the tree
What! *h.* a man for going mad! *Pat.* 23
To *h.* their momentary fires *Q.V.* 15
The fruits that *h.* on pleasure's flowery stem *R.* 179
That thieves at home must *h.,* but he that puts *T.* i 736
And *h.* his head, to think himself a man? *T.* ii 28
H. over mortal eyes, blind from the birth *T.* iii 234
That day and night are exercised, and *h. T.* iii 549
And cherries *h.* her twigs. Geranium boasts *T.* iii 577
To stroke the prickly grievance, and to *h. T.* v 329
And *h.* it up in honour of a man?) *T.* vi 641

Some shout him, and some *h.* upon his car *T.* vi 698
Spring *h.* her infant blossoms on the trees *Tir.* 43
He blushes, *h.* his head, is shy and strange *Tir.* 568

HANGED.

And who is *h.,* and who is brought to bed *Con.* 396

HANGING.

Those *h.* with their worn-out graces *M.F.* 5
Arms *h.* idly down, hands clasped below *R.* 286

HAPLESS.

Where oft the bitch-fox hides her *h.* brood *N.A.* 4
" Ah, *h.* wretch! condemned to dwell *P.* 5
With tears o'er *h.* favorites shed *T.B.* 2

HAPLY.

He claps his lens, if *h.* they may see *Ch.* 385
With less excuse, and, *h.,* worse effect?" *F.A.* 17
His dangers or escapes, and *h.* find *T.* ii 309

HAPPENED.

('Tis a case that has *h.,* and may do again) *A.C.* 18
It *h.* on a solemn eventide *Con.* 505

HAPPIER.

"Nymphs quite as fair, and *h.* once than you *A.T.*110
Would feel herself *h.* here *C.* 28
While Conscience, *h.* than in ancient years *Ch.* 274
At any poet's *h.* lays *Dr.* 15
He found the laurel only—*h.* you *Ex.* 600
From *h.* scenes, to make your land a prey *H.* 478
Still *h.,* if he till a thankful soil *H.* 760
But *h.* far, who comfort those that wait *H.* 762
(And thou wast *h.* than myself the while *M.P.* 78
Of *h.* times, appear *N.* 22
Happy if full of days—but *h.* far *R.* 45
But farewell promises of *h.* fruits *R.* 241
In *h.* days, to brighter prospects born! *S.* ii 5
Maturer years shall *h.* stores produce *T.* 495
Was bliss reserved for *h.* days;—so slow *T.* i 83
The envied tenants of some *h.* spot *T.* i 610
Would I had fallen upon those *h.* days *T.* iv 513
Shows somewhat of that *h.* life to come *T.* vi 907
The prize of *h.* times, will serve thee now *T.T.* 371
Thou surpassest, *h.* far *Trans.* iii 19
Already by some *h.* bard 1789, 10

HAPPIEST.

On man's most dignified and *h.* state *Ch.* 2
Its *h.* soil in the serenest minds? *Con.* 594
And *h.* he that groans beneath his weight *R.* 156
Than ye, when *h.,* and enlightened most *R.* 675
Its *h.* seasons, and a peaceful close *R.* 750
The *h.* of the great *M.B.* 16
The kindest and the *h.* pair *M.F.* 37
Beyond the *h.* lot *O.* i 22
There they are *h.* who dissemble best *T.* ii 639
Infect his *h.* moments, he forebodes *T.* v 606
Now *h.* they that occupy the scenes *T.* vi 397
Feels all his *h.* privileges lost *Tir.* 574
H. grasshoppers that are *Trans.* iii 20

HAPPILY.

Some minds are tempered *h.,* and mixed *T.* ii 788

HAPPINESS.

And make colloquial *h.* your care *Con.* 82
Where 'tis an angel's *h.* to stray) *Con.* 472
Domestic *h.* and rural joy *Ex.* 535
Taste *h.,* or know what pleasure means *H.* 10
His *h.,* her dear, her only aim *H.* 64
That lasting *h.,* a thankful heart *H.* 160
In part abate, that *h.* were small *N.A.* 112
No *h.* is felt, except the true *R.* 461

Some seeking *h.* not found below *R.* 604
Grasp seeming *H.*, and find it Pain *R.* 756
Consulting England's *h.* at home *T.* ii 246
Domestic *H.*, thou only bliss *T.* iii 41
In chase of fancied *h.*, still wooed *T.* iii 126
Substantial *h.* for transient joy *T.* iii 300
Fireside enjoyments, homeborn *h. T.* iv 140
Finds *h.* unblighted; or, if found *T.* iv 334
We miss'd that *h.* we might have found ! *T.* vi 28
Nor feels their *h.* augment his own *T.* vi 326
A far superior *h.* to theirs *T.* vi 346
Prepare for *h.*; bespeak him one *T.* vi 912
He seek his proper *h.* by means *T.* vi 954
Blest England, if this *h.* be thine ! *T.T.* 82
Thus *h.* depends as Nature shows *T.T.* 246
All hope of *h.* below 1789, 53
The *h.* of answered prayers 1789, 64

HAPPY.

And finds a changing clime a *h.* source *Con.* 387
His *h.* eloquence seemed there at home *Con.* 622
While all the *h.* man possessed before *Con.* 895
Oh, *h.* Britain ! we have not to fear *E.* iii 54
All speak her *h.*:—let the Muse look round *Ex.* 27
Returned them *h.* to the land they loved *Ex.* 76
H. to fill Religion's vacant place *Ex.* 121
H. the man there seeking and there found *Ex.* 652
H. the nation where such men abound ! *Ex.* 653
Lived *h.* prisoners there *F.B.* 6
This man was *h.*—had the world's good word *H.* 678
H. the bard, (if that fair name belong *H.* 754
I mourn, or, since thrice *h.* thou must be *J.T.* 9
Ere yet with ruthless joy the *h.* hound *N.A.* 33
None here is *h.* but in part *N.Y.G.* 13
Illustrious drop ! and *h.* then *O.* i 21
H. if full of days—but happier far *R.* 45
He proves, less *h.* than his favoured brute *R.* 633
O *h.* shades !—to me unblest *S.* 1
O *h.* peasant ! O unhappy bard ! *T.* 331
Feels herself *h.* amidst all her grief *T.* 456
Trembling yet *h.*, confident yet meek *T.* 572
In Albion's *h.* isle. The lumber stood *T.* i 58
Delight us, *h.* to renounce awhile *T.* i 515
And *h.* in their unforeseen release *T.* ii 126
H. the man who sees a God employed *T.* ii 161
That lost in his own musings, *h.* man ! *T.* iii 301
Not slothful; *h.* to deceive the time *T.* iii 362
Whose only *h.* are their wasted hours *T.* iv 225
O *h.* ! and, in my account, denied *T.* iv 357
Refinement is endued; thrice *h.* thou ! *T.* iv 359
Whose *h.* skill and industry combined *T.* iv 30
This folio of four pages, *h.* work ! *T.* iv 50
Thee I account still *h.*, and the chief *T.* v 460
" Radiant with joy towards the *h.* land *T.* v 836
H. who walks with him ! whom what he finds *T.* vi 247
All *h.*, and all perfect in their kind *T.* vi 354
H. to rove among poetic flowers *T.* vi 752
He is the *h.* man whose life e'en now *T* vi 906
H. the state that has not these to fear *T.T.* 167
Is always *h.*, reign whoever may *T.T.* 238
The mind attains, beneath her *h.* reign *T.T.* 262
Back to the season of life's *h.* spring *Tir.* 132
As *h.* as we once to kneel and draw *Tir.* 306
Ah, *h.* designation, prudent choice *Tir.* 342
Thrice *h.* bird ! I too have seen *Tran.* ii 31

HARANGUE.

But all he gains for his *h.* is;—" Well ! *Ch.* 393
The clear *h.*, and cold as it is clear *P.E.* 19
Than all invective is his bold *h. T.* ii 354
The popular *h.*, the tart reply *T.* iv 31

HARANGUED.

H. him thus, right eloquent *N.G.* 14

HARASSED.

Provoked and *h.*, in return plagued thee *Ex.* 533

HARBINGER.

A *h.* of endless good *E.* i 90
Prolific all, and *h.* of more *T.* iii 531
Always *h.* of good *Tran.* iii 4

HARBOUR.

Hearts may be found that *h.* at this hour *Con.* 561

HARD. [*A.T.* ii 4

With as many *h.* names as would line a good trunk
Begone ! the whip and bell in that *h.* hand *Ch.* 212
'Tis *h.* if all is false that I advance *Con.* 95
'Tis *h.*, indeed, if nothing will defend *Con.* 173
How credibly, 'tis *h.* for me to state) *Con.* 816
Who labour *h.* to allure and draw *E.* i 23
That *h.* by nature, and of stubborn will *E* ii 21
Such *h.* and arbitrary measure here *E.* iii 55
Oppression labouring *h.* to grind the poor *Ex.* 40
Of all their *h.* oppressors valued most *Ex.* 172
H. task indeed o'er arctic seas to roam ! *H.* 548
H. task ! for one who lately knew no care *H.* 696
But for one piece they thought it *h. L.W.* 11
" Child ! 1 am rather *h.* of hearing" *M.F.* 24
Winks *h.*, and talks of darkness at noonday *P.E.* 451
'Twas *h.* to tell, of streets or squares *Q.V.* 9
Cowper, whose silver voice, tasked sometimes *h. S.* i 1
H. lot of man, to toil for the reward *T.* 11
Of virtue, and yet lose it ! Wherefore *h.* ? *T.* 12
The growth of what is excellent; so *h. T.* i 84
H. fare ! but such as boyish appetite *T.* i 123
His *h.* condition with severe constraint *T.* i 612 [323
Laughed at, he laughs again; and stricken *h. T.* ii
And neatly fitted, it compresses *h. T.* ii 587
'Twas *h.* perhaps on here and there a waif *T.* iii 80
A dry but independent crust, *h.* earned *T.* iv 409
Contrives, *h.* shifting, and without her tools *T.* v 417
Swears 'tis a bargain, rails at his *h.* fate *T.* vi 293
The heart is *h.* in nature, and unfit *T.* vi 321
He deems it *h.* to vegetate alone *Tir.* 724
Not *h.* by nature, in a feeling part *V.* 42

HARDEN.

Was formed to *h.* hearts and shock the sight *Ex.* 495
Prepares it for its ruin, *h.*, blinds *T.* ii 690

HARDENED.

Till *h.* his heart's temper in the forge *T.* v 664

HARDENING.

There *h.* by degrees, till double steeled *P.E.* 590

HARDER.

And *h.* to withstand *B.R.* 4
A life of ease would make them *h.* still *E.* ii 22
And *h.* still as learnt beneath despair *H.* 697
If cushion might be called, what *h.* seemed *T.* 155

HARD-FARING.

From his accustomed perch. *H.* race ! *T.* i 564

HARD-HANDED.

That lean *h.* Poverty inflicts *T.* iii 827

HARDNESS.

He hates the *h.* of a Balaam's heart *T.* vi 467

HARDSHIPS. [*P.A.* 3

What I hear of their *h.*, their tortures, their groans

HARDY.

If after all, some headstrong *h.* lout *H.* 314
The *h.* chief, upon the rugged rock *T.* i 12
Thy frame, robust and *h.*, feels indeed *T.* iv 360

HARE.
Was still a wild Jack *h. Ep.* ii 8 [334
Well—one at least is safe. One sheltered *h. T.* iii
I knew at least one *h.* that had a friend *T.* iii 351
These shades are all my own. The timorous *h. T.* vi 305

HAREM.
" Seraglios sing, and *h.* dance for joy ! *A.T.* 108
Where chanticleer amidst his *h.* sleeps *T.* iv 447

HARK !
H. ! the Gaul is at her gates ! *B.* 20
H. ! 'tis the music of a thousand rills *Ch.* 367
H. ! He answers,—Wild tornadoes *N.C.* 33
H. ! how it floats upon the dewy air ! *P.E.* 63 [ii 351
But *h.*—the Doctor's voice !—fast wedged between *T.*
H. ! universal Nature shook and groaned *T.* 563
H. ! 'tis the twanging horn o'er yonder bridge *T.* iv 1
H. ! how the sire of chits, whose future share *Tir.* 318

HARLOT.
Seest thou yon *h.*, wooing all she meets *T.* 507
And some street-pacing *h.* his first love *Tir.* 217

HARM.
And thou couldst laugh away the fear of *h. Ex.* 705
His sacred head from *h. M.* ii 8
Enamoured of its *h.* ! *St.* v 14
There only minds like yours can do no *h. T.* i 759
Than hellish foes, confederate for his *h. T.* v 735
Or *h.* them there is guilty of a wrong *T.* vi 578

HARMLESS.
The *h.* play of pleasantry and mirth *E.* iii 39
Though loose, as *h.* as an infant's play *H.* 613
'Tis innocent, and *h.*, and refined *P.E.* 179
Of *h.* Nature, dumb, but yet endued *T.* iii 329
Or *h.* flocks, is hazardous and bold *T.* iv 575
His ignorance and *h.* manners too *T.* iv 651
And *h.* pleasures, in the thronged abode *T.* iv 782
So Eden was a scene of *h.* sport *T.* vi 364
H., and safe, and natural, as they are *Tir.* 565

HARMLESSLY.
Unnumbered pleasures *h.* pursued *R.* 784

HARMONIOUS.
Nor more *h.* or compact *Mrs. M—* 40
Sweet birds in concert with *h.* streams *R.* 259
Our more *h.* notes: the thrush departs *T.* i 767
And the *h.* order of them all *Tir.* 635
In praise *h.* the first air he drew *Y.O.* 155

HARMONIST.
Sweet *h.* of Flora's court ! *Dr.* 3

HARMONY.
Love graced the theme, and *h.* the song *A.T.* 198
H...the path to fame *B.* 24
Not more distinct from *h.* divine *Con.* 9
Forget his *h.*, with rapture heard *Con.* 447
Instead of *h.*, 'tis jar *M.F.* 47
'Tis *H.* from yon sequestered bower *P.E.* 65
Sweet *H.* that soothes the midnight hour *P.E.* 66
Heaven's *h.* is universal love *P.E.* 78
Love, joy, and peace make *h.* more meet *P.E.* 140
Each yielding *h.*, disposed aright *R.* 326
Its wasted tones and *h.* unheard *T.* iv 480
Again the *h.* comes o'er the vale *T.* vi 65
Thus *h.* and family accord *T.* vi 379
Deaf as the dead to *h.*, forgets *T.* vi 646
But all is *h.* and love. Disease *T.* vi 788
Then Pope, as *h.* itself exact *T.T.* 646
H. strength, words exquisitely sought *T.T.* 701

HARP. [496
Thy Druids struck the well strung *h.* they bore *Ex.*
Muse, hang this *h.* upon yon aged beech *Ex.* 718
Man is a *h.* whose chords elude the sight *R.* 325
Sweet is the *h.* of prophecy ; too sweet *T.* vi 747

HARPSICHORD.
If he the tinkling *h.* regards *P.E.* 148

HARRY.
" Dismiss poor H.! " he replies *M.F.* 19

HARSH.
But angry, coarse, and *h.* expression *M.F.* 59
Sounds inharmonious in themselves and *h. T.* 207
Religion *h.*, intolerant, austere *T.T.* 612 [vi 1012
Roved far, and gathered much ; some *h.*, 'tis true *T.*

HARSHLY.
Sounds *h.* in so delicate an ear *R.* 250
Not *h.* thundered forth, or rudely pressed *T.* vi 503

HARVEST.
The abundant *h.*, recompense divine *H.* 770
Through the ripe *h.* lies their destined road *Her.* 54
The golden *h.*, of a mellow brown *T.* iv 314
And plenteous *h.*, to the prayer he makes *T.* vi 947
The peasants urge their *h.*, ply the fork *T.T.* 214
And view with tears the expected *h.* lost *V.* 57

HASSOCKS.
And knees and *h.* are well nigh divorced *T.* i 748

HASTE.
With all the flowers he found, he wove in *h. A.T.* 13
Bade rise in *h.* a dark and drizzling fog *A.T.* 94
Their *h.* himself condemn *Cast.* 32
And up he got, in *h.* to ride *J.G.* 47
I am in *h.* to dine *J.G.* 198
But though the birds were thus in *h. P.T.* 45
Then swift descending with a seaman's *h. R.* 435
Friends not adopted with a schoolboy's *h. R.* 725
He 'gan in *h.* the drawers explore *R.C.* 92
Is hackneyed home unlackeyed ; who, in *h. T.* ii 652
H. now, philosopher, and set him free *T.* v 670 [v 819
With which Heaven rang, when every star in *h. T.*
H., then, and wheel away a shattered world *T.* vi 823
Summer in *h.* the thriving charge receives *Tir.* 45
I seize thy name in *h. U.* 20

HASTEN.
And new or old, still *h.* to a close *Con.* 238
A falling empire, *h.* its decay *R.* 384

HASTENED.
So have I seen (and *h.* to the sight *Ch.* 547

HASTENING.
Revived, are *h.* into fresh repute *Con.* 818

HASTILY.
I *h.* seized it, unfit as it was *The Rose* 0

HASTING.
My fugitive years are all *h.* away *P.F.* 13
And *h.* to a grave, yet doomed to rise *T.* v 830

HASTY.
Nor noise was heard but of the *h.* brook *N.A.* 39
That pressed the beach, and, *h.* to depart *T.* ii 118
And death still future. Not a *h.* stroke *T.* v. 608

HAT.
And has him safe beneath his *h. E.* iv 56
Away went *h.* and wig *J.G.* 98
My *h.* and wig will soon be here *J.G.* 175
Whence straight he came with *h.* and wig *J.G.* 181

HAT—HEAD

A *h.* not much the worse for wear *J.G.* 183
Went Gilpin's *h.* and wig *J.G.* 210
With lace, and *h.* with splendid riband bound *T.* i 536
One hand secures his *h.*, save when with both *T.* iv 354
Sheepish he doffs his *h.*, and mumbling swears *T.* iv 628
His *h.*, or his plumed helmet, with a grace *T.* iv 643
To pitch the ball into the grounded *h. Tir.* 308

HATCH.
Should never game-fowl *h.* her eggs again *T.* iii 312

HATCHED.
H. by the beams of truth, denies him rest *P.E.* 241
These *h.*, and those resuscitated worms *R.* 64

HATE.
Reviled by those that *h.* her, prays for them *Ch.* 425
Preserve me from the thing I dread and *h. Con.* 83
H. their own likeness in a brother's face *Con.* 158
Out of the very flames of rage and *h. Con.* 186
(I *h.* long arguments verbosely spun) *E.* iii 44
The treacherous smile, a mask for secret *h. Ex.* 42
Viewed a deliverer with disdain and *h. Ex.* 217
And charged Hostility and *H.* to roar *Ex.* 566
And *h.* him for encroaching *F.* 84
H. with a deep sincerity the true *H.* 642
Of fools that *h.* thee and delight in sin *H.* 745
A land that distant tyrants *h.* in vain *Her.* 89
He that *h.* truth shall be the dupe of lies *P.E.* 607
And *h.* the tumult half the world enjoys *R.* 176
Sly circumvention, unrelenting *h. T.* i 615 [*T.* ii 644
And *h.* their coming. They (what can they less?)
And bow obsequious, hide their *h.* of her *T.* ii 646
All *h.* the rank society of weeds *T.* iii 670 [464
He gave them in his children's veins, and *h. T.* iv
He *h.* the field, in which no fife or drum *T.* iv 646
He *h.* the hardness of a Balaam's heart *T.* vi 467
A world that does not dread and *h.* his laws *T.* vi 826
Those arts be theirs that *h.* his gentle reign *T.T.* 89
And *h.* it with the malice of a Jew *Tir.* 168
And emulation, as engendering *h. Tir.* 497

HATED.
Reminds them of their *h.* inmate, Sin *E.* ii 36
Reminds him of religion, *h.* theme! *H.* 218
He loved the world that *h.* him; the tear *H.* 574
Oh! welcome now the sun's once *h.* light *H.* 736
Shine not, or undesired and *h.* shine *R.* 351
He *h.*, hoped, and loved! *St.* iii 22
For which we shunned and *h.* thee before *T.* v 882

HATEFUL.
Are *h.* ensigns of usurped command *Ch.* 213
Thenceforth 'tis *h.*, for it smells of you *Con.* 44
Safe policy, but *h. F.* 183
His court, the dissolute and *h.* school *T.T.* 626

HATING.
For thou art meek and constant, *h.* change *T.* iii 55

HATRED.
For the *h.* she ever has shown *M.D.* 46
And the world's *h.*, as its sure effect *T.* 282
(And no man's *h.* ever wronged her yet) *T.* iii 101
Of envy, *h.*, jealousy, and pride *Tir.* 467

HAUGHTY.
Dismissed with grave, not *h.* looks *Mrs. M—* 38
Perhaps the self-approving *h.* world *T.* vi 940

HAUGHTILY.
When did the waves so *h.* o'erleap *T.* ii 55

HAUNT.
Still *h.*, in hope to dream of youth again *Ex.* 26
These and a thousand plagues that *h.* the breast *R.* 763

From such unpleasing sounds as *h.* the ear *T.* i 229
On pleasure, *h.* the capital, and thus *T.* iv 590
The cheerful *h.* of man; to wield the axe *T.* v 42
Defies the check of winter, *h.* of deer *T.* vi 110 [355
The creatures, summon'd from their various *h. T.* vi
Nor plagues that *h.* the rich man's door *Trans. H.* 11

HAVEN.
In some safe *h.* of our western world *Ch.* 444
To the fair *h.* of my native home *R.* 385

HAVOC.
H. and devastation in the van *Her.* 21

HAWS.
I fed on scarlet hips and stony *h. T.* i 120

HAWTHORN.
On twigs of *h.* he regaled *Ep.* ii 17
Not yet the *h.* bore her berries red *N.A.* 19
So stooping down from *h.* top *N.G.* 11 [114
Peeps through the moss that clothes the *h.* root *T.* vi

HAY.
Dry fern or littered *h.*, that may imbibe *T.* iii 476

HAYFIELD. [295
There from the sunburnt *h.* homeward creeps *T.* i

HAZARD.
And *h.* life for any or no cause *Con.* 184

HAZARDING.
Contusion *h.* of neck or spine *N.A.* 7.

HAZARDOUS.
Of this world's *h.* and headlong shore *St.* ii 14
Or harmless flocks, is *h.* and bold *T.* iv 575

HAZELS. [10
Where the *h.* afford him a screen from the heat *P.F.*

HEAD.
A fancied *h.* against a fancied post *A.T.* 45
So polished and compact from *h.* to heel *A.T.* 184
Worms may be caught by either *h.* or tail *Ch.* 528
Flings at your *h.* conviction in the lump *Con.* 153
Its *h.* as guarded as its base is sure *Con.* 556 [626
When some green *h.*, as void of wit as thought *Con.*
That truth itself is in her *h.* as dull *Con.* 779
His *h.* and his heart are both likely to ache *F.M.* 15
"For lift thy palsied *h.*, shake off the gloom *H.* 37
The coronet, placed idly at their *h. H.* 268
They were by nature, atheists, *h.* and heart *H.* 498
His eyes are sunk, arms folded, *h.* reclined *H.* 689
When, turning round his *h.* he saw *J.G.* 51
His reeking *h.* full low *J.G.* 122
My *h.* is twice as big as yours *J.G.* 187
He meant not to forbid the *h. L.W.* 18
His sacred *h.* from harm *M.* ii 8
He rears unchanged his barren *h. Miss—* 39 [*M.P.* 79
Wouldst softly speak, and stroke my *h.* and smile)
But lovely spring peeps o'er his *h. N.* 15
Oaks intersperse it, that had once a *h. N.A.* 11
In praise applied to the same part—his *h. P.E.* 533
With a turf on my breast, and a stone at my *h. P.F.* 15
With helmet *h.*, and dragon-scales adorned *R.* 69
'Tis not, as *h.* that never ache suppose *R.* 323
Not sounder he that on the mainmast *h. R.* 431
What obvious truths the wisest *h.* may miss! *R.* 458
Habits of close attention, thinking *h. R.* 705
With this reflection in his *h. R.C.* 108 [10
Both heart and *h.*; and couldst with music sweet *S.* i
The Bramin kindles on his own bare *h. T.* 99
Her *h.* erect, her fan upon her lips *T.* 134
And sails with lappet *h.* and mincing airs *T.* 139
To nourish pride, or turn the weakest *h. T.* 366
The tedious rector drawling o'er his *h. T.* i 95

Above the reach of man : his hoary *h. T.* i 520
And hang his *h.*, to think himself a man? *T.* ii 28
From such apostles, O ye mitred *h. T.* ii 392
Drink, when we choose it, at the fountain *h. T.* ii 502
There dwelt a sage called Discipline. His *h. T.* ii 702
The *h.* of modest and ingenuous worth *T.* ii 711
They would be, were not madness in the *h. T.* iii 741
And his *h.* thumps, to feed upon the breath *T.* iv 47
Her *h.*, adorned with lappets pinned aloft *T.* iv 540
Beneath one *h.* for purposes of war *T.* iv 666
His wonted strut ; and, wading at their *h. T.* v 74
May give an useful lesson to the *h. T.* vi 86
In *h.* replete with thoughts of other men *T.* vi 90
Now sanguine, and her beauteous *h.* now set *T.* vi 158
God set the diadem upon his *h. T.* vi 351
That finds out every crevice of the *h. T.* vi 707
His *h.* alone remained to tell *T.B.* 65
Round Thurlow's *h.* in early youth *Th.* 1
And weighed down its beautiful *h. The Rose* 4
The wisest *h.* might agitate in vain *Tir.* 130 [444
Young *h.* are giddy, and young hearts are warm *Tir.*
He blushes, hangs his *h.*, is shy and strange *Tir.* 568
And lay thine hand upon his flaxen *h. Tir.* 848
And others to his *h. Trans.* i. 8
And such a *h.* between 'em *Trans.* ii 36
Liberty blushed, and hung her drooping *h. T.T.* 324
He laid his *h.* in Luxury's soft lap *T.T.* 678
And flings his *h.* before *Y.D.* 30

HEADACHES.

Whose *h.* nail them to a noonday bed *T.* i 500

HEADLESS.

Some *h.* hero, or some Cæsar shows *P.E.* 395

HEADLONG.

Washed *h.* from on board *Cast.* 4
Not e'en the vigorous and *h.* rage *Con.* 45
For persevering chase, and *h.* leaps *P.E.* 86
Of this world's hazardous and *h.* shore *St.* ii 14
He seeks them *h.*, and is seen no more *T.* i 454
The rocks fall *h.*, and the valleys rise *T.* ii 95
A silent witness of the *h.* rage *T.* iii 218

HEADSTRONG.

Of *h.* youth were broken ; bars and bolts *T.* ii 745
Lascivious, *h.*, or all these at once *Tir.* 202

HEAL.

Would *h.* his heart, and melt his chains away *Ch.* 229
No cure for such, till God who makes them *h. R.* 342
Have wounds which only God can *h. St.* vi 19
Need other physic none to *h.* the effects *T.* i 590
Or *h.* it, makes it languish or rejoice *T.* ii 70
Suspend the effect, or *h.* it ? Has not God *T.* ii 197
Shall give him consequence, *h.* all defects *Tir.* 392

HEALED.

They saw distemper *h.*, and life restored *Ex.* 153
He drew them forth, and *h.*, and bade me live *T.* iii 116

HEALING.

By way of balm for *h. F.* 96
Sweet as the privilege of *h.* woe *J.T.* 17

HEALTH.

Some men employ their *h.*, an ugly trick *Con.* 311
I ike conservators of the public *h. Con.* 390
That, while in *h.*, the ground of her support *Con.* 771
Our *h.*, the weather, and the news *E.* i. 5 [4
Seems it to say —" *H.* here has long to reign ? " *Ep.* i.
What *h.* and sober appetite demand *H.* 158
Must go to heaven—and I must drink his *h. H.* 412
But youth, *h.*, vigour to expend *Mor.* 33 [*P.E.* 246
Good sense, good *h.*, good conscience, and good fame ?
'Tis exercise, and *h.*, and length of days ; *P.E.* 91

Emblems of *h.* and heavenly aid *Q.V.* 47
When *h.* required it, would consent to roam *R.* 517
No present *h.* can *h.* insure *St.* i. 25
An infidel in *h.* ;—" But what when sick ? " *T.* 309
That Nature rides upon, maintains her *h. T.* i 369
Good *h.*, and, its associate in the most *T.* i 399
H. suffers, and the spirits ebb ; the heart *T.* i 466
Such *h.* and gaiety of heart enjoy *T.* i 587
What wonder then that *h.* and virtue, gifts *T.* i 750
And putrefy the breath of blooming *H.*—*T.* ii 184 [691
H., leisure, means to improve it, friendship, peace *T.* iii
Hail, therefore, patroness of *h.* and ease *T.* iv 780
The fatal issue to his *h.*, fame, peace *T.* v 601
The sum is this. If man's convenience, *h. T.* vi 581
Threaten his *h.*, his fortune, and his fame *Tir.* 532
When *h.* demands it, of athletic sort *Tir.* 653
H.'s last farewell, a staff of thine old age *Tir.* 878
He may be called to give up *h.* and gain *V.* 63
If God give *h.*, that sunshine of our days ! *V.* 88

HEALTHFUL.

Tastes of its *h.* origin, and flows *Con.* 565
Temperance and Peace insure its *h.* state *Con.* 603
Yet fear, youth ofttimes *h.* and at ease *Ep.* i 7
His cheek recovers soon its *h.* hue *T.* i 441
All *h.*, are the employs of rural life *T.* iii 625
H. and undisturbed by factious fumes *T.* v 513

HEAP.

Like a loose *h.* of ribbon, a glittering show *F.M.* 6
The stable yields a stercoraceous *h. T.* iii 463

HEAR.

Never *h.* the sweet music of speech *A.S.* 11
To *h.* them tell of parentage and birth *Con.* 210
With strains it was a privilege to *h. Con.* 618
Where Venus *h.* the lover's tender vow *Con.* 824
Shall *h.* of this thy deed *D.W.* 38
Which, couched in prose, they will not *h. E.* i 22
Will *h.* perhaps thy salutary strain *Ex.* 453
That few will *h.*, and fewer heed the strain *Ex.* 725
For tattlers, will be sure to *h. F.* 98
" Say little, and *h.* all you can " *F.* 182
He *h.* the notice of the clock, perplexed *H.* 700
To *h.* plain truth at Judah's hallowed gate *H.* 763
The goddess chanced to *h. L.R.* 18
'Twas Liberty only to *h. M.D.* 24
What shall I do to make you *h.* ? *M.F.* 18
I tell you, you can't *h.* at all ! " *M.F.* 28
No matter if you *h.* or no ! *M.F.* 30 [groans *P.A.* 3
What I *h.* of their hardships, their tortures, their
And helpless, hopeless, *h.* thee say *O.* ii 23
He *h.* the herbs and flowers rejoicing all *N.A.* 60
But ah ! those dreadful yells what soul can *h. N.A.* 99
H. him again. He calls it a delight *P.E.* 163
Like fabled Tantalus, condemned to *h. P.E.* 231
Imbibes and copies what she *h.* and sees *P.E.* 356
H. the just law—the judgment of the skies ! *P.E.* 606
And *h.* the million hum *Q.V.* 42
Till authors *h.* at length one general cry *R.* 707
H. the sweet accents of his tuneful voice *R.* 771
H. him, o'erwhelmed with sorrow, yet rejoice *R.* 772
H. it often as we may *St.* iv 26
Reformed and well instructed ? You shall *h. T.* 130
He *h.* the tempest howling in the trees *T.* 254
H. him, himself the poet and the theme *T.* 404
H. then how Mercy, slighted and defied *T.* 501
To *h.* his creaking panniers at the door *T.* i 245 [396
Were he on earth, would *h.*, approve, and own *T.* ii
Adore him? Will he *h.*, accept, and bless ? *T.* ii 515
As aught occurs that she may smile to *h. T.* iii 395
To *h.* the roar she sends through all her gates *T.* iv 91
H. the faint echo of those brazen throats *T.* iv 104
To *h.* that ye were fallen at last ; to know *T.* v 390

HEAR—HEART

Charm the deaf serpent wisely. Make him *h. T.* v 671
That *h.* not, or receive not their report *T.* v 855
A voice is heard that mortal ears *h.* not *T.* v 886
Which he that *h.* it with a shout repeats *T.* v 889
By the impure, and *h.* his power denied *T.* v 895
Some chord in unison with what we *h. T.* vi 4
Commemoration mad; content to *h. T.* vi 635
In vain the poet sings, and the world *h. T.* vi 1018
They *h.* him speak—the oracle of law *Tir.* 363
H. Nature plead, show mercy to thy son *Tir.* 756
To *h.* it called extravagance and waste *T.T.* 163
I *h.* as mute as if a Syren sung *T.T.* 199
He *h.* the thunder ere the tempest lowers *T.T.* 496
At first he aims at what he *h. Tran.* iv 19
In pulpit none shall *h. Y.D.* 58

HEARD.

These valleys and rocks never *h. A.S.* 30
A trumpet that was *h.* through all the land *A.T.* 162
Against my orders, whom you *h. Beau* 7
A louder voice than yours I *h. B.R.* 3
The longer I *h.* I esteemed *C.* 21
Had *h.* his voice in every blast *Cast.* 45
Forget his harmony, with rapture *h. Con.* 447
And blest reforms that I have never *h. Con.* 804
The moment when I *h.* from you *E.* iv 24
Nor ear *h.* huntsman's halloo *Ep.* ii 4
He *h.* the wheels of an avenging God *Ex.* 57
Wept till all Israel *h.* his bitter cry *Ex.* 63
I *h.* and acquiesced: then to and-fro *F.A.* 18
Then praise is *h.* instead of reasoning pride *H.* 143
'Tis *h.* where England's Eastern glory shines *H.* 457
Or voice of turtle in your land is *h. H.* 470
Had *h.* a lion roar *J.G.* 206
Was *h.*, one genial summer's day *J.P.* 31
The sweetest that ear ever *h. M.D.* 18
H. shouts that ascended the sky *M.D.* 39
"Where'er is *h.* a groan *Miss* — 88
With me but roughly since I *h.* thee last *M.P.* 2
I *h.* the bell tolled on thy burial day *M.P* 28
Where once we dwelt our name is *h.* no more *M.P.* 46
Nor noise was *h.* but of the hasty brook *N.A.* 39
And from within the wood that crash was *h. N.A.* 45
"Friends! we have lived too long. I never *h. N.A.* 83
Or *h.* we that tremendous bray alone *N.A.* 93
While thus she spake, I fainter *h.* the peals *N.A.* 123
The songster *h.* his short oration *N.G.* 23
Was *h.*—though never *h.* before *P.* 2
Dick *h.*, and tweedling, ogling, bridling *P.T.* 38
H. an inexplicable scratching *R.C.* 78
Thou was not *h.* with drowsy disregard *S.* i 5
These alone, so often *h. St.* iv 30
Yet *h.* in scenes where peace for ever reigns *T.* 208
'Tis done—the raging storm is *h.* no more *T.* 275
She, never *h.* of half a mile from home *T.* 334 [567
What! silent? Is your boasting *h.* no more? *T.*
H. the sweet moan with pity, and devised *T.* i 74
She *h.* the doleful tidings of his death *T.* i 545
And *h.* our music; are they simple friends *T.* i 645
H. at conventicle, where worthy men *T.* ii 437
Played on his lips, and in his speech was *h. T.* ii 707
Has never *h.* the sanguinary yell *T.* iii 335 [848
For whom God *h.* his Abraham plead in vain *T.* iii
Resounding oft, and never *h.* in vain *T.* iv 356
Of midnight murder was a wonder *h. T.* iv 563
And ever as the sullen sound is *h. T.* v 405
Till Thou art *h.*, imaginations vain *T.* v 861
A voice is *h.* that mortal ears hear not *T.* v 886
Where memory slept. Wherever I have *h. T.* vi 12
Which heaven has *h.* for ages, have an end *T.* vi 730
Is *h.* salvation. Eastern Java there *T.* vi 810 [497
Beats back the roaring surge, scarce *h.* so high *T.* vi
And *h.* the voice of love *The Doves* 6

And I recorded what I *h. The Doves* 39
But reason *h.*, and nature well perused *Tir.* 89
H. to articulate like other men *Tir.* 667 [231
Is seldom felt, though sometimes seen and *h. T.T.*
As if he *h.* his king say, "Slave, be free!" *T.T.* 245
In him, Demosthenes was *h.* again *T.T.* 342
And ages ere the Mantuan Swan was *h. T.T.* 557

HEARERS.

He ties up all his *h.* in suspense *Con.* 130
Their peevish *h.* almost wish they had *Con.* 324
Or seldom such, the *h.* of his song *T.* ii 305
On thy distorted root, with *h.* none *Y.O.* 140

HEARING.

H. a lawyer, grave in his address *Con.* 69
"Child! I am rather hard of *h.*" *M.F.* 26
He has no *h.* on the prudent side *P.E.* 549

HEARSE.

I saw the *h.* that bore thee slow away *M.P.* 29

HEART. [there? *A.T.* 118

"Find out her treacherous *h.*, and plant a dagger
His tender *h.* victoriously impressed *A.T.* 4 [*A.T.* 22
And graved it on a gem, and wore it next his *h.*
"Seduce our husbands, and estrange their *h. A.T.* 114
To other *h.*, must have thee in his own *Ch.* 10 [54
That stripped him bare, and broke his honest *h. Ch.*
That has a *h.* and life in it, "Be free!" *Ch.* 170
Would heal his *h.*, and melt his chains away *Ch.* 229
Teach mercy to ten thousand *h.* that share *Ch.* 278
Has still a veil of midnight on his *h. Ch.* 376
Each *h.* would quit its prison in the breast *Ch.* 610
A difference strikes at length the musing *h. Comp.* i 8
The vainest corner of our own vain *h. Con.* 366
Man's *h.* had been impenetrably sealed *Con.* 427
Warming his *h.*, should at his lips transpire? *Con.* 484
Your *h.* shall yield a life-renewing stream *Con.* 503
A deep memorial graven on their *h, Con.* 514
Did not our *h.* feel all He deigned to say *Con.* 535
H. may be found that harbour at this hour *Con.* 561
And while at *h.* sin unrelinquished lies *Con.* 673
Of *h.* in union mutually disclosed *Con.* 680 [682
Those *h.* should be reclaimed, renewed upright *Con.*
Sad as it is, his undissembling *h. Con.* 712
And one in *h.*, in interest, and design *Con.* 701
He knows that God demands his *h.* entire *Con.* 759
Than while his conduct proves his *h.* sincere *Con.* 766
That in her *h.* the Christian she reveres *Con.* 787
Though, could our *h.* repine *Dr.* 14
The centre of a glowing *h. E.* i 14 [ii 19
But He who knew what human *h.* would prove *E.*
But distance only cannot change the *h. E.* iii 2
"Yea marry shalt thou, and with all my *h. E.* iii 29
Broad-cloth without, and a warm *h.* within *E.* iii 63
That beams delight? a *h.* untaught to sigh? *Ep.* i 6
My *h.* of thoughts that made it ache *Ep.* ii 35
Self-idolized, and yet a knave at *h. Ex.* 94 [625
Their streaming *h.* poured freely when they died *Ex.*
The web of every scheme they have at *h. Ex.* 331
To quell the valour of the stoutest *h. Ex.* 358 [396
Hast thou, with *h.* perverse and conscience seared *Ex.*
For ears and *h.* that he can hope to please? *Ex.* 451
Was formed to harden *h.* and shock the sight *Ex.* 495
Wisdom and Goodness are twin-born one *h. Ex.* 634
And bind the task assigned thee to thine *h. Ex.* 651
Of Liberality of *h. F.* 5 [659
Or his, who touched their *h.* with hallowed fires? *Ex.*
Illuminating *h.* or mind *F.* 8
And held accustomed conference with my *h. F.A.* 9
His head and his *h.* are both likely to ache *F.M.* 15
That lasting happiness, a thankful *h. H.* 160
Nor set a price upon a willing *h. H.* 337

The writer well remarks, a *h.*, that knows *H.* 429
They were by nature, atheists, head and *h. H.* 498
Had each a brother's interest in his *h. H.* 579
Powers of the mind, and feelings of the *h. H.* 654
And writes a Doomsday sentence on his *h. H.* 693
'Tis God himself triumphant in his *h. H.* 735
But pleasure wins his *h. H.F.* 12
After long sleep, of passion in the *h. J.T.* 42
Have wound themselves about this *h. M.* 19
Thy worn-out *h.* will break at last *M.* 51.
Proves that the *h.* is none of his *M.F.* 61
And dwells there in a female *h. Miss* — 1
No bribes the *h.* can win *Miss* — 58
And fashioning my softened *h. Miss* — 91
With all a tender *h.* can feel *Miss* — 103
I would not trust my *h.*—the dear delight *M.P.* 82
With present ills his *h.* must ache *N.* 11
Only by a broken *h. N.C.* 48
To thy whole *h.* desire ? *N.Y.G.* 12
There dwells some wish in every *h. N.Y.G.* 15
Once more in this sad *h. O.* ii 3
The sight our foolish *h.* inflames *P.B.* 31
The serpent Error twines round human *h. P.E.* 43
And has the Ladies' Etiquette by *h. P.E.* 196
These both are pleasures to the feeling *h. P.E.* 254
The *h.*, surrendered to the ruling power *P.E.* 275
To taint his *h.*, was worthy of thine own! *P.E.* 346
His stock, a few French phrases got by *h. P.E.* 375
Inveterate habits choke the unfruitful *h. R.* 41
The roving eye misleads the careless *h. R.* 126
May feel a *h.* enriched by what it pays *R.* 209
'Tis consecration of his *h.*, soul, time, *R.* 223
No longer give an image all thine *h. R.* 276 [307
Blessed, rather cursed, with *h.* that never feel *R.*
And staunch the bleedings of a broken *h. R.* 322
With aching *h.*, and discontented looks *R.* 471
His countenance, his purse, his *h.*, his hand *R.* 595
From vulgar minds, have honour much at *h. R.* 728
No, not a moment, in his royal *h. R.* 774
His noble *h.* went pit-a-pat *R.C.* 79
And *h.* that cannot rest, agree ! *S.* 4 [i 10
Both *h.* and head; and couldst with music sweet *S.*
So prays your Clerk with all his *h. St.* i 33
But when his *h.* had roved *St.* iii 24
Strange fondness of the human *h. St.* v 13
Prompt every movement of his *h.* and mind *T.* 194
One act, that from a thankful *h.* proceeds *T.* 223
And, pleased at *h.*, because on holy ground *T.* 232
By some kind, hospitable *h.* possessed *T.* 251
What glowing thanks his lips and *h.* employ *T.* 255
Lies down secure, her *h.* and pocket light *T.* 322
He, lost in errors his vain *h.* prefers *T.* 335
Strength in his *h.*, dominion in his nod *T.* 409
His conduct, to the test, but tries his *h. T.* 562
That they proceeded from a grateful *h. T.* 580
With acrid salts, his very *h.* athirst *T.* i 448
Health suffers, and the spirits ebb ; the *h. T.* i 466
The mouth with blasphemy, the *h.* with woe *T.* i 505
Such health and gaiety of *h.* enjoy *T.* i 587
I cannot think thee yet so dull of *h. T.* i 651
There is no flesh in man's obdurate *h. T.* ii 8
With stripes, that Mercy, with a bleeding *h. T.* ii 24
No : dear as freedom is, and in my *h.'s T.* ii 33
And bids the world take *h.* and banish fear *T.* ii 195
Thy joys and sorrows, with as true a *h. T.* ii 220
Put so much of his *h.* into his act *T.* ii 249 [ii 320
What vice has it subdued ? whose *h.* reclaimed *T.*
I venerate the man whose *h.* is warm *T.* ii 372
Reclaims the wanderer, binds the broken *h. T.* ii 344
When sent with God's commission to the *h. T.* ii 471
O Popular Applause ! what *h.* of man *T.* ii 481
Upon the roving and untutored *h. T.* ii 570
The occupation dearest to his *h. T.* ii 709

What provocation to the indignant *h. T.* iii 65
So hollow and so false—I feel my *h. T.* iii 182 [241
Through all the *h.'s* dark chambers, and reveal *T.* iii
Reflections such as meliorate the *h. T.* iii 304 [322
Delights which who would leave, that has a *h. T.* iii
That has a *h.*, and keeps it ; has a mind *T.* iii 374
With her who shares his pleasures and his *h. T.* iii 390
And folly in the *h.*; were England now *T.* iii 742
By which he speaks the language of his *h. T.* iv 105
Discover countries, with a kindred *h. T.* iv 116
Ensanguined *h.*, clubs typical of strife *T.* iv 218
And have a friend in every feeling *h. T.* iv 376 [517
Nymphs were Dianas then, and swains had *h. T.* iv
The *h.* of merit in the meaner class *T.* iv 618
To break some maiden's or his mother's *h. T.* iv 656
He gives a tongue to enlarge upon, a *h. T.* iv 794
Than human passion please. In every *h. T.* v 205
The scorn of danger, and united *h. T.* v 377
Ye horrid towers, the abode of broken *h. T.* v 385
There's not an English *h.* that would not leap *T.* v 389
All *h.* to sadness, and none more than mine *T.* v 464
And sickly, while her champions wear their *h. T.* v511
Were sons indeed ; they felt a filial *h. T.* v 518
'Tis Liberty of *H.*, derived from Heaven *T.* v 545
Whose lying *h.* disputes against a God *T.* v 568
Propense his *h.* to idols, he is held *T.* v 585
" We find sound argument, we read the *h.*" *T* v 654
Till hardened his *h.'s* temper in the forge *T.* v 664
Whose *h.* with praise, and whose exalted mind *T.* v 751
Thine eye shall be instructed, and thine *h. T.* v 782
Possess the *h.*, and fables false as hell *T.* v 862
Is touch'd within us, and the *h.* replies *T.* vi 5 [87
May think down hours to moments. Here the *h. T.* vi
The *h.* is hard in nature, and unfit *T.* vi 321 [328
When none pursues, through mere delight of *h. T.* vi
No cruel purpose lurk'd within his *h. T.* vi 362 [372
Thy groves and lawns then witness'd! Every *h. T.* vi
Man may dismiss compassion from his *h. T.* vi 442
He hates the hardness of a Balaam's *h. T.* vi 467
The *h.'s* insanity admits no cure *T.* vi 523
The charity that warmed his *h.* was moved *T.* vi 498
To steel their *h.* against the dread of death" *T.* vi 511
That piety has still in human *h. T.* vi 683 [786
The breath of Heaven has chased it. In the *h. T.* vi
And e'en the joy that haply some poor *h. T.* vi 832
Thy saints proclaim thee king; and in their *h. T.* vi 861
He by the test of conscience ; and a *h. T.* vi 988 [895
With conscience and with thee. Lust in their *h. T.* vi
To charm his ear, whose eye is on the *h. T.* vi 1022
This widowed *h.* would break" *The Doves* 36
Regardless of wringing and breaking a *h. The Rose* 15
To press the important question on his *h. Tir.* 57
And not with curses on his *h.*, who stole *Tir.* 151
Assert the native evil of his *h. Tir.* 162
The practice was a bond upon his *h. Tir.* 177
But taverns teach the knowledge of the *h. Tir.* 213
Shall win his *h.*, and have his drunken praise *Tir.* 215
The scene is touching, and the *h.* is stone *Tir.* 298
Christian in name, and infidel in *h. Tir.* 421 [444
Young heads are giddy, and young *h.* are warm *Tir.*
'Twere wiser sure to inspire a little *h. Tir.* 454
Against a *h.* depraved and temper hurt *Tir.* 489
He will not blush, that has a father's *h. Tir.* 547
How does it lacerate both your *h.* and his ! *Tir.* 558
Unless thy conscious *h.* acknowledge none *Tir.* 580
The mind and *h.* of every sprightly boy *Tir.* 598
To teach his *h.* to glow with generous flame *Tir.* 644
An upright *h.*, and cultivated mind *Tir.* 722 [*Tir.* 801
Whose *h.* will ache, once told what ills may reach
Thou canst not ! Nature, pulling at thine *h. Tir.* 865
His *h.*, now passive, yields to thy command *Tir.* 885
One comfort yet shall cheer thine aged *h. Tir.* 897
Thou hast all thine *h.* desire *Trans.* iii 16

Tells of a few stout h. that fought and died T.T. 23
Patriots, who love good places at their h. T.T. 191
The poet's h.; he looks to distant storms T.T. 495 [380
The stream that feeds the wellspring of the h. T.T.
That, like some cottage beauty strikes the h. T.T. 524
In Eden, ere yet innocence of h. T.T. 584
And every warbler has his tune by h. T.T. 655
Should be the poet's h. U. 26
Farewell, false h.! whose best affections fail V. 1
Your altered h.—and so, my Lord, farewell! V 26
Might prove a welcome gift, and touch thine h. V. 41
Should be renewed in nature, pure in h. V. 60
The h. of man, for such a task too frail V. 67
Union of h. without a flaw between V. 86
Content of h., more praises still are due V. 90
And giving one, whose h. is in the skies V. 93
Each h. as heavy as a log Y.D. 15

HEART-CHILLING.
Expects in darkness and h. fears H. 714

HEART-CONSOLING.
And contemplation, h. joys T. iv 781

HEART-DISTENDING.
Of silent tears and h. sighs! T. iii 331

HEART-FELT.
A scene of fancied bliss and h. care H. 5
Of h. joys, succeeds not soon again Her. 64
Indulges all a father's h. glee Tir. 321

HEARTH.
Feeds a blue flame, and makes a cheerful h. T. iii 33
The glowing h. may satisfy awhile T. iv 273
Chirping on my kitchen h. Trans. iii 2

HEARTILY.
And in due time feeds h. on both Con. 338
Will h. thank us, no doubt, for our pains P.A. 10
Lived long, wrote much, laughed h. and died T. 307

HEART-SEARCHING.
Sincerity towards the h. God Con. 753

HEART-SHAKING.
With such h. music, who can say T. iv 24

HEART-SICK.
And Chatham h. of his country's shame T. ii 244

HEART-STRINGS.
Upon his h., trembling with delight T. v 414

HEARTY.
And now a h. smack Trans. iv 18

HEAT.
For him, though chased with furious h. Beau 11
Nice in its choice, and of a tempered h. J.T. 36 [10
Where the hazels afford him a screen from the h. P.F.
Her summer h., her fruits, and her perfumes R. 196
The auspicious moment, when the tempered h. T.iii508
The process. H. and cold, and wind and steam T. iii 554
Till Autumn's fiercer h. and plenteous dews Tir. 47
In Afric's torrid clime, or India's fiercest h. T.T. 297
Destroys them—skies uncertain, now the h. Y.O. 74

HEATH.
The h. uncovered and the moors A Tale 17
Groves, h., and smoking villages, remote T. i 176
Near yonder h.; where Industry misspent T. iii 643

HEATHEN.
The h. lawgivers of ancient days Con. 35
Are bringing into vogue their h. train Con. 821
The gross idolatry blind h. teach H. 499

Let h. worthies, whose exalted mind T. 525
(For was it less, what h. would have dared T. vi 639

HEATHY.
Then neither h. wilds, nor scenes as fair R. 331

HEAVE.
"And still the sigh responsive h. Miss — 87
Will weep indeed, and h. a pitying groan T. 177
Tormented into billows, h. and swells T. ii 101 [429
With bleeding sides and flanks that h. for life T. vi
He h. up many a sigh Y.D. 12

HEAVED.
She teemed and h. with an infernal birth Her. 13
But when he felt it, h. a sigh St. iii 27
A bosom h. with never ceasing sighs T. i 552

HEAVEN.
H. awards the vengeance due B. 42
Nor felt but in the soul that H. selects Ch. 8
Through fear, not love; and H. abhors the fee Ch. 46
Of H.'s mysterious purposes and ways Ch. 58
H. speed the canvas, gallantly unfurled Ch. 123
Remember, H. has an avenging rod Ch. 216
The poor thy clients, and H.'s smile thy fee Ch. 312
That H. spreads wide before the view of man Ch. 324
H. held his hand, the likeness must be true Ch. 434
That in the h. of h., that space He deems Ch. 589
And H. reflected in her face Comp. ii 10
That H. and Hell, and righteousness and sin Con. 469
O days of h., and nights of equal praise! Con. 567
Who waits for h. ere he becomes divine Con. 584
Can hopes of H., bright prospects of an hour Con. 591
For which H. formed the faculty divine Con. 898
Where under H. is Pleasure more pursued Ex. 7
With all that man e'er wished, or H. bestowed? Ex.196
If we escaped not, if H. spared not us Ex. 245 [390
Hast thou, when H. has clothed thee with disgrace Ex.
Brought fire from H., the sex-abusing crime Ex. 415
Their hope in H., servility their scorn Ex. 440
While his own h. surveys the troubled scene Ex. 586
Marked with the signature and stamp of H.—Ex. 685
Which make that H., if thou desire it, thine Ex. 687
By which H. rules the mixed affairs of man H. 16
That H.'s intentions are not what they seem H. 66
Revere the laws they dream that H. ordains H. 241
The tidings of unpurchased H. create H. 343 [366
That H. will weigh man's virtues and his crimes H.
I glide and steal along with h. in view H. 379
Then h. enjoins the fallible and frail H. 391
Must go to h.—and I must drink his health H. 412
To take with gratitude what h. bestows H. 430
And he that finds his H. must lose his sins H. 638
'Tis H., all H., descending on the wings H. 732
And h. is all departed as a scroll H. 747
The breath of h. must swell the sail H.F. 23 [19
That privilege was thine; H. gave thee means J.T.
Thine had a value in the scales of H.—J.T. 29
By bounteous h. designed Miss — 2
Mankind received from h. Miss — 24
And fixed by H.'s decree Miss — 46
"Oh! grant, kind H. to me Miss — 66
This artless vow may H. receive Miss — 93 [73
Not scorned in H., though little noticed here M.P.
His lamp now planted on H.'s topmost arch N.A. 30
The H. that thou alone canst make? O. ii 14 [165
When the glad soul is made H.'s welcome guest P.E.
H. from above, and Conscience from within P.E. 37
H.'s harmony is universal love P.E. 78 [P.E. 216
H. blessed the youth, and made him fresh and fair
Envy the beast, then, on whom H. bestows P.E. 267
Kneels and asks H. to bless the dear deceit P.E. 525
Till yonder h. and earth shall mingle P.T. 33
Amid the vault of h. Q.V. 16

H. grant us no such future sight *Q.V.* 79
For *H.'s* high purposes, and not his own *R.* 18
Ask wealth of *H.*, and gain a real prize *R.* 162
Then *H.*, eclipsed so long, and this dull earth *R.* 355
Nor seldom, as propitious *H.* might send *R.* 377
Could I, from *H.* inspired, as sure presage *St.* ii 1
All *H.* unfolded to my eyes *St.* iii 11
Called up from Earth to *H. St.* iii 30
Death and Judgment, *H.* and Hell *St.* iv 29
H.'s easy, artless, unencumbered plan ! *T.* 22 [34
" *H.* on such terms !" they cry with proud disdain *T.*
H. turns from with abhorrence and disdain *T.* 72
As stoop from *H.* to sell the proud a throne *T.* 78
Have purchased *H.*, and prove my title good *T.* 96
Thus *H.* approves, as honest and sincere *T.* 225
And *h.*, no doubt shall be their home at last *T.* 296
One pleasure lost, lose *h.* without regret *T.* 342
Shall fall on her, when *H.* denies it thee *T.* 512
Kindled in *H.*, that it burns down to earth *T.* ii 134
That live an atheist life ; involves the *H.*—*T.* ii 180
Are all such teachers ? Would to *H.* all were! *T.* ii 350
Since *H.* would grow weary of a world *T.* ii 583 [788
Just when it meets his hopes, and proves the *H.*—*T.* iii
Unless by *H.'s* peculiar grace, escape *T.* ii 632 [221
God never meant that man should scale the *H.*—*T.* iii
Than all that held their routs in Juno's *h.* ! *T.* ii 660
Has made a *H.* on earth ; with suns and moons *T.* iii 645
One drop of *H.'s* sweet mercy in his cup *T.* iii 804
H., earth, and ocean, plunder'd of their sweets *T.* iv 82
From *H.* to Earth, of lambent flame serene *T.* v 153
And tremble at vain dreams ? *H.* grant I may! *T.* v 492
Was registered in *H.* ere time began *T.* v 530
'Tis Liberty of Heart, derived from *H.*—*T.* v 545
In other *h.* than these that we behold *T.* v 571
And chased them up to *H.* Their ashes flew *T.* v 726
Can lift to *H.* an unpresumptuous eye *T.* v 746 [796
Not so the mind that has been touched from *H.*—*T.* v
Much conversant with *H.*, she often holds *T.* v 815
With which *H.* rang, when every star, in haste *T.* v 819
"And to possess a brighter *H.* than yours? *T.* v 831
Breaks on the soul, and by a flash from *H.*—*T.* v 884
Is register'd in *h.* ; and these no doubt *T.* vi 440 [844
" And that, infused from *H.*, must thither tend " *T.* v
By which *H.* moves in pardoning guilty man *T.* vi 597
Which *h.* has heard for ages, have an end *T.* vi 730
The breath of *H.* has chased it. In the heart *T.* vi 786
Saw never, such as *H.* stoops down to see *T.* vi 817
Derives from *H.*, pure as the fountain is *T.* vi 833
She makes familiar with a *H.* unseen *T.* vi 926 [547
Was now to learn that *H.*, though slow to wrath *T.* vi
Were all that *H.* required of human kind *Tir.* 85
What if thine *H.* be overcast *Trans. H.* 25
His portion in the good that *H.* bestows *T.T.* 20
May she ! and, if offended *H.* be still *T.T.* 406 [460
Earth shakes beneath them, and *H.* roars above *T.T.*
Brings colours dipped in *H.*, that never die *T.T.* 703
Touched with a coal from *H.*, assume the lyre *T.T.* 735
With truth from *h.*, created thing adore *Y.O.* 7
With love and wisdom, rendered back to *H.*—*Y.O.* 154
One breath of *H.*, that cried—" Restore ! " 1789, 40

HEAVEN-BORN.
H., and destined to the skies again *T.* iii 50

HEAVEN-DEFYING.
When Perjury, that *H.* vice *T.T.* 418

HEAVENLY.
Resides in that *h.* word ! *A.S.* 26
Inform his mind ; one flash of *h.* day *Ch.* 228
Philosophy, without his *h.* guide *Ch.* 375
Serene and peaceful as those *h.* days *Con.* 568
" What, always dreaming over *h.* things *Con.* 575

Of joys they meet with in their *h.* range *Con.* 694
Know then, that *H.* Wisdom on this ball *Ex.* 314
Religion, if in *h.* truths attired *Ex.* 492
Though *h.* in pretension, fleeced thee well *Ex.* 515
The beams of *h.* truth have swelled the debt! *Ex.* 611
Save for the fruits his *h.* beams produce *H.* 82
Born capable indeed of *h.* truth *H.* 231
(Yet charge not *h.* skill with having planned *H.* 542
Where'er the *h.* Nymph is seen *Miss* — 69
The peacock sends his *h.* dyes *Mrs. M*— 3
With a whole gamut filled of *h.* notes *N.A.* 26
Emblems of health and *h.* aid *Q.V.* 47
Souls that have long despised their *h.* birth *R.* 35
Instruct me, guide me to that *h.* day *R.* 95
O that unwelcome voice of *h.* love *T.* 463
In science, win one inch of *h.* ground *T.* 338
Not so ; the silver trumpet's *h.* call *T.* 349
Of *h.* temper, furnishes with arms *T.* ii 346
And rustic coarseness would. A *h.* mind *T.* ii 457
Can lodge a *h.* mind—demands a doubt *T.* ii 462
The eclipse that intercepts truth's *h.* beam *T.* v 683
A ray of *h.* light gilding all forms *T.* v 810
In *h.* truth ; evincing, as she makes *T.* vi 183
Betimes into the mould of *h.* truth *Tir.* 106

HEAVEN-PROTECTED.
O place me in some *H.* isle *Her.* 83

HEAVEN-RENOUNCING.
In *h.* exile, he endures *T.* v 598

HEAVENWARD.
With anxious meaning, *H.* turn his eye ! *St.* ii 8 [818
Thus *H.* all things tend. For all were once *T.* vi

HEAVIER.
They only weigh the *h. Y.D.* 48

HEAVIEST.
Till the best tongue, or *h.* hand, prevails *H.* 196
And *h.*, light of foot steals fast away *T.* iv 442
Comes *h.* to the ground *Trans. H.* 15

HEAVILY.
Groan *h.* along the distant road *Ex.* 58
The wain goes *h.*, impeded sore *T.* iv 343

HEAVINGS.
Soft airs and gentle *h.* of the wave *Ch.* 127

HEAVY.
'Tis *h.*, bulky, and bids fair to prove *Con.* 307
If chance, on *h.* pinions slowly borne *H.* 716
Galled by affliction's *h.* chain *St.* v 11
And, *h.* laden, brings his beverage home *T.* i 242
Each heart as *h.* as a log *Y.D.* 15

HEBERDEN.
Virtuous and faithful *H.*, whose skill *R.* 279

HEBREW.
H., or Syriac, shall be forced to bend *P.E.* 499

HEBRUS.
On Thracian *H.* side *T.B.* 63

HEDGE.
When scarlet fruits the russet *h.* adorn *A.T.* 72
O'er *h.* and ditch, through gaps and mews *E.* iv 52
Where frequent *h.* intercept the eye *T.* i 514
They pick their fuel out of every *h. T.* i 565
Enjoy close shelter, wall, or reeds, or *h. T.* iii 474
Woe to the gardener's pale, the farmer's *h. T.* iv 436
Beneath the *h.*, or near the stream *Trans.* i 1

HEDGEROW.
As *h.* in the wild *A Tale* 8

Her h. shrubs, a variegated store R. 419
Of h. beauties numberless, square tower T. i 173

HEED.

That few will hear, and fewer h. the strain Ex. 725
With caution and good h. J.G. 80
But ah! by constant h. I know M. 45
Warily therefore, and with prudent h. T. iii 470
Nor h. what guests there enter and abide Tir. 888

HEEDLESS.

H. of a soldier's name B. 22
Though Wisdom hail them, h. of her call Ch. 406
They fix attention, h. of your pain Con. 63
Bent all on pleasure, h. of its end E. ii 18
The tide of pleasure, h. of his frown Ex. 683
And h. whither, to that field I came N.A. 32
Viewed from a distance, and with h. eyes P.E. 202
She shines but little in his h. eyes R. 405
H. of his loudest lay St. iv 3 [487
And therefore h., can withstand thy power? T. ii
Or h. folly, by which thousands die T. iii 219 [148
Cough their own knell, while, h. of the sound T. iv
H. of all his pranks, the sturdy churl T. v 52
And doom him for perhaps a h. word T. v 440
Ruminate h. of the scene outspread T. v 788
The uninformed and h. souls of men T. v 864

HEEL.

So polished and compact from head to h. A.T. 184
Went postboy at his h. J.G. 230
For Reynard, close attended at his h. N.A. 124
A business with an income at its h. R. 615
Had made the vessel h. R.G. 7
With slipshod h., and dewdrop at his nose T. 144
A growing dread of vengeance at his h. T. 258
With belted waist and pointed at their h. T. ii 753
He climbs, he pants, he grasps them! At his h. T. iv 60
Close at his h., a demagogue ascends T. iv 61 [iv 546
Ill propped upon French h.; she might be deemed T.
Expect her soon with footboy at her h. T. iv 550
His dog attends him. Close behind his h. T. v 47
To madness; while the savage at his h. T. vi 422
Some royal mastiff panting at their h. T.T. 35 [vi 332
Then stops and snorts, and, throwing high his h. T.

HEIGHT.

Hangs out her lamp in yon cærulean h. A.T. 138
Duly, as ever on the mountain's h. Ch. 260
That throned above all h. He condescends Ch. 587
The Lily's h. bespoke command L.R. 13
Like sunbeams on the golden h. Mrs. M— 35
And he shall gild yon mountain's h. again P.E. 69
And posted on this speculative h. T. i 289
To an enormous and o'erbearing h. T. ii 112
To shake thy senate, and from h. sublime T. ii 216
To the sharp peak of her sublimest h. T. iii 157
To some secure and more than mortal h. T. iv 96
To some not steep, though philosophic h. Tir. 631
Fond of the speculative h. Tran. ii 13

HEIR.

Is still the progeny and h. of sin Ch. 344 [Tir. 356
Whose h., their honours none, their incomes small
For thou art born sole h., and single E. iv 3 [Tir. 708
And, as thou wouldst the advancement of thine h.
Than how to enrich thyself, and next, thine h. Tir.661

HELD.

He breaks the cord that h. him at the rack Ch. 173
Heaven h. his hand, the likeness must be true Ch. 434
H. within modest bounds, the tide of speech Con. 889
Seized fast his hand, h. out to set them free Ex. 219

By joys possessed, and joys still h. in chase Ex. 669
H. by the tenure of his will alone Ex. 673 [9
And h. accustomed conference with my heart F.A.
They could have h. the conduct they pursue H. 256
He h. them up, and in his turn J.G. 185
I always h. them in the right Pat. 7
But all unconscious whom it h. R.C 52
His fingers h. the pen R.G. 22
He h. the thunder. But the monarch owes T. i 382
Than all that h. their routs in Juno's heaven! T. ii 660
The mind was well-informed, the passions h. T. ii 715
Long h., and scarcely disengaged at last T. iii 16
And sealed with the same token. It is h. T. v 547
Propense his heart to idols, he is h. T. v 585 [574
Not so when, h. within their proper bounds T. vi
Which having served us, perish, we are h. T. vi 604
The auburn nut that h. thee, swallowing down Y.O. 20

HELICON.

"Who throw their H. about E. iv 85
To turn the course of H. that way T.T. 183

HELL. [469

That Heaven and H., and righteousness and sin Con.
Call legions up from H. to back the deed Con. 691
And H.'s close mischief naked in his sight Ex. 339
Legates and delegates, with powers from h. Ex. 514
From earth or h., we can but plunge at last " N.A. 122
Those awful syllables, H., Death, and Sin H. 690
Diffused, make Earth the vestibule of H.—P.E. 465
Death and the pains of H. attend him there P.E. 547
Delusions strong as H. shall bind him fast P.E. 609
Death and Judgment, Heaven and H. St. iv 29
He reads his sentence at the flames of H.—T. 10 [686
Tempered in h., invades the throbbing breast T. iii
Of Earth and H. confederate take away T. v 541
Possess the heart, and fables false as h. T. v 862
Asked, when in H., to see the royal jail T.T. 94

HELLISH.

" O cursed Hypothesis! your h. arts A.T. 113
With such a jest as filled with h. glee Con. 737
That h. foes, confederate for his harm T. v 735

HELM.

And darting through his h. an eagle's eye A.T. 148
Buckled his h., and to his steed repaired A.T. 172
And hoped to seize his abdicated h. Ex. 577

HELMET.

With h. heads, and dragon-scales adorned R. 69
His hat, or his plumed h., with a grace T. iv 643
Of trophied h., spears, and shields 1789, 4

HELP.

Entreated " H.!" or cried—" Adieu!" Cast. 42
Quickens a market, and h. off the trash Ch. 522
By Contemplation's h., not sought in vain M.P. 114
Need h., let honest industry provide P.E. 252
Need h., denies them nothing but his name T. iv 428
Not more in human h., than we on theirs T. vi 609
Where Discipline h. opening buds of sense T.T. 508

HELPLESS.

Thou tutelary friend of h men? Ch. 42
And h., hopeless, hear thee say— O. ii 23
Thus some retire to nourish h. woe R. 603
Thine h. charge, dependent on thy care T. iv 369
But h., in few years shall find their hands T. iv 423
And h. victims with a sense so keen T. vi 475
In aiding h. indigence, in works T. vi 964

HEMS.

Or oaken fence that h. the paddock round T.T. 583

HEMMED.
h comfortless existence! *h.* around *T.* v 432

HERALD.
h. of God's love to pagan lands *Ch.* 136
he busy *h.* hang the sable scene *H.* 264
hat *h.* ere designed *Q.V.* 24
e comes, the *h.* of a noisy world *T.* iv 5

HERB.
ips meek infusions of a milder *h. Con.* 268
nd drought on all the drooping *h.* around *E.* ii 50
ith every *h.* that blunts the sense *Miss* — 23 [38
he *h.* as soft, while nibbling strayed the rest *N.A.*
e bears the *h.* and flowers rejoicing all *N.A.* 60
he grain, or *h.*, or plant that each demands *R.* 788
mells fresh, and, rich in odoriferous *h. T.* i 531
Iis favourite *h.*; while all the leafless groves *T.* iv 319
rom every *h.* and every spiry blade *T.* v 9 [762
What are the casements lined with creeping *h. T.* iv
Beneath the frozen clod: all seeds of *h. T.* v 81
And eyes intent upon the scanty *h. T.* v 786

HERBAGE.
Vines, olives, *h.*, forests disappear *Her.* 23
Upon the yielding *h.* (so they sing) *T.* iv 521

HERCULANEAN.
Models of *H.* pots and pans *P.E.* 398
Not formed like us, with such *H.* powers *T.T.* 235

HERD.
Henceforth associate in one common *h. Con.* 76
That fed the flocks and *h.* of wealthy Lot *Ex.* 419
Nor *h.* have ye to boast, nor bleating flocks *H.* 466
The lawless *h.*, with fury blind *M.* ii 13
And hills that echo to the distant *h. R.* 184
I was a stricken deer that left the *h. T.* iii 108
Unpeople all our counties of such *h. T.* iii 831
The total *h.* receiving first from one *T.* vi 335 [688
There, in his commerce with the liveried *h. Tir.*
Swarmed with a scribbling *h.*, as deep inlaid *T.T* 628

HERDSMAN.
That screen the *h.'s* solitary hut *T.* i 168

HERESY.
Then Truth is hushed, that *H.* may preach *Ex.* 107

HERMIT.
A *H.* (or if 'chance you hold *Mor.* 1
As *H.* could have well desired *Mor.* 4
Your *h.*, young and jovial sirs! *Mor.* 23
See the sage *h.*, by mankind admired *T.* 87
Ten starveling *h.* suffer less than he *T.* 112 [168
Where *h.* and where Bramins meet with theirs *T.*

HERO.
And tears by bards or *h.* shed *Cast.* 53
That now and then a *h.* must decease *Con.* 175
The reeking, roaring *h.* of the chase *Con.* 405
H. and worthies of days past, thy sires? *Ew.* 658
What are ye, monarchs, laurelled *h.*, say *Her.* 77
Some headless *h.*, or some Cæsar shows *P.E.* 395
Of *h.* little known, and call the rant *T.* iii 140
To Nature's praises. *H.* and their feats *T.* iv 705
Of *h.*, whose infirm and baby minds *T.* v 190
Were burnished into *h.*, and became *T.* v 280
The minor *h.* view with envious eyes *Tir.* 223
The feats of *h.* and the wrath of kings *T.T.* 597

HEROIC.
As ever mingled with *h.* dust *Ch.* 24
A stream of liberal and *h.* deeds *Ch.* 245
Than that *h.* strut assumed before *Con.* 490
Impelled thee more to that *h.* course *J.T.* 34
Of patriots, bursting with *h.* rage *T.* iv 48

That takes not fire at their *h.* deeds *T.T.* 26
H. song from thy free touch acquires *T.T.* 292
Make their *h.* powers your own at once *T.T.* 570

HEROSHIP.
And, his three years of *h.* expired *T.* iv 644

HESITATE.
No muse can *h.*, or linger long) *Tir.* 291

HESITATION.
With *h.* admirably slow *Con.* 123
To banish *h.*, and proclaim *H.* 63

HETEROGENEOUS.
Their *h.* politics *F.* 128

HEW.
To enrich thy walls; but thou didst *h.* the floods *T.* v133

HEWED. [*Tir.* 303
Though mangled, hacked, and *h.*, not yet destroyed
And *h.* them link from link. There Albion's sons *T.* v [517

HEWING.
At *h.* mountains into men, and some *T.* v 178

HEWN.
Oaks fell not, *h.* by thousands, to supply *Y.O.* 101

HID.
Has he not *h.* thee, and thy favoured land *Ex.* 562
Our friend's defect long *h.* from sight *F.* 149
That remedy, not *h.* in deeps profound *H.* 111
There *h.* in loathed obscurity, removed *R.* 563
Long *h.* by interposing hill or wood *T.* 249
As, *h.* from ages past, God now displays *Tir.* 638
Of treeship—first a seedling *h.* in grass *Y.O.* 61

HIDDEN.
Like *h.* lamps in old sepulchral urns *Con.* 358
And *h.* as it is, and far remote *T.* i 228
In cities, vice is *h.* with most ease *T.* i 689

HIDE.
Not even birds can *h. A Tale* 66
He *h.* behind a magisterial air *Ch.* 493
And *h.* past folly from all-seeing eyes? *Ex.* 405 [481
Taught thee to clothe thy pinked and painted *h. Ex.*
Where oft the bitch-fox *h.* her hapless brood *N.A.* 4
And *h.* the ruin that it feeds upon *P.E.* 286
Themselves will *h.* its coarseness with a veil *P.E.* 292
To *h.* the shocking features of her face *P.E.* 298
Beneath your shades your grey possessor *h. R.* 368
Dewdrops may deck the turf that *h.* the bones *St.* ii 31
Crush me, ye rocks; ye falling mountains *h. T.* 269
And *h.* his hands to keep his fingers warm *T.* 148
With base materials, sat on well-tanned *h. T.* i 51
That *h.* the seamew in his hollow clefts *T.* i 519
The livelong night. A tattered apron *h. T.* i 549
Worn as a cloak, and hardly *h.*, a gown *T.* i 550
And bow obsequious, *h.* their hate of her *T.* ii 646
And bid them *h.* themselves in earth beneath *T.* iii 213
These on the warm and genial earth that *h. T.* iii 516
Here every drop of honey *h.* a sting *T.* vi 830
That *h.* divinity from mortal eyes *T.* vi 877
And badger-colored *h. T.B.* 36 [422
When Avarice starves, and never *h.* his face *T.T.*

HIDEOUS.
With all these *h.* howlings to the skies *N.A.* 88
More *h.* foes than fancy can devise *R.* 68
Or with vortiginous and *h.* whirl *T.* ii 102
Would find them *h.* nurseries of the spleen *T.* iii 318
Is Winter *h.* in a garb like this? *T.* iv 194

HIDING.
The neat conveyance *h.* all the offence *T.* vi 980

HIGH.
And on her wickerwork *h.* mounted *A Fable* 3
But suddenly a wind, as *h. A Fable* 10
To exalt a people, and to place them *h. Con.* 519
And *h.* in pedigree *D.W.* 6
They knew, by sure prognostics seen on *h. Ex.* 157
Leaped out of nothing, called by the most *H. Ex.* 639
With ribbon-bound tassel on *h. Gr.* 2 [*H.* 312
That all might mark—knight, menial, *h.*, and low
Stood pilloried on infamy's *h.* stage *H.* 556 [*N.A.* 25
With tails *h.* mounted, ears hung low, and throats
Is there One who reigns on *h.* ? *N.C.* 26
Now, while the poison all *h.* life pervades *P.E.* 347
And steeples towering *h.*, much like our own *P.E.* 382
The ocean serves, on *h. Q.V.* 18
For Heaven's *h.* purposes, and not his own *R.* 18
Would mock the majesty of man's *h.* birth *R.* 71
Nightly lifts his voice on *h. St.* iv 6
Thankless for favours from on *h. St.* v 1
H. in demand, though lowly in pretence *T.* 93
And bruised the side, and, elevated *h. T.* i 66
Upridged so *h.*, and sent on such a charge *T.* ii 116
And roofs embattled *h.*, the gloomy scenes *T.* ii 122
Delicious, when her patriots of *h.* note *T.* iv 170
No less than hers, not worn indeed on *h. T.* iv 255
Sofa, and couch, and *h.* built throne august *T.* v.164
Here glittering turrets rise, upbearing *h. T.* v 110
At building human wonders mountain *h. T.* v 179
Beat *h.* within them at a mother's wrongs *T.* v 519
His *h.* endeavour, and his glad success *T.* v 901 [vi 332
Then stops and snorts, and throwing *h.* his heels *T.*
The very kine that gambol at *h.* noon *T.* vi 334
(As if barbarity were *h.* desert) *T.* vi 435 [*T.* vi 497
Beats back the roaring surge, scarce heard so *h.*
No need of lightnings from on *h. The Doves* 33
Patient, affectionate, of *h.* command *Tir.* 602
No. His *h.* mettle, under good control *T.T.* 308
Have raised you *h.* as talents can ascend *V.* 13

HIGH-BRED.
His *h.* steed expands his nostrils wide *A.T.* 163

HIGHER.
But *h.* far my proud pretensions rise *M.P.* 110
Her smile his aim, all *h.* aims farewell *R.* 246
A *h.* than a mere plebeian fame *Tir.* 691

HIGHEST.
Around their flight who *h.* soar) *Mrs. M—* 48
Whose *h.* praise is that they live in vain *R.* 23
And *h.* in renown, can justly boast *R.* 676
Now which stands *h.* in your serious thought ? *T.* 221
The balance in the *h.* place *Th.* 11
Stooped from its *h.* pitch to pounce a wren *T.T.* 553

HIGH-FINISHED.
Thou polished and *h.* foe to truth *P.E.* 341

HIGH-LIFTED.
While the billows *h.* the boat *M.D.* 7

HIGHLY.
And only there, please *h.* for their sake *T.* 209

HIGH-MINDED.
H., foaming out their own disgrace *T.* vi 898

HIGH-RAISED.
Or with the *h.* horn's melodious clang *N.A.* 35

HIGH-SOUNDING.
Ah, tinkling cymbal and *h.* brass *T.* v 681

HIGHT.
October *h.*, but mild and fair as May *A.T.* 71

HIGHWAYMAN.
"Stop thief! stop thief!—a *h.*!" *J.G.* 237

HIGHWAY-SIDE.
Suburban villas, *h.* retreats *R.* 481

HILL.
H., valleys, rivers, and the boundless sea *A.T.* 49
But groves, *h.*, and valleys diffuse *C.* 39 [*Ch.* 368
Some through the groves, some down the sloping *h.*
Perched on the top of yonder *h. E.* i 44
One story more, dear *H.*, and I have done *E.* iii 45
She spreads the morning over eastern *h. H.* 41
And from the trees that fringed his *h. Mor.* 14 [34
Told *h.* and dale that Reynard's track was found *N.A.*
And *h.* that echo to the distant herds *R.* 184
Nor soft declivities with tufted *h. R.* 333
And bid her mountains and her *h.* rejoice *R.* 362
Long hid by interposing *h.* or wood *T.* 249 [113
O'er *h.*, through valleys, and by river's brink *T.* i
'Tis perched upon the green *h.* top, but close *T.* i 222
Of *h.* and valley interposed between *T.* i 322
The air salubrious of her lofty *h. T.* i 428
The *h.* move lightly, and the mountains smoke *T.* ii 91
That draw the sportsman over *h.* and dale *T.* iii 310
Woods vanish, *h.* subside, and valleys rise *T.* iii 775
Noiseless, appears a moving *h.* of snow *T.* iv 346
The *h.* and valleys with their ceaseless songs *T.* v 78
These meadows and that range of *h.* his own *T.* v 223
Of no mean city, planned or ere the *h. T.* v 764
Upon the southern side of the slant *h. T.* vi 59
Would creep into the bowels of the *h. T.* vi 867

HILLOCKS.
Our foot half sunk in *h.* green and soft *T.* i 272

HINDER.
No noise is here, or none that *h.* thought *T.* vi 76
That may advance, but cannot *h.*, thine *T.* vi 955

HINDRANCE.
And meets with *h.* in the smoothest way *P.E.* 443
If *h.* obstruct thy way *Trans. H.* 31

HINDS.
Knew their own masters, and laborious *h. T.* iii 747

HINGE.
Swinging the parlour door upon its *h. E.* iii 21
Say on what *h.* does his obedience move ? *T.* 207

HINT.
I am no preacher; let this *h.* suffice *P.E.* 621
He cultivates. These serve him with a *h. T.* iv 758

HIPS.
Her elbows pinioned close upon her *h. T.* 133
I fed on scarlet *h.* and stony haws *T.* i 120

HIRE.
Who vote for *h.*, or point it with lampoon *Con.* 29
"Do they themselves, who undertake for *h. T.* v 644
Why *h.* a lodging in a house unknown *Tir.* 555

HIRED. [89
The nurse sleeps sweetly, *h.* to watch the sick *T.* i
To more than he is *h.* or bound to teach *Tir.* 732

HIRELING.
Scorns the base *h.*, and the slavish drudge *T.* 228
The wearied *h.* finds it a release *T.* v. 411

HISS.
Would *h.* the cherub Mercy from the stage *T.* 478

HISSED.
All mercy from his lips, and sneered and *h. H.* 561

HISSING.
And while the bubbling and loud h. urn T. iv 38

HISTORIAN.
The poet's or h.'s page by one T. iv 158

HISTORIC.
In vain recorded in h. page B.B. 3
Their names to the sweet lyre. The H. Muse T. v 707
And the sixth Edward's, grace the h. page T.T. 106
In many a page h. strayed 1789, 22

HISTORICAL.
Her utmost reach, h. assent Con. 777

HISTORY.
This h. chanced of late A Tale 10
This h. of a wedded pair A Tale 11
Ask now of H.'s authentic page Ex. 161
The Saviour's h. makes known F. 206
'Tis now become a h. little known M.P. 52
A h.: describe the man, of whom T. iii 141
And H., so warm on meaner themes T. v 729
And when recording H. displays T.T. 21
Then leave their crimes for H. to scan T.T. 119
Is truth, if h. itself be true T.T. 399
The clock of h., facts and events Y.O. 46
With problems. H. not wanted yet Y.O. 159

HISTRIONIC.
And h. mummery, that let down T. ii 563
Illustrious h. patentee V. 29

HIT.
And therefore 'tis a mark fools never h. Con. 880

HITCH.
Knots and impediments make something h. Con. 108

HIVES.
And bees in h. as idly wait N. 3
Our public h. of puerile resort Tir. 458

HOARD.
What pleasure can the miser's fondled h. J.T. 15
The squirrel here his h. provides M.B. 5
And h. them in her sleeve; but needful food T. i 554

HOARSENESS.
And by the h. of his note Trans. ii 2

HOARY.
Sat the Druid, h. chief B. 6
Such freedom is ;—and Windsor's h. towers Ex. 596
Above the reach of man : his h. head T. i 520
That at the sound of Winter's h. wing T. iii 830

HODGE.
The morning came, when neighbour H.—A Fable 24
Dame Gurton thus, and H. her son E. iv 39
While eager H. beholds the prize E. iv 43

HOG.
From the whole h. to be debarred L.W. 12
Mahometans eat up the h. L.W. 22

HOIST.
Now h. the sail, and let the streamers float T. ii 255

HOLD.
When one that h. communion with the skies Ch. 435
H. a usurped dominion o'er his tongue Con. 462 [606
The churches warmed, they would no longer h. Ch.
She boasts a confidence she does not h. Con. 768
Must h. both sisters, never seen apart Ex. 635
She h. a Paradise of rich delight H. 60

His offspring h. in his paternal care H. 140
Hope, as an anchor firm and sure, h. fast H. 167
Even till his spacious hall would h. no more H. 309
To h. the liquor that she loved J.G. 67
A Hermit (or if 'chance you h. Mor. 1
I h. it therefore wisest and most fit N.A. 103
Nor h. forbidden joys in view O. ii 5
And through life's labyrinth h. fast the clue P.E. 357
For 'tis a rule that h. for ever true P.E. 534
To h. discourse, at least in fable P.T. 4
And h. the world indebted to your aid R. 665
He h. no parley with unmanly fears R.H. 5
And h. them dangling at arm's length in scorn T. 164
The paralytic, who can h. her cards T. i 472
That life h. out to all, should most abound T. i 752
Who then that has thee, would not h. thee fast T. ii 129
The earth shall shake him out of all his h. T. ii 146
The mirror of the mind, and h. them fast T. ii 291
Exposes, and h. up to broad disgrace T. ii 553
A relaxation of Religion's h. T. ii 569
They gaze upon the links that h. them fast T. ii 664
That h. mankind together, to a scourge T. ii 687
Which not e'en critics criticise: that h. T. iv 51
Perched on the signpost, h. with even hand T. iv 483
Your self-denying zeal, that h. it good T. v 328
Eradicate him, tear him from his h. T. v 437
With ease, and is at large. The oppressor h. T. v 774
Much conversant with Heaven, she often h. T. v 815
And seeking grace to improve the prize they h. T. vi 55
H. an unthinking multitude enthrall'd T. vi 101
The charter was conferred, by which we h. T. vi 451
Supplied such relics as devotion h. T. vi 689
H. its due course, nor fears the frost of age T. vi 790
H. no ignoble, though a slighted, place T. vi 971
H. fast her office here, can ne'er forget Tir. 134
Maintains its h. with such unfailing sway Tir. 316
Either his gratitude shall h. him fast Tir. 893
He that h. fast the golden mean Trans. H. 7 [273
Free to prove all things, and h. fast the best T.T.
That h. in view the good of man U. 24
H. up the cloth before Y.D. 44
The stubborn soil, and h. thee still erect Y.O. 119

HOLDING.
Then h. the spectacles up to the Court A.C. 13

HOLD'ST.
And dreaded as thou art! Thou h. the sun T. iv. 129

HOLES.
And drilled in h., the solid oak is found T. i 26 [86
Thins all their numerous flocks. In chinks and h. T. v

HOLIDAY.
On all the wings of h. delight) Ch. 548
No h. have seen J.G. 8
Humour in h., and sightly trim T.T. 643

HOLINESS.
With h. and consecrated rest P.E. 158

HOLLOW.
And had a h. with a wheel A Tale 35
With h. form, and gesture, and grimace Ex. 122
Weighing them in the h. of his hand Ex. 343
A h. scooped, I judge, in ancient time N.A. 17
That hides the seamew in his h. clefts T. i 519
She quakes at his appproach. Her h. womb T. ii 88
So h. and so false—I feel my heart T. iii 182
Its h. glens, its thickets, and its plains T. vi 402

HOLLOW'D.
That age or injury has h. deep T. vi 311

HOLLOW-EYED.
H. Abstinence, and lean Despair H. 58

HOLLOW-TRUNKED.
A shattered veteran, *h*. perhaps *Y.O.* 4

HOLY.
The temple and its *h*. rites profaned *Ex.* 145
Thy services, once *h*. without spot *Ex.* 261
H. and unpolluted : are thine such ? *Ex.* 447
Those *h*. men, so full of truth and grace *Ex.* 618
God's *h*. word, once trivial in his view *H.* 706
And pleased at heart, because on *h*. ground *T.* 232
Hence a demeanour *h*. and unspecked *T.* 281
Of *h*. writ, she has presumed to annul *T.* i 741
With what intent I touch that *h*. thing) *T.* ii 328
Of *h*. discipline, to glorious war *T.* ii 348
Truths undiscerned but by that *h*. light *T.* iii 242
That makes a minister in *h*. things *T.* iii 280
Whose eye they fill with tears of *h*. joy *T.* v 750
That His most *h*. book, from whom it came *T.* vi 650

HOMAGE.
The lambent *h*. of his arrowy tongue *T.* vi 782

HOME.
Their roofless *h*. they fixed *A Tale* 38
To wing all her moments at *h*. *C.* 50
His floating *h*. for ever left *Cast.* 6
At my best *h*., if not exiled from thee " *Ch.* 243
From Sparta hither, and art here at *h*. *Ch.* 271
To traverse seas, range kingdoms, and bring *h*. *Ch.* 301
Has left some hundreds without *h*. or food *Ch.* 466
H. to the goal where it began the race *Ch.* 566
Called on a friend, drank tea, stepped *h*. again *Con.* 278
But when you knock, it never is at *h*. *Con.* 304
As from a seven years' transportation *h*. *Con.* 400
Discourse, as if released and safe at *h*. *Con.* 571
His happy eloquence seemed there at *h*. *Con.* 622
Make every parish but their own their *h*. *Con.* 860
"Nay—stay at *h*.—you're always going out " *E.* iii 25
He finds his long, last *h*. *Ep.* ii 38 [*Con.* 529
That reaching *h*., "The night," they said, "is near
And having trucked thy soul, brought *h*. the fee *Ex.* 374
And all at *h*. is pleasure, wealth, and ease *Ex.* 583
Reclaim the wandering thousands and bring *h*. *Ex.* 728
Is Hope exotic ? Grows it not at *h*. ? *H.* 549
Engaged myself to be at *h*. *M.F.* 12
Thy morning bounties ere I left my *h*. *M.P.* 60
Forced from *h*. and all its pleasures *N.C.* 1
A little nearer *h*. *Pat.* 4
Like a slain deer, the tumbrel brings him *h*. *P.E.* 94
Their answer to the call it—" Not at *h*." *P.E.* 168
From school to Cam or Isis, and thence *h*. *P.E.* 369
Excels a dunce that has been kept at *h*. *P.E.* 416
If a wish wander that way, call it *h*. *P.E.* 586
To the fair haven of my native *h*. *R.* 385
Revered at *h*., and felt in foreign lands *R.* 412
Obsequious when abroad, though proud at *h*. *R.* 440
Else more attached to pleasures found at *h*. *R.* 518
Start it at *h*., and hunt it in the dark *R.* 693
Have found their *h*., the grave *St.* i 4
" My *h*. henceforth is in the skies *St.* iii 9
Soon the grave must be your *h*. *St.* iv 15
Or ford the rivulets, are best at *h*. *T.* 217
Then welcome refuge, and a peaceful *h*. *T.* 267
And heaven, no doubt, shall be their *h*. at last *T.* 296
She, never heard of half a mile from *h*. *T.* 334
Still hungering, pennyless, and far from *h*. *T.* i 119
And, heavy laden, brings his beverage *h*. *T.* i 242
Who scorns it, starves deservedly at *h*. *T.* i 435
That thieves at *h*. must hang, but he that puts *T.* i 736
We have no slaves at *h*.: —Then why abroad ? *T.* ii 37
Consulting England's happiness at *h*. *T.* ii 246
And show the name ye might conceal at *h*. *T.* ii 279
But rare at *h*., and never at his books *T.* ii 383
Is hackneyed *h*. unlackeyed ; who, in haste *T.* ii 652

Have we not tracked the felon *h*., and found *T.* ii 813
His devious course uncertain, seeking *h*. *T.* iii 3
That brings the planets *h*. into the eye *T.* iii 230
Innocent partner of my peaceful *h*. *T.* iii 337
Delightful industry enjoyed at *h*. *T.* iii 356
His warm but simple *h*., where he enjoys *T.* iii 389
May turn the clod, and wheel the compost *h*. *T.* iii 637
Runs the great circuit, and is still at *h*. *T.* iv 119 [236
Which seen delights him not; then coming *h*. *T.* iv
That sweeps the bolted shutter, summons *h*. *T.* iv 304
Neglected pine at *h*., themselves, as more *T.* iv 456
To swear, to game, to drink ; to show at *h*. *T.* iv 652
Chains nowhere patiently, and chains at *h*. *T.* v 478
" Ordained to guide the embodied spirit *h*. *T.* v 840
Below the skies, but having there his *h*. *T.* vi 914
With what intense desire he wants his *h*. *Tir*. 562
Thus bringing *h*. to him the most remote *Tir.* 643
Not occupied in day-dreams, as at *h*. *Tir.* 775 [757
Saved from his *h*., where every day brings forth *Tir.*
When thou, transplanted from thy genial *h*. *Tir.* 850
What burns at *h*., or threatens from afar *T.T.* 447
This Bedlam part ; and others nearer *h*. *T.T.* 609
Then let the boobies stay at *h*. *Y.D.* 65

HOME-BORN.
Fireside enjoyments, *h*. happiness *T.* iv 140

HOMELESS.
The *h*. birds a nest ? *A Tale* 28

HOMELY.
Serves, in a plain and *h*. way *E.* i 3

HOMELY-FEATURED.
Like *h*. Night, of clustering gems *T.* iv 252

HOMER.
Or can, the more than *H.* of his age ? *T.* vi 647
What need of *H.*'s verse, or Tully's prose *Tir.* 399
Ages elapsed ere *H.*'s lamp appeared *T.T.* 556

HOMESTALL. [i 64
And *h*. thatched with leaves. But hast thou found *T.*

HOMEWARD.
There from the sunburnt hayfield *h*. creeps *T.* i. 295
Bound *h*., and in hope already there *T.* i 522

HOMOGENEAL.
Of *h*. and discordant springs *T.* ii 190

HONEST.
That stripped him bare, and broke his *h*. heart *Ch.* 54
And *h*. Merit stands on slippery ground *Ch.* 284
Would hang an *h*. man, and save a thief *Con.* 128
Never, if *h*. ones, when death is sure *Con.* 408
An *h*. man, close-buttoned to the chin *E.* iii 62
Act but an *h*. and a faithful part *Ex.* 556
If *h*. eulogy can spare thee room *H.* 589
Whose lines uniting by an *h*. art *H.* 756
As *h*. and more eloquent than mine *J.T.* 8
Need help, let *h*. industry provide *P.E.* 252
Thus Heaven approves, as *h*. and sincere *T.* 225
I see thee weep, and thine are *h*. tears *T.* i 657
That he is *h*. in the sacred cause *T.* ii 375
And all their *h*. pleasures. Mansions once *T.* iii 746
So he may wrap himself in *h*. rags *T.* iii 806
To soothe their *h*. pride, that scorns to beg *T.* iv 405
If, therefore, e'en when *h*. in design *Tir.* 452

HONESTY.
H. shines with great advantage there *H.* 402
A knave when tried on *h*.'s plain rule *H.* 566

HONEY.
But we that make no *h*., though we sting *Con.* 289

HONEY—HOPE

The h. on his tongue *M.* ii 16
Can gather h. from a weed *P.B.* 36
And spreads the h. of his deep research *T.* iv 112
Here every drop of h. hides a sting *T.* vi 830

HONEYED.
Those open on the spot their h. store *P.E.* 49

HONOUR.
" H., esteem and confidence forgot *A.T.* 111
The Point of H. has been deemed of use *Con.* 163
Whatever Use may urge, or H. plead *Con* 189
To take his h.'s orders, cap in hand *Con.* 416
That 'tis an h. and a joy to pay *Con.* 646
Conspire to h. thee *Dr.* 4
While H., Virtue, Piety, bear sway *Ex.* 326
Designed, in h. of his endless love *H.* 121
A right to the meek h. of her name) *H.* 236
All the grim h. of his ghastly court *H.* 261
Ye monarchs, whom the lure of h. draws *Her.* 41
Who bidst me h. with an artless song *M.P.* 13
Such h. to thee as my numbers may *M.P.* 71
From vulgar minds, have h. much at heart *R.* 728
Have changed the woods, in scarlet h. bright *T.* i 320
Whom we call gay? That h. has been long *T.* i 491
And liberty, and oft-times h. too *T.* i 734
Farewell those h., and farewell with them *T.* ii 239
The h. of the turf as all our own *T.* ii 277
Of h., perjury, corruption, frauds *T.* ii 669
Of h., dignity, and fair renown! *T.* iii 59
Her sex's h., was renounced herself *T.* iii 77
Men too, were nice in h. in those days *T.* iii 85
Her crimson h.; and the spangled beau *T.* iii 578
Of h., or emolument, or fame *T.* iv 785
At random, without h., hope, or peace *T.* v 899
Then each, in its peculiar h. clad *T.* vi 147
The h.'s of his matchless horse his own *T.* vi 438
Deserving h., but for wisdom more *T.* vi 491
Wins public h.; and ten thousand sit *T.* vi 633
And hang it up in h. of a man?) *T.* vi 641
Her h., her emoluments, her joys *T.* vi 923
The h. of his ebon poll *T.B.* 13   [356
Whose heirs, their h. none, their income small *Tir.*
His wealth, fame, h., all that I intend *Tir.* 389
Least qualified in h., learning, worth *Tir.* 413
Some give that h. to his tail *Trans.* i 7
In H.'s field advancing his firm foot *T.T.* 16
For senatorial h. Thus to Time *Y.O.* 103

HONOURABLE.
They wept the wrongs of h. love *A.T.* 98
In h. bumps his rich amends *Con.* 200
And fruit reward his h. toil *H.* 761
Though I revere your h. names *R.* 663
Such squalid sloth to h. soil! *T.* i 579
The world accounts an h. man *Tir.* 738
Men well endowed, of h. parts *Tir.* 836

HONOURED.
Hail, h. land! a desert where *A Tale* 65
Canst thou, and h. with a Christian name *Ch.* 180
And add Right Reverend to Smug's h. name *H.* 438
Thy generous powers, but silence h. thee *S.* i 7
Was sacred, and was h., loved, and wept *T.* ii 786

HOOD-WINKED.
Surrender judgment, h. Some the style *T.* vi 102

HOOF.
Or e'er his h. had pressed the crumbling verge *T.* vi 519
With pointed h. dibbling the glebe prepared *Y.O.* 26

HOOK.
And baits its h. with prodigies and lies *Con.* 224
To snare the mole, or with ill-fashioned h. *R.* 401

Nor baited h. deceive the fish's eye *T.* iii 313
H. disappointment on the public wheels *T.T.* 146

HOOPS.
And filleted about with h. of brass *T.* v 402

HOPE.
And spread her golden h. below *A Fable* 15
Vain our delusive h. of constant knights *A.T.* 100
And may his h. be true! *A Tale* 64
With little to h. or to fear *C.* 54
Of friends, of h., of all bereft *Cast.* 5
The fears and h. of a commercial care *Ch.* 279
Thrives against H., and in the rudest scene *Ch.* 575
In h. to gain, what else I must have lost *Ch.* 630
And when I h. his blunders are all out *Con.* 117
He humbly h.—presumes—it may be so *Con.* 124
Some handsome present, as your h. presage *Con.* 306
You speak with life, in h. to entertain *Con.* 327
Your h. to please him vain on every plan *Con.* 341
Physicians write in h. to work a cure *Con.* 407
Their object, and their subject, and their h. *Con.* 542
Can h. of Heaven, bright prospects of an hour *Con.* 591
Oh! I have seen (nor h. perhaps in vain *Con.* 605
And, farewell else all h. of pure delight *Con.* 681
Their h., desires, and purposes estranged *Con.* 725
Her h. presumption, and her faith a lie *Con.* 774
Still haunts, in h. to dream of youth again *Ex.* 26
When we were visited, what h. for you? *Ex.* 248
Their h. in Heaven, servility their scorn *Ex.* 440
For ears and hearts that he can h. to please? *Ex.* 451
In h. of permanent delight *F.* 68
With still less h. of thriving *F.* 144
To recommence life's trial, in the h. *F.A.* 4
And h., in due time, to behold *Gr.* 31
The inquirer's aim, that remedy, is H.—*H.* 114
Of sensual evil, and thus H. is born *H.* 152
H. sets the stamp of vanity on all *H.* 153
H., with uplifted foot, set free from earth *H.* 161
H., as an anchor firm and sure, holds fast *H.* 167
H.! nothing else can nourish and secure *H.* 169
H.! let the wretch, once conscious of the joy *H.* 171
Forgiveness, and the privilege of h. *H.* 214
Nor h. have they, nor fear of aught to come *H.* 254
Life without h. can close but in despair *H.* 274
Thus h. of every sort, whatever sect *H.* 294
The Christian H. is—Waiter, draw the cork *H.* 361
Shall answer—" H., sweet H., has set me free *H.* 536
Is H. exotic? Grows it not at home? *H.* 549
Your H. shall stand unblamed, perhaps admired *H.* 616
If not that H. the Scripture has required *H.* 617
All h. despair, that stands not on his cross *H.* 632
That folly ends where genuine H. begins *H.* 637
Parent of H., immortal Truth! make known *H.* 663
Must spring that H. he pants to make his own *H.* 709
When H., long lingering, at last yields the ghost *H.* 723
Of him whom H. has with a touch made whole *H.* 731
That H. which can alone exclude despair *H.* 751
The peasant's h., and not in vain, assured *Her.* 9
In h. to bask a little yet *Mor.* 21
There no delusive h. invites despair *P.E.* 617
Scorned by the rest, with patient h. they wait *R.* 165
Whatever h. a change of scene inspires *R.* 679
His soul exults, H. animates his lays *R.* 777
He has no h. who never had a fear *T.* 298
The Scripture yields) or h. to find, a friend? *T.* 440
Truth, H., and Charity, and touched with awe *T.* i 2
Bound homeward, and in h. already there *T.* i 522
With conflict of contending h. and fears *T.* i 668
By other h. and richer fruits than yours *T.* i 677
By frequent lapse, can h. no triumph there *T.* i 691
The h. of such hereafter! They have fallen *T.* ii 240
Should speak to purpose, or with better h. *T.* iii 25

HOPE—HOST

And find the total of their *h*. and fears *T*. iii 132 [788
Just when it meets his *h*., and proves the Heaven *T*. iii
And spreads his *h*. before the blaze of day *T*. iii 445
To his young *h*., requires discreet delay *T*. iii 504
The *h*. of better things, the chance to win *T*. iii 828
And I can weep, can *h*., and can despond *T*. iii 841
That flattered me with *h*. of earthly bliss *T*. iv 696
Had found me, or the *h*. of being free *T*. iv 699
Of freedom, in that *h*. itself possess *T*. v 375
And then alternate, with a sickly *h*. *T*. v 428
That he at last forgets it. All his *h*. *T*. v 591
So I with animated *h*. behold *T*. v 837
At random, without honour, *h*., or peace *T*. v 899
Must drop indeed the *h*. of public praise *T*. vi 973
And his end sure, without one glimpse of *h*. *Tir*. 427
To such base *h*., in many a sordid soul *Tir*. 460 [359
They risk their *h*., their dearest treasure, there? *Tir*.
But though the joys he *h*. beneath your roof *Tir*. 563
And hopest thou not ('tis every father's *h*.) *Tir*. 875
And *h*. in spite of pain *Trans*. *H*. 21
Nor judge by statute a believer's *h*. *T.T*. 72
Must *h*. to look upon their like again *T.T*. 661
We hug the *h*. of constancy and truth *V*. 53
All *h*. of happiness below 1789, 53

HOPED.
And *h*. to seize his abdicated helm *Ex*. 577
Jack knew his friend, but *h*. in that disguise *R*. 587
He hated, *h*., and loved *St*. iii 22
Nor *h*., but in thy righteousness divine *T*. 576

HOPEFUL.
With show of love, at least with *h*. proof *T*. ii 558
With *h*. gems. The rest, no portion left *T*. iii 421

HOPELESS.
Perish, *h*. and abhorr'd *B*. 15
"My dear deliverer out of *h*. night *Ch*. 234
Makes contradiction such a *h*. case *Con*. 60
A *h*. task, and damns them if they fail *H*. 392
And helpless, *h*., hear thee say— *O*. ii 23
With *h*. wish one looks and lingers *P.B*. 33
And *h*. of repose *St*. v 12
Now drenched throughout, and *h*. of his case *T*. 246
Solicit pleasure, *h*. of success *T*. ii 635
H. indeed that dissipated minds *T*. iii 695
Inveterate, *h*. of a cure, conspires *T*. iv 577
Cruelly spared, and *h*. of escape! *T*. v 399
Ages of *h*. misery. Future death *T*. v 607

HOPEST.
And *h*. thou not ('tis every father's hope) *Tir*. 875

HOPHNI.
H. and Phineas may describe the rest *Ex*. 449

HOPING.
But me, scarce *h*. to attain that rest *M.P*. 100

HOPKINS.
Hail, Sternhold then, and *H*., hail! Amen *T.T*. 760

HORACE.
Anacreon, *H*., played in Greece and Rome *T.T*. 608

HORATIO.
"A friend!" *H*. cried, and seemed to start *E*. iii 28
H.'s servant once, with bow and cringe *E*. iii 20

HORIZON.
Seen in the dim *h*., turns thee pale *T*. i 667
That skirt the *h*., wore a sable hue *T*. iv 320
Ascending, fires the *h*.; while the clouds *T*. v 2

HORN.
Poured out from Plenty's overflowing *h*. *Ex*. 10

To sound his *h*., and publish it abroad *H*. 311
Or with the high-raised *h*.'s melodious clang *N.A*. 35
Beneath a pane of thin translucent *h*. *Tir*. 120
Hark! 'tis the twanging *h*. o'er yonder bridge *T*.iv 1

HORRIBLE.
Than reign in this *h*. place *A.S*. 8
His *h*. intent, again he sought *T*. vi 525

HORRID.
Whose *h*. perpetration stamps disgrace *Ex*. 416
And *h*. brambles intertwine below *N.A*. 16
Abrupt and *h*. as the tempest roars *R*. 533
To *h*. sounds of hostile feet within *T*. iv 571
Ye *h*. towers, the abode of broken hearts *T*. v 384

HORRORS.
Minute the *h*. that ensued *T.B*. 52
And hang their *h*. in the neighbouring skies *Her*. 16

HORSE.   [169
"To *h*.!" he cried, "or by this good right hand *A.T*.
Was equal to the swiftness of his *h*. *A.T*. 194
Whose only fit companion is his *h*. *Con*. 412
Can quell the love of freedom in a *h*. *Ch*. 172
If neither *h*. nor groom affect the squire *Con*. 419
Will lend his *h*. to go" *J.G*. 24
John Gilpin at his *h*.'s side *J.G*. 45
His *h*., who never in that sort *J.G*. 93
Which made his *h*.'s flanks to smoke *J.G*. 127
But yet his *h*. was not a whit *J.G*. 149
His *h*. at last stood still *J.G*. 160
"I came because your *h*. would come *J.G*. 173
So turning to his *h*., he said *J.G*. 197
Whereat his *h*. did snort, as he *J.G*. 205
The postboy's *h*. right glad to miss *J.G*. 231
'Twas but a mile; your favorite *h*. *M.F*. 23
By panting dog, tired man, and spattered *h*. *N.A*. 125
And always, ere he mounted, kissed his *h*. *R*. 578
He that would win the race, must guide his *h*. *T*. 13
His *h*. and him, unconscious of them all *T*. iv 22
The *h*. as wanton, and almost as fleet *T*. vi 330
That wait on man, the flight performing *h*. *T*. vi 426
The honours of his matchless *h*. his own *T*. vi 438
His *h*., as he had caught his master's mood *T*. vi 549
Agreed. But would you sell or slay your *h*. *T.T*. 304
A king, that would, might recommend his *h*. *Tir*. 417
A kick that scarce would move a *h*. *Y.D*. 63

HORSEBACK.
On *h*. after we" *J.G*. 16

HOSANNA.
A loud *h*. sent from all thy works *T*. v 888
Earth rolls the rapturous *h*. round *T*. vi 797

HOSPITABLE.
By some kind, *h*. heart possessed *T*. 251
What England was, plain, *h*., kind *T*. iii 743

HOSPITALITY.
Where peace and *h*. might reign *T*. ii 617

HOSPITALS.
Or building *h*. on English ground? *Ch*. 44

HOST.
Their *h*. to move, and when it stayed to rest *Ex*. 180
Thy Levites, once a consecrated *h*. *Ex*. 263
The sacramental *h*. of God's elect *T*. ii 349
Shouting for joy.—"Tell me, ye shining *h*. *T*. v 822
His *h*. of wooden warriors to and fro *T*. vi 266
Where all the attention of his faithful *h*. *Tir*. 769
Prowess to dissipate a *h*. 1789, 6
A long despised, but now victorious *h*. *T.T*. 473

HOSTILE.

Whose deeds had left, in spite of *h.* arts *Con.* 513
To horrid sounds of *h.* feet within *T.* iv 571

HOSTILITY.

And charged H. and Hate to roar *Ex.* 566
By weakness, and *h.* by love *T.* v 703

HOT.

Reports it *h.* or cold, or wet or dry *Con.* 386
Were basking *h.*, and all in blow *P.B.* 2
His *h.* displeasure against foolish men *T.* ii 179 [742
When sin hath moved him, and his wrath is *h. T.* vi
The little ones, unbutton'd, glowing *h. Tir.* 304

HOUND.

Here lies, whom *h.* did ne'er pursue *Ep.* ii 1
Ere yet with ruthless joy the happy *h. N.A.* 33
Though not a *h.* from whom it burst appeared *N.A.* 46
So sweet to huntsman, gentleman, and *h. N.A.* 131
True beagle as the staunchest *h.* he keeps *P.E.* 87

HOUR.

Fancy endued her in her natal *h.*) *A.T.* 92
He long survives, who lives an *h. Cast.* 37
And at this *h.* the conqueror feels the proof *Ch.* 60
We feel thy force still active, at this *h. Ch.* 272
H. after *h.*, the yet unlettered boy *Con.* 12
Thy worst effect is banishing for *h. Con.* 253
Know, your arrears with every *h.* accrue *Con.* 491
Hearts may be found that harbour at this *h. Con.* 561
And chase the splenetic dull *h.* away *Con.* 582 [591
Can hopes of Heaven, bright prospects of an *h. Con.*
To tremble (as the creature of an *h. Con.* 657
Brings forth that unexpected *h. E.* i 30
Sheds every *h.* a clearer light *E.* i 61
A tedious *h.*—and now we never meet! *E.* iii 5
His frisking was at evening *h. Ep.* ii 25
With self-indulgence winged the fleeting *h. Ex.* 71
That balances the wings of every *h. Ex.* 321
In lighter diet at a later *h. Ex.* 403
And to this *h.*, to keep it fresh in mind *Ex.* 516
H. after *h.*, thy gratitude and love *Ex.* 561
Can pause one *h.* to read a serious rhyme *Ex.* 605
Not that his *h.* devoted all to Care *H.* 57
To spend two *h.* in dressing for the day *H.* 80
Transient indeed, as is the fleeting *h. H.* 119
But Conscience, in some awful, silent *h. H.* 215
His *h.* no longer pass unmarked away *H.* 698
Their *h.*, their days, in listening to his joy *H.* 739
Join me, amid your silent *h. Miss* — 19
So may the rosy-fingered *h. Miss* — 97
His *h.* of study closed at last *Mor.* 5
Could Time, his flight reversed, restore the *h. M.P.*74
To crown the smiling *h. N.* 20
Sweet Harmony, that soothes the midnight *h.!P.E.* 66
Of Sabbath *h.* with plausible excuse? *P.E.* 145
Of some ungoverned passion every *h. P.E.* 276
How to secure, in some propitious *h. R.* 141
And every *h.* sweeps multitudes away *R.* 158
His *h.* of leisure and recess employs *R.* 215
H. after *h.* delightfully allot *R.* 373
What early philosophic *h.* he keeps *R.* 429
And talks and laughs away his vacant *h. R.* 452
Is occupied as well, employs his *h. R.* 507
Behold in these what leisure *h.* demand *R.* 701
For yet an *h.* to come *St.* i 26
O most delightful *h.* by man *St.* iii 1
The *h.* that terminates his span *St.* iii 3
"When my last *h.* arrives" *St.* iii 34
Recoil from weary life's best *h. St.* v 19
Then boast (but wait for that unhoped for *h.*) *T.* 401
Since the dear *h.* that brought me to thy foot *T.* 573
Who quits the coachbox at the midnight *h. T.* i 91

Nor his who quits the box at midnight *h. T.* i 98
Of *h.* that sorrow since has much endeared *T.* i 117
From strenuous toil his *h.* of sweetest ease *T.* i 388
And now perhaps the glorious *h.* is come *T.* iii 790
And therefore more obnoxious at this *h. T.* iii 846
Compensating his loss with added *h. T.* iv 134
Of undisturbed Retirement, and the *h. T.* iv 142
Whose only happy are their wasted *h. T.* iv 225
And whether I devote thy gentle *h. T.* iv 261
Not undelightful is an *h.* to me *T.* iv 277
Thus oft reclined at ease, I lose an *h. T.* iv 302
All has its date below; the fatal *h. T.* v 529 [vi 85
May think down *h.* to moments. Here the heart *T.*
Were driven from Paradise; and in that *h. T.* vi 380
An unsuspected storm. His *h.* was come *T.* vi 545
Receives advantage from his noiseless *h. T.* vi 944
If man be what he seems, this *h.* a slave *Tir.* 59
At stated *h.*, his freakish thoughts engage *Tir.* 606
And say, My boy, the unwelcome *h.* is come *Tir.* 849
The glass that bids man mark the fleeting *h. T.T.* 41
The crisis of a dark decisive *h. T.T.* 359
He thought the dying *h.* already come *T.T.* 392
That *h.* elapsed, the incurable revolt *T.T.* 402
In penury consumed his idle *h. T.T.* 673
Who fret their *h.* and are forgotten things *V.* 46

HOUR-BELL.

To count the *h.*, and expect no change *T.* v 404

HOUR-GLASS.

What should be, and what was an *h.* once *T.* iv 220

HOURLY.

Is that which angles *h.* for surprise *Con.* 223
H. allurements on his passions press *P.E.* 61
To *h.* use applied *St.* iii 20

HOUSE.

Resort on Sundays to the *h.* of prayer *H.* 242
Ethelred's *h.*, the centre of six ways *H.* 302
"Stop, stop, John Gilpin!—Here's the *h.*!" *J.G.* 145
For why?—his owner had a *h. J.G.* 151
But to the *h.* went in *J.G.* 180
What a mere dungeon is this *h.*! *M.F.* 2
That once we called the pastoral *h.* our own *M.P.* 53
Your *h.* about your ears *Pat.* 16
Who deem his *h.* a useless place *St.* vi 21 [210
He likes your *h.*, your housemaid, and your pay *T.*
Or make his *h.* his grave: nor so contend *T.* ii 147
May be indifferent to her *h.* of clay *T.* ii 458
That sits a stigma on his father's *h. T.* ii 760
H. in ashes, and the fall of stocks *T.* iv 16
Stealing a sidelong glance at a full *h. T.* iv 201
Soothed with a waking dream of *h.*, towers *T.* iv 287
Her *h.* of bondage, worse than that of old *T.* v 382
So in the chapel of old Ely *H.T.* vi 658
Above, below, in all the *h. T.B.* 19
In sacrilege, in God's own *h.* profaned *Tir.* 409
Why hire a lodging in a *h.* unknown *Tir.* 555
Or is thine *h.*, though less superb thy rank *Tir.* 751

HOUSED.

But corn was *h.*, and beans were in the stack *N.A.* 23

HOUSEHOLD.

We sacrifice to dress, till *h.* joys *T.* ii 613
Thy days roll on exempt from *h.* care *T.* iv 366

HOUSELESS.

The *h.* rovers of the sylvan world *T.* i 588

HOUSEMAID.

He likes your house, your *h.*, and your pay *T.* 210

HOUSEWIFE.
But well thou playedst the *h.'s* part *M.* 17
The frugal *h.* trembles when she lights *T.* iv 380
Come trooping at the *h.'s* well known call *T.* v 61

HOUSEWIFELY.
When in came, *h.* inclined *R.C.* 49

HOVEL.
And slight the *h.* as beneath her care *T.* ii 459
Nor does the boarded *h.* better guard *T.* iv 443

HOVER.   [own? *Tir.* 556
For one whose tenderest thoughts all *h.* round your

HOVERED.
H. thy spirit o'er thy sorrowing son *M.P.* 23

HOVERING.
The screaming nations, *h.* in mid air *H.* 353
Or kites are *h.* near *The Doves* 22

HOWARD.
I must incur, forgetting *H.'s* name *Ch.* 296

HOWL.
And, *h.* and roar as likes them, uncontrol'd *T.* vi 404

HOWLING.
And Danish *h.* scared thee as they passed *Ex.* 471
Me *h.* blasts drive devious, tempest-tossed *M.P.* 102
With all these hideous *h.* to the skies *N.A.* 88
He hears the tempest *h.* in the trees *T.* 254
By drunken *h.*; and the chilling tale *T.* iv 562

HOYS.
In coaches, chaises, caravans, and *h. R.* 521

HUDDLE.
Just fifteen minutes, *h.* up their work *T.* ii 412

HUDDLING.
All *h.* into phalanx, stood and gazed *N.A.* 48

HUE.
And verse, more lasting, *h.* that never fade *Ch.* 108
That souls have no discriminating *h. Ch.* 202
He talks of light, and the prismatic *h. Ch.* 391
Its odour perished, and its charming *h. Con.* 43
And never of a sabler *h.* than now) *Ex.* 395
Thus things terrestrial wear a different *h. H.* 69
They raised the *h.* and cry *J.G.* 236
"Yours is," she said, "the nobler *h. L.R.* 21
Presents it decked with every *h. Mor.* 30
The birds put off their every *h. Mrs. M—* 1
Knows what the freshness of their *h.* implies *N.A.* 61
Though each its *h.* peculiar; paler some *T.* i 308
His cheek recovers soon its healthful *h. T.* i 441
And sorted *h.* (each giving each relief *T.* iii 634
That skirt the horizon, wore a sable *h. T.* iv 320
And, tingeing all with his own rosy *h. T.* v 8 [vi 161
Which *h.* she most approved, she choose them all *T.*
Lamps gracefully disposed, and of all *h. T.* v. 149
Their balmy odours, and imparts their *h. T.* vi 243
His bosom of the *h. T.B.* 15   [*Tir.* 447
Whose scent and *h.* are rather guessed than known
Works magic wonders, adds a brighter *h. Tir.* 23
Dye them at last in all their glowing *h. Tir.* 48
Seem graced with a livelier *h. W.N.* 22
(For feats of sanguinary *h.* 1789, 25

HUG.
We *h.* the hopes of constancy and truth *V.* 53

HUGE.
Discover *h.* cathedrals built with stone *P.E.* 381
The seas globose and *h.*, the o'erarching vault *R.* 552
A *h.* throat calling to the clouds for drink *Y.O.* 112

HUM.
And hears the million *h. Q.V.* 42

HUMAN.
That forms and rites are tricks of *h.* law *A.T.* 62
And softens *h.* rock-work into men *Ch.* 96
What *h.* wisdom cannot but oppose *Ch.* 340
But God o'errules all *h.* follies still *Ch.* 463
To see a God stretch forth his *h.* hand *Ch.* 581
Sacred interpreter of *h.* thought *Con.* 23
Pronounce your *h.* form a false pretence *Con.* 78
That odious libel on a *h.* voice? *Con.* 450
And yet, God knows, look *h.* nature through *Con.* 749
The monuments of *h.* strength *E.* i 82   [19
But He who knew what *h.* hearts would prove *E.* ii
Strange fluctuation of all *h.* things! *E.* iii 9
Baboons are free from, upon *h.* race? *Ex.* 417
With fingers deeply dyed in *h.* gore *Ex.* 497
And make a calm of *h.* life *F.* 134
My gravelly bounds, from self to *h.* kind *F.A.* 20
Ask what is *h.* life—the sage replies *H.* 1
Chargeable only with a *h.* shape *H.* 514
That sorest ill of *h.* life *M.F.* 32
Obtrude on *h.* notice more *Mrs. M—* 34
Prove that you have *h.* feelings *N.C.* 55
The serpent Error twines round *h.* hearts *P.E.* 4
Lights of the world, and stars of *h.* race *P.E.* 97
To the wild wave, or wilder *h.* breast *P.E.* 601
That yields not to the touch of *h.* skill *R.* 344
But reveries (for *h.* minds will act) *R.* 637
To dance on earth, and charm all *h.* eyes *R.* 796
Strange fondness of the *h.* heart *St.* v 13
Sees, far as *h.* optics may command *T.* 3
To soothe and satisfy the *h.* ear *T.* 199
The self-restoring arm of *h.* power *T.* 402
In *h.* mould, should brutalize by choice *T.* i 575
As *h.* nature's broadest, foulest blot *T.* ii 22
And having *h.* feelings, does not blush *T.* ii 27
And agonies of *h.* and of brute *T.* ii 105
That fear no discipline of *h.* hands *T.* ii 325
Ah spare your idol! think him *h.* still *T.* ii 496
As sweet as charity from *h.* breasts *T.* iii 197
By strides of *h.* wisdom. In his works *T.* iii 222
All that is *h.* in me, to protect *T.* iii 347
Not waste it, and aware that *h.* life *T.* iii 363
And magnified beyond all *h.* size *T.* iv 542
The course of *h.* things from good to ill *T.* iv 578
In *h.* bosoms, quench it or abate *T.* iv 747
On *h.* grandeur and the courts of kings *T.* v 172
At building *h.* wonders mountain high *T.* v 179
Than *h.* passion please. In every heart *T.* v 205
Should ever drivel out of *h.* lips *T.* v 285
There dwell the most forlorn of *h.* kind *T.* v 397
Challenging *h.* scrutiny, and proved *T.* v 868
For *h.* fellowship, as being void *T.* vi 322
Were sown in *h.* nature's fruitful soil *T.* vi 383
He sees that *h.* equity is slack *T.* vi 472
Not more on *h.* help, than we on theirs *T.* vi 609
That piety was still in *h.* hearts *T.* vi 683
Of this tempestuous state of *h.* things *T.* vi 737
From touch of *h.* lips at best impure *T.* vi 835
But they have *h.* feelings—turn to them *Tir.* 806
Two or three millions of the *h.* race *T.T.* 423
If *h.* woes her soft attention claim *T.T.* 484 [497
And armed with strength surpassing *h.* powers *T.T.*
Man lavished all his thoughts on *h.* things *T.T.* 596
Oh friendship! cordial of the *h.* breast! *V.* 49

HUMANE.
Affects indeed a most *h.* concern *Ch.* 495
H. as they would seem, not always show *T.* iv 373
From Nature's bounty—that *h.* address *T.* v 469

HUMANITY.
I am out of *H.'s* reach *A.S.* 9

HUMANITY—HURRYING

No Cotton, whose *h*. sheds rays *H.* 205
But he that has *h*., forewarn'd *T.* vi 566

HUMANIZING.
The wonder; *h*. what is brute *T.* v 700

HUMANKIND.
What shall the man deserve of *h. T.* 429
Were all that Heaven required of *h. Tir.* 85
See what contempt is fallen on *h. Tir.* 814

HUMBLE.
Would *h*. many a towering poet's pride *Ch.* 536
A Persian, *h*. servant of the sun *Con.* 67
Came, not expected in that *h*. guise *Ex.* 87
Affable, *h*., diffident, and mild *P.E.* 537
To cherish Virtue in an *h*. state *R.* 789
And oh! that *h*. as my lot *St.* i 29
You think him *h*.—God accounts him proud *T.* 92
She, for her *h*. sphere by nature fit *T.* 323
The theme though *h*., yet august and proud *T.* i 6
Of dayspring overshoot his *h*. nest *T.* i 496
And *h*. learners of a Saviour's worth *T.* ii 542
Perhaps by moonlight, at their *h*. doors *T.* iv 171
Wisdom is *h*. that he knows no more *T.* vi 97
And I, contented with an *h*. theme *T.* vi 719
His sphere though *h*., if that *h*. sphere *T.* vi 960
Within some pious pastor's *h*. cot *Tir.* 760
However *h*. and confined the sphere *T.T.* 166
Backed with a modest sheet of *h*. prose *V.* 20

HUMBLEBEE.
That's worse—the drone-pipe of an *h. Con.* 330

HUMBLER.
Now seek repose upon an *h*. theme *T.* i 5
And of an *h*. growth, the other tall *T.* vi 152
Teach *h*. thoughts to you *Trans.* i 26

HUMBLY.
He *h*. hopes—presumes—it may be so *Con.* 124

HUMDRUM.
And lulled by her own *h*. song *R.C.* 46

HUMID.
Fearless of *h*. air and gathering rains *T.* 212

HUMILITY.
H. the parent of the first *Con.* 377
H. is gentle, apt to learn *Ex.* 454
H. may clothe an English Dean *T.* 118
H. is crowned, and Faith receives the prize *T.* 589

HUMMING.
From cities *h*. with a restless crowd *R.* 21

HUMOUR.
A story in which native *h*. reigns *Con.* 203
The freakish *h*. of the present time *Con.* 866
Perhaps 'twas mere good *h*. gave it birth *E.* iii 38
I kept him for his *h*.'s sake *Ep.* ii 33
Their *h*. yet so various *F.* 111
And in her *h*., when she frowned *J.P.* 9
That *h*. interposed too often makes *M.P.* 67
Some to comply with *h*., and a mind *R.* 605
Those *h*., tart as wines upon the fret *R.* 761
That his own *h*. dictates, from the clutch *T.* v 317
The playful *h*.; he could now endure *T.* vi 47
The dark and sullen *h*. of the time *T.T.* 616
H. in holiday and sightly trim *T.T.* 643

HUMOROUS. [137
Whose *h*. vein, strong sense, and simple style *Tir.*
His *h*. talent next employs *Trans.* iv 26

HUMPHREY.
Sir H., shooting in the dark *M.F.* 9

HUNDRED.
Has left some *h*. without home or food *Ch.* 466
Eight *h*. of the brave *R.G.* 5
With twice four *h*. men *R.G.* 24
And He and his Eight *H.*—*R.G.* 35
Some fifty or a *h*. lustrums hence *T.* ii 579
Her dear five *h*. friends, contemns them all *T.* ii 643

HUNG.
H. not far off upon a myrtle bough *A.T.* 174
With doleful rumour and sad presage *h. Ex.* 357
And his that seraphs tremble at is *h. Ex.* 662
And *h*. a bottle on each side *J.G.* 71
Some clouds which had over us *h. M.D.* 21
A scourge *h*. with lashes he bore *M.D.* 30 [*N.A.* 25
With tails high mounted, ears *h*. low, and throats
Else He that *h*. there suffered all his pain *P.E.* 623
Where the prisoned lark is *h. St.* iv 2   [v 107
And see where it has *h*. the embroider'd banks *T.*
That pressed it, and the feet *h*. dangling down *T.* i 47
Trembling, as if eternity were *h. T.* vi 270 [*T.* vi 685
The mulberry-tree was *h*. with blooming wreaths
On fire with curses, and with nonsense *h. Tir.* 832
Liberty blushed, and *h*. her drooping head *T.T.* 324

HUNGER.
With *h*. pinched, and pinched for room *R.C.* 73 [555
Though pressed with *h*. oft, or comelier clothes *T.* i
And introduces *h*., frost, and woe *T.* ii 616
That *h*., and supplies it; and who seeks *T.* iii 375
Fails for the craving *h*. of the state *T.* v 459
" To gratify the *h*. of his wish *T.* v 637
Of *h*. unassuaged, has interposed *T.* vi 463
(What will not *h*.'s cruel rage?) *T.B.* 5

HUNGERING.
Still *h*., pennyless, and far from home *T.* i 119
Their wonted fodder; not like *h*. man *T.* v 30

HUNGRY.
Gone thither armed and *h*., returned full *Ex.* 368
Be in a *h*. case" *J.G.* 192
When I am *h*. for the bread of life? *T.* ii 426
With an old tavern quill, is *h*. yet *T.* ii 628
It is a *h*. vice;—it eats up all *T.* ii 680
His *h*. acres, stinks and is no use *T.* iv 503
Were e'er such *h*. folk? *Y.D.* 38

HUNT.
Would *h*. a Saracen through fire and flood *Ex.* 521
Start it at home, and *h*. it in the dark *R.* 693
There they are privileged; and he that *h. T.* vi 577
The nations *h*., all mark thee for a prey *T.T.* 364

HUNTSMAN.
Nor ear heard *h*.'s halloo *Ep.* ii 4
But when the *h*. with distended cheek *N.A.* 43
So sweet to *h*., gentleman, and hound *N.A.* 131
A cassocked *h*., and a fiddling priest *P.E.* 111

HURLED.
Dying, *h*. them at the foe *B.* 40

HURRIED.
And *h*., but with unsuccessful speed *T.* 245

HURRY.
Soon *h*. me back to despair *A.S.* 48   [372
With needless *h*. whirled from place to place *T.* iv

HURRYING.
And *h*. him, impatient of his stay *T.* iv 132

HURT. [458

Whom man, for his own *h*., permits to reign *Con.*
It *h*. our pride, and moves our envy less *H*. 553
Was *h*., disgusted, mortified *P*. 19
Might soothe a soul less *h*. than mine *S*. 7
Nor can example *h*. them: what they see *T*. ii 794
Been *h*.by the archers. In his side He bore *T*. iii 113
Is evil; *h*. the faculties, impedes *T*. v 450
Against a heart depraved and temper *h*. *Tir*. 489
H. too perhaps for life; for early wrong *Tir*. 490

HURTFUL.

Are *h*. is a truth confessed by all *P.E*. 226
Still *h*. in the abuse, or by the excess *P.E*. 228
With *h*. error, prejudice, and dreams *T*. ii 504
For dissolution, *h*. to the main *T*. iv 675

HUSBAND.

" Seduce our *h*., and estrange their hearts *A.T*. 114
For *h*. there and wife may boast *A Tale* 5
The tender ties of father, *h*., friend *Ch*. 141
Her tender *h*., wondering much *J.G*. 143
Her *h*. posting down *J.G*. 214
My *h*. safe and well " *J.G*. 220
Wives beggar *h*., *h*. starve their wives *T*. ii 656

HUSH.

H.—silent readers profit most *A Tale* 29
But *h*.!—the muse perhaps is too severe *T*. vi 653

HUSHED.

And all her fears were *h*. together *A Fable* 17
Were *h*. in favour of thy generous plea *Ch*. 311
Then Truth is *h*., that Heresy may preach *Ex*. 107

HUSKS.

The total grist unsifted, *h*. and all *T*. vi 110

HUT.

That screen the herdsman's solitary *h*. *T*. i 168

HYMEN.

And *H*., trimming his dim torch anew *A.T*. 201
The jocund Loves in *H*.'s band *Miss* — 73

HYMENEAL.

" In vain," they cried, " are *h*. rites *A.T*. 99

HYMN'D.

The mulberry-tree was *h*. with dulcet airs *T*. vi 687

HYPERBOLE.

Is this *h*.? The world well known *P.E*. 488

HYPERBOLICAL.

Her notions *h*. *R.C*. 104

HYPERICUM.

H. all bloom, so thick a swarm *T*. vi 165

HYPOCRISY.

And finds H. close lurking there *Con.* 746
H., formality in prayer *Ex*. 43
Is to renounce *h*.; to draw *Ex*. 408
With which *H*. for ever teems *H*. 619
H., detest her as we may *T*. iii 100

HYPOCRITE.

A mere church-juggler, *h*. and slave *P.E*. 109
A *h*.'s pretence! *St*. vi 24
Sometimes a canting *h*. is found *T*. 233

HYPOTHESIS.

The land of dreams, H. her name *A.T*. 6
And for *H*. was somewhat long *A.T*. 19
H. (for with such magic power *A.T*. 91
" O cursed *H*.! your hellish arts *A.T*. 113
When some *h*. absurd and vain *P.E*. 444

HYSSOP.

The cedar and the *h*. on the wall *H*. 287

I.

IBERIA.

" Art thou too fallen, *I*.? Do we see *Ch*. 67

ICE. [16

Of eastern groves, and oceans floored with *i*. *Ex*.
I. upon *i*., the well-adjusted parts *T*. v 146
From many a twig the pendent drops of *i*. *T*. vi 81

ICY.

On *i*. plains, and in eternal snows *H*. 464 [vi 137
Of leaf and flower? It sleeps; and the *i*. touch *T*.
And fledged with *i*. feathers, nod superb *T*. v 26

IDEAL.

There Fancy nursed her in *i*. bowers *A.T*. 7
Friendship a false *i*. good *F*. 29

IDIOT.

So should an *i*., while at large he strays *Con*. 899
We can escape from Custom's *i*. sway *R*. 49

IDLE.

As *i*. as the chattering of a daw *A.T*. 63
Dozing out all his *i*. noons *Ep*. ii 31
Might shine in fable, and grace *i*. themes *Ex*. 233

See it an uninformed and *i*. mass *Her*. 26
O'erheard and checked this *i*. talk *P*. 40
Condemn the prattler, for his *i*. pains *R*. 547
Of *i*. mirth and affectation coy *S*. ii 10
She begs an *i*. pin of all she meets *T*. i 553
Is squandered in pursuit of *i*. sports *T*. ii 758
Calls *i*., and who justly, in return *T*. iii 353
Will he be *i*.who has much to enjoy? *T*. iii 360 [224
To his true worth, most pleased when *i*. most *T*. iv
Paint cards and dolls, and every *i*. thing *T*. iv 241
Nor envies he aught more their *i*. sport *T*. vi 272
And *i*. tinkling of a minstrel's lyre *T*. vi 1021
Account him no just mark for *i*. wit *Tir*. 726
In penury consumed his *i*. hours *T.T*. 673

IDLENESS.

As silly pride and *i*. produce *Ex*. 50
Which *I*. and Weariness beget *R*. 762
But that of *i*., and taste no scenes *T*. i 756
That *i*. has ever yet contrived *T*. iv 208
By lewdness, *i*., and sabbath-breach *T*. iv 653

IDLER.

An *i*. is a watch that wants both hands *R*. 681
Esteems that busy world an *i*. too! *T*. iii 354
Of little worth, an *i*. in the best *T*. vi 952

IDLEST.
" To escape him at the *i.* time *E.* iv 76

IDLY.
The coronet, placed *i.* at their head *H.* 268
Arms hanging *i.* down, hands clasped below *R.* 286
Thus *i.* do we waste the breath of praise *T.* vi 711

IDOL.
Then kiss their *i.*, and pronounce her fair *P.E.* 300
Farthest retires—an *i.*, at whose shrine *T.* i 410.
Ah, spare your *i.*! think him human still *T.* ii 496
Improvement too, the *i.* of the age *T.* iii 764
Propense his heart to *i.*, he is held *T.* v 585
The *i.* of our worship while he lived *T.* vi 666
Or, if to see the name of *i.* Self *T.T.* 744

IDOLATER.
Tender *i.* of absent charms *R.* 220

IDOLATRY.
The gross *i.* blind heathens teach *H.* 499
Thou god of our *i.*, the Press? *P.E.* 461
The god of our *i.* once more *T.* vi 667
It seems *i.* with some excuse *Y.O.* 9

IDOL-GOD.
They set up self, that *i.*, within *Ex.* 216

IDOLIZED.
To war with pleasure, *i.* before *Ex.* 410

IGNOBLE.
To names *i.*, born to be forgot! *B.B.* 2
To smother in *i.* rest *Miss* — 7
And we that worship him, *i.* graves *T.* iii 265
Holds no *i.*, though a slighted, place *T.* vi 971

IGNOBLER.
Spared yet again the *i.* for his sake *T.* vi 530

IGNOMINIOUS.
Doomed to a no less *i.* fate *Tir.* 498

IGNORANCE.
Sin forged, and *I.* made fast, the chain *Ch.* 237
From pride, in league with *i.*, have sprung! *Ch.* 462
Known by thy bleating, *I.* thy name *Con.* 588
The pride of lettered *i.*, that binds *H.* 483
And *i.* of better things makes man *R.* 503
Such lunacy is *i.* alone *T.* 450
For *i.* of what they could not know? *T.* 518
And well prepared, by *i.* and sloth *T.* ii 388
Of solemn farce, where *I.* in stilts *T.* ii 736
A weight of *i.*; in that, of pride *T.* iv 485
Of *i.*, till then she overlooked *T.* v 809
Blest with an infant's *i.* of all *T.* iv 624
His *i.* and harmless manners too *T.* iv 651
Let reverend churls his *i.* rebuke *Tir.* 401

IGNORANT.
Sordid as active, *i.* as loud *R.* 22
And *i.*, except of outward show) *T.* i 650
As nations *i.* of God contrive *T.* ii 574

IGNORANTLY.
Nor *i.* wandering miss the skies *Tir.* 108

ILIAD.
My *I.* and Odyssey too *Gr.* 32
An *I.*, only not in verse, ensues *H.* 194

ILL.
O most degrading of all *i.* that wait *Ch.* 155
But *i.* of every shape and every name *E.* ii 37
To urge reformation of national *i.* *F.M.* 14
And cure of every *i.*! *G.* 15

I. fated race! how deeply must they rue *Her.* 51
And still to love, though pressed with *i.* *M.* 41
That sorest *i.* of human life *M.F.* 32
With present *i.* his heart must ache *N.* 11
Exempt from every *i.* beside *P.* 54   [545
To fatal *i.*; that though the path he treads *P.E.*
And in a world where, other *i.* apart *R.* 125
And thou, sad sufferer under nameless *i.* *R.* 343
To snare the mole, or with *i.* fashioned hook *R.* 401
The unpitied victim of *i.* judged expense *R.* 512
Recompense *i.*? He trembles at the thought *T.* 192
In all the good and *i.* that chequer life! *T.* ii 162
We may with patience bear our moderate *i.* *T.* iv 339
The course of human things from good to *i.* *T.* iv 578
That even servitude, the worst of *i.* *T.* v 302
Or nothing much, his constancy in *i.* *T.* v 667
By budding *i.*, that ask a prudent hand *T.* vi 591
" Those *i.* that wait on all below *The Doves* 17
Quick-sighted arbiter of good and *i.* *Tir.* 31
With all varieties of *i.* by turns *Tir.* 475 [*Tir.* 801
Whose hearts will ache, once told what *i.* may reach
Much trash unuttered, and some *i.* undone *Tir.* 733
Beset with every *i.* but that of fear *T.T.* 363

ILL-CHOSEN.
" Nor suffered one *i.* rhyme *E.* iv 75
But proud of his uncouth, *i.* task *T.* iii 644

ILL-CLAD.
I. and fed but sparely, time to cool *T.* iv 379

ILLIBERAL.
These move the censure and *i.* grin *H.* 744

ILLUME.
I. the land's remotest part 1789, 61

ILLUMINATES.
And so *i.* the path of life *T.* ii 529
I. thy lamp, mysterious Word! *T.* v 846

ILLUMINATING.
I. heart or mind *F.* 8
Like his to shed *i.* rays *T.T.* 712

ILLUMINATION.
With faint *i.*, that uplifts *T.* iv 274

ILLUMINE.
To *i.* with delight the saddest scenes *J.T.* 20
Makes more conspicuous, and *i.* more *T.* vi 175

ILLUMINED.
I. every side; a watery light *T.* v 150
As more *i.*, and with nobler truths *T.* iv 192

ILLUSIVE.
I. of philosophy, so called *T.* ii 505

ILLUSTRATE.
With simile to *i.* it *E.* iv 62
Must lend its aid to *i.* all their charms *T.* iii 591

ILLUSTRATED.
Explained, *i.*, and searched so well *Con.* 527

ILLUSTRATION.
May furnish *i.*, well applied *Con.* 206

ILLUSTRIOUS.
There goes the parson—O *i.* spark! *B.B.* 13
And there, scarce less *i.*, goes the clerk *B.B.* 14
Hence authors of *i.* name *F.* 85
I. drop! and happy their *O.* i 21
Of objects, more *i.* in her view *T.* vi 916
But families of less *i.* fame *Tir.* 354
In less *i.* bards his beauty shone *T.T.* 574

I. histrionic patentee *V.* 29

IMAGE.
Then God's own *i.* on the soul impressed *Ex.* 109
Yesterday's face turn *i.* of to-day *H.* 102
Against thine *i.*, in thy saint, O Lord *H.* 593
Till Cæsar's *i.* is effaced at last *P.E.* 280
And stamp their *i.* in each other's mint *P.E.* 567
Nor Ouse on his bosom their *i.* receives *P.F.* 4
Pastoral *i.* and still retreats *R.* 257
No longer give an *i.* all thine heart *R.* 276
To arrest the fleeting *i.* that fill *T.* ii 290
By every pleasing *i.* they present *T.* iii 303
These, and a thousand *i.* of bliss *T.* vi 341
They fear'd, and as his perfect *i.* loved *T.* vi 400
A soul, an *i.* of Himself, and therefore true *V.* 98

IMAGINATION.
I. to his view *Mor.* 29
I. scattering round *Mrs. M—* 27
Till Thou art heard, *i.* vain *T.* v 861
I. noxious and perverse *Tir.* 599
Of wild *i.*, and there reeled *T.T.* 605

IMAGINED.
I. Sanctity. The conscience, yet *Y.O.* 11

IMBIBE.
So barren sands *i.* the shower *F.* 184
I. and copies what she hears and sees *P.E.* 356
Dry fern or littered hay, that may *i. T.* iii 476

IMBRUED.
With blood of his subjects *i. M.D.* 36

IMBRUTES.
His every action, and *i.* the man *T.* iv 461

IMBUE.
She should *i.* the tongue with what she sips *Con.* 441

IMBUED.
Relics of ages! Could a mind, *i. Y.O.* 6

IMITATION.
Provoke to *i. F.* 9

IMITATIVE.
But *i.* strokes can do no more *T.* i 426
While servile trick and *i.* knack *T.T.* 666

IMMACULATE.
And kept the faith *i.* and pure *Ex.* 208
And burghers, men *i.* perhaps *T.* iv 672

IMMEASURABLE.
For such *i.* woe appears *T.* i 459

IMMEDIATE.
Of an *i.* conjugation *P.T.* 41
And need not his *i.* hand, who first *T.* vi 203

IMMENSE.
At one *i.* explosion *F.* 66
On steady wing sails through the *i.* abyss *H.* 163
Sucks down its prey insatiable. *I.—T.* ii 103
That seems half quenched in the *i.* abyss *T.* iii 216
Mine, spindling into longitude *i. T.* v 11

IMMENSITY.
Absorbed in that *i.* I see *R.* 93

IMMERSED.
In the soft medium, till they stand *i. T.* iii 520
Sheer o'er the craggy barrier, and *i. T.* vi 554

IMMORTAL.
Verse, like the laurel, its *i.* meed *Ch.* 292
I. fragrance fills the circuit wide *Ch.* 439
Although *i.*, may be pricked or scratched *Ch.* 512
Till tuned at length to some *i.* song *Con.* 907
That won a nymph on that *i.* plain *Ex.* 598
And yet the seed of an *i.* flower *H.* 120
Parent of Hope, *i.* Truth! make known *H.* 663
In youth *i.* warm *Miss —* 78
Had shed *i.* glories on your brow *T.* 569
On such a Stool *i.* Alfred sat *T.* i 22
Has man within him an *i.* seed ? *T.* ii 517
I. Hale! for deep discernment praised *T.* iii 258
Enchanting music and *i.* wreaths *T.* iv 687
Our claim to feed upon *i.* truth *T.* v 721
Or what achievements of *i.* fame *T.* vi 933
To palates that can taste *i.* truth *T.* vi 1015

IMMORTALITY.
Some thought of *i.* remains *T.* 39

IMMORTALIZE.
Alike *i.* the dead *Cast.* 54
(Blest be the art that can *i. M.P.* 8
So strong the zeal to *i.* himself *T.* i 284
Shortlived themselves to *i.* their bones *T.* v 184
To guard them, and to *i.* her trust *T.* v 711

IMMUNITY.
Enjoy *i.* from priestly power *Ch.* 273
A long *i.* from grief and pain *Ex.* 82
And full *i.* from penal woe *T.* v 580

IMMURED.
That man *i.* in cities, still retains *T.* iv 766
I. though unaccused, condemned untried *T.* v 398

IMPAIR.
Those truths, which neither use nor years *i. Ex.* 626

IMPAIRED.
A blemish, or a sense *i. M.F.* 43
Mine have not pilfered yet; nor yet *i. T.* i 140
I. by age, his unrelenting hand *T.* iii 416

IMPALED.
With blood of their inhabitants *i. T.* vi 391

IMPART.
That sight *i.* a never-dying flame *Ch.* 593
Will speak without disguise, and must *i. Con.* 711
Forgot the blush that virgin fears *i. Ex.* 47
The choicest raptures to *i. Miss —* 3
Earn if you want; if you abound, *i. P.E.* 253
With much to learn, but nothing to *i. P.E.* 376
I. to things inanimate a voice *R.* 361
And wherefore ? Will not God *i.* his light *T.* iii 272
His glory, and his nature to *i. T.* iii 274
Their balmy odours, and *i.* their hues *T.* vi 243
I. to the benevolent, who wish *T.* vi 344
That pedantry is all that schools *i. Tir.* 212
But poor in knowledge, having none to *i. Tir.* 663
Watch every beam Philosophy *i. T.T.* 70
The Muse *i.*, and can command the lyre *T.T.* 481

IMPARTED.
In selfish silence, but *i.* oft *T.* iii 394

IMPARTIALLY.
He will be found *i.* severe *Ex.* 255

IMPARTING.
I. substance to an empty shade *T.* iv 257
Nature *i.* her satiric gift *T.T.* 656

IMPATIENT.
And shines as if *i.* to bestow *Ch.* 591
I. swim to meet *D.W.* 34
I. to descry the flags of France *Ex.* 291
And all, *i.* of dry land, agree *R.* 523
Vociferous, and *i.* of delay *T.* i 299
As bashful, yet *i.* to be seen *T.* i 325
And crowd the roads, *i.* for the town! *T.* iii 319

IMPATIENT—IMPOSTORS

The *i.* fervour which it first conceives *T.* iii 502
And hurrying him, *i.* of his stay *T.* iv 132

IMPEACH.
Prove, rather than *i.*, the just remark *Tir.* 842

IMPEDE.
Catharina, did nothing *i. C.* 27
I. the bark that ploughs the deep serene *Ch.* 132
And never checked by what *i.* the wise *T.* 373
Is evil; hurts the faculties, *i. T.* v 450
While no base fear *i.* her in her course *T.T.* 267

IMPEDED.
None ever yet *i.* what He wrought *Ex.* 336
Too oft, and much *i.* in its work *T.* iii 370
The wain goes heavily, *i.* sore *T.* iv 343

IMPEDIMENTS.
Knots and *i.* make something hitch *Con.* 108

IMPEL.
I. the fleet whose errand is to save *Ch.* 128
That fire abated which *i.* rash youth *Con.* 641

IMPELLED.
I. me to the deed *B.R.* 8
A task I venture on, *i.* by thee *Ch.* 6
That men engage in it, *i.* by force *Con.* 179
I. thee more to that heroic course *J.T.* 34
I. through regions dense and rare *O.* i 15.
By no malignity *i.-R.C.* 51
So vast in its demands, unless *i. T.* vi 218

IMPENDING.
A drawer *i.* o'er the rest *R.C.* 39
And overbuilt with most *i.* brows *T.* iii 193
To escape the *i.* famine, often scared *T.* v 68

IMPENETRABLE.
" And dost thou dream," the *i.* man *T.* vi 505

IMPENETRABLY.
Man's heart had been *i.* sealed *Con.* 427

IMPERCEPTIBLE.
Through the *i.* meandering veins *T.* vi 136

IMPERFECT.
Weak and *i.* in all grace beside *Con.* 758
A kind release from their *i.* state *R.* 166
My prayers and alms, *i.* and defiled *T.* 577

IMPERIAL.
As vain *i.* Philip on his own *Ch.* 52
A fair *i.* flower *L.R.* 14
I. mistress of the fur-clad Russ! *T.* v 129

IMPERTINENCE.
And deaf to all the *i.* of tongue *R.* 549

IMPERVIOUS.
I. to the wind. First he bids spread *T.* iii 475
Or shed *i.* to the blast. Resigned *T.* v 72

IMPETUOUS.
Again, *i.* to the field he flies *P.E.* 92
These like a deluge with *i.* force *R.* 77
He sprang *i.* forth *Ch.* 14

IMPIOUS.
Nor do we madly, like an *i.* world *T.* iv 177
The *i.* challenger of power divine *T.* vi 546
Less *i.* than absurd, and owing more *T.* vi 656

IMPLACABLE.
Thy foes *i.*, thy land at rest *Ex.* 581
Object of my *i.* disgust *T.* ii 418

IMPLEMENT.
Account them *i.* of mischief still *Ch.* 556
Too often proves an *i.* of play *Con.* 17
The sacred *i.* I now employ *P.E.* 301
In London. Where her *i.* exact *T.* i 715

IMPLIED.
Mutual attention is *i. F.* 49

IMPLY.
Self-knowledge truly learned of course *i. Ch.* 359
I. no trespass against Love Divine) *Ch.* 488
Knows what the freshness of their hue *i. N.A.* 61
I. authority that never can *P.E.* 602
On word and deed, *i. St.* vi 30
Seems to *i.* a censure on the rest *T.T.* 92

IMPORT.
I. what others have invented well *Ch.* 117
For matters of more grave *i. E.* iv 66
And *i.*, of their oracles divine *Ex.* 126
With such address from themes of sad *i. T.* ii 300
Of theological and grave *i.*) *T.* v 662

IMPORTANCE.
And if it weigh the *i.* of a fly *Con.* 21
Who deal with Scripture, its *i.* felt *Con.* 729
A dark *i.* saddens every day *H.* 699
And his *i.* of such weight *R.C.* 112

IMPORTANT.
Alike *i.* in their Maker's view *Ch.* 203
The *i.* letters that include the rest *Ch.* 523
I. triflers! have more smoke than fire *Con.* 250
But fear to call a more *i.* cause *Con.* 397
Events of most *i.* use *E.* i 76
Forgetting its *i.* weight *F.* 70
If thus the *i.* cause is to be tried *H.* 373
Go now, and with *i.* tone demand *H.* 528
A quarry more *i.* still than you *P.E.* 332
Our most *i.* are our earliest years *P.E.* 354
From mighty means to more *i.* ends *R.* 112
And search the themes, *i.* above all *R.* 137
Your useful labours, and *i.* aims *R.* 664
Employs, shut out from more *i.* views *R.* 803
The most *i.* and effectual guard *T.* ii 335
But O the *i.* budget! ushered in *T.* iv 23
Gloriously drunk, obey the *i.* call! *T.* iv 510
To press the *i.* question on his heart *Tir.* 57
Are not *i.* always as dear-bought *Tir.* 74
But 'tis her own *i.* charge *Trans.* iv 10

IMPORTING.
The punishment *i.* this, no doubt *E.* iii 52

IMPORTUNITY.
To clamorous *i.* in rags *T.* iv 414

IMPOSE.
Successive loads succeeding broils *i. Ex.* 308
In misery fools upon themselves *i. T.* 126
The ascending damps; then leisurely *i. T.* iii 477

IMPOSED.
First wish to be *i.* on, and then are *P.E.* 290
I. a gay delirium for a truth *T.* iv 528

IMPOSSIBLE.
Specious in show, *i.* in fact *R.* 638
" Incredible, *i.*, and vain! " *T.* 35
The last *i.*, he fears the first *T.* 265
I. when Virtue is so scarce *T.* iv 531
Do I forebode *i.* events *T.* v 491

IMPOSTORS.
He stripped the *i.* in the noonday sun *Ex.* 141

IMPOSTURE.
The Bible an *i.* and a cheat? *T.* 432

IMPOTENCE.
Conscious of *i.* they soon grow drunk *T.* v 255

IMPOVERISHED.
A little Naiad her *i.* urn *T.* i 328
The *i.* earth; an overbearing race *T.* iii 672

IMPREGNATED.
While airs *i.* with incense play *M.P.* 94
Their wishes all *i.* with earth *R.* 36
I. with quick fermenting salts *T.* iii 464

IMPRESS.
With adjurations every word *i. Con.* 70
Faintly *i.* the mind, or not at all *T.* vi 24
How shall a verse *i.* thee? By what name *Ex.* 654
To *i.* a value, not to be erased *Tir.* 613

IMPRESSED.
His tender heart victoriously *i. A.T.* 4
Then God's own image on the soul *i. Ex.* 109
For truth self-evident, with pomp *i. H.* 109
Except the few his God may have *i. H.* 633
If scorn of God's commands, *i. St.* vi 29
Just then, by adverse fate *i. T.B.* 43
The grand retreat from injuries *i. T.* i 280
And natural in gesture; much *i. T.* ii 402
The footsteps of Simplicity *i. T.* iv 520
Of unprolific winter has *i. T.* vi 138
The stamp of artless piety *i. Tir.* 153
Not yet perhaps incurably *i. Tir.* 764

IMPRESSIBLE.
The mind, *i.* and soft, with ease *P.E.* 355

IMPRESSION.
Are mere *i.* on the passive mind *A.T.* 43
And all their deep *i.*, wear away *P.E.* 278
The *i.* of the blast with proud disdain *T.* i 380
The stamp and clear *i.* of good sense *T.* vi 983

IMPRINT.
Nature *i.* upon whate'er we see *Ch.* 169
The mind and conduct mutually *i. P.E.* 566

IMPRISONED.
Again the mountain feels the *i.* foe *Her.* 37
Something *i.* in the chest *R.C.* 84
He does not scorn it, who, *i.* long *T.* i 436
I burn to set the *i.* wranglers free *T.* iv 34
Earth yields them nought: the *i.* worm is safe *T.* v 80

IMPROBABLE.
Events *i.* and strange as these *Tir.* 370

IMPROVE.
To *i.* the fortitude that bears the load *Ch.* 160
Else who would lose, that had the power to *i. Ch.* 224
Let him *i.* his talent if he can *Con.* 425
As Time *i.* the grape's authentic juice *Con.* 643
Man may *i.* the crisis, or abuse *P.E.* 26
The suitor's air indeed he soon *i. R.* 237
I. the kind occasion, understand *R.* 345
I. the remnant of his wasted span *R.* 13
As wisely, and as much *i.* his powers *R.* 508
Would he *i.* the boon *St.* v 4
Even here: while sedulous I seek to *i. T.* iii 367 [691
Health, leisure, means to *i.* it, friendship, peace *T.* iii
To *i.* and cultivate their just demesne *T.* v 226
And seeking grace to *i.* the prize they hold *T.* vi 55
To *i.* this diet, at no great expense *Tir.* 628

IMPROVED.
I. thee far beyond his own intent *Ex.* 489
I. the simple plan; made three legs four *T.* i 29

IMPROVEMENT.
He catches all *i.* in his flight *Ch.* 115
His great *i.* and new lights he draws *P.E.* 402
I. too, the idol of the age *T.* iii 764
Less for *i.* than to tickle spite *Tir.* 481

IMPRUDENT.
Condemns the unfatherly, the *i.* part *T.* 866

IMPUDENT.
And stands an *i.* and fearless mark *T.* ii 812
I. blasphemy! So Folly pleads *Ch.* 194

IMPULSE.
All feel the freshening *i.*, and are cleansed *T.* i 376
Such is the *i.* and the spur he feels *T.* vi 755
But worn by frequent *i.*, to the cause *Y.O.* 84

IMPUNITY.
That none shall with *i.* neglect *Ch.* 36
Is never with *i.* defied *T.* vi 548

IMPURE.
Infectious as *i.*, your blighting power *Con.* 41
Of all that was absurd, profane, *i. Con.* 888
Called to the temple of *i.* delight *P.E.* 584
Of pride, ambition, or *i.* desires *R.* 110
For gamesters, jockeys, brothellers *i. T.* ii 751
By the *i.*, and hears his power denied *T.* v 895
From touch of human lips at best *i. T.* vi 835
From vicious inmates and delights *i. Tir.* 892

IMPURITY.
Draws gross *i.*, and likes it well *T.* vi 979

IMPUTED.
But still the *i.* tints are those alone *H.* 73

INABILITY.
Through downright *i.* to rise *T.* i 480

INADVERTENT.
An *i.* step may crush the snail *T.* vi 564

INANIMATE.
Impart to things *i.* a voice *R.* 361
Nature *i.* employs sweet sounds *T.* 197

INATTENTIVE.
And all in sight of *i.* man? *T.* vi 120

INBORN.
His *i.* inextinguishable thirst *T.* iv 767

INCAS.
Oh! could their ancient *I.* rise again *Ch.* 65

INCAUTIOUS.
To draw the *i.* minnow from the brook *R.* 402
Or too *i.*, to preserve thy sweets *T.* iii 45
Commits her eggs, *i.*, to the dust *Tir.* 791

INCENSE.
While airs impregnated with *i.* play *M.P.* 94

INCESSANT.
I., clinking hammers, grinding wheels *T.* i 231

INCH.
In science, win one *i.* of heavenly ground *T.* 338

INCIDENT.
The language plain, and *i.* well linked *Con.* 236
Which this day's *i.* began? *E.* i 84
It is an evil *i.* to man *F.A.* 30

INCISION.
With nice *i.* of her guided steel *T.* i 708
INCLEMENCY.
The rude *i.* of wintry skies *T.* 138
INCLEMENT.
Whether *i.* seasons recommend *T.* iii 388
INCLINATION.
(Hardly the effect of *i. E.* i 99
May taste, whate'er his *i. L.W.* 5
Of habit, *i.*, temper, taste *Tir.* 441
INCLINES.
And each *i.* its votary to retreat *R.* 174
INCLINED.
Two bosom friends, each pensively *i. Con.* 507
I. to tarry there *J.G.* 150
By nature weak, or viciously *i. P.E.* 432
When in came, housewifely *i. R.C.* 49
To thrift and parsimony much *i. T.* 141
Serve to compose a spirit well *i. T.* v 657
Serene, and to his duties much *i. Tir.* 774
Fulfilled with ease had you been so *i. V.* 22
INCLUDE.
The important letters that *i.* the rest *Ch.* 523
I. creation in her close embrace *Ch.* 598
And bathes their eyes with nectar, and *i. T.* vi 244
INCOME.
A business with an *i.* at its heels *R.* 615   [356
Whose heirs, their honours none, their *i.* small *Tir.*
INCOMMODIOUSLY.
Complained, though *i.* pent in *T.* i 69
INCOMPARABLE.
I. gem! thy worth untold *T.T.* 330
INCOMPATIBLE.
And *i.* with serious thought *T.* iv 622
INCONSTANT.
But she, *i.* as the beams that play *A.T.* 23
INCONTINENCE.
That lewd *i.*, and lawless rape *A.T.* 64
By riot and *i.* the worst *T.* i 699
INCONVENIENT.
In contact *i.*, nose to nose *Con.* 270
INCORPORATED.
I., seem at once to lose *T.* iv 678
INCORRIGIBLY.
The *i.* wrong, the deaf, the dead! *Tir.* 780
INCREASE.
To teach the wanderer, as his woes *i. Ch.* 161
To *i.* a stranger's treasures *N.C.* 3   [421
Shall much befriend you. Time shall give *i. T.* iv
I. of power begets *i.* of wealth *T.* iv 580
And endless her *i.* Thy rams are there *T.* vi 804
His spirits rising as his toils *i. T.T.* 279
INCREASED.
Whether *i.* momentum, and the force *P.E.* 405
From anxious thoughts how wealth may be *i. R.* 140
INCREASING.
Daily derive *i.* light and force *Con.* 697
I. commerce and reviving art *Her.* 73
The rising waves obey the *i.* blast *R.* 532

I. London? Babylon of old *T.* i 722
I. taxes and the nation's debt *T.T.* 177
INCREDIBLE.
Is it *i.*, or can it seem *Con.* 481
"*I.*, impossible, and vain!" *T.* 35
INCREDULOUS.
That the *i.* themselves may see *J.T.* 49
INCULCATED.
Were precious, and *i.* with care *T.* ii 701
INCUMBER.
Does but *i.* whom it seems to enrich *T.* vi 95
INCUMBRANCE.
To thrive in; an *i.* ere half spent *H.* 98
The *i.* of his own concerns, and spare *T.* vi 206
Excused the *i.* of more solid worth *Tir.* 347
INCUR.
I must *i.*, forgetting Howard's name *Ch.* 296
I. resentment for the love he shows *H.* 285
I. derision for his easy faith *T.* v 500
A necessary act *i.* no blame *T.* vi 573
INCURABLE.
I. obduracy evinced *T.* vi 532
That hour elapsed, the *i.* revolt *T.T.* 402
INCURABLY.
Not yet perhaps *i.* impressed *Tir.* 764
INCURRED.
Though blameless, had *i.* perpetual strife *Con.* 512
Stand now and judge thyself.—Hast thou *i. Ex.* 340
As to be wantonly *i. M.F.* 34
Conscious of jeopardy *i. R.C.* 76
He has *i.* a long arrear *St.* v 31
Ambition, Avarice, Penury *i. T.* iii 811
INCURRING.
I. short fatigue; and though our years *T.* i 129
IND.
The looms of Ormus, and the mines of *I.*—*T.* vi 806
INDEBTED.
The blessings of the most *i.* land *Ex.* 164
Countries *i.* to thy power, that shine *Ex.* 280
And hold the world *i.* to your aid *R.* 665
Scorned in a world, *i.* to that scorn *R.* 751
Grant her *i.* to what zealots call *T.* 483
Its bergamot, or aids the *i.* eye *T.* ii 452
A sliding car, *i.* to no wheels *T.* iv 126
I. to some smart wig-weaver's hand *T.* iv 543
INDECENT.
When wine has given *i.* language birth *Con.* 263
INDENTED.
Two leaves produced, two rough *i.* leaves *T.* iii 526
The *i.* stick, that loses day by day *Tir.* 559
INDEPENDENT.
A dry but *i.* crust, hard earned *T.* iv 409
INDIA.
The gems of *I.*, Nature's rarest birth *Ch.* 134
The sun matures on *I.*'s spicy shores *Ch.* 442
Pulled down the tyrants *I.* served with dread *Ex.* 366
From *I.*, for the ladies' use *R.C.* 38   [39
Now came the cane from *I.*, smooth and bright *T.* i
Of Portugal and Western *I.* there *T.* iii 572
Is *I.* free? and does she wear her plumed *T.* iv 28
In Afric's torrid clime, or *I.*'s fiercest heat *T.T.* 297

INDIAN.
Was glued to the sword-hilt with *I.* gore *Ch.* 50
The fervour and the force of *I.* skies *Ex.* 12
Supple and flexible as *I.* cane *H.* 602
All tribes beside of *I.* name *Mrs. M—* 9
An *I.* mystic, or a French recluse *T.* 128
And range an *I.* waste without a tree *T.* i 261
The wealth of *I.* provinces, escapes *T.* i 738
Of *I.* fume, and guzzling deep, the boor *T.* iv 473
Like a swarth *I.* with his belt of beads *T.* iv 749

INDICATE.
As meant to *i.* a God to man *T.* iii 246
That turns and turns, to *i. Trans.* ii 8

INDIFFERENCE.
My form with *i.* see *A.S.* 14
Scorns with the same *i.* frowns and smiles *H.* 650
I. may repel *Miss —* 42

INDIFFERENT.
Or pride can look at with *i.* eyes *H.* 52
To please her sated and *i.* lord ? *P.E.* 258
Ye ladies ! (for, *i.* in your cause *P.E.* 510
May be *i.* to her house of clay *T.* ii 458
To him *i.* whether grief or joy *T.* iv 15

INDIGENCE.
And years of pining *i.* must show *Her.* 65
To *i.* and rapine; till at last *T.* iv 497
In aiding helpless *i.*, in works *T.* vi 964

INDIGENT.
(Toilsome and *i.*), she renders much *T.* 326

INDIGNANT.
He spoke *i.*, and his spurs applied *A.T.* 191
Sought, with an *i.* mien *B.* 3
He seems indeed *i.*, and to feel *T.* i 379
What provocation to the *i.* heart *T.* iii 65
Returns *i.* to the slighted plough *T.* iv 645

INDIGNATION.
Fire *i.* and a sense of scorn *T.T.* 489
Moves *i.*, makes the name of king *T.* v 442

INDIRECT.
And thus gives Virtue *i.* applause *T.* iii 104

INDISCRETION.
Past *i.* is a venial crime *T.* 491

INDISCRIMINATELY.
If all men *i.* share *T.T.* 256

INDISPOSED.
A mind unnerved, or *i.* to bear *R.* 677
Pregnant, or *i.* alike to all *T.* iv 281

INDISTINCT.
Their views, indeed, were *i.* and dim *Con.* 539
Thy *i.* expressions seem *M.* 21

INDITE.
I. much metre with much pains *O.* i 3

INDIVIDUAL.
Each *i.*, suffering a constraint *Con.* 383
An *i.* is a sacred mark *Ex.* 434

INDOLENCE.
Starved by that *i.* their minds create *Ch.* 64
The yawning chasm of *i.* supply ! *P.E.* 172
With *i.* and luxury, is trash *P.E.* 428
Blames his own *i.*, observes, though late *R.* 477
(Life spent in *i.* and therefore sad) *T.* v 181

INDOLENT.
His active years with *i.* repose *R.* 618
In *i.* vacuity of thought *T.* iv 297

INDUCED.
I. a splendid cover, green and blue *T.* i 32

INDULGE.
I *i.* my poetical moods *Gr.* 51
The Poet's treasure, silence, and *i. T.* i 235
On petty robbers, and *i.* life *T.* i 733
What !—will a man play tricks, will he *i. T.* ii 419
I. all a father's heartfelt glee *Tir.* 321
To *i.* his genius, after long fatigue *T.T.* 153
If he *i.* a cultivated taste *T.T.* 161

INDULGED.
Might also have *i.* with an escape *H.* 513
And pleased with novelty, might be *i. T.* i 508
I. in what they wish, they soon supply *T.* iii 534

INDULGENCE.
For such *i.* gilding all thy years *Ex.* 609
Or lust engenders, and *i.* feeds *R.* 644

INDULGENT.
Perhaps *i.* Nature meant *Trans.* i 13

INDURATED.
I. and fixed, the snowy weight *T.* v 98

INDUSTRIOUS.
Not more *i.* are the just and true *P.E.* 293
Plies all the sinews of *i.* toil *Her.* 69
Of temperate wishes and *i.* hands *T.* i 599
Some, more acute and more *i.* still *T.* iii 155
Vainly *i.*, a disgraceful prize *T.* iii 385
Poor, yet *i.*, modest, quiet, neat *T.* iv 371

INDUSTRIOUSLY.
While every worm *i.* weaves *Tir.* 595

INDUSTRY.
Thou hadst an *i.* in doing good *J.T.* 23
Need help, let honest *i.* provide *P.E.* 252
Where Power secures what *I.* has won *Her.* 87
What happy skill and *i.* combined *T.* 430
Delightful *i.* enjoyed at home *T.* iii 356
Near yonder heath ; where *I.* misspent *T.* iii 643
Or female *i.*: the threaded steel *T.* iv 165
Desire of more ; and *i.* in some *T.* v 225
Who, just when *i.* begins to snore *Tir.* 745
Guards well what Arts and *I.* have won *T.T.* 280

INEBRIATE.
That cheer but not *i.*, wait on each *T.* iv 40

INEFFECTUAL.
Of Revelation's *i.* beam *Con.* 830
Most part an empty *i.* sound *T.* iii 22
Slides *i.* down the snowy vale *T.* v 7

INERT.
Can boast but little virtue ; and *i. T.* i 623

INESTIMABLE.
The fragrant grove, the *i.* mine *H.* 177
The *i.* estimate of Brown *T.T.* 384

INEXORABLY.
There find a judge *i.* just *H.* 227

INEXPERIENCE.
Exposed their *i.* to the snare *T.* ii 801
(Through *i.*, as we now perceive) *T.* vi 27
That sanguine *i.* loves to make *V.* 56

INEXPERIENCED.
Seek to supplant his *i.* youth *P.E.* 59

INEXPERT.
With all his canvass set, and *i. T.* ii 486

INEXPLICABLE.
Heard an *i.* scratching *R.C.* 78

INEXTINGUISHABLE.
In beams of *i.* light *H.* 134
His inborn *i.* thirst *T.* iv 767

INFALLIBLE.
And prove it in the *i.* result *T.* iii 180

INFAMOUS.
When *i.* Venality, grown bold *T.T.* 416

INFAMY.
The flower of Israel's *i.* full blown *Ex.* 222
Stood pilloried on *i.*'s high stage *H.* 556
With *i.* too nauseous to be named *Tir.* 828
But let eternal *I.* pursue *T.T.* 29

INFANCY.
Nor age nor *i.* could find thee there *Ch.* 48
Credulous *i.*, or age as weak *Con.* 225
From *i.* through childhood's giddy maze *H.* 187

INFANT.
Though loose, as harmless as an *i.*'s play *H.* 613
Till, all my stock of *i.* sorrow spent *M.P.* 43
Both baby-featured, and of *i.* size *P.E.* 201
That shines and rests, as *i.* smile and sleep *R.* 528
And, like an *i.*, troublesome awake *T.* 427
And swayed the sceptre of his *i.* realms *T.* i 23
And *i.* clamorous whether pleased or pained *T.* i 232
She brings her *i.* forth with many smiles *T.* iii 437
And while her *i.* race, with outspread hands *T.* iv 384
Blest with an *i.*'s ignorance of all *T.* iv 624
The *i.* elements received a law *T.* vi 200
And smiles to see, her *i.*'s playful hand *T.* vi 779
Spring hangs her *i.* blossoms on the trees *Tir.* 43
To feed our *i.* minds with proper fare *Tir.* 116
Before whose *i.* eyes the flatterer bows *T.T.* 123

INFATUATES.
I., and through labyrinths and wilds *T.* vi 104

INFECT.
I. his happiest moments, he forebodes *T.* v 606

INFECTED.
I. with the manners and the modes *T.* iv 693

INFECTIOUS.
I. as impure, your blighting power *Con.* 41

INFERIOR.
Mounts from *i.* beings up to God *R.* 114
The *i.* wonders of an artist's hand *T.* i 419
That man inflicts on all *i.* kinds *T.* vi 385

INFERNAL.
He bruised beneath his feet the *i.* powers *Ch.* 584
That, with a black, *i.* train *E.* iv 15
She teemed and heaved with an *i.* birth *Her.* 13
Each sire and dam, of an *i.* race *P.E.* 568

INFERRED. [431
The reasoning power vouchsafed of course *i. Con.*

INFEST.
To poison vermin that *i.* his plants *Con.* 256

This of all maladies that man *i. R.* 301
From pangs arthritic that *i.* the toe *T.* i 105
Mourns because every plague that can *i. T.* ii 815
With what vermin else *i. Trans.* iii 13

INFIDEL.
That *i.* may prove their title good *Ex.* 380
An *i.* in health;—"But what when sick?" *T.* 309
That, through profane and *i.* contempt *T.* i 740
The *i.* has shot his bolts away *T.* vi 872
Christian in name, and *i.* in heart *Tir.* 421
With Gospel lore, turn *i.* themselves *Tir.* 826

INFIDELITY.
By *i.* and love o' the world *T.* ii 389
In *i.* and lewdness men *Tir.* 209

INFINITE.
Were fountains fed with *i.* supplies *Ex.* 34
(*I.* skill) in all that He has made *R.* 52
Man's obligations *i.*, of course *T.* 197
Mercy is *i.*, and man is weak *T.* 294
And goodness *i.*, but speak in ears *T.* v 854

INFIRM.
Or tasting long enjoy thee; too *i. T.* iii 44
Of the *i.*, is wholesome air to thee *T.* iv 365
Of heroes, whose *i.* and baby minds *T.* v 190

INFIRMITIES.
But if *i.* that fall *M.F.* 41

INFIXED.
Long since: with many an arrow deep *i. T.* iii 109

INFLAMED.
Nor yet the mariner, his blood *i. T.* i 447

INFLAMES.
The sight our foolish heart *i. P.B.* 31
From what debilitates and what *i. R.* 20

INFLAMMATORY.
Howe'er disguised the *i.* tale *P.E.* 327

INFLATED.
I. and astrut with self-conceit *T.* v 268

INFLICT.
As Vengeance can *i.*, or sinners fear *T.* 554
That lean hard-handed Poverty *i. T.* 827
That man *i.* on all inferior kinds *T.* vi 385
The rottenness which time is charged to *i. Y.O.* 67

INFLICTED.
Weeps when she sees *i.* on a beast *T.* ii 25

INFLUENCE.
To thwart its *i.*, and its end defeat *Ch.* 38
In vain warm suns their *i.* shed *Miss —* 37
Their lustre to his *i.* owe *Mrs. M—* 54
The comet's baneful *i.* is a dream *P.E.* 100
From Fancy's *i.*, and intemperate zeal *P.E.* 455
Exert their *i.*, and advance their cause *P.E.* 463
I., and power, were all at his command *R.* 596
She loses all her *i.* Cities then *T.* iii 729
The soothing *i.* of the wafted strains *T.* vi 68
His *i.*, if that *i.* all be spent *T.* vi 962

INFLUENCED.
For this, of all that ever *i.* man *H.* 643
I. mightily the rest *P.T.* 43

INFOLD.
The pheasant plumes which round *i. Mrs. M—* 5

INFORM.
I. his mind; one flash of heavenly day *Ch.* 228.
The gale i. us, laden with the scent *Ch.* 446
And while they captivate, i. the mind *H.* 759
A terrible sagacity i. *T.T.* 494

INFORMATION.
Let all your rays of i. meet *Con.* 240
The dearth of i. and good sense *T.* iv 71

INFORMED.
I., He gathered up the broken thread *Con.* 525
Yet age, by long experience well i. *Con.* 639
Faithful, and faithfully i., unfold *Ex.* 647
By curious eyes and judgments ill i. *T.* ii 435
His mind i., his morals undefiled *Tir.* 683

INFUSE.
Could i. into numbers of mine *C.* 20
I. lies and errors of his own *Ex.* 102

INFUSED.
He mounts at once—such confidence i. *A.T.* 175
I. at the creation of the kind *T.* iv 733   [844
" And that, i. from Heaven, must thither send " *T.* v

INFUSIONS.
Sips meek i. of a milder herb *Con.* 268

INGENIOUS.
I. Art, with her expressive face *Ch.* 97
Howe'er i. on his darling theme *Con.* 137
Or more i., or more freed *N.Y.G.* 7
Thus men go wrong with an i. skill *P.E.* 556
I. to diversify dull life *R.* 520
Peace to the artist whose i. thought *T.* 210
I. Fancy, never better pleased *T.* i 72
I. Parsimony takes, but just *T.* iv 400
I. Cowley! and though now reclaimed *T.* iv 723
To such amusements as i. woe *T.* v 416
I. dreamer, in whose well-told tale *Tir.* 135

INGENUITY.
To artists i. and skill *T.* iv 797

INGENUOUS.
The head of modest and i. worth *T.* ii 711
A father blest with an i. son *Tir.* 543

INGLORIOUS.
The i. feat, and, clamorous in praise *T.* vi 436

INGOT.
When a bar of pure silver or i. of gold *F.M.* 1

INGREDIENT.
A principal i. *F.* 204
Make works a vain i. in the case *H.* 360
And though the world may think the i. odd *R.* 729
With such i. of good sense and taste *T.* ii 789
Is an i. in the compound, man *T.* iv 732

INHABIT.
To i. a mansion remote *C.* 45

INHABITANTS.
That there are blest i. of earth *Con.* 723
Thy racked i. repine, complain *Ex.* 304
The poor reclaimed i., his eyes *H.* 532
Divide the frail i. of earth *R.* 648
Fall prone; the pale i. come forth *T.* ii 125
Its foul i. But to assuage *T.* iii 501
With blood of their i. impaled *T.* vi 391

INHALING.
That play of lungs, i. and again *T.* i 137

INHARMONIOUS.
Sounds i. in themselves and harsh *T.* 207

INHERIT.
The works of man i., as is just *Con.* 553

INHOSPITABLE.
Stand starved at your i. door? *P.E.* 250

INIMITABLE.
Performing such i. feats *T.* v 125
Uninjured, with i. art *T.* vi 195
He stood, as some i. hand *T.T.* 348

INITIATED.
Once simple, are i. in arts *T.* iv 493

INJURE.
Poor man! what a pity to i. him so! *P.A.* 34

INJURED.
And i., makes forgiveness her delight *Ch.* 431
In just resentment of his i. laws *Ex.* 328
Then Nature, i., scandalized, defiled *Ex.* 424
That feels for i. love! but I disdain *T.* iii 66
Their vigour, i. soon, not soon restored *T.* iii 608
To the deliverer of an i. land *T.* iv 793

INJURIOUS.
The subtle and i. may be just *Con.* 809
Condemns the i. deed, the slanderous tongue *T.* 559
The i. trampler upon Nature's law *T.* vi 465

INJURY.
Of the rude i. it late sustained *Con.* 906
Where only Vice and I. are tied *Ex.* 594
Who scorns to do an i. by stealth *H.* 411
The grand retreat from i. impressed *T.* i 280
Forgets in peace the i. of war *T.* ii 269
That age or i. has hollow'd deep *T.* vi 311
Of i., with such knowledge of their strength *T.* vi 476

INJUSTICE.
Considers all i. with a frown *Ch.* 210

INK.
A poet's drop of i.? *O.* i 12

INKY.
Or wrap himself in Hamlet's i. cloak *T.* vi 675

INLAID.
Swarmed with a scribbling herd, as deep i. *T.T.* 628

INLAND.   [117
Possessed an i. scene. Where now the throng *T.* ii
From i. regions to the distant main *T.* v 790

INLAYS.
That, as with molten glass, i. the vale *T.* i 170

INMATE.
Reminds them of their hated i., Sin *E.* ii 36
From vicious i. and delights impure *Tir* 892
Little i., full of mirth *Trans.* iii 1

INN.
Is to conduct it to the destined i. *T.* iv 10

INNOCENCE.
Trade in the blood of i., and plead *Ch.* 182
But let insolvent i. go free " *Ch.* 289
Oh come not ye near i. and truth *Con.* 39
With tortured i. in Mary's court *Ex.* 613
Folly and I. are so alike *P.E.* 203
But I., sedate, serene, erect *P.E.* 207
Steal to the closet of young i. *P.E.* 316

INNOCENCE—INSPIRE

When boyish *i.* was all my praise!) *R.* 372
Lost *i.*, or cancel follies past *T.* iii 678
That felt their virtues; *I.*, it seems *T.* iv 518
On fancied *I.* Again he falls *T.* v 623
Waged with defenceless *i.*, while he *T.* vi 393
" While *i.* without disguise *The Doves* 13
In Eden, ere yet *i.* of heart *T.T.* 584

INNOCENT.
But *i.* was all his sport *Beau* 15
Against an *i.*, unconscious breast *Ex.* 431
While one as *i.* regards *L.W.* 27
'Tis *i.*, and harmless, and refined *P.E.* 179
I.! oh! if venerable Time *P.E.* 181
To teach the canvass *i.* deceit *R.* 797
Deception *i.*—give ample space *T.* i 353
The *i.* are gay—the lark is gay *T.* i 493
I. partner of my peaceful home *T.* iii 337
Oh *i.*, compared with arts like these *T.* iii 801
But many a crime deem'd *i.* on earth *T.* vi 439
Of *i.* commercial Justice red *T.* iv 683
Our *i.* sweet simple years again *Tir.* 313
To joys less *i.*, as less refined *T.T.* 601

INOFFENSIVE.
A Christian's wit is *i.* light *Con.* 599
As *i.*, what offence in cards? *P.E.* 149
I., welcome guest! *Trans.* iii 10

INQUEST.
And in the furious *i.* that it makes *T.* ii 135

INQUIRE.
Was much addicted to *i. R.C.* 3
We next *i.*, but softly and by stealth *Con.* 389 [818
Sweet conference; *i.* what strains were they *T.* v
And not a tongue *i.* how, where, or when *T.T.* 424

INQUIRER.
The *i.'s* aim, that remedy, is Hope *H.* 114
Or negligent *i.*, not a spark *T.* iii 276
Learn from expert *i.* after truth *Tir.* 192

INQUIRING.
Downs that almost escape the *i.* eye *R.* 423

INQUIRY.
Whatever steep *i.* recommends *Ch.* 316
'Twere vain *i.* to what port she went *Ch.* 445
The cause perhaps *i.* may descry *Con.* 363
Oh vain *i.*! they without remorse *Ex.* 462
Where bold *I.*, diving out of sight *H.* 443
Pushing her bold *i.* to the date *R.* 669
In vain they push'd *i.* to the birth *T.* ii 511
Before the keen *i.* of her thought *T.T.* 493

INQUISITIVE.
I. attention, while I read *T.* iv 52
I., the less ambiguous past *Y.O.* 44

INQUISITOR.
No grand *i.* could worse invent *T.* 103

INROADS.
Make cruel *i.* in my brain *E.* iv 16

INSANITY.
The heart's *i.* admits no cure *T.* vi 523

INSATIABLE.
Sucks down its prey *i.* Immense *T.* ii 103

INSCRIBED.
I. above the portal, from afar *T.* 28

INSCRIPTION.
Points to *i.* whereso'er they tread *P.E.* 391

INSECT.
To wonder at a thousand *i.* forms *R.* 63
Who gives its lustre to an *i.'s* wing *T.* v 813
To show him in an *i.* or a flower *Tir.* 636

INSENSIBILITY.
Peace (if *i.* may claim) *H.* 235

INSENSIBLE.
I. of Truth's almighty charms *H.* 655

INSEPARABLY.
And cleaves through life *i.* close *T.* ii 761

INSERTED.
The bud *i.* in the rind *U.* 13

INSIDIOUS.
The *i.* witch that had his wits abused *A.T.* 176

INSIGNIFICANT.
Witness its *i.* result *Con.* 16

INSIGNIFICANTLY.
And anger *i.* fierce *T.* vi 320

INSINCERE.
Are *i.*, meant only to conceal *Con.* 785
Unworthy, base, and *i. F.* 215
But to the proud, uncandid, *i. T.* iii 275

INSINUATING.
The poisonous, black, *i.* worm *P.E.* 7

INSINUATION.
I scorn your coarse *i. P.* 27

INSIPID.
To which the *i.* citizen resorts *T.* iii 642
I. else, and sure to be despised *T.* vi 1016

INSIST.
I. on, as if each were his own pope *H.* 213
Still I *i.*, though music heretofore *P.E.* 138

INSOLENCE.
That air of *i.* affronts your God *Con.* 487
'Tis not however, *i.* and noise *T.T.* 408

INSOLENT.
Her women, *i.* and self-caressed *Ex.* 45
The rugged frowns and *i.* rebuffs *T.* iv 411

INSOLVENCIES.
Yet hence, alas! *i.*, and hence *R.* 511

INSOLVENT.
But let *i.* innocence go free " *Ch.* 289

INSPIRATION.
They scorned his *i.*, and his theme *Ex.* 69
Or *I.* teaches; and enclosed *T.* i 628

INSPIRE.
'Tis thus the tenderness that Love *i. A.T.* 29
And with scenes that new raptnre *i. C.* 51
The founder of that name alone *i. Ch.* 600
The language of the land she seeks *i. Con.* 886
The mischiefs your ambitious pride *i.*! *Her.* 46
And wit that puppet prompters might *i. R.* 312
Nature in every form *i.* delight *R.* 417
Whatever hopes a change of scene *i. R.* 679
What fear he feels his gratitude *i. T.* 190
And well tried virtues, could alone *i. T.* i 148
I. the News, his trumpet. Keener far *T.* ii 353
To break a jest, when pity would *i. T.* ii 468
With eloquence that agonies *i. T.* iii 330
Of his unrival'd pencil. He *i. T.* vi 242
'Twere wiser sure to *i.* a little heart *Tir.* 454
Whose fair example may at once *i. Tir.* 648
Hence Liberty, sweet Liberty, *i. T.T.* 222

Its clearest tone, the rapture it *i.* *T.T.* 293
I. the song, and that his name is Love *T.T.* 739

INSPIRED.
'Tis to believe what men *i.* of old *Ex.* 646
From thousands with rapture *i.* *M.D.* 40
Could I, from heaven *i.*, as sure presage *St.* ii 1
With all that bigotry adopts, *i.* *T.* 88
But who, with filial confidence *i.* *T.* v 745
What knavish priests promulgate as *i.* *Tir.* 186
Which first *i.* the flame, decays *M.F.* 54

INSPIRER.
Their great *i.* call *J.P.* 30
Be thou the great *i.* of my strains *R.* 202

INSPIRING.
And makes the task his own. *I.* dumb *T.* vi 474

INSTANCE.
But (I might *i.* in St. Patrick's dean) *Ch.* 499

INSTANT.
The wreath he won drew down an *i.* curse *Ch.* 61
An *i.*'s pause, and lives but while she moves *T.* i 371
That *i.* he becomes the serjeant's care *T.* iv 631
That *i.* upon all his future pains *Tir.* 715

INSTINCT.
With genial *i.* filled *A Tale* 14
As all by *i.*, like the bees *Q.V.* 43
When led by *i.* sharp and sure *T.B.* 32
Yet feel the burning *i.*: over-head *T.* iv 773
As *i.* prompts; self-buried ere they die *T.* v 88
Yours, a blind *i.*, crouches to the rod *T.* v 355
In measure, as by force of *i.* drawn *T.* vi 412
While meaner things, whom *i.* leads *The Doves* 3
Swelling with vegetative force *i.* *Y.O.* 34

INSTINCTIVE.
Much of her vigilant *i.* dread *T.* iii 340
A jealousy and an *i.* fear *T.* vi 374

INSTITUTED.
That certain feasts are *i.* now *Con.* 823

INSTITUTIONS.
Shall royal *i.* miss the bays *Tir.* 503

INSTRUCT.
I. us how to love! *A Tale* 80
If he wish to *i.*, he must learn to delight *F.M.* 17
I. me, guide me to that heavenly day *R.* 95
And loose example, whom he should *i.* *T.* ii 552
She next *i.* him in the kiss *Trans.* iv 16

INSTRUCTED.
But let the wise and well *i.* hand *Con.* 903
Thus fell the best *i.* in her day *Ex.* 225
I. him at length to gain *F.B.* 17
Reformed and well *i.* ? You shall hear *T.* 130
Thine eye shall be *i.*, and thine heart *T.* v 782
The Muse *i.* a well-nurtured train *T.T.* 634

INSTRUCTION.
Thy lips have shed *i.* as the dew *Ch.* 238
With rich *i.*, and a soul enlarged *Ch.* 322
Spirit of *i.*! come *St.* iv 35
I., and inventing to ourselves *T.* v 875
And all the *i.* of thy son's best friend *Tir.* 717

INSTRUCTIVE.
With social converse and *i.* ease *T.* iv 135

INSTRUCTORS.
Of all these sepulchres, *i.* true *St.* ii 34
To quadruped *i.*, many a good *T.* vi 622

INSTRUMENT.
As a mere *i.* in hands divine *Ex.* 319
'Gan make his *i.* of music speak *N.A.* 44
An *i.* whose chords, upon the stretch *T.* 384
And having found his *i.*, forgets *T.* ii 176
" Is but an *i.* on which the priest *T.* v 651
But read the *i.*, and mark it well *T.* vi 454
All are his *i.*; each form of war *T.T.* 446

INSTRUMENTAL.
From *i.* causes proud to draw *T.* iii 238

INSUFFICIENT
Doomed it, as *i.* for his praise *T.* v 565

INSULT.
When lawless mobs *i.* the Court *Pat.* 9
And the fool with it, who *i.* his Lord *T.* 504

INSULTED.
I. and traduced, are cast aside *T.* vi 879

INSUPPORTABLE.
The *i.* fatigue of thought *T.* vi 106

INSURANCE.
Like Hand-in-Hand *i.* plates *F.* 106

INSURE.
Temperance and Peace *i.* its healthful state *Con.* 603
No present health can health *i.* *St.* i 25
To *i.* a side-box station at half price *T.* ii 624

INTEGRITY.
Had once his *i.* put to the test *P.A.* 22
And sound *i.*, not more than famed *T.* iii 259
Their sober zeal, *i.*, and worth *T.T.* 377

INTELLECT.
Their want of light and *i.* supplied *Con.* 147
Adorn his *i.* as well as shelves *T.* 423
Our wayward *i.*, the more we learn *T.* iii 236
Bestial, a meagre *i.*, unfit *T.* v 454
With *i.* bemazed in endless doubt *T.* v 848
Who feed a pupil's *i.* with store *Tir.* 622

INTELLECTUAL.
An *i.* kingdom, all her own *Tir.* 12

INTELLIGENCE.
The meek *i.* of those dear eyes *M.P.* 7
Bears proof of an *i.* divine *R.* 208
He sucks *i.* in every clime *T.* iv 111
By one of sound *i.* rehearsed *T.* vi 480

INTELLIGENT.
Are more *i.* at least,—try them " *Ex.* 461
Far more *i.*, and better taught *R.* 673
Thus form'd, thus placed, *i.*, and taught *Tir.* 53
Not more *i.* than loose and gay *Tir.* 530
At once, upstood *i.*, surveyed *Y.O.* 150

INTEMPERATE.
From Fancy's influence, and *i.* zeal *P.E.* 455

INTEND.
But Charity not feigned *i.* alone *Ch.* 449
Springs from the mischief it *i.* to cure *Con.* 170
The stroke that a vindictive God *i.* *Ex.* 407
Whatever parents, guardians, schools *i.* *P.E.* 424
Did not his eye rule all things, and *i.* *T.* ii 166
Fresh for his task, *i.* what task he may *T.* iii 387
His wealth, fame, honours, all that I *i.* *Tir.* 389
Too busy to *i.* a meaner care *Tir.* 660

INTENDANTS.
Have ye, ye sage *i.* of the whole *Tir.* 265

INTENDED.
And the Nose was as plainly *i.* for them " *A.C.* 24
They drew a curse from an *i.* good *Ex.* 129
It err but little from the *i.* line *P.E.* 574

INTENSE.
And, in the glow of her *i.* desires *Ch.* 402
With visions prompted by *i.* desire *T.* i 451
He burns with most *i.* and flagrant zeal *T.* iii 794
With what *i.* desire he wants his home *Tir.* 562

INTENT.
Propitious to his fond *i.* there grew *A.T.* 80
I. upon her destined course *Comp.* ii 6
Some never seem so wide of their *i. Con.* 857
Their beauties I *i.* surveyed *D.W.* 15
Improved thee far beyond his own *i. Ex.* 489
To prove at last my main *i. F.* 139
Some foe to his upright *i. H.F.* 9
Shall recompense his mere *i. Mor.* 56
The worm, aware of his *i. N.G.* 13
The worst is—Scripture warped from its *i. P.E.* 437
With what *i.* I touch that holy thing) *T.* ii 328
Desert their office; and themselves *i. T.* iv 589
And eyes *i.* upon the scanty herb *T.* v 786
And no distrust of his *i.* in theirs *T.* vi 363
His horrible *i.*, again he sought *T.* vi 525
Force not my drift beyond its just *i. Tir.* 505

INTENTIONS.
That Heaven's *i.* are not what they seem *H.* 66

INTERCEPT.
How dark the veil that *i.* the blaze *Ch.* 57
Where frequent hedges *i.* the eye *T.* i 514
The eclipse that *i.* truth's heavenly beam *T.* v 683

INTERCEPTING.
And, *i.* in their silent fall *T.* vi 74

INTERCOURSE.
This genial *i.*, and mutual aid *Ch.* 93
With frequent *i.*, and always sweet *E.* iii 3
Sure there is need of social *i. T.* ii 48
His *i.* with peers and sons of peers *Tir.* 393

INTERDASHED.
A prologue *i.* with many a stroke *T.T.* 538

INTERDICTS.
And *i.* its growth. Thence straight succeed *T.* iii 529

INTEREST.
And begged an *i.* in his frequent prayers *Con.* 74
And one in heart, in *i.*, and design *Con.* 701
The soul's sure *i.* in the good she seeks *Con.* 728
As *I.* biased knaves, or Fashion fools *Ex.* 38
So rich an *i.* in Almighty love? *Ex.* 166
Thou hast as bright an *i.* in her rays *Ex.* 590
If *I.* move thee, to persuade e'en thee *Ex.* 667
That stands on sordid *i. F.* 38
To passion, *i.*, pleasure, whim, resigned *H.* 212
Had each a brother's *i.* in his heart *H.* 579
Their real *i.* to discern *N.G.* 28
The point of *i.* or the post of power *R.* 142
His master's *i.* and his own combined *T.* 193
Consults all day your *i.* and your ease *T.* 217
For though the Pope has lost his *i.* here *T.* 289
For *i.* sake, the living to the dead *T.* iii 661
Her *i.*, or that gives her sacred cause *T.* iii 792
For *i.* sake, or swarming into clans *T.* iv 665
And by an emphasis of *i.* his *T.* v 749
Are yet his care, and have an *i.* all *T.* vi 448

Connexion formed for *i.*, and endeared *Tir.* 495
That God and nature, and your *i.* too *Tir.* 553

INTERESTING.
Filled up at last with *i.* news *Con.* 394

INTERFERE.
Hence all that *i.*, and dares to clash *P.E.* 427
To *i.* though in so just a cause *T.* vi 473
Or safety *i.*, his rights and claims *T.* vi 582

INTERFERENCE.
Forbids their *i.*, looking on *T.* v 523

INTERFUSED.
Than water *i.* to make them one *T.* v 148

INTERIOR.
Glorious as Solyma's *i.* shrine *T.* 388
He that attends to his *i.* self *T.* iii 373

INTERJECTED.
Strange! how the frequent *i.* dash *Ch.* 521

INTERJECTIONS.
Sweet *i.*! if he learn but those? *Tir.* 400

INTERLACED.
That *i.* each other, these supplied *T.* i 41

INTERMEDDLING.
Nor stranger *i.* with my joy *T.* vi 298

INTERMINABLE.
That finding an *i.* space *T.* v 556

INTERMINGLING.
With all my purpose *i. E.* i 26
Shadow and sunshine *i.* quick *T.* i 347
The amomum there with *i.* flowers *T.* iii 576

INTERPOSE.
An envious world will *i.* its frown *E.* ii 33
None *i.* now to succour thee *Ex.* 279
And marks whatever clouds may *i. T.T.* 707

INTERPOSED.
That humour *i.* too often makes *M.P.* 67
Or should the brambles, *i.*, our fall *N.A.* 111
Of hill and valley *i.* between *T.* i 322
Abhor each other. Mountains *i. T.* ii 17
Of hunger unassuaged, has *i. T.* vi 463

INTERPOSING.
The pipe, with solemn *i.* puff *Con.* 245
Long hid by *i.* hill or wood *T.* 249

INTERPRET.
Than to *i.* by the letter *P.T.* 6
I. to the marking eye distress *R.* 287
I. her more truly) of a rank *T.* iv 548

INTERPRETER.
Sacred *i.* of human thought *Con.* 23
A lewd *i.* is never just *P.E.* 459
His black *i.* the charge disdained *T.T.* 99

INTERRED.
When some stranger is *i. St.* iv 32

INTERRUPT.
I *i.* him with a sudden bow *Con.* 281
As once in Gibeon, *i.* the race *T.* vi 126

INTERRUPTION.
It suffers *i.* and delay *P.E.* 442

INTERSECTED.
Lands *i.* by a narrow frith *T.* ii 16

INTERSPERSE.
Oaks *i.* it, that had once a head *N.A.* 11

INTERSPERSED.
Nor gardens *i.* with flowery beds *R.* 336
INTERTEXTURE.
And skirted thick with *i.* firm *T.* i 111
INTERTWINE.
And horrid brambles *i.* below *N.A.* 16
INTERVAL.
And while, at *i.*, a cold blast sings *Ex.* 720
That meet (no barren *i.* between) *T.* iii 409
Falling at *i.* upon the ear *T.* vi 7
These were the chief; each *i.* of night *T.T.* 572
INTERVENE.
Or scorned where business never *i. R.* 122
But judge, where so much evil *i. Tir.* 486
Aware then how much danger *i. Tir.* 883
But Providence himself will *i. T.T.* 444
INTERVENING.
A transient visit *i. E.* i 97
INTERVIEW.
At every *i.* their route the same *Con.* 213
INTERWOVEN.
Close *i.*, where they meet the vase *T.* iii 612
INTESTINE.
No thunders shook with deep *i.* sound *Her.* 5
And tumult, and *i.* war *M.F.* 48
A cold stagnation on the *i.* tide *T.* vi 139
INTIMATE.
I crown thee king of *i.* delights *T.* iv 139
INTOLERANT.
Religion, harsh, *i.*, austere *T.T.* 612
INTOXICATE.
Was sure to *i.* the brows it bound *T.* v 245
INTOXICATION.
Where once *i.* pressed the ground *Con.* 808
I. and delirium wild *T.* ii 510
INTREPID.
Sound sense, *i.* spirit, manly grace *V.* 12
INTRICATE.
Contrivance *i.* expressed with ease *R.* 55
INTRIGUE.
Where dreams of dress, *i.*, and pleasure reign *R.* 642
By diving into cabinet *i. T.T.* 154
INTRINSIC.
To your *i.* merit true *E.* i 27
INTRINSICALLY.
I. precious; to the foot *T.* v 175
INTRODUCE.
With such as merchants *i. R.C.* 37
And *i.* hunger, frost, and woe *T.* ii 616
INTROVERTED.
Self-searching with an *i.* eye *Con.* 364
His awkward gait, his *i.* toes *T.* iv 633
INTRUDE.
Or where does cold Reflection less *i.? Ex.* 8
A thought *i.*, that says, or seems to say *H.* 372
And bar the door the moment they *i. P.E.* 160
Truth will *i.*—she bids him yet beware *T.* 471
Woe to the tyrant, if he dare *i. T.* vi 406
And charged perhaps with venom, that *i. T.* vi 569

INTRUDER.
That made them an *i.* on their joys *T.* iv 179
INTRUSION.
His bold *i.* on their dark retreat *H.* 356
Risk an *i.* on thy pensive mood *R.* 255
INTRUSTED.
Life an *i.* talent, or a toy? *R.* 650
INTUITION.
He spells them true by *i.*'s light *N.A.* 69
INURED.
The poor, *i.* to drudgery and distress *H.* 7
The man feels least, as more *i.* than she *T.* iv 387
INVADE.
To quit the forest and *i.* the fold *Ch.* 185
The worst that can *i.* a sickly brain *Con.* 222
Bids rottenness *i.*, and bring to dust *Ex.* 332
I., possesses, and o'erwhelms the soul *H.* 730
Taught the raised shoulders to *i.* the ears *T.* i 67
Which winds and waves obey, *i.* the shore *T.* ii 114
That no rude savour maritime *i. T.* ii 258
Tempered in hell, *i.* the throbbing breast *T.* iii 686
To *i.* another's rights, or guard their own *T.* iv 560
Winter *i.* the spring, and often pours *T.T.* 210
INVALID.
As the leaf that enfolds what an *i.* swallows *F.M.* 22
INVECTIVE.
Than all *i.* is his bold harangue *T.* ii 354
INVENT.
And of all arts sagacious dupes *i. P.E.* 435
No grand inquisitor could worse *i. T.* 103
From all that Science traces, Art *i. T.* i 627
With all that Fancy can *i.* to please *T.T.* 765
INVENTED.
Imports what others have *i.* well *Ch.* 117
Thus first Necessity *i.* Stools *T.* i 86
The curbs *i.* for the mulish mouth *T.* ii 744
Thus kings were first *i.*, and thus kings *T.* v 279
Priests have *i.*, and the world admired *Tir.* 185
INVENTING.
Instruction, and *i.* to ourselves *T.* v 875
INVENTION.
Or taxed *i.* for a fresh supply *Ch.* 514
Beggars *I.*, and makes Fancy lame *R.* 710
The birthday of *I.*; weak at first *T.* i 17
And some ascribe the *i.* to a priest *T.* i 62
The expedients and *i.* multiform *T.* ii 287
INVENTIVE.
Which busy man's *i.* brain *E.* i 65
INVENTOR.
The sword and falchion their *i.* claim *T.* v 218
INVENTORY.
Saves the small *i.*, bed, and stool *T.* iv 401
INVERTED.
O Winter, ruler of the *i.* year *T.* iv 120
Such reasoning falls like an *i.* cone *T.T.* 53
INVEST.
With clasping tendrils, and *i.* his branch *T.* iii 666
'Tis plain the creature, whom he chose to *i. Tir.* 95
INVESTING.
With blushing wreaths, *i.* every spray *T.* vi 169

INVETERATE.
I. habits choke the unfruitful heart *R.* 41
And their *i.* habits, all forbid *T.* i 490
I., hopeless of a cure, conspires *T.* iv 577

INVIGORATE.
And youth *i.* that frame again *H.* 34
Not more *i.* life's noblest part *T.T.* 381
I. by turns the springs of life *Y.O.* 78

INVINCIBLE.
None *i.* as they " *B.* 32
Baptized her fleet I. in vain *Ex.* 569

INVISIBLE.
Their own defect *i.* to them *Con.* 155
Certain *i.* as shrewd as he *Con.* 738
The I. in things scarce seen revealed *R.* 61
" Distinctly scenes *i.* to man *T.* v 826

INVITATION.
Man, Nature's guest by *i.* sweet *P.E.* 209

INVITE.
His wit *i.* you by his looks to come *Con.* 303
I. thee, woo thee, to the bliss they share *Ex.* 627
The open windows seemed to *i. F.B.* 19
Without a soil to *i.* the tiller's care *Her.* 27
There no delusive hope *i.* despair *P.E.* 617
I. us. Monument of ancient taste *T.* i 253
Soft fomentation, and *i.* the seed *T.* iii 510
Then spread the rich discovery, and *i. T.T.* 752

INVITED.
I. her to slumber there *R.C.* 42
Kings are *i.*, and would kings obey *T.* 351

INVITING.
Dressed to his taste, *i.* him abroad *T.* iii 358

INVOLVED.
Obscurest night *i.* the sky *Cast.* 1
There sit, *i.* and lost in curling clouds *T.* iv 472

INVOLVES.
That live an atheist life ; *i.* the Heaven *T.* ii 180
I. the combatants; each claiming Truth *T.* iii 162

IRIS.
To form an I. in the skies *O.* i 19

IRISH.
(As I. bogs are always green) *F.* 122

IRON.
The studs that thick emboss his *i.* door *T.* v 426

IRON-HEARTED.
Think, ye masters *i. N.C.* 21

IRRATIONAL.
I. in what they thus prefer *Tir.* 795

IRREGULAR.
All is *i.*, and out of course *P.E.* 449
The onset, and *i.* At length *T.* v 230

IRRESOLUTE.
Weak and *i.* is man *H.F.* 1

IRREVOCABLE.
Alike *i.* both when past *Comp.* i 5

IRRITATE.
Not to molest, or *i.*, or raise *R.* 317

ISAAC.
Like I., with a mind applied *Mor.* 11   [538
Such was Sir I., and such Boyle and Locke *P.E.*

ISAAC-LIKE.
When, I., the solitary saint *T.* vi 948

ISIS.   [369
From school to Cam or I., and thence home *P.E.*

ISLAND.
This *i.*, spot of unreclaimed rude earth *Ex.* 468
To a slave-cultured *i.* we came *M.D.* 26
A flowery *i.*, from the dark green lawn *T.* iii 630

ISLE.
The simple native of the new found *i. Ch.* 30
An *i.* possessed by creatures of our kind *Ch.* 381
From side to side of her delightful *i. Ex.* 3
Yet Truth is yours, remote unenvied *i.* ! *H.* 481
O place me in some heaven-protected *i. Her.* 83
In Britain's *i.*, beneath a George's reign ! *Her.* 90
So then—the Vandals of our I.—*M.* i 1
Shoots into port at some well-havened *i. M.P.* 90
We find a little *i.*, this life of man *R.* 148
In Albion's happy *i.* The lumber stood *T.* i 58 [620
Towards the Antarctic. Even the favoured *i. T.* i
And we the righteous, whose fast-anchored *i. T.* ii 151
And fill with discontent a British *i. T.T.* 253
Emerged all splendour in our *i.* at last *T.T.* 565
To the delicate growth of our *i. W.N.* 2
O Queen of Albion, queen of *i.* ! 1789, 56

ISLINGTON.
Thus all through merry I.—*J.G.* 133

ISRAEL.
How would they take up I.'s taunting strain ! *Ch.* 66
If I.'s Lord be God, then serve the Lord *Con.* 852
The prophet wept for I. ; wished his eyes *Ex.* 33
For I. dealt in robbery and wrong *Ex.* 35
Wept till all I. heard his bitter cry *Ex.* 63
People and priest, the sons of I. were *Ex.* 124
The flower of I.'s infamy full blown *Ex.* 222
O I., of all nations most undone ! *Ex.* 257

ISSUE.
Thy tears all *i.* from a source divine *E.* ii 47
The fatal *i.* to his health, fame, peace *T.* v 601

ISSUED.
When all his glowing language *i.* forth *Con.* 709
Now therefore *i.* forth the spotted pack *N.A.* 24
That beak, whence *i.* many a lay *T.B.* 56

ISSUING.
Of stale debauch, forth *i.* from the styes *T.* iv 470

ITALIAN.
He from I. songsters takes his cue *P.E.* 112
That make I. flowers so sweet and fair *P.E.* 410
And throws I. light on English walls *T.* i 425

ITALY.
O I. ! thy sabbaths will be soon *P.E.* 152
He sunk in Greece, in I. he rose *T.T.* 563

ITCH.
Denominates an *i.* for writing *E.* i 18   [111
And many a dunce, whose fingers *i.* to write *T.T*

ITCHING.
Should feel that *i.* and that tingling *E.* i 25
Is but to gratify an *i.* ear *T.* vi 643

ITCHY.
Excess, the scrofulous and *i.* plague *T.* iv 582

ITEM.
And *i.* down the victims of the past *St.* ii 4

But that she fasts, and, *i.*, goes to church T. 152
Drained to the last poor *i.* of his wealth T. iii 784

IVORY.
Was smooth and even as an *i.* ball *A.T.* 47
Four *i.* eggs soon pave its floor *A Tale* 41
As alphabets in *i.* employ *Con.* 11
Or twining silken threads round *i.* reels T. iv 264
With *i.* teeth, or ploughs it with his snout T. v 50

In streaming gold; syringa, *i.* pure T. vi 150
To trivial toys, and, pushing *i.* balls T. vi 274

IVY.
As creeping *i.* clings to wood or stone *P.E.* 285
His brows with *i.*, rushed into the field *T.T.* 604

IVY-MANTLED.
Calls Nature from her *i.* den *Ch.* 95

J.

JACHIN.
The *J.* and the Boaz of them all *Tir.* 500

JACK.
Or giant-killing *J.* would please no more *Con.* 244
Was still a wild *j.* hare *Ep.* ii 8
The man that hails you Tom or *J.*—*F.* 169
Poor *J.*—no matter who—for when I blame *R.* 575
J. vanished, was regretted and forgot *R.* 581 [*R.* 599
J. bowed and was obliged—confessed 'twas strange
J. knew his friend, but hoped in that disguise *R.* 587
'Twas he, the same, the very *J.* he knew *R.* 592

JACQUES.
I shall not ask Jean *J.* Rousseau *P.T.* 1

JAIL.
Asked, when in Hell, to see the royal *j. T.T.* 94
Begs a warm office, doomed to a cold *j.* T. iii 820

JAPAN.
No matter where, in China or *J.*—*E.* iii 47

JAR.
The clash of arguments and *j.* of words *Con.* 85
And grins with wonder at the *j.* he makes *Con.* 902
Thy senate is a scene of civil *j. Ex.* 294
Instead of harmony, 'tis *j. M.F.* 47

JARGON.
To them, the sounding *j.* of the schools T. 367

JARRING.
Hence *j.* sectaries may learn *N.G.* 27
O blest seclusion from a *j.* world T. iii 675
A *j.* note. Themes of a graver tone T. iv 181

JASMINE.
The *J.*, throwing wide her elegant sweets T. vi 173

JAVA.
Is heard salvation. Eastern *J.* there T. vi 810

JAY. [*Y.O.* 18
Which babes might play with; and the thievish *j.*
The *j.*, the pie, and even the boding owl T. 205

JEALOUS.
He did it with a *j.* look *Ep.* ii 11
And *j.* of the blessing. Spread it then T. ii 44
Does law, so *j.* in the cause of man T. vi 432
And Equity: not *j.* more to guard T. vi 850

JEALOUSY.
So *J.* looks forth distressed *F.* 80
A *j.* and an instinctive fear T. vi 374
Of envy, hatred, *j.*, and pride *Tir.* 467

JEAN.
I shall not ask *J.* Jacques Rousseau *P.T.* 1

JEHOVAH. [908
It sounds *J.*'s name, and pours his praise along *Con.*
Are part of a *J.*'s cares *E.* i 58
From Sinai's top *J.* gave the law T. 549

JEJUNE.
Till farce itself, most mournfully *j. R.* 711

JEOPARDY.
Conscious of *j.* incurred *R.C.* 76

JERK. [62
And with a dexterous *j.* soon twists him down T. iv

JERUSALEM.
J. a prey, her glory soiled *Ex.* 61

JESSAMINE.
The violet, the pink, the *j. M.P.* 76
Their *j.*, her *j.* remote T. iii 584

JEST.
With such a *j.* as filled with hellish glee *Con.* 737
And having felt the pangs you deem a *j. Con.* 497
Becomes a mockery and a standing *j. Ex.* 110
And say he wounded you in *j. F.* 95
Or laugh or mourn with me, the rueful *j. P.E.* 110
Could argue once, could *j.*, or join the song *R.* 290
The Scripture was his *j.* book, whence he drew T. 308
No smartness in the *j.*, and wonders why T. i 469
To break a *j.*, when pity would inspire T. ii 468
The tasselled cap and the spruce band a *j.* T. ii 749
His pupil, and his torment, and his *j.* T. iv 632
And he abhors the *j.* by which he shines T. v 617
So that the *j.* is clearly to be seen *T.T.* 540
Come, ponder well, for 'tis no *j. Y.D.* 1

JESTER.
No *j.*, and yet lively in discourse *Tir.* 668

JET.
The bramble, black as *j.*, or sloes austere T. i 122

JEW.
Had Paul of Tarsus lived and died a *J.*—*H.* 257
Bon mots to gall the Christian and the *J.*—T. 308
But God will never. When he charged the *J.*—T.vi 443
And hates it with the malice of a *J.*—*Tir.* 168
The leathern ears of stockjobbers and *J.*—*T.T.* 187

JEWEL.
He sought the *j.* in his neighbour's shame *Ch.* 540
That *j.* of the purest flame *F.* 11
That picked the *j.* out of England's crown T. ii 265
Unquestioned, though the *j.* be but glass *Tir.* 463

JEWELED.
And *j.* turban with a smile of peace T. iv 29

JEWISH.
The favours poured upon the J. name *Ex.* 170
So when the J. leader stretched his arm *T.* ii 825

JINGLE.
Of dear Mat Prior's easy j. *E.* iv 4

JINGLING.
Sportive and j. her poetic bells *T.* iv 702
True to the j. of our leader's bells *Tir.* 254

JOB.
And asked him to go and assist in the j. *P.A.* 24
J. felt it, when he groaned beneath the rod *R.* 303
Friends such as his for modern J. prepare *R.* 306

JOCKEY.
Prepares for meals as j. take a sweat *P.E.* 221
For gamesters, j., brothellers impure *T.* ii 751
And, while the playful j. scours the room *Tir.* 366

JOCKEYSHIP.
Where can at last his j. retire? *Con.* 420
At least superior j., and claim *T.* ii 276

JOCULAR.
To conquer those by j. exploits *T.* ii 479

JOCUND.
The j. Loves in Hymen's band *Miss —* 73
To theatre, or j. feast, or ball *T.* v 410

JOG.
For then the farmers come j., j. *Y.D.* 13

JOHN. [*A.T.* iii 3
Should J. wed a score, O the claws and the scratches!
If J. marries Mary, and Mary alone *A.T.* iii 1
'Tis a very good match between Mary and J. *A.T.* iii 2
And all the love of the beloved J.—*H.* 625
J. Gilpin was a citizen *J.G.* 1
J. Gilpin's spouse said to her dear *J.G.* 5
J. Gilpin kissed his loving wife *J.G.* 29
J. Gilpin at his horse's side *J.G.* 45
So, "Fair and softly," J. he cried *J.G.* 85
But J. he cried in vain *J.G.* 86   [145
"Stop, stop, J. Gilpin!—Here's the house!" *J.G.*
Said J., "It is my wedding day *J.G.* 193
J. coming back amain *J.G.* 222

JOIN. [*H.* 741
Rocks, groves, and streams, must j. him in his praise
And wilt thou j. to this bold enterprise *Ex.* 698
Did j. in the pursuit *J.G.* 240
J. me, amid your silent hours *Miss —* 19
Could argue once, could jest, or j. the song *R.* 290
To j. a traveller, of far different note *T.* vi 489

JOINED.
A stranger j. them, courteous as a friend *Con.* 522
The gentler virtues too are j. *Miss —* 77
He blamed and protested, but j. in the plan *P.A.* 43
In one procession j. *Q.V.* 22
Strength j. with beauty, dignity with grace *Tir.* 2

JOINER.
As smiths or j. perfect a design *Con.* 790
Smith, cobbler, j., he that plies the shears *T.* iv 476

JOINING.
And j. the freethinker's brutal roar *P.E.* 593

JOINT.
Thy bones not fashioned, and thy j. not knit *Ex.* 475
What j. the prophet had in mind) *L.W.* 14
The shapely limb and lubricated j. *R.* 57
The uplifted frame, compact at every j. *T.* iii 484
And nimble motion of those restless j. *T.* iii 762

JOINT-STOOLS.
J. were then created, on three legs *T.* i 19

JOKE.
And loved a timely j. *J.G.* 170
Their sovereign nostrum is a clumsy j. *R.* 313
From repartee, with j. that he disdains *Tir.* 728
An art contrived to advertise a j. *T.T.* 539
It is no time to j. *Y.D.* 40

JONQUIL.
That poor J., with almost every breath *H.* 89

JORDAN.
A J. for the ablution of our woes *Con.* 566

JOSEPH.
Dear J.—five and twenty years ago *E.* iii 1

JOTHAM.
J. ascribed to his assembled trees *T.* v 322

JOURNAL.
A tasteless j. of the day before *Con.* 276

JOURNEY.
I must finish my j. alone *A.S.* 10
That cheers the silent j. of the night *Ch.* 320
Both speed their j. with a restless stream *Comp.* i 2
Ere yet they brought their j. to an end *Con.* 521
Feel less the j.'s roughness and its length *Con.* 699
His j. to begin *J.G.* 50
Wretch even then, life's j. just begun! *M.P.* 24
All these, life's rambling j. done *St.* i 3
Yet thousands still desire to j. on *T.* i 470
Æthereal j., submarine exploits *T.* iv 85
Shortening his j. between morn and noon *T.* iv 131
Short as in retrospect the j. seems *T.* vi 19

JOURNEYED.
He j.; and his chance was as he went *T.* vi 488

JOVE.
Like Pallas springing armed from J. *Mrs. M—* 26
The moons of J., and Saturn's belted ball *Tir.* 634
To strip J.'s statue of his oaken wreath *T.* vi 640

JOVIAL.
Your hermit, young and j. sirs! *Mor.* 2
Lolling at your j. boards *N.C.* 22
A corresponding tone in j. souls *T.* iii 333

JOY.
"Seraglios sing, and harems dance for j.! *A.T.* 108
We come with j. from our eternal rest *Ch.* 73
While life's sublimest j. are overlooked *Ch.* 219
Farewell, my former j.! I sigh no more *Ch.* 240
And Thornton is familiar with the j. *Ch.* 253
J. doubly sweet to feelings quick as thine *Ch.* 298
Her eager thought, and feeds her flowing j. *Ch.* 405
Unfriendly to society's chief j. *Con.* 252
Oh! to the club, the scene of savage j. *Con.* 421
That 'tis an honour and a j. to pay *Con.* 646   [708
Lives the dear thought of j. he once possessed *Con.*
Of j. they meet with in their heavenly range *Con.* 694
Chill blasts of trouble nip their springing j. *E.* ii 32
And after all the j. that Plenty leads *Ex.* 83
Beheld with j. the lovely scene defaced *Ex.* 426
Domestic happiness and rural j. *Ex.* 535
By J. possessed, and j. still held in chase *Ex.* 669
Secure the favour, and enhance the j. *Ex.* 678
May suddenly your j. disperse *F.* 65
O ye, who never taste the j. *F.B.* 31   [36
J. always prized, when placed within our reach *H.*
Plucks amaranthine j. from bowers of bliss *H.* 164

JOY—JUDGMENT

Hope! let the wretch, once conscious of the *j. H.* 171
A pale procession of past sinful *j. H.* 221
And with it every *j.* it can afford *H.* 679
J., far superior *J.*, that much outweighs *H.* 728
Their hours, their days, in listening to his *j. H.* 739
Of heartfelt *j.*, succeeds not soon again *Her.* 64
From generous sympathy what *j. Miss* — 15
No *j.* can ever dwell *Miss* — 44
And every *j.* which now is yours *Miss* — 99
Adds *j.* to duty, makes me glad to pay *M.P.* 70
That thought is *j.*, arrive what may to me *M.P.* 107
To have renewed the *j.* that once were mine *M.P.* 116
A glimpse of *j.* that we have met *N.* 23
Ere yet with ruthless *j.* the happy hound *N.A.* 33
Nor hold forbidden *j.* in view *O.* ii 5
To *j.* forbidden man aspires *P.B.* 15
Enthusiasts drunk with an unreal *j. P.E.* 76
The *j.*, the danger and the toil o'erpays *P.E.* 90
Love, *j.*, and peace make harmony more meet *P.E.* 140
Witness of *j.* that shun the sight of noon *P.E.* 174
He snuffs far off the anticipated *j. P.E.* 219
Forbids him none but the licentious *j. P.E.* 237
To express unwieldy *j. Q.V.* 20
He may possess the *j.* he thinks he sees *R.* 11
In drawing pictures of forbidden *j. R.* 216
But feels while grasping at his faded *j. R.* 473
Fly to the coast for daily, nightly *j. R.* 522 [593
O'erwhelmed at once with wonder, grief, and *j. R.*
To taste a *j.* like that he has bestowed *R.* 632
And share the *j.* your bounty may create *R.* 790 [ii 9
Time then would seem more precious than the *j. St.*
To thine;—best gift the unfailing source of *j. S.* ii 13
"His *j.* be mine," each Reader cries *St.* iii 33
Of giddy *j.* comprised *St.* vi 10
While danger passed is turned to present *j. T.* 256
Weeps tears of *j.*, and bursts into a song *T.* 458
All *j.* to the believer! He can speak *T.* 571
Witness a *j.* that thou hast doubled long *T.* i 149
He walks, he leaps, he runs—is winged with *j. T.* i 443
And tasteless of the same repeated *j. T.* i 463
As dear to thee as once? And have thy *j. T.* i 647
Thy *j.* and sorrows, with as true a heart *T.* ii 220
Such *j.* has he that sings. But ah! not such *T.* ii 304
We sacrifice to dress, till household *j. T.* ii 613
Of riper *j.*, and commerce with the world *T.* ii 763
J. that her stormy raptures never yield *T.* iii 57
The grand effect; acknowledges with *j. T.* iii 227
To them that ask it?—Freely—'Tis his *j. T.* iii 273
The *j.* of many, and the dread of more *T.* iii 281
Substantial happiness for transient *j. T.* iii 300
Should seek the guiltless *j.* that I describe *T.* iii 698
Perhaps to thousands, and of *j.* to some *T.* iv 14
To him indifferent whether grief or *j. T.* iv 15
That made them an intruder on their *j. T.* iv 179
Sees not a countenance there that speaks of *j. T.* iv 205
But dying soon, like all terrestrial *j. T.* iv 382
The *j.* half lost, because not sooner found *T.* iv 717
And contemplation, heart-consoling *j. T.* iv 781
Then shakes his powdered coat, and barks for *j. T.* v 51
Whose eye they fill with tears of holy *j. T.* v 750
Shouted for *j.* - "Tell me, ye shining hosts *T.* v 822
"Radiant with *j.* towards the happy land *T.* v 836
Fires all the faculties with glorious *j. T.* v 885
Across a velvet level, feel a *j. T.* vi 275
Nor stranger intermeddling with my *j. T.* vi 298
The comfort of a reasonable *j. T.* vi 347 [361
He ruled with meekness, they obey'd with *j. T.* vi
Their kerchiefs, and old women weep for *j. T.* vi 700
His soul refreshed with foretaste of the *j.? T.* vi 762
From distant mountains catch the flying *j. T.* vi 795
Flows into her; unbounded is her *j. T.* vi 803
To see thy beauty, and to share thy *j. T.* vi 815
And e'en the *j.* that haply some poor heart *T.* vi 832

Her honours, her emoluments, her *j. T.* vi 923
Would die at last in comfort, peace, and *j. Tir.* 150
Oh 'tis a sight to be with *j.* perused *Tir.* 537 [*Tir.* 746
Flies, winged with *j.*, to some coach-crowded door
But though the *j.* he hopes beneath your roof *Tir.* 563
To speak its excellence; I danced for *j. T.* iv 712
Is odious, and their wages all their *j. Tir.* 824
With *j.* beyond what Victory bestows *T.T.* 80
We never feel the alacrity and *j. T.T.* 242
Communicates with *j.*, the good she finds *T.T.* 275
The tempest of tumultuary *j. T.T.* 409
The storms that overset the *j.* of life *T.T.* 449
To *j.* less innocent, as less refined *T.T.* 601
Then peace and *j.* again possessed 1789, 46
Such *j.* and peace as can be known 1789, 48
With *j.* not unallied to thine 1789, 59

JOYFUL.

Unless, when rising on a *j.* wing *Con.* 716
But with a *j.* tear *Q.V.* 54
Which *j.* I will oft record 1789, 34

JOYLESS.

Still to reflect, that though a *j.* note *T.* v 406

JUDAH.

To hear plain truth at *J.*'s hallowed gate *H.* 763
See *J.*'s promised king, bereft of all *R.* 767

JUDGE.

To *j.* the lands, to purge atrocious crimes *A.T.* 141
And, Avarice being *j.*, with ease succeeds *Ch.* 195
The *j.* of all men owes them no regard *Ch.* 572
Will *j.* himself deceived, and prove it too *Con.* 112
A fool with *j.*, amongst fools a *j. Con.* 300
The noble beast *j.* otherwise, his groom *Con.* 414
They best can *j.* a poet's worth *Dr.* 5 [340
Stand now and *j.* thyself.—Hast thou incurred *Ex.*
Then *j.* yourself, and prove your man *F.* 151
There find a *j.* inexorably just *H.* 227
No *j.*, sure, were e'er so mad *J.P.* 25
A hollow scooped, I *j.*, in ancient time *N.A.* 17
And *j.* you from the kennel and the stye *P.E.* 262
J. his own ways, and sigh for a return *P.E.* 611
And Conscience and our conduct *j.* us all? *R.* 660
But, with averted eyes, the omniscient *j. T.* 227
Their *j.* was Conscience, and her rule their law *T.* 535
'Twas the last trumpet—see the *J.* enthroned *T.* 564.
That He will *j.* the earth, and call the fool *T.* iii 178
Sarcastic, would exclaim, and *j.* the song *T.* iii 563
To monarchs dignity; to *j.* sense *T.* iv 796
That oft the beast has seem'd to *j.* the man *T.* vi 478
She *j.* of refinement by the eye *T.* vi 987
But *j.*, where so much evil intervenes *Tir.* 486
Nor *j.* by statute a believer's hope *T.T.* 72

JUDGED.

He *j.* them with as terrible a frown *Ex.* 131
Who, strange to tell, all *j.* it wrong *J.P.* 19
The well *j.* purchase, and the gift *M.* i 7
The unpitied victim of ill *j.* expense *R.* 512
Who *j.* the Pharisee? What odious cause *T.* 44
And *j.* offenders well. Then he that sharp'd *T.* iii 86
Then skilful most when most severely *j. T.* v 869
And seem, if *j.* by their expressive looks *Tir.* 288
I *j.* a man of sense could scarce do worse *T.T.* 518
J. every effort of the Muse a crime *T.T.* 617

JUDGING.

J., in charity no doubt, the town *H.* 250

JUDGMENT.

Where men of *j.* creep, and feel their way *Con.* 145
Man's favourable *j.*, but his own *Con.* 764

J., however tardy, mends her pace *Ex.* 151
Of talents, j., mercies, better far *F.A.* 15
And differing j. serve but to declare *H.* 423
Enslaves the will, nor leaves the j. free *P.E.* 270
But if to wrong the j. and abuse *P.E.* 304
And j. drunk, and bribed to lose his way *P.E.* 450
Hear the just law—the j. of the skies ! *P.E.* 606
Strong J. labouring in the scripture mine *R.* 698
Death and J., Heaven and Hell *St.* iv 29
'Tis J. shakes him; there's the fear *St.* v 29
His will and j. at continual strife *T.* 467
That even a j., making way for thee *T.* ii 131
By curious eyes and j. ill informed *T.* ii 435
Of j. and of mercy, should beware *T.* ii 465
By a just j. strip and starve themselves *T.* iii 759
Soon, by a righteous j., in the line *T.* v 211
And sober j. that he is but man *T.* v 265   [102
Surrender j., hood-winked. Some the style *T.* vi
To want of j. than to wrong design *T.* vi 657
For her the J., umpire in the strife *Tir.* 29
So take my j. in his language dressed *Tir.* 507
And yet his j. was not framed amiss *T.T.* 390

JUDGMENT-PROOF.

The reprobated race grows j. *T.T.* 459

JUDICIALLY.

And that, j. withdrawn, disgrace *Ex.* 692

JUDICIOUS.

A tale should be j., clear, succinct *Con.* 235
In reason, is j., manly, free *T.* v 354

JUICE.

As Time improves the grape's authentic j. *Con.* 643
Like that of salts with lemon j. *F.* 130
'Tis not alone the grape's enticing j. *P.E.* 271
And meliorate the well concocted j. *T.* 496

JUICY.

And when his j. salads failed *Ep.* ii 19

JULY.

Broiling beneath a J. sun *E.* iv 50
With all a J. sun's collected rays *R.* 484

JUMP.

And gains remote conclusions at a j. *Con.* 154

JUNE.

When gently, as in J., the rivers glide *A.T.* 74
" With J.'s undoubted right *J.P.* 36

JUNIORS.

So much thy j., who, their birth received *Y.O.* 135

JUNO.   [ii 660

Than all that held their routs in J.'s heaven ! *T.*

JUPITER.

And J. bids fair to rule again *Con.* 822

JURY.

The j. meet, the coroner is short *T.* 447

JUST.   [*A.T.* ii 9

It has always been reckoned a j. cause of strife
Truth armed it with a point so keen, so j. *A.T.* 145
And reddening with a j. and generous pride *A.T.* 204
When Cook—lamented, and with tears as j. *Ch.* 23
But grant the plea, and let it stand for j. *Ch.* 196
Let j. Restraint, for public peace designed *Ch.* 286
Though Vice derided with a j. design *Ch.* 487
No skill in swordsmanship, however j. *Ch.* 509
Affords a plea allowable, or j. *Con.* 47
For want of prominence and j. relief *Con.* 127
The works of man inherit, as is j. *Con.* 553
And gives him all his j. demands require *Con.* 760

The subtle and injurious may be j. *Con.* 809   [904
Once take the shell beneath his j. command *Con.*
Too j. to wink, or speak the guilty clear " *Ex.* 256
In j. resentment of his injured laws *Ex.* 328
Of his j. praise, to lavish it on them ? *Ex.* 349
Candid and j., with no false aim in view *Ex.* 648
Candid, and generous, and j. *F.* 19
A tax upon their own j. praise *F.* 89
That friends should be sincere and j. *F.* 158
The j. Creator condescends to write *H.* 133
There find a judge inexorably j. *H.* 227
No ! the decree was j. and without flaw *H.* 318
And silence every fear with—God is j. *H.* 370
A lawyer's dealing should be j. and fair *H.* 401 [47
Fast by the stream that bounds your j. domain *Her.*
Is far too j. to pass the trifler by *P.E.* 200
Not more industrious are the j. and true *P.E.* 293
A j. deportment, manners graced with ease *P.E.* 421
Hear the j. law—the judgment of the skies ! *P.E.* 606
A lewd interpreter is never j. *P.E.* 459
'Tis God's j. claim, prerogative divine *R.* 278
But never marked her with so j. a sight *R.* 418
Skilful alike to seem devout and j. *R.* 689
Let verse at length yield thee thy j. reward *S.* i 4
Some lead a life unblameable and j. *T.* 283
J. estimation prized above all price *T.* ii 34
Thy follies too; and with a j. disdain *T.* ii 222
And j. proportion, fashionable mien *T.* ii 421
Make j. reprisals, and with cringe and shrug *T.* ii 645
The charms of virtue in their j. esteem *T.* ii 796
Our British Themis gloried with j. cause *T.* iii 257
To its j. point—the service of mankind *T.* iii 372
By j. degrees, an overhanging breadth *T.* iii 482
Yet j. arrangement, rarely brought to pass *T.* iii 588
Sightly, and in j. order, ere he gives *T.* iii 649 [759
By a j. judgment strip and starve themselves *T.* iii
To improve and cultivate their j. demesne *T.* v 226
Abridge him of his j. and native rights *T.* v 436
Its only j. proprietor in him *T.* v 804
And j. in his account, why bird and beast *T.* vi 389
To interfere though in so j. a cause *T.* vi 473
And j. direction sacred, to a thing *T.* vi 713
The praise bestowed was j. and wise *Th.* 13
With j. abhorrence of so mean a part *Tir.* 455
Force not my drift beyond its j. intent *Tir.* 505
And schools, that have outlived all j. esteem *Tir.* 704
Respect, as is but rational and j. *Tir.* 710
Account him no j. mark for idle wit *Tir.* 726
Prove, rather than impeach, the j. remark *Tir.* 842
To pour in Virtue's lap her j. reward *T.T.* 65
When he usurped Authority's j. place *T.T.* 320 [640
Whipped out of sight, with satire j. and keen *T.T.*
Vouchsafes to man a poet's j. pretence *T.T.* 699
Distorted from its use and j. design *T.T.* 754

JUSTER.

The mark at which my j. aim I take *Con.* 105
The glowing tablets with a j. skill *Ex.* 232

JUSTICE.

And Vengeance executes what J. wills *Ch.* 82
Or how do j. in this case ? *E.* iv 72
That Scripture, J., and Good Sense disown *Ex.* 593
Makes J. still the guide of his career *Ex.* 715
Thus between J., as my prime support *H.* 377
Was one, whom J., on an equal plan *H.* 511
And when, as J. has long since decreed *H.* 748
Glory your aim, but J. your pretence *Her.* 44
In j. to the various powers *Miss* — 17
And J., guardian of the dread command *T.* 277
To J. she may make her bold appeal *T.* 498
Of innocent commercial J. red *T.* iv 683
So God wrought double j. ; made the fool *T.* vi 557

Suffer his *j.* in a world to come *Tir.* 102
To him that fights with *J.* on his side *T.T.* 12
Plants it upon the line that *J.* draws *T.T.* 17
There is a time, and *J.* marks the date *T.T.* 400

JUSTIFIED.
Who when occasion *j.* its use *Con.* 613

JUSTIFY.
There stand, and *j.* the foul abuse *P.E.* 144
To *j.* it by a thousand lies *P.E.* 284
Nor Cunning *j.* the proud man's wrong *T.* vi 844

JUTTING.
Upon their *j.* chests. He formed to bear *T.* iv 350

K.

KATE. [*T.* i 556
Though pinched with cold, asks never.—*K.* is crazed!

KATERFELTO.
And *K.*, with his hair on end *T.* iv 86

KEDAR.
Nebaioth, and the flocks of *K.* there *T.* vi 805

KEEN.
Occasion prompt, and appetite so *k. A.T.* 90
Truth armed it with a point so *k.*, so just *A.T.* 145
The *k.* demands of appetite *N.G.* 6
Like thine, her appetite is *k. P.B.* 27 [640
Whipped out of sight, with satire just and *k. T.T.*
Surveys his fair reversion with *k.* eye *T.* ii 601
By tricks and lies as numerous and as *k. T.* ii 671
K. enough, wise and skilful as thou art *T.* iii 207
His broad *k.* knife into the solid mass *T.* v 35
To a *k.* edge and made it bright for war *T.* v 216
And helpless victims with a sense so *k. T.* vi 475
K. in pursuit, and vigorous to retain *Tir.* 524
Before the *k.* inquiry of her thought *T.T.* 493

KEENER.
Inspires the news, his trumpet. *K.* far *T.* ii 353
Beguile the night, and set a *k.* edge *T.* iv 164

KEENEST.
The *k.* frost that binds the stream *N.* 5
Place me where Winter breathes his *k.* air *T.T.* 294

KEEN-EYED.
Exact yet not precise, though meek *k. Con.* 610
On special search, the *k.* eagle blind *Ex.* 631

KEEP.
Why such a one should *k.* himself away *Con.* 294
K. still the dear companion at their side? *Con.* 734
K. wisdom, or meet vengeance in your turn! *Ex.* 244
And to this hour, to *k.* it fresh in mind *Ex.* 516
Whoever *k.* an open ear *F.* 97
These curtains, that *k.* the room warm *Gr.* 37
And *k.* it safe and sound *J.G.* 68
That memory *k.* of all thy kindness there *M.P.* 55
Than that to which he *k.* confined *Mrs. M.* — 41
True beagle as the staunchest hound he *k. P.E.* 87
By his good will would *k.* us single *P.T.* 32
What early philosophic hours he *k. R.* 429
And *k.* the polish of the manners clean *R.* 733
And hides his hands to *k.* his fingers warm *T.* 148
Some youthful grace that age would gladly *k. T.* i 32
And *k.* our larder lean; puts out our fires *T.* ii 615
That has a heart, and *k.* it; has a mind *T.* iii 374
With packhorse constancy we *k.* the road *Tir.* 252
Still *k.* a seat or two for worth and grace *Tir.* 433
And *k.* him warm and filial to the last *Tir.* 894
To cultivate and *k.* the morals clean *Tir.* 920
K. Vice restrained behind a double guard *T.T.* 66
To *k.* the matrimonial bond unstained *T.T.* 74
And *k.* alive his fierce but noble fires *T.T.* 223

KEEPING.
But not a friend worth *k. F.* 78
Her want of care, screening and *k.* warm *T.* iii 440

KEMPENFELT.
Brave *K.* is gone *R.G.* 14
When *K.* went down *R.G.* 23
But *K.* is gone *R.G.* 33

KENNEL.
And judge you from the *k.* and the sty *P.E.* 262

KEPT.
Relate how many weeks they *k.* their bed *Con.* 315
I *k.* him for his humour's sake *Ep.* ii 33
Their prayers made public, their excesses *k. Ex.* 143
And *k.* the faith immaculate and pure *Ex.* 208
Why, having *k.* good faith, and often shown *Ex.* 276
Yet blessed the guardian care that *k. M.* ii 7
Excels a dunce that has been *k.* at home *P.E.* 416
And tells of laws despised, at least not *k. H.* 220
K. snug in caskets of close-hammered steel *R.* 308
In which are *k.* our arrows! Rusting there *T.* ii 804
Or having, *k.* concealed. Some drill and bore *T.* iii 150
The frequent flakes has *k.* a path for me *T.* vi 75
Is *k.* and guarded as a sacred thing *T.* v 304
Is *k.* to strut, look big, and talk away *T.T.* 233

KERCHIEFS.
How smooth these *k.*, and how sweet! *R.C.* 59
Their *k.*, and old women weep for joy *T.* vi 700

KERNEL.
We slight the precious *k.* of the stone *P.E.* 419

KETTLE.
'Their miserable meal. A *k.*, slung *T.* i 560

KEY.
She guides the finger o'er the dancing *k. Ch.* 109
Serve as a *k.* to those that are suppressed *Ch.* 524
You fall at once into a lower *k. Con.* 329
An office *k.*, a picklock to a place *Ex.* 379
The warder at the door his *k.* applies *H.* 720
Alighting, turns the *k.* in her own door *T.* ii 653
Secure it thine, its *k.* is in thine hand *Tir.* 886 [188
Vouchsafe, at least, to pitch the *k.* of rhyme *T.T.*

KICK.
The creature is so sure to *k.* and bite *P.E.* 540
In counterpoise, flies up and *k.* the beam *T.* 356
A *k.* that scarce would move a horse *Y.D.* 63

KILL.
Nor did you *k.* that you might eat *Beau* 9
Vociferated logic *k.* me quite *Con.* 113 [115
Meantime, noise *k.* not. Be it Dapple's bray *N.A.*
Then *k.* a constable, and drink five more *P.E.* 194
K. too the flowery weeds, where'er they grow *T.* 461
But, once delivered, *k.* them with a frown *T.* iii 438
May *k.* a sound divine *Y.D.* 64

KILLED.
But you have k. a tiny bird *Beau* 5

KILLING.
If k. birds be such a crime *B.R.* 25
What think you, Sir, of k. *Time B.R.* 27
A cold misgiving, and a k. dread *Con.* 770

KILWICK.
Adjoining close to K.'s echoing wood *N.A.* 3
All K. and all Dinglederry rang *N.A.* 36

KIND.
That substances, and modes of every k. *A.T.* 42
And she regardless of her softer k. *A.T.* 177
As she had changed her k. *A Tale* 46
One man the common father of the k. *Ch.* 18
She still is k., and still she perseveres *Ch.* 415
Though feeble in degree, in k. the same *Ch.* 594
As to depise the glory of our k. *Con.* 258
And asked them, with a k., engaging air *Con.* 523
Their very language of a k. that speaks *Con* 727
Old Tiny, surliest of his k. *Ep.* ii 5
My gravelly bounds, from self to human k. *F.A.* 20
And foe of our perishing k. *Gr.* 46
K. souls! to teach their tenantry to prize *H.* 252
Distinguish every cultivated k. *H.* 291
And sure it is as k. to smile and give *H.* 328
Her grave concern, her k. suspicions, there *H.* 516
Throughout mankind, the Christian k. at least *H.* 635
Each comely in its k. *J.G.* 184
They gentle called, and k. and soft *J.P.* 21
But steadfast principle, and, in its k. *J.T.* 43
The same k. office for me still *M.* 14
'Tis gentle, delicate, and k. *M.F.* 55
"Oh! grant, k. Heaven to me *Miss* — 66|
To me their peace by k. contagion spread *N.A.* 42
He scans of every locomotive k. *N.A.* 64
Than the colour of our k. *N.C.* 52
Solicits k. attention to his dream *P.E.* 523
A k. release from their imperfect state *R.* 166
Improve the k. occasion, understand *R.* 345
In k. compassion of his failing strength *R.* 626
There feels a pleasure perfect in its k. *R.* 629
Calls for the k. assistance of a tune *R.* 712
With linen of the softest k. *R.C.* 36
By some k., hospitable heart possessed *T.* 251
And strength is lord of all; but gentle, k. *T.* i 603
One common Maker bound me to the k.? *T.* iii 209
Should some contagion, k. to the poor brutes *T.* iii 308
Discharge but these k. offices, (and who *T.* iii 618
So manifold, all pleasing in their k. *T.* iii 624
What England was, plain, hospitable, k. iii 743
Infused at the creation of the k. *T.* iv 733
There dwell the most forlorn of human k. *T.* v 397
"So frail a k., and then enacting laws *T.* v 640
In the lost k., extracting from the lips *T.* v 701
With which k. nature graces every scene *T.* vi 342
All happy, and all perfect in their k. *T.* vi 354
That man inflicts on all inferior k.'s *T.* vi 385 [504
But like his purpose, gracious, k., and sweet *T.* vi
Vast in its powers, ethereal in its k. *Tir.* 6
By k. tuition on his yielding breast *Tir.* 154
By no k. arts his confidence again *Tir.* 586
The ostrich, silliest of the feathered k. *Tir.* 789
Is base in k., and born to be a slave *T.T.* 28
K. Providence attends with gracious aid *T.T.* 249
Must she perform the same k. office now? *T.T.* 405
Is profanation of the basest k. *T.T.* 758
Adorns, though differing in its k. *U.* 15

KINDER.
Proved k. to them than the coast *A Tale* 31

KINDEST.
The k. and the happiest pair *M.F.* 37

KINDLE.
Teach me to k. at thy gentle fires *Ch.* 12
Though nothing have occurred to k. strife *E.* iii 15
And k. in his soul a treacherous fire *P.E.* 40
As axles sometimes k. as they go *P.E.* 407
While morning k. with a wirdy red *R.* 432
The sense of mercy k. into praise *R.* 778
The Bramin k. on his own bare head *T.* 99
K. a fiery boil upon the skin *T.* ii 183
Are sown the sparks that k. fiery war *T.* v 206
"Love k. as I gaze. I feel desires *T.* v 842
That k. up the skies *Trans.* i 10
Acts with a force, and k. with a zeal *T.T.* 482

KINDLED. [*T.* i 566
Which, k. with dry leaves, just saves unquenched
Like him, the soul, thus k. from above *Ch.* 595
The light they walk by, k. from above *T.* 369
Have k. beacons in the skies, and the old *T.* ii 59
K. in Heaven, that it burns down to earth *T.* ii 134
Whose fire was k. at the prophet's lamp *T.* vi 732
But still, while Virtue k. his delight *T.T.* 598

KINDLING.
Who, k. a combustion of desire *P.E.* 319
Swells at the thought, and k. into rage *T.* 477
And no such lights are k. in their stead *Tir.* 285
And tell the world still k. as he sung *T.T.* 736

KINDLY.
Down to the rosy west; but k. still *T.* iv 133
Ah, treat them k.! rude as thou appearest *T.* iv 370

KINDNESS.
That memory keeps of all thy k. there *M.P.* 55
Where k. on his part, who ruled the whole *T.* vi 365
The k. of a friend *U.* 2

KINDRED.
The tender argument of k. blood *Ch.* 32 |289
What parts the k. tribes of weeds and flowers? *H.*
He followed Paul, his zeal a k. flame *H.* 582
Forsaking country, k., friends, and ease *H.* 585
Not k. minds alone are called to employ *H.* 738
Till sympathy contract a k. pain *R.* 299
No mean advantage from a k. cause *T.* i 387
Like k. drops been mingled into one *T.* ii 19
Bone of my bone, and k. souls to mine *T.* iii 220
Discover countries, with a k. heart *T.* iv 116
Scarce noticed in the k. dusk of eve *T.* iv 321
A k. melody, the scene recurs *T.* vi 13
A k. spark: they burn to do the like *Tir.* 233
As in Dodona once thy k. trees *Y.O.* 41

KINE.
The very k. that gambol at high noon *T.* vi 334

KING.
Not Mexico could purchase k. a claim *Ch.* 214
Their God their captain, lawgiver and k. *Ex.* 190
Of the glad legions of the K. of kings *H.* 733
Now let us sing, long live the k. *J.G.* 249
Ye k. and rulers, what have courts to show? *R.* 104
See Judah's promised k., bereft of all *R.* 767
What purpose has the K. of saints in view? *T.* 179
K. are invited, and would k. obey *T.* 351
So sit two k. of Brentford on one throne *T.* i 78
Of gratulation and delight, her K.? *T.* ii 84
I crown thee k. of intimate delights *T.* iv 139
On human grandeur and the courts of k. *T.* v 172
K. would not play at. Nations would do well *T.* v 188

For skill in government, at length made *k*. *T*. v 241
K. was a name too proud for man to wear *T*. v 242
Thus *k*. were first invented, and thus *k*. *T*. v 279
The *k*. who loves the law, respects his bounds *T*. v 332
We trust him not too far. *K*. though he be *T*. v 336
And *k*. in England too, he may be weak *T*. v 337
Of *k*., between your loyalty and ours *T*. v 347
We, for the sake of liberty, a *k*. *T*. v 351 [*T*. vi 674
Shall stuff his shoulders with *K*. Richard's hunch
I would not be a *k*. to be beloved *T*. v 359 [vi 861
Thy saints proclaim thee *k*. ; and in their hearts *T*.
Moves indignation, makes the name of *k*. *T*. v 442
(Of *k*. whom such prerogative can please) *T*. v 443
When he was crown'd as never *k*. was since *T*. vi 350
Sung to the praise and glory of *K*. George ! *T*. vi 663
Thy saints proclaim thee *k*.; and thy delay *T*. vi 864
A *k*., that would, might recommend his horse *Tir*. 417
With the *k*. shoulder-knot and gay cockade *T.T*. 44
K. do but reason on the self-same plan *T.T*. 48
Man made for *k*. ! those optics are but dim *T.T*. 55
"But where, good sir, do you confine your *k*." *T.T*. 79
K. then, at last, have but the lot of all *T.T*. 107
I pity *k*. whom worship waits upon *T.T*. 121
Sighing, I say again, I pity *k*. ! *T.T*. 140 [*Y.O*. 50
Time made thee what thou wast, *k*. of the woods
(For what *k*. deem a toil, as well they may *T.T*. 155
As if he heard his *k*. say, "Slave, be free !" *T.T*. 245
The feats of heroes and the wrath of *k*. *T.T*. 597
And strutting in thy school of Queens and *k*. *V*. 45

KINGCUPS.
To gather *k*. in the yellow mead *T*. vi 302

KINGDOM.
Shook principalities and *k*. down *Ch*. 77
To traverse seas, range *k*., and bring home *Ch*. 301
Life and a *k*. upon worms below *Ch*. 592
His mind his *k*., and his will his law *T*. 406
All *k*. and all princes of the earth *T*. vi 801
An intellectual *k*., all her own *Tir*. 12
The worth of his three *k*. I defy *T.T*. 85
So stands a *k*., whose foundation yet *Y.O*. 120

KING-ENNOBLING.
That were indeed a *k*. thought *T.T*. 57

KINGLY.
Blest country, where these *k*. glories shine ! *T.T*. 81
If this be *k*., then farewell for me *T.T*. 149
Leave *k*. backs to cope with *k*. cares *T.T*. 174

KINGSHIP.
Were *k*. as true treasure as it seems *T*. v 357
With *k*. and dominion o'er the rest *Tir*. 96
All *k*., and may I be poor and free ! *T.T*. 150

KISS.
Soon her pride shall *k*. the ground *B*. 19
Bid suffer it awhile, and *k*. the rod *Ch*. 166 [389
K. the book's outside, who ne'er look within ? *Ex*.
And chirp, and *k*., he seemed to say *F.B*. 26
Perhaps thou gavest me, though unfelt, a *k*. *M.P*. 25
Then *k*. their idol, and pronounce her fair *P.E*. 300
A Father's frown, and *k*. his chastening hand *R*. 346
Kneels, *k*. hands, and shines again in place *R*. 480
She next instructs him in the *k*. *Trans*. iv 16

KISSED.
I only *k*. his ruffled wing *B.R*. 19
John Gilpin *k*. his loving wife *J.G*. 29
And always, ere he mounted, *k*. his horse *R*. 578

KITCHEN.
Chirping on my *k*. hearth *Trans*. iii 2

KITE.
Such is the clamour of rooks, daws, and *k*. *H*. 349
But cawing rooks, and *k*. that swim sublime *T*. 203
Or *k*. are hovering near *The Doves* 22
Or *k*. with cruel beak *The Doves* 34

KNACK.
While servile trick and imitative *k*. *T.T*. 666

KNAVE.
The ring a bauble, and the priest a *k*. *A.T*. 66
Shall stand proscribed, a madman or a *k*. *Con*. 476
Self-idolized, and yet a *k*. at heart *Ex*. 94
As Interest biased *k*., or Fashion fools *Ex*. 38
So may a tradesman, if not quite a *k*. *H*. 210
A *k*., when tried on honesty's plain rule *H*. 566
No *k*., but boldly will pretend *F*. 13 [*k*. *P.A*. 2
And fear those who buy them and sell them, are
What atheists call him, a designing *k*. *P.E*. 108
Of *k*. in office, partial in the work *T*. iv 412

KNAVISH.
Praise is the medium of a *k*. trade *E*. ii 6
What *k*. priests promulgate as inspired *Tir*. 186

KNEADS.
And he that *k*. the dough; all loud alike *T*. iv 477

KNEE.
And gammer finds it on her *k*. *E*. iv 45
The Roman taught thy stubborn *k*. to bow *Ex*. 476
Thy parliaments adored, on bended *k*. *Ex*. 538
Then place it once again between my *k*. *Ex*. 730
Could bend one *k*., engage one votary there *H*. 506
And *k*. and hassocks are well nigh divorced *T*. i 748
And crowded *k*., sit cowering o'er the sparks *T*. iv 385
Bent *k*., round shoulders, and dejected looks *T*. iv 634
A power, confessed so lately on his *k*. *Tir*. 180
With his own likeness placed on either *k*. *Tir*. 320
His favourite stand between his father's *k*. *Tir*. 570
Oh ! if Servility with supple *k*. *T.T*. 127

KNEEL.
Forgot to curse, and only *k*. to pray *Con*. 814
They learn to bow, to *k*., to sit, to stand *Ex*. 120
K. now, and lay thy forehead in the dust *Ex*. 554
K. and ask Heaven to bless the dear deceit *P.E*. 525
K., kisses hands, and shines again in place *R* 480
K. with the native of the farthest west *T*. vi 811 [433
With woes, which who that suffers would not *T. T*. v
Worthy, compared with sycophants who *k*. *T*. vi 886
As happy as we once to *k*. and draw *Tir*. 306
I might with reverence *k*., and worship thee *Y.O*. 8

KNEELED. [374
Confessed a God; they *k*. before they fought *T.T*.

KNEE-TIMBER.
Warped into tough *k*., many a load ! *Y.O*. 99

KNELL.
Never sighed at the sound of a *k*. *A.S*. 31 [iv 148
Cough their own *k*., while, heedless of the sound *T*.

KNEW.
Regions Cæsar never *k*. *B*. 29
But he, they *k*., worship nor shore *Cast*. 29
Whose Love *k*. no beginning, knows no end *Ch*. 400
The bright original was one he *k*. *Ch*. 433
Well known, or such as no man ever *k*. *Con*. 62
Knows what he knows, as if he *k*. it not *Con*. 131
But he who *k*. what human hearts would prove *E*. ii 19
I *k*. the man, and *k*. his nature mild *E*. iii 32
Bespoke at least a man that *k*. mankind *E*. iii 41
They *k*., by sure prognostics seen on high *Ex*. 157

But that delight they never k. F.B. 11 [519]
Were trained beneath his lash, and k. the smack Ex.
That truth lies somewhere, if we k. but where H. 424
His crimes were such as Sodom never k. H. 562
Hard task! for one who lately k. no care H. 696
Yet loss of pence, full well he k. J.G. 55
Thy constant flow of love, that k. no fall M.P. 65
And thought again—but k. not what to think N.A. 54
And k. the glowworm by his spark N.G. 10
But other magic there, she k. Q.V. 61
His flock the chief concern he ever k. R. 404
Jack k. his friend, but hoped in that disguise R. 587
'Twas he, the same, the very Jack he k. R. 592
But k. no medium between guzzling beer R. 601
At length a voice which well he k. R.C. 87
A truth the brilliant Frenchman never k. T. 328
They k. not, what some bishops may not know T. 451
Celestial, though they k. not whence it came T. 532
Our fathers k. the value of a screen T. i 255 [v 538
From what they k., to what they wished to know T.
I k. at least one hare that had a friend T. iii 351
K. their own masters, and laborious hinds T. iii 747
It k. not once, the country wins me still T. iv 694
Whom flowers alone I k. would little please T. vi 1010
To Nature's scenes, than Nature ever k. Tir. 24
Ye k. at least, by constant proofs addressed Tir. 273
Gold, purer far than Ophir ever k. V. 97

KNIFE.

Save when the k. is at your throat P. 52
Flies to the tempting pool, or felon k. T. 446
By rural carvers, who with k. deface T. i 281
Dooms to the k.; nor does he spare the soft T. iii 417
Must fly before the k.; the withered leaf T. iii 614
His broad keen k. into the solid mass T. v 35

KNIGHT.

Airy del Castro was as bold a k. A.T. 1
Full many a k. had been entangled there A.T. 35
"Fair fall the deed!" the k. exulting cried A.T. 68
"Vain our delusive hope of constant k. A.T. 100
"Will none arise, no k. who still retains A.T. 115
"A k.—(can he that serves the fair do less) A.T. 119
K. of the Silver Moon, Sir Marmadan A.T. 136
Oh spare them, ye k. of the boot Gr. 19 [815
The world of wandering k. and squires to town T. iii
That all might mark—k., menial, high, and low H. 312

KNIGHTHOOD.

Enticed him from his oaths if k. far A.T. 27
A courteous k., caught the generous flame A.T. 134
"Oh, shame to k.!" his assailant cried A.T. 179

KNIT.

And k. the unsocial climates into one Ch. 126
But we, in mutual bondage k. Dr. 17
Not that I mean, while thus I k. E. iv 5 [475
Thy bones not fashioned, and thy joints not k. Ex.

KNOCK.

But when you k., it never is at home Con. 304
K. at the gates of nations, rouse their fears Ex. 269

KNOLL.

Nor are these all. To deck the shapely k. T. iii 628

KNOT.

K. and impediments make something hitch Con. 108
The closest k. that may be tied F. 62
K. worthy of solution, which alone T. ii 520
Can seize the slippery prey, unties the k. T. ii 685

KNOTTED.

The sheep here smoothes the k. thorn M.B. 9
Ask him, if your k. scourges N.C. 29

Under dissection of the k. scourge T. vi 419
A quarry of stout spurs and k. fangs Y.O. 117

KNOW.

The point in dispute was, as all the world k. A.C. 3
Then shifting his side as a lawyer k. how A.C. 25
But what were his arguments few people k. A.C. 27
On the banks of our river, I k. C. 30
A Briton k., or if he k. it not Ch. 200
And k. that falling he shall rise no more Ch. 347
A sense they k. not, to the wondering crowd Ch. 390
Whose Love knew no beginning, k. no end Ch. 400
What few can learn, and all suppose they k. Ch. 627
K. what he k., as if he knew it not Con. 131
Tell not as new what everybody k. Con. 237
Recovering what we lost we k. not how Con. 402
K. then, and modestly let fall your eyes Con. 485
K., your arrears with every hour accrue Con. 491
And yet, God k., look human nature through Con. 749
(And in due time the world shall k. it too) Con. 750
He k. that God demands his heart entire Con. 759
And k. no other fear The Doves 24
And this is what the world, who k. E. i 15
Good lack, we k. not what to-morrow brings E. iii 8
When God and you k. I have neither E. iv 8
Since twenty sheets of lead, God k. E. iv 27
K. then, that Heavenly Wisdom on this ball Ex. 314
But k., that Wrath Divine, when most severe Ex. 715
I k. the warning song is sung in vain Ex. 724
K. he his origin? can he ascend F.A. 22
Taste happiness, or k. what pleasure means H. 10
An ordinance it concerned them much to k. H. 313
The writer well remarks, a heart, that k. H. 429
As all the world doth k. J.G. 22
But ah! by constant heed I k. M. 45
Eternal winter doomed to k. Miss — 35
The sordid never k. Miss — 54 [59
That thou mightest k. me safe and warmly laid M.P.
The Plume and Poet both we k. Mrs. M — 53
K. what the freshness of their hue implies N.A. 61
The ass; for he, we k., has lately strayed N.A. 96
(As who k. but perhaps it may?) Pat. 3
But k., the law that bids the drunkard die P.E. 199
Discoverers of they k. not what, confined P.E. 476
The scholar's pitch (the scholar best k. why) P.E. 505
None but an author k. an author's cares P.E. 516
And e'en the child who k. no better P.T. 5
Bare trees and shrubs but ill, you k. P.T. 52
The servant of the public never k. R. 370
He k. indeed that whether dressed or rude R. 415
I k. not where she caught the trick R.C. 7
Hardly k. that he has sung St. iv 4
Just k., and k. no more, her Bible true T. 327 [451
They knew not, what some bishops may not k. T.
For ignorance of what they could not k.? T. 518
From what they knew, to what they wished to k. T. 538
And dream of transports she was not to k. T. i 544
In chariots and sedans, k. no fatigue T. i 755
A brave man k. no malice, but at once T. ii 268
Which only poets k. The shifts and turns T. ii 286
What man that lives, and that k. how to live T. ii 618
Few k. thy value, and few taste thy sweets T. iii 293
Grudge not the cost. Ye little k. the cares T. iii 547
And the loud laugh—I long to k. them all T. iv 33
Of long uninterrupted evening k. T. iv 143 [237
Describes and prints it, that the world may k. T. iv
That never felt a stupor, k. no pause T. iv 283
To do he k. not what. The task performed T. iv 630
They k. not what it is to feel within T. v 250
To hear that ye were fallen at last; to k. T. v 390
His body bound, but k. not what a range T. v 775
"That navigate a sea that k. no storms T. v 823
Wisdom is humble that he k. no more T. vi 97

KNOW—LABOUR

An agency divine, to make him *k. T.* vi 129
That *k.* no measure, by the scanty rule *T.* vi 213
She scorns his pleasures, for she *k.* them not *T.* vi 719
The parson *k.* enough who *k.* a duke *Tir.* 403
From constant converse with I *k.* not whom *Tir.* 854
That slaves, howe'er contented, never *k. T.T.* 261
I *k.* the mind that feels indeed the fire *T.T.* 480
I sent you verse, and, as your Lordship *k. V.* 19
And well he may, for well he *k. Y.D.* 25

KNOWEST.
Thou *k.* my praise of Nature most sincere *T.* i 150

KNOWING.
Well *k.* him a sacred thing *B.R.* 17
Without the means of *k.* right from wrong *Con.* 149
That sick, she trembles, *k.* she must die *Con.* 773
Who, *k.* them, can tell *Miss —* 14
Not *k.* thee, we reap, with bleeding hands *R.* 753
What causes move us, *k.*, as we must *Tir.* 292
Not *k.*, and too oft not caring, why *Tir.* 794

KNOWLEDGE.
But *k.* such as only dungeons teach *Ch.* 303
And, from a *k.* of her own disease *Ch.* 410
Though all accomplishments, all *k.* meet *Ch.* 601
Good sense and *k.* of mankind *F.* 200
K. of good and evil is from thee *P.E.* 469
Amusement and true *k.* hand in hand *R.* 702
Long *k.* and the scrutiny of years *T.* i 179
Grace, *k.*, comfort—an unfathomed store? *T.* ii 538
Their thirst of *k.*, and their candour too! *T.* ii 544
And lack of *k.*, and with cause enough *T.* v 501
K. and wisdom far from being one *T.* vi 88
Have oft-times no connexion. *K.* dwells *T.* vi 89
K., a rude unprofitable mass *T.* vi 92
K. is proud that he has learn'd so much *T.* vi 96
Of injury, with such *k.* of their strength *T.* vi 476
But taverns teach the *k.* of the heart *Tir.* 213
The *k.* of the World, and dull of thought *Tir.* 380
Such *k.*, gained betimes, and which appears *Tir.* 650
But poor in *k.*, having none to impart *Tir.* 663

KNOWN.
But the strife is the strangest that ever was *k. A.T.* [ii 11
Who seeks to praise thee, and to make thee *k. Ch.* 9
This is indeed Philosophy; this *k. Ch.* 349
Well *k.*, or such as no man ever knew *Con.* 62

In making *k.* how oft they have been sick *Con.* 312
K. by thy bleating, Ignorance thy name *Con.* 588
And, with a fearless confidence, make *k. Con.* 695
Who oft themselves have *k. Dr.* 6
And howsoever *k. Dr.* 22
Say, Anna, had you never *k. E.* i 67
Some few that I have *k.* in days of old *E.* iii 58
(For thou hast *k.* eclipses, and endured *Ex.* 392
Freedom, in other lands scarce *k.* to shine *Ex.* 588
True freedom is where no restraint is *k. Ex.* 592
Some blemish in due time made *k. F.* 146
The Saviour's history makes *k. F.* 206
By good vouchsafed makes *k.* superior good *H.* 147
Parent of Hope, immortal Truth! make *k. H.* 663
Now let the bright reverse be *k.* abroad *H.* 710
And dangers little *k. H.F.* 18
Her frowns were seldom *k.* to last *J.P.* 15
'Tis now become a history little *k. M.P.* 52
Is this hyperbole? The world well *k. P.E.* 488
Had *k.* their sovereign come *Q.V.* 44
That I may catch a fire but rarely *k. R.* 205
And while I teach an art too little *k. R.* 807
For 'tis a truth well *k.* to most *R.C.* 95
These truths, though *k.*, too much forgot *St.* i 31
And, proud to make his firm attachment *k. T.* 219
Reverse the sentence, let the truth be *k. T.* 449
Sweets tasted here, and left as soon as *k. T.* i 653
Of goddesses yet *k.*, and costlier far *T.* ii 659
What chance that I, to fame so little *k. T.* iii 23
Thou art not *k.* where Pleasure is adored *T.* iii 51
Of heroes little *k.*, and call the rant *T.* iii 140 [144
As they had *k.* him from his mother's womb *T.* iii
I studied, prized, and wished that I had *k. T.* iv 722
Come trooping at the housewife's well *k.* call *T.* v 61
In scenes which, having never *k.* me free *T.* v 489
Ere yet he starts is *k. Th.* 18
Are rarely *k.* to stray *The Doves* 4 [*Tir.* 447
Whose scent and hues are rather guessed than *k.*
This fond attachment to the well *k.* place *Tir.* 314
Unpatronized, and therefore little *k. Tir.* 674
A worm is *k.* to stray *Trans.* i 2
And having *k.* thee bearded and full grown *V.* 37
One who has *k.*, and has escaped mankind *V.* 78
With him, perhaps with her (for men have *k. V.* 81
Such joy and peace as can be *k.* 1789, 48

KNUCKLE.
The chalky ring, and *k.* down at taw *Tir.* 307

L.

LABORIOUS.
Display with busy and *l.* hand *Ex.* 163
That, while *l.* and quick-thoughted man *Ex.* 316
Yet man, *l.* man, by slow degrees *Her.* 67
Me, therefore, studious of *l.* ease *T.* iii 361
And more *l.*; cares on which depends *T.* iii 607
Knew their own masters, and *l.* hinds *T.* iii 747
As too *l.* and severe a task *T.* vi 210
L., yet unconscious of her toil *Tir.* 18

LABOUR.
Visiting every flower with *l.* meet *Con.* 439
No longer *l.* merely to produce *Con.* 891
By *l.* of their own *Dr.* 8
Who *l.* hard to allure and draw *E.* i 23
" Sure so much *l.*, so much toil *E.* iv 81
Taxed till the brow of *L.* sweats in vain *Ex.* 305
Seem the *l.* of Mulciber's hands *Gr.* 40
Business is *l.*, and man's weakness such *H.* 19

Pleasure is *l.* too, and tires as much *H.* 20
Nor *l.* they, nor time nor talents waste *H.* 766
Who, if from *l.* eased *Miss —* 62
Which *L.* of his frown beguile *Mrs. M—* 29
Forget their *l.*, and yet find no rest *R.* 496
He finds the *l.* of that state exceed *R.* 619
Your useful *l.*, and important aims *R.* 664
Forgets her *l.* as she toils along *T.* 457
Than by the *l.* and the skill it cost *T.* ii 297 [*T.* ii 434
Though learned with *l.*, and though much admired
Of lubbard *L.* needs his watchful eye *T.* iii 400
Fair recompense of *l.* well bestowed *T.* iii 430
He shuts it close, and the first *l.* ends *T.* iii 489
The vigilance, the *l.*, and the skill *T.* iii 548
Of too much *l.*, worthless when produced *T.* iii 565
Emerging, must be deemed a *l.* due *T.* iii 631
Warmed, while it lasts, by *l.*, all day long *T.* iv 377
And *l.* too. Meanwhile ye shall not want *T.* iv 424
Repays their *l.* more; and perched aloft *T.* v 91

From *l.*; and the lover, who has chid *T.* v 412
Not so the *l.* of his love: they shine *T.* v 570
Whose work is without *l.*; whose designs *T.* vi 228
The *l.*, were a task more arduous still *T.* vi 758
See Salem built, the *l.* of a God! *T.* vi 799
His fervent spirit *l.* There he fights *T.* vi 936
That form, the *l.* of Almighty skill *Tir.* 7
And *l.* to surpass him day and night *Tir.* 480
E'en when he *l.* for his country's good *T.T.* 142
When *L.* and when Dulness, club in hand *T.T.* 526
The fruit of all her *l.* is whipped cream *T.T.* 551
Achieved a *l.* which bad, far and wide *Y.O.* 108

LABOURED.

Like him he *l.*, and like him content *H.* 586
L., and many a night pursued in dreams *T.* iii 787

LABOURING.

Oppression, *l.* hard to grind the poor *Ex.* 40
A conflagration *l.* in her womb *Her.* 12
Strong Judgment *l.* in the scripture mine *R.* 698
His *l.* team that swerved not from the track *T.* i 161

LABURNUM.

Its family and tribe. *L.* rich *T.* vi 149

LABYRINTH.

And through life's *l.* holds fast the clue *P.E.* 357
Infatuates, and through *l.* and wilds *T.* vi 103
And, warp'd into the *l.* of lies *Tir.* 157

LACE.

With *l.*, and hat with splendid riband bound *T.* i [536

LACERATE.

How does it *l.* both your heart and his! *Tir.* 558

LACK.

"Good *l.*!" quoth he, "yet bring it me *J.G.* 61
And *l.* of knowledge, and with cause enough *T.* v 501

LACQUEY.

His palace, and his *l.*, and "My Lord" *T.* 122 [474
The *l.*, and the groom; the craftsman there *T.* iv

LADDERS.

Church *l.* are not always mounted best *Tir.* 381

LADEN.

The gale informs us, *l.* with the scent *Ch.* 446
Thus *l.*, dream that they are rich and great *R.* 155
And, heavy *l.*, brings his beverage home *T.* i 242
An ass's burden, and, when *l.* most *T.* iv 441
Though *l.*, not encumbered with her spoil *Tir.* 17

LADY.

As ever earned a *l.'s* love in fight *A.T.* 2
There goes my *l.*, and there goes the squire *B.B.* 12
The *l.* thus addressed her spouse *M.F.* 1
"You are so deaf," the *l.* cried *M.F.* 15
And as for you, my *L.* Squeamish *P.* 55
And has the *L.'s* Etiquette by heart *P.E.* 196
Ye *l.*! (for, indifferent in your cause *P.E.* 510
From India, for the *l.'s* use *R.C.* 38
And ill at ease behind. The *l.* first *T.* i 70
Our palaces, our *l.*, and our pomp *T.* i 643
Frequent in Park with *l.* at his side *T.* ii 381
A soldier's feather, or a *l.'s* glove *T.T.* 549
A slave at court, elsewhere a *l.'s* man *Tir.* 423

LADYLIKE.

Fops at all corners, *l.* in mien *Tir.* 829

LADYSHIP.

"An't please your *l.*" quoth I—*E.* iv 79
Of *l.*, a stranger to the poor *T.* ii 386

LAGS.

The Tempest itself *l.* behind *A.S.* 43

LAID.

The beast is *l.* down in his lair *A.S.* 50
And *l.* her soft in amaranthine flowers *A.T.* 8
Thy pomp is in the grave, thy glory *l. Ch.* 71
That after man's defection *l.* all waste *Con.* 752
And waits, in snug concealment *l. Ep.* ii 39 [*Ex.* 427
And praised the wrath that *l.* her beauties waste
And when he *l.* them on the scent of blood *Ex.* 520
L. down his pipe, flew to the gate *J.G.* 163 [*M.P.* 59
That thou mightest know me safe and warmly *l.*
What then!—are appetites and lust *l.* down *P.E.* 102
Remorse, the fatal egg by Pleasure *l. P.E.* 239
And now in the grass behold they are *l. P.F.* 7
And *l.* her on her side *R.G.* 8
Think on the grave where He was *l. St.* v 35
Where man, by nature fierce, has *l.* aside *T.* i 594
And fairly *l.* the zodiac in the dust *T.* iii 647 [697
But there I *l.* the scene. There early strayed *T.* iv
The egg was *l.* from which he sprung *T.B.* 8
He *l.* his head in Luxury's soft lap *T.T.* 678
Fails not, in virtue and in wisdom *l. Y.O.* 121

LAIR.

The beast is laid down in his *l. A.S.* 50
'Tis he, the Nimrod of the neighbouring *l. P.E.* 84

LAITY.

The *l.* run wild.—But do they now? *T.* ii 572

LAKE.

From many a steaming *l.* and reeking bog *A.T.* 93
His conscience, like a glassy *l.* before *T.* 259
Else noxious: oceans, rivers, *l.*, and streams *T.* i 375
He speaks. The *l.* in front becomes a lawn *T.* iii 774

LAMA.

L. Sabacthani before their eyes *H.* 630

LAMB.

And sheep-walks populous with bleating *l. T.* vi 111
"Worthy the *L.*, for he was slain for us!" *T.* vi 792

LAMBENT.

From Heaven to Earth, of *l.* flame serene *T.* v 153
The *l.* homage of his arrowy tongue *T.* vi 782

LAMBKIN.

Lapdog and *l.* with black, staring eyes *T.* i 37

LAME.

The repetition makes attention *l. Con.* 214
Beggars Invention, and makes Fancy *l. R.* 710
Resistless in so bad a cause, but *l. T.* iv 439

LAMENT.

My soul shall sigh in secret, and *l. Ex.* 722
Pierced with the woes that she *l.* in vain *R.* 300
I cannot but *l.* thy splendid wit *T.* iv 725

LAMENTED.

When Cook—*l.*, and with tears as just *Ch.* 23
L. change! to which full many a cause *T.* iv 576

LAMP.

Hangs out her *l.* in yon cærulean height *A.T.* 138
The *l.* of revelation only shows *Ch.* 339
Like hidden *l.* in old sepulchral urns *Con.* 358 [500
Who brought the *l.* that with awaking beams *Ex.*
With mournful scutcheons, and dim *l.* between *H.* 265
His *l.* now planted on Heaven's topmost arch *N.A.* 30
"Did you admire my *l.*," quoth he *N.G.* 15
And with a clear and shining *l.* supplied *P.E.* 558
Then Loyalty, with all her *l. Q.V.* 5

LAMP—LANGUAGE

The splendour of your *l*., they but eclipse *T*. i 765
The little wick of life's poor shallow *l*. *T*. iii 164
Needs he the tragic fur, the smoke of *l*. *T*. iv 195
L. gracefully disposed, and of all hues *T*. v 149
So reads he Nature, whom the *l*. of truth *T*. v 845
Illuminates. Thy *l*., mysterious Word! *T*. v 846
Whose fire was kindled at the prophet's *l*. *T*. vi 732
By such a *l*. bestowed *Trans*. i 14
Ages elapsed ere Homer's *l*. appeared *T.T*. 556

LAMPOON.

Who vote for hire, or point it with *l*. *Con*. 29

LANCE.

The well-poised *l*. that quivered at his side *A.T*. 144
But he, the virtues of his *l*. to show *A.T*. 165
Barren as *l*., among which the wind *T*. vi 142

LAND.

Of a *l*. I shall visit no more *A.S*. 36
When I think of my own native *l*. *A.S*. 45
In fairy *l*. was born the matchless dame *A.T*. 5
The *l*. of dreams, Hypothesis her name *A.T*. 6
To judge the *l*., to purge atrocious crimes *A.T*. 141
A trumpet that was heard through all the *l*. *A.T*. 162
Hail, honoured *l*.! a desert where *A Tale* 65
From the forests of our *l*. *B*. 26
Those twinkling, tiny lustres of the *l*. *B.B*. 5
Rolled over all our desolated *l*. *Ch*. 76
No *l*. but listens to the common call *Ch*. 91
A herald of God's love to Pagan *l*. *Ch*. 136
A rich deposit, on the bordering *l*. *Ch*. 249
Thy rights have suffered, and our *l*., too long *Ch*. 277
And *l*. some grave optician on the shore *Ch*. 384 [i 10
How laughs the *l*. with various plenty crowned! *Comp*.
And while it shows the *l*. the soul desires *Con*. 885
The language of the *l*. she seeks inspires *Con*. 886
To steer it close to *l*. *D.W*. 18
Leads to the *l*. where sorrow is unknown *E*. ii 10
Flow in a foreign *l*., but not in vain *E*. ii 46
Returned them happy to the *l*. they loved *Ex*. 76
The blessings of the most indebted *l*. *Ex*. 164 [186
While they passed through to their appointed *l*. *Ex*.
And the most favoured *l*., look where we may *Ex*. 226
To pour down wrath upon a thankless *l*. *Ex*. 254
He brought thy *l*. a blessing when he came *Ex*. 481
Who poises and proportions sea and *l*. *Ex*. 342
Soon raised a cloud that darkened every *l*. *Ex*. 509
Has he not hid thee, and thy favoured *l*. *Ex*. 562
Thy foes implacable, thy *l*. at rest *Ex*. 581
Freedom, in other *l*. scarce known to shine *Ex*. 588
Had he the gems, the spices, and the *l*. *H*. 175
And yet our lot is given us in a *l*. *H*. 439
Or voice of turtle in your *l*. is heard *H*. 470
From happier scenes, to make your *l*. a prey *H*. 478
Of one, whose birth was in a *l*. of light *H*. 535
A *l*. that distant tyrants hate in vain *Her*. 89
But soon as approaching the *l*. *M.D*. 33
To fairy *l*. be driven *Miss* — 22
And where the *l*. slopes to its watery bourn *N.A*. 13
Let Comus rise Archbishop of the *l*. *P.E*. 184
It stabs at once the morals of a *l*. *P.E*. 306
Far, far away, these flesh-flies of the *l*. *P.E*. 324
Sets off a wanderer into foreign *l*. *P.E*. 378 [464
By thee worse plagues than Pharaoh's *l*. befell *P.E*.
From urns that never fail, through every *l*. *R*. 76
Revered at home, and felt in foreign *l*. *R*. 412 [*R*.421
Green balks and furrowed *l*., the stream that spreads
Begins a long look out for distant *l*. *R*. 433
And all, impatient of dry *l*., agree *R*. 523
Flowers of rank odour upon thorny *l*. *R*. 754
To give dissimilar yet fruitful *l*. *R*. 787
A sleeping fog, and fancies it dry *l*. *T*. 4

As leanest *l*. supplies the richest wine *T*. 364
The sloping *l*. recedes into the clouds *T*. i 171
Each to his choice, soon whiten all the *l*. *T*. i 294
The Ouse, dividing the well-watered *l*. *T*. i. 323
The dregs and feculence of every *l*. *T*. i 684
L. intersected by a narrow frith *T*. ii 16
Reflect dishonour on the *l*. I love *T*. ii 224
In character has littered all the *l*. *T*. ii 676
And the *l*. stank—so numerous was the fry *T*. ii 832
Caffraria; foreigners from many *l*. *T*. iii 585
From flower to flower, so he from *l*. to *l*. *T*. iv 108
Though faded; and the *l*. where lately waved *T*.iv 313
Village, or hamlet, of this merry *l*. *T*. iv 467
To the deliverer of an injured *l*. *T*. iv 793
And shrubs of fairy *l*. The crystal drops *T*. v 113
Himself the only freeman of his *l*.? *T*. v 312
Old or of later date, by sea or *l*. *T*. v 381
And for a time ensure, to his loved *l*. *T*. v 716
"Radiant with joy towards the happy *l*. *T*. v 836
Their way was on the margin of the *l*. *T*. v 495
Laughs with abundance; and the *l*., once lean *T*.vi766
Flock to that light; the glory of all *l*. *T*. vi 802
Into all *l*. From every clime they come *T*. vi 814
His life a lesson to the *l*. he sways *T.T*. 76 [*Tir*.900
Pull down the schools—what! all the schools in the *l*.
As dwell at large in Britain's chartered *l*. *T.T*. 259
When Providence means mercy to a *l*. *T.T*. 355
Bespeaks a *l*., once Christian, fallen and lost *T.T*.428
Are but his rods to scourge a guilty *l*. *T.T*. 450
Perched on the meagre produce of the *l*. *T.T*. 580
Illume the *l*.'s remotest part 1789, 61

LAND-BREEZE.

A *l*. shook the shrouds *R.G*. 9

LANDING.

And may ye, sometimes *l*. here *A Tale* 79

LANDSCAPE.

Where late we saw the mimic *l*. glow *H*. 263
Or lay the *l*. on the snowy sheet *R*. 798
Estates are *l*., gazed upon awhile *T*. iii 755
With what he views. The *l*. has his praise *T*. v 792

LANES.

Of all that deck the *l*., the fields, the bowers *H*. 288
For I have loved the rural walk through *l*. *T*. i 109
And *l*. in which the primrose ere her time *T*. vi 112

LANGFORD.

As duly as the *L*. of the show *T*. vi 287

LANGUAGE.

Differing in *l*., manners, or in face *Ch*. 21
In *l*. warm as all that love inspires *Ch*. 401
So *l*. in the mouths of the adult *Con*. 15
The *l*. plain, and incidents well linked *Con*. 236
When wine has given indecent *l*. birth *Con*. 263
When all his glowing *l*. issued forth *Con*. 709
Their very *l*. of a kind that speaks *Con*. 727
The *l*. of the land she seeks inspires *Con*. 886
Howe'er it was, his *l*., in my mind *E*. iii 40
"That, while the *l*. lives shall last" *E*. iv 78
Thy *l*. at this distant moment shows *Ex*. 480
All speak one *l*., all with one sweet voice *H*. 53
All speakers, yet all *l*. at a loss *H*. 345
Their *l*. simple, as their manners meek *H*. 764
Like *l*. uttered in a dream *M*. 22
Oh that those lips had *l*.! Life has passed *M.P*. 1
If *l*. and copies all cry, "No!" *P.E*. 500
Teaches his eyes a *l*., and no less *R*. 239
That Chatham's *l*. was his mother tongue *T*. ii 237
In doctrine uncorrupt; in *l*. plain *T*. ii 400

LANGUAGE—LAST

In *l.* soft as Adoration breathes! *T.* ii 495
By which he speaks the *l.* of his heart *T.* iv 105
L., above all teaching, or if taught *T.T.* 586
So take my judgment in his *l.* dressed *Tir.* 507
The *l.* and the tone *Trans.* iv 33

LANGUID.

But relaxation of the *l.* frame *T.* i 81
The tone of *l.* Nature. Mighty winds *T.* i 183
For none they need: the *l.* eye, the cheek *T.* i 391
That palls and satiates, and makes *l.* life *T.* i 464
My *l.* limbs, when summer sears the plains *T.* iii 30
The citizen, and brace his *l.* frame! *T.* iv 752

LANGUISH.

Or heals it, makes it *l.* or rejoice *T.* ii 70
While morals *l.*, a despised concern *Tir.* 514

LANGUISHED.

Then Study *l.*, Emulation slept *T.* ii 734

LANGUISHING.

Receive me, *l.* for that repose *R.* 369

LANK.

From him who rears a poem *l.* and long *T.T.* 532

LANTERN.

And, at the watchman's *l.* borrowing light *T.* ii 654

LAP.

O folly worthy of the nurse's *l. Con.* 479
Upon the *l.* of covenanted rest *Con.* 574
Lay his old age upon the *l.* of Ease *R.* 12
And one in council. Wolfe, upon the *l. T.* ii 242
Shakes her encumbered *l.*, and casts them out *T.* iv 499
To pour in Virtue's *l.* her just reward *T.T.* 65
He laid his head in Luxury's soft *l. T.T.* 678

LAP-DOG.

L. and lambkin with black, staring eyes *T.* i 37

LAPPET.

And sails with *l.* head and mincing airs *T.* 139
Her head, adorned with *l.* pinned aloft *T.* iv 540

LAPSE.

The *l.* of time and rivers is the same *Comp.* i 1
Well—what are ages, and the *l.* of time *Con.* 547
By frequent *l.*, can hope no triumph there *T.* i 691
Descending, and with never ceasing *l. T.* iv 327

LARDED.

As meal and *l.* locks can make him; wears *T.* iv 642

LARDER.

And keeps our *l.* lean; puts out our fires *T.* ii 615

LARGE.

L. population on a liberal plan *A.T.* 157
On points which God has left at *l. F.* 136
And thus he left the point at *l. L.W.* 8
By no means *l.* enough; and was it *M.F.* 3
I mean to tread. I feel myself at *l. T.* iii 18
L. expectation, he disposes neat *T.* iii 423
L. foliage, overshadowing golden flowers *T.* iii 535
Ten thousand rovers in the world at *l. T.* v 408 [112
L. growth of what may seem the sparkling trees *T.* v
L. prelibation oft to saints below *T.* v 574
L. built and latticed well *T.B.* 24
Then ask not, whether limited or *l.? Tir.* 511
Surpassed in frenzy by the mad at *l. Tir.* 820
As dwell at *l.* in Britain's chartered land *T.T.* 259

LARGELY.

And she gives *l.* more than he requires *H.* 56

LARGER.

Extend a *l.* sphere *Miss* — 100

LARGESS.

The *l.* He bestows, prescribes the terms *H.* 325
How glad they catch the *l.* of the skies *N.A.* 62

LARK.

Just when the *l.*, and when the shepherds rise *H.* 86
Where the prisoned *l.* is hung *St.* iv 2
The innocent are gay—the *l.* is gay *T.* i 493

LARUM.

And the first *l.* of the cock's shrill throat *T.* iv 569

LASCIVIOUS.

The Fauns, and Satyrs, a *l.* race *A.T.* 199
L., headstrong, or all these at once *Tir.* 202
To the *l.* pipe and wanton song *T.T.* 462
The victim of his own *l.* fires *T.T.* 606

LASH. [*Ex.* 519

Were trained beneath his *l.*, and knew the smack
Wait but the *l.* of a wintry storm *H.* 185
A scourge hung with *l.* he bore *M.D.* 30

LASHED.

L. into foaming waves, begins to roar *T.* 260

LASS.

The full-blown rose, the shepherd and his *l. T.* i 36
No: we are polished now! The rural *l. T.* iv 534
Give him his *l.*, his fiddle, and his frisk *T.T* 237

LAST.

Has burnt to tinder a stale *l.* year's news *B.B.* 10
The *l.* evening-ramble we made *C.* 9 [604
Were Love, in these the world's *l.* doting years *Ch.*
The *l.* by Vanity produced and nursed *Con.* 378
In the *l.* scene of her six thousand years *Con.* 456
Till the *l.* fire burn all between the poles *Con.* 756
"That, while the language lives shall *l.*" *E.* iv 78
He finds his long, *l.* home *Ep.* ii 38
The *l.* of nations now, though once the first *Ex.* 242
And Mercy, fled to as the *l.* resort *H.* 378 [*H.* 746
But these shall *l.* when night has quenched the pole
When on a day, like that of the *l.* doom *Her.* 11
Her frowns were seldom known to *l. J.P.* 15
Ah would that this might be the *l.! M.* 3
But he, whom e'en in life's *l.* stage *Mor.* 49
Or, if it does not, brands him to the *l. P.E.* 107
And he that will be cheated to the *l. P.E.* 608
A *l.* year's bird, who ne'er had tried *P.T.* 28
In the *l.* scene of such a senseless play *R.* 32
His *l.* sea-fight is fought *R.G.* 15
To whom the rising year shall prove his *l. St.* ii 2
"When my *l.* hour arrives" *St.* iii 34
The *l.* impossible, he fears the first *T.* 265
View him at Paris in his *l.* career *T.* 311 [564
'Twas the *l.* trumpet—see the Judge enthroned! *T.*
And strained to the *l.* screw that he can bear *T.* 385
Angry and sad, and his *l.* crust consumed *T.* i 246
Their *l.* poor pittance—Fortune, most severe *T.* ii 658
Sells the *l.* scantling, and transfers the price *T.* iii 753
Drained to the *l.* poor item of his wealth *T.* iii 784
At his *l.* gasp; but could not for a world *T.* iii 807
Of the *l.* meal commence. A Roman meal *T.* iv 168
Warmed, while it *l.*, by labour, all day long *T.* iv 377
And force the beggarly *l.* doit, by means *T.* v 316
The dawn of thy *l.* advent, long desired *T.* vi 866
The features of the *l.* degenerate times *T.* vi 900
Due to thy *l.* and most effectual work *T.* vi 904
That first, or *l.*, hereafter, if not here *Tir.* 99
Their breath a sample of *l.* night's regale *Tir.* 834
Health's *l.* farewell, a staff to thine old age *Tir.* 878
The dark appearance will not *l. Trans. H.* 26

And the *l.* left the scene when Chatham died *T.T.* 339
Gives Liberty the *l.*, the mortal shock *T.T.* 476
Hackneyed and worn to the *l.* flimsy thread *T.T.* 727
Lest this should prove the *l. U.* 22
I bid you both a long and *l.* adieu *V.* 5
With prominent wens globose, till at the *l. Y.O.* 66

LASTING.

But waged with Death a *l.* strife *Cast.* 17
A *l.*, a sacred delight *C.* 40
And verse, more *l.*, hues that never fade *Ch.* 108
Matched against truths as *l.* as sublime ? *Con.* 548
That *l.* happiness, a thankful heart *H.* 160
Is virtue ; the only *l.* treasure, truth *T.* iii 269
And trivial favours, *l.* as the life *T.* vi 630
To fame as *l.* as the earth pretend *V.* 17

LATE.

'Tis well if, looked for at so *l.* a day *R.* 31
Yet e'en in transitory life's *l.* day *Tir.* 143

LATE-BLOWING.

The charms of the *l.* rose *W.N.* 21

LATELY.

Starts from the down on which she *l.* slept *H.* 219
The ass; for he, we know, has *l.* strayed *N.A.* 96
I sing the Sofa. I who *l.* sang *T.* i 1
So *l.* found, although the constant sun *T.* i 621
A power, confessed so *l.* on his knees *Tir.* 180
When Tumult *l.* burst his prison door *T.T.* 318

LATER.

In lighter diet at a *l.* hour *Ex.* 403
A quickness, which in *l.* life is lost *Tir.* 110
Old or of *l.* date, by sea or land *T.* v 381

LATEST.

And make it brightest at its *l.* date *Con.* 604
But down to *l.* age, from earliest youth *H.* 232
The Love that cheers life's *l.* stage *M.F.* 49
And still to be so to my *l.* age *M.P.* 69
He begs their flattery with his *l.* breath *T.* 315
To *l.* times; and Scripture, in her turn *T.* v 709
Down to the sunset of their *l.* day *Tir.* 82
We feel it e'en in age, and at our *l.* day *Tir.* 317
Shall cheer our *l.* age *The Doves* 12

LATIN.

We give some *L.*, and a smatch of Greek *P.E.* 365
That they must soon learn *L.*, and to box *Tir.* 323
Small skill in *L.*, and still less in Greek *Tir.* 385

LATINISTS.

By learned clerks, and *L.* professed *Tir.* 382

LATITUDE.

Thy yet close-folded *l.* of boughs *Y.O.* 21

LATTICED.

Large built and *l.* well *T.B.* 24
Well *l.*—but the grate alas! *T.B.* 25

LATTICE-WORK.

Of texture firm a *l.*, that braced *T.* i 42

LAUDABLE.

Endeavours *l.* engage *Mor.* 50

LAUGH.

L. at their only remedy, and die *Ch.* 419   [i 10
How *l.* the land with various plenty crowned! *Comp.*
And thou couldst *l.* away the fear of harm *Ex.* 705
He *l.*, whatever weapon Truth may draw *H.* 596
And raise a *l.*) pass unmolested by *H.* 621
You *l.*—'tis well—the tale applied *L.W.* 23
May make you *l.* on t'other side *L.W.* 24

Or *l.* or mourn with me, the rueful jest *P.E.* 110
Then *l.* at all you trembled at before *P.E.* 592
A *l.* at his expense, is slender praise *R.* 318
And talks and *l.* away his vacant hours *R.* 452
L. at the reputations she has torn *T.* 163
Laughed at, he *l.* again; and stricken hard *T.* ii 323
Till they can *l.* at virtue, mock the fools *T.* ii 692
I think, articulate, I *l.* and weep *T.* iii 198
That pleasest and yet shock'st me, I can *l. T.* iii 840
And the loud *l.*—I long to know them all *T.* iv 33
L. ye, who boast your more mercurial powers *T.* iv 282
L.'s at the frantic sufferer's fury, spent *T.* vi 423
L. with abundance; and the land, once lean *T.* vi 766
And Nature *l.* again *Trans. H.* 24
And *l.* the sense of misery far away *T.T.* 239
To *l.* it would be wrong *Y.D.* 2

LAUGHED.   [*H.* 517

The wretch, who once sang wildly, danced, and *l.*
He *l.* and trifled, made him welcome there *H.* 685
Built God a church, and *l.* his word to scorn *R.* 688
Lived long, wrote much, *l.* heartily and died *T.* 307
By rigour? or whom *l.* into reform? *T.* ii 321
L. at, he laughs again; and stricken hard *T.* ii 323

LAUGHING.

The weekly censor of a *l.* Town *V.* 38

LAUGHTER.

And *l.*, all their work, is life misspent *Con.* 876
And *l.* sounds like madness in his ear *H.* 703
Of *l.* his compunctions are sincere *T.* v 616

LAUNCHED.

Now see him *l.* into the world at large *H.* 197

LAUREATE.

True. While they live, the courtly *l.* pays *T.T.* 109

LAUREL.

Verse, like the *l.*, its immortal meed *Ch.* 292
He found the *l.* only—happier you *Ex.* 600
The unfading *l.*, and the virgin too! *Ex.* 601
And pluck each other's *l. F.* 90
Who sell their *l.* for a myrtle wreath *T.* ii 229
The *l.* that a Cæsar reaps are weeds *T.* vi 939
The *l.* that the very lightning spares *T.T.* 6
Let *l.* drenched in pure Parnassian dews *T.T.* 13
The *l.* seemed to wait on his command *T.T.* 688

LAURELLED.

What are ye, monarchs, *l.* heroes, say *Her.* 77

LAUREL-WREATH.

" Theirs be the *l.* decreed *E.* iv 83

LAVENDER.

With *l.*, and sprinkle liquid sweets *T.* ii 257

LAVES.

Her peaceful bosom *l. Q.V.* 72
And owns her power on every shore he *l.? Tir.* 40

LAVISH.

Of his just praise, to *l.* it on them? *Ex.* 349
L. of life, to win an empty tomb *Ex.* 522

LAVISHED.

They *l.* all on her *J.P.* 28
Man *l.* all his thoughts on human things *T.T.* 596

LAVISHLY.

But poets having *l.* long since *T.* vi 716

LAW.

While Chief Baron Ear sat to balance the *l. A.C.* 7
And *l.* and duties are neglected things *A.T.* 33

LAW—LAZILY

That forms and rites are tricks of human *l. A.T.* 62
When Roman rapine, by no *l.* withheld *A.T.* 126
Vice passing current by the stamp of *l. A.T.* 156
He flew to reach it, by a *l. A Tale* 51
But though some nobler minds a *l.* respect *Ch.* 35
'Tis thus Omnipotence his *l.* fulfils *Ch.* 81
Unless his *l.* be trampled on,—in vain? *Ch.* 191
The world is charmed, and Scrib escapes the *l. Ch.* 526
His evidence, if he were called by *l. Con.* 125
At least to trample on our Maker's *l. Con.* 183
As if 'twere treason against English *l. Con.* 398
A dark confederacy against the *l. Con.* 685
Else, could a *l.* like that which I relate *E.* iii 56
Were trusted with his own engraven *l. Ex.* 199
In just resentment of his injured *l. Ex.* 328
Thy life upon the pattern of the *l. Ex.* 409
Time wasted, violated *l.*, abuse *F.A.* 14
And tells of *l.* despised, at least not kept *H.* 220
Revere the *l.* they dream that Heaven ordains *H.* 241
And he that made had right to make the *l. H.* 319
As when a felon, whom his country's *l. H.* 712
Sworn foes to sense and *l. M.* i 2
'Tis Nature bids, and whilst the *l. Miss* — 49
But know, the *l.* that bids the drunkard die *P.E.* 199
By thee, Religion, Liberty, and *L.—P.E.* 462
Hear the just *l.*—the judgment of the skies *P.E.* 606
Our conduct with the *l.* engraven there *R.* 132
Exposed him to the vengeance of the *l.? T.* 45
The *l.* grown clamorous, though silent long *T.* 261
His mind his kingdom, and his will|his *l. T.* 406 [535
Their judge was conscience, and her rule their *l. T.*
From Sinai's top Jehovah gave the *l. T.* 549
The *l.* by which all creatures else are bound *T.* i 385
To avenge than to prevent the breach of *l. T.* i 731
By necessary *l.* their sure effects *T.* ii 192
By him, the violated *l.* speaks out *T.* ii 340
By forgery, by subterfuge of *l. T.* ii 670 [*T.* iii 97
Transgress what *l.* they may. Well-dressed, well-bred
In playing tricks with Nature, giving *l. T.* iii 165
Against the *l.* of love, to measure lots *T.* iv 337
Oh for a *l.* to noose the villain's neck *T.* iv 462 [471
That *l.* has licensed, as makes temperance reel *T.* iv
The king who loves the *l.*, respects his bounds *T.* v 332
" So frail a kind, and then enacting *l. T.* v 640
The sweets of Liberty and equal *l. T.* v 717
To mix her wild vagaries with thy *l. T.* v 873
The infant elements received a *l. T.* vi 200
Dull as it is, and satisfy a *l. T.* vi 217
Or bounded only by a *l.*, whose force *T.* vi 358
And own, the *l.* of universal love *T.* vi 360
Does *l.*, so jealous in the cause of man *T.* vi 432
The injurious trampler upon Nature's *l. T.* vi 465
A world that does not dread and hate his *l. T.* vi 826
More than the perquisite: where *L.* shall speak *T.* vi 848
One step beyond the boundary of the *l. T.T.* 228
Spoke from his lips, and in his looks gave *l. T.T.* 245
Let active *L.* apply the needful curb *T.T.* 314
In all its parts, times, ministry, and *l. T.T.* 427
(A dire effect, by one of Nature's *l. T.T.* 442
E'en on the fools that trampled on their *l. T.T.* 651
The wildest scorner of his Maker's *l. Tir.* 55
They hear him speak—the oracle of *l. Tir.* 363
Church, army, physic, *l. Trans.* ii 27

LAWFUL.

Dooms and devotes him as his *l.* prey *T.* ii 15

LAWGIVER.

The heathen *l.* of ancient days *Con.* 35
Their God their captain, *l.*, and king *Ex.* 190

LAWLESS.

That lewd incontinence, and *l.* rape *A.T.* 64
To bind the *l.*, and to punish guilt *Ch.* 281

A *l.* brood, and curse thee to thy face *Ex.* 283
The *l.* herd, with fury blind *M.* ii 13
When *l.* mobs insult the Court *Pat.* 9
The Will made subject to a *l.* force *P.E.* 448
One *l.* particle to thwart his plan *T.* ii 170
To all the violence of *l.* hands *T.* iv 591

LAWN.

And wood and *l.* in dusky folds enclosed *A.T.* 96
A Turkey carpet was his *l. Ep.* ii 21
For clumps, and *l.*, and temples, and cascades *H.* 247
For all that pleased in wood or *l. S.* 13
A flowery island, from the dark green *l. T.* iii 630
He speaks. The lake in front becomes a *l. T.* iii 774
Wrought patiently into the snowy *l. T.* iv 152 [372
Thy groves and *l.* then witness'd! Every heart *T.* vi

LAWYER.

So Tongue was the *l.*, and argued the cause *A.C.* 5
Then shifting his side as a *l.* knows how *A.C.* 25
Hearing a *l.*, grave in his address *Con.* 69
If *l.*, loud whatever cause he plead *H.* 201
A *l.'s* dealings should be just and fair *H.* 401
That sage they seemed, as *l.* o'er a doubt *N.A.* 77
The statesman, *l.*, merchant, man of trade *R.* 5
Great *l.*, *l.* without study made *Tir.* 822

LAX.

Stiff in the letter, *l.* in the design *Ex.* 125

LAY. [*A.T.* 79

L. snug and warm; 'twas Summer's farewell peep!
To where the fond Sir Airy *l.* entranced *A.T.* 150
Expert to swim, he *l. Cast.* 14
Thus have I sought to grace a serious *l. Ch.* 628
And either warps or *l.* it useless by *Con.* 670
Usurps God's office, *l.* his bosom bare *Con.* 745
At any poet's happier *l. Dr.* 15
A stranger's purpose in these *l. E.* ii 1
War *l.* a burden on the reeling state *Ex.* 306
To waste thy life in arms, or *l.* it down *Ex.* 531
Kneel now, and *l.* thy forehead in the dust *Ex.* 554
L. bleeding under that soft hand of thine *P.E.* 338
With reverend tutor, clad in habit *l. P.E.* 371
L. his old age upon the lap of Ease *R.* 12
In spiral rings ascends the trunk, and *l. R.* 231
Or *l.* the landscape on the snowy sheet *R.* 798
Heedless of his loudest *l. St.* iv 3
On God's behalf, *l.* waste his fairest works *T.* ii 136
Presume to *l.* their hand upon the ark *T.* ii 231
Preserve the church! and *l.* not careless hands *T.* ii 393
And *l.* it at its ease with gentle care *T.* ii 449
Her undecisive scales. In this she *l. T.* iv 484
The magisterial sword in vain, and *l. T.* iv 596
Except what wisdom *l.* on evil men *T.* v 449
Die too: the deep foundations that we *l. T.* v 532
That beak, whence issued many a *l. T.B.* 56
Again she *l.* them slumbering on the shore *Tir.* 26
There waiter Dick, with bacchanalian *l. Tir.* 214
His soul exults, Hope animates his *l. R.* 777
And *l.* thine hand upon his flaxen head *Tir.* 848
L. such a stake upon the losing side *Tir.* 863
Nor say, go thither, conscious that there *l. Tir.* 869
And *l.* his arrows by *Trans. H.* 30
The post-horns of all Europe, *l.* her waste *T.T.* 32
Is genius only found in epic *l.? T.T.* 568
Whose worth deserves as warm a *l. U.* 3

LAYMEN.

L. have leave to dance, if parsons play *P.E.* 151

LAZILY.

Oft loitering *l.* if not o'erseen *T.* iii 401

LAZINESS.

The effect of *l.* or sottish waste T. iv 431

LAZY.

Freshening his *l.* spirits as he ran P.E. 411
Of *l.* nurse who snores the sick man dead T. i 97
The sedentary stretch their *l.* length T. i 389
The tædium that the *l.* rich endure T.T. 742

LEAD.

Since twenty sheets of *l.*, God knows E. iv 27
But 'tis not timber, *l.*, and stone F. 163
By cold submersion, razor, rope, or *l.* R. 584
And move the lips of poets cast in *l.* T.T. 203
May rove at will, where appetite shall *l.* A.T. 60
To measure the life that she *l.*·C. 48
Owes all its weight, like loaded dice, to *l.* Con. 302
L. to the land where sorrow is unknown E. ii 10
And after all the joys that Plenty *l.* Ex. 83
Then Ceremony *l.* her bigots forth Ex. 115 [464
Where beckoning Pleasure *l.* them, wildly stray Ex.
As in a dance the pair that take the *l.* H. 13
L. on the various year Miss — 98
Or *l.* him devious from the path of truth P.E. 60
L. to the bliss she promises the wise P.E. 73
Footing it in the dance that Fancy *l.* P.E. 308
Serves but to *l.* philosophers astray P.E. 433 [477
Within no bounds—the blind that *l.* the blind P.E.
Tell him he wanders, that his error *l.* P.E. 544
While meaner things, whom instinct *l.* The Doves 3
Nereids or Dryads, as the fashion *l.* R. 537
A temper rustic as the life we *l.* R. 732
Grace *l.* the right way; if you choose the wrong T. 17
Some *l.* a life unblameable and just T. 283
To bind the roving appetite, and *l.* T. ii 525
To him that *l.* it, wise, and to be praised T. iii 380
The road that *l.* from competence and peace T. iv 496
Of error *l.* them by a tune entranced T. vi 104
That *l.* the dance a summons to be gay T. vi 336
To take the *l.* and be the foremost still Tir. 377
To *l.* his son, for prospects of delight Tir. 630
That wants no driving and disdains the *l.* T.T. 134
Spreads the fresh verdure of the field and *l.* T.T. 692

LEADER.

Yet Fashion, *l.* of a chattering train Con. 457
Their *l.* armed with meekness, zeal and love Ex. 187
So when the Jewish *l.* stretched his arm T. ii 825
Was chosen *l.*; him they served in war T. v 233
True to the jingling of our *l.*'s bells Tir. 254

LEADING.

One that still needs his *l.* string and bib P.E. 531
From education, as the *l.* cause Tir. 911

LEAF.

Shook the young *l.* about her ears A Fable 12
Through the dry *l.*, and pants upon the strings Ex. 721
As the *l.* that enfolds what an invalid swallows F.M. 22
With her chill hand, the mellow *l.* away N.A. 22
The winds play no longer and sing in the *l.* P.F. 3
The *l.* came on not quite so fast P.T. 45 [T. i 641
And homes all thatched with *l.* But hast thou found
And all their *l.* fast fluttering, all at once T. i 189
And poplar that with silver lines his *l.* T. i 310 [566
Which, kindled with dry *l.* just saves unquenched T. i
And darkening and enlightening, as the *l.* T. i 348
The sleeping *l.*, is all the light they wish T. i 763
For ere the beech and elm have cast their *l.* T. iii 466
Two *l.* produced, two rough indented *l.* T. iii 526
The spiry myrtle with unwithering *l.* T. iii 570
The gay diversities of *l.* and flower T. iii 590
All plants, of every *l.*, that can endure T. iii 580
Must fly before the knife; the withered *l.* T. iii 614
The scent regaled, each odoriferous *l.* T. iii 621
Stripped of her ornaments, her *l.*, and flowers! T. iii 728
His patrimonial timber cast its *l.* T. iii 752
Unfolds its bosom, buds, and *l.*, and sprigs T. iv 153
That tinkle in the wither'd *l.* below T. vi 82 [137
Of *l.* and flower? It sleeps; and the icy touch T. vi
That scarce a *l.* appears; mezereon too T. vi 167
The deep dark green of whose unvarnish'd *l.* T. vi 174
Where, on his bed of wool and matted *l.* T. vi 312
Beneath the shade of her expanded *l.* Tir. 46 [Rose 5
The cup was all filled, and the *l.* were all wet The
And winds his web about the rivelled *l.* Tir. 596
A *l.* succeeded, and another *l.* Y.O. 37
Time was when, settling on thy *l.*, a fly Y.O. 91

LEAFLESS.

A *l.* branch thy sceptre, and thy throne T. iv 125
His favourite herb; while all the *l.* groves T. iv 319
Seen through the *l.* wood. His slanting ray T. v 6
Though *l.*, well attired, and thick beset T. vi 168

LEAFY.

Her golden tassels on the *l.* sprays T. 232

LEAGUE. [462

From pride in *l.* with ignorance, have sprung! Ch.
Conspicuous many a *l.*, the mariner T. i 521

LEAGUED.

Bid nations *l.* against thee stand aloof Ex. 565
But man associated and *l.* with man T. iv 663

LEAK.

She sprang no fatal *l.* R.G. 19

LEAN.

For whose *l.* country much disdain A Tale 73
By *l.* despair upon an empty purse Ch. 506
Hollow-eyed Abstinence, and *l.* Despair H. 58 [117
Pride may be pampered while the flesh grows *l.* T.
Decrepitude, and in the looks of *l.* T. ii 489
And keeps our larder *l.*; puts out our fires T. ii 615
That *l.* hard-handed Poverty inflicts T. iii 827 [468
Though *l.* and beggared, every twentieth pace T. iv
Transformed to a *l.* shank. The shapeless pair T. v 16
Shaggy, and *l.*, and shrewd, with pointed ears T. v 45
L. pensioners upon the traveller's track T. v 93 [766
Laughs with abundance; and the land, once *l.* T. vi
With *l.* performance ape the work of Love! T. vi 854
Of the mere schoolboy's *l.* and tardy growth Tir. 657

LEANED. [160

L. on her elbow, watching Time, whose course Y.O.

LEANEST.

As *l.* land supplies the richest wine T. 364

LEANING.

And when the Stuart, *l.* on the Scot Ex. 574
That to the wrong side *l.* O. i 2
The boorish driver *l.* o'er his team T. i 298
And wandering eyes, still *l.* on the arm T. iii 53
Lest storms should overset the *l.* pi.e T. v 39

LEAP.

That life to save, we *l.* into the pit" N.A. 104
" How! *l.* into the pit our life to save! N.A. 107
To save our life *l.* all into the grave! N.A. 108
For persevering chase, and headlong *l.* P.E. 86
L. every fence but one, there falls and dies P.E. 93
That mounts the stile with ease, or *l.* the fence T. i 136
He walks, he *l.*, he runs—is winged with joy T. i 443
Not so where, scornful of a check, it *l.* T. v 101
There's not an English heart that would not *l.* T. v 389
Whose word *l.* forth at once to its effect T. v 686
The dreadful *l.*, more rational his steed T. vi 517

LEAPED.

L. out of nothing, called by the most High *Ex.* 639

LEARN.

Might *l.* from the wisdom of age *A.S.* 23
Alternately the nations *l.* and teach *Ch.* 120
Whate'er she *l., l.* nothing as she ought *Ch.* 338
L. to compassionate the sick she sees *Ch.* 411
That men, if gently tutored, will not *l. Ch.* 496
What few can *l.*, and all suppose they know *Ch.* 627
To *l.* the twittering of a meaner bird ? *Con.* 448
And Echo *l.* politely to repeat *Con.* 827
How slow to *l.* the dictates of his love *E.* ii 20
They *l.* to bow, to kneel, to sit, to stand *Ex.* 120 [243
They warn and teach the proudest, would they *l. Ex.*
Humility is gentle, apt to *l. Ex.* 454
To *l.* in God's own school the Christian part *Ex.* 650
For who but *l.* in riper years *F.* 22
If he wish to instruct, he must *l.* to delight *F.M.* 17
L. something from whate'er occurs *Mor.* 24
Hence jarring sectaries may *l. N.G.* 27
With much to *l.*, but nothing to impart *P.E.* 376
Will *l.* in school of tribulation *R.C.* 115
L. then, ye living ! by the mouths be taught *St.* ii 33
Make us *l.* that we must die *St.* iv 36 [i 595
His fierceness, having learnt, though slow to *l. T.*
Of wisdom, proves a school in which he *l. T.* i 614
And *l.*, though late, the genuine cause of all *T.* ii 205
Or unenlightened, and too proud to *l. T.* ii 549
On skulls that cannot teach, and will not *l. T.* ii 394
She needs herself correction ; needs to *l. T.* ii 776
Extract a register, by which we *l. T.* iii 152
Our wayward intellect, the more we *l. T.* iii 236
L. every trick, and soon play all the game *T.* iv 231
But none with readier skill !—'Tis here they *l. T.* iv 495
Unapt to *l.*, and formed of stubborn stuff *T.* iv 636
New faculties, or *l.* at least to employ *T.* v 806 [547
Was now to *l.* that Heaven, though slow to wrath *T.* vi
That whom it teaches it makes prompt to *l. T.* v 859
And pedantry that coxcombs *l.* with ease *T.* vi 290
We could not teach, and must despair to *l. T.* vi 620
But *l.* we might, if not too proud to stoop *T.* vi 621
And suffer for its crime ; would *l.* how fair *T.* vi 827
That 'tis our shame and misery not to *l. Tir.* 78
And *l.* with wonder how this world began *Tir.* 127
L. from expert inquirers after truth *Tir.* 192
There shall he *l.*, ere sixteen winters old *Tir.* 210
That they must soon *l.* Latin, and to box *Tir.* 323
Sweet interjections ! if he *l.* but those *Tir.* 400 [811
Who, wise yourselves, desire your son should *l. Tir.*
L. much, and to a thousand listening minds *T.T.* 274
O *l.*, from our example and our fate *T.T.* 436
L. wisdom and repentance ere too late " *T.T.* 437
But *l.* his error in maturer years *Tir.* 449
If anxious only that their boys may *l. Tir.* 513

LEARNED.

I have read the Review ; it is *l.* and wise *A.T.* iv 1
Self-knowledge truly *l.* of course implies *Ch.* 359
No *l.* disputants would take the field *Ch.* 620
Words *l.* by rote a parrot may rehearse *Con.* 7
Grave without dulness, *l.* without pride *Con.* 609
L. at the bar, in the palæstra bold *Con.* 842
And *l.* as 'tis sweet *Dr.* 12
The virtue they had *l.* in scenes of woe *Ex.* 80
Hast thou not *l.*, what thou art often told *Ex.* 350
Proclaim the remedy, ye *l.*, next *H.* 108
And he that stole has *l.* to steal no more *H.* 523
Politely *l.*, and of a gentle race *H.* 682
And the sad lesson must be *l.* once more *Her.* 75
My mother ! when I *l.* that thou wast dead *M.P.* 21
I *l.* at last submission to my lot *M.P.* 44
For many a grave and *l.* clerk *P.* 31

Candid and *l.*, dispassionate and free *P.E.* 453
And *l.* in future to be wiser *P.T.* 60
To *l.* cares or philosophic toil *R.* 662
Nor those of *l.* philologists, who chase *R.* 691
Or else she *l.* it of her master *R.C.* 10
That self-renouncing wisdom *l.* before *T.* 568
To those that need it. Folly is soon *l. T.* ii 283 [434
Though *l.* with labour, and though much admired *T.* ii
That grave and *l.* clerks should need such aid *T.* ii 368
Than in the bounds of duty ? What was *l. T.* ii 754
If aught was *l.* in childhood, is forgot *T.* ii 755
Great contest follows, and much *l.* dust *T.* iii 161
Dissolve in pity, and account the *l. T.* iii 183
And oft at last in vain. The *l.* and wise *T.* iii 562
The *l.* finger never need explore *T.* iv 362
All *l.*, and all drunk ! the fiddle screams *T.* iv 478
Knowledge is proud that he has *l.* so much *T.* vi 96
Truths that the *l.* pursue with eager thought *Tir.* 73
By *l.* clerks, and Latinists professed *Tir.* 382
And better never *l.*, or left behind *Tir.* 584
On all around him ; *l.* not by degrees *Y.O.* 147

LEARNERS.

And humble *l.* of a Saviour's worth *T.* ii 542

LEARNING.

With a great deal of skill, and a wig full of *l. A.C.* 6
Their *l.* legendary, false, absurd *Ex.* 127
Well tutored *L.*, from his books *Mrs. M—* 37
There Genius, *L.*, Fancy, Wit *Mrs. M—* 45
While *l.*, once the man's exclusive pride *P.E.* 429
L. itself, received into a mind *P.E.* 431
Admire his *l.*, and almost adore *P.E.* 507
Manly designs, and *l.*'s grave pursuits *R.* 242
But such as *L.* without false pretence *R.* 695
L. is one, and wit, however rare *R.* 302
When *l.*, virtue, piety, and truth *T.* ii 700
Close to his side that pleased him. *L.* grew *T.* ii 713
If this be *l.*, most of all deceived *T.* iii 184
L. has borne such fruit in other days *T.* iii 248
That *l.* is too proud to gather up *T.* iii 286
And *l.* wiser grow without his books *T.* vi 88
With wholesome *l.*, yet acquired with ease *Tir.* 118
Least qualified in honour, *l.*, worth *Tir.* 413
And you are staunch indeed in *l.*'s cause *Tir.* 492
Prepared by taste, by *l.*, and true worth *Tir.* 678

LEARNT.

And harder still as *l.* beneath despair *H.* 697 [595
His fierceness, having *l.*, though slow to learn *T.* i

LEATHERN.

My *l.* belt likewise *J.G.* 62
With *l.* girdle braced *J.G.* 130
The *l.* ears of stockjobbers and Jews *T.T.* 187

LEAVE.

Neglected, *l.* a dreary waste behind *Comp.* i 12
L. saints to enjoy those altitudes they teach *Con.* 585
Babbler of ancient fables, *l.* a doubt *Ex.* 503
Or expectation of the next, give *l. Ex.* 607
Remain with thee, or *l.* thee at his word *Ex.* 675
But if He *l.* thee, though the skill and power *Ex.* 702
And of the worst, that unexplored he *l. F.A.* 31
To *l.* his friend behind *F.B.* 24 [*H.* 275
'Twas there we found them, and must *l.* them there
L. Vice and Folly unsubdued behind *P.E.* 81
Laymen have *l.* to dance, if parsons play *P.E.* 151
Enslaves the will, nor *l.* the judgment free *P.E.* 270
And suck, and *l.* a craving maggot there ! *P.E.* 326
Take *l.* of nature's God, and God revealed *P.E.* 591
'Tis criminal to *l.* a sinking state *R.* 478
Oh ! grant a poet *l.* to recommend *R.* 541
That *l.* no stain upon the wing of Time *R.* 800

He drops the rein, and *l.* him to his pace *T.* 247
And *l.* to mercy, with a tranquil mind, *T.* 499 [322
Delights which who would *l.*, that has a heart *T.* iii
At least neglect not, or *l.* unemployed *T.* iii 368 [785
He sighs, departs, and *l.* the accomplished plan *T.* iii
From his pernicious force. Nor will he *l. T.* iv 445
Takes a Lethean *l.* of all his toil *T.* iv 475
Freely and with delight, who *l.* us free *T.* v 334
Nor ask his *l.* to slumber or to play *T.* vi 405
No cat had *l.* to dwell *T.B.* 21
Then *l.* their crimes for History to scan *T.T.* 119
L. kingly backs to cope with kingly cares *T.T.* 174

LEAVING.

The pannels, *l.* an obscure, rude name *T.* i 282
Forth goes the woodman, *l.* unconcerned *T.* v 41
L. the poor no remedy but tears *T.* vi 845

LEBANON.

For cedars famed, fair *L.* supplied *A.T.* 143

LECTURE.

He reads wise *l.*, and describes aloud *Ch.* 389
To read wise *l.*, vanity the text *H.* 107
A mother's *l.* and a nurse's care *Tir.* 196
Is Nature's progress, when she *l.* man *T.* vi

LED.

Are gloomy thoughts *l.* on by Spleen *E.* iv 20
Captivity *l.* captive, rose to claim *Ch.* 585
If, *l.* from earthly things to things divine *H.* 141
Following, that *l.* me to my own abode *N.A.* 128
Not to be *l.* in chains, but to subdue *R.* 266
L. them, however faltering, faint and slow *T.* 537
When *l.* by instinct-sharp and sure *T.B.* 32

LEECH. [*T.* iii 817

And the shark's prey; the spendthrift, and the *l.*

LEES.

Quite to the *l.*? And has religion none? *P.E.* 260
Pure from the *l.*, which often more enhanced *T.* ii 508

LEUWENHOEK.

E'en *L.* himself would stand aghast *P.E.* 485

LEFT.

They *l.* these bodily concerns at large *A.T.* 130
Is doubtless *l.* behind *A Tale* 48
You *l.* when he was slain *Beau* 12
But has *l.* a regret and esteem *C.* 7
His floating home for ever *l. Cast.* 6
Nor ever ship *l.* Albion's coast *Cast.* 9
They *l.* their outcast mate behind *Cast.* 23
What has he *l.* that he can yet forego? *Ch.* 150
Has *l.* some hundreds without home or food *Ch.* 466
Whose deeds had *l.*, in spite of hostile arts *Con.* 513
The scene of all those sorrows *l.* behind *Con.* 508 [534
And *l.* them both exclaiming "'Twas the Lord! *Con.*
And plunging *l.* the shore *D.W.* 32 [*Ex.* 175
For them, the states they *l.* made waste and void
Who *l.* them still a tributary state *Ex.* 217
But *l.* their virtues and thine own behind *Ex.* 373
It sparkles with the gems he *l.* behind *Ex.* 483
He found thee savage, and he *l.* thee tame *Ex.* 485
Some twigs of that old scourge are *l.* behind *Ex.* 517
They *l.* their bones beneath unfriendly skies *Ex.* 524
On points which God has *l.* at large *F.* 136 [29
To unriddle, and have *l.* them mysteries still *F.A.*
"The wine is *l.* behind!" *J.G.* 60
That failing *l.* untold *J.P.* 24
And thus be *l.* the point at large *L.W.* 8
Thy morning bounties ere I *l.* my home *M.P.* 60
Myself removed, thy power to soothe me *l. M.P.* 121
Afric's coast I *l.* forlorn *N.C.* 2

Give wit, that what is *l.* may shine *O.* i 27
Of the plague spread by bundles *l.* behind *P.E.* 352
L. out his linchpin, or forgot his tar *P.E.* 441
But not the mischiefs; they still *l.* behind *P.E.* 554
From pleasures *l.*, but never more be loved *R.* 564
She *l.* the cares of life behind *R.C.* 47
"The open drawer was *l.* I see *R.C.* 55
He *l.* his bed, he trod the floor *R.C.* 91
Can e'er forget the charms he *l.* behind *S.* ii 3
Charge not, with light sufficient and *l.* free *T.* 19
And prejudice have *l.* a passage clear) *T.* 114
Is *l.* to sleep for peace and quiet sake *T.* 428
Fair fields appear below, such as he *l. T.* i 452
L. sensuality and dross behind *T.* 526
With one who *l.* her, went to sea, and died *T.* i 538
Sweets tasted here, and *l.* as soon as known *T.* i 653
My country! and while yet a nook is *l. T.* ii 207
Or all that we have *l.*, is empty talk *T.* ii 253 [523
L. them as dark themselves. Their rules of life *T.* ii
Finds a cold bed her only comfort *l. T.* ii 655
As *l.* him not, till penitence had won *T.* ii 723
And *l.* them to an undirected choice *T.* ii 802
I was a stricken deer that *l.* the herd *T.* iii 108
Some traces of her youthful beauty *l.*) *T.* iii 299
With hopeful gems. The rest, no portion *l. T.* iii 421
When having no stake *l.*, no pledge to endear *T.* iii 791
The few small embers *l.* she nurses well *T.* iv 383
Foh!'twas a bribe that *l.* it: he has touched *T.* iv 609
And sighs for the smart comrades he has *l. T.* iv 648
The deluge washed it out; but *l.* unquenched *T.* v 209
Then what were *l.* of roughness in the grain *T.* v 480
Fame had not *l.* the venerable man *T.* vi 492
Of good Evander, still where he was *l. T.* vi 537
He *l.* poor Bully's beak *T.B.* 54 [7
To weep for the buds it had *l.* with regret *The Rose*
And better never learned, or *l.* behind *Tir.* 584
Their offspring, *l.* upon so wild a beach *Tir.* 802
And give thy life its only cordial *l.*? *Tir.* 882 [339
And the last *l.* the scene when Chatham died *T.T.*
Are we then *l.*—not wholly in the dark *T.T.* 662
Was *l.* to spring by vigour of his own *T.T.* 675 [125
Thine arms have *l.* thee. Windshave rent them off *Y.O.*
The task was *l.* to whittle thee away *Y.O.* 104 [*Y.O.* 127
With bow and shaft have burnt them. Some have *l.*

LEG.

One *l.* by truth supported, one by lies *P.E.* 561
Joint-stools were then created, on three *l. T.* i 19
Upborne they stood. Three *l.* upholding firm *T.* i 20
Improved the simple plan, made three *l.* four *T.* i 29
His *l.* depending at the open door *T.* i 93
Preposterous sight! the *l.* without the man *T.* v 20
Though Vestris on one *l.* still shine below *Tir.* 542
So in they come—each makes his *l. Y.D.* 29

LEGATE.

L., and delegates, with powers from hell *Ex.* 514
The *l.* of the skies!—His theme divine *T.* ii 338

LEGATEE.

No.—Mammon makes the world his *l. Ch.* 45

LEGENDARY.

Their learning *l.*, false, absurd *Ex.* 127
An ancient, not a *l.* tale *T.* vi 479
But now farewell all *l.* tales *Tir.* 181

LEGENDS.

L. prolix delivers in the ears *S.* i 2

LEGIBLE.

All this still *l.* in Memory's page *M.P.* 68
Such as, when *l.*, were never read *P.E.* 392
L. only by the light they give *T.* 30
Is *l.* and plain *Trans.* i 22

LEGIONS.
Disbanded *l.* freely might depart *Ch.* 618
Call *l.* up from Hell to back the deed *Con.* 691
Beckons the *l.* of his storms away *H.* 477
Of the glad *l.* of the King of kings *H.* 733
The trumpet sounds, your *l.* swarm abroad *Her.* 53

LEGISLATURE.
The *l.* called it May *A Fable* 9

LEGITIMATE.
Of its *l.*, peculiar powers) *T.* ii 333
Now the *l.* and rightful lord *T.* iii 749

LEISURE.
And chattels of *l.* and ease *Gr.* 50
But *l.*, silence, and a mind released *R.* 139
His hours of *l.* and recess employs *R.* 215
And he that deems his *l.* well bestowed *R.* 505
But not to manage *l.* with a grace *R.* 622
Behold in these what *l.* hours demand *R.* 701
Domestic life in rural *l.* passed ! *T.* iii 292 [*T.* iii 691
Health, *l.*, means to improve it, friendship, peace
A wish for ease and *l.*, and ere long *T.* iv 800
Found here that *l.* and that ease I wished *T.* iv 801

LEISURELY.
The ascending damps; then *l.* impose *T.* iii 477

LEMON.
Like that of salts with *l.* juice *F.* 130

LEND.
Let supposition *l.* her aid once more *Ch.* 383
To listen is to *l.* him aid *F.* 101   [*H.* 260
They die.—Death *l.* them, pleased, and as in sport
Will *l.* his horse to go" *J.G.* 24
And *l.* celestial fire *Miss* — 82
But does a mischief while she *l.* a grace *R.* 233 [591
Must *l.* its aid to illustrate all their charms *T.* iii
Need no such aids as Superstition *l. T.* vi 510 [669
The strength they borrow with the grace they *l. T.*iii

LENGTH.
Decide no question with their tedious *l. Con.* 87
Can *l.* of years on God himself exact *Con.* 549
Feel less the journey's roughness and its *l. Con.* 699
Is sent to be flatted or wrought into *l. F.M.* 2
Bound on a voyage of awful *l. H.F.* 17
'Tis exercise, and health, and *l.* of days *P.E.* 91
Expending late on all that *l.* of plea *S.* i 6
And holds them dangling at arm's *l.* in scorn *T.* 164
Their *l.* and colour from the locks they spare *T.* i 134
Not distant far, a *l.* of colonnade *T.* i 252
The sedentary stretch their lazy *l. T.* i 389
That with its wearisome but needful *l. T.* iv 2
He brandishes his pliant *l.* of whip *T.* iv 355
Stretches a *l.* of shadow o'er the field *T.* v 10
Shoot into pillars of pellucid *l. T.* v 115
Mov'd many a sigh at its dishcart'ning *l. T.* vi 22
The roof, though movable through all its *l. T.* vi 74
To carry nature *l.* unknown before *T.T.* 558

LENGTHENING.
Punctually paid for *l.* out disease *H.* 204

LENIENT.
With *l.* balm may Oberon hence *Miss* — 21
And *l.* as soft opiates to the mind *P.E.* 80

LENS.
He claps his *l.*, if haply they may see *Ch.* 385

LENT.   [*P.F.* 8
And the tree is my seat that once *l.* me a shade

LEPROSY.
'Tis in the church the *l.* begins *Ex.* 96

LESSENS.
And *l.* to the sight *A Tale* 44

LESSON.
And the sad *l.* must be learned once more *Her.* 75
This *l.* seems to carry *P.T.* 63
Admires the work but slips the *l.* by *R.* 214
May give an useful *l.* to the head *T.* vi 86
A *l.* for mankind *The Doves* 40
His *l.* tire, his mild rebukes offend *Tir.* 716
His life a *l.* to the land he sways *T.T.* 76

LET.
Nor write on each—This building to be *l. Tir.* 916

LETHARGIC.
Conceals the mood *l.* with a mask *T.* iv 299

LETHÆAN.
L. gulfs receive them as they fall *B.B.* 7
Takes a L. leave of all his toil *T.* iv 475

LETTER.
How I shall hammer out a *l. E.* iv 34
Stiff in the *l.*, lax in the design *Ex.* 125
The important *l.* that include the rest *Ch.* 523 [348
Write, if thou canst, one *l.* from the shades *P.E.*
Than to interpret by the *l. P.T.* 6
A man of *l.* and of manners too ! *T.* ii 782
The royal *l.* are a thing of course *Tir.* 416
A man of *l.*, manners, morals, parts *Tir.* 673

LETTERED.
The pride of *l.* ignorance, that binds *H.* 483
That graced his *l.* store *M.* i 8
Where beauty oft and *l.* worth consume *T.* ii 123

LETTING.
By *l.* poetry alone *E.* iv 10
In *l.* fall the curtain of repose *T.* iv 248

LETTUCES.
Thistles, or *l.* instead *Ep.* ii 15

LEUCONOMUS.
L. (beneath well sounding Greek *H.* 554

LEVANTINE.
L. regions these, the Azores send *T.* iii 583

LEVEE.
Flies to the *l.*, and, received with grace *R.* 479
The *l.* swarms, as if in golden pomp *T.* iii 822

LEVEL.
Here Ouse, slow winding through a *l.* plain *T.* i 163
The pulpit to the *l.* of the stage *T.* ii 564
Across a velvet *l.*, feel a joy *T.* vi 275
Stand on a *l.*, and you prove too much *T.T.* 255

LEVELLED.
The explosion of the *l.* tube excites *H.* 350

LEVIATHAN.
Alas ! L. is not so tamed *T.* ii 322

LEVIED.
L. a tax of wonder and applause *T.T.* 650

LEVITES.
Thy L., once a consecrated host *Ex.* 263
No longer L., and their lineage lost *Ex.* 264

LEVYING.
And *l.* thus, and with an easy sway *Tir.* 611

LEWD.
That *l.* incontinence, and lawless rape *A.T.* 64

LEWD—LIE

L., avaricious, arrogant, unjust *Ex.* 56
By some *l.* earl, or rakehell baronet *P.E.* 314
A *l.* interpreter is never just *P.E.* 459
In which *l.* sensualists print out themselves *R.* 684
Perverting often, by the stress of *l. T.* ii 551 [764
The *l.* vain world that must receive him soon *T.* ii
And surfeited *l.* town with her fair dues *T.* iii 758
Those habits of profuse and *l.* expense *Tir.* 350
Complain not if attachments *l.* and base *Tir.* 889

LEWDNESS.
By *l.*, idleness, and sabbath-breach *T.* iv 653
In infidelity and *l.* men *Tir.* 209
That *L.* had usurped and worn so long *T.T.* 637

LIBATION.
And weeps a sad *l.* in despair *R.* 226

LIBBARD.
The lion, and the *l.*, and the bear *T.* vi 773

LIBEL.
That odious *l.* on a human voice ? *Con.* 450

LIBERAL.
Large population on a *l.* plan *A.T.* 157
A stream of *l.* and heroic deeds *Ch.* 245
A hand as *l.* as the light of day *H.* 408
For Nature, nice, as *l.* to dispense *P.E.* 213
And mortifies the *l.* hand of love *T.* ii 757
So *l.* in construction, and so rich *T.* iii 94
Pure is the nymph, though *l.* of her smiles *T.* iii 712
Of distribution ; *l.* of their aid *T.* iv 413
L. in all things else, yet Nature here *T.T.* 208

LIBERALITY.
Of *L.* of heart *F.* 5
Yet was thy *l.* discreet *J.T.* 35

LIBERATES.
That *l.* and exempts me from them all *T.* iv 97

LIBERTINE.
The praises of the *l.* professed *T.* 433
Of *l.* excess. The Sofa suits *T.* i 106

LIBERTY.
Thine altar, sacred *L.*, should stand *Ch.* 256
Culprit his *l.* regains *E.* iv 59
Strangers to *l.* 'tis true *F.B.* 10
To *L.* without *F.B.* 36
But these excuse, the *l.* I take *H.* 435
And methought while she *L.* sung *M.D.* 23
'Twas *L.* only to hear *M.D.* 24
By thee. Religion, *L.*, and Laws *P.E.* 462
A moment's *l.* to speak *P.T.* 20
Ranges at *l.*, and snuffs the wind *R.* 630
Thought, word, and deed, his *l.* evince *T.* 195
Escapes at last to *l.* and light *T.* i 440
By culture tamed, by *l.* refreshed *T.* i 606
And *l.*, and oft-times honour too *T.* i 734
My fancy, ere yet *l.* of choice *T.* iv 698
We, for the sake of *l.*, a king *T.* v 351
The State that strives for *l.*, though foiled *T.* v 367
For he who values *L.* confines *T.* v 393
'Tis *L.* alone that gives the flower *T.* v 446
Of *L.*, themselves the slaves of lust *T.* v 499
But there is yet a *L.* unsung *T.* v 538
A *L.* which persecution, fraud *T.* v 542
'Tis *L.* of Heart, derived from Heaven *T.* v 545
The sweets of *L.* and equal laws *T.* v 717
A *l.* like his, who unimpeached *T.* v 759
Is *L.* : a flight into his arms *T.* v 577
Then we are free. Then *L.* like day *T.* v 883
Hence *L.*, sweet *L.*, inspires *T.T.* 222
L. chases all that gloom away *T.T.* 271
O *L.* ! the prisoner's pleasing dream *T.T.* 288

And I will sing, if *L.* be there *T.T.* 295
And I will sing, at *L.*'s dear feet *T.T.* 296
And *L.*, preserved from wild excess *T.T.* 316
L. blushed, and hung her drooping head *T.T.* 324
L. taught him her Athenian strain *T.T.* 343
Gives *L.* the last, the mortal shock *T.T.* 476

LIBIDINOUS.
(As often as *l.* discourse *T.* v 660

LICE.
Than abstinence, and beggary and *l. T.* 124

LICENCE.
The *l.* of the lowest in degree *T.* iv 588

LICENSED.
That law has *l.*, as makes temperance reel *T.* iv 471

LICENTIOUS.
And forced the floodgates of *l.* mirth *Con.* 264
Forbids him none but the *l.* joy *P.E.* 237

LICENTIOUSNESS.
And fierce *L.* should bear the blame *T.T.* 329

LICK. [iii 342
Yes—thou mayst eat thy bread, and *l.* the hand *T.*
And *l.* the foot that treads it in the dust *T.* v 356

LICKED.
And *l.* his feathers smooth *B.R.* 20

LIDS. [859
Canst thou, the tear just trembling on thy *l. Tir.*

LIE.
When Scandal has new minted an old *l. Ch.* 513
What monstrous *l.* some travellers will tell " *Ch.* 394
The scales are false, or algebra a *l. Con.* 22
And baits its hook with prodigies and *l. Con.* 224
And while at heart sin unrelinquished *l. Con.* 673
Her hope presumption, and her faith a *l. Con.* 774
Here *l.*, whom hound did ne'er pursue *Ep.* ii 1
Infuses *l.* and errors of his own *Ex.* 102
But here again a danger *l. F.* 25
To search forbidden deeps where mystery *l. F.A.* 33
In which, or astronomy *l. Gr.* 15
Can only say,—" Nobility *l.* here " *H.* 271
But here alas ! the fatal difference *l. H.* 282 [424
That truth *l.* somewhere, if we knew but where *H.*
Thy deep repentance of thy thousand *l. H.* 590
To sweep away all refuges of *l. H.* 628 [54
Through the ripe harvest *l.* their destined road *Her.*
Brutes capable would tell you 'tis a *l. P.E.* 261
To justify it by a thousand *l. P.E.* 204
Thou ever bubbling spring of endless *l. P.E.* 467
One leg by truth supported, one by *l. P.E.* 561
That Scripture *l.*, and blasphemy is sense *P.E.* 595
He that hates truth shall be the dupe of *l. P.E.* 607
And I must ere long *l.* as lowly as they *P.F.* 14
A sepulchre in which the living *l. R.* 737
L. down secure, her heart and pocket light *T.* 322
L. scattered where the shapely column stood *T.* ii 76
By tricks and *l.* as numerous and as keen *T.* ii 671
Ten thousand *l.* in wait to thwart *T.* iii 553
The verdure of the plain *l.* buried deep *T.* v 21
L. covered close ; and berry-bearing thorns *T.* v 82
L. undissolved; while silently beneath *T.* v 99
And, warp'd into the labyrinth of *l. Tir.* 157
To lure me to the baseness of a *l. T.T.* 86
And, of all *l.* (be that one poet's boast) *T.T.* 87
The *l.* that flatters I abhor the most *T.T.* 88
Stamps God's own name upon a *l.* just made *T.T.* 420
In wisdom, wealth, in fortune, and in *l. T.T.* 469
He scolds, and gives the *l. Trans.* iv 27

LIFE

LIFE. [A.T. 127
Lest Rome should end with her first founder's *l.*
To measure the *l.* that she leads C. 48
She will have just the *l.* she prefers C. 53
Supported by despair of *l.* Cast. 18
While Cook is loved for savage *l.* he saved Ch. 39
That has a heart and *l.* in it, "Be free!" Ch. 170
While *l.'s* sublimest joys are overlooked Ch. 219
L. and a kingdom upon worms below Ch. 592
Some men have surely then a peaceful *l.*! Con. 56
And hazard *l.* for any or no cause Con. 184
Am I to set my *l.* upon a throw Con. 191
You speak with *l.*, in hopes to entertain Con. 327
They spake of him they loved, of him whose *l.* Con. 511
Whose wisdom, drawn from the deep well of *l.* Con. 564
Ere *l.* go down, to see such sights again) Con. 606
Is madly to forget that *l.* is short Con. 772 [638
Crowned with the garland of *l.'s* blooming years Con.
And laughter, all their work, is *l.* misspent Con. 876
But though *l.'s* valley be a vale of tears Con. 881
A *l.* of ease would make them harder still E. ii 22
Whence comes it then, that in the wane of *l.* E. iii 14
Consult L.'s silent clock, thy bounding vein Ep. i 3
The graces of a *l.* that wins the skies Ex. 112
They saw distemper healed, and *l.* restored Ex. 153
Might give more *l.* to marble, or might fill Ex. 231
Thy *l.* upon the pattern of the law Ex. 409
Lavish of *l.*, to win an empty tomb Ex. 522
To waste thy *l.* in arms, or lay it down Ex. 536
Nor spare a *l.* too short to reach the skies Ex 623
And truth alone, where'er my *l.* be cast Ex. 732
They manifest their whole *l.* through F. 112
And make a calm of human *l.* F. 134
To recommence *l.'s* trial, in the hope F.A. 4
Ask what is human *l.*—the sage replies H. 1 [24
Through *l.'s* sad remnant, what no sighs restore H.
Is such a *l.*, so tediously the same H. 87
By which he reads, that *l.* without a plan H. 95
L. is his gift, from whom whate'er *l.* needs H. 115
Men deal with *l.* as children with their play H. 127
His date of *l.*, so likely to be short H. 208
And *l.* abused, and not to be suborned H. 224
L. without hope can close but in despair H. 274
With him the Donor of eternal *l.* H. 323
And grace be grace indeed, and *l.* a gift H. 531
Deem *l.* a blessing with its numerous woes H. 546
His only answer was a blameless *l.* H. 577
He draws upon *l.'s* map a zig-zag line H. 607
Which most should sweeten his untroubled *l.* H. 681
The *l.* of multitudes, a nation's bread! Her. 56
That sorest ill of human *l.* M.F. 32
The love that cheers *l.'s* latest stage M.F. 49
Each tender tie of *l.* defied Miss — 29
Give *l.* her every charm Miss — 80
Ere long approach *l.'s* evening shades Mor. 35
But he, whom e'en in *l.'s* last stage Mor. 49
Oh that those lips had language! L. has passed M.P. 1
Wretch even then, *l.'s* journey just begun? M.P. 24
But no—what here we call our *l.* is such M.P. 84
Of *l.*, long since has anchored by thy side M.P. 99
That *l.* to save, we leap into the pit" N.A. 104
How! leap into the pit our *l.* to save! N.A. 107
To save our *l.* leap all into the grave! N.A. 108
Till *l.'s* poor transient night is spent N.G. 32
Thus *l.* is spent (oh fie upon 't!) P. 37
That Virtue points to? Can a *l.* thus spent P.E. 72
Charged with the folly of his *l.'s* mad scene P.E. 88
Now, while the poison all high *l.* pervades P.E. 347
And through *l.'s* labyrinth holds fast the clue P.E. 357
Nor rested till the Gods had given it *l.* P.E. 529
Faults in the *l.* breed errors in the brain P.E. 564
Though his *l.* be a dream, his enjoyments, I see P.F. 19
But which, when *l.* at ebb runs weak and low R. 3

If, ere we yet discern *l.'s* evening star R. 46
New *l.* ordained and brighter scenes to share R. 65
Compared with this sublimest *l.* below R. 103
We find a little isle, this *l.* of man R. 148
Nor these alone prefer a *l.* recluse R. 169
Can call up *l.* into his faded eye R. 339
Yet seek him, in his favour *l.* is found R. 353
Are *l.'s* prime pleasures in his simple view R. 403
The tide of *l.*, swift always in its course R. 453
Seems at the best but dreaming *l.* away R. 468
Ingenious to diversify dull *l.* R. 520
A *l.* of ease a difficult pursuit R. 634
L. an intrusted talent, or a toy? R. 650
A temper rustic as the *l.* we lead R. 732
Or shine the dulness of still *l.* away R. 746
O sacred art! to which alone *l.* owes R. 749
To close *l.* wisely, may not waste my own R. 808
She left the cares of *l.* behind R.C. 47
Sweet moralist! afloat on *l.'s* rough sea R.H. 3
All these, *l.'s* rambling journey done St. i 3
Die self-accused of *l.* run all to waste? St. ii 28
Again *l.'s* dreary waste St. iii 6
"Such only be your *l.*" St. iii 36
Would gladly stretch *l.* little span St. v 7
Recoil from weary *l.'s* best hour St. v 19
Whence *l.* can be supplied St. vi 4
But *l.*, within a narrow ring St. vi 9
Can *l.* in them deserve the name St. vi 13
And endless *l.* above? St. vi 16
With *l.* that cannot die St. vi 32
Wearing out *l.* in his religious whim T. 89 [198
His *l.* should prove that he perceives their force T.
To save your *l.* would nobly risk his own T. 220
A soul redeemed demands a *l.* of praise T. 279
Some lead a *l.* unblameable and just T. 283
Shows them the shortest way to *l.* and love T. 370
Thus often Unbelief, grown sick of *l.* T. 445
That civil war embitters all his *l.* T. 468
That man is dead in sin, and *l.* a gift T. 514
L. for obedience, death for every flaw T. 550
As *l.* declines, speed rapidly away T. i 130
If Solitude make scant the means of *l.* T. i 248
Not such the alert and active. Measure *l.* T. i 396
That palls and satiates, and makes languid *l.* T. i 464
Themselves love *l.*, and cling to it, as he T. i 483
The spark of *l.* The sportive wind blows wide T. i 567
The manners and the arts of civil *l.* T. i 596
The gifts of Providence, and squander *l.* T. i 638
And genial soil of cultivated *l.* T. i 679
On petty robbers, and indulges *l.* T. i 733
That *l.* holds out to all, should most abound T. i 752
L. in the unproductive shades of death T. ii 124
L.'s necessary means, but he must die T. ii 141
In all the good and ill that chequer *l.*! T. ii 162
That live an atheist *l.*; involves the Heaven T. ii 180
He feels the anxieties of *l.*, denied T. ii 302 [T. ii 373
Whose hands are pure; whose doctrine and whose *l.*
When I am hungry for the bread of *l.*? T. ii 426 [523
Left them as dark themselves. Their rules of *l.* T. ii
And so illuminates the path of *l.* T. ii 529
Variety's the very spice of *l.* T. ii 606
And cleaves through *l.* inseparably close T. ii 761
Than once, and others of a *l.* to come T. iii 123
The little wick of *l.'s* poor shallow lamp T. iii 164
Ah! what is *l.* thus spent? and what are they T. iii 173
Domestic *l.* in rural leisure passed! T. iii 292
Not waste it, and aware that human *l.* T. iii 363
A social, not a dissipated *l.* T. iii 376
A *l.* all turbulence and noise may seem T. iii 379
All healthful, are the employs of rural *l.* T. iii 625
Abroad, and desolating public *l.* T. iii 683
What is it but a map of busy *l.* T. iv 55 [iv 187
Unlooked for, *l.* preserved, and peace restored T.

LIFE—LIGHT

Against the charities of domestic *l. T.* iv 677
Thee too enamoured of the *l.* I loved *T.* iv 718
The most unfurnished with the means of *l. T.* iv 770
Of multitudes unknown. Hail! rural *l.! T.* iv 783
That lifts him into *l.*, and lets him fall *T.* iv 791
In the low vale of *l.*, that early felt *T.* iv 799
Some have amused the dull sad years of *l. T.* v 180
(*L.* spent in indolence and therefore sad) *T.* v 181
He deems a thousand or ten thousand *l. T.* v 276
His thousands, weary of penurious *l. T.* v 319
Who lives, and is not weary of a *l. T.* v 365
By him of Babylon, *l.* stands a stump *T.* v 401
Upon the endearments of domestic *l. T.* v 438
Of fleeting *l.* its lustre and perfume *T.* v 447
And plausible that social *l.* requires *T.* v 466
That can ennoble man, and make frail *l. T.* v 603
And no condition of this changeful *l. T.* v 768
"From toilsome *l.* to never ending rest *T.* v 841
From thee is all that soothes the *l.* of man *T.* v 900
How gladly would the man recall to *l. T.* vi 42 [181
From dearth to plenty, and from death to *l. T.* vi 1000
Sustains, and is the *l.* of all that lives *T.* vi 222
With sight of animals enjoying *l. T.* vi 325 [vi 429
With bleeding sides and flanks that heave for *l. T.*
O'er all we feed on power of *l.* and death *T.* vi 453
As free to live, and to enjoy that *l. T.* vi 585
And trivial favours, lasting as the *l. T.* vi 630
He is the happy man whose *l.* e'en now *T.* vi 906
Shows somewhat of that happier *l.* to come *T.* vi 907
Nor, though he tread the secret path of *l. T.* vi 956
He sits secure, and in the scale of *l. T.* vi 970
So *l.* glides smoothly and by stealth away *T.* vi 995
So glide my *l.* away! and so at last *T.* vi 1000
Resolved a union formed for *l. The Doves* 27 [30
That grace and Nature have to wage through *l. Tir.*
'Tis true that, if to trifle *l.* away *Tir.* 81
A quickness, which in later *l.* is lost *Tir.* 110
Back to the season of *l.*'s happy spring *Tir.* 132
Yet e'en in transitory *l.*'s late day *Tir.* 143
When first we started into *l.*'s long race *Tir.* 315
With all the adventures of his early *l. Tir.* 325
Hurt too perhaps for *l.*; for early wrong *Tir.* 490
Which, oft neglected, in *l.*'s waning years *Tir.* 589
Chained to the routs that she frequents for *l. Tir.* 744
To you, then, tenants of *l.*'s middle state *Tir.* 807
And give thy *l.* its only cordial left? *Tir.* 882
His *l.* a lesson to the land he sways *T.T.* 76
Respect, while stalking o'er *l.* narrow stage *T.T.* 118
Not more invigorates *l.*'s noblest part *T.T.* 381
The storms that overset the joys of *l. T.T.* 449
And all the crowds that bustle *l.* away *V.* 74
Beget no thunder-clouds to trouble *l. V.* 76
Down to the close of *l.*'s fast fading scene *V.* 85
Sits half the pleasures of short *l.* away *Y.O.* 32
Invigorate by turns the springs of *l. Y.O.* 78
Yet *L.* still lingers in thee, and puts forth *Y.O.* 130
Drew not his *l.* from woman; never gazed *Y.O.* 145

LIFE-RENEWING.

Your heart shall yield a *l.* stream *Con.* 503

LIFE-RESTORING.

The trumpet of a *l.* day *H.* 456

LIFT.

Then *l.* it gently from the ground *E.* iv 57
"For *l.* thy palsied head, shake off the gloom *H.* 37
Nightly *l.* his voice on high *St.* iv 6 [*T.* vi 925
Whose power is such, that whom she *l.* from earth
Can *l.* herself above corporeal things *T.* 487
Till the stout bearers *l.* the corpse again *T.* i 481
That *l.* him into life, and lets him fall *T.* iv 791
Strange that such folly as *l.* bloated man *T.* v 283

Can *l.* to Heaven an unpresumptuous eye *T.* v 746
Where Violence shall never *l.* the sword *T.* vi 843

LIFTED.

A few forsake the throng; with *l.* eyes *R.* 161
L. at length, by dignity of thought *T.T.* 676

LIGHT.

And the swift-winged arrows of *L.*—*A.S.* 44
No *l.* propitious shone *Cast.* 62
The sword shall *l.* upon thy boasted powers *Ch.* 79
From her the canvass borrows *l.* and shade *Ch.* 107
Whose bounty bought me but to give me *l. Ch.* 235
The peep of morning shed a dawning *l. Ch.* 261
Drinks wisdom at the milky stream of *l. Ch.* 319
With a new medium and a purer *l. Ch.* 330
They cannot give it, or make darkness *l. Ch.* 388
He talks of *l.*, and the prismatic hues *Ch.* 391
Unless a love of virtue *l.* the flame *Ch.* 491
Their want of *l.* and intellect supplied *Con.* 147
Quite as absurd, though not so *l.*, as he *Con.* 296
The southern sash admits too strong a *l. Con.* 331
The fixed fee-simple of the vain and *l.? Con.* 590
A Christian's wit is inoffensive *l. Con.* 599
'Tis such a *l.* as putrefaction breeds *Con.* 675
Daily derive increasing *l.* and force *Con.* 697
And through the scenes of toil-renewing *l. Con.* 732
Whose glory, with a *l.* that never fades *Con.* 883
Sheds every hour a clearer *l. E.* i 61
As often as too little *l. E.* iv 64 [281
With *l.* derived from thee, would smother thine *Ex.*
Where sharp and solid, phlegmatic and *l. Ex.* 296
Darkness itself before his eye is *l. Ex.* 338
His victory was that of orient *l. Ex.* 478 [504
But still *l.* reached thee; and those gods of thine *Ex.*
By such a change, thy darkness is made *l. Ex.* 640
Them without *l.*, and thee without a cloud *Ex.* 717
Sometime occasion brings to *l. F.* 148
In beams of inextinguishable *l. H.* 134 [178
Were *l.*, when weighed against one smile of thine *H.*
That cannot bear the blaze of Scripture *l. H.* 298
A hand as liberal as the *l.* of day *H.* 408
Brings many a precious pearl of truth to *l. H.* 444
But above all, in her own *l.* arrayed *H.* 447
Of one, whose birth was in a land of *l. H.* 535
And *l.* and shade, and every stroke be thine *H.* 673
Oh! welcome now the sun's once hated *l. H.* 736
Than golden beams of orient *l. M.* 27
Shed *l.*, like a sun on the waves *M.D.* 14
Around her, fanning *l.* her streamers gay *M.P.* 95
He spells them true by intuition's *l. N.A.* 69
That you with music, I with *l. N.G.* 21
And only pervious to the *l. P.B.* 10
That not a glimpse of genuine *l.* pervades *P.E.* 6
L. of the world, and stars of human race *P.E.* 97
But show peculiar *l.*, by many a grin *P.E.* 383
His great improvement and new *l.* he draws *P.E.* 402
The sun, a world whence other worlds drink *l. R.* 81
And sees, by no fallacious *l.* or dim *R.* 115
Give useful *l.* though I should miss renown *R.* 206
Seem drops descending in a shower of *l. R.* 350
We seek it, ere it come to *l. R.C.* 97
Observe the dappled foresters, how *l. St.* ii 21
All evils then seem *l.*, compared *St.* v 27
Charge not, with *l.* sufficient and left free *T.* 19
Legible only by the *l.* they give *T.* 30
The foam upon the waters not so *l. T.* 43
Lies down secure, her heart and pocket *l. T.* 322
The *l.* they walk by, kindled from above *T.* 369
"Truly not I! The partial *l.* men have *T.* 521
Derived from the same source of *l.* and grace *T.* 533
How airy and how *l.* the graceful arch *T.* i 341
Brushed by the wind. So sportive is the *l. T.* i 345

LIGHT—LINE

And throws Italian *l.* on English walls *T.* i 425
Escapes at last to liberty and *l. T.* i 440   [152
Moved not, while theirs was rocked like a *l.* skiff *T.* ii
The sleeping leaves, is all the *l.* they wish *T.* i 763
That each may find its most propitious *l. T.* ii 295
Of *L.* Divine. But Egypt, Greece, and Rome *T.* ii 500
And, at the watchman's lantern borrowing *l. T.* ii 654
Rotation; from what fountain flowed their *l. T.* iii 160
Truths undiscerned but by that holy *l. T.* iii 242
And wherefore? Will not God impart His *l. T.* iii 272
With *l.*, by clear reflection multiplied *T.* iv 268
The frugal housewife trembles when she *l. T.* iv 380
And heaviest, *l.* of foot steals fast away *T.* iv 442
By modern *l.* from an erroneous taste *T.* iv 724
Can but arrest the *l.* and smoky mist *T.* v 105
Illumined every side: a watery *l. T.* v 150
A ray of heavenly *l.* gilding all forms *T.* v 810
With those fair ministers of *l.* to man *T.* v 816
Pleased with his solitude, and flitting *l. T.* vi 79
Her silver globes, *l.* on the foamy surf *T.* vi 155
Though poor in skill to rear them, *l.* at last *T.* vi 753
Flock to that *l.*; the glory of all lands *T.* vi 802
And no such *l.* are kindling in their stead *Tir.* 285
Was graced with many an undulating *l. T.T.* 573
Fair Science poured the *l.* of truth *Th.* 3   [1009
With that *l.* task; but soon, to please her more *T.* vi
Gives him a modicum of *l. Trans.* i 11
Nor crush a worm, whose useful *l. Trans.* i 17
Affection *l.* a brighter flame *U.* 27
Whose noblest coin is *l.* and brittle man *V.* 96
Loved not the *l.*, but, gloomy, into gloom *Y.O.* 14

LIGHT-CREATING.
Dwelt visibly the *l.* God *T.* 390

LIGHTENED.
The loaded wain, while *l.* of its charge *T.* i 296

LIGHTER.
In *l.* diet at a later hour *Ex.* 403

LIGHTEST.
The breathings of the *l.* air that blows *R.* 530

LIGHT-HEARTED.
He whistles as he goes, *l.* wretch *T.* iv 12

LIGHTLY.
The hills move *l.*, and the mountains smoke *T.* ii 91
And *l.*, shaking it with agile hand *T.* iii 478
He places *l.*, and as time subdues *T.* iii 518

LIGHTNESS.
Of *l.* in his speech. 'Tis pitiful *T.* ii 466

LIGHTNING.
Upon his dungeon walls the *l.* play *H.* 718
In dazzling streaks the vivid *l.* play *Her.* 18
Swift beyond thought the *l.* dart away *T.* 243
And perilous *l.* from the angry clouds *T.* iii 212
The laurel that the very *l.* spares *T.T.* 6
"When *l.* flash among the trees *The Doves* 21
No need of *l.* from on high *The Doves* 33

LIKE.
He *l.* yours little, and his own still less *Con.* 344
Yet *l.* a slice as well as he *L.W.* 36
He *l.* the country, but in truth must own *R.* 573
Most *l.* it, when he studies it in town *R.* 574   [210
He *l.* your house, your housemaid, and your pay *T.*
Grows conscious of a change, and *l.* it well *T.* iv 638
And howl and roar as *l.* them, uncontrol'd *T.* vi 404
Draws gross impurity, and *l.* it well *T.* vi 979

LIKED.
But N. *l.* it never the better for that *A.T.* ii 6

LIKENESS.
Heaven held his hand, the *l.* must be true *Ch.* 434
Hate their own *l.* in a brother's face *Con.* 158
Begets its *l.*   Rank abundance breeds *T.* i 686
A faithful *l.* of the forms he views *T.* ii 293
The *l.* of some object seen before *T.* v 121
With his own *l.* placed on either knee *Tir.* 320

LILAC.
The *l.*, various in array, now white *T.* vi 157

LILY.
His *l.* newly blown *D.W.* 14
I saw him, with that *l.* cropped *D.W.* 33
The rose or *l.* appears blue or green *H.* 72
The *L.* and the Rose *L.R.* 8
The *L.*'s height bespoke command *L.R.* 13
As with the diamond on his *l.* hand *T.* ii 424
And *l.* for the brows of faded age *T.* iv 80

LIMB.
Such feebleness of *l.* thou provest *M.* 37
The shapely *l.* and lubricated joint *R.* 57
With *l.* of British oak, and nerves of wire *R.* 311
By soft recumbency of outstretched *l. T.* i 82
The gouty *l.*, 'tis true; but gouty *l. T.* i 107   [581
They swathe the forehead, drag the limping *l. T.* i
My languid *l.*, when summer sears the plains *T.* iii 30
I view the muscular proportioned *l. T.* v 15
Would cheerfully these *l.* resign *Trans.* ii 34

LIME.
For the close-woven arches of *l. C.* 29
For baking earth, or burning rock to *l. N.A.* 18
Of ash, or *l.*, or beech, distinctly shine *T.* i 303
Prolific, and the *l.* at dewy eve *T.* i 316
The ruddier orange and the paler *l. T.* iii 573

LIMIT.
Within the scanty *l.* of the mind *Ch.* 247
To *l.* thought, by Nature prone to stray *R.* 127
The *l.* of control, his gentle eye *T.* ii 719

LIMITATION.
And righteous *l.* of its act *T.* vi 596

LIMITED.
Then ask not, whether *l.* or large? *Tir.* 511
Discreetly *l.* to two at most *Tir.* 770

LIMITING.
Circling around and *l.* his years *R.* 150

LIMPID.
And fit the *l.* element for use *T.* i 374

LIMPING.
They swathe the forehead, drag the *l.* limb *T.* i 581

LINCHPIN.
Left out his *l.*, or forgot his tar *P.E.* 441

LINE.   [*A.T.* ii 4
With as many hard names as would *l.* a good trunk
A poet does not work by square or *l. Con.* 789
That Robert's *l.* are easy too *E.* iv 70
He draws upon life's map a zigzag *l. H.* 607
Whose *l.* uniting by an honest art *H.* 756
Bricks *l.* the sides, but shivered long ago *N.A.* 15
As bloated spiders draw the flimsy *l. P.E.* 495
It err but little from the intended *l. P.E.* 574
Unlike the enigmatic *l. Q.V.* 49
And poring on thy page, whose every *l. R.* 207
Long *l.* of ancestry, renowned of old *Tir.* 817
These chestnuts ranged in corresponding *l. T.* i 263
And poplar that with silver *l.* his leaf *T.* i 310

Soon, by a righteous judgment, in the *l. T.* v 211
Plants it upon the *l.* that Justice draws *T.T.* 17
Along the nerve of every feeling *l. T.T.* 487 [522
Give me the *l.* that ploughs its stately course *T.T.*
No Muses on these *l.* attend *U.* 29

LINEAGE.
No longer Levites, and their *l.* lost *Ex.* 264

LINEAMENT.
And *l.* divine I trace a hand *T.* iii 722
Exhibit every *l.* of these *T.* vi 901

LINED.
A drawer, it chanced, at bottom, *l. R.C.* 35 [762
What are the casements *l.* with creeping herbs *T.* iv
In coach with purple *l.*, and mitres on its side *Tir.* 369
The diadem, with mighty projects *l. T.T.* 59

LINEN.
With *l.* of the softest kind *R.C.* 36

LINEN-DRAPER.
I am a *l.* bold *J.G.* 21

LINGER.
With hopeless wish one looks and *l. P.B.* 33
No muse can hesitate, or *l.* long) *Tir.* 291
Yet Life still *l.* in thee and puts forth *Y.O.* 130

LINGERING.
When Hope, long *l.*, at last yields the ghost *H.* 723

LINK.
To loose the *l.* that galled mankind before *T.* 185
They gaze upon the *l.* that hold them fast *T.* ii 664
To cut the *l.* of brotherhood, by which *T.* iii 208
And hewed them *l.* from *l.* Then Albion's sons *T.* v 517

LINKED.
The language plain, and incidents well *l. Con.* 236

LINKING.
Sits *l.* cherry-stones, or platting rush *R.* 398

LINNET.
The *l.* twittered out his parting song *A.T.* 76
And when your *l.* on a day *B.R.* 13

LION.
Had heard a *l.* roar *J.G.* 206
And wilds familiar with a *l.'s* roar *R.* 779
The *l.* tells him—I am monarch here ! *T.* vi 408
The unfledged raven and the *l.'s* whelp *T.* vi 461
The *l.*, and the libbard, and the bear *T.* vi 773

LIP.
Thy *l.* have shed instruction as the dew *Ch.* 238
God's name so much upon his *l.*, a priest *Con.* 72
But being tied, it dies upon the *l. Con.* 355
And shed the balmy blessing on the *l. Con.* 442 [484
Warming his heart, should at his *l.* transpire ? *Con.*
And *l.* unstained by folly or by strife *Con.* 563
Those breathed from *l.* of everlasting love *E.* ii 30
And the dull service of the *l.* were there *Ex.* 44
The purple bumper trembling at his *l. H.* 358 [454
Live from his *l.*, and spread the glorious sound *H.*
All mercy from his *l.*, and sneered, and hissed *H.* 561
Oh that those *l.* had language ! Life has passed *M.P.* 1
Those *l.* are thine—thy own sweet smile I see *M.P.* 3
The parting word shall pass my *l.* no more ! *M.P.* 35
L. busy, and eyes fixed, foot falling slow *R.* 285
Her head erect, her fan upon her *l. T.* 134
What glowing thanks his *l.* and heart employ *T.* 255
And Chatham's eloquence to marble *l. T.* i 704
Blows mildew from between his shrivelled *l. T.* ii 186
Praise from the rivelled *l.* of toothless, bald *T.* ii 488

Played on his *l.*, and in his speech was heard *T.* ii 707
Drops from the *l.* a disregarded thing *T.* ii 565
Has flowed from *l.* wet with Castalian dews *T.* iii 251
Some note of Nature's music from his *l. T.* iii 600
Thy breath congealed upon thy *l.*, thy cheeks *T.* iv 122
Should ever drivel out of human *l. T.* v 285
In the lost kind, extracting from the *l. T.* v 701
From touch of human *l.* at best impure *T.* vi 835
And move the *l.* of poet's cast in lead *T.T.* 203
Spoke from his *l.*, and in his looks gave law *T.T.* 245

LIP-DEEP.
L. in what he longs for, and yet curst *P.E.* 233

LIQUID.
With lavender, and sprinkle *l.* sweets *T.* ii 257
That in its fall the *l.* sheet throws wide *T.* v 106
Recovering fast its *l.* music, prove *T.* vi 261

LIQUOR.
To hold the *l.* that she loved *J.G.* 67

LISPING.
L. our syllables, we scramble next *Tir.* 125

LIST.
Were I empowered to regulate the *l. Con.* 195
And frolic where they *l. F.B.* 9
I would not enter on my *l.* of friends *T.* vi 560

LISTEN.
No land but *l.* to the common call *Ch.* 91
Speak but the word, will *l.* and return *Ex.* 455
To *l.* is to lend him aid *F.* 101
Speaks with reserve, and *l.* with applause *R.* 448

LISTENING.
Placed with advantage at his *l.* ear *A.T.* 181
Yet, though he tease and baulk your *l.* ear *Con.* 135
That fills the *l.* lover with delight *Con.* 446
Their hours, their days, in *l.* to his joy *H.* 739
Greybeard corrupter of our *l.* youth *P.E.* 342
Just undulates upon the *l.* ear *T.* i 175
And soothed the *l.* dove *The Doves* 8
Then turning, he regales his *l.* wife *Tir.* 324
Learns much, and to a thousand *l.* minds *T.T.* 274
And, *l.* close with both his ears *Trans.* iv 20

LISTLESS.
Falls soporific on the *l.* ear *P.E.* 20
Hence an unfurnished and a *l.* mind *T.E.* 425
Fastidious, or else *l.*, or perhaps *T.* ii 306

LITERARY.
When, 'scaped from *l.* cares *D.W.* 3
The Frenchman first in *l.* fame *T.* 303
In all true worth and *l.* skill ? *Tir.* 378

LITTERED.
Dry fern or *l.* hay, that may imbibe *T.* iii 476

LITTERING.
Wandering, and *l.* with unfolded silks *T.* vi 280

LITTLE.
My *l.* garrison of sense *E.* iv 18
In dying sighs my *l.* breath *G.* 11
The *l.* Greeks look trembling at the scales *H.* 195
Thy hands thy *l.* force resign *M.* 34
Distant a *l.* mile he spied *Mor.* 17
Spontaneous, take but *l.* pains to sow *P.E.* 364
We find a *l.* isle, this life of man *R.* 148
Would gladly stretch life's *l.* span *St.* v 7
And drank the *l.* bumper every day *T.* 158
Pillow and bobbins all her *l.* store *T.* 318
Has *l.* understanding, and no wit *T.* 324
A *l.* Naiad her impoverished urn *T.* i 328

Can boast but *l.* virtue ; and inert *T.* i 623
The *l.* wick of life's poor shallow lamp *T.* iii 164
With all her *l.* ones, a sportive train *T.* vi 301
Of *l.* worth, an idler in the best *T.* vi 952   [19
And the tear that is wiped with a *l.* address *The Rose*
In *l.* bosoms such achievements strike *Tir.* 232
The *l.* ones, unbuttoned, glowing hot *Tir.* 304
They dream of *l.* Charles or William graced *Tir.* 360
'Twere wiser sure to inspire a *l.* heart *Tir.* 454
L. inmate, full of mirth *Trans.* iii 1
'Tis now a *l.* one, like Miss *Trans.* iv 17
The *l.* and the great *Trans. H.* 9
At Westminster, where *l.* poets strive *T.T.* 506
Spread *l.* wings, and rather skip than fly *T.T.* 579
She fills profuse ten thousand *l.* throats *T.T.* 694
The *l.* boy and all ? *Y.D.* 34
The great and *l.* of thy lot, thy growth *Y.O.* 87

LITURGY.
He drew the *l.*, and framed the rights *T.* vi 679

LIVE.
He long survives, who *l.* an hour *Cast.* 37   [609
And e'en the dipped and sprinkled *l.* in peace *Ch.*
That the surviving world may *l.* in peace *Con.* 176
L. the dear thought of joys he once possessed *Con.* 708
"That, while the language *l.* shall last" *E.* iv 78
You must not *l.* alone *F.B.* 27
L. to no sober purpose, and contend *H.* 129
Who *l.* in pleasure, dead e'en while they *l. H.* 230
As with a frown to say, "Do this, and *l.*" *H.* 329 [454
L. from his lips, and spread the glorious sound *H.*
Some wiser rule must teach him how to *l. H.* 600
Shall *l.* exempt from weakness and decay *H.* 752 [30
Clothes it with earth, and bids the produce *l. Her.*
Now let us sing, long *l.* the king *J.G.* 249
And Gilpin, long *l.* he *J.G.* 250
And something every day they *l. M.F.* 39
But *l.* when that exterior grace *M.F.* 53
To *l.*, unblessed, in torpid ease *Miss* — 27
Perceives in everything that *l.* a tongue *N.A.* 56
L. till to-morrow, will have passed away *N.A.* 133
That thy worst part, thy principles, *l.* yet *P.E.* 350
Whose highest praise is that they *l.* in vain *R.* 23
The love of change that *l.* in every breast *R.* 171
Some pleasures *l.* a month, and some a year *R.* 459
Worthy to *l.*, and of eternal use *R.* 700
He *l.* who *l.* to God, alone *St.* vi 1
To *l.* to God is to requite *St.* vi 5
Who only *l.* to prove *St.* vi 14   [31
Stand the soul-quickening words—Believe and *l. T.*
The book shall teach you; read, believe, and *l.!* *T.* 274
Oh! may I *l.* exempted (while I *l. T.* i 103   [371
An instant's pause, and *l.* but while she moves *T.* i
Yet scorn the purposes for which they *l. T.* i 486 [116
He drew them forth, and healed, and bade me *l. T.* iii
That *l.* an atheist life ; involves the Heaven *T.* ii 180
What man that *l.*, and that knows how to *l. T.* ii 618
"'Twere well, could you permit the world to *l. T.* iii 194
How then should I and any man that *l. T.* iii 200
L. by contriving delicates for you) *T.* iii 546   [582
L. there, and prosper. Those Ausonia claims *T.* iii
They *l.*, and *l.* without extorted alms *T.* iv 403 [759
That Nature *l.* ; that sight-refreshing green *T.* iv
Who *l.*, and is not weary of a life *T.* v 365   [403
Still *l.*, though all its pleasant boughs are gone *T.* v
To *l.* on terms of amity with vice *T.* v 658   [184
The grand transition, that there *l.* and works *T.* vi
Sustains, and is the life of all that *l. T.* vi 222
Or by necessity constrained, they *l. T.* vi 413
He *l.*, and o'er his brimming beaker boasts *T.* vi 434
Will tread aside, and let the reptile *l. T.* vi 567
As free to *l.*, and to enjoy that life *T.* vi 585
For these they *l.*, they sacrifice to these *T.* vi 893

True. While they *l.*, the courtly laureate pays *T.T.* 109
His right of empire over all that *l. Tir.* 4
And useless while he *l.* and when he dies *Tir.* 71
To *l.* estranged from God his total scope *Tir.* 426
L. not, aged though he be *Trans.* iii 31
So shalt thou *l.* beyond the reach *Trans. H.* 2
And *l.* contentedly between *Trans. H.* 8
To *l.* by buskin, sock, and raree-show *V.* 34
In all that *l.*, plant, animal, and man *Y.O.* 79

LIVED.
And I have *l.* recluse in rural shades *Con.* 801 [451
And too short *l.* to reach the realms of peace *Ch.*
L. happy prisoners there *F.B.* 6
Had Paul of Tarsus *l.* and died a Jew *H.* 257
A man once young, who *l.* retired *Mor.* 3
I seem to have *l.* my childhood o'er again *M.P.* 115
"Friends! we have *l.* too long. I never heard *N.A.* 83
And having *l.* a trifler, die a man *R.* 14
L. in his saddle, loved the chase, the course *R.* 577
Such *l.* Aspasio ; and at last *St.* iii 29   [306
L. long, wrote much, laughed heartily, and died *T.*
To a sharp reckoning that has *l.* in vain *T.* iii 179
Yet few remember them. They *l.* unknown *T.* v 724
The idol of our worship while he *l. T.* vi 666
Such Mary's true love, that has *l. W.N.* 19 [*Y.O.* 40
Who *l.* when thou wast such? oh couldst thou speak
That once *l.* here thy brethren! at my birth *Y.O.* 2

LIVELIER.
Seem graced with a *l.* hue *W.N.* 22
In matted grass, that with a *l.* green *T.* 195

LIVELONG.
Will the sweet warbler of the *l.* night *Con.* 445
The *l.* night : nor these alone, whose notes *T.* 201
Shuffling her threads about the *l.* day *T.* 320
The dreary waste ; there spends the *l.* day *T.* i 547
The *l.* night. A tattered apron hides *T.* i 549

LIVELY.
Or *l.* fancy guess *Miss* — 104
No jester, and yet *l.* in discourse *Tir.* 668

LIVERIED.
There, in his commerce with the *l.* herd *Tir.* 688

LIVERY.
Is still the *l.* she delights to wear *T.* iv 760

LIVERY-NAGS.
Or throw them up to *l.* and grooms *Tir.* 901

LIVID.
Pale, wan, and *l.*, but assuming soon *T.* iii 523

LIVING.
A sepulchre in which the *l.* lie *R.* 737
Learn thou, ye *l.!* by the mouths be taught *St.* ii 33
Where should the *l.*, weeping o'er his woes *T.* 435
For interest sake, the *l.* to the dead *T.* iii 661
Feed on the slain, but spare the *l.* brute! *T.* vi 458
But all are capable of *l.* well *Tir.* 510
To set some *l.* worthy in his view *Tir.* 647

LOAD.
To improve the fortitude that bears the *l. Ch.* 160
Thy rulers *l.* thy credit, year by year *Ex.* 284
Successive *l.* succeeding broils impose *Ex.* 308 [8
True to his charge, the close packed *l.* behind *T.* iv
By congregated *l.* adhering close *T.* iv 344
Society, grown weary of the *l. T.* iv 498
No longer blushing for her awkward *l. T.* iv 551 [33
He from the stack carves out the accustomed *l. T.* v
Shall be dismantled of its fleecy *l. T.* vi 179
Warped into tough knee-timber, many a *l.! Y.O.* 99

LOADED—LONG

LOADED.
They should encounter with well *l*. fists *Con.* 196
Owes all its weight, like *l*. dice, to lead *Con.* 302
The *l*. wain, while lightened of its charge *T.* i 296
The *l*. soil, and ye may waste much good *T.* v 756

LOAF. [393
Just when the day declined, and the brown *l. T.* iv

LOAMY.
Deep in the *l*. bank. Uptorn by strength *T.* iv 438
Thou fellest mature; and, in the *l*. clod *Y.O.* 33

LOAN.
Is but a *l*., to be repaid with use *T.* iii 364
Supplies his need with a usurious *l. T.* iii 798

LOATHE.
He takes what he at first professed to *l. Con.* 337
They love it, and yet *l*. it; fear to die *T.* i 485
And serves the altar, in my soul I *l. T.* ii 416

LOATHED. [206
The spot he *l*. so much for ever cleansed away *A.T.*
There hid in *l*. obscurity, removed *R.* 563
And *l*. the thought of sin *St.* iii 28
Precipitate the *l*. abode of man *T.* vi 376

LOATHSOME.
Who drive a *l*. traffic, gauge and span *Ch.* 139
Succesfully conceals her *l*. form *P.E.* 8
Of *l*. diet, penury, and cold *T.* i 591
Becomes a *l*. body, only fit *T.* iv 674
The creeping vermin, *l*. to the sight *T.* vi 568
And *l*. Ribaldry has done his worst *T.T.* 729

LOBES. [522
And spreading wide their spongy *l*., at first *T.* iii
Now stars; two *l*., protruding, paired exact *Y.O.* 36

LOCAL.
Truth is not *l*., God alike pervades *R.* 119
He gives the *l*. bias all its sway *Tir.* 334

LOCK.
Thy silver *l*., once auburn bright *M.* 25
Fleecy *l*. and black complexion *N.C.* 13
A tooth or auburn *l*., and by degrees *T.* i 133 [134
Their length and colour from the *l*. they spare *T.* i
An eyebrow, next compose a straggling *l. T.* ii 446
With spatter'd boots, strapp'd waist and frozen *l.T.*iv6
As meal and larded *l*. can make him; wears *T.* iv 642
And tells them, as he strokes their silver *l. Tir.* 322
Slips the slave's collar on, and snaps the *l. T.T.* 477

LOCKE. [538
Such was Sir Isaac, and such Boyle and *L.* — *P.E.*

LOCKED.
Fast *l*. in mine, with pleasure such as Love *T.* i 146

LOCKETS.
Sees watches, bracelets, rings and *l. P.B.* 25

LOCOMOTIVE.
He scans of every *l*. kind *N.A.* 64

LODGE.
Who long had marked her airy *l. A Fable* 25 [531
Plunged in the stream, they *l*. upon the mind *Ch.*
I called the low-roofed *l*. the Peasant's nest *T.* i 227
Oh for a *l*. in some vast wilderness *T.* ii 1
Can *l*. a heavenly mind—demands a doubt *T.* ii 462

LODGED.
L. with convenience in the fork *R.C.* 13
L. on the shelf; half-eaten without sauce *T.* iv 394

Doomed to the dust, or *l*. already there *T.* vi 714
A mind well *l*., and masculine of course *T.T.* 221

LODGING.
Why hire a *l*. in a house unknown *Tir.* 555

LOFTIEST.
The subtlest serpent with the *l*. crest *T.* 476
Of wintry blasts; the *l*. tower *Trans. H.* 14

LOFTY.
An apple tree, or *l*. pear *R.C.* 12
The air salubrious of her *l*. hills *T.* i 428
O'ertop the *l*. wood that skirts the wild *T.* i 558
Such *l*. strains embellish what you teach *T.T.* 478

LOG.
The well-stacked pile of riven *l*. and roots *T.* iv 444
Each heart as heavy as a *l. Y.D.* 15

LOGIC.
Vociferated *l*. kills me quite *Con.* 113
His cap well-lined with *l*. not his own *T.* ii 737
The *l*., and the wisdom, and the wit *T.* iv 32
This once believed, 'twere *l*. misapplied *Tir.* 103
Seldom, alas! the power of *l*. reigns *T.T.* 51

LOINS. [109
From *l*. enthroned, and rulers of the earth *M.P.*
Distressed the weary *l*. that felt no ease *T.* i 45

LOIRE.
Are come from distant *L.* to choose *E.* i 47

LOITERERS.
The *l*. I never saw *E.* i 24
Remarks two *l*. that have lost their way *P.E.* 386

LOITERING.
Oft *l*. lazily if not o'erseen *T.* iii 401
Of fluttering, *l*., cringing, begging, loose *T.* iii 832

LOLLS.
L. at his ease behind four handsome bays *R.* 392

LOLLING.
L. at your jovial boards *N.C.* 22

LONDON.
Though the pleasures of *L.* exceed *C.* 25
Of famous *L.* town *J.G.* 4
Set *L.* in a glow *Q.V.* 8
Such *L.* is, by taste and wealth proclaimed *T.* i 697
In *L.* Where her implements exact *T.* i 715
In *L.* Where has commerce such a mart *T.* i 719
As *L.*, opulent, enlarged, and still *T.* i 721
Increasing *L.*? Babylon of old *T.* i 722
L. engulphs them all! The shark is there *T.* iii 816
And wanton vagrants, as make *L.*, vast *T.* iii 833
The villas with which *L.* stands begirt *T.* iv 748
And blazing *L.* seemed a second Troy *T.T.* 323

LONELY.
Taking my *l*. winding walk, I mused *F.A.* 8
To distant caves the *l*. wanderer flies *R.* 769

LONG.
Who *l*. had marked her airy lodge *A Fable* 25
And for Hypothesis was somewhat *l. A.T.* 19
Not *l*. beneath the whelming brine *Cast.* 13
He *l*. survives, who lives an hour *Cast.* 37
And so *l*. he, with unspent power *Cast.* 39
Thy rights have suffered, and our land, too *l. Ch.* 277
But sedentary weavers of *l*. tales *Con.* 207
Yet Age, by *l*. experience well informed *Con.* 639
And gods and goddesses discarded *l. Con.* 819
Grace him again with *l*. forgotten arts *Con.* 839

LONG—LOOK

I thence withdrew, and followed *l. D.W.* 27
Ears *l.* accustomed to the pleasing lute *Ex.* 68
L. time Assyria bound them in her chain *Ex.* 73
A *l.* immunity from grief and pain *Ex.* 82
Where Policy is busied, all night *l. Ex.* 300
And *l.* provoked, repaid thee to thy face *Ex.* 391
How much, though *l.* neglected, shining yet *Ex.* 610
By *l.* fidelity and love *E.* i 104
(I hate *l.* arguments verbosely spun) *E.* iii 44 [i 4
Seems it to say—" Health here has *l.* to reign ?" *Ep.*
He finds his *l.*, last home *Ep.* ii 38
Our friend's defect *l.* hid from sight *F.* 149
Is not the pardon of thy *l.* arrear *F.A.* 13
Had been their mutual solace *l. F.B.* 5
Though short, too *l.*, the price he pays for all *H.* 200
Of critics now alive or *l.* since dead *H.* 426 [723
When Hope, *l.* lingering, at last yields the ghost *H.*
And when, as Justice has *l.* since decreed *H.* 748
'Twas *l.* before the customers *J.G.* 57
His *l.* red cloak, well brushed and neat *J.G.* 75
Like streamer *l.* and gay *J.G.* 102
Now let us sing, *l.* live the king *J.G.* 249
And Gilpin, *l.* live he *J.G.* 250
After *l.* sleep, of passion in the heart *J.T.* 42
L. beards, *l.* noses, and pale faces *M.F.* 6
Ere *l.* approach life's evening shades *Mor.* 35
Affectionate, a mother lost so *l. M.P.* 14
A *l., l.* sigh, and wept a last adieu ! *M.P.* 31
What ardently I wished, I *l.* believed *M.P.* 38
Of life, *l.* since has anchored by thy side *M.P.* 99
After *l.* drought, when rains abundant fall *N.A.* 59
"Friends ! we have lived too *l.* I never heard *N.A.* 83
A nightingale, that all-day *l. N.G.* 1
Disputes, though short, are far too *l. P.* 45
We *l.* for pineapples in frames *P.B.* 32
Sing, Muse, (if such a theme, so dark, so *l. P.E.* 1
L. ere the charioteer of day had run *P.E.* 67
Lip-deep in what he *l.* for, and yet curst *P.E.* 233
Ere *l.* some bowing, smirking, smart Abbé *P.E.* 385
Men loved their own productions *l.* ago *P.E.* 527
He cannot *l.* be safe whose wishes roam *P.E.* 587
But, Muse, forbear; *l.* flights forebode a fall *P.E.* 604
And I must ere *l.* lie as lowly as they *P.F.* 14
When, *l.* sequestered from his throne *Q.V.* 1
Those the *l.* milky way *Q.V.* 12
Where all his *l.* anxieties forgot *R.* 7
Though *l.* rebelled against, not yet suppressed *R.* 16
Souls that have *l.* despised their heavenly birth *R.* 35
Begins a *l.* look out for distant land *R.* 433
Recumbent at her ease, ere *l. R.C.* 45
A *l.* and melancholy mew *R.C.* 88
He has incurred a *l.* arrear *St.* v 31
Sit *l.* and late at the carousing board ? *T.* 50
And sore tormented *l.* before his time *T.* 84
His voluntary pains, severe and *l. T.* 101
L. hid by interposing hill or wood *T.* 249 [306
Lived *l.*, wrote much, laughed heartily, and died *T.*
The law grown clamorous, though silent *l. T.* 261
But made *l.* since, like Babylon of old *T.* 391
L. time elapsed or e'er our rugged sires *T.* i 68
His wasted spirits quickly, by *l.* toil *T.* i 128
Confirmed by *l.* experience of thy worth *T.* i 147
Witness a joy that thou hast doubled *l. T.* i 149
L. knowledge and the scrutiny of years *T.* i 179
And *l.* protracted bowers, enjoyed at noon *T.* i 257
Whom we call gay ? That honour has been *l. T.* i 491
As one who *l.* in thickets and in brakes *T.* iii 1
Or having *l.* in' miry ways been foiled *T.* iii 4
L. held, and scarcely disengaged at last *T.* iii 16
L. since : with many an arrow deep infixed *T.* iii 109
Whom ten *l.* years' experience of my care *T.* iii 338
And fruitful soil, that has been treasured *l. T.* iii 514
And which no care can obviate. It were *l. T.* iii 558

Too *l.*, to tell the expedients and the shifts *T.* iii 559
Ficoides, glitters bright the winter *l. T.* iii 579 [786
That he has touched, retouched, many a *l.* day *T.* iii
And the loud laugh—I *l.* to know them all *T.* iv 33
Of *l.* uninterrupted evening know *T.* iv 143
Warmed, while it lasts, by labour, all day *l. T.* iv 377
Their *l.* complaints, is self-inflicted woe *T.* iv 430
A wish for ease and leisure, and ere *l. T.* iv 800
The *l.* protracted rigour of the year *T.* v 85
For grandeur or for use. L. wavy wreaths *T.* v 158
His art survived the waters ; and ere *l. T.* v 220
He gulps the windy diet, and ere *l. T.* v 269
A course of *l.* observance for its use *T.* v 301
Its *l.* delay, feels every welcome stroke *T.* v 413
" As one who *l.* detained on foreign shores *T.* v 832
His *l.* love-ditty for my near approach *T.* vi 309
Narrow and *l.*, o'erlooks the western wave *T.* vi 484
She *l.* to yield, no sooner woo'd than won *Tir.* 172
No muse can hesitate, or linger *l.*) *Tir.* 291
When first we started into life's *l.* race *Tir.* 315
That here begins with most that *l.* complaint *Tir.* 587
L. lines of ancestry, renowned of old *Tir.* 817
To indulge his genius, after *l.* fatigue *T.T.* 153
From him who rears a poem lank and *l. T.T.* 532
Then like a bow *l.* forced into a curve *T.T.* 622
From these a *l.* succession, in the rage *T.T.* 630
That Lewdness had usurped and worn so *l. T.T.* 637
Satire has *l.* since done his best, and curst *T.T.* 728
I bid you both a *l.* and last adieu *V.* 5
Graced with the name of a *l.* absent friend *V.* 40
And *l.* before the day appears *Y.D.* 11
L. since, and rovers of the forest wild *Y.O.* 126
Much ancient chronicle, and *l.* 1789, 2
An era cherished *l.* by me 1789, 33

LONG-AGITATED.
Our Queen's *l.* breast 1789, 47

LONGER.
The *l.* I heard, I esteemed *C.* 21
His birthright shaken, and no *l.* clear *Con.* 765
No *l.* Levites, and their lineage lost *Ex.* 264
The Sacred Book no *l.* suffers wrong *H.* 449
The world, no *l.* thy abode, not thee *J.T.* 10
Deem our nation brutes no *l. N.C.* 49
No *l.* give an image all thine heart *R.* 276
To bid Affliction's eye no *l.* stream *S.* ii 12
And covet *l.* woe ? *St.* v 20
Then anxious to be *l.* spared *St.* v 25
Or charmed me young, no *l.* young I find *T.* i 142
A *l.* respite, unaccomplished yet *T.* ii 67
A wooden one, so we, no *l.* taught *T.* ii 575
No *l.* blushing for her awkward load *T.* iv 551
But violence can never *l.* sleep *T.* v 204
Which whoso sees no *l.* wanders lost *T.* v 847
A *l.* date to the far nobler beast *T.* vi 529
Till Reason, now no *l.* overawed *Tir.* 187
No *l.* takes, as once, with fearless ease *Tir.* 569

LONGEST.
What *l.* binds the closet, forms secure *T.* iii 480
That flutters least is *l.* on the wing *T.* vi 931

LONGITUDE.
Mine, spindling into *l.* immense *T.* v 11

LONG-SURVIVING.
Lord of the woods, the *l.* oak *T.* i 313

LONG-TIME.
L. a breeding-place they sought *A Tale* 21

LOOK.
To *l.* at him who formed us and redeemed *Ch.* 579
His wit invites you by his *l.* to come *Con.* 303

And yet, God knows,*l.* human nature through *Con.*749
Such drunken reelings, have an awkward *l. Con.* 862
He did it with a jealous *l. Ep.* ii 11
All speak her happy :—let the Muse *l.* round *Ex.* 27
And the most favoured land, *l.* where we may *Ex.* 221
Kiss the book's outside, who ne'er *l.* within *Ex.* 389
Where shall a teacher *l.,* in days like these *Ex.* 450
" L. to the poor ; the simple and the plain *Ex.* 452
So Jealousy *l.* forth distressed *F.* 80
Or pride can *l.* at with indifferent eyes *H.* 52
The little Greeks *l.* trembling at the scales *H.* 195
A transport glows in all he *l.* and speaks *H.* 726
Transforms thy smiles to *l.* of woe *M.* 47
Will never *l.* one hair the worse " *M.F.* 24
Dismissed with grave, not haughty *l. Mrs. M—* 38
The *l.* and gestures of their griefs and fears *N.A.* 67
You speak very fine, and you *l.* very grave *P.A.* 29
With hopeless wish one *l.* and lingers *P.B.* 33 [129
All elbows shake. L. in, and you would swear *P.E.*
L. where he comes; in this embowered alcove *R.* 283
Begins a long *l.* out for distant land *R.* 433
With aching heart, and discontented *l. R.* 471
Nature indeed *l.* prettily in rhyme *R.* 567
And *l.* on Folly's pageantry with scorn *S.* ii 8
Frown at effeminates, whose very *l. T.* ii 223
May feel it too; affectionate in *l. T.* ii 405
Decrepitude, and in the *l.* of lean *T.* ii 489
Bent knees, round shoulders, and dejected *l. T.* iv 634
He *l.* abroad into the varied field *T.* v. 738
But well compensating her sickly *l. T.* vi 163
With *l.* of some complacence he resumed *T.* vi 535
*L.*where he will,the wonders God hath wrought *Tir.*54
And seem, if judged by their expressive *l. Tir.* 288
The exalted prize demands an upward *l. Tir.* 383
L. round you on a world perversely blind *Tir.* 813
Now *l.* on him, whose very voice in tone *Tir.* 845
L. up—your brains begin to swim *Trans.* ii 10
While condescending majesty *l.* on *T.T.* 138
Is kept to strut, *l.* big, and talk away *T.T.* 233
Spoke from his lips, and in his *l.* gave law *T.T.* 245
And dared to *l.* his master in the face *T.T.* 321
The poet's heart; he *l.* to distant storms *T.T.* 495
Must hope to *l.* upon their like again *T.T.* 661
L. to the westward from the dappled east *T.T.* 706
And *l.* as if he came to beg *Y.D.* 31

LOOKED. [425

Unveiled her blushing cheek, *l.* on, and smiled *Ex.*
'Tis well if, *l.* for at so late a day *R.* 31
Curried his nag and *l.* another way *R.* 390
L. to the sea for safety ? They are gone *T.* ii 119
Or *l.* for now, the fault must be his own *Tir.* 243

LOOKING.

By *l.* on the bud, descry *E.* i 70
And stood *l.* out for his prey *M.D.* 31
When, *l.* eagerly around *N.G.* 7
Forbids their interference, *l.* on *T.* v 523

LOOM.

For the unscented fictions of the *l. T.* i 416
Through every change that Fancy, at the *l. T.* ii 608
The *l.* of Ormus, and the mines of Ind *T.* vi 806

LOOP.

Till, *l.* and button failing both *J.G.* 103

LOOPHOLES.

'Tis pleasant, through the *l.* of retreat *T.* iv 88

LOOSE.

" And flutters *l.,* the sport of every wind *A.T.* 102
L. fly his forelock and his ample mane *Ch.* 176
Much to the purpose, if our tongues were *l. Con.* 354
And wanting him to *l.* the sacred seal *Con.* 544

That Sin let *l.* speaks Punishment at hand *Ex.* 160
That flutter *l.* on golden wing *F.B.* 8
Like a *l.* heap of ribbon, a glittering show *F.M.* 6
Though *l.,* as harmless as an infant's play *H.* 613
Ten thousand thousand strings at once go *l. R.* 520
To *l.* the links that galled mankind before *T.* 185
Upon *l.* pebbles, lose themselves at length *T.* 194
But *l.* in morals, and in manners vain *T.* ii 378
And *l.* example, whom he should instruct *T.* ii 552
No *l.* or wanton, though a wandering Muse *T.* iii 692
Of fluttering, loitering, cringing, begging, *l. T.* iii 832
So *l.* to private duty, that no brain *T.* v 512
The gilded equipage, and turning *l. T.* vi 702
For *l.* expense and fashionable waste *Tir.* 204
Not more intelligent, than *l.* and gay *Tir.* 530
Extravagant or sober, *l.* or chaste *Tir.* 914 [327
Worse than the deeds of galley-slaves broke *l. T.T.*

LOOSED.

That parts us, are emancipate and *l. T.* ii 39

LORD. [109

"For British nymphs, whose *l.* were lately true *A.T.*
I am *l.* of the fowl and the brute *A.S.* 4 [193
The barb sprang forward, and his *l.*, whose force *A.T.*
" Shall mourn her absent *l.,* for he is gone *A.T.* 104
That flies, like Gabriel on his *L.'s* commands *Ch.* 135
And left them both exclaiming,"'Twas the *L.*! *Con.*534
If Israel's *L.* be God, then serve the *L. Con.* 852
L. of the conquered soil, there rooted fast *Ex.* 192
Unblest, and that the battle is the *L.'s ? Ex.* 353
Thy chiefs, the *l.* of many a petty fee *Ex.* 532
Like angels in the service of their *L. Ex.* 674
L. paramount of the surrounding plains *H.* 305
Just made fifth chaplain of his patron *l. H.* 414
Against thine image, in thy saint, O *L.*! " *H.* 593
To please her sated and indifferent *l. ? P.E.* 258
My *L.,* alighting at his usual place *R.* 585
But when his *l.* would quit the busy road *R.* 631 [51
(Such were the sins with which he charged his *L.*) *T.*
His palace, and his lacqueys, and " My *L.*" *T.* 122
Asserts the rights of his offended *L.—T.* 263
And the fool with it, who insults his *L.—T.* 504
L. of the woods, the long-surviving oak *T.* i 313
But that the *l.* of this enclosed demesne *T.* i 331
Binds man, the *l.* of all. Himself derives *T.* i 386
And strength is *l.* of all; but gentle, kind *T.* i 605
Now the legitimate and rightful *l. T* iii 749
The *L.* of all, himself through all diffused *T.* vi 221
Ungratified: for there some noble *l. T.* vi 673 [871
" Where is the promise of your *L.'s* approach ?" *T.* vi
One *L.,* one Father. Error has no place *T.* vi 784
Witty, and well employed, and, like thy *L. Tir.* 139
Your altered heart—and so, my *L.,* farewell! *V.* 26

LORDLY.

Free as the *l.* bull that ranges o'er the mead *A.T.* 61

LORDSHIP. [14

"Your *l.* observes they are made with a straddle *A.C.*
And your *l.*," he said," will undoubtedly find *A.C.* 10
" Again, would your *l.* a moment suppose *A.C.* 17
So his *l.* decreed, with a grave solemn tone *A.C.* 29
I sent you verse, and, as your *L.* knows *V.* 19 [397
Your *L.,* and your Grace! what school can teach *Tir.*
And, like his *L.,* cast thy friend away *V.* 48

LORE.

With Gospel *l.,* turn infidels themselves *Tir.* 826

LOSE.

L. in tears the far receding shore *Ch.* 147 [224
Else who would *l.,* that had the power to improve *Ch.*
Relenting forms would *l.* their power, or cease *Ch.*608

LOSE—LOT

"Adieu, dear Sir! lest you should *l*. it now" *Con*.282
L. at once all value and esteem *Ex*. 113
And he that finds his Heaven must *l*. his sins *H*. 638
The nymph must *l*. her female friend *L.R*. 1
I would not *l*. it to be styed *M.B*. 15
He will *l*. none by me, though I get a few" *P.A*. 40
And judgment drunk, and bribed to *l*. his way *P.E*.450
Secure of nothing, but to *l*. the race *P.E*. 563
Of virtue, and yet *l*. it! Wherefore hard? *T*. 12
Upon loose pebbles, *l*. themselves at length *T*. 194
One pleasure lost, *l*. heaven without regret *T*. 342
Through plenty, *l*. in morals what they gain *T*. i 625
Freedom! whom they that *l*. thee so regret *T*. ii 130
The sons of Albion; fearing each to *l*. *T*. iii 599
L. its treasure of salubrious salts *T*. iii 610
She *l*. all her influence. Cities then *T*. iii 729
And wins them, but to *l*. them in his turn *T*. iv 63
Thus oft reclined at ease, I *l*. an hour *T*. iv 302
Incórporated, seem at once to *l*. *T*. iv 678
She *l*. in such storms her very name *T.T*. 328
Soon *l*. their credit, and are all effaced *Tir*. 200
The indented stick, that *l*. day by day *Tir*. 559

LOSING.

Lay such a stake upon the *l*. side *Tir*. 863
And some wits flag through fear of *l*. it *T.T*. 521
Who *l*., or supposing lost 1789, 50

LOSS.

All speakers, yet all language at a *l*. *H*. 345
To prove that without Christ all gain is *l*. *H*. 631
So down he came; for *l*. of time *J.G*. 53
Yet *l*. of pence, full well he knew *J.G*. 55
The *l*. was his alone *M*. i 10
O'er Murray's *l*. the Muses wept *M*. ii 5
Bewildered once, must he bewail his *l*. *P.E*. 612
That purity, whose *l*. was *l*. of all *T*. iii 84
Compensating his *l*. with added hours *T*. iv 134
Of rural scenes, compensating his *l*. *T*. iv 768
And pity for her *l*. But that's a cause *T*. v 370
To France than all her *l*. and defeats *T*. v 380 [457
With all thy *l*. of empire, and though squeezed *T*. v
Would not reproach me with the *l*. I felt *T*. v 490
Fortune and dignity; the *l*. of all *T*. v 602
To meaner music, and not suffer *l*. *T*. vi 750
As God's expedient to retrieve his *l*. *Tir*. 166
With *l*. of what she least could spare 1789, 38

LOST.

" The marriage bond has *l*. its power to bind *A.T*.101
In hopes to gain, what else I must have *l*. *Ch*. 630
With one he stumbled on, and *l*. his walk *Con*. 280
Recovering what we *l*. we know not how *Con*. 402
That in the valley of decline are *l*. *Con*. 636
Now wantoned *l*. in flags and reeds *D.W*. 9
But ah! 'tis *l*. as soon as found *E*. iv 58
For then he *l*. his fear *Ep*. ii 26
No longer Levites, and their lineage *l*. *Ex*. 264 [579
"What tidings?" and the surge replied, "All *l*.!" *Ex*.
Youth *l*. in dissipation, we deplore *H*. 23
When captivating lusts have *l*. their power *H*. 216
Both may be *l*., yet each in his own way *H*. 277
Was—welladay, the title page was *l*. *H*. 428
If then, just then, all thoughts of mercy *l*. *H*. 722
Or all the toil is *l*. *H.F*. 24
He *l*. them sooner than at first *J.G*. 211
And, next, commemorating worthies *l*. *J.T*. 3
To urge the fruitless chase be *l*. *Mor*. 42
Affectionate, a mother *l*. so long *M.P*. 14 [*M.P*. 103
Sails ripped, seams opening wide, and compass *l*.
And being *l*., perhaps, and wandering wide *N.A*. 97
Remarks two loiterers that have *l*. their way *P.E*. 386
L., till he tune them, all their power and use *R*. 330
In Freedom *l*. so long, now repossessed *R*. 410

The spot he loved has *l*. the power to please *R*. 466
Pants to be told of battles won or *l*. *R*. 476
Lucrative offices are seldom *l*. *R*. 611
L. by abandoning her own relief *R*. 758
That whatsoever thing is *l*. *R.C*. 96
Has *l*. its beauties and its powers *S*. 16
His ship half foundered, and his compass *l*. *T*. 2
Despise the plain direction, and are *l*. *T*. 33
For though the Pope has *l*. his interest here *T*. 289
He, *l*. in errors his vain heart prefers *T*. 335
One pleasure *l*., lose heaven without regret *T*. 342
Restore to man the glories he has *l*. *T*. 398
" And is the soul indeed so *l*."—she cries *T*. 479
Ten thousand sages *l*. in endless woe *T*. 517
There, *l*. behind a rising ground, the wood *T*. i 305
By short transition we have *l*. his glare *T*. i 336
L. nothing by comparison with ours? *T*. i 648
True, we have *l*. an empire—let it pass *T*. ii 263
That *l*. in his own musings, happy man! *T*. ii 301
L. favour back again, and closed the breach *T*. ii 724
And specious semblances have *l*. their use *T*. iii 107
Each in his own delusions; they are *l*. *T*. iii 125
Has made at last familiar; she has *l*. *T*. iii 339
Distempered, or has *l*. prolific powers *T*. iii 415
And purified, rejoices to have *l*. *T*. iii 500
L. innocence, or cancel follies past *T*. iii 678
In which all comprehension wanders *l*. *T*. iv 75
Has *l*. its terrors ere it reaches me *T*. iv 101 [301
Were tasked to his full strength, absorbed and *l*. *T*. iv
There sit, involved and *l*. in curling clouds *T*. iv 472
Is seen no more. The character is *l*.! *T*. iv 539
But with his clumsy port the wretch has *l*. *T*. iv 650
The joy half *l*., because not sooner found *T*. iv 717
For a *l*. world in solitude and verse *T*. iv 730
The streams are *l*. amid the splendid blank *T*. v 96
Of his *l*. bees to her maternal ear *T*. v 137
And if I must bewail the blessing *l*. *T*. v 485
In the *l*. kind, extracting from the lips *T*. v 701
Which whoso sees no longer wanders *l*. *T*. v 847
From thee departing, they are *l*., and rove *T*. v 898
Of poetry not *l*., if verse of mine *T*. vi 726 [*T*. vi 146
Shall boast new charms, and more than they have *l*.
A quickness, which in later life is *l*. *Tir*. 110
What sums he *l*. at play, and how he sold *Tir*. 330
Feels all his happiest privileges *l*. *Tir*. 574
Of filial frankness *l*., and love grown faint *Tir*. 588
L. without thee the ennobling powers of verse *T.T*.291
Bespeaks a land, once Christian, fallen and *l.T.T*.428
And view with tears the expected harvest *l*. *V*. 57
And one of pigs that he has *l*. *Y.D*. 55
Who losing, or supposing *l*. 1789, 50

LOT.

And reconciles man to his *l*. *A.S*. 56
" Feel all the meanness of your slavish *l*. *A.T*. 112
Oh fond attempt to give a deathless *l*. *B.B*. 1
May it still be her *l*. to possess *C*. 43
Ah! be not sad, although thy *l*. be cast *E*. ii 41
That fed the flocks and herds of wealthy *L*. *Ex*. 419
Compliance with his will your *l*. ensures *H*. 326
Of all it ever was my *l*. to read *H*. 425
And yet our *l*. is given us in a land *H*. 439
And should my future *l*. be cast *M*. 49
In common to the *l*. of all *M.F*. 42
I learned at last submission to my *l*. *M.P*. 44
Beyond the happiest *l*. *O*. i 22
That never ought to be the *l*. of man *P.E*. 603
'Tis wild good nature's never failing *l*. *R*. 582
And oh! that humble as my *l*. *St*. i 29
That, soon or late, death also is your *l*. *St*. ii 35
Hard *l*. of man, to toil for the reward *T*. 11
Receives no praise, but though her *l*. be such *T*. 325
Possess for me their undisputed *l*. *T*. 527

From rickets and distortion, else our *l. T.* ii 592
With eyes of anguish, execrate their *l. T.* ii 665
Against the law of love, to measure *l. T.* iv 337
'Tis therefore, many whose sequestered *l. T.* v 522
God drave asunder, and assigned their *l. T.* v 198
And dint of genius, to an affluent *l. T.T.* 677
And scorn thy present *l. The Doves* 32
Kings, then at last, have but the *l.* of all *T.T.* 107
The great and little of thy *l.*, thy growth *Y.O.* 87

LOTHARIO.
L. cries, "What philosophic stuff! *H.* 28

LOTION.
Her form with dress and *l.* they repair *P.E.* 299

LOUD.
If lawyer, *l.* whatever cause he plead *H.* 201
As *l.* as he could bawl *J.G.* 112
Did sing most *l.* and clear *J.G.* 204
Sordid as active, ignorant as *l. R.* 22
The *l.* demand, from year to year the same *R.* 709
In still repeated circles screaming *l. T.* 204 [iii 740
And thundering *l.*, with his ten thousand wheels ? *T.*
Thrown up by wintry torrents roaring *l. T.* i 14
These speak a *l.* memento. Yet even these *T.* i 482
L. when they beg, dumb only when they steal *T.* i 573
And the *l.* laugh—I long to know them all *T.* iv 33
And while the bubbling and *l.* hissing urn *T.* iv 38
And he that kneads the dough; all *l.* alike *T.* iv 477
Designed by *l.* declaimers on the part *T.* v 498
That scruple checks him. Riot is not *l. T.* v 614
A *l.* Hosanna sent from all thy works *T.* v 888
Now pealing *l.* again, and louder still *T.* vi 9 [490
The strings are swept with such a power, so *l. T.T.*
Urged *l.* a claim to be rehearsed 1789, 14

LOUDER.
A *l.* voice than yours I heard *B.R.* 3
Now pealing loud again, and *l.* still *T.* vi 9

LOUDEST.
(For stormy troubles *l.* roar *Mrs. M—* 47
Heedless of his *l.* lay *St.* iv 3
Be *l.* in their praise who do no more *T.* ii 314 [650
"Nay—conduct hath the *l.* tongue. The voice *T.* v

LOUDLY.
L. resent the stranger's freedom there *H.* 354
These call him *l.* to pursuit of more *P.E.* 50
And *l.* wondering at the sudden change *T.* iv 451

LOUT.
If after all, some headstrong hardy *l. H.* 314

LOVE.
Society, Friendship, and *L.—A.S.* 17
As ever earned a lady's *l.* in fight *A.T.* 2
'Tis thus the tenderness that *l.* inspires *A.T.* 29
They wept the wrongs of honourable *l. A.T.* 98
L. graced the theme, and harmony the song *A.T.* 198
Of never-failing *l. A Tale* 52
Instruct us how to *l.* ! *A Tale* 80
'Tis Nature alone that we *l. C.* 36
Whether we name thee Charity or *L.—Ch.* 3 [46
Through fear, not *l.*; and Heaven abhors the fee *Ch.*
A herald of God's *l.* to pagan lands *Ch.* 136
Of her he *l.*, and never can forget *Ch.* 146
Can quell the *l.* of freedom in a horse *Ch.* 172
And *L.* Divine has paid one price for all *Ch.* 205
The occasion of transmuting fear to *l.* ? *Ch.* 225
While Gratitude and *L.* made service sweet *Ch.* 233
Whose *L.* knew no beginning, knows no end *Ch.* 400
The Truth she *l.* a sightless world blaspheme *Ch.* 416
Not less effectual than what *L.* bestows *Ch.* 483
Implies no trespass against *L.* Divine) *Ch.* 488

Unless a *l.* of virtue light the flame *Ch.* 491
Perhaps, enchanted with the *l.* of fame *Ch.* 539
Nor spring from *l.* to God, or *l.* to man *Ch.* 560
Fed by the *L.* from which it rose at first *Ch.* 574
Spreads wide her arms of universal *l. Ch.* 596 [604
Were *L.*, in these the world's last doting years *Ch.*
A vehicle of virtue, truth, and *l. Ch.* 624
The emphatic speaker dearly *l.* to oppose *Con.* 269
An absent friend's fidelity and *l. Con.* 308
Fruits of his *l.* and wonders of his might *Con.* 473
That man should *l.* his Maker, and that fire *Con.* 483
That *l.* of Christ in all its quickening power *Con.* 562
To supplicate his mercy, *l.* his ways *Con.* 661
Concludes his unfeigned *l.* of him, a feint *Con.* 748
And all her *l.* of God a groundless claim *Con.* 781
To show a *l.* as prompt as thine *D.W.* 43
By long fidelity and *l. E.* i 104
How slow to learn the dictates of his *l. E.* ii 20
Those breathed from lips of everlasting *l. E.* ii 30
As if not *L.*, but Wrath, had brought Him down *Ex.* 132
So rich an interest in Almighty *l.* ? *Ex.* 166 [187
Their leader armed with meekness, zeal, and *l. Ex.*
Their usefulness ensured by zeal and *l. Ex.* 443
Hour after hour, thy gratitude and *l. Ex.* 561
Their *l.* is so precarious *F.* 114
Designed, in honour of his endless *l. H.* 121 [135
His names of wisdom, goodness, power, and *l. H.*
Incurs resentment for the *l.* he shows *H.* 285
L. is not pedler's trumpery, bought and sold *H.* 320
Because the deed, by which his *l.* confirms *H*, 324
Can see his *l.*, though secret evil lurks *H.* 544
Paul's *l.* of Christ, and steadiness unbribed *H.* 580
And all the *l.* of the beloved John *H.* 625
Friendship and *L.* seem tenderly at strife *H.* 680
To him whose works bespeak his nature, *L.—J.T.* 46
Some *l.* a concert or a race *L.W.* 31
And still to *l.*, though pressed with ill *M.* 41
The *L.* that cheers life's latest stage *M.F.* 49
Shows *L.* to be a mere profession *M.F.* 60
The jocund *L.* in Hymen's band *Miss —* 73
Whate'er you wish or *l.*, *Miss —* 96
Thy constant flow of *l.*, that knew no fall *M.P.* 65
In wedded *l.* already blest *N.Y.G.* 11
By pity, sympathy, and *l. P.* 62
If *L.* reward him, or if Vengeance strike *P.E.* 31
L. makes the music of the blest above *P.E.* 77
Heaven's harmony is universal *l. P.E.* 78 [140
L., joy, and peace make harmony more meet *P.E.*
That virtue has a title to your *l. P.E.* 248
Assembled on affairs of *l. P.T.* 14
How much the object of her *l. Q.V.* 31
Save *l.* of George alone *Q.V.* 64
Remind him of his Maker's power and *l. R.* 30 [164
Sealed with his signet whom they serve and *l. R.*
The *l.* of change that lives in every breast *R.* 171
So *L.*, that clings around the noblest minds *R.* 235
And forms it to the taste of her he *l. R.* 238
The *l.* of virtue, and the fear of God! *R.* 730
'Tis *l.* like his that can alone defeat *R.* 781
But *l.* of-change, it seems, has place *R.C.* 21
His *l.*, as best we may *St.* vi 6
Or, if a chain, the golden one of *l. T.* 188
Has he a world of gratitude and *l.* ? *T.* 208
The work of generous *l.* and filial fear *T.* 226
Shows them the shortest way to life and *l. T.* 371
O that unwelcome voice of heavenly *l. T.* 463
Some *l.* of virtue, and some power to praise *T.* 486
The atonement a Redeemer's *l.* has wrought *T.* 505
He bids him glow with unremitting *l. T.* 557 [446
Fast locked in mine, with pleasure such as *L.—T.* i
Reproach their owner with that *l.* of rest *T.* i 394
To which he forfeits even the rest he *l. T.* i 395
The *l.* of Nature, and the scenes she draws *T.* i 412

LOVE—LOVER

Themselves *l.* life, and cling to it, as he *T.* i 483
They *l.* it, and yet loathe it ; fear to die *T.* i 485
Not senseless of its charms, what still we *l. T.* i 516
A serving-maid was she, and fell in *l. T.* i 537
Thee, gentle savage! whom no *l.* of thee *T.* i 633
And brethren in calamity should *l. T.* ii 74 [*T.* ii 209
Shall be constrained to *l.* thee. Though thy clime
England, with all thy faults, I *l.* thee still *T.* ii 206
Reflect dishonour on the land I *l. T.* ii 224 [*T.* ii 230
And *l.* when they should fight; when such as these
By infidelity and *l.* o' the world *T.* ii 389 [ii 543
Preach it who might. Such was their *l.* of truth *T.*
With show of *l.*, at least with hopeful proof *T.* ii 558
Paternal sweetness, dignity, and *l. T.* ii 708
And mortifies the liberal hand of *l. T.* ii 757
And finding in the calm of truth-tried *l. T.* iii 56
That feels for injured *l.*! but I disdain *T.* iii 66
In the pure fountain of eternal *l. T.* iii 244 [320
They *l.* the country, and none else, who seek *T.* iii
Thine unsuspecting gratitude and *l. T.* iii 348
Who *l.* a garden, *l.* a greenhouse too *T.* iii 566 [619
Would spare, that *l.* them, offices like these ?) *T.* iii
Scenes that I *l.*, and with regret perceive *T.* iii 710
Abandoned as unworthy of our *l. T.* iii 731
A moment's operation on his *l. T.* iii 793
Much that I *l.*, and more that I admire *T.* iii 838
I *l.* thee, all unlovely as thou seem'st *T.* iv 128
Exciting oft our gratitude and *l. T.* iv 182
Fruits of omnipotent eternal *l. T.* iv 188
That I, and mine, and those we *l.*, enjoy *T.* iv 193
Against the law of *l.*, to measure lots *T.* iv 337
Nor comfort else, but in their mutual *l. T.* iv 406
And wrongs the woman he has sworn to *l.*! *T.* iv 465
'Tis born with all: the *l.* of Nature's works *T.* iv 731
We too are friends to loyalty. We *l. T.* v 331
The king who *l.* the law, respects his bounds *T.* v 332
Mark now the difference, ye that boast your *l. T.* v 346
We *l.* the man ; the paltry pageant you *T.* v 348
Our *l.* is principle, and has its root *T.* v 353
Where *l.* is mere attachment to the throne *T.* v 331
Yet being free, I *l.* thee : for the sake *T.* v 473
Where private was not ? Can he *l.* the whole *T.* v 503
Who *l.* no part ? He be a nation's friend *T.* v 504
Not so the labours of his *l.* : they shine *T.* v 570
By weakness, and hostility by *l. T.* v 703
With worthy thoughts of that unwearied *L.*—*T.* v 752
" *L.* kindles as I gaze. I feel desires *T.* v 842
Made such by thee, we *l.* thee for that cause *T.* v 881
Was but the graver countenance of *l. T.* vi 32 [324
To *l.* and friendship both, that is not pleased *T.* vi
And own, the law of universal *l. T.* vi 360
All, in the universal Father's *l. T.* vi 449 [588
Ye, therefore, who *l.* mercy, teach your sons *T.* vi
To *l.* it too. The spring-time of our years *T.* vi 589
Propitious in his chariot paved with *l. T.* vi 744
But all is harmony and *l.* Disease *T.* vi 788
With lean performance ape the work of *L.*! *T.* vi 854
Dipped in the fountain of eternal *l. T.* vi 863 [885
Blind, and in *l.* with darkness! Yet e'en these *T.* vi
And heard the voice of *l. The Doves* 6
Opposed against the pleasures Nature *l.*! *Tir.* 170
And some street-pacing harlot his first *l. Tir.* 217
We *l.* the playplace of our early days *Tir.* 297
Of *l.* by absence chilled into respect *Tir.* 576
Of filial frankness lost, and *l.* grown faint *Tir.* 588
The force of discipline when backed by *l. Tir.* 681
That any thing but vice could win thy *l. Tir.* 742
With close fidelity and *l.* unfeigned *T.T.* 73
But he that *l.* him has no need to feign *T.T.* 90
To doubt the *l.* his favourites may pretend *T.T.* 159
Patriots, who *l.* good places at their hearts *T.T.* 191
'Tis found as everlasting as his *l. T.T.* 595 [*T.T.* 461
But nothing scares them, from the course they *l.*

Inspires the song, and that his name is *L.*—*T.T.* 739
As that of true fraternal *l. U.* 12
That sanguine inexperience *l.* to make *V.* 56
A thousand ways the force of genuine *l. V.* 62
Faithless alike in friendship and in *l. V.* 72
Such Mary's true *l.*, that has lived *W.N.* 19 [154
With *l.* and wisdom, rendered back to heaven *Y.O.*

LOVED.

He *l.* them both, but both in vain *Cast.* 11
While Cook is *l.* for savage lives he saved *Ch.* 39
For Africa's once *l.*, benighted shore *Ch.* 241 [511
They spake of him they *l.*, of him whose life *Con.*
But to treat justly what he *l.* so well *Con.* 624
Whereon he *l.* to bound *Ep.* ii 22
Returned them happy to the land they *l. Ex.* 76
He *l.* the world that hated him : the tear *H.* 574
To hold the liquor that she *l. J.G.* 67
And *l.* a timely joke *J.G.* 170
Reviled and *l.*, renounced and followed *L.W.* 33
So little to be *l.*, and thou so much *M.P.* 85
And thy *l.* consort on the dangerous tide *M.P.* 98
Whate'er I *l.* before *O.* ii 21
Men *l.* their own productions long ago *P.E.* 527
Was *l.* by all beside *Q.V.* 32
The spot he *l.* has lost the power to please *R.* 436
Lived in his saddle, *l.* the chase, the course *R.* 577
He hated, hoped, and *l. St.* iii 22
For I have *l.* the rural walk through lanes *T.* i 109
Of thorny boughs: have *l.* the rural walk *T.* i 112
And all were swift to follow whom all *l. T.* ii 251
Was sacred, and was honoured, *l.*, and wept *T.* ii 786
Thee too enamoured of the life I *l. T.* iv 718
And for a time ensure, to his *l.* land *T.* v 716
We *l.*, but not enough, the gentle hand *T.* vi 37
They fear'd, and as his perfect image *l. T.* vi 400
I disregard as much as once I *l. V.* 8
L. not the light, but, gloomy, into gloom *Y.O.* 14

LOVE-DITTY.

His long *l.* for my near approach *T.* vi 309

LOVELIER.

But Nature's works far *l.* I admire *T.* i 421

LOVELIEST.

Earth seems a garden in its *l.* dress *Her.* 57
The richest scenery and the *l.* forms *T.* i 711
Still wants a grace, the *l.* it could show *T.* iii 782

LOVELY.

Beheld with joy the *l.* scene defaced *Ex.* 426
Sweet scent, or *l.* form, or both combined *H.* 290
Appeared two *l.* foes *L.R.* 6
And still more *l.* in my sight *M.* 26
With me is to be *l.* still *M.* 49
But *l.* Spring peeps o'er his head *N.* 15
And woman, *l.* woman, does the same *P.E.* 274
Nature assuming a more *l.* face *R.* 357
Scrawled upon glass Miss Bridget's *l.* name *T.* 156
L. indeed the mimic works of Art *T.* i 420
Prospects, however *l.*, may be seen *T.* i 509
How *l.*, and the moral sense how sure *T.* v 673
Among her *l.* works with a secure *T.* vi 722 [654
Would make him—what some *l.* boys have been *Tir.*
Thus *l.* halcyons dive into the main *T.T.* 566

LOVER.

Nor soft enough to suit a *l.'s* tongue *A.T.* 20
That fills the listening *l.* with delight *Con.* 446
Where Venus hears the *l.'s* tender vow *Con.* 824
The *L.* too shuns business and alarms *R.* 219
And *l.*, of all creatures, tame or wild *R.* 251

With transports such as favoured *l*. feel *T*. iv 721
From labour; and the *l*., who has chid *T*. v 412

LOVEST.
Upheld by two; yet still thou *l*. *M*. 39

LOVING.
If a man must be scolded for *l*. his own *A.T*. ii 12
Yet parent of this *l*. pair *A Tale* 67
John Gilpin kissed his *l*. wife *J.G*. 29
At Edmonton, his *l*. wife *J.G*. 141
Him answered then his *l*. mate and true *N.A*. 105

LOW.
L. in the pits thine avarice has made *Ch*. 72
The practice dastardly, and mean and *l*. *Con*. 178
Verse cannot stoop so *l*. as thy desert *Ex*. 547
His reeking head full *l*. *J.G*. 122 [*H*. 312
That all might mark—knight, menial, high, and *l*.
'Twas my distress that brought thee *l*. *M*. 7
Then, with a voice exceeding *l*. *M.F*. 29
Which breathes the *l*. desire *Miss* — 10 [*N.A*. 25
With tails high mounted, ears hung *l*., and throats
Let no *l*. thought suggest the prayer *Miss* — 65
But which, when life at ebb runs weak and *l*. *R*. 3
With handkerchief in hand depending *l*. *T*. ii 450
In the *l*. vale of life, that early felt *T*. iv 799
Careless of their Creator. And that *l*. *T*. v 587
L. in the world, because he scorns its arts *Tir*. 672
To dally much with subjects mean and *l*. *T.T*. 544
By *l*. ambition and the thirst of praise *T.T*. 591
Who, born a gentleman, has stooped too *l*. *V*. 33

LOWER.
You fall at once into a *l*. key *Con*. 329 [vi 33
Whose favour, like the clouds of spring, might *l*. *T*.
But if you please, some fathoms *l*. down *T*. 170
They sink and settle *l*. than they need *T*. v 249
He hears the thunder ere the tempest *l*. *T.T*. 496

LOWERING.
With disappointment *l*. in his eyes *H*. 2
The *l*. eye, the petulance, the frown *T*. i 456

LOWEST.
Turn downward, and the *l*. pair succeed *H*. 14
Sir Smug," he cries (for *l*. at the board *H*. 413
The *l*. first, and without stop *R.C*. 93
The licence of the *l*. in degree *T*. iv 588
Sells oaths by tale, and at the *l*. price *T.T*. 419

LOWLY.
And I must ere long lie as *l*. as they *P.F*. 14
High in demand, though *l*. in pretence *T*. 93
And *l*. creeping, modest and yet fair *T*. iii 663
And all the comforts that the *l*. roof *T*. iv 141

LOW-ROOFED.
I called the *l*. lodge the Peasant's nest *T*. i 227

LOWTH.
We sometimes see a *L*. or Bagot there *Tir*. 435

LOYAL.
The simple clerk, but *l*., did announce *T*. vi 661

LOYALTY.
Then *L*., with all her lamps *Q.V*. 5
We too are friends to *l*. We love *T*. v 331
Of kings, between your *l*. and ours *T*. v 347

LUBBARD.
Of *l*. Labour needs his watchful eye *T*. iii 400

LUBRICATE.
Meanders *l*. the course they take *T*. iv 65

LUBRICATED.
The shapely limb and *l*. joint *R*. 57

LUBRICITY.
The same *l*. was found in all *T*. v 165

LUCID.
A *l*. mirror, in which Nature sees *T*. i 701
Coincident, exhibit *l*. proof *T*. ii 374
That shows by night a *l*. beam *Trans*. i 3

LUCK.
How he was flogged, or had the *l*. to escape *Tir*. 329

LUCKLESS.
Ah! *l*. speech, and bootless boast *J.G*. 201
Patron of all those *l*. brains *O*. i 1

LUCKY.
Gives him at length the *l*. pat *E*. iv 55

LUCRATIVE.
L. offices are seldom lost *R*. 611
In *l*. concerns. Examine well *T*. iv 606

LUCRE.
Though motives of mere *l*. sway the most *Tir*. 518

LUCULLUS.
Our habits, costlier than *L*. wore *T*. ii 596

LUDICROUS.
Me oft has Fancy, *l*. and wild *T*. iv 286

LUGGING.
Each *l*. out his bag *Y.D*. 52

LULL.
To *l*. the painful malady with alms *Ch*. 448
And *l*. the spirit while they fill the mind *T*. i 187

LULLABY.
Is like a nurse's *l*. at night *Con*. 242
Exclaimed, "that me, the *l*. of age *T*. vi 506

LULLED. [6
Thus, while gray evening *l*. the wind and called *F.A*.
And *l*. by her own humdrum song *R.C*. 46
That winds and waters, *l*. by magic sounds *T*. ii 261

LUMBER.
Like useless *l*., or a stroller's song *Con*. 820
In Albion's happy isle. The *l*. stood *T*. i 58
Was *l*. in an age so void of taste *T.T*. 619

LUMBERING.
The *l*. of the wheels *J.G*. 232
News from all nations *l*. at his back *T*. iv 7

LUMINOUS.
Though fair without, and *l*. within *Ch*. 343
Could you, though *l*. your eye *E*. i 69
The gem, though *l*. before *Mrs. M*— 33
The parallax of yonder *l*. point *T*. iii 215

LUMP.
Flings at your head conviction in the *l*. *Con*. 153

LUMPISH.
And *l*. still as ever *Y.D*. 46

LUNACY.
And *l*. the verdict of the court *T*. 448
Such *l*. is ignorance alone *T*. 450

LUNG.
Of demons uttered, from whatever *l*. *N.A*. 118
That play of *l*., inhaling and again *T*. i 137
Slaves cannot breathe in England; if their *l*. *T*. ii 40

LUNG—LYRE

Should ever tease the *l*. and blear the sight *T*. iii 168
To range the fields and treat their *l*. with air *T*. iv 772

LURCHER.
And tail cropped short, half *l*. and half cur *T*. v 46

LURE.
Ye monarchs, whom the *l*. of honour draws *Her*. 41
Discern the fraud, beneath the specious *l*. *P.E.* 17
The *l*. of avarice, or the pompous prize *R*. 177
Yet deemed oracular, *l*. down to death *T*. v 863
To *l*. me to the baseness of a lie *T.T.* 85

LURK.
Suspicion *l*. not in her artless breast *Ch*. 426
A mere disguise, in which a devil *l*. *Con*. 79
Snares in his path, and foes that *l*. within *Con*. 470
Can see his love, though secret evil *l*. *H*. 544 [5
Tell where she *l*., beneath what flowery shades *P.E.*
L. in the serpent now; the mother sees *T*. vi 778
Some sneaking virtue *l*. in him, no doubt *Tir*. 244
L. the contagion chiefly to be feared *Tir*. 689

LURKED.
The croaking nuisance *l*. in every nook *T*. ii 830
No cruel purpose *l*. within his heart *T*. vi 362

LURKING.
And finds Hypocrisy close *l*. there *Con*. 746

LUST.
For making speech the pamperer of *l*. *Con*. 48
And he grown chaste that was the soul of *l*. *Con*. 810
He saw his people slaves to every *l*. *Ex*. 55
Or, waking at the call of *l*. alone *Ex*. 101
To punish *l*., or pluck presumption down *Ex*. 250
To vanquish *l*., and wear its yoke no more *Ex*. 411
Themselves the slaves of bigotry or *l*. *Ex*. 529
When captivating *l*. have lost their power *H*. 216
If appetite, or what divines call *l*. *H*. 385
And reconcile his *l*. with saving grace *H*. 605
This only spares no *l*., admits no plea *H*. 645
What then!—are appetites and *l*. laid down *P.E.* 102
Ambition, avarice, and the *l*. of fame *P.E.* 273
And relish of their pleasure all to *l*. *P.E.* 330
Flee from the domineering power of *L*.—*P.E.* 458
Hence the same word, that bids our *l*. obey *P.E.* 496
Or *l*. engenders, and indulgence feeds *R*. 644
In gross and pampered cities, sloth and *l*. *T*. i 687
Profusion, deluging a state with *l*. *T*. ii 688
By endless riot, Vanity, the *L*.—*T*. iii 812
Of elements tumultuous, in whom *l*. *T*. v 308
Of Liberty, themselves the slaves of *l*. *T*. v 499
A clear escape from tyrannizing *l*. *T*. v 579
What does he not, from *l*. opposed in vain *T*. v 599
Of *l*., and on the anvil of despair *T*. v 665 [vi 895
With conscience and with thee. *L*. in their hearts *T*.
With every *l*. with which frail Nature burns *Tir*. 65
But that effeminacy, folly, *l*. *T.T.* 394
With brutal *l*. as ever Circe made *T.T.* 629
If Flattery, Folly, *L*., employ the pen *T.T.* 761

LUSTRE.
Those twinkling, tiny *l*. of the land *B.B.* 5
The stench remains, the *l*. dies away *Con*. 678
"And thus o'er all a *l*. cast *E*. iv 77
And rival in *l*. of that *Gr*. 14
Their *l*. to his influence owe *Mrs. M*— 54

Give Truth a *l*., and make Wisdom smile *R*. 718
Of fleeting life its *l*. and perfume *T*. v 447
Who gives its *l*. to an insect's wing *T*. v 813
With such a *l*., he that runs may read *Tir*. 80

LUSTRE-BEAMING.
With *l*. eye *Miss* — 70

LUSTRUMS.
Some fifty or a hundred *l*. hence *T*. ii 579

LUTE.
"Ye fair Circassians! all your *l*. employ *A.T.* 107
Ears long accustomed to the pleasing *l*. *Ex*. 68

LUXURIANT.
As richest soil the most *l*. weeds *Ex*. 214
Shall grow the myrtle, and *l*. yew" *H*. 527
Pride has attained its most *l*. growth *T*. 115
Bore on his branch, *l*. then and rude *T*. 493
Her blossoms; and *l*. above all *T*. vi 172
If unrestrained, into *l*. growth *T*. vi 593

LUXURIOUS.
In manners—victims of *l*. ease *T*. i 625
Nor habits of *l*. city-life *T*. iv 745

LUXURY.
She strikes out all that *L*. can ask *Ch*. 103
Yet above all, his *l*. supreme *Con*. 619
A new-found *l*., not seen in her? *Ex*. 6
That Fashion, Taste, or *L*. suggest *H*. 446
The *l*. within *Miss* — 60
A day of *l*., observed aright *P.E.* 164
With indolence and *l*., is trash *P.E.* 428
Are *l*. excelling all the glare *R*. 185
L. gives the mind a childish cast *R*. 703
And *L*. the accomplished Sofa last *T*. i 88
With *l*. of unexpected sweets *T*. i 533
Grudge not, ye rich, (since *L*. must have *T*. iii 544
Wealth *l*., and *l*. excess *T*. iv 581
'Twas thus till *L*. seduced the mind *T.T.* 600
He laid his head in *L*.'s soft lap *T.T.* 678

LYING.
Whose *l*. heart disputes against a God *T*. v 568

LYMPH. [391
Sweet converse, sipping calm the fragrant *l*. *T*. iii
While summer was, the pure and subtile *l*. *T*. vi 135

LYRE.
Of his sweet but awful *l*. *B*. 36
With her book, and her voice, and her *l*. *C*. 49
The painter's pencil, and the poet's *l*. *Ch*. 106
Find the sweet *l*. on which an artist plays *Con*. 900
Though Phœbus string the *l*. *Miss* — 12
The Muses sweep the *l*. *Miss* — 84
Still as I touch the *l*., do thou expand *R*. 203 [iv 160
The sprightly *l*., whose treasure of sweet sounds *T*.
By magic summons of the Orphean *l*. *T*. iii 587 [704
No bard could please me but whose *l*. was tuned *T*. iv
Their names to the sweet *l*. The Historic Muse *T*. v 707
And idle tinkling of a minstrel's *l*. *T*. vi 1021
The Muse imparts, and can command the *l*. *T.T.* 481
He struck the *l*. in such a careless mood *T.T.* 686
The poet's *l*., to fix his fame *U*. 25 [735
Touched with a coal from Heaven, assume the *l*. *T.T.*

M.

MA'AM. [381
"Yes, *m.*," and "No, *m.*," uttered soft y, show *Con.*

MACE.
Becomes a dicebox, and a billiard *m. T.* iv 221

MACHIAVEL.
Might burn his useless *M.*, and sleep *Ch.* 613

MACHINE.
The new *m.*, and it became a Chair *T.* i 43
M. themselves, and governed by a clock *Tir.* 625

MAD.
As if Cheapside were *m. J.G.* 44
No judges, sure, were e'er so *m. J.P.* 25
Who say the mob are *m.* outright *Pat.* 19
What! hang a man for going *m.*! *Pat.* 23
Charged with the folly of his life's *m.* scene *P.E.* 88
Conclusion retrograde, and *m.* mistake *T.* iii 239
Commemoration *m.*; content to hear *T.* vi 635 [509
Drink and be *m.* then; 'tis your country bids! *T.* iv
Surpassed in frenzy by the *m.* at large *Tir.* 820 [435
"Stop, while ye may; suspend your *m.* career *T.T.*
With *m.* rapidity and unconcern *T.T.* 464

MADAM.
Take, *M.*, the reward of all your prayers *T.* 167
And how does miss and *m.* do *Y.D.* 33

MADE. [*A.C.* 14
"Your lordship observes they are *m.* with a straddle
Ye winds that have *m.* me your sport *A.S.* 33 [23
That the spectacles plainly were *m.* for the Nose *A.C.*
And *m.* her dupes see all things with her eyes *A.T.* 39
That man by Faith and Truth is *m.* a slave *A. T.* 66
M. half their maids, sans ceremony, wives *A.T.* 128
The last evening-ramble we *m. C.* 9
He *m.* at first, though free and unconfined *Ch.* 17
Low in the pits thine avarice has *m. Ch.* 72
And *m.* the mountains tremble at his frown? *Ch.* 78
So may the wolf, whom famine has *m.* bold *Ch.* 184
While Gratitude and Love *m.* service sweet *Ch.* 233
Sin forged, and Ignorance *m.* fast, the chain *Ch.* 237
And if perhaps *m.* angry, soon appeased *Ch.* 429
By softer methods, must be *m.* ashamed *Ch.* 498
Having unloaded and *m.* many stare *Con.* 230
Calls gentleman whom she has *m.* a fool *Con.* 466
And *m.* so welcome at their simple feast *Con.* 532
Has *m.* the new-born creature her abode *Con.* 754
Is *m.* subservient to the grand design *Con.* 897
And *m.* almost without a meaning *E.* i 98 [*E.* iii 37
His grief might prompt him with the speech he *m.*
My heart of thoughts that *m.* it ache *Ep.* ii 35
Their prayers *m.* public, their excesses kept *Ex.* 143
M. sure by prodigies till then unknown *Ex.* 174 [175
For them, the states they left *m.* waste and void *Ex.*
And *m.* the symbols of atoning grace *Ex.* 378
M. thee at last a warrior like his own *Ex.* 491
When persecuting zeal *m.* royal sport *Ex.* 612
By such a change, thy darkness is *m.* light *Ex.* 640
And must be *m.* the basis *F.* 57
Some blemish in due time *m.* known *F.* 146
And having *m.* election *F.* 153 [*H.* 497
What were they? What some fools are *m.* by art
Such stuff the world is *m.* of; and mankind *H.* 211
And he that *m.* had right to make the law *H.* 319
Just *m.* fifth chaplain of his patron lord *H.* 414
And *m.* all pleasures else mere dross to me" *H.* 537

He laughed and trifled, *m.* him welcome there *H.* 685
Of him whom Hope has with a touch *m.* whole *H.* 731
Which *m.* his horse's flanks to smoke *J.G.* 127
And *m.* him faster run *J.G.* 228
And, though God *m.* thee of a nature prone *J.T.* 31
Autumnal rains had *m.* it chill *Mor.* 13 [fair *P.E.* 216
Heaven blessed the youth, and *m.* him fresh and
Thy nightly visits to my chamber *m. M.P.* 58
Should deem it by our old companion *m. N.A.* 95
The sacred function in your hands is *m. P.E.* 122
M. nothing but a brute, the slave of sense *P.E.* 214
In every bosom where her nest is *m. P.E.* 240 [165
When the glad soul is *m.* Heaven's welcome guest *P.E*
The Will *m.* subject to a lawless force *P.E.* 448
Where George, recovered, *m.* a scene *Q.V.* 27
(Infinite skill) in all that He has *m.*! *R.* 52
Earth *m.* for man, and man himself for him *R.* 116
With mouths *m.* only to grin wide and eat *R.* 309
This observation, as it chanced, not *m. R.* 463
Enriched with the discoveries ye have *m. R.* 666
Had *m.* the vessel heel *R.G.* 7
Was man (frail always) *m.* more frail *St.* i 5
M. all his virtues gewgaws of no price *T.* 55
But *m.* long since, like Babylon of old *T.* 391 [29
Improved the simple plan; *m.* three legs four *T.* i
But softened into mercy; *m.* the pledge *T.* i 365
The Earth was *m.* so various, that the mind *T.* i 506
God *m.* the country, and man *m.* the town *T.* i 749
Has *m.*, what enemies could ne'er have done *T.* i 772
They *m.* us many soldiers. Chatham, still *T.* ii 245
Spent all his force, and *m.* no proselyte) *T.* ii 321
By nature, or by flattery *m.* so, taught *T.* ii 546
Finds one ill *m.*, another obsolete *T.* ii 602 [*T.* ii 198
Still wrought by means since first He *m.* the world?
Forsaking thee, what shipwreck have we *m. T.* iii 58
That He who *m.* it, and revealed its date *T.* iii 153
Has *m.* at last familiar; she has lost *T.* iii 339 [iii 645
Has *m.* a Heaven on earth; with suns and moons *T.*
That, like the multitude *m.* faction-mad *T.* iii 673
M. vocal for the amusement of the rest *T.* iv 159
That *m.* them an intruder on their joys *T.* iv 179
Exposed than others, with less scruple *m. T.* iv 457
The great proficiency he *m.* abroad *T.* iv 654 [iv 123
Fringed with a beard, *m.* white with other snows *T.*
Clean riddance quickly *m.*, one only care *T.* v 70
(*M.* by a monarch) on her own estate *T.* v 171
To a keen edge and *m.* it bright for war *T.* v 216
M. others covet what they saw so fair *T.* v 227 [239
Of virtue, *m.* one chief, whom times of peace *T.* v
For skill in government, at length *m.* king *T.* v 241
The world was *m.* in vain, if not for him *T.* v 271
And quake before the Gods themselves had *m. T.* v 292
Compounded and *m.* up like other men *T.* v 307
Is *m.* familiar, watches his approach *T.* v 423
And *m.* so sparkling what was dark before *T.* v 558
Is work for him that *m.* him. He alone *T.* v 697
And smiling say—My Father *m.* them all!" *T.* v 747
M. pure, shall relish with divine delight *T.* v 783
M. such by thee, we love thee for that cause *T.* v 881
His presence, who *m.* all so fair, perceived *T.* vi 253
The new *m.* monarch, while before him pass'd *T.* vi 353
So God wrought double justice; *m.* the tool *T.* vi 557
Who in his sovereign wisdom *m.* them all *T.* vi 587
And thou hast *m.* it thine by purchase since *T.* vi 859
Oh, had he *m.* that too his prey! *T.B.* 55 [vi 665
When time hath somewhat mellow'd it, and *m. T.*
Received his nobler nature, and was *m. Tir.* 97 [128
Who *m.*, who marred, and who has ransomed man *Tir.*

M. just the adept that you designed your son *Tir.* 237
Say, muse (for education *m.* the song *Tir.* 290
He had not *m.* his own with more address *Tir.* 582
Great lawyers, lawyers without study *m. Tir.* 822
'Tis your belief the world was *m.* for man *T.T.* 47
Vigilant over all that he has *m. T.T.* 248 [50
Who think, or seem to think, man *m.* for them *T.T.*
Stamps God's own name upon a lie just *m. T.T.* 420
That *m.* the vaulted roofs of Pleasure ring *T.T.* 625
With brutal lust as ever Circe *m. T.T.* 629 [*Tir.* 129
Points, which, unless the Scripture *m.* them plain
M. poetry a mere mechanic art *T.T.* 654 [*Tir.* 231
Transport them, and are *m.* their favourite themes
M. you a Peer, but spoiled you for a friend! *V.* 14
Born from above and *m.* divinely wise *V.* 94
Oh! why are farmers *m.* so coarse *Y.D.* 61
Or clergy *m.* so fine? *Y.D.* 62 [50
Time *m.* thee what thou wast, king of the woods *Y.O.*
And Time hath *m.* thee what thou art—a cave *Y.O.* 51
By man performed, *m.* all the forest ring *Y.O.* 109

MADLY.
Is *m.* to forget that life is short *Con.* 772
Nor do we *m.*, like an impious world *T.* iv 177

MADMAN.
Can be secure against a *m.'s* thrust *Ch.* 510
On Reason's verdict is a *m.'s* deed *Con.* 190
Shall stand proscribed, a *m.* or a knave *Con.* 476
Pushed with a *m.'s* fury. Fancy shrinks *T.* vi 513

MADNESS.
And wild as *m.* in the world's esteem *Con.* 666
And sucked in dizzy *m.* with his draught *H.* 518
And laughter sounds like *m.* in his ear *H.* 703
The sin and *m.* of mankind *P.B.* 14
Even Bacchanalian *m.* has its charms *P.E.* 56
Sorrow might muse herself to *m.* then *T.* 441
They would be, were not *m.* in the head *T.* iii 741
To *m.*; while the savage at his heels *T.* vi 422

MADRIGAL.
One *m.* of theirs is worth them all *T.T.* 767

MAGGOT.
In fly-blown flesh, whereon the *m.* feeds *Con.* 676
And suck, and leave a craving *m.* there! *P.E.* 326
By *m.* at the tail *Y.D.* 56

MAGIC.
Hypothesis (for with such *m.* power *A.T.* 91
But Rome, with sorceries and *m.* wand *Ew.* 508
And all thy threads with *m.* art *M.* 18
Then with his silver beard and *m.* wand *P.E.* 183
But other *m.* there, she knew *Q.V.* 61
The fiercest animals with *m.* charms) *R.* 254
Of other's speech, but *m.* of thy own *S.* i 14
Whence has the world her *m.* power? *St.* v 17
None more admires, the painter's *m.* skill *T.* i 422
That winds and waters, lulled by *m.* sounds *T.* ii 261
With *m.* wand. So potent is the spell *T.* ii 630
By *m.* summons of the Orphean lyre *T.* iii 587
By which the *m.* art of shrewder wits *T.* vi 99
Works *m.* wonders, adds a brighter hue *Tir.* 23

MAGICIAN.
And seemed by some *m.'s* art *Q.V.* 59
The omnipotent *m.*, Brown, appears! *T.* iii 766

MAGISTERIAL.
He hides behind a *m.* air *Ch.* 493
The *m.* sword in vain, and lays *T.* iv 596

MAGISTRATES.
Let *m.* alert perform their parts *T.T.* 311

MAGNANIMITY.
Thy *m.* in fight *M.B.* 19
Thy *m.* display *Trans. H.* 32
By silent *m.* alone *T.T.* 68

MAGNET.
Touched with the *m.*, had attracted his *Con.* 272
That his example had a *m.'s* force *T.* ii 250

MAGNIFICENT.
The song *m.*, the theme a worm! *T.* 412
Of her *m.* and awful cause? *T.* ii 232
Thy most *m.* and mighty freak *T.* v 130
And yet *m.*—a God the theme! *T.T.* 593
Slow, into such *m.* decay *Y.O.* 90

MAGNIFIED.
And *m.* beyond all human size *T.* iv 542

MAGNIFIES.
Each vainly *m.* his own success *Tir.* 476

MAGNITUDE.
Of such *m.* and weight *St.* iv 22
All distance, motion, *m.*, and now *T.* i 717

MAHOMET.
Such *M.'s* mysterious charge *L.W.* 7

MAHOMETANS.
M. eat up the hog *L.W.* 22

MAID.
"Now is the time to make the *m.* a bride!" *A.T.* 69
Made half their *m.*, sans ceremony, wives *A.T.* 128
Apt emblem of a virtuous *m. Comp.* ii 2
Adorning May, that peevish *m. J.P.* 35
Come, then fair *m.* (in nature wise) *Miss* — 13
And you, fond *m.*, approve *Miss* — 94
The *m.* who views with pensive air *P.B.* 23
"Then came the *m.*, and it was closed *R.C.* 58
Belinda's *m.* are soon preferred *Trans.* iv 7

MAIDEN.
Then sang the married and the *m.* throng *A.T.* 197
Thy *m.* grieved themselves at my concern *M.P.* 36
Like a coy *m.*, Ease, when courted most *T.* i 409
To break some *m.'s* and his mother's heart *T.* iv 656
To gaze in his eyes and bless him. *M.* wave *T.* vi 699

MAIL.
If the new *m.* thy merchants now receive *Ew.* 606

MAIN.
Thou self-entitled ruler of the *m. Ew.* 549
To prove at last my *m.* intent *F.* 139
Crossing in your barks the *m. N.C.* 44
And plough the distant *m. R.G.* 32
But was a wholesome rigour in the *m. T.* iii 82
For dissolution, hurtful to the *m. T.* iv 675
From inland regions to the distant *m. T.* v 790
But truths on which depends our *m.* concern *Tir.* 77
Thus lovely halcyons dive into the *m. T.T.* 566

MAINLY.
And anxious *m.* that the flock he feeds *T.* ii 404

MAINMAST.
Not sounder he that on the *m.* head *R.* 431

MAINTAIN.
But Fate reserved Sir Airy to *m. A.T.* 56
Man to *m.*, and such as God approves *Con.* 538
What dotage will not vanity *m.? Ew.* 628
Yet half mankind *m.* a churlish strife *H.* 322
No blinder bigot, I *m.* it still *H.* 594
She thus *m.* divided sway *Mrs. M—* 51
That Nature rides upon, *m.* her health *T.* i 369

MAINTAIN—MAKE

M. its hold with such unfailing sway *Tir.* 316
Or tell me, if you can, what power *m. T.T.* 200

MAINTAINED.
Had they *m.* allegiance firm and sure *Ex.* 207
By which the mighty process is *m. T.* vi 225

MAINTAINING.
M. yours, you cannot theirs condemn *T.T.* 49

MAJESTIC.
M. in its own simplicity *T.* 27
In nature, from the broad *m.* oak *T.* vi 250
No bard, howe'er *m.*. old or new *T.T.* 180

MAJESTY.
Would mock the *m.* of man's high birth *R.* 71
Much of the power and *m.* of God *R.* 526
A monarch clothed with *m.* and awe *T.* 405
With all its *m.* of thundering pomp *T.* iv 686
And crown'd it with the *m.* of man *Tir.* 52
The fleeting forms of *m.* engage *T.T.* 117
While condescending *M.* looks on *T.T.* 138

MAKE.   [ii 10
For a man to *m.* free with another man's wife *A.T.*
" Now is the time to *m.* the maid a bride! " *A.T.* 69
Who seeks to praise thee, and to *m.* thee known *Ch.* 9
No.—Mammon *m.* the world his legatee *Ch.* 45 [244
Some men *m.* gain a fountain, whence proceeds *Ch.*
That man *m.* man his prey, because he must *Ch.* 197
Who *m.* some rich for the supply of all *Ch.* 251
M. wisdom, worthy of the name, his own *Ch.* 350
They cannot give it, or *m.* darkness light *Ch.* 388
She *m.* excuses where she might condemn *Ch.* 424
And injured, *m.* forgiveness her delight *Ch.* 431
That brass and steel should *m.* so fine a show *Ch.* 554
To *m.* the shining prodigy complete *Ch.* 602
That Zeal, not Vanity, has chanced to *m. Ch.* 635
M. contradiction such a hopeless case *Con.* 60
And *m.* colloquial happiness your care *Con.* 82
To brush the surface, and to *m.* it flow *Con.* 102
Knots and impediments *m.* something hitch *Con.* 108
He *m.* one useful point exceeding clear *Con.* 136
The repetition *m.* attention lame *Con.* 214
M. half a sentence at a time enough *Con.* 246
But we that *m.* no honey, though we sting *Con.* 289
What *m.* some sick, and others à-la-mort *Con.* 292
To *m.* a blaze—that's roasting him alive *Con.* 334
The fear of being silent *m.* us mute *Con.* 352
Or *m.* the parrot's mimicry his choice *Con.* 449
That *m.* seas stable, and dissolves the rock *Con.* 502
Or *m.* that fiction which was once a fact? *Con.* 550
Who *m.* no bustle with his soul's affairs *Con.* 580
And purifying, *m.* it shine the more *Con.* 598
And *m.* it brightest at its latest date *Con.* 604
Mellows and *m.* the speech more fit for use *Con.* 644
And, with a fearless confidence, *m.* known *Con.* 695
M. him athletic as in days of old *Con.* 841
M. every parish but their own their home *Con.* 860
And grins with wonder at the jar he *m. Con.* 902
Will *m.* the dark enigma clear *E.* i 54
A life of ease would *m.* them harder still *E.* ii 22
M. cruel inroads in my brain *E.* iv 16
Which *m.* that Heaven, if thou desire it thine *Ex.* 687
M. Justice still the guide of his career *Ex.* 715
Will seldom scruple to *m.* free *F.* 92
And *m.* a calm of human life *F.* 134
The Saviour's history *m.* known *F.* 206
Too many, yet too few to *m.* us wise *H.* 26
To *m.* the sun a bauble without use *H.* 81
By good vouchsafed *m.* known superior good *H* 147
That *m.* superior skill his second praise *H.* 206
And he that made had right to *m.* the law *H.* 319
M. works a vain ingredient in the case *H.* 360

Who *m.* the good Creator on their plan *H.* 383
From happier scenes, to *m.* your land a prey *H.* 478
But *m.* him, if at all, completely free *H.* 646
Parent of Hope, immortal Truth! *m.* known *H.* 663
Must spring that Hope he pants to *m.* his own *H.* 709
To *m.* his balance true *J.G.* 72
" Shall *m.* your scribbling fingers ache *J.P.* 39
Thy bounties all were Christian, and I *m. J.T.* 47
May *m.* you laugh on t'other side *L, W.* 24
Each thinks his neighbour *m.* too free *L.W.* 35
" I go to *m.* Freemen of Slaves " *M.D.* 16
M. answer quite beside the mark *M.F.* 10
What shall I do to *m.* you hear? " *M.F.* 18
That humour interposed too often *m. M.P.* 67
Adds joy to duty, *m.* me glad to pay *M.P.* 70
'Gan *m.* his instrument of music speak *N.A.* 44
M. the plant for which we toil? *N.C.* 18
Who studiously *m.* peace their aim *N.G.* 36
Return and *m.* thy downy nest *O.* ii 2
The Heaven that thou alone canst *m.*? *O.* ii 14
To *m.* them grow just where she chooses *P.* 24
Love *m.* the music of the blest above *P.E.* 77
Love, joy, and peace *m.* harmony more meet *P.E.* 140
Then to the dance, and *m.* the sober moon *P.E.* 173
But he can draw a pattern, *m.* a tart *P.E.* 195
That *m.* Italian flowers so sweet and fair *P.E.* 410
Diffused, *m.* Earth the vestibule of Hell *P.E.* 465
From every hair-brained proselyte he *m. P.E.* 491
Soothe thee to *m.* thee but a surer prey *R.* 263 [67
Whose shape would *m.* them, had they bulk and size *R.*
No cure for such, till God who *m.* them heals *R.* 342
And *m.* the course he recommends my choice *R.* 388
And ignorance of better things *m.* man *R.* 503
Beggars Invention, and *m.* Fancy lame *R.* 710
Give Truth a lustre, and *m.* Wisdom smile *R.* 718
'Tis manly music, such as martyrs *m. R.* 775
The foes of man, or *m.* a desert sweet *R.* 782
M. us learn that we must die *St.* iv 36
To *m.* his precepts our delight *St.* vi 7
Of ancient growth, *m.* music not unlike *T.* 185
And, proud to *m.* his firm attachment known *T.* 219
To Justice she may *m.* her bold appeal *T.* 498
Respiring freely the fresh air, that *m. T.* i 138
If Solitude *m.* scant the means of life *T.* i 248
That palls and satiates, and *m.* languid life *T.* i 464
Beguile their woes, and *m.* the woods resound *T.* i 586
That can alone *m.* sweet the bitter draught *T.* i 751
M. enemies of nations who had else *T.* ii 18
Or heals it, *m.* it languish or rejoice *T.* ii 70
And in the furious inquest that it *m. T.* ii 135
Or *m.* his house his grave: nor so content *T.* ii 147
To *m.* God's work a sinecure; a slave *T.* ii 390
Now *m.* our own.   Posterity will ask *T.* ii 577
M. just reprisals, and with cringe and shrug *T.* ii 645
M. men mere vermin, worthy to be trapped *T.* ii 683
Feeds a blue flame, and *m.* a cheerful hearth *T.* iii 33
That *m.* a minister in holy things *T.* iii 280 [iii 432
M. needful still; whose Spring is but the child *T.*
That metropolitan volcanoes *m. T.* iii 737
And wanton vagrants, as *m.* London, vast *T.* iii 833
And avarice that *m.* man a wolf to man *T.* iv 103
Or *m.* me so.   Composure is thy gift *T.* iv 260
I slight thee not, but *m.* thee welcome still *T.* iv 266
That law has licensed, as *m.* temperance reel *T.* iv 471
As meal and larded locks can *m.* him; wears *T.* iv 642
And *m.* thy marble of the glassy wave *T.* v 134
Than water interfused to *m.* them one *T.* v. 148
And *m.* the sorrows of mankind their sport *T.* v 186
Moves indignation, *m.* the name of king *T.* v 442
That can ennoble man, and *m.* frail life *T.* v 603
" Dishonours God, and *m.* a slave of man *T.* v 643
Charm the deaf serpent wisely. *M.* him here *T.* v 671
Grace *m.* the slave a freeman. "Tis a change *T.* v 683

MAKE—MAN

He is the freeman whom the Truth *m.* free *T.* v 733
Brings its own evil with it, *m.* it less *T.* v 770
That whom it teaches it *m.* prompt to learn *T.* v 859
And *m.* the world the wilderness it is *T.* vi 53 [876
Gods such as guilt *m.* welcome ; gods that sleep *T.* v
An agency divine, to *m.* him know *T.* vi 129
M. wintry music, sighing as it goes *T.* vi 143
M. more conspicuous, and illumines more *T.* vi 175
In heavenly truth; evincing, as she *m. T.* vi 183
That *m.* so gay the solitary place *T.* vi 187
M. all still fairer. As with him no scene *T.* vi 254
Regardless of their plaints. To *m.* him sport *T.*vi 386
And *m.* the task his own. Inspiring dumb *T.* vi 474
In modern eyes), shall *m.* the doctrine clear *T.* vi 482
She *m.* familiar with a Heaven unseen *T.* vi 926
And plenteous harvest, to the prayer he *m. T.* vi 947
No polish can *m.* sterling ; and that vice *T.* vi 990
The swains their baskets *m. T.B.* 30 [*T.* vi 910
Would *m.* his fate his choice ; whom peace, the fruit
He too might *m.* his author's wisdom clear *Tir* 100
May teach the gayest, *m.* the gravest smile *Tir.* 138
Religion *m.* the free by nature slaves *Tir.* 184
Should *m.* the little ye retain still less *Tir.* 278
And *m.* mistakes for manhood to reform *Tir.* 445
Where early rest *m.* early rising sure *Tir.* 765 [654
Would *m.* him—what some lovely boys have been *Tir.*
Yet *m.* their progeny their dearest care *Tir.* 800
And *m.* him quite a wit *Trans.* iv 12
Would strive to *m.* a Paul or Tully stand *T.T.* 349
And *m.* his pupils proud with silver pence *T.T.* 509
And truth cut short to *m.* a period round *T.T.* 517
Proves that the mind is weak, or *m.* it so *T.T.* 545
M. their heroic powers your own at once *T.T.* 570
To *m.* the pitiful possessor shine *T.T.* 755
That sanguine inexperience loves to *m. V.* 56
To *m.* their payments good *Y.D.* 16
So in they come—each *m.* his leg *Y.D.* 29

MAKER.

Alike important in their *M.'s* view *Ch.* 203
At least to trample on our *M.'s* laws *Con.* 183
Had not his *M.'s* all-bestowing hand *Con.* 429
That man should love his *M.*, and that fire *Con.* 483
She mocks her *M.*, and herself deceives *Con.* 776
Thy *M.* fills the nations with alarm *Ex.* 585
Than this his *M.* has seen fit to give *H.* 601
Remind him of his *M.'s* power and love *R.* 30
Resign our own and seek our *M.'s* will *R.* 130
That builds its glory on its *M.'s* praise *R.* 210
Yield only discord in his *M.'s* ear *T.* 386
His *M.* has no beauty in his sight *T.* 414
He mocks his *M.*, prostitutes and shames *T.* ii 427
Where must he find his *M.* ? With what rites *T.* ii 514
One common *M.* bound me to the kind ? *T.* iii 209
And though the Almighty *M.* has throughout *T.*iv734
The wildest scorner of his *M.'s* laws *Tir.* 55 [88
And man would breathe but for his *M.'s* shame *Tir.*
But moulded by his *M.* into man *Y.O.* 149

MAKING.

A poet's name by *m.* thee the theme *Ch.* 14
For *m.* speech the pamperer of lust *Con.* 48
Still *m.* probability your clue *Con.* 218
In *m.* known how oft they have been sick *Con.* 312
That even a judgment, *m.* way for thee *T.* ii 131
And *m.* prize of all that he condemns *T.* ii 604
" The use of his own bounty ?—*m.* first *T.* v 639
See great commanders *m.* war a trade *Tir.* 821

MALADY.

To lull the painful *m.* with alms *Ch.* 448
This, of all *m.* that man infest *R.* 301

MALE.

But goes the *m.* ? Far wiser, he *A Tale* 47
Female and *m.*, Pomona, Pales, Pan *T.* vi 233

MALICE.

The very dart that *M.* ever shot *H.* 559
Of *m.* fed while flesh is mortified *T.* 166
A brave man knows no *m.*, but at once *T.* ii 268
And hates it with the *m.* of a Jew *Tir.* 168

MALIGNANT.

The more *m.* If he spared not them *T.* ii 158

MALIGNITY.

By no *m.* impelled *R.C.* 51

MALLET. [10

The thump after thump of a gold-beater's *m. F.M.*
With the double employment of *m.* and mill *F.M.* 16

MAMMON.

No,—*M.* makes the world his legatee *Ch.* 45

MAN.

The *m.* that's strangled by a hair *A Fable* 35
They are so unacquainted with *m. A.S.* 15
Divinely bestowed upon *m. A.S.* 18
And reconciles *m.* to his lot *A.S.* 56
But *m.*, within a wider pale enclosed *A.T.* 58 [66
That *m.* by Faith and Truth is made a slave *A.T.*
And woman trembling at the foot of *m. A.T.* 158 [10
For a *m.* to make free with another *m.'s* wife *A.T.* ii
If a *m.* must be scolded for loving his own *A.T.* ii 12
In company with *m. A Tale* 72
So much resemble *m.* ? *Beau* 20
On *m.'s* most dignified and happiest state *Ch.* 2
By various ties attaches *m.* to *m. Ch.* 16
One *m.* the common father of the kind *Ch.* 18
Wherever he found *m.* to nature true *Ch.* 27
The rights of *m.* were sacred in his view *Ch.* 28
Thou tutelary friend of helpless *m.* ? *Ch.* 42
Wherever found (and all *m.* need thy care) *Ch.* 47
And softens human rock-work into *m. Ch.* 96
And buy the muscles and the bones of *m.* ? *Ch.* 140
On *m.*, a mourner in his best estate ! *Ch.* 156
That *m.* make *m.* his prey, because he must *Ch.* 197
But marks the *m.* that treads his fellow down *Ch.* 211
Patron of else the most despised of *m. Ch.* 290 [244
Some *m.* make gain a fountain, whence proceeds *Ch.*
M. to the centre of the common cause *Ch.* 328 [324
That Heaven spreads wide before the view of *m. Ch.*
That *m.*, in Nature's richest mantle clad *Ch.* 341
For self to self, and God to *m.* revealed *Ch.* 361
As *m.* of depth in erudition use *Ch.* 392
That *m.*, if gently tutored, will not learn *Ch.* 496
Perhaps the *m.* was in a sportive fit *Ch.* 537
Nor spring from love to God, or love to *m. Ch.* 560
The judge of all *m.* owes them no regard *Ch.* 572
And slaying *m.* would cease to be an art *Ch.* 619
To every *m.* his modicum of sense *Con.* 2 [37
Would drive them forth from the resort of *m. Con.*
Some *m.* have surely then a peaceful life ! *Con.* 56
Well known, or such as no *m.* ever knew *Con.* 62
Supposed the *m.* a bishop, or at least *Con.* 71
A disputable point is no *m.'s* ground *Con.* 99
A noisy *m.* is always in the right *Con.* 114
Dubius is such a scrupulous good *m. Con.* 119 [145
Where *m.* of judgment creep, and feel their way *Con.*
Would hang an honest *m.*, and save a thief *Con.* 128
That *m.* engage in it impelled by force *Con.* 179
A moral, sensible, and well-bred *m. Con.* 193
Of all ambitions *m.* may entertain *Con.* 221
Some *m.* employ their health, an ugly trick *Con.* 311
I pity bashful *m.*, who feel the pain *Con.* 347
Till none but beasts acknowledge him a *m. Con.* 426
M.'s heart had been impenetrably sealed *Con.* 427

MAN

No—Nature, unsophisticate by m. Con. 451 [458
Whom m., for his own hurt, permits to reign Con.
That m. should love his Maker, and that fire Con. 483
M. to maintain, and such as God approves Con. 538
The works of m. inherit, as is just Con. 553 [611
A m. that would have foiled at their own play Con.
And wiser m.'s ability, pretence Con. 628
Such m. are not forgot as soon as cold Con. 630
Convicts a m. fanatic in the extreme Con. 665
Its sordid nourishment from m.'s applause Con. 672
True bliss, if m. may reach it, is composed Con. 679
That after m.'s defection laid all waste Con. 752 [683
Bad m., profaning friendship's hallowed name Con.
M.'s favourable judgment, but his own Con. 764
May Mercury once more embellish m. Con. 838 [875
For tell some m. that pleasure, all their bent Con.
And first, let no m. charge me, that I mean Con. 871
While all the happy m. possessed before Con. 895
Of m.'s superior breed D.W. 40
Far more alive than other m. E. i 10
Which busy m.'s inventive brain E. i 65
The works of m. tend, one and all E. i 79
From m. to m., or e'en to woman paid E. ii 5
I knew the m., and knew his nature mild E. iii 32
Bespoke at least a m. that knew mankind E. iii 41
Once on a time an Emperor, a wise m. E. iii 46
An honest m., close-buttoned to the chin E. iii 62
Each m. of common sense agrees E. iv 68
All m. of common sense allow E. iv 69
But m. is frail, and can but ill sustain Ex. 81
In form a m., in dignity a God Ex. 86
Rhetoric is artifice, the work of m. Ex. 136 [Ex. 196
With all that m. e'er wished or Heaven bestowed ?
That Truth and Mercy had revealed to m. Ex. 236
That, while laborious and quick-thoughted m. Ex. 316
The m. that dares traduce, because he can Ex. 432
With safety to himself, is not a m. Ex. 433
As meek as the m. Moses, and withal Ex. 444
Those holy m., so full of truth and grace Ex. 618
'Tis to believe what m. inspired of old Ex. 646
Happy the m. there seeking and there found Ex. 652
Happy the nation where such m. abound Ex. 653
But m. unqualified and base F. 2
That m., when smoothest he appears F. 23
An envious m., if you succeed F. 76
A m. renowned for repartee F. 91
Then judge yourself, and prove your m. F. 151
The m. that hails you Tom or Jack F. 169
The m. I trust, if shy to me F. 187 [21
I passed, and next considered—What is m. ? F.A.
It is an evil incident to m. F.A. 30 [36
With ease, and find them nutriment : but m. F.A.
By which Heaven rules the mixed affairs of m. H. 16
Business is labour, and m.'s weakness such H. 19
With smiles alluring her admirer, m. H. 40
M. feels the spur of passions and desires H. 55 [127
M. deal with life as children with their play H.
Bestowed on m., like all that we partake H. 117
When God and m. stand opposite in view H. 131
M.'s disappointment must of course ensue H. 132
That m. have deemed substantial since the fall H. 154
M. is the genuine offspring of revolt H. 181
To m. of pedigree, their noble race H. 237
Each m.'s belief is right in his own eyes H. 283
That m. will freely take an unbought bliss H. 335
A being of less equity than m. H. 384 [H. 366
That Heaven will weigh m.'s virtues and his crimes
Which m. comply with e'en because they must H. 386
"Fallible m.," the church-bred youth replies H. 421
The best of every m.'s performance here H. 499
Not e'en the glorious sun, though m. revere H. 501
Denouncing death upon the sins of m. H. 512 [560
The m. that mentioned him, at once dismissed H.

Reveal (the m. is dead) to wondering eyes H. 572
A M. arise, a m. whom God has taught H. 623
For this, of all that ever influenced m. H. 643 [678
This m. was happy—had the World's good word H.
Hence all that is in m.,—pride, passion, art H. 653
Say m.'s a worm, and power belongs to God H. 711
It marches o'er the prostrate works of m. Her. 22
Yet m., laborious m., by slow degrees Her. 67
Weak and irresolute is m. H.F. 1
M. vainly trusts his own H.F. 20
How in a trice the turnpike m. J.G. 119
Praising the Author of all good in m. J.T. 2
That all the true delights of m. Miss — 47
A m. once young, who lived retired Mor. 3
The real worth of m.'s pursuits Mor. 26
But m., all feeling and awake N. 9
The m. to solitude accustomed long N.A. 55 [125
By panting dog, tired m., and spattered horse N.A.
M. from England bought and sold me N.C. 5 [27
Besides the m.'s poor, his orchard's bread P.A.
Poor m. ! what a pity to injure him so ! P.A. 34 [35
Poor m. ! I would save him his fruit if I could P.A.
He shared in the plunder, but pitied the m. P.A. 44
That m. shall be my toast Pat. 10
What ! hang a m. for going mad ! Pat. 73
To joys forbidden m. aspires P.B. 15
M. may improve the crisis, or abuse P.E. 26
Say to what bar amenable were m. ? P.E. 28
M. thus endued with an elective voice P.E. 45 [103
With the same ease that m. puts on his gown ? P.E.
M., Nature's guest by invitation sweet P.E. 209
Is m. then only for his torment placed P.E. 229
M.'s coltish disposition asks the thong P.E. 360
Praise his proficiency, and dub him m. P.E. 368
For m. of their appearance and address P.E. 388
Unfolded genially and spread the m. P.E. 412 [429
While learning, once the m.'s exclusive pride P.E.
M. loved their own productions long ago P.E. 527
A muleteer's the m. to set him right P.E. 541
Thus m. go wrong with an ingenious skill P.E. 556
That never ought to be the lot of m. P.E. 603
To muse on the perishing pleasures of m. P.F. 18
An aspect stern on m.'s affairs P.T. 48
The statesman, lawyer, merchant, m. of trade R. 5
And having lived a trifler, die a m. R. 14
Where works of m. are clustered close around R. 25
Conversant only with the ways of m. R. 39
Would mock the majesty of m.'s high birth R. 71
That m. erroneously their glory call R. 100
Earth made for m., and m. himself for him R. 116
We find a little isle, this life of m. R. 148
Woe to the m. whose wit disclaims its use R. 211
This of all maladies that m. infest R. 301
He that has not usurped the name of m. R. 319
M. is a harp whose chords elude the sight R. 325
Nor guiltless of corrupting other m. R. 382
A m. whom marks of condescending grace R. 445
The m. of business and his friends compressed R. 495
And ignorance of better things makes m. R. 503
Thought to the m. that never thinks may seem R. 635
M. shall be summoned and the dead attend ? R. 654
The foes of m., or make a desert sweet R. 782
The m. who dreams himself so great R.C. 111
With twice four hundred m. R.G. 24
Was m. (frail always) made more frail St. i 5
O most delightful hour by m. St. iii 1
He was a m. among the few St. iii 17
M. thinks he fades too soon St. v 2
M. mourns his fleeting breath St. v 26
The better part of m. unblessed St. vi 31
Till m. resigns his breath St. vi 34
M. on the dubious waves of error tossed T. 1
Hard lot of m., to toil for the reward T. 11

MAN

Oh how unlike the complex works of m. T. 21
Or stabbed a m. to serve some private end ? T. 47
No—the m.'s morals were exact; what then? T. 52
'Twas his ambition to be seen of m. T. 53
What is all righteousness that m. devise T. 75
M.'s obligations infinite, of course T. 197
Forth steps the m.—an emblem of myself! T. 213
Mercy is infinite, and m. is weak T. 294
That question has its answer—What is m.? T. 382
Restore to m. the glories he has lost T. 398
But what is m. in his own proud esteem ? T. 403
What shall the m. deserve of human kind T. 429
The worst of m., and curses of the best T. 434
And seeking exile from the sight of m. T. 442
That m. is dead in sin, and life a gift T. 514
"Truly not I! The partial light m. have T. 521
And m. might safely trifle with his name T. 556
Of lazy nurse who snores the sick m. dead T. i 97
Beats in the breast of m., that even a few T. i 285
Binds m., the lord of all. Himself derives T. i 386
And music of the woods—no works of m. T. i 430
Of desultory m., studious of change T. i 507
Above the reach of m.: his hoary head T. i 520
Where m., by nature fierce, has laid aside T. i 594
God made the country, and m. made the town T. i 749
There is no flesh in m.'s obdurate heart T. ii 8
It does not feel for m. The natural bond T. ii 9
Thus m. devotes his brother, and destroys T. ii 20
Then what is m.? And what m., seeing this T. ii 26
And hang his head, to think himself a m.? T. ii 28
The minister of m., to serve his wants T. ii 138
Happy the m. who sees a God employed T. ii 161
His hot displeasure against foolish m. T. ii 179
To fill the ambition of a private m. T. ii 236
A brave m. knows no malice, but at once T. ii 268
That lost in his own musings, happy m.! T. ii 301
I venerate the m. whose heart is warm T. ii 372
A messenger of grace to guilty m. T. ii 407 [T. ii 512
And spring-time of the world; asked, Whence is m.?
In m. or woman, but far most in m. T. ii 414
And most of all in m. that ministers T. ii 415 [419
What!—will a m. play tricks, will he indulge T. ii
Heard at conventicle, where worthy m. T. ii 437
O Popular Applause! what heart of m. T. ii 481
He that negotiates between God and m. T. ii 463
Has m. within him an immortal seed ? T. ii 517
My m. of morals, nurtured in the shades T. ii 532
Of m.'s occasions, when in him reside T. ii 537
M. that, if now alive, would sit content T. ii 541
The brightest truths that m. has ever seen T. ii 555
While prejudice in m. of stronger minds T. ii 567
What m. that lives, and that knows how to live T. ii 618
A m. o' the town dines late, but soon enough T. ii 622
Makes m. mere vermin, worthy to be trapped T. ii 683
And warps the consciences of public m. T. ii 691
Peace to the memory of a m. of worth T. ii 781
A m. of letters and of manners too! T. ii 782
Of what is excellent in m., they thirst T. ii 790
Nor conversant with m. or manners much T. iii 24
M. too were nice in honour in those days T. iii 85
(And no m.'s hatred ever wronged her yet) T. iii 101
With other views of m. and manners now T. iii 122
A history: describe the m., of whom T. iii 141
While thoughtful m. is plausibly amused T. iii 186
And exercise all functions of a m. T. iii 199 [T. iii 221
God never meant that m. should scale the Heavens
How then should I and any m. that lives T. iii 200
As meant to indicate a God to m. T. iii 246
The m. we celebrate must find a tomb T. iii 264
What pearl is it that rich m. cannot buy T. iii 285
Oh friendly to the best pursuits of m. T. iii 290
But foolish m. foregoes his proper bliss T. iii 296
Of cruel m., exulting in her woes T. iii 336

The morning finds the self-sequestered m. T. iii 386
Cannot indeed to guilty m. restore T. iii 677
Is free to all m.—universal prize T. iii 724 [T. iv 265
When they command whom m. was born to please
And avarice that make m. a wolf to m. T. iv 103
On bird and beast, the other charged for m. T. iv 249
Of deep deliberation, as the m. T. iv 300
The m. feels least, as more inured than she T. iv 387
I mean the m. who, when the distant poor T. iv 427
His every action, and imbrutes the m. T. iv 461
M. in society is like a flower T. iv 659   [iv 559
The unguarded door was safe; m. did not watch T.
But m. associated and leagued with m. T. iv 663
And burghers, m. immaculate perhaps T. iv 672
For mercy and the common rights of m. T. iv 680
Is an ingredient in the compound, m. T. iv 732
That m., immured in cities, still retains T. iv 766
Sad witnesses how close-pent m. regrets T iv 777
Great talents: and God gives to every m. T. iv 739
Preposterous sight! the legs without the m. T. v 20
Their wonted fodder; not like hungering m. T. v 30
The cheerful haunts of m.; to wield the axe T. v 42
Because a novelty, the work of m. T. v 128
At hewing mountains into m., and some T. v 178
Because m. suffer it, their toy the World T. v 192
The seeds of murder in the breast of m. T. v 210
When m. was multiplied and spread abroad T. v 221
King was a name too proud for m. to wear T. v 242
With gazing, when they see an able m. T. v 256
And sober judgment that he is but m. T. v 265
Strange that such folly as lifts bloated m. T. v 233
Such dupes are m. to custom, and so prone T. v 299
Of rational discussion, that a m. T. v 306
Compounded and made up like other m. T. v 307
But recollecting still that he is m. T. v 335
We love the m.; the paltry pageant you T. v 343
Sterling, and worthy of a wise m.'s wish T. v 358
Not to the m. who fills it as he ought T. v 362
The sighs and groans of miserable m.! T. v 388
Wherever pleaded. 'Tis the cause of m. T. v 393
That m. should thus encroach on fellow m. T. v 435
Except what wisdom lays on evil m. T. v 449
To be the tenant of m.'s noble form T. v 455 [505
Who is, in truth, the friend of no m. there? T. v
'Tis therefore sober and good m. are sad T. v 509
But these are not his glory. M., 'tis true T. v 559
Chains are the portion of revolted m. T. v 581
That can ennoble m., and make frail life T. v 603
What none but bad m. wish exploded, must T. v 613
" Hath God indeed given appetites to m. T. v 635J
" Dishonours God, and makes a slave of m. T. v 64
But transformation of apostate m. T. v 695
So clothed with beauty, for rebellious m.? T. v 754
Of usurpation, and to no m.'s wrong T. v 760
M. views it and admires, but rests content T. v 791
With those fair ministers of light to m. T. v 816
" Distinctly scenes invisible to m. T. v 820
The uninformed and heedless souls of m. T. v 864
From thee is all that soothes the life of m. T. v 900
How gladly would the m. recall to life T. vi 42
In heads replete with thoughts of other m. T. vi 90
And all in sight of inattentive M.?—T. vi 122
Is Nature's progress, when she lectures m. T. vi 182
So m., the moth, is not afraid, it seems T. vi 211
Precipitate the loathed abode of m. T. vi 376 [vi 256
Though winter had been none, had m. been true T
Where cruel m. defeats not her design T. vi 343
M. scarce had risen, obedient to his call T. vi 348
But sin marr'd all; and the revolt of m. T. vi 368
That m. inflicts on all inferior kinds T. vi 385
Unvisited by m. There they are free T. vi 403 [426
That wait on m., the flight performing horse T. vi
Dependent upon m.; those in his fields T. vi 414

Does law, so jealous in the cause of *m*. *T*. vi 432 [478
That oft the beast has seem'd to judge the *m*. *T*. vi
M. may dismiss compassion from his heart *T*. vi 442
Fame had not left the venerable *m*. *T*. vi 492 [505
"And dost thou dream"' the impenetrable *m*. *T*. vi
(As is the course of rash and fiery *m*.) *T*. vi 542
Yet wanting sensibility) the *m*. *T*. vi 562 [597
By which Heaven moves in pardoning guilty *m*. *T*. vi
The sum is this. If *m*.'s convenience, health *T*. vi 581
That *m*.'s attainments in his own concerns *T*. vi 613
And figure of the *m*., his secret aim *T*. vi 618
M. praises *m*. Desert in arts or arms *T*. vi 632
And hang it up in honour of a *m*.?) *T*. vi 641
To buckram out the memory of a *m*. *T*. vi 652
M. praises *m*.; and Garrick's memory next *T*. vi 664
M. praises *m*. The rabble, all alive *T*. vi 694
For *m*.'s revolt, shall with a smile repair *T*. vi 746
Antipathies are none. No foe to *m*. *T*. vi 777
All creatures worship *m*., and all mankind *T*. vi 783
In nooks obscure, far from the ways of *m*. ! *T*. vi 842
Nor Cunning justify the proud *m*.'s wrong *T*. vi 844
Thy name adoring, and then preach the *m*. ! *T*. vi 887
He is the happy *m*. whose life e'en now *T*. vi 906
The *m*., whose virtues are more felt then seen *T*. vi 972
Of God and *m*., and peaceful in its end *T*. vi 999
M. yet mistakes his way *The Doves* 2
That *m*., the master of this globe, derives *Tir*. 3
And crown'd it with the majesty of *m*. *Tir*. 52
If *m*. be what he seems, this hour a slave *Tir*. 59
And *m*. would breathe but for his Maker's shame *Tir*. 88
Revere the *m*. whose Pilgrim marks the road *Tir*. 145
The *m*. approving what had charm'd the boy *Tir*. 149
Replete with dreams, unworthy of a *m*. *Tir*. 160
In infidelity and lewdness *m*. *Tir*. 209 [*Tir*. 128
Who made, who marred, and who has ransomed *m*.
Boys as ye were, the gravity of *m*. *Tir*. 272
A slave at court, elsewhere a lady's *m*. *Tir*. 423
Caught from the deeds of *m*. of ancient fame *Tir*. 645
Art thou a *m*. professionally tied *Tir*. 658
Heard to articulate like other *m*. *Tir*. 667
A *m*. of letters, manners, morals, parts *Tir*. 673 [700
Are such *m*. rare ? perhaps they would abound *Tir*.
A *m*. deemed worthy of so dear a trust *Tir*. 711
The world accounts an honourable *m*. *Tir*. 738
But courage, *m*.! methought the muse replied *Tir*. 786
M. well endowed, of honourable parts *Tir*. 836
But, being *m*., and therefore frail, he may ?) *Tir*. 896
Much of the vanities of *m*. *Trans*. ii 32
Far beyond the date of *m*. *Trans*. iii 28
Wretched *m*., whose years are spent *Trans*. iii 29 [11
Nor plagues that haunt the rich *m*.'s door *Trans*. H.
The deeds that *m*. admire as half divine *T.T*. 3
I grant that *m*. continuing what they are *T.T*. 9
'Tis to the virtues of such *m*., *m*. owes *T.T* 19
The *m*. that is not moved with what he reads *T.T*. 25
The glass that bids *m*. mark the fleeting hour *T.T*. 41
'Tis your belief the world was made for *m*. *T.T*. 47
Who think, or seem to think, *m*. made for them *T.T*. 50
M. made for kings! those optics are but dim *T.T*. 55
Poets, of all *m*., ever least regret *T.T*. 176 [120
And ask, with busy scorn," Was this the *m*. ?" *T.T*.
If all *m*. indiscriminately share *T.T*. 256 [*T.T*. 168
Thus *m*., whose thoughts contemplative have dwelt
She rears her favourite *m*. of all mankind *T.T*. 217
Such *m*. are raised to station and command *T.T*. 354
Seizes events as yet unknown to *m*. *T.T*. 498
I judged a *m*. of sense could scarce do worse *T.T*. 518
The *m*. that means success should soar above *T.T*. 548
M. lavished all his thoughts on human things *T.T*. 596
Vouchsafes to *m*. a poet's just pretence *T.T*. 699
Thus graced, the *m*. asserts a poet's name *T.T*. 714
That holds in view the good of *m*. *U*. 24
Forgetful of the *m*. whom once ye chose *V*. 3

The heart of *m*., for such a task too frail *V*. 67 [81
With him, perhaps with her (for *m*. have known *V*.
Whose noblest coin is light and brittle *m*. *V*. 96
Quoth one a rarer *m*. than you *Y D*. 57
In all that live, plant, animal, and *m*. *Y.O*. 79
By *m*. performed, made all the forest ring *Y.O*. 109
One *m*. alone, the father of us all *Y.O*. 144
But moulded by his Maker into *m*. *Y.O*. 149

MANACLES.
Exposed to *m*., deserves them well *T* v. 366

MANAGE.
But not to *m*. leisure with a grace *R*. 622
To *m*. with address, to seize with power *T.T*. 358

MANAGEABLE.
Conducted on a *m*. scale *Tir*. 703

MANAGED.
Thy soldiery, the Pope's well *m*. pack *Ex*. 518
Whose wit well *m*., and whose classic style *R*. 717
Beyond a size that can be *m*. well *Tir*. 502
Or better *m*., or encouraged less *Tir*. 922

MANAGEMENT.
Can least brook *m*., however mild *R*. 252
The *m*. of tyros of eighteen *Tir*. 220

MAN-DEGRADING.
To the *m*. mart *N.C*. 46

MANE.
Loose fly his forelock and his ample *m*. *Ch*. 176
Seized fast the flowing *m*. *J.G*. 46
He grasped the *m*. with both his hands *J.G*. 91

MANFULLY.
He *m*. did throw *J.G*. 76

MANGLED.
Their pages *m*., burnt, and torn *M*. i 9 [*Tir*. 303
Though *m*., hacked, and hewed, not yet destroyed

MANHOOD.
One proof at least of *m*.! while the friend *T*. ii 594
Then shame to *m*., and opprobrious more *T*. v 379
And make mistakes for *m*. to reform *Tir*. 445
See womanhood despised, and *m*. shamed *Tir*. 827

MANIACS.
So many *m*. dancing in their chains *T*. ii 663

MANICHEAN.
As dreadful as the *M*. God *T*. v 444

MANIFEST.
They *m*. their whole life through *F*. 112

MANIFOLD.
And *m*. results, into the will *T*. ii 164
So *m*., all pleasing in their kind *T*. iii 624
So *m*. in cares, whose every day *T*. v 769

MANKIND.
To associate all the branches of *m*. *Ch*. 84
Chain up the wolves and tigers of *m*. *Ch*. 287
And wins *m*., as his attempts prevail *Ch*. 335
And Commerce partially reclaims *m*. *Ch*. 372
M. from quarrels, but their fatal end *Con*. 174
To cheer the rude forefathers of *m*. *Con*. 454
To rescue from the ruins of *m*. *E*. ii 24
Bespoke at least a man that knew *m*. *E*. iii 41
They, and they only, amongst all *m*. *Ex*. 197
A blessing to my country and *m*. *Ex*. 727
Good sense and knowledge of *m*. *F*. 200
To catch the wandering notice of *m*. *H*. 137
Such stuff the world is made of; and *m*. *H*. 211
Yet half *m*. maintain a churlish strife *H*. 322

MANKIND—MARBLE

Throughout *m.*, the Christian kind at least *H.* 635
Seek to delight, that they may mend *m. H.* 758
M. received from heaven *Miss* — 24
That serve *m.*, or shun them, wild or tame *N.A.* 66
The sin and madness of *m. P.B.* 14
One sad epistle thence, may cure *m. P.E.* 351
Till half *m.* were like himself possessed *P.E.* 471
See the sage hermit, by *m.* admired *T.* 87
To loose the links that galled *m.* before *T.* 185
The worthless and unfruitful of *m.*" *T.* 500
He, not unlike the great ones of *m. T.* i 274
Is felt, *m.* may feel her mercy too *T.* ii 47
That holds *m.* together, to a scourge *T.* ii 687
With the vain stir. I sum up half *m. T.* iii 130
To its just point—the service of *m. T.* iii 372
Chequered with all complexions of *m. T.* iii 836
And make the sorrows of *m.* their sport *T.* v 186
Still stranger much that when at length *m. T.* v 287
Bought with His blood who gave it to *m. T.* v 546
On Noah, and in him on all *m. T.* vi 450
All creatures worship man, and all *m. T.* vi 783
A lesson for *m. The Doves* 40
M. are various, and the world is wide *Tir.* 788
That occupy *m.* below *Trans.* ii 17
To catch renown by ruining *m. T.T.* 60
She rears her favourite man of all *m. T.T.* 217
The noblest cause *m.* can have at stake *T.T.* 285
Skilled in the characters that form *m. T.T.* 705
M. to share in the divine delight *T.T.* 753
One who has known, and has escaped *m. V.* 78

MANLINESS.

He bears it with meek *m.* of soul *T.T.* 225

MANLY.

M. deportment, gallant, easy, gay *H.* 407
M. designs, and learning's grave pursuits *R.* 242
All such as *m.* and great souls produce *R.* 699
'Tis *m.* music, such as martyrs make *R.* 775
In reason, is judicious, *m.*, free *T.* v 354
His *m.* forehead to the fiercest foe *T.T.* 277
Sound sense, intrepid spirit, *m.* grace *V.* 12

MAN-MONSTER.

At sight of the *m.* With a smile *T.* vi 499

MANNA.

His *m.* from the ground, or starve and die *F.A.* 38
And fed on *m.*! And such thine, in whom *T.* iii 256

MANNER.

Differing in language, *m.*, or in face *Ch.* 21
His *m.* with his fate, puts on the brute *Ch.* 154
To teach good *m.*, and to curb abuse *Con.* 164
Our polished *m.* are a mask we wear *Con.* 166
Great changes and new *m.* have occurred *Con.* 803
So *m.* decent and polite *F.* 178
And finds the modish *m.* of the day *H.* 612
Their language simple, as their *m.* meek *H.* 764
Of *m.* rough, and coarse athletic cast *P.E.* 187
A just deportment, *m.* graced with ease *P.E.* 421
With what success let modern *m.* show *R.* 686
And keep the polish of the *m.* clean *R.* 733
The *m.* and the arts of civil life *T.* i 596
In *m.*—victims of luxurious ease *T.* i 625
Where English minds and *m.* may be found *T.* ii 208
But loose in morals, and in *m.* vain *T.* ii 378
And plain in *m.*; decent, solemn, chaste *T.* ii 401
A man of letters and of *m.* too! *T.* ii 782
Of *m.* sweet as Virtue always wears *T.* ii 783
Nor conversant with men or *m.* much *T.* iii 24
With other views of men and *m.* now *T.* iii 122
His *m.*, and with rapture tastes his style *T.* iii 228
For sanctity of *m.* undefiled *T.* iii 260

The *m.*, customs, policy of all *T.* iv 109
And *m.* profligate, were rarely found *T.* iv 523
Her artless *m.*, and her neat attire *T.* iv 536
Scenes rarely graced with rural *m.* now! *T.* iv 557
His ignorance and harmless *m.* too *T.* iv 651
Infected with the *m.* and the modes *T.* iv 693
Thine unadulterate *m.* are less soft *T.* v 465
A stranger to the *m.* of the youth *T.* vi 493 [vi 561
(Though graced with polished *m.* and fine sense *T.*
A man of letters, *m.*, morals, parts *Tir.* 673
Else coarse and rude in *m.*, and their tongue *Tir.* 831
Thence the prevailing *m.* take their cast *Tir.* 913
M. is all in all, whate'er is writ *T.T.* 542
Parent of *m.* like herself severe *T.T.* 613
The *m.*, not the morals, of the day *V.* 80

MANNISH.

Else of a *m.* growth, and five in ten *Tir.* 208

MANSION.

The winged *m.* move *A Tale* 50
To inhabit a *m.* remote *C.* 45
So he who seeks a *m.* in the sky *P.E.* 576
Some *m.* neat and elegantly dressed *T.* 250
And such in ancient halls and *m.* drear *T.* i 24
And all their honest pleasures. *M.* once *T.* iii 746
With those whose *m.* glitter in his sight *T.* v 740

MANTLE.

His snowy *m.* o'er his shoulders threw *A.T.* 202
That man in Nature's richest *m.* clad *Ch.* 341
In scarlet *m.* warm and velvet capped *M.P.* 51
Gladly the thickening *m.*, and the green *T.* iv 330
While Earth wears a *m.* of snow *W.N.* 13

MANTLED.

Darkness the skies had *m.* o'er *Q.V* 33
With woodbine and wild roses *m.* o'er *R.* 420

MANTLE-TREE.

Except in porcelain on her *m. Ch.* 460

MANTLING.

His *m.* neck with downy gold *Mrs. M—* 6

MANTUAN.

Their eulogy, those sang the *M.* bard *T.* iii 453
And ages ere the *M.* Swan was heard *T.T.* 557

MANURE.

The smoking *m.*, and overspreads it all *T.* iii 517

MANUSCRIPT.

To zigzag *m.* and cheats the eyes *T.* ii 364

MAP.

He draws upon life's *m.* a zigzag line *H.* 607
Opening the *m.* of God's extensive plan *R.* 147
O'er these but far beyond a spacious *m. T.* i 321
What is it but a *m.* of busy life *T.* iv 55
(As in a *m.* the voyager his course) *T.* vi 17

MAPLE.

Book, beads, and *m.* dish, his meagre stock *T.* 80
The *m.*, and the beech of oily nuts *T.* i 315

MAR. [272

Unnerves the moral powers, and *m.* their use *P.E.*
Ye novelists, who *m.* what ye would mend *P.E.* 309
And *m.* the face of Beauty, when no cause *T.* i 458
And slumbering oscitancy *m.* the brood? *T.* ii 774
To *m.* delights superior to its own *E.* ii 34 [80
And in conclusion *m.* them. Nature's threads *Y.O.*

MARBLE.

No; *m.* and recording brass decay *Con.* 551

Might give more life to *m.*, or might fill *Ex.* 231
The *m.* breathes, the canvass glows *Miss* — 83
And Chatham's eloquence to *m.* lips *T.* i 704
And make thy *m.* of the glassy wave *T.* v 134
No *m.* tells us whither. With their names *T.* v 727
As fix'd as *m.*, with a forehead ridged *T.* vi 268

MARCH.
A cloud to measure out their *m.* by day *Ex.* 177
The sun accomplishing his early *m. N.A.* 29
Begin their *m.* to meet thee at the bar *H.* 226
It *m.* o'er the prostrate works of man *Her.* 22
Attends him; drives his cattle to a *m. T.* iv 647
Proud of the treasure, *m.* with it down *T.* v 708
The dust that waits upon his sultry *m. T.* vi 741

MARCHING.
M. and countermarching, with an eye *T.* vi 267

MARGIN.
Their way was on the *m.* of the land *T* vi 495

MARIA.
Catharina, *M.*, and I *C.* 10
Less sweet to *M.* and me *C.* 15
M.! I have every good *N.Y.G.* 1
Oh! share *M.*'s grief *T.B.* 3
M. weeps—the Muses mourn *T.B.* 61

MARINER.
Thy *m.* explore the wild expanse *Ex.* 290
Oft pacing, as the *m.* his deck *F.A.* 19
Nor yet the *m.*, his blood inflamed *T.* i 447
Conspicuous many a league, the *m T.* i 521

MARITIME.
That no rude savour *m.* invade *T.* ii 258

MARK.
But *m.* the man that treads his fellow down *Ch.* 211
The *m.* at which my juster aim I take *Con.* 105
And bear the *m.* upon a blushing face *Con.* 349
Than rove and stagger with no *m.* in view *Con.* 864
And therefore 'tis a *m.* fools never hit *Con.* 880
And *m.* the bounds of our abode *E.* i 38 [*H.* 225
"*M.* these," she says, "these, summoned from afar
An individual is a sacred *m. Ex.* 434 [312
That all might *m.*—knight, menial, high, and low *H.*
Makes answer quite beside the *m. M.F.* 10 [76
Stamped on each countenance such *m.* of mind *N.A.*
None sends his arrow to the *m.* in view *P.E.* 570
A man whom *m.* of condescending grace *R.* 445
M. well the finished plan without a fault *R.* 551
To *m.* the matchless workings of the Power *R.* 791
Death at hand—yourselves his *m. St.* iv 11
M. what a sumptuous Pharisee is he! *T.* 59
She has her praise. Now *m.* a spot or two *T.* i 725
Of wrath obnoxious, God may choose his *m. T.* ii 156
And stands an impudent and fearless *m. T.* ii 812
Moves right toward the *m.*; nor stops for aught *T.* v53
Beyond that *m.* is treason. He is ours *T.* v 341 [346
M. now the difference, ye that boast your love *T.* v
He *m.* the bounds which Winter may not pass *T.* vi 192
But read the instrument, and *m.* it well *T.* vi 454
M. now the proof I give thee, that the brave *T* vi 509
Right to his *m.* the monster went *T.B.* 50
Revere the man whose Pilgrim *m.* the road *Tir.* 145
Account him no just *m.* for idle wit *Tir.* 726
The glass that bids man *m.* the fleeting hour *T.T.* 41
The Nations hunt, all *m.* thee for a prey *T.T.* 364
There is a time, and Justice *m.* the date *T.T.* 400 [457
And *m.* them with a seal of wrath pressed down *T.T.*
And *m.* whatever clouds may interpose *T.T.* 708

MARKED.
Who long had *m.* her airy lodge *A Fable* 25

Beau *m.* my unsuccessful pains *D.W.* 21
M. with the signature and stamp of Heaven *Ex.* 685
But never *m.* her with so just a sight *R.* 418
And some are *m.* to fall *St.* i 14 [88
Was *m.* and shunned as odious. He that sold *T.* iii

MARKET.
Quickens a *m.*, and helps off the trash *Ch.* 522
Or sell their glory at a *m.* price *Con.* 28

MARKING.
Interpret to the *m.* eye distress *R.* 287

MARMADAN.
The trumpet now spoke *M.* at hand *A.T.* 161

MARO.
And those Arcadian scenes that *M.* sings *T.* iv 515

MARRED.
Fades rapidly, and by compression *m. T.* iv 669
But sin *m.* all; and the revolt of man *T.* vi 368 [128
Who made, who *m.*, and who has ransomed man *Tir.*

MARRIAGE.
Are *m.* in its true and proper shape *A.T.* 65
"The *m.* bond has lost its power to bind *A.T.* 101
What *m.* means, thus pert replied *P.T.* 29
Births, deaths, and *m.*, epistles wet *T.* iv 17

MARRIED.
Then sang the *m.* and the maiden throng *A.T.* 197

MARRY.
"Yea *m.* shalt thou, and with all my heart *E.* iii 29
I *m.* without more ado *P.T.* 36
But proper time to *m. P.T.* 65
If John *m.* Mary, and Mary alone *A.T.* iii 1

MARRYING.
And Christians *m.* may convert the Turks *A.T.* 160

MARSHALS.
And *m.* all the order of the year *T.* vi 191

MARSHALLED.
Suffice to give the *m.* ranks the grace *T.* iii 604

MARSHALLING.
M. all his terrors as he came *T.* 547

MARSHES.
Of Tiber's *m.* and the papal bog *Ex.* 511

MART.
To the man-degrading *m. N.C.* 46 [719
In London. Where has commerce such a *m. T.* i
Oh thou resort and *m.* of all the earth *T.* iii 835

MARTHA.
Thus *M.*, even against her will *E.* i 43

MARTIAL.
He steps right onward, *m.* in his air *T.* iv 640
With melting airs, or *m.*, brisk, or grave *T.* vi 3
Playing at beat of drum, their *m.* pranks *T.T.* 136

MARTYR.
'Tis manly music, such as *m.* make *R.* 775
But *M.* struggle for a brighter prize *T.* v 718
Deny thy Godhead with a *m.*'s zeal *T.* vi 883

MARTYRDOM.
Received the seal of *m.* in blood *Ex.* 617
Prepared for *m.*, and strong to prove *V.* 61

MARVELLED.
I *m.* much that, at so ripe an age *T.* iv 713

MARY.

If John marries *M.*, and *M.* alone *A.T.* iii 1 [iii 2
'Tis a very good match between *M.* and John *A.T.*
With tortured innocence in *M.*'s court *Ex.* 613
Bids me and *M.* mourn *N.* 14
Which *M.* to Anna conveyed *The Rose* 2
My *M.*! *To Mary*
See, *M.*, what beauties I bring *W.N.* 5
Such *M.*'s true love, that has lived *W.N.* 19

MASCULINE.

Or if in *m.* debate he shared *H.* 686
A mind well lodged, and *m.* of course *T.T.* 221

MASK.

Our polished manners are a *m.* we wear *Con.* 166
A shallow brain behind a serious *m. Con.* 297
The treacherous smile, a *m.* for secret hate *Ex.* 42
The *m.* from faces never seen before *Ex.* 140
And finds it a mere *m.* of sly grimace *Con.* 744 [105
But she has burned her *m.*, not needed here *T.* iii
Conceals the mood lethargic with a *m. T.* iv 229
Not skulk, or put on a prudential *m. T.T.* 312

MASQUERADE.

Till gowns at length are found mere *m. T.* ii 748
But the World's Time is Time in *m.*! *T.* iv 213

MASS

See it an uninformed and idle *m. Her.* 26 [*T.* iii 492
Slow gathering in the midst, through the square *m.*
His broad keen knife into the solid *m. T.* v 35
That being parcel of the common *m. T.* v 247
Knowledge, a rude unprofitable *m. T.* vi 94

MASSY.

A *m.* slab, in fashion square or round *T.* i 21
Ponderous, and fixed by its own *m.* weight *T.* i 59
Grew rusty by disuse; and *m.* gates *T.* ii 746

MAST.

The tree they call a *m. A Tale* 34

MASTER.

Their skill a truth, his *m.*'s a pretence *Con.* 418
Think, ye *m.* iron-hearted *N.C.* 21
He takes the field, the *m.* of the pack *P.E.* 114
M. of all the enjoyments he designed *R.* 427
Or else she learned it of her *m. R.C.* 10
Within her *m.*'s snug abode *R.C.* 34
His *m.*'s interest and his own combined *T.* 193
But by a *m.*'s hand, disposing well *T.* iii 589
Knew their own *m.*, and laborious hinds *T.* iii 747
His horse, as he had caught his *m.*'s mood *T.* vi 549
That man, the *m.* of this globe, derives *Tir.* 3
As Poll can *m.* it *Trans.* iv 9
And dared to look his *m.* in the face *T.T.* 321

MASTER-LUST.

Remorse begets reform. His *m. T.* v 618

MASTER-SPRING.

As if one *m.* controlled them all *T.* iv 203

MASTER-STROKES.

His *m.*, and draw from his design *T.* ii 398

MASTERY.

Ensured us *m.* there, we yet retain *T.* ii 274

MASTIFF.

Some royal *m.* panting at their heels *T.T.* 35

MAT.

Of dear *M.* Prior's easy jingle *E.* iv 4 [iii 525
Strained through the friendly *m.*, a vivid green *T.*

MATCH. [iii 2

'Tis a very good *m.* between Mary and John *A.T.*
It can't be a *m.*—tis a bundle of *m.*'s *A.T.* iii 4
And stirs his own to *m.* them, or excel *Ch.* 118
M., blood-extorting screws *N.C.* 30
A wrestling *m.*, a footrace, or a fair *T.* iv 626

MATCHED.

And even Virtue, so unfairly *m. Ch.* 511
M. against truths as lasting as sublime? *Con.* 548
Was quickly distanced, *m.* against a peer's *R.* 580
Here also grateful mixture of well *m. T.* iii 633 [614
M. with the expertness of the brutes in theirs *T.* vi
To meet with such a well *m.* pair *Trans.* iv 32

MATCHLESS.

In fairy land was born the *m.* dame *A.T.* 5
Weep upon thy *m.* wrongs *B.* 10
To mark the *m.* workings of the Power *R.* 791 [229
" Where dwell these *m.* saints ?" old Curio cries *T.*
The honours of his *m.* horse his own *T.* vi 438
Of *m.* grandeur, and declension thence *Y.O.* 89

MATE.

A chaffinch and his *m. A Tale* 12
They left their outcast *m.* behind *Cast.* 23
Him answered then his loving *m.* and true *N.A.* 105
Choose not alone a proper *m. P.T.* 64
More delicate his timorous *m.* retires *T.* 214
The turtle thus addressed her *m. The Doves* 7

MATERIAL.

That forms *m.*, whatsoe'er we dream *A.T.* 40
Formed with *m.* neat and soft *A Tale* 39
And bends the tough *m.* to his will *Ch.* 464
His rich *m.*, and regale your ear *Con.* 617
With what *m.*, on what ground, you please *H.* 615
With base *m.*, sat on well-tanned hides *T.* i 51
And slippery the *m.*, yet frostbound *T.* v 155
The mere *m.* with which wisdom builds *T.* vi 93
Exhausted all *m.* of the art *T.* vi 717

MATERNAL.

Ah, that *m.* smile! it answers—" Yes " *M.P.* 27
M. nature had reversed its course *T.* iii 436
Of his lost bees to her *m.* ear *T.* v 137

MATHEMATIC.

Sure ne'er to want them, *m.* truths *N.A.* 80

MATRIMONIAL.

Your *m.* plan *A Tale* 70
To keep the *m.* bond unstained *T.T.* 74

MATRON.

Whom *m.* now, of character unsmirched *T.* iii 73
With *m.* step slow moving, while the Night *T.* iv 216

MATTED.

In *m.* grass, that with a livelier green *T.* 195
Where, on his bed of wool and *m.* leaves *T.* vi 312

MATTER. [845

The change shall please, nor shall it *m.* aught *Con.*
No *m.* where, in China or Japan *E.* iii 47
For *m.* of more grave import *E.* iv 66
No *m.* if you hear or no " *M.F.* 30
No *m.* when--a poet's Muse is *P.* 23
Began to agitate the *m. P.T.* 16
Poor Jack—no *m.* who—for when I blame *R.* 575
But how should *m.* occupy a charge *T.* vi 216 [770
No *m.*;—we could shift when they were not *T.T.*
In my own ear such *m.* as I may *Y.O.* 143

MATTHEW.

That *M.'s* numbers run with ease *E.* iv 67
" *M.*," says Fame, "with endless pains *E.* iv 73

MATURE.

The sun *m.* on India's spicy shores *Ch.* 442
And like the stores autumnal suns *m. Con.* 649
Can even now when they are grown *m. T.* v 296
Thou fellest *m.*; and, in the loamy clod *Y.O.* 33

MATURED.

In peace upon her sloping sides *m. Her.* 10
And all her fruits by radiant truth *m. T.* i 607
That toiling ages have but just *m. T.* iii 450

MATURER.

M. years shall happier stores produce *T.* 495
But learns his error in *m.* years *Tir.* 449

MATURITY.

And, as *m.* of years comes on *Tir.* 236

MAUL.

Poets, are sometimes apt to *m.* the thing *Con.* 290

MAUSOLEAN.

By pyramids and *m.* pomp *T.* v 183

MAW.

With sand to scour his *m. Ep.* ii 16

MAY.

The legislature called it *M.*—*A Fable* 9
October hight, but mild and fair as *M.*—*A.T.* 71
" Adorning *M.*, that peevish maid *J.P.* 35
Then April with her sister *M.*—*N.* 17
But warm, and bright, and calm as *M.*—*P.T.* 10 [62
And as the warmth of *M.* The vault is blue *T.* vi
On the beautiful bosom of *M.*—*W.N.* 16

MAZE.

From infancy through childhood's giddy *m. H.* 187

MAZY.

Can trace her *m.* windings to their end *P.E.* 16

MEAD. [61

Free as the lordly bull that ranges o'er the *m. A.T.*
Pursued the swallow o'er the *m. D.W.* 11 [46
The yellow tilth, green *m.*, rocks, rising ground *H.*
Old Winter, halting o'er the *m. N.* 13
That murmurs through the dewy *m. O.* ii 16
Its cooling vapour o'er the dewy *m. R.* 422
And turned into the park or *m.* to graze *R.* 627
Now in the floods, now panting in the *m. R.* 538
Of spacious *m.* with cattle sprinkled o'er *T.* i 164
To gather kingcups in the yellow *m. T.* vi 302
The dancing Naiads through the dewy *m. T.T.* 693

MEADOW.

Wasting towns, plantations, *m. N.C.* 35
A variegated show; the *m.* green *T.* iv 312
These *m.* and that range of hills his own *T.* v 223
That skims the spacious *m.* at full speed *T.* vi 331
Oft water fairest *m.*, and the bird *T.* vi 930

MEAGRE.

Book, beads, and maple dish, his *m.* stock *T.* 80
He calls for Famine, and the *m.* fiend *T.* ii 185
Bestial, a *m.* intellect, unfit *T.* v 454
Perched on the *m.* produce of the land *T.T.* 580

MEAL.

Prepares for *m.* as jockeys take a sweat *P.E.* 221
How regular his *m.*, how sound he sleeps! *R.* 430
Their miserable *m.* A kettle, slung *T.* i 560
The bee transports the fertilizing *m. T.* iii 538

Of the last *m.* commence. A Roman *m. T.* iv 168
As *m.* and larded locks can make him; wears *T.* iv 642
Doom him not then to solitary *m. Tir.* 719

MEAN.

Wise to promote whatever end he *m. Ch.* 87
And wound the grace I *m.* to recommend *Ch.* 486
But still remember, if you *m.* to please *Con.* 103 [149
Without the *m.* of knowing right from wrong *Con.*
The practice dastardly, and *m.*, and low *Con.* 178
They *m.* to try what may at last be done *Con.* 833
And first, let no man charge me, that I *m. Con.* 871
Not that I deem, or *m.* to call *E.* i. 91
Not that I *m.*, while thus I knit *E.* iv 5
The fierce banditti which I *m. E.* iv 19 [*Ex.* 402
What *m.* they ? Canst thou dream there is a power
And, tainted by the very *m.* of cure *Ex.* 104
Are far too *m.* for Him that rules the skies *Ex.* 138
From *m.* self-interest and ambition clear *Ex.* 439
Or *m.* self-love erected *F.* 39
I will by no *m.* entertain *F.* 191
Taste happiness, or know what pleasure *m. H.* 10
My creed (whatever some creed-makers *m. H.* 393
Thy *m.* so feeble, and despised so much *H.* 666
That privilege was thine; Heaven gave thee *m. J.T.* 19
By no *m.* large enough; and was it *M.F.* 3
Are the *m.* that duty urges *N.C.* 31
He takes offence, and wonders what you *m. P.E.* 89
Than Vices *m.* and disingenuous race *P.E.* 297
What marriage *m.*, thus pert replied *P.T.* 29
From mighty *m.* to more important ends *R.* 112
Not that I *m.* to approve, or would enforce *R.* 117
The portion of a *m.* or vulgar mind *R.* 502
What *m.* the drama by the world sustained ? *R.* 646
Content though *m.*, and cheerful if not gay *T.* 319
And sinks, while favoured with the *m.* to rise *T.* 544
If Solitude make scant the *m.* of life *T.* i 248
No *m.* advantage from a kindred cause *T.* i 387
M. self-attachment, and scarce aught beside *T.* i 616
Life's necessary *m.*, but he must die *T.* ii 141 [ii 198
Still wrought by *m.* since first He made the world ?*T.*
And did He not of old employ his *m. T.* ii 199
Than a capacious reservoir of *m. T.* ii 201 [*T.* iii 691
Health, leisure, *m.* to improve it, friendship, peace
I *m.* to tread. I feel myself at large *T.* iii 18
To no *m.* hand, and asks the touch of taste *T.* iii 632
I *m.* the man who, when the distant poor *T.* iv 427
The most unfurnished with the *m.* of life *T.* iv 770
And destitute of *m.* to raise themselves *T.* v 248
And force the beggarly last doit, by *m. T.* v 316
"And stored the earth so plenteously with *m. T.* v636
And He by *m.* in philosophic eyes *T.* v 698
Of no *m.* city, planned or ere the hills *T.* v 764
With *m.* that were not till by thee employed *T.* v 850
Of what he deems no *m.* or trivial trust *T.* vi 607
He seek his proper happiness by *m. T.* vi 954 [406
Pressed on his part by *m.* that would disgrace *Tir.*
With just abhorrence of so *m.* a part *Tir.* 455
The end, though plausible, not worth the *m. Tir.* 487
His post not *m.*, his talents not unknown *Tir.* 723
Where vile example (yours I chiefly *m. Tir.* 761
To compass that good end, forecast the *m. Tir.* 884
He that holds fast the golden *m. Trans. H.* 7
When Providence *m.* mercy to a land *T.T.* 355
M. you to prophesy, or but to preach ? *T.T.* 479
To dally much with subjects *m.* and low *T.T.* 544
The man that *m.* success, should soar above *T.T.* 548

MEANDERS.

M. lubricate the course they take *T.* iv 65

MEANDERING.

Her wooed Sir Airy, by *m.* streams *A.T.* 11

Take of the crimson stream *m.* there *T.* iii 202
Through the imperceptible *m.* veins *T.* vi 136

MEANER.

And once more mingles with us *m.* things *Ch.* 437
To learn the twittering of a *m.* bird ? *Con.* 448
The want of both denotes a *m.* breed *H.* 292
A *m.* than himself shall gain the prize *T.* 16
And seems to say—" Ye *m.* fowl, give place *T.* 64
No *m.* hand may discipline the shoots *T.* iii 413
The ambition of one *m.* far, whose powers *T.* iii 458
With *m.* objects even the few she finds ! *T.* iii 727
The heart of merit in the *m.* class *T.* iv 618
And History, so warm on *m.* themes *T.* v 729
Proved he not plainly that his *m.* works *T.* vi 447
To *m.* music, and not suffer loss *T.* vi 750
While *m.* things, whom instinct leads *The Doves* 3
Too busy to intend a *m.* care *Tir.* 660
Next, busy actor on a *m.* stage *V.* 27

MEANEST.

" Smoothed and refined the *m.* strains *E.* iv 74
Else they are all—the *m.* things that are *T.* vi 584

MEANING.

And made almost without a *m. E.* i 98
And little or no *m. O.* i 4
With anxious *m.*, Heavenward turn his eye ! *St.* ii 8
His mind with *m.* that he never had *T.* iii 149
There forests of no *m.* spread the page *T.* iv 74

MEANNESS.

" Feel all the *m.* of your slavish lot *A.T.* 112
Patience itself is *m.* in a slave *Ch.* 164
Nor taint his speech with *m.*, designed *Tir.* 686

MEANT. [778

The doctrines warped to what they never *m. Con.*
Are insincere, *m.* only to conceal *Con.* 785
As when returning to the theme they *m. Con.* 858
But not performing what he *m. J.G.* 225
He *m.* not to forbid the head *L.W.* 18
A brighter prize than that he *m. Mor.* 55
The plant he *m.* grew not far off *P.* 17
But Granby was, *m.* truly what he said *R.* 598
That scorns afflictions mercifully *m. R.* 760
The very elements, though each be *m. T.* ii 137
Upon thy foes, was never *m.* my task *T.* ii 218
As *m.* to indicate a God to man *T.* iii 246 [iii 221
God never *m.* that man should scale the Heavens *T.*
M. it eternal, had he not himself *T.* v 562
But still in vain. The Providence that *m. T.* vi 528
Was never *m.*, was never used before *T.* vi 651
Perhaps indulgent Nature *m. Trans.* i 13 [*T.* vi 659
When wandering Charles, who *m.* to be the third
Whate'er she *m.*, this truth divine *Trans.* i 21
And never *m.* the rule should be applied *T.T.* 11
The growth that Nature *m.* she should attain *T.T.* 203

MEASURE.

To *m.* the life that she leads *C.* 48
Whether he *m.* earth, compute the sea *Ch.* 353
They fill their *m.*, and receive their due *Con.* 34
Such hard and arbitrary *m.* here *E.* iii 55
A cloud to *m.* out their march by day *Ex.* 177
Their *m.* filled, they too shall pay the debt *Ex.* 712
To *m.* all that passes in the breast *R.* 133
Not such the alert and active. *M.* life *T.* i 396
M. an atom, and now girds a world ? *T.* i 718
Against the law of love, to *m.* lots *T.* iv 337
But above *m.* strange, that neither proof *T.* v 293
And folly in as ample *m.* meet *T.* v 309
To span omnipotence, and *m.* might *T.* vi 212
That knows no *m.*, by the scanty rule *T.* vi 213
In *m.*, as by force of instinct drawn *T.* vi 412

And *m.* of the offence, rebukes a deed *T.* vi 655
Behold the *m.* of the promise filled *T.* vi 798
'Tis not in artful *m.*, in the chime *T.* vi 1020
But *m.* planned and executed well *T.T.* 386
Art has in a *m.* supplied *W.N.* 3

MEASURED.

At *m.* distances, that air and sun *T.* iii 424
His *m.* step were governed by his ear *T.* 63
Beating alternately, in *m.* time *T.T.* 528

MECHANIC.

Not as if raised by mere *m.* powers *Con.* 706
Some plain *m.*, who, without pretence *R.* 449
Made poetry a mere *m.* art *T.T.* 654

MECHANICAL.

In an engine of utmost *m.* strength *F.M.* 4

MECHANICALLY.

If guards, *m.* formed in ranks *T.T.* 135

MEDALS.

And sells them *m.*, which, if neither rare *P.E.* 399

MEDICINE.

Grief is itself a *m.*, and bestowed *Ch.* 159
No *m.*, though it oft can cure *St.* i 27
By *m.* well applied, but without grace *T.* vi 522

MEDIOCRITY.

In modest *m.*, content *T.* i 50

MEDITATE.

That thought that *m.* a brother's wrong *T.* 560
Walks forth to *m.* at eventide *T.* vi 949

MEDITATION.

Charms more than silence. *M.* here *T.* vi 84

MEDIUM.

With a new *m.* and a purer light *Ch.* 330
To find the *m.* asks some share of wit *Con.* 879
Praise is the *m.* of a knavish trade *E.* ii 6
The *m.* represents, and not their own *H.* 74
Seen through the *m.* of a cloud like thine *R.* 352
But knew no *m.* between guzzling beer *R.* 601
In the soft *m.*, till they stand immersed *T.* iii 520

MEED.

Verse, like the laurel, its immortal *m. Ch.* 292
It were to weep that goodness has its *m. J.T.* 12
Of amnesty, the *m.* of blood divine *Y.O.* 13

MEEK.

Sips *m.* infusions of a milder herb *Con.* 268   [610
Exact, yet not precise, though *m.*, keen-eyed *Con.*
As *m.* as the man Moses, and withal *Ex.* 444
M., modest, venerable, wise, sincere *Ex.* 620
A right to the *m.* honours of her name) *H.* 236
Is sober, *m.*, benevolent, and prays *H.* 520
Their language simple, as their manners *m. H.* 764
The *m.* intelligence of those dear eyes *M.P.* 7
Trembling yet happy, confident yet *m. T.* 572
His eye was *m.* and gentle, and a smile *T.* ii 706[55
For thou art *m.* and constant, hating change *T.* iii
I praise you much, ye *m.* and patient pair *T.* iv 407
Fretful if unsupplied ; but silent, *m. T.* v 31
The *m.* and modest Truth, and forcing her *T.* vi 840
The *m.* and bashful boy will soon be taught *Tir.* 338
He bears it with *m.* manliness of soul *T.T.* 225

MEEKNESS.

Their leader armed with *m.*, zeal, and love *Ex.* 187
With modesty and *m.*, and the crown *T.* v 243
He ruled with *m.*, they obey'd with joy *T.* vi 361

MEET.

And *m.* perhaps never again *C.* 2
In baser souls unnumbered evils *m. Ch.* 37 [*Ch.* 148
But not the thought that they must *m.* no more
Prepared to poniard whomsoe'er they *m. Ch.* 508
They *m.* with little pity, no redress *Ch.* 530 [601
Though all accomplishments, all knowledge *m. Ch.*
Let all your rays of information *m. Con.* 240
Visiting every flower with labour *m. Con.* 439 [694
Of joys they *m.* with in their heavenly range *Con.*
M. their opposers with united strength *Con.* 700
Impatient swim to *m. D.W.* 34
Shall *m.,* unite, and part no more *E.* i 32
A tedious hour—and now we never *m.*! *E.* iii 5
Her vaults below, where every vintage *m. Ex.* 22
Discordant atoms *m.,* ferment, and fight *Ex.* 297
The great and small but rarely *m. F.* 115 [244
"Keep wisdom, or *m.* vengeance,in your turn! *Ex.*
How freely will they *m.* and charge! *F.* 137
The youth did ride, and soon did *m. J.G.* 221 [*H.* 49
From the blue rim, where skies and mountains *m.*
Begin their march to *m.* thee at the bar *H.* 226
When wit and genius *m.* their doom *M.* ii 1
May I but *m.* thee on that peaceful shore *M.P.* 34
Farewell! we *m.* no more? *O* ii 24
Or present, or in prospect, *m.* his sight *P.E.* 48
Love,joy, and peace make harmony more *m. P.E* 140
Surprised at all they *m.,* the gosling pair *P.E.* 379
And *m.* with hindrance in the smoothest way *P.E.*443
New-raised objections with new quibbles *m. P.E.*551
No mockery *m.* you. no deception there *P E.* 618
The subject upon which we *m. P.T.* 24
Discordant motives in one centre *m. R.* 173
We *m.* at last in one sincere desire *R.* 389
Thy fame diffuse, praised not for utterance *m. S.* i 13
The jury *m.,* the coroner is short *T.* 447 [*T.* 168
Where hermits and where Brahmins *m.* with theirs
Seest thou yon harlot, wooing all she *m. T.* 507
The wain that *m.* it passes swiftly by *T.* i 297
She begs an idle pin of all she *m. T.* i 553
Swarms in all quarters; *m.* the eye, the ear *T.* ii 818
That *m.* (no barren interval between) *T.* iii 409
Close interwoven, where they *m.* the vase *T.* iii 612
And folly in as ample measure *m. T.* v 309 [*T.* iii 788
Just when it *m.* his hopes, and proves the Heaven
To *m.* with such a well matched pair *Trans.* iv 32
Virtue indeed *m.* many a rhyming friend *T.T.* 620

MELANCHOLY.

To give the *m.* theme *Cast.* 57
I could expound the *m.* tone *N.A.* 94
Gives *M.* up to Nature's care *R.* 281
A long and *m.* mew *R.C.* 88

MELIORATE.

To *m.* and tame the stubborn soil *R.* 786
And *m.* the well concocted juice *T.* 496
Reflections such as *m.* the heart *T.* iii 304

MELLIFLUOUS.

Of such *m.* tone *T.B.* 57

MELLOW.

M. and makes the speech more fit for use *Con.* 644
With her chill hand, the *m.* leaves away *N.A.* 22
The golden harvest, of a *m.* brown *T.* iv 314

MELLOW'D. [665

When time hath somewhat *m.* it, and made *T.* vi
Beneath thy parent tree *m.* the soil *Y.O.* 24

MELODIOUS.

Or with the high-raised horn's *m.* clang *N.A.* 35
Of other tenants than *m.* birds *T.* iv 574

MELODY.

The *m.* that was at first designed *Con.* 453
Fled, chased by her *m.* clear *M.D.* 22 [*P.F.* 11
And the scene where his *m.* charmed me before.
A kindred *m.,* the scene recurs *T.* vi 13
M. throughout the year *Trans.* iii 24

MELT. [229

Would heal his heart, and *m.* his chains away *Ch.*
That *m.* and fade into the distant sky *R.* 424

MELTING.

"Still may my *m.* bosom cleave *Miss* — 85
With *m.* airs, or martial, brisk, or grave *T.* vi 3

MEMENTO.

These speak aloud *m.* Yet even these *T.* i 482

MEMORABLE.

In *m.* eighty-nine 1789, 31

MEMORANDUM-BOOK.

With *m.* for every town *P.E.* 373

MEMORIAL.

A deep *m.* graven on their hearts *Con.* 514
Perhaps a frail *m.,* but sincere *M.P.* 72
A sad *m.,* and subjoin his own *T.* v 420
And some *m.* none where once they grew *Y.O.* 129

MEMORY.

And, like the graver's *m.,* pass away *Con.* 552
Their fragrant *m.* will outlast their tomb *Con.* 631
There *M.,* like the bee that's fed *M.* ii 9
That *m.* keeps of all thy kindness there *M.P.* 55
All this still legible in *M.'s* page *M.P.* 68
But every tear shall scald thy *m. P.E.* 336
For her, the *M.* fills her ample page *T.* 13
In faithful *m.* she records the crimes *T.* 160
And bred, within the *m.* of no few *T.* ii 677
Peace to the *m.* of a man of worth *T.* ii 781
While we retrace with *M.'s* pointing wand *T.* iv 183
Where *M.* slept. Wherever I have heard *T.* vi 12
To buckram out the *m.* of a man *T.* vi 652
Man praises man; and Garrick's *m.* next *T.* vi 664
I pleased remember, and, while *m.* yet *Tir.* 133
Reward his *m.,* dear to every Muse *T.T.* 14

MENACED.

Much *m.,* nothing dread *St.* vi 18

MENAGERIES.

That these *m.* all fail their trust *Tir.* 293

MEND.

Judgment, however tardy, *m.* her pace *Ex.* 151
By useless censure, whom we cannot *m. H.* 273
But speaks with plainness art, could never *m. H.* 451
Seek to delight, that they may *m.* mankind *H.* 758
Ye novelists, who mar what ye would *m. P.E.* 309

MENDED. [824

"Battered and bankrupt fortunes *m.* here" *T.* iii

MENDICANTS.

As *m.,* whose business is to roam *Con.* 859

MENIAL. [312

That all might mark—knight, *m.,* high, and low *H.*

MENTAL.

What virtue, or what *m.* grace *F.* 1
For such is all the *m.* food purveyed *Tir.* 620

MENTION. [*T.* 304

("*M.* him if you please;—Voltaire?"—"The same"

MENTIONED.
The man that *m.* him, at once dismissed *H.* 560

MENTOR.
Sticks close, a *M.* worthy of his charge *T.* ii 595
With some such *M.* always at his side *Tir.* 699

MERCENARY.
Built by no *m.* vulgar hand *Ch.* 257
His soul abhors a *m.* thought *H.* 332
Excels ten thousand *m.* deeds *T.* 224

MERCER. [279
To Miss, the *m.'s* plague, from shop to shop *T.* vi

MERCHANT.
Or was the *m.* charged to bring *A Tale* 27
For *m.* rich in cargoes of despair *Ch.* 138
If the new mail thy *m.* now receive *Ex.* 606
The statesman, lawyer, *m.*, man of trade *R.* 5
With such as *m.* introduce *R.C.* 37
Hence *m.*, unimpeachable of sin *T.* iv 676

MERCIFUL.
And—God is *m.*—sets all to rights *H.* 376

MERCIFULLY.
That scorns afflictions *m.* meant *R.* 760

MERCURIAL.
Laugh ye, who boast your more *m.* powers *T.* iv 282

MERCURY.
May *M.* once more embellish man *Con.* 838

MERCY.
There is *M.* in every place *A.S.* 53
And *M.*, encouraging thought! *A.S.* 54
Alike the wrath and *m.* of the skies *Ch.* 70
Teach *m.* to ten thousand hearts that share *Ch.* 278
As little *m.* as the grubs and worms! *Con.* 260
For *m.* shown, while wrath is justly due *Con.* 492
To supplicate his *m.*, love his ways *Con.* 661
That Truth and *M.* had revealed to man *Ex.* 236
Is wooing *m.* by renewed offence *Ex.* 413
Of talents, judgment, *m.*, better far *F.A.* 15
And *M.*, fled to as the last resort *H.* 378
See *M.'s* grand apocalypse displayed *H.* 448
The dire effect of *M.* without price *H.* 496
All *m.* from his lips, and sneered and hissed *H.* 561
If then, just then, all thoughts of *m.* lost *H.* 722
Who fasten without *m.* on the fair *P.E.* 325
The sense of *m.* kindles into praise *R.* 778
And *m.* cast away *St.* vi 40
M. receives him on her peaceful shore *T.* 276
M. is infinite, and man is weak *T.* 294
Sad messenger of *m.* from above *T.* 464
Would hiss the cherub *M.* from the stage *T.* 478
And leave to *M.*, with a tranquil mind *T.* 499
Hear then how *M.*, slighted and defied *T.* 501
But softened into *m.*; made the pledge *T.* i 365
With stripes, that *M.*, with a bleeding heart *T.* ii 24
Is felt, mankind may feel her *m.* too *T.* ii 47
Seems, in their eyes, a *m.*, for thy sake *T.* ii 132
Of judgment and of *m.*, should beware *T.* ii 465
To seek him rather where his *m.* shines *T.* iii 224
One drop of Heaven's sweet *m.* in his cup *T.* iii 804
Yet show that thou hast *m.*, which the great *T.* iv 371
For *m.* and the common rights of man *T.* iv 680
Of royal *m.*, and through generous scorn *T.* vi 410
So little *m.* shows who needs so much! *T.* vi 431
Ye, therefore, who love *m.*, teach your sons *T.* vi 588
M. to him that shows it, is the rule *T.* vi 595
Shall visit earth in *m.*; shall descend *T.* vi 743
Though *m.* for thyself thou canst have none *Tir.* 755

Hear Nature plead, show *m.* to thy son *Tir.* 756
When Providence means *m.* to a land *T.T.* 355
If *M.* then put by the threatening blow *T.T.* 404

MERETRICIOUS.
No *m.* graces to beguile *T.* 23

MERIDIAN.
The blaze of a *m.* day *E.* i 78
M. sunbeams tempt him to unfold *T.* 60
The sun's *m.* disk, and at the back *T.* iii 473

MERIT.
And honest *M.* stands on slippery ground *Ch.* 234
To your intrinsic *m.* true *E.* i 27
How he esteems your *m. F.* 171
Who write in blood the *m.* of your cause *Her.* 42
May claim this *m.* still—that she admits *T.* iii 102
The heart of *m.* in the meaner class *T.* iv 618
Try now the *m.* of this blest exchange *Tir.* 173

MERITORIOUS.
Then, conscious of her *m.* zeal *T.* 497

MERRILY.
And eke did rear right *m.*, two staves *T.* vi 662

MERRIMENT.
Filled with as much true *m.* and glee *T.T.* 244

MERRY.
But what old Chaucer's *m.* page befits *A.T.* 84
Thus all through *m.* Islington *J.G.* 133
In *m.* guise, he spoke *J.G.* 172
His friend in *m.* pin *J.G.* 178
Or *m.* turn in all he ever wrote *T.* ii 473
With *m.* descants on a nation's woes *T.* iv 77
Village, or hamlet, of this *m.* land *T.* iv 467
The priest he *m.* is and blithe *Y.D.* 5

MESSAGE.
Reports a *m.* with a pleasing grace *T.* 205

MESSENGER.
Sad *m.* of mercy from above *T.* 464
There stands the *m.* of truth; there stands *T.* ii 337
A *m.* of grace to guilty men *T.* ii 407
Cold and yet cheerful: *m.* of grief *T.* iv 13

MESSIAH.
M.'s eulogy for Handel's sake *T.* vi 637

MET.
She came—she is gone—we have *m. C.* 1
The world and I fortuitously *m. Con.* 795
As if they *m.* around a father's bier *Con.* 874
When minds that never *m.* before *E.* i 31
A glimpse of joy, that we have *m. N.* 23
Except that they had ever *m. P.T.* 59

METEOR.
Fires from beneath, and *m.* from above *T.* ii 57
Another moon new risen, or *m.* fallen *T.* v 152
The *m.* of the Gospel dies away *Tir.* 190
A *M.*, or a star; in these, the sun *T.T.* 575

METHINKS.
"*M.*," I said, "in thee I find *P.B.* 13
"*M.* the gentleman," quoth she *P.T.* 30
M. I see thee straying on the beach *T.* i 654
M. I see thee in the streaky west *T.* iv 245
But less, *m.*, than sacrilege might serve *T.* vi 638
But yet, *m.* to tell you true *Y.D.* 59

METHOD.
By softer *m.*, must be made ashamed *Ch.* 498
The *m.* clear, and argument exact? *T.* iii 279
Approved their *m.* in all other things *T.T.* 95

METHOUGHT.
But courage, man! *m.* the muse replied *Tir.* 786

METRE.
Indite much *m.* with much pains *O.* i 3

METROPOLITAN.
Grand *M.* of all the tribe *P.E.* 186
That *m.* volcanoes make *T.* iii 737

METTLE.
No. His high *m.*, under good control *T.T.* 308

MEW.
O'er hedge and ditch, through gaps and *m. E.* iv 52
A long and melancholy *m. R.C.* 88

MEXICO.
Not *M.* could purchase kings a claim *Ch.* 214

MEZEREON.
That scarce a leaf appears; *m.* too *T.* vi 167

MICE.   [flies *T.* iii 555
Moisture and drought, *m.*, worms, and swarming
Yet gnats have had, and frogs and *m.*, long since *T.*

MICROSCOPIC.   [iii 452
Such *m.* proof of skill and power *Tir.* 637

MID.
The screaming nations, hovering in *m.* air *H.* 353

MIDAS.
Touched by the *M.* finger of the state *T.* iv 507

MIDDLE.
The *m.* of my song *J.G.* 156
The *m.* field; but scattered by degrees *T.* i 293
To you, then, tenants of life's *m.* state *Tir.* 807

MIDNIGHT.
Has still a veil of *m.* on his heart *Ch.* 376
As *m.*, and despairing of a morn *J.T.* 22
Sweet Harmony that soothes the *m.* hour *P.E.* 66
Pardon me, ye that give the *m.* oil *R.* 661
Who quits the coach-box at the *m.* hour *T.* i 91
Nor his who quits the box at *m.* hour *T.* i 98
Of *m.* murder was a wonder heard *T.* iv 563
As set the *m.* riot in a blaze *Tir.* 287

MIEN.
Sought, with an indignant *m. B.*·3
And yours the statelier *m. L.R.* 22
Ecstasy sets her stamp on every *m. P.E.* 136
He, Christianlike, retreats with modest *m. T.* 68
Grace in his *m.*, and glory in his eyes *T.* 407
And just proportion, fashionable *m. T.* ii 421
Fops at all corners, ladylike in *m. Tir.* 829

MIGHT.
Fruits of his love and wonders of his *m. Con.* 473
Thy chaos order, and thy weakness *m. Ex.* 641
And eke with all his *m. J.G.* 92
And gallop'd off with all his *m. J.G.* 207
To span omnipotence, and measure *m. T.* v 212
Of all-creating energy and *m. T.* v 554
But this is sure—the hand of *m. Trans.* i 9

MIGHTIER.
A *m.* cried—"Proceed"—*B.R.* 6

MIGHTIEST.
We turn to dust, and all our *m.* works *T.* v 531

MIGHTILY.
Influenced *m.* the rest *P.T.* 43

MIGHTY.
On every mind some *m.* spell she cast *A.T.* 37
Are *m.* mischiefs, not to be withstood *Ch.* 283
Weak to perform, though *m.* to pretend *P.E.* 15
The *m.* myriads, now securely scorned *R.* 70
From *m.* means to more important ends *R.* 112
M. to parry and push-by God's word *H.* 659
His *m.* work, who speaks and it is done *R.* 60
The tone of languid Nature. *M.* winds *T.* i 183
Not by a *m.* wind, but by that voice *T.* ii 113
Thy most magnificent and *m.* freak *T.* v 130
By which the *m.* process is maintain'd *T.* vi 225
The diadem, with *m.* projects lined *T.T.* 59
The *m.* plan, oracular, in verse *T.T.* 179
On other *m.* ones, found also thee *Y.O.* 68

MIGRATES.
M. uplifted, and, with all its soil *T.* ii 108

MILD.
October hight, but *m.* and fair as May *A.T.* 71
Pure in her aim, and in her temper *m. Ch.* 422
I knew the man, and knew his nature *m. E.* iii 32
Had both alike been *m. J.P.* 6
Affable, humble, diffident, and *m. P.E.* 537
Can least brook management, however *m. R.* 252
But though true worth and virtue, in the *m. T.* i 678
For oft, as if in her the stream of *m. T.* iii 435 [443
As the sun peeps, and vernal airs breathe *m. T.* iii
His lessons tire, his *m.* rebukes offend *Tir.* 716

MILDER.
Sips meek infusions of a *m.* herb *Con.* 268
M., among a people less austere *T.* v 488

MILDEST.
Their *m.* physic is a farrier's purge *Ch.* 502

MILDEW.
Blows *m.* from between his shrivelled lips *T.* ii 186
One talks of *m.* and of frost *Y.D.* 53

MILE.
Full ten *m.* off, at Ware *J.G.* 152
'Twas but a *m.*; your favorite horse *M.F.* 23
Distant a little *m.* he spied *Mor.* 17
She, never heard of half a *m.* from home *T.* 334

MILESTONE.
The second *m.* fronts the garden gate *R.* 490

MILITARY.
To let the *m.* deluge pass *Ex.* 60

MILK.
The *m.* of their good purpose all to curd *Ch.* 504
And *m.*, and oats, and straw *Ep.* ii 14
Much. I was born of woman, and drew *m. T.* iii 196

MILKWHITE.
His *m.* hand; the palm is hardly clean *T.* iv 607

MILKY.
Drinks wisdom at the *m.* stream of light *Ch.* 319
Those the long *m.* way *Q.V.* 12

MILL.   [16
With the double employment of mallet and *m. F.M.*
Nor view of waters turning busy *m. R.* 334

MILLDAM.
The *m.*, dashes on the restless wheel *T.* v 102

MILLENNIUM.
Half a *m.* since the date of thine *Y.O.* 136

MILLIONS.

And sighing m. prophecy the close *Ex.* 309
Those rights that m. envy thee appear *Ex.* 681
Combined with m. more *O.* i 18
And hears the m. hum *Q.V.* 42
Earth's m. daily fed, a world employed *R.* 553
Dreams empty dreams. The m. flit as gay *T.* iii 133
Two or three m. of the human race *T.T.* 423
Confine the m. in the beaten track *T.T.* 667

MILTON.

M., whose genius had angelic wings *T.* iii 255
Then M. had indeed a poet's charms *T.* iv 709
To give a M. birth, asked ages more *T.T.* 559

MIMIC.

Where late we saw the m. landscape glow *H.* 263
And I can view this m. show of thee *M.P.* 119
Lovely indeed the m. works of Art *T.* i 420
The worth of what she m. with such care *T.* iii 103
Sweet Poll! the m. bird replies *Trans.* iv 14

MIMICRY.

Or make the parrot's m. his choice *Con.* 449

MINCING.

And sails with lappet head and m. airs *T.* 139

MIND. [12

Which amounts to possession time out of m." *A.C.*
How fleet is a glance of the M.—*A.S.* 41
On every m. some mighty spell she cast *A.T.* 37
Are mere impressions on the passive m. *A.T.* 43
Far other dreams his feverish m. employed *A.T.* 153
So it is, when the m. is endued *C.* 33
But though some nobler m. a law respect *Ch.* 35
He feels his body's bondage in his m. *Ch.* 152
Inform his m.; one flash of heavenly day *Ch.* 228
Within the scanty limits of the m. *Ch.* 247
But time that should enrich the nobler m. *Comp.* i 11
And show the softest m. and fairest forms *Con.* 259
The M. despatched upon her busy toil *Con.* 437
Its happiest soil in the serenest m.? *Con.* 594
Is the false fire of an o'erheated m. *Con.* 668
Upon the surface of the m. *E.* i 8
When m. that never met before *E.* i 31
Howe'er it was, his language, in my m. *E.* iii 40
Received the transcript of the Eternal M.—*Ex.* 198
With Asiatic vices stored thy m. *Ex.* 372
And to this hour, to keep it fresh in m. *Ex.* 516
To every pang that racks an anxious m. *Ex.* 571
Illuminating heart or m. *F.* 8
As similarity of m. *F.* 175
Or seeking with a biassed m. *F.* 209
Much less could he alter her m. *Gr.* 43
For he, with all his follies, has a m. *H.* 91
Their m. a wilderness through want of care *H.* 233
What simplest m. can soonest comprehend *H.* 452
In chains of error our accomplished m. *H.* 484
Powers of the m., and feelings of the heart *H.* 654
Alas, how changed! Expressive of his m. *H.* 688
Not kindred m. alone are called to employ *H.* 738
And while they captivate, inform the m. *H.* 759
She had a frugal m. *J.G.* 32
Were suited to their m. *J.G.* 58
Of close alliance to the Eternal M.—*J.T.* 44
What joint the prophet had in m.) *L.W.* 14
Like Isaac, with a m. applied *Mor.* 11
And "Hence," he said, "my m. computes *Mor.* 25
Is paid at least in peace of m. *Mor.* 51
The various treasures of his m. *Mrs. M*— 42
But, with precision nicer still, the m. *N.A.* 63
M. are never to be sold *N.C.* 8 [*N.A.* 76
Stamped on each countenance such marks of m.

Come, peace of m., delightful guest! *O.* ii 1
The noblest m. their virtue prove *P.* 61
Your scruples and arguments bring to my m. *P.A.* 17
Might well alarm the most unguarded m. *P.E.* 58
And lenient as soft opiates to the m. *P.E.* 80
The balm of care, Elysium of the m. *P.E.* 180
The M., impressible and soft, with ease *P.E.* 355
Hence an unfurnished and a listless m. *P.E.* 425
Learning itself, received into a m. *P.E.* 431
The m. and conduct mutually imprint *P.E.* 566
Delivered briefly thus his m. *P.T.* 22
But 'tis not easy with a m. like ours *R.* 123
But leisure, silence, and a m. released *R.* 139
Some m. by nature are averse to noise *R.* 175
So Love, that clings around the noblest m. *R.* 235
And m. that deem derided pain a treat *R.* 310
No rough annoyance rankling in his m. *R.* 428
The portion of a mean or vulgar m. *R.* 502
Some to comply with humour, and a m. *R.* 605
A m. quite vacant is a m. distressed *R.* 624
But reveries (for human m. will act) *R.* 637
A m. employed on so sublime a theme *R.* 668
A m. unnerved, or indisposed to bear *R.* 677
Luxury gives the m. a childish cast *R.* 703
The m., relaxing into needful sport *R.* 715
From vulgar m., have honour much at heart *R.* 728
And puss came into m. no more *R.C.* 71
Oh, tell thy thoughtless sex, the virtuous m. *S.* ii 6
Prompt every movement of his heart and m. *T.* 194
His m. his kingdom, and his will his law *T.* 406 [411
So sings he, charmed with his own m. and form *T.*
And leave to Mercy, with a tranquil m. *T.* 499
Let heathen worthies, whose exalted m. *T.* 525
And lull the spirit while they fill the m. *T.* i 187
The Earth was made so various, that the m. *T.* i 506
In cities foul example on most m. *T.* i 685
There only m. like yours can do no harm *T.* i 759
Where English m. and manners may be found *T.* ii 208
To which the m. resorts, in chase of terms *T.* ii 288
The mirror of the m., and hold them fast *T.* ii 291
Are occupations of the poet's m. *T.* ii 298 [457
And rustic coarseness would. A heavenly m. *T.* ii
Can lodge a heavenly m.—demands a doubt *T.* ii 462
While prejudice in men of stronger m. *T.* ii 567
Some m. are tempered happily, and mixed *T.* ii 788
The m. was well-informed, the passions held *T.* ii 715
His m. with meanings that he never had *T.* iii 149
The m. indeed, enlightened from above *T.* iii 225
Compose the passions, and exalt the m. *T.* iii 305
Susceptible of pity, or a m. *T.* iii 323 [369
The m. He gave me; driving it, though slack *T.* iii
That has a heart, and keeps it; has a m. *T.* iii 374
Of thought, the creature of a polished m. *T.* iii 640
But it has peace, and much secures the m. *T.* iii 679
Hopeless indeed that dissipated m. *T.* iii 695
Suits well the thoughtful or unthinking m. *T.* iv 279
The m. contemplative, with some new theme *T.* iv 280
Behold the schools in which plebeian m. *T.* iv 492
To me an unambitious m., content *T.* iv 798 [iv 740
And all can taste them: m. that have been formed *T.*
Of heroes, whose infirm and baby m. *T.* v 190 [751
Whose heart with praise, and whose exalted m. *T.* v
In those that suffer it, a sordid m. *T.* v 453 [v 796
Not so the m. that has been touched from Heaven *T.*
Thou art the source and centre of all m. *T.* v 896
And, as the m. is pitch'd, the ear is pleased *T.* vi 2
Faintly impress the m., or not at all *T.* vi 24
Wisdom in m. attentive to their own *T.* vi 92 [262
Who then, that has a m. well strung and tuned *T.* vi
Food chiefly for the m. *T.B.* 42
Some act by the delicate m. *The Rose* 14
That form, indeed, the associate of a m. *Tir.* 5
The present Muse of every pensive m. *Tir.* 22

MIND—MIRY

At once the dreaming m. is disabused *Tir.* 90
Proofs of the wisdom of the all-seeing m. *Tir.* 94
That we are bound to cast the m. of youth *Tir.* 105
To feed our infant m. with proper fare *Tir.* 116
The most disinterested and virtuous m. *Tir.* 438[583
Though some, perhaps, that shock thy feeling m.*Tir.*
The m. and heart of every sprightly boy *Tir.* 598
No nourishment to feed his growing m. *Tir.* 618
His m. informed, his morals undefiled *Tir.* 683
An upright heart, and cultivated m. *Tir.* 722
Where, stillness aiding study, and his m. *Tir.* 773
And formed of God without a parent's m. *Tir.* 790
A m. well lodged, and masculine of course *T.T.* 221
The m. attains, beneath her happy reign *T.T.* 262
Learns much, and to a thousand listening m. *T.T.* 274
The m. that slumbers sweetly in her snares *T.T.* 439
I know the m. that feels indeed the fire *T.T.* 480
Proves that the m. is weak, or makes it so *T.T.* 545
'Twas thus till Luxury seduced the m. *T.T.* 600 [623
The m., released from too constrained a nerve *T.T.*
To polish, furnish, and delight the m. *T.T.* 645
A soul exalted above Earth, a m. *T.T.* 704
Proof of a trifling and a worthless m. *T.T.* 759
Not to recall a promise to your m. *V.* 21
Relics of ages! could a m., imbued *Y.O.* 6   [158
With the thought-tracing quill or tasked his m. *Y.O.*

MINE.
Starved by that indolence their m. create *Ch.* 64
"'Tis ready polished from the m." *E.* iv 90
With sums Peruvian m. could never clear *Ex.* 235
That proved a mint of wealth, a m. to Rome *Ex.* 523
The fragrant grove, the inestimable m. *H.* 177
And in the gulfs of her Cornubian m. *H.* 458
(Unfelt the fury of those bursting m.) *Her.* 8
Surpassing all that m. or mint had given *J.T.* 30
His unexhausted m., the sordid vice *P.E.* 51   [698
Strong Judgment labouring in the Scripture m. *R.*
And taints|the golden ear. He springs the m. *T.*ii 187
A m. to satisfy the enormous cost *T.* iii 783
Or if that m. be shut, some private purse *T.* iii 797
The looms of Ormus, and the m. of Ind *T.* vi 806

MINER.
Raised by the mole, the m. of the soil *T.* i 273

MINGLE.
And once more m. with us meaner things *Ch.* 437
No Envy m. with our praise *Dr.* 13
Till yonder heaven and earth shall m. *P.T.* 33
And m. with our cup *R.G.* 27
That m. all my brown with sober gray *Tir.* 144

MINGLED.
As ever m. with heroic dust *Ch.* 24
And will not punish, in one m. crowd *Ex.* 716
Her m. suits and sequences, and sits *T.* i 475
Like kindred drops been m. into one *T.* ii 19
To them it flowed much m. and defiled *T.* ii 503
His sprightly m. with a shade of sad *Tir.* 665

MINIATURE.
Thyself in m., thy flesh, thy bone? *Tir.* 874

MINISTER.
The m. of man, to serve his wants *T.* ii 138
And most of all in man that m. *T.* ii 415
That makes a m. in holy things *T.* iii 280
Bleed gold for m. to sport away *T.* iv 508
With those fair m. of light to man *T.* v 816
When m. and ministerial arts *T.T.* 191
Prize it, ye m.; ye monarchs, spare *T.T.* 324

MINISTERIAL.
To serve his country. M. grace *T.* iii 795
When ministers and m. arts *T.T.* 190

MINISTRY.
In all its parts, times, m. and laws *T.T.* 427

MINNOW.   [483
M. and gudgeons gorge the unwholesome food *P.E.*
To draw the incautious m. from the brook *R.* 402

MINOR.
The m. heroes view with envious eyes *Tir.* 223

MINORITY.
M. No tutor charged his hand *Y.O.* 157

MINSTREL.
Afford the smaller m. no supply *T.* v 84
And idle tinkling of a m.'s lyre *T.* vi 1021

MINSTRELSY.
"As much as I your m. *N.G.* 16

MINT.   [iv 756
That here and there some sprigs of mournful m. *T.*
That proved a m. of wealth, a mine to Rome *Ex.* 523
Surpassing all that mine or m. had given *J.T.* 30
And stamp their image in each other's m. *P.E.* 567

MINTED.
When Scandal has new m. an old lie *Ch.* 513

MINUTE.
And ever as the m. flew *Cast.* 41
Every five m. how the m. go *Con.* 382
To trace in Nature's most m. design *R.* 53
Just fifteen m., huddle up their work *T.* ii 412
M. as dust and numberless, oft work *T.* iii 556
Terrestrial, in the vast and the m. *T.* v 811
M. the horrors that ensued *T.B.* 52

MINUTIÆ.
From mere m. can educe *E.* i 75

MINX.
"The m. shall, for your folly's sake *J.P.* 37

MIRACLE.
All we behold is m.; but, seen *T.* vi 132
So duly, all is m. in vain *T.* vi 133

MIRACULOUSLY.
Muscle and nerve m. spun *R.* 59

MIRROR.
This table and m. within *Gr.* 21
A lucid m., in which Nature sees *T.* i 701
The m. of the mind, and hold them fast *T.* ii 291
Forth comes the pocket m.—First we stroke *T.*ii 445
From many a m. in which he of Gath *T.* iv 269
Blushed on the pannels. M. needed none *T.* v 160

MIRTH.
And forced the floodgates of licentious m. *Con.* 264
Though future pain may serve for present m. *Con.* 494
Then m. is sin, and we should always cry *Con.* 878
The harmless play of pleasantry and m. *E.* iii 39
Business or vain amusement, care or m. *R.* 647
Of idle m. and affectation coy *S.* ii 10
There is a public mischief in your m. *T.* i 769
Of fancy, or proscribes the sound of m. *T.* iv 176
And m. without offence. No few return'd *T.* vi 692
Little inmate, full of m. *Trans.* iii 1
Her serious m., to Arbuthnot and Swift *T.T.* 657

MIRTHFUL.
Can change their whine into a m. note *T.* i 583

MIRY.
Or having long in m. ways been foiled *T.* iii 4
Along the m. road *Y.D.* 14

MISAGATHUS.
Dwelt young *M.*; a scorner he *T.* vi 485

MISAPPLIED.
Lest, having *m.* our eyes *F.* 26
Is *m.* to sanctify their sway *P.E.* 497
Who pant with application *m. T.* vi 273
This once believed, 'twere logic *m. Tir.* 103
How are the powers of genius *m.! T.T.* 749

MISAPPLYING.
Or *m.* his unskilful strength *T.* iii 402

MISARRANGEMENT.
(Fantastic *m.*)! on the roof *T.* v 111

MISCARRIAGE.
The way to glory by *m.* foul *T.* iii 506
Exults in his *m.* if he fail *Tir.* 478

MISCARRY.
Lest they *m.* of what seems their due *Con.* 372

MISCHIEF.
Are mighty *m.*, not to be withstood *Ch.* 283
Account them implements of *m.* still *Ch.* 556
Springs from the *m.* it intends to cure *Con.* 170
And Hell's close *m.* naked in his sight *Ex.* 339
His aim was *m.* and his zeal pretence *H.* 564
The *m.* your ambitious pride inspires! *Her.* 46
Might prove a *m.*, or at best a toy *P.E.* 302
But not the *m.*: they still left behind *P.E.* 554
But does a *m.* while she lends a grace *R.* 233
A den of *m.* never to be told *T.* 392
That may record the *m.* he has done *T.* i 277
There is a public *m.* in your mirth *T.* i 769
Of such deep *m.* has itself a cause *T.* ii 698
Of that calamitous *m.* has been found *T.* ii 821
Are gratified with *m.*, and who spoil *T.* v 191
And *m.* in their hands, they roam the earth *T.* vi 896
If, author of no *m.* and some good *T.* vi 953
Childish in *m.* only and in noise *Tir.* 207 [249
Though from ourselves the *m.* more proceeds *Tir.*
Such *m.* after it, with much applause *Tir.* 494
Find it expedient, come what *m.* may *Tir.* 692
Some *m.* fatal to his future worth *Tir.* 758

MISCHIEVOUS.
Works the deplored and *m.* effect *T.* iv 616

MISDEEMS.
M. it, dazzled by its bright array *T.* iv 685

MISEMPLOY'D.
Power *m.*, munificence misplaced *Tir.* 50

MISER.
Charity may relax the *m.'s* fist *Con.* 812
What pleasure can the *m.'s* fondled hoard *J.T.* 15
Ye patriots, guard it with a *m.'s* care *T.T.* 335

MISERABLE.
Their *m.* meal. A kettle, slung *T.* i 560
The sighs and groans of *m.* men! *T.* v 388

MISERY.
But *m.* still delights to trace *Cast.* 59
By the *m.* that we tasted *N.C.* 43
It thrives in *m.*, and abundant grows *T.* 125
In *m.* fools upon themselves impose *T.* 126
Ages of hopeless *m.* Future death *T.* v 607
That 'tis our shame and *m.* not to learn *Tir.* 38
And laughs the sense of *m.* far away *T.T.* 239

MISGIVING.
A cold *m.*, and a killing dread *Con.* 770

MISGUIDED.
Blind was he born, and his *m.* eyes *Ch.* 357

MISHAPS.
And now—alas, for unforeseen *m.*! *Con.* 321

MISLEAD.
The roving eye *m.* the careless heart *R.* 126

MISLED.
M. by custom, strain celestial themes *T.* ii 438

MISPLACED.
And gave *m.* applause *J.P.* 20
Power misemploy'd, munificence *m. Tir.* 50
See wealth abused, and dignities *m. Tir.* 815
The globe and sceptre in such hands *m. T.T.* 39

MISS. [75
And only *m.* the flowers that graced their side *A.T.*
Transformed to blessings, *m.* their cruel aim *E.* ii 38
The postboy's horse right glad to *m, J.G.* 231
Whose corresponding *m.* fill the ream *P.E.* 311
M.! the tale that I relate *P.T.* 62
Give useful light though I should *m.* renown *R.* 206
The good we never *m.* we rarely prize *R.* 406 [458
What obvious truths the wisest heads may *m.*! *R.*
Scrawled upon glass *M.* Bridget's lovely name *T.* 156
E'en *m.*, at whose age their mothers wore *T.* iv 226
Nor ignorantly wandering *m.* the skies *Tir.* 108 [279
To *M.*, the mercer's plague, from shop to shop *T.* vi
Shall royal institutions *m.* the bays *Tir.* 503
'Tis now a little one, like *M.*—*Trans.* iv 17
And how does *m.* and madam do *Y.D.* 33

MISSED.
And therefore never *m. F.B.* 12
We *m.* that happiness we might have found! *T.* vi 28

MISSPENT.
And laughter, all their work, is life *m. Con.* 876
The shameful close of all his *m.* years *H.* 715
Thee to deplore were grief *m.* indeed *J.T.* 11
Near yonder heath; where Industry *m. T.* iii 643

MISSTATED.
Recovering and *m.* setting right *Y.O.* 48

MIST.
And snorts aloud to cast the *m.* aside *A.T.* 164
The rustling straw sends up a frequent *m. T.* i 360
Can but arrest the light and smoky *m. T.* v 105
The sun proceeds, I wander. Neither *m. T.* vi 296

MISTAKE.
Let Charity forgive me a *m. Ch.* 634
But sage observers oft *m.* the flame *Con.* 655
If I *m.* not—Blockhead! with a fork! *H.* 362
But if the wanderer his *m.* discern *P.E.* 610
Conclusion retrograde, and mad *m. T.* iii 239
Adopting their *m.*, profoundly thinks *T.* v 270
Man yet *m.* his way *The Doves* 2
And make *m.* for manhood to reform *Tir.* 445
But soon, alas! detect the rash *m. V.* 55

MISTAKEN.
To Moses, was *m.* in its age *T.* iii 154

MISTRESS.
M., at least while Providence shall please *Ex.* 274
Now *m.* Gilpin (careful soul!) *J.G.* 65
Now *m.* Gilpin, when she saw *J.G.* 213
And she, once *m.* of the realms around *T.* 393
Such as the *m.* of the world once found *T.* iv 169
Ere yet her ear was *m.* of their powers *T.* iv 703
Imperial *m.* of the fur-clad Russ! *T.* v 129
Sweet Poll! his doting *m.* cries *Trans.* iv 13

MISUSE.
Who first *m.*, then cast their toys away *H.* 128

MITE.
Adds as he can, his tributary *m. T.T.* 112

MITRED.
But not the *m.* few, the soul their charge *A.T.* 129
From such apostles, O ye *m.* heads *T.* ii 392

MITRES.
In coach with purple lined, and *m.* on its side *Tir.* [369

MIX.
The soul can *m.* with the celestial bands *Con.* 717
Courtier and Patriot cannot *m. F.* 127
By deeds in which the world must never *m. P.E.* 162
M. with the world, but with its wiser part *R.* 275
To *m.* her wild vagaries with thy laws *T.* v 873

MIXED.
Bents, wool, and feathers *m. A Tale* 40
'Tis wrong to bring into a *m.* resort *Con.* 291
By which Heaven rules the *m.* affairs of man *H.* 16
Pleasure and wonder in his features *m. T.* 416
Some minds are tempered happily, and *m. T.* ii 788
With colours *m.* for a far different use *T.* iv 240

MIXTURE.
Here also grateful *m.* of well matched *T.* iii 633

MOAN.
Heard the sweet *m.* with pity, and devised *T.* i 74

MOB.
When lawless *m.* insult the Court *Pat.* 9
Who say the *m.* are mad outright *Pat.* 19
Train him in public with a *m.* of boys *Tir.* 206

MOCK.
Touched by that power that you have dared to *m.* [*Con.* 501
She *m.* her Maker, and herself deceives *Con.* 776
Flits out of sight, and *m.* his pains *E.* iv 60
Would *m.* the majesty of man's high birth *R.* 71
He *m.* his Maker, prostitutes and shames *T.* ii 427
Till they can laugh at virtue, *m.* the fools *T.* ii 692
As they designed to *m.* me, at my side *T.* v 17
Thus Nature works as if to *m.* at Art *T.* v 122

MOCKERY.
Becomes a *m.* and a standing jest *Ex.* 110
No *m.* meets you, no deception there *P.E.* 618
A *m.* of the world! What need of these *T.* ii 750

MODE.
That substances, and *m.* of every kind *A.T.* 42
And sought it in the likeliest *m. R.C.* 33
And centering all authority in *m. T.* i 745
And *m.* of its conveyance, by such tricks *T.* ii 561
Infected with the manners and the *m. T.* iv 693
The slaves of custom and established *m. Tir.* 251
Not that he peevishly rejects a *m. T.* vi 981

MODELS.
M. of Herculanean pots and pans *P.E.* 398

MODERATE.
We may with patience bear our *m.* ills *T.* iv 339

MODERN.
The chaster Muse of *m.* days omits *A.T.* 85
A dozen would-bes of the *m.* day *Con.* 612
Digression is so much in *m.* use *Con.* 855
At least, we *m.*, our attention less *Con.* 791
What web too weak to catch a *m.* brain? *Ex.* 629
Friends such as his for *m.* jobs prepare *R.* 306
Your prudent grandmammas, ye *m.* belles *R.* 515
With what success let *m.* manners show *R.* 686

Down into *m.* use; transforms old print *T.* ii 363
Like those which *m.* senators employ *T.* iv 490
By *m.* lights from an erroneous taste *T.* iv 724
In *m.* eyes), shall make the doctrine clear *T.* vi 482
To combat atheists with in *m.* days *Tir.* 639
I was a poet too: but *m.* taste *T.T.* 510
Sufficient to redeem the *m.* race *T.T.* 664
To *m.* times, with Truth to guide 1789, 11

MODEST.
Held within *m.* bounds, the tide of speech *Con.* 839
To *m.* cheeks, and borrowed one from Art *Ex.* 48
Meek, *m.*, venerable, wise, sincere *Ex.* 620
But *m.*, sober, cured of all *R.C.* 103
He, Christianlike, retreats with *m.* mien *T.* 68
In *m.* mediocrity, content *T.* i 50
The head of *m.* and ingenuous worth *T.* ii 711
And lowly creeping, *m.* and yet fair *T.* iii 663
The *m.* speaker is ashamed and grieved *T.* iv 66
With *m.* grandeur in thy purple zone *T.* iv 257
Poor, yet industrious, *m.*, quiet, neat *T.* iv 374
The meek and *m.* Truth, and forcing her *T.* vi 840
Of *m.* truth for wit's eccentric range *Tir.* 174
Backed with a *m.* sheet of humble prose *V.* 20

MODESTLY.
Know then, and *m.* let fall your eyes *Con.* 485
Those winding *m.* a silent course *R.* 78

MODESTY.
To press your point with *m.* and ease *Con.* 104
True *M.* is a discerning grace *Con.* 373
Whom once her virgin *m.* and grace *T.* iv 535
With *m.* and meekness, and the crown *T.* v 243
Offend not him, whom *m.* restrains *Tir.* 727

MODICUM.
To every man his *m.* of sense *Con.* 2
Gives him a *m.* of light *Trans.* i 11

MODISH.
And finds the *m.* manners of the day *H.* 612

MODULATING.
With music *m.* all their notes *T.T.* 695

MOGUL.
Fed from the richest veins of the *M. Ex.* 369

MOIST.
And all was *m.* to the warm touch; a scene *T.* v 166

MOISTURE.
M. and drought, mice, worms, and swarming flies *T.* [iii 555
Soft airs and genial *m.* feed and cheer *H.* 489
And drunk no *m.* from the dripping clouds *T.* iii 515
The plentiful *m.* encumbered the flower *The Rose* 3
Calm and alternate storm, *m.* and drought *Y.O.* 77

MOLE.
The *m.* and bats in full assembly find *Ex.* 630
To snare the *m.*, or with ill-fashioned hook *R.* 401
Raised by the *m.*, the miner of the soil *T.* i 273
As useless to the *m.* and to the bats *T.* vi 880
Were brighter than the sleekest *m. T.B.* 14

MOLEST.
Not to *m.*, or irritate, or raise *R.* 317

MOLTEN.
That, as with *m.* glass, inlays the vale *T.* i 170

MOMENT.
"Again, would your lordship a *m.* suppose *A.C.* 17
In a *m.* I seem to be there *A.S.* 46
The sun of that *m.* is set *C.* 3
To wing all her *m.* at home *C.* 50
All bonds of nature in that *m.* end *Ch.* 142

And snap the chain the *m.* when you may *Ch.* 168
And every *m.'s* calm, that soothes the breast *E.* ii 39
But somewhat at that *m.* pinched him close *E.* iii 34
The *m.* when I heard from you *E.* iv 24
Demands one *m.* of thy fleeting time *Ep.* i 2
Thy language at this distant *m.* shows *Ex.* 480
At length his destined *m.* to be born? *F.A.* 26
As useless as the *m.* it began *H.* 96
And the *m.* the monster expired *M.D.* 38
Your golden *m.* bless *Miss* — 102
And bar the door the *m.* they intrude *P.E.* 160
A *m.* liberty to speak *P.T.* 20
God in a *m.* executes with ease) *R.* 328
No, not a *m.*, in his royal heart *R.* 774
Play wanton, every *m.*, every spot *T.* i 349
Receive our air, that *m.* they are free *T.* ii 41
Of smiling Victory that *m.* won *T.* ii 243
And at this *m.* unassayed in song *T.* iii 451 [508
The auspicious *m.*, when the tempered heat *T.* iii
A *m.'s* operation on his love *T.* iii 793
To engross a *m.* notice ; and yet begs *T.* iv 67
To him whose *m.* all have one dull pace *T.* v 407
Infect his happiest *m.*, he forebodes *T.* v 606
In that blest *m.*, Nature throwing wide *T.* v 891
That in a few short *m.* I retrace *T.* vi 16 [85
May think down hours to *m.* Here the heart *T.* vi
His *m.* when to sink and when to rise *T.* vi 130
Can cheat, or move a *m.'s* fear in me? *T.* vi 508
Finds in a sober *m.* time to pause *Tir.* 56
Weigh, for a *m.*, classical desert *Tir.* 488 [*Tir.* 614
On *m.* squandered else, and running all to waste
That unimproved those many *m.* fly? *Tir.* 616
Deem it of no great *m.* whose or where *Tir.* 784

MOMENTARY.

A *m.* dream, that thou art she *M.P.* 20
To hang their *m.* fires *Q.V.* 15

MOMENTUM.

Whether increased *m.*, and the force *P.E.* 405

MONARCH.

I am *m.* of all I survey *A.S.* 1
She, with all a *m.'s* pride *B.* 37
Thy *m.* arbitrary, fierce, unjust *Ex.* 528
Her gloomy *m.*, doubtful, and resigned *Ex.* 570
The *m.* most that seldom will appear *H.* 502
Ye *m.*, whom the lure of honour draws *Her.* 41
What are ye, *m.*, laurelled heroes, say *Her.* 77
A *m.* clothed with majesty and awe *T.* 405
He held the thunder. But the *m.* owes *T.* i 382
To *m.* dignity ; to judges sense *T.* iv 796
(Made by a *m.*) on her own estate *T.* v 171
That *m.* have supplied, from age to age *T.* v 386
Which *m.* cannot grant, nor all the powers *T.* v 540
The new made *m.*, while before him pass'd *T.* vi 353
The lion tells him—I am *m.* here ! *T.* vi 408
A *m.* errors are forbidden game *T.T.* 114
Prize it, ye ministers; ye *m.'s*, spare *T.T.* 334

MONARCHY.

If *m.* consist in such base things *T.T.* 139

MONASTIC.

A superstitious and *m.* course *R.* 118

MONEY.

Deals him out *m.* from the public chest *T.* iii 796
Spendthrift alike of *m.* and of wit *T.T.* 684
The *m.* chinks, down drop their chins *Y.D.* 51

MONITOR.

The faithful *m.'s* and poet's part *H.* 757
A *m.'s*, though not a poet's praise *R.* 806
By *m.* that mother church supplies *T.* ii 576

What was a *M.* in George's days? *T.* ii 580
A *M.* is wood—plank shaven thin *T.* ii 585

MONITORY.

Pause here, and think ! A *m.* rhyme *Ep.* i 1
But the *m.* strain *St.* iv 17

MONK.

So he called him a bigot, a wrangler, a *m. A.T.* ii 3

MONKISH.

Wast thou in *m.* cells and nunneries found *Ch.* 43

MONMOUTH.

Send your dishonoured gown to *M.* Street *P.E.* 121

MONOPOLISTS.

Suppose themselves *m.* of sense *Con.* 627

MONSTER.

And quell the shapeless *m.* of the times *A.T.* 142
And the moment the *m.* expired *M.D.* 38
This more than *m.* in his proper guise *H.* 573
Come fiend, come fury, giant, *m.*, blast *N.A.* 121
Right to his mark the *m.* went *T.B.* 50
Chief *m.* that has plagued the nations yet ! *T.T.* 38

MONSTROUS.

What *m.* lies some travellers will tell " *Ch.* 394
For *m.* novelty and strange disguise *T.* ii 612
And give your *m.* project all its force *Tir.* 239

MONTAGU.

To dress a room for *M.*—*Mrs. M*— 2
Safe with protecting *M.*—*Mrs. M*— 20
All these to a *M.'s* repair *Mrs. M*— 43

MONTH.

Some pleasures live a *m.*, and some a year *R.* 459
And novels (witness every *m.'s* Review) *R.* 713
Learn then, ye living ! by the *m.* be taught *St.* ii 33
The regular return of genial *m. T.* vi 123
But let the *m.* go round, a few short *m. T.* vi 140

MONUMENT.

Not the proud *m.* of Greece or Rome *Ch.* 302
Where stands that *m.* of ancient power *Ch.* 549
The *m.* of human strength *E.* i 82
Invites us. *M.* of ancient taste *T.* i 253

MONUMENTAL.

Toils much to earn a *m.* pile *T.* i 276
With schemes of *m.* fame ; and sought *T.* v 182

MOOD.

Played only gambols in a frantic *m. H.* 541
I indulge my poetical *m. Gr.* 51
And though she changed her *m.* so oft *J.P.* 23
Both sad and in a cheerful *m. N.Y.G.* 3
Risk an intrusion on thy pensive *m. R.* 255
Of churlish Winter, in her froward *m. T.* iii 433
Conceals the *m.* lethargic with a mask *T.* iv 299
The night was winter in his roughest *m. T.* vi 57
His horse, as he had caught his master's *m. T.* vi 549
And thou at best, and in thy soberest *m. Tir.* 753
He struck the lyre in such a careless *m. T.T.* 686

MOON.

Knight of the Silver *M.*, Sir Marmadan *A.T.* 136
Eight years and five round-rolling *m. Ep.* ii 29
States thrive or wither, as *m.* wax and wane *Ex.* 324
Then to the dance, and make the sober *m. P.E.* 173
In rushes Folly with a full *m.* tide *P.E.* 282
The crescent *m.*, the diadem of night *R.* 82
The purple evening and resplendent *m. R.* 348
While thirteen *m.* saw smoothly run *St.* i 1
That hails the rising *m.*, have charms for me *T.* 206
But change with every *m.* The sycophant *T.* ii 599

Suffices thee ; save that the *m.* is thine *T.* iv 254[645
Has made a Heaven on earth ; with suns and *m. T.* iii
Bestrides the wintry flood, in which the *m. T.* iv 3
Another *m.* new risen, or meteor fallen *T.* v 152
Enchanting novelty, that *m.* at full *T.* vi 706
Why takes the gentler *M.* her turn to rise *Tir.* 38
The *m.* of Jove, and Saturn's belted ball *Tir.* 634

MOONBEAM.

The *m.* sliding softly in between *T.* i 762

MOONLIGHT.

Perhaps by *m.*, at their humble doors *T.* iv 171

MOORS.

The heaths uncovered and the *m. A Tale* 17

MOP.

Just like unto a trundling *m. J.G.* 139

MORAL.

A *m.*, sensible, and well-bred man *Con.* 193
And give the *m.* springs their proper play *Con.* 832
Not of the *m.*, but the dancing school *P.E.* 190
Unnerves the *m.* powers, and mars their use *P.E.* 272
It stabs at once the *m.* of a land *P.E.* 306
With some cold *m.* think to quench the fire *P.E.* 320
Then pour it on the *m.* of thy son *P.E.* 345
No— the man's *m.* were exact ; what then ? *T.* 52
Through plenty, lose in *m.* what they gain *T.* i 624
But loose in *m.*, and in manners vain *T.* ii 378
My man of *m.*, nurtured in the shades *T.* ii 532
Seem most at variance with all *m.* good *T.* iv 621
Of rectitude and fitness, *m.* truth *T.* v 672
How lovely, and the *m.* sense how sure *T.* v 673
Through *m.* narrative, or sacred text *Tir.* 126
While *m.* languish, a despised concern *Tir.* 514
A man of letters, manners, *m.*, parts *Tir.* 673
His mind informed, his *m.* undefiled *Tir.* 683
To cultivate and keep the *m.* clean *Tir.* 920
The song was *m.*, and so far was right *T.T.* 599
The manners, not the *m.*, of the day *V.* 80

MORALIST.

Sweet *m.* ! afloat on life's rough sea *R.H.* 3
The saint or *m.* should tread *S.* 17
And stately tone of *m.*, who boast *T.* v 690

MORALITY.

"Adieu to all *m.*, if Grace *H.* 359
What are they now ?—*M.* may spare *H.* 515
Gave Virtue and *M.* a grace *T.T.* 648

MORALIZE.

But not to *m.* too much, and strain *E.* iii 42

MORN.

Yes, but an object bright as orient *m. H.* 550
A tempest usher in the dreaded *m. H.* 717
As midnight, and despairing of a *m. J.T.* 22
And here I wander eve and *m. M.B.* 11
Ask not the boy, who when the breeze of *m. R.* 395
The sprightly *m.* her cause renewed *R.C.* 69
Or pass unheeded this auspicious *m. S.* ii 4
Herself from *m.* to night, from night to *m. T.* 509
She tells me, too, that duly every *m. T.* i 663 [131
Shortening his journey between *m.* and noon *T.* iv
From *m.* to eve his solitary task *T.* v 44

MORNING.

The *m.* came, when neighbour Hodge *A Fable* 24
Snuffs up the *m.* air, forgets the rain *Ch.* 175
The peep of *m.* shed a dawning light *Ch.* 261
Whose foot ne'er tainted *m.* dew *Ep.* ii 3
My drink the *m.* dew *G.* 3
She spreads the *m.* over eastern hills *H.* 41
The *m.* came, the chaise was brought *J.G.* 33
Thy *m.* bounties ere I left my home *M.P.* 60
His *m.* course, the enchantment was begun *P.E.* 68
While *m.* kindles with a windy red *R.* 432
Would ye, when rambling in your *m.* ride *R.* 545
Duly as clink of bell to *m.* prayers *T.* 140
Whose flambeaux flash against the *m.* skies *T.* ii 648
The *m.* finds the self-sequestered man *T.* iii 386
'Tis *m.* ; and the sun, with ruddy orb *T.* v 1
The *m.* sharp and clear. But now at noon *T.* vi 58

MOROSE.

Else he was seldom bitter or *m. E.* iii 35

MORRIS-DANCE.

Than caper in the *m.* of verse *T.T.* 519

MORSEL.

Receives the *m.*—flesh obscene of dog *T.* i 562

MORTAL.

Worse than the *m.* brunt of rival swords *Con.* 86
M. whose pleasures are their only care *P.E.* 289
Felt each a *m.* stab in her own breast *P.E.* 339
And *m.* nuisance into all the air *T.* ii 98
Hangs over *m.* eyes, blind from the birth *T.* iii 234
To some secure and more than *m.* height *T.* iv 96
A voice is heard that *m.* ears hear not *T.* v 886
Not to be wronged by a mere *m.* touch *T.* vi 748
That hides divinity from *m.* eyes *T.* vi 877
Gives Liberty the last, the *m.* shock *T.T.* 476
With more than *m.* music on his tongue *T.T.* 737

MORTALITY.

Ere yet *m.'s* fine threads give way *T.* v. 578

MORTIFIED.

Was hurt, disgusted, *m. P.* 19
Of malice fed while flesh is *m. T.* 166

MORTIFY.

My dog shall *m.* the pride *D.W.* 39
To *m.* and grieve me *F.* 213
And *m.* the liberal hand of love *T.* ii 757

MORTIFYING.

And is it not a *m.* thought *T.* 339
Alas ! 'twas but a *m.* stroke *T.* v 169

MOSES.

As meek as the man *M.*, and withal *Ex.* 444
To *M.*, was mistaken in its age *T.* iii 154

MOSS. [*T.* vi 113

Peeps through the *m.* that clothes the hawthorn root
Thick overspread with *m.* and silky grass *N.A.* 2
Hence, ankle-deep in *m.* and flowery thyme *T.* i 270

MOSS-CUSHIONED.

Of girth enormous, with *m.* root *Y.O.* 64

MOSS-GROWN.

This *m.* alley, musing, slow *S.* 18

MOSSY.

Where Nature has her *m.* velvet spread *E.* ii 15

MOTH.

So man, the *m.*, is not afraid, it seems *T.* vi 211

MOTHER.

Affectionate, a *m.* lost so long *M.P.* 14
My *m.* ! when I learned that thou wast dead *M.P.* 21
Soon every father-bird and *m. P.T.* 56
That Chatham's language was his *m.* tongue *T.* ii 237
By monitors that *m.* church supplies *T.* ii 576 [144
As they had known him from his *m.'s* womb *T.* iii
E'en misses, at whose age their *m.* wore *T.* iv 226

MOTHER—MOVE

To break some maiden's and his *m.'s* heart *T.* iv 656
Beat high within them at a *m.'s* wrongs *T.* v 519
The boy's neglected sire! a *m.* too *T.* vi 43
Lurks in the serpent now: the *m.* sees *T.* vi 778
A *m.'s* lecture and a nurse's care *Tir.* 196

MOTHER-BIRD.
The *m.* is gone to sea *A Tale* 45

MOTION.
All distance, *m.*, magnitude, and now *T.* i 717
Shall counterfeit the *m.* of the flood *T.* ii 148
Friendly to vital *m.*, may afford *T.* iii 509
The nimble *m.* of those restless joints *T.* iii 762

MOTIONLESS.
Stand *m.* expectants of its fall *T.* v 528
Fixed *m.*, and petrified with dread *T.* vi 538

MOTIVE.
From *m.* such as his, though not the best *Ch.* 481
Such as our *m.* is our aim must be *Ch.* 567
And still by *m.* of religious force *J.T.* 33
Here various *m.* his ambition raise *P.E.* 53
Discordant *m.* in one centre meet *R.* 173
The principle and *m.* all in all *T.* 200
Though *m.* of mere lucre sway the most *Tir.* 518

MOTLEY.
Vicissitude wheels round the *m.* crowd *H.* 17 [154
Preaching and pranks will share the *m.* scene *P.E.*
That spreads his *m.* wings in the eye of noon *T.* iii 135
The world, with all its *m.* rout. *Trans.* ii 26 [215
With *m.* plumes; and, where the peacock shows *T.* iv

MOTS.
Bon *m.* to gall the Christian and the Jew *T.* 308

MOULD.
In such a *m.* philosophique *R.C.* 9
In human *m.*, should brutalize by choice *T.* i 575
Betimes into the *m.* of heavenly truth *Tir.* 106
Verse in the finest *m.* of fancy cast *T.T.* 618

MOULDED.
But *m.* by his Maker into man *Y.O.* 149

MOULDERING.
Where *m.* abbey walls o'erhang the glade *H.* 351
To view some rugged rock or *m.* tower *T.* iv 235

MOULDY.
To read, engraven on the *m.* walls *T.* v 418

MOUND.
Grow freakish, and o'erleaping every *m. T.T.* 302

MOUNT.
He *m.* at once—such confidence infused *A.T.* 175
Sounds forth the signal, as she *m.* her car *H.* 647
M. from inferior beings up to God *R.* 114
Doubts not hereafter with the saints to *m. T.* 150
That *m.* the stile with ease, or leaps the fence *T.* i 136
We *m.* again, and feel at every step *T.* i 271
The things that *m.* the rostrum with a skip *T.* ii 409
He settles next upon the sloping *m. T.* iii 486

MOUNTAIN.
And made the *m.* tremble at his frown? *Ch.* 78
Duly, as ever on the *m.'s* height *Ch.* 260
From the blue rim, where skies and *m.* meet *H.* 49
And bids the *m.* he has built, stand fast *H.* 476
Slept unperceived, the *m.* yet entire *Her.* 2
Again the *m.* feels the imprisoned foe *Her.* 37
Some Alpine *m.*, wrapped in snow *Miss —* 33
And he shall gild yon *m.'s* height again *P.E.* 69
Where *m.*, river, forest, field, and grove *R.* 29

And bid her *m.* and her hills rejoice *R.* 362
Crush me, ye rocks; ye falling *m.*, hide *T.* 269
Thou climbest the *m.* top, with eager eye *T.* i 664
Abhor each other. M. interposed *T.* ii 17
The hills move lightly, and the *m.* smoke *T.* ii 91
At hewing *m.* into men, and some *T.* v 178
At building human wonders *m.* high *T.* v 179
His are the *m.*, and the valleys his *T.* v 742
Shout to each other, and the *m.* tops *T.* vi 794
From distant *m.* catch the flying joy *T.* vi 795
The bolts that spare the *m.'s* side *Trans. H.* 16

MOUNTAINOUS.
Here runs the *m.* and craggy ridge *T.* iv 57

MOUNTAIN-TOP.
Brutes graze the *m.*, with faces prone *T.* v 785

MOUNTEBANK.
God's worship and the *m.* between *P.E.* 156

MOUNTED.
And on her wickerwork high *m. A Fable* 3
Now see him *m.* once again *J.G.* 77 [25
With tails high *m.*, ears hung low, and throats *N.A.*
And always, ere he *m.*, kissed his horse *R.* 578
Church ladders are not always *m.* best *Tir.* 381

MOURN.
"Shall *m.* her absent lord, for he is gone *A.T.* 104
I *m.*; or, since thrice happy thou must be *J.T.* 9
But ages yet to come shall *m. M.* i 11
Bids me and Mary *m. N.* 14
Or laugh or *m.* with me, the rueful jest *P.E.* 110
Man *m.* his fleeting breath *St.* v 26
Ye fallen avenues! once more I *m. T.* i 338 [814
His birth-place and his dam? The country *m. T.* ii
M. because every plague that can infest *T.* ii 815
Grieves, but alarms me not. I *m.* the pride *T.* iv 102
The cattle *m.* in corners, where the fence *T.* v 27
Maria weeps—the Muses *m.*—*T.B.* 61

MOURNER.
On man, a *m.* in his best estate! *Ch.* 156
And crowns the soul, while yet a *m.* here *H.* 165
And waft it to the *m.* as he roves *R.* 338

MOURNFUL.
With *m.* scutcheons, and dim lamps between *H.* 265
And oaks coeval spread a *m.* shade *H.* 352
How each would trembling wait the *m.* sheet *St.* ii 5
That here and there some sprigs of *m.* mint *T.* iv 756

MOURNFULLY.
Till farce itself, most *m.* jejune *R.* 711

MOUSE.
And where, secure as *m.* in chink *R.C.* 5
Dire foe alike of bird and *m. T.B.* 20
And the *m.* with curious snout *Trans.* iii 12

MOUTH.
So language in the *m.* of the adult *Con.* 15
Give it the breast, or stop its *m.* with pap! *Con.* 480
With *m.* made only to grin wide and eat *R.* 309
The *m.* with blasphemy, the heart with woe *T.* i 505
The curbs invented for the mulish *m. T.* ii 744
Hence, in a Roman *m.*, the graceful name *T.T.* 500
The future, best unknown, but at thy *m. Y.O.* 43

MOVE.
The winged mansion *m. A Tale* 50
It *m.* me more perhaps than Folly ought *Con.* 625
In England's case to *m.* the Muse to tears? *Ex.* 2
In England's case to *m.* the Muse to tears? *Ex.* 31
Their host to *m.*, and when it stayed to rest *Ex.* 180

MOVE—MUSE

If Interest m. thee, to persuade e'en thee *Ex.* 667
But they that wore them, m. not at the sound *H.* 267
It hurts our pride, and m. our envy less *H.* 553
These m. the censure and illiberal grin *H.* 744 [25
Which, though new-born, with vigour m. *Mrs. M—*
Ordained to m. when others please *P.* 7
A trifle if it m. but to amuse *P.E.* 303
Stand close concealed, and see a statue m. *R.* 284
Must m. and act for him alone *R.C.* 114
No more m. us than the bell *St.* iv 31
M. without noise, and swift as an express *T.* 204
Say on what hinge does his obedience m. ? *T.* 207
An instant's pause, and lives but while she m. *T.* i 371
As m. derision, or by foppish airs *T.* ii 562 [91
The hills m. lightly, and the mountains smoke *T.* ii
M. right toward the mark; nor stops for aught *T.* v 53
For their conception, which they cannot m. *T.* v 254
M. indignation, makes the name of king *T.* v 442
The great artificer of all that m. *T.* vi 207 [*T.* v 666
He slights the strokes of conscience. Nothing m.
Of that controlling ordinance they m. *T.* vi 202 [597
By which Heaven m. in pardoning guilty man *T.* vi
Can cheat, or m. a moment's fear in me ? *T.* vi 508
Can m. or warp ; and gratitude for small *T.* vi 629
Should m. a sneer at thy deserved fame *Tir.* 142
What causes m. us, knowing, as we must *Tir.* 292
And m. the lips of poets cast in lead *T.T.* 203
A kick that scarce would m. a horse *Y.D.* 63

MOVEABLE.
This m. structure of shelves *Gr.* 25
The roof, though m. through all its length *T.* vi 72

MOVED. [232
" Yes "(rather m.) " I saw it with these eyes ! " *Con.*
And Cyrus, with relenting pity m. *Ex.* 75   [152
M. not, while theirs was rocked like a light skiff *T.* ii
Grew tremulous, and m. derision more *T.* ii 729 [566
The weak prehaps are m., but are not taught *T.* ii
More briskly m. by his severer toil *T.* iv 389
M. many a sigh at its disheart'ning length *T.* vi 22
Where now the vital energy that m. *T.* vi 134
The charity that warmed his heart was m. *T.* vi 498
When sin hath m. him, and his wrath is hot *T.* vi 742
The man that is not m. with what he reads *T.T.* 25

MOVEMENT.
Prompt every m. of his heart and mind *T* 194
His form, and m. ; is as smart above *T.* iv 641

MOVEST.
That now at every step thou m. *M.* 38

MOVING.
That m. signal summoning, when best *Ex.* 179
With opera glass to watch the m. scene *T.* ii 453
With matron step slow m., while the Night *T.* iv 246
Noiseless, appears a m. hill of snow *T.* iv 346

MUD. [*Ch.* 531
Plunged in the stream, they lodge upon the m.
Darts to the m., and finds his safety there *P.E.* 503

MUDDY.
Spawned in the m. beds of Nile, came forth *T.* ii 827

MULBERRY-TREE.
The m. was hung with blooming wreaths *T.* vi 685
The m. stood centre of the dance *T.* vi 686
The m. was hymn'd with dulcet airs *T.* vi 687
And from his touchwood trunk the m. *T.* vi 688

MULCIBER.
Seem the labour of *M.'s* hands *Gr.* 40

MULETEER.
A m.'s the man to set him right *P.E.* 541

MULISH.
That m. folly, not to be reclaimed $C_{h.}$ 497
The curbs invented for the m. m

MULTIFORM.
The expedients and inventions m. *T.* ii 237
And tortures and groans will be m. still *P.A.* 12
And by caprice as m. as his *T.* ii 597
With lights, by clear reflection m. *T.* iv 268
When man was m. and spread abroad *T.* v 221

MULTITUDE.
So fares it with the m. beguiled *H.* 278
The life of m., a nation's bread ! *Her.* 56
" We do "—a m. replies *L.W.* 26
And every hour sweeps m. away *R.* 153
M., fugitive on every side *T.* ii 106
That, like the m. made faction-mad *T.* iii 673
Of m. unknown ! Hail, rural life ! *T.* iv 783
With all his roaring m. of waves *T.* v 766
Holds an unthinking m. enthrall'd *T.* vi 100

MUM.
I pity them greatly, but I must be m. *P.A.* 5

MUMBLING.
Sheepish he doffs his hat, and m. swears *T.* iv 628

MUMMERY.
By m. He that dwelt in it disdained *Ex.* 146
Our sabbaths closed with m. and buffoon *P.E.* 153
And histrionic m., that let down *T.* ii 563

MUNIFICENCE.
Powers misemploy'd, m. misplaced *Tir.* 50

MURDER.
Of midnight m. was a wonder heard *T.* iv 563
The seeds of m. in the breast of man *T.* v 210

MURDERER.
The robber and the m. weak as we ? *Ch.* 68
And the first smith was the first m.'s son *T.* v 219
His m. on his back, and, push'd all day *T.* vi 428

MURMUR.
O salutary streams, that m. there! *E.* ii 28
Could he with reason m. at his case *H.* 316
That m. through the dewy mead *O.* ii 16
'Gan m., as became the softer sex *T.* i 71
Snore to the m. of the Atlantic wave ? *T.* iv 27
Falls a soft m. on the uninjured ear *T.* iv 93

MURMURING.
M. and weary of our daily toil *Ch.* 221
Still m. with the solemn truths I teach *Ex.* 719
M. and ungrateful Discontent *R.* 759
Now m. soft, now roaring in cascades *T.* iii 779

MURRAY.
And *M.* sighs o'er Pope, and Swift *M.* i 5
O'er *M.'s* loss the Muses wept *M.* ii 5

MUSCLE.
And buy the m. and the bones of man ? *Ch.* 140
M. and nerve miraculously spun *R.* 59
And withered m., and the vapid soul *T.* i 393
Proportioned well, half m. and half bone *T.T.* 219

MUSCULAR.
I view the m. proportioned limb *T.* v 15

MUSE.
The chaster *M.* of modern days omits *A.T.* 85
That I presume to address the *M.*—*E.* iv 12 [*Ex.* 1
Why weeps the *M.* for England ? What appears

In England's case to move the M. to tears ? *Ex.* 2
All speak her happy :—let the M. look round *Ex.* 27
In England's case to move the M. to tears ? *Ex.* 32
M., hang this harp upon yon aged beech *Ex.* 718 [19
But oh ! what M., and in what powers of song *Her.*
O'er Murray's loss the M. wept M. ii 5
The angry M. thus sings thee forth *M.B.* 23
Awaking, how could I but m. *M.D.* 41
The M. sweep the lyre *Miss* — 84
No matter when—a poet's M. is *P.* 23
Sing M., (if such a theme, so dark, so long *P.E.* 1
May find a M. to grace it with a song) *P.E.* 2
But the M., eagle-pinioned, has in view *P.E.* 331
Petronius ! all the M. weep for thee *P.E.* 335 [604
But, M., forbear ; long flights forebode a fall *P.E.*
To m. on the perishing pleasures of man *P.F.* 18
Then sweet to m. upon his skill displayed *R.* 51
Sorrow might m. herself to madness then *T.* 441
To m. in silence, or at least confine *T.* iii 36 [692
No loose or wanton, though a wandering M.—*T.* iii
The firstborn efforts of my youthful m. *T.* iv 701
Ah, M. ! forbear to speak *T.B.* 51 [v 707
Their names to the sweet lyre. The historic M.—*T.*
But hush !—the m. perhaps is too severe *T.* vi 653
Maria weeps—the M. mourn *T.B.* 61
The present M. of every pensive mind *Tir.* 22
Say, m., (for education made the song *Tir.* 290
No m. can hesitate, or linger long) *Tir.* 291 [787
But courage, man ! methought the M. replied *Tir.*
You think, no doubt, he sits and m. *Trans.* ii 19
Awakes sometimes the M. too *Trans. H.* 29
Reward his memory, dear to every M.—*T.T.* 14
The poet's m., his passion, and his theme *T.T.* 289
The M. imparts, and can command the lyre *T.T.* 481
Else summoning the M. to such a theme *T.T.* 550
Judged every effort of the M. a crime *T.T.* 617
The M. instructed a well nurtured train *T.T.* 634
He snatched it rudely from the M.'s hand *T.T.* 689
And every M. attend her in her way *T.T.* 719
No M. on these lines attend *U.* 29

MUSED.

Taking my lonely winding walk, I m. *F.A.* 8
Awhile they m. ; surveying every face *N.A.* 73
Catching its ardour as I m. along *R.* 376

MUSIC.

Never hear the sweet m. of speech *A.S.* 11
Hark ! 'tis the m. of a thousand rills *Ch.* 367
Like m. it tinkles and rings in your ears *F.M.* 7
Sweet m. is no longer m. here *H.* 702
'Gan make his instrument of m. speak *N.A.* 44
That you with m., I with light *N.G.* 21
Love makes the m. of the blest above *P.E.* 77
Set Paul to m., he shall quote him too *P.E.* 113
Still I insist, though m. heretofore *P.E.* 138
To waste unheard the m. of his strains *R.* 548
'Tis manly m., such as martyrs make *R.* 775[*S.* i 10
Both heart and head ; and couldst with m. sweet
He treads as if, some solemn m. near *T.* 62
Of ancient growth, make m. not unlike *T.* i 185
And m. of her woods—no works of man *T.* i 430
Is famished—finds no m. in the song *T.* i 468
And m. of the bladder and the bag *T.* i 585
And heard our m. ; are thy simple friends *T.* i 645
Birds warbling all the m. We can spare *T.* i 764
Some note of Nature's m. from his lips *T.* iii 600
With such heart-shaking m., who can say *T.* iv 24
To books, to m., or the poet's toil *T.* iv 262
Enchanting m. and immortal wreaths *T.* iv 687
With m. such as suits their sovereign ears *T.* v 387
Account it m. ; that it summons some *T.* v 409 [647
"Attend to their own m. ? Have they faith *T.* v
Smitten in vain ! such m. cannot charm *T.* v 682
How soft the m. of those village bells *T.* vi 6
Whence all the m. I again perceive *T.* vi 67
Makes wintry m., sighing as it goes *T.* vi 143
Recovering fast its liquid m., prove *T.* vi 261
(O wonderful effect of m.'s power !) *T.* vi 636
To meaner m., and not suffer loss *T.* vi 750 [491
The storm of m. shakes the astonished crowd *T.T.*
With m. modulating all their notes *T.T.* 695
With more than mortal m. on his tongue *T.T.* 737

MUSICAL.

As only her m. tongue *C.* 19
M. as the chime of tinkling rills *P.E.* 14
Are m. enough in Thomson's song *R.* 570
As ornamental, m., polite *T.* iv 489
But he (his m. finesse was such) *T.T.* 652

MUSIC-DRAWING.

Of drunkards, or the m. bow *St.* ii 12

MUSICIAN.

And give the day to a m.'s praise *T.* vi 644

MUSING.

In daily m. and in nightly dreams *A.T.* 12
A difference strikes at length the m. heart *Comp.* i 8
In m. worthy of the great event *Con.* 510
This moss-grown alley, m., slow *S.* 18
That lost in his own m., happy man ! *T.* ii 301
And settle in soft m. as I tread *T.* vi 69

MUSSULMAN.

" Good M., abstain from pork *L.W.* 2

MUSTERING.

When most severe, and m. all its force *T.* vi 31

MUTABILITY.

Witnessed, of m. in all *Y.O.* 70

MUTATION.

And studious of m. still, discard *T.* ii 610

MUTE.

The fear of being silent makes us m. *Con.* 352
That fables old, that seemed for ever m. *Con.* 817
Ensured him m. attention and regard *H.* 687
Not one of them was m. *J.G.* 238
M. as e'er gazed on orator or bard *S.* i 8
Scared, and the offended nightingale is m. *T.* i 768
And though by nature m. *T.B.* 9
I hear as m. as if a Syren sung *T.T.* 199
With m. unconsciousness of what he saw *Y.O.* 143

MUTILATED.

A m. structure, soon to fall *T.* i 774

MUTINY.

He gives the word, and M. soon roars *T.T.* 452

MUTTON.

When thus a m. statelier than the rest *N.A.* 81

MUTUAL.

This genial intercourse, and m. aid *Ch.* 93
But we, in m. bondage knit *Dr.* 17
M. attention is implied *F.* 49
Had been their m. solace long *F.B.* 5
Benevolence, and peace, and m. aid *T.* ii 48
Nor comfort else, but in their m. love *T.* iv 406
" Our m. bond of faith and truth *The Doves* 9

MUTUALLY.

Of hearts in union m. disclosed *Con.* 680
The mind and conduct m. imprint *P.E.* 566

MYRIADS.

The mighty m., now securely scorned *R.* 70

How find the *m.*, that in summer cheer *T.* v 77
The propagated *m.* spread so fast *P.E.* 484
She *m.* found below *Q.V.* 76

MYRTLE.
Hung not far off upon a *m.* bough *A.T.* 174
Shall grow the *m.*, and luxuriant yew " *H.* 527
Once more the spiry *m.* crowns the glade *Her.* 31
Of golden fruitage, and her *m.* bowers *T.* ii 215
Who sell their laurel for a *m.* wreath *T.* ii 229
The spiry *m.* with unwithering leaf *T.* iii 570
Of orange, *m.*, or the fragrant weed *T.* iv 764

MYSTERY. [*F.A.* 28
Deep *m.* both! which schoolmen must have toiled
To unriddle, and have left them *m.* still *F.A.* 29
To search forbidden deeps where *m.* lies *F.A.* 33

M. are food for angels; they digest *F.A.* 35
Explains all *m.*, except her own *T.* ii 528
And all the *m.* to faith proposed *T.* vi 878

MYSTERIOUS.
Of Heaven's *m.* purposes and ways *Ch.* 58
M. are his ways whose power *E.* i 29
Such Mahomet's *m.* charge *L.W.* 7
On subjects more *m.*, they were yet *T.* v 290
Illuminates. Thy lamp, *m.* Word! *T.* v 846

MYSTIC.
An Indian *m.*, or a French recluse *T.* 128

MYTHOLOGIC.
And taught at schools much *m.* stuff *Tir.* 197

N.

NABAIOTH.
N., and the flocks of Kedar there *T.* vi 805

NAG.
Curried his *n.* and looked another way *R.* 590

NAIAD.
A little *N.* her impoverished urn *T.* i 328
The dancing *N.* through the dewy meads *T.T.* 693

NAIL.
Whose headaches *n.* them to a noonday bed *T.* i 500

NAILED.
From a worse yoke, and *n.* it to the tree *Ex.* 220

NAKED.
Sea-beaten rocks and *n.* shores *A Tale* 19
And Hell's close mischief *n.* in his sight *Ex.* 339
Those *n.* acres to a sheltering grove *T.* iii 773
And all shall be restored. These *n.* shoots *T.* vi 141

NAME.
The land of dreams, Hypothesis her *n. A.T.* 6 [ii 4
With as many hard *n.* as would line a good trunk *A.T.*
Heedless of a soldier's *n. B.* 22
To *n.* ignoble, born to be forgot! *B.B.* 2
That tells his *n.*, his worth, his age *Cast.* 51
Whether we *n.* thee Charity or Love *Ch.* 3
A poet's *n.*, by making thee the theme *Ch.* 14
Canst thou, and honoured with a Christian *n. Ch.* 180
I must incur, forgetting Howard's *n. Ch.* 296
Makes wisdom, worthy of the *n.*, his own *Ch.* 350
Flavia, most tender of her own good *n. Ch.* 453
A thousand *n.* are tossed into the crowd *Ch.* 517
The wreath He won so dearly in our *n. Ch.* 586
The founder of that *n.* alone inspires *Ch.* 600
Whoever boasts that *n.*—behold a cheat! *Ch.* 603
N. almost worthy of a Christian's praise *Con.* 36
God's *n.* so much upon his lips, a priest *Con.* 72
By Fashion taught, forbade them once to *n. Con.* 496
Known by thy bleating, Ignorance thy *n. Con.* 588
And give true piety that odious *n. Con.* 656 [683
Bad men, profaning friendship's hallowed *n. Con.*
The praise of *n.* for ages obsolete *Con.* 828 [*Con.* 908
It sounds Jehovah's *n.*, and pours his praise along
But ills of every shape and every *n. E.* ii 37
The favours poured upon the Jewish *n. Ex.* 170
Their *n.* far published, and revered as far *Ex.* 194
How shall a verse impress thee ? By what *n. Ex.* 654

Their *n.*, alas! in vain reproach an age *Ex.* 660
Hence authors of illustrious *n. F.* 85
His *n.* of wisdom, goodness, power, and love *H.* 135
Or, more provoking still, of nobler *n. H.* 192
A right to the meek honours of her *n.*, *H.* 236 [438
And add Right Reverend to Smug's honoured *n. H.*
I slur a *n.* a poet must not speak) *H.* 555
Happy the bard, (if that fair *n.* belong *H.* 754
Oppression his terrible *n. M.D.* 28
All tribes beside of Indian *n. Mrs. M—* 9 [46
Where once we dwelt our *n.* is heard no more *M.P.*
Those Christians best deserve the *n. N.G.* 35
Birds of all feather, beasts of every *n. N.A.* 65
Retires to blazon his own worthless *n. R.* 217
Thyrsis, Alexis, or whatever *n. R.* 247
He that has not usurped the *n.* of man *R.* 319
To carve his rustic *n.* upon a tree *R.* 400
I pity, and must therefore sink the *n. R.* 576
Though I revere your honourable *n. R.* 663
Belie their *n.*, and offer nothing new *R.* 714
Too rigid, in my view, that *n.* to one *R.* 720
Flowers by that *n.* promiscuously we call *R.* 723
Can life in them deserve tho *n. St.* vi 13
Your sentence and mine differ. What's a *n.* ? *T.* 107
Scrawled upon glass Miss Bridget's lovely *n. T.* 156
And man might safely trifle with his *n. T.* 556
The panels, leaving an obscure, rude *n. T.* i 282
And theirs alone seems worthy of the *n. T.* i 398
The boast of mere pretenders to the *n. T.* i 492
How, in the *n.* of soldiership and sense *T.* ii 225 [238
And Wolfe's great *n.* compatriot with his own *T.* ii
And show the *n.* ye might conceal at home *T.* ii 279
The pulpit, therefore, (and I *n.* it filled *T.* ii 326
Oh *n.* it not in Gath! it cannot be *T.* ii 367
And vicious pleasures; buys the boy a *n. T.* ii 759
His *n.* a theme for praise and for reproach ? *T.* iii 282
Start at his awful *n.*, or deem his praise *T.* iv 180
Need help, denies them nothing but his *n. T.* iv 428
King was a *n.* too proud for man to wear *T.* v 242
Moves indignation, makes the *n.* of king *T.* v 442
Such reasonings (if that *n.* must needs belong *T.* v 655
Their *n.* to the sweet lyre. The Historic Muse *T.* v 707
No marble tells us whither. With their *n. T.* v 727
Some to the fascination of a *n. T.* vi 103
Nature is but a *n.* for an effect *T.* vi 223
With self-taught rites, and under various *n. T.* vi 232
Each animal, of every *n.*, conceived *T.* vi 373
Thy *n.* adoring, and then preach thee man! *T.* vi 887

NAME—NATURE

While Alfred's n., the father of his age *T.T.* 105
She loses in such storms her very n. *T.T.* 328
But when a country (one that I could n.) *T.T.* 414
Stamps God's own n. upon a lie just made *T.T.* 420
What follows next, let cities of great n. *T.T.* 430
Hence, in a Roman mouth, the graceful n. *T.T.* 500
Inspires the song, and that his n. is Love *T.T.* 739
Thus graced, the man asserts the poet's n. *T.T.* 714
Or, if to see the n. of idol self *T.T.* 744
I n. thee not, lest so despised a n. *Tir.* 141
The very n. we carved subsisting still *Tir.* 301
Retracing thus his frolics ('tis a n. *Tir.* 332
Whose chief distinction is their spotless n. *Tir.* 353
Christian in n., and infidel in heart *Tir.* 421
And emulation is its specious n. *Tir.* 469
Such vicious habits as disgrace his n. *Tir.* 531
Thy n. omitted, in a page *U.* 5
I seize thy n. in haste *U.* 20
But not hereafter to the n. of friend! *V.* 18
Graced with the n. of a long absent friend *V.* 40
To each his n. significant, and, filled *Y.O.* 153

NAMED.

N. with emphatic dignity, "The Tower" *Ch.* 550
Be never n. in ears esteemed polite *Con.* 474
Is falsely n., and no such thing *St.* vi 11
Him, Tubal n., the Vulcan of old times *T.* v 217
With infamy too nauseous to be n. *Tir.* 828

NAMELESS.

Are all the n. sweets of friendship fled? *P.E.* 244
And thou, sad sufferer under n. ill *R.* 343

NAMING.

But, n. none, the Voice now speaks to all *St.* ii 20

NAP.

And took too often there his easy n. *T.T.* 679

NARRATIVE.

Of n. sincere *Cast.* 50
The path of n. with care pursue *Con.* 217
Some write a n. of wars and feats *T.* iii 139
Through moral n., or sacred text *Tir.* 126

NARROW.

'Tis n., selfish, arrogant, and draws *Con.* 671
A n. brook, by rushy banks concealed *N.A.* 9
Himself a wanderer from the n. way *P.E.* 118
But life, within a n. ring *St.* vi 9
To n. bounds. The Grove receives us next *T.* i 354
Lands intersected by a n. frith *T.* ii 16
No n. bounds; her cause engages him *T.* v 395
No nook so n. but he spreads them there *T.* v 773
N. and long, o'erlooks the western wave *T.* vi 484
Respect, while stalking o'er life's n. stage *T.T.* 118

NASAL.

To me is odious as tho n. twang *T.* ii 436

NATAL.

Fancy endued her in her n. hour) *A.T.* 92

NATION.

Alternately the n. learn and teach *Ch.* 120
Or scare the n. with its big contents *Ch.* 617
When n. are to perish in their sins *Ex.* 95
What n. will you find, whose annals prove *Ex.* 165
In vain the n., that had seen them rise *Ex.* 203
The last of n. now, though once the first *Ex.* 242
O Israel, of all n. most undone! *Ex.* 257
Knock at the gates of n., rouse their fears *Ex.* 269
And in whose awful sight all n. seem *Ex.* 344
When other n. flew from coast to coast *Ex.* 552
Bid n. leagued against thee stand aloof *Ex.* 565

The Maker fills the n. with alarm *Ex.* 585
Happy the n. where such men abound *Ex.* 653
Of n., sworn to spoil thee and devour *Ex.* 703
What n. amongst all my foes is free *Ex.* 710
A n. scourged, yet tardy to repent *Ex.* 723
The screaming n., hovering in mid air *H.* 353
A n. dwells, not envious of your throne *Her.* 49
The life of multitudes, a n.'s bread! *Her.* 56
Deem our n. brutes no longer *N.C.* 49
That water all the n.'s *O.* i 6
Seas on which every n. spreads her sails *R.* 80
Make enemies of n. who had else *T.* ii 18
That's noble, and bespeaks a n. proud *T.* ii 43
Between the n., in a world that seems *T.* ii 50
And desolates a n. at a blast *T.* ii 188
As n. ignorant of God contrive *T.* ii 574
With things so sacred as a n.'s trust *T.* ii 778
News from all n. lumbering at his back *T.* iv 7
With merry descants or a n.'s woes *T.* iv 77
Kings would not play at. N. would do well *T.* v 188
To all the n. Ample was the boon *T.* v 199
Among the n., seeing thou art free *T.* v 461
Who loves no part? He be a n.'s friend *T.* v 504
One song employs all n.; and all cry *T.* vi 791
Till, n. after n. taught the strain *T.* vi 796
The wisdom of great n., now no more *Tir.* 16
Chief monster that has plagued the n. yet! *T.T.* 38
Increasing taxes and the n.'s debt *T.T.* 177
And weighs the n. in an even scale *T.T.* 251
The n. hunt, all mark thee for a prey *T.T.* 364
And that a n. shamefully debased *T.T.* 396
The standards of all n. are unfurled *T.T.* 454

NATIONAL.

To urge reformation of n. ill *F.M.* 14

NATIVE.

When I think of my own n. land *A.S.* 45
The simple n. of the new-found isle *Ch.* 30
I was a bondman on my n. plain *Ch.* 236
A story in which n. humour reigns *Con.* 203
For ever in my n. shell *P.* 6
To the fair haven of my n. home *R.* 385
Fast by their n. shore! *R.G.* 4
By n. power and energy her own *T.* 396
Thus fare the shivering n. of the north *T.* i 617
Forth from thy n. bowers, to show thee here *T.* i 636
Blown in its n. bed; 'tis there alone *T.* iv 660
Abridge him of his just and n. rights *T.* v 436
My n. nook of earth! Thy clime is rude *T.* v 462
Kneels with the n. of the farthest west *T.* vi 811
Assert the n. evil of his heart *Tir.* 162
A n. of the gorgeous East *Trans.* iv 2

NATURAL.

"Her n. ally *Miss* — 90
As n. as when asleep to dream *R.* 636
It does not feel for man. The n. bond *T.* ii 9
And n. in gesture; much impressed *T.* ii 402
Harmless, and safe, and n., as they are *Tir.* 565
Alas, poor boy!—the n. effect *Tir.* 575
Of n. pity, send him not to school *Tir.* 872
Was n. as in the flowing stream *T.T.* 592
'Tis but the n. effect 1789, 68

NATURE.

'Twas N., sir, whose strong behest *B.R.* 7
Yet much as N. I respect *B.R.* 9
Tis N. alone that we love *C.* 36
Wherever he found man to n. true *Ch.* 27
God opens fruitful N.'s various scenes *Ch.* 88
Calls N. from her ivy-mantled den *Ch.* 95
The gems of India, N.'s rarest birth *Ch.* 134
All bonds of n., in that moment end *Ch.* 142

NATURE

Puts off his generous *n*., and, to suit *Ch.* 153
N. imprints upon whate'er we see *Ch.* 169
Walks arm in arm with *N.* all his way *Ch.* 314
That man, in *N.*'s richest mantle clad *Ch.* 341
(Two themes to *N.*'s eye for ever sealed) *Ch.* 362
The ties of *N.* do but feebly bind *Ch.* 371
Endued with reason, yet by *n.* blind *Ch.* 382
Though *N.* weigh our talents, and dispense *Con.* 1
No—*N.*, unsophisticate by man *Con.* 451
And yet, God knows, look human *n.* through *Con.* 749
Pursues the course that truth and *n.* teach *Con.* 890
The gift of *n.*, or the classic store *Con.* 896
Derived from *n.*'s noblest part *E.* i 13
Like some of *N.*'s sweetest flowers *E.* i 94
Where *N.* has her mossy velvet spread *E.* ii 15
That hard by *n.*, and of stubborn will *E.* ii 21
I knew the man, and knew his *n.* mild *E.* iii 32
Can *N.* add a charm, or Art confer *Ex.* 5
Then *N.*, injured, scandalized, defied *Ex.* 424
Ere *N.* rose from her eternal sleep *Ex.* 637
But *n.* works in every breast *F.B.* 13
See *N.* gay as when she first began *H.* 39
N., employed in her allotted place *H.* 145
To enjoy cool *n.* in a country seat *H.* 245
If wild in *n.*, and not duly found *H.* 296
N. indeed vouchsafes for our delight *H.* 487
They were by *n.*, atheists, head and heart *H.* 498
Wild as if *n.* there, void of all good *H.* 540
Contrived to suit frail *n.*'s crazy case *H.* 604
N. opposes with her utmost force *H.* 639
Unconscious *n.*, all that he surveys *H.* 740
Sweet *N.*, stripped of her embroidered robe *Her.* 79
And, though God made thee of a *n.* prone *J.T.* 31
To Him whose works bespeak his *n.*, Love *J.T.* 46
Its *n.* to forego *Miss* — 6
Come, then, fair maid (in *n.* wise) *Miss* — 13
'Tis *N.* bids, and whilst the laws *Miss* — 49
Of *N.* we retain *Miss* — 50
Cannot forfeit *N.*'s claim *N.C.* 14
Why did all-creating *N.*—*N.C.* 17
The gifts of *N.* and of Grace *N.G.* 34
Man, *N.*'s guest by invitation sweet *P.E.* 209
For *N.*, nice, as liberal to dispense *P.E.* 213
Chafed him, and brought dull *n.* to a glow *P.E.* 408
By *n.* weak, or viciously inclined *P.E.* 432
Take leave of *n.*'s God, and God revealed *P.E.* 591
To trace in *N.*'s most minute design *R.* 53
To limit thought, by *N.* prone to stray *R.* 127
Some minds by *n.* are averse to noise *R.* 175
N. in all the various shapes she wears *R.* 193
O *N.*! whose Elysian scenes disclose *R.* 199
Who studies *N.* with a wanton eye *R.* 213
Gives Melancholy up to *N.*'s care *R.* 281
Parks in which Art preceptress *N.* weds *R.* 335
N. in every form inspires delight *R.* 417
(A poet fond of *N.* and your friend) *R.* 542
N. assuming a more lovely face *R.* 357
N. indeed looks prettily in rhyme *R.* 567
'Tis wild good *n.*'s never failing lot *R.* 582
To social scenes by *n.* disinclined *R.* 606
Must change her *n.*, or in vain retires *R.* 680
Sends *N.* forth, the daughter of the skies *R.* 795
N. perhaps herself had cast her *R.C.* 8
N. inanimate employs sweet sounds *T.* 197
But animated *N.* sweeter still *T.* 198
She, for her humble sphere by *n.* fit *T.* 323
As *N.* at her own peculiar cost *T.* 397
Hark! universal *N.* shook and groaned *T.* 563
With *N.*'s varnish; severed into stripes *T.* i 40
Thou knowest my praise of *N.* most sincere *T.* i 150
The tone of languid *N.* Mighty winds *T.* i 183
That *N.* rides upon, maintains her health *T.* i 369
The love of *N.*, and the scenes she draws *T.* i 412

But *N.*'s works far lovelier. I admire *T.* i 421 [413
Is *N.*'s dictate. Strange! there should be found *T.* i
Than please the eye—sweet *N.* every sense *T.* i 427
To gaze at *N.* in her green array *T.* i 449
His *n.*, and though capable of arts *T.* i 576
Where man, by *n.* fierce, has laid aside *T.* i 594
A lucid mirror, in which *N.* sees *T.* i 701
As human *n.*'s broadest, foulest blot *T.* ii 22
And *N.* with a dim and sickly eye *T.* ii 64
In *N.*'s tendencies, oft overlooks *T.* ii 175
The source of the disease that *N.* feels *T.* ii 194
Blind *n.* to a God not yet revealed *T.* ii 526
By *n.*, or by flattery made so, taught *T.* ii 546
Of grossest *n.* and of worst effects *T.* ii 689
Contrive creation; travel *n.* up *T.* iii 156
In playing tricks with *N.*, giving laws *T.* iii 165
Of *N.*, overlooks her author more *T.* iii 237
His glory, and his *n.* to impart *T.* iii 274
Of harmless *N.*, dumb, but yet endued *T.* iii 329
And *N.* in her cultivated trim *T.* iii 357
Maternal *n.* had reversed its course *T.* iii 436
Then acts in *N.*'s office, brings to pass *T.* iii 542
Some note of *N.*'s music from his lips *T.* iii 600
N., enchanting *N.*, in whose form *T.* iii 721
Attract us, and neglected *N.* pines *T.* iii 730
The charms of *N.* 'Tis the cruel gripe *T.* iii 826
Of universal *n.* undergoes *T.* iv 325
The clown, the child of *n.*, without guile *T.* iv 623
Their *n.*; and, disclaiming all regard *T.* iv 679
To *N.*'s praises. Heroes and their feats *T.* iv 705
'Tis born with all: the love of *N.*'s works *T.* iv 731
That *N.* lives; that sight-refreshing green *T.* iv 759
A peep at *N.*, when he can no more *T.* iv 779
Thus *N.* works as if to mock at Art *T.* v 122
'Twas transient in its *n.*, as in show *T.* v 173
From *N.*'s bounty—that humane address *T.* v 469
Of British *n.*, wanting its excuse *T.* v 481
Till *N.*, unavailing *n.*, foiled *T.* v 627
The shag of savage *n.*, and were each *T.* v 693
Of *N.*, and though poor perhaps compared *T.* v 739
Appropriates *n.* as his Father's work *T.* v 761
So reads he *N.*, whom the lamp of truth *T.* v 845
In that blest moment, *N.* throwing wide *T.* v 891
And in the constancy of *N.*'s course *T.* vi 122
Is *N.*'s progress, when she lectures man *T.* vi 182
N. is but a name for an effect *T.* vi 223
Rules universal *n.* Not a flower *T.* vi 240
In *n.*, from the broad majestic oak *T.* vi 250
The heart is hard in *n.*, and unfit *T.* vi 321
With which kind *n.* graces every scene *T.* vi 342
Were sown in human *n.*'s fruitful soil *T.* vi 383
The injurious trampler upon *N.*'s law *T.* vi 465
Disturbs the economy of *N.*'s realm *T.* vi 579
The vale of *N.*, where it creeps and winds *T.* vi 721
The groans of *N.* in this nether world *T.* vi 729
By ancient covenant ere *N.*'s birth *T.* vi 858
And though by *n.* mute *T.B.* 9
To *N.*'s scenes, than *N.* ever knew *Tir.* 24 [30
That Grace and *N.* have to wage through life *Tir.*
With every lust with which frail *N.* burns *Tir.* 66
Then he, of all that *N.* has brought forth *Tir.* 69
But reason heard, and *n.* well perused *Tir.* 89
Received his nobler *n.*, and was made *Tir.* 97
Touch but his *n.* in its ailing part *Tir.* 161
How weak the barrier of mere *N.* proves *Tir.* 169
Opposed against the pleasures *N.* loves! *Tir.* 170
Religion makes the free by *n.* slaves *Tir.* 184
Or if, by *n.* sober, ye had then *Tir.* 271
That God and *n.*, and your interest too *Tir.* 553
Hear *N.* plead, show mercy to thy son *Tir.* 756
Designed by *N.* wise, but self-made fools *Tir.* 837
Thou canst not! *N.*, pulling at thine heart *Tir.* 865
Thou wouldst not, deaf to *N.*'s tenderest plea *Tir.* 867

NATURE—NEED

Perhaps indulgent N. meant *Trans.* i 13
And N. laughs again *Trans. H.* 24
Liberal in all things else, yet N. here *T.T.* 208
Thus happiness depends, as N. shows *T.T.* 246
The growth that N. meant she should attain *T.T.* 263
(A dire effect, by one of N.'s laws *T.T.* 442
N. in arms, her elements at strife *T.T.* 448
To carry n. lengths unknown before *T.T.* 558
N. imparting her satiric gift *T.T.* 656
N. exerting an unwearied power *T.T.* 690
As if produced by N. there *U.* 18
Not hard by n., in a feeling part *V.* 42
Should be renewed in n., pure in heart *V.* 60
He gives, what bankrupt n. never can *V.* 95
What N., alas! has denied *W.N.* 1
And in conclusion mar them. N.'s threads *Y.O.* 80

NAUGHT.

She whispered still that he had n. to fear *A.T.* 182
The faculties that seemed reduced to n. *Con.* 403
That all was n. within, and all found out *E.* iii 53
Away went Gilpin, neck or n. *J.G.* 97
With n. in charge, he could betray no trust *P.E.* 29
We travel far, 'tis true, but not for n. *T.* i 675
Stark n., because corrupt in their design *T.T.* 4
The wretch, to n. but his ambition true *T.T* 30

NAUSEA.

And unless you adorn it, a n. follows *F.M.* 24

NAUSEOUS.

'Tis n. as the vapour of a vault *Con.* 50
The full-gorged savage, at his n. feast *H.* 509
O n.!—an emetic for a whet! *P.E.* 222
The n. task to paint her as she is *T.* iii 67
Pick up their n. dole, though sweet to them *T.* v 94
With infamy too n. to be named *Tir.* 828

NAVAL.

The feats of Vestris, or the n. force *Con.* 58

NAVIES.

They trust in n., and their n. fail *T.T.* 466

NAVIGATE.

"That n. a sea that knows no storms *T.* v 823

NAVIGATORS.

By n. uninformed as they *T.* i 630

NEAR.

But the Chief Shepherd even there is n. *E.* ii 44
N. barren rocks, in palaces, or cells *R.* 540 [*T.* iv 295
Though still deceived, some stranger's n. approach
His long love-ditty for my n. approach *T.* vi 309
But 'twas a transient calm. A storm was n. *T.* vi 544
So sure to spoil him, and so n. at hand *Tir.* 697

NEARER.

A little n. home *Pat.* 4
Convinced at last, upon a n. view *R.* 591

NEAREST.

Emulous always of the n. place *H.* 238

NEAT.

Formed with materials n. and soft *A Tale* 39
There centering in a focus round and n. *Con.* 239
His long red cloak, well brushed and n. *J.G.* 75
Some mansion, n. and elegantly dressed *T.* 250
Large expectation, he disposes n. *T.* iii 423 [iii 278
And him who writes it, though the style be n. *T.*
Poor, yet industrious, modest, quiet, n. *T.* iv 374
Her artless manners, and her n. attire *T.* iv 536
The n. conveyance hiding all the offence *T.* vi 980

Behold that figure, n., though plainly clad *Tir.* 664
Prevented much by diet n. and plain *Tir.* 767

NEATLY.

Tight boxes n. sashed, and in a blaze *R.* 483
And n. fitted, it compresses hard *T.* ii 587
Which n. she prepares; then to his book *T.* iii 392
Of the smooth-shaven prop, and n. tied *T.* iii 659
Plashed n., and secured with driven stakes *T.* iv 437
With which when n. peeled and dried *T.B.* 29
N. secured from being soiled or torn *Tir.* 119

NEATNESS.

Washed with a n. scrupulously nice *Ex.* 149
Swept with a woman's n., breeding else *T.* iii 616
Sacred to n. and repose, the alcove *T.* vi 571

NECESSARY.

Life's n. means, but he must die *T.* ii 141
By n. laws their sure effects *T.* ii 192
A n. act incurs no blame *T.* vi 573

NECESSITY.

Not only fill's N.'s demand *Ch.* 99
Through mere n. to close his eyes *H.* 85
Thus first N. invented Stools *T.* i 86
As the n. their authors feel *T.* ii 672
To sad n., the cock foregoes *T.* v 73
Or by n. constrained, they live *T.* vi 413

NECK. [*Ex.* 53

They stretched the n., and rolled the wanton eye
Away went Gilpin, n. or naught *J.G.* 97
For all might see the bottle n. *J.G.* 131
His mantling n. with downy gold *Mrs. M—* 6
Contusion hazarding of n. or spine *N.A.* 7
Ere our n. received the chain *N.C.* 42 [380
With awkward gait, stretched n. and silly stare *P.E.*
With bony and unkerchiefed n. defies *T.* 137
Oh for a law to noose the villain's n. *T.* iv 462
To stroke his azure n., or to receive *T.* vi 781
And bend her polished n. beneath his hand *T.T.* 441

NECTAR. [244

And bathes their eyes with n., and includes *T.* vi

NECTAREOUS.

N. essences, Olympian dews *T.* iv 83
Where most n. sweets abound *1789*, 20

NEED. [88

Small n. of Prayer Book, or of priest, I ween *A.T.*
Though little n., to his good palfrey's side *A.T.* 192
Wherever found (and all men n. thy care) *Ch.* 47
Each climate n. what other climes produce *Ch.* 89
And what dilates the powers must n. refine *Ch.* 332
He feels his n. of an unerring guide *Ch.* 346
Such virtues had n. prove their own reward *Ch.* 571
The sight's enough—no n. to smell a beau *Con.* 285
You n. his pardon, and provoke his rod *Con.* 488
And you, though you must n. prefer *E.* i 45
As n. they must, from great to small! *E.* i 80
"Nor n. his genuine ore refine! *E.* iv 89
N. only to be seen to be admired *Ex.* 493
N. no expense of argument *F.* 140
Is such a friend that one had n. *F.* 172
"No n.," he cries, " of gravity, stuffed out *H.* 105
Life is his gift, from whom whate'er life n. *H.* 115
Pious enough, and having n. of none *H.* 251
So stooping down, as n. he must *J.G.* 89
They therefore n. must fit *J.G.* 188
Such strings for all who n. 'em *Pat.* 22
N. help, let honest industry provide *P.E.* 252
One that still n. his leading string and bib *P.E.* 531
And n. no glossary to set him right *N.A.* 70

To wish thee fairer is no n. N.Y.G. 5
We therefore n. not part O. ii 6
Her works must n. excel who fashioned you R. 544
Still n. repeated warnings, and at last St. ii 26
I dare not—" And you n. not," God replies T. 272
Is not for you—the righteous n. it not T. 506
Rouse all your courage at your utmost n. T. 565[391
For none they n.: the languid eye, the cheek T. i
N. other physic none to heal the effects T. i 590
Sure there is n. of social intercourse T. ii 48 [ii 368
That grave and learned clerks should n. such aid T.
To those that n. it. Folly is soon learned T. ii 283
The wisest and the best feel urgent n. T. ii 483
Of whom I n. must argue better things T. ii 582
A mockery of the world! What n. of these T. ii 750
She n. herself correction; n. to learn T. ii 776
Of lubbard Labour n. his watchful eye T. iii 400
And seem to smile at what they n. not fear T. iii 575
Supplies his n. with a usurious loan T. iii 798
N. he the tragic fur, the smoke of lamps T. iv 195
Nor n. one; I am conscious and confess T. iv 284
The learned finger never n. explore T. iv 362
N. help, denies them nothing but his name T. iv 428
Occasion n. but fan them, and they blaze T. v 207
They sink and settle lower than they n. T. v 249
And thou hast n. of discipline and art T. v 467[655
Such reasonings (if that name must n. belong T. v
And n. not his immediate hand, who first T. vi 203
So little mercy shows who n. so much! T. vi 431
N. no such aids as Superstition lends T. vi 510
The garden fears no blight, and n. no fence T. vi 771
What n. of Homer's verse, or Tully's prose Tir. 399
Will n. no stress of argument to enforce Tir. 803
And thou wilt n. some comfort to assuage Tir. 877
"No n. of lightnings from on high The Doves 33
But he that loves him has no n. to feign T.T. 96
The country's n. have scantily supplied T.T. 338
Enervate and enfeeble, and n. must T.T. 395

NEEDED.
Nor Sofa then I n. Youth repairs T. i 127
But she has burned her mask, not n. here T. iii 105
Blushed on the panels. Mirror n. none T. v 160

NEEDFUL.
This truth premised was n. as a text N.A. 71
Especially sugar, so n. we see? P.A. 7
The mind, relaxing into n. sport R. 713
And hoards them in her sleeve; but n. food T. i 554
Not n. here, beneath a roof like mine T. iii 341[636
Is n. Strength may wield the ponderous spade T. iii
Makes n. still; whose Spring is but the child T. iii 432
That with its wearisome but n. length T. iv 2
Let active Laws apply the n. curb T.T. 314

NEEDING.
And n. none assistance of the storm T. ii 144
Not sumptuously adorned, nor n. aid T. iv 251

NEEDLE.
That useful thing, her n., gone E. iv 40
True as a n. to the pole F. 110
The n.'s deviations too F. 113
Thy n., once a shining store M. 9
But here the n. plies its busy task T. iv 150

NEEDLESS.
Of n. shame, and self-imposed disgrace Con. 350
I soon recover from these n. frights H. 375
With n. hurry whirled from place to place T. iv 372
He severs it away: no n. care T. v 38
N., and first torments ere he devours T. vi 396
This second weaning, n. as it is Tir. 557

NEEDLESSLY.
Who n. sets foot upon a worm T. vi 563

NEEDLEWORK.
And woven close, or n. sublime T. i 34

NEGATIVE.
Dreading a n., and overawed E. iii 22
A flat and fatal n. obtains Tir. 714

NEGLECT.
That none shall with impunity n. Ch. 36
Than to n. a good adviser P.T. 61
Not more affronted by avowed n. T. 73
Than in a churchman slovenly n. T. ii 456
Unmixed with drops of bitter, which n. T. iii 46
At least n. not, or leave unemployed T. iii 368
That self-condemned they must n. the prize T. iii 700
Against unkindness, absence, and n. T. vi 627
A friend, whate'er he studies or n. Tir. 391
But, watch they strictly, or n. their charge? Tir. 512
From youthful folly than the same n.? Tir. 713

NEGLECTED.
And laws and duties are n. things A.T. 33
N., leaves a dreary waste behind Comp. i 12
How much, though long n., shining yet Ex. 610
Like a n. forester, runs wild P.E. 362
The Bible only stands n. there T. 425
So colleges and halls n. much T. ii 731
Attract us, and n. Nature pines T. iii 730
N. pine at home, themselves, as more T. iv 456
The boy's n. sire! a mother too T. vi 43
Which, oft n., in life's waning years Tir. 589
N. talents rust into decay T.T. 546

NEGLECTING.
Drop one by one from Fame's n. hand B.B. 6

NEGLIGENCE.
Beware no n. of yours F. 154
Small thanks to those whose n. or sloth T. ii 800
'Twas n. in him, not want of worth T.T. 681

NEGLIGENT.
Or n. inquirer, not a spark T. iii 276

NEGLIGENTLY.
Not quickly found, if n. sought Ex. 695

NEGOTIATES.
He that n. between God and man T. ii 463

NEIGH.
Responsive to the distant neigh he n. Ch. 177

NEIGHBOUR.
The morning came, when n. Hodge A Fable 24
He sought the jewel in his n.'s shame Ch. 540
As if the gnomon on his n.'s phiz Con. 271
Adultery neighing at his n.'s door Ex. 39
Studious of peace, their n. and their own Her. 50
His n. in such trim J.G. 162
What! rob our good n.! I pray you don't go P.A. 26
Each thinks his n. makes too free L.W. 35
Some more aspiring, catch the n. shrub T. iii 665
And stuns the n. round Trans. iv 24
" Come, n., we must wag" Y.D. 50

NEIGHBOURING.
Or taste the fountain in the n. glade Ch. 223
And hang their horrors in the n. skies Her. 16
Reserved to solace many a n. squire N.A. 5
'Tis he, the Nimrod of the n. lairs P.E. 84
Nor can he much affect the n. peer R. 441
Of n. fountain, or of rills that slip T. 192

But barren, at the expense of *n.* twigs *T.* iii 419
Now from the roost, or from thè *n.* pale *T.* v 58
Of *n.* cypress, or more sable yew *T. vi* 154 [317
Ascend the *n.* beech; there whisks his brush *T.* vi
Than yonder upstarts of the *n.* wood *Y.O.* 134

NEIGHING.
Adultery, *n.* at his neighbour's door *Ex.* 39

NEN.
The *N.'s* barge-laden wave *St.* i 2

NEREIDS.
N. or Dryads, as the fashion leads *R.* 537

NERVE.
Muscle and *n.* miraculously spun *R.* 59 [*T.* i 350
And now, with *n.* new braced and spirits cheered
With limbs of British oak, and *n.* of wire *R.* 311
His every *n.* in action and at stretch *T.* iii 90
Along the *n.* of every feeling line *T.T.* 487 [622
The mind, released from too constrained a *n. T.T.*

NEST.
But the sea-fowl is gone to her *n. A.S.* 49
They paired, and would have built a *n. A Tale* 15
The homeless birds a *n.* ? *A Tale* 28
Return and make thy downy *n. O.* ii 2
In every bosom where her *n.* is made *P.E.* 240
All paired, and each pair built a *n. P.T.* 44
Stepping into their *n.,* they paddled *P.T.* 54
" Merely to prove a *n.* for me *R.C.* 56 [227
I called the low-roofed lodge the Peasant's *n. T.* i
So farewell envy of the Peasant's *N.* ! *T.* i 247
Of dayspring overshoot his humble *n. T.* i 496

NET.
Caught in a delicate, soft, silken *n. P.E.* 313
To weaving *n.* for bird-alluring fruit *T.* iv 263

NETHER.
To attain perfection in this *n.* world *T.* i 85
" Have reached this *n.* world, ye spy a face *T.* v 828
The groans of Nature in this *n.* world *T.* vi 729

NEVER-DYING.
That sight imparts a *n.* flame *Ch.* 593

NEW.
And from a chance so *n. A Tale* 62
And with scenes that *n.* rapture inspire *C.* 51
The simple native of the *n.* found isle *Ch.* 30
And gains *n.* vigour at her endless task *Ch.* 104
Still prompt him, with a pleasure always *n. Ch.* 326
With a *n.* medium and a purer light *Ch.* 330
A Trojan combat would be something *n. Con.* 197
Tell not as *n.* what everybody knows *Con.* 237
And *n.* or old, still hasten to a close *Con.* 238
The *n.* acquaintance soon became a guest *Con.* 531
Partakers of a *n.* ethereal birth *Con.* 724 [809
Great changes and *n.* manners have occurred *Con.*
This page of providence quite *n. E.* i 49
Their very garments sacred, old yet *n. Ex.* 183
If the *n.* mail thy merchants now receive *Ex.* 606
My strains for ever *n. G.* 6
This earth shall blaze, and a *n.* world succeed *H.* 749
It boasts a splendour ever *n. Mrs. M—* 19 [402
His great improvement and *n.* lights he draws *P.E.*
N. raised objections with *n.* quibbles meets *P.E.* 551
N. trimmed, a gallant show ! *Q.V.* 6
N. life ordained and brighter scenes to share *R.* 65
From all he sees he catches *n.* delight *R.* 189
That does not charm the more for being *n. R.* 462
Belie their name and offer nothing *n. R.* 714
The task of *n.* discoveries falls on me *T.* 218
With its *n.* foliage on *St.* i 18

N. as ever seem our sins *St.* iv 27 [*T.* i 350
And now, with nerves *n.* braced and spirits cheered
The *n.* machine, and it became a Chair *T.* i 48
A *n.* possessor, and survives the change *T.* ii 110
If toil await me, or if dangers *n. T.* iii 20
Of old achievements, and despair of *n. T.* ii 254
And pregnant with discoveries *n.* and rare *T.* iii 138
The mind contemplative, with some *n.* theme *T.* iv 280
N. to my taste his Paradise surpassed *T.* iv 710
Another moon *n.* risen, or meteor fallen *T.* v 152
N. faculties, or learns at least to employ *T.* v 806
N. situations give a different cast *Tir.* 440 [*T.* vi 146
Shall boast *n.* charms, and more than they have lost
The *n.* made monarch, while before him pass'd *T.* vi 353
No bard, howe'er majestic, old or *n. T.T.* 180
The varied fields of science, ever *n. T.T.* 264 [733
Whate'er we write, we bring forth nothing *n. T.T.*
'Twere *n.* indeed to see a bard all fire *T.T.* 734

NEW-BORN.
To spread the *n.* glories in their view *Con.* 546
Has made the *n.* creature her abode *Con.* 754
His *n.* virtues, and preserve him pure *H.* 170
Which, though *n.,* with vigour move *Mrs. M—* 25

NEW-CREATED.
To gratulate the *n.* earth *T.* v 820

NEW-FANGLED.
N. sentiment, the boasted grace *Tir.* 539

NEW-FOUND.
A *n.* luxury, not seen in her ? *Ex.* 6

NEW-LAID.
Her *n.* eggs she fondly pressed *A Fable* 2

NEWLY.
His lilies *n.* blown *D.W.* 14
Is but a transient guest, *n.* arrived *T.* iii 750

NEWS.
Has burnt to tinder a stale last year's *n. B.B.* 10
Filled up at last with interesting *n. Con.* 394
Our health, the weather, and the *n. E.* i,5
To read the *n.,* or fiddle, as seems best *H.* 76
" What *n.* ? what *n.* ? your tidings tell *J.G.* 165
But soon my ear caught the glad *n. M.D.* 43
Inspires the *n.*, his trumpet. Keener far *T.* ii 353
N. from all nations lumbering at his back *T.* iv 7
Is balloted, and trembles at the *n. T.* iv 627 [660
Had fled from William, and the *n.* was fresh *T.* vi

NEWTON.
Such was thy wisdom, *N.,* childlike sage ! *T.* iii 252

NIBBLING.
The herb as soft, while *n.* strayed the rest *N.A.* 38
Of grassy swarth, close cropped by *n.* sheep *T.* i 110

NICE.
Washed with a neatness scrupulously *n. Ex.* 149
With *n.* attention in a righteous scale *H.* 367
By this, with *n.* precision of design *H.* 606
N. in its choice, and of a tempered heat *J.T.* 36
" Some people are more *n.* than wise *M.F.* 20
For Nature, *n.,* as liberal to dispense *P.E.* 213
But chosen with a *n.* discerning taste *R.* 726
With *n.* incision of her guided steel *T.* i 708
The nose of *n.* nobility. Breathe soft *T.* ii 259
Men too were *n.* in honour in those days *T.* iii 85
Some show that *n.* sagacity of smell *T.* vi 616
(So *n.* his ear, so delicate his touch) *T.T.* 653

NICE-FINGERED.
N. art must emulate in vain *T.* 202

NICELY.
And periwig n. adjust *Gr.* 24
This fits not n., that is ill-conceived *T.* ii 603

NICENE.
By Athanasian nonsense, or N.) *H.* 394

NICER.
From which our n. optics turn away *H.* 494
But, with precision n. still, the mind *N.A.* 63

NICEST.
To steer with n. art betwixt the extreme *S.* ii 9

NICHE.
Just in the n. he was ordained to fill *T.* iv 792

NICHOL. [36
Where N. swung the birch and twined the bays *V.*

NIGER.
First, farewell N.! whom now duly proved *V.* 7

NIGHT.
Oft as his patroness who rules the n. *A.T.* 137
Obscurest n. involved the sky *Cast.* 1
" My dear deliverer out of hopeless n. *Ch.* 234
That cheers the silent journey of the n. *Ch.* 320
So, when the cold damp shades of n. prevail *Ch* 527
Is like a nurse's lullaby at n. *Con.* 242   [*Con.* 529
That reaching home, " The n.," they said " is near
You rise and drop the curtain—now 'tis n. *Con.* 332
Will the sweet warbler of the livelong n. *Con.* 445
O days of heaven, and n. of equal praise! *Con.* 567
And half the n. ? fanatic and absurd ! *Con.* 578
And in the silent watches of the n. *Con.* 731 [iii 30
" And fetch my cloak ; for though the n. be raw *E.*
His pittance every n. *Ep.* ii 10
And every n. at play *Ep.* ii 32
By n. a fire, to cheer the gloomy way *Ex.* 178
Where Policy is busied, all n. long *Ex.* 300   [479
When the Sun's shafts disperse the gloom of n. *Ex.*
But thine, as dark as witcheries of the n. *Ex.* 494
Earth glitters with the drops the n. distils *H.* 42
The sweet vicissitudes of day and n. *H.* 488 [*H.* 746
But these shall last when n. has quenched the pole
All n., me resting quiet in the fold *N.A.* 92
Might beautify and cheer the n." *N.G.* 22
Till life's poor transient n. is spent *N.G.* 32   [177
Where N., down-stooping from her ebon throne *P.E.*
Yet glad she came that n. to prove *Q.V.* 29
That n. except her own *Q.V.* 40
Arrived, a n. like noon she sees *Q.V.* 41
The n. his city fell *Q.V.* 52
Yet let the glories of a n. *Q.V.* 77
The crescent moon, the diadem of n. *R.* 82
The stars that, sprinkled o'er the vault of n. *R.* 349
The n. rolled tardily away *R.C.* 67
That n., by chance, the poet watching *R.C.* 77
Sport for a day, and perish in a n. *T.* 42
The livelong n. : nor these alone, whose notes *T.* 201
Just earns a scanty pittance, and at n. *T.* 321
Herself from morn to n., from n. to morn *T.* 509
Of cheerful days, and n. without a groan *T.* i 366
The livelong n. A tattered apron hides *T.* i 549
To dream all n. of what the day denied *T.* i 671
At evening, and at n. retire secure *T.* iii 344
That day and n. are exercised, and hang *T.* iii 549
Laboured, and many a n. pursued in dreams *T.* iii 787
Beguile the n., and set a keener edge *T.* iv 164
Of card devoted Time, and n. by n. *T.* iv 229 [246
With matron step slow moving, while the N.—*T.* iv
Like homely-featured N., of clustering gems *T.* iv 252
The pelting brunt of the tempestuous n. *T.* iv 351
Such claim compassion in a n. like this *T.* iv 375
But farewell now to unsuspicious n. *T.* iv 565
The n. was winter in his roughest mood *T.* vi 57
So soon succeeding such an angry n. *T.* vi 259
N. veiled the pole ; all seemed secure *T.B.* 31
And labours to surpass him day and n. *Tir.* 480
Their breath a sample of last n.'s regale *Tir.* 834
That shows by n. a lucid beam *Trans.* i 3
To show a stumbling stone by n. *Trans.* i 19
Neither n. nor dawn of day *Trans.* iii 25
These were the chief; each interval of n. *T.T.* 572
From total n. and absolute disgrace *T.T.* 665

NIGHT-BOLT.
And drop the n. ;—ruffians are abroad *T.* iv 568

NIGHTCAP.
They put on a damp n., and relapse *Con.* 322

NIGHTINGALE.
By the n. warbling nigh *C.* 12
A n., that all day long *N.G.* 1
Scared, and the offended n. is mute *T.* i 768
The n. may claim the topmost bough *T.T.* 576

NIGHTLY.
In daily musings and in n. dreams *A.T.* 12
Thy n. visits to my chamber made *M.P.* 58
Fly to the coast for daily, n. joys *R.* 522
N. lifts his voice on high *St.* iv 6
Now goes the n. thief prowling abroad *T.* iv 432
That fill the skies n. with silent pomp *T.* v 817

NIGHTSHADE.
Of n., or valerian, grace the well *T.* iv 757

NILE. [827
Spawned in the muddy beds of N., came forth *T.* ii

NIMBLE.
Their n. nonsense takes a shorter course *Con.* 152
Upon his n. steed *J.G.* 78
The n. motion of those restless joints *T.* iii 762
Follow the n. finger of the fair *T.* iv 155
Not of a n. tongue, though now and then *Tir.* 666

NIMBLEST.
Proceeding with his n. pace *Mor.* 20

NIMROD.
'Tis he, the N. of the neighbouring lairs *P.E.* 84

NINE.
Nor would the N. consent the sacred tide *T.T.* 184

NINEVEH.
N., Babylon, and ancient Rome *T.T.* 432

NIOBE.
Channel her cheeks, a N. appears *T.* 174

NIP. [32
Chill blasts of trouble n. their springing joys *E.* ii
And social, n. his fruitfulness and use *T.* v 439

NITROUS.
And sheltered Sofa, while the n. air *T.* iii 32

NOAH.
To Gaul, to Greece, and into N.'s ark *R.* 694
On N., and in him on all mankind *T.* vi 450

NOBILITY.
Can only say,—" N. lies here " *H.* 271
But royalty, n., and state *T.* 353
The nose of nice n. Breathe soft *T.* ii 259

NOBLE.
Should be the guerdon of a n. deed *Ch.* 293

NOBLE—NORTH

Pants to communicate her *n.* fires *Ch.* 403
The *n.* beast judge otherwise, his grooms *Con.* 414
Through all He spoke a *n.* plainness ran *Ex.* 135
Profusion apes the *n.* part *F.* 4
And yield so much to *n.* folk *F.* 118
Fires all his feelings with a *n.* scorn *H.* 151
To men of pedigree, their *n* race *H.* 237
But ask the *n.* drudge in state affairs *R.* 407
His *n.* heart went pit-a-pat *R.C.* 79
Not many wise, rich, *n.*, or profound *T.* 337
That's *n.*, and bespeaks a nation proud *T.* ii 43
Where once your *n.* fathers won a crown ! *T.* ii 281
His *n.* office, and, instead of truth *T.* ii 428
A *n.* show ! while Roscius trod the stage *T.* iii 597
A *n.* cause, which none who bears a spark *T.* iv 614
To be the tenant of man's *n.* form *T.* v 455
Ungratified; for there some *n.* lord *T.* vi 673
Their *n.* qualities all quenched and cold *Tir.* 818
And keeps alive his fierce but *n.* fires *T.T.* 223
The *n.* sweep of all their privilege *T.T.* 475

NOBLER.

But though some *n.* minds a law respect *Ch.* 35
To seek a *n.* amidst scenes of woe *Ch.* 300
The rich possession of a *n.* prize *Ch.* 360
But time that should enrich the *n.* mind *Comp.* i 11
" The rich, the produce of a *n.* stem *Ex.* 460
Or, more provoking still, of *n.* name *H.* 192
" Yours is," she said, "the *n.* hue *L.R.* 21
Have burnt to dust a *n.* pile *M.* i 3
Scorned by the *n.* tenants of the flood *P.E.* 482
As more illumined, and with *n.* truths *T.* iv 192
A longer date to the far *n.* beast *T.* vi 529
Received his *n.* nature, and was made *Tir.* 97
Done to the *n.* part affects it long *Tir.* 491
To fit thee for a *n.* post than thine *V.* 32

NOBLEST.

Derived from nature's *n.* part *E.* i 13
The *n.* Friendship ever shown *F.* 205
Poets attempt the *n.* task they can *J.T.* 1
On application to its *n.* end *J.T.* 28
The *n.* minds their virtue prove *P.* 61
Conscious of weakness in its *n.* powers *R.* 124
So Love, that clings around the *n.* minds *R.* 235
The *n.* function, and discredits much *T.* ii 554
In confirmation of the *n.* claim *T.* v 720
He too is witness, *n.* of the train *T.* vi 425
The *n.* cause mankind can have at stake *T.T.* 285
Not more invigorates life's *n.* part *T.T.* 381
Whose *n.* coin is light and brittle man *V.* 96

NOBLY.

N. distinguished above all the six *P.E.* 161
To save your life would *n.* risk his own *T.* 220
To serve him *n.* in the common cause *T.* v 344
Bled *n.*, and their deeds, as they deserve *T.* v 705

NOCTURNAL.

Soft airs, *n.* vigils, and day dreams *R.* 260
By works of darkness and *n.* wrong *T.* iv 435

NOD.

Carelessly *n.* and sleeps upon the brink *Ex.* 99
The Babylonian tyrant writh a *n.* *P.E.* 130
Strength in his heart, dominion in his *n.* *T.* 409
And fledged with icy feathers, *n.* superb *T.* v 26

NOISE.

The school of coarse good fellowship and *n.* *Con.* 422
Of Friendship, satisfied with *n.* *F.B.* 32
Shows with a pointing finger, but no *n.* *H.* 221
With senseless *n.*, his argument the sword *H.* 660
Nor *n.* was heard but of the hasty brook *N.A.* 39
Meantime, *n.* kills not. Be it Dapple's bray *N.A.* 115

Some minds by nature are averse to *n.* *R.* 175
And prayer more seasonable than the *n.* *St.* ii 11
Moves without *n.*, and swift as an express *T.* 204
A life all turbulence and *n.* may seem *T.* iii 379
No *n.* is here, or none that hinders thought *T.* vi 76
Childish in mischief only and in *n.* *Tir.* 207
'Tis not, however, insolence and *n.* *T.T.* 408

NOISELESS.

N., appears a moving hill of snow *T.* iv 346
Receives advantage from his *n.* hours *T.* vi 944
N., an atom, and an atom more *Y.O.* 106

NOISOME.

As to a common and most *n.* sewer *T.* i 683
N., and ever greedy to exhaust *T.* iii 671

NOISY.

A *n.* man is always in the right *Con.* 114
He comes, the herald of a *n.* world *T.* iv 5

NONSENSE.

Their nimble *n.* takes a shorter course *Con.* 152
By Athanasian *n.*, or Nicene) *H.* 394
On fire with curses, and with *n.* hung *Tir.* 832

NOOK.

Within its customary *n.* *Mor.* 8
Struggling, detained in many a petty *n.* *N.A.* 40
For *n.* to which she might retire *R.C.* 4
My country ! and while yet a *n.* is left *T.* ii 207
The croaking nuisance lurked in every *n.* *T.* ii 830
Remains to each, the search of sunny *n.* *T.* v 71
My native *n.* of earth ! Thy clime is rude *T.* v 462
No *n.* so narrow but he spreads them there *T.* v 773
In *n.* obscure, far from the ways of men *T.* vi 842

NOON.

'Twas on the *n.* of an autumnal day *A.T.* 70
The *n.* was shady, and soft airs *D.W.* 1
The virtuoso thus, at *n.* *E.* iv 49
Dozing out all his idle *n.* *Ep.* ii 31
To rise at *n.*, sit slipshod and undressed *H.* 75
Why, stooping from the *n.* of day *O.* i 9
Witness of joys that shun the sight of *n.* *P.E.* 174
Arrived, a night like *n.* she sees *Q.V.* 41
To thee the dayspring, and the blaze of *n.* *R.* 347
Returns at *n.* to billiards, or to books *R.* 472
And long protracted bowers, enjoyed at *n.* *T.* i 257
Our groves were planted to console at *n.* *T.* i 760
That spreads his motley wings in the eye of *n.* *T.*iii135
Shortening his journey between morn and *n.* *T.*iv 131
The morning sharp and clear. But now at *n.* *T.* vi 58
Nor deems he wiser him, who gives his *n.* *T.* vi 278
The very kine that gambol at high *n.* *T.* vi 334 [774
Graze with the fearless flocks; all bask at *n.* *T.* vi

NOONDAY.

Reflect the *n.* glory of the skies *Ch.* 398
He stripped the impostors in the *n.* sun *Ex.* 141
His *n.* beams were never half so bright *H.* 737
Winks hard, and talks of darkness at *n.* *P.E.* 451
While he that scorns the *n.* beam, perverse *T.* 523
Of atoms, sparkling in the *n.* beam *T.* i 361
Whose headaches nail them to a *n.* bed *T.* i 500

NOONTIDE.

Traduce the splendour of a *n.* ray *T.* 540

NOOSE.

Oh for a law to *n.* the villain's neck *T.* iv 462

NORTH.

Her sons to pour it on the farthest *n.* *H.* 460
I care not whether east or *n.* *M.B.* 21
Now shifted east, and east by *n.* *P.T.* 51

Thus fare the shivering natives of the *n. T.* i 617
It may enjoy the advantage of the *n. T.* iii 771
The wonder of the *N.* No forest fell *T.* v 131
If Winter bellow from the *n. Trans. H.* 22

NORTHERN.
And where the woods fence off the *n.* blast *T.* vi 60

NORWEGIAN.
Was rocked by many a rough *N.* blast *Ex.* 470

NOSE. [*A.C.* 23
That the spectacles plainly were made for the *N.*—
Between *N.* and Eyes a strange contest arose *A.C.* 1
That the *N.* has had spectacles always in wear *A.C.* 11
" In behalf of the *N.*, it will quickly appear *A.C.* 9
As wide as the bridge of the *N.* is; in short *A.C.* 15
That the visage or countenance had not a *N.*—*A.C.* 19
And the *N.* was as plainly intended for them" *A.C.* 24
That, whenever the *N.* put his spectacles on *A.C.* 31
Assert the *n.* upon his face his own *Con.* 122
In contact inconvenient, *n.* to *n. Con.* 270
Who thrusts his *n.* into a raree-show? *Con.* 286
N., ears, and eyes seem present on the spot *Con.* 318
Claps spectacles on her sagacious *n. Con.* 742
" And pinch your *n.* blue " *J.P.* 40
Long beards, long *n.*, and pale faces *M.F.* 6
Defective only in his Roman *n. P.E.* 396
With slipshod heels, and dewdrop at his *n. T.* 144
The *n.* of nice nobility. Breathe soft *T.* ii 259
The better hand, more busy, gives the *n. T.* ii 451
Terribly arched and aquiline his *n. T.* iii 192
Conducts the unguarded *n.* to such a whiff *T.* iv 469
That fumes beneath his *n.*; the trailing cloud *T.* v 56
One wipes his *n.* upon his sleeve *Y.D.* 41

NOSEGAY.
For a *n.*, so dripping and drowned *The Rose* 10

NOSTRIL.
His high-bred steed expands his *n.* wide *A.T.* 163
Through the pressed *n.*, spectacle-bestrid *T.* ii 439
The toiling steeds expand the *n.* wide *T.* iv 347

NOSTRUM.
Swallow the two grand *n.* they dispense *P.E.* 594
Their sovereign *n.* is a clumsy joke *R.* 313

NOTCH.
N. after *n.*, till all are smoothed away *Tir.* 560

NOTE.
And by Philomel's annual *n. C.* 47
And pours a torrent of sweet *n.* around *Ch.* 111
Faint as a chicken's *n.* that has the pip *Con.* 356
Is *n.* for *n.* delivered in our ears *Con.* 455
With a whole gamut filled of heavenly *n.*'s *N.A.* 26
Nor yet at eve his *n.* suspended *N.G.* 3
Me poetry (or rather *n.* that aim *R.* 801   [i 201
The livelong night: nor these alone, whose *n. T.*
Can change their whine into a mirthful *n. T.* i 583
Of public *n.*, they reach their perfect size *T.* i 696
Our more harmonious *n.*: the thrush departs *T.* i 767
They never undertook, they little *n. T.* ii 308
N. their extravagance, and be convinced *T.* ii 573
His own coevals took but little *n. T.* iii 142
Some *n.* of Nature's music from his lips *T.* iii 600
Delicious, when her patriots of high *n. T.* iv 170
A jarring *n.* Themes of a graver tone *T.* iv 181
Still to reflect, that though a joyless *n. T.* v 40 [78
With slender *n.*, and more than half suppress'd *T.* vi
He *n.* it in his book, then raps his box *T.* vi 292
To join a traveller, of far different *n. T.* vi 489
Its various parts to his attentive *n. Tir.* 642
And by the hoarseness of his *n. Trans.* ii 2
With music modulating all their *n. T.T.* 695

NOTHING.
Whom *n.* could divide *A Tale* 68
Yet from a richer *n.* gain *A Tale* 75
Let *n.* adverse, *n.* unforeseen *Ch.* 131
Whate'er she learns, learns *n.* as she ought *Ch.* 338
N. is slightly touched, much less forgot *Con.* 317
So self starts *n.*, but what tends apace *Ch.* 565
Though *n.* have occurred to kindle strife *E.* iii 15
That yields them chaff and dust and *n.* more *Ex.* 303
And Peace does *n.* to relieve the weight *Ex.* 307
Leaped out of *n.*, called by the Most High *Ex.* 639
Who found thee *n.*, formed thee for his praise *Ex.* 643
Once thought of *n.*, and now thinks in vain *H.* 30
Hope! *n.* else can nourish and secure *H.* 169
Adds *n.* now to the degraded dead *H.* 269
With *n.* here that wants to be concealed *H.* 406
" You shapeless *n.* in a dish *P.* 25
Yet *n.* feel in that rough coat *P.* 51
Made *n.* but a brute, the slave of sense *P.E.* 214
Saints offer *n.*, in their warmest prayers *R.* 221
Belie their name and offer *n.* new *R.* 714
There, wanting *n.* save a fan *R.C.* 17
And forth he peeped, but *n.* spied *R.C.* 82
Lost *n.* by comparison with ours? *T.* i 648
Aware of *n.* arduous in a task *T.* ii 307
And growing old in drawing *n.* up!" *T.* iii 190
N. is proof against the general curse *T.* iii 266
How far he went for what was *n.* worth *T.* iv 238
Need help, denies them *n.* but his name *T.* iv 428
Where *n.* feeds it. Neither business crowds *T.* iv 744
A garden in which *n.* thrives, has charms *T.* iv 754
Or *n.* much, his constancy in ill *T.* v 667   [v 666
He slights the strokes of conscience. *N.* moves *T.*
And seems it *n.* in a father's eye *Tir.* 615
Or doing *n.* with a deal of skill *T.T.* 193   [461
But *n.* scares them, from the course they love *T.T.*
Whate'er we write, we bring forth *n.* new *T.T.* 733

NOTICE.
They court the *n.* of a future age *B.B.* 4
Has one that *n.* his silent grief *Ch.* 207
To catch the wandering *n.* of mankind *H.* 137
He hears the *n.* of the clock, perplexed *H.* 700
Obtrude on human *n.* more *Mrs. M*— 34
And call her charms to public *n.* forth *P.E.* 296
The Crown, took *n.* of an ostler's face *R.* 586
Wins no *n.*, wakes no fears *St.* iv 20
Advance it into *n.*, that its worth *T.* iii 703
To engross a moment's *n.*; and yet begs *T.* iv 67
And gathering, at short *n.*, in one group *T.* iv 136
Step forth to *n.*; and, besotted thus *T.* v 257
Scarce deign to *n.* him, or, if she see *T.* vi 942
Engage no *n.*, and enjoy much ease *T.* vi 957
Our early *n.* of truth, disgraced *Tir.* 199

NOTICED.   [73
Not scorned in Heaven, though little *n.* here *M.P.*
Scare *n.* in the kindred dusk of eve. *T.* iv 321

NOTING.
Thy prophets speak of such; and *n.* down *T.* vi 899

NOTIONS.
Her *n.* hyperbolical *R.C.* 104
And teach him *n.* splendid as themselves *T.* 424

NOTORIOUS.
Else sure *n.* fact, and proof so plain *Tir.* 259

NOUNS.
But conjugated verbs and *n.* declined *Tir.* 619

NOURISH.
May blow up self-conceit, and *n.* pride *Ch.* 376
Hope! nothing else can *n.* and secure *H.* 169

Thus some retire to n. helpless woe R. 603
But not like me to n. woe ! S. 20
More n. pride, that condescending vice T. 123
To n. pride, or turn the weakest head T. 366

NOURISHING.
Threatening at once and n. the plant T. vi 36

NOURISHMENT.
Its solid n. from man's applause Con. 672
Or turn to n., digested well T. iii 396
No n. to feed his growing mind Tir. 618

NOVEL.
Admiring, terrified, the n. strain N.A. 49
And n. (witness every month's Review) R. 713

NOVELISTS.
Ye n., who mar what ye would mend P.E. 309

NOVELTY.
Please daily, and whose n. survives T. i 178
And pleased with n., might be indulged T. i 503
For monstrous n. and strange disguise T. ii 612
Of N., her fickle, frail support T. iii 54
Because a n., the work of man T. v 128
Enchanting n., that moon at full T. vi 706

NOVEMBER.
Deciduous, when now N. dark T. iii 467

NOXIOUS.
Their n. growth, starve every better seed R. 44
Else n.: oceans, rivers, lakes, and streams T. i 375
Imaginations n. and perverse Tir. 599

NUISANCE.
The worn-out n. of the public streets T. 508
And mortal n. into all the air T. ii 98
The croaking n. lurked in every nook T. ii 830
Is but a garnished n., fitter far T. vi 993
The encroaching n. asks a faithful hand Tir. 601

NULLITY.
And He, whose power mere n. obeys Ew. 642
From almost n. into a state Y.O. 88

NUMBER.
My n. that day she had sung C. 17
Could infuse into n. of mine C. 20
In n. the days of the year C. 26
That Matthew's n. run with ease E. iv 67
Such honours to thee as my n. may M.P. 71
As I can n. in my punctual page St. ii 3
And in thy n., Philips, shines for aye T. iii 455
By flowing n. and a flowery style T.T. 741 [764
Though Butler's wit, Pope's n., Prior's ease T.T.
(Since which I n. threescore winters past Y.O. 3

NUMBERING.
To wear out time in n. to and fro T. v 425

NUMBERLESS.
Of hedge-row beauties n., square tower T. i 173
Minute as dust and n., oft work T. iii 556

NUMEROUS.
Though n. once, reduced to few or none? E. iii 17
Through n. generations till he found F.A. 25
Deem life a blessing with its n. woes H. 546
Of n. charms possessed J.P. 2
By tricks and lies as n. and as keen T. ii 671
And the land stank—so n. was the fry T. ii 832
His dainties, and the World's more n. half T. iii 545
And all your n. progeny, well trained T. iv 422 [86
Thins all their n. flocks. In chinks and holes T. v
O'erwatch the n. and unruly clan Tir. 262

So n. are the follies that T ir.
O'erhung the campaign; and the n. flock Y.O. 53

NUNNERIES.
Wast thou in monkish cells and n. found Ch. 43

NURSE.
Is like a n.'s lullaby at night Con. 242
O folly worthy of the n.'s lap Con. 479
Though, clasped and cradled in his n.'s arms H. 179
The n. sleeps sweetly, hired to watch the sick T. i 8J
Of lazy n. who snores the sick man dead T. i 97
Grand caterer and dry n. of the church ! T. ii 371
Now blame we most the nurslings or the n.? T. ii 771
The n., no doubt. Regardless of her charge T. ii 775
Thou art the n. of Virtue. In thine arms T. iii 4S
Scenes formed for contemplation, and to n. T. iii 301
The few small embers left she n. well T. iv 383
A mother's lecture and a n.'s care Tir. 196
To n. with tender care the thriving Arts T.T. 69
Genius is thine, and thou art Fancy's n. T.T. 290

NURSED.
There Fancy n. her in ideal bowers A.T. 7
True Charity, a plant divinely n. Ch. 573
The last by Vanity produced and n. Con. 378
Who, n. with tender care Ep. ii 6

NURSERY.
And, turning from my n. window, drew M.P. 30
Children not thine have trod my n. floor M.P. 47
I do confess them n. of the arts T. i 693
Would find them hideous n. of the spleen T. iii 318
And wisely store the n. by degrees Tir. 117
Ye n. of our boys, we owe to you Tir. 248
And, while on public n. they rely Tir. 793

NURSLINGS.
Now blame we most the n. or the nurse ? T. ii 771

NURTURE.
The n. of her youth, her dearest pledge T. ii 779

NURTURED.
My man of morals, n. in the shades T. ii 532
The Muse instructed a well n. train T.T. 634

NUTS.
The maple, and the beech of oily n. T. i 315 [20
The auburn n. that held thee, swallowing down Y.O.

NUTRIMENT.
With ease, and find them n. : but man F.A. 36

NUTRITIOUS.
And draining its n. powers to feed R. 43
If fanned by balmy and n. air T. iii 524

NYMPH. [A.T. 180
" Oh, shame!" ten thousand echoing n. replied
" For British n.,whose lords were lately true A.T.109
"N. quite as fair, and happier once than you A.T. 110
(Two n. adorned with every grace D.W. 7
That won a n. on that immortal plain Ew. 598
Two n., both nearly of an age J.P. 1
The n. referred the cause J.P. 18
" My favourite N. to slight J.P. 34
The n. must lose her female friend L.R. 1
Where'er the heavenly N. is seen Miss — 69
The n. between two chariot glasses P.B. 20
To seem some n. in her sedan R.C. 18
How many self-deluded n. and swains T. iii 316
Pure is the n., though liberal of her smiles T. iii 712
Or n. responsive, equally affect T. iv 21 [517
N. were Dianas then, and swains had hearts T. iv
Ye n.! if e'er your eyes were red T.B. 1

O.

OAK.
Sage beneath the spreading o. *B.* 5
Steered Britain's o. into a world unknown *Ch.* 23
And o. coeval spread a mournful shade *H.* 352
Of rugged o. for worms *M.B.* 8
O. intersperse it, that had once a head *N.A.* 11
With limbs of British o., and nerves of wire *R.* 311
And drilled in holes, the solid o. is found *T.* i 26 [56
Than the firm o. of which the frame was formed *T.* i
Lord of the woods, the long surviving o. *T.* i 313
By restless undulation; even the o. *T.* i 377
And under an old o.'s domestic shade *T.* iv 172
The walk, still verdant, under o. and elms *T.* vi 70
In nature, from the broad majestic o. *T.* vi 250
When our forefathers Druids in their o. *Y.O.* 10
O. fell not, hewn by thousands, to supply *Y.O.* 101

OAKEN.
To strip Jove's statue of his o. wreath *T.* vi 640
Or o. fence that hems the paddock round *T.T.* 583

OAR.
That ever dragged a chain, or tugged an o. *Ex.* 527
But o. alone can ne'er prevail *H.F.* 21
Hackneyed in business, wearied at that o. *R.* 1

OATH.
Enticed him from his o. of knighthood far *A.T.* 27
O. terminate, as Paul observes, all strife *Con.* 55
With o. like rivets forced into the brain *Con.* 64
O. used as playthings or convenient tools *Ex.* 37
By an o. dipped in sacramental blood? *Ex.* 381
The cheek-distending o., not to be praised *T.* iv 488
Whose o. is rhetoric, and who swear for fame *T.* iv 491
By the unimpeachable and awful o. *T.* v 549
Much less transfix his feelings with an o. *Tir.* 729
Sells o. by tale, and at the lowest price *T.T.* 419

OATS.
And milk, and o., and straw *Ep.* ii 14

OBDURACY
O. itself must yield the rest *Ex.* 559
Incurable o. evinced *T.* vi 532
O. takes place; callous and tough *T.T.* 458

OBDURATE.
O. and unyielding, glassy smooth *T.* i 52
There is no flesh in man's o. heart *T.* ii 8

OBEDIENCE.
Let my o. then excuse *B.R.* 21
Say on what hinge does his o. move? *T.* 207
Life for o., death for every flaw *T.* 550

OBEDIENT.
The sun, o., at her call appears *H.* 43
The youth, o. to his sire's commands *P.E.* 377
Drives to their dens the o. beasts of prey *R.* 766
Man scarce had risen, o. to his call *T.* vi 348
I played awhile, o. to the fair *T.* vi 1008
O. to the customs of the course *T.* 14
Tom quits you, with—"Your most o., Sir" *T.* 212

OBERON.
With lenient balm may O. hence *Miss* — 21

OBEY.
And He, whose power mere nullity o. *Ex.* 642
I will o., not willingly alone *M.P.* 15   [496
Hence the same word, that bids our lusts o. *P.E.*
To serve the Sovereign we were born to o. *R.* 50
The rising waves o. the increasing blast *R.* 532
Rebel, because 'tis easy to o. *T.* 36
Kings are invited, and would kings o. *T.* 351 [114
Which winds and waves o., invades the shore *T.* ii
Gloriously drunk, o. the important call! *T.* iv 510
His pride, that scorns to o. or to submit *Tir.* 226

OBEYED.
Consulted and o., to guide his steps *T.* v 674
He ruled with meekness, they o. with joy *T.* vi 361

OBJECT.
Their o., and their subject, and their hope *Con.* 542
Yes, but an o. bright as orient morn *H.* 550
His o. chosen, wealth or fame *Mor.* 27
A vicious o. still is worse *Mor.* 47
Must be supplied with o. of his choice *P.E.* 46
From o. too much dreaded or desired *R.* 144
Be still a pleasing o. in my view *T.* i 250
O. of my implacable disgust *T.* ii 418
With meaner o. even the few she finds! *T.* iii 727
Assimilates all o. Earth receives *T.* iv 329
The likeness of some o. seen before *T.* v 121
Of o., more illustrious in her view *T.* vi 916
How much the o. of her love *Q.V.* 31

OBJECTIONS.
New raised o. with new quibbles meets *P.E.* 551

OBLIGATIONS.
Man's o. infinite, of course *T.* 197

OBLIGED.   [*R.* 599
Jack bowed, and was o.;—confessed 'twas strange

OBLIQUITY.
The least o. is fatal here *P.E.* 579

OBLITERATE.
The future shall o. the past *T.* 295
Ensuing seemed to o. the past *T.* vi 540

OBLIVION.
And dark o. soon absorbs them all *B.B.* 8
Of blank o., seem a glorious prize *T.* i 287
With sweet o. of the cares of day *T.* iv 250

OBNOXIOUS.
Of wrath o., God may choose his mark *T.* ii 156
And therefore more o. at this hour *T.* iii 846

OBSCENE.
O., to swill and swallow at a trough? *P.E.* 266
Guiltless of pampered appetite o.) *T.* i 104
Receives the morsel—flesh o. of dog *T.* i 562
And waved his rod divine, a rod o. *T.* ii 826
Is difficult, their punishment o. *Tir.* 221
Foul with excess, and with discourse o. *Tir.* 736

OBSCENITY.
Of rank o., debauched their age *T.T.* 631

OBSCURE.
O. or quench a faculty that finds *Con.* 593
But as too much o. the sight *E.* iv 63
Amazed that shadows should o. the sight *H.* 534
Though plain to others, is o. to him *P.E.* 447
The panels, leaving an o., rude name *T.* i 282
In nooks o., far from the ways of men *T.* vi 842
Who, doomed to an o. but tranquil state *T.* vi 908

OBSCURED.
Dimness and anguish, all thy beams *o*. *Ex*. 393

OBSCUREST.
O. night involved the sky *Cast*. 1

OBSCURITY.
O. with splendour *F*. 120
There hid in loathed *o*., removed *R*. 563
In which *o*. has wrapped them up *T*. iii 146

OBSEQUIOUS.
O. when abroad, though proud at home *R*. 440
And bow *o*., hide their hate of her *T*. ii 646
Who, with bare-headed and *o*. bows *T*. iii 819
O., from the cradle to the throne *T.T*. 122

OBSERVANCE.
A course of long *o*. for its use *T*. v 301

OBSERVATION.
For our dim-sighted *o*. *E*. i 86
Are *o*. on the case *F*. 160
And *o*. taught me, I would teach *P.E*. 12
This *o*., as it chanced, not made *R*. 463
Of *O*., and discovers, else *T*. iii 231

OBSERVE. [*A.C*. 14
"Your lordship *o*. they are made with a straddle
Oaths terminate, as Paul *o*., all strife *Con*. 55
O. each face, how sober and demure! *P.E*. 134
Blames his own indolence, *o*., though late *R*. 477
O. the dappled foresters, how light *St*. ii 21

OBSERVED.
A day of luxury, *o*. aright *P.E*. 164
At Popish practices *o*. within *P.E*. 384
O. as prodigies, and soon reclaimed *T*. iv 524

OBSERVER.
"Can this be true?"—an arch *o*. cries *Con*. 231
But sage *o*. oft mistake the flame *Con*. 655

OBSERVING.
He might escape the most *o*. eyes *R*. 588

OBSOLETE.
The praise of names for ages *o*. *Con*. 828
The *o*. prolixity of shade *T*. i 265
Finds one ill made, another *o*. *T*. ii 602

OBSTINACY.
When *O*. once has conquered Grace *Ex*. 152
Where *O*. takes his sturdy stand *Ex*. 298

OBSTINATE.
Then *o*. Self-will confirms him so *P.E*. 543
Is *o*., and cure beyond our reach *T*. iii 40

OBSTINATELY.
Praise him on earth, or *o*. dumb *Tir*. 101

OBSTRUCT.
If hindrances *o*. thy way *Trans. H*. 31

OBTAIN.
Dearly *o*. the refuge it affords *T*. i 238
Seek and *o*., and often find unsought? *T*. iii 288
Twins at all points—yet this *o*. in all *T*. iv 738
And there *o*. fresh triumphs o'er himself *T*. vi 937
And does but at the goal *o*. *Th*. 19
That, viewing it, we seem almost to *o*. *Tir*. 312
Add too, that, thus estranged, thou canst *o*. *Tir*. 585
A flat and fatal negative *o*. *Tir*. 714

OBTAINED.
A despot big with power *o*. by wealth *Ex*. 370
And that *o*. by rapine and by stealth? *Ex*. 371
And pocketed a prize by fraud *o*. *T*. iii 87
Asks egress; which *o*., the overcharged *T*. iii 497

OBTRUDE.
O. on human notice more *Mrs. M* — 34

OBTUSE.
By repetition palled, by age *o*. *H*. 22 [ii 808
Their points *o*., and feathers drunk with wine! *T*.

OBVIATE.
And which no care can *o*. It were long *T*. iii 558

OBVIOUS.
What *o*. truths the wisest heads may miss! *R*. 438
Is *o*., placed within the easy reach *T*. i 598

OCCASION.
O. prompt, and appetite so keen *A.T*. 90
The *o*. of transmuting fear to love? *Ch*. 225
Who when *o*. justified its use *Con*. 613
Too small perhaps the slight *o*. *E*. i 85
Sometimes *o*. brings to light *F*. 148
Will find *o*. to forbear *M.F*. 38
And have most plentiful *o*. *P*. 28
Improve the kind *o*., understand *R*. 345
The *o*.—for the Fair commands the song *T*. i 7
To serve *o*. of poetic pomp *T*. i 152
When safe *o*. offers; and with dance *T*. i 584
Of man's *o*., when in him reside *T*. ii 537
To seize the fair *o*.; well they eye *T*. v 66
O. needs but fan them, and they blaze *T*. v 207
The *o*. it presents of doing good *T*. vi 847
O bright *o*. of dispensing good *T.T*. 63

OCCASIONAL.
These, therefore, are *o*., and pass *T*. v 566

OCCIDUUS.
O. is a pastor of renown *P.E*. 124
Has charmed me much (not even *O*. more) *P.E*. 130

OCCUPATION.
Absence of *o*. is not rest *R*. 623
Are *o*. of the poet's mind *T*. ii 298
Waste youth in *o*. only fit *T*. ii 636
The *o*. dearest to his heart *T*. ii 709
Can he want *o*. who has these? *T*. iii 359
And constant *o*. without care *T*. iii 693
Were *o*. easier to be found *Tir*. 701
The same their *o*. and success *T.T*. 46

OCCUPIED.
Is *o*. as well, employs his hours *R*. 507
He that is ever *o*. in storms *T*. iii 383
Which he, thus *o*., enjoys! Retreat *T*. iii 676
And, *o*. as earnestly as she *T*. vi 917
Not *o*. in day dreams, as at home *Tir*. 775

OCCUPY.
Whatever subject *o*. discourse *Con*. 57
Error and darkness *o*. their place *Ex*. 693
Nor yet the swarms that *o*. the brain *R*. 641
Nor does the chisel *o*. alone *T*. i 705
But how should matter *o*. a charge *T*. vi 216
Now happiest they that *o*. the scenes *T*. vi 397
To *o*. a sacred, awful post *Tir*. 414
That *o*. mankind below *Trans*. ii 17

OCCURRENCE.
To express the *o*. of the day *E*. i 4

OCCURS.
"And he that does not, whatsoe'er *o*. *A.T*. 121
Learns something from whate'er *o*. *Mor*. 24
As aught *o*. that she may smile to hear *T*. iii 395
Great cause *o*. to save him from a band *Tir*. 696

OCCURRED.
Great changes and new manners have *o*. *Con*. 803

Though nothing have o. to kindle strife E. iii 15
Or if the thought o. not duly weighed R. 464

OCEAN.
In o. self-upheld Cast. 38
And a wide o. swallows both at last Comp. i 6
Of eastern groves, and o. floored with ice Ex. 16
I dreamed that, on o. afloat M.D. 5 [89
(The storms all weathered and the o. crossed M.P.
Ah! why, since o., rivers, streams O. i 5
O. exhibits, fathomless and broad R. 525
Or bury me in o.'s angry tide! T. 270
The dash of O. on his winding shore T. i 186
Else noxious: o., rivers, lakes, and streams T. i 375
In boundless o., never to be passed T. i 629
O. has caught the frenzy, and upwrought T. ii 111
Heaven, earth, and o., plundered of their sweets T. iv 82
The o. serves, on high Q.V. 18 [39
Whom O. feels through all his countless waves Tir.

OCTAVOS.
And charged with o. and twelves Gr. 27

OCTOBER.
O. hight, but mild and fair as May A. T. 71

ODD. [R. 729
And though the world may think the ingredients o.

ODE.
His quitrent o., his peppercorn of praise T.T. 110

ODIOUS.
See Cortez o. for a world enslaved! Ch. 40
That o. libel on a human voice? Con. 450
And give true piety that o. name Con. 656
To me is o. as the nasal twang T. ii 436 [88
Was marked and shunned as o. He that sold T. iii
Who judged the Pharisee? What o. cause T. 44
Is o., and their wages all their joy Tir. 824

ODORIFEROUS.
His o. attempts to please Con. 287
Smells fresh, and, rich in o. herbs T. i 531
The scent regaled, each o. leaf T. iii 621

ODOUR.
Its o. perished, and its charming hue Con. 43
Fresh o. from the shrubbery at my side F.A. 7
Flowers of rank o. upon thorny lands R. 754
Diffusing o.; nor unnoted pass T. i 317
Renounce the o. of the open field T. i 415
With o., and profligate as sweet T. ii 228
With never cloying o., early and late T. vi. 164
Their balmy o., and imparts their hues T. vi 243
Its o. o'er the Christian's thorny road! T. 454

ODYSSEY.
My Iliad and O. too Gr. 32

O'ERARCHING.
The seas globose and huge, the o. vault R. 552

O'ERBEARING.
To an enormous and o. height T. ii 112

O'ERCHARGED. [757
The country starves, and they that feed the o. T. iii

O'ERCLOUDED.
Yet still, o. with a constant frown Con. 339

O'ERCOME.
Had found one city not to be o. Ex. 210
And own his crab-computing powers o. P.E. 487

O'ERFLOWING.
The o. well of Charity springs here! Ch. 366

O'ERHANG.
Where mouldering abbey walls o. the glade H. 351

O'ERHEARD.
O. and checked this idle talk P. 40

O'ERHEATED.
Is the false fire of an o. mind Con. 668

O'ERHUNG.
O. the campaign; and the numerous flock Y.O. 53

O'ERJOYED.
O. was he to find J.G. 30

O'ERLEAP.
When did the waves so haughtily o. T. ii 55

O'ERLEAPED.
A faithful barrier, not o. with ease T. iii 681

O'ERLEAPING.
Grow freakish, and o. every mound T.T. 302

O'ERLOOK.
Will Providence o. the wasted good? P.E. 223
Narrow and long, o. the western wave T. vi 484
The world o. him in her busy search T. vi 915
Though more sublimely, he o. the world T. vi 918

O'ERLOOKED.
O. and unemployed, fell sick, and died T. ii 733

O'ERPAYS.
The joy, the danger and the toil o. P.E. 90

O'ERRULES.
But God o. all human follies still Ch. 463

O'ERSEEN.
Oft loitering lazily if not o. T. iii 401

O'ERSHADE.
And sullen sadness, that o., distort T. i 457

O'ERSPREAD.
To see again my day o. St. iii 7

O'ERTAKE.
The waves o. them in their serious play R. 157

O'ERTAKEN.
He walked abroad, o. in the rain Con. 277

O'ERTHROWN.
Upon the guiltless passenger o. T. vi 424

O'ERTOP.
O. the lofty wood that skirts the wild T. i 558

O'ERVALUED.
Pleasure o., and his grace despised Ex. 252

O'ERWATCH.
O. the numerous and unruly clan Tir. 262

O'ERWHELM.
Invades, possesses, and o. the soul H. 730
Storms rise to o. him; or if stormy winds T. ii 142

O'ERWHELMED.
O. at once with wonder, grief, and joy R. 593
Hear him, o. with sorrow yet rejoice R. 772

O'ERWHELMING.
O. all distinction. On the flood T. v 97

OFFENCE.
His own o., and strips others bare Ch. 494
All zeal for a Reform that gives o. Ch. 533

Through constant dread of giving Truth o. *Con.* 129
Were sin in me, and an o. to you *E.* ii 4
Is wooing mercy by renewed o. *Ex.* 413
He takes o., and wonders what you mean *P.E.* 89
As inoffensive, what o. in cards ? *P.E.* 149
Whatever shocks, or gives the least o. *P.E.* 512
To birth or wit ; nor gives nor takes o. *R.* 450
On which he rode. Her opportune o. *T.* vi 470
And guiltless of o., they range the air *T.* vi 573
And measure of the o., rebukes a deed *T.* vi 655
And mirth without o. No few return'd *T.* vi 692
The neat conveyance hiding all the o. *T.* vi 980
That neither gave nor would endure o. *T.T.* 639
Yet not to give o. or grieve *Y.D.* 43

OFFEND.

Decreed that whosoever should o. *E.* iii 48
Peace to all such,—'twere pity to o. *H.* 272
May least o. against so pure a flame *R.* 248
Whence springs the conduct that o. you so *T.* 237
They never sin—or if (as all o.) *T.* 283
Now this is fulsome ; and o. me more *T.* ii 455
His lessons tire, his mild rebukes o. *Tir.* 716
O. not him, whom modesty restrains *Tir.* 727

OFFENDED. [591

Which, aimed at him, have pierced the o. skies *H.*
Deserves not, if so soon o. *P.* 43
Asserts the rights of his o. Lord *T.* 263
Scared, and the o. nightingale is mute *T.* i 768
Covering his shame from his o. sight *T.* v 634
May she ! and if o. Heaven be still *T.T.* 406

OFFENDERS.

And judged o. well. Then he that sharped *T.* iii 86

OFFENDING.

As fearful of o. whom he wished *T.* vi 501

OFFENSIVE.

The rivers die into o. pools *T.* ii 96
Found too where most o., in the skirts *T.* ii 822

OFFER.

And o. something to the general use *Ch.* 90
Saints o. nothing, in their warmest prayers *R.* 221
Belie their name, and o. nothing new *R.* 714
How ill the scene that o. rest *S.* 3
O. him warmth, security, and rest *T.* 252
When safe occasion o. ; and with dance *T.* i 584
Polite Refinement o. him in vain *T.* vi 977

OFFERED.

Forget to enjoy the palm-tree's o. shade *Ch.* 222

OFFERING.

On Fortune's velvet altar o. up *T.* ii 657

OFFICE.

Except that O. clips it as it goes *Ch.* 484
Usurps God's o., lays his bosom bare *Con.* 745
The priest, whose o. is, with zeal sincere *Ex.* 97
An o. key, a picklock to a place *Ex.* 379
" Your o. is to winnow false from true *H.* 417
Now Truth, perform thine o. ; waft aside *H.* 570
The same kind o. for me still *M.* 14
Renounced alike its o. and its sport *R.* 293
Escaped from o. and its constant cares *R.* 408
Lucrative o. are seldom lost *R.* 611
His o. sacred, his credentials clear *T.* ii 339
His noble o., and, instead of truth *T.* ii 428
Absurdly, not his o., but himself *T.* ii 548
Forgot their o., opening with a touch *T.* ii 747
Then acts in Nature's o., brings to pass *T.* iii 542
Discharge but these kind o., (and who *T.* iii 618

Would spare, that loves them, o. like these ?) *T.* iii 619
Begs a warm o., doomed to a cold jail *T.* iii 820
The seals of o. glitter in his eyes *T.* iv 59
Of knaves in o., partial in the work *T.* iv 412
Desert their o. ; and themselves intent *T.* iv 589
Some must be great. Great o. will have *T.* iv 788
That o. served, they must be swept away *T.* v 564
" The teacher's o., and dispense at large *T.* v 643
Where he, that fills an o., shall esteem *T.* vi 846
And quit their o. for their error's sake *T.* vi 884
Its destined o., yet with gentle stroke *T.* vi 1003
Must she perform the same kind o. now ? *T.T.* 403
The gift whose o. is the Giver's praise ! *T.T.* 750
Holds fast her o. here, can ne'er forget *Tir.* 134
Ghostly in o., earthly in his plan *Tir.* 422
Great titles, o. and trusts disgraced *Tir.* 816
Starts from its o. like a broken bow *V.* 70

OFFSPRING.

His o. hold in his paternal care *H.* 140
Man is the genuine o. of revolt *H.* 181
And Peace the genuine o. of her smile *H.* 482
Is it that Adam's o. may be saved *T.* 183
Their o., left upon so wild a beach *Tir.* 802

OFT-TIMES.

And liberty, and o. honour too *T.* i 734
Is o. proof of wisdom, when the fault *T.* iii 39
But o. deaf to suppliants who would blush *T.* iv 413
Are o. vanquished and thrown far behind *T.* vi 615

OGLES.

While Cynthio o., as she passes *P.B.* 19

OGLING.

Dick heard, and tweedling, o., bridling *P.T.* 38

OIL.

Our wasted o. unprofitably burns *Con.* 357
Furnishes always o. for its own wheels *R.* 616
Pardon me, ye that give the midnight o. *R.* 661

OILY.

The maple, and the beech of o. nuts *T.* i 315
Here rills of o. eloquence in soft *T.* iv 64

OLD.

They teach both conjurers and o. women *A Fable* 21
But what o. Chaucer's merry page befits *A.T.* 84
When Scandal has new minted an o. lie *Ch.* 513
Like hidden lamps in o. sepulchral urns *Con.* 358
There he was copious as o. Greece or Rome *Con.* 621
And new or o., still hasten to a close *Con.* 238 [623
Though Time will wear us, and we must grow o. *Con.*
And say as stern Elijah said of o. *Con.* 850 [*Con.* 741
The World grown o. her deep discernment shows
That fables o., that seemed for ever mute *Con.* 817
The virtues of o. Rome for English use *Con.* 836
Make him athletic as in days of o. *Con.* 841
Some few that I have known in days of o. *E.* iii 58
In o. grimalkin's glaring eyes *E.* iv 44
O. Tiny, surliest of his kind *Ep.* ii 5
Their very garments sacred, o. yet new *Ex.* 183
A truth still sacred, and believed of o. *Ex.* 351
Hast thou within thee sin, that in o. time *Ex.* 414
Some twigs of that o. scourge are left behind *Ex.* 517
'Tis to believe what men inspired of o. *Ex.* 646
Proof against sickness and o. age *M.F.* 50
With such as its o. tenants are *M.B.* 3
That title now too trite and o.) *Mor.* 2
O. Winter, halting o'er the mead *N.* 13 [53
They gathered close around the o. pit's brink *N.A.*
Should deem it by our o. companion made *N.A.* 95
Lay his o. age upon the lap of Ease *R.* 12 [602
And his o. stint—three thousand pounds a year *R.*

In an *o.* empty watering pot *R.C.* 16
And the *o.* utensil of tin *R.C.* 27   [cries *T.* 229
" Where dwell these matchless saints ? " *o.* Curio
But made long since, like Babylon of *o. T.* 391
Sprightly, and *o.* almost without decay *T.* i 408
Increasing London? Babylon of *o. T.* i 722   [59
Have kindled beacons in the skies, and the *o. T.* ii
And did he not of *o.* employ his means *T.* ii 199
Of *o.* achievements, and despair of new *T.* ii 254
Down into modern use; transforms *o.* print *T.* ii 363
For second childhood; and devote *o.* age *T.* ii 637
With an *o.* tavern quill, is hungry yet *T.* ii 628
A priesthood such as Baal's was of *o. T.* ii 678 [732
Their good *o.* friend, and Discipline at length *T.* ii
Virtue and vice had boundaries in *o.* time *T.* iii 75
And growing *o.* in drawing nothing up ! " *T.* iii 190
Are wedded thus, like beauty to *o.* age *T.* iii 660
And under an *o.* oak's domestic shade *T.* iv 172 [402
Skillet, and *o.* carved chest, from public sale *T.* iv
Than the fair shepherdess of *o.* romance *T.* iv 538
Him, Tubal named, the Vulcan of *o.* times *T.* v 217
Say ye, who (with less prudence than of *o. T.* v 321
O. or of later date, by sea or land *T.* v 381   [382
Her house of bondage, worse than that of *o. T.* v
And seeing the *o.* castle of the state *T.* v 525 [v 515
Such were not they of *o.*, whose tempered blades *T.*
With shallow shifts and *o.* devices, worn *T.* v 632
So in the chapel of *o.* Ely House *T.* vi 658   [700
Their kerchiefs, and *o.* women weep for joy *T.* vi
Encomium in *o.* time was poet's work *T.* vi 715 [737
And thou a wretch, whom, following her *o.* plan *Tir.*
There shall he learn, ere sixteen winters *o. Tir.* 210
Long lines of ancestry, renowned of *o. Tir.* 817 [878
Health's last farewell, a staff to thine *o.* age *Tir.*
A querulous *o.* woman's voice *Trans.* iv 25
No bard, howe'er majestic, *o.* or new *T.T.* 180
Proof of an *o.* affection still alive *V.* 24

OLIVE.
Her unctuous *o.*, and her purple vines *Her.* 7
Vines, *o.*, herbage, forests disappear *Her.* 23
Like gleanings of an *o.* tree they show *T.* 379

OLYMPIAN.
Nectareous essences, *O.* dews *T.* iv 83

OLYMPIC.   [309
Gives him *O.* speed, and shoots him to the goal *T.T.*

OLYMPUS.
That all *O.* through the country roves *Con.* 825

OMEN.
(For ravens, though, as birds of *o. A Fable* 20

OMINOUS.
Prodigies *o.*, and viewed with fear *P.E.* 99
A presage *o.*, portending still *T.* v 625

OMISSION.
By trespass or *o. F.* 147

OMITS.
The chaster Muse of modern days *o. A.T.* 85

OMITTED.
Thy name *o.*, in a page *U.* 5

OMNIPOTENCE.
'Tis thus *O.* his law fulfils *Ch.* 81
To span *o.*, and measure might *T.* vi 212

OMNIPOTENT.
Just so the *O.*, who turns *E.* i 73
The *o.* magician, Brown, appears! *T.* iii 766

Fruits of *o.* eternal love *T.* iv 188
An Orpheus, and *o.* in song *T.* v 694

OMNISCIENT.
But, with averted eyes, the *o.* Judge *T.* 227

ONION.
And, feasting on an *o.* and a crust *T.T.* 241

ONSET.
And feeble *o.* of a pigmy rush *Ex.* 707
The *o.* and irregular. At length *T.* v 230

OPAQUE.
As diamonds, stripped of their *o.* disguise *Ch.* 307
Her veil *o.*, discloses with a smile *T.* v 892

OPEN.
And set the unseemly pair in *o.* day *A.T.* 168
God *o.* fruitful Nature's various scenes *Ch.* 88
Winding a secret or an *o.* course *Ch.* 369
Whoever keeps an *o.* ear *F.* 97
Enjoyed the *o.* air *F.B.* 3
The *o.* windows seemed to invite *F.B.* 19
And they might enter at his *o.* door *H.* 308
Their gates wide *o.* threw *J.G.* 120
Flew *o.* in short space *J.G.* 212
Those *o.* on the spot their honeyed store *P.E.* 49
Half *o.* in the topmost chest *R.C.* 40
" The *o.* drawer was left, I see *R.C.* 55
'Tis *o.*, and ye cannot enter—why ? *T.* 357
His legs depending at the *o.* door *T.* i 93
Renounce the odours of the *o.* field *T.* i 415
Beneath the *o.* sky she spreads the feast *T.* i 433
With easy force it *o.* all the cells *T.* vi 11
Forms, *o.*, and gives scent to every flower *T.T.* 691

OPENED.
Were built, the fountains *o.*, or the sea *T.* v 765

OPENING.   [884
Shoots between scattered rocks and *o.* shades *Con.*
And now just *o.* to our view *E.* i 50   [103
Sails ripped, seams *o.* wide, and compass lost *M.P.*
Entreated, *o.* wide his beak *P.T.* 19   [281
The breach, though small at first, soon *o.* wide *P.E.*
O. the map of God's extensive plan *R.* 147
Forgot their office, *o.* with a touch *T.* ii 747
Each *o.* blossom, freely breathes abroad *T.* iii 622
O. and wider *o.* on her view *T.T.* 265
Where Discipline helps *o.* buds of sense *T.T.* 503
And the next *o.* grave may yawn for you *St.* ii 36

OPERA.
With *o.* glass to watch the moving scene *T.* ii 453

OPERATION.
A moment's *o.* on his love *T.* iii 793

OPHIR.
Gold, purer far than *O.* ever knew *V.* 97

OPIATES.
And lenient as soft *o.* to the mind *P.E.* 80

OPINION.
(For opposition gives *o.* strength) *Con.* 88
Set your *o.* at whatever pitch *Con.* 107
His sole *o.*, whatsoe'er befall *Con.* 133
In vain *o.* waste and dangerous wild *H.* 279
To streams of popular *o.* drawn *P.E.* 478

OPIUM.
Or do they still, as if with *o.* drugged *T.* iv 26

OPPORTUNE.
On which he rode. Her *o.* offence *T.* vi 470

OPPORTUNITY.
Than o. vouchsafed to err *F.A.* 16
A splendid o. to die? *T.* v 320

OPPOSE.
What human wisdom cannot but o. *Ch.* 340
The emphatic speaker dearly loves to o. *Con.* 269
Nature o. with her utmost force *H.* 639
Pride above all o. her design *T.* 474
No sycophant or slave, that dared o. *T.T.* 350

OPPOSED.
That strength would fail, o. against the push *Ex.* 706
Is weakness when o.; conscious of wrong *T.* v 372
What does he not, from lusts o. in vain *T.* v 599
O. against the pleasures Nature loves! *Tir.* 170

OPPOSERS.
Meet their o. with united strength *Con.* 700

OPPOSITE.
When God and man stand o. in view *H.* 131
" O. in the apple-tree *P.T.* 31

OPPOSITION.
(For o. gives opinion strength) *Con.* 88

OPPRESSOR.
To see the o. in his turn oppressed *Ch.* 74
Of all their hard o. valued most *Ex.* 172
With ease, and is at large. The o. holds *T.* v 774

OPPRESSED.
To see the oppressor in his turn o. *Ch.* 74
Where the betrayed, forsaken and o. *T.* 437

OPPRESSION.
O., labouring hard to grind the poor *Ex.* 40
O. his terrible name *M.D.* 28
Where rumour of o. and deceit *T.* ii 3
O., prisons, have no power to bind *T.* v 543
The o. of a tyrannous control *T.* vi 455

OPPROBRIOUS.
Then shame to manhood, and o. more *T.* v 379
O. residence, he finds them all *T.* v 584

OPTICIAN.
And land some grave o. on the shore *Ch.* 384

OPTICS.
From which our nicer o. turn away *H.* 494
Sees, far as human o. may command *T.* 3
Man made for kings! those o. are but dim *T.T.* 55

OPULENCE.
The smile of o. in sorrow's face *Ch.* 130
Denied that earthly o. they choose *Ex.* 458
(Such is his thirst of o. and ease) *Her.* 68

OPULENT.
As London, o., enlarged, and still *T.* i 721
That seizes first the o., descends *T.* iv 583

ORACLE.
An o. within an empty cask *Con.* 298
And import, of their o. divine *Ex.* 126
" Spoke like an o.," they all exclaim *H.* 437
Of o. like these? Great pity too *T.* iii 169
They hear him speak—the o. of law *Tir.* 363
Myself the o., and will discourse *Y.O.* 142

ORACULAR.
Where, in his own o. abode *T.* 389
Yet deemed o., lure down to death *T.* v 863
The mighty plan, o., in verse *T.T.* 179
O., I would not curious ask *Y.O.* 42

ORANGE.
The ruddier o. and the paler lime *T.* iii 573
Of o., myrtle, or the fragrant weed *T.* iv 764

ORATION.
The songster heard his short o. *N.G.* 23

ORATOR.
Mute as e'er gazed on o. or bard *S.* i 8

ORATORY.
Where flails of o. thresh the floor *Ex.* 302

ORB.
And, though the soul shall seek superior o. *Ch.* 563
The rising or the setting o. of day *R.* 191
'Tis morning; and the sun with ruddy o. *T.* v 1

ORBIT.
Ye clergy, while your o. is your place *P.E.* 96

ORCHARD.
His comrades had plotted an o. to rob *P.A.* 23
In many an o., copse, and grove *P.T.* 13

ORDAIN.
As He o. things sordid in their birth *Ch.* 561
E'en as his will and his decrees o. *Ex.* 325
Revere the laws they dream that Heaven o. *H.* 241
To take the bend his appetites o. *H.* 603

ORDAINED.
It seems as if we Britons were o. *Con.* 360
O. perhaps, ere summer flies *O.* i 17
O. to move when others please *P.* 7
New life o. and brighter scenes to share *R.* 65
Whence, and what are we? to what end o.? *R.* 645
And virtue, and those scenes which God o. *T.* iii 703
Just in the niche he was o. to fill *T.* iv 792
" O. to guide the embodied spirit home *T.* v 840

ORDER.
Against my o., whom you heard *Beau* 7
To take his honour's o., cap in hand *Con.* 416
And plans and o. our connexions *E.* i 36
He sowed the seeds of o. where he went *Ex.* 488
Thy chaos o., and thy weakness might *Ex.* 641
Their o. on his shelves exact *Mrs. M—* 39
Go, cast your o. at your bishop's feet *P.E.* 120
The rest in o. to the top *R.C.* 94
Who trample o.; and the day *St.* vi 25
He graced a college, in which o. yet *T.* ii 785
Sightly, and in just o., ere he gives *T.* iii 649
Disturb good o., and degrade true worth *T.* iii 674
Of o., from the chariot to the plough *T.* iv 586
Where all was vitreous; but in o. due *T.* v 161
Of these the first in o., and the pledge *T.* v 575
And marshals all the o. of the year *T.* vi 191
And the harmonious o. of them all *Tir.* 635

ORDERED.
Thus genius rose and set at o. times *T.T.* 560

ORDINANCE.
An o. it concerned them much to know *H.* 313
The total o. and will of God *T.* i 743
Of that controlling o. they move *T.* vi 202
Where no regard of o. is shown *Tir.* 242

ORE.
The recollection, like a vein of o. *Con.* 515
" Nor needs his genuine o. refine! *E.* iv 89

ORGAN.
While, through that public o. of report *T.* ii 355

ORIENT.
His victory was that of o. light *Ex.* 478
Yes, but an object bright as o. morn *H.* 550
Than golden beams of o. light *M.* 27

ORIGIN.
Tastes of its healthful o., and flows *Con.* 565
Knows he his o. ? can he ascend *F.A.* 22
Some say that in the o. of things *T.* vi 198

ORIGINAL.
The bright o. was one he knew *Ch.* 433
Review thy dim o. and prime *Ex.* 467

ORIGINATE.
The greatest oft o.) could Chance *T.* ii 168

ORMUS.
The looms of O., and the mines of Ind *T.* vi 806

ORNAMENT.
No shining o. have they to seek *H.* 765
No clustering o. to clog the pile *T.* 24
And decks itself with o. of gold *T.* i 529
Support, and o. of Virtue's cause *T.* ii 336
Stripped of her o., her leaves, and flowers *T.* iii 728
Studious of o., yet unresolved *T.* vi 160

ORNAMENTAL.
As o., musical, polite *T.* iv 489

ORPHEAN.
By magic summons of the O. lyre *T.* iii 587

ORPHEUS.
An O., and omnipotent in song *T.* v 694
The tree-enchanter O. fell *T.B.* 64

OSCITANCY.
And slumbering o. mars the brood ? *T.* ii 774

OSIERS.
Streams edged with o., fattening every field *H.* 47

OSTENT.
Of God and goodness, atheist in o. *T.* vi 486

OSTENTATION.
From o., as from weakness, free *T.* 25
Less o., and yet studded thick *T.* iii 420

OSTENTATIOUS.
With o. pageantry, but set *T.* iv 256

OSTLER.
The Crown, took notice of an o.'s face *R.* 586

OSTRICH.
The o., silliest of the feathered kind *Tir.* 789

OUSE.
Swept O.'s silent tide *D.W.* 2
It was the time when O. displayed *D.W.* 13
A cottage on the banks of O.—*E.* i 48
Nor O. on his bosom their image receives *P.F.* 4
Fast by the banks of the slow-winding O.—*R.* 804
Here O., slow-winding through a level plain *T.* i 163
The O., dividing the well-watered land *T.* i 323
But smooth with wands from O.'s side *T.B.* 28

OUTCAST.
They left their o. mate behind *Cast.* 23

OUTCRIES.
Though Appetite raise o. at the cost ? *T.* ii 621

OUTLAST.
Their fragrant memory will o. their tomb *Con.* 631

OUTLINE.
And o. of the present transient state *R.* 670

OUTLIVED.
And schools, that have o. all just esteem *Tir.* 704
No flock frequents thee now. Thou hast o. *Y.O.* 56

OUTLIVES.
Still o. many a storm that has effaced *M.P.* 56

OUT-MANTLE.
Till it o. all the pride of verse *T.* v 680

OUTRAGE.
Of wrong and o. with which earth is filled *T.* ii 7
And conscious of the o. he commits *T.* vi 599

OUTRAGEOUS.
Charge not a God with such o. wrong" *T.* 520

OUTRIGHT.
Who say the mob are mad o. *Pat.* 19

OUTSCOLDS.
O. the ranting actor on the stage *T.* iv 45

OUTSIDE.
Less dainty than becomes his grave o. *T.* iv 605

OUTSLEPT.
He has o. the winter, ventures forth *T.* vi 313

OUTSPREAD.
And while her infant race with o. hands *T.* iv 384
Ruminate heedless of the scene o. *T.* v 788
Whose o. branches overarch the glade *T.* vi 71

OUTSTRETCHED.
By soft recumbency of o. limbs *T.* i 82

OUTWARD.
And ignorant, except of o. show) *T.* i 650

OUTWEIGHS.
Joy, far superior Joy, that much o. *H.* 723

OUTWITTED.
And by themselves o. *F.* 72

OVEN-WOOD.
But now wear crests of o. instead *N.A.* 12

OVERARCH.
Whose outspread branches o. the glade *T.* vi 71

OVERAWED.
Dreading a negative, and o. *E.* iii 22
Thus free from censure o. by fear *T.T.* 115
Till Reason, now no longer o. *Tir.* 187

OVERBEARING.
The impoverished earth; an o. race *T.* iii 672

OVERBUILT.
And o. with most impending brows *T.* iii 193

OVERCAST.
Since first our sky was o. *M.* 2
What if thine Heaven be o. *Trans. H.* 25

OVERCHARGED.
Asks egress; which obtained, the o. *T.* iii 497

OVERCHARGES.
But o. her capacious hand *Ch.* 100

OVERFLOWING.
Poured out from Plenty's o. horn *Ex.* 10

OVERGORGED.
Into his *o.* and bloated purse *T.* i 737
To turn purveyor to an *o. T.* v 421

OVERGROWN.
The common *o.* with fern, and rough *T.* i 526

OVERHANG.
That *o.* the borders of thy tomb *H.* 38
That *o.* the thatch, itself unseen *T.* i 224
That *o.* a torrent, to a twig *T.* i 484

OVERHANGING.
By just degrees, an *o.* breadth *T.* iii 482

OVER-HEAD.
Yet feel the burning instinct: *o. T.* iv 773

OVERLAID.
And *o.* with clear translucent glass *T.* iii 485

OVERLEAPED.
That one among so many *o. T.* ii 718

OVERLEAPING.
Nor stops, till, *o.* all delays *Ch.* 178

OVERLOOKED.
While life's sublimest joys are *o. Ch.* 219
Shall be despised and *o.* no more *R.* 359
Stand, never *o.,* our favourite elms *T.* i 167
Of ignorance, till then she *o. T.* v 809

OVERLOOKS.
In Nature's tendencies, oft *o. T.* ii 175
Of Nature, *o.* her author more *T.* iii 237

OVERNICE.
That with a world, not often *o. Tir.* 464

OVERPAID.
And *o.* its value with thy blood *T.* vi 860

OVERPOWERING.
Of asps their venom, *o.* strength *T.* v 702

OVERSET.
And she was *o. R.G.* 10
Lest storms should *o.* the leaning pile *T.* v 39
The storms that *o.* the joys of life *T.T.* 449

OVERSHADOWING.
Large foliage, *o.* golden flowers *T.* iii 535

OVERSHOOT.
Proud of his speed, to *o.* the truth *Con.* 642
Of dayspring *o.* his humble nest *T.* i 496

OVERSPREAD.
So then;—as darkness *o.* the deep *Ex.* 636
Thick *o.* with moss and silky grass *N.A.* 2
The smoking manure, and *o.* it all *T.* iii 517

OVERTHROW.
The tumult and the *o.,* the pangs *T.* ii 104

OVERTHWART.
While far beyond, and *o.* the stream *T.* i 169

OVERWHELM.
They *o.* me with the spleen " *M.F.* 8

OWE.
The judge of all men *o.* them no regard *Ch.* 572
O. all its weight, like loaded dice, to lead *Con.* 302
How much the country to the conqueror *o. Ex.* 481
This cap to my cousin I *o. Gr.* 5
All these are not half that I *o. Gr.* 41
Their lustre to his influence *o. Mrs. M—* 54
Such writers, and such readers, *o.* the gust *P.E.* 329
O sacred art! to which alone life *o. R.* 749
The tears that England *o. R.G.* 28
He held the thunder. But the monarch *o. T.* i 382
That *o.* its pleasures to another's pain *T.* iii 327
That oft we *o.* our safety to a skill *T.* vi 619
Of which she little dreams. Perhaps she *o. T.* vi 945
'Tis to the virtues of such men, man *o. T.T.* 19
He speaks, and they appear; to him they *o. T.T.* 356
Ye nurseries of our boys, we *o.* to you *Tir.* 248
O. their repute in part, but not the whole *Tir.* 461
Instead of paying what he *o. Y.D.* 27
Of their best tone their dissolution *o. Y.O.* 85

OWED.
I *o.* a trifle, and have paid the debt *Con.* 796
Nor *o.* articulation to his ear *Y.O.* 148

OWING.
Less impious than absurd, and *o.* more *T.* vi 656

OWL.
The jay, the pie, and even the boding *o. T.* 205 [52
For *o.* to roost in. Once thy spreading boughs *Y.O.*

OWN.
O. no superior but the God she fears *Ch.* 275
His conscience *o.* it true *H.F.* 16
That *o.* a carcass, and not quake for fear? *N.A.* 100
And *o.* his crab-computing powers o'ercome *P.E.* 487
Shall *o.* itself a stammerer in that cause *R.* 413
He likes the country, but in truth must *o. R.* 573
Communicative of the good he *o. T.* i 332   [74
And chaste themselves, are not ashamed to *o. T.* iii
Were he on earth, would hear, approve, and *o. T.* ii 396
And *o.,* the law of universal love *T.* vi 360
And *o.* her power on every shore he laves *Tir.* 40

OWNED.
The estate his sires had *o.* in ancient years *R.* 579
More worthily the powers she *o.* before *T.* v 807

OWNER.
For why?—his *o.* had a house *J.G.* 151
And prove their *o.* half divine " *P.* 64
Reproach their *o.* with that love of rest *T.* i 394
Even as he bids! The enraptured *o.* smiles *T.* iii 780
Might have bloomed with its *o.* awhile *The Rose* 18

OX.   [420
Witness the patient *o.,* with stripes and yells *T.* vi

OYSTER.
An *o.,* cast upon the shore *P.* 1

P.

PACE.
Are taught by rays that fly with equal *p. Ch.* 363
The silent *p.* with which they steal away *Comp.* i 3
Judgment, however tardy, mends her *p. Ex.* 151
Proceeding with his nimblest *p. Mor.* 20
They sidle to the goal with awkward *p. P.E.* 562
He drops the rein, and leaves him to his *p. T.* 247
Swift *p.* or steep ascent no toil to me *T.* i 139
How oft upon yon eminence our *p. T.* i 154
But now with pleasant *p.* a cleanlier road *T.* iii 17
To the clogged wheels; and in its sluggish *p. T.* iv 345
Though lean and beggared, every twentieth *p. T.* iv 468
To him whose moments all have one dull *p. T.* v 407

PACING.
Oft *p.*, as the mariner his deck *F.A.* 19
Full slowly *p.* o'er the stones *J.G.* 79

PACK.
Thy soldiery, the Pope's well managed *p. Ex.* 518
Now therefore issued forth the spotted *p. N.A.* 24
He takes the field, the master of the *p. P.E.* 114
A pedlar's *p.*, that bows the bearer down *T.* i 465
For all the savage din of the swift *p. T.* iii 325
The puppy *p.* that had defiled the scene *T.T.* 641

PACKED.
Close *p.* and smiling, in a chaise and one *T.* i 80
True to his charge, the close *p.* load behind *T.* iv 8

PACKHORSE.
With *p.* constancy we keep the road *Tir.* 252

PADDLE.
Ducks *p.* in the pond, before the door *R.* 499

PADDLED.
Stepping into their nests, they *p. P.T.* 54

PADDOCK.
Or oaken fence that hems the *p.* round *T.T.* 583

PAGAN.
A herald of God's love to *p.* lands *Ch.* 136

PAGE.
But what old Chaucer's merry *p.* befits *A.T.* 84
In vain recorded in historic *p. B.B.* 3
No poet wept him; but the *p. Cast.* 49
Or from philosophy's enlightened *p. Con.* 616
This *p.* of providence quite new *E.* i 49
Ask now of History's authentic *p. Ex.* 161
Was—welladay, the title *p.* was lost *H.* 428
Thee, Thornton! worthy in some *p.* to shine *J.T.* 7
Appealed to many a poet's *p. L.R.* 11
Their *p.* mangled, burnt, and torn *M.* i 9
All this still legible in Memory's *p. M.P.* 68
Nor touch the *p.* he cannot but profane) *P.E.* 457
To spread the *p.* of Scripture, and compare *R.* 131
And poring on thy *p.*, whose every line *R.* 207
With which I charge my *p. St.* i 22
As I can number in my punctual *p. St.* ii 3
Which future *p.* yet are doomed to share *T.* 146
For her, the Memory fills her ample *p. Tir.* 13
'Tis called a book, though but a single *p.*) *Tir.* 122
This folio of four *p.*, happy work! *T.* iv 50
There forests of no meaning spread the *p. T.* iv 74
The poet's or historian's *p.* by one *T.* iv 158
'Tis not enough that Greek or Roman *p. Tir.* 605
And the sixth Edward's, grace the historic *p. T.T.* 106

Thy name omitted, in a *p. U.* 5
In many a *p.* historic strayed 1789, 22

PAGEANT.
We love the man; the paltry *p.* you *T.* v 348
A pompous and slow-moving *p.* comes *T.* vi 697
Had all the *p.* of the world *Q.V.* 21

PAGEANTRY.
And look on Folly's *p.* with scorn *S.* ii 8
Could *p.* and dance, and feast and song *T.* iii 314
With ostentatious *p.*, but set *T.* iv 256

PAID.
And Love Divine has *p.* one price for all *Ch.* 205
She deems all safe, for she has *p.* the price *Ch.* 458
The visit *p.*, with ecstasy we come *Con.* 399
I owed a trifle, and have *p.* the debt *Con.* 796
From man to man, or e'en to woman *p. E.* ii 5
If *p.* in any other coin *E.* iv 26
Punctually *p.* for lengthening out disease *H.* 204
For which he *p.* full dear *J.G.* 202
Is *p.* at least in peace of mind *Mor.* 51
P. my price in paltry gold *N.C.* 6
Pay!—follow Christ, and all is *p. St.* v 33
His praise postponed, and never to be *p. T.* 86 [91
P. with the blood that he had basely spared *T.* iii
But fairer wreaths are due, though never *p. T.* v 712
For wages so unlikely to be *p. Tir.* 457

PAIN.
With many a freakish trick deceived his *p. A.T.* 25
And ease a doggish *p. Beau* 10
I see you after all my *p. Beau* 19
And I might spare myself the *p.* to show *Ch.* 626
They fix attention, heedless of your *p. Con.* 63
I pity bashful men, who feel the *p. Con.* 347 [494
Though future *p.* may serve for present mirth *Con.*
Beau marked my unsuccessful *p. D.W.* 21
Employs our present thoughts and *p. E.* i 51
Flits out of sight, and mocks his *p. E.* iv 60
"Matthew," says Fame, "with endless *p. E.* iv 73
But age in spite of weakness and of *p. Ex.* 25
Pleasure is deaf when told of future *p. Ex.* 66
A long immunity from grief and *p. Ex.* 82
And at last is of service in sickness or *p. F.M.* 11
If sentence of eternal *p.* belong *H.* 389
If ever thou hast felt another's *p. H.* 674
Woven with *p.* into his plan *H.F.* 3
On *p.* of excommunication" *L.W.* 6
A pleasure from its *p. Miss —* 52
Indite much metre with much *p. O.* i 3
Will heartily thank us, no doubt, for our *p. P.A.* 10
Remorse, and Sorrow, and vindictive *P.—P.E.* 44
Ere yet the pleasing toil becomes a *p. P.E.* 70
Spontaneous, take but little *p.* to sow *P.E.* 364
Death and the *p.* of Hell attend him there *P.E.* 547
Else He that hung there suffered all his *p. P.E.* 623
Grasp seeming Happiness, and find it *P.—R.* 756
Till Sympathy contract a kindred *p. R.* 299
And minds that deem derided *p.* a treat *R.* 310
Condemn the prattler, for his idle *p. R.* 547
To ages in a world of *p. St.* v 9
His voluntary *p.*, severe and long *T.* 101
Escaped with *p.* from that adventurous flight *T.* i 4
From gaiety that fills the bones with *p. T.* i 504
There is a pleasure in poetic *p. T.* ii 285
That owes its pleasures to another's *p, T.* iii 327
That sensibility of *p.* with which *T.* iv 358

And shock me. I should then with double *p*. *T.* v 483
And win it with more *p*. Their blood is shed *T.* v 719
For he has wings that neither sickness, *p*. *T.* v 771
And with it all its pleasures and its *p*. *T.* vi 14
The stress of a continual act, the *p*. *T.* vi 208
Hence date the persecution and the *p*. *T.* vi 384 [63
With passions, just that he may prove, with *p. Tir.*
A childish waste of philosophic *p. Tir.* 76
That instant upon all his future *p. Tir.* 715
Would deem it no abuse, or waste of *p. Tir.* 627
And hopes in spite of *p. Trans. H.* 21   [536
Or, having whelped a prologue with great *p. T.T.*
To exchange content for trouble, ease for *p. V.* 64

PAINED.

And infants clamorous whether pleased or *p. T.* i 232
Might never reach me more! My ear is *p. T.* ii 5

PAINFUL.

To lull the *p*. malady with alms *Ch.* 443
A *p*. passage o'er a restless flood *H.* 3
These ask with *p*. shyness, and, refused *T.* iv 418

PAINT.

Poetry may, but colours cannot *p. Con.* 384
Artist, attend! your brushes and your *p. T.* 171
Thus Fancy *p*. thee, and though apt to err *T.* i 661
Perhaps errs little when she *p*. thee thus *T.* i 662
To tell its slumbers, and to *p*. its dreams *T.* iii 13
The nauseous task to *p*. her as she is *T.* iii 67 [214
Theirs, should I *p*. him, has his pinions fledged *T.* iv
And *p*. his person, character and views *T.* iii 143
P. cards and dolls, and every idle thing *T.* iv 241

PAINTED.

Taught thee to clothe thy pinked and *p*. hide *Ex.* 486
The *p*. tablets, dealt and dealt again! *P.E.* 170
Save their own *p*. shins, our sires had none *T.* i 9
In *p*. plumes superbly dressed *Trans.* iv 1
That, quite eclipsing Pleasure's *p*. face *T.T.* 649

PAINTER.

The *p.*'s pencil, and the poet's lyre *Ch.* 106
A *p.*'s skill into a poet's hand *H.* 670
None more admires, the *p.*'s magic skill *T.* i 422

PAINTING.

Far other *p*. grace the chamber now *H.* 262

PAIR.

Forms or no forms, pluralities or *p. A.T.* 131
And set the unseemly *p*. in open day *A.T.* 168
This history of a wedded *p. A Tale* 11
Yet parent of this loving *p. A Tale* 67
As in a dance the *p*. that take the lead *H.* 13
Turn downward, and the lowest *p*. succeed *H.* 14
All in a chaise and *p. J.G.* 12
The kindest and the happiest *p. M.F.* 37
Surprised at all they meet, the gosling *p. P.E.* 379
All paired, and each *p*. built a nest *P.T.* 44
I praise you much, ye meek and patient *p. T.* iv 407
Transformed to a lean shank. The shapeless *p. T.* v 16
For such a *p*. of wings as thine *Trans.* ii 35
To meet with such a well-matched *p. Trans.* iv 32

PAIRED.

They *p*., and would have built a nest *A Tale* 15
All *p*., and each pair built a nest *P.T.* 44
Now stars; two lobes, protruding, *p*. exact *Y.O.* 36

PALACE.

The *p*. were but half complete *F.* 166
Near barren rocks, in *p*, or cells *R.* 540
His *p*., and his lacqueys, and "My Lord" *T.* 122
Our *p*., our ladies, and our pomp *T.* i 643

Her *p*. are dust. In all her streets *T.* ii 77
Nor *p*., nor even chambers, 'scaped *T.* ii 831
But tasteless. Springs a *p*. in its stead *T.* iii 769
In such a *p*. Aristæus found *T.* v 135
In such a *p*. Poetry might place *T.* v 138

PALAESTRA.

Learned at the bar, in the *p*. bold *Con.* 843

PALATE.

To cover a pill for a delicate *p. F.M.* 12
Disdains not, nor the *p*., undepraved *T.* i 124
So grateful to the *p*., and when rare *T.* iii 447
To *p*. that can taste immortal truth *T.* vi 1015

PALE.

But man, within a wider *p*. enclosed *A.T.* 59
A *p*. procession of past sinful joys *H.* 221
Long beards, long noses, and *p*. faces *M.F.* 6
And if he but suspects a frown turns *p. T.* 216
Seen in the dim horizon, turns thee *p. T.* i 667
Fall prone; the *p*. inhabitants come forth *T.* ii 125
P., wan, and livid, but assuming soon *T.* iii 523 [58
Now from the roost, or from the neighbouring *p. T.*v
Woe to the gardener's *p*., the farmer's hedge *T.* iv 436
For England's glory, seeing it wax *p. T.* v 510[162
Copious of flowers the woodbine, *p*. and wan *T.* iv
Now flushed with drunkenness, now with whoredom *p.*
                                                    [*Tir.* 833

PALER.

Though each its hue peculiar; *p*. some *T.* i 308
The ruddier orange and the *p*. lime *T.* iii 573

PALES.

Female and male, Pomona, *P*., Pan *T.* vi 233

PALFREY.

Though little need to his good *p.*'s side *A.T.* 192

PALLAS.

Like *P*. springing armed from Jove *Mrs. M—* 26

PALLED.

By repetition *p*., by age obtuse *H.* 22

PALLET.

So I, with brush in hand and *p*. spread *T.* iv 239

PALLIATE.

To *p*. dullness, and give time a shove *T.* iv 210
That *p*. deeds of folly and of shame) *Tir.* 333

PALLS.

That *p*. and satiates, and makes languid life *T.* i 464

PALM.

Slides guinea behind guinea in his *p. Ch.* 474
Thy cocoas and bananas, *p*. and yams *T.* i 640
His milkwhite hand; the *p*. is hardly clean *T.* iv 607
And bear the *p*. away *Th.* 12
And claim the *p*. for purity of song *T.T.* 636

PALMISTRY.

Great skill have they in *p*., and more *T.* i 570

PALM-TREE.

Forget to enjoy the *p.*'s offered shade *Ch.* 222

PALSIED.

"For lift thy *p*. head, shake off the gloom *H.* 37

PALSY.

A *p*. struck his arm, his sparkling eye *T.* ii 727

PAMPERED.

Pride may be *p*. while the flesh grows lean *T.* 117
(Guiltless of *p*. appetite obscene) *T.* i 104
In gross and *p*. cities, sloth, and lust *T.* i 687

And bloated spider, till the *p*. pest *T*. v 423
If the gilt carriage, and the *p*. steed *T.T*. 133

PAMPERER.
For making speech the *p*. of lust *Con*. 48

PAN.
Models of Herculanean pots and *p. P.E*. 398
Female and male, Pomona, Pales, *P.—T*. vi 233

PANE.
To every *p*. his trunk applied *P.B*. 8
From the dashed *p*. the deluge as its falls *T*. iii 488
Beneath a *p*. of thin translucent horn *Tir*. 120

PANEGYRIC.
Have poured my stream of *p*. down. *T*. vi 720

PANELS.
The *p*., leaving an obscure, rude name *T*. i 282

PANG.
Flies to save some, and feels a *p*. for all *Ch*. 407
And having felt the *p*. you deem a jest *Con*. 497
The *p*. of a poetic birth *Dr*. 7
And many a *p*., experienced still within *E*. ii 35
To every *p*. that racks an anxious mind *Ex*. 571
On *p*. enforced with God's severest stroke *R*. 314
Grow frantic with her *p*., and bite the ground *T*. 444
From *p*. arthritic that infest the toe *T*. i 105
Flash desperation, and betray their *p. T*. i 502
The tumult and the overthrow, the *p. T*. ii 104
And beg for exile, or the *p*. of death ? *T*. v 434
Adds tenfold bitterness to death by *p. T*. vi 395
Plead not in vain for pity on the *p. T*. vi 462

PANNELS.
Blushed on the *p*. Mirror needed none *T*. v 160

PANNIERS.
To hear his creaking *p*. at the door *T*. i 245

PANOPLY.
And armed himself in *p*. complete *T*. ii 345

PANT.
P. to communicate her noble fires *Ch*. 403 [721
Through the dry leaves, and *p*. upon the strings *Ex*.
P. for the place of her ethereal birth *H*. 162
Must spring that Hope he *p*. to make his own *H*. 709
And *p*. for brighter days *N*. 12
P. for the refuge of some rural shade *R*. 6
Who will may *p*. for glory and excel *R*. 245
P. to be told of battles won or lost *R*. 476
P. for it, aims at it, enters it, and dies *T*. 6 [iv 60
He climbs, he *p*., he grasps them ! At his heels *T*.
P. for the praise of dressing to the taste *T*. iii 460
" *P*. to return, and when he sees afar *T*. v 833
Who *p*. with application misapplied *T*. vi 273

PANTED.
And sucked a breast that *p*. with alarms *Ex*. 473
For thee I *p*., thee I prized *O*. ii 19

PANTING.
And *p*. pressed the floor *B.R*. 16
By *p*. dog, tired man, and spattered horse *N.A*. 125
Now in the floods, now *p*. in the meads *R*. 538
A *p*. syllable through time and space *R*. 692
My *p*. side was charged, when I withdrew *T*. iii 110
Some royal mastiff *p*. at their heels *T.T*. 35

PAP. [480
Give it the breast, or stop its mouth with *p*. ! *Con*.

PAPAL.
Of Tiber's marshes and the *p*. bog *Ex*. 511

PAPER.
I pricked them into *p*. with a pin *M.P*. 77

PAPER-KITE.
Rose like a *p*., and charmed the town *T.T*. 385

PAPIST.
No *P*. more desirous to compound *T*. 201

PARABLES.
Speaking in *p*. his slighted word *Tir*. 140

PARADE.
To flourish and *p*. with at the bar *Ex*. 665

PARADISE.
Where *P*. seemed still vouchsafed on earth *Ex*. 429
She holds a *P*. of rich delight *H*. 60
O charming *P*. of shortlived sweets ! *Her*. 34
Can British *P*. no scenes afford *P.E*. 257
When he designed a *P*. below *R*. 270
Disclosing *P*. where'er He treads ? *T*. ii 87
Of *P*. that has survived the fall ! *T*. iii 42
Though placed in *P*., (for earth has still *T*. iii 298
New to my taste his *P*. surpassed *T*. iv 710
And fade not. There is *P*. that fears *T*. v 572
The *P*. he sees, he finds it such *T*. v 794
Were driven from *P*. : and in that hour *T*. vi 380

PARALLAX.
The *p*. of yonder luminous point *T*. iii 215

PARALYTIC.
The *p*., who can hold her cards *T*. i 472

PARAMOUNT.
Lord *p*. of the surrounding plains *H*. 305
Are *p*., and must extinguish theirs *T*. vi 583

PARCEL.
'Tis like a *p*. sent you by the stage *Con*. 305
That being *p*. of the common mass *T*. v 247

PARCELLED.
Ours *p*. out, as thine have ever been *P.E*. 155

PARCH.
Sent us a wind to *p*. us at a blast ? *P.E*. 256

PARDON.
You need his *p*., and provoke his rod *Con*. 488
To *p*. or to bear it *F*. 174
Is not the *p*. of thy long arrear *F.A*. 13
And—*p*. me, the bottle stands with you " *H*. 320
The sound of *p*. pierce his startled ear *H*. 724
P. me, ye that give the midnight oil *R*. 661
And *p*. are not sold as once they were *T*. 290
The solitary Shilling. *P*. then *T*. iii 456

PARDONING.
By which Heaven moves in *p*. guilty man *T*. vi 597

PARENT.
Yet *p*. of this loving pair *A Tale* 67
To be resolved into their *p*. earth *Ch*. 562
Humility the *p*. of the first *Con*. 377
The fruitful *p*. of abuse and wrong *Con*. 461
P. of Hope, immortal Truth ! make known *H*. 663
The son of *p*. passed into the skies *M.P*. 111
Whatever *p*., guardians, schools, intend *P.E*. 424
And such expense as pinches *p*. blue *T*. ii 756
And feel a *p*.'s presence no restraint *T*. vi 49
The young to let the *p*. bird go free *T*. vi 446
Our *p*. yet exert a prudent care *Tir*. 115
A *p*. pours into regardless ears *Tir*. 590
And formed of God without a *p*.'s mind *Tir*. 780

P. of manners like herself severe *T.T.* 613
Beneath thy p. tree mellowed the soil *Y.O.* 24

PARENTAGE.
To hear them tell of p. and birth *Con.* 210

PARENTAL.
Which only a p. eye foresees *Tir.* 371

PARIS.
View him at P. in his last career *T.* 311

PARISH.
Make every p. but their own their home *Con.* 860

PARK.
P. in which Art preceptress Nature weds *R.* 335
And turned into the p. or mead to graze *R.* 627
Frequent in P. with lady at his side *T.* ii 381

PARLEY.
He holds no p. with unmanly fears *R.H.* 5

PARLIAMENTS.
Thy p. adored, on bended knees *Ex.* 538

PARLOUR.
Swinging the p. door upon its hinge *E.* iii 21
There prisoned in a p. snug and small *R.* 493
So spent in p. twilight; such a gloom *T.* iv 278
Briskly, astride upon the p. broom *Tir.* 367

PARNASSIAN.
Let laurels drenched in pure P. dews *T.T.* 13

PARROT.
Words learned by rote a p. may rehearse *Con.* 7
Or make the p.'s mimicry his choice *Con.* 449
Trivial as a p.'s prate? *St.* iv 24
And p. with twin cherries in their beak *T.* i 38
With p. tongue performed the scholar's part *T.* ii 738
And in his cage, like p. fine and gay *T.T.* 232

PARRY.
Mighty to p. and push-by God's word *H.* 659
With such artillery armed. Vice p. wide *T.* ii 810

PARSIMONY.
To thrift and p. much inclined *T.* 141
Ingenious P. takes, but just *T.* iv 400

PARSON.
There goes the p.—O illustrious spark! *B.B.* 13
Laymen have leave to dance, if p. play *P.E.* 151
Nor yet the p.'s, who would gladly come *R.* 439
The plump convivial p. often bears *T.* iv 595 [124
Which children use, and p.—when they preach *Tir.*
The p. knows enough who knows a duke *Tir.* 403

PART. [53
And promised they should act the wild goose p. *A.T.*
Where seas or deserts p. them from the rest *Ch.* 20
But while his province is the reasoning p. *Ch* 375
Close to the p. where vision ought to be *Ch.* 386
Though each resemble each in every p. *Comp.* i 7
And Conversation, in its better p. *Con.* 3 [216
And in the saddest p. cry—"Droll indeed!" *Con.*
Concealed within an unsuspected p. *Con.* 365
Reclaim his taste, and brighten up his p. *Con.* 840
Best for the public, and my wisest p. *Con.* 870
Derived from nature's noblest p. *E.* i 13
Shall meet, unite, and p. no more *E.* i 32
Are p. of a Jehovah's cares *E.* i 58 [iii 10
True. Changes will befall, and friends may p. *E.*
With powers urpassing theirs, performed her p. *Ex.* 230
And teach the combatant a woman's p.? *Ex.* 359
Act but an honest and a faithful p. *Ex.* 556 [650
To learn in God's own school the Christian p. *Ex.*

Profusion apes the noble p. *F.* 4 [*H.* 289
What p. the kindred tribes of weeds and flowers?
Will trust him for a faithful generous p. *H.* 336
That conscience there performs her proper p. *H.* 692
'Tis more—'tis God diffused through every p. *H.* 734
The faithful monitor's and poet's p. *H.* 757
Renew the quarrel on the conqueror's p. *Her.* 74
Finds out his weaker p. *H.F.* 10
There is a p. in every swine *L.W.* 3
(Had he the sinful p. expressed *L.W.* 9
But well thou playedst the housewife's p. *M.* 17
"So Pity shall take Virtue's p. *Miss* — 89
In p. abate, that happiness were small *N.A.* 112
None here is happy but in p. *N.Y.G.* 13
We therefore need not p. *O.* ii 6
That thy worst p. Thy principles, live yet *P.E.* 350
In praise applied to the same p.—his head *P.E.* 533
It was a scene in every p. *Q.V.* 57
Their fibres penetrate its tenderest p. *R.* 42
Mix with the world, but with its wiser p. *R.* 275
To assuage the throbbings of the festered p. *R.* 321
No womanish or wailing grief has p. *R.* 773
Begs you for once to take his p. *St.* i 35
The better p. of man unblessed *St.* vi 31
Brings not alone the more conspicuous p. *T.* 561
Howe'er performed, it was their brightest p. *T.* 579
The slippery seat betrayed the sliding p. *T.* i 46
That p. us, are emancipate and loosed *T.* ii 39
Of his own works, his dreadful p. alone *T.* ii 82
Be fickle, and thy year, most p., deformed *T.* ii 210
And play his brilliant p. before my eyes *T.* ii 425
With some sincerity, on the giver's p. *T.* ii 559 [738
With parrot tongue performed the scholar's p. *T.* ii
Most p. an empty ineffectual sound *T.* iii 22
It seems the p. of wisdom, and no sin *T.* iv 336
Ice upon ice, the well adjusted p. *T.* v 146
Designed by loud declaimers on the p. *T.* v 498
Who loves no p.? He be a nation's friend *T.* v 504
Takes p. with Appetite, and pleads the cause *T.* v 630
To excuses in which reason has no p.) *T.* v 656 [365
Where kindness on his p., who ruled the whole *T.* vi
Such teachable and apprehensive p. *T.* vi 612 [13
"And such," I exclaimed, "is the pitiless p. *The Rose*
Touch but his nature in its ailing p. *Tir.* 161
A pledge he gave for a consistent p. *Tir.* 178
A rhetoric equal to those p. of speech? *Tir.* 398
Pressed on his p. by means that would disgrace *Tir.* 406
Behold your bishop! well he plays his p. *Tir.* 420
With just abhorrence of so mean a p. *Tir.* 455
Owe their repute in p., but not the whole *Tir.* 461
Done to the nobler p. affects it long *Tir.* 491
To take in childish plays a childish p. *Tir.* 548
Its various p. to his attentive note *Tir.* 642
A man of letters, manners, morals, p. *Tir.* 673
Men well endowed, of honourable p. *Tir.* 836
Condemns the unfatherly, the imprudent p. *Tir.* 866
Howe'er he slight thee, thou hast done thy p. *Tir.* 898
P. of the captain's precious store *Trans.* iv 5
Each character in every p. *Trans.* iv 34
Let magistrates alert perform their p. *T.T.* 311
Not more invigorates life's p. *T.T.* 381
In all its p., times, ministry, and laws *T.T.* 427
This Bedlam p.; and others nearer home *T.T.* 609
Pretend to all that p. have e'er acquired *V.* 15
Not hard by nature, in a feeling p. *V.* 42
Whoever undertakes a friend's great p. *V.* 59
Illume the land's remotest p. 1789, 61

PARTAKE.
Must soon p. his grave *Ep.* ii 44
Bestowed on man, like all that we p. *H.* 117
The great, the gay, shall they p. *O.* ii 13
But I can feel thy fortunes, and p. *T.* ii 219

Which all might view with envy, none p. *T.* iii 718
And, summoned to p. its fellow's woe *V.* 69

PARTAKER.
P. of a new ethereal birth *Con.* 724
P. of thy sad decline *M.* 33

PARTED.
We must not now be p., sojourn here" *Con.* 530
P. without the least regret *P.T.* 58

PARTERRE.
The pride of the p. *L.R.* 20

PARTICLE.
One lawless p. to thwart his plan *T.* ii 170

PARTING.
The linnet twittered out his p. song *A.T.* 76
The p. word shall pass my lips no more! *M.P.* 35

PARTNER.
And p. once of Tiny's box *Ep.* ii 43
But genuine, and art p. of them all *T.* i 153
My p. in retreat. Disgust concealed *T.* iii 38
My former p. of my peopled scene *T.* iii 119
Innocent p. of my peaceful home *T.* iii 337
Thy schoolfellow and p. of thy plays *V.* 35

PARTY.
Where p. are agreed, retired the scene *A.T.* 89
The snug, close p., or the splendid hall *P.E.* 176

PASS.
That will not so suddenly p. *C.* 8
A toy to sport with, and p. time away *Con.* 18
And, like the graver's memory, p. away *Con.* 552
To let the military deluge p. *Ex.* 60
A p. between his wires *F.B.* 18
Which they that woo preferment rarely p. *H.* 420
And raise a laugh) p. unmolested by *H.* 621
His hours no longer p. unmarked away *H.* 698
Revolving seasons, fruitless as they p. *Her.* 25
The parting word shall p. my lips no more! *M.P.* 35
There is a field, through which I often p. *N.A.* 1
While Cynthio ogles, as she p. *P.B.* 19
Is far too just to p. the trifler by *P.E.* 200
But if you p. the threshold, you are caught *P.E.* 588
To measure all that p. in the breast *R.* 133
That p. all he sees unheeded by *R.* 340
Or p. unheeded this auspicious morn *S.* ii 4
We p. a gulf in which the willows dip *T.* i 268
The wain that meets it p. swiftly by *T.* i 297
Diffusing odours; nor unnoted p. *T.* i 317
True, we have lost an empire—let it p. *T.* ii 263
And let that p.—'twas but a trick of state *T.* ii 267
And gild our chamber ceilings as they p. *T.* ii 649
No :—let her p., and charioted along *T.* iii 69
To p. us readily through every door *T.* iii 99
Then acts in Nature's office, brings to p. *T.* iii 542
Yet just arrangement, rarely brought to p. *T.* iii 588
And having dropped the expected bag, p. on *T.* iv 11
That it foretells us always comes to p. *T.* iv 72 [466
P. where we may, through city or through town *T.* iv
Time, as he p. us, has a dove's wing *T.* iv 211 [iv 771
And they that never p. their brick-wall bounds *T.*
There, therefore, are occasional, and p. *T.* v 566
That he has let it p.—But never bids *T.* vi 294 [192
He marks the bounds which Winter may not p. *T.* vi
A public school shall bring to p. with ease *Tir.* 372
A principle, whose proud pretensions p. *Tir.* 462

PASSAGE.
A painful p. o'er a restless flood *H.* 3
And prejudice have left a p. clear) *T.* 114

PASSED.
Through which the tackle p. *A Tale* 36
Perhaps, however, as some years have p. *Con.* 799
It p. unnoticed, as the bird *E.* i 87 [186
While they p. through to their appointed land *Ex.*
And Danish howlings scared thee as they p. *Ex.* 471
Of p. experience, and the wisdom gleaned *F.A.* 2
I p., and next considered—what is man ? *F.A.* 21
It is p. between cylinders often, and rolled *F.M.* 3
Soon p. the wiry grate *G.* 12
Riches are p. away from hand to hand *H.* 11 [568
The world's best comfort was, his doom was p. *H.*
And all and each that p. that way *J.G.* 239 [1
Oh that those lips had language! Life has p. *M.P.*
The son of parents p. into the skies *M.P.* 111
Live till to-morrow, will have p. away *N.A.* 133
Of all that ever p. my pen *O.* i 23
Perceived the fragrance as he p. *P.B.* 4
So coin grows smooth, in traffic current p. *P.E.* 279
Beauties he lately slighted as he p. *R.* 425
I p.—and they were gone *St.* i 20
The gulf of death triumphant p. *St.* iii 31
While danger p. is turned to present joy *T.* 256
E'er since, a truant boy, I p. my bounds *T.* i 114
In boundless oceans, never to be p. *T.* i 629
Not to be p.: and she that had renounced *T.* iii 76
Domestic life in rural leisure p.! *T.* iii 292 [353
The new-made monarch, while before him p. *T.* vi
And, tedious years of Gothic darkness p. *T.T.* 564

PASSENGER.
Upon the guiltless p. o'erthrown *T.* vi 424

PASSING.
Vice p. current by the stamp of law *A.T.* 156
P. his prison door *B.R.* 14
Sighs unregarded to the p. wind *Ex.* 30
" How sweet, how p. sweet is solitude ! *R.* 740
Soft as the p. wind *The Loves* 38
Fine p. thought, e'en in her coarsest works *Y.O.* 81

PASSION.
To bring the p. under sober sway *Con.* 831
Man feels the spur of p. and desires *H.* 55
His p., like the watery stores that sleep *H.* 183
While P. turns aside from its due scope *H.* 113
To p., interest, pleasure, whim, resigned *H.* 212
Hence all that is in man—pride, p., art *H.* 653
But p. rudely snaps the string *H.F.* 7
After long sleep, of p. in the heart *J.T.* 42
To gratify a fretful p. *M.F.* 35
As Reason, or as P. takes the reins *P.E.* 36
Hourly allurements on his p. press *P.E.* 61
Of some ungoverned p. every hour *P.E.* 276
Church-quacks, with p. under no command *P.E.* 474
The storm of p., and say," Peace, be still ! " *P.E.* 599
To spare no p., and no favourite sin *R.* 136
That p.'s force, and so did she *R.C.* 24
His p. tamed, and all at his control *T.* 417
Just please us while the p. is at full *T.* ii 598
The mind was well-informed, the p. held *T.* ii 715
Compose the p., and exalt the mind *T.* iii 305
Than human p. please. In every heart *T.* v 205
No p. touches a discordant string *T.* vi 787
With p., just that he may prove, with pain *Tir.* 63
The poet's muse, his p., and his theme *T.T.* 289

PASSIONATE.
A temper p. and fierce *F.* 64

PASSIVE.
Are mere impressions on the p. mind *A.T.* 43

Where find ye *p*. fortitude? Whence springs *T*. v 327
His heart, now *p*., yields to thy command *Tir*. 885

PAST.

At length his transient respite *p*. *Cast*. 43
Alike irrevocable both when *p*. *Comp*. i 5
Of dangers *p*., and wonders yet to come *Con*. 572
Like other scenes already *p*. *E*. i 56
And hide *p*. folly from all-seeing eyes? *Ex*. 405
Heroes and worthies of days *p*., thy sires? |*Ex*. 658
This wisdom, and but this, from all the *p*.? *F.A.* 12
Whose eye reverted weeps o'er all the *p*. *H*. 31
A pale procession of *p*. sinful joys *H*. 221
The twentieth year is well-nigh *p*. *M*. 1
With much resemblance of the *p*. *M*. 50
Well, I protest 'tis *p*. all bearing!" *M.F.* 25
And like a summer brook are *p*. away *R*. 296
These tell me of enjoyments *p*. *S*. 23
And item down the victims of the *p*. *St*. ii 4
With all the gloomy *p*. *St*. iii 8
"*P*. all dispute, yon anchorite," say you *T*. 106
The future shall obliterate the *p*. *T*. 295
P. indiscretion is a venial crime *T*. 491
Those barbarous ages *p*., succeeded next *T*. i 16
The dream is *p*.; and thou hast found again *T*. i 639
Bespoke him *p*. the bounds of freakish youth *T*. ii 704
Lost innocence, or cancel follies *p*. *T*. iii 678
That calls the *p*. to our exact review *T*. iv 184
But the age of virtuous politics is *p*. *T*. v 493
Yet, feeling present evils, while the *p*. *T*. vi 23
Ensuing seemed to obliterate the *p*. *T*. vi 540
Of barrenness is *p*. The fruitful field *T*. vi 765
As, hid from ages *p*., God now displays *Tir*. 638
Of pleasures *p*., or follies yet to come *Tir*. 776
Since which I number threescore winters *p*. *Y.O.* 3
Inquisitive, the less ambiguous *p*. *Y.O.* 44

PASTIME.

No *p*. but with her he deigned to take *A.T.* 17
P. and business both, it should exclude *P.E.* 159
Or take their *p*. in the spacious field *T*. vi 576
E'en in his *p*. he requires a friend *Tir*. 607

PASTOR.

Occiduus is a *p*. of renown *P.E.* 124
And thus it is. The *p*., either vain *T*. ii 545
And what they will. All *p*. are alike *T*. vi 890
Within some pious *p*.'s humble cot *Tir*. 760

PASTORAL.

That once we called the *p*. house our own *M.P.* 53
P images and still retreats *R*. 257
Time was when in the *p*. retreat *T*. iv 558

PASTURE.

He finds the *p*. where his fellows graze *Ch*. 179
The glimpse of a green *p*., how they cheer *T*. iv 751

PAT.

Gives him at length the lucky *p*. *E*. iv 55
A story so *p*., you may think it is coined *P.A.* 18
Or drive it devious with a dextrous *p*. *Tir*. 309

PATCH.

Retrench a sword-blade, or displace a *p*. *T*. ii 318
Shows all its rents and *p*. to the world *Tir*. 451

PATE.

Employs his philosophic *p*. *Trans*. ii 23
With rueful faces and bald *p*. *Y.D.* 23

PATENTEE.

Illustrious histrionic *p*. *V*. 29

PATERNAL.

These have an ear for his *p*. call *Ch*. 250

His offspring hold in his *p*. care *H*. 140
Thine, and upheld by thy *p*. care *R*. 89
P. sweetness, dignity, and love *T*. ii 708

PATH.

Harmony the *p*. to fame *B*. 24
The *p*. of wisdom, all whose *p*. of peace *Ch*. 162
Taught me what *p*. to shun, and what pursue *Ch*. 239
The *p*. of narrative with care pursue *Con*. 217
Snares in his *p*., and foes that lurk within *Con*. 470
The *p*. of sorrow, and that *p*. alone *E*. ii 9
Or lead him devious from the *p*. of truth *P.E.* 60
Is this the rugged *p*., the steep ascent *P.E.* 71
Is this the *p*. of sanctity? Is this *P.E.* 116
The fatal ills; that though the *p*. he treads *P.E.* 545
The *p*. to bliss abounds with many a snare *T*. 301
Though halt, and weary of the *p*. they tread *T*.i 471
And so illuminates the *p*. of life *T*. ii 529
By the wayside, or stalking in the *p*. *T*. v 92
The windings of my *p*. through many years *T*. vi 18
It seem'd not always short; the rugged *p*. *T*. vi 20
The frequent flakes has kept a *p*. for me *T*. vi 77
That crawls at evening in the public *p*. *T*. vi 565
Nor, though he tread the secret *p*. of life *T*. vi 956
Shine by the side of every *p*. we tread *Tir*. 79

PATHETIC.

P. exhortation; and to address *T*. ii 469
P. in its praise, in its pursuit *T*. iv 719

PATHLESS.

To *p*. wilds and unfrequented plains *A.T.* 26 [iv 573
Through *p*. wastes and woods, unconscious once *T*.

PATIENCE.

P. itself is meanness in a slave *Ch*. 164
Give me the fidgets, and my *p*. fails *Con*. 208
All sustained by *p*., taught us *N.C.* 47
We may with *p*. bear our moderate ills *T*. iv 339

PATIENT.

P. of contradiction as a child *P.E.* 536
Its *p*. drudges with dry chaff and weeds *R*. 48
Scorned by the rest, with *p*. hope they wait *R*. 165
And sends the *p*. into purer air *R*. 282
Nor his, who *p*. stands till his feet throb *T*. iv 46
I praise you much, ye meek and *p*. pair *T*. iv 407
And *p*. of the slow-paced swain's delay *T*. v 32
Witness the *p*. ox, with stripes and yells *T*. vi 420
P., affectionate, of high command *Tir*. 602
P. of constitutional control *T.T.* 224

PATRICK.

But (I might instance in St. *P*.'s dean) *Ch*. 499

PATRIMONIAL.

"My *p*. treasure and my pride *R*. 367
His *p*. timber cast its leaf *T*. iii 752

PATRIOT.

The boldest *p*. might be proud to feel *Ch*. 308
Courtier and *P*. cannot mix *F*. 127
A rope! I wish we *p*. had *Pat*. 21
For once I can approve the *p*.'s voice *R*. 387
A *p*.'s for his country; thou art sad *T*. i 658
Of *p*. eloquence to flash down fire *T*. ii 217
Of *p*., bursting with heroic rage *T*. iv 48
Delicious, when her *p*. of high note *T*. iv 170
By some whose *p*. virtue has prevailed *T*. v 295
P. are grown too shrewd to be sincere *T*. v 495
P. have toiled, and in their country's cause *T*. v 704
Have fallen in her defence. A *P*.'s blood *T*. v 714
To see a band, called *p*., for no cause *T.T.* 143
P., who love good places at their hearts *T.T.* 191

Ye *p.*, guard it with a miser's care *T.T.* 335
P. alas! the few that have been found *T.T.* 336

PATRIOTIC.
Guard what you say. The *p.* tribe *T.T.* 83

PATRON.
P. of else the most despised of men *Ch.* 290
Just made fifth chaplain of his *p.* lord *H.* 414
P. of all those luckless brains *O.* i 1
To his own pleasure and his *p.*'s pride *T.* ii 391
And groat per diem, if his *p.* frown *T.* iii 821
We the chief *p.* of the commonwealth *T.* v 349

PATRONESS.
Oft as his *p.* who rules the night *A.T.* 137
To the same *P.* resort *Mrs. M—* 21
Hail, therefore, *p.* of health and ease *T.* iv 780

PATTERN.
Thy life upon the *p.* of the law *Ex.* 409
These stoves that for *p.* and form *Gr.* 39
But he can draw a *p.*, make a tart *P.E.* 195
The *p.* grows, the well depicted flower *T.* iv 151
Becomes their *p.*, upon whom they fix *Tir.* 224
P. of every virtue, every grace *T.T.* 373

PAUL.
Oaths terminate, as *P.* observes, all strife *Con.* 55
As bold as, in Agrippa's presence, *P.—Ex.* 445
Had *P.* of Tarsus lived and died a Jew *H.* 257
P.'s love of Christ, and steadiness unbribed *H.* 580
He followed *P.*, his zeal a kindred flame *H.* 582
Set *P.* to music, he shall quote him too *P.E.* 113
Would I describe a preacher, such as *P.—T.* ii 395
P. should himself direct me. I would trace *T.* ii 397
So did not *P.*   Direct me to a quip *T.* ii 472
How oft, when *P.* has served us with a text *T.* ii 539
Would strive to make a *P.* or Tully stand *T.T.* 349

PAUSE.
Then *p.* and puff—and speak, and *p.* again *Con.* 248
P. here, and think: a monitory rhyme *Ep.* i 1
Can *p.* one hour to read a serious rhyme *Ex.* 605
Forced to a *p.*, would feel it good to think *St.* ii 15
Has slackened to a *p.*, and we have borne *T.* i 155
Suffer a syncope and solemn *p. T.* ii 80   [371
An instant's *p.*, and lives but while she moves *T.* i
That never felt a stupor, know no *p. T.* iv 283[108
And swallowing, therefore, without *p.* or choice *T.* vi
Finds in a sober moment time to *p. Tir.* 56

PAUSED.
We *p.* under many a tree *C.* 13

PAVE.
Four ivory eggs soon *p.* its floor *A Tale* 41

PAVED.
Propitious in his chariot *p.* with love *T.* vi 744

PAVILION.
As he that slumbers in *p.* graced *R.* 509
To grace the full *p.*   His design *T.* iii 716

PAW.
Conjecture gripes the victims in his *p. Ch.* 525

PAWNED.
That authors are most useful *p.* or sold *Tir.* 211

PAY.
That 'tis an honour and a joy to *p. Con.* 646   [712
Their measure filled, they too shall *p.* the debt *Ex.*
Though short, too long, the price he *p.* for all *H.* 200
And Folly *p.*, resound at your return *Her.* 62
Adds joy to duty, makes me glad to *p. M.P.* 70
P. tribute to thy glorious beams *O.* i 7

May feel a heart enriched by what it *p. R.* 209
And must despair to *p. St.* v 32
P.!—follow Christ, and all is paid *St.* v 33   [210
He likes your house, your housemaid, and your *p. T.*
P. contribution to the store he gleans *T.* iv 110
Propitious, *p.* his tribute, game or fish *T.* iv 611
And Sabo's spicy groves, *p.* tribute there *T.* vi 807
To entertain a thief or two in *p. Tir.* 693   [907
And feed him well, and give him handsome *p. Tir.*
P. me for thy warm retreat *Trans.* iii 5   [109
True.   While they live, the courtly laureate *p. T.T.*
Firm friends to peace, to pleasure, and good *p. T.T.* 195
When he that takes, and he that *p. Y.D.* 19
Without the clowns that *p. Y.D.* 68

PAYING.
Instead of *p.* what he owes *Y.D.* 27

PAYMENT.
Could you contrive the *p.*, and rehearse *T.T.* 178
To make their *p.* good *Y.D.* 16

PEACE.
The path of wisdom, all whose paths are *p. Ch.* 162
Let just Restraint, for public *p.* designed *Ch.* 286
That pleads for *p.* till it disturbs the state *Ch.* 310
Whoever threatens war, to speak of *p. Ch.* 421
And too short lived to reach the realms of *p. Ch.* 451
To *P.* and Charity, is mere pretence *Ch.* 534
And e'en the dipped and sprinkled live in *p. Ch.* 609
That the surviving world may live in *p. Con.* 176
Temperance and *P.* insure its healthful state *Con.* 603
And had the grace in scenes of *p.* to show *Ex.* 79
In *p.* possessing what they won by war *Ex.* 193
And *p.* does nothing to relieve the weight *Ex.* 307
P. be to those (such *p.* as Earth can give) *H.* 229
P. (if insensibility may claim) *H.* 235
P. to all such—'twere pity to offend *H.* 272
And *P.* the genuine offspring of her smile *H.* 482
In *p.* upon her sloping sides matured *Her.* 10   [50
Studious of *p.*, their neighbour's and their own *Her.*
Where *P.*, and Equity, and Freedom smile *Her.* 84
Like her a friend to *p. M.B.* 12
P. to the phlegm of sullen elves *Miss —* 61
Is paid at least in *p.* of mind *Mor.* 51
To me their *p.* by kind contagion spread *N.A.* 42
Of *p.* or ease to creatures clad as we *N.A.* 114
Who studiously make *p.* their aim *N.G.* 36
P., both the duty and the prize *N.G.* 37
Come, *p.* of mind, delightful guest! *O.* ii 1
P. follows Virtue as its sure reward *P.E.* 42
Love, joy, and *p.* make harmony more meet *P.E.* 140
The storm of passion, and say, "*P.* be still!" *P.E.* 599
Truth, wisdom, grace, and *p.*, like that above *R.* 163
Conspire against thy *p.* with one design *R.* 262
To seek that *p.* a tyrant's frown denies *R.* 770
Friendly to *p.*, but not to me *S.* 2
While *P.* possessed these silent bowers *S.* 14
His death your *p.* ensures *St.* v 34
Yet heard in scenes where *p.* for ever reigns *T.* 208
P. to the artist whose ingenious thought *T.* 210
Is left to sleep for *p.* and quiet sake *T.* 428
Benevolence, and *p.*, and mutual aid *T.* ii 49
To what no few have felt, there should be *p. T.* ii 73
Forgets in *p.* the injuries of war *T.* ii 269
Where *p.* and hospitality might reign *T.* ii 617
P. to the memory of a man of worth *T.* ii 781 [iii 69
Health, leisure, means to improve it, friendship, *p. T.*
Friendly to thought, to virtue, and to *p. T.* iii 291
But it has *p.*, and much secures the mind *T.* iii 679
And jewelled turban with a smile of *p. T.* iv 29 [187
Unlooked for, life preserved, and *p.* restored *T.* iv
Come, evening, once again, season of *p. T.* iv 243

The road that leads from competence and p. T. iv 496
As angels use, the Gospel whispers p. T. ii 342 [v 202
P. was awhile their care: they ploughed and sowed T.
And equal; and he bade them dwell in p. T. v 201
And him in p., for sake of warlike deeds T. v 234
Of virtue, made one chief, whom times of p. T. v 239
In fancied p. beneath his dangerous branch T. v 325
The fatal issue to his health, fame, p. T. v 601 [v 620
And seems dethroned and vanquished. P. ensues T.
At random, without honour, hope, or p. T. v 899
Would die at last in comfort, p., and joy Tir. 150
P. to them all! those brilliant times are fled Tir. 284
Firm friends to p., to pleasure, and good pay T.T. 195
Glorious in war, but for the sake of p. T.T. 278
To guard the P. that Riot would disturb T.T. 315
Then p. and joy again possessed 1779, 46 [T. vi 910
Would make his fate his choice; whom p., the fruit
Such joy and p. as can be known 1789, 48

PEACEABLE.
Called thee away from p. employ Ex. 534

PEACEABLY-DISPOSED.
And put the p. to death Con. 90

PEACEFUL.
Some men have surely then a p. life! Con. 56
Serene and p. as those heavenly days Con. 568
Her p. shores, where busy Commerce waits Ex. 13
Within the garden's p. scene L.R. 5
May I but meet thee on that p. shore M.P. 34
All seemed so p., that from them conveyed N.A. 41
Her p. bosom laves Q.V. 72
Its happiest seasons, and a p. close R. 750
Then welcome refuge, and a p. home T. 267
Mercy receives him on her p. shore T. 276
Oft have I wished the p. covert mine T. i 233
Innocent partner of my p. home T. iii 337
So let us welcome p. evening in T. iv 41
Of God and man, and p. in its end T. vi 999

PEACE-RESTORING.
To sheath it, in the p. close T.T. 79

PEACH.
The bud of p. or rose U. 14

PEACOCK.
The p. sends his heavenly dyes Mrs. M— 3
The self-applauding bird, the p. see T. 58 [215
With motley plumes; and where the p. shows T. iv

PEAK.
To the sharp p. of her sublimest height T. iii 157

PEAL.
While thus she spake, I fainter heard the p. N.A. 123
P. upon p. redoubling all around T. 240

PEALING.
Now p. loud again, and louder still T. vi 9

PEAR.
If not, you shall have neither apple nor p." P.A. 32
An apple-tree, or lofty p. R.C. 12

PEARL.
Is a p. cast, completely cast, away H. 259
Brings many a precious p. of truth to light H. 444
What p. is it that rich men cannot buy T. iii 285
But wisdom is a p. with most success T. iii 381
Show thou hast sense enough to prize the p. Tir. 707

PEASANT.
P. and children all around us E. i 40
The p.'s hopes, and not in vain, assured Her. 9

As ever recompensed the p.'s care R. 332
O happy p.! O unhappy bard! T. 331
I called the low-roofed lodge the P.'s nest T. i 227
So farewell envy of the P.'s Nest! T. i 247
The p. too, a witness of his song T. i 497
That like the filth with which the p. feeds T. iv 502
The p. urge their harvest, ply the fork T.T. 214

PEBBLE.
Some shining p., and some weeds and shells R. 154
Upon loose p., lose themselves at length T. 194

PEBBLY.
And wantons in the p. gulf below T. v 103

PECCANCY.
And stand exposed by common p. T. ii 72

PECKED.
Grew quarrelsome, and p. each other P.T. 57

PECULATION.
That waste our vitals; p., sale T. ii 668

PECULATORS.
To p. of the public gold T. i 735

PECULIAR.
And Virtue with p. charms appears Con. 637
P. is the grace by thee possessed Ex. 580
Fired with a zeal p , they defy H. 461
But show p. light, by many a grin P.E. 383
As Nature at her own p. cost T. 397
Though each its hue p.; paler some T. i 308
P. and exclusively her own T. i 432
Of its legitimate, p. powers) T. ii 333
Unless by Heaven's p. grace, escape T. ii 632
These therefore are his own p. charge T. iii 412
Was but to boast his own p. good T. iii 717
Are they not his by a p. right T. v 748
Then each, in its p. honours clad T. vi 147

PEDAGOGUE.
Of the robed p.! Else let the arraigned T. ii 823
The p., with self-complacent air Tir. 527

PEDANTIC.
Of dreaming study and p. rust T.T. 171

PEDANTRY.
And p. that coxcombs learn with ease T. vi 290
That p. is all that schools impart Tir. 212

PEDESTAL.
Exalted on his p. of pride T. 313
Build him a p., and say, "Stand there T. v 258

PEDIGREE.
And high in p. D W. 6
To men of p., their noble race H. 237
The vellum of the p. they claim T. i 569

PEDLER.
Love is not p.'s trumpery, bought and sold H. 320
A p.'s pack, that bows the bearer down T. i 465

PEEL.
On pippins' russet p. Ep. ii 18

PEELED.
P., scattered, and exterminated thus Ex. 246
With which when neatly p. and dried T.B. 29

PEEP. [A.T. 79
Lay snug and warm;—'twas Summer's farewell p.!
The p. of morning shed a dawning light Ch. 261
But lovely Spring p. o'er his head N. 15

P. at the vale below; so thick beset T. i 225
As the sun p., and vernal airs breathe mild T. iii 443
P. through their polished foliage at the storm T iii 574
A p. at Nature, when he can no more T. iv 779 [65
The sparrows p., and quit the sheltering eaves T. v
To p. at such a world; to see the stir T. iv 89 [vi 113
P. through the moss that clothes the hawthorn root T.
But never p. beyond the thorny bound T.T. 582

PEEPED.
And forth he p., but nothing spied R.C. 82

PEEPING.
To show the p. down upon his chin Tir. 235

PEER.
Nor can he much affect the neighbouring p. R. 441
Was quickly distanced, matched against a p.'s R. 580
P. are not always generous as well-bred R. 597
(Attentive when thou readest) of p. S. i 3
His intercourse with p. and sons of p. Tir. 393
If smiling peeresses, and simpering p. T.T. 131
Made you a P., but spoiled you for a friend! V. 14

PEERESSES.
If smiling p., and simpering peers T.T. 133

PEERING.
Ascends his topmast, through his p. eyes T. iv 115

PEEVISH.
Their p. hearers almost wish they had Con. 324
" Adorning May, that p. maid J.P. 35

PEEVISHLY.
Not that he p. rejects a mode T. vi 981

PELLUCID.
Shoot into pillars of p. length T. v 115

PELTING.
P. each other for the public good Ch. 623
And bore the p. scorn of half an age H. 557
The p. brunt of the tempestuous night T. iv 351

PEN.
Accept the tribute of a stranger's p. Ch. 291
But when a poet takes the p. B. i 9
Of all that ever passed my p. O. i 23
His fingers held the p. R.G. 22
And, ere he quits the p. St. i 34 [384
Or with his p., save when he scrawls a card T. ii
Friends, books, a garden, and perhaps his p. T. iii 355
The pencil or the p., may trace the scene! T. v 109
Thy title is engraven with a p. T. vi 862
If Flattery, Folly, Lust, employ the p. T.T. 761 [769
To dash the p. through all that you proscribe T.T.

PENAL.
And full immunity from p. woe T. v 580

PENALTIES.
He was excused the p. of dull Y.O. 156

PENCE.
Till perjuries are common as bad p. Ex. 387
Yet loss of p., full well he knew J.G. 55
And makes his pupils proud with silver p. T.T. 509

PENCIL.
The painter's p., and the poet's lyre Ch. 106
The p. or the pen, may trace the scene! T. v 109
Of his unrival'd p. He inspires T. vi 242

PENCILLED.
Who, satisfied with only p. scenes T. i 417
And force them sit, till he has p. off T. ii 292

PENDENT.
Their p. boughs, stooping as if to drink T. i 269
From many a twig the p. drops of ice T. vi 81

PENDULOUS.
P., and foreboding, in the view T. iv 293

PENETRATE.
Rejects all treaty, p. all wiles H. 649
Their fibres p. its tenderest part R. 42

PENITENCE.
Till p. had purged the public stain Ex. 74
As left him not, till p. had won T. ii 723
Unless sweet P. her powers renew T.T. 398

PENITENTIAL.
My p. stripes, my streaming blood T. 95
Prayer only, and the p. tear T.T. 412

PENNED.
And many a compliment politely p. T.T. 721
As ever Friendship p. U. 4

PENNY.
To turn a p. in the way of trade T.T. 421

PENNYLESS.
Still hungering, p., and far from home T. i 119

PENSIONERS.
Lean p. upon the traveller's track T. v 93

PENSIVE.
The maid who views with p. air P.B. 23
Risk an intrusion on thy p. mood R. 255
The p. wanderer in their shades. At eve T. i 761
The present Muse of every p. mind Tir. 22

PENSIVELY.
Two bosom friends, each p. inclined Con. 507

PENT.
Could I believe, that winds for ages p. N.A. 85
Complained, though incommodiously p. in T. i 69

PENTATEUCH.
Who starve upon a dog's-eared P. Tir. 402

PENT-UP.
The p. breath of an unsavoury throng T. iv 196

PENURIOUS.
His thousands, weary of p. life T. v 319

PENURY.
A blessed effect of p. and want T. 361
Of loathsome diet, p., and cold T. i 591
Ambition, Avarice, P. incurred T. iii 811
Where p. is felt the thought is changed T. iv 397
Nor p., can cripple or confine T. v 772
In p. consumed his idle hours T.T. 673

PEONY.
There might ye see the p. spread wide T. i 35

PEOPLE.
But what were his arguments few p. know A.C. 27
To exalt a p., and to place them high Con. 519
He saw his p. slaves to every lust Ex. 55
P. and priest, the sons of Israel were Ex. 124
A p. planted, watered, blest as they? Ex. 168
Which here p. call a buffet Gr. 34
Then might all p. well discern J.G. 105
"Some p. are more nice than wise M.F. 20
Reproach a p. with his single fall T. 234
A prince with half his p.! Ancient towers T. ii 121
A p. such as never was till now T. ii 679
Milder, among a p. less austere T. v 488

To see a *p*. scattered like a flock *T.T.* 34
And if He doom that *p*. with a frown *T.T.* 456

PEOPLED.
My former partners of my *p*. scene *T.* iii 119

PEOPLING.
And Flora, and Vertumnus, *p*. earth *T.* vi 234

PEPPERCORN.
His quitrent ode, his *p*. of praise *T.T.* 110

PERCEIVE.
He now *p*. where earthly pleasure ends *H.* 695
P. in everything that lives a tongue *N.A.* 56
His life should prove that he *p*. their force *T.* 198
Whose arm this twentieth winter I *p*. *T.* i 145
Scenes that I love, and with regret *p*. *T.* iii 710
Thou shalt *p*. that thou wast blind before *T.* v 781
(Through inexperience, as we now *p*.) *T.* vi 27
Whence all the music. I again *p*. *T.* vi 67

PERCEIVED.
P. the fragrance as he passed *P.B.* 4
His presence, who made all so fair, *p*. *T.* vi 253

PERCH.   [iv 443
In unsuspecting pomp. Twitched from the *p. T.*
From his accustomed *p*. Hard-faring race! *T.* i 564
Where, bishoplike, he finds a *p. Trans.* ii 5

PERCHED.
P. on the top of yonder hill *E.* i 44
I *p*. at will on every spray *G.* 4
'Tis *p*. upon the greenhill top, but close *T.* i 222
P. on the signpost, holds with even hand *T.* iv 483
Repays their labour more; and *p*. aloft *T.* v 91
P. on the meagre produce of the land *T.T.* 580

PERCHING.
Then, *p*. at his consort's side *A Tale* 53

PER DIEM.
And groat *p*., if his patron frown *T.* iii 821

PERDITION.
Be punished with *p*., who is pure? *H.* 387

PEREMPTORY.
He would not, with a *p*. tone *Con.* 121

PERFECT.
For all is *p*. that God works on earth *Con.* 433
As smiths or joiners *p*. a design *Con.* 790
A beautiful and *p*. whole *E.* i 64
He first conceives, then *p*. his design *Ex.* 318
With every good and *p*. gift, proceeds *H.* 116
There feels a pleasure *p*. in its kind *R.* 629
How *p*. the composure of his soul *T.* 418
He gives a *p*. rule—what can He less? *T.* 552
Of public note, they reach their *p*. size *T.* i 696
All affectation! 'Tis my *p*. scorn *T.* ii 417
"So strict, that less than *p*. must despair? *T.* v 641
P. and unimpeachable of blame *T.* v 867
All happy, and all *p*. in their kind *T.* vi 354
They fear'd, and as his *p*. image loved *T.* vi 400
That is not sound and *p*., hath in theirs *T.* vi 708
P., and all must be at length restored *T.* vi 819

PERFECTION.
Forms rise, to quick *p*. wrought *Mrs. M—* 24
His bright *p*. at whose word they rose *R.* 200
To attain *p*. in this nether world *T.* i 85

PERFIDY.
True, we may thank the *p*. of France *T.* ii 264

PERFORATED.
May still be seen; but *p*. sore *T.* i 25

PERFORM.
Now, Truth, *p*. thine office; waft aside *H.* 570
That conscience there *p*. her proper part *H.* 692
Weak to *p*., though mighty to pretend *P.E.* 15
Dull in design, and clumsy to *p*. *T.* i 18
While God *p*., upon the trembling stage *T.* ii 81
But much *p*. himself. No works, indeed *T.* iii 404
What prodigies can power divine *p*. *T.* vi 118
May some disease, not tardy to *p*. *T.* vi 1002
Let magistrates alert *p*. their parts *T.T.* 311
Must she *p*. the same kind office now? *T.T.* 405
Or prompter, save the scene, I will *p*. *Y.O.* 141

PERFORMANCE.
The best of every man's *p*. here *H.* 499
Prefer to the *p*. of a God *T.* i 418
Scoffs at her own *p*. Reason now *T.* v 629
With lean *p*. ape the work of Love! *T.* vi 854

PERFORMED.
His vow was (and he well *p*. his vow) *A.T.* 139
With power surpassing theirs, *p*. her part *Ex.* 230
Howe'er *p*., it was their brightest part *T.* 579
That task *p*., relapse into themselves *T.* ii 441
Then, with an air most gracefully *p*. *T.* ii 447
With parrot tongue *p*. the scholar's part *T.* ii 738
Nor even then, dismissing as *p*. *T.* iii 655
Which even now, though silently *p*. *T.* iv 323
To do he knows not what. The task *p*. *T.* iv 630
By man *p*., made all the forest ring *Y.O.* 109

PERFORMING.
But not *p*. what he meant *J.G.* 225
P. such inimitable feats *T.* v 125
That wait on man, the flight *p*. horse *T.* vi 426

PERFUME.
A fine puss-gentleman that's all *p. Con.* 284
Embalmed for ever in its own *p. Con.* 632
Her summer heats, her fruits, and her *p. R.* 196
Of fleeting life its lustre and *p*. *T.* v 447

PERFUMED.
Though well *p*. and elegantly dressed *T.* vi 991

PERILOUS.
And *p*. lightnings from the angry clouds *T.* iii 212

PERIOD.
Sad *p*. to a pleasant course! *St.* vi 37
Fast as the *p*. from his fluent quill *T.* iv 19
Puts a *p*. to thy play *Trans.* iii 26
And truth cut short to make a *p*. round *T.T.* 517
Adorn the polished *p*. as they fall *T.T.* 766

PERISH.
Rome shall *p*.—write that word *B.* 13
P., hopeless and abhorr'd *B.* 15
When nations are to *p*. in their sins *Ex.* 95
And *p*. there, as all presumption must" *H.* 228
Take it and *p*.; but restrain your tongue *T.* 18
Sport for a day, and *p*. in a night *T.* 42
"*P.* the virtue, as it ought, abhorred *T.* 503
Can dig, beg, rot, and *p*., well content *T.* iii 805
Which having served us, *p*., we are held *T.* vi 604
Then *p*. on futurity's wide shore *Tir.* 83
And will prevail or *p*. in her cause *T.T.* 18

PERISHED.
We *p*., each alone *Cast.* 64
Its odour *p*., and its charming hue *Con.* 43

PERISHING.
And foe of our *p*. kind *Gr.* 46
To muse on the *p*. pleasures of man *P.F.* 18

PERIWIG.
And *p*. nicely adjust *Gr.* 24
Their *p*. of wool and fears combined *N.A.* 75

PERJURY.
Till *p*. are common as bad pence *Ex.* 387
And P. stood up to swear all true *H.* 563
Of honour, *p*., corruption, frauds *T.* ii 669
When P., that Heaven-defying vice *T.T.* 418

PERKS. [318
And *p*.'s his ears, and stamps, and cries aloud *T.* vi

PERMANENT.
In hopes of *p*. delight *F.* 68
Though fair in promise, *p*. and sound *Tir.* 437

PERMIT.
Whom man, for his own hurt, *p*. to reign *Con.* 458
"'Twere well, could you *p*. the world to live *T.* iii 194

PERNICIOUS.
P. weed! whose scent the fair annoys *Con.* 251
Pronounced by greybeards a *p*. dream *Ex.* 114
Your zeal, and *p*. in the extreme *P.E.* 101
From his *p*. force. Nor will he leave *T.* iv 445

PERPETRATION.
Whose horrid *p*. stamps disgrace *Ex.* 416

PERPETUAL.
Though blameless, had incurred *p*. strife *Con.* 512
Is she not clothed with a *p*. smile? *Ex.* 4
Burning and scorched into *p*. dearth *Ex.* 421
With prohibition and *p*. thirst? *P.E.* 234
And in their service wage *p*. war *T.* vi 894

PERPLEXED.
He hears the notice of the clock, *p. H.* 700
Undaunted still, though wearied and *p. T.T.* 366

PERQUISITE.
More than the *p*.: where Law shall speak *T.* vi 848

PERSECUTE.
We *p*., annihilate the tribes *T.* iii 309
Who starves his own; who *p*. the blood *T.* iv 463

PERSECUTED.
Thou that hast set the *p*. free *Ex.* 278

PERSECUTING.
When *p*. zeal made royal sport *Ex.* 612

PERSECUTION.
A Liberty which *p*., fraud *T.* v 542
Till P. dragged them into fame *T.* v 725
Hence date the *p*. and the pain *T.* vi 384

PERSEVERANCE.
To ensure the *p*. of his course *Tir.* 238

PERSEVERED.
Despising all rebuke, still *p. Ex.* 397

PERSEVERES.
She still is kind, and still she *p. Ch.* 415

PERSEVERING.
Where nought eludes the *p*. quest *H.* 445
For *p*. chase, and headlong leaps *P.E.* 86

PERSIAN.
A P., humble servant of the sun *Con.* 67

PERSON.
And paint his *p*., character and views *T.* iii 143

PERSUADE.
No wealth can bribe, no prayers *p*. to stay *Comp.* i 4
Prompt to *p*., expostulate, and warn *Ex.* 441
If Interest move thee, to *p*. e'en thee *Ex.* 667
As youth or age *p*., and neither true *H.* 70
My creed *p*. me, well employed, may save *T.* 522
Much to *p*., he plied his ear with truths *T.* vi 502

PERSUASION.
My firm *p*. is, at least sometimes *H.* 365

PERT.
What marriage means, thus *p*. replied *P.T.* 29
No powdered *p*. proficient in the art *T.* iv 145
As oft return a *p*. voracious kind *T.* v 69
The squirrel, flippant, *p*., and full of play *T.* vi 315
The youth now bearded, and yet *p*. and raw *Tir.* 155
The *p*. made perter, and the tame made wild *Tir.* 345

PERTER.
The pert made *p*., and the tame made wild *Tir.* 345

PERTINENT.
To themes more *p*., if less sublime *T.T.* 190

PERUSE.
P. closely the true Christian's face *Con.* 743
This is a sight for Pity to *p. R.* 297

PERUSED.
Well-chosen, and not sullenly *p. T.* iii 393
But reason heard, and nature well *p. Tir.* 89
Oh 'tis a sight to be with joy *p. Tir.* 537

PERUVIAN.
With sums P. mines could never clear *Ex.* 285

PERVADE.
Which seldom a distinct report *p. Con.* 802
That not a glimpse of genuine light *p. P.E.* 6
Now, while the poison all high life *p. P.E.* 347
Truth is not local, God alike *p. R.* 119
A tender sympathy *p*. the frame *T.T.* 485

PERVERSE. [396
Hast thou, with heart *p*. and conscience seared *Ex.*
Safe from the clamours of *p*. dispute *R.* 145
While he that scorns the noonday beam, *p. T.* 523
Than reverence, in *p*. rebellious youth *T.* ii 730
Imaginations noxious and *p. Tir.* 599

PERVERSELY.
And teach the world, if not *p*. blind *H.* 138
P., which of late she so condemned *T.* v 631
Look round you on a world *p*. blind *Tir.* 813

PERVERTED.
When gifts *p*., or not duly prized *Ex.* 251

PERVERTING.
P. often, by the stress of lewd *T.* ii 551

PERVERTS.
And while she polishes, *p*. the taste *R.* 704

PERVIOUS.
And only *p*. to the light *P.B.* 10

PEST. [ii 829
Were covered with the *p*.; the streets were filled *T.*
To advertise in verse a public *p. T.* iv 501
To be a *p*. where he was useful once *T.* iv 657
And bloated spider, till the pampered *p. T.* v 422

PESTILENCE.
Famine, and P., her first-born son *Her.* 59
That creeping *p.* is driven away *T.* vi 785

PESTILENT.
A *p.* and most corrosive steam *T.* iii 494

PETRIFIED.
Blush, if thou canst; not *p.*, thou must *Ex.* 555
Screens them, and seem half *p.* to sleep *T.* v 28
Fixed motionless, and *p.* with dread *T.* vi 538

PETRONIUS!
P.! all the Muses weep for thee *P.E.* 335

PETTY.
Thy chiefs, the lords of many a *p.* fee *Ex.* 532
Struggling, detained in many a *p.* nook *N.A.* 40
On *p.* robbers, and indulges life *T.* i 733

PETULANCE.
The lowering eye, the *p.*, the frown *T.* i 456

PEW.
The brief proclaimed, it visits every *p. Ch.* 469

PHÆDRUS.
Æsop, and *P.*, and the rest?—Why not? *Tir.* 546

PHALANX.
All huddling into *p.*, stood and gazed *N.A.* 48

PHANTOM.
Fond of the *p.* of an earthly rest *R.* 764
Then grace the bony *p.* in their stead *T.T.* 43

PHARAOH. [464
By thee, worse plagues than *P.'s* land befell *P.E.*
Which God avenged on *P.*—the Bastille *T.* v 383

PHARISEE.
The *p.* the dupe of his own art *Ex.* 93
Mark what a sumptuous *P.* is he! *T.* 59
Who judged the *P.*? What odious cause *T.* 44

PHEASANT.
The *p.* plumes which round infold *Mrs. M—* 5
Not so the *p.* on his charms presumes *T.* 66

PHILIP.
As vain imperial *P.* on his own *Ch.* 52
And in thy numbers, *P.*, shines for aye *T.* iii 455

PHILISTIA.
As Dagon in *P.* long before *Ex.* 507

PHILLYREA.
And *p.* of a golden green *A.T.* 83

PHILOLOGISTS.
Nor those of learned *p.*, who chase *R.* 691

PHILOMEL.
And by *P.'s* annual note *C.* 47

PHILOSOPHER.
(A fault *p.* might blame *A Fable* 5
Serves but to lead *p.* astray *P.E.* 433
P., who darken and put out *P.E.* 472
Forth steps the spruce *p.*, and tells *T.* ii 189
Haste now, *p.*, and set him free *T.* v 670
That babblers, called *p.*, devise *Tir.* 158
The well-informed *p. Trans. H.* 19

PHILOSOPHIC.
Where others toil with *p.* force *Con.* 151

With cold disgust, or *p.* pride *Ex.* 691
Lothario cries, What *p.* stuff! *H.* 28
What early *p.* hours he keeps *R.* 429
To learned cares or *p.* toil *R.* 662
His well built systems, *p.* dreams *T.* 8
But never yet did *p.* tube *T.* iii 229
In wisdom, and with *p.* deeps *T.* v 297
And He by means in *p.* eyes *T.* v 698
A childish waste of *p.* pains *Tir.* 76
To some not steep, though *p.*, height *Tir.* 631
Employs his *p.* pate *Trans.* ii 23
In such a mould *p. R.C.* 9

PHILOSOPHY.
P., that does not dream or stray *Ch.* 313
And graced with all *P.* can add *Ch.* 342
This is indeed *P.*; this known *Ch.* 349
P., without his heavenly guide *Ch.* 373
A sceptic in *p.* may seem *Con.* 138
Or from *p.'s* enlightened page *Con.* 616
As Tully with *p.* once dealt *Con.* 730
P. indeed on Grecian eyes *Ex.* 227
'Tis grave *P.'s* absurdest dream *H.* 65
And teach *P.* a smile *Mrs. M—* 30
Are sweet *p.'s* enjoyments run *P.E.* 259
Where finds *P.* her eagle eye *T.* i 712
This truth, *P.*, though eagle-eyed *T.* ii 174
Illusive of *p.*, so called *T.* ii 505
Then all is plain. *P.* baptized *T.* iii 243
The shadows fly, *p.* prevails *Tir.* 182
Watch every beam *P.* imparts *T.T.* 70

PHINEAS.
And, *P.* like, transfixed them at a blow *A.T.* 196
Hophni and *P.* may describe the rest *Ex.* 449

PHIZ.
As if the gnomon on his neighbour's *p. Con.* 271

PHLEGM.
Peace to the *p.* of sullen elves *Miss —* 61

PHLEGMATIC.
Where sharp and solid, *p.* and light *Ex.* 296

PHŒBUS.
Like her the fabled *P.* wooed in vain *Ex.* 599
Though *P.* string the lyre *Miss —* 12
And she the works of *P.* aiding *Mrs. M—* 55
P., if such be thy design *O.* i 25

PHRASE.
His stock, a few French *p.* got by heart *P.E.* 375
Elegant *p.*, and figure formed to please *P.E.* 422
Of Attic *p.* and senatorial tone *S.* i 11
His *p.* well chosen, clear, and full of force *Tir.* 669

PHTHISIC. [392
And coughs, and rheums, and *p.*, and catarrh *Con.*

PHYSIC.
Their mildest *p.* is a farrier's purge *Ch.* 502
Need other *p.* none to heal the effects *T.* i 590
Church, army, *p.*, law *Trans.* ii 27

PHYSICIAN.
P. write in hopes to work a cure *Con.* 407
Perhaps a grave *p.*, gathering fees *H.* 203

PICK.
And Chloe from her garland *p.* the weed *H.* 293
They *p.* their fuel out of every hedge *T.* i 565
He *p.* clean teeth, and, busy as he seems *T.* ii 627
P. up their nauseous dole, though sweet to them *T.* v 94
And prink their hair with daisies, or to *p. T.* vi 303

PICKED.
That *p.* the jewel out of England's crown *T.* ii 265
P. from the thorns and briars of reproof *T.* vi 1013

PICKLOCK.
An office key, a *p.* to a place *Ex.* 379

PICTURE.
In drawing *p.* of forbidden joys *R.* 216
Behold the *p.*!—is it like ?—Like whom ? *T.* ii 408
Thus blest, I draw a *p.* of that bliss *T.* iii 694
Sat for the *p.*; and the poet's hand *T.* iv 526

PIE.
The jay, the *p.*, and even the boding owl *T.* 205

PIECE.
A smaller *p.* amidst the precious store *Ch.* 476
But for one *p.* they thought it hard *L.W.* 11
A *p.* of mere church furniture at best *Tir.* 425

PIERCE.
The sound of pardon *p.* his startled ear *H.* 724
Be strangers to each other ? *P.* my vein *T.* iii 201

PIERCED.
Not to be *p.* in play, or in the dark *Ex.* 435
P. to the very centre of the realm *Ex.* 576 [591
Which, aimed at him, have *p.* the offended skies *H.*
P. with the woes that she laments in vain *R.* 300

PIERCING.
The *p.* cold, but feels it unimpaired *T.* iv 361

PIETY.
And give true *p.* that odious name *Con.* 656
Their *p.* a system of deceit *Ex.* 91
While Honour, Virtue, P., bear sway *Ex.* 326
True *P.* is cheerful as the day *T.* 176
When learning, virtue, *p.*, and truth *T.* ii 700
On all her branches. *P.* has found *T.* iii 249
The cause of *p.*, and sacred truth *T.* iii 707
Evander, famed for *p.*, for years *T.* vi 490
That *p.* has still in human hearts *T.* vi 683
The stamp of artless *p.* impress'd *Tir.* 153

PIGEON.
Like angel-heads in stone with *p.* wings ? *Con.* 576

PIGMY.
And feeble onset of a *p.* rush *Ex.* 707

PIGS.
And one of *p.* that he has lost *Y.D.* 55

PILATE. [270
But what is truth ? 'Twas *P.*'s question put *T.* iii

PILE.
P. up his stores amidst the frozen waste *H.* 475
Have burnt to dust a nobler *p.* *M.* i 3
No clustering ornaments to clog the *p.* *T.* 24
Or velvet soft, or plush with shaggy *p.* *T.* i 11
Toils much to earn a monumental *p.* *T.* i 276
The agglomerated *p.*, his frame may front *T.* iii 472
Down falls the venerable *p.*, the abode *T.* iii 767
The well stacked *p.* of riven logs and roots *T.* iv 444
Lest storms should overset the leaning *p.* *T.* v 39
And prop the *p.* they but adorned before *T.* v 116

PILFERED.
Mine I ave not *p.* yet ; nor yet impaired *T.* i 140

PILFERS.
And not a year but *p.* as he goes *T.* i 131

PILGRIM.
As when two *p.* in a forest stray *H.* 276
Revere the man whose *P.* marks the road *Tir.* 145

PILGRIMAGE.
In *p.* to bow before his shrine *T.* vi 669

PILL.
Now the distemper, spite of draught or *p.* *Con.* 319
To cover a *p.* for a delicate palate *F.M.* 12

PILLAR.
The *p.* of the eternal plan appears *Con.* 558
The *p.* of support in which they trust *Ex.* 333
And *p.* of our planet seem to fail *T.* ii 63
Shoot into *p.* of pellucid length *T.* v 115

PILLORIED.
Stood *p.* on infamy's high stage *H.* 556

PILLOW.
Their fleece his *p.* and his weekly drawl *H.* 199
P. and bobbins all her little store *T.* 318

PIMPLE.
A *p.* that portends a future sprout *T.* iii 528

PIMPS.
Ye *p.*, who, under virtue's fair pretence *P.E.* 315

PIN.
His friend in merry *p.* *J.G.* 178
I pricked them into paper with a *p.* *M.P.* 77
She begs an idle *p.* of all she meets *T.* i 553
In balance on his conduct of a *p.*? *T.* vi 271

PINCH.
" And *p.* your noses blue " *J.P.* 40
And such expense as *p.* parents blue *T.* ii 756
Cautious he *p.* from the second stalk *T.* iii 527
Feels not the wants that *p.* the poor *Trans. H.* 10

PINCHED.
P. close between his finger and his thumb *Ch.* 477
But somewhat at that moment *p.* him close *E.* iii 34
With hunger *p.*, and *p.* for room *R.C.* 73 [*T.* i 556
Though *p.* with cold, asks never—Kate is crazed !

PINE.
As Envy *p.* at good possessed *F.* 79
The tallest *p.* feel most the power *Trans. H.* 13
This glassy stream, that spreading *p.* *S.* 5 [*H.* 59
The wretch may *p.*, while to his smell, taste, sight
Attract us, and neglected Nature *p.* *T.* iii 730
Neglected *p.* at home, themselves as more *T.* iv 456

PINEAPPLE.
The *P.* in triple row *P.B.* 1
She is the *P.*, and he *P.B.* 21
We long for *p.* in frames *P.B.* 32

PINE-TREE.
Sits cooing in the *p.*, nor suspends *T.* vi 308

PINING.
The cankered spoil corrodes the *p.* state *Ch.* 63
In scenes of plenty, or the *p.* waste *Ex.* 733
And years of *p.* indigence must show *Her.* 65

PINIONS.
On waxen *p.* soar without a fall *A.T.* 54
If chance, on heavy *p.* slowly borne *H.* 716
Pleased Fancy claps her *p.* at the sight *R.* 190 [214
Theirs, should I paint him, has his *p.* fledged *T.* iv

PINIONED.
Her elbows *p.* close upon her hips *T.* 133

PINK.
The violet, the p., the jessamine *M.P.* 76
These p. are as fresh, and as gay *W.N.* 14

PINKED.
Taught thee to clothe thy p. and painted hide *Ex.* [486

PINNED.
Her head, adorned with lappets p. aloft *T.* iv 540

PIOUS.
May such success attend the p. plan *Con.* 837
P. enough, and having need of none *H.* 251
Re-echoing p. anthems! while beneath *T.* i 343
Still sacred, and preserves with p. care *T.* vi 690
Within some p. pastor's humble cot *Tir.* 760

PIOUSLY.
And p. prefer the tail *L.W.* 20

PIP.
Faint as a chicken's note that has the p. *Con.* 356

PIPE.
The p., with solemn interposing puff *Con.* 245
Laid down his p., flew to the gate *J.G.* 163
Fatigued me, never weary of the p. *T.* iv 706
To the lascivious p. and wanton song *T.T.* 462

PIPING.
When p. winds shall soon arise *T.B.* 17

PIPPINS.
On p.s' russet peel *Ep.* ii 18

PISTOL. [802
Crape and cocked p., and the whistling ball *T.* iii
Guns, halberts, swords and p., great and small *Ch.* 551

PIT.
Low in the p., thine avarice has made *Ch.* 72 [53
They gathered close around the old p.'s brink *N.A.*
That life to save, we leap into the p." *N.A.* 104
How! leap into the p. our life to save! *N.A.* 107

PIT-A-PAT.
His noble heart went p. *R.C.* 79

PITCH.
Set your opinion at whatever p. *Con.* 107
No flights above the p. of prose *E.* i 16 [505
The scholar's p. (the scholar best knows why *P.E.*
Vouchsafe, at least, to p. the key of rhyme *T.T.* 188
Stooped from its highest p. to pounce a wren *T.T.* 553
To p. the ball into the grounded hat *Tir.* 308

PITCH'D.
And, as the mind is p., the ear is pleased *T.* vi 2

PITCHER.
And watered duly. There the p. stands *T.* iv 775

PITCHKETTLED.
I fairly find myself p. *E.* iv 32

PITEOUS.
Most p. to be seen *J.G.* 126
Plaintive and p., as it wept and wailed *T.* iv 479

PITIED.
Much to be p. or commended *P.* 44
He shared in the plunder, but p. the man *P.A.* 44

PITIFUL.
Of lightness in his speech. 'Tis p. *T.* ii 466
To make the p. possessor shine *T.T.* 755

PITILESS.
"Ruffians, p. as proud *B.* 41

That, p. perforce *Cast.* 22 [13
"And such," I exclaimed, "is the p. part *The Rose*

PITTANCE.
His p. every night *Ep.* ii 10
Just earns a scanty p., and at night *T.* 321
Their last poor p.—Fortune, most severe *T.* ii 658

PITY.
Still there is room for p. to abate *Ch.* 198
The swell of p., not to be confined *Ch.* 246
They meet with little p., no redress *Ch.* 530
I p. bashful men, who feel the pain *Con.* 347
In p. to the souls his grace designed *E.* ii 23
And Cyrus, with relenting p. moved *Ex.* 75
Peace to all such,—'twere p. to offend *H.* 272
Glistening at once with p. and surprise *H.* 533
That P. had engendered, drop one here *H.* 677
Ah! I could p. thee exiled *M.B.* 13
To p. and perhaps forgive *M.F.* 40
With P.'s watery sight *Miss* — 76
"So P. shall take Virtue's part *Miss* — 89
By p., sympathy, and love *P.* 62
Is almost enough to draw p. from stones *P.A.* 4
I p. them greatly, but I must be mum *P.A.* 5
Poor man! what a p. to injure him so! *P.A.* 34
Have you no touch of p. that the poor *P.E.* 249
This is a sight for P. to peruse *R.* 297
I p., and must therefore sink the name *R.* 576
Heard the sweet moan with p., and devised *T.* i 74
These therefore I can p., placed remote *T.* i 626
To break a jest, when p. would inspire *T.* ii 468
Is't not a p. now, that tickling rheums *T.* iii 167
Of oracles like these? Great p. too *T.* iii 169
Dissolve in p., and account the learn'd *T.* iii 183
Susceptible of p., or a mind *T.* iii 323
Feel wrath and p., when I think on thee! *T.* iii 842
Did p. of their sufferings warp aside *T.* iv 453
And p. for her loss. But that's a cause *T.* v 370
Plead not in vain for p. on the pangs *T.* vi 462
And teach one tyrant p. for his drudge *T.* vi 723
Of natural p., send him not to school *Tir.* 872
I p. kings whom worship waits upon *T.T.* 121
Sighing I say again, I p. kings! *T.T.* 140
P. Religion has so seldom found *T.T.* 716

PITYING.
Will weep indeed, and heave a p. groan *T.* 177

PLACE.
Than reign in this horrible p. *A.S.* 8
There is mercy in every p. *A.S.* 53 [*A.T.* 200
Shrieked at the sight, and, conscious, fled the p.
Afford them p. of rest? *A Tale* 26
And only blushes in the proper p. *Con.* 374
To exalt a people, and to p. them high *Con.* 519
Where then the preference shall we p. *E.* iv 71
Happy to fill Religion's vacant p. *Ew.* 121
An office key, a picklock to a p. *Ex.* 379
Error and darkness occupy their p. *Ex* 693
Then p. it once again between my knees *Ex.* 730
All shining in their p. *F.* 60
Nature, employed in her alloted p. *H.* 145
Pants for the p. of her ethereal birth *H.* 162
Emulous always of the nearest p. *H.* 238
To p. you where his saints his presence share *H.* 339
And p., instead of quirks themselves devise *H.* 629
O p. me in some Heaven-protected isle *Her.* 83
The pleasures of this p. *M.B.* 2
And right toward the favoured p. *Mor.* 19
To p. it in thy bow *O.* i 26
Ye clergy, while your orbit is your p. *P.E.* 96
Will Avarice, and Concupiscence give p. *P.E.* 104
Accomplishments have taken Virtue's p. *P.E.* 417

Stars countless, each in his appointed p. R. 83
Teach, while they flatter him, his proper p. R. 446
Kneels, kisses hands, and shines again in p. R. 480
My Lord, alighting at his usual p. R. 585
'Tis easy to resign a toilsome p. R. 621
But love of change, it seems, has p. R C. 21
Some p. of more serene repose R.C. 30
And wishing for a p. of rest R.C. 105
Who deem his house a useless p. St. vi 21
And seems to say—" Ye meaner fowl give p. T. 64
Expert in all the duties of his p. T. 206
Conveying worthless dross into its p. T. i 572
Find p. in his dominion, or dispose T. ii 169
Then compromise had p., and scrutiny T. ii 740
And when I p. thee in it, sighing say T. iii 350
He p. lightly, and as time subdues T. iii 518
With needless hurry whirled from p. to p. T. iv 372
In such a palace Poetry might p. T. v 138
Till smooth'd and squar'd and fitted to its p. T. vi 94
That makes so gay the solitary p. T. vi 187
Some p., a spark or two not yet extinct T. vi 684
His steeds, usurp a p. they well deserve T. vi 703
One Lord, one Father. Error has no p. T. vi 784
Holds no ignoble, though a slighted, p. T. vi 971
The balance in the highest p. Th. 11
This fond attachment to the well known p. Tir. 314
I give the bauble but the second p. Tir. 388
A scrivener's clerk, or footman out of p. Tir. 407
In spite of all the wrigglers into p. Tir. 432
Of those who never feel in the right p. Tir. 540
Supplant thee in it, and usurp thy p. Tir. 890
A plan well worthy to supply their p. Tir. 918
Patriots, who love good p. at their hearts T.T. 191
P. me where Winter breathes his keenest air T.T. 294
When he usurped Authority's just p. T.T. 320
Obduracy takes p.; callous and tough T.T. 458 [471
When He commands in whom they p. no trust T.T.
And p. it in this first essay U. 21

PLACED.

P. with advantage at his listening ear A.T. 181
That every tribe, though p. as he sees best Ch. 19
The Scripture p. within his reach, he ought Ch. 201
Fate having p. all truth above his reach Con. 142
And p. it in our power to prove E. i 103 [586
And plucks the fruit p. more within his reach" Con.
Joys always prized, when p. within our reach H. 36
The coronet, p. idly at their head H. 268
P. for his trial on this bustling stage P.E. 23
Is man then only for his torment p. P.E. 229
Well born, well disciplined, who, p. apart R. 727
Though p. in golden Durham's second stall T. 120
These for the rich: the rest, whom Fate had p. T. i 49
Is obvious, p. within the easy reach T. i 598
These therefore I can pity, p. remote T. i 626
Though p. in Paradise (for earth has still T. iii 298
P. at some vacant corner of the board T. iv 230
Thus form'd, thus p., intelligent, and taught Tir. 53
Reflect his attributes who p. them there Tir. 92
With his own likeness p. on either knee Tir. 320
Securely p. between the small and great Tir. 808
Where Duty p. them, at their country's side T.T. 24

PLACEMAN.

The dear-bought p., and the cheap buffoon Con. 30
Or p., all tranquillity and smiles T. iv 49

PLACID.

Some are so p. and serene F. 121

PLAGUE.

The fretting p. is in the public purse Ch. 62
'Tis gone again—p. on't! I thought E. iv 37
Let Egypt's p., and Canaan's woes proclaim Ex. 169

Of the p. spread by bundles left behind P.E. 352
By thee, worse p. than Pharaoh's land befell P.E. 464
These and a thousand p. that haunt the breast R. 763
Did Famine or did P. prevail St. i 7
Nor P. nor Famine came St. i 10
A p. so little to be feared M.F. 33
It p. your country. Folly such as yours T. i 770
A p. into his blood; and cannot use T. ii 140
And gives them all their fury; bids a p. T. ii 182
Now basket up the family of p. T. ii 667
Mourns because every p. that can infest T. ii 815
Excess, the scrofulous and itchy p. T. iv 582 [671
Hence chartered boroughs are such public p. T. iv
Far worse than all the p. with which his sins T. v 605
To Miss, the Mercer's p., from shop to shop T. vi 279
Nor p. that haunt the rich man's door Trans. H. 11

PLAGUED.

Provoked and harassed, in return p. thee Ex. 533
Chief monster that has p. the nations yet! T.T. 38

PLAGUY.

You sell it p. dear Y.D. 60

PLAIN.

The beasts that roam over the p. A.S. 13
To pathless wilds and unfrequented p. A.T. 26
I was a bondman on my native p. Ch. 236
Suggests it safe, or dangerous, to be p. Ch. 520
The cause is p., and not to be denied Con. 159
The language p., and incidents well linked Con. 236
If this be p., 'tis plainly understood Con. 435
For us p. folks, and all who side with us Con. 848
Serves, in a p. and homely way E. i 3
The world may dance along the flowery p. E. ii 13
Look to the poor; the simple and the p. Ex. 452
That won a nymph on that immortal p. Ex. 598
Lord paramount of the surrounding p. H. 305
This only can; for this p. cause, expressed H. 340
In terms as p., himself has shut the rest H. 341
On icy p., and in eternal snows H. 464
A knave when tried on honesty's p. rule H. 566
Scripture indeed is p., but God and he H. 598
To hear p. truth at Judah's hallowed gate H. 763
Rebuilds the towers that smoked upon the p. Her. 71
Whilst beauty decks the p. Miss -- 40
Speckle the bosom of the distant p. P.E. 83
O the dear pleasures of the velvet p. P.E. 169
Though p. to others, is obscure to him P.E. 447
Some p. mechanic, who, without pretence R. 449
Despise the p. direction, and are lost T. 33
Their sin is p., but what have we to fear T. 129
See where it smokes along the sounding p. T. 238
Here Ouse, slow-winding through a level p. T. i 163
Thy simple fare, and all thy p. delights T. i 646
In doctrine uncorrupt; in language p. T. ii 400
And p. in manner; decent, solemn, chaste T. ii 401
Polluting Egypt: gardens, fields, and p. T. ii 828
My languid limbs, when summer sears the p. T. iii 30
Then all is p. Philosophy baptized T. iii 243
What England was, p., hospitable, kind T. iii 743
The verdure of the p. lies buried deep T. v 21
Its hollow glens, its thickets, and its p. T. vi 402
So the best courser on the p. Th. 17 [Tir. 129
Points, which, unless the Scripture made them p.
'Tis p. the creature, whom he chose to invest Tir. 95
Else sure notorious fact, and proof so p. Tir. 259
Which, though in p. plebeians we condemn Tir. 352
Prevented much by diet neat and p. Tir. 767
Is legible and p. Trans. i 22
He break away, and seek the distant p. ? T.T. 307

PLAINER.

'Tis granted, and no p. truth appears P.E. 353

PLAINNESS.

Through all He spoke a noble *p.* ran *Ex.* 135
But speaks with *p.* art could never mend *H.* 451

PLAINTIVE.

Thy tender sorrows and thy *p.* strain *E.* ii 45
P. and piteous, as it wept and wailed *T.* iv 479
Cyrene, when he bore the *p.* tale *T.* v 136

PLAINTS.

Regardless of their *p.* To make him sport *T.* vi 386

PLAN.

Large population on a liberal *p. A.T.* 157
Your matrimonial *p. A Tale* 70
God, working ever on a social *p. Ch.* 15
The treasured sweets of the capacious *p. Ch.* 323
That square not truly with the Scripture *p. Ch.* 559
Your hope to please him vain on every *p. Con.* 341
Starts not aside from her Creator's *p. Con.* 452
The pillar of the eternal *p.* appears *Con.* 558
May such success attend the pious *p. Con.* 837
And *p.* and orders our connections *E.* i 36
But who can tell how vast the *p. E.* i 83
'Twas theirs alone to dive into the *p. Ex.* 235 [237
And while the world beside, that *p.* unknown *Ex.*
Snuffs up the praise of what he seems to *p. Ex.* 317
Some act upon this prudent *p. F.* 181
So shifting and so various is the *p. H.* 15
By which he reads, that life without a *p. H.* 95
Who make the good Creator on their *p. H.* 383
Was one, whom Justice, on an equal *p. H.* 511
Build by whatever *p.* caprice decrees *H.* 614
Woven with pains into his *p. H.F.* 3
'Tis woven in the world's great *p. Miss* — 45
Contribute to the gorgeous *p. Mrs. M*— 13   [43
He blamed and protested, but joined in the *p. P.A.*
Else, on the fatalists' unrighteous *p. P.E.* 27
Exhibits elevations, drawings, *p. P.E.* 397
Opening the map of God's extensive *p. R.* 147
Mark well the finished *p.* without a fault *R.* 551
Heaven's easy, artless, unencumbered *p.! T.* 22
How readily, upon the Gospel *p. T.* 381
Improved the simple *p.*; made three legs four *T.* i 29
One lawless particle to thwart his *p. T.* ii 170 [iii 785
He sighs, departs, and leaves the accomplished *p. T.*
I never framed a wish, or formed a *p. T.* iv 695
Almost without an effort, *p.* too vast *T.* v 253
Had not its author dignified the *p. Tir.* 51
And all the *p.* their destiny design'd *Tir.* 86
Blasphemes his creed, as founded on a *p. Tir.* 159
Ghostly in office, earthly in his *p. Tir.* 422   [737
And thou a wretch, whom, following her old *p. Tir.*
A *p.* well worthy to supply their place *Tir.* 918
Kings do but reason on the self-same *p. T.T.* 48
To win no *p.* when well-wrought *p.* prevail *T.T.* 157
The mighty *p.*, oracular, in verse *T.T.* 179
And darts his soul into the dawning *p. T.T.* 499
'Tis where it should be in a *p. U.* 23

PLANET.

And pillars of our *p.* seemed to fail *T.* ii 63
That brings the *p.* home into the eye *T.* iii 230

PLANETARY.

Sees *p.* wonders smoothly roll *Ch.* 317
And *p.* some; what gave them first *T.* iii 159

PLANK.

A Monitor is wood—*p.* shaven thin *T.* ii 585

PLANKED.   [*Y.O.* 95

That might have ribbed the sides and *p.* the deck

PLANNED.

To disconcert what Policy has *p. Ex.* 299
(Yet charge not heavenly skill with having *p. H.* 542
That *p.*, and built, and still upholds a world *T.* v 753
Of no mean city, *p.* or ere the hills *T.* v 764
But measures *p.* and executed well *T.T.* 386

PLANT.   [there! *A.T.* 118

" Find out her treacherous heart, and *p.* a dagger
True Charity, a *p.* divinely nursed *Ch.* 573
To poison vermin that infest his *p. Con.* 256
I *p.* my foot upon this ground of trust *H.* 369
And *p.* successfully sweet Sharon's rose *H.* 463
Make the *p.* for which we toil ? *N.C.* 18
The *p.* he meant grew not far off *P.* 17
Did *p.* called sensitive grow there ? " *P.* 22
If all the *p.* that can be found *P.* 57   [359
P. raised with tenderness are seldom strong *P.E.*
As woodbine weds the *p.* within her reach *R.* 229
The seed sown there, how vigorous is the *p.* ? *T.* 362
The grain, or herb, or *p.* that each demands *R.* 788
Beneath his care, a thriving vigorous *p. T.* ii 714
Checks vegetation in the torpid *p. T.* iii 468
All *p.*, of every leaf, than can endure *T.* iii 580
Threatening at once and nourishing the *p. T.* vi 36
P. behind *p.* aspiring, in the van *T.* iii 593
Sure to exhaust the *p.* on which they feed *Tir.* 604
P. it upon the line that Justice draws *T.T.* 17
In all that live, *p.*, animal, and man *Y.O.* 79

PLANTATIONS.

Wasting towns, *p.*, meadows *N.C.* 35

PLANTED.

A people *p.*, watered, blest as they ? *Ex.* 168
His lamp now *p.* on Heaven's topmost arch *N.A.* 30
Our groves were *p.* to console at noon *T.* i 760
Suspend their crazy boxes, *p.* thick *T.* iv 774

PLASHED.

P. neatly, and secured with driven stakes *T.* iv 437

PLASTERED.

The cottage, wulk along the *p.* wall *T.* v 19

PLATE.

Like figures drawn upon a dial *p. Con.* 380
Like Hand-in-Hand Insurance *p. F.* 106   [280
In foreign eyes!—be grooms, and win the *p. T.* ii
Above the steeple shines a *p. Trans.* ii 7

PLATO.

Has Epictetus, P., Tully, preached! *T.* ii 540

PLATTED.   [239

Who wore the *p.* thorns with bleeding brows *T.* vi

PLATTING.

Sits linking cherry-stones, or *p.* rush *R.* 398

PLAUSIBLE.

Of sabbath hours with *p.* excuse ? *P.E.* 145
And *p.* than social life requires *T.* v 466
The end, though *p.*, not worth the means *Tir.* 487
While thoughful man is *p.* amused *T.* iii 186

PLAY.

But she, inconstant as the beams that *p. A.T.* 23
Too often proves an implement of *p. Con.* 17
Religion curbs indeed its wanton *p. Con.* 595 [611
A man that would have foiled at their own *p. Con.*
And give the moral springs their proper *p. Con.* 832
Find the sweet lyre on which an artist *p. Con.* 900
The harmless *p.* of pleasantry and mirth *E.* iii 39
And every night at *p. Ep.* ii 32

Not to be pierced in *p.*, or in the dark *Ex.* 435
So settling in his cage, by *p. F.B.* 25
Men deal with life as children with their *p. H.* 127
Froward at school, and fretful in his *p. H.* 188
Though loose, as harmless as an infant's *p. H.* 613
Upon his dungeon walls the lightning *p. H.* 718
In dazzling streaks the vivid lightnings *p. Her.* 18
These gambols he did *p. J.G.* 134
Or a wild goose at *p. J.G.* 140
Can see no evil in a *p. L.W.* 30
While airs impregnated with incense *p. M.P.* 94
To *p.* the fool on Sundays, why not we ? *P.E.* 147
Laymen have leave to dance, if parsons *p. P.E.* 151
But, if he *p.* the glutton and exceed *P.E.* 211   [3
The winds *p.* no longer and sing in the leaves *P.F.*
In the last scene of such a senseless *p. R.* 32
The waves o'ertake them in their serious *p. R.* 157
And *p.* the fool, but at a cheaper rate *R.* 562
The rest might then seem privileged to *p. St.* ii 19
Dishonour with unhallowed *p. St.* vi 27
To watch yon amorous couple in their *p. T.* 136
No, not a spark—'tis all mere sharper's *p. T.* 209
Now flashing wide, now glancing as in *p. T.* 242
That *p.* of lungs, inhaling and again *T.* i 137
P. wanton, every moment, every spot *T.* i 349
But cannot *p.* them, borrows a friend's hand *T.* i 473
And silent cipher, while her proxy *p. T.* i 477
What!—will a man *p.* tricks, will he indulge *T.* ii 419
And *p.* his brilliant parts before my eyes *T.* ii 425
Nor such as with a frown forbids the *p. T.* iv 175
Learn every trick, and soon *p.* all the game *T.* iv 231
The sooty films that *p.* upon the bars *T.* iv 292 [v 188
Kings would not *p.* at. Nations would do well *T.*
May *p.* what tune he pleases. In the deed *T.* v 652
The squirrel, flippant, pert, and full of *p. T.* vi 315
Nor ask his leave to slumber or to *p. T.* vi 405
In bilking tavern bills, and spouting *p. Tir.* 327
What sums he lost at *p.*, and how he sold *Tir.* 330
Behold your bishop! well he *p.* his part *Tir.* 420
Allows short time for *p.*, and none for sloth *Tir.* 484
To take in childish *p.* a childish part *Tir.* 548
A tax of profit from his very *p. Tir.* 612   [*Tir.* 335
Resolves that where he played his sons shall *p.*
Puts a period to thy *p. Trans.* iii 26
To him is relaxation and mere *p.*) *T.T.* 156
Too apt to *p.* the wanton with her powers *T.T.* 301
I *p.* with syllables, and sport in song *T.T.* 505
And every effort ends in push-pin *p. T.T.* 547
In tales, in trifles, and in children's *p. T.T.* 731
Thy schoolfellow and partner of thy *p. V.* 35 [*Y.O.* 18
Which babes might *p.* with; and the thievish jay

PLAYED.   [*p. T.* v 177
Great princes have great playthings. Some have
P. only gambols in a frantic mood *H.* 541
P. on his lips, and in his speech was heard *T.* ii 707
P. by the creatures of a Power who swears *T.* iii 177
I *p.* awhile, obedient to the fair *T.* vi 1008   [268
Went with him, and saw all the game he *p.* ? *Tir.*
Resolves that where he *p.* his sons shall play *Tir.* 335
Anacreon, Horace, *p.* in Greece and Rome *T.T.* 608

PLAYEDST.

But well thou *p.* the housewife's part *M.* 17

PLAYFUL.

So when a child, as *p.* children use *B.B.* 9
The *p.* humour; he could now endure *T.* vi 47
And smiles to see, her infant's *p.* hand *T.* vi 779
And, while the *p.* jockey scours the room *Tir.* 366

PLAYING.   [75

When, *p.* with thy vesture's tissued flowers *M.P.*
Of some tall temple *p.* bright *Mrs. M—* 36

In *p.* tricks with Nature, giving laws *T.* iii 165
P. our games, and on the very spot *Tir.* 305
P., at beat of drum, their martial pranks *T.T.* 136

PLAY-PLACE.

And had no other *p.* for his wit *Ch.* 538
We love the *p.* of our early days *Tir.* 297

PLAYTHING.

And was his *p.* often when a child *E.* iii 33
Oaths used as *p.* or convenient tools *Ex.* 37
A *p.* world, unworthy of his hand) *H.* 543
Not as the *p.* of a froward child *R.* 107   [v 177
Great princes have great *p.* Some have played *T.*

PLAYTIME.

E'en in the spring and *p.* of the year *T.* vi 299

PLEA.

Prosper (I press thee with a powerful *p.*) *Ch.* 5
But grant the *p.*, and let it stand for just *Ch.* 196
Were hushed in favour of thy generous *p. Ch.* 311
Affords a *p.* allowable, or just *Con.* 47
Pleasure herself perhaps suggests a *p. Ex.* 666
This only spares no lust, admits no *p. H.* 645
Expending late on all that length of *p. S.* i 6
The *p.* of works, as arrogant and vain *T.* 71
That *p.* refuted, other quirks they seek *T.* 293
I cast them at thy feet—my only *p. T.* 583
But still in virtue of a Saviour's *p. T.* 529 [*Tir.* 867
Thou wouldst not, deaf to Nature's tenderest *p.*

PLEAD.

Trade in the blood of innocence, and *p. Ch.* 182
Impudent blasphemy! So Folly *p. Ch.* 194
That *p.* for peace till it disturbs the state *Ch.* 310
Whatever Use may urge, or Honour *p. Con.* 189
If lawyer, loud whatever cause he *p. H.* 201   [43
Who strike the blow, then *p.* your own defence *Her.*
Go, fool; and, arm in arm with Clodio, *p. P.E.* 197
Thus Conscience *p.* her cause within the breast *R.* 15
Or *p.* its silence as its best applause *R.* 414
Now summon every virtue, stand and *p. T.* 567
For whom God heard His Abraham *p.* in vain *T.* iii 848
To reverence what is ancient, and can *p. T.* v 300
Takes part with Appetite, and *p.* the cause *T.* v 630
P. not in vain for pity on the pangs *T.* vi 462
(If such who *p.* for Providence may seem *T.* vi 481
Hear Nature *p.*, show mercy to thy son *Tir.* 756

PLEADED.

He *p.* again in behalf of the eyes *A.C.* 26
Wherever *p.* 'Tis the cause of man *T.* v 396

PLEADING.

No subterfuge, or *p. F.* 189
To bid the *p.* of Self-love be still *R.* 129

PLEASANT.

And ours would be *p.* as hers *C.* 55
From such communion in their *p.* course *Con.* 698
Now Gilpin had a *p.* wit *J.G.* 169
So *p.* it seemed as I lay *M.D.* 4
Could those few *p.* days again appear *M.P.* 80
Sad period to a *p.* course! *St.* vi 37
But now with *p.* pace a cleanlier road *T.* iii 17
His *p.* work, may he suppose it done *T.* iii 656
'Tis *p.*, through the loopholes of retreat *T.* iv 88
Still lives, though all its *p.* boughs are gone *T.* v 403
Of Avon, famed in song. Ah *p.* proof *T.* vi 682
How *p.* in itself what pleases him *T.* vi 829

PLEASANTRY.

The harmless play of *p.* and mirth *E.* iii 39

PLEASANTRY—PLEASURE

While fields of p. amuse us there T. iv 76
Then decent p. and sterling sense T.T. 638

PLEASE.

That, while they p., possess us with alarms Ch. 546
Rove where you p., 'tis common all around Con. 100
But still remember, if you mean to p. Con. 103
Who to p. others will themselves disgrace Con. 227
Yet p. not, but affront you to your face Con. 228
Or giant-killing Jack, would p. no more Con. 244
His odoriferous attempts to p. Con. 287
Your hope to p. him vain on every plan Con. 341
The change shall p., nor shall it matter aught Con.845
"An't p. your ladyship," quoth I E. iv 79 [E. iii 27
"For what?" "And p. you, sir, to see a friend"
Mistress, at least while Providence shall p. Ex. 274
For ears and hearts that he can hope to p.? Ex. 451
The sovereignty they were convened to p. Ex. 539
The sound of truth will then be sure to p. Ex. 731
With what materials, on what ground, you p. H. 615
"Oh! if my Sovereign Author p. Miss — 25
Ordained to move when others p. P. 7
To p. her sated and indifferent lord? P.E. 258
Elegant phrase, and figure formed to p. P.E. 422
The screws reversed (a task which if He p. R. 327
The spot he loved has lost the power to p. R. 466
And p., if anything could p. S. 8
But, if you p., some fathoms lower down T. 170
And only there, p. highly for their sake T. 209
Richly rewarded if he can but p. T. 218 [T. 304
("Mention him if you p.;—Voltaire?" "The same"
P. daily, and whose novelty survives T. i 178
Than p. the eye—sweet Nature every sense T. i 427
Then forests, or the savage rock, may p. T. i 518
May punish, if he p., the less, to warn T. ii 157
Just p. us while the passion is at full T. ii 598 [195
As the world p. What's the world to you?" T. iii
A bible-oath to be whate'er they p. T. iv 629 [265
When they command whom man was born to p. T. iv
No bard could p. me but whose lyre was tuned T.iv704
Than human passion p. In every heart T. v 205
Should, when he p., and on whom he will T. v 313
(Of king whom such prerogative can p.) T. v 443
"May play what tune he p. In the deed T. v 652
Is dreary, so with him all seasons p. T. vi 255
How pleasant in itself what p. him T. vi 829 [1009
With that light task; but soon, to p. her more T. vi
Whom flowers alone I knew would little p. T. vi 1010
A book (to p. us at a tender age Tir. 121
That youth takes pleasure in, to p. his boy Tir. 550
Not English stiff, but frank, and formed to p. Tir. 671
'Tis in the clouds—that p. him Trans. ii 11
Whose trade it is to smile, to crouch, to p. T.T. 123
Sing where you p., in such a cause I grant T.T. 298
With all that Fancy can invent to p. T.T. 765
That p. and yet shocks me, I can laugh T. iii 840

PLEASED.

All prompt his p. pursuit, and to pursue Ch. 325
We therefore p. extol thy song Dr. 9
Sliced carrot p. him well Ep. ii 20 [260
They die.—Death lends them, p., and as in sport H.
By this he forms, as p. he sports along H. 610
The carriage bowls along and all are p. P.E. 438
P. she beheld aloft portrayed Q.V. 45
P. Fancy claps her pinions at the sight R. 190
On whom he rests well p. his weary powers R. 451
For all that p. in wood or lawn S. 13
And, p. at heart, because on holy ground T. 232
Ingenious Fancy, never better p. T. i 72
And infants clamorous whether p. or pained T. i 232
And p. with novelty, might be indulged T. i 508
Close to his side that p. him. Learning grew T. ii 713

Well they reward the toil. The sight is p. T. iii 620
To his true worth, most p. when idle most T. iv 224
And such well p. to find it, asks no more T. v 795
And, as the mind is pitch'd, the ear is p. T. vi 2
P. with his solitude, and flitting light T. vi 79
To love and friendship both, that is not p. T. vi 324
All that are capable of pleasure p. T. vi 345 [vi 533
His rage grew cool; and p. perhaps to have earned T.
Is p. with it, and, were he free to choose T. vi 909
I p. remember, and, while memory yet Tir. 133
Their childhood p. them at a riper age Tir. 143

PLEASING.

Much less of p. expectation) E. i 100
Ears long accustomed to the p. lute Ex. 68
Of p., which you share Miss — 18
Ere yet the p. toil becomes a pain P.E. 70
Reports a message with a p. grace T. 205
Be still a p. object in my view T. i 250
So p., and that steal away the thought T. ii 299
By every p. image they present T. iii 303
So manifold, all p. in their kind T. iii 624
The p. spectacle at once excites Tir. 310
O Liberty! the prisoner's p. dream T.T. 288

PLEASURE.

(So vanishes P. alas!) C. 6
Though the p. of London exceed C. 25
God's gift with p. in his praise employ Ch. 252
Still prompt him, with a p. always new Ch. 326
The attention P. has so much engrossed Ch. 631
His only p. is to be displeased Con. 346
And prize them above p., wealth or praise Con. 662
For tell some men that p., all their bent Con. 875
Bent all on p., heedless of its end E. ii 18
Where under Heaven is P. more pursued Ex. 7
P. is deaf when told of future pain Ex. 66
P. o'ervalued, and his grace despised Ex. 252
To war with p., idolized before Ex. 410
Where beckoning P. leads them, wildly stray Ex. 464
And all at home is p., wealth, and ease Ex. 583
Now think, if P. have a thought to spare Ex. 602
P. herself perhaps suggests a plea Ex. 666
The tide of p., heedless of his frown Ex. 683
A mere Utopian p. F. 30
Taste happiness, or know what p. means H. 10
P. is labour too, and tires as much H. 20
To passion, interest, p., whim, resigned H. 212
Who live in p., dead e'en while they live H. 230
His sovereign power and p. unrestrained H. 320
And made all p. else mere dross to me" H. 537
Than he who must have p., come what will H. 595
He now perceives where earthly p. ends H. 695
But p. wins his heart H.F. 12
That, though on p. she was bent J.G. 31
'Twas for your p. you came here J.G. 199
What p. can the miser's fondled hoard J.T. 15
The p. of this place M.B. 2
Thy p. is to show M.B. 18
Whence social p. spring Miss — 30
A p. from its pain Miss — 52
Forced from home and all its p. N.C. 1
And p.'s fatal wiles? O. ii 9
And P. brings as surely in her train P.E. 43
Nor these alone, whose p. less refined P.E. 57
O the dear p. of the velvet plain P.E. 169
Slain at the foot of P. be no crime P.E. 182
That p., therefore, or what such we call P.E. 225
Remorse the fatal egg by P. laid P.E. 239
No p.! Are domestic comforts dead? P.E. 243
These both are p. to the feeling heart P.E. 254
No p.! Has some sickly eastern waste P.E. 255
Your p. with no curses in the close P.E. 268

PLEASURE—PLUMAGE

P. admitted in undue degree *P.E.* 269
Mortals whose *p.* are their only care *P.E.* 289
And relish of their *p.* all to lust *P.E.* 330
To muse on the perishing *p.* of man *P.F.* 18
The dupes of *p.*, or the slaves of gain *R.* 24
The fruits that hang on *p.*'s flowery stem *R.* 179
Are life's prime *p.* in his simple view *R.* 403
Some *p.* live a month, and some a year *R.* 459
Else more attached to *p.* found at home *R.* 518
Votaries of *P.* still, where'er she dwells *R.* 539
From *p.* left, but never more beloved *R.* 564
There feels a *p.* perfect in its kind *R.* 629
Where dreams of dress, intrigue and *p.* reign *R.* 612
Unnumbered *p.* harmlessly pursued *R.* 784
The guide to *p.* which can never cease *S.* ii 14
P.'s call attention wins *St.* iv 25
Think with what *p.*, safe and at his ease *T.* 253
One *p.* lost, lose heaven without regret *T.* 342
P. and wonder in his features mixed *T.* 416
Crippling his *p.* with the cramp of fear *T.* 466
Fast locked in mine, with *p.* such as Love *T.* i 146
Thence with what *p.* have we just discerned *T.* i 159
There is a *p.* in poetic pains *T.* ii 285
To his own *p.* and his patron's pride *T.* ii 391
Solicit *p.*, hopeless of success *T.* ii 635
And vicious *p.*; buys the boy a name *T.* ii 759
And winds his way with *p.* and with ease *T.* iii 10
Thou art not known where *P.* is adored *T.* iii 51
That owes its *p.* to another's pain *T.* iii 327
With her who shares his *p.* and his heart *T.* iii 390
With *p.* more than even their fruits afford *T.* iii 410
And all their honest *p.* Mansions once *T.* iii 746
Of *p.* and variety, dispatch *T.* iii 813
My *p.* to begin. But me, perhaps *T.* iv 272
And sweet colloquial *p.* are but few ! *T.* iv 398
On *p.*, haunt the capital, and thus *T.* iv 590
But his own simple *p.*; now and then *T.* iv 625
And harmless *p.*, in the thronged abode *T.* iv 782
And sweetness, without which no *p.* is *T.* v 470
And with it all its *p.* and its pains *T.* vi 14
All that are capable of *p.* pleased *T.* vi 345
Two gods divide them all—*P.* and Gain *T.* vi 892
She scorns his *p.*, for she knows them not *T.* vi 919
Opposed against the *p.* Nature loves! *Tir.* 170
That youth takes *p.* in, to please his boy *Tir.* 550
O'er all his *p.* gently to preside *Tir.* 609
To double all thy *p.* in thy child *Tir.* 682
If not a scene of *p.*, a mere blank *Tir.* 752
Of *p.* past, or follies yet to come *Tir.* 776
Firm friends to peace, to *p.*, and good pay *T.T.* 195
Alas! the tide of *p.* sweeps along *T.T.* 368
That made the vaulted roofs of *P.* ring *T.T.* 625
That, quite eclipsing *P.*'s painted face *T.T.* 649
Votaries of business and of *p.* prove *V.* 71
Sits half the *p.* of short life away! *Y.O.* 32

PLEBEIAN.
P. must surrender *F.* 117
Behold the schools in which *p.* minds *T.* iv 462
Which, though in plain *p.* we condemn *Tir.* 352
A higher than a mere *p.* fame *Tir.* 691
And set *p.* thousands in a roar *T.T.* 319

PLEDGE.
But softened into mercy; made the *p. T.* i 365
The nurture of her youth, her dearest *p. T.* ii 779
When having no stake left, no *p.* to endear *T.* iii 791
Of these the first in order, and the *p. T.* v 575
A *p.* he gave for a consistent part *Tir.* 178
A blessing, freedom is the *p.* of all *T.T.* 287

PLEDGED.
For I have gained thy confidence, have *p. T.* iii 346

PLENTEOUS.
And o'er the seat, with *p.* wadding stuffed *T.* i 31
The *p.* bloom, that no rough blast may sweep *T.* iii 441
And *p.* harvest, to the prayer he makes *T.* vi 947
Till Autumn's fierce heats and *p.* dews *Tir.* 47

PLENTEOUSLY.
" And stored the earth so *p.* with means *T.* v 636

PLENTIFUL.
And have most *p.* occasion *P.* 28
The *p.* moisture encumbered the flower *The Rose* 3

PLENTY.
And if a boundless *p.* be the robe *Ch.* 85 [*Comp.* i 10
How laughs the land with various *p.* crowned!
Poured out from *P.*'s overflowing horn *Ex.* 10
And after all the joys that *P.* leads *Ex.* 83
In scenes of *p.*, or the pining waste *Ex.* 733
A calm succeeds—but *P.*, with her train *Her.* 63
In gathering *p.* yet to be enjoyed *R.* 554
Not all the *p.* of a Bishop's board *T.* 121
To call up *P.* from the teeming earth *T.* 181
Through *p.*, lose in morals what they gain *T.* i 624
With blushing fruits, and *p.* not his own *T.* iii 429
And reaped their *p.* without grudge or strife *T.* v 203
From dearth to *p.*, and from death to life *T.* vi 181

PLIANT.
He brandishes his *p.* length of whip *T.* iv 355

PLIED. [502
Much to persuade, he *p.* his ear with truths *T.* vi

PLODS.
Presented bare against the storm, *p.* on *T.* iv 353

PLOTTED.
His comrades had *p.* an orchard to rob *P.A.* 23

PLOTTING.
Disfigures Earth, and, *p.* in the dark *T.* i 275

PLOUGH.
Were not afraid to *p.* the brine *A Tale* 71
Impede the bark that *p.* the deep serene *Ch.* 132
The *p.* of wisdom never entering there *H.* 234
And *p.* the distant main *R.G.* 32
Must *p.* the wave no more *R.G.* 36
P. up the roots of a believer's care *T.* 460
The distant *p.* slow-moving, and beside *T.* i 160
She *p.* a brazen field, and clothes a soil *T.* i 709
Of order from the chariot to the *p. T.* iv 586
Returns indignant to the slighted *p. T.* iv 645
With ivory teeth, or *p.* it with his snout *T.* v 50
Time *p.* them up, and not a trace remains *T.* v 533
Give me the line that *p.* its stately course *T.T.* 522

PLOUGHED.
Or *p.* perhaps by British bark again *T.* i 631 [v 202
Peace was awhile their care: they *p.* and sowed *T.*

PLUCK. [586
And *p.* the fruit placed more within his reach " *Con.*
To punish lust, or *p.* presumption down *Ex.* 250
And *p.* each other's laurel *F.* 90
P. amaranthine joys from bowers of bliss *H.* 164

PLUCKED. [Ex. 579
He that had raised thee, could have *p.* thee down

PLUM.
The biscuit, or confectionary *p. M.P.* 61

PLUMAGE.
Thus taught, down falls the *p.* of his pride *Ch.* 345

My form genteel, my *p.* gay *G.* 5
But gaudy *p.*, sprightly strain *G.* 7
This *p.*, neither dashing shower *Mrs. M—* 15
Their ruffled *p.* calm refit *Mrs. M—* 46
For Bully's *p.* sake *T.B.* 27

PLUME.

No crested warrior dips his *p.* in blood *Her.* 86
The pheasant *p.* which round infold *Mrs. M—* 5
The P. and Poet both we know *Mrs. M—* 53
Both Poet saves and P. from fading *Mrs. M—* 55
Though he too has a glory in his *p. T.* 67 [215
With motley *p.*; and, where the peacock shows *T.* iv
In painted *p.* superbly dressed *Trans.* iv 1
Then show far off their shining *p.* again *T.T.* 567

PLUMED.

Is India free? and does she wear her *p. T.* iv 28
His hat, or his *p.* helmet, with a grace *T.* iv 643

PLUMP.

The seed, selected wisely, *p.*, and smooth *T.* iii 511
The *p.* convivial parson often bears *T.* iv 595

PLUNDER.

He shared in the *p.*, but pitied the man *P.A.* 44
For *p.*; much solicitous how best *T.* iv 433

PLUNDERED.

Heaven, earth, and ocean, *p.* of their sweets *T.* iv 82

PLUNGE.

From earth or hell, we can but *p.* at last" *N.A.* 122
The rage of fermentation, *p.* deep *T.* iii 519
Conscious and fearful of too deep a *p. T.* v 64

PLUNGED.

P. in the stream, they lodge upon the mud *Ch.* 531

PLUNGING.

And *p.* left the shore *D.W.* 32
P., and half despairing of escape *T.* iii 6
Deep *p.*, and again deep *p.* oft *T.* v 34
Of folly, *p.* in pursuit of death *T.* v 595

PLURALITIES.

Forms or no forms, *p.* or pairs *A.T.* 131

PLUSH.

Or velvet soft, or *p.* with shaggy pile *T.* i 11.

PLY.

P. all the sinews of industrious toil *Her.* 69
Spreads all his canvass, every sinew *p. T.* 5
But here the needle *p.* its busy task *T.* iv 150
Smith, cobbler, joiner, he that *p.* the shears *T.* iv 476
The peasants urge their harvest, *p.* the fork *T.T.* 214

POCKET.

But sighs at thought of empty *p. P.B.* 26
Lies down secure, her heart and *p.* light *T.* 322 [445
Forth comes the *p.* mirror.—First we stroke *T.* ii

POCKETED.

And *p.* a prize by fraud obtained *T.* iii 87

POCKET-STORE.

How oft, my slice of *p.* consumed *T.* i 118

POEM.

" Lets fall a *p. en passant E.* iv 88
My *p.* enchanted I view *Gr.* 30
From him who rears a *p.* lank and long *T.T.* 532

POET.

So tuneful a *p.* before *C.* 24
No *p.* wept him; but the page *Cast.* 49

A *p.*'s name, by making thee the theme *Ch.* 14
The painter's pencil, and the *p.*'s lyre *Ch.* 106
Would humble many a towering *p.*'s pride *Ch.* 536
And spare the *p.* for his subject's sake *Ch.* 636
P., are sometimes apt to maul the thing *Con.* 290
A *p.* does not work by square or line *Con.* 789
Two P. (*p.*, by report *Dr.* 1
They best can judge a *p.*'s worth *Dr.* 5
At any *p.*'s happier lays *Dr.* 15
But when a *p.* takes the pen *E.* i 9
Alas for the *p.*! who dares undertake *F.M.* 13
P.'s goods are not often so fine *Gr.* 54
The *p.* will swear that I dream *Gr.* 55
I slur a name a *p.* must not speak) *H.* 555
A painter's skill into a *p.*'s hand *H.* 670
The faithful monitor's and *p.*'s part *H.* 757
To *p.* of renown in song *J.P.* 17
P. attempt the noblest task they can *J.T.* 1
Appealed to many a *p.*'s page *L.R.* 11
The Plume and P. both we know *Mrs. M—* 53
Both P. saves and Plume from fading *Mrs. M—* 55
A *p.*'s drop of ink? *O.* i 12
No matter when—a *p.*'s Muse is *P.* 23
A *p.*, in his evening walk *P.* 39
So, ancient *p.* say, serene *Q.V.* 69
At such a sight to catch the *p.*'s flame *R.* 85
For such a cause the P. seeks the shade *R.* 188
Yet let a *p.* (Poetry disarms *R.* 253
Oh! grant a *p.* leave to recommend *R.* 541
(A *p.* fond of Nature and your friend) *R.* 542
A monitor's, though not a *p.*'s praise *R.* 806
A *p.*'s cat, sedate and grave *R.C.* 1
As *p.* well could wish to have *R.C.* 2
That night, by chance, the *p.* watching *R.C.* 77
Then stepped the *p.* into bed *R.C.* 107
Hear him, himself the *p.* and the theme *T.* 404
The P.'s treasure, silence, and indulge *T.* i 235
Which only *p.* know. The shifts and turns *T.* ii 286
Are occupations of the *p.*'s mind *T.* ii 298
The *p.*'s or historian's page by one *T.* iv 158
To books, to music, or the *p.*'s toil *T.* iv 262
That *p.* celebrate; those golden times *T.* iv 514
Sat for the picture; and the *p.*'s hand *T.* iv 526
Then Milton had indeed a *p.*'s charms *T.* iv 709
By *p.*, and by senators unpraised *T.* v 539
Encomium in old time was *p.*'s work *T.* vi 715
But *p.*, having lavishly long since *T.* vi 716
Foretold by prophets, and by *p.* sung *T.* vi 731
But when a *p.*, or when one like me *T.* vi 751
In vain the *p.* sings, and the world hears *T.* vi 1018
Of *p.* raised by you, and statesmen, and divines *Tir.* 283
And, of all lies (be that one *p.* boast) *T.T.* 87
P., of all men, ever least regret *T.T.* 176 [198
When themes like these employ the *p.*'s tongue *T.T.*
And move the lips of *p.* cast in lead *T.T.* 203
The *p.*'s muse, his passion, and his theme *T.T.* 289
An English *p.*'s privilege to rant *T.T.* 299
Of prophet and of *p.* was the same *T.T.* 501
At Westminster, where little *p.*'s strive *T.T.* 506
I was a *p.* too: but modern taste *T.T.* 510
The *p.*'s heart; he looks to distant storms *T.T.* 495
Hence British *p.* to the priesthood shared *T.T.* 502
As if the *p.*, purposing to wed *T.T.* 554
Vouchsafes to man a *p.*'s just pretence *T.T.* 699
Thus graced, the man asserts the *p.*'s name *T.T.* 714
The *p.*'s lyre, to fix his fame *U.* 25
Should be the *p.*'s heart *U.* 26
I sink the *p.* in the friend *U.* 30

POETIC.

The pangs of a *p.* birth *Dr.* 7
With all the embroidery of *p.* dreams *Ex.* 234
Saluting his *p.* ears *R.C.* 89

POETIC—POLITE

Streams tinkle sweetly in *p.* chime *R.* 568
Feebly and vainly, at *p.* fame) *R.* 802
To serve occasions of *p.* pomp *T.* i 152
There is a pleasure in *p.* pains *T.* ii 285
Ye sage dispensers of *p.* fame *T.* iii 457
And Sidney, warbler of *p.* prose *T.* iv 516
Sportive and jingling her *p.* bells *T.* iv 702
And with *p.* trappings grace thy prose *T.* v 679
Happy to rove among *p.* flowers *T.* vi 752
A skilful guide into *p.* ground ! *T.T.* 717
'Twould thin the ranks of the *p.* tribe *T.T.* 768

POETICAL.

I indulge my *p.* moods *Gr.* 51

POETRY.

P. may, but colours cannot paint *Con.* 384
By letting *p.* alone! *E.* iv 10
Yet let a poet (*P.* disarms *R.* 253
Me *p.* (or rather notes that aim *R.* 801
In such a palace *P.* might place *T.* v 138
Of *p.* not lost, if verse of mine *T.* vi 726
Had faded, *p.* was not an art *T.T.* 585
Made *p.* a mere mechanic art *T.T.* 654
Which now and then sweet *P.* may cure *T.T.* 743
A theme for *p.* divine 1789, 29

POINT.

The *p.* in dispute was, as all the world knows *A.C.* 3
Armed at all *p.*, with terror on his brow *A.T.* 140
Truth armed it with a *p.* so keen, so just *A.T.* 145
Struck thrice the *p.* upon his saddle bow *A.T.* 166
The turns are quick, the polished *p.* surprise *Ch.* 544
Who vote for hire, or *p.* it with lampoon *Con.* 29
A disputable *p.* is no man's ground *Con.* 99
To press your *p.* with modesty and ease *Con.* 104
He makes one useful *p.* exceeding clear *Con.* 136
The *P.* of Honour has been deemed of use *Con.* 163
As bastions set *p.* blank against God's will *Con.* 688
On *p.* which God has left at large *F.* 136
Where Science *p.* her telescopic eye *H.* 441
And thus he left the *p.* at large *L.W.* 8
That Virtue *p.* to? Can a life thus spent *P.E.* 72
P. to inscriptions wheresoe'er they tread *P.E.* 391
Within the small dimensions of a *p. R.* 58
Wherever freakish Fancy *p.* the way *R.* 128
The *p.* of interest or the post of power *R.* 142
P. out a conflict with thyself, the worst *R.* 268 [92
For he has touched them. From the extremest *p. T.* ii
In vain he *p.* his powers against the skies *T.* 469 [808
Their *p.* obtuse, and feathers drunk with wine ! *T.* ii
The parallax of yonder luminous *p. T.* iii 215
To its just *p.*—the service of mankind *T.* iii 372 [44
And bored with elbow *p.* through both his sides *T.* iv
At the sword's *p.*, and dyeing the white robe *T.* iv 682
Twins at all *p.*—yet this obtains in all *T.* iv 738
Their only *p.* of rest, Eternal Word ! *T.* v 897 [129
P., which, unless the Scripture made them plain *Tir.*
P. to the cure, describe a Saviour's cross *Tir.* 165
Subsist and centre in one *p.*—a friend *Tir.* 390
A *p.* secured, if once he be supplied *Tir.* 698
From what *p.* blows the weather *Trans.* ii 9
As one at *p.* to die *Y.D.* 10

POINTED.

A trick upon the canvass, *p.* flame *Con.* 782
Shaggy, and lean, and shrewd, with *p.* ears *T.* v 45
And blunts his *p.* fury ; in its case *T.* vi 193
With *p.* hoof dibbling the glebe, prepared *Y.O.* 26

POINTERS.

With belted waist and *p.* at their heels *T.* ii 753

POINTING.

Shows with a *p.* finger, but no noise *H.* 221
While we retrace with Memory's *p.* wand *T.* iv 183

POISE.

Who *p.* and proportions sea and land *Ex.* 342
And smiles delighted with the eternal *p. T.* iv 486

POISED.

His well *p.* estimate of right and wrong *H.* 611

POISING.

And after *p.* her adventurous wings *R.* 671

POISON.

To *p.* vermin that infest his plants *Con.* 256
While others *p.* what the flock must drink *Ex.* 100
Now, while the *p.* all high life pervades *P.E.* 347

POISONED.

And *p.* every virtue in them both *T.* 116

POISONING.

P. the waters where their swarms abound *P.E.* 481

POISONOUS.

The *p.*, black, insinuating worm *P.E.* 7

POLAR.

The rage and rigour of a *p.* sky *H.* 462

POLE.

His freeborn brethren of the southern *p. Ch.* 34
To give the *p.* the produce of the sun *Ch.* 125
Till the last fire burn all between the *p. Con.* 756
From the world's girdle to the frozen *p. Ex.* 20
True as a needle to the *p. F.* 110   [*H.* 746
But these shall last when night has quenched the *p.*
Between two *p.* upon a stick transverse *T.* i 561
Night veiled the *p.* ; all seemed secure *T.B.* 31

POLICY.

To disconcert what *P.* has planned *Ex.* 299
Where *P.* is busied, all night long *Ex.* 300
Safe *p.*, but hateful *F.* 183
Of the edifice that *p.* has raised *T.* ii 817
The manners, customs, *p.* of all *T.* iv 109

POLISH.

And toil to *p.* its rough coat alone *P.E.* 420
And, while she *p.*, perverts the taste *R.* 704
And keep the *p.* of the manners clean *R.* 733
No *p.* can make sterling ; and that vice *T.* vi 990
To *p.*, furnish, and delight the mind *T.T.* 645

POLISHED.

So *p.* and compact from head to heel *A.T.* 184
The turns are quick, the *p.* points surprise *Ch.* 544
Our *p.* manners are a mask we wear *Con.* 166
'Tis ready *p.* from the mine " *E,* iv 90
If every *p.* gem we find *F,* 7
Cards with what rapture, and the *p.* die *P.E.* 171
Thou *p.* and high-finished foe to truth *P.E.* 341
But the same word that, like *p.* share *T.* 459
And though himself so *p.*, still reprieves *T.* i 264
Peep through their *p.* foliage at the storm *T.* iii 574
Of thought, the creature of a *p.* mind *T.* iii 640
No : we are *p.* now !   The rural lass *T.* iv 534
See that your *p.* arms be primed with care *T.* iv 567
The *p.* counter, and approving none *T.* vi 281 [561
(Though graced with *p.* manners and fine sense *T.*vi
And stroke his *p.* cheek of purest red *Tir,* 847
And bend her *p.* neck beneath his hand *T.T.* 441
Adorn the *p.* periods as they fall *T.T,* 766

POLITE.

Be never named in ears esteemed *p. Con.* 474
So manners decent and *p. F.* 178
Poured forth by Beauty splendid and *p. T.* ii 494
Their weariness ; and they the most *p. T.* ii 640

POLITE—POPE

As ornamental, musical, *p. T.* iv 489
P. Refinement offers him in vain *T.* vi 977
Or hadst thou a *p.*, card-playing wife *Tir.* 743
P., yet virtuous, who has brought away *V.* 79

POLITELY.
And Echo learns *p.* to repeat *Con.* 827
P. learned, and of a gentle race *H.* 682
And many a compliment *p.* penned *T.T.* 721

POLITER.
Which some may practise with *p.* grace *T.* iv 494
To give thee what *p.* France receives *T.* v 468

POLITESSE.
And being always primed with *p. P.E.* 387

POLITIC.
The threads of *p.* and shrewd design *T.* iii 147
In *p.* convention) put your trust *T.* v 323

POLITICS.
Their heterogeneous *p. F.* 128
But the age of virtuous *p.* is past *T.* v 493

POLL.
With golden wing and satin *p. P.T.* 27
The honours of his ebon *p. T.B.* 13
P. gains at length the British shore *Trans.* iv 4
As *P.* can master it *Trans.* iv 9
Sweet *P.*! his doting mistress cries *Trans.* iv 13
Sweet *P.*! the mimic bird replies *Trans.* iv 14
Poor *P.* is like to die! *Trans.* iv 30

POLLUTING.
P. Egypt: gardens, fields, and plains *T.* ii 828

POMONA.
Female and male, *P.*, Pales, Pan *T.* vi 233

POMP. [*P.E.* 54
Power, *P.*, and Splendour, and the Thirst of Praise
Thy *p.* is in the grave, thy glory laid *Ch.* 71
The *p.* of sound, or tinkle without use *Con.* 892
Mere shadows now, their ancient *p.* forgot *Ex.* 262
For truth self-evident, with *p.* impressed *H.* 109
To serve occasions of poetic *p. T.* i 152
Our palaces, our ladies, and our *p. T.* i 643
The Levee swarms, as if in golden *p. T.* iii 822 [448
In unsuspecting *p.* Twitched from the perch *T.* iv
With all its majesty of thundering *p. T.* iv 686
By pyramids and mausolean *p. T.* v 183
That fill the skies nightly with silent *p. T.* v 817
Or bids the rocks in ruder *p.* arise *Tir.* 28

POMPOUS.
The lure of avarice, or the *p.* prize *R.* 177
A *p.* and slow-moving pageant comes *T.* vi 697
Proving at last, though told in *p.* strains *Tir.* 75

POND.
Ducks paddle in the *p.*, before the door *R.* 499

PONDER.
Come, *p.* well, for 'tis no jest *Y.D.* 1

PONDERED.
Is adverse Providence when *p.* well *Ex.* 310 [33
They spoke, and Tom *p.*—"I see they will go *P.A.*

PONDEROUS.
P., and fixed by its own massy weight *T.* i 59 [636
Is needful. Strength may wield the *p.* spade *T.* iii
In *p.* boots beside his reeking team *T.* iv 342

PONIARD.
Prepared to *p.* whomsoe'er they meet *Ch.* 508
Worse than a *p.* in the basest hand *P.E.* 305

PONY.
To cross his ambling *p.* day by day *R.* 467

POOL.
Flies to the tempting *p.*, or felon knife *T.* 446
The rivers die into offensive *p. T.* ii 96
Pure, from so foul a *p.*, to shine abroad *T.* ii 798
From *p.* and ditches of the commonwealth *T.* iii 809

POOR.
"And now," quoth *p.* unthinking Ralph *A Fable* 18
He found it inconvenient to be *p. Ch.* 189
To smite the *p.* is treason against God *Ch.* 217 [312
The *p.* thy clients, and Heaven's smile thy fee! *Ch.*
Must cease for ever when the *p.* shall cease *Ch.* 452
Her superfluity the *p.* supplies *Ch.* 455
His Budget, often filled, yet always *p. Ch.* 614
Oppression, labouring hard to grind the *p. Ex.* 40
To tempt the *p.* to sell himself to thee? *Ex.* 375
"Look to the *p.*; the simple and the plain *Ex.* 452
The *p.*, inured to drudgery and distress *H.* 7
The rich grow *p.*, the *p.* become purse-proud *H.* 18
That *p.* Jonquil, with almost every breath *H.* 89
The *p.* reclaimed inhabitant, his eyes *H.* 532
The comfort of a few *p.*, added days *H.* 729
"Dismiss *p.* Harry!" he replies *M.F.* 19
Till life's *p.* transient night is spent *N.G.* 32
If we do not buy the *p.* creatures, they will *P.A.* 11
Besides the man's *p.*, his orchard's his bread *P.A.* 27
P. man! what a pity to injure him so! *P.A.* 34
Have you no touch of pity that the *p. P.E.* 249
With all the simple and unlettered *p. P.E.* 506
P. Jack—no matter who—for when I blame *R.* 575
For what *p.* toys they can disclaim *St.* vi 15
The *p.* are near at hand, the charge is small *T.* 287
The *p.* should gain it, and the rich should not? *T.* 340
Sounds for the *p.*, but sounds alike for all *T.* 350
Of ladyships, a stranger to the *p. T.* ii 386 [658
Their last *p.* pittance—Fortune, most severe *T.* ii
The little wick of life's *p.* shallow lamp *T.* iii 164
But which the *p.*, and the despised of all *T.* iii 287
Should some contagion, kind to the *p.* brutes *T.* iii 308
Drained to the last *p.* item of his wealth *T.* iii 784
Begs a propitious ear for his *p.* thoughts *T.* iv 68
Thy waggon is thy wife, and the *p.* beasts *T.* iv 367
P., yet industrious, modest, quiet, neat *T.* iv 374
I mean the man who, when the distant *p. T.* iv 427
Disgraced as thou hast been, *p.* as thou art *T.* v 475
Of Nature, and though *p.* perhaps compared *T.* v 739
Give what Thou canst, without thee we are *p. T.* v 905
Of the *p.* brute, seems wisely to suppose *T.* vi 437
Though *p.* in skill to rear them, lights at last *T.* vi 753
And e'en the joy that haply some *p.* heart *T.* vi 832
Leaving the *p.* no remedy but tears *T.* vi 845
A dream disturbed *p.* Bully's rest *T.B.* 44
He left *p.* Bully's beak *T.B.* 54
Alas, *p.* boy!—the natural effect *Tir.* 575
But *p.* in knowledge, having none to impart *Tir.* 663
P. Poll is like to die! *Trans.* iv 30
Feels not the wants that pinch the *p. Trans. H.* 10
All kingship, and may I be *p.* and free! *T.T.* 150
P. England! thou art a devoted deer *T.T.* 362
While the *p.* grasshopper must chirp below *T.T.* 577

POOREST.
Alas, not so! the *p.* of the flock *Ex.* 456

POPE.
Thy soldiery, the *P.'s* well-managed pack *Ex.* 518
Insist on, as if each were his own *p. H.* 213
And Murray sighs o'er *P.*, and Swift *M.* i 5 [*R.* 572
When *P.* describes them, have a thousand sweets
Girt with a bell-rope that the *p.* has blessed *T.* 82
For though the *P.* has lost his interest here *T.* 289

I praise a school as *P*. a government *Tir.* 506
Then *P*., as harmony itself exact *T.T.* 646   [764
Though Butler's wit, *P.'s* numbers, Prior's ease *T.T.*

POPISH.
At *P.* practices observed within *P.E.* **384**

POPLAR.
The *p.* are felled ;—farewell to the shade *P.F.* 1
And *p.* that with silver lines his leaf *T.* i 310

POPULAR.
To streams of *p.* opinion drawn *P.E.* 478
O *P.* Applause! what heart of man *T.* ii 481
Of *p.* disgust, yet boldly still *T.* iii 706
The *p.* harangue, the tart reply *T.* iv 31
But that they catch at *p.* applause *T.T.* 144

POPULARITY.
Thy *p.*, and art become *Y.O.* 57

POPULATION.
Large *p.* on a liberal plan *A.T.* 157

POPULOUS.
And sheep-walks *p.* with bleating lambs *T.* vi 111

PORCELAIN.
Except in *p.* on her mantle-tree *Ch.* 460

PORING.
And *p.* on thy page, whose every line *R.* 207
In the red cinders, while with *p.* eye *T.* iv 289
Not to be found by *p.* on a book *Tir.* 384

PORK.
Good Mussulman, abstain from *p. L.W.* 2

PORT.
'Twere vain inquiry to what *p.* she went *Ch.* 445
Shoots into *p.* at some well-havened isle *M.P.* 90
Always from *p.* withheld, always distressed *M.P.* 101
But with his clumsy *p.* the wretch has lost *T.* iv 650
And read with such discernment, in the *p. T.* vi 617

PORTAL.
Inscribed above the *p.*, from afar *T.* 28

PORTENDS.
A pimple that *p.* a future sprout *T.* iii 528

PORTENDING.
A presage ominous, *p.* still *T.* v 625

PORTENTOUS.
P., unexampled, unexplained *T.* ii 58

PORTION.
The *p.* of a mean or vulgar mind *R.* 502
Your *p.* is with them; nay, never frown *T.* 169
With hopeful gems. The rest, no *p.* left *T.* iii 421
Chains are the *p.* of revolted man *T.* v 581
His *p.* in the good that Heaven bestows *T.T.* 20

PORTRAIT.
Such was the *p.* an apostle drew *Ch.* 432

PORTRAYED.
Pleased she beheld aloft *p. Q.V.* 45

PORTUGAL.
Of *P.* and Western India there *T.* iii 572

POSITION.
Flew to its first *p.*, with a spring *T.T.* 623

POSITIVE.
The *p.* pronounce without dismay *Con.* 146

POSSESS.
May it still be her lot to *p. C.* 43
That, while they please, *p.* us with alarms *Ch.* 546
Invades, *p.*, and o'erwhelms the soul *H.* 730
He may *p.* the joys he thinks he sees *R.* 11
Believe, rush forward, and *p.* the prize *T.* 374
P. herself of all that's good or true *T.* 489
P. for me their undisputed lot *T.* 527
Here, I have said, at least I should *p. T.* i 234
P. ye, therefore, ye who, borne about *T.* i 754
But such as Art contrives, *p.* ye still *T.* i 757
What could I wish, that I *p.* not here? *T.* iii 690
Of freedom, in that hope itself *p. T.* v 375
"And to *p.* a brighter Heaven than yours? *T.* v 831
P. the heart, and fables false as hell *T.* v 862

POSSESSED.
An isle *p.* by creatures of our kind *Ch.* 381
Lives the dear thought of joys he once *p. Con.* 703
While all the happy man *p.* before *Con.* 895
Peculiar is the grace by thee *p. Ex.* 580
By joys *p.*, and joys still held in chase *Ex.* 669
As Envy pines at good *p. F.* 79
Of numerous charms *p. J.P.* 2
What favour then not yet *p. N.Y.G.* 9
Till half mankind were like himself *p. P.E.* 471
While Peace *p.* these silent bowers *S.* 14
So spake Aspasio, firm *p. St.* iii 13
By some kind, hospitable heart *p. T.* 251
Upon the ship's tall side he stands, *p. T.* i 450
P. an inland scene. Where now the throng *T.* ii 117
But if he grant a friend, that boon *p. V.* 91
Then peace and joy again *p.* 1789, 46

POSSESSING.
In peace *p.* what they won by war *Ex.* 193
Determined, and *p.* it at last *T.* iv 720
If all we find *p.* earth, sea, air *Tir.* 91
P. nought but the scooped rind that seems *Y.O.* 111

POSSESSION.
Which amounts to *p.* time out of mind" *A.C.* 12
The rich *p.* of a nobler prize *Ch.* 360
Will boast it their *p.? F.* 3
Shortlived *p.*! but the record fair *M.P.* 54
Surveyed the scene, and took *p. R.C.* 44

POSSESSOR.
Beneath your shades your grey *p.* hide *R.* 368
A new *p.*, and survives the change *T.* ii 110
That soothe the rich *p.*; much consoled *T.* iv 755
And that, *p.* of a soul refined *Tir.* 721
Wouldst thou, *p.* of a flock, employ *Tir.* 905
To make the pitiful *p.* shine *T.T.* 755

POST.
A fancied head against a fancied *p. A.T.* 45
The *p.* that at his bidding speeds away *Ex.* 355 [374
And every *p.*, and where the chaise broke down *P.E.*
The point of interest or the *p.* of power *R.* 142
P. away swiftly to more active scenes *R.* 273
He chides the tardiness of every *p. R.* 475
For want of powers proportionate to the *p. R.* 612
Advancing Fashion to the *p.* of Truth *T.* i 744
To occupy a sacred, awful *p. Tir.* 414
His *p.* not mean, his talents not unknown *Tir.* 723
To fit thee for a nobler *p.* than thine *V.* 32

POSTBOY.
Went *p.* at his heels *J.G.* 230
The *p.'s* horse right glad to miss *J.G.* 231
With *p.* scampering in the rear *J.G.* 235

POSTED.
And *p.* on this speculative height *T.* i 289
To those who, *p.* at the shrine of Truth *T.* v 713

POSTERITY.
Thy p. shall sway B. 30
Now make our own. P. will ask T. ii 577
(If e'er p. see verse of mine) T. ii 578

POST-HORNS.
The p. of all Europe, lays her waste T.T. 32

POSTING.
Her husband p. down J.G. 214

POSTPONED.
His praise p., and never to be paid T. 86

POSTURE.
Now, in a p. that becomes you more Con. 489

POSY.
He called her P., with an amorous art A.T. 21

POT.
Models of Herculanean p. and pans P.E. 398
In an old empty watering p. R.C. 16
And glossy, he commits to p. of size T. iii 512

POTENT.
With magic wand. So p. is the spell T. ii 630
And p. to resist the freezing blast T. iii 465

POUNCE.
Stooped from its highest pitch to p. a wren T.T. 553

POUND.
"'Tis for a thousand p.!" J.G. 116
And his old stint—three thousand p. a year R. 602

POUR. [Con. 908
It sounds Jehovah's name, and p. his praise along
And p. a torrent of sweet notes around Ch. 111
Than those a brighter season p. around Con. 648
To p. his golden tide through all her gates Ex. 14
To p. down wrath upon a thankless land Ex. 253
He p. contempt on them, and on their cause Ex. 329
P. out a flood of splendour upon thine Ex. 589
Her sons to p. it on the farthest north H. 460
Again p. ruin on the vale below Her. 38
Where no volcano p. his fiery flood Her. 85
Then p. it on the morals of thy son P.E. 345
P. out its fleecy tenants o'er the glebe T. i 291
P. she not all her choicest fruits abroad T. ii 85
A parent p. into regardless ears Tir. 590
To p. in Virtue's lap her just reward T.T. 65
Winter invades the spring, and often p. T.T. 210
Vengeance at last p. down upon their coast T.T. 47
She p. a sensibility divine T.T. 486

POURED.
P. out from Plenty's overflowing horn Ex. 10
The favours p. upon the Jewish name Ex. 170
Had p. the day, and cleared the Roman skies Ex. 228
Their streaming hearts p. freely when they died Ex. 625
Ten thousand rivers p. at his command R. 75
P. forth by Beauty splendid and polite T. ii 494
Have p. my stream of panegyric down T. vi 720
Fair science p. the light of truth Th. 3
With truths p. down from every distant age Tir. 14

POVERTY.
No soil like p. for growth divine T. 363
And craving P., and in the bow T. ii 490
That lean hard-handed P. inflicts T. iii 827
But p., with most who whimper forth T. iv 429
Of P., that thus he may procure T. v 318
Is cause of half the p. we feel T. vi 52

POWDERED.
No p. pert proficient in the art T. iv 145
Then shakes his p. coat, and barks for joy T. v 51

POWER.
Hypothesis (for with such magic p. A.T. 91
"The marriage bond has lost its p. to bind A.T. 101
And so long he, with unspent p. Cast. 39
The sword shall light upon thy boasted p. Ch. 79
He from whose hands alone all p. proceeds Ch. 208
Enjoy immunity from priestly p. Ch. 273 [224
Else who would lose, that had the p. to improve Ch.
He too has a connecting p., and draws Ch. 327
And what dilates the p. must needs refine Ch. 332
Unless the p. that bade him stand, restore Ch. 348
Where stands that monument of ancient p. Ch. 549
He bruised beneath his feet the infernal p. Ch. 584
Relenting forms would lose their p. or cease Ch. 608
Infectious as impure, your blighting p. Con. 41 [431
The reasoning p. vouchsafed of course inferred Con.
Ye p. who rule the tongue, if such there are Con. 81
The p. to clothe that reason with his word Con. 432
And speech may praise the p. that bids it flow Con. 444
Ought at the view of an Almighty p. Con. 658 [501
Touched by that p. that you have dared to mock Con.
That love of Christ in all its quickening p. Con. 562
That comes to waft us out of sorrow's p. Con. 592
Not as if raised by mere mechanic p. Con. 706
Mysterious are his ways whose p. E. i 29
Or guess, with a prophetic p. E. i 71
And placed it in our p. to prove E. i 103
By p. divine, and skill that could not err Ex. 206
With p. surpassing theirs, performed her part Ex. 230
Countries indebted to thy p., that shine Ex. 280
Blind to the working of that secret P. Ex. 320 [402
What mean they? Canst thou dream there is a p. Ex.
A despot big with p. obtained by wealth Ex. 370
Legates and delegates, with p. from hell Ex. 514
Found thee a goodly sponge for P. to press Ex. 531
O slave! with p. thou didst not dare exert Ex. 546
And He, whose p. mere nullity obeys Ex. 642 [568
His p. secured thee, when presumptuous Spain Ex.
Stood trembling at the boldness of thy p. Ex. 597
But if He leave thee, though the skill and p. Ex. 702
His names of wisdom, goodness, p., and love H. 135
When captivating lusts have lost their p. H. 216
His sovereign p. and pleasure unrestrained H. 320
P. of the mind, and feelings of the heart H. 654
The silent progress of thy p. is such H. 665
His grief the world of all her p. disarms H. 704
Say man's a worm, and p. belongs to God H. 711
But oh! what Muse, and in what p. of song Her. 19
Where P. secures what Industry has won Her. 87
Its use and p. exemplified in thee J.T. 50
The sceptre of her p. L.R. 16
In justice to the various p. Miss — 17
His p. of best exertion there Mor. 32
Thyself removed, thy p. to soothe me left M.P. 121
Tarnish all your boasted p. N.C. 54
For 'twas the self-same P. Divine N.G. 19
Nor riches I, nor p. pursue O. ii 4 [P.E. 54
P., Pomp, and Splendour, and the Thirst of Praise
Unnerves the moral p., and mars their use P.E. 272
The heart, surrendered to the ruling p. P.E. 275
Oh that a verse had p., and could command P.E. 323
But teems with p. he never felt before P.E. 404
Free from the domineering p. of Lust P.E. 458
How shall I speak thee, or thy p. address P.E. 460
And own his crab-computing p. o'ercome P.E. 487
Die then, if p. Almighty save you not P.E. 589
There, and there only, is the p. to save P.E. 616
Remind him of his Maker's p. and love R. 30
And draining its nutritious p. to feed R. 43

The signature and stamp of *p.* divine *R.* 54
Thy *p.* divine, and bounty beyond thought *R.* 91
Conscious of weakness in its noblest *p. R.* 124
The point of interest or the post of *p. R.* 142
Next to that *p.* who formed thee and sustains *R.* 201
And feed the fire that wastes thy *p.* away *R.* 264
Lost, till he tune them, all their *p.* and use *R.* 330
On whom he rests well pleased his weary *p. R.* 451
The spot he loved has lost the *p.* to please *R.* 466
As wisely, and as much improves his *p. R.* 508
Much of the *p.* and majesty of God *R.* 526
Influence, and *p.*, were all at his command *R.* 596
For want of *p.* proportioned to the post *R.* 612
To mark the matchless workings of the *P.—R.* 791
Has lost its beauties and its *p. S.* 16
Thy generous *p.*, but silence honoured thee *S.* i 7
And still has *p.* to charm *St.* v 16
Whence has the world her magic *p.? St.* v 17
By native *p.* and energy her own *T.* 396
The self-restoring arm of human *p. T.* 402
In vain he points his *p.* against the skies *T.* 469
Some love of virtue, and some *p.* to praise *T.* 486
Still soothing, and of *p.* to charm me still *T.* i 143
The *p.* of fancy and strong thought are theirs *T.* i 402
May rival these; these all bespeak a *p. T.* i 431
From which no *p.* of thine can raise her up *T.* i 660
The *p.* of sculpture, but the style as much *T.* i 706
Not coloured like his own, and having *p. T.* ii 13
Of all your empire; that where Britain's *p. T.* ii 46
Denies the *p.* that wields it. God proclaims *T.* ii 178
Of its legitimate, peculiar *p.*) *T.* ii 333 [487
And therefore heedless, can withstand thy *p.? T.* ii
That bids defiance to the united *p. T.* ii 769
Played by the creatures of a *P.* who swears *T.* iii 177
Such *p.* I boast not—neither can I rest *T.* iii 217
Distempered, or has lost prolific *p. T.* iii 415
The ambition of one meaner far, whose *p. T.* iii 458
Than Sodom in her day had *p.* to be *T.* iii 847 [282
Laugh ye, who boast your more mercurial *p. T.* iv
The recollected *p.*, and snapping short *T.* iv 305
Increase of *p.* begets increase of wealth *T.* iv 580
Ere yet her ear was mistress of their *p. T.* iv 703
With forms so various, that no *p.* of art *T.* v 108
And in defiance of her rival *p. T.* v 123
May exercise amiss his proper *p. T.* v 339
Not often unsuccessful: *p.* usurped *T.* v 371
Which monarchs cannot grant, nor all the *p. T.* v 540
Oppression, prisons, have no *p.* to bind *T.* v 543
And sordid gravitation of his *p. T.* v 588
Spare not in such a cause. Spend all the *p. T.* v 676
More worthily the *p.* she owned before *T.* v 807
They are thy witnesses, who speak thy *p. T.* v 853
Thy Providence forbids that fickle *p. T.* v 871
(If *p.* she be that works but to confound) *T.* v 872
By the impure, and hears his *p.* denied *T.* v 895
What prodigies can *p.* divine perform *T* vi 118
Vast was his empire, absolute his *p. T.* vi 357
O'er all we feed on *p.* of life and death *T.* vi 453
The impious challenger of *p.* divine *T.* vi 546
(O wonderful effect of music's *p.*!) *T.* vi 636 [vi 925
Whose *p.* is such, that whom she lifts from earth *T.*
Vast in its *p.*, ethereal in its kind *Tir.* 6
And owns her *p.* on every shore he laves? *Tir.* 40
P. misemploy'd, munificence misplaced *Tir.* 50
Sit for the *p.* in which he stands array'd *Tir.* 98
A *p.*, confessed so lately on his knees *Tir.* 180 [188
Resumes her *p.*, and spurns the clumsy fraud *Tir.*
Lest *p.* exerted, but without success *Tir.* 277
Such microscopic proof of skill and *p. Tir.* 637
'Tis *p.* almighty bids him shine *Trans.* i 23
Of adverse fortune's *p. Trans. H.* 3
The tallest pines feel most the *p. Trans. H.* 13
Or tell me, if you can, what *p.* maintains *T.T.* 200

Seldom, alas! the *p.* of logic reigns *T.T.* 51 [*T.T.* 42
And Death's own scythe would better speak his *p.*
Not formed like us, with such Herculean *p. T.T.* 235
His fostering *p.*, and tutelary care *T.T.* 257
Lost without thee the ennobling *p.* of verse *T.T.* 291
Too apt to play the wanton with her *p. T.T.* 301
To manage with address, to seize with *p. T.T.* 358
The *p.* that Sin has brought to a decline *T.T.* 383
Unless sweet Penitence her *p.* renew *T.T.* 398 [490
The strings are swept with such a *p.*, so loud *T.T.*
Make their heroic *p.* your own at once *T.T.* 570 [497
And armed with strength surpassing human *p. T.T.*
The proud Protector of the *p.* he gained *T.T.* 611
Churchill, himself unconscious of his *p. T.T.* 672
Nature exerting an unwearied *p. T.T.* 690 [*T.T.* 610
When Cromwell fought for *p.*, and while he reigned
Fancy has sported all her *p.* away *T.T.* 730
How are the *p.* of genius misapplied! *T.T.* 749

POWERFUL.

Prosper (I press thee with a *p.* plea) *Ch.* 5
The spur is *p.*, and I grant its force *Tir.* 482

PRACTICE.

Reduced to *p.*, his beloved rule *Con.* 139
The *p.* dastardly, and mean, and low *Con.* 178
At Popish *p.* observed within *P.E.* 384
The *p.* was a bond upon his heart *Tir.* 177
Nor gambling *p.* can find it out *Tir.* 246

PRACTISE.

Which some may *p.* with politer grace *T.* iv 494

PRACTISED.

The same we *p.* at first sight *F.* 179
And start theatric, *p.* at the glass! *T.* ii 431

PRAISE.

Who seeks to *p.* thee, and to make thee known *Ch.* 9
God's gift with pleasure in his *p.* employ *Ch.* 252
My soul should yield thee willing thanks and *p. Ch.* 264
But that were sacrilege;—*p.* is not thine *Ch.* 266
But though we *p.* the exact designer's skill *Ch.* 555
Names almost worthy of a Christian's *p. Con.* 36 [444
And speech may *p.* the power that bids it flow *Con.*
O days of heaven, and nights of equal *p.! Con.* 567
And prize them above pleasure, wealth, or *p. Con.* 662
The *p.* of names for ages obsolete *Con.* 828
No envy mingles with our *p. Dr.* 13 [*Con.* 908
It sounds Jehovah's name, and pours his *p.* along
Is to congratulate, not to *p. E.* ii 2
P. is the medium of a knavish trade *E.* ii 6
Snuffs up the *p.* of what he seems to plan *Ex.* 317
Of his just *p.*, to lavish it on them? *Ex.* 349 [643
Who found thee nothing, formed thee for his *p. Ex.*
To *p.* him is to serve him, and fulfil *Ex.* 644
A tax upon their own just *p. F.* 89 [*H.* 741
Rocks, groves, and streams, must join him in his *p.*
Then *p.* is heard instead of reasoning pride *H.* 143
That make superior skill his second *p. H.* 206
And echoing *p.*, such as fiends might earn *Her.* 61
P. his proficiency, and dub him man *P.E.* 368 [54
Power, Pomp, and Splendour, and the thirst of *p. P.E.*
The *p.* of wisdom, comeliness, and worth *P.E.* 295
And *p.* his genius, he is soon repaid *P.E.* 532
In *p.* applied to the same part—his head *P.E.* 533
Whose highest *p.* is that they live in vain *R.* 23
That builds its glory on its Maker's *p. R.* 210
A laugh at his expense, is slender *p. R.* 318
When boyish innocence was all my *p.*!) *R.* 372
Till Gratitude grew vocal in the *p. R.* 555
I *p.* the Frenchman, his remark was shrewd *R.* 739
The sense of mercy kindles into *p. R.* 778
A monitor's, though not a poet's *p. R.* 806

PRAISE—PRAYER

His p. postponed, and never to be paid T. 86
A soul redeemed demands a life of p. T. 279
Receives no p., but, though her lot be such T. 325
The p. of the libertine professed T. 433
Some love of virtue, and some power to p. T. 486
Thou knowest my p. of Nature most sincere T. i 150
P. justly due to those that I describe T. i 180
She has her p., Now mark a spot or two T. i 725
Time was, when it was p. and boast enough T. ii 233
That we were born her children. P. enough T. ii 235
Go then, well worthy of the p. ye seek T. ii 278
P. from the rivelled lips of toothless, bald T. ii 488
Be loudest in their p. who do no more T. ii 314 [712
That blushed at its own p.; and press the youth T. ii
His name a theme for p. and for reproach? T. iii 282
Gives him his p., and forfeits not her own T. iii 247
Pant for the p. of dressing to the taste T. iii 460
What we admire we p., and when we p. T. iii 702
Sweet bashfulness! it claims at least this p. T. iv 70
Start at his awful name, or deem his p. T. iv 180
I p. you much, ye meek and patient pair T. iv 407
To Nature's p. Heroes and their feats T. iv 705
Pathetic in its p., in its pursuit T. iv 719
And·be our admiration and our p." T. v 259
His thorns with streamers of continual p.? T. v 330
Causeless, and daubed with undiscerning p. T. v 360
Doomed it, as insufficient for his p. T. v 565
But gives the glorious sufferers little p. T. v 732
Whose heart with p., and whose exalted mind T. v 751
Of rant and rhapsody in virtue's p. T. v 677 [v 792
With what he views. The landscape has his p. T.
Much more who fashioned it, he gives it p. T. v 801
P. that from earth resulting, as it ought T. v 802
A teaching voice; but 'tis the p. of thine T. v 858
And adds his rapture to the general p. T. v 890
The inglorious feat, and, clamorous in p. T. vi 436
Man p. man. Desert in arts or arms T. vi 632
And give the day to a musician's p. T. vi 644
Yes—we remember him; and while we p. T. vi 648
Sung to the p. and glory of King George! T. vi 663
Man p. man; and Garrick's memory next T. vi 664
Man p. man. The rabble, all alive T. vi 694
Thus idly do we waste the breath of p. T. vi 711
To give it p. proportioned to its worth T. vi 756
P. is in all her gates: upon her walls T. vi 808
Must drop indeed the hope of public p. T. vi 973
But all is in His hand, whose p. I seek T. vi 1017
The p. bestowed was just and wise Th. 13
P. him on earth, or, obstinately dumb Tir. 101
Shall win his heart, and have his drunken p. Tir. 215
Be it a weakness, it deserves some p. Tir. 296
And small academies win all the p.? Tir. 504
I p. a school as Pope a government Tir. 506
Claims more than half the p. as his due share Tir. 528
Thus thy p. shall be expressed Trans. iii 9
Covetous only of a virtuous p. T.T. 75
His quitrent ode, his peppercorn of p. T.T. 110 [157
To win no p. when well-wrought plans prevail T.T.
Subserviency his p., and that alone T.T. 361
Prove this, and forfeit all pretence to p. T.T. 569
By low ambition and the thirst of p. T.T. 591
The gift whose office is the Giver's p. T.T. 750
'Tis grace, 'tis bounty, and it calls for p. V. 87
Content of heart, more p. still are due V. 90
In p. harmonious the first air he drew Y.O. 155

PRAISED. [427

And p. the wrath that laid her beauties waste Ex.
Adored and p. in all that thou hast wrought R. 92
Thy fame diffuse, p. not for utterance meet S. i 13
And smothered in't at last, is p. to death T. 316
He, p. perhaps for ages yet to come T. 333
Immortal Hale! for deep discernment p. T. iii 258

To him that leads it, wise, and to be p. T. iii 380
The cheek-distending oath, not to be p. T. iv 488
They now are deemed the faithful, and are p. T. vi 881
And p for virtues that they scorn to wear T.T. 116
And p. him in the victories He wrought T.T. 375

PRAISING.

P. the Author of all good in man J.T. 2

PRANKS. [154

Preaching and p. will share the motley scene P.E.
Heedless of all his p., the sturdy churl T. v 52
Watch, seals, and all,—till all his p. are told Tir. 331
Playing, at beat of drum, their martial p. T.T. 136

PRATE.

They drop through mere desire to p. F. 71
Trivial as a parrot's p.? St. iv 24
When birds are to be taught to p. Trans. iv 41
And p. and preach about what others prove T.T. 172

PRATTLER.

Condemn the p., for his idle pains R. 547

PRATTLING.

Ambling and p. scandal as he goes T. ii 382

PRAY. [A.C. 20

P. who would, or who could, wear spectacles then?
Reviled by those that hate her, p. for them Ch. 425
Forgot to curse, and only kneel to p. Con. 814
And seem to p., for good example's sake H. 249
Is sober, meek, benevolent, and p. H. 520 [P.A. 26
What! rob our good neighbour! I p. you don't go
P. tell me why we may not also go snacks? P.A. 16
So p. your Clerk with all his heart St. i 33
And one who wears a coronet and p. T. 378
The few that p. at all p. oft amiss T. vi 54
With decent duty, not ashamed to p. Tir. 176

PRAYED. [125

When he has p. and preached the sabbath down P.E.

PRAYER.

Small need of P. Book, or of priest, I ween A.T. 88
But ah! what wish can prosper, or what p. Ch. 137
No wealth can bribe, no p. persuade to stay Comp. i 4
And begged an interest in his frequent p. Con. 74
Mine be the friend less frequent in his p. Con. 579
Hypocrisy, formality in p. Ex. 43
Their p. made public, their excesses kept Ex. 143
They breathed in faith their well directed p. Ex. 239
Resort on Sundays to the house of p. H. 242
Fasting and p. sit well upon a priest H. 403
To form the better p. Miss — 20
Let no low thought suggest the p. Miss — 65
None else, except in p. for him Q.V. 55
Saints offer nothing, in their warmest p. R. 221
And p. more seasonable than the noise St. ii 11
His p. preferred to saints that cannot ail T. 85
Duly at clink of bell to morning p. T. 140 [T. 344
P. would add faith, and faith would fix them there
Take, Madam, the reward of all your p. T. 167
Regret would rouse them, and give birth to p. T. 343
My p. and alms, imperfect and defiled T. 577
The emphasis in score, and gives to p. T. ii 360 [250
Friends in the friends of science, and true p. T. iii
And plenteous harvest, to the p. he makes T. vi 947
Presents the p. the Saviour deigned to teach Tir. 123
P. to the winds, and caution to the waves Tir. 183
As must create an appetite for p.? Tir. 374
Accessible, and p. prevail, she will T.T. 407
P. only, and the penitential tear T.T. 412
The happiness of answered p. 1789, 64

PRAYING.
A *p.*, synagogue-frequenting beau *T.* 57

PREACH. [ii 53
To *p.* the general doom. When were the winds *T.*
Then Truth is hushed, that Heresy may *p. Ex.* 107
Some, decent in demeanour while they *p. T.* ii 440
P. it who might. Such was their love of truth *T.* ii 543
Thy name adoring, and then *p.* thee man! *T.* vi 887
Which children use, and parsons—when they *p. Tir.* 124
And prate and *p.* about what others prove *T.T.* 172
Mean you to prophesy or but to *p.? T.T.* 479 [vi 889
The world takes little thought. Who will may *p. T.*

PREACHED. [125
When he has prayed and *p.* the sabbath down *P.E.*
Has Epictetus, Plato, Tully, *p.! T.* ii 540

PREACHER.
God gives the word, the *p.* throng around *H.* 453
" Renounce the world "—the *p.* cries *L.W.* 25
I am no *p.*; let this hint suffice *P.E.* 621
Would I describe a *p.*, such as Paul *T.* ii 395

PREACHING.
P. and pranks will share the motley scene *P.E.* 154

PRECARIOUS.
Their love is so *p. F.* 114
O bliss *p.*, and unsafe retreats! *Her.* 33
The chase for sustenance, *p.* trust! *T.* i 611

PRECAUTION.
And wise *p.*, which a clime so rude *T.* iii 431

PRECEDENCE.
Became stone blind; *p.* went in truck *T.* ii 741
Asserts *p.*, and bespeaks control *Tir.* 9

PRECEDENTS.
To follow foolish *p.*, and wink *Tir.* 255

PRECEPT.
Her *p.* for your sake *B.R.* 12
But gladly, as the *p.* were her own *M.P.* 16
The *p.* that enjoins him abstinence *P.E.* 236
To make his *p.* our delight *St.* vi 7

PRECEPTOR.
And under such *p.*, who can fail? *T.* ii 284
Appointed sage *p.* to the Will *Tir.* 32

PRECEPTRESS.
Parks in which Art *p.* Nature weds *R.* 335
Experience, slow *p.*, teaching oft *T.* iii 505

PRECIOUS.
More *p.* than silver and gold *A.S.* 27
All truth is *p.*, if not all divine *Ch.* 331
A smaller piece amidst the *p.* store *Ch.* 476
Brings many a *p.* pearl of truth to light *H.* 444
Six *p.* souls and all agog *J.G.* 39
The *p.* stream still purling in his ear *P.E.* 232
We slight the *p.* kernel of the stone *P.E.* 419
Like something *p.* ventured far from shore *P.E.* 520
Time then would seem more *p.* than the joys *St.* ii 9
Were *p.*, and inculcated with care *T.* ii 701
Intrinsically *p.*; to the foot *T.* v 175
Part of the captain's *p.* store *Trans.* iv 5

PRECIPICE.
He spoke, and to the *p.* at hand *T.* vi 512

PRECIPITATE.
His sun *p.* descend *Mor.* 54
P. the loathed abode of man *T.* vi 376

PRECISE.
ract yet not *p.*, though meek keen-eyed *Con.* 610

PRECISION.
By this, with nice *p.* of design *H.* 606
But, with *p.* nicer still, the mind *N.A.* 63
All creatures, with *p.* understood *Y.O.* 151

PRECONCEIVED.
Shall break into its *p.* display *T.* iii 652

PREDECESSOR.
His *p.*'s coat advanced to wear *T.* 145
In staggering types, his *p.*'s tale *T.* v 419

PREDOMINANCE.
His zeal for her *p.* within *T.* v 394

PREDOMINATES.
Even where Death *p.* The spring *Y.O.* 132

PRE-EMINENCE.
Some small *p.*; we justly boast *T.* ii 275

PREFER.
She will have just the life she *p. C.* 53
P. his fellow grooms, with much good sense *Con.* 417
And you, though you must needs *p. E.* i 45
And piously *p.* the tail *L.W.* 20
Nor these alone *p.* a life recluse *R.* 169
He, lost in errors his vain heart *p. T.* 335
P. the twilight of a darker time *T.* 541
P. to the performance of a God *T.* i 418
Self-banished from society, *p. T.* i 578
Irrational in what they thus *p. Tir.* 795

PREFERENCE.
Where then the *p.* shall we place *E.* iv 71

PREFERMENT.
Which they that woo *p.* rarely pass *H.* 420
Ambitious of *p.* for its gold *T.* ii 387

PREFERRED.
Go, quit the rank to which ye stood *p. Con.* 75
A prison to a friend *p. F.B.* 35
His prayer to saints that cannot aid *T.* 85
To be *p.* to smoke, to the eclipse *T.* iii 736
Belinda's maids are soon *p. Trans.* iv 7

PREGNANT.
P. with celestial fire *B.* 34
And *p.* with discoveries new and rare *T.* iii 138
P., or indisposed alike to all *T.* iv 281

PREJUDICE.
The curtain drawn by *P.* and Pride *H.* 571
And *p.* have left a passage clear) *T.* 114
With hurtful error, *p.*, and dreams *T.* ii 504
While *p.* in men of stronger minds *T.* ii 567
Custom and *p.* shall bear no sway *T.* vi 838

PRELIBATION.
Large *p.* oft to saints below *T.* v 574

PRELIMINARIES.
Thus, the *p.* settled *E.* iv 31

PREMATURELY.
Her chickens *p.* counted *A Fable* 4

PREMISED.
This truth *p.* was needful as a text *N.A.* 71

PREPARE.
Exclaims " *P.* thee for an early shroud " *Ep.* i 10
" *P.* it for the sky " *Miss* — 92
For whom, alas! dost thou *p. O.* ii 10
P. for meals as jockeys take a sweat *P.E.* 221
Friends such as his for modern Jobs *p. R.* 306
P. it for its ruin; hardens, blinds *T.* ii 690

Which neatly she *p.*; then to his book *T.* iii 392
P. for happiness; bespeak him one *T.* vi 912
Not only Vice disposes and *p. T.T.* 438

PREPARED.

P. to poniard whomsoe'er they meet *Ch.* 508
P. to fight for shadows of no worth *Ex.* 116
That there is bliss *p.* in yonder sky *J.T.* 13
And sends thee to thy cabin, well *p. T.* i 670
And well *p.*, by ignorance and sloth *T.* ii 388
P. by taste, by learning, and true worth *Tir.* 678
Unless the world were all *p.* to embrace *Tir.* 917
P. for martyrdom, and strong to prove *V.* 61
With pointed hoof dibbling the glebe *p. Y.O.* 26

PREPONDERATING.

Are such a dead, *p.* weight *T.* 354

PREPOSTEROUS.

P. sight! the legs without the man *T.* v 20

PREROGATIVE.

'Tis God's just claim, *p.* divine *R.* 278
(Of king whom such *p.* can please) *T.* v 443
Thus proud *P.*, not much revered *T.T.* 230

PRESAGE.

Some handsome present, as your hopes *p. Con.* 306
With doleful rumour and sad *p.* hung *Ex.* 357
Could I, from Heaven inspired, as sure *p. St.* ii 1
The surest *p.* of the good they seek *T.* v 378
A *p.* ominous, portending still *T.* v 625
And screaming at the sad *p. T.B.* 47

PRESAGED.

She now *p.* approaching doom *R.C.* 74

PRESCRIBE.

Some farrier should *p.* his proper course *Con.* 411
P. the theme, the tone, and the grimace *Con.* 464
The largess He bestows, *p.* the terms *H.* 325
Prevent the danger, or *p.* the cure *P.E.* 18
Let him your rubric and your feasts *p. P.E.* 185

PRESCRIBED.

P. their course, to regulate it now *T.* vi 204

PRESENCE.

The sex whose *p.* civilizes ours *Con.* 254
Before his *p.*, at whose awful throne *Con.* 659
As bold as, in Agrippa's *p.*, Paul *Ex.* 445
To place you where his saints his *p.* share *H.* 339
And pretty face, in *p.* of his God? *T.* ii 422
Resign the scenes their *p.* might protect *T.* iv 592
And feel a parent's *p.* no restraint *T.* vi 49
His *p.*, who made all so fair, perceived *T.* vi 253
A ubiquarian *p.* and control *Tir.* 266
Awe-struck, before thy *p.* bend 1789, 67

PRESENT.

Some handsome *p.*, as your hopes presage *Con.* 306
Nose, ears, and eyes seem *p.* on the spot *Con.* 318
Though future pain may serve for *p.* mirth *Con.* 494
The freakish humour of the *p.* time *Con.* 866
Employs our *p.* thoughts and pains *E.* i 51
P. it decked with every hue *Mor.* 30
With *p.* ills his heart must ache *N.* 11
Or *p.*, or in prospect, meet his sight *P.E.* 48
An outline of the *p.* transient state *R.* 670
No *p.* health can health insure *St.* i 25
While danger passed is turned to *p.* joy *T.* 256
By every pleasing image they *p. T.* iii 303
Yet, feeling *p.* evils, while the past *T.* vi 23
Prompts with remembrance of a *p.* God *T.* vi 252
Patiently *p.* at a sacred song *T.* vi 634

The occasion it *p.* of doing good *T.* vi 847
And scorn thy *p.* lot *The Doves* 32
The *p.* Muse of every pensive mind *Tir.* 22
P. the prayer the Saviour deigned to teach *Tir.* 123
A *p.* to his toast *Trans.* iv 6
Speak to the *p.* times and times to come *T.T.* 433
The shipwright's darling treasure, did'st *p. Y.O.* 97

PRESENTED.

P. bare against the storm, plods on *T.* iv 353

PRESERVE.

But his who gave thee, and *p.* thee mine *Ch.* 267
P. me from the thing I dread and hate *Con.* 83
To watch the fountain, and *p.* it clear *Ex.* 98
His new-born virtues, and *p.* him pure *H.* 170
P. the church! and lay not careless hands *T.* ii 393
Or too incautious, to *p.* thy sweets *T.* iii 45 [83
And taught the unblemished to *p.* with care *T.* iii
That salt *p.* thee; more corrupted else *T.* iii 845
Still sacred, and *p.* with pious care *T.* vi 690

PRESERVED.

P. by virtue from declension *M.F.* 51
Nor ancient, will be so *p.* with care *P.E.* 400
Unlooked for, life *p.*, and peace restored *T.* iv 187
P. from guilt by salutary fears *Tir.* 111
And Liberty, *p.* from wild excess *T.T.* 316

PRESIDE.

That to suppose a scene where she *p. T.* iv 532
O'er all his pleasures gently to *p. Tir.* 609

PRESS.

Prosper (I *p.* thee with a powerful plea) *Ch.* 5
Did Charity prevail, the *p.* would prove *Ch.* 623
To *p.* your point with modesty and ease *Con.* 104
Found thee a goodly sponge for Power to *p. Ex.* 531
May *p.* the eye too closely to be borne *H.* 551
Yet gently pressed, *p.* gently mine *M.* 35
Hourly allurements on his passions *p. P.E.* 61
Thou god of our idolatory, the *P.? P.E.* 461 [ii 6
On which the *p.* might stamp him next to die *St.*
Come hither, ye that *p.* your beds of down *T.* i 362
And *p.* thy wedded side *The Doves* 26 [*T.* ii 712
That blushed at its own praise; and *p.* the youth
To *p.* the important question on his heart *Tir.* 57
The abuses of her sacred charge, the *p. T.T.* 633
To *p.* with energy your ardent thought *V.* 10

PRESSED.

Her new-laid eggs she fondly *p. A Fable* 2
And panting *p.* the floor *B.R.* 16
Where once intoxication *p.* the ground *Con.* 808
The more 'twere *p.* the firmer it would stand *Ex.* 287
Yet gently *p.*, press gently mine *M.* 35
And still to love, though *p.* with ill *M.* 41 [*N A.* 37
Sheep grazed the field; some with soft bosom *p.*
Were witnesses how cordially I *p. R.* 379
He *p.* him much to quit his base employ *R.* 594
That *p.* it, and the feet hung dangling down *T.* i 47
Receding wide, they *p.* against the ribs *T.* i 65
Though *p.* with hunger oft, or comelier clothes *T.* i 554
That *p.* the beach, and hasty to depart *T.* ii 118
Through the *p.* nostril, spectacle-bestrid *T.* ii 439
Not harshly thundered forth, or rudely *p. T.* vi 503
Or e'er his hoof had *p.* the crumbling verge *T.* vi 519
P. on his part by means that would disgrace *Tir.* 406
And mark them with a seal of wrath *p.* down *T.T.* 457

PRESSURE.

And, warmed by the *p.*, is all in a glow *F.M.* 8
But now and then with *p.* of his thumb *T.* v 54
And under *p.* of some conscious cause? *T.* vi 220

PRESUME.

He humbly hopes—*p*.—it may be so *Con*. 124
P. itself chief favourite of the skies *Con*. 674
That I *p*. to address the Muse *E*. iv 12
Not so the pheasant on his charms *p*. *T*. 66
P. to lay their hand upon the ark *T*. ii 231
Whose only care, might truth *p*. to speak *Tir*. 193

PRESUMED.

Of holy writ, she has *p*. to annul *T*. i 741
I thought the volume I *p*. to send *V*. 39

PRESUMING.

P. an attempt not less sublime *T*. iii 459

PRESUMPTION.

Her hope *p*., and her faith a lie *Con*. 774
To punish lust, or pluck *p*. down *Ex*. 250
And perish there, as all *p*. must " *H*. 228

PRESUMPTUOUS.

His power secured thee, when *p*. Spain *Ex*. 568
Or disregards, or more *p*. still *T*. ii 177

PRESUMPTUOUSLY.

Nor could he dare *p*. displease *Tir*. 179

PRETENCE.

Here see, acquitted of all vain *p*. *Ch*. 412
To Peace and Charity, is mere *p*. *Ch*. 534
Pronounce your human form a false *p*. *Con*. 78
Their skill a truth, his master's a *p*. *Con*. 418
And wiser men's ability, *p*. *Con*. 628
And hast thou sworn on every slight *p*. *Ex*. 386
All fasting else, whate'er be the *p*. *Ex*. 412
His aim was mischief and his zeal *p*. *H*. 564
Glory your aim, but Justice your *p*. *Her*. 44
Ye pimps, who, under virtue's fair *p*. *P.E.* 315
Some plain mechanic, who, without *p*. *R*. 440
But such as Learning without false *p*. *R*. 695
A hypocrite's *p*.! *St*. vi 24
High in demand, though lowly in *p*. *T*. 93
Wage war, with any or with no *p*. *T*. v 314
And we are deep in that of cold *p*. *T*. v 494
Prove this, and forfeit all *p*. to praise *T.T.* 569
Vouchsafes to man a poet's just *p*. *T.T.* 699

PRETEND.

No knave but boldly will *p*. *F*. 13
P. a zeal for godliness and grace *H*. 661
Weak to perform, though mighty to *p*. *P.E.* 15
To doubt the love his favourites may *p*. *T.T.* 159
P. to all that parts have e'er acquired *V*. 15
To fame as lasting as the earth *p*. *V*. 17

PRETENDERS.

The boast of mere *p*. to the name *T*. i 492

PRETENSIONS.

Without it, his *p*. were as vain *Con*. 761
Though heavenly in *p*., fleeced thee well *Ex*. 515
But higher far my proud *p*. rise *M.P.* 110
A principle, whose proud *p*. pass *Tir*. 462

PRETTIEST.

My spaniel, *p*. of his race *D.W.* 5

PRETTILY.

Nature indeed looks *p*. in rhyme *R*. 567

PRETTINESS.

With all the *p*. of feign'd alarm *T*. vi 319

PRETTY.

And *p*. face, in presence of his God ? *T*. ii 422
Boys are, at best, but *p*. buds unblown *Tir*. 446

PREVAIL.

And wins mankind, as his attempts *p*. *Ch*. 335
So, when the cold damp shades of night *p*. *Ch*. 527
Did Charity *p*., the press would prove *Ch*. 623
And e'en when sober truth *p*. throughout *Con*. 65
Till the best tongue, or heaviest hand, *p*. *H*. 196
And save or damn as these or those *p*. *H*. 368
But oars alone can ne'er *p*. *H.F.* 21
Did Famine or did Plague *p*. *St*. i 7
And barbarous climes, where violence *p*. *T*. i 604
Sweet fiction and sweet truth alike *p*. *Tir*. 136
The shadows fly, philosophy *p*. *Tir*. 182
Deems his reward too great if he *p*. *Tir*. 479
Disputes have been, and still *p*. *Trans*. i 5
And will *p*. or perish in her cause *T.T.* 18   [157
To win no plans when well-wrought plans *p*. *T.T.*
Bids equity throughout his works *p*. *T.T.* 250
Accessible, and prayer *p*., she will *T.T.* 407

PREVAILED.

But so the furious blast *p*. *Cast*. 21
By some whose patriot virtue has *p*. *T*. v 295

PREVAILING.

With gentle yet *p*. force *Comp*. ii 5
Thence the *p*. manners take their cast *Tir*. 913

PREVARICATION.

Where no *p*. shall avail *R*. 657

PREVENT.

P. the danger, or prescribe the cure *P.E.* 18
Such friends *p*. what else would soon succeed *R*. 731
To avenge than to *p*. the breach of law *T*. i 731
May here and there *p*. erroneous choice *Tir*. 798

PREVENTED.

P. much by diet neat and plain *Tir*. 767

PREY.

Forbidding you the *p*. *Beau* 8
That man make man his *p*., because he must *Ch*.197
No longer *p*. upon our annual rents *Ch*. 616
To captivate the tempting *p*. *T*. iv 54
Jerusalem a *p*., her glory soiled *Ex*. 61
From happier scenes, and making your land a *p*. *H*. 478
And stood looking out for his *p*. *M.D.* 31
Now stoops upon it, and now grasps the *p*. *P.E.* 334
Soothe thee to make thee but a surer *p*. *R*. 263
Drives to their dens the obedient beasts of *p*. *R*. 766
In some unwholesome dungeon, and a *p*. *T*. i 437
Dooms and devotes him as his lawful *p*. *T*. ii 15
Sucks down its *p*. insatiable. Immense *T*. ii 103
Can seize the slippery *p*., unties the knot *T*. ii 685
Not satisfied to *p*. on all around *T*. vi 394 [*T*. iii 817
And the shark's *p*.; the spendthrift, and the leech
To *p*. upon each other: stubborn, fierce *T*. vi 897
Oh, had he made that too his *p*. ! *T.B.* 55
The Nations hunt, all mark thee for a *p*. *T.T.* 364

PRICE.

And Love Divine has paid one *p*. for all *Ch*. 205
She deems all safe, for she has paid the *p*. *Ch*. 458
Or sell their glory at a market *p*. *Con*. 28
It is indeed above all *p*. *F*. 56
Though short, too long, the *p*. he pays for all *H*. 200
Nor set a *p*. upon a willing heart *H*. 337
The dire effect of Mercy without *p*. ! *H*. 496
Paid my *p*. in paltry gold *N.C.* 6
Avarice shows, and virtue is the *p*. *P.E.* 52
Such previous woe the *p*. ! *Q.V.* 80
Made all his virtues gewgaws of no *p*. *T*. 55
Just estimation prized above all *p*. *T*. ii 34 [iii 800
Well-managed shall have earned its worthy *p*. *T*.
To insure a side-box station at half *p*. *T*. ii 624

PRICE—PRINCIPLE

The *p.* of his default. But now—yes, now *T. iii* 92
Sells the last scantling, and transfers the *p. T. iii* 753
Sells oaths by tale, and at the lowest *p. T.T.* 419

PRICE-DECIDING.
Oft as the *p.* hammer falls *T.* vi 291

PRICKED.
Although immortal, may be *p.* or scratched *Ch.* 512
I *p.* them into paper with a pin *M.P.* 77

PRICKLY.
With *p.* gorse, that shapeless and deformed *T.* i 527
To raise the *p.* and green-coated gourd *T. iii* 446
To stroke the *p.* grievance, and to hang *T.* v 329

PRICKS.
It *p.* the genius forward in its course *Tir.* 483

PRIDE.
And reddening with a just and generous *p. A.T.* 204
Soon her *p.* shall kiss the ground *B.* 19
She, with all a monarch's *p. B.* 37.   [462
From *p.* in league with ignorance, have sprung ! *Ch.*
Thus taught, down falls the plumage of his *p. Ch.* 345
May blow up self-conceit and nourish *p. Ch.* 376
Would humble many a towering poet's *p. Ch.* 536
By sparks Absurdity strikes out of *P. Con.* 148
The proud are always most provoked by *p. Con.* 160
By way of wholesome curb upon our *p. Con.* 361
Grave without dulness, learned without *p. Con.* 609
Sincerity ! why 'tis his only *p. Con.* 757
My dog shall mortify the *p. D.W.* 39
As silly *p.* and idleness produce *Ex.* 50
The filth of rottenness and worm of *p. Ex.* 90
And grace thy figure with a soldier's *p. Ex.* 487
With cold disgust, or philosophic *p. Ex.* 691
Caledonia's traffic and *p.* ! *Gr.* 18
Or *p.* can look at with indifferent eyes *H.* 52
Then praise is heard instead of reasoning *p. H.* 143
The *p.* of lettered ignorance, that binds *H.* 483
It hurts our *p.*, and moves our envy less *H.* 553
The curtain drawn by Prejudice and *P.—H.* 571
Hence all that is in man,—*p.*, passion, art *H.* 653
The mischiefs your ambitious *p.* inspires ! *Her.* 46
The *p.* of the parterre *L.R.* 20
While learning, once the man's exclusive *p. P.E.* 429
In vain : the slave of arrogance and *p. P.E.* 548
Of *p.*, ambition, or impure desires *R.* 110
" My patrimonial treasure and my *p. R.* 367
The *p.* of arrogant distinctions fall *R.* 659
His virtues were his *p.* ; and that one vice *T.* 54
P. has attained its most luxuriant growth *T.* 115
P. may be pampered while the flesh grows lean *T.* 117
More nourish *p.*, that condescending vice *T.* 123
Such are the fruits of sanctimonious *p. T.* 165
Exalted on his pedestal of *p. T.* 313
To nourish *p.*, or turn the weakest head *T.* 366
P. above all opposes her design *T.* 474
P., of a growth superior to the rest *T.* 475
Retorts the affront against the crown of *P.—T.* 502
P. falls unpitied, never more to rise *T.* 588
That crowns it ! yet not all its *p.* secures *T.* i 279
To his own pleasure and his patron's *p. T.* ii 391
Grieves, but alarms me not. I mourn the *p. T.* iv 102
To soothe their honest *p.*, that scorns to beg *T.* iv 405
A weight of ignorance; in that, of *p. T.* iv 485
Of self-congratulating *P.*, begot *T.* v 622
Till it out-mantle all the *p.* of verse *T.* v 680   [163
His *p.* resents the charge, although the proof *Tir.*
His *p.*, that scorns to obey or to submit *Tir.* 226
Of envy, hatred, jealousy, and *p. Tir.* 467
Debased to servile purposes of *P.—T.T.* 748

PRIEST.
The ring a bauble, and the *p.* a knave *A.T.* 66
Small need of Prayer Book, or of *p.*, I ween *A.T.* 88
Died by the sentence of a shaven *p. Ch.* 55
God's name so much upon his lips, a *p. Con.* 72
The *p.*, whose office is, with zeal sincere *Ex.* 97
People and *p.*, the sons of Israel were *Ex.* 124 [512
Then *p.* with bulls, and briefs, and shaven crowns *Ex.*
If *p.*, supinely droning o'er his charge *H.* 198
Fasting and prayer sit well upon a *p. H.* 403
A cassocked huntsman, and a fiddling *p. P.E.* 111
Abhorred the sacrifice, and cursed the *p. P.E.* 340
Whoever errs, the *p.* can ne'er be wrong *P.E.* 508
And some ascribe the invention to a *p. T.* i 62
"Is but an instrument on which the *p. T.* v 651
P. have invented, and the world admired *Tir.* 185
What knavish *p.* promulgate as inspired *Tir.* 186
The father, who designs his babe a *p. Tir.* 364
Dumb as a senator, and as a *p. Tir.* 424
The troubles of a worthy *p. Y.D.* 3
The *p.* he merry is and blithe *Y.D.* 5

PRIESTHOOD.
A *p.* such as Baal's was of old *T.* ii 678
Hence British poets too the *p.* shared *T.T.* 502

PRIESTLY.
Enjoy immunity from *p.* power *Ch.* 273
Theirs were the prophets, theirs the *p.* call *Ex.* 201
The *p.* brotherhood, devout, sincere *Ex.* 438
The veil is rent, rent too by *p.* hands *T.* vi 876

PRIMAL.
Before he eats it.—'Tis the *p.* curse *T.* i 364

PRIME.
And to say truth, though in its early *p. Con.* 633
Review thy dim original and *p. Ex.* 467
Thus between Justice, as my *p.* support *H.* 377
Are life's *p.* pleasures in his simple view *R.* 403
Where Flora is still in her *p. W.N.* 10

PRIMED.
And being always *p.* with politesse *P.E.* 387   [567
See that your polished arms be *p.* with care *T.* iv

PRIMROSE.
And lanes in which the *p.* ere her time *T.* vi 113

PRINCE.   [*T.* v 177
Great *p.* have great playthings. Some have played
Their *p.*, as justly seated on his throne *Ch.* 51
Her *p.* captive, and her treasures spoiled *Ex.* 62
His freedom is the freedom of a *p. T.* 196
A *p.* with half his people ! Ancient towers *T.* ii 121
Not as the *p.* in Shushan, when he called *T.* iii 714
All kingdoms and all *p.* of the earth *T.* vi 801

PRINCELY.
Called for his arms, and for his *p.* steed *A.T.* 124
He gives the *p.* bird, with all his wives *T.* iv 449

PRINCESS.
"*P.* ! if our aged eyes *B.* 9

PRINCIPAL.
A *p.* ingredient *F.* 204

PRINCIPALITIES.
Shook *p.* and kingdoms down *Ch.* 77

PRINCIPLE.
And savage in its *p.* appears *Con.* 171
But steadfast *p.*, and, in its kind *J.T.* 43
That thy worst part, thy *p.*, live yet *P.E.* 350
The *p.* and motive all in all *T.* 200

And *p.* ; of causes, how they work *T.* ii 191
His *p.*, and tempt him into sin *T.* iv 454
On *p.*, where foppery atones *T.* iv 689
Our love is *p.*, and has its root *T.* v 353
O for a world in *p.* as chaste *T.* vi 836
A *p.*, whose proud pretensions pass *Tir.* 462
On selfish *p.*, is shame and guilt *T.T.* 2

PRINK.

And *p.* their hair with daisies, or to pick *T.* vi 303

PRINT.

But I can assure you I saw it in *p. P.A.* 20
And therefore *p.*, himself but half deceived *P.E.* 492
In which lewd sensualists *p.* out themselves *R.* 684
Down into modern use; transforms old *p. T.* ii 363
Describes and *p.* it, that the world may know *T.* iv 237

PRIOR.

Of dear Mat *P.'s* easy jingle *E.* iv 4   [764
Though Butler's wit, Pope's numbers, *P.'s* ease *T.T.*

PRISMATIC.

He talks of light, and the *p.* hues *Ch.* 391

PRISON.

Passing his *p.* door *B.R.* 14
P. expect the wicked, and were built *Ch.* 280
Each heart would quit its *p.* in the breast *Ch.* 610
A *p.* with a friend preferred *F.B.* 35
Oppression, *p.*, have no power to bind *T.* v 543
When Tumult lately burst his *p.* door *T.T.* 318

PRISONED.

There *p.* in a parlour snug and small *R.* 493
Where the *p.* lark is hung *St.* iv 2

PRISONER.

Lived happy *p.* there *F.B.* 6
Had been your *p.* still *G.* 18
A *p.* in the yet undawning east *T.* iv 130
O Liberty! the *p.'s* pleasing dream *T.T.* 288

PRISON-HOUSE.

And from their *p.* below arise *N.A.* 87
So fare we in this *p.*, the world *T.* ii 661

PRIVATE.

As *p.* as the chambers where they slept *Ex.* 144
Or stabbed a man to serve some *p.* end? *T.* 47
To fill the ambition of a *p.* man *T.* ii 236
Or if that mine be shut, some *p.* purse *T.* iii 797
In all their *p.* functions, once combined *T.* iv 673
Where *p.* was not? Can he love the whole *T.* v 503
So loose to *p.* duty, that no brain *T.* v 512

PRIVILEGE.

Oh! 'tis a godlike *p.* to save *Ch.* 226
No!—there I grant the *p.* I claim *Con.* 98
Expression and the *p.* of thought *Con.* 404
With strains it was a *p.* to hear *Con.* 618
Forgiveness, and the *p.* of hope *H.* 214
Sweet as the *p.* of healing woe *J.T.* 17
That *p.* was thine; Heaven gave thee means *J.T.* 19
Though 'tis his *p.* to die *St.* v 3
'Twas his sublimest *p.* to feel *T.* vi 359
Feels all his happiest *p.* lost *Tir.* 574
An English poet's *p.* to rant *T.T.* 299
The noble sweep of all their *p. T.T.* 475

PRIVILEGED.

The rest might then seem *p.* to play *St.* ii 19
Even age itself seems *p.* in them *T.* i 403
There they are *p.*; and he that hunts *T.* vi 577

PRIZE.

And bore the worthless *p.* away *A Fable* 29

Than when he tows a *p. A Tale* 60
Sounds not arms shall win the *p. B.* 23
The rich possession of a nobler *p. Ch.* 360   [662
And *p.* them above pleasure, wealth, or praise *Con.*
But still the *p.*, though nearly caught *D.W.* 19
That seemed to promise no such *p. E.* i 96
While eager Hodge beholds the *p. E.* iv 43
His worthless absolution all the *p. Ex.* 525   [622
They could not purchase earth with such a *p. Ex.*
Our years, a fruitless race without a *p. H.* 25
Kind souls! to teach their tenantry to *p. H.* 252
A brighter *p.* than that he meant *Mor.* 55
Peace, both the duty and the *p. N.G.* 37
That *p.* belongs to none but the sincere *P.E.* 578
Ask wealth of Heaven, and gain a real *p. R.* 162
The lure of avarice, or the pompous *p. R.* 177
The good we never miss we rarely *p. R.* 406
A meaner than himself shall gain the *p. T.* 16
Believe, rush forward, and possess the *p. T.* 374
Humility is crowned, and Faith receives the *p. T.* 589
Of blank oblivion, seem a glorious *p. T.* i 287
And pocketed a *p.* by fraud obtained *T.* ii 87
And making *p.* of all that he condemns *T.* ii 604
Vainly industrious, a disgraceful *p. T.* iii 385
Wafts the rich *p.* to its appointed use *T.* iii 540 [700
That self-condemned they must neglect the *p. T.* iii
Is free to all men—universal *p. T.* iii 724
But Martyrs struggle for a brighter *p. T.* v 718 [55
And seeking grace to improve the *p.* they hold *T.* vi
Secure of conquest where the *p. Th.* 15
That candidates for such a *p.* should feel *Tir.* 376
The exalted *p.* demands an upward look *Tir.* 383
The *p.* of beauty in a woman's eyes *Tir.* 472
Not brighter than in theirs the scholar's *p. Tir.* 473
Show thou hast sense enough to *p.* the pearl *Tir.* 707
P. it, ye ministers; ye monarchs, spare *T.T.* 334
The *p.* of happier times, will serve thee now *T.T.* 371
Then suddenly regain the *p.* 1789, 54

PRIZED.

When gifts perverted, or not duly *p. Ex.* 251
Joys always *p.*, when placed within our reach *H.* 36
For thee I panted, thee I *p. O.* ii 19
That rule he *p.*, by that he feared *St.* iii 21
Just estimation *p.* above all price *T.* iii 34
By all that *p.* it; not for prudery's sake *T.* iii 78
I studied, *p.*, and wished that I had known *T.* iv 722
More to be *p.* and coveted than yours *T.* iv 191

PROBABILITY.

Still making *p.* your clue *Con.* 218

PROBATIONARY.

Like Eden's dread *p.* tree *P.E.* 468

PROBITY.

Famed for thy *p.* from shore to shore *J.T.* 6

PROBLEMS.

With *p.* History, not wanted yet *Y.O.* 159

PROCEED.

A mightier cried—"*P.*"—*B.R.* 6
He from whose hands alone all power *p. Ch.* 208
Some men make gain a fountain, whence *p. Ch.* 244
And having struck the balance, now *p. Con.* 798
With every good and perfect good, *p. H.* 116
One act, that from a thankful heart *p. T.* 223
Flies swiftly, and unfelt the task *p. T.* iv 166
Where shall I find an end, or how *p*.? *T.* iv 233
The sun *p.*, I wander. Neither mist *T.* vi 296
Too careless often, as our years *p. Tir.* 113

PROCEED—PROFIT

Though from ourselves the mischief more *p. Tir.* 249
From whence his rays *p. Trans.* i 6

PROCEEDED.
That they *p.* from a grateful heart *T.* 580

PROCEEDING.
A spy on my *p. F.* 192
P. with his nimblest pace *Mor.* 20
P. soon a graduated dunce *T.* ii 739

PROCESS.
This *p.* achieved, it is doomed to sustain *F.M.* 9
The *p.* Heat and cold, and wind and steam *T.* iii 554
By which the mighty *p.* is maintain'd *T.* vi 225

PROCESSION.
A pale *p.* of past sinful joys *H.* 221
In one *p.* joined *Q.V.* 22
He sets the bright *p.* on its way *T.* vi 190

PROCLAIM.
Let Egypt's plagues, and Canaan's woes *p. Ex.* 169
To banish hesitation, and *p. H.* 63
P. the remedy, ye learned, next *H.* 103
P. their titles to the crowd around *H.* 266
P. the soil a conquest he has won *H.* 479
Returning, he *p.*, by many a grace *P.E.* 413
Yearly in my song *p. St.* iv 10
Denies the power that wields it. God *p. T.* ii 178
Till Thou *p.* thyself. Theirs is indeed *T.* v 857
Thy saints *p.* thee king ; and in their hearts *T.* vi 861
Thy saints *p.* thee king ; and thy delay *T.* vi 864
P. him born to sway *Th.* 10
A subject's faults a subject may *p. T.T.* 113
And regions long since desolate *p. T.T.* 431

PROCLAIMED.
The brief *p.*, it visits every pew *Ch.* 469
Such London is, by taste and wealth *p. T.* i 697

PROCREATION.
To check the *p.* of a breed *Tir.* 603

PROCURE.
P. him many a curse. By slow degrees *T.* iv 635
Of Poverty, that thus he may *p. T.* v 318

PRODIGAL.
Divert the champions *p.* of breath *Con.* 89
Or spendthrift's *p.* excess afford *J.T.* 16

PRODIGY.
To make the shining *p.* complete *Ch.* 602
And baits its hook with *p.* and lies *Con.* 224
Made sure by *p.* till then unknown *Ex.* 174
P. ominous, and viewed with fear *P.E.* 99
Observed as *p.*, and soon reclaimed *T.* iv 524
So stood the brittle *p.* ; though smooth *T.* v 154
What *p.* can power divine perform *T.* vi 118
Your son come forth a *p.* of skill *Tir.* 525

PRODUCE.
Each climate needs what other climes *p. Ch.* 89
To give the pole the *p.* of the sun *Ch.* 125
Whate'er this world *p.*, it absorbs *Ch.* 564
Thy thirst-creating steams at length *p. Con.* 262
We sometimes think we could a speech *p. Con.* 353
Had wit as bright as ready to *p. Con.* 614
And whether Roman rites may not *p. Con.* 835
No longer labours merely to *p. Con.* 891
As silly pride and idleness *p. Ex.* 50
"The rich, the *p.* of a nobler stem *Ex.* 460
Which does not yet like that *p. F.* 131
The gayest I had to *p. Gr.* 28
Save for the fruits his heavenly beams *p. H.* 82

Clothes it with earth, and bids the *p.* live *Her.* 30
Demons *p.* them doubtless, brazen-clawed *N.A.* 101
All such as manly and great souls *p. R.* 699
But why before us Protestants *p. T.* 127
P. them—take a chair—now draw a Saint *T.* 172
Maturer years shall happier stores *p. T.* 495
More grand than it *p.* year by year *T.* vi 119
Blushed that effects like these she should *p. T.T.* 326
Perched on the meagre *p.* of the land *T.T.* 580

PRODUCED.
The last by Vanity *p.* and nursed *Con.* 378
P. a friendship then begun *E.* i 101
Two leaves *p.*, two rough indented leaves *T.* iii 526
Of too much labour, worthless when *p. T.* iii 565
As if *p.* by Nature there *U.* 18

PRODUCTION.
Men loved their own *p.* long ago *P.E.* 527

PRODUCTIVE.
P. only of a race like ours *T.* ii 584

PROFANATION.
When *p.* of the sacred cause *T.T.* 426
Is *p.* of the basest kind *T.T.* 758

PROFANE.
Of all that was absurd, *p.*, impure *Con.* 888
Delights like these, ye sensual and *p. P.E.* 263
Nor touch the page he cannot but *p.*) *P.E.* 457
That, through *p.* and infidel contempt *T.* i 740
Then were not all effaced ; then speech *p. T.* iv 522

PROFANED.
The temple and its holy rites *p. Ex.* 145
Sabbaths *p.* without remorse *St.* vi 39
Him blind antiquity *p.*, not served *T.* vi 231
In sacrilege, in God's own house *p. Tir.* 409
And dizzy with delight, *p.* the sacred wires *T.T.* 607

PROFANING.
Bad men, *p.* friendship's hallowed name *Con.* 683

PROFESS.
Is not to find what they *p.* to seek *Tir.* 194

PROFESSED.
He takes what he at first *p.* to loathe *Con.* 337
The praises of the libertine *p. T.* 433
Where science and where virtue are *p.* ? *T.* ii 766
By learned clerks, and Latinists *p. Tir.* 382
So little felt, so fervently *p.* ! *V.* 50

PROFESSING.
Betray thee, while *p.* to defend *T.T.* 333

PROFESSION.
Shows Love to be a mere *p. M.F.* 60
Perhaps, though by *p.* ghostly pure *T.* iv 603

PROFESSIONALLY.
Art thou a man *p.* tied *Tir.* 658

PROFICIENCY.
O blessed *p.* ! surpassing all *R.* 99
Praise his *p.*, and dub him man *P.E.* 368
The great *p.* he made abroad *T.* iv 654

PROFICIENT.
True, I am no *p.*, I confess *T.* iii 210
No powdered pert *p.* in the art *T.* iv 145

PROFIT.
Hush—silent readers *p.* most *A Tale* 29
What neither yields us *p.* nor delight *Con.* 241
By which the world might *p.*, and himself *T.* i 577

But censure *p.* little : vain the attempt *T.* iv 500
A tax of *p.* from his very play *Tir.* 612

PROFITABLE.
The strenuous use of *p.* thought *R.* 674
With odours, and *p.* as sweet *T.* ii 228
And *p.* abusers of a world *T.* iii 696
And manners *p.*, were rarely found *T.* iv 523

PROFOUND.
That remedy, not hid in deeps *p. H.* 111
And beaus, adepts in every thing *p. H.* 347
Not many wise, rich, noble, or *p. T.* 337
Bury herself in solitude *p. T.* 443
" 'Twere well," says one sage, erudite, *p. T.* iii 191

PROFOUNDER.
To reach a depth *p.* still, and still *T.* v 593
P., in the fathomless abyss *T.* v 594

PROFOUNDLY.
Adopting their mistakes, *p.* thinks *T.* v 270

PROFUSE.
Thought is so rare, and fancy so *p. Con.* 856
Of what He gives, unsparing and *p. Ex.* 677
Extreme, at once rapacious and *p. T.* ii 380
That ye may garnish your *p.* regales *T.* iii 551
Those habits of *p.* and lewd expense *Tir.* 350
She fills *p.* ten thousand little throats *T.T.* 694

PROFUSION.
R. apes the noble part *F.* 4
At the right door. *P.* is the sire *T.* ii 674
P. unrestrained, with all that's base *T.* ii 675
P., deluging a state with lusts *T.* ii 688
This does *P.*, and the accursed cause *T.* ii 697
P. breeds them; and the cause itself *T.* ii 820
The bright *p.* of her scatter'd stars *T.* vi 176
'Twere wild *p.* all, and bootless waste *Tir.* 49

PROGENITOR.
Even as his first *p.*, and quits *T.* iii 297

PROGENY.
Then the *p.* that springs *B.* 25
Is still the *p.* and heir of sin *Ch.* 344
And all your numerous *p.*, well trained *T.* iv 422
Of his descending *p.* was found *T.* v 212
Yet make their *p.* their dearest care *Tir.* 800

PROGNOSTICS.
They knew, by sure *p.* seen on high *Ex.* 157

PROGRESS.
Our *p.* was often delayed *C.* 11
And catch in its *p.* a sensible glow *F.M.* 20
The silent *p.* of thy power is such *H.* 665
The folded gates would bar my *p.* now *T.* i 330
Their *p.* in the road of science; blinds *T.* v 451
Is Nature's *p.*, when she lectures man *T.* vi 182
And guides the *p.* of a soul to God *Tir.* 146
Beheld their *p.* with the deepest dread *T.T.* 325

PROGRESSIVE.
At first, *p.* as a stream, they seek *T.* i 292

PROHIBITION.
With *p.* and perpetual thirst ? *P.E.* 234

PROJECT.
The wildest *p.* of her teeming brain *A.T.* 57
The statesman, skilled in *p.* dark and deep *Ch.* 612
The strange conceits, vain *p.*, and wild dreams *H.* 618
And give your monstrous *p.* all its force *Tir.* 239
The diadem, with mighty *p.* lined *T.T.* 59

PROJECTED.
Sheltering the base with its *p.* eaves *T.* iii 483

PROJECTORS.
Confederacy of *p.* wild and vain *T.* v 194

PROLIFIC.
P., and the lime at dewy eve *T.* i 316
Distempered, or has lost *p.* powers *T.* iii 415
P. all, and harbingers of more *T.* iii 531

PROLIX.
Legends *p.* delivers in the ears *S.* i 2
With wig *p.*, down flowing to his waist *Tir.* 361

PROLIXITY.
The obsolete *p.* of shade *T.* i 265

PROLOGUE.
Or, having whelped a *p.* with great pains *T.T.* 536
A *p.* interdashed with many a stroke *T.T.* 538

PROMINENCE.
For want of *p.* and just relief *Con.* 127

PROMINENT.
The *p.* and most unsightly bones *T.* ii 588
With *p.* wens globose; till at the last *Y.O.* 66

PROMISCUOUSLY.
Flowers by that name *p.* we call *R.* 723

PROMISE.
That seemed to *p.* no such prize *E.* i 96
Of all the ways that seem to *p.* fair *H.* 338
Oft gave me *p.* of thy quick return *M.P.* 37
Lead to the bliss she *p.* the wise *P.E.* 73
But farewell *p.* of happier fruits *R.* 241
His *p.* our stay *St.* vi 8
That field of *p.*, how it flings abroad *T.* 453
And *p.* of a God. His other gifts *T.* v 550
Behold the measure of the *p.* filled *T.* vi 798 [871
" Where is the *p.* of your Lord's approach?" *T.* vi
P. a work of which they must despair *Tir.* 264
Though fair in *p.*, permanent and sound *Tir.* 437
Not to recall a *p.* to your mind *V.* 21
The *p.* of delicious fruit appears *V.* 52

PROMISED.
And *p.* they should act the wild goose part *A.T.* 53
Taints in its rudiments the *p.* flower *Con.* 42
See Judah's *p.* king, bereft of all *R.* 767
That *p.* once more firmness, so assailed *T.* v 526
The time of rest, the *p.* Sabbath, comes *T.* vi 733

PROMISING.
Or *p.* with smiles to call again *T.* vi 282

PROMOTE.
Wise to *p.* whatever end he means *Ch.* 87 [709
Should best secure them, and *p.* them most *T.* iii

PROMPT.
Occasion *p.*, and appetite so keen *A.T.* 90
Come, *p.* me with benevolent desires *Ch.* 11
All *p.* his pleased pursuit, and to pursue *Ch.* 325
Still *p.* him, with a pleasure always new *Ch.* 326
There sits and *p.* him with his own disgrace *Con.* 463
Found him as *p.*, as their desire was true *Con.* 545
To show a love as *p.* as thine *D.W.* 43 [iii 37
His grief might *p.* him with the speech he made *E.*
P. to persuade, expostulate, and warn *Ex.* 441
Warns him or *p.*, approves him or restrains *P.E.* 35
His wish and mine both *p.* me to retire" *R.* 390
That *p.* the wish to stay *St.* v 30
P. every movement of his heart and mind *T.* 194
Good temper; spirits *p.* to undertake *T.* i 400
That she is slack in discipline; more *p. T.* i 730

Must p. him, and admonish how to catch T. iii 507
Call comedy, to p. him with a smile ? T. iv 199
Of ruinous ebriety that p. T. iv 460
As instinct p.; self-buried ere they die T. v 88
That whom it teaches it makes p. to learn T. v 859
P. with remembrance of a present God T. vi 252
Seldom, and never but as Wisdom p. T. vi 849
Courage in arms, and ever p. to show T.T. 276
P. his endeavour, and engage his aim T.T. 747

PROMPTED.
With visions p. by intense desire T. i 451
Not p., as in our degenerate days T.T. 590
Or else vain-glory, p. us to draw T. i 635

PROMPTER.
And wit that puppet p. might inspire R. 312
Or p., save the scene, I will perform Y.O. 141

PROMULGATE.
What knavish priests p. as inspired Tir. 186

PRONE.
Are sadly p. to quarrel F. 87
And, though God made thee of a nature p. J.T. 31
Once p. on earth, now buoyant upon air R. 66
To limit thought, by Nature p. to stray R. 127
Fall p.; the pale inhabitants come forth T. ii 125
Such dupes are men to custom, and so p. T. v 299
'Tis pusillanimous and p. to flight T. v 373 [785
Brutes graze the mountain-top, with faces p. T. v

PRONOUNCE.
P. your human form a false pretence Con. 78
The positive p. without dismay Con. 146
Then kiss their idol and p. her fair P.E. 300
And then skip down again ; p. a text T. ii 410
The creature is that God p. good T. vi 828

PRONOUNCED.
P. him frantic, and his fears a dream Ex. 70
P. by greybeards a pernicious dream Ex. 114
P. it transient, glorious as it is T. v 563

PROOF.
No spell or charm was p. against the thrust A.T. 146
And at this hour the conqueror feels the p. Ch. 60
To swallow much upon much weaker p. Con. 722
With p., that we, and our affairs E. i 57
One p. should serve—a reference to you E. iii 13
There, p. against prosperity, awhile Ex. 77
Given thee his blessing on the clearest p. Ex. 564
Of fewer errors, in a second p. ! F.A. 5
P. against sickness and old age M.F. 50
Bears p. of an intelligence divine R. 208
Coincident, exhibit lucid p. T. ii 374
Grow wanton, and give p. to every eye T. ii 443
Is p. against thy sweet seducing charms ? T. ii 482
With show of love, at least with hopeful p. T. ii 558
One p. at least of manhood ! while the friend T. ii 594
Is oft-times p. of wisdom, when the fault T. iii 39
Nothing is p. against the general curse T. iii 266
The Frenchman's darling? Are they not all p. T.iv 765
But above measure strange, that neither p. T. v 293
Mark now the p. I give thee, that the brave T. vi 509
By any change of fortune; p. alike T. vi 626
Of Avon, famed in song. Ah pleasant p. T. vi 682
P. of the wisdom of the all-seeing mind Tir. 94 [163
His pride resents the charge, although the p. Tir.
Else sure notorious fact, and p. so plain Tir. 259
Ye knew at least, by constant p. addressed Tir. 273
Bid fair enough to answer in the p. Tir. 564
Such microscopic p. of skill and power Tir. 637
P. of a trifling and a worthless mind T.T. 759
P. of an old affection still alive V. 24
P. not contemptible of what she can Y.O. 131

PROP.
Is it a time to wrangle, when the p. T. ii 62
Of the smooth-shaven p., and neatly tied T. iii 659
And p. the pile they but adorned before T. v 116
On p. of smoothest shaven wood T.B. 23
The p. of such proud seminaries fall Tir. 499

PROPAGATED.
The p. myriads spread so fast P.E. 484

PROPENSE.
P. his heart to idols, he is held T. v 585

PROPER.
Are marriage in its true and p. shape A.T. 65
And fear, not courage, is its p. source Con. 180
And only blushes in the p. place Con. 374
Some farrier should prescribe his p. course Con. 411
And give the moral springs their p. play Con. 832
This more than monster in his p. guise H. 573
That conscience there performs her p. part H. 692
Choose not alone a p. mate P.T. 64
But p. time to marry P.T. 65
Who seek retirement for its p. use R. 170
And woo and win thee to thy p. good R. 256
Teach, while they flatter him, his p. place R. 446
Here virtue thrives as in her p. soil T. i 600
But foolish man foregoes his p. bliss T. iii 296
Shine out; there only reach their p. use T. iv 662
May exercise amiss his p. powers T. v 339
Not so when, held within their p. bounds T. vi 574
He seek his p. happiness by means T. vi 954
To feed our infant minds with p. fare Tir. 116
Wanting its p. base to stand upon T.T. 54

PROPERTY.
For p. stripped off by cruel chance T. i 503
The tasted sweets of p. begat T. v 224
It is the abject p. of most T. v 246
Their purport, uses, p., resigned Y.O. 152

PROPHECY.
The word of p., those truths divine Ex. 686
As well for them had p. been dumb H. 255
More distant, and that p. demands T. ii 66
Sweet is the harp of p.; too sweet T. vi 747

PROPHESY.
Can't p. themselves at all) A Fable 23
And sighing millions p. the close Ex. 309
Mean you to p., or but to preach ? T.T. 499

PROPHESYING.
Of superstition, p. still T. iv 294

PROPHET.
The p. wept for Israel ; wished his eyes Ex. 33
Their were the p., theirs the priestly call Ex. 201
Come, p., drink, and tell us what think you " H. 418
Well spake the p.,—" Let the desert sing H. 524
Thus says the p. of the Turk L.W. 1
What joint the p. had in mind) L.W. 14
What says the p. ? Let that day be blest P.E. 157
And, p. as he was, he might not strike T. vi 468
Foretold by p., and by poets sung T. vi 731
Whose fire was kindled at the p.'s lamp T. vi 732
Thy p. speak of such ; and, noting down T. vi 899
Of p. and of poet was the same T.T. 501

PROPHETIC.
Such the Bard's p. words B. 33
Or guess, with a p. power E. i 71
And sounds p. are too rough to suit Ex. 67
Ah self-deceived ! Could I, p., say St. ii 17
But no p. fires to me belong T.T. 504

PROPITIOUS.

P. to his fond intent there grew *A.T.* 80
Blessed the glad beams of that *p.* day *A.T.* 205
No light *p.* shone *Cast.* 62
P. Spirit! yet expunge a wrong *Ch.* 276
How to secure, in some *p.* hour *R.* 141
Nor seldom, as *p.* Heaven might send *R.* 377
That each may find its most *p.* light *T.* ii 295
Unconscious of a less *p.* clime *T.* iii 567
Begs a *p.* ear for his poor thoughts *T.* iv 68
P., pays his tribute, game or fish *T.* iv 611
P. in his chariot paved with love *T.* vi 744
In that bright quarter his *p.* skies *Tir.* 395
With more than a *p.* gale *Trans. H.* 35
Fostering *p.*, thou becamest a twig *Y.O.* 39

PROPOUND.

"And gesture, they *p.* to our belief? *T.* v 649

PROPORTION.

Who poises and *p.* sea and land *Ex.* 342
And just *p.*, fashionable mien *T.* ii 421

PROPORTIONED.

For want of powers *p.* to the post *R.* 612
I view the muscular *p.* limb *T.* v 15
To give it praise *p.* to its worth *T.* vi 756
P. to his size *Trans.* i 12
P. well, half muscle and half bone *T.T.* 219

PROPOSED.

And truth, *p.* to reasoners wise as they *H.* 258
And all the mysteries to faith *p. T.* vi 878

PROPPED. [iv 546

Ill *p.* upon French heels; she might be deemed *T.*

PROPRIETOR.

Its only just *p.* in him *T.* v 804

PROPRIETY.

With a *p.* that none can feel *T.* v 744

PROSCRIBE.

Of fancy, or *p.* the sound of mirth *T.* iv 176
To dash the pen through all that you *p. T.T.* 769

PROSCRIBED.

Shall stand *p.*, a madman or a knave *Con.* 476
Of fruit *p.*, as to a refuge, fled *Y.O.* 16

PROSE.

P. answers every common end *E.* i 2
No flights above the pitch of *p. E.* i 16
Which, couched in *p.*, they will not hear *E.* i 22
(I would say twenty sheets of *p.*) *E.* iv 28
And Sidney, warbler of poetic *p. T.* iv 516
And with poetic trappings grace thy *p. T.* v 679
What need of Homer's verse, or Tully's *p. Tir.* 399
Backed with a modest sheet of humble *p. V.* 20

PROSELYTE.

From every hair-brained *p.* he makes *P.E.* 491
Spent all his force, and made no *p.*) *T.* ii 331

PROSPECT.

Can hopes of Heaven, bright *p.* of an hour *Con.* 591
How bright soe'er the *p.* seems *F.* 73
Whose *p.* shows thee a disheartening waste *H.* 32
Or present, or in *p.*, meet his sight *P.E.* 48
The *p.*, such as might enchant despair *R.* 469
Me fruitful scenes and *p.* waste *S.* 21
In happier days, to brighter *p.* born! *S.* ii 5
My relish of fair *p.*; scenes that soothed *T.* i 141
P., however lovely, may be seen *T.* i 509
And *p.* oft so dreary and forlorn *T.* vi 21

Though but in distant *p.*, and not feel *T.* vi 761
To lead his son, for *p.* of delight *Tir.* 630
An ell or two of *p.* we command *T.T.* 581

PROSPER. [ii 226

Should England *p.*, when such things, as smooth *T.*
P. (I press thee with a powerful plea) *Ch.* 5
But ah! what wish can *p.*, or what prayer *Ch.* 137
Perhaps might *p.* with a swarm of bees *Con.* 288
Live there, and *p.* Those Ausonia claims *T.* iii 582
Whose approbation—*p.* even thine *T.* vi 1024

PROSPERITY.

There proof against *p.*, awhile *Ex.* 77

PROSPEROUS.

Claimed all the glory of thy *p.* wars? *Ex.* 347
Sets me more distant from a *p.* course *M.P.* 105
She ventures onward with a *p.* force *T.T.* 266

PROSTITUTE.

Who *p.* it in the cause of vice *Con.* 27
He mocks his Maker, *p.* and shames *T.* ii 427

PROSTITUTION.

Till *p.* elbows us aside *T.* iii 60
In barbarous *p.* of your son *Tir.* 405
In *p.* sinks the sense of shame *T.T.* 415

PROSTRATE.

It marches o'er the *p.* works of man *Her.* 22

PROTECT.

Esteem them, sow them, rear them, and *p. H.* 295
So sophistry cleaves close to and *p. P.E.* 287
All that is human in me, to *p. T.* iii 347
Resign the scenes their presence might *p. T.* iv 592

PROTECTOR.

The proud P. of the power he gained *T.T.* 611

PROTECTING.

Safe with *p.* Montagu *Mrs. M*—20

PROTECTION.

He sells *p.* Witness at his foot *T.* vi 417

PROTEST.

Well, I *p.* 'tis past all bearing!" *M.F.* 25

PROTESTANTS.

But why before us P. produce *T.* 127

PROTESTED.

He blamed and *p.*, but joined in the plan *P.A.* 43

PROTRACTED.

And long *p.* bowers, enjoyed at noon *T.* i 257
The long *p.* rigour of the year *T.* v 85

PROTRUDING.

Now stars; two lobes, *p.*, paired exact *Y.O.* 36

PROUD.

"Ruffians, pitiless as *p. B.* 41
Not the *p.* monuments of Greece or Rome *Ch.* 302
The boldest patriot might be *p.* to feel *Ch.* 308
The *p.* are always most provoked by pride *Con.* 160
P. of his speed, to overshoot the truth *Con.* 642
Then the *p.* eagles of all-conquering Rome *Ex.* 209
Cry to the *p.*, the cruel, and unjust *Ex.* 268
P. of thy fleets and armies, stolen the gem *Ex.* 348
Are *p.*, and set their faces as a rock *Ex.* 457
Should say that she was *p. J.G.* 36
But higher far my *p.* pretensions rise *M.P.* 110
P. to advance it all they can *Mrs. M*—14
Obsequious when abroad, though *p.* at home *R.* 44

Yet not in cities oft: in p., and gay T. i 681 [T. 34
Heaven on such terms!" they cry with p. disdain
As stoop from Heaven to sell the p. a throne T. 78
You think him humble—God accounts him p. T. 92
And, p. to make his firm attachment known T. 219
But what is man in his own p. esteem? T. 403
The theme though humble, yet august and p. T. i 6
The summit gained, behold the p. Alcove T. i 278
The impression of the blast with p. disdain T. i 380
Who, self-imprisoned in their p. saloons T. i 414
That's noble, and bespeaks a nation p. T. ii 43
Or unenlightened, and too p. to learn T. ii 549
From instrumental causes p. to draw T. iii 238
But to the p., uncandid, insincere T. ii 275
That learning is too p. to gather up T. iii 286 [408
P. of his well-spread walls, he views his trees T. iii
But p. of his uncouth ill-chosen task T. iii 644
Too p. for dairy work or sale of eggs T. iv 549
King was a name too p. for man to wear T. v 242
Receive p. recompense. We give in charge T. v 706
P. of the treasure, marches with it down T. v 708
Knowledge is p. that he has learn'd so much T. vi 96
But learn we might, if not too p. to stoop T. vi 621
Nor Cunning justify the p. man's wrong T. vi 844
A principle, whose p. pretensions pass Tir. 462
The props of such p. seminaries fall Tir. 499 [785
Too p. to adopt the thoughts of one unknown Tir.
Ye p. and wealthy, let this theme Trans. i 25
Fierce, avaricious, p., there must be war T.T. 10
Thus p. Prerogative, not much revered T.T. 230[523
Like a p. swan, conquering the stream by force T.T.
And makes his pupils p. with silver pence T.T. 509
The p. Protector of the power he gained T.T. 611
Too p. for art, and trusting in mere force T.T. 683

PROUDER.

A p. station on the general scale Ch. 336
The p. sashes fronted with a range T. iv 763

PROUDEST.

Swift as the p. gander of them all A.T. 55 [243
They warn and teach the p., would they learn Ex.
But p. of the worst, if that succeed H. 202
A form as splendid as the p. there T. ii 620
Whose frown can disappoint the p. strain T. vi 1023

PROUDLY.

Ere you p. question ours! N.C. 56

PROVE

The same resource to p. A Tale 78
Such virtues had need p. their own reward Ch. 571
Did Charity prevail, the press would p. Ch. 623
And p. too weak for so divine a theme Ch. 633
Too often p. an implement of play Con. 17
Will judge himself deceived, and p. it too Con. 112
Would only p. him a consummate fool Con. 140
P. after all a wind-gun's airy charge Con. 271
'Tis heavy, bulky, and bids fair to p. Con. 307
Than while his conduct p. his heart sincere Con. 766
May p., though much besides the rules of art Con. 869
And yet may p., when understood E. i 89
And placed it in our power to p. E. i 103 [ii 19
But He who knew what human hearts would p. E.
And were I called to p. the assertion true E. iii 12
To p. an evil of which all complain T. iii 43
What nation will you find, whose annals p. Ex. 11
That infidels may p. their title good Ex. 380
Then thou art bound to serve him, and to p. Ex. 560
'Twas but to p. how quickly, with a frown Ex. 578
P. it;—if better, I submit and bow Ex. 633
But p. as ready to believe F. 17
May p. a dangerous foe indeed F. 77
To p. at last my main intent F. 139

Then judge yourself, and p. your man F. 151
And p. by thumps upon your back F. 170
May p. the task, a task indeed F. 196
To p. that what she gives she gives sincere H. 62
His gracious attributes, and p. the share H. 139
To p. that without Christ all gain is lost H. 631
To p. you their destroyers, as ye are Her. 82
"Still p. herself a shrew J.P. 38
To p. her right to reign L.R. 12
P. that the heart is none of his M.F. 61
P. that you have human feelings N.C. 55
The noblest minds their virtue p. P. 61
And p. their owner half divine" P. 64
And p. a raging scorpion in his breast P.E. 241
All these belong to virtue, and all p. P.E. 247
Might p. a mischief, or at best a toy P.E. 302
Though all your engineering p. in vain P.E. 321
Yet glad she came that night to p. Q.V. 29
He p., less happy than his favoured brute R. 633
Seeming a sanctuary, p. a grave R. 736
Merely to p. a nest for me R.C. 56
To whom the rising year shall p. his last St. ii 2
Who only live to p. St. vi 14
Have purchased Heaven, and p. my title good T. 96
The freeborn Christian has no chains to p. T. 187
His life should p. that he perceives their force T. 198
Shall p. (what argument could never yet) T. 431
Of wisdom, p. a school in which he learns T. i 614
And binds the shoulders flat. We p. its use T. ii 589
Eternity for bubbles p. at last T. iii 175
And p. it in the infallible result T. iii 180 [T. iii 788
Just when it meets his hopes, and p. the Heaven
Search it, and p. now if it be not blood T. iii 204
May p. a trumpet, summoning your ear T. iv 570
He too may have his vice, and sometimes p. T. iv 604
P. it. A breath of unadulterate air T. iv 750
What none can p. a forgery, may be true T. v. 612
Recovering fast its liquid music, p. T. vi 261
They p. too often at how dear a rate T. vi 416 [63
With passions, just that he may p., with pain Tir.
To p. a consequence by none denied Tir. 104
How weak the barrier of mere Nature p. Tir. 169
Should p. your ruin, and his own at last Tir. 205
His counsellor and bosom friend shall p. Tir. 216
Beneath thy roof, beneath thine eye to p. Tir. 680
Though thou hadst never grace enough to p. Tir.741
P., rather than impeach, the just remark Tir. 842
Or, if he p. unkind (as who can say) Tir. 895
And prate and preach about what others p. T.T. 172
Stand on a level, and you p. too much T.T. 255
Free to p. all things, and hold fast the best T.T. 273
P. that the mind is weak, or makes it so T.T. 545
P. this, and forfeit all pretence to praise T.T. 569
And may as rich in comfort p. U. 11
Lest this should p. the last U. 22 [41
Might p. a welcome gift, and touch thine heart V.
Prepared for martyrdom, and strong to p. V. 61
Votaries of business and of pleasure p. V. 71

PROVED.

P. kinder to them than the coast A Tale 31 [498
Have p. them truths too big to be expressed Con.
That having p. the weakness, it should seem Con. 829
That p. a mint of wealth, a mine to Rome Ex. 523
And never p. severe J.P. 16
Somebody p. it, centuries ago P.E. 501
Braved and defied, and in our own sea p. T. ii 272
Defective and unsanctioned, p. too weak T. ii 524
Challenging human scrutiny, and p. T. v 868
P. he not plainly that his meaner works T. vi 447
And now, his prowess p., and his sincere T. vi 531
He seeks not hers, for he has p. them vain T. vi 920
First, farewell Niger! whom now duly p. V. 7

PROVEST.
Such feebleness of limbs thou *p. M.* 37

PROVIDE.
P. the faculties an ampler range *Ch.* 334
The squirrel here his hoard *p. M.B.* 5
Sits banqueting, and God *p.* the feast *P.E.* 166
Need help, let honest industry *p. P.E.* 252
Cause to *p.* for a great future day *R.* 652
That appetite can ask, or wealth *p. R.* 744
Subsistence to *p. T B* 33

PROVIDENCE.
'Tis P. alone secures *A Fable* 30
While P. enjoins to every soul *Ch.* 121
Should range where P. has blessed the soil *Con.* 438
This page of *p.* quite new *E.* i 49
Mistress, at least while P. shall please *Ex.* 274
Is adverse P., when pondered well *Ex.* 310
P. adverse in events like these ? *Ex.* 313
And God's disposing *p.* confessed *Ex.* 558
Will P. o'erlook the wasted good ? *P.E.* 223
The gifts of P., and squander life *T.* i 638
Thy P. forbids that fickle power *T.* v 871
(If such who plead for P. may seem *T.* vi 481
But still in vain. The P. that meant *T.* vi 528
For P., that seems concerned to exempt *Tir.* 430
Kind P. attends with gracious aid *T.T.* 249
When P. means mercy to a land *T.T.* 355
But P. himself will intervene *T.T.* 443

PROVINCE.
But while his *p.* is the reasoning part *Ch.* 375
Say, botanist, within whose *p.* fall *H.* 286
Each *p.* of her art her equal care *T.* i 707
The wealth of Indian *p.*, escapes *T.* i 738
To each some *p.*, garden, field, or grove *T.* vi 237

PROVING.
From all assaults of evil, *p.* still *T.* iii 680
P. at last, though told in pompous strains *Tir.* 75

PROVOCATION.
On every trivial *p.* ? *M.F.* 36
What *p.* to the indignant heart *T.* iii 65
Of *p.* given or wrong sustained *T.* v 315

PROVOKE.
You need his pardon, and *p.* his rod *Con.* 488
P. the vengeance of his righteous hand *Ex.* 253
P. to imitation *F.* 9
P. me to a smile. With eye askance *T.* v 14

PROVOKED.
Not soon *p.*, however stung and teased *Ch.* 428
The proud are always most *p.* by pride *Con.* 160
And long *p.*, repaid thee to thy face *Ex.* 391
P. and harassed, in return plagued thee *Ex.* 533

PROVOKING.
Or, more *p.* still, of nobler name *H.* 192

PROWESS.
Thy *p.*—therefore, go ! *M.B.* 20
As he whose *p.* had subdued their foes ? *T.* v 237
And now, his *p.* proved, and his sincere *T.* vi 531
P. to dissipate a host 1789, 6

PROWLING.
Now goes the nightly thief *p.* abroad *T.* iv 432

PROXY.
And silent cipher, while her *p.* plays *T.* i 477
In him thy well appointed *p.* see *Tir.* 676

PRUDE.
Yon ancient *p.*, whose withered features show *T.* 131

PRUDENCE.
With *p.* always ready at our call *H.* 431
Say ye, who (with less *p.* than of old *T.* v 321

PRUDENT.
Some act upon this *p.* plan *F.* 181
More *p.*, or more sprightly *N.Y.G.* 6
He has no hearing on the *p.* side *P.E.* 549
Your *p.* grandmammas, ye modern belles *R.* 515
And, doubtful what, with *p.* care *R.C.* 85
Warily therefore, and with *p.* heed *T.* iii 470
By budding ills, that ask a *p.* hand *T.* vi 591
Our parents yet exert a *p.* care *Tir.* 115
Ah, happy designation, *p.* choice *Tir.* 342

PRUDENTIAL.
Not skulk, or put on a *p.* mask *T.T.* 312

PRUDERY.
By all that prized it ; not for *p.*'s sake *T.* iii 78

PRURIENCE.
There is a *p.* in the speech of some *Con.* 31

PSALM.
And while the clerk just puzzles out the *p. Ch.* 473

PSALTERY.
P. and sackbut, dulcimer and flute *P.E.* 133

PUBLIC.
The fretting plague is in the *p.* purse *Ch.* 62
Let just Restraint, for *p.* peace designed *Ch.* 286
That grief, sequestered from the *p.* stage *Ch.* 305
Most satirists are indeed a *p.* scourge *Ch.* 501
Pelting each other for the *p.* good *Ch.* 622
We dare not risk them into *p.* view *Con.* 371
Like conservators of the *p.* health *Con.* 390
Best for the *p.*, and my wisest part *Con.* 870
Till penitence had purged the *p.* stain *Ex.* 74
Their prayers made *p.*, their excesses kept *Ex.* 143
But *p.* censure speaks a *p.* foe *Ex.* 436
(Though other follies strike the *p.* eye *H.* 620
Drew me to school along the *p.* way *M.P.* 49
And call her charms to *p.* notice forth *P.E.* 296
Committed once into the *p.* arms *P.E.* 518
The servant of the *p.* never knows *R.* 370
The worn-out nuisance of the *p.* streets *T.* 508
Of *p.* note, they reach their perfect size *T.* i 696
To peculators of the *p.* gold *T.* i 735
There is a *p.* mischief in your mirth *T.* i 769
While, through that *p.* organ of report *T.* ii 355
Would fail to exhibit at the *p.* shows *T.* ii 619
And warps the consciences of *p.* men *T.* iii 691
In guilty splendour, shake the *p.* ways *T.* iii 70
Abroad, and desolating *p.* life *T.* iii 683
Deals him out money from the *p.* chest *T.* iii 796
Skillet, and old carved chest, from *p.* sale *T.* iv 402
To advertise in verse a *p.* pest *T.* iv 501
Of *p.* virtue ever wished removed *T.* iv 615 [671
Hence chartered boroughs are such *p.* plagues *T.* iv
By *p.* exigence, till annual food *T.* v 458
For when was *p.* virtue to be found *T.* v 502
Shone brighter still, once called to *p.* view *T.* v 521
That crawls at evening in the *p.* path *T.* vi 565
Wins *p.* honour ; and ten thousand sit *T.* vi 633
The task now falls into the *p.* hand *T.* vi 718
Must drop indeed the hope of *p.* praise *T.* vi 973
Train him in *p.* with a mob of boys *Tir.* 206
For *p.* schools 'tis *p.* folly feeds *Tir.* 250
A *p.* school shall bring to pass with ease *Tir.* 372
Our *p.* hives of puerile resort *Tir.* 458
By *p.* hackneys in the schooling trade *Tir.* 621
And, while on *p.* nurseries they rely *Tir.* 793

The p. character its colours draws *Tir.* 912
Hook disappointment on the p. wheels *T.T.* 146

PUBLICLY.
And, silence p. enjoined *P.T.* 21

PUBLISH.
To sound his horn, and p. it abroad *H.* 311
Shall p., even to the distant eye *T.* vi 148

PUBLISHED.
Their name far p., and revered as far *Ex.* 194

PUBLISHING.
P. to all aloud *St.* iv 14

PUCKERED.
With half-shut eyes and p. cheeks and teeth *T.* iv 352

PUERILE.
Our public hives of p. resort *Tir.* 458

PUFF.
The pipe, with solemn interposing p. *Con.* 245 [248
Then pause and p.—and speak and pause again *Con.*

PUFFED.
P. up with gifts they never understood *Ex.* 130

PUISSANT.
He couched it firm upon his p. thigh *A.T.* 147

PULING.
While yet thou wast a grovelling, p. chit *Ex.* 474

PULL.
Who constitutionally p. *Pat.* 15   [land *Tir.* 900
P. down the schools—what! all the schools in the

PULLED.
P. down the tyrants India served with dread *Ex.* 366
She p. out half-a-crown *J.G.* 216

PULLING.
Thou canst not! Nature, p. at thine heart *Tir.* 865

PULPIT.
The p., therefore, (and I name it filled *T.* ii 326
The p. (when the satirist has at last *T.* ii 329
I say the p. (in the sober use *T.* ii 332
The p. to the level of the stage *T.* ii 564
Since p. fail, and sounding boards reflect *T.* iii 21
In p. none shall hear *Y.D.* 58

PULSE.
Daniel ate p. by choice—example rare! *P.E.* 215
Thy vigorous p., and the unhealthful East *T.* iv 363
Of voided p. or half-digested grain *T.* v 95

PULVERIZED.
P. of venality, a shell *Y.O.* 123

PUNCH.
The p. goes round, and they are dull *Y.D.* 45

PUNCTUAL.
As I can number in my p. page *St.* ii 3
Dependent on the baker's p. call *T.* i 244
Of the undeviating and p. sun *T.* vi 129
Timing more p., unrecorded facts *Y.O.* 47

PUNCTUALLY.
P. paid for lengthening out disease *H.* 204

PUNISH.
To bind the lawless, and to p. guilt *Ch.* 281
To p. lust, or pluck presumption down *Ex.* 250

And will not p., in one mingled crowd *Ex.* 716
May p., if he please, the less, to warn *T.* ii 157

PUNISHED.
Be p. with perdition, who is pure? *H.* 387
And earth be p. for its tenants' sake *T.* vi 257
Was p. with revolt of his from him *T.* vi 370
Is p., and down comes the thunderbolt *T.T.* 403

PUNISHMENT.
Effects of p. and wrath divine *A.T.* 51
The p. importing this, no doubt *E.* iii 52
That Sin let loose speaks P. at hand *Ex.* 160
Is difficult, their p. obscene *Tir.* 221
For more than common p., it shall *Tir.* 411

PUNY.
The p. tyrant burns to subjugate *H.* 189   [189
To extort their truncheons from the p. hands *T.* v
But spurious and short-lived; the p. child *T.* v 621
And, all the elements thy p. growth *Y.O.* 38

PUPIL.
Of womanhood, fit p. in the school *T.* iv 228
His p., and his torment, and his jest *T.* iv 632
Your p. strike upon have struck yourselves *Tir.* 270
Who feed a p.'s intellect with store *Tir.* 622
And makes his p. proud with silver pence *T.T.* 509

PUPPET.
And wit that p. prompters might inspire *R.* 312

PUPPY.
And puzzling set his p. brains *D.W.* 23
While colts and p. cost us so much care? *Tir.* 295
The p. pack that had defiled the scene *T.T.* 641

PURCHASE.
Not Mexico could p. kings a claim *Ch.* 214
They could not p. earth with such a prize *Ex.* 622
The well judged p., and the gift *M.* i 7
I own I am shocked at the p. of slaves *P.A.* 1
That all your virtues cannot p. now *T.* 570
Are there who p. of the Doctor's ware? *T.* ii 366
Spent in the p. of renown for him *T.* v 277
And thou hast made it thine by p. since *T.* vi 859
And thinking I might p. it too dear *T.T.* 515
To p., at the fool-frequented fair *T.T.* 756

PURCHASED.
Their freedom p. for them, at the cost *Ex.* 171
Have p. Heaven, and prove my title good *T.* 96

PURCHASING.
But while they get riches by p. blacks *P.A.* 15

PURE.
P. in her aim, and in her temper mild *Ch.* 422
Has filled his urn where these p. waters rise *Ch.* 436
And, farewell else all hope of p. delight *Con.* 681
His unsuspecting sheep, believe it p. *Ex.* 103
And kept the faith immaculate and p. *Ex.* 208 [442
Their wisdom p., and given them from above *Ex.*
When a bar of p. silver or ingot of gold *F.M.* 1
His new-born virtues, and preserve him p. *H.* 170
Be punished with perdition, who is p.? *H.* 387
For when it streams from that p. source *Miss* — 57
Oh fie! 'Tis evangelical and p. *P.E.* 133
May least offend against so p. a flame *R.* 248 [*T.* ii 373
Whose hands are p., whose doctrine and whose life
P. from the lees, which often more enhanced *T.* ii 508
P., from so foul a pool, to shine abroad *T.* ii 798
Though few now taste thee unimpaired and p. *T.* iii 43
In the p. fountain of eternal love *T.* iii 244   [712
P. is the nymph, though liberal of her smiles *T.* iii

PURE—PURSUING

Perhaps, though by profession ghostly *p. T.* iv 603
Made *p.*, shall relish with divine delight *T.* v 783
Thy purity, till *p.* as Thou art *p. T.* v 880
While summer was, the *p.* and subtile lymph *T.* vi 135
In streaming gold; syringa, ivory *p. T.* vi 150
Is not: the *p.* and uncontaminate blood *T.* vi 789
Derives from Heaven, *p.* as the fountain is *T.* vi 833
Let laurels drenched in *p.* Parnassian dews *T.T.* 13
Should be renewed in nature, *p.* in heart *V.* 60

PURE-BOSOMED.

P. as that watery glass *Comp.* ii 9

PURER.

With a new medium and a *p.* light *Ch.* 330
And sends the patient into *p.* air *R.* 282
Gold, *p.* far than Ophir ever knew *V.* 97

PUREST.

That jewel of the *p.* flame *F.* 11
And stroke his polished cheek of *p.* red *Tir.* 847

PURGE.

To judge the lands, to *p.* atrocious crimes *A.T.* 141
Their mildest physic is a farrier's *p. Ch.* 502
To *p.* and skim away the filth of vice *P.E.* 343
That so much beauty would do well to *p. T.* i 726

PURGED.

Till penitence had *p.* the public stain *Ex.* 74

PURIFIED.

And *p.*, rejoices to have lost *T.* iii 500

PURIFYING.

And *p.*, makes it shine the more *Con.* 598

PURITY.

That *p.*, whose loss was loss of all *T.* iii 84
Thy *p.*, till pure as Thou art pure *T.* v 880
And claim the palm for *p.* of song *T.T.* 636

PURL.

Should *p.* amidst the traffic of Cheapside *T.T.* 185

PURLING.

The precious stream still *p.* in his ear *P.E.* 232

PURLOINED.

Or vermin, or at best of cock *p. T.* i 563
Seeking her food, with ease might have *p. Y.O.* 19

PURPLE.

The *p.* bumper trembling at his lips *H.* 358
Her unctuous olives, and her *p.* vines *Her.* 7
The *p.* evening and resplendent moon *R.* 348
With modest grandeur in thy *p.* zone *T.* iv 257
With *p.* spikes pyramidal, as if *T.* vi 159
Althæa with the *p.* eye; the broom *T.* vi 170 [369
In coach with *p.* lined, and mitres on its side *Tir.* 73

PURPORT.

The *p.* of his deep decrees *E.* i 60
Their *p.*, uses, properties, resigned *Y.O.* 152

PURPOSE.

I therefore *p.* not, or dream *Cast.* 55
Of Heaven's mysterious *p.* and ways *Ch.* 58
The milk of their good *p.* all to curd *Ch.* 504
Resumed his *p.*, had a world of talk *Con.* 279
Much to the *p.*, if our tongues were loose *Con.* 354
Their hopes, desires, and *p.* estranged *Con.* 725
With all my *p.* intermingling *E.* i 26
A stranger's *p.* in these lays *E.* ii 1
Frames many a *p.*, and God works his own *Ex.* 323
Live to no sober *p.*, and contend *H.* 129

Is handmaid to the *p.* of grace *H.* 146
The *p.* of to-day *H.F.* 2
On *p.* to answer you, out of my mint *P.A.* 19
While, all his *p.* and steps to guard *P.E.* 41
Must watch his *p.* with a stedfast eye *P.E.* 577
For Heaven's high *p.*, and not his own *R.* 18
What *p.* has the King of Saints in view? *T.* 179
Yet scorn the *p.* for which they live *T.* i 486
The bias of the *p.* How much more *T.* ii 493
Should speak to *p.*, or with better hope *T.* iii 25
Convened for *p.* of empire less *T.* iii 62
That ran through all his *p.*, and charge *T.* iii 148
Beneath one head for *p.* of war *T.* iv 666
Great *p.* with ease, that turns and wields *T.* v 252
The triple *p.* In that sickly, foul *T.* v 583
No cruel *p.* lurk'd within his heart *T.* vi 362
But like his *p.*, gracious, kind, and sweet *T.* vi 504
No. Doth he *p.* its salvation? No *T.* vi 705
He *p.*, and he shall answer—None *T.* vi 934
A devil's *p.* with an angel's face *T.T.* 130
Debased to servile *p.* of Pride *T.T.* 748
Fulfil the *p.*, and appeared design'd *Tir.* 93
Egregious *p.*! worthily begun *Tir.* 404

PURPOSED.

So God has greatly *p.*; who would else *T.* vi 820

PURPOSING.

As if the poet *p.* to wed *T.T.* 554

PURRED.

Nor slept a single wink, or *p. R.C.* 75

PURSE.

The fretting plague is in the public *p. Ch.* 62
His glittering *p.*, that envy of all eyes *Ch.* 472
By lean despair upon an empty *p. Ch.* 506
His countenance, his *p.*, his heart, his hand *R.* 595
Into his overgorged and bloated *p. T.* i 737
And he was competent whose *p.* was so *T.* ii 742
Or if that mine be shut, some private *p. T.* iii 797

PURSE-PROUD.

The rich grow poor, the poor become *p. H.* 18

PURSUE.

Should wiser be, than to *p. Beau* 3
Taught me what path to shun, and what *p. Ch.* 239
All prompt his pleased pursuit, and to *p. Ch.* 325
Perhaps—whatever end he might *p. Ch.* 541
The path of narrative with care *p. Con.* 217
P. the course that truth and nature teach *Con.* 890
The gilded butterfly *p. E.* iv 51
Here lies, whom hound did ne'er *p. Ep.* ii 1
That He bids thousands fly when none *p. Ex.* 360
P. the search, and you will find *F.* 199
They could have held the conduct they *p. H.* 256
Nor riches I, nor power *p. O.* ii 4
P. their sport, and follow to the deep *R.* 160
P. the track of his directing wand *T.* iii 777 [328
When none *p.*, through mere delight of heart *T.* vi
Truths that the learned *p.* with eager thought *Tir.* 73
But let eternal Infamy *p. T.T.* 29

PURSUED.

P. the swallow o'er the meads *D.W.* 11
Where under Heaven is Pleasure more *p. Ex.* 7
Trifles *p.*, whate'er the event *Mor.* 45
Like trout *p.*, the critic in despair *P.E.* 502
Unnumbered pleasures harmlessly *p. R.* 784
These, these are arts *p.* without a crime *R.* 799
That rule, *p.* with reverence and with awe *T.* 536
Laboured, and many a night *p.* in dreams *T.* iii 787

PURSUING.

P. gilded flies; and such he deems *T.* vi 922

PURSUIT.
All prompt his pleased p., and to pursue *Ch.* 325
A vain p. of fugitive, false good *H.* 4
Did join in the p. *J.G.* 240
The real worth of man's p. *Mor.* 26
Folly the spring of his p. *P.B.* 17
These call him loudly to p. of more *P.E.* 50
At least are friendly to the great p. *R.* 146
Manly designs, and learning's grave p. *R.* 242
A life of ease a difficult p. *R.* 634
Is squandered in p. of idle sports *T.* ii 758
Oh friendly to the best p. of man *T.* iii 290
Pathetic in its praise, in its p. *T.* iv 719
Address himself who will to the p. *T.* iv 784
Of folly, plunging in p. of death *T.* v 595
Keen in p., and vigorous to retain *Tir.* 524

PURVEYED.
For such is all the mental food p. *Tir.* 620

PURVEYOR.
To turn p. to an overgorged *T.* v 421

PUSH.
Forbid in vain to p. his daring way *Ex.* 17 [706
That strength would fail, opposed against the p. *Ex.*

PUSH-BY.
Mighty to parry and p. God's word *H.* 659

PUSHED.
Are never long vouchsafed, if p. aside *Ex.* 690
In vain they p. inquiry to the birth *T.* ii 511
His murderer on his back, and, p. all day *T.* vi 428
P. with a madman's fury. Fancy shrinks *T.* vi 513
While thus through all the stages thou hast p. *Y.O.* 60

PUSHING.
P. her bold inquiry to the date *R.* 669
To trivial toys, and p. ivory balls *T.* vi 274

PUSH-PIN.
And every effort ends in p. play *T.T.* 547

PUSILLANIMOUS.
'Tis p. and prone to flight *T.* v 373

PUSS.
Till gentler P. shall come *Ep.* ii 40
P. with delight beyond expression *R.C.* 43
Awakened by the shock (cried P.) *R.C.* 53
And P. remained still unattended *R.C.* 66
And p. came into mind no more *R.C.* 71

PUSS-GENTLEMAN.
A fine p. that's all perfume *Con.* 284

PUT.
He thought to p. him in his crop *N.G.* 12
In politic convention) p. your trust *T.* v 323

PUTREFACTION.
'Tis such a light as p. breeds *Con.* 675

PUTREFY.
And p. the breath of blooming Health *T.* ii 184

PUTRID. [97
And, charged with p. verdure, breathe a gross *T.* ii

PUZZLE.
And while the clerk just p. out the psalm *Ch.* 473
Which, puzzling long, at last they p. out *N.A.* 78

PUZZLED.
They disentangle from the p. skein *T.* iii 145

PUZZLING.
And p. set his puppy brains *D.W.* 23
Sorting and p. with a deal of glee *Con.* 13
Which, p. long, at last they puzzle out *N.A.* 78

PYRAMID.
She towered a cloud-capped p. of snow *Her.* 4
By p. and mausolean pomp *T.* v 183

PYRAMIDAL.
With purple spikes p., as if *T.* vi 159

Q.

QUADRANGULAR.
With spots q. of diamond form *T.* iv 217

QUADRILLE.
Blame, cynic, if you can, q. or ball *P.E.* 175

QUADRUPED.
To q. instructors, many a good *T.* vi 622

QUAGS. [253
Crooked or straight, through q. or thorny dells *Tir.*

QUAINT.
And q. in its deportment and attire *T.* ii 461

QUAKE.
That owns a carcass, and not q. for fear? *N.A.* 100
She q. at his approach. Her hollow womb *T.* ii 88
The silent circle fan themselves, and q. *T.* iv 149
Retires, content to q., so they be warmed *T.* iv 386
And q. before the gods themselves had made *T.* v 292

QUAKING.
Unmoved and without q. *F.* 126

QUALIFIED.
Least q. in honour, learning, worth *Tir.* 413
But since although well q. by age *Y.O.* 137

QUALIFY.
To q. him more at large *Trans.* iv 11

QUALITY.
But we, as if good q. would grow *P.E.* 363
Are q. that seem to comprehend *P.E.* 423
Where all good q. grow sick and die *R.* 738
And useful q., and virtue too *T.* vi 623
Their noble q. all quenched and cold *Tir.* 818
In thee some virtuous q. combine *V.* 31

QUALMS. [447
Some seek, when queasy conscience has its q. *Ch.*

QUARREL.
M. q. with N. because M. wrote a book *A.T.* ii 1
Mankind from q., but their fatal end *Con.* 174
Are sadly prone to q. *F.* 87
Renew the q. on the conqueror's part *Her.* 74
To tease for cash, and q. with all day *P.E.* 372
Robbery of gardens, q. in the streets *Tir.* 229

QUARRELSOME.
Grew q., and pecked each other *P.T.* 57

QUARRY.
A q. more important still than you *P.E.* 332   [132
When thou wouldst build; no q. sent its stores *T.* v
A q. of stout spurs and knotted fangs *Y.O.* 117

QUARTER.
Winds from all q. agitate the air *T.* i 373
Swarms in all q.; meets the eye, the ear *T.* ii 818
In that bright q. his propitious skies *Tir.* 395
Three q. of a year *Y.D.* 6

QUARTER-STROKES.
But such mere q. are not for me *T.T.* 531

QUARTO.   [745
Stamped on the well-bound q., grace the shelf *T.T.*

QUAVERING.
Q. and semiquavering care away *P.E.* 127

QUEASY.   [447
Some seek, when q. conscience has its qualms *Ch.*

QUEEN.
When the British warrior q. *B.* 1
And trident-bearing q. of the wide seas *Ex.* 275
Aspiring to the rank of Q.—*L.R.* 7
Let each be deemed a Q." *L.R.* 24
A train, attendant on their q. *Miss*— 71
For no such sight had England's Q.—*Q.V.* 25
Darkness, O Q.! ne'er called before *Q.V.* 35
And show this q. of cities, that so fair *T.* i 727
And strutting in thy school of Q. and Kings *V.* 45
Our Q.'s long-agitated breast 1789, 47
O Q. of Albion, q. of isles! 1789, 56
But she is something more than Q. 1789, 70

QUELL.
And q. the shapeless monsters of the times *A.T.* 142
Can q. the love of freedom in a horse" *Ch.* 172
To q. the valour of the stoutest heart *Ex.* 358
To q. the faction that affronts the throne *T.T.* 67

QUELLED.
Be q. in all our summer-months' retreats *T.* iii 315

QUENCH.
Obscure or q. a faculty that finds *Con.* 593
With some cold moral think to q. the fire *P.E* 320
To q. it) here shines on me still the same *M.P.* 10
No Fear attends to q. his glowing fires *T.* 189
In human bosoms, q. it or abate *T.* iv 747
Unwelcome vapours q. autumnal beams *T.T.* 212

QUENCHED.   [746
But these shall last when night has q. the pole *H.*
Was q. in rheums of age, his voice, unstrung *T.*|ii 728
That seems half q. in the immense abyss *T.* iii 216
Their noble qualities all q. and cold *Tir.* 818

QUENCHING.
In soothing sorrow, and in q. strife *T.* vi 963
Now q. in a boundless sea of clouds *Y.O.* 76

QUENCHLESS.
Cruel is all he does. 'Tis q. thirst *T.* iv 459

QUERULOUS.
O q. and weak!—whose useless brain *H.* 29
A q. old woman's voice *Trans.* iv 25

QUEST.
" To distant wilds in q. of other game *A.T.* 106
Where nought eludes the persevering q. *H.* 445

QUESTION.
Decide no q. with their tedious length *Con.* 87
Ere you proudly q. ours! *N.C.* 56
That q. has its answer—What is man? *T.* 382
But what is truth? 'Twas Pilate's q. put *T.* iii 270
Of its own taunting q., asked so long *T.* vi 870
To press the important q. on his heart *Tir.* 57
A captious q., sir (and yours is one) *Tir.* 903

QUEVEDO.
Q., as he tells his sober tale *T.T.* 93

QUIBBLES.
New raised objections with new q. meets *P.E.* 551

QUICK.
Joys doubly sweet to feelings q. as thine *Ch.* 298
The turns are q., the polished points surprise *Ch.* 544
My q. approach, and soon he dropped *D.W.* 35
Forms rise, to q. perfection wrought *Mrs. M* — 24
Oft gave me promise of thy q. return *M.P.* 37
Oh, then, a text would touch him at the q.! *T.* 310
Shadow and sunshine intermingling q. *T.* i 347
Impregnated with q. fermenting salts *T.* iii 464
Then rise the tender germs, upstarting q. *T.* iii 521
Here, Sally, Susan, come, come q. *Trans.* iv 29

QUICKEN.
Q. a market, and helps off the trash *Ch.* 522   [503
And though his beams, that q. where they shine *H.*
Than Virtue q., with a warmth divine *T.T.* 382

QUICKENING.
That love of Christ in all its q. power *Con.* 562

QUICKLY.
'Twas but to prove how q., with a frown *Ex.* 578
Not q. found, if negligently sought *Ex.* 695
Was q. distanced, matched against a peer's *R.* 580
His wasted spirits q., by long toil *T.* i 128
Clean riddance q. made, one only care *T.* v 70

QUICKNESS.
A q., which in later life is lost *Tir.* 110

QUICKSAND.
Till sinking in the q. he defends *P.E.* 552
A brood of asps, or q in his way *Tir.* 870

QUICK-SIGHTED.
Q. arbiter of good and ill *Tir.* 31

QUICK-SILVER.
Like q., the rhetoric they display *P.E.* 21

QUICK-THOUGHTED.
That, while laborious and q. man *Ex.* 316

QUIESCENT.
There sits q. on the floods that show *M.P.* 92
Nor less amused, have I q. watched *T.* iv 291

QUIET.
And with a q., which no fumes disturb *Con.* 267
All night, we resting q. in the fold *N.A.* 92
Is left to sleep for peace and q. sake *T.* 428
Poor, yet industrious, modest, q., neat *T.* iv 374

QUILL.

With an old tavern q., is hungry yet T. ii 628
Fast as the periods from his fluent q. T. iv 19 [158
With the thought-tracing q. or tasked his mind Y.O.

QUINTESSENCE.

The q. of all be read M. ii 11

QUIP.

So did not Paul. Direct me to a q. T. ii 472

QUIRKS.

And place, instead of q. themselves devise H. 629
His still-refuted q. he still repeats P.E. 550
That plea refuted, other q. they seek T. 293

QUIT.

To q. the forest and invade the fold Ch. 185
To q. the bliss thy rural scenes bestow Ch. 299
Each heart would q. its prison in the breast Ch. 610
Go, q. the rank to which ye stood preferred Con. 75
Which is, that I may fairly q. E. iv 22
Nor would he q. that chosen stand F.B. 28
And wilt thou q. the stream O. ii 15
Which thousands once fast chained to q. no more R. 2
Nor q. till evening watch his giddy stand R. 434
He pressed him much to q. his base employ R. 594
But when his lord would q. the busy road R. 631
And, ere he q. the pen St. i 34 [212
Tom q. you, with—" Your most obedient, sir" T.
Who q. the coachbox at the midnight hour T. i 91
Nor his who q. the box at midnight hour T. i. 98
In tempests; q. his grasp upon the winds T. ii 181
Even as his first progenitor, and q. T. iii 297 [v 65
The sparrows peep, and q. the sheltering eaves T.
And q. their office for their error's sake T. vi 884
And not to q. a score Y.D. 32

QUITRENT.

His q. ode, his peppercorn of praise T.T. 110

QUIVER.

See then the q. broken and decayed T. ii 803
Till, his exhausted q. yielding none T. vi 873

QUIVERED.

The well-poised lance that q. at his side A.T. 144

QUIVERING.

Those alders q. to the breeze S. 6
Dancing uncouthly to the q. flame T. iv 276

QUOTE.

Set Paul to music, he shall q. him too P.E. 113

QUOTH.

"And now," q. poor unthinking Ralph A Fable 18
" An't please your ladyship," q. I—E. iv 79
Q. Mrs. Gilpin,—" That's well said J.G. 25
" Good lack ! " q. he, " yet bring it me J.G. 61
"Did you admire my lamp," q. he N.G. 15
" Methinks the gentleman," q. she P.T. 30
Q. one a rarer man than you Y.D. 57

R.

RABBLE. [T.T. 322

When the rude r.'s watchword was—" Destroy !"
Man praises man. The r., all alive T. vi 694

RACE.

The Fauns and Satyrs, a lascivious r. A.T. 199
Might feel themselves allied to all the r. Ch. 22
Steps forth to fashion and refine the r. Ch. 98
Home to the goal where it began the r. Ch. 566
Gird up each other to the r. divine Con. 702
My spaniel, prettiest of his r. D.W. 5
Where will you find a r. like theirs endowed Ex. 195
Their glory faded, and their r. dispersed Ex. 241
Baboons are free from, upon human r. ? Ex. 417
Seem to reflection of a different r. Ex. 619
Our years, a fruitless r. without a prize H. 25
To men of pedigree, their noble r. H. 237
Politely learned, and of a gentle r. H. 682
Ill fated r.! how deeply must they rue Her. 51
" He carries weight ! " " He rides a r.!" J.G. 115
That Gilpin rode a r. J.G. 244
Some love a concert or a r. L.W. 31
Creatures of gentler r. M.B. 4
Thou hadst supposed them of superior r. N.A. 74
For with a r. like theirs no chance I see N.A. 113
Lights of the world, and stars of human r. P.E. 97
Than Vice's mean and disingenuous r. P.E. 297
Secure of nothing, but to lose the r. P.E. 563
Each sire and dam, of an infernal r. P.E. 568
The busy r. examine and explore R. 151
Not only in our wiser r. R.C. 22
And ardour in the Christian r. St. vi 23
He that would win the r., must guide his horse T. 13
That guides the Christian in his swifter r. T. 534
That yet a remnant of your r. survives T. i 340
Productive only of a r. like ours T. ii 584 [i 564
From his accustomed perch. Hard-faring r.! T.
And waved his rod divine, a r. obscene T. ii 826
The impoverished earth; and overbearing r. T. iii 672
Of our forefathers—a grave, whiskered r. T. iii 768
"Have reached this nether world, ye spy a r. T. v 828
As once in Gibeon, interrupt the r. T. vi 126 [384
And while her infant r., with outspread hands T. iv
Starts to the voluntary r. again T. vi 333
Our ancestry, a gallant Christian r. T.T. 372
Two or three millions of the human r. T.T. 423
The reprobated r. grows judgment proof T.T. 459
Sufficient to redeem the modern r. T.T. 664
Ere yet his r. begins, its glorious close T.T. 708
When first we started into life's long r. Tir. 315
The boughs in which are bred the unseemly r. Tir. 594

RACER.

This r. of the sea A Tale 30

RACK.

He breaks the cord that held him at the r. Ch. 173
To every pang that r. an anxious mind Ex. 571

RACKED.

Thy r. inhabitants repine, complain Ex. 304

RADIANT.

His r. glories, azure, green, and gold T. 61
And all her fruits by r. truth matured T. i 607
" R. with joy towards the happy land T. v 836
Receive yet one, as r. as the rest T. vi 903

RADISH.
Enjoyed, spare feast! a r. and an egg! *T.* iv 173

RAGE.
Full of r. and full of grief *B.* 8
Of controversial r. emits *F.* 104 [earned *T.* vi 533
His r. grew cool; and pleased perhaps to have
Not e'en the vigorous and hateful r. *Con.* 45
Out of the very flames of r. and hate *Con.* 186
The r. and rigour of a polar sky *H.* 462
The Rose soon reddened into r. *L.R.* 9
Swells at the thought, and kindling into r. *T.* 477
Or when rough winter r., on the soft *T.* iii 31
A silent witness of the headlong r. *T.* iii 218
The r. of fermentation, plunges deep *T.* iii 519
Of patriots, bursting with heroic r. *T.* iv 48
Arms, through the vanity and brainless r. *T.* iv 619
The season smiles resigning all its r. *T.* vi 61
Snorting, and starting into sudden r. *T.* vi 550
From these a long succession, in the r. *T.T.* 630
(What will not hunger's cruel r.?) *T.B.* 5
Feel all the r. that female rivals feel *Tir.* 471

RAGGED.
Wide yawns a gulf beside a r. thorn *N.A.* 14

RAGING.
O'er the r. billows borne *N.C.* 4
And proves a r. scorpion in his breast *P.E.* 241
'Tis done—the r. storm is heard no more *T.* 275
By vicious Custom, r. uncontrolled *T.* iii 682
R. abroad, and the rough wind, endear *T.* iv 309

RAGS.
Their fluttering r., and shows a tawny skin *T.* i 568
So he may wrap himself in honest r. *T.* iii 806
To clamorous importunity in r. *T.* iv 414

RAIL.
Too often r. to gratify his spleen *Ch.* 500
While others at that doctrine r. *L.W.* 19
Swears 'tis a bargain, r. at his hard fate *T.* vi 293

RAIMENT.
And cast his filthy r. at them all *T.* 235

RAIN.
He walked abroad, o'ertaken in the r. *Con.* 277
Himself as bountiful as April r. *H.* 304
Autumnal r. had made it chill *Mor.* 13
After long drought, when r. abundant fall *N.A.* 59
Could shelter them from r. or snow *P.T.* 53
Fearless of humid air and gathering r. *T.* 212
Blown all aslant, a driving, dashing r. *T.* 239
With dripping r., or withered by a frost *T.* ii 211
Her sunshine and her r., her blooming spring *T.* vi 946
But Fate thy growth decreed; autumnal r. *Y.O.* 23

RAINBOWS.
His r. and his starry eyes *Mrs. M—* 4

RAISE.
But r. the shrillest cry in British ears *Ex.* 271
And r. a laugh) pass unmolested by *H.* 621
Would r. her voice, and roar *J.P.* 10
Here various motives his ambition r. *P.E.* 53
To r. such wonders in her view *Q.V.* 63
Not to molest, or irritate, or r. *R.* 317
Content if thus sequestered I may r. *R.* 805
From which no power of thine can r. her up *T.* i 660
Though Appetite r. outcries at the cost? *T.* ii 621
To r. the prickly and green-coated gourd *T.* iii 446
And destitute of means to r. themselves *T.* v 248
Shall r. no feuds for armies to suppress *T.T.* 317
May r. such fruits as shall reward his care *Tir.* 771

RAISED.
Not as if r. by mere mechanic powers *Con.* 706
And r. thyself, a greater, in their stead? *Ex.* 367
Soon r. a cloud that darkened every land *Ex.* 509
They r. the hue and cry *J.G.* 236 [*Ex.* 579
He that had r. thee, could have plucked thee down
(And r. her voice, and frowned beside) *M.F.* 16
Plants r. with tenderness are seldom strong *P.E.* 359
New r. objections with new quibbles meets *P.E.* 551
Taught the r. shoulders to invade the ears *T.* i 67
R. by the mole, the miner of the soil *T.* i 273
Of the edifice that policy has r. *T.* ii 817
And ribands streaming gay, superbly r. *T.* iv 541
As if exalting him they r. themselves *T.* v 263
Ask him, indeed, what trophies he has r. *T.* vi 932
Such men are r. to station and command *T.T.* 354
Shifted the wind that r. it, and it fell *T.T.* 337
With droll sobriety they r. a smile *T.T.* 658 [283
Of poets r. by you, and statesmen, and divines *Tir.*
Have r. you high as talents can ascend *V.* 13

RAKE.
R. well the cinders, sweep the floor *E.* iv 41

RAKEHELL.
By some lewd earl, or r. baronet *P.E.* 314

RALPH.
"And now," quoth poor unthinking *R.—A Fable* 18

RAM. [804
And endless her increase. Thy r. are there *T.* vi
A r., the ewes and wethers, sad, addressed *N.A.* 82

RAMBLE.
My r. ended, I returned *D.W.* 29
To enjoy a r. on the banks of Thames *T.* i 115
Yields no unpleasing r.; there the turf *T.* i 530

RAMBLED.
Have r. wide. In country, city, seat *T.* iii 14

RAMBLING.
Would ye, when r. in your morning ride *R.* 545
All these, life's r. journey done *St.* i 3

RAN.
Through all He spoke a noble plainness r. *Ex.* 135
Down r. the wine into the road *J.G.* 125
Freshening his lazy spirits as he r. *P.E.* 411
She r. upon no rock *R.G.* 20 [148
That r. through all his purposes, and charge *T.* iii

RANDOM.
And all at r., fabulous and dark *T.* ii 522
They shame their shooters with a r. flight *T.* ii 807
By these fortuitous and r. strokes *T.* v 124
At r., without honour, hope, or peace *T.* v 899
And, like a scattered seed at r. sown *T.T.* 674

RANG.
All Kilwick and all Dingloderry r. *N.A.* 36 [v 819
With which Heaven r., when every star in haste *T.*

RANGE.
Free as the lordly bull that r. o'er the mead *A.T.* 61
To traverse seas, r. kingdoms, and bring home *Ch.* 301
Provides the faculties an ampler r. *Ch.* 334 [438
Should r. where Providence has blessed the soil *Con.*
Of joys they meet with in their heavenly r. *Con.* 694
R. at liberty, and snuffs the wind *R.* 630
And r. an Indian waste without a tree *T.* i 261
The prouder sashes fronted with a r. *T.* iv 763
To r. the fields and treat their lungs with air *T.* iv 772
These meadows and that r. of hills his own *T.* v 223

His body bound, but knows not what a r. T. v 775
And 'guiltless of offence, they r. the air T. vi 575
Of modest truth for wit's eccentric r. Tir. 174

RANGED.
These chestnuts r. in corresponding lines T. i 263
So once were r. the sons of ancient Rome T. iii 596

RANGERS.
And thus the r. of the western world T. i 618

RANK.
R. its abuse among the foulest deeds Ch. 209
Go, quit the r. to which ye stood preferred Con. 75
And where unsightly and r. thistles grew H. 526
Aspiring to the r. of Queen L.R. 7
The r. debauch suits Clodio's filthy taste P.E. 188
Flowers of r. odour upon thorny lands R. 754
Like regimented coxcombs r. and file T. 422
Begets its likeness. R. abundance breeds T. i 686
Assuming thus a r. unknown before T. ii 370
Suffice to give the marshalled r. the grace T. iii 604
All hate the r. society of weeds T. iii 670
Interprets her more truly) of a r. T. iv 548
To the next r. contagious, and in time T. iv 584
If guards, mechanically formed in r. T.T. 135
Of r. obscenity, debauched their age T.T. 631
'Twould thin the r. of the poetic tribe T.T. 768
Rise in his forehead, and seem r. enough Tir. 164
R. as a virtue, and is yet a vice Tir. 465
Or is thine house, though less superb thy r. Tir. 751

RANKLING.
No rough annoyance r. in his mind R. 428

RANSACKED.
I r., for a theme of song 1789, 1

RANSOMED.
Who made, who marred, and who has r. man Tir. 128

RANT.
Of heroes little known, and call the r. T. iii 140
Of r. and rhapsody, in virtue's praise T. v 677
An English poet's privilege to r. T.T. 299

RANTING.
Outscolds the r. actor on the stage T. iv 45

RAPACIOUS.
Extreme, at once r. and profuse T. ii 380

RAPE.
That lewd incontinence, and lawless r. A.T. 64

RAPID.
Sinuous or straight, now r. and now slow T. iii 778
But trees, and rivulets whose r. course T. vi 109

RAPIDITY.
With mad r. and unconcern T.T. 464

RAPIDLY.
As life declines, speed r. away T. i 130
Fades r., and by compression marred T. iv 669

RAPINE.
When Roman r., by no laws withheld A.T. 126
And that obtained by r. and by stealth? Ex. 371
To indigence and r.; till at last T. iv 497

RAPS.
He notes it in his book, then r. his box T. vi 292

RAPT.
Fearless, and r. away from all his cares T. iii 311

RAPTURE.
And with scenes that new r. inspire C. 51
Forget his harmony, with r. heard Con. 447
From thousands with r. inspired M.D. 40
The choicest r. to impart Miss — 3
Cards with what r., and the polished die P.E. 171
And with a r. like his own exclaim R. 86
And that my r. are not conjured up T. i 151
Joys that her stormy r. never yield T. iii 57
His manner, and with r. tastes his style T. iii 228
That errs not, and find r. still renewed T. iii 723
And adds his r. to the general praise T. v 890
Akin to r., when the bauble finds T. vi 276
Its clearest tone, the r. it inspires T.T. 293

RAPTUROUS.
Earth rolls the r. hosanna round T. vi 797

RARE.
And false ones are as r. almost A Tale 7
Thought is so r., and fancy so profuse Con. 856
An acquisition rather r. F. 31
Not e'en the sun, desirable as r. H. 505
Impelled through regions dense and r. O. i 15
Daniel ate pulse by choice—example r.! P.E. 215
And sells them medals, which, if neither r. P.E. 399
Become more r. as dissipation spreads R. 706
Learning is one, and wit, however r. T. 302
But r. at home, and never at his books T. ii 383
And pregnant with discoveries new and r. T. iii 138
So grateful to the palate, and when r. T. iii 447 [434
And therefore 'tis, that, though the sight be r. Tir.
Are such men r.? perhaps they would abound Tir. 700
Such r. exceptions, shining in the dark Tir. 841
Belinda and her bird! 'tis r. Trans. iv 31

RAREE-SHOW.
Who thrusts his nose into a r.? Con. 286
The bustle and the r. Trans. ii 16
To live by buskin, sock, and r. V. 34

RARER.
Quoth one a r. man than you Y.D. 57

RAREST.
The gems of India, Nature's r. birth Ch. 134

RASED.
Thy temple, once thy glory, fallen and r. Ex. 259

RASH.
That fire abated which impels r. youth Con. 641 [901
With r. and awkward force the chords he shakes Con.
(As is the course of r. and fiery men) T. vi 542
But soon alas! detect that r. mistake V. 55

RASHLY.
Not r. or in sport U. 8

RAT.
A r. fast clinging to the cage T.B. 46
While the r. is on the scout Trans. iii 11

RATE.
And play the fool, but at a cheaper r. R. 562
They prove too often at how dear a r. T. vi 416

RATED.
Shall find them r. at their full amount T. 545

RATIFY.
That none could frame or r. but she Con. 468

RATIONAL.
Strange! that a creature r., and cast T. i 574
Of r. discussion, that a man T. v 306
The dreadful leap, more r. his steed T. vi 517
Respect, as is but r. and just Tir. 710

RATTLE.
The stones did r. underneath J.G. 43

RATTLING.
Till half the world comes r. at his door H. 77
No r. wheels stop short before these gates T. iv 144

RAVE.
Yon roaring boys, who r. and fight Pat. 5
There, and there only (though the deist r. P.E. 614
For solitude, however some may r. R. 735

RAVEN.
A r., while with glossy breast A Fable 1
(For r., though, as birds of omen A Fable 20
The unfledged r. and the lion's whelp T. vi 461

RAVING.
The r. storm and dashing wave defies Con. 559

RAVISH.
May no foes r. thee, and no false friend T.T. 332

RAW. [iii 30
'And fetch my cloak; for though the night be r. E.
The youth now bearded, and yet pert and r. Tir. 155

RAY.
Are taught by r. that fly with equal pace Ch. 363
Let all your r. of information meet Con. 240
Thou hast as bright an interest in her r. Ex. 590
But now and then perhaps a feeble r. H. 93
No Cotton, whose humanity sheds r. H. 205
Diverging each from each, like equal r. H. 303
With all a July sun's collected r. R. 484
Traduce the splendour of a noontide r. T. 540 [v 6
Seen through the leafless wood. His slanting r. T.
But if his word once teach us, shoot a r. T. iii 240
A r. of heavenly light gilding all form's T. v 810
Like his to shed illuminating r. T.T. 712
And Genius shed his r. Th. 4
Our striplings shine indeed, but with such r. Tir. 286
From whence his r. proceed Trans. i 6

RAZOR.
By cold submersion, r., rope, or lead R. 584

REACH.
I am out of Humanity's r. A.S. 9
He flew to r. it, by a law A Tale 51
The Scripture placed within his r., he ought Ch. 201
And only sympathy like thine could r. Ch. 304
And too short lived to r. the realms of peace Ch. 451
Fate having placed all truth above his r. Con. 142
True bliss, if man may r. it, is composed Con. 679
Her utmost r., historical assent Con. 777 [586
And plucks the fruit placed more within his r." Con.
And all is trash that Reason cannot r. Ex. 108
Nor spare a life too short to r. the skies Ex. 623
Joys alwaye prized, when placed within our r. H. 36
Was too refined for them, beyond their r. H. 500
To r. the distant coast H.F. 22
Truths that the theorist could never r. P.E. 11
As woodbine weds the plant within her r. R. 229
Above the r. of man : his hoary head T. i 520
Is obvious, placed within the easy r. T. i 598
Of public note, they r. their perfect size T. i 696
Might never r. me more! My ear is pained T. ii 5
Shall roll themselves ashore, and r. him there T. ii 145
Is obstinate, and cure beyond our r. T. iii 40
Has lost its terrors ere it r. me T. iv 101
Shine out; there only r. their proper use T. iv 662
As she with all her rules can never r. T. v 126
To r. a depth profounder still, and still T. v 593
To contemplation, and within his r. T. vi 263
And, trust me, his utility may r. Tir. 731 [Tir. 801
Whose hearts will ache, once told what ills may r.
So shalt thou live beyond the r. Trans. H. 2

REACHED.
No traveller ever r. that blest abode E. ii 11 [504
But still light r. thee; and those gods of thine Ex.
Directs thee to that eminence they r. Ex. 657
For saddletree scarce r. had he J.G. 49
Just r. it when the sun was set Mor. 22 [96
So thou, with sails how swift! hast r. the shore M.P.
His censure r. them as he dealt it P. 65
Had r. the sinewy firmness of their youth T. v 288
" Have r. this nether world, ye spy a race T. v 828
Rushed to the cliff, and having r. it, stood T. vi 552

REACHING. [529
That r. home, "The night," they said, "is near Con.

REACTION.
Of action and r. He has found T. ii 193

READ.
I have r. the Review; it is learned and wise A.T. iv 1
He r. the skies, and, watching every change Ch. 333
He r. wise lectures, and describes aloud Ch. 389
Well r., well tempered, with religion warmed Con. 640
Thou canst not r., with readiness and ease Ex. 312
Can pause one hour to r. a serious rhyme Ex. 605
To r. the news, or fiddle, as seems best H. 76
By which he r., that life without a plan H. 95
To r. wise lectures, vanity the text H. 107
Of all it ever was my lot to r. H. 425
The quintessence of all he r. M. ii 11
Ye writers of what none with safety r. P.E. 307
Such as, when legible, were never r. P.E. 392
R., ye that run, the awful truth St. i 21
He r. his sentence at the flames of Hell T. 10 [274
The book shall teach you; r., believe, and live!" T.
And in that charter r., with sparkling eyes T. 329
Inquisitive attention, while I r. T. iv 52 [358
He teaches those to r., whom schools dismissed T. ii
To r., engraven on the mouldy walls T. v 418
" We find sound argument, we r. the heart " T. v 654
To r. his wonders, in whose thought the world T. v 798
So r. he Nature, whom the lamp of truth T. v 845
But r. the instrument, and mark it well T. vi 454
And r. with such discernment, in the port T. vi 617
The man that is not moved with what he r. T.T. 25
And mine can r. them there The Doves 16
With such a lustre, he that runs may r. Tir. 80 [114
What friends we sort with, or what books we r. Tir.
I r. of bright embattled fields 1789, 3

READER.
Hush—silent r. profit most A Tale 29
Such writers, and such r., owe the just P.E. 329
" His joys be mine," each R. cries St. iii 33
My very gentle r. yet unborn T. ii 581
Sagacious r. of the works of God T. iii 253

READEST.
(Attentive when thou r.) of England's peers S. i 3

READIER. [495
But none with r. skill!—'Tis here they learn T. iv

READINESS.
Thou canst not read, with r. and ease Ex. 312
With unsuspecting r. he takes T. vi 427

READING.
And r. here his sentence, how replete St. ii 7
Cry—hem! and r. what they never wrote T. ii 411

READY.
Had wit as bright as r. to produce Con. 614
" 'Tis r. polished from the mine " E. iv 90
But prove as r. to believe F. 17

READY—RECEIVE

To me ever r. to show Gr. 43
With prudence always r. at our call H. 431
Thus showed his r. wit J.G. 186
And r. to be borne to court R.C. 20
Formed for his use, and r. at his will? T. ii 202

REAL.
A r. and a sound one F. 15
Seeking a r. friend, we seem F. 142
From emptiness itself a r. use H. 156
The r. worth of man's pursuits Mor. 26
Their r. interest to discern N.G. 28
Yours r., and pernicious in the extreme P.E. 101
Ask wealth of Heaven, and gain a r. prize R. 162
Or r., or fictitious, of the times T. 162
A r. elegance, a little used T. ii 611
And, common sense diffusing r. day Tir. 189

REALITY.
And earth has no r. but woe " H. 68
And in r. to find no friend T.T. 160

REALM.
In Scotland's r., where trees are few A Tale 1
In Scotland's r., forlorn and bare A Tale 9
" This triple r. adores thee;—thou art come Ch. 270
And too short lived to reach the r. of peace Ch. 451
Pierced to the very centre of the r. Ex. 576
Cry to her universal r., " Rejoice!" H. 54
Drives through the r. of Sin, where Riot reels H. 651
And she, once mistress of the r. around T. 393
And swayed the sceptre of his infant r. T. i 23
Disturbs the economy of Nature's r. T. vi 579

REAM.
Whose corresponding misses fill the r. P.E. 311

REAP.
Not knowing thee, we r. with bleeding hands R. 753
Yes—ye may fill your garners, ye that r. T. v 755
The laurels that a Cæsar r. are weeds T. vi 939

REAPED.
And r. their plenty without grudge or strife T. v 203

REAR.
Which seems by the crest that it r. Gr. 3
Esteem them, sow them, r. them, and protect H. 295
With post-boy scampering in the r. J.G. 235
He r. unchanged his barren head Miss — 39
The dwarfish, in the r. retired, but still T. iii 594
Though poor in skill to r. them, lights at last T. vi 753
And eke did r. right merrily, two staves T. vi 662
She r. her favourite man of all mankind T.T. 217
From him who r. a poem lank and long T.T. 532

REARED.
That r. us. At a thoughtless age, allur'd T. vi 38

REASCEND.
As soon shall rise and r. the throne T. 395

REASCENT.
And such the r.; between them weeps T. i 327

REASON.
But R. still, unless divinely taught Ch. 337
Endued with r., yet by nature blind Ch. 382
Religion, Virtue, R., Common Sense Con. 77
On R.'s verdict is a madman's deed Con. 190
The power to clothe that r. with his word Con. 432
Then there's another r. yet E. iv 21
And all is trash that R. cannot reach Ex. 108
Could he with r. murmur at his case H. 316
And when by that of r., a mere fool H. 567
Till some r. ye shall find N.C. 50

As R., or as Passion, takes the reins P.E. 36
Is there, as R., Conscience, Scripture say R. 651
And is this all? Can R. do no more R.H. 1
In r., is judicious, manly, free T. v 354
Scoffs at her own performance. R. now T. v 629
To excuses in which r. has no part) T. v 656
Distinguished much by r., and still more T. vi 601
Kings do but r. on the self-same plan T.T. 48
Could they, or would they, r. as they ought T.T. 58
Endued with r. only to descry Tir. 61
But r. heard, and nature well perused Tir. 89
Till R., now no longer overawed Tir. 187
With so much r. all expect from them Tir. 353

REASONABLE.
With r. forecast and dispatch T. ii 623
The comfort of a r. joy T. vi 347

REASONERS.
And truth, proposed to r. wise as they H. 258
Ye r. broad awake, whose busy search Y.O. 30

REASONING.
With a r. the Court will never condemn A.C. 22
But while his province is the r. part Ch. 375
The r. power vouchsafed of course inferred Con. 431
Then praise is heard instead of r. pride H. 143
R. at every step he treads The Doves 1
Such r. (if that name must needs belong T. v 655
Such r. falls like an inverted cone T.T. 53

REBEL.
R., because 'tis easy to obey T. 36

REBELLED.
Though long r. against, not yet suppressed R. 16

REBELLION.
His speech r. against common sense H. 565
R. is my theme all day Pat. 1

REBELLIOUS.
Than reverence, in perverse r. youth T. ii 730
So clothed with beauty, for r. man? T. v 754

REBOUND.
From stuccoed walls smart arguments r. H. 346

REBUFFS.
The rugged frowns and insolent r. T. iv 411

REBUILDS.
R. the towers that smoked upon the plain Her. 71

REBUKE.
Despising all r., still persevered Ex. 397
But gently to r. his awkward fear H. 61
Grew stern, and darted a severe r. T. ii 720
Falls first before his resolute r. T. v 619
The blameless animal, without r. T. vi 469
And measure of the offence, r. a deed T. vi 655
Let reverend churls his ignorance r. Tir. 401
His lessons tire, his mild r. offend Tir. 716

RECALL.
How gladly would the man r. to life T. vi 42
Not to r. a promise to your mind V. 21

RECEDES.
The sloping land r. into the clouds T. i 171

RECEDING.
Loses in tears the far r. shore Ch. 147
R. wide, they pressed against the ribs T. i 65

RECEIPT.
A satisfactory r. in full Con. 202

RECEIVE.
Lethæan gulfs r. them as they fall B.B. 7

And in return *r.* supply from all *Ch.* 92
And still enlarged as she *r.* the grace *Ch.* 597
They fill their measure, and *r.* their due *Con.* 34
Thus touched, the tongue *r.* a sacred cure *Con.* 887
If the new mail thy merchants now *r. Ex.* 606
This artless vow may Heaven *r. Miss* — 93
R. from her both appetite and treat *P.E.* 210
Nor Ouse on his bosom their image *r. P.F.* 4
Claims most compassion, and *r.* the least *R.* 302
R. me, languishing for that repose *R.* 369
R. me now, not uncorrupt as then *R.* 381
Mercy *r.* him on her peaceful shore *T.* 276
R. no praise, but, though her lot be such *T.* 325
Humility is crowned, and Faith *r.* the prize *T.* 589
To narrow bounds. The Grove *r.* us next *T.* i 354
R. the morsel—flesh obscene of dog *T.* i 562
R. our air, that moment they are free *T.* ii 41 [83
How does the earth *r.* him?—with what signs *T.* ii
The lewd, vain world that must *r.* him soon *T.* ii 764
Assimilates all objects. Earth *r. T.* iv 329
To give thee what politer France *r. T.* v 468
R. proud recompense. We give in charge *T.* v 706
The soul that sees him, or *r.* sublimed *T.* v 805
That hear not, or *r.* not their report *T.* v 855
To stroke his azure neck, or to *r. T.* vi 781
R. yet one, the crown of all the earth *T.* vi 856
R. yet one, as radiant as the rest *T.* vi 903
R. advantage from his noiseless hours *T.* vi 944
Summer in haste the thriving charge *r. Tir.* 45
In return thou shalt *r. Trans.* iii 7
R., dear friend, the truths I teach *Trans. H.* 1

RECEIVED.

R. the transcript of the Eternal Mind *Ex.* 198
If Vice *r.* her retribution due *Ex.* 247
The cradle that *r.* thee at thy birth *Ex.* 469
R. the seal of martyrdom in blood *Ex.* 617
Mankind *r.* from heaven *Miss* — 24
Ere our necks *r.* the chain *N.C.* 42
Learning itself, *r.* into a mind *P.E.* 431
Flies to the levee, and, *r.* with grace *R.* 479
And in the midst an elbow, it *r. T.* i 76
Desirous to return, and not *r. T.* iii 81
The infant elements *r.* a law *T.* vi 200
R. his nobler nature, and was made *Tir.* 97 [156
Regards with scorn, though once *r.* with awe *Tir.*
So much thy juniors, who their birth *r. Y.O.* 135

RECEIVING.

The total herd *r.* first from one *T.* vi 335
R. benefits and rendering none *T.* vi 959

RECEPTACLE.

The soft *r.*, in which, secure *Y.O.* 27

RECESS.

Since then in the rural *r. C.* 41
Forcibly drawn from many a close *r. Ch.* 529
To them the deep *r.* of dusky groves *R.* 181
His hours of leisure and *r.* employs *R.* 215
His dwelling a *r.* in some rude rock *T.* 79
How calm is my *r.*, and how the frost *T.* iv 308
None that, in thy domestic snug *r. Tir.* 581

RECIPROCALLY.

And these, *r.*, those again *P.E.* 565

RECIPROCATED.

R. duties *F.* 48

RECIPROCATING.

'Tis thus, *r.* each with each *Ch.* 119

RECITAL.

And give us, in *r.* of disease *Con.* 313
Strange the *r.!* from whatever cause *P.E.* 401

RECKON.

Who *r.* every touch a blemish *P.* 56
Will *r.* with us roundly for the abuse *T.* vi 606

RECKONED.

It has always been *r.* a just cause of strife *A.T.* ii 9

RECKONING.

To a sharp *r.* that has lived in vain *T.* iii 179
An easy *r.*, and they think the same *T.* v 278

RECLAIM.

And Commerce partially *r.* mankind *Ch.* 372
R. his taste, and brighten up his parts *Con.* 840
R. the wandering thousands, and bring home *Ex.* 728
R. the wanderer, binds the broken heart *T.* ii 344
That would *r.* a vicious age *U.* 6

RECLAIMED.

That mulish folly, not to be *r. Ch.* 497
A mere fox-follower never is *r. Con.* 410 [682
Those hearts should be *r.*, renewed, upright *Con.*
The poor *r.* inhabitant, his eyes *H.* 532
What vice has it subdued? whose heart *r. T.* ii 320
Observed as prodigies, and soon *r. T.* iv 524
Ingenious Cowley! and though now *r. T.* iv 723
Or in one article of vice *r. Tir.* 241

RECLINED.

His eyes are sunk, arms folded, head *r. H.* 689
Thus oft *r.* at ease, I lose an hour *T.* iv 302
In the shadow of a bramble, and *r. T.* v 324

RECLUSE.

And I have lived *r.* in rural shades *Con.* 801
Nor these alone prefer a life *r. R.* 169
An Indian mystic, or a French *r. T.* 128

RECOGNISE.

And *r.* the slow retiring fair *T.* ii 454

RECOIL.

R. from weary life's best hour *St.* v 19
R. from its own choice—at the full feast *T.* i 467

RECOILED.

He gleans the blunted shafts that have *r. T.* vi 874

RECOLLECT.

(As you perhaps may *r.*) *B.R.* 11
To *r.* that in a form like ours *Ch.* 583
Conscious of age, she *r.* her youth *T.* 153
But *r.* that he has sense, and feels *Tir.* 720

RECOLLECTED.

Or *r.* only to gild o'er *R.* 9
The *r.* powers, and snapping short *T.* iv 305

RECOLLECTING.

But *r.*, with a sudden thought *N.A.* 51
But *r.* still that he is man *T.* v 335

RECOLLECTION.

But alas! *R.* at hand *A.S.* 47
The *r.*, like a vein of ore *Con.* 515
Such *r.* of our own delights *Tir.* 311

RECOMMENCE.

To *r.* life's trials, in the hope *F.A.* 4

RECOMMEND.

Whatever steep inquiry *r. Ch.* 316
And wound the grace I mean to *r. Ch.* 486
And make the course he *r.* my choice *R.* 388
Oh! grant a poet leave to *r. R.* 541
If sufferings Scripture nowhere *r. T.* 109
Whether inclement seasons *r. T.* iii 388
I therefore *r.*, though at the risk *T.* iii 705
A king, that would, might *r.* his horse *Tir.* 417

RECOMPENSE.

The abundant harvest, r. divine *H.* 770
Shall r. his mere intent *Mor.* 56
His r. in both unjust alike *P.E.* 32
The r. that arts or arms can yield *R.* 101
R. ill? He trembles at the thought *T.* 192
Fair r. of labour well bestowed *T.* iii 430
Receive proud r. We give in charge *T.* v 706
He serves his country, r. well *T.* vi 968
That then, in r. of all thy cares *Tir.* 879

RECOMPENSED.

She did me wrong, I r. the deed *Con.* 797
As ever r. the peasant's care *R.* 332
And I am r., and deem the toils *T.* vi 725

RECOMPENSING.

And fragrant chaplet, r. well *T.* iii 668

RECONCILE.

And r. man to his lot *A.S.* 56
And r. his lusts with saving grace *H.* 605
Whom famine cannot r. to filth *T.* iv 417

RECONCILED.

Thus soothed and r., each seeks *L.R.* 25

RECORD.

Could fetch from r. of an earlier age *Con.* 615
This r. of thee for the Gospel's sake *J.T.* 48
Short-lived possession! but the r. fair *M.P.* 54
In faithful memory she r. the crimes *T.* 161
That may r. the mischiefs he has done *T.* i 277
Have each their r., with a curse annex'd *T.* vi 441
Nor can the wonders it r. be sung *T.* vi 749
Which joyful I will oft r. 1789, 34

RECORDED.

In vain r. in historic page *B.B.* 3
And worthy thus to be r. *P.* 4
And I r. what I heard *The Doves* 39

RECORDING.

No; marble and r. brass decay *Con.* 551
And when r. History displays *T.T.* 21

RECOVER.

I soon r. from these needless frights *H.* 375
His cheek r. soon its healthful hue *T.* i 441

RECOVERED.

Where George, r., made a scene *Q.V.* 27

RECOVERING.

R. what we lost we know not how *Con.* 402
R. fast its liquid music, prove *T.* vi 261
R. and misstated setting right *Y.O.* 48

RECOVERY.

Ourselves, and our r. from our fall *R.* 138
And a complete r. struck him dumb *T.T.* 393

RECREANT.

"Is r., and unworthy of his spurs" *A.T.* 122

RECTITUDE.

Some beams of r. she yet displays *T.* 485
Of r. and fitness, moral truth *T.* v 672

RECTOR.

The tedious r. drawling o'er his head *T.* i 95

RECUMBENCY.

By soft r. of outstretched limbs *T.* i 82

RECUMBENT.

The sheep r., and the sheep that grazed *N.A.* 47

R. at her ease, ere long *R.C.* 45
It yields them, or r. on its brow *T.* v 787

RECURS.

A kindred melody, the scene r. *T.* vi 13

RED.

His long r. cloak, well brushed and neat *J.G.* 75
Not yet the hawthorn bore her berries r. *N.A.* 19
While morning kindles with a windy r. *R.* 432
Drops the r. vengeance from his willing hand *T.* 278
Yellow and r., of tapestry richly wrought *T.* i 33
His azure eyes, is tinctured black and r. *T.* iv 216
In the r. cinders, while with poring eye *T.* iv 289
Of innocent commercial Justice r. *T.* iv 683
The scentless and the scented rose; this r. *T.* vi 151
Ye nymphs! if e'er your eyes were r. *T.B.* 1
And stroke his polished cheek of purest r. *Tir.* 847

REDBREAST.

The r. warbles still, but is content *T.* vi 77

REDCAP.

My dear Dick R., what say you? *P.T.* 37

REDDENED.

The Rose soon r. into rage *L.R.* 9

REDDENING.

And r. with a just and generous pride *A.T.* 204

REDEEM.

And, though disgraced and slighted, to r. *Ch.* 13
Or blade that might r. it from despair *Her.* 28
Rarely r. the short remaining ten *R.* 40
Not to r. his time, but his estate *R.* 561
Sufficient to r. the modern race *T.T.* 664

REDEEMED.

To look at him who formed us and r. *Ch.* 579
A soul r. demands a life of praise *T.* 279

REDEEMER.

The atonement a R.'s love has wrought *T.* 505

REDOUBLING.

Peal upon peal r. all around *T.* 240

REDOUBT.

Enlarge and fortify the dread r. *Con.* 689

REDRESS.

They meet with little pity, no r. *Ch.* 530
To feel, and courage to r. her wrongs *T.* iv 795
Dishonour, and be wronged without r. *T.* vi 822
Nor ceased till, ever anxious to r. *T.T.* 632

REDRESSED.

The frenzy of the brain may be r. *T.* vi 521

REDUCE.

R. his wages, or get rid of her *T.* 211

REDUCED.

R. to practice, his beloved rule *Con.* 139
The faculties that seemed r. to naught *Con.* 403
Though numerous once, r. to few or none? *E.* iii 17

REDUNDANT.

With foliage of such dark r. growth *T.* i 226

RE-ECHOING.

R. pious anthems! while beneath *T.* i 343

REEKING.

From many a steaming lake and r. bog *A.T.* 93
The r., roaring hero of the chase *Con.* 405
His r. head full low *J.G.* 122

Within its r. bosom, threatening death T. iii 503
In ponderous boots beside his r. teem T. iv 342
REEDS.
Now wantoned lost in flags and r. D.W. 9
Enjoy close shelter, wall, or r., or hedge T. iii 474
REEL. [651
Drives through the realms of Sin, where Riot r. H.
Or twining silken threads round ivory r. T. iv 264
That law has licensed, as makes temperance r. T.iv 471
REELED.
Of wild imagination, and there r. T.T. 605
REELING.
Such drunken r., have an awkward look Con. 862
War lays a burden on the r. state Ex. 306
That r. goddess with the zoneless waist T. iii 52
REFECTORY.
The chamber, or r., may die T. vi 572
REFERENCE.
One proof should serve—a r. to you E. iii 13
REFERRED.
The Nymphs r. the cause J.P. 18
REFINE.
"Nor needs his genuine ore r.! E. iv 89
Steps forth to fashion and r. the race Ch. 98
And what dilates the powers must needs r. Ch. 332
That, while thy truths my grosser thoughts r. R. 97
R. his speech, and fashions his address R. 240
REFINED.
"Smoothed and r. the meanest strains E. iv 74
Expressive, energetic, and r. Ex. 482
Was too r. for them, beyond their reach H. 500
To feel the most r. Miss — 4
Nor even these, whose pleasures less r. P.E. 57
'Tis innocent, and harmless, and r. P.E. 179
That, so r., it might the more entice P.E. 344
Though busy, trifling; empty, though r. P.E. 426
At length a generation more r. T. i 28
Half so r. or so sincere as ours T. iv 206
By footman Tom for witty and r. Tir. 687
And that, possessor of a soul r. Tir. 721
Is so r., and delicate, and chaste T.T. 511
To joys less innocent, as less r. T.T. 601
REFINEMENT.
R. is endued, thrice happy thou! T. iv 359
Polite R. offers him in vain T. vi 977
She judges of r. by the eye T. vi 987
REFIT.
Their ruffled plumage calm r. Mrs. M— 46
REFLECT.
R. the noonday glory of the skies Ch. 398
R. that these, and all that seems thine own Ex. 672
But above all r., how cheap soe'er Ex. 680
R. dishonour on the land I love T. ii 224
Since pulpits fail, and sounding boards r. T. iii 21
Still to r., that though a joyless note T. v 406
R. his attributes who placed them there Tir. 92
REFLECTED.
And Heaven r. in her face Comp. ii 10
Her beauteous form r. clear below M.P. 93
All her r. features. Bacon there T. i 702
Sees her unwrinkled face r. bright T. iv 4
REFLECTING.
And unambitious course, r. clear T. vi 723

REFLECTION.
Of wise r. and well timed discourse Con. 388
Or where does cold R. less intrude? Ex. 8
Seem to r. of a different race Ex. 619
With this r. in his head R.C. 108
R. and remorse, the fear of shame T. i 489
R. such as meliorate the heart T. iii 304
With lights, by clear r. multiplied T. iv 268
REFLUENT.
Gone with the r. wave into the deep T. ii 120
REFORM.
All zeal for a R. that gives offence Ch. 533
And blest r. that I have never heard Con. 804
By rigour? or whom laughed into r.? T. ii 321
Remorse begets r. His master-lust T. v 618
And make mistakes for manhood to r. Tir. 445
REFORMATION.
To urge r. of national ill F.M. 14
REFORMED.
R. and well instructed? You shall hear T. 130
Enraged the more by what might have r. T. vi 524
REFRAIN.
But above all (or let the wretch r.) P.E. 456
REFRESH.
Nor cheer the spirit, nor r. the sight H. 299
R., where it winds, the faded green J.T. 39
REFRESHED.
By culture tamed, by liberty r. T. i 606
Courageous, and r. for future toil T. iii 19
And sleeps and is r. Meanwhile the face T. iv 298
Doubtless much edified, and all r. T. vi 693
His soul r. with foretaste of the joy? T. vi 762
REFRESHING.
R. change! where now the blazing sun? T. i 335
REFRESHMENT.
When Custom bids, but no r. find T. i 390
REFUGE.
To sweep away all r. of lies H. 628
Pants for the r. of some rural shade R. 6
Then welcome r., and a peaceful home T. 267
Dearly obtains the r. it affords T. i 238
Sleep seems their only r.: for, alas! T. iv 396
To fly for r. from distracting thought T. v 415
Drawn from his r. in some lonely elm T. vi 310
To seek a r. from the tongue of Strife T. vi 841
Of fruit proscribed, as to a r., fled Y.O. 16
REFUNDED.
To be r. duly, when his vote T. iii 799
REFUSE.
Nor some reproof yourself r. B.R. 23
God's better gift they scoff at, and r. Ex. 459
Gleans up the r. of the general spoil Her. 70
Free in his will to choose or to r. P.E. 25
If stubborn Greek r. to be his friend P.E. 498
REFUSED.
These ask with painful sadness, and, r. T. iv 418
REFUSING.
Yet thus we dote, r. while we can T. v 874
REFUTE.
And cavil at with ease, but none r. T. 360
Stand up unconscious, and r. the charge T. ii 824
And we can readily r. it here T.T. 104

REFUTED.
That plea r., other quirks they seek T. 293
And Victory r. all he said T.T. 389

REGAIN.
Culprit his liberty r. E. iv 59
Then suddenly r. the prize 1789, 54

REGAL.
By r. warrant or self-joined by bond T. iv 664

REGALE.
His rich materials, and r. your ear Con. 617
Nor grateful eglantine r. the smell H. 471
And fungous fruits of earth, r. the sense T. i 532
That ye may garnish your profuse r. T. iii 551
Then turning, he r. his listening wife Tir. 324
Their breath a sample of last night's r. Tir. 834

REGALED.
On twigs of hawthorn he r. Ep. ii 17
The scent r., each odoriferous leaf T. iii 621

REGARD.
The judge of all men owes them no r. Ch. 572
Ensured him mute attention and r. H. 687
While one as innocent r. L.W. 27
If he the tinkling harpsichord r. P.E. 148
Their nature; and disclaiming all r. T. iv 679
Worthier of r., and stronger N.C. 51
If he r. not, though divine the theme T. vi 1019 [156
R. with scorn, though once received with awe Tir.
Where no r. of ordinances is shown Tir. 242

REGARDLESS.
And she r. of her softer kind A.T. 177
Or does he sit r. of his works? T. ii 516
The nurse, no doubt.   R. of her charge T. ii 775
You the r. author of its woes T. v 350
R. of their plaints.   To make him sport T. vi 386
R. of wringing and breaking a heart The Rose 15
A parent pours into r. ears Tir. 590

REGENT.
With yon bright r. of the day Mrs. M – 52
But one, the rose, the r. of them all) R. 724

REGIMENTED.
Like r. coxcombs rank and file T. 422

REGION.
R. Cæsar never knew B. 29
To succour wasted r., and replace Ch. 129
Deplores the wasted r. of her globe Her. 80
Impelled through r. dense and rare O. i 15
To r. where, in spite of sin and woe R. 27
Levantine r. these, the Azores send T. iii 583
From inland r. to the distant main T. v 790
And r. long since desolate, proclaim T.T. 431
Ennobling every r. that he chose T.T. 562

REGISTER.
Extract a r., by which we learn T. iii 152

REGISTERED.
Was r. in Heaven ere time began T. v 530
Is r. in heaven; and these no doubt T. vi 440

REGRET.
But has left a r. and esteem C. 7
The sable warrior, frantic with r. Ch. 145
And if a tear, that speaks r. N. 21
One, and one only, charged with deep r. P.E. 349
Parted without the least r. P.T. 58
One pleasure lost, lose heaven without r. T. 342
R. would rouse them, and give birth to prayer T. 343

And still remember, nor without r. T. i 116
And spiritless, as never to r. T. i 652
Freedom! whom they that lose thee so r. T. ii 130
Scenes that I love, and with r. perceive T. iii 710
Sad witnesses how close-pent man r. T. iv 777
That converse which we now in vain r. T. vi 41
Abandoned, and, which still I more r. T. iv 692
And still admiring, with r. supposed T. iv 716
To weep for the buds it had left with r. The Rose 7
Poets, of all men, ever least r. T.T. 176

REGRETTED.
Ye saw me once (ah, those r. days R. 371
Jack vanished, was r. and forgot R. 581

REGULAR.
How r. his meals, how sound he sleeps! R. 430
And dress the r. yet various scene T. iii 592
The r. return of genial months T. vi 123
Exact and r. the sounds will be T.T. 530

REGULATE.
Were I empowered to r. the lists Con. 195
The freaks of fashion, r. the dress T. ii 317
Prescribed their course, to r. it now T. vi 204

REHEARSE.
Their zeal begotten, as their works r. Ch. 505
Words learned by rote a parrot may r. Con. 7
Could you contrive the payment and r. T.T. 178

REHEARSED.
By one of sound intelligence r. T. vi 480
Urged loud a claim to be r. 1789, 14

REIGN.
Than r. in this horrible place A.S. 8
The r. of genuine Charity commence Ch. 413
A story in which native humour r. Con. 203
Whom man, for his own hurt, permits to r. Con. 458
Seems it to say—"Health here has long to r.?" Ep. i 4
Would age in thee resign his wintry r. H. 33
And tells you where ye have a right to r. Her. 48
In Britain's isle, beneath a George's r.! Her. 90
To prove her right to r. L R. 12
They r. united there L.R. 28
Is there one who r. on high? N.C. 26
Yet heard in scenes where peace for ever r. T. 203
Where peace and hospitality might r. T. ii 617 [642
Where dreams of dress, intrigue, and pleasure r. R.
The spleen is seldom felt where Flora r. T. i 455
And r. content within them: him we serve T. v 333
Seldom, alas! the power of logic r. T.T. 51
Those arts be theirs that hate his gentle r. T.T. 89
Is always happy, r. whoever may T.T. 238
The mind attains, beneath her happy r. T.T. 262
That he who died below, and r. above T.T. 738
Entitled here to r. Q.V. 4
The symbol of a righteous r. 1789, 44

REIGNED
When Cromwell fought for power, and while he r. [T.T. 610
So 'twas a hallow'd time; decorum r. T. vi 691
"Few, fellow!—there are all that ever r. T.T. 100

REIGNEST.
But Chance is not; or is not where thou r. T. v 870

REIN.
Snuffs up the morning air, forgets the r. Ch. 175
In spite of curb and r. J.G. 88
By catching at his r. J.G. 224
As Reason, or as Passion, takes the r. P.E. 36 [535
Till He that rides the whirlwind checks the r. R.
He drops the r., and leaves him to his pace T. 247
Or if, when ridden with a careless r. T.T. 306

REITERATED.
R. as the wheel of time *T.* iii 626

REJECT.
R. all treaty, penetrates all wiles *H.* 649
Thee we *r.*, unable to abide *T.* v 879
Not that he peevishly *r.* a mode *T.* vi 981

REJECTED.
Great schools *r.* then, as those that swell *Tir.* 501

REJECTING.
Who, constant only in *r.* thee *T.* vi 882

REJOICE.
Catharina alone can *r. C.* 42
R. with a wholesome fear *Trans. H.* 20
Cry to her universal realm, "*R.!*" *H.* 54
And bid her mountains and her hills *r. R.* 362
Who cannot much, *r.* in what he can *R.* 504
Hear him, o'erwhelmed with sorrow, yet *r. R.* 772
Your fate unmerited, once more *r. T.* i 339
Or heals it, makes it languish or *r. T.* ii 70
And purified, *r.* to have lost *T.* iii 500
R. in him, and celebrate his sway *T.* v 326
The event is sure; expect it, and *r.!* *Tir.* 343

REJOICING.
He hears the herbs and flowers *r.* all *N.A.* 60

RELAPSE.
They put on a damp nightcap, and *r. Con.* 322
That task performed, *r.* into themselves *T.* ii 441
Its own dishonour by a worse *r. T.* v 626

RELATE.
R. how many weeks they kept their bed *Con.* 315
Else, could a law like that which I *r. E.* iii 56
Misses! the tale that I *r. P.T.* 62

RELATIONS.
The soft *r.*, which, combined *Miss* — 79

RELAX.
Charity may *r.* the miser's fist *Con.* 812

RELAXATION.
But *r.* of the languid frame *T.* i 81
A *r.* of Religion's hold *T.* ii 569
To him is *r.* and mere play) *T.T.* 156

RELAXED.
R. into a universal grin *T.* iv 204

RELAXING.
The mind, *r.* into needful sport *R.* 715

RELEASE.
A kind *r.* from their imperfect state *R.* 166
And happy in their unforeseen *r. T.* ii 126
Than to *r.* the adultress from her bond *T.* iii 63
The wearied hireling finds it a *r. T.* v 411

RELEASED.
Discourse, as if *r.* and safe at home *Con.* 571
R. him as my story tells *N.G.* 25
But leisure, silence, and a mind *r. R.* 139
The mind, *r.* from too constrained a nerve *T.T.* 622

RELENTING.
R. forms would lose their power, or cease *Ch.* 608
And Cyrus, with *r.* pity moved *Ex.* 75
Or guilty soon *r.* into tears *Tir.* 112

RELICS.
Supplied such *r.* as devotion holds *T.* vi 689
R. of ages! Could a mind, imbued *Y.O.* 6

RELIED.
When most *r.* on is most sure to fail *V.* 68

RELIEF. [206
The wretch that works and weeps without *r. Ch.*
For want of prominence and just *r. Con.* 127
Would give *r.* of bed and board to none *H.* 306
Fancy shall weave a charm for my *r. M.P.* 18
Lost by abandoning her own *r. R.* 758
The soul reposing on assured *r. T.* 455
And sorted hues (each giving each *r. T.* iii 634

RELIEVE.
And Peace does nothing to *r.* the weight *Ex.* 307

RELIGION.
In the ways of *r.* and truth *A.S.* 22
R.! what treasure untold *A.S.* 25
R., Virtue, Reason, Common Sense *Con.* 77
R. curbs indeed its wanton play *Con.* 595
Well read, well tempered, with *r.* warmed *Con.* 640
Of virtue, and *r.'s* glorious cause *Con.* 686
And chiefly when *R.* leads the way *Con.* 704
Happy to fill *R.'s* vacant place *Ex.* 121
R., if in heavenly truths attired *Ex.* 492
R should extinguish strife *F.* 133
R. ruling in the breast *F.* 203
Reminds him of *r.*, hated theme! *H.* 218
A false *r.*, is unknown to you *H.* 486
And, while *r.* seems to be her view *H.* 641
Wit flashing on *R.'s* side *Mrs. M—* 31
Quite to the lees? And has *r.* none? *P.E.* 260
By thee, *R.*, Liberty, and Laws *P.E.* 462
And stab *R.* with a sly side-thrust *R.* 690
R. does not censure or exclude *R.* 783
A relaxation of *R.'s* hold *T.* ii 569
Who deem *R.* frenzy, and the God *T.* iv 178
To give *R.* her unbridled scope *T.T.* 71
R., richest favour of the skies *T.T.* 268
R., virtue, truth, whate'er we call *T.T.* 286
R. harsh, intolerant, austere *T.T.* 612
Pity *R.* has so seldom found *T.T.* 716
R. weaves for her, and half undressed *T.T.* 723
R. makes the free by nature slaves *Tir.* 184
And sound *r.* sparingly enough *Tir.* 198

RELIGIOUS.
And still by motives of *r.* force *J.T.* 33
Wearing out life in his *r.* whim *T.* 89
Till his *r.* whimsy wears him out *T.* 90

RELISH.
And *r.* of their pleasure all to lust *P.E.* 330
My *r.* of fair prospect; scenes that soothed *T.* i 141
And tutored with a *r.* more exact *T.* iv 741
But none without some *r.*, none unmoved *T.* iv 742
Some *r.*, till the sum, exactly found *T.* v 430
Made pure, shall *r.* with divine delight *T.* v 783

RELUMINES.
His eye *r.* its extinguished fires *T.* i 442

RELY.
And, while on public nurseries they *r. Tir.* 793

REMAIN.
My dog! what remedy *r. Beau* 17
The stench *r.*, the lustre dies away *Con.* 678
R. with thee, or leave thee at his word *Ex.* 675
Some thought of immortality *r. T.* 39
Of their complete effect. Much yet *r. T.* iii 605
R. to each, the search of sunny nook *T.* v 71
Time ploughs them up, and not a trace *r. T.* v 533
Over a sinful world; and what *r. T.* vi 736
Two thirds of all the virtue that *r. Tir.* 810

REMAINED.
And Puss r. still unattended R.C. 66
His head alone r. to tell T.B. 65

REMAINING.
To consecrate our few r. groves Con. 826
Rarely redeem the short r. ten R. 40
And add two-thirds of the r. half T. iii 131

REMARK.
A bold r., but which, if well applied Ch. 535
But merely to r., that ours E. i 93
The writer well r., a heart, that knows H. 429
R. two loiterers that have lost their way P.E. 386
I praise the Frenchman, his r. was shrewd R. 739
R. that gall so many, to the few T. iii 37
In spite of gravity and sage r. T. v 12
Prove, rather than impeach, the just r. Tir. 842
Conjecture and r., however shrewd T.T. 205

REMEDY.
My dog! what r. remains Beau 17
Laugh at their only r., and die Ch. 419
The very r., however sure Con. 169
Sure to succeed, the r. they found Con. 500
Proclaim the r., ye learned, next H. 108
That r., not hid in deeps profound H. 111
The inquirer's aim, that r., is Hope H. 114
"The r. you want I freely give T. 273
Leaving the poor no r. but tears T. vi 845

REMEMBER.
R., Heaven has an avenging rod Ch. 216
But still r., if you mean to please Con. 103
What he r. seems to have forgot Con. 132
R., if He guard thee and secure Ex. 700
And still r., nor without regret T. i 116
Yet few r. them. They lived unknown T. v 724
R. Handel? Who, that was not born T. vi 645
Yes—we r. him; and while we praise T. vi 648
A talent so divine, r. too T. vi 649
I pleased r., and, while memory yet Tir. 133
You told me, I r., glory built T.T. 1

REMEMBRANCE.
Prompts with r. of a present God T. vi 252

REMEMBRANCER.
Faithful r. of one so dear M.P. 11

REMIND.
R. them of their hated inmate, sin! E. ii 36
R. him of religion, hated theme! H. 218
R. him of his Maker's power and love R. 30

REMINISCENCE.
By r. to his earliest date? F.A. 23

REMNANT.
Through life's sad r., what no sighs restore H. 24
Improve the r. of his wasted span R. 13
That yet a r. of your race survives T. i 340
Smooth as a wall the upright r. stands T. v 36

REMORSE.
Oh vain inquiry! they without r. Ex. 462
What they themselves, without r., despise H. 253
R., and Sorrow, and vindictive Pain P.E. 43
R., the fatal egg by Pleasure laid P.E. 239
Sabbaths profaned without r. St. vi 39
Reflection and r., the fear of shame T. i 489
R. begets reform. His master-lust T. v 618

REMOTE.
To inhabit a mansion r. C. 45

And gains r. conclusions at a jump Con. 154
Yet Truth is yours, r., unenvied isle! H. 481
Groves, heaths, and smoking villages, r. T. i 176
And hidden as it is, and far r. T. i 228
(If e'er she spring spontaneous) in r. T. i 603
These therefore I can pity, placed r. T. i 626
Their jessamine, her jessamine r. T. iii 584
The most r. from his abhor'd resort T. vi 398
Since then, with few associates, in r. T. iii 117
Thus bringing home to him the most r. Tir. 643
So, when r. futurity is brought T.T. 492

REMOTER.
And what could a r. scene show more? R. 500

REMOTEST.
Illume the land's r. part 1789, 61

REMOVED.
Thyself r., thy power to soothe me left M.P. 121
There hid in loathed obscurity, r. R. 563
Of public virtue ever wished r. T. iv 615

REND.
To-morrow r. away H.F. 4
Angelic gratulations r. the skies T. 587
To r. a victim trembling at his foot T. vi 411

RENDER.
But r. neither fruit nor flower F. 185
His utmost he can r. is but small T. 199
(Toilsome and indigent), she r. much T. 326
To such I r. more than mere respect T. ii 376
Not rich, I r. what I may U. 19

RENDERED.
With love and wisdom, r. back to Heaven Y.O. 154

RENDERING.
Receiving benefits and r. none T. vi 959

RENEW. [395
The soul, whose sight all-quickening grace r. Ch.
R. the quarrel on the conqueror's part Her. 74
And while that face r. my filial grief M.P. 17
Her tale of guilt r. St. v 22
Unless sweet Penitence her powers r. T.T. 398

RENEWED. [682
Those hearts should be reclaimed, r., upright Con.
Is wooing mercy by r. offence Ex. 413
R. desire would grace with other speech H. 35
To have r. the joys that once were mine M.P. 116
The sprightly morn her cause r. R.C. 69
'Tis free to all—'tis every day r. T. i 434
The soil must be r., which often washed T. iii 609
That errs not, and find raptures still r. T. iii 723
Should be r. in nature, pure in heart V. 60

RENOUNCE.
Is to r. hypocrisy; to draw Ex. 408
"R. the world"—the preacher cries L.W. 25
R. the odours of the open field T. i 415 [487
Then wherefore not r. them? No—the dread T. i
Delight us, happy to r. awhile T. i 515

RENOUNCED.
Reviled and loved, r. and followed L.W. 33
R. alike its office and its sport R. 293
A secret thirst of his r. employs R. 474
Not to be passed: and she that had r. T. iii 76
Her sex's honour, was r. herself T. iii 77
By ev'ry gilded folly, we r. T. vi 39

RENOVATION.
And r. of a faded world T. vi 124

RENOWN.
Of credit and r. *J.G.* 2
To poets of r. in song *J.P.* 17
Occiduus is a pastor of r. *P.E.* 124
Give useful light though I should miss r. *R.* 206
And highest in r., can justly boast *R.* 676
Of honour, dignity, and fair r.! *T.* iii 59
Spent in the purchase of r. for him *T.* v 277
As if, like him of fabulous r. *T.* v 691
So cheaply the r. of that attempt *T.* vi 534 [22
Feats of r., though wrought in ancient days *T.T.*
To catch r. by ruining mankind *T.T.* 60
Deeds of unperishing r. 1789, 15

RENOWNED.
Rome, for empire far r. *B.* 17
A man r. for repartee *F.* 91
That Britannia r. o'er the waves *M.D.* 45
Like thy r. forefathers, far and wide *S.* i 12
And so, while Garrick, as r. as he *T.* iii 598
R. in ancient song; not vexed with care *T.* vi 997
Long lines of ancestry, r. of old *Tir.* 817

RENT.
When all disguises shall be r. away *Ch.* 558
No longer prey upon our annual r. *Ch.* 616
Anticipated r., and bills unpaid *R.* 559 [*Y.O.* 125
Thine arms have left thee. Winds have r. them off
The veil is r., r. too by priestly hands *T.* vi 876
Shows all its r. and patches to the world *Tir.* 451

REPAID.
And long provoked, r. thee to thy face *Ex.* 391
And praise his genius, he is soon r. *P.E.* 532
Is but a loan, to be r. with use *T.* iii 364
All well r., demand him, he attends *T.* iii 398
Might have r. him well, I wote *T.B.* 58

REPAIR.
And I to my cabin r. *A.S.* 52
And we will then r. *J.G.* 10
All these to a Montagu's r. *Mrs. M—* 43
Her form with dress and lotion they r. *P.E.* 299
Nor sofa then I needed. Youth r. *T.* i 127
A cottage, whither oft we since r. *T.* i 221
For man's revolt, shall with a smile r. *T.* vi 746
To which the unwashed artificer r. *T.T.* 152

REPAIRED.
Buckled his helm, and to his steed r. *A.T.* 172

REPARTEE.
A man renowned for r. *F.* 91
From r., with jokes that he disdains *Tir.* 728

REPAST.
And finished his concise r. *Mor.* 6
At his return—a rich r. for me *T.* iv 113

REPAY.
Though Scorn r. her sympathetic tears *Ch.* 414
R. their work—the gleaning only mine *H.* 771
Yet so will God r. *St.* vi 38
R. their labour more; and perched aloft *T.* v 91
Unwin, I should but ill r. *U.* 1

REPEALED.
Their woes, not yet r., thence date them all *Ex.* 224
Exults to see its thistly curse r. *T.* vi 768

REPEAT.
And Echo learns politely to r. *Con.* 827
And seem to warn him never to r. *H.* 355
His still-refuted quirks he still r. *P.E.* 550
Which he that hears it with a shout r. *T.* v 889

REPEATED.
Still need r. warnings, and at last *St.* ii 26

Oft r. in your ears *St.* iv 18
In still r. circles, screaming loud *T.* 204
And tasteless of the same r. joys *T.* i 463

REPEL.
Indifference may r. *Miss —* 42

REPELLED.
His destiny r. *Cast.* 40

REPENT. [399
That cried " R. !"—and gloried in thy choice? *Ex.*
A nation scourged, yet tardy to r. *Ex.* 723

REPENTANCE.
Thy deep r. of thy thousand lies *H.* 590
Learn wisdom and r. ere too late " *T.T.* 437

REPETITION.
The r. makes attention lame *Con.* 214
By r. palled, by age obtuse *H.* 22

REPINE.
Though, could our hearts r. *Dr.* 14
Thy racked inhabitants r., complain *Ex.* 304

REPINING.
In r. discontent *Trans.* iii 30

REPLACE.
To succour wasted regions, and r. *Ch.* 129
R. the wandering comet in his sphere *T.* 400

REPLACED.
Stoppled his cruise, r. his book *Mor.* 7

REPLETE.
Forth skipped the cat, but now r. *R.C.* 99
And reading here his sentence, how r. *St.* ii 7
The supposition is r. with sin *T.* 347
R. with vapours, and disposes much *T.* v 463
In heads r. with thoughts of other men *T.* vi 90
R. with dreams, unworthy of a man *Tir.* 160

REPLIED. [*A.T.* 180
" Oh, shame !" ten thousand echoing nymphs r.
When from within it thus a voice r. *F.A.* 10 [573
" What tidings ?" and the surge r.—" All lost ! *Ex.*
He soon r.,—" I do admire *J.G.* 17
And with asperity r. *P.* 20
What marriage means, thus pert r. *P.T.* 29
" Indeed," r. the Don, " there are but few " *T.T.* 98
But courage, man! methought the muse r. *Tir.* 787

REPLY.
R. discreetly—" To be sure—no doubt !" *Con.* 118
Their wisdom bursts into this sage r. *Con.* 877
(For 'tis my business to r.) *E.* iv 80
Ask what is human life—the sage r. *H.* 1
" Fallible man," the Church-bred youth r. *H.* 421
" We do "—a multitude r *L.W.* 26
" Dismiss poor Harry !" he r. *M.F.* 19
" They shall be yours," my Verse r. *St.* iii 35
I dare not—" And you need not," God r. *T.* 272
" Because ye will not," Conyers would r. *T.* 358
To Truth itself, that deigned him no r. *T.* iii 271
The popular harangue, the tart r. *T.* iv 31
The Sabine bard. O evenings, I r. *T.* iv 190
Is touch'd within us, and the heart r. *T.* vi 5
Sweet Poll! the mimic bird r. *Trans.* iv 14

REPORT.
Some cordial endearing r. *A.S.* 35
R. it hot or cold, or wet or dry *Con.* 386
Which seldom a distinct r. pervades *Con.* 802
Two Poets, (poets, by r. *Dr.* 1
R. a message with a pleasing grace *T.* 205
It is not seemly, nor of good r. *T.* i 729

My soul is sick, with every day's *r. T.* ii 6
While, through that public organ of *r. T.* ii 355
Allured by my *r.*: but sure no less *T.* iii 699
That hear not, or receive not their *r. T.* v 855
And worships. Her *r.* has travelled forth *T.* vi 813
That are of chief and most approved *r. Tir.* 459

REPOSE.
Contrived both for toil and *r. Gr.* 10
Secure of their *r. N.* 8
Receive me, languishing for that *r. R.* 369
His active years with indolent *r. R.* 618
She might *r.*, or sit and think *R.C.* 6
Some place of more serene *r. R.C.* 30
And hopeless of *r. St.* v 12
Now seek *r.* upon an humbler theme *T.* i 5
Compared with the *r.* the Sofa yields *T.* i 102
And charmed with rural beauty, to *r. T.* iii 28
In letting fall the curtain of *r. T.* iv 248
'Tis thus the understanding takes *r. T.* iv 296
But ere he gain the comfortless *r. T.* v 596
Sacred to neatness and *r.*, the alcove *T.* vi 571

REPOSED.   [95
That curtained round the scene where they *r. A.T.*
Fearless of wrong, *r.* his weary strength *T.* i 15

REPOSING.
The soul *r.* on assured relief *T.* 455

REPOSSESSED.
In Freedom lost so long, now *r. R.* 410

REPREHENSION.
An evidence and *r.* both *Tir.* 656

REPRESENTS.
The medium *r.*, and not their own *H.* 74

REPRIEVES.
And, though himself so polished, still *r. T.* i 264

REPRIMAND.
To *r.* them all *J.P.* 32

REPRISALS.
Make just *r.*, and with cringe and shrug *T.* ii 645

REPROACH.
Their names, alas! in vain *r.* an age *Ex.* 660
R. a people with his single fall *T.* 234
R. their owner with that love of rest *T.* i 394
Or seen with least *r.*; and virtue, taught *T.* i 690
His name a theme for praise and for *r.? T.* iii 282
Would not *r.* me with the loss I felt *T.* v 490
And clothe all climes with beauty; the *r. T.* vi 764
The whole *r.*, the fault was all his own *Tir.* 536

REPROBATE.
"And doth he *r.* and will he damn *T.* v 638

REPROBATED.
The *r.* race grows judgment-proof *T.T.* 459

REPROOF.
Nor some *r.* yourself refuse *B.R.* 23
Picked from the thorns and briars of *r. T.* vi 1013

REPTILE.
Will tread aside, and let the *r.* live *T.* vi 567
Since such a *r.* has its gem *Trans.* i 27

REPUBLIC.
The free *r.* of the whip-gig state *H.* 190

REPUTATION.
Laughs at the *r.* she has torn *T.* 163
Thus *r.* is a spur to wit *T.T.* 520

REPUTE.
Revived, are hastening into fresh *r. Con.* 818
Owe their *r.* in part, but not the whole *Tir.* 461

REQUIRE.
And gives him all his just demands *r. Con.* 760
An architect *r.* alone *F.* 164
And she gives largely more than he *r. H.* 56
Can I for thee *r. N.Y.G.* 10
And he soon finds the talents it *r. R.* 614
This annual tribute Death *r. St.* i 11
To his young hopes, *r.* discreet delay *T.* iii 504
And plausible that social life *r. T.* v 466
E'en in his pastimes he *r.* a friend *Tir.* 607

REQUIRED.
If not that Hope the Scripture has *r. H.* 617
When health *r.* it, would consent to roam *R.* 517
His country, or was slack when she *r. T.* iii 89
Were all that Heaven *r.* of humankind *Tir.* 85

REQUISITES.
The *r.* that form a friend *F.* 14

REQUITE.
That I should ill *r.* thee, to constrain *M.P.* 86
To live to God is to *r. St.* vi 5
The feller's toil which thou could'st ill *r. Y.O.* 115

RESCUE.
Alone could *r.* them *Cast.* 34
To *r.* from the ruins of mankind *E.* ii 24
(Unless verse *r.* thee awhile) a thing *Y.C.* 58

RESEARCH.
And spreads the honey of his deep *r. T.* iv 112

RESEMBLANCE.
Takes the *r.* of the good she views *Ch.* 396
With much *r.* of the past *M.* 50

RESEMBLE.
So much *r.* man? *Beau* 20
Though each *r.* each in every part *Comp.* i 7
I may *r.* Thee, and call Thee mine" *R.* 98
Till she *r.* faintly what she views *R.* 298
R. most some city in a blaze *T.* v 5
No few, that would seem wise, *r.* her *Tir.* 796

RESEMBLING.
These most *r.* clustered stars *Q.V.* 11

RESENT.
Loudly *r.* the stranger's freedom there *H.* 354
With well considered steps, seems to *r. T.* v 75
His pride *r.* the charge, although the proof *Tir.* 163
R. his fellow's, wishes it were less *Tir.* 477

RESENTFUL.
But dignity's, *r.* of the wrong *T.* iii 79

RESENTMENT.
'Tis because *r.* ties *B.* 11
In just *r.* of his injured laws *Ex.* 328
Incurs *r.* for the love he shows *H.* 285

RESERVE.
A decent caution and *r.* at least *H.* 404
Speaks with *r.*, and listens with applause *R.* 448
In converse, either starved by cold *r. T.* v 471

RESERVED.
But Fate *r.* Sir Airy to maintain *A.T.* 56
Shall find me as *r.* as he *F.* 188
R. to solace many a neighbouring squire *N.A.* 5
Was bliss *r.* for happier days;—so slow *T.* i 83

RESERVOIR.
Than a capacious *r.* of means *T.* ii 201

RESIDE.
R. in that heavenly word! *A.S.* 26
But how? *r.* such virtue in that air *Tir.* 373
Of man's occasions, when in him *r. T.* ii 537

RESIDENCE.
Once the blest *r.* of truth divine *T.* 387

That royal *r*. might well befit *T*. v 157
Opprobrious *r*. he finds them all *T*. v 584

RESIDENT.
Though *r*., and witness of the wrong *T*. iv 594

RESIGN.
And ye, who, rather than *r*. *A Tale* 69
Blessed with all wealth can give thee, to *r*. *Ch*. 297
Would age in thee *r*. his wintry reign *H*. 33
Thy hands their little force *r*. *M*. 34
R. our own and seek our Maker's will *R*. 130
'Tis easy to *r*. a toilsome place *R*. 621
" I will *r*. myself to rest *R.C*. 61
Till man *r*. his breath *St*. vi 34
R. the scenes their presence might protect *T*. iv 592
And when descending he *r*. the skies *Tir*. 37
Then why *r*. into a stranger's hand *Tir*. 551
Would cheerfully these limbs *r*. *Trans*. ii 34

RESIGNED.
Yes, to deep sadness sullenly *r*. *Ch*. 151
Her gloomy monarch, doubtful, and *r*. *Ex*. 570
To passion, interest, pleasure, whim, *r*. *H*. 212
Or shed impervious to the blast. *R*.—*T*. v 72
Already to sorrow *r*. *The Rose* 16
Their purport, uses, properties, *r*. *Y.O*. 152

RESIGNING.
The season smiles, *r*. all its rage *T*. vi 61

RESIST.
Whate'er was asked, too timid to *r*. *Ex*. 540
And potent to *r*. the freezing blast *T*. iii 465

RESISTLESS.
R. Never such a sudden flood *T*. ii 115
R. in so bad a cause, but lame *T*. iv 439
R. from the centre he should seek *T*. v 590

RESOLUTE.
Falls first before his *r*. rebuke *T*. v 619

RESOLVED.
To be *r*. into their parent earth *Ch*. 562
Deeply *r*. to shut a Saviour out *Con*. 690   [682
And though *r*. to risk them, and swim down *Ex*.
Or so *r*. to err *J.P*. 26
R. to be unknown *Q.V*. 58
R. it should continue there *R.C*. 86
The scattered grain, and thievishly *r*. *T*. v 67
Their efforts, yet *r*. with one consent *T*. vi 338
To wandering sheep, *r*. to follow none *T*. vi 891
R. a union formed for life *The Doves* 27

RESOLVES.
R. to have none of her own *M.D*. 48   [335
R. that where he played his sons shall play *Tir*

RESOLVING.
R. all events, with their effects *T*. ii 163

RESORT.
Would drive them forth from the *r*. of men *Con*. 37
'Tis wrong to bring into a mixed *r*. *Con*. 291
The scenes to which not youth alone *r*. *Ex*. 24
R. on Sundays to the house of prayer *H*. 242
And Mercy, fled to as the last *r*. *H*. 378
To which the mind *r*., in chase of terms *T*. ii 288
If Christ, then why *r*. at every turn *T*. ii 535
To which the insipid citizen *r*. *T*. iii 642
Oh thou *r*. and mart of all the earth *T*. iii 835
Exhausted, he *r*. to solemn themes *T*. v 661
The most remote from his abhor'd *r*. *T*. vi 398
To the same Patroness *r*. *Mrs. M*.— 21
R. to this example as a rock *P.E*. 143
Our public hives of puerile *r*. *Tir*. 458

RESOUND.
And Folly pays, *r*. at your return *Her*. 62
R. with his sweet-flowing ditty no more *P.F*. 12
Thump after thump *r*. the constant flail *T*. i 357
Beguile their woes, and make the woods *r*. *T*. i 586

RESOUNDING.
R. oft, and never heard in vain *T*. iv 356

RESOURCE.
The same *r*. to prove *A Tale* 78

RESPECT.
Yet much as Nature I *r*. *B.R*. 9
But though some nobler minds a law *r*. *Ch*. 35
How few *r*., or use thee, as they ought ! *Con*. 24
But veneration or *r*. finds none *Con*. 739
Delights us, by engaging our *r*. *P.E*. 208
Than by the mere dissembler's feigned *r*. *T*. 74
To such I render more than mere *r*. *T*. ii 376
Whose actions say that they *r*. themselves *T*. ii 377
The king who loves the law, *r*. his bounds *T*. v 332
R., while stalking o'er life's narrow stage *T.T*. 118
Of love by absence chilled into *r*. *Tir*. 576
R., as is but rational, and just *Tir*. 710
Thy child shall show *r*. to thy gray hairs *Tir*. 880
Of grandeur that insures *r*. 1789, 69

RESPECTFUL.
R. of the smutched artificer *T*. ii 491

RESPECTING.
R. in each other's case *N. G*. 33

RESPIRATION.
While every breath, by *r*. strong *T*. iv 348

RESPIRING.
R. freely the fresh air, that makes *T*. i 138

RESPITE.
At length his transient *r*. past *Cast*. 43
A longer *r*., unaccomplished yet *T*. ii 67

RESPLENDENT.
The purple evening and *r*. moon *R*. 348
R. less, but of an ampler round *T*. iv 258
And the *r*. rivers. His to enjoy *T*. v 743

RESPONSIVE.
R. to the distant neigh he neighs *Ch*. 177
" And still the sigh *r*. heave *Miss* — 87
Or nymphs *r*., equally affect *T*. iv 21

REST.
Even here is a season of *r*. *A.S*. 51
Many he sought, but one above the *r*. *A.T*. 3
The *r*., alert and active, as became *A.T*. 133
Afford them place of *r*.? *A Tale* 26   [20
Where seas or deserts part them from the *r*. *Ch*.
We come with joy from our eternal *r*. *Ch*. 73
The important letters that include the *r*. *Ch*. 523
And flow in free communion with the *r*. *Ch*. 611
Upon the lap of convenanted *r*. *Con*. 574
Is given in earnest of eternal *r*. *E*. ii 40   [180
Their host to move, and when it stayed to *r*. *Ec*
Hophni and Phineas may describe the *r*. *Ex*. 449
And b'ushing at the tameness of the *r*. *Ex*. 543
Obduracy itself must yield the *r*. *Ex*. 559
Thy foes implacable, thy land at *r*. *Ex*. 581
And, after summing all the *r*. *F*. 202
Is vanity surpassing all the *r*." *H*. 110
In terms as plain, himself has shut the *r*. *H*. 341
And death's a doom sufficient for the *r*." *H*. 396 [510
Spent half the darkness, and snored out the *r*. *H*.
A tenfold frenzy seizes all the *r*. *H*. 634
They might with safety eat the *r*. *L.W*. 10

To smother in ignoble *r. Miss* — 7
But me, scarce hoping to attain that *r. M.P.* 100
The herb as soft, while nibbling strayed the *r. N.A.* 38
When thus a mutton statelier than the *r. N.A.* 81
A youngster at school more sedate than the *r. P.A.* 21
With holiness and consecrated *r. P.E.* 158 [240
Hatched by the beams of truth, denies him *r. P.E*
No wild enthusiast ever yet could *r. P.E.* 470
Influenced mightily the *r. P.T.* 43 [165
Scorned by the *r.*, with patient hope they wait *R.*
Genius, and temper, and desire of *r. R.* 172 [451
On whom he *r.* well pleased his weary powers *R.*
Forget their labours, and yet find no *r. R.* 496 [528
That shines and *r.*, as infants smile and sleep *R.*
Absence of occupation is not *r. R.* 623
Will stand advanced a step above the *r. R.* 722
Fond of the phantom of an earthly *r. R.* 764
A drawer impending o'er the *r. R.C.* 39
will resign myself to *r. R.C.* 61
The *r.* in order to the top *R.C.* 94
And wishing for a place of *r. R.C.* 105
How ill the scene that offers *r. S.* 3
And heart that cannot *r.* agree! *S.* 4 [ii 23
One falls—the *r.*, wide-scattered with affright *St.*
The *r.* might then seem privileged to play *St.* ii 19
Then breathed his soul into his *r. St.* iii 15
The *r.* too busy, or too gay, to wait *T.* 40
Offer him warmth, security, and *r. T.* 252
The thousands whom the world forbids to *r. T.* 438
Pride, of a growth superior to the *r. T.* 475 [T. i 49
These for the rich : the *r.*, whom Fate had placed
Reproach their owner with that love of *r. T.* i 394
To which he forfeits even the *r.* he loves *T.* i 395
But far beyond the *r.*, and with most cause *T.* i 632
More frequent, and foregone her usual *r. T.* ii 61
The *r.* are sober dreamers, grave and wise *T.* iii 137
Such powers I boast not—neither can I *r. T.* iii 217
With hopeful gems. The *r.*, no portion left *T.* iii 421
Sublime above the *r.*, the statelier stand *T.* iii 595
he *r.* appears a wilderness of strange *T.* iv 78
Made vocal for the amusement of the *r. T.* iv 159
His reverence and his worship both to *r. T.* iv 597
But faster far, and more than all the *r. T.* iv 613
Like flowers selected from the *r.*, and bound *T.* iv 667
And coarser grass, upspearing o'er the *r. T.* v 23
One eminent above the *r.* for strength *T.* v 231
Familiar, serve to emancipate the *r.*! *T.* v 298
To seek no sublunary *r.* beside *T.* v 476
And confident assurance of the *r. T.* v 576
Man views it and admires, but *r.* content *T.* v 791
From toilsome life to never ending *r. T.* v 841
Their only point of *r.*, Eternal Word ! *T.* v 897 [80
From spray to spray, where'er he *r.* he shakes *T.* vi
The time of *r.*, the promised Sabbath, comes *T.* vi 733
Before a calm, that rocks itself to *r. T.* vi 739
Receive yet one, as radiant as the *r. T.* vi 903
. dream disturbed poor Bully's *r. T.B.* 44
With kingship and dominion o'er the *r. Tir.* 96
To ears and eyes, the vices of the *r. Tir.* 274 [546
Æsop, and Phædrus, and the *r.* ?—Why not ? *Tir.*
There early *r.* makes early rising sure *Tir.* 765
The *r.* will slight thy counsel, or condemn *Tir.* 805
Seems to imply a censure on the *r. T.T.* 92
Indeed is treasure, and crowns all the *r. V.* 92
Disjoining from the *r.*, has unobserved *Y.O.* 107
But *r.* on none till that be found 1789, 19

RESTED.
For *r.* till the Gods had given it life *P.E.* 529

RESTING.
All night, me *r.* quiet in the fold *N.A.* 92

RESTITUTION.
And death or *r.* is the word *T.* 264

RESTLESS.
A ship !—Could such a *r.* thing *A Tale* 25
Both speed their journey with a *r.* stream *Comp.* i 2
What ails thee, *r.* as the waves that roar *Ex.* 272
A painful passage o'er a *r.* flood *H.* 3
For my sake *r.* heretofore *M.* 10
R. as his who toils and sweats for food *J.T.* 24
From cities humming with a *r.* crowd *R.* 21
But *r.* was the Chair ; the back erect *T.* i 44
The chequered earth seems *r.* as a flood *T.* i 344
By *r.* undulation ; even the oak *T.* i 377
Thrice must the voluble and *r.* earth *T.* iii 490
And nimble motion of those *r.* joints *T.* iii 762
The milldam, dashes on the *r.* wheel *T.* v 102

RESTORE.
Unless the power that bade him stand, *r. Ch.* 348
Through life's sad remnant, what no sighs *r. H.* 24
That only future ages can *r. Her.* 40 [74
Could Time, his flight reversed, *r.* the hours *M.P.*
R. to man the glories he has lost *T.* 398
Exhilarate the spirit, and *r. T.* i 182
He stablishes the strong, *r.* the weak *T.* ii 343
Cannot indeed to guilty man *r. T.* iii 677
Her brittle toys, *r.* me to myself *T.* iv 307
One breath of Heaven, that cried—" *R* !" 1789, 40

RESTORED.
Of rights *r.*, variety enjoyed *A.T.* 154
They saw distemper healed, and life *r. Ex.* 153
Their vigour, injured soon, not soon *r. T.* iii 608
Unlooked for, life preserved, and peace *r. T.* iv 187
And all shall be *r.* These naked shoots *T.* vi 141
Perfect, and all must be at length *r. T.* vi 819

RESTRAIN.
Warns him or prompts, approves him or *r. P.E.* 35
Take it and perish ; but *r.* your tongue *T.* 18
Perhaps timidity *r.* his arm *T.* iv 599
Offend not him, whom modesty *r. Tir.* 727

RESTRAINED.
We are *r.* indeed, but not subdued *Con.* 168
Keep Vice *r.* behind a double guard *T.T.* 66

RESTRAINT.
Let just *R.*, for public peace designed *Ch.* 286
True freedom is where no *r.* is known *Ex.* 592
From all the rigours of *r.*, enjoy *T.* ii 127
That no *r.* can circumscribe them more *T.* ii 792
And feel a parent's presence no *r. T.* vi 49
Though want of due *r.* alone have bred *Tir.* 533

RESULT.
Witness its insignificant *r. Con.* 16
And manifold *r.*, into the will *T.* ii 164
And prove it in the infallible *r. T.* iii 181
And most attractive is the fair *r. T.* iii 639
The excise is fattened with the rich *r. T.* iv 504

RESULTING.
Praise that from earth *r.*, as it ought *T.* v 802

RESUME.
And there *r.* an unembarrassed brow *Con.* 401 [188
R. her powers, and spurns the clumsy fraud *Tir.*

RESUMED.
R. his purpose, had a world of talk *Con.* 279
With looks of some complacence he *r. T.* vi 535

RESUSCITATED.
These hatch'd, and those *r.* worms *R.* 64

RETAILER.
A great *r.* of the curious ware *Con.* 229

RETAIN.

"Will none arise, no knight who still *r. A.T.* 115
Of Nature we *r. Miss* — 50
Ensured us mastery there, we yet *r. T.* ii 274
That man immured in cities, still *r. T.* iv 766
Should make the little ye *r.* still less *Tir.* 278
Keen in pursuit, and vigorous to *r. Tir.* 524
Whose character, yet undebauched, *r. Tir.* 809

RETIRE.

Where can at last his jockeyship *r.? Con.* 420
And when I bend, *r.*, and shrink *P.* 35
R. to blazon his own worthless name *R.* 217
His wish and mine both prompt me to *r." R.* 390
Shakes hands with business, and *r.* indeed *R.* 514
Thus some *r.* to nourish helpless woe *R.* 603
Must change her nature, or in vain *r. R.* 680
For nooks to which she might *r. R.C.* 4
Farthest *r.*—an idol, at whose shrine *T.* i 410
Their wonted entertainment, all *r. T.* ii 303
At evening, and at night *r.* secure *T.* iii 344
More delicate his timorous mate *r. T.* 214
Now glitters in the sun and now *r. T.* i 325
R., content to quake, so they be warmed *T.* iv 386
Because deserving, silently *r. T.* iv 419

RETIRED.

Where parties are agreed, *r.* the scene *A.T.* 89
A man once young, who lived *r. Mor.* 3
A soul serene, and equally *r. R.* 143
That so *r.* he should not wish a change *R.* 600
The dwarfish, in the rear *r.*, but still *T.* iii 594
I still revere thee, courtly though *r. T.* iv 727
The Author of her beauties, who, *r. T.* v 893
R. from all the circles of the gay *V.* 73

RETIREMENT.

Who seek *r.* for its proper use *R.* 170
O sweet *r.*! who would balk the thought *R.* 487
That could afford *r.*, or could not? *R.* 488
But few that court *R.* are aware *R.* 609
Of undisturbed *R.*, and the hours *T.* iv 142

RETIRING.

And recognize the slow *r.* fair *T.* ii 454

RETORT.

R. the charge, and let the World be told *Con.* 767
R. the affront against the crown of Pride *T.* 502

RETOUCHED.

That he has touched, *r.*, many a long day *T.* iii 786

RETRACE.

While we *r.* with Memory's pointing wand *T.* iv 183
That in a few short moments I *r. T.* vi 16

RETRACING.

R. thus his frolics ('tis a name *Tir.* 332

RETREAT.

Could yield them no *r. A Tale* 20
Enjoy the stillness of some close *r. Con.* 570
My shrubs displaced from that *r. F.B.* 2
Themselves, perhaps, when weary they *r. H.* 244
His bold intrusion on their dark *r. H.* 356
O bliss precarious, and unsafe *r.! Her.* 33
From his secure *r. M.B.* 14
The blackbird has fled to another *r. P.F.* 9
Forsaken her *r. Q.V.* 26
And each inclines its votary to *r. R.* 174
Pastoral images and still *r. R.* 257
Suburban villas, highway-side *r. T.* 481   [571
And Cobham's groves, and Windsor's green *r. T.*
But grant me still a friend in my *r. R.* 741
" Oh what a delicate *r.! R.C.* 60
He, Christianlike, *r.* with modest mien *T.* 68
Vain thought! the dweller in that still *r. T.* i 237
The grand *r.* from injuries impressed *T.* i 280
My partners in *r.* Disgust concealed *T.* iii 38
Be quelled in all our summer-months' *r. T.* iii 315
Which he, thus occupied, enjoys! *R.*—*T.* iii 676
'Tis pleasant, through the loopholes of *r. T.* iv 88
Time was when in the pastoral *r. T.* iv 558
Dismiss me weary to a safe *r. T.* vi 1004
And eyes the door, and watches a *r. Tir.* 572
Pay me for thy warm *r. Trans.* iii 5
A fortress to which she *r. W.N.* 11

RETRENCH.

R. a swordblade, or displace a patch *T.* ii 318

RETRENCHED.

His altered gait and stateliness *r. T.* v 76

RETRIBUTION.

If Vice received her *r.* due *Ex.* 247

RETRIEVE.

As God's expedient to *r.* his loss *Tir.* 166

RETROGRADE.

Conclusion *r.*, and mad mistake *T.* iii 239

RETROSPECT.

Short as in *r.* the journey seems *T.* vi 19

RETURN.

And in *r.* receives supply from all *Ch.* 92
And brings, at his *r.*, a bosom charged *Ch.* 321
Their author's frailty, and *r.* to dust *Con.* 554 [293
R. ashamed, without the wreaths they sought *Ex.*
Speak but the word, will listen and *r. Ew.* 455
Provoked and harassed, in *r.* plagued thee *Ew.* 533
And Folly pays, resound at your *r. Her.* 62
Oft gave me promise of thy quick *r. M.P.* 87
And whispers your *r. N.* 16
R. and make thy downy nest *O.* ii 2
Judge his own ways, and sigh for a *r. P.E.* 611
Wins in *r.* an answer of disdain *R.* 228
R. at noon to billiards, or to books *R.* 472
No Sofa then awaited my *r. T.* i 126
Would oft anticipate his glad *r. T.* i 543
Desirous to *r.*, and not received *T.* iii 81
Calls idle, and who justly, in *r. T.* iii 353
At his *r.*—a rich repast for me *T.* iv 113
R., sweet Evening, and continue long! *T.* iv 244
R. indignant to the slighted plough *T.* iv 645
As oft *r.* a pert voracious kind *T.* v 69
" Pants to *r.*, and when he sees afar *T.* v 833
The regular *r.* of genial months *T.* vi 123
Shall sigh at their exclusion, and *r. T.* vi 672
Down to the gulf from which is no *r. T.T.* 46'
In *r.* thou shalt receive *Trans.* iii 7

RETURNED.

My ramble ended, I *r. D.W.* 29
R. them happy to the land they loved *Ex.* 76
Gone thither armed and hungry, *r.* full *Ex.* 368
R. him to his own *F.B.* 30
R. him not a single word *J.G.* 179
Rude as thou art (for we *r.* thee rude *T.* i 649
And mirth without offence. No few *r. T.* vi 692

RETURNING.

As when *r.* to the theme they meant *Con.* 858
R., he proclaims, by many a grace *P.E.* 413

REVEAL.

R. (the man is dead) to wondering eyes *H.* 572 [241
Through all the heart's dark chambers, and *r. T.* iii

REVEALED.

For self to self, and God to man *r. Ch.* 361

That Truth and Mercy had *r*. to man *Ex*. 236
Has ne'er been *r*. to us yet *Gr*. 36
That bliss, *r*. in Scripture, with a glow *H*. 149
Take leave of nature's God, and God *r*. *P.E.* 591
The Invisible in things scarce seen *r*. *R*. 61
Blind nature to a God not yet *r*. *T*. ii 526
That He who made it, and *r*. its date *T*. iii 153
And shows him glories yet to be *r*. *T*. vi 927
Stands most *r*. before the freeman's eyes *T.T.* 269

REVELATION.

The lamp of *r*. only shows *Ch*. 339
Go seek on *R*.'s hallowed ground *Con*. 499
Of *R*.'s ineffectual beam *Con*. 830
'Tis *R*. satisfies all doubts *T*. ii 527

REVELRY.

Are silent. *R*., and dance, and show *T*. ii 79

REVELS.

Her theatres, her *r*., and her sports *Ex*. 23

REVENGE.

War followed for *r*., or to supplant *T*. i 609
And such sagacity to take *r*. *T*. vi 477
And taught a brute the way to safe *r*. *T*. vi 559

REVERE.

That in her heart the Christian she *r*. *Con*. 787
R. the laws they dream that Heaven ordains *H*. 241
Not e'en the glorious sun, though men *r*. *H*. 501
Though I *r*. your honourable names *R*. 663
Surrounding throngs the demigod *r*. *T*. 312
I still *r*. thee, courtly though retired *T*. iv 727
R. the man whose Pilgrim marks the road *Tir*. 145

REVERED.

Their name far published, and *r*. as far *Ex*. 194
R. at home, and felt in foreign lands *R*. 412
Thus proud Prerogative not much *r*. *T.T.* 230

REVERENCE. [*P.E.* 105

Charmed by the sounds, "Your *R*." or "Your Grace"?
And claims a *r*. in its shortening day *Con*. 645
That rule, pursued with *r*. and with awe *T*. 536
Than *r*., in perverse rebellious youth *T*. ii 730
His *r*. and his worship both to rest *T*. iv 597
To *r*. what is ancient, and can plead *T*. v 300
What none could *r*. all might justly blame *Tir*. 87
Through *r*. of the censor of thy son *Tir*. 734
I might with *r*. kneel, and worship thee *Y.O.* 8

REVERENCED.

R. no less. Who could with him compare? *T*. v 235

REVEREND.

Right *r*. Sirs! was no concern of theirs *A.T.* 132
And add Right *R*. to Smug's honoured name *H*. 438
With *r*. tutor, clad in habit lay *P.E.* 371
Let *r*. churls his ignorance rebuke *Tir*. 401

REVERIE.

Shall steep me in Elysian *r*. *M.P.* 19
But *r*. (for human minds will act) *R*. 637
"From *r*. so airy, from the toil *T*. iii 188

REVERSE.

Now let the bright *r*. be known abroad *H*. 710
R. the sentence, let the truth be known *T*. 449

REVERSED.

That show *r*. the villas on their side *H*. 468
Has wept a silent flood, *r*. his ways *H*. 519
Could Time, his flight *r*., restore the hours *M.P.* 74
The screws *r*. (a task which if He please *R*. 327
Maternal nature had *r*. its course *T*. iii 436
Soon shows the strong similitude *r*. *Tir*. 443

REVERSION.

Surveys his fair *r*. with keen eye *T*. ii 601

REVERTED.

Whose eye *r*. weeps o'er all the past *H*. 31

REVIEW.

I have read the *R*.; it is learned and wise *A.T.* iv 1
R. thy dim original and prime *Ex*. 467
And novels (witness every month's *R*.) *R*. 713
That calls the past to our exact *r*. *T*. iv 184

REVILED.

R. by those that hate her, prays for them *Ch*. 425
R. and loved, renounced and followed *L.W.* 33

REVIVED.

R., are hastening into fresh repute *Con*. 818
And arts *r*. beneath a softer day *T.T.* 621

REVIVES.

And it *r*. again *H.F.* 8

REVIVING.

Increasing commerce and *r*. art *Her*. 73

REVOKED.

How readily we wish time spent *r*. *T*. vi 25

REVOLT.

Man is the genuine offspring of *r*. *H*. 181
But sin marr'd all; and the *r*. of man *T*. vi 368
Was punish'd with *r*. of his from him *T*. vi 370
For man's *r*., shall with a smile repair *T*. vi 746
That hour elapsed, the incurable *r*. *T.T.* 402

REVOLTED.

If clemency *r*. by abuse *P.E.* 596
Chains are the portion of *r*. man *T*. v 581

REVOLUTION.

It is the constant *r*., stale *T*. i 462

REVOLVENCY.

Its own *r*. upholds the world *T*. i 372

REVOLVING.

R. seasons, fruitless as they pass *Her*. 25

REWARD.

Such virtues had need prove their own *r*. *Ch*. 571
And fruit *r*. his honourable toil *H*. 761
If Love *r*. him, or if Vengeance strike *P.E.* 31
Peace follows Virtue as its sure *r*. *P.E.* 42
Success in rhyme his glory and *r*. *R*. 198
Let verse at length yield thee thy just *r*. *S.* i 4
Take, Madam, the *r*. of all your prayers *T*. 167
His the mere tinsel, hers the rich *r*. *T*. 332
And take unenvied the *r*. they sought *T*. 528
Hard lot of man, to toil for the *r*. *T*. 11   [620
Well they *r*. the toil. The sight is pleased *T*. iii
Deems his *r*. too great if he prevail *Tir*. 479
May raise such fruits as shall *r*. his care *Tir*. 771
R. his memory, dear to every Muse *T.T.* 14
To pour in Virtue's lap her just *r*. *T.T.* 65

REWARDED.

Richly *r*. if he can but please *T*. 218

REYNARD.

Told hill and dale that *R*.'s track was found *N.A.* 34
For *R*., close attended at his heels *N.A.* 124

REYNOLDS.

There touched by *R*., a dull blank becomes *T*. i 700

RHAPSODY.

Of rant and *r*. in virtue's praise *T*. v 677

RHAPSODIES.
Such *r*. our shrewd discerning youth *Tir*. 191

RHENUS.
Where *R*. strays his vines among *T.B.* 7

RHETORIC.
R. is artifice, the work of man *Ex*. 136
Like quicksilver, the *r*. they display *P.E.* 21
Whose oath is *r*., and who swear for fame *T.* iv 491
A *r*. equal to those parts of speech? *Tir*. 398

RHEUMS. [392
And coughs, and *r*., and phthisic, and catarrh *Con*.
Is't not a pity now, that tickling *r. T.* iii 167 [ii 728
Was quenched in *r*. of age, his voice, unstrung *T*.

RHYME.
No wonder I, who scribble *r. E.* i 19
"Nor suffered one ill-chosen *r. E.* iv 75
Pause here, and think! a monitory *r. Ep.* i 1
Can pause one hour to read a serious *r. Ex.* 605
But never yet in *r. N.Y.G.* 4
Success in *r*. his glory and reward *R*. 198
Nature indeed looks prettily in *r. R.* 567
Vouchsafe, at least, to pitch the key of *r. T.T.* 188
The clockwork tintinabulum of *r. T.T.* 529

RHYMING.
Virtue indeed meets many a *r*. friend *T.T.* 620

RIBALDRY.
And loathsome *R*. has done his worst *T.T.* 729

RIBAND.
With lace, and hat with splendid *r*. bound *T.* i 536
And *r*. streaming gay, superbly raised *T.* iv 541

RIBBED. [Y.O. 95
That might have *r*. the sides and planked the deck

RIBBON.
Like a loose heap of *r*., a glittering show *F.M.* 6
The *r*. with which it is tied *Gr*. 8

RIBBON-BOUND.
With *r*. tassel on high *Gr*. 2

RIBS.
Receding wide, they pressed against the *r. T.* i 65

RICH.
For merchants *r*. in cargoes of despair *Ch*. 138
With *r*. instruction, and a soul enlarged *Ch*. 322
The *r*. possession of a nobler prize *Ch*. 360
A *r*. deposit, on the bordering lands *Ch*. 249
Who makes some *r*. for the supply of all *Ch*. 251
In honourable bumps his *r*. amends *Con*. 200
His *r*. materials, and regale your ear *Con*. 617
R. in embellishment as strong *Dr*. 11
Her fields, a *r*. expanse of wavy corn *Ex*. 9
So *r*. an interest in Almighty love? *Ex*. 166
The *r*., the produce of a nobler stem *Ex*. 460
R. are passed away from hand to hand *H*. 11 [18
The *r*. grow poor, the poor become purse-proud *H*.
She holds a Paradise of *r*. delight *H*. 60
Whate'er they boast of *r*. and gay *Mrs. M*— 12
Nor *r*. I, nor power pursue *O*. ii 4
But while they get *r*. by purchasing blacks *P.A.* 15
Thus laden, dream that they are *r*. and great *R*.155
His the mere tinsel, hers the *r*. reward *T*. 332 [i 49
These for the *r*.: the rest, whom Fate had placed *T*.
Not many wise, *r*., noble, or profound *T*. 337 [340
The poor should gain it, and the *r*. should not? *T*.
We boast some *r*. ones whom the Gospel sways *T*.377
Smells fresh, and, *r*. in odoriferous herbs *T*. i 531

So *r*., so thronged, so drained, and so supplied *T.* i 720
So liberal in construction, and so *r. T.* iii 94
R. have wings, and grandeur is a dream *T.* iii 263
What pearl is it that *r*. men cannot buy *T.* iii 285
Hence Summer has her *r*., Autumn hence *T.* iii 427
Wafts the *r*. prize to its appointed use *T.* iii 540
Grudge not, ye *r*., (since Luxury must have *T.* iii 544
The wings that waft our *r*. out of sight *T.* iii 760
At his return—a *r*. repast for me *T.* iv 113
The excise is fattened with the *r*. result *T.* iv 504
The *r*., and they that have an arm to check *T.* iv 587
Not unemployed, and finding *r*. amends *T.* iv 729
That soothe the *r*. possessor; much consoled *T.* iv 755
And with thee *r*., take what Thou wilt away *T.* v 906
Its family and tribe. Laburnum *r. T.* v 147
The great indeed, by titles, *r*., birth *Tir*. 346
Or art thou (as though *r*., perhaps thou art) *Tir*. 662
Nor plagues that haunt the *r*. man's door *Trans.H.*11
The tædium that the lazy *r*. endure *T.T.* 742
Then speed the *r*. discovery, and invite *T.T.* 752
And may as *r*. in comfort prove *U*. 11
Not *r*., I render what I may *U*. 19

RICHARD. [674
Shall stuff his shoulders with king *R*.'s hunch *T.* vi

RICHER.
Yet from a *r*. nothing gain *A Tale* 75
By other hopes and *r*. fruits than yours *T.* i 677
And has a *r*. use of yours than you *T.* v 762

RICHEST.
That man, in Nature's *r*. mantle clad *Ch*. 341
As *r*. soil the most luxuriant weeds *Ex*. 214
Fed from the *r*. veins of the Mogul *Ex*. 369
The *r*. earthly boon his hands afford *R*. 271
As leanest land supplies the *r*. wine *T*. 364
The *r*. scenery and the loveliest forms *T.* i 711
Religion, *r*. favour of the skies *T.T.* 268
And far the *r*. crown on earth 1789, 42

RICKETS.
From *r*. and distortion, else our lot *T.* ii 592

RID.
Reduce his wages, or get *r*. of her *T.* 211

RIDDANCE.
Clean *r*. quickly made, one only care *T.* v 70
For cleanly *r*. than for fair attire *T.* vi 994

RIDDEN.
Or if, when *r*. with a careless rein *T.T.* 306

RIDE.
The social walk, or solitary *r. Con*. 733
Escaped from a cross country *r. Gr*. 20
Will fill the chaise; so you must *r. J.G.* 15
And up he got, in haste to *r. J.G.* 47
"He carries weight!" "He *r*. a race!" *J.G.* 115
To see how he did *r. J.G.* 144
The youth did *r*., and soon did meet *J.G.* 221
And when he next doth *r*. abroad *J.G.* 251
And what if he did *r*. whip and spur *M.F.* 22
The sea-maid *r*. the waves *Q.V.* 70
Till He that *r*. the whirlwind, checks the rein *R*. 535
Would ye, when rambling in your morning *r. R.* 545
That Nature *r*. upon, maintains her health *T.* i 369
In fancy sees him more superbly *r. Tir*. 368

RIDER.
Baffled his *r*., saved against his will *T.* vi 520

RIDGE.
Here runs the mountainous and craggy *r. T.* iv 57

RIDGED—RIOTOUS

RIDGED.
As fix'd as marble, with a forehead r. T. vi 268

RIDICULE.
That turns to r. the turgid speech T. v 689

RIG.
Of running such a r. J.G. 100

RIGHT.
My r. there is none to dispute A.S. 2
R. reverend Sirs! was no concern of theirs A.T. 132
Of r. restored, variety enjoyed A.T. 154 [A.T. 169
"To horse!" he cried, "or by this good r. hand
The r. of man were sacred in his view Ch. 28
Unless his r. to rule it be dismissed? Ch. 193
Thy r. have suffered, and our land, too long Ch. 277
She rather waives than will dispute her r. Ch. 430
A fool must now and then be r. by chance Con. 96
A noisy man is always in the r. Con. 114 [149
Without the means of knowing r. from wrong Con.
And those the most, where neither has a r. Con. 162
Is sparkling wit the world's exclusive r. Con. 589
And claim a r. to scamper and run wide Con. 793
In setting r. what Faction has set wrong Ex. 301
Strikes the rough thread of error r. athwart Ex. 330
And claims for ever, as his royal r. Ex. 362
Those r. that millions envy thee appear Ex. 681
A r. to the meek honours of her name) H. 236
Each man's belief is r. in his own eyes H. 283
And he that made had r. to make the law H. 319
And—God is merciful—sets all to r. H. 376
"R.," says an ensign, "and for aught I see H. 397
And add R. Reverend to Smug's honoured name H.438
May claim some r. to be esteemed divine H. 504
His well poised estimate of r. and wrong H. 611
And tells you where ye have a r. to reign Her. 48
The calender, r. glad to find J.G. 177
The postboy's horse r. glad to miss J.G. 231
" With June's undoubted r. J.P. 36
To prove her r. to reign L.R. 12
And r. toward the favoured place Mor. 19
And needs no glossary to set him r. N.A. 70
What are England's r., I ask N.C. 10
Harangued him thus, r. eloquent N.G. 14
I always held them in the r. Pat 7
A muleteer's the man to set him r. P.E. 541
He that abstains, and he alone, does r. P.E. 585
By r. of worth, not blood alone Q.V. 3
In every cranny but the r. R.C. 98 [T. 17
Grace leads the r. way; if you choose the wrong
Asserts the r. of his offended Lord T. 263
Else his own glorious r. He would disclaim T. 555
At the r. door. Profusion is the sire T. ii 674
He steps r. onward, martial in his air T. iv 640
For mercy and the common r. of man T. iv 680 [v 53
Moves r. toward the mark; nor stops for aught T.
Abridge him of his just and native r. T. v 436
Are they not his by a peculiar r. T. v 748
Or safety interfere, his r. and claims T. vi 582
And eke did roar r. merrily, too staves T. vi 662
He drew the liturgy, and framed the r. T. vi 679
R. to his mark the monster went T.B. 50
His r. of empire over all that lives Tir. 4
Of those who never feel in the r. place Tir. 540
To invade another's r., or guard their own T. iv 560
The song was moral, and so far was r. T.T. 599
Recovering and misstated setting r. Y.O. 48

RIGHTEOUS.
Provoke the vengeance of his r. hand Ex. 253
With nice attention in a r. scale H. 367
Is not for you—the r. need it not T. 506
And we the r., whose fast-anchored isle T. ii 151
Ten r. would have saved a city once T. iii 843
And thou hast many r.—Well for thee! T. iii 844
Soon, by a r. judgment, in the line T. v 211
And r. limitation of its act T. vi 596
The symbol of a r. reign 1789, 44

RIGHTEOUSNESS.
That Heaven and Hell, and r. and sin Con. 469
What is all r. that men devise T. 75
Nor hoped, but in thy r. divine T. 576

RIGHTFUL.
Now the legitimate and r. lord T. iii 749

RIGID.
Too r., in my view, that name to one R. 720
That she is r. in denouncing death T. i 732

RIGOROUS.
That wedlock is not r., as supposed A.T. 58
And brings the trifler under r. sway Con. 596

RIGOUR.
Through wintry r. unimpaired endure Con. 650
The rage and r. of a polar sky H. 462
From all the r. of restraint, enjoy T. ii 127
By r.? or whom laughed into reform? T. ii 321
But was a wholesome r. in the main T. iii 82
The long protracted r. of the year T. v 85
Feel all the r. of thy fickle clime T. v 484
Thus with a r., for his good designed T.T. 216

RILL.
Hark! 'tis the music of a thousand r. Ch. 367
As in some solitude the summer r. J.T. 38
Musical as the chime of tinkling r. P.E. 14
Of neighbouring fountain, or of r. that slip T. 192
Here r. of oily eloquence in soft T. iv 64

RIM. [H. 49
From the blue r., where skies and mountains meet

RIND.
The bud inserted in the r. U. 13 [Y.O. 111
Possessing nought but the scooped r. that seems

RING.
They sport like wanton doves in airy r. A.T. 32
The r. a bauble, and the priest a knave A.T. 66
Like music it tinkles and r. in your ears F.M. 7
Sees watches, bracelets, r. and lockets P.B. 25
In spiral r. ascends the trunk, and lays R. 231
R. with ecstatic sounds unheard before R. 780
But life, within a narrow r. St. vi 9
Environed with a r. of branching elms T. i 223
That none, decoyed into that fatal r. T. ii 631
And still are disappointed. R. the world T. iii 129
Till the street r.; no stationary steeds T. iv 147
The chalky r., and knuckle down at taw Tir. 307
That made the vaulted roofs of Pleasure r. T.T. 625
By man performed, made all the forest r. Y.O. 109

RINGLETS.
Teeth for the toothless, r. for the bald T. iv 81

RIOT. [651
Drives through the realms of Sin, where R. reels H.
And r. in the sweets of every breeze T. i 444
By r. and incontinence the worst T. i 699
To fill with r., and defile with blood T. iii 307
By endless r., Vanity, the Lust T. iii 812
Of all this r.: and ten thousand casks T. iv 505
That scruple checks him. R. is not loud T. v 614
In senseless r.; but ye will not find T. v 757
As set the midnight r. in a blaze Tir. 287
To guard the Peace that R. would disturb T.T. 315

RIOTOUS.
They dare not wait the r. abuse Con. 261

RIPE—ROAD

RIPE. [54
Through the r. harvest lies their destined road *Her.*
I marvelled much that, at so r. an age *T.* iv 713
And he that shows none, being r. in years *T.* vi 598

RIPER.
For who but learns in r. years *F.* 22
Of r. joys, and commerce with the world *T.* ii 763
Their childhood pleased them at a r. age *Tir.* 148

RIPPED. [103
Sails r., seams opening wide, and compass lost *M.P.*

RIPPLING.
On r. waters in an April day *A.T.* 24

RISE.
Bade r. in haste a dark and drizzling fog *A.T.* 94
Oh! could their ancient Incas r. again *Ch.* 65
And knows that falling he shall r. no more *Ch.* 347
Has filled his urn where these pure waters r. *Ch.* 436
You r. and drop the curtain—now 'tis night *Con.* 332
In vain the nations, that had seen them r. *Ex.* 203
To r. at noon, sit slipshod and undressed *H.* 75 [86
Just when the larks, and when the shepherds r. *H.*
Dark and voluminous the vapours r. *Her.* 15
The sun would r. in vain for me *M.* 31
Where r. and where sets the day *Mrs. M—* 11
Forms r., to quick perfection wrought *Mrs. M—* 24
But higher far my proud pretensions r. *M.P.* 110
Let Comus r. Archbishop of the land *P.E.* 184
The trumpet—will it sound? the curtain r.? *R.* 655
Told that his setting sun must r. no more *St.* ii 16
As soon shall r. and reascend the throne *T.* 395
Fallen from her glory, and too weak to r. *T.* 480
And sinks, while favoured with the means to r. *T.* 544
Pride falls unpitied, never more to r. *T.* 588
Through downright inability to r. *T.* i 480
The rocks fall headlong, and the valleys r. *T.* ii 95
R. not, the waters of the deep shall r. *T.* ii 143 [142
Storms r. to o'erwhelm him; or if stormy winds *T.* ii
Those suns are set. Oh, r. some other such! *T.* ii 252
And faithful to the foot, his spirits r. *T.* iii 8
The shapely side, that as it r. takes *T.* iii 481
Then r. the tender germs, upstarting quick *T.* iii 521
Woods vanish, hills subside, and valleys r. *T.* iii 775
Here glittering turrets r., upbearing high *T.* v 110
"And hasting to a grave, yet doomed to r. *T.* v 830
His moment when to sink and when to r. *T.* vi 130
To assist his foe's down-fallen beast to r. *T.* vi 444
At her command winds r. and waters roar *Tir.* 25
Why takes the gentler Moon her turn to r. *Tir.* 38
R. in his forehead, and seem rank enough *Tir.* 164
Shall blush betimes, and there his glory r. *Tir.* 396
The wretch shall r., and be the thing on earth *Tir.* 412

RISEN.
And seems to have r. in vain *C.* 4
Have r. at length on your admiring eyes *H.* 492
Another moon new r., or meteor fallen *T.* v 152
Man scarce had r., obedient to his call *T.* vi 348

RISING.
Unless, when r. on a joyful wing *Con.* 716 [46
The yellow tilth, green meads, rocks, r. grounds *H.*
The r. or the setting orb of day *R.* 191
The r. waves obey the increasing blast *R.* 532
To whom the r. year shall prove his last *St.* ii 2
That hails the r. moon, have charms for me *T.* i 206
There, lost behind a r. ground, the wood *T.* i 305
Like a gross fog Bœotian, r. fast *T.* iii 495
Where early rest makes early r. sure *Tir.* 765
His spirits r. as his toils increase *T.T.* 279
And as the sun in r. beauty dressed *T.T.* 706

RISK. [*Tir.* 359
They r. their hopes, their dearest treasure, there?
We dare not r. them into public view *Con.* 371
Would run most dreadful r. of catching cold *E.* iii 59
R. an intrusion on thy pensive mood *R.* 255 [682
And though resolved to r. them, and swim down *Ex.*
To save your life would nobly r. his own *T.* 220
I therefore recommend, though at the r. *T.* iii 705
And while the dreadful r. foreseen forbids *Tir.* 860

RITES.
That forms and r. are tricks of human law *A.T.* 62
"In vain," they cried, "are hymeneal r. *A.T.* 99
And whether Roman r. may not produce *Con.* 835
The temple and its holy r. profaned *Ex.* 145 [514
Where must he find his Maker? With what r. *T.* ii
The volume closed, the customary r. *T.* iv 167 [232
With self-taught r., and under various names *T.* vi

RIVAL.
Worse than the mortal brunt of r. swords *Con.* 86
Discerns a r. in a friend *F.* 83
And r. in lustre of that *Gr.* 14
May r. these; these all bespeak a power *T.* i 431
And in defiance of her r. powers *T.* v 123
Feel all the rage that female r. feel *Tir.* 471

RIVELLED.
Praise from the r. lips of toothless, bald *T.* ii 488
And winds his web about the r. leaves *Tir.* 596

RIVEN.
The well-stacked pile of r. logs and roots *T.* iv 444

RIVER.
Hills, valleys, r., and the boundless sea *A.T.* 49
When gently, as in June, the r. glide *A.T.* 74
On the banks of our r., I know *C.* 30
The lapse of time and r. is the same *Comp.* i 1
Ah! why, since oceans, r., streams *O.* i 5
Where mountain, r., forest, field, and grove *R.* 29
Ten thousand r. poured at his command *R.* 75
O'er hills, through valleys, and by r.'s brink *T.* i 113
Else noxious: oceans, r., lakes, and streams *T.* i 375
The r. die into offensive pools *T.* ii 96
And the resplendent r. His to enjoy *T.* v 743
R. of gladness water all the earth *T.* vi 763

RIVER-BLANCHED.
And, r., the swan his snow *Mrs. M—* 8

RIVET.
With oaths like r. forced into the brain *Con.* 64
They may confirm his habits, r. fast *T.* ii 767

RIVING.
This r. stroke, this ultimate divorce *H.* 640

RIVULETS.
Or ford the r., are best at home *T.* 217
But trees, and r. whose rapid course *T.* vi 109
Which it would give in r. to thy root *Y.O.* 113

ROAD.
Directs us in our distant r. *E.* i 37
Who found not thorns and briars in his r. *E.* ii 12
Groan heavily along the distant r. *Ex.* 58
He sent a servant forth by every r. *H.* 310 [54
Through the ripe harvest lies their destined r. *Her.*
But finding soon a smoother r. *J.G.* 81
Down ran the wine into the r. *J.G.* 125
They are upon the r." *J.G.* 176
Six gentlemen upon the r. *J.G.* 233
The flock grew calm again, and I, the r. *N.A.* 127
To stand a way-mark in the r. to bliss? *P.E.* 117
But when his lord would quit the busy r. *R.* 631
Its odour o'er the Christian's thorny r.! *T.* 454

But now with pleasant pace a cleanlier *r.* *T.* iii 17
And crowd the *r.*, impatient for the town! *T.* iii 319
The *r.* that leads from competence and peace *T.*iv 496
Their progress in the *r.* of science; blinds *T.* v 451
But runs the *r.* of wisdom. Thou hast built *T.* v 849
His *r.*, deriding much the blank amaze *T.* vi 536
Revere the man whose Pilgrim marks the *r. Tir.* 145
With packhorse constancy we keep the *r. Tir.* 252
Perhaps some courser who disdains the *r. T.T.* 668
Along the miry *r. Y.D.* 14

ROAM.

The beasts that *r.* over the plain *A.S.* 13
As oft as it suits her to *r. C.* 52
As mendicants whose business is to *r. Con.* 859
A flock so scattered, and so wont to *r. Ex.* 729
Hard task indeed o'er arctic seas to *r.*! *H.* 548
How much a dunce that has been sent to *r. P.E.* 415
He cannot long be safe whose wishes *r. P.E.* 587
When health required it, would consent to *r. R.* 517
Alike admonish not to *r. S.* 22 [896
And mischief in their hands, they *r.* the earth *T.* vi
And never smiled again! and now she *r. T.* i 456

ROAR.

What ails thee, restless as the waves that *r. Ex.* 272
And charged Hostility and Hate to *r. Ex.* 566
To frown and *r.*, and shake his feeble form *H.* 186
Had heard a lion *r. J.G.* 206
Would raise her voice and *r. J.P.* 10
(For stormy troubles loudest *r. Mrs. M—* 47 [97
"Where tempests never beat nor billows *r.*" *M.P.*
And, joining the freethinkers' brutal *r. P.E.* 593
Abrupt and horrid as the tempest *r. R.* 533
And wilds familiar with a lion's *r. R.* 779
Nor less composure waits upon the *r. T.* 190
Lashed into foaming waves, begins to *r. T.* 260
And fiery caverns, *r.* beneath his foot *T.* ii 90 [91
To hear the *r.* she sends through all her gates *T.* iv
And howl and *r.* as likes them, uncontrol'd *T.* vi 404
And set plebeian thousands in a *r. T.T.* 319 [*T.T.* 460
Earth shakes beneath them, and Heaven *r.* above
He gives the word, and Mutiny soon *r. T.T.* 452
At her command winds rise and waters *r. Tir.* 25

ROARED.
The Atlantic billows *r. Cast.* 2

ROARING.

The reeking, *r.* hero of the chase *Con.* 405
Yon *r.* boys, who rave and fight *Pat.* 5
Thrown up by wintry torrents *r.* loud *T.* i 14
Now murmuring soft, now *r.* in cascades *T.* iii 779
With all his *r.* multitude of waves *T.* v 766 [497
Beats back the *r.* surge, scarce heard so high *T.* vi

ROASTING.
To make a blaze—that's *r.* him alive *Con.* 334

ROB.
'Tis not that I design to *r. E.* iv 1 [*P.A.* 26
What! *r.* our good neighbour! I pray you don't go
His comrades had plotted an orchard to *r. P.A.* 23

ROBBED.
His victims, *r.* of their defenceless all *T.* iv 458

ROBBER.
The *r.* and the murderer weak as we? *Ch.* 68
On petty *r.*, and indulges life *T.* i 733

ROBBERY.
For Israel dealt in *r.* and wrong *Ex.* 35
R. of gardens, quarrels in the streets *Tir.* 229

ROBE.
And if a boundless plenty be the *r. Ch.* 85
To fling his glories, o'er the *r.* she wears *H.* 44 [79
Sweet Nature, stripped of her embroidered *r. Her.*
The snowy *r.* her wintry state assumes *R.* 195
Appears a spot upon a vestal's *r. T.* iv 554 [682
At the sword's point, and dyeing the white *r. T.* iv

ROBED. [823
Of the *r.* pedagogue! Else let the arraigned *T.* ii

ROBERT.
That *R.*'s lines are easy too *E.* iv 70
"Friend *R.*, thus like *chien savant E.* iv 87

ROBIN.
And where the gardener *R.*, day by day *M.P.* 48

ROBUST.
That ask *r.*, tough sinews, bred to toil *T.* iii 405
Thy frame, *r.* and hardy, feels indeed *T.* iv 360
His form *r.* and of elastic tone *T.T.* 218
To the four-quartered winds, *r.* and bold *Y.O.* 98

ROCK. [
These valleys and *r.* never heard *A.S.* 30 [*Con.* 884
Shoots between scattered *r.* and opening shades
Sea-beaten *r.* and naked shores *A Tale* 19 [502
That makes seas stable, and dissolves the *r. Con.*
For them, the *r.* dissolved into a flood *Ex.* 181
Are proud, and set their faces as a *r. Ex.* 457 [*H.*46
The yellow tilth, green meads, *r.*, rising grounds
O blessed within the enclosure of your *r. H.* 465
To wish myself the *r.* I view *P.* 29 [*H.* 741
R., groves, and streams, must join him in his praise
For baking earth, or burning *r.* to lime *N.A.* 18
Resort to this example as a *r. P.E.* 143
Your blunderer is as sturdy as a *r. P.E.* 539
Near barren *r.*, in palaces, or cells *R.* 540
She ran upon no *r. R.G.* 20
His dwelling a recess in some rude *r. T.* 79 [i 193
Through the cleft *r.*, and, chiming as they fall *T.*
Crush me, ye *r.*; ye falling mountains, hide *T.* 269
The hardy chief, upon the rugged *r. T.* i 12
Then forests, or the savage *r.*, may please *T.* i 518
The *r.* fall headlong, and the valleys rise *T.* ii 95
To view some rugged *r.* or mouldering tower *T.* iv 235
Firm as a *r.* Nor wanted aught within *T.* v 156
We build with what we deem eternal *r. T.* v 534
Before a calm, that *r.* itself to rest *T.* vi 739 [v 834
"His country's weather-bleached and battered *r. T.*
O'er the green summit of the *r.*, whose base *T.* vi 496
The dwellers in the vales and on the *r. T.* vi 793
And flee for safety to the falling *r. T.* vi 868
Think yourself stationed on a towering *r. T.T.* 33
Or bids the *r.* in ruder pomp arise *Tir.* 28
Yet is thy root sincere, sound as the *r. Y.O.* 116

ROCKED. [ii 152
Moved not, while theirs was *r.* like a light skiff *T.*
Was *r.* by many a rough Norwegian blast *Ex.* 470
R. in the cradle of the western breeze *Tir.* 44

ROCKETS.
And *r.* flew, self-driven *Q.V.* 14

ROCK-WORK.
And softens human *r.* into men *Ch.* 96

ROD.
Bleeding from the Roman *r. B.* 2
Bid suffer it awhile, and kiss the *r. Ch.* 166
Remember, Heaven has an avenging *r. Ch.* 216
You need his pardon, and provoke his *r. Con.* 488
When He that ruled them with a shepherd's *r. Ex.*85
Job felt it, when he groaned beneath the *r. R.* 303
Of faith's supporting *r. St.* iii 14
And waved his *r.* divine, a race obscene *T.* ii 826

Yours, a blind instinct, crouches to the *r.* T. v 355
Of flowers, like flies clothing her slender *r.* T. vi 166
Are but his *r.* to scourge a guilty land T.T. 450

RODE.
That Gilpin *r.* a race J.G. 244
On which he *r.* Her opportune offence T. vi 470

ROGUE. [Con. 415
Yet e'en the *r.* that serves him, though he stand
But if the *r.* be gone a cup too far P.E. 440
You have two servants,—Tom an arch, sly *r.* T. 201

ROLL.
Sees planetary wonders smoothly *r.* Ch. 317 [ii 145
Shall *r.* themselves ashore, and reach him there T
Whom the winds waft where'er the billows *r.* Ex. 19
Thy days *r.* on exempt from household care T. iv 366
They *r.* themselves before him in the dust T. v 260
Earth *r.* the rapturous hosanna round T. vi 797
Or ere the wheels of verse begin to *r.* T.T. 711

ROLLED.
R. over all our desolated land Ch. 76 [53
They stretched the neck, and *r.* the wanton eye Ex.
It is passed between cylinders often, and *r.* F.M. 3
The night *r.* tardily away R.C. 67 [91
Yourselves have seen, what time the thunders *r.* N.A.
Then twig; then sapling; and, as century *r.* Y.O. 62

ROLLING.
Fixed in the *r.* flood of endless years Con. 557 [499
Upon the *r.* chords rung out his dying breath Ex.
And wheels his throne upon the *r.* worlds T. v 814
Turn him adrift upon a *r.* sea Tir. 868

ROMAN.
When R. rapine, by no laws withheld A.T. 126
Bleeding from the R. rods B. 2
Other R. shall arise B. 21
And whether R. rites may not produce Con. 835
Had poured the day, and cleared the R. skies Ex. 228
The R. taught thy stubborn knee to bow Ex. 476
As ever R. had in Rome's best days Ex. 591
Than ever R. saw! M. i 4
Defective only in his R. nose P.E. 396
Of the last meal commence. A R. meal T. iv 168
'Tis not enough that Greek or R. page Tir. 605
Hence, in a R. mouth, the graceful name T.T. 500

ROMANCE.
Than the fair shepherdess of old *r.* T. iv 538

ROME. [A.T. 127
Lest R. should end with her first founders' lives
R. shall perish—write that word B. 13
R., for empire far renowned B. 17
Not the proud monuments of Greece or R.—Ch. 302
There he was copious as old Greece or R.—Con. 621
The virtues of old R. for English use Con. 836
Then the proud eagles of all-conquering R.—Ex. 209
But R., with sorceries and magic wand Ex. 508
That proved a mint of wealth, a mine to R. Ex. 523
As ever Roman had in R.'s best days Ex. 591
They tell us of the fate of R.—M. ii 3 [370
And thence with all convenient speed to R.—P.E.
Of Light Divine. But Egypt, Greece, and R.—T. ii 500
To Athens or to R., for wisdom short T. ii 536
So once were ranged the sons of ancient R.—T. iii 596
Nineveh, Babylon, and ancient R.—T.T. 432 [608
Anacreon, Horace, played in Greece and R.—T.T.

ROOF.
Bright shone the *r.*, the domes, the spires Q.V. 13
Yet awful as the consecrated *r.* T. i 342
And *r.* embattled high, the gloomy scenes T. ii 122

Not needful here, beneath a *r.* like mine T. iii 341
And all the comforts that the lowly *r.* T. iv 141
The slope of faces, from the floor to the *r.* T. iv 202
(Fantastic misarrangement)! on the *r.* T. v 111
The *r.*, though movable through all its length T. vi 72
These at his crib, and some beneath his *r.* T. vi 415
But though the joys he hopes beneath your *r.* Tir. 563
Beneath thy *r.*, beneath thine eye, to prove Tir. 680
That made the vaulted *r.* of Pleasure ring T.T. 625

ROOFLESS.
Their *r.* home they fixed A Tale 38

ROOKS.
Such is the clamour of *r.*, daws, and kites H. 349
But cawing *r.*, and kites that swim sublime T. 203
The very *r.* and daws forsake the fields T. v 89

ROOM.
Still there is *r.* for pity to abate Ch. 198
I cannot talk with civet in the *r.* Con. 283
These curtains, that keep the *r.* warm Gr. 37
If honest eulogy can spare thee *r.* H. 589
Yet this dull *r.*, and that dark closet M.F. 4
To dress a *r.* for Montagu Mrs. M— 2
With hunger pinched, and pinched for *r.* R.C. 73
Others are dragged into the crowded *r.* T. i 478
Just when our drawing *r.* begin to blaze T. iv 267
And, while the playful jockey scours the *r.* Tir. 366
Or turn them into shops and auction *r.*? Tir. 902

ROOST. [v 58
Now from the *r.*, or from the neighbouring pale T.
For owls to *r.* in. Once thy spreading boughs Y.O. 52

ROOT.
And Faith, the *r.* whence only can arise Ex. 111
And at the *r.* of age St. i 24
Ploughs up the *r.* of a believer's care T. 460
And cut up all my follies by the *r.* T. 574
Takes deeper *r.*, confirmed by what they see T. ii 568
The crowded *r.* demand enlargement now T. iii 532
And disappoints the *r.*; the slender *r.* T. iii 611 [90
Where neither grub, nor *r.*, nor earth-nut now T. v
The well-stacked pile of riven logs and *r.* T. iv 444
Our love is principle, and has its *r.* T. v 353 [T. vi 113
Peeps through the moss that clothes the hawthorn *r.*
Who with a courage of unshaken *r.* T.T. 15
Of girth enormous, with moss-cushioned *r.* Y.O. 64
Could shake the tother.—and time has been Y.O. 92
Which it would give in rivulets to thy *r.* Y.O. 113
Yet is thy *r.* sincere, sound as the rock Y.O. 116
On thy distorted *r.*, with hearers none Y.O. 140

ROOTED.
Lords of the conquered soil, there *r.* fast Ex. 192
Fast *r.* against every rub" P. 161
Delighted. There, fast *r.* in their bank T. i 166
Grows fluid; and the fixed and *r.* earth T. ii 100

ROPE.
And that a *r.* must cure them Pat. 20
A *r.*! I wish we patriots had Pat. 21
By cold submersion, razor, *r.*, or lead R. 584

ROSCIUS.
A noble show! while R. trod the stage T. iii 597

ROSE.
Fed by the Love from which it *r.* at first Ch. 574
Captivity led captive, *r.* to claim Ch. 585
Still to that element from which she *r.* Con. 266
R. from a seed of tiny size E. i 95
The beauties of a *r.* full blown E. i 68
Ere Nature *r.* from her eternal sleep Ex. 637
The *r.* or lily appears blue or green H. 72

And plant successfully sweet Sharon's *r*: *H.* 463
The Lily and the *R.*—*L.R.* 8
The *R.* soon reddened into rage *L.R.* 9 [thorn *S.* ii 1
Deem not, sweet *r.*, that bloomest 'midst many a
Wild *r.* over furrowed ground *Mrs. M*— 28
His bright perfections at whose word they *r. R.* 200
With woodbine and wild *r.* mantled o'er *R.* 420
But one, the *r.*, the regent of them all) *R.* 724
The full-blown *r.*, the shepherd and his lass *T.* i 36
By *r.*, and clear suns though scarcely felt *T.* iii 733
But gay confusion; *r.* for the cheeks *T.* iv 79
Silently as a dream the fabric *r. T.* v 144
The scentless and the scented *r.*; this red *T.* vi 151
Her sacred cause, but trembled when he *r. T.T.* 351
R. like a paper-kite, and charmed the town *T.T.* 385
Thus genius *r.* and set at ordered times *T.T.* 560
He sunk in Greece, in Italy he *r. T.T.* 563 [*The Rose* 1
The *r.* had been washed (just washed in a shower)
This elegant *r.*, had I shaken it less *The Rose* 17
The bud of peach or *r. U.* 14
The charms of the late-blowing *r. W.N.* 21

ROSTRUM.
The things that mount the *r.* with a skip *T.* ii 409

ROSY.
She saw, and turned her *r.* cheek away *A.T.* 87
(Her *r.* chorus) fly *Miss* — 72
Beneath the *r.* cloud, while yet the beams *T.* i 495
Down to the *r.* west, but kindly still *T.* iv 133
And, tinging all with his own *r.* hue *T.* v 8

ROSY-FINGERED.
So may the *r.* hours *Miss* — 97

ROT.
The foul forerunner of a general *r. Ex.* 106
Can dig, beg, *r.*, and perish, well content *T.* iii 805

ROTATION.
A dull *r.*, never at a stay *H.* 101
Constant *r.* of the unwearied wheel *T.* i 368
R.; from what fountain flowed their light *T.* iii 160

ROTE.
Words learned by *r.* a parrot may rehearse *Con.* 7

ROTTEN.
Sin's *r.* trunk, concealing its defects *P.E.* 288

ROTTENNESS.
The filth of *r.* and worm of pride *Ex.* 90
Bids *r.* invade, and bring to dust *Ex.* 332
The *r.*, which time is charged to inflict *Y.O.* 67

ROUGH.
And sounds prophetic are too *r.* to suit *Ex.* 67
Strikes the *r.* thread of error right athwart *Ex.* 330
Was rocked by many a *r.* Norwegian blast *Ex.* 470
Yet nothing feel in that *r.* coat *P.* 51
Of manners *r.*, and coarse athletic cast *P.E.* 187
And toil to polish its *r.* coat alone *P.E.* 420
No *r.* annoyance rankling in his mind *R.* 428 [230
R. elm, or smooth-grained ash, or glossy beech *R.*
Sweet moralist! afloat on life's *r.* sea *R.H.* 3
The common overgrown with fern, and *r. T.* i 506
Or when *r.* winter rages, on the soft *T.* iii 31 [iii 441
The plenteous bloom, that no *r.* blast may sweep *T.*
Two leaves produced, two *r.* indented leaves *T.* iii 526
Raging abroad, and the *r.* wind, endear *T.* iv 309
Not *r.* with wire of steel or brass *T.B.* 26 [341
Great schools suit best the sturdy and the *r. Tir.*
Drew a *r.* copy of the Christian face *T.T.* 614

ROUGHENED.
Ne'er *r.* by those cataracts and breaks *M.P.* 66

ROUGHER.
But I beneath a *r.* sea *Cast.* 65
Divest the *r.* sex of female airs *Con.* 843

ROUGHEST.
The night was winter in his *r.* mood *T.* vi 57

ROUGHLY.
With me but *r.* since I heard thee last *M.P.* 2

ROUGHNESS.
Feel less the journey's *r.* and its length *Con.* 699
Then what were left of *r.* in the grain *T.* v 480

ROUND.
From the centre all *r.* to the sea *A.S.* 3
R. other systems under her control *Ch.* 318
There centering in a focus *r.* and neat *Con.* 239
All speak her happy :—let the Muse look *r. Ex.* 27
Smack went the whip, *r.* went the wheels *J.G.* 41
The serpent Error twines *r.* human hearts *P.E.* 4
Where the watchman in his *r. St.* iv 5
A massy slab, in fashion square or *r. T.* i 21
Constant at routs, familiar with a *r. T.* ii 385
Resplendent less, but of an ampler *r. T.* iv 258
Bent knees, *r.* shoulders, and dejected looks *T.* iv 634
Declined the death, and wheeling swiftly *r. T.* vi 518
Earth rolls the rapturous hosanna *r. T.* vi 797
Conjectured, sniffing *r.* and *r. T.B.* 40
R. Thurlow's head in early youth *Th.* 1
And truth cut short to make a period *r. T.T.* 517
Or oaken fence that hems the paddock *r. T.T.* 583
The punch goes *r.*, and they are dull *Y.D.* 45

ROUNDABOUT.
He sees that this great *r. Trans.* ii 25

ROUND-ROLLING.
Eight years and five *r.* moons *Ep.* ii 29

ROUSE. [343
Regret would *r.* them, and give birth to prayer *T.*
Knock at the gates of nations, *r.* their fears *Ex.* 269
R. all your courage at your utmost need *T.* 565

ROUSSEAU.
I shall not ask Jean Jacques *R.*—*P.T.* 1

ROUT.
Fandango, ball, and *r.*! *F.B.* 33
Constant at *r.*, familiar with a round *T.* ii 385
The *R.* is Folly's circle, which she draws *T.* ii 629
Than all that held their *r.* in Juno's heaven! *T.* ii 660
Chained to the *r.* that she frequents for life *Tir.* 744
The world, with all its motley *r. Trans.* ii 26

ROUTE.
At every interview their *r.* the same *Con.* 213

ROVE.
May *r.* at will, where appetite shall lead *A.T.* 60
R. where you please, 'tis common all around *Gon.* 100
That all Olympus through the country *r. Con.* 825
Than *r.* and stagger with no mark in view *Con.* 861
Ten thousand *r.* the brakes and thorns among *H.* 280
Or forest where the deer securely *r. R.* 182
And waft it to the mourner as he *r. R.* 338
And even to a clown.—Now *r.* the eye *T.* i 288
But truce with censure. Roving as I *r. T.* iv 232
Happy to *r.* among poetic flowers *T.* vi 752
From thee departing, they are lost and *r. T.* v 898

ROVED. [1011
Let fall the unfinished wreath, and *r.* for fruit *T.* vi
But when his heart had *r. St.* iii. 24 [vi 1012
R. far, and gathered much: some harsh, 'tis true *T.*

ROVERS.
Food for the famished *r.* of the flood *Ch.* 532
The houseless *r.* of the sylvan world *T.* i 588

Ten thousand r. in the world at large T. v 408
Long since, and r. of the forest wild Y.O. 126

ROVING.

The flame extinct, he views the r. fire B.B. 11
The r. eye misleads the careless heart R. 126
To bind the r. appetite, and lead T. ii 525
Upon the r. and untutored heart T. ii 570
But truce with censure. R. as I rove T. iv 232
The r. thought and fix it on themselves T. vi 117
For her the Fancy, r. unconfined Tir. 21

ROW.

The Pineapples in triple r. P.B. 1

ROWELS.

With sounding whip, and r. dyed in blood T. vi 527

ROYAL.

And claims for ever, as his r. right Ex. 362
When persecuting zeal made r. sport Ex. 612
No, not a moment, in his r. heart R. 774
Down went the R. George R.G. 11
That r. residence might well befit T. v 157
All bear the r. stamp that speaks them his T. v. 551
Of r. mercy, and through generous scorn T. vi 410
The r. letters are a thing of course Tir. 416
Shall r. institutions miss the bays Tir. 503
Some r. mastiff panting at their heels T.T. 35
With much sufficiency in r. brains T.T. 52
Asked, when in Hell, to see the r. jail T.T. 94

ROYALLY.

R., freely, for his bounty's sake H. 118

ROYALTY.

Tricked out of all his r. by art Ch. 53
But r., nobility, and state T. 353
Must follow r., then welcome ease T.T. 165

RUB.

Fast rooted against every r" P. 16

RUBRIC.

Let him your r. and your feasts prescribe P.E. 185

RUDDIER.

The r. orange and the paler lime T. iii 573

RUDDY.

'Tis morning; and the sun with r. orb T. v 1

RUDE.

Lest the r. blast should snap the bough A Fable 14
Then, whether embellished or r. C. 35
And at the bottom barbarous still and r. Con. 167
Because a bear is r. and surly? No Con. 192
To cheer the r. forefathers of mankind Con. 454
Of the r. injuries it late sustained Con. 906
This island, spot of unreclaimed r. earth Ex. 468
They felt the r. alarm M. ii 6
He knows indeed that, whether dressed or r. R. 415
His dwelling a recess in some r. rock T. 79
The r. inclemency of wintry skies T. 138
Suppose, unlooked for in a scene so r. T. 248
Bore on his branch, luxuriant then and r. T. 493
But r. at first, and not with easy slope T. i 64
The panels, leaving an obscure, r. name T. i 282
Thrives by the r. concussion of the storm T. i 378
Not r. and surly, and beset with thorns T. i 601
R. as thou art (for we returned thee r. T. i 649
Alas for Sicily! r. fragments now T. ii 75
That no r. savour maritime invade T. ii 258
And wise precaution, which a clime so r. T. iii 431
Ah, treat them kindly! r. as thou appearest T. iv 370
My native nook of earth! Thy clime is r. T. v 462
Russet and r., folds up the tender germ T. vi 194

The r. companion smiled, as if transformed T. vi 543
The r. will scuffle through with ease enough Tir. 340
Else coarse and r. in manners, and their tongue Tir. 831
Knowledge, a r. unprofitable mass T. vi 92 [T.T. 322
When the r. rabble's watchword was—"Destroy!"

RUDENESS.

Whose wit is r., whose good breeding tires R. 438

RUDER.

Of r. shape, and feeling none P. 12
Or bids the rocks in r. pomp arise Tir. 28

RUDEST.

Thrives against Hope, and in the r. scene Ch. 575

RUDIMENTS.

Taints in its r. the promised flower Con. 42
The r. should sleep the winter through Y.O. 28

RUE.

Ill-fated race! how deeply must they r. Her. 51

RUEFUL.

Or laugh or mourn with me, the r. jest P.E. 110
With r. faces and bald pates Y.D. 23

RUFFIAN.

"R., pitiless as proud B. 41
So may the r., who with ghostly glide Ch. 186
And drop the night-bolt;—r. are abroad T. iv 568

RUFFLED.

I only kissed his r. wing B.R. 19
Their r. plumage calm refit Mrs. M— 46
Her elbows r., and her tottering form T. iv 545

RUFFLING.

The r. wind, scarce conscious that it blew T. i 156

RUFILLUS.

R., exquisitely formed by rule P.E. 189

RUGGED.

Of r. oaks for worms M.B. 8
Is this the r. path, the steep ascent P.E. 71
The hardy chief, upon the r. rock T. i 12
Long time elapsed or e'er our r. sires T. i 68
To view some r. rock or mouldering tower T. iv 235
The r. frowns and insolent rebuffs T. iv 411
It seem'd not always short; the r. path T. vi 20

RUIN.

Deep in r. as in guilt B. 16
Shame and r. wait for you" B. 44
Our self-importance r. its own scheme Con. 368
To rescue from the r. of mankind E. ii 24
Again pours r. in the vale below Her. 38
That wealth within is r. at the door Her. 76
And hides the r. that it feeds upon P.E. 286
Prepares it for its r.; hardens, blinds T. ii 690
Should prove your r., and his own at last Tir. 205
And spread the r. round Trans. H. 18

RUINING.

To catch renown by r. mankind T.T. 60

RUINOUS.

Of r. ebriety that prompts T. iv 460

RULE.

Oft as his patroness who r. the night A.T. 137
Unless his right to r. it be dismissed? Ch. 193 [81
Ye powers who r. the tongue, if such there are Con.
Reduced to practice, his beloved r. Con. 139
And Jupiter bids fair to r. again Con. 822   [869
May prove, though much beside the r. of art Con.
Are far too mean for Him that r. the skies Ex. 138

By which Heaven r. the mixed affairs of man H. 16
A knave when tried on honesty's plain r. H. 566
Some wiser r. must teach him how to live H. 600
What scourges are the gods that r. below Her. 66
Rufillus, exquisitely formed by r. P.E. 189
For 'tis a r. that holds for ever true P.E. 534 [557
Bend the straight r. to their own crooked will P.E.
That r. he prized, by that he feared St. iii 21 [535
Their judge was Conscience, and her r. their law T.
That r., pursued with reverence and with awe T. 536
He gives a perfect r.—what can He less? T. 552
Did not his eye r. all things, and intend T. ii 166
Bright as his own, and trains by every r. T. ii 347
Left them as dark themselves. Their r. of life T.ii 523
Discover him that r. them; such a veil T. iii 233
As she with all her r. can never reach T. v 126
As in the bosoms of the slaves he r. T. v 310
That knows no measure, by the scanty r. T. vi 213
R. universal Nature. Not a flower T. vi 240
Mercy to him that shows it, is the r. T. vi 595
Then, only governed by the self-same r. Tir. 871
And never meant the r. should be applied T.T. 11
Of Wantonness, where vice was taught by r. T.T.627
And so disdained the r. he understood T.T. 687

RULED.

When He that r. them with a shepherd's rod Ex.85
And while he r. thee by the sword alone Ex. 490
He r. with meekness, they obey'd with joy T. vi 361
Where kindness on his part, who r. the whole T. vi365

RULER.

Thy r. load thy credit, year by year Ex. 284
Thou self-entitled r. of the main Ex. 549
From loins enthroned, and r. of the earth M.P. 109
Ye kings and r., what have courts to show? R. 104
O Winter, r. of the inverted year T. iv 120

RULING.

Religion r. in the breast F. 203
The heart, surrendered to the r. power P.E. 275

RUM.

For how could we do without sugar and r.? P.A. 6

RUMINATE.

Here much I r., as much I may T. iii 121
R. heedless of the scene outspread T. v 788

RUMINATING.

On southern banks the r. sheep A.T. 78
And r. flocks enjoy the shade Her. 32
From thoughtless youth to r. age P.E. 24

RUMOUR.

With doleful r. and sad presage hung Ex. 357
Where r. of oppression and deceit T. ii 3

RUMP.

And swing his r. around Ep. ii 24

RUN.

And claim a right to scamper and r. wide Con. 793
Would r most dreadful risk of catching cold E. iii 59
That Matthew's numbers r. with ease E. iv 67
And made him faster r. J.G. 228 [112
And now, Farewell.—Time unrevoked has r. M.P.
R. in a bottom, and divides the field N.A. 10
Shines as it r., but grasped at, slips away P.E. 22
Long ere the charioteer of day had r. P.E. 67
Are sweet philosophy's enjoyments r. P.E. 259
Like a neglected forester, r. wild P.E. 362
But which, when life at ebb r. weak and low R. 3
The sound shall r. along the winding vales R. 363
May r. in cities with a brisker force R. 454

While thirteen moons saw smoothly r. St. i 1
Read, ye that r., the awful truth St. i 21
Die self-accused of life r. all to waste? St. ii 28
He walks, he leaps, he r.—is winged with joy T. i 443
The laity r. wild.—But do they now? T. ii 572
That gives it all its flavour. We have r. T. ii 607
R. round; still ending, and beginning still T. iii 627
R. the great circuit, and is still at home T. iv 119
Here r. the mountainous and craggy ridge T. iv 57
The worse for what it soils. The fashion r. T. iv 555
But r. the road of wisdom. Thou hast built T. v 849
Driven to the slaughter, goaded, as he r. T. vi 421
With such a lustre, he that r. may read Tir. 80
Merely to sleep, and let them r. astray Tir. 908
Short his career, indeed, but ably r. T.T. 671

RUNG. [461

How many deeds with which the world has r. Ch.
Upon the rolling chords r. out his dying breath Ex.499

RUNNING.

Of r. such a rig J.G. 100 [614
On moments squandered else, and r. all to waste Tir.

RURAL.

Since then in the r. recess C. 41
To quit the bliss thy r. scenes bestow Ch. 299
And I have lived recluse in r. shades Con. 801
Domestic happiness and r. joy Ex. 535
Which r. gentlemen call sport divine N.A. 8
Pants for the refuge of some r. shade R. 6
Or half so clear, as in the r. scene R. 456
But still 'tis r.—trees are to be seen R. 497
For I have loved the r. walk through lanes T. i 109
Of thorny boughs: have loved the r. walk T. i 112
Nor r. sights alone, but r. sounds T. i 181
By r. carvers, who with knives deface T. i 281
And charmed with r. beauty, to repose T. iii 28
Domestic life in r. leisure passed! T. iii 292
All healthful, are the employs of r. life T. iii 625
No: we are polished now! The r. lass T. iv 534
Down into scenes still r.; but, alas! T. iv 556
Scenes rarely graced with r. manners now! T. iv 557
My very dreams were r.: r. too T. iv 700
Of r. scenes, compensating his loss T. iv 768
Of multitudes unknown. Hail! r. life! T. iv 783

RUSH.

To r. into a fixed eternal state Con. 185
And feeble onset of a pigmy r. Ex. 707
And r. into dissension F. 102 [N.A. 117
And r. those other sounds, that seem by tongues
In r. Folly with a full moon tide P.E. 282
Sits linking cherry-stones, or platting r. R. 398
With one consent to r. into the sea R. 524
Believe, r. forward, and possess the prize T. 374

RUSHED.

R. with a whirlwind's fury on the foe A.T. 195
R. to battle, fought, and died B. 39
R. to the cliff, and having reached it, stood T. vi 552
His brows with ivy, r. into the field T.T. 604

RUSHY.

A narrow brook, by r. banks concealed N.A. 9

RUSS.

Imperial mistress of the fur-clad R.! T. v 129

RUSSET.

When scarlet fruits the r. hedge adorn A.T. 72
With r. specks bedight A Tale 42
On pippins' r. peel Ep. ii 18
Whom fiery suns, that scorch the r. spice Ex. 15
R. and rude, folds up the tender germ T. vi 194

RUST.

By *r.* unperishable or by stealth *J.T.* 26
Now *r.* disused, and shine no more *M.* 11
And eats into his bloody sword like *r. T.T.* 8
Of dreaming study and pedantic *r. T.T.* 171
Neglected talents *r.* into decay *T.T.* 546

RUSTIC.

To carve his *r.* name upon a tree *R.* 400
A temper *r.* as the life we lead *R.* 732
A sudden steep upon a *R.* Bridge *T.* i 267
And *r.* coarseness would. A heavenly mind *T.* ii 457

The *r.* throng beneath his favourite beech *T.* iv 708

RUSTING.

In which are kept our arrows. *R.* there *T.* ii 804

RUSTLING.

The *r.* straw sends up a frequent mist *T.* i 360

RUSTY.

Grew *r.* by disuse; and massy gates *T.* ii 746

RUTHLESS.

Ere yet with *r.* joy the happy hound *N.A.* 33

S.

SABA.

And *S.'s* spicy groves, pay tribute there *T.* vi 807

SABACTHANI.

Lama *S.* before their eyes *H.* 630

SABBATH.

Or smiled when a *s.* appeared *A.S.* 32   [125
When he has prayed and preached the *s.* down *P.E.*
For *s.* evenings, and perhaps as sweet *P.E.* 141
Of *s.* hours with plausible excuse? *P.E.* 145
O Italy!—Thy *s.* will be soon *P.E.* 152
Our *s.*, closed with mummery and buffoon *P.E.* 153
S. profaned without remorse *St.* vi 39
The time of rest, the promised *s.*, comes *T.* vi 733

SABBATH-BREACH.

By lewdness, idleness and *s. T.* iv 653

SABBATH-RITES.

And customs of her own, till *s. T.* i 746

SABINE.   [*A.T.* 125

So swarmed the *S.* youth, and grasped the shield
The *S.* bard. O evenings I reply *T.* iv 190

SABLE.

The *s.* warrior, frantic with regret *Ch.* 145
To close in *s.* every social scene *Con.* 872
The busy heralds hang the *s.* scene *H.* 264
That skirt the horizon, wore a *s.* hue *T.* iv 320
Of neighbouring cypress, or more *s.* yew *T.* vi 154

SABLER.

And never of a *s.* hue than now) *Ex.* 395

SACK.

And calls aloud for *s. Trans.* iv 15

SACKBUT.

Psaltery and *s.*, dulcimer and flute *P.E.* 133

SACRAMENTAL.

By an oath dipped in *s.* blood? *Ex.* 381
The *s.* host of God's elect *T.* ii 349

SACRED.

Well knowing him a *s.* thing *B.R.* 17
A lasting, a *s.* delight *C.* 40
The rights of man were *s.* in his view *Ch.* 28
Thine altar, *s.* Liberty, should stand *Ch.* 256
S. interpreter of human thought *Con.* 23
And wanting him to loose the *s.* seal *Con.* 544
And spread the *s.* treasures of the breast *Con.* 573
Thus touched, the tongue receives a *s.* cure *Con.* 887
Their very garments *s.*, old yet new *Ex.* 183
A truth still *s.*, and believed of old *Ex.* 351
An individual is a *s.* mark *Ex.* 434
The *S.* Book, its value understood *Ex.* 616

That blessings truly *s.*, and when given *Ex.* 684
That secrets are a *s.* trust *F.* 157
The *S.* Book no longer suffers wrong *H.* 449
His *s.* head from harm *M.* ii 8
Whose fires to *s.* Truth applied *Mrs. M—* 32
The *s.* function, in your hands is made *P.E.* 122
The *s.* implement I now employ *P.E.* 301
A critic on the *s.* book should be *P.E.* 452
Faithfully, fairly, by that *s.* test *R.* 134
Of sorrow, sorrow is a *s.* thing *R.* 316
O *s.* art! to which alone life owes *R.* 749
From the strict duties of the *s.* day? *T.* 49
The *s.* fire, self-torturing his trade *T.* 100
His office *s.*, his credentials clear *T.* ii 339
That he is honest in the *s.* cause *T.* ii 375
Of union, and converts the *s.* band *T.* ii 686
With things so *s.* as a nation's trust *T.* ii 778
Was *s.*, and was honoured, loved, and wept *T.* ii 786
The cause of piety, and *s.* truth *T.* iii 707
Her interests, or that gives her *s.* cause *T.* iii 792
Is kept and guarded as a *s.* thing *T.* v 304
And in the school of *s.* wisdom taught *T.* v 797
S. to neatness and repose, the alcove *T.* vi 571
Patiently present at a *s.* song *T.* vi 634
Still *s.*, and preserves with pious care *T.* vi 690
And just direction *s.*, to a thing *T.* vi 713
Bright as a sun the *s.* city shines *T.* vi 800
Through moral narrative, or *s.* text *Tir.* 126
To occupy a *s.*, awful post *Tir.* 414
But, if thou guard its *s.* chambers sure *Tir.* 891
Nor would the Nine consent the *s.* tide *T.T.* 184
Her *s.* cause, but trembled when he rose *T.T.* 351
When profanation of the *s.* cause *T.T.* 426 [607
And dizzy with delight, profaned the *s.* wires *T.T.*
The abuses of her *s.* charge, the press *T.T.* 633

SACRIFICE.

Abhorred the *s.*, and cursed the priest *P.E.* 340
Who oftenest *s.* are favoured least *T.* i 411
We *s.* to dress, till household joys *T.* ii 613
For these they live, they *s.* to these *T.* vi 893
Is but the fire without the *s. T.T.* 379

SACRIFICED.

For thee I gladly *s. O.* ii 20
If sentiment were *s.* to sound *T.T.* 516

SACRILEGE.

But that were *s.*;—praise is not thine *Ch.* 266
Hast thou (a *s.* his soul abhors) *Ex.* 346
Sad *s.*! no function, but a trade! *P.E.* 123
But less, methinks, than *s.* might serve *T.* vi 638
In *s.*, in God's own house profaned *Tir.* 409

SAD.

And soothe the sorrows of so *s.* a state *Ch.* 199

SAD—SAID

S. as it is, his undissembling heart *Con.* 712
Ah! be not *s.*, although thy lot be cast *E.* ii 41
Thence date their *s.* declension, and their fall *Ex.* 223
With doleful rumour and *s.* presage hung *Ex.* 357
Through life's *s.* remnant, what no sighs restore *H.* 24
Partakers of thy *s.* decline *M.* 33 [75
And the *s.* lesson must be learned once more *Her.*
Thus many a *s.* to-morrow came and went *M.P.* 42
Both *s.* and in a cheerful mood *N.Y.G.* 3 [82
A ram, the ewes and wethers, *s.*, addressed *N.A.*
Once more in this *s.* heart *O.* ii 3
S. sacrilege! no function but a trade! *P.E.* 123
One *s.* epistle thence, may cure mankind *P.E.* 351
And weeps a *s.* libation in despair *R.* 226
And thou, *s.* sufferer under nameless ill *R.* 343
S. waste! for which no after-thrift atones *St.* ii 29
Nor ever frowned, or *s.* appeared *St.* iii 23
S. period to a pleasant course! *St.* vi 37
And screaming at the *s.* presage *T.B.* 47
On the *s.* theme, their everlasting state *T.* 41
Oh sorrowful and *s.*! the streaming tears *T.* 173
S. messenger of mercy from above *T.* 464
Angry and *s.*, and his last crust consumed *T.* i 246
Spectatress both and spectacle, a *s. T.* i 476
A patriot's for his country; thou art *s. T.* i 658
With such address from themes of *s.* import *T.* ii 300
S. witnesses how close-pent man regrets *T.* iv 777
To *s.* necessity, the cock forgoes *T.* v 73
Some have amused the dull *s.* years of life *T.* v 180
(Life spent in indolence and therefore *s.*) *T.* v 181
Of *s.* experience, nor examples set *T.* v 294
A *s.* memorial, and subjoin his own *T.* v 420
'Tis therefore sober and good men are *s. T.* v 509
His sprightly mingled with a shade of *s. Tir.* 665
And 'tis the *s.* complaint, and almost true *T.T.* 732

SADDENS.

A dark importance *s.* every day *H.* 699

SADDEST.

And in the *s.* part cry—"Droll indeed!" *Con.* 216
To illumine with delight the *s.* scenes *J.T.* 20

SADDLE.

Designed to sit close to it just like a *s. A.C.* 16
Struck thrice the point upon his *s.* bow *A.T.* 166
Seized fast the *s.* and sprang up behind *A.T.* 178
Lived in his *s.*, loved the chase, the course *R.* 577

SADDLETREE.

For *s.* scarce reached had he *J.G.* 49

SADNESS.

Yes, to deep *s.* sullenly resigned *Ch.* 151
How oft the *s.* that I show *M.* 46
Shows the same *s.* every where *S.* 11
And sullen *s.*, that o'ershade, distort *T.* i 457
In unrecumbent *s.* There they wait *T.* v 29
All hearts to *s.*, and none more than mine *T.* v 464

SAFE.

"'Tis over, and the brood is *s.*" *A Fable* 19
In some *s.* haven of our western world *Ch.* 444
She deems all *s.*, for she has paid the price *Ch.* 458
Suggests it *s.*, or dangerous, to be plain *Ch.* 520
Discourse, as if released and *s.* at home *Con.* 571
And has him *s.* beneath his hat *E.* iv 56
For ages *s.* beneath his sheltering hand *Ex.* 563
S. policy, but hateful *F.* 183
My creed is, he is *s.* that does his best *H.* 395
That shows how far 'tis *s.* to follow sin *H.* 608
And keep it *s.* and sound *J.G.* 68
My husband *s.* and well" *J.G.* 220
S. with protecting Montagu *Mrs. M—* 20

Shine *s.* without a fear to fade *Mrs. M—* 50 [*M.P.* 59
That thou mightest know me *s.* and warmly laid
Yet oh the thought, that thou art *s.*, and he! *M.P.* 106
S. in themselves, but dangerous in the excess *P.E.* 62
He cannot long be *s.* whose wishes roam *P.E.* 587
S. from the clamours of perverse dispute *R.* 145
You find *s.* shelter in the next stage-coach *R.* 492
Think with what pleasure, *s.* and at his ease *T.* 253
She, *s.* in the simplicity of hers *T.* 336
When *s.* occasion offers; and with dance *T.* i 584
That they are *s.*, sinners of either sex *T.* iii 96
Well one at least is *s.* One sheltered hare *T.* iii 334
Perhaps may crown us, but to fly is *s. T.* iii 688
At a *s.* distance, where the dying sound *R.* iv 92
Here grotto within grotto *s.* defies *T.* v 117 [iv 559
The unguarded door was *s.*; men did not watch *T.*
Dismiss me weary to a *s.* retreat *T.* vi 1004 [*s. T.* v 80
Earth yields them naught: the imprisoned worm is
And taught a brute the way to *s.* revenge *T.* vi 559
Harmless, and *s.*, and natural, as they are *Tir.* 565
S. under such a wing, his boy shall show *Tir.* 684
Uncrowded, yet *s.* sheltered from the storm *Y.O.* 55

SAFETY.

S. consists not in escape *A Fable* 32
With *s.* to himself, is not a man *Ex.* 433
They might with *s.* eat the rest *L.W.* 10
Ye writers of what none with *s.* reads *P.E.* 307
Darts to the mud, and finds his *s.* there *P.E.* 503
Looked to the sea for *s.*? They are gone *T.* ii 110
Or *s.* interfere, his rights and claims *T.* vi 582
That oft we owe our *s.* to a skill *T.* vi 619
And flee for *s.* to the falling rocks *T.* vi 868
And trust for *s.* to a stranger's care *Tir.* 852

SAGACIOUS.

Claps spectacles on her *s.* nose *Con.* 742
And of all arts *s.* dupes invent *P.E.* 435
S. reader of the works of God *T.* iii 253
And in his word *s.* Such too thine *T.* iii 254
Start up *s.*, covered with the dust *T.T.* 170

SAGACITY.

And such *s.* to take revenge *T.* vi 477
Some show that nice *s.* of smell *T.* vi 616
A terrible *s.* informs *T.T.* 494

SAGE.

That *s.* have seen in thy face? *A.S.* 6
S. beneath the spreading oak *B.* 5
The dozing *s.* drop the drowsy strain *Con.* 247
But *s.* observers oft mistake the flame *Con.* 655
Their wisdom bursts into this *s.* reply *Con.* 877
Ask what is human life—the *s.* replies *H.* 1 [77
That *s.* they seemed, as lawyers o'er a doubt *N.A.*
Though *s.* advice of friends the most sincere *R.* 249
See the *s.* hermit, by mankind admired *T.* 87
Ten thousand *s.* lost in endless woe *T.* 517
But falsely. *S.* after *s.* strove *T.* ii 506 [702
There dwelt a *s.* called Discipline. His head *T.* ii
"'Twere well," says one *s.*, erudite, profound *T.* iii 191
Such was thy wisdom, Newton, childlike *s.*! *T.* iii 252
Ye *s.* dispensers of poetic fame *T.* iii 457
In spite of gravity and *s.* remark *T.* v 12
The experienced and the *s. Th.* 6
Appointed *s.* preceptor to the Will *Tir.* 32
Have ye, ye *s.* intendants of the whole *Tir.* 265

SAID. [*A.C.* 10

And your lordship," he *s.*, "will undoubtedly find
Embellished with—" He *s.*," and," So *s.* I" *Con.* 212
He says but little, and that little *s. Con.* 301
And say as stern Elijah *s.* of old *Con.* 850 [*Con.* 529
That reaching home, " The night," they *s.*, " is near

370 SAID—SALUTARY

And, Truth and Wisdom gracing all He s. Con. 526
And s.,"Go spend them in the vale of tears" E. ii 26
John Gilpin's spouse s. to her dear J.G. 5
Quoth Mrs. Gilpin,—"That's well s. J.G. 25
As hath been s. or sung J.G. 108
S. Gilpin—"So am I!" J.G. 148
S. John,—"It is my wedding day J.G. 193
So turning to his horse, he s. J.G. 197
And thus unto the youth she s. J.G. 217
"Since thus ye have combined," he s. J.P. 33
"Yours is," she s., "the nobler hue L.R. 21
By some 'tis confidently s. L.W. 17
And "Hence," he s., "my mind computes Mor. 25
Much more in behalf of your wish might be s. P.A. 14
"Methinks," I s., "in thee I find P.B. 13
And to himself he s.—"What's that?" R.C. 80
But Granby was, meant truly what he s. R. 598
Here, I have s., at least I should possess T. i 234
And Victory refuted all he s. T.T. 339   [T.T. 97
"There," s. his guide, "the group is full in view"

SAIL.   [M.P. 96
So thou, with s. how swift! hast reached the shore
On steady wing s. through the immense abyss H.163
The breath of heaven must swell the s. H.F. 23 [103
S. ripped, seams opening wide, and compass lost M.P.
Seas on which every nation spreads her s. R. 80 [333
Down, down the wind, she swims, and s. away P.E.
And s. with lappet head and mincing airs T. 139
O'er all his thoughts, and swelled his easy s. T. 420
Now hoist the s., and let the streamers float T. ii 255
When disposition, like a s. unfurled Tir. 450
But oh! if Fortune fill thy s. Trans. H. 34
God's curse can cast away ten thousand s. T.T. 467

SAILED.
Far hence to the westward I s. M.D. 6

SAILOR.
At what a s. suffers; Fancy too T. i 541

SAINT.   [585
Leaves s. to enjoy those altitudes they teach Con.
To place you where his s. his presence share H. 339
Against thine image, in thy s., O Lord! H. 593
To forestall sweet S. Valentine P.T. 12   [P.E. 115
Cries—"Well done, s.!" and claps him on the back
S. offer nothing, in their warmest prayers R. 221
The s. or moralist should tread S. 17
His prayer preferred to s. that cannot aid T. 85
Doubts not hereafter with the s. to mount T. 150
Produce them—take a chair—now draw a s. T. 172
Is this a S.? Throw tints and all away T. 175 [T. 229
"Where dwell these matchless s.?" old Curio cries
What purpose has the King of S. in view? T. 179
Large prelibation oft to s. below T. v 574   [861
Thy s. proclaim thee king; and in their hearts T. vi
Thy s. proclaim thee king; and thy delay T. vi 864
When, Isaaclike, the solitary s. T. vi 948

ST. DUNSTAN'S.
Like the two figures at St. D.'s stand T.T. 527

SAINTLIER.
Which is the s. worthy of the two? T. 105

SAINTSHIP.
Give s., then all Europe must agree T. 111

SAKE.
And if he studied, studied for her s. A.T. 18
Her precept for your s. B.R. 12
And spare the poet for his subject's s. Ch. 636
Is contradiction for its own dear s. Con. 106
I kept him for his humour's s. Ep. ii 33

Royally, freely, for his bounty's s. H. 118
And seem to pray, for good example's s. H. 249
I wave just now, for conversation's s. H. 436
"The minx shall for your folly's s. J.P. 37
This record of thee for the Gospel's s. J.T. 48
For my s. restless heretofore M. 10
Tis valued for the danger's s. the more P.E. 521
His only bliss is sorrow for her s. R. 244
Suffering with gladness for a Saviour's s. R. 776
And scorn, for its own s., the gracious way T. 37
And only there, please highly for their s. T. 209
Seems, in their eyes, a mercy, for thy s. T. ii 132
Is left to sleep for peace and quiet s. T. 428   [793
Than they themselves by choice, for wisdom's s. T. ii
By all that prized it; not for prudery's s. T. iii 78
For their own s. its silence and its shade T. iii 321
For interest s., the living to the dead T. iii 661
For interest s. or swarming into clans T. iv 665
And him in peace, for s. of warlike deeds T. v. 234
We, for the s. of liberty, a king T. v 351
You chains and bondage for a tyrant's s. T. v 352
Yet being free, I love thee: for the s. T. v 473
Who slights the charities for whose dear s. T. v 507
Not for its own s. merely, but for his T. v 800
And Earth be punish'd for its tenants' s. T. vi 257
Spared yet again the ignobler for his s. T. vi 530
From creatures that exist but for our s. T. vi 603
Messiah's eulogy for Handel's s. T. vi 637
And quit their office for their error's s. T. vi 884
He puts it on, and, for decorum s. T. vi 985
For Bully's plumage s. T.B. 27
Who for the s. of filling with one blast T.T. 31
Glorious in war, but for the s. of peace T.T. 278
For that dear sorrow's s. forego 1789, 52

SALAD.
And when his juicy s. failed Ep. ii 19
A cheap but wholesome s. from the brook T. vi 304

SALE.
That waste our vitals, peculation, s. T. ii 668
Skillet, and old carved chest, from public s. T. iv 402
Too proud for dairy work, or s. of eggs T. iv 549

SALEM.
See S. built, the labour of a God! T. vi 799

SALLIED.
A beast forth s. on the scout T.B. 34

SALLIES.
And be cheered by the s. of youth A.S. 24

SALLOW.
To s. sickness, which the vapours, dank T. i 437

SALLY.
Here, S., Susan, come, come quick Trans. iv 29

SALOONS.
Who, self-imprisoned in their proud s. T. i 414

SALT.
Like that of s. with lemon juice F. 130
With acrid s., his very heart athirst T. i 448
Impregnated with quick fermenting s. T. iii 464
Loses its treasure of salubrious s. T. iii 610   [845
That s. preserves thee; more corrupted else T. iii

SALUBRIOUS.
The air s. of her lofty hills T. i 428
Loses its treasure of s. salts T. iii 610

SALUTARY.
Where'er it winds, the s. stream Con. 893

O s. streams, that murmur there! *E.* ii 28
Will hear perhaps thy s. strain *Ex.* 453
Preserved from guilt by s. fears *Tir.* 111

SALUTING.
S. his poetic ears *R. C.* 89

SALVATION.
That sound bespeaks S. on her way *H.* 455
No. Doth he purpose its s. ? No *T.* vi 705
Is heard s. Eastern Java there *T.* vi 810

SAMPLE.
These s.—for alas! at last *F.* 193
These are but s., and a taste *F.* 194
Though sickly s. of the exuberant whole *T.* iv 761
Their breath a s. of last night's regale *Tir.* 834

SAMSON.
With as much ease as S. his green withes *T.* v 737

SANCERRE.
The fairer scenes of sweet S.—*E.* i 46

SANCTIFY.
Scripture employed to s. the cheat *Ex.* 92
Is misapplied to s. their sway *P.E.* 497
No bard embalms and s. his song *T.* v 728
Where Fashion shall not s. abuse *T.* vi 852

SANCTIMONIOUS.
Such are the fruits of s. pride *T.* 165

SANCTION.
Once have the s. of our triple state *E.* iii 57
And guards it with a s. as severe *T.* 553

SANCTIONED.
By charter, and that charter s. sure *T.* v 548

SANCTITY.
Is this the path of s. ? Is this *P.E.* 116
For s. of manners undefiled *T.* iii 260
Imagined s. The conscience, yet *Y.O.* 11

SANCTUARY.
Seeming a s., proves a grave *R.* 736

SAND.
Disdains the Bank, and throws the golden s. *Ch.* 248
With s. to scour his maw *Ep.* ii 16
So barren s. imbibe the shower *F.* 184
In grains as countless as the seaside s. *T.* vi 245

SANG.
Then s. the married and the maiden throng *A.T.* 197
They s. as blithe as finches sing *F.B.* 7 [*H.* 517
The wretch, who once s. wildly, danced and laughed
I sing the Sofa. I who lately s. *T.* i 1
Their eulogy; those s. the Mantuan bard *T.* iii 453
Of Tityrus, assembling, as he s. *T.* iv 707
Thus s. the sweet sequestered bird *The Doves* 37

SANGUINARY.
" The s. schemes that some devise *H.* 382
Has never heard the s. yell *T.* iii 335
(For feats of s. hue 1789, 25

SANGUINE.
Now s., and her beauteous head now set *T.* vi 158
That s. inexperience loves to make *V.* 56

SANK.
The stifling wave and then he s. *Cast.* 48

SAPIENCE.
Just as the s. of an author's brain *Ch.* 519

SAPIENT.
Now tell me, dignified and s., sir *T.* ii 531

SAPLESS.
The s. wood, divested of the bark *Con.* 53
Must smooth be shorn away; the s. branch *T.* iii 613

SAPLING.
Then twig; then s.; and, as century rolled *Y.O.* 62

SAPS.
Society, and that s. and worms the base *T.* ii 816

SARACEN.
Would hunt a S. through fire and flood *Ex.* 521

SARCASM.
I grant the s. is too severe *T.T.* 103

SARCASTIC.
S., would exclaim, and judge the song *T.* iii 563

SASH.
The southern s. admits too strong a light *Con.* 331
And fast condensed upon the dewy s. *T.* iii 496
The prouder s. fronted with a range *T.* iv 763

SASHED.
Tight boxes neatly s., and in a blaze *R.* 483

SAT.
While Chief Baron Ear s. to balance the laws *A.C.* 7
S. the Druid, hoary chief *B.* 6
Fair Cassiopëia s. *Gr.* 16
How much his feelings suffered, s. Sir Smug) *H.* 416
She s., and a shield at her side *M.D.* 13
On such a Stool immortal Alfred s. *T.* 22
With base materials, s. on well-tanned hides *T.* i 51
S. for the picture; and the poet's hand *T.* iv 526
The bench on which we s. while deep employed *Tir.* 302
S. fast on George's brows again 1789, 45

SATED.
To please her s. and indifferent lord ? *P.E.* 258

SATELLITE.
Our softer s. Your songs confound *T.* i 766

SATIATE.
" S. of her, and weary of the same *A.T.* 105
That palls and s., and makes languid life *T.* i 464

SATIN.
With golden wing and s. poll *P.T.* 27
As yet black breeches were not, s. smooth *T.* i 10
Saw better clad, in cloak of s. trimmed *T.* i 535

SATIRE.
S. is, more than those he brands, to blame *Ch.* 492
'Tis called a s., and the World appears *Ch.* 515
Yet what can s., whether grave or gay ? *T.* ii 315
Whipped out of sight, with s. just and keen *T.T.* 640
S. has long since done his best, and curst *T.T.* 728

SATIRIC.
Crack the s. thong ? 'Twere wiser far *T.* iii 26
Nature imparting her s. gift *T.T.* 656

SATIRIST.
Most s. are indeed a public scourge *Ch.* 501
The pulpit (when the s. has at last *T.* ii 329

SATISFACTORY.
A s. receipt in full *Con.* 202

SATISFIED.
Of Friendship, s. with noise *F.B.* 32

SATISFIED—SAW

Who, s. with only pencilled scenes *T.* i 417
Not s. to prey on all around *T.* vi 394
While others, not so s., unhorse *T.* vi 701

SATISFY.
To soothe and s. the human ear *T.* 199
'Tis Revelations. all doubts *T.* ii 527
A mine to s. the enormous cost *T.* iii 783
The glowing heart may s. awhile *T.* iv 273
Dull as it is, and s. a law *T.* vi 217

SATURATE.
That dries his feathers, s. with dew *T.* i 494

SATURATED
From the full fork, the s. straw *T.* iii 479

SATURN.
The moons of Jove, and *S.*'s belted ball *Tir.* 634

SATYRS.
The Fauns and *S.*, a lascivious race *A.T.* 199
And shut up every s. in his den *Con.* 38

SAUCE.
With sophistry their s. they sweeten *L.W.* 37
Lodged on the shelf, half-eaten without s. *T.* iv 394

SAUL.
Driven out an exile from the face of *S.*—*R.* 768

SAVAGE.
While Cook is loved for s. lives he saved *Ch.* 39
And s. in its principle appears *Con.* 171
Oh! to the club, the scene of s. joys *Con.* 421
He found thee s., and he left thee tame *Ex.* 485
The full-gorged s., at his nauseous feast *H.* 509
Then forests, or the s. rock, may please *T.* i 518
War and the chase engross the s. whole *T.* i 608
Thee, gentle s.! whom no love of thee *T.* i 633
For all the s. din of the swift pack *T.* iii 325
And those in self-defence. *S.* at first *T.* v 229
The shag of s. nature, and were each *T.* v 693
To madness; while the s. at his heels *T.* vi 422
With all the s. thirst a tiger feels *T.T.* 36

SAVAGE-FIERCE.
Vicious in act, in temper s. *T.* vi 487

SAVE.
Impel the fleet whose errand is to s. *Ch.* 128
Oh! 'tis a godlike privilege to s. *Ch.* 226
Flies to s. some, and feels a pang for all *Ch.* 407
Would hang an honest man, and s. a thief *Con.* 128
From which no care can s. *Ep.* ii 42
S. as He will, by many or by few *Ex.* 361
Must s. it from declension *F.* 180
S. for the fruits his heavenly beams produce *H.* 82
And s. or damn as these or those prevail *H.* 368
And flew to s., ere yet too late *L.R.* 19
Both Poet s. and Plume from fading *Mrs. M—* 55
That life to s., we leap into the pit" *N.A.* 104
How! leap into the pit our life to s.! *N.A.* 107
To s. our life leap all into the grave! *N.A.* 108
S. when the knife is at your throat *P.* 52 [35
Poor man! I would s. him his fruit if I could *P.A.*
S. that his scent is less acute than theirs *P.E.* 85
Die then, if power Almighty s. you not *P.E.* 589
There and there only, is the power to s. *P.E.* 616
Can s. us always from a tedious day *R.* 745
To s. your life would nobly risk his own *T.* 220
My creed persuades me, well employed, may s. *T.* 522
S. their own painted skins, our sires had none *T.* i 9
But s. me from the gaiety of those *T.* i 499 [*T.* i 566
Which, kindled with dry leaves, just s. unquenched
And s. me too from theirs whose haggard eyes *T.* i 501

S. the small inventory, bed, and stool *T.* iv 401 [iii 411
Which, s. himself who trains them, none can feel *T.*
One hand secures his hat, s. when with both *T.* iv 354
Thus dream they, and contrive to s. a God *T.* vi 205
Great cause occurs to s. him from a band *Tir.* 696
And s. him from a fall *Trans.* i 20 [*T.T.* 367
Once Chatham saved thee, but who s. thee next?

SAVED.   [state? *T.* vi 704
Why? What has charmed them? Hath he s. the
While Cook is loved for savage lives he s. *Ch.* 39
Ten righteous would have s. a city once *T.* iii 843
S. him, or the unrelenting seer had died *T.* vi 471
Is it that Adam's offspring may be s. *T.* 183 [757
S. from his home, where every day brings forth *Tir.*
Baffled his rider, s. against his will *T.* vi 520 [367
Once Chatham s. thee, but who saves thee next? *T.T.*

SAVING.
And reconcile his lusts with s. grace *H.* 605

SAVIOUR.
Deeply resolved to shut a *S.* out *Con.* 690
And every drop bespeaks a *S.* thine *E.* ii 48
And theirs, by birth, the *S.* of us all *Ex.* 202
The *S.*'s feast, his own blest bread and wine *Ex.* 377
The *S.*'s history makes known *F.* 206
Suffering with gladness for a *S.*'s sake *R.* 776
But still in virtue of a *S.*'s plea *T.* 529
And humble learners of a *S.*'s worth *T.* ii 542
Presents the prayer the *S.* deigned to teach *Tir.* 123
Point to the cure, describe a *S.*'s cross *Tir.* 165

SAVOUR.
That s. much of commonplace *F.* 161
That no rude s. maritime invade *T.* ii 258

SAVOURY.
Of s. cheese, or butter costlier still *T.* iv 395
With s. truth and wholesome common sense *Tir.* 629

SAW.
She s., and turned her rosy cheek away *A.T.* 87
No! Soon as from ashore he s. *A Tale* 49
To swear to some enormity he s. *Con.* 126 [*Con.* 232
"Yes" (rather moved) "I s. it with these eyes!"
Who never s. the sword he could not wield *Con.* 608
I s. him, with that lily cropped *D.W.* 33
The loiterers I never s. *E.* i 24
"I'll see him too—the first I ever s." *E.* iii 31
He thus s. steal away *Ep.* ii 30
He s. his people slaves to every lust *Ex.* 55
S. Babylon set wide her two-leaved brass *Ex.* 59
They s. distemper healed, and life restored *Ex.* 153
Where late we s. the mimic landscape glow *H.* 263
When, turning round his head, he s. *J.G.* 51
Now Mistress Gilpin, when she s. *J.G.* 213
Then ever Roman s.! *M.* i 4
In the steerage a woman I s. *M.D.* 9
I s. him both sicken and die *M.D.* 37
I s. the hearse that bore thee slow away *M.P.* 29
But I can assure you I s. it in print *P.A.* 20
Ye s. me once (ah, those regretted days *R.* 371
While thirteen moons s. smoothly run *St.* i 1
S. better clad, in cloak of satin trimmed *T.* i 535
And soon to be supplanted. He that s. *T.* iii 751
I gazed, myself creating what I s. *T.* iv 290
I s. the woods and fields at close of day *T.* iv 311
I s. far off the weedy fallows smile *T.* iv 316
The taper soon extinguished, which I s. *T.* iv 391
No sound of hammer or of s. was there *T.* v 145
Made others covet what they s. so fair *T.* v 227 [817
S. never, such as Heaven stoops down to see *T.* vi
Went with him, and s. all the game he played? *Tir.* 268

With mute unconsciousness of what he *s. Y.O.* 146
The eyes, that never *s.* thee, shine 1789, 58

SAY.

'Twas April as the bumpkins *s. A Fable* 8
Suffice it then in decent terms to *s. A.T.* 86
Then would he *s.,* submissive at thy feet *Ch.* 232
Else I would *s.,* and as I spake bid fly *Ch.* 268
An argument of cogence, we may *s. Con.* 293
He *s.* but little, and that little said *Con.* 301
Did not our hearts feel all he deigned to *s. Con.* 535
And to *s.* truth, though in its early prime *Con.* 633
And *s.* as stern Elijah said of old *Con.* 850
S., Anna, had you never known *E.* i 67
As some grave gentleman in Terence *s. E.* iii 6
(I would *s.* twenty sheets of prose) *E.* iv 28 [*Ep.* i 4
Seems it to *s.*—" Health here has long to reign ?"
" Matthew," *s.* Fame, "with endless pains *E.* iv 73
S. Wrath is coming, and the storm appears *Ex.* 270
S. not (and if the thought of such defence *Ex.* 708
And *s.* he wounded you in jest *F.* 95
"*S.* little, and hear all you can" *F.* 182
And chirp, and kiss, he seemed to *s. F.B.* 26 [*H* 225
"Mark these," she *s.,* "these, summoned from afar
Can only *s.,*—"Nobility lies here" *H.* 271
S., botanist, within whose province fall *H.* 286
As with a frown to *s.,* "Do this, and live" *H.* 329
A thought intrude, that *s.,* or seems to *s. H.* 372
" Right," *s.* an ensign, "And for aught I see *H.* 397
And *s.*—"Blot out my sin, confessed, deplored *H.*592
S. man's a worm, and power belongs to God *H.* 711
What are ye, monarchs, laurelled heroes, *s. Her.* 77
Should *s.* that she was proud *J.G.* 36
S. why bareheaded you are come *J.G.* 167
Thus *s.* the prophet of the Turk *L.W.* 1
And one whatever you may *s. L.W.* 29
Voice only fails, else how distinct they *s. M.P.* 5
S., wast thou conscious of the tears I shed ? *M.P.* 22
And helpless, hopeless, hear thee *s. O.* ii 23
S.—"Well, 'tis more than one would think!" *P.* 36
Who *s.* the mob are mad outright *Pat.* 19
S. to what bar amenable were man ? *P.E.* 28 [599
The storm of passion, and *s.,* "Peace, be still!" *P.E.*
What *s.* the prophet ? Let that day be blest *P.E.* 157
My dear Dick Redcap, what *s.* you? *P.T.* 37
So, ancient poets *s.,* serene *Q.V.* 69
Is there, as Reason, Conscience, Scripture *s. R.* 651
Ah, self-deceived ! Could I, prophetic, *s. St.* ii 17
And seems to *s.*—" Ye meaner fowl, give place *T.* 64
" Past all dispute, yon anchorite," *s.* you *T.* 106
I *s.* the Bramin has the fairer claim *T.* 108 [*T.* 222
" Charles without doubt," *s.* you,—and so he ought
S. on what hinge does his obedience move? *T.* 207
And he *s.* much that many may dispute *T.* 359
But elbows still were wanting ; these, some *s. T.* i 60
I *s.* the pulpit (in the sober use *T.* ii 332 [377
Whose actions *s.* that they respect themselves *T.* ii
" Defend me therefore, Common Sense," *s.* I *T.* iii 187
"'Twere well," *s.* one sage, erudite, profound *T.*iii191
And when I place thee in it, sighing *s. T.* iii 350
With such heart-shaking music, who can *s. T.* iv 24
Build him a pedestal, and *s.,* "Stand there *T.* v 258
S. ye, who (with less prudence than of old *T.* v 321
Some *s.* that in the origin of things *T.* vi 198 [747
And smiling *s.*—" My Father made them all!" *T.* v
S., muse (for education made the song *Tir.* 290
S., what accomplishments, at school acquired *Tir.* 577
And *s.,* My boy, the unwelcome hour is come *Tir.* 849
Nor *s.,* Go thither, conscious that there lay *Tir.* 869
Or, if he prove unkind (as who can *s. Tir.* 895
And *s.*—what *s.* he ?—Caw *Trans.* ii 30
That tell you so—*s.,* rather, they for him *T.T.* 56
Guard what you *s.* ; the patriotic tribe *T.T.* 83
Sighing, I *s.* again, I pity kings! *T.T.* 140
As if he heard his king *s.,* "Slave, be free!" *T.T.* 245
'Twould cost him, I dare *s. Y.D.* 66

SCALD.

But every tear shall *s.* thy memory *P.E.* 336

SCALE.

A prouder station on the general *s. Ch.* 336
The *s.* are false, or algebra a lie *Con.* 22
The little Greeks look trembling at the *s. H.* 195
With nice attention in a righteous *s. H.* 367
Thine had a value in the *s.* of Heaven *J.T.* 29
But as a *s.,* by which the soul ascends *R.* 111
Turns to the stroke his adamantine *s. T.* ii 324
Her undecisive *s.* In this she lays *T.* iv 484 [*T.* iii 221
God never meant that man should *s.* the Heavens
Taints downward all the graduated *s. T.* iv 585
He sits secure, and in the *s.* of life *T.* vi 970
Conducted on a manageable *s. Tir.* 703
And weighs the nations in an even *s. T.T.* 251

SCALY.

What though in *s.* armour dressed *Miss* — 41

SCAMPER.

And claim a right to *s.* and run wide *Con.* 793
To send our sons to scout and *s.* there *Tir.* 294

SCAMPERING.

With postboy *s.* in the rear *J.G.* 235
Wide *s.,* snatches up the drifted snow *T.* v 49

SCAN.

He *s.* of every locomotive kind *N.A.* 64
But he, not wise enough to *s. St.* v 5
With which she calculates, computes, and *s. T.* i 716
Then leave their crimes for History to *s. T.T.* 119

SCANDAL.

When *S.* has new minted an old lie *Ch.* 513
Assailed by *s.* and the tongue of strife *H.* 576
Books, therefore, not the *s.* of the shelves *R.* 683
Ambling and prattling *s.* as he goes *T.* ii 382

SCANDALIZED.

Then Nature, injured, *s.,* defiled *Ex.* 424

SCANT.

If Solitude make *s.* the means of life *T.* i 248

SCANTILY.

Or if yourself, too *s.* supplied *P.E.* 251
The country's need have *s.* supplied *T.T.* 338

SCANTLING.

Sells the last *s.,* and transfers the price *T.* iii 753

SCANTY.

Within the *s.* limits of the mind *Ch.* 247
Too *s.* for the exertion of his beams *Ch.* 590
Just earns a *s.* pittance and at night *T.* 321
Her *s.* stock of brushwood, blazing clear *T.* iv 381
And eyes intent upon the *s.* herb *T.* v 786
That knows no measure, by the *s.* rule *T.* vi 213

'SCAPED.

When, '*s.* from literary cares *D.W.* 3
Nor palaces, nor even chambers, '*s. T.* ii 831
The dangers we have '*s.,* the broken snare *T.* iv 185

'SCAPES. [230

His hairbreadth '*s.,* and all his daring schemes *Tir.*

SCARE.

Or *s.* the nation with its big contents *Ch.* 617 [461
But nothing *s.* them, from the course they love *T.T.*

SCARED.

Sir Airy, not a whit dismayed or *s. A.T.* 171
And Danish howlings *s.* thee as they passed *Ex.* 471
S., and the offended nightingale is mute *T.* i 768
To escape the impending famine, often *s. T.* v 68

SCARLET.

When *s.* fruits the russet hedge adorn *A.T.* 72
Where, flaming in *s.* and gold *Gr.* 29
In *s.* mantle warm, and velvet capped *M.P.* 51
Or *s.* crewel, in the cushion fixed *T.* i 54
I fed on *s.* hips and stony haws *T.* i 120   [320
Have changed the woods, in *s.* honours bright *T.* i

SCARS.

And in his hands and feet, the cruel *s. T.* iii 114

SCATTERED.   [884

Shoots between *s.* rocks and opening shades *Con.*
Peeled, *s.*, and exterminated thus *Ex.* 246
A flock so *s.*, and so wont to roam *Ex.* 729
Collect the *s.* truths that Study gleans *R.* 274
Now *s.* wide, and nowhere to be found *T.* 394
The middle field ; but *s.* by degrees *T.* i 293
Lie *s.* where the shapely column stood *T.* ii 76
Thy *s.* hair with sleet like ashes filled *T.* iv 121
The *s.* grain, and thievishly resolved *T.* v 67
The bright profusion of her *s.* stars *T.* vi 176
To see a people *s.* like a flock *T.T.* 34
And, like a *s.* seed at random sown *T.T.* 674

SCATTERING.

Imagination *s.* round *Mrs. M—* 27

SCENE.

Where parties are agreed, retired the *s. A.T.* 89 [95
That curtained round the *s.* where they reposed *A.T.*
The *s.* of her sensible choice ! *C.* 44
And with *s.* that new rapture inspire *C.* 51
God opens fruitful Nature's various *s. Ch.* 88
To quit the bliss thy rural *s.* bestow *Ch.* 299
To seek a nobler amidst *s.* of woe *Ch.* 300
Thrives against Hope, and in the rudest *s. Ch.* 575
To uphold the boundless *s.* of his command *Ch.* 582
So withered stumps disgrace the sylvan *s. Con.* 51
Oh ! to the club, the *s.* of savage joys *Con.* 421
In the last *s.* of her six thousand years *Con.* 456
The *s.* of all those sorrows left behind *Con.* 308
And through the *s.* of toil-renewing light *Con.* 732
To close in sable every social *s. Con.* 872
A brighter *s.* beyond that vale appears *Con.* 882
The fairer *s.* of sweet Sancerre *E.* i 46
Like other *s.* already past *E.* i 56
The *s.* to which not youth alone resorts *Ex.* 24
And had the grace in *s.* of peace to show *Ex.* 79
The virtue they had learned in *s.* of woe *Ex.* 80
Thy senate is a *s.* of civil jar *Ex.* 294
Beheld with joy the lovely *s.* defaced *Ex.* 426 [586
While his own heaven surveys the troubled *s. Ex.*
In *s.* of plenty, or the pining waste *Ex.* 733
A *s.* of fancied bliss and heart-felt care *H.* 5
And nowhere, but in feigned Arcadian *s. H.* 9
The busy heralds hang the sable *s. H.* 264
From happier *s.*, to make your land a prey *H.* 478
These, amidst *s.* as waste as if denied *H.* 538
Ten thousand swains the wasted *s.* deplore *Her.* 39
To illumine with delight the saddest *s. J.T.* 20
Within the garden's peaceful *s. L.R.* 5
Are such an antiquated *s. M.F.* 7
The gloomy *s.* surveys *N.* 10
Embellishing the *s.* around *P.* 58
Charged with the folly of his life's mad *s. P.E.* 88
Can British Paradise no *s.* afford *P.E.* 257   [154
Preaching and pranks will share the motley *s. P.E.*

Where George, recovered, made a *s. Q.V.* 27   [11
And the *s.* where his melody charmed me before *P.F.*
It was a *s.* in every part *Q.V.* 57
And fearless of the billowy *s. Q.V.* 71
In the last *s.* of such a senseless play *R.* 32
New life ordained and brighter *s.* to share *R.* 65
And may be feared amid the busiest *s. R.* 121
From *s.* of sorrow into glorious day *R.* 168
O Nature ! whose Elysian *s.* disclose *R.* 199
Post away swiftly to more active *s. R.* 273
Then neither heathy wilds, nor *s.* as fair *R.* 331
Or half so clear, as in the rural *s. R.* 456
And what could a remoter *s.* show more ? *R.* 500
Sighs o'er the beauties of the charming *s. R.* 566
To social *s.* by nature disinclined *R.* 606
Whatever hopes a change of *s.* inspires *R.* 679
As theirs who bustle in the busiest *s. R.* 734
Surveyed the *s.*, and took possession *R.C.* 44
How ill the *s.* that offers rest *S.* 3
And slights the season and the *s. S.* 12
Me fruitful *s.* and prospects waste *S.* 21
Yet heard in *s.* where peace for ever reigns *T.* 208
Suppose, unlooked for in a *s.* so rude *T.* 248
My relish of fair prospect ; *s.* that soothed *T.* i 141
And still unsated, dwelt upon the *s. T.* i 158
S. must be beautiful which, daily viewed *T.* i 177
Nor less attractive is the woodland *s. T.* i 300
The love of Nature, and the *s.* she draws *T.* i 412
Who, satisfied with only pencilled *s. T.* i 417
Fastidious, seeking less familiar *s. T.* i 512
But that of idleness, and taste no *s. T.* i 756
And fugitive in vain. The sylvan *s. T.* ii 107 [117
Possessed an inland *s.* Where now the throng *T.* ii
And roofs embattled high, the gloomy *s. T.* ii 122
And with a well-bred whisper close the *s.* ! *T.* ii 413
With opera glass to watch the moving *s. T.* ii 453
And Virtue fled. The schools became a *s. T.* ii 735
For me, enamoured of sequestered *s. T.* iii 27
My former partners of my peopled *s. T.* iii 119
S. formed for contemplation, and to nurse *T.* iii 301
S. such as these, 'tis his supreme delight *T.* iii 306
And dress the regular yet various *s. T.* iii 592
Without it, all is gothic as the *s. T.* iii 641   [708
And virtue, and those *s.* which God ordained *T.* iii
Forecasts the future whole ; that when the *s. T.* iii 65
S. that I love, and with regret perceive *T.* iii 710
And those Arcadian *s.* that Maro sings *T.* iv 515
That to suppose a *s.* where she presides *T.* iv 532
Down into *s.* still rural ; but, alas ! *T.* iv 556
S. rarely graced with rural manners now ! *T.* iv 557
Resign the *s.* their presence might protect *T.* iv 592
But there I laid the *s.* There early strayed *T.* iv 697
Of rural *s.*, compensating his loss *T.* iv 768
The pencil or the pen, may trace the *s.* ! *T.* v 109
And all was moist to the warm touch ; a *s. T.* v 166
In *s.* which, having never known me free *T.* v 480
Smit with the beauty of so fair a *s. T.* v 560
Ruminate heedless of the *s.* outspread *T.* v 788
" Distinctly *s.* invisible to man *T.* v 826
A kindred melody, the *s.* recurs *T.* vi 13
The dazzling splendour of the *s.* below *T.* vi 64
And all this uniform uncolour'd *s. T.* vi 178
Makes all still fairer. As with him no *s. T.* vi 254
A *s.* so friendly to his favorite task *T.* vi 264
With which kind nature graces every *s. T.* vi 342
So Eden was a *s.* of harmless sport *T.* vi 364
Now happiest they that occupy the *s. T.* vi 397
A visitor unwelcome, into *s. T.* vi 570
O *s.* surpassing fable, and yet true *T.* vi 759   [760
S. of accomplish'd bliss ! which who can see *T.* vi
To Nature's *s.*, than Nature ever knew *Tir.* 24
The *s.* is touching, and the heart is stone *Tir.* 298
Just in the *s.* where he displayed his own *Tir.* 337

If not a s. of pleasure, a mere blank *Tir.* 752
And the last left the s. when Chatham died *T.T.* 339
To throw his dark displeasure o'er the s. *T.T.* 445
The puppy pack that had defiled the s. *T.T.* 641
On every s. and subject it surveys *T.T.* 713 [*T.T.* 696
And charms the woodland s., and wilds unknown
To s. where competition, envy, strife *V.* 75
Down to the close of life's fast fading s. *V.* 85
Or prompter, save the s., I will perform *Y.O.* 141

SCENERY.
The richest s. and the loveliest forms *T.* i 711
Calls the delightful s. all his own *T.* v 741

SCENT.
The gale informs us, laden with the s. *Ch.* 446
Pernicious weed! whose s. the fair annoys *Con.* 251
And when he laid them on the s. of blood *Ex.* 520
Sweet s., or lovely form, or both combined *H.* 290
Save that his s. is less acute than theirs *P.E.* 85
Nor gales that catch the s. of blooming groves *R.* 337
For aided both by ear and s. *T.B.* 49
The s. regaled, each odoriferous leaf *T.* iii 621
Of flavour or of s. in fruit or flower *T.* vi 248 [*Tir.* 447
Whose s. and hues are rather guessed than known
Forms, opens, and gives s. to every flower *T.T.* 691

SCENTED.
As ever dressed a bank, or s. summer air *Ch.* 259
Curled, s., furbelowed, and flounced around *Ex.* 51
The scentless and the s. rose; this red *T.* vi 151

SCENTING.
Streams far behind him, s. all the air *T.* v 57

SCENTLESS.
The s. and the scented rose; this red *T.* vi 151

SCEPTRE.
Thy diadem displaced, thy s. gone *Ex.* 258
The s. of her power *L.R.* 16
And swayed the s. of his infant realms *T.* i 23
A leafless branch thy s., and thy throne *T.* iv 125
The globe and s. in such hands misplaced *T.T.* 39

SCEPTIC.
A s. in philosophy may seem *Con.* 138.
And shakes the s. in the scorner's chair *T.* 472

SCHEME.
Our self-importance ruins its own s. *Con.* 368
The web of every s. they have at heart *Ex.* 331
"The sanguinary s. that some devise *H.* 382
Then farewell all self-satisfying s. *T.* 7
His hairbreadth 'scapes, and all his daring s. *Tir.* 230
Exchanged for the secure domestic s. *Tir.* 705
With s. of monumental fame; and sought *T.* v 182

SCHOLAR.
The s.'s pitch (the s. best knows why) *P.E.* 505
With parrot tongue performed the s.'s part *T.* ii 738
Not brighter than in theirs the s.'s prize *Tir.* 473

SCHOLARSHIP.
Undoubted s. and genuine worth *Tir.* 280

SCHOOL.
The s. of coarse good fellowship and noise *Con.* 422
And when accomplished in her wayward s. *Con.* 465
To learn in God's own s. the Christian part *Ex.* 650
Froward at s., and fretful in his plays *H.* 188
Drew me to s. along the public way *M.P.* 49
A youngster at s. more sedate than the rest *P.A.* 21
Not of the moral, but the dancing s. *P.E.* 190
From s. to Cam or Isis, and thence home *P.E.* 369
Whatever parents, guardians, s. intend *P.E.* 424

Will learn in s. of tribulation *R.C.* 115
To them, the sounding jargon of the s. *T.* 367
Of wisdom, proves a s. in which he learns *T.* i 614
Strutting and vapouring in an empty s. *T.* ii 330
He teaches those to read, whom s. dismissed *T.* ii 358
Is Christ the abler teacher, or the s. ? *T.* ii 534
And Virtue fled. The s. became a scene *T.* ii 735
Of womanhood, fit pupils in the s. *T.* iv 228
Behold the s. in which plebeian minds *T.* iv 492
Is but a s., where thoughtlessness is taught *T.* iv 688
Entangled in the cobwebs of the s. *T.* iv 726
And in the s. of sacred wisdom taught *T.* v 797
And taught at s. much mythologic stuff *Tir.* 197
That pedantry is all that s. impart *Tir.* 212
S., unless discipline were doubly strong *Tir.* 218
Great s. suit best the sturdy and the rough *Tir.* 341
A public s. shall bring to pass with ease *Tir.* 372
For public s. 'tis public folly feeds *Tir.* 250 [*Tir.* 397
Your Lordship, and your Grace! what s. can teach
Great s. rejected then, as those that swell *Tir.* 501
I praise a s. as Pope a government *Tir.* 506
Say, what accomplishments, at s. acquired *Tir.* 577
And s., that have outlived all just esteem *Tir.* 704
All these, and more like these, were bred at s. *Tir.* 838
Of natural pity, send him not to s. *Tir.* 872 [900
Pull down the s.—what! all the s. in the land *Tir.*
Survey our s. and colleges, and see *Tir.* 909
His court, the dissolute and hateful s. *T.T.* 626
And strutting in thy s. of Queens and Kings *V.* 45

SCHOOLBOY.
Friends, not adopted with a s.'s haste *R.* 725
Of the mere s.'s lean and tardy growth *Tir.* 657

SCHOOL-BRED.
That though s. the boy be virtuous still *Tir.* 840

SCHOOLFELLOW.
Thy s. and partner of thy plays *V.* 35

SCHOOL-FRIENDSHIPS.
Besides, s. are not always found *Tir.* 436

SCHOOLING.
By public hackneys in the s. trade *Tir.* 621

SCHOOLMEN. [*F.A.* 28
Deep mysteries both! which s. must have toiled

SCIENCE.
Those seeds of s. called his ABC *Con.* 14
Where S. points her telescopic eye *H.* 441
In s., win one inch of heavenly ground *T.* 338
From all that S. traces, Art invents *T.* i 627
Where s. and where virtue are professed ? *T.* ii 766
Friends in the friends of s., and true prayer *T.* iii 250
Their progress in the road of s.; blinds *T.* v 451
Fair s. poured the light of truth *Th.* 3
The varied fields of s., ever new *T.T.* 264

SCOFF.
God's better gift they s. at, and refuse *Ex.* 459
The s. of withered age and beardless youth *H.* 743
S. at her own performance. Reason now *T.* v. 629

SCOLD.
The flippant and the s. *J.P.* 22
He s., and gives the lie *Trans.* iv 27

SCOLDED.
If a man must be s. for loving his own *A.T.* ii 12

SCOOPED.
A hollow s., I judge, in ancient time *N.A.* 17 [111
Possessing nought but the s. rind that seems *Y.O.*

SCOPE.

Christ and his character their only *s. Con.* 541
While Passion turns aside from its due *s. H.* 113
To live estranged from God his total *s. Tir.* 426
To give Religion her unbridled *s. T.T.* 71

SCORCH.

Whom fiery suns, that *s.* the russet spice *Ex.* 15

SCORCHED.

Burning and *s.* into perpetual dearth *Ex.* 421

SCORE. [*A.T.* iii 3

Should John wed a *s.*, oh the claws and the scratches!
He cannot drink five bottles, bilk the *s. P.E.* 193
The emphasis in *s.*, and gives to prayer *T.* ii 360
Some half a dozen, and some half a *s. Tir.* 695
And not to quit a *s. Y.D.* 32

SCORN.

And he that *s.* it is himself a slave *Ch.* 227
Though *S.* repay her sympathetic tears *Ch.* 413
Of fancied *s.* and undeserved disdain *Con.* 348
And while she seems to *s.* him, only fears *Con.* 788
Admonished, *s.* the caution and the friend *E.* ii 17
Their hope in Heaven, servility their *s. Ex.* 440
Fires all his feelings with a noble *s. H.* 151
Who *s.* to do an injury by stealth *H.* 411
And *s.* to share it with the distant sun *H.* 480
And bore the pelting *s.* of half an age *H.* 557 [650
S. with the same indifference frowns and smiles *H.*
And felt the sneer with *s.* enough *P.* 18
I *s.* your·coarse insinuation *P.* 27 [688
Built God a church, and laughed his word to *s. R.*
Scorned in a world, indebted to that *s. R.* 751
That *s.* afflictions mercifully meant *R.* 760
And look on Folly's pageantry with *s. S.* ii 8
If *s.* of God's commands, impressed *St.* vi 29
And *s.*, for its own sake, the gracious way *T.* 37
And holds them dangling at arms' length in *s. T.* 164
S. the base hireling, and the slavish drudge *T.* 228
Where deists, always foiled, yet *s.* to yield *T.* 372
Her own abhorrence, and as much your *s. T.* 510
While he that *s.* the noonday beam, perverse *T.* 523
His firm stability to what he *s. T.* i 383
Who *s.* it, starves deservedly at home *T.* i 435
He does not *s.* it, who, imprisoned long *T.* i 436
He does not *s.* it, who has long endured *T.* i 445
Yet *s.* the purposes for which they live *T.* i 486
All affectation. 'Tis my perfect *s. T.* ii 417
To soothe their honest pride, that *s.* to beg *T.* iv 405
The *s.* of danger, and united hearts *T.* v 377
Of royal mercy, and through generous *s. T.* vi 410
She *s.* his pleasures, for she knows them not *T.* vi 919
And *s.* thy present lot *The Doves* 32 [156
Regards with *s.*, though once received with awe *Tir.*
His pride, that *s.* to obey or to submit *Tir.* 226
That *s.* of all delights but those of sense *Tir.* 351
Low in the world, because he *s.* its arts *Tir.* 672
A Briton's *s.* of arbitrary chains? *T.T.* 201 [116
And praised for virtues that they *s.* to wear *T.T.*
And ask, with busy *s.*, " Was this the man ? " *T.T.* 120
Fire indignation and a sense of *s. T.T.* 489

SCORNED.

What is fanatic frenzy, *s.* so much *Con.* 651
They *s.* his inspiration, and his theme *Ex.* 69
And having chosen evil, *s.* the voice *Ex.* 398
Whom all tho vanities they *s.* engage *Ex.* 661
All witnesses of blessings foully *s. H.* 223 [73
Not *s.* in Heaven, though little noticed here *M.P.*
S. by the nobler tenants of the flood *P.E.* 482

The mighty myriads, now securely *s. R.* 70
Or *s.* where business never intervenes *R.* 122
S. by the rest, with patient hope they wait *R.* 165
S. in a world, indebted to that scorn *R.* 751
And *s.* as is my strain *St.* i 30.
A thousand awful admonitions *s. St.* ii 27
The good he *s.*, all carried to account" *T.* 546
Now *s.*, but worthy of a better fate *T.* i 254

SCORNER. [36

There were the *s.*'s and the slanderer's tongue *Ex.*
And shakes the sceptic in the *s.*'s chair *T.* 472
Dwelt young Misagathus; a *s.* he *T.* vi 485
The wildest *s.* of his Maker's laws *Tir.* 55

SCORNFUL.

Not so where, *s.* of a check, it leaps *T.* v 101

SCORNING.

For *s.* what they taught him to detest *Ch.* 56

SCORPION.

And proves a raging *s.* in his breast *P.E.* 241

SCOT.

And when the Stuart, leaning on the *S.*—*Ex.* 574

SCOTLAND.

In *S.*'s realm, where trees are few *A Tale* 1
In *S.*'s realm, forlorn and bare *A Tale* 9

SCOUR.

With sand to *s.* his maw *Ep.* ii 16
He wipes and *s.* the silver cup in vain *Ex.* 385
And, while the playful jockey *s.* the room *Tir.* 366

SCOURGE.

To *s.* him, weariness his only blame *Ch.* 215
Most satirists are indeed a public *s. Ch.* 501
Some twigs of that old *s.* are left behind *Ex.* 517
What *s.* are the gods that rule below *Her.* 66
A *s.* hung with lashes he bore *M.D.* 30
The *s.* he let fall from his hand *M.D.* 35
Ask him, if your knotted *s. N.C.* 29
That holds mankind together, to a *s. T.* ii 687
Under dissection of the knotted *s. T.* vi 419
Are but his rods to *s.* a guilty land *T.T.* 450

SCOURGED.

A nation *s.*, yet tardy to repent *Ex.* 723

SCOUT.

A beast forth sallied on the *s. T.B.* 34
To send our sons to *s.* and scamper there *Tir.* 294
While the rat is on the *s. Trans.* iii 11

SCOWLS.

Not so when winter *s.* Assistant Art *T.* iii 541

SCRAMBLE.

Lisping our syllables, we *s.* next *Tir.* 125

SCRAPE.

"But let me *s.* the dirt away *J.G.* 189
What shifts he used, detected in a *s. Tir.* 328

SCRATCHED.

Although immortal, may be pricked or *s. Ch.* 512

SCRATCHES. [*A.T.* iii 3

Should John wed a score, oh the claws and the *s.*!

SCRATCHING.

Heard an inexplicable *s. R.C.* 78

SCRAWLED.

S. upon glass Miss Bridget's lovely name *T.* 156

SCRAWLS.
Or with his pen, save when he *s.* a card *T.* ii 384

SCREAM.
"Yes, truly—one must *s.* and bawl *M.F.* 27
All learned, and all drunk! the fiddle *s. T.* iv 478

SCREAMED.
The dogs did bark, the children *s. J.G.* 109

SCREAMING.
The *s.* nations, hovering in mid air *H.* 353
When Betty *s.* came down stairs *J. G.* 59
In still repeated circles, *s.* loud *T.* 204
And *s.* at the sad presage *T.B.* 47

SCREEN. [10
Where the hazels afford him a *s.* from the heat *P.F.*
That *s.* the herdsman's solitary hut *T.* i 168
Our fathers knew the value of a *s. T.* i 255
Of other *s.*, the thin umbrella spread *T.* i 260
S. them, and seem half petrified to sleep *T.* v 28

SCREENED. [581
The winter's frown, if *s.* from his shrewd bite *T.* iii
But *s.* from every storm that blows *Mrs. M—* 18

SCREENING.
Her want of care, *s.* and keeping warm *T.* iii 440

SCREW.
Matches, blood-extorting *s. N.C.* 30
The *s.* reversed (a task which if He please *R.* 327
And strained to the last *s.* that he can bear *T.* 385

SCRIB. [526
The world is charmed, and *S.* escapes the law *Ch.*

SCRIBBLE.
No wonder I, who *s.* rhyme *E.* i 19
In which I both *s.* and dose *Gr.* 12
To *s.* as you scribbled, at fifteen *P.E.* 318

SCRIBBLED.
To scribble as you *s.*, at fifteen *P.E.* 318

SCRIBBLING.
" Shall make your *s.* fingers ache *J.P.* 39
Swarmed with a *s.* herd, as deep inlaid *T.T.* 628

SCRIPTURE.
The *S.* placed within his reach, he ought *Ch.* 201
That square not truly with the *S.* plan *Ch.* 559
Who deal with *S.*, its importance felt *Con.* 729
S. employed to sanctify the cheat *Ex.* 92
That *S.*, Justice, and Good Sense disown *Ex.* 593
That bliss, revealed in *S.*, with a glow *H.* 149
That cannot bear the blaze of *S.* light *H.* 298
S. indeed is plain, but God and he *H.* 598
On *S.* ground are sure to disagree *H.* 599
If not that Hope the *S.* has required *H.* 617
The worst is—*S.* warped from its intent *P.E.* 437
Nor has, nor can have, *S.* on its side *P.E.* 515
That *S.* lies, and blasphemy is sense *P.E.* 595
To spread the page of *S.*, and compare *R.* 131
Is there, as Reason, Conscience, *S.* say *R.* 651
Strong Judgment labouring in the *S.* mine *R.* 698
And all his strength from *S.* drew *St.* iii 19
If sufferings *S.* no where recommends *T.* 109
The *S.* was his jest book, whence he drew *T.* 308
The *S.* yields) or hope to find, a friend? *T.* 440
That *S.* is the only cure of woe *T.* 452
S. is still a trumpet to his fears *T.* v 611 [129
Points, which, unless the *S.* made them plain *Tir.*

SCRIVENER.
A *s.*'s clerk, or footman out of place *Tir.* 407

SCROFULOUS.
Excess, the *s.* and itchy plague *T.* iv 582

SCROLL.
And heaven is all departed as a *s. H.* 747

SCRUPLE.
Will seldom *s.* to make free *F.* 92
Your *s.* and arguments bring to my mind *P.A.* 17
His *s.* thus silenced, Tom felt more at ease *P.A.* 41
Exposed than others, with less *s.* made *T.* iv 457
That *s.* checks him. Riot is not loud *T.* v 614
Strange doctrine this! that without *s.* tears *T.T.* 5

SCRUPULOUS.
Dubius is such a *s.* good man *Con.* 119

SCRUPULOUSLY.
Washed with a neatness *s.* nice *Ex.* 149

SCRUTINY.
Perhaps at last close *s.* may show *Con.* 177
The *s.* of those all-seeing eyes *T.* 271
Long knowledge and the *s.* of years *T.* i 179
Then compromise had place, and *s. T.* ii 740
Challenging human *s.*, and proved *T.* v 868

SCUDDED.
And *s.* still before the wind *Cast.* 24

SCUFFLE.
The rude will *s.* through with ease enough *Tir.* 340

SCULPTURE.
The powers of *s.*, but the style as much *T.* i 706
To latest times; and *S.*, in her turn *T.* v 709

SCUTCHEONS.
With mournful *s.*, and dim lamps between *H.* 265

SCYTHE.
A stroke as fatal as the *s.* of Death *Ch.* 144
Well does the work of his destructive *s. T.* iv 222
But oh! it cuts him like a *s. Y.D.* 7 [*T.T.* 42
And Death's own *s.*, would better speak his power
With his sly *s.*, whose ever-nibbling edge *Y.O.* 105

SEA.
From the centre all round to the *s. A.S.* 3
Hills, valleys, rivers, and the boundless *s. A.T.* 49
This racer of the *s. A Tale* 30
The mother-bird is gone to *s. A Tale* 45
Aware that flight, in such a *s. Cast.* 33
But I beneath a rougher *s. Cast.* 65 [301
To traverse *s.*, range kingdoms, and bring home *Ch.*
Where *s.* or deserts part them from the rest *Ch.* 20
Whether he measure earth, compute the *s. Ch.* 353
That makes *s.* stable, and dissolves the rock *Con.* 502
And trident-bearing queen of the wide *s. Ex.* 275
Who poises and proportions *s.* and land *Ex.* 342
To trace thee to the date when yon fair *s. Ex.* 550
Thy thunders travel over earth and *s. Ex.* 582
Hard task indeed o'er arctic *s.* to roam! *H.* 548
Like him, crossed cheerfully tempestuous *s. H.* 584
That shook the circling *s.* and solid earth *Her.* 14
Strewing yonder *s.* with wrecks *N.C.* 34
S. on which every nation spreads her sails *R.* 80
With one consent to rush into the *s. R.* 524 [552
The *s.* globose and huge, the o'erarching vault *R.*
Sweet moralist! afloat on life's rough *s. R.H.* 3
Earth, *s.*, and sun, adieu! *St.* iii 10
Washed by the *s.*, or on the gravelly bank *T.* i 13
With one who left her, went to *s.*, and died *T.* i 538
Looked to the *s.* for safety? They are gone *T.* ii 119
Braved and defied, and in our own *s.* proved *T.* ii 272
Old or of later date, by *s.* or land *T.* v 381
" That navigate a *s.* that knows no storms *T.* v 823
Were built, the fountains opened, or the *s. T.* v 765

Is merely as the working of a *s. T.* vi 738
If all we find possessing earth, *s.,* air *Tir.* 91
Turn him adrift upon a rolling *s. Tir.* 868
Now quenching in a boundless *s.* of clouds *Y.O.* 76

SEA-BEATEN.
S. rocks and naked shores *A Tale* 19

SEA-BORN.
For *s.* Venus her attachment shows *Con.* 265

SEA-FOWL.
But the *s.* is gone to her nest *A.S.* 49

SEA-FIGHT.
His last *s.* is fought *R.G.* 15

SEAL.
And wanting him to loose the sacred *s. Con.* 544
Received the *s.* of martyrdom in blood *Ex.* 617
The *s.* of office glitter in his eyes *T.* iv 59 [457
And mark them with a *s.* of wrath pressed down *T.T.*
Watch, *s.,* and all,—till all his pranks are told *Tir.* 331

SEALED.
(Two themes to Nature's eye for ever *s.*) *Ch.* 362
Man's heart had been impenetrably *s. Con.* 427
S. with his signet whom they serve and love *R.* 164
And *s.* with the same token. It is held *T.* v 547

SEA-MAID.
The *s.* rides the waves *Q.V.* 70

SEAMAN.
Then swift descending with a *s.'s* haste *R.* 435
The *s.,* with sincere delight *A Tale* 57
For *s.* much believe in signs *A Tale* 61

SEAMEW.
That hides the *s.* in his hollow clefts *T.* i 519

SEAMS. [103
Sails ripped, *s.* opening wide, and compass lost *M.P.*

SEARCH.
To sift and *s.* them with unerring eyes *Ex.* 88
On special *s.,* the keen-eyed eagle blind *Ex.* 631
Pursue the *s.,* and you will find *F.* 199
To *s.* forbidden deeps, where mystery lies *F.A.* 33
And *s.* the themes, important above all *R.* 137
Though not a grace appears on strictest *s. T.* 151
S. it, and prove now if it be not blood *T.* iii 204
That breathes the spleen, and *s.* every bone *T.* iv 364
Remains to each, the *s.* of sunny nook *T.* v 71
The world o'erlooks him in her busy *s. T.* vi 915 [204
The cause, though worth the *s.,* may yet elude *T.T.*
My busy *s.,* I next applied 1789, 12
Ye reasoners broad awake, whose busy *s. Y.O.* 30

SEARCHED.
Explained, illustrated, and *s.* so well *Con.* 527
And *s.* for crannies in the frame *P.B.* 6
And in the dust, sifted and *s.* in vain *T.* v 536

SEARED. [396
Hast thou, with heart perverse and conscience *s. Ex.*

SEARS. [30
My languid limbs, when summer *s.* the plains *T.* iii

SEASIDE.
In grains as countless as the *s.* sands *T.* vi 245

SEASON.
Even here is a *s.* of rest *A.S.* 51
Than those a brighter *s.* pours around *Con.* 648
Or cool, as the *s.* demands *Gr.* 38
Revolving *s.,* fruitless as they pass *Her.* 25
'Twas in the glad *s.* of spring *M.D.* 1
Where spices breathe and brighter *s.* smile *M.P.* 91
Its happiest *s.,* and a peaceful close *R.* 750
And slights the *s.* and the scene *S.* 12
At such a *s.,* and with such a charge *T.* 219
Cheer all their *s.* with a grateful smile *T.* i 622
To sport their *s.,* and be seen no more *T.* iii 136
Whether inclement *s.* recommend *T.* iii 388
Which he that fights a *s.* so severe *T.* iii 560
Come, Evening, once again, *s.* of peace *T.* iv 243
They brave the *s.,* and yet find at eve *T.* iv 378
That in due *s.* he forgets it too *T.* v 267
The *s.* smiles, resigning all its rage *T.* vi 61
And, ere one flowery *s.* fades and dies *T.* vi 196
Is dreary, so with him all *s.* please *T.* vi 255
The various *s.* woven into one *T.* vi 769
And that one *s.* an eternal spring *T.* vi 770
Ye slow-revolving *s.!* We would see *T.* vi 842
Why do the *s.* still enrich the year *Tir.* 41
Back to the *s.* of life's happy spring *Tir.* 132

SEASONABLE.
And prayer more *s.* than the noise *St.* ii 11

SEAT.
The greenhouse is my summer *s. F.B.* 1
To enjoy cool nature in a country *s. H.* 245
Which galled him in his *s. J.G.* 84
The *s.* of empire is her cheeks *L.R.* 27
And the tree is my *s.* that once lent me a shade *P.F.* 8
George took his *s.* again *Q.V.* 2
Umbrageous walks and solitary *s. R.* 258 [31
And o'er the *s.,* with plenteous wadding stuffed *T.* i
The slippery *s.* betrayed the sliding part *T.* i 46
Fall back into our *s.,* extend an arm *T.* ii 448
Have rambled wide. In country, city, *s. T.* iii 14
Convivial table and commodious *s. T.* v 162 [*T.* v 163
(What seemed at least commodious *s.*) were there
Still keeps a *s.* or two for worth and grace *Tir.* 433
But seeks the corner of some distant *s. Tir.* 571

SEATED.
Their prince, as justly *s.* on his throne *Ch.* 51
Between supporters: and, once *s.,* sit *T.* i 479
May be expected from thee, *s.* here *Y.O.* 139

SECLUSION.
Oh blest *s.* from a jarring world *T.* iii 675

SECOND.
Of fewer errors, on a *s.* proof! *F.A.* 5
That make superior skill his *s.* praise *H.* 206
Thy sight now *s.* not thy will *M.* 15
Shall seem to start into a *s.* birth *R.* 356
The *s.* milestone fronts the garden gate *R.* 490
Though placed in golden Durham's *s.* stall *T.* 120
For *s.* childhood; and devote old age *T.* ii 637
Cautious he pinches from the *s.* stalk *T.* iii 527
I give the bauble but the *s.* place *Tir.* 388
This *s.* weaning, needless as it is *Tir.* 557
And blazing London seemed a *s.* Troy *T.T.* 323
But when the *s.* Charles assumed the sway *T.T.* 620

SECONDED.
When fierce Temptation, *s.* within *T.* iii 684

SECRET.
Winding a *s.* or an open course *Ch.* 369
Who yet betrays his *s.* by his works *Con.* 80
The treacherous smile, a mask for *s.* hate *Ex.* 42
Blind to the working of that *s.* Power *Ex.* 320 [337
None bars Him out from his most *s.* thought *Ex.*

My soul shall sigh in s., and lament *Ex.* 722
The s. just committed *F.* 69
That s. are a sacred trust *F.* 157
Can see his love, though s. evil lurks *H.* 544
And though in act unwearied, s. still *J.T.* 37
To dive into the s. deeps within *R.* 135
Both fail beneath a fever's s. sway *R.* 295
A s. thirst of his renounced employs *R.* 474
They seek like me the s. shade *S.* 19
Betrays the s. of their silent course *T.* 196
The undiscoverable s. sleeps *T.* v 537
Whose cause is God. He feeds the s. fire *T.* vi 224
And figure of the man, his s. aim *T* vi 618
Nor, though he tread the s. path of life *T.* vi 956

SECT.
Thus hopes of every sort, whatever s. *H.* 294

SECTARIES.
Hence jarring s. may learn *N.G.* 27

SECURE.
'Tis Providence alone s. *A Fable* 30
Can be s. against a madman's thrust *Ch.* 510
But Truth divine for ever stands s. *Con.* 555
S. the favour, and enhance the joy *Ex.* 678
Remember, if He guard thee and s. *Ex.* 700
They sleep s. from waking *F.* 123
S. from collision and dust *Gr.* 22
Hope! nothing else can nourish and s. *H.* 169
Where Power s. what Industry has won *Her.* 87
From this s. retreat *M.B.* 14
S. of favour at her Court *Mrs. M—* 22
S. of their repose *N.* 8
S. of nothing, but to lose the race *P.E.* 563
How to s., in some propitious hour *R.* 141
And where, s. as mouse in chink *R.C.* 5
Lies down s., her heart and pocket light *T.* 322
To sleep within the carriage more *s. T.* i 92
To slumber in the carriage more *s. T.* i 99
The dreams of fancy, tranquil and s. *T.* i 236
That crowns it! yet not all its pride s. *T.* i 279
By wealth or dignity, who dwells s. *T.* i 593
Sovereign, and most effectual, to s. *T.* ii 590
At evening, and at night retire s. *T.* iii 344
What longest binds the closest, forms s. *T.* iii 480
Whose sharp declivity shoots off s. *T.* iii 487
But it has peace, and much s. the mind *T.* iii 679
Should best s. them, and promote them most *T.* iii 709
And groves, if unharmonious yet s. *T.* iii 734
To some s. and more than mortal height *T.* iv 96
One hand s. his hat, save when with both *T.* iv 354
Among her lovely works with a s. *T.* vi 722
He sits s., and in the scale of life *T.* vi 970
Night veiled the pole; all seemed s. *T.B.* 31
S. of conquest where the prize *Th.* 15
Exchanged for the s. domestic scheme *Tir.* 705
S. it thine, its key is in thine hand *Tir.* 886
S. and at his ease *Trans.* ii 18
The soft receptacle, in which, s. *Y.O.* 27

SECURED.
Themselves s. beneath the Almighty wing *Ex.* 189
His power s. thee, when presumptuous Spain *Ex.* 568
S. it by an unforgiving frown *T.* ii 247
Plashed neatly, and s. with driven stakes *T.* iv 437
Unwrenched the door, however well s. *T.* iv 446
Neatly s. from being soiled or torn *Tir.* 119
A point s., if once he be supplied *Tir.* 698

SECURELY.
With unshod feet they yet s. tread *E.* ii 16
The mighty myriads, now s. scorned *R.* 70
S., though by steps but rarely trod *R.* 113
Or forest where the deer s. roves *R.* 182
S. placed between the small and great *Tir.* 803
And thence s. sees *Trans.* ii 15

SECURITY.
Offer him warmth, s., and rest *T.* 252
Convenience, and s., and use *T.* ii 682

SEDAN.
To seem some nymph in her s. *R.C.* 18
In chariots and s., know no fatigue *T.* i 755
With half the chariots and s. in town *Tir.* 748

SEDATE.
But Innocence, s., serene, erect *P.E.* 207
A poet's cat, s. and grave *R.C.* 1

SEDENTARY.
But s. weavers of long tales *Con.* 207
The s. stretch their lazy length *T.* i 389

SEDUCE. [114
" S. our husbands, and estrange their hearts *A.T.*
That can s. him not to spare *Mor.* 31
Glittering in vain, or only to s. *R.* 212
While sloth s. more, too weak to bear *T.* vi 10;

SEDUCED.
Had he s. a virgin, wronged a friend *T.* 46
Nor him who, by his vanity s. *T.* vi 283
Twas thus till Luxury s. the mind *T.T.* 600

SEDUCING.
Is proof against thy sweet s. charms? *T.* ii 482
The most s., and the oftenest seen) *Tir.* 762

SEDULOUS.
Even here: while s. I seek to improve *T.* iii 367

SEE.
My form with indifference s. *A.S.* 14
Though a friend I am never to s. *A.S.* 40 ·[*A.T.* 39
And made her dupes s. all things with her eyes)
Each trifle that he s. *Beau* 4
I s. you after all my pains *Beau* 19
(Which I can hardly s.) *B.R.* 26 [19
That every tribe, though placed as he s. best *Ch.*
S. Cortez odious for a world enslaved! *Ch.* 40
" Art thou too fallen, Iberia? Do we s. *Ch.* 67
To s. the oppressor in his turn oppressed *Ch.* 74
Nature imprints upon whate'er we s. *Ch.* 169
S. planetary wonders smoothly roll *Ch.* 317
He claps his lens, if haply they may s. *Ch.* 385
She s. a world stark blind to what employs *Ch.* 404
Learns to compassionate the sick she s. *Ch.* 411
Here s., acquitted of all vain pretence *Ch.* 412
To s. a God stretch forth his human hand *Ch.* 581
A graver coxcomb we may sometimes s. *Con.* 295
Ere life go down, to s. such sights again) *Con.* 606
A thought—I have it—let me s. *E.* iv 36 [*E.* iii 27
" For what?"—" An' please you, sir, to s. a friend "
" I'll s. him too—the first I ever saw " *E.* iii 31
And cannot s., though few s. better *E.* iv 33
In every shining straw she s. *E.* iv 46
Anticipates a day it never s. *Ep.* i 8
S. Nature gay as when she first began *H.* 39
Now s. him launched into the world at large *H.* 197
" Right," says an ensign, " and for aught I s. *H.* 397
S. Mercy's grand apocalypse displayed! *H.* 448
And still it spreads. S. Germany send forth *H.* 459
Here s. the encouragement Grace gives to vice *H.* 495
Can s. his love, though secret evil lurks *H.* 544
Oh! s. me sworn to serve thee, and command *H.* 669
S. it an uninformed and idle mass *Her.* 26
Now s. him mounted once again *J.G.* 77

For all might s. the bottle necks J.G. 131
To s. how he did ride J.G. 144
The calender, amazed to s. J.G. 161
May I be there to s.! J.G. 252
That the incredulous themselves may s. J.T. 49
Can s. no evil in a play L.W. 30
I s. thee daily weaker grow M. 6
What sight worth seeing could I s.? M. 30
Those lips are thine—thy own sweet smile I s. M.P.3
For with a race like theirs no chance I s. N.A. 113
And shall I s. thee start away O. ii 22
Especially sugar, so needful we s.? P.A. 7
S. watches, bracelets, rings, and lockets P.B. 25
Imbibes and copies what she hears and s. P.E. 356
Be flowery, and he s. no cause of fear P.E. 546 [19
Though his life be a dream, his enjoyments, I s. P.F.
Arrived, a night like noon she s. Q.V. 41
He may possess the joys he thinks he s. R. 11
Where unassisted sight no beauty s. R. 56
Absorbed in that immensity I s. R. 93
And s., by no fallacious light or dim R. 115
From all he s. he catches new delight R. 189
That passes all he s. unheeded by R. 340 [409
What charms he s. in Freedom's smile expressed R.
Stand close concealed, and s. a statue move R. 284
He views it not, or s. no beauty there R. 470
" The open drawer was left, I s. R.C. 55
To s. again my day o'erspread St. iii 7
S., far as human optics may command T. 3
It stands, like the cerulean arch we s. T. 26
The self-applauding bird, the peacock, s. T. 58
S. the sage hermit, by mankind admired T. 87
S. where it smokes along the sounding plain T. 238
S. where he sits, contemplative and fixed T. 415
Not blind by choice, but destined not to s. T. 530 [564
'Twas the last trumpet—s. the Judge enthroned! T.
There might ye s. the peony spread wide T. i 35 [363
And sleep not; s. him sweating o'er his bread T. i
Who shows me that which I shall never s. T. i 423
I s. a column of slow-rising smoke T. i 557
Methinks I s. thee straying on the beach T. i 654
I s. thee weep, and thine are honest tears T. i 657
A lucid mirror, in which Nature s. T. i 701
Weeps when she s. inflicted on a beast T. ii 25
Happy the man who s. a God employed T. ii 161 [568
Takes deeper root, confirmed by what they s. T. ii
(If e'er posterity s. verse of mine) T. ii 578
Nor can example hurt them: what they s. T. ii 794
S. then the quiver broken and decayed T. ii 803
I s. that all are wanderers, gone astray T. iii 124
A senseless bargain. When I s. such games T. iii 176
Has eyes indeed; and viewing all she s. T. iii 245
And 'tis a fearful spectacle to s. T. ii 662 [iii 648
He, therefore, who would s. his flowers disposed T.
And spotted with all crimes; in whom I s. T. iii 837
S. her unwrinkled face reflected bright T. iv 4 [205
S. not a countenance there that speaks of joy T. iv
That tempts ambition. On the summit s. T. iv 58
Methinks I s. thee in the streaky west T. iv 245
To peep at such a world; to s. the stir T. iv 89 [567
S. that your polished arms be primed with care T. iv
With gazing, when they s. an able man T. v 256 [107
And s. where it has hung the embroider'd banks T. v
The Paradise he s., he finds it such T. v 794
The soul that s. him, or receives sublimed T. v 805
Which whoso s. no longer wanders lost T. v 847
S. nought to wonder at. Should God again T. vi 126
Where no eye s. them. And the fairer forms T. vi 188
He s. me, and at once, swift as a bird T. vi 316
To s. their sov'reign, and confess his sway T. vi 356
He s. that human equity is slack T. vi 472 [760
Scenes of accomplish'd bliss! which who can s. T. vi
Exults to s. its thistly curse repealed T. vi 768

Lurks in the serpent now: the mother s. T. vi 778
And smiles to s., her infant's playful hand T. vi 779
S. Salem built, the labour of a God! T. vi 799
To s. thy beauty, and to share thy joy T. vi 815 [817
Saw never, such as Heaven stoops down to s. T. vi
Ye slow-revolving seasons! we would s. T. vi 824
Gives courage to their foes, who, could they s. T.vi 865
Scarce deigns to notice him, or, if she s. T. vi 942
" S.!" with united wonder, cried Th. 5
Soon s. your wish fulfilled in either child Tir. 344
In fancy s. him more superbly ride Tir. 368 [362
They s. the attentive crowds his talents draw Tir.
We sometimes s. a Lowth or Bagot there Tir. 435
The symptoms that you s. with so much dread Tir.534
In him thy well appointed proxy s. Tir. 676
S. what contempt is fallen on human kind Tir. 814
S. wealth abused, and dignities misplaced Tir. 815
S. Bedlam's closeted and handcuffed charge Tir. 819
S. great commanders making war a trade Tir. 821
S. womanhood despised, and manhood shamed Tir.827
S. volunteers in all the vilest arts Tir. 835
Survey our schools and colleges, and s. Tir. 909
And thence securely s. Trans. ii 15
He s. that this great roundabout Trans. ii 25
To s. a people scattered like a flock T.T. 34
Asked, when in Hell, to s. the royal jail T.T. 94
To s. a band, called patriot, for no cause T.T. 143
Contemporaries all surpassed, s. one T.T. 670
'Twere new indeed to s. a bard all fire T.T. 734
Or, if to s. the name of idol self T.T. 744
S., Mary, what beauties I bring W.N. 5
S. how they have safely survived W.N. 17

SEED.

Those s. of science called his ABC Con. 14
Rose from a s. of tiny size E. i 95
He sowed the s. of order where he went Ex. 488
The thistle's downy s. my fare G. 2
And yet the s. of an immortal flower H. 120
Their noxious growth, starve every better s. R. 44
That shuts within its s. the future flower R. 792
The s. sown there, how vigorous is the plant! T. 362
Has man within him an immortal s.? T. ii 518
The growing s. of wisdom; that suggest T. iii 302
Soft fomentation, and invite the s. T. iii 510
The s., selected wisely, plump, and smooth T. iii 511
The beds the trusted treasure of their s. T. iii 650
Beneath the frozen clod; all s. of herbs Y. 81
The s. of murder in the breast of man T. v 210
The s. of cruelty, that since have swell'd T. vi 381
And, like a scattered s. at random sown T.T. 674

SEEDLING.

Of treeship—first a s. hid in grass Y.O. 61

SEEING.

Thus s. Gilpin fly J.G. 234
What sight worth s. could I see? M. 30
Then what is man? And what man, s. this T. ii 26
Among the nations, s. thou art free T. v 461
For England's glory, s. it wax pale T. v 510
And s. the old castle of the state T. v 525

SEEK.

Who s. to praise thee, and to make thee known Ch.9
To s. a nobler amidst scenes of woe Ch. 300 [447
Some s., when queasy conscience has its qualms Ch.
And though the soul shall s. superior orbs Ch. 563
Are fittest auditors for such to s. Con. 226
Go s. on Revelation's hallowed ground Con. 499
The soul's sure interest in the good she s. Con. 728
The language of the land she s. inspires Con. 886
Who s. a friend should come disposed F. 43
That form the character he s. F. 46

SEEK—SEEM

S. to delight, that they may mend mankind *H.* 758
No shining ornaments have they to *s. H.* 765
Thus soothed and reconciled, each *s. L.R.* 25
S. to supplant his inexperienced youth *P.E.* 59
So he who *s.* a mansion in the sky *P.E.* 576
Resign our own and *s.* our Maker's will *R.* 130
Who *s.* retirement for its proper use *R.* 170
For such a cause the poet *s.* the shade *R.* 188
Yet *s.* him, in his favour life is found *R.* 353
But wisely *s.* a more convenient friend *R.* 443
To *s.* that peace a tyrant's frown denies *R.* 770
We *s.* it, ere it come to light *R.C.* 97
They *s.* like me the secret shade *S.* 19
That plea refuted, other quirks they *s. T.* 293
Now *s.* repose upon an humbler theme *T.* i 5
At first, progressive as a stream, they *s. T.* i 292
He *s.* them headlong, and is seen no more *T.* i 454
Go then, well worthy of the praise ye *s. T.* ii 278
Or will he *s.* to dazzle me with tropes *T.* ii 423
I *s.* divine simplicity in him *T.* ii 432
To *s.* a tranquil death in distant shades *T.* iii 3
To *s.* him rather where his mercy shines *T.* iii 224
S. and obtain, and often find unsought? *T.* iii 288
They love the country, and none else, who *s. T.* iii 320
Even here: while sedulous I *s.* to improve *T.* iii 367
That hungers, and supplies it; and who *s. T.* iii 375
He *s.* a favoured spot; that where he builds *T.* iii 471
Should *s.* the guiltless joys that I describe *T.* iii 698
Corruption! Whoso *s.* an audit here *T.* iv 610
Ten thousand *s.* an unmolested end *T.* v 87
Capricious, in which fancy *s.* in vain *T.* v 120
Some *s.* diversion in the tented field *T.* v 185
The surest presage of the good they *s. T.* v 378
To *s.* no sublunary rest beside *T.* v 476
Resistless from the centre he should *s. T.* v 590
He *s.*, an acquiescence of his soul *T.* v 597
Shall *s.* it, and not find it, in his turn *T.* vi 600
To *s.* a refuge from the tongue of Strife *T.* vi 841
He *s.* not hers, for he has proved them vain *T.* vi 920
He *s.* his proper happiness by means *T.* vi 954
But all is in His hand, whose praise I *s. T.* vi 1017
Is not to find what they profess to *s. Tir.* 194
Is more than adequate to all I *s. Tir.* 386
For there the game they *s.* is easiest found *Tir.* 520
But *s.* the corner of some distant seat *Tir.* 571
Who *s.* it in his climate and his frame *T.T.* 207
He break away, and *s.* the distant plain? *T.T.* 307

SEEKING.

Happy the man there *s.* and there found *Ex.* 652
S. a real friend, we seem *F.* 142
Or *s.* with a biassed mind *F.* 209
Some *s.* happiness not found below *R.* 604
And, *s.* exile from the sight of men *T.* 442
Fastidious, *s.* less familiar scenes *T.* i 512
His devious course uncertain, *s.* home *T.* iii 3
And *s.* grace to improve the prize they hold *T.* vi 55
S. her food, with ease might have purloined *Y.O.* 19

SEEM.

In a moment I *s.* to be there *A.S.* 46
Are not at all, or are not what they *s. A.T.* 41
And *s.* to have risen in vain *C.* 4
Her wisdom *s.* the weakness of a child *Ch.* 423
But lest I *s.* to sin against a friend *Ch.* 485
What he remembers *s.* to have forgot *Con.* 132
A sceptic in philosophy may *s. Con.* 138
Nose, ears, and eyes *s.* present on the spot *Con.* 318
It *s.* as if we Britons were ordained *Con.* 360
Lest they miscarry of what *s.* their due *Con.* 372
Is it incredible, or can it *s. Con.* 481
Or *s.* to boast a fire he does not feel *Con.* 714 [829
That having proved the weakness, it should *s. Con.*
And while she *s.* to scorn him, only fears *Con.* 788

Some never *s.* so wide of their intent *Con.* 857
But now, to gather up, what *s.* dispersed *Con.* 867
In gentle sounds it *s.* as it complained *Con.* 905 [i 4
S. it to say—"Health here has long to reign?" *Ep.*
Snuffs up the praise of what he *s.* to plan *Ex.* 317
And in whose awful sight all nations *s. Ex.* 344
S. to reflection of a different race *Ex.* 619
Reflect that these, and all that *s.* thine own *Ex.* 672
How bright soe'er the prospect *s. F.* 73
On good that *s.* approaching *F.* 81
Seeking a real friend, we *s. F.* 142
Have not, it *s.*, discerned it *F.* 210
Which *s.* by the crest that it rears *Gr.* 3
S. the labour of Mulciber's hands *Gr.* 40
And fancies I fear they will *s. Gr.* 53
That Heaven's intentions are not what they *s. H.* 66
To read the news, or fiddle, as *s.* best *H.* 76
No trifle, howsoever short it *s. H.* 123
And *s.* to pray, for good example sake *H.* 249
Of all the ways that *s*, to promise fair *H.* 338
And *s.* to warn him never to repeat *H.* 355
A thought intrude, that says, or *s.* to say *H.* 372
And, while religion *s.* to be her view *H.* 641
S., as it is, the fountain whence alone *H.* 708
The thunder *s.* to summon him away *H.* 719
Earth *s.* a garden in its loveliest dress *Her.* 57
Vice *s.* already slain *H.F.* 6
Thy indistinct expressions *s. M.* 21
S. so to be desired, perhaps I might *M.P.* 83 [117
And rush those other sounds, that *s.* by tongues *N.A.*
I *s.* to have lived my childhood o'er again *M.P.* 115
Are qualities that *s.* to comprehend *P.E.* 423 [132
So well that thought the employment *s.* to suit *P.E.*
And some that *s.* to threaten virtue less *P.E.* 227
S. verging fast towards the female side *P.E.* 430
This lesson *s*, to carry *P.T.* 63
All wish, or *s.* to wish, they could forego *R.* 4
On earth what is, *s.* formed indeed for us *R.* 106
S. drops descending in a shower of light *R.* 350
S. through the medium of a cloud like thine *R.* 352
Shall *s.* to start into a second birth *R.* 356
But versed in arts that while they *s.* to stay *R.* 383
S. all created since he travelled last *R.* 426
S. at the best but dreaming life away *R.* 468
Ye want but that to *s.* indeed divine *R.* 558
Thought to the man that never thinks may *s. R.* 635
Skilful alike to *s.* devout and just *R.* 689
To *s.* some nymph in her sedan *R.C.* 18
But love of change, it *s.*, has place *R.C.* 21 [ii 9
Time then would *s.* more precious than the joys *St.*
The rest might then *s.* privileged to play *St.* ii 19
S. to sound too much in vain *St.* iv 19
New as ever *s.* our sins *St.* iv 27
All evils then *s.* light, compared *St.* v 27
And *s.* to say—"Ye meaner fowl give place *T.* 64
That endless bliss (how strange soe'er it *s.*) *T.* 355
S. what it is, a cap and bells for fools *T.* 368
Of blank oblivion, *s.* a glorious prize *T.* i 287 [306
S. sunk, and shortened to its topmost boughs *T.* i
The chequered earth *s.* restless as a flood *T.* i 344
That *s.* to swing uncertain, and yet falls *T.* i 358
He *s.* indeed indignant, and to feel *T.* i 379
And theirs alone *s.* worthy of the name *T.* i 398
Even age itself *s.* privileged in them *T.* i 403
Between the nations, in a world that *s. T.* ii 50
And pillars of our planet *s.* to fail *T.* ii 63
S., in their eyes, a mercy, for thy sake *T.* ii 132
He picks clean teeth, and, busy as he *s. T.* ii 627
In all our crowded streets; and senates *s. T.* iii 61
That *s.* half quenched in the immense abyss *T.* iii 216
A life all turbulence and noise may *s. T.* iii 379
And *s.* to smile at what they need not fear *T.* iii 575
'Tis finished, and yet, finished as it *s. T.* iii 781

The globe and its concerns, I *s*. advanced *T*. iv 95
It *s*. the part of wisdom, and no sin *T*. iv 336
Humane as they would *s*., not always show *T*. iv 373
Sleep *s*. their only refuge: for, alas! *T*. iv 396
That felt their virtues; Innocence it *s*. *T*. iv 518
S. most at variance with all moral good *T*. iv 621
Incorporated, *s*. at once to lose *T*. iv 678
Screens them, and *s*. half petrified to sleep *T*. v 28
With well considered steps, *s*. to resent *T*. v 75 [112
Large growth of, what may *s*. the sparkling trees *T*.v
Were kingship as true treasure as it *s*. *T*. v 357
Short as in retrospect the journey *s*. *T*. vi 19 [v 620
And *s*. dethroned and vanquished. Peace ensues *T*.
Does but incumber whom it *s*. to enrich *T*. vi 97
So man, the moth, is not afraid, it *s*. *T*. vi 211
Of the poor brute, *s*. wisely to suppose *T*. vi 437
(If such who plead for Providence may *s*. *T*. vi 481
If man be what he *s*., this hour a slave *Tir*. 59
Rise in his forehead, and *s*. rank enough *Tir*. 164
And *s*., if judged by their expressive looks *Tir*. 288
That, viewing it, we *s*. almost to obtain *Tir*. 312
But, fair although and feasible it *s*. *Tir*. 428 [430
For Providence, that *s*. concerned to exempt *Tir*.
S. with one voice to delegate to you? *Tir*. 554
And *s*. it nothing in a father's eye *Tir*. 615
No few, that would *s*. wise, resemble her *Tir*. 796
S. to imply a censure on the rest *T.T.* 92 [50
Who think, or *s*. to think, man made for them *T.T.*
But then, it *s*. (what cannot grandeur do *V*. 43
S. graced with a livelier hue *W.N.* 22
It *s*. idolatry with some excuse *Y.O.* 9 [111
Possessing nought but the scooped rind that *s*. *Y.O.*

SEEMED.
And e'en to myself never *s*. *C*. 23
Nor, cruel as it *s*., could he *Cast*. 31
God stood not, though he *s*. to stand, aloof *Ch*. 59
Victorious *s*., and now the doctor's skill *Con*. 320
The faculties that *s*. reduced to naught *Con*. 403
His happy eloquence *s*. there at home *Con*. 622
That fables old, that *s*. for ever mute *Con*. 817
Yet to consult a little *s*. no crime *Con*. 865.
That *s*. to promise no such prize *E*. i 96
No; gold they *s*., but they were never such *E*. iii 19
"A friend!" Horatio cried, and *s*. to start *E*. iii 28
Showed that they followed all they *s*. to shun *Ex*. 142
Where Paradise *s*. still vouchsafed on earth *Ex*. 420
The open windows *s*. to invite *F.B.* 19
And chirp, and kiss, he *s*. to say *F.B.* 26
Friendship and Love *s*. tenderly at strife *H*. 680
But still he *s*. to carry weight *J.G.* 129
She *s*. designed for Flora's hand *L.R.* 15
So pleasant it *s*. as I lay *M.D.* 4
All *s*. so peaceful, that from them conveyed *N.A.* 41
That sage they *s*., as lawyers o'er a doubt *N.A.* 77
And *s*. by some magician's art *Q.V.* 59 [v 151
Gleamed through the clear transparency that *s*. *T*.
If cushion might be called, what harder *s*. *T*. i 55
(What *s*. at least commodious seat) were there *T*. v 163
'Twas durable, as worthless as it *s*. *T*. v 174
It *s*. not always short; the rugged path *T*. vi 20
That oft the beast has *s*. to judge the man *T*. vi 478
Ensuing *s*. to obliterate the past *T*. vi 540
Night veiled the pole: all *s*. secure *T.B.* 31
In sleep he *s*. to view *T.B.* 45
And it *s*. to a fanciful view *The Rose* 6
And he that *s*. our counterpart at first *Tir*. 442
And blazing London *s*. a second Troy *T.T.* 323
The laurel *s*. to wait on his command *T.T.* 688

SEEMING.
The *s*. virtue weighed against the vice *Ch*. 457
S. a sanctuary, proves a grave *R*. 736
Grasp *s*. Happiness, and find it Pain *R*. 756

Society for me! Thou *s*. sweet *T*. i 249
And when I weigh this *s*. wisdom well *T*. iii 180
Not slothful he, though *s*. unemployed *T*. vi 928

SEEMLY.
It is not *s*., nor of good report *T*. i 729
And 'tis but *s*., that where all deserve *T*. ii 71

SEEM'ST.
I love thee, all unlovely as thou *s*. *T*. iv 123

SEEN.
That sages have *s*. in thy face? *A.S.* 6
Oh! never *s*. but in thy blest effects *Ch*. 7
That earth has *s*., or fancy can devise *Ch*. 234
So have I *s*. (and hastened to the sight *Ch*. 547
S. in another they at once condemn *Con*. 156
I could not, had I *s*. it with my own" *Con*. 234
Oh! I have *s*. (nor hope perhaps in vain *Con*. 605
A new-found luxury, not *s*. in her? *Ex*. 6
The mask from faces never *s*. before *Ex*. 140
They knew, by sure prognostics *s*. on high *Ex*. 157
In vain the nations, that had *s*. them rise *Ex*. 203
Needs only to be *s*. to be admired *Ex*. 493
Must hold both sisters, never *s*. apart *Ex*. 635
Where'er they flow, now *s*. and now concealed *H*. 48
So Flora's wreath through coloured crystal *s*. *H*. 71
And bliss not *s*. by blessings understood *H*. 148
Than this his Maker has *s*. fit to give *H*. 601
No holiday have *s*. *J.G.* 8
Most piteous to be *s*. *J.G.* 126 [*N.A.* 91
Yourselves have *s*., what time the thunders rolled
Where'er the heavenly Nymph is *s*. *Miss* — 69
Chins fallen, and not an eye-ball to be *s*. *P.E.* 137
The Cross once *s*. is death to every vice *P.E.* 622
Like that, once *s*., suffice *Q.V.* 78
Traces of Eden are still *s*. below *R*. 28
The Invisible in things scarce *s*. revealed *R*. 61
How dimly *s*., how faintly understood! *R*. 88
But still 'tis rural—trees are to be *s*. *R*. 497
The gay, the thoughtless, have I *s*. *St*. i 19
'Twas his ambition to be *s*. of men *T*. 53
And shines without desiring to be *s*. *T*. 70
May still be *s*.; but perforated sore *T*. i 25
As bashful, yet impatient to be *s*. *T*. i 325
He seeks them headlong, and is *s*. no more *T*. i 454
Prospects, however lovely, may be *s*. *T*. i 509 [642
Their former charms? And having *s*. our state *T*. i
S. in the dim horizon, turns thee pale *T*. i 667 [690
Or *s*. with least reproach; and virtue, taught *T*. i
The brightest truths that man has ever *s*. *T*. ii 555
Spendthrifts, and booted sportsmen, oftener *s*.*T*.ii 752
To sport their season, and be *s*. no more *T*. iii 136
And covetous of Shakespeare's beauty, *s*. *T*. iii 601
Like virtue thriving most where little *s*. *T*. iii 664
Which *s*. delights him not; then coming home *T*. iv 236
Goliath, might have *s*. his giant bulk *T*. iv 270
Is *s*. no more. The character is lost! *T*. iv 539
S. through the leafless wood. His slanting ray *T*.v 6
The likeness of some object *s*. before *T*. v 121
There, like the visionary emblem *s*. *T*. v 400
All we behold is miracle; but *s*. *T*. vi 132 [972
The man, whose virtues are more felt than *s*. *T*. vi
And more than one perhaps that I have *s*. *Tir*. 655
The most seducing, and the oftenest *s*.) *Tir*. 762
Civited fellows, smelt ere they are *s*. *Tir*. 830
Thrice happy bird! I too have *s*. *Trans*. ii 31
And, sick of having *s*. 'em *Trans*. ii 33
And let thy strength be *s*. *Trans. H.* 33 [231
Is seldom felt, though sometimes *s*. and heard *T.T.*
So that the jest is clearly to be *s*. *T.T.* 540
Who is beloved where never *s*. 1789, 71

SEER.
Saved him, or the unrelenting *s*. had died *T*. vi 471

SEEST.
S. thou yon harlot, wooing all she meets *T.* 507

SEIZE.
Sir, when I flew to *s.* the bird *B.R.* 1
And hoped to *s.* his abdicated helm *Ex.* 577
A tenfold frenzy *s.* all the rest *H.* 634 [42
And went with his comrades the apples to *s. P.A.*
Can *s.* the slippery prey, unties the knot *T.* ii 685
Of vanity, that *s.* all below *T.* iii 267
That *s.* first the opulent, descends *T.* iv 583
To *s.* the fair occasion; well they eye *T.* v 66
By slow solicitation, *s.* at once *T.* vi 116
I fear lest thee alone they *s. The Doves* 23
To manage with address, to *s.* with power *T.T.* 358
S. events as yet unknown to man *T.T.* 498
I *s.* thy name in haste *U.* 20

SEIGE.
S. after *s.*, fight after fight 1789, 23

SEIZED.
Fear *s.* the trembling sex; in every grove *A.T.* 97
S. fast the saddle and sprang up behind *A.T.* 178
S. fast his hand, held out to set them free *Ex.* 219
S. fast the flowing mane *J.G.* 46
And when the bush exploring boy, that *s. T.* vi 445
I hastily *s.* it, unfit as it was *The Rose* 9
The brimming goblet, *s.* the Thyrsus bound *T.T.* 603

SELECTED.
The seed, *s.* wisely, plump, and smooth *T.* iii 511
Like flowers *s.* from the rest, and bound *T.* iv 667

SELECTING.
By flocks, fast feeding and *s.* each *T.* iv 318

SELECTS.
Nor felt but in the soul that Heaven *s. Ch.* 8

SELF.
For *s.* to *s.*, and God to man revealed *Ch.* 361
So *S.* starts nothing, but what tends apace *Ch.* 565
If *S.* employ us, whatsoe'er is wrought *Ch.* 569
We glorify that *S.*, not him we ought *Ch.* 570
My gravelly bounds, from *s.* to human kind *F.A.* 20
Devised by *s.* to answer selfish ends *T.* 110
He that attends to his interior *s. T.* iii 373
Embowelled now, and of thy ancient *s. Y.O.* 110

SELF-ACCUSED.
Die *s.* of life run all to waste ? *St.* ii 28

SELF-APPLAUDING.
The *s.* bird, the peacock, see *T.* 58

SELF-APPROVING.
Our *s.* bosom draws *Miss —* 51
Perhaps the *s.* haughty world *T.* vi 940

SELF-ATTACHMENT.
Mean *s.*, and scarce aught beside *T.* i 616

SELF-BANISHED.
S. from society, prefer *T.* i 578

SELF-BETRAYED.
While *s.*, and wilfully undone *Tir.* 171

SELF-BURIED.
As instinct prompts; *s.* ere they die *T.* v 88

SELF-CARESSED.
Her women, insolent and *s. Ex.* 45

SELF-CHEATED.
Thus by degrees *s.* of their sound *T.* v 264

SELF-COMPLACENCE.
While Fame and *s.* are the bribe *Ch.* 408

SELF-COMPLACENT.
The *s.* actor, when he views *T.* iv 200
The pedagogue, with *s.* air *Tir.* 527

SELF-CONCEIT.
May blow up *s.*, and nourish pride *Ch.* 376
As erst with airy *s. R.C.* 100
Inflated and astrut with *s. T.* v 268

SELF-CONDEMNED.
That *s.* they must neglect the prize *T.* iii 700

SELF-CONGRATULATING.
Of *s.* Pride, begot *T.* v 622

SELF-DECEIVED.
Ah *s.*! Could I, prophetic, say *St.* ii 17

SELF-DEFENCE.
And those in *s.* Savage at first *T.* v 229

SELF-DELUDED.
How many *s.* nymphs and swains *T.* iii 316

SELF-DENYING.
Your *s.* zeal, that holds it good *T.* v 328

SELF-DEPRIVED.
We bear our shades about us; *s. T.* i 259

SELF-DESERTED.
Despondence, *s.* in her grief *R.* 757

SELF-DISGRACING.
No—shame upon a *s.* age *Con.* 735

SELF-DRIVEN.
And rockets flew, *s. Q.V.* 14

SELF-ENTITLED.
Thou *s.* ruler of the main *Ex.* 549

SELF-EVIDENT.
For truth *s.*, with pomp impressed *H.* 109

SELF-EXALTING.
If *s.* claims be turned adrift *H.* 530

SELF-IDOLIZED.
And though *s.* in every case *Con.* 157
S., and yet a knave at heart *Ex.* 94

SELF-IMPEACHED.
Stands *s.* the creature of least worth *Tir.* 70

SELF-IMPORTANCE.
Our *s.* ruins its own scheme *Con.* 368

SELF-IMPOSED.
Of needless shame, and *s.* disgrace *Con.* 350

SELF-IMPOVERISHED.
Some *s.* and because they must *R.* 608

SELF-IMPRISONED.
Who, *s.* in their proud saloons *T.* i 414

SELF-INDULGENCE.
With *s.* winged the fleeting hours *Ex.* 71

SELF-INFLICTED.
Their long complaints, is *s.* woe *T.* iv 430

SELF-INTEREST.
From mean *s.* and ambition clear *Ex.* 439

SELFISH.
'Tis narrow, *s.*, arrogant, and draws *Con.* 671
Calls him away from *s.* ends and aims *R.* 19
Devised by self to answer *s.* ends *T.* 111
Since all alike are *s.*, why not they ? *T.* ii 696
In *s.* silence, but imparted oft *T.* iii 394
As this is gross and *s.*! over which *T.* vi 837
By *s.* views, thus censured and cashiered *Tir.* 496
On *s.* principles, is shame and guilt *T.T.* 2

SELF-JOINED.
By regal warrant, or *s.* by bond *T.* iv 661

SELF-KNOWLEDGE.
S. truly learned of course implies *Ch.* 359

SELF-LOVE.
Or mean s. erected *F.* 39
To bid the pleadings of S. be still *R.* 129

SELF-MADE.
Designed by Nature wise, but s. fools *Tir.* 837

SELF-PROCLAIMED.
Then view him, s. in a gazette *T.T.* 37

SELF-RENOUNCING.
That s. wisdom, learned before *T.* 568

SELF-REPROACHING.
And s. conscience? He foresees *T.* v 600

SELF-RESTORING.
The s. arm of human power *T.* 402

SELF-SAME.
The s. gale that wafts the fragrance round *Her.* 35
For 'twas the s. Power Divine *N.G.* 19
Kings do but reason on the s. plan *T.T.* 48
He trod the very s. ground you tread *T.T.* 388
Then, only governed by the s. rule *Tir.* 871

SELF-SATISFYING.
Then farewell all s. schemes *T.* 7

SELF-SEARCHING.
S. with an introverted eye *Con.* 364

SELF-SEQUESTERED.
The morning finds the s. man *T.* iii 386

SELF-SUPPORTED.
Few s. flowers endure the wind *T.* iii 657

SELF-TAUGHT.
With s. rites, and under various names *T.* vi 232

SELF-TORTURING.
The sacred fire, s. his trade *T.* 100

SELF-UPHELD.
In ocean s. *Cast.* 38

SELF-WILL.
Then obstinate s. confirms him so *P.E.* 543

SELL.
Or s. their glory at a market price *Con.* 28
To tempt the poor to s. himself to thee? *Ex.* 375
Has He bid you buy and s. us *N.C.* 27   [*P.A.* 2
And fear those who buy them and s. them, are knaves
And s. them medals, which, if neither rare *P.E.* 399
As stoop from Heaven to s. the proud a throne *T.* 78
Who s. their laurel for a myrtle wreath *T.* ii 229
And colleges, untaught; s. accent, tone *T.* ii 359
S. the last scantling, and transfers the price *T.* iii 753
He s. protection. Witness at his foot *T.* vi 417
Just what the toy will s. for, and no more *T.T.* 62
Agreed. But would you s. or slay your horse *T.T.* 304
S. oaths by tale, and at the lowest price *T.T.* 419
You s. it plaguy dear *Y.D.* 60

SEMBLANCE.
Its s. in another's case *Cast.* 60
And specious s. have lost their use *T.* iii 107
Stands now, and s. only of itself! *Y.O.* 124

SEMINARIES.
The props of such proud s. fall *Tir.* 499

SEMIQUAVERING.
Quavering and s. care away *P.E.* 127

SEMPITERNAL.
All truth is from the s. source *T.* ii 499

SENATE.
Thy s. is a scene of civil jar *Ex.* 294
The bar, the s., or the tented field *R.* 102

To shake thy s., and from heights sublime *T.* ii 216
In all our crowded streets; and s. seem *T.* iii 61

SENATOR.
Like those which modern s. employ *T.* iv 490
By poets, and by s. unpraised *T.* v. 539
Dumb as a s., and as a priest *Tir.* 424

SENATORIAL.
Of Attic phrase and s. tone *S.* i 11
Your s. dignity of face *V.* 11
For s. honours. Thus to Time *Y.O.* 103

SEND.
My friends, do they now and then s. *A.S.* 37
Or s. another shivering to the bar *Con.* 187
And still it spreads. See Germany s. forth *H.* 459
The peacock s. his heavenly dyes *Mrs. M—* 3 [121
S. your dishonoured gown to Monmouth Street *P.E.*
None s. his arrow to the mark in view *P.E.* 570
And s. the patient into purer air *R.* 282
Nor seldom, as propitious Heaven might s. *R.* 377
S. Nature forth, the daughter of the skies *R.* 795
The rustling straw s. up a frequent mist *T.* i 360
And s. thee to thy cabin, well-prepared *T.* i 670
Levantine regions these, the Azores s. *T.* iii 583
To hear the roar she s. through all her gates *T.* iv 91
Nor what a wealthier than ourselves may s. *T.* iv 426
No forfeiture, and of its fruits he s. *T.* v 573
Like that which s. him to the dusty grave *T.* v 609
S. him to college. If he there be tamed *Tir.* 240
To s. our sons to scout and scamper there *Tir.* 294
Of natural pity, s. him not to school *Tir.* 872
Tyranny s. the chain that must abridge *T.T.* 474
I thought the volume I presumed to s. *V.* 39

SENIOR.
Attendant at the S.'s side *Mor.* 40

SENSE.   [390
A s. they know not, to the wondering crowd *Ch.*
To every man his modicum of s. *Con.* 2
Religion, Virtue, Reason, Common S.—*Con.* 77 [417
Prefers his fellow grooms, with much good s. *Con.*
Suppose themselves monopolists of s. *Con.* 627
Though common s., allowed a casting voice *Con.* 663
My little garrison of s. *E.* iv 18
The s. was dark; 'twas therefore fit *E.* iv 61
Each man of common s. agrees *E.* iv 68
All men of common s. allow *E.* iv 69
That Scripture, Justice, and Good S. disown *Ex.* 593
Good s. and knowledge of mankind *F.* 200
The very s. of it foregoes its use *H.* 21
His speech rebellion against common s. *H.* 565
Good breeding and good s. gave all a grace *H.* 683
Sworn foes to s. and law *M.* i 2
A blemish, or a s. impaired *M.F.* 43
With every herb that blunts the s. *Miss—* 23
And s. of having well designed *Mor.* 52
"And your fine s.," he said, "and yours" *P.* 41
Made nothing but a brute, the slave of s. *P.E.* 214
No, wrangler,—destitute of shame and s. *P.E.* 235
To virtue, delicacy, truth, or s. *P.E.* 513 [*P.E.* 246
Good s., good health, good conscience and good fame?
That Scripture lies, and blasphemy is s. *P.E.* 595
A s. of elegance we rarely find *R.* 501
The friend of Truth, the associate of sound S.—*R.* 696
The s. of mercy kindles into praise *R.* 778
Beware of too sublime a s. *R.C.* 109
To blend good s. and elegance and ease *S.* ii 11
Faith, want of common s. *St.* vi 22
Of all his conduct this the genuine s. *T.* 94
Sinful and weak, in every s. a wretch *T.* 383
Than please the eye—sweet Nature every s. *T.* i 427
And fungous fruits of earth, regales the s. *T.* i 532
How, in the name of soldiership and s. *T.* ii 225

With such ingredients of good *s*. and taste *T*. ii 789
" Defend me therefore, Common *S*.," say I *T*. iii 187
The dearth of information and good *s*. *T*. iv 71
How lovely, and the moral *s*. how sure *T*. v 673
And helpless victims with a *s*. so keen *T*. vi 475
To monarchs dignity; to judges *s*. *T*.iv 796 [*T*.vi 561
(Though graced with polished manners and fine *s*.
The stamp and clear impression of good *s*. *T*. vi 983
And, common *s*. diffusing real day *Tir*. 189 [*Tir*. 137
Whose humorous vein, strong *s*., and simple style
Except of caution and of common *s*. *Tir*. 258
That scorn of all delights but those of *s*. *Tir*. 351
With savoury truth and wholesome common *s*.*Tir*.629
Show thou hast *s*. enough to prize the pearl *Tir*. 707
But recollect that he has *s*., and feels *Tir*. 720
And laughs the *s*. of misery far away *T.T.* 239
In prostitution sinks the *s*. of shame *T.T.* 415
Fire indignation and a *s*. of scorn *T.T.* 489
Where Discipline helps opening buds of *s*. *T.T.*508
I judged a man of *s*. could scarce do worse *T.T.* 518
The substitute for genius, *s*., and wit *T.T.* 543
Then decent Pleasantry and sterling *s*. *T.T.* 638
Sound *s*., intrepid spirit, manly grace *V*. 12

SENSELESS.
Deified useless wood or *s*. stone *Ew*. 238
'Tis *s*. arrogance to accuse *F*. 52
With *s*. noise, his argument the sword *H*. 660
In the last scene of such a *s*. play *R*. 32
Not *s*. of its charms, what still we love *T*. i 516
A *s*. bargain. When I see such games *T*. iii 176
Or flushed with fierce dispute, a *s*. brawl *T*. v 472
In *s*. riot; but ye will not find *T*. v 757

SENSIBLE.
The scene of her *s*. choice! *C*. 44
A moral, *s*., and well-bred man *Con*. 193
And catch in its progress a *s*. glow *F.M.* 20

SENSIBILITY.
Our *s*. are so acute *Con*. 351
" Sweet *S*." *Miss* — 68
And *s*. so fine! *P*. 14
That *s*. of pain with which *T*. iv 358
Yet wanting *s*.) the man *T*. vi 562
She pours a *s*. divine *T.T.* 486

SENSITIVE.
Did plants called *s*. grow there?" *P*. 22

SENSUAL.
Of *s*. evil, and thus Hope is born *H*. 152
Delights like these, ye *s*. and profane *P.E.* 263
Her golden tube, through which a *s*. world *T*. vi 978

SENSUALIST.
Between the sot and *s*. *F*. 41
In which lewd *s*. print out themselves *R*. 684

SENSUALITY.
Left *s*. and dross behind *T*. 526

SENT.
With warmer wishes *s*. *Cast*. 10
'Tis like a parcel *s*. you by the stage *Con*. 305 [518
S. to do more than He appeared to have done *Con*.
Is *s*. to be flatted or wrought into length *F.M.* 2
He *s*. a servant forth by every road *H*. 310
S. us a wind to parch us at a blast? *P.E.* 256 [803
S. through the traveller's temples! He that finds*T*. iii
How much a dunce that has been *s*. to roam *P.E.* 415
Upridged so high, and *s*. on such a charge *T*. ii 116
When *s*. with God's commission to the heart *T*. ii 471
A loud Hosanna *s*. from all thy works *T*. v 888 [132
When thou wouldst build; no quarry *s*. its stores *T*. v
S. forth a voice, and all the sons of God *T*. v 821
I *s*. you verse, and, as your Lordship knows *V*. 19

SENTENCE.
Died by the *s*. of a shaven priest *Ch*. 55
Makes half a *s*. at a time enough *Con*. 246
If *s*. of eternal pain belong *H*. 389
And writes a Doomsday *s*. on his heart *H*. 693
And reading here his *s*., how replete *St*. ii 7
He reads his *s*. at the flames of Hell *T*. 10
Your *s*. and mine differ. What's a name? *T*. 107
Reverse the *s*., let the truth be known *T*. 449

SENTIMENT.
My threadbare *s*. together *E*. iv 6
Their *s*. so well expressed *P.T.* 42
By all whom *s*. has not abused *Tir*. 538
New-fangled *s*., the boasted grace *Tir*. 539
If *s*. were sacrificed to sound *T.T.* 516

SENTIMENTAL.
With *s*. frippery, and dream *P.E.* 312

SEPARATES.
Then, as a shepherd *s*. his flock *T*. v 196

SEPULCHRAL.
Like hidden lamps in old *s*. urns *Con*. 358

SEPULCHRE.
A *s*. in which the living lie *R*. 737
Of all these *s*., instructors true *St*. ii 34

SEQUENCES.
Her mingled suits and *s*., and sits *T*. i 475

SEQUESTERED.
That grief, *s*. from the public stage *Ch*. 305
The grove, and the *s*. shed *O*. ii 17
'Tis Harmony from yon *s*. bower *P.E.* 65
When, long *s*. from his throne *Q.V.* 1
Amid the charms of a *s*. spot *R*. 8
Content if thus *s*. I may raise *R*. 805
To the close copse, or far *s*. green *T*. 69
For me, enamoured of *s*. scenes *T*. iii 27
'Tis therefore, many whose *s*. lot *T*. v 522
Thus sang the sweet *s*. bird *The Doves* 37

SERAGLIOS.
" *S*. sing, and harems dance for joy! *A.T.* 108

SERAPHS.
And his that *s*. tremble at, is hung *Ex*. 662

SERENE.
Impede the bark that ploughs the deep *s*. *Ch*. 132
S. and peaceful as those heavenly days *Con*. 568
And feel's no change, unshaken and *s*. *Ex*. 587
Some are so placid and *s*. *F*. 121
But Innocence, sedate, *s*., erect *P.E.* 207
So, ancient poets say, *s*. *Q.V.* 69
A soul *s*., and equally retired *R*. 143
But nowhere with a current so *s*. *R*. 455
Some place of more *s*. repose *R.C.* 30
From Heaven to Earth, of lambent flame *s*. *T*. v 153
S., and to his duties much inclined *Tir*. 774

SERENEST.
Its happiest soil in the *s*. minds? *Con*. 594

SERGEANT.
That instant he becomes the *s*.'s care *T*. iv 631

SERIOUS.
Thus have I sought to grace a *s*. lay *Ch*. 628
A shallow brain behind a *s*. mask *Con*. 297
Can pause one hour to read a *s*. rhyme *Ex*. 605
That their Creator had no *s*. end *H*. 130
To *s*. thought at evening-tide *Mor*. 12
The waves o'ertake them in their *s*. play *R*. 157
Now which stands highest in your *s*. thought? *T*. 221
No: he was *s*. in a *s*. cause *T*. ii 476
And incompatible with *s*. thought *T*. iv 622
Her *s*. mirth, to Arbuthnot and Swift *T.T.* 657

SERMONS.
S., and city feasts, and favourite airs *T.* iv 84

SERPENT.
The *s.* Error twines round human hearts *P.E.* 4
The subtlest *s.* with the loftiest crest *T.* 476
Charm the deaf *s.* wisely. Make him hear *T.* v 671
Lurks in the *s.* now : the mother sees *T.* vi 778

SERVANT.
A Persian, humble *s.* of the sun *Con.* 67
Horatio's *s.* once, with bow and cringe *E.* iii 20
He sent a *s.* forth by every road *H.* 310
The *s.* of the public never knows *R.* 370
You have two *s.*,—Tom, an arch, sly rogue *T.* 201
But Discipline, a faithful *s.* long *T.* ii 725

SERVE.
"A knight—(can he that *s.* the fair do less) *A.T.* 119
S. as a key to those that are suppressed *Ch.* 524
S. him with venison, and he chooses fish *Con.* 335 [415
Yet e'en the rogue that *s.* him, though he stand *Con.*
Though future pain may *s.* for present mirth *Con.* 494
God's work may *s.* an ape upon a stage *Con.* 736
If Israel's Lord be God, then *s.* the Lord *Con.* 852
S., in a plain and homely way *E.* i 3
One proof should *s.*—a reference to you *E.* iii 13
Then thou art bound to *s.* him, and to prove *Ex.* 560
To praise him is to *s.* him, and fulfil *Ex.* 644
Or *s.* the champion in forensic war *Ex.* 664
S. merely as a soil for discontent *H.* 97
And differing judgments *s.* but to declare *H.* 423
Oh! see me sworn to *s.* thee, and command *H.* 669
That *s.* mankind, or shun them, wild or tame *N.A.* 66
Had summoned them to *s.* his golden god *P.E.* 131
S. but to lead philosophers astray *P.E.* 433
So one, whose story *s.* at least to show *P.E.* 526
The ocean *s.*, on high *Q.V.* 18
To *s.* the Sovereign we were born to obey *R.* 50
Sealed with his signet whom they *s.* and love *R.* 164
Or stabbed a man to *s.* some private end? *T.* 47
To *s.* occasions of poetic pomp *T.* i 152
The minister of man, to *s.* his wants *T.* ii 138
And *s.* the altar, in my soul I loathe *T.* ii 416
To *s.* his country. Ministerial grace *T.* iii 795
He cultivates. These *s.* him with a hint *T.* iv 758
Familiar, *s.* to emancipate the rest! *T.* v 298
And reigns content within them : him we *s.* *T.* v 333
To *s.* him nobly in the common cause *T.* v 344
Comes at his call, and *s.* him for a friend *T.* v 424
Stripes, and a dungeon ; and his body *s.* *T.* v 582
S. to compose a spirit well inclined *T.* v 657
His strength to suffer, and his will to *s.* *T.* v 902
But less, methinks, than sacrilege might *s.* *T.* vi 638
Much less might *s.*, when all that we design *T.* vi 642
He *s.* his country, recompenses well *T.* vi 968
S. but to show how black is all beside *Tir.* 844
Might *s.*, however small *Trans.* i 18 [371
The prize of happier times, will *s.* thee now *T.T.*
Your sullen silence *s.* at least to tell *V.* 25

SERVED.
It *s.* them with a tree *A Tale* 32 [361
Pulled down the tyrants India *s.* with dread *Ex.*
Which *s.* my weak thought for a guide *M.D.* 44
The dinner *s.*, Charles takes his usual stand *T.* 213
How oft, when Paul has *s.* us with a text *T.* ii 539
Who had survived the father, *s.* the son *T.* iii 748
Was chosen leader ; him they *s.* in war *T.* v 233
That office *s.*, they must be swept away *T.* v 569
Him blind antiquity profaned, not *s.* *T.* vi 231
Which, having *s.* us, perish, we are held *T.* vi 604

SERVICE.
While Gratitude and Love made *s.* sweet *Ch.* 233
And the dull *s.* of the lip were there *Ex.* 44
Thy *s.*, once holy without spot *Ex.* 261
Like angels in the *s.* of their Lord *Ex.* 674
And at last is of *s.* in sickness or pain *F.M.* 11
Sick of the *s.* of a world that feeds *R.* 47
Exempt from future *s.* all his days *R.* 628
But strong for *s.* still, and unimpaired *T.* ii 705
To its just point—the *s.* of mankind *T.* iii 372
And sweating in his *s.* ; his caprice *T.* v 274
And tattered in the *s.* of debauch *T.* v 633
To ceaseless *s.* by a ceaseless force *T.* vi 219
And in their *s.* wage perpetual war *T.* vi 894
Framed for the *s.* of a freeborn will *Tir.* 8

SERVILE.
If this be *s.*, that can ne'er be free *Ch.* 568
From *s.* fear, or be the more enslaved ? *T.* 184
S. employ ; but such as may amuse *T.* iii 406
While *s.* trick and imitative knack *T.T.* 666
Debased to *s.* purposes of Pride *T.T.* 748

SERVILITY.
Their hope in Heaven, *s.* their scorn *Ex.* 440
Oh! if *S.* with supple knees *T.T.* 127

SERVING.
S. a benefactor, I am free *Ch.* 242 [747
And, *s.* God herself through mere constraint *Con.*

SERVING-MAID.
A *s.* was she, and fell in love *T.* i 537

SERVITUDE.
That even *s.*, the worst of ills *T.* v 302

SET.
The spectacles *s.* them unhappily wrong *A.C.* 2
And *s.* the unseemly pair in open day *A.T.* 168
And *s.* up his back, and clawed like a cat *A.T.* ii 5
The sun of that moment is *s.* *C.* 3
S. your opinion at whatever pitch *Con.* 107
Am I to *s.* my life upon a throw *Con.* 191 [688
As bastions *s.* point blank against God's will *Con.*
And puzzling *s.* his puppy brains *D.W.* 23
Saw Babylon *s.* wide her two-leaved brass *Ex.* 59
They *s.* up self, that idol-god, within *Ex.* 216 [219
Seized fast his hand, held out to *s.* them free *Ex.*
Thou that hast *s.* the persecuted free *Ex.* 278
In setting right what Faction has *s.* wrong *Ex.* 301
Are proud, and *s.* their faces as a rock *Ex.* 457
Hope *s.* the stamp of vanity on all *H.* 153
Hope with uplifted foot, *s.* free from earth *H.* 161
And—God is merciful—*s.* all to rights *H.* 376
Nor *s.* a price upon a willing heart *H.* 337 [*H.* 536
Shall answer,—" Hope, sweet Hope, has *s.* me free
He little dreamt, when he *s.* out *J.G.* 99
And *s.* their wit at work to find *L.W.* 13
And, staff in hand, *s.* forth to share *Mor.* 9
Just reached it when the sun was *s.* *Mor.* 22 [105
S. me more distant from a prosperous course *M.P.*
Where rises and where *s.* the day *Mrs. M*— 11
And needs no glossary to *s.* him right *N.A.* 70
S. Paul to music, he shall quote him too *P.E.* 113
Ecstasy *s.* her stamp on every mien *P.E.* 136
S. off a wanderer into foreign lands *P.E.* 378
A muleteer's the man to *s.* him right *P.E.* 541
S. London in a glow *Q.V.* 8
The terrors of the day that *s.* them free *T.* ii 128
Those suns are *s.* Oh, rise some other such ! *T.* ii 252
With all his canvas *s.*, and inexpert *T.* iii 486
I burn to *s.* the imprisoned wranglers free *T.* iv 34
Beguile the night, and *s.* a keener edge *T.* iv 164
With ostentatious pageantry, but *s.* *T.* iv 256 [600
When he should strike, he trembles and *s.* free *T.* iv
So dazzling in their eyes who *s.* it on *T.* v 244
Haste now, philosopher, and *s.* him free *T.* v 670
Of sad experience, nor examples *s.* *T.* v 294 [vi 158
Now sanguine, and her beauteous head now *s.*, *T.*

He *s.* the bright procession on its way *T.* vi 190
God *s.* the diadem upon his head *T.* vi 351
Who needlessly *s.* foot upon a worm *T.* vi 563
As *s.* the midnight riot in a blaze *Tir.* 287
Than *s.* your son to work at a vile trade *Tir.* 456
To *s.* some living worthy in his view *Tir.* 647
And *s.* plebeian thousands in a roar *T.T.* 319
To *s.* a distich upon six and five *T.T.* 507
Thus genius rose and *s.* at ordered times *T.T.* 560
That constellation *s.*, the world in vain *T.T.* 660

SETTEE.
The soft *S.*; one elbow at each end *T.* i 75

SETTING.
In *s.* right what Faction has set wrong *Ex.* 301
The rising or the *s.* orb of day *R.* 191
Told that his *s.* sun must rise no more *St.* ii 16 [433
Where England, stretch'd towards the *s.* sun *T.* vi
Recovering and misstated *s.* right *Y.O.* 48

SETTLE.
He *s.* next upon the sloping mount *T.* iii 486
They sink and *s.* lower than they need *T.* v 249
And *s.* in soft musings as I tread *T.* vi 69

SETTLED.
Thus we were *s.* when you found us *E.* i 39
Thus, preliminaries *s. E.* iv 31
In *s.* habit and decided taste *Tir.* 778

SETTLING.
So *s.* on his cage, by play *F.B.* 25
S. at last upon eternal things *R.* 672
Time was when, *s.* on thy leaf, a fly *Y.O.* 91
Till *s.* on the current year 1789, 27

SEVEN.
As from a *s.* years' transportation, home *Con.* 400
As twice *s.* years, his beauties had then first *T.* iv 714

SEVER.
Me from my delights to *s. N.C.* 11
He *s.* it away : no needless care *T.* v 38
That the wind *s.* from the broken wave *T.* vi 156

SEVERE.
And give good company a face *s. Con.* 873
He will be found impartially *s. Ex.* 255
But know, that Wrath Divine, when most *s. Ex.* 714
And never proved *s. J.P.* 16
For which, alas! my destiny *s. N.A.* 27
His utmost faculties, *s.* indeed *R.* 620
His voluntary pains, *s.* and long *T.* 101
And guards it with a sanction as *s. T.* 553
His hard condition with *s.* constraint *T.* i 612
Their last poor pittance—Fortune, most *s. T.* ii 658
Grew stern, and darted a *s.* rebuke *T.* ii 720
Which he that fights a season so *s. T.* iii 560
When most *s.*, and must'ring all its force *T.* vi 31
As too laborious and *s.* a task *T.* vi 210
But hush!—the muse perhaps is too *s. T.* vi 653
I grant the sarcasm is too *s. T.T.* 103
Parent of manners like herself *s. T.T.* 613
The frowns of a sky so *s. W.N.* 18

SEVERED.
With Nature's varnish ; *s.* into stripes *T.* i 40
Of brotherhood is *s.* as the flax *T.* ii 10

SEVERELY.
Then skilful most when most *s.* judged *T.* v 869

SEVERER.
More briskly moved by his *s.* toil *T.* iv 389

SEVEREST.
On pangs enforced with God's *s.* stroke *R.* 314

SEVERITY.
Of undesigned *s.*, that glanced *T.* v 170
With stern *s.* deals out the year *T.T.* 209

SEWER.
As to a common and most noisome *s. T.* i 683

SEX. [97
Fear seized the trembling *s.*; in every grove *A.T.*
The *s.* whose presence civilizes ours *Con.* 254
Divest the rougher *s.* of female airs *Con.* 843
Oh, tell thy thoughtless *s.*, the virtuous mind *S.* ii 6
'Gan murmur, as became the softer *s. T.* i 71
Her *s.*'s honour, was renounced herself *T.* iii 77
That they are safe, sinners of either *s. T.* iii 96 [537
These have their *s.* ; and when summer shines *T.* iii

SEX-ABUSING.
Brought fire from Heaven, the *s.* crime *Ex.* 415

SHACKLES.
They touch our country, and their *s.* fall *T.* ii 42
Dispersed the *s.* of usurped control *T.* v 516

SHADE.
Cheers what were else a universal *s. Ch.* 94
From her the canvass borrows light and *s. Ch.* 107
Forget to enjoy the palm-tree's offered *s. Ch.* 222
So, when the cold damp *s.* of night prevail *Ch.* 527
And I have lived in rural *s. Con.* 801 [884
Shoots between scattered rocks and opening *s.Con.*
But now, beneath this walnut *s. Ep.* ii 37
And oaks coeval spread a mournful *s. H.* 352
And light and *s.*, and every stroke be thine *H.* 673
And ruminating flocks enjoy the *s. Her.* 32
S. slanting at the close of day *Mor.* 15
Ere long approach life's evening *s. Mor.* 35
Tell where she lurks, beneath what flowery *s. P.E.* 5
Write, if thou canst, one letter from the *s. P.E.* 348
The poplars are felled ;—farewell to the *s. P.F.* 1
And the tree is my seat that once lent me a *s. P.F.* 8
Pants for the refuge of some rural *s. R.* 6
And fills the world of traffic and the *s. R.* 120
For such a cause the poet seeks the *s. R.* 188
Beneath your *s.* your grey possessor hide *R.* 368
Force many a shining youth into the *s. R.* 560
O happy *s.*!—to me unblest *S.* 1
They seek like me the secret *s. S.* 19 [ii 2
Thy friend, though to a cloister's *s.* consigned *S.*
Vanish at once into the darkest *s. St.* ii 24
We bear our *s.* about us; self-deprived *T.* i 259
The obsolete prolixity of *s. T.* i 265
Within the twilight of their distant *s. T.* i 304
The pensive wanderer in their *s.* At eve *T.* i 761
Some boundless contiguity of *s. T.* ii 3
Life in the unproductive *s.* of death *T.* ii 124
My man of morals, nurtured in the *s. T.* ii 532
To seek a tranquil death in distant *s. T.* iii 3
For their own sake its silence and its *s. T.* iii 321
They form one social *s.*, as if convened *T.* iii 586
And under an old oak's domestic *s. T.* iv 172
Imparting substance to an empty *s. T.* iv 527
That I myself am but a fleeting *s. T.* v 13 [305
These *s.* are all my own. The timorous hare *T.* vi
Together, or all gambol in the *s. T.* vi 775
Beneath the *s.* of her expanded leaves *Tir.* 46
His sprightly mingled with a *s.* of sad *Tir.* 665
No *s.* of superstition blot the day *T.T.* 270
Of thickest *s.*, like Adam after taste *Y.O.* 15

SHADED.
From sultry suns, and in their *s.* walks *T.* i 256

SHADOW.
Exuberant is the *s.* it supplies *Ch.* 577
Prepared to fight for *s.* of no worth *Ex.* 116
Mere *s.* now, their ancient pomp forgot *Ex.* 262
That only *s.* are dispensed below *H.* 67
Amazed that *s.* should obscure the sight *H.* 534
All bliss beside a *s.* or a sound *R.* 354

SHADOW—SHARE

S. and sunshine intermingling quick *T.* 347
The *s.* to the ceiling, there by fits *T.* iv 275
Stretches a length of *s.* o'er the field *T.* v 10
In the *s.* of a bramble, and reclined *T.* v 324
The state, beneath the *s.* of whose vine *T.* vi 969
The *s.* fly, philosophy prevails *Tir.* 182

SHADOWY.
And, howsoever *s.*, no dream *H.* 124

SHADY.
The noon was *s.*, and soft airs *D.W.* 1

SHAFT. [*Y.O.* 127
With bow and *s.* have burnt them. Some have left
When the Sun's *s.* disperse the gloom of night *Ex.* 479
The *s.* of woe—in such a breast *Miss —* 43
For though, ere yet the *s.* is on the wing *P.E.* 572
Between the upright *s.* of whose tall elms *T.* i 355
Stand chargeable with guilt, and to the *s. T.* ii 155
He gleans the blunted *s.* that have recoiled *T.* vi 874

SHAG.
The *s.* of savage nature, and were each *T.* v 693

SHAGGY.
Or velvet soft, or plush with *s.* pile *T.* i 11 [45
S., and lean, and shrewd, with pointed ears *T.* v

SHAKE. [901
With rash and awkward force the chords he *s. Con.*
He *s.* with cold—you stir the fire and strive *Con.* 333
It *s.* the sides of splenetic Disdain *Ex.* 548
" For lift thy palsied head, *s.* off the gloom *H.* 37
To frown and roar, and *s.* his feeble form *H.* 186
And *s.* with fury to the ground *J.P.* 11
Nor blasts that *s.* the dripping bower *Mrs. M—* 16
All elbows *s.* Look in, and you would swear *P.E.* 129
First *s.* the glittering drops from every thorn *R.* 396
S. hands with business, and retires indeed *R.* 514
'Tis Judgment *s.* him; there's the fear *St.* v 29
S. it again, and faster, to the ground *T.* 241
And *s.* the sceptic in the scorner's chair *T.* 472
The earth shall *s.* him out of all his holds *T.* ii 146
To *s.* thy senate, and from heights sublime *T.* ii 216
Then *s.* them in despair, and dance again *T.* ii 666
In guilty splendour, *s.* the public ways *T.* iii 70 [161
The touch from many a trembling cord *s.* out *T.* iv
S. her encumbered lap, and casts them out *T.* iv 499
Then *s.* his powdered coat, and barks for joy *T.* v 51
From spray to spray, where'er he rests he *s. T.* vi 80
In all her gates, and *s.* her distant shores *T.T.* 453
That all its tempest-beaten turrets *s. T.* v 527 [460
Earth *s.* beneath them, and Heaven roars above *T.T.*
The storm of music *s.* the astonished crowd *T.T.* 491
Could *s.* thee to the root—and time has been. *Y.O.* 92

SHAKEN.
His birthright *s.*, and no longer clear *Con.* 765
This elegant rose, had I *s.* it less *The Rose* 17

SHAKESPEARE.
And covetous of *S.'s* beauty, seen *T.* iii 601

SHAKING.
And crazy earth has had her *s.* fits *T.* ii 60
And lightly, *s.* it with agile hand *T.* iii 478

SHALLOW.
A *s.* brain behind a serious mask *Con.* 297
Deposit in those *s.* all their spawn *P.E.* 479
The little wick of life's poor *s.* lamp *T.* iii 164
With *s.* shifts and old devices, worn *T.* v 632
Like *s.* brooks which summer suns exhale! *V.* 2

SHAME. [179
" Oh, *s.* to knighthood!" his assailant cried *A.T.*
S. and ruin wait for you" *B.* 44 [*A.T.* 180
" Oh, *s.*!" ten thousand echoing nymphs replied
Buy what is woman-born, and feel no *s.? Ch.* 181

I may alarm thee, but I fear the *s. Ch.* 294
He sought the jewel in his neighbour's *s. Ch.* 540
Of needless *s.*, and self-imposed disgrace *Con.* 350
Where 'tis a *s.* to be ashamed to appear *Con.* 376
Acquainted with the woes that fear or *s. Con.* 495
Well spoken, advocate of sin and *s. Con.* 587
Form, in its stead, a covenant of *s. Con.* 684
No—*s.* upon a self-disgracing age *Con.* 735 [811
Arts once esteemed may be with *s.* dismissed *Con.*
And do his errand of disgrace and *s. Ex.* 334
Shall I abjure thee not to court thy *s.? Ex.* 655
Thy glory, and thy *s.* if unimproved) *Ex.* 689
To bear it, suffered *s.* where'er he went *H.* 587
Must cause him *s.* or discontent *Mor.* 46
No, wrangler,—destitute of *s.* and sense *P.E.* 235
Has time worn out, or fashion put to *s. P.E.* 245
Reflection and remorse, the fear of *s. T.* i 489
And Chatham heart-sick of his country's *s. T.* ii 244
He hails the clergy, and defying *s. T.* ii 356
He mocks his Maker, prostitutes and *s. T.* ii 427
They *s.* their shooters with a random flight *T.* ii 807
Cruel, abandoned, glorying in her *s.! T.* iii 68
Then *s.* to manhood, and opprobrious more *T.* v 379
Covering his *s.* from his offended sight *T.* v 634
That 'tis our *s.* and misery not to learn *Tir.* 78 [88
And man would breathe but for his Maker's *s. Tir.*
That palliates deeds of folly and of *s.*) *Tir.* 333
On selfish principles, is *s.* and guilt *T.T.* 2
In prostitution sinks the sense of *s. T.T.* 415

SHAMED.
And *s.* as we have been, to the very beard *T.* ii 271
See womanhood despised, and manhood *s. Tir.* 827

SHAMEFACED.
The squire, once bashful, is *s.* no more *P.E.* 403

SHAMEFUL.
The *s.* close of all his misspent years *H.* 715

SHAMEFULLY.
And that a nation *s.* debased *T.T.* 396

SHANK. [16
Transformed to a lean *s.* The shapeless pair *T.* v

SHAPE.
From dangers of a frightful *s. A Fable* 33
Are marriage in its true and proper *s. A.T.* 65
Who shifts and changes all things but his *s. Con.* 459
But ills of every *s.* and every name *E.* ii 37
Chargeable only with a human *s. H.* 514
Of ruder *s.*, and feeling none *P.* 12 [*R.* 67
Whose *s.* would make them, had they bulk and size
Nature in all the various *s.* she wears *R.* 193
The growing wonder takes a thousand *s. T.* v 119
Though in voice and *s.* they be *Trans.* iii 17

SHAPELESS.
And quell the *s.* monsters of the times *A.T.* 142
" You *s.* nothing in a dish *P.* 25
With prickly gorse, that *s.* and deformed *T.* i 527
Transformed to a lean shank. The *s.* pair *T.* v 16

SHAPELY.
Hers is the spacious arch, the *s.* spire *Ch.* 105
The *s.* limb and lubricated joint *R.* 57
Lie scattered where the *s.* column stood *T.* ii 76
The *s.* side, that as it rises takes *T.* iii 481
Nor are these all. To deck the *s.* knoll *T.* iii 628

SHARE.
Teach mercy to ten thousand hearts that *s. Ch.* 278
What their affliction was, and begged a *s. Con.* 524
To find the medium, asks some *s.* of wit *Con.* 879
Invite thee, woo thee, to the bliss they *s. Ex.* 627
His gracious attributes, and prove the *s. H.* 139
To place you where his saints his presence *s. H.* 339

SHARE—SHELTER

And scorns to *s.* it with the distant sun *H.* 480 [750
Then these thy glorious works, and they who *s. H.*
Go! thou art all unfit to *s. M.B.* 1
Of pleasing, which you *s. Miss* — 18
And, staff in hand, set forth to *s. Mor.* 9
The sweets that I was wont to *s. O.* ii 11 [154
Preaching and pranks will *s.* the motley scene *P.E.*
New life ordained and brighter scenes to *s. R.* 65
The world can boast, and her chief favourites *s.R.*186
And *s.* the joys your Bounty may create *R.* 790
Which future pages yet are doomed to *s. T.* 146
But the same word that, like polished *s. T.* 459
Admits me to a *s.* : the guiltless eye *T.* i 333
But let not him that *s.* a brighter day *T.* 539
With her who *s.* his pleasures and his heart *T.* iii 390
Suffer his woes, and *s.* in his escapes *T.* iv 117
Upturned so lately by the forceful *s. T.* iv 315
To see thy beauty, and to *s.* thy joy *T.* vi 815
My *s.* of duties decently fulfilled *T.* vi 1001
Oh! *s.* Maria's grief *T.B.* 3
And thus, well tutored only while we *s. Tir.* 195
Hark! how the sire of chits, whose future *s. Tir.* 318
Claims more than half the praise as his due *s. Tir.* 528
Who, if their sons some slight tuition *s. Tir.* 783
If all men indiscriminately *s. T.T.* 256
Mankind to *s.* in the divine delight *T.T.* 753

SHARED.
Or if in masculine debate he *s. H.* 686
As being *s.* with thee *The Doves* 20
Hence British poets too the priesthood *s. T.T.* 502
And if he add, a blessing *s.* by few *V.* 89
But none I found, or found them *s.* 1789, 9

SHARK. [*T.* iii 817
And the *s.'s* prey; the spendthrift, and the leech
London engulphs them all! The *s.* is there *T.* iii 816

SHARON.
And plant successfully sweet *S.'s* rose *H.* 463

SHARP.
Where *s.* and solid, phlegmatic and light *Ex.* 296
By ceaseless *s.* corrosion *F.* 63
And deems her *s.* artillery mere straw *H.* 597
Hence the declivity is *s.* and short *T.* i 326
To the *s.* peak of her sublimest height *T.* iii 157
To a *s.* reckoning that has lived in vain *T.* iii 179
Whose *s.* declivity shoots off secure *T.* iii 487
The morning *s.* and clear. But now at noon *T.* vi 58
When led by instinct *s.* and sure *T.B.* 32

SHARPED. [86
And judged offenders well. Then he that *s. T.* iii

SHARPER.
No, not a spark—'tis all mere *s.'s* play *T.* 209
To some shrewd *s.*, ere it buds again *T.* iii 754

SHATTERED.
Were *s.* at a blow *J.G.* 124
Haste, then, and wheel away a *s.* world *T.* vi 823
A *s.* veteran, hollow-trunked perhaps *Y.O.* 4

SHAVE.
At which I oft *s.* cheek and chin *Gr.* 23

SHAVEN.
But such a tree! 'twas *s.* deal *A Tale* 33
Died by the sentence of a *s.* priest *Ch.* 55 [*Ex.* 512
Then priests with bulls, and briefs, and *s.* crowns
A monitor is wood—plank *s.* thin *T.* ii 585
On props of smoothest *s.* wood *T.B.* 23

SHEARS.
Smith, cobbler, joiner, he that plies the *s. T.* iv 476

SHEATH.
His sword was in the *s. R.G.* 21
To *s.* it, in the peace-restoring close *T.T.* 79

SHED.
And tears by bards or heroes *s. Cast.* 53
Thy lips have *s.* instruction as the dew *Ch.* 238
The peep of morning *s.* a dawning light *Ch.* 261
And *s.* the balmy blessing on the lips *Con.* 442
S. every hour a clearer light *E.* i 61
When Sin has *s.* dishonour on thy brow *Ex.* 394
No Cotton, whose humanity *s.* rays *H.* 205
S. light, like a sun on the waves *M.D.* 14
In vain warm suns their influence *s. Miss* — 37
Say, wast thou conscious of the tears I *s.* ? *M.P.* 22
The grove, and the sequestered *s. O.* ii 17
Had *s.* immortal glories on your brow *T.* 569
Or Temper *s.* into thy crystal cup *T.* iii 47
Or *s.* impervious to the blast. Resigned *T.* v 72
Cain had already *s.* a brother's blood *T.* v 208 [719
And win it with more pain. Their blood is *s. T.* v
With tears o'er hapless favorites *s. T.B.* 2
And Genius *s.* his rays *Th.* 4
Like his to *s.* illuminating rays *T.T.* 712
From the shelter of that sunny *s. W.N.* 6

SHEEP.
On southern banks the ruminating *s. A.T.* 78
His unsuspecting *s.* believe it pure *Ex.* 103
The *s.* here smooths the knotted thorn *M.B.* 9 [37
S. grazed the field; some with soft bosom pressed *N.A.*
The *s.* recumbent, and the *s.* that grazed *N.A.* 47
Much wondered that the silly *s.* had found *N.A.* 129
His silly *s.*, what wonder if they stray? *P.E.* 119
Will not the sickliest *s.* of every flock *P.E.* 142 [110
Of grassy swarth, close cropped by nibbling *s. T.* i
To wandering *s.*, resolved to follow none *T.* vi 891

SHEEPFOLD.
Exults in its command. The *s.* here *T.* i 290

SHEEPISH.
S. he doffs his hat, and mumbling swears *T.* iv 628

SHEEP-WALKS.
And *s.* populous with bleating lambs *T.* vi 112

SHEER.
S. o'er the craggy barrier, and immersed *T.* vi 554

SHEET.
Since twenty *s.* of lead, God knows *E.* iv 27
(I would say twenty *s.* of prose) *E.* iv 28
Or lay the landscape on the snowy *s. R.* 798 [ii 5
How each would trembling wait the mournful *s. St.*
That in its fall the liquid *s.* throws wide *T.* v 106
Backed with a modest *s.* of humble prose *V.* 20

SHELF.
Lodged on the *s.*, half-eaten without sauce *T.* iv 394
This moveable structure of *s. Gr.* 25
Their order on his *s.* exact *Mrs. M*— 39
Books, therefore, not the scandal of the *s. R.* 683
Adorn his intellects as well as *s. T.* 423 [745
Stamped on the well-bound quarto, graced the *s.T.T.*
Yes—ye are conscious[; and on all the *s. Tir.* 269
Who, far enough from furnishing their *s. Tir.* 825
The *s.* are full, all other themes are sped *T.T.* 726

SHELL.
Once take the *s.* beneath his just command *Con.* 904
For ever in my native *s. P.* 6
Some shining pebbles, and some weeds and *s. R.* 154
Pulverized of venality, a *s. Y.O.* 123

SHELTER.
Ambitious of a *s.* there *Mrs. M*— 44
Could *s.* them from rain or snow *P.T.* 58
You find safe *s.* in the next stage-coach *R.* 492
Oh for a *s.* from the wrath to come! *T.* 268 [519
From courts dismissed, found *s.* in the groves *T.* iv
Enjoy close *s.*, wall, or reeds, or hedge *T.* iii 474
From the *s.* of that sunny shed *W.N.* 6

SHELTERED.
Then snug enclosures in the s. vale *T.* i 513
And s. Sofa, while the nitrous air *T.* iii 32
Well—one at least is safe. One s. hare *T.* iii 334
Uncrowded, yet safe s. from the storm *Y.O.* 55

SHELTERING.
For ages safe beneath his s. hand *Ex.* 563
S. the base with its projected eaves *T.* iii 483
Those naked acres to a s. grove *T.* iii 773
The sparrows peep, and quit the s. eaves *T.* v 65
His s. side, and wilfully forewent *T.* vi 40

SHEPHERD.
No s.'s tents within thy view appear *E.* ii 43
But the Chief S. even there is near *E.* ii 44
When He that ruled them with a s.'s rod *Ex.* 85
And Bonner, blithe as s. at a wake *Ex.* 614
Just when the larks, and when the s. rise *H.* 86
The full-blown rose, the s. and his lass *T.* i 36
Then, as a s. separates his flock *T.* v 196

SHEPHERDESS.
Than the fair s. of old romance *T.* iv 538

SHIELD.   [*A.T.* 125
So swarmed the Sabine youth, and grasped the s.
She sat, and a s. at her side *M.D.* 13
And aims them at the s. of Truth again *T.* vi 875
Of trophied helmets, spears, and s. 1789, 4

SHIFT.   [459
Who s. and changes all things but his shape *Con.*
Which only poets know. The s. and turns *T.* ii 286
Where Vice has such allowance, that her s. *T.* iii 106
Too long, to tell the expedients and the s. *T.* iii 559
By supplemental s., the best he may ? *T.* iv 769
With shallow s. and old devices, worn *T.* v 632
What s. he used, detected in a scrape *Tir.* 328
No matter;—we could s. when they were not *T.T.* 770

SHIFTED.
Now s. east, and east by north *P.T.* 51
S. the wind that raised it, and it fell *T.T.* 387

SHIFTING.
Then s. his side as a lawyer knows how *A.C.* 25
So s. and so various is the plan *H.* 15
Contrives, hard s., and without her tools *T.* v 417
Thyself meanwhile e'en s. as thou mayst *Tir.* 749

SHILLING.
The solitary S. Pardon then *T.* iii 456

SHINE.
But s. with cruel and tremendous charms *Ch.* 545
And s. as if impatient to bestow *Ch.* 591
Content on earth in earthly things to s. *Con.* 583
And purifying, makes it s. the more *Con.* 598
Ambitious, not to s. or to excel *Con.* 623
S. in the dark, but ushered into day *Con.* 677
Might s. in fable, and grace idle themes *Ex.* 233
Countries indebted to thy power, that s. *Ex.* 280
Freedom, in other lands scarce known to s. *Ex.* 588
Who bids him s., or if he s. or not *H.* 84
On all that blooms below, or s. above *H.* 136
He s. with all a cherub's artless charms *H.* 180
Honesty s. with great advantage there *H.* 402 [*H.* 503
And though his beams, that quicken where they s.
'Tis heard where England's Eastern glory s. *H.* 457
Thee, Thornton! worthy in some page to s. *J.T.* 7
Now rust disused, and s. no more *M.* 11
To quench it) here s. on me still the same *M.P.* 10
That glossy s., or vivid flame *Mrs. M*—10
S. safe without a fear to fade *Mrs. M*—50
Shall s. and dry the tear *N.* 24
Taught you to sing, and me to s. *N.G.* 20
But sing and s. by sweet consent *N.G.* 31
Give wit, that what is left may s. *O.* i 27
S. as it runs, but grasped at, slips away *P.E.* 22
S. not, or undesired and hated s. *R.* 351
She s. but little in his heedless eyes *R.* 405
Kneels, kisses hands, and s. again in place *R.* 480
That s. and rests, as infants smile and sleep *R.* 528
Or s. the dulness of still life away *R.* 746 [*R.* 557
Graced with such wisdom, how would beauty s. !
And s. without desiring to be seen *T.* 70
Of ash, or lime, or beech, distinctly s. *T.* i 303
Your element; there only ye can s. *T.* i 758
And s. by situation, hardly less *T.* ii 296
Pure, from so foul a pool, to s. abroad *T.* ii 798
To seek him rather where his mercy s. *T.* iii 224
And in thy numbers, Philips, s. for aye *T.* iii 455
These have their sexes, and when summer s. *T.* iii 537
S. there, and flourishes. The golden boast *T.* iii 571
The wish to s., the thirst to be amused *T.* iii 829
S. out; there only reach their proper use *T.* iv 662
Of late unsightly and unseen, now s. *T.* v 24
Not so the labours of his love : they s. *T.* v 570
And he abhors the jest by which he s. *T.* v 617
Bright as a sun the sacred city s. *T.* vi 800
S. with his fair example, and though small *T.* vi 961
S. by the side of every path we tread *Tir.* 79
And in the firmament of fame still s. *Tir.* 281
Our striplings s. indeed, but with such rays *Tir.* 286
Must s. by true desert, or not at all *Tir.* 357
Though Vestris on one leg still s. below *Tir.* 542
Blest country, where these kingly glories s. ! *T.T.* 81
To make the pitiful possessor s. *T.T.* 755
'Tis power almighty bids him s. *Trans.* i 23
Nor bids him s. in vain *Trans.* i 24
Above the steeple s. a plate *Trans.* ii 7
The eyes, that never saw thee, s. 1789, 58

SHINING.
To make the s. prodigy complete *Ch.* 602
In every s. straw she sees *E.* iv 46
How much, though long neglected s. yet *Ex.* 610
All s. in their places *F.* 60
No s. ornaments have they to seek *H.* 765
And the sun gilds the s. spires again *Her.* 72
Thy needles, once a s. store *M.* 9
And with a clear and s. lamp supplied *P.E.* 558
Some s. pebbles, and some weeds and shells *R.* 154
Force many a s. youth into the shade *R.* 560
Some glossy-leaved, and s. in the sun *T.* i 314
And by contrasted beauty s. more) *T.* iii 635
Not such his evening, who with s. face *T.* iv 42
And s. each in his domestic sphere *T.* v 520
Shouted for joy.—" Tell me, y s. hosts *T.* v 822
Such rare exceptions, s. in the dark *Tir.* 841
Then show far off their s. plumes again *T.T.* 567

SHIP.
At length a s. arriving brought *A Tale* 23
A s. !—Could such a restless thing *A Tale* 25
Nor ever s. left Albion's coast *Cast.* 9
But he, they knew, nor s. nor shore *Cast.* 29
So when a s., well freighted with the stores *Ch.* 441
The cry in all thy s. is still the same *Ex.* 288
His s. half foundered, and his compass lost *T.* 2
For sight of s. from England. Every speck *T.* i 666
Upon the s.'s tall side he stands, possessed *T.* i 450

SHIPMATES.
His feathered s. eyes *A Tale* 58

SHIPWRECK.
But s., earthquake, battle, fire, and flood *Ch.* 282
Forsaking thee, what s. have we made *T.* iii 58

SHIPWRIGHT.
The s.'s darling treasure, didst present *Y.O.* 97

SHIRT.
In *s.* of hair, and weeds of canvass dressed *T.* 81

SHIVER.
With double toil, and *s.* at their work *T.T.* 215

SHIVERED.
Bricks line the sides, but *s.* long ago *N.A.* 15

SHIVERING.
Or send another *s.* to the bar *Con.* 187
The *s.* urchin, bending as he goes *T.* 143
Thus fare the *s.* natives of the north *T.* i 617
Stands in the desert *s.* and forlorn *T.T.* 724

SHOCK.
He, still more aged, feels the *s. Ep.* ii 41   [495
Was formed to harden hearts and *s.* the sight *Ex.*
Whatever *s.,* or gives the least offence *P.E.* 512
Awakened by the *s.* (cried Puss) *R.C.* 53
No tempest gave the *s. R.G.* 18
But is it fit, or can it bear the *s. T.* v 305
And *s.* me. I should then with double pain *T.* v 483
At once the *s.* unseated him : he flew *T.* vi 553 [583
Though some, perhaps, that *s.* thy feeling mind *Tir.*
Gives Liberty the last the mortal *s. T.T.* 476

SHOCKED.   [*P.A.* 25
He was *s.,* sir, like you, and answered—"Oh no!"
I own I am *s.* at the purchase of slaves *P.A.* 1
Too many, *s.* at what should charm them most *T.* 32
That would have *s.* Credulity herself *T.* ii 694
That pleasest and yet *s.* me, I can laugh *T.* iii 840

SHOCKING.
Their tameness is *s.* to me *A.S.* 16
To hide the *s.* features of her face *P.E.* 298

SHOD.
Beneath his well *s.* feet *J.G.* 82

SHONE.
No light propitious *s. Cast.* 62   [63
By thy own hand, till fresh they *s.* and glowed *M.P.*
Bright *s.* the roofs, the domes, the spires *Q.V.* 13
S. brighter still, once called to public view *T.* v 521
In less illustrious bards his beauty *s. T.T.* 574

SHOOK.
S. the young leaves about her ears *A Fable* 12
S. principalities and kingdoms down *Ch.* 77
'Tis e'en as if an angel *s.* his wings *Ch.* 438
No thunders *s.* with deep intestine sound *Her.* 5
That *s.* the circling seas and solid earth *Her.* 14
Which *s.* Belshazzar at his wine *Q.V.* 51
A land-breeze *s.* the shrouds *R.G.* 9
Hark! universal Nature *s.* and groaned *T.* 563
S. the delinquent with such fits of awe *T.* ii 722

SHOOT. [884
S. between scattered rocks and opening shades *Con.*
Of distant wisdom *s.* across his way *H.* 94
That *s.* into your darkest caves the day *H.* 493
S. back the bolt, and all his courage dies *H.* 721
S. into port at some well-havened isle *M.P.* 90
Or *s.* the careless with a surer aim *R.* 218
But if his word once teach us, *s.* a ray *T.* iii 240
No meaner hand may discipline the *s. T.* iii 413
Whose sharp declivity *s.* off secure *T.* iii 487
And all shall be restored. These naked *s. T.* vi 141
To check them. But, alas! none sooner *s. T.* vi 592
S. into pillars of pellucid length *T.* v 115   [309
Gives him Olympic speed, and *s.* him to the goal *T.T.*

SHOOTERS.
They shame their *s.* with a random flight *T.* ii 807

SHOOTING.
And others *s.* and the chase *L.W.* 32
Sir Humphrey, *s.* in the dark *M.F.* 9

SHOP.
To Miss, the mercer's plague, from *s.* to *s. T.* vi 279
Or turn them into *s.* and auction rooms *Tir.* 902

SHORE.
Convey to this desolate *s. A.S.* 34
Sea-beaten rocks and naked *s. A Tale* 19
The vessel weighs, forsakes the *s. A Tale* 43
But he, they knew, nor ship nor *s. Cast.* 29
Loses in tears the far receding *s. Ch.* 147
For Africa's once loved, benighted *s. Ch.* 241
And land some grave optician on the *s. Ch.* 384
The sun matures on India's spicy *s. Ch.* 442
And plunging left the *s. D.W.* 32
Her peaceful *s.,* where busy Commerce waits *Ex.* 13
And fling their foam against thy chalky *s.? Ex.* 273
That clips thy *s.,* had no such charms for thee *Ex.* 551
Where else they would, but not upon thy *s.? Ex.* 567
And all from *s.* to *s.* is free beside *Ex.* 595
Famed for thy probity from *s.* to *s. J.T.* 6
From Africa's sorrowful *s. M.D.* 32   [*M.P.* 96
So thou, with sails how swift! hast reached the *s.*
May I but meet thee on that peaceful *s. M.P.* 34
An oyster cast upon the *s. P.* 1   [520
Like something precious ventured far from *s. P.E.*
Each creek and cavern of the dangerous *s. R.* 152
Thunder and flash upon the steadfast *s. R.* 534
Fast by their native *s.! R.G.* 4
Than bid me shun the deep, and dread the *s.? R.H.* 2
Of this world's hazardous and headlong *s. St.* ii 14
Mercy receives him on her peaceful *s. T.* 276
The dash of Ocean on his winding *s. T.* i 186
To distant *s.,* and she would sit and weep *T.* i 540
If ever it has washed our distant *s. T.* i 656
Which winds and waves obey, invades the *s. T.* ii 114
May bear us smoothly to the Gallic *s. T.* ii 262
"As one who long detained on foreign *s. T.* v 832
Again she lays them slumbering on the *s. Tir.* 26
And owns her power on every *s.* he laves? *Tir.* 40
Then perish on futurity's wide *s. Tir.* 83
Poll gains at length the British *s. Trans.* iv 4
Along the treacherous *s. Trans. H.* 6
In all her gates, and shakes her distant *s. T.T.* 453

SHORN. [613
Must smooth be *s.* away; the sapless branch *T.* iii

SHORT.
As wide as the bridge of the Nose is; in *s. A.C.* 15
And too *s.* lived to reach the realms of peace *Ch.* 451
The time is *s.,* and there are souls on earth *Con.* 493
Is madly to forget that life is *s. Con.* 772
"Go, fellow!—whither?—turning *s.* about *E.* iii 24
We have our similes cut *s. E.* iv 65
Nor spare a life too *s.* to reach the skies *Ex.* 623
No trifle, howsoever *s.* it seem *H.* 123
Though *s.,* too long, the price he pays for all *H.* 200
His date of life, so likely to be *s. H.* 208
Flew open in *s.* space *J.G.* 242
In *s.,* the charms her sister had *J.P.* 27
The songster heard his *s.* oration *N.G.* 23
Disputes, though *s.,* are far too long *P.* 45
Turning *s.* round, strutting, and sideling *P.T.* 39
Rarely redeem the *s.* remaining ten *R.* 40
Its brisker and its graver strains fall *s. R.* 294
But *s.* the date of all we gather here *R.* 460
The jury meet, the coroner is *s. T.* 447
Incurring *s.* fatigue: and though our years *T.* i 129
Hence the declivity is sharp and *s. T.* i 326
By. *s.* transition we have lost his glare *T.* i 336
That such *s.* absence may endear it more *T.* i 517
To Athens or to Rome, for wisdom *s. T.* ii 536
And gathering, at *s.* notice, in one group *T.* iv 136
No rattling wheels stop *s.* before these gates *T.* iv 144
The recollected powers, and snapping *s. T.* iv 305

And tail cropped s., half lurcher and half cur T. v 46
To adjust the fragrant charge of a s. tube T. v 55
S. as it is, supportable. Still worse T. v 604
That in a few s. moments I retrace T. vi 16
S. as in retrospect the journey seems T. vi 19
It seem'd not always s.; the rugged path T. vi 20
But let the months go round, a few s. months T. vi 140
Allows s. time for play, and none for sloth Tir. 484
Encompassing his throne a few s. years T.T. 132
And truth cut s. to make a period round T.T. 517
S. his career, indeed, but ably run T.T. 671
Sits half the pleasures of s. life away! Y.O. 32

SHORTENED.
Seems sunk, and s. to its topmost boughs T. i 306

SHORTENING.
And claims a reverence in its s. day Con. 645
S. his journey between morn and noon T. iv 131

SHORTER.
Their nimble nonsense takes a s. course Con. 152

SHORTEST.
Shows them the s. way to life and love T. 370

SHORTLIVED.
O charming Paradise of s. sweets! Her. 34
S. possession! but the record fair M.P. 54
S. themselves to immortalize their bones T. v 184
But spurious and s.; the puny child T. v 621

SHOT.
The very dart that malice ever s. H. 559
S. by an archer strong J.G. 154 [346
S. through the boughs, it dances as they dance T. i
The infidel has s. his bolts away T. vi 872
And s. a dayspring into distant climes T.T. 561

SHOULDERS.
His snowy mantle o'er his s. threw A.T. 202
His s. witnessing by many a shrug H. 415
Taught the raised s. to invade the ears T. i 67
And binds the s. flat. We prove its use T. ii 589
Bent knees, round s., and dejected looks T. iv 634
Shall stuff his s. with King Richard's hunch T. vi 674

SHOULDERING.
That govern all things here, s. aside T. vi 839
S., and standing as if struck to stone T.T. 137

SHOULDER-KNOT.
With the king's s. and gay cockade T.T. 44

SHOUT.
Which he that hears it with a s. repeats T. v 889
Some s. him, and some hang upon his car T. vi 698
S. to each other, and the mountain tops T. vi 794
With which he s. and carols, "Vive le Roy!" T.T. 243

SHOUTED.
He s.; nor his friends had failed Cast. 19
S. for joy.—"Tell me, ye shining hosts T. v 822

SHOVE.
To palliate dullness and give time a s. T. iv 210

SHOVED.
Hast thou, by statute, s. from its design Ex. 376

SHOW. [21
"On the whole it appears, and my argument s. A.C.
But he, the virtues of his lance to s. A.T. 165
We English often s. A Tale 74
Than aught that the city can s. C. 32
The lamp of revelation only s. Ch. 339
That brass and steel should make so fine a s. Ch. 554
And I might spare myself the pains to s. Ch. 626
Perhaps at last close scrutiny may s. Con. 177
Then each might s., to his admiring friends Con. 199
And s. the softest minds and fairest forms Con. 259

For sea-born Venus her attachment s. Con. 265 [741
The World grown old her deep discernment s. Con.
And while it s. the land the soul desires Con. 885
To s. a love as prompt as thine D.W. 43 [Con. 381
"Yes, ma'am," and "No, ma'am," uttered softly, s.
But half a coat, and s. his bosom bare E. iii 51
To s. my genius or my wit E. iv 7
And had the grace in scenes of peace to s. Ex. 79
Thy language at this distant moment s. Ex. 480
Enjoyed the s. and danced about the stake Ex. 615
Like a loose heap of ribbon, a glittering s. F.M. 6
To me ever ready to s. Gr. 43
Whose prospect s. thee a disheartening waste H. 32
S. with a pointing finger, but no noise H. 221
Incurs resentment for the love he s. H. 285
That s. reversed the villas on their side H. 468
That s. how far 'tis safe to follow sin H. 608
And years of pining indigence must s. Her. 65
How oft the sadness that I s. M. 46
Thy pleasure is to s. M.B. 18
S. Love to be a mere profession M.F. 60
There sits quiescent on the floods that s. M.P. 92
And I can view this mimic s. of thee M.P. 119
The cock his arched tail's azure s. Mrs. M— 7
Avarice s., and virtue is the price P.E. 52
But s. peculiar light, by many a grin P.E. 383
Some headless hero, or some Cæsar, s. P.E. 395
So one, whose story serves at least to s. P.E. 526
New trimmed, a gallant s.! Q.V. 6
She viewed the sparkling s. Q.V. 74
Ye kings and rulers, what have courts to s.? R. 104
And what could a remoter scene s. more? R. 500
Specious in s., impossible in fact R. 638
And s. the august tribunal of the skies R. 656
With what success let modern manners s. R. 686
S. the same sadness everywhere S. 11
He wore them as fine trappings for a s. T. 56 [131
Yon ancient prude, whose withered features s. T.
Attend;—an apt similitude shall s. T. 236
S. them the shortest way to life and love T. 370
Like gleanings of an olive tree they s. T. 379
The veteran s., and gracing a grey beard T. i 406
Who s. me that which I shall never see T. i 423
A girdle of half-withered shrubs he s. T. i 524
Their fluttering rags, and s. a tawny skin T. i 568
And ignorant, except of outward s.) T. i 650 [636
Forth from thy native bowers, to s. thee here T. i
And s. this queen of cities, that so fair T. i 727
Are silent. Revelry, and dance, and s. T. ii 79
And s. the name ye might conceal at home T. ii 279
With s. of love, at least with hopeful proof T. ii 558
Would fail to exhibit at the public s. T. ii 619
A noble s.! while Roscius trod the stage T. iii 597
But elegance, chief grace the garden s. T. iii 638
Still wants a grace, the loveliest it could s. T. iii 782
A variegated s.; the meadows green T. iv 312 [215
With motley plumes, and where the peacock s. T. iv
Yet s. that thou hast mercy, which the great T. iv 371
Humane as they would seem not always s. T. iv 373
To swear, to game, to drink; to s. at home T. iv 652
'Twas transient in its nature, as in s. T. v 173
"That s. like beacons in the blue abyss T. v 839
A father, whose authority, in s. T. vi 30 [241
But s. some touch, in freckle, streak, or stain T. vi
As duly as the Langford of the s. T. vi 287
So little mercy s. who needs so much! T. vi 431
Mercy to him that s. it, is the rule T. vi 595
And he that s. none, being ripe in years T. vi 598
Some s. that nice sagacity of smell T. vi 616
To s. the world how Garrick did not act T. vi 677
S. somewhat of that happier life to come T. vi 907
And s. him glories yet to be revealed T. vi 927
To s. the peeping down upon his chin Tir. 235

SHOW—SHUT

Soon s. the strong similitude reversed *Tir.* 443
S. all its rents and patches to the world *Tir.* 451
A sight surpassed by none that we can s. *Tir.* 541
To s. him in an insect or a flower *Tir.* 636
Safe under such a wing, his boy shall s. *Tir.* 684
S. thou hast sense enough to prize the pearl *Tir.* 707
Hear Nature plead, s. mercy to thy son *Tir.* 756
Serves but to s. how black is all beside *Tir.* 844
Thy child shall s. respect to thy gray hairs *Tir.* 880
That s. by night a lucid beam *Trans.* i 3
To s. a stumbling stone by night *Trans.* i 19
Thus happiness depends, as Nature s. *T.T.* 246
No. Freedom has a thousand charms to s. *T.T.* 260
Courage in arms, and ever prompt to s. *T.T.* 276
Then s. far off their shining plumes again *T.T.* 567
Wit now and then, struck smartly, s. a spark *T.T.* 663
And the winter of sorrow best s. *W.N.* 23
That gild thy features, s. in theirs 1789, 65

SHOWED. [142
S. that they followed all they seemed to shun *Ex.*
Thus s. his ready wit *J.G.* 186
And each by shrinking s. he felt it *P.* 66

SHOWER.
Should flow like waters after summer s. *Con.* 705
But most before approaching s. *Ep.* ii 27
So barren sands imbibe the s. *F.* 184
This plumage, neither dashing s. *Mrs. M—* 15
Seem drops descending in a s. of light *R.* 350
A step if fair, and if a s. approach *R.* 491
The gracious s., unlimited and free *T.* 511 ·[*Rose* 1
The Rose had been washed (just washed in a s.) *The*
Fast falls a fleecy s.: the downy flakes *T.* iv 326

SHOW-GLASS.
The s. fraught with glittering ware *P.B.* 24

SHOWN.
In other eyes our talents rarely s. *Con.* 369
For mercy s., while wrath is justly due *Con.* 492
Or such as might be better s. *E.* iv 9
Why, having kept good faith, and often s. *Ex.* 276
The noblest Friendship ever s. *F.* 205
And I, if you had s. me less *G.* 17
For the hatred she ever has s. *M.D.* 46
And tamer far for so much fury s. *T.* vi 541
Where no regard of ordinances is s. *Tir.* 242
And destines their bright genius to be s. *Tir.* 336
No firmer friendships than the fair have s.) *V.* 82

SHREW.
"Still prove herself a s. *J.P.* 38
With all the cunning of an envious s. *T.* ii 266

SHREWD.
Certain invisibles as s. as he *Con.* 738
I praise the Frenchman, his remark was s. *R.* 739
The threads of politic and s. design *T.* iii 147 [iii 581
The winter's frown, if screened from his s. bite *T.*
To some s. sharper, ere it buds again *T.* iii 754
Shaggy, and lean, and s., with pointed ears *T.* v 45
The first artificer of death; the s. *T.* v 213
Patriots are grown too s. to be sincere *T.* v 495
Such rhapsodies our s. discerning youth *Tir.* 191
If s., and of a well constructed brain *Tir.* 523
Conjecture and remark, however s. *T.T.* 205

SHREWDER.
By which the magic art of s. wits *T.* vi 99

SHRIEK.
They s. and sink, survivors start and weep *R.* 159
That feeds upon the sobs and dying s. *T.* iii 328

SHRIEKED. [200
S. at the sight, and, conscious, fled the place *A.T.*

SHRILL.
And the first larum of the cock's s. throat *T.* iv 569
Unimpaired, and s., and clear *Trans.* iii 23

SHRILLEST.
But raise the s. cry in British ears *Ex.* 271

SHRINE.
Woden and Thor, each tottering in his s. *Ex.* 505
The Graces too, while Virtue at their s. *P.E.* 337
Glorious as Solyma's interior s. *T.* 388
Farthest retires—an idol, at whose s. *T.* i 410
To those who, posted at the s. of Truth *T.* v 713
In pilgrimage to bow before his s. *T.* vi 669

SHRINK.
The soldier thus endowed, who never s. *H.* 409
And when I bend, retire, and s. *P.* 35
I s. abased, and yet aspire to Thee *R.* 94
Pushed with a madman's fury. Fancy s. *T.* vi 513

SHRINKING.
And each by s. showed he felt it *P.* 66

SHRIVELLED.
Blows mildew from between his s. lips *T.* ii 186

SHROUD.
Exclaims, "Prepare thee for an early s." *Ep.* i 10
A land-breeze shook the s. *R.G.* 9
And your only suit, a s. *St.* iv 16

SHRUB.
Nor even s. abound *A Tale* 2
My s. displaced from that retreat *F.B.* 2
Not animals alone, but s. and trees *N.A.* 57
I envy that unfeeling s. *P.* 15
Bare trees and s. but ill, you know *P.T.* 52
Her hedge-row s., a variegated store *R.* 419
A girdle of half-withered s. he shows *T.* i 524
Some more aspiring, catch the neighbour s. *T.* iii 665
And s. of fairy land. The crystal drops *T.* v 113

SHRUBBERY.
Fresh odours from the s. at my side *F.A.* 7

SHRUG.
His shoulders witnessing by many a s. *H.* 415
By s. and strange contortions of his face *P.E.* 414
Make just reprisals, and with cringe and s. *T.* ii 645

SHRUNK.
Deserted of its bloom, the flaccid, s. *T.* i 392

SHUFFLE.
To deal and s., to divide and sort *T.* i 474

SHUFFLING.
S. her threads about the livelong day *T.* 320

SHUN. [142
Showed that they followed all they seemed to s. *Ex.*
Taught me what path to s., and what pursue *Ch.* 239
That serve mankind, or s. them, wild or tame *N.A.* 66
Witness of joys that s. the sight of noon *P.E.* 174
The Lover too s. business and alarms *R.* 219
Than bid me s. the deep, and dread the shore? *R.H.* 2
Scarce s. me; and the stockdove unalarm'd *T.* vi 307

SHUNNED.
Was marked and s. as odious. He that sold *T.* iii 88
For which we s. and hated thee before *T.* v 882

SHUSHAN.
Not as the prince in S., when he called *T.* iii 714

SHUT. [32
By daylight or candlelight—Eyes should be s. *A.C.*
And s. up every satyr in his den *Con.* 38
Deeply resolved to s. a Saviour out *Con.* 690
Would disobey, though sure to be s. out *H.* 315
In terms as plain, himself has s. the rest *H.* 341
His eyes s. fast, his fingers in his ears *H.* 658

That *s.* within its seed the future flower *R.* 792
Employs, *s.* out from more important views *R.* 803
The chambermaid, and *s.* it fast *R.C.* 50
He *s.* it close, and the first labour ends *T.* iii 489
Or if that mine be *s.*, some private purse *T.* iii 797

SHUTTER.
Now stir the fire, and close the *s.* fast *T.* iv 36
That sweeps the bolted *s.*, summons home *T.* iv 304

SHY.
The man I trust, if *s.* to me *F.* 187
Not *s.*, as in the world, and to be won *T.* vi 115
He blushes, hangs his head, is *s.* and strange *Tir.* 563

SHYNESS.
These ask with painful *s.*, and, refused *T.* iv 418

SICILIAN.
And all the charms of a *S.* year *Her.* 21

SICILY.
Alas for *S.*! rude fragments now *T.* ii 75

SICK.
Learns to compassionate the *s.* she sees *Ch.* 411
What makes some *s.*, and others à-la-mort *Con.* 292
In making known how oft they have been *s. Con.* 312
That *s.*, she trembles, knowing she must die *Con.* 773
S. of the service of a world that feeds *R.* 47
S. of a thousand disappointed aims) *R.* 366
Where all good qualities grow *s.* and die *R.* 738
An infidel in health,—" But what when *s.* ? " *T.* 309
Thus often Unbelief, grown *s.* of life *T.* 445 [i 89
The nurse sleeps sweetly, hired to watch the *s. T.*
Of lazy man who snores the *s.* man dead *T.* i 97
My soul is *s.*, with every day's report *T.* ii 6 [733
O'erlooked and unemployed, fell *s.*, and died *T.* ii
And, *s.* of having seen 'em *Trans.* ii 33
And now he sings, and now is *s. Trans.* iv 28

SICKENING.
Sordid and *s.* at his own success *T.* iii 810

SICKENS.
The young apostate *s.* at the view *Tir.* 167

SICKLIEST.
Will not the *s.* sheep of every flock *P.E.* 142

SICKLY.
The worst that can invade a *s.* brain *Con.* 222
No pleasure! Has some *s.* eastern waste *P.E.* 255
He just endures and with a *s.* spleen *R.* 565
And Nature with a dim and *s.* eye *T.* ii 64
Though *s.* samples of the exuberant whole *T.* iv 761
And then alternate, with a *s.* hope *T.* v 428 [511
And *s.*, while her champions wear their hearts *T.* v
The triple purpose. In that *s.*, foul *T.* v 583
But well compensating her *s.* looks *T.* vi 163

SICKNESS.
And at last is of service in *s.* or pain *F.M.* 11
Perhaps when *s.*, or some fearful dream *H.* 217
Proof against *s.* and old age *M.F.* 50
To sallow *s.*, which the vapours, dank *T.* i 438
Yet even these, though, feigning *s.* oft *T.* i 580
For he has wings that neither *s.*, pain *T.* v 771

SIDE.
Then shifting his *s.* as a lawyer knows how *A.C.* 25
And only miss the flowers that grace their *s. A.T.* 75
The well-poised lance that quivered at his *s. A.T.* 144
Though little need to his good palfrey's *s. A.T.* 192
He turned and viewed it oft on every *s. A Tale* 203
Then, perching at his consort's *s. A Tale* 53
Both *s.* deceived, if rightly understood *Ch.* 622
A graver fact, enlisted on your *s. Con.* 205
'Tis always active on the *s.* of Truth *Con.* 602
Keep still the dear companion at their *s. Con.* 734

For us plain folks, and all who *s.* with us *Con.* 848
I wandered on his *s. D.W.* 4
From *s.* to *s.* of her delightful isle *Ex.* 3
It shakes the *s.* of splenetic Disdain *Ex.* 548
And equal truth on either *s. F.* 50
Fresh odours from the shrubbery at my *s. F.A.* 7
Suppose the beam should dip on the wrong *s. H.* 374
In peace upon her sloping *s.* matured *Her.* 10
That show reversed the villas on their *s. H.* 468
John Gilpin at his horse's *s. J.G.* 45
And hung a bottle on each *s. J.G.* 71
A bottle swinging at each *s. J.G.* 107
On both *s.* of the way *J.G.* 138
May make you laugh on t'other *s. L.W.* 24
And woodpeckers explore the *s. M.B.* 7
A western bank's still sunny *s. Mor.* 18
Attendant at the senior's *s. Mor.* 40
Of life, long since has anchored by thy *s. M.P.* 99
Wit flashing on Religion's *s. Mrs. M—* 31
Bricks line the *s.*, but shivered long ago *N.A.* 15
That to the wrong *s.* leaning *O.* i 2
On the other *s.* the Atlantic *Pat.* 6
Urged his attempt on every *s. P.B.* 7
Seems verging fast towards the female *s. P.E.* 430
Nor has, nor can have, Scripture on its *s. P.E.* 515
He has no hearing on the prudent *s. P.E.* 540
With some unmeaning coxcomb at your *s. R.* 546
He drew the curtain at his *s. R.C.* 81
And laid her on her *s. R.G.* 8
Sincere on Virtue's *s. St.* iii 18
Even at your *s.*, Sir, and before your eyes *T.* 230
And fumed with frankincense on every *s. T.* 314
And bruised the ash, and elevated high *T.* i 66
Displaying, on its varied *s.*, the grace *T.* i 172
Upon the ship's tall *s.* he stands, possessed *T.* i 450
Multitudes, fugitive on every *s. T.* ii 106
Frequent in Park with lady at his *s. T.* ii 381
Your only one, till *s.* and benches fail *T.* ii 475 [713
Close to his *s.* that pleased him. Learning grew *T.* ii
My panting *s.* was charged, when I withdrew *T.* iii 110
Been hurt by the *s.*. In his *s.* He bore *T.* iii 113
The shapely *s.*, that as it rises takes *T.* iii 481 [iv 44
And bored with elbow points through both his *s. T.*
Without some thistly sorrow at its *s. T.* iv 335
As they designed to mock me, at my *s. T.* v 17
His sheltering *s.*, and wilfully forewent *T.* vi 40
Upon the southern *s.* of the slant hills *T.* vi 59
Of smiling day, they gossip'd *s.* by *s. T.* v 60
Illumined every *s.*; a watery light *T.* v 150 [vi 429
With bleeding *s.* and flanks that heave for life *T.*
But smooth with wands from Ouse's *s. T.B.* 28
On Thracian Hebrus' *s. T.B.* 63
And press thy wedded *s. The Doves* 26
Shine by the *s.* of every path we tread *Tir.* 79 [369
In coach with purple lined, and mitres on its *s. Tir.*
With some such Mentor always at his *s. Tir.* 699
And stood the test, perhaps on the wrong *s. Tir.* 740
The bolts that spare the mountain's *s. Trans. H.* 16
To him that fights with Justice on his *s. T.T.* 12
Where Duty placed them, at their country's *s. T.T.* 24
Upheaved above the soil, and *s.* embossed *Y.O.* 65
Lay such a stake upon the losing *s. Tir.* 863 [*Y.O.* 95
That might have ribbed the *s.* and planked the deck

SIDE-BOX.
To insure a *s.* station at half-price *T.* ii 624

SIDELING.
Turning short round, strutting, and *s. P.T.* 39

SIDELONG.
Stealing a *s.* glance at a full house *T.* iv 201

SIDE-THRUST.
And stab Religion with a sly *s. R.* 690

SIDLE.
They s. to the goal with awkward pace *P.E.* 562

SIDNEY.
For which our Hampdens and our *S.* bled *T.* v 486
And *S.*, warbler of poetic prose *T.* iv 516

SIFT.
And s. the dust behind the door *E.* iv 42
To s. and search them with unerring eyes *Ex.* 88

SIFTED.
And in the dust, s. and searched in vain *T.* v 536

SIGH.
Farewell, my former joys! I s. no more *Ch.* 240
That beams delight? a heart untaught to s.? *Ep.* i 6
S. unregarded to the passing wind *Ex.* 30
My soul shall s. in secret, and lament *Ex.* 722
In dying s. my little breath *G.* 11   [24
Through life's sad remnant, what no s. restore *H.*
S. for his exit, vulgarly called death *H.* 90
And Murray s. o'er Pope, and Swift *M.* i 5
" And still the s. responsive heave *Miss* -- 87
A long, long s., and wept a last adieu! *M.P.* 31
S. must fan it, tears must water *N.C.* 19
But s. at thought of empty pockets *P.B.* 26
Judge his own ways, and s. for a return *P.E.* 611
In s. he worships his supremely fair *R.* 225
He s.,—for after all, by slow degrees *R.* 465
S. o'er the beauties of the charming scene *R.* 566
But when he felt it, heaved a s. *St.* iii 27
S. if perhaps your appetite should fail *T.* 215
Of silent tears and heart-distending s. *T.* iii 331
Vain tears, alas! and s. that never find *T.* iii 332
A bosom heaved with never ceasing s. *T.* i 552 [785
He s., departs, and leaves the accomplished plan *T.* iii
Or charged with amorous s. of absent swains *T.* iv 20
And s., but never tremble at the sound *T.* iv 106
And eaten with a s., than to endure *T.* iv 410
And s. for the smart comrades he has left *T.* iv 648
The s. and groans of miserable men! *T.* v 388
Mov'd many a s. at its disheart'ning length *T.* vi 22
Shall s. at their exclusion, and return *T.* vi 672
To echo s. for s., and groan for groan *V.* 65
He heaves up many a s. *Y.D.* 12

SIGHED.
Never s. at the sound of a knell *A.S.* 31
And s. for every fool that fluttered by *Ex.* 54
If ever when he s., hast s. again *H.* 675

SIGHING.
And s. millions prophesy the close *Ex.* 309
S. and smiling as he takes his glass *H.* 419
And when I place thee in it, s. say *T.* iii 350
Makes wintry music, s. as it goes *T.* vi 143
S., I say again, I pity kings! *T.T.* 140

SIGHT.   [*A.T.* 200
Shrieked at the s., and, conscious, fled the place
And lessens to the s. *A Tale* 44
Scarce less exulting in the s. *A Tale* 59
Spreads foreign wonders in his country's s. *Ch.* 116
Aiding a dubious and deficient s. *Ch.* 329
But finds that though his tubes assist the s. *Ch.* 387
So have I seen (and hastened to the s. *Ch.* 547 [395
The soul, whose s. all-quickening grace renews *Ch.*
That s. imparts a never-dying flame *Ch.* 593
The s.'s enough—no need to smell a beau *Con.* 285
A beam that aids, but never grieves the s. *Con.* 600
Ere life go down, to see such s. again) *Con.* 606
Now starting into s. *D.W.* 10   [37
Charmed with the s., " The World," I cried *D.W.*
In aid of our defective s. *E.* i 62
Flits out of s., and mocks his pains *E.* iv 60
But as too much obscures the s. *E.* iv 63
And Hell's close mischief naked in his s. *Ex.* 339
And in whose awful s. all nations seem *Ex.* 344 [495
Was formed to harden hearts and shock the s. *Ex.*
Our friend's defect long hid from s. *F.* 149
The same we practised at first s. *F.* 179
Must tinkle and glitter like gold to the s. *F.M.* 19
The wretch may pine, while to his smell, taste, s. *H.* 59
Nor cheer the spirit, nor refresh the s. *H.* 299
Where bold Inquiry, diving out of s. *H.* 443
Amazed that shadows should obscure the s. *H.* 534
Thy s. now seconds not thy will *M.* 15
And still more lovely in my s. *M.* 26
What s. worth seeing could I see? *M.* 30
With Pity's watery s. *Miss* — 76
The s. our foolish heart inflames *P.B.* 31
Or present, or in prospect meet his s. *P.E.* 48
Witness of joys that shun the s. of noon *P.E.* 174
'Tis a s. to engage me, if anything can *P.F.* 17
For no such s. had England's queen *Q.V.* 25
Heaven grant us no such future s. *Q.V.* 79
Where unassisted s. no beauty sees *R.* 56
At such a s. to catch the poet's flame *R.* 85
Pleased Fancy claps her pinions at the s. *R.* 190
This is a s. for Pity to peruse *R.* 297
Man is a harp whose chords elude the s. *R.* 325
But never marked her with so just a s. *R.* 418
I have no s. for you" *St.* iii 12
To your weak s. her telescopic eye *T.* 98
His Maker has no beauty in his s. *T.* 414
And seeking exile from the s. of men *T.* 442
Nor rural s. alone, but rural sounds *T.* i 181
Till half their beauties fade; the weary s. *T.* i 510
And terrible to s., as when she springs *T.* i 602
For s. of ship from England. Every speck *T.* i 666
Should ever tease the lungs and blear the s. *T.* iii 168
Well they reward the toil. The s. is pleased *T.* iii 620
The wings that waft our riches out of s. *T.* iii 760
Preposterous s.! the legs without the man *T.* v 20
Covering his shame from his offended s. *T.* v 634
With those whose mansions glitter in his s. *T.* v 740
And all in s. of inattentive man? *T.* vi 120
Who sleeps not, is not weary; in whose s. *T.* vi 223
With s. of animals enjoying life *T.* vi 325
At s. of the man-monster. With a smile *T.* vi 499
The creeping vermin, loathsome to the s. *T.* vi 568
(A s. to which our eyes are strangers yet) *T.* vi 825
That feels not at that s., and feels at none *Tir.* 299
Oh 'tis a s. to be with joy perused *Tir.* 537   [434
And therefore.'tis, that, though the s. be rare *Tir.*
A s. surpassed by none that we can show *Tir.* 541
A s. not much unlike my simile *Tir.* 910
Whipped out of s. with satire just and keen *T.T.* 640
He trembles at the s. *Y.D.* 24

SIGHTLESS.
The Truth she loves a s. world blaspheme *Ch.* 416

SIGHTLY.
S., and in just order, ere he gives *T.* iii 649
Humour in holiday, and s. trim *T.T.* 643

SIGHT-REFRESHING.
That Nature lives; that s. green *T.* iv 759

SIGN.
For seamen much believe in s. *A Tale* 61
The constant creaking of a country s. *Con.* 10 [ii 83
How does the earth receive him?—with what s. *T.*
Here unmolested, through whatever s. *T.* vi 295
A glory, bright as that of all the s. *Tir.* 282

SIGNAL.
As soldiers watch the s. of command *Ex.* 119
That moving s. summoning, when best *Ex.* 179
Sounds forth the s., as she mounts her car *H.* 647
Still they are frowning s., and bespeak *T.* ii 68

SIGNATURE.
Marked with the *s.* and stamp of Heaven *Ex.* 685
The *s.* and stamp of power divine *R.* 54

SIGNET.
Sealed with his *s.* whom they serve and love *R.* 164

SIGNIFICANT.
The solemn fop, *s.* and budge *Con.* 299
To each his name *s.*, and, filled *Y.O.* 153

SIGNPOST.
Perched on the *s.*, holds with even hand *T.* iv 483

SILENCE.
And *s.* every fear with—God is just *H.* 370 [598
Some dream that they can *s.*, when they will *P.E.*
And, *s.* publicly enjoined *P.T.* 21
But leisure, *s.*, and a mind released *R.* 139
Or plead its *s.* as its best applause *R.* 414
Thy generous powers, but *s.* honoured thee *S.* i 7
The Poet's treasure, *s.*, and indulge *T.* i 235
To muse in *s.*, or at least confine *T.* iii 36
For their own sake its *s.* and its shade *T.* iii 321
In selfish *s.*, but imparted oft *T.* iii 394
From clamour, and whose very *s.* charms *T.* iii 735
Fast bound in chains of *s.*, which the fair *T.* iv 53
The *s.* and the warmth enjoyed within *T.* iv 310
Charms more than *s.* Meditation here *T.* vi 85
Your sullen *s.* serves at least to tell *V.* 25

SILENCING.
For *s.* so sweet a throat *T.B.* 59

SILENT.
Fate steals along with *s.* tread *A Fable* 36
Hush—*s.* readers profit most *A Tale* 29
Has one that notices his *s.* grief *Ch.* 207
That cheers the *s.* journey of the night *Ch.* 320
The *s.* pace with which they steal away *Comp.* i 3
S. and chaste she steals along *Comp.* ii 3
The fear of being *s.* makes us mute *Con.* 352
The circle formed, we sit in *s.* state *Con.* 379
And in the *s.* watches of the night *Con.* 731
If he be *s.*, faith is all a whim *Con.* 853
Swept Ouse's *s.* tide *D.W.* 2
Consult Life's *s.* clock, thy bounding vein *Ep.* i 3
But Conscience, in some awful, *s.* hour *H.* 215
Has wept a *s.* flood, reversed his ways *H.* 519
The *s.* progress of thy power is such *H.* 665
There was a time when Ætna's *s.* fire *Her.* 1
Join me, amid your *s.* hours *Miss* — 19
Those winding modestly a *s.* course *R.* 78
That tongue is *s.* now ; that *s.* tongue *R.* 289
While Peace possessed these *s.* bowers *S.* 14
Betrays the secret of their *s.* course *T.* 196
The law grown clamorous, though *s.* long *T.* 261
What ! *s.* ? Is your boasting heard no more ? *T.* 567
And *s.* cipher, while her proxy plays *T.* i 477
Are *s.* Revelry, and dance, and show *T.* ii 79
And *s.* woods I wander, far from those *T.* iii 118
A *s.* witness of the headlong rage *T.* iii 218
Of *s.* tears and heart-distending sighs ! *T.* iii 331
No unimportant, though a *s.* task *T.* iii 378
The *s.* circle fan themselves and quake *T.* iv 149
Fretful if unsupplied ; but *s.*, meek *T.* v 31 [iv 728
Though stretched at ease in Chertsey's *s.* bowers *T.*
That till the skies nightly with *s.* pomp *T.* v 817
And, intercepting in their *s.* fall *T.* vi 75
One *s.* eve I wandered late *The Doves* 5
By *s.* magnanimity alone *T.T.* 68

SILENTLY.
With tiptoe-step Vice *s.* succeeds *Ex.* 84
Which even now, though *s.* performed *T.* iv 323
Because deserving, *s.* retire *T.* iv 419

Lies undissolved ; while *s.* beneath *T.* v 99
S. as a dream the fabric rose *T.* v 144

SILK. [941
That as she sweeps him with her whistling *s. T.* vi
Wandering, and littering with unfolded *s. T.* vi 280

SILKEN.
Caught in a delicate, soft, *s.* net *P.E.* 313
Unsoiled and swift, and of a *s.* sound *T.* iv 212
Or twining *s.* threads round ivory reels *T.* iv 264

SILKY.
Thick overspread with moss and *s.* grass *N.A.* 2

SILLIEST.
The ostrich, *s.* of the feathered kind *Tir.* 789

SILLY.
As *s.* pride and idleness produce *Ex.* 50 [129
Much wondered that the *s.* sheep had found *N.A.*
The *s.* unsuccessful Bee *P.B.* 22 [380
With awkward gait, stretched neck, and *s.* stare *P.E.*
His *s.* sheep, what wonder if they stray ? *P.E.* 119
A *s.* fond conceit of his fair form *T.* ii 420
In *s.* dotage on created things *T.* v 586

SILVER.
More precious than *s.* and gold *A.S.* 27
Knight of the *s.* Moon, Sir Marmadan *A.T.* 136
He wipes and scours the *s.* cup in vain *Ex.* 385
When a bar of pure *s.* or ingot of gold *F.M.* 1
Thy *s.* locks, once auburn bright *M.* 25
Then, with his *s.* beard and magic wand *P.E.* 183
Cowper, whose *s.* voice, tasked sometimes hard *S.* i 1
Not so ; the *s.* trumpet's heavenly call *T.* 349
And poplar that with *s.* lines his leaf *T.* i 310
Her *s.* globes, light as the foamy surf *T.* vi 155
And tells them, as he strokes their *s.* locks *Tir.* 322
The God that strings the *s.* bow *Trans. H.* 28
And makes his pupils proud with *s.* pence *T.T.* 509

SILVER-END.
Deep in the abyss of *S.*—*E.* i 42

SILVERED.
Not yet by time completely *s.* o'er *T* ii 703

SIMILAR.
Deserves an answer *s.*, or none *Tir.* 904

SIMILARITY.
As *s.* of mind *F.* 175

SIMILE.
This *s.* were apt enough *E.* iv 47
With *s.* to illustrate it *E.* iv 62
We have our *s.* cut short *E.* iv 65
A sight not much unlike my *s. Tir.* 910

SIMILITUDE.
Attend ;—an apt *s.* shall show *T.* 236
Soon shows the strong *s.* reversed *Tir.* 443

SIMPERING.
A *s.* countenance, and a trifling air *P.E.* 206
If smiling peeresses, and *s.* peers *T.T.* 131

SIMPLE.
How *s.* wedlock fornication works *A.T.* 159
The *s.* native of the new found isle *Ch.* 30
And made so welcome at their *s.* feast *Con.* 532
" Look to the poor ; the *s.* and the plain *Ex.* 452
Their language *s.*, as their manners meek *H.* 764
With all the *s.* and unlettered poor *P.E.* 506
Are life's prime pleasures in his *s.* view *R.* 403
Improved the *s.* plan ; made three legs four *T.* i 29
And heard our music ; are thy *s.* friends *T.* i 645
Thy *s.* fare, and all thy plain delights *T.* i 646
I would express him *s.*, grave, sincere *T.* ii 399
His warm but *s.* home, where he enjoys *T.* iii 389
Once *s.*, are initiated in arts *T.* iv 493

SIMPLE—SINGLE

But his own s. pleasures; now and then T. iv 625
The s. clerk, but loyal, did announce T. vi 661 [137
Whose humorous vein, strong sense, and s. style Tir.
Our innocent sweet s. years again Tir. 313
He drinks his s. beverage with a gust T.T. 240

SIMPLEST.
What s. minds can soonest comprehend H. 452

SIMPLICITY.
Majestic in its own s. T. 27
She, safe in the s. of hers T. 336
I seek divine s. in him T. ii 432
The footsteps of S., impressed T. iv 520
Elegant as s., and warm T.T. 588

SIN.
Others, that earth, ere s. had drowned it all A.T. 46
S. forged, and Ignorance made fast, the chain Ch.237
Is still the progeny and heir of s. Ch. 344
But lest I seem to s. against a friend Ch. 485 [469
That Heaven and Hell, and righteousness and s. Con.
Well spoken, advocate of s. and shame Con. 587
And while at heart s. unrelinquished lies Con. 673
Then mirth is s., and we should always cry Con. 878
Were s. in me, and an offence to you E. ii 4
Reminds them of their hated inmate s. E. ii 36
Had grace for others' s., but none for theirs Ex. 12
When nations are to perish in their s. Ex. 95
That S. let loose speaks Punishment at hand Ex. 160
Cured of the golden calves, their fathers' s. Ex. 215
While thousands careless, of the damning s. Ex. 388
When s. has shed dishonour on thy brow Ex. 394
Hast thou within thee s., that in old time Ex. 414
Denouncing death upon the s. of man H. 512 [592
And say;—" Blot out my s., confessed, deplored H.
That shows how far 'tis safe to follow s. H. 608
And he that finds his Heaven must lose his s. H. 638
Of fools that hate thee and delight in s. H. 745 [651
Drives through the realms of s., where Riot reels H.
Those awful syllables, Hell, Death, and S.—H. 690
Without the s. of violating thine M.P. 117
The s. and madness of mankind P.B. 14
Cry in his startled ear, " Abstain from s.!" P.E. 38
S.'s rotten trunk, concealing its defects P.E. 288
To regions where, in spite of s. and woe R. 27
To spare no passion, and no favourite s. R. 136
The grave admits no cure for guilt or s. St. ii 30
And loathed the thought of s. St. iii 28
New as ever seem our s. St. iv 27
Was blasphemy his s.? Or did he stray T. 48 [51
(Such were the s. with which he charged his Lord) T.
Their s. is plain, but what have we to fear T. 129
They never s.—or if (as all offend) T. 285
The supposition is replete with s. T. 347
That man is dead in s., and life a gift T. 514
Such evil S. hath wrought, and such a flame T. ii 133
It seems the part of wisdom, and no s. T. iv 336
His principle, and tempt him into s. T. iv 454
Hence merchants, unimpeachable of s. T. iv 676 [605
Far worse than all the plagues with which his s. T. v
And s. without disturbance. Often urged T. v 659
But s. marr'd all ; and the revolt of man T. vi 368
Thanks for thy food. Carnivorous, through s. T. vi457
When s. hath moved him, and his wrath is hot T.vi742
It may succeed; and, if his s. should call Tir. 410
The powers that S. has brought to a decline T.T. 383

SINAI.
From S.'s top Jehovah gave the law T. 549

SINCERE.
The seaman, with s. delight A Tale 57
Of narrative s. Cast. 50
Than while his conduct proves his heart s. Con. 766
The priest, whose office is, with zeal s. Ex. 97
The priestly brotherhood, devout, s. Ex. 438
Meek, modest, venerable, wise, s. Ex. 620
That friends should be s. and just F. 158
Was much too generous and s. F.B. 23
To prove that what she gives she gives s. H. 62
That dropped upon his Bible was s. H. 575
Perhaps a frail memorial but s. M.P. 72
That prize belongs to none but the s. P.E. 578
Though sage advice of friends the most s. R. 249
We meet at last in one s. desire R. 389
S. on Virtue's side St. iii 18
Thus Heaven approves, as honest and s. T. 225
Thou knowest my praise of Nature most s. T. i 150
I would express him simple, grave, s. T. ii 399
Half so refined or so s. as ours T. iv 206
Patriots are grown too shrewd to be s. T. v 495
Of laughter his compunctions are s. T. v 616
And now, his prowess proved, and his s. T. vi 531
And constancy s. The Doves 14
Yet is thy root s., sound as the rock Y.O. 116

SINCERITY.
S. towards the heart-searching God Con. 753
S.! why 'tis his only pride Con. 757
But will s. suffice? F. 55
Hates with a deep s. the true H. 642
Of some s., on the giver's part T. ii 559

SINECURE.
To make God's work a s.; a slave T. ii 390

SINEW.
Plies all the s. of industrious toil Her. 69
Spreads all his canvass, every s. plies T. 5
That s. bought and sold have ever earned T. ii 32
That ask robust, tough s., bred to toil T. iii 405

SINEWY.
Had reached the s. firmness of their youth T. v 288

SINFUL.
A pale procession of past s. joys H. 221
(Had he the s. part expressed L.W. 9
S. and weak, in every sense a wretch T. 383
Over a s. world; and what remains T. vi 736

SING.
" Seraglios s., and harems dance for joy! A.T. 108
And while, at intervals, a cold blast s. Ex. 720
They sang as blithe as finches s. F.B. 7
When I s. of the splendour of mine Gr. 56
Well spake the prophet,—" Let the desert s. H. 524
Did s. most loud and clear J.G. 204
Now let us s., long live the King J.G. 249
The angry Muse thus s. thee forth M.B. 23
I dreamed what I cannot but s. M.D. 3
Taught you to s., and me to shine N.G. 20
But s. and shine by sweet consent N.G. 31
S., Muse, (if such a theme, so dark, so long P.E. 1
The winds play no longer and s. in the leaves P.F. 3
So s. he, charmed with his own mind and form T. 411
I s. the Sofa. I who lately sang T. i 1
Such joys has he that s. But ah ! not such T. ii 304
And yet ambitious not to s. in vain T. ii 312
And those Arcadian scenes, that Maro s. T. iv 515
Upon the yielding herbage (so they s.) T. iv 521
In vain the poet s., and the world hears T. vi 1018
S., then—and extend thy span Trans. iii 27
And now he s., and now is sick Trans. iv 28
And I will s., if Liberty be there T.T. 295
And I will s., at Liberty's dear feet T.T. 296
S. where you please, in such a cause I grant T.T. 298

SINGING.
The voice of s. and the sprightly cord T. ii 78

SINGLE.
For thou art born sole heir, and s. E. iv 3

Find not, or hardly find, a *s.* friend *Ex.* 118
Were all collected in thy *s.* arm *Ex.* 704
Returned him not a *s.* word *J.G.* 179
By his good will would keep us *s. P.T.* 32
Nor slept a *s.* wink, or purred *R.C.* 75
Reproach a people with his *s.* fall *T.* 234
'Tis called a book, though but a *s.* page) *Tir.* 122
No; not a *s.* thought like that *Trans.* ii 22
Of chiefs whose *s.* arm could boast 1789, 5.

SINISTER.
Another of *s.* views *F.* 53

SINK.
They shriek and *s.*, survivors start and weep *R.* 159
I pity, and must therefore *s.* the name *R.* 576
And *s.*, while favoured with the means to rise *T.* 544
They *s.* and settle lower than they need *T.* v 249
Tend downward; his ambition is to *s. T.* v 592
His moment when to *s.* and when to rise *T.* vi 130
In prostitution *s.* the sense of shame *T.T.* 415
I *s.* the poet in the friend *U.* 30

SINKING.
Till *s.* in the quicksand he defends *P.E.* 552
'Tis criminal to leave a *s.* state *R.* 478

SINNER.
So fares it with the *s.*, when he feels *T.* 257
Than some grave *s.* upon English ground *T.* 292
That bind the *s.*'s Bacchanalian brow *T.* 462
As Vengeance can inflict, or *s.* fear *T.* 554
That they are safe, *s.* of either sex *T.* iii 96

SINUOUS.
Conducts the eye along his *s.* course *T.* i 165
S. or straight, now rapid and now slow *T.* iii 778

SION.
The song of *S.* is a tasteless thing *Con.* 715
O *S.!* an assembly such as earth *T.* vi 816

SIPPING. [391
Sweet converse, *s.* calm the fragrant lymph *T.* iii

SIPS.
S. meek infusions of a milder herb *Con.* 268 [441
She should imbue the tongue with what she *s. Con.*
"Adieu," Vinosa cries, ere yet he *s. H.* 357
He that *s.* often, at last drinks it up *P.E.* 581
Assiduous *s.* at every flower 1789, 18

SIR. [no!" *P.A.* 25
He was shocked, *s.*, like you, and answered—"Oh
Her wooed *S.* Airy, by meandering streams *A.T.* 11
But Fate reserved *S.* Airy to maintain *A.T.* 56 [132
Right reverend *S.!* was no concern of theirs *A.T.*
Knight of the Silver Moon, *S.* Marmadan *A.T.* 136
To where the fond *S.* Airy lay entranced *A.T.* 150
S. Airy, not a whit dismayed or scared *A.T.* 171 [187
"By Dian's beams," *S.* Marmadan exclaimed *A.T.*
S., when I flew to seize the bird *B.R.* 1
'Twas Nature, *s.*, whose strong behest *B.R.* 7
What think you, *s.*, of killing Time *B.R.* 27
Oh! thwart me not, *S.* Soph, at every turn *Con.* 91
"*S.!* I believe it on that ground alone *Con.* 233 [282
"Adieu, dear *S.!* lest you should lose it now" *Con.*
"'Tis but a step, *s.*, just at the street's end" *E.* iii 26
Mere folly and delusion—*S.*, your toast *H.* 364 [*E.* iii 27
"For what?"—"An' please you, *s.*, to see a friend"
S. Smug," he cries (for lowest at the board *H.* 413
How much his feelings suffered, sat *S.* Smug) *H.* 416
S. Humphrey, shooting in the dark *M.F.* 9 [538
Such was *S.* Isaac, and such Boyle and Locke *P.E.*
Your hermit, young and jovial *s.! Mor.* 23 [212
Tom quits you, with—"Your most obedient, *S.*" *T.*

Even at your side, *S.*, and before your eyes *T.* 230
Now tell me, dignified and sapient *s. T.* ii 531 [96
"But where, good *s.*, do you confine your kings?" *T.T.*
A captious question, *s.* (and yours is one) *Tir.* 903

SIRE.
Beyond the example of our *s.* digress *Con.* 792
Heroes and worthies of days past, thy *s.? Ex.* 658
The youth, obedient to his *s.*'s commands *P.E.* 377
Each *s.* and dam, of an infernal race *P.E.* 568
The estate his *s.* had owned in ancient years *R.* 579
No; these were vigorous as their *s. St.* i 9
Save their own painted skins, our *s.* had none *T.* i 9
Long time elapsed or e'er our rugged *s. T.* i 68
At the right door. Profusion is the *s. T.* ii 674
Discovering much the temper of her *s. T.* iii 434
Because delivered down from *s.* to son *T.* v 303
The boy's neglected *s.!* a Mother too *T.* vi 43 [318
Hark! how the *s.* of chits, whose future share *Tir.*

SISTER.
Is rather careless of her *s.*'s fame *Ch.* 454
Must hold both *s.*, never seen apart *Ex.* 635
My *s.*, and my *s.* child *J.G.* 13
In short, the charms her *s.* had *J.P.* 27
Then April with her *s.* May *N.* 17

SIT. [*Con.* 463
There *s.* and prompts him with his own disgrace
Designed to *s.* close to it just like a saddle *A.C.* 16
The circle formed, we *s.* in silent state *Con.* 379
They learn to bow, to kneel, to *s.*, to stand *Ex.* 120
To rise at noon, *s.* slipshod and undressed *H.* 75
Fasting and prayer *s.* well upon a priest *H.* 403
S. absolute on his unshaken throne *H.* 474
Who cannot *s.* upright *J.G.* 90
There *s.* quiescent on the floods that show *M.P.* 92
S. banquetting, and God provides the feast *P.E.* 166
Gorgonius *s.*, abdominous and wan *P.E.* 217
S. linking cherry-stones, or platting rush *R.* 398
She might repose, or *s.* and think *R.C.* 6
He who *s.* from day to day *St.* iv 1
S. long and late at the carousing board? *T.* 50
See where he *s.*, contemplative and fixed *T.* 415
So *s.* two Kings of Brentford on one throne *T.* i 78
Her mingled suits and sequences, and *s. T.* i 475
Between supporters; and, once seated, *s. T.* i 479
To distant shores, and she would *s.* and weep *T.* i 540
And force them *s.*, till he has pencilled off *T.* ii 292
Or does he *s.* regardless of his works? *T.* ii 516
Men that if now alive, would *s.* content *T.* ii 541
That *s.* a stigma on his father's house *T.* ii 760 [385
And crowded knees, *s.* cowering o'er the sparks *T.* iv
There *s.*, involved and lost in curling clouds *T.* iv 472
Or disregard our follies, or that *s. T.* v 877
S. cooing in the pine-tree, nor suspends *T.* v 308
Wins public honour; and ten thousand *s. T.* vi 633
He *s.* secure, and in the scale of life *T.* vi 970
And, if admitted at thy board he *s. Tir.* 725
You think, no doubt, he *s.* and muses *Trans.* ii 19
The dinner comes, and down they *s. Y.D.* 37
S. half the pleasures of short life away! *Y.O.* 32

SITE.
Its elevated *s.* forbids the wretch *T.* i 239

SITTEST.
Cry aloud, thou that *s.* in the dust *Ex.* 267

SITTING.
Thus *s.*, and surveying thus at ease *T.* iv 94

SITUATION.
And shine by *s.*, hardly less *T.* ii 296
New *s.* give a different cast *Tir.* 440
On *s.* that they never felt *T.T.* 169

SIX.
In the last scene of her s. thousand years *Con.* 456
Ethelred's house, the centre of s. ways *H.* 302
S. precious souls, and all agog *J.G.* 39
S. gentlemen upon the road *J.G.* 233
Nobly distinguished above all the s. *P.E.* 161
S. thousand years of sorrow have well nigh *T.* vi 734
To set a distich upon s. and five *T.T.* 507

SIXTEEN.
There shall he learn, 'ere s. winters old *Tir.* 210

SIXTH. [106
And the s. Edward's, grace the historic page *T.T.*

SIZE.
Rose from a seed of tiny s. *E.* i 95
Both baby-featured, and of infant s. *P.E.* 201
Then welcome errors, of whatever s. *P.E.* 283
Halting on crutches of unequal s. *P.E.* 560 [s. *R.* 67
Whose shape would make them, had they bulk and
Fruits of a blighted s., austere and crude *T.* 494
Of public note, they reach their perfect s. *T.* i 696
And glossy, he commits to pots of s. *T.* iii 512
And magnified beyond all human s. *T.* iv 542
And with a gravity beyond the s. *T.* vi 654
The stout tall captain, whose superior s. *Tir.* 222
Beyond a s. that can be managed well *Tir.* 502
Different in s., but in effect the same *Tir.* 516 [633
Yon circling worlds, their distance, and their s. *Tir.*
Proportioned to his s. *Trans.* i 12

SKEIN.
They disentangle from the puzzled s. *T.* iii 145

SKIFF. [*T.* ii 152
Moved not, while theirs was rocked like a light s.

SKILFUL.
As if, like arches built with s. hand *Ex.* 286
S. alike to seem devout and just *R.* 689
Keen enough, wise and s. as thou art *T.* iii 207
Then s. most when most severely judged *T.* v 869
A s. guide into poetic ground! *T.T.* 717

SKILL. [*A.C.* 6
With a great deal of s., and a wig full of learning
The solemn trifler, with his boasted s. *Ch.* 355
No s. in swordmanship, however just *Ch.* 509
But though we praise the exact designer's s. *Ch.* 555
Victorious seemed, and now the doctor's s. *Con.* 320
Their s. a truth, his master's a pretence *Con.* 418
They build each other up with dreadful s. *Con.* 687
By power divine, and s. that could not err *Ex.* 206
The glowing tablets with juster s. *Ex.* 232 [702
But if He leave thee, though the s. and power *Ex.*
That make superior s. his second praise *H.* 206 [542
(Yet charge not heavenly s. with having planned *H.*
A painter's s. into a poet's hand *H.* 670
Thus men go wrong, with an ingenious s. *P.E.* 556
Then sweet to muse upon his s. displayed *R.* 51
(Infinite s.) in all that He has made! *R.* 52
Virtuous and faithful Heberden, whose s. *R.* 279
That yields not to the touch of human s. *R.* 344
What happy s. and industry combined *T.* 430
None more admires, the painter's magic s. *T.* i 422
Great s. have they in palmistry, and more *T.* i 570
With what superior s. we can abuse *T.* i 637
'Tis generous to communicate your s. *T.* ii 282
Than by the labour and the s. it cost *T.* ii 297
Not tire, demanding rather s. than force *T.* iii 407
The vigilance, the labour, and the s. *T.* iii 548
To artists ingenuity and s. *T.* iv 797 [iv 495
But none with readier s.!—'Tis here they learn *T.*
For s. in government, at length made king *T.* v 241
That oft we owe our safety to a s. *T.* vi 619 [753
Though poor in s. to rear them, lights at last *T.* vi
That, if his country stand not by his s. *T.* vi 975

With all the s. of age *Th.* 8
That form, the labour of Almighty s. *Tir.* 7
The wall on which we tried our graving s. *Tir.* 300
His s. in coachmanship, or driving chaise *Tir.* 326
In all true worth and literary s.? *Tir.* 378
Small s. in Latin, and still less in Greek *Tir.* 385
Your son come forth a prodigy of s. *Tir.* 525
Such microscopic proof of s. and power *Tir.* 637
Or doing nothing with a deal of s. *T.T.* 193 [357
S. to direct, and strength to strike the blow *T.T.*

SKILLED.
The statesman, s. in projects dark and deep *Ch.* 612
If smooth Dissimulation, s. to grace *T.T.* 129
S. in the characters that form mankind *T.T.* 705

SKILLET.
S., and old carved chest, from public sale *T.* iv 402

SKIM.
To purge and s. away the filth of vice *P.E.* 343
That s. the spacious meadow at full speed *T.* vi 331
He cannot s. the ground like summer birds *T.* vi 921

SKIN.
S. may differ, but affection *N.C.* 15
Save their own painted s., our sires had none *T.* i 9
Their fluttering rags, and shows a tawny s. *T.* i 538
He finds his fellow guilty of a s. *T.* ii 12
Kindle a fiery boil upon the s. *T.* ii 183

SKIN-PIERCING.
S. volley, blossom-bruising hail *T.* v 141

SKIP.
To s. and gambol like a fawn *Ep.* ii 23
The things that mount the rostrum with a s. *T.* ii 409
And then s. down again; pronounce a text *T.* ii 410
Spread little wings, and rather s. than fly *T.T.* 579

SKIPPED.
Forth s. the cat, but now replete *R.C.* 99

SKIPPING.
Designed thy cradle; and a s. deer *Y.O.* 25

SKIRT. [184
That sweep the s. of some far-spreading wood *T.* i
O'ertop the lofty wood that s. the wild *T.* i 558
Found too where most offensive, in the s. *T.* ii 822
That s. the horizon, wore a sable hue *T.* iv 320

SKIRTED.
And s. thick with intertexture firm *T.* i 111

SKITTISH.
The s. fancy with facetious tales *T.* i 470

SKULK. [375
But counterfeit is blind, and s. through fear *Con.*
Not s., or put on a prudential mask *T.T.* 312

SKULL.
And carry, in contusions of his s. *Con.* 201
And useless as a candle in a s. *Con.* 780
Must have a most uncommon s. *P.T.* 8
On s. that cannot teach, and will not learn *T.* ii 394

SKY.
As ever swept a winter s. *A Fable* 11
Obscurest night involved the s. *Cast.* 1
Alike the wrath and mercy of the s. *Ch.* 70
Oh! could I worship aught beneath the s. *Ch.* 254
A captive bird into the boundless s. *Ch.* 269
He reads the s., and, watching every change *Ch.* 333
Reflect the noonday glory of the s. *Ch.* 398
When one that holds communion with the s. *Ch.* 435
Its fruit on earth, its growth above the s. *Ch.* 578
As if in close committee on the s. *Con.* 385 [486
And veil your daring crest that braves the s. *Con.*
Built by that architect who built the s. *Con.* 560

Presumes itself chief favourite of the *s. Con.* 674
It is the allotment of the *s. E.* i 33
And bid a dawning *s.* display *E.* i 77
The fervour and the force of Indian *s. Ex.* 12
The graces of a life that wins the *s. Ex.* 112
Are far too mean for Him that rules the *s. Ex.* 138
The future tone and temper of the *s. Ex.* 158 [228
Had poured the day, and cleared the Roman *s. Ex.*
To charm to sleep the threatening of the *s. Ex.* 404
They left their bones beneath unfriendly *s. Ex.* 524
Nor spare a life too short to reach the *s. Ex.* 623
And this delightful earth, and that fair *s. Ex.* 638
A bolder still, a contest with the *s.? Ex.* 699
Ambitious of brushing the *s. Gr.* 4 [*H.* 49
From the blue rim, where *s.* and mountains meet
Familiar with the wonders of the *s. H.* 442
The rage and rigour of a polar *s. H.* 462 [*H.* 591
Which, aimed at him, have pierced the offended *s.*
But brighter beams than his who fires the *s. H.* 491
But while they speak the wisdom of the *s. H.* 768
And hang their horrors in the neighbouring *s. Her.* 16
That there is bliss prepared in yonder *s. J.T.* 13
Since first our *s.* was overcast *M.* 2
Heard shouts that ascended the *s. M.D.* 39
" Prepare it for the *s.*" *Miss* — 92
The son of parents passed into the *s. M.P.* 111
How glad they catch the largess of the *s. N.A.* 62
With all these hideous howlings to the *s. N.A.* 88
Speaking from his throne, the *s.? N.C.* 28
To form an Iris in the *s. O.* i 19 [*P.E.* 74
Detach the soul from earth and speed her to the *s.?*
Or whether clearer *s.* and softer air *P.E.* 409
So he who seeks a mansion in the *s. P.E.* 576
Hear the just law—the judgment of the *s.! P.E.* 606
Darkness the *s.* had mantled o'er *Q.V.* 33
One Georgian star adorns the *s. Q.V.* 75
That melt and fade into the distant *s. R.* 424
And show the august tribunal of the *s. R.* 656
Sends Nature forth, the daughter of the *s. R.* 795
" My home henceforth is in the *s. St.* iii 9
What but a sordid bargain for the *s.? T.* 76
The rude inclemency of wintry *s. T.* 138
Her title to a treasure in the *s. T.* 330
Supreme on earth, and worthy of the *s. T.* 408
In vain he points his powers against the *s. T.* 469
Assert the *s.*, and vindicate her due *T.* 490
The wretch who slights the bounty of the *s. T.* 543
Angelic gratulations rend the *s. T.* 587
Beneath the open *s.* she spreads the feast *T.* i 433
Have kindled beacons in the *s.*, and the old *T.* ii 59
I would not yet exchange thy sullen *s. T.* ii 212
The legate of the *s.*!—His theme divine *T.* ii 338
Whose flambeaux flash against the morning *s. T.* ii 648
Heaven-born, and destined to the *s.* again *T.* iii 50
Sought in still water, and beneath clear *s. T.* iii 382
I would at least bewail it under *s. T.* v 487
To soar, and to anticipate the *s. T.* v 723
That fill the *s.* nightly with silent pomp *T.* v 817
Yet not in vengeance ; as his smiling *s. T.* vi 258
Nor freezing *s.* nor sultry, checking me *T.* vi 297
Below the *s.*, but having there his home *T.* vi 914
With which Aurora decks the *s. T.B.* 16
And when descending he resigns the *s. Tir.* 37
Brings into doubt the wisdom of the *s. Tir.* 72
Nor ignorantly wandering miss the *s. Tir.* 108
In that bright quarter his propitious *s. Tir.* 395
That kindles up the *s. Trans.* i 10
Expect a brighter *s. Trans. H.* 27
Religion, richest favour of the *s. T.T.* 268
Courage, ungraced by these, affronts the *s. T.T.* 378
Fancy that from the bow that spans the *s. T.T.* 702
And giving one, whose heart is in the *s. V.* 93
The frowns of a *s.* so severe *W.N.* 18

Destroys them—*s.* uncertain, now the heat *Y.O.* 74
And flash thanksgivings to the *s.*! 1789, 55

SLAB.

A massy *s.*, in fashion square or round *T.* i 21

SLACK.

That she is *s.* in discipline; more prompt *T.* i 730
His country, or was *s.* when she required *T.* iii 89
The mind He gave me; driving it, though *s. T.* iii 369
He sees that human equity is *s. T.* vi 472

SLACKENED.

Has *s.* to a pause, and we have borne *T.* i 155

SLAIN.

You left where he was *s. Beau* 12
Vice seems already *s. H.F.* 6
Like a *s.* deer, the tumbrel brings him home *P.E.* 94
S. at the foot of Pleasure be no crime *P.E.* 182
Feed on the *s.*, but spare the living brute! *T.* vi 458
" Worthy the Lamb, for he was *s.* for us!" *T.* vi 792

SLAKED.

The thirst than *s.* it, and not seldom bred *T.* ii 509

SLANDER.

The very butt of *s.*, and the blot *H.* 558
If Acrimony, *S.*, and Abuse *T.T.* 762

SLANDERER.

There were the scorner's and the *s.*'s tongue *Ex.* 36

SLANDEROUS.

Condemns the injurious deed, the *s.* tongue *T.* 559

SLANT.

Upon the southern side of the *s.* hills *T.* vi 59

SLANTING.

Shades *s.* at the close of day *Mor.* 15
Seen through the leafless wood. His *s.* ray *T.* v 6

SLAUGHTER.

Driven to the *s.*, goaded as he runs *T.* vi 421

SLAVE.

That man by Faith and Truth is made a *s. A.T.* 66
Patience itself is meanness in a *s. Ch.* 164
And he that scorns it is himself a *s. Ch.* 227
And *s.*, by truth enlarged, are doubly freed *Ch.* 231
And he grown chaste that was the *s.* of lust *Con.* 810
He saw his people *s.* to every lust *Ex.* 55
Thou wast the veriest *s.*, in days of yore *Ex.* 526
Themselves the *s.*, of bigotry or lust *Ex.* 529 [546
O *s.*! with powers thou didst not dare exert *Ex.*
" I go to make Freemen of *S.*" *M.D.* 16
She sung of the *s.*'s broken chain *M.D.* 19
To the black-sceptred rulers of *s. M.D.* 47
But though *s.* they have enrolled me *N.C.* 7
S. of gold, whose sordid dealings *N.C.* 53
I own I am shocked at the purchase of *s. P.A.* 1
A mere church-juggler,—hypocrite and *s. P.E.* 109
Made nothing but a brute, the *s.* of sense *P.E.* 214
In vain : the *s.* of arrogance and pride *P.E.* 548
And atheist, if Earth bear so base a *s.*) *P.E.* 615
The dupes of pleasure, or the *s.* of gain *R.* 24
No *s.* on earth more welcome were than they *T.* 352
I would not have a *s.* to till my ground *T.* ii 29
I had much rather be myself the *s. T.* ii 35 [37
We have no *s.* at home:—Then why abroad? *T.* ii
S. cannot breathe in England ; if their lungs *T.* ii 40
To make God's work a sinecure; a *s. T.* ii 390
As in the bosoms of the *s.* he rules *T.* v 310
True to the death, but not to be his *s. T.* v 345 [374
But *s.* that once conceive the glowing thought *T.* v
Of Liberty, themselves the *s.* of lust *T.* v 499
" Dishonours God, and makes a *s.* of man *T.* v 643
Grace makes the *s.* a freeman. 'Tis a change *T.* v 688
And all are *s.* beside. There's not a chain *T.* v 734

If man be what he seems, this hour a *s. Tir.* 59
Religion makes the free by nature *s. Tir.* 184
The *s.* of custom and established mode *Tir.* 251
A *s.* at court, elsewhere a lady's man *Tir.* 423
Is base in kind, and born to be a *s. T.T.* 28
No sycophant or *s.,* that dared oppose *T.T.* 350
Freeman and *s.* then, if the case be such *T.T.* 254
As if he heard his king say, " *S.,* be free! " *T.T.* 245
That *s.,* howe'er contented, never know *T.T.* 261
S. fight for what were better cast away *T.T.* 282
Slips the *s.*'s collar on, and snaps the lock *T.T.* 477

SLAVE-CULTURED.
To a *s.* island we came *M.D.* 26

SLAVERY.
But *s.!*—Virtue dreads it as her grave *Ch.* 163
Exported *s.* to the conquered East? *Ex.* 365
He can encourage *s.* to a smile *T.T.* 252

SLAVISH.
" Feel all the meanness of your *s.* lot *A.T.* 112
Scorns the base hireling, and the *s.* drudge *T.* 228
The *s.* dread of solitude, that breeds *T.* i 488

SLAY.
The hand that slew till it could *s.* no more *Ch.* 49
Agreed. But would you sell or *s.* your horse *T.T.* 301

SLAYING.
And *s.* man would cease to be an art *Ch.* 619

SLEEKEST.
Were brighter than the *s.* mole *T.B.* 14

SLEEP.
Might burn his useless Machiavel, and *s. Ch.* 613
Carelessly nods and *s.* upon the brink *Ex.* 99
To charm to *s.* the threatening of the skies *Ex.* 404
Ere Nature rose from her *s. Ex.* 637
They *s.* secure from waking *F.* 123
His passions, like the watery stores that *s. H.* 183
After long *s.,* of passion in the heart *J.T.* 42
How regular his meals, how sound he *s.! R.* 430
That shines and rests, as infants smile and *s. R.* 528
Then all the world of waters *s.* again *R.* 536
And slept as she would *s.* her last *R.C.* 48
Is left to *s.* for peace and quiet sake *T.* 428
The nurse *s.* sweetly, hired to watch the sick *T.* i 89
To *s.* within the carriage more secure *T.* i 92
Sweet *s.* enjoys the curate in his desk *T.* i 94
And sweet the clerk below. But neither *s. T.* i 96
Nor *s.* enjoyed by curate in his desk *T.* i 100
And *s.* not ; see him sweating o'er his bread *T.* i 363
To carry me, to fan me while I *s. T.* ii 30
Great crimes alarm the conscience, but it *s. T.* iii 185
And *s.* and is refreshed. Meanwhile the face *T.* iv 298
S. seems their only refuge: for, alas! *T.* iv 396
Where chanticleer amidst his harem *s. T.* iv 447
Then *s.* was undisturbed by Fear, unscared *T.* iv 561
And slumbers unalarmed ! Now, ere you *s. T.* iv 566
Authority herself not seldom *s. T.* iv 593
Screens them, and seems half petrified to *s. T.* v 28
But violence can never longer *s. T.* v 204
The undiscoverable secret *s. T.* v 537   [876
Gods such as guilt makes welcome ; gods that *s. T.* v
'Tis desperate, and he *s.* the *s.* of death *T.* v 669
Of leaf and flower ? It *s.* ; and the icy touch *T.* vi 137
Who *s.* not, is not weary ; in whose sight *T.* vi 226
In *s.* he seemed to view *T.B.* 45
Merely to *s.,* and let them run astray ? *Tir.* 908
The rudiments should *s.* the winter through *Y.O.* 28

SLEEPING.
A *s.* fog, and fancies it dry land *T.* 4
The *s.* leaves, is all the light they wish *T.* i 763

SLEET.
Except with snow and *s. A Tale* 18
Thy scattered hair with *s.* like ashes filled *T.* iv 121
The gloomy clouds, find weapons, arrowy *s. T.* v 140

SLEEVE.
And hoards them in her *s.* ; but needful food *T.* i 554
One wipes his nose upon his *s. Y.D.* 41

SLENDER.
A laugh at his expense, is *s.* praise *R.* 318
And disappoints the roots ; the *s.* roots *T.* iii 611
With *s.* notes, and more than half suppress'd *T.* vi 78
Of flowers, like flies clothing her *s.* rods *T.* vi 166
By *s.* threads, and swinging in the breeze *Tir.* 592

SLEPT.
As private as the chambers where they *s. Ex.* 144
S. he in Adam ? And in those from him *F.A.* 24
Starts from the down on which she lately *s. H.* 219
S. unperceived, the mountain yet entire *Her.* 2
And *s.* as she would sleep her last *R.C.* 48
Nor *s.* a single wink, or purred *R.C.* 75
Then Study languished, Emulation *s. T.* ii 734
Where memory *s.* Wherever I have heard *T.* vi 12

SLEW.
The hand that *s.* till it could slay no more *Ch.* 49

SLICE.
Yet likes a *s.* as well as he *L.W.* 36
How oft, my *s.* of pocket-store consumed *T.* i 118

SLICED.
S. carrot pleased him well *Ep.* ii 20

SLIDE.
S. guinea behind guinea in his palm *Ch.* 474
Too well acquainted with their smiles, *s.* off *T.* i 511
S. ineffectual down the snowy vale *T.* v 7
And soon to *s.* into a stream again *T.* v 168

SLIDING.
The slippery seat betrayed the *s.* part *T.* i 46
The moonbeam, *s.* softly in between *T.* i 762
A *s.* car, indebted to no wheels *T.* iv 126

SLIGHT.
And hast thou sworn on every *s.* pretence *Ex.* 386
Too small perhaps the *s.* occasion *E.* i 85
" My favorite Nymph to *s. J.P.* 34
For one *s.* trespass all this stir ? *M.F.* 21
We *s.* the precious kernel of the stone *P.E.* 419
And *s.* the season and the scene *S.* 12
A *s.* gratuity atones for all *T.* 288   [666
He *s.* the strokes of conscience. Nothing moves *T.* v
The wretch who *s.* the bounty of the skies *T.* 543
And *s.* the hovel as beneath her care *T.* ii 459
I *s.* thee not, but make thee welcome still *T.* iv 266
Who *s.* the charities for whose dear sake *T.* v 507
Familiar with th' effect we *s.* the cause *T.* vi 121
Who, if their sons some *s.* tuition share *Tir.* 783
The rest will *s.* thy counsel, or condemn *Tir.* 805
Howe'er he *s.* thee, thou hast done thy part *Tir.* 898

SLIGHTED.
And, though disgraced and *s.,* to redeem *Ch.* 13
He spurned the wretch that *s.,* or withstood *Ch.* 31
Beauties he lately *s.* as he passed *R.* 425
Her *s.* works to your admiring view *R.* 543
Hear then now mercy, *s.* and defied *T.* 501
Returns indignant to the *s.* plough *T.* iv 645
But *s.* as it is, and by the great *T.* iv 691
Till time has stolen away the *s.* good *T.* vi 51
Holds no ignoble, though a *s.,* place *T.* vi 971
Speaking in parables his *s.* word *Tir.* 140

SLIGHTEST.
For such a cause, to feel the *s.* fear *N.A.* 90

SLIGHTING.
His more sublime vagaries s. *E.* i 17
SLIGHTLY.
Nothing is s. touched, much less forgot *Con.* 317
SLIP.
To every sudden s. and transient wrong *H.* 390
Shines as it runs, but grasped at s. away *P.E.* 22
Admires the work but s. the lesson by *R.* 214
S. to his hammock, and forgets the blast *R.* 436
Of neighbouring fountain, or of rills that s. *T.* 192
Some trivial s. their daily walk attend *T.* 286
Let s. with such a warrant to destroy? *T.* ii 54
S. the slave's collar on, and snaps the lock *T.T.* 477
SLIPPER.
Who stole her s., filled it with Tokay *T.* 157
SLIPPERY.
And honest Merit stands on s. ground *Ch.* 284
The s. seat betrayed the sliding part *T.* i 46
Can seize the s. prey, unties the knot *T.* ii 685
But urged by storms along its s. way *T.* iv 127
And s. the materials, yet frostbound *T.* v 155
SLIPSHOD.
To rise at noon, sit s. and undressed *H.* 75
With s. heels, and dewdrop at his nose *T.* 144
SLOES.
The bramble, black as jet, or s. austere *T.* i 122
SLOPE.
But rude at first, and not with easy s. *T.* i 64
And where the land s. to its watery bourn *N.A.* 13
The s. of faces, from the floor to the roof *T.* iv 202
SLOPING. [*Ch.* 368
Some through the groves, some down the s. hills
In peace upon her s. sides matured *Her.* 10
The s. land recedes into the clouds *T.* i 171
He settles next upon the s. mount *T.* iii 486
SLOTH.
Such squalid s. to honourable toil! *T.* i 579
In gross and pampered cities, s., and lust *T.* i 687
And well prepared, by ignorance and s. *T.* ii 388
Small thanks to those whose negligence or s. *T.* ii 800
He may compensate for a day of s. *T.* iv 434
On the same cushion of habitual s. *T.* iv 598
While s. seduces more, too weak to bear *T.* vi 105
Allows short time for play, and none for s. *Tir.* 484
SLOTHFUL.
Not s.; happy to deceive the time *T.* iii 362
Not s. he, though seeming unemployed *T.* vi 928
SLOUCH.
He stands erect; his s. becomes a walk *T.* iv 639
SLOUGH.
And sore discomfited, from s. to s. *T.* iii 5
SLOVENLY.
Than in a churchman s. neglect *T.* ii 456
Surly and s., and bold and coarse *T.T.* 682
SLOW.
With s. deliberation he unties *Ch.* 471
With hesitation admirably s. *Con.* 123
For God unfolds by s. degrees *E.* i 59
How s. to learn the dictates of his love *E.* ii 20
Till I, with s. and cautious hand *F.B* 29
Yet man, laborious man, by s. degrees *Her.* 67
I saw the hearse that bore thee s. away *M.P.* 29
Lips busy, and eyes fixed, foot falling s. *R.* 285
He sighs,—for after all, by s. degrees *R.* 465
Led them, however faltering, faint, and s. *T.* 537
Was bliss reserved for happier days;—so s. *T.* i 83
With curvature of s. and easy sweep *T.* i 352 [i595
His fierceness, having learnt, though s. to learn *T.*

And recognise the s. retiring fair *T.* ii 454 [*T.* iii 492
S. gathering in the midst, through the square mass
In volumes wheeling s., the vapour dank *T.* iii 499
Experience, s. preceptress, teaching oft *T.* iii 505
And to the stir of Commerce, driving s. *T.* iii 739
Sinuous or straight, now rapid and now s. *T.* iii 778
With matron step s. moving, while the Night *T.* iv 246
Procure him many a curse. By s. degrees *T.* iv 635
He yet by s. degrees puts off himself *T.* iv 637 [48
Now creeps he s.; and now, with many a frisk *T.* v
By s. solicitation, seize at once *T.* vi 116 [*T.* vi 547
Was now to learn that Heaven, though s. to wrath
S. circling ages are as transient days *T.* vi 227
S. after century, a giant bulk *Y.O.* 63
S., into such magnificent decay *Y.O.* 90
SLOWER.
With scarce a s. flight *D.W* 12
SLOWLY.
And while the victim s. bled to death *Ex.* 498
If chance, on heavy pinions s. borne *H.* 716
Full s. pacing o'er the stones *J.G.* 79
The clouds that flit, or s. float away *R.* 192
And s., and by most unfelt, the face *T.* iv 321
SLOW-MOVING.
The distant plough s., and beside *T.* i 160
A pompous and s. pageant comes *T.* vi 697
SLOW-PACED.
And patient of the s. swain's delay *T.* v 32
SLOW-REVOLVING.
Ye s. seasons! We would see *T.* vi 824
SLOW-RISING.
I see a column of s smoke *T.* i 557
SLOW-WINDING.
Fast by the banks of the s. Ouse *R.* 804
Here Ouse, s. through a level plain *T.* i 163
SLUGGISH.
To the clogged wheels; and in its s. pace *T.* iv 345
SLUMBER.
And s. on in state *Miss* — 28
As he that s. in pavilions graced *R.* 509
Invited her to s. there *R.C.* 42
To s. in the carriage more secure *T.* i 99
To tell its s., and to paint its dreams *T.* iii 13
To thy straw couch, and s. unalarmed *T.* iii 345
And s. unalarmed! Now, ere you sleep *T.* iv 566
Nor ask his leave to s. or to play *T.* vi 405
The mind that s. sweetly in her snares *T.T.* 439
SLUMBERING.
And s. oscitancy mars the brood? *T.* ii 774
Again she lays them s. on the shore *Tir.* 26
SLUNG.
The bottles he had s. *J.G.* 106
Their miserable meal. A kettle, s. *T.* i 560
SLUR.
I s. a name, a poet must not speak) *H.* 565
SLY.
And finds it a mere mask of s. grimace *Con.* 744
And stab Religion with a s. side-thrust *R.* 690 [201
You have two servants,—Tom, an arch, s. rogue *T.*
S. circumvention, unrelenting hate *T.* i 615 [105
With his s. scythe, whose ever-nibbling edge *Y.O.*
SMACK. [519
Were trained beneath his lash, and knew the s. *Ex.*
S. went the whip, round went the wheels *J.G.* 41
And now a hearty s. *Trans.* iv 18
SMALL. [83
S. need of Prayer Book, or of priest, I ween *A.T.*

SMALL—SMILING 403

Guns, halberts, swords and pistols, great and s. *Ch* 551
As needs they must, from great to s.! *E.* i 80
Too s. perhaps the slight occasion *E.* i 85
Friendship a blessing cheap or s. *E.* i 92
Thy soul as ample as thy bounds are s. *Ex.* 696
The great and s. but rarely meet *F.* 115 [*P.E.* 281
The breach, though s. at first, soon opening wide
In part abate, that happiness were s. *N.A.* 112
Within the s. dimensions of a point *R.* 58
There prisoned in a parlour snug and s. *R.* 493
His utmost he can render is but s. *T.* 199
The poor are near at hand, the charge is s. *T.* 287
Come, then—a still, s. whisper in your ear *T.* 297
Envy, ye great, the dull unlettered s. *T.* 375
Some s. pre-eminence; we justly boast *T.* ii 275
S. thanks to those whose negligence or sloth *T.* ii 800
The few s. embers left she nurses well *T.* iv 383
The still s. voice is wanted. He must speak *T.* v 685
Can move or warp; and gratitude for s. *T.* vi 629
The theatre, too s., shall suffocate *T.* vi 670
Shine with his fair example, and though s. *T.* vi 961
S. skill in Latin, and still less in Greek *Tir.* 385 [356
Whose heirs, their honours none, their income s. *Tir.*
Saves the s. inventory, bed, and stool *T.* iv 401
And s. academies win all the praise? *Tir.* 504 [515
The great and s. deserve one common blame *Tir.*
Securely placed between the s. and great *Tir.* 808
Might serve, however s. *Trans.* i 18
Contemplating with s. delight 1789, 24

SMALLER.
A s. piece amidst the precious store *Ch.* 476
Afford the s. minstrels no supply *T.* v 84

SMART.
From stuccoed walls s. arguments rebound *H.* 346
The bow well bent, and s. the spring *H.F.* 5
Ere long some bowing, smirking, s. Abbé *P.E.* 385
Strange world, that costs it so much s. *St.* v 15
To thaw him into feeling; or the s. *T.* iv 197
Indebted to some s. wig-weaver's hand *T.* iv 543
His form, and movement; is as s. above *T.* iv 641
And sighs for the s. comrades he has left *T.* iv 648

SMARTED.
Think how many backs have s. *N.C.* 23

SMARTLY.
Wit now and then, struck s., shows a spark *T.T.* 663

SMARTNESS.
No s. in the jest, and wonders why *T.* i 469

SMATCH.
We give some Latin, and a s. of Greek *P.E.* 365

SMELL.
Thenceforth 'tis hateful, for it s. of you *Con.* 44
The sight's enough—no need to s. a beau *Con.* 285
Nor grateful eglantine regales the s. *H.* 471 [59
The wretch may pine, while to his s., taste, sight *H.*
In colour these, and those delight the s. *R.* 794
S. fresh, and, rich in odoriferous herbs *T.* i 531
Some show that nice sagacity of s. *T.* vi 616

SMELT.
Civited fellows, s. ere they are seen *Tir.* 830

SMILE.
He soothed with gifts, and greeted with a s. *Ch.* 29
The s. of opulence in sorrow's face *Ch.* 130 [312
The poor thy clients, and Heaven's s. thy fee! *Ch.*
A teacher should be sparing of his s. *Ch.* 490
And force me to a s. *Ep.* ii 36
Is she not clothed with a perpetual s.? *Ex.* 4
The treacherous s., a mask for secret hate *Ex.* 42
They stood the test of her ensnaring s. *Ex.* 78
By every charm that s. upon her face *Ex.* 668
With s. alluring her admirer, man *H.* 40

Were light, when weighed against one s. of thine *H.* 178
And sure it is as kind to s. and give *H.* 323
And Peace the genuine offspring of her s. *H.* 482
Scorns with the same indifference frowns and s. *H.* 650
Where Peace, and Equity, and Freedom s. *Her.* 84
But one, although her s. was sweet *J.P.* 7
Transforms thy s. to looks of woe *M.* 47 [*M.P.* 79
Wouldst softly speak, and stroke my head and s.
Those lips are thine—thy own sweet s. I see *M.P.* 3
Ah, that maternal s.! it answers—"Yes" *M.P.* 27
Where spices breathe and brighter seasons s. *M.P.* 91
And teach Philosophy a s. *Mrs. M*— 30
The banquet of thy s.? *O.* ii 12
The baby seems to s. with added charms *P.E.* 519
And add a s. to what was sweet before *R.* 10
Her s. his aim, all higher aims farewell! *R.* 246 [403
What charms he sees in Freedom's s. expressed *R.*
That shines and rests, as infants s. and sleep *R.* 528
Give Truth a lustre, and make Wisdom s. *R.* 718
Her animating s. withdrawn *S.* 15
For other's woes, but s. upon her own *T.* 178 [407
With youthful s., descends towards the grave *T.* i
Sweet s., and bloom less transient than her own *T.* i 461
Too well acquainted with their s., slides off *T.* i 511
Cheer all their seasons with a grateful s. *T.* i 622
Who squander time and treasure with a s. *T.* ii 641
His eye was meek and gentle, and a s. *T.* ii 706
When gay Goodnature dresses her in s. *T.* ii 784
She s., appearing, as in truth she is *T.* iii 49
As aught occurs that she may s. to hear *T.* iii 395
She brings her infants forth with many s. *T.* iii 437
And seem to s. at what they need not fear *T.* iii 575
Pure is the nymph, though liberal of her s. *T.* iii 712
Even as he bids! The enraptured owner s. *T.* iii 780
And jewel'd turban with a s. of peace *T.* iv 29
Or placemen, all tranquillity and s. *T.* iv 49
Call comedy, to prompt him with a s.? *T.* iv 199
I saw far off the weedy fallows s. *T.* iv 316
And s. delighted with the eternal poise *T.* iv 486
Provokes me to a s. With eye askance *T.* v 14
Her veil opaque, discloses with a s. *T.* v 892
The season s., resigning all its rage *T.* vi 61
Or promising with s. to call again *T.* vi 282
At sight of the man-monster. With a s. *T.* vi 499
For man's revolt, shall with a s. repair *T.* vi 746
And s. to see, her infant's playful hand *T.* vi 779
May be followed perhaps by a s." *The Rose* 20
May teach the gayest, make the gravest s. *Tir.* 138
Whose trade it is to s., to crouch, to please *T.T.* 128
He can encourage slavery to a s. *T.T.* 252
Without the s., the sweetness, or the grace *T.T.* 615
With droll sobriety they raised a s. *T.T.* 658
And winter is decked with a s. *W.N.* 4
Since all thy tears were changed to s. 1789, 57

SMILED.
Or s. when a sabbath appeared *A.S.* 32
Delighted with her babe the enchantress s. *A.T.* 9
Unveiled her blushing cheek, looked on, and s. *Ex.* 425
Frowned oftener than she s. *J.P.* 8
Not altogether s. on theirs *P.T.* 49
And never s. again! and now she roams *T.* i 456
Treacherous and false; it s. and it was cold *T.* v 176
The rude companion s., as if transformed *T.* vi 543

SMILING.
Beneath the s. surface of the deep *H.* 184
Sighing and s. as he takes his glass *H.* 419
And s. divinely, she cried *M.D.* 15
The arts come s. in the close *Miss* — 81
To crown the s. hours *N.* 20
Close packed and s., in a chaise and one *T.* i 80
Of s. Victory that moment won *T.* ii 213
Of s. day, they gossip'd side by side *T.* v 60

And s. say—"My Father made them all!" *T.* v 747
Yet not in vengeance; as this s. sky *T.* vi 258
If s. peeresses, and simpering peers *T.T.* 131
Can call her s. down, and fix her here *T.T.* 413

SMIRKING.
Ere long some bowing, s., smart Abbé *P.E.* 385

SMIT.
S. with the beauty of so fair a scene *T.* v 560

SMITE. [170
"And better spear I s. you where you stand" *A.T.*
To s. the poor is treason against God *Ch.* 217 [627
And s. the untempered wall 'tis death to spare *H.*
The axe will s. at God's command *St.* i 15
And soon shall s. us all *St.* i 16
Displeasure in his breast who s. the earth *T.* ii 69
Not seldom, his avenging arm, to s. *T.* vi 464

SMITH.
As s. or joiners perfect a design *Con.* 790
S., cobbler, joiner, he that plies the shears *T.* iv 476
And the first s. was the first murderer's son *T.* v 219

SMITTEN.
S. in vain! such music cannot charm *T.* v 682

SMOKE.
Important triflers! have more s. than fire *Con.* 250
It is combining fire with s. *F.* 119
Which made his horse's flanks to s. *J.G.* 127
In catching s. and feeding upon air *R.* 38
See where it s. along the sounding plain *T.* 238
I see a column of slow-rising s. *T.* i 557
The hills move lightly, and the mountains s. *T.* ii 91
But frantic who thus spend it all for s.? *T.* iii 174
To be preferred to s., to the eclipse *T.* iii 736
Needs he the tragic fur, the s. of lamps *T.* iv 195

SMOKED.
Rebuilds the towers that s. upon the plain *Her.* 71

SMOKING.
Groves, heaths, and s. villages, remote *T.* i 176
The s. manure, and overspreads it all *T.* iii 517

SMOKY.
Can but arrest the light and s. mist *T.* v 105

SMOOTH.
Was s. and even as an ivory ball *A.T.* 47
And licked his feathers s. *B.R.* 20
Might s. her feathers, and enjoy her cage *Ch.* 306
S., ductile, and even his fancy must flow *F.M.* 18
The sheep here s. the knotted thorn *M.B.* 9
So coin grows s., in traffic current passed *P.E.* 279
Rough elm, or s. grained ash, or glossy beech *R.* 230
'Tis such an easy walk, so s. and straight *R.* 489
"How s. these kerchiefs, and how sweet! *R.C.* 59
As yet black breeches were not, satin s. *T.* i 10
Now came the cane from India, s. and bright *T.* i 39
Obdurate and unyielding, glossy s. *T.* i 52
Alike yet various. Here the grey s. trunks *T.* i 302
The s. and equal course of his affairs *T.* ii 173 [ii 226
Should England prosper, when such things, as s.*T.*
If chance at length he find a greensward s. *T.* iii 7
The seed, selected wisely, plump and s. *T.* iii 511
Must s. be shorn away; the sapless branch *T.* iii 613
S. as a wall the upright remnant stands *T.* v 36
So stood the brittle prodigy; though s. *T.* v 154
They had indeed ability to s. *T.* v 692 [853
Nor s. good-breeding (supplemental grace) *T.* vi
But s. with wands from Ouse's side *T.B.* 28
Your s. eulogium, to one crown addressed *T.T.* 91
If s. Dissimulation, skilled to grace *T.T.* 129

SMOOTHED.
S. and refined the meanest strains *E.* iv 74

Till s. and squared and fitted to its place *T.* vi 95
Notch after notch, till all are s. away *Tir.* 560

SMOOTHER.
But finding soon a s. road *J.G.* 81

SMOOTHEST.
That man, when s. he appears *F.* 23
And meets with hindrance in the s. way *P.E.* 443
On props of s. shaven wood *T.B.* 23

SMOOTHLY.
Sees planetary wonders s. roll *Ch.* 317
While thirteen moons saw s. run *St.* i 1
May bear us s. to the Gallic shore *T.* ii 262
So life glides s. and by stealth away *T.* vi 995

SMOOTHNESS.
Without a creamy s. has no charms *T.T.* 513

SMOOTH-SHAVEN.
Of the s. prop, and neatly tied *T.* iii 659

SMOTE. [65
But wept, and stamped, and s. his thigh in vain *Ex.*
Stamped with his foot, and s. upon his thigh *Ex.* 64

SMOTHER. [281
With light derived from thee, would s. thine *Ex.*
To s. in ignoble rest *Miss* — 7
Whatever else they s. of true worth *T.* iv 746

SMOTHERED.
And thine was s. in the stench and fog *Ex.* 510
And s. in't at last, is praised to death *T.* 316

SMUG. [433
And add Right Reverend to *S.*'s honoured name *H.*

SMUTCH.
But here and there an ugly s. appears *T.* iv 608

SMUTCHED
Respectful of the s. artificer *T.* ii 491

SNACKS.
Pray tell me why we may not also go s.? *P.A.* 16

SNAIL.
An inadvertent step may crush the s. *T.* vi 564

SNAP.
Lest the rude blast should s. the bough *A Fable* 14
And s. the chain the moment when you may *Ch.* 168
But passion rudely s. the string *H.F.* 7
Slips the slave's collar on, and s. the lock *T.T.* 477

SNAPPED.
Your thread of argument is s. again *Con.* 110
Soon follows, and the curb of conscience s. *T.* ii 571
I s. it, it fell to the ground *The Rose* 12

SNAPPING.
The recollected powers, and s. short *T.* iv 305

SNAPPISH.
And s. dialogue, that flippant wits *T.* iv 198

SNARE.
S. in his path, and foes that lurk within *Con.* 470
Whate'er enchants them, are no s. to them *R.* 180
To s. the mole, or with ill-fashioned hook *R.* 401
The path to bliss abounds with many a s. *T.* 301
Exposed their inexperience to the s. *T.* ii 801 [185
The dangers we have 'scaped, the broken s. *T.* iv
The mind that slumbers sweetly in her s. *T.T.* 439

SNATCHED.
When, s. from all effectual aid *Cast.* 63
And unregretted are soon s. away *R.* 167
He s. it rudely from the Muse's hand *T.T.* 689

SNATCHES.
Wide scampering, s. up the drifted snow *T.* v 49

SNEAKING.
Some *s.* virtue lurks in him, no doubt *Tir.* 244

SNEER. [*Con.* 182
Lest fops should censure us, and fools should *s.*
Tell her again, the *s.* upon her face *Con.* 783
And felt the *s.* with scorn enough *P.* 18
Will *s.*, and charge you with a bribe *T.T.* 84
Should move a *s.* at thy deserved fame *Tir.* 142

SNEERED.
All mercy from his lips, and *s.*, and hissed *H.* 561

SNIFFING.
Conjectured, *s.* round and round *T.B.* 40

SNIVELING.
S. and driveling folly without end *P.E.* 310

SNORE.
Of lazy nurse who *s.* the sick man dead *T.* i 97
S. to the murmurs of the Atlantic wave *T.* iv 27
Who, just when industry begins to *s. Tir.* 745

SNORED.
Spent half the darkness, and *s.* out the rest *H.* 510

SNORING.
Whom *s.* she disturbs. As sweetly he *T.* i 90

SNORT.
And *s.* aloud to cast the mist aside *A.T.* 164
Whereat his horse did *s.*, as he *J.G.* 205 [vi 332
Then stops and *s.*, and throwing high his heels *T.*

SNORTING.
The *s.* beast began to trot *J.G.* 83
S., and starting into sudden rage *T.* vi 550

SNOUT.
Till quite from tail to *s.* 'tis eaten *L.W.* 38
With ivory teeth, or ploughs it with his *s. T.* v 50
Long backed, long tailed, with whiskered *s. T.B.* 35
And the mouse with curious *s. Trans.* iii 12

SNOW.
Except with *s.* and sleet *A Tale* 18
On icy plains, and in eternal *s. H.* 464
She towered a cloud-capped pyramid of *s. Her.* 4
Some Alpine mountain wrapped in *s. Miss* — 33
And, river-blanched, the swan his *s. Mrs. M*— 8
Could shelter them from rain or *s. P.T.* 53 [iv 123
Fringed with a beard made white with other *s. T.*
While the winds whistle, and the *s.* descend *T.* iii 569
Noiseless, appears a moving hill of *s. T.* iv 346 [49
Wide scampering, snatches up the drifted *s. T.* v
And *s.*, that often blinds the traveller's course *T.* v 142
And these dissolving *s.*, and this clear stream] *T.* vi 260
While Earth wears a mantle of *s. W.N.* 13

SNOWY.
His *s.* mantle o'er his shoulders threw *A.T.* 202
The *s.* robe her wintry-state assumes *R.* 195
Or lay the landscape on the *s.* sheet *R.* 798
Wrought patiently into the *s.* lawn *T.* iv 152
Slides ineffectual down the *s.* vale *T.* v 7
Indurated and fixed, the *s.* weight *T.* v 98
A splintered stump bleached to a *s.* white *Y.O.* 128

SNUFF.
S. up the morning air, forgets the rein *Ch.* 175
S. up the praise of what he seems to plan *Ex.* 317
Dangling his cane about, and taking *s. H.* 27
He *s.* far off the anticipated joy *P.E.* 219
Ranges at liberty, and *s.* the wind *R.* 630
S. up the wind and flings himself abroad *T.T.* 669

SNUG. [*A.T.* 79
Lay *s.* and warm;—'twas Summer's farewell peep!
And waits, in *s.* concealment laid *Ep.* ii 39
A *s.* and friendly game at cards *L.W.* 28
The *s.*, close party, or the splendid hall *P.E.* 176

Kept *s.* in caskets of close-hammered steel *R.* 308
There prisoned in a parlour *s.* and small *R.* 493
Within her master's *s.* abode *R.C.* 34
Then *s.* enclosures in the sheltered vale *T.* i 513
There blooms exotic beauty, warm and *s. T.* iii 568
None that, in thy domestic *s.* recess *Tir.* 581

SOAK.
When Winter *s.* the fields, and female feet *T.* 215

SOAR.
On waxen pinions *s.* without a fall *A.T.* 54
Around their flight who highest *s.*) *Mrs. M*— 48
To *s.*, and to anticipate the skies *T.* v 723 [548
The man that means success, should *s.* above *T.T.*

SOARING.
And *s.* on her own unborrowed wings *T.* 488

SOBER.
Again, when evening in her *s.* vest *Ch.* 262
And e'en when *s.* truth prevails throughout *Con.* 65
To bring the passions under *s.* sway *Con.* 831
Live to no *s.* purpose, and contend *H.* 129
What health and *s.* appetite demand *H.* 158
Is *s.*, meek, benevolent, and prays *H.* 520
The *s.* cordial of sweet air *Mor.* 10
Observe each face, how *s.* and demure? *P.E.* 134
Then to the dance, and make the *s.* moon *P.E.* 173
If Tom be *s.*, and the wheels well greased *P.E.* 439
Your *s.* thoughts will hardly find it one *P.E.* 489
But modest, *s.*, cured of all *R.C.* 103
These are the *s.*, in whose cooler brains *T.* 38
I say the pulpit (in the *s.* use *T.* ii 332
The rest are *s.* dreamers, grave and wise *T.* iii 137
Cultured and capable of *s.* thought *T.* iii 324
And *s.* judgment that he is but man *T.* v 265
'Tis therefore *s.* and good men are sad *T.* v 509
(Himself grown *s.* in the vale of tears) *T.* vi 48
Finds in a *s.* moment time to pause *Tir.* 56
That mingles all my brown with *s.* gray *Tir.* 144
Or if, by nature *s.*, ye had then *Tir.* 271
Not very *s.* though, nor very chaste *Tir.* 750
Extravagant or *s.*, loose or chaste *Tir.* 914
Quevedo, as he tells his *s.* tale *T.T.* 93
Their *s.* zeal, integrity, and worth *T.T.* 377

SOBEREST.
And thou at best, and in thy *s.* mood *Tir.* 753

SOBERLY.
But that disease, when *s.* defined *Con.* 667

SOBERNESS.
Whom Truth and *S.* assailed in vain *T.* ii 480

SOBRIETY.
S. perhaps may now be found *Con.* 807
With droll *s.* they raised a smile *T.T.* 658

SOBS.
That feeds upon the *s.* and dying shrieks *T.* iii 328

SOCIAL.
God, working ever on a *s.* plan *Ch.* 15
The *s.* walk, or solitary ride *Con.* 733
To close in sable every *s.* scene *Con.* 872
Whence *s.* pleasures spring *Miss* — 30
To *s.* scenes by nature disinclined *R.* 606
Sure there is need of *s.* intercourse *T.* ii 48
A *s.*, not a dissipated life *T.* iii 376
They form one *s.* shade, as if convened *T.* iii 586
With *s.* converse and instructive ease *T.* iv 135
And *s.*, nip his fruitfulness and use *T.* v 439
And plausible than *s.* life requires *T.* v 466

SOCIETY.
S., Friendship, and Love *A.S.* 17
Unfriendly to *s.'s* chief joys *Con.* 252

There, in the sweet *s* of those *Con.* 423
If dear *s.* be worth a thought *Ex.* 670
S. for me! Thou seeming sweet *T.* i 249
Self-banished from *s.*, prefer *T.* i 578
That gives *s.* its beauty, strength *T.* ii 681
S., and that saps and worms the base *T.* ii 816
All hate the rank *s.* of weeds *T.* iii 670
S., grown weary of the load *T.* iv 498
Man in *s.* is like a flower *T.* iv 659

SOCK.
To live by buskin, *s.*, and raree-show *V.* 34

SODOM.
His crimes were such as *S.* never knew *H.* 562
Than *S.* in her day had power to be *T.* iii 847

SOFA.
I sing the *S.* I who lately sang *T.* i 1
And Luxury the accomplished *S.* last *T.* i 88
Compared with the repose the *S.* yields *T.* i 102
Of libertine excess. The *S.* suits *T.* i 106
Though on a *S.*, may I never feel *T.* i 108
No *S.* then awaited my return *T.* i 126
Nor *S.* then I needed. Youth repairs *T.* i 127
To adorn the *S.* with eulogium due *T.* iii 12
And sheltered *S.*, while the nitrous air *T.* iii 32
Let fall the curtains, wheel the *s.* round *T.* iv 37
S., and couch, and high built throne august *T.* v 164
To dress a *S.* with the flowers of verse *T.* vi 1007

SOFT.
And laid her *s.* in amaranthine flowers *A.T.* 8
Nor *s.* enough to suit a lover's tongue *A.T.* 20
Formed with materials neat and *s. A Tale* 39
S. airs and gentle heavings of the wave *Ch.* 127
The noon was shady, and *s.* airs *D.W.* 1
Yet He was gentle as *s.* summer airs *Ex.* 133
These carpets, so *s.* to the foot *Gr.* 17
S. airs and genial moisture feed and cheer *H.* 489
They gentle called, and kind and *s. J.P.* 21
The *s.* relations, which, combined *Miss* — 79 [*N.A.* 37
Sheep grazed the field; some with *s.* bosom pressed
The herb as *s.*, while nibbling strayed the rest *N.A.* 38
And lenient as *s.* opiates to the mind *P.E.* 80
Caught in a delicate, *s.*, silken net *P.E.* 313
Lay bleeding under that *s.* hand of thine *P.E.* 338
The mind, impressible and *s.*, with ease *P.E.* 355
S. airs, nocturnal vigils, and day dreams *R.* 260
Nor *s.* declivities with tufted hills *R.* 333
Her voice is terrible though *s. St.* v 23
Or velvet *s.*, or plush with shaggy pile *T.* i 2
The *s.* Settee; one elbow at each end *T.* i 75
By *s.* recumbency of outstretched limbs *T.* i 82
Our foot half sunk in hillocks green and *s. T.* i 272
The nose of nice nobility. Breathe *s. T.* ii 259
In language *s.* as Adoration breathes! *T.* ii 495
Or when rough winter rages, on the *s. T.* iii 31 [417
Dooms to the knife; nor does he spare the *s. T.* iii
S. fomentation; and invite the seed *T.* iii 510
In the *s.* medium, till they stand immersed *T.* iii 520
Now murmuring *s.*, now roaring in cascades *T.* iii 779
Here rills of oily eloquence *s. T.* iv 64
Falls a *s.* murmur, on the uninjured ear *T.* iv 93
Thine unadulterate manners are less *s. T.* v 465
Deep in his *s.* credulity the stamp *T.* v 497
How *s.* the music of those village bells *T.* vi 6
And settle in *s.* musings as I tread *T.* vi 69
Stillness, accompanied with sounds so *s. T.* vi 83
S. as the passing wind *The Doves* 38
With a song more *s.* and sweet *Trans.* iii 6
If human woes her *s.* attention claim *.T.T.* 484
He laid his head in Luxury's *s.* lap *T.T.* 678
The *s.* receptacle, in which, secure *Y.O.* 27

SOFTENED.
"And fashioning my *s.* heart *Miss* — 91
But *s.* into mercy; made the pledge *T.* i 365

SOFTENS.
And *s.* human rock-work into men *Ch.* 96

SOFTER.
And she regardless of her *s.* kind *A.T.* 177
By *s.* methods, must be made ashamed *Ch.* 498
And teach the *s.* not to copy theirs *Con.* 844
Or whether clearer skies and *s.* air *P.E.* 409
Of distant floods, or on the *s.* voice *T.* 191
'Gan murmur, as became the *s.* sex *T.* i 71
Our *s.* satellite. Your songs confound *T.* i 766
Ye clarionets, and *s.* still, ye flutes *T.* ii 260
That *s.* friend, perhaps more gladly still *T.* vi 44
Born in a climate *s.* far than ours *T.T.* 234
And arts revived beneath a *s.* day *T.T.* 621

SOFTEST.
And show the *s.* minds and fairest forms *Con.* 259
With linen of the *s.* kind *R.C.* 36

SOFTLY. [*Con.* 381
"Yes, ma'am," and "No, ma'am," uttered *s.*, show
Some whispered *s.*, and some twanged aloud *Ch.* 518
We next inquire, but *s.* and by stealth *Con.* 389
So, "Fair and *s.*," John, he cried *J.G.* 85 [*M.P.* 79
Wouldst *s.* speak, and stroke my head and smile)
The moonbeam, sliding *s.* in between *T.* i 762
That *s.* swelled and gaily dressed appears *T.* iii 629
S. alighting upon all below *T.* iv 328

SOIL.
We wander o'er a sunburnt thirsty *s. Ch.* 220
On culture, and the sowing of the *s. Con.* 6 [*Con.* 438
Should range where Providence has blessed the *s.*
Its happiest *s.* in the serenest minds? *Con.* 594
The flinty *s.* indeed their feet annoys *E.* ii 31
"Bespeak at least a stubborn *s. E.* iv 82
Lords of the conquered *s.*, there rooted fast *Ex.* 192
As richest *s.* the most luxuriant weeds *Ex.* 214
Serves merely as a *s.* for discontent *H.* 97
Proclaims the *s.* a conquest he has won *H.* 479
Still happier, if he till a thankful *s. H.* 760
Without a *s.* to invite the tiller's care *Her.* 27
Sweat of ours must dress the *s. N.C.* 20
To meliorate and tame the stubborn *s. R.* 786
No *s.* like poverty for growth divine *T.* 363
Raised by the mole, the miner of the *s. T.* i 273
Here virtue thrives as in her proper *s. T.* i 600
And genial *s.* of cultivated life *T.* i 679 [*s. T.* iii 646
Of close-rammed stones has charged the encumbered
She ploughs a brazen field, and clothes a *s. T.* i 709
Migrates uplifted; and, with all its *s. T.* ii 108
And fruitful *s.*, that has been treasured long *T.* iii 514
The *s.* must be renewed, which often washed *T.* iii 609
Some clothe the *s.* that feeds them, far diffused *T.* iii 662
The worse for what it *s.* The fashion runs *T.* iv 555
The loaded *s.*, and ye may waste much good *T.* v 756
Were sown in human nature's fruitful *s. T.* vi 883
Must find a colder *s.* and bleaker air *Tir.* 851
Beneath thy parent tree mellowed the *s. Y.O.* 24
Upheaved above the *s.*, and sides embossed *Y.O.* 65
The stubborn *s.*, and hold thee still erect *Y.O.* 119

SOILED.
Jerusalem a prey, her glory *s. Ex.* 61
Neatly secured from being *s.* or torn *Tir.* 119

SOJOURN.
We must not now be parted, *s.* here" *Con.* 530
Content indeed to *s.* while he must *T.* vi 913

SOL.
"Till *S.*, declining in the west *R.C.* 62

SOLACE.
Had been their mutual s. long *F.B.* 5
Reserved to s. many a neighbouring squire *N.A.* 5
Sometimes her ease and s. sought *R.C.* 15

SOLACED.
The same that oft in childhood s. me *M.P.* 4

SOLAR.
Transmitting cloudless, and the s. beam *Y.O.* 75

SOLD.
Love is not pedler's trumpery bought and s. *H.* 330
Men from England bought and s. me *N.C.* 5
Minds are never to be s. *N.C.* 8   [s. *T.T.* 331
Cheap though blood-bought, and thrown away when
And pardons are not s. as once they were *T.* 290
That sinews bought and s. have ever earned *T.* ii 32
Was marked and shunned as odious. He that s. *T.*iii 88
That authors are most useful pawned or s. *Tir.* 211
What sums he lost at play, and how he s. *Tir.* 330
Writes on his bosom, "To be let or s." *T.T.* 417

SOLDIER.
Heedless of a s.'s name *B.* 22
As s. watch the signal of command *Ex.* 119
And grace thy figure with a s.'s pride *Ex.* 487
A s. may be anything, if brave *H.* 209
A s.'s best is courage in the field *H.* 405
The s. thus endowed, who never shrinks *H.* 409
They made us many s. Chatham, still *T.* ii 245
A s.'s feather, or a lady's glove *T.T.* 549

SOLDIERSHIP.
How, in the name of s. and sense *T.* ii 225
'Tis universal s. has stabbed *T.* iv 617

SOLDIERY.
Thy s., the Pope's well managed pack *Ex.* 518

SOLE.
His s. opinion, whatsoe'er befall *Con.* 133   [336
With s.—that's just the sort he would not wish *Con.*
For thou art born s. heir, and single *E.* iv 3
Himself s. author of his own disgrace? *H.* 317
Unmasked, vouchsafing this their s. excuse *T.* ii 695
Are his s. aim, and all his glory now *T.* iv 658
Survivor s., and hardly such, of all *Y.O.* 1

SOLEMN.   [29
So his lordship decreed, with a grave s. tone *A.C.*
The s. trifler, with his boasted skill *Ch.* 355
Toils much, and is a s. trifler still *Ch.* 356
The pipe, with s. interposing puff *Con.* 245
The s. fop, significant and budge *Con.* 299
It happened on a s. eventide *Con.* 505
Still murmuring with the s. truths I teach *Ex.* 719
He treads as if, some s. music near *T.* 62
Tho s. chords, and with a trembling hand *T.* i 3
Suffer a syncope and s. pause *T.* ii 80
With s. awe, that bids me well beware *T.* ii 327
And plain in manner; decent, s., chaste *T.* ii 401
Of s. farce, where Ignorance in stilts *T.* ii 736
Exhausted, he resorts to s. themes *T.* v 661
And s. ceremonial of the day *T.* vi 680

SOLEMNITY.
"In what, with such s. of tone *T.* v 648

SOLICIT.
The world around s. his desire *P.E.* 39
S. kind attention to his dream *P.E.* 523
S. pleasure, hopeless of success *T.* ii 635

SOLICITATION.
By slow s., seize at once *T.* vi 117

SOLICITING.
With gentle force s. the darts *T.* iii 115

SOLICITOUS.
For plunder; much s. how best *T.* iv 433

SOLID.
Compress the sum into its s. worth *Con.* 20
Where sharp and s., phlegmatic and light *Ex.* 296
That shook the circling seas and s. earth *Her.* 14
And drilled in holes, the s. oak is found *T.* i 26
What s. was, by transformation strange *T.* ii 99
The s. earth, and from the strata there *T.* iii 151
His broad keen knife into the s. mass *T.* v 35
Excused the incumbrance of more s. worth *Tir.* 347
Though s., not too weighty for his years *Tir.* 651
Thou hadst within thy bole s. contents *Y.O.* 94

SOLITARY.
The social walk, or s. ride *Con.* 733
A s. thing—" *Miss* — 32
Umbrageous walks and s. seats *R.* 258
That screen the herdsman's s. hut *T.* i 168
The s. Shilling. Pardon then *T.* iii 456
From morn to eve his s. task *T.* v 44
That makes so gay his s. place *T.* vi 187
When, Isaaclike, the s. saint *T.* vi 948
Doom him not then to s. meals *Tir.* 719

SOLITUDE.
O *S.*! where are the charms *A.S.* 5
As in some s. the summer rill *J.T.* 38
The man to s. accustomed long *N.A.* 55
For s., however some may rave *R.* 735
"How sweet, how passing sweet is s.! *R.* 740
Whom I may whisper—s. is sweet" *R.* 742
Bury herself in s. profound *T.* 443
If *S.* make scant the means of life *T.* i 248
The slavish dread of s., that breeds *T.* i 488
For a lost world in s. and verse *T.* iv 730
To barrenness, and s., and tears *T.* v 441
Pleased with his s., and flitting light *T.* vi 79

SOLOMON.
That *S.* has wisely spoken *E.* i 105

SOLUTION.
Knots of worthy s., which alone *T.* ii 520

SOLVE.
A Deity could s. Their answers, vague *T.* ii 521

SOLVED.
Not to be s., and useless if it might *F.A.* 34

SOLYMA.
Glorious as *S.*'s interior shrine *T.* 388

SOMEBODY.
S. proved it centuries ago *P.E.* 501

SON
Dame Gurton thus, and Hodge her s. *E.* iv 39
People and priest, the s. of Israel were *Ex.* 124
Her s. to pour it on the farthest north *H.* 460
Famine, and Pestilence, her firstborn s. *Her.* 59
Hovered thy spirit o'er thy sorrowing s. *M.P.* 23
The s. of parents passed into the skies *M.P.* 111
Afric's s. should undergo *N.C.* 37
Then pour it on the morals of thy s. *P.E.* 345 [596
So once were ranged the s. of ancient Rome *T.* iii
The s. of Albion; fearing each to lose *T.* iii 599
Who had survived the father, served the s. *T.* iii 748
And the first smith was the first murderer's s. *T.* v 219
Because delivered down from sire to s. *T.* v 303 [517
And hewed them link from link. Then Albion's s. *T.* v
Were s. indeed; they felt a filial heart *T.* v 518
Sent forth a voice, and all the s. of God *T.* v 821 [29
Some friend is gone, perhaps his s.'s best friend! *T.* vi
Ye, therefore, who love mercy, teach your s. *T.* vi 588
Would you your s. should be a sot or dunce *Tir.* 201

408 SON—SORE

Made just the adept that you designed your s. Tir.237
To send our s. to scout and scamper there Tir. 294
Resolves that where he played his s. shall play Tir.335
His intercourse with peers and s. of peers Tir. 393
In barbarous prostitution of your s. Tir 405
Than set your s. to work at a vile trade Tir. 456
Your s. come forth a prodigy of skill Tir. 525
A father blest with an ingenuous s. Tir. 543
Thou well deservest an alienated s. Tir. 579
And is he well content his s. should find Tir. 617
To form thy s., to strike his genius forth Tir. 679
And all the instructions of thy s.'s best friend Tir.717
Through reverence of the censor of thy s. Tir. 734
Hear Nature plead, show mercy to thy s. Tir. 756
Who, if their s. some slight tuition share Tir.783
To lead his s., for prospects of delight Tir. 630 [811
Who, wise yourselves, desire your s. should learn Tir.
And Freedom claims him for her firstborn s. T.T. 281

SONG.

The linnet twittered out his parting s. A.T. 76 [198
Love graced the theme, and harmony the s. A.T.
And cheered her with a s. A Tale 56
The s. of Sion is a tasteless thing Con. 715
Like useless lumber, or a stroller's s. Con. 820
Till tuned at length to some immortal s. Con. 907
We therefore pleased extol thy s. Dr. 9
I know the warning s. is sung in vain Ex. 724
Two goldfinches, whose sprightly s. F.B. 4
To him that blends no fable with his s.) H. 755 [19
But oh! what Muse, and in what powers of s. Her.
The middle of my s. J.G. 156
To poets of renown in s. J.P. 17
Who bidst me honour with an artless s. M.P. 13
Had cheered the village with his s. N.G. 2
As much as I to spoil your s. N.G. 18
May find a Muse to grace it with a s. P.E. 2
The fall of waters, and the s. of birds R. 183
Could argue once, could jest, or join the s. R. 290
And cultivate a taste for ancient s. R. 375
Are musical enough in Thomson's s. R. 570
And lulled by her own humdrum s. R.C. 46
Yearly in my s. proclaim St. iv 10
Would give a barbarous air to British s. T. 102
The s. magnificent, the theme a worm T. 412
Weeps tears of joy, and bursts into a s. T. 458
The occasion—for the Fair commands the s. T. i 7
Is famished—finds no music in the s. T. i 468
Or seldom such, the hearers of his s. T. ii 305
But is amusement all? Studious of s. T. ii 311 [314
Could pageantry and dance, and feast and s. T. iii
And at this moment unassayed in s. T. iii 451
Sarcastic, would exclaim, and judge the s. T. iii 563
The hills and valleys with their ceaseless s. T. v 78
An Orpheus, and omnipotent in s. T. v 694
No bard embalms and sanctifies his s. T. v 728
In feast or in the chase, in s. or dance T. v 758 [887
Till thou hast touched them, 'tis the voice of s. T. v
One s. employs all nations; and all cry T. vi 791
Patiently present at a sacred s. T. vi 634
Of Avon, famed in s. Ah pleasant proof T. vi 682
Renowned in ancient s.; not vexed with care T. vi 997
Say, Muse, for education made the s. Tir. 290
With a s. more soft and sweet Trans. iii 6
Theirs is but a summer's s. Trans. iii 21
Heroic s. from thy free touch acquires T.T. 292
All that should be the boast of British s. T.T. 369
To the lascivious pipe and wanton s. T.T. 462
I play with syllables, and sport in s. T.T. 505
To him who strains his all into a s. T.T. 533
The s. was moral, and so far was right T.T. 599
And claim the palm for purity of s. T.T. 636
Inspires the s., and that his name is Love T.T. 739

The burden of my s. Y.D. 4
I ransacked, for a theme of s. 1789, 1

SONGSTER.

The s. heard his short oration N.G. 23
He from Italian s. takes his cue P.E. 112
Himself a s., is as gay as he T. i 498

SONOROUS.

Clear and s., as the gale comes on! T. vi 10

SOOTHE.

And s. the sorrows of so sad a state Ch. 199   [39
And every moment's calm, that s. the breast E. ii
Thyself removed, thy power to s. me left M.P. 121
Sweet Harmony that s. the midnight hour P.E. 66
S. thee to make thee but a surer prey R. 263
Might s. a soul less hurt than mine S. 7
To s. and satisfy the human ear T. 199
From thee is all that s. the life of man T. v 900
To s. their honest pride, that scorns to beg T. iv 405
That s. the rich possessor; much consoled T. iv 755

SOOTHED.

He s. with gifts, and greeted with a smile Ch. 29
Thus s. and reconciled, each seeks L.R. 25
My relish of fair prospect; scenes that s. T. i 141
S. with a waking dream of houses, towers T. iv 287
And s. into a dream that he discerns T. vi 284
And s. the listening dove The Doves 8

SOOTHING.

Till others have the s. tale believed P.E. 493
Still s., and of power to charm me still T. i 143
The s. influence of the wafted strains T. vi 68
In s. sorrow, and in quenching strife T. vi 963

SOOTY.

The s. films that play upon the bars T. iv 292

SOPH.

Oh! thwart me not, Sir S., at every turn Con. 91

SOPHISTRY.

With s. their sauce they sweeten L.W. 37
So s. cleaves close to and protects P.E. 237

SOPORIFIC.

Falls s. on the listless ear P.E. 20

SORCERESS.

" And guard behind the s. at thy back!" A.T. 190

SORCERIES.

But Rome, with s. and magic wand Ex. 508

SORDID.

As He ordains things s. in their birth Ch. 561
Its s. nourishment from man's applause Con. 672
That stands on s. interest F. 38
The s. never know Miss — 54
Slaves of gold, whose s. dealings N.C. 53
His unexhausted mine, the s. vice P.E. 51
S. as active, ignorant as loud R. 22
What, but a s. bargain for the skies? T. 76
Of critic appetite, no s. fare T. iii 461
S. and sickening at his own success T. iii 810
In those that suffer it, a s. mind T. v 453
And s. gravitation of his powers T. v 588
To such base hopes, in many a s. soul Tir. 460

SORE.

Although it grieved him s. J.G. 54
And s. against his will J.G. 158
And s. tormented long before his time T. 84
May still be seen; but perforated s. T. i 25
And vex their flesh with artificial s. T. i 582
And s. discomfited, from slough to slough T. iii 5
The wain goes heavily, impeded s. T. iv 343
Which filthily bewray and s. disgrace Tir. 593

SOREST.
That s. ill of human life *M.F.* 32

SORROW.
My s. I then might assuage *A.S.* 21
The smile of opulence in s.'s face *Ch.* 130
All other s. virtue may endure *Ch.* 157
And soothe the s. of so sad a state *Ch.* 199
The scene of all those s. left behind *Con.* 508
That comes to waft us out of s.'s power *Con.* 592
The s. Sympathy esteems its own *Con.* 696
The path of s., and that path alone *E.* ii 9
Leads to the land where s. is unknown *E.* ii 10
Thy tender s. and thy plaintive strain *E.* ii 45
From east to west, no s. can be found *Ex.* 28
Till, all my stock of infant s. spent *M.P.* 43
Remorse, and *S.*, and vindictive Pain *P.E.* 44
From scenes of s. into glorious day *R.* 168
His only bliss is s. for her sake *R.* 244
Or charm the s. of a drooping friend *R.* 292
Of s., is is a sacred thing *R.* 316
Hear him, o'erwhelmed with s., yet rejoice *R.* 772
And those of s. yet to come *S.* 24
S. might muse herself to madness then *T.* 441
Of hours that s. since has much endeared *T.* i 117
Thy joys and s., with as true a heart *T.* ii 220
Without some thistly s. at its side *T.* iv 335
And make the s. of mankind their sport *T.* v. 186
S. has, since they went, subdued and tamed *T.* vi 46
Six thousand years of s. have well nigh *T.* vi 734
In soothing s., and in quenching strife *T.* vi 963
Already to s. res gned *The Rose* 16
And wet his cheeks with s. not his own *V.* 66
And the winter of s. best shows *W.N.* 23
In sooth the s. of such days *Y.D.* 17
For that dear s.'s sake forego 1789, 52

SORROWFUL.
From Africa's s. shore *M.D.* 32
Oh s. and sad ! the streaming tears *T.* 173

SORROWING.
Hovered thy spirit o'er thy s. son *M.P.* 23

SORT.
Nor was he of the thievish s. *Beau* 13 [336
With sole—that's just the s. he would not wish *Con.*
Thus hopes of every s., whatever sect *H.* 294
His horse, who never in that s. *J.G.* 93
The text that s. not with his darling whim *P.E.* 446
Should turn to writers of an abler s. *R.* 716
Apparelled in exactest s. *R.C.* 19
To deal and shuffle, to divide and s. *T.* i 474
Or growl'd defiance in such angry s. *T.* vi 377 [114
What friends we s. with, or what books we read *Tir.*
When health demands it, of athletic s. *Tir.* 653
And faithful in its s. *U.* 10

SORTED.
And s. hues (each giving each relief *T.* iii 634

SORTING.
S. and puzzling with a deal of glee *Con.* 13
In s. flowers to suit a fickle taste *H.* 767

SOT.
Between the s. and sensualist *F.* 41
Would you your son should be a s. or dunce *Tir.* 201

SOTTISH.
The effect of laziness or s. waste *T.* iv 431

SOUGHT.
Many he s., but one above the rest *A.T.* 3
Long-time a breeding-place they s. *A Tale* 21
S., with an indignant mien *B.* 3
And in his country's glory s. his own *Ch.* 26
He s. the jewel in his neighbour's shame *Ch.* 540
Thus have I s. to grace a serious lay *Ch.* 628
S. their own village, busied as they went *Con.* 509
With cane extended far I s. *D.W.* 17
Had s. to crush them, guarded as they were *Ex.* 205
Return ashamed, without the wreaths they s. *Ex.* 293
Not quickly found, if negligently s. *Ex.* 695
We s. without attaining *F.* 36
Yet seldom s. where only to be found *H.* 112
But guests that s. it in the appointed One *H.* 307
By contemplation's help, not s. in vain *M.P.* 114
Or s. with energy, must fill the void *R.* 748
Sometimes her ease and solace s. *R.C.* 15
And s. it in the likeliest mode *R.C.* 33
And take unenvied the reward they s. *T.* 528
S. in still water, and beneath clear skies *T.* iii 382
With schemes of monumental fame; and s. *T.* v 182
And forced to abandon what she bravely s. *T.* v 368
His horrible intent, again he s. *T.* vi 525
Deep in the flood found, when he s. it not *T.* vi 555
Harmony, strength, words exquisitely s. *T.T.* 701
I s. an eligible theme 1789, 8

SOUL. [*Con.* 707
The Christian, in whose s., though now distressed
But not the mitred few, the s. their charge *A.T.* 129
Nor felt but in the s. that Heaven selects *Ch.* 8
In baser s. unnumbered evils meet *Ch.* 37
While Providence enjoins to every s. *Ch.* 121 [*Ch.*264
My s. should yield thee willing thanks and praise
That s. have no discriminating hue *Ch.* 202
With rich instruction, and a s. enlarged *Ch.* 322 [395
The s., whose sight all-quickening grace renews *Ch.*
But still a s. thus touched can never cease *Ch.* 420
And though the s. shall seek superior orbs *Ch.* 563
Like him, the s. thus kindled from above *Ch.* 595
Given him a s., and bade him understand *Con.* 430
The time is short, and there are s. on earth *Con.* 493
When s. drawn upwards in communion sweet *Con.* 569
Who makes no bustle with his s.'s affairs *Con.* 580
But s. that carry on a blest exchange *Con.* 693
The s. can mix with the celestial bands *Con.* 717
The s.'s sure interest in the good she seeks *Con.* 728
Nor shall be found in unregenerate s. *Con.* 755
And while it shows the land the s. desires *Con.* 885
And spreads, at length, before the s. *E.* i 63
In pity to the s. his Grace designed *E.* ii 23
Then God's own image on the s. impressed *Ex.* 109
Hast thou (a sacrilege his s. abhors) *Ex.* 346
And if some Spartan s. a doubt expressed *Ex.* 542
Thy s. as ample as thy bounds are small *Ex.* 696 [374
And having trucked thy s., brought home the fee *Ex.*
My s. shall sigh in secret, and lament *Ex.* 722
But every virtue of the s. *F.* 58
Some fickle creatures boast a s. *F.* 109
O Friendship! if my s. forego *F.* 211
And crowns the s., while yet a mourner here *H.* 165
Kind s. ! to teach their tenantry to prize *H.* 252
Nor animate the s. to Christian deeds *H.* 300
His s. abhors a mercenary thought *H.* 332
Invades, possesses, and o'erwhelms the s. *H.* 730
Six precious s., and all agog *J.G.* 39
Now mistress Gilpin (careful s.!) *J.G.* 65
And every s. cried out, " Well done ! " *J.G.* 111
Perhaps a tear, if s. can weep in bliss *M.P.* 26 [99
But ah! those dreadful yells what s. can hear *N.A.*
Consumes his s. with vain desires *P.B.* 16 [*P.E.* 74
Detach the s. from earth, and speed her to the skies
And kindles in his s. a treacherous fire *P.E.* 40
But as a scale, by which the s. ascends *R.* 3 [*P.E.*165
When the glad s. is made Heaven's welcome guest
S. that have long despised their heavenly birth *R.*35
A s. serene, and equally retired *R.* 143
'Tis consecration of his heart, s., time *R.* 223

Forbids the advancement of the *s*. he binds *R*. 236
But with a *s*. that ever felt the sting *R*. 315
All such as manly and great *s*. produce *R*. 699
His *s*. exults, Hope animates his lays *R*. 777
Might soothe a *s*. less hurt than mine *S*. 7
Then breathed his *s*. into his rest *St*. iii 15
A *s*. redeemed demands a life of praise *T*. 279
How perfect the composure of his *s*.! *T*. 418
The *s*. reposing on assured relief *T*. 455
"And is the *s*. indeed so lost"—she cries *T*. 479
And withered muscle, and the vapid *s*. *T*. i 393
My *s*. is sick, with every day's report *T*. ii 6
And serves the altar, in my *s*. I loathe *T*. ii 416
To court a grin, when you should woo a *s*. *T*. ii 467
Bone of my bone, and kindred *s*. to mine *T*. iii 220
A corresponding tone in jovial *s*. *T*. iii 333
Fearless, a *s*. that does not always think *T*. iv 285
Becomes the *s*. that animates them all *T*. v 275
He seeks, and acquiescence of his *s*. *T*. v 597
And chills and darkens a wide-wandering *s*. *T*. v 684
The *s*. that sees him, or receives sublimed *T*. v 805
The uninformed and heedless *s*. of men *T*. v 864
Breaks on the *s*., and by a flash from Heaven *T*. v 884
There is in *s*. a sympathy with sounds *T*. vi 1
A *s*. in all things, and that *s*. is God *T*. vi 185
His *s*. refreshed with foretaste of the joy? *T*. vi 762
But borrows all its grandeur from the *s*. *Tir*. 10
And guides the Progress of a *s*. to God *Tir*. 146
The gem of truth from his unguarded *s*. *Tir*. 152
To such base hopes, in many a sordid *s*. *Tir*. 460
And that, possessor of a *s*. refined *Tir*. 721
He bears it with meek manliness of *s*. *T.T.* 225
The *s*., emancipated, unoppressed *T.T.* 272
And darts his *s*. into the dawning plan *T.T.* 499
A *s*. exalted above Earth, a mind *T.T.* 704
A *s*., an image of Himself, and therefore true *V*. 98

SOUL-QUICKENING.
Stand the *s*. words—Believe and Live *T*. 31

SOUL-REVIVING.
O balmy gales of *s*. air! *E*. ii 27

SOUND.
I start at the *s*. of my own *A.S.* 12
But the *s*. of the church-going bell *A.S.* 29
Never sighed at the *s*. of a knell *A.S.* 31
S. not arms shall win the prize *B*. 23
Could catch the *s*. no more *Cast*. 46
Fast as the thirsting ear can drink the *s*. *Ch*. 112
The fruits of age, less fair, are yet more *s*. *Con*. 647
The pomp of *s*., or tinkle without use *Con*. 892
In gentle *s*. it seems as it complained *Con*. 905 [908
It *s*. Jehovah's name, and pours his praise along *Con*.
And *s*. prophetic are too rough to suit *Ex*. 67
The *s*. of truth will then be sure to please *Ex*. 731
A real and a *s*. one *F*. 15   [sprightly *s*. *H*. 45
Banks clothed with flowers, groves filled with
But they that wore them, move not at the *s*. *H*. 267
To *s*. his horn, and publish it abroad *H*. 311
Die of disdain, or whistle off the *s*. *H*. 348
Live from his lips, and spread the glorious *s*. *H*. 454
That *s*. bespeaks Salvation on her way *H*. 455
No groves have ye; nor cheerful *s*. of bird *H*. 469
S. forth the signal, as she mounts her car *H*. 647
Starts at her first approach, and *s*. to arms! *H*. 656
And laughter *s*. like madness in his ear *H*. 703
The *s*. of pardon pierce his startled ear *H*. 724
No thunders shook with deep intestine *s*. *Her*. 5
Brings to the distant ear a sullen *s*. *Her* 36
The trumpet *s*., your legions swarm abroad *Her*. 53
And keep it safe and *s*. *J.G.* 68
Adieus and farewells are a *s*. unknown *M.P.* 33
S. such as these, so worthy to be feared *N.A.* 84 [117
And rush those other *s*., that seem by tongues *N.A.*

S. are but *s*., and till the cause appear *N.A.* 119
Such cause of terror in an empty *s*. *N.A.* 130 [*P.E.* 79
And earthly *s*., though sweet and well combined
Her timbers yet are *s*. *R.G.* 29 [Grace?" *P.E.* 103
Charmed by the *s*., "Your Reverence," or "Your
And the whispering *s*. of the cool colonnade *P.F.* 2
S. harshly in so delicate an ear *R*. 250
All bliss beside a shadow or a *s*. *R*. 354
The *s*. shall run along the winding vales *R*. 363
How regular his meals, how *s*. he sleeps! *R*. 430
The trumpet—will it *s*.? the curtain rise? *R*. 655
The friend of Truth, the associate of *s*. Sense *R*. 696
Ring with ecstatic *s*. unheard before *R*. 780
None, accustomed to the *s*. *St*. iv 7
Seems to *s*. too much in vain *St*. iv 19
Nature inanimate employs sweet *s*. *T*. 197
S. inharmonious in themselves and harsh *T*. 207
S. for the poor, but *s*. alike for all *T*. 350   [174
Tall spire, from which the *s*. of cheerful bells *T*. i
Nor rural sights alone, but rural *s*. *T*. i 181
From such unpleasing *s*. as haunt the ear *T*. i 229
That winds and waters, lulled by magic *s*. *T*. ii 261
Most part an empty ineffectual *s*. *T*. iii 22
And *s*. integrity, not more than famed *T*. iii 259
That at the *s*. of Winter's hoary wing *T*. iii 830
At a safe distance, where the dying *s*. *T*. iv 92
The tumult and am still. The *s*. of war *T*. iv 100
And sigh, but never tremble at the *s*. *T*. iv 106 [148
Cough their own knell, while, heedless of the *s*. *T*. iv
The sprightly lyre, whose treasure of sweets *s*. *T*. iv 160
Of fancy, or proscribes the *s*. of mirth *T*. iv 176
Unsoiled and swift, and of a silken *s*. *T*. iv 212
Dire is the frequent curse, and its twin *s*. *T*. iv 487
To horrid *s*. of hostile feet within *T*. iv 571
No *s*. of hammer or of saw was there *T*. v 145
Thus by degrees self-cheated of their *s*. *T*. v 264
And ever as the sullen *s*. is heard *T*. v 405
"We find *s*. argument, we read the heart" *T*. v 654
There is in souls a sympathy with *s*. *T*. vi 1
Stillness, accompanied with *s*. so soft *T*. vi 83
By one of *s*. intelligence rehearsed *T*. iv 480
That is not *s*. and perfect, hath in theirs *T*. vi 708
Well taught, he all the *s*. expressed *T.B.* 11
And *s*. religion sparingly enough *Tir*. 198
Though fair in promise, permanent and *s*. *Tir*. 437
Just catches at the *s*. *Trans*. iv 21
If sentiment were sacrificed to *s*. *T.T.* 516
Exact and regular the *s*. will be *T.T.* 530
S. sense, intrepid spirit, manly grace *V*. 12
May kill a *s*. divine *Y.D.* 64
Yet is thy root sincere, *s*. as the rock *Y.O.* 116

SOUNDER.
Not *s*. he that on the mainmast head *R*. 431

SOUNDING.
Leuconomus (beneath well *s*. Greek *H*. 554
See where it smokes along the *s*. plain *T*. 238
To them, the *s*. jargon of the schools *T*. 367
Since pulpits fail, and *s*. boards reflect *T*. iii 21
Of *s*. an alarm assaults these doors *T*. iv 146
With *s*. whip, and rowels dyed in blood *T*. vi 527

SOURCE.
And all supplied from an eternal *s*. *Ch*. 370
And fear, not courage, is its proper *s*. *Con*. 180
And finds a changing clime a happy *s*. *Con*. 387
Thy tears all issue from a *s*. divine *E*. ii 47
Traced easily to its true *s*. above *J.T.* 45
For when it streams from that pure *s*. *Miss* — 57
"These are thy glorious works, thou *S*. of good *R*. 87
Is thine;—best gift, the unfailing *s*. of joy *S*. ii 12
For other *s*. than God is none *St*. vi 3
Himself so much the *s*. of his delight *T*. 413
Derived from the same *s*. of light and grace *T*. 533

The s. of the disease that Nature feels *T.* ii 194
All truth is from the sempiternal s. *T.* ii 499
Thou art the s. and centre of all minds *T.* v 896
That s. of evils not exhausted yet *T.* vi 369

SOUTHERN.
On s. banks the ruminating sheep *A.T.* 78
His freeborn brethren of the s. pole *Ch.* 34
The s. sash admits too strong a light *Con.* 331
Like bottled wasps upon a s. wall *R.* 494
Upon the s. side of the giant hills *T.* vi 59

SOVEREIGN.
His s. power and pleasure unrestrained *H.* 320
"Oh! if my s. author please *Miss* — 25
Had known their s. come *Q.V.* 44
To serve the S. we were born to obey *R.* 50
Their s. nostrum is a clumsy joke *R.* 313
When the great S. would his will express *T.* 551
S., and most effectual, to secure *T.* ii 590
With music such as suits their s. ears *T.* v 387
To earth's acknowledged S., finds at once *T.* v 803
To see their s., and confess his sway *T.* vi 356
Who in his s. wisdom made them all *T.* vi 587
Her s.'s tutelary care 1789, 39

SOVEREIGNTY.
Or if the will and s. of God *Ch.* 165
The s. they were convened to please *Ex.* 539

SOW.
Esteem them, s. them, rear them, and protect *H.* 295
Spontaneous, take but little pains to s. *P.E.* 364

SOWED. [*T.* v 202
Peace was awhile their care; they ploughed and s.
He s. the seeds of order where he went *Ex.* 488

SOWING.
On culture, and the s. of the soil *Con.* 6

SOWN.
And thou thyself o'er every country s. *Ex.* 265
Like thistle-seeds, are s. by every wind *P.E.* 555
The seed s. there, how vigorous is the plant! *T.* 362
Are s. the sparks that kindle fiery war *T.* v 206
Were s. in human nature's fruitful soil *T.* vi 383
And, like a scattered seed at random s. *T.T.* 674

SPACE. [589
That in the heaven of heavens, that s. He deems *Ch.*
Whether the s. between the stars and us *Ch.* 352
Flew open in short s. *J.G.* 242
Fast anchored in the deep abyss of s. *R.* 84
A panting syllable through time and s. *R.* 692
Deception innocent—give ample s. *T.* i 353
And transplantation in an ampler s. *T.* iii 533
That finding an interminable s. *T.* v 556

SPACIOUS.
Hers is the s. arch, the shapely spire *Ch.* 105
Even his hall would hold no more *H.* 309
Of s. meads with cattle sprinkled o'er *T.* i 164
O'er these, but far beyond, a s. map *T.* i 321
That skims the s. meadow at full speed *T.* vi 331
Or take their pastime in the s. field *T.* vi 576
And in her streets, and in her s. courts *T.* vi 809

SPADE. [*T.* iii 636
Is needful. Strength may wield the ponderous s.
And s., the emblem of untimely graves *T.* iv 219

SPAIN. [*Ex.* 568
His power secured thee, when presumptuous *S.*—

SPAKE.
Else I would say, and as I s., bid fly *Ch.* 268
They s. of him they loved, of him whose life *Con.* 511
Well s. the prophet,—"Let the desert sing *H.* 524
For while he s., a braying ass *J.G.* 203

While thus she s., I fainter heard the peals *N.A.* 123
So s. Aspasio, firm possessed *St.* iii 13

SPAN.
Who drive a loathsome traffic, gauge and s. *Ch.* 139
Improve the remnant of his wasted s. *R.* 13
The hour that terminates his s. *St.* iii 3
Would gladly stretch life's little s. *St.* v 7
To s. omnipotence, and measure might *T.* vi 212
Sing, then—and extend thy s. *Trans.* iii 27
Half a s., compared with thee *Trans.* iii 32
Fancy that from the bow that s. the sky *T.T.* 702

SPANGLED.
Her crimson honours; and the s. beau *T.* iii 578

SPANIEL.
A s., Beau, that fares like you *Beau* 1
My s., prettiest of his race *D.W.* 5
That s. found for me) *D.W.* 8
The s. dying for some venial fault *T.* vi 418

SPANNED.
Who s. her waist, and who, where'er he came *T.* 155

SPARE.
An earthquake may be bid to s. *A Fable* 34
And I might s. myself the pains to show *Ch.* 623
And s. the poet for his subject's sake *Ch.* 636
Now think, if Pleasure have a thought to s. *Ex.* 602
Nor s. a life too short to reach the skies *Ex.* 623
Oh s. them, ye knights of the boot *Gr.* 19
The bolts that s. the mountain's side *Trans.* H. 16
What are they now?—Morality may s. *H.* 515
If honest eulogy can s. thee room *H.* 589 [627
And smite the untempered wall 'tis death to s. *H.*
This only s. no lust, admits no plea *H.* 645
That can seduce him not to s. *Mor.* 31
To s. no passion, and no favourite sin *R.* 136
And such emollients as his friends could s. *R.* 305
Of depth enough, and none to s. *R.C.* 41 [134
Their length and colour from the locks they s. *T.* i
Thanks to Benevolus—he s. me yet *T.* i 262
Birds warbling all the music. We can s. *T.* i 764
Far guiltier England! lest he s. not thee *T.* ii 160
Ah s. your idol! think him human still *T.* ii 496
Dooms to the knife; nor does he s. the soft *T.* iii 417
Would s., that loves them, offices like these?) *T.* iii 619
Enjoyed, s. feast! a radish and an egg! *T.* iv 173
What, conscious of your virtues, we can s. *T.* iv 425
S. not in such a cause. Spend all the powers *T.* v 676
The incumbrance of his own concerns, and s. *T.* vi 206
And, if he s. him, s. him in the terms *T.* vi 409
Feed on the slain, but s. the living brute! *T.* vi 458
The laurel that the very lightning s. *T.T.* 6
Prize it, ye ministers; ye monarchs, s. *T.T.* 334
With loss of what she least could s. 1789, 38

SPARED.
If we escaped not, if Heaven s. not us *Ex.* 245
If even her face he has s. *Gr.* 47
Are crimes so little to be s. *M.F.* 44
Then anxious to be longer s. *St.* v 25
The more malignant. If he s. not them *T.* ii 158
Paid with the blood that he had basely s. *T.* iii 91
Cruelly s., and hopeless of escape! *T.* v 399
S. yet again the ignobler for his sake *T.* vi 530
But the axe s. thee. In those thriftier days *Y.O.* 100

SPARELY.
Ill-clad and fed but s. time to cool *T.* iv 379

SPARING.
A teacher should be s. of his smile *Ch.* 490

SPARINGLY.
Feeds s., communicates his store *H.* 521
And sound religion s. enough *Tir.* 198

SPARK.
Three s. ensued that chased it all away *A.T.* 167
There goes the parson—O illustrious s.! *B.B.* 13
Grows fungous, and takes fire at every s. *Con.* 54
By s. Absurdity strikes out of Pride *Con.* 148
The s. of disputation *F.* 105
And knew the glowworm by his s. *N.G.* 10
And many a gay unlettered s. *P.* 32
No, not a s.—'tis all mere sharper's play *T.* 209
Has she no s. that may be deemed her own ? *T.* 482
The s. of life. The sportive wind blows wide *T.* i 567
Or negligent inquirer, not a s. *T.* iii 276
And crowded knees, sit cowering o'er the s. *T.* iv 385
A noble cause, which none who bears a s. *T.* iv 614
Are sown the s. that kindle fiery war *T.* v 206
Some place, a s. or two not yet extinct *T.* vi 684
A kindred s.: they burn to do the like *Tir.* 233
Wit now and then, struck smartly, shows a s. *T.T.* 663

SPARKLES.
It s. with the gems he left behind *Ex.* 483

SPARKLING.
Is s. wit the world's exclusive right *Con.* 589
She viewed the s. show *Q.V.* 74
And in that charter reads, with s. eyes *T.* 329
Of atoms, s. in the noonday beam *T.* i 361
A s. eye beneath a wrinkled front *T.* i 405
A palsy struck his arm, his s. eye *T.* ii 727
Large growth of what may seem the s. trees *T.* v 112
And made so s. what was dark before *T.* v 558

SPARROWS.
The s. peep, and quit the sheltering eaves *T.* v 65

SPARTA.
From *S.* hither, and art here at home *Ch.* 271

SPARTAN.
And if some *S.* soul a doubt expressed *Ex.* 542

SPATTERED.
By panting dog, tired man, and s. horse *N.A.* 125
With s. boots, strapp'd waist, and frozen locks *T.* iv 6

SPAWN.
Deposit in those shallows all their s. *P.E.* 479

SPAWNED.
S. on the muddy beds of Nile, came forth *T.* ii 827

SPEAK.
S. a divine ambition, and a zeal *Ch.* 307
She s. of Him, her author, guardian, friend *Ch.* 399
Whoever threatens war, to s. of peace *Ch.* 421 [248
Then pause and puff—and s., and pause again *Con.*
You s. with life, in hopes to entertain *Con.* 327
Will s. without disguise, and must impart *Con.* 711
Their very language of a kind that s. *Con.* 727
All s. her happy: let the Muse look round *Ex.* 27
That Sin let loose s. Punishment at hand *Ex.* 160
Too just to wink, or s. the guilty clear *Ex.* 256
But public censure s. a public foe *Ex.* 436
S. but the word, will listen and return " *Ex.* 455
All s. one language, all with one sweet voice *H.* 53
S., for he can, and none so well as he *H.* 173
But s. with plainness art could never mend *H.* 451
I slur a name a poet must not s.) *H.* 555
A transport glows in all he looks and s. *H.* 726
But while they s. the wisdom of the skies *H.* 768
And if a tear, that s. regret *N.* 21 [*M.P.* 79
Wouldst softly s., and stroke my head and smile
'Gan make his instrument of music s. *N.A.* 44
Are the voice with which He s. *N.C.* 36
You s. very fine, and you look very grave *P.A.* 29
How shall I s. thee, or thy power address *P.E.* 460
A moment's liberty to s. *P.T.* 20
His mighty work, who s. and it is done *R.* 60
S. with reserve, and listens with applause *R.* 448
But, naming none, the voice now s. to all *St.* ii 20
S. him a criminal, assured *St.* vi 35
All joy to the believer! He can s. *T.* 571
These s. a loud memento. Yet even these *T.* i 482
By him, the violated law s. out *T.* ii 340
Should s. to purpose, or with better hope *T.* iii 25
He s.. The lake in front becomes a lawn *T.* iii 774
By which he s. the language of his heart *T.* iv 105
Sees not a countenance there that s. of joy *T.* iv 205
To s. its excellence; I danced for joy *T.* iv 712
All bear the royal stamp that s. them his *T.* v 551
The still small voice is wanted. He must s. *T.* v 685
They are thy witnesses, who s. thy power *T.* v 853
And goodness infinite, but s. in ears *T.* v 854 [128
How would the world admire! But s. it less *T.* vi
More than the'perquisite: where Law shall s. *T.* vi 848
Thy prophets s. of such; and, noting down *T.* vi 899
Whose only care, might truth presume to s. *Tir.* 193
They hear him s.—the oracle of law *Tir.* 363 [*T.T.* 42
And death's own scythe would better s. his power
He s., and they appear; to him they owe *T.T.* 356
S. to the present times, and times to come *T.T.* 433
Ah, Muse! forbear to s. *T.B.* 51 [s. *Y.O.* 40
Who lived when thou wast such ? Oh, couldst thou
Desperate attempt, till trees shall s. again *Y.O.* 49

SPEAKER.
The emphatic s. dearly loves to oppose *Con.* 269
All s., yet all language at a loss *H.* 345
The modest s. is ashamed and grieved *T.* iv 66

SPEAKING.
S. from his throne, the sky ? *N.C.* 28
S. in parables his slighted word *Tir.* 140

SPEAR. [170
" And better s. I smite you where you stand " *A.T.*
That no success attends on s. and swords *Ex.* 352
Of trophied helmets, s., and shields 1789, 4

SPECIAL.
On s. search, the keen-eyed eagle blind *Ex.* 631

SPECIOUS.
Discern the fraud, beneath the s. lure *P.E.* 17
And covered with a fine-spun s. veil *P.E.* 328
S. in show, impossible in fact *R.* 638
And s. semblances have lost their use *T.* iii 107
And emulation is its s. name *Tir.* 469

SPECK.
With russet s. bedight *A Tale* 42
For sight of ship from England. Every s. *T.* i 666
Without a cloud, and white without a s. *T.* vi 63

SPECKLE.
S. the bosom of the distant plain *P.E.* 83

SPECTACLE.
The s. set them unhappily wrong *A.C.* 2
To which the said s. ought to belong *A.C.* 4
That the Nose has had s. always in wear *A.C.* 11
Then holding the s. up to the Court *A.C.* 13 [20
Pray who would, or who could, wear s. then ? *A.C.*
That the s. plainly were made for the Nose *A.C.* 23
That, whenever the Nose put his s. on *A.C.* 31
Claps s. on her sagacious nose *Con* 742
Spectatress both and s., a sad *T.* i 476
And 'tis a fearful s. to see *T.* ii 662
The pleasing s. at once excites *Tir.* 310
Not better much than s. a brute *Tir.* 782

SPECTACLE-BESTRID.
Through the pressed nostril, s. *T.* ii 439

SPECTATORS.
Amused s. of this bustling stage *T.* v 878

SPECTATRESS.
S. both and spectacle, a sad *T.* i 476

SPECULATIST.
Fresh confidence the s. takes *P.E.* 490

SPECULATIVE.
And posted on this s. height *T.* i 289
Fond of the s. height *Trans.* ii 13

SPED.
How an emetic or cathartic s. *Con.* 316 [*P.E.* 406
With which from clime to clime he s. his course
The shelves are full, all other themes are s. *T.T.* 726

SPEECH.
Never hear the sweet music of s. *A.S.* 11
There is a prurience in the s. of some *Con.* 31
For making s. the pamperer of lust *Con.* 48
Useless in him alike both brain and s. *Con.* 141
We sometimes think we could a s. produce *Con.* 353
And s. may praise the power that bids it flow *Con.* 444
Mellows and makes the s. more fit for use *Con.* 644
Held within modest bounds, the tide of s. *Con.* 889
Renewed desire would grace with other s. *H.* 35 [37
His grief might prompt him with the s. he made *E.* iii
His s. rebellion against common sense *H.* 565
Ah! luckless s., and bootless boast *J.G.* 201
Have s. for him, and understood with ease *N.A.* 58
Complaining in a s. well worded *P.* 3
Refines his s. and fashions his address *R.* 240
Of others' s., but magic of thy own *S.* i 14
That s. betrays at once a bigot's tongue *T.* 519
Of lightness in his s. 'Tis pitiful *T.* ii 466
Played on his lips, and in his s. was heard *T.* ii 707
Then were not all effaced; then s. profane *T.* iv 522
That turns to ridicule the turgid s. *T.* v 689
A rhetoric equal to those parts of s.? *Tir.* 398
Nor taint his s. with meannesses designed *Tir.* 686
His s., his form, his action, full of grace *T.T.* 346

SPEED.
Compared with the s. of its flight *A.S.* 42 [i 2
Both s. their journey with a restless stream *Comp.*
Heaven s. the canvass, gallantly unfurled *Ch.* 123
We bustle up with unsuccessful s. *Con.* 215
Proud of his s., to overshoot the truth *Con.* 642
"Who both write well, and write full s.! *E.* iv 84
"S. us away to battle and to fame!" *Ex.* 289
The post that at his bidding s. away *Ex.* 355 [*P.E.* 74
Detach the soul from earth, and s. her to the skies?
And thence with all convenient s. to Rome *P.E.* 370
And hurried but with unsuccessful s. *T.* 245
As life declines, s. rapidly away *T.* i 130
Wildfowl or venison, and his errand s. *T.* iv 612
That skims the spacious meadow at full s. *T.* vi 331
Their strength, or s., or vigilance, were given *T.* vi 610
Always at s., and never drawing bit *T.T.* 685 [309
Gives him olympic s., and shoots him to the goal *T.T.*

SPELL.
On every mind some mighty s. she cast *A.T.* 37 [146
No s. or charm was proof against the thrust *A.T.*
To guess and s. what it contains *E.* i 52
So dimly writ, or difficult to s. *Ex.* 311
He s. them true by intuition's light *N.A.* 69 [619
The s. and charms that blinded you before *P.E.*
So difficult to s. *Q.V.* 50
With magic wand. So potent is the s. *T.* ii 630
Books are not seldom talismans and s. *T.* vi 100
When children first begin to s. *Trans.* iv 37
In characters uncouth, and s. amiss *T.* i 283

SPEND.
And said, "Go s. them in the vale of tears" *E.* ii 26
To s. two hours in dressing for the day *H.* 80
The dreary waste; there s. the livelong day *T.* i 457

And Truth disclaiming both; and thus they s. *T.* iii 163
But frantic who thus s. it all for smoke? *T.* iii 174
Spare not in such a cause. S. all the powers *T.* v 676
The force he s. against their fury vain *Tir.* 64
Thought cannot s. itself, comparing still *Y.O.* 86

SPENDTHRIFT.
Or s.'s prodigal excess afford *J.T.* 15
S., and booted sportsmen, oftener seen *T.* ii 752
And the shark's prey; the s., and the leech *T.* iii 817
S. alike of money and of wit *T.T.* 684

SPENT.
To thrive in, an incumbrance ere half s. *H.* 98
S. half the darkness, and snored out the rest *H.* 510
Till, all my stock of infant sorrow s. *M.P.* 43
Till life's poor transient night is s. *N.G.* 32
Thus life is s. (oh fie upon 't!) *P.* 37
That Virtue points to? Can a life thus s. *P.E.* 72
And not soon s., though in an arduous task *T.* i 401
S. all his force, and made no proselyte) *T.* ii 331 [173
Ah! what is life thus s.? and what are they *T.* iii
So s. in parlour twilight; such a gloom *T.* iv 278
(Life s. in indolence and therefore sad) *T.* v 181
S. in the purchase of renown for him *T.* v 277
Well s. in such a strife, may earn indeed *T.* v 715
How readily we wish time s. revoked *T.* vi 25
Laughs at the frantic sufferer's fury, s. *T.* vi 423
His influence, if that influence all be s. *T.* vi 962
Feels himself s., and fumbles for his brains *T.T.* 537
Wretched man whose years are s. *Trans.* iii 29

SPHERE.
Is to discharge the duties of his s. *H.* 400
Extend a larger s. *Miss* — 100
But if eccentric ye forsake your s. *P.E.* 98
She, for her humble s. by nature fit *T.* 323
Replace the wandering comet in his s. *T.* 400
And shining each in his domestic s. *T.* v 520
His s. though humble, if that humble s. *T.* vi 960
However humble and confined the s. *T.T.* 166

SPICE.
Whom fiery suns, that scorch the russet s. *Ex.* 15
Had he the gems, the s., and the land *H.* 175
Where s. breathe and brighter seasons smile *M.P.* 91
Variety's the very s. of life *T.* ii 606

SPICY.
The sun matures on India's s. shores *Ch.* 412
And Saba's s. groves, pay tribute there *T.* vi 807

SPIDERS.
As bloated s. draw the flimsy line *P.E.* 495
And bloated s., till the pampered pest *T.* v 422

SPIED.
From the balcony s. *J.G.* 142
Distant a little mile he s. *Mor.* 17
He s. far off, upon the ground *N.G.* 8
And forth he peeped, but nothing s. *R.C.* 82

SPIKE.
With purple s. pyramidal, as if *T.* vi 159

SPILT.
In the blood that she has s. *B.* 14

SPIN.
S. round upon her axle, ere the warmth *T.* iii 491

SPINDLING.
Mine, s. into longitude immense *T.* v 11

SPINE.
Contusion hazarding of neck or s. *N.A.* 7

SPIRAL.
In s. rings ascends the trunk, and lays *R.* 231

SPIRE.
Hers is the spacious arch, the shapely *s. Ch.* 105
And the sun gilds the shining *s.* again *Her.* 72
Bright shone the roofs, the domes, the *s. Q.V.* 13
Tall *s.*, from which the sound of cheerful bells *T.* i174

SPIRIT.
Propitious *S.!* yet expunge a wrong *Ch.* 276
Except a few with Eli's *s.* blest *Ex.* 448
With wreaths like those triumphant *s.* wear *H.* 166
Nor cheer the *s.*, nor refresh the sight *H.* 299
Thy *s.* have a fainter flow *M.* 5
Hovered thy *s.* o'er thy sorrowing son *M.P.* 23
Thy unbound *s.* into bonds again *M.P.* 87
Freshening his lazy *s.* as he ran *P.E.* 411
That cordial thought her *s.* cheered *Q.V.* 65
No wounds like those a wounded *s.* feels *R.* 341
S. of instruction! Come *St.* iv 35
With *s.*, genius, eloquence, supplied *T.* 305
His wasted *s.* quickly, by long toil *T.* i 128
Exhilarate the *s.*, and restore *T.* i 182
And lull the *s.* while they fill the mind *T.* i 187 [i 350
And now, with nerves new braced and *s.* cheered *T.*
Good temper; *s.* prompt to undertake *T.* i 400
Health suffers, and the *s.* ebb; the heart *T.* i 466
And faithful to the foot, his *s.* rise *T.* iii 8
All that the contest calls for; *s.*, strength *T.* v 376
Serve to compose a *s.* well inclined *T.* v 657
His *s.* takes, unconscious of a chain *T.* v 776
" Ordained to guide the embodied *s.* home *T.* v 840
Such comprehensive views the *s.* takes *T.* vi 15
But all are under one. One *s.* His *T.* vi 238
And *s.* buoyant with excess of glee *T.* vi 329
The very *s.* of the world is tired *T.* vi 869
His fervent *s.* labours. There he fights *T.* vi 936
Such youths of *s.*, and that *s.* too *Tir.* 247
The *s.* of that competition burns *Tir.* 474
His *s.* rising as his toils increase *T.T.* 279
Sound sense, intrepid *s.*, manly grace *V.* 12
To teach, no *S.* dwells in thee, nor voice *Y.O.* 138

SPIRITLESS.
And *s.*, as never to regret *T.* i 652

SPIRY. [525
Where sprang the thorn, the *s.* fir shall spring *H.*
Once more the *s.* myrtle crowns the glade *Her.* 31
The *s.* myrtle with unwithering leaf *T.* iii 570
From every herb and every *s.* blade *T.* v 9

SPIT.
Weigh sunbeams, carve a fly, or *s.* a flea *Ch.* 354
And *s.* abhorrence in the Christian's face *H.* 662
One *s.* upon the floor *Y.D.* 42

SPITE.
In *s.* of your command *B.R.* 2
Few competitions but engender *s. Con.* 161
Now the distemper, *s.* of draught or pill *Con.* 319
Whose deeds had left, in *s.* of hostile arts *Con.* 513
But age in *s.* of weakness and of pain *Ex.* 25
A blot that will be still a blot, in *s. Ex.* 382
In *s.* of curb and rein *J.G.* 88
To regions where, in *s.* of sin and woe *R.* 27
In *s.* of gravity and sage remark *T.* v 12
In *s.* of all the wrigglers into place *Tir.* 432
Less for improvement than to tickle *s. Tir.* 481
Though there, in *s.* of all that care can do *Tir.* 521
And hopes in *s.* of pain *Trans. H.* 21

SPLEEN.
Too often rails to gratify his *s. Ch.* 500
Are gloomy thoughts led on by *S.—E.* iv 20
He just endures and with a sickly *s. R.* 565
They overwhelm me with the *s.*" *M.F.* 8
The *s.* is seldom felt where Flora reigns *T.* i 455

Would find them hideous nurseries of the *s. T.* iii 318
That breathes the *s.*, and searches every bone *T.* iv 364

SPLENDID.
Become at length so *s.* in our own *Con.* 370
The snug, close party, or the *s.* hall *P.E.* 176
On many a *s.* wall *Q.V.* 46
And teach him notions *s.* as themselves *T.* 424
Induced a *s.* cover, green and blue *T.* i 32
With lace, and hat with *s.* ribbon bound *T.* i 536
Poured forth by Beauty *s.* and polite *T.* ii 494
A form as *s.* as the proudest there *T.* ii 620
I cannot but lament thy *s.* wit *T.* iv 725
The streams are lost amid the *s.* blank *T.* v 96
A *s.* opportunity to die? *T.* v 320

SPLENDOUR.
The future *s.* of the flower? *E.* i 72
Pours out a flood of *s.* upon thine *Ex.* 589
Obscurity with *s. F.* 120
When I sing of the *s.* of mine *Gr.* 56
That decks, with all the *s.* of the true *H.* 485
It boasts a *s.* ever new *Mrs. M—* 19 [54
Power, Pomp, and *S.*, and the thirst of Praise *P.E.*
" I am all *s.*, dignity, and grace!" *T.* 65
Traduce the *s.* of a noontide ray *T.* 540
The *s.* of your lamps; they but eclipse *T.* i 765
To gaze at his own *s.*, and to exalt *T.* ii 547
In guilty *s.*, shake the public ways *T.* iii 70
The dazzling *s.* of the scene below *T.* vi 64
Hers is the state, the *s.*, and the throne *Tir.* 11
There dawns the *s.* of his future years *Tir.* 394
And boasts its *s.* too *Trans.* i 28
Emerged all *s.* in our isle at last *T.T.* 565

SPLENETIC.
And chase the *s.* dull hours away *Con.* 582
It shakes the sides of *s.* Disdain *Ex.* 548

SPLINTERED.
A *s.* stump bleached to a snowy white *Y.O.* 128

SPLIT.
And he that *s.* his cranium, breaks at most *A.T.* 44
Was *s.* into diversity of tongues *T.* v 195

SPOIL.
The cankered *s.* corrodes the pining state *Ch.* 63
Of nations, sworn to *s.* thee and devour *Ex.* 703
Gleans up the refuse of the general *s. Her.* 70
As much as I to *s.* your song *N.G.* 18
Dote not too much, nor *s.* what ye admire *T.* ii 498
His folly, but to *s.* him is a task *T.* ii 768
To better deeds, he bundles up the *s. T.* iv 440
Are gratified with mischief, and who *s. T.* v 191 [228
Thus war began on earth: these fought for *s. T.* v
Though laden, not encumbered with her *s. Tir.* 17
So sure to *s.* him, and so near at hand *Tir.* 697
Every dish, and *s.* the best *Trans.* iii 14

SPOILED.
Her princes captive, and her treasures *s. Ex.* 62
Made you a Peer, but *s.* you for a friend! *V.* 14

SPOILER.
On eager wing the *s.* came *P.B.* 5

SPOKE.
The trumpet now *s.* Marmadan at hand *A.T.* 161
He *s.* indignant, and his spurs applied *A.T.* 191
Every burning word he *s. B.* 7
Through all He *s.* a noble plainness ran *Ex.* 135
" *S.* like an oracle," they all exclaim *H.* 437
In merry guise, he *s. J.G.* 172 [*P.A.* 33
They *s.*, and Tom pondered—" I see they will go
He *s.*, and to the precipice at hand *T.* vi 512
S. from his lips, and in his looks gave law *T.T.* 245
Felt himself crushed at the first word he *s. T.T.* 353

SPOKEN.
Well s., advocate of sin and shame *Con.* 587
That Solomon has wisely s. *E.* i 105
And having s. wisely, at the close *T.* ii 442

SPONGE.
Found thee a goodly s. for Power to press *Ex.* 531

SPONGY.
And spreading wide their s. lobes, at first *T.* iii 522

SPONTANEOUS.
S., take but little pains to sow *P.E.* 364
(If e'er she spring s.) in remote *T.* i 603

SPORT.
Ye winds that have made me your s. *A.S.* 33
They s. like wanton doves in airy rings *A.T.* 32
"And flutters loose, the s. of every wind *A.T.* 102
But innocent was all his s. *Beau* 15
A toy to s. with, and pass time away *Con.* 18
Her theatres, her revels, and her s. *Ex.* 23
When persecuting zeal made royal s. *Ex.* 612
If arms engage him, he devotes to s. *H.* 207 [*H.* 260
They die.—Death lends them, pleased and as in s.
By this he forms, as pleased he s. along *H.* 610
The zephyrs s. in vain *Miss —* 38
Which rural gentlemen call s. divine *N.A.* 8
If breaking windows be the s. *Pat.* 11
Pursue their s., and follow to the deep *R.* 160
Renounced alike its office and its s. *R.* 293
Is duty a mere s., or an employ? *R.* 649
The mind, relaxing into needful s. *R.* 715
In which he s. away the treasure now *St.* ii 10
S. for a day, and perish in a night *T.* 42
Of equipage, our gardens, and our s. *T.* i 644
The s. of every wave? No: none are clear *T.* ii 153
He doubtless is in s., and does but droll *T.* ii 369
To s. which only childhood could excuse *T.* ii 638
Is squandered in pursuit of idle s. *T.* ii 758
To s. their season, and be seen no more *T.* iii 136
And clamours of the field? Detested s. *T.* iii 326
Bleed gold for ministers to s. away *T.* iv 508
And make the sorrows of mankind their s. *T.* v 186
Nor envies he aught more their idle s. *T.* vi 272
So Eden was a scene of harmless s. *T.* vi 364 [386
Regardless of their plaints. To make him s. *T.* vi
Sweet in itself, and not forbidding s. *Tir.* 652
And I play with syllables, and s. in song *T.T.* 505
Not rashly or in s. *U.* 8
Both in their toils and at their s. 1789, 63

SPORTED.
Fancy has s. all her powers away *T.T.* 730

SPORTING.
That it is dangerous s. with the world *T.* ii 777

SPORTIVE.
Perhaps the man was in a s. fit *Ch.* 537
Crushed by the wind. So s. is the light *T.* i 345
The spark of life. The s. wind blows wide *T.* i 567
S. and jingling her poetic bells *T.* iv 702
With all her little ones, a s. train *T.* vi 301
And in his s. days *Th.* 2

SPORTSMAN.
Grey dawn appears; the s. and his train *P.E.* 82
Spendthrifts, and booted s., oftener seen *T.* ii 752
That draw the s. over hill and dale *T.* iii 310

SPOT. [*A.T.* 206
The s. he loathed so much for ever cleansed away
Nose, ears, and eyes seem present on the s. *Con.* 318
Catch from each other a contagious s. *Ex.* 105
Thy services, once holy without s. *Ex.* 261
Think on the fruitful and well-watered s. *Ex.* 418
This island, s. of unreclaimed rude earth *Ex.* 468

A world is up in arms, and thou, a s. *Ex.* 694
Those open on the s. their honeyed store *P.E.* 49
Amid the charms of a sequestered s. *R.* 8
The s. he loved has lost the power to please *R.* 466
Play wanton, every moment, every s. *T.* i 349
The envied tenants of some happier s. *T.* i 610
Undazzled, and detects and counts his s.? *T.* i 714
She has her praise. Now mark a s. or two *T.* i 725
But in a distant s., where, more exposed *T.* iii 770
He seeks a favoured s.; that where he builds *T.* iii 471
With s. quadrangular of diamond form *T.* iv 217
Appears a s. upon a vestal's robe *T.* iv 554
Playing our games, and on the very s. *Tir.* 305
No s. contracted among grooms below *Tir.* 685
Find him a better in a distant s. *Tir.* 759
Let me enjoy, in some unthought of s. *V.* 83

SPOTLESS.
Whose chief distinction is their s. name *Tir.* 355

SPOTTED.
Now therefore issued forth the s. pack *N.A.* 21
And s. with all crimes; in whom I see *T.* iii 837

SPOUSE.
John Gilpin's s. said to her dear *J.G.* 5
The lady thus addressed her s. *M.F.* 1

SPOUT.
"As freely as a conduit s.! *E.* iv 86

SPOUTING.
In bilking tavern bills, and s. plays *Tir.* 327

SPOUTLESS.
A fragment, and the s. teapot there *T.* iv 776

SPRANG. [193
The barb s. forward, and his lord, whose force *A.T.*
Seized fast the saddle and s. up behind *A.T.* 178
Where s. the thorn, the spiry fir shall spring *H.* 525
She s. no fatal leak *R.G.* 19
He s. impetuous forth *Th.* 14

SPRAY.
With many a wild, indeed, but flowery s. *Ch.* 629
I perched at will on every s. *G.* 4
Nor Autumn yet had brushed from every s. *N.A.* 21
Her golden tassels on the leafy s. *R.* 232
From s. to s., where'er he rests he shakes *T.* vi 81
With blushing wreaths, investing every s. *T.* vi 169

SPREAD.
And s. her golden hopes below *A Fable* 15
S. foreign wonders in his country's sight *Ch.* 116
That Heaven s. wide before the view of man *Ch.* 324
S. wide her arms of universal love *Ch.* 596
To s. the newborn glories in their view *Con.* 546
And s. the sacred treasures of the breast *Con.* 573
And s., at length, before the soul *E.* i 63
Where Nature has her mossy velvet s. *E.* ii 15
She s. the morning over eastern hills *H.* 41
To me their peace by kind contagion s. *N.A.* 42
And oaks coeval s. a mournful shade *H.* 352
Live from his lips, and s. the glorious sound *H.* 454
And still it s. See Germany send forth *H.* 459
His fame soon s. around *J.G.* 114
Of the plague s. by bundles left behind *P.E.* 352
Unfolded genially, and s. the man *P.E.* 412
The propagated myriads s. so fast *P.E.* 484
Seas on which every nation s. her sails *R.* 80
To s. the page of Scripture, and compare *R.* 131
Become more rare as dissipation s. *R.* 706 [*R.* 421
Green balks and furrowed lands, the stream that s.
S. all his canvass, every sinew plies *T.* 5
There might ye see the peony s. wide *T.* i 35
Of other screen, the thin umbrella s. *T.* i 260
Beneath the open sky she s. the feast *T.* i 433

SPREAD—SQUANDER

And jealous of the blessing. *S.* it then *T.* ii 44 [135
That *s.* his motley wings in the eye of noon *T.* iii
And *s.* his hopes before the blaze of day *T.* iii 445
Impervious to the wind. First he bids *s. T.* iii 475
There forests of no meaning *s.* the page *T.* iv 74
And *s.* the honey of his deep research *T.* iv 112
So I, with brush in hand and pallet *s. T.* iv 239
When man was multiplied and *s.* abroad *T.* v 221
No nook so narrow but he *s.* them there *T.* v 773
And more aspiring, and with ampler *s. T.* vi 145
And Æthiopia *s.* abroad the hand *T.* vi 812
To *s.* the earth before him, and commend *Tir.* 640
And *s.* the ruin round *Trans. H.* 18
S. anarchy and terror all around? *T.T.* 303
S. little wings, and rather skip than fly *T.T.* 579
S. the fresh verdure of the field, and leads *T.T.* 692
Then *s.* the rich discovery, and invite *T.T.* 752

SPREADING.
Sage beneath the *s.* oak *B.* 5
This glassy stream, that *s.* pine *S.* 5
And *s.* wide their spongy lobes, at first *T.* iii 522
For owls to roost in. Once thy *s.* boughs *Y.O.* 52

SPRIGHTLINESS.
Youth has a *s.* and fire to boast *Con.* 635

SPRIGHTLY.
S. and fresh, enriches every theme *Con.* 894
Cheered as they go by many a *s.* strain *E.* ii 14
Two goldfinches, whose *s.* song *F.B.* 4
But gaudy plumage, *s.* strain *G.* 7 [sounds *H.* 45
Banks clothed with flowers, groves filled with *s.*
More prudent, or more *s. N.Y.G.* 6
The *s.* morn her course renewed *R.C.* 69
S., and old almost without decay *T.* i 408
The voice of singing and the *s.* chord *T.* ii 78
The *s.* lyre, whose treasure of sweet sounds *T.* iv 160
The mind and heart of every *s.* boy *Tir.* 598
His *s.* mingled with a shade of sad *Tir.* 665

SPRIGS. [756
That here and there some *s.* of mournful mint *T.* iv
Unfolds its bosom, buds, and leaves, and *s. T.* iv 153

SPRING.
The *s.* drew near, each felt a breast *A Tale* 13
Then the progeny that *s. B.* 25
The o'erflowing well of Charity *s.* here! *Ch.* 366
S. in due time supply for the distressed *Ch.* 482
Nor *s.* from love to God, or love to man *Ch.* 560
And give the moral *s.* their proper play *Con.* 832
S. from the mischief it intends to cure *Con.* 170
Should *s.* within thy bosom, drive it thence) *Ex.* 709
Where sprang the thorn, the spiry fir shall *s. H.* 525
Must *s.* that Hope he pants to make his own *H.* 709
The bow well bent, and smart the *s. H.F.* 5
'Twas in the glad season of *s. M.D.* 1
Whence social pleasures *s. Miss —* 30
No genial *s.* to taste *Miss —* 36
Should *s.* from sympathy *Miss —* 48
The call of early *S.—N.* 4
But lovely *S.* peeps o'er his head *N.* 15
Folly the *s.* of his pursuit *P.B.* 17
Thou ever bubbling *s.* of endless lies *P.E.* 467
Whence *s.* the conduct that offends you so *T.* 237
The elastic *s.* of an unwearied foot *T.* i 135
And terrible to sight, as when she *s. T.* i 602
(If e'er she *s.* spontaneous) in remote *T.* i 603
And taints the golden ear. He *s.* his mines *T.* ii 187
Of homogeneal and discordant *s. T.* ii 190 [432
Makes needful still; whose *S.* is but the child *T.* iii
But tasteless. *S.* a palace in its stead *T.* iii 769
Where find ye passive fortitude? Whence *s. T.* v 327
Whose favour, like the clouds of *s.*, might lower *T.* vi 33
E'en in the *s.* and playtime of the year *T.* vi 299

And that one season an eternal *s. T.* vi 770
Her sunshine and her rain, her blooming *s. T.* vi 946
S. hangs her infant blossoms on the trees *Tir.* 43
Back to the season of life's happy *s. Tir.* 132
Soon the sweet *S.* comes dancing forth *Trans. H.* 23
Winter invades the *s.*, and often pours *T.T.* 210
Flew to its first position, with a *s. T.T.* 624
Was left to *s.* by vigour of his own *T.T.* 675[*T.T.*718
The flowers would *s.* where'er she deigned to stray
Where the flowers have the charms of the *s. W.N.* 7
Invigorate by turns the *s.* of life *Y.O.* 78
Even where Death predominates. The *s. Y.O.* 132
The *s.* of eighty-nine shall be 1789, 32

SPRINGING.
Chill blasts of trouble nip their *s.* joys *E.* ii 32
Like Pallas *s.* armed from Jove *Mrs. M—* 26

SPRING-TIME. [512
And *s.* of the world; asked, Whence is man? *T.* ii
To love it too. The *s.* of our years *T.* vi 589

SPRINKLE.
With lavender, and *s.* liquid sweets *T.* ii 257
The forms with which he *s.* all the earth *T.* vi 246

SPRINKLED.
And e'en the dipped and *s.* live in peace *Ch.* 609
The stars that, *s.* o'er the vault of night *R.* 349
Of spacious meads with cattle *s.* o'er *T.* i 164

SPROUT.
A pimple that portends a future *s. T.* iii 528

SPRUCE.
Forth steps the *s.* philosopher, and tells *T.* ii 189
The tasselled cap and the *s.* band a jest *T.* ii 749

SPRUNG. [462
From pride in league with ignorance, have *s.*! *Ch.*
Blasphemed the authority from which it *s. Ex.* 156
The egg was laid from which he *s. T.B.* 8

SPUN.
(I hate long arguments verbosely *s.*) *E.* iii 44
Hence comment after comment, *s.* as fine *P.E.* 494
Muscle and nerve miraculously *s. R.* 59

SPUR.
" Is recreant, and unworthy of his *s.*" *A.T.* 122
He spoke indignant, and his *s.* applied *A.T.* 191
Man feels the *s.* of passions and desires *H.* 55
And what if he did ride whip and *s. M.F.* 22
Such is the impulse and the *s.* he feels *T.* vi 755
The *s.* is powerful, and I grant its force *Tir.* 482
Thus reputation is a *s.* to wit *T.T.* 520
A quarry of stout *s.* and knotted fangs *Y.O.* 117

SPURIOUS.
S., and only current with the blind *E.* ii 8
But *s.* and short-lived; the puny child *T.* v 621

SPURN.
Nor *s.* away a gift a God bestows *H.* 547 [183
Resumes her powers, and *s.* the clumsy fraud *Tir.*

SPURNED.
He *s.* the wretch that slighted, or withstood *Ch.* 31

SPY. [823
A *s.* on my proceeding *F.* 192
" Have reached this nether world, ye *s.* a race *T.* v

SQUAB.
Like a fat *s.* upon a Chinese fan *P.E.* 218

SQUALID.
Such *s.* sloth to honourable toil! *T.* i 579

SQUANDER.
The gifts of Providence, and *s.* life *T.* i 633
Who *s.* time and treasure with a smile *T.* ii 641

SQUANDERED.
Is *s.* in pursuit of idle sports *T.* ii 758
On moments *s.* else, and running all to waste *Tir.* 614

SQUARE.
That *s.* not truly with the Scripture plan *Ch.* 559
A poet does not work by *s.* or line *Con.* 789
'Twas hard to tell, of streets or *s. Q.V.* 9
A massy slab, in fashion *s.* or round *T.* i 21 [492
Slow gathering in the midst, through the *s.* mass *T.* iii
Of hedge-row beauties numberless, *s.* tower *T.* i 173

SQUAR'D.
Till smooth'd and *s.* and fitted to its place *T.* vi 94

SQUEAMISH.
And as for you, my Lady *S.*— *P.* 55

SQUEEZED.
Thus tortured and *s.*, at last it appears *F.M.* 5
Sweats in the crowded theatre and *s. T.* iv 43
With all thy loss of empire, and though *s. T.* v 457
Its *s.* contents, and more than it admits *T.* vi 671

SQUIRE.
There goes my lady, and there goes the *s. B.B.* 12
But first the *s.'s*, a compliment but due *Ch.* 470
How the good *s.* gives never less than gold *Ch.* 480
If neither horse nor groom affect the *s. Con.* 419
Reserved to solace many a neighbouring *s. N.A.* 5
The *s.*, once bashful, is shamefaced no more *P.E.* 403
He chooses company but not the *s.'s R.* 437 [815
The world of wandering knights and *s.* to town *T.* iii

SQUIRREL.
Climbed like a *s.* to his dray *A Fable* 28
The *s.* here his hoard provides *M.B.* 5
The *s.*, flippant, pert, and full of play *T.* vi 315

STAB.
It *s.* at once the morals of a land *P.E.* 306
Felt each a mortal *s.* in her own breast *P.E.* 339
And *s.* Religion with a sly side-thrust *R.* 690

STABBED.
Or *s.* a man to serve some private end? *T.* 47
'Tis universal soldiership has *s. T.* iv 617

STABILITY.
His firm *s.* to what he scorns *T.* i 383

STABLE.
That makes seas *s.*, and dissolves the rock *Con.* 502
The *s.* yields a stercoraceous heap *T.* iii 463

STABLISHES.
He *s.* the strong, restores the weak *T.* ii 343

STACK. [23
But corn was housed, and beans were in the *s. N.A.*
He from the *s.* carves out the accustomed load *T.* v 33

STAFF.
And, *s.* in hand, set forth to share *Mor.* 9
Health's last farewell, a *s.* to thine old age *Tir.* 878

STAGE.
That grief, sequestered from the public *s. Ch.* 305
'Tis like a parcel sent you by the *s. Con.* 305
God's work may serve an ape upon a *s. Con.* 736
Stood pilloried on infamy's high *s. H.* 556
The love that cheers life's latest *s. M.F.* 49
But he, whom e'en in life's last *s. Mor.* 49
Placed for his trial on this bustling *s. P.E.* 23
Nor those in which the *s.* gives vice a blow *R.* 685
Would hiss the cherub Mercy from the *s. T.* 478
While God performs, upon the trembling *s. T.* ii 81
The pulpit to the level of the *s. T.* ii 564
A noble show! while Roscius trod the *s. T.* iii 597
Outscolds the ranting actor on the *s. T.* iv 45
Amused spectators of this bustling *s. T.* v 878

Respect, while stalking o'er life's narrow *s. T.T.* 118
Though the chief actor died upon the *s. T.T.* 341
Next, busy actor on a meaner *s. V.* 27 [60
While thus through all the *s.* thou hast pushed *Y.O.*

STAGE-COACH.
You find safe shelter in the next *s. R.* 492

STAGGER.
Than rove and *s.* with no mark in view *Con.* 864

STAGGERING.
In *s.* types, his predecessor's tale *T.* v 419

STAGNATION.
A cold *s.* on the intestine tide *T.* vi 139

STAIN.
Till penitence had purged the public *s. Ex.* 74
And though a Bishop toil to cleanse the *s. Ex.* 384
That leave no *s.* upon the wing of Time *R.* 800 [241
But shows some touch, in freckle, streak, or *s. T.* vi
The town has tinged the country; and the *s. T.* iv 553
Of abler votaries to cleanse the *s. T.T.* 635

STAINED.
Or *s.* with guilt, beneficent, approved *T.* vi 998

STAIRS.
When Betty screaming came down *s. J.G.* 59
To be the Table Talk of clubs up *s. T.T.* 151

STAKE.
Enjoyed the show, and danced about the *s. Ex.* 615
When having no *s.* left, no pledge to endear *T.* iii 791
Plashed neatly, and secured with driven *s. T.* iv 437
Lay such a *s.* upon the losing side *Tir.* 863
The noblest cause mankind can have at *s. T.T.* 285

STALE.
Has burnt to tinder a *s.* last year's news *B.B.* 10
It is the constant revolution, *s. T.* i 462
Of *s.* debauch, forth issuing from the styes *T.* iv 470

STALK.
Cautious he pinches from the second *s. T.* iii 527
Ill fares the traveller now, and he that *s. T.* iv 341

STALKING.
By the wayside, or *s.* in the path *T.* v 92
Respect, while *s.* o'er life's narrow stage *T.T.* 118

STALL. [695
From tippling benches, cellars, *s.*, and styes *T.* vi
Though placed in golden Durham's second *s. T.* 120

STAMMER.
And *s.* out a syllable *Trans.* iv 38

STAMMERER.
Shall own itself a *s.* in that cause *R.* 413

STAMMERING.
Ghastly in feature, and his *s.* tongue *Ex.* 356

STAMP.
Vice passing current by the *s.* of law *A.T.* 156
With God's deep *s.* upon its current worth *Con.* 710
Whose horrid perpetration *s.* disgrace *Ex.* 416
Marked with the signature and *s.* of Heaven *Ex.* 685
Hope sets the *s.* of vanity on all *H.* 153
Ecstasy sets her *s.* on every mien *P.E.* 136
And *s.* their image in each other's mint *P.E.* 567
The signature and *s.* of power divine *R.* 54
On which the press might *s.* him next to die *St.* ii 6
All bear the royal *s.* that speaks them his *T.* v 551
And perks his ears, and *s.*, and cries aloud *T.* vi 318
Deep in his soft credulity the *s. T.* v 497 [vi 676
And strut, and storm, and straddle, *s.*, and stare *T.*
The *s.* and clear impression of good sense *T.* vi 983
The *s.* of artless piety impress'd *Tir.* 153
S. God's own name upon a lie just made *T.T.* 420

STAMPED.

S. with his foot, and smote upon his thigh *Ex.* 64
But wept, and s., and smote his thigh, in vain *Ex.* 65
In all we touch, s. plainly on his works *H.* 545
S. on each countenance such marks of mind *N.A.* 76
May never more be s. upon his breast *Tir.* 763 [745
S. on the well-bound quarto, grace the shelf *T.T.*

STAND. [170

" And better spear I smite you where you s." *A.T.*
God stood not, though he seemed to s., aloof *Ch.* 59
But grant the plea, and let it s. for just *Ch.* 196
Thine altar, sacred Liberty, should s. *Ch.* 256
And honest Merit s. on slippery ground *Ch.* 284
Unless the power that bade him s., restore *Ch.* 348
Where s. that monument of ancient power *Ch.* 549
We wonder, as we gazing s. below *Ch.* 553 [*Con.*415
Yet e'en the rogue that serves him, though he s.
Shall s. proscribed, a madman or a knave *Con.* 476
But Truth divine for ever s. secure *Con.* 555
'Tis time, however, if the case s. thus *Con.* 847
" The strife now s. upon a fair award *Con.* 851
They learn to bow, to kneel, to sit, to s. *Ex.* 120
Streams swelled above the bank, enjoined to s. *Ex.*185
The more 'twere pressed the firmer it would s. *Ex.*287
Where Obstinacy takes his sturdy s. *Ex.* 298 [340
S. now and judge thyself.—Hast thou incurred *Ex.*
Bid nations leagued against thee s. aloof *Ex.* 565
That s. on sordid interest *F.* 38
Nor would he quit that chosen s. *F.B.* 28
When God and man s. opposite in view *H.* 131
And—pardon me, the bottle s. with you " *H.* 380
Where busy arts are never at a s. *H.* 440
And bids the mountains he has built s. fast *H.* 476
On what foundation virtue is to s. *H.* 529 [616
Your Hope shall s. unblamed, perhaps admired *H.*
All hope despair, that s. not on his cross *H.* 632
Fancy may s. aloof from the design *H.* 672
And s. a witness at Truth's awful bar *Her.* 81
To s. a way-mark in the road to bliss ? *P.E.* 117
There s., and justify the foul abuse *P.E.* 144
S. starved at your inhospitable door ? *P.E.* 250
E'en Leeuwenhoek himself would s. aghast *P.E.* 485
S. close concealed, and see a statue move *R.* 284
Nor quits till evening watch his giddy s. *R.* 434
Yet let me s. excused, if I esteem *R.* 667
As useless if it goes as when it s. *R.* 682
Will s. advanced a step above the rest *R.* 722
Like crowded forest-trees we s. *St.* i 13
It s., like the cerulean arch we see *T.* 26 [31
S. the soul-quickening words—Believe and Live *T.*
The dinner served, Charles takes his usual s. *T.* 213
Now which s. highest in your serious thought ? *T.*221
The Bible only s. neglected there *T.* 425
Now summon every virtue, s. and plead *T.* 566
S., never overlooked, our favourite elms *T.* i 167
Upon the ship's tall side he s., possessed *T.* i 450
S. chargeable with guilt, and to the shafts *T.* ii 155
And s. exposed by common peccancy *T.* ii 72 [334
Must s. acknowledged, while the world shall s. *T.* ii
There s. the messenger of truth; there s. *T.* ii 337
Two empirics he s., and with swoln cheeks *T.* ii 352
And s. an impudent and fearless mark *T.* ii 812
S. up unconscious, and refute the charge *T.* ii 824
In the soft medium, till they s. immersed *T.* iii 520
Sublime above the rest, the statelier s. *T.* iii 595
Nor his, who patient s. till his feet throb *T.* iv 46
He s. erect; his slouch becomes a walk *T.* iv 639
The villas with which London s. begirt *T.* iv 748
And watered duly. There the pitcher s. *T.* iv 775
Smooth as a wall the upright remnant s. *T.* v 36
Build him a pedestal, and say, " S. there *T.* v 258
By him of Babylon, life s. a stump *T.* v 401
S. motionless expectants of its fall *T.* v 528
May s. between an animal and woe *T.* vi 727
That, if his country's. not by his skill *T.* vi 975 [70
S. self-impeached the creature of least worth *Tir.*
Fit for the power in which he s. array'd *Tir.* 98
His favourite s. between his father's knees *Tir.* 570
Wanting its proper base to s. upon *T.T.* 54
By their own conduct they must s. or fall *T.T.* 108
S. on a level, and you prove too much *T.T.* 255
S. most revealed before the freeman's eyes *T.T.* 269
Would strive to make a Paul or Tully s. *T.T.* 349
Like the two figures at St. Dunstan's s. *T.T.* 527
S. in the desert shivering and forlorn *T.T.* 724
So s. a kingdom, whose foundation yet *Y.O.* 120
S. now, and semblance only of itself! *Y.O.* 124

STANDARD.

And the twelve s. of the tribes unfurled *Ex.* 211
And s. of his own, that is to-day *T.* vi 214
The s. of all nations are unfurled *T.T.* 454

STANDING.

Becomes a mockery and a s. jest *Ex.* 110
We have at least commodious s. here *N.A.* 120
Shouldering, and s. as if struck to stone *T.T.* 137
When admirals, extolled for s. still *T.T.* 192

STAND'ST.

They swarm around thee, and thou s. at bay *T.T.* 365

STANK.

And the land s.—so numerous was the fry *T.* ii 832

STAR.

Whether the space between the s. and us *Ch.* 352
And e'en the s., that glitters on the bier *H.* 270
Lights of the world, and s. of human race *P.E.* 97
These most resembling clustered s. *Q.V.* 11
One Georgian s. adorns the skies *Q.V.* 75
If, ere we yet discern life's evening s. *R.* 46
S. countless, each in his appointed place *R.* 83
The s. that, sprinkled o'er the vault of night *R.* 349
Conspicuous as the brightness of a s. *T.* 29 [iii 158
And tell us whence the s.; why some are fixed *T.*
A s. or two, just twinkling on thy brow *T.* iv 253
The bright profusion of her scatter'd s. *T.* vi 176 [819
With which Heaven rang, when every s. in haste *T.* v
As here and there a twinkling s. descried *Tir.* 843
A meteor, or a s.; in these, the sun *T.T.* 575 [36
Now s.; two lobes, protruding, paired exact *Y.O.*

STARE.

Fix on the wainscot a distressful s. *Con.* 116
Having unloaded and made many s. *Con.* 230
And all the world would s. *J.G.* 194
" When, cry the botanists, and s. *P.* 21
Yet Folly ever has a vacant s. *P.E.* 205 [*P.E.* 330
With awkward gait, stretched neck, and silly s.
Therefore, avaunt all attitude, and s. *T.* ii 430 [vi 676
And strut, and storm, and straddle, stamp, and s. *T.*

STARING.

Lap-dog and lambkin with black, s. eyes *T.* i 37

STARK.

She sees a world s. blind to what employs *Ch.* 404
S. naught, because corrupt in their design *T.T.* 4

STARRY.

In s. forms disposed upon the wall *Ch.* 552
His rainbows and his s. eyes *Mrs. M*— 4

START.

I s. at the sound of my own *A.S.* 12
" S. at the call of beauty in distress *A.T.* 120
The wild assassins s. into the street *Ch.* 507
So Self s. nothing, but what tends apace *Ch.* 565
S. not aside from her Creator's plan *Con.* 452 [28
" A friend!" Horatio cried, and seemed to s. *E.* iii

S. from the down on which she lately slept *H.* 219
S. at her first approach, and sounds to arms ! *H.*656
Such was thy charity ; no sudden *s. J.T.* 41
And shall I see thee *s.* away *O.* ii 22
They shriek and sink, survivors *s.* and weep *R.* 159
Shall seem to *s.* into a second birth *R.* 356
S. it at home, and hunt it in the dark *R.* 693
And *s.* theatric, practised at the glass ! *T.* ii 431
S. at his awful name, or deem his praise *T.* iv 180
S. to the voluntary race again *T.* vi 333
Ere yet he *s.* is known *Th.* 18
S. up sagacious, covered with the dust *T.T.* 170
S. from its office like a broken bow *V.* 70

STARTED.
When all creation *s.* into birth *T.* vi 199
When first we *s.* into life's long race *Tir.* 315

STARTING.
Now *s.* into sight *D.W.* 10
Snorting, and *s.* into sudden rage *T.* vi 550

STARTLED.
The sound of pardon pierce his *s.* ear *H.* 724
Cry in his *s.* ear, " Abstain from sin !" *P.E.* 38

STARVE.   [*T.* ii 656
Wives beggar husbands, husbands *s.* their wives
His manna from the ground, or *s.* and die *F.A.* 38
Their noxious growth, *s.* every better seed *R.* 44
Who scorns it, *s.* deservedly at home *I.* 435
Displaying his own beauty, *s.* his flock ! *T.* ii 429[757
The countrys.,and they that feed the o'ercharged *T.*iii
By a just judgment, strip and *s.* themselves *T.* iii 597
Who *s.* his own ; who persecutes the blood *T.* iv 463
Who *s.* upon a dog's-eared Pentateuch *Tir.* 402
When Avarice *s.*, and never hides his face *T.T.* 422

STARVED.
S. by that indolence their mines create *Ch.* 64
For caught and caged, and *s.* to death *G.* 10
Stand *s.* at your inhospitable door ? *P.E.* 250
In converse, either *s.* by cold reserve *T.* v 471
Or, if it enter, soon *s.* out again *Tir.* 768

STARVELING.
Ten *s.* hermits suffer less than he *T.* 112

STATE.
Tramples on a thousand *s. B.* 18
On man's most dignified and happiest *s. Ch.* 2
The cankered spoil corrodes the *s. Ch.* 63
And soothe the sorrows of so sad a *s. Ch.* 199
That pleads for peace till it disturbs the *s. Ch.* 310
To rush into a fixed eternal *s. Con.* 185
The circle formed, we sit in silent *s. Con.* 379 [603
Temperance and Peace insure its healthful *s. Con.*
How credibly, 'tis hard for me to *s.*) *Con.* 816
Once have the sanction of our triple *s. E.* iii 57 [175
For them, the *s.* they left made waste and void *Ex.*
For them, the *s.* to which they went destroyed *Ex.*176
Who left them still a tributary *s. Ex.* 218
War lays a burden on the reeling *s. Ex.* 306
S. thrive or wither, as moons wax and wane *Ex.* 324
The free republic of the whip-gig *s. H.* 190
The comfort of the wedded *s. M.F.* 46
And slumber on in *s. Miss —* 28
The swallows in their torpid *s. N.* 1
A kind release from their imperfect *s. R.* 166
The snowy robe her wintry *s.* assumes *R.* 195
The disencumbered Atlas of the *s. R.* 394
But ask the noble drudge in *s.* affairs *R.* 407
'Tis criminal to leave a sinking *s. R.* 478
He finds the labours of that *s.* exceed *R.* 619
And outline of the present transient *s. R.* 670
To cherish Virtue in an humble *s. R.* 789
Like thee, content in every *s.* may find *S.* ii 7

On the sad theme, their everlasting *s. T.* 41
And he that never doubted of his *s. T.* 299 [i 642
Their former charms ? And having seen our *s. T.*
At thought of her forlorn and abject *s. T.* i 659
And let that pass—'twas but a trick of *s. T.* ii 237
Profusion, deluging a *s.* with lusts *T.* ii 683
Touched by the Midas finger of the *s. T.* iv 507
To administer, to guard, to adorn the *s. T.* v 342
The *S.* that strives for liberty, though foiled *T.* v 367
Fails for the craving hunger of the *s. T.* v 459
And seeing the old castle of the *s. T.* v 525
His freedom is the same in every *s. T.* v 767
But royalty, nobility, and *s. T.* 353 [the *s. ? T.* vi 704
Why ? What has charmed them ? Hath he saved
Of this tempestuous *s.* of human things *T.* vi 737
Who, doomed to an obscure but tranquil *s. T.* vi 903
Account him an encumbrance on the *s. T.* vi 958
The *s.*, beneath the shadow of whose vine *T.* vi 969
Hers is the *s.*, the splendour, and the throne *Tir.* 11
To you, then, tenants of life's middle *s. Tir.* 807
Embittering all his *s. Trans. H.* 12
Whom Education stiffens into *s. T.T.* 125
Happy the *s.* that has not these to fear *T.T.* 167
From almost nullity into a *s. Y.O.* 88
That threatened England's trembling *s.* 1789, 37
If they who on thy *s.* attend 1789, 65

STATED.
At *s.* hours, his freakish thoughts engage *Tir.* 606

STATELIER.
And yours the *s.* mien *L.R.* 22
When thus a mutton *s.* than the rest *N.A.* 81
Sublime above the rest, the *s.* stand *T.* iii 595

STATELINESS.
His altered gait and *s.* retrenched *T.* v 76

STATELY.
This cap, that so *s.* appears *Gr.* 1
And *s.* tone of moralists, who boast *T.* v 690
Give me the line that ploughs its *s.* course *T.T.* 522

STATESMAN.
The *s.*, skilled in projects dark and deep *Ch.* 612
The *s.*, lawyer, merchant, man of trade *R.* 5
" Ye groves " (the *s.* at his desk exclaims *R.* 365
Were charactered on every *s.*'s door *T.* iii 823
Swarm in the streets. The *s.* of the day *T.* vi 696
Of poets raised by you, and *s.*, and divines *Tir.* 283

STATION.
A prouder *s.* on the general scale *Ch.* 336
To insure a side-box *s.* at half-price *T.* ii 624
Such men are raised to *s.* and command *T.T.* 354

STATIONARY.
Till the street rings ; no *s.* steeds *T.* iv 147

STATION'D.
Frequents the crowded auction : *s.* there *T.* vi 286
Think yourself *s.* on a towering rock *T.T.* 33

STATUE.
Wooed an unfeeling *s.* for his wife *P.E.* 528
Stand close concealed, and see a *s.* move *R.* 284
To strip Jove's *s.* of his oaken wreath *T.* vi 640

STATUTE.
Hast thou, by *s.*, shoved from its design *Ex.* 573
Nor judge by *s.* a believer's hope *T.T.* 72

STAUNCH.
And *s.* the bleedings of a broken heart *R.* 322
And you are *s.* indeed in learning's cause *Tir.* 492

STAUNCHEST.
True beagle as the *s.* hound he keeps *P.E.* 87

STAVES.
And eke did roar right merrily two *s. T.* vi 662

STAY. [*Con.* 32
Wrath *s.* him, or else God would strike them dumb
Here *s.* thy foot; how copious, and how clear *Ch.* 365
No wealth can bribe, no prayers persuade to *s. Comp.* i 4
A dull rotation, never at a *s. H.* 101 [iii 25
"Nay, *s.* at home—you're always going out!" *E.*
But versed in arts that while they seem to *s. R.* 383
That prompts the wish to *s. St.* v 30
His promises our *s. St.* vi 8
And hurrying him, impatient of his *s. T.* iv 132
Will win her visits or engage her *s. T.T.* 411
Then let the boobies *s.* at home *Y.D.* 65

STAYED.
Their host to move, and when it *s.* to rest *Ex.* 180
So three doors off the chaise was *s. J.G.* 37

STAYING.
But *s.* behind will do him no good *P.A.* 36

STEAD.
Form, in its *s.*, a covenant of shame *Con.* 684
And raised thyself, a greater, in their *s. ? Ex.* 367
Ere another such grove shall arise in its *s. P.F.* 16
But tasteless. Springs a palace in its *s. T.* iii 769
And no such lights are kindling in their *s. Tir.* 285
Then grace the bony phantom in their *s. T.T.* 43

STEADFAST.
But *s.* principle, and, in its kind *J.T.* 43
Must watch his purpose with a *s.* eye *P.E.* 577
Thunder and flash upon the *s.* shores *R.* 534
Our arch of empire, *s.* but for you *T.* i 773

STEADINESS.
Paul's love of Christ, and *s.* unbribed *H.* 580

STEADY.
On *s.* wing sails through the immense abyss *H.* 163

STEAL.
Fate *s.* along with silent tread *A Fable* 36
Dagger in hand, *s.* close to your bedside *Ch.* 187
The silent pace with which they *s.* away *Comp.* i 3
Silent and chaste she *s.* along *Comp.* ii 3
He thus saw *s.* away *Ep.* ii 30
I glide and *s.* along with heaven in view *H.* 379
And he that stole has learned to *s.* no more *H.* 523
S. to the closet of young innocence *P.E.* 316 [573
Loud when they beg, dumb only when they *s. T.* i
So pleasing, and that *s.* away the thought *T.* ii 299
And heaviest, light of foot *s.* fast away *T.* iv 442
And unperceived the current *s.* away *T.* v 100

STEALING.
S. a sidelong glance at a full house *T.* iv 201

STEALTH.
We next inquire, but softly and by *s. Con.* 389
And that obtained by rapine and by *s. ? Ex.* 371
Who scorns to do an injury by *s. H.* 411
By rust unperishable or by *s. J.T.* 26
So life glides smoothly and by *s.* away *T.* vi 995

STEAM.
Thy thirst-creating *s.* at length produce *Con.* 262
A pestilent and most corrosive *s. T.* iii 494 [554
The process. Heat and cold, and wir d and *s. T.* iii

STEAMING.
From many a *s.* lake and reeking bog *A.T.* 93

STEAMY.
Throws up a *s.* column, and the cups *T.* iv 39

STEED.
Called for his arms, and for his princely *s. A.T.* 124
His high-bred *s.* expands his nostrils wide *A.T.* 163
Buckled his helm, and to his *s.* repaired *A.T.* 172

From the clatter of street-pacing *s. C.* 46
Upon his nimble *s. J.G.* 78
The frighted *s.* he frighted more *J.G.* 227
The veteran *s.* excused his task at length *R.* 625
Ere yet it came, the traveller urged his *s. T.* 244
He cherups brisk his ear-erecting *s. T.* iii 9
Till the street rings; no stationary *s. T.* iv 147
The toiling *s.* expand the nostril wide *T.* iv 347
The dreadful leap, more rational his *s. T.* vi 517
His *s.*, usurp a place they well deserve *T.* vi 703
If the gilt carriage, and the pampered *s. T.T.* 133

STEEL.
That he was cased in such enchanted *s. A.T.* 183
That brass and *s.* should make so fine a show *Ch.* 554
Kept snug in caskets of close-hammered *s. R.* 308
With nice incision of her guided *s. T.* i 708 [414
None but his *s.* approach them. What is weak *T.* iii
On female industry: the threaded *s. T.* iv 165 [511
To *s.* their hearts against the dread of death" *T.* vi
And forced the blunt and yet unblooded *s. T.* v 215
Not rough with wire of *s.* or brass *T.B.* 26

STEELED.
There hardening by degrees, till double *s. P.E.* 590

STEEP.
Whatever *s.* inquiry recommends *Ch.* 316
Shall *s.* me in Elysian reverie *M.P.* 19
Is this the rugged path, the *s.* ascent *P.E.* 71
Swift pace or *s.* ascent no toil to me *T.* i 139
A sudden *s.* upon a Rustic Bridge *T.* i. 267
To some not *s.*, though philosophic height *Tir.* 631

STEEPLE.
And *s.* towering high, much like our own *P.E.* 382
Above the *s.* shines a plate *Trans.* ii 7

STEER.
To *s.* it close to land *D.W.* 18
Where Duty bids he confidently *s. R.H.* 6
To *s.* with nicest art betwixt the extreme *S.* ii 9

STEERED.
S. Britain's oak into a world unknown *Ch.* 25

STEM.
"The rich, the produce of a nobler *s. Ex.* 460
The fruits that hang on pleasure's flowery *s. R.* 179

STENCH.
The *s.* remains, the lustre dies away *Con.* 678
And thine was smothered in the *s.* and fog *Ex.* 510

STEP.
S. forth to fashion and refine the race *Ch.* 98
"'Tis but a *s.*, sir, just at the street's end" *E* iii 26
And if success his *s.* attend *F.* 82
Dare *s.* across his arbitrary views *H.* 193
At every *s.* beneath their feet they tread *Her.* 55
That now at every *s.* thou movest *M.* 38
Beware of desperate *s.* The darkest day *N.A.* 132
While all his purposes and *s.* to guard *P.E.* 41
Securely, though by *s.* but rarely trod *R.* 113
With eager *s.*, and carelessly arrayed *R.* 187
'Tis done;—he *s.* into the welcome chaise *R.* 391
A *s.* if fair, and if a shower approach *R.* 491
Will stand advanced a *s.* above the rest *R.* 722
His measured *s.* were governed by his ear *T.* 63
Forth *s.* the man—an emblem of myself! *T.* 213
We mount again, and feel at every *s. T.* i 271 [246
With matron *s.* slow moving, while the Night *T.* iv
Forth *s.* the spruce philosopher, and tells *T.* ii 189
He *s.* right onward, martial in his air *T.* iv 640
Take *s.* for *s.*; and, as I near approach *T.* v 18
With well-considered *s.*, seems to resent *T.* v 75

S. forth to notice ; and, besotted thus *T.* v 257
Consulted and obeyed, to guide his *s. T.* v 674
An inadvertent *s.* may crush the snail *T.* vi 564
Reasoning at every *s.* he treads *The Doves* 1
Would turn our *s.* into a wiser train *Tir.* 260
One *s.* beyond the boundary of the laws *T.T.* 228

STEPPED.
Called on a friend, drank tea, *s.* home again *Con.* 278
Then *s.* the poet into bed *R.C.* 107
And *s.* at once into a cooler clime *T.* i 337

STEPPING.
S. into their nests, they paddled *P.T.* 54.

STERCORACEOUS.
The stable yields a *s.* heap *T.* iii 463

STERILE.
So *s.* with what charms soe'er she will *T.* i 710

STERLING.
S., and worthy of a wise man's wish *T.* v 358
No polish can make *s.*, and that vice *T.* vi 990
Then decent Pleasantry and *s.* Sense *T.T.* 638

STERN.
And say as *s.* Elijah said of old *Con.* 850
An aspect *s.* on man's affairs *P.T.* 48
Grew *s.*, and darted a severe rebuke *T.* ii 720
With *s.* severity deals out the year *T.T.* 209

STERNHOLD.
Hail, *S.* then ; and, Hopkins, hail ! Amen *T.T.* 760

STEWS.
Of fashion, dissipation, taverns, *s. T.* ii 770

STICK.
Between two poles upon a *s.* transverse *T.* i 561
S. close, a Mentor worthy of his charge *T.* ii 595
The indented *s.*, that loses day by day *Tir.* 559

STICKLER.
And every venal *s.* for the yoke *T.T.* 352

STIFF.
Such frozen figures, *s.* as they are cold *Ch.* 607
S. in the letter, lax in the design *Ex.* 125   [671
Not English *s.*, but frank, and formed to please *Tir.*

STIFFENS.
Whom Education *s.* into state *T.T.* 125

STIFFER.
No combatants are *s. F.* 138

STIFLING.
The *s.* wave and then he sank *Cast.* 48
Even in the *s.* bosom of the town *T.* iv 753

STIGMA.
That sits a *s.* on his father's house *T.* ii 760

STILE.   [136
That mounts the *s.* with ease, or leaps the fence *T.* i

STILL.
To bid the pleadings of self-love be *s. R.* 129
Pastoral images and *s.* retreats *R.* 257
Or shine the dullness of *s.* life away *R.* 746
Sought in *s.* water, and beneath clear skies *T.* iii 382
The *s.* small voice is wanted. He must speak *T.* v 685

STILLEST.
And censured oft as useless. *S.* streams *T.* vi 929

STILLNESS.
Enjoy the *s.* of some close retreat *Con.* 570
S., accompanied with sounds so soft *T.* vi 84
Where, *s.* aiding study, and his mind *Tir.* 773

STILL-REFUTED.
His *s.* quirks he still repeats *P.E.* 550

STILTS.
Of solemn farce, where Ignorance in *s. T.* ii 736

STING.
But we that make no honey, though we *s. Con.* 289
But with a soul that ever felt the *s. R.* 315
Here every drop of honey hides a *s. T.* vi 830

STINKS.
His hungry acres, *s.* and is no use *T.* iv 503

STINT.
And his old *s.*— three thousand pounds a year *R.* 602
Friends (for I cannot *s.* as some have done *R.* 719

STIPULATES.
He *s.*, indeed, but merely this *H.* 334

STIR.
And *s.* his own to match them, or excel *Ch.* i 18 [333
He shakes with cold—you *s.* the fire and strive *Con.*
For one slight trespass all this *s.* ? *M.F.* 21
With the vain *s.* I sum up half mankind *T.* iii 130
And to the *s.* of Commerce, driving slow *T.* iii 739
Now *s.* the fire, and close the shutters fast *T.* iv 36
To peep at such a world ; to see the *s. T.* iv 89

STIRRED.
Their acrid temper turns, as soon as *s. Ch.* 503

STOCK.
While conversation, an exhausted *s. H.* 103
Till, all my *s.* of infant sorrow spent *M.P.* 43
His *s.* a few French phrases got by heart *P.E.* 375
Book, beads, and maple dish, his meagre *s. T.* 80
Houses in ashes, and the fall of *s. T.* iv 16
Her scanty *s.* of brushwood, blazing clear *T.* iv 381
The *s.* whereon it grows *U.* 16

STOCKDOVE.
Scarce shuns me : and the *s.* unalarm'd *T.* vi 307

STOCKJOBBERS.
The leathern ears of *s.* and Jews *T.T.* 187

STOLE.
And he that *s.* has learned to steal no more *H.* 523
Who *s.* her slipper, filled it with Tokay *T.* 157
And not with curses on his heart, who *s. Tir.* 151

STOLEN.
Proud of thy fleets and armies, *s.* the gem *Ex.* 348
Apollo, hast thou *s.* away *O.* i 11
Till time has *s.* away the slighted good *T.* vi 51

STOMACH.
Which stuck in M.'s *s.* as cross as a bone *A.T.* ii 8

STONE.   [310
To find it stuffed with brickbats, earth, and *s. Con.*
Like angel-heads in *s.* with pigeon wings ? *Con.* 576
By stout, substantial gods of wood and *s. Con.* 834
Doified useless wood or senseless *s. Ex.* 238
But 'tis not timber, lead, and *s. F.* 163
The *s.* did rattle underneath *J.G.* 43
Had two *s.* bottles found *J.G.* 66
Full slowly pacing o'er the *s. J.G.* 79
Is almost enough to draw pity from *s. P.A.* 4
As creeping ivy clings to wood or *s. P.E.* 285
Discover huge cathedrals built with *s. P.E.* 381
We slight the precious kernel of the *s. P.E.* 419 [15
With a turf on my breast, and a *s.* at my head *P.F.*
Gives more than female beauty to a *s. T.* i 703
Became *s.* blind ; precedence went in truck *T.* ii 741
'Twere better to be born a *s. P.* 11   [*T.* iii 646
Of close-rammed *s.* has charged the encumbered soil
Gives bond in *s.* and ever-during brass *T.* v 710
The scene is touching, and the heart is *s. Tir.* 298
To show a stumbling *s.* by night *Trans.* i 19
Shouldering, and standing as if struck to *s. T.T.* 137

STONY.
I fed on scarlet hips and s. haws T. i 120

STOOD.
God s. not, though he seemed to stand, aloof Ch. 59
Go, quit the rank to which ye s. preferred Con. 75
Can gold grow worthless that has s. the touch E. iii 18
They s. the test of her ensnaring smile Ex. 78
S. trembling at the boldness of thy powers Ex. 597
S. pilloried on infamy's high stage H. 556
And Perjury s. up to swear all true H. 563
If ever on thy eyelid s. the tear H. 676
His horse at last s. still J.G. 160
Where a demon, her enemy, s. M.D. 27
All huddling into phalanx, s. and gazed N.A. 48
Upborne they s. Three legs upholding firm T. i 20
In Albion's happy isle. The lumber s. T. i 58
Lie scattered where the shapely column s. T. ii 76
So s. the brittle prodigy; though smooth T. v 154
A distant age asks where the fabric s. T. v 535
And angel choirs attended. Wondering s. T. vi 352
Rushed to the cliff, and having reached it, s.T. vi 552
The mulberry-tree s. centre of the dance T. vi 686
And Bully's cage supported s. T.B. 22
And s. the test, perhaps on the wrong side Tir. 740
He s., as some inimitable hand T.T. 348
That grazed it s. beneath that ample cope Y.O. 54

STOOL.
On such a s. immortal Alfred sat T. i 22
Thus first Necessity invented S.—T. i 86
Saves the small inventory, bed, and s. T. iv 401

STOOP.
Verse cannot s. so low as thy desert Ex. 547
While yet he dwells below, must s. to glean F.A. 37
Now s. upon it, and now grasps the prey P.E. 334
As s. from Heaven to sell the proud a throne T. 78
That he had ta'en in charge. He would not s. T. ii 478
But learn we might, if not too proud to s. T. vi 621
Saw never, such as Heaven s. down to see T. vi 817
To s. to Tyranny's usurped command T.T. 440

STOOPED.
S. from its highest pitch to pounce a wren T.T. 553
Who, born a gentleman, has s. too low V. 33

STOOPING.
So s. down, as needs he must J.G. 89
So s. down from hawthorn top N.G. 11
Why, s. from the noon of day O. i 9
Their pendant boughs, s. as if to drink T. i 269
Whole without s., towering crest and all T. iv 271

STOP.
Nor s., till, overleaping all delays Ch. 178
Give it the breast, or s. its mouth with pap! Con. 480
" S., s., John Gilpin!—Here's the house!" J.G. 145
And s. and eat, for well you may J.G. 191
Whom in a trice he tried to s. J.G. 223
" S. thief! s. thief!—a highwayman!" J.G. 237
The lowest first, and without s. R.C. 93 [332
Then s. and snorts, and throwing high his heels T. vi
No rattling wheels s. short before these gates T. iv 144
Moves right toward the mark; nor s. for aught T. v 53
"S., while ye may; suspend your mad career T.T. 435

STOPPED.
Nor s. till where he had got up J.G. 247

STOPPLED.
S. his cruise, replaced his book Mor. 7

STORE.
Than she supplies from her abounding s. Ch. 102
So when a ship, well freighted with the s. Ch. 441
A smaller piece amidst the precious s. Ch. 476
And like the s. autumnal suns mature Con. 649
The gift of nature, or the classic s. Con. 896
His passions, like the watery s. that sleep H. 183
Doubtless it is. To which, of my own s. H. 433
Piles up his s. amidst the frozen waste H. 475
Feeds sparingly, communicates his s. H. 521
Thy needles, once a shining s. M. 9
That graced his lettered s. M. i 8
From Flora's balmy s. M. ii 10
Those open on the spot their honeyed s. P.E. 49
Her hedge-row shrubs, a variegated s. R. 419
Pillow and bobbins all her little s. T. 318
Maturer years shall happier s. produce T. 495 [ii 538
Grace, knowledge, comfort—an unfathomed s. ? T.
Pay contribution to the s. he gleans T. iv 110 [132
When thou wouldst build; no quarry sent its s. T. v
For her, amasses an unbounded s. Tir. 15
And wisely s. the nursery by degrees Tir. 117
Who feed a pupil's intellect with s. Tir. 622
Part of the captain's precious s. Trans. iv 5
Is worth, with all its gold and glittering s. T.T. 61

STORED.
With Asiatic vices s. thy mind Ex. 372 [636
" And s. the earth so plenteously with means T. v

STORKS. [v 282
S. among frogs, that have but croaked and died T.

STORM.
Frowns in the s. with angry brow A Fable 38
And, such as s. allow Cast. 26
No voice divine the s. allayed Cast. 61
S. but enliven its unfading green Ch. 576
The raving s. and dashing wave defies Con. 559
Or when a s. drew near Ep. ii 28
Say Wrath is coming, and the s. appears Ex. 270
Wait but the lashes of a wintry s. H. 185
Beckons the legions of his s. away H. 477
To s. the citadels they build in air H. 626
Aware of wintry s. M.B. 6
But screened from every s. that blows Mrs. M—18
Still outlives many a s. that has effaced M.P. 56
(The s. all weathered and the ocean crossed) M.P. 89
The s. of passion, and say, "Peace, be still!" P.E. 599
Frowning in s., or breathing gentle airs R. 194
'Tis done—the raging s. is heard no more T. 275
Thrives by the rude concussion of the s. T. i 378
S. rise to o'erwhelm him; or if stormy winds T. ii 142
And needing none assistance of the s. T. ii 144
He that is ever occupied in s. T. iii 383 [574
Peep through their polished foliage at the s. T. iii
But urged by s. along its slippery way T. iv 127
Presented bare against the s., plods on T. iv 353
Lest s. should overset the leaning pile T. v 39
" That navigate a sea that knows no s. T. v 823
And furrow'd into s., and with a hand T. vi 269
But 'twas a transient calm. A s. was near T. vi 544
An uncrowded s. His hour was come T. vi 545 [676
And strut, and s., and straddle, stamp, and stare T. vi
And what his s. have blasted and defaced T. vi 745
She loses in such s. her very name T.T. 328
The s. that overset the joys of life T.T. 449 [491
The s. of music shakes the astonished crowd T.T.
The poet's heart; he looks to distant s. T.T. 495
And one of s. of hail Y.D. 54
Uncrowded, yet safe sheltered from the s. Y.O. 55
Calm and alternate s., moisture and drought Y.O.77

STORMY.
(For s. troubles loudest roar Mrs. M— 47 [142
Storms rise to o'erwhelm him; or if s. winds T. ii
Joys that her s. raptures never yield T. iii 57

STORY.
A s. in which native humour reigns Con. 203

One *s.* more, dear Hill, and I have done *E.* iii 45
Released him as my *s.* tells *N.G.* 25
So one, whose *s.* serves at least to show *P.E.* 526
A *s.* of a cock and bull *P.T.* 7

STOUT.
By *s.* substantial gods of wood and stone *Con.* 834
Till the *s.* bearers lift the corpse again *T.* i 481
The *s.* tall captain, whose superior size *Tir.* 222
Tells of a few *s.* hearts that fought and died *T.T.* 23
A quarry of *s.* spurs and knotted fangs *Y.O.* 117

STOUTEST.
To quell the valour of the *s.* heart *Ex.* 358

STOVES.
These *s.* that for pattern and form *Gr.* 39

STRADDLE. [*A.C.* 14
"Your lordship observes they are made with a *s.*
And strut, and storm, and *s.*, stamp and stare *T.* vi 676

STRAGGLING.
An eyebrow, next compose a *s.* lock *T.* ii 446

STRAIGHT.
Whence *s.* he came with hat and wig *J.G.* 181
Much controversy *s.* arose *L.W.* 15
Bend the *s.* rule to their own crooked will *P.E.* 557
'Tis such an easy walk, so smooth and *s. R.* 489 [529
And interdicts its growth. Thence *s.* succeed *T.* iii
Sinuous or *s.*, now rapid and now slow *T.* iii 778
Crooked or *s.*, through quags or thorny dells *Tir.* 253

STRAIN.
How would they take up Israel's taunting *s.*! *Ch.* 66
The dozing sages drop the drowsy *s. Con.* 247
With *s.* it was a privilege to hear *Con.* 618
And give the *s.* the compass it demands *Con.* 718
Cheered as they go by many a sprightly *s. E.* ii 14
Thy tender sorrows and thy plaintive *s. E.* ii 45
But not to moralize too much, and *s. E.* iii 42
Smoothed and refined the meanest *s. E.* iv 74
Will hear perhaps thy salutary *s. Ex.* 453
That few will hear, and fewer heed the *s. Ex.* 725
My *s.* for ever new *G.* 6
But gaudy plumage, sprightly *s. G.* 7
Then raising her voice to a *s. M.D.* 17
Far be the thought, and far the *s. Miss* — 9
Admiring, terrified, the novel *s. N.A.* 49
Be thou the great inspirer of my *s. R.* 202
Its brisker and its graver *s.* fall short *R.* 294 [411
The tongue whose *s.* were cogent as commands *R.*
To waste unheard the music of his *s. R.* 548
And scorned as is my *s. St.* i 30
But the monitory *s. St.* iv 17
Its thunders; and by him, in *s.* as sweet *T.* ii 341
Misled by custom, *s.* celestial themes *T.* ii 438
And these the Grecian in ennobling *s. T.* iii 454
"Their weekly dole of edifying *s. T.* v 646 [818
Sweet conference; inquires what *s.* were they *T.* v
The soothing influence of the wafted *s. T.* vi 68
Till, nation after nation taught the *s. T.* vi 796 [1023
Whose frown can disappoint the proudest *s. T.* vi
Proving at last, though told in pompous *s. Tir.* 75
Such a *s.* as I can give *Trans.* iii 8
Liberty taught him her Athenian *s. T.T.* 343
Such lofty *s.* embellish what you teach *T.T.* 478
To him who *s.* his all into a song *T.T.* 533

STRAINED.
And *s.* to the last screw that he can bear *T.* 385
S. through the friendly mats, a vivid green *T.* iii 525

STRAITENING.
S. its growth by such a strict embrace *R.* 234

STRANGE.
Between Nose and Eyes a *s.* contest arose *A.C.* 1
S. ! how the frequent interjected dash *Ch.* 521
S. tidings these to tell a world who treat *Con.* 719
S. fluctuation of all human things! *E.* iii 9 [618
The *s.* conceits, vain projects, and wild dreams *H.*
Who, *s.* to tell, all judged it wrong *J.P.* 19
S. the recital! from whatever cause *P.E.* 401
By shrugs and *s.* contortions of his face *P.E.* 414
Jack bowed and was obliged—confessed 'twas *s. R.* 599
S. fondness of the human heart *St.* v 13
S. world, that costs it so much smart *St.* v 15
That endless bliss (how *s.* soe'er it seem *T.* 355 [413
Is Nature's dictate. *S.* ! there should be found *T.* i
S.! that a creature rational, and cast *T.* i 574
What solid was, by transformation *s. T.* ii 99
For monstrous novelty and *s.* disguise *T.* ii 612
S. that so fair a creature should yet want *T.* iii 725
The rest appears a wilderness of *s. T.* iv 78
Trees, churches, and *s.* visages, expressed *T.* iv 288
S. that such folly as lifts bloated man *T.* v 283
But above measure *s.*, that neither proof *T.* v 293
Though wild their *s.* vagaries, and uncouth *T.* vi 337
Events improbable and *s.* as these *Tir.* 370
He blushes, hangs his head, is shy and *s. Tir.* 568
S. doctrine this! that without scruple tears *T.T.* 5

STRANGER.
Accept the tribute of a *s.*'s pen *Ch.* 291
A *s.* joined them, courteous as a friend *Con.* 522
A *s.*'s purpose in these lays *E.* ii 1
S. to liberty 'tis true *F.B.* 10
Loudly resent the *s.*'s freedom there *H.* 354
A *s.* to superior strength. *H.F.* 19
To increase a *s.*'s treasures *N.C.* 3
When some *s.* is interred *St.* iv 32
They, *s.* to the controversial field *T.* 371
Of ladyships—a *s.* to the poor *T.* ii 386
Be *s.* to each other? Pierce my vein *T.* iii 201 [295
Though still deceived, some *s.*'s near approach *T.* iv
Still *s.* much that when at length mankind *T.* v 237
Nor *s.* intermeddling with my joy *T.* vi 298
A *s.* to the manners of the youth *T.* vi 493
(A sight to which our eyes are *s.* yet) *T.* vi 825
Then why resign into a *s.*'s hand *Tir.* 551
And trust for safety to a *s.*'s care *Tir.* 852
And *s.* to the air of courts 1789, 62

STRANGEST. [11
But the strife is the *s.* that ever was known *A.T.* ii

STRANGLED.
The man that's *s.* by a hair *A Fable* 35

STRAPP'D. [iv 6
With spatter'd boots, *s.* waist, and frozen locks *T.*

STRATA.
The solid earth, and from the *s.* there *T.* iii 151

STRATAGEM.
For *s.*, or courage, or for all *T.* v 232

STRAW.
In every shining *s.* she sees *E.* iv 46
And milk, and oats, and *s. Ep.* ii 14
And deems her sharp artillery mere *s. H.* 597
The rustling *s.* sends up a frequent mist *T.* i 360
The undreaded volley with a sword of *s. T.* ii 811
To thy *s.* couch, and slumber unalarmed *T.* iii 345
From the full fork, the saturated *s. T.* iii 479

STRAY.
Philosophy, that does not dream or *s. Ch.* 313
Where 'tis an angel's happiness to *s. Con.* 472
So should an idiot, while at large he *s. Con.* 899 [464
Where beckoning Pleasure leads them, wildly *s. Ex.*

As when two pilgrims in a forest *s. H.* 276
His silly sheep, what wonder if they *s.? P.E.* 119
To limit thought, by Nature prone to *s. R.* 127
Was blasphemy his sin? or did he *s. T.* 48
That fools discover it, and *s.* no more *T.* ii 530
Where Rhenus *s.* his vines among *T.B.* 7
Are rarely known to *s. The Doves* 4
A worm is known to *s. Trans.* i 2   [*s. T.T.* 718
The flowers would spring where'er she deigned to

STRAYED.
The herb as soft, while nibbling *s.* the rest *N.A.* 38
The ass; for he, we know, has lately *s. N.A.* 96
But there I laid the scene. There early *s. T.* iv 697
Elisha's eye, that, when Gehazi *s. Tir.* 267
In many a page historic *s.* 1789, 22

STRAYING.
Methinks I see thee *s.* on the beach *T.* i 654

STREAK.
In dazzling *s.* the vivid lightnings play *Her.* 18 [241
But shows some touch, in freckle, *s.*, or stain *T.* vi

STREAKY.
Methinks I see thee in the *s.* west *T.* iv 245

STREAM.
Her wooed Sir Airy, by meandering *s. A.T.* 11
A *s.* of liberal and heroic deeds *Ch.* 245
Drinks wisdom at the milky *s.* of light *Ch.* 319
Plunged in the *s.*, they lodge upon the mud *Ch.* 531
Both speed their journey with a restless *s. Comp.* i 2
S. never flow in vain; where *s.* abound *Comp.* i 9
Sweet *s.* that winds through yonder glade *Comp.* ii 1
Your heart shall yield a life-renewing *s. Con.* 503
Where'er it winds, the salutary *s. Con.* 893
The windings of the *s. D.W.* 28
O salutary *s.*, that murmur there! *E.* ii 28
S. swelled above the bank, enjoined to stand *Ex.* 185
S. edged with osiers, fattening every field *H.* 47
No fertilizing *s.* your fields divide *H.* 467   [*H.* 741
Rocks, groves, and *s.*, must join him in his praise
Fast by the *s.* that bounds your just domain *Her* 47
For when it *s.* from that pure source *Miss* — 57
The keenest frost that binds the *s. N.* 5
Ah! why, since oceans, rivers, *s. O.* i 5
And wilt thou quit the *s. O.* ii 15
The precious *s.* still purling in his ear *P.E.* 232
Called to these crystal *s.*, do ye turn off *P.E.* 265
The dribbling *s.* ne'er puts it out again *P.E.* 322
To *s.* of popular opinion drawn *P.E.* 478
Sweet birds in concert with harmonious *s. R.* 259
S. tinkle sweetly in poetic chime *R.* 568   [*R.*421
Green balks and furrowed lands, the *s.* that spreads
This glassy *s.*, that spreading pine *S.* 5
To bid Affliction's eye no longer *s. S.* ii 12
While far beyond, and overthwart the *s. T.* i 169
At first, progressive as a *s.*, they seek *T.* i 292
Else noxious: oceans, rivers, lakes, and *s. T.* i 375
Drew from the *s.* below. More favoured, we *T.* ii 501
Take of the crimson *s.* meandering there *T.* iii 202
For oft, as if in her the *s.* of mild *T.* iii 435
And *s.*, as if created for his use *T.* iii 776
S. far behind him, scenting all the air *T.* v 57
The *s.* are lost amid the splendid blank *T.* v 96
Of evanescent glory, once a *s. T.* v 167
And soon to slide into a *s.* again *T.* v 168   [260
And these dissolving snows, and this clear *s. T.* vi
Should suffer torture, and the *s.* be dyed *T.* vi 390
Have poured my *s.* of panegyric down *T.* vi 720 [776
Of the same grove, and drink one common *s. T.* vi
Is sullied in the *s.*, taking a taint *T.* vi 834
And censured oft as useless. Stillest *s. T.* vi 929
Are a *s.* choked, or trickling to no end *Tir.* 718

Beneath the hedge, or near the *s. Trans.* i 1
Ungenial blasts attending curl the *s. T.T.* 213 [380
The *s.* that feeds the wellspring of the heart *T.T.*
Was natural as in the flowing *s. T.T.* 592   [523
Like a proud swan, conquering the *s.* by force *T.T.*

STREAMER
Like *s.* long and gay *J.G.* 102
Around her, fanning light her *s.* gay *M.P.* 95
Now hoist the sail, and let the *s.* float *T.* ii 255
His thorns with *s.* of continual praise? *T.* v 330

STREAMING.
Their *s.* hearts poured freely when they died *Ex.* 625
My penitential stripes, my *s.* blood *T.* 95
Oh sorrowful and sad! the *s.* tears *T.* 173
And ribands *s.* gay, superbly raised *T.* iv 541
In *s.* gold; syringa, ivory pure *T.* vi 150

STREET.
The wild assassins start into the *s. Ch.* 507   [121
Send your dishonoured gown to Monmouth *S.—P.E.*
"'Tis but a step, sir, just at the *s.*'s end" *E.* iii 26
The chariots bounding in her wheel-worn *s. Ex.* 21
'Twas hard to tell, of *s.* or squares *Q.V.* 9   [482
That dread the encroachment of our growing *s. R.*
The worn-out nuisance of the public *s. T.* 508
Her palaces are dust. In all her *s. T.* ii 77   [829
Were covered with the pest; the *s.* were filled *T.* ii
In all our crowded *s.*; and senates seem *T.* iii 61
Till the *s.* rings; no stationary steeds *T.* iv 147
Swarm in the *s.* The statesmen of the day *T.* vi 696
And in her *s.*, and in her spacious courts *T.* vi 809
Robbery of gardens, quarrels in the *s. Tir.* 229

STREET-PACING.
From the clatter of *s.* steeds *C.* 46
And some *s.* harlot his first love *Tir.* 217

STRENGTH.
Had fluttered all his *s.* away *B.R.* 15
Nor soon he felt his *s.* decline *Cast.* 15
(For opposition gives opinion *s.*) *Con.* 88
Meet their opposers with united *s. Con.* 700
The monuments of human *s. E.* i 82
Of the chief *s.* and glory of the frame *Ex.* 335 [706
That *s.* would fail, opposed against the push *Ex.*
In an engine of utmost mechanical *s. F.M.* 4
A stranger to superior *s. H.F.* 19
In kind compassion of his failing *s. R.* 626
And all his *s.* from Scripture drew *St.* iii 19
S. in his heart, dominion in his nod *T.* 409
Fearless of wrong, reposed his weary *s. T.* i 15
And *s.* is lord of all; but gentle, kind *T.* i 605
That gives society its beauty, *s. T.* ii 681
Or misapplying his unskilful *s. T.* iii 402   [iii 636
Is needful. *S.* may wield the ponderous spade *T.*
The *s.* they borrow with the grace they lend *T.* iii 669
Were tasked to his full *s.*, absorbed and lost *T.* iv 301
Deep in the loamy bank. Uptorn by *s. T.* iv 438
One eminent above the rest for *s. T.* v 231
All that the contest calls for; spirit, *s. T.* v 376
Of asps their venom, overpowering *s. T.* v 702 [851
Worlds that had never been hadst Thou in *s. T.* v
His *s.* to suffer, and his will to serve *T.* v 902
Of injury, with such knowledge of their *s. T.* vi 476
Their *s.*, or speed, or vigilance, were given *T.* vi 610
S. joined with beauty, dignity with grace *Tir.* 2
That, since thy *s.* must with thy years elope *Tir.* 876
And let thy *s.* be seen *Trans. H.* 33   [497
And armed with *s.* surpassing human powers *T.T*
Skill to direct, and *s.* to strike the blow *T.T.* 357
Harmony, *s.*, words exquisitely sought *T.T.* 701

STRENUOUS.
The *s.* use of profitable thought *R.* 674

From s. toil his hours of sweetest ease *T.* i 388
Can he be s. in his country's cause *T.* v 503

STRESS.
Perverting often, by the s. of lewd *T.* ii 551
The s. of a continual act, the pain *T.* vi 208
Will need no s. of argument to enforce *Tir.* 803

STRETCH.
To see a God s. forth his human hand *Ch.* 581
Far as the faculty can s. away *R.* 74
Would gladly s. life's little span *St.* v 7
An instrument whose cords, upon the's. *T.* 384
The sedentary s. their lazy length *T.* i 389
His every nerve in action and at s. *T.* iii 90
S. a length of shadow o'er the field *T.* v 10

STRETCHED.
They s. the neck, and rolled the wanton eye *Ex.* 53
With awkward gait, s. neck, and silly stare *P.E.* 380
So when the Jewish leader s. his arm *T.* ii 825 [728
Though s. at ease in Chertsey's silent bowers *T.* iv
Where England, s. towards the setting sun *T.* vi 483
S. forth to dally with the crested worm *T.* vi 780

STRETCHING.
Beneath, beyond, and s. far away *T.* v 789

STREW.
Upon the wanton breezes. S. the deck *T.* ii 256
Must be detached, and where it s. the floor *T.* iii 615

STREWING.
S. yonder sea with wrecks *N.C.* 34

STRICKEN.
Laughed at, he laughs again; and s. hard *T.* ii 323
I was a s. deer that left the herd *T.* iii 108

STRICT.
Straitening its growth by such a s. embrace *R.* 234
From the s. duties of the sacred day? *T.* 49 [641
" So s., that less than perfect must despair? *T.* v

STRICTEST.
Though not a grace appears on s. search *T.* 151

STRICTLY. [512
But, watch they s., or neglect their charge? *Tir.*

STRIDES.
By s. of human wisdom. In his works *T.* iii 222

STRIFE. [ii 9
It has always been reckoned a just cause of s. *A.T.*
But waged with Death a lasting s. *Cast.* 17 [ii 11
But the s. is the strangest that ever was known *A.T.*
Oaths terminate, as Paul observes, all s. *Con.* 55
Though blameless, had incurred perpetual s. *Con.* 512
And lips unstained by folly or by s. *Con.* 563
" The s. now stands upon a fair award *Con.* 851
Though nothing have occurred to kindle s. *E.* iii 15
Religion should extinguish s. *F.* 133
Yet half mankind maintain a churlish s. *H.* 322
But oh! the s., the bickering, and debate *H.* 342
Assailed by scandal and the tongue of s. *H.* 576
Friendship and Love seemed tenderly at s. *H.* 680
Alas! and is domestic s. *M.F.* 31
His will and judgment at continual s. *T.* 467
And in the charming s. triumphant still *T.* iv 163
Ensanguined hearts, clubs typical of s. *T.* iv 218
And reaped their plenty without grudge or s. *T.* v 203
Well spent in such a s., may earn indeed *T.* v 715
To seek a refuge from the tongue of S.—*T.* vi 841
In soothing sorrow, and in quenching s. *T.* vi 963
For her the Judgment, umpire in the s. *Tir.* 29
Nature in arms, her elements at s. *T.T.* 448
To scenes where competition, envy, s. *V.* 75

STRIKE.
But in the sunshine s. the blow *A Fable* 39
She s. out all that Luxury can ask *Ch.* 103 [*Con.* 32
Wrath stays him, or else God would s. them dumb
A difference s. at length the musing heart *Comp.* i 8
By sparks Absurdity s. out of Pride *Con.* 148
S. the rough thread of error right athwart *Ex.* 330
(Though other follies s. the public eye *H.* 620
And cries, " Perhaps eternity s. next!" *H.* 701 [43
Who s. the blow, then plead your own defence *Her.*
Precisely when the clock s. four " *M.F.* 14
If Love reward him, or if Vengeance s. *P.E.* 31
S. up the fiddles, let us all be gay! *P.E.* 150
The difference, though essential, fails to s. *P.E.* 204
S. on the deep-toned chord the sum of all *P.E.* 605
When he should s., he trembles and sets free *T.* iv 600
And, prophet as he was, he might not s. *T.* vi 468
In little bosoms such achievements s. *Tir.* 232
Your pupil s. upon have struck yourselves *Tir.* 270
To form thy son, to s. his genius forth *Tir.* 679
Wit, undistinguishing, is apt to s. *T.T.* 101
Skill to direct, and strength to s. the blow *T.T.* 357
That like some cottage beauty, s. the heart *T.T.* 524

STRING. [721
Through the dry leaves, and pants upon the s. *Ex.*
But passion rudely snaps the s. *H.F.* 7
Though Phœbus s. the lyre *Miss* — 12
Such s. for all who need 'em *Pat.* 22
One that still needs his leading s. and bib *P.E.* 531
Or when it first forsakes the elastic s. *P.E.* 573
Ten thousand thousand s. at once go loose *R.* 329
No passion touches a discordant s. *T.* vi 787
The God that s. the silver bow *Trans. H.* 28 [490
The s. are swept with such a power, so loud *T.T.*

STRIP.
His own offences, and s. others bare *Ch.* 494
To s. them off, 'tis being flayed alive *P.E.* 583 [759
By a just judgment s. and starve themselves *T.* iii
To s. Jove's statue of his oaken wreath *T.* vi 640

STRIPE.
Adust with s. told out for every crime *T.* 83
My penitential s., my streaming blood *T.* 95
With Nature's varnish; severed into s. *T.* i 40
With s., that Mercy, with a bleeding heart *T.* ii 24
S., and a dungeon; and his body serves *T.* v 582
Witness the patient ox, with s. and yells *T.* vi 420

STRIPLING.
That in good time the s.'s finished taste *Tir.* 203
Our s. shine indeed, but with such rays *Tir.* 286

STRIPPED.
That s. him bare, and broke his honest heart *Ch.* 54
As diamonds, s. of their opaque disguise *Ch.* 397
He s. the impostors in the noonday sun *Ex.* 141
Sweet Nature, s. of her embroidered robe *Her.* 79
For property s. off by cruel chance *T.* i 503 [728
S. of her ornaments, her leaves, and flowers *T.* iii

STRIVE. [333
He shakes with cold—you stir the fire and s. *Con.*
Habits are soon assumed, but when we s. *P.E.* 582
The State that s. for liberty, though foiled *T.* v 367
Would s. to make a Paul or Tully stand *T.T.* 349
At Westminster, where little poets s. *T.T.* 506

STROKE.
A s. as fatal as the scythe of Death *Ch.* 144
At every s. Wit flashes in our eyes *Ch.* 543
The s. that a vindictive God intends *Ex.* 407
This riving s., this ultimate divorce *H.* 640 [79
Wouldst softly speak, and s. my head and smile) *M.P.*
And light and shade, and every s. be thine *H.* 673

On pangs enforced with God's severest s. R. 314
But imitative s. can do no more T. i 426
Turns to the s. his adamantine scales T. ii 324 [445
Forth comes the pocket mirror.—First we s. T. ii
Was to encourage goodness. He would s. T. ii 710
Discriminated each from each, by s. T. iv 735
By these fortuitous and random s. T. v 124
Alas! 'twas but a mortifying s. T. v 169 [T. v 666
He slights the s. of conscience. Nothing moves
To s. the prickly grievance, and to hang T. v 329
Its long delay, feels every welcome s. T. v 413
And death still future. Not a hasty s. T. v 608
To s. his azure neck, or to receive T. vi 781
Its destined office, yet with gentle s. T. vi 1003
And tells them, as he s. their silver locks Tir. 322
And s. his polished cheek of purest red Tir. 847
A prologue interdashed with many a s. T.T. 538

STROLLER.
Like useless lumber, or a s.'s song Con. 820

STRONG.
'Twas Nature, sir, whose s. behest B.R. 7
Herself as weak as her support is s. Ch. 408
They always are decisive, clear and s. Con. 150
The southern sash admits too a light Con. 331
Rich in embellishment as s. Dr. 11
But with a cherup clear and s. D.W. 25
Shot by an archer s. J.G. 154
S. genius, from whose forge of thought Mrs. M—23
Plants raised with tenderness are seldom s. P.E. 359
Delusions s. as Hell shall bind him fast P.E. 609
The warblings of the blackbird, clear and s. R. 569
S. Judgment labouring in the Scripture mine R. 698
So s. the zeal to immortalize himself T. i 284 [402
The powers of fancy and s. thought are theirs T. i
He stablishes the s., restores the weak T. ii 343
But s. for service still, and unimpaired T. ii 705
While every breath, by respiration s. T. iv 348
Adored through fear, s. only to destroy T. v 445
Been less, or less benevolent than s. T. v 852
His teeth were s., the cage was wood T.B. 53 [137
Whose humorous vein, s. sense, and simple style Tir.
Schools, unless discipline were doubly s. Tir. 218
Soon shows the s. similitude reversed Tir. 443
Prepared for martyrdom, and s. to prove V. 61

STRONGER.
Worthier of regard, and s. N.C. 51
While prejudice in men of s. minds T. ii 567

STROVE.
But falsely. Sages after sages s. T. ii 506

STRUCK.
S. thrice the point upon his saddle bow A.T. 166
And having s. the balance, now proceed Con. 798
Thy Druids s. the well strung harps they bore Ex. 496
A palsy s. his arm, his sparkling eye T. ii 727
Your pupil strike upon have s. yourselves Tir. 270
Shouldering, and standing as if s. to stone T.T. 137
And a complete recovery s. him dumb T.T. 393 [663
Wit now and then, s. smartly, shows a spark T.T.
He s. the lyre in such a careless mood T.T. 686

STRUCTURE.
This moveable s. of shelves Gr. 25
A mutilated s., soon to fall T. i 774

STRUGGLE.
Too weak to s. with tenacious clay T. 216
But Martyrs s. for a brighter prize T. v 718

STRUGGLING.
S., detained in many a petty nook N.A. 40
While s. in the vale of tears below T. 585

To his voracious bag, s. in vain T. iv 450
The s. efforts of my boyish tongue T. iv 711

STRUMPET. [245
Where neither s.'s charms, nor drinking bout Tir.

STRUNG. [496
Thy Druids struck the well s. harps they bore Ex.
Who then, that has a mind well s. and tuned T. vi 262

STRUT. [T. vi 676
And s., and storm, and straddle, stamp, and stare
Than that heroic s. assumed before Con. 490
His wonted s.; and, wading at their head T. v 74
Is kept to s., look big, and talk away T.T. 233

STRUTTING.
Turning short round, s., and sideling P.T. 39
S. and vapouring in an empty school T. ii 330
And s. in thy school of Queens and Kings V. 45

STUART.
And when the S., leaning on the Scot Ex. 574

STUBBORN.
That hard by nature, and of s. will E. ii 21
" Bespeak at least a s. soil E. iv 82
The Roman taught thy s. knee to bow Ex. 476
S. and sturdy, a wild ass's colt H. 182
If s. Greek refuse to be his friend P.E. 498
To meliorate and tame the s. soil R. 786
Unapt to learn, and formed of s. stuff T. iv 636
To prey upon each other: s., fierce T. vi 897
The s. soil, and hold thee still erect Y.O. 119

STUCCOED.
From s. walls smart arguments rebound H. 346

STUCK.
Which s. in M.'s stomach as cross as a bone A.T. ii 8
Fast s. within his own T.B. 60

STUDDED.
Less ostentatious, and yet s. thick T. iii 420

STUDENT.
Deceive no s. Wisdom there and truth T. vi 114

STUDIED.
And if he s., s. for her sake A.T. 18
Thus s., used and consecrated thus R. 105
I s., prized, and wished that I had known T. iv 722

STUDIOUS.
S. of peace, their neighbours' and their own Her. 50
Burly and big, and s. of his ease T. i 63
Of desultory man, s. of change T. i 507
But is amusement all? S. of song T. ii 311
And, s. of mutation still, discard T. ii 610
Me, therefore, s. of laborious ease T. iii 361
S. of ornament, yet unresolved T. vi 160

STUDIOUSLY.
Who s. make peace their aim N.G. 36

STUDS.
The s. that thick emboss his iron door T. v 426

STUDY.
Grown dim in trifling s., blind he dies Ch. 358
Might swing at ease behind his s. door Ch. 615
His hours of s. closed at last Mor. 5
Who s. Nature with a wanton eye R. 213
Collect the scattered truths that S. gleans R. 274
To s. then familiar, since forgot R. 374
Most likes it, when he s. it in town R. 574
To s. culture, and with artful toil R. 785
Then S. languished, Emulation slept T. ii 734
He, entering at the s. door T.B. 37
A friend, whate'er he s. or neglects Tir. 391
Where, stillness aiding s., and his mind Tir. 773

Great lawyers, lawyers without *s.* made *Tir.* 822
Of dreaming *s.* and pedantic rust *T.T.* 171
STUDYING.
This wheel-footed *s.* chair *Gr.* 9

STUFF. [vi 674
Shall *s.* his shoulders with King Richard's hunch *T.*
Lothario cries, "What philosophic *s.* ! *H.* 28
Such *s.* the world is made of ; and mankind *H.* 211
Unapt to learn, and formed of stubborn *s. T.* iv 636
And taught at schools much mythologic *s. Tir.* 197

STUFFED. [310
To find it *s.* with brickbats, earth, and stones *Con.*
"No need," he cries, " of gravity, *s.* out *H.* 105
And o'er the seat, with plenteous wadding *s. T.* i 31

STUMBLED.
With one he *s.* on, and lost his walk *Con.* 280

STUMBLES.
Is tramontane, and *s.* all belief *T.* iv 533

STUMBLING.
To show a *s.* stone by night *Trans.* i 19

STUMP.
So withered *s.* disgrace the sylvan scene *Con.* 51
By him of Babylon, life stands a *s. T.* v 401
A splintered *s.* bleached to a snowy white *Y.O.* 128

STUNG.
Not soon provoked, however *s.* and teased *Ch.* 428

STUNS.
And *s.* the neighbours round *Trans.* iv 24

STUPID.
Discerns in all things what, with *s.* gaze *T.* v 808

STUPIDITY.
And deem his base *s.* no crime *T.* 542

STUPOR.
That never felt a *s.*, know no pause *T.* iv 283

STURDY.
Where Obstinacy takes his *s.* stand *Ex.* 298
Stubborn and *s.*, a wild ass's colt *H.* 182
Your blunderer is as *s.* as a rock *P.E.* 539
The *s.* swain diminished to a boy ! *T.* i 162
The branches, *s.* to his utmost wish *T.* iii 530
Heedless of all his pranks, the *s.* churl *T.* v 52
Great schools suit best the *s.* and the rough *Tir.* 341
But bends his *s.* back to any toy *Tir.* 549

STY. [695
From tippling benches, cellars, stalls, and *s.* vi
And judge you from the kennel and the *s. P.E.* 262
Of stale debauch, forth issuing from the *s. T.* iv 470

STYED.
I would not lose it to be *s. M.B.* 15

STYGIAN. [iii 738
Whose *S.* throats breathe darkness all day long *T.*
While through the *S.* veil that blots the day *Her.* 17

STYLE. [102
Surrender judgment hood-winked. Some the *s. T.* vi
Once more I would adopt the graver *s. Ch.* 489
Whose wit well managed, and whose classic *s. R.* 717
His books well trimmed, and in the gayest *s. T.* 421
The powers of sculpture, but the *s.* as much *T.* i 706
His manner, and with rapture tastes his *s. T.* iii 223
And him who writes it, though the *s.* be neat *T.* iii 278
By flowing numbers and a flowery *s. T.T.* 741 [137
Whose humorous vein, strong sense, and simple *s. Tir.*

SUBDUE.
Not to be led in chains, but to *s. R.* 266
He places lightly, and as time *s. T.* iii 518

SUBDUED.
For then, by toil *s.*, he drank *Cast.* 47
We are restrained indeed, but not *s. Con.* 168
Wild without art, or artfully *s. R.* 416
What vice has it *s.* ? whose heart reclaimed *T.* ii 320
As he whose prowess had *s.* their foes ? *T.* v 237
Sorrow has, since they went, *s.* and tamed *T.* vi 46

SUBJECT.
And spare the poet for his *s.*'s sake *Ch.* 636
Whatever *s.* occupy discourse *Con.* 57
Their object, and their *s.*, and their hope *Con.* 542
Save from the *s.* of that work alone *Con.* 740
And touch the *s.* I designed at first *Con.* 868
Dared to suppose the *s.* had a choice *Ex.* 544
Is yet no *s.* of despair *F.* 32
With blood of his *s.* imbrued *M.D.* 36
The Will made *s.* to a lawless force *P.E.* 448
The *s.* upon which we meet *P.T.* 24
The weight of *s.* worthiest of her care *R.* 678
But war's a game which, were their *s.* wise *T.* v 187
On *s.* more mysterious, they were yet *T.* v 290
A *s.* faults a *s.* may proclaim *T.T.* 113
They have their weight to carry, *s.* theirs *T.T.* 175
To dally much with *s.* mean and low *T.T.* 544
On every scene and *s.* it surveys *T.T.* 713

SUBJOIN.
A sad memorial, and *s.* his own *T.* v 420

SUBJUGATE.
The puny tyrant burns to *s. H.* 189

SUBLIME.
Matched against truths as lasting as *s.* ? *Con.* 543
His more *s.* vagaries slighting *E.* i 17
Now borne upon the wings of Truth *s. Ex.* 466
A mind employed on so *s.* a theme *R.* 668
Beware of too *s.* a sense *R.C.* 109
But cawing rooks, and kites that swim *s. T.* 203
And woven close, or needlework *s. T.* i 34
To shake thy senate, and from heights *s. T.* ii 216
Presuming an attempt not less *s. T.* iii 459
S. above the rest, the statelier stand *T.* iii 595
To themes more pertinent, if less *s. T.T.* 190

SUBLIMED.
The soul that sees him, or receives *s. T.* v 805

SUBLIMELY.
Be most *s.* good, verbosely grand *T.* v 678
Though more *s.*, he o'erlooks the world *T.* vi 918

SUBLIMER.
But where are its *s.* trophies found ? *T.* ii 319

SUBLIMEST.
While life's *s.* joys are overlooked *Ch.* 219
Compared with this *s.* life below *R.* 103
To the sharp peak of her *s.* height *T.* iii 157
'Twas his *s.* privilege to feel *T.* vi 359

SUBLIMITY.
S. and attic taste combined *T.T.* 644

SUBLUNARY.
Or other *s.* game *Mor.* 28
Had I the choice of *s.* good *T.* iii 689
To seek no *s.* rest beside *T.* v 476

SUBMARINE.
Æthereal journeys, *s.* exploits *T.* iv 85

SUBMERSION.
By cold *s.*, razor, rope, or lead *R.* 584

SUBMISSION.
And find s. more than half a cure Ch. 158
I learned at last s. to my lot M.P. 44
SUBMISSIVE.
Then would he say, s. at thy feet Ch. 232
SUBMIT.
Prove it;—if better, I s. and bow Ex. 633
His pride, that scorns to obey or to s. Tir. 226
SUBMITTED.
It turns s. to my view, turns round T. iv 98
SUBORDINATE.
S., and diligence was choice T. ii 716
SUBORNED.
And life abused, and not to be s. H. 224
SUBSCRIBE.
Extravagance and Avarice shall s. Ch. 467
SUBSERVIENCY.
S. his praise, and that alone T.T. 361
SUBSERVIENT.
Is made s. to the grand design Con. 897
SUBSIDE.
And captious cavil and complaint s. H. 144
Woods vanish, hills s., and valleys rise T. iii 775
SUBSIST.
Built a brave world, which cannot yet s. Ch. 192
Nor such as may awhile s. F. 40
By ceaseless action all that is s. T. i 367
Due sustenance, or where s. they now? T. v 79
S. and centre in one point—a friend Tir. 390
Change is the diet on which all s. Y.O. 72
SUBSISTENCE.
S. to provide T.B. 33
SUBSISTING.
The very name we carved s. still Tir. 301
SUBSTANCE.
That s., and modes of every kind A.T. 42
Imparting s. to an empty shade T. iv 527
SUBSTANTIAL.
By stout s. gods of wood and stone Con. 834
That men have deemed s. since the fall H. 154
S. happiness for transient joy T. iii 300
SUBSTANTIALLY.
Your faith and mine s. agree H. 398
SUBSTITUTE.
The s. for genius, sense, and wit T.T. 543
SUBTERFUGE.
No s., or pleading F. 189
By forgery, by s. of law T. ii 670
SUBTILE.
While summer was, the pure and s. lymph T. vi 135
SUBTLE.
The s. and injurious may be just Con. 809
SUBTLEST.
The s. serpent with the loftiest crest T. 476
SUBTLETY.
What edge of s. canst thou suppose T. iii 203
SUBURBAN.
S. villas, highway-side retreats R. 481
SUCCEED.
And, Avarice being judge, with ease s. Ch. 195
Sure to s., the remedy they found Con. 500
And, cursed with conquest, finally s. Con. 692
With tiptoe-step Vice silently s. Ex. 84
An envious man, if you s. F. 76

In which 'tis much if we s. F. 197
Turn downward, and the lowest pair s. H. 14
But proudest of the worst, if that s. H. 202
This earth shall blaze, and a new world s. H. 749
A calm s.—but Plenty, with her train Her. 63
Of heartfelt joys, s. not soon again Her. 64
Where to s. is not to be undone Her. 88 [529
And interdicts its growth. Thence straight s. T. iii
Such friends prevent what else would soon s. R. 731
And still they dream that they shall still s. T. iii 128
It may s.; and, if his sins should call Tir. 410
SUCCEEDED.
Time has but half s. in his theft M.P. 120
Those barbarous ages past, s. next T. i 16
A leaf s., and another leaf Y.O. 37
SUCCEEDING.
Successive loads s. broils impose Ex. 308
So soon s. such an angry night T. vi 259
SUCCESS.
May such s. attend the pious plan Con. 837
That no s. attends on spears and swords Ex. 352
Whoe'er assails thee, thy s. is sure Ex. 701
And if s. his steps attend F. 82
S. in rhyme his glory and reward R. 198
With what s. let modern manners show R. 686
Solicit pleasure; hopeless of s. T. ii 635
But wisdom is a pearl with most s. T. iii 381
To combat may be glorious, and s. T. iii 687
Sordid and sickening at his own s. T. iii 810
With most s. when all besides decay T. iv 157
Thwart his attempt, or envy his s. T. iv 787
" That give assurance of their own s. T. v 843
His high endeavour, and his glad s. T. v 901
Lest power exerted, but without s. Tir. 277
Are best disposed of where with most s. Tir. 348
Each vainly magnifies his own s. Tir. 476
The same their occupation and s. T.T. 46
Thus all s. depending on an ear T.T. 514
The man that means s., should soar above T.T. 548
SUCCESSFUL.
But yet s., being aimed at him Con. 540
S. there, he wins a curse Mor. 48
Beyond the achievement of s. flight T. i 692
Of unsuccessful or s. war T. ii 4
SUCCESSFULLY.
And plant s. sweet Sharon's rose H. 463
S. conceals her loathsome form P.E. 8
SUCCESSION.
From these a long s., in the rage T.T. 630
SUCCESSIVE.
S. loads succeeding broils impose Ex. 308
SUCCINCT.
A tale should be judicious, clear, s. Con. 235
SUCCOUR.
Some s. yet they could afford Cast. 25
To s. wasted regions, and replace Ch. 129
None interposes now to s. thee Ex. 279
SUCCULENT.
And s., that feeds its giant growth T. iii 418
SUCK.
And s., and leave a craving maggot there P.E. 326
If some mere driveller s. the sugared fib P.E. 530
S. down its prey insatiable. Immense T. ii 103
That s. him; there the sycophant, and he T. iii 818
He s. intelligence in every clime T. iv 111
SUCKED.
And s. a breast that panted with alarms Ex. 473
And s. in dizzy madness with his draught H. 518

SUCKLED. [364
Hast thou, though *s.* at fair Freedom's breast *Ex.*

SUDDEN.
I interrupt him with a *s.* bow *Con.* 281
To every *s.* slip and transient wrong *H.* 390
Such was thy charity ; no *s.* start *J.T.* 41
But recollecting, with a *s.* thought *N.A.* 51
A *s.* steep upon a Rustic Bridge *T.* i 267
Resistless. Never such a *s.* flood *T.* ii 115
And loudly wondering at the *s.* change *T.* iv 451
Snorting, and starting into *s.* rage *T.* vi 550

SUDDENLY.
But *s.* a wind, as high *A Fable* 10
May *s.* your joys disperse *F.* 65
Then *s.* regain the prize 1789, 54

SUFFER.
Bid *s.* it awhile, and kiss the rod *Ch.* 166
The Sacred Book no longer *s.* wrong *H.* 449
It *s.* interruption and delay *P.E.* 442
Than he contrives to *s.* well content *T.* 104
Ten starveling hermits *s.* less than he *T.* 112
Health *s.*, and the spirits ebb ; the heart *T.* i 466
At what a sailor *s.* ; Fancy too *T.* i 541
S. a syncope and solemn pause *T.* ii 80
S. his woes, and share in his escapes *T.* iv 117
Because men *s.* it, their toy the World *T.* v 192 [433
With woes, which who that *s.* would not kneel *T.* v
In those that *s.* it, a sordid mind *T.* v 453
His strength to *s.*, and his will to serve *T.* v 902
Should *s.* torture, and the streams be dyed *T.* vi 390
To meaner music, and not *s.* loss *T.* vi 750
And *s.* for its crime ; would learn how fair *T.* vi 827
S. his justice in a world to come *Tir.* 102

SUFFERANCE.
Whose freedom is by *s.*, and at will *T.* v 363

SUFFERED.
Thy rights have *s.*, and our land, too long *Ch.* 277
"Nor *s.* one ill-chosen rhyme *E.* iv 75
How much his feelings *s.*, sat Sir Smug *H.* 416
To bear it, *s.* shame where'er he went *H.* 587
S. by virtue combating below ? *J.T.* 18
Else He that hung there *s.* all his pain *P.E.* 623

SUFFERER.
And thou, sad *s.* under nameless ill *R.* 343
But gives the glorious *s.* little praise *T.* v 732
Laughs at the frantic *s.*'s fury, spent *T.* vi 423
By *s.* like herself alone 1789, 49

SUFFERING.
Each individual, *s.* a constraint *Con.* 383
"*S.* the vengeance of eternal fire" *Ex.* 423
Doing and *s.*, his unquestioned will *Ex.* 645
But Ætnas of the *s.* world ye sway ? *Her.* 78
"To *s.* not my own *Miss* — 86
By our *s.*, since ye brought us *N.C.* 45
S. with gladness for a Saviour's sake *R.* 776
If *s.* Scripture nowhere recommends *T.* 109
And sympathize with others *s.* more *T.* iv 310
Did pity of their *s.* warp aside *T.* iv 453

SUFFICE.
S. it then in decent terms to say *A.T.* 86
But will sincerity *s.* ? *F.* 55
I am no preacher ; let this hint *s.* *P.E.* 621
Like that, once seen, *s.* *Q.V.* 78
S. to give the marshalled ranks the grace *T.* iii 604
S. thee ; save that the moon is thine *T.* iv 254
And his own cattle must *s.* him soon *T.* vi 710

SUFFICED.
As the wind sways it, has yet well *s.* *T.* vi 73

SUFFICIENCY.
With much *s.* in royal brains *T.T.* 52

SUFFICIENT.
And death's a doom *s.* for the rest *H.* 396
Charge not, with light *s.* and left free *T.* 19
S. to redeem the modern race *T.T.* 664

SUFFOCATE.
And *s.* the breath at every turn *T.* ii 819
The theatre, too small, shall *s.* *T.* vi 670

SUGAR.
For how could we do without *s.* and rum ? *P.A.* 6
Especially *s.*, so needful we see ? *P.A.* 7

SUGARED.
If some mere driveller suck the *s.* fib *P.E.* 530

SUGGEST.
S. it safe, or dangerous, to be plain *Ch.* 520
S. the expedient of a yearly fast *Ex.* 401
Pleasure herself perhaps *s.* a plea *Ex.* 666
That Fashion, Taste, or Luxury *s.* *H.* 446
Let no low thought *s.* the prayer *Miss* — 65
The growing seeds of wisdom ; that *s.* *T.* iii 302

SUGGESTED.
The worst *s.*, she believes the best *Ch.* 427
Convenience next *s.* Elbow Chairs *T.* i 87

SUICIDE.
Your wilful *s.* on God's decree *T.* 20

SUIT.
Nor soft enough to *s.* a lover's tongue *A.T.* 20
As oft as it *s.* her to roam *C.* 52
Puts off his generous nature, and, to *s.* *Ch.* 153
And sounds prophetic are too rough to *s.* *Ex.* 67
Contrived to *s.* frail nature's crazy case *H.* 604
In sorting flowers to *s.* a fickle taste *H.* 767 [*P.E.* 132
So well that thought the employment seems to *s.*
The rank debauch *s.* Clodio's filthy taste *P.E.* 188
And your only *s.*, a shroud *St.* iv 16
The truth is (if the truth may *s.* your ear *T.* 113
Of libertine excess. The Sofa *s.* *T.* i. 106
Her mingled *s.* and sequences, and sits *T.* i. 475
S. well the thoughtful or unthinking mind *T.* iv 279
With music such as *s.* their sovereign ears *T.* v 387
Would urge a wiser *s.* than asking more *T.* vi 56 [341
Great schools *s.* best the sturdy and the rough *Tir.*
Whom care and cool deliberation *s.* *Tir.* 781

SUITED.
Were *s.* to their mind *J.G.* 58

SUITOR.
The *s.*'s air indeed he soon improves *R.* 237

SULLEN.
Brings to the distant ear a *s.* sound *Her.* 36
Peace to the phlegm of *s.* elves *Miss* — 61
And *s.* sadness, that o'ershade, distort *T.* i 457
I would not yet exchange thy *s.* skies *T.* ii 212
And ever, as the *s.* sound is heard *T.* v 405
The dark and *s.* humour of the time *T.T.* 616
Your *s.* silence serves at least to tell *V.* 25

SULLENLY.
Yes, to deep sadness *s.* resigned *Ch.* 151
Well-chosen, and not *s.* perused *T.* iii 393

SULLIED.
Is *s.* in the stream, taking a taint *T.* vi 834

SULLY.
These are the charms that *s.* and eclipse *T.* iii 823

SULTRY.
From *s.* suns, and in their shaded walks *T.* i 256

Nor freezing sky nor *s.*, checking me *T.* vi 297
The dust that waits upon his *s.* march *T.* vi 741

SUM.
He half exhibits, and then drops the *s. Ch.* 478
Compress the *s.* into its solid worth *Con.* 20
His ambiguities his total *s. Con.* 143
With *s.* Peruvian mines could never clear *Ex.* 235
Employed to calculate the enormous *s. P.E.* 486
Strike on the deep-toned chord the *s.* of all *P.E.* 605
With the vain stir.   I *s.* up half mankind *T.* iii 130
Some relish, till the *s.*, exactly found *T.* v 430 [581
The *s.* is this. If man's convenience, health *T.* vi
What *s.* he lost at play, and how he sold *Tir.* 330
Less trouble taking twice the *s. Y.D.* 67

SUMMER. [*A.T.* 79
Lay snug and warm;—'twas *s.'s* farewell peep!
As ever dressed a bank, or scented *s.* air *Ch.* 259
Should flow like waters after *s.* showers *Con.* 705
Yet He was gentle as soft *s.* airs *Ex.* 133
The greenhouse is my *s.* seat *F.B.* 1
Was heard, one genial *s.'s* day *J.P.* 31
As in some solitude the *s.* rill *J.T.* 38
Ordained perhaps, ere *s.* flies *O.* i 17
Her *s.* heats, her fruits, and her perfumes *R.* 196
And like a *s.* brook are past away *R.* 296
All *s.* long, which winter fills again *T.* i 329
My languid limbs, when *s.* sears the plains *T.* iii 30
Hence *S.* has her riches, Autumn hence *T.* iii 427
These have their sexes; and when *s.* shines *T.* iii 537
With *s.* fruits, brought forth by wintry suns *T.* iii 552
How find the myriads that in *s.* cheer *T.* v 77
While *s.* was, the pure and subtile lymph *T.* vi 135
He cannot skim the ground like *s.* birds *T.* vi 921
S. in haste the thriving charge receives *Tir.* 45
Theirs is but a *s.* song *Trans.* iii 27
A chilling flood on *s.'s* drooping flowers *T.T.* 211
Like shallow brooks which *s.* suns exhale! *V.* 2

SUMMER-MONTHS'.
Be quelled in all our *s.* retreats *T.* iii 315

SUMMING.
And, after *s.* all the rest *F.* 202

SUMMIT.
The *s.* gained, behold the proud Alcove *T.* i 278
Blown on the *s.* of the apparent fruit *T.* iii 536
That tempts Ambition. On the *s.* see *T.* iv 58
O'er the green *s.* of the rocks, whose base *T.* vi 496

SUMMON.
The thunder seems to *s.* him away *H.* 719
Now *s.* every virtue, stand and plead *T.* 566
By magic *s.* of the Orphean lyre *T.* iii 587
That sweeps the bolted shutter, *s.* home *T.* iv 304
Account it music; that it *s.* some *T.* v 409
That leads the dance a *s.* to be gay *T.* vi 336

SUMMONED. [225
"Mark these," she says, "these, *s.* from afar *H.*
Had *s.* them to serve his golden god *P.E.* 131
Man shall be *s.* and the dead attend? *R.* 654
The creatures, *s.* from their various haunts *T.* vi 355
And, *s.* to partake its fellow's woe *V.* 69

SUMMONING.
That moving signal *s.*, when best *Ex.* 179
May prove a trumpet, *s.* your ear *T.* iv 570
Else, *s.* the muse to such a theme *T.T.* 550

SUMPTUOUS.
Mark what a *s.* Pharisee is he! *T.* 59
Time was, when clothing, *s.* or for use *T.* i 8

SUMPTUOUSLY.
Not *s.* adorned, nor needing aid *T.* iv 251

SUN.
The *s.* of that moment is set *C.* 3
To give the pole the produce of the *s. Ch.* 125
The *s.* matures on India's spicy shores *Ch.* 442
A Persian, humble servant of the *s. Con.* 67
And like the stores autumnal *s.* mature *Con.* 649
Broiling beneath a July *s. E.* iv 50   [*Ex.* 479
When the *s.'s* shafts disperse the gloom of night
Whom fiery *s.*, that scorch the russet spice *Ex.* 15
He stripped the impostors in the noonday *s. Ex.* 141
The *s.*, obedient, at her call appears *H.* 43
To make the *s.* a bauble without use *H.* 81
And scorns to share it with the distant *s. H.* 480
Not e'en the glorious *s.*, though men revere *H.* 501
Not e'en the *s.*, desirable as rare *H.* 505
Oh! welcome now the *s.'s* once hated light *H.* 736
And the *s.* gilds the shining spires again *Her.* 72
The *s.* would rise in vain for me *M.* 31
Shed light, like a *s.* on the waves *M.D.* 14
In vain warm *s.* their influence shed *Miss* — 37
And *s.* to come, as round they wheel *Miss* — 101
Just reached it when the *s.* was set *Mor.* 22
His *s.* precipitate descend *Mor.* 54
The *s.* accomplishing his early march *N.A.* 29 [81
The *s.*, a world whence other worlds drink light *R.*
With all a July *s.'s* collected rays *R.* 484
The evening came, the *s.* descended *R.C.* 65
Told that his setting *s.* must rise no more *St.* ii 16
Earth, seas, and *s.*, adieu! *St.* iii 10
From sultry *s.*, and in their shaded walks *T.* i 256
Some glossy-leaved, and shining in the *s. T.* i 314
Now glitters in the *s.* and now retires *T.* i 324 [335
Refreshing change! where now the blazing *s.? T.* i
So lately found, although the constant *s. T.* i 621
Those *s.* are set. Oh, rise some other such! *T.* ii 252
At measured distances, that air and *s. T.* iii 424 [443
As the *s.* peeps, and vernal airs breathe mild *T.* iii
The *s.'s* meridian disk, and at the back *T.* iii 473 [552
With summer fruits brought forth by wintry *s. T.* iii
'Tis morning; and the *s.* with ruddy orb *T.* v 1 [645
Has made a Heaven on earth; with *s.* and moons *T.* iii
By roses, and clear *s.* though scarcely felt *T.* iii 733
And dreaded as thou art; Thou hold'st the *s. T.* iv 129
Of the undeviating and punctual *s. T.* vi 129
And is not ere to-morrow's *s.* go down *T.* vi 215
To the green blade that twinkles in the *s. T.* vi 251
The *s.* proceeds, I wander. Neither must *T.* vi 296
To frisk awhile, and bask in the warm *s. T.* vi 314
Bright as a *s.* the sacred city shines *T.* vi 800 [vi 483
Where England, stretch'd towards the setting *s. T.*
To yon fair *S.* and his attendant Earth? *Tir.* 36
A meteor, or a star; in these, the *s. T.T.* 575
And as the *s.* in rising beauty dressed *T.T.* 706
Like shallow brooks which summer *s.* exhale! *V.* 2

SUNBEAM.
Weigh *s.*, carve a fly, or spit a flea *Ch.* 354
Like *s.* on the golden height *Mrs. M*— 35
Meridian *s.* tempt him to unfold *T.* 60
The *s.*; there embossed and fretted wild *T.* v 118

SUNBURNT.
We wander o'er a *s.* thirsty soil *Ch.* 229
There from the *s.* hayfield homeward creeps *T.* i 295

SUNDAY.
Resort on *S.* to the house of prayer *H.* 242
To play the fool on *S.*, why not we? *P.E.* 147

SUNG.
My numbers that day she had *s. C.* 17
I know the warning song is *s.* in vain *Ex.* 724
As hath been said or *s. J.G.* 108
And methought while she Liberty *s. M.D.* 23
Hardly knows that he has *s. St.* iv 4

SUNG—SUPPORT

s. to the praise and glory of King George! *T.* vi 663
Foretold by prophets, and by poets *s. T.* vi 731
Nor can the wonders it records be *s. T.* vi 749
I hear as mute as if a Syren *s. T.T.* 199
And tell the world, still kindling as he *s. T.T.* 736

SUNK.
His eyes are *s.*, arms folded, head reclined *H.* 689
All *s.* beneath the wave *R.G.* 3
Our foot half *s.* in hillocks green and soft *T.* i 272
Seems *s.*, and shortened to its topmost boughs *T.* i 306
He *s.* in Greece, in Italy he rose *T.T.* 563

SUNNY.
A western bank's still *s.* side *Mor.* 18
They bound, and airy, o'er the *s.* glade *St.* ii 22
Remains to each, the search of *s.* nook *T.* v 71
From the shelter of that *s.* shed *W.N.* 6

SUNSET.
Down to the *s.* of their latest day *Tir.* 82

SUNSHINE.
But in the *s.* strikes the blow *A Fable* 39]
Shadow and *s.* intermingling quick *T.* i 347
Her *s.* and her rain, her blooming spring *T.* vi 946
If God give health, that *s.* of our days! *V.* 88

SUPERADD.
I *s.* a few essentials more *H.* 434

SUPERB.
And fledged with icy feathers, nod *s. T.* v 26
Or is thine house, though less *s.* thy rank *Tir.* 751

SUPERBLY.
And ribands streaming gay, *s.* raised *T.* iv 541
In fancy sees him more *s.* ride *Tir.* 368
In painted plumes *s.* dressed *Trans.* iv 1

SUPERCILIOUS.
Then let the *s.* great confess *T.* vi 967

SUPERFLUITY.
Her *s.* the poor supplies *Ch.* 455

SUPERFLUOUS.
Cards were *s.* here, with all the tricks *T.* iv 207

SUPERIOR.
Owns no *s.* but the God she fears *Ch.* 275
And though the soul shall seek *s.* orbs *Ch.* 563
Of man's *s.* breed *D.W.* 40
To mar delights *s.* to its own *E.* ii 34
By good vouchsafed makes known *s.* good *H.* 147
That make *s.* skill his second praise *H.* 206
Joy, far *s.* joy, that much outweighs *H.* 728
A stranger to *s.* strength *H.F.* 19
Thou hadst supposed them of *s.* race *N.A.* 74
Pride, of a growth *s.* to the rest *T.* 475
With what *s.* skill we can abuse *T.* i 637
At least *s.* jockeyship, and claim *T.* ii 276
Of a *s.*, he is never free *T.* v 364
A far *s.* happiness to theirs *T.* vi 343
S. as we are, they yet depend *T.* vi 608
Attends *s.* worth *Th.* 16
The stout tall captain, whose *s.* size *Tir.* 222

SUPERSTITION.
Of *s.*, prophesying still *T.* iv 294
Need no such aids as *s.* lends *T.* vi 510
No shades of *s.* blot the day *T.T.* 270

SUPERSTITIOUS.
A *s.* and monastic course *R.* 118

SUPERSTRUCTURE.
Though all the *s.*, by the tooth *Y.O.* 122

SUPINE,
Take, if ye can, ye careless and *s. P.E.* 9

SUPINELY.
If priest, *s.* droning o'er his charge *H.* 198

SUPPER.
And found a *s.* somewhere else *N.G.* 26
" Shall call to *s.*, when, no doubt *R.C.* 63

SUPPLANT.
Seek to *s.* his inexperienced youth *P.E.* 59
War followed for revenge, or to *s. T.* i 609
S. thee in it, and usurp thy place *Tir.* 890

SUPPLANTED.
And soon to be *s.* He that saw *T.* iii 751

SUPPLE.
S. and flexible as Indian cane *H.* 602
Oh! if Servility with *s.* knees *T.T.* 127

SUPPLEMENTAL.
By *s.* shifts, the best he may? *T.* iv 769
Nor smooth good-breeding (*s.* grace) *T.* vi 853

SUPPLIANTS.
But oft-times deaf to *s.* who would blush *T.* iv 415

SUPPLICATE.
To *s.* his mercy, love his ways *Con.* 661

SUPPLIED.
For cedars famed, fair Lebanon *s. A.T.* 143
And all *s.* from an eternal source *Ch.* 370
That tells us whence his treasures are *s. Ch.* 440
Their want of light and intellect *s. Con.* 147
Must be *s.* with objects of his choice *P.E.* 46
Or if yourself, too scantily *s. P.E.* 251
And with a clear and shining lamp *s. P.E.* 558
Whence life can be *s. St.* vi 4
With spirit, genius, eloquence, *s. T.* 305
That interlaced each other, these *s. T.* i 41
So rich, so thronged, so drained, and so *s. T.* i 720
That monarchs have *s.*, from age to age *T.* v 386
S. such relics as devotion holds *T.* vi 689
" Ambition in a boy *s. Th.* 7
When copiously *s.*, then most enlarged *Tir.* 19
A point secured, if once he be *s. Tir.* 698
The country's need have scantily *s. T.T.* 338
Art has in a measure *s. W.N.* 3

SUPPLY.
And in return receives *s.* from all *Ch.* 92
Than she *s.* from her abounding store *Ch.* 102
Who makes some rich for the *s.* of all *Ch.* 251
Her superfluity the poor *s. Ch.* 455
Springs in due time *s.* for the distressed *Ch.* 482
Or taxed invention for a fresh *s. Ch.* 514
Exuberant is the shadow it *s. Ch.* 577
Ambrosial gardens, in which Art *s. Ex.* 11.
Were fountains fed with infinite *s. Ex.* 34
The yawning chasm of indolence *s.! P.E.* 172
As leanest land *s.* the richest wine *T.* 364
His wants, indeed, are many; but *s. T.* i 597
By monitors that mother church *s. T.* ii 576
Exhausted, has had genius to *s. T.* ii 609
That hungers, and *s.* it; and who seeks *T.* iii 375
He, therefore, timely warned, himself *s. T.* iii 439
Indulged in what they wish, they soon *s. T.* iii 534
S. his need with a usurious loan *T.* iii 798
Afford the smaller minstrels no *s. T.* v 84
With flower and fruit the wilderness *s. Tir.* 27
A plan well worthy to *s.* their place *Tir.* 918
S. with warm activity and force *T.T.* 220
Oaks fell not, hewn by thousands, to *s. Y.O.* 101
Eventful, should *s.* her with a theme ... *Y.O.* 161

SUPPORT.
Herself as weak as her *s.* is strong *Ch.* 408

That, while in health, the ground of her s. *Con.* 771
The pillars of s. in which they trust *Ex.* 333
Thus between Justice, as my prime s. *H.* 377
S., and ornament of Virtue's cause *T.* ii 336
Of novelty, her fickle, frail s. *T.* iii 54
For their s., so destitute. But they *T.* iv 455

SUPPORTABLE.
Short as it is, s. Still worse *T.* v 604

SUPPORTED.
S. by despair of life *Cast.* 18
And constantly s. *F.* 51
One leg by truth s., one by lies *P.E.* 561

SUPPORTERS.
Between s.; and, once seated, sit *T.* i 479

SUPPORTING.
Of faith's s. rod *St.* iii 14

SUPPOSE.
"Again, would your lordship a moment s. *A.C.* 17
S. (when thought is warm, and fancy flows *Ch.* 379
What will not argument sometimes s.?) *Ch.* 380
What few can learn, and all s. they know *Ch.* 627
S. themselves monopolists of sense *Con.* 627
Dared to s. the subject had a choice *Ex.* 544
S. the beam should dip on the wrong side *H.* 374
'Tis not, as heads that never ache s. *R.* 323
S., unlooked for in a scene so rude *T.* 248
What edge of subtlety canst thou s. *T.* iii 206
His pleasant work, may he s. it done *T.* iii 656
That to s. a scene where she presides *T.* iv 532
That feed the thrush (whatever some s.) *T.* v 83
Might well s. the artificer divine *T.* v 561
Of the poor brute, seems wisely to s. *T.* vi 437
Less on exterior things than most s. *T.T.* 247

SUPPOSED.
That wedlock is not rigorous, as s. *A.T.* 58
S. the man a bishop, or at least *Con.* 71
At length, when all had long s. him dead *R.* 583
Thou hadst s. them of superior race *N.A.* 74
Might be s. to clamour for a guide *N.A.* 98
And still admiring, with regret s. *T.* iv 716
Might be s. a crow *Trans.* ii 3

SUPPOSING.
Who losing, or s. lost 1789, 50

SUPPOSITION.
Let s. lend her aid once more *Ch.* 383
The s. is replete with sin *T.* 347

SUPPRESS.
Shall raise no feuds for armies to s. *T.T.* 317

SUPPRESSED.
Serve as a key to those that are s. *Ch.* 524
With force not easily s. *F.B.* 14
Though long rebelled against, not yet s. *R.* 16
With slender notes, and more than half s. *T.* vi 80
To ecstasy too big to be s. *T.* vi 340

SUPREME.
Yet above all, his luxury s. *Con.* 619
He views it with complacency s. *P.E.* 522
S. on earth, and worthy of the skies *T.* 403
And arbitration wise of the S.—*T.* ii 165
Scenes such as these, 'tis his s. delight *T.* iii 306

SUPREMELY.
The hand of the S. Wise *E.* i 34
In sighs he worships his s. fair *R.* 225

SURCHARGED.
Still to be fed, and not to be s. *Tir.* 20

SURE.
Gold, to be s.!—Throughout the town 'tis told *Ch.* [479

S. not to conquer, and s. not to yield *Ch.* 621
Reply discreetly—"To be s.—no doubt!" *Con.* 118
The very remedy, however s. *Con.* 169
Never, if honest ones, when death is s. *Con.* 408
S. to succeed, the remedy they found *Con.* 500
Its head as guarded as its base is s. *Con.* 556
The soul's s. interest in the good she seeks *Con.* 728
"S. so much labour, so much toil *E.* iv 81
They knew, by s. prognostics seen on high *Ex.* 157
Made s. by prodigies till then unknown *Ex.* 174
Had they maintained allegiance firm and s. *Ex.* 207
The event and s. decision of the fight? *Ex.* 363
Whoe'er assails thee, thy success is s. *Ex.* 701
The sound of truth will then be s. to please *Ex.* 731
For tattlers, will be s. to hear *F.* 98
Hope, as an anchor firm and s., holds fast *H.* 167
Would disobey, though s. to be shut out *H.* 315
And s. it is as kind to smile and give *H.* 323
Then theirs, no doubt, as well as mine is s. *H.* 388
On Scripture ground are s. to disagree *H.* 599
No judges, s., were e'er so mad *J.P.* 25
S. ne'er to want them, mathematic truths *N.A.* 80
Peace follows Virtue as its s. reward *P.E.* 42
The creature is so s. to kick and bite *P.E.* 540
Could I, from Heaven inspired, as s. presage *St.* ii 1
And the world's hatred, as its s. effect *T.* 282
S. there is need of social intercourse *T.* ii 48
By necessary laws their s. effects *T.* ii 192
Allured by my report: but s. no less *T.* iii 699
Was s. to intoxicate the brows it bound *T.* v 245
By charter, and that charter sanctioned s. *T.* v 543
How lovely, and the moral sense how s. *T.* v 673
Insipid else, and s. to be despised *T.* vi 1016
When led by instinct sharp and s. *T.B.* 2
Else s. notorious fact, and proof so plain *Tir.* 239
The event is s.; expect it, and rejoice! *Tir.* 343
And his end s., without one glimpse of hope *Tir.* 427
'Twere wiser s. to inspire a little heart *Tir.* 454
S. to exhaust the plant on which they feed *Tir.* 604
So s. to spoil him, and so near at hand *Tir.* 697
Were education, else so s. to fail *Tir.* 702
Where early rest makes early rising s. *Tir.* 765
But, if thou guard its sacred chambers s. *Tir.* 801
But this is s.—the hand of might *Trans.* i 9
When most relied on is most s. to fail *V.* 68

SURER.
Or shoot the careless with a s. aim *R.* 218
Soothe thee to make thee but a s. prey *R.* 263

SUREST.
The s. presage of the good they seek *T.* v 378

SURETY.
Soon after He that was our s. died *Con.* 506

SURF.
Her silver globes, light as the foamy s. *T.* vi 155

SURFACE.
To brush the s., and to make it flow *Con.* 102
Upon the s. of the mind *E.* i 8
Beneath the smiling s. of the deep *H.* 184
Diffused, attain the s.; when, behold! *T.* iii 493

SURFEITED.
And s. lewd town with her fair dues *T.* iii 758

SURGE. [*Ex.* 573
"What tidings?" and the s. replied—"All lost!"
And asking of the s. that bathes thy foot *T.* i 655
Beats back the roarings., scarce heard so high *T.* vi 497

SURGEON.
Deeper in none than in their s.'s books *Tir.* 289

SURLIEST.
Old Tiny, s. of his kind *Ep.* ii 5

SURLY.
Because a bear is rude and s.? No *Con.* 192
Not rude and s., and beset with thorns *T.* i 601
S. and slovenly, and bold and coarse *T.T.* 682

SURMOUNTS.
And trusting in his God, s. them all *R.H.* 8

SURPASS.
And till a third s. you *L.R.* 23
And labours to s. him day and night *Tir.* 480

SURPASSED.
New to my taste his Paradise s. *T.* iv 710
A sight s. by none that we can show *Tir.* 541
S. in frenzy by the mad at large *Tir.* 820
Contemporaries all s., see one *T.T.* 670

SURPASSEST.
Thou s., happier far *Trans.* iii 19

SURPASSING.
With power s. theirs, performed her part *Ex.* 230
Is vanity s. all the rest " *H.* 110
S. all that mine or mint had given *J.T.* 30
O blessed proficiency! s. all *R.* 99
O scenes s. fable, and yet true *T.* vi 759
And armed with strength s. human powers *T.T.* 497

SURPRISE.
The turns are quick, the polished points s. *Ch.* 544
Is that which angles hourly for s. *Con.* 223
Glistening at once with pity and s. *H.* 533

SURPRISED.
S. at all they meet, the gosling pair *P.E.* 379
Then God might be s., and unforeseen *T.* ii 171

SURRENDER.
Plebeians must s. *F.* 117
S. judgment, hood-wink'd. Some the style *T.* vi 102

SURRENDERED.
The heart, s. to the ruling power *P.E.* 275

SURROUNDING.
Lord paramount of the s. plains *H.* 305
S. throngs the demigod revere *T.* 312

SURVEY.
I am monarch of all I s. *A.S.* 1
That all the various beauties we s. *A.T.* 48
While his own heaven s. the troubled scene *Ex.* 586
Unconscious nature, all that he s. *H.* 740
The gloomy scene s. *N.* 10
Then with a glance of Fancy to s. *R.* 73
S. his fair reversion with keen eye *T.* ii 601
S. our schools and colleges, and see *Tir.* 909
On every scene and subject it s. *T.T.* 713

SURVEYED.
Their beauties I intent s. *D.W.* 15
S. the scene, and took possession *R.C.* 44
At once, upstood intelligent, s. *Y.O.* 150

SURVEYING.
Awhile they mused; s. every face *N.A.* 73
Thus sitting, and s. thus at ease *T.* iv 94

SURVIVE.
He long s., who lives an hour *Cast.* 37
Please daily, and whose novelty s. *T.* i 178
That yet a remnant of your race s. *T.* i 340
A new possessor, and s. the change *T.* ii 110
Or does the tomb take all? If he s. *T.* ii 518
If I s. thee, I will dig thy grave *T.* iii 349

SURVIVED.
Of Paradise that has s. the fall! *T.* iii 42
Who had s. the father, served the son *T.* iii 748

His art s. the waters; and ere long *T.* v 220
See how they have safely s. *W.N.* 17

SURVIVING.
That the s. world may live in peace *Con.* 176

SURVIVOR.
They shriek and sink, s. start and weep *R.* 159
S. sole, and hardly such, of all *Y.O.* 1

SUSAN.
" S. will come and let me out " *R.C.* 64
Here, Sally, S., come, come quick *Trans.* iv 29

SUSCEPTIBLE.
S. of pity, or a mind *T.* iii 323

SUSPECT.
And if he but s. a frown, turns pale *T.* 216
" Falsehood! which whoso but s. of truth *T.* v 642

SUSPECTED.
Is most to be s.? *F.* 24
To be s., thwarted, and withstood *T.T.* 141

SUSPEND.
The fast that wins deliverance, and s. *Ex.* 406
S. the effect, or heal it? Has not God *T.* ii 197
S. their crazy boxes, planted thick *T.* iv 774
Sits cooing in the pine-tree, nor s. *T.* vi 308
" Stop, while ye may; s. your mad career *T.T.* 435

SUSPENDED.
Nor yet at eve his note s. *N.G.* 3

SUSPENSE.
He ties up all his hearers in s. *Con.* 130
Upon the ticklish balance of s. *T.* iii 550

SUSPICION.
S. lurks not in her artless breast *Ch.* 426
And even from s. *F.* 150
Her grave concern, her kind s., there *H.* 516

SUSTAIN.
But man is frail, and can but ill s. *Ex.* 81
This process achieved, it is doomed to s. *F.M.* 9
Next to that power who formed thee and s. *R.* 201
For more than half the tresses it s. *T.* iv 544
S., and is the life of all that lives *T.* vi 222
Unenvied there, he may s. alone *Tir.* 535
Delight in agitation, yet s. *Y.O.* 82

SUSTAINED.
Of the rude injuries it late s. *Con.* 906
All s. by patience, taught us *N.C.* 47
Created and s. *Q.V.* 60
What means the drama by the world s.? *R.* 646
Of provocation given or wrong s. *T.* v 315
S. with so much grace and art *Trans.* iv 35

SUSTENANCE.
The chase for s., precarious trust! *T.* i 611
Due s., or where subsist they now? *T.* v 79

SWAIN.
Thanks, gentle s., for all my woes *G.* 13
Let cottagers, and unenlightened s. *H.* 240
Ten thousand s. the wasted scene deplore *Her.* 39
The sturdy s. diminished to a boy! *T.* i 162
How many self-deluded nymphs and s. *T.* iii 316
Or charged with amorous sighs of absent s. *T.* iv 20
Nymphs were Dianas then, and s. had hearts *T.* iv 517
And patient of the slow-paced s.'s delay *T.* v 32
The s. their baskets make *T.B.* 30
The clumsy s. alight *Y.D.* 22

SWALLOW.
And a wide ocean s. both at last *Comp.* i 6
He does not s., but he gulps it down *Con.* 340

434 SWALLOWED—SWEET

To s. much upon much weaker proof Con. 722
Pursued the s. o'er the meads D.W. 11
As the leaf that enfolds what an invalid s. F.M. 22
The s. in their torpid state N. 1
Obscene, to swill and s. at a trough? P.E. 266
S. the two grand nostrums they dispense P.E. 594
As duly as the s. disappear T. iii 814
Ye all can s., and she asks no more T. iv 512

SWALLOWED.
Thus bit by bit the world is s. L.W. 34

SWALLOWING.
And s., therefore, without pause or choice T. vi 107
The auburn nut that held the s. down Y.O. 20

SWAMP.
The arbiters of this terraqueous s. T. v 281

SWAN.
And, river-blanched, the s. his snow Mrs. M — 8 [523
Like a proud s., conquering the stream by force T.T.
And ages ere the Mantuan S. was heard T.T. 557

SWARM.
Perhaps might prosper with a s. of bees Con. 288
The trumpet sounds, your legions s. abroad Her. 53
Poisoning the waters where their s. abound P.E. 481
Nor yet the s. that occupy the brain R. 641
S. in all quarters; meets the eye, the ear T. ii 818
The Levee s., as if in golden pomp T. iii 822
Hypericum all bloom, so thick a s. T. vi 165
S. in the streets. The statesmen of the day T. vi 696
They s. around thee, and thou stand'st at bay T.T. 365

SWARMED. [125
So s. the Sabine youth, and grasped the shield A.T.
S. with a scribbling herd, as deep inlaid T.T. 628

SWARMING. [iii 555
Moisture and drought, mice, worms, and s. flies T.
For interest sake or s. into clans T. iv 665

SWARTH. [110
Of grassy s., close-cropped by nibbling sheep T. i
Like a s. Indian with his belt of beads T. iv 749

SWATHE.
He s. about the swelling of the deep R. 527
They s. the forehead, drag the limping limb T. i 581

SWAY.
Thy posterity shall s. B. 30
And brings the trifler under rigorous s. Con. 596
To bring the passions under sober s. Con. 831
While Honour, Virtue, Piety, bear s. Ex. 326
But Ætnas of the suffering world ye s.? Her. 78
In his hand, as the sign of his s. M.D. 29
She thus maintains divided s. Mrs. M— 51 [277
Finds, by degrees, the truths that once bore s. P.E.
Is misapplied to sanctify their s. P.E. 497
We can escape from Custom's idiot s. R. 49
Both fail beneath a fever's secret s. R. 295
We boast some rich ones whom the Gospel s. T. 377
Rejoice in him, and celebrate his s. T. v 326
As the wind s. it, has yet well sufficed T. vi 73
To see their sovereign, and confess his s. T. vi 356
Custom and prejudice shall bear no s. T. vi 838
Proclaim him born to s. Th. 10
Maintains its hold with such unfailing s. Tir. 316
He gives the local bias all its s. Tir. 334
Though motives of mere lucre s. the most Tir. 518
And levying thus, and with an easy s. Tir. 611
Unless the s. of custom warp thy course Tir. 862
His life a lesson to the land he s. T.T. 76
The chain that binds them, and a tyrant's s. T.T. 283
But when the Second Charles assumed the s. T.T. 620

SWAYED.
Some s. by fashion, some by deep disgust R. 607
And s. the sceptre of his infant realms T. i 23

SWEAR.
They s. it, till affirmance breeds a doubt Con. 66
To s. to some enormity he saw Con. 126
The poets will s. that I dream Gr. 55
And Perjury stood up to s. all true H. 563 [129
All elbows shake. Look in, and you would s. P.E.
Played by the creatures of a Power who s. T. iii 177
Whose oath is rhetoric, and who s. for fame T. iv 491
Sheepish he doffs his hat, and mumbling s. T. iv 628
To s., to game, to drink; to show at home T. iv 652
S. 'tis a bargain, rails at his hard fate T. vi 293

SWEAT.
Taxed till the brow of Labour s. in vain Ex. 315
Restless as his who toils and s. for food J.T. 24
S. of ours must dress the soil N.C. 20
Prepares for meals as jockeys take a s. P.E. 221
Chains him, and tasks him, and exacts his s. T. ii 23
S. in the crowded theatre, and squeezed T. iv 43

SWEATED.
Contriver who first s. at the forge T. v 214

SWEATING.
And sleep not; see him s. o'er his bread T. i 363
And s. in his service; his caprice T. v 274

SWEEP.
Rake well the cinders, s. the floor E. iv 41
To s. away all refuges of lies H. 628
The Muses s. the lyre Miss — 84
And every hour s. multitudes away R. 158
That s. the skirt of some far-spreading wood T. i 184
With curvature of slow and easy s. T. i 352 [iii 441
The plenteous bloom, that no rough blast may s. T.
That s. the bolted shutter, summons home T. iv 304
That as she s. him with her whistling silks T. vi 941
To s. away the dew T.B. 18
Alas! the tide of pleasure s. along T.T. 368
The noble s. of all their privilege T.T. 475

SWEEPING.
Treads on thy s. train; one hand employed T. iv 247

SWEET.
Never hear the s. music of speech A.S. 11
Of his s. but awful lyre B. 36
Less s. to Maria and me C. 15 [41
Where wast thou then, s. Charity? Where then Ch.
And pours a torrent of s. notes around Ch. 111
While Gratitude and Love made service s. Ch. 233
Joys doubly s. to feelings quick as thine Ch. 298
The treasured s. of the capacious plan Ch. 323 [ii 1
S. stream that winds through yonder glade Comp.
There, in the s. society of those Con. 423
And gathering all her treasures, s. by s. Con. 440
Will the s. warbler of the livelong night Con. 445
When souls drawn upwards in communion s. Con. 569
Find the s. lyre on which an artist plays Con. 900
S. harmonist of Flora's Court! Dr. 3
And learned as 'tis s. Dr. 12
The fairer scenes of s. Sancerre E. i 46
With frequent intercourse, and always s. E. iii 3
All speak one language, all with one s. voice H. 53
S. scent, or lovely form, or both combined H. 290
And plant successfully s. Sharon's rose H. 463
The s. vicissitudes of day and night H. 488 [536
Shall answer—"Hope, s. Hope, has set me free H.
S. music is no longer music here H. 702
O charming Paradise of shortlived s.! Her. 34
S. Nature, stripped of her embroidered robe Her. 79
But one, although her smile was s. J.P. 7
S. as the privilege of healing woe J.T. 17

SWEET—SWEET

How s. soe'er the verse complain *Miss* — 11
"S. sensibility" *Miss* — 68
The sober cordial of s. air *Mor.* 10
Those lips are thine—thy own s. smile I see *M.P.* 3
So s. to huntsman, gentleman, and hound *N.A.* 131
For the s. your cane affords *N.C.* 24
But sing and shine by s. consent *N.G.* 31
The s. that I was wont to share *O.* ii 11 [*P.E.* 79
And earthly sounds, though s. and well combined
S. Harmony that soothes the midnight hour *P.E.* 66
For sabbath evenings, and perhaps as s. *P.E.* 141
Man, Nature's guest by invitation s. *P.E.* 209
Are all the nameless s. of friendship fled ? *P.E.* 244
Are s. philosophy's enjoyments run *P.E.* 259
That make Italian flowers so s. and fair *P.E.* 410
With caution taste the s. Circean cup *P.E.* 580
To forestall s. St. Valentine *P.T.* 12
S. always doubly s. *Q.V.* 28
And add a smile to what was s. before *R.* 10
Then s. to muse upon his skill displayed *R.* 51
S. birds in concert with harmonious streams *R.* 259
O s. retirement ! who would balk the thought *R.* 487
When Pope describes them, have a thousand s. *R.*572
"How s., how passing s. is solitude ! *R.* 740
Whom I may whisper—solitude is s." *R.* 742
Hear the s. accents of his tuneful voice *R.* 771
The foes of man, or make a desert s. *R.* 782
"How smooth these kerchiefs, and how s. ! *R.C.* 59
S. moralist ! afloat on life's rough sea *R.H.* 3 [i 10
Both heart and head ; and couldst with music s. *S.*
Nature inanimate employs s. sounds *T.* 197 [*S.* ii 1
Deem not, s. rose, that bloomest midst many a thorn
Heard the s. moan with pity, and devised *T.* i 74
S. sleep enjoys the curate in his desk *T.* i 94
And s. the clerk below. But neither sleep *T.* i 96
Nor yet the dozings of the clerk, are s. *T.* i 101
To drink s. waters of the crystal well *T.* i 240
Society for me ! Thou seeming s. *T.* i 249
Than please the eye—s. Nature every sense *T.* i 427
And riots in the s. of every breeze *T.* i 444 [i 461
S. smiles, and bloom less transient than her own *T.*
With luxury of unexpected s. *T.* i 533
S. tasted here, and left as soon as known *T.* i 653
That can alone make s. the bitter draught *T.* i 751
With odours, and profligate as s. *T.* ii 228
With lavender, and sprinkle liquid s. *T.* ii 257
Its thunders; and by him, in strains as s. *T.* ii 341
Is proof against thy s. seducing charms ? *T.* ii 482
Of manners s. as Virtue always wears *T.* ii 783
Or too incautious, to preserve thy s. *T.* iii 45
As s. as charity from human breasts *T.* iii 197 [391
S. converse, sipping calm the fragrant lymph *T.* iii
Few know thy value and few taste thy s. *T.* iii 293
Its gratitude, and thanks him with its s. *T.* iii 623
One drop of Heaven's s. mercy in his cup *T.* iii 804
My charmer is not mine alone ; my s. *T.* iii 719
S. bashfulness ! it claims at least this praise *T.* iv 70
Heaven, earth, and ocean, plundered of their s. *T.*iv82
The sprightly lyre, whose treasure of s. sounds *T.*iv160
Return, s. Evening, and continue long ! *T.* iv 244
With s. oblivion of the cares of day *T.* iv 250
And s. colloquial pleasures are but few ! *T.* iv 398
Pick up their nauseous dole, though s. to them *T.* v94
The tasted s. of property begat *T.* v 224 [v 707
Their names to the s. lyre. The Historic Muse *T.*
The s. of Liberty and equal laws *T.* v 717 [v 818
S. conference ; inquires what strains were they *T.*
In cadence s., now dying all away *T.* vi 8
The jasmine, throwing wide her elegant s. *T.* vi 173
But like his purpose, gracious, kind, and s. *T.* vi 504
S. is the harp of prophecy ; too s. *T.* vi 747
For silencing so s. a throat *T.B.* 59
Thus sang the s. sequestered bird *The Doves* 37

S. fiction and s. truth alike prevail *Tir.* 136
Our innocent s. simple years again *Tir.* 313
S. interjections ! if he learn but those ? *Tir.* 400
S. in itself, and not forbidding sport *Tir.* 652
S. Poll ! his doting mistress cries *Trans.* iv 13
S. Poll ! the mimic bird replies *Trans.* iv 14 [23
Soon the s. Spring comes dancing forth *Trans.* H.
Hence Liberty, s. Liberty, inspires *T.T.* 222
Unless s. Penitence her powers renew *T.T.* 398
Which now and then s. Poetry may cure *T.T.* 743
With a song more soft and s. *Trans.* iii 6
With flower as s., or fruit as fair *U.* 17
'Tis a bower of Arcadian s. *W.N.* 9
Finds thee not less alive to her s. force *Y.O.* 133
Where most nectareous s. abound 1789, 20

SWEETEN.
Which most should s. his untroubled life *H.* 681
With sophistry their sauce they s. *L.W.* 37
And she that s. all my bitters too *T.* iii 720
Brings he, to s. fruits so undesired ? *Tir.* 578

SWEETER.
Are s. to her many times *C.* 31
But if a s. voice, and one designed *Ex.* 726
But animated Nature s. still *T.* 198

SWEETEST.
Like some of Nature's s. flowers *E.* i 94
The s. that ear ever heard *M.D.* 18
From strenuous toil his hours of s. ease *T.* i 388
Her s. flowers, her aromatic gums *T.* ii 86
Worms wind themselves into our s. flowers *T.* vi 831
As the fairest and s. that blow *W.N.* 15

SWEET-FLOWING.
Resounds with his s. ditty no more *P.F.* 12

SWEETLY.
Streams tinkle s. in poetic chime *R.* 568
The nurse sleeps s., hired to watch the sick *T.* i 89
Whom snoring she disturbs. As s. he *T.* i 90
The mind that slumbers s. in her snares *T.T.* 439

SWEETNESS.
Has God then given its s. to the cane *Ch.* 190
Paternal s., dignity, and love *T.* ii 708
And s., without which no pleasure is *T.* v 470
Without the smile, the s. or the grace *T.T.* 615

SWELL.
The s. of pity, not to be confined *Ch.* 246
The breath of heaven must s. the sail *H.F.* 23
The glowing bosom s. *Miss* — 16
The full concerto s. upon your ear *P.E.* 128
S. at the thought, and kindling into rage *T.* 477
Tormented into billows, heaves and s. *T.* ii 101
Great schools rejected then, as those that s. *Tir.* 501

SWELLED.
Streams s. above the bank, enjoined to stand *Ex.* 185
The beams of heavenly truth have s. the debt ! *Ex.*611
O'er all his thoughts, and s. his easy sail *T.* 420
But s. into a gust—who then, alas ! *T.* ii 485
That softly s. and gaily dressed appears *T.* iii 629
The seeds of cruelty, that since have s. *T.* vi 381

SWELLING.
And s. with disdain *L.R.* 10
He swathes about the s. of the deep *R.* 527
And ventilate and warm the s. buds *T.* iii 426
S. with vegetative force instinct *Y.O.* 34

SWEPT.
As ever s. a winter sky *A Fable* 11
Bending as he s. the chords *B.* 35
S. Ouse's silent tide *D.W.* 2
S. with a woman's neatness, breeding else *T.* iii 616

That office served, they must be *s.* away *T.* v 569
The strings are *s.* with such a power, so loud *T.T.* 490

SWERVE. [*T.* vi 201
From which they *s.* not since.   That under force

SWERVED. [161
His labouring team that *s.* not from the track *T.* i

SWIFT.
S. as the proudest gander of them all *A.T.* 55
So like an arrow *s.* he flew *J.G.* 153
And Murray sighs o'er Pope and *S.*—*M.* i 5 [*M.P.* 96
So thou, with sails how *s.*! hast reached the shore
Then *s.* descending with a seaman's haste *R.* 435
The tide of life, *s.* always in its course *R.* 453
Moves without noise, and *s.* as an express *T.* 204
S. beyond thought the lightnings dart away *T.* 243
S. pace or steep ascent no toil to me *T.* i 139
And all were *s.* to follow whom all loved *T.* ii 251
In arts like yours.   I cannot call the *s. T.* iii 211
For all the savage din of the *s.* pack *T.* iii 325
Unsoiled and *s.*, and of a silken sound *T.* iv 212
He sees me, and at once, *s.* as a bird *T.* vi 316
Her serious mirth, to Arbuthnot and *S.*—*T.T.* 657

SWIFTER.
Nor *s.* greyhound follow *Ep.* ii 2
That guides the Christian in his *s.* race *T.* 534

SWIFTLY.
Thus *s.* dividing the flood *M.D.* 25
Post away *s.* to more active scenes *R.* 273
The wain that meets it passes *s.* by *T.* i 297
Flies *s.*, and unfelt the task proceeds *T.* iv 166
Declined the death, and wheeling *s.* round *T.* vi 518

SWIFTNESS.
Was equal to the *s.* of his horse *A.T.* 194

SWIFT-WINGED.
And the *s.* arrows of Light *A.S.* 44

SWILL.
Obscene, to *s.* and swallow at a trough? *P.E.* 266

SWIM.
Expert to *s.*, he lay *Cast.* 14
Impatient *s.* to meet *D.W.* 34 [682
And though resolved to risk them, and *s.* down *Ex*
Down, down the wind, she *s.*, and sails away *P.E.* 333
But cawing rooks, and kites that *s.* sublime *T.* 203
Look up—your brains begin to *s. Trans.* ii 10

SWINE.
There is a part in every *s. L.W.* 3

SWING.
Might *s.* at ease behind his study door *Ch.* 615
And *s.* his rump around *Ep.* ii 24
That seems to *s.* uncertain, and yet falls *T.* i 358

SWINGING.
S. the parlour door upon its hinge *E.* iii 21
A bottle *s.* at each side *J.G.* 107
And *s.* it rudely, too rudely, alas! *The Rose* 11
By slender threads, and *s.* in the breeze *Tir.* 592

SWOLN.
Two empirics he stands, and with *s.* cheeks *T.* ii 352

SWORD.
The *s.* shall light upon thy boasted powers *Ch.* 79
And waste them, as thy *s.* has wasted ours" *Ch.* 80
Guns, halberts, *s.* and pistols, great and small *Ch.* 551
Worse than the mortal brunt of rival *s. Con.* 86
Who never saw the *s.* he could not wield *Con.* 608
That no success attends on spears and *s. Ex.* 352
And while he ruled thee by the *s.* alone *Ex.* 490
With senseless noise, his argument the *s. H.* 660
Attend to finish what the *s.* begun *Her.* 60

In which I bear my trusty *s. J.G.* 63
His *s.* was in its sheath *R.G.* 21
Graced with a *s.*, and worthier of a fan *T.* i 771
The undreaded volley with a *s.* of straw *T.* ii 811
The magisterial *s.* in vain, and lays *T.* iv 596
At the *s.* point, and dyeing the white robe *T.* iv 682
The *s.* and falchion their inventor claim *T.* v 218
Where violence shall never lift the *s. T.* vi 843
And eats into his bloody *s.* like rust *T.T.* 8
To touch the *s.* with conscientious awe *T.T.* 77

SWORDBLADE.
Retrench a *s.*, or displace a patch *T.* ii 318

SWORD-HILT.
Was glued to the *s.* with Indian gore *Ch.* 50

SWORDMANSHIP.
No skill in *s.*, however just *Ch.* 509

SWORN.
(*S.* foes to every thing that's witty!) *E.* iv 14
And hast thou *s.* on every slight pretence *Ex.* 386
Of nations, *s.* to spoil thee and devour *Ex.* 703
Oh! see me *s.* to serve thee, and command *H.* 669
S. foes to sense and law *M.* i 2
First Appetite enlists him Truth's *s.* foe *P.E.* 512
And wrongs the woman he has *s.* to love! *T.* iv 465

SWUNG. [36
Where Nichol *s.* the birch and twined the bays *V.*

SYCAMORE.
The *s.*, capricious in attire *T.* i 318

SYCOPHANT.
But change with every moon.   The *s. T.* ii 599
That sucks him; there the *s.*, and he *T.* iii 818
Worthy, compared with *s.*, who kneel *T.* vi 886
No *s.* or slave, that dared oppose *T.T.* 350

SYLLABLE.
Those awful *s.*, Hell, Death, and Sin *H.* 690
A panting *s.* through time and space *R.* 692
Lisping our *s.*, we scramble next *Tir.* 125
And stammer out a *s. Trans.* iv 38
I play with *s.*, and sport in song *T.T.* 505

SYLLOGISMS.
Though *s.* hang not on my tongue *Con.* 93

SYLVAN.
So withered stumps disgrace the *s.* scene *Con.* 51
The houseless rovers of the *s.* world *T.* i 588
And fugitive in vain.   The *s.* scene *T.* ii 107

SYMBOL.
And made the *s.* of atoning grace *Ex.* 378
The *s.* of a righteous reign 1789, 44

SYMPATHETIC.
Though Scorn repay her *s.* tears *Ch.* 414

SYMPATHISE.
And *s.* with others suffering more *T.* iv 340

SYMPATHY.
And only *s.* like thine could reach *Ch.* 304
The sorrows *s.* esteems it own *Con.* 696
From generous *s.* what joys *Miss —* 15
Should spring from *s. Miss —* 48
And will, with *s.*, endure *M.F.* 57
By pity, *s.*, and love *P.* 62
Till *s.* contract a kindred pain *R.* 299
There is in souls a *s.* with sounds *T.* vi 1
Of *s.*, and therefore dead alike *T.* vi 323
A tender *s.* pervades the frame *T.T.* 485

SYMPHONIOUS.
And the clear voice, *s.*, yet distinct *T.* iv 162

SYMPTOM—TAKE

SYMPTOM.
Such as its *s.* can alone express *R.* 288
The *s.* that you see with so much dread *Tir.* 534

SYNAGOGUE-FREQUENTING.
A praying, *s.* beau *T.* 57

SYNCOPE.
Suffer a *s.* and solemn pause *T.* ii 80

SYNTAX.
Of *s.*, truly, but with little more *Tir.* 623

SYREN.
I hear as mute as if a *s.* sung *T.T.* 199

SYRIAC.
Hebrew, or *S.*, shall be forced to bend *P.E.* 499

SYRINGA.
In streaming gold; *s.*, ivory pure *T.* vi 150

SYSTEM.
Round other *s.* under her control *Ch.* 318
The *s.* of a world's concerns *E.* i 74
Their piety a *s.* of deceit *Ex.* 91
His well-built *s.*, philosophic dreams *T.* 8
A thousand *s.*, each in his own way *T.* iii 171
And *s.* of whose birth no tidings yet *T.* v 827

T.

TABLE.
This *t.* and mirror within *Gr.* 21
Convivial *t.* and commodious seat *T.* v 162
But, if thy *t.* be indeed unclean *Tir.* 735
To be the *t.* talk of clubs upstairs *T.T.* 151

TABLET.
The glowing *t.* with a juster skill *Ex.* 232
The painted *t.*, dealt and dealt again *P.E.* 170

TACKLE.
Through which the *t.* passed *A Tale* 36

TÆDIUM.
The *t.* that the lazy rich endure *T.T.* 742

TA'EN.   [ii 478
What he had *t.* in charge. He would not stoop *T.*

TAIL.
Worms may be caught by either head or *t. Ch.* 528
And piously prefer the *t. L.W.* 20   [*N.A.* 25
With *t.* high mounted, ears hung low, and throats
Till quite from *t.* to snout 'tis eaten *L.W.* 38
The cock his arched *t.'s* azure show *Mrs. M*—7 [46
And *t.* cropped short, half lurcher and half cur *T.* v
Some give that honour to his *t. Trans.* i 7
By maggots at the *t. Y.D.* 56

TAILED.
Long backed, long *t.*, with whiskered snout *T.B.* 35

TAINT.
T. in its rudiments the promised flower *Con.* 42
And free from every *t.* but that of vice *Ex.* 150
To *t.* his heart, was worthy of thine own *P.E.* 346
And *t.* the golden ear. He springs his mines *T.* ii 187
T. downward all the graduated scale *T.* iv 585
Is sullied in the stream, taking a *t. T.* vi 834
Nor *t.* his speech with meannesses, designed *Tir.* 686

TAINTED.
And, *t.* by the very means of cure *Ex.* 104
Whose foot ne'er *t.* morning dew *Ep.* ii 3

TAKE.
No pastime but with her he deigned to *t. A.T.* 17 [66
How would they *t.* up Israel's taunting strain! *Ch.*
T. the resemblance of the good she views *Ch.* 396
No learned disputants would *t.* the field *Ch.* 620
Grows fungous, and *t.* fire at every spark *Con.* 54
The mark at which my juster aim I *t. Con.* 105
Their nimble nonsense *t.* a shorter course *Con.* 152
He *t.* what he at first professed to loathe *Con.* 337
To *t.* his honour's orders, cap in hand *Con.* 416
Once *t.* the shell beneath his just command *Con.* 904

What walks we *t.*, what books we choose *E.* i 6
But when a poet *t.* the pen *E.* i 9
Where Obstinacy *t.* his sturdy stand *Ex.* 298
To *t.* for truth what cannot but be true *Ex.* 649
As in a dance the pair that *t.* the lead *H.* 13
And while she *t.*, as at a father's hand *H.* 157
May now and then their velvet cushions *t. H.* 248
That man will freely *t.* an unbought bliss *H.* 335
Sighing and smiling as he *t.* his glass *H.* 419
To *t.* with gratitude what heaven bestows *H.* 430
But these, excuse the liberty I *t. H.* 435
To *t.* the bend his appetites ordain *H.* 603
So Pity shall *t.* Virtue's part *Miss* — 89
T., if ye can, ye careless and supine *P.E.* 9
As Reason, or as Passion, *t.* the reins *P.E.* 36
He *t.* offence, and wonders what you mean *P.E.* 89
He from Italian songsters *t.* his cue *P.E.* 112
He *t.* the field, the master of the pack *P.E.* 114
Prepares for meals as jockeys *t.* a sweat *P.E.* 221
Spontaneous, *t.* but little pains to sow *P.E.* 364
Fresh thoughts the speculatist *t. P.E.* 490
First put it out, then *t.* it for a guide *P.E.* 559
T. leave of Nature's God, and God revealed *P.E.* 591
To birth or wit; nor gives nor *t.* offence *R.* 450
Begs you for once to *t.* his part *St.* i 35
T. it and perish; but restrain your tongue *T.* 18
T., Madam, the reward of all your prayers *T.* 167
Produce them—*t.* a chair—now draw a Saint *T.* 172
The dinner served, Charles *t.* his usual stand *T.* 213
And *t.* unenvied the reward they sought *T.* 528
And so two citizens who *t.* the air *T.* i 79
And bids the world *t.* heart and banish fear *T.* ii 195
And I consent you *t.* it for your text *T.* ii 474
Or does the tomb *t.* all? If he survive *T.* ii 518
T. deeper root, confirmed by what they see *T.* ii 568
T. of the crimson stream meandering there *T.* iii 202
The shapely side, that as it rises *t. T.* iii 481
Meanders lubricate the course they *t. T.* iv 65
'Tis thus the understanding *t.* repose *T.* iv 296
Ingenious Parsimony *t.*, but just *T.* iv 400
T. a Lethean leave of all his toil *T.* iv 475
T. step for step; and, as I near approach *T.* v 18
The growing wonder *t.* a thousand shapes *T.* v 119
And we too wise to trust them. He that *t. T.* v 496
Of Earth and Hell confederate *t.* away *T.* v 541
T. part with Appetite, and pleads the cause *T.* v 630
His spirit *t.*, unconscious of a chain *T.* v 776
And with thee rich, *t.* what Thou wilt away *T.* v 906
Such comprehensive views the spirit *t. T.* vi 15
With unsuspecting readiness he *t. T.* vi 427
And such sagacity to *t.* revenge *T.* vi 477

Or *t.* their pastime in the spacious field *T.* vi 576[889
The world *t.* little thought. Who will may preach *T.*vi
That *t.* not fire at their heroic deeds *T.T.* 26
They *t.* perhaps a well directed aim *T.T.* 206
Obduracy *t.* place; callous and tough *T.T.* 458
Why *t.* the gentler Moon her turn to rise *Tir.* 38
The tomb *t.* all, and all be blank beyond *Tir.* 68
To *t.* the lead and be the foremost still *Tir* 377
So *t.* my judgment in his language dressed *Tir.* 507
To *t.* in childish plays a childish part *Tir.* 548
That youth *t.* pleasure in, to please his boy *Tir.* 550
No longer *t.*, as once, with fearless ease *Tir.* 569
Thence the prevailing manners *t.* their cast *Tir.* 913
T. half thy canvass in *Trans. H.* 36
When he that *t.*, and he that pays *Y.D.* 19

TAKEN.
And *t.* trash for treasure *F.* 27
Accomplishments have *t.* Virtue's place *P.E.* 417

TAKING.
T. my lonely winding walk, I mused *F.A.* 8
Dangling his cane about, and *t.* snuff *H.* 27
Is sullied in the stream, *t.* a taint *T.* vi 834
Less trouble *t.* twice the sum *Y.D.* 67

TALE.
In every *t.* they tell, or false or true *Con.* 61
But sedentary weavers of long *t. Con.* 207
A *t.* should be judicious, clear, succinct *Con.* 235
You laugh—'tis well—the *t.* applied *L.W.* 23
Howe'er disguised the inflammatory *t. P.E.* 327
Till others have the soothing *t.* believed *P.E* 493
Misses! the *t.* that I relate *P.T.* 62
Her *t.* of guilt renews *St.* v 22
The skittish fancy with facetious *t. T.* ii 470
By drunken howlings; and the chilling *t. T.* iv 562
Cyrene, when he bore the plaintive *t. T.* v 136
In staggering types, his predecessor's *t. T.* v 419
An ancient, not a legendary *t. T.* vi 479
Quevedo, as he tells his sober *t. T.T.* 93
Sells oaths by *t.* and at the lowest price *T.T.* 419
In *t.*, in trifles, and in children's play *T.T.* 731
Ingenious dreamer, in whose well told *t. Tir.* 135
But now farewell all legendary *t. Tir.* 181
How! turn again to *t.* long since forgot *Tir.* 545

TALENT.
So famed for his *t.* in nicely discerning *A.C.* 8
His time, his *t.*, and his ceaseless care *A.T.* 15
Though Nature weigh our *t.* and dispense *Con.* 1
In other eyes our *t.* rarely shown *Con.* 369
Let him improve his *t.* if he can *Con.* 425
Of *t.*, judgment, mercies, better far *F.A.* 15
Nor labour they, nor time nor *t.* waste *H.* 766
And he soon finds the *t.* it requires *R.* 614
Life an intrusted *t.*, or a toy? *R.* 650
And give the world their *t.* and themselves *T.* ii 799
Great *t.* : and God gives to every man *T.* iv 789
And with the boon gives *t.* for its use *T.* v 860
A *t.* so divine, remember too *T.* vi 649
They see the attentive crowds his *t.* draw *Tir.* 312
Few boys are born with *t.* that excel *Tir.* 509
His post not mean, his *t.* not unknown *Tir.* 723
His humorous *t.* next employs *Trans.* iv 26
Neglected *t.* rust into decay *T.T.* 516
Have raised you high as *t.* can ascend *V.* 13

TALISMANS.
Books are not seldom *t.* and spells *T.* vi 98

TALK.
He *t.* of light, and the prismatic hues *Ch.* 391
Resumed his purpose, had a world of *t. Con.* 279
I cannot *t.* with civet in the room *Con.* 283
O'erheard and checked this idle *t. P.* 40
Winks hard, and *t.* of darkness at noonday *P.E.* 451
And *t.* and laughs away his vacant hours *R.* 452
Or all that we have left, is empty *t. T.* ii 253
To be the Table *T.* of clubs up stairs *T.T.* 151
Is kept to strut, look big, and *t.* away *T.T.* 233
One *t.* of mildew and of frost *Y.D.* 53

TALKATIVE.
In vain the *t.* unite *F.* 67

TALKING.
But *t.* is not always to converse *Con.* 8
There's little *t.*, and no wit *Y.D.* 39

TALL.
Of some *t.* temple playing bright *Mrs. M*— 36 [i 174
T. spire, from which the sound of cheerful bells *T.*
Between the upright shafts of whose *t.* elms *T.* i 355
Upon the ship's *t.* side he stands, possessed *T.* i 450
And of an humbler growth, the other *t. T.* vi 152
The stout *t.* captain, whose superior size *Tir.* 222

TALLEST.
The *t.* pines feel most the power *Trans. H.* 13

TAME.
He found thee savage, and he left thee *t. Ex.* 485
That serve mankind, or shun them, wild or *t. N.A.*66
And lovers, of all creatures, *t.* or wild *R.* 251
To meliorate and *t.* the stubborn soil *R.* 786
The pert made perter, and the *t.* made wild *Tir.* 345

TAMED.
And though the fox he follows may be *t. Con.* 409
His passions *t.*, and all at his control *T.* 417
By culture *t.*, by liberty refreshed *T.* i 606
Alas! Leviathan is not so *t. T.* ii 322   [46
Sorrow has, since they went, subdued and *t. T.* vi
Send him to college. If he there be *t. Tir.* 240

TAMELY.
But if a deed not *t.* to be borne *T.T.* 488

TAMENESS.
And blushing at the *t.* of the rest *Ex.* 543
Their *t.* is shocking to me *A.S.* 16

TAMER.
And *t.* far for so much fury shown *T.* vi 541

TAMPERING.
Vain *t.* has but fostered his disease *T.* v 668

TANTALUS.
Like fabled *T.*, condemned to hear *P.E.* 231

TAPER.
The *t.* soon extinguished, which I saw *T.* iv 391

TAPESTRY.
Yellow and red, of *t.* richly wrought *T.* i 33

TAR.
Left out his linchpin, or forgot his *t. P.E.* 441

TARDILY.
The night rolled *t.* away *R.C.* 67

TARDINESS.
He chides the *t.* of every post *R.* 475

TARDY.
Judgment, however *t.*, mends her pace *Ex.* 151
A nation scourged, yet *t.* to repent *Ex.* 723
Fulfill'd their *t.* and disastrous course *T.* vi 735
May some disease, not *t.* to perform *T.* vi 1002
Of the mere schoolboy's lean and *t.* growth *Tir.* 657

TARNISH.
T. all your boasted powers *N.C.* 54

TARRY.
Inclined to *t.* there *J.G.* 150

TARSUS.
Had Paul of *T*. lived and died a Jew *H*. 257

TART.
But he can draw a pattern, make a *t*. *P.E.* 195
Those humours, *t*. as wines upon the fret *R*. 761
The popular harangue, the *t*. reply *T*. iv 31

TASK.
A *t*. I venture on, impelled by thee *Ch*. 6
And gains new vigour at her endless *t*. *Ch*. 104
And bind the *t*. assigned thee to thine heart *Ex*. 651
May prove the *t*., a *t*. indeed *F*. 196
A hopeless *t*., and damns them if they fail *H*. 392
Hard *t*. indeed o'er arctic seas to roam! *H*. 548
Hard *t*.! for one who lately knew no care *H*. 696
Poets attempt the noblest *t*. they can *J.T*. 1
Me to torture, me to *t*.? *N.C*. 12
With much compassion undertakes the *t*. *P.E*. 389
Attempts no *t*. it cannot well fulfil *R*. 280
The screws 'reversed (a *t*. which if He please *R*. 327
The veteran steed excused his *t*. at length *R*. 625
The *t*. of new discoveries falls on me *T*. 218
We may discern the thresher at his *t*. *T*. i 356
And not soon spent, though in an arduous *t*. *T*. i 401
Chains him, and *t*. him, and exacts his sweat *T*. ii 23
Upon thy foes, was never meant my *t*. *T*. ii 218
Aware of nothing arduous in a *t*. *T*. ii 307
That *t*. performed, relapse into themselves *T*. ii 441
His folly, but to spoil him is a *t*. *T*. ii 768
The nauseous *t*. to paint her as she is *T*. iii 67
No unimportant, though a silent *t*. *T*. iii 378
Fresh for his *t*., intend what *t*. he may *T*. iii 387
Exposed to his cold breath, the *t*. begins *T*. iii 469
But proud of his uncouth ill-chosen *t*. *T*. iii 644
But here the needle plies its busy *t*. *T*. iv 150
Flies swiftly, and unfelt the *t*. proceeds *T*. iv 166
To do he knows not what. The *t*. performed *T*. iv 630
From morn to eve his solitary *t*. *T*. v 44
By dint of change to give his tasteless *t*. *T*. v 429
As too laborious and severe a *t*. *T*. vi 210 [vi 1009
With that light *t*.; but soon, to please her more *T*.
A scene so friendly to his favourite *t*. *T*. vi 264
And makes the *t*. his own. Inspiring dumb *T*. iv 474
The *t*. now falls into the public hand *T*. vi 718
The labour, were a *t*. more arduous still *T*. vi 758
As if their duty were a desperate *t*. *T.T*. 313
A *t*. as much within your own command *Tir*. 552
The heart of man, for such a *t*. too frail *V*. 67
The *t*. was left to whittle thee away *Y.O*. 104

TASKED.
Cowper, whose silver voice, *t*. sometimes hard *S*. i 1
Were *t*. to his full strength, absorbed and lost *T*. iv 301
With the thought-tracing quill or *t*. his mind *Y.O*. 158

TASSEL.
With ribbon-bound *t*. on high *Gr*. 2
Her golden *t*. on the leafy sprays *R*. 232

TASSELLED.
The *t*. cap and the spruce band a jest *T*. ii 749

TASTE.
How soon would I *t*. you again! *A.S*. 20
With a well-judging *t*. from above *C*. 34
Capricious *T*. itself can crave no more *Ch*. 101
Or *t*. the fountain in the neighbouring glade *Ch*. 223
T. of its healthful origin, and flows *Con*. 565
Reclaim his *t*., and brighten up his parts *Con*. 840
These are but samples, and a *t*. *F*. 194
O ye, who never *t*. the joys *F.B* 31 [*H*. 59
The wretch may pine, while to his smell, *t*., sight
T. happiness, or know what pleasure means *H*. 10
That Fashion, *T*., or Luxury suggest *H*. 446
Wine has no *t*., and beauty has no charms *H*. 705

In sorting flowers to suit a fickle *t*. *H*. 767
May *t*. whate'er his inclination *L.W*. 5
But thou canst *t*. no calm delight *M.B*. 17
No genial spring to *t*. *Miss* — 36
A Bee of most discerning *t*. *P.B*. 3
The rank debauch suits Clodio's filthy *t*. *P.E*. 188
The centre of delights he may not *t*.? *P.E*. 230
With caution *t*. the sweet Circean cup *P.E*. 580
And forms it to the *t*. of her he loves *R*. 238
And cultivate a *t*. for ancient song *R*. 375
With all the charms of an accomplished *t*. *R*. 510
To *t*. a joy like that he has bestowed *R*. 632
And while she polishes, perverts the *t*. *R*. 704
But chosen with a nice discerning *t*. *R*. 726
Invites us. Monument of ancient *t*. *T*. i 253 [697
Such London is, by *t*. and wealth proclaimed *T*. i
But that of idleness, and *t*. no scenes *T*. i 756
With such ingredients of good sense and *t*. *T*. ii 789
Though few now *t*. thee unimpared and pure *T*. iii 43
His manner, and with rapture *t*. his style *T*. iii 228
Few know thy value, and few *t*. thy sweets *T*. iii 293
Dressed to his *t*., inviting him abroad *T*. iii 358 [317
Who dream they have a *t*. for fields and groves *T*. iii
Pant for the praise of dressing to the *t*. *T*. iii 460
Nor *t*. alone and well-contrived display *T*. iii 603
To no mean hand, and asks the touch of *t*. *T*. iii 632
And what they will not *t*. must yet approve *T*. iii 701
New to my *t*. his Paradise surpassed *T*. iv 710
By modern lights from an erroneous *t*. *T*. iv 724
If he indulge a cultivated *t*. *T.T*. 161 [*T*. iv 740
And all can *t*. them; minds that have been formed
The virtue, temper, understanding, *t*. *T*. iv 790
Which whoso *t*. can be enslaved no more *T*. v 544
Acquaint thyself with God, if thou wouldst *t*. *T*. v 779
Some *t*. of comfort in a world of woe *T*. vi 966
To palates that can *t*. immortal truth *T*. vi 1015
I was a poet too: but modern *t*. *T.T*. 510
Was lumber in an age so void of *t*. *T.T*. 619
Sublimity and attic *t*. combined *T.T*. 644
That in good time the stripling's finished *t*. *Tir*. 203
Of habit, inclination, temper, *t*. *Tir*. 441
Prepared by *t*., by learning, and true worth *Tir*. 678
In settled habit and decided *t*. *Tir*. 778
Of thickest shades, like Adam after *t*. *Y.O*. 15

TASTED.
By the miseries that we *t*. *N.C*. 43
Sweets *t*. here, and left as soon as known *T*. i 653
The *t*. sweets of property begat *T*. v 224

TASTELESS.
A *t*. journal of the day before *Con*. 276
The song of Sion is a *t*. thing *Con*. 715
And *t*., of the same repeated joys *T*. i 463
But *t*. Springs a palace in its stead *T*. iii 769
By dint of change to give his *t*. task *T*. v 429

TASTING.
Or *t*. long enjoy thee; too infirm *T*. iii 44

TATTERED.
More *t*. still; and both but ill conceal *T*. i 551
The livelong night. A *t*. apron hides *T*. i 549
To wear a *t*. garb however coarse *T*. iv 416
And *t*. in the service of debauch *T*. v 633

TATTLERS.
For *t*. will be sure to hear *F*. 98

TAUGHT.
For scorning what they *t*. him to detest *Ch*. 56
T. me what path to shun, and what pursue *Ch*. 239
But Reason still, unless divinely *t*. *Ch*. 337
Thus *t*., down falls the plumage of his pride *Ch*. 345
Are *t*. by rays that fly with equal pace *Ch*. 363
By Fashion *t*., forbade them once to name *Con*. 496

The Roman t. thy stubborn knee to bow Ex. 476
T. thee to clothe thy pinked and painted hide Ex. 486
A man arise, a man whom God has t. H. 622   [11
"Couldst thou in truth ? and art thou t. at length F.A.
Ne'er t. me by woman before M.D. 12   [H. 668
And none can teach them but whom thou hast t.
All sustained by patience, t. us N.C. 47
T. you to sing, and me to shine N.G. 20
And observation t. me, I would teach P.E. 12
Far more intelligent, and better t. R. 673
Learn then, ye living ! by the mouths be t. St. ii 33
T. the raised shoulders to invade the ears T. i 67
Or seen with least reproach ; and virtue, t. T. i 690
Or ask of whomsoever he has t. T. ii 204
By nature, or by flattery made so, t. T. ii 546
The weak perhaps are moved, but are not t. T. ii 566
A wooden one, so we, no longer t. T. ii 575   [83
And t. the unblemished to preserve with care T. iii
Is but a school, where thoughtlessness is t. T. iv 688
And in the school of sacred wisdom t. T. v 797
As t. him too to tremble in his turn T. vi 378
And t. a brute the way to safe revenge T. vi 559
Till, nation after nation t. the strain T. vi 796
Well t., he all the sounds expressed T.B. 11
Thus form'd, thus placed, intelligent, and t. Tir. 53
That t. of God they may indeed be wise Tir. 107
And t. at schools much mythologic stuff Tir. 197
The meek and bashful boy will soon be t. Tir. 338
As, wheresoever t., so formed, he will Tir 526
When birds are to be t. to prate Trans. iv 41
Liberty t. him her Athenian strain T.T. 343
Language, above all teaching, or if t. T.T. 586 [V. 9
Your brain well furnished, and your tongue well t.
Of Wantonness, where vice was t. by rule T.T. 627

TAUNTING.
How would they take up Israel's t. strain ! Ch. 66
Of its own t. question, asked so long T. vi 870

TAVERN.
With an old t. quill, is hungry yet T. ii 628
Of fashion, dissipation, t., stews T. ii 770
But t. teach the knowledge of the heart Tir. 213
In bilking t. bills, and spouting plays Tir. 327

TAW.
The chalky ring, and knuckle down at t. Tir. 307

TAWNY.
Now green, now t., and ere autumn yet T. i 319
Their fluttering rags, and shows a t. skin T. i 568

TAX.
A t. upon their own just praise F. 89
A t. of profit from his very play Tir. 612
Increasing t. and the nation's debt T.T. 177
Levied a t. of wonder and applause T.T. 650

TAXED.
Or t. Invention for a fresh supply Ch. 514
T. till the brow of Labour sweats in vain Ex. 305

TEA.   [Con. 278
Called on a friend, drank t., stepped home again
What, give up our desserts, our coffee, and t. ! P.A. 8

TEACH.   [38
Some she would t. (for she was wondrous wise A.T.
They t. both conjurors and old women A Fable 21
Since t. you all I can Beau 18
T. me to kindle at thy gentle fires Ch. 12
Alternately the nations learn and t. Ch. 120
To t. the wanderer, as his woes increase Ch. 161
T. mercy to ten thousand hearts that share Ch. 278
But knowledge such as only dungeons t. Ch. 303
To t. good manners, and to curb abuse Con. 164 [585
Leaves saints to enjoy those altitudes they t. Con.

And t. the softer not to copy theirs Con. 844 [890
Pursues the course that truth and nature t. Con.
And t. the combatant a woman's part ? Ex. 359 [243
They warn and t. the proudest, would they learn Ex.
Still murmuring with the solemn truths I t. Ex. 719
And t. the world, if not perversely blind H. 138
Kind souls ! to t. their tenantry to prize H. 252
The gross idolatry blind heathens t. H. 499
Some wiser rule must t. him how to live H. 600
And t. Philosophy a smile Mrs. M— 30   [H. 668
And none can t. them but whom thou hast taught
And observation taught me, I would t. P.E. 12
And t. her, unexperienced yet and green P.E. 317
T. him to fence and figure twice a week P.E. 366
T. his eyes a language, and no less R. 239
T., while they flatter him, his proper place R. 446
To t. the canvass innocent deceit R. 797
And while I t. an art too little known R. 807
I may not t. in vain St. i 32
The book shall t. you ; read, believe, and live T. 274
And t. him notions splendid as themselves T. 424
Or Inspiration t. ; and enclosed T. i 628   [358
He t. those to read, whom schools dismissed T. ii
On skulls that cannot t., and will not learn T. ii 394
Or vicious, and not therefore apt to t. T. ii 550
But if his word once t. us, shoot a ray T. iii 240
That whom it t. it makes prompt to learn T. v 859
Ye, therefore, who love mercy, t. your sons T. vi 588
We could not t., and must despair to learn T. vi 620
And t. one tyrant pity for his drudge T. vi 728 [123
Presents the prayer the Saviour deigned to t. Tir.
May t. the gayest, make the gravest smile Tir. 138
But taverns t. the knowledge of the heart Tir. 213
To warn, and t. him safely to unbend Tir. 608
To t. his heart to glow with generous flame Tir. 644
To more than he is hired or bound to t. Tir. 732
T. humbler thoughts to you Trans. i 26 [t. Tir. 397
Your Lordship, and your Grace ! what school can
To t. him now and then a word Trans. iv 8
Receive, dear friend, the truths I t. Trans. H. i
Such lofty strains embellish what you t. T.T. 478
To t., no Spirit dwells in thee, nor voice Y.O. 138

TEACHABLE.
Such t. and apprehensive parts T. vi 612

TEACHER.
A t. should be sparing of his smile Ch. 490
Such, when the T. of his church was there Ex. 123
Where shall a t. look, in days like these Ex. 450 [351
Are all such t. ?   Would to Heaven all were ! T. ii
Is Christ the abler t., or the schools ? T. ii 534
And woman are the t. Trans. iv 42
" The t.'s office, and dispense at large T. v 645
Much zeal in virtue's cause all t. boast Tir. 517

TEACHING.
Or academic tutors, t. youths N.A. 79
Experience, slow preceptress, t. oft T. iii 505
A t. voice ; but 'tis the praise of thine T. v 858
Language, above all t., or if taught T.T. 586

TEAM.   [i 161
His labouring t. that swerved not from the track T.
The boorish driver leaning o'er his t. T. i 298
In ponderous boots beside his reeking t. T. iv 342

TEAPOT.
A fragment, and the spoutless t. there T. iv 776

TEAR.
Is wet with Anson's t. Cast. 52
And t. by bards or heroes shed Cast. 53
When Cook—lamented, and with t. as just Ch. 23
Loses in t. the far receding shore Ch. 147
Though Scorn repay her sympathetic t. Ch. 414

TEAR—TEMPER

But though life's valley be a vale of t. *Con.* 881[26
And said, " Go spend them in the vale of t." *E.* ii
Thy t. all issue from a source divine *E.* ii 47
In England's case to move the Muse to t. ? *Ex.* 2
In England's case to move the Muse to t. ? *Ex.* 32
He loved the world that hated him ; the t. *H.* 574
If ever on thy eyelid stood the t. *H.* 676
And the first thankful t. bedew his cheeks *H.* 727
And ecstasy attends the t. *Miss* — 55
Say, wast thou conscious of the t. I shed ? *M.P.* 22
Perhaps a t., if souls can weep in bliss *M.P.* 26
And if a t., that speaks regret *N.* 21
Shall shine and dry the t. *N.* 24
Sighs must fan it, t. must water *N.C.* 19
But every t. shall scald thy memory *P.E.* 336
But with a joyful t. *Q.V.* 54
The t. that England owes *R.G.* 28
But t. of godly grief ne'er flow within *St.* ii 32
With t. o'er hapless favourites shed *T.B.* 2 [*Rose* 19
And the t. that is wiped with a little address *The*
Oh sorrowful and sad ! the streaming t. *T.* 173
Weeps t. of joy, and bursts into a song *T.* 458
While struggling in the vale of t. below *T.* 585
I see thee weep, and thine are honest t. *T.* i 657
Of silent t. and heart-distending sighs ! *T.* iii 331
Vain t., alas ! and sighs that never find *T.* iii 332
To barrenness, and solitude, and t. *T.* v 441 [iv 18
With t., that trickled down the writer's cheeks *T.*
Eradicate him, t. him from his hold *T.* v 437
Whose eye they fill with t. of holy joy *T.* v 750
(Himself grown sober in the vale of t.) *T.* vi 48
Leaving the poor no remedy but t. *T.* vi 845
Or guilty soon relenting into t. *Tir.* 112
Canst thou, the t. just trembling on thy lids *Tir.* 859
Strange doctrine this ! that without scruple t. *T.T.* 5
Prayer only, and the penitential t. *T.T.* 412
And view with t. the expected harvest lost *V.* 57
Since all thy t. were changed to smiles 1789, 57

TEASE. [135

Yet, though he t. and baulk your listening ear *Con.*
To t. for cash, and quarrel with all day *P.E.* 372
Should ever t. the lungs and blear the sight *T.* iii 168

TEASED.

Not soon provoked, however stung and t. *Ch.* 428
Thus always teasing others, always t. *Con.* 345

TEASING.

Thus always t. others, always teased *Con.* 345

TEDIOUS.

Decide no question with their t. length *Con.* 87
A t. hour—and now we never meet ! *E.* iii 5
These twice ten t. years, yet we *J.G.* 7
Can save us always from a t. day *R.* 745
The t. rector drawling o'er his head *T.* i 95
We think them t. creatures *Trans.* iv 39
And, t. years of Gothic darkness passed *T.T.* 564

TEDIOUSLY.

Is such a life, so t. the same *H.* 87

TEEMED.

She t. and heaved with an infernal birth *Her.* 13

TEEMING.

The wildest project of her t. brain *A.T.* 57
To call up Plenty from the t. earth *T.* 181

TEEMS.

With which Hypocrisy for ever t. *H.* 619
But t. with powers he never felt before *P.E.* 404

TEETH. [iv 352

With half-shut eyes and puckered cheeks and t. *T.*
His t. were strong, the cage was wood *T.B.* 53
He picks clean t., and, busy as he seems *T.* ii 627

T. for the toothless, ringlets for the bald *T.* iv 81
With ivory t., or ploughs it with his snout *T.* v 50

TELESCOPIC.

Where science points her t. eye *H.* 441
To your weak sight her t. eye *T.* 98

TELL.

To t. us what is to befall *A Fable* 22
Oh ! t. me I yet have a friend *A.S.* 39
That t. his name, his worth, his age *Cast* 51 [394
What monstrous lies some travellers will t." *Ch.*
That t. us whence his treasures are supplied *Ch.* 440
In every tale they t., or false or true *Con.* 61
To hear them t. of parentage and birth *Con.* 210
T. not as new what everybody knows *Con.* 237 [719
Strange tidings these to t. a world who treat *Con.*
T. her again, the sneer upon her face *Con.* 783 [875
For t. some men that pleasure, all their bent *Con.*
And t. them truths divine and clear *E.* i 21
But who can t. how vast the plan *E.* i 83
Blush when I t. you how a bird *F.B.* 34
And t. of laws despised, at least not kept *H.* 220[418
Come, prophet, drink, and t. us what think you" *H.*
Though whispered, plainly t. what works within *H.* 691
And t. you where ye have a right to reign *Her.* 48
What news ? what news ? Your tidings t. *J.G.* 165
T. me you must and shall *J.G.* 166
Who, strange to t., all judged it wrong *J.P.* 19
They t. us of the fate of Rome *M.* ii 3
I t. you, you can't hear at all ! " *M.F.* 28
Who, knowing them, can t. *Miss* — 14
Is there, as ye sometimes t. us *N.C.* 25
Released him as my story t. *N.G.* 25
Pray t. me why we may not also go snacks ? *P.A.* 16
Brutes capable would t. you 'tis a lie *P.E.* 261 [*P.E.* 5
T. where she lurks, beneath what flowery shades
To t. them more than they have wit to ask *P.E.* 390
T. him he wanders, that his error leads *P.E.* 544
'Twas hard to t., of streets or squares *Q.V.* 9
These t. me of enjoyments past *S.* 23
Oh, t. thy thoughtless sex, the virtuous mind *S.* ii 6
And t., not always with an eye to truth *T.* 154
She t. me, too, that duly every morn *T.* i 663
Forth steps the spruce philosopher, and t. *T.* ii 189
Now t. me, dignified and sapient sir *T.* ii 531 [iii 158
And t. us whence the stars ; why some are fixed *T.*
To t. its slumbers, and to paint its dreams *T.* iii 13
T. me—and I will t. thee what is Truth *T.* iii 289
Too long, to t. the expedients and the shifts *T.* iii 559
No marble t. us whither. With their names *T.* v 727
Shouted for joy.—" *T.* me, ye shining hosts *T.* v 822
The lion t. him—I am monarch here ! *T.* vi 408
His head alone remained to t. *T.B.* 65
And t. them, as he strokes their silver locks *Tir.* 322
T. of a few stout hearts that fought and died *T.T.* 23
That t. you so say, rather, they for him *T.T.* 50
Quevedo, as he t. his sober tale *T.T.* 93
Or t. me, if you can, what power maintains *T.T.* 200
And t. the world, still kindling as he sung *T.T.* 736
Your sullen silence serves at least to t. *V.* 25
But yet, methinks to t. you true *Y.D.* 59

TEMPER.

Pure in her aim, and in her t. mild *Ch.* 422
Their acrid t. turns, as soon as stirred *Ch.* 503
Some fretful t. wince at every touch *Con.* 325
The future tone and t. of the sky *Ex.* 158
A fretful t. will divide *F.* 61
A t. passionate and fierce *F.* 64
Whose t. was the best *J.P.* 4
From t. flaws unsightly *N.Y.G.* 8
Genius, and t., and desire of rest *R.* 172
A t. rustic as the life we lead *R.* 732

Of *t.* as envenomed as an asp *T.* 159
Good *t.*; spirits prompt to undertake *T.* i 400
Of heavenly *t.*, furnishes with arms *T.* ii 346
Or *T.* sheds into thy crystal cup *T.* iii 47
Discovering much the *t.* of her sire *T.* iii 434
The virtue, *t.*, understanding, taste *T.* iv 790
Till hardened his heart's *t.* in the forge *T.* v 664
Vicious in act, in *t.* savage-fierce *T.* vi 487
Of habit, inclination, *t.*, taste *Tir.* 441
Against a heart depraved and *t.* hurt *Tir.* 489

TEMPERANCE.
T. and Peace insure its healthful state *Con.* 603
That gratitude and *t.* in our use *Ex.* 676
T. were no virtue if He could *P.E.* 224
That law has licensed, as makes *t.* reel *T.* iv 471

TEMPERATE.
Of *t.* wishes and industrious hands *T.* i 599

TEMPERED.
Well read, well *t.*, with religion warmed *Con.* 640
Nice in its choice, and of a *t.* heat *J.T.* 36
Some minds are *t.* happily, and mixed *T.* ii 788
The auspicious moment, when the *t.* heat *T.* iii 508
T. in hell, invades the throbbing breast *T.* iii 686
Such were not they of old, whose *t.* blades *T.* v 515

TEMPEST.
The *t.* itself lags behind *A.S.* 43
A *t.* usher in the dreaded morn *H.* 717
"Where *t.* never beat nor billows roar" *M.P.* 97
Abrupt and horrid as the *t.* roars *R.* 533
No *t.* gave the shock *R.G.* 18
He hears the *t.* howling in the trees *T.* 254
In *t.*; quits his grasp upon the winds *T.* ii 181
The *t.* of tumultuary joys *T.T.* 409
He hears the thunder ere the *t.* lowers *T.T.* 496
When *t.* could not. At thy firmest age *Y.O.* 93

TEMPEST-BEATEN.
That all its *t.* turrets shake *T.* v 527

TEMPEST-TOSSED.
Me howling blasts drive devious, *t. M.P.* 102

TEMPESTUOUS.
'Tis thus, extending his *t.* arm *Ex.* 584
Like him, crossed cheerfully *t.* seas *H.* 584
The pelting brunt of the *t.* night *T.* iv 351
Of this *t.* state of human things *T.* vi 737

TEMPLE.
The *t.* and its holy rights profaned *Ex.* 145
Thy *t.*, once thy glory, fallen and rased *Ex.* 259
For clumps, and lawns, and *t.*, and cascades *H.* 247
Of some tall *t.* playing bright *Mrs. M—* 36
Called to the *t.* of impure delight *P.E.* 584 [iii 803
Sent through the traveller's *t.*! He that finds *T.*

TEMPT.
To *t.* the poor to sell himself to thee? *Ex.* 375
Whose fruit, though fair, *t.* only to destroy *P.E.* 238
Meridian sunbeams *t.* him to unfold *T.* 60
To *t.* us in thy country. Doing good *T.* i 673
That *t.* Ambition. On the summit see *T.* iv 58
His principle, and *t.* him into sin *T.* iv 454
Not always *t.* the distant deep *Trans. H.* 4

TEMPTATION.
When fierce *T.*, seconded within *T.* iii 684

TEMPTEST.
Thou *t.* none, but rather much forbiddest *Y.O.* 114

TEMPTING.
To captivate the *t.* prey *E.* iv 54
Flies to the *t.* pool, or felon knife *T.* 446

TEN. [*A.T.* 180
"Oh, shame!" *t.* thousand echoing nymphs replied
"Come *t.*, come twenty,—should an army call *A.T.* 185

Teach mercy to *t.* thousand hearts that share *Ch.* 278
T. thousand charms, that only fools despise *H.* 51
T. thousand rove the brakes and thorns among *H.* 280
T. thousand swains the wasted scene deplore *Her.* 39
These twice *t.* tedious years, yet we *J.G.* 7
Full *t.* miles off, at Ware *J.G.* 152
Rarely redeem the short remaining *t. R.* 40
T. thousand rivers poured at his command *R.* 75
T. thousand thousand strings at once go loose *R.* 329
T. starveling hermits suffer less than he *T.* 112
T. thousand warblers cheer the day, and one *T.* 200
Excels *t.* thousand mercenary deeds *T.* 224
T. thousand sages lost in endless woe *T.* 517 [iii 740
And thundering loud, with his *t.* thousand wheels? *T.*
Whom *t.* long years' experience of my care *T.* iii 338
T. thousand dangers lie in wait to thwart *T.* iii 553
T. righteous would have saved a city once *T.* iii 843
Of all this riot: and *t.* thousand casks *T.* iv 505
T. thousand seek an unmolested end *T.* v 87
He deems a thousand or *t.* thousand lives *T.* v 276
T. thousand rovers in the world at large *T.* v 408
Wins public honour; and *t.* thousand sit *T.* vi 633
Else of a mannish growth, and five in *t. Tir.* 208
God's curse can cast away *t.* thousand sail! *T.T.* 467
She fills profuse *t.* thousand little throats *T.T.* 694

TENACIOUS.
Too weak to struggle with *t.* clay *T.* 216

TENANT.
With such as its old *t.* are *M.B.* 3
Scorned by the nobler *t.* of the flood *P.E.* 482
Pours out its fleecy *t.* o'er the glebe *T.* i 291
The envied *t.* of some happier spot *T.* i 610
Of other *t.* than melodious birds *T.* iv 574
To be the *t.* of man's noble form *T.* v 455
And earth be punished for it's *t.* sake *T.* vi 257
To you, then, *t.* of life's middle state *Tir.* 807

TENANTRY.
Kind souls! to teach their *t.* to prize *H.* 252

TEND. [*T.* v 844
"And that, infused from Heaven, must thither *t.*"
So Self starts nothing, but what *t.* apace *Ch.* 565
The works of man *t.*, one and all *E.* i 79 [*T.* vi 818
Thus Heavenward all things *t.* For all were once
T. downward; his ambition is to sink *T.* v 592

TENDENCIES.
In Nature's *t.*, oft overlooks *T.* ii 175

TENDER.
His *t.* heart victoriously impressed *A.T.* 4
The *t.* argument of kindred blood *Ch.* 32
The *t.* ties of father, husband, friend *Ch.* 141
Flavia, most *t.* of her own good name *Ch.* 453
The *t.* theme on which they chose to dwell *Con.* 528
Where Venus hears the lover's *t.* vow *Con.* 824
Thy *t.* sorrows and thy plaintive strain *E.* ii 45
Who, nursed with *t.* care *Ep.* ii 6
Her *t.* husband, wondering much *J.G.* 143
Each *t.* tie of life defied *Miss —* 29
With all a *t.* heart can feel *Miss —* 103
T. idolator of absent charms *R.* 220
And *t.* as a girl, all essenced o'er *T.* ii 227
And *t.* in address, as well becomes *T.* ii 406
Then rise the *t.* germs, upstarting quick *T.* iii 521
Devises, while he guards his *t.* trust *T.* iii 561
And *t.* blade, that feared the chilling blast *T.* iv 331
Russet and rude, folds up the *t.* germ *T.* vi 194
A book (to please us at a *t.* age *Tir.* 121
To nurse with *t.* care the thriving Arts *T.T.* 69
A *t.* sympathy pervades the frame *T.T.* 485

TENDEREST. [*Tir.* 556
For one whose *t.* thoughts all hover round your own?

Their fibres penetrate its *t.* part *R.* 42
Thou wouldst not, deaf to Nature's *t.* plea *Tir.* 867
TENDERLY.
Friendship and Love seemed *t.* at strife *H.* 680
TENDERNESS.
'Tis thus the *t.* that love inspires *A.T.* 29
Than with a *t.* like mine *P.* 13
Plants raised with *t.* are seldom strong *P.E.* 359
TENDRILS.
With clasping *t.*, and invest his branch *T.* iii 666
And curling *t.*, gracefully disposed *T.* iv 154
TENFOLD.
A *t.* frenzy seizes all the rest *H.* 634
Or curse the desert with a *t.* dearth ? *T.* 182
Adds *t.* bitterness to death by pangs *T.* vi 395
TENTED.
The bar, the senate, or the *t.* field *R.* 102
Some seek diversion in the *t.* field *T.* v 185
TENT.
No shepherd's *t.* within thy view appear *E.* ii 43
TENURE.
Held by the *t.* of his will alone *Ex.* 673
TERENCE.
As some grave gentleman in *T.* says *E.* iii 6
TERENTIUS.
T., once my friend, farewell to thee ! *V.* 30
TERM.
Suffice it then in decent *t.* to say *A.T.* 86
On *t.* of amity complete *F.* 116   [*T.* 34
" Heaven on such *t.* ! " they cry with proud disdain
The largess He bestows, prescribes the *t. H.* 325
In *t.* as plain, himself has shut the rest *H.* 341
To which the mind resorts, in chase of *t. T.* ii 288
And understood too well the weighty *t. T.* ii 477
To live on *t.* of amity with vice *T.* v 658
And, if he spare him, spares him on the *t.* vi 409
TERMINATE.
Oaths *t.*, as Paul observes, all strife *Con.* 55
The hour that *t.* his span *St.* iii 3
His virtuous toil may *t.* at last *Tir.* 777
TERRAQUEOUS.
A union with the vast *t.* whole *Ch.* 122
The arbiters of this *t.* swamp *T.* v 281
TERRESTRIAL.
From things *t.*, and divinely changed *Con.* 726
Thus things *t.* wear a different hue *H.* 69
But dying soon, like all *t.* joys *T.* iv 382
T., in the vast and the minute *T.* v 811
TERRIBLE.
He judged them with as *t.* a frown *Ex.* 131
Oppression his *t.* name *M.D.* 28
Her voice is *t.* though soft *St.* v 23
And *t.* to sight, as when she springs *T.* i 602
Garden of God, how *t.* the change *T.* vi 371
A *t.* sagacity informs *T.T.* 494
TERRIBLY.
T. arched and aquiline his nose *T.* iii 192
TERRIFIED.
Admiring, *t.*, the novel strain *N.A.* 49
TERROR.
Armed at all points, with *t.* on his brow *A.T.* 140
All the *t.* of our tongues *B.* 12
But Winter, armed with *t.* here unknown *H.* 473
Such cause of *t.* in an empty sound *N.A.* 130
Marshalling all his *t.* as he came *T.* 547
The *t.* of the day that sets them free *T.* ii 128

His frown was full of *t.*, and his voice *T.* ii 721
Has lost its *t.* ere it reaches me *T.* iv 101
Himself enslaved by *t.* of the band *T.* iv 601
Spread anarchy and *t.* all around ? *T.T.* 303
TEST.
They stood the *t.* of her ensnaring smile *Ex.* 78
No friendship will abide the *t. F.* 37
Had once his integrity put to the *t. P.A.* 22   [34
Brings every thought, word, action to the *t. P.E.*
Faithfully, fairly, by that sacred *t. R.* 134
His conduct, to the *t.*, but tries his heart *T.* 562
He by the *t.* of conscience, and a heart *T.* vi 988
And stood the *t.*, perhaps on the wrong side *Tir.* 740
TESTIFY.
In vain thy creatures *t.* of thee *T.* v 856
TEXT.
To read wise lectures, vanity the *t. H.* 107
This truth premised was needful as a *t. N.A.* 71
The *t.* that sorts not with his darling whim *P.E.* 446
Oh, then, a *t.* would touch him at the quick ! *T.* 310
And then skip down again; pronounce a *t. T.* ii 410
And I consent you take it for your *t. T.* ii 474
How oft, when Paul has served us with a *t. T.* ii 539
Through moral narrative, or sacred *t. Tir.* 126
TEXTURE.
Of *t.* firm a lattice-work, that braced *T.* i 42
THAMES.
To enjoy a ramble on the banks of *T.—T.* i 115
THANK.   [264
My soul should yield thee willing *t.* and praise *Ch.*
T., gentle swain, for all my woes *G.* 13
And *t.* for this effectual close *G.* 14
Will heartily *t.* us, no doubt, for our pains *P.A.* 10
What glowing *t.* his lips and heart employ *T.* 255
T. to Benevolus—he spares me yet *T.* i 262
True, we may *t.* the perfidy of France *T.* ii 264
Small *t.* to those whose negligence or sloth *T.* ii 800
Its gratitude, and *t.* him with its sweets *T.* iii 623
T. for thy food. Carnivorous, through sin *T.* vi 457
THANKFUL.
That lasting happiness, a *t.* heart *H* 160
And the first *t.* tears bedew his cheeks *H.* 727
Still happier, if he till a *t.* soil *H.* 760
One act, that from a *t.* heart proceeds *T.* 223
And *t.* at my frugal board 1789, 35
THANKLESS.
To pour down wrath upon a *t.* land *Ex.* 253
That *t.* waste and wild abuse destroy *Ex.* 679
T. for favours from on high *St.* v 1
How does it grate upon his *t.* ear *T.* 465
THANKSGIVINGS.
And flash *t.* to the skies ! 1789, 55
THATCH.
That overhang the *t.*, itself unseen *T.* i 224
THATCHED.   [*T.* i 641
And homestall *t.* with leaves. But hast thou found
THAW.
To *t.* him into feeling; or the smart *T.* iv 197
THEATRE.
Her *t.*, her revels, and her sports *Ex.* 23
Sweats in the crowded *t.*, and squeezed *T.* iv 43
To *t.*, or jocund feast, or ball *T.* v 410
The *t.*, too small, shall suffocate *T.* vi 670
THEATRIC.
And start *t.*, practised at the glass ! *T.* ii 431
THEFT.
Time has but half succeeded in his *t. M.P.* 120

THELYPTHORA
Clean, candid, and witty—*T.* dies *A.T.* iv 2

THEME.
Love graced the *t.*, and harmony the song *A.T.* 198
To give the melancholy *t. Cast.* 57
A Poet's name by making thee the *t. Ch.* 14
(Charity chosen as my *t.* and aim) *Ch.* 295
(Two *t.* to Nature's eye for ever sealed) *Ch.* 362
And prove too weak for so divine a *t. Ch.* 633
Howe'er ingenious on his darling *t. Con.* 137
His whispered *t.*, dilated and at large *Con.* 273
That *t.* exhausted, a wide chasm ensues *Con.* 393
Prescribes the *t.*, the tone, and the grimace *Con.* 464
The tender *t.* on which they chose to dwell *Con.* 528
And his chief glory, was the Gospel *t. Con.* 620
But conversation, choose what *t.* we may *Con.* 703
As when returning to the *t.* they meant *Con.* 858
Sprightly and fresh, enriches every *t. Con.* 894
They scorned his inspiration, and his *t. Ex.* 69
Might shine in fable, and grace idle *t. Ex.* 233
Shall be my chosen *t.*, my glory to the last *Ex.* 734
Reminds him of religion, hated *t.*! *H.* 218
Yet me they charm, whate'er the *t. M.* 23
A thousand other *t.* less deeply traced *M.P.* 57
Rebellion is my *t.* all day *Pat.* 1
Sing, Muse, (if such a *t.*, so dark, so long *P.E.* 1
And George the *t.* of all *Q.V.* 48
And search the *t.*, important above all *R.* 137
A mind employed on so sublime a *t. R.* 668
A *t.* for all the world's attention *R.C.* 102
Now seek repose upon an humbler *t. T.* i 5
The *t.* though humble, yet august and proud *T.* i 6
On the sad *t.*, their everlasting state *T.* 41
Hear him, himself the poet and the *t. T.* 404
The song magnificent, the *t.* a worm! *T.* 412
With such address from *t.* of sad import *T.* ii 300
The legate of the skies!—His *t.* divine *T.* ii 338
Misled by custom, strain celestial *t. T.* ii 438
So I, designing other *t.*, and called *T.* iii 11
The adultress: what a *t.* for angry verse! *T.* iii 64
His name a *t.* for praise and for reproach? *T.* iii 282
Cold as its *t.*, and like its *t.* the fruit *T.* iii 564
A jarring note. *T.* of a graver tone *T.* iv 181 [481
Fierce the dispute whate'er the *t.*; while she *T.* iv
The mind contemplative, with some new *t. T.* iv 280
Exhausted, he resorts to solemn *t. T.* v 661
And History, so warm on meaner *t. T.* v 729
So on they fared. Discourse on other *t. T.* vi 539
And I, contented with an humble *t. T.* vi 719
On some fair *t.*, some *t.* divinely fair *T.* vi 754
If he regard not, though divine the *t. T.* vi 1019 [231
Transport them, and are made their favourite *t. Tir.*
Ye proud and wealthy, let this *t. Trans.* i 25
To *t.* more pertinent, if less sublime *T.T.* 190 [198
When *t.* like these employ the poet's tongue *T.T.*
That were a *t.* might animate the dead *T.T.* 202
The poet's muse, his passion, and his *t. T.T.* 289
Whate'er the *t.*, that others never feel *T.T.* 483
Else summoning the Muse to such a *t. T.T.* 550
And yet magnificent—a God the *t.*! *T.T.* 593
That *t.* on earth exhausted, though above *T.T.* 594
The shelves are full, all other *t.* are sped *T.T.* 726
Eventful, should supply her with a *t. Y.O.* 161
I ransacked, for a *t.* of song 1789, 1
I sought an eligible *t.* 1789, 8
So I, from *t.* to *t.* displayed 1789, 21
A *t.* for poetry divine 1789, 29
A *t.* to ennoble even mine 1789, 30

THEMIS.
Our British *T.* gloried with just cause *T.* iii 257

THEOLOGICAL.
Of *t.* and grave import) *T.* v 662

THEORIST.
Truths that the *t.* could never reach *P.E.* 11

THICK.
To dash throught *t.* and thin *J.G.* 40
T. overspread with moss and silky grass *N.A.* 2
And skirted *t.* with intertexture firm *T.* i 111
Peeps at the vale below; so *t.* beset *T.* i 225
Less ostentatious, and yet studded *t. T.* iii 420
Suspend their crazy boxes, planted *t. T.* iv 774
The studs that *t.* emboss his iron door *T.* v 426
Hypericum all bloom, so *t.* a swarm *T.* vi 165
Though leafless, well attired, and *t.* beset *T.* vi 168

THICKENING.
Gladly the *t.* mantle; and the green *T.* iv 330

THICKEST.
An arbour near at hand of *t.* yew *A.T.* 81
Of *t.* shades, like Adam after taste *Y.O.* 15

THICKETS.
As one who long in *t.* and in brakes *T.* iii 1
Its hollow glens, its *t.*, and its plains *T.* vi 402

THIEF. [508
True Christians are, dissemblers, drunkards, *t. H.*
Would hang an honest man, and save a *t. Con.* 128
"Stop *t.*! stop *t.*!—a highwayman!" *J.G.* 237 [736
That *t.* at home must hang, but he that puts *T.* i
Now goes the nightly *t.* prowling abroad *T.* iv 432
Assassined by a *t.*! *T.B.* 6
To entertain a *t.* or two in pay *Tir.* 693

THIEVISH.
Nor was he of the *t.* sort *Beau* 13 [18
Which babes might play with; and the *t.* jay *Y.O.*

THIEVISHLY.
The scattered grain, and *t.* resolved *T.* v 67

THIGH. [165
But wept, and stamped, and smote his *t.* in vain *Ex.*
He couched it firm upon his puissant *t. A.T.* 147
Stamped with his foot, and smote upon his *t. Ex.* 64

THIN.
After all he must beat it as *t.* and as fine *F.M.* 21
To dash through thick and *t. J.G.* 40 [*T.* v 86
T. all their numerous flocks. In chinks and holes
Of other screen, the *t.* umbrella spread *T.* i 260
A monitor is wood—plank shaven *t. T.* ii 585
Beneath a pane of *t.* translucent horn *Tir.* 120
'Twould *t.* the ranks of the poetic tribe *T.T.* 768

THING.
And laws and duties are neglected *t. A.T.* 33
And made her dupes see all *t.* with her eyes) *A.T.* 39
Some better *t.* are found *A Tale* 4
A ship! Could such a restless *t. A Tale* 25
Well knowing him a sacred *t. B.R.* 17
And once more mingles with us meaner *t. Ch.* 437
As He ordains *t.* sordid in their birth *Ch.* 561
Preserve me from the *t.* I dread and hate *Con.* 83
Poets, are sometimes apt to maul the *t. Con.* 290
Who shifts and changes all *t.* but his shape *Con.* 459
"What, always dreaming over heavenly *t. Con.* 575
Content on earth in earthly *t.* to shine *Con.* 583
The song of Sion is a tasteless *t. Con.* 715
From *t.* terrestrial, and divinely changed *Con.* 726
Strange fluctuation of all human *t.*! *E.* iii 9
(Sworn foes to every *t.* that's witty!) *E.* iv 14
That useful *t.*, her needle gone *E.* iv 40
While truths on which eternal *t.* depend *Ex.* 117
Thus *t.* terrestrial wear a different hue *H.* 69

THING—THOMSON　　　　445

If, led from earthly t. to t. divine H. 141
And beaus, adepts in every t. profound H. 347
What t. upon his back had got J.G. 95
A solitary t. Miss — 32
Perceives in every t. that lives a tongue N.A. 56
'Tis a sight to engage me, if any t. can P.F. 17
The Invisible in t. scarce seen revealed R. 61
Of sorrow, sorrow is a sacred t. R. 316
Impart to t. inanimate a voice R. 361
And ignorance of better t. makes man R. 503
Settling at last upon eternal t. R. 672
That whatsoever t. is lost R.C. 96
Any t. rather than a chest R.C. 106
And please, if any t. could please S. 8
Is falsely named, and no such t. St. vi 11
Can lift herself above corporeal t. T. 487 [T. ii 226
Should England prosper, when such t., as smooth
Did not his eye rule all t., and intend T. ii 166
With what intent I touch that holy t.) T. ii 328
The t. that mount the rostrum with a skip T. ii 409
Who handles t. divine ; and all beside T. ii 433
Drops from the lips a disregarded t. T. ii 565
Of whom I needs must argue better t. T. ii 582
With t. so sacred as a nation's trust T. ii 778
And dark in t. divine. Full often too T. iii 235
That makes a minister in holy t. T. iii 280
The hope of better t., the chance to win T. iii 828
Paint cards and dolls, and every idle t. T. iv 241
The course of human t. from good to ill T. iv 578
Is kept and guarded as a sacred t. T. v 304
In silly dotage on created t. T. v 586
Who calls for t. that are not, and they come T. v 687
Discerns in all t. what, with stupid gaze T. v 808
A soul in all t., and that soul is God T. vi 185
Some say that in the origin of t. T. vi 198
Else they are all—the meanest t. that are T. vi 584
And just direction sacred, to a t. T. vi 713 [vi 818
Thus Heavenward all t. tend. For all were once T.
Of this tempestuous state of human t. T. vi 737
That govern all t. here, shouldering aside T. vi 839
While meaner t., whom instinct leads The Doves 3
The wretch shall rise, and be the t. on earth Tir. 412
The royal letters are a t. of course Tir. 416
That any t. but vice could win thy love Tir. 742
Approved their method in all other t. T.T. 95
If monarchy consist in such base t. T.T. 139
Liberal in all t. else, yet Nature here T.T. 208
Less on exterior t. than most suppose T.T. 247
Free to prove all t., and hold fast the best T.T. 273
Man lavished all his thoughts on human t. T.T. 596
Who fret their hour and are forgotten t. V. 46
With truth from heaven, created t. adore Y.O. 7
(Unless verse rescue thee awhile) a t. Y.O. 58

THINK.　　　[28
For the Court did not t. they were equally wise A.C.
When I t. of my own native land A.S. 45
What t. you, Sir, of killing time B.R. 27
We sometimes t. we could a speech produce Con. 353
Pause here, and t.: a monitory rhyme E. i 1
T. on the fruitful and well watered spot Ex. 418
Now t., if Pleasure have a thought to spare Ex. 602
Oh t., if chargeable with deep arrears Ex. 608
Act without aim, t. little, and feel less H. 8 [418
Come, prophet, drink, and tell us what t. you " H.
Once thought of nothing, and now t. in vain H. 30
Nor closets up his thoughts, whate'er he t. H. 410
Each t. his neighbour makes too free L.W. 35 [54
And thought again—but knew not what to t. N.A.
T., ye masters iron-hearted N.C. 21
T. how many backs have smarted N.C. 23
Says—" Well, 'tis more than one would t.!" P. 36
A story so pat, you may t. it is coined P.A. 18

Then t. of his children, for they must be fed " P.A. 28
But since they will take them, I t. I'll go too P.A. 39
With some cold moral t. to quench the fire P.E. 320
And having done, we t., the best we can P.E. 367
He may possess the joys he t. he sees R. 11 [729
And though the world may t. the ingredients odd R.
Thought to the man that never t. may seem R. 635
She might repose, or sit and t. R.C. 6
Forced to a pause, would feel it good to t. St. ii 15
Man t. he fades too soon St. v 2
T. on the grave where He was laid St. v 35
You t. him humble—God accounts him proud T. 92
T. with what pleasure, safe and at his ease T. 253
I cannot t. thee yet so dull of heart T. i 651
And hang his head, to t. himself a man ? T. ii 28
Ah spare your idol ! t. him human still T. ii 496
You t., perhaps, so delicate his dress T. ii 625
I t., articulate, I laugh and weep T. iii 198
Feel wrath and pity when I t. on thee ! T. iii 842
Fearless, a soul that does not always t. T. iv 285
Adopting their mistakes, profoundly t. T. v 270
An easy reckoning, and they t. the same T. v 278
And t. on her, who t. not for herself T. vi 950 [vi 85
May t. down hours to moments. Here the heart T.
With both our eyes, is easier than to t. Tir. 256
You t., no doubt, he sits and muses Trans. ii 19
We t. them tedious creatures Trans. iv 39
T. yourself stationed on a towering rock T.T. 33
Who t., or seem to t., man made for them T.T. 50

THINKING.
The toll-men t. as before J.G. 243
Habits of close attention, t. heads R. 705
And t. I might purchase it too dear T.T. 515

THIRD.
And, till a t. surpasses you L.R. 23 [T. vi 659
When wandering Charles, who meant to be the t.
Two t. of all the virtue that remains Tir. 810

THIRST.　　　[P.E. 54
Power, Pomp, and Splendour, and the t. of Praise
(Such is his t. of opulence and ease) Her. 68
With prohibition and perpetual t. ? P.E. 234
A secret t. of his renounced employs R. 474 [544
Their t. of knowledge, and their candour too ! T. ii
The t. than slaked it, and not seldom bred T. ii 509
Of what is excellent in man, they t. T. ii 790
The wish to shine, the t. to be amused T. iii 829
Cruel is all he does. 'Tis quenchless t. T. iv 459
His inborn inextinguishable t. T. iv 767
With all the savage t. a tiger feels T.T. 36
By low ambition and the t. of praise T.T. 591

THIRST-CREATING.
Thy t. steams at length produce Con. 262

THIRSTING.
Fast as the t. ear can drink the sound Ch. 112

THIRSTY.
We wander o'er a sunburnt t. soil Ch. 220

THIRTEEN.
While t. moons saw smoothly run St. i 1

THISTLE.
T., or lettuces instead Ep. ii 15
The t.'s downy seed my fare G. 2
And where unsightly and rank t. grew H. 526

THISTLE-SEEDS.
Like t., are sown by every wind P.E. 555

THISTLY.
Without some t. sorrow at its side T. iv 335
Exults to see its t. curse repealed T. vi 768

THOMSON.
Are musical enough in T.'s song R. 570

THONG.
Man's coltish disposition asks the *t. P.E.* 360
Crack the satiric *t.?* 'Twere wiser far *T.* iii 26

THOR.
Woden and *T.*, each tottering in his shrine *Ex.* 505

THORN.
And floating films envelope every *t. A.T.* 73
Who found not *t.* and briars in his road *E.* ii 12
Ten thousand rove the brakes and *t.* among *H.* 280
Where sprang the *t.*, the spiry fir shall spring *H.* 525
The sheep here smooths the knotted *t. M.B.* 9
Wide yawns a gulf beside a ragged *t. N.A.* 14 [*S.* ii 1
Deem not, sweet rose, that bloomest midst many a *t.*
First shakes the glittering drops from every *t. R.* 396
Not rude and surly, and beset with *t. T.* i 601
Lie covered close; and berry-bearing *t. T.* v 82 [239
Who wore the platted *t.* with bleeding brows *T.* vi
His *t.* with streamers of continual praise? *T.* v 330
Picked from the *t.* and briars of reproof *T.* vi 1013
A wintry figure like a withered *t. T.T.* 725

THORNTON.
And *T.* is familiar with the joy *Ch.* 253
Thee, *T.!* worthy in some page to shine *J.T.* 7

THORNY.
Flowers of rank odour upon *t.* lands *R.* 754
Its odour o'er the Christian's *t.* road! *T.* 454
Of *t.* boughs: have loved the rural walk *T.* i 112
In such a world, so *t.*, and where none *T.* iv 333 [253
Crooked or straight, through quags or *t.* dells *Tir.*
But never peep beyond the *t.* bound *T.T.* 582

THOUGHT.
A wish or a *t.* after me? *A.S.* 38
And Mercy, encouraging *t.! A.S.* 54
But not the *t.* that they must meet no more *Ch.* 148
Suppose (when *t.* is warm, and fancy flows *Ch.* 379
Her eager *t.*, and feeds her flowing joys *Ch.* 405
Sacred interpreter of human *t. Con.* 23 [323
They *t.* they must have died, they were so bad *Con.*
Expression and the privilege of *t. Con.* 404
They *t.* him, and they justly *t.* him one *Con.* 517
When some green heads, as void of wit as *t. Con.* 626
Lives the dear *t.* of joys he once possessed *Con.* 708
T. is so rare, and fancy so profuse *Con.* 856
And all the floating *t.* we find *E.* i 7
Employs our present *t.* and pains *E.* i 51
Are gloomy *t.* led on by Spleen *E.* iv 20
First, for a *t.*—since all agree—*E.* iv 35
A *t.*—I have it—let me see—*E.* iv 36
'Tis gone again—plague on't! I *t. E.* iv 37
My heart of *t.* that made it ache *Ep.* ii 35
None bars Him out from his most secret *t. Ex.* 337
Far be the *t.* from any verse of mine *Ex.* 423
Now think, if Pleasure have a *t.* to spare *Ex.* 602
If dear society be worth a *t. Ex.* 670
Say not (and if the *t.* of such defence *Ex.* 708
All *t.* of friendship are but dreams *F.* 74
The *t.* of conflagration *F.* 108
Once *t.* of nothing, and now thinks in vain *H.* 30
Quite to forget, or deem it worth no *t. H.* 83
Its value, what no *t.* can ascertain *H.* 125
His soul abhors a mercenary *t. H.* 332
A *t.* intrude, that says, or seems to say *H.* 372
Nor closets up his *t.*, whate'er he thinks *H.* 410
And if, unblameable in word and *t. H.* 622
If then, just then, all *t.* of mercy lost *H.* 722
But for one piece they *t.* it hard *L.W.* 11
Far be the *t.*, and far the strain *Miss* — 9
Let no low *t.* suggest the prayer *Miss* — 65
To serious *t.* at evening-tide *Mor.* 12
Yet oh the *t.*, that thou art safe, and he! *M.P.* 106

That *t.* is joy, arrive what may to me *M.P.* 107
Which served my weak *t.* for a guide *M.D.* 44
Strong genius, from whose forge of *t.* Mrs. *M—* 23
But recollecting, with a sudden *t. N.A.* 51
And *t.* again—but knew not what to think *N.A.* 54
Still in *t.* as free as ever *N.C.* 9
He *t.* to put him in his crop *N.G.* 12
Brings every *t.*, word, action, to the test *P.E.* 34 [132
So well that *t.* the employment seems to suit *P.E.*
Turtle and venison all his *t.* employ *P.E.* 220
Your sober *t.* will hardly find it one *P.E.* 489
But sighs at *t.* of empty pockets *P.B.* 26
That cordial *t.* her spirit cheered *Q.V.* 65
Thy power divine, and bounty beyond *t. R.* 91
That, while thy truths my grosser *t.* refine *R.* 97
To limit *t.*, by Nature prone to stray *R.* 127 [140
From anxious *t.* how wealth may be increased *R.*
And every *t.* that wanders is a crime *R.* 224
Or if the *t.* occurred not duly weighed *R.* 464
O sweet retirement! who would balk the *t. R.* 487
T., to the man that never thinks, may seem *R.* 635
Attain not to the dignity of *t. R.* 640
The strenuous use of profitable *t. R.* 674
And loathed the *t.* of sin *St.* iii 28
Some *t.* of immortality remains *T.* 39
Recompense ill! He trembles at the *t. T.* 192
T., word, and deed, his liberty evince *T.* 195
Peace to the artist whose ingenious *t. T.* 210
Now which stands highest in your serious *t.? T.* 221
Swift beyond *t.* the lightnings dart away *T.* 243
And is it not a mortifying *t. T.* 339
O'er all his *t.*, and swelled his easy sail *T.* 420
Swells at the *t.*, and kindling into rage *T.* 477
The *t.* that meditates a brother's wrong *T.* 560
Vain *t.!* the dweller in that still retreat *T.* i 237
The powers of fancy and strong *t.* are theirs *T.* i 402
At *t.* of her forlorn and abject state *T.* i 659
So pleasing, and that steal away the *t. T.* ii 299
Friendly to *t.*, to virtue, and to peace *T.* iii 291
Cultured and capable of sober *t. T.* iii 324
Of *t.*, the creature of a polished mind *T.* iii 640
Begs a propitious ear for his poor *t. T.* iv 68
The family dispersed, and fixing *t. T.* iv 137
In indolent vacuity of *t. T.* iv 297
Where penury is felt the *t.* is changed *T.* iv 397
And incompatible with serious *t. T.* iv 622 [374
But slaves that' once conceive the glowing *t. T.* v
To fly for refuge from distracting *t. T.* v 415
With worthy *t.* of that unwearied Love *T.* v 752
To read his wonders, in whose *t.* the world *T.* v 798
No noise is here, or none that hinders *t. T.* vi 76
In heads replete with *t.* of other men *T.* vi 90
The insupportable fatigue of *t. T.* vi 106
The roving *t.* and fix it on themselves *T.* vi 117
And the blood thrills and curdles at the *t. T.* vi 514
(Forgive a transient *t.*) *The Doves* 30 [889
The world takes little *t.* Who will may preach *T.* vi
Truths that the learned pursue with eager *t. Tir.* 73
The knowledge of the World, and dull of *t. Tir.* 380
Teach humbler *t.* to you *Trans.* i 23 [*Tir.* 556
For one whose tenderest *t.* all hover round your own?
At stated hours, his freakish *t.* engage *Tir.* 606
Too proud to adopt the *t.* of one unknown *Tir.* 785
No; not a single *t.* like that *Trans.* ii 22
That were indeed a king-ennobling *t. T.T.* 57 [168
Thus men, whose *t.* contemplative have dwelt *T.T.*
He *t.* the dying hour already come *T.T.* 392
Before the keen enquiry of her *t. T.T.* 493
Only by gratitude and glowing *t. T.T.* 587
Man lavished all his *t.* on human things *T.T.* 596
Lifted at length, by dignity of *t. T.T.* 676
Fervency, freedom, fluency of *t. T.T.* 700
To press with energy your ardent *t. V.* 10

I *t.* the volume I presumed to send *V.* 39
Fine passing *t.*, e'en in her coarsest works *Y.O.* 81

THOUGHTFUL.
While *t.* man is plausibly amused *T.* iii 186
Suits well the *t.* or unthinking mind *T.* iv 279

THOUGHTLESS.
From *t.* youth to ruminating age *P.E.* 24
Oh, tell thy *t.* sex, the virtuous mind *S.* ii 6
The gay, the *t.*, have I seen *St.* i 19
That reared us. At a *t.* age, allur'd *T.* vi 38

THOUGHTLESSNESS.
Is but a school, where *t.* is taught *T.* iv 688

THOUGHT-TRACING.
With the *t.* quill, or tasked his mind *Y.O.* 158

THOUSAND.
And filled her with a *t.* fears *A Fable* 13 [180
"Oh, shame!" ten *t.* echoing nymphs replied *A.T.*
Tramples on a *t.* states *B.* 18
Teach mercy to ten *t.* hearts that share *Ch.* 278
Hark! 'tis the music of a *t.* rills *Ch.* 367
A *t.* names are tossed into the crowd *Ch.* 517
In the last scene of her six *t.* years *Con.* 456
Crowned with a *t.* victories, and at last *Ex.* 191
That he bids *t.* fly when none pursue *Ex.* 360
While *t.*, careless of the damning sin *Ex.* 388
Reclaim the wandering *t.*, and bring home *Ex.* 728
Ten *t.* charms, that only fools despise *H.* 51
To exchange the centre of a *t.* trades *H.* 246
Ten *t.* rove the brakes and thorns among *H.* 280
Thy deep repentance of thy *t.* lies *H.* 590
Ten *t.* swains the wasted scene deplore *Her.* 39
"'Tis for a *t.* pound!" *J.G.* 116
From *t.* with rapture inspired *M.D.* 40
A *t.* other themes less deeply traced *M.P.* 57
To justify it by a *t.* lies *P.E.* 284
Which *t.* once fast chained to quit no more *R.* 2
To wonder at a *t.* insect forms *R.* 63
Ten *t.* rivers poured at his command *R.* 75
Ten *t.* strings at once go loose *R.* 329
Sick of a *t.* disappointed aims) *R.* 366
When Pope describes them, have a *t.* sweets *R.* 572
And his old stint—three *t.* pounds a year *R.* 602
Nor his who for the bane of *t.* born *R.* 687
These and a *t.* plagues that haunt the breast *R.* 763
Faces a *t.* dangers at her call *R.H.* 7
A *t.* awful admonitions scorned *St.* ii 27
Ten *t.* warblers cheer the day, and one *T.* 200
Excels ten *t.* mercenary deeds *T.* 224
The *t.* whom the world forbids to rest *T.* 438
Ten *t.* sages lost in endless woe *T.* 517
Yet *t.* still desire to journey on *T.* i 470
Conceiving thunders, through a *t.* deeps *T.* ii 89
Of gallery critics by a *t.* arts *T.* ii 365
A *t.* systems, each in his own way *T.* iii 171
Or heedless folly, by which *t.* die *T.* iii 219
Ten *t.* dangers lie in wait to thwart *T.* iii 553 [740
And thundering loud, with his ten *t.* wheels? *T.* iii
Perhaps to *t.*, and of joy to some *T.* iv 14
Of all this riot: and ten *t.* casks *T.* iv 505
Ten *t.* seek an unmolested end *T.* v 87
The growing wonder takes a *t.* shapes *T.* v 119
He deems a *t.* or ten *t.* lives *T.* v 276
His *t.*, weary of penurious life *T.* v 319
Ten *t.* rovers in the world at large *T.* v 408
These, and a *t.* images of bliss *T.* vi 341
Wins public honour; and ten *t.* sit *T.* vi 633
Six *t.* years of sorrow have well nigh *T.* vi 734
No. Freedom has a *t.* charms to show *T.T.* 260
Learns much, and to a *t.* listening minds *T.T.* 274
And set plebeian *t.* in a roar *T.T.* 319

God's curse can cast away ten *t.* sail! *T.T.* 467
He fills profuse ten *t.* little throats *T.T.* 694
A *t.* ways the force of genuine love *V.* 62
Oaks fell not, hewn by *t.*, to supply *Y.O.* 101
Which, crooked into a *t.* whimsies, clasp *Y.O.* 118

THRACIAN.
On *T.* Hebrus' side *T.B.* 63

THREAD.
Your *t.* of argument is snapped again *Con.* 110
Informed, he gathered up the broken *t. Con.* 525
Strikes the rough *t.* of error right athwart *Ex.* 330
And all thy *t.* with magic art *M.* 18
Shuffling her *t.* about the livelong day *T.* 320
The *t.* of politic and shrewd design *T.* iii 147
Or twining silken *t.* round ivory reels *T.* iv 264
The glassy *t.* with which the Fancy weaves *T.* iv 306
Ere yet mortality's fine *t.* give way *T.* v 578
By slender *t.*, and swinging in the breeze *Tir.* 592
Hackneyed and worn to the last flimsy *t. T.T.* 727
And in conclusion mar them. Nature's *t. Y.O.* 80

THREADBARE.
My *t.* sentiments together *E.* iv 6

THREADED.
On female industry: the *t.* steel *T.* iv 165

THREAT.
Fidelity that neither bribe nor *t. T.* vi 628

THREATEN.
And daily *t.* to drive thence *E.* iv 17
Whoever *t.* war, to speak of peace *Ch.* 421
And some that seem to *t.* virtue less *P.E.* 227
T. his health, his fortune, and his fame *Tir.* 532
What burns at home; or *t.* from afar *T.T.* 447

THREATENED.
And least be *t.* in the fields and groves? *T.* i 753
That *t.* England's trembling state 1789, 37

THREATENING.
To charm to sleep the *t.* of the skies *Ex.* 404
Within its reeking bosom, *t.* death *T.* iii 503
T. at once and nourishing the plant *T.* vi 36
If Mercy then put by the *t.* blow *T.T.* 404

THREE.
T. sparks ensued that chased it all away *A.T.* 167
Myself, and children *t. J.G.* 14
So *t.* doors off the chaise was stayed *J.G.* 37
T. customers came in *J.G.* 52
And his old stint—*t.* thousand pounds a year *R.* 602
Joint-stools were then created, on *t.* legs *T.* i 19
Upborne they stood. *T.* legs upholding firm *T.* i 20
Improved the simple plan; made *t.* legs four *T.* i 29
Greets with *t.* cheers exulting. At his waist *T.* i 523
And his *t.* years of heroship expired *T.* iv 644
The worth of his *t.* kingdoms I defy *T.T.* 85
Two or *t.* millions of the human race *T.T.* 423
T. quarters of a year *Y.D.* 6

THREEFOLD.
"A *t.* cord is not soon broken" *E.* i 106

THREESCORE.
For *t.* years employed with ceaseless care *R.* 37
Since which I number *t.* winters past *Y.O.* 3

THRESH.
When flails of oratory *t.* the floor *Ex.* 302

THRESHER.
We may discern the *t.* at his task *T.* i 356

THRESHOLD.
But if you pass the *t.*, you are caught *P.E.* 588

THREW.
His snowy mantle o'er his shoulders t. *A.T.* 202
And he that forged, and he that t. the dart *H.* 578
Their gates wide open t. *J.G.* 120
And there he t. the Wash about *J.G.* 137
If brighter beams than all he t. not forth *T.T.* 680

THRICE.
Struck t. the point upon his saddle bow *A.T.* 166
I mourn; or, since t. happy thou must be *J.T.* 9
T. must the voluble and restless earth *T.* iii 490
Refinement is endued! t. happy thou! *T.* iv 359
And t. in every winter throngs thine own *Tir.* 747
T. happy bird! I too have seen *Trans.* ii 31

THRIFT.
To t. and parsimony much inclined *T.* 141
To her who, frugal only that her t. *T.* ii 650
With all this t. they thrive not. All the care *T.* iv 399

THRIFTIER.
But the axe spared thee. In those t. days *Y.O.* 100

THRILLS.
And the blood t. and curdles at the thought *T.* vi 514

THRIVE.
These are the gifts of Art; and Art t. most *Ch.* 113
T. against Hope, and in the rudest scene *Ch.* 575
States t. or wither, as moons wax and wane *Ex.* 324
To t. in; an incumbrance ere half spent *H.* 98
It t. in misery, and abundant grows *T.* 125
T. by the rude concussion of the storm *T.* i 378
Here virtue t. as in her proper soil *T.* i 600
T. most, and may perhaps t. only there *T.* i 680
With all this thrift they t. not. All the care *T.* iv 399
A garden in which nothing t. has charms *T.* iv 754

THRIVING.
With still less hope of t. *F.* 144
Beneath his care, a t. vigorous plant *T.* ii 714
Like virtue t. most where little seen *T.* iii 664
Summer in haste the t. charge receives *Tir.* 45
To nurse with tender care the t. Arts *T.T.* 69

THROAT.
Of epidemic t., if such there are *Con.* 391   [25
With tails high mounted, ears hung low, and t. *N.A.*
Save when the knife is at your t. *P.* 52   [738
Whose Stygian t. breathe darkness all day long *T.* iii
Hear the faint echo of those brazen t. *T.* iv 104
Her cause demands the assistance of your t. *T.* iv 511
And the first larum of the cock's shrill t. *T.* iv 569
For silencing so sweet a t. *T.B.* 59
She fills profuse ten thousand little t. *T.T.* 694
A huge t. calling to the clouds for drink *Y.O.* 112

THROB.
Nor his, who patient stands till his feet t. *T.* iv 46

THROBBING.
To assuage the t. of the festered part *R.* 321
Tempered in hell, invades the t. breast *T.* iii 686

THRONE.
Their prince, as justly seated on his t. *Ch.* 51
Before his presence, at whose awful t. *Con.* 659
To any t., except the t. of grace *H.* 239
Sits absolute on his unshaken t. *H.* 474
A nation dwells, not envious of your t. *Her.* 49
Speaking from his t., the sky? *N.C.* 28   [177
Where Night, down-stooping from her ebon t. *P.E.*
When, long sequestered from his t. *Q.V.* 1
As stoop from Heaven to sell the proud a t. *T.* 78
As soon shall rise and reascend the t. *T.* 395
So sit two kings of Brentford on one t. *T.* i 78
A leafless branch thy sceptre and thy t. *T.* iv 125
Sofa, and couch, and high built t. august *T.* v 164

Where love is mere attachment to the t. *T.* v 361
And wheels his t. upon the rolling worlds *T.* v 814
Hers is the state, the splendour, and the t. *Tir.* 11
To quell the faction that affronts the t. *T.T.* 67
Obsequious, from the cradle to the t. *T.T.* 122
Encompassing his t. a few short years *T.T.* 132

THRONED.
That t. above all height He condescends *Ch.* 587

THRONG.
Then sang the married and the maiden t. *A.T.* 197
Far from the world's gay busy t. *Comp.* ii 4
God gives the word, the preachers t. around *H.* 453
And through the cumbrous t. *Q.V.* 66
A few forsake the t.; with lifted eyes *R.* 161
Surrounding t. the demigod revere *T.* 312   [117
Possessed an inland scene. Where now the t. *T.* ii
The pent-up breath of an unsavoury t. *T.* iv 196
The rustic t. beneath his favourite beech *T.* iv 708
And thrice in every winter t. thine own *Tir.* 747

THRONG'D.
So rich, so t., so drained, and so supplied *T.* i 720
And harmless pleasures, in the t. abode *T.* iv 782

THROW.
Disdains the Bank, and t. the golden sands *Ch.* 248
Am I to set my life upon a t. *Con.* 191
Who t. their Helicon about *E.* iv 85
He manfully did t. *J.G.* 76
Is this a Saint? T. tints and all away *T.* 175
And t. Italian light on English walls *T.* i 425   [29
Where chance may t. me, beneath elm or vine *T.* iii
T. up a steamy column, and the cups *T.* iv 39
That in its fall the liquid sheet t. wide *T.* v 106
To t. his dark displeasure o'er the scene *T.T.* 445
If thou desert thy charge, and t. it wide *Tir.* 887
Or t. them up to livery-nags and grooms *Tir.* 901

THROWING.
In that blest moment Nature, t. wide *T.* v 891
And t. up into the darkest gloom *T.* vi 153
The jasmine, t. wide her elegant sweets *T.* vi 173
Then stops and snorts, and t. high his heels *T.* vi 332

THROWN.   [*T.T.* 331
Cheap though blood-bought, and t. away when sold
T. up by wintry torrents roaring loud *T.* i 14
Are oft-times vanquished and t. far behind *T.* vi 615

THRUSH.
Our more harmonious notes: the t. departs *T.* i 767
That feed the t. (whatever some suppose) *T.* v 83

THRUST.
No spell or charm was proof against the t. *A.T.* 146
Can be secure against a madman's t. *Ch.* 510
Who t. his nose into a raree-show? *Con.* 286
To t. the charge of deeds that I detest *Ex.* 430
Will t. a dagger at your breast *F.* 94

THUMB.
Pinched close between his finger and his t. *Ch.* 477
I twirl my t., fall back into my chair *Con.* 115
Down to his finger and his t. *E.* i 12
But now and then with pressure of his t. *T.* v 54

THUMP.
And proves by t. upon your back *F.* 170
The t. after t. of a gold-beater's mallet *F.M.* 10
T. after t. resounds the constant flail *T.* i 357
And his head t., to feed upon the breath *T.* iv 47

THUNDER.
Armed with t., clad with wings *B.* 27
Art thou the God, the t. of whose hand *Ch.* 75
Thy t. travel over earth and seas *Ex.* 582
The t. seems to summon him away *H.* 719
No t. shook with deep intestine sound *Her.* 5

Yourselves have seen, what time the *t*. rolled *N.A.* 91
T. and flash upon the steadfast shores *R*. 534
Full charged with England's *t*. *R.G.* 31
T., and earthquake, and devouring flame *T*. 548
He held the *t*. But the monarch owes *T*. i 382
Conceiving *t*., through a thousand deeps *T*. ii 89
Its *t*.; and by him, in strains as sweet *T*. ii 341
Cataracts of declamation *t*. here *T*. iv 73
He hears the *t*. ere the tempest lowers *T.T.* 496

THUNDERBOLT.
And, *t*. excepted, quite a God ! *T*. 410
Is punished, and down comes the *t*. *T.T.* 403

THUNDER-CLOUDS.
Beget no *t*. to trouble life *V*. 76

THUNDERED.
Not harshly *t*. forth, or rudely pressed *T*. vi 503

THUNDERER.
As any *t*. there. And I can feel *T*. ii 221

THUNDERING.
And *t*. loud, with his ten thousand wheels ? *T*. iii 740
With all its majesty of *t*. pomp *T*. iv 686

THURLOW.
Round *T*.'s head in early youth *Th*. 1

THWART.
To *t*. its influence, and its end defeat *Ch*. 38
Oh! *t*. me not, Sir Soph, at every turn *Con*. 91
His creature *t*. not his august design *H*. 142
One lawless particle to *t*. his plan *T*. ii 170
Ten thousand dangers lie in wait to *t*. *T*. iii 553
T. his attempts, or envy his success *T*. iv 787
No flaw deforms, no difficulty *t*. *T*. vi 229

THWARTED.
To be suspected, *t*., and withstood *T.T.* 141

THWARTING.
And day by day some current's *t*. force *M.P.* 104

THYME.
Hence, ankle-deep in moss and flowery *t*. *T*. i 270

THYRSIS.
T., Alexis, or whatever name *R*. 247.

THYRSUS.
The brimming goblet, seized the *t*., bound *T.T.* 603

TIBER.
Of *T*.'s marshes and the papal bog *Ex*. 511

TICKET.
Well-equipaged, is *t*. good enough *T*. iii 98

TICKLE.
T. and entertain us, or we die *R*. 708
Less for improvement than to *t*. spite *Tir*. 481

TICKLING.
Is't not a pity now, that *t*. rheums *T*. iii 167

TICKLISH.
Upon the *t*. balance of suspense *T*. iii 550

TIDE.
Held within modest bounds, the *t*. of speech *Con*. 889
From them to thee, conveyed along the *t*. *Ex*. 624
The *t*. of pleasure, heedless of his frown *Ex*. 683
Swept Ouse's silent *t*. *D.W.* 2
To pour his golden *t*. through all her gates *Ex*. 14
And thy loved consort on the dangerous *t*. *M.P.* 98
Wherever driven by wind or *t*. *P*. 53
In rushes Folly with a full moon *t*. *P.E.* 282
The *t*. of life, swift always in its course *R*. 453
Or bury me in ocean's angry *t*. ! *T*. 270
A cold stagnation on the intestine *t*. *T*. vi 139
Watch his emotions, and control their *t*. *Tir*. 610

Nor would the Nine consent the sacred *t*. *T.T.* 184
Alas! the *t*. of pleasure sweeps along *T.T.* 368

TIDINGS.
Strange *t*. these to tell a world who treat *Con*. 719
The *t*. of unpurchased Heaven create *H*. 343 [573
" What *t*. ?" and the surge replied—" All lost !" *Ex*.
" What news ? what news ? your *t*. tell " *J.G.* 165
She heard the doleful *t*. of his death *T*. i 545
What are its *t*. ? have our troops awaked ? *T*. iv 25
" And systems of whose birth no *t*. yet *T*. v 827

TIE.
'Tis because resentment *t*. *B*. 11
By various *t*. attaches man to man *Ch*. 16
The tender *t*. of father, husband, friend *Ch*. 141
The *t*. of nature do but feebly bind *Ch*. 371
He *t*. up all his hearers in suspense *Con*. 130
Of friendship's closest *t*. *Dr*. 18
Each tender *t*. of life defied *Miss* — 29

TIED.
But being *t*., it dies upon the lip *Con*. 355
Where only vice and injury are *t*. *Ex*. 594
The closest knot that may be *t*. *F*. 62
The ribbon with which it is *t*. *Gr*. 8
Of the smooth-shaven prop, and neatly *t*. *T*. iii 659
Art thou a man professionally *t*. *Tir*. 658

TIGER.
Chain up the wolves and *t*. of mankind *Ch*. 287
With all the savage thirst a *t*. feels *T.T.* 36

TIGHT.
But still in vain, the frame was *t*. *P.B.* 9
T. boxes neatly sashed, and in a blaze *R*. 483
All *t*. and well. And how do you *Y.D.* 35

TILL.
Still happier, if he *t*. a thankful soil *H*. 760
I would not have a slave to *t*. my ground *T*. ii 29

TILLER.
Yet much depends, as in the *t*.'s toil *Con*. 5
Without a soil to invite the *t*.'s care *Her*. 27

TILTH. [46
The yellow *t*., green meads, rocks, rising ground *H*.

TIMBER.
But 'tis not *t*., lead, and stone *F*. 163
Her *t*. yet are sound *R.G.* 29
No want of *t*. then was felt or feared *T*. i 57
His patrimonial *t*. cast its leaf *T*. iii 752

TIME.
Which amounts to possession *t*. out of mind " *A.C.* 12
His *t*., his talents, and his ceaseless care *A.T.* 15
" Now is the *t*. to make the maid a bride !" *A.T.* 69
And quell the shapeless monsters of the *t*. *A.T.* 142
What think you, sir, of killing *T*.—*B.R.* 27
Are sweeter to her many *t*. *C*. 31
Springs in due *t*. supply for the distressed *Ch*. 482
The lapse of *t*. and rivers is the same *Comp*. i 1
But *t*. that should enrich the nobler mind *Comp*. i 11
A toy to sport with, and pass *t*. away *Con*. 18
Makes half a sentence at a *t*. enough *Con*. 246
And in due *t*. feeds heartily on both *Con*. 338 [629
Though *T*. will wear us, and we must grow old *Con*.
The *t*. is short, and there are souls on earth *Con*. 493
Well—what are ages, and the lapse of *t*. *Con*. 547
As *T*. improves the grape's authentic juice *Con*. 643
(And in due *t*. the world shall know it too) *Con*. 750
'Tis *t*., however, if the case stands thus *Con*. 847
The freakish humour of the present *t*. *Con*. 866
It was the *t*. when Ouse displayed *D.W.* 13
To catch the triflers of the *t*. *E*. i. 20
Alas, how *t*. escapes !—'tis even so *E*. iii 2
Once on a *t*. an Emperor, a wise man *E*. iii 46

" To escape him at the idlest *t. E.* iv. 76
Demands one moment of thy fleeting *t. Ep.* i 2
Long *T.* Assyria bound them in her chain *Ex.* 73
Uplifted hands, that, at convenient *t. Ex.* 147
And *T.* forbid to touch them as he flew *Ex.* 184
Hast thou within thee sin, that in old *t. Ex.* 414
If business, constant as the wheels of *t. Ex.* 604
Some blemish in due *t.* made known *F.* 146
T. wasted, violated laws, abuse *F.A.* 14
T. was when I was free as air *G.* 1
And hope, in due *t.*, to behold *Gr.* 31
For *T.*, the destroyer declared *Gr.* 45
Nor labour they, nor *t.* nor talents waste *H.* 766
There was a *t.* when Ætna's silent fire *Her.* 1
Yet *t.* at length (what will not *t.* achieve?) *Her.* 29
So down he came; for loss of *t. J.G.* 53
But whether all the *t.* it cost *Mor.* 41
The art that baffles *T.*'s tyrannic claim *M.P.* 9 [74
Could *T.*, his flight reversed, restore the hours *M.P.*
And now, farewell.—*T.* unrevoked has run *M.P.* 112
T. has but half succeeded in his theft *M.P.* 120
Of happier *t.*, appear *N.* 22
A hollow scooped, I judge, in ancient *t. N.A.* 17
For thee wished many a *t. N.Y.G.* 2 [*N.A.* 91
Yourselves have seen, what *t.* the thunders rolled
Innocent! Oh! if venerable *T.*—*P.E.* 181
Has *t.* worn out, or fashion put to shame *P.E.* 245
But proper *t.* to marry *P.T.* 65
'Tis consecration of his heart, soul, *t. R.* 223
Not to redeem his *t.*, but his estate *R.* 561
A panting syllable through *t.* and space *R.* 692
That leave no stain upon the wing of *T.*—*R.* 800 [ii 9
T. then would seem more precious than the joys *St.*
Duly at my *t.* I come *St.* iv 13
And sore tormented long before his *t. T.* 84
Or real, or fictitious, of the *t. T.* 162
And if the youth, unmellowed yet by *t. T.* 492
Prefer the twilight of a darker *t. T.* 541
T. was, when clothing, sumptuous or for use *T.* i 8
Long *t.* elapsed or e'er our rugged sires *T.* i 68
Is it a *t.* to wrangle, when the props *T.* ii 62 [233
T. was, when it was praise and boast enough *T.* ii
Who squander *t.* and treasure with a smile *T.* ii 641
Not yet by *t.* completely silvered o'er *T.* ii 703
Virtue and vice had boundaries in old *t. T.* iii 75
Not slothful; happy to deceive the *t. T.* iii 362
He places lightly, and as *t.* subdues *T.* iii 518
Reiterated as the wheel of *t. T.* iii 626 [iii 772
And aguish east, till *t.* shall have transformed *T.*
To palliate dullness and give *t.* a shove *T.* iv 210
T., as he passes us, has a dove's wing *T.* iv 211
But the world's *T.* is *T.* in masquerade! *T.* iv 213
Of card devoted *T.*, and night by night *T.* iv 229
Ill-clad and fed but sparely, *t.* to cool *T.* iv 379
But be ye of good courage. *T.* itself *T.* iv 420 [421
Shall much be friend you. *T.* shall give increase *T.* iv
That poets celebrate; those golden *t. T.* iv 514
T. was when in the pastoral retreat *T.* iv 558
To the next rank contagious, and in *t. T.* iv 584
Him, Tubal named, the Vulcan of old *t. T.* v 217
Of virtue, made one chief, whom *t.* of peace *T.* v 239
To wear out *t.* in numbering to and fro *T.* v 425
Was registered in heaven ere *t.* began *T.* v 530
T. ploughs them up, and not a trace remains *T.* v 533
To latest *t.*; and sculpture, in her turn *T.* v 709
And for a *t.* ensure, to his loved land *T.* v 716
How readily we wish *t.* spent revoked *T.* vi 25
Till *t.* has stolen away the slighted good *T.* vi 51
And lanes, in which the primrose ere her *t. T.* vi 112
So 'twas a hallow'd *t.*: decorum reign'd *T.* vi 691
Encomium in old *t.* was poet's work *T.* vi 715 [665
When *t.* hath somewhat mellow'd it, and made *T.* vi
The *t.* of rest, the promised Sabbath, comes *T.* vi 733

The features of the last degenerate *t. T.* vi 900
No *t.* shall disengage *The Doves* 10
Finds in a sober moment *t.* to pause *Tir.* 56
T. was he closed as he began the day *Tir.* 175
That in good *t.* the stripling's finished taste *Tir.* 203
Peace to them all! those brilliant *t.* are fled *Tir.* 234
In early years connected, *t.* unbinds *Tir.* 439
Allows short *t.* for play, and none for sloth *Tir.* 484
Thus genius rose and set at ordered *t. T.T.* 560
The prize of happier *t.*, will serve thee now *T.T.* 371
There is a *t.*, and Justice marks the date *T.T.* 400
Speak to the present *t.* and *t.* to come *T.T.* 433
In all its parts, *t.*, ministry, and laws *T.T.* 427
Beating alternately in measured *t. T.T.* 528
The dark and sullen humour of the *t. T.T.* 616
Decayed by *t.*, or withered by a frost *V.* 58
When tithing *t.* draws near *Y.D.* 8
It is no *t.* to joke *Y.D.* 40
At length the busy *t.* begins *Y.D.* 49 [50
T. made thee what thou wast, king of the woods *Y.O.*
And *T.* hath made thee what thou art, a cave *Y.O.* 51
The rottenness, which *t.* is charged to inflict *Y.O.* 67
T. was when, settling on thy leaf, a fly *Y.O.* 91 [92
Could shake thee to the root—and *t.* has been *Y.O.*
For senatorial honours. Thus to *T.*—*Y.O.* 103
To modern *t.* with truth to guide 1789, 11 [*Y.O.* 160
Leaned on her elbow, watching *T.*, whose course

TIMED.
Of wise reflection and well *t.* discourse *Con.* 388

TIMELY.
And loved a *t.* joke *J.G.* 170
He, therefore, *t.* warned, himself supplies *T.* iii 439

TIMID.
Whate'er was asked, too *t.* to resist *Ex.* 540

TIMIDITY.
Perhaps *t.* restrains his arm *T.* iv 599

TIMING.
T. more punctual, unrecorded facts *Y.O.* 47

TIMOROUS.
More delicate his *t.* mate retires *T.* 214
These shades are all my own. The *t.* hare *T.* vi 305

TIMOROUSLY.
Nor always *t.* creep *Trans. H.* 5

TIN.
And the old utensil of *t. R.C.* 27

TINCTURED.
His azure eyes, is *t.* black and red *T.* iv 216

TINDER.
Has burnt to *t.* a stale last year's news *B.B.* 10

TINGED.
The town has *t.* the country; and the stain *T.* iv 553

TINGING.
And, *t.* all with his own rosy hue *T.* v 8

TINGLING.
He feels a gentle *t.* come *E.* i 11
Should feel that itching and that *t. E.* i 25

TINKLE.
The pomp of sound or *t.* without use *Con.* 892
Like music it *t.* and rings in your ears *F.M.* 7
Must *t.* and glitter like gold to the sight *F.M.* 19
Streams *t.* sweetly in poetic chime *R.* 568
That *t.* in the wither'd leaves below *T.* vi 82
Or *t.* in 'Change Alley, to amuse *T.T.* 186

TINKLING.
Musical as the chime of *t.* rills *P.E.* 14
If he the *t.* harpsichord regards *P.E.* 148

Ah, *t.* cymbal and high-sounding brass *T.* v 681
And idle *t.* of a minstrel's lyre *T.* vi 1021

TINSEL.
His the mere *t.*, hers the rich reward *T.* 332

TINTS.
But still the imputed *t.* are those alone *H.* 73
Is this a saint ? Throw *t.* and all away *T.* 175

TINTINABULUM.
The clockwork *t.* of rhyme *T.T.* 529

TINY.
Those twinkling, *t.* lustres of the land *B.B.* 5
But you have killed a *t.* bird *Beau* 5
Rose from a seed of *t.* size *E.* i 95
Old *T.*, surliest of his kind *Ep.* ii 5
And partner once of *T.*'s box *Ep.* ii 43

TIPPLING.
From *t.* benches, cellars, stalls, and styes *T.* vi 695

TIPTOE-STEP.
With *t.* Vice silently succeeds *Ex.* 84

TIRE.
Pleasure is labour too, and *t.* as much *H.* 20
Whose wit is rudeness, whose good breeding *t. R.* 438
Not *t.*, demanding rather skill than force *T.* iii 407
That never *t.*, soon fans them all away *T.* iii 763
His lessons *t.*, his mild rebukes offend *Tir.* 716

TIRED.
Till both grew vexed and *t. A Tale* 22
" The dinner waits, and we are *t.*" *J.G.* 147   [125
By panting dog, *t.* man, and spattered horse *N.A.*
The very spirit of the world is *t. T.* vi 869

TISSUED.
When, playing with thy vesture's *t.* flowers *M.P.* 75

TITHING.
When *t.* time draws near *Y.D.* 8

TITLE.
Their *t.* to a country not their own *Ex.* 173
That infidels may prove their *t.* good *Ex.* 380
Proclaim their *t.* to the crowd around *H.* 266
Was—welladay, the *t.* page was lost *H.* 428
That *t.* now too trite and old) *Mor.* 2
That virtue has a *t.* to your love *P.E.* 248
Have purchased Heaven, and prove my *t.* good *T.* 96
Her *t.* to a treasure in the skies *T.* 330
Thy *t.* is engraven with a pen *T.* vi 862
The great indeed, by *t.*, riches, birth *Tir.* 346
Great *t.*, offices, and trusts disgraced *Tir.* 816
In all that wars against that *t.* most *T.T.* 429

TITYRUS.
Of *T.*, assembling, as he sang *T.* iv 707

TOAST.
Mere folly and delusion—Sir, your *t. H.* 364
That man shall be my *t. Pat.* 10
A present to his *t. Trans.* iv 6

TO-DAY.
Which flew not till *t. Beau* 6
Yesterday's face turn image of *t. H.* 102
The purpose of *t. H.F.* 2
And standard of his own, that is *t. T.* vi 214

TOE.
Equipped from top to *t. J.G.* 74
Whose *t.* of emulation treads too near *R.* 442
From top to *t.* the Geta now in vogue *T.* 202
From pangs arthritic that infest the *t. T.* i 105
His awkward gait, his introverted *t. T.* iv 633

TOIL.
Forgetful of the glorious *t.* of war *A.T.* 28

For then, by *t.* subdued, he drank *Cast.* 47
Murmuring and weary of our daily *t. Ch.* 221
T. much, and is a solemn trifler still *Ch.* 356
Yet much depends, as in the tiller's *t. Con.* 5
Where others *t.* with philosophic force *Con.* 151
The Mind despatched upon her busy *t. Con.* 437
T. to anticipate in vain *E.* i 66
" Sure so much labour, so much *t. E.* iv 81
And though a Bishop *t.* to cleanse the stain *Ex.* 384
Contrived both for *t.* and repose *Gr.* 10
And fruit reward his honourable *t. H.* 761
Plies all the sinews of industrious *t. Her.* 69
Or all the *t.* is lost *H.F.* 24
Restless as his who *t.* and sweats for food *J.T.* 24
Make the plant for which we *t.? N.C.* 18
Ere yet the pleasing *t.* becomes a pain *P.E.* 70
The joy, the danger and the *t.* o'erpays *P.E.* 90
And *t.* to polish its rough coat alone *P.E.* 420
Of half the *t.* they must encounter there *R.* 610
To learned cares or philosophic *t. R.* 662
To study culture, and with artful *t. R.* 785
Hard lot of man, to *t.* for the reward *T.* 11
Forgets her labour as she *t.* along *T.* 457
His wasted spirits quickly, by long *t. T.* i 128
Swift pace or steep ascent no *t.* to me *T.* i 139
T. much to earn a monumental pile *T.* i 276
From strenuous *t.* his hours of sweetest ease *T.* i 388
Such squalid sloth to honourable *t.! T.* i 579
Courageous, and refreshed for future *t. T.* iii 19
If *t.* await me, or if dangers new *T.* iii 20 [620
Well they reward the *t.* The sight is pleased *T.* iii
That ask robust, tough sinews, bred to *t. T.* iii 405
To books, to music, or the poet's *t. T.* iv 262
More briskly moved by his severer *t. T.* iv 389
Takes a Lethean leave of all his *t. T.* iv 475
And I am recompensed, and deem the *t. T.* vi 725
Laborious, yet unconscious of her *t. Tir.* 18
From reveries so airy, from the *t. T.* iii 188
His virtuous *t.* may terminate at last *Tir.* 777
(For what kings deem a *t.*, as well they may *T.T.* 155
With double *t.*, and shiver at their work *T.T.* 215
His spirits rising as his *t.* increase *T.T.* 279
The feller's *t.* which thou could'st ill requite *Y.O.* 115
Both in their *t.* and at their sports 1789, 63

TOILED.   [*t. F.A.* 28
Deep mysteries both ! which school-men must have
Patriots have *t.*, and in their country's cause *T.* v 704

TOILET.
And whether at the *t.* of the fair *H.* 684

TOILING.
That *t.* ages have but just matured *T.* iii 450
The *t.* steeds expand the nostril wide *T.* iv 347

TOIL-RENEWING.
And through the scenes of *t.* light *Con.* 732

TOILSOME.
'Tis easy to resign a *t.* place *R.* 621
(*T.* and indigent), she renders much *T.* 326
" From *t.* life to never-ending rest *T.* v 841

TOKAY.
Who stole her slipper, filled it with *T.—T.* 157

TOKEN.
And sealed with the same *t.* It is held *T.* v 547

TOLD.
Retort the charge, and let the World be *t. Con.* 767
It has indeed been *t.* me (with what weight *Con.* 815
Pleasure is deaf when *t.* of future pain *Ex.* 66 [479
Gold, to be sure!—Throughout the town 'tis *t. Ch.*
Hast thou not learned, what thou art often *t. Ex.* 350
Pants to be *t.* of battles won or lost *R.* 476   [31
T. hill and dale that Reynard's track was found *N.A.*
T. that his setting sun must rise no more *St.* ii 16

Adust with stripes *t.* out for every crime *T.* 83
A den of mischiefs never to be *t. T.* 392 [331
Watch, seals, and all,—till all his pranks are *t. Tir.*
With doubtful credit, *t.* to frighten babes *T.* iv 564
Proving at last, though *t.* in pompous strains *Tir.* 75
Ingenious dreamer, in whose well *t.* tale *Tir.* 135
You *t.* me, I remember, glory built *T.T.* 1 [*Tir.* 801
Whose hearts will ache, once *t.* what ills may reach

TOLL.
T. for the brave ! *R.G.* 1
T. for the brave ! *R.G.* 13
To *t.* the death-bell of its own decease *T.* ii 51

TOLLED.
I heard the bell *t.* on thy burial day *M.P.* 28

TOLL-MEN.
The *t.* thinking as before *J.G.* 243

TOM.
The man that hails you *T.* or Jack *F.* 169 [41
His scruples thus silenced, *T.* felt more at ease *P.A.*
But *T.* was still confused *F.B.* 21 [*P.A.* 33
They spoke, and *T.* pondered—" I see they will go
If *T.* be sober, and the wheels well greased *P.E.* 439
You have two servants,—*T.*, an arch, sly rogue *T.*201
By footman *T.* for witty and refined *Tir.* 687 [212
T. quits you, with—" Your most obedient, Sir " *T.*

TOMB.
Their fragrant memory will outlast their *t. Con.* 631
And many a *t.*, like Hamilton's aloud *Ep.* i 9
Lavish of life, to win an empty *t. Ex.* 522
That overhangs the borders of thy *t. H.* 38
Blush, Calumny ! and write upon his *t. H.* 588
Can always balk the *t. St.* i 28
Oh then, ere the turf or *t. St.* iv 33
Or does the *t.* take all ? If he survive *T.* ii 518
The man we celebrate must find a *t. T.* iii 264
And wraps him in an unexpected *t. T.* v 143
The *t.* take all, and all be blank beyond *Tir.* 68

TOMES.
Through *t.* of fable and of dream 1789, 7

TO-MORROW.
Good lack, we know not what *t.* brings *E.* iii 8
T. rends away *H.F.* 4
T. is our wedding-day *J.G.* 9
Dupe of *t.* even from a child *M.P.* 41
Thus many a sad *t.* came and went *M.P.* 42
Live till *t.*, will have passed away *N.A.* 133
T. brings a change, a total change ! *T.* iv 322
And is not ere *t.'s* sun go down *T.* vi 215

TONE.
And much was she charmed with a *t. C.* 14 [29
So his lordship decreed, with a grave solemn *t. A.C.*
He would not, with a peremptory *t. Con.* 121 [464
Prescribes the theme, the *t.*, and the grimace *Con.*
The future *t.* and temper of the sky *Ex.* 158
Go now, and with important *t.* demand *H.* 528
With all Elijah's dignity of *t. H.* 624
I could expound the melancholy *t. N.A.* 94
Wonders at Clodio's follies, in a *t. P.E.* 191
Of attic phrase and senatorial *t. S.* i 11
The *t.* of languid Nature. Mighty winds *T.* i 183
And colleges, untaught ; sells accent, *t. T.* ii 359
A corresponding *t.* in jovial souls *T.* iii 333
A jarring note. Themes of a graver *t. T.* iv 181
Its wasted *t.* and harmony unheard *T.* iv 480
" In what, with such solemnity of *t. T.* v 648
And stately *t.* of moralists, who boast *T.* v 690
Of such mellifluous *t. T.B.* 57
Now look on him, whose very voice in *t. Tir.* 815
The language and the *t. Trans.* iv 33
His form robust and of elastic *t. T.T.* 218

Its clearest *t.* the rapture it inspires *T.T.* 293
Of their best *t.* their dissolution owe *Y.O.* 85

TONGUE.
So *T.* was the lawyer, and argued the cause *A.C.* 5
Nor soft enough to suit a lover's *t. A.T.* 20
All the terrors of our *t.'s B.* 12
As only her musical *t. C.* 19
Who dare dishonour, or defile, the *t. Con.* 26
Ye powers who rule the *t.*, if such there are *Con.* 81
Though syllogisms hang not on my *t. Con.* 93
Much to the purpose, if our *t.* were loose *Con.* 354
She should imbue the *t.* with what she sips *Con.* 441
Holds a usurped dominion o'er his *t. Con.* 462 [36
There were the scorner's and the slanderer's *t. Ex.*
Thus touched, the *t.* receives a sacred cure *Con.* 887
Confessed the wonder, and with daring *t. Ex.* 155
Ghastly in feature, and his stammering *t. Ex.* 356
Disgracefully on every trifler's *t. Ex.* 663
Till the best *t.*, or heaviest hand, prevails *H.* 196
Bound in the fetters of an unknown *t. H.* 450
Assailed by scandal and the *t.* of strife *H.* 576
And while his *t.* the charge denies *H.F.* 15
The honey on his *t. M.* ii 16
Perceives in everything that lives a *t. N.A.* 56 [117
And rush those other sounds, that seem by *t. N.A.*
With such fine words familiar to his *t. P.E.* 509
A Finch, whose *t.* knew no control *P.T.* 26
That *t.* is silent now ; that silent *t. R.* 289 [411
The *t.* whose strains were cogent as commands *R.*
And deaf to all the impertinence of *t. R.* 549
Take it and perish ; but restrain your *t. T.* 18
That speech betrays at once a bigot's *t. T.* 519 [559
Condemns the injurious deed, the slanderous *t. T.*
That Chatham's language was his mother *t. T.* ii 237
With parrot *t.* performed the scholar's part *T.* ii 738
The struggling efforts of my boyish *t. T.* iv 711
He gives a *t.* to enlarge upon, a heart *T.* iv 794
Was split into diversity of *t. T.* v 195
" Nay—conduct hath the loudest *t.* The voice *T.* v 650
And *t.* accomplish'd in the fulsome cant *T.* vi 289
The lambent homage of his arrowy *t. T.* vi 782
To seek a refuge from the *t.* of strife *T.* vi 841
With all their flippant fluency of *t. T.T.* 147
When themes like these employ the poet's *t. T.T.* 198
And not a *t.* inquires how, where, or when *T.T.* 424
With more than mortal music on his *t. T.T.* 737 [9
Your brain well furnished, and your *t.* well taught *V.*
Not of a nimble *t.*, though now and then *Tir.* 666
Else coarse and rude in manners, and their *t. Tir.* 831

TOOK.
Though duly from my hand he *t. Ep.* ii 9 [*N.A.* 126
Through mere good fortune, *t.* a different course
George *t.* his seat again *Q.V.* 2 [5
Twelve years have elapsed since I last *t.* a view *P.F.*
The Crown, *t.* notice of an ostler's face *R.* 586
Surveyed the scene, and *t.* possession *R.C.* 44
His own coevals *t.* but little note *T.* iii 142
And *t.*, too often, there his easy nap *T.T.* 679

TOOL.
Oaths, used as playthings or convenient *t. Ex.* 37
Contrives, hard shifting, and without her *t. T.* v 417

TOOTH.
Not destined to my *t. B.R.* 18
A *t.* or auburn lock, and by degrees *T.* i 133
Though all the superstructure, by the *t. Y.O.* 122

TOOTHLESS.
Praise from the rivelled lips of *t.*, bald *T.* ii 488
Teeth for the *t.*, ringlets for the bald *T.* iv 81

TOP.
Perched on the *t.* of yonder hill *E.* i 44
Equipped from *t.* to toe *J.G.* 74
So stooping down from hawthorn *t. N.G.* 11

TOP—TOUGH 453

The rest in order to the *t. R.C.* 94
From *t.* to toe the Geta now in vogue *T.* 202
From Sinai's *t.* Jehovah gave the law *T.* 549 [664
Thou climbest the mountain *t.*, with eager eye *T.* i
'Tis perched upon the green hill *t.*, but close *T.* i 222
Shout to each other, and the mountain *t. T.* vi 794

TOPMAST.
Ascends his *t.*, through his peering eyes *T.* iv 115

TOPMOST.
His lamp now planted on Heaven's *t.* arch *N.A.* 31
Half open in the *t.* chest *R.C.* 40
Here and there one upon the *t.* bough *T.* 380
Seems sunk, and shortened to its *t.* boughs *T.* i 306
The nightingale may claim the *t.* bough *T.T.* 576

TORCH.
And Hymen, trimming his dim *t.* anew *A.T.* 201
With *t.* ever bright *Miss* — 74

TORE.
The astonished vulgar trembled while he *t. Ex.* 139

TORMENT.
Is man then only for his *t.* placed *P.E.* 229
His pupil, and his *t.*, and his jest *T.* iv 632
Needless, and first *t.* ere he devours *T.* vi 396

TORMENTED.
And sore *t.* long before his time *T.* 84
T. into billows, heaves and swells *T.* ii 101

TORN.
Whom you have *t.* for yours *Beau* 16
Their pages mangled, burnt, and *t. M.* i 9
Laughs at the reputations she has *t. T.* 163
So when by Bacchanalians *t. T.B.* 62
Neatly secured from being soiled or *t. Tir.* 119

TORNADOES.
Hark! He answers—Wild *t. N.C.* 33

TORPID.
To live, unblessed, in *t.* ease *Miss* — 27
The swallows in their *t.* state *N.* 1
T. and dull beneath a frozen zone *T.* 481
Checks vegetation in the *t.* plant *T.* iii 468

TORRENT.
And pours a *t.* of sweet notes around *Ch.* 111
Can trace the *t.* as it burns along? *Her.* 20
Thrown up by wintry *t.* roaring loud *T.* i 14
That overhangs a *t.*, to a twig *T.* i 484

TORRID.
In Afric's *t.* clime, or India's fiercest heat *T.T.* 297

TORTUOUS.
Of some flagged admiral; and *t.* arms *Y.O.* 96

TORTURE.
Me to *t.*, me to task? *N.C.* 12 [*P.A.* 3
What I hear of their hardships, their *t.*, their groans
And *t.* and groans will be multiplied still *P.A.* 12
Should suffer *t.*, and the streams be dyed *T.* vi 390

TORTURED.
With *t.* innocence in Mary's Court *Ex.* 613
Thus *t.* and squeezed, at last it appears *F.M.* 5

TOSS.
The flirted fan, the bridle, and the *t. H.* 344

TOSSED.
A thousand names are *t.* into the crowd *Ch.* 517
But *t.* and buffeted about *P.* 9
Man on the dubious waves of error *t. T.* 1
By many a billow *t. Trans.* iv 3

TOTAL.
His ambiguities his *t.* sum *Con.* 143
The *t.* ordinance and will of God *T.* i 743
And find the *t.* of their hopes and fears *T.* iii 132
To-morrow brings a change, a *t.* change *T.* iv 322
The *t.* grist unsifted, husks and all *T.* vi 108

The *t.* herd receiving first from one *T.* vi 335
To live estranged from God his *t.* scope *Tir.* 426
From *t.* night and absolute disgrace *T.T.* 665

TOTTERING.
Woden and Thor, each *t.* in his shrine *Ex.* 505
Her elbows ruffled, and her *t.* form *T.* iv 545

TOUCH.
But if she *t.* a character, it dies *Ch.* 456
Some fretful tempers wince at every *t. Con.* 325
And dreaded more than a contagious *t.? Con.* 652
And *t.* the subject I designed at first *Con.* 868 [18
Can gold grow worthless that has stood the *t. E.* iii
With feet too delicate to *t.* the ground *Ex.* 52
And Time forbid to *t.* them as he flew *Ex.* 184
Should fly the world's contaminating *t. Ex.* 446
With curious *t.* examines me *P.* 33
Who reckon every *t.* a blemish *P.* 56
Exposed to view, but not to *t. P.B.* 30
Have you no *t.* of pity that the poor *P.E.* 249
Nor *t.* the page he cannot but profane) *P.E.* 457
In all we *t.*, stamped plainly on his works *H.* 545
Of him whom Hope has with a *t.* made whole *H.* 731
Still as I *t.* the lyre, do thou expand *R.* 203
That yields not to the *t.* of human skill *R.* 344
Oh, then, a text would *t.* him at the quick! *T.* 310
And dangerous to the *t.*, has yet its bloom *T.* i 528
To conjure clean away the gold they *t. T.* i 571
That falls asunder at the *t.* of fire *T.* ii 11 [161
The *t.* from many a trembling chord shakes out *T.* iv
They *t.* our country, and their shackles fall *T.* ii 42
With what intent I *t.* that holy thing) *T.* ii 328
Forgot their office, opening with a *t. T.* ii 747
To no mean hand, and asks the *t.* of taste *T.* iii 632
And *t.* of his hand, with so much art *T.* iv 736
And all was moist to the warm *t.*; a scene *T.* v 166
Of leaf and flower? It sleeps; and the icy *t. T.* vi 137
Not to be wronged by a mere mortal *t. T.* vi 748
No passion *t.* a discordant string *T.* vi 787 [241
But shows some *t.*, in freckle, streak, or stain *T.* vi
From *t.* of human lips at best impure *T.* vi 835
T. but his nature in its ailing part *Tir.* 161
To *t.* the sword with conscientious awe *T.T.* 77
Heroic song from thy free *t.* acquires *T.T.* 292
So nice his ear, so delicate his *t.*) *T.T.* 653
Might prove a welcome gift, and *t.* thine heart *V.* 41

TOUCHED.
But still a soul thus *t.* can never cease *Ch.* 420 [501
T. by that power that you have dared to mock *Con.*
T. with the magnet, had attracted his *Con.* 272
Nothing is slightly *t.*, much less forgot *Con.* 317
Thus *t.*, the tongue receives a sacred cure *Con.* 887
In being *t.*, and crying—"Don't!" *P.* 38 [659
Or his, who *t.* their hearts with hallowed fires? *Ex.*
Truth, Hope, and Charity, and *t.* with awe *T.* i 2
There *t.* by Reynolds, a dull blank becomes *T.* i 700
For he has *t.* them. From the extremest point *T.* ii 92
That he has *t.*, retouched, many a long day *T.* iii 786
T. by the Midas finger of the State *T.* iv 507 [796
Not so the mind that has been *t.* from Heaven *T.* v
Foh! 'twas a bribe that left it: he has *t. T.* iv 609
Till Thou hast *t.* them; 'tis the voice of song *T.* v 887
Is *t.* within us, and the heart replies *T.* vi 5
T. with a coal from Heaven, assume the lyre *T.T.* 735

TOUCHING.
The scene is *t.*, and the heart is stone *Tir.* 298

TOUCHWOOD.
And from his *t.* trunk the mulberry-tree *T.* vi 688

TOUGH.
And bends the *t.* materials to his will *Ch.* 464
That ask robust, *t.* sinews, bred to toil *T.* iii 405

Obduracy takes place ; callous and *t. T.T.* 458
Warped into *t.* knee-timber, many a load ! *Y.O.* 99

TOWER.
Named with emphatic dignity, "The *T.*" *Ch.* 556
Till the foe found them, and down fell the *t. Ex.* 72
Such freedom is,—and Windsor's hoary *t. Ex.* 596
Rebuilds the *t.* that smoked upon the plain *Her.* 71
Of hedge-row beauties numberless, square *t. T.* i 173
A prince with half his people ! Ancient *t. T.* ii 121
To view some rugged rock or mouldering *t. T.* iv 235
Soothed with a waking dream of houses, *t. T.* iv 287
Ye horrid *t.*, the abode of broken hearts *T.* v 384
And through the trees I view the embattled *t. T.* vi 66
Of wintry blasts; the loftiest *t. Trans. H.* 14

TOWERED.
She *t.* a cloud-capped pyramid of snow *Her.* 4

TOWERING.
Would humble many a *t.* poet's pride *Ch.* 536
And steeples *t.* high, much like our own *P.E.* 382
Whole without stooping ; *t.* crest and all *T.* iv 271
Think yourself stationed on a *t.* rock *T.T.* 33

TOWN.
Gold, to be sure !—Throughout the *t.* 'tis told *Ch.* 479
Judging, in charity no doubt, the *t. H.* 250
Of famous London *t. J.G.* 4
For he got first to *t. J.G.* 246
Wasting *t.*, plantations, meadows *N.C.* 35
With memorandum-book for every *t. P.E.* 373
Most likes it, when he studies it in *t. R.* 574
In village or in *t.*, the bay of curs *T.* i 230 [*T.* iii 815
The world of wandering knights and squires to *t.*
God made the country, and man made the *t. T.* i 749
A man o' the *t.* dines late, but soon enough *T.* ii 622
And crowd the road, impatient for the *t.* ! *T.* iii 319
And surfeited lewd *t.* with her fair dues *T.* iii 758
Even in the stifling bosom of the *t. T.* iv 753 [553
The *t.* has tinged the country ; and the stain *T.* iv
Therefore in *t.* and cities they abound *Tir.* 519 [iv 466
Pass where we may, through city or through *t. T.*
With half the chariots and sedans in *t. Tir.* 748
Rose like a paper-kite and charmed the *t. T.T.* 385
The weekly censor of a laughing *T.—V.* 38

TOWS.
Than when he *t.* a prize *A Tale* 60

TOY.
A *t.* to sport with, and pass time away *Con.* 18
Who first misuse, then cast their *t.* away *H.* 128
Might prove a mischief, or at best a *t. P.E.* 302
Life an intrusted talent, or a *t.* ? *R.* 650
For what poor *t.* they can disclaim *St.* vi 15
Devised the Weatherhouse, that useful *t.* ! *T.* 211
Her brittle *t.*, restores me to myself *T.* iv 307
Because men suffer it, their *t.* the world *T.* v 192
To trivial *t.*, and, pushing ivory balls *T.* vi 274
But bends his sturdy back to any *t. Tir.* 549
Just what the *t.* will sell for, and no more *T.T.* 62

TRACE.
But misery still delights to *t. Cast.* 59
To *t.* thee to the date when yon fair sea *Ex.* 550
That while I trembling *t.* a work divine *H.* 671
Can *t.* the torrent as it burns along ? *Her.* 20
Can *t.* her mazy windings to their end *P.E.* 16
T. of Eden are still seen below *R.* 28
To *t.* in Nature's most minute design *R.* 53
From all that Science is, Art invents *T.* i 627
Paul should himself direct me. I would *t. T.* ii 397
Some *t.* of her youthful beauty left) *T.* iii 299
And lineaments divine I *t.* a hand *T.* iii 722
The pencil or the pen, may *t.* the scene ! *T.* v 109

Time ploughs them up, and not a *t.* remains *T.* v 533
It is not from his form, in which we *t. Tir.* 1
To *t.* him in his word, his works, his ways ! *T.T.* 751

TRACED.
The farther *t.*, enriched them still the more *Con.* 516
A thousand other themes less deeply *t. M.P.* 57
T. easily to its true source above *J.T.* 45

TRACK.
Told hill and dale that Reynard's *t.* was found *N.A.* 34
Pursue the *t.* of his directing wand *T.* iii 777 [i 161
His labouring team, that swerved not from the *t. T.*
Lean pensioners upon the traveller's *t. T.* v 93
Confine the million in the beaten *t. T.T.* 667

TRACKED.
Have we not *t.* the felon home, and found *T.* ii 813

TRADE.
T. is the golden girdle of the globe *Ch.* 86
T. in the blood of innocence, and plead *Ch.* 182
Praise is the medium of a knavish *t. E.* ii 6
Aspersion is the babbler's *t. F.* 100
To exchange the centre of a thousand *t. H.* 246
If foreigners likewise would give up the *t. P.A.* 13
Sad sacrilege ! no function, but a *t.* ! *P.E.* 123
The statesman, lawyer, merchant, man of *t. R.* 5
The sacred fire, self-torturing his *t. T.* 100
Disinterested good, is not our *t. T.* i 674
Build factories with blood, conducting *t. T.* iv 681
Than set your son to work at a vile *t. Tir.* 456
By public hackneys in the schooling *t. Tir.* 621
See great commanders making war a *t. Tir.* 821
Whose *t.* it is to smile, to crouch, to please *T.T.* 128
To turn a penny in the way of *t. T.T.* 421

TRADESMAN.
So may a *t.*, if not quite a knave *H.* 210

TRADITION.
T., now decrepid and worn out *Ex.* 502

TRADUCE.
The man that dares *t.*, because he can *Ex.* 432
T. the splendour of a noontide ray *T.* 540
Give it a charge to blacken and *t. T.T.* 763

TRADUCED.
Insulted and *t.*, are cast aside *T.* vi 879

TRAFFIC.
Who drive a loathsome *t.*, gauge and span *Ch.* 139
Caledonia's *t.* and pride ! *Gr.* 18
So coin grows smooth, in *t.* current passed *P.E.* 279
And fills the world of *t.* and the shades *R.* 120
Should purl amidst the *t.* of Cheapside *T.T.* 185

TRAGIC.
Needs he the *t.* fur, the smoke of lamps *T.* iv 195

TRAGICAL.
As *t.*, as others at his own *P.E.* 192

TRAILING.
That fumes beneath his nose, the *t.* cloud *T.* v 56

TRAIN.
Fairest and foremost of the *t.* that wait *Ch.* 1
Yet Fashion, leader of a chattering *t. Con.* 457
Are bringing into vogue their heathen *t. Con.* 821
That, with a black, infernal *t. E.* iv 15
A calm succeeds—but Plenty, with her *t. Her.* 63
A *t.*, attendant on their queen *Miss* — 71 [iii 411
Which, save himself who *t.* them, none can feel *T.*
And Pleasure brings as surely in her *t. P.E.* 43
Grey dawn appears ; the sportsman and his *t. P.E.* 82
Bright as his own, and *t.* by every rule *T.* ii 347
Her *t.* and her umbrella all her care *T.* iv 552 [247
Treads on thy sweeping *t.* ; one hand employed *T.* iv

With all her little ones, a sportive t. *T.* vi 301
He too is witness, noblest of the t. *T.* vi 425
T. him in public with a mob of boys *Tir.* 206
Would turn our steps into a wiser t. *Tir.* 260
The Muse instructed a well nurtured t. *T.T.* 634

TRAINBAND.
A t. captain eke was he *J.G.* 3

TRAINED. [519
Were t. beneath his lash and knew the smack *Ex.*
And all your numerous progeny, well t. *T.* iv 422

TRAITOR.
He was a t. by the general voice *Ex.* 545
By t. Appetite, and armed with darts *T.* iii 685

TRAMONTANE.
Is t., and stumbles all belief *T.* iv 533

TRAMPLE.
T. on a thousand states *B.* 18
At least to t. on our Maker's laws *Con.* 183
Who t. order; and the day *St.* vi 25

TRAMPLED.
Unless his laws be t. on,—in vain ? *Ch.* 191
Will be despised and t. on at last *T.T.* 397
E'en on the fools that t. on their laws *T.T.* 651

TRAMPLER.
The injurious t. upon Nature's law *T.* vi 465

TRANQUIL.
And leave to Mercy, with a t. mind *T.* 499
The dreams of fancy, t. and secure *T.* i 236
To seek a t. death in distant shades *T.* iii 111
Begat a t. confidence in all *T.* vi 366
Who, doomed to an obscure but t. state *T.* vi 908

TRANQUILLITY.
Or placemen, all t. and smiles *T.* iv 49

TRANSCENDING.
Charged with a freight t. in its worth *Ch.* 133

TRANSCENDS.
And are august, but this t. them all *T.* v 552

TRANSCRIBED.
Were copied close in him, and well t. *H.* 581

TRANSCRIPT.
Received the t. of the Eternal Mind *Ex.* 198

TRANSFERS.
Sells the last scantling, and t. the price *T.* iii 753

TRANSFIX.
Much less t. his feelings with an oath *Tir.* 729

TRANSFIXED.
And, Phineas-like, t. them at a blow *A.T.* 196

TRANSFORMATION.
What solid was, by t. strange *T.* ii 99
But t. of apostate man *T.* v 695

TRANSFORMED.
T. to blessings, miss their cruel aim *E.* ii 38
And aguish east, till time shall have t. *T.* iii 772
T. to a lean shank. The shapeless pair *T.* v 16
The rude companion smiled, as if t. *T.* vi 543

TRANSFORMS.
T. thy smiles to looks of woe *M.* 47
Down into modern use; t. old print *T.* ii 363

TRANSGRESS. [*T.* iii 97
T. what laws they may. Well-dressed, well-bred
" Favoured as ours, t. from the womb *T.* v 829

TRANSIENT.
At length his t. respite past *Cast.* 43
A t. visit intervening *E.* i 97
And of a t. date *G.* 9

T. indeed, as is the fleeting hour *H.* 119
To every sudden slip and t. wrong *H.* 390
Till life's poor t. night is spent *N.G.* 32
And outline of the present t. state *R.* 670
Few t. years, won from the abyss abhorred *T.* i 286
Substantial happiness for t. joy *T.* iii 300 [461
Sweet smiles, and bloom less t. than her own *T.* i
Is but a t. guest, newly arrived *T.* iii 750
'Twas t. in its nature, as in show *T.* v 173
Pronounced it t., glorious as it is *T.* v 563
Slow circling ages are as t. days *T.* vi 227
But 'twas a t. calm. A storm was near *T.* vi 544
(Forgive a t. thought) *The Doves* 30

TRANSITION.
By short t. we have lost his glare *T.* i 336
The grand t., that there lives and works *T.* vi 184

TRANSITORY.
Yet e'en in t. life's late day *Tir.* 143

TRANSLUCENT.
And overlaid with clear t. glass *T.* iii 485
Beneath a pane of thin t. horn *Tir.* 120

TRANSMITTING.
T. cloudless, and the solar beam *Y.O.* 75
The occasion of t. fear to love ? *Ch.* 225

TRANSPARENCY.
Gleamed through the clear t. that seemed *T.* v 151

TRANSPIRE.
Warning his heart, should at his lips t.? *Con.* 484

TRANSPLANTED.
When thou, t. from thy genial home *Tir.* 850

TRANSPLANTATION.
And t. in an ampler space *T.* iii 533

TRANSPORT.
A t. glows in all he looks and speaks *H.* 726
All, all alike, t. the glowing bard *R.* 197
And dream of t. she was not to know *T.* i 544
The bee t. the fertilizing meal *T.* iii 538
With t. such as favoured lovers feel *T.* iv 721
T. them, and are made their favourite themes *Tir.* 231
T. not chargeable with art 1789, 60

TRANSPORTATION.
As from a seven years' t., home *Con.* 400

TRANSVERSE.
Between two poles upon a stick t. *T.* i 561

TRAPPED.
Makes men mere vermin, worthy to be t. *T.* ii 683

TRAPPINGS.
He wore them as fine t. for a show *T.* 56
And with poetic t. grace thy prose *T.* v 679

TRAPS.
T. to catch youth are most abundant too *Tir.* 522

TRASH.
Quickens a market, and helps off the t. *Ch.* 522
And all is t. that Reason cannot reach *Ex.* 108
And taken t. for treasure *F.* 27
With indolence and luxury is t. *P.E.* 428
Much t. unuttered, and some ills undone *Tir.* 733

TRAVEL.
Thy thunders t. over earth and seas *Ex.* 582
We t. far, 'tis true, but not for naught *T.* i 675
In every clime, and t. where we might *T.* ii 234
Contrive creation; t. nature up *T.* iii 156
He t. and expatiates, as the bee *T.* iv 107
He t., and I too. I tread his deck *T.* iv 114
As he that t. far, oft turns aside *T.* iv 234

TRAVELLED.
Seem all created since he t. last *R.* 426
And worships. Her report has t. forth *T.* vi 813

TRAVELLER.
What monstrous lies some *t.* will tell" *Ch.* 394
No *t.* ever reached that blest abode *E.* ii 11
Ere yet it came, the *t.* urged his steed *T.* 244
Sent through the *t.'s* temples! He that finds *T.* iii 803
Ill fares the *t.* now, and he that stalks *T.* iv 341
Lean pensioners upon the *t.'s* track *T.* v 93
And snow, that often blinds the *t.'s* course *T.* v 142
To join a *t.*, of far different note *T.* vi 489
To bid the *t.*, as he went *Trans.* i 15

TRAVERSE.
To *t.* seas, range kingdoms, and bring home *Ch.* 301
Might *t.* England safely to and fro *E.* iii 61

TREACHEROUS. [*A.T.* 118
" Find out her *t.* heart, and plant a dagger there?
The *t.* smile, a mask for secret hate *Ex.* 42
And kindles in his soul a *t.* fire *P.E.* 40
T. and false; it smiled and it was cold *T.* v 176
Along the *t.* shore *Trans. H.* 6

TREAD.
Fate steals along with silent *t. A Fable* 36
But marks the man that *t.* his fellow down *Ch.* 211
With unshod feet they yet securely *t. E.* ii 16
That *t.* the circuit of the cistern wheel! *H.* 100
At every step beneath their feet they *t. Her.* 55
Points to inscriptions wheresoe'er they *t. P.E.* 391
The fatal ills; that though the path he *t. P.E.* 545
Whose toe of emulation *t.* too near *R.* 442
The saint or moralist should *t. S.* 17
" Worlds should not bribe me back to *t. St.* iii 5
He *t.* as if, some solemn music near *T.* 62 [351
We *t.* the Wilderness, whose well-rolled walks *T.* i
Though halt, and weary of the path they *t. T.* i 471
Disclosing Paradise where'er He *t.? T.* ii 87
I mean to *t.* I feel myself at large *T.* iii 18
He travels, and I too. I *t.* his deck *T.* iv 114 [247
T. on thy sweeping train; one hand employed *T.* iv
And licks the foot that *t.* it in the dust *T.* v 356
And settle in soft musings as I *t. T.* vi 69
Will *t.* aside, and let the reptile live *T.* vi 567
Nor, though he *t.* the secret path of life *T.* vi 956
Reasoning at every step he *t. The Doves* 1
Shine by the side of every path we *t. Tir.* 79
To him that *t.* upon his free-born toe *T.T.* 227
He trod the very self-same ground you *t. T.T.* 388

TREAT.
But to *t.* justly what he loved so well *Con.* 624
Strange tidings these to tell a world who *t. Con.* 719
Receives from her both appetite and *t. P.E.* 210
" My friends! be cautious how ye *t. P.T.* 23
And minds that deem derided pain a *t. R.* 310 [772
To range the fields and *t.* their lungs with air *T.* iv
And *t.* them kindly! rude as thou appearest *T.* iv 370

TREASON.
To smite the poor is *t.* against God *Ch.* 217
As if 'twere *t.* against English laws *Con.* 398
Beyond that mark is *t.* He is ours *T.* v 341

TREASURE.
And destined all the *t.* there *A Fable* 26
Religion! what *t.* untold *A.S.* 25
That tells us whence his *t.* are supplied *Ch.* 440
And gathering all her *t.*, sweet by sweet *Con.* 440
And spread the sacred *t.* of the breast *Con.* 573
The *t.* at my feet *D.W.* 36
Her princes captive, and her *t.* spoiled *Ex.* 62
And taken trash for *t. F.* 27
What *t.* centre, what delights, in thee *H.* 174
That boasts the *t.*, all at his command *H.* 176
And many a *t.* more *M.* i 6
The various *t.* of his mind *Mrs. M—* 42

To increase a stranger's *t. N.C.* 3
" My patrimonial *t.* and my pride *R.* 367
In which he sports away the *t.* now *St.* ii 10
Her title to a *t.* in the skies *T.* 330
The Poet's *t.*, silence, and indulge *T.* i 235
Who squander time and *t.* with a smile *T.* ii 641
Is virtue; the only lasting *t.*, truth *T.* iii 269
Loses its *t.* of salubrious salts *T.* iii 610
The beds the trusted *t.* of their seeds *T.* iii 650 [160
The sprightly lyre, whose *t.* of sweet sounds *T.* iv
Were kingship as true *t.* as it seems *T.* v 357
Proud of the *t.*, marches with it down *T.* v 708
But not to understand a *t.'s* worth *T.* vi 50 [359
They risk their hopes, their dearest *t.* there? *Tir.*
Indeed is *t.*, and crowns all the rest *V.* 92
The shipwright's darling *t.*, didst present *Y.O.* 97
I found the far-sought *t.* near 1789, 28

TREASURED.
The *t.* sweets of the capacious plan *Ch.* 323
Had *t.* up before *M.* ii 12
And fruitful soil, that has been *t.* long *T.* iii 514

TREATY.
Rejects all *t.*, penetrates all wiles *H.* 649

TREE.
In Scotland's realm, where *t.* are few *A Tale* 1
It served them with a *t. A Tale* 32
But such a *t.*! 'twas shaven deal *A Tale* 33
The *t.* they call a mast *A Tale* 34
We paused under many a *t. C.* 13
From a worse yoke, and nailed it to the *t. Ex.* 220
And from the *t.* that fringed his hill *Mor.* 14
Not animals alone, but shrubs and *t. N.A.* 57
Like Eden's dread probationary *t. P.E.* 468 [*P.A.* 38
His apples might hang till they dropped from the *t.*
Opposite in the apple *t. P.T.* 31 [8
And the *t.* is my seat that once lent me a shade *P.F.*
Bare *t.* and shrubs but ill, you know *P.T.* 52
To carve his rustic name upon a *t. R.* 400
But still 'tis rural—*t.* are to be seen *R.* 497
An apple *t.*, or lofty pear *R.C.* 12
Green as the bay *t.*, ever green *St.* i 17
He hears the tempest howling in the *t. T.* 254
Like gleanings of an olive *t.* they show *T.* 379
And range an Indian waste without a *t. T.* i 261
Diversified with *t.* of every growth *T.* i 301 [408
Proud of his well-spread walls, he views his *t. T.* iii
No *t.* in all the grove but has its charms *T.* i 307
Jotham ascribed to his assembled *t. T.* v 322 [288
T., churches, and strange visages, expressed *T.* iv
But *t.*, and rivulets whose rapid course *T.* vi 109
When lightnings flash among the *t. The Doves* 21
Spring hangs her infant blossoms on the *t. Tir.* 43
Like caterpillars, dangling under *t. Tir.* 591 [v 112
Large growth of what may seem the sparkling *t. T.*
Beneath thy parent *t.* mellowed the soil *Y.O.* 24
As in Dodona once thy kindred *t. Y.O.* 41 [66
And through the *t.* I view th' embattled tower *T.* vi
Desperate attempt, till *t.* shall speak again *Y.O.* 49

TREE-ENCHANTER.
The *t.* Orpheus fell *T.B.* 64

TREESHIP.
Of *t.*—first a seedling, hid in grass *Y.O.* 61

TREMBLE.
And made the mountains *t.* at his frown? *Ch.* 78
To *t.* (as a creature of an hour *Con.* 657
All *t.* in all worlds, except our own *Con.* 660
That sick, she *t.*, knowing she must die *Con.* 773
And his that seraphs *t.* at, is hung *Ex.* 662
Recompense ill? He *t.* at the thought *T.* 192
And *t.* when I wake, for all the wealth *T.* ii 31

T. and be amazed at thine escape *T.* ii 159
And sigh, but never *t.* at the sound *T.* iv 106
The frugal housewife *t.* when she lights *T.* iv 380
When he should strike, he *t.* and sets free *T.* iv 600
Is balloted, and *t.* at the news *T.* iv 627 [492
And *t.* at vain dreams? Heaven grant I may! *T.* v
As taught him too to *t.* in his turn *T.* vi 378
In which the best and worthiest *t.* most *Tir.* 415
He *t.* at the sight *Y.D.* 24

TREMBLED.
The astonished vulgar *t.*, while he tore *Ex.* 13
Then laugh at all you *t.* at before *P.E.* 592
Her sacred cause, but *t.* when he rose *T.T.* 351

TREMBLING.
Fear seized the *t.* sex; in every grove *A.T.* 97
And woman *t.* at the foot of man *A.T.* 158
Stood *t.* at the boldness of thy powers *Ex.* 597
The little Greeks look *t.* at the scales *H.* 195
The purple bumper *t.* at his lips *H.* 358
That while I *t.* trace a work divine *H.* 671
How each would *t.* wait the mournful sheet *St.* ii 5
The dying, *t.* at the awful close *T.* 436
T. yet happy, confident yet meek *T.* 572
The solemn chords, and with a *t.* hand *T.* i 3
While God performs, upon the *t.* stage *T.* ii 81
The touch from many a *t.* chord shakes out *T.* iv 161
Upon his heart-strings, *t.* with delight *T.* v 414
T., as if eternity were hung *T.* vi 270
To rend a victim *t.* at his foot *T.* vi 411
Canst thou, the tear just *t.* on thy lids *Tir.* 859
That threatened England's *t.* state 1789, 37

TREMENDOUS.
But shine with cruel and *t.* charms *Ch.* 545
Or heard we that *t.* bray alone *N.A.* 93
The victim of his own *t.* choice *T.* vi 558

TREMULOUS.
Grew *t.*, and moved derision more *T.* ii 729

TRESPASS.
Implies no *t.* against Love Divine) *Ch.* 488
Lest he should *t.*, begged to go abroad *E.* iii 23
By *t.* or omission *F.* 147
For one slight *t.* all this stir *M.F.* 21

TRESSES.
For more than half the *t.* it sustains *T.* iv 544

TRIAL.
To recommence life's *t.*, in the hope *F.A.* 4
Placed for his *t.* on this bustling stage *P.E.* 23

TRIBE.
That every *t.*, though placed as he sees best *Ch.* 19
And the twelve standards of the *t.* unfurled *Ex.* 211
All *t.* beside of Indian name *Mrs. M—* 9 [289
What parts the kindred *t.* of weeds and flowers? *H.*
Grand Metropolitan of all the *t. P.E.* 186
A vagabond and useless *t.* there eat *T.* i 559
We persecute, annihilate the *t. T.* iii 309
The feathered *t.* domestic. Half on wing *T.* v 62
In *t.* and clans, and had begun to call *T.* v 222
Its family and *t.* Laburnum rich *T.* vi 149
Guard what you say; the patriotic *t. T.T.* 83
'Twould thin the ranks of the poetic *t. T.T.* 768

TRIBULATION.
Will learn in school of *t. R.C.* 115

TRIBUNAL.
And show the august *t.* of the skies *R.* 656

TRIBUTARY.
Who left them still a *t.* state *Ex.* 218
Adds, as he can, his *t.* mite *T.T.* 112

TRIBUTE.
Accept the *t.* of a stranger's pen *Ch.* 291
Pay *t.* to thy glorious beams *O.* i 7
This annual *t.* Death requires *St.* i 11
Propitious, pays his *t.*, game or fish *T.* iv 611
And dedicate a *t.*, in its use *T.* vi 712
And Saba's spicy groves, pay *t.* there *T.* vi 807

TRICE.
How in a *t.* the turnpike men *J.G.* 119
Whom in a *t.* he tried to stop *J.G.* 223

TRICK.
With many a freakish *t.* deceived his pains *A.T.* 25
That forms and rites are *t.* of human law *A.T.* 62
Some men employ their health, an ugly *t. Con.* 311
A *t.* upon the canvass, pointed flame *Con.* 782
And *t.* and turns, that Fancy may devise *Ex.* 137
I know not where she caught the *t. R.C.* 7
And let that pass—'twas but a *t.* of state *T.* ii 267
What!—will a man play *t.*, will he indulge *T.* ii 419
And mode of its conveyance, by such *t. T.* ii 561
By *t.* and lies as numerous and as keen *T.* ii 671
In playing *t.* with Nature, giving laws *T.* iii 165
Learn every *t.*, and soon play all the game *T.* iv 231
Cards were superfluous here, with all the *t. T.* iv 207
Quite unindebted to the *t.* of art *T.T.* 525
While servile *t.* and imitative knack *T.T.* 666
Their whole attention, and ape all his *t. Tir.* 225

TRICKED.
T. out of all his royalty by art *Ch.* 53
Like an unburied carcass *t.* with flowers *T.* vi 992

TRICKLE.
That *t.* down the branches, fast congealed *T.* v 114

TRICKLED.
With tears, that *t.* down the writer's cheeks *T.* iv 18

TRICKLING.
Are a stream choked, or *t.* to no end *Tir.* 718

TRIDENT-BEARING.
And *t.* queen of the wide seas *Ex.* 275

TRIED.
T., as it should be, by the fruit it bears *Con.* 172
If thus the important cause is to be *t. H.* 373
A knave when *t.* on honesty's plain rule *H.* 566
Whom in a trice he *t.* to stop *J.G.* 223
A last year's bird, who ne'er had *t. P.T.* 28
Whose courage well was *t. R.G.* 6
And well *t.* virtues, could alone inspire *T.* i 148
The wall on which we *t.* our graving skill *Tir.* 300
Or rather a gross compound, justly *t. Tir.* 466
Because forsooth thy courage has been *t. Tir.* 739

TRIFLE.
Each *t.* that he sees *Beau* 4
I owed a *t.*, and have paid the debt *Con.* 796
Here just such *t.*, without worth or use *Ex.* 49
No *t.*, howsoever short it seem *H.* 123
T. pursued, whate'er the event *Mor.* 45
A *t.* if it move but to amuse *P.E.* 303
And man might safely *t.* with his name *T.* 556
I would not *t.* merely, though the world *T.* ii 313
'Tis true that, if to *t.* life away *Tir.* 81
In tales, in *t.*, and in children's play *T.T.* 731

TRIFLED.
He laughed and *t.*, made him welcome there *H.* 685

TRIFLER.
The solemn *t.*, with his boasted skill *Ch.* 355
Toils much, and is a *t.* still *Ch.* 356
Important *t.*! have more smoke than fire *Con.* 250
And brings the *t.* under rigorous sway *Con.* 596
To catch the *t.* of the time *E.* i 20

The busy *t.* dreams himself alone *Ex.* 322
Disgracefully on every *t.'s* tongue *Ex.* 663
But *t.* are engaged and cannot come *P.E.* 167
Is far too just to pass the *t.* by *P.E.* 200
And having lived a *t.*, die a man *R.* 14
Then doubtless many a *t.*, on the brink *St.* ii 13
A *t.* vain, and empty of all good *Tir.* 754

TRIFLING.
Grown dim in *t.* studies, blind he dies *Ch.* 358
A simpering countenance, and a *t.* air *P.E.* 206
Though busy, *t.*; empty, though refined *P.E.* 426
To distant worlds, and *t.* in their own *T.* iii 166
Proof of a *t.* and a worthless mind *T.T.* 759
Amusement-monger of a *t.* age *V.* 28

TRIM.
His neighbour in such *t. J.G.* 162
But how a body so fantastic, *t. T.* ii 460
And Nature in her cultivated *t. T.* iii 357
Humour in holiday, and sightly *t. T.T.* 643

TRIMMED.
He *t.* his flight another way *P.B.* 12
New *t.*, a gallant show! *Q.V.* 6
His books well *t.*, and in the gayest style *T.* 421
Saw better clad, in cloak of satin *t. T.* i 535

TRIMMING.
And Hymen, *t.* his dim torch anew *A.T.* 201

TRIPLE.
"This *t.* realm adores thee;—thou art come *Ch.* 270
Once have the sanction of our *t.* state *E.* iii 57
The Pineapples in *t.* row *P.B.* 1
The *t.* purpose. In that sickly, foul *T.* v 583

TRIPPING.
Yes—you may catch him *t.*, if you can *Con.* 120

TRITE.
That title now too *t.* and old) *Mor.* 2

TRIUMPH.
Thy deathless wreaths, and *t.* all thine own *H.* 664
By frequent lapse, can hope no *t.* there *T.* i 691
And there obtains fresh *t.* o'er himself *T.* vi 937
Our fathers' *t.* and our own 1789, 16

TRIUMPHANT.
With wreaths like those *t.* spirits wear *H.* 166
'Tis God himself *t.* in his heart *H.* 735
The gulf of death *t.* passed *St.* iii 31
And in the charming strife *t.* still *T.* iv 163

TRIVIAL.
God's holy word, once *t.* in his view *H.* 706
On every *t.* provocation? *M.F.* 36
T. as a parrot's prate? *St.* iv 24
Some *t.* slips their daily walk attend *T.* 286
However *t.* all that he conceives *T.* iv 69
Discourse ensues, not *t.*, yet not dull *T.* iv 174
T. and worthy of disdain, achieves *T.* v 639
To *t.* toys, and, pushing ivory balls *T.* vi 274
Of what he deems no mean or *t.* trust *T.* vi 607
And *t.* favours, lasting as the life *T.* vi 630

TROD.
Securely, though by steps but rarely *t. R.* 113 [47
Children not thine have *t.* my nursery floor *M.P.*
He left his bed, he *t.* the floor *R.C.* 91
A noble show! while Roscius *t.* the stage *T.* iii 597
Beneath the turf that I have often *t. T.* vi 1005
Be careful where he *t. Trans.* i 16
He *t.* the very self-same ground you tread *T.T.* 388

TROJAN.
A *T.* combat would be something new *Con.* 197

TROOPS.
What are its tidings? have our *t.* awaked? *T.* iv 25
The armoury of Winter; where his *t. T.* v 139

TROOPING.
Come *t.* at the housewife's well known call *T.* v 61

TROPES.
Or will he seek to dazzle me with *t. T.* ii 423

TROPHIED.
Of *t.* helmets, spears and shields 1789, 4

TROPHY.
But where are its sublimer *t.* found? *T.* ii 319
Ask him, indeed, what *t.* he has raised *T.* vi 932
Brings down the warrior's *t.* to the dust *T.T.* 7

TROT.
The snorting beast began to *t. J.G.* 83
That *t.* became a gallop soon *J.G.* 87

TROTTING.
Beau *t.* far before *D.W.* 30

TROUBLE.
T. is grudgingly and hardly brooked *Ch.* 218
A doctor's *t.*, but without the fees *Con.* 314
Chill blasts of *t.* nip their springing joys *E.* ii 32
Would *t.* him much more *J.G.* 56
(For stormy *t.* loudest roar *Mrs. M—* 47
Or *t.* it at all *Trans.* ii 24
To exchange content for *t.*, ease for pain *V.* 64
Beget no thunder-clouds to *t.* life *V.* 76
The *t.* of a worthy priest *Y.D.* 3
Less *t.* taking twice the sum *Y.D.* 67

TROUBLED.
While his own heaven surveys the *t.* scene *Ex.* 586

TROUBLESOME.
And, like an infant, *t.* awake *T.* 427

TROUGH.
Obscene, to swill and swallow at a *t.*? *P.E.* 266

TROUT.
Like *t.* pursued, the critic in despair *P.E.* 502

TROY.
And blazing London seemed a second *T.—T.T.* 323

TRUANT.
E'er since, a *t.* boy, I passed my bounds *T.* i 114

TRUCE.
But *t.* with censure. Roving as I rove *T.* iv 232

TRUCK.
Became stone blind; precedence went in *t. T.* ii 741

TRUCKED. [374
And having *t.* thy soul, brought home the fee *Ex.*

TRUE. [*A.T.* 109
"For British nymphs, whose lords were lately *t.*
And may his hopes be *t.*! *A Tale* 64
Are marriage in its *t.* and proper shape *A.T.* 65
Wherever he found man to nature *t. Ch.* 27 [434
Heaven held his hand, the likeness must be *t. Ch.*
T. charity, a plant divinely nursed *Ch.* 573
In every tale they tell, or false or *t. Con.* 61
Admit it *t.*, the consequence is clear *Con.* 165
"Can this be *t.*!"— an arch observer cries *Con.* 231
T. modesty is a discerning grace *Con.* 373
Found him as prompt, as their desire was *t. Con.* 545
And give *t.* piety that odious name *Con.* 656
T. bliss, if man may reach it, is composed *Con.* 679
Peruses closely the *t.* Christian's face *Con.* 743
And I had rather creep to what is *t. Con.* 863
To your intrinsic merit *t. E.* i 27
T., changes will befall, and friends may part *E.* iii 10

TRUE—TRUSTING

And were I called to prove the assertion *t. E.* iii 12
And the *t.* God, the God of truth, was theirs *Ex.* 240
T. freedom is where no restraint is known *Ex.* 592
To take for truth what cannot but be *t. Ex.* 649
T. as a needle to the pole *F.* 110
Strangers to liberty 'tis *t. F.B.* 10
As youth or age persuades, and neither *t. H.* 70
" Your office is to winnow false from *t. H.* 417
That decks, with all the splendour of the *t. H.* 485
And Perjury stood up to swear all *t. H.* 563 [*H.* 508
T. Christians are, dissemblers, drunkards, thieves
Hates with a deep sincerity the *t. H.* 642
Now by the voice of his experience *t. H.* 707
His conscience owns it *t. H.F.* 16
To make his balance *t. J.G.* 72
Traced easily to its *t.* source above *J.T.* 45
That all the *t.* delights of man *Miss —* 47
" *T.*," answered an angelic guide *Mor.* 39
He spells them *t.* by intuition's light *N.A.* 69
Him answered then his loving mate and *t. N.A.* 105
T. beagle as the staunchest hound he keeps *P.E.* 87
Not more industrious are the just and *t. P.E.* 293
That education gives her, false or *t. P.E.* 358
For 'tis a rule that holds for ever *t. P.E.* 534
T., Wisdom will attend his feeble call *R.* 33
No happiness is felt except the *t. R.* 461
Amusement and *t.* knowledge hand in hand *R.* 702
Of all these sepulchres, instructors *t. St.* ii 34
T. piety is cheerful as the day *T.* 176
Just knows, and knows no more, her Bible *t. T.* 327
Possess herself of all that's good or *t. T.* 489
The gouty limb, 'tis *t.* ; but gouty limb *T.* i 107
By its *t.* worth, the comforts it affords *T.* i 397
We travel far, 'tis *t.*, but not for naught *T.* i 675
But though *t.* worth and virtue, in the mild *T.* i 678
Thy joys and sorrows, with as *t.* a heart *T.* ii 220
T., we have lost an empire—let it pass *T.* ii 263
T., we may thank the perfidy of France *T.* ii 264
Of academies, is this false or *t.? T.* ii 533   [224
To his *t.* worth, most pleased when idle most *T.* iv
T., I am no proficient, I confess *T.* iii 210 [iii 250
Friends in the friends of science, and *t.* prayer *T.*
Disturb good order, and degrade *t.* worth *T.* iii 674
T. to his charge, the close packed load behind *T.* iv 8
Whatever else they smother of *t.* worth *T.* iv 746
T. to the death, but not to be his slaves *T.* v 345
Were kingship as *t.* treasure as it seems *T.* v 357
But these are not his glory. Man, 'tis *t. T.* v 559
What none can prove a forgery, may be *t. T.* v 612
O scenes surpassing fable, and yet *t. T.* vi 759 [256
Though winter had been none, had man been *t. T.* vi
And be not costly more than of *t.* worth *T.* vi 984
Awoke and found it *t. T.B.* 48   [*T.* vi 1012
Roved far, and gathered much ; some harsh, 'tis *t.*
'Tis *t.* that, if to trifle life away *Tir.* 81
T. to the jingling of our leader's bells *Tir.* 254
Must shine by *t.* desert, or not at all *Tir.* 357
In all *t.* worth and literary skill ? *Tir.* 378   [109
T. While they live, the courtly laureate pays *T.T.*
Prepared by taste, by learning, and *t.* worth *Tir.* 678
The wretch, to nought but his ambition *t. T.T.* 30
Filled with as much *t.* merriment and glee *T.T.* 244
Is truth, if history itself be *t. T.T.* 399
And 'tis the sad complaint, and almost *t. T.T.* 732
As that of *t.* fraternal love *U.* 12
A soul, an image of Himself and therefore *t. V.* 98
Such Mary's *t.* love, that has lived *W.N.* 19
But yet, methinks to tell you *t. Y.D.* 59

TRULY.

Self-knowledge *t.* learned of course implies *Ch.* 359
That square not *t.* with the Scripture plan *Ch.* 559
That blessings *t.* sacred, and when given *Ex.* 684

" Yes, *t.*—one must scream and bawl *M.F.* 27
These, these are feelings *t.* fine *P.* 63
But Granby was, meant *t.* what he said *R.* 598
" *T.*, not I! The partial light men have *T.* 521
Interprets her more *t.*) of a rank *T.* iv 548
Of syntax, *t.*, but with little more *Tir.* 623

TRUMPERY.

Love is not pedler's *t.*, bought and sold *H.* 330

TRUMPET.

The *t.* now spoke Marmadan at hand *A.T.* 161
A *t.* that was heard through all the land *A.T.* 162
The *t.* of contention *F.* 99
The *t.* of a life-restoring day *H.* 456
The *t.* sounds, your legions swarm abroad *Her.* 53
The *t.*—will it sound ? the curtain rise ? *R.* 655
Not so ; the silver *t.*'s heavenly call *T.* 349
'Twas the last *t.*—see the Judge enthroned! *T.* 564
Inspires the news, his *t.* Keener far *T.* ii 353
May prove a *t.*, summoning your ear *T.* iv 570
Scripture is still a *t.* to his fears *T.* v 611

TRUNCHEONS.

To extort their *t.* from the puny hands *T.* v 189

TRUNDLING.

Just like unto a *t.* mop *J.G.* 139

TRUNK.

To every pane his *t.* applied *P.B.* 8   [*A.T.* ii 4
With as many hard names as would line a good *t.*
Sin's rotten *t.*, concealing its defects *P.E.* 288
In spiral rings ascends the *t.*, and lays *R.* 231 [688
And from his touchwood *t.* the mulberry-tree *T.* vi
Alike yet various. Here the grey smooth *t. T.* i 302

TRUST.

To call the few that *t.* in him his friends *Ch.* 588
The pillars of support in which they *t. Ex.* 333
Boys care but little whom they *t. F.* 20
That secrets are a sacred *t. F.* 157
The man I *t.*, if shy to me *F.* 187
Will *t.* him for a faithful generous part *H.* 336
I plant my foot upon this ground of *t. H.* 369
Man vainly *t.* his own *H.F.* 20
I would not *t.* my heart—the dear delight *M.P.* 82
Their own dear virtue their unshaken *t. T.* 284 [29
With naught in charge, he could betray no *t. P.E.*
The chase for sustenance, precarious *t.! T.* i 611
That *t.* them, and in the end disclose a face *T.* ii 693
With things so sacred as a nation's *t. T.* ii 778
Devises, while he guards his tender *t. T.* iii 561
In politic convention) put your *t. T.* v 323
We *t.* him not too far. King though he be *T.* v 336
And we too wise to *t.* them. He that takes *T.* v 496
To guard them, and to immortalize her *t. T.* v 711
Of what he deems no mean or trivial *t. T.* vi 607
That these menageries fail their *t. Tir.* 293
A man deemed worthy of so dear a *t. Tir.* 711
And, *t.* me, his utility may reach *Tir.* 731
Forgetful that the foot may crush the *t. Tir.* 792
Great titles, offices, and *t.* disgraced *Tir.* 816
And *t.* for safety to a stranger's care *Tir.* 852
They *t.* in navies, and their navies fail *T.T.* 466
They *t.* in armies, and their courage dies *T.T.* 468
But all they *t.* in withers, as it must *T.T.* 470 [471
When He commands in whom they place no *t. T.T.*

TRUSTED.

Were *t.* with his own engraven laws *Ex.* 199
I never *t.* in an arm but thine *T.* 575
The beds the *t.* treasure of their seeds *T.* iii 650

TRUSTING.

And *t.* in his God, surmounts them all *R.H.* 8
Too proud for art, and *t.* in mere force *T.T.* 683

TRUSTY.

In which I bear my *t.* sword *J.G.* 63
Can dream them *t.* to the general weal *T.* v 514

TRUTH.

In the ways of religion and *t. A.S.* 22
That man by Faith and *T.* is made a slave *A.T.* 66
T. armed it with a point so keen, so just *A.T.* 145
And slaves, by *t.* enlarged, are doubly freed *Ch.* 231
All *t.* is precious, if not all divine *Ch.* 331
'Tis *t.* divine, exhibited on earth *Ch.* 377
The *T.* she loves a sightless world blaspheme *Ch.* 416
A vehicle of virtue, *t.*, and love *Ch.* 624
Oh come not ye near innocence and *t. Con.* 39
And e'en when sober *t.* prevails throughout *Con.* 65
Through constant dread of giving *T.* offence *Con.* 129
Fate having placed all *t.* above his reach *Con.* 142
On all the vestiges of *t.* attend *Con.* 219
Their skill a *t.*, his master's a pretence *Con.* 418
Have proved them *t.* too big to be expressed *Con.* 498
And, *T.* and Wisdom gracing all He said *Con.* 526
Matched against *t.* as lasting as sublime? *Con.* 548
But *T.* divine for ever stands secure *Con.* 555
'Tis always active on the side of *T.—Con.* 602
And to say *t.*, though in its early prime *Con.* 633
Proud of his speed, to overshoot the *t. Con.* 642
It views the *t.* with a distorted eye *Con.* 669
That *t.* itself is in her head as dull *Con.* 779
Pursues the course that *t.* and nature teach *Con.* 890
And tell them *t.* divine and clear *E.* i 21
Then *T.* is hushed, that Heresy may preach *Ex.* 107
While *t.* on which eternal things depend *Ex.* 117
That *T.* and Mercy had revealed to man *Ex.* 236
And the true God, the God of *t.*, was theirs *Ex.* 240
A *t.* still sacred, and believed of old *Ex.* 351 [277
Friendship and *t.* to others, findest thou none? *Ex.*
Now borne upon the wings of *T.* sublime *Ex.* 466
Religion, if in heavenly *t.* attired *Ex.* 492 [611
The beams of heavenly *t.* have swelled the debt! *Ex.*
Those holy men, so full of *t.* and grace *Ex.* 618
Those *t.*, which neither use nor years impair *Ex.* 626
To take for *t.* what cannot but be true *Ex.* 649
The word of prophecy, those *t.* divine *Ex.* 686
Still murmuring with the solemn *t.* I teach *Ex.* 719
The sound of *t.* will then be sure to please *Ex.* 731
And *t.* alone, where'er my life be cast *Ex.* 732
And equal *t.* on either side *F.* 50 [*F.A.* 11
"Couldst thou in *t.*? and art thou taught at length
T. useful and attainable with ease *F.A.* 32
For *t.* is unwelcome, however divine *F.M.* 23
Benignity, friendship, and *t. Gr.* 44
For *t.* self-evident, with pomp impressed *H.* 109
Born capable indeed of heavenly *t. H.* 231
And *t.*, proposed to reasoners wise as they *H.* 258
That *t.* lies somewhere, if we knew but where *H.* 424
Brings many a precious pearl of *t.* to light *H.* 444
Yet *T.* is yours, remote, unenvied isle! *H.* 481
Now, *T.*, perform thine office; waft aside *H.* 570
He laughs, whatever weapon *T.* may draw *H.* 596
Insensible of *T.'s* almighty charms *H.* 655
Parent of Hope, immortal *T.!* make known *H.* 663
These are thy glorious works, eternal *T.—H.* 742
To hear plain *t.* at Judah's hallowed gate *H.* 763
And stands a witness at *T.'s* awful bar *Her.* 81
Whose fires to sacred *T.* applied *Mrs. M—* 32
This *t.* premised was needful as a text *N.A.* 71
Sure ne'er to want them mathematic *t. N.A.* 80
But they whom *T.* and Wisdom lead *P.B.* 35
T. that the theorist could never reach *P.E.* 11
Or lead him devious from the path of *t. P.E.* 60
Are hurtful is a *t.* confessed by all *P.E.* 226 [277
Finds, by degrees, the *t.* that once bore sway *P.E.*
Hatched by the beams of *t.*, denies him rest *P.E.* 241

Thou polished and high-finished foe to *t. P.E.* 341
'Tis granted, and no plainer *t.* appears *P.E.* 353
Eternal *t.* by everlasting doubt *P.E.* 473
First Appetite enlists him *T.'s* sworn foe *P.E.* 542
One leg by *t.* supported, one by lies *P.E.* 561
To virtue, delicacy, *t.*, or sense *P.E.* 513
He that hates *t.* shall be the dupe of lies *P.E.* 607
That, while thy *t.* my grosser thoughts refine *R.* 97
T. is not local, God alike pervades *R.* 119
T., wisdom, grace, and peace like that above *R.* 163
Collect the scattered *t.* that Study gleans *R.* 274
What obvious *t.* the wisest heads may miss! *R.* 458
He likes the country, but in *t.* must own *R.* 573
The friend of *T.*, the associate of sound Sense *R.* 696
Give *T.* a lustre, and make Wisdom smile *R.* 718
For 'tis a *t.* well known to most *R.C.* 95
Read, ye that run, the awful *t. St.* i 21
These *t.*, though known, too much forgot *St.* i 31
Can a *T.*, by all confessed *St.* iv 21
The *t.* is (if the *t.* may suit your ear *T.* 113
And tells, not always with an eye to *t. T.* 154
A *t.* the brilliant Frenchman never knew *T.* 328
Once the blest residence of *t.* divine *T.* 387
Reverse the sentence, let the *t.* be known *T.* 449
T. will intrude—she bids him yet beware *T.* 471
Though various foes against the *T.* combine *T.* 473
T., Hope, and Charity, and touched with awe *T.* i 2
And all her fruits by radiant *t.* matured *T.* i 607
Advancing Fashion to the post of *T.—T.* i 744
This *t.*, Philosophy, though eagle-eyed *T.* ii 174
His noble office, and, instead of *t. T.* ii 428 [337
There stands the messenger of *t.*; there stands *T.* ii
Whom *T.* and Soberness assailed in vain *T.* ii 480
All *t.* is from the sempiternal source *T.* ii 499 [543
Preach it who might. Such was their love of *t. T.* ii
The brightest *t.* that man has ever seen *T.* ii 555
When learning, virtue, piety, and *t. T.* ii 700
She smiles, appearing, as in *t.* she is *T.* iii 49 [162
Involves the combatants; each claiming *T.—T.* iii
T. undiscerned but by that holy light *T.* iii 242 [163
And *T.* disclaiming both; and thus they spend *T.* iii
Is virtue; the only lasting treasure, *t. T.* iii 269
To *T.* itself, that deigned him no reply *T.* iii 271
Tell me—and I will tell thee what is *T.—T.* iii 289
The cause of piety, and sacred *t. T.* iii 707 [270
But what is *t.*? 'Twas Pilate's question put *T.* iii
As more illumined, and with nobler *t. T.* iv 192
Imposed a gay delirium for a *t. T.* iv 528
Who is, in *t.*, the friend of no man there? *T.* v 505
"Falsehood! which whoso but suspects of *t. T.* v 642
Of rectitude and fitness, moral *t. T.* v 672 [683
The eclipse that intercepts *t.'s* heavenly beam *T.* v
To those who, posted at the shrine of *T.—T.* v 713
Our claim to feed upon immortal *t. T.* v 721
He is the freeman whom the *T.* makes free *T.* v 733
So reads he Nature, whom the lamp of *t. T.* v 845
Deceive no student. Wisdom there and *t. T.* vi 116
In heavenly *t.*; evincing, as she makes *T.* vi 183
Much to persuade, he plied his ear with *t. T.* vi 502
The meek and modest *T.*, and forcing her *T.* vi 840
And aims them at the shield of *T.* again *T.* vi 875
To palates that can taste immortal *t. T.* vi 1015
Fair science poured the light of *t. Th.* 3
" Our mutual bond of faith and *t. The Doves* 9 [73
T. that the learned pursue with eager thought *Tir.*
With *t.* poured down from every distant age *Tir.* 14
But *t.* on which depends our main concern *Tir.* 77
Betimes into the mould of heavenly *t. Tir.* 106
Sweet fiction and sweet *t.* alike prevail *Tir.* 136
The gem of *t.* from his unguarded soul *Tir.* 152
Of modest *t.* for wit's eccentric range *Tir.* 174
Learn from expert inquirers after *t. Tir.* 192
Whose only care, might *t.* presume to speak *Tir.* 193

Our early notices of t., disgraced *Tir.* 199   [629
With savoury t. and wholesome common sense *Tir.*
Whate'er she meant, this t. divine *Trans.* i 21
Receive, dear friend, the t. I teach *Trans. H.* 1
Religion, virtue, t., whate'er we call *T.T.* 286
Is t., if history itself be true *T.T.* 399
And t. cut short to make a period round *T.T.* 517
We hug the hopes of constancy and t. *V.* 53
The t. of a friend such as you *W.N.* 24
With t. from heaven, created thing adore *Y.O.* 7
To modern times, with *T.* to guide 1789, 11

TRUTH-TRIED.
And finding in the calm of t. love *T.* iii 56

TRY.   [vi 26
That we might t. the ground again, where once *T.*
They mean to t. what may at last be done *Con.* 833
Are more intelligent at least,—t. them " *Ex.* 461
(*T.* the criterion, 'tis a faithful guide) *P.E.* 514
His conduct, to the test, but t. his heart *T.* 562
T. now the merits of this blest exchange *Tir.* 173

TUBAL.
Him, *T.* named, the Vulcan of old times *T.* v 217

TUBE.
But finds that though his t. assist the sight *Ch.* 387
Such often, like the t. they so admire *Con.* 249
The explosion of the levelled t. excites *H.* 350
But never yet did philosophic t. *T.* iii 229   [978
Her golden t. through which a sensual world *T.* vi
To adjust the fragrant charge of a short t. *T.* v 55

TUCKED.
Carries her Bible t. beneath his arm *T.* 147

TUFT.
With here and there a t. of crimson yarn *T.* i 53

TUFTED.
Nor soft declivities with t. hills *R.* 333

TUGGED.
That ever dragged a chain, or t. an oar *Ex.* 527

TUITION.
By kind t. on his yielding breast *Tir.* 154
Who, if their sons some slight t. share *Tir.* 783

TULLY.
As *T.* with philosophy once dealt *Con.* 730
Has Epictetus, Plato, *T.*, preached ! *T.* ii 540
What need of Homer's verse, or *T.*'s prose *Tir.* 399
Would strive to make a Paul or *T.* stand *T.T.* 349

TUMBREL.
Like a slain deer, the t. brings him home *P.E.* 94

TUMULT.
And t., and intestine war *M.F.* 48
And hate the t. half the world enjoys *R.* 176
The t. and the overthrow, the pangs *T.* ii 254
The t. and am still. The sound of war *T.* iv 100
When *T.* lately burst his prison door *T.T.* 318

TUMULTUARY.
The tempest of t. joys *T.T.* 409

TUMULTUOUS.
Of elements t., in whom lust *T.* v 308

TUNBRIDGE WELLS.
Content with Bristol, Bath, and *T.*—*R.* 516

TUNE.
Lost, till he t. them, all their power and use *R.* 330
Calls for the kind assistance of a t. *R.* 712
" May play what t. he pleases. In the deed *T.* v 652
Of error leads them by a t. entranced *T.* vi 105
And every warbler has his t. by heart *T.T.* 655

TUNED.   [iv 704
No bard could please me but whose lyre was t. *T.*
Who then, that has a mind well strung and t. *T.* vi 262
Till t. at length to some immortal song *Con.* 907

TUNEFUL.
So t. a poet before *C.* 24
Hear the sweet accents of his t. voice *R.* 771

TURBAN.
And jewel'd t. with a smile of peace *T.* iv 29

TURBULENCE.
A life all t. and noise may seem *T.* iii 379

TURBULENT.
Through many a t. year *W.N.* 20

TURF.
Down to the very t. beneath Thy feet *H.* 50   [258
With fragrant t., and flowers as wild and fair *Ch.*
Oh then, ere the t. or tomb *St.* iv 33   [*P.F.* 15
With a t. on my breast, and a stone at my head
Yields no unpleasing ramble ; there the t. *T.* i 530
The honours of the t. as all our own *T.* ii 277 [ii 31
Dewdrops may deck the t. that hides the bones *St.*
Beneath the t. that I have often trod *T.* vi 1005

TURGID.
That turns to ridicule the t. speech *T.* v 689

TURKS.
Thus says the prophet of the *T.*—*L.W.* 1   [160
And Christians marrying may convert the *T.*—*A.T.*

TURKEY.
A *T.* carpet was his lawn *Ep.* ii 21

TURN.
To see the oppressor in his t. oppressed *Ch.* 74
Their acrid temper t., as soon as stirred *Ch.* 503
Oh! thwart me not, Sir Soph, at every t. *Con.* 91
Just so the Omnipotent, who t. *E.* i 73   [544
The t. are quick, the polished points surprise *Ch.*
And tricks and t., that Fancy may devise *Ex.* 137
T. downward, and the lowest pair succeed *H.* 14
And just when evening t. the blue vault grey *H.* 79
While Passion t. aside from its due scope *H.* 113
From which our nicer optics t. away *H.* 494   [244
" Keep wisdom, or meet vengeance in your t. ! *Ex.*
He held them up, and in his t. *J.G.* 185
Where'er he t., enjoyment and delight *P.E.* 47
Called to these crystal streams, do ye t. off *P.E.* 265
Should t. to writers of an abler sort *R.* 716   [ii 8
With anxious meaning, Heavenward t. his eye ! *St.*
Heaven t. from with abhorrence and disdain *T.* 72
T. eastward now, and Fancy shall apply *T.* 97
And if he but suspects a frown, t. pale *T.* 216
To nourish pride, or t. the weakest head *T.* 366
Seen in the dim horizon, t. thee pale *T.* i 667
Which only poets know. The shifts and t. *T.* ii 230
T. to the stroke his adamantine scales *T.* ii 324
Or merry t. in all he ever wrote *T.* ii 473
If Christ, then why resort at every t. *T.* ii 535
Alighting, t. the key in her own door *T.* ii 653
And suffocates the breath at every t. *T.* ii 819
Or t. to nourishment, digested well *T.* iii 396 [637
May t. the clod, and wheel the compost home *T.* iii
And wins them, but to lose them in his t. *T.* iv 63
It t. submitted to my view, t. round *T.* iv 98
As he that travels far, oft t. aside *T.* iv 234   [252
Great purposes with ease, that t. and wields *T.* v
To t. purveyor to an overgorged *T.* v 421
We t. to dust, and all our mightiest works *T.* v 531
That t. to ridicule the turgid speech *T.* v 689
To latest times ; and Sculpture, in her t. *T.* v 709
As taught him too to tremble in his t. *T.* vi 378
Shall seek it, and not find it, in his t. *T.* vi 600

Why takes the gentler Moon her *t.* to rise *Tir.* 38
And if, soon after having burned, by *t. Tir.* 65
Would *t.* our steps into a wiser train *Tir.* 260
With all varieties of ill by *t. Tir.* 475
How! *t.* again to tales long since forgot *Tir.* 545
But they have human feelings—*t.* to them *Tir.* 806
Your wisdom and your ways—to you I *t. Tir.* 812
With Gospel lore, *t.* infidels themselves *Tir.* 826
What character, what *t.* thou wilt assume *Tir.* 853
T. him adrift upon a rolling sea *Tir.* 868
Or *t.* them into shops and auction rooms *Tir.* 902
That *t.* and *t.*, to indicate *Trans.* ii 8
To *t.* the course of Helicon that way *T.T* 183
To *t.* a penny in the way of trade *T.T.* 421
Cold in my *t.*, and unconcerned like you *V.* 6
Invigorate by *t.* the springs of life *Y.O.* 78

TURNED.
She saw, and *t.* her rosy cheek away *A.T.* 87
He *t.* and viewed it oft on every side *A.T.* 203
Though some have *t.* and *t.* it *F.* 207
If self-exalting claims be *t.* adrift *H.* 530
And *t.* into the park or mead to graze *R.* 627
While danger passed is *t.* to present joy *T.* 256

TURNING.
"Go, fellow!—whither?"—*t.* short about *E.* iii 24
When, *t.* round his head, he saw *J.G.* 51
So *t.* to his horse, he said *J.G.* 197
And, *t.* from my nursery window, drew *M.P.* 30
T. short round, strutting, and sideling *P.T.* 39
Nor view of waters *t.* busy mills *R.* 334
The gilded equipage, and *t.* loose *T.* vi 702
Then *t.*, he regales his listening wife *Tir.* 324

TURNPIKE.
How in a trice the *t.* men *J.G.* 119

TURNPIKE-GATES.
And now the *t.* again *J.G.* 241

TURNPIKE-ROAD.
In contemplation of a *t. R.* 506

TURRETS.
Here glittering *t.* rise, upbearing high *T.* v 110
That all its tempest-beaten *t.* shake *T.* v 527

TURTLE.
Or voice of *t.* in your land is heard *H.* 470
T. and venison all his thoughts employ *P.E.* 220
The *t.* thus addressed her mate *The Doves* 7

TUTELARY.
Thou *t.* friend of helpless men? *Ch.* 42
With *t.* goddesses and gods *T.* vi 235
His fostering power, and *t.* care *T.T.* 257
Her sovereign's *t.* care 1789, 39

TUTOR.
Or academic *t.*, teaching youths *N.A.* 79
With reverend *t.*, clad in habit lay *P.E.* 371
Father, and friend, and *t.*, all in one *Tir.* 544
Minority. No *t.* charged his hand *Y.O.* 157

TUTORED.
She *t.* some in Dædalus's art *A.T.* 52
That men, if gently *t.*, will not learn *Ch.* 496
Well *t.* Learning, from his books *Mrs. M—* 37
And *t.* with a relish more exact *T.* iv 741
And thus, well *t.* only while we share *Tir.* 195

TWAIN.
The bottles *t.* behind his back *J.G.* 123
United yet divided, *t.* at once *T.* i 77

TWANG.
To me is odious as the nasal *t. T.* ii 436

TWANGED.
Some whispered softly, and some *t.* aloud *Ch.* 518

TWANGING.
Hark! 'tis the *t.* horn o'er yonder bridge *T.* iv 1

TWEEDLING.
Dick heard, and *t.*, ogling, bridling *P.T.* 38

TWELVE.
And the *t.* standards of the tribes unfurled *Ex.* 211
And charged with octavos and *t. Gr.* 27
T. years have elapsed since I last took a view *P.F.* 5

TWENTIETH.
The *t.* year is well nigh past *M.* 1
Whose arm this *t.* winter I perceive *T.* i 145
Though lean and beggared, every *t.* pace *T.* iv 468

TWENTY.
"Come ten, come *t.*—should an army call *A.T.* 185
Dear Joseph—five and *t.* years ago *E.* iii 1
Since *t.* sheets of lead, God knows *E.* iv 27
(I would say *t.* sheets of prose) *E.* iv 28

TWICE.
Though *t.* a Cæsar could not bend thee now *Ex.* 477
These *t.* ten tedious years, yet we *J.G.* 7
"My head is *t.* as big as yours *J.G.* 187
Teach him to fence and figure *t.* a week *P.E.* 366
With *t.* four hundred men *R.G.* 24 [714
As *t.* seven years, his beauties had then first *T.* iv
Less trouble taking *t.* the sum *Y.D.* 67

TWIG.
On *t.* of hawthorn he regaled *Ep.* ii 17
Some *t.* of that old scourge are left behind *Ex.* 517
That overhangs a torrent, to a *t. T.* i 484 [419
But barren, at the expense of neighbouring *t. T.* iii
And cherries hang her *t.* Geranium boasts *T.* iii 577
From many a *t.* the pendent drops of ice *T.* vi 81
Fostering propitious, thou becamest a *t. Y.O.* 39
Then *t.*; then sapling; and, as century rolled *Y.O.* 62

TWILIGHT.
Prefer the *t.* of a darker time *T.* 541
Within the *t.* of their distant shades *T.* i 304
So spent in parlour *t.*, such a gloom *T.* iv 278

TWIN.
Yesterday's face *t.* image of to-day *H.* 102
And parrots with *t.* cherries in their beak *T.* i 38
Dire is the frequent curse, and its *t.* sound *T.* iv 487
T. at all points—yet this obtains in all *T.* iv 738
Clothe the *t.* brethren in each others' dress *T.T.* 45
Didst burst thine egg, as thine the fabled *t. Y.O.* 35

TWIN-BORN.
Wisdom and Goodness are *t.*, one heart *Ex.* 634

TWINE.
Who would not *t.* a wreath for Thee *Dr.* 23
The serpent Error *t.* round human hearts *P.E.* 34

TWINED. [36
Where Nichol swung the birch and *t.* the bays *V.*

TWINGES.
Though conscience will have *t.* now and then *T T.*425

TWINING.
Or *t.* silken threads round ivory reels *T.* iv 264

TWINKLE.
To the green blade that *t.* in the sun *T.* vi 251

TWINKLING.
Those *t.*, tiny lustres of the land *B.B.* 5
A star or two, just *t.* on thy brow *T.* iv 253
As here and there a *t.* star descried *Tir.* 843

TWIRL.
I *t.* my thumbs, fall back into my chair *Con.* 115

TWISTED.
Gave them a *t.* form vermicular *T.* i 30 [772
The children, crooked, and *t.*, and deformed *T.* ii

TWISTS.
And with a dexterous jerk soon *t*. him down *T*. iv 62
TWITCHED.
In unsuspecting pomp. *T*. from the perch *T*. iv 448
TWITTER.
And with much *t*., and much chatter *P.T.* 15
TWITTERED.
The linnet *t*. out his parting song *A.T.* 76
TWITTERING.
To learn the *t*. of a meaner bird? *Con*. 448
TWO.
(*T*. themes to Nature's eye for ever sealed) *Ch*. 362
T. bosom friends, each pensively inclined *Con*. 507
T. Poets, (poets, by report *Dr*. 1
(*T*. nymphs adorned with every grace *D.W.* 7
T. goldfinches, whose sprightly song *F.B.* 4
To spend *t*. hours in dressing for the day *H*. 80
As when *t*. pilgrims in a forest stray *H*. 276
Had *t*. stone bottles found *J.G.* 66
T. nymphs, both nearly of an age *J.P.* 1
Appeared *t*. lovely foes *L.R.* 6
Upheld by *t*.; yet still thou lovest *M*. 39 [594
Swallow the *t*. grand nostrums they dispense *P.E.*
Though ears she gave me *t*., gave me no ear *N.A.* 28
The nymph between *t*. chariot glasses *P.B.* 20
Remarks *t*. loiterers that have lost their way *P.E.*, 386
Which is the saintlier worthy of the *t*.? *T*. 105
You have *t*. servants,—Tom, an arch, sly rogue *T*. 201
So sit *t*. kings of Brentford on one throne *T*. i 78
And so *t*. citizens who take the air *T*. i 79
Between *t*. poles upon a stick transverse *T*. i 561
She has her praise. Now mark a spot or *t*. *T*. i 725
T. leaves produced, *t*. rough indented leaves *T*. iii 526
A star or *t*., just twinkling on thy brow *T*. iv 253
Diversified, that *t*. were never found *T*. iv 737 [352
T. empirics he stands, and with swoln cheeks *T*. ii
And eke did roar right merrily, *t*. staves *T*. vi 662
Some place, a spark or *t*. not yet extinct *T*. vi 684
T. gods divide them all—Pleasure and Gain *T*. vi 892
Still keeps a seat or *t*. for worth and grace *Tir*. 433
To entertain a thief or *t*. in pay *Tir*. 693
Discreetly limited to *t*. at most *Tir*. 770
T. or three millions of the human race *T.T.* 423
Like the *t*. figures at St. Dunstan's stand *T.T.* 527
An ell or *t*. of prospect we command *T.T.* 581
Now stars, *t*. lobes, protruding, paired exact *Y.O.* 36
TWO-LEAVED.
Saw Babylon set wide her *t*. brass *Ex*. 59
TWO-THIRDS.
And add *t*. of the remaining half *T*. iii 131
T. of all the virtue that remains *Tir*. 810
TYPES.
In staggering *t*., his predecessor's tale *T*. v 419
TYPICAL.
Ensanguined hearts, clubs *t*. of strife *T*. iv 218
TYRANNIC.
The art that baffles Time's *t*. claim *M.P.* 9
TYRANNIZING.
A clear escape from *t*. lust *T*. v 579
TYRANNOUS.
The oppression of a *t*. control *T*. vi 455
TYRANNY.
The *t*. that doomed them to the fire *T*. v 731
T. sends the chain that must abridge *T.T.* 474
To stoop to *T*.'s usurped command *T.T.* 440
TYRANT.
The fear of *t*. custom, and the fear *Con*. 181
Pulled down the *t*. India served with dread *Ex*. 366
The puny *t*. burns to subjugate *H*. 189
A land that distant *t*. hate in vain *Her*. 89
Fixed their *t*. habitations *N.C.* 38
The Babylonian *t*. with a nod *P.E.* 130
To seek that peace a *t*.'s frown denies *R*. 770
You chains and bondage for a *t*.'s sake *T*. v 352
Woe to the *t*., if he dare intrude *T*. vi 406
And teach one *t*. pity for his drudge *T*. vi 728
The chain that binds them, and a *t*.'s sway *T.T.* 283
TYROS.
The management of *t*. of eighteen *Tir*. 220

U.

UBIQUARIAN.
A *u*. presence and control *Tir*. 266
UGLY.
Some men employ their health, an *u*. trick *Con*. 311
But here and there an *u*. smutch appears *T*. iv 608
ULTIMATE.
This riving stroke, this *u*. divorce *H*. 640
UMBRAGEOUS.
U. walks and solitary seats *R*. 258
And ash far-stretching his *u*. arm *T*. i 311
UMBRELLA.
Of other screen, the thin *u*. spread *T*. i 260
Her train and her *u*. all her care *T*. iv 552
UMPIRE.
For her the Judgment, *u*. in the strife *Tir*. 29
UNABLE.
Thee we reject, *u*. to abide *T*. v 879
UNACCOMPLISHED.
A longer respite, *u*. yet *T*. ii 67
UNACCUSED.
Immured though *u*., condemned untried *T*. v 398
UNACQUAINTED.
They are so *u*. with man *A.S.* 15
UNADORNED.
Else *u*., with many a gay festoon *T*. iii 667
UNADULTERATE.
Prove it. A breath of *u*. air *T*. iv 750
Thine *u*. manners are less soft *T*. v 465
UNALARMED.
To thy straw couch, and slumber *u*. *T*. iii 345
And slumbers *u*.! Now, ere you sleep *T*. iv 566
Scarce shuns me; and the stockdove *u*. *T*. vi 307
UNALLIED.
With joy not *u*. to thine 1789, 59
UNALLOY'D.
Yellow and bright, as bullion *u*. *T*. vi 171
UNALTERABLE.
'Tis an *u*. fixed decree *Con*. 467
But fixed, *u*. care *S*. 9

UNAMBIGUOUS.
The *u.* footsteps of the God *T.* v 812
UNAMBITIOUS.
To me an *u.* mind, content *T.* iv 798
And *u.* course, reflecting clear *T.* vi 723
UNAPT.
U. to learn, and formed of stubborn stuff *T.* iv 636
UNASSAYED.
And at this moment *u.* in song *T.* iii 451
UNASSISTED.
Where *u.* sight no beauty sees *R.* 56
UNASSUAGED.
Of hunger *u.*, has interposed *T.* vi 463
UNATTENDED.
And Puss remained still *u. R.C.* 66
UNATTIRED.
But, *u.* in that becoming vest *T.T.* 722
UNAVAILING.
Till Nature, *u.* Nature, foiled *T.* v 627
UNAVOIDABLY.
Most *u.* creates *F.* 107
UNBALANCED.
Deciduous, or its own *u.* weight *T.* v 40
UNBELIEF.
Thus often *U.*, grown sick of life *T.* 445
UNBEND.
With whom, dismissing forms, he may *u. R.* 444
To warn, and teach him safely to *u. Tir.* 608
UNBIDDEN.
U., and not now to be controlled *T.* vi 551
UNBINDS.
In early years connected, time *u. Tir.* 439
UNBLAMEABLE.
But if, *u.* in word and thought *H.* 622
Some lead a life *u.* and just *T.* 283
UNBLAMED.
Your Hope shall stand *u.*, perhaps admired *H.* 616
UNBLEMISHED.
And taught the *u.* to preserve with care *T.* iii 83
UNBLESSED.
To live, *u.*, in torpid ease *Miss* — 27
The better part of man *u. St.* vi 31
UNBLEST.
U., and that the battle is the Lord's ? *Ex.* 353
O happy shades!—to me *u. S.* 1
UNBLIGHTED.
Finds happiness *u.*; or, if found *T.* iv 334
UNBLOODIED.
And forced the blunt and yet *u.* steel *T.* v 215
UNBLOWN.
Boys are, at best, but pretty buds *u. Tir.* 446
UNBORN.
My very gentle reader yet *u. T.* ii 581
UNBORROWED.
And soaring on her own *u.* wings *T.* 488
UNBOUGHT.
That man will freely take an *u.* bliss *H.* 335
UNBOUND.
Thy *u.* spirit into bonds again *M.P.* 87
UNBOUNDED.
Flows into her; *u.* is her joy *T.* vi 803
For her, amasses an *u.* store *Tir.* 15

UNBRIBED.
Paul's love of Christ, and steadiness *u. H.* 580
UNBRIDLED.
To give Religion her *u.* scope *T.T.* 71
UNBURIED.
Like an *u.* carcass tricked with flowers *T.* vi 992
UNBUTTONED.
The little ones, *u.*, glowing hot *Tir.* 304
UNCANDID.
But to the proud, *u.*, insincere *T.* iii 275
UNCERTAIN.
That seems to swing *u.*, and yet falls *T.* i 358
His devious course *u.*, seeking home *T.* iii 3
Destroys them.—Skies *u.*, now the heat *Y.O.* 74
UNCHANGEABLY.
U. connected with its cause) *T.T.* 443
UNCHANGED.
He rears *u.* his barren head *Miss* — 39
UNCHASTE.
"But oh! if, fickle and *u. The Doves* 29
UNCLEAN.
But, if thy table be indeed *u. Tir.* 735
UNCOLOUR'D.
And all this uniform *u.* scene *T.* vi 178
UNCOMMON.
Must have a most *u.* skull *P.T.* 8
UNCONCERN.
With mad rapidity and *u. T.T.* 464
UNCONCERNED.
And whistling, as if *u.* and gay *R.* 589
Forth goes the woodman, leaving *u. T.* v 41
But not its Author. *U.* who formed *T.* v 793
Cold in my turn, and *u.* like you *V.* 6
UNCONFINED.
He made at first, though free and *u. Ch.* 17
And chaste, though *u.*, whom I extol *T.* iii 713
For her the Fancy, roving *u. Tir.* 21
UNCONSCIOUS.
Against an innocent *u.* breast *Ex.* 431
U. nature, all that he surveys *H.* 740
But all *u.* whom it held *R.C.* 52
Frowning as if in his *u.* arm *T.* i 381
Stand up *u.*, and refute the charge *T.* ii 824
U. of a less propitious clime *T.* iii 567
His horse and him, *u.* of them all *T.* iv 22
Through pathless wastes and woods, *u.* once *T.* iv 573
His spirit takes, *u.* of a chain *T.* v 776
Laborious, yet *u.* of her toil *Tir.* 18
Churchill, himself *u.* of his powers *T.T.* 672
UNCONSCIOUSNESS.
With mute *u.* of what he saw *Y.O.* 146
UNCONTAMINATE.
Is not : the pure and *u.* blood *T.* vi 789
UNCONTROLLED.
By vicious Custom, raging *u. T.* iii 682
And howl and roar as likes them, *u. T.* vi 404
UNCORRUPT.
Receive me now, not *u.* as then *R.* 381
In doctrine *u.*; in language plain *T.* ii 400
UNCOUTH.
In characters *u.*, and spelt amiss *T.* i 283
But proud of his *u.*, ill-chosen task *T.* iii 644 [337
Though wild their strange vagaries, and *u. T.* vi

UNCOUTHLY.
Dancing u. to the quivering flame T. iv 276
UNCOVERED.
The heaths u. and the moors A Tale 17
UNCROWDED.
U., yet safe sheltered from the storm Y.O. 55
UNCTUOUS.
Her u. olives, and her purple vines Her. 7
UNCURED.
Such want it;—and that want, u. St. vi 33
UNDAUNTED.
U. still, though wearied and perplexed T.T. 366
UNDAWNING.
A prisoner in the yet u. east T. iv 130
UNDAZZLED.
U., and detects and counts his spots? T. i 714
UNDEBAUCHED.
And u. But we have bid farewell T. iii 744
Whose character, yet u., retains Tir. 809
UNDECISIVE.
Her u. scales. In this she lays T. iv 484
UNDEFILED.
Their union u. A Tale 6
For sanctity of manners u. T. iii 260
His mind informed, his morals u. Tir. 683
UNDELIGHTFUL.
Not u. is an hour to me T. iv 277
UNDEPRAVED.
Disdains not, nor the palate, u. T. i 124
UNDERGO.
Afric's sons should u. N.C. 37
Of universal nature u. T. iv 325
UNDERSTAND.
Given him a soul, and bade him u. Con. 430
But, grave dissemblers! could not u. Ex. 159
Improve the kind occasion, u. R. 345
To u. and choose thee for their own T. iii 295
But not to u. a treasure's worth T. vi 50
UNDERSTANDING.
Has little u., and no wit T. 324
'Tis thus the u. takes repose T. iv 296
The virtue, temper, u., taste T. iv 790
UNDERSTOOD.
Both sides deceived, if rightly u. Ch. 622
If this be plain, 'tis plainly u. Con. 435
And yet may prove, when u. E. i 89
Puffed up with gifts they never u. Ex. 130
The Sacred Book, its value u. Ex. 616
And bliss not seen by blessings u. H. 148
Have speech for him, and u. with ease N.A. 58
How dimly seen, how faintly u.! R. 88
And u. too well the weighty terms T. ii 477
How seldom used, how little u.! T.T. 64
And so disdained the rules he u. T.T. 687
All creatures with precision u. Y.O. 151
UNDERTAKE.
Alas for the poet! who dares u. F.M. 13
With much compassion u. the task P.E. 389
Good temper; spirits prompt to u. T. i 400
"Do they themselves, who u. for hire T. v 644
But they that fight for freedom, u. T.T. 284
Whoever u. a friend's great part V. 59
UNDERTOOK.
They never u., they little note T. ii 308

UNDESCRIED.
A witness u. Q.V. 30
UNDESERVED.
Of fancied scorn and u. disdain Con. 348
Grace u., yet surely not for all T. 484
UNDESIGNED.
Of u. severity, that glanced T. v 170
UNDESIRED.
Shine not, or u. and hated shine R. 351
Brings he, to sweeten fruits so u.? Tir. 578
UNDEVIATING.
With such u. and even force T. v 37
Of the u. and punctual sun T. vi 127
UNDIRECTED.
And left them to an u. choice T. ii 802
UNDISCERNED.
Truths u. but by that holy light T. iii 242
UNDISCERNING.
Causeless, and daubed with u. praise T. v 360
UNDISCOVERABLE.
The u. secret sleeps T. v 537
UNDISPUTED.
Possess for me their u. lot T. 527
UNDISSEMBLING.
Sad as it is, his u. heart Con. 712
His u. virtue to my breast R. 380
UNDISSOLVED.
Lies u.; while silently beneath T. v 99
UNDISTINGUISHED.
Blest he, though u. from the crowd T. i 592
UNDISTINGUISHING.
Wit, u., is apt to strike T.T. 101
UNDISTURBED.
There, u. by Folly, and apprised T. iii 34
Of u. Retirement, and the hours T. iv 142
Healthful and u. by factious fumes T. v 513
Then sleep was u. by Fear, unscared T. iv 561
UNDOES.
Depreciates and u. us in our own? T. iii 284
UNDONE.
O Israel, of all nations most u.! Ex. 257
Where to succeed is not to be u. Her. 88
While self-betrayed, and wilfully u. Tir. 171
Much trash unuttered, and some ills u. Tir. 733
UNDOUBTED.
"With June's u. right J.P. 36
U. scholarship and genuine worth Tir. 280
UNDREADED.
The u. volley with a sword of straw T. ii 811
UNDRESSED.
To rise at noon, sit slipshod and u. H. 75
Religion weaves for her, and half u. T.T. 723
UNDUE.
Pleasure admitted in u. degree P.E. 269
UNDULATES.
Just u. upon the listening ear T. i 175
UNDULATING.
Was graced with many an u. light T.T. 573
UNDULATION.
By restless u.; even the oak T. i 377
UNEMBARRASSED.
And there resume an u. brow Con. 401

UNEMPLOYED.
O'erlooked and *u*., fell sick, and died *T*. ii 733
At least neglect not, or leave *u*. *T*. iii 368
Not *u*., and finding rich amends *T*. iv 729
Not slothful he, though seeming *u*. *T*. vi 928

UNENCUMBERED.
Heaven's easy, artless, *u*. plan! *T*. 22

UNENLIGHTENED.
Let cottagers, and *u*. swains *H*. 240
Or *u*., and too proud to learn *T*. ii 549

UNENVIED.
Yet Truth is yours, remote *u*. isle! *H*. 481
And take *u*. the reward they sought *T*. 528
U. there, he may sustain alone *Tir*. 535

UNEQUAL.
Halting on crutches of *u*. size *P.E.* 560

UNEQUALLED.
Else, though *u*. to the goal he flies *T*. 15

UNEQUIVOCAL.
"The *u*., authentic deed *T*. v 653

UNERRING.
He feels his need of an *u*. guide *Ch*. 346
To sift and search them with *u*. eyes *Ex*. 88
And the foe's *u*. aim *St*. iv 12

UNEXAMPLED.
Portentous, *u*., unexplained *T*. ii 58

UNEXHAUSTED.
His *u*. mine, the sordid vice *P.E.* 51

UNEXPECTED.
Brings forth that *u*. hour *E*. i 30
O welcome guest, though *u*. here! *M.P.* 12
With luxury of *u*. sweets *T*. i 533
And wraps him in an *u*. tomb *T*. v 143
Arrived, he feels an *u*. change *Tir*. 567

UNEXPERIENCED.
And teach her, *u*. yet and green *P.E.* 317

UNEXPLAINED.
Portentous, unexampled, *u*. *T*. ii. 58

UNEXPLORED.
And of the worst, that *u*. he leaves *F.A.* 31

UNFADING.
Storms but enliven its *u*. green *Ch*. 576
The *u*. laurel, and the virgin too! *Ex*. 601

UNFAILING.
Is thine;—best gift, the *u*. source of joy *S*. ii 13
Maintains its hold with such *u*. sway *Tir*. 316

UNFAIRLY.
And even Virtue, so *u*. matched *Ch*. 511

UNFATHERLY.
Condemns the *u*., the imprudent part *Tir*. 866

UNFATHOMED.
Grace, knowledge, comfort—an *u*. store? *T*. ii 538

UNFATIGUED.
His warfare is within. There *u*. *T*. vi 935

UNFEELING.
I envy that *u*. shrub *P*. 15
Wooed an *u*. statue for his wife *P.E.* 528

UNFEIGNED.
Concludes his *u*. love of him, a feint *Con*. 748
With close fidelity and love *u*. *T.T.* 73

UNFELT.
(*U*. the fury of those bursting mines) *Her*. 8
Perhaps thou gavest me, though *u*., a kiss *M.P.* 25
Shall fill thee with delights *u*. before *R*. 360

Flies swiftly, and *u*. the task proceeds *T*. iv 166
And slowly, and by most *u*., the face *T*. iv 324 [784
Till then *u*., what hands divine have wrought *T*. v

UNFINISHED.
Let fall the *u*. wreath, and roved for fruit *T*. vi 1011

UNFIT.
Go! thou art all *u*. to share *M.B.* 1
In wild disorder, and *u*. for use *T*. ii 805
Bestial, a meagre intellect, *u*. *T*. v 454
The heart is hard in nature, and *u*. *T*. vi 321
I hastily seized it, *u*. as it was *The Rose* 9

UNFLEDGED.
The *u*. raven and the lion's whelp *T*. vi 461

UNFOLD.
For God *u*. by slow degrees *E*. i 59
Faithful, and faithfully informed, *u*. *Ex*. 647
U. his flock, then under bank or bush *R*. 397
Meridian sunbeams tempt him to *u*. *T*. 60
U. its bosom; buds, and leaves, and sprigs *T*. iv 153

UNFOLDED.
U. genially and spread the man *P.E.* 412
All Heaven *u*. to my eyes *St*. iii 11
Wandering, and littering with *u*. silks *T*. vi 280

UNFORESEEN.
Let nothing adverse, nothing *u*. *Ch*. 131
And now—alas, for *u*. mishaps! *Con*. 321
And happy in their *u*. release *T*. ii 126
Then God might be surprised, and *u*. *T*. ii 171

UNFORGIVING.
Secured it by an *u*. frown *T*. ii 247

UNFREQUENTED.
To pathless wilds and *u*. plains *A.T.* 26

UNFRIENDLY.
U. to Society's chief joys *Con*. 252
They left their bones beneath *u*. skies *Ex*. 524

UNFRUITFUL.
Inveterate habits choke the *u*. heart *R*. 41
The worthless and *u*. of mankind" *T*. 500

UNFURLED.
Heaven speed the canvass, gallantly *u*. *Ch*. 123
And the twelve standards of the tribes *u*. *Ex*. 211
And all the banners been *u*. *Q.V.* 23
When disposition, like a sail *u*. *Tir*. 450
The standards of all nations are *u*. *T.T.* 454

UNFURNISHED.
Hence an *u*. and a listless mind *P.E.* 425
To fill the void of an *u*. brain *T*. iv 209
The most *u*. with the means of life *T*. iv 770

UNGENIAL.
U. blasts attending curl the streams *T.T.* 213

UNGOVERNED.
Of some *u*. passion every hour *P.E.* 276

UNGRACED.
Courage, *u*. by these, affronts the skies *T.T.* 378

UNGRATEFUL.
Unpleasant and *u*. *F*. 186
Murmuring and *u*. Discontent *R*. 759

UNGRATIFIED.
U.: for there some noble lord *T*. vi 673

UNGUARDED.
Might well alarm the most *u*. mind *P.E.* 58
Conducts the *u*. nose to such a whiff *T*. iv 469
The *u*. door was safe; men did not watch *T*. iv 559
The gem of truth from his *u*. soul *Tir*. 152

UNHALLOWED.
Dishonour with *u*. play *St*. vi 27

UNHAPPILY.
But if, *u.* deceived, I dream *Ch.* 632
UNHAPPY.
O happy peasant! O *u.* bard! *T.* 331
UNHARMONIOUS.
And groves, if *u.* yet secure *T.* iii 734
UNHEALTHFUL.
Thy vigorous pulse, and the *u.* East *T.* iv 363
UNHEARD.
That cleaves the yielding air *u. E.* i 88
And cheers the drooping flowers, *u.*, unseen *J.T.* 40
To waste *u.* the music of his strains *R.* 548
Ring with ecstatic sounds *u.* before *R.* 780
Its wasted tones and harmony *u. T.* iv 480
UNHEEDED.
That passes all he sees *u.* by *R.* 340
Or pass *u.* this auspicious morn *S.* ii 4
UNHOPED-FOR.
Then boast (but wait for that *u.* hour) *T.* 401
UNHORSE.
While others, not so satisfied, *u. T.* vi 701
UNHURT.
Escapes *u.* beneath so warm a veil *T.* iv 332
UNIFORM.
And all this *u.* uncolour'd scene *T.* vi 178
UNIMPAIRED.
Through wintry rigours *u.* endure *Con.* 650
But strong for service still, and *u. T.* ii 705
Though few now taste thee *u.* and pure *T.* iii 43
The piercing cold, but feels it *u. T.* iv 361
U., and shrill, and clear *Trans.* iii 23
The force that agitates not *u. Y.O.* 83
UNIMPEACHABLE.
Hence merchants, *u.* of sin *T.* iv 676
By the *u.* and awful oath *T.* v 549
Perfect and *u.* of blame *T.* v 867
UNIMPEACHED.
By theirs whose bright example, *u. Ex.* 656
A liberty like his, who *u. T.* v 759
UNIMPORTANT.
No *u.*, though a silent task *T.* iii 378
UNIMPROVED.
Thy glory, and thy shame if *u.) Ex.* 689
Shall find the blessing *u.*, a curse *T.* 524
That *u.* those many moments fly? *Tir.* 616
UNINCUMBERED.
And conscious of an *u.* back *Ch.* 174
UNINDEBTED.
Quite *u.* to the tricks of art *T.T.* 525
UNINFORMED.
See it an *u.* and idle mass *Her.* 26
By navigators *u.* as they *T.* i 630
The *u.* and heedless souls of men *T.* v 864
UNINJURED.
U., but expect the upholding aid *T.* iii 658
Falls a soft murmur on the *u.* ear *T.* iv 93
U., with inimitable art *T.* vi 195
UNINTERRUPTED.
Of long *u.* evening know *T.* iv 143
UNION.
Their *u.* undefiled *A Tale* 6
A *u.* with the vast terraqueous whole *Ch.* 122
Of hearts in *u.* mutually disclosed *Con.* 680
For 'tis a *u.* that bespeaks *F.* 47
Of *u.*, and converts the sacred band *T.* ii 686
Resolved a *u.* formed for life *The Doves* 27
A *u.* formed as mine with thee *U.* 7
U. of hearts without a flaw between *V.* 86
UNISON.
Some chord in *u.* with what we hear *T.* vi 4
And both in *u. Trans.* iv 36
UNITE.
Shall meet, *u.*, and part no more *E.* i 32
In vain the talkative *u. F.* 67
UNITED.
Meet their opposers with *u.* strength *Con.* 700
They reign *u.* there *L.R.* 28
U. yet divided, twain at once *T.* i 77
That bids defiance to the *u.* powers *T.* ii 769
The scorn of danger, and *u.* hearts *T.* v 377
"See!" with *u.* wonder, cried *Th.* 5
UNITING.
Whose lines *u.* by an honest art *H.* 756
UNIVERSAL.
Cheers what were else a *u.* shade *Ch.* 94
Spreads wide her arms of *u.* love *Ch.* 596
Cry to her *u.* realm "Rejoice!" *H.* 54
Of an eternal, *u.* war *H.* 648
Heaven's harmony is *u.* love *P.E.* 78
This *u.* frame, thus wondrous fair *R.* 90
Hark! *u.* Nature shook and groaned *T.* 563
Is free to all men—*u.* prize *T.* iii 724
Relaxed into a *u.* grin *T.* iv 204
Of *u.* nature undergoes *T.* iv 325
'Tis *u.* soldiership has stabbed *T.* iv 617
Rules *u.* nature. Not a flower *T.* vi 240
And own, the law of *u.* love *T.* vi 360
All, in the *u.* Father's love? *T.* vi 449
UNJAUNDICED.
With an *u.* eye *Dr.* 20
UNJUST.
Lewd, avaricious, arrogant, *u. Ex.* 56
Cry to the proud, the cruel, and *u. Ex.* 268
Thy monarchs arbitrary, fierce, *u. Ex.* 528
His recompense in both *u.* alike *P.E.* 32
UNKERCHIEFED.
With bony and *u.* neck defies *T.* 137
UNKIND.
Thou couldst become *u.* at last *The Doves* 31
Or, if he prove *u.* (as who can say *Tir.* 895
UNKINDNESS.
Against *u.*, absence, and neglect *T.* vi 627
UNKNOWN.
Steered Britain's oak into a world *u. Ch.* 25
But gives it usefulness *u.* before *Con.* 597
Leads to the land where sorrow is *u. E.* ii 10
Made sure by prodigies till then *u. Ex.* 174
And while the world beside, that plan *u. Ex.* 237
Bound in the fetters of an *u.* tongue *H.* 450
But Winter, armed with terrors here *u. H.* 473
A false religion, is *u.* to you *H.* 486
Adieus and farewells are a sound *u. M.P.* 33
Resolved to be *u. Q.V.* 38
Eternity's *u.* expanse appears *R.* 149
The Christian has an art *u.* to thee *R.H.* 4
Once went I forth, and found, till then *u. T.* 220
Assuming thus a rank *u.* before *T.* ii 370
Of multitudes *u.*! Hail, rural life! *T.* iv 783
Yet few remember them. They lived *u. T.* v 724
Why hire a lodging in a house *u. Tir.* 555
His post not mean, his talents not *u. Tir.* 723
Too proud to adopt the thoughts of one *u. Tir.* 785

UNKNOWN—UNQUENCHED

Is all chance-medley, and *u*., to me *Tir.* 858
Seizes events as yet *u*. to man *T.T.* 498
To carry nature lengths *u*. before *T.T.* 558 [*T.T.*696
And charms the woodland scenes, and wilds *u*.
The future, best *u*., but at thy mouth *Y.O.* 43

UNLACKEYED.
Is hackneyed home *u*.; who, in haste *T.* ii 652

UNLETTERED.
Hour after hour, the yet *u*. boy *Con.* 12
And many a gay *u*. spark *P.* 32
With all the simple and *u*. poor *P.E.* 506
Envy, ye great, the dull *u*. small *T.* 375

UNLIMITED.
The gracious showers, *u*. and free *T.* 511

UNLOADED.
Having *u*. and made many stare *Con.* 230

UNLOOKED.
Suppose, *u*. for in a scene so rude *T.* 248
U. for, life preserved, and peace restored *T.* iv 187

UNLOVELY.
I love thee, all *u*. as thou seem'st *T.* iv 128

UNMANACLED.
As ecstasy, *u*. by form *T.T.* 589

UNMANLY.
He holds no parley with *u*. fears *R.H.* 5

UNMARKED.
His hours no longer pass *u*. away *H.* 698

UNMASKED.
U., vouchsafing this their sole excuse *T.* ii 695

UNMEANING.
With some *u*. coxcomb at your side *R.* 546

UNMELLOWED.
And if the youth, *u*. yet by time *T.* 492

UNMENTIONED.
Of evils yet *u*. *F.* 195

UNMERITED.
Your fate *u*., once more rejoice *T.* i 339

UNMISSED.
U. but by his dogs and by his groom *P.E.* 95

UNMIXED.
U. with drops of bitter, which neglect *T.* iii 46

UNMOLESTED.
And raise a laugh) pass *u*. by *H.* 621
Ten thousand seek an *u*. end *T.* v 87
Here *u*., through whatever sign *T.* vi 295

UNMOVED.
U. and without quaking *F.* 126
U. with all the world beside *Miss* — 31
But none without some relish, none *u*. *T.* iv 742
At folly's cost, themselves *u*. the while *T.T.* 659

UNNATURAL.
With all the guilt of such *u*. war *Con.* 188

UNNERVES.
U. the moral powers, and mars their use *P.E.* 272

UNNERVED.
A mind *u*., or indisposed to bear *R.* 677

UNNOTED.
Diffusing odours; nor *u*. pass *T.* i 317

UNNOTICED.
It passed *u*., as the bird *E.* i. 87
Like him *u*., I, and such as I—*T.T.* 578

UNNUMBERED.
In baser souls *u*. evils meet *Ch.* 37

U. pleasures harmlessly pursued *R.* 784
U. branches waving in the blast *T.* i. 188

UNOBSERVED.
Disjoining from the rest, has *u*. *Y.O.* 107

UNOCCUPIED.
U., has filled the void so well *T.* v 557

UNOPPRESSED.
The soul, emancipated, *u*. *T.T.* 272

UNPACKED.
But when *u*. your disappointment groans *Con.* 309

UNPAID.
Anticipated rents, and bills *u*. *R.* 559

UNPARTICIPATED.
Your *u*. cares *F.* 125

UNPATRONIZED.
U., and therefore little known *Tir.* 674

UNPEOPLE.
Despise his bulwarks, and *u*. earth *R.* 72
U. all our counties of such herds *T.* iii 831

UNPERCEIVED.
Slept *u*., the mountain yet entire *Her.* 2
And *u*. the current steals away *T.* v 100

UNPERFUMED.
But are not wholesome airs, though *u*. *T.* iii 732

UNPERISHABLE.
By rust *u*. or by stealth *J.T.* 26

UNPERISHING.
Deeds of *u*. renown 1789, 15

UNPITIED.
The *u*. victim of ill judged expense *R.* 512
Pride falls *u*., never more to rise *T.* 588

UNPLEASANT.
U. and ungrateful *F.* 186

UNPLEASED.
Unpleasing and *u*. *Miss* — 64

UNPLEASING.
U. and unpleased *Miss* — 64
From such *u*. sounds as haunt the ear *T.* i 229
Yields no *u*. ramble; there the turf *T.* i 530

UNPOLLUTED.
Holy and *u*.: are thine such? *Ex.* 447

UNPRAISED.
By poets, and by senators *u*. *T.* v 539

UNPRESUMPTUOUS.
Can lift to Heaven an *u*. eye *T.* v 746

UNPRODUCTIVE.
Life in the *u*. shades of death *T.* ii 124

UNPROFITABLE.
With verdure not *u*., grazed *T.* iv 317
Knowledge, a rude *u*. mass *T.* vi 92

UNPROFITABLY.
Our wasted oil *u*. burns *Con.* 357

UNPROLIFIC.
Of *u*. Winter has impress'd *T.* vi 138

UNPURCHASED.
The tidings of *u*. Heaven create *H.* 343

UNPURIFIED.
U. by an authentic act *Y.O.* 12

UNQUALIFIED.
But men *u*. and base *F.* 2

UNQUENCHED. [566
Which, kindled with dry leaves, just saves *u*. *T.* i
The deluge washed it out; but left *u*. *T.* v 209

UNQUESTIONED.
Doing and suffering, his *u.* will *Ex.* 645
U., though the jewel be but glass *Tir.* 463

UNREAL.
Enthusiasts drunk with an *u.* joy *P.E.* 76

UNRECLAIMED.
This island, spot of *u.* rude earth *Ex.* 468

UNRECORDED.
Timing more punctual, *u.* facts *Y.O.* 47

UNRECUMBENT.
In *u.* sadness. There they wait *T.* v 29

UNREGARDED.
Sighs *u.* to the passing wind *Ex.* 30

UNREGENERATE.
Nor shall be found in *u.* souls *Con.* 755

UNREGRETTED.
And *u.* are soon snatched away *R.* 167

UNRELENTING.
And griping fists, and *u.* frowns *Ex.* 513
Sly circumvention, *u.* hate *T.* i 615
Impaired by age, his *u.* hand *T.* iii 416
Saved him, or the *u.* seer had died *T.* vi 471

UNRELINQUISHED.
And while at heart sin *u.* lies *Con.* 673

UNREMITTED.
Of *u.* vigilance and care *T.* vi 209

UNREMITTING.
He bids him glow with *u.* love *T.* 557

UNREPEALABLE.
But *u.* enduring death *T.* v 610

UNRESERVED.
They gain at last his *u.* assent *T.* v 663

UNRESOLVED.
Studious of ornament, yet *u. T.* vi 160

UNRESPECTED.
Have dwindled into *u.* forms *T.* i 747

UNRESTRAINED.
His sovereign power and pleasure *u. H.* 320
Profusion *u.*, with all that's base *T.* ii 675
If *u.*, into luxuriant growth *T.* vi 593

UNREVOKED.
And now, Farewell.—Time *u.* has run *M.P.* 112

UNRIDDLE.
To *u.*, and have left them mysteries still *F.A.* 29

UNRIGHTEOUS.
Else, on the fatalist's *u.* plan *P.E.* 27

UNRIVAL'D.
Of his *u.* pencil. He inspires *T.* vi 242

UNRULY.
O'erwatch the numerous and *u.* clan *Tir.* 262

UNSAFE.
O bliss precarious, and *u.* retreats! *Her.* 33

UNSANCTIONED.
Defective and *u.*, proved too weak *T.* ii 524

UNSATED.
And still *u.*, dwelt upon the scene *T.* i 158

UNSAVOURY.
By culinary arts, *u.* deems *T.* i 125
The pent-up breath of an *u.* throng *T.* iv 196

UNSCARED.
Then sleep was undisturbed by Fear, *u. T.* iv 561

UNSCENTED.
For the *u.* fictions of the loom *T.* i 416

UNSEATED.
At once the shock *u.* him: he flew *T.* vi 553

UNSEEMLY.
And set the *u.* pair in open day *A.T.* 168
The boughs in which are bred the *u.* race *Tir.* 594

UNSEEN. [40
And cheers the drooping flowers, unheard, *u. J.T.*
By what *u.* and unsuspected arts *P.E.* 3
That overhang the thatch, itself *u. T.* i 224
Of late unsightly and *u.*, now shine *T.* v 24
Behind his own creation, works *u. T.* v 894
She makes familiar with a Heaven *u. T.* vi 926

UNSHAKEN.
And feels no change, *u.* and serene *Ex.* 587
Sits absolute on his *u.* throne *H.* 474
Their own dear virtue their *u.* trust *T.* 284
Who with a courage of *u.* root *T.T.* 15

UNSHOD.
With *u.* feet they yet securely tread *E.* ii 16

UNSIFTED.
The total grist *u.*, husks and all *T.* vi 108

UNSIGHTLY.
And where *u.* and rank thistles grew *H.* 526
From temper flaws *u. N.Y.G.* 8
The prominent and most *u.* bones *T.* ii 588
Of late *u.* and unseen, now shine *T.* v 24

UNSKILFUL.
Or misapplying his *u.* strength *T.* iii 402

UNSMIRCHED.
Whom matrons now, of character *u. T.* iii 73

UNSOCIAL.
And knit the *u.* climates into one *Ch.* 126

UNSOILED.
U., and swift, and of a silken sound *T.* iv 212

UNSOPHISTICATE.
No, Nature—*u.* by man *Con.* 451

UNSOUGHT.
Seek and obtain, and often find *u.? T.* iii 288

UNSPARING.
Of what He gives, *u.* and profuse *Ex.* 677

UNSPECKED.
Hence a demeanour holy and *u. T.* 281

UNSPENT.
And so long he, with *u.* power *Cast.* 39

UNSTAINED.
And lips *u.* by folly or by strife *Con.* 563
And when *u.* with any grosser crime *Con.* 634
To keep the matrimonial bond *u. T.T.* 74

UNSTRUNG. [728
Was quenched in rheums of age, his voice, *u. T.* ii

UNSUBDUED.
Leave Vice and Folly *u.* behind *P.E.* 81

UNSUCCESSFUL.
We bustle up with *u.* speed *Con.* 215
Beau marked my *u.* pains *D.W.* 21
The silly *u.* Bee *P.B.* 22
And hurried, but with *u.* speed *T.* 245
Of *u.* or successful war *T.* ii 4
Well may the Church wage *u.* war *T.* ii 809
Not often *u.*: power usurped *T.* v 371

UNSULLIED.
" Beneath a vault *u.* with a cloud *T.* v 824

UNSUNG.
U., and many cares are yet behind *T.* iii 606
But there is yet a Liberty *u. T.* v 538

UNSUPPLIED.
Fretful if *u.*; but silent, meek *T.* v 31

UNSUSPECTED.
Concealed within an *u.* part *Con.* 365
By what unseen and *u.* arts *P.E.* 3
An *u.* storm. His hour was come *T.* vi 545

UNSUSPECTING.
His *u.* sheep believe it pure *Ex.* 103
Thine *u.* gratitude and love *T.* iii 348
In *u.* pomp. Twitched from the perch *T.* iv 448
With *u.* readiness he takes *T.* vi 427
Thy blossoms deck our *u.* years *V.* 51

UNSUSPICIOUS.
But farewell now to *u.* nights *T.* iv 565

UNTAUGHT.
That beaus delight? a heart *u.* to sigh? *Ep.* i 6
And colleges, *u.*; sells accent, tone *T.* ii 359
Ah, blind to bright futurity, *u. Tir.* 379

UNTEMPERED.
And smite the *u.* wall 'tis death to spare *H.* 627

UNTHINKING.
"And now," quoth poor *u.* Ralph *A Fable* 18
Suits well the thoughtful or *u.* mind *T.* iv 279
Holds an *u.* multitude enthrall'd *T.* vi 100

UNTHOUGHT-OF.
Let me enjoy, in some *u.* spot *V.* 83

UNTIES.
With slow deliberation he *u. Ch.* 471
Can seize the slippery prey, *u.* the knot *T.* ii 685

UNTIMELY.
And spades, the emblem of *u.* graves *T.* iv 219

UNTOLD.
Religion! what treasure *u. A.S.* 25
That failing left *u. J.P.* 24
Incomparable gem! thy worth *u. T.T.* 330

UNTRIED. [398
Immured though unaccused, condemned *u. T.* v

UNTROUBLED.
Which most should sweeten his *u.* life *H.* 681

UNTRUE.
Whose hand is feeble, or his aim *u. P.E.* 571

UNTUTORED.
Upon the roving and *u.* heart *T.* ii 570

UNUTTERED.
Much trash *u.*, and some ills undone *Tir.* 733

UNVARNISHED.
The deep dark green of whose *u.* leaf *T.* vi 174

UNVEILED. [425
U. her blushing cheek, looked on, and smiled *Ex.*

UNVISITED.
U. by man. There they are free *T.* vi 403

UNWARILY.
We should *u.* conclude *F.* 28

UNWASHED.
To which the *u.* artificer repairs *T.T.* 152

UNWEARIED.
By Vanity's *u.* finger dressed *Ex.* 46
And though in act *u.*, secret still *J.T.* 37
The elastic spring of an *u.* foot *T.* i 135
Constant rotation of the *u.* wheel *T.* i 368

With worthy thoughts of that *u.* Love *T.* v 752
Nature exerting an *u.* power *T.T.* 690

UNWELCOME.
For truth is *u.*, however divine *F.M.* 23
O that *u.* voice of heavenly love *T.* 463
A visitor *u.*, into scenes *T.* vi 570
And say, My boy, the *u.* hour is come *Tir.* 849
U. vapours quench autumnal beams *T.T.* 212
Now, all *u.*. at his gates *Y.D.* 21

UNWHOLESOME.
Minnows and gudgeons gorge the *u.* food *P.E.* 483
In some *u.* dungeon, and a prey *T.* i 437

UNWIELDY.
To express *u.* joy *Q.V.* 20

UNWIN.
U., I should but ill repay *U.* 1

UNWITHERING.
The spiry myrtle with *u.* leaf *T.* iii 570

UNWONTED.
That calls the *u.* villager abroad *T.* vi 300

UNWORTHY.
"Is recreant, and *u.* of his spurs" *A.T.* 122
U. of his own *Dr.* 24
U., base, and insincere *F.* 215
A plaything world, *u.* of his hand) *H.* 543
Not else *u.* to be feared *Q.V.* 67
Abandoned as *u.* of our love *T.* iii 731
Replete with dreams, *u.* of a man *Tir.* 160
U. of the blessings of the brave *T.T.* 27

UNWRENCHED.
U. the door, however well secured *T.* iv 446

UNWRINKLED.
Sees her *u.* face reflected bright *T.* iv 4

UNYIELDING.
Obdurate and *u.*, glassy smooth *T.* i 52

UPBEARING.
Here glittering turrets rise, *u.* high *T.* v 110

UPBORNE.
U. into the viewless air *O.* i 13
U. they stood. Three legs upholding firm *T.* i 20

UPHEAVED.
U. above the soil, and sides embossed *Y.O.* 65

UPHELD.
U. by two; yet still thou lovest *M.* 39
Thine, and *u.* by thy paternal care *R.* 89

UPHOLD. [582
To *u.* the boundless scenes of his command *Ch.*
Its own revolvency *u.* the world *T.* i 372 [753
That planned, and built, and still *u.* a world *T.* v

UPHOLDING.
Upborne they stood. Three legs *u.* firm *T.* i 20
Uninjured, but expect the *u.* aid *T.* iii 658

UPLAND.
These to the *u.*, to the valley those *T.* v 197

UPLIFTED.
U. hands, that, at convenient times *Ex.* 147
Hope, with *u.* foot, set free from earth *H.* 161
Migrates *u.*, and, with all its soil *T.* ii 108
The *u.* frame, compact at every joint *T.* iii 484

UPLIFTS.
With faint illumination, that *u. T* iv 274

UPRIDGED.
U. so high, and sent on such a charge *T.* ii 116

UPRIGHT. [682
Those hearts should be reclaimed, renewed, *u. Con.*
Some foe to his *u.* intent *H.F.* 9

Who cannot sit *u. J.G.* 90
Between the *u.* shafts of whose tall elms *T.* i 355
Smooth as a wall the *u.* remnant stands *T.* v 36
An *u.* heart, and cultivated mind *Tir.* 722

UPSPEARING.
And coarser grass, *u.* o'er the rest *T.* v 23

UPSPOUTED.
U. by a whale in air *Q.V.* 19

UPSTARTS.
Than yonder *u.* of the neighbouring wood *Y.O.* 134

UPSTARTING.
Then rise the tender germs, *u.* quick *T.* iii 521

UPSTOOD.
At once, *u.* intelligent, surveyed *Y.O.* 150

UPTORN.
Deep in the loamy bank. *U.* by strength *T.* iv 438

UPTURNED.
U. so lately by the forceful share *T.* iv 315

UPWARD.
The exalted prize demands an *u.* look *Tir.* 3 83

UPWROUGHT.
Ocean has caught the frenzy, and *u. T.* ii 111

URCHIN.
The shivering *u.*, bending as he goes *T.* 143

URGE.
Whatever Use may *u.*, or Honour plead *Con.* 189
To *u.* reformation of national ill *F.M.* 14
To *u.* the fruitless chase be lost *Mor.* 42
Are the means that duty *u. N.C.* 31
Would *u.* a wiser suit than asking more *T.* vi 56
The peasants *u.* their harvest, ply the fork *T.T.* 214

URGED. [52
That flight in circles *u.* advanced them nought *N.A.*
U. his attempt on every side *P.B.* 7
Ere yet it came, the traveller *u.* his steed *T.* 244
But *u.* by storms along its slippery way *T.* iv 127
And sin without disturbance. Often *u. T.* v 659
U. loud a claim to be rehearsed, 1789, 14

URGENT.
The wisest and the best feel *u.* need *T.* ii 483

URN. [436
Has filled his *u.* where these pure waters rise *Ch.*
Like hidden lamps in old sepulchral *u. Con.* 358
From *u.* that never fail, through every land *R.* 76
A little naiad her impoverished *u. T.* i 328
And while the bubbling and loud hissing *u. T.* iv 38

USE.
So when a child, as playful children *u. B.B.* 9
And offers something to the general *u. Ch.* 90
As men of depth in erudition *u. Ch.* 392
How few respect, or *u.* thee, as they ought ! *Con.* 24
The point of honour has been deemed of *u. Con.* 163
Whatever *U.* may urge, or Honour plead *Con.* 189
What *u.* of his boon the giver would *Con.* 436
Who when occasion justified its *u. Con.* 613 [644
Mellows and makes the speech more fit for *u. Con.*
The virtues of old Rome for English *u. Con.* 836
Digression is so much in modern *u. Con.* 855
The pomp of sound or tinkle without *u. Con.* 892
Events of most important *u. E.* i 76 [*Ex.* 626
Those truths, which neither *u.* nor years impair
A coin by Craft for Folly's *u.* designed *E.* ii 7
Were just such trifles, without worth or *u. Ex.* 49
That gratitude and temperance in our *u. Ex.* 676
I could be well content, allowed the *u. F.A.* 1
For its beauty admired and its *u. Gr.* 26

The very sense of it foregoes its *u. H.* 21
To make the sun a bauble without *u. H.* 81
From emptiness itself a real *u. H.* 156
To guide our *u.* of it, is all in all *H.* 432
Its *u.* and power exemplified in thee *J.T.* 50
Agents of his will to *u.* ? *N.C.* 32 [272
Unnerves the moral powers, and mars their *u. P.E.*
Who seek retirement for its proper *u. R.* 170
Woe to the man whose wit disclaims its *u. R.* 211
Lost, till he tune them, all their power and *u. R.* 330
The strenuous *u.* of profitable thought *R.* 674
Worthy to live, and of eternal *u. R.* 700
From India, for the ladies' *u. R.C.* 38
To hourly *u.* applied *St.* iii 20
Time was, when clothing, sumptuous or for *u. T.* i 8
And fit the limpid element for *u. T.* i 374
A plague into his blood ; and cannot *u. T.* ii 140
Formed for his *u.*, and ready at his will ? *T.* ii 202
I say the pulpit (in the sober *u. T.* ii 332
As angels *u.*, the Gospel whispers peace *T.* ii 342
Down into modern *u.* ; transforms old print *T.* ii 363
And binds the shoulders flat. We prove its *u. T.* ii 589
Convenience, and security, and *u. T.* ii 682
In wild disorder, and unfit for *u. T.* ii 805
And specious semblances have lost their *u. T.* iii 107
Is but a loan, to be repaid with *u. T.* iii 364
Wafts the rich prize to its appointed *u. T.* iii 540
And streams, as if created for his *u. T.* iii 776
With colours mixed for a far different *u. T.* iv 240
His hungry acres, stinks and is no *u. T.* iv 503 [662
Shine out ; there only reach their proper *u. T.* iv
For grandeur or for *u.* Long wavy wreaths *T.* v 158
A course of long observance for its *u. T.* v 301
And social, nip his fruitfulness and *u. T.* v 439
" The *u.* of his own bounty ?—making first *T.* v 639
And has a richer *u.* of yours than you *T.* v 762
And with the boon gives talents for its *u. T.* v 860
And dedicate a tribute, in its *u. T.* vi 712 [*Tir.* 124
Which children *u.*, and parsons—when they preach
Distorted from its *u.* and just design *T.T.* 754
Their purport, *u.*, properties, resigned *Y.O.* 152

USED.
Oaths *u.* as playthings or convenient tools *Ex.* 37
Thus studied, *u.* and consecrated thus *R.* 105
A real elegance, a little *u. T.* ii 611
Was never meant, was never *u.* before *T.* vi 651
What shifts he *u.*, detected in a scrape *Tir.* 328
How seldom *u.*, how little understood ! *T.T.* 64

USEFUL.
Graceful and *u.* all she does *Comp.* ii 7
He makes one *u.* point exceeding clear *Con.* 136
Is often *u.*, always entertains *Con.* 204
That *u.* thing, her needle gone *E.* iv 40
Truths *u.* and attainable with ease *F.A.* 32
Give *u.* light though I should miss renown *R.* 206
Your *u.* labours, and important aims *R.* 664
Devised the Weatherhouse, that *u.* toy ! *T.* 211
To be a pest where he was *u.* once *T.* iv 657
May give an *u.* lesson to the head *T.* vi 86
And *u.* quality, and virtue too *T.* vi 623
That authors are most *u.* pawned or sold *Tir.* 211
Nor crush a worm, whose *u.* light *Trans.* i 17

USEFULNESS.
But gives it *u.* unknown before *Con.* 597
Their *u.* ensured by zeal and love *Ex.* 443

USELESS.
Might burn his *u.* Machiavel, and sleep *Ch.* 613
U. in him alike both brain and speech *Con.* 141
And either warps or lays it *u.* by *Con.* 670
And *u.* as a candle in a skull *Con.* 780
Like *u.* lumber, or a stroller's song *Con.* 820

USELESS—VAIN

Deified *u*. wood or senseless stone *Ex*. 238
Not to be solved, and *u*. if it might *F.A*. 34
O querulous and weak!—whose *u*. brain *H*. 29
As *u*. as the moment it began *H*. 96
By *u*. censure, whom we cannot mend *H*. 273
Compose their *u*. wing *N*. 2
Nor such as *u*. conversation breeds *R*. 643
As *u*. if it goes as when it stands *R*. 682
Who deem his house a *u*. place *St*. vi 21
A vagabond and *u*. tribe there eat *T*. i 559
As *u*. to the moles and to the bats *T*. vi 880
And censured oft as *u*. Stillest streams *T*. vi 929
And *u*. while he lives, and when he dies *Tir*. 71

USHER.
A tempest *u*. in the dreaded morn *H*. 717

USHERED.
Shines in the dark, but, *u*. into day *Con*. 677
But O the important budget! *u*. in *T*. iv 23

USUAL.
My lord, alighting at his *u*. place *R*. 585
The dinner served, Charles takes his *u*. stand *T*. 213
More frequent, and foregone her *u*. rest *T*. ii 61

USURIOUS.
Supplies his need with a *u*. loan *T*. iii 798

USURP.
U. God's office, lays his bosom bare *Con*. 745
His steeds, *u*. a place they well deserve *T*. vi 703
Supplant thee in it, and *u*. thy place *Tir*. 890

USURPATION.
Of *u*., and to no man's wrong *T*. v 760

USURPED.
Are hateful ensigns of *u*. command *Ch*. 213
Holds a *u*. dominion o'er his tongue *Con*. 462
He that has not *u*. the name of man *R*. 319
Not often unsuccessful: power *u*. *T*. v 371
Dispersed the shackles of *u*. control *T*. v 516
When he *u*. Authority's just place *T.T*. 320
To stoop to Tyranny's *u*. command *T.T*. 440
That Lewdness had *u*. and worn so long *T.T*. 637

UTENSIL.
And the old *u*. of tin *R.C*. 27

UTILITY.
So void of all *u*. or aim *H*. 88
And, trust me, his *u*. may reach *Tir*. 731

UTOPIAN.
A mere *U*. pleasure *F*. 30

UTTER.
And *u*. now and then an awful voice *T*. vi 34

UTTERANCE.
Thy fame diffuse, praised not for *u*. meet *S*. i 13
And give them voice and *u*. once again *T*. iv 35
To give such act and *u*. as they may *T*. vi 339

UTTERED. [*Con*. 381
"Yes, ma'am," and "No, ma'am," *u*. softly, show
Like language *u*. in a dream *M*. 22
Of demons *u*., from whatever lungs *N.A*. 118

V.

VACANT.
Happy to fill Religion's *v*. place *Ex*. 121
Yet Folly ever has a *v*. stare *P.E*. 205
And talks and laughs away his *v*. hours *R*. 452
A mind quite *v*. is a mind distressed *R*. 624
Placed at some *v*. corner of the board *T*. iv 230

VACUITY.
To fill the dull *v*. till four *H*. 78
In indolent *v*. of thought *T*. iv 297

VAGABOND.
A *v*. and useless tribe there eat *T*. i 559

VAGARIES.
His more sublime *v*. slighting *E*. i 17
To mix her wild *v*. with thy laws *T*. v 873
Though wild their strange *v*., and uncouth *T*. vi 337

VAGRANTS.
And wanton *v*., as make London, vast *T*. iii 833

VAGUE.
A Deity could solve. Their answers, *v*. *T*. ii 521

VAIN.
"In *v*.," they cried, "are hymeneal rites *A.T*. 99
"V. our delusive hope of constant knights *A.T*. 100
In *v*. recorded in historic page *B.B*. 3
And seems to have risen in *v*. *C*. 4
He loved them both, but both in *v*. *Cast*. 11
As *v*. imperial Philip on his own *Ch*. 52
Unless his laws be trampled on,—in *v*.? *Ch*. 191
Here see, acquitted of all *v*. pretence *Ch*. 412
'Twere *v*. inquiry to what port she went *Ch*. 445
Adopt his own, 'tis equally in *v*. *Con*. 109 [*Comp*. i 9
Streams never flow in *v*.; where streams abound
Your hope to please him *v*. on every plan *Con*. 341
The vainest corner of our own *v*. heart *Con*. 366
The fixed fee-simple of the *v*. and light? *Con*. 590
Oh! I have seen (nor hope perhaps in *v*. *Con*. 605
Without it, his pretensions were as *v*. *Con*. 761
Toils to anticipate in *v*. *E*. i 66
Flow in a foreign land, but not in *v*. *E*. ii 46
And, after many a *v*. essay *E*. iv 53
Forbid in *v*. to push his daring way *Ex*. 17 [*Ex*. 65
But wept, and stamped, and smote his thigh in *v*.
In *v*. the nations, that had seen them rise *Ex*. 203
Taxed till the brow of Labour sweats in *v*. *Ex*. 305
He wipes and scours the silver cup in *v*. *Ex*. 385
Oh *v*. inquiry! they without remorse *Ex*. 462
Baptized her fleet Invincible in *v*. *Ex*. 569
Like her the fabled Phœbus wooed in *v*. *Ex*. 599
Their names, alas! in *v*. reproach an age *Ex*. 660
I know the warning song is sung in *v*. *Ex*. 724
In *v*. the talkative unite *F*. 67
That, after many an effort *v*. *F.B*. 16
And form genteel were all in *v*. *G*. 8
A *v*. pursuit of fugitive, false good *H*. 4
Once thought of nothing, and now thinks in *v*. *H*. 30
In *v*. opinion's waste and dangerous wild *H*. 279
Make works a *v*. ingredient in the case *H*. 360 [618
The strange conceits, *v*. projects, and wild dreams *H*.
The peasant's hopes, and not in *v*., assured *Her*. 9
A land that distant tyrants hate in *v*. *Her*. 89
But John he cried in *v*. *J.G*. 86
The sun would rise in *v*. for me *M*. 31
In *v*. warm suns their influence shed *Miss* — 37
The zephyrs sport in *v*. *Miss* — 38
By contemplation's help, not sought in *v*. *M.P*. 114
But still in *v*., the frame was tight *P.B*. 9

VAIN—VANISH

Consumes his soul with *v.* desires *P.B.* 16
Though all your engineering proves in *v. P.E.* 321
When some hypothesis absurd and *v. P.E.* 444
In *v.* : the slave of arrogance and pride *P.E.* 548
Bled, groaned, and agonized, and died in *v. P.E.* 624
Whose highest praise is that they live in *v. R.* 23
Glittering in *v.*, or only to seduce *R.* 212
Adores a creature, and devout in *v. R.* 227
Pierced with the woes that she laments in *v. R.* 300
Business or *v.* amusement, care or mirth *R.* 647
Must change her nature, or in *v.* retires *R.* 680
And while Experience cautions us in *v. R.* 755
I may not teach in *v. St.* i 32
Seems to sound too much in *v. St.* iv 19
"Incredible, impossible, and *v.*!" *T.* 35
The plea of works, as arrogant and *v. T.* 71
Nice-fingered Art must emulate in *v. T.* 202
He, lost in errors his *v.* heart prefers *T.* 335
In *v.* he points his powers against the skies *T.* 469
In *v.* he closes or averts his eyes *T.* 470
Anxious in *v.* to find the distant floor *T.* i 48
V. thought! the dweller in that still retreat *T.* i 237
And fugitive in *v.* The sylvan scene *T.* ii 107
And yet ambitious not to sing in *v. T.* ii 312
But loose in morals, and in manners *v. T.* ii 378
Whom Truth and Soberness assailed in *v. T.* ii 480
In *v.* to filter off a crystal draught *T.* ii 507
In *v.* they pushed inquiry to the birth *T.* ii 511
And thus it is. The pastor, either *v. T.* ii 545 [764
The lewd *v.* world that must receive him soon *T.* ii
With the *v.* stir. I sum up half mankind *T.* iii 130
To a sharp reckoning that has lived in *v. T.* iii 179
V. tears, alas! and sighs that never find *T.* iii 332
By causes not to be divulged in *v. T.* iii 371
And oft at last in *v.* The learned and wise *T.* iii 562
Created fair so much in *v.* for them *T.* iii 697 [848
For whom God heard his Abraham plead in *v. T.* iii
Resounding oft, and never heard in *v. T.* iv 356
To his voracious bag, struggling in *v. T.* iv 450
But censure profits little : *v.* the attempt *T.* iv 500
V. wish! those days were never; airy dreams *T.* iv 525
The magisterial sword in *v.*, and lays *T.* iv 596
Capricious, in which fancy seeks in *v. T.* v 120
Confederacy of projectors wild and *v. T.* v 194
The world was made in *v.*, if not for him *T.* v 271
And *v.* enough to be ambitious still *T.* v 338 [v 492
And tremble at *v.* dreams? Heaven grant I may! *T.*
And in the dust, sifted and searched in *v. T.* v 536
What does he not, from lusts opposed in *v. T.* v 599
So oft, and wearied in the *v.* attempt *T.* v 628
V. tampering has but fostered his disease *T.* v 668
Smitten in *v.*! such music cannot charm *T.* v 682
And that to bind him is a *v.* attempt *T.* v 777
In *v.* thy creatures testify of thee *T.* v 856
Till Thou art heard, imaginations *v. T.* v 861
That converse which we now in *v.* regret *T.* vi 41
So duly, all is miracle in *v. T.* vi 133
Plead not in *v.* for pity on the pangs *T.* vi 462
But still in *v.* The Providence that meant *T.* vi 528
He seeks not hers, for he has proved them *v. T.* vi 920
Polite Refinement offers him in *v. T.* vi 977
In *v.* the poet sings, and the world hears *T.* vi 1018
The force he spends against their fury *v. Tir.* 64
The wisest heads might agitate in *v. Tir.* 130
A trifler *v.*, and empty of all good *Tir.* 754
That constellation set, the world in *v. T.T.* 660
Nor bids him shine in *v. Trans.* i 24

VAINEST.
The *v.* corner of our own vain heart *Con.* 366

VAINGLORIOUS.
V. of her charms, his Vashti forth *T.* iii 715

VAIN-GLORY.
Or else *v.*, prompted us to draw *T.* i. 635

VAINLY.
Feebly and *v.*, at poetic fame) *R.* 802
V. industrious, a disgraceful prize *T.* iii 385
Each *v.* magnifies his own success *Tir.* 476

VALE.
But though life's valley be a *v.* of tears *Con.* 881
A brighter scene beyond that *v.* appears *Con.* 882
And said, "Go spend them in the *v.* of tears" *E.* ii 26
Again pours ruin on the *v.* below *Her.* 38
The cloud-surmounting Alps, the fruitful *v. R.* 79
The sound shall run along the winding *v. R.* 363
While struggling in the *v.* of tears below *T.* 585
That, as with molten glass, inlays the *v. T.* i 170
Peeps at the *v.* below; so thick beset *T.* i 225
The cheering fragrance of her dewy *v. T.* i 429
Then snug enclosures in the sheltered *v. T.* i 513
Declined at length into the *v.* of years *T.* ii 726
In the low *v.* of life, that early felt *T.* iv 799
Slides ineffectual down the snowy *v. T.* v 7
(Himself grown sober in the *v.* of tears) *T.* vi 48
Again the harmony comes o'er the *v. T.* vi 65 [72
The *v.* of Nature, where it creeps and winds *T.* v
The dwellers in the *v.* and on the rocks *T.* vi 793

VALENTINE.
To forestall sweet St. *V.*—*P.T.* 12

VALERIAN.
Of nightshade, or *v.*, grace the well *T.* iv 757

VALLEY.
These *v.* and rocks never heard *A.S.* 30
Hills, *v.*, rivers, and the boundless sea *A.T.* 49
But groves, hills, and *v.* diffuse *C.* 39
That in the *v.* of decline are lost *Con.* 636
But though life's *v.* be a vale of tears *Con.* 881
O'er hills, through *v.*, and by river's brink *T.* i 113
Of hill and *v.* interposed between *T.* i 322
The rocks fall headlong, and the *v.* rise *T.* ii 95
Woods vanish, hills subside, and *v.* rise *T.* iii 775
The hills and *v.* with their ceaseless songs *T.* v 78
These to the upland, to the *v.* those *T.* v 197
His are the mountains, and the *v.* his *T.* v 742

VALOUR.
To quell the *v.* of the stoutest heart *Ex.* 358

VALUE.
No Charity but alms aught *v.* she *Ch.* 459
Loses at once all *v.* and esteem *Ex.* 113
The Sacred Book, its *v.* understood *Ex.* 616
Its *v.*, what no thought can ascertain *H.* 125
Thine had a *v.* in the scales of Heaven *J.T.* 29
Our fathers knew the *v.* of a screen *T.* i 255 [293
Few know thy *v.*, and few taste thy sweets *T.* iii
For he who *v.* Liberty confines *T.* v 393
And overpaid its *v.* with thy blood *T.* vi 860
To impress a *v.*, not to be erased *Tir.* 613

VALUED.
Of all their hard oppressors *v.* most *Ex.* 172
'Tis *v.* for the danger's sake the more *P.E.* 521
What once I *v.* and could boast, a friend *R.* 37
If *v.* by its wearer's worth 1789, 43
The good on earth they *v.* most 1789, 51

VAN.
Havoc and devastation in the *v. Her.* 21
Plant behind plant aspiring, in the *v. T.* iii 593

VANDALS.
So then—the *V.* of our Isle *M.* i 1

VANISH.
(So *v.* Pleasure alas!) *C.* 6
All *v.* there, and fascinate no more *P.E.* 620
V. at once into the darkest shade *St.* ii 24
Woods *v.*, hills subside, and valleys rise *T.* iii 775
Nor frown, unless he *v.* with the cloth *Tir.* 730

VANISHED.
He blessed the bread, but *v.* at the word *Con.* 533
Jack *v.*, was regretted and forgot *R.* 581

VANITY.
The last by *V.* produced and nursed *Con.* 378
And *v.* absorbs at length *E.* i 81
By *V.'s* unwearied finger dressed *Ex.* 46
What dotage will not *v.* maintain? *Ex.* 628
That Zeal, not *V.*, has chanced to mate *Ch.* 635
Whom all the *v.* they scorned engaged *Ex.* 661
To read wise lectures, *v.* the text *H.* 107
Is *v.* surpassing all the rest" *H.* 110
Hope sets the stamp of *v.* on all *H.* 153
Of *v.*, that seizes all below *T.* iii 267
By endless riot, *V.*, the Lust *T.* iii 812
Arms, through the *v.* and brainless rage *T.* iv 619
Nor him who, by his *v.* seduced *T.* vi 283
Much of the *v.* of men *Trans.* ii 32
Of *V.*, a wreath for self to wear *T.T.* 757

VANQUISH.
To *v.* lust, and wear its yoke no more *Ex.* 411

VANQUISHED.   [620
And seems dethroned and *v.* Peace ensues *T.* v
Are oft-times *v.* and thrown far behind *T.* vi 615

VAPID.
And withered muscle, and the *v.* soul *T.* i 393

VAPOUR.
'Tis nauseous as the *v.* of a vault *Con.* 50
Dark and voluminous the *v.* rise *Her.* 15
It floats a *v.* now *O.* i 14
Its cooling *v.* o'er the dewy meads *R.* 422
To sallow sickness, which the *v.*, dank *T.* i 438
In volumes wheeling slow, the *v.* dank *T.* iii 499
Replete with *v.*, and disposes much *T.* v 463
Unwelcome *v.* quench autumnal beams *T.T.* 212

VAPOURING.
Strutting and *v.* in an empty school *T.* ii 330

VARIANCE.
Seem most at *v.* with all moral good *T.* iv 621

VARIED.
Displaying, on its *v.* side, the grace *T.* i 172
He looks abroad into the *v.* field *T.* v 738
The *v.* fields of science, ever new *T.T.* 264

VARIEGATED.
Her hedge-row shrubs, a *v.* store *R.* 419
A *v.* show; the meadows green *T.* iv 312

VARIETY.
Of rights restored, *v.* enjoyed *A.T.* 154
V.'s the very spice of life *T.* ii 606
Of pleasure and *v.*, dispatch *T.* iii 813
And flush into *v.* again *T.* vi 180
With all *v.* of ill by turns *Tir.* 475

VARIOUS.
That all the *v.* beauties we survey *A.T.* 48
By *v.* ties attaches man to man *Ch.* 16
God opens fruitful Nature's *v.* scenes *Ch.* 88 [i 10
How laughs the land with *v.* plenty crowned! *Comp.*
Though *v.* yet complete *Dr.* 10
Their humour yet so *v.* *F.* 111
So shifting and so *v.* is the plan *H.* 15
In justice to the *v.* powers *Miss* — 17
Lead on the *v.* year *Miss* — 98
The *v.* treasures of his mind *Mrs. M*— 42
Here *v.* motives his ambition raise *P.E.* 53
Nature in all the *v.* shapes she wears *R.* 193
Though *v.* foes against the truth combine *T.* 473
Alike yet *v.* Here the grey smooth trunks *T.* i 302
The earth was made so *v.*, that the mind *T.* i 506
How *v.* his employments whom the world *T.* iii 352
And dress the regular yet *v.* scene *T.* iii 592
With forms so *v.*, that no powers of art *T.* v 108

The lilac, *v.* in array, now white *T.* vi 157   [232
With self-taught rites, and under *v.* names *T.* vi
The *v.* seasons woven into one *T.* vi 769   [vi 355
The creatures, summon'd from their *v.* haunts *T.*
Its *v.* parts to his attentive note *Tir.* 642
Mankind are *v.*, and the world is wide *Tir.* 788
What exhibitions *v.* hath the world *Y.O.* 69

VARNISH.
With Nature's *v.*; severed into stripes *T.* i 40

VASE.
Close interwoven, where they meet the *v.* *T.* iii 612
And bundled close to fill some crowded *v.* *T.* iv 668

VASHTI.
Vainglorious of her charms, his *V.* forth *T.* iii 715

VAST.
A union with the *v.* terraqueous whole *Ch.* 122
But who can tell how *v.* the plan *E.* i 83
V. as it is, it answers, as it flows *R.* 529
Oh for a lodge in some *v.* wilderness *T.* ii 1
And wanton vagrants, as make London, *v.T.* iii 833
Its fluctuations, and its *v.* concerns? *T.* iv 56
Almost without an effort, plans too *v.* *T.* v 253
Terrestrial, in the *v.* and the minute *T.* v 811
So *v.* in its demands, unless impell'd *T.* vi 218
V. was his empire, absolute his power *T.* vi 357
V. in its powers, ethereal in its kind *Tir.* 6

VASTNESS.
And all thine embryo *v.*, at a gulp *Y.O.* 22

VAULT.
'Tis nauseous as the vapour of a *v.* *Con.* 50
Her *v.* below, where every vintage meets *Ex.* 22
And just when evening turns the blue *v.* grey *H.* 79
The stars that, sprinkled o'er the *v.* of night *R.* 349
The seas globose and huge, the o'erarching *v. R.* 552
" Beneath a *v.* unsullied with a cloud *T.* v 824 [62
And has the warmth of May. The *v.* is blue *T.* vi
Amid the *v.* of heaven *Q.V.* 16

VAULTED.
That made the *v.* roofs of Pleasure ring *T.T.* 625

VEGETATE.
He deems it hard to *v.* alone *Tir.* 724

VEGETATION.
Checks *v.* in the torpid plant *T.* iii 468

VEGETATIVE.
Swelling with *v.* force instinct *Y.O.* 34

VEHICLE.
A *v.* of virtue, truth, and love *Ch.* 624

VEIL.   [*Her.* 17
While through the Stygian *v.* that blots the day
How dark the *v.* that intercepts the blaze *Ch.* 57
Has still a *v.* of midnight on his heart *Ch.* 376 [486
And *v.* your daring crest that braves the skies *Con.*
Themselves will hide its coarseness with a *v. P.E.* 292
And covered with a fine-spun specious *v. P.E.* 328
Discover him that rules them; such a *v. T.* iii 233
Escapes unhurt beneath so warm a *v. T.* iv 332
Her *v.* opaque, discloses with a smile *T.* v 892
The *v.* is rent, rent too by priestly hands *T.* vi 876
To *v.* a deed of thine! *Q.V.* 36

VEILED.
Night *v.* the pole; all seemed secure *T.B.* 31

VEIN.
" The blood of ancient worthies in his *v. A.T.* 116
The recollection, like a *v.* of ore *Con.* 515
Consult Life's silent clock, thy bounding *v. Ep.* i 3
Fed from the richest *v.* of the Mogul *Ex.* 369
And let it circulate through every *v. T.* ii 45 [201
Be strangers to each other? Pierce my *v. T.* iii
He gave them in his children's *v.*, and hates *T.*iv 464

To winter, and the current in his *v. T.* iv 388 [137
Whose humorous *v.*, strong sense, and simple style *Tir.*
Through the imperceptible meandering *v. T.* vi 136

VELLUM.
The *v.* of the pedigree they claim *T.* i 569

VELVET.
Where Nature has her mossy *v.* spread *E.* ii 15
May now and then their *v.* cushions take *H.* 248
In scarlet mantle warm, and *v.* capped *M.P.* 51
() the dear pleasures of the *v.* plain *P.E.* 169
Or *v.* soft, or plush with shaggy pile *T.* i 11
On Fortune's *v.* altar offering up *T.* ii 657
Across a *v.* level, feel a joy *T.* vi 275

VENAL.
And every *v.* stickler for the Yoke *T.T.* 352

VENALITY.
When infamous *V.*, grown bold *T.T.* 416
Pulverized of *v.*, a shell *Y.O.* 123

VENERABLE.
Meek, modest, *v.*, wise, sincere *Ex.* 620
Innocent! Oh! if *v.* Time *P.E.* 181
Down falls the *v.* pile, the abode *T.* iii 767
Fame had not left the *v.* man *T.* vi 492

VENERATE.
I *v.* the man whose heart is warm *T.* ii 372

VENERATION.
But *v.* or respect finds none *Con.* 739

VENGEANCE.
Heaven awards the *v.* due *B.* 42
And *V.* executes what Justice wills *Ch.* 82
"Keep wisdom, or meet *v.* in your turn! *Ex.* 244
Provoke the *v.* of his righteous hand *Ex.* 253
"Suffering the *v.* of eternal fire" *Ex.* 423
If Love reward him, or if *V.* strike *P.E.* 31
Exposed him to the *v.* of the laws? *T.* 45
A growing red of *v.* at his heels *T.* 258
Drops the dread *v.* from his willing hand *T.* 278
As *V.* can inflict, or sinners fear *T.* 554
Yet not in *v.*: as this smiling sky *T.* vi 258
V. at last pours down upon their coast *T.T.* 472

VENIAL.
Past indiscretion is a *v.* crime *T.* 491
The spaniel dying for some *v.* fault *T.* vi 418

VENISON.
Serve him with *v.*, and he chooses fish *Con.* 335
Turtle and *v.* all his thoughts employ *P.E.* 220
Wildfowl or *v.*, and his errand speeds *T.* iv 612

VENOM.
Of asps their *v.*, overpowering strength *T.* v 702
And charged perhaps with *v.*, that intrudes *T.* vi 569

VENT. [86
In earth's dark womb have found at last a *v. N.A.*

VENTILATE.
And *v.* and warm the swelling buds *T.* iii 426

VENTURE.
A task I *v.* on, impelled by thee *Ch.* 6
He has outslept the winter, *v.* forth *T.* vi 313
She *v.* onward with a prosperous force *T.T.* 266

VENTURED.
I *v.* once to break *B.R.* 10
Like something precious *v.* far from shore *P.E.* 520

VENUS.
For sea-born *V.* her attachment shows *Con.* 265
Where *V.* hears the lover's tender vow *Con.* 824

VERBOSELY.
(I hate long arguments *v.* spun) *E.* iii 44
Be most sublimely good, *v.* grand *T.* v 678

VERBS.
But conjugated *v.*, and nouns declined? *Tir.* 619

VERDANT.
The walk, still *v.*, under oaks and elms *T.* vi 70

VERDICT.
On Reason's *v.* is a madman's deed *Con.* 190
And lunacy the *v.* of the Court *T.* 448

VERDURE.
And, charged with putrid *v.*, breathe a gross *T.* ii 97
With *v.* not unprofitable, grazed *T.* iv 317
The *v.* of the plain lies buried deep *T.* v 21
Spreads the fresh *v.* of the field, and leads *T.T.* 692

VERGE. [519
Or e'er his hoof had pressed the crumbling *v. T.* vi

VERGING.
Seems *v.* fast towards the female side *P.E.* 430

VERIEST.
Thou wast the *v.* slave, in days of yore *Ex.* 526

VERNAL.
As the sun peeps, and *v.* airs breathe mild *T.* iii 443

VERMICULAR.
Gave them a twisted form *v. T.* i 30

VERMIN.
To poison *v.* that infest his plants *Con.* 256
Of *v.*, or at best of cock purloined *T.* i 563
Makes men mere *v.*, worthy to be trapped *T.* ii 683
The creeping *v.*, loathsome to the sight *T.* vi 568
With what *v.* else infest *Trans.* iii 13

VERSE.
With *v.* addressed to me? *B.R.* 28
And *v.*, more lasting, hues that never fade *Ch.* 108
V., like the laurel, its immortal meed *Ch.* 292
Far be the thought from any *v.* of mine *Ex.* 428
V. cannot stoop so low as thy desert *Ex.* 547 [654
How shall a *v.* impress thee? By what name *Ex.*
An Iliad, only not in *v.*, ensues *H.* 194
How sweet soe'er the *v.* complain *Miss* — 11
Oh that a *v.* had power, and could command *P.E.* 323
Let *v.* at length yield thee thy just reward *S.* i 4
"They shall be yours," my *V.* replies *St.* iii 35
(If e'er posterity see *v.* of mine) *T.* ii 578
The adultress! what a theme for angry *v.*! *T.* iii 64
And *v.* of mine shall never brand the wretch *T.* iii 72
To advertise in *v.* a public pest *T.* iv 501
For a lost world in solitude and *v. T.* iv 730
Till it out-mantle all the pride of *v. T.* v 680
Of poetry not lost, if *v.* of mine *T.* vi 726
To dress a Sofa with the flowers of *v. T.* vi 1007
The mighty plan, oracular, in *v. T.T.* 179 [291
Lost without thee the ennobling powers of *v. T.T.*
That *v.*, whatever fire the fancy warms *T.T.* 512
Than caper in the morris-dance of *v. T.T.* 519
V. in the finest mould of fancy cast *T.T.* 618
In *v.* well disciplined, complete, compact *T.T.* 647
Or ere the wheels of *v.* begin to roll *T.T.* 711
What need of Homer's *v.*, or Tully's prose *Tir.* 399
I sent you *v.*, and, as your Lordship knows *V.* 19
(Unless *v.* rescue thee awhile) a thing *Y.O.* 58

VERSED.
But *v.* in arts that while they seem to stay *R.* 383

VERSE-MAN.
So your *V.* I, and Clerk *St.* iv 9

VERTUMNUS.
And Flora, and *V.*; peopling earth *T.* vi 234

VESSEL.
The *v.* weighs, forsakes the shore *A Tale* 43

To check the *v.'s* course *Cast.* 20
The Christian *v.*, and defies the blast *H.* 168
Had made the *v.* heel *R.G.* 7
Weigh the *v.* up *R.G.* 25
VEST.
Again, when evening in her sober *v. Ch.* 262
But, unattired in that becoming *v. T.T.* 722
VESTAL.
Appears a spot upon a *v.'s* robe *T.* iv 554
VESTIBULE.
Diffused, make Earth the *v.* of Hell *P.E.* 465
VESTIGES.
On all the *v.* of truth attend *Con.* 219
VESTRIS.
The feats of *V.*, or the naval force *Con.* 58
Though *V.* on one leg still shine below *Tir.* 542
VESTURE.
When, playing with thy *v.'s* tissued flowers *M.P.* 75
VETERAN.
A *v.* warrior in the Christian field *Con.* 607
The *v.* steed excused his task at length *R.* 625
The *v.* shows, and gracing a grey beard *T.* i 406
A shattered *v.*, hollow-trunked perhaps *Y.O.* 4
VEX.
And *v.* their flesh with artificial sores *T.* i 582
VEXATIOUS.
He, foreseeing what *v. N.C.* 37
VEXED.
Till both grew *v.* and tired *A Tale* 22   [997
Renowned in ancient song; not *v.* with care *T.* vi
VICE.
V. passing current by the stamp of law *A.T.* 156
The seeming virtue weighed against the *v. Ch.* 457
(Though *V.* derided with a just design *Ch.* 487
Who prostitute it in the cause of *v. Con.* 27
With tiptoe-step *V.* silently succeeds *Ex.* 84
And free from every taint but that of *v. Ex.* 150
If *V.* received her retribution due *Ex.* 247
With Asiatic *v.* stored thy mind *Ex.* 372
Where only *V.* and Injury are tied *Ex.* 594
As fortune, *v.*, or folly may command *H.* 12
Here see the encouragement Grace gives to *v. H.* 495
V. seems already slain *H.F.* 6
His unexhausted mine, the sordid *v. P.E.* 51
Leave *V.* and Folly unsubdued behind *P.E.* 81
Than *V.'s* mean and disingenuous race *P.E.* 297
To purge and skim away the filth of *v. P.E.* 343
The Cross once seen is death to every *v. P.E.* 622
Nor those in which the stage gives *v.* a blow *R.* 685
His virtues were his pride; and that one *v. T.* 54
More nourish pride, that condescending *v. T.* 123
In cities, *v.* is hidden with most ease *T.* i 689 [ii 320
What *v.* has it subdued? whose heart reclaimed *T.*
It is a hungry *v.*;—it eats up all *T.* ii 680
Of *v.* in others but enhancing more *T.* ii 795
With such artillery armed. *V.* parries wide *T.* ii 810
Virtue and *v.* had boundaries in old time *T.* iii 75
Where *V.* has such allowance, that her shifts *T.* iii 106
He too may have his *v.*, and sometimes prove *T.* iv 604
For folly, gallantry for every *v. T.* iv 690
To live on terms of amity with *v. T.* v 658
No polish can make sterling, and that *v. T.* vi 990
Or in one article of *v.* reclaimed *Tir.* 241
To ears and eyes, the *v.* of the rest *Tir.* 274
Ranks as a virtue, and is yet a *v. Tir.* 465
That any thing but *v.* could win thy love *Tir.* 742
Keep *V.* restrained behind a double guard *T.T.* 66
When Perjury, that Heaven-defying *v. T.T.* 418

Not only *v.* disposes and prepares *T.T.* 438
Of Wantonness, where *v.* was taught by rule *T.T.* 627
VICINITY.
Their only crime, *v.* to you! *Her.* 52
VICIOUS.
For *v.* ends connected *F.* 42
A *v.* object still is worse *Mor.* 47
Or *v.*, and not therefore apt to teach *T.* ii 550
And *v.* pleasures; buys the boy a name *T.* ii 759
By *v.* Custom, raging uncontrolled *T.* iii 682
V. in act, in temper savage-fierce *T.* vi 487
Such *v.* habits as disgrace his name *Tir.* 531
From *v.* inmates and delights impure *Tir.* 892
That would reclaim a *v.* age *U.* 6
VICIOUSLY.
By nature weak, or *v.* inclined *P.E.* 432
VICISSITUDE.
V. wheels round the motley crowd *H.* 17
The sweet *v.* of day and night *H.* 488
VICTIM.
Conjecture gripes the *v.* in his paw *Ch.* 525
And while the *v.* slowly bled to death *Ex.* 498
The unpitied *v.* of ill-judged expense *R.* 512
And item down the *v.* of the past *St.* ii 4
In manners—*v.* of luxurious ease *T.* i 625
Is fed with many a *v.* Lo, he comes! *T.* iii 765
His *v.*, robbed of their defenceless all *T.* iv 458
To rend a *v.* trembling at his foot *T.* vi 411
And helpless *v.* with a sense so keen *T.* vi 475
The *v.* of his own tremendous choice *T.* vi 558
The *v.* of his own lascivious fires *T.T.* 606
VICTORIOUS.
V. seemed, and now the doctor's skill *Con.* 320
A long despised, but now *u.*, host *T.T.* 473
VICTORIOUSLY.
His tender heart *v.* impressed *A.T.* 4
VICTORY.
Crowned with a thousand *v.*, and at last *Ex.* 191
His *v.* was that of orient light *Ex.* 478
His *v.* are o'er *R.G.* 34
Of smiling *V.* that moment won *T.* ii 243
With joy beyond what *v.* bestows *T.T.* 80
So Gideon earned a *v.* not his own *T.T.* 360
And praised him in the *v.* He wrought *T.T.* 375
And *V.* refuted all he said *T.T.* 389
VIEW.
But where, however bleak the *v. A Tale* 3
The flame extinct, he *v.* the roving fire *B.B.* 11
Might we *v.* her enjoying it here *C.* 56
The rights of man were sacred in his *v. Ch.* 28
Alike important in their Maker's *v. Ch.* 203   [324
That Heaven spreads wide before the *v.* of man *Ch.*
Takes the resemblance of the good she *v. Ch.* 396
The cause of Virtue could not be his *v. Ch.* 542
His wise forbearance has their end in *v. Con.* 33
We dare not risk them into public *v. Con.* 371
Their *v.*, indeed, were indistinct and dim *Con.* 539
To spread the newborn glories in their *v. Con.* 546
Ought at the *v.* of an Almighty power *Con.* 658
It *v.* the truth with a distorted eye *Con.* 669
Than rove and stagger with no mark in *v. Con.* 864
And now just opening to our *v. E.* i 50
No shepherds' tents within thy *v.* appear *E.* ii 43
'Tis not with either of these *v. E.* iv 11
Candid and just, with no false aim in *v. Ex.* 648
Another of sinister *v. F.* 53
My poems enchanted I *v. Gr.* 30
When God and man stand opposite in *v. H.* 131
Dare step across his arbitrary *v. H.* 193

VIEW—VINTAGE

I glide and steal along with heaven in *v*. *H*. 379
And, while religion seems to be her *v*. *H*. 641
God's holy word, once trivial in his *v*. *H*. 706
Through all his art we *v*. *H.F.* 14
'Twas wonderful to *v*. *J.G.* 118
For, could I *v*. nor them nor thee *M*. 29
Imagination to his *v*. *Mor*. 29
And I can *v*. this mimic show of thee *M.P.* 119
Nor hold forbidden joys in *v*. *O*. ii 5
To wish myself the rock I *v*. *P*. 29
The maid who *v*. with pensive air *P.B.* 23
Exposed to *v*., but not to touch *P.B.* 30
V. constellations brighter than her own *P.E.* 178
But the muse, eagle-pinioned, has in *v*. *P.E.* 331
He *v*. it with complacency supreme *P.E.* 522
None sends his arrow to the mark in *v*. *P.E.* 570
To raise such wonders in her *v*. *Q.V.* 63 [*P.F.* 5
Twelve years have elapsed since I last took a *v*.
Up!—God has formed thee with a wiser *v*. *R*. 265
Till she resemble faintly what she *v*. *R*. 298
Nor *v*. of waters turning busy mills *R*. 334
Are life's prime pleasures in his simple *v*. *R*. 403
He *v*. it not, or sees no beauty there *R*. 470
Her slighted works to your admiring *v*. *R*. 543
Convinced at last, upon a nearer *v*. *R*. 591
Too rigid, in my *v*., that name to one *R*. 720
Employs, shut out from more important *v*. *R*. 803
Deceitful *v*. of future bliss, farewell! *T*. 9
What purpose has the King of Saints in *v*.? *T*. 179
V. him at Paris in his last career *T*. 311
Be still a pleasing object in my *v*. *T*. i 250
A faithful likeness of the forms he *v*. *T*. ii 293
With other *v*. of men and manners now *T*. iii 122
And paint his person, character and *v*. *T*. iii 143
V. him in all; ascribes to the grand cause *T*. iii 226
Proud of his well-spread walls, he *v*. his trees *T*. iii 408
Which all might *v*. with envy, none partake *T*. iii 718
It turns submitted to my *v*., turns round *T*. iv 98
The self-complacent actor, when he *v*. *T*. iv 200 [235
To *v*. some rugged rock or mouldering tower *T*. iv
Pendulous, and foreboding, in the *v*. *T*. iv 293
I *v*. the muscular proportioned limb *T*. v 15 [521
Shone brighter still, once called to public *v*. *T*. v
Man *v*. it and admires, but rests content *T*. v 791
With what he *v*. The landscape has his praise *T*. v 792
"If from your elevation, whence ye *v*. *T*. v 825
Such comprehensive *v*. the spirit takes *T*. vi 15[vi 66
And through the trees I *v*. the embattled tower *T*.
Or what he *v*. of beautiful or grand *T*. vi 249
Whose face too was familiar to his *v*. *T*. vi 494
Of objects, more illustrious in her *v*. *T*. vi 916
In sleep he seemed to *v*. *T.B.* 45
The young apostate sickens at the *v*. *Tir*. 167
The minor heroes *v*. with envious eyes *Tir*. 223
To set some living worthy in his *v*. *Tir*. 647 [*Tir*. 855
Who there will court thy friendship, with what *v*.
By selfish *v*., thus censured and cashiered *Tir*. 496
And it seemed to a fanciful *v*. The Rose 6 [*T.T.* 07
"There," said his guide, "the group is full in *v*.
Then *v*. him, self-proclaimed in a gazette *T.T.* 37
Opening and wider opening on her *v*. *T.T.* 265
That holds in *v*. the good of man *U*. 24
And *v*. with tears the expected harvest lost *V*. 57
Not always glitter in my *v*.) 1789, 26

VIEWED.
He turned and *v*. it oft on every side *A.T.* 203
V. a deliverer with disdain and hate *Ex*. 217
Prodigies ominous, and *v*. with fear *P.E.* 99
V. from a distance, and with heedless eyes *P.E.* 202
That goddess-like woman he *v*. *M.D.* 34
She *v*. the sparkling show *Q.V.* 74
Scenes must be beautiful which, daily *v*. *T*. i 177

VIEWING.
Has eyes indeed; and *v*. all she sees *T*. iii 245
That, *v*. it, we seem almost to obtain *Tir*. 312

VIEWLESS.
Upborne into the *v*. air *O*. i 13

VIGIL.
Soft airs, nocturnal *v*., and day dreams *R*. 260

VIGILANCE.
The *v*., the labour, and the skill *T*. iii 548
Of unremitted *v*. and care *T*. vi 209
Their strength, or speed, or *v*., were given *T*. vi 610

VIGILANT.
Much of her *v*. instinctive dread *T*. iii 340
V. over all that he has made *T.T.* 248

VIGOROUS.
Not e'en the *v*. and headlong rage *Con*. 45
V. in age as in the flush of youth *Con*. 601
No; these were *v*. as their sires *St*. i 9
The seed sown there, how *v*. is the plant! *T*. 362
Beneath his care, a thriving *v*. plant *T*. ii 714
Thy *v*. pulse, and the unhealthful East *T*. iv 363
Keen in pursuit, and *v*. to retain *Tir*. 524

VIGOUR.
And gains new *v*. at her endless task *Ch*. 104
Hast thou the *v*. of thy youth? an eye *Ep*. i 5
But youth, health, *v*. to expend *Mor*. 33
Which, though new-born, with *v*. move *Mrs. M*— 25
Their *v*., injured soon, not soon restored *T*. iii 608
Was left to spring by *v*. of his own *T.T.* 675

VILE.
To a *v*. clod, so draws him, with such force *T*. v 589
Than set your son to work at a *v*. trade *Tir*. 456
Where *v*. example (yours I chiefly mean *Tir*. 761

VILEST.
See volunteers in all the *v*. arts *Tir*. 835

VILLAGE.
Sought their own *v*., busied as they went *Con*. 509
Had cheered the *v*. with his song *N.G.* 2
Groves, heaths, and smoking *v*., remote *T*. i 176
In *v*. or in town, the bay of curs *T*. i 230
V., or hamlet, of this merry land *T*. iv 467
How soft the music of those *v*. bells *T*. vi 6

VILLAGER.
That calls the unwonted *v*. abroad *T*. vi 300

VILLAIN.
Oh for a law to noose the *v*.'s neck *T*. iv 462

VILLAS.
That show reversed the *v*. on their side *H*. 468
Suburban *v*., highway-side retreats *R*. 481
The *v*. with which London stands begirt *T*. iv 748

VINDICATE.
Assert the skies, and *v*. her due *T*. 490

VINDICTIVE.
The stroke that a *v*. God intends *Ex*. 407
Remorse, and Sorrow, and *v*. Pain *P.E.* 44

VINE.
Her unctuous olives, and her purple *v*. *Her*. 7
V., olives, herbage, forests disappear *Her*. 23 [iii 29
Where chance may throw me, beneath elm or *v*. *T*.
With all her *v*.; nor for Ausonia's groves *T*. ii 214
The state, beneath the shadow of whose *v*. *T*. vi 969
Where Rhenus strays his *v*. among *T.B.* 7

VINOSA.
"Adieu," *V*. cries, ere yet he sips *H*. 357

VINTAGE.
Her vaults below, where every *v*. meets *Ex*. 22

VIOLATED.
Time wasted, *v.* laws, abuse *F.A.* 14
By him, the *v.* law speaks out *T.* ii 340

VIOLATING.
Without the sin of *v.* thine *M.P.* 117

VIOLENCE.
And barbarous climes, where *v.* prevails *T.* i 604
To all the *v.* of lawless hands *T.* iv 591
But *v.* can never longer sleep *T.* v 204
Where *V.* shall never lift the sword *T.* vi 843

VIOLET.
The *v.*, the pink, the jessamine *M.P.* 76

VIRGIN.
Forgot the blush that *v.* fears impart *Ex.* 47
The unfading laurel, and the *v.* too! *Ex.* 601
But now alike, gay widow, *v.*, wife *R.* 519
Had he seduced a *v.*, wronged a friend *T.* 46
Whom once her *v.* modesty and grace *T.* iv 535

VIRTUE.
Of *v.* too well fenced to fear a flaw *A.T.* 155
But he, the *v.* of his lance to show *A.T.* 165
All other sorrows *v.* may endure *Ch.* 157
But slavery!—*V.* dreads it as her grave *Ch.* 163
The foe of *v.* has no claim to thee *Ch.* 288
The seeming *v.* weighed against the vice *Ch.* 457
Unless a love of *v.* light the flame *Ch.* 491
And even *V.*, so unfairly matched *Ch.* 511
The cause of *V.* could not be his view *Ch.* 542
Such *v.* had need prove their own reward *Ch.* 571
A vehicle of *v.*, truth, and love *Ch.* 624
Religion, *V.*, Reason, Common Sense *Con.* 77
And *V.* with peculiar charms appears *Con.* 637
Of *v.*, and religion's glorious cause *Con.* 686
The *v.* of old Rome for English use *Con.* 836
The *v.* they had learned in scenes of woe *Ex.* 80
While Honour, *V.*, Piety, bear sway *Ex.* 326
But left their *v.* and thine own behind *Ex.* 373
Unless a zeal for *v.* guide the blow *Ex.* 437
What *v.*, or what mental grace *F.* 1
But every *v.* of the soul *F.* 58
Yet has the wondrous *v.* to educe *H.* 155
His new-born *v.*, and preserve him pure *H.* 170
On what foundation *v.* is to stand *H.* 529 [*H.* 366
That Heaven will weigh man's *v.* and his crimes
A distant *v.* we can all confess *H.* 552
V. engages his assent *H.F.* 11
Suffered by *v.* combating below? *J.T.* 18
Preserved by *v.* from declension *M.F.* 51
When *v.* bids it flow *Miss* — 56
The gentler *V.* too are joined *Miss* — 77
"So Pity shall take *V.*'s part *Miss* — 89
The noblest minds their *v.* prove *P.* 61
Peace follows *V.* as its sure reward *P.E.* 42
Avarice shows, and *v.* is the price *P.E.* 52
That *V.* points to? Can a life thus spent *P.E.* 72
Temperance were no *v.* if he could *P.E.* 224
And some that seem to threaten *v.* less *P.E.* 227
All these belong to *v.*, and all prove *P.E.* 247
That *v.* has a title to your love *P.E.* 248
To give to *V.* what is *V.*'s due *P.E.* 294
Ye pimps, who, under *V.*'s fair pretence *P.E.* 315
The Graces, too, while *V.* at their shrine *P.E.* 337
Accomplishments have taken *V.*'s place *P.E.* 417
To *v.*, delicacy, truth, or sense *P.E.* 513
His undissembling *v.* to my breast *R.* 380
The love of *v.*, and the fear of God! *R.* 730
To cherish *V.* in an humble state *R.* 789
Sincere on *V.*'s side *St.* iii 18
Of *v.*, and yet lose it! Wherefore hard? *T.* 12
His *v.* were his pride; and that one vice *T.* 54
Made all his *v.* gewgaws of no price *T.* 55
And poisoned every *v.* in them both *T.* 116
Their own dear *v.* their unshaken trust *T.* 284
Some love of *v.*, and some power to praise *T.* 486
"Perish the *v.*, as it ought, abhorred *T.* 503
"Is *v.* then, unless of Christian growth *T.* 515
But still in *v.* of a Saviour's plea *T.* 529
Now summon every *v.*, stand and plead *T.* 566
That all your *v.* cannot purchase now *T.* 570
And well tired *v.*, could alone inspire *T.* i 148
Can boast but little *v.*; and inert *T.* i 623
Here *v.* thrives as in her proper soil *T.* i 600
But though true worth and *v.*, in the mild *T.* i 678
Or seen with least reproach; and *v.*, taught *T.* i 690
What wonder then that health and *v.*, gifts *T.* i 750
Support, and ornament of *V.*'s cause *T.* ii 336
Till they can laugh at *v.*, mock the fools *T.* ii 692
When learning, *v.*, piety, and truth *T.* ii 700
And *V.* fled. The schools became a scene *T.* ii 735
Where science and where *v.* are professed? *T.* ii 766
Of manners sweet as *V.* always wears *T.* ii 783
The charms of *v.* in their just esteem *T.* ii 796
Thou art the nurse of *V.* In thine arms *T.* iii 48
V. and vice had boundaries in old time *T.* iii 75
And thus gives *V.* indirect applause *T.* iii 104
Is *v.*; the only lasting treasure, truth *T.* iii 269
Friendly to thought, to *v.*, and to peace *T.* iii 291
Like *v.* thriving most where little seen *T.* iii 664
And *v.*, and those scenes which God ordained *T.* iii 703
To all the *v.* of those better days *T.* iii 745
What, conscious of your *v.*, we can spare *T.* iv 425
That felt their *v.*; Innocence, it seems *T.* iv 518
Impossible when *V.* is so scarce *T.* iv 531
Of public *v.* ever wished removed *T.* iv 615
The *v.*, temper, understanding, taste *T.* iv 790
Of *v.*, made one chief, whom times of peace *T.* v 239
By some whose patriot *v.* has prevailed *T.* v 295
For when was public *v.* to be found *T.* v 502
And useful quality, and *v.* too *T.* vi 623
Of rant and rhapsody in *v.*'s praise *T.* v 677
If not the *v.*, yet the worth of brutes *T.* vi 724
Of *v.*, and whom *v.*, fruit of faith *T.* vi 911
The man, whose *v.* are more felt than seen *T.* vi 972
Some sneaking *v.* lurks in him, no doubt *Tir.* 244
But how? resides such *v.* in that air *Tir.* 373
Ranks as a *v.*, and is yet a vice *Tir.* 465
Much zeal in *v.*'s cause all teachers boast *Tir.* 517
Two-thirds of all the *v.* that remains *Tir.* 810
'Tis to the *v.* of such men, man owes *T.T.* 19
To pour in *V.*'s lap her just reward *T.T.* 65
And praised for *v.* that they scorn to wear *T.T.* 116
Religion, *v.*, truth, whate'er we call *T.T.* 286
Not so. The *v.* still adorns our age *T.T.* 340
Than *V.* quickens, with a warmth divine *T.T.* 382
Patterns of every *v.*, every grace *T.T.* 373
But still, while *V.* kindled his delight *T.T.* 598
V. indeed meets many a rhyming friend *T.T.* 620
Gave *V.* and morality a grace *T.T.* 648
Fails not, in *v.* and in wisdom laid *Y.O.* 121

VIRTUOSO.
The *v.* thus, at noon *E.* iv 49

VIRTUOUS.
Apt emblem of a *v.* maid *Comp.* ii 2
And glory for the *v.* when they die *J.T.* 14
No *v.* wish can bear a date *Mor.* 57
V. and faithful Heberden, whose skill *R.* 279
Oh, tell thy thoughtless sex, the *v.* mind *S.* ii 6
But the age of *v.* politics is past *T.* v 493
The most disinterested and *v.* minds *Tir.* 438
His *v.* toil may terminate at last *Tir.* 777
That though school-bred the boy be *v.* still *Tir.* 840
Covetous only of a *v.* praise *T.T.* 75

In thee some *v.* qualities combine *V.* 31
Polite, yet *v.*, who has brought away *V.* 79
VISAGE.
That the *v.* or countenance had not a nose *A.C.* 19
Trees, churches, and strange *v.*, expressed *T.* iv 288
VISIBLE.
Not *v.*, his family of worlds *T.* iii 232
His other works, the *v.* display *T.* v 553
VISIBLY.
Dwelt *v.* the light-creating God *T.* 390
VISION.
Close to the part where *v.* ought to be *Ch.* 386
With *v.* prompted by intense desire *T.* i 451
VISIONARY.
There, like the *v.* emblem seen *T.* v 400
VISIT.
Of a land I shall *v.* no more *A.S.* 36
Whate'er they gave, should *v.* more *Cast.* 30
The brief proclaimed, it *v.* every pew *Ch.* 469
The *v.* paid, with ecstasy we come *Con.* 399
A transient *v.* intervening *E.* i 97
Thy nightly *v.* to my chamber made *M.P.* 58
My *v.* still, but never mine abode *T.* i 251
Shall *v.* earth in mercy; shall descend *T.* vi 743
Will win her *v.* or engage her stay *T.T.* 411
VISITED.
When we were *v.*, what hope for you ? *Ex.* 248
VISITING.
V. every flower with labour meet *Con.* 439
VISITOR.
A *v.* unwelcome, into scenes *T.* vi 570
VITAL.
That waste our *v.*; peculation, sale *T.* ii 668
Friendly to *v.* motion, may afford *T.* iii 509
Where now the *v.* energy that mov'd *T.* vi 134
VITREOUS.
Where all was *v.*; but in order due *T.* v 161
"VIVE LE ROY!"
With which he shouts and carols " *V.* ! " *T.T.* 243
VIVID.
In dazzling streaks the *v.* lightnings play *Her.* 18
That glossy shine, or *v.* flame *Mrs. M—* 10 [iii 525
Strained through the friendly mats a *v.* green *T.*
VOCAL.
Till Gratitude grew *v.* in the praise *R.* 555
Made *v.* for the amusement of the rest *T.* iv 159
VOCIFERATED.
V. logic kills me quite *Con.* 113
VOCIFEROUS.
V., and impatient of delay *T.* i 299
VOGUE.
Are bringing into *v.* their heathen train *Con.* 821
From top to toe the Geta now in *v. T.* 202
VOICE.
A louder *v.* than yours I heard *B.R.* 3
With her book, and her *v.*, and her lyre *C.* 49
Had heard his *v.* in every blast *Cast.* 45
No *v.* divine the storm allayed *Cast.* 61
Oh that the *v.* of clamour and debate *Ch.* 309
Your elevated *v.* goes through the brain *Con.* 328
That odious libel on a human *v.* ? *Con.* 450
Though common sense, allowed a casting *v. Con.* 663
And having chosen evil, scorned the *v. Ex.* 398
He was a traitor by the general *v. Ex.* 545
But if a sweeter *v.*, and one designed *Ex.* 726
When from within it thus a *v.* replied *F.A.* 10

All speak one language, all with one sweet *v. H.* 53
Or *v.* of turtle in your land is heard *H.* 470
Now by the *v.* of his experience true *H.* 707
Would raise her *v.*, and roar *J.P.* 10
Then raising her *v.* to a strain *M.D.* 17
(And raised her *v.*, and frowned beside) *M.F.* 16
Then, with a *v.* exceeding low *M.F.* 29
V. only fails, else how distinct they say *M.P.* 5
Are the *v.* with which He speaks *N.C.* 36
Counsel and caution from a *v.* like mine ! *P.E.* 10
Man thus endued with an elective *v. P.E.* 45
Impart to things inanimate a *v. R.* 361
For once I can approve the patriot's *v. R.* 387
Hear the sweet accents of his tuneful *v. R.* 771
At length a *v.* which well he knew *R.C.* 87
Cowper, whose silver *v.*, tasked sometimes hard *S.* i 1
Thou art not *v.* alone, but hast beside *S.* i 9
But, naming none, the *v.* now speaks to all *St.* ii 20
Nightly lifts his *v.* on high *St.* iv 6
Her *v.* is terrible though soft *St.* v 23
Of distant floods, or on the softer *v. T.* 191 [*T.* ii 351
But hark—the doctor's *v.*!—fast wedged between
O that unwelcome *v.* of heavenly love *T.* 463 [ii 728
Was quenched in rheums of age, his *v.*, unstrung *T.*
The *v.* of singing and the sprightly chord *T.* ii 78
Not by a mighty wind, but by that *v. T.* ii 113
His frown was full of terror, and his *v. T.* ii 721
Each for itself, and all as with one *v. T.* iii 653
And give them *v.* and utterance once again *T.* iv 35
And the clear *v.*, symphonious, yet distinct *T.* iv 162
And by the *v.* of all its elements *T.* ii 52 [*T.* v 650
"Nay—conduct hath the loudest tongue. The *v.*
The still small *v.* is wanted. He must speak *T.* v 685
Sent forth a *v.*, and all the sons of God *T.* v 821
A teaching *v.*; but 'tis the praise of thine *T.* v 858
A *v.* is heard that mortal ears hear not *T.* v 886 [887
Till Thou hast touched them, 'tis the *v.* of song *T.* v
And utter now and then an awful *v. T.* vi 34
And heard the *v.* of love *The Doves* 6   [418
And deans, no doubt, and chapters, with one *v. Tir.*
Condemns, approves, and with a faithful *v. Tir.* 33
Seem with one *v.* to delegate to you ? *Tir.* 554
But all are not alike. Thy warning *v. Tir.* 797
Now look on him, whose very *v.* in tone *Tir.* 845
Though in *v.* and shape they be *Trans.* iii 17
A querulous old woman's *v. Trans.* iv 25
To teach, no Spirit dwells in thee, nor *v. Y.O.* 138
VOID.   [*Con.* 626
When some green heads, as *v.* of wit as thought
So *v.* of all utility or aim *H.* 88   [*Ex.* 175
For them, the states they left made waste and *v.*
Wild as if Nature there, *v.* of all good *H.* 540
Or sought with energy, must fill the *v. R.* 748
To fill the *v.* of an unfurnished brain *T.* iv 209
Unoccupied, has filled the *v.* so well *T.* v 557
For human fellowship, as being *v. T.* vi 322
Was lumber in an age so *v.* of taste *T.T.* 619
VOIDED.
Of *v.* pulse or half-digested grain *T.* v 95
VOLCANO.
Where no *v.* pours his fiery flood *Her.* 85
That metropolitan *v.* make *T.* iii 737
VOLLEY.
The undreaded *v.* with a sword of straw *T.* ii 811
Skin-piercing *v.*, blossom-bruising hail *T.* v 141
VOLTAIRE.   [*T.* 304
(" Mention him, if you please ;—*V.* ?" "The same ")
VOLUBLE.
Thrice must the *v.* and restless earth *T.* iii 490
VOLUME.
In *v.* wheeling slow, the vapour dank *T.* iii 499

The v. closed, the customary rites *T.* iv 167
I thought the v. I presumed to send *V.* 39
VOLUMINOUS.
Dark and v. the vapours rise *Her.* 15
VOLUNTARY.
His v. pains, severe and long *T.* 101
Starts to the v. race again *T.* vi 333
VOLUNTEERS.
See v. in all the vilest parts *Tir.* 835
VOLUPTUARIES.
No;—the v., who ne'er forget *T.* 341
VORACIOUS.
By worms v. eating through and through *T.* i 27
To his v. bag, struggling in vain *T.* iv 450
As oft return, a pert v. kind *T.* v 69
VORTIGINOUS.
Or with v. and hideous whirl *T.* ii 102
VOTARY.
Too oft betrays the v. of his fires *A.T.* 30
And would degrade her v. to an ape *Con.* 460
Could bend one knee, engage one v. there *H.* 506
And each inclines its v. to retreat *R.* 174
V. of Pleasure still, where'er she dwells *R.* 539
Come then, and thou shalt find thy v. calm *T.* iv 259
Of abler v. to cleanse the stain *T.T.* 635
V. of business and of pleasure prove *V.* 71
VOTE.
Who v. for hire, or point it with lampoon *Con.* 29
To be refunded duly, when his v. *T.* iii 799

VOUCHSAFES.
Nature indeed, v. for our delight *H.* 487
V., at least, to pitch the key of rhyme *T.T.* 188
V. to man a poet's just pretence *T.T.* 699
VOUCHSAFED.
The reasoning power v. of course inferred *Con.* 431
Where Paradise seemed still v. on earth *Ex.* 420
Are never long v., if pushed aside *Ex.* 690
Than opportunity v. to err *F.A.* 16
By good v. makes known superior good *H.* 147
VOUCHSAFING.
Unmasked, v. this their sole excuse *T.* ii 695
VOW.
His v. was (and he well performed his v.) *A.T.* 139
Where Venus hears the lover's tender v. *Con.* 824
This heartless v. may Heaven receive *Miss —* 93
VOYAGE.
Bound on a v. of awful length *H.F.* 17
VOYAGER.
(As in a map the v. his course) *T.* vi 17
VULCAN.
Him, Tubal named, the *V.* of old times *T.* v 217
VULGAR.
Built by no mercenary v. hand *Ch.* 257
The astonished v. trembled, while he tore *Ex.* 13
The portion of a mean or v. mind *R.* 502
From v. minds, have honour much at heart *R.* 728
Food for the v. merely—is an art *T.* iii 449
VULGARLY.
Sighs for his exit, v. called death *H.* 90

W.

WADDED.
Wide-elbowed, and w. with hair *Gr.* 11
WADDING.
And o'er the seat, with plenteous w. stuffed *T.* i 31
WADING.
His wonted strut; and, w. at their head *T.* v 74
WAFT.
That comes to w. us out of sorrow's power *Con.* 592
Whom the winds w. where'er the billows roll *Ex.* 19
Now Truth, perform thine office, w. aside *H.* 570 [35
The selfsame gale that w. the fragrance round *Her.*
And w. it to the mourner as he roves *R.* 338
W. the rich prize to its appointed use *T.* iii 540
The wings that w. our riches out of sight *T.* iii 760
WAFTED.
The soothing influence of the w. strains *T.* vi 68
WAG.
"Come, neighbours, we must w.—" *Y.D.* 50
WAGE.
A warm dispute once chanced to w. *J.P.* 3
Reduce his w., or get rid of her *T.* 211
Well may the Church w. unsuccessful war *T.* ii 809
W. war, with any or with no pretence *T.* v 314
And in their service w. perpetual war *T.* vi 894 [30
That Grace and Nature have to w. through life *Tir.*
For w. so unlikely to be paid *Tir.* 457
Is odious, and their w. all their joy *Tir.* 824
WAGED.
But w. with Death a lasting strife *Cast.* 17
W. with defenceless innocence, while he *T.* vi 393
The bottomless demands of contest w. *Y.O.* 102

WAGGON.
Thy w. is thy wife, and the poor beasts *T.* iv 367
WAIF.
'Twas hard perhaps on here and there a w. *T.* iii 80
WAILED.
Plaintive and piteous, as it wept and w. *T.* iv 479
WAILING.
No womanish or w. grief has part *R.* 773
WAIN.
The loaded w., while lightened of its charge *T.* i 296
The w. that meets it passes swiftly by *T.* i 297
The w. goes heavily, impeded sore *T.* iv 343
WAINSCOAT.
Fix on the w. a distressful stare *Con.* 116
WAIST. [*T.* iv 6
With spatter'd boots, strapp'd w., and frozen locks
Wreaths for her brow, and girdles for her w. *A.T.* 14
Still dangling at his w. *J.G.* 132 [155
Who spanned her w., and who, where'er he came *T.*
Greets with three cheers exulting. At his w. *T.* i 523
With belted w. and pointers at their heels *T.* ii 753
That reeling goddess with the zoneless w. *T.* iii 52
With wig prolix, down flowing to his w. *Tir.* 361
WAIT.
Shame and ruin w. for you" *B.* 44
Fairest and foremost of the train that w. *Ch.* 1
O most degrading of all ills that w. *Ch.* 155
W. for the dawning of a brighter day *Ch.* 167
They dare not w. the riotous abuse *Con.* 261
Who w. for heaven ere he becomes divine *Con.* 584
And w., in snug concealment laid *Ep.* ii 39

Her peaceful shores, where busy commerce'w. *Ex.*13
W. but the lashes of a wintry storm *H.* 185
The common care that w. on all beside *H.* 539
But happier far, who comfort those that w. *H.* 762
"The dinner w., and we are tired" *J.G.* 147
And bees in hives as idly w. *N.* 3   [*T.* ii 5
How each would trembling w. the mournful sheet
Scorned by the rest, with patient hope they w. *R.* 165
The rest too busy, or too gay, to w. *T.* 40
Nor less composure w. upon the roar *T.* 190
Then boast (but w. for that unhoped-for hour) *T.* 401
Far fetched and little worth, nor seldom w. *T.* i 243
To w. the close of all ? But grant her end *T.* ii 65
Who w. to dress us, arbitrates their date *T.* ii 600
Ten thousand dangers lie in w. to thwart *T.* iii 553
That cheer but not inebriate, w. on each *T.* iv 40
In unrecumbent sadness. There they w. *T.* v 29
That w. on man, the flight performing horse *T.* vi 426
The dust that w. upon his sultry march *T.* vi 741
"Those ills that w. on all below *The Doves* 17
A disappointment w. him even there *Tir.* 566
I pity kings whom worship w. upon *T.T.* 121
For long forbearing Clemency to w. *T.T.* 401
The laurel seemed to w. on his command *T.T.* 688

WAITER.
The Christian Hope is—*W.*, draw the cork *H.* 361
There w. Dick, with bacchanalian lays *Tir.* 214

WAIVES.
She rather w. than will dispute her right *Ch.* 430

WAKE.
And Bonner, blithe as shepherd at a w. *Ex.* 614
W. the sooner for his cry *St.* iv 8
Wins no notice, w. no fears *St.* iv 20
And tremble when I w., for all the wealth *T.* ii 31

WAKING.
Or, w. at the call of lust alone *Ex.* 101
They sleep secure from w. *F.* 123
Soothed with a w. dream of houses, towers *T.* iv 287

WALK.
W. arm in arm with Nature all his way *Ch.* 314
With one he stumbled on, and lost his w. *Con.* 280
The social w., or solitary ride *Con.* 733
What w. we take, what books we choose *E.* i 6
Taking my lonely winding w., I mused *F.A.* 8
Of those that w. at evening where ye dwell *H.* 472
A poet, in his evening w. *P.* 39
Umbrageous w. and solitary seats *R.* 258
'Tis such an easy w., so smooth and straight *R.* 489
Some trivial slips their daily w. attend *T.* 286
The light they w. by, kindled from above *T.* 369
For I have loved the rural w. through lanes *T.* i 109
Of thorny boughs : have loved the rural w. *T.* i 112
And witness, dear companion of my w. *T.* i 144
From sultry suns, and in their shaded w. *T.* i 256
We tread the Wilderness, whose well-rolled w. *T.* i 351
He w., he leaps, he runs—is winged with joy *T.* i 443
But thus admonished, we can w. erect *T.* ii 593
Even daylight has its dangers; and the w. *T.* iv 572
He stands erect; his slouch becomes a w. *T.* iv 639
The cottage, w. along the plastered wall *T.* v 19
To w. with God, to be divinely free *T.* v 722   [247
Happy who w. with him ! whom what he finds *T.* vi
The w., still verdant, under oaks and elms *T.* vi 70
W. forth to meditate at eventide *T.* vi 949

WALKED.
He w. abroad, o'ertaken in the rain *Con.* 277

WALL.
In starry forms disposed upon the w. *Ch.* 552
The cedar and the hyssop on the w. *H.* 287   [351
Where mouldering abbey w. o'erhang the glade *H.*
From stuccoed w. smart arguments rebound *H.* 346

And smite the untempered w.'tis death to spare *H.* 627
Upon his dungeon w. the lightning play *H.* 718
On many a splendid w. *Q.V.* 46
Like bottled wasps upon a southern w. *R.* 494
And throws Italian light on English w. *T.* i 425 [408
Proud of his well-spread w., he views his trees *T.* iii
Enjoy close shelter, w., or reeds, or hedge *T.* iii 474
The cottage, walk along the plastered w. *T.* v 19
Smooth as a w. the upright remnant stands *T.* v 36
To read, engraven on the mouldy w. *T.* v 418 [133
To enrich thy w. : but thou didst hew the floods *T.* v
Praise is in all her gates : upon her w. *T.* vi 808
The w. on which we tried our graving skill *Tir.* 306

WALNUT.
But now, beneath this w. shade *Ep.* ii 37

WAN.
Gorgonius sits, abdominous and w. *P.E.* 217
Pale, w., and livid, but assuming soon *T.* iii 523 [162
Copious of flowers the woodbine, pale and w. *T.* vi

WAND.
But Rome, with sorceries and magic w. *Ex.* 508
Then with his silver beard and magic w. *P.E.* 183
With magic w. So potent is the spell *T.* ii 630
Pursue the track of his directing w. *T.* iii 777 [183
While we retrace with Memory's pointing w. *T.* iv
But smooth with w. from Ouse's side *T.B.* 28

WANDER.
We w. o'er a sunburnt thirsty soil *Ch.* 220
And here I w. eve and morn *M.B.* 11
Tell him he w., that his error leads *P.E.* 544
If a wish w. that way, call it home *P.E.* 586
And every thought that w. is a crime *R.* 224
There often w. one, whom better days *T.* i 534
And silent woods I w., far from those *T.* iii 118
In which all comprehension w. lost *T.* iv 75
Which whoso sees no longer w. lost *T.* v 847
The sun proceeds, I w. Neither mist *T.* vi 296

WANDERED.
I w. on his side *D.W.* 4
One silent eve I w. late *The Doves* 5

WANDERER.
To teach the w., as his woes increase *Ch.* 161
Himself a w. from the narrow way *P.E.* 118
Sets off a w. into foreign lands *P.E.* 378
But if the w. his mistake discern *P.E.* 610
To distant caves the lonely w. flies *R.* 769
The pensive w. in their shades. At eve *T.* i 761
Reclaims the w., binds the broken heart *T.* ii 344
I see that all are w., gone astray *T.* iii 124

WANDERING.
Reclaim the w. thousands, and bring home *Ex.* 728
To catch the w. notice of mankind *H.* 137
And being lost, perhaps, and w. wide *N.A.* 97
Replace the w. comet in his sphere *T.* 400
And breathing wholesome air, and w. much *T.* i 589
And w. eyes, still leaning on the arm *T.* iii 53 [815
The world of w. knights and squires to town *T.* iii
No loose or wanton, though a w. Muse *T.* iii 692
W., and littering with unfolded silks *T.* vi 280 [659
When w. Charles, who meant to be the third *T.* vi
To w. sheep, resolved to follow none *T.* vi 891
Nor ignorantly w. miss the skies *Tir.* 108

WANE.   [14
Whence comes it then, that in the w. of life *E.* iii
States thrive or wither, as moons wax and w. *Ex.* 324
Wrought this disturbance. But the w. is near *T.* vi 709

WANING.
Which, oft neglected, in life's w. years *Tir.* 589

WANNISH.
And of a w. grey ; the willow such *T.* i 309

WANT.

As frequent as the *w.* of it appears *Ch.* 605
Discourse may *w.* an animated—No *Con.* 101
For *w.* of prominence and just relief *Con.* 127
Their *w.* of light and intellect supplied *Con.* 147
Thou art indeed the drug a gardener *w. Con.* 255
Their mind a wilderness through *w.* of care *H.* 233
The *w.* of both denotes a meaner breed *H.* 292
With nothing here that *w.* to be concealed *H.* 406
And learned too late, it *w.* the grace *Mor.* 37
Sure ne'er to *w.* them, mathematic truths *N.A.* 80
But apples we *w.*, and apples we'll have *P.A.* 30
Earn if you *w.*; if you abound, impart *P.E.* 253
Ye *w.* but that to seem indeed divine *R.* 558
For *w.* of powers proportioned to the post *R.* 612
An idler is a watch that *w.* both hands *R.* 681
Faith, *w.* of common sense *St.* vi 22
Such *w.* it;—and that *w.*, uncured *St.* vi 33
Feels not the *w.* that pinch the poor *Trans. H.* 10
That *w.* no driving and disdains the lead *T.T.* 134
"The remedy you *w.* I freely give *T.* 273
O blessed effect of penury and *w. T.* 361
No *w.* of timber then was felt or feared *T.* i 57
His *w.*, indeed, are many; but supply *T.* i 597
The minister of man, to serve his *w. T.* ii 138 [773
Through *w.* of care; or her whose winking eye|*T.* ii
Can he *w.* occupation who has these ? *T.* iii 359 [440
Her *w.* of care, screening and keeping warm *T.* iii
Strange that so fair a creature should yet *w. T.* iii 725
Still *w.* a grace, the loveliest it could show *T.* iii 782
And labour too. Meanwhile ye shall not *w. T.* iv 424
To *w.* of judgment than to wrong design *T.* vi 657
With what intense desire he *w.* his home *Tir.* 562
Though *w.* of due restraint alone have bred *Tir.* 533
'Twas negligence in him, not *w.* of worth *T.T.* 681

WANTED.

Now N. had a wife, and he *w.* but one *A.T.* ii 7
He *w.*, for a wealthier to enjoy! *T.* iii 789
Firm as a rock. Nor *w.* aught within *T.* v 156
The still small voice is *w.* He must speak *T.* v 685
With problems. History not *w.* yet *Y.O.* 159

WANTING.

And *w.* him to loose the sacred seal *Con.* 544
There, *w.* nothing save a fan *R.C.* 17
But elbows still were *w.*; these, some say *T.* i 60
Of British natures, *w.* its excuse *T.* v 481
Yet *w.* sensibility) the man *T.* vi 562
W. its proper base to stand upon *T.T.* 54

WANTON.

They sport like *w.* doves in airy rings *A.T.* 32
Religion curbs indeed its *w.* play *Con.* 595   [53
They stretched the neck, and rolled the *w.* eye *Ex.*
Who studies Nature with a *w.* eye *R.* 213
Too rudely *w.* with her hair *R.C.* 32
Play *w.*, every moment, every spot *T.* i 349
Upon the *w.* breezes. Strew the deck *T.* ii 256
Grow *w.*, and give proof to every eye *T.* ii 443
No loose or *w.*, though a wandering Muse *T.* iii 692
And *w.* vagrants, as make London, vast *T.* iii 833
And *w.* in the pebbly gulf below *T.* v 103
The horse as *w.*, and almost as fleet *T.* vi 330
But if Authority grow *w.*, woe *T.T.* 226
Too apt to play the *w.* with her powers *T.T.* 301
To the lascivious pipe and *w.* song *T.T.* 462

WANTONED.

Now *w.* lost in flags and reeds *D.W.* 9

WANTONLY.

As to be *w.* incurred *M.F.* 34

WANTONNESS.

But *w.* and woe *A Tale* 76

And *w.*, and gluttonous excess *T.* i 688
Of *W.*, where vice was taught by rule *T.T.* 627

WAR.

Forgetful of the glorious toils of *w. A.T.* 28
Whoever threatens *w.*, to speak of peace *Ch.* 421
With all the guilt of such unnatural *w. Con.* 188
In peace possessing what they won by *w. Ex.* 193
Chaos of contrarieties at *w. Ex.* 295
W. lays a burden on the reeling state *Ex.* 306
Claimed all the glory of thy prosperous *w. ? Ex.* 347
To *w.* with pleasure, idolized before *Ex.* 410
Or serves the champion in forensic *w. Ex.* 664
Of an eternal, universal *w. H.* 648
And tumult, and intestine *w. M.F.* 48
That brother should not *w.* with brother *N.G.* 29
That civil *w.* embitters all his life *T.* 468
W. and the chase engross the savage whole *T.* i 608
W. followed for revenge, or to supplant *T.* i 609
Of unsuccessful or successful *w. T.* ii 4
Forgets in peace the injuries of *w. T.* ii 269
Of holy discipline, to glorious *w. T.* ii 348   [809
Well may the Church wage unsuccessful *w. T.* ii
Some write a narrative of *w.* and feats *T.* iii 139
The tumult and am still. The sound of *w. T.* iv 100
Beneath one head for purposes of *w. T.* iv 666 [187
But *w.'s* a game which, were their subjects wise *T.* v
Are sown the sparks that kindle fiery *w. T.* v 206
To a keen edge and made it bright for *w. T.* v 216
Thus *w.* began on earth : these fought for spoil *T.* v 228
Was chosen leader; him they served in *w. T.* v 233
Thus *w.* affording field for the display *T.* v 238
Wage *w.*, with any or with no pretence *T.* v 314
Earth groans beneath the burden of a *w. T.* vi 392
And in their service wage perpetual *w. T.* vi 894
See great commanders making *w.* a trade *Tir.* 821
Fierce, avaricious, proud, there must be *w. T.T.* 10
Glorious in *w.*, but for the sake of peace *T.T.* 278
In all that *w.* against that title most *T.T.* 429
All are his instruments; each form of *w. T.T.* 446

WARBLER.

Will the sweet *w.* of the livelong night *Con.* 445
Ten thousand *w.* cheer the day, and one *T.* 200
And Sidney, *w.* of poetic prose *T.* iv 516
And every *w.* has his tune by heart *T.T.* 655

WARBLES.

The redbreast *w.* still, but is content *T.* vi 78

WARBLING.

By the nightingale *w.* nigh *C.* 12
And *w.* out his approbation *Iv.G.* 24
The *w.* of the blackbird, clear and strong *R.* 569
Birds *w.* all the music. We can spare *T.* i 764

WARDER.

The *w.* at the door his key applies *H.* 720

WARE.

A great retailer of the curious *w. Con.* 229
Full ten miles off, at *W.*—*J.G.* 152
And I should dine at *W.*"—*J.G.* 196
The show-glass fraught with glittering *w. P.B.* 24
Are there who purchase of the Doctor's *w. ? T.* ii 366

WARFARE.

His *w.* is within. There unfatigued *T.* vi 935

WARILY.

W. therefore, and with prudent heed *T.* iii 470

WARLIKE.

And him in peace, for sake of *w.* deeds *T.* v 234

WARM.   [*A.T.* 79

Lay snug and *w.*;—'twas Summer's farewell peep!
Suppose (when thought is *w.*, and fancy flows *Ch.* 379
In language *w.* as all that love inspires *Ch.* 401 [63
Broad-cloth without, and a *w.* heart within *E.* iii

WARM—WASTE

These curtains, that keep the room w. *Gr.* 37
A w. dispute once chanced to wage *J.P.* 3
In vain w. suns their influence shed *Miss* — 37
In youth immortal w. *Miss* — 78
In scarlet mantle w., and velvet capped *M.P.* 51
But w., and bright, and calm as May *P.T.* 10
And hides his hands to keep his fingers w. *T.* 148
Of w. encouragement, and in the eye *T.* i 695
I venerate the man whose heart is w. *T.* ii 372
His w. but simple home, where he enjoys *T.* iii 389
And ventilate and w. the swelling buds *T.* iii 426
Her want of care, screening and keeping w. *T.* iii 440
These on the w. and genial earth that hides *T.* iii 516
There blooms exotic beauty, w. and snug *T.* iii 568
Begs a w. office, doomed to a cold jail *T.* iii 820
Escapes unhurt beneath so w. a veil *T.* iv 332 [166
And all was moist to the w. touch; a scene *T.* v
And History, so w. on meaner themes *T.* v 729
To frisk awhile, and bask in the w. sun *T.* vi 314
Supplies with w. activity and force *T.T.* 220
That verse, whatever fire the fancy w. *T.T.* 512
Elegant as simplicity, and w. *T.T.* 588 [*Tir.* 444
Young heads are giddy, and young hearts are w.
And keep him w. and filial to the last *Tir.* 894
Pay me for thy w. retreat *Trans.* iii 5
Whose worth deserves as w. a lay *U.* 3

WARMED.
The churches w., they would no longer hold *Ch.* 606
Well read, well tempered, with religion w. *Con.* 640
And, w. by the pressure, is all in a glow *F.M.* 8
Had we their wisdom, should we, often w. *St.* ii 25
W., while it lasts, by labour, all day long *T.* iv 377
Retires, content to quake, so they be w. *T.* iv 386
The charity that w. his heart was moved *T.* vi 498

WARMER.
With w. wishes sent *Cast.* 10 [213
And fields without a flower, for w. *France T.* ii

WARMEST.
Saints offer nothing, in their w. prayers *R.* 221
Delusive most where w. wishes are *T.* i 542

WARMING.
W. his heart, should at his lips transpire? *Con.* 484

WARMLY. [59
That thou mightest know me safe and w. laid *M.P*

WARMTH.
Offer him w., security, and rest *T.* 252
Spin round upon her axle, ere the w. *T.* iii 491
The silence and the w. enjoyed within *T.* iv 310
Of flowers that feared no enemy but w. *T.* v 159
And has the w. of May. The vault is blue *T.* vi 62
Than Virtue quickens, with a w. divine *T.T.* 382

WARN. [*Ex.* 243
They w. and teach the proudest would they learn
Prompt to persuade, expostulate, and w. *Ex.* 441
And seem to w. him never to repeat *H.* 355 [35
W. him or prompts, approves him or restrains *P.E.*
May punish, if he please, the less, to w. *T.* ii 157
To w., and teach him safely to unbend *Tir.* 608

WARNED.
He, therefore, timely w., himself supplies *T.* iii 439

WARNING.
I know the w. song is sung in vain *Ex.* 724
Still need repeated w., and at last *St.* ii 26
But all are not alike. Thy w. voice *Tir.* 797

WARP.
And either w. or lays it useless by *Con.* 670
And w. the consciences of public men *T.* ii 691
Did pity of their sufferings w. aside *T.* iv 453
But not to w. or change it. We are his *T.* v 343
Can move or w.; and gratitude for small *T.* vi 629
Unless the sway of custom w. thy course *Tir.* 862

WARPED. [778
The doctrines w. to what they never meant *Con.*
The worst is—Scripture w. from its intent *P.E.* 437
And, w. into the labyrinth of lies *Tir.* 157
W. into tough knee-timber, many a load! *Y.O.* 99

WARRANT.
Expedience as a w. for the deed? *Ch.* 183
Let slip with such a w. to destroy? *T.* ii 54
By regal w., or self-joined by bond *T.* iv 664
Can find no w. there. Feed then, and yield *T.* vi 456

WARRING.
Had bid defiance to the w. world *Ex.* 212

WARRIOR.
When the British w. queen *B.* 1
A veteran w. in the Christian field *Con.* 607
The sable w., frantic with regret *Ch.* 145
Made thee at last a w. like his own *Ex.* 491
No crested w. dips his plume in blood *Her.* 86
His host of wooden w. to and fro *T.* vi 266
Brings down the w. trophy to the dust *T.T.* 7

WARWICK.
Guy Earl of W. and fair Eleanore *Con.* 243

WASH.
Until he came unto the W.—*J.G.* 135
And there he threw the W. about *J.G.* 137

WASHED.
W. with a neatness scrupulously nice *Ex.* 149
W. headlong from on board *Cast.* 4
W. by the sea, or on the gravelly bank *T.* i 13
If ever it has w. our distant shore *T.* i 656
The frequency of crimes has w. them white *T.* iii 71
The soil must be renewed, which often w. *T.* iii 609
The deluge w. it out; but left unquenched *T.* v. 209
The Rose had been w. (just w. in a shower) *The Rose* 1

WASP.
Like bottled w. upon a southern wall *R.* 494
Censorious, and her every word a w. *T.* 160

WASTE.
And w. them, as thy sword has wasted ours" *Ch.* 80
Neglected, leaves a dreary w. behind *Comp.* i 12
That after man's defection laid all w. *Con.* 752
Far from the flock, and in a boundless w. *E.* ii 42 [175
For them, the states they left made w. and void *Ex.*
His anger who can w. thee with a word *Ex.* 341 [427
And praised the wrath that laid her beauties w. *Ex.*
To w. thy life in arms, or lay it down *Ex.* 536
That thankless w. and wild abuse destroy *Ex.* 679
In scenes of plenty, or the pining w. *Ex.* 733 [32
Whose prospect shows thee a disheartening w. *H.*
In vain opinion's w. and dangerous wild *H.* 279
Piles up his stores amidst the frozen w. *H.* 475
These, amidst scenes as w. as if denied *H.* 538
Nor labour they, nor time nor talents w. *H.* 766
No pleasure! Has some sickly eastern w. *P.E.* 255
And feed the fire that w. thy powers away *R.* 264
Curling and whitening over all the w. *R.* 531
To w. unheard the music of his strains *R.* 548
To close life wisely, may not w. my own *R.* 808
The fruitful scenes and prospects w. *S.* 21
Die self-accused of life run all to w.? *St.* ii 28
Sad w.! for which no after-thrift atones *St.* ii 29
Again life's dreary w. *St.* iii 6
And range an Indian w. without a tree *T.* i 261
Commits no wrong, nor w. what it enjoys *T.* i 334
The dreary w.; there spends the livelong day *T.* i 457
Exploring far and wide the watery w. *T.* i 665
On God's behalf, lays w. his fairest works *T.* ii 136
W. youth in occupations only fit *T.* ii 636
That w. our vitals; peculation, sale *T.* ii 668
Not w. it, and aware that human life *T.* iii 363
The effect of laziness or sottish w. *T.* iv 431 [iv 573
Through pathless w. and woods unconscious once *T.*

WASTE—WAVY

The loaded soil, and ye may w. much good *T.* v 756
Would w. attention at the checker'd board *T.* vi 265
Thus idly do we w. the breath of praise *T.* vi 711
'Twere wild profusion all, and bootless w. *Tir.* 49
A childish w. of philosophic pains *Tir.* 76 [*Tir.*614
On moments squandered else, and running all to w.
For loose expense and fashionable w. *Tir.* 204
Would deem it no abuse, or w. of pains *Tir.* 627
The post-horns of all Europe, lays her w. *T.T.* 32
To hear it called extravagance and w. *T.T.* 163
And w. it at the bidding of his hand *T.T.* 451

WASTED.
Thou that hast w. earth, and dared despise *Ch.* 69
And waste them, as thy sword has w. ours " *Ch.* 80
To succour w. regions, and replace *Ch.* 129
Our w. oil unprofitably burns *Con.* 357
Time w., violated laws, abuse *F.A.* 14
Ten thousand swains the w. scene deplore *Her.* 39
Deplores the w. regions of her globe *Her.* 80
By our blood in Afric w. *N.C.* 41
Thus having w. half the day *P.B.* 11
Wilt Providence o'erlook the w. good? *P.E.* 223
Improve the remnant of his w. span *R.* 13
His w. spirits quickly, by long toil *T.* i 128
Whose only happy are their w. hours *T.* iv 225
Its w. tones and harmony unheard *T.* iv 480

WASTING.
W. towns, plantations, meadows *N.C.* 35

WATCH.
And in the silent w. of the night *Con.* 731
To w. the fountain, and preserve it clear *Ex.* 98
As soldiers w. the signal of command *Ex.* 119
The very children w. for thy disgrace *Ex.* 282
Sees w., bracelelts, rings, and lockets *P.B.* 25
Must w. his purpose with a steadfast eye *P.E.* 577
Nor quits till evening w. his giddy stand *R.* 434
An idler is a w. that wants both hands *R.* 681
To w. yon amorous couple in their play *T.* 136
W. your eye, anticipates command *T.* 214 [89
The nurse sleeps sweetly, hired to w. the sick *T.* i
With opera glass to w. the moving scene *T.* ii 453
The unguarded door was safe; men did not w. *T.*iv 559
Is made familiar, w. his approach *T.* v 423
W., seals, and all—till all his pranks are told *Tir.*331
And eyes the door, and w. a retreat *Tir.* 572 [512
But, w. they strictly, or neglect their charge? *Tir*
W. his emotions, and control their tide *Tir.* 610
W. every beam Philosophy imparts *T.T.* 70

WATCHED.
She w. the gardener at his work *R.C.* 14
Nor less amused, have I quiescent w. *T.* iv 291

WATCHFUL.
Of lubbard Labour needs his w. eye *T.* iii. 400

WATCHING.
He reads the skies, and, w. every change *Ch.* 333
That night, by chance, the poet w. *R.C.* 77
Leaned on her elbow, w. time, whose course *Y.O.* 160

WATCHMAN.
Where the w. in his round *St.* iv 5
And, at the w.'s lantern borrowing light *T.* ii 654

WATCHWORD. [322
When the rude rabble's w. was—" Destroy!" *T.T.*

WATER.
On rippling w. in an April day *A.T.* 24
Has filled his urn where these pure w. rise *Ch.* 436
Should flow like w. after summer showers *Con.* 705
The fragrant w. on my cheeks bestowed *M.P.* 62
Sighs must fan it, tears must w. *N.C.* 19
That w. all the nations *O.* i 6
Now in the w. and now out *P.* 10

Poisoning the w. where their swarms abound *P.E.* 481
So, fire with w. to compare *Q.V.* 17
The fall of w., and the song of birds *R.* 183
Nor view of w. turning busy mills *R.* 334
Then all the world of w. sleeps again *R.* 536
The foam upon the w. not so light *T.* 43
To drink sweet w. of the crystal well *T.* i 240
Rise not, the w. of the deep shall rise *T.* ii 143
That winds and w., lulled by magic sounds *T.* ii 261
Sought in still w., and beneath clear skies *T.* iii 382
Than w. interfused to make them one *T.* v 148
His heart survived the w. ; and ere long *T.* v 220
Rivers of gladness w. all the earth *T.* vi 763
Oft w. fairest meadows, and the bird *T.* vi 930
At her command winds rise and w. roar *Tir.* 25

WATERED.
Think on the fruitful and well w. spot *Ex.* 418
A people, planted, w., blest as they? *Ex.* 168
And w. duly. There the pitcher stands *T.* iv 775

WATERING.
In an old empty w. pot *R.C.* 16

WATERY.
Pure-bosomed as that w. glass *Comp.* ii 9
His passions, like the w. stores that sleep *H.* 183
With Pity's w. sight *Miss* — 76
And where the land slopes to its w. bourn *N.A.* 13
Soon w. grew her eyes and dim *Q.V.* 53
Exploring far and wide the w. waste *T.* i 665
Illumined every side; a w. light *T.* v 150

WAVE.
The stifling w. and then he sank *Cast.* 48
Soft airs and gentle heavings of the w. *Ch.* 127
The raving storm and dashing w. defies *Con.* 559
What ails thee, restless as the w. that roar *Ex.* 272
Asked of the w. that broke upon his coast *Ex.* 572
I w. just now, for conversation's sake *H.* 436
Shed light, like a sun on the w. *M.D.* 14
That Britannia renowned o'er the w. *M.D.* 45
To the wild w., or wilder human breast *P.E.* 601
The sea-maid rides the w. *Q.V.* 70
The w. o'ertake them in their serious play *R.* 157
The rising w. obey the increasing blast *R.* 532
All sunk beneath the w. *R.G.* 3
Must plough the w. no more *R.G.* 36
The Nen's barge-laden w. *St.* i 2
And never w. his claim *St.* i 12
Lashed into foaming w., begins to roar *T.* 260
Man on the dubious w. of error tossed *T.* 1
Her Fancy followed him through foaming w. *T.* i 539
And they themselves once ferried o'er the w. *T.* ii 38
When did the w. so haughtily o'erleap *T.* ii 55
Which winds and w. obey, invades the shore *T.* ii 114
Gone with the refluent w. into the deep *T.* ii 120
The sport of every w.? No: none are clear *T.* ii 153
Snore to the murmurs of the Atlantic w.? *T.* iv 27
And make thy marble of the glassy w. *T.* v 134
With all his roaring multitude of w. *T.* v 766
" From the green w. emerging, darts an eye *T.* v 835
That the wind severs from the broken w. *T.* vi 156
Narrow and long, o'erlooks the western w. *T.* vi 484
To gaze in his eyes and bless him. Maidens w. *T.*vi 699
Whom Ocean feels through all his countless w. *Tir.*39
Prayer to the winds, and caution to the w. *Tir.* 183

WAVED.
And w. his rod divine, a race obscene *T.* ii 826 [313
Though faded; and the lands where lately w. *T.* iv

WAVING.
Unnumbered branches w. in the blast *T.* i 188

WAVY.
Her fields, a rich expanse of w. corn *Ex.* 9
For grandeur or for use. Long w. wreaths *T.* v 158

WAX. [324]

States thrive or wither, as moons w. and wane *Ex.*
For England's glory, seeing it w. pale *T.* v 510

WAXEN.

On w. pinions soar without a fall *A.T.* 54

WAY. [145]

In the w. of religion and truth *A.S.* 22
Where men of judgment creep, and feel their w. *Con.*
Of Heaven's mysterious purposes and w. *Ch.* 58
Walks arm in arm with Nature all his w. *Ch.* 314
By w. of wholesome curb upon our pride *Con.* 361
Did they not burn within us by the w. ?" *Con.* 536
To supplicate his mercy, love his w. *Con.* 661
And chiefly when Religion leads the w. *Con.* 704
Serves, in a plain and homely w. *E.* i 3
Mysterious are his w. whose power *E.* i 29
Forbid in vain to push his daring w. *Ex.* 18
By night a fire, to cheer the gloomy w. *Ex.* 178
By w. of balm for healing *F.* 96
And Dick, although his w. was clear *F.B.* 22
Of distant wisdom shoots across his w. *H.* 94
Both may be lost, yet each in his own w. *H.* 277
Ethelred's house, the centre of six w. *H.* 302
Of all the w. that seem to promise fair *H.* 338
That sound bespeaks Salvation on her w. *H.* 455
Has wept a silent flood, reversed his w. *H.* 519
On both sides of the w. *J.G.* 138
And all and each that passed that w. *J.G.* 239
Chilled more his else delightful w. *Mor.* 16
Drew me to school along the public w. *M.P.* 49
He trimmed his flight another w. *P.B.* 12 [443
And meets with hindrance in the smoothest w. *P.E.*
Himself a wanderer from the narrow w. *P.E.* 118
Remarks two loiterers that have lost theirs *P.E.* 386
Where children would with ease discern the w. *P.E.* 434
If a wish wander that w., call it home *P.E.* 586 [450
And judgment drunk, and bribed to lose his w. *P.E.*
Judge his own w., and sigh for a return *P.E.* 611
Those the long milky w. *Q.V.* 12
Conversant only with the w. of men *R.* 39
Wherever freakish Fancy points the w. *R.* 128
Of God, beneficent in all His w. *R.* 556
Curried his nag and looked another w. *R.* 590 [*T.* 17
Grace leads the right w. ; if you choose the wrong
And scorn, for its own sake, the gracious w. *T.* 37
Shows them the shortest w. to life and love *T.* 370
That even a judgment, making w. for thee *T.* ii 131
Entangled, winds now this w. and now that *T.* iii 2
Or having long in miry w. been foiled *T.* iii 4 [10
And winds his w. with pleasure and with ease *T.* iii
In guilty splendour, shake the public w. *T.* iii 70
A thousand systems, each in his own w. *T.* iii 171
The w. to glory by miscarriage foul *T.* iii 506
But urged by storms along its slippery w. *T.* iv 127
Ere yet mortality's fine threads give w. *T.* v 578
He sets the bright procession on its w. *T.* vi 190
Their w. was on the margin of the land *T.* vi 495
And taught a brute the w. to safe revenge *T.* vi 559
In nooks obscure, far from the w. of men *T.* vi 842
Man yet mistakes his w. *The Doves* 2
Your wisdom and your w.—to you I turn *Tir.* 812
A brood of asps, or quicksands in his w. *Tir.* 870
If hindrances obstruct thy w. *Trans. H.* 31
To turn the course of Helicon that w. *T.T.* 183
To turn a penny in the w. of trade *T.T.* 421
And every Muse attend her in her w. *T.T.* 619
To trace him in his word, his works, his w. *T.T.* 751
A thousand w. the force of genuine love *V.* 62

WAY-MARK.

To stand a w. in the road to bliss ? *P.E.* 117

WAYSIDE.

By the w., or stalking in the path *T.* v 92

WAYWARD.

Nor he alone addressed the w. fair *A.T.* 34
And when accomplished in her w. school *Con.* 465
Free from the w. bias bigots feel *P.E.* 454
Our w. intellect, the more we learn *T.* iii 236

WEAK.

The robber and the murderer w. as we ? *Ch.* 68
Herself as w. as her support is strong *Ch.* 408
And prove too w. for so divine a theme *Ch.* 633
Credulous infancy, or age as w. *Con.* 225
W. and imperfect in all grace beside *Con.* 758
What web too w. to catch a modern brain ? *Ex.* 629
O querulous and w. !—whose useless brain *H.* 29
W. and irresolute is man *H.F.* 1
Which served my w. thought for a guide *M.D.* 44
W. to perform, though mighty to pretend *P.E.* 15
By nature w., or viciously inclined *P.E.* 432
But which, when life at ebb runs w. and low *R.* 3
To your w. sight her telescopic eye *T.* 98
Too w. to struggle with tenacious clay *T.* 216
Mercy is infinite, and man is w. *T.* 294
Sinful and w., in every sense a wretch *T.* 383
Fallen from her glory, and too w. to rise *T.* 480
The birthday of Invention, w. at first *T.* i 17
Too w. for those decisive blows that once *T.* ii 273
He stablishes the strong, restores the w. *T.* ii 343
Defective and unsanctioned, proved too w. *T.* ii 524
The w. perhaps are moved, but are not taught *T.* ii 566
And king in England too, he may be w. *T.* v 337 [414
None but his steel approach them. What is w. *T.* iii
While sloth seduces more, too w. to bear *T.* vi 105
How w. the barrier of mere nature proves *Tir.* 169
Proves that the mind is w., or makes it so *T.T.* 545

WEAKER.

To swallow much upon much w. proof *Con.* 722
Finds out his w. part *H.F.* 10
I see thee daily w. grow *M.* 6

WEAKEST.

To nourish pride, or turn the w. head *T.* 366

WEAKNESS.

Her wisdom seems the w of a child *Ch.* 423
That having proved the w., it should seem *Con.* 829
But age in spite of w. and of pain *Ex.* 25
Thy chaos order, and thy w. might *Ex.* 641
Business is labour, and man's w. such *H.* 19
Shall live exempt from w. and decay *H.* 752
From ostentation, as from w., free *T.* 25
Conscious of w. in its noblest powers *R.* 124
Even in the cradled w. of the world ! *T.* v 286
Is w. when opposed ; conscious of wrong *T.* v 372
By w., and hostility by love *T.* v 703
Be it a w., it deserves some praise *Tir.* 296

WEAL.

His ashes, where, and in what w. or woe ? *T.* ii 519
Can dream them trusty to the general w. *T.* v 514

WEALTH. [*Comp.* i 4]

No w. can bribe, no prayers persuade to stay
Blessed with all w. can give thee, to resign *Ch.* 297
And prize them above pleasure, w., or praise *Con.* 662
A despot big with power obtained by w., *Ex.* 370
That proved a mint of w., a mine to Rome *Ex.* 523
And all at home is pleasure, w. and ease, *Ex.* 583
That w. within is ruin at the door *Her.* 76
Avarice in thee was the desire of w. *J.T.* 25
His object chosen, w. or fame *Mor.* 27
Ask w. of Heaven, and gain a real prize *R.* 162 [140
From anxious thoughts how w. may be increased *R.*
That appetite can ask, or w. provide *R.* 744
By w. or dignity, who dwells secure *T.* i 593
Such London is, by taste and w. proclaimed *T.* i 697
The w. of Indian provinces, escapes *T.* i 738
And tremble when I wake, for all the w. *T.* ii 31

Drained to the last poor item of his *w. T.* iii 784
Increase of power begets increase of *w. T.* iv 580
W. luxury, and luxury excess *T.* iv 581
His *w.*, fame, honours, all that I intend *Tir.* 389
See *w.* abused, and dignities misplaced *Tir.* 815
In wisdom, *w.*, in fortune, and in lies *T.T.* 469

WEALTHIER.
He wanted, for a *w.* to enjoy! *T.* iii 789
Nor what a *w.* than ourselves may send *T.* iv 426

WEALTHY.
That fed the flocks and herds of *w. Lot Ex.* 419
Ye proud and *w.*, let this theme *Trans.* i 25

WEANED.
Attachment never to be *w.* or changed *T.* vi 625

WEANING.
This second *w.*, needless as it is *Tir.* 557

WEAPON.
He laughs, whatever *w.* Truth may draw *H.* 596
The gloomy clouds, find *w.*, arrowy sleet *T.* v 140

WEAR. [*A.C.* 20
Pray who would, or who could, *w.* spectacles then?
That the Nose has had spectacles always in *w. A.C.* 11
Our polished manners are a mask we *w. Con.* 166
Convicted once, should ever after *w. E.* iii 50 [629
Though Time will *w.* us, and we must grow old *Con.*
To vanquish lust, and *w.* its yoke no more *Ex.* 411
To fling his glories o'er the robe she *w. H.* 44
Thus things terrestrial *w.* a different hue *H.* 69
With wreaths like those triumphant spirits *w. H.* 166
A hat not much the worse for *w. J.G.* 183
But now *w.* crests of oven-wood instead *N.A.* 12
And all their deep impressions *w.* away *P.E.* 278
Nature in all the various shapes she *w. R.* 193
Till his religious whimsy *w.* out him *T.* 90
His predecessor's coat advanced to *w. T.* 145
And one who *w.* a coronet and prays *T.* 378
And *w.* the bonds, than fasten them on him *T.* ii 36
We *w.* it at our backs. There, closely braced *T.* ii 586
To him that *w.* it. What can after-games *T.* ii 762
Of manners sweet as Virtue always *w. T.* ii 783
Is India free? and does she *w.* her plumed *T.* iv 28
To *w.* a tattered garb however coarse *T.* iv 416
As meal and larded locks can make him; *w. T.* iv 642
Is still the livery she delights to *w. T.* iv 760 [v 511
And sickly, while her champions *w.* their hearts *T.*
King was a name too proud for man to *w. T.* v 242
To *w.* out time in numbering to and fro *T.* v 425
Can *w.* it e'en as gracefully as she *T.* vi 986 [116
And praised for virtues that they scorn to *w. T.T.*
Of Vanity, a wreath for self to *w. T.T.* 757
While Earth *w.* a mantle of snow *W.N.* 13

WEARER.
If valued by its *w.*'s worth 1789, 43

WEARIED.
Hackneyed in business, *w.* at that oar *R.* 1
The *w.* hireling finds it a release *T.* v 411
So oft, and *w.* in the vain attempt *T.* v 628
Undaunted still, though *w.* and perplexed *T.T.* 366

WEARINESS.
To scourge him, *w.* his only blame *Ch.* 215
O *w.* beyond what asses feel *H.* 99
Which Idleness and *W.* beget *R.* 762
Their *w.*; and they the most polite *T.* ii 640

WEARING.
W. out life in his religious whim *T.* 89

WEARISOME.
From all his *w.* engagements freed *R.* 513
That with its *w.* but needful-length *T.* iv 2

WEARY.
"Satiate of her, and *w.* of the same *A.T.* 105
Murmuring and *w.* of our daily toil *Ch.* 221

Themselves, perhaps, when *w.* they retreat *H.* 244
Becomes not *w.* of attention *M.F.* 52
On whom he rests well pleased his *w.* powers *R.* 451
Recoil from *w.* life's best hour *St.* v 19
Fearless of wrong, reposed his *w.* strength *T.* i 15
Distressed the *w.* loins that felt no ease *T.* i 45
Though halt, and *w.* of the path they tread *T.* i 471
Till half their beauties fade; the *w.* sight *T.* i 510
Since Heaven would grow *w.* of a world *T.* ii 583
Society, grown *w.* of the load *T.* iv 498
Fatigued me, never *w.* of the pipe *T.* iv 706
His thousands, *w.* of penurious life *T.* v 319
Who lives, and is not *w.* of a life *T.* v 365
Who sleeps not, is not *w.*; in whose sight *T.* vi 226
Dismiss me *w.* to a safe retreat *T.* vi 1004

WEATHER.
But just at eve the blowing *w. A Fable* 16
Our health, the *w.*, and the news *E.* i 5
From what point blows the *w. Trans.* ii 9

WEATHER-BLEACHED.
"His country's *w.* and battered rocks *T.* v 834

WEATHERED.
(The storms all *w.* and the ocean crossed) *M.P.* 89

WEATHERHOUSE.
Devised the *W.*, that useful toy! *T.* 211

WEAVE.
Fancy shall *w.* a charm for my relief *M.P.* 18
And *w.* fresh garlands every day *N.* 19
Yon cottager, who *w.* at her own door *T.* 317 [306
The glassy threads with which the Fancy *w. T.* iv
While every worm industriously *w. Tir.* 595
Religion *w.* for her, and half undressed *T.T.* 723

WEAVERS.
But sedentary *w.* of long tales *Con.* 207

WEAVING.
To *w.* nets for bird-alluring fruit *T* iv 263.

WEB. [639
Those flimsy *w.* that break as soon as wrought *R.*
The *w.* of every scheme they have at heart *Ex.* 331
What *w.* too weak to catch a modern brain? *Ex.* 629
And winds his *w.* about the riveled leaves *Tir.* 596

WED. [scratches! *A.T.* iii 3
Should John *w.* a score, Oh the claws and the
Who danced with whom, and who are like to *w. Con.* 395
As woodbine *w.* the plant within her reach *R.* 229
Parks in which Art preceptress Nature *w. R.* 335
As if the poet, purposing to *w. T.T.* 554

WEDDED.
This history of a *w.* pair *A Tale* 11
"Though *w.* we have been *J.G.* 6
The comfort of the *w.* state *M.F.* 46
In *w.* love already blest *N.Y.G.* 11
Are *w.* thus, like beauty to old age *T.* iii 660
And press thy *w.* side *The Doves* 26

WEDDING.
To-morrow is our *w.* day *J.G.* 9
Said John,—"It is my *w.* day *J.G.* 193

WEDGE.
And drive the *w.* in yonder forest drear *T.* v 43

WEDGED. [ii 351
But hark—the Doctor's voice!—fast *w.* between *T.*

WEDLOCK.
That *w.* is not rigorous, as supposed *A.T.* 58
How simple *w.* fornication works *A.T.* 159

WEED. [251
Pernicious *w.*! whose scent the fair annoys *Con.*
As richest soil the most luxuriant *w. Ex.* 214 [*H.* 289
What parts the kindred tribes of *w.* and flowers?
And Chloe from her garland picks the *w. H.* 293

(Oh cast them from thee!) are w., arrant w. H. 301
Can gather honey from a w. P.B. 36
Its patient drudges with dry chaff and w. R. 48 [154
Some shining pebbles, and some w. and shells R.
In shirt of hair, and w. of canvass dressed T. 81
Kills too the flowery w., where'er they grow T. 461
All hate the rank society of w. T. iii 670
Of orange, myrtle, or the fragrant w. T. iv 764
And we are w. without it. All constraint T. v 448
The laurels that a Cæsar reaps are w. T. vi 939
WEEDY.
He dips his bowl into the w. ditch T. i 241
I saw far off the w. fallows smile T. iv 316
WEEK.
Relate how many w. they kept their bed Con. 315
Teach him to fence and figure twice a w. P.E. 366
WEEKLY.
Their fleece his pillow, and his w. drawl H. 199
" Their w. dole of edifying strains T. v 646
The w. censor of a laughing Town V. 38
WEEN. [88
Small need of Prayer Book, or of priest, I w. A.T.
WEEP.
W. upon thy matchless wrongs B. 10 [206
The wretch that works and w. without relief Ch.
Why w. the Muse for England ? What appears Ex. 1
Then wherefore w. for England ? What appears Ex.30
Whose eye reverted w. o'er all the past H. 31
It were to w. that goodness has its meed J.T. 12
Perhaps a tear, if souls can w. in bliss M.P. 26
Petronius! all the Muses w. for thee P.E. 335
They shriek and sink, survivors start and w. R. 159
And w. a sad libation in despair R. 226
Will w. indeed, and heave a pitying groan T. 177
W. tears of joy, and bursts into a song T. 458
And such the reascent ; between them ψ. T. i 327
To distant shores, and she would sit and w. T. i 540
I see thee w., and thine are honest tears T. i 657
W. when she sees inflicted on a beast T. ii 25
I think, articulate, I laugh and w. T. iii 198
And I can w., can hope, and can despond T. iii 841
Their kerchiefs, and old women w. for joy T. vi 700
Maria w.—the Muses mourn T.B. 61
To w. for the buds it had left with regret The Rose 7
WEEPING.
Where should the living, w. o'er his woes T. 435
WEIGH.
The vessel w., forsakes the shore A Tale 43
W. sunbeams, carve a fly, or spit a flea Ch. 354
Though Nature w. our talents, and dispense Con. 1
And if it w. the importance of a fly Con. 21 [366
That Heaven will w. man's virtues and his crimes H.
W. the vessel up R.G. 25
And when I w. this seeming wisdom well T. iii 180
W., for a moment, classical desert Tir. 488
And w. the nations in an even scale T.T. 251
They only w. the heavier Y.D. 48
WEIGHED.
And w. down its beautiful head The Rose 4
The seeming virtue w. against the vice Ch. 457 [178
Were light, when w. against one smile of thine H.
Or if the thought occurred not duly w. R. 464
WEIGHING.
W. them in the hollow of his hand Ex. 343
WEIGHT.
Owes all its w., like loaded dice, to lead Con. 302
It has indeed been told me (with what w. Con. 815
The partial balance, and deceitful w. Ex. 41
And Peace does nothing to relieve the w. Ex. 307
Forgetting its important w. F. 70
" He carries w.!" " He rides a race!" J.G. 115

But still he seemed to carry w. J.G. 129
And happiest he that groans beneath his w. R. 156
The w. of subjects worthiest of her care R. 678
And his importance of such w. R.C. 112
Of such magnitude and w. St. iv 22
Are such a dead, preponderating w. T. 354
Ponderous, and fixed by its own massy w. T. i 59
A w. of ignorance ; in that, of pride T. iv 485
Deciduous, or its own unbalanced w. T. v 40
Indurated and fixed, the snowy w. T. v 98
They have their w. to carry, subjects theirs T.T. 175
WEIGHTY.
And understood too well the w. terms T. ii 477
Though solid, not too w. for his years Tir. 651
WELCOME.
And made so w. at their simple feast Con. 532
He laughed and trifled, made him w. there H. 685
Oh! w. now the sun's once hated light H. 736
O w. guest, though unexpected here ! M.P. 12
Then w. errors, of whatever size P.E. 283 [165
When the glad soul is made Heaven's w. guest P.E.
'Tis done—he steps into the w. chaise R. 391
Then w. refuge, and a peaceful home T. 267
No slaves on earth more w. were than they T. 352
Is oft too w., and may much disturb T. ii 492
The w. call, conscious how much the hand T. iii 399
So let us w. peaceful evening in T. iv 41
I slight thee not, but make thee w. still T. iv 266
Its long delay, feels every w. stroke T. v 413 [876
Gods such as guilt makes w. ; gods that sleep T. v
Inoffensive, w. guest! Trans. iii 10
Must follow royalty, then w. ease T.T. 165
Might prove a w. gift, and touch thine heart V. 41
WELL. [564
Whose wisdom, drawn from the deep w. of life Con.
The o'erflowing w. of Charity springs here ! Ch. 366
My husband safe and w." J.G. 220
To drink sweet waters of the crystal w. T. i 240
Of dropping buckets into empty w. T. iii 189
Of nightshade, or valerian, grace the w. T. iv 757
WELLADAY.
Was—w., the title page was lost H. 428
WELL-BOUND.
Stamped on the w. quarto, grace the shelf T.T. 745
WELL-BRED. [T. iii 97
Transgress what laws they may. Well-dressed, w.
And with a w. whisper close the scene ! T. ii 413
WELL-CHOSEN.
W., and not sullenly perused T. iii 393
WELL-CONTRIVED.
Nor taste alone and w. display T. iii 603
WELL-DRESSED. [97
Transgress what laws they may. W., well-bred T. iii
WELL-EQUIPAGED.
W., is ticket good enough T. iii 98
WELL-HAVENED.
Shoots into port at some w. isle M.P. 90
WELL-INFORMED.
The mind was w., the passions held T. ii 715
The w. philosopher Trans. H. 19
WELL-INTENTIONED.
However w. F. 198
WELL-JUDGING.
With a w. taste from above C. 34
WELL-KNOWN.
Against the w. duties of a friend E. iii 49
WELL-LINED.
His cap w. with logic not his own T. ii 737
WELL-MANAGED.
W. shall have earned its worthy price T. iii 800

WELL-POISED.
The w. lance that quivered at his side *A.T.* 144
WELL-PREPARED.
Diminutive, well filled with w. *T.* iii 513
WELL-ROLLED.
We tread the Wilderness, whose w. walks *T.* i 351
WELL-SPREAD.
Proud of his w. walls, he views his trees *T.* iii 408
WELLSPRING.
The stream that feeds the w. of the heart *T.T.* 380
WELL-STACKED.
The w. pile of riven logs and roots *T.* iv 444
WELL-TANNED.
With base materials, sat on w. hides *T.* i 51
WELL-WATERED.
The Ouse, dividing the w. land *T.* i 323
WELL-WROUGHT.
To win no praise when w. plans prevail *T.T.* 157
WENS.
With prominent w. globose; till at the last *Y.O.* 66
WENT.
Than he with whom he w. *Cast.* 8   [171
For them, the states to which they w. destroyed *Ex.*
'Twere vain inquiry to what port she w. *Ch.* 445
Sought their own village, busied as they w. *Con.* 509
He sowed the seeds of order where he w. *Ex.* 488
To bear it, suffered shame where'er he w. *H.* 587
Smack w. the whip, round w. the wheels *J.G.* 41
Away w. Gilpin, neck or naught *J.G.* 97
Away w. hat and wig *J.G.* 98
Away w. Gilpin—who but he? *J.G.* 113
And now, as he w. bowing down *J.G.* 121
Away w. Gilpin, out of breath *J.G.* 157
But to the house w. in *J.G.* 180
Away w. Gilpin, and away *J.G.* 209
W. Gilpin's hat and wig *J.G.* 210
Away w. Gilpin, and away *J.G.* 229
W. postboy at his heels *J.G.* 230   [42
And w. with his comrades the apples to seize *P.A.*
Thus many a sad to-morrow came and w. *M.P.* 42
His noble heart w. pit-a-pat *R.C.* 79
Down w. the Royal George *R.G.* 11
When Kempenfelt w. down *R.G.* 23   [220
Once w. I forth, and found, till then unknown *T.*
With one who left her, w. to sea and died *T.* i 538
How far he w. for what was nothing worth *T.* iv 238
Sorrow has, since they w., subdued and tamed *T.*vi 46
He journeyed; and his chance was as he w. *T.* vi 488
Right to his mark the monster w. *T.B.* 50   [268
W. with him, and saw all the game he played? *Tir.*
To bid the traveller, as he w. *Trans.* i 15
WEPT.
They w. the wrongs of honourable love *A.T.* 98
No poet w. him; but the page *Cast.* 49
The prophet w. for Israel; wished his eyes *Ex.* 33
W. till all Israel heard his bitter cry *Ex.* 63   [641
But w., and stamped, and smote his thigh, in vain *Ex.*
Has w. a silent flood, reversed his ways *H.* 519
O'er Murray's loss the Muses w. *M.* ii 5
A long, long sigh, and w. a last adieu! *M.P.* 31 [786
Was sacred, and was honoured, loved, and w. *T.* ii
Plaintive and piteous, as it w. and wailed *T.* iv 479
WEST.
Drew the grey curtain of the fading w. *Ch.* 263
From East to W., no sorrow can be found *Ex.* 28
Till Sol, declining in the w. *R.C.* 62
Down to the rosy w., but kindly still *T.* iv 133
Methinks I see thee in the streaky w. *T.* iv 245
Kneels with the native of the farthest w. *T.* vi 811

WESTERN.
In some safe haven of our w. world *Ch.* 444
A w. bank's still sunny side *Mor.* 18
And thus the rangers of the w. world *T.* i 618
Of Portugal and W. India there *T.* iii 572
Narrow and long, o'erlooks the w. wave *T.* vi 484
Rock'd in the cradle of the w. breeze *Tir.* 44
WESTMINSTER.
At W., where little poets strive *T.T.* 506
WESTWARD.
Some eastward, and some w., and all wrong *H.* 281
Far hence to the w. I sailed *M.D.* 6
Looks to the w. from the dappled east *T.T.* 706
WET.
Is w. with Anson's tear *Cast.* 52   [*The Rose* 5
The cup was all filled, and the leaves were all w.
Reports it hot or cold, or w. or dry *Con.* 386 [251
Has flowed from lips w. with Castalian dews *T.* iii
Births, deaths, and marriages, epistles w. *T.* iv 17
And w. his cheeks with sorrows not his own *V.* 66
WETHERS.
A ram, the ewes and w., sad, addressed *N.A.* 82
WHALE.
Up-spouted by a w. in air *Q.V.* 19
WHAT-D'YE-CALL.
Good Mr. W.? *Y.D.* 36
WHEATEN.
His diet was of w. bread *Ep.* ii 13
WHEEL.
And had a hollow with a w. *A Tale* 35
He heard the w. of an avenging God *Ex.* 57
If Business, constant as the w. of time *Ex.* 604
Vicissitude w. round the motley crowd *H.* 17
That tread the circuit of the cistern w.! *H.* 100 [652
And grinds his crown beneath her burning w.! *H.*
Smack went the whip, round went the w. *J.G.* 41
The lumbering of the w. *J.G.* 232
And suns to come, as round they w. *Miss* — 101
If Tom be sober, and the w. well greased *P.E.* 439
On borrowed w. away she flies *Q.V.* 37
Furnishes always oil for its own w. *R.* 616
Incessant, clinking hammers, grinding w. *T.* i 231
Constant rotation of the unwearied w. *T.* i 368
Reiterated as the w. of time *T.* iii 626   [iii 740
And thundering loud, with his ten thousand w.? *T.*
May turn the clod, and w. the compost home *T.* iii 637
Let fall the curtains, w. the sofa round *T.* iv 37
A sliding car, indebted to no w. *T.* iv 126   [144
No rattling w. stop short before these gates *T.* iv
To the clogged w.; and in its sluggish pace *T.* iv 345
The milldam, dashes on the restless w. *T.* v 102
And w. his throne upon the rolling worlds *T.* v 814
Haste, then, and w. away a shattered world *T.* vi 823
Hook disappointment on the puplic w. *T.T.* 146
Or ere the w. of verse begin to roll *T.T.* 711
WHEEL-FOOTED.
This w. studying chair *Gr.* 9
WHEELING.
In volumes w. slow, the vapour dank *T.* iii 499
Declined the death, and w. swiftly round *T.* vi 518
WHEEL-WORN.
The chariots bounding in her w. streets *Ex.* 21
WHELMED.
And w. in deeper gulfs than he *Cast.* 66
WHELMING.
Not long beneath the w. brine *Cast.* 13
WHELP.
The unfledged raven and the lion's w. *T.* vi 461

WHELPED.
Or, having w. a prologue with great pains *T.T.* 536

WHET.
O nauseous!—an emetic for a w.! *P.E.* 222

WHIFF.
Conducts the unguarded nose to such a w. *T.* iv 469

WHIM.
If he be silent, faith is all a w. *Con.* 853
To passion, interest, pleasure, w. resigned *H.* 212
The text that sorts not with his darling w. *P.E.* 446
Wearing out life in his religious w. *T.* 89

WHIMPER.
But poverty with most who w. forth *T.* iv 429

WHIMSY.
Till his religious w. wears out him *T.* 90
Which, crooked into a thousand w., clasp *Y.O.* 118

WHINE.
Can change their w. into a mirthful note *T.* i 583

WHINING.
Canting and w. out all day the word *Con.* 577

WHIP.
Begone! the w. and bell in that hard hand *Ch.* 212
Smack went the w., round went the wheels *J.G.* 41
And what if he did ride w. and spur *M.F.* 22
He brandishes his pliant length of w. *T.* iv 355
With sounding w., and rowels dyed in blood *T.* vi 527

WHIP-GIG.
The free republic of the w. state *H.* 190

WHIPPED.
The fruit of all her labour is w. cream *T.T.* 551
W. out of sight, with satire just and keen *T.T.* 640

WHIRL.
That w. away from business and debate *R.* 393
Or with vortiginous and hideous w. *T.* ii 102

WHIRLED.
With needless hurry w. from place to place *T.* iv 372

WHIRLING.
Thus braves the w. blast *Miss —* 34

WHIRLWIND.
Rushed with a w.'s fury on the foe *A.T.* 195
Till He that rides the w., checks the rein *R.* 535
Where his w. answer—"No" *N.C.* 40

WHISKERED.
Of our forefathers—a grave, w. race *T.* iii 768
Long backed, long tailed, with w. snout *T.B.* 35

WHISKS. [*T.* vi 317
Ascends the neighbouring beech; there w. his brush

WHISPER.
And w. your return *N.* 16
Whom I may w.—solitude is sweet" *R.* 742
Come, then—a still, small w. in your ear *T.* 297
As angels use, the Gospel w. peace *T.* ii 342
And with a well-bred w. close the scene! *T.* ii 413

WHISPERED.
She w. still that he had naught to fear *A.T.* 182
Some w. softly, and some twanged aloud *Ch.* 518
His w. theme, dilated and at large *Con.* 273
Though w., plainly tell what works within *H.* 691

WHISPERING.
And the w. sound of the cool colonnade *P.F.* 2

WHISTLE.
Die of disdain, or w. off the sound *H.* 348
While the winds w., and the snows descend *T.* iii 569
He w. as he goes, light-hearted wretch *T.* iv 12
Or only with a w. blessed *T.B.* 10

WHISTLING.
And w., as if unconcerned and gay *R.* 589

Crape and cocked pistol, and the w. ball *T.* iii 802
That as she sweeps him with her w. silks *T.* vi 941

WHIT.
Sir Airy, not a w. dismayed or scared *A.T.* 171
But yet his horse was not a w. *J.G.* 149

WHITE. [iv 123
Fringed with a beard made w. with other snows *T.*
Dwells in w. and black the same *N.C.* 16
The frequency of crimes has washed them w. *T.* iii 71
At the sword's point, and dyeing the w. robe *T.* iv 682
Without a cloud, and w. without a speck *T.* vi 63
The lilac, various in array, now w. *T.* vi 157
A splintered stump bleached to a snowy w. *Y.O.* 128

WHITEN.
Each to his choice, soon w. all the land *T.* i 294

WHITENING.
Curling and w. over all the waste *R.* 531

WHITTLE.
The task was left to w. thee away *Y.O.* 104

WHOLE. [21
" On the w. it appears, and my argument shows *A.C*
A union with the vast terraqueous w. *Ch.* 122
A beautiful and perfect w. *E.* i 64
Must constitute the charming w. *F.* 59
They manifest their w. life through *F.* 112
Of him whom Hope has with a touch made w. *H.* 731
From the w. hog to be debarred *L.W.* 12
With a w. gamut filled of heavenly notes *N.A.* 26
To thy w. heart's desire? *N.Y.G.* 12 [65]
Forecasts the future w.; that when the scene *T.* iii
War and the chase engross the savage w. *T.* i 608
W. without stooping, towering crest and all *T.* iv 271
Though sickly samples of the exuberant w. *T.* iv 761
Where private was not? Can he love the w. *T.* v 503
Where kindness on his part, who ruled the w. *T.* vi 365
Their w. attention, and ape all his tricks *Tir.* 225
Have ye, ye sage intendants of the w. *Tir.* 265
Owe their repute in part, but not the w. *Tir.* 461

WHOLESOME.
By way of w. curb upon our pride *Con.* 361
And breathing w. air, and wandering much *T.* i 589
But was a w. rigour in the main *T.* iii 82
But are not w. airs, though unperfumed *T.* iii 732
Of the infirm, is w. air to thee *T.* iv 365
A cheap but w. salad from the brook *T.* vi 304
But w., well digested; grateful some *T.* vi 1014
With w. learning, yet acquired with ease *Tir.* 118
With savoury truth and w. common sense *Tir.* 629
Let Discipline employ her w. arts *T.T.* 310
Rejoices with a w. fear *Trans. H.* 20

WHOREDOM. [*Tir.* 833
Now flushed with drunkenness, now with w. pale

WICK.
The little w. of life's poor shallow lamp *T.* iii 164

WICKED.
Prisons expect the w., and were built *Ch.* 280
What then? Were they the w. above all *T.* ii 150

WICKERWORK.
And on her w. high mounted *A Fable* 3

WIDE. [324
That Heaven spreads w. before the view of man *Ch.*
As w. as the bridge of the Nose is; in short *A.C.* 15
His high-bred steed expands his nostrils w. *A.T.* 163
Immortal fragrance fills the circuit w. *Ch.* 439
Spreads w. her arms of universal love *Ch.* 596
And a w. ocean swallows both at last *Comp.* i 6
That theme exhausted, a w. chasm ensues *Con.* 393
And claim a right to scamper and run w. *Con.* 793
Some never seem so w. of their intent *Con.* 857

Saw Babylon set w. her two-leaved brass *Ex.* 59
And trident-bearing queen of the w. seas *Ex.* 275
Their gates w. open threw *J.G.* 120   [*M.P.* 103
Sails ripped, seams opening w., and compass lost
W. yawns a gulf beside a ragged thorn *N.A.* 14
And being lost, perhaps, and wandering w. *N.A.* 97
It falls at last, far w. of his design *P.E.* 575 [*P.E.* 281
The breach, though small at first, soon opening w.
Entreated, opening w. his beak *P.T.* 19
With mouths made only to grin w. and eat *R.* 309
Like thy renowned forefathers, far and w. *S.* i 12
Now flashing w., now glancing as in play *T.* 242
Now scattered w., and nowhere to be found *T.* 394
There might ye see the peony spread w. *T.* i 35
Receding w., they pressed against the ribs *T.* i 65
Full on the destined ear. W. flies the chaff *T.* i 359
Exploring far and w. the watery waste *T.* i 665 [567
The spark of life. The sportive wind blows w. *T.* i
With such artillery armed. Vice parries w. *T.* ii 810
Have rambled w. In country, city, seat *T.* iii 14
And spreading w. their spongy lobes, at first *T.* iii 522
The toiling steeds expand the nostril w. *T.* iv 347
W. scampering, snatches up the drifted snow *T.* v 49
That in its fall the liquid sheet throws w. *T.* v 106
In that blest moment Nature, throwing w. *T.* v 891
The jasmine, throwing w. her elegant sweets *T.* vi 173
Then perish on futurity's w. shore *Tir.* 83
Mankind are various, and the world is w. *Tir.* 788
If thou desert thy charge, and throw it w. *Tir.* 887
Achieved a labour which had, far and w. *Y.O.* 108

WIDE-ELBOWED.
W., and wadded with hair *Gr.* 11

WIDER.
But man, within a w. pale enclosed *A.T.* 58
Shall a w. world command *B.* 28
Opening and w. opening on her view *T.T.* 265

WIDE-SCATTERED.
One falls—the rest, w. with affright *St.* ii 23

WIDE-WANDERING.
And chills and darkens a w. soul *T.* v 684

WIDOW.
But now alike, gay w., virgin, wife *R.* 519

WIDOWED.
This w. heart would break " *The Doves* 36

WIELD.   [*T.* iii 636
Is needful. Strength may w. the ponderous spade
Who never saw the sword he could not w. *Con.* 608
Denies the power that w. it. God proclaims *T.* ii 178
The cheerful haunts of man ; to w. the axe *T.* v 42
Great purposes with ease, that turns and w. *T.* v 252

WIELDED.
That having w. th' elements, and built *T.* iii 170

WIFE.
For husband there and w. may boast *A Tale* 5
Made half their maids, sans ceremony, w. *A.T.* 128
Now N. had a w., and he wanted but one *A.T.* ii 7
John Gilpin kissed his loving w. *J.G.* 29   [ii 10
For a man to make free with another man's w. *A.T.*
At Edmonton, his loving w. *J.G.* 141
If w. should dine at Edmonton *J.G.* 195
Wooed an unfeeling statue for his w. *P.E.* 528
But now alike, gay widow, virgin, w. *R.* 519   [656
W. beggar husbands, husbands starve their w. *T.* ii
Thy waggon is thy w., and the poor beasts *T.* iv 367
He gives the princely bird, with all his w. *T.* iv 449
" 'Tis then I feel myself a w. *The Doves* 25
Then turning, he regales his listening w. *Tir.* 324
Or hadst thou a polite, card-playing w. *Tir.* 743
Should carve himself a w. in gingerbread *T.T.* 555

WIG.   [*A.C.* 6
With a great deal of skill, and a w. full of learning
Away went hat and w. *J.G.* 98
My hat and w. will soon be here *J.G.* 175
Whence straight he came with hat and w. *J.G.* 181
A w. that flowed behind *J.G.* 182
Went Gilpin's hat and w. *J.G.* 210
With w. prolix, down flowing to his waist *Tir.* 361

WIG-WEAVER.
Indebted to some smart w.'s hand *T.* iv 543

WILD.
To pathless w. and unfrequented plains *A.T.* 26 [53
And promised they should act the w. goose part *A.T.*
" To distant w. in quest of other game *A.T.* 106
As hedgerows in the w. *A Tale* 8   [258
With fragrant turf, and flowers as w. and fair *Ch.*
The w. assassins start into the street *Ch.* 507
With many a w., indeed, but flowery spray *Ch.* 629
And w. as madness in the world's esteem *Con.* 666
Was still a w. Jack hare *Ep.* ii 8
Thy mariners explore the w. expanse *Ex.* 290
That thankless waste and w. abuse destroy *Ex.* 679
Stubborn and sturdy, a w. ass's colt *H.* 182
In vain opinion's waste and dangerous w. *H.* 279
If w. in nature, and not duly found *H.* 296
W. as if nature there, void of all good *H.* 540 [618
The strange conceits, vain projects, and w. dreams *H.*
Or a w. goose at play *J.G.* 140
W. roses over furrowed ground *Mrs. M—* 28 .[66
That serve mankind, or shun them, w. or tame *N.A.*
Hark ! He answers—W. tornadoes *N.C.* 33
Like a neglected forester, runs w. *P.E.* 362
No w. enthusiast ever yet could rest *P.E.* 470
To the w. wave, or wilder human breast *P.E.* 601
And lovers, of all creatures, tame or w. *R.* 251
Then neither heathy w., nor scenes as fair *R.* 331
W. without art, or artfully subdued *R.* 416
With woodbine and w. roses mantled o'er *R.* 420
'Tis w. good nature's never failing lot *R.* 582
And w. familiar with a lion's roar *R.* 779
O'ertop the lofty wood that skirts the w. *T.* i 558
Intoxication and delirium w. *T.* ii 510
The laity run w.— But do they now ? *T.* ii 572
Me oft has Fancy, ludicrous and w. *T.* iv 286 [118
The sunbeam ; there, embossed and fretted w. *T.* v
Confederacy of projectors w. and vain *T.* v 194
To mix her w. vagaries with thy laws *T.* v 873 [337
Though w. their strange vagaries, and uncouth *T.* vi
Infatuates, and through labyrinths and w. *T.* vi 103
Within the confines of their w. domain *T.* vi 407
'Twere w. profusion all, and bootless waste *Tir.* 49
His w. excursions, window-breaking feats *Tir.* 228
The pert made perter, and the tame made w. *Tir.* 345
Their offspring, left upon so w. a beach *Tir.* 802
And Liberty, preserved from w. excess *T.T.* 316
Of w. imagination, and there reeled *T.T.* 605
In w. disorder, and unfit for use *T.* ii 805 [*T.T.* 696
And charms the woodland scenes, and w. unknown
Long since, and rovers of the forest w. *Y.O.* 126

WILDER.
To the wild wave, or w. human breast *P.E.* 601

WILDERNESS.
We tread the W., whose well-rolled walks *T.* i 351
Oh for a lodge in some vast w. *T.* ii 1
The rest appears a w. of strange *T.* iv 78
And makes the world the w. it is *T.* vi 53
The beauties of the w. are his *T.* vi 186
The w. is theirs with all its caves *T.* vi 401
Their mind a w. through want of care *H.* 233
Before them, and behind a w. *Her.* 58
With flower and fruit the w. supplies *Tir.* 27

WILDEST.
The w. project of her teeming brain *A.T.* 57
The w. wind that blows *N.* 6
The w. scorner of his Maker's laws *Tir.* 55

WILDFOWL.
W. or venison, and his errand speeds *T.* iv 612

WILDLY. [*H.* 517
The wretch, who once sang w., danced and laughed
Where beckoning Pleasure leads them w. stray *Ex.* 464

WILES.
Rejects all treaty, penetrates all w. *H.* 649
And pleasure's fatal w.? *O.* ii 9

WILFUL.
Your w. suicide on God's decree *T.* 20

WILFULLY.
His sheltering side, and w. forewent *T.* vi 40
While self-betrayed, and w. undone *Tir.* 171

WILL.
May rove at w., where appetite shall lead *A.T.* 60
And Vengeance executes what Justice w. *Ch.* 82
Or if the w. and sovereignty of God *Ch.* 165
And bends the tough materials to his w. *Ch.* 464
As bastions set point blank against God's w. *Con.* 688
Thus Martha, even against her w. *E.* i 43
That hard by nature, and stubborn w. *E.* ii 21
E'en as his w. and his decrees ordain *Ex.* 325
Doing and suffering, his unquestioned w. *Ex.* 645
Held by the tenure of his w. alone *Ex.* 673
I perched at w. on every spray *G.* 4
Compliance with his w. your lot ensures *H.* 326
And sore against his w. *J.G.* 158
Thy sight now seconds not thy w. *M.* 15
Agents of his w. to use? *N.C.* 32
Free in his w. to choose or to refuse *P.E.* 25 [270
Enslaves the w., nor leaves the judgment free *P.E.*
The W. made subject to a lawless force *P.E.* 448
By his good w. would keep us single *P.T.* 32 [557
Bend the straight rule to their own crooked w. *P.E.*
Resign our own and seek our Maker's w. *R.* 130
His mind his kingdom, and his w. his law *T.* 406
His w. and judgment at continual strife *T.* 467 [551
When the great Sovereign would his w. express *T.*
The total ordinance and w. of God *T.* i 743
And manifold results, into the w. *T.* ii 164
Formed for his use, and ready at his w.? *T.* ii 202
Whose freedom is by sufferance, and at w. *T.* v 363
His strength to suffer, and his w. to serve *T.* v 902
Baffled his rider, saved against his w. *T.* vi 520
Framed for the service of a free-born w. *Tir.* 8
Appointed sage preceptor to the W.—*Tir.* 32

WILLIAM.
Had fled from W., and the news was fresh *T.* vi 660
They dream of little Charles or W. graced *Tir.* 360

WILLING. [264
My soul should yield thee w. thanks and praise *Ch.*
Nor set a price upon a w. heart *H.* 337
Drops the red vengeance from his w. hand *T.* 278

WILLINGLY.
I will obey, not w. alone *M.P.* 15

WILLOW.
We pass a gulf in which the w. dip *T.* i 268
And of a wannish grey; the w. such *T.* i 309

WIN.
Sounds not arms shall w. the prize *B.* 23
And w. mankind, as his attempts prevail *Ch.* 335
The graces of a life that w. the skies *Ex.* 112
The fast that w. deliverance, and suspends *Ex.* 406
Lavish of life, to w. an empty tomb *Ex.* 522
Shall w. my confidence again *F.* 190
But pleasure w. his heart *H.F.* 12

No bribes the heart can w. *Miss*— 58
Successful there, he w. a curse *Mor.* 48
To w. due credence to what follows next *N.A.* 72
W. in return an answer of disdain *R.* 228
And woo and w. thee to thy proper good *R.* 256
W. no notice, wakes no fears *St.* iv 20 [280
In foreign eyes!—be grooms, and w. the plate *T.* ii
Pleasure's call attention w. *St.* iv 25 [*T.* 13
He that would w. the race, must guide his horse
In science, w. one inch of heavenly ground *T.* 338
Though apt, yet coy, and difficult to w. *T.* ii 289
The hope of better things, the chance to w. *T.* iii 828
And w. them, but to lose them in his turn *T.* iv 63
It knew not once, the country w. me still *T.* iv 694
W. public honour; and ten thousand sit *T.* vi 633
And w. it with more pain. Their blood is shed *T.* v 719
But he may boast, what few that w. it can *T.* vi 974
Shall w. his heart, and have his drunken praise *Tir.* 215
And small academies w. all the praise? *Tir.* 504
That anything but vice could w. thy love *Tir.* 742
Will w. her visits or engage her stay *T.T.* 411 [157
To w. no praise when well-wrought plans prevail *T.T.*

WINCE.
Some fretful tempers w. at every touch *Con.* 325

WIND.
But suddenly a w., as high *A Fable* 10
Ye w. that have made me your sport *A.S.* 33
"And flutters loose, the sport of every w. *A.T.* 102
And scudded still before the w. *Cast.* 24 [ii 1
Sweet stream that w. through garden glade *Comp.*
Where'er it w., the salutary stream *Con.* 893 [iii 60
While you, my friend, whatever w. should blow *E.*
Whom the w. waft where'er the billows roll *Ex.* 19
Sighs unregarded to the passing w. *Ex.* 30 [*F.A.* 6
Thus, while gray evening lulled the w. and called
The w. did blow, the cloak did fly *J.G.* 101
Refreshes, where it w., the faded green *J.T.* 39
The wildest w. that blows *N.* 6
Could I believe, that w. for ages pent *N.A.* 85
By all the w.'s that blow *O.* i 16
Wherever driven by w. or tide *P.* 53
Sent us a w. to parch us at a blast? *P.E.* 256 [333
Down, down the w., she swims, and sails away *P.E.*
Like thistle-seeds, are sown by every w. *P.E.* 555
The w. play no longer and sing in the leaves *P.F.* 3
The w., of late breathed gently forth *P.T.* 50
Ranges at liberty, and snuffs the w. *R.* 630
Exposed her too much to the w. *R.C.* 26 [156
The ruffling w., scarce conscious that it blew *T.*
The tone of languid Nature. Mighty w. *T.* i 183
Brushed by the w. So sportive is the light *T.* i 345
The spark of life. The sportive w. blows wide *T.* i 567
W. from all quarters agitate the air *T.* i 373 [ii 53
To preach the general doom. When were the w. *T.*
Not by a mighty w., but by that voice *T.* ii 113
Which w. and waves obey, invades the shore *T.* ii 114
In tempests; quits his grasp upon the w. *T.* ii 181
That w. and waters, lulled by magic sounds *T.* iii 261
Entangled, w. now this way and now that *T.* iii 2
And w. his way with pleasure and with ease *T.* iii 10
Like the fair flower dishevelled in the w. *T.* iii 262
Impervious to the w. First he bids spread *T.* iii 475
While the w. whistle, and the snows descend *T.* iii 569
Few self-supported flowers endure the w. *T.* iii 657
Raging abroad, and the rough w., endear *T.* iv 309
That crowd away before the driving w. *T.* v 3 [554
The process. Heat and cold, and w. and steam *T.* iii
Can w. around him, but he casts it off *T.* v 736 [142
Storms rise to o'erwhelm him; or if stormy w. *T.* ii
As the w. sways it, has yet well sufficed *T.* vi 73
Barren as lances, among which the w. *T.* vi 142
That the w. severs from the broken wave *T.* vi 156
The vale of Nature, where it creeps and w. *T.* vi 721

WIND—WINTRY

For He, whose car the w. are, and the clouds T. vi 740
When piping w. shall soon arise T.B. 17 [vi 831
Worms w. themselves into our sweetest flowers T.
And something in the w. T.B. 39
Soft as the passing w. The Doves 38 [Y.O. 125
Thine arms have left thee. W. have rent them off
At her command w. rise and waters roar Tir. 25
Prayer to the w., and caution to the waves Tir. 183
And w. his web about the riveled leaves Tir. 596
Shifted the w. that raised it, and it fell T.T. 387
Snuffs up the w. and flings himself abroad T.T. 669
To the four-quartered w., robust and bold Y.O. 98

WIND-GUN.
Proves after all a w.'s airy charge Con. 274

WINDING.
W. a secret or an open course Ch. 369
The w. of the stream D.W. 28
Taking my lonely w. walk, I mused F.A. 8
Can trace her mazy w. to their end P.E. 16
Those w. modestly a silent course R. 78
The sound shall run along the w. vales R. 363
The dash of ocean on his w. shore T. i 186
The w. of my path through many years T. vi 18

WINDOW.
The open w. seemed to invite F.B. 19
Up flew the w. all J.G. 110
And, turning from my nursery w., drew M.P. 30
If breaking w. be the sport Pat. 11
From every w., and the fields are green R. 498

WINDOW-BREAKING.
His wild excursions, w. feats Tir. 228

WINDSOR.
Such freedom is;—and W.'s hoary towers Ex. 596
And Cobham's groves, and W.'s green retreats R. 571

WINDY.
While morning kindles with a w. red R. 432
He gulps the w. diet, and ere long T. v 269

WINE.
When w. has given indecent language birth Con. 263
And for that w. is dear J.G. 26 [377
The Saviour's feast, his own blest bread and w. Ex.
W. has no taste, and beauty has no charms H. 705
"The w. is left behind!" J.G. 60
Down ran the w. into the road J.G. 125
Which shook Belshazzar at his w. Q.V. 51
Those humours, tart as w. upon the fret R. 761
As leanest land supplies the richest w. T. 364 [808
Their points obtuse, and feathers drunk with w.! T. ii

WING.
Oh! had I the w. of a dove A.S. 19
Borne far away on elevated w. A.T. 31
On all the w. of chivalry advanced A.T. 149
Armed with thunder, clad with w. B. 27
I only kissed his ruffled w. B.R. 19
To w. all her moments at home C. 50
'Tis e'en as if an angel shook his w. Ch. 438
On all the w. of holiday delight) Ch. 548
Like angel-heads in stone with pigeon w.? Con. 576
Unless, when rising on a joyful w. Con. 716 [189
Themselves secured beneath the Almighty w. Ex.
That balances the w. of every hour Ex. 321
Now borne upon the w. of truth sublime Ex. 466
That flutter loose on golden w. F.B. 8 [163
On steady w. sails through the immense abyss H.
'Tis Heaven, all Heaven, descending on the w. H. 732
And while the w. of fancy still are free M.P. 118
Compose their useless w. N. 2
On eager w. the spoiler came P.B. 5
For though, ere yet the shaft is on the w. P.E. 572
With golden w. and satin pole P.T. 27

And after poising her adventurous w. R. 671
That leave no stain upon the w. of time R. 800
And soaring on her own unborrowed w. T. 488 [135
That spreads his motley w. in the eye of noon T. iii
Milton, whose genius had angelic w. T. iii 255
Riches have w., and grandeur is a dream T. iii 263
The w. that waft our riches out of sight T. iii 760
That at the sound of Winter's hoary w. T. iii 830
Time, as he passes us, has a dove's w. T. iv 211
The feathered tribes domestic. Half on w. T. v 62
For he has w. that neither sickness, pain T. v 771
Who gives its lustre to an insect's w. T. v 813
That flutters least is longest on the w. T. vi 931
Oh thou, whom, borne on fancy's eager w. Tir. 131
Safe under such a w., his boy shall show Tir. 684
Thither he w. his airy flight Trans. ii 14
For such a pair of w. as thine Trans. ii 35
Spread little w., and rather skip than fly T.T. 579

WINGED.
The w. mansion move A Tale 50 [746
Flies, w. with joy, to some coach-crowded door Tir.
With self-indulgence w. the fleeting hours Ex. 71
He walks, he leaps, he runs—is w. with joy T. i 443

WINK.
Too just to w., or speak the guilty clear" Ex. 256
W. hard, and talks of darkness at noonday P.E. 451
Nor slept a single w., or purred R.C. 75
To follow foolish precedents, and w. Tir. 255

WINKING.
Through want of care; or her whose w. eye T. ii 773

WINNOW.
"Your office is to w. false from true H. 417

WINTER.
As ever swept a w. sky A Fable 11
But W., armed with terrors here unknown H. 473
Eternal w. doomed to know Miss — 35
Old w., halting o'er the mead N. 13
It chanced then on a w. day P.T. 9
I fear we shall have w. yet" P.T. 25
When W. soaks the fields, and female feet T. 215
Go, bid the w. cease to chill the year T. 399
Whose arm this twentieth w. I perceive T. i 145
All summer long, which w. fills again T. i 329
Or when rough w. rages, on the soft T. iii 31
And hence even W. fills his withered hand T. iii 428
Of churlish W., in her froward moods T. iii 433
Not so when w. scowls. Assistant Art T. iii 541
Ficoides, glitters bright the w. long T. iii 579 [581
The w.'s frown, if screened from his shrewd bite T. iii
That at the sound of W.'s hoary wing T. iii 830
O W., ruler of the inverted year T. iv 120
Is W. hideous in a garb like this? T. iv 194
To w., and the current in his veins T. iv 388
The armoury of W.; where his troops T. v 139
The night was w. in his roughest mood T. vi 57
Defies the check of w., haunts of deer T. vi 110
Of unprolific w. has impress'd T. vi 138 [192
He marks the bounds which W. may not pass T. vi
Though w. had been none, had man been true T. vi 256
He has outslept the w., ventures forth T. vi 313
There shall he learn, ere sixteen w. old Tir. 210
And thrice in every w. throngs thine own Tir. 747
Thine endures the w. long Trans. iii 22
If W. bellow from the north Trans. H. 22
W. invades the spring, and often pours T.T. 210
Place me where W. breathes his keenest air T.T. 294
And w. is decked with a smile W.N. 4
And the w. of sorrow best shows W.N. 23
(Since which I number threescore w. past Y.O. 3
The rudiments should sleep the w. through Y.O. 28

WINTRY.
A conflagration, or a w. flood Ch. 465

Whose wit can brighten up a *w.* day *Con.* 581
Through *w.* rigours unimpaired endure *Con.* 650
Would age in thee resign his *w.* reign *H.* 33
Wait but the lashes of a *w.* storm *H.* 185
In *w.* age to feel no chill *M.* 42
Aware of *w.* storms *M.B.* 6
With which the fieldfare, *w.* guest, is fed *N.A.* 20
The snowy robe her *w.* state assumes *R.* 195
The rude inclemency of *w.* skies *T.* 138
Thrown up by *w.* torrents roaring loud *T.* i 14 [552
With summer fruits brought forth by *w.* suns *T.* iii
Bestrides the *w.* flood, in which the moon *T.* iv 3
Makes *w.* music, sighing as it goes *T.* vi 143
Of *w.* blasts; the loftiest tower *Trans. H.* 14
A *w.* figure like a withered thorn *T.T.* 725

WIPED. [*Rose* 19
And the tear that is *w.* with a little address *The*

WIPES.
He *w.* and scours the silver cup in vain *Ex.* 385
One *w.* his nose upon his sleeve *Y.D.* 41

WIRE.
A pass between his *w. F.B.* 18
With *w.* and catgut he concludes the day *P.E.* 126
With limbs of British oak, and nerves of *w. R.* 311
Not rough with *w.* of steel or brass *T.B.* 26   [607
And dizzy with delight, profaned the sacred *w.T.T.*

WIRY.
Soon passed the *w.* grate *G.* 12

WISDOM.
Might learn from the *w.* of age *A.S.* 23
The path of *w.*, all whose paths are peace *Ch.* 162
Drinks *w.* at the milky stream of light *Ch.* 319
What human *w.* cannot but oppose *Ch.* 340
Makes *w.*, worthy of the name, his own *Ch.* 350
Though *W.* hail them, heedless of her call *Ch.* 406
Her *w.* seems the weakness of a child *Ch.* 423
And, Truth and *W.* gracing all he said *Con.* 526
Whose *w.*, drawn from the deep well of life *Con.* 564
Their *w.* bursts into this sage reply *Con.* 877 [244
" Keep *w.*, or meet vengeance in your turn! *Ex.*
Know then, that heavenly *W.* on this ball *Ex.* 314
Their *w.* pure, and given them from above *Ex.* 442
W. and Goodness are twin-born, one heart *Ex.* 634
Of passed experience, and the *w.* gleaned *F.A.* 2
This *w.*, and but this, from all the past ? *F.A.* 12
Of distant *w.* shoots across his way *H.* 94
His names of *w.*, goodness, power, and love *H.* 135
The plough of *w.* never entering there *H.* 234
But while they speak the *w.* of the skies *H.* 768
The praise of *w.*, comeliness, and worth *P.E.* 295
And *W.* falls before exterior grace *P.E.* 418
But they whom Truth and *W.* lead *P.B.* 35
More years and *w.* than the most *P.T.* 18
True *w.* will attend his feeble call *R.* 33
Truth, *w.*, grace, and peace like that above *R.* 163
Give Truth a lustre, and make *W.* smile *R.* 718 [557
Graced with such *w.*, how would beauty shine! *R.*
Had we their *w.*, should we, often warned *St.* ii 25
Of all that *W.* dictates this the drift *T.* 513
Their fortitude and *w.* were a flame *T.* 531
That self-renouncing *w.*, learned before *T.* 568
Of *w.*, proves a school in which he learns *T.* i 614
To Athens or to Rome, for *w.* short *T.* ii 536 [793
Than they themselves by choice, for *w.*'s sake *T.* ii
Is oft-times proof of *w.*, when the fault *T.* iii 39
And when I weigh this seeming *w.* well *T.* iii 180
By strides of human *w.* In his works *T.* iii 222
Such was thy *w.*, Newton, childlike sage ! *T.* iii 252
The growing seeds of *w.* ; that suggest *T.* iii 302
But *w.* is a pearl with most success *T.* iii 381
The logic, and the *w.*, and the wit *T.* iv 32
It seems the part of *w.*, and no sin *T.* iv 336

In *w.*, and with philosophic deeps *T.* v 297
Except what *w.* lays on evil men *T.* v 449
And in the school of sacred *w.* taught *T.* v 797
But runs the road of *w.* Thou hast built *T.* v 849
Knowledge and *w.* far from being one *T.* vi 90
W. in minds attentive to their own *T.* vi 91
The mere materials with which *w.* builds *T.* vi 93
W. is humble that he knows no more *T.* vi 98
Deceive no student. *W.* there and truth *T.* vi 114
Deserving honour, but for *w.* more *T.* vi 491
Who in his sovereign *w.* made them all *T.* vi 587
Seldom, and never but as *W.* prompts *T.* vi 849
The *w.* of great nations, now no more *Tir.* 16
Brings into doubt the *w.* of the skies *Tir.* 72
Proofs of the *w.* of the all-seeing mind *Tir.* 94
He too might make his author's *w.* clear *Tir.* 100
Your *w.* and your ways—to you I turn *Tir.* 812
Learn *w.* and repentance ere too late " *T.T.* 437
In *w.*, wealth, in fortune, and in lies *T.T.* 469
Fails not, in virtue and in *w.* laid *Y.O.* 121
With love and *w.* rendered back to Heaven *Y.O.* 154

WISE. [*A.C.* 28
For the court did not think they were equally *w.*
The hand of the Supremely *W.—E.* i 34   [38
Some she would teach (for she was wondrous *w. A.T.*
W. to promote whatever end he means *Ch.* 87 [iv 1
I have read the Review ; it is learned and *w. A.T.*
He reads *w.* lectures, and describes aloud *Ch.* 389
His *w.* forbearance has their end in view *Con.* 33
Of *w.* reflection and well-timed discourse *Con.* 388
And she may now be as discreet and *w. Con.* 805
But let the *w.* and well-instructed hand *Con.* 903
Once on a time an Emperor, a *w.* man *E.* iii 46
Meek, modest, venerable, *w.*, sincere *Ex.* 620
Nor is it *w.* complaining *F.* 33
Too many, yet too few to make us *w. H.* 26
To read *w.* lectures, vanity the text *H.* 107
And truth, proposed to reasoners *w.* as they *H.* 258
" Is still found fallible, however *w. H.* 422
'Tis here the folly of the *w. H.F.* 13
" Some people are more nice than *w. M.F.* 20
Come, then, fair maid (in nature *w.*) *Miss* — 13
Lead to the bliss she promises the *w. P.E.* 73 [466
Thou fountain at which drink the good and *w. P.E.*
But he, not *w.* enough to scan *St.* v 5
Not many *w.*, rich, noble, or profound *T.* 337
And never checked by what impedes the *w. T.* 373
May yet be foul ; so witty, yet not *w. T.* i 728
And arbitration *w.* of the Supreme *T.* ii 165
There we grow early grey, but never *w. T.* ii 633
The rest are sober dreamers, grave and *w. T.* iii 137
Keen enough, *w.* and skilful as thou art *T.* iii 207
To him that leads it, *w.*, and to be praised *T.* iii 380
And *w.* precaution, which a clime so rude *T.* iii 431
And oft at last in vain. The learned and *w. T.* iii 562
But war's a game which, were their subjects *w. T.* v 187
Sterling, and worthy of a *w.* man's wish *T.* v 358
And we too *w.* to trust them. He that takes *T.* v 496
From fool to *w.*, from earthly to divine *T.* v 682
The praise bestowed was just and *w. Th.* 13 [*Tir.* 811
Who, *w.* yourselves, desire your sons should learn
That taught of God they may indeed be *w. Tir.* 107
W. for himself and his few friends alone *Tir.* 675
No few, that would seem *w.*, resemble her *Tir.* 796
Designed by Nature *w.*, but self-made fools *Tir.* 837
Born from above and made divinely *w. V.* 94

WISELY.
That Solomon has *w.* spoken *E.* i 105
But *w.* seeks a more convenient friend *R.* 443
As *w.*, and as much improves his powers *R.* 508
To close life *w.*, may not waste my own *R.* 808
And having spoken *w.*, at the close *T.* ii 442

The seed, selected *w.*, plump, and smooth *T. iii* 511
Charm the deaf serpent *w.* Make him hear *T. v* 671
Of the poor brute, seems *w.* to suppose *T. vi* 437
And *w.* store the nursery by degrees *Tir.* 117

WISER.
But goes the male? Far *w.*, he *A Tale* 47
Should *w.* be, than to pursue *Beau* 3
And *w.* men's ability, pretence *Con.* 628
And did they dream, and art thou *w.* now? *Ex.* 632
Some *w.* rule must teach him how to live *H.* 600
And learned in future to be *w. P.T.* 60
Up!—God has formed thee with a *w.* view *R.* 265
Mix with the world, but with its *w.* part *R.* 275
Not only in our *w.* race *R.C.* 22
Crack the satiric thong? 'Twere *w.* far *T. iii* 26
Would urge a *w.* suit than asking more *T. vi* 56
And Learning *w.* grow without his books *T. vi* 87
Nor deems he *w.* him, who gives his vow *T. vi* 278
Would turn our steps into a *w.* train *Tir.* 260
'Twere *w.* sure to inspire a little heart *Tir.* 454

WISEST.
Best for the public, and my *w.* part *Con.* 870
I hold it therefore *w.* and most fit *N.A.* 103
What obvious truths the *w.* heads may miss! *R.* 458
The *w.* and the best feel urgent need *T. ii* 483
The *w.* heads might agitate in vain *Tir.* 130

WISH.
A *w.* or a thought after me? *A.S.* 38
With warmer *w.* sent *Cast.* 10   [137
But ah! what *w.* can prosper, or what prayer *Ch.*
Their peevish hearers almost *w.* they had *Con.* 324
If he *w.* to instruct, he must learn to delight *F.M.* 17
Dwells there a *w.* in such a breast *Miss* — 5   [336
With sole—that's just the sort he would not *w. Con.*
Whate'er you *w.* or love *Miss* — 96
No virtuous *w.* can bear a date *Mor.* 57   [*M.P.* 81
Might one *w.* bring them, would I *w.* them here?
To *w.* thee fairer is no need *N.Y.G.* 5
There dwells some *w.* in every heart *N.Y.G.* 15
That *w.* on some fair future day *N.Y.G.* 17
I *w.* it all fulfilled *N.Y.G.* 20
To *w.* myself the rock I view *P.* 29   [14
Much more in behalf of your *w.* might be said *P.A.*
I only *w.* 'twould come *Pat.* 2
A rope! I *w.* we patriots had *Pat.* 21
First *w.* to be imposed on, and then are *P.E.* 290
If a *w.* wander that way, call it home *P.E.* 586
He cannot long be safe whose *w.* roam *P.E.* 587
With hopeless *w.* one looks and lingers *P.B.* 33
All *w.*, or seem to *w.*, they could forego *R.* 4
Their *w.* all impregnated with earth *R.* 36
Girt with a chain he cannot *w.* to break *R.* 243
His *w.* and mine both prompt me to retire" *R.* 390
That so retired he should not *w.* a change *R.* 600
As poet well could *w.* to have *R.C.* 2
That prompts the *w.* to stay *St.* v 30
Delusive most where warmest *w.* are *T. i* 542
Of temperate *w.* and industrious hands *T. i* 599
The sleeping leaves, is all the light they *w. T. i* 763
The branches, sturdy to his utmost *w. T. iii* 530
Indulged in what they *w.*, they soon supply *T. iii* 534
What could I *w.*, that I possess not here? *T. iii* 690
The *w.* to shine, the thirst to be amused *T. iii* 829
I never framed a *w.* or formed a plan *T. iv* 695 [525
Vain *w.*! those days were never; airy dreams *T. iv*
A *w.* for ease and leisure, and ere long *T. iv* 800
Sterling, and worthy of a wise man's *w. T. v* 358
What none but bad men *w.* exploded, must *T. v* 613
"To gratify the hunger of his *w. T. v* 637
"And many an aching *w.*, your beamy fires *T. v* 838
How readily we *w.* time spent revoked *T. vi* 25
Impart to the benevolent, who *w. T. vi* 344

Soon see your *w.* fulfilled in either child *Tir.* 344
Resents his fellow's, *w.* it were less *Tir.* 477
A *w.* to copy what he must admire *Tir.* 649
(Forgive the crime) I *w.* them, I confess *Tir.* 921

WISHED.
And one I *w.* my own *D.W.* 16
The prophet wept for Israel; *w.* his eyes *Ex.* 33
What ardently I *w.*, I long believed *M.P.* 38   [196
With all that man e'er *w.*, or Heaven bestowed? *Ex.*
His wonted course, yet what I *w.* is done *M.P.* 113
For thee *w.* many a time *N.Y.G.* 2
She therefore *w.* instead of those *R.C.* 29   [538
From what they knew, to what they *w.* to know *T.*
Oft have I *w.* the peaceful covert mine *T. i* 233
Of public virtue ever *w.* removed *T. iv* 615
Found here that leisure and that ease I *w. T. iv* 801
As fearful of offending whom he *w. T. vi* 501
I studied, prized, and *w.* that I had known *T. iv* 722

WISHING.
And *w.* for a place of rest *R.C.* 105
With few associates, and not *w.* more *T. iii* 120

WIT.
The insidious witch that had his *w.* abused *A.T.* 176
And had no other play-place for his *w. Ch.* 538
At every stroke *w.* flashes in our eyes *Ch.* 543
But are we so to *w.* and beauty blind *Con.* 257
His *w.* invites you by his looks to come *Con.* 303
Whose *w.* can brighten up a wintry day *Con.* 581
Is sparkling *w.* the world's exclusive right *Con.* 589
A Christian's *w.* is inoffensive light *Con.* 599
Had *w.* as bright as ready to produce *Con.* 614
To find the medium, asks some share of *w. Con.* 879
Can gaze on even Darwin's *w. Dr.* 19   [*Con.* 626
When some green heads, as void of *w.* as thought
To show my genius or my *w. E. iv* 7
To deem the *w.* a friend displays *F.* 88
Now Gilpin had a pleasant *w. J.G.* 169
Thus showed his ready *w. J.G.* 186
And set their *w.* at work to find *L.W.* 13
When *w.* and genius meet their doom *M. ii* 1
W. flashing on Religion's side *Mrs. M—* 31
There Genius, Learning, Fancy, *W. Mrs. M—* 45
Give *w.*, that what is left may shine *O. i.* 27
To tell them more than they have *w.* to ask *P.E.* 390
Woe to the man whose *w.* disclaims its use *R.* 211
And *w.* that puppet prompters might inspire *R.* 312
To birth or *w.*, nor gives nor takes offence *R.* 450
Learning is one, and *w.*, however rare *T.* 302 [438
Whose *w.* is rudeness, whose good breeding tires *R.*
Has little understanding, and no *w. T.* 324   [717
Whose *w.* well managed, and whose classic style *R.*
The logic, and the wisdom, and the *w. T. iv* 32
And snappish dialogue, that flippant *w. T. iv* 198
I cannot but lament thy splendid *w. T. iv* 725
By which the magic art of shrewder *w. T. vi* 99
Of modest truth for *w.*'s eccentric range *Tir.* 174
With them is courage; his effrontery *w. Tir.* 227
Account him no just mark for idle *w. Tir.* 726
And make him quite a *w. Trans. iv* 12
W., undistinguishing, is apt to strike *T.T.* 101
Thus reputation is a spur to *w. T.T.* 520 [*T.T.* 663
W. now and then, struck smartly, shows a spark
And some *w.* flag through fear of losing it *T.T.* 521
The substitute for genius, sense and *w. T.T.* 543
Spendthrift alike of money and of *w. T.T.* 684
There's little talking, and no *w. Y.D.* 39   [*T.T.* 764
Though Butler's *w.*, Pope's numbers, Prior's ease

WITCH.
The insidious *w.* that had his wits abused *A.T.* 176

WITCHERIES.
But thine, as dark as *w.* of the night *Ex.* 494

WITHDRAWS—WOMAN

WITHDRAWS.
Who comes when called, and at a word *w. R.* 447

WITHDRAWN.
And that, judicially *w.*, disgrace *Ex.* 692
Her animating smile *w. S.* 15
The fence *w.*, he gives them every beam *T.* iii 444

WITHDREW.
I thence *w.*, and followed long *D.W.* 27
My panting side was charged, when I *w. T.* iii 110

WITHER.
States thrive or *w.*, as moons wax and wane *Ex.* 324
Should droop and *w.* where they grow *P.* 59
But all they trust in *w.* as it must *T.T.* 470

WITHERED.
So *w.* stumps disgrace the sylvan scene *Con.* 51
The scoff of *w.* age and beardless youth *H.* 743
Yon ancient prude, whose *w.* features show *T.* 131
And *w.* muscle, and the vapid soul *T.* i 393
With dripping rains, or *w.* by a frost *T.* ii 211
And hence even Winter fills his *w.* hand *T.* iii 428
Must fly before the knife; the *w.* leaf *T.* iii 614
That tinkle in the *w.* leaves below *T.* vi 82
A wintry figure like a *w.* thorn *T.T.* 725
Decayed by time, or *w.* by a frost *V.* 58

WITHERING. [938
And never *w.* wreaths, compared with which *T.* vi

WITHES.
With as much ease as Samson his green *w. T.* v 737

WITHHELD.
When Roman rapine, by no laws *w. A.T.* 126
Always from port *w.*, always distressed *M.P.* 101

WITHHOLD.
He will give freely, or he will *w. H.* 331

WITHSTAND. [*A.T.* 186
"Thee to the field, thou shouldst *w.* them all"
And harder to *w. B.R.* 4 [487
And therefore heedless, can *w.* thy power ? *T.* ii

WITHSTOOD.
He spurned the wretch that slighted, or *w. Ch.* 31
Are mighty mischiefs, not to be *w. Ch.* 283
To be suspected, thwarted, and *w. T.T.* 141

WITNESS.
W. its insignificant result *Con.* 16
All *w.* of blessings foully scorned *H.* 222
And stands a *w.* at Truth's awful bar *Her.* 81
W. of joys that shun the sight of noon *P.E.* 174
A *w.* undescried *Q.V.* 30
Were *w.* how cordially I pressed *R.* 379
And novels (*w.* every month's Review) *R.* 713
And *w.*, dear companion of my walks *T.* i 144
W. a joy that thou hast doubled long *T.* i 149
The peasant too, a *w.* of his song *T.* i 497
A silent *w.* of the headlong rage *T.* iii 218
Though resident, and *w.* of the wrong *T.* iv 594
Sad *w.* how close-pent man regrets *T.* iv 777
They are thy *w.*, who speak thy power *T.* v 853
He sells protection. *W.* at his foot *T.* vi 417
W. the patient ox, with stripes and yells *T.* vi 420
He too is *w.*, noblest of the train *T.* vi 425
Bears *w.*, long ere his dismission come *Tir.* 561

WITNESSED.
Who so lately had *w.* her own *C.* 16 [372
Thy groves and lawns then *w.*! Every heart *T.* vi
W. of mutability in all *Y.O.* 70

WITNESSING.
His shoulders *w.* by many a shrug *H.* 415

WITTY.
Clean, candid, and *w.*—Thelypthora dies *A.T.* iv 2
(Sworn foes to every thing that's *w.*!) *E.* iv 14

May yet be foul; so *w.*, yet not wise *T.* i 728
W., and well employed, and, like thy Lord *Tir.* 139
By footman Tom for *w.* and refined *Tir.* 687

WODEN.
W. and Thor, each tottering in his shrine *Ex.* 505

WOE.
But wantonness and *w. A Tale* 76
To teach the wanderer, as his *w.* increase *Ch.* 161
To seek a nobler amidst scenes of *w. Ch.* 300
Acquainted with the *w.* that fear or shame *Con.* 495
A Jordan for the ablution of our *w. Con.* 566 [169
Let Egypt's plagues, and Canaan's *w.* proclaim *Ex.*
The virtue they had learned in scenes of *w. Ex.* 80
Thanks, gentle swain, for all my *w. G.* 13 [224
Their *w.*, not yet repealed, thence date them all *Ex.*
And earth has no reality but *w.*" *H.* 68
Deem life a blessing with its numerous *w. H.* 546
Sweet as the privilege of healing *w. J.T.* 17
Transforms thy smiles to looks of *w. M.* 47
At once both bliss and *w.*! *Miss* — 8
The shafts of *w.*—in such a breast *Miss* — 43
Such previous *w.* the price! *Q.V.* 80
To regions where, in spite of sin and *w. R.* 27
W. to the man whose wit disclaims its use *R.* 211
Pierced with the *w.* that she laments in vain *R.* 300
Forgery of fancy, and a dream of *w. R.* 324
Thus some retire to nourish helpless *w. R.* 603
But not like me to nourish *w.*! *S.* 20
His folly, and his *w.*! *St.* iii 4
And covet longer *w.*? *St.* v 20
For other's *w.*, but smiles upon her own *T.* 178
Where should the living, weeping o'er his *w. T.* 435
That Scripture is the only cure of *w. T.* 452
Ten thousand sages lost in endless *w. T.* 517 [505
The mouth with blasphemy, the heart with *w. T.* i
For such immeasurable *w.* appears *T.* i 459 [586
Beguile their *w.*, and make the woods resound *T.* i
His ashes, where, and in what weal or *w.*? *T.* ii 519
And introduces hunger, frost, and *w. T.* ii 616
Of cruel man, exulting in her *w. T.* iii 336
With merry descants on a nation's *w. T.* iv 77
Suffer his *w.*, and share in his escapes *T.* iv 117
Their long complaints, is self-inflicted *w. T.* iv 430
You the regardless author of its *w. T.* v 350 [436
W. to the gardener's pale, the farmer's hedge *T.* iv
To such amusements as ingenious *w. T.* v 416 [433
With *w.*, which who that suffers would not kneel *T.* v
And full immunity from penal *w. T.* v 580
W. to the tyrant, if he dare intrude *T.* vi 406
May stand between an animal and *w. T.* vi 727
Some taste of comfort in a world of *w. T.* vi 966
And if Authority grow wanton, *w. T.T.* 226
If human *w.* her soft attention claim *T.T.* 484
Cold in his cause, and careless of his *w. V.* 4
And, summoned to partake its fellow's *w. V.* 69

WOLF.
So may the *w.*, whom famine has made bold *Ch.* 184
Chain up the *w.* and tigers of mankind *Ch.* 287
And avarice that make man a *w.* to man *T.* iv 103

WOLFE. [238
And *W.*'s great name compatriot with his own *T.* ii
And one in council. *W.*, upon the lap *T.* ii 242 [248
If any wronged her. *W.*, where'er he fought *T.* ii

WOMAN.
They teach both conjurers and old *w. A Fable* 21
And *w.* trembling at the foot of man *A.T.* 158
From man to man, or e'en to *w.* paid *E.* ii 5
Her *w.*, insolent and self-caressed *Ex.* 45
And teach the combatant a *w.*'s part? *Ex.* 359
In the steerage a *w.* I saw *M.D.* 9
Ne'er taught me by *w.* before *M.D.* 12

That goddess-like w. he viewed *M.D.* 34
And w., lovely w., does the same *P.E.* 274
W., whom custom has forbid to fly *P.E.* 504
W. indeed, a gift he would bestow *R.* 269
In man or w., but far most in man *T.* ii 414
Much. I was born of w., and drew milk *T.* iii 196
Swept with a w.'s neatness, breeding else *T.* iii 616
And wrongs the w. he has sworn to love ! *T.* iv 465
Their kerchiefs, and old w. weep for joy *T.* vi 700
The prize of beauty in a w.'s eyes *Tir.* 472
A querulous old w.'s voice *Trans.* iv 25
And w. are the teachers *Trans.* iv 42
Drew not his life from w., never gazed *Y.O.* 145

WOMAN-BORN.
Buy what is w., and feel no shame ? *Ch.* 181

WOMANHOOD.
Of w., fit pupils in the school *T.* iv 228
See w. despised, and manhood shamed *Tir.* 827

WOMANISH.
No w. or wailing grief has part *R.* 773

WOMANKIND.
Of w. but one *J.G.* 18

WOMB.
Or was he not, till fashioned in the w. ? *F.A.* 27
A conflagration labouring in her w. *Her.* 12
In earth's dark w. have found at last a vent *N.A.* 86
She quakes at his approach. Her hollow w. *T.* ii 88
As they had known him from his mother's w. *T.* iii 144
"Favoured as ours, transgressors from the w. *T.* v 829

WON.
The wreath he w. drew down an instant curse *Ch.* 61
The wreath He w. so dearly in our name *Ch.* 586
We find the friends we fancied we had w. *E.* iii 16
In peace possessing what they w. by war *Ex.* 193
That w. a nymph on that immortal plain *Ex.* 598
Proclaims the soil a conquest he has w. *H.* 479
Where Power secures what Industry has w. *Her.* 87
And so he did, and w. it too *J.G.* 245
Pants to be told of battles w. or lost *R.* 476 [i 286
Few transient years, w. from the abyss abhorred *T.*
Of smiling Victory that moment w. *T.* ii 243 [281
Where once your noble fathers w. a crown ! *T.* ii
As left him not, till penitence had w. *T.* ii 723
And never w. Dream after dream ensues *T.* iii 127
Not shy, as in the world, and to be w. *T.* vi 115
She longs to yield, no sooner woo'd than w. *Tir.* 172
Guards well what Arts and Industry have w. *T.T.* 280
Here cities w., and fleets dispersed 1789, 13

WONDER.
May even our w. excite *C.* 38
Spreads foreign w. in his country's sight *Ch.* 116
Sees planetary w. smoothly roll *Ch.* 317
We w., as we gazing stand *Ch.* 553
Himself should work that w. if he can *Con.* 342
Fruits of his love and w. of his might *Con.* 473
Of dangers past, and w. yet to come *Con.* 572
Who works the w., if it be but wrought *Con.* 846
And grins with w. at the jar he makes *Con.* 902
No w. I, who scribble rhyme *E.* i 19
Confessed the w., and with daring tongue *Ex.* 155
No w. Friendship does the same *F.* 10
Familiar with the w. of the sky *H.* 442
That few believe the w. thou hast wrought *H.* 667
The brightest w. of an endless day *H.* 753
Did w. more and more *J.G.* 96
He takes offence, and w. what you mean *P.E.* 89
His silly sheep, what w. if they stray ? *P.E.* 119
W. at Clodio's follies, in a tone *P.E.* 191
To raise such w. in her view *Q.V.* 63
To w. at a thousand insect forms *R.* 63
O'erwhelmed at once with w., grief, and joy *R.* 593

Pleasure and w. in his features mix *T.* 416
The inferior w. of an artist's hand *T.* i 419
No smartness in the jest, and w. why *T.* i 469
What w. then that health and virtue, gifts *T.* i 750
What w., if discharged into the world *T.* ii 806
At his own w., wondering for his bread *T.* iv 87
Of midnight murder was a w. heard *T.* iv 563
Engaged my w., and admiring still *T.* iv 715
The growing w. takes a thousand shapes *T.* v 119
The w. of the North. No forest fell *T.* v 131
At building human w. mountain high *T.* v 179
The w.; humanizing what is brute *T.* v 700
To read his w., in whose thought the world *T.* v 798
See nought to w. at. Should God again *T.* vi 125
Designs the blooming w. of the next *T.* vi 197
Nor can the w. it records be sung *T.* vi 749
"See !" with united w., cried *Th.* 5
Works magic w., adds a brighter hue *Tir.* 23
Look where he will, the w. God has wrought *Tir.* 54
And learn with w. how this world began *Tir.* 127
Levied a tax of w. and applause *T.T.* 650

WONDERED.
Above all else, and w. He should die *Con.* 520
Much w. that the silly sheep had found *N.A.* 129

WONDERFUL.
'Twas w. to view *J.G.* 118
(O w. effect of music's power !) *T.* vi 636

WONDERING.
A sense they know not, to the w. crowd *Ch.* 390
Reveal (the man is dead) to w. eyes *F.* 572
Her tender husband, w. much *J.G.* 143
At his own wonders, w. for his bread *T.* iv 87
And loudly w. at the sudden change *T.* iv 451
And angel choirs attended. W. stood *T.* vi 352
Thence to exhibit to his w. eyes *Tir.* 632

WONDROUS.
Some she would teach (for she was w. wise *A.T.* 38
Yet has the w. virtue to educe *H.* 155
This universal frame, thus w. fair *R.* 90
Though w., He commands us, in his word *T.* iii 223

WONT.
A flock so scattered, and so w. to roam *Ex.* 729
The sweets that I was w. to share *O.* ii 11

WONTED.
His w. course, yet what I wished is done *M.P.* 113
Their w. entertainment, all retire *T.* ii 303
Their w. fodder; not like hungering man *T.* v 30
His w. strut; and, wading at their head *T.* v 74

WOO.
Invite thee, w. thee, to the bliss they share *Ex.* 627
Which they that w. preferment rarely pass *H.* 420
There Beauty w. him with expanded arms *P.E.* 55
And w. and win thee to thy proper good *R.* 256
To court a grin, when you should w. a soul *T.* ii 467

WOOD.
With many a chorister the w. among *A.T.* 77
And w. and lawn in dusky folds enclosed *A.T.* 96
The sapless w., divested of the bark *Con.* 53
By stout substantial gods of w. and stone *Con.* 834
Deified useless w. or senseless stone *Ex.* 238
Adjoining close to Kilwick's echoing w. *N.A.* 3
And from within the w. that crash was heard *N.A.* 45
As creeping ivy clings to w. or stone *P.E.* 285
For all that pleased in w. or lawn *S.* 13
Long hid by interposing hill or w. *T.* 249 [184
That sweep the skirt of some far-spreading w. *T.* i
There, lost behind a rising ground, the w. *T.* i 305
Lord of the w., the long-surviving oak *T.* i 313 [320
Have changed the w., in scarlet honours bright *T.* i
And music of the w.—no works of man *T.* i 430

WOOD—WORK

O'ertop the lofty w. that skirts the wild T. i 558
Beguile their woes, and make the w. resound T. i 586
And silent w. I wander, far from those T. iii 118
W. vanish, hills subside, and valleys rise T. iii 775
I saw the w. and fields at close of day T. iv 311
A Monitor is w.—plank shaven thin T. ii 585 [iv 573
Through pathless wastes and w., unconscious once T.
Seen through the leafless w. His slanting ray T. v 6
And where the w. fence off the northern blast T. vi 60
On props of smoothest shaven w. T.B. 23
His teeth were strong, the cage was w. T.B. 53 [50
Time made thee what thou wast, king of the w. Y.O.
Than yonder upstarts of the neighbouring w. Y.O. 134

WOODBINE.
As w. weds the plant within her reach R. 229
With w. and wild roses mantled o'er R. 420
Copious of flowers one w., pale and wan T. vi 162

WOODEN.
A w. one, so we, no longer taught T. ii 575
His host of w. warriors to and fro T. vi 266

WOODLAND.
Nor less attractive is the w. scene T. i 300 [696
And charms the w. scenes, and wilds unknown T.T.

WOODMAN.
Forth goes the w., leaving unconcerned T. v 41

WOODPECKERS.
And w. explore the sides M.B. 7

WOOED.
Her w. Sir Airy, by meandering streams A.T. 11
But still, whoever w. her, or embraced A.T. 36
Like her the fabled Phœbus w. in vain Ex. 599
W. an unfeeling statue for his wife P.E. 528
In chase of fancied happiness, still w. T. iii 126
She longs to yield, no sooner w. than won Tir. 172

WOOING.
Is w. mercy by renewed offence Ex. 413
Seest thou yon harlot, w. all she meets T. 507

WOOL.
Bents, w., and feathers mixed A Tale 40
Their periwigs of w. and fears combined N.A. 75
Where, on his bed of w. and matted leaves T. vi 312

WORD.
Resides in that heavenly w.! A.S. 26
Every burning w. he spoke B. 7
Rome shall perish—write that w. B. 13
Such the Bard's prophetic w. B. 33
W. learned by rote a parrot may rehearse Con. 7
With adjurations every w. impress Con. 70
The clash of arguments and jar of w. Con. 85
The power to clothe that reason with his w. Con. 432
He blessed the bread, but vanished at the w. Con. 533
Canting and whining out all day the w. Con. 577
And yet exalted above God's own w. Ex. 128
In answer to the fiat of his w. Ex. 154
His anger, who can waste thee with a w. Ex. 341
Speak but the w., will listen and return" Ex. 455
Or, in his w. who damned the base desire Ex. 422
Remain with thee, or leave thee at his w. Ex. 675
The w. of prophecy, those truths divine Ex. 686
God gives the w., the preachers throng around H. 453
And if unblameable in w. and thought H. 622
Mighty to parry and push-by God's w. H. 659 [678
This man was happy—had the World's good w. H.
God's holy w., once trivial in his view H. 706
Returned him not a single w. J.G. 179
The parting w. shall pass my lips no more! M.P. 35
Brings every thought, w., action, to the test P.E. 34
Hence the same w., that bids our lusts obey P.E. 496
With such fine w. familiar to his tongue P.E. 509
Thy w., more clearly than thy works, display R. 96
His bright perfections at whose w. they rose R. 200

Who comes when called, and at a w. withdraws R. 447
Built God a church, and laughed his w. to scorn R. 688
On w. and deed, imply St. vi 30 [31
Stand the soul-quickening w.—Believe and Live T
Censorious, and her every w. a wasp T. 160
Thought, w., and deed, his liberty evince T. 195
And death or restitution is the w. T. 264 [459
But the same w. that, like the polished share T.
Though wondrous, He commands us, in his w. T.iii 223
But if his w. once teach us, shoot a ray T. iii 240
And in his w. sagacious. Such too thine T. iii 254
To teach him now and then a w. Trans. iv 8
And doom him for perhaps a heedless w. T. v 440
Whose w. leaps forth at once to its effect T. v 686
Illuminates. Thy lamp, mysterious W.!—T. v 846
Their only point of rest, eternal W.!—T. v 897
Are grand, no doubt, and worthy of the W.—T. v 555
Thy w. fulfilled, the conquest of a world! T. vi 905
Speaking in parables his slighted w. Tir. 140 [353
Felt himself crushed at the first w. he spoke T.T.
He gives the w., and Mutiny soon roars T.T. 452
Not in the w.—but in the gap between T.T. 541
Harmony, strength, w. exquisitely sought T.T. 701
To trace him in his w., his works, his ways T.T. 751

WORDED.
Complaining in a speech well w. P. 3

WORE. [A.T. 22
And graved it on a gem, and w. it next [his heart
But they that w. them, move not at the sound H. 267
The garland that she w. J.P. 12
Such at least was the form that she w. M.D. 10
He w. them as fine trappings for a show T. 56
Our habits, costlier than Lucullus w. T. ii 596
E'en misses, at whose age their mothers w. T. iv 226
That skirt the horizon, w. a sable hue T. iv 320 [239
Who w. the platted thorns with bleeding brows T. vi

WORK.
How simple wedlock fornication w. A.T. 159
The w. of my Fancy the more C. 22 [206
The wretch that w. and weeps without relief Ch.
Their zeal begotten, as their w. rehearse Ch. 505
No w. shall find acceptance, in that day Ch. 557
Who yet betrays his secret by his w. Con. 80
Himself should w. that wonder if he can Con. 342
Physicians write in hopes to w. a cure Con. 407
For all is perfect that God w. on earth Con. 433
The w. of man inherit, as is just Con. 553
God's w. may serve an ape upon a stage Con. 736
Save from the subjects of that w. alone Con. 740
And all her censures of the w. of grace Con. 784
A poet does not w. by square or line Con. 789
Who w. the wonder, if it be but wrought Con. 846
And laughter, all their w., is life misspent Con. 876
The w. of man tend, one and all E. i 79
Rhetoric is artifice, the w. of man Ex. 136
Frames many a purpose, and God w. his own Ex. 323
But nature w. in every breast F.B. 13
Make w. a vain ingredient in the case H. 360
Without good w., whatever some may boast H. 363
In all we touch, stamped plainly on his w. H. 545
That while I trembling trace a w. divine H. 671
Though whispered, plainly tell what w. within H. 691
These are thy glorious w., eternal Truth H. 742 [750
Then these thy glorious w., and they who share H.
Repays their w.—the gleaning only mine H. 771
It marches o'er the prostrate w. of man Her. 22
To Him whose w. bespeak his nature, Love J.T. 46
And set their wit at w. to find L.W. 13
And she the w. of Phœbus aiding Mrs. M— 55
Where w. of man are clustered close around R. 25
And w. of God are hardly to be found R. 26
His mighty w., who speaks and it is done R. 60

Admires the w., but slips the lesson by R. 214 [87
"These are thy glorious w., thou Source of good R.
Thy words, more clearly than thy w., display R. 96
Borrowing a beauty from the w. of grace R. 358
Her slighted w. to your admiring view R. 543
Her w. must needs excel who fashioned you R. 544
She watched the gardener at his w. R.C. 14
His w. of glory done R.G. 16
Oh how unlike the complex w. of man T. 21
The plea of w., as arrogant and vain T. 71
His w., his abstinence, his zeal allowed T. 91
The w. of generous love and filial fear T. 226
Lovely indeed the mimic w. of Art T. i 420
But Nature's w. far lovelier. I admire T. i 421
And music of the woods—no w. of man T. i 430
Of his own w., his dreadful part alone T. ii 82
On God's behalf, lays waste his fairest w. T. ii 136
And principles; of causes, how they w. T. ii 191
To make God's w. a sinecure; a slave T. ii 390
Just fifteen minutes, huddle up their w. T. ii 412
Or does he sit regardless of his w.? T. ii 516
By strides of human wisdom. In his w. T. iii 222
Sagacious reader of the w. of God T. iii 253
Too oft, and much impeded in its w. T. iii 370 [404
But much performs himself. No w., indeed T. iii
Minute as dust and numberless, oft w. T. iii 556
His pleasant w., may he suppose it done T. iii 656
This folio of four pages, happy w.! T. iv 50
Well does the w. of his destructive scythe T. iv 222
Of knaves in office, partial in the w. T. iv 412
By w. of darkness and nocturnal wrong T. iv 435
Too proud for dairy w., or sale of eggs T. iv 549
W. the deplored and mischievous effect T. iv 616
'Tis born with all: the love of Nature's w. T. iv 731
That all discern a beauty in his w. T. iv 739
Thus Nature w. as if to mock at Art T. v 122
Because a novelty, the w. of man T. v 128
We turn to dust and all our mightiest w. T. v 531
His other w., the visible display T. v 553
Is w. for him that made him. He alone T. v 697
Appropriates Nature as his Father's w. T. v 761
His w. Admitted once to his embrace T. v 780
The glory of thy w., which yet appears T. v 866
(If power she be that w. but to confound) T. v 872
A loud Hosanna sent from all thy w. T. v 888
Behind his own creation, w. unseen T. v 894 [184
The grand transition, that there lives and w. T. vi
Whose w. is without labour; whose designs T. vi 228
Proved he not plainly that his meaner w. T. vi 447
Encomium in old time was poet's w. T. vi 715
Among her lovely w. with a secure T. vi 722
In his dishonour'd w. himself endure T. vi 821
With lean performance ape the w. of love! T. vi 854
Due to thy last and most effectual w. T. vi 904
Deems him a cipher in the w. of God T. vi 943
In aiding helpless indigence, in w. T. vi 964
W. magic wonders, adds a brighter hue Tir. 23
Promise a w. of which they must despair Tir. 264
Than set your son to w. at a vile trade Tir. 456
Armed for a w. too difficult for thee Tir. 677
His galleries with the w. of art well graced T.T. 162
With double toil, and shiver at their w. T.T. 215
Bids equity throughout his w. prevail T.T. 250
To train him in his word, his w., his ways! T.T.751
Fine passing thought, e'en in her coarest w. Y.O.81

WORKING.

God, w. ever on a social plan Ch. 15
Blind to the w. of that secret Power Ex. 320
To mark the matchless w. of the Power R. 791
Is merely as the w. of a sea T. vi 738

WORLD.

The point in dispute was, as all the w. knows. A.C. 3
Shall a wider w. command B. 28
Steered Britain's oak into a w. unknown Ch. 25
See Cortez odious for a w. enslaved! Ch. 40
No.—Mammon makes the w. his legatee Ch. 45
To furnish and accommodate a w. Ch. 124
Built a brave w., which cannot yet subsist Ch. 192
She sees a w. stark blind to what employs Ch. 404
The truth she loves a sightless w. blaspheme Ch. 416
In some safe haven of our western w. Ch. 444 [461
How many deeds with which the w. has rung Ch.
'Tis called a satire, and the w. appears Ch. 515
Whate'er this w. produces, it absorbs Ch. 564 [526
The w. is charmed, and Scrib escapes the law Ch.
Were Love, in these the w.'s last doting years Ch. 604
Far from the w.'s gay busy throng Comp. ii. 4
That the surviving w. may live in peace Con. 176
Resumed his purpose, had a w. of talk Con. 279
For ever aiming at the w.'s esteem Con. 367
Is sparkling wit the w.'s exclusive right? Con. 589
All tremble in all w., except our own Con. 660
And wild as madness in the w.'s esteem Con. 666
Strange tidings these to tell a w. who treat Con. 719
The w grown old her deep discernment shows Con. 741
As, having it, he deems the w.'s disdain Con. 762
Retort the charge, and let the w. be told Con. 767
(And in due time the w. shall know it too) Con. 750
The w. and I fortuitously met Con. 795
Charmed with the sight, "The w.," I cried D.W. 37
And this is what the w., who knows E. i 15
The system of a w.'s concerns E. i 74
The w. may dance along the flowery plain E. ii 13
An envious w. will interpose its frown E. ii 33
From the w.'s girdle to the frozen pole Ex. 20
Had bid defiance to the warring w. Ex. 212
And while the w. beside, that plan unknown Ex. 237
Should fly the w.'s contaminating touch Ex. 446
A w. is up in arms, and thou, a spot Ex. 694
And all the w. admits them F. 162
Till half the w. comes rattling at his door H. 77
But Ætnas of the suffering w. ye sway? Her. 78
And teach the w., if not perversely blind H. 138
Now see him launched into the w. at large H. 197
Such stuff the w. is made of; and mankind H. 211
The book of all the w. that charmed me most H. 427
A plaything w., unworthy of his hand H. 543 [568
The w.'s best comfort was, his doom was passed H.
He loved the w. that hated him; the tear H. 574
Since Abel worshipped, or the w. began H. 644 [678
This man was happy—had the w.'s good word H.
His grief the w. of all her power disarms H. 704
This earth shall blaze, and a new w. succeed H. 749
As all the w. doth know J.G. 22
And all the w. would stare J.G. 194
The w., no longer thy abode, not thee J.T. 10
"Renounce the w."—the preacher cries L.W. 25
Thus, bit by bit, the w. is swallowed L.W. 34
Unmoved with all the w. beside Miss — 31
'Tis woven in the w.'s great plan Miss — 45
The w. around solicits his desire P.E. 39
Lights of the w., and stars of human race P.E. 97
By deeds in which the w. must never mix P.E. 162
To cheat themselves and gain the w.'s assent P.E. 436
Who fill the w. with doctrines contraband P.E. 475
Is this hyperbole? The w. well known P.E. 488
Had all the pageants of the w. Q.V. 21
Sick of the service of a w. that feeds R. 47
The sun, a w. whence other w. drink light R. 81
And fills the w. of traffic and the shades R. 120
And in a w. where, other ills apart R. 125
And hate the tumult half the w. enjoys R. 176 [186
The w. can boast, and her chief favourites share R.
Mix with the w., but with its wiser part R. 275
Then all the w. of waters sleeps again R. 536
Earth's millions daily fed, a w. employed R. 553

What means the drama by the *w*. sustained ? *R*. 646
And hold the *w*. indebted to your aid *R*. 665 [*R*.729
And though the *w*. may think the ingredients odd
Scorned in a *w*., indebted to that scorn *R*. 751
A theme for all the *w*.'s attention *R.C*. 102
Of this *w*.'s hazardous and headlong shore *St*. ii 14
" *W*. should not bribe me back to tread *St*. iii 5
To ages in a *w*. of pain *St*. v 9
Strange *w*., that costs it so much smart *St*. v 15
Whence has the *w*. her magic power ? *St*. v 17
Has he a *w*. of gratitude and love ? *T*. 208
And the *w*.'s hatred, as its sure effect *T*. 282
The thousands whom the *w*. forbids to rest *T*. 438
To attain perfection in this nether *w*. *T*. i 85
Its own revolvency upholds the *w*. *T*. i 372
By which the *w*. might profit, and himself *T*. i 577
And thus the rangers of the western *w*. *T*. i 618
Measures an atom, and now girds a *w*. ? *T*. i 718
A more accomplished *w*.'s chief glory now *T*. i 724
Between the nations, in a *w*. that seems *T*. ii 50
And bids the *w*. take heart and banish fear *T*. ii 195
The houseless rovers of the sylvan *w*. *T*. i 588 [*T*. ii 198
Still wrought by means since first He made the *w*. ?
I would not trifle merely, though the *w*. *T*. ii 313
The fairest capital of all the *w*. *T*. i 698 [*T*. ii 334
Must stand acknowledged, while the *w*. shall stand
Announces to the *w*. his own and theirs *T*. ii 357
By infidelity and love o' the *w*. *T*. ii 389 [*T*. ii 512
And spring-time of the *w*.; asked, Whence is man ?
Since Heaven would grow weary of a *w T*. ii 583
So fare we in this prison-house, the *w*. *T*. ii 661
A mockery of the *w*.! What need of these *T*. ii 750
Of riper joys, and commerce with the *w*. *T*. ii 763
The lewd vain *w*. that must receive him soon *T*. ii 764
That it is dangerous sporting with the *w*. *T*. ii 777
And give the *w*. their talents and themselves *T*. ii 799
What wonder, if discharged into the *w*. *T*. ii 806
And still are disappointed. Brings the *w*. *T*. iii 129
To distant *w*., and trifling in their own *T*. iii 166
"'Twere well, could you permit the *w*. to live *T*. iii 194
As the *w*. pleases. What's the *w*. to you ?" *T*. iii 195
Not visible, his family of *w*. *T*. iii 232 [iii 545
His dainties, and the *W*.'s more numerous half *T*.
How various his employments whom the *w*. *T*. iii 352
Esteems that busy *w*. an idler too! *T*. iii 354
Oh blest seclusion from a jarring *w*. *T*. iii 675
And profligate abusers of a *w*. *T*. iii 696 [*T*. iii 815
The *w*. of wandering knights and squires to town
At his last gasp; but could not for a *w*. *T*. iii 807
He comes, the herald of a noisy *w*. *T*. iv 5
Such as the mistress of the *w*. once found *T*. iv 169
Nor do we madly, like an impious *w*. *T*. iv 177 [213
But the *W*.'s Time is Time in masquerade! *T*. iv
To peep at such a *w*.; to see the stir *T*. iv 89 [iv 223
Thus decked, he charms a *w*. whom Fashion blinds *T*.
In such a *w*., so thorny, and where none *T*. iv 333
Describes and prints it, that the *w*. may know *T*.iv237
Hence to the field of glory, as the *w*. *T*. iv 684
For a lost *w*. in solitude and verse *T*. iv 730
Because men suffer it, their toy the *w*. *T*. v 192
The *w*. was made in vain, if not for him *T*. v 271
Even in the cradled weakness of the *w*.! *T*. v 286
Ten thousand rovers in the *w*. at large *T*. v 408 [753
That planned, and built, and still upholds a *w*. *T*. v
To read his wonders, in whose thought the *w*. *T*. v 798
And wheels his throne upon the rolling *w*. *T*. v 814
" Have reached this nether *w*., ye spy a race *T*. v 828
And makes the *w*. the wilderness it is *T*. vi 53 [851
W. that had never been hadst Thou in strength *T*. v
Not shy, as in the *w*., and to be won *T*. vi 115
And renovation of a faded *w*. *T*. vi 124 [128
How would the *w*. admire! but speaks it less *T*. vi
Shall have its altar; and the *w*. shall go *T*. vi 668
To show the *w*. how Garrick did not act *T*. vi 677
And call'd the *w*. to worship on the banks *T*. vi 681
The groans of Nature in this nether *w*. *T*. vi 729
Over a sinful *w*.; and what remains *T*. vi 736 [823
Haste, then, and wheel away a shattered *w*. *T*. vi
A *w*. that does not dread and hate his laws *T*. vi 826
O for a *w*. in principle as chaste *T*. vi 836
The very spirit of the *w*. is tired *T*. vi 869 [*T*. vi 889
The *w*. takes little thought. Who will may preach
The *w*. o'erlooks him in her busy search *T*. vi 915
Thy word fulfilled, the conquest of a *w*.! *T*. vi 905
Though more sublimely, he o'erlooks the *w*. *T*. vi 918
Perhaps the self-approving haughty *w*. *T*. vi 940
Some taste of comfort in a *w*. of woe *T*. vi 966 [978
Her golden tube, through which a sensual *w*. *T*. vi
Because that *w*. adopts it. If it bear *T*. vi 982
In vain the poet sings, and the *w*. hears *T*. vi 1018
Suffer his justice in a *w*. to come *Tir*. 102
And learn with wonder how this *w*. began *Tir*. 127
Priests have invented, and the *w*. admired *Tir*. 185
The knowledge of the *w*., and dull of thought *Tir*.380
Shows all its rents and patches to the *w*. *Tir*. 451
That with a *w*., not often over nice *Tir*. 464 [633
Yon circling *w*., their distance, and their size *Tir*.
Low in the *w*., because he scorns its arts *Tir*. 672
The *w*. accounts an honourable man *Tir*. 738
Mankind are various, and the *w*. is wide *Tir*. 788
Look round you on a *w*. perversely blind *Tir*. 813
Unless the *w*. were all prepared to embrace *Tir*. 917
'Tis your belief the *w*. was made for man *T.T*. 47
As if the *w*. and they were hand and glove *T.T*. 173
She has one foe, and that one foe, the *w*. *T.T*. 455
That constellation set, the *w*. in vain *T.T*. 660
And the *w*. cheerfully admits the claim *T.T*. 715
And tell the *w*., still kindling as he sung *T.T*. 736
The *w*., with all its motley rout *Trans*. ii 26
What exhibitions various hath the *w*. *Y.O*. 69

WORM.
W. may be caught by either head or tail *Ch*. 528
Life and a kingdom upon *w*. below *Ch*. 592
Ye *w*. that eat into the bud of youth! *Con*. 40
As little mercy as the grubs and *w*. ? *Con*. 260
The filth of rottenness and *w*. of pride *Ex*. 90
Say man's a *w*., and power belongs to God *H*. 711
Of rugged oaks for *w*. *M.B*. 8
The *w*., aware of his intent *N.G*. 13
The poisonous, black, insinuating *w*. *P.E*. 7
These hatched, and those resuscitated *w*. *R*. 64
A *w*. is in the bud of youth *St*. i 23 [*T*. iii 555
Moisture and drought, mice, *w*., and swarming flies
The song magnificent, the theme a *w*.! *T*. 412
By *w*. voracious eating through and through *T*. i 27
Society, and that saps and *w*. the base *T*. ii 816
Who needlessly sets foot upon a *w*. *T*. vi 563 [*T*. v 80
Earth yields them nought: the imprisoned *w*. is safe
Stretch'd forth to dally with the crested *w*. *T*. vi 780
W. wind themselves into our sweetest flowers *T*. vi 831
While every *w*. industriously weaves *Tir*. 595
A *w*. is known to stray *Trans*. i 2
Nor crush a *w*., whose useful light *Trans*. i 17

WORN.
Tradition, now decrepid and *w*. out *Ex*. 502
Has time *w*. out, or fashion put to shame *P.E*. 245
But being cankered now, and half *w*. out *P.E*. 393
W. as a cloak, and hardly hides, a gown *T*. i 550
No less than hers, not *w*. indeed on high *T*. iv 255
With shallow shifts and old devices, *w*. *T*. v 632
That lewdness had usurped and *w*. so long *T.T*. 637
Hackneyed and *w*. to the last flimsy thread *T.T*. 727
But *w*. by frequent impulse, to the cause *Y.O*. 84

WORN-OUT.
From *w*. follies, now acknowledged such *F.A*. 3
Thy *w*. heart will break at last *M*. 51

Those hangings with their *w.* graces *M.F.* 5
The *w.* nuisance of the public streets *T.* 508
WORRY.
And *w.* and devour each other *N.G.* 30
WORSE.
W. than the mortal brunt of rival swords *Con.* 86
That's *w.*—the drone-pipe of an humblebee *Con.* 330
From a *w.* yoke, and nailed it to the tree *Ex.* 220
With less excuse, and, haply, *w.* effect?" *F.A.* 17
A hat not much the *w.* for wear *J.G.* 184
Will never look one hair the *w.*" *M.F.* 24
A vicious object still is *w. Mor.* 47
W. than a poniard in the basest hand *P.E.* 305 [464
By thee, *w.* plagues than Pharaoh's land befell *P.E.*
No grand inquisitor could *w.* invent *T.* 103
And *w.* than all, and most to be deplored *T.* ii 21
The *w.* for what it soils. The fashion runs *T.* iv 555
From ill to *w.*, is fatal, never fails *T.* iv 579
Her house of bondage, *w.* than that of old *T.* v 382
Short as it is, supportable. Still *w. T.* v 604 [605
Far *w.* than all the plagues with which his sins *T.* v
Its own dishonour by a *w.* relapse *T.* v 626 [327
W. than the deeds of galley-slaves broke loose *T.T*
I judged a man of sense could scarce do *w. T.T.* 518
WORSHIP.
Oh! could I *w.* aught beneath the skies *Ch.* 254
Then Baal is the God, and *w.* him" *Con.* 854
God's *w.* and the mountebank between *P.E.* 156
In sighs he *w.* his supremely fair *R.* 225
And *w.* chance alone! *St.* vi 28
And we that *w.* him, ignoble graves *T.* iii 265
His reverence and his *w.* both to rest *T.* iv 597
The idol of our *w.* while he lived *T.* vi 666
And call'd the world to *w.* on the banks *T.* vi 681
All creatures *w.* man, and all mankind *T.* vi 783
And *w.* Her report was travelled forth *T.* vi 813
I pity kings whom *w.* waits upon *T.T.* 121
I might with reverence kneel, and *w.* thee *Y.O.* 8
WORSHIPPED.
Since Abel *w.*, or the world began *H.* 644
WORSHIPPER.
And thou a *w.* e'en where thou mayst *Ex.* 260
For Garrick was a *w.* himself *T.* vi 678
WORST.
The *w.* suggested, she believes the best *Ch.* 427
The *w.* that can invade a sickly brain *Con.* 222
Thy *w.* effect is banishing for hours *Con.* 253
Could act extortion and the *w.* of crimes *Ex.* 148
And of the *w.*, that unexplored he leaves *F.A.* 31
But proudest of the *w.*, if that succeed *H.* 202
That thy *w.* part, thy principles, live yet *P.E.* 350
The *w.* is—Scripture warped from its intent *P.E.* 437
Points out a conflict with thyself, the *w. R.* 268
And having well deserved, expects the *w. T.* 266
The *w.* of men, and curses of the best *T.* 434
By riot and incontinence the *w. T.* i 699
Of grossest nature and of *w.* effects *T.* ii 689
That even servitude, the *w.* of ills *T.* v 302
And loathsome Ribaldry has done his *w. T.T.* 729
WORTH.
That tells his name, his *w.*, his age *Cast.* 51
Charged with a freight transcending in its *w. Ch.* 133
Compress the sum into its solid *w. Con.* 20
With God's deep stamp upon its current *w. Con.* 710
They best can judge a poet's *w. Dr.* 5
Can ne'er be deemed *w.* half so much *E.* iv 29
Were just such trifles, without *w.* or use *Ex.* 49
Prepared to fight for shadows of no *w. Ex.* 116
If dear society be *w.* a thought *Ex.* 670
But not a friend *w.* keeping *F.* 78
Quite to forget, or deem it *w.* no thought *H.* 83
The *w.* of each had been complete *J.P.* 5
And if the genuine *w.* of gold depend *J.T.* 27

What sight *w.* seeing could I see? *M.* 30
The real *w.* of man's pursuits *Mor.* 26
Must be decided by the *w. Mor.* 43
The praise of wisdom, comeliness and *w. P.E.* 295
By right of *w.*, not blood alone *Q.V.* 3
Of your own *w.* and consequence *R.C.* 110
Confirmed by long experience of thy *w. T.* i 147
Far fetched and little *w.*; nor seldom waits *T.* i 243
By its true *w.*, the comforts it affords *T.* i 397
But though true *w.* and virtue, in the mild *T.* i 678
Where beauty oft and lettered *w.* consume *T.* ii 123
And humble learners of a Saviour's *w. T.* ii 542
The head of modest and ingenuous *w. T.* ii 711
Peace to the memory of a man of *w. T.* ii 781
The *w.* of what she mimics with such care *T.* iii 103
That, while it gives us *w.* in God's account *T.* iii 283
Disturb good order, and degrade true *w. T.* iii 674
Advance it into notice, that its *w. T.* iii 703 [224
To his true *w.*, most pleased when idle most *T.* iv
How far he went for what was nothing *w. T.* iv 238
Whatever else they smother of true *w. T.* iv 746
But not to understand a treasure's *w. T.* vi 50
If not the virtues, yet the *w.* of brutes *T.* vi 724
To give it praise proportioned to its *w. T.* vi 756
Of little *w.*, an idler in the best *T.* vi 952
And be not costly more than of true *w. T.* vi 984
Attends superior *w. Th.* 16
Stands self-impeached the creature of least *w. Tir.* 70
Undoubted scholarship and genuine *w. Tir.* 280
Excused the incumbrance of more solid *w. Tir.* 347
In all true *w.* and literary skill? *Tir.* 378
Least qualified in honour, learning, *w. Tir.* 413
Still keeps a seat or two for *w.* and grace *Tir.* 433
The end, though plausible, not *w.* the means *Tir.* 487
Prepared by taste, by learning, and true *w. Tir.* 678
Some mischief fatal to his future *w. Tir.* 758
Is *w.*, with all its gold and glittering store *T.T.* 61
The *w.* of his three kingdoms I defy *T.T.* 85 [204
The cause, though *w.* the search, may yet elude *T.T.*
Incomparable gem! thy *w.* untold *T.T.* 330
Their sober zeal, integrity, and *w. T.T.* 377
'Twas negligence in him, not want of *w. T.T.* 681
One madrigal of theirs is *w.* them all *T.T.* 767
Whose *w.* deserves as warm a lay *U.* 3
If valued by its wearer's *w.* 1789, 43
WORTHIER.
W. of regard, and stronger *N.C.* 51
Graced with a sword, and *w.* of a fan *T.* i 771
WORTHIEST.
The weight of subjects *w.* of her care *R.* 678
In which the best and *w.* tremble most *Tir.* 415
WORTHILY.
More *w.* the powers she owned before *T.* v 807
Egregious purpose! *W.* begun *Tir.* 404
WORTHLESS.
And bore the *w.* prize away *A Fable* 29 [18
Can gold grow *w.* that has stood the touch! *E.* iii
Retires to blazon his own *w.* name *R.* 217
His *w.* absolution all the prize *Ex.* 525
The *w.* and unfruitful of mankind" *T.* 500
Conveying *w.* dross into its place *T.* i 572
Of too much labour, *w.* when produced *T.* iii 565
'Twas durable; as *w.* as it seemed *T.* v 174
A *w.* form, than to decide aright *T.* vi 851
Proof of a trifling and a *w.* mind *T.T.* 759
WORTHY.
" The blood of ancient *w.* in his veins *A.T.* 116
Makes wisdom, *w.* of the name, his own *Ch.* 350
Names almost *w.* of a Christian's praise *Con.* 36
O folly *w.* of the nurse's lap *Con.* 479
In musings *w.* of the great event *Con.* 510
Heroes and *w.* of days past, thy sires? *Ex.* 658
And, next, commemorating *w.* lost *J.T.* 3

Thee, Thornton! *w*. in some page to shine *J.T.* 7
Sounds such as these, so *w*. to be feared *N.A.* 84
And *w*. thus to be recorded *P.* 4
To taint his heart, was *w*. of thine own *P.E.* 346
W. to live, and of eternal use *R.* 700
Which is the saintlier *w*. of the two? *T.* 105
Supreme on earth, and *w*. of the skies *T.* 408
Though that of all most *w*. of his care *T.* 426
Let heathen *w*., whose exalted mind *T.* 525
Now scorned, but *w*. of a better fate *T.* i 254
And theirs alone seems *w*. of the name *T.* i 398
To enforce the wrong, for such a *w*. cause *T.* ii 14
Go then, well *w*. of the praise ye seek *T.* ii 278
Heard at conventicle, where *w*. men *T.* ii 437
Knots *w*. of solution, which alone *T.* ii 520
Sticks close, a Mentor *w*. of his charge *T.* ii 595
Makes men mere vermin, *w*. to be trapped *T.* ii 683
Well-managed shall have earned its *w*. price *T.* iii 800
O evenings *w*. of the gods! exclaimed *T.* iv 189
For ye are *w*.; choosing rather far *T.* iv 408
Less *w*. of applause, though more admired *T.* v 127
Or who so *w*. to control themselves *T.* v 236
Sterling, and *w*. of a wise man's wish *T.* v 358
Are grand, no doubt, and *w*. of the Word *T.* v 555
Trivial and *w*. of disdain, achieves *T.* v 699
With *w*. thoughts of that unwearied Love *T.* v 752
" *W*. the Lamb, for he was slain for us!" *T.* vi 792
Thou who alone art *w*.! It was thine *T.* vi 857
W., compared with sycophants, who kneel *T.* vi 886
To set some living *w*. in his view *Tir.* 647
A man deemed *w*. of so dear a trust *Tir.* 711
A plan well *w*. to supply their place *Tir.* 918
The troubles of a *w*. priest *Y.D.* 3

WOTE.
Might have repaid him well, I *w*. *T.B.* 58

WOULD-BES.
A dozen *w*. of the modern day *Con.* 612

WOUND.
And *w*. the grace I mean to recommend *Ch.* 486
Have *w*. themselves about this heart *M.* 19
No *w*. like those a wounded spirit feels *R.* 341
Have *w*. which only God can heal *St.* vi 19

WOUNDED.
And say he *w*. you in jest *F.* 95
No wounds like those a *w*. spirit feels *R.* 341
When Freedom, *w*. almost to despair *T.T.* 196

WOVE.
With all the flowers he found, he *w*. in haste *A.T.* 13

WOVEN.
W. with pains into his plan *H.F.* 3
'Tis *w*. in the world's great plan *Miss* — 45
And *w*. close, or needlework sublime *T.* i 34
The various seasons *w*. into one *T.* vi 769

WRANGLE.
Is it a time to *w*., when the props *T.* ii 62

WRANGLER.
So he called him a bigot, a *w*., a monk *A.T.* ii 3
The *w*., rather than accord with you *Con.* 111
No, *w*.,—destitute of shame and sense *P.E.* 235
I burn to set the imprisoned *w*. free *T.* iv 34

WRAP.
So he may *w*. himself in honest rags *T.* iii 806
And *w*. him in an unexpected tomb *T.* v 143
Or *w*. himself in Hamlet's inky cloak *T.* vi 675

WRAPPED.
Some Alpine mountain *w*. in snow *Miss* — 33
Delighted with my bauble coach, and *w*. *M.P.* 50
In which obscurity has *w*. them up *T.* iii 146 [124
Than those of age, thy forehead *w*. in clouds *T.* iv

WRATH.
Effects of punishment and *w*. divine *A.T.* 51
For mercy shown, while *w*. is justly due *Con.* 492

Alike the *w*. and mercy of the skies *Ch.* 70 [*Con.* 32
W. stays him, or else God would strike them dumb
As if not Love, but *W*., had brought Him down *Ex.* 132
To pour down *w*. upon a thankless land *Ex.* 253
Say *W*. is coming, and the storm appears *Ex.* 270
And praised the *w*. that laid her beauties waste *Ex.* 427
But know, that *W*. Divine, when most severe *Ex.* 714
And where his danger and God's *w*. begin *H.* 609
Oh for a shelter from the *w*. to come! *T.* 268
His *w*. is busy, and his frown is felt *T.* ii 94
Of *w*. obnoxious, God may choose his mark *T.* ii 156
Feel *w*. and pity, when I think on thee! *T.* iii 842
To gratify the frenzy of his *w*. *T.* vi 387 [*T.* vi 547
Was now to learn that Heaven, though slow to *w*.
When sin hath moved him, and his *w*. is hot *T.* vi 742
And mark them with a seal of *w*. pressed down *T.T.* 457
The feats of heroes and the *w*. of kings *T.T.* 597

WREATH.
W. for her brow, and girdles for her waist *A.T.* 14
The *w*. he won drew down an instant curse *Ch.* 61
The *w*. He won so dearly in our name *Ch.* 586
Who would not twine a *w*. for Thee *Dr.* 23
The floating *w*. again discerned *D.W.* 31 [293
Return ashamed, without the *w*. they sought *Ex.*
So Flora's *w*. through coloured crystal seen *H.* 71
With *w*. like those triumphant spirits wear *H.* 166
Thy deathless *w*., and triumphs all thine own *H.* 664
Who sell their laurel for a myrtle *w*. *T.* ii 229
A *w*. that cannot fade, of flowers that blow *T.* iv 156
Enchanting music and immortal *w*. *T.* iv 687
For grandeur or for use. Long wavy *w*. *T.* v 158
But fairer *w*. are due, though never paid *T.* v 712
With blushing *w*., investing every spray *T.* v 169
To strip Jove's statue of his oaken *w*. *T.* vi 640 [685
The mulberry-tree was hung with blooming *w*. *T.* vi
And never withering *w*., compared with which *T.* vi 938
Let fall the unfinished *w*., and roved for fruit *T.* vi 1011
And binds a *w*. about their baby brows *T.* 124
'Tis not the *w*. that once adorned thy brow *T.T.* 370
Of Vanity, a *w*. for self to wear *T.T.* 757

WREATHED.
W. into an elegant bow *Gr.* 7

WRECK.
Strewing yonder sea with *w*. *N.C.* 34
The *w*. of what I was, fatigued I come *R.* 386

WREN. [553
Stooped from its highest pitch to pounce a *w*. *T.T.*

WRESTLING.
A *w*. match, a footrace, or a fair *T.* iv 626

WRETCH. [*H.* 517
The *w*., who once sang wildly, danced, and laughed
When such a destined *w*. as I *Cast.* 3 [31
He spurned the *w*. that slighted, or withstood *Ch.*
The *w*. that works and weeps without relief *Ch.* 206
The *w*. may pine, while to his smell, taste, sight *H.* 59
Hope! let the *w*., once conscious of the joy *H.* 171
W. even then, life's journey just begun? *M.P.* 24
" Ah, hapless *w*.! condemned to dwell *P.* 5
But above all (or let the *w*. refrain,) *P.E.* 456
Sinful and weak, in every sense a *w*. *T.* 383
The *w*. who slights the bounty of the skies *T.* 543
Its elevated site forbids the *w*. *T.* i 239
And verse of mine shall never brand the *w*. *T.* iii 72
He whistles as he goes, light-hearted *w*. *T.* iv 12
But with his clumsy port the *w*. has lost *T.* iv 650
The *w*. shall rise, and be the thing on earth *Tir.* 412
And thou a *w*., whom, following her old plan *Tir.* 737
The *w*., to nought but his ambition true *T.T.* 30

WRETCHED.
W. Man, whose years are spent *Trans.* iii 29

WRIGGLERS.
In spite of all the *w*. into place *Tir.* 432

WRIGGLING.
The w. fry soon fill the creeks around P.E. 480
WRINGING.
Regardless of w. and breaking a heart *The Rose* 15
WRINKLED.
A sparkling eye beneath a w. front T. i 405
WRIT.
So dimly w., or difficult to spell *Ex*. 311
Of holy w., she has presumed to annul T. i 741
Manner is all in all, whate'er is w. T.T. 542
WRITE.
Rome shall perish—w. that word B. 13
Physicians w. in hopes to work a cure *Con*. 407
" Who both w. well, and w. full speed! E. iv 84
Of all that grave apologists may w. *Ex*. 383
The first creator condescends to w. H. 133
Blush, Calumny! and w. upon his tomb H. 588
And w. a Doomsday sentence on his heart H. 693
Who w. in blood the merits of your cause *Her*. 42
W., if thou canst, one letter from the shades P.E. 348
Some w. a narrative of wars and feats T. iii 139 [278
And him who w. it, though the style be neat T. iii
Nor w. on each—This building to be let *Tir*. 916
And many a dunce, whose fingers itch to w. T.T. 111
W. on his bosom, "To be let or sold" T.T. 417 [733
Whate'er we w., we bring forth nothing new T.T.
WRITER.
The w. well remarks, a heart, that knows H. 429
Ye w. of what none with safety reads P.E. 307
Such w., and such readers, owe the gust P.E. 329
Should turn to w. of an abler sort R. 716   [iv 18
With tears, that trickled down the w.'s cheeks T.
WRITING.
Denominates an itch for w. E. i 18
WRONG.
The spectacles set them unhappily w. A.C. 2
They wept the w. of honourable love A.T. 98
Weep upon thy matchless w. B. 10
Propitious spirit! Yet expunge a w. *Ch*. 276
But all shall give account of every w. *Con*. 25
I am not surely always in the w. *Con*. 94   [149
Without the means of knowing right from w. *Con*.
'Tis w. to bring into a mixed resort *Con*. 291
The fruitful parent of abuse and w. *Con*. 461
She did me w., I recompensed the deed *Con*. 797
For Israel dealt in robbery and w. *Ex*. 35
In setting right what Faction has set w. *Ex*. 301 [281
Some eastward, and some westward, and all w. H.
The w. was his who wrongfully complained H. 321
Suppose the beam should dip on the w. side H. 374
To every sudden slip and transient w. H. 390
The Sacred Book no longer suffers w. H. 449
His well poised estimate of right and w. H. 611
Who, strange to tell, all judged it w. J.P. 19
Have done him cruel w. M. ii 14
You would abhor to do me w. N.G. 17
That to the w. side leaning O. i 2
Where both alike are in the w. P. 46
But if to w. the judgment and abuse P.E. 304
Whoever errs, the priest can ne'er be w. P.E. 508
Thus men go w. with an ingenious skill P.E. 556
That, while it courts, affronts and does you w. R. 550
Grace leads the right way; if you choose the w. T. 17
Arraigns him, charges him with every w. T. 262
Charge not a God with such outrageous w. T. 520
That thought which meditates a brother's w. T. 560
Fearless of w., reposed his weary strength T. i 15
Commits no w., nor wastes what it enjoys T. i 334
Of w. and outrage with which earth is filled T. ii 7
To enforce the w., for such a worthy cause T. ii 14
But dignity's, resentful of the w. T. iii 79
By works of darkness and nocturnal w. T. iv 435
And w. the woman he has sworn to love ! T. iv 465
Though resident, and witness of the w. T. iv 594
To feel, and courage to redress her w. T. iv 795
Of provocation given or w. sustained T. v 315 [372
Is weakness when opposed; conscious of w. T. v
Beat high within them at a mother's w. T. v 519
Of usurpation, and to no man's w. T. v 760
Or harms them there is guilty of a w. T. vi 578
To want of judgment than to w. design T. vi 657
Nor cunning justify the proud man's w. T. vi 844
Hurt too perhaps for life; for early w. *Tir*. 490
And stood the test, perhaps on the w. side *Tir*. 740
The incorrigibly w., the deaf, the dead ! *Tir*. 780
Most confident, when palpably most w. T.T. 148
To laugh it would be w. Y.D. 2
WRONGED.
Had he seduced a virgin, w. a friend T. 46
If any w. her. Wolfe, where'er he fought T. ii 248
(And no man's hatred ever w. her yet) T. iii 101
Not to be w. by a mere mortal touch T. vi 748
Dishonour, and be w. without redress T. vi 822
WRONGFULLY.
The wrong was his who w. complained H. 321
WROTE.   [306
Lived long, w. much, laughed heartily, and died T.
M. quarrels with N. because M. w. a book A.T. ii 1
Cry— hem! and reading what they never w. T. ii 411
Or merry turn in all he ever w. T. ii 473
WROUGHT.
If self employ us, whatsoe'er is w. *Ch*. 569
Who works the wonder, if it be but w. *Con*. 846
None ever yet impeded what He w. *Ex*. 336
Is sent to be flatted or w. into length F.M. 2
That few believe the wonders thou hast w. H. 667
Forms rise, to quick perfection w. *Mrs. M*— 24
Adored and praised in all that thou hast w. R. 92
Those flimsy webs that break as soon as w. R. 639
Shall he, for such deliverance freely w. T. 191
The atonement a Redeemer's love has w. T. 505
Yellow and red, of tapestry richly w. T. i 33
Such evil Sin hath w., and such a flame T. ii 133
W. patiently into the snowy lawn T. iv 152 [T. ii 198
Still w. by means since first He made the world?
Till then unfelt, what hands divine have w. T. v 784
So God w. double justice; made the fool T. vi 557
W. this disturbance. But the wane is near T. vi 709
At least his follies have not w. her fall T. vi 976
Look where he will, the wonders God has w. *Tir*. 54
Feats of renown, though w. in ancient days T.T. 22
And praised him in the victories He w. T.T. 375

Y.

YAMS.
Thy cocoas and bananas, palms and y. T. i 640
YARN.
With here and there a tuft of crimson y. T. i 53
YAWN.
Wide y. a gulf beside a ragged thorn N.A. 14
And the next opening grave may y. for you St. ii 36
YAWNING.
The y. chasm of indolence supply! P.E. 172
YEAR.
Be it your fortune, y. by y. *A Tale* 77
Has burnt to tinder a stale last y.'s news B.B. 10
In number the days of the y. C. 26   [274
While Conscience, happier than in ancient y. *Ch*.

Were Love, in these the world's last doting y. *Ch.* 604
As from a seven y. transportation, home *Con.* 400
Whose friendship from his boyish y. he chose *Con.* 424
In the last scene of her six thousand y. *Con.* 456
Can length of y. on God himself exact *Con.* 549
Fixed in the rolling flood of endless y. *Con.* 557 [638
Crowned with the garland of life's blooming y. *Con.*
Perhaps, however, as some y. have passed *Con.* 799
But day by day, and y. by y. *E.* i 53
Called for a cloud to darken all their y. *E.* ii 25
Dear Joseph—five and twenty y. ago *E.* iii 1
Eight y. and five round-rolling moons *Ep.* ii 29
Thy rulers load thy credit, y. by y. *Ex.* 284
For such indulgence gilding all thy y. *Ex.* 609 [626
Those truths, which neither use nor y. impair *Ex.*
For who but learns in riper y. *F.* 22
Our y., a fruitless race without a prize *H.* 25
The shameful close of all his misspent y. *H.* 715
And all the charms of a Sicilian y. *Her.* 24
And y. of pining indigence must show *Her.* 65
These twice ten tedious y., yet we *J.G.* 7
The twentieth y. is well nigh past *M.* 1
Lead on the various y. *Miss* — 98
Our most important are our earliest y. *P.E.* 354 [5
Twelve y. have elapsed since I last took a view *P.F.*
My fugitive y. are all hasting away *P.F.* 13
More y. and wisdom than the most *P.T.* 18
A last y.'s bird, who ne'er had tried *P.T.* 28 [37
For threescore y. employed with ceaseless care *R.*
Circling around and limiting his y. *R.* 150
Some pleasures live a month, and some a y. *R.* 459
The estate his sires had owned in ancient y. *R.* 579
And his old stint—three thousand pounds a y. *R.* 602
His active y. with indolent repose *R.* 618
The loud demand, from y. to y. the same *R.* 709
Than in foregoing y. ? *St.* i 6
To whom the rising y. shall prove his last *St.* ii 2
She might be young some forty y. ago *T.* 132
Go, bid the winter cease to chill the y. *T.* 399
Maturer y. shall happier stores produce *T.* 495
Incurring short fatigue : and though our y. *T.* i 129
And not a y. but pilfers as he goes *T.* i 131
Long knowledge and the scrutiny of y. *T.* i 179 [286
Few transient y., won from the abyss abhorred *T.* i
Be fickle, and thy y., most part, deformed *T.* ii 210
Declined at length into the vale of y. *T.* ii 726
Whom ten long y. experience of my care *T.* iii 338
O Winter, ruler of the inverted y. *T.* iv 120 [423
But helpless, in few y. shall find their hands *T.* iv
And, his three y. of heroship expired *T.* iv 644 [714
As twice seven y., his beauties had then first *T.* iv
The long protracted rigour of the y. *T.* v 85
Some have amused the dull sad y. of life *T.* v 180
The windings of my path through many y. *T.* vi 18
More grand than it produces y. by y. *T.* vi 119
And marshals all the or ler of the y. *T.* vi 191
E'en in the spring and playtime of the y. *T.* vi 299
Evander, famed for piety, for y. *T.* vi 490
To love it too. The springtime of our y. *T.* vi 589
And he that shows none, being ripe in y. *T.* vi 598
Six thousand y. of sorrow have well nigh *T.* vi 734
Why do the seasons still enrich the y. *Tir.* 41
Too careless often, as our y. proceed *Tir.* 113
And, as maturity of y. comes on *Tir.* 236
Our innocent sweet simple y. again *Tir.* 313
There dawns the splendour of his future y. *Tir.* 394
In early y. connected, time unbinds *Tir.* 439
But learns his error in maturer y. *Tir.* 449   876
That, since thy strength must with thy y. elope *Tir.*
Which, oft neglected, in life's waning y. *Tir.* 589
Though solid, not too weighty for his y. *Tir.* 651
Melody throughout the y. *Trans.* iii 24
Wretched man, whose y. are spent *Trans.* iii 29
Encompassing his throne a few short y. *T.T.* 132

With stern severity deals out the y. *T.T.* 209
And, tedious y. of Gothic darkness passed *T.T.* 564
Thy blossoms deck our unsuspecting y. *V.* 51
Through many a turbulent y. *W.N.* 20
Three quarters of a y. *Y.D.* 6
Till settling on the current y. 1789, 27

YEARLY.
Suggests the expedient of a y. fast *Ex.* 401
Y. in my song proclaim *St.* iv 10

YELL. [99
But ah! those dreadful y. what soul can hear *N.A.*
Has never heard the sanguinary y. *T.* iii 335
Witness the patient ox, with stripes and y. *T.* vi 420

YELLOW. [46
The y. tilth, green meads, rocks, rising grounds *H.*
Y. and red, of tapestry richly wrought *T.* i 33
Y. and bright, as bullion unalloy'd *T.* vi 171
To gather kingcups in the y. mead *T.* vi 302

YESTERDAY.
Y.'s face twin image of to-day *H.* 102

YEW.
An arbour near at hand of thickest y. *A.T.* 81
Shall grow the myrtle, and luxuriant y." *H.* 527
Of neighbouring cypress, or more sable y. *T.* vi 154

YIELD.
Could y. them no retreat *A Tale* 20 [264
My soul should y. thee willing thanks and praise *Ch.*
Sure not to conquer, and sure not to y. *Ch.* 621
What neither y. us profit nor delight *Con.* 241
Your heart shall y. a life-renewing stream *Con.* 503
Obduracy itself must y. the rest *Ex.* 559 [303
That y. them chaff and dust, and nothing more *Ex.*
And y. so much to noble folk *F.* 118 [723
When Hope, long lingering, at last y. the ghost *H.*
The recompense that arts or arms can y. *R.* 101
That y. not to the touch of human skill *R.* 344
Let verse at length y. thee thy just reward *S.* i 4
Where deists, always foiled, yet scorn to y. *T.* 372
Y. only discord in his Maker's ear *T.* 386
The Scripture y.) or hope to find, a friend ? *T.* 440
Compared with the repose the Sofa y. *T.* i 102
Y. no unpleasing ramble; there the turf *T.* i 530
Joys that her stormy raptures never y. *T.* iii 57
The stable y. a stercoraceous heap *T.* iii 463 [v 80
Earth y. them nought : the imprisoned worm is safe *T.*
It y. them, or recumbent on its brow *T.* v 787 [456
Can find no warrant there. Feed then, and y. *T.* vi
She longs to y., no sooner woo'd than won *Tir.* 172
His heart, now passive, y. to thy command *Tir.* 885

YIELDING.
That cleaves the y. air unheard *E.* i 88
Each y. harmony, disposed aright *R.* 326
Upon the y. herbage (so they sing) *T.* iv 521
Till, his exhausted quiver y. none *T.* vi 873
By kind tuition on his y. breast *Tir.* 154

YOKE.
From a worse y., and nailed it to the tree *Ex.* 220
To vanquish lust, and wear its y. no more *Ex.* 411
Have burst the bands, and cast the y. away *Ex.* 465
And every venal stickler for the y. *T.T.* 352

YOKED.
As well be y. by Despotism's hand *T.T.* 258

YORE.
Thou wast the veriest slave, in days of y. *Ex.* 526
A form, not now gymnastic as of y. *T.* ii 591

YOUNG.
Shook the y. leaves about her ears *A Fable* 12
A man once y., who lived retired *Mor.* 3
Your hermit, y. and jovial sirs! *Mor.* 23
Steal to the closet of y. innocence *P.E.* 316
She might be y. some forty years ago *T.* 132

Or charmed me y., no longer y., I find *T.* i 142
To his y. hopes, requires discreet delay *T.* iii 504
The y. to let the parent bird go free *T.* vi 446
Dwelt y. Misagathus; a scorner he *T.* vi 485
Fruitful and y. as in their first career? *Tir.* 42
The y. apostate sickens at the view *Tir.* 167
Y. heads are giddy, and y. hearts are warm *Tir.* 444

YOUNGSTER.
A y. at school more sedate than the rest *P.A.* 21

YOUTH. [*A.T.* 125
So swarmed the Sabine y., and grasped the shield
And be cheered by the sallies of y. *A.S.* 24
Ye worms that eat into the bud of y." *Con.* 40
Vigorous in age as in the flush of y. *Con.* 601
Y. has a sprightliness and fire to boast *Con.* 635
That fire abated which impels rash y. *Con.* 641
Hast thou the vigour of thy y.? An eye *Ep.* i 5
Yet fear. Y. ofttimes healthful and at ease *Ep.* i 7
The scenes to which not y. alone resorts *Ex.* 24
Still haunts, in hope to dream of y. again *Ex.* 26
To one, from our earliest y. *Gr.* 42
Y. lost in dissipation, we deplore *H.* 23
And y. invigorate that frame again *H.* 34
As y. or age persuades, and neither true *H.* 70
But down to latest age, from earliest y. *H.* 232
"Fallible man," the church-bred y. replies *H.* 421
The scoff of withered age and beardless y. *H.* 743
And thus unto the y. she said *J.G.* 217
The y. did ride, and soon did meet *J.G.* 221
In y. immortal warm *Miss —* 78
But y., health, vigour to expend *Mor.* 33
Or academic tutors, teaching y. *N.A.* 79 [*P.E.* 216
Heaven blessed the y., and made him fresh and fair

From thoughtless y. to ruminating age *P.E.* 24
Seek to supplant his inexperienced y. *P.E.* 59
Greybeard corrupter of our listening y. *P.E.* 342
The y., obedient to his sire's commands *P.E.* 377
Force many a shining y. into the shade *R.* 560
A worm is in the bud of y. *St.* i 23
Conscious of age, she recollects her y. *T.* 153
And if the y., unmellowed yet by time *T.* 492
Nor Sofa then I needed. Y. repairs *T.* i 127
Waste y. in occupations only fit *T.* ii 636 [ii 712
That blushed at its own praise! and press the y. *T.*
Bespoke him past the bounds of freakish y. *T.* ii 704
Than reverence, in perverse rebellious y. *T.* ii 730
Of headstrong y. were broken; bars and bolts *T.* ii 745
The nurture of her y., her dearest pledge *T.* ii 779
Had reached the sinewy firmness of their y. *T.* v 288
A stranger to the manners of the y. *T.* vi 493
Round Thurlow's head in early y. *Th.* 1
Those blessings of our early y. *The Doves* 11
That we are bound to cast the minds of y. *Tir.* 105
The y. now bearded, and yet pert and raw *Tir.* 155
Such rhapsodies our shrewd discerning y. *Tir.* 191
Such y. of spirit, and that spirit too *Tir.* 247
Traps to catch y. are most abundant too *Tir.* 522
That y. takes pleasure in, to please his boy *Tir.* 550
Such is the folly of our dreaming y. *V.* 54
Forgotten as the foliage of thy y. *Y.O.* 59

YOUTHFUL.
Some y. grace that age would gladly keep *T.* i 132
With y. smiles, descends towards the grave *T.* i 407
Some traces of her y. beauty left) *T.* iii 299
The firstborn efforts of my y. muse *T.* iv 701
From y. folly than the same neglect? *Tir.* 713

Z.

ZEAL.
Speaks a divine ambition, and a z. *Ch.* 307
Their z. begotten, as their works rehearse *Ch.* 505
All z. for a Reform that gives offence *Ch.* 533
That z., not vanity, has chanced to make *Ch.* 635
Abhors constraint, and dares not feign a z. *Con.* 713
The priest, whose office is, with z. sincere *Ex.* 97 [187
Their leader armed with meekness, z., and love *Ex.*
Unless a z. for virtue guide the blow *Ex.* 437
Their usefulness ensured by z. and love *Ex.* 443
When persecuting z. made royal sport *Ex.* 612
Fired with a z. peculiar, they defy *H.* 461
His aim was mischief and his z. pretence *H.* 564
He followed Paul, his z. a kindred flame *H.* 582
Pretends a z. for godliness and grace *H.* 661
From Fancy's influence, and intemperate z. *P.E.* 455
That he devotes not with a z. like theirs *R.* 222
And such as, in the z. of good design *R.* 697
His works, his abstinence, his z. allowed *T.* 91
Then, conscious of her meritorious z. *T.* 497
So strong the z. to immortalize himself *T.* i 284
With such a z. to be what they approve *T.* ii 791
He burns with most intense and flagrant z. *T.* iii 794
Your self-denying z., that holds it good *T.* v 328
His z. for her predominance within *T.* v 394

Destruction, with a z. to be destroyed *T.* vi 526
Deny thy Godhead with a martyr's z. *T.* vi 883
And will it breathe into him all the z. *Tir.* 375
Boys, once on fire with that contentious z. *Tir.* 470
Much z. in virtue's cause all teachers boast *Tir.* 517
Their sober z., integrity, and worth *T.T.* 377
Acts with a force, and kindles with a z. *T.T.* 482

ZEALOTS.
Grant her indebted to what z. call *T.* 483

ZEPHYRS.
The z. sport in vain *Miss —* 38

ZIGZAG.
Though such continual z. in a book *Con.* 861
He draws upon life's map a z. line *H.* 607
To z. manuscript, and cheats the eyes *T.* ii 364

ZODIAC.
And fairly laid the z. in the dust *T.* iii 647

ZONE.
Torpid and dull beneath a frozen z. *T.* 481
With modest grandeur in thy purple z. *T.* iv 257

ZONELESS.
That reeling goddess with the z. waist *T.* iii 52